Tolley's Value Added Tax 2005

Second Edition

by
Robert Wareham BSc (Econ) FCA
and
Alan Dolton MA (Oxon)

LexisNexis®
® Tolley

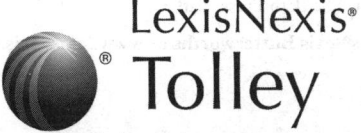

Members of the LexisNexis Group worldwide

United Kingdom	LexisNexis Butterworths, a Division of Reed Elsevier (UK) Ltd, Halsbury House, 35 Chancery Lane, LONDON, WC2A 1EL, and RSH, 1–3 Baxter's Place, Leith Walk, EDINBURGH EH1 3AF
Argentina	LexisNexis Argentina, BUENOS AIRES
Australia	LexisNexis Butterworths, CHATSWOOD, New South Wales
Austria	LexisNexis Verlag ARD Orac GmbH & Co KG, VIENNA
Canada	LexisNexis Butterworths, MARKHAM, Ontario
Chile	LexisNexis Chile Ltda, SANTIAGO DE CHILE
Czech Republic	Nakladatelství Orac sro, PRAGUE
France	Editions du Juris-Classeur SA, PARIS
Germany	LexisNexis Deutschland, Gmbh, FRANKFURT and MUNSTER
Hong Kong	LexisNexis Butterworths, HONG KONG
Hungary	HVG-Orac, BUDAPEST
India	LexisNexis Butterworths, NEW DELHI
Italy	Giuffrè Editore, MILAN
Malaysia	Malayan Law Journal Sdn Bhd, KUALA LUMPUR
New Zealand	LexisNexis Butterworths, WELLINGTON
Poland	Wydawnictwo Prawnicze LexisNexis, WARSAW
Singapore	LexisNexis Butterworths, SINGAPORE
South Africa	LexisNexis Butterworths, DURBAN
Switzerland	Stämpfli Verlag AG, BERNE
USA	LexisNexis, DAYTON, Ohio

Published by LexisNexis Butterworths

A CIP Catalogue record for this book is available from the British Library.

ISBN 07545 28790

Typeset by Kerrypress Ltd, Luton, Beds

Printed and bound in Great Britain by The Bath Press, Bath

Visit LexisNexis Butterworths at www.lexisnexis.co.uk

About This Book

Value added tax commenced in the United Kingdom on 1 April 1973. Since that date a mass of legislation, Orders, Regulations, law cases and Customs notices support a system which has become increasingly complex. Tolley's Value Added Tax seeks to aid practitioners and traders by being their first point of reference on this tax.

This edition includes the current law and practice of value added tax up to 1 July 2005 including the provisions of the Finance (No 2) Act 2005. Relevant statutory instruments, tribunal, and court cases, Customs notices, information sheets, and business briefs are also covered.

Chapters in this book are in alphabetical order for ease of reference to a particular subject and cross-references, an index and a table of statutes provide further ways of quickly finding the matter required.

Comments on this annual publication and suggestions for improvements are always welcomed.

LEXISNEXIS TOLLEY

Contents

Abbreviations and References

ABBREVIATIONS

All ER	=	All England Law Reports, (LexisNexis UK, Halsbury House, 35 Chancery Lane, London WC2A 1EL).
Art	=	Article
C & E	=	H.M. Customs and Excise
CA	=	Court of Appeal
CCAB	=	Consultative Committee of Accountancy Bodies
CEMA	=	Customs and Excise Management Act 1979
Ch D	=	Chancery Division
CIR	=	Commissioners of Inland Revenue
CJEC	=	Court of Justice of the European Communities
CS	=	Court of Session (Scotland)
EC	=	European Community
EEC	=	European Economic Community
ESC	=	Extra-statutory concession
FA	=	Finance Act
F(No 2)A	=	Finance (No 2) Act
HC	=	High Court
HL	=	House of Lords
HMRC	=	Her Majesty's Revenue and Customs
ICTA	=	Income and Corporation Taxes Act
IMA 1979	=	Isle of Man Act 1979
NI	=	Northern Ireland
p	=	Page
QB	=	Queen's Bench Division
Reg	=	Regulation
s	=	Section
Sch	=	Schedule
Sec	=	Section
SI	=	Statutory Instrument
STC	=	Simon's Tax Cases, (LexisNexis UK, as above).
STI	=	Simon's Tax Intelligence, (LexisNexis UK, as above).
t/a	=	Trading as
VATA 1994	=	Value Added Tax Act 1994
VTD	=	VAT Tribunal decision

Court cases. Citation where appropriate is of Simon's Tax Cases and is preceded by the Court and year of the decision (if different from the citation).

Tribunal cases. Citation is by reference to the number assigned to the decision by the VAT Tribunals Headquarters (e.g. *(VTD 18775)*). In all tribunal cases only the appellant or applicant is named.

Tolley's VAT cases. All case citations include a reference to any summary of that case in Tolley's VAT Cases 2005 (e.g (TVC 39.52)). References ending with a letter (e.g. (TVC 39.52A)) are to cases subsequent to the publication of Tolley's VAT Cases 2005 in a bound book format and are only available in the electronic version of that book.

1 Introduction and General Principles

De Voil Indirect Tax Service. See V1.101.

1.1 VAT LAW AND INTERPRETATION

Value added tax (VAT) was introduced in the UK on 1 April 1973.

European Community legislation. The overriding law on VAT throughout the European Community (EC) is in the EC *Directives*, notably the *6th VAT Directive*. The form and method of compliance is left to individual EC countries but, where any of the provisions are mandatory, EC law takes precedence if there are any inconsistencies with national law. See 22 EUROPEAN COMMUNITY LEGISLATION for further details.

UK legislation. VAT was initially introduced into UK legislation by the *Finance Act 1972*. Subsequent amendments to the UK legislation were first consolidated in the *Value Added Tax Act 1983* (*VATA 1983*) and subsequently in the *Value Added Tax Act 1994* (*VATA 1994*). Changes to *VATA 1994* are made by successive *Finance Acts*.

Although *VATA 1994* provides the main framework of the tax, much of the detail is to be found in statutory instruments (SIs), either in the form of *Orders* made by the Treasury or *Regulations* made by HM Revenue and Customs (previously Customs and Excise). SIs both create law in their own right and amend existing law (both SIs and, occasionally, statutes). The principal *Regulations* made by HMRC are the VAT Regulations (*SI 1995/2518*).

1.2 Interpretation of the law by HMRC

HMRC currently publish in excess of 130 Notices and Leaflets affecting VAT. With certain exceptions (as indicated in the text), these are not part of the law but explain how HMRC interpret the law. They also publish VAT Information Sheets, VAT Notes and Business Briefs.

The fact that HMRC publications largely only interpret the law should be borne in mind where this book indicates a Notice, etc as source material.

1.3 Court and tribunal decisions

If a business disagrees with HMRC's interpretation of the law, it has a right of appeal, in certain cases, to a VAT tribunal. In England and Wales, either party can then appeal from that decision to the High Court and, with leave, on to the Court of Appeal and House of Lords. In Scotland, appeals from a tribunal go to the Court of Session and, with leave, directly to the House of Lords. A tribunal or Court may also refer a question to the Court of Justice of the European Communities (CJEC).

Tribunals and even Court decisions relating to VAT do not create law but merely interpret it. They may, however, cause HMRC to change the way that they interpret the law and may lead to amendments being made to the legislation by statute or statutory instrument.

See 5 APPEALS generally.

1.4 GENERAL PRINCIPLES OF VAT

VAT is a tax on consumer expenditure and is collected on business transactions and imports.

The basic principle is to charge VAT at each stage in the supply of goods and services (output tax). If the customer is registered for VAT and uses the supplies for business purposes, he will receive credit for this VAT (input tax). The broad effect is that businesses are not affected and VAT is actually borne by the final consumer.

1.5 **Scope of VAT**

A transaction is within the scope of UK VAT if all the following conditions are met.

- *It is a supply of goods or services.* The term 'supply' is not defined in the legislation but is broadly interpreted. See 64.2 SUPPLY for the meaning of supply and 64.3 and 64.4 SUPPLY for supplies of goods and services respectively. Certain transactions, although supplies, are regarded as supplies of neither goods nor services and are outside the scope of UK VAT. See 64.5 SUPPLY.
- *It takes place in the UK.*
- *It is made by a taxable person.* A taxable person is an individual, firm or company, etc which is registered for VAT or which is required to register for VAT but has failed to do so. See 1.13 below.
- *It is made in the course or furtherance of any business carried on by that person.* See 8.1 to 8.3 BUSINESS for the interpretation of 'business'.

A transaction which does not meet all of the above conditions is outside the scope of UK VAT.

1.6 **Place of supply**

To be within the charge to UK VAT, a supply must be made in the UK. Supplies made outside the UK are outside the scope of UK VAT (although they may be liable to VAT in another country).

Separate rules apply for determining the place of supply of goods and services. See 64.8 and 64.18 SUPPLY for the place of supply of goods and services respectively.

1.7 **Time of supply (tax point)**

The time at which a supply of goods is treated as taking place is called the tax point. VAT must normally be accounted for in the VAT period (see 1.18 below) in which the tax point occurs and at the rate of VAT (see 1.11 below) in force at that time. Small businesses can, however, account for VAT on the basis of cash paid and received (see 1.21 below).

Basic tax point. The basic tax point for a supply of goods is the date the goods are removed (ie sent to, or taken by, the customer). If the goods are not removed, it is the date they are made available for his use.

The basic tax point for a supply of services is the date the services are performed.

Actual tax points. In the case of both goods and services, where a VAT invoice is raised or payment is made *before* the basic tax point, there is an earlier actual tax point at the time the invoice is issued or payment received, whichever occurs first.

There is also generally an actual tax point where a VAT invoice is issued within 14 days *after* the basic tax point. This overrides the basic tax point but not the actual tax point created by the issue of an invoice or payment before the basic tax point.

There are also special provisions for particular supplies of goods and services.

For further details see 64.32–64.57 SUPPLY.

1.8 **Value of supply**

The value of a supply is the value on which VAT is due. The amount of VAT is then the value multiplied by the VAT rate (see 1.11 below).

The value of a supply normally depends upon what is given in exchange for the supply (ie the consideration). If this is wholly in money, the value will be based on that amount. If not, the value is the monetary equivalent of the consideration.

There are special rules relating to discounts offered, transactions between connected persons and values expressed in foreign currencies. Imports (see 1.14 below) and acquisitions from other EC countries (see 1.16 below) also have their own valuation rules.

See 69 VALUATION for further details.

1.9 **Output tax**

Output tax is the VAT due on taxable supplies and is normally the liability of the person making the supply. In addition to straightforward business transactions, output tax may also be due on business gifts and private use of own goods and services.

A particular supply may be complicated by being a mixed supply where a single inclusive price is charged for a number of separate supplies. Where these supplies are taxable at different rates, a fair and justifiable apportionment of the total price must be made.

See 47 OUTPUT TAX for further details.

Special schemes for retailers. Traders registered for VAT normally issue an invoice for each sale made in order to have the necessary records to calculate output tax. As this may be difficult or impossible where goods are sold directly to the public, special schemes are available for use by retailers only. See 60 RETAIL SCHEMES for further details.

Second-hand goods. There are special provisions for second-hand goods. Subject to certain conditions being satisfied, under the Margin Scheme VAT is only chargeable on the amount by which the selling price of a particular item exceeds the price paid when it was obtained. The scheme extends to almost the full range of second-hand goods. There is also a Global Accounting Scheme which is a simplified scheme for VAT on low value, bulk volume second-hand goods. Under this scheme, VAT is accounted for on the difference between the total purchases and sales of eligible goods in each VAT period rather than on an item by item basis. See 61 SECOND-HAND GOODS for further details.

Flat-rate scheme for small businesses. Small businesses with taxable turnover and total turnover below specified annual limits can opt to join a flat-rate scheme under which they calculate net VAT due by applying a flat-rate percentage to tax-inclusive turnover. The flat-rate percentage varies with the trade sector into which a business falls. See 63.15 SPECIAL SCHEMES.

Flat-rate scheme for farmers. Farmers who are certified under the scheme do not have to account for VAT on sales of goods and services within designated activities but are not able to recover input tax incurred on purchases. To compensate for this, farmers in the scheme may charge (and retain) a fixed flat-rate addition of 4% on top of the sale price. The customer can recover the addition as if it were VAT. See 63.25 to 63.30 SPECIAL SCHEMES for further details.

1.10 **Input tax**

A taxable person is entitled to reclaim input tax suffered on goods and services supplied to him, imports from outside the EC (see 1.14 below) and acquisition of goods from other EC countries (see 1.16 below) provided that the input tax relates to

- taxable business supplies made by him; or
- supplies made by him which are outside the scope of UK VAT but which would have been taxable if made in the UK; or
- certain supplies by him of exempt insurance and financial services to persons belonging outside the EC.

Taxable supplies are those chargeable at the standard, reduced or zero rate.

VAT cannot be recovered on goods and services which are not used for business purposes (eg for private use). Where goods are used partly for business and partly for non-business purposes, the VAT incurred is normally apportioned.

VAT incurred on a number of items is non-deductible. These include motor cars (with certain exceptions), business entertainment, goods sold under one of the second-hand schemes and certain articles installed in buildings by builders.

Where input tax has been claimed but the consideration for the supply is not paid within six months, the input tax must be repaid to HMRC.

Special rules also apply to input tax incurred before registration for VAT and after deregistration.

See 35 INPUT TAX for further details.

1.11 **VAT rates**

There are currently three main rates of VAT, a standard rate of 17.5%, a reduced rate of 5% and a zero rate. See 58 REDUCED RATE SUPPLIES and 72 ZERO-RATED SUPPLIES (and supporting chapters) for goods and services which are currently zero-rated.

The effect of a supply being zero-rated is as follows.

- The amount of VAT on the supply is nil but it is still a taxable supply.
- As a taxable supply, it must be taken into account in determining whether registration is required (see 1.13 below).
- Input tax may be reclaimed subject to the same rules as for standard-rated supplies.
- Where a supply could be either zero-rated or exempt (see 1.12 below), zero-rating takes priority.

1.12 **Exempt supplies**

Certain supplies are exempt from VAT. See 24 EXEMPT SUPPLIES and supporting chapters. This means that no VAT is chargeable but, unlike zero-rated supplies, related input tax is not recoverable.

Where a person makes both taxable supplies and exempt supplies, he is partially exempt and may or may not be able to recover all his input tax. All input tax directly attributable to taxable supplies can be reclaimed but none of the input tax directly attributable to exempt supplies (subject to a *de minimis* limit). Special rules then apply to work out how much input tax can be reclaimed on general overheads, etc. See 49 PARTIAL EXEMPTION.

1.13 Registration

Where a person is in business and making taxable supplies, the value of these supplies is his taxable turnover. If, at the end of any month,

- taxable turnover in the year then ended has exceeded a specified limit, or
- there are reasonable grounds for believing that the value of taxable supplies in the next 30 days will exceed a specified limit,

that person normally becomes a taxable person and must notify HMRC of his liability to register for VAT. There are financial penalties for failing to do so. Where, however, only zero-rated supplies are made, HMRC have a discretion to exempt a person from registration.

Even if taxable turnover is below the specified limit, a person who makes taxable business supplies can request voluntary registration.

A person who is registered for VAT ceases to be liable to be registered and can apply to be deregistered if the VAT-exclusive value of supplies in the next twelve months will not exceed a specified limit.

See 59.1 to 59.10 REGISTRATION for further details including how to apply for registration and deregistration.

See also

- 8.5 BUSINESS for anti-avoidance measures to combat business splitting and the conditions for the separation of a previously single business into independent parts for registration purposes;
- 31.1 to 31.5 GROUPS OF COMPANIES for group registration;
- 48.1 to 48.4 OVERSEAS TRADERS for registration by overseas traders; and
- 59.37 REGISTRATION for divisional registration by companies.

Even where there is no liability to register for VAT in respect of UK supplies of goods or services, a liability may arise in respect of

- 'distance selling' to non-taxable persons in the UK by suppliers in other EC countries (see 59.11 to 59.17 REGISTRATION); or
- acquisitions of goods in the UK from other EC countries (see 59.18 to 59.25 REGISTRATION).

1.14 Imports

Unless special relief applies, VAT is charged and payable on the importation of goods into the UK from outside the EC. The rate of VAT is the same as if the goods had been supplied in the UK.

Unless the goods are placed under customs or excise warehousing or certain customs arrangements (eg free zones, inward processing relief or Community Transit arrangements) any VAT due must normally either be paid at the time of importation or deferred with any duty if the importer or his agent are approved for deferment. VAT paid on the importation of goods can be claimed as input tax, subject to the normal rules.

See 34 IMPORTS for further details.

1.15 Exports

Provided various conditions are met, goods exported outside the EC are zero-rated. See 25 EXPORTS for further details.

1.16 Transactions with other EC countries

The concepts of 'imports' and 'exports' of goods apply only to transactions with countries outside the EC. For intra-EC movements of goods, the terms 'acquisitions' and 'supplies' are used. It is not necessary to make an import declaration on an acquisition of goods in the UK from another EC country or to pay VAT at the frontier.

Supplies of goods to a customer registered for VAT in another EC country can be zero-rated provided certain conditions are met. These include obtaining the customer's VAT registration number and showing it on the VAT invoice. The customer then accounts for VAT at the appropriate rate on the goods in the EC country of destination. If the conditions cannot be met, VAT must be charged in the country of origin at the rate applicable to the goods in that country.

VAT must also be charged on supplies of goods to non-registered customers in other EC countries. Where, however, the supplier is also responsible for the delivery of the goods, once the value of such 'distance' sales to any particular EC country exceeds an annual threshold set by that country, the supplier is automatically liable to register for VAT in that other country. VAT on any further sales is then due in the EC country of destination.

Special rules apply to transfers of own goods between EC countries, goods installed or assembled at the customer's premises, new means of transport and goods subject to excise duty purchased by non-taxable persons. There are also special rules for 'triangulation' (ie where a chain of supplies of goods involves three parties and, instead of goods physically passing from one party to the next, they are delivered from the first party to the last party in the chain).

See 23 EUROPEAN COMMUNITY: SINGLE MARKET for further details.

1.17 Invoices

A registered taxable person must issue a VAT invoice where he makes a standard or reduced-rated supply to another taxable person in the UK or a standard, reduced or zero-rated supply to a person in another EC country.

See 40 INVOICES for further details including the particulars required to be shown on the invoice and special invoices which may be issued by retailers and cash and carry wholesalers.

1.18 Returns and payment of VAT

Every taxable person must keep a VAT account summarising the output tax and input tax for each VAT period. See 56.12 RECORDS. A VAT period is normally three months but a one-month period is also allowed, particularly where input tax is likely to exceed output tax on a regular basis.

The information in the VAT account, plus certain statistical information, must then be shown on a VAT return for that period. The return must be sent to HMRC, and any VAT due to HMRC paid, no later than one month after the end of the period. The due date for payment will be extended by seven days where payment is made by credit transfer. Certain large VAT payers must make monthly payments on account.

See 2 ACCOUNTING PERIODS AND RETURNS and 51.1 to 51.4 PAYMENT OF VAT for further details.

Annual accounting. Smaller businesses with turnover below an annual limit may apply to join the annual accounting scheme. This allows them to complete one VAT return each year. Monthly, or with the agreement of HMRC, quarterly interim payments on account are required based on an estimate of the amount of VAT due. The annual VAT return must be completed and sent to HMRC, with any balancing payment, within two months of the end of the annual VAT accounting period. See 63.9 to 63.14 SPECIAL SCHEMES for further details.

1.19 Records

Every taxable person must keep such records as HMRC require. Specifically, these include business and accounting records, the VAT account (see 1.18 above), copies of all VAT invoices and credit notes issued and received, and documentation relating to imports, exports, acquisitions of goods from other EC countries and goods dispatched to other EC countries. All such records must be kept for six years unless HMRC agree to a shorter period.

See 56 RECORDS for further details.

1.20 Bad debts

VAT is normally due by reference to the tax point (see 1.7 above). The supplier must therefore account to HMRC for the VAT even if the debt, including the VAT, is not paid. By way of relief, VAT can be reclaimed where a debt has been written off and six months has elapsed from the date of supply and the date payment is due. See 7 BAD DEBT RELIEF.

The problem of VAT on bad debts can also be removed by using the cash accounting system (see 1.21 below).

1.21 Cash accounting

Provided turnover is below an annual limit, a taxable person may, subject to conditions, account for and pay VAT on the basis of cash or other consideration paid and received. The main advantages of the scheme are automatic bad debt relief and the deferral of the time for payment of VAT where extended credit is given. See 63.2 to 63.8 SPECIAL SCHEMES for further details.

1.22 Assessments

HMRC are given powers to raise an assessment where VAT returns have not been made or it appears to them that returns are incomplete or incorrect. The assessment must normally be made within two years from the end of the return period in question or, if later, within one year of the facts on which the assessment is based coming to their knowledge. An assessment cannot be raised more than three years after the end of the return period except in cases of fraud when the period is extended to 20 years. Where the taxable person has died, an assessment cannot be made more than three years after death or relate to a period more than three years before death.

See 6 ASSESSMENTS for further details.

1.23 **Interest and penalties**

Interest is chargeable in certain circumstances where VAT has been underdeclared or overclaimed. See 51.14 PAYMENT OF VAT. On the other hand, repayment supplement is due where HMRC do not make a repayment on time and interest can be paid to the taxpayer where VAT has been overpaid or underclaimed as a result of error by HMRC. See 51.15 and 51.16 PAYMENT OF VAT.

There is an extensive range of criminal and civil penalties including the following.

Offence	Maximum penalty
Criminal	
Fraudulent evasion of VAT	Unlimited fine or 7 years imprisonment
Producing false documents	Unlimited fine or 7 years imprisonment
Civil	
Evasion of VAT	Amount of VAT evaded
Misdeclaration or neglect	15% of the VAT which would have been lost
Repeated misdeclarations	15% of the VAT which would have been lost
Failure to register	15% of the VAT which would have been due
Failure to keep records	£500
Default surcharge	15% of the unpaid VAT

See 52 PENALTIES for further details of these and other penalties. Liability for certain civil penalties can be avoided where there is reasonable excuse for conduct and penalties can be mitigated by HMRC or a VAT tribunal.

1.24 **Appeals**

An appeal against a decision of HMRC on certain matters may be made to a VAT and Duties tribunal and from there, on a point of law, to the High Court (Court of Session in Scotland) and continued up to the House of Lords under normal procedure. The matters on which an appeal to a tribunal may be made are restricted and certain conditions must be complied with. Notably, unless HMRC agree otherwise, the appellant must have made all the returns he is required to make and paid over the VAT due according to those returns. Notice of the appeal must be served within 30 days of the disputed decision.

See 5 APPEALS for further details.

2 Accounting Periods and Returns

Cross-references. See 51 PAYMENT OF VAT; 52 PENALTIES; 56 RECORDS; 63.9 SPECIAL SCHEMES for annual VAT returns.

De Voil Indirect Tax Service. See V5.101–108.

The contents of this chapter are as follows

2.1 MAKING RETURNS

A taxable person must account for and pay VAT by reference to VAT periods. For this purpose, he must make a return to HMRC, not later than the last day of the month following the end of the return period, showing the amount of VAT payable by or to him and containing full information in respect of other matters specified in the return. [*VATA 1994, s 25*(*1*)*; SI 1995/2518, Reg 25*(*1*)*; SI 2000/258, Reg 3*].

Online VAT services (eVAT). A VAT-registered business can use HMRC's eVAT service to submit its returns on-line rather than sending them by post.

Accessing the service. In order to get access to the service, a business must:

- *Sign up.* Go to the HMRC website and enter personal details (including setting a password). A User ID will then be displayed for future use.
- *Enrol.* Login with the User ID and password and select 'Enrol for eVAT services'. Then supply the information requested which is available from the certificate of registration and the last VAT return.
- *Activate.* An activation pin will be sent, normally within seven days. To activate the service, go to the Government Gateway at

  www.gateway.gov.uk

  and Login, select the 'Activate' link and enter the activation pin.

A business can then Login to the HMRC website to access its VAT return. Once a business has enrolled for online VAT services, HMRC expect it to continue to use the service and not use paper returns unless it has problems using the site.

Authorisation. When the online application has been successfully completed, the business is authorised to use the service although HMRC reserve the right to deny access to the service where they consider it necessary for the protection of the revenue. Unless permission to use the service has been granted (and not revoked), any return made using the service is treated as not having been made. A person is not treated as being authorised to use the service only because of

- being registered under *SI 1995/2518, Reg 6* in substitution for another person who has been so authorised on the transfer of a business as a going concern (see 59.36 REGISTRATION); or
- acting in a representative capacity and being required by HMRC under *SI 1995/2518, Reg 30* to comply with the VAT requirements relating to accounting, payment and records (see 19.1 and 19.2 DEATH AND INCAPACITY and 36.1 INSOLVENCY).

Sending returns. If transmission of an eVAT return is successful, the business will receive an electronic acknowledgement from HMRC. This is evidence that the business has met its legal responsibility to submit a return. It is therefore recommended that a copy of the acknowledgement is printed and retained in the records. The acknowledgement also shows a unique reference for each return sent which should be quoted in any queries about the return. If an electronic acknowledgement is not received, the business should presume that the return has not been received.

[*SI 1995/2518, Reg 25(4A)–(4M); SI 2000/258; SI 2004/1675*].

Payment of VAT. A condition of using the eVAT service is that any VAT due on the return is also paid by an approved electronic payment method. [*SI 1995/2518, Reg 40(2A); SI 2000/258*]. See 51.2 PAYMENT OF VAT for methods of paying electronically.

2.2 **ACCOUNTING PERIODS**

Subject to the exceptions below, returns must be completed for three-monthly periods ending on the dates notified in the certificate of registration (or otherwise). [*SI 1995/2518, Reg 25(1); SI 2000/258, Reg 3*].

In order to spread the flow of returns over the year, taxable persons are allocated to one of the three groups of VAT periods ('VAT periods') as follows.

- Three-month periods ending on 30 June, 30 September, 31 December and 31 March.
- Three-month periods ending on 31 July, 31 October, 31 January and 30 April.
- Three-month periods ending on 31 August, 30 November, 28 February and 31 May.

(VAT Notice 700, para 20.5).

A taxable person who was, or is, required to be registered (but has not done so) will, unless HMRC otherwise allow, be allocated to the first group.

Exceptions. The following are exceptions to the above rules.

(*a*) **Annual returns**. See 63.9 SPECIAL SCHEMES.

(*b*) **Monthly returns**. HMRC may allow or direct a person to complete returns for periods of one month and to submit these within one month of the period to which they relate. [*SI 1995/2518, Reg 25(1)(a)*]. If repayments are expected to be received (eg because most of the outputs are zero-rated) this method of accounting is advantageous. Where monthly VAT returns are prepared and the business changes from receiving repayments to making payment of VAT, it may have to change to three-monthly VAT periods. (VAT Notice 700, para 20.5).

(*c*) **The first return period** commences on the effective date on which the taxable person was, or should have been, registered. [*SI 1995/2518, Reg 25*(*1*)(*b*); *SI 2000/794*].

(*d*) **HMRC may vary the length of any period** or the date on which any return is to be submitted. This applies whether or not the varied period has ended. [*SI 1995/2518, Reg 25*(*1*)(*c*)]. There is no appeal against their decision to the VAT tribunal under *VATA 1994, s 83*(*a*) (*Punchwell Ltd, (VTD 1085)(TVC 57.2)*; *Selected Growers Ltd (VTD 10)(TVC 57.1)*).

In particular:

- Written application may be made (quoting registration number and dates) to have VAT periods corresponding with the financial year of the business.
- Where there is a new registration either because of a transfer of a going concern or a change in circumstances of a registered business (see 59.36 and 59.7 REGISTRATION respectively) application can be made to retain the VAT periods of the previous registration.
- Special consideration will also be given, **where accounting systems are not based on calendar months,** to arrangements for VAT periods to fit in with the particular system. For example, quarterly VAT periods ending within 14 days of the end of the standard period *or* monthly VAT periods ending within 7 days of the end of the calendar month (14 days for a four-weekly accounting cycle) are acceptable.
- Any other arrangement will be specially considered.

(VAT Notice 700, para 20.5).

(*e*) **Where control of the assets of any registered person passes** to a trustee in bankruptcy, administrative receiver, liquidator or person otherwise acting in a representative capacity, the current VAT period in which the date of the receiving order, appointment of administrative receiver or provisional liquidator or winding up order, etc (the '*relevant date*') occurs is divided into two periods. The first period ends on the day prior to the relevant date and the appropriate return must be submitted by the last day of the following month. The second period commences on the relevant date and ends (and all subsequent periods end) on the normal last day for the VAT periods. [*SI 1995/2518, Reg 25*(*3*)].

(*f*) **Final return.** Any person who

- ceases to be liable to be registered, or
- ceases to be entitled to be registered under *VATA 1994, Sch 1 para 9* or *VATA 1994, Sch 1 para 10* (see 59.2 REGISTRATION)

must submit a final return on Form VAT 193 *unless* the registration is allocated to the purchaser on the transfer of a business as a going concern (see 59.36 REGISTRATION). Unless HMRC allow otherwise, the return must contain full information of the matters specified in the form and a declaration, signed by the taxpayer, that the return is true and complete. The return must be furnished by a person who was or is registered within one month of the effective date for cancellation of registration and by any other person within one month of the date on which he ceases to be liable to be registered. [*SI 1995/2518, Reg 25*(*4*)].

2.3 VAT RETURNS

The prescribed forms are

- **Form VAT 193** (or the Welsh version Form VAT 193(W)) in the circumstances under 2.2(*f*) above; and
- **Form VAT 100** (or the Welsh version Form VAT 100(W))for use in all other cases.

2.4 ESTIMATED RETURNS

Where HMRC are satisfied that a person is not able to account for the exact amount of output tax chargeable or claim the exact amount of input tax to be deducted in any VAT period, that person may estimate a part of his output tax or input tax for that period provided

- the estimate is adjusted and exactly accounted for in the next VAT period; or
- if the exact amount is still not known and HMRC are satisfied that it could not with due diligence be ascertained, the estimate is adjusted in the next but one VAT period.

[*SI 1995/2518, Regs 28, 29*(*3*)].

Permission for estimated returns must be obtained in advance. If the estimated return is submitted, and the VAT shown paid, by the due date, the taxpayer will not be in default for the purposes of the default surcharge provisions (see 52.15 PENALTIES). Permission will still be considered after the due date has passed, but it will not affect any default which has already been recorded. (VAT Notice 700, para 21.2).

Local authorities. See 43.10 LOCAL AUTHORITIES AND PUBLIC BODIES for special estimation schemes for local authorities.

De Voil Indirect Tax Service. See V3.505.

2.5 COMPLETION OF RETURN FORM 100 (OR WELSH VERSION VAT 100(W))

The procedure outlined in 2.6 to 2.15 below should be adopted for the completion of return Form 100. [*SI 1995/2518, Reg 39*]. (VAT Notice 700/12/02).

Nil returns. If the business has not traded in the period and has no input tax to recover or output tax to declare, a VAT return must still be submitted with all boxes completed as 'None' ('0.00' if the return is sent electronically).

Assessments. When sending in a return after paying an assessment, the VAT return should be completed as usual without adjusting any of the figures to offset what has already been paid by assessment. If the value of Box 5 is more than the assessment, just the extra should be paid. If it is less than the assessment, no payment should be made and HMRC will pay or credit the business with the difference.

If a Notice of assessment and/or overdeclaration has been received to correct mistakes found by an HMRC officer, these should not be reflected on the next VAT return.

(VAT Notice 700/12/02, paras 7.2, 7.3).

Declaration. The return must contain full information in respect of the matters specified in the return and a declaration, signed by the taxpayer, that the return is true and complete. [*SI 1995/2518, Reg 25(1); SI 2000/258, Reg 3*]. This declaration must be unqualified (*DK Wright and Associates Ltd, (VTD 203)(TVC 2.112)*).

2.6 **Box 1**

Enter the total VAT due on sales and other outputs for the VAT period for which the return is submitted.

In addition to VAT on sales and other taxable business income in the period, VAT is also due on the following.

- Supplies to staff (eg canteen meals, goods at reduced prices, sales from vending machines, payments from staff for use of cars and telephones)
- Sales of business assets or capital equipment in most situations (eg office equipment and commercial vehicles) but note that special rules apply to a transfer of an asset as part of the transfer of a business as a going concern (see 8.10 BUSINESS)
- Fuel used for private motoring using a scale charge (see 45.16 MOTOR CARS)
- Gifts of goods costing more than £50 excluding VAT (see 47.6 OUTPUT TAX)
- Goods or services for own use taken out of the business (see 47.7 OUTPUT TAX)
- The full value of goods sold where something has been taken in part exchange (see 69.7 VALUATION)
- Commission received for selling something on behalf of someone else (other than financial or insurance commissions which are exempt)
- Supplies of goods to unregistered customers in other EC countries (see 23.10 EUROPEAN COMMUNITY: SINGLE MARKET)
- Self-billing invoices received

Any VAT on credit notes issued to customers during the period should be deducted. If for this or any other reason a minus figure needs to be entered in Box 1, it should be shown in brackets (by using a minus sign in electronic returns).

Errors in output tax in earlier periods (subject to the three-year time limit) may be entered provided the net effect of all earlier errors in input tax and output tax discovered in the period of the return does not exceed £2,000 (see 56.11 RECORDS).

For sales under the cash accounting scheme (see 63.2 SPECIAL SCHEMES) this box should be completed on the basis of payments received and *not* invoices issued.

2.7 **Box 2**

Enter VAT due on acquisitions from other EC countries (see 23.3 EUROPEAN COMMUNITY: SINGLE MARKET). Errors in VAT on acquisitions in earlier periods (subject to the three-year time limit) may be entered provided the net effect of all earlier errors in input tax and output tax discovered in the period of the return does not exceed £2,000 (see 56.11 RECORDS). If for any reason a minus figure needs to be entered in Box 2, it should be shown in brackets (by using a minus sign in electronic returns).

2.8 **Box 3**

Insert total of Boxes 1 and 2 (ie total output tax). For electronic returns this will be completed automatically.

2.9 **Box 4**

Enter VAT reclaimed in the period on purchases and other inputs (ie the aggregate of all entries in the VAT allowable portion of the VAT account (see 56.12 RECORDS) for the VAT period for which the return is furnished). This includes VAT on imports and removals from HMRC warehouse or from a free zone, and VAT deductible on acquisitions of goods from other EC countries and services under the 'reverse charge' procedure. VAT cannot be reclaimed on the following.

- Goods and services where a proper VAT invoice is not held. Letters, bills, receipts, order forms, statements and pro forma invoices are not VAT invoices (see 56.7 RECORDS)
- Purchases for purely private or personal use (eg private telephone calls). See 35.7 INPUT TAX for apportionment where goods or services are used for business and non-business purposes
- Purchases, acquisitions or importations of most ordinary business cars (other than taxis, driving school and self-drive hire cars or cars where there is no use for private motoring), see 45.3 MOTOR CARS
- BUSINESS ENTERTAINMENT (9)
- Goods bought under one of the schemes for SECOND-HAND GOODS (61)
- Imported goods before the relevant import VAT certificate is received
- Goods imported for use in another person's business (even if the VAT mistakenly appears on the import VAT certificate)
- VAT on self-billing invoices raised by the business where the supplier is not registered for VAT

Any VAT on credit notes issued by suppliers during the period should be deducted.

Errors in input tax in earlier periods (subject to the three-year time limit) may be entered provided the net effect of all earlier errors in input tax and output tax discovered in the period of the return does not exceed £2,000 (see 56.11 RECORDS).

If, after taking account of errors, credit notes, etc a minus figure needs to be entered in Box 4, it should be shown in brackets (by using a minus sign in electronic returns).

For purchases under the cash accounting scheme (see 63.2 SPECIAL SCHEMES) this box should be completed on the basis of payments made and *not* invoices received.

Also use this box to claim VAT under the special rules for BAD DEBT RELIEF (7).

2.10 **Box 5**

Insert difference between Box 3 and Box 4. For electronic returns this will be done automatically. If less than £1, no payment should be sent (and no repayment will be made) but the return should still be sent.

2.11 **Box 6**

Insert value of total sales/outputs (excluding VAT) including

- standard-rated supplies (including road fuel scale charges)
- supplies to VAT-registered traders in other EC countries
- supplies to non VAT-registered or private individuals in other EC countries (distance sales)
- zero-rated supplies, including exports
- exempt supplies
- any other business income
- 'reverse charge' transactions
- purchases under the special accounting scheme for gold (see 30.9 GOLD AND PRECIOUS METALS)
- supplies which are outside the scope of VAT under the place of supply rules (see 64.7–64.38 SUPPLY)
- any own goods transferred to other EC countries
- sales to customers in other EC countries on a sale or return basis
- deposits for which an invoice has been issued

Any amount entered in Box 8 below must also be entered in Box 6.

If the cash accounting scheme is used (see 63.2 SPECIAL SCHEMES), figures should be based on payments received and *not* invoices issued.

2.12 **Box 7**

Insert value of total purchases/inputs excluding VAT (including imports, acquisitions and 'reverse charge' transactions) and other business expenses. Any amount entered in Box 9 must also be entered in Box 7.

If the cash accounting scheme is used (see 63.2 SPECIAL SCHEMES), figures should be based on payments made and *not* invoices received.

2.13 **Boxes 6 and 7**

The following should be left out.

- VAT itself
- Wages and salaries, PAYE and NIC
- Money put into or taken out of the business by the trader
- Loans, dividends and gifts of money
- Insurance claims
- Stock Exchange dealings (unless a financial institution)
- MOT certificates
- Motor vehicle licence duty

- Local authority rates
- Income which is outside the scope of VAT because it is not consideration for a supply

Figures should be net of any credits received but cash discounts should not be taken off. If accounts are kept net of cash discounts a reasonable amount should be added back for any discounts given or received.

2.14 **Box 8**

Insert the total value of all supplies of *goods* (and directly related services) to other EC countries. This must include the value of goods despatched from the UK to a destination in another EC country, even if no actual sale is involved or the sale is being invoiced to a person located outside the EC. Include

- supplies of goods to VAT-registered persons in other EC countries
- transfers of own goods from the UK to other EC countries (see 23.23 EUROPEAN COMMUNITY: SINGLE MARKET)
- consignment stocks transferred from the UK to other EC countries (see 23.23 EUROPEAN COMMUNITY: SINGLE MARKET)
- goods supplied to VAT-registered customers in other EC countries on a call-off basis (see 23.30 EUROPEAN COMMUNITY: SINGLE MARKET)
- goods supplied to customers in other EC countries on sale or return, approval or similar basis (see 23.27 EUROPEAN COMMUNITY: SINGLE MARKET)
- goods despatched from the UK for installation or assembly in other EC countries (see 23.29 EUROPEAN COMMUNITY: SINGLE MARKET)
- distance sales to unregistered customers in other EC countries where on or above the distance selling threshold for that country (or the seller has voluntarily registered in that country) (see 23.18 EUROPEAN COMMUNITY: SINGLE MARKET)
- supplies of new means of transport to unregistered customers in other EC countries (see 23.32 EUROPEAN COMMUNITY: SINGLE MARKET)
- process work carried out in the UK for customers in other EC countries (include only the value of the process work, not the value of the goods themselves)

Separate supplies of services to other EC countries should only be included in Box 6.

The value to be included is the invoice (or contract) price, including directly related services such as freight and insurance charges associated with the goods. The supply of other services (eg legal or financial services) should not be included.

2.15 **Box 9**

Insert the total value of acquisitions of *goods* from other EC countries, including any goods removed to the UK from another EC country even if no actual purchase takes place (eg goods transferred between divisions of the same company) or the person invoiced is located outside the EC. Included are supplies of goods installed or assembled in the UK which have been despatched from another EC country and the value of acquisitions of process work from other EC countries (include only the value of the process work, not the value of the goods themselves).

The value to be included is the invoice (or contract) price, including directly related services such as freight and insurance charges associated with the goods. The receipt of other services should not be included.

2.16 HOW TO COMPLETE VAT RETURNS IF DISAGREEING WITH A DECISION OF HMRC

Where a business disagrees with a decision by HMRC on the VAT treatment of a supply, or on entitlement to input tax, it should still complete VAT returns in line with HMRC's decision. This applies even where

(*a*) HMRC have been asked to reconsider its decision (see 5.1 APPEALS);

(*b*) an appeal has been lodged to a VAT tribunal or higher court; or

(*c*) a decision is being awaited in an appeal by another business.

If returns are not completed in this way, HMRC may assess for the VAT underdeclared. If any such VAT proves to be due to HMRC, the business may also be liable to a misdeclaration penalty (see 52.10 PENALTIES).

It is important to register any claim against HMRC (even where (*b*) or (*c*) above applies) in writing. This action will preserve entitlement to a refund or payment of disputed VAT up to three years old should HMRC's decision be overturned. See 51.7–51.12 PAYMENT OF VAT.

Following any appeal to a VAT tribunal,

- *If the business is successful*, HMRC will give further advice on how to complete returns. The business may not be obliged to complete further returns in line with HMRC's over-ruled decision, but this will depend on the circumstances of the case and whether HMRC appeal to a higher court against the ruling.
- *If HMRC are successful*, the business should complete its returns in line with HMRC's earlier decision unless they advise otherwise. (This also applies to any businesses who have appealed to a tribunal on the same grounds or who have not appealed at all.)

Following any further appeal to the High Court,

- *If the business is successful*, HMRC will act in line with the court's ruling and review any assessment decision or claim registered by the business which the ruling affects. The business is no longer obliged to complete returns in line with HMRC's overturned decision and may be entitled to claim interest from HMRC.

  If HMRC decide to appeal against the ruling to a higher court, they will normally still pay the business any amounts (including interest) that arise from valid claims (subject to the three-year time limit). But if the higher court rules that HMRC's original decision was correct, the business must repay these amounts and HMRC may also charge default interest. For this reason, the business can ask HMRC to retain any payment due by way of a claim until the disputed decision is finally resolved in the courts. Then, if HMRC's original decision is overturned, the business can claim interest for the period it has been disadvantaged.
- *If HMRC are successful*, the business should complete returns in line with HMRC's earlier decision even if it decides to contest the decision to a higher court. (This applies also to those businesses who had appealed on the same grounds or have not appealed at all.)

(VAT Notice 700/45/02, paras 8.1–8.6).

2.17 INCORRECT AND INCOMPLETE RETURNS OR FAILURE TO MAKE A RETURN

Any error in accounting for VAT or in the return generally must be corrected as required by HMRC. [*SI 1995/2518, Reg 35*]. See 56.11 RECORDS.

The consequences of an incorrect return or failure to make a return are as follows.

- HMRC may assess the amount of VAT due to the best of their judgment (see 6.1 ASSESSMENTS). HMRC have indicated that incomplete or incorrect returns will be returned for correction. Traders classified as 'payment traders' will be assessed and the notice of assessment will accompany the rejected return with an error-return notice. For traders classified as 'repayment traders' the period will remain open until an acceptable return is received. Repayments will not be made until the error has been corrected.
- A VAT tribunal cannot normally entertain an appeal unless the appellant has submitted the relevant return and paid the VAT due (see 5.4 APPEALS).
- Criminal or civil penalties may be incurred for failure to comply with the necessary requirements. See 52 PENALTIES and particularly 52.10 for penalties for misdeclaration or neglect resulting from understatements or overclaims and 52.15 for default surcharge for failure to submit returns on time or pay the VAT due.

2.18 RETURNS BY PERSONS SELLING UNDER A POWER OF SALE

Where a business is carried on by a taxable person and goods forming part of the business are sold by another person under any power exercisable by him in satisfaction of a debt owed by the taxable person, the goods are deemed to be supplied by the taxable person in the course or furtherance of his business. Land forming part of the assets of the business is treated as if it were goods and any sale includes a reference to a grant or assignment of any interest in, right over or licence to occupy the land concerned.

The auctioneer (on a sale by auction) or the person selling the goods must, *whether or not registered*, within 21 days of the sale, send the VAT and a statement on Form VAT 833 to VAT Central Unit at Southend-on-Sea showing

- his name, address and registration number (if registered);
- the name, address and registration number of the taxable person;
- the date of sale;
- the description and quantity of goods sold at each rate of VAT; and
- the sales proceeds and the VAT charged at each rate.

The auctioneer or person selling the goods must also send a copy of the statement to the taxable person within the same time limit. Both parties must then exclude the VAT chargeable from their normal returns, if any. [*VATA 1994, Sch 4 paras 7, 9, Sch 11 para 2(12); SI 1995/2518, Reg 27*].

The auctioneer, etc must also issue a VAT invoice but giving the name, address and VAT registration number of the supplier. He need not be registered to issue it and should not ask the supplier for a VAT invoice.

This procedure does not normally apply to liquidators, administrative receivers or trustees in bankruptcy (see 36.1 INSOLVENCY), who continue to account for VAT in the normal way.

(VAT Notice 700, para 18.4).

De Voil Indirect Tax Service. See V5.142.

2.19 EC SALES LISTS

Under powers given to them in *VATA 1994, Sch 11 para 2(3)*, HMRC require a business registered for VAT in the UK which

- makes supplies of goods to traders registered for VAT in other EC countries,
- transfers its own goods from the UK to another EC country, or
- is the intermediary in triangular transactions between VAT-registered traders in other EC countries

to submit statements containing particulars of the transactions involved. Other EC countries have similar requirements. In the UK, these statements are known as EC sales lists (ESLs) but in other EC countries the forms are referred to as 'recapitulative statements' or 'summary statements'. The information provided is used to ensure that VAT has been correctly accounted for.

Penalties. See 52.18 and 52.19 PENALTIES respectively for inaccuracies in, and failure to submit, ESLs.

(VAT Notice 725, paras 14.2–14.4).

De Voil Indirect Tax Service. See V5.271.

2.20 Obtaining forms

A business will automatically be sent an ESL (Form VAT 101 or Welsh version VAT 101(W)) by HMRC if at any time it has completed Box 8 of its VAT return (total value of supplies of goods to other EC countries). The form is sent separately from the VAT return.

The form can also be obtained from the National Advice Service (tel: 0845 010 9000) or can be downloaded from the HMRC website at:

www.hmrc.gov.uk

The following can also be obtained from either of these sources.

- EC Sales List Continuation Sheet (Form 101A or Welsh version Form 101A(W)).
- EC Sales Correction Sheet (Form 101B or Welsh version Form 101B(W)).
- Helpful Hints VAT 101/VAT 101A for the completion of the ESL and Continuation Sheet.
- Helpful Hints VAT 101B for the completion of the ESL Correction Sheet.

(VAT Notice 725, paras 14.5, 14.6).

2.21 **Return periods and submission dates**

Subject to the exceptions below, every business which has, in any calendar quarter, made a supply of, or dispatched, transported or transferred, goods to a person registered in another EC country must submit an ESL within 42 days of the end of the quarter.

Exceptions. HMRC may vary the requirements to prepare ESLs as follows.

(*a*) *Monthly periods*. HMRC may allow a business to submit ESLs for monthly periods, in which case the ESL must be submitted within 42 days of the end of the calendar quarter in which the month occurs. Application to prepare monthly ESLs should be made to the National Advice Service.

(*b*) *Persons with low turnover*. Where a business satisfies HMRC that

(i) *either* at the end of any month the value of its taxable supplies in the period of one year then ending is less than the 'relevant figure' *or* at any time there are reasonable grounds for believing that the value of its taxable supplies in the period of one year beginning at that or any later time will not exceed the relevant figure, *and*

(ii) *either* at the end of any month the value of its supplies to persons registered in other EC countries in the period of one year then ending is less than £11,000 *or* at any time there are reasonable grounds for believing that the value of its supplies to such persons in the period of one year beginning at that or any later time will not exceed £11,000, *and*

(iii) it has not supplied a new means of transport (see 23.31 EUROPEAN COMMUNITY: SINGLE MARKET) to any person for the purpose of acquisition by that person in another EC country (in which case a quarterly return for the relevant quarter *must* be prepared)

HMRC may allow the business to submit an annual ESL. If so, full details of values of goods supplied to each EC customer need not be disclosed (see 2.22(*d*) below).

An annual ESL must be submitted within 42 days of the end of the year to which it relates.

'*Relevant figure*' is the compulsory VAT registration threshold (see 59.3 REGISTRATION) plus £25,500.

(*c*) *Businesses preparing annual VAT returns, etc.* Where HMRC have allowed a business to prepare VAT returns for periods longer than three months (ie normally annual returns but including any other non-standard return period) and the business satisfies HMRC that

(i) *either* at the end of any month, the value of its taxable supplies in the period of one year then ending is less than £145,000 *or* at any time there are reasonable grounds for believing that the value of its taxable supplies in the period of one year beginning at that or any later time will not exceed £145,000, *and*

(ii) *either* at the end of any month the value of its supplies to persons registered in other EC countries in the period of one year then ending is less than £11,000 *or* at any time there are reasonable grounds for believing that the value of its supplies to such persons in the period of one year beginning at that or any later time will not exceed £11,000, *and*

(iii) it has not supplied a new means of transport (see 23.31 EUROPEAN COMMUNITY: SINGLE MARKET) to any person for the purpose of acquisition by that person in another EC country (in which case a quarterly return for the relevant quarter *must* be prepared)

HMRC may allow the business to submit an ESL for the same period as its VAT return. The return must be submitted within 42 days of the end of the period for which the VAT return is required. Application to prepare such ESLs should be made to the National Advice Service.

(*d*) *Monthly or quarterly non-standard VAT periods.* If a business has agreed non-standard monthly or quarterly VAT return periods, it can apply to the National Advice Service for a similar concession for its ESLs. If agreed, the centrally issued ESLs will still show the standard period dates which should not be altered. ESLs must be submitted within 42 days of the end of the quarter.

Changing VAT periods. It is also possible for a business to change its VAT return period to coincide with the calendar quarterly ESL period. Application should be made to the National Registration Service.

[*SI 1995/2518, Regs 21, 22*(*1*)(*2*)(*6*)*; SI 1996/210*]. (VAT Notice 725, paras 14.7–14.9).

2.22 Information to be disclosed

Unless HMRC allow otherwise, the ESL must contain the following information.

(*a*) The name, address and VAT registration number of the taxable person. The prefix GB must be shown before the VAT registration number. (This is pre-printed on Form VAT 101.)

(*b*) The date of submission of the ESL and the last day of the period to which the ESL refers.

(*c*) A two-letter prefix code identifying the customer's country and the VAT registration number of each person acquiring, or deemed to have acquired, goods in the period. The codes are

Austria	AT
Belgium	BE
Cyprus	CY
Czech Republic	CZ
Denmark	DK
Estonia	EE
Finland	FI
France	FR
Germany	DE
Greece	EL
Hungary	HU
Ireland	IE
Italy	IT
Latvia	LV
Lithuania	LT

Luxembourg	LU
Malta	MT
Netherlands	NL
Poland	PL
Portugal	PT
Slovak Republic	SK
Slovenia	SI
Spain	ES
Sweden	SE

See 21.7–21.30 EUROPEAN COMMUNITY: GENERAL for the only acceptable format of EC VAT numbers in the various countries.

Where the VAT registration number in another EC country contains alphabetical as well as numerical characters, alphabetical characters should be underlined to reduce the possibility of misinterpretation.

(*d*) The 'total value' of the goods supplied in the period to each person in (*c*) above (rounded down to the nearest £). Where a business has been allowed to complete a simplified annual ESL under 2.21(*b*) above, the value of goods supplied does not have to be inserted. Instead, the figure '1' should be inserted in the value column.

'*Total value*' means the consideration for the supply including costs of any freight transport services and ancillary transport services (eg insurance) charged by the supplier of the goods to the customer.

The ESL should not include

- supplies to non-registered customers in other EC countries where the supplier is responsible for delivery (distance sales);
- supplies to registered customers in other EC countries where their VAT number is not known (and the supply has therefore been taxed);
- supplies of services only;
- goods sent for processing in another EC country;
- temporary movements of own goods to another EC country unless the conditions relating to the transfer change (see 23.24 EUROPEAN COMMUNITY: SINGLE MARKET); or
- details for the Canaries, Cyprus, the Channel Islands, Gibraltar, Malta, Norway or Switzerland, or any other countries which are outside the EC.

Credit notes. The value of any credit note should be deducted from the values of the supplies made to the customer. If this results in a negative value, the resulting negative figure should be included in brackets (and not with a minus sign).

Goods supplied free of charge. If a business supplies goods free of charge and they do not qualify as samples (see 47.8(23) OUTPUT TAX), there is a deemed supply of goods which must be included in the EC sales list at the cost of the goods to the business.

(*e*) If a business is an intermediary in a triangular transaction within the EC (see 23.22 EUROPEAN COMMUNITY: SINGLE MARKET), it must include the information under (*a*)–(*d*) above separately on a different line from the total of normal direct supplies to each EC customer. The figure '2' should be inserted in the indicator box on Form VAT 101 to show that the information describes triangular trade.

A business must complete an ESL even if its only EC supplies are triangular. It should contact the National Advice Service who will arrange for ESLs to be sent to the business automatically.

Continuation sheets (Form VAT 101A) are available from the National Advice Service (tel: 0845 010 9000). If required, the top of the form should be completed with the same pre-printed information that is shown on the Form VAT 101.

Nil returns. If no relevant intra-EC transaction has taken place during a return period, there is no need to submit a return and a penalty will not be imposed.

[*SI 1995/2518, Reg 21, Reg 22(3)(5); SI 1996/210*]. (VAT Notice 725, paras 14.11, 14.20, 14.25–14.28; Form VAT 101 Notes on Completion).

2.23 **Method of sending**

Form VAT 101. HMRC automatically send a Form VAT 101, separately from the VAT return, for use as an ESL where they have identified a business as being required to submit a return. On completion, it should be returned, again separately from the VAT return, in the white prepaid envelope marked 'ECSL'.

Electronic data interchange, etc. A business can submit its data electronically using a variety of transmission methods, including Value Added Networks (VANs), the public X400 facilities, port DTI communities and magnetic tape or diskette. Further details about electronic submission are available from the National Advice Service.

Plain paper returns. A business can submit ESLs on plain paper returns produced by its own computer provided it first obtains the agreement of the EASy Team in Southend. (This concession may be withdrawn when HMRC have developed an internet solution for the submission of ESLs.). The application, with an example of a plain paper ESL, should be sent to

HM Revenue and Customs
Plain Paper Unit
VCU EASy Team
7th Floor NW
Alexander House
Southend-on-Sea
SS99 1AA

Tel: 01702 366402

ESLs need to stand up to manual processing and microfilming procedures and are keyed at high speed. In order to be approved, plain paper ESLs must be very like the Forms VAT 101 and VAT 101A in style and format particularly in the following ways.

- There must be a space measuring at least 2 × 10 cms for microfilm purposes in the top right hand corner.
- The VAT registration number, the branch or subsidiary identifier and the calendar quarter must be in the same positions in relation to each other.

- There must be a space under the calendar quarter for VAT Central Unit to note the date when they receive the form.
- Each page must have a space to note the number of 'lines completed' on that individual page.
- The first page of the plain paper ESL must have spaces for the number of 'pages completed', for a declaration and for a contact's name and number.
- The paper must be plain, light coloured, A4 upright and weigh a minimum of $80g/m^2$ (ie the same quality as the Form VAT 101).
- The printing must be of better quality and on one side of the paper only.
- The typeface should be clear, no less than 12 point in size and with no more than ten characters per inch.
- There must be no more than 15 data lines per page and the data lines should be double spaced or, as on Form VAT 101, separated by lines across the page.
- There should be no upright dividing lines between digits.
- Continuation sheets must be very like the Form VAT 101A in layout.

(VAT Notice 725, paras 14.5, 14.13–14.15).

2.24 **Correction of errors**

Errors discovered by the business. HMRC must be informed of errors or omissions on an ESL where

- errors exceed £100;
- an incorrect VAT registration number has been quoted; or
- a business has incorrectly stated that its supplies to a customer were part of a triangular transaction.

Errors must be disclosed by completion of a Form VAT 101B obtainable from the National Advice Service (tel: 0845 010 9000). This form must be used whatever method is used to send in the ESL.

Help on the correction of errors is available from the ESL Correction Unit on 0151 703 8737/8789 or by e-mailing:

ESL.helpdesk@hmrc.gsi.gov.uk.

Errors discovered by HMRC. HMRC will notify a business of any errors that they identify on Form VAT 104 (EC Sales List Error Report). The form will show the error lines and the reasons for the errors. The errors must be corrected in the spaces provided and the form returned within 21 days of receipt to the address shown.

(VAT Notice 725, paras 14.19, 14.21).

2.25 **Branch and group registration**

Written application may be made for

- individual branches of a business, or
- individual companies within a group registration

to send in separate ESLs. Each branch or company must then use a separate three digit identifier when completing its own ESL.

Divisions of a company registered separately for VAT *must* send in separate ESLs.

(VAT Notice 725, para 14.22).

2.26 **Final statements**

A business which ceases to be registered for VAT under *VATA 1994, Sch 1* must submit a final ESL *unless* the registration is allocated to the purchaser on the transfer of a business as a going concern (see 59.36 REGISTRATION). Unless HMRC allow otherwise, the ESL must contain full information normally required and be submitted within 42 days of the date from which the VAT registration is cancelled. [*SI 1995/2518, Reg 23; SI 1996/210*].

2.27 **INTRASTAT**

Intrastat is the name given to the system for collecting statistics on the trade in goods between EC countries. Businesses which are not registered for VAT, and private individuals who move goods within the EC, have no obligations under the Intrastat system.

The statistics are collected from two sources.

(1) **The VAT return**

All VAT-registered businesses must complete Boxes 8 and 9 on the VAT return showing details of goods supplied to ('dispatches') and acquired from ('arrivals') other EC countries.

(2) **Supplementary declarations (SDs)**

If the annual value of intra-EC trade of a business is below the thresholds in the table below, it can be treated as supplying 'simplified information' to HMRC for Intrastat purposes and is not required to prepare SDs. The threshold separately applies to its

- dispatches of goods to other EC countries; and
- arrivals of goods from other EC countries.

HMRC can treat '*simplified information*' as being the value of supplies of goods (and related costs) to, and the value of acquisitions of goods (and related costs) from, other EC countries as collected on VAT returns.

Where the level of its dispatches or arrivals (or both) is above the threshold, the business must prepare SDs.

[*SI 1992/2790, Reg 3; SI 2000/3227; SI 2003/3131; SI 2004/3284*].

Calendar year	
2000–2003	£233,000
2004–2005	£221,000

Additionally, if a business is not required to provide SDs from the start of a **calendar year but the cumulative total of dispatches or arrivals from 1 January in the current calendar year exceeds the threshold for the current year, SDs must** be submitted for the rest of the calendar year, commencing with the month in which the threshold is reached. Under these circumstances, the business should inform HMRC in writing at HM Revenue and Customs, Statistics and Analysis of Trade Unit, Intrastat Team, 3rd Floor South East, Alexander House, 21 Victoria Avenue, Southend-on-Sea, Essex SS99 1AA, stating the month the threshold for dispatches or arrivals (or both) was exceeded.

For full details about the preparation of SDs, see Customs Notice 60.

3 Agents

Cross-references. See 11.6, 11.7 and 11.8 CATERING for catering in factories, hospitals and schools respectively supplied by agents.

De Voil Indirect Tax Service. See V3.221.

The contents of this chapter are as follows.

3.1 MEANING OF AGENT

There is no definition of 'agent' in the legislation. An agent is someone who acts for, or represents, someone else (the principal) in arranging supplies of goods and services. Supplies arranged by an agent are made by or to the principal represented. The principal cannot avoid any liability to account for VAT on supplies, or to pay VAT on purchases, by using an agent. However, whether or not a person is an agent for another person depends upon the actual arrangement between them and not simply upon the trading titles adopted. For example, 'motor agents and distributors' usually trade as principals and travel agents and employment agencies are not usually agents in all their activities. Solicitors and architects are normally principals but may occasionally arrange supplies as agents for their clients.

An agent/principal relationship exists if both parties agree that it does *and* the agent has agreed with the principal *to act on his behalf* in relation to the particular transaction concerned. The agreement may be written, oral or merely inferred from their general relationship and the way their business is conducted. Whatever form this relationship takes, the following conditions must be satisfied.

(*a*) It must always be clearly established between the agent and principal, and acceptable to HMRC, that the agent is arranging transactions for the principal, rather than trading on his own account.

(*b*) The agent must never be the owner of the goods or use any of the services bought or sold for the principal.

(*c*) The agent must not alter the nature or value of any of the supplies made between the principal and third parties.

(VAT Notice 700, para 22.2).

In *C & E Commrs v Johnson, QB [1980] STC 624 (TVC 1.1)* Woolf J took agency as the 'relationship which exists between two persons, one of whom expressly or impliedly consents that the other should represent him or act on his behalf and the other of whom similarly consents to represent the former or so to act'.

Whether acting as agent or principal — case law. For decisions in specific cases as to whether a person was acting as agent or principal see *JK Hill & Co v C & E Commrs, QB [1988] STC 424 (TVC 1.6)* (sales of craft pottery); *C & E Commrs v Paget and Another, QB [1989] STC 773 (TVC 1.56)*, *Flashlight Photography Ltd (VTD 9088)(TVC 65.46)* and *H Tempest Ltd (VTD 201)(TVC 65.22)* (school photographs—see also 20.18 EDUCATION); *C & E Commrs v Music & Video Exchange Ltd, QB [1992] STC 220 (TVC 1.7)* (second-hand musical equipment); *Bagshawe (JNS) and Walker (CAE) (VTD 1762)(TVC 1.2)* (art dealers); *National Bus Company (VTD 2530) (TVC 1.34)* (refreshments sold by hostesses on buses); *Dr R Nader (t/a Try Us) (VTD 4927)(TVC 1.4)* (meals delivered by taxi); *Prontobikes Ltd (VTD 13213) (TVC 1.26)* (motorcycle courier service); *Cornhill Management Ltd (VTD 5444)(TVC 1.8)* (company investing money deposited by clients); *LS & A International Ltd (VTD 3717) (TVC 1.14)* (purchases of paper); *Jocelyn Feilding Fine Arts Ltd (VTD 652)(TVC 58.7)* (auctioneers); *Leapmagic Ltd (VTD 6441)(TVC 60.253)* (hostesses at night club); and *Ivychain Ltd (VTD 5627)(TVC 60.285)* (service washes at launderette). For a fuller list, see Tolley's VAT Cases.

HMRC's approach to distinguishing agency. HMRC take the following approach to determine whether a business acts as agent or principal.

(1) Assemble a package of information including a copy of any written contract or agreement governing the conduct of the two parties (otherwise precise written details of what was agreed orally between the two parties); correspondence; normal commercial documentation (eg invoices, orders, statements, promotional and advertising material, and the profit and loss account and business accounts of both parties); and practical arrangements (eg receipt of payments, responsibility for bad debts, etc).

(2) Consider the written agreement between the two parties (if no written agreement exists, proceed directly to (3)). It must be clear from the reading of it that the parties have consented to act as agent and principal.

(3) Consider the following six indicating factors which are normally present in an agent/principal relationship.

- *Title*. This is the most important consideration when dealing with supplies of goods. In a true agency relationship, title always remains with the principal. The agent never assumes ownership of the principal's goods, but merely buys and sells them on the principal's behalf.

- *Identity*. The goods or services bought or sold by the agent on behalf of the principal must be clearly identifiable.

- *Value*. The principal must know the exact value at which goods or services have been bought or sold on his behalf and any discounts which the agent obtains must be passed back to the principal.

- *Separation*. The agreement between the parties must make it clear that a charge is to be made and establish the basis of its calculation. The value of the agent's service must be separately identifiable from the main supply and should normally be known to the principal (although the fact that the exact amount of the agent's commission is not disclosed to the principal would not, of itself, invalidate an agency arrangement).

- *No change*. The direction of the main supply between buyer and seller cannot be altered by the intervention of the agent.
- *Nature and value*. Agents cannot alter the nature or value of supplies which they arrange for their principal although the principal may give his authority for the agent to negotiate a different price.

If these indicating factors do not conclusively determine the VAT position, HMRC will look beyond the agreements and consider all the facts, including the trader's working practices, to reach a decision about agent/principal status.

(4) The double-check on consistency. Even if satisfied that a written agreement creates an agent/principal relationship, HMRC will examine the conduct of both parties to confirm that it remains in accordance with the agreement. If not, the agreement does not reflect reality and may be a facade to create an artificial impression of agency (although the onus is on HMRC to prove this).

(Internal Guidance V1–5, Chapter 2 para 2.8).

3.2 AGENTS AND VAT

An agent will usually be involved in at least two separate supplies at any one time.

- The supply of own services to the principal for which the agent charges a fee or commission.
- The supply made between the principal and the third party.

The VAT liability on the supply of agent's services will not necessarily be the same as the liability of the supply between the principal and the third party.

(VAT Notice 700, paras 22.3, 22.4).

Registration. In determining whether an agent is liable to be registered for VAT, turnover includes the value of services to the principal and the value of any supplies which the agent is treated as making through acting in his own name (see under 3.4 below). (VAT Notice 700, para 22.7).

3.3 Agents acting in the name of their principals

An agent may only take a minor role in a transaction and simply introduce the principal to potential clients or suppliers. Alternatively, the agent may be more closely involved and receive/deliver goods, make/receive payment and possibly hold stocks of goods on behalf of the principal. However, provided that the invoicing for the supply is between the principal and the customer, the only VAT supply made by the agent is the provision of services to the principal. (VAT Notice 700, para 22.5).

3.4 Agents acting in their own name (undisclosed agents)

An agent may be empowered by a principal to enter into contracts with a third party on behalf of the principal. In such cases, particularly where the principal wishes to remain unnamed or undisclosed, the agent may receive and issue invoices in his own name for the supplies concerned. In such circumstances, although in commercial terms the transaction remains between the principal and third party, for VAT purposes special rules apply as set out below. (VAT Notice 700, para 22.6).

Goods. Where an agent acts in his own name in relation to a supply and either

(*a*) goods are imported from outside the EC by a taxable person who supplies them as agent for a non-taxable person, or (*b*) goods are acquired from another EC country by a non-taxable person and a taxable person acts as agent in relation to the acquisition, and then supplies the goods as agent for that non-taxable person, or

(*c*) where neither (*a*) nor (*b*) above applies in relation to a supply, goods are supplied through an agent

then the goods *must* be treated, as the case may be, as imported and supplied by the agent, acquired and supplied by the agent or supplied to and by the agent as principal. For these purposes, a person who is not resident in the UK and whose place (or principal place) of business is outside the UK may be treated as being a non-taxable person if as a result he will not be required to be registered under *VATA 1994*. [*VATA 1994, s 47(1)(2)(2A); FA 1995, s 23*].

Accounting for VAT

- *Non-EC and intra-EC supplies.* In order to put the VAT treatment of UK undisclosed agents on the same footing as that for commissionaires elsewhere in the EC, an undisclosed agent who is involved in non-EC or intra-EC supplies is seen as taking a full part in the underlying supply of any goods. There is no separate supply of the agent's own services to his principal and the commission retained is seen as subsumed in the value of the onward underlying supply. This treatment is for VAT purposes only and has no impact on the legal status of agents or the way in which they are treated for the purposes of other taxes or legislation.

Example

A UK undisclosed agent sells goods to final customer for £100. He retains £20 as commission and pays £80 back to his overseas principal. All figures are net of VAT.

If the goods are imported, the VAT value at importation is arrived at in the normal way. If the goods are acquired from a principal in another EC country, the VAT value at acquisition is £80 based on the value of the invoice raised by the principal to the agent. The agent must account for VAT on the acquisition.

The agent can recover import/acquisition VAT, subject to the normal rules. He then makes an onward supply in his own name to the customer for £100, and accounts for output tax. The commission of £20 is treated as subsumed in the value of the onward supply of the goods and is not treated as a separate supply of own services to the non-UK principal.

Cost incurred in the UK (eg warehousing and handling) can be treated as supplied to the agent who can recover the input tax on them (subject to the normal rules).

- *Domestic supplies.* Subject to below, there is an underlying supply between the principal and customer and a separate supply of agent's services to the principal. The agent reclaims input tax and must account for output tax on the supply of the goods but as the nature or value of the supply is unchanged the amount of input and output tax is normally the same. The deemed supplies to and by the agent are simultaneous and he cannot reclaim the input tax on the supply to him in one period but defer the time when he is required to account for output tax to a later period in which he invoices the supply made by him (*Metropolitan Borough of Wirral v C & E Commrs, QB [1995] STC 597 (TVC 1.64)*). The VAT liability of the supply of agent's services is not necessarily the same as the liability of the supply of goods.

However, if he wishes, an undisclosed agent may also adopt the VAT treatment set out above for non-EC and intra-EC supplies for his domestic transactions.

Services. Where an agent who acts in his own name arranges a supply of taxable services and both the agent and supplier are registered for VAT, HMRC *may*, if they think fit, treat the supply both as a supply to the agent and by the agent. [*VATA 1994, s 47(3); FA 1995, s 23*]. (VAT Notice 700, para 22.6).

Accounting for VAT

- *International supplies of services.* In order to put the VAT treatment of UK undisclosed agents on the same footing as that for commissionaires elsewhere in the EC, where an agent is involved in international services the services are treated as supplied to the UK agent as though he was a principal and supplied on by him. The agent's commission is seen as subsumed in the value of the onward supply and he is not regarded as making a separate supply of his own services to the principal. This applies to services being supplied both to and from the UK.

  Where the international services are treated as supplied where the supplier belongs, as a UK undisclosed agent is treated as the supplier, the supply takes place in the UK and will be subject to UK VAT. For international services listed in *VATA 1994, Sch 5* which are treated as supplied where the customer belongs (see 64.26 SUPPLY), a UK undisclosed agent is treated as receiving the supplies and must therefore account for VAT under the reverse charge. The agent then makes an onward supply in the UK and accounts for output tax in the normal way.

- *Domestic supplies.* Subject to below, there is an underlying supply between the principal and customer and a separate supply of agent's services to the principal. The agent reclaims input tax and must account for output tax on the supply of the main services but as the nature or value of the supply is unchanged the amount of input and output tax is normally the same. The deemed supplies to and by the agent are simultaneous and he cannot reclaim the input tax on the supply to him in one period but defer the time when he is required to account for output tax to a later period in which he invoices the supply made by him (*Metropolitan Borough of Wirral v C & E Commrs, QB [1995] STC 597 (TVC 1.64)*). The VAT liability of the supply of agent's services is not necessarily the same as the liability of the supply of the main services.

  However, if he wishes, an undisclosed agent may also adopt the VAT treatment set out above for international supplies of services for his domestic supplies.

Second-hand goods. Where any supplies by an agent acting in his own name are eligible goods under one of the second-hand goods schemes, the agent may be able to include the value of services to the principal (ie commission, etc) in calculating the VAT due. All the conditions of the scheme must be satisfied. See 61 SECOND-HAND GOODS for full details.

Supplies for travellers. The above arrangements cannot be used for supplies which are for the benefit of travellers (eg supplies of accommodation or passenger transport).

(VAT Notice 700, paras 22.6, 24.1, 24.2; Business Brief 9/2000; VAT Information Sheet 3/00).

De Voil Indirect Tax Service. See V3.423.

3.5 Invoices for supplies made through a selling agent not using a margin scheme

Where an agent is registered for VAT and is acting in his own name, the procedure outlined in 3.4 above may be used. Otherwise, if the principal is registered for VAT either the principal must issue a VAT invoice to the agent or the agent can use the self-billing procedure (see 40.6 INVOICES). The agent must account for output tax on his onward supply to his customer and, if the customer is registered, issue a VAT invoice to him.

Where an agent is acting in the name of his principal, the procedures depend upon whether or not the principal is registered for VAT.

- If the principal is registered for VAT, the principal must issue the invoice made out to the customer. This can be issued direct to the customer or can be passed to the agent for onward transmission. If the agent is VAT-registered, he need only account for VAT on services to the principal.
- If the principal is not registered for VAT, no VAT is due on the supply arranged by the agent.

A registered agent must account for output tax on his supply of services to the principal. The agent must also have evidence that he is arranging the supply on behalf of the principal and the supply should be readily distinguishable in his records from supplies on which VAT is charged. The evidence may be a standing agreement between agent and principal or a signed declaration from the principal giving his name and address and confirming that he is not a registered person making a supply in the course of business.

(VAT Notice 700, para 23.1).

3.6 Invoices for supplies obtained through a buying agent not using a margin scheme

Where an agent is registered for VAT and is acting in his own name, the procedure outlined in 3.4 above may be used. Otherwise, if the supplier is registered for VAT, the supplier must issue a VAT invoice to the agent who may reclaim the VAT as input tax. The agent must account for output tax on his onward supply to the buyer and, if the buyer is registered, issue a VAT invoice to him. The principal (the buyer) should be able to know the price paid by his agent in obtaining the supply.

Where an agent is acting in the name of his principal, the procedures depend upon whether or not the supplier is registered for VAT.

- If the supplier is registered, the supplier should issue the VAT invoice made out to the principal. This can be issued direct to the principal or can be passed to the agent for onward transmission. If the agent is VAT-registered, he need only account for VAT on services to the principal.
- If the supplier is not registered for VAT, no VAT is due on the supply arranged by the agent. A registered agent must account for output tax on his supply of services to the principal.

(VAT Notice 700, para 23.2).

3.7 DISBURSEMENTS

Where a supplier incurs incidental costs (eg travelling expenses, postage, telephone) in the course of making the supply and charges these items separately on the invoice to the client, such costs must be included in the value when VAT is calculated. See *Rowe & Maw v C & E Commrs, QB [1975] STC 340 (TVC 60.44)* (travelling expenses billed by solicitors to client), *Shuttleworth & Co (VTD 12805) (TVC 60.307)* (bank transfer fees re-charged to client) and *National Transit Insurance Co Ltd v C & E Commrs, QB 1974, [1975] STC 35 (TVC 1.71)* (fee for handling insurance claim). However, where amounts are paid to third parties as agent of a client, such payments may be treated as disbursements if all the following conditions are satisfied.

(*a*) The agent acted for his client when paying the third party.

(*b*) The client actually received and used the goods or services provided by the third party. This condition usually prevents the agent's own travelling expenses, telephone bills, postage, etc being treated as disbursements for VAT purposes.

(*c*) The client was responsible for paying the third party.

(*d*) The client authorised the agent to make the payment on his behalf.

(*e*) The client knew that the goods or services would be provided by a third party.

(*f*) The agent's outlay must be separately itemised when invoicing the client.

(*g*) The agent must recover only the exact amount he paid to the third party.

(*h*) The goods or services paid for must be clearly additional to the supplies made to the client.

If a payment qualifies as a disbursement, it can be treated in either of the following ways.

- The disbursement can be passed on to the client as a VAT-inclusive amount (if taxable) and excluded when calculating any VAT due on the main supply to the client. The agent cannot reclaim VAT on the supply (since no goods or services have been supplied to him). Unless the VAT invoice for the disbursement is addressed directly to the client, the client is also prevented from reclaiming input tax as he does not hold a valid invoice. Generally, therefore, it is only advantageous to treat a disbursement in this way if no VAT is chargeable on the supply by the third party or the client is not entitled to reclaim the VAT.

  If an agent does treat a payment as a disbursement in this way, he must keep evidence to enable him to show that he was entitled to exclude the payment from the value of his supply to his client. He must also be able to show that he did not reclaim input tax on the supply by the third party.

- The goods or services can be treated as supplied to and by the agent under 3.4 above. The agent can then reclaim the related input tax (subject to the normal rules) and charge VAT on the onward supply if appropriate.

(VAT Notice 700, para 25.1).

Disbursements in particular cases

(1) *Counsel's fees.* A concessionary treatment has been agreed with HMRC for counsel's fees. The agent (usually a solicitor or accountant) may treat the counsel's advice as supplied directly to the client and the settlement of the fees as a disbursement. Counsel's VAT invoice may be amended by adding the name

and address of the client to it and inserting 'per' before the agent's own name and address. The fee note from counsel will then be recognised as a valid VAT invoice in the hands of the client. Where the agent considers that the services of counsel, if supplied directly to the client, would be outside the scope of UK VAT, he may certify the counsel's fee note to this effect and pay the counsel only the net of VAT fee. (Tax Faculty of the ICAEW Guidance Notes 15/94, paras 23–26).

(2) *Debt collectors.* See 3.16 below.

(3) *Estate agents.* Estate agents often separately itemise their costs when they prepare an invoice for the vendor on whose behalf they act. Such costs might include photographs, advertising, provision of notice boards, etc. However, these cannot be treated as disbursements as they are received and used by the estate agent, not by the client. In particular, commercial estate agents may obtain printed brochures giving details of their clients' property. The supply to the estate agent may be zero-rated as printed matter, but that supply is used by the estate agent to help procure a sale, and must therefore be passed on with VAT when the charge to the vendor is made.

(4) *MOT tests.* See 47.8(13) OUTPUT TAX.

(5) *Postal charges.* See 47.8(18) OUTPUT TAX.

(6) *Private investigators.* Where private investigators incur expenses for items such as travel, postage, or the swearing of an oath in the presence of a solicitor, the supply is to them, not to their client. They must therefore include these costs in the value of their supply and charge VAT accordingly. However, where private investigators pay 'conduct money' to meet the expenses of witnesses attending court, this represents the refunding of the cost of supplies which were made direct to those witnesses. Private investigators therefore act as agent for the client in paying this conduct money, and can treat the payment as a disbursement, provided that they only recover from the client the exact amount which was paid to the witness. (Internal Guidance V1–5, Chapter 2 para 2.16).

(7) *Search agencies.* See 3.17 below.

(8) *Solicitors.* The following charges are usually eligible to be treated as disbursements by solicitors on behalf of their clients.

- Statutory charges such as court fees, estate duty, incorporation fees, probate fees, stamp duty, etc. In such cases, the supply by the statutory body is to the client who has the statutory liability.
- Charges for the professional services of a third party. For example, on the sale of a property a solicitor normally presents a bill to the vendor for both his own services and the commission payable to the estate agent. The supply of the estate agent's services is to the vendor, not the solicitor, and so the solicitor may treat this as a disbursement for VAT purposes. The fees of notaries, surveyors, or witnesses, and charges for police and medical reports may also fall into this category.
- Postal search fees. In agreement with the Law Society, where a solicitor pays a fee for a *postal* search, this may be treated as a disbursement as the solicitor merely obtains a document on behalf of the client (whether the solicitor passes the document obtained from a postal search to a Building Society or bank or to the client direct). Where a solicitor pays a fee for a *personal* search of official records (such as are held by local authorities) in

order to extract information needed to advise the client, this cannot be treated as a disbursement for VAT purposes. The fee is charged for the supply of access to the official record and it is the solicitor rather than the client who receives that service.

- Fees for office copy entries on the land register. Where a vendor's solicitor obtains an office copy entry of his client's title from the Land Registry and recharges the fee to his client, he may treat it as a disbursement. If the cost of the office copy entry is passed on to the purchaser's solicitor who, in turn, charges his client, the fee would not be eligible for treatment as a disbursement since it would not meet the above requirements.
- Accommodation and/or transport provided by the client at his own expense. Where a solicitor incurs accommodation and/or travelling expenses in the course of a taxable supply of legal services to a client, the charge made to the client for such expenses is part of the consideration for the supply of those services and must be included in the value for VAT. Where, however, clients provide accommodation and/or transport necessary for the performance of a solicitor's services at their own expense, the cost of these items will not be included in any account rendered by the solicitor. In such circumstances, it has been agreed with the Law Society that HMRC will not seek to include the value of these items as part of the consideration for the solicitor's supply. This agreement also extends to the situation where a solicitor has his client's authority to use money being held for the client to obtain such incidentals of transport and/or accommodation.

Charges *not eligible* for disbursement treatment include

- charges from third parties which were actually incurred for the solicitor's own purposes (eg telegraphic transfer fees or CHAPS fees, see *Shuttleworth & Co* above); and
- general expenses (eg travel (see *Rowe & Maw* above), accommodation, and telephone and telex charges) borne by a solicitor or his staff (but see above where travel and accommodation expenses are provided to solicitors by clients at their own expense).

(Internal Guidance V1–5, Chapter 2 paras 2.17, 2.17.1; V1–12, para 7.21).

3.8 VAT REPRESENTATIVES AND AGENTS FOR OVERSEAS PRINCIPALS

Direction to appoint by HMRC. HMRC may direct a person to appoint a VAT representative to act on his behalf for VAT purposes in the UK where that person

(*a*) is a taxable person or, without being a taxable person, makes taxable supplies or acquires goods in the UK from one or more other EC countries;

(*b*) is not established, and does not have a 'fixed establishment', in the UK;

(*c*) is established in a country or territory

- which is neither an EC country nor part of such a country; and
- with which it appears to HMRC that there is no provision for mutual assistance similar in scope to the assistance provided between the UK and other EC countries under *FA 2002, s 134* and *Sch 39* (recovery of VAT due in other EC countries, see 17.2 CUSTOMS: POWERS), *FA 2003, s 197* (exchange of information between tax authorities of EC countries, see

15.7 CUSTOMS: ADMINISTRATION) and *EC Council Regulation 1798/2003* (on administrative co-operation in the field of VAT); and

(*d*) in the case of an individual, does not have his 'usual place of residence' in the UK.

See 64.19 SUPPLY for a consideration of where a business is established, 'fixed establishment' and 'usual place of residence'.

A person is treated as having been directed to appoint a VAT representative if HMRC have served notice of the direction on him or have taken all such other steps as appear to them to be reasonable to bring the direction to his attention.

Voluntary appointment. A person who has not been directed by HMRC to appoint a VAT representative to act on his behalf under the above provisions, but who satisfies the conditions in (*a*), (*b*) and (*d*) above, may with the agreement of HMRC appoint a VAT representative to act on his behalf.

[*VATA 1994, s 48(1)(1A)(1B)(2)(2A)(8); FA 2001, s 100; FA 2003, s 197; SI 2003/3092*].

3.9 **Effect of appointment**

Subject to below, any person appointed as a VAT representative

- is entitled to act on his principal's behalf for all purposes relating to VAT;
- must ensure (if necessary by acting on his behalf) that his principal complies with, and discharges, all his obligations and liabilities relating to VAT; and
- is jointly and severally liable with his principal for complying with UK VAT law.

A VAT representative is not, by virtue of the above, guilty of any offence committed by his principal unless he has consented to it or connived in its commission, its commission is attributable to any neglect on his part, or the offence is a contravention by the VAT representative of an obligation which, under those provisions, is imposed on both him and his principal.

[*VATA 1994, s 48(3)(5)*].

3.10 **Failure to appoint a VAT representative**

Where a person fails to appoint a VAT representative when directed to do so, HMRC may require him to provide such security, or further security, as they think appropriate for the payment of any VAT which is or may become due from him. A person is treated as having been required to provide security if HMRC have served notice of the requirement on him or have taken all such other steps as appear to them to be reasonable for bringing the requirement to his attention. Where any such security has been required and is not lodged, it can be recovered by distraint on goods (in Scotland through diligence) as if it were VAT due. See 17.4 and 17.5 CUSTOMS: POWERS. There may also be a liability to a criminal penalty under 52.6 PENALTIES. [*VATA 1994, s 48(7)(7A)(8), Sch 11 para 5(10); FA 1997, s 53(6)*].

3.11 **Notification of appointment and changes**

Any person appointed a VAT representative of another must notify his appointment to HMRC on the appropriate form within 30 days of the appointment first becoming effective. Evidence of the appointment must also be sent. The principal being represented must complete the normal VAT registration forms (Form VAT 1 and, if a partnership, Form VAT 2) and both the principal and tax representative must complete a Form VAT 1TR (or Welsh version Form VAT 1TR(W)) authorising HMRC to accept that the representative is acting on the principal's behalf. HMRC must then register the name of the VAT representative against that of his principal in the register kept for the purposes of *VATA 1994*.

Once appointed, the VAT representative must, within 30 days, notify HMRC in writing of any changes in the name, constitution or ownership of his business or of his ceasing to act as his principal's VAT representative or of any other event which would require a change in the register.

The date of cessation is the earliest of the times when

- HMRC receive notification from the principal of the cessation of the existing tax representative or the appointment of a different tax representative,
- HMRC receive notification of the appointment of a different tax representative or the cessation of the existing tax representative under the above provisions, or
- a tax representative dies, becomes insolvent or becomes incapacitated (which, in the case of a company, includes going into liquidation or receivership or administration)

although if HMRC has received no notification but another person has actually been appointed as VAT representative, HMRC may treat the date of cessation of the existing tax representative as being the date of appointment of that other person.

[*SI 1995/2518, Reg 10; SI 2003/2096, Art 57*].

3.12 **Records to be kept**

Although his principal is established abroad, a VAT representative must keep all the RECORDS (56) required to be kept under UK law as the principal is making taxable supplies in the UK. The VAT representative must set up and maintain a separate VAT account for each principal represented and keep documents such as VAT invoices to show how the VAT account is built up.

3.13 **EMPLOYMENT BUREAUX**

The bureau will act in one of the following ways.

(*a*) **As a principal**, supplying its own staff to the client. Workers may be employed by the bureau under a contract of service or may be self-employed and engaged by the bureau under a contract for services. In either case, they supply their services to the bureau which makes an onward supply as principal to the client. There is a continuing contractual relationship between bureau and worker which will be reflected in both the promotional literature (which may use terms such as 'our staff') and the agreement between bureau and client. The client is charged an overall sum by the bureau and is thus not aware of what proportion of this charge is retained by the worker. See, for example, *MG Parkinson (VTD 6017)(TVC 31.3)*.

The bureau makes one supply of staff which is normally standard-rated. Output tax is due on the full charge made to the client. Where the client asks the bureau to act on its behalf in paying the travelling and subsistence expenses of candidates attending interviews, the bureau may treat these payments as disbursements for VAT purposes under 3.7 above. But where expenses are paid to interview candidates from within the bureau's agreed commission, these may not be treated as disbursements.

3.13 Agents

The *Conduct of Employment Agencies and Employment Business Regulations 2003*, made by the Department of Trade and Industry and applying with effect from 6 July 2004, set out new rules governing the conduct of employment businesses and the rights of workers using them. Under normal circumstances *any* temporary workers supplied by an employment bureau will have a contractual relationship with the bureau supplying them (either being an employee of the bureau under a contract of service or self-employed and engaged by the agency under a contract for services) and not the client hiring them. In either case, the bureau will be acting as a principal for VAT purposes and VAT will be due on the full amount received from the client, including salary and associated costs in relation to the temporary worker.

HMRC have announced that it will carry out a review of the impact of the *Regulations* on the VAT treatment of employment agencies and employment businesses. The review will not commence until 18 months after the DTI regulations came into effect on 6 July 2004. Until the review is completed, the staff hire concession (which allows employment bureau hiring out its own staff not to charge VAT on salary costs if the client pays the staff direct, see 44.4 MANAGEMENT SERVICES AND SUPPLIES OF STAFF for details) will continue to apply. (Business Brief 2/04).

HMRC also intend to introduce an ESC to coincide with the introduction of revised treatment which will allow all businesses providing *home care services* to exclude the salary and related costs (NI contributions, pension costs, etc) of home care workers from the value of their supplies. This will allow agencies providing home care to charge VAT only on their commission. To qualify for the concession, businesses must retain evidence that the client was in need of the services provided. The concession will apply to home care services where there is a risk to the recipients' physical or mental health or welfare because they are unable to carry out domestic or personal tasks safely or adequately, or without significant pain or discomfort. The concession will cover personal care, such as bathing, as well as practical tasks such as house cleaning. The scope of the concession will be consistent with the existing VAT relief for home care provided by charities (see 12.11 CHARITIES). (Business Brief 3/2000).

(*b*) **As agent for the client**, finding workers who enter into a direct contractual relationship with the client. The only document prepared for the worker's benefit is one by which control is passed over to the client. After that, the bureau takes its introductory fee and, where it has supplied permanent staff, ends its involvement. Where it has supplied temporary staff, the bureau may agree, for the sake of convenience, to pay the wages of the worker on the employer's behalf.

In this situation, the continuing contractual relationship is between the bureau and the client which will make clear that the worker is employed by the client, and that the client must therefore bear all the obligations of an employer. If the bureau has assumed responsibility for paying the worker's wages, a specific clause of the agreement should make clear that this is a service performed for the employer, not a part of the bureau's normal responsibilities. All parties (worker, bureau, and employer) must be fully aware of how much is paid to the worker, and how much commission is retained by the bureau.

The bureau must account for VAT on the commission charged to the client. Any payments of a worker's wages by the bureau are made on behalf of the client and may be treated as disbursements by the bureau under 3.7 above.

HMRC have confirmed that there will be no change to the above arrangements until such time as they have completed their review (see (*a*) above), even though the *Regulations* may mean that a bureau is, in reality, acting as principal. (Business Brief 10/04).

(*c*) **As agent for the worker**, finding employment openings for the worker who then enters directly into a contractual relationship with his or her new employer. (Note that social legislation prohibits most bureaux from making charges to employees. One exception where charges can be made is to fashion models.) The main indicator of this situation is that the continuing contractual relationship is between the bureau and the worker. This should be clearly stated in the agreement between them and reflected in the agreement between bureau and client. The bureau may collect the worker's wages and deduct its agency commission at source, passing the balance to the worker, but the agreement must clearly state that this is the worker's money and the bureau is merely acting on his or her behalf.

Output tax is due only on the commission charged to the worker for the bureau's supply of services. Where the worker is not registered for VAT, the bureau must not issue VAT invoices or charge VAT for the supplies made by the worker to the client. However, some workers may be registered for VAT and in such cases the bureau may issue VAT invoices on their behalf under the provisions in *VATA 1994, s 47(3)* (see 3.4 above). This applies mainly to fashion models, where social legislation does not prevent the bureau charging a commission to the worker and where earnings are more likely to be high enough to exceed the VAT registration threshold.

(*d*) **As agent for both the employer and the worker**, supplying its agency service to both parties. Once it has brought the parties together, it usually withdraws and the continuing contractual relationship is directly between worker and employer. This situation is comparatively rare but does occur with medical agencies. The indicators to look for will be a combination of those in (*b*) and (*c*) above.

VAT must be accounted for on the bureau's charges made to both parties, although, where this situation occurs, the bureau normally only charges commission to the employer and the supply to the worker is made for no consideration.

Determining which of (*a*)-(*d*) above applies to a particular bureau will depend upon the facts derived from documentation and bureau's working practices. Relevant documentation includes

- advertising, marketing and promotional material used to attract the worker and the employer to the bureau;
- the agreement ('terms and conditions') between the worker and the bureau (including scales of pay) and the agreement between the bureau and the employer (including scales of charges);
- time-sheets and pay-slips; and
- invoices raised to the client.

(VAT Notice 700/34/05, para 3.9; Internal Guidance V1–5, Chapter 3, paras 3.21–3.23, Appendix K).

3.14 TRAVEL AGENCIES

How a travel agency accounts for VAT depends upon its relationship with the customer. It may act in either of the following ways.

(*a*) **As a principal**, ie supplying travel packages (including transport or accommodation), part of which is bought in from other businesses, although part of which may be supplied in-house from own resources. The travel agency must be able to demonstrate this, normally by holding commercial documentary evidence (eg an agreement or contract). In these circumstances, the agency must account for VAT using the TOUR OPERATORS' MARGIN SCHEME (66).

(*b*) **In its own name**, ie the ultimate provider of the goods or services (eg the travel or accommodation provider) remains undisclosed to the customer. Again the travel agency must be able to demonstrate this, normally by holding commercial documentary evidence (eg an agreement or contract). In these circumstances, the travel agency must account for VAT on its commission (profit margin) under the TOUR OPERATORS' MARGIN SCHEME (66).

(*c*) **As an agent, ie intermediary**. A travel agency will be acting as an intermediary if

- both the travel agency and its principal have agreed that it will act as their intermediary (agent). The travel agency must be able to demonstrate this, normally by holding commercial documentary evidence (eg agreement or contract);
- it routinely fully discloses the name of the principal it is acting for (eg on all tickets it issues or in its booking terms and conditions); and
- it is not taking any significant commercial risk in relation to the services it is arranging.

As an intermediary, the value of a travel agency's supplies upon which any VAT may be due is the amount of commission due from its principal, or any fee that it charges, excluding any VAT itself. It is the travel agency's responsibility to issue invoices for its supplies, although it is common practice in the travel industry for tour operators to use a self-billing system (see 40.6 INVOICES).

Place of supply of services. Once it is established that a travel agency is acting as an intermediary, it is then necessary to determine whether the place of supply of its services is in the UK. For a detailed consideration of the place of supply of services generally, see 64.18–64.31 SUPPLY. If the place of supply of the services is outside the UK, the services are outside the scope of UK VAT, although if the place of supply is in another EC country

- the travel agency may be liable to register and account for VAT in that country; or
- if its principal is registered for VAT in a different EC country to the travel agency, the principal may be responsible for accounting for the VAT under the 'reverse charge' procedure. See 39.4 INTERNATIONAL SERVICES.

Insurance and financial services. If a travel agency makes arrangements for the supply of insurance or makes a charge for exchanging currency or travellers' cheques, the place of supply of services is

- where the customer belongs if the customer belongs outside the EC or in another EC country and receives the supply of services for business purposes; and
- where the travel agency belongs in all other cases.

Where the place of supply is in the UK,

- any charges for exchanging currency are exempt under *VATA 1994, Sch 9 Group 5 Item 1* (see 27.8 FINANCIAL SERVICES); and
- the supply of arranging travel insurance is exempt if supplied
  - (i) in isolation of any travel; or
  - (ii) in relation to a supply of travel on which no UK VAT is payable; or
  - (iii) in relation to a sale of travel services which bears UK VAT provided that the travel agent notifies the traveller, in writing, of the price of the insurance as due under the contract of insurance *and* any fee related to that insurance charged over and above the premium.

  See 37.17 INSURANCE.

Passenger transport services. If a travel agency acts as the *initial* intermediary in arranging zero-rated passenger transport, such as

- scheduled flights,
- journeys from a place within to a place outside the UK and vice versa, and
- most UK transport in vehicles with a carrying capacity of not less than ten people

then its services of arranging the transport are also zero-rated.

See 68.14 to 68.23 TRANSPORT AND FREIGHT for a more detailed consideration of passenger transport and 68.30 TRANSPORT AND FREIGHT for services of agents in providing transport generally.

Designated travel services. If a travel agency is acting as an intermediary for a tour operator who is established (or has a fixed establishment) in the UK, then its services are standard-rated.

Sub-agents. If a travel agency is acting as a sub-agent (ie is an intermediary acting for another intermediary), then its services which are supplied in the UK are standard-rated.

Recovering input tax. Where a travel agency is acting as an intermediary, it can normally reclaim VAT, subject to the normal rules, which is chargeable and invoiced to it by UK VAT-registered suppliers if it relates to

- taxable (including zero-rated) supplies;
- supplies made outside the UK that would have been taxable (including zero-rated) if made in the UK; or
- supplies of services to a person who belongs outside the EC, or the making of arrangements for such supplies, provided that the supply is an

exempt insurance service or certain specified exempt financial service, or would have been if made in the UK.

(VAT Notice 709/6/02).

3.15 AUCTIONEERS

Agent or principal. The main activity of an auctioneer is to act as agent for the vendor of the goods and arrange for a sale to be made to the highest bidder. However, an auctioneer occasionally acts as principal and buys and sells goods in his own right. The key to distinguishing agent and principal activities is that only when title to the goods has passed to the auctioneer does the auctioneer become a principal.

Adopting uncollected goods. An auctioneer who adopts uncollected goods acts as a principal rather than as agent. This usually occurs because an auctioneer pays vendors the net proceeds of the sale before the end of the period in which the purchaser must pay for those goods and collect them. Where the purchaser does not collect and pay for those goods, the auctioneer adopts them at the price realised on the abortive sale. On a subsequent sale, the auctioneer must account for VAT on the full sale price unless the goods are being sold under one of the second-hand schemes (see below).

Accounting for VAT. The rules in 3.2–3.7 above apply to auctioneers if they offer goods for sale as agents of the seller. If an auctioneer issues an invoice for goods or demands payment in his own name, the goods are treated as supplied to the auctioneer by the vendor and by the auctioneer to the buyer. The auctioneer is liable to account for VAT on the supply of the goods (regardless of the VAT status of the vendor) as well as on the commission charged to the seller and, if applicable, on any fee charged to the buyer (the 'buyer's premium'). However, where an auctioneer arranges supplies of second-hand goods, works of art or collectors' items, he may be able to use the special accounting scheme for auctioneers. This scheme allows auctioneers to calculate their VAT on a margin basis. The margin on such sales is normally equal to the commission and associated charges and the amount of output tax due is largely unchanged in comparison to supplies by auctioneers made before that date. See 61.53 SECOND-HAND GOODS for further details.

(VAT Notice 700, para 25.2; Internal Guidance V1–5, Chapter 3 para 3.5).

See 2.18 ACCOUNTING PERIODS AND RETURNS where an auctioneer arranges sales of goods in satisfaction of a debt (eg under a court order) of a registered person and the goods sold are part of the debtor's business assets. The procedures outlined above for agents must not be followed.

3.16 DEBT COLLECTION AGENCIES

The following VAT treatment applies to debt collectors who act as agents.

(*a*) **Court fees**. Amounts paid by collectors to solicitors in respect of court fees may be treated as disbursements on behalf of the creditor. Any amount recovered from debtors in respect of such fees and retained by collectors may then be regarded as reimbursement of the amount disbursed and outside the scope of VAT.

(*b*) **Legal fees**. Two options are open to collectors in respect of VAT charged by solicitors for their services.

- Collectors may choose not to recover the VAT as input tax and treat the charges as disbursements under 3.7 above. If so, where the agreement with the creditor provides that the collector bears the cost of solicitors' services but may retain, as reimbursement of his costs, any amounts recovered from the debtor in respect of solicitors' scale charges awarded by the court, such amounts may be treated as outside the scope of VAT.

- Collectors may choose to recover the VAT as input tax, subject to the normal rules, but recharge the legal fees, plus VAT, to the creditor under *VATA 1994, s 47(3)* (see 3.4 above). The scale charges retained represent payment of the fees recharged.

If a debt collector considers that he is acting as a principal, any VAT charged to him by a solicitor is recoverable as input tax, subject to the normal rules. However, any amounts recovered by the collector from the debtor in respect of court fees and/or solicitors' scale charges and retained represents consideration for the collector's supply of services to the creditor. Output tax must be accounted for on all such amounts in the normal way. This treatment does not apply if the collector has received an equitable or legal assignment of the debts, whether in whole or in part. Such an assignment is an exempt supply of services to the collector and the collection of the debts is outside the scope of VAT.

(VAT Notice 700, para 25.6).

3.17 SEARCH AGENCIES

HMRC regard the fiche or document obtained from a source such as Companies House as a piece of information rather than a tangible object. The recharge of a search fee to the customer for the provision of a fiche or document may be treated as a disbursement under 3.7 above provided

- the information is passed on without analysis or comment; or
- the agency carries out a process on the fiche or document (eg conversion of a fiche to hard copy or provision of typewritten extracts) but does not use the data to inform an opinion or report.

Where the agency analyses, comments on, or produces a report on a fiche or document, or otherwise uses the information obtained on a search to make a report, the search fee is not a disbursement but a component part of the cost of providing the service to the customer, and is taxable at the standard rate.

(VAT Notice 700, para 25.5).

3.18 'PARTY PLAN' AND 'DIRECT' SELLING

See 69.23 VALUATION for supplies of goods made to non-taxable persons for retail sale.

See also *Churchway Crafts Ltd (No 1) (VTD 782)(TVC 1.80)*and *(No 2) (VTD 1186)(TVC 65.33)*; *C & E Commrs v Pippa-Dee Parties Ltd, QB [1981] STC 495 (TVC 65.31)* and *Younger (VTD 1173)(TVC 1.81)*. For a discussion of the nature of the distributor/dealer relationship, see *P & R Potter v C & E Commrs, CA 1984, [1985] STC 45 (TVC 1.79)* where the relationship was found to be that of principal to principal and VAT payable on the recommended retail price. See also *Betterware Products Ltd v C & E Commrs, QB [1985] STC 648 (TVC 1.84)*.

For the VAT position of any incentive gifts to encourage individuals to act as agents for mail order concerns, see 47.6 OUTPUT TAX and *GUS Merchandise Corporation Ltd v C & E Commrs, CA [1981] STC 569 (TVC 56.1)*.

4 Anti-Avoidance

4.1 GENERAL APPROACH OF THE COURTS

Direct tax cases. The classical interpretation of the constraints upon the Courts in deciding cases involving tax avoidance schemes is summed up in Lord Tomlin's statement in *Duke of Westminster v CIR HL 1935, 19 TC 490* case that '.. every man is entitled if he can to order his affairs so that the tax attaching .. is less than it otherwise would be.' The judgment was concerned with the tax consequences of a single transaction, but in *W T Ramsay Ltd v CIR, Eilbeck v Rawling HL 1981, 54 TC 101*, and subsequently in *Furniss v Dawson (and related appeals) HL 1984, 55 TC 324*, the House of Lords set bounds to the ambit within which this principle can be applied in relation to modern sophisticated and increasingly artificial arrangements to avoid tax. In *CIR v McGuckian HL 1997, 69 TC 1*, it was observed that while Lord Tomlin's words in the *Duke of Westminster* case 'still point to a material consideration, namely the general liberty of the citizen to arrange his financial affairs as he thinks fit, they have ceased to be canonical as to the tax consequences of a tax avoidance scheme'. It was further observed that the *Ramsay* principle was 'more natural and less extreme' than the majority decision in *Duke of Westminster*.

Ramsay concerned a complex 'circular' avoidance scheme at the end of which the financial position of the parties was little changed, but it was claimed that a large capital gains tax loss had been created. It was held that where a preconceived series of transactions is entered into to avoid tax, and with the clear intention to proceed through all stages to completion once set in motion, the *Duke of Westminster* principle does not compel a consideration of the individual transactions and of the fiscal consequences of such transactions taken in isolation.

The HL opinions in *Furniss v Dawson* are of outstanding importance, and establish, *inter alia*, that the *Ramsay* principle is not confined to 'circular' devices, and that if a series of transactions is 'preordained', a particular transaction within the series, accepted as genuine, may nevertheless be ignored if it was entered into solely for fiscal reasons and without any commercial purpose other than tax avoidance, even if the series of transactions as a whole has a legitimate commercial purpose.

However, in *Craven v White and related appeals HL 1988, 62 TC 1* the House of Lords indicated that for the *Ramsay* principle to apply all the transactions in a series have to be pre-ordained with such a degree of certainty that, at the time of the earlier transactions, there is no practical likelihood that the transactions would not take place. It is not sufficient that the ultimate transaction is simply of a kind that was envisaged at the time of the earlier transactions.

In the unanimous decision of the House of Lords in *Ensign Tankers (Leasing) Ltd v Stokes HL 1992, 64 TC 617*, the lead judgment drew a clear distinction between 'tax avoidance' and 'tax mitigation', it being said that the *Duke of Westminster* principle is accurate as far as the latter is concerned but does not apply to the former.

The inheritance tax case *Countess Fitzwilliam and others v CIR (and related appeals) HL 1993, 67 TC 614* appears to further restrict the application of the *Ramsay* principle, in that the HL found for the taxpayer in a case in which all their Lordships agreed that, once the scheme was embarked upon, there was no real possibility that the later transactions would not be proceeded with. There is, however, some suggestion that a decisive factor was that the first step in the transactions took place before the rest of the scheme had been formulated.

In *MacNiven v Westmoreland Investments Ltd HL 2001, 73 TC 1* the House of Lords held that the *Ramsay* principle did not apply where a company loaned money to a subsidiary to enable it to pay up outstanding interest and thus crystallise tax losses. Lord Nicholls held that 'the very phrase "the *Ramsay* principle" is potentially misleading. In *Ramsay* the House did not enunciate any new legal principle. What the House did was to highlight that, confronted with new and sophisticated tax avoidance devices, the courts' duty is to determine the legal nature of the transactions in question and then relate them to the fiscal legislation'. Lord Hoffmann held that 'what Lord Wilberforce was doing in the *Ramsay* case was no more .. than to treat the statutory words "loss" and "disposal" as referring to commercial concepts to which a juristic analysis of the transaction, treating each step as autonomous and independent, might not be determinative'. Lord Hutton held that 'an essential element of a transaction to which the *Ramsay* principle is applicable is that it should be artificial'.

Indirect tax cases. VAT planning does not, in the main, involve complicated schemes designed solely for the purpose of making a VAT liability disappear. Such schemes may give rise to one-off gains (although a significant number have been found by the courts to be ineffective) but in the longer term may simply complicate the administration and collection of the tax. Indeed, it is the creation and aggressive marketing of artificial schemes for avoiding VAT (in a similar way to what happened in the middle 1970s when artificial schemes to avoid direct tax were in vogue) which is leading to increasingly complex anti-avoidance provisions.

Historically, HMRC have sought, largely unsuccessfully, to apply the direct tax principles of *Furniss v Dawson*, *Ramsay*, *Westmoreland* and *McGuckian* above to VAT. Instead, the arguments in the tribunals and courts have revolved mainly around the technical implementation of planning arrangements.

However, in *Halifax plc v C & E Commrs (and related appeals), CJEC Case C–255/02, 7 April 2005 (unreported)* Customs chose not to argue the technical points, but instead argued that the transactions involved in the planning arrangements should be disregarded on the grounds that they had been entered into solely for a VAT avoidance motive (which the taxpayer accepted as being the case). The tribunal held that the sole purpose of the various parties was tax avoidance to enable Halifax to recover VAT otherwise irrecoverable and there was no business or commercial rationale for the relevant transactions. However, it directed that the case should be referred to the CJEC. The Advocate-General has expressed the opinion that a person who relies upon the literal meaning of a Community law provision to claim a right that runs counter to its purposes does not deserve to have that right upheld. In such circumstances, the legal provision at issue must be interpreted, contrary to its literal meaning, as actually not conferring the right. Legal certainty must be balanced against other values of the legal system. Tax law should not become a sort of legal 'wild-west' in which virtually every sort of opportunistic behaviour has to be tolerated so long as it conforms with a strict formalistic interpretation of the relevant tax provisions. The *EC Sixth Directive* should be interpreted as *not* conferring the right to deduct or recover input VAT (under the doctrine of abuse of rights) if two elements are found to be present by the national courts. First, that the aims and results pursued by the legal provisions formally giving rise to the right would be frustrated if the right claimed were actually conferred. Secondly, that the right invoked derives from activities for which there is no other explanation than the creation of the right claimed.

BUPA Hospitals Ltd v C & E Commrs; Goldsborough Developments Ltd v C & E Commrs; CJEC Case C–419/02; 7 April 2005 (unreported) (which the Advocate-General heard with *Halifax* above) involved a prepayment scheme to crystallise an entitlement to input tax before the abolition of zero-rating for drugs and prostheses supplied to hospital in-patients with effect from 1 January 1998. Customs rejected the input tax claims, considering that, in making the purported supplies, the recipients of the prepayments were not carrying out any economic or business activities. The Advocate-General expressed the opinion that that the arrangements facilitated the recovery of input VAT on the acquisition of goods during a period when that right was no longer available. *EC Sixth Directive, Art 10(2)* referred to situations where a payment is to be made on account before the goods are delivered or the services are performed. Properly construed, this required that those goods or services must be specifically identified when the payment on account took place. A mere payment on account for goods generically indicated in a list, from which the buyer could choose in the future one or more items (or none at all) and in circumstances in which the buyer was able to terminate the agreement unilaterally at any time and recover the unused balance of the prepayment made, did not suffice to characterise that prepayment as a payment on account within the meaning of the *EC Sixth Directive, Art 10(2)*. Even if the referring court considered that the facts of the case were incompatible with this suggested interpretation of *EC Sixth Directive, Art 10(2)*, it would still be open to them to take into account the doctrine of abuse of rights. In the Advocate-General's opinion, such an abuse existed if the prepayment arrangements put into effect were entered into with no other explanation (in terms to be objectively assessed by the national court) but to achieve a practical result that frustrated the objectives pursued by the change in the legislation after 1 January 1998, namely exemption without the right to deduct.

In *Blackqueen Ltd (VTD 17680) (TVC 60.144)*, a scheme was devised (which would no longer be effective following the insertion of *VATA 1994, Sch 3A* by *FA 2000, s 136*) to make use of the provisions of the *EC Eighth Directive* for the refund of VAT to taxable persons not established in EC. The tribunal held that the relevant transactions did not constitute 'supplies' for the purposes of VAT, since 'the series of transactions entered into by the group was wholly alien to the provisions of the *Sixth Directive*. Furthermore, the applications had been an 'abuse of rights', applying the decision in *Emsland-Stärke GmbH v Hauptzollamt Hamburg-Jonas, CJEC [2001] All ER(D) 34(Jan)*.

In *Optigen Ltd (and related appeals), CJEC Case C–354/03, 16 February 2005 (unreported) (TVC 21.81A)* Customs rejected claims for input tax on the basis that purchases formed part of a 'carousel missing trader fraud', designed to obtain a substantial repayment of sums which had never been paid as output tax. The tribunal dismissed the companies' appeals, observing that 'a circular series of transactions comprising the carousel fraud where the goods enter and leave the UK at the same price certainly does not look like an economic transaction'. On appeal, the Ch D directed that the case should be referred to the CJEC for a ruling on the interpretation of an 'economic activity' in the *EC Sixth Directive, Art 4*. The Advocate-General has expressed the opinion that the CJEC should not consent to the combating of carousel fraud by limiting the scope of the VAT system. In order to determine whether a transaction in a supply chain qualifies as an economic activity within the meaning of *EC Sixth Directive, Art 4(2)*, the transaction must be considered individually and *per se*. Transactions forming part of a circular supply chain in which a trader misappropriates the amounts paid to it as VAT instead of accounting for those amounts to the tax authorities do not, on that account, cease to constitute an economic activity.

The tribunal allowed the companies' appeals in *RBS Property Developments; Royal Bank of Scotland Group plc (No 5) (VTD 17789) (TVC 60.148)*. HMRC rejected a claim for input tax by two associated companies (which were not in the same VAT group) on the basis that the transactions were carried out for tax avoidance purposes and, applying *Halifax*, did not constitute supplies for VAT purposes. The tribunal held that although the series of transactions had a substantial element of tax mitigation, they were not *solely* directed to tax avoidance. As there were real and understandable business purposes for structuring the transactions, it could not be said that they were artificial. A taxpayer was entitled to so construct his activities as to obtain favourable tax consequences. The transactions were not an 'abuse of rights' as there was nothing improper, illegal or artificial about the transactions in question so the principles in *Emsland-Stärke GmbH v Hauptzollamt Hamburg-Jonas* above did not apply.

There have been two results of the proliferation of avoidance schemes.

- HMRC have set up special units to monitor tax avoidance and have indicated that they intend to take a much more robust line in dealing with such artificial arrangements.
- The use of certain avoidance schemes and arrangements has to be notified to HMRC (see 4.2 *et seq* below).

4.2 DISCLOSURE OF VAT AVOIDANCE SCHEMES

Taxpayers using certain VAT avoidance schemes must disclose their use to HMRC. The requirements apply to schemes used in VAT periods starting on or after 1 August 2004 (including schemes that started before that date). The measures are designed to provide greater information to HMRC about the take-up of avoidance schemes of which they are already aware and early notice of new, potentially damaging, schemes.

There are two categories of schemes that must be notified.

- **Listed schemes**. Certain schemes are 'designated' schemes for these purposes and are named and described in the legislation (by statutory instrument). A business whose annual turnover exceeds £600,000 must notify HMRC if it makes a VAT return or claim (such as a voluntary declaration) which is affected by its use of a listed scheme. See 4.3 to 4.6 below for the detailed provisions. Failure to notify incurs a penalty of 15% of the VAT avoided. See 52.21 PENALTIES.
- **Hallmarked schemes**. Certain features that are regularly associated with avoidance schemes are designated in the law (by statutory instrument). They can relate to the adoption of schemes or be components of them. Hallmarked schemes are those schemes that include at least one of the designated provisions. A business whose annual turnover exceeds £10 million must notify HMRC if it has entered into a scheme for the purposes of securing a tax advantage, the scheme contains one or more of the hallmarks of avoidance, and it makes a return or claim which is affected by the use of the hallmarked scheme.

  There is also a voluntary facility for anyone, including those who devise and market avoidance schemes, to register hallmarked schemes. A business using a registered hallmarked scheme will not normally have separately to notify its use.

See 4.7 to 4.11 below for the detailed provisions. Failure to notify incurs a flat-rate penalty of £5,000. See 52.21 PENALTIES.

[*VATA 1994, s 58A, Sch 11A; FA 2004, s 19, Sch 2; SI 2004/1934*].

'Scheme' includes any arrangement, transaction or series of transactions. [*VATA 1994, Sch 11A para 1; FA 2004, Sch 2 para 2*].

It is not a scheme *in itself* to

- engage someone to ensure that all the input tax entitlement is claimed,
- utilise an extra-statutory concession open to all,
- use the grouping provisions and make changes to the VAT group structure, or
- negotiate a new partial exemption method

even if it involves a hallmark of avoidance. However, these features may form part of a scheme.

(VAT Notice 700/8/04, para 2.2).

4.3 **Listed schemes**

The Treasury can designate a scheme for the purposes of these provisions if it appears to them that

- a scheme of a particular description has been, or might be, entered into for the purpose of enabling any person to 'obtain a tax advantage', and
- that it is unlikely that persons would enter into a scheme of that description unless the main purpose, or one of the main purposes, of doing so was the obtaining by any person of a tax advantage.

A scheme may be designated even though the Treasury are of the opinion that no scheme of that description could, as a matter of law, result in the obtaining by any person of a tax advantage (ie they consider it to be legally ineffective).

Each listed scheme must be allocated a reference number.

[*VATA 1994, Sch 11A para 3; FA 2004, Sch 2 para 2*].

Obtaining a tax advantage. A *taxable person* obtains a tax advantage if

- in any VAT period, the excess of output tax accounted for by him over input tax deducted by him is less than it otherwise would be;
- he obtains a VAT credit when he would not otherwise do so, or obtains a larger or earlier VAT credit than would otherwise be the case;
- in a case where he recovers input tax as a recipient of a supply before the supplier accounts for the output tax, the period between the time when the input tax is recovered and the time when the output tax is accounted for is greater than would otherwise be the case; or
- with effect from a date to be appointed, the amount of his 'non-deductible tax' is less than it would otherwise be.

  '*Non-deductible tax*' means

  (i) input tax for which he is not entitled to credit under *VATA 1994, s 25*; and

(ii) VAT on any supply of goods or services to him, or on the acquisition or importation of goods by him, which is not input tax and in respect of which he is entitled to a refund from HMRC under any provision of *VATA 1994*.

With effect from a date to be appointed, a *non-taxable person* obtains a tax advantage if his 'non-refundable tax' is less than it would otherwise be. '*Non-refundable tax*' means the VAT on any supply of goods or services to him, or on the acquisition or importation of goods by him, other than VAT in respect of which he is entitled to a refund from HMRC under any provision of *VATA 1994*.

[*VATA 1994, Sch 11A paras 2, 2A; FA 2004, Sch 2 para 2; F(No 2)A 2005, Sch 1 paras 3, 4*].

4.4 *Liability to notify listed schemes*

A taxable person must notify the use of a scheme when all of the following conditions are met (even if HMRC already know that he is using the scheme).

(*a*) The total value of his VAT-exclusive taxable supplies and exempt supplies exceeded:

(i) £600,000 in the year immediately prior to

- the 'affected VAT return period'; or
- any of the VAT return periods that are the subject of an 'affected claim'; or

(ii) the 'appropriate proportion' of £600,000 in the VAT return period immediately prior to

- the affected VAT return period; or
- any of the VAT return periods that are the subject of an affected claim.

The '*appropriate proportion*' means the proportion which the length of that VAT period bears to twelve months (ie one quarter where quarterly VAT returns are prepared and one twelfth where monthly VAT returns are prepared).

See (*c*) below for '*affected VAT return period*' and '*affected claim*'.

See 4.12 below for powers given to HMRC to prevent any artificial separation of business activities in an attempt to reduce turnover below the above limits.

Group undertakings. If the taxable person is a 'group undertaking', the conditions must be met by the taxable person *plus* every other group undertaking (ie the criteria apply to the group as a whole). Group undertaking for these purposes is defined in *Companies Act 1985, s 259* (and does not simply mean a member of the same VAT group).

'*Group undertaking*' in relation to an undertaking means an undertaking which is

- a 'parent undertaking' or a 'subsidiary undertaking' of that undertaking; or
- a subsidiary undertaking of any parent undertaking of that undertaking.

An undertaking is a '*parent undertaking*' in relation to another undertaking (a '*subsidiary undertaking*') if

- it holds the majority of the voting rights in the undertaking;
- it is a member of the undertaking and has the right to appoint or remove a majority of its board of directors;
- it has the right to exercise a dominant influence over the undertaking by virtue of either provisions in the undertaking's memorandum or articles or of a 'control contract' (as defined); or
- it is a member of the undertaking and controls alone, pursuant to an agreement with other shareholders or members, a majority of the voting rights; or
- it has a 'participating interest' in the undertaking and *either* it actually exercises a dominant influence over it *or* the two undertakings in question are managed on a unified basis.

A '*participating interest*' means an interest in shares of another undertaking held on a long-term basis for the purposes of exercising control or influence over that undertaking's activities. Unless the contrary is shown, a holding of 20% or more of the shares of an undertaking is presumed to be a participating interest.

An '*undertaking*' means a body corporate (companies and other bodies with legal personality) or partnership, or an unincorporated association carrying on a trade or business. The term does not include individuals acting as sole traders.

(*b*) The scheme used is a listed scheme under 4.6 below.

(*c*) Either

- in a return for a VAT period (the '*affected VAT return period*') beginning after 31 July 2004, the amount of VAT shown as payable by/to the taxable person is less than/greater than it would be but for the use of a listed scheme to which he is party,
- the taxable person makes a claim (the '*affected claim*') for the repayment of output tax or an increase in credit for input tax for any VAT period beginning after 31 July 2004 in respect of which he has previously delivered a return and the amount claimed is greater than it would be but for a listed scheme, or
- with effect from a date to be appointed, the amount of the taxable person's non-deductible tax in respect of any VAT period (the '*affected VAT return period*') is less than it would be but for a listed scheme.

(*d*) The taxable person has not on a previous occasion

- notified HMRC as required under these provisions that he is using the scheme; or
- with effect from a date to be appointed, provided HMRC with prescribed information in relation to the scheme under 4.8 below when it was a hallmarked scheme and before it became a listed scheme.

Where a scheme is designed to give an ongoing VAT benefit over future VAT periods, a taxable person is only required to notify the scheme once. However, if he starts a new set of arrangements using the same type of scheme (either whilst any existing scheme is in place or after it has finished) he must, subject to the necessary conditions being met, notify the use of the revised scheme. (VAT Notice 700/8/04, para 3.6).

[*VATA 1994, Sch 11A paras 6, 7; FA 2004, Sch 2 para 2; F(No 2)A 2005, Sch 1 paras 5, 6*].

Use of multiple schemes. If a return is affected by the use of more than one listed scheme, there is an obligation to notify all of those schemes (subject to (*d*) above).

Schemes involving several parties. If a listed scheme involves more than one party, all the parties to that scheme are obliged to notify HMRC if they meet the conditions set out above. In such a case, the parties concerned can make a joint notification.

(VAT Notice 700/8/04, para 3.5).

4.5 *Notifying listed schemes to HMRC*

Time limit for notification. A taxable person must notify HMRC of the use of a listed scheme within 30 days from the end of

- the last day for submission of the affected VAT return;
- the date the affected claim is made; or
- where HMRC make a direction under 4.12 below (artificial splitting of business), the last day for submission of the first VAT return made to HMRC following the direction.

[*VATA 1994, Sch 11A para 6; FA 2004, Sch 2 para 2; SI 2004/1929*].

Method of notification. The following provisions relating to notification as set out in VAT Notice 700/8 have the force of law.

HMRC must be notified of the use of a listed scheme either

- by e-mail to vat.avoidance.disclosures.bst@hmrc.gsi.gov.uk

  or

- in writing to

  HM Revenue and Customs
  VAT Avoidance Disclosures Unit
  Room 3/39
  1 Parliament Street
  London SW1A 2BQ

Notification sent to any other address (eg a local VAT office or the National Advice Service) is not proper notification and may give rise to a penalty.

The notification should be prominently headed

Disclosure of use of listed scheme – Notification under paragraph 6(2) of Schedule 11A to the VAT Act 1994

and give details of business name, address and VAT registration number.

Otherwise, the only information that is required is the number of the listed scheme (see 4.6 below). [*SI 2004/1929*]. If a taxable person is required to notify the use of more than one scheme with the same number, he must inform HMRC how many schemes of that number are being used. Similarly, if he is using a number of schemes with different scheme numbers which affect a VAT return, he must inform HMRC about all of them.

HMRC will acknowledge receipt of notifications received at the above addresses. They will consider what action, if any, should be taken in respect of the notification and the taxable person will be contacted as necessary. If HMRC are already investigating use of the scheme notified, that action will continue as appropriate.

(VAT Notice 700/8/04, paras 4.1–4.6).

4.6 *The listed schemes*

The Treasury have designated the schemes detailed below (with the reference numbers as indicated) as listed schemes. The interpretation and examples within boxes are not part of the legislation but taken from VAT Notice 700/8.

Where a taxable person treats a scheme as having a feature described in the law, that scheme will fall within the description given, even if, either as a matter of law or for any other reason, the feature is not present. [*SI 2004/1933*]. HMRC give the example of where a scheme relies on a transaction being a supply for VAT purposes but they argue, when challenging the scheme, that there has been no supply as a matter of law. For the purposes of deciding whether a scheme fits the scheme description, what matters is not what HMRC contend about a scheme transaction, but what the user of the scheme believes that transaction to be.

1 *First grant of a major interest in a building*

Any scheme comprising or including the first grant of a major interest in any building of a description falling within *VATA 1994, Sch 8 Group 5 item 1*(*a*) (see 42.13 LAND AND BUILDINGS) where

(*a*) the grant is made to a person 'connected with' the grantor; and

(*b*) the grantor, or any body corporate treated as a member of a VAT group (see 31 GROUPS OF COMPANIES) of which the grantor is a member, attributes to that grant input tax incurred by him

(i) in respect of a service charge relating to the building; or

(ii) in connection with any extension, enlargement, repair, maintenance or refurbishment of the building, other than for remedying defects in the original construction.

A person is '*connected with*' another for the above purposes where

- one of them is an 'undertaking' in relation to which the other is a 'group undertaking', or
- both of them are connected to the same trust

and a person is connected to a trust where

- he is the settlor of the trust, a trustee or beneficiary of it; or
- he holds any shares in a company in accordance with the terms of the trust, or is a person on whose behalf such shares are held.

See 4.4(*a*) above for the meaning of '*undertaking*' and '*group undertaking*'.

These are schemes that aim to remove the VAT cost of extending, enlarging, repairing, refurbishing or servicing a building by attributing the VAT incurred to a zero-rated major interest grant in the building to a connected person by a person with 'person constructing' status.

> *Example*
>
> - A housing landlord may seek to use such a scheme to recover input tax on the major refurbishment of houses which he had constructed several years earlier. The landlord sells them to a subsidiary in such a way that he attributes the VAT on the refurbishment to that zero-rated disposal (either before or after the grant). The subsidiary may simply lease the houses back to the landlord so that he can then let them on again to tenants.
> - The builder of new halls of residence may try to recover future input tax on repairs and maintenance on the buildings, even though his income from the property at that time will be exempt, by building into the initial zero-rated sale a payment for, and agreement to provide, maintenance in the future.

2 *Payment handling service*

Any scheme comprising or including a retail supply of goods or services together with a 'linked supply' to the same customer, where the total consideration for the retail supply and the linked supply is no different, or not significantly different, from what would be payable for the retail sale alone.

'Linked supply' means a supply by the retailer or any other person that

(*a*) relates to the means of payment used for the retail supply; and

(*b*) is a supply of a description falling within *VATA 1994, Sch 9 Group 5* (see 27 FINANCIAL SERVICES).

These are schemes that aim to reduce the VAT due on the advertised price for retail goods or services.

> *Example*
>
> When a customer presents his goods at the till, he may be informed that an element of the price is being paid to a separate company as an exempt payment handling service for processing or accepting his credit card as the means of payment. The price paid for the retail supply remains the same if the customer chooses to pay by cash.

3 *Value shifting*

Any scheme comprising or including a 'retail supply' of goods or services together with a linked supply to the same customer where (*a*) the 'linked supply' is a separate supply under the terms of any agreement made by the customer;

(*b*) part of the total consideration for the retail supply and the linked supply is attributed to the linked supply by the terms of any such agreement; and

(*c*) the total consideration for the retail supply and the linked supply is no different, or not significantly different, from what it would be for the retail supply alone.

'*Retail supply*' means a supply by retail upon which VAT is charged at standard rate.

'*Linked supply*' means a supply of goods or services made by the retailer or any other person which is zero-rated or exempt.

These are schemes that aim to transfer value from standard-rated retail supplies into linked zero-rated or exempt supplies. The customer will pay the same or similar overall price whether or not he accepts the linked supply. This separation of the consideration across the two supplies is alleged to be supported by agreements signed or agreed by the customer at the point of sale.

Examples

- *Notification required.* A retail customer making a purchase is offered, at the point of sale, an insurance product with the goods. Rather than paying an additional amount for this cover, the customer is informed that the ticket price will be apportioned to cover both the goods and the insurance. If the customer then declines the insurance, there is no reduction of the ticket price to reflect this. The overall price paid by the customer remains the same whether he takes the insurance or not.
- *Notification not required.* Notification is not required where the linked goods/services are supplied 'free', with no part of the price being attributed to that supply. Notification will also not be required for normal business promotion arrangements. For example, a retailer offers a 'meal deal' where customers can buy a sandwich, a soft drink and packet of crisps for a single price that is lower than the normal combined price of the three items. When apportioning the cost between the zero-rated and standard-rated items the retailer spreads the discount across all the goods supplied. These arrangements are not notifiable as each linked supply would not normally be subject to a separate agreement with the customer.

4 *Leaseback agreement*

Any scheme comprising or including the supply of goods, or the leasing or letting on hire of goods ('the relevant supply') by a taxable person to a connected relevant person where

(*a*) the taxable person or another taxable person connected with him, including the relevant person, is entitled to credit for all the input tax arising on the purchase of the goods;

(*b*) the relevant person uses the goods in the course or furtherance of a business carried on by him, and for the purpose of that business, otherwise than for the purpose of selling or leasing or letting on hire the goods; and

(*c*) the relevant person or a person connected with him has directly or indirectly provided funds for meeting more than 90% of the cost of the goods.

'*Relevant person*' means any person who, in respect of the relevant supply, is not entitled to credit for all the input tax wholly attributable to the supplies he makes.

The provision of funds includes

- the making of a loan of funds; and
- the provision of any consideration for the issue of any shares or other securities issued wholly or partly for raising the funds.

The grant, assignment or surrender of a major interest in land is not a supply of goods for the purposes of this scheme.

See 1 above for the meaning of '*connected persons*'.

These are schemes that aim to defer or reduce the VAT cost of acquiring goods by a business that cannot recover all of the input tax charged to it on those goods. The business arranges a sale or lease and leaseback of the goods with a connected person which enables full initial input tax recovery on the acquisition of the goods, with a 'drip feed' of the VAT cost over the lease period.

Examples

- *Notification required.* A partly-exempt bank requires new computer equipment. The bank's corporate group purchases the equipment outright but, in order to reduce or remove the VAT effect of the irrecoverable input tax, the group acquires the computers in a subsidiary, which then leases them to the bank. Depending on the values and length of the lease, the intention is to spread the irrecoverable VAT cost, or to avoid a proportion of it altogether.
- *Notification not* required. Notification is not required for leasing arrangements between unconnected parties. For example, an insurance company (A) requires a new computerised telephone system for its call centres. Rather than buy the equipment outright it decides to lease it and contracts with an unconnected commercial leasing business (B) to lease the equipment for a five-year period. As B has no expertise in sourcing the equipment required, it is agreed that A will purchase the equipment from its usual supplier. A is then to sell the equipment to B who will then lease it to A.

5 *Extended approval period*

Any scheme comprising or including a retail supply of goods whereby

(*a*) the goods are sent or taken on approval or sale or return or similar terms;

(*b*) payment for the supply is required in full by the retailer before the expiry of any approval, return or similar period; and

(*c*) for the purposes of accounting for VAT, the retailer treats the goods as supplied on a date after the date on which payment is received in full.

These are schemes that aim to defer accounting for output tax on the supply of retail goods until an adoption period has been completed, or title transfers to the customer, by arranging for the goods to be sent or taken on approval or sale or return or similar terms, whereas payment is required in full before such a time.

> *Example*
>
> A customer orders goods from an internet retailer. The retailer is paid on-line when the order is placed by the customer and delivery follows shortly thereafter. The retailer, either due to various guarantees or specific terms and conditions, will seek to account for VAT on the transaction at a later date, claiming the supply was on 'approval' or 'sale or return', despite the fact that payment has been received, delivery taken place and, in some cases, the goods have been consumed or used by the customer before the retailer regards the goods as having been adopted.

6 *Groups: third party suppliers*

Any scheme comprising or including supplies made to one or more group members by a 'specified body' in relation to which the 'benefits condition' is not satisfied. See 31.2 GROUPS OF COMPANIES for whether a body is a '*specified body*' and whether the '*benefits condition*' is satisfied in relation to it.

These are schemes that aim to reduce or remove the VAT incurred on bought in taxable services (including outsourced services) by a user that cannot recover all of the input tax charged to it for those services. The user arranges to include a corporate body in its VAT group with an activity of supplying the services. This corporate body is set up so that the majority of the benefits of the activity accrue to a third party service provider and its corporate group rather than the user. The aim is that very little VAT is charged to the user as supplies within a VAT group are disregarded, but the third party provider (who in practice manages the activity of providing the service) receives the profits and other benefits from the activity.

> *Example*
>
> A partly exempt insurance company (A) wishes to buy in computer services from a third party company (B) but wants to reduce the irrecoverable VAT cost of doing this. A and B establish another company (C). A controls C by owning 51% of its shares and includes C in its VAT group. B owns the remaining shares, but these shares confer rights to 99% of the dividends declared by C and 99% of the assets on winding up. C holds the contract to provide the computer services required by A from B and employs the staff to provide the service. Besides the dividends, B also receives benefits from C in the form of a management charge for managing C's activity of providing computer services. As a result almost all of the benefits of C's activity accrue to B. Thus, B has access to the

profits and benefits of the computing activity, and A hopes to avoid a large VAT cost as there will be no VAT charged within the VAT group.

7 *Exempt education or vocational training by a non-profit making body*

Any scheme comprising or including the conduct of a 'relevant business' by a 'non-profit making body' where

- it receives a 'relevant supply' from a connected taxable person who is not an 'eligible body'; and
- in any one prescribed accounting period the value of all such relevant supplies is equal to or more than 20% of the cost of making the supplies comprising the relevant business.

'*Relevant business*' means a business whose activities consist wholly or mainly of the supply of education or vocational training to persons who are not taxable persons.

'*Non-profit making body*' means a body within *VATA 1994, Sch 9 Group 6 Note 1*(*e*) (see 20.3(*e*) EDUCATION) which is not otherwise within 20.3(*a*)–(*f*) EDUCATION.

'*Relevant supply*' means the supply, including the leasing or letting on hire, for use in a relevant business of

- a capital item used in the course or furtherance of the relevant business, and for the purpose of that business, otherwise than solely for the purpose of selling the item;
- staff;
- management services;
- administration services; or
- accountancy services.

'*Eligible body*' has the meaning in *VATA 1994, Sch 9 Group 6 Note* (*1*) (see 20.3 EDUCATION).

'*Vocational training*' has the meaning in *VATA 1994, Sch 9 Group 6 Note* (*3*) (see 20.7 EDUCATION) but does not include vocational training of a description falling within

- *VATA 1994, Sch 9 Group 6 Item 5* (vocational training where the consideration is ultimately a charge to funds provided under *Employment and Training Act 1973, s 2, Employment and Training Act* (*NI*) *1950, s 1A* or *Enterprises and New Towns* (*Scotland*) *Act 1990, s 2*); or
- *VATA 1994, Sch 9 Group 6 Item 5A* (vocational training where the consideration is ultimately a charge to funds provided by the Learning and Skills Council for England or the National Council for Education and Training for Wales under *Learning and Skills Act 2000, Parts I* or *II*).

See 1 above for '*connected persons*'.

These are schemes that aim to allow a business to retain, from the fees received from customers for its services, that element of the fees that it would normally have paid as output VAT. The customers for the services are mainly or wholly private individuals. The scheme generally involves the establishment of a non-profit making body to be an eligible body, that takes on the business and then provides the training and education services exempt from VAT. The non-profit making body will receive supplies for one or more key supplies (eg property and asset leases, staff, management) from the business that originally provided the services or another person. The non-profit making body and the providers of the services are connected persons. The effect of this is that the profits of the non-profit making body are still available to the other business by means of the supplies made to it, despite the non-profit making body being technically unable to make distributions.

> *Example*
>
> A training company which normally trains private individuals and accounts for VAT out of its income, sets up a non-profit making body to provide the training in future, exempt from VAT. However, if the new body really is a non-profit making body, it will not be able to distribute its profits and the shareholders of the existing business will lose out. Various agreements are put in place, including a lease for the business premises. The rent is set so that it is directly related to the turnover or profit of the non-profit making body and thus acts as a mechanism to return those profits to the original training company.

8 *Taxable education or vocational training by a non-eligible body*

Any scheme comprising or including the conduct of a 'relevant business' by a non-eligible body connected to an 'eligible body' where

- the non-eligible body benefits or intends to benefit the eligible body by way of gift, dividend or otherwise; or
- the eligible body makes any supply to the non-eligible body which is a relevant supply and, in any one prescribed accounting period, the value of all such relevant supplies is equal to or more than 20% of the cost of making the supplies comprising the relevant business.

'*Eligible body*' has the meaning in *VATA 1994, Sch 9 Group 6 Note* (*1*) (see 20.3 EDUCATION).

'*Relevant business*' means a business whose activities consist wholly or mainly of the taxable supply of education or vocational training.

'*Vocational training*' has the meaning in *VATA 1994, Sch 9 Group 6 Note* (*3*) (see 20.7 EDUCATION).

'*Relevant supply*' means the supply, or leasing or letting on hire, for use in a relevant business of

- a capital item used in the course or furtherance of the relevant business, and for the purpose of that business, otherwise than solely for the purpose of selling the item;
- staff;
- management services;

- administration services; or
- accounting services.

See 1 above for '*connected persons*'.

These are schemes that aim to enable eligible bodies to avoid incurring irrecoverable input VAT. A business which is not an eligible body is established to provide taxable training or education services to persons who are able to recover the tax on those supplies from HMRC. The typical customers involved would be bodies such as NHS Trusts and Local Authorities, but can also include normal commercial bodies. The non-eligible body is connected to an eligible body (probably as its subsidiary) from which it will receive a range of supplies which enable it to carry out the training or education business. It is expected that the non-eligible body will distribute its profits to the connected eligible body (eg by way of Gift Aid).

> *Example*
>
> A university has a contract to provide training to employees of a NHS Trust. To provide this training, it needs to build a new facility but wishes to reduce the cost of the irrecoverable VAT on the building. Normally, the training would be exempt from VAT and thus the VAT on costs involved in providing it would not be recoverable. The university establishes a subsidiary which is expressly allowed to distribute its profits and thus not qualify for exemption for its training supplies. The subsidiary may have little or no resources and will need to be provided with those resources by the university under various contracts and agreements. The university may also want to access any profits from this activity and may choose to do this by having the subsidiary gift those profits to it under the Gift Aid relief. As a result, the university hopes to transform the training into a fully taxable activity and recover the input tax on the new facility, together with other taxable costs, in the subsidiary.

[*SI 2004/1933*]. (VAT Notice 700/8/04, paras 5.1–5.9).

4.7 Hallmarked schemes

In addition to the listed schemes falling within the provisions in 4.3 to 4.6 above, the Treasury can designate certain provisions (including any agreements, transactions, acts or courses of conduct) that it appears to them are, or are likely to be, included in (or associated with) schemes entered into for the purpose of enabling any person to obtain a tax advantage. See 4.3 above for the meaning of '*obtaining a tax advantage*'.

The Treasury can designate a provision even though it considers that the provision is likely to be a feature of schemes that are not tax avoidance schemes.

[*VATA 1994, Sch 11A paras 2, 4, 5; FA 2004, Sch 2 para 2; F(No 2)A 2005, Sch 1 paras 3, 4*].

4.8 *Liability to notify hallmarked schemes*

A taxable person is liable to notify HMRC of the use of a hallmarked scheme when all of the following conditions are met.

(*a*) The total value of his VAT-exclusive taxable supplies and exempt supplies exceeded:

(i) £10 million in the year immediately prior to

- the 'affected VAT return period'; or
- any of the VAT return periods that are the subject of an 'affected claim'; or

(ii) the 'appropriate proportion' of £10 million in the VAT return period immediately prior to

- the affected VAT return period; or
- any of the VAT return periods that are the subject of an affected claim.

The '***appropriate proportion***' means the proportion which the length of that VAT period bears to twelve months (ie one quarter where quarterly VAT returns are prepared and one twelfth where monthly VAT returns are prepared).

See (*d*) below for '*affected VAT return period*' and '*affected claim*'.

See 4.12 below for powers given to HMRC to prevent any artificial separation of business activities in an attempt to reduce turnover below the above limits.

Group undertakings. If the taxable person is a 'group undertaking', the conditions must be met by the taxable person *plus* every other group undertaking (ie the criteria apply to the group as a whole). Group undertaking for these purposes is defined in *Companies Act 1985, s 259* (and does not simply mean a member of the same VAT group). See 4.4 above.

(*b*) The taxable person is a party to a scheme that is not a listed scheme (see 4.3 to 4.6 above).

(*c*) The main purpose, or one of the main purposes, of the scheme is to obtain a tax advantage. See 4.3 above for the meaning of 'obtaining a tax advantage'.

(*d*) Either

- in a return (the '*affected VAT return period*') for a VAT period beginning after 31 July 2004, the amount of VAT shown as payable by/to the taxable person is less than/greater than it would be but for the use of a hallmarked scheme to which he is party,
- the taxable person makes a claim (the '*affected claim*') for the repayment of output tax or an increase in credit for input tax for any VAT period beginning after 31 July 2004 in respect of which he has previously delivered a return and the amount claimed is greater than it would be but for such a scheme, or
- with effect from a date to be appointed, the amount of the taxable person's non-deductible tax in respect of any VAT period (the '*affected VAT return period*') is less than it would be but for such a scheme.

(*e*) The scheme contains one or more of the hallmarks of avoidance. See 4.11 below.

(*f*) The taxable person has not on a previous occasion provided HMRC with prescribed information under these provisions.

A scheme need only be notified once. If a taxable person starts a new scheme that is 'structured in the same way' as a previously notified scheme, he need not notify this new scheme. By 'structured in the same way', HMRC mean that the details of the scheme required to be notified under 4.9 below are the same as a previously notified scheme, even though the parties to the scheme and the hallmarks may be different.

However, if a taxable person starts a new scheme that is structured in a different way to a previously notified scheme, he must, subject to the necessary conditions being met, notify use of that scheme, irrespective of whether the hallmarks are the same.

(VAT Notice 700/8/04, para 6.5).

(*g*) The taxable person has not been provided with a scheme number by someone who has registered the scheme with HMRC.

If someone has already registered the hallmarked scheme being used under the voluntary registration scheme (see 4.10 below) and has advised the taxable person of the scheme reference number allocated to it by HMRC, the taxable person is not required to notify HMRC. (VAT Notice 700/8/04, para 6.6).

[*VATA 1994, Sch 11A paras 6, 7; FA 2004, Sch 2 para 2; F(No 2)A 2005, Sch 1 paras 5, 6*].

Use of multiple schemes. If a return is affected by the use of more than one scheme containing or associated with a hallmark, there is an obligation to notify all of those schemes (subject to (*f*) above).

Schemes involving several parties. If a hallmarked scheme involves more than one party, all the parties to that scheme are obliged to notify HMRC if they meet the conditions set out above. In such a case, the parties concerned can make a joint notification.

(VAT Notice 700/8/04, para 6.4).

4.9 *Notifying use of hallmarked schemes to HMRC*

Time limit for notification. HMRC must be notified of the use of a hallmarked scheme within 30 days from the end of

- the last day for submission of the affected VAT return;
- the date the affected claim is made; or
- where HMRC make a direction under 4.12 below (artificial splitting of business), the last day for submission of the first VAT return made to HMRC following the direction.

[*VATA 1994, Sch 11A para 6; FA 2004, Sch 2 para 2; SI 2004/1929*].

Method of notification. The following provisions relating to notification as set out in VAT Notice 700/8 have the force of law.

HMRC must be notified of the use of a listed scheme either

- by e-mail to vat.avoidance.disclosures.bst@hmrc.gsi.gov.uk

  or

- in writing to

4.9 Anti-Avoidance

HM Revenue and Customs
VAT Avoidance Disclosures Unit
4th Floor West
New King's Beam House
22 Upper Ground
London SE1 9PJ

Notification sent to any other address (eg a local VAT office or the National Advice Service) is not proper notification and may give rise to a penalty.

The notification should be prominently headed

Disclosure of use of hallmarked scheme – Notification under paragraph 6(3) of Schedule 11A to the VAT Act 1994

and give details of business name, address and VAT registration number.

Information to be notified. All of the following information must be provided.

(*a*) A statement as to which hallmark or hallmarks listed in 4.11 below are included in or associated with the scheme being notified.

This need not be a standalone part of the notification and can be included as part of the general explanation of the working of the scheme.

(*b*) How the scheme gives rise to a 'tax advantage', including, to the extent that it is material to the tax advantage:

- A description of each arrangement, transaction or series of transactions.

  Sufficient information must be provided to allow HMRC to understand how the tax advantage is obtained. The degree of information to be provided will vary from scheme to scheme but often the inclusion of a summary of the aims of the scheme and a diagrammatic representation of its structure, showing the participants, transaction flows, etc will be of assistance. Only generic information need be provided, not detail that is specific to the particular circumstances (eg a step of the scheme could be described as 'building is leased to Company A' rather than '1 High Street is leased to Bank plc'. Copies of contracts and other documents do not need to be submitted. However, if it is easier to explain the scheme by referring to the specific detail, this may be done and supplementary documentation may be submitted if preferred.

- The sequence of those arrangements, etc.

  The precise sequence should be made clear. HMRC recommend listing these as 'Step 1', 'Step 2', etc.

- The timing, or the intervals between, those arrangements, etc.

  Explanation should be given, for example, if transactions are

  (i) due to take place within a short period of time of each other to take advantage of a VAT rule;

  (ii) due to take place over a long period to cause a VAT 'drip feed' effect; or

  (iii) timed to miss or bridge accounting periods.

- The goods or services involved.

(*c*) How the involvement of any party to the scheme contributes to the obtaining of the tax advantage.

(*d*) Any provision having the force of law in the UK or elsewhere relied upon as giving rise the tax advantage.

There is no obligation to quantify the amount or expected amount of the tax advantage.

See 4.3 above for the meaning of obtaining a '*tax advantage*'. For these purposes, a tax advantage is considered to be obtained (and any arrangement, transaction or series of transactions is considered to take place) provided a taxable person treats it as having been obtained or taken place for the purposes of a VAT return or a claim for repayment of output tax or an increase in credit for input tax.

Acknowledgement by HMRC. HMRC will acknowledge notifications received at the above addresses. If all the required information is not received, the taxable person will be asked to produce the information needed to meet his statutory obligation. If this information is not supplied within the time limit for making a notification (see above), the taxable person will be liable to a penalty. See 52.21 PENALTIES.

HMRC will consider what action, if any, should be taken in respect of the notification and the taxable person will be contacted as necessary. If HMRC are already investigating use of the scheme notified, that action will continue as appropriate.

[*SI 2004/1929*]. (VAT Notice 700/8/04, paras 7.1–7.9).

4.10 *Voluntary registration of hallmarked schemes*

Any person may, at any time, make a voluntary notification to HMRC of the details of a hallmarked scheme (eg a business that devises or markets a scheme may wish to do this to relieve its clients of the obligation of having to notify HMRC of the use of the scheme). To do so, the person should notify HMRC, and provide them with the information, as set out in 4.9 above. The notification should make clear that it is a voluntary notification.

HMRC will acknowledge the notification within ten working days of its receipt and indicate the reference number they have allocated to the scheme.

[*VATA 1994, Sch 11A para 9; FA 2004, Sch 2 para 2; SI 2004/1929*].

4.11 *The hallmarks*

The Treasury have designated the following as provisions associated with, or as the case may be, included in schemes.

A provision is treated as fitting a description listed even if it, or any feature of it, is not actually present (whether as a matter of law or for any other reason), provided a taxable person has treated that feature as being present for the purpose of making a VAT return or a claim for the repayment of output tax or an increase in credit for input tax. [*SI 2004/1933*].

Provisions associated with schemes

(1) *Confidentiality condition*

An agreement preventing or limiting the disclosure of how a scheme gives rise to a tax advantage.

Such an agreement is frequently imposed before a potential user has the workings of a scheme explained to them.

(2) *The sharing of the tax advantage with another party to the scheme or with the promoter*

An agreement that the tax advantage to a person accruing from the operation of the scheme be shared to any extent with another party to it or another person promoting it.

A person is a '*promoter of a scheme*' if, in the course of a trade, profession or business which involves the provision to other persons of services relating to taxation

- he is to any extent responsible for the design of the proposed arrangements; or
- he invites persons to enter into contracts for the implementation of the proposed arrangements.

(3) *Fee payable to a promoter which is in whole or in part contingent on tax savings from the scheme*

An agreement that payment to a promoter of the scheme be contingent in whole or in part on the tax advantage accruing from the operation of the scheme.

See (2) above for the meaning of '*promoter of a scheme*'.

Provisions included in schemes

(1) *Prepayment between connected parties*

A payment for a supply of goods or services between connected persons

(*a*) before the basic tax point for the supply (see 64.39 SUPPLY for supplies of goods and 64.49 SUPPLY for supplies of services) or, where applicable, the special tax point that applies to goods supplied on sale or return (see 64.43 SUPPLY); or

(*b*) where the supply is a 'continuous supply' and the payment is before the goods or services are provided.

A supply is a '*continuous supply*' if it is a supply to which any of the following applies:

- *SI 1995/2518, Reg 85* (leases treated as supplies of goods, see 64.44 SUPPLY).
- *SI 1985/2518, Reg 86* (supplies of water, gas or any form of power, heat, refrigeration or ventilation, see 64.46 SUPPLY).
- *SI 1985/2518, Reg 90* (continuous supply of services, see 64.50 SUPPLY).
- *SI 1985/2518, Reg 91* (royalties and similar payments, see 64.51 SUPPLY).
- *SI 1985/2518, Reg 93* (supplies in the construction industry, see 42.29 LAND AND BUILDINGS).

For the purposes of (*b*) above goods or services are provided at the time when, and to the extent that, the recipient receives the benefit of them.

A person is '*connected with*' another for the above purposes where

- one of them is an 'undertaking' in relation to which the other is a 'group undertaking', or
- both of them are connected to the same trust

and a person is connected to a trust where

- he is the settlor of the trust, a trustee or beneficiary of it; or
- he holds any shares in a company in accordance with the terms of the trust, or is a person on whose behalf such shares are held.

See 4.4(*a*) above for the meaning of '*undertaking*' and '*group undertaking*'.

(2) *Funding by loan, share subscription or subscription in securities*

The funding (in whole or in part) of a supply of goods or services between connected persons by means of a loan between connected persons or the subscription for shares in, or securities issued by, a connected person.

See (1) above for the meaning of '*connected persons*'.

(3) *Off-shore loops*

A supply of 'relevant services' which is used or intended to be used, in whole or in part, directly or indirectly, in making to a person belonging in the UK, a supply which is zero-rated, exempt or treated as made in another country (and not in the UK) by virtue of *VATA 1994, s 7(10)* (place of supply of services, see 64.20 SUPPLY).

'*Relevant services*' are either

(*a*) services which are exempt insurance services or exempt financial services (other than the management of an authorised unit trust scheme or an open-ended investment company) and which are

(i) supplied to a person who belongs outside the EC; or

(ii) directly linked to the export of goods to a place outside the EC, insofar as they are supplies falling within *VATA 1994, Sch 9 Group 5 item 2* (the making of any advance or any credit, see 27.11 FINANCIAL SERVICES); or

(iii) consist of the provision of intermediary insurance services within *VATA 1994, Sch 9 Group 2 item 4* (see 37.13 INSURANCE) or intermediary financial services within *VATA 1994, Sch 9 Group 5 item 5* (see 27.25 FINANCIAL SERVICES) in relation to any transaction within (i) or (ii) above; or

(*b*) a supply falling within *VATA 1994, Sch 5 paras 1–8* (see 64.27 SUPPLY) where the recipient of that supply belongs in a country, other than the Isle of Man, which is not an EC country.

(4) *Property transactions between connected persons*

A 'relevant grant' where

- the grantor or grantee of the interest or right is a person who is not entitled to credit for all the input tax wholly attributable to the supplies he makes;

- any work of construction, alteration, demolition, repair, maintenance or civil engineering has been or is to be carried out on the land; and
- the grant is made to a person connected with the grantor.

'*Relevant grant*' means the grant of any interest in or right over land or of any licence to occupy land or, in relation to land in Scotland, any personal right to call for or be granted any such interest or right, other than a grant of a description falling within *VATA 1994, Sch 8 Group 5 Item 1* (first grant of a major interest by a person constructing a building designed for dwelling, or intended for use solely for residential or charitable purposes; or by a person converting a non-residential building to residential use, see 42.13 LAND AND BUILDINGS) or *VATA 1994, Sch 8 Group 6 Item 1* (first grant of a major interest in a protected building by a person reconstructing it, see 42.14 LAND AND BUILDINGS).

'*Grant*' includes an assignment or surrender and the supply made by the person to whom an interest is surrendered when there is a reverse surrender.

See (1) above for '*connected persons*'.

4.12 **Power of HMRC to exclude exemption from duty to notify**

Under normal circumstances, a taxable person does not have to disclose the use of a listed or hallmarked scheme where turnover is below certain limits (see 4.4(*a*) and 4.8(*a*) above respectively).

The following provisions are, however, designed to prevent the maintenance or creation of any 'artificial' separation of business activities carried on by two or more persons from resulting in any avoidance of the obligations to notify schemes. In determining whether any separation of business activities is '*artificial*', consideration must be given to the extent to which the different persons carrying on those activities are closely bound to one another by financial, economic and organisational links. See 8.7 BUSINESS for examples illustrating the types of factors indicative of these links.

HMRC may make a direction under which the persons specified therein become treated as a single taxable person carrying on the activities of a business described in the direction with effect from the date of the direction or such later date as is specified. Where this is done, if that single taxable person would not be excluded from notifying a scheme, then the persons named in the direction cannot be excluded.

The direction must be served on each person named in it and remains in force until it is revoked or replaced by a further direction.

Before making a direction naming any person, HMRC must be satisfied that

- he is making or has made taxable or exempt supplies;
- the activities in the course of which he makes those supplies form only part of certain activities, the other activities being carried on concurrently or previously (or both) by one or more other persons; and
- if all the taxable and exempt supplies of the business described in the direction were taken into account, the turnover would exceed the minimum turnover limits.

[*VATA 1994, Sch 11A para 8; FA 2004, Sch 2 para 2*].

4.13 SPECIFIC ANTI-AVOIDANCE PROVISIONS

Anti-avoidance legislation is intended to counteract transactions designed to avoid taxation, but *bona fide* transactions may sometimes be caught also. The main provisions relating to VAT are listed below.

Provisions in VATA 1994

- Groups supplies using an overseas member. [*VATA 1994, s 43(2A)–(2E)*]. See 31.6 GROUPS OF COMPANIES.
- Groups of companies – eligibility rules. [*VATA 1994, s 43D*]. See 31.2 GROUPS OF COMPANIES.
- Acquisition of a business as a going concern by a partly-exempt group. [*VATA 1994, s 44*]. See 31.7 GROUPS OF COMPANIES.
- Joint and several liability for unpaid VAT. [*VATA 1994, s 77A*]. See 17.3 CUSTOMS: POWERS.
- Place of supply of services – transitional provisions. [*VATA 1994, s 97A*]. See 64.18 SUPPLY.
- Disaggregation of business activities (business splitting). [*VATA 1994, Sch 1 para 1A*]. See 8.5 BUSINESS.
- Registration by overseas traders in respect of disposals of assets for which a VAT repayment is claimed. [*VATA 1994, Sch 3A*]. See 59.26 REGISTRATION.
- Telecommunications services. [*VATA 1994, Sch 5 para 7A*]. See 64.27 SUPPLY.
- Transactions between connected persons. [*VATA 1994, Sch 6 para 1*]. See 69.19 VALUATION.
- Demonstration cars. [*VATA 1994, Sch 6 para 1A*]. See 45.7 MOTOR CARS.
- Direct (party plan) selling. [*VATA 1994, Sch 6 para 2*]. See 69.23 VALUATION.
- Heated water. [*VATA 1994, Sch 8 Group 2 Item 2(c)*]. See 72.2 ZERO-RATED SUPPLIES.
- Groups of companies – registration. [*VATA 1994, Sch 9A*]. See 31.5 GROUPS OF COMPANIES.
- Option to tax (election to waive exemption for) land and buildings. [*VATA 1994, Sch 10 paras 2, 3, 3A, 9*]. See 42.9 LAND AND BUILDINGS.
- Face value vouchers. [*VATA 1994, Sch 10A*]. See 67.11 TRADE PROMOTION SCHEMES.
- Power to require security. [*VATA 1994, Sch 11 para 4*]. See 17.1 CUSTOMS: POWERS.
- Duty to notify certain avoidance schemes. [*VATA 1994, Sch 11A*]. See 4.3 above.

Provisions in the VAT Regulations 1995

- Construction industry stage payments. [*SI 1995/2518, Reg 93*]. See 42.29 LAND AND BUILDINGS.
- Assignment of debts. [*SI 1995/2518, Reg 94A*]. See 64.37 SUPPLY.

- Continuous supplies of services – time of supply. [*SI 1995/2518, Reg 94B*]. See 64.50 SUPPLY.
- Grants of land – time of supply. [*SI 1995/2518, Reg 94B*]. See 64.44 SUPPLY.
- Long leases and tenancies – time of supply. [*SI 1995/2518, Reg 94B*]. See 64.44 SUPPLY.
- Power, heat, water and gas – time of supply. [*SI 1994/2518, Reg 94B*]. See 64.46 SUPPLY.
- Partial exemption – special method over-ride. [*SI 1995/2518, Regs 102A–102C*]. See 49.6 PARTIAL EXEMPTION.
- Partial exemption – standard method over-ride. [*SI 1995/2518, Regs 107A–107C*]. See 49.5 PARTIAL EXEMPTION.
- Attribution of input tax – financial services. [*SI 1995/2518, Reg 103(B)*]. See 49.8 PARTIAL EXEMPTION.
- Capital goods scheme generally and specifically disposals of capital items during the period of adjustment. [*SI 1995/2518, Regs 112–116*]. See 10 CAPITAL GOODS SCHEME and specifically 10.7 CAPITAL GOODS SCHEME.
- Bad debt relief – repayment of refund on assigned debts. [*SI 1995/2518, Reg 171*]. See 7.12 BAD DEBT RELIEF.

Other provisions

- Telecommunications services. [*SI 1992/3121, Art 7*]. See 64.27 SUPPLY.
- Margin scheme supplies acquired as part of a TOGC. [*SI 1992/3122, Art 8*]. See 61.4 SECOND-HAND GOODS.
- Leased cars. [*SI 1992/3222, Art 7*]. See 45.11 MOTOR CARS.
- Private use of services following a TOGC. [*SI 1993/1507*]. See 47.7 OUTPUT TAX.
- Land, buildings and civil engineering works used for private purposes – use of *Lennartz* mechanism for recovery of input tax. [*SI 1993/1507*]. See 35.7 INPUT TAX and 47.7 OUTPUT TAX.
- Margin scheme supplies acquired as part of a TOGC – motor cars. [*SI 1995/1268, Art 12*]. See 61.4 SECOND-HAND GOODS.

5 Appeals

Cross-references. See 6.8 ASSESSMENTS for correction of assessments on appeal by tribunals; 8.9 BUSINESS for appeals regarding registration of two or more persons as one taxable person; 31.5 GROUPS OF COMPANIES; 35.12 INPUT TAX for appeals in respect of input tax; 52.22 PENALTIES for mitigation of penalties by a tribunal on appeal.

De Voil Indirect Tax Service. See V5.4.

The contents of this chapter are as follows.

5.1 RECONSIDERATIONS

When a person disagrees with a decision made by HMRC, he may ask them to reconsider it. This is an informal process of looking again at the decision and will be carried out internally by HMRC but by an officer independent of the officer who made the original decision. The role of the review officer is not to defend the appealed decision but rather to consider the appellant's case objectively and attempt to resolve the dispute. The officer will be seeking to avoid a formal appeal except in cases of genuine disagreement and has considerable scope for negotiation and compromise. This may mean overturning or varying the original decision.

A person should ask HMRC to reconsider a decision if he can provide further information or there are facts which he thinks have not been fully taken into account. Asking for a reconsideration does not deny the right of an appeal to a VAT tribunal and HMRC will discuss or review a case at any time, even though an appeal may have already been lodged with the VAT tribunal. HMRC aim to complete a reconsideration within 45 days of the request.

Although a reconsideration can be requested at any time, a notice of appeal to a VAT tribunal must normally be served within 30 days of the date of the disputed decision (see 5.6 below). If a reconsideration is requested within the 30-day time limit for an appeal, and the reconsideration then exhausts that 30-day period, HMRC can (*a*) confirm the original decision, in which case the trader has a further 21 days from the date of confirmation to lodge an appeal with a VAT tribunal; or

(*b*) send a revised decision, in which case he has a further 30 days from the date of that decision to lodge an appeal.

In any case, the trader should ask HMRC to extend the time limit for appealing against the decision in case agreement cannot be reached.

If a reconsideration is requested after the 30-day time limit for an appeal, HMRC have no equivalent powers to grant an extension of time and the trader must apply to the tribunal for an extension (see 5.6 below).

(VAT Notice 700, paras 28.2, 28.5; Internal Guidance V1–29, paras 1.8, 2.3, 2.6).

5.2 APPEALS AND APPLICATIONS TO VAT TRIBUNALS

An appeal against a decision of HMRC on certain matters may be made to a VAT tribunal and from there, *on a point of law only*, to the High Court (Court of Session in Scotland) and continued up to the House of Lords under normal procedure. The matters on which an appeal to a tribunal may be made are restricted (see 5.3 below) and certain conditions must be complied with (see 5.4 below).

Public funding (formerly legal aid) is not generally available for appeals to tribunals. However, funding may be available for legal advice prior to the tribunal and legal representation at the tribunal where

- the proceedings concern penalties which the courts have declared to be criminal within the terms specified by the European Convention on Human Rights or where an applicant seeks to argue that issue; and
- it is in the interests of justice for an applicant to be legally represented.

In practice, funding is most likely to be available where a penalty, which is substantial either in terms of its amount or its impact, is being contested and where the amount imposed is beyond the assessed liability. The applicant must be financially eligible for funding. Applicants on Income Support and income-based Jobseekers' Allowance are automatically financially eligible. Each application is considered on an individual basis and is subject to the statutory tests of the applicant's means and the merits of the case.

Applications for funding should be made to the Legal Services Commission, 62–68 Hills Road, Cambridge, CB2 1LA via a solicitor or another authorised organisation. Solicitors who carry out public-funded work can be found in the Community Legal Service Directory (available in most local libraries), on the CLS website at www.justask.org.uk or by telephoning the CLS Helpline on 0845 608 1122.

Constitution. The functions of the VAT tribunals are carried out by a President, a panel of chairmen and a panel of other members.

The tribunals are run by the Court Service Agency (in Scotland, the Scottish Office) and they work under the supervision of the Council on Tribunals, 22 Kingsway, London WC2B 6LE and of its Scottish Committee, 20 Walker Street, Edinburgh, EH3 7HS.

[*VATA 1994, Sch 12 paras 1-7*].

Procedural rules. The Lord Chancellor after consultation with the Lord Advocate may make rules with respect to the procedure to be followed on appeals to, and in other proceedings before, tribunals and such rules may include provisions for

- limiting the time within which appeals may be brought, see 5.6 below;
- enabling hearings to be held in private, see 5.23 below;
- parties to the proceedings to be represented by such persons as may be determined, see 5.23 below;
- requiring persons to attend and give evidence, see 5.20 below;
- discovery and for requiring persons to produce documents, see 5.17 below;
- the payment of expenses and allowances to persons attending as witnesses or producing documents, see 5.20 below;
- the award and recovery of costs, see 5.25 below; and
- authorising the administration of oaths to witnesses, see 5.23 below.

[*VATA 1994, Sch 12 para 9*].

Penalties. A person who fails to comply with a direction or summons issued by a VAT tribunal is liable to a penalty not exceeding £1,000. The penalty may be awarded summarily by the tribunal notwithstanding that no proceedings for its recovery have been commenced. Appeal lies to the High Court (Court of Session in Scotland) which court may confirm or reverse the decision of the tribunal and reduce or increase the penalty. Any penalty so awarded is recoverable as VAT due from the person liable. [*VATA 1994, Sch 12 para 10*].

5.3 Appealable matters

An appeal to a tribunal against a decision of HMRC may only be made on the following matters.

(*a*) The registration or cancellation of registration of any person.

(*b*) The VAT chargeable on the supply of any goods or services, on the acquisition of goods from another EC country or, subject to (ii) below, on the importation of goods from a place outside the EC. A tribunal has no jurisdiction in relation to future supplies (*Allied Windows (S Wales) Ltd v C & E Commrs, QB April 1983 (unreported) (TVC 2.1)*; *Odhams Leisure Group Ltd v C & E Commrs, QB [1992] STC 332 (TVC 2.3)*).

(*c*) The amount of any input tax which may be credited to a person.

(*d*) Any claim for a refund by virtue of regulations made under *VATA 1994, s 13(5)* (acquisitions of goods from another EC country where VAT has also been paid in that other country).

(*da*) A decision by HMRC under *VATA 1994, s 18A* on the approval of a person as a fiscal warehousekeeper or the withdrawal of such approval or the fiscal warehouse status from any premises. See 70.13 WAREHOUSED GOODS AND FREE ZONES.

(*e*) The proportion of input tax allowable under *VATA 1994, s 26*.

(*f*) A claim by a taxable person under *VATA 1994, s 27* (goods imported for another person for private purposes, see 35.8 INPUT TAX).

(*fza*) A decision of HMRC refusing or withdrawing authorisation (i) to use the flat-rate scheme for small businesses or (ii) as to the appropriate percentage(s) to be used under the scheme, see 63.15 SPECIAL SCHEMES.

(*fa*) A decision by HMRC that an election under *SI 1993/2001, Art 12A* (right to elect under the payments on account provisions to pay actual liability for the preceding month rather than the predetermined amount) shall cease to have effect. See 51.4 PAYMENT OF VAT.

(*g*) The amount of any refunds under *VATA 1994, s 35* (construction of certain buildings otherwise than in the course of a business by 'do-it-yourself' builders, see 42.34 LAND AND BUILDINGS).

(*h*) A claim for a refund under *VATA 1994, s 36* or earlier provisions (see 7 BAD DEBT RELIEF).

(*j*) The amount of any refunds under *VATA 1994, s 40* (supplies of new means of transport to other EC countries by non-taxable persons, see 23.34 EUROPEAN COMMUNITY: SINGLE MARKET).

(*k*) Any refusal of an application under *VATA 1994, s 43B* (applications re group treatment, see 31.3 GROUPS OF COMPANIES).

(*ka*) Notice by HMRC under *VATA 1994, s 43C* terminating group membership (see 31.3 GROUPS OF COMPANIES).

(*l*) The requirement of any security under *VATA 1994, s 48(7)* or *VATA 1994, Sch 11 para 4(1A)(2)* (for the payment of VAT due or which may become due, see 17.1 CUSTOMS: POWERS).

(*m*) Any refusal or cancellation of certification under *VATA 1994, s 54* or any refusal to cancel such certification (flat-rate scheme for farmers, see 63.25 SPECIAL SCHEMES).

(*n*) Any liability to a penalty or surcharge under *VATA 1994, ss 59–69A* (see 52.9–52.15 and 52.18-52.20 PENALTIES). See also 52.22 PENALTIES for mitigation by the tribunal.

(*o*) A decision of HMRC under *VATA 1994, s 61* (liability of a director where the conduct of a company gives rise to a penalty for VAT evasion, see 52.9 PENALTIES).

(*p*) The making or amount of an assessment under *VATA 1994, s 73(1)(2)* for any period for which the appellant has made a return or under *VATA 1994, s 73(7)(7A)(7B)* or *VATA 1994, s 75* (see 6.1(*b*)-(*g*) ASSESSMENTS).

(*q*) The amount of any penalty, interest or surcharge specified in an assessment under *VATA 1994, s 76* (see 6.3 ASSESSMENTS). But without prejudice to the tribunals powers of mitigation (see 52.22 PENALTIES), the tribunal may only vary the amount assessed insofar as it is necessary to reduce it to the amount which is appropriate under the relevant penalty, etc provision.

(*r*) The making of an assessment, on the basis set out in *VATA 1994, s 77(4)*, outside the normal time limit where it is believed that VAT may have been lost through fraud, conduct involving dishonesty, failure to notify liability to be registered or unauthorised issue of VAT invoices. See 6.4 ASSESSMENTS.

(*ra*) Any liability arising under *VATA 1994, s 77A* (joint and several liability for unpaid VAT, see 17.3 CUSTOMS: POWERS).

(*s*) Any liability of HMRC to pay interest under *VATA 1994, s 78* or the amount of the interest payable (see 51.16 PAYMENT OF VAT).

(*sa*) An assessment under *VATA 1994, s 78A* (interest overpayments) or the amount of such an assessment (see 6.5 ASSESSMENTS).

(*t*) A claim for the crediting or repayment of overstated or overpaid VAT under *VATA 1994, s 80* (see 51.8 PAYMENT OF VAT), an assessment under *VATA 1994, s 80(4A)* (repayment to HMRC of overpaid refund, see 6.5 ASSESSMENTS) or the amount of such an assessment.

(*ta*) An assessment under *VATA 1994, s 80B(1)* or *(1B)* (recovery by HMRC under the unjust enrichment provisions of credits or repayments made to a taxpayer) or the amount of such an assessment (see 6.5 ASSESSMENTS).

(*u*) Any direction or supplementary direction under *VATA 1994, Sch 1 para 2* (registration of two or more persons as one taxable person, see 8.5 BUSINESS).

(*v*) Any direction under *VATA 1994, Sch 6 para 1, para 1A* or *para 2* or under *VATA 1983, Sch 4 para 2* (VAT on transactions between connected persons and supplies of goods to non-taxable persons for retail sale and, see 69.19, 69.23, and 69.30 VALUATION respectively).

(*w*) Any direction under *VATA 1994, Sch 7 para 1* (VAT on acquisitions of goods between connected persons to be charged on the open market value, see 69.12 VALUATION).

(*wa*) Any direction or assessment under *VATA 1994, Sch 9A* (anti-avoidance provisions for groups, see 31.5 GROUPS OF COMPANIES).

(*x*) Any refusal to permit the value of supplies to be determined by a method described in a VAT Notice published under *VATA 1994, Sch 11 para 2(6)* (see 60.1 RETAIL SCHEMES).

(*y*) Any refusal of authorisation or termination of authorisation in connection with the scheme under *VATA 1994, Sch 11 para 2(7)* (cash accounting scheme, see 63.2 SPECIAL SCHEMES).

(*z*) Any requirement imposed by HMRC in a particular case under *VATA 1994, Sch 11 para 2B(2)(c)* (self-billed invoices, see 40.6 INVOICES) or *para 3(1)* (production of VAT invoices by computer, see 40.10 INVOICES).

(*za*) A direction under *VATA 1994, Sch 11A para 8* (power of HMRC to exclude exemption from duty to notify a VAT avoidance scheme in cases of business splitting, see 4.12 ANTI-AVOIDANCE).

(*zb*) Any liability to a penalty under *VATA 1994, Sch 11A para 10(1)* (penalty for failure to notify use of a notifiable avoidance scheme, see 52.21 PENALTIES), any assessment of such a penalty under *VATA 1994, Sch 11A para 12(1)* (see 6.3 ASSESSMENTS) or the amount of such an assessment. But without prejudice to the tribunals powers of mitigation (see 52.22 PENALTIES), the tribunal may only vary the amount assessed insofar as it is necessary to reduce it to the amount as correctly calculated under the provisions.

(*zz*) A decision of HMRC on a review under *SI 2003/3075, Reg 21* (money laundering regulations).

[*VATA 1994, ss 83, 84(6)(6A); FA 1996, s 31(3), Sch 3 para 12; FA 1997, s 45(2)(5), s 46(3)(4), s 47(7)(9); FA 1999, Sch 2 para 3; FA 2000, s 137(5); FA 2002, s 23(2); FA 2003, ss 17(6), 18(2); FA 2004, s 22(3), Sch 2 paras 4, 5; F(No 2)A 2005, s 4(5); SI 1997/2542; SI 2001/3641, Reg 17; SI 2003/3075*].

An appeal may also be made against an assessment to recover an incentive payment for the submission of a VAT return electronically, the amount of such an assessment or a decision by HMRC that the conditions of entitlement to an incentive payment have not been met, see 6.7 ASSESSMENTS. [*SI 2001/759*].

No appeal lies to a tribunal on

(i) any matter which is outside (*a*) to (*zz*) above (subject to below); or

(ii) any decision which HMRC can be required to review under *FA 1994, s 14* (decisions relating to customs duty or the Community Customs Code or made under *CEMA 1979*) unless no request for a review has been made or the decision relates only to whether or not zero-rating applies to the importation of the goods in question and/or the rate of VAT charged on the goods.

[*VATA 1994, s 84(9)*].

Where an appeal is against a decision of HMRC which depended upon a prior decision taken by them in relation to the appellant, the fact that the prior decision was not within (*a*) to (*zz*) above (eg the exercise of a discretion by HMRC) does not prevent the tribunal from allowing the appeal on the grounds that it would have allowed an appeal against the prior decision. [*VATA 1994, s 84(10)*]. This follows the decision in *C & E Commrs v JH Corbitt (Numismatists) Ltd, HL [1980] STC 231 (TVC 58.1)*.

Extra-statutory concessions. In *RW Shepherd (VTD 11753) (TVC 24.29)*, the tribunal held that HMRC were bound to have regard to the terms of their concessions and while the tribunal could not interfere with those terms, it was entitled to consider whether those terms had been complied with. A similar conclusion was reached in *British Teleflower Service Ltd (VTD 13756) (TVC 38.50)*. However, it has been held in *Dr BN Purdue (VTD 13430) (TVC 2.74)* and subsequently in *C & E Commrs v Arnold, QB [1996] STC 1271 (TVC 2.75)* that a tribunal has no jurisdiction in relation to non-statutory arrangements or concessions which are a matter for HMRC. In *Arnold*, Hidden J, disapproving of the decision in *British Teleflower Service Ltd*, held that the provisions of *VATA 1994, s 84(10)* (see above) only applied to a case where there were two separate decisions (as had been the case in *JH Corbitt (Numismatists) Ltd*) and did not apply in the present case where there had only been one decision.

The decision in *Arnold* was distinguished in the subsequent case of *R (oao Greenwich Property Ltd) v C & E Commrs, Ch D [2002] STC 618 (TVC 2.77)*. The appellant had granted an underlease to a university (of which the appellant was a wholly owned subsidiary) and had treated it as a zero-rated supply. The university had issued a zero-rating certificate to the appellant in reliance on guidelines agreed between Customs and the Committee of Vice Chancellors and Principals of the Universities of the UK. Customs ruled that the certificate should not have been issued and raised an assessment to recover input tax. On appeal, the tribunal held that it had no jurisdiction to review the application of a concession. The appellant applied for judicial review. Collins J held that it would be 'unfair and so unlawful for Customs not to apply the concession .. provided that the taxpayer had complied with its terms'. Customs were not entitled to raise the assessment and the appellant was entitled to rely on the concession.

De Voil Indirect Tax Service. See V5.404–406.

5.4 **Conditions for hearing an appeal**

No appeal will be entertained unless the following conditions are satisfied.

(*a*) The appellant has made all the returns which he is required to make and has paid the amounts shown in those returns as payable by him. [*VATA 1994, s 84(2); FA 1995, s 31*]. The tribunal has no power to waive this requirement. If the condition is not satisfied, HMRC can apply to the tribunal for the appeal to be struck out or dismissed, although it need not do so and can allow the appeal to proceed (*Stilwell Darby & Co Ltd (VTD 35) (TVC 2.109)*; *Gittins, t/a Robinsons Ironmongery (VTD 87) (TVC 2.110)*).

However, in *PW Coleman, (VTD 15906, VTD 16178) (TVC 2.17)* the tribunal held that an appellant had a directly enforceable right under the *EC 6th Directive* to have an appeal heard and this right overrode the conditions in *VATA 1994, s 84(2)*. Following that case, HMRC now accept that the condition that *all* returns and payments have to be up-to-date is contrary to the EC principle of proportionality. Pending any change in the UK legislation, HMRC will not apply for appeals to be struck out solely because returns and payments are outstanding for VAT periods which are not under dispute. They will continue to make applications where a return has not been rendered for a VAT period subject to a disputed assessment or where the VAT in dispute has not been paid. (Business Brief 23/99).

(*b*) In the case of an appeal on matters under 5.3(*b*), (*n*), (*p*), (*q*), (*ra*), (*sa*) or (*zb*) above,

(i) the amount which HMRC have determined to be payable as VAT (or, in the case of 5.3(*sa*) have notified by assessment) has been paid or deposited with them; or

(ii) on being satisfied that the appellant would otherwise suffer hardship, HMRC agree, or the tribunal decides, that the appeal be entertained notwithstanding non-payment (see 5.11 below). Note that if the hardship application is granted but, subsequently, the appeal is lost, default interest on the amount of the disputed VAT may be payable. Conversely, if the hardship application is lost but, subsequently, the appeal is won, HMRC are liable to pay interest on any amount of disputed VAT paid or deposited with them which is repayable (see 51.16 PAYMENT OF VAT).

The tribunal in *PW Coleman (VTD 15906, VTD 16178) (TVC 2.17)* held that the condition in (i) above was acceptable and did not conflict with *EC 6th Directive* because of the hardship provision under (ii) above and because HMRC's decision on that is reviewable by the tribunal.

[*VATA 1994, s 84(3)(3A); FA 1997, s 45(3)(5); FA 2003, s 18(3); FA 2004, Sch 2 para 5*].

(*c*) The appellant has a sufficient interest in maintaining the appeal. (See *Williams and Glyn's Bank Ltd (VTD 118) (TVC 26.1)*). The appellant is not required to be the supplier (*Canterbury Hockey Club; Canterbury Ladies Hockey Club (VTD 19086) (TVC 2.45A)* or a taxable person accountable for the VAT in dispute (eg he may be an unregistered recipient of taxable supplies) but where he is the recipient of a supply, he should wherever possible seek the consent of the supplier to the appeal being brought jointly (*Processed Vegetable Growers Association Ltd (VTD 25) (TVC 2.41)*). For other cases where a tribunal allowed an appeal by the recipient of a supply, see *Dr Cameron (VTD 41) (TVC 31.38)*; *Gilbourne (VTD 109) (TVC 2.42)*; and *Beckley (JR) (VTD 114) (TVC 2.44)*.

(*d*) In appeals involving group registrations (see 31 GROUPS OF COMPANIES), only the representative member may appeal.

(*e*) Where HMRC have obtained a final judgment against the appellant for VAT on an assessment, the tribunal has no jurisdiction to entertain an appeal unless the applicant first procures the High Court judgment against him to be set aside (*Digwa (TS) (VTD 612) (TVC 2.179)*).

When an appeal is about a penalty, surcharge or an amount of interest, the appellant does not have to pay it before the appeal can be heard.

De Voil Indirect Tax Service. See V5.402; V5.421–423.

5.5 **Categories of appeal**

There are three different categories of appeal to the tribunals and procedure differs with each.

Category 1. Penalty for VAT evasion appeal. This is an appeal against

- an assessment to a penalty under *VATA 1994, ss 60* or *61* (on the grounds that the taxpayer, or a director or similar person, has been guilty of dishonest conduct, see 52.9 PENALTIES) or *FA 2003, ss 25* or *28* (evasion of import VAT, see 52.24 PENALTIES) which is not solely a mitigation appeal (see Category 2 below); and
- any accompanying appeal against an assessment for the amount of VAT alleged to have been evaded by the same conduct as in the appeal against the assessment to a penalty.

In a Category 1 appeal the burden of proof initially lies with HMRC.

Category 2. General penalty appeals (mitigation appeals and reasonable excuse appeals). A '*mitigation appeal*' is an appeal to a tribunal to reduce the amount of a penalty for

- conduct involving dishonesty under *VATA 1994, s 60* (see 52.9 PENALTIES) (an appeal against liability to the penalty is a Category 1 appeal);
- misdeclaration or neglect under *VATA 1994, ss 63, 64* (see 52.10 and 52.11 PENALTIES);
- late registration for VAT or unauthorised issue of invoices under *VATA 1994, s 67* (see 52.12 PENALTIES);
- breach of record-keeping requirements in relation to transactions in gold under *VATA 1994, s 69A* (see 52.20 PENALTIES); or
- evading import VAT under *FA 2003, s 29* (see 52.24 PENALTIES).

A '*reasonable excuse*' appeal is an appeal against any liability to, or the amount of

- a penalty for misdeclaration or neglect under *VATA 1994, ss 63, 64* (see 52.10 and 52.11 PENALTIES) on the grounds of reasonable excuse;
- a penalty for late registration for VAT or unauthorised issue of invoices under *VATA 1994, s 67* (see 52.12 PENALTIES) on the grounds of reasonable excuse;
- a penalty for breach of a walking possession agreement under *VATA 1994, s 68* (see 52.13 PENALTIES) on the grounds of reasonable excuse;
- a penalty for breach of regulatory provisions under *VATA 1994, s 69* (see 52.14 PENALTIES) on the grounds of reasonable excuse;

- a default surcharge for late submission of returns or late payment of VAT under *VATA 1994, s 59* (see 52.15 PENALTIES) on the grounds of reasonable excuse or because the return or VAT was posted in time to get to VAT Central Office by the due date;
- a penalty for giving or preparing an incorrect certificate as to zero-rating under *VATA 1994, s 62* (see 52.17 PENALTIES) on the grounds of reasonable excuse;
- a penalty for inaccuracies in EC sales lists under *VATA 1994, s 65* (see 52.18 PENALTIES) on the grounds of reasonable excuse;
- a penalty for failure to submit an EC sales lists under *VATA 1994, s 66* (see 52.19 PENALTIES) on the grounds of reasonable excuse; or
- a penalty for evasion of import VAT under *FA 2003, s 27* (see 52.25 PENALTIES).

In a Category 2 appeal the burden of proof lies with the appellant.

Category 3. Assessment and all other issues. This category covers all matters except those solely concerning reasonable excuses or penalties. Common examples of appeals within this category are appeals against HMRC decisions regarding

- assessments to VAT;
- refusals to allow claims for input tax;
- rulings as to liability for tax on supplies of goods or services;
- refusal to allow bad debt relief;
- requirements to provide security as a condition of continuing to trade; and
- refusals to allow a special scheme to be used.

In a Category 3 appeal the burden of proof lies with the appellant, although in appeals against VAT assessments the tribunal must first be satisfied that the assessment was made to the best judgement of HMRC.

[*SI 1986/590, Rule 2; SI 1994/2617; SI 1997/255; SI 2003/2757*].

Appeals falling into more than one category. The following guidelines apply.

- If an appeal involving dishonest conduct is against both an assessment of arrears of VAT and the accompanying penalty, the appeal falls within Category 1 above.
- If an appeal involving dishonest conduct is against the assessment of a penalty and also on the grounds of mitigation, the appeal falls within Category 2 above.
- If the appeal is against the liability for, or the amount of, a civil penalty or surcharge and also on the grounds of reasonable excuse, the appeal falls within Category 3 above.

5.6 Time limit for appealing

A notice of appeal must be served at the appropriate tribunal centre within 30 days after the date of the document containing the disputed decision of HMRC. If, during that 30 days, HMRC so notify the appellant by letter, his time to appeal is extended until the expiration of 21 days after the date set out in that letter (or to be set out in a further letter). Where, in relation to evasion of import VAT, a decision of HMRC is deemed to have been confirmed under *FA 2003, s 35(4)* (see 52.26 PENALTIES), a notice of appeal must be served at the appropriate tribunal centre within 75 days of the day on which the review was required. [*SI 1986/590, Rule 4; SI 2003/2757*].

A tribunal may of its own motion, or on application of either party, extend the time limit for doing anything in relation to the appeal. [*SI 1986/590, Rule 19*(*1*)]. Once the 30-day period above (or any extended period) has expired, only a tribunal can grant a further extension. Any notice of appeal to the tribunal should be served together with a notice of application for an extension of time, setting out the reason for the delay.

An extension has been allowed where the appellant was mistakenly under the impression that the matter was being handled by his accountants (*Hallam (WR) (VTD 683) (TVC 2.164)*) and where the appeal was delayed through the illness of a partner (*Hornby (WW & JH) (VTD 155) (TVC 2.176)*). Application was refused, although within the discretion of the tribunal, where to admit it would be to enable the applicant to recover VAT paid voluntarily under a mistake of law (*Kyffin (R) (VTD 617) (TVC 2.175)*). In *WJ Price (VTD 559) (TVC 2.163)* an extension was allowed where, although no real excuse for delay existed, there was evidence that the taxpayer intended to appeal, but this decision was not followed in *Wan & Wan (VTD 14829) (TVC 2.168)* on the grounds that the earlier tribunal's reasoning was inconsistent with subsequent decisions of the Court of Appeal including that in *Norwich & Peterborough Building Society v Steed, CA [1991] 1 WLR 449; [1991] 2 All ER 880.*

De Voil Indirect Tax Service. See V5.411.

5.7 **Making an appeal**

An appeal to a tribunal is brought by a notice of appeal being served at the '*appropriate tribunal centre*'. This is normally the centre for the area covering the address to which HMRC's disputed decision was sent. [*SI 1986/590, Rule 2*]. Application may be made (on *Form Trib 5*) to the appropriate tribunal centre for the transfer of an appeal to another tribunal centre. [*SI 1986/590, Rule 15*]. The tribunal centres and the areas which they cover are:

London Tribunal Centre, 15/19 Bedford Avenue, London W1B 3AS (Tel: 020 7631 4242; Fax No: 020 7436 4150/1).

The London tribunal centre deals with appeals against decisions sent to addresses covered by VAT offices at Bath, Bedford, Brighton, Bristol, Canterbury, Cardiff, Carmarthen, Colchester, Croydon, Enfield, Exeter, Finchley, Gloucester, Hammersmith, Harlow, Holborn, Ipswich, Kennington, Kingston-upon-Thames, London (City), London (West End), Luton, Maidenhead, Maidstone, Northampton, Norwich, Orpington, Oxford, Peterborough, Plymouth, Poole, Portsmouth, Reading, Reigate, Romford, Southampton, Southend, Stratford, Swansea, Taunton, Wembley, Westminster and Woking.

It also deals with appeals against decisions sent to addresses in Northern Ireland and addresses outside the UK or the Isle of Man.

Manchester Tribunal Centre, Warwickgate House, Warwick Road, Manchester M16 0GP (Tel: (0161) 872 6471; Fax No: (0161) 876 4479).

The Manchester tribunal centre deals with appeals against decisions sent to addresses covered by VAT offices at Birmingham, Bradford, Bury, Carlisle, Colwyn Bay, Cheadle, Chester, Chesterfield, Coventry, Derby, Doncaster, Droitwich, Dudley, Grimsby, Halifax, Hull, Leeds, Leicester, Liverpool, Lytham-St-Annes, Manchester, Middlesbrough, Newcastle-under-Lyme, Newcastle upon Tyne, Nottingham, Oldham, Sheffield, Washington, Wigan and Wolverhampton.

It also deals with appeals against decisions sent to addresses in the Isle of Man.

Edinburgh Tribunal Centre, 44 Palmerston Place, Edinburgh EH12 5BJ (Tel: (0131) 226 3551; Fax No: (0131) 220 6817).

The Edinburgh tribunal centre deals with appeals against decisions sent to addresses in Scotland.

Standard forms. The following standard forms for use in connection with appeals (and applications) to a tribunal are available from any tribunal office or the National Advice Service (tel: 0845 010 9000).

Form Trib 1	Notice of Appeal (see 5.8 below)
Form Trib 2	List of Documents (see 5.17 below)
Form Trib 3/3a	Witness Statement and Continuation (see 5.18 below)
Form Trib 4	Notice of Objection (to Witness Statement) (see 5.18 below)
Form Trib 5	Notice of Application (see 5.11 below)
Form Trib 6	Notice of Application for an appeal to be heard without payment or deposit of VAT (see 5.11 below)

It is not essential to use the printed forms but any notice or document served must contain all information required to be set out under the *VAT Tribunal Rules* (*SI 1986/590*).

One or more partners in a firm which is not a distinct legal person may appeal in the name of the firm, unless a tribunal directs otherwise, but with the same consequences as would have ensued if brought in the names of the partners. [*SI 1986/590, Rule 12; SI 1994/2617*].

On the death or insolvency of an appellant, if his liability or interest passes to another person (the 'successor'), the tribunal may direct, on the application of HMRC or the successor, that the successor is substituted for the original appellant. Written consent is required from the successor. Where this is not received within two months of being requested by the tribunal, the tribunal may, of its own motion or on application by HMRC, and after having given written notice to the successor, dismiss the appeal. It may similarly dismiss any appeal where it is satisfied that there is no person interested in it in succession to the original appellant. [*SI 1986/590, Rule 13; SI 1994/2617*].

5.8 *Contents of notice*

A notice of appeal (on *Form Trib 1*) must be signed by or on behalf of the appellant and must

- state the name and address of the appellant;
- state the date (if any) with effect from which the appellant was registered for VAT and the nature of his business;
- state the address of the HMRC office from which the disputed decision was sent;
- state the date of the document containing the disputed decision and the address to which it was sent; and
- have attached a document containing the disputed decision;

- set out, or have a document attached containing, the grounds of the appeal, including in a Category 2 appeal (see 5.5 above), particulars of the excuse relied upon (eg the date the return was posted or the reason why a penalty should be mitigated); and
- have attached to it a copy of any letter from HMRC extending the appellant's time to appeal against the disputed decision and any further letter from them notifying the appellant of a date from which his time to appeal against the disputed decision is to run.

[*SI 1986/590, Rule 3; SI 1994/2617*].

Representatives of the appellant may be authorised in the notice of appeal to receive acknowledgement of service of appeal and subsequent communications. [*SI 1986/590, Rule 32; SI 1991/186, Rule 24*].

De Voil Indirect Tax Service. See V5.411.

5.9 *Service and acknowledgment of notice*

The completed notice of appeal should be handed, or sent by post, fax, telex or other electronic means, to the appropriate tribunal centre. See 5.7 above for addresses of principal VAT tribunal centres and VAT offices covered. It is important to send the notice of appeal to the correct tribunal centre. If it is sent to another tribunal centre, although that tribunal centre may send it on to the correct tribunal centre, it can also hand or send back the notice of appeal to the person from whom it was received. This delay may be critical. [*SI 1986/590, Rules 2, 31; SI 1991/186; SI 1997/255; SI 2003/2757; SI 2004/1032*].

The notice of appeal must be acknowledged by a proper officer of the tribunal centre who will also send a copy of the notice and accompanying documents to HMRC. The acknowledgement and copy must state the date of service and the date of notification of the notice of appeal to HMRC. [*SI 1986/590, Rule 5; SI 1991/186*]. It will also show the tribunal reference number to be quoted in future correspondence.

5.10 Striking off, dismissing or amending an appeal

On application by HMRC. Where HMRC contend that

(*a*) an appeal does not lie to a tribunal (see 5.3 above), or

(*b*) an appeal cannot be entertained by a tribunal because the conditions of appeal have not been satisfied (see 5.4 above)

they must serve a notice to that effect at the appropriate tribunal centre containing the grounds for such contention and applying for the appeal to be stuck off or dismissed. A copy of the disputed decision must also be sent unless it has previously been served at the tribunal centre. An officer of the tribunal must send a copy of the notice and any accompanying documents to the appellant.

Where, at a hearing, HMRC's contention is proved to the satisfaction of the tribunal, the tribunal must strike out an appeal where (*a*) above applies and dismiss an appeal where (*b*) above applies.

In a Category 2 appeal (see 5.5 above) the hearing of HMRC's application can immediately precede the hearing of the substantive appeal.

[*SI 1986/590, Rules 6, 18(1)*].

By the tribunal. A tribunal may dismiss an appeal for want of prosecution where the appellant (or the person to whom his interest or liability has been assigned or transmitted) has been guilty of inordinate and inexcusable delay. However, unless the parties have settled the appeal by agreement (see 5.14 below) an appeal cannot be struck out or dismissed under this provision without a hearing. [*SI 1986/590, Rule 18*(*2*)(*3*)].

Amendment to notice of appeal. The tribunal may, at any time, either on its own motion or on the application of any party, direct that a notice of appeal be amended on such terms as it thinks fit. [*SI 1986/590, Rule 14*].

De Voil Indirect Tax Service. See V5.412.

5.11 **Making an application for a direction**

Before an appeal is heard, either party may apply to the tribunal for a preliminary direction. An application can be made for any of the following purposes.

- The hearing of an appeal without payment or deposit of VAT (a 'hardship application'). A tribunal cannot hear an appeal which relates to disputed VAT unless either the VAT in dispute has been paid or deposited or the tribunal or HMRC have waived that requirement. If paying the VAT would cause financial hardship, the appellant should first write to HMRC asking them to waive the requirement. He should demonstrate his financial position with evidence of assets, liabilities, income and expenditure and, if appropriate, bank statements. If HMRC do not agree to waive the requirement, the appellant may apply to the tribunal.
- The substitution of a person interested for an appellant or an applicant who has died or become bankrupt (see 5.7 above).
- The amendment of a notice of appeal (see 5.10 above), notice of application (see below), statement of case (see 5.16 below), defence, reply, particulars or other document in the proceedings.
- The transfer of an appeal or an application to another tribunal centre (see 5.7 above).
- The granting of an extension of time within which a person is required or authorised to do anything in relation to the appeal or application, for example, the time for the service of a notice of appeal or notice of application for relief from payment or deposit of VAT (see 5.6 above).
- A direction as to the conduct of, or as to any matter or thing in connection with, the appeal or application which the tribunal may think necessary or expedient to ensure the speedy and just determination of the appeal, including the joining of other persons to the appeal. [*SI 1986/590, Rule 19*(*3*)*; SI 1994/2617*]. Specific provision is made for

  (*a*) either party to serve further particulars of its case (see 5.16 below);

  (*b*) joinder of evasion penalty appeals brought by different persons relating to a penalty notice [*SI 1986/590, Rule 19*(*3*)*; SI 1994/2617*];

  (*c*) the postponement or adjournment of the hearing of any appeal or application [*SI 1986/590, Rule 27*(*5*)(*6*)]; and

  (*d*) the payment of costs (see 5.25 below).

- To waive any breach or non-observance of the rules of procedure or of any decision or direction of the tribunal. [*SI 1986/590, Rule 19*(*5*)].
- That the other party must serve a list of documents, or any class of documents, which are or have been in his possession, custody or power (see 5.17 below).
- For directions in relation to affidavits and depositions made in other legal proceedings (see 5.19 below).
- The issue of a witness summons or the setting aside of the issue of a witness summons (see 5.20 below).
- That the hearing, or any part of the hearing, of an appeal shall take place in private (see 5.23 below).
- The reinstatement of an appeal or application dismissed or struck out in the absence of both parties when the appeal or application was called on for hearing (see 5.23 below).
- That a decision or direction made in the absence of one party be set aside (see 5.23 below).
- For a certificate that the tribunal's decision involves a point of law relating wholly or mainly to the construction of an enactment, statutory instrument, EC treaty or EC instrument (see 5.30 below).
- The inspection of any document necessary for the purpose of the hearing which is in the possession, custody or power of any other person in the UK or the Isle of Man, whether or not such other person is a party to that appeal or application (see 5.20 below).

Contents, service and acknowledgment of application for a direction. An application to a tribunal, made otherwise than at a hearing, must

- state the name and address of the applicant;
- state the direction sought or details of the witness summons sought to be issued or set aside;
- set out, or have a document attached containing, the grounds for the application; and
- if served by an intending appellant
  - (i) state the address of HMRC from which the disputed decision was sent, the date of the decision and the address to which it was sent;
  - (ii) set out shortly the disputed decision or attach a copy of the document containing it; and
  - (iii) have attached a copy of any letter from HMRC extending the time limit for appeal or notifying the date from which the time limit runs.

The completed notice of application should be handed, or sent by post, fax, telex or other electronic means, to the appropriate tribunal centre. See 5.7 above for addresses of principal VAT tribunal centres and VAT offices covered. It is important to send the notice to the correct tribunal centre. If it is sent to another tribunal centre, although that tribunal centre may send it on to the correct tribunal centre, it can also hand or send back the notice to the person from whom it was received. This delay may be critical. [*SI 1986/590, Rules 2, 31; SI 1991/186; SI 1997/255; SI 2003/2757; SI 2004/1032*]. Application may be made (on *Form Trib 5*) to the appropriate tribunal centre for the transfer of an application to another tribunal centre. [*SI 1986/590, Rule 15*]. See 5.7 above for the tribunal centres and the areas which they cover. In the case of an application for a hardship direction, the notice must be served within the period for the service of a notice of appeal (see 5.6 above).

Except for the special rules for summonses in 5.20 below, a proper officer of the tribunal centre must acknowledge the application and send a copy of it, together with any attachments, to the other party, stating the date of service and date of notification of the notice of application. That other party must then, within 14 days of the date of notification, indicate whether or not he consents to the application and, if not, his reasons.

[*SI 1986/590, Rule 11; SI 1991/186, Rules 7–9*].

Amendment of an application. The tribunal may, at any time, either on its own motion or on the application of any party, direct that a notice of application be amended on such terms as it thinks fit. [*SI 1986/590, Rule 14*].

Power to extend time. A tribunal may on the application of any party, or of its own motion, extend the time limit for doing anything in relation to the application upon such terms as it thinks fit. [*SI 1986/590, Rule 19(1)–(3); SI 1994/2617*].

One or more partners in a firm which is not a distinct legal person may make an application in the name of the firm, unless a tribunal directs otherwise, but with the same consequences as would have ensued if brought in the names of the partners. [*SI 1986/590, Rule 12; SI 1994/2617*].

On the death or insolvency of an applicant, if his liability or interest passes to another person (the 'successor'), the tribunal may direct, on the application of HMRC or the successor, that the successor is substituted for the original applicant. Written consent is required from the successor. Where this is not received within two months of being requested by the tribunal, the tribunal may, of its own motion or on application by HMRC, and after having given written notice to the successor, dismiss the application. It may similarly dismiss any application where it is satisfied that there is no person interested in it in succession to the original applicant. [*SI 1986/590, Rule 13; SI 1994/2617*].

De Voil Indirect Tax Service. See V5.431-V5.435.

5.12 Withdrawal of an appeal or application

An appellant or applicant may at any time withdraw his appeal or application by serving notice in writing, signed by him or on his behalf, at the appropriate tribunal centre. A proper officer of the tribunal must send a copy of the notice to other parties. The withdrawal of an appeal or application does not prevent a party to the appeal from applying for an award of costs or interest (see 5.25 and 5.26 below) or a tribunal from making such award as it thinks fit. [*SI 1986/590, Rule 16; SI 1994/2617; SI 1997/255*]. If an appellant or applicant decides to withdraw after the date for a hearing has been fixed, he should advise the tribunal centre immediately by telephone or fax. HMRC may ask for costs if they attend a mutually agreed hearing where the other party fails to appear.

If an appellant notifies HMRC, whether orally or in writing, that he does not wish to proceed with the appeal, then unless HMRC object in writing to the withdrawal of the appeal within 30 days of notification, the provisions relating to settling appeals by agreement (see 5.14 below) are treated as having effect as if, at the date of the appellant's notification, the appellant and HMRC had come to an agreement, orally or in writing as the case may be, that the decision under appeal should be upheld without variation. [*VATA 1994, s 85(4)*].

De Voil Indirect Tax Service. See V5.461.

5.13 **Review of decision by HMRC**

HMRC officers carry out an internal review of disputed decisions to consider objectively both the appellant's case against HMRC's decision and the most effective way to settle the dispute. The review normally takes place in the 15 days following the service of the notice of appeal (see 5.9 above). This is to allow the Solicitor's Office enough time to prepare the statement of case if the appeal is to continue. If further time for review is required, the Solicitor's Office may make an application for an extension of time in which to serve the statement of case.

In particular, HMRC consider the following matters.

(*a*) *The decision.* Was the decision legally and technically valid, taking into account all relevant information and consulting, where necessary, with all those who have an interest in the appeal? In particular, officers are advised to

- check that the decision and the circumstances leading up to it are fully documented;
- confirm the calculations and logic of the decision;
- ensure that it is supportable in law, and
- consider the possibility of misunderstanding (ie where a trader has genuinely misunderstood official guidance) or misdirection (ie where HMRC is responsible, by act or omission, for misleading a trader about a liability to charge or deduct VAT). In the later case, although misdirection is not an appealable matter, if a tribunal finds that the appellant was misdirected, HMRC may be required to remit the VAT due even if the appeal is dismissed.

(*b*) *The appellant's case.* Officers are advised to

- confirm and evaluate the appellant's argument, ie check the facts and consider whether the arguments are supportable in law, and identify the strengths and weaknesses of the case; and
- consider the circumstances surrounding the dispute.

(*c*) *Consider how best to proceed with the dispute.* If the decision is to be defended at a hearing, an officer will prepare instructions to enable the Solicitor's Office to present the statement of case (see 5.16 below). Otherwise, if it appears that

- the decision should be withdrawn,
- there is room for negotiation and the dispute can be settled by agreement, or
- the decision should stand but on the facts, especially the overall cost, it is not worth defending at a hearing

an attempt may be made to settle the appeal be agreement (see 5.14 below).

5.14 **Settling an appeal or application by agreement**

HMRC's overall approach to an appeal is to look as the dispute objectively and find the most efficient method of resolving it. A tribunal hearing should only be required when a genuine disagreement remains. If there is a reasonable chance of reaching agreement, HMRC may apply for the appeal to be stood over (in Scotland, sisted) to allow further time for discussion. (Internal Guidance V1–29, paras 7.1, 7.3).

Where a person has given notice of appeal and, before the appeal is determined by a tribunal, HMRC and the appellant come to an agreement under which the decision under appeal is to be treated as

- upheld without variation,
- varied in a particular manner, or
- discharged or cancelled,

the agreement is binding as if a tribunal had determined the appeal in accordance with the terms of the agreement (including any terms as to costs). Where the parties have reached such an agreement, a tribunal will not continue the appeal purely in relation to an award of costs (*The Cadogan Club Ltd (VTD 548) (TVC 2.404)*).

The appellant may, however, within 30 days of the agreement, give written notice to HMRC that he desires to repudiate or resile from the agreement.

The agreement need not be in writing but, if it is not, the fact that an agreement was reached and the terms of that agreement must be confirmed in writing by HMRC to the appellant (or *vice versa*). The time of the agreement is then treated as the date of giving that notice of confirmation.

A person may act through an agent in all matters relating to settling appeals by agreement.

[*VATA 1994, s 85(1)–(3)(5)*].

Where the parties to an appeal have agreed on the terms of any decision or direction to be given by a tribunal, a tribunal may give such decision or direction without a hearing. [*SI 1986/590, Rule 17*].

Compounding agreement. Where HMRC and the taxpayer reach a compounding agreement, the dispute between the parties is resolved and any assessments raised effectively treated as discharged. Any outstanding appeal must be treated as having been settled by agreement (*Cummings (C) (VTD 14870) (TVC 2.192)*).

5.15 **Preparation for the hearing of an appeal or application**

The formal procedures set out in 5.16 to 5.21 below are designed to make hearings as open and fair as possible.

5.16 *Statement of case in an appeal*

Different provisions apply depending upon the category of appeal.

(*a*) *Category 1 appeals* (see 5.5 above). Unless the tribunal directs otherwise, HMRC must, within 42 days of the date of notification of

- the notice of appeal, or
- if later, the notice of withdrawal or dismissal of any application made by them under *Rule 6* (see 5.10 above)

serve at the appropriate tribunal centre a statement of case setting out, in numbered paragraphs, the matters and facts on which they rely for making the penalty assessment (or ascertaining the penalty) and, where also disputed, the making of the assessment (or the ascertainment of) for the VAT alleged to have been evaded. The statement of case must include full particulars of the alleged dishonesty and state the relevant statutory provision. It must be accompanied by a copy of the disputed decision unless a copy has previously been served by either party. An officer of the tribunal centre must acknowledge the service of the statement of case and send a copy of it, and any accompanying documents, to the appellant.

The appellant must, within 42 days of the date of notification of HMRC's statement of case, serve at the appropriate tribunal centre a defence thereto setting out, in numbered paragraphs, the facts on which he relies for his defence. (At the hearing, the burden of proof falls on HMRC but they will not be required to prove, or bring evidence relating to, any matter or fact admitted by the appellant in his defence.) An officer of the tribunal centre must acknowledge the service of the statement of case and send a copy of it, and any accompanying documents, to HMRC. See, however, *Patel (VTD 17248) (TVC 2.140)* where the tribunal did not see how the requirement to set out a defence could be reconciled with the *European Convention on Human Rights* and the implicit right to silence except on the footing that the appellant is not obliged to state any matters or facts which do not advance his case.

HMRC *may*, within 21 days of the date of notification of such defence, serve a reply to the defence. They *must* serve a reply where it is necessary to set out specifically any matter or fact

- showing illegality;
- which they allege makes the defence not maintainable;
- which might otherwise take the appellant by surprise; or
- which raises any issue of fact not arising out of the statement of case.

(*b*) *Category 2 appeals* (see 5.5 above). No statement of case is required in such appeals as particulars are set out in the Notice of Appeal (see 5.8 above).

(*c*) *Category 3 appeals* (see 5.5 above). Unless the tribunal directs otherwise, HMRC must within 30 days of the latest of

- the date of notification of the notice of appeal,
- the date of notification of withdrawal or dismissal of any application under *Rule 6* (see 5.10 above), or
- the date on which a direction dismissing any such application is released by the tribunal

serve at the appropriate tribunal centre a statement of case setting out the matters and facts on which they rely to support the disputed decision and the statutory provision under which the VAT or penalty is assessed or demanded or the decision is made. The statement of case must be accompanied by a copy of the disputed decision unless a copy has previously been served by either party.

An officer of the tribunal centre must acknowledge the service or the statement of case and send a copy of it, and any accompanying documents, to the appellant.

Where, in an appeal regarding an assessment or demand notice or the amount of an assessment, HMRC wish to contend that the amount specified in the assessment or demand notice is less than it ought to have been, their statement of case must indicate the amount of the alleged deficiency and the method of calculation.

[*SI 1986/590, Rules 2, 7, 8, 8A, 10; SI 1991/186, Rules 3, 5, 6; SI 1994/2617; SI 1997/255; SI 2003/2757*].

Further particulars. The tribunal may, at any time, direct a party to the appeal to serve further particulars of its case with at least 14 days' notice. [*SI 1986/590, Rule 9; SI 1997/255*].

Amendment of statement of case. A tribunal may, at any time, either on its own motion or on the application of any party, direct that a statement of case be amended on such terms as it thinks fit. [*SI 1986/590, Rule 14*].

Late statement of case. If HMRC are late in serving their statement of case and apply for an extension of time, this will normally be granted where there is no obvious injustice to the appellant. The period during which the documents should have been, but were not, served may be ignored in calculating interest on any VAT which may ultimately be due (*Dormer Builders (London) Ltd (VTD 2044)*).

De Voil Indirect Tax Service. See V5.412; V5.415.

5.17 *Disclosure, inspection and production of documents*

Each party to a Category 1 or Category 3 appeal (see 5.5 above) and an application for a hardship direction (see 5.11 above) must serve at the appropriate tribunal centre a list of the documents it proposes to produce at the hearing of the appeal or application

- in the case of a Category 1 appeal within 15 days after the last date for the service of HMRC's reply to the appellant's defence (ie within 36 days of the date of service of the appellant's defence);
- in the case of a Category 3 appeal, within 30 days of the date of notification of notice of the appeal or, if later, the date of notification of withdrawal or dismissal of an application by HMRC under *Rule 6* (see 5.10 above); and
- in the case of a hardship application, within 30 days after the date of notification of the application.

It is important to list all the documents that are to be produced. If an appellant or applicant introduces further documents at the hearing of which the other party is unaware, this may result in a time-wasting adjournment and he may be ordered to pay the costs of the wasted hearing. (Tribunals Explanatory Leaflet, para 23).

In Category 2 appeals (see 5.5 above) it is not compulsory to disclose documents in advance but the appellant will need to take to the appeal hearing any documents he is relying on to show reasonable excuse or that any return was posted on time.

The tribunal may also, on application of one party, direct the other party to serve a list (verified by affidavit if so ordered) of documents which have been or are in the possession of the other party relating to any question in issue in the appeal. (By preparing such a list, the other party effectively states that there are no other relevant documents.) If the other party wishes to claim that any document in such a list is privileged from production in the appeal, the claim and grounds for privilege must be made in the list.

A copy of any list of documents must be sent by an officer of the tribunal centre to the other party who may inspect the documents and take copies of them (unless privileged) at a time and place mutually agreed (or as directed by the tribunal).

In practice, *Form Trib 2* should normally be used to prepare such a list of documents and also state where and when the other party can inspect the documents and take copies.

All documents included in such a list must be available for production at the hearing (unless privileged).

[*SI 1986/590, Rule 20; SI 1991/186; SI 1994/2617; SI 1997/255; SI 2003/2757*].

De Voil Indirect Tax Service. See V5.413; V5.419.

5.18 *Witness statements*

Each party to an appeal may serve at the tribunal centre a statement in writing (a 'witness statement') containing evidence proposed to be given by any person at the hearing. The witness statement must contain the name, address and description of the person proposing to give the evidence contained therein and must be signed by the witness. The time limit for serving a witness statement is

- in a Category 1 appeal (see 5.5 above), within 21 days after the last date for the service of HMRC's reply to the appellant's defence (ie within 42 days of the date of service of the appellant's defence);
- in a Category 2 appeal (see 5.5 above), within 21 days after the date of the notification of the notice of appeal; and
- in a Category 3 appeal (see 5.5 above), within 21 days after the date of notification of HMRC's statement of case.

An officer of the tribunal centre must than send a copy of the witness statement to the other party. Unless that other party gives notice of objection within 14 days of its notification to him, the witness statement will be admitted as evidence at the hearing without the witness giving oral evidence. If notice of objection is given, the witness statement cannot be read but the person who signed it can attend the hearing and give evidence orally. Where, however, the matter under appeal is such that the case should be treated as a criminal one for the purposes of *European Convention on Human Rights, Art 6* (right to a fair trial) the tribunal is entitled to read a witness statement despite any notice of objection. See *Murrell (VTD 16878) (TVC 32.10)* where a serious misdeclaration penalty was imposed under *VATA 1994, s 61* and the appellant was in Australia at the time of the hearing. (The provisions of the *European Convention on Human Rights* are incorporated in *Human Rights Act 1998, Sch 1.*)

[*SI 1986/590, Rule 21; SI 1991/186; SI 1994/2617; SI 1997/255*].

Standard *Forms Trib 3/3a* and *Trib 4* may be used for the witness statement and the notice of objection respectively.

In a case which depends upon the date of posting a return, evidence in person from the individual who actually posted the envelope is likely to be essential to the appellant's case. (Tribunals Explanatory Leaflet, para 24).

De Voil Indirect Tax Service. See V5.414; V5.457.

5.19 *Affidavits and depositions made in other legal proceedings*

Affidavits and depositions made in other legal proceedings are admissible at a hearing of an appeal or application as evidence of any fact stated therein where

- oral evidence of the facts stated by the person who made the affidavit or deposition would be admissible; and
- that person is dead, outside the UK, medically or mentally unfit to attend as a witness or, despite reasonable diligence, cannot be traced.

Notice of intention to use such a document must be served within 21 days of the date of notification of the notice of appeal of notice of application. Any party objecting to its use must serve a notice of application for directions with regard to it at the appropriate tribunal centre within 21 days of notification of its intended use. At the hearing of such an application, a tribunal may give directions as to whether, and if so on what conditions, the affidavit or deposition may be admitted as evidence and, where applicable, the manner in which it is to be proved.

[*SI 1986/590, Rule 21A; SI 1991/186*].

De Voil Indirect Tax Service. See V5.457.

5.20 *Witness summonses and summonses to third parties*

A tribunal chairman or the Registrar of the VAT and Duties Tribunal may, at the request of a party to an appeal or application,

(*a*) issue a summons to a witness anywhere in the UK or Isle of Man requiring him to attend at a hearing and give oral evidence or produce any documents in his possession; or

(*b*) issue a summons to any person in the UK or Isle of Man requiring him to

- meet with that party at such date, time and place as the chairman or Registrar directs in order to produce, for inspection and copying, documents in his possession which are necessary for the hearing; or
- post such documents by first class mail to that party at an address in the UK or Isle of Man.

Any such summons must be signed by the chairman or Registrar and served

- in the case of an individual, by leaving a copy of the summons with him and showing him the original, and
- in the case of a body corporate, by sending a copy of the summons by post to, or leaving it at, its registered or principal office in the UK or Isle of Man

not less than four days before the date on which the attendance of the witness or third party, or posting of the document, is required. The summons must contain a statement, or be accompanied by a note, to the effect that the witness or third party may apply for a direction to the tribunal centre from which the summons was issued for the summons to be set aside.

No person can be required to attend and give evidence or to produce any document

- which he could not be compelled to give or produce by a court of law; and

- unless a reasonable and sufficient sum of money to defray the expenses of attending any hearing or meeting are tendered at the time the summons is served.

[*SI 1986/590, Rule 22; SI 1991/186; SI 1994/2617*].

Failure to comply with a summons renders a person liable to a penalty not exceeding £1,000. [*VATA 1994, Sch 12 para 10*].

De Voil Indirect Tax Service. See V5.419.

5.21 *Agreed statement of facts*

An appellant may approach HMRC to discuss the case with them and possibly produce an agreed statement of facts, an agreed bundle of documents, agreed accounts or a summary of those matters not agreed. This will simplify preparations for the hearing and save time and money. The tribunal will also find agreed statements, etc useful. (Tribunals Explanatory Leaflet, para 25).

5.22 **Notice and location of a hearing**

At least 14 days before the hearing (unless the parties agree otherwise), a proper officer of the tribunal must send notice of the date, time and place of the hearing to

- in the case of an appeal, or a hearing for the purposes of giving directions relating to an appeal, to the parties to the appeal;
- in the case of an application for the issue of a witness summons, to the applicant;
- in the case of an application to set aside a witness summons, to the applicant and the party who obtained the issue of the witness summons; and
- in the case of any other application, to the parties to the applications.

Unless a tribunal directs otherwise, an application made at a hearing is heard forthwith and no notice is sent to the parties to the appeal.

[*SI 1986/590, Rule 23; SI 1997/255*].

Hearings normally take place at the London, Manchester or Edinburgh tribunal centre (see 5.7 above) but the tribunal also arranges to hear appeals and applications in other places (eg Belfast, Birmingham and Cardiff) on request. If the appellant or applicant has moved to a new address, he can have his appeal or application heard at the nearest practicable tribunal centre. (Tribunals Explanatory Leaflet, para 17).

Postponement. A tribunal is reluctant to postpone a hearing but if it is essential to do so, the appellant or applicant (or his representative) should

- contact the tribunal listing office by telephone within 14 days of receiving the notice, followed by a letter or fax;
- give reasons for asking for the postponement;
- be prepared to agree an alternative hearing date when he and any witnesses will be ready; and
- be prepared to supply a medical certificate if the reason for the postponement is illness.

An engagement elsewhere is not normally sufficient reason for a postponement and the appellant should be ready to explain why another engagement takes priority. In any event, it should not be assumed that a hearing will be cancelled because a postponement has been requested. The hearing will stand unless the tribunal states otherwise.

De Voil Indirect Tax Service. See V5.441; V5.443.

5.23 Procedure at the hearing

A tribunal consists of a chairman sitting alone (where it appears that only a question of law is involved) or with one or two other members (where questions of fact may be in issue). [*VATA 1994, Sch 12 para 5(1)*].

Public or private. An appeal is heard in public unless a tribunal directs otherwise on application by a party to the appeal. [*SI 1986/590, Rule 24*]. An application for a private appeal may be made in advance by serving *Form Trib 5* (Notice of Application) at the appropriate tribunal centre or may be made at the hearing without notice. A direction will only be made in exceptional circumstances, eg where the disclosure of confidential information would harm the appellant's business or his competitive position (*Consortium International Ltd (VTD 824) (TVC 2.221)*). Where the appeal is held in private, expert witnesses from both sides may attend throughout (*R v Manchester VAT Tribunal (ex p C & E), QB 1982 (unreported) (TVC 2.223)*).

Unless a tribunal directs otherwise, the hearing of an application made otherwise than at or subsequent to the hearing of an appeal takes place in private.

Representatives. The appellant or applicant may conduct his own case or be represented by any person he appoints. HMRC may be represented by any person they appoint. [*SI 1986/590, Rule 25*].

Failure to appear at a hearing. If when an appeal or application is called for hearing,

- no party appears in person or by his representative, the tribunal may dismiss or strike out the appeal or application, but it may reinstate it on application, within 14 days after its decision or direction is released, by either party or any person interested; and
- one party fails to appear, the tribunal may proceed in his absence but may set aside any decision if the absent party or other person interested makes an application to have the case reinstated within 14 days after the written decision of the tribunal is released. However, where the applicant does not attend the hearing of that application, he is not entitled to apply to have a decision or direction of the tribunal on the hearing of that application set aside.

[*SI 1986/590, Rule 26; SI 1991/186, Rule 17; SI 1994/2617*].

Applications should be made on *Form Trib 5* (see 5.6 above) and should give the reasons for non-attendance on the hearing date. (Tribunals Explanatory Leaflet, para 20).

Procedure. At the hearing of an application or of an appeal other than a Category 1 appeal (see 5.5 above) the tribunal must allow the following procedure.

- The appellant or applicant (or his representative) to open his case. An appellant should explain what the case is about, giving a summary of the facts and indicating how the law applies to them. He should explain what has been already been agreed, what is in dispute, what evidence will be put forward and the basic points being made. He should state clearly why HMRC's decision was wrong. Where the appellant or applicant is not used to court proceedings, the chairman will help with the case as far as possible. But the chairman will have no knowledge of the case before the hearing and will not have seen correspondence between the appellant or applicant and HMRC. If it helps, the chairman may ask HMRC's representative to explain initially the basis of their decision.

- The appellant or applicant (or his representative) to give evidence in support of the appeal or application and to produce documentary evidence.
- The appellant or applicant (or his representative) to call other witnesses to give evidence in support of the appeal or application or to produce documentary evidence.
- HMRC's representative to cross-examine any witness called (including the appellant or applicant).
- The appellant or applicant (or his representative) to re-examine any witness following his cross-examination.
- HMRC's representative to open his case.
- HMRC's representative to give evidence in opposition to the appeal or application and to produce documentary evidence.
- HMRC's representative to call other witnesses to give evidence in opposition to the appeal or application or to produce documentary evidence.
- The appellant or applicant (or his representative) to cross-examine any witness called (including the other party to the appeal or application).
- HMRC's representative to re-examine any witness following his cross-examination.
- HMRC's representative to make a second address closing his case.
- The appellant or applicant (or his representative) to make a final address closing the case. New issues should not be raised unless the tribunal allows.

In an appeal other than a Category 1 appeal, the onus of adducing evidence and satisfying the tribunal the assessment, penalty or decision is wrong lies on the appellant (*Tynewydd Labour Working Men's Club and Institute Ltd v C & E Commrs, QB [1979] STC 570 (TVC 23.8)*; *Grunwick Processing Laboratories Ltd v C & E Commrs, CA [1987] STC 357 (TVC 2.215)*).

In a Category 1 appeal, the burden of proof lies upon HMRC. Their representative is obliged, therefore, to begin the hearing. The procedure is as set out above but reading 'HMRC's representative' for 'the appellant or applicant (or his representative)' and 'the appellant or his representative' for 'HMRC's representative'.

Subject to the above provisions, a tribunal may regulate its own proceedings as it thinks fit and the chairman or any other member of the tribunal may put any question to any witness called to give evidence (including a party to the appeal if he gives evidence).

[*VATA 1994, s 60(7); SI 1986/590, Rule 27; SI 1994/2617*]. (Tribunals Explanatory Leaflet, paras 26, 27).

Evidence may consist of oral evidence of witnesses, production of documents set out in list served under 5.17 above, statements read contained in witness statements (see 5.18 above) and any other evidence admitted by the tribunal. The tribunal cannot refuse evidence on the grounds only that it would be inadmissible in a court of law. See *Bord (VTD 7946) (TVC 2.222)*. It may require oral evidence of a witness to be given on oath or affirmation. [*SI 1986/590, Rule 28; SI 1991/186*]. Hearsay evidence may be introduced if not objected to by the other party or excluded by the chairman (*Wayne Farley Ltd and Another v C & E Commrs, QB [1986] STC 487 (TVC 2.225)*).

De Voil Indirect Tax Service. See V5.446–448; V5.451; V5.452; V5.456.

5.24 **Decision of the tribunal**

The tribunal reaches its decision not only on the basis of all the evidence put before it but also on a broad basis of common sense.

(*a*) **Appeal hearings**. At the conclusion of the hearing of an appeal, the chairman may announce the tribunal's decision or may reserve it to be given later in writing. In either case, most decisions must be recorded in a written document, signed by the chairman, containing the findings of fact by the tribunal and its reasons for the decision. A copy of this decision must be sent to each party to the appeal. However, if at the end of a Category 2 appeal (see 5.5 above) the chairman announces the tribunal's decision, he may ask the parties present at the hearing whether they require the decision to be recorded in such a written document and if they do not, the chairman will instead only issue a brief direction recording the outcome.

(*b*) **Hearings of applications**. At the conclusion of an application, the chairman may give or announce the tribunal's decision. In any event, the outcome of the application and any award or direction given by the tribunal must be recorded in a written direction, signed by the chairman. If a party to the application so requests within 14 days of the release of the application, the tribunal's decision must be recorded in a fuller written document, signed by the chairman, containing the findings of fact by the tribunal and its reasons for the decision. A copy of the decision and any direction must be sent to each party to the appeal.

The chairman may correct any clerical mistake or other error in a decision or direction, in which case a corrected copy must be sent to each party.

Where a copy of a decision or direction, either dismissing an application or containing a decision or direction made in the absence of a party, is sent to a party entitled to have the appeal or application reinstated under *Rule 26* for failing to appear (see 5.23 above), the copy must contain or be accompanied by a note to that effect.

[*SI 1986/590, Rule 30; SI 1991/186, Rules 19–22; SI 1994/2617*].

Although tribunals frequently follow previous tribunal decisions, they are not obliged to do so.

Voting procedure. If the tribunal does not consist of the chairman sitting alone, its decision may be taken by a majority of votes. Where the tribunal chairman is sitting with one other lay member, the chairman has a casting vote so that his conclusion determines the outcome of the appeal. [*VATA 1994, Sch 12 para 5*(*2*)]. See also *Rahman (t/a Khayam Restaurant) v C & E Commrs, QB [1998] STC 826 (TVC 2.254)*.

De Voil Indirect Tax Service. See V5.469.

5.25 *Costs*

Award by tribunal. A tribunal may direct a party or applicant to pay to the other party to the appeal or application a sum it may specify on account of that party's costs of appeal or application. Alternatively, it may direct such costs to be assessed by a Taxing Master of the Supreme Court or a district judge of the High Court by way of a detailed assessment (in Scotland taxed by the Auditor of the Court of Session and in

Northern Ireland taxed by the Taxing Master of the Supreme Court of Northern Ireland). Any sum awarded is recoverable as a civil debt. [*SI 1986/590, Rule 29; SI 1991/186, Rule 18; SI 1994/2617; SI 2003/2757*]. Where either party to an appeal or application does ask for costs, it must give clear details as to how they are made up. Costs allowed include reasonable barristers', solicitors' and accountants' fees and costs and expenses of employees attending hearings. For a consideration of what is 'reasonable' and not excessive, see *VSP Marketing Ltd (No 3) (VTD 13587) (TVC 2.400)*.

Where an appeal relates to two or more distinct issues or assessments which could have been heard separately, an appellant may be awarded costs in respect of a successful appeal on one assessment even if overall VAT is due to HMRC (*EA Kilburn (VTD 4866) (TVC 2.333)*).

The tribunal's power to award costs is confined to those costs recoverable at common law. As these are recoverable by way of indemnity only, where there is no liability on the appellant to pay his costs there is no basis for an award of costs. See *C & E Commrs v Vaz, QB 1994, [1995] STC 14 (TVC 2.329)* where there was an agreement to limit fees to the amount, if any, recovered by way of an award of costs so that, without such an award, no fees were payable.

The *Litigant in Person* (*Costs and Expenses*) *Act 1975* does not apply to VAT tribunals (*C & E Commrs v Ross and Others, QB [1990] STC 353 (TVC 2.332)*). Costs can only, therefore, be awarded to such a person on the common law basis that a litigant in person is entitled only to out-of-pocket expenses and not costs in respect of time spent preparing for the hearing. See also *Nader (t/a Try Us) v C & E Commrs, CA [1993] STC 806 (TVC 2.322)* where the court rejected claims for loss of business income. In *G A Boyd Building Services Ltd (VTD 9788) (TVC 2.393)* a limited company was held not to be a litigant in person because it must be represented by one of its officers or a third party. Time spent by a director in preparing for the company's case was therefore taken into account in determining costs. In *Rupert Page Developments Ltd (VTD 9823) (TVC 2.321)* the tribunal held that there was no logical distinction between a company and a litigant in person for these purposes so that the company was not entitled to claim costs in respect of time expended by its chairman, only out-of-pocket expenses. This contention was in turn rejected in *Alpha International Coal Ltd (VTD 11441) (TVC 2.375)* where the company was represented by its company secretary (a certified accountant) who was not a shareholder.

HMRC's costs. As a general rule, HMRC do not seek costs against unsuccessful appellants. They do, however, ask for costs in certain cases so as to provide protection for public funds and the general body of taxpayers. For instance, they will seek costs at those exceptional tribunal hearings of substantial and complex cases where large sums are involved and which are comparable with High Court cases, unless the appeal involves an important general point of law requiring clarification. See, for example, *University of Reading (VTD 15387) (TVC 2.298)*. HMRC will also consider seeking costs where the appellant has misused the tribunal procedure, eg in frivolous or vexatious cases, where he has failed to appear or to be represented at a mutually arranged hearing without sufficient explanation, or where he has first produced at a hearing relevant evidence which ought properly to have been disclosed at an earlier stage and which could have saved public funds had it been produced timeously. Appeals against penalties under *VATA 1994, s 60* on the grounds that a person has evaded VAT and his conduct has involved dishonesty are comparable with High Court cases. Where such appeals are unsuccessful, HMRC will normally seek an award of costs. (Hansard 24 July 1986, cols 459, 460; C & E Press Notice 1132, 5 August 1986).

A tribunal may, however, make an award of costs to HMRC even though no application for costs has been made (*Houston Stewart (VTD 9526) (TVC 2.406)*). The tribunal has frequently awarded costs to HMRC where appellants have abandoned appeals at the last moment or failed to attend to pursue their appeals or applications without reasonable explanation. See, for example, *Santi (VTD 954) (TVC 2.292)*.

De Voil Indirect Tax Service. See V5.481–485.

5.26 *Award of interest*

Where a tribunal decides that any 'VAT paid or deposited' should be repaid to the appellant or any amount of input tax should be paid to him, it may direct that the amount is repaid with interest at such rate as it may specify.

Similarly, where an appeal has been entertained despite the fact that VAT determined by HMRC to be payable has not been paid or deposited (see 5.11 above) and it is found on the appeal that that amount is due, the tribunal may direct that that amount must be paid with interest at such rate as the tribunal may specify.

[*VATA 1994, s 84(8)*].

'*Tax paid or deposited*' includes paying VAT charged on a supply 'without prejudice' should the VAT be found not to be payable (*Mahoney (VTD 258) (TVC 2.419)*).

No rate of interest is laid down and this has been subject to a variety of treatments by tribunals.

De Voil Indirect Tax Service. See V5.487–489.

5.27 *Enforcement of decisions*

Where, as a result of the tribunal's decision, any amount of VAT due or recoverable from any person or any costs are awarded to HMRC, then the decision may

- in England and Wales be registered by HMRC under the rules of court and enforced by the High Court as if due to HMRC in pursuance of a judgment or order of the High Court;
- in Scotland be recorded for execution in the Books of Council and Session and enforced accordingly; and
- in Northern Ireland be enforced by the Enforcement of Judgments Office under *Judgments Enforcement (Northern Ireland) Order 1981, Art 2(2)*.

[*VATA 1994, s 87*].

For this purpose, a party to the appeal may request, in writing within one year of the date on which the decision is released, that the outcome of the appeal and any award of costs or interest is recorded in a written direction signed by the Chairman or Registrar. [*SI 1986/590, Rule 30; SI 1991/186, Rule 19*]. This will enable a decision to be registered at less administrative cost.

5.28 *Recommendations by the tribunal*

The tribunal may recommend time to pay arrangements or a reduction in the amount due. Although it has no power to direct that any of its recommendations be accepted, or that HMRC should refrain from collecting VAT which is lawfully due, HMRC officers are advised to give consideration to any recommendation by the tribunal because

- it is likely to be referred to by the appellant in later dealings with them after the tribunal hearing; and

- it may become a matter of political or press interest.

(Internal Guidance V1–29, para 10.5).

5.29 *Action by HMRC on receipt of tribunal decision*

The written tribunal decision is sent to HMRC's Solicitor's Office who will pass on a copy to the VAT office concerned. The action taken by that office depends upon the decision.

(*a*) Where the decision requires any repayment to the appellant

(i) if the appellant was completely successful on all counts, immediate steps will be taken to repay the amount in dispute including any interest due (even in cases where HMRC may decide to appeal to the High Court);

(ii) if the appellant was partially successful, action as in (i) above will be taken where it is possible to determine the amount to be repaid. Where it is not, HMRC will take immediate steps to obtain all the information required and, if necessary, agree the amount with the appellant; and

(iii) if the appellant was the recipient of the supply and the appeal was not about input tax, the supplier's VAT office will inform the supplier of the decision, authorise him to credit the appellant (and any other customer affected by the decision) with the VAT involved and ensure that the supplier makes the necessary adjustments to his VAT account.

(*b*) Where the appeal is upheld, the VAT officer in charge will consult with the Solicitor's Office and, if appropriate, HQ Divisions on any clemency recommendation by the tribunal (see 5.28 above) and the possibility of any appeal to the High Court.

(*c*) If an assessment has been reduced or nullified, the appropriate action will be taken to amend HMRC's records and the appellant will be notified accordingly.

(*d*) If the appeal is dismissed, the appellant will be allowed 56 (42 days in NI) days from the date of the decision to appeal to a higher court. If he does not, HMRC will resume debt management action but if he does appeal, action will be deferred until the outcome is known.

(Internal Guidance V1–29, paras 10.4, 17).

5.30 APPEALS TO THE HIGH COURT

An appeal to the High Court cannot be made unless the matter has already been considered by a tribunal or at judicial review.

Appeals from a tribunal to the High Court. If any party to proceedings before the tribunal is dissatisfied on a *point of law* with a decision of the tribunal, he may either appeal to the High Court or require the tribunal to state and sign a case for the opinion of the High Court. In Scotland, the appeal lies to the Court of Session. [*Tribunal and Inquiries Act 1992, s 11*].

The decision of the tribunal on a *question of fact* is final. The leading case on the question of the distinction between fact and law is *Edwards v Bairstow & Harrison, HL 1955, 36 TC 207.*

There may be a possible further appeal from the High Court to the Court of Appeal and then the House of Lords. The Court of Appeal may, in certain circumstances, be 'leap-frogged'. In Scotland, appeals go directly from the Court of Session to the House of Lords.

Appeals from a tribunal direct to the Court of Appeal. In England and Wales, if any party to proceedings before the tribunal is dissatisfied on a *point of law* with a decision of the tribunal, he may appeal direct to the Court of Appeal provided the parties consent and the tribunal endorses its decision with a certificate that the decision involves a point of law relating wholly or mainly to the construction of an Act, statutory instrument or EC Treaty or Instrument which has been fully argued before it and considered by it.

The party wishing to appeal must apply to the tribunal for the certificate at the conclusion of the hearing or within 21 days after the date on which the tribunal's decision is released.

[*VATA 1994, s 86; SI 1986/590, Reg 30A; SI 1986/2288; SI 1986/2290; SI 1994/1978; SI 1994/2617*].

Costs. The general rule in appeal courts is that the losing party risks having to pay the other side's costs. However, HMRC may consider waiving their claim in particular where they are appealing against an adverse decision. Influential factors include the risk of financial hardship to the other party and whether the case is one of significant interest to taxpayers as a whole, turning on a point of law in need of clarification. If HMRC do come to such an arrangement, they would expect to do so in advance of the hearing and following an approach by the taxpayer.(Hansard 12 March 1980, Vol 980, col 572).

De Voil Indirect Tax Service. See V5.476.

5.31 REFERENCES TO THE EUROPEAN COURT OF JUSTICE

A tribunal or higher court may refer a question to the CJEC if a decision on that matter is necessary to enable it to give judgment. [*EC Treaty Art 177*]. Whether or not to refer a question is a matter within the discretion of the tribunal or court and it cannot be compelled to do so. It is not a matter for the parties to the case, although their views are no doubt taken into account. If one of the parties is dissatisfied with a refusal to refer a point to the CJEC, it must appeal under national law and has no right of access to the CJEC direct.

The national court has three options.

- It may decide that a decision on the question is unnecessary and that the case may, for example, be decided on the basis of national law which makes the question of EC law irrelevant.
- It may decide the question of EC law itself. This may be done, for example, where the point has been settled in previous CJEC decisions or where the circumstances of the case make a reference inconvenient.
- It may make a reference to the CJEC.

The courts have applied the following guidelines in exercising their discretion whether or not to make a reference.

- The point must be conclusive since the purpose of a ruling is to enable judgment to be given.

5.31 Appeals

- There must have been no previous ruling which decides or substantially decides the point.
- If the point is reasonably clear and free from doubt it may not be necessary to interpret but simply apply the EC law.
- It is necessary to decide the facts first.
- The question to be referred is a matter of some importance.

The CJEC cannot interpret national law or apply its interpretation of EC law to the facts of the case. Its sole function is to decide what the EC law is, and leave the national courts to implement its ruling.

6 Assessments

Cross-references. See 5 APPEALS; 31.5 GROUPS OF COMPANIES; 51 PAYMENT OF VAT.

De Voil Indirect Tax Service. See V5.131–140A.

The contents of this chapter are as follows.

6.1 ASSESSMENTS OF VAT DUE

VAT is normally paid (without any assessment being made) on the submission of a return for a VAT period.

However, subject to the time limits in 6.2 below, HMRC are given power to raise assessments where the following circumstances apply.

(*a*) *Returns have not been made*. Assessments will generally be based on centrally stored data concerning the trader's business and VAT history and will normally be withdrawn if an acceptable return is made and the VAT declared on it paid.

(*b*) *Documents have not been kept* and facilities have not been afforded to verify returns.

(*c*) *It appears to HMRC that the returns are incomplete or incorrect*. This will most frequently happen following control visits by HMRC officers.

(*d*) *Incorrect VAT credits*, ie where for any VAT period an amount has been paid or credited to any person as either a repayment or refund of VAT or as being due as a VAT credit and the amount ought not to have been paid or credited. This is further extended to cover an amount which would not have been so paid or credited had the facts been known or been as they later turn out to be (eg where bad debt relief has been claimed and subsequently the debt, or part, has been repaid without the VAT element being paid to HMRC). There are conflicting court judgments as to the period HMRC should assess (which is important, particularly in view of the two-year time limit under 6.2 below). HMRC have taken the view that the period to assess is the period for which a return was made that contained the incorrect claim or, following the judgment in *C & E Commrs v The Croydon Hotel & Leisure Co Ltd, CA [1996] STC 1105 (TVC 3.42)*, the period in which a voluntary disclosure containing the incorrect claim was made. However, the judgment in *C & E Commrs v Laura Ashley Ltd, Ch D 2003, [2004] STC 635 (TVC 3.43)* was that the period to assess should be the period to which the relevant VAT related, ie an assessment to recover a repayment or credit wrongly given following a voluntary disclosure of an error in an earlier period should have been made for that earlier period. Finally, in *C & E Commrs v DFS Furniture Co plc, CA [2004] STC 559 (TVC 3.104)* the court took the view, in similar although not identical circumstances, that the period to assess was the period current when the repayment was made.

(*e*) *Failure to account for goods*, ie where goods have, in the course or furtherance of a business, been supplied to a taxable person, acquired or obtained by him from another EC country or imported by him from a place outside the EC and he is unable to prove to HMRC that the goods

- have been, or are available to be, supplied by him;
- have been exported or otherwise removed from the UK without being exported or so removed by way of supply; or
- have been lost or destroyed.

(*f*) *A fiscal warehousekeeper has failed to pay VAT* required under *VATA 1994, s 18E* on any missing or deficient goods or it appears to HMRC that goods have been removed from a warehouse or fiscal warehouse without payment of the VAT required under *VATA 1994, s 18(4)* or *s 18D*.

(*g*) *Goods subject to excise duty or new means of transport* have been acquired in the UK from another EC country by a person who at that time was not a taxable person and

(i) no notification of that acquisition has been given to HMRC by the person required to give it;

(ii) HMRC are not satisfied that the particulars in a notification are accurate or complete; or

(iii) there has been a failure to supply HMRC with the information necessary to verify the particulars contained in the notification.

See 23.9 and 23.35 EUROPEAN COMMUNITY: SINGLE MARKET for general provisions relating to such acquisition of dutiable goods and new means of transport respectively.

Any amount assessed and notified under these provisions is deemed to be an amount of VAT due and, if the person fails to pay, enforcement action can be taken to recover the debt.

(*h*) *VAT has been lost as a result of conduct involving dishonesty* within *VATA 1994, s 60* (see 52.9 PENALTIES), conduct for which a person has been convicted of fraud, or registration irregularities or unauthorised issue of VAT invoices under *VATA 1994, s 67* (see 52.12 PENALTIES).

An amount assessed and notified to a person under any of the above provisions is, subject to appeal, deemed to be an amount of VAT due and is recoverable unless the assessment is subsequently withdrawn or reduced.

Where a person is assessed under either of (*a*) to (*c*) *and* (*d*) above for the same VAT period, assessments may be combined and notified to the person in one assessment.

[*VATA 1994, s 73(1)–(4)(7)(7A)(7B)(9), s 75(1)(3), s 77(4); FA 1996, Sch 3 paras 10, 11; FA 2000, s 136(4)*].

HMRC may raise a single or 'global' assessment covering more than one accounting period (*SJ Grange Ltd v C & E Commrs, CA 1978, [1979] STC 183 (TVC 3.107)*). This power may be necessary where it is impossible or impracticable to identify the specific accounting periods for which the VAT claimed is due but is not restricted to such cases. It is a question of fact (important for time limit purposes) whether there is one global assessment or a number of separate assessments notified together. In *Razaq and Bashir (t/a/ Streamline Taxis) (VTD 17537) (TVC 45.14)* Customs incorrectly issued the registration certificate in the names of Razaq and Shabir and subsequently issued a global assessment covering the period 1 November 1994 to 1 November 1998.

The tribunal held that the certificate was invalid. The effect of *SI 1995/2518, Reg 25(1)* was that the partnership was required to be registered and make quarterly returns from 1 November 1984 but since there was no valid certificate of registration, the effect of *VATA 1994, s 73* was that Customs had to assess accounting period by accounting period and could not make a valid global assessment for the overall period.

The Form on which HMRC notify assessments is clearly intended to be used for either a single or a number of assessments and the fact therefore that demands for multiple accounting periods are included on the same form does not necessarily constitute a single global assessment (*C & E Commrs v Le Rififi Ltd, CA 1994, [1995] STC 103 (TVC 3.84)* not following the earlier decision in *Don Pasquale (a firm) v C & E Commrs, CA [1990] STC 556 (TVC 2.137)*).

The assessment, to be valid, must show the period covered not just the end of that period (*RE Bell (VTD 761) (TVC 3.123)*) although the information need not necessarily be on the assessment itself. See *House (PJ) (t/a P & J Autos) v C & E Commrs, CA 1995, [1996] STC 154 (TVC 3.116)* where the dates covered by the assessment were left blank but the period assessed was indicated by accompanying schedules. A notice of assessment issued 'without prejudice' is not invalid (*McCafferty (VTD 483) (TVC 3.47)*).

Where an assessment has been made as a result of a person's failure to submit a return for a VAT period and, although the VAT assessed has been paid, no proper return has been made for that period, if HMRC find it necessary to raise assessments for later periods due to the failure to submit returns by that person or a representative of his (see 6.9 below) then HMRC may raise the later assessments for amounts greater than that which they would otherwise consider to be appropriate. [*VATA 1994, s 73(8)*].

Subject to the foregoing, assessments under (*a*) to (*c*) and (*e*) to (*g*) above must be made to the best of HMRC's judgment. [*VATA 1994, s 73(1)(7)(7A)(7B), s 75(1); FA 1996, Sch 3 para 10*]. HMRC must exercise their powers honestly and bona fide and there must be material before them on which to make their judgment. Although their decisions must be reasonable and not arbitrary, they are under no obligation to do the work of a taxpayer by carrying out exhaustive investigations but if they do make investigations, they must take into account material disclosed by them (*Van Boeckel v C & E Commrs, QB 1980, [1981] STC 290 (TVC 3.1)*). The function of the tribunal is supervisory. An assessment should only be held to fail the 'best judgment' test if made dishonestly, vindictively or capriciously, where it is a spurious estimate or guess in which all the elements of judgment are missing, or where it is wholly unreasonable. Short of such a finding there is no justification for setting aside an assessment. In the normal case, the important issue is the amount of the assessment (*MH Rahman (t/a Khayam Restaurant) v C & E Commrs, QB [1998] STC 826 (TVC 3.10)*and see also *C & E Commrs v Pegasus Birds Ltd, [2004] STC 1509 (TVC 3.19)*) and once the tribunal has accepted that Customs were entitled to make that assessment, the amount is for the tribunal to decide (*Murat v C & E Commrs, QB [1998] STC 923 (TVC 3.137)*). The function of the tribunal is to decide what information Customs relied upon to make the assessment and then make a value judgment as to how they arrived at the assessment. It is not a function of the tribunal to engage in a process that looks afresh at all the evidence before it (*Georgiou and another (t/a Mario's Chippery) v C & E Commrs, QB [1995] STC 1101 (TVC 3.6)*). See also *Seto v C & E Commrs, CS 1980, [1981] STC 698 (TVC 3.2)*. An assessment must be considered as a whole and if it is not made to the best of HMRC's judgment, then it is wholly invalid and void and cannot be corrected by any subsequent amendment to it or treated as partly valid. See *Barber (JH) (VTD 7727) (TVC 3.36)* where an assessment partly covered a period for which a previous assessment had already been raised.

Where an earlier assessment has been held to be defective because it was not made to the best of HMRC's judgment, HMRC are not estopped from issuing a replacement assessment by the principle of '*res judicata*', ie that an issue which a court has decided in an action between the parties cannot be questioned in a later action between the same parties (*Bennett v C & E Commrs (No 2), Ch D [2001] STC 137 (TVC 2.108)*).

Once an assessment has been raised, it is not open to HMRC to seek to treat that assessment, on fresh evidence, as an assessment for some other purpose. In *Ridgeons Bulk Ltd v C & E Commrs, QB [1994] STC 427 (TVC 3.151)*, Customs initially raised an assessment for overclaimed input tax but subsequently, when that could not be supported, sought to treat the assessment as one for undeclared output tax for a different amount. The court held that the correct procedure would have been to issue a further assessment under 6.6 below (which was not possible as the time limit had expired).

De Voil Indirect Tax Service. See V5.132; V5.133; V5.139; V5.239; V5.261; V5.267.

6.2 Time limits

The time limits for assessments under 6.1 above in respect of any VAT period are as follows.

(*a*) Under 6.1(*a*)–(*d*), subject to the provisions relating to death below, an assessment for any VAT period cannot be made after the later of

(i) two years after the end of the VAT period; or

(ii) one year after evidence of fact, sufficient in the opinion of HMRC to justify the making of an assessment, comes to their knowledge

but in any case not more than three years after the end of the VAT period. See 6.6 below for further assessments.

Where a single global assessment is made because it is not possible to identify a specific period for which VAT is due, the time limit in (i) above runs from the end of the *first* VAT period it covers (*International Language Centres Ltd v C & E Commrs, QB, [1983] STC 394 (TVC 3.40)*). Where a global assessment is raised out of time on this basis, it is a nullity *ab initio* even if the taxpayer failed to lodge an appeal against it in due time with a VAT tribunal (*Lord Advocate v Shanks (t/a Shanks & Co), CS [1992] STC 928 (TVC 2.181)*). See, however, 6.1 above for the different interpretation of what constitutes a global assessment following the decision in *C & E Commrs v Le Rififi Ltd, CA 1994, [1995] STC 103 (TVC 3.84)*.

A tribunal considering the possible application of (ii) above must decide what were the facts which, in the opinion of the officer making the assessment on behalf of HMRC, justified the making of the assessment and then decide when the last of these facts came to the knowledge of the officer. The period of one year then runs from that date (*Heyfordian Travel Ltd (VTD 774) (TVC 3.122)*). Similarly, in *Pegasus Birds Ltd v C & E Commrs, CA [2000] STC 91 (TVC 3.57)* the court observed that provided Customs acquired the last piece of evidence of sufficient weight to justify an assessment within the one-year time limit, the test in (ii) above is satisfied. 'Evidence of facts' means what it says; the words do not encompass constructive knowledge (*Spillane v C & E Commrs, QB 1989, [1990] STC 212 (TVC 3.4)*). This was confirmed in *C & E Commrs v Post Office, QB [1995] STC 749 (TVC 3.55)* where it was held that the relevant date was not when any error should have been discovered but when evidence of facts actually came to the knowledge of Customs. Nothing in the statutory provisions encompasses constructive knowledge. There is no obligation on HMRC to be alert to discover a mistake (*FC Milnes (Bradford) Ltd (VTD 478) (TVC 3.46)*). Following the rule in *C & E Commrs v J H Corbitt (Numismatists) Ltd, HL [1980] STC 231 (TVC 58.1)*, the Court is prevented from substituting its opinion for that of HMRC and therefore it can only interfere if there is material to show that an officer's failure to make an earlier assessment was perverse (*Cumbrae Properties (1963) Ltd v C & E Commrs, QB [1981] STC 799 (TVC 60.23)*).

Where returns which are clearly incorrect are in the hands of HMRC, assessments are out of date if made outside the two year period in (i) above and no evidence of new facts have come to HMRC's attention to bring the case within (ii) above (*Lord t/a Lords Electrical and Fancy Goods (VTD 320) (TVC 3.69)*).

(*b*) Under 6.1(*e*)(*f*) above, subject to the provisions relating to death below, an assessment cannot be made more than three years after the end of the VAT period or importation or acquisition concerned.

(*c*) Under 6.1(*g*) above, subject to the provisions relating to death below, an assessment cannot be made after the later of

(i) two years after the time of notification to HMRC of the acquisition of the goods in question; or

(ii) one year after evidence of fact, sufficient in the opinion of HMRC to justify the making of an assessment, comes to their knowledge

but in any case not more than three years after the end of the VAT period. See 6.6 below for further assessments.

(*d*) Under 6.1(*h*) above, subject to the provisions relating to death below, an assessment cannot be made more than 20 years after the end of the relevant period or two years after the VAT due for the relevant period has been finally determined.

The legislation specifies time limits for the 'making' of an assessment rather than the 'notification' of that assessment to the taxpayer. For a consideration of when an assessment is made (as distinct from notified) see *Cheeseman (t/a Well in Tune) v C & E Commrs, Ch D [2000] STC 1119 (TVC 3.82)*. However, to avoid any uncertainty, for all assessments issued on or after 1 March 2001, HMRC will apply the time limit rule to the 'notified' date rather than the earlier 'made' date. See 6.7 below.

Death. Where the taxable person has died, any assessment cannot be made more than three years after death. In addition, for assessments within 6.1(*h*) above, the 20 year time limit above is reduced to three years but any assessment which, from the point of view of time limits, could have been made immediately after death may be made at any time within three years after it.

[*VATA 1994, s 73(6), s 75(2), s 77(1)(4)(5); FA 1997, s 47(10)*].

De Voil Indirect Tax Service. See V5.136.

6.3 ASSESSMENTS OF PENALTIES, INTEREST AND SURCHARGES

HMRC may assess and notify any amount due by way of

(*a*) default surcharge under *VATA 1994, ss 59, 59A* (see 52.15 and 52.16 PENALTIES), (*b*) penalty under *VATA 1994, ss 60-69A* (see 52.9 to 52.14 and 52.18 to 52.20 PENALTIES),

(*c*) interest under *VATA 1994, s 74* (see 51.14 PAYMENT OF VAT), or

(*d*) penalty under *VATA 1994, Sch 11A* (see 4.2 ANTI-AVOIDANCE)

except that a penalty under 52.14(*b*)(vi)–(x) PENALTIES can only be assessed if, within the two years preceding the date of the assessment, HMRC have issued a written warning of the consequences of a continuing failure to comply with the relevant requirement.

Unless the assessment is withdrawn or reduced, the amount is recoverable as if it were VAT due. The fact that the conduct giving rise to any penalty under (*b*) or (*d*) above may have ceased before an assessment is made does not affect the powers of HMRC to make an assessment.

Combining assessments. Where for a particular accounting period a person is assessed for VAT due under 6.1(*a*)–(*g*) as well as surcharge, penalty or interest under these provisions, HMRC may combine the assessments but the amount of the penalty, interest or surcharge should be shown separately.

Allocation of VAT between periods. Where any penalty, etc must be calculated by reference to VAT which was paid late or avoided and that VAT cannot be readily attributed to one or more VAT periods, HMRC are empowered to allocate the VAT due to such period or periods as they determine to the best of their judgment.

Penalties, interest accruing on daily basis. Where a penalty or interest accrues on a daily basis, the assessment must specify a date (not later than the date of the notice) to which the penalty or interest is calculated. If the penalty or interest continues to accrue after that date, a further assessment or assessments may be made in respect of amounts so accruing. HMRC, however, may notify the person liable of a period during which he may remedy the failure or default which caused the penalty or pay the amount on which interest was charged. If the person meets this requirement, no further penalty or interest accrues after the date specified in the assessment.

Penalties for tax avoidance. Where HMRC notify a person of a penalty under (*d*) above the assessment must specify the amount of the penalty, the reasons for the imposition of the penalty, how the penalty has been calculated, and any mitigation of the penalty under *VATA 1994, s 70* (see 52.22 PENALTIES).

[*VATA 1994, s 76, Sch 11A para 12; FA 1996, s 35*(*7*), *Sch 3 para 11; FA 2000, s 137*(*4*); *FA 2004, Sch 2; F*(*No 2*)*A 2005, Sch 1 para 8*].

De Voil Indirect Tax Service. See V5.132.

6.4 Time limits

An assessment for any relevant period under 6.3 above cannot be made after the following times or, where there is an alternative, the *earlier* of such times.

(*a*) Where VAT has been lost as a result of conduct falling within *VATA 1994, s 60*(*1*) (VAT evasion: conduct involving dishonesty, see 52.9 PENALTIES) or conduct for which a person has been convicted of fraud

- 20 years after the end of the relevant period; or
- two years after the VAT due for the relevant period has been finally determined.

(*b*) Where VAT has been lost in circumstances giving rise to a penalty under *VATA 1994, s 67* (registration irregularities and unauthorised issue of VAT invoices, see 52.12 PENALTIES) 20 years after the event giving rise to the penalty.

(*c*) For assessments under *VATA 1994, s 59* (default surcharge, see 52.15 PENALTIES), *VATA 1994, s 63* (misdeclaration, see 52.10 PENALTIES) or *VATA 1994, s 74* (interest on VAT, see 51.14 PAYMENT OF VAT)

- three years after the end of the relevant period; or
- two years after the VAT due for the relevant period has finally been determined.

(*d*) For assessments under *VATA 1994, s 62* (incorrect certificates of zero-rating, see 52.17 PENALTIES), *VATA 1994, s 64* (repeated misdeclaration, see 52.11 PENALTIES), *VATA 1994, s 68* (breaches of walking possession agreements, see 52.13 PENALTIES) or *VATA 1994, s 69* (breaches of regulatory provisions, see 52.14 PENALTIES) three years after the event giving rise to the penalty.

(*e*) For assessments under *VATA 1994, s 65* (inaccuracies in EC sales statements, see 52.18 PENALTIES) or *VATA 1994, s 66* (failure to submit EC sales statements, see 52.19 PENALTIES)

- three years after the event giving rise to the penalty; or
- two years after the time when sufficient facts came to the knowledge of HMRC to indicate that, as the case may be, the statement had a material inaccuracy or there had been a default in the submission of a sales statement.

In law these time limits have effect in relation to penalties becoming due on or after 27 July 1999 although HMRC's policy has always been to apply such time limits since the penalties were introduced.

(*f*) For assessments under *VATA 1994, s 69A* (breach of record-keeping requirements in relation to transactions in gold, see 52.20 PENALTIES)

- three years after the transaction giving rise to the penalty; or
- two years after HMRC have evidence of facts '*sufficient in their opinion to justify the making of the assessment*' ie facts sufficient both to indicate that there has been a failure to comply with the provisions and to determine the value of the transaction concerned.

(*g*) For assessments under *VATA 1994, Sch 11A para 12* (failure to notify certain VAT avoidance schemes, see 4.2 ANTI-AVOIDANCE) two years after the time when sufficient facts come to the knowledge of HMRC to indicate that there has been a failure to comply with those provisions in relation to a notifiable scheme.

The legislation specifies time limits for the 'making' of an assessment rather than the 'notification' of that assessment to the taxpayer. For a consideration of when an assessment is made (as distinct from notified) see *Cheeseman (t/a Well in Tune) v C & E Commrs, Ch D [2000] STC 1119 (TVC 3.82)*. However, to avoid any uncertainty, for all assessments issued on or after 1 March 2001, HMRC will apply the time limit rule to the 'notified' date rather than the earlier 'made' date. See 6.7 below.

Death. Where the taxable person has died, any assessment under (*a*)–(*e*) above cannot be made more than three years after death. In addition, for assessments within (*a*) or (*b*) above, the 20 year time limit is reduced to three years but any assessment which, from the point of view of time limits, could have been made immediately after death may be made at any time within three years after it.

[*VATA 1994, ss 69A(4)(5), 77(1)–(5), Sch 11A para 12(4); FA 1997, s 47(10); FA 1999, s 18; FA 2000, s 137(2); FA 2004, Sch 2*].

De Voil Indirect Tax Service. See V5.136.

6.5 ASSESSMENTS FOR OVERPAID INTEREST AND REPAYMENTS

HMRC may raise recovery assessments to the best of their judgment in the following circumstances and notify the person accordingly.

(*a*) Where they have paid interest under *VATA 1994, s 78* (see 51.16 PAYMENT OF VAT) to any person who was not entitled to it, they may assess the amount paid.

(*b*) Where they have credited a person with an amount under *VATA 1994, s 80(1)* or (*1A*) (see 51.8(*a*) and (*b*) PAYMENT OF VAT) in excess of the amount for which they were liable at that time, they may assess the excess credited. *For claims made before 26 May 2005*, HMRC may raise recovery assessments where they made a repayment in excess of their repayment liability at that time.

(*c*) Where any person is liable under *Regulations* made under *VATA 1994, s 80A* to pay to HMRC any VAT previously repaid by HMRC to them on the understanding that it would be reimbursed to customers (see 51.9 PAYMENT OF VAT), they may assess the amount due.

(*d*) Where

(i) they have credited a person with an amount ('the gross credit') under *VATA 1994, s 80(1)* or (*1A*) (see 51.8(*a*) and (*b*) PAYMENT OF VAT),

(ii) any sums were set against that amount by HMRC, and

(iii) the amount reimbursed to customers was less than the gross credit,

they may assess so much of the gross credit as exceeds the amount reimbursed to customers. No liability can arise on the same amount under both (*c*) above and this provision.

Unless the assessment is withdrawn or reduced, the amount is recoverable as if it were VAT due.

Time limits. Any such assessment cannot be made more than two years after evidence of facts, sufficient in the opinion of HMRC to justify the making of an assessment, comes to their knowledge. 'Evidence of facts' does not include court judgments and their effects. See *C & E Commrs v DFS Furniture Co plc, CA [2004] STC 559 (TVC 3.104)* where an HMRC assessment raised in 2001 to recover VAT relating to periods from April 1993 to June 1996 was held to be invalid even though it was within two years of the decision by the CJEC in *C & E Commrs v Primback Ltd, CJEC [2001] STC 803 (TVC 21.168)* (which overruled the 1996 decision by the CA in that case on the basis of which a repayment had been made to *DFS Furniture*).

Interest. The provisions of *VATA 1994, s 74* (interest payable on VAT, see 51.14 PAYMENT OF VAT) apply to such an assessment except that in the calculation of the period of interest, interest runs from the date the assessment is notified until the date of payment.

HMRC may assess and notify any amount due by way of interest on a recovery assessment but (without prejudice to the power to make assessments for interest for later periods) the assessment is restricted to interest for a period of no more than two years ending with the time when the assessment to interest is made. The assessment must specify a date (not later than the date of the notice) to which the interest is calculated. If the interest continues to accrue after that date, a further assessment or assessments may be made in respect of the amounts so accruing. HMRC, however, may notify the person liable of a period during which he may pay the underlying assessment and, if the person meets this requirement, no further interest accrues after the date specified in the assessment.

Further assessments. See 6.6(*b*) below.

Notification of an assessment to a personal representative, trustee in bankruptcy, interim or permanent trustee, receiver, liquidator or person otherwise acting in a representative capacity is treated as notification to the person on whose behalf he acts.

[*VATA 1994, s 78A, s 80(4A)(4C), s 80B; FA 1997, s 45(1)(4), s 46(2)(4), s 47(6)(9); F(No 2)A 2005, ss 3(9), 4(4)*].

6.6 FURTHER ASSESSMENTS

HMRC may make further assessments in the following circumstances.

(*a*) Where, after an assessment has been made under 6.1(*a*)–(*d*) or (*g*) above, further 'evidence of facts', sufficient in the opinion of HMRC to justify the making of an assessment, comes to their knowledge. [*VATA 1994, s 73(6), s 75(2)*]. The further assessment must also be within the time limit (see 6.2 above). Contents of nil returns submitted by a taxpayer do not amount to 'evidence of facts' justifying a further assessment (*Parekh & another v C & E Commrs, QB [1984] STC 284 (TVC 3.73)*). In that case, Woolf J also observed that, where the two-year time limit for an assessment has elapsed. HMRC should only be allowed to make a further assessment in relation to the VAT due based on the evidence which has come to their knowledge since the earlier assessment. Where, however, the two-year period has not elapsed, HMRC are not prevented from withdrawing the earlier assessment and replacing it by another.

(*b*) If, otherwise than in circumstances falling within (*a*) above, it appears to HMRC that the amount which ought to have been assessed under any of the provisions of 6.1, 6.3 or 6.5 above exceeds the amount which was so assessed, then a supplementary assessment of the amount of the excess may be made and notified to the person concerned under the same provisions and within the same time limits as the original assessment. [*VATA 1994, s 77(6), s 78A(6); FA 1997, s 45(1)*]. Note that there is no requirement for further evidence as in (*a*) above.

De Voil Indirect Tax Service. See V5.134.

6.7 THE ASSESSMENT PROCESS

Unless there is a danger of losing VAT because of the imminence of a time limit or unless the nature of the irregularity is agreed and already clear, HMRC will normally write to the taxpayer in advance of making an assessment for underdeclared or overclaimed VAT, setting out why they believe an assessment to be necessary and detailing the calculation of arrears. This letter does not constitute the 'making' of an assessment but gives the taxpayer the chance to bring further information to the attention of HMRC and help resolve any misunderstanding or disagreement before the assessment is made. Normally, HMRC give the taxpayer three weeks to reply.

The assessment process itself is made up of three stages.

(*a*) *The decision to assess.*

(*b*) *The making of the assessment.* This process includes deciding in principle to assess, the quantification of arrears and any necessary checking of arrears calculations. It ends when the HMRC officer has taken all steps necessary to establish to the best of his judgement that the taxpayer owes a quantified sum for a given reason. That officer, and any checking officer, will sign and date any schedules of calculation. HMRC will normally provide copies of these schedules to the taxpayer to help explain the basis of the assessment.

(*c*) *The notification of that amount.* HMRC must formally notify the taxpayer by way of assessment of the amount of VAT due [*VATA 1994, s 73(1)*] but there is no express provision as to the manner in which this is to be done. In practice, the taxpayer will be notified in one of two ways.

- Normally, an internal Form VAT 641 is completed, signed and dated. This form is the means of inputting an assessment on to HMRC's computer system which then generates Form VAT 655, the notice of assessment to be issued to the taxpayer. The Form VAT 655 is sent from the central computer centre to the local VAT office where it is checked and then dated and sent to the taxpayer.
- In certain circumstances, for example, where there is some risk of an assessment which has been made in time not being notified to the taxpayer until after the time limit has expired, the assessing officer will send a dated notification of assessment by letter to the taxpayer. The computer generated Form VAT 655 will then normally be issued in due course.

The legislation specifies time limits for the making of an assessment under (*b*) above (see 6.2 and 6.4 above) but there are no time limits rules for notifications under (*c*) above. The date an assessment is made is not normally communicated to the taxpayer. To avoid any uncertainty, for all assessments issued on or after 1 March 2001, where, for example, an assessment is 'made' in time but not notified until after the time limit for assessing has expired, HMRC will always apply the time limit rules to the 'notified date' rather than the earlier 'made date'. The 'notified date' for this purpose is the date on which the assessment is sent by HMRC to the taxpayer. The date will be shown on the letter or other formal notification of the assessment.

(Customs Notice 915, paras 1.2, 2.1, 4.1–4.4).

Any notice for VAT purposes can be served on a person by sending it by post in a letter addressed to him or his VAT representative (see 3.8 AGENTS) at the last or usual residence or place of business of that person or representative. [*VATA 1994, s 98*]. See 50.5 PARTNERSHIPS AND JOINT VENTURES for the special provisions for serving notice on partners and 6.9 below for service on representatives.

An assessment which is incorrectly notified (eg by being sent to the taxpayer's solicitors without authority) is not invalid but simply unenforceable until properly notified to the taxpayer (*Grunwick Processing Laboratories Ltd v C & E Commrs, QB [1986] STC 441 (TVC 3.59)*).

De Voil Indirect Tax Service. See V5.137; V5.138.

6.8 CORRECTIONS OF ASSESSMENTS BY TRIBUNALS

Where on an appeal against a decision within 6.1(*b*)-(*e*) above it is found that the amount specified in the assessment is less than it ought to have been, the tribunal may give a direction specifying the correct amount. The appellant is deemed to have been notified of the revised amount. [*VATA 1994, s 84(5)*]. A tribunal may exercise its power to increase an assessment in order to correct arithmetical errors or where HMRC have argued at the hearing that the assessment should be increased. A tribunal does not have a free-standing power to increase an assessment entirely of its own initiative. Furthermore, if a tribunal was contemplating increasing an assessment, the appellant should be given a fair opportunity (by adjournment, if necessary) to consider the position (*Elias Gale Racing v C & E Commrs, QB [1999] STC 66 (TVC 3.140)*).

A tribunal may reduce or discharge an assessment on appeal. See 5 APPEALS.

6.9 ASSESSMENTS ON, AND NOTIFICATION TO, REPRESENTATIVES

Where a person required to make a return as a personal representative, trustee in bankruptcy, receiver, liquidator or otherwise in a representative capacity fails to make that return or makes a return which appears to HMRC to be incomplete or incorrect, assessments (including assessments of penalties, interest or surcharges) may be made by HMRC on that person in his representative position and a notification to him is treated as also notifying the person for whom he acts. [*VATA 1994, s 73(5)(10), s 76(10); FA 1997, s 45(6)*].

Similar provisions apply to assessments on, and notifications to, such persons in respect of acquisitions of goods subject to excise duty or new means of transport under 6.1(*g*) above. [*VATA 1994, s 75(4)*].

7 Bad Debt Relief

Cross-references. See 59.36 REGISTRATION for effect of transfer of registration with a business as a going concern; 60.21(6) RETAIL SCHEMES for bad debt relief for mail order businesses.

De Voil Indirect Tax Service. See V5.156; V5.157.

The contents of this chapter are as follows.

7.1 INTRODUCTION

Where a business has made supplies of goods or services to customers and has not been paid, it can claim bad debt relief in respect of the unpaid VAT provided certain conditions are met. In particular, relief depends upon the supply being written off as a bad debt in the books of the claimant and a period of six months having elapsed since the date payment became due. See 7.2 below for full details. If, following a claim, the bad debt is paid, any refund received from HMRC must be repaid to them. See 7.12 below. There are also implications for a customer if he does not pay the supplier within six months. See 7.13 below.

Use of credit notes. A business cannot issue a credit note to a customer for unpaid VAT (instead of claiming bad debt relief) simply because he has not paid for a supply. A credit note can only be issued where there is a genuine mistake or overcharge or an agreed reduction in the value of the supply. (VAT Notice 700/18/02, para 5.6). See also *Peter Cripwell & Associates (VTD 660) (TVC 38.74)* and *Temple Gothard & Co (VTD 702) (TVC 38.80)*.

Appeals. Where a claim to bad debt relief is refused, an appeal may be made to a VAT tribunal. [*VATA 1994, s 83*(*h*)]. See 5.3(*h*) APPEALS.

7.2 CONDITIONS FOR RELIEF

A business is entitled, on making a claim, to a refund of VAT where the following conditions are satisfied.

(*a*) It has supplied goods or services and has accounted for and paid the VAT on the supply.

Relief can be claimed whether the payment due is in money or in goods or services to be provided under a barter arrangement.

Normally, only the actual supplier can claim. There are two exceptions to this rule.

- *Transfer of VAT registration number.* Where a business has been transferred and the transferee takes over the VAT registration of the seller, the transferee acquires the seller's entitlement to any bad debt relief on supplies made by the seller. (VAT Notice 700/18/02, para 5.1).

- *Gas and electricity suppliers.* With effect from 2 August 2004, by concession, a supplier of gas and/or electricity can obtain relief from VAT on debts owed by a domestic customer where the supplier has accepted the transfer of that customer and his debts from another supply company. See 29.8(9) FUEL AND POWER for full details.

(*b*) The whole or part of the consideration for the supply has been written off in the accounts as a bad debt. This involves writing the debt off in the day-to-day VAT accounts and transferring it to a separate 'refunds for bad debts account' which must be kept (see 7.4 below).

(*c*) The debt must be over six months old, ie six months must have elapsed from

- the date of supply; and
- the time when the consideration became due and payable to (or to the order of) the supplier.

(*d*) The value of the supply must not exceed its open market value. HMRC interpret this as meaning that the value of the supply must not be more than the customary selling price.

(*e*) *For supplies made before 1 January 2003*, where the customer was a taxable person, the claimant had to give written notice to the customer of

- the date of issue of the notice;
- the date of the claim;
- the date and number of any VAT invoice issued for each relevant supply included in the claim;
- the amount of consideration for each relevant supply which the claimant had written off as a bad debt; and
- the amount of the claim (except where the claim was for a supply accounted for under a margin scheme, see 7.9 below).

This notice had to be given not before, but within seven days from, the making of the claim. The date a claim was made was the date the relevant VAT return including the claim (see 7.5 below) was sent to HMRC.

(*f*) The debt must not have been paid, sold or factored under a valid legal assignment (see 7.11(2) below).

The normal provisions as to the time of supply of goods or services apply for determining when a supply is treated as taking place for the above purposes. See 64.32 *et seq.* SUPPLY.

[*VATA 1994, s 36(1)(2)(4)(8); FA 1997, s 39(1); FA 1998, s 23; SI 1995/2518, Regs 6(3), 166A, 172(1)(1A)(2); SI 1996/2960; SI 1997/1086, Regs 3, 12, 14; SI 2002/3027, Reg 3*]. (VAT Notice 700/18/02, paras 2.2, 2.6, 2.7).

7.3 WHEN TO CLAIM RELIEF

A claim in respect of a relevant supply cannot be made until six months has elapsed from the later of

- the date on which the consideration (or part) which has been written off as a bad debt became due and payable to, or to the order of, the person who made the relevant supply; and
- the date of supply

but must be made within three years and six months from the later of those dates.

A business entitled to a refund which has not made a claim by the end of that period is regarded as having ceased to be so entitled.

[*VATA 1994, s 36(1); SI 1995/2518, Regs 165A, 172(1A); SI 1996/2960; SI 1997/1086, Regs 10, 14*].

A claim is made on the date that the VAT return including the claim is sent to HMRC. (VAT Notice 700/18/02, para 2.6).

7.4 RECORDS REQUIRED

Evidence required. Unless HMRC allow otherwise, before submitting a claim the claimant must hold the following in respect of every relevant supply.

- A copy of any VAT invoice provided or, where there was no obligation to provide a VAT invoice, a document showing the time and nature of the supply, purchaser and consideration.
- Records, or any other document, showing that VAT has been accounted for and paid on the supply and that the consideration has been written off in his accounts as a bad debt.

[*SI 1995/2518, Reg 167*].

Records required. Any business making a claim for bad debt relief must keep a record of that claim and, unless HMRC allow otherwise, that record must consist of the following information in respect of each claim made.

- In respect of each relevant supply for that claim
  - (i) the amount of the VAT chargeable;
  - (ii) the VAT period in which the VAT chargeable was accounted for and paid to HMRC;
  - (iii) the date and number of any invoice issued or, where there is no such invoice, such information as is necessary to identify the time, nature and purchaser; and
  - (iv) any payment received for the supply (including any payment received by the claimant or by a person to whom a right to receive it has been assigned and any payment made by any person by way of consideration for the supply regardless of whether such payment extinguishes the purchaser's debt to the claimant or not).
- The 'outstanding amount' to which the claim relates (see 7.6 below).
- The amount of the claim.
- The VAT period in which the claim was made.
- A copy of any notice to the customer required under 7.2(*e*) above.

Any records created under these provisions must be kept in a single account to be known as the '*refunds for bad debts account*'.

[*FA 1999, s 15(4); SI 1995/2518, Regs 165, 168; SI 1997/1086, Reg 13; SI 1999/3029*].

Preservation of evidence and documents. Unless HMRC allow otherwise, the claimant must preserve the evidence and records required above for a period of four years from the date of making the claim. He must also produce them, on demand, for inspection by an authorised person and permit that person to remove them at a reasonable time and for a reasonable period. [*SI 1995/2518, Reg 169*]. This requirement does not alter the standard requirement to retain records for six years (see 56.3 RECORDS).

7.5 HOW TO MAKE THE CLAIM

If all the conditions in 7.2 above are satisfied, a claim may be made for refund of the VAT on the bad debt. The claim is made by including the correct amount of the refund in Box 4 on the VAT return for the VAT period in which entitlement to the claim arises or, subject to 7.3 above, any later return.

Claimants no longer registered. If at the time the claimant becomes entitled to a refund he is no longer required to make returns, he should write to his VAT office giving details of

- former VAT registration number;
- name and address of the debtor(s);
- amount of refund claimed;
- copies of supporting evidence (eg invoices);
- proof that the debt has remained unpaid for six months from the date payment became due and payable or, if later, the time of supply; and
- proof that he possesses a separate bad debt ledger.

For supplies made to VAT-registered customers before 1 January 2003, the claimant still had to comply with 7.2(*e*) above even though no longer registered.

[*SI 1995/2518, Reg 166; SI 1997/1086, Reg 11*]. (VAT Notice 700/18/02, para 5.3).

Annual returns. By concession, where a business accounts for VAT using annual returns, it can claim bad debt relief on debts over six months old on the same return as that on which VAT on the debt is accounted for. (VAT Notice 700/18/02, para 5.5).

7.6 AMOUNT OF THE CLAIM

A business is entitled, on making a claim, to a refund of VAT by reference to 'the outstanding amount'. '*The outstanding amount*' means the consideration for the supply written off in the accounts as a bad debt *less* any part of that consideration 'received' before the time of the claim. '*Received*' means received by the claimant or by a person to whom a right to receive the whole or any part of the consideration written off has been assigned.

Where the whole or any part of the consideration for the supply does not consist of money, the amount in money that is taken to represent any non-monetary part of the consideration is so much of the amount made up of

- the value of the supply, and

- the VAT charged on the supply

as is attributable to the non-monetary consideration in question.

[*VATA 1994, s 36(2)(3)(3A); FA 1998, s 23; FA 1999, s 15*].

Where, under a voluntary arrangement, creditors receive shares in full satisfaction of outstanding debts, there is no longer an '*outstanding amount*' and bad debt relief cannot be claimed (*AEG (UK) Ltd (VTD 11428) (TVC 4.9)*).

The effect of the above is that

- where no payment has been received in respect of a supply or supplies, the claim will be for the amount of VAT accounted for and paid to HMRC; and
- where a part payment has been received in respect of a supply or supplies, a refund can be claimed relating to the amount of VAT that is still outstanding.

Special rules apply to determine the amount of the claim where

- part payments are received relating to more than one supply (see 7.7 below);
- payments are received under hire purchase or conditional or credit sale agreements (see 7.8(1) below); and
- supplies are made under the margin scheme for second-hand goods or the tour operators' margin scheme (see 7.9 below).

7.7 Attributing part payments

Subject to 7.8(1) below, where

- the claimant has made more than one supply (whether taxable or not) to the purchaser, and
- a 'payment' is received in relation to those supplies,

then, unless the purchaser has specified that the payment is for a particular supply and pays for that supply in full, in calculating any VAT due on the outstanding debt the payment is attributed to earliest supplies first. Supplies made on the same day are aggregated and treated as one, the payment being rateably apportioned. [*SI 1995/2518, Reg 170; SI 2002/3027, Reg 4*].

'*Payment*' means any payment or part payment which is made by any person to any person by way of consideration for a supply, regardless of whether such payment extinguishes the purchaser's debt to the claimant or not. [*FA 1999, s 15(4); SI 1995/2518, Reg 165; SI 1999/3029*]. This definition is widely drawn and includes payment in the form of

- any non-monetary payments (eg goods or services provided in exchange);
- third party payments received;
- the proceeds from the sale of repossessed goods under finance agreements (see 7.8(2) below);
- payments received from a guarantor of the customer (see 7.10(1) below);
- payments made by the *customer's* insurers (but not by the *claimant's* insurers where it has taken out bad debts insurance) (see 7.10(2) below);
- mutual debts (see 7.10(3) below); and

- the value of any enforceable security (see 7.10(5) below).

Example 1

A claimant has made the following supplies to the purchaser.

Date of supply	*Supply*	*VAT-exclusive*	*VAT*	*VAT-inclusive*
		£	£	£
30.6.02	1	1,000	Zero-rated	1,000
28.7.02	2	1,000	175	1,175
25.8.02	3	2,000	350	2,350
29.9.02	4	350	Exempt	350
27.10.02	5	800	140	940
24.11.02	6	3,000	525	3,525
		£8,150	£1,190	£9,340

A payment of only £3,500 is received. As the payment has not been allocated by the customer, it is allocated to the earliest supplies and treated as relating to supplies 1, 2 and part of 3 as follows.

Supply	*VAT-inclusive*
	£
1	1,000
2	1,175
3 (part)	1,325
Amount of payment	£3,500

The VAT-inclusive debt outstanding on supply 3 is therefore £1,025 (£2,350 – £1,325) and the VAT outstanding on the supply is £152.66 (£1,025 × 4/47).

The outstanding amount of £5,840 (£9,340 – £3,500) and the bad debt relief that can be claimed is as follows.

Supply	*VAT-inclusive*	*VAT*
	£	£
3 (part)	1,025	152.66
4	350	Exempt
5	940	140.00
6	3,525	525.00
	5,840	£817.66

Example 2

The figures are as in *Example 1* above except that supplies 1, 2 and 3 were all made on the same day and are therefore treated as a single supply.

The debt outstanding on supplies 1, 2 and 3 is £1,025 (£4,525 – £3,500) and the proportion of VAT included is

$$\frac{\text{VAT in supplies 1, 2 and 3}}{\text{Total VAT} - \text{inclusive value of supplies 1, 2 and 3}} \times \text{debt outstanding}$$

= 525/4,525 × £1,025 = £118.92

The outstanding amount of £5,840 (£9,340 – £3,500) and the bad debt relief that can be claimed is as follows.

Supply	*VAT-inclusive*	*VAT*
	£	£
1–3 (part)	1,025	118.92
4	350	Exempt
5	940	140.00
6	3,525	525.00
	£5,840	£783.92

(VAT Notice 708/18/02, paras 3.3, 3.4).

7.8 **Goods supplied with associated finance**

(1) **Attribution of payments to goods or finance**

Bad debt relief is available on supplies of goods made by way of hire purchase or conditional or credit sale agreements where the customer has defaulted. Such supplies have two components, a taxable supply of goods and an exempt supply of associated financial services. The time of supply for goods is typically when they are made available to the customer [*VATA 1994, s 6*] and the time of supply of the financial services is when payment is made. [*SI 1995/2518, Reg 9*]. Therefore, unless the supplier seeks an agreement with HMRC to treat the supply of finance as occurring at the same time as the supply of goods, in applying the part payment rules in 7.6 above, strictly, the supplier should allocate any payments received from their customer first to the supply of the goods and only then to the supply of financial services after the goods element has been 'paid in full'. The provisions detailed below have been implemented in order to avoid this.

Where

- the claimant made a supply of goods and, in connection with that supply, a supply of credit,
- those supplies were made under a hire purchase, conditional sale or credit sale agreement, and

- a payment is received in relation to those supplies (other than a payment of an amount upon which interest is not charged, eg a deposit),

the payment is attributed

(i) as to the supply of credit, by multiplying the payment by the fraction

$$\frac{A}{B}$$

where

A = the total of the interest on the credit provided under the agreement (determined as at the date of the making of the agreement); and

B = is the total amount payable under the agreement, less any amount upon which interest is not charged; and

(ii) as to the balance, to the supply of goods.

Where an agreement provides for variation of the rate of interest after the date of the making of the agreement then, for the purposes of the above calculation, it is assumed that the rate is not varied.

Example 1

A car is sold on hire purchase. The cost of the car is £8,000 and interest over the life of the agreement is £2,000, making the total HP price £10,000. The customer makes payments totalling £3,000 and then defaults.

The payments of £3,000 are allocated in the ratio 8,000:2,000, ie 80% to the goods (£2,400) and 20% to interest (£600). A bad debt claim can be made (subject to the normal conditions) of

(£8,000 – £2,400) × 7/47 = £834.04

Example 2

A car is sold on hire purchase. The cost of the car is £8,000. A deposit of £1,000 is paid and the balance of £7,000 attracts interest of £1,750 under the hire purchase agreement. The customer pays the deposit of £1,000 and £2,000 under the hire purchase agreement and then defaults.

The deposit of £1,000 is attributed wholly to the goods. The payments of £2,000 under the hire purchase agreement are allocated in the ratio 7,000:1,750, ie 80% to the goods (£1,600) and 20% to interest (£400). A bad debt claim can be made (subject to the normal conditions) of

(£8,000 – £1,000 – £1,600) × 7/47 = £804.26

[*SI 1995/2518, Reg 170A; SI 2002/3027, Reg 5*]. (VAT Notice 700/18/02, para 3.5).

The above method of apportionment allocates interest equally to instalments over the life of the agreement (the 'straightline' method) although, in practice, many finance companies allocate a greater proportion of interest to the earlier instalments (the 'rule of 78' method). In *Abbey National plc v C & E Commrs, Ch D [2005] All ER(D) 94 (Jun) (TVC 4.26)* the High Court upheld the decision of the tribunal that the straightline method was the method laid down by the *Regulations* and, unless that method was irrational to the point that no person acting reasonably would use it (which was not the case), it had to be used.

(2) **Repossessed goods**

Where goods are supplied with finance, if the customer does not make the required payments the seller may have the right to repossess the goods and sell them to recover all or part of the debt due from the customer. The disposal of these second-hand repossessed goods is normally subject to VAT but is outside the scope of VAT provided

- they are sold in the same condition as when repossessed;
- in the case of goods other than motor cars, if the defaulting customer had sold them VAT would not have been chargeable or would have been chargeable on less than full value (eg because the goods had not been acquired for business purposes or they were margin scheme supplies); and
- in the case of motor cars, the defaulting customer had not been allowed to deduct some or all of the input tax charged on the car.

See 27.15 FINANCIAL SERVICES for full details.

In determining the outstanding amount on which bad debt relief can be claimed

(i) *if the sale of the repossessed goods is not subject to VAT*, any relief should be based on the amount remaining unpaid, if any, after taking into account payments by the customer and the proceeds from the sale; and

(ii) *if the sale of the repossessed goods is subject to VAT*, with effect from 6 December 2001 only payments by the customer have to be deducted. Before 6 December 2001, both payments by the customer and the proceeds of sale had to be deducted.

(VAT Notice 700/18/02, para 3.6; Business Brief 19/01).

7.9 **Second-hand goods and tour operators' margin scheme**

Bad debt relief may be claimed in respect of supplies made under the margin schemes for SECOND-HAND GOODS (61) or the TOUR OPERATORS' MARGIN SCHEME (66) as follows.

- If the debt is equal to or less than the profit margin, bad debt relief may be claimed on the VAT fraction of the debt.
- If the debt is greater than the profit margin, bad debt relief is limited to the VAT fraction of the profit margin (ie the amount of VAT which the supplier has paid to HMRC).

Debt for the above purposes means full consideration for the relevant supply *less* any payment received in respect of it. Payment means any payment which is made by any person to any person by way of consideration for a supply, regardless of whether such payment extinguishes the purchaser's debt to the claimant or not. [*FA 1999, s 15(4); SI 1995/2518, Reg 165; SI 1999/3029*].

Example

Second-hand goods purchased for £400 are sold for £500 (ie the profit margin is £100). The customer only pays (a) £450 and (b) £350. Bad debt relief is calculated as follows.

(*a*) The debt is £50 which is less than the profit margin of £100. Bad debt relief can be claimed on

7/47 × £50 = £7.45

(*b*) The debt is £150 which is greater than the profit margin. Bad debt relief can be claimed on

7/47 × £100 = £14.89

[*SI 1995/2518, Regs 172A, 172B; SI 1997/1086, Reg 15*]. (VAT Notice 700/18/02, paras 5.7, 5.8).

7.10 **Amount of claim — miscellaneous matters**

(1) **Guarantors, etc of debts**

Where a supplier receives payment, in full or in part, from a guarantor or other person (eg a director of the debtor company), entitlement to relief is reduced by the amount paid. If full payment is made by the guarantor or third party there is no entitlement to bad debt relief.

(VAT Notice 700/18/02, para 3.10).

(2) **Insured debts**

(*a*) Where the claimant has insured its debts, any payment by the insurers does not affect entitlement to relief.

(*b*) Where the debtor is insured for the costs of the supply (eg when a garage repairs a damaged vehicle), for convenience the insurer may pay the supplier direct. If the insured is VAT-registered, the VAT-exclusive amount is usually paid, leaving the customer to pay the VAT element. The supplier can only claim relief on the actual balance written off.

(VAT Notice 700/18/02, paras 3.9, 3.11).

(3) **Mutual debts**

Where the claimant owes an amount of money to the purchaser which can be set off, the consideration written off in the accounts must be reduced by the amount so owed.

> *Example*
>
> A bad debt has arisen in respect of a supply for which the claimant has charged £705 (£600 + VAT). The claimant also owes £235 (£200 + VAT) to the debtor.
>
> The amount of the debt for relief purposes is £705 – £235 = £470
>
> The amount of the bad debt relief is
>
> £470 × 7/47 = £70

[*SI 1995/2518, Reg 172(3)*]. (VAT Notice 700/18/02, para 3.7).

(4) **Non-payment of VAT only**

If

- a customer refuses to pay the VAT charged on an invoice, or
- the claimant did not charge VAT on a supply but issues a supplementary invoice to recover the VAT and this is not paid,

the claim to relief is limited to the VAT element of the total debt. For example, where a customer was originally charged £100 (which the customer paid) and the claimant then unsuccessfully attempts to recover the £17.50 VAT charge originally omitted, the claimant is only entitled to claim the VAT fraction of £17.50 as bad debt relief.

(VAT Notice 708/18/02, para 3.13).

In *Enderby Transport Ltd (VTD 1607) (TVC 4.1)* the customer paid the full price for the goods (£10,200) but not the VAT (£816). The tribunal held that as the amount of the debt outstanding was £816, the VAT element of this was £106.43 (3/23rds when the standard rate of VAT was 15%) and bad debt relief should be restricted to this amount. In *Palmer (t/a R & K Engineering) (VTD 11739) (TVC 4.4)* the tribunal allowed full bad debt relief where, following registration with retrospective effect, an invoice was raised charging VAT on supplies originally invoiced (and paid) without VAT and the customer went into receivership without paying the VAT. The tribunal did, however, comment that Customs had been dilatory in dealing with registration and the position might be different where late registration is due to the trader's own default.

(5) **Security for debts**

Where the claimant holds an enforceable security against the purchaser, the consideration written off must be reduced by the value of the security. [*SI 1995/2518, Reg 172(4)*]. If the claimant holds a security which cannot be enforced, he can write off the full amount of the debt and base his claim to relief on that amount. (VAT Notice 708/18/02, para 3.8).

7.11 TREATMENT OF BAD DEBT RELIEF IN PARTICULAR CASES

(1) **Cash accounting scheme**

Subject to conditions, including an annual turnover limit, a business may account for and pay VAT by reference to the time when the consideration for the supply is received. See 63.2 SPECIAL SCHEMES. The adoption of such a scheme removes the problem of VAT on bad debts from the supplier.

(*b*) a payment is, under 7.7 or 7.8(1) above, treated as attributed to the relevant supply; or

(*c*) the claimant fails to comply with the requirements of 7.4, 7.7 or 7.8(1) above.

Under (*a*) and (*b*) above the amount of the repayment is

$$\frac{\text{Amount of payment received or attributed}}{\text{Amount of outstanding consideration}} \times \text{Amount of refund}$$

Under (*c*) above repayment must be made of the full amount of the refund obtained from HMRC by the claim to which the failure to comply relates.

> *Example*
>
> A business sells goods for £117.50 (£100 plus £17.50 VAT). It receives no payment by the relevant date and claims bad debt relief of £17.50. It subsequently receives £75.00 from the customer for the goods.
>
> The business must repay to HMRC the VAT element of the £75 received, calculated as follows.
>
> £75.00 ÷ £117.50 × £17.50 = £11.17

The repayment is made by including the appropriate amount in Box 1 on the VAT return for the VAT period in which the payment is received under (*a*) or (*b*) or as designated by HMRC under (*c*). If, at that time, the claimant is no longer required to make returns, the repayment must still be made and the supplier should contact HMRC.

For these purposes, payment does not include a payment received by a person to whom a right to receive it has been assigned. Claimants are not therefore required to repay bad debt relief in respect of payments received by assignees after a refund has been claimed. However, as an anti-avoidance measure, in the case of assignments made after 10 December 2003, this does not apply (and repayment of the VAT refund is still required) where the person to whom the right to receive a payment has been assigned (whether by the claimant or any other person) is connected to the claimant. See 69.19 VALUATION for connected persons.

[*SI 1995/2518, Reg 171; SI 1999/3029; SI 2002/3027, Reg 6; SI 2003/3220, Regs 22, 23*]. (VAT Notice 700/18/02, paras 3.14, 3.15).

7.13 REPAYMENT OF INPUT TAX BY PURCHASER

In relation to supplies made on or after 1 January 2003, there are general provisions requiring input tax to be repaid where a customer has not paid the supplier within six months of the date of supply or, if later, the date payment is due. These provisions apply whether or not the supplier makes a claim for bad debt relief. See 35.4 INPUT TAX.

For supplies made before 1 January 2003, where

- a valid claim to VAT bad debt relief has been made; and
- the purchaser has claimed deduction of the whole or part of the VAT on the relevant supply as input tax

then, from the date of the bad debt claim, the purchaser is taken not to be entitled to credit for input tax in respect of the VAT which has been refunded to the supplier on the claim.

The supplier must notify the purchaser of the claim (see 7.2(*e*) above) and the purchaser must make a negative entry in Box 4 of his VAT return for the VAT period in which the supplier claims bad debt relief. The amount of that negative entry is calculated by the formula

$$\frac{\text{Amount of the VAT claim by the supplier}}{\text{VAT on the relevant supply}} \times \text{Input tax claimed}$$

Such an entry is not treated as a voluntary disclosure of an error for the purposes of *SI 1995/2518, Reg 34* (see 56.11 RECORDS).

Example

A business B sells goods for £1,175.00 (£1,000 plus £175.00 VAT). By the relevant date, the customer C has only paid £500 and so B claims bad debt relief on the outstanding amount (£675) of £100.53 (£675 × 7/47).

Assuming C is fully taxable, it would have been originally entitled to deduct £175.00. Following the notification of the bad debt claim by B, C must repay to HMRC

£100.53 ÷ £117.50 × £117.50 = £100.53

Where a business has been transferred as a going concern and the transferee takes on the transferor's VAT registration number, the transferee takes over the transferor's obligation to make any repayments of input tax under these provisions.

[*VATA 1994, s 36(4A); FA 1997, s 39(2); SI 1995/2518, Regs 6(3), 172C, 172D; SI 1997/1086, Regs 3, 15, 16*].

Insolvency. By concession, an insolvency practitioner need not repay input tax under the above provisions where, after an 'insolvency procedure' has been commenced, the practitioner receives notice of a claim to VAT bad debt relief from a supplier in respect of pre-insolvency transactions provided

- HMRC have been properly notified of the insolvency (see 36.2 INSOLVENCY); and
- the application of the concession does not give rise to tax avoidance.

The concession applies whether or not the business of the insolvent person is carried on.

The '*insolvency procedures*' to which the concession applies are bankruptcies, compulsory liquidations, creditors' and members' voluntary liquidations, administrative receiverships, administration orders, individual and company voluntary arrangements, Scottish trust deeds, deeds of arrangement, partnership voluntary arrangements and liquidations, partnership administration orders, sequestrations, county court administration orders, schemes of arrangement, and deceased persons' administration orders.

The effective date for the application of the concession is the date of HMRC's claim in the insolvency (ie the relevant date of the insolvency and the date of the insolvency meeting if applicable or, in the case of an administration order, the date of that order). The concession only applies to a provisional liquidation if it is followed by a permanent liquidation although, in such a case, the concession takes effect from the date of the provisional liquidation.

If an insolvency arrangement fails, the requirement to account for clawback is reinstated.

(VAT Notice 48, ESC 3.20).

Restoration of entitlement to input tax. Where

- the purchaser has made a negative entry in a VAT return under the above provisions (the 'input tax repayment') and has paid any VAT due in respect of that period, and
- subsequently, a payment has been made in respect of the supply so that the supplier has made a repayment to HMRC of all or part of the bad debt refund under 7.12 above,

the purchaser can make a positive entry in Box 4 of his VAT return for the VAT period in which the repayment is made. The amount of that positive entry is calculated by the formula

$$\frac{\text{Amount of the VAT repaid by the supplier}}{\text{Total amount of the claim}} \times \text{Input tax repayment}$$

Such an entry is not treated as a voluntary disclosure of an error for the purposes of *SI 1995/2518, Reg 34* (see 56.11 RECORDS).

[*SI 1995/2518, 172C, 172E; SI 1997/1086, Reg 16*].

8 Business

Cross-reference. See 71.6 WORKS OF ART for sales of antiques, etc from stately homes.

De Voil Indirect Tax Service. See V2.2.

The contents of this chapter are as follows.

8.1 GENERAL MEANING OF 'BUSINESS'

EC legislation. The *EC 6th Directive* adopts the term 'economic activity' rather than business. See 22.6 EUROPEAN COMMUNITY LEGISLATION. Unless a decision of the CJEC provides otherwise, the meaning of economic activity is not materially different from the meaning of 'business' in the UK legislation.

UK legislation. The proper identification of an activity as a 'business' activity is fundamental to the operation of VAT. Output tax must be charged on any taxable supply of goods or services made in the UK by a taxable person *in the course or furtherance of any business* carried on by him. [*VATA 1994, s 4(1)*]. Similarly, input tax must relate to supplies of goods and services to a taxable person (and, where relevant, acquisitions and importations of goods by him) used or to be used *for the purpose of any business* carried on or to be carried on by him. [*VATA 1994, s 24(1)*].

Despite the importance of the meaning of '*business*', it is not comprehensively defined in UK (or EC) legislation. *VATA 1994, s 94* gives the following guidance as to what the term encompasses and excludes. If a particular activity is not covered, then it is necessary to apply the 'business test' developed by the Courts (see 8.2 below).

(*a*) It includes any trade, profession or vocation.

(*b*) The following (without prejudice to the generality of anything else in *VATA 1994*) are deemed to be the carrying on of a business.

  (i) The provision by a club, association or organisation (for a subscription or other consideration) of the facilities or advantages available to its members (but see (*c*) below). See also 14.1 CLUBS AND ASSOCIATIONS.

  (ii) The admission, for a consideration, of persons to any premises (see *The Eric Taylor Testimonial Match Committee (VTD 139) (TVC 7.83)*).

(*c*) Where a person accepts any office in the course or furtherance of a trade, profession or vocation, services supplied by him as holder of that office are treated as supplied in the course or furtherance of that trade, profession or vocation. See 8.4(11) below, 44.8 MANAGEMENT SERVICES AND SUPPLIES OF STAFF and 50.6 PARTNERSHIPS AND JOINT VENTURES.

(*d*) Anything done in connection with the termination or intended termination of a business is treated as being done in the course or furtherance of that business.

(*e*) The disposition of a business as a going concern, or of its assets or liabilities (whether or not in connection with its reorganisation or winding up) is a supply made in the course or furtherance of the business (but see 8.10 below).

De Voil Indirect Tax Service. See V2.202.

8.2 **The business test**

When considering whether an activity is to be treated as a business, if it is not one of the deemed businesses under 8.1 above then the 'business test' must be applied. This test is derived from decisions of the VAT tribunals and Courts.

The following principles, as summarised in *C & E Commrs v Lord Fisher, QB [1981] STC 238 (TVC 7.6)* are a guide as to whether an activity is a business although the absence of one common attribute of ordinary businesses (eg the pursuit of profit) does not necessarily mean that the activity is not a business and the criteria are not therefore conclusive in every case.

(*a*) By providing in *VATA 1994, s 94* (see 8.1 above) that business *includes* any trade, profession or vocation, it is clear that a wide meaning of 'business' is intended.

(*b*) In determining whether any particular activity constitutes a business it is necessary to consider the whole of that activity.

(*c*) A business activity can generally be identified from the answers to the following criteria (as laid down in *C & E Commrs v Morrison's Academy Boarding Houses Association, CS 1977, [1978] STC 1 (TVC 7.1)*).

(i) Is the activity a 'serious undertaking earnestly pursued' or a 'serious occupation not necessarily confined to commercial or profit making undertakings'?

(ii) Is the activity an occupation or function actively pursued with reasonable or recognisable continuity?

A one-off supply or a series of infrequent, unconnected supplies is not normally a business activity in its own right although it is important to consider the nature of the activity. For example, occasional sales by small speculative builders and property developers are business activities.

(iii) Does the activity have a certain measure of substance as measured by the quarterly or annual value of taxable supplies made?

(iv) Is the activity conducted in a regular manner and on sound and recognised business principles?

(v) Is the activity predominantly concerned with the making of taxable supplies to consumers for a consideration?

This is perhaps the most important point to establish, bearing in mind that 'consideration' need not necessarily be monetary. If a trader is carrying on an activity which does not involve the making of any supplies for a consideration and there is no intention in the future of doing so, then the activity is unlikely to be regarded as business even if all the other criteria are met.

In *C & E Commrs v The Apple and Pear Development Council, HL [1988] STC 221 (TVC 21.55)* the Council's principal activity was to advertise English apples and pears, which activity was financed by a statutory levy on growers. The CJEC ruled that the levy was not consideration because there was no direct link between the payments and the benefits of individual growers on which basis the House of Lords concluded that the activity was not 'business' in the VAT sense. Similarly, a charity raising funds in a 'business-like' manner from its activities was held not to be running a business unless taxable supplies, made for a consideration, formed the basis of the fund raising (*C & E Commrs v Royal Exchange Theatre Trust, QB [1979] STC 278 (TVC 7.5)*).

Where an activity is just beginning and no supplies are being made at the time but there is a clear intention to do so at some time in the future, then the activity may qualify as a business. See *Rompelman v Minister van Financien, CJEC [1985] 3 CMLR 202; [1985] ECR 655 (TVC 21.71)* and *Merseyside Cablevision Ltd (VTD 2419) (TVC 34.464)*.

(vi) Are the taxable supplies of a kind which are commonly made by those who seek to profit by them?

If a person is carrying on an activity and it is not clear whether it amounts to a business, it is more likely to be regarded as such if others are carrying on the same type of activity and are clearly doing so on a commercial basis. See *Church of Scientology of California (No 1) v C & E Commrs, CA 1980, [1981] STC 65 (TVC 7.4)* where courses in the study of its beliefs provided by the Church, some of which competed with those offered by trained psychologists and psychiatrists, were found to be business activities.

(*d*) Whether the activity is pursued for profit or some other private purpose or motive is not decisive in determining whether the activity is a business.

(*e*) If all or a sufficient number of the above criteria are satisfied in sufficient measure to override any contra-indications which might be seen in the facts, then as a matter of law the activity must be held to be a business.

The carrying on, by a regulatory authority, of a statutory licensing activity to protect the public interest is not a business activity even though carried on for a consideration. See *Institute of Chartered Accountants in England and Wales v C & E Commrs, HL [1999] STC 398 (TVC 60.140)* in respect of the Institute's authorisation to issue licences to auditors, insolvency practitioners and persons carrying on investment business.

See the chapter *Business* in *Tolley's VAT Cases* for tribunal and court decisions involving the general meaning of 'business'.

De Voil Indirect Tax Service. See V2.202–V2.209.

8.3 BUSINESS AND NON-BUSINESS ACTIVITIES

Businesses with more than one activity. Where a taxable person undertakes distinct and separate activities, some of these may be business and others non-business. A non-business activity may be a private activity (eg a hobby, see below) or, particularly in the grant-funded and voluntary sectors, it might be an activity which forms part of the overall organisational objectives but be non-business for VAT purposes (see, for example, 12.5 CHARITIES for business and non-business activities of charities). In either case, the business test must be applied to each activity. For cases where the VAT tribunals have been concerned with multiple activities, see *Rainheath Ltd (VTD 1249) (TVC 7.33)* (yacht purchased by a farming business); *DA Walker (VTD 240) (TVC 7.16)* (accountant with furnished letting income); and *RW & AAW Williamson (VTD 555) (TVC 7.22)* (retail partnership also renting out lock-up garages).

Hobbies. Activities of pleasure and social enjoyment, though organised in a business-like way, do not amount to a 'business' if no taxable supplies are made for a consideration (*C & E Commrs v Lord Fisher, QB [1981] STC 238 (TVC 7.6)*).

Traders may sometimes have hobbies that involve the making of taxable supplies (eg repairing cars or selling stamps). These supplies are not automatically made in the course or furtherance of business and the business test must be applied. Hobbies which involve a registered trader making minimal supplies are unlikely to be seen as business. However, in some cases, a hobby can involve a trader making substantial supplies and may grow to become a business activity. See, for example, *Haydon-Baillie (VTD 2072) (TVC 34.470)*. When judging whether a hobby should be seen as a business, HMRC officers are recommended to enquire whether the activity is taxable for income tax purposes under Schedule D.

Disposal of private assets. This is normally a non-business activity. Where, however, the assets are disposed of through the trader's own business the disposal may occasionally be treated as business. See, for example, *Mittu (VTD 1275) (TVC 60.65)* where a jeweller sold items of jewellery belonging to his wife through the business and paid the proceeds into the business account.

When deciding if a sale is private or business the following questions should be considered.

- Are the goods of a type normally sold through the business?
- Was the sale dependent upon the contacts and reputation of the business?
- How were the receipts dealt with and accounted for?

The independent disposal of private assets merely to raise funds for a business is non-business and outside the scope of VAT. See *RWK Stirling (VTD 1963) (TVC 60.66)*.

(Internal Guidance V1–6, paras 4.1–4.4).

Apportionment of input tax. Where a business incurs VAT on goods and services which it intends to use for both business activities and non-business activities, it is unlikely that it will be able to treat all the VAT as input tax and some form of apportionment will be required. See 35.7 INPUT TAX.

8.4 PARTICULAR PROBLEM AREAS

(1) Bloodstock

(*a*) **Breeders.** The principal aim of a breeder is to breed thoroughbred racehorses for sale. VAT registration is required (or allowed voluntarily) where a business of breeding horses for sale exists. As it is normally advantageous for a breeder to obtain registration for VAT (because most breeders will be in a repayment position), HMRC will seek to establish that a breeder is carrying on, or intending to carry on, a business activity as opposed to breeding horses for own use and recreation (ie a 'hobby' breeder).

Breeding is a long term activity and a breeder will normally need to own several mares before supplies (sale of offspring) can be made with any degree of regularity. However, HMRC would normally accept there was a business activity where a breeder acquires one or two well-bred mares, covers them by an expensive stallion, and sells the offspring for substantial amounts.

Following the introduction of the Registration Scheme for racehorse owners (see 63.31 SPECIAL SCHEMES) HMRC accept that where breeders engage in racing activities with the intention of enhancing the value of their stock and/or general standing in the business, they do so in the course and furtherance of business. Racing stock includes colts, fillies and home-bred geldings. Where breeders have acquired non-home-bred geldings for racing purposes, they may still be treated as part of the VAT registration provided they comply with the conditions of the scheme (such as seeking sponsorship).

(Internal Guidance V1–6, paras 15.1, 15.3, 15.4).

(*b*) **Trainers**. VAT registration is required (or allowed voluntarily) where a business exists of providing training services to owners. HMRC accept that a trainer who has an unrestricted licence to train horses owned by unconnected persons is making standard-rated supplies of training in the course and furtherance of a business.

HMRC also accept that where racehorses are both owned and trained by a trainer, any related costs are regarded as business expenditure for VAT purposes providing the number of horses involved is not disproportionate to the training activity.

Trainers who own racehorses on their own account, or with others, and which are not trained by them cannot recover VAT incurred under the above rules but they may qualify to do so under the Registration Scheme for racehorse owners (see 63.31 SPECIAL SCHEMES).

(Internal Guidance V1–6, paras 12.3, 16.1).

(*c*) **Dealers**. HMRC regard persons engaged in the purchase and sale of horses in the course and furtherance of a business as liable or eligible for VAT registration. The racing, for business purposes, of racehorses held as trading stock by a VAT-registered dealer is accepted as part of the trading activity whilst the stock remains available for sale, and any VAT incurred can be claimed as input tax in accordance with the normal rules.

Dealers who purchase racehorses on their own account, or with others, for racing purposes only may not recover VAT incurred under the above rules but they may qualify to do so under the Registration Scheme for racehorse owners (see 63.31 SPECIAL SCHEMES).

(Internal Guidance V1–6, para 12.3).

(*d*) **Stallion syndicates**. When a colt is to become a stallion standing at stud, it is often syndicated, usually into 40 shares. A share entitles its owner to one nomination each breeding season. The syndicate appoints a secretary, usually a bloodstock agency or firm of solicitors, to deal with the financial and practical arrangements.

The sale of additional nominations are treated as supplies in the course of business by the syndicate and, if such sales exceed the VAT registration threshold, the syndicate is required (subject to below) to register for VAT as a partnership.

However, as an alternative to registering, where the syndicate secretary is VAT-registered, he can be accepted as an agent acting in his own name on behalf of the syndicate. The secretary is required to raise an invoice in his own name for the full value of the nomination (plus VAT). Any syndicate member who is VAT-registered must provide the secretary with a VAT invoice for his share, which the secretary can use to recover the VAT element as input tax. (The tax point for the supply by the member to the secretary is the same as that for the supply by the secretary to the purchaser of the nomination.) The secretary can recover input tax on costs incurred on behalf of the syndicate (subject to the normal rules). Such costs must then be charged on by secretary to the members who, in turn, will be able to recover the VAT if registered.

(Internal Guidance V1–6, para 15.8).

(2) **Boats**

Where a boat owner independently pursues the activity of letting boats to the public, the basic test in 8.2 above must be applied to determine whether a business is being carried on. The supply on hire of a single boat may amount to a business if actively and continuously carried on throughout the season. See, for example, *C R King and Partners (Holdings) Ltd (VTD 6695) (TVC 7.39)*. Following the decision in *Lennartz v Finanzamt Munchen, CJEC [1995] STC 514 (TVC 21.297)* a business may also exist where the predominant use of the boat is for non-business purposes (although in such a case the non-business use must be treated as a taxable supply of services).

Use of boat hire companies. Boat hire companies let on hire to the public both their own and other boats, and are normally in business on their own account.

Where an owner uses a boat hire company but retains control and management of his boat(s), the company is likely to be acting as agent of the owner. In such cases, the question of whether or not the owner is in business is determined as above, applying the basic test.

Where, however, an owner leases a boat to a boat hire company (which becomes totally responsible for all aspects of its management) and the company lets the boat to the public as principal, the long term supply of the boat by the owner to the company is a single supply of letting for the period of the agreement. Such an isolated supply is not normally regarded as a business activity. See *Coleman (KG) (VTD 242) (TVC 7.28)* and *Berwick (M & C) (VTD 17686) (TVC 7.43)*. HMRC regard these decisions as applying equally to any person who lets out two boats on hire. Even in such circumstances, it may still be possible for the owner to satisfy the business test

- because of the scale of the activity;
- because, in addition to the letting of the boat to a hire company, the owner also lets it out direct to the public for part of the year (although where such activity is minimal – as a rule of thumb where no more than 3 weeks lettings in a 12 month period – this may not satisfy the test of being seriously pursued) or is actively involved in the business run by the boat hire company; or

- because the boat owner has other business activities and the letting on hire can be regarded as forming part of the overall business.

Where three or more boats are let on hire to a boat hire company, the scale of the activity is more likely to be considered sufficient to allow the owner to be regarded as carrying on a business. It is important, however, that decisions as to whether boat owners are carrying on a business are not based simply on the number of boats involved, but on the extent to which the vessel(s) are actually exploited to make taxable supplies.

Boats purchased for use by associated businesses. Boats are often used as a means of providing business entertainment or corporate hospitality. Although input tax is not deductible on goods purchased for the purpose of providing business entertainment, the supply of goods or services to be used for business entertainment is a business activity with the right to deduct input tax. Associated persons can therefore arrange for one party to purchase a boat, recover the associated input tax, and hire the boat out to the associated parties for their use in business entertainment. The VAT charged on the hire fee would not be recoverable by the associated parties but the arrangement would provide scope for the recovery of input tax on the purchase and upkeep of a boat, even though it may be used mainly for business entertainment. HMRC will, however, be concerned to see that the hire fee is realistic in relation to the value of the boat, the period of hire etc.

(Internal Guidance V1–6, paras 11.2–11.5).

(3) **Light aircraft**

Similar guidance applies as for boats under (2) above. See also *Three H Aircraft Hire v C & E Commrs, QB [1982] STC 653 (TVC 7.7).*

(4) **Charities**

See 12.4 CHARITIES.

(5) **Clubs and associations**

See 14.1 CLUBS AND ASSOCIATIONS.

(6) **Education**

See 20.2 EDUCATION.

(7) **Local authorities**

See 43.3 and 43.4 LOCAL AUTHORITIES AND PUBLIC BODIES and for government departments and health authorities see 43.11 LOCAL AUTHORITIES AND PUBLIC BODIES.

(8) **Shooting rights**

See 57.16 RECREATION AND SPORT.

(9) **Office holders**

Under *VATA 1994, s 94(4)* where a person in the course or furtherance of a trade, profession or vocation accepts any office, services supplied by him as the holder of that office are treated as supplied in the course or furtherance of the trade, profession or vocation. Both public and private office holders can be affected. The appointments will generally be held for an indefinite period (often on a part-time basis). Payment is normally in the form of fees and expenses or an annual retainer. The status of the office holder is not affected by fees being described as a salary.

The provisions only apply to persons such as solicitors, accountants and other practising consultants in business to provide professional services and who continue to supply their services and skills in the course of their duties as office holders. HMRC do not regard the provisions as applying to the following categories of office holders whose services as such are treated as outside the scope of VAT.

- Persons who can demonstrate that their appointment to an office was offered and accepted in writing before their business consultancy began. See *Gardner (JJ) (VTD 3687) (TVC 60.150)*.
- Persons appointed on grounds of their personal merit, occupational expertise or experience, or standing in the community as distinct from professional expertise as solicitors, etc as above.
- Persons who do not otherwise provide professional services.
- Persons who practice their profession solely as partners in a firm providing professional services and who accept the appointment in a purely private capacity.
- Persons who are genuinely retired from active professional business and who supply their professional services solely as office holders.
- Persons whose status is that of an employee or who by virtue of their conditions of appointment as office holders are effectively employees (eg they have conditioned hours of work, leave and sick leave entitlement, superannuation benefits, etc).

See also 44.8 MANAGEMENT SERVICES AND SUPPLIES OF STAFF for directors or employees or a company, sole traders and partners as office holders.

(Internal Guidance V1–6, paras 6.1, 6.3, 6.4. See also Internal Guidance V1–6, paras 6.7 and 6.8 for special rules applying to ecclesiastical legal appointments, judicial appointments, Legal Aid Committee members, Notaries Public and Commissioners for Oaths and services provided in connection with debt recovery).

(10) **Works of art – disposals from stately homes**

See 71.6 WORKS OF ART, ETC.

(11) **Grant-funded bodies**

Some traders receive grants (eg from central government, local authorities or the national lottery) to support their activities. Although such grants are normally outside the scope of VAT, in some circumstances they can be seen as direct or third party consideration for a supply.

The receipt of outside the scope income does not automatically mean that an activity is non-business. Each grant-funded activity should be looked at separately and the business test applied.

- If an activity involves the making of no taxable supplies for consideration and is entirely funded by outside the scope income, it is non-business (and no VAT relating to it can be treated as input tax). See also *West Central Halifax Partnership Ltd (VTD 16570) (TVC 7.107)*.

- If an activity involves the making of some taxable supplies and the receipt of some outside the scope income, then the treatment depends upon the application of the business test. The receipt of money to act as a subsidy for a loss-making commercial activity need not result in input tax restriction. However, in many cases the outside the scope income is indicative of the existence of a non-business activity and an apportionment is needed.

(Internal Guidance V1–6, para 8.1).

(12) Museums and galleries

Although the main activity of most museums and galleries is the public display of a collection, many have a number of other activities and it is necessary to identify all activities and consider the business/non-business nature of each.

Admission charges. Where a museum, etc makes a general admission charge for the public to enter its premises, this constitutes a 'deemed' business activity under *VATA 1994, s 94* (see 8.1(*b*)(ii) above). In general, the full amount of any admission charge is standard-rated. However, admission charges to museums and galleries by certain eligible bodies are exempt and voluntary donations in lieu of admission charges are outside the scope of VAT. See 57.6 RECREATION AND SPORT.

A museum or gallery which admits the public free of charge is not carrying on a business activity. Consequently, under the normal rules any VAT it incurs in relation to the provision of free rights of admission cannot be recovered. See, however, 35.13(16A) INPUT TAX for a special scheme allowing certain non-charging national museums and galleries to recover related input tax.

Examples of other potential business activities include

- charges for special exhibitions
- retail and catering outlets (self-administered, concessions or shop rental)
- car parking
- reproduction rights
- publications
- collection loans made for consideration
- premises rental/corporate entertaining
- slot machines, rides, charged 'experiences'
- membership scheme or friends organisation
- consultancy for a charge
- supplies of staff
- sponsorship

Examples of potential non-business activities include

- academic research
- free loans of objects
- free educational activities
- free 'treasure trove' work
- free consultancy
- free photographic archives
- establishment of internet site, virtual museum or archive

(Internal Guidance V1–6, paras 9.1, 9.2).

(13) **Groundwork Trusts**

Goundwork Trusts exist as a result of government policy towards promoting urban renewal and post-industrial renewal. Rather than see such work as being solely the responsibility of local authorities, the objective is to encourage partnerships between local communities, local businesses and national government. The Federation of Groundwork Trusts (operating under the style of 'Groundwork UK') acts as the central distributor for government funds to Trusts. Individual Trusts undertake different types of projects and, although autonomous in nature and in terms of management, must submit copies of its audited accounts to Groundwork UK and the auditors must be satisfied that all public money has been properly expended. In addition, each Trust is required to maintain and comply with specific rules set by the government and monitored by Groundwork UK.

A substantial proportion of funding for any Trust comes centrally from Groundwork UK but funds for projects are also received from local authorities, National Lottery money, Regional Development funds from the EU, English Partnerships, The Countryside Commission, etc.

VAT treatment. The organisation of a Trust is such that all of its activities can be allocated to specific projects. Consequently, a Trust will not normally have any general non-business activity (eg consisting of general management or administration) separate from its project activities. The Trust's business/non-business position will therefore depend entirely upon an analysis of its various projects.

For an activity to be seen as business for VAT purposes it must involve the making of supplies to somebody for consideration. That activity is then wholly business. Output tax is due on the full consideration received, both from the recipient (normally the landowner) and from third parties, which directly relates to that supply. In practice, any grants or subsidies received by a Trust, either from Groundwork UK or from other sources, that are specific to a project will normally form part of the consideration for that project. (Grants and subsidies which a Trust receives in the way of general support of its activities and that are not specific to any project are outside the scope of VAT.) All of the VAT incurred on the project is input tax, whether or not the project is partly funded by income that is outside the scope of VAT.

Whether there has been a supply for consideration depends upon the specific facts of each project, applying the usual tests of what constitutes a supply for consideration. Broadly, if the Trust acts like a commercial builder and undertakes a project for which there is a specific client who commissions and pays for the work in full, the project is clearly a business supply. Projects, on the other hand, that are designed to be of benefit to the community as a whole, and do not involve a supply to any specific organisation or individual, will be non-business. In practice, the answers to both of the following questions must be 'yes' if the project is to be considered business. Otherwise, the project is non-business.

- Has the Trust entered a contractual relationship with the landowner, or another person, to do something tangible for them from which they derive some direct benefit? In considering whether there is a contract, it is important to distinguish between cases where the landowner simply gives permission for a Trust to enter onto the land and those where the landowner receives a material benefit from the work that is undertaken.
- Does the Trust receive payment which is directly linked to doing that 'something', even if that payment comes from a third party?

Examples

(1) A landowner allows work to be undertaken that is intended to encourage a particular form of wildlife.

This does not, of itself, mean that there is a supply to the landowner (even if the landowner makes a contribution to the cost). There would, however, be a supply if the work provided some form of benefit to the landowner, for example, being able to better exploit the land for hunting or fishing purposes.

(2) A local authority agrees to the planting of trees on its land for the benefit of the community at large.

The local authority is unlikely to be receiving a supply unless it has specifically commissioned the Trust to undertake that work or has a statutory duty to ensure that it is carried out.

(3) A factory owner contributes to the cost of refurbishment of the external factory walls.

He will normally be receiving a supply even if a significant part of the cost is met from grant funding.

Example of a mixed-funded business project

A Trust carries out a project to build a wall around an unsightly factory in order to screen it off. The funding of the project is as follows:

(*a*) The factory owner is obliged to pay £20,000.

(*b*) Groundwork UK provides a grant of £80,000.

(*c*) The local authority provides a grant of £15,000.

(*d*) The Trust provides £5,000 from a general fund made up from bequests and donations.

All payments are inclusive of VAT, where appropriate.

There is clearly a supply to the factory owner, even though the Trust's motivation in carrying out the work and arranging the financing may well be to improve the environment of the adjoining community.

Payments (*a*), (*b*) and (*c*) are all part of the consideration for the supply because they are all payments to the Trust specifically for the wall to be built. Item (*d*) is not such a payment and is not part of the consideration. The total consideration is therefore £115,000.

The invoice to the landowner should read:

	£
To environmental services	97,872.34
VAT	17,127.66
Total due	115,000.00
Less paid by way of subsidy	95,000.00
Net sum now due	£20,000.00

(Internal Guidance V1–6, paras 10.1–10.6).

8.5 DISAGGREGATION OF BUSINESS ACTIVITIES

EC legislation. See 22.6 EUROPEAN COMMUNITY LEGISLATION.

The following provisions are designed to prevent the maintenance or creation of any 'artificial' separation of business activities carried on by two or more persons from resulting in the avoidance of VAT. In determining whether any separation of business activities is '*artificial*', consideration must be given to the extent to which the different persons carrying on those activities are closely bound to one another by financial, economic and organisational links.

HMRC may make a direction under which the persons specified therein become treated as a single taxable person carrying on the activities of a business described in the direction. That taxable person is then liable to be registered under *VATA 1994, Sch 1* with effect from the date of the direction or such later day as is specified. The direction must be served on each person named in it.

If, immediately before the direction (or any supplementary direction below) any person named therein is already registered in respect of taxable supplies made by him, he ceases to be liable to be registered from the date of the direction or, if later, the date with effect from which the single taxable person concerned became liable to be registered.

Supplementary directions. HMRC may subsequently make and serve a supplementary direction adding a further person's name to those detailed in the earlier direction where that person appears to HMRC to be making taxable supplies in the course of the activities of the business previously specified. The name is added from the date on which he began making those taxable supplies or, if later, the date with effect from which the single taxable person referred to in the earlier direction became liable to be registered under *VATA 1994, Sch 1*.

[*VATA 1994, Sch 1 para 1A, para 2(1)(3)–(5); FA 1997, s 31(1)(2)(4)*].

De Voil Indirect Tax Service. See V2.190C.

8.6 **Preconditions for making a direction**

Before making a direction naming any person HMRC must be satisfied that

(*a*) he is making or has made taxable supplies;

(*b*) the activities in the course of which he makes or made those supplies form only part of certain activities, the other activities being carried on concurrently or previously (or both) by one or more other persons; and

(*c*) if all the taxable supplies of the business described in the direction were taken into account, a person carrying on that business would at the time of the direction be liable to be registered under the normal registration rules.

[*VATA 1994, Sch 1 para 2*(*2*); *FA 1997, s 31*(*2*)(*4*)].

8.7 **HMRC's policy**

Artificial separation. In deciding whether or not to make a direction, HMRC will be concerned with separations which are devices contrived to circumvent the normal VAT registration rules. Whether any particular separation is artificial will, in most cases, depend upon the facts. The following are examples of where HMRC would at least make further enquiries.

- Separate entities supply registered and unregistered customers.
- The same equipment/premises is used by different entities on a regular basis. This may occur, for example, in launderettes, food take-aways or mobile catering equipment.
- Splitting up of what is usually a single supply, eg bed and breakfast and the livery trade.
- Artificially separated businesses which maintain the appearance of a single business, eg bar sales and catering in a public house (although the relationship between the parties is important here as truly franchised 'shop within a shop' arrangements will not normally be considered artificial).
- One person has a controlling influence in a number of entities which all make the same type of supply in diverse locations.

Financial, economic and organisational links. Again these will depend upon the specific circumstances but the following examples illustrate the types of factors indicative of the necessary links.

(*a*) *Financial links*

- Financial support given by one part to another.
- One part would not be financially viable without support from another.
- Common financial interest in the proceeds of the business.

(*b*) *Economic links*

- Seeking to realise the same economic objective.
- The activities of one part benefit the other part.
- Supplying the same circle of customers.

(*c*) *Organisational links*

- Common management.
- Common employees.
- Common premises.
- Common equipment.

(VAT Notice 700/1/02, paras 14.5, 14.6).

8.8 **Effect of a direction**

The effects of a direction on the '*constituent members*' (ie all those named in the direction and any supplementary direction) are as follows.

(*a*) The taxable person carrying on the specified business is registrable in such name as the persons named in the direction jointly nominate in writing within 14 days of the direction. Otherwise the taxable person is registrable in such name as may be specified in the direction.

(*b*) Any supply of goods or services by or to one of the constituent members in the course of the specified business is treated as a supply by or to the taxable person.

(*c*) Any acquisition of goods from another EC country by one of the constituent members in the course of the specified business is treated as an acquisition by the taxable person.

(*d*) Each of the constituent members is jointly and severally liable for any VAT due from the taxable person.

(*e*) Without prejudice to (*d*) above, any failure by a taxable person to comply with any VAT requirement is treated as a failure by each of the constituent members severally.

(*f*) Subject to (*a*)–(*e*) above, the constituent members are treated as a partnership carrying on the specified business and any question as to the scope of that business at any time is determined accordingly.

HMRC may subsequently give notice that one of the constituent members is no longer to be regarded as such for the purposes of (*d*) or (*e*) above. He then ceases to have any liability for those purposes after a date specified in the notice and, from the same date, ceases to be regarded as a member of the partnership referred to in (*f*) above.

[*VATA 1994, Sch 1 para 2*(*6*)–(*8*)].

8.9 **Appeals**

An appeal may be made against a direction or supplementary direction but the tribunal cannot allow the appeal unless it considers that HMRC could not reasonably have been satisfied that there were grounds for making that direction or supplementary direction. [*VATA 1994, s 84*(*7*); *FA 1997, s 31*(*3*)].

For cases where HMRC's direction was upheld, see *Chamberlain v C & E Commrs, QB [1989] STC 505 (TVC 55.29)* (associated companies operating launderettes); *Osman v C & E Commrs, QB [1989] STC 596 (TVC 55.33)* (husband and wife acting as tax consultants from the same office); *TSD & Mrs M E Williams (VTD 2445) (TVC 55.35)* (married couple carrying on business as a café and bread shop from the same premises); *MJ & P Summers (VTD 3498) (TVC 55.38)* (health studio operated by married couple and son); *P & RJ Jervis (VTD 3920) (TVC 55.41)* (catering at a public house); *West End Health and Fitness Club (VTD 4070) (TVC 55.40)* (company operating a fitness club and a director and his wife operating a beauty salon in partnership from the same premises); *Old Farm Service Station Ltd & L Williams (VTD 4261) (TVC 55.45)* (company operating a service station and a director's son running a video club at the same premises); *Allerton Motors (VTD 9427) (TVC 55.51)* (car sales and car washing at same premises); *EM, PG & CP Evans (VTD 10532) (TVC 55.52)* (fairground amusement operators); and *A & S Essex (t/a Essex Associates) (VTD 15072) (TVC 55.53)* (married couple providing computer programming services via a partnership and supplying computer hardware via a limited company).

For cases where the appellants were successful, see *D & Mrs LM Horsman (VTD 5401) (TVC 55.64)* (farming and pony trekking carried on by married couple); *P, C & J Allen (VTD 12209) (TVC 55.66)* (where, to avoid inheritance tax, a husband, who ran a bookselling business and three launderettes, took his wife into partnership in the bookselling business, transferred one of the launderettes to her and took his son into partnership in another of the launderettes); *I Reayner, J Colegate & A Reayner (VTD 15396) (TVC 55.67)* (dry-cleaning businesses operated from separate premises by a mother, her son and his common law wife); and *Trippitt (S & AJ) (VTD 17340) (TVC 55.60)* (wife of publican providing bed and breakfast facilities and paying 35% of income to husband).

8.10 TRANSFER OF A BUSINESS AS A GOING CONCERN ('TOGC')

EC legislation. See 22.7 EUROPEAN COMMUNITY LEGISLATION.

The TOGC provisions have two main purposes.

- To help businesses by improving their cash flow and avoiding the need to separately value assets, which may be liable at different rates or exempt, and which have been sold as a whole.
- To protect the revenue by removing a charge to VAT and entitlement to input tax where the output tax may not be paid to HMRC (eg where a business charges VAT which is claimed as input tax by the new business but never declared or paid by the old business).

Typical cases which may be covered by the provisions are where

- the assets of a business are bought by another person and the existing business ceases to trade;
- the existing owner of a business dies or retires and the business assets are taken over by another person;
- part of an existing business is sold to another person; and
- the assets of a business are transferred to a new legal entity, for example, a sole proprietor may take on a partner, or form a limited company.

There is no TOGC simply because of a change in the constitution of a partnership or the transfer of shares in a limited company from one person to another.

If all the conditions in 8.11 below are met, the transfer is not a taxable supply and VAT must not be charged on the assets transferred (except, in certain circumstances as indicated in 8.12 below, on the land and buildings used in the business).

If VAT is charged when it should not have been:

- The seller must cancel any VAT invoice issued and provide the new owner with a refund of the VAT charged (normally by issue of a credit note or document giving similar effect).
- If any VAT is incorrectly shown on a VAT invoice which is not cancelled, it is recoverable by HMRC from the seller, see 17.2 CUSTOMS: POWERS.
- The new owner will not be able to reclaim this amount as input tax (even if he has paid it to the vendor in good faith) because there was no taxable supply. But where HMRC are wholly satisfied that the amount of 'VAT' has been both declared and paid to them by the seller, they may allow the new owner to recover it as if it were input tax.

The TOGC rules are compulsory and so it is very important to establish from the outset whether the business is being sold as a going concern.

(VAT Notice 700/9/02, paras 1.2–1.5, 2.2; Internal Guidance V1–10, Chapter 2 para 3.2).

De Voil Indirect Tax Service. See V2.226; V3.116.

8.11 Conditions for transfer not to be a taxable supply

Subject to 8.12 below, the supply by a person of the assets of his business to a person to whom he transfers that business (or part thereof) as a going concern is neither a supply of goods nor a supply of services provided all the following conditions are satisfied.

(*a*) The assets are to be used by the transferee in carrying on the same kind of business, whether or not as part of an existing business, as that carried on by the transferor in relation to the whole or part transferred. [*SI 1995/1268, Art 5*(*1*)]. But the buyer does not need to have been pursuing the same type of business as the seller before the transfer (*Zita Modes Sàrl v Administration de l'enregistrement et des domaines, CJEC Case C–497/01; [2003] All ER(D) 411(Nov)*).

Common areas of difficulty include companies which have more than one trading activity. For example, a brewery is in business selling beers, wines and spirits to the public via their managed house outlets. It is also in business renting properties to tenants (where the tenants are selling to the public). If a brewery was leasing a pub to tenants, and then sold the business to someone who was to run the pub himself, there would not be a TOGC. The brewery had a business of renting the property, the new owner has a business of running a pub.

HMRC accept that there can be a TOGC where a business is sold to someone who intends to restructure it so that it will not be the same type of business but who continues with the existing business, even if for a very short period of time.

The same kind of business has been held to be carried on where a public house was subsequently aimed at different clientele and sold different beer (*G Draper (Marlow) Ltd (VTD 2079) (TVC 63.3)*) and where an Indian restaurant became an Italian restaurant (*Tahmassebi (t/a Sale Pepe) (VTD 13177) (TVC 63.89)*). There is not necessarily a different kind of business because the seller made supplies to wholesalers and the purchaser sells to retail customers. See, for example, *Village Collection Interiors Ltd (VTD 6146) (TVC 63.23)*.

If the new owner is to use the assets to carry on a different kind of business, VAT must be charged in the normal way.

It is implied that the transferor had to have been carrying on the business, or part of the business, transferred. See *Kwik Save Group plc (VTD 12749) (TVC*

63.77) where a holding company carrying on the business of food retailers purchased foodstores (not a taxable supply) and then transferred them to a subsidiary which carried on a similar business but without itself in the meantime having traded at those foodstores (a taxable supply).

(*b*) In a case in which the transferor is a taxable person (ie registered or liable to be registered for VAT), the transferee must already be a taxable person or immediately become, as a result of the transfer, a taxable person (or Isle of Man equivalent). [*SI 1995/1268, Art 5*(*1*)]. In determining whether the transferee is a taxable person, the turnover of the seller must also be taken into account. See 59.3 REGISTRATION.

This condition is not met if the buyer is not registered or required to be registered for VAT, for example, because

- at the date the transfer takes place, the buyer does not expect the value of his taxable supplies in the next 12 months to be above the deregistration limit since he intends to reduce trading by introducing shorter working hours; or
- the seller was registered voluntarily at the date of the transfer so that the buyer is not required to register because the value of his taxable supplies in the 12 month period then ended is not above the registration limit.

In such circumstances, unless the buyer is accepted for voluntary registration, the TOGC conditions are not met and the sale takes its normal liability.

(*c*) In relation to a part transfer, that part is capable of separate operation. [*SI 1995/1268, Art 5*(*1*)]. It does not matter whether it will, in fact, be operated separately from any other business the new owner carries on. (VAT Notice 700/9/02, para 2.3).

(*d*) The effect of the transfer must be to put the new owner in possession of a business which can be operated as such. A sale of capital assets is not in itself a TOGC but if the effect is to put the purchaser in possession of a business, then it is such a transfer even if the assets are transferred on different dates. (VAT Notice 700/9/02, para 2.3).

(*e*) The business, or part, transferred must be a 'going concern' at the time of transfer. This does not necessarily imply that the business is commercially viable. It may have been scaled down due to financial difficulties or in anticipation of sale or be trading under a liquidator or administrative receiver. See, for example, *Baltic Leasing Ltd (VTD 2088) (TVC 63.17)* and *C & E Commrs v Dearwood Ltd, QB [1986] STC 327 (TVC 63.12)*.

In order for a business to be regarded as 'dead', HMRC would normally expect such evidence as all employees having been made redundant, orders no longer being accepted/sought, supplies ceasing, etc. The effect of a break in trading before sale will depend upon the kind of business involved. For example, a seasonal business which has been closed during what is normally the closed season may still be a going concern because it is advertising for customers, accepting bookings, etc.

(VAT Notice 700/9/02, para 2.3; Internal Guidance V1–10, Chapter 2 para 2.6).

In *JMA Spijkers v Gevroeders Benedik Abattoir CV, CJEC [1986] 2 CMLR 296 (TVC 21.92)* it was held that there could be a TOGC even if there had been a cessation of trading before the date on which the transfer took place provided the wherewithal to carry on the business, such as plant, building and employees, were available and were transferred.

(*f*) There must not be a series of immediately consecutive transfers of the business. Where A sells its assets to B who immediately sells those assets to C, B has not carried on the business. As a result, B can neither receive nor make an onward supply of the assets under the special provisions. In relation to property transactions, such immediate transfers often occur where A contracts to sell property to B, and B sells on to C with both contracts being completed by a single transfer from A to C. There is an exception to this for the transfer of a property rental business in Scotland where, subject to the provisions relating to land and buildings in 8.13 below, the disposition of the *dominium utile* may be seen to be direct from A to C. (VAT Notice 700/9/02, para 2.3).

(*g*) There should be no significant break in the normal trading pattern before or immediately after the transfer. A short period of closure which does not significantly disrupt the existing trading pattern, eg for redecoration, will be ignored. (VAT Notice 700/9/02, para 2.3).

In deciding whether a transaction amounts to a TOGC, regard must be had to its substance rather than its form, and consideration must be given to the whole of the circumstances, weighing the factors which point in one direction against those which point in another. In the end, the vital consideration is whether the effect of the transaction was to put the transferee in possession of a going concern, the activities of which he could carry on without interruption. Many factors may be relevant to this decision though few will be conclusive in themselves. Thus, if the transferee carries on the business in the same manner as before, this will point to the existence of a transfer, but the converse is not necessarily true, because the transfer may be complete even though the transferee does not choose to avail himself of all the rights which he acquires thereunder. Similarly, an express assignment of goodwill is strong evidence of a transfer of a business, but the absence of such an assignment is not conclusive the other way. The absence of the assignment of premises, stock or outstanding contracts will likewise not be conclusive, if the particular circumstances of the transferee enable him to carry on substantially the same business as before. (*Kenmir Ltd v Frizzell, QB [1968] 1 All ER 414*).

HMRC officers are advised to take to following into account when determining whether there has been a TOGC although is not possible to say that the presence or absence of a particular factor means that a transaction is or is not such a transfer.

- *Goodwill.* Whilst its absence from any transfer does not imply that no TOGC has taken place, its presence normally gives a very good indication that it has. This is so even if the contract for sale attributes only a nominal value to goodwill. See, for example, *Quadrant Stationers (VTD 1599) (TVC 63.9).*

- *Whether the business name has been transferred.*

- *Customer lists, knowledge of customers and common directors.* The sale of a list of previous or potential customers is a good indication of a TOGC. However, a transfer of a customer list alone is not likely to be the transfer of a business, even in the case of a service business whose only real asset of worth it may be.

- *Transfer of contracts and work in progress.* If a purchaser takes over contracts with suppliers, buys work in progress or takes over obligations under contracts with customers, this is a good indication that he is to carry on the business of the seller.

- *Stock*. The transfer of stock to a single purchaser can indicate a TOGC; the sale of a small proportion of stock is less likely to, unless the effect is to put the purchaser in possession of an identifiable business.
- *Plant and equipment*. The transfer of the equipment needed to carry on the business is an indication that there is a TOGC. However, if it is not transferred, the transaction can still be a TOGC, especially if the purchaser already owns similar equipment.
- *Premises*. The transfer of premises is significant for two reasons. First, some businesses are so closely linked to the premises from which they are run that, if they are not transferred, it is unlikely or even impossible that the business has been transferred (eg a property letting business, theatre, bowling alley). Secondly, goodwill often attaches to the premises (eg in retail businesses where the location of the premises is significant) so that their transfer is a good indication of a TOGC.
- *Staff*. If the new business takes over the contracts of existing staff, or even re-employs staff made redundant, this will suggest a TOGC.
- *Restrictive covenants*. The presence of a restrictive covenant in the contract of sale (eg preventing the seller from trading in the same business in the same area) is a good indicator that a TOGC has taken place.
- *The contract of sale and other documentation* although statements in the contract that a transaction is, or is not, a TOGC are not conclusive. See also *C & E Commrs v Padglade Ltd, QB [1995] STC 602 (TVC 63.48)*.
- *Consensus* between the vendor and purchaser.
- *Advertisements*. The way in which a sale is advertised is an indication of the vendor's intentions. HMRC may also look at any advertisements issued announcing the purchase. Phrases such as 'Under new management' will indicate the same type of business is being carried on and there has been a TOGC.

(Internal Guidance V1–10, Chapter 2 para 2.5).

For cases held to fall within the special provisions (so that VAT charged was not recoverable by the purchaser) see *E & E Phillips (VTD 1130) (TVC 63.1)*, *Advanced Business Technology Ltd (VTD 1488) (TVC 63.8)*, and *C & E Commrs v Dearwood Ltd, QB [1986] STC 327 (TVC 63.12)*. For cases held not to fall within the special provisions (so that VAT was chargeable by the vendor and recoverable by the purchaser), see *Eric Ladbroke (Holbeach) Ltd (VTD 1557) (TVC 63.52)*, *Computech Developments Ltd (VTD 9798) (TVC 63.42)* and *E J Caunt (t/a Edward James Confectionery) (VTD 1561) (TVC 63.37)*.

8.12 Land and buildings

A TOGC often involves the transfer of land and buildings. In such cases, there are extra rules to determine whether VAT should be charged on the transfer of the land and buildings, even if the rest of the transfer does qualify for TOGC treatment.

A supply of assets as part of the supply of a business is not treated as a TOGC under the rules in 8.11 above to the extent that it consists of

- a grant of land or buildings, the supply of which would be exempt under *VATA 1994, Sch 9 Group 1* but for an option to tax which the *transferor* has made (see 42.8 LAND AND BUILDINGS), or

- a grant of the fee simple in new and uncompleted buildings liable to VAT at the standard rate under 42.3(*a*) LAND AND BUILDINGS

unless the following conditions have been met no later than the '*relevant date*', ie the date upon which the grant would have been treated as having been made or, if there is more than one such date, on the earliest of them.

(*a*) The *transferee* must have opted to tax the land or buildings concerned and must have given written notification of the election to HMRC.

C& E take this to mean that, for the TOGC provisions to apply, the option must be notified to HMRC in writing no later than the time of the supply. This is normally the date of the transfer but also includes receipt of a deposit which may otherwise have created a tax point. A tax point is not created by the receipt of a deposit by a third party acting as an independent stakeholder (as opposed to an agent of the vendor) until the money is released to the vendor.

Following the decision in *Chalegrove Properties Ltd (VTD 17151) (TVC 63.84)* HMRC accept that, where the written notification of the election is sent to HMRC by mail, the notification must be properly addressed, pre-paid and posted on or before the time of supply. The transferee is advised to retain evidence of posting. (VAT Notice 700/9/02, para 2.4; Internal Guidance V1–10, Chapter 2 para 5.3). See also *Higher Education Statistics Agency Ltd v C & E Commrs, QB [2000] STC 332 (TVC 63.83).*

(*b*) With effect from 18 March 2004, the transferee must have notified the transferor that his option to tax the land or buildings concerned will not be disapplied. To do this, the transferee must be satisfied that the following scenario does *not* apply to him, namely that:

(i) the land transferred to him would, in relation to him, become a capital item within the CAPITAL GOODS SCHEME (10) (whether the transfer to him were to be treated as neither a supply of goods nor a supply of services under a TOGC, or otherwise); and

(ii) his supplies of that land will, or would fall, to be exempt supplies by virtue of the disapplication of the option to tax under the anti-avoidance rules in *VATA 1994, Sch 10 para 2(3AA)* (see 42.9(*g*) LAND AND BUILDINGS).

Interim provisions. Although this extra condition applies with effect from 18 March 2004:

- Where a payment on exchange of contracts was made before 18 March 2004 but completion took place on or after that date, HMRC will accept that the payment made on completion can be treated under the same rules as the payment made on exchange, ie only the condition in (*a*) above has to be satisfied. Both parties must agree to this.
- For sales made between 18 March 2004 and 30 June 2004, where the transferee's option to tax is not disapplied under this condition and all other conditions for the sale to be treated as a TOGC are met, HMRC will permit the sale to be treated as a TOGC even if the transferee has actually not notified the transferor. Both parties must agree that the transaction should remain treated as a TOGC.

[*VATA 1994, s 5(3); SI 1995/1268, Art 5(2)(3); SI 2004/779*].

The transferor is responsible for applying the correct amount of VAT and HMRC may require him to support his decision. It is prudent for the transferor to

- ask the transferee for evidence that his option to tax is in place by the relevant date (eg a copy of the notification letter); and
- ask for written confirmation the transferee's option to tax will not be disapplied.

If it subsequently turns out that an incorrect notification was given, HMRC will not seek to recover any uncharged output tax from the transferor and the supply will remain a TOGC. However, HMRC will look closely at the circumstances that led to that event and this, in turn, may lead to further investigations.

(VAT Notice 700/9/02, para 2.4; Business Brief 12/04; Business Brief 15/04).

Where the above conditions are not met, the transfer of the land and buildings is a supply and VAT is due at the standard rate.

8.13 Transfer of a property rental business

HMRC give the following examples of circumstances concerning the transfer of land and buildings where there may be a transfer of a business of property rental as a going concern. Provided the conditions in 8.12 above relating to land and buildings and the general conditions in 8.11 above are satisfied, the supply of the assets can then be ignored for VAT purposes.

Examples where a business can be transferred as a going concern

1. Freehold property is owned and is sold with the benefit of an existing lease (or where a leasehold interest is owned and assigned with the benefit of a sub-lease), even if the property is only partly tenanted.
2. A building is owned which is being let but is sold during an initial rent-free period.
3. A lease has been granted in respect of a building but the tenants are not yet in occupation.
4. A property is owned and tenants have been found but the property is transferred to a third party with the benefit of a prospective tenancy before a lease agreement has been signed.
5. A property developer sells a site as a package (to a single buyer) which is a mixture of let and unlet, finished and unfinished properties, and the sale of the site would otherwise have been standard-rated, provided the purchaser elects to waive exemption for the *whole* site.
6. A property is owned by a member of a VAT group and a tenant who is a member of either the outgoing landlord's VAT group or the purchaser's VAT group is one of a number of tenants of the property. The presence of a tenant or tenants outside the group means that the whole transaction can still be treated as a TOGC.

There is not a transfer of a going concern in the following circumstances

1. A property developer sells a property which he has built and which
   - he has allowed someone to occupy temporarily (without any right to occupy after the proposed sale); or
   - he is 'actively marketing' in search of a tenant.

This is because a property rental business is not being carried on.

2. A freehold property is owned and a lease is granted, or where a headlease is owned and a sub-lease granted (because there is no transfer of a business, just the creation of a new asset).

3. A property is sold and a lease previously granted is surrendered immediately before the sale (because the property rental business ceases when the lease is surrendered).

4. A property is sold to an existing tenant who leases the whole premises from the seller (because the tenant cannot carry on the same business of property rental).

5. Where the purchaser of the property rental business is a member of the same VAT group as the existing tenant. This is because the property rental business ceases after the transfer because the tenant and new landlord effectively become one taxable person.

6. Where a member of a VAT group sells a property, which is being rented to another member of the group, to a third party. This is because HMRC believe that no business exists which is making relevant taxable supplies capable of a transfer as a going concern.

(VAT Notice 700/9/02, paras 2.5, 4.3, 7.1–7.3; Business Brief 26/98).

Nominee transferee. Strictly, a transfer of a going concern cannot occur where the transferee is a nominee for a beneficial owner because the beneficial owner will be the person carrying on the business, not the nominee. However, where the legal title in land is to be held by a nominee for a *named* beneficial owner, that beneficial owner (and not the nominee) may optionally, for the purposes of establishing the transfer of a property letting business as a going concern, be considered to be the transferee. The transferor, nominee and beneficial owner must agree to this optional treatment in writing. Examples of where a nominee might hold property for a beneficial owner are where the legal title is held on trust for a partnership, unincorporated association or pension fund. (VAT Notice 700/9/02, paras 2.5, 9.1–9.3). Para 9.3 contains an example format that the parties can use to record their agreement.

The option does not need to apply to transactions where the nominee is the transferor of the legal title. In these cases, *VATA 1994, Sch 10 para 8* deems the beneficial owner to be the transferor. See 42.5 LAND AND BUILDINGS.

8.14 Other assets

Unidentifiable goodwill. The sale of unidentifiable goodwill (ie the difference between the value of a business as a whole and the sum of the values of its identifiable assets) is treated as a taxable supply unless brought outside the scope of VAT by satisfying the provisions in 8.11 above. Sales of goodwill which can be specifically identified as an asset of the business (eg the use of a trade mark, sole right to trade in a particular area, lists of customers, etc) are taxable supplies of services. (C & E Press Notice 790, 10 December 1982).

8.15 Miscellaneous aspects

Registration. See 59.3 REGISTRATION for circumstances where the transferee is liable to be registered at the time the business is transferred. See also 59.36 REGISTRATION for the re-allocation of the transferor's registration number.

Flat-rate scheme for small businesses. See 63.23 SPECIAL SCHEMES for the consequences of a business that is using the flat-rate scheme transferring its business as a going concern.

Deduction of related input tax. Although a transfer of a going concern is not a supply for VAT purposes, this does not prevent the deduction of input tax on related expenses. There is, however, a distinction between the extent to which the transferor and the transferee can deduct that input tax.

- For the position of the transferee following the decision in *C & E Commrs v UBAF Bank Ltd*, see 49.8(5) PARTIAL EXEMPTION.
- In the case of the transferor, since the sale of the business as a going concern is not a supply, the input tax incurred on the costs of selling the business cannot be attributed to a supply by the transferor. In *Abbey National plc v C & E Commrs, CJEC [2001] STC 297 (TVC 21.278)* the CJEC confirmed that, in such circumstances, the transferor's costs form part of his overheads and thus, in principle, have a direct and immediate link with the whole of his economic activity so that he can deduct a proportion of the input tax attributable to taxable supplies under his partial exemption method. See also VAT Notice 700/9/02, para 2.8. However, the CJEC also indicated that if the transferor's costs have a direct and immediate link with a *clearly defined part* of his economic activities, so that the costs form part of the overheads of that part of the business, and all the transactions relating to that part of the business are subject to VAT, he may deduct all the VAT charged on his costs of acquiring those services.

  Following the *Abbey National* decision, HMRC take the view that, in respect of transfers taking place after 31 July 2001,

  (*a*) VAT incurred on services that have a direct and immediate link with the transferred part of a business should be treated as an overhead of that part of the business;

  (*b*) where that part of the business makes only taxable supplies, then the VAT incurred is deductible;

  (*c*) where that part of the business makes only exempt supplies, then the VAT incurred is not deductible; and

  (*d*) in instances where both taxable and exempt supplies are made by that part of the business, the VAT incurred is partly deductible by reference to the partial exemption method in place. If the partial exemption method fails to achieve a fair and reasonable result, HMRC may be prepared to approve an alternative method.

  Businesses may, if they wish, apply the revised policy from an earlier date but any business wishing to do so must apply the new treatment consistently from the date it makes the retrospective change. Claims will be subject to the normal three-year time limit on refunds and claimants will need to produce the necessary records for the claim to be verified.

  (VAT Notice 700/9/02, para 2.8; Business Brief 8/01).

Retention of records. Business records generally have to be kept for six years. Where a business is transferred as a going concern, any records relating to the seller's business, which under the six-year rule are required to be kept for a period after the transfer, must be preserved by the purchaser unless HMRC allow otherwise. [*VATA 1994, s 49(1)(b)*].

In practice, this transfer of records is unlikely to happen for good commercial reasons but it remains the seller's responsibility to ask HMRC that he may be allowed to retain the records. HMRC's policy is to allow him to do so unless there are compelling revenue reasons otherwise. Where a business using the margin scheme for SECOND-HAND GOODS (61) is sold as a going concern, the purchaser needs the original purchase invoices to identify that the goods are eligible for the margin scheme and to calculate the margin on which VAT is due. In these circumstances, where there are compelling reasons for the seller to retain the purchase invoices, HMRC may agree to copies of the invoices being held by the purchaser. This agreement must be in writing and both parties should retain copies of it for future assurance purposes.

(Internal Guidance V1–10, Chapter 2 para 3.9).

Supplies to partly-exempt VAT groups. On certain transfers of businesses to partly-exempt VAT groups, the chargeable assets transferred are treated as being supplied to and by the representative member of the group at the open market value. See 31.7 GROUPS OF COMPANIES.

Capital goods scheme. Where a business is sold as a going concern and the assets transferred include land or buildings or a civil engineering work worth £250,000 or more and/or computer equipment worth £50,000 or more, the new owner takes over responsibility for applying the capital goods scheme. See 10.12(4) CAPITAL GOODS SCHEME.

Anti-avoidance provisions — subsequent free supply. Where goods or services are transferred as part of a TOGC and the transferor (or any previous owner) has deducted input tax on those goods or services, output tax is chargeable on any subsequent free supply of those goods or services by the transferee. See 47.6 and 47.7 OUTPUT TAX.

9 Business Entertainment

De Voil Indirect Tax Service. See V3.446.

The contents of this chapter are as follows.

9.1 **SUPPLIES TO A TAXABLE PERSON**

VAT charged on any goods or services supplied to a taxable person, or on any goods acquired or imported by him, is excluded from any credit where the goods or services in question are used or to be used for the purpose of 'business entertainment'. [*SI 1992/3222, Art 5(1)*].

'*Business entertainment*' means entertainment (including hospitality of any kind) provided by a taxable person in connection with a business carried on by him, but does not include the provision of any such entertainment for either or both

- employees of the taxable person; or
- if the taxable person is a company, its directors or persons engaged in the management of the company

unless the provision of entertainment for such persons is incidental to its provision for others. [*SI 1992/3222, Art 5(3)*].

9.2 **General scope**

Following on from the definition in 9.1 above, HMRC regard business entertainment as including

- provision of food and drink;
- provision of accommodation (hotels, etc.);
- provision of theatre and concert tickets;
- entry to sporting events and facilities;
- entry to clubs, nightclubs, etc; and
- use of capital goods such as yachts and aircraft for the purpose of entertaining.

Where the cost of providing hospitality is passed on as part of the overall charge for a taxable supply, VAT incurred in providing the hospitality cannot be reclaimed.

(VAT Notice 700/65/02, para 2.2; Internal Guidance V1–13, para 16.3).

See *C & E Commrs v Shaklee International and Another, CA [1981] STC 776 (TVC 8.3)* for the provision of food and accommodation for self-employed agents undergoing training; *BMW (GB) Ltd v C & E Commrs, QB [1997] STC 82 (TVC 8.32)* for hospitality provided to dealers and potential customers at 'track days' where vehicles could be test driven; *Medicare Research Ltd (VTD 1045) (TVC 8.6)* for refreshments and hospitality provided at business discussion meetings in the course of making taxable supplies; *Webster Communications International Ltd (VTD 14753) (TVC 8.37)* for meals and refreshments provided at sponsored conferences to delegates nominated by the sponsor and attending free of charge; *Wilsons Transport Ltd (VTD 1468) (TVC 8.10)* for launching parties; *Polash Tandoori Restaurant (VTD 10903) (TVC 8.22)* for free drinks supplied to customers; and *William Matthew Mechanical Services Ltd (VTD 1210) (TVC 8.8)* for subscription for theatre seats used to extend hospitality and entertainment to clients. However, if the entertainment is not given gratuitously but is provided under a contractual obligation, it does not fall within the scope of the provision. See *Celtic Football and Athletic Club Ltd v C & E Commrs, CS [1983] STC 470 (TVC 8.34)* and *C & E Commrs v Kilroy Television Company Ltd, QB [1997] STC 901 (TVC 8.45)*.

9.3 Employees

For business entertainment purposes, HMRC regard '*employee*' as including

- directors or anyone engaged in the management of the business (including partners);
- self-employed persons (subsistence expenses only) treated by the employer in the same way for subsistence purposes as an employee; and
- helpers, stewards and other people essential to the running of sporting or similar events

but not as including pensioners and former employees, job applicants and interviewees, and shareholders (who are not also employees).

(VAT Notice 700/65/02, paras 2.3, 2.4).

Staff entertainment. Following the decision in *Ernst & Young (VTD 15100) (TVC 8.42)* HMRC accept that where an employer provides entertainment for the benefit of its employees (eg to reward them for good work or to maintain and improve staff morale), it does so wholly for business purposes. Thus, the VAT incurred on entertainment of employees (eg staff parties, team building exercises, staff outings and similar events) is input tax and is not blocked from recovery under the business entertainment rules. There are two exceptions to this general rule.

- Where entertainment is provided only for directors, partners or sole proprietors of a business, the VAT incurred is not input tax as the goods or services are not used for a business purpose. But where directors, etc attend staff parties together with other employees, HMRC accept that the VAT incurred is input tax and is not blocked from recovery.
- Where employees act as hosts to non-employees, the costs are incurred solely for the purpose of entertaining the non-employees and the input tax is blocked under the business entertainment rules.

(VAT Notice 700/65/02, paras 3.1–3.3).

Subsistence expenses. Where meals etc are provided away from the place of work on a business trip, the VAT incurred on the employee's meal can be claimed as input tax under the subsistence rules (see 35.13(21) INPUT TAX). (VAT Notice 700/65/02, para 2.5).

Staff parties with guests, etc. Where a business entertains both employees and non-employees, it can only recover as input tax the VAT it incurs on entertaining its employees. The portion of the input tax incurred in entertaining others is blocked under the business entertainment rules. (VAT Notice 700/65/02, para 3.4). In *KPMG (No 2) (VTD 14962) (TVC 8.33)* an accountancy firm organised dinner dances for its

bodies choose, from affiliated clubs, individual amateur sports persons to represent their country or county, the persons selected are not full subscribing members of the representative body and therefore the provisions applying to clubs above cannot apply. By concession HMRC have agreed that input tax necessarily incurred on the provision of accommodation and meals for team members selected by such representative bodies, and committee members of that body, may be deductible as input tax. The concession does not cover alcoholic drinks and tobacco. (VAT Notice 48, ESC 3.10).

9.7 SUPPLIES BY A TAXABLE PERSON

Special provisions as below apply where, as a result of 9.1 above, no input tax on goods or services used for business entertaining has been claimed and the taxable person subsequently supplies the goods or services in question.

Supplies of goods. Following the decision in *EC Commission v Italian Republic, CJEC [1997] STC 1062 (TVC 21.238)*, where, as a result of 9.1 above, no input tax has been claimed by a taxable person on a supply, acquisition or importation of any *goods*, the disposal of those goods is an exempt supply under *VATA 1994, Sch 9 Group 14*, regardless of whether they are sold at a profit or loss. See 24.4 EXEMPT SUPPLIES.

It should be noted that the provisions only apply where *no* input tax has been claimed (eg where a yacht or private aircraft is used solely for entertaining). Where, however, the asset was used for both entertaining and business purposes, on resale VAT must be accounted for on the full selling price. (VAT Notice 700/65/02, para 2.8).

Supplies of services. Where, as a result of 9.1 above, a taxable person has claimed no input tax on a supply of any services to him, VAT must be charged on a supply by him of those services as if made for a consideration equal to the excess of

(*a*) the consideration for which the services are supplied by him, over

(*b*) the consideration for which they were supplied to him.

Where (*b*) is greater than (*a*), the supply is treated as outside the scope of VAT.

[*SI 1992/3222, Art 5(2); SI 1999/2930*].

10 Capital Goods Scheme

Cross-references. See 38.1 INTERACTION WITH OTHER TAXES for the effect on capital allowances where adjustments are made to input tax deduction under the capital goods scheme.

De Voil Indirect Tax Service. See V3.470–478.

The contents of this chapter are as follows.

10.1 INTRODUCTION

The capital goods scheme applies to certain items of capital expenditure on computer equipment, land and buildings, civil engineering works and refurbishments and fitting-out works which are acquired or brought into use after 31 March 1990 and which are not used wholly for making taxable supplies. The scheme recognises that such items of capital expenditure can be used by a business over a number of years and that there may be variation over those years in the extent to which the items are used to make taxable supplies. It provides a mechanism whereby the initial input tax claimed can be adjusted over a period of up to ten years.

When a capital item within the scheme (see 10.2 below) is acquired, the normal rules for claiming input tax apply, ie

- if it is used wholly in making taxable supplies, input tax is recoverable in full;
- if it is used wholly in making exempt supplies, none of the input tax is recoverable; and
- if it is used for making taxable and exempt supplies, a proportion of the input tax may be claimed under the partial exemption rules.

Where, subsequently, in the adjustment period for that item (see 10.3 below) there is a change in the extent of taxable use, an input tax adjustment has to be made to take account of this. If taxable use increases, a further amount of input tax can be claimed and, if it decreases, some of the input tax already claimed must be repaid.

10.2 CAPITAL ITEMS WITHIN THE SCHEME

Capital items to which the capital goods scheme applies are any items within (*a*)-(*g*) below which the owner uses in the course or furtherance of a business carried on by him, and for the purpose of that business. The scheme does not apply to assets acquired or expenditure on assets held solely for resale (eg stock-in-trade). However, if an asset is used in the business before it is sold, it is no longer treated as an asset held solely for resale and the capital goods scheme will apply; conversely if a capital item is acquired for use in the business but is sold before being used, it is no longer treated as a capital item.

All values are VAT-exclusive. Where any capital item is only partly used for business purposes, if all the VAT incurred is treated as input tax and output tax is accounted for on the non-business use (the 'Lennartz approach', see 35.7 INPUT TAX), the value of the capital item is the full tax-exclusive value of the item. Otherwise, if VAT incurred is apportioned between business and non-business use, the value of the capital item is the VAT-exclusive value of the part attributed to business activities.

(*a*) A computer, or an item of computer equipment, worth £50,000 or more supplied to, or acquired or imported by, the owner.

Any delivery or installation costs should be included unless invoiced separately. If imported, the value for VAT at importation (including import duty) should be taken.

The scheme applies only to individual computers and items of computer equipment, not to complete networks. *Excluded* are

- computerised equipment. eg a computerised telephone exchange or computer-controlled blast furnace; and
- computer software.

(*b*) Land, a building or part of a building or a civil engineering work or part of a civil engineering work where the value of the interest supplied to the owner, by a taxable supply other than a zero-rated supply, is £250,000 or more. When determining whether the value of the supply is £250,000 or more

- any part of that value consisting of rent (including charges reserved as rent) is excluded provided that it is neither payable nor paid more than twelve months in advance nor invoiced for a period in excess of twelve months; and
- any associated costs (eg legal or estate agency fees) should be excluded.

(*c*) A building or part of a building where the owner's interest in, right over or licence to occupy it is treated as self-supplied to him under the provisions in 42.12 LAND AND BUILDINGS (change of use of residential or charitable buildings).

The value of the supply, as determined under the respective provisions, must be £250,000 or more. See also *C & E Commrs v Trustees for R & R Pension Fund, QB [1996] STC 889 (TVC 6.34)*.

(*d*) A building or part of a building where the owner's interest in, right over or licence to occupy was, on or before 1 March 1997, treated as supplied to him under the developer's self-supply charge and the value of that supply was £250,000 or more.

(*e*) A building not falling, or capable of falling, within (*c*) or (*d*) above constructed by the owner and first brought into use by him after 31 March 1990 where the aggregate of

- the value of taxable grants relating to the land on which the building is constructed made to the owner after that date, and
- the value of all the taxable supplies of goods and services, other than any that are zero-rated, made or to be made to him for, or in connection with, the construction of the building after that date

is £250,000 or more.

(*f*) A building which the owner alters, or an extension or an annexe which he constructs, where additional floor area is created in the altered building, extension or annexe, of 10% or more of the original floor area before the work was carried out. The value of all taxable supplies of goods and services, other than any that are zero-rated, made or to be made to the owner after 31 March 1990 for, or in connection with, the alteration, etc must be £250,000 or more.

(*g*) A civil engineering work constructed by the owner and first brought into use by him after 2 July 1997 where the aggregate of

- the value of taxable grants relating to the land on which the civil engineering work is constructed made to the owner after that date, and
- the value of all the taxable supplies of goods and services, other than any that are zero-rated, made or to be made to him for, or in connection with, the construction of the civil engineering work after that date

is £250,000 or more.

Civil engineering work should be given its everyday meaning and includes such items as roads, bridges, golf courses, running tracks and installation of pipes for connection to mains services.

(*h*) A building which the owner refurbishes or fits out where the value of capital expenditure on the taxable supplies of services and of 'goods affixed' to the building, other than any that are zero-rated, made or to be made to the owner for, or in connection with, the refurbishment or fitting out in question after 2 July 1997 is £250,000 or more.

'*Goods affixed*' should be given its everyday meaning. Usually, this includes items of fixtures and fittings and interior decoration that are not easily portable or easily removed. In general terms, these are items that would be sold with the property. Common inclusions (although the deciding factor will be whether the item becomes part of the fabric of the building) are

- materials to build internal and external walls, roofs and ceilings and floors and hard flooring;
- permanent partitioning;
- windows;
- lifts;
- 'built-in' storage such as cupboards or shelving;
- air conditioning;
- lighting; and
- decorative features.

It excludes items secured to the floor for safety or security reasons. Common exclusions are

- office furniture;
- storage unless 'built in';
- carpets;
- computers and computer equipment; and
- factory and office machinery.

Where it is difficult or costly to identify the value of goods affixed from the value of other goods which do not become affixed to the property, by concession, businesses may include any additional amount of capital expenditure (over and above that incurred on items affixed to the building) incurred in connection with the refurbishment, etc in the total value of capital expenditure for the purposes of the capital goods scheme. The concessionary value must then be used in calculating adjustments to the claimed input tax for the whole of the adjustment period. This applies even if those items not affixed have been disposed of (unless they are disposed of as part of the disposal of the whole interest in the building when a final adjustment must be made in the normal way). Businesses must keep a record of the concessionary value of the capital expenditure, including full details of the supplies on which the value was determined. HMRC may withdraw the concession or restrict its use if it considers that it is being used to avoid VAT.

Phased refurbishments are those undertaken in stages. Whether, for the purposes of the capital goods scheme, a phased refurbishment should be treated as a whole or as more than one refurbishment will usually be a matter of fact. Indicators that there is more than one refurbishment might be

- separate contracts for each phase of the work or a contract where each phase is a separate option which can be selected; and
- each phase is completed before work on the next phase starts.

If the refurbishment is of one building only and is only 'phased' because the contractors have to do one floor at a time since the building remains occupied throughout, this would usually indicate there is only one refurbishment.

What is capital expenditure? When considering whether expenditure constitutes 'capital expenditure' HMRC will normally accept the accounting treatment adopted by the business. If the expenditure is treated as a cost in arriving at the profit and loss of the business, the expenditure will not be capital expenditure. If, on the other hand, the expenditure is added to the cost of assets for accounting purposes, it will be capital expenditure. Subject to this, the costs under (*e*)-(*h*) above include all those involved in making the building ready for occupation or the costs involved in the civil engineering work, for example

- professional and management services including architects, surveyors and site management;
- demolition and site clearance;
- building and civil engineering contractors' services;
- materials used in the construction;
- security;
- equipment hire;
- haulage;
- landscaping; and
- fitting out, including the value of any fixtures.

Estimated values. Where it is not known whether a project will exceed the value threshold for the capital goods scheme until all invoices have been received (eg certain construction projects and refurbishments where input tax is incurred over a period of time and contracts that include a retention clause) it will be necessary to estimate the value of the supplies. If the estimate is that the value of relevant supplies will exceed the value threshold, the item becomes a capital item and remains so, even if subsequently the value does not reach the threshold. Any adjustments due under the scheme should continue to be made as necessary. All documents on which the estimate was based must be kept for possible inspection by HMRC.

[*SI 1995/2518, Regs 112, 113; SI 1997/1614, Reg 10*]. (VAT Notice 48, ESC 3.22; VAT Notice 706/2/02, paras 3.4, 3.5, 4.1–4.4, 4.10–4.13, 4.15).

10.3 **THE ADJUSTMENT PERIOD**

The adjustment period is the period of time in which the business must review the extent to which a capital item is used in making taxable supplies. It consists of

- five successive intervals for
  - (i) computers, etc under 10.2(*a*) above, and
  - (ii) land, buildings and civil engineering works under 10.2(*b*) above where the interest has less than ten years to run at the time it is supplied to the owner (eg an eight-year lease); and
- ten successive intervals for all other land and buildings not within (ii) above.

[*SI 1995/2518, Reg 114(3); SI 1997/1614, Reg 11*].

10.4 **First interval**

Subject to the special case below, the rules relating to the transfer of a business as a going concern (see 10.12(4) below) and the rules relating the groups of companies (see 10.12(5) below), the first interval commences, as the case may be,

- where the owner is a registered person when he imports, acquires or is supplied with the item as a capital item (or when he appropriates an item to use as a capital item), the date of importation, acquisition, supply or appropriation,
- where the capital item falls within 10.2(*c*) above, on the date of the self-supply under those provisions,
- where the capital item falls within 10.2(*d*) above, on the later of 1 April 1990 and the day the owner first used the building (or part of the building),
- where the capital item falls within 10.2(*e*)–(*h*) above, on the date that the owner first uses the building, altered building, extension, annexe, civil engineering work or building which has been refurbished or fitted out

and ends on the day before the start of the owner's tax year following that date, ie it normally runs to the following 31 March, 30 April or 31 May depending upon his VAT periods, see 49.9 PARTIAL EXEMPTION.

'*Use*' includes any use in the business. For buildings, it usually consists of the granting of a lease or physical occupation. 'First use' will be the time that any part of the constructed, altered, extended, refurbished or fitted out building is used.

Where the owner is not registered when he first uses an item as a capital item

- if he subsequently becomes a registered person, the first interval commences on his effective date of registration and ends on the following 31 March, 30 April or 31 May depending upon the VAT period allocated to him; and

- if he is subsequently treated as a member of a group for VAT purposes (see 31 GROUPS OF COMPANIES), the first interval corresponds with, or is that part still remaining of, the then current tax year of the group.

[*SI 1995/2518, Reg 114(4); SI 1997/1614, Reg 11*]. (VAT Notice 706/2/02, para 5.3).

Special case — extended first interval. Where

- the extent to which a capital item is used in making taxable supplies does not change between what would otherwise have been the first interval and the first subsequent interval under 10.5 below, and
- the length of the two intervals taken together does not exceed twelve months

the first interval applicable to the capital item ends on what otherwise would have been the end of the first subsequent interval, ie the two periods are combined to become the first interval.

[*SI 1995/2518, Reg 114(5B); SI 1997/1614, Reg 11*].

10.5 **Subsequent intervals**

Subject to the rules relating to the transfer of a business as a going concern (see 10.12(4) below) and the rules relating the groups of companies (see 10.12(5) below), each subsequent interval after the first interval corresponds with a longer period applicable to the owner or, if no longer period applies, a tax year. In either case this will normally run to the following 31 March, 30 April or 31 May depending upon the owner's VAT periods, but see 49.9 PARTIAL EXEMPTION for exceptions. [*SI 1995/2518, Reg 114(5); SI 1997/1614, Reg 11*].

10.6 METHOD OF ADJUSTMENT

Where the extent to which a capital item is used in a subsequent interval increases or decreases from the extent to which it was so used (or to be used) at the time the original entitlement to deduction of the input tax was determined under the partial exemption rules, an adjustment is required. This is calculated by the formula

$$\frac{\text{'Total input tax on the capital item'}}{A} \times \text{'the adjustment \%'}$$

where

A = 5 or 10 depending on the number of intervals in the period of adjustment (see 10.3 above)

'*Total input tax on the capital item*' means

- for a capital item within 10.2(*a*) or (*b*) above, VAT charged on the supply, acquisition or importation. Any VAT charged on rent (including charges reserved as rent) is excluded unless it is payable or paid more than twelve months in advance or invoiced for a period in excess of twelve months;
- for a capital item within 10.2(*c*) or 10.2(*d*) above, the VAT charged on the supply which the owner is treated as making to himself; and
- for a capital item under 10.2(*e*)-(*h*) above, the aggregate of the VAT charged on the supplies described, other than VAT charged on rent (if any)

and includes any VAT treated as input tax under the rules relating to pre-registration or pre-incorporation input tax (see 35.10 INPUT TAX).

'*The adjustment %*' is the difference (if any), expressed as a percentage, between the extent to which the capital item

- was used or to be used for making taxable supplies at the time the original entitlement to deduction of the input tax was determined under the partial exemption rules (for subsequent intervals beginning before 10 March 1999, to which the capital item was used, or regarded as used, in making taxable supplies in the first interval); and
- is so used, or treated as used as the result of a disposal under 10.7 below, in the subsequent interval in question.

Where the owner of a building within these provisions grants or assigns a tenancy or lease in the whole or part of the building and the premium (or if no premium is payable the first payment of rent) is zero-rated, any subsequent exempt supply arising from the grant (eg rent) is disregarded in determining the extent to which the building is used in making taxable supplies.

The percentage is

- 100% where the item is used wholly for making taxable supplies;
- 0% where it is used wholly for making exempt supplies; and
- where it is used for making both taxable and exempt supplies, normally the claimable percentage of residual input tax following the partial exemption annual adjustment for the respective year (see 49.9 PARTIAL EXEMPTION) (although HMRC may allow, or direct, the use of another method). Where the standard method is used (see 49.4 PARTIAL EXEMPTION) the same percentage applies to the whole of the residual input tax. If a special method is used (see 49.6 PARTIAL EXEMPTION) involving different calculations for different parts of the business, the percentage to be used is that which applies to the part of the business in which the capital item is used.

Where different percentages are used for different parts of the business, the percentage to be used is that for the part of the business in which the item is used.

[*SI 1995/2518, Reg 115(1)(2)(5), Reg 116; SI 1995/3147; SI 1997/1614, Regs 12, 13; SI 1999/599*]. (VAT Notice 706/2/02, para 6.5).

10.7 Disposals of capital items during the adjustment period

If a capital item is sold without ever having been used, HMRC do not regard it as a capital item for the purposes of the capital goods scheme. Otherwise, where, during an interval other than the last interval, the owner of a capital item either

- supplies it, or
- is deemed to supply it on ceasing to be a taxable person (see 59.34 REGISTRATION), or
- would have been deemed to supply it on ceasing to be a taxable person but for the fact that VAT on the deemed supply would not have been more than the amount specified in 59.34(*c*) REGISTRATION (whether by virtue of its value or because it is zero-rated or exempt),

then

(*a*) if that supply is a taxable supply, the owner is treated as having used the capital item for each of the remaining *complete* intervals wholly in the making of taxable supplies; and

(*b*) if that supply is an exempt supply, he is treated as not using the capital item for each of the remaining *complete* intervals in making any taxable supplies.

The effect of this is as follows.

- *For the interval in which the capital item is sold*, the adjustment is calculated (or, if it is the first interval, input tax is reclaimed) in the normal way under 10.6 above *as if the capital item had been in use for the whole of that interval.*
- *For any remaining complete intervals in the adjustment period*, the recovery percentage will be 100% where (*a*) above applies or 0% where (*b*) above applies, but subject to the following two provisos.

  (1) The aggregate of the amounts which may be deducted in respect of the remaining complete intervals cannot exceed the output tax chargeable on the supply of the capital item.

  (2) Unless HMRC allow otherwise (see below), a 'disposal test' applies. Where the total amount of input tax deducted or deductible by the owner of a capital item as a result of

  - the input tax initially recovered on the capital item;
  - any adjustments already made under the capital goods scheme; and
  - any final adjustment that is required as a result of the sale of the item

  would exceed the output tax chargeable on the supply of the capital item, then the owner must pay to HMRC, or as the case may be may deduct, such an amount as results in the total input tax deducted or deductible being equal to the output tax chargeable on the supply of the capital item.

  The 'disposal test' is an anti-avoidance measure to ensure that partly exempt businesses such as banks, insurance companies, educational establishments, sports clubs and providers of private healthcare do not obtain an unjustified tax advantage, for example, by making a substantial exempt supply of a long lease of a property followed immediately by the taxable disposal of the freehold for low consideration. HMRC do not intend that the disposal test should be applied to *bona fide* commercial transactions. Given the policy objective, the disposal test will not be applied

  - to sales of computer equipment;
  - where the owner disposes of an item at a loss due to the market conditions (such as a general downturn in property prices);
  - where the value of the capital item has depreciated (as is normally the case with computers);
  - where the value of the capital item is reduced for other legitimate reasons (such as accepting a low price for a quick sale);
  - where the amount of output tax on disposal is less than the total input tax only because of a reduction in the VAT rate; and

- where the item is used only for taxable (including zero-rated) purposes throughout the adjustment period (which includes the final disposal).

Where there is no unjustified tax advantage, a business need not apply these provisions and it is not necessary to apply to HMRC for a specific ruling. Where there is an unjustified tax advantage, a business must calculate the net tax advantage (ie the overall benefit derived from the avoidance device, normally the amount of input tax that would still be subject to adjustment under the scheme were it not for the sale of the capital item less any output tax due on the sale) and then work out how much of the net tax advantage is unjustified. Normally this could be achieved by using the ratio that the value of the final taxable sale bears to the value of both the exempt supply and the final taxable sale.

Example 1

The facts are the same as in the example in 10.6 above except that the computer is sold in interval 4 for £10,000, the current market value.

Intervals 1 to 3

No change

Interval 4

Input tax repayable to HMRC

17,500 ÷ 5 × (48 – 45)% = £105

Interval 5

Additional input tax claimed from HMRC

17,500 ÷ 5 × (100 – 48)% = £1,820

but restricted under proviso (1) above to £10,000 × 17.5% = £1,750

A final adjustment of £1,645 (£1,750 – £105) should be made in respect of interval 4.

Example 2

A developer, whose tax year ends on 31 March, completes a commercial development on 1 June 1998 at a cost of £25 million plus VAT of £4,375,000. The developer opts to tax the property and leases it for two years to a third party tenant at market value plus VAT. On 1 June 2000 the developer grants a 99 year lease at a premium of £24 million and a peppercorn rent to its wholly-owned subsidiary which is wholly exempt. On 1 May 2001 the developer sells the freehold, subject to the 99 year lease, for £250,000 plus VAT of £43,750 to the wholly owned subsidiary.

Interval 1 (to 31 March 1999). The developer can initially deduct all the VAT incurred on the development because of the option to tax.

Interval 2 (to 31 March 2000). No adjustment is required for interval 2 as the building continues to be let under a taxable lease.

Interval 3 (to 31 March 2001). On the grant of the lease, *VATA 1994, Sch 10 para 2(3AA)* (see 42.9(*g*) LAND AND BUILDINGS) operates so as to disapply the developer's option to tax and the premium is not subject to VAT. An adjustment in respect of 1/10th (£437,500) of the initial input tax incurred is required at the end of interval 3. On the basis of that during that interval the property was used for taxable purposes for two months and exempt purposes of ten months, VAT of £364,583 (305/366 × £437,500) must be paid back to HMRC.

Interval 4 (to 31 March 2002). The sale of the property on 1 May 2001 is compulsorily standard-rated under *VATA 1994, Sch 9 Group 1 Item 1(a)* as it is less than three years old (see 42.3(*a*) LAND AND BUILDINGS). Output tax is therefore due of £43,750 (£250,000 × 17.5%). Since the building is only used for exempt purposes up to the sale, an adjustment in respect of the full 1/10th (£437,500) of the initial input tax incurred is required.

Intervals 5-10. Since the output tax on the sale of the freehold is less than the input tax claimed in the adjustment period, the disposal test applies. In this instance there is an unjustified tax advantage because the high value exempt grant in interval 3 enables a low value taxable sale of the freehold. At the same time the taxable sale enables full recovery of input tax in respect of the six remaining intervals 5–10. In principle £3,529,167 would be due as follows

Interval	*Input tax claim*	*Output tax declared*	*Cumulative difference*
	£	£	£
1	4,375,000	-	4,375,000
2	-	-	4,375,000
3	(364,583)		4,010,417
4	(437,500)	(43,750)	3,529,167
5–10			3,529,167

However, the net tax advantage is that the developer is able to secure the amount of input tax that would still be subject to adjustment under the scheme for intervals 5–10 were it not for the sale of the property (6/10ths of £4,375,000 = £2,625,000) by making a taxable supply giving rise to output tax of £43,750. The net tax advantage is therefore £2,581,250.

Some form of fair and reasonable apportionment needs to be applied to work out how much of the net tax advantage is unjustified. This could be achieved by using the ratio that the value of the exempt supply bears to the value of both the exempt supply and the final taxable sale, ie

24,000,000 ÷ 24,250,000 × £2,554,639

Thus, in practice the disposal test would be applied, but the amount due to HMRC would be the value of the unjustified tax advantage, ie £2,554,639.

[*SI 1995/2518, Reg 115(3)(3A)(3B); SI 1997/1614, Reg 12; SI 2000/258, Reg 5*]. (VAT Notice 706/2/02, paras 8.1–8.7; Business Brief 30/97).

10.8 **Lost, stolen, destroyed or expired assets**

If, during the adjustment period, a capital item is

- irretrievably lost or stolen or is totally destroyed, or
- an interest in land or buildings which expires (eg a short lease)

no further adjustment must be made in respect of the remaining *complete* intervals applicable to it. [*SI 1995/2518, Reg 115*(*4*)].

The normal scheme adjustment is made for the interval of loss, etc as if the capital item had been used for the whole interval.

Where a capital item is lost, stolen or destroyed, any evidence of the loss (eg an insurance claim) should be kept for possible inspection by a visiting VAT officer.

See also 10.12(3) below for 'rolling reburbishments' where the original refurbishments are stripped out and replaced before the end of the adjustment period.

(VAT Notice 706/2/02, para 8.8).

10.9 **Capital items temporarily not used**

Once the capital goods scheme has started, if a capital item is not used for a period of time (eg a computer is overhauled) it is treated as still being used during that period for the same purpose as it was previously used. But if a capital item is never used in the business, HMRC do not regard it as an asset for the purposes of the capital goods scheme. (VAT Notice 706/2/02, paras 6.13, 8.7).

10.10 **VAT returns**

Where an adjustment is required under 10.6 to 10.9 above, it should be included in the return for the second VAT period following the interval to which the adjustment relates or in which the supply as a result of sale, or deemed supply as a result of deregistration, takes place. This is the period after the one in which the partial exemption annual adjustment is made for the year. The adjustment should be included in Box 4 of the VAT return.

Where an interval has come to an end because

- the owner of the capital item has ceased to be a member of a group (see 10.12(5) below), or
- the owner (who remains a taxable person) has transferred part of his business as a going concern (see 10.12(4) below),

the adjustment for that interval must be included in the return for the group or transferor (as the case may be) for the second VAT period after the end of the tax year of the group/transferor in which the interval in question fell.

HMRC may allow any adjustment to be made in a later return but only if it is a return for a VAT period commencing within three years of the end of the period when the adjustment should have been made.

If VAT registration has been cancelled, the adjustment should be entered on the final VAT return for the period ending with the effective date of deregistration.

[*SI 1995/2518, Reg 115*(*6*)-(*8*); *SI 1997/1086, Reg 8; SI 1997/1614, Reg 12*]. (VAT Notice 706/2/02, para 7.1).

10.11 **RECORDS**

See 56 RECORDS for general requirements for records. In respect of each capital item, the records kept must enable a business to work out the capital goods scheme adjustment for each subsequent interval in the adjustment period and should therefore include

- a description of the capital item;
- its value;
- the amount of input tax incurred on it;
- the amount of input tax reclaimed on it;
- the start and end date of each interval, including the first;
- when adjustments are due; and
- the date and value of disposal if the item is sold before the end of the adjustment period.

Although, by law, records only have to be kept for six years, businesses are advised to keep records of *all* capital items in case a capital goods scheme adjustment becomes necessary. It is also important to keep detailed records because if

- the capital item is sold as part of the transfer of a business as a going concern (see 10.12(4) below), or
- the owner moves in or out of a VAT group (see 10.12(5) below),

the new owner is responsible for any adjustments for the remainder of the adjustment period.

(VAT Notice 706/6/02, paras 2.1, 2.2).

10.12 **TREATMENT IN PARTICULAR CASES**

(1) **Input tax incurred before the first interval**

Where a business incurs input tax before the first interval, it must work out the overall initial claimable percentage against which it can measure the percentage of taxable use in subsequent periods. This could be done, for example, by expressing the total input tax recovered as a percentage of the input tax incurred on the capital item.

Example

A business constructs a new head office and incurs input tax of £500,000 in its tax year ending 31 March 2001 (in which its reclaimable percentage is 75%) and £250,000 in its tax year ending 31 March 2002 (in which its reclaimable percentage is 80%). It occupies the building for use in its partly exempt business as from 1 September 2001.

The first interval runs from 1 September 2001 to 31 March 2002. The average reclaimable percentage for subsequent intervals is

Total input tax reclaimed ÷ Total input tax incurred × 100%

= [(£500,000 × 75%) + (£250,000 × 80%)] ÷ (£500,000 + £250,000) × 100%

= £575,000 ÷ £750,000 × 100% = 76.67%

(VAT Notice 706/2/02, para 6.2).

(2) **Input tax incurred after the first interval**

Some projects, for example, construction projects and refurbishments where the work is carried out over a period of time, may result in additional input tax being incurred after the first interval. This may also occur where a contract includes a retention clause. Input tax incurred in the second interval does not form part of the capital goods scheme adjustment in the second interval but should be adjusted where necessary from the third interval onwards.

(VAT Notice 706/2/02, para 6.3). See VAT Notice 706/2/02, para 6.4 for examples of how to calculate the adjustments due using the 'combined adjustments' and 'parallel adjustments' methods.

(3) **Rolling refurbishments**

Rolling refurbishments occur where a property is refurbished on a regular basis and some or all of the original refurbishments are replaced. If a second refurbishment is undertaken before the original adjustment period has ended

- where the original refurbishment is completely stripped out or replaced, it should be treated as destroyed (see 10.8 above) and no further adjustments made to the input tax on that refurbishment; or
- where elements of the original refurbishment are retained, adjustments to the original input tax must still be made for the remainder of the adjustment period of that refurbishment.

(VAT Notice 706/2/02, para 4.14).

(4) **Transfer of a business as a going concern**

Where a business or part of a business is transferred as a going concern (see 8.10 BUSINESS), any capital items included as part of the transfer are not 'sold' for the purposes of the capital goods scheme and therefore 10.7 above does not apply. The responsibility for applying the capital goods scheme to any capital item transferred passes to the new owner for any remaining intervals. The timing of intervals depends upon whether the new owner takes over the original owner's VAT registration number.

- *If the new owner takes over the seller's VAT registration number*, the interval during which the business is transferred does not end at the time of the transfer and continues without a break. The seller does not need to make any adjustments for that interval. The interval ends on the last day of the new owner's longer period ending immediately after the transfer (or if no longer period then applies, on the last day of his tax year following the day of transfer). The new owner must make any adjustment for that interval and any remaining intervals in the normal way. Longer periods and tax years both normally run to the following 31 March, 30 April or 31 May depending upon the owner's VAT periods, but see 49.9 PARTIAL EXEMPTION for exceptions.
- *If the new owner does not take over the seller's VAT registration number*, the interval applying to the capital item ends on the day before the transfer

takes place. The seller should make any adjustment for that interval on his VAT return for the second period after the end of his tax year in the normal way or, if he is cancelling his registration, he can make any adjustment on his final return. The new owner is responsible for the next interval which runs from the date of transfer to the anniversary date and any other remaining intervals which run for 12 months from each anniversary date. Subsequent intervals applicable to the transferred item may or may not coincide with the new owner's partial exemption tax year. If they do not, the new owner will need to agree a way of calculating subsequent intervals with HMRC.

As the new owner takes over responsibility for applying the capital goods scheme, for each relevant capital item the original owner must supply

- a description of the capital item;
- the date of acquisition and number of remaining intervals in the period of adjustment;
- the total input tax incurred; and
- the percentage of that input tax which was claimed on the item in the first interval.

[*SI 1995/2518, Reg 114(5A)(7); SI 1997/1614, Reg 11*]. (VAT Notice 706/2/02, para 9.4).

(5) **VAT groups**

On the first occasion during an adjustment period applicable to a capital item that the owner of the item

- being VAT-registered subsequently becomes a member of a group of companies for VAT purposes (see 31 GROUPS OF COMPANIES), or
- being a member of a group for VAT purposes ceases to be a member of that group (whether or not it immediately becomes a member of another such group)

the interval then applying ends on the day before the owner becomes a member of the group or the day the owner ceases to be a member of the group (as the case may be). The original owner of the capital item must make any adjustment for this interval. The new owner becomes responsible for subsequent intervals (if any) applicable to the capital item which end on the successive anniversaries of that day (irrespective of whether there are any further movements into or out of VAT groups since this provision only applies on the *first* occasion of joining or leaving a group). The new owner will need to agree a way of calculating adjustments for any such intervals with HMRC in the likely event that these intervals do not coincide with its longer periods.

As the new owner takes over responsibility for applying the capital goods scheme, for each relevant capital item the original owner must supply

- a description of the capital item;
- the date of acquisition and number of remaining intervals in the period of adjustment;
- the total input tax incurred; and

- the percentage of that input tax which was claimed on the item in the first interval.

[*SI 1995/2518, Reg 114(5A); SI 1997/1614, Reg 11*]. (VAT Notice 706/2/02, paras 10.1–10.3).

11 Catering

De Voil Indirect Tax Service. See V4.227.

Note. The provisions in this chapter deal with the VAT liability of food and drink supplied in the course of any catering business. The rules do not apply to food or drink supplied as groceries, for which see 28 FOOD. Where overnight accommodation is also provided, see 33 HOTELS AND HOLIDAY ACCOMMODATION.

The contents of the chapter are as follows.

11.1 SUPPLIES IN THE COURSE OF CATERING

A supply of food and drink in the course of 'catering' is standard-rated. [*VATA 1994, Sch 8 Group 1(a)*].

To decide whether any supply is in the course of catering, the following three questions should be considered in turn.

- Is it within the ordinary meaning of catering?
- Is it for 'on premises' consumption?
- Is it hot take-away food?

If the answer is 'yes' at any stage the supply is a standard-rated supply of catering (but see 11.7 and 11.8 below for certain supplies made in hospitals and schools or similar establishments respectively which may be exempt).

Catering. Where a supply can be identified as catering in its everyday meaning, it is *per se* standard-rated and it is not necessary to consider the problems relating to 'premises' and 'hot take-away food'. This point was clarified in *C & E Commrs v Cope, QB [1981] STC 532 (TVC 27.42)*.

The word 'catering' is not defined in the legislation but in its ordinary meaning includes the supply of prepared food and drink

- incidental to another activity or function such as business activities, sporting or social events (eg wedding receptions, parties, dinner dances, exhibitions, conferences and the theatre), see *Cope* above;
- that is not incidental to an event or function but is so similar that it is treated in the same way (eg the inclusion of delivery, cutlery, crockery, napkins and staff and/or the fact that complete ready meals are delivered to customers are all indicators that a supply is one of catering); or
- supplied as part of a contract to supply catering. (Supplies to customers not covered by the contract will only be standard-rated if they are consumed on the premises or are hot take-away food, see below.)

Catering also includes the supply of cooking and/or preparing food provided by a customer, such as a dinner party at the customer's home.

Catering may take place at the caterer's premises or where the event is held and includes any meals, snacks, etc delivered to customers for a function or similar event.

HMRC consider the following questions as pointers to help in clarifying whether a supply is one of catering.

- Is the supply linked to an event, function or social occasion?
- Does the trader by his trading name or advertising indicate that he is a caterer?
- Is there a menu?
- Does the supply require some preparation of the food?
- Is the food presented in a way to make it different from food sold in a supermarket or grocer's shop?
- Is the supply to the final consumer or a person receiving it on behalf of the final consumer?
- Is the food, whether hot or cold, supplied for immediate consumption?
- Is there provision of tables and chairs, cutlery, plates, napkins, or condiments, etc?
- Is there an element of service provided to the customer? This could vary from a full waiter/waitress service to simply laying out sandwiches on a platter.
- If the food is delivered, is there only minimal preparation required by the customer?
- If an invoice is raised is it on a per person basis rather than per item?

The list is not exhaustive but if the answers are 'yes' to most of these questions then HMRC are likely to regard the supply as being in the course of catering. If the answer to any question is 'no' (eg there is no menu or no invoice has been raised), the supply may still be in the course of catering depending on the facts of the individual case, particularly if it is linked to an occasion.

Food for customer preparation. The supply of food which customers must prepare themselves before it can be consumed is not a supply in the course of catering. This applies whether the food is delivered to, or collected by, the customers. For these purposes, 'preparation' includes thawing frozen food, cooking food, reheating food and arranging food on serving plates.

Delivered sandwiches and groceries. Where sandwiches, or other items of food and drink, are taken to buildings in order to sell them,

- if the supplier has no contract or agreement to do so, this is not a supply in the course of catering and any item can be zero-rated if eligible (see 28.3–28.13 FOOD); and
- if the supplier is supplying the food under a contract to do so, this is a supply in the course of catering and all supplies are standard-rated.

See *Zeldaline Ltd (VTD 4388) (TVC 27.28).*

Delivered food such as milk, bread and other groceries are zero-rated unless they are certain goods which are always standard-rated (see 28.3–28.13 FOOD).

See 47.8(18) OUTPUT TAX for the treatment of any delivery charge.

Grocery items sold from a catering outlet. Provided these items are in the same form as when sold by a grocer or supermarket, and are clearly not intended for on premises consumption, they need not be treated as being made in the course of catering. Examples of items that are clearly not intended for on premises consumption include packets of tea, coffee, sugar, loaves of bread and cartons of factory sealed milk.

Packed lunches. Where packed meals are provided for an event or a function (eg coach parties or race meetings), HMRC consider the meals are supplied in the course of catering and should be standard-rated.

Where there is no link to an event/function and consumption is off the supplier's premises, the supply will normally be of zero-rated cold foodstuffs unless comprising items which are always standard-rated (see 28.3–28.13 FOOD). This includes packed lunches provided by hotels and similar establishments for which a separate charge is made. (Where the supply by a hotel consists of accommodation and meals at an inclusive price, for example, full board, half board, or bed and breakfast, this should be treated as a single standard-rated supply even if any of the meals are taken as packed lunches.)

(VAT Notice 709/1/02, paras 1.3, 2.1; Internal Guidance V1–7, Chapter 1 paras 14.3, 17.6).

Cold take-away buffets. A problem often arises in deciding whether a supply of a cold buffet platters, etc is a standard-rated supply of catering or simply a supply of zero-rated food items. There is no definitive guide to this and each case should be decided on its own facts. There have been a number of tribunal decisions. In *Out to Lunch (a firm) (VTD 13031) (TVC 27.10)* and *Happy Place Ltd (t/a The Munch Box) (VTD 17654) (TVC 27.9)* it was held that the supply of sandwich platters comprising sandwiches, fruit, cakes, etc available for take-away or delivery from the shop was not in the course of catering even though described as 'for meetings'. Compare, however, *Wendy's Kitchen (VTD 15531) (TVC 27.14)* and *PJ & LJ Lawson (t/a Country Fayre) (VTD 14903) (TVC 27.12)* where on the evidence, including advertising material, 'finger buffets' supplied to local offices were held to be supplies in the course of catering. See also *C & E Commrs v Safeway Stores plc, QB 1996, [1997] STC 163 (TVC 27.8)* for 'party trays' of food sold from delicatessen counters. For a general consideration of delivered cold meals, etc, see *C Chasney Ltd (VTD 4136) (TVC 27.6)*.

Food and drink for consumption on the premises. Any supply of food and drink for consumption on the premises in which it is supplied is standard-rated. [*VATA 1994, Sch 8 Group 1 Note 3(a)*]. 'Premises' are widely defined. See 11.2 below.

Hot take-away food. Any supply of 'hot food' for consumption off the premises on which it is supplied is standard-rated. See 11.2 below for premises.

'*Hot food*' means food which, or any part of which,

- has been heated for the purposes of enabling it to be consumed at a temperature above the ambient air temperature; and
- is above that temperature at the time it is provided to the customer (before 1 January 2005, at the time of supply).

[*VATA 1994, Sch 8 Group 1 Note 3(b); SI 2004/3343*].

The change in the legislation with effect from 1 January 2005 is to remove any doubt that, where payment for hot take-away food is made in advance (eg when ordering) of the basic tax point when the food leaves the shop, this establishes a time of supply before the food is cooked. This would lead to the conclusion that the food is not above the ambient air temperature when it is paid for, and so is not hot food.

Included in standard-rating when sold hot are fish/chicken and chips; chips sold on their own; Chinese, Indian, Greek, Italian and similar take-away meals and dishes; baked potatoes with hot or cold filling; hot dogs and hamburgers; pies, sausage rolls, pasties and similar items (but see below if sold freshly cooked); toasted sandwiches; cups of tea, coffee, chocolate and other hot drinks; cups of soup; and roasted chestnuts.

Hot and cold ingredients supplied together. If an item of hot food has an ingredient which is cold as a single item, the whole supply is standard-rated (see *Marshall (t/a Harry Ramsbottom's) (VTD 13766) (TVC 27.56)*). This includes anything in a bun, bap, baguette or other speciality bread with any hot filling such as a sausage, reheated cheese and ham, pastrami, etc. Examples include hot dogs, hamburgers, bacon sandwiches, chip butties, baked potatoes with a cold filling, hot steak sandwiches and kebabs.

Freshly cooked products. Some products which may be eaten while still hot are also bought like other grocery items for consumption later, either cold or after re-heating. Examples include pies, pasties, sausage rolls and similar savoury products, cooked chickens or joints of meat, bread products and croissants. The liability of such items will depend on the way in which they are sold.

- If they are *either* sold warm simply because they happen to be freshly baked and are not intended to be eaten while hot *or* are sold cold or chilled at the time of purchase, the supply can be zero-rated.
- If they are sold specifically for consumption while still hot (as a result of being freshly baked, cooked or reheated) the supply is standard-rated. This includes where the business has an established hot take-away trade, any hot food sold as part of that trade.

Indicators of a standard-rated supply of hot take-away food include the following.

- The outlet is advertised as a take-away food outlet.
- The food is advertised or promoted (eg by in-store signs or wording on the packaging) to indicate that it should be eaten while still hot.
- Food is packaged to retain heat. (The reverse does not apply as food intended for immediate consumption is often sold in packaging that is not heat-retentive.)
- Availability of condiments, napkins and utensils.
- The food is generally accepted as unpalatable when cold. (The reverse does not necessarily apply: the fact that an item remains palatable when cold does not preclude the possibility that it has been heated in order to be consumed hot.)
- Food is thrown away once cold.
- Food is microwaved (or otherwise heated) by the trader on request.
- Food spoils on re-heating.
- Use of heat-retentive containers between the time the food is cooked/heated and handed to the customer.
- Trader reheats or replaces food on complaint that it is too cold.

Indicators of a zero-rated supply include the following.

- It is made clear to the customer that they should reheat the food and instructions are given.
- Food is kept at a minimum temperature for hygiene reasons and is too cold to eat at the time of sale.
- Lack of heat-retentive containers.
- Food is not re-heated.

HMRC accept that, in some cases, food may be kept hot partly for the purposes of complying with food hygiene regulations. However, the requirement to comply with such regulations will often not be the aim in itself for the supplier, but merely a consequence of supplying food for consumption whilst hot or warm. In such a case, the supply is standard-rated.

Use of microwave oven on premises by customers. If food is sold to be taken away for consumption elsewhere but a microwave oven is made available for customers to heat up the food (either before or after the till point) the supply is one of hot food and must be standard-rated (whether or not a charge is made for the use of the oven).

Hot and cold food sold at the same time. Where a mixture of standard-rated and zero-rated items is sold for an inclusive price for consumption off the premises, the price may be apportioned to calculate the tax value of each supply (see 47.3 OUTPUT TAX). Examples of mixed supplies include

- burger, chips and a milkshake;
- a cup of tea with a biscuit; or
- a meal consisting of hot and cold items or dishes supplied in separate containers.

A supply is normally considered to be a mixed supply if each of the items in the inclusively-priced package can be purchased separately from the menu. This is not the same as a single item of food that happens to have hot and cold ingredients for which one charge is made (see above).

Condiments, etc. Any minor items for which no charge is made (eg salt, pepper, vinegar or mustard) should be ignored.

(VAT Notice 709/1/02, paras 4.1–4.9; Internal Guidance V1–7, Chapter 1 paras 15.2–15.6; Business Brief 4/05).

In *John Pimblett & Sons Ltd v C & E Commrs, CA 1987, [1988] STC 358 (TVC 27.52)* it was held that for supplies of freshly baked pies to be taxed as hot take-away food, it had to be shown that the predominant subjective purpose of the seller in heating the food was to enable it to be consumed while still hot. If the seller's predominant purpose was to assure customers that it had been freshly baked, the food was not standard-rated, even though some customers consumed the food while still hot.

In *The Lewis's Group Ltd (VTD 4931) (TVC 27.64)* it was held that the supply of hot freshly-roasted chickens from the food department was not a supply in the course of catering because it was not the supplier's predominant purpose, in heating the chicken, to enable customers to eat it at any particular temperature. However, in *Malik (t/a Hotline Foods) v C & E Commrs, QB [1998] STC 537 (TVC 27.70)* the court dismissed the appellant's contentions that standard-rating only applied where the food had been heated as opposed to cooked. The court held that the trader had heated the food with a dual purpose and her supplies were therefore standard-rated.

In *Pret A Manger (Europe) Ltd (VTD 16246) (TVC 27.60)* the tribunal rejected the argument that filled croissants were heated to keep them fresh and to prevent them from hardening. On the evidence, it found that the company's predominant purpose in cooking the savoury croissants and presenting them for sale hot was so that they could be consumed at a temperature above the ambient air temperature. However, in *The Great American Bagel Factory Ltd (VTD 17018) (TVC 27.61)* the tribunal accepted that the purpose of toasting bagels was to create a crunchy interior and promote freshness rather than enable them to be consumed hot.

Vending machines. Vending machine supplies follow the same general principles as food and drink supplied from catering outlets.

- If there is an agreement or arrangement to provide food and drink for a particular group of people, the supplies are standard-rated, whether hot or cold and wherever the food is consumed.
- All supplies of food and drink that is to be consumed on the premises where the machine is placed are standard-rated, whether hot or cold. See 11.2 below for 'premises'.
- If the food and drink is not intended for consumption on the site where the machine is placed then supplies may be zero-rated apart from certain items which are always standard-rated (see 28.3–28.13 FOOD).

See 11.8 below if the machine is on a university campus and is run by the students' union.

(VAT Notice 709/1/02, para 2.3).

See also 47.8(30) OUTPUT TAX for hiring of vending machines.

Supplies to persons making catering supplies. A supply in the course of catering is, for VAT purposes, to be taken as a supply to the final consumer or to a person receiving it on behalf of the final consumer. Where a trader supplies prepared cold food and drink to a customer who then sells it in the course of catering, the first supply is not regarded as being made in the course of catering. Examples are bulk supplies of sandwiches, salads and prepared meals requiring cooking or re-heating.

However, it should be borne in mind that

- some items are always standard-rated (see 28.3–28.13 FOOD);
- if food is prepared on the premises where it is to be eaten then the supply is regarded as being in the course of catering and standard-rated (see above); and
- if the food is supplied hot to be eaten while still hot then the supply is in the course of catering and standard-rated (see above).

(Internal Guidance V1–7, Chapter 1 para 17.11).

Catering on aircraft, ships, etc. Where the catering is an adjunct to the supply of the transport and no separate charge is made for it, the consideration for the ticket need not be apportioned. The catering is treated as part of the supply of the passenger transport (*British Airways plc v C & E Commrs, CA [1990] STC 643 (TVC 64.8)*). Otherwise HMRC treat catering as a supply of *goods* which is

- outside the scope of UK under *VATA 1994. s 7(2)* when supplied on a journey to a country outside the EC; and
- outside the scope under *SI 2004/3148, Art 6* when supplied for consumption on board intra-EC transport.

11.2 Catering

In *Faaborg-Gelting Linien A/S v Finanzamt Flensburg, CJEC [1996] STC 774 (TVC 21.105)*, the CJEC held that catering supplied on board a ferry travelling between Denmark and Germany was a supply of *services*, supplied where the supplier had his established place of business under *EC Sixth Directive, Art 9(1)*. However, many EC countries, including the UK, have not implemented this judgment.

(VAT Notice 709/1/02, para 2.4; Internal Guidance V1–4, Chapter 2 para 10.8).

11.2 Premises

Standard-rating applies to

- hot and cold food and drink for consumption on the premises where supplied; and
- hot food for consumption off the premises where supplied.

It is clearly important therefore to determine what is meant by 'premises' in relation to the supply of catering. The correct interpretation of 'premises' has been debated in many court and tribunal decisions and its application can still cause problems.

HMRC's view is that the wording ensures that all meals supplied in premises such as restaurants, cafés and canteens are, as Parliament intended, excluded from zero-rating. However, 'premises' can mean more than just the outlet where food or drink is sold. Catering outlets can be part of a larger site, eg an office block or shopping centre. In such cases, they can be distinguished between those in places to which the public have unrestricted access and those to which they do not. The practical effect of this distinction is that

- where public access to the site or building is unrestricted (eg shopping malls, hospitals, bus stations and railway stations) the premises is limited to the catering outlet itself plus any associated facilities such as tables and chairs provided for the use of customers, whether or not such facilities are owned or provided by the outlet; and
- where public access to the site or building is restricted (such as a sports stadium, club, amusement park, cinema, concert hall or secure office building) because public entry is limited in some way by, for example, payment or security pass, the premises is the whole building or site. (But see below for the distinction where an office building has multiple tenancy.)

HMRC's treatment of common examples of premises is set out below. It should be borne in mind that it is the actual circumstances rather than the generic description which will be the deciding factor and in some cases it is necessary to consider whether there is catering *per se* (see 11.1 above).

Agricultural shows and markets	'Closed' shows are one set of premises. In 'open' shows only the catering outlet and facilities for consumption are premises

Airports, amusement parks, bus and railway stations	Areas with restriction of access to the public are premises. In areas with no restriction of access only the catering outlet and facilities for consumption are premises. See *Whitbread Group plc v C & E Commrs, Ch D [2005] STC 539 (TVC 27.19)* for sandwiches sold in airport departure lounges
Building sites	The whole of the site is one set of premises
Clubs	The building and its curtilage are the premises. See *Ivy Café Ltd (VTD 288) (TVC 27.37)*
Coaches, trains, ships and aircraft	All are premises but supplies may be incidental to the main supply
Exhibition halls	The whole of the exhibition hall is one set of premises
Factories	The whole factory site is one set of premises
Film and TV location sets	This is normally catering *per se*
Football grounds and sports stadia	The whole ground including its adjacent car parks is premises. See *C & E Commrs v Cope, QB [1981] STC 532 (TVC 27.42)* and *Bristol City Football Supporters Club (VTD 164) (TVC 27.35)*
Holiday camps, caravan parks and camping sites	The open grounds of a site are to be treated as if they were a public space. However, food supplied for consumption in any building in which it is supplied is standard-rated
Hospitals	A single site is usually premises. See *Ashby Catering Ltd (VTD 4220) (TVC 27.29)*
Hotels, hostels, motels and the like	Each establishment is one set of premises
Industrial estates	Each unit rather than the estate is a set of premises
Markets and covered shopping areas	Unless there is a discrete area for consumption these are treated as public open spaces. See *Armstrong (M) (VTD 1609) (TVC 27.24)* and *Crownlion (Seafood) Ltd (VTD 1924) (TVC 27.45)*

11.2 Catering

Military bases	See *Bishop & Elcocks (VTD 17620) (TVC 27.34)* where the tribunal ruled that 'premises' meant the canteen and not the entire naval station. Previously, HMRC regarded the whole base as one set of premises (but excluding residential areas such as married quarters)
Mobile outlets in public open spaces	Only the outlet and facilities like counter, tables and chairs are treated as premises. See *Fresh Sea Foods (Barry) Ltd (VTD 6658) (TVC 27.31)* and *Skilton and Gregory (VTD 11723) (TVC 27.44)*
Motorway service areas	Catering outlets and associated facilities are treated as premises. The rest of the service area is a public open space
Office buildings - single occupancy	The whole building is one set of premises. See *Bergonzi (t/a Beppi's Buffet Service) (VTD 12122) (TVC 27.50)*
- multiple occupancy	The part occupied by each individual tenant is premises. See *R v C & E (ex p Sims (t/a Supersonic Snacks)), QB [1988] STC 210 (TVC 27.26)*
Piers	One set of premises if there is restricted access
Public buildings	Where the building has single occupancy eg a museum or library the building and its curtilage form one set of premises. Where there is multiple occupancy eg a county hall which incorporates some retail outlets each outlet is separate premises
Public car parks	No premises — this is a public open space
Restaurants, cafés, pubs and similar outlets	The whole outlet, including any forecourt or garden, is premises
Schools and colleges	Are mostly one set of premises. See, however, *St Benedict Trading Ltd (VTD 12915) (TVC 27.32)*. Supplies may be incidental and therefore exempt or non-business

Showgrounds	Areas with restricted public access are premises. Where there is no restriction only the food outlet and facilities for consumption are premises. But in connection with events consider catering *per se*

(Internal Guidance V1–7, Chapter 1 Part C paras 3.5, 3.6; VAT Notice 709/1/02, paras 3.1, 3.2).

11.3 ACCOUNTING FOR VAT

The owner of catering facilities must account for VAT on any supplies of catering or hot take-away food and can reclaim any VAT charged as input tax, subject to the normal rules.

Retail scheme calculations. If each sale can be recorded as it takes place, the normal method of accounting can be used. This applies whether sales are only standard-rated or a mixture of standard-rated and zero-rated.

If each sale cannot be recorded as it takes place, then the Point of Sale scheme must normally be used (see 60.14 RETAIL SCHEMES) unless the catering adaptation described below can be used. (It is not normally possible to use the Apportionment or Direct Calculation schemes. These assume that goods bought at one rate of VAT will be sold at the same rate and food bought at the zero rate often becomes standard-rated when supplied in the course of catering.)

Catering adaptation. A caterer may use a special catering adaptation to account for VAT provided

- he can satisfy HMRC that it is impracticable to keep records to operate the Point of Sale scheme;
- he has reasonable grounds for believing that the VAT-exclusive value of standard-rated and zero-rated catering supplies will not exceed £1 million in the next twelve months; and
- the use of the catering adaptation produces a fair and reasonable result in any period.

If the conditions (which have the force of law) are met, he must notify HMRC that he intends to operate the catering adaptation and may then begin to operate it as soon as acknowledgement of the letter is received.

To calculate output tax for each VAT period

Step 1	Add up daily gross takings	A
Step 2	Calculate the percentage of total supplies of catering made at the standard rate (see below)	B%
Step 3	Apply the percentage at Step 2 to the daily gross takings in Step 1	
Step 4	To calculate output tax, multiply the total at Step 3 by the VAT fraction	

In algebraic form, output tax is

$A \times (B \div 100) \times V$

See 60.8 and 60.9 RETAIL SCHEMES for general rules applying to the calculation of daily gross takings. Service charges (but not tips) and the value of any meals or drinks given in exchange for an identifiable benefit to the business (see 11.4 below) should be included. It is not necessary to include the cost of food or drink used for free meals for family and staff but the full cost of any standard-rated items of food taken out of business stock for own or family use should be included (see 11.4 below).

The percentage of total supplies of catering made at the standard rate must be based on a sample of actual sales for a representative period. The period depends on the nature of the business but HMRC must be satisfied that it takes account of hourly, daily and seasonal fluctuations. Details of the sample, including dates and times, must be retained and a new calculation must be carried out in each tax period.

If the conditions of the adaptation are not complied with, HMRC may assess for any undeclared VAT and/or refuse use of the adaptation for future periods.

(VAT Notice 727, paras 8.3–8.8 which have the force of law).

Other retail supplies. Where other retail non-catering supplies are made, it may be possible to run separate retail schemes for each part of the business provided separate books are kept. See 60.4 RETAIL SCHEMES.

11.4 **Free supplies of catering**

Catering for employees. Where employees are provided with food or drink free of charge (including supplies from vending machines), the consideration for the supply is taken to be nil (and no VAT is chargeable). Where there is any consideration, in cash or otherwise (eg deduction from wages) the supply, valued at the amount of the payment or deduction, is standard-rated. [*VATA 1994, Sch 6 para 10*(*1*)(*2*)]. HMRC accept that where employees are paid a minimum wage under a *Wages Order* for an industry and that *Order* allows for appropriate reductions to be made for catering and accommodation, these calculations are steps in arriving at the amount of the weekly wage to be paid and are not monetary consideration on which the employer is liable to VAT (*RW & MJ Goodfellow (VTD 2107) (TVC 60.13)* and VAT Notice 709/1/02, para 5.8).

Catering for self and family. Where the proprietor of a restaurant, cafe or other catering establishment provides meals for himself or his family, these are not regarded as catering and VAT need not be accounted for on them. But VAT must be accounted for on the full cost of any standard-rated items which are taken out of business stock for own or family use. See 28.3–28.13 FOOD for standard-rated items of food. (VAT Notice 709/1/02, para 5.8).

Catering for customers and friends. Free meals or drink provided for customers or friends are regarded as business entertainment and any input tax incurred in the provision of the meal or the purchase of the drink is non-deductible. See also 9 BUSINESS ENTERTAINMENT. Free sweets or drinks provided as part of a meal which a customer pays for (eg mints or liqueurs with the bill) can be treated as attributable to the taxable supply of the meal and any input tax recovered.

Where meals or drinks are given in exchange for an identifiable benefit to the business (eg coach drivers or group organisers in return for bringing a party to the establishment) any VAT incurred can be deducted but output tax must also be accounted for. Output tax should be calculated on the cost of the goods purchased or, if this cannot be established, on the cost of producing the goods.

(VAT Notice 709/1/02, para 5.7).

11.5 **Service charges and tips**

Service charges are standard-rated but any tips given freely are outside the scope of VAT. (VAT Notice 700, para 8.14; VAT Notice 709/1/02, para 2.2).

11.6 **Contract catering**

1. **Catering provided by a catering contractor acting as principal**

A catering contractor running catering facilities on someone else's premises as a principal must account for VAT at the standard-rate on the following.

- Any supplies of catering or hot take-away food under the rules explained in 11.1 and 11.2 above. VAT charged on supplies is deductible under the normal rules.
- Any fee to the owner of the catering facility.
- Any subsidy received from the owner of the catering facilities. This subsidy should include payments received to balance a profit and loss account.

VAT must be charged on these supplies even if the owner of the facilities makes exempt supplies (see, for example, 11.7 and 11.8 below).

2. **Catering provided by a catering contractor acting as agent**

Although such a person runs the canteen etc, the food and drink is supplied by the owner of the catering facilities (the principal). The owner must account for VAT on the supplies of catering or hot take-away food (unless they make exempt supplies as in 11.7 and 11.8 below).

The catering contractor should act as follows.

- *Invoices made out to the principal.* If the contractor buys goods or services for his principal and they are invoiced to the principal, the supplier should send the invoices direct to the principal who can reclaim the VAT subject to the normal rules. The contractor should show a VAT-inclusive amount against the purchase of the item in his profit and loss account.
- *Invoices made out to the contractor.* If the contractor buys goods or services for his principal and they are invoiced to the contractor, the contractor should re-invoice them to his principal and account for VAT on them. If the contractor buys goods or services from unregistered suppliers, the principal must be aware that the contractor will have to charge VAT where appropriate. The contractor can reclaim the VAT on the invoice subject to the normal rules.

  Provided the contractor issues a separate VAT invoice for these goods or services when charging them on to the principal, the contractor should merely record the VAT-inclusive amount in his profit and loss account. However, if it is the contractor's normal practice to issue a single document to serve as both the VAT invoice and the profit and loss account, he must clearly show the dual purpose of the document and keep the VAT invoice details separate from the other information.

- *Contractor's fee for services to his principal.* The contractor must account for VAT on the fee charged for running the catering facilities. The canteen owner can reclaim the VAT charged subject to the normal rules.
- *Profit and loss account.* If the contractor provides the canteen owner with a profit and loss account, he must show the VAT-inclusive amounts spent on food and received from supplies of meals. If there is a profit that the agent pays to the canteen owner or a loss reimbursed by the canteen owner to the contractor, these amounts are outside the scope of VAT.

3. **Catering provided by a catering contractor acting as both principal and agent**

If a catering contractor supplies food and drink to the owner of the catering facilities and then prepares and serves it to the users of the canteen etc on the owner's behalf, the contractor is acting both as a principal in his own right and as an agent of the owner. The contractor must account for VAT on both

- his supplies of prepared food and drink to the owner (reclaiming any VAT invoiced to him subject to the normal rules); and
- his fee for services to the owner of the catering facilities for running the canteen.

Although under these arrangements the contractor runs the canteen, he is supplying the food and drink to the canteen owner and the owner supplies the food and drink to the users of the canteen. The owner must therefore account for VAT on standard-rated supplies of catering and hot take-away food under the rules in 11.1 and 11.2 above, unless the owner makes exempt supplies as in 11.7 and 11.8 below.

(VAT Notice 709/1/02, paras 5.2–5.4).

Memorandum of understanding on VAT practice between HMRC and the Contract Caterers Forum of the British Hospitality Association. A memorandum of understanding on VAT practice has been agreed between HMRC and the Contract Caterers Forum of the British Hospitality Association. In addition to the general principles outlined above, the memorandum also covers the following points.

Indications of principal/agency status. The following factors are indicative of whether a catering contractor is acting as a principal or agent.

(i) *Control over pricing.* If a contractor has total control over pricing policy it would be indicative that the contractor is the principal. At the very least, as principal it must have some degree of discretion over pricing, quality of service, etc. A high level of control by the client over the pricing policy indicates that the contractor is acting as agent.

(ii) *Control of premises.* If acting as a principal, the contract should demonstrate that the contractor has some form of control over the running of the premises demised (eg a formal lease or a licence to occupy a specific area of the premises). In addition the contractor might be responsible for insuring the stock. If the contractor is acting as an agent, management and control of any premises it occupies should normally remain with the client.

(iii) *Purchases of food and drink.* Agency status for the purchase of food stocks, etc will be supported if

- the contracts explicitly state this to be the case;

- contracts and agreements with suppliers and clients include statements such as 'the contractor shall purchase on behalf of';
- discounts are available to the clients on whose behalf the contractor acts in placing the orders; and
- the client is entitled to take action against the supplier if poor quality food stocks are supplied.

Principal status for the purchase of food stocks, etc will be supported if

- the contracts explicitly state this to be the case;
- contracts and agreements with food suppliers are with the contract caterer;
- the supply agreement disqualifies the contractor from entitlement to discounts if it buys as agent for a third party, or the discounts are exclusive to the contractor when purchasing in its own name;
- the contractor (and not the client) is entitled to take action against the supplier if poor quality food stocks are supplied;
- where (3) above applies, the contract provides for the transfer of ownership of the food stocks, etc to the client prior to preparation and defines the time at which title passes; and
- where (3) above applies, until such time as the client takes title to the stock, the contractor is entitled to move stock freely between various clients' premises without requiring the client's permission.

(iv) *Control and ownership of stock.* A contractor acting as principal must own all stock at the time of supply to the consumer and must be entitled to move stock freely between various clients' premises without requiring the client's permission. If unsold food stock is owned by the client, this is indicative of the client being principal.

Wages concession in relation to staff employed in restaurants, canteens and dining facilities. Where the contractor acts as agent of the client but uses its own staff who are employed solely to serve that particular client, the contractor may, by concession, treat the wages as a non-VATable disbursement provided it clearly identifies the staff wages in the profit and loss accounts and/or invoices to the client. The concession does not apply to staff who work in respect of more than one client or to staff employed in licensed bars, cleaning, security, etc.

Discounts. If the contractor is buying food stocks on behalf of the client as agent, the discounts would normally be passed back to the client. If there is provision within the contract for the contractor to retain the discount, this is further consideration for the management service and subject to VAT at the standard rate. Normal rules apply to discounts where the contractor is buying food stocks as principal (see 69.24 VALUATION).

Advance payments. Where a contract caterer receives advance payments from the client which form part of the consideration for the contract caterer's supply, they create a tax point for VAT purposes when they are received. This can include advance payment of the subsidy due from the client under a principal contract, or an advance of the contract caterer's management fee under an agency agreement. Under an agency agreement, the amount received might include an element which is not subject to VAT. The contract caterer may therefore need to agree with HMRC the basis on which the VAT liability is to be calculated in such circumstances.

11.7 Catering

Tax points. It is standard practice for contractors to invoice on a four or five weekly basis for all purchases and sales in that period. Goods purchased by the contractor in that period are sold to the client, notwithstanding that they may not have been consumed. Any reference to 'total consumption in the period' in 4/5 weekly statements and VAT invoices means stock purchased for use in the client's canteen, etc.

Although the basic tax point is the date of delivery of the stock to the client's premises, the supplies are not invoiced or paid for (apart from any deposits above) until the 4/5 weekly invoice is issued. Contract caterers need to obtain written approval from HMRC for monthly invoicing to permit the tax point to be linked to the issue of the invoice.

Free/internal issues. Where a contractor is required to provide any meals, snacks, etc outside the normal catering arrangements (eg food provided at a function, special event or on client entertaining) or certain client's staff receive free meals or refreshments

- under principal contracts, the contractor invoices the value of the supply of catering at an agreed price and charges VAT on that full value; and
- under agency contracts, the contractor is providing the food as agent for the client. Therefore, VAT is charged by the contractor on the supply of services to the client and, where applicable, any food, drinks, and other items supplied to the client which do not qualify for zero-rating (ie this is not a supply of catering).

Price capping and performance guarantees, etc. Some contracts include price capping or guaranteed price conditions that limit the costs to be incurred by the client, normally by fixing in advance the subsidy under principal contracts or the management fee where the contract caterer is acting as an agent. Where, however, it involves the payment of a rebate to the client at the end of a specific period, this will normally represent a reduction in the consideration for the contract caterer's supply to the client. Normal VAT credit note procedures apply to any adjustments, including the option under which both parties may agree not to adjust any VAT previously accounted for (see 40.15 INVOICES). Contractors affected by this and who require further guidance (eg where the rebate includes consumables subject to mixed rates of VAT) should contact HMRC.

Profit share. If a contractor acting as a principal under the contract is obliged to pay a proportion (or all) of any operating profits to the client, its VAT treatment is determined by how it is characterised in the agreement. If a contract caterer acting as an agent *receives* a share of any profits realised, this normally represents additional consideration for the supply of agency services and is taxable at the standard rate.

Vending machines. The status of the contractor under the contract will determine which party is liable to account for any VAT due on sales made from vending machines.

11.7 Catering in hospitals, clinics, nursing homes, etc.

Care provided in a hospital or other statutorily-registered institution is exempt from VAT (see 32.11 HEALTH AND WELFARE). This exemption includes the supply by such institutions of prepared food and drink directly to their patients in the course of care.

Supplies of catering to other persons such as staff and visitors are not exempt and the hospital, etc must account for VAT on such sales.

(VAT Notice 709/1/02, para 2.6).

11.8 **Catering in schools, universities, colleges, etc.**

Certain supplies of education, training and research are exempt from VAT. Where an educational institution provides exempt education to its own pupils and students, then the supply of catering they make can also be exempt. See 20.8 EDUCATION. If the supply of education is non-business, as in the case of a local authority school, the supply of catering will also be non-business, provided it is made at, or below, cost.

Whichever treatment is appropriate, it applies to anything provided by way of catering. This includes food supplied at mealtimes and break times from the refectory, canteen or other similar outlet but not items purchased from a university campus shop, as they are not provided by way of catering.

Food and drink supplied at or below cost from a tuck shop run by the school itself takes on the same liability as the education.

VAT must be accounted for on supplies of catering to staff and visitors (except visiting students).

Catering provided by student unions in universities and other higher education establishments. Where a student union supplies catering or hot take-away food to students both on behalf, and with the agreement, of the parent institution, as a concession it can treat its supplies in the same way as the parent institution itself. This means that a student union can treat its supplies as exempt when made at universities and other institutions supplying exempt education and outside the scope of VAT when supplied at further education and sixth form colleges.

As a result, most supplies of food and drink made by a students union will be exempt, wherever they are consumed within the educational establishment's premises, ie it covers food and drink sold from canteens, refectories, vending machines and other catering outlets.

The concession does not cover food and drink sold from campus shops, bars, tuck shops or other similar outlets because they are not considered supplies that are made in the course of catering. In addition, the concession does not cover any other goods or services supplied by the student unions.

(VAT Notice 709/1/02, paras 2.5, 5.5).

11.9 **FRANCHISED CATERING IN CLUBS**

It is common for clubs to have their catering undertaken by a franchised caterer, often the club steward or their spouse acting as a self-employed person (who may, or may not, be VAT-registered).

Generally, HMRC consider VAT incurred by the club on goods and services in connection with catering (eg fuel and kitchen equipment) is the club's input tax because the catering is part of the facilities and advantages to subscribing members. However, the precise extent to which the club may recover input tax depends upon the nature of the supplies made by the club.

Where the club simply rents the kitchen premises to the caterer, it makes an exempt supply (subject to the option to tax the rents) and the normal partial exemption rules apply.

Where the club does not rent any part of the premises to the caterer but simply enters into a franchise agreement setting out what is to be provided, the agreement normally makes the club responsible for providing heat, light, and kitchen equipment.

- If the club makes a taxable charge to the franchisee for the right to use its facilities, the club may recover the input tax incurred on the overheads and will have no liability to output tax on any deemed non-business use.
- If the club makes no charge for the use of its facilities, the treatment is as follows.

  (*a*) *Gas and electricity* used by the caterer is not used for a business purpose by the club. The simplest way to deal with these supplies of goods is to agree some reasonable apportionment of input tax between the proportion of fuel used by the caterer and the remainder used by the club. (Strictly, as goods are involved, the club could follow the *Lennartz* approach (see 35.7 INPUT TAX) and claim all input tax but this would give the same VAT result as output tax would then have to be accounted for on supplies to the caterer each VAT period.)

  (*b*) *Kitchen equipment* (cookers, microwaves). As the club pays for and owns such items (which may be used by a number of successive caterers) HMRC accept that the equipment is bought for the purposes of the club's business. VAT incurred is input tax and deductible by the club. Output tax is, however, due from the club under *VATA 1994, Sch 4 para 5* for each VAT period during which the goods are used by the caterer. See 47.7 OUTPUT TAX.

  (*c*) *Building services*. As the building is an asset of the club and used by the members, HMRC consider that VAT incurred on building works is input tax and deductible. Strictly the provisions of *SI 1993/1507* (services put to non-business use, see 47.7 OUTPUT TAX) could apply in respect of VAT incurred on building repairs and maintenance to areas of a club's premises used only by the caterer but such sums would usually be so small as to be *de minimis*. If a club builds an extension to house a kitchen for use by the caterer, then the club should account for output tax under *SI 1993/1507* but note that once output tax paid under those provisions equals the input tax incurred, there is no further VAT due.

(Internal Guidance V1–13, para 23.6).

12 Charities

Cross-references. See 29 FUEL AND POWER for reduced rate on supplies to charities for non-business use.

The contents of this chapter are as follows.

12.1 CHARITY, CHARITABLE PURPOSES — GENERAL PRINCIPLES

The term 'charity' has no precise meaning in law. Under the *Recreational Charities Act 1958, s 1* the provision, in the interest of social welfare, of facilities for recreation or other leisure time occupation, is deemed to be charitable (subject to the principle that, unless the trust is for the relief of poverty (*Dingle v Turner, HL [1972] 1 All ER 878*), a trust or institution to be charitable must be for the public benefit).

In England and Wales, most charities are registered with the Charity Commission under the *Charities Act 1993* (which confirms their charitable status) but certain charities (eg universities, churches and other places of worship and certain small charities with annual income below £1,000) are exempt from such registration. They are still, however, charities. Charities in Scotland and Northern Ireland are not required to register with the Charity Commissioners. HMRC accept that a body has charitable status in those countries if the Inland Revenue has accepted that it does. The Office of the Scottish Charities Regulator opened in December 2003 and it is anticipated that charitable bodies in Scotland will be required to register with that Regulator. HMRC will then accept that such bodies have charitable status.

Subject to the above, what is a charity rests largely on judicial interpretation. A leading case is *Special Commrs v Pemsel, HL [1891] 3 TC 53* in which Lord Macnaghten laid down that 'charity' should be given its technical meaning under English law and comprises 'four principal divisions; trusts for the relief of poverty, trusts for the advancement of education, trusts for the advancement of religion and trusts beneficial to the community and not falling under any of the previous heads. The trusts last referred to are not the less charitable ... because incidentally they affect the rich as well as the poor'. Included are trusts for the relief of sickness and infirmity, nature conservation trusts and trusts for support of the arts.

There is no distinction for VAT purposes between those charities registered with one of the charity regulators and those that are not. However, unregistered charities claiming VAT relief may need to demonstrate that they have 'charitable status'. This may be achieved from their written 'objects' or by the recognition of their charitable status by the Inland Revenue. (VAT Notice 701/1/04, para 2.2). For guidelines issued by HMRC to establish charitable status, see Internal Guidance V1–9, paras 5.1–5.12.

12.2 CHARITIES AND VAT

Since the introduction of VAT, the law has provided a range of special reliefs which cover many supplies to and by charities. Zero-rating applies to some supplies to charities and there are some exemptions, zero-rating and other concessions for business supplies by charities. However, there is no general relief from VAT for goods supplied to charities and in general the normal VAT rules apply to business supplies made by charities.

Under charity law, charities can carry out '*primary purpose trading*', ie trading activities in the course of carrying out their primary purpose (eg the holding of an art exhibition by a charitable art gallery or museum in return for admission charges).

But charities may also wish to carry out '*non-primary purpose trading*' as a way of raising money (eg a charity whose primary purpose is providing education may sell Christmas cards and gifts through a catalogue). Charity law does not permit charities to carry out non-primary purpose trading in their own right on a substantial basis. In order to carry out non-primary purpose trading on a significant scale, charities have to establish 'subsidiary trading companies'. These are trading companies controlled by one or more charities but are not themselves charities. Although profits of these subsidiaries can be passed to the charity free of corporation tax, they are not charities and most of the VAT reliefs available to charities are not available to subsidiary trading companies.

Where a charity and its trading subsidiaries are VAT-registered it may be possible, under certain conditions, for them to register as a VAT group. see 31 GROUPS OF COMPANIES.

(VAT Notice 701/1/04, para 2.3).

Business activities. It is important not to confuse the term 'trading' as frequently used by a charity to describe its non-charitable commercial fund-raising activities with 'business' as used for VAT purposes. Although trading activities will invariably be business activities, 'business' for VAT purposes can have a much wider application and include some or all of the charity's primary or charitable activities. See 12.4 and 12.5 below for further consideration of business and non-business activities.

One-off extra-statutory concessions. These are only available in extremely limited circumstances and cannot be used as a means of extending reliefs. This would too easily set a precedent and other charities would demand similar relief. Individual ESCs have been allowed only in special and unique cases where a relief clearly exists for the goods or services but, because of the particular circumstances or the way in which the charity organised the matter, the supply did not qualify for relief. Any claims for concessional treatment should be made to HMRC who will refer the matter to the VAT Policy Directorate, Charities Branch. (Internal Guidance V1–9, para 1.8).

12.3 REGISTRATION AND BASIC PRINCIPLES

Registration. Any business (including a charity or its trading subsidiary) that makes taxable supplies in excess of the VAT registration threshold (see 59.3 REGISTRATION) must register for VAT. Taxable supplies are business transactions that are liable to VAT at the standard rate, reduced rate or zero rate. See 12.4 below for a consideration of what are business activities generally and 12.5 below for common business and non-business activities of charities.

If a charity's income from taxable supplies is below the VAT registration threshold it can voluntarily register for VAT (see 59.2 REGISTRATION) but a charity that makes no taxable supplies (either because it has no business activities or because its supplies or income are exempt from VAT) cannot register.

Charging VAT. Where a VAT-registered charity makes supplies of goods and services in the course of its business activities, the VAT liability of those supplies is, in general, determined in the normal way as for any other business. See, however, 12.6 below for certain supplies by charities which are zero-rated and 12.10 below for certain exempt supplies by charities. Even if VAT-registered, a charity should not charge VAT on any non-business supplies or income.

Reclaiming VAT. The first stage in determining the amount of VAT which a VAT-registered charity can reclaim is to eliminate all the VAT incurred that relates to its non-business activities. It cannot reclaim any VAT it is charged on purchases that *directly* relate to non-business activities. It will also not be able to reclaim a proportion of the VAT on its general expenses (eg telephone and electricity) that relate to those non-business activities. See 35.7 INPUT TAX for various methods which can be used to calculate this proportion.

Once this has been done, the remaining VAT relating to the charity's business activities is input tax.

- It can reclaim all the input tax it has been charged on purchases which *directly* relate to standard-rated, reduced-rated or zero-rated goods or services it supplies.
- It cannot reclaim any of the input tax it has been charged on purchases that relate *directly* to exempt supplies.

It also cannot claim a proportion of input tax on general expenses (after adjustment for non-business activities) that relates to exempt activities unless this amount, together with the input tax relating directly to exempt supplies, is below a *de minimis* limit. See 49.3 to 49.7 PARTIAL EXEMPTION.

12.4 BUSINESS AND NON-BUSINESS ACTIVITIES

An organisation such as a charity that is run on a non-profit-making basis may still be regarded as carrying on a business activity for VAT purposes. This is unaffected by the fact that the activity is performed for the benefit of the community. It is therefore important for a charity to determine whether any particular activity is a 'business' or a 'non-business' activity. This applies both when considering registration (if there is no business activity a charity cannot be registered and therefore cannot recover any input tax) and after registration.

If registered, a charity must account for VAT on taxable supplies it makes by way of business. Income from any non-business activities is not subject to VAT and affects the amount of VAT reclaimable as input tax (see 12.3 above).

'*Business*' has a wide meaning for VAT purposes based upon the *EC Sixth Directive* (which uses the term 'economic activity' rather than 'business'), UK VAT legislation and decisions by the Courts and VAT Tribunals. See 8.1 to 8.3 BUSINESS for a fuller consideration of the meaning of 'business' and in particular the business test in 8.2 BUSINESS.

An activity may still be business if the amount charged does no more than cover the cost to the charity of making the supply or where the charge made is less than cost (but see non-business supplies of welfare services in 12.5 below). If the charity makes no charge at all the activity is unlikely to be considered business.

An area of particular difficulty for charities when considering whether their activities are in the course of business is receipt of grant funding (see 12.5 below).

(VAT Notice 701/1/04, para 4.1).

12.5 **COMMON INCOME/ACTIVITIES OF CHARITIES**

This paragraph considers the VAT treatment of some of the more common income-producing activities of charities.

(1) **Admission to premises**

Where a charity admits visitors to places of interest, gardens, exhibitions, entertainment, functions, etc for a charge, this is a business activity.

Fixed admission charges. A VAT-registered charity must account for VAT on this income at the standard rate unless

- the income is for admittance to a qualifying fund-raising event, in which case it is exempt from VAT (see 12.10 below); or
- the income is covered by the exemption for admission to museums, galleries, art exhibitions, zoos and theatrical, musical or choreographic performances (see 57.6(3) RECREATION AND SPORT).

Donations in lieu of admission. True donations are outside the scope of VAT. If admission to the premises is not dependent on a payment then the monies received are donations but if admission is conditional upon payment, VAT must be accounted for at the standard rate.

A charity which 'suggests' an amount that visitors may wish to contribute, but does not insist on payment of that amount before allowing admission, can treat the amounts received as donations. An admission fee of £20 plus a 'minimum voluntary contribution' of £30 has been held to fail this test, implying that the £30 donation was compulsory (*Glasgow's Miles Better Mid Summer 5th Anniversary Ball (VTD 4460) (TVC 65.136)*).

No charge for admission. If no charge is made for admission, there is no business activity and any monies received can be treated as donations and outside the scope of VAT.

(VAT Notice 701/1/04, para 5.1).

(2) **Advertising in brochures, programmes, annual reports, etc**

The sale of such advertising space is a business activity and is normally standard-rated with the following exceptions.

(*a*) By concession, provided 50% or more of the total number of advertisements in a publication are clearly placed by private individuals, the charity can treat *all* sums received from advertisers as non-business and outside the scope of VAT. A private advertisement must make no reference to a business. An example of a private advertisement is one that says 'Good wishes from John and Susan Smith'; but not one taken out by 'John and Susan Smith, Grocers, 49 High Street'.

(*b*) The supply of advertising to another charity can be zero-rated (see 12.7(*f*) below).

(*c*) The sale of advertising space in brochures or programmes for a fund-raising event is exempt (see 12.10 below) unless overridden by zero-rating under (*b*) above.

(VAT Notice 701/1/04, para 5.2).

(3) **Affinity credit cards**

A charity may receive payments from a bank, building society or other financial institution in return for the charity endorsing that institution's credit card and recommending its use to the charity's members or supporters. This is a business activity and the payments would normally be treated as standard-rated marketing services provided to the financial institution. However, HMRC recognise that a large element of such payments could be charitable and not payment for services rendered. Provided the charity is not acting as an intermediary between the card provider and the applicant (see below), HMRC allow charities to treat part of these payments as standard-rated and the remainder as outside the scope of VAT. Note that this treatment only applies to income from affinity credit cards and does not extend to any other financial products.

Typically, a card provider will pay a fixed amount to the charity (or its trading subsidiary) on the issue of each new card and a percentage of the turnover (value of purchases) on the card.

To benefit from this treatment there must be two separate agreements.

- One agreement, between the charity (or its trading subsidiary) and the card provider should provide for the supply by the charity (or its trading subsidiary) of the necessary marketing and publicity services, access to membership lists and other promotional activity for the card (marketing services). These supplies are taxable at the standard rate.
- A second and separate agreement between the charity and the card provider should provide for contributions to be made by the card provider in respect of the use only of the charity's name and/or logo. Contributions made under this agreement can be treated as outside the scope.

Part (at least 20%) of the initial payment is then treated as the consideration for the standard-rated business supplies by the charity. The remaining 80% (or less) of the initial payment and all subsequent payments based on turnover are outside the scope of VAT.

Intermediary services. A charity acts as an intermediary in arranging a contract between its members and a credit card provider where it

- stands between the parties to a contract in the performance of a distinct act of negotiation, without having any interest of its own in the terms of the contract;
- brings the two parties to the contract together; and
- undertakes preparatory work, such as completing or assisting with completion of application forms, forwarding forms to the credit card company, and making representations on behalf of either party.

If a charity is providing intermediary services the payment they receive from the credit card provider is exempt from VAT. HMRC do not see clerical tasks (eg providing a list of names or access to a database) as intermediary services.

See also *BAA plc v C & E Commrs, CA 2002, [2003] STC 35 (TVC 26.19); Institute of Directors v C & E Commrs, CA 2002, [2003] STC 35 (TVC 26.20)*. Following these cases, charities should consider whether supplies involving affinity credit cards are exempt although HMRC have confirmed that, if they wish, charities can continue to treat their income as before. (Business Brief 18/03).

(VAT Notice 701/1/04, paras 5.3, 8.1, 8.2).

(4) Charity shops and sales of goods

The sale of donated and bought-in goods by charities and their trading subsidiaries is a business activity.

- *Donated goods*. The sale, hire or export of donated goods by a charity and, in most instances, its trading subsidiary is zero-rated. See 12.6(*a*) and (*b*) below. This also applies where the goods are sold at a qualifying fund-raising event (see 12.10 below).
- *Bought-in goods*. If a charity buys in goods for resale, it must account for VAT at the standard rate on the sale unless the goods are zero-rated or reduced-rated under the general provisions (eg children's clothes, books, etc). Bought-in goods sold at qualifying fund-raising events are exempt (see 12.10 below).

(VAT Notice 701/1/04, para 5.5).

(5) Catering

Catering is normally a business activity liable to VAT at the standard rate. See 11 CATERING. But some catering can be exempt from VAT when carried out by a charity, eg

- catering supplied as part of welfare services (see (21) below), such as meals for residents of care homes, and supplies of food and drink (but not alcohol) from trolleys, canteens and shops to patients in hospitals or inmates in prisons; and
- catering provided as part of a qualifying fund-raising event (see 12.10 below).

Catering may also be non-business when it forms part of a non-business supply of welfare (see (21) below).

(VAT Notice 701/1/04, para 5.6).

(6) Donations

A donation which

- is freely given; and
- does not entitle the donor to any further benefit

is not consideration for a supply and is outside the scope of VAT. The giving of a low value token as an acknowledgement of the donation is not treated as a supply for a consideration, provided no minimum payment is specified.

> *Example*
>
> A charity sells tokens to members of the public specifying a minimum price. The price is consideration for the supply of goods (the token) and liable to VAT at the standard rate. Purchasers may choose to give a sum in excess of the minimum price, in which case the excess can be treated as a donation and outside the scope of VAT.
>
> Note that if the charity had arranged with a sponsor to produce the tokens and donate them to the charity free of charge, the sale by the charity could be zero-rated as donated goods (see (4) above).

(VAT Notice 701/1/04, para 5.9; Internal Guidance V1–9, paras 4.7, 4.8).

(7) **Dividends and interest**

Dividends received on shares, and interest received from banks, building societies and other financial institutions, are outside the scope of VAT and regarded as part of the charity's non-business income.

(8) **Education, research and training**

See 20 EDUCATION.

(9) **Free export of goods**

The export of *any* goods by a charity (ie including goods exported free of charge, usually in the form of relief-aid) to a place outside the EC is treated as a business activity. See 12.6(*b*) below.

(10) **Free supplies**

- *Free supply of services* is a non-business activity and outside the scope of VAT. This may cover many of the services typically provided by a charity (eg first aid at public functions, rescue at sea). If the recipient makes a financial contribution towards the work of the charity this does not turn the activity into a business activity, provided it is freely given.
- *Free supply of goods* is also usually a non-business activity (but see (9) above for the free export of goods).

(11) **Fund-raising**

Fund-raising covers a wide range of activities which must be judged to be business or non-business under normal rules. Some of the most common methods are:

(*a*) *Donations*. These are outside the scope of VAT if freely given. See (6) above.

(*b*) *Qualifying fund-raising events*. Subject to conditions and exclusions, the supply of certain goods and services in connection with a qualifying event whose primary purpose is the raising of money is exempt from VAT. See 12.10 below.

(*c*) *Sponsored events in the UK*. Many charities organise walks, runs, swims and other similar sponsored events or arrange for teams of representatives to participate in these events in order to raise funds.

If a charity is organising and promoting the event it may be able to take advantage of the fund-raising exemption. See 12.10 below.

Sometimes a charity may organise an exempt fund-raising event in association with a different event which may or may not be an exempt fund-raising event in its own right (eg a charity may have a marquee and hold an auction of sporting memorabilia at a national sporting event). The charity can use the fund-raising exemption provided the event it is organising meets the conditions set out in 12.10 below.

There are, however, many events that individuals take part in to raise funds for charity that do not fall within the fund-raising exemption (eg a commercially organised sports event such as a marathon). Charities may pay for places within such events and then offer those places to individuals.

Where a charity allows individuals to take part in the event regardless of the amount they raise, and the individuals do not receive any benefits in return, the monies they raise can be treated as a donation and outside the scope of VAT. HMRC do not consider the following to be benefits.

- Provision of free training and health advice.
- A free t-shirt, running vest or similar which clearly portrays the charity that the individual is representing.
- Free massages and support for physical well-being during the event.
- Free pre-event meeting, which may include free professional advice or support, a simple meal, energy drinks and encouragement from the charity and other participants.
- Free post-event meeting, which may include medical treatment or advice, changing facilities, light refreshments and gives the charity the opportunity to thank participants.

If the charity provides free travel or accommodation and other benefits or gifts (eg bicycles or watches) the amount raised by the participant is taxable at the standard rate.

If a charity requires individuals to pay a registration fee or insists that they raise a minimum amount of sponsorship before they can take part in the event, this is effectively an entry fee and is taxable at the standard rate. Any payment in excess of the minimum amount can be treated as a donation and outside the scope of VAT.

If a charity asks individuals to 'pledge' or 'commit' to raise a certain amount of sponsorship, but do not insist on any payment before allowing the individual to take part in the event, the total amounts raised can be treated as donations and outside the scope of VAT. A charity can encourage individuals to pass on sponsorship money as they receive it, but cannot insist on receiving a certain amount before allowing the individual to take part.

Some charities offer prizes to top fund-raisers. These are not benefits for VAT purposes and do not affect the VAT treatment of income from participants.

(*d*) *Charity challenge events.* Charities frequently organise treks, bike rides and other sponsored events in order to raise funds. These are usually arranged to include travel and accommodation and are often known as 'charity challenge events'. Any fund-raising events that include

- both travel and accommodation, or
- more than two nights accommodation

do not qualify for fund-raising exemption. The provision of travel and accommodation is also likely to bring the event within the TOUR OPERATORS' MARGIN SCHEME (66).

(*e*) *Sponsorship of a charity*. Many charities receive money, goods or services from sponsors.

- If the charity is obliged to provide the sponsor with a significant benefit in return the sponsorship (eg free tickets, free advertising space in a charity event programme), this is a business activity and is taxable at the standard rate.
- If the sponsor receives no significant benefits in return for its contribution, the charity may be able to treat the income as non-business. HMRC accept that giving a flag or sticker to a donor, or naming a donor in a list of supporters is insignificant.

See 57.18 RECREATION AND SPORT for further details.

(VAT Notice 701/1/04, para 5.9).

(12) **Grant funding**

Charities often receive funding to support their charitable activities. If funding is freely given, with nothing supplied in return, then no VAT is due. The funding is not consideration for any supply and is therefore outside the scope of VAT. But if funding is given in return for goods or services supplied by the charity, such funding is consideration for a supply and VAT may be due on the income if the goods and/or services supplied by the charity in return are taxable at either the standard or reduced rate.

To decide whether funding is consideration for a supply, a charity should consider the following questions.

- Does the donor receive anything in return for the funding? (Certain 'benefits' to the donor, such as copies of reports, are seen as necessary safeguards to ensure the money is spent correctly and that the end product is put to proper use; they can be ignored where they are incidental to the primary purpose of the project and are minimal in relation to the amount of funding.)
- If the donor does not benefit, does a third party benefit instead? And if so, is there a direct link between the money paid by the funder and the supply received by the third party?
- Are any conditions attached to the funding, which go beyond the requirement to account for the funds (commonly referred to as 'good housekeeping')?

If the answer to any of the above questions is 'yes', this is an indication that the funding *may* not be freely given and may be consideration for a supply.

Where a charity is supported by outside the scope funding, this does not determine the nature of any supplies it makes (ie it does not follow that outside the scope income means that the charity will only have non-business activities).

(VAT Notice 701/1/04, para 5.10).

(13) **Hiring out buildings, including village halls**

The hiring out of a building for a fee is normally a business activity. The fees received are exempt from VAT unless the charity has opted to tax the building. If so, the fees received are standard-rated except where the option to tax cannot be applied because the hirer is intending to use it

- as a dwelling (eg a residential flat above a charity shop);
- for a relevant charitable purpose (eg as a village hall or similarly, or for a non-business purpose); or
- for a relevant residential purpose (eg a residential home for children or disabled people, or a hospice),

in which case the fees remain exempt.

See 42.2 LAND AND BUILDINGS for exempt supplies of land and 42.8 *et seq* LAND AND BUILDINGS for the option to tax.

Where the hire of the building (or part of a building) is incidental to the provision of facilities (eg the hiring of facilities for playing sport), the supply is normally standard-rated. However, where rooms are hired as facilities for playing sport for a period exceeding 24 hours or for a series of ten or more sessions, the supply may be exempt. See 57.7 *et seq* RECREATION AND SPORT.

(14) **Legacies**

The receipt of a legacy or bequest is non-business. Income from the sale of bequeathed goods is not a business activity. (Business Brief 12/92; Internal Guidance V1–9, para 4.11).

(15) **Meals on Wheels**

The local authority is responsible for ensuring that a meals on wheels service is available to those who need it. Where meals are delivered by a charity on behalf of a local authority,

- any charge made to the recipient of the meal by the local authority is treated as part of the local authority's non-business income and is not a consideration paid to the charity; and
- any charge made by the charity to the local authority for running the service is standard-rated. It cannot be treated as exempt welfare services because the charity is only providing a delivery service. HMRC take this view even if the charge to the local authority is below cost or there is an incidental element of care provided to the recipient of the meal by the charity.

(Internal Guidance V1–9, para 17.3).

(16) **Museums and galleries**

Where a charity running a museum or gallery makes a charge for admission, the normal rules in (1) above apply.

Admission to a museum or gallery for no charge is a non-business activity. Normally, this means that no input tax can be reclaimed. See, however, 35.13(16A) INPUT TAX for a special scheme allowing certain non-charging national museums and galleries to recover related input tax.

Other activities (eg catering and the sale of books and postcards) must be considered separately.

(17) **Membership subscriptions**

The provision of membership benefits to members is a business activity and the VAT liability of a membership subscription depends on the benefits being supplied. Normally, this means that the provider must decide whether it is making a single or multiple supply and tax the subscription accordingly. However, as a concession, a charity may, if it wishes, treat a single supplies of membership benefits as a multiple supply. The VAT treatment of each benefit can then be considered separately and the subscription charge apportioned so that, for example, the supply of magazines or handbooks to members can be zero-rated. See 14.2 CLUBS AND ASSOCIATIONS for further details.

(17A) **Nursery and crèche facilities**

In *C & E Commrs v Yarburgh Children's Trust, Ch D 2001, [2002] STC 207 (TVC 15.61)* the charity undertook to provide nursery and crèche facilities for pre-school age children as part of its charitable objectives. It charged fees for its services but these were set at a level designed to ensure that it merely covered its costs. The Court decided that the charity was not making supplies by way of business. Despite that decision, Customs' position remained that the provision of nursery and crèche facilities in such circumstances was a business activity for VAT purposes. However, in the subsequent case of *C & E Commrs v St Paul's Community Project Ltd, Ch D 2004, [2005] STC 95 (TVC 15.62)* in similar circumstances the Court again decided in favour of the charity. It found that the intrinsic nature of the enterprise was not the carrying on of a business, identifying the distinguishing features as the social concern for the welfare of disadvantaged children, lack of commerciality in setting fees and the overall intention simply to cover costs.

Although HMRC do not agree that these features point to the activities being non-business, considering that the charities are making supplies of services for consideration in much the same way as a commercial nursery, they have decided not to appeal further and now accept that the provision of nursery and crèche facilities by charities, along the same lines as those in the *Yarburgh* and *St Paul's* cases, is not a business activity for VAT purposes. In cases that are not broadly in line with the *Yarburgh* or *St Paul's* cases, HMRC will continue to apply the business test, in order to determine whether the supplies concerned are being made by way of business.

(Business Brief 2/05).

(18) **Patron and supporter schemes**

Many charities operate patron or supporter schemes offering benefits (eg free admission to special exhibitions, the right to receive regular publications, discounts on shop purchases, etc) in return for a minimum payment. The minimum payment is business income and is standard-rated, although if one of the benefits to patrons or supporters is the right to receive publications, it may be possible to treat part of the payment as zero-rated.

If a patron or supporter pays more than the minimum amount, the excess can be treated as a donation and outside the scope of VAT provided the patron or supporter is aware that scheme benefits are available for a given amount, and that anything in excess of that amount is a voluntary donation. This should be explicit in the patron or supporter scheme literature.

(VAT Notice 701/1/04, para 5.14).

(19) **Secondment of staff to other charities**

Income received for the supply of staff is a business activity and is normally taxable at the standard rate. However:

- If staff are jointly employed there is no supply of staff for VAT purposes. See 44.6 MANAGEMENT SERVICES AND SUPPLIES OF STAFF.
- By concession, where staff are seconded from one charity or non-profit-making 'voluntary organisation' to another, the income from the hire or loan can be treated as non-business and outside the scope of VAT provided

  (i) the employee seconded has been engaged only in the non-business activities of the lending charity/organisation and is being seconded to assist in such activities of the borrowing organisation; and

  (ii) the payment for the supply of the employee's services does not exceed 'normal remuneration' (calculated *pro rata* for part-time secondments). '*Normal remuneration*' means the total cost incurred by the lending charity/organisation including salary, NIC, pension costs, etc.

  A '*voluntary organisation*' is a body that operates otherwise than for profit, but does not include any public or local authority.

(VAT Notice 701/1/04, para 5.17).

(20) **Share dealing**

The acquisition or disposal of shares and other securities by a charity is not a business activity. Any VAT incurred in connection with such acquisition or disposal, or the management of the investments, cannot be treated as input tax. See *National Society for the Prevention of Cruelty to Children (VTD 9325) (TVC 11.40)* where the tribunal held that the charity's investment activities, although having a turnover in excess of £7 million, did not amount to a business as the charity was not predominantly concerned with those supplies. See also *The Wellcome Trust Ltd v C & E Commrs, CJEC [1996] STC 945 (TVC 21.78)* where the court confirmed that the concept of an economic activity is to be interpreted as not including the purchase and sale of shares and other securities by a trustee in the course of the management of the assets of a charitable trust.

(21) **Welfare**

The supply of welfare services by a charity are normally business and exempt from VAT. Similar provisions now apply to such supplies made by public bodies and state-regulated private welfare institutions. See 32.14 HEALTH AND WELFARE.

Non-business welfare services. By concession, charities that provide welfare services at 'significantly below cost', to 'distressed' persons for the relief of their distress, *may* treat these supplies as non-business and outside the scope of VAT. To qualify:

- There must be a deliberate policy to subsidise the welfare services by at least 15%, ie the subsidy should not be achieved as a result of circumstance or unintentionally.
- The subsidy must be available to all distressed persons, ie both to those who can and cannot afford to pay the full rate.
- The subsidy must not be applied conditionally (eg only during cold weather or only to persons in certain areas or of a certain age).
- The services must be provided to the distressed individual (and not, for example, to a local authority).

See 32.14 HEALTH AND WELFARE for the definition of '*welfare services*'.

'*Significantly below cost*' means subsidised by at least 15%. Cost should be calculated to include all out-of-pocket expenses incurred by the charity but to exclude capital expenditure, depreciation charges and the creation of financial reserves. No value should be placed on unpaid volunteer labour or donated goods used.

'*Distressed*' means suffering pain, grief, anguish, severe poverty, etc.

(VAT Notice 701/1/04, para 5.18; Internal Guidance V1–9, para 4.9.3).

12.6 ZERO-RATED SUPPLIES BY CHARITIES

Certain supplies by charities are zero-rated not because of the charitable status of the supplier but because they are covered by general application. See 72.1 ZERO-RATED SUPPLIES. In addition, the following zero-rating provisions apply specifically to charities.

(*a*) **Sale of donated goods**. Subject to below, zero-rating applies to the sale or letting on hire of any 'goods' donated to

- a charity, or
- a taxable person who is a 'profits-to-charity' person in respect of the goods

where the goods are donated for sale, letting or any combination of these two and export.

'*Goods*' means goods in the normal sense of the word. It does not, in particular, include anything that is not goods, even though *VATA 1994* or any other enactment provides that the supply of it is, or is treated as, a supply of goods. Land, for example, is therefore excluded from zero-rating under these provisions.

Goods are donated for letting only if they are donated for letting, re-letting after the end of any first or subsequent letting *and* sale, export or disposal as waste if not, or when no longer, used for letting.

'*Profits-to-charity*' person. A taxable person is a profits-to-charity person in respect of any goods if

- he has agreed in writing (whether or not by deed) to transfer to a charity his profits from supplies and lettings of the goods; or
- his profits from supplies and lettings of the goods are 'otherwise payable' to a charity.

HMRC regard *'otherwise payable'* as including documents and unwritten arrangements which oblige the taxable person to pay the profits to charity, but which are not (strictly speaking) agreements to transfer profits. This may include: a trust document; the taxable person's memorandum and articles of association; and ownership by a charity of 100% of the taxable person's shares. (Internal Guidance V1–9, para 6.6).

Zero-rating does not apply

(i) unless the sale or letting takes place as a result of the goods having been made available for purchase or hire (whether in a shop or elsewhere such as a charity auction) to

- the general public; or
- two or more persons who are handicapped (ie chronically sick or disabled) and/or entitled to receive one or more means-tested benefits (income support, housing benefit, council tax benefit, income-based jobseeker's allowance, any element of child tax credit other than the family element, or working tax credit);

(ii) if the sale or letting takes place as a result of any arrangements (whether legally binding or not) relating to the goods and entered into, before the goods were made available as under (i) above, by

- each of the parties to the sale or letting; or
- the donor of the goods and either or both of those parties; or

(iii) to any sale or letting of particular donated goods if the goods, at any time after they are donated but before they are sold, exported or disposed of as waste, are whilst unlet used for any purpose other than being available for purchase, hire or export.

[*VATA 1994, Sch 8 Group 15 Items 1, 1A; Tax Credits Act 2002, Sch 3 para 49; SI 2000/805, Arts 6, 8*].

By concession, zero-rating also applies where the goods, although of a kind made available for purchase by the general public under (i) above, are by reason of their poor quality not fit to be so made available. This concession will benefit many charities, particularly those selling scrap clothing to rag merchants or those who are prevented under safety legislation from selling certain goods to the public (eg second-hand electrical goods and toys). (VAT Notice 48, ESC 3.21; Business Brief 13/97).

It must be the intention of both the donor and the charity or taxable person that the donated goods are to be sold, hired or exported (see (*b*) below). The donor's intention may be implicit (eg by leaving clothing in a charity shop doorway).

The relief does not apply to

- goods which are donated for sale or hire but which are diverted to a charity's own use;
- goods which have been donated to a charity for its own use but which it is subsequently decided should be sold;
- goods donated as raffle prizes; or
- donated goods which are used to make other goods for sale. In these circumstances neither the donation of the goods, nor the sale of the

manufactured goods, will be eligible for zero-rating. For example, if an artist donates a painting to a charity and, rather than sell the painting outright, the charity arranges for prints to be made of the painting which are then sold. The donation by the artist cannot be zero-rated because the painting is not to be sold. The sale of the prints cannot be zero-rated because they were not donated to the charity.

(Internal Guidance V1–9, paras 6.7, 6.8).

(*b*) **Export of any goods by a charity** is zero-rated. [*VATA 1994, Sch 8 Group 15 Item 3*]. Proof of export is required. See 25.24 EXPORTS.

The export is treated as a supply made by the charity in the UK and in the course or furtherance of a business carried on by the charity. [*VATA 1994, s 30(5); FA 1995, s 28*]. This enables a charity to reclaim any VAT paid on the purchase of the goods and any overheads of exporting them (or to register for VAT in order to do so) where the VAT would not otherwise be deductible (eg where the goods are given away overseas as part of a non-business activity such as relief aid).

De Voil Indirect Tax Service. See V4.266.

12.7 ZERO-RATED SUPPLIES TO OR FOR CHARITIES

The following supplies to charities are zero-rated.

(*a*) **Talking books for the blind and disabled**. The supply to the Royal National Institute for the Blind, the National Listening Library or other similar charity of

(i) magnetic tape specially adapted for the recording and reproduction of speech for the blind or severely handicapped;

(ii) apparatus designed or specially adapted for the making on magnetic tape, by way of transfer of recorded speech from another magnetic tape, of a recording as in (vi) below;

(iii) apparatus designed or specially adapted for transfer to magnetic tapes of a recording made by apparatus within (ii) above;

(iv) apparatus for rewinding magnetic tape described in (vi) below;

(v) apparatus designed or specially adapted for the reproduction from recorded magnetic tape of speech for the blind or severely handicapped which is not available for use otherwise than by them;

(vi) magnetic tape on which has been recorded speech for the blind or severely handicapped, such recording being suitable for reproduction only in the apparatus mentioned in (v) above;

(vii) apparatus solely for the making on a magnetic tape of a sound recording which is for use by the blind or severely handicapped;

(viii) parts and accessories (other than a magnetic tape for use with apparatus in (vii) above) for goods comprised in (i) to (vii) above; and

(ix) the supply of a service of repair or maintenance of any goods within (i) to (viii) above.

Included is the letting on hire of eligible goods under (i) to (vii) above. [*VATA 1994, Sch 8 Group 4 Item 1*].

(*b*) **Wireless sets for the blind**. Wireless receiving sets or apparatus solely for the making and reproduction of sound recording on a magnetic tape permanently contained on a cassette. In each case, the goods must be solely for gratuitous loan to the blind. Included is the letting on hire of eligible goods. [*VATA 1994, Sch 8 Group 4 Item 2*].

(*c*) **Aids for disabled persons**. Certain goods to be made available to persons with disabilities and services of adapting, repairing and installing goods for such persons. See 32.16 to 32.35 HEALTH AND WELFARE.

(*d*) **Donations of goods**. The donation of any 'goods' for sale, export or letting by

- a charity; or
- a taxable person who is a 'profits-to-charity' person in respect of the goods.

'*Goods*' means goods in the normal sense of the word. It does not, in particular, include anything that is not goods, even though *VATA 1994* or any other enactment provides that the supply of it is, or is treated as, a supply of goods. Land, for example, is therefore excluded from zero-rating under these provisions.

Goods are donated for letting only if they are donated for letting, re-letting after the end of any first or subsequent letting *and* sale, export or disposal as waste if not, or when no longer, used for letting.

A taxable person is a '*profits-to-charity*' person in respect of any goods if

- he has agreed in writing (whether or not by deed) to transfer to a charity his profits from supplies and lettings of the goods; or
- his profits from supplies and lettings of the goods are otherwise payable to a charity.

[*VATA 1994, Sch 8 Group 15 Item 2; SI 2000/805, Arts 6, 8*].

(*e*) **Lifeboats**. Lifeboats, including repairs and maintenance and spares and accessories, supplied to a charity providing rescue and assistance at sea. See 68.13 TRANSPORT AND FREIGHT.

(*f*) **Advertising**. Subject to the exclusions below, the supply to a charity of

(i) a right to make known an advertisement by means of any medium of communication with the 'public';

(ii) making known an advertisement by means of such a medium;

(iii) services of design or production of an advertisement that is, or was intended to be, made known by means of such a medium (eg the design of a poster or the filming or recording of an advertisement to be broadcast); and

(iv) goods closely related to a supply within (iii) above. This would include

- a finished article like a film or recorded cassette;
- an element to be incorporated in the advertisement such as a photograph, picture or a sound track; or

- all alternative versions of an advertisement produced, to see which works best, even if it is the intention that only one version will be used.

(VAT Notice 701/58/02, para 4.2).

Exclusions. Zero-rating does not apply in the following cases.

- Neither (i) or (ii) above includes a supply where any of the members of the public (whether individuals or other persons) who are reached though the medium are 'selected' by or on behalf of the charity. '*Selected*' includes selection by address (whether postal address or telephone number, e-mail address or other address for electronic communications purposes) or at random.

  Selected people could be individually named people, all those at the same address (eg family groups) or everyone in a particular building. Advertisements targeted at general groups (eg readers of a trade or religious magazine) are not considered to be selected. Neither are groups in particular parts of the country who are, for example, targeted for a general poster campaign in their area. (VAT Notice 701/58/02, paras 3.2, 3.3).

  Direct mail (by post, fax and e-mail) and telesales are both excluded from zero-rating because they are not a supply of advertising time or space but are marketing and advertising addressed to selected individuals or groups. (Individual elements of a postal package may qualify for zero-rating as PRINTED MATTER, ETC. (54) or under the class concession for goods used by charities in connection with collecting monetary donations (see (*g*) below).) (VAT Notice 701/58/02, para 3.4).

- None of (i)–(iv) above include any supply used to create, or contribute to, a website that is the charity's own. For this purpose, a website is the charity's own even though hosted by another person. Zero-rating does not therefore apply to advertising in, on or through a charity's own website whether or not the website is owned, rented or loaned to the charity. (VAT Notice 701/58/02, para 3.7).

- Neither of (iii) or (iv) above include a supply to a charity that is used directly by the charity to design or produce an advertisement.

- Where the supply is not directly to a charity but to one of its trading companies, eg a wholly-owned subsidiary.

- Any method of advertising which is not a supply of someone else's advertising time and space or is in the form of general marketing and promotion, including direct mail and telesales (see above); anything on the charity's own website (see above); advertisements where there is no supply of time and space to the charity (eg advertisements on a charity's own greetings cards); exhibition stands and space; services of distribution; and commemorative items whether or not they bear the charity's logo (eg pens and adult clothing). (VAT Notice 701/58/02, para 3.8).

[*VATA 1994, Sch 8 Group 15 items 8–8C; SI 2000/805*].

The relief covers all types of advertisement on any subject, including staff recruitment. There is no requirement that they mention the name of the charity or show its logo to obtain relief. The wide relief is allowed in the expectation that charities will only place advertisements which comply with their charitable objects. The relief does not override charity law or the need to comply with the British Codes of Advertising or any other relevant regulations.

Zero-rating applies to advertisements placed in any medium which communicates with the public, including conventional advertising media such as television, cinema, billboards, sides of vehicles, newspapers and printed publications. The important factor is whether the advertisement is placed in someone else's time or space. If space is sold to a charity for advertising on other items, such as beer mats, calendars, till rolls, etc this will be covered by the zero rate although the sale of the items themselves is not zero-rated (unless qualifying in their own right, eg advertising on books or children's clothing).

(VAT Notice 701/58/02, paras 2.3, 3.1).

Services involving advertising agencies. If a charity uses an advertising agency instead of contacting the suppliers of advertising or printing direct, the VAT liability depends on whether the agency is acting as a principal or an agent and normal VAT rules for agent/principal agreements apply. See 3 AGENTS generally but broadly

- where an advertising agency is the principal, the advertising agency's supply of qualifying advertising time or space (eg television broadcasting time) and associated production costs to the charity are zero-rated but supplies to the agency are standard-rated; and
- where an advertising agency acts solely as an agent, the agency fees, charged to the charity, are standard-rated. The supply of the advertising time or space is direct to the charity and eligible for zero-rating under this relief in the normal way.

(VAT Notice 701/58/02, para 4.4).

Claiming relief. A supplier is responsible for determining the liability of the supplies he makes and must be sure that all the relevant conditions for relief are met. He must take reasonable steps to check with the charity any condition which he cannot verify for himself. For this reason, it is recommended that a charity gives its supplier a declaration that the specific conditions for the claimed relief are fulfilled. See VAT Notice 701/58/02, Part 10 for a suggested form of declaration. Other types of declaration (whether in paper form, faxed or electronic) that contain sufficient verifiable information to accurately identify the customer are acceptable to HMRC. Declarations are not always required, eg when a charity requests repeat orders and the information contained in a declaration for the first order has not changed. If a supplier has taken reasonable steps to check the validity of a declaration but fails to identify an inaccuracy and in good faith makes the supplies concerned at the zero rate, HMRC will not seek to recover the VAT due from the supplier. See Customs ESC 3.11. (VAT Notice 701/58/02, paras 10.1–10.5).

(*g*) **Goods used by charities in connection with collecting monetary donations**. By concession, supplies of the following goods to a charity may be treated as if they were zero-rated.

(i) Lapel stickers or attachments designed to be worn on the lapel, which are of no intrinsic value, low cost to the charity and are given as a token in acknowledgement of a donation.

Included are paper stickers, ribbons, artificial flowers (if used as a symbol of the charity) and metal pins and badges. Large items for decorating buildings, vehicles, monuments, etc are not eligible for relief even if bigger versions of a lapel badge.

Emblems or badges given in return for any non-specified donation or a suggested donation of up to £1 are considered to be of no intrinsic value or low cost. Lapel attachments which are offered for a fixed price, even if this is less than £1, do no qualify for relief because they are not given away freely. Relief will apply if a charity suggests a donation of £1.

If a charity makes its own lapel attachments, equipment for manufacturing badges is not covered by the concession but where it buys identifiable constituent parts which it will assemble into badges in-house, these come within the concession.

(ii) Component parts of items described in (i) above when supplied for self-assembly.

(iii) Any form of receptacle which

- is manufactured specifically for the purpose of collecting donated money;
- is used solely for collecting money for charity;
- is, or will be, clearly marked as collecting for a named charity; and
- can be secured by lock or tamper evident seal.

Examples of receptacles which might be made to comply with the above requirements are pre-printed card collecting boxes, moulded plastic collecting boxes, and models in any material including hollow plaster, wood, base metal or glass. Boxes may be of types that are hand held, floor standing, wall mounted or for placing on a table-top or shop counter. Boxes of greater value, such as those made of precious metal, are not zero-rated. Boxes where a simple balance mechanism moves money from one level to another or the weight of the coin causes it to roll helter-skelter fashion into the box are included; but more elaborate boxes which have additional purposes (eg gaming or quiz machines) or have some form of mechanical entertainment are not covered by the concession.

All boxes must bear the name of the charity, for example, by indelible printing or embossing or having raised letters, or allow for the charity name to be added later.

(iv) Bucket lids, designed to fit buckets and provide a secure seal, for use solely in connection with collecting money for charity.

(v) Pre-printed letters the primary purpose of which is to appeal for money for the charity (not necessarily including the addressees' particulars).

(vi) Envelopes used in conjunction with letters in (v) above for forwarding donations, provided that they are over-printed with an appeal request related to that contained in the letter.

(vii) Outer envelopes used in conjunction with letters in (v) above provided that they are over-printed with an appeal request related to that contained in the letter.

(viii) Pre-printed collecting envelopes appealing for money (of the type used by the welfare charities and which are usually hand delivered to domestic premises).

(ix) Stewardship envelopes used for planned giving which, as a minimum requirement, are pre-printed with the name of the relevant place of worship or other charity.

Plain envelopes bearing only a symbol such as a cross printed on them, and available from retailers as general stationery, do not qualify.

The Commissioners may withdraw or restrict the application of this concession if they have reasonable cause to believe that it is being abused.

(VAT Notice 48, ESC 3.3).

There is a separate concession (the 'package test') for determining the liability of a mixed supply of printed items (eg items for a mailshot). *With effect from 1 August 2003*, that concession has been extended to some of the charity stationery zero-rated under the concession for charities above. *Before that date*, charity stationery zero-rated under the above concession was not counted as zero-rated for that test. See 54.16 PRINTED MATTER, ETC.

(VAT Notice 701/58/02, paras 6.2, 6.4, 7.1–7.3, 7.5, 8.1, 8.3, 8.4, Part 12).

Claiming relief. A supplier is responsible for determining the liability of the supplies he makes and must be sure that all the relevant conditions for relief are met. He must take reasonable steps to check with the charity any condition which he cannot verify for himself. For this reason, it is recommended that a charity gives its supplier a declaration that the specific conditions for the claimed relief are fulfilled. See VAT Notice 701/58/02, Part 10 for a suggested form of declaration. Other types of declaration (whether in paper form, faxed or electronic) that contain sufficient verifiable information to accurately identify the customer are acceptable to HMRC. Declarations are not always required, eg when a charity requests repeat orders and the information contained in a declaration for the first order has not changed. If a supplier has taken reasonable steps to check the validity of a declaration but fails to identify an inaccuracy and in good faith makes the supplies concerned at the zero rate, HMRC will not seek to recover the VAT due from the supplier. See Customs ESC 3.11. (VAT Notice 701/58/02, paras 10.1–10.5).

(*h*) **Medicinal products**. The supply to a charity

(i) providing care or medical or surgical treatment for human beings or animals; or

(ii) engaging in medical or veterinary research

of a 'medicinal product' where the supply is solely for use by the charity in such care, treatment or research.

'*Medicinal product*' means any 'substance' or article (not being an instrument, apparatus or appliance) which is for use wholly or mainly in either or both of the following ways, viz. by being 'administered' to one or more human beings or animals for 'medicinal purposes' or as an 'ingredient' in the preparation of a substance or article to be so administered.

'*Substance*' means any natural or artificial substance, whether in solid or liquid form or in the form of a vapour or gas.

'*Administer*' means administering whether orally, by injection or by introduction into the body in any other way, or by external application, whether by direct contact with the body or not and includes both administering a substance in its existing state or after it has been dissolved, diluted or mixed with some other substance used as a vehicle.

Use for '*medicinal purpose*' includes use for treating or preventing of disease; diagnosing disease or ascertaining physiological condition; contraception; inducing anaesthesia; or otherwise bringing about some alteration in the physical or physiological state of the patient or animal.

'*Ingredient*', in relation to the manufacture or preparation of a substance, includes anything which is the sole active ingredient of that substance as manufactured or prepared.

[*VATA 1994, Sch 8 Group 15 Item 9; Medicines Act 1968, s 130(2)(9), s 132*].

HMRC use the following guidelines.

- *Medical and veterinary research* should be given its technical meaning ie it is restricted to activities which are directed towards opening up new areas of knowledge or understanding, or initial development of new techniques, rather than towards mere quantitative additions to human knowledge.
- *Medical or veterinary treatment* includes the administration of medicines, physiotherapy and surgery.

(Internal Guidance V1–9, para 11.3).

(*j*) **Substances for medical or veterinary research**. The supply to a charity of a 'substance' directly used for synthesis or testing in the course of medical or veterinary research. See (*h*) above for '*substance*'. [*VATA 1994, Sch 8 Group 15 Item 10*].

(*k*) **Major interests in land and buildings**. The grant by a person constructing a building of a major interest in it provided the building is intended solely for use for a relevant residential purpose or use for a relevant charitable purpose. See 42.13 LAND AND BUILDINGS.

(*l*) **Construction services**. Supplies to a charity of services in the course of construction of a new building intended solely for use for a relevant residential purpose or use for a relevant charitable purpose. See 42.18 LAND AND BUILDINGS.

Proof of zero-rating. Zero-rating of items under (*a*), (*b*), (*e*), (*h*) and (*j*) above may depend on the *use* rather than the nature of the item. The charity must, therefore, give the supplier a certified declaration that the goods are to be used for the specified purpose. Declaration forms are not supplied by HMRC but examples can be found in VAT Notice 701/6 Supplement. These can be reproduced in any convenient way, eg by incorporating them in any order form. It is the supplier's responsibility to take reasonable steps to satisfy himself that the charity is entitled to zero-rating and the declaration is correct. Where, however, despite taking all reasonable steps, nonetheless the supplier fails to identify the inaccuracy and in good faith makes the supplies concerned at the zero rate, HMRC will not seek to recover the VAT due from the supplier. (VAT Notice 48, ESC 3.11).

Importation. Imports by charities of any goods within (*a*), (*b*), (*e*), (*h*) and (*j*) above can be zero-rated under the same conditions as supplies made to them in the UK. The appropriate declaration (see under *Proof of zero-rating* above) must be presented with the customs entry form.

De Voil Indirect Tax Service. See V4.262; V4.266.

12.8 **Charity-funded equipment for medical, veterinary uses, etc**

The following supplies are zero-rated.

(*a*) Relevant goods (see (1) below) supplied *for donation* to a nominated eligible body (see (2) below). To qualify for relief

- the funds for the purchase (or the letting or hire) must be provided by a charity or from voluntary contributions (see (3) below); and
- where the *donee* of the goods is not a charity, it must not have contributed, wholly or in part, to the purchase (or hiring) of the goods.

[*VATA 1994, Sch 8 Group 15, Item 4 and Notes* (*5A*),(*6*) *and* (*9*)].

This *Item* zero-rates qualifying goods and services when they are supplied to any person, body or organisation for donation to an eligible body. (VAT Notice 701/6/03, para 6.1).

(*b*) Relevant goods (see (1) below) supplied to an eligible body (see (2) below). To qualify for relief

- the eligible body must pay for the relevant goods (or hire them) with funds provided by a charity or from voluntary contributions (see (3) below); and
- where the eligible body is not a charity, it must not have contributed, wholly or in part, to the purchase (or hiring) of the goods.

[*VATA 1994, Sch 8 Group 15, Item 5 and Notes* (*7*) *and* (*9*)].

(*c*) Relevant goods (see (1) below) supplied (or hired) to an eligible body which is a charitable institution providing care or medical or surgical treatment (see (4) below) for handicapped persons (see (5) below). [*VATA 1994, Sch 8 Group 15, Item 5* and *Note* (*9*)].

(*d*) The repair and maintenance of relevant goods (see (1) below) owned by an eligible body (see (2) below), and any goods supplied in connection with the repair and maintenance, provided

- the supply is paid for with funds which have been provided by a charity or from voluntary contributions (see (3) below); and
- where the owner (or hirer) of the goods repaired or maintained is not a charity, it must not have contributed, wholly or in part, to those funds.

[*VATA 1994, Sch 8 Group 15, Items 6, 7 and Note* (*8*)].

(*e*) By concession, relevant goods (see (1) below) supplied to a charity

(i) whose sole purpose and function is to provide a range of care services to meet the personal needs of handicapped people (see (5) below) (eg a charity established to: provide care or welfare services to disabled people; lobby on behalf of disabled people; or fund medical research into the causes, prevention or cure of disablement); or

(ii) which provides transport services predominantly to handicapped people.

Zero-rating also applies to the repair and maintenance of those goods and the supply of any further goods in connection with that repair and maintenance.

In theory, any relevant goods can be supplied at the zero rate under this concession. In practice, the type of relevant goods which are most likely to be purchased by these charities are motor vehicles adapted for use by disabled passengers (with space for at least one wheelchair user) or a motor vehicle to transport mainly blind, deaf, mentally impaired or terminally sick persons. Boats that are designed or permanently adapted for use by disabled people are also eligible for zero-rating.

It is the responsibility of the purchasing charity to prove that it is entitled to buy the relevant goods at the zero rate. To avoid charities having to keep detailed records simply to prove eligibility, HMRC will use records and documentation already kept by the charity for non-VAT purposes, for example,

- its charitable aims and objectives;
- its publicity and advertising material;
- any documents issued for the purpose of obtaining funds from a third party such as a local authority;
- evidence of its day-to-day operations; and
- any other relevant evidence.

When a charity claims zero-rating on an adapted motor vehicle (or any other relevant goods), it must issue a certificate to the supplier claiming eligibility for zero-rating and, where required, it must attach documentary evidence (as outlined above) to support the claim. (Some documents, particularly funding documents or aims and objectives, are lengthy. A charity need not provide the whole document, but it should provide the parts which will enable it to make the declaration for relief.) The charity should make up two sets of the documents listed above, one set for itself and one to present to *each* supplier. This means the charity in reality has to search for and collate the information only once. It can then be retained by the charity for any future supplies. A charity need only provide the supporting evidence once to each supplier unless there have been relevant changes to its operation.

(VAT Notice 48, ESC 3.19; VAT Information Sheet 8/98, paras 3.3–3.5; VAT Notice 701/6/03, para 3.4.1). See Annexes B to E of the VAT Information Sheet for examples of documents which might be produced by charities intending to purchase an adapted motor vehicle.

(1) **Relevant goods**

These comprise the following.

(*a*) *Medical, scientific, computer, video, sterilising, laboratory or refrigeration equipment* for use in

- medical or veterinary research (ie original research into disease and injury of human beings or animals);
- medical or veterinary training (ie training doctors, nurses, surgeons (including dental and veterinary surgeons) and other professionals involved in medical or veterinary diagnosis or treatment. The overall programme of training must include the physical application by the students of theoretical knowledge so that the teaching of subjects such as biology and zoology, where the trainee has no practical medical or veterinary involvement with patients, is not regarded as training for these purposes); or

- medical or veterinary diagnosis or treatment (ie the diagnosis and treatment of a physical or mental abnormality by a medical or paramedical practitioner or a veterinary surgeon).

Included are parts and accessories for use with any such equipment.

[*VATA 1994, Sch 8 Group 15, Note (3)(a)(c)*]. (VAT Notice 701/6/03, para 4.3).

'*Equipment*' means articles designed for a specific purpose. It will usually be durable but certain disposable items (eg syringes which are designed to be used once only) may still be equipment. *Not included* are

- bulk materials (eg liquids, powders, sheets, pellets, and granules);
- clothing (other than specialist medical equipment such as surgical masks, gowns and gloves); and
- consumables (eg chemical reagents, fuel, ink, medicines, oil, paper, and cleaning and sterilising fluids).

(VAT Notice 701/6/03, para 4.2.1).

'*For use in*'. The equipment only qualifies for relief if purchased for use in medical or veterinary research, etc. Where equipment is to be used partly for a qualifying use and partly for other use, it is only eligible for relief where its main use is a qualifying use. In this context, 'main' means real, substantial and continuing. (VAT Notice 701/6/03, para 4.3).

Medical equipment is equipment that has features or characteristics that identify it as having been designed for a medical (including dental) purpose or function, such as the diagnosis or treatment of patients. *Eligible* are anaesthetic apparatus; aprons (lead lined for X-ray protection); bandages; bedpans; highly specialised beds (eg net suspension beds, medical water beds); catheters; medical clamps; dental chairs, drills, mirrors and spittoons; drip poles; endoscopes; electro-cardiographs; eye test charts; adjustable examination couches; first aid kits (supplied as pre-packaged units); forceps; surgical gloves; heart pacemakers; hypodermic needles; identification bracelets for patients; kidney bowls; mattresses specially designed for the relief/prevention of pressure sores; medicine measures (graduated); operating lights; patient trolleys and stretchers; specialised physiotherapy equipment (other than gymnasium equipment); orthopaedic pillows specially designed and used for neck or spinal injuries; radiography equipment; renal dialysis units; resuscitation equipment; scalpels; sphygmomanometers; splints; stethoscopes; surgical gloves, gowns and masks; suture needles; swabs; clinical thermometers; tongue depressors; wound dressings; X-ray films and plates; medical X-ray machines and X-ray viewers. *Not eligible* are alarm bracelets; aprons (not lead lined); blankets; cotton wool; disinfectants; drugs trolleys; gloves (other than surgical); gymnasium equipment; hearing aids; nurse call systems; occupational therapy materials; overbed tables; pagers; pillows (other than specially designed orthopaedic pillows as above); screens; towels; and uniforms. (VAT Notice 701/6/03, paras 4.2.2, 4.11).

Dental simulation equipment and artificial heads for use in training dentists have both been held to be medical equipment. See *The Anglodent Company (VTD 16891) (TVC 11.3)* and *Medical & Dental Staff Training Ltd (VTD 17031) (TVC 11.4)*.

Scientific equipment is equipment designed to perform a scientific function. It includes precision measuring equipment and analytical equipment. Equipment that is not designed to perform a scientific function, but merely works on a scientific principle, is not scientific equipment. *Eligible* are barometers; centrifuges; microscopes; non-clinical thermometers; spectrometers; weighing machines; and non-medical X-ray machines. (VAT Notice 701/6/03, paras 4.2.3, 4.11).

Computer equipment includes computer hardware. Machinery or other equipment, that is either operated by computer or has computerised components, is not computer equipment. *Eligible* are computer keyboards; computer disks, tapes, mouses, printers, screens, and screen filters (as accessories to computer equipment); and computer servers. *Not eligible* is computer stationery. (VAT Notice 701/6/03, paras 4.2.4, 4.11). See (*g*) below for certain computer software.

Video equipment includes video recording and playback equipment. *Eligible* are video cameras, tapes, players and monitors. (VAT Notice 701/6/03, paras 4.2.6, 4.11).

Sterilising equipment includes specialised equipment using steam or other high temperature processes. *Eligible* are autoclaves and bedpan washers with sterilising steam cycles. *Not eligible* are microwave ovens and other cooking appliances even if they can be used to sterilise; and sterilising solutions. (VAT Notice 701/6/03, paras 4.2.7, 4.11).

Laboratory equipment includes equipment designed for use in a laboratory. *Eligible* are Bunsen burners; centrifuges; cryostats; fume cupboards; laboratory benches and glassware; microscopes; microtomes; pipettes; specialised sinks and catchpots; and test tubes. *Not eligible* are ordinary cupboards, lockers, seats and other furniture even if used to equip a laboratory; bulk materials such as liquids, powders, sheets, pellets, granules; general purpose items used to equip a laboratory; consumables such as chemical reagents, medicines, and cleaning and sterilising fluids; and laboratory animals. (VAT Notice 701/6/03, paras 4.2.8, 4.11).

In *Research Establishment (VTD 19095) (TVC 11.7A)* a ventilation system was held to qualify as laboratory equipment as it had been specifically designed to control not only temperature and humidity but also pressure, allowing experiments to take place under laboratory conditions controlled to the highest practicable level.

Following the decision in *Supplier Ltd (VTD 18247) (TVC 11.11)* HMRC accept that cage and tray liners and research grade litter, bedding and nesting materials are accessories (see below) when designed for use in or with specialised laboratory caging. (Business Brief 21/03).

Refrigeration equipment includes all cooling and freezing equipment, whether designed for industrial, domestic or any other purpose. *Eligible* are deep freezer and ice-making machines. (VAT Notice 701/6/03, paras 4.2.9, 4.11).

Parts means integral components without which the equipment is incomplete. (VAT Notice 701/6/03, para 4.5.2).

Accessories means optional extras that are not necessary for the equipment to operate in its normal course, but which are used to

- improve the operation of the equipment; or
- enable it to be used, or be used to better effect, in particular circumstances.

This would include, for example, a printer for use with a computer; a specially designed camera for use with a microscope; or a rack for holding test tubes.

Not included are items which have independent uses (eg televisions); accessories to accessories; and generic bulk substances (eg liquids, powders, sheets, pellets and granules).

(VAT Notice 701/6/03, para 4.5.2).

Whether an item is an accessory is to be judged subjectively and the fact that the item can also be used otherwise than with relevant goods does not necessarily mean that it fails to qualify as an accessory. See *Royal Midland Counties Home for Disabled People v C & E Commrs, Ch D 2001, [2002] STC 395 (TVC 11.10)* where a stand-by generator, bought as a precaution against power failure, was held to be an accessory where most of the patients were dependant on electrically-powered medical equipment, even though the generator would also power lights, televisions, etc in the event of a power failure.

Ineligible equipment. Equipment purchased or hired for any other use than medical or veterinary research, training, diagnosis or treatment is not eligible for zero-rating under this provision. This includes equipment for

- general biological studies;
- environmental research;
- research into animal husbandry or food production;
- general administration; or
- domestic or leisure purposes.

Examples of ineligible equipment include air conditioners; security and smoke alarms; still cameras; catering equipment; cleaning equipment; closed circuit television systems; curtains; fuel; lockers; overhead projecting units; stationery; tape recorders; television sets; waste disposal bags, boxes, jars and sacks; and waste disposal machinery.

(VAT Notice 701/6/03, paras 4.3, 4.11).

(*b*) *Ambulances* (including parts and accessories). [*VATA 1994, Sch 8 Group 15, Note* (*3*)(*b*)(*c*)].

An '*ambulance*' is an emergency vehicle used for transporting sick and injured people or animals. It includes specially equipped air ambulances or watercraft. The vehicle must have

- the front and both sides permanently fitted with signs indicating that the vehicle is an ambulance;
- in the case of an ambulance for transporting human patients, adequate door space for the loading of a patient on a stretcher;
- seating at the rear of the driver or pilot for at least one attendant; and

- at least one stretcher that, with handles extended, measures at least 2.28 metres, together with permanent fittings to hold it in position. (This size specification applies only to ambulances that transport human patients. For ambulances that transport animals, any reasonable lifting or carrying equipment is acceptable.)

'*Parts*' are integral components without which the ambulance is incomplete. '*Accessories*' means optional extras that are not necessary for the ambulance to operate but are used to improve the operation or enable the ambulance to be used, or be used to better effect, in particular circumstances.

(VAT Notice 701/6/03, para 4.4).

(*c*) *Goods used by people with disabilities of a kind described in VATA 1994, Sch 8 Group 12 Item 2*. [*VATA 1994, Sch 8 Group 15, Note* (*3*)(*d*)].

This covers medical and surgical appliances; certain electrically or mechanically adjustable beds, sanitary devices, chair or stair lifts, hoists and lifters; motor vehicles capable of carrying up to 12 people designed, or substantially and permanently adapted, for the carriage of a person in a wheelchair or on a stretcher; boats designed, or substantially and permanently adapted, for use by a disabled person; and other equipment and appliances designed solely for use by a chronically sick or disabled person. See 32.17–32.26 HEALTH AND WELFARE for full details.

(*d*) *Motor vehicles* (other than vehicles with more than 50 seats) designed or substantially and permanently adapted for the safe carriage of a handicapped person (see (5) below) in a wheelchair provided that

- vehicles with 17 to 26 seats have provision for at least two such persons;
- vehicles with 27 to 36 seats have provision for at least three such persons;
- vehicles with 37 to 46 seats have provision for at least four such persons; and
- vehicles with 47 to 50 seats have provision for at least five such persons.

The vehicle must have either a fitted electrically or hydraulically operated lift or, in the case of a vehicle with less than 17 seats, a fitted ramp to provide access for a passenger in a wheelchair.

[*VATA 1994, Sch 8 Group 15, Note* (*3*)(*e*)].

(*e*) *Motor vehicles* with 7 to 50 seats for use by an eligible body (see (2) below) providing care for blind, deaf, mentally handicapped or terminally sick persons mainly to transport such persons. [*VATA 1994, Sch 8 Group 15, Note* (*3*)(*f*)].

(*f*) *Telecommunication, aural, visual, light enhancing or heat detecting equipment* (not being equipment ordinarily supplied for private or recreational use) solely for use for the purpose of rescue or first aid services undertaken by a charitable institution providing such services. [*VATA 1994, Sch 8 Group 15, Note* (*3*)(*g*)].

Eligible are image intensifiers, heat seekers and similar specialist equipment used to locate casualties; flares used to illuminate large areas for search purposes; and two-way radios that are pre-calibrated to the emergency frequency. *Not eligible* are general items such as mobile phones and pagers, binoculars, torches, searchlights and loudhailers. (VAT Notice 701/6/03, para 4.8).

Early warning sirens were held to be aural equipment in *Severnside Siren Trust Ltd (VTD 16640) (TVC 11.12)*.

(*g*) *Computer software* when purchased by an eligible body (see (2) below) solely for use in medical research, diagnosis or treatment. [*VATA 1994, Sch 8 Group 15, Note* (*10*)].

Zero-rating does not apply to computer software or programs that are purchased

- for a purpose other than medical research, diagnosis or treatment; or
- by a person, body or organisation other than an eligible body (even if purchased for *donation* to a nominated eligible body).

(*h*) *Resuscitation training models.* By concession, human resuscitation training models (ie models which include a head and torso) acquired for use in first-aid training in either 'cardiopulmonary resuscitation' or defibrillation techniques or both, together with parts and accessories for training models used for such purposes. '*Cardiopulmonary resuscitation*' means a combination of expired air ventilation and chest compression. (VAT Notice 748, ESC 3.25). Other resuscitation dummies, including intravenous cannulation models, blood transfusion models and static anatomical models are not within the scope of the concession and therefore not eligible for relief. (Business Brief 10/99).

Installation. If the normal selling price of the relevant goods includes an amount for fixing or connecting to mains services and/or testing the equipment on site, the whole selling price can be included in the relief. Any building work (eg removal of walls or reinforcing floors) necessary in order to install large items of equipment is standard-rated even if carried out by the supplier of the equipment. (VAT Notice 701/6/03, para 4.10).

(2) **Eligible body**

Eligible body means any of the following.

- A Strategic Health Authority (previously Health Authority) or Special Health Authority in England.
- A Health Authority, Special Health Authority or Local Health Authority in Wales.
- A Health Board in Scotland.
- A Health and Social Services Board in Northern Ireland.
- A hospital or research institution whose activities are 'not carried on for profit'.

'*Not carried on for profit*' means that the hospital or research establishment

(i) cannot, and does not, distribute any profit achieved; and

(ii) applies any surplus that arises from supplies of hospital or research services to the furtherance of its objectives.

- A charitable institution providing care or medical or surgical treatment (see (4) below) for handicapped persons which satisfies one of the following conditions.

  (i) It provides the care or medical or surgical treatment in a relevant establishment (see (6) below), the relevant goods are used in that establishment, and the majority of persons who receive the care or treatment there are handicapped (see (5) below).

  HMRC accept that a charitable institution may still be an eligible body if, for a temporary period, handicapped people form less than 50% of the recipients of care or treatment services provided that, over an extended period, the majority of recipients are handicapped.

  (ii) It provides medical care (see (7) below) to handicapped persons (see (5) below) in their own homes, the relevant goods are medical equipment falling within (1)(*a*) above or are parts or accessories for use in or with such equipment, and the goods are used in, or in connection with, the provision of that care.

- The Common Services Agency for the Scottish Health Service, the Northern Ireland Central Services Agency for Health and Social Services, or the Isle of Man Health Services Board.
- A charitable institution providing rescue or first-aid services. Rescue services do not include the operation of a website to help practitioners involved in paediatric medicine to diagnose potential complications (*Isabel Medical Charity (VTD 18209) (TVC 11.18)*).
- A NHS trust established under *National Health Service and Community Care Act 1990, Part I* or *National Health Service (Scotland) Act 1978.*
- A Primary Care Trust established under *National Health Service Act 1977, s 16A.*

Non-eligible bodies under these provisions include day centres, residential care homes or providers of home care services

- that are not charities; or
- where over an extended period the majority of the recipients of care provided are not chronically sick or disabled people (see (5) below).

Animal charities qualify as eligible bodies if

- they are animal *hospitals* providing 'in-patient' facilities; or
- they provide rescue or first-aid services to animals.

Animal clinics or surgeries are not eligible bodies unless they are part of an animal hospital or are run by a charity that also provides rescue or first-aid services.

[*VATA 1994, Sch 8 Group 15 Items 4, 4A, 5A, 5B; FA 1997, s 34; SI 2000/503; SI 2002/2813*]. (VAT Notice 701/6/03, paras 3.3, 3.4.1, 3.5, 3.6).

(3) **Voluntary contributions**

Where a person, group or organisation contributes funds to an eligible body, and does not receive anything in return, this is a voluntary contribution or donation. Lottery funding is also regarded as a voluntary contribution for the purposes of this relief. (VAT Notice 701/6/03, para 5.1).

(4) **Care or medical or surgical treatment**

This includes protection, treatment, supervision, control or guidance that is provided to meet medical, physical, personal or domestic needs of an individual. Care or treatment will usually involve some personal contact between the provider and recipient. Examples include

- helping a person with daily personal needs (eg bathing, dressing, feeding or toileting);
- medical or surgical treatment;
- nursing sick or injured patients in a hospital, hospice or nursing home; and
- looking after or supervising vulnerable people.

Not included are catering, laundry and other services that do not require direct contact with the recipient.

(VAT Notice 701/6/03, para 3.4.2).

(5) **Handicapped**

Handicapped means chronically sick or disabled. [*VATA 1994, Sch 8 Group 15, Note* (*5*)].

Chronic sickness is a condition regarded as such by the medical profession. Disability is a physical or mental impairment that has a substantial and long-term adverse effect on a person's ability to carry out day-to-day activities. Frail elderly people who are not disabled, or people whose mobility is temporarily impaired by short-term illness or injury are not chronically sick or disabled for the purposes of this VAT relief. (VAT Notice 701/6/03, para 3.4.3).

(6) **Relevant establishment**

Relevant establishment means either of the following.

- A day centre other than one that exists primarily as a place for activities that are social or recreational or both.

  Examples of day centres which would qualify include charitable physiotherapy centres for disabled children and charitable centres that run daily rehabilitation or training classes for disabled adults.

- An institution which is approved, licensed or registered under the relevant social legislation or which is exempt from any such requirement by that legislation.

  Examples include charitable hospices and residential care homes.

[*VATA 1994, Sch 8 Group 15, Note* (*4B*); *FA 1997, s 34*]. (VAT Notice 701/6/03, para 3.4.1).

(7) **Medical care**

Medical care includes medical treatment and the sort of care that a nurse might carry out or supervise (eg washing or feeding a patient, helping a patient out of bed, and administering drugs). It does not include assistance with general domestic tasks such as cooking, cleaning or shopping.

(VAT Notice 701/6/03, para 3.4.4).

Evidence of eligibility. The supplier is responsible for ensuring that all the conditions for zero-rating are met. As this may not always be evident at the time of supply, HMRC recommend that suppliers obtain a written declaration of eligibility from each customer who claims entitlement to VAT relief. The declaration should

- contain sufficient information to demonstrate that the conditions for the relief are satisfied; and
- be separate, or clearly distinguishable from, any order form or invoice against which the goods or services are supplied (ie a customer signing an order should not automatically be signing a declaration of eligibility for VAT relief).

Examples of declarations that might be obtained from a customer are reproduced in a Supplement to VAT Notice 701/7 dated April 1997. Any other declaration form used must require the purchaser to provide the same information.

In addition to a written declaration, suppliers may require evidence that the purchaser is an eligible body. This may include in the case of

- a charitable body, evidence that it is a charity;
- domiciliary care agencies, day centres or other establishments, evidence that care or treatment services are provided mainly to chronically sick or disabled people;
- charitable transport providers, evidence that transport services are provided mainly to disabled people;
- other charities, evidence that its sole purpose is the provision of services for, or on behalf of, chronically sick or disabled people.

Suppliers must retain evidence that any supply was eligible for relief.

The receipt of a declaration and/or other evidence from a customer does not authorise the zero-rating of a supply. A supplier must take reasonable steps to check any apparent inconsistencies and to confirm that any information given by the customer is correct. However, the purchaser has a responsibility to make truthful statements and to provide appropriate documentation to support this. HMRC will not, therefore, seek to recover VAT due from a supplier who has taken reasonable steps to check the validity of a declaration, but has failed to identify an inaccuracy, and, in good faith, has zero-rated a supply.

(VAT Notice 48, ESC 3.11; VAT Notice 701/6/03, paras 8.1–8.4).

Imports. Goods that meet all the conditions for zero-rating when purchased in the UK can be zero-rated on importation. Importers should lodge the relevant declaration of eligibility (see above) with HMRC at the point of importation. Special provisions apply to the importation of computer software. See 34.33 IMPORTS. (VAT Notice 701/6/03, para 7.1).

Acquisitions from other EC countries. Where a VAT-registered eligible body acquires goods from another EC country, the normal rules for acquisitions apply. If the supply meets all the conditions for relief, no VAT is due. Eligibility declarations do not need to be provided to the overseas supplier but evidence that the supply is correctly zero-rated should be retained.

Where an eligible body is not VAT-registered, any goods acquired from another EC country are subject to VAT at the rate in force in that country. The UK relief for charity-funded equipment does not apply.
(VAT Notice 701/6/03, para 7.2).

Supplies to eligible bodies outside the UK. Apart from the specific UK Health Boards, etc, there is no requirement in the legislation that an eligible body must be within the UK. Therefore

- where a supply is made to an eligible body (ie a qualifying hospital, research institution or charitable institution) based in another EC country and that body is not VAT-registered there, this relief can be used to zero-rate the supply provided all the conditions are met; and
- if the customer is VAT-registered in another EC country or is outside the EC, the supply of goods can be zero-rated under the normal rules.

(VAT Notice 701/6/03, para 7.3).

De Voil Indirect Tax Service. See V4.266.

12.9 EXEMPT SUPPLIES BY CHARITIES

Certain supplies by charities are exempt from VAT not because of the charitable status of the supplier but because they are covered by general application. See 24 EXEMPT SUPPLIES. In addition, the exemptions in 12.10 and 12.11 below apply specifically to charities and certain other qualifying bodies.

12.10 Fund-raising events by charities and other qualifying bodies

Subject to the exclusions below, the supply of goods and services in connection with an 'event' whose primary purpose is the raising of money and which is promoted as such is exempt from VAT where

- the supply of goods and services is by a 'charity' and the event is organised for charitable purposes by one or more charities;
- the supply of goods and services is by a 'qualifying body' and the event is organised exclusively for the body's own benefit; or
- the supply of goods and services is by a charity or a qualifying body and the event is organised, jointly by one or more charities and the qualifying body, exclusively for charitable purposes or that body's own benefit or a combination of those purposes.

[*VATA 1994, Sch 9 Group 12 Items 1 and 2; SI 2000/802*].

Evidence that an event was primarily organised to raise funds includes minutes of meetings, costings and similar documents. In order to show that the event is promoted for fund-raising purposes, the publicity material, ticket, etc should clearly refer to fund-raising such as 'fund-raising for', 'in aid of', 'help us to build' or 'help us to raise money for'. Examples should be retained as evidence. (Leaflet CWL4, para 3.16).

The exemption applies to

- all admission charges;

- the sale of commemorative brochures unless zero-rated under 54.4 PRINTED MATTER, ETC;
- the sale of advertising space in those brochures;
- any other items sold by the charity or qualifying body at the event (eg T-shirts, non-donated auctioned goods, etc) unless the items would normally be zero-rated (eg children's T-shirts) in which case zero-rating applies; and
- sponsorship payments directly connected with the qualifying event.

The exemption does not apply to commemorative goods and souvenirs sold for a period after the qualifying fund-raising event. For example,

- video and audio recordings of the event, surplus T-shirts, mugs, etc will be standard-rated;
- commemorative programmes and children's T-shirts will remain zero-rated; and
- donated goods for sale may still be sold VAT-free provided the normal conditions are met.

(Leaflet CWL4, paras 4.7, 4.8).

'*Event*' includes an event accessed (wholly or partly) by means of electronic communications including an electronic communications network (such as the internet). [*VATA 1994, Sch 9 Group 12 Note 1; Communications Act 2003, Sch 17 para 129; SI 2000/802*]. HMRC regard an event as an incident with an outcome or a result so that activities of a semi-regular or continuous nature (eg the frequent operation of a shop or bar) cannot be an event. The relief is not intended to exempt normal trading activities. Events which may qualify include

- a ball, dinner dance, disco or barn dance;
- a performance (eg a concert or stage production);
- the showing of a film;
- a fete, fair or festival;
- a horticultural show;
- an exhibition, including art, history, science, etc;
- a bazaar, jumble sale, car boot sale or good-as-new sale;
- sporting participation (including spectators) such as a sponsored walk or swim;
- sporting performances;
- games of skill, contests and quizzes;
- participation in an endurance event;
- a fireworks display;
- a dinner, lunch or barbecue; or
- an auction of bought-in goods (auction of donated goods is zero-rated).

(Leaflet CWL4, paras 3.2, 3.3).

'*Charity*' includes a body corporate which is wholly-owned by the charity if

- the body has agreed in writing (whether or not by deed) to transfer its profits from whatever source to a charity; or
- the body's profits from whatever source are otherwise payable to a charity.

[*VATA 1994, Sch 9 Group 12 Note 2; SI 2000/802*].

A '*qualifying body*' is

- a non-profit making body within 14.7(*a*)–(*f*) CLUBS AND ASSOCIATIONS;
- any eligible body as defined in 57.9 RECREATION AND SPORT whose principal purpose is the provision of facilities for persons to take part in sport and physical recreation; or
- any body which is an eligible body for the purposes of *VATA 1994, Sch 9 Group 13 Item 2* (exempt admission charges to entertainment, cultural activities, etc) as defined in 57.6 RECREATION AND SPORT.

[*VATA 1994, Sch 9 Group 12 Note 3; SI 2000/802*].

Exclusions. The following events are excluded from exemption.

(*a*) *Multiple events of the same kind at the same location.* Exemption does not apply to *any* event where in its financial year a charity or qualifying body organises (whether alone or in association with another charity or qualifying body) more than 15 events of the same kind in the same 'location' (ie if a charity or body organises 16 similar events in the same location in its financial year, none of those events are exempt). In determining whether the limit of 15 events has been exceeded, there can be disregarded any event of that kind at that location in a week during which the aggregate gross takings from events involving the charity or body of that kind in that location do not exceed £1,000.

Where a charity's or body's financial year is longer or shorter than a year, the maximum number of events qualifying for exemption is

15 × number of days in financial year ÷ 365

expressed to the nearest whole number.

[*VATA 1994, Sch 9 Group 12 Notes 4–7; SI 2000/802*].

'*Location*'. Similar kinds of events held in different locations qualify for exemption provided all the other conditions are met. For example, 20 balls held by a national charity in the same financial year, each in a different town, would all qualify for relief. In determining whether two events are held at the same location

- where events need to be held on special premises (eg a sports ground, swimming pool or theatre), each of these premises is a separate location;
- where an event is held in a complex of cinemas, theatres or concert halls, the location is the specific cinema, etc in which the fund-raising event takes place; and
- a charity's entire website is regarded as a location for events held over the internet.

These rules are designed to be generous to charities that may hold a number of events of the same type in different locations but in the same town. HMRC will not accept arrangements such as weekly car boot sales, each held in different but adjacent fields, as constituting a separate location without considering whether such an arrangement is potentially distorting competition (see (*c*) below).

In determining the number of events held in any location, where an event such as a concert is repeated over successive evenings, each performance counts as a separate event. A single event which takes place at the same location for more than one day (eg a golf tournament) is accepted as one event.

(Leaflet CWL4, paras 3.5, 3.6).

(*b*) *Events where accommodation also provided.* An event does not qualify for exemption where accommodation in connection with the event is provided, directly or indirectly, by

- any of the charities or the qualifying body organising the event, or
- any charity connected with any charity organising the event

unless the accommodation so provided does not exceed two nights in total (whether or not consecutive) *and* the supply of accommodation does not fall within the TOUR OPERATORS' MARGIN SCHEME (66).

[*VATA 1994, Sch 9 Group 12 Notes 8, 9; SI 2000/802*].

(*c*) *Distortion of competition.* An event does not qualify for exemption if it is likely to cause distortion of competition and place a commercial enterprise carried on by a taxable person at a disadvantage.

[*VATA 1994, Sch 9 Group 12 Note 11; SI 2000/802*].

Fund-raising over the internet. Fund-raising events held over the internet which meet all the conditions set out above qualify for exemption. HMRC regard a charity's entire website as a location (see under (*a*) above). An internet auction (which usually takes place over a number of days and may include a variety of items (or lots) for sale) can be a single event provided

- there is a specified closing date;
- bidding closes at this date; and
- goods are not sold before the closing date.

Where these conditions are not met, HMRC regard the sale of each item (or lot) as a separate event.

Trading subsidiaries of charities. In order to be eligible to hold VAT exempt fund-raising events, a charity's trading subsidiary must be wholly owned by the charity and transfer all profits, from whatever source, to the charity (see above). By retaining profits, a trading subsidiary could, therefore, find itself ineligible to hold exempt fund-raising events. However, HMRC accept that, for the purposes of this exemption, the 'transfer of profits' condition is met if

- the arrangements are compatible with charity law;
- profits are paid to the charity;
- the only profit retained annually by the subsidiary is not subject to corporation tax (ie does not exceed the upper profit limit for the starting rate band for corporation tax purposes);
- the profit is retained for development which has the clear aim of increasing funds going to the charity; and

- the subsidiary is not involved in any abuse or avoidance.

HMRC may review this approach if the amount or proportion of profits that is eligible for corporation tax relief changes or abuse occurs.

(Internal Guidance V1–9, paras 8.1–8.6).

Non-qualifying events. Supplies made by a charity or qualifying body at a fund-raising event which does not qualify for exemption are subject to VAT in the normal way. See 12.5(1) above.

De Voil Indirect Tax Service. See V4.171.

12.11 **Welfare services**

The supply by a charity of welfare services, and of goods supplied in connection with those services, is exempt. [*VATA 1994, Sch 9 Group 7, Item 9*].

Identical provisions apply to such supplies made by public bodies, state-regulated private welfare institutions (from 21 March 2002) and state-regulated private welfare agencies (from 31 January 2003). See 32.14 HEALTH AND WELFARE for full details.

See 12.5(21) above for welfare services supplied consistently below cost.

12.12 REDUCED RATE SUPPLIES TO CHARITIES

(*a*) **Fuel and power.** Supplies of fuel and power can be subject to the reduced rate in certain circumstances. These include

- use in a dwelling or a building used for a relevant residential purpose; and
- use by a charity otherwise than in the course or furtherance of a business.

See 29 FUEL AND POWER.

(*b*) **Energy-saving materials.** The installation of certain energy saving materials in a building used solely for a relevant charitable purpose is liable to VAT at the reduced rate. See 58.2 REDUCED RATE SUPPLIES.

12.13 RELIEF FOR IMPORTATIONS

No VAT is payable on the importation of certain goods by or for charities and other philanthropic organisations. See 34.15(6) IMPORTS.

12.14 NEW BUILDING PROJECTS ON A SELF-BUILD OR SELF-HELP BASIS

Refunds of VAT may be available to a charity involved in a self-build project of a building intended solely for use for a relevant charitable purpose. See 42.33 LAND AND BUILDINGS.

13 Clothing and Footwear

De Voil Indirect Tax Service. See V4.287

The contents of this chapter are as follows.

13.1 INTRODUCTION

Zero-rating applies to

- articles of clothing or footwear designed for young children and not suitable for older children (see 13.2 to 13.7 below); and
- certain supplies of protective boots and helmets (see 13.8 below).

Other supplies of clothing and footwear are standard-rated.

13.2 YOUNG CHILDREN'S CLOTHING AND FOOTWEAR

Articles designed as clothing (including hats and other headgear) or footwear for young children and not suitable for older persons are zero-rated. [*VATA 1994, Sch 8 Group 16 Item 1 and Note 1*]. Special provisions apply to clothing made wholly or partly of fur (see 13.4 below).

In order to qualify for zero-rating, an article must therefore satisfying all of the following conditions.

- It must be an article of clothing or footwear. See 13.3 below.
- It must not be made of fur (with minor exceptions). See 13.4 below.
- It must be designed for young children. See 13.5 below.
- It must only be suitable for young children. See 13.6 below.

(VAT Notice 714, para 1.3).

13.3 What qualifies as clothing and footwear

The word 'clothing' must be given its ordinary meaning and whether an item is clothing or not is a question of fact. To have a function as clothing, an item should provide cover for the body (either for decency or protection from the elements). But the purpose for which an item was intended to be used is not conclusive and a garment designed primarily for another purposes (see, for example, safety aids below), but also fulfilling a clothing function, can still qualify for zero-rating (*British Vita Co Ltd (VTD 322) (TVC 12.3)*).

For a consideration of the phrase 'articles designed as clothing' see *C & E Commrs v Ali Baba Tex Ltd, QB [1992] STC 590 (TVC 12.4)*.

If an item is not an article of clothing or footwear it is standard-rated. HMRC have expressed their view on the following items.

13.3 Clothing and Footwear

(1) Clothing in general

As well as all the obvious garments, clothing includes items such as hats, caps, braces, belts, garters and scarves. Ties, although purely ornamental, are also accepted as clothing.

Not included are clothing accessories and items of haberdashery sold separately, such as

- sporrans and other types of purses, pouches and sashes;
- shoulder pads, textile lengths;
- cricket pads;
- motorcyclists' chest protectors;
- items of Guide and Scout uniform comprising belt pouches, pins, woggles and sash pins (see *BG Supplies (Birmingham) Ltd (VTD 11663) (TVC 12.6)*);
- fastenings such as buckles, buttons and zips;
- badges, collars, cuffs, patches and other sew-on or iron-on items;
- hand muffs and ear muffs; and
- wristbands for sport, etc (see *Vidhani Brothers Ltd (VTD 18997) (TVC 12.5A)*).

(2) Baby wear

Most items of baby wear (eg bonnets, bootees and matinee jackets) can be clearly recognised as clothing, but the following less obvious items are also considered to be articles of clothing.

- Bibs, including plastic bibs with a curved tray at the base.
- Hooded rain covers for pushchairs, provided they are suitable for the baby to wear as a rain cape when out of the pushchair.
- Nappies (and nappy liners), both disposable and re-usable, provided they are held out for sale appropriately.
- Babies' shawls, provided they are designed and held out as such.
- Padded sleeping garments, similar in construction to sleeping bags, but shaped at the neck and armholes or having sleeves and/or legs.
- Towelling bathrobes designed with a hood or sleeves enabling the baby to be wrapped in them as a garment.

The following are *not* considered to be baby clothing and are standard-rated.

- Pram and pushchair covers not designed to serve as rain capes outside the pram or chair.
- Disposable nappy material sold in a continuous role from which individual nappies are cut.
- 'Mother-and-baby' shawls intended to wrap around both mother and child.

- Sleeping bags not designed with neck and arm holes or sleeves and/or legs.

See also *Mothercare Ltd (VTD 323) (TVC 12.1)* and *Little Rock Ltd (VTD 424) (TVC 12.2)*.

(3) **Footwear**

Articles of footwear include

- boots, shoes, sandals and slippers, even if they are designed for special purposes (such as ballet shoes or studded football boots); and
- ice-skating or roller-skating boots, with or without skating blades or rollers attached;

but do not include

- blades or rollers sold on their own, or platform type roller skates for attaching to normal shoes; and
- shoelaces, insoles, heel protectors and stick-on soles sold as separate items.

(4) **Headgear**

HMRC consider items of headgear to be clothing if they cover the whole head in the same way as a traditional hat or cap (eg first communion veil and head-dress sets). but not where they cover only part of the head (eg bridesmaids' head-dresses, yarmulkes (Jewish skull caps), sunvisors and ear muffs). Headbands are not regarded as clothing (see *Cassidy (t/a Balou) (VTD 5760) (TVC 12.5)*).

(5) **Safety aids**

Clothing includes items that, although primarily designed as safety aids, have the form and function of clothing (eg waistcoat-style lifejackets or safety overvests with reflective strips for cyclists). Other safety aids which have no clothing functions (eg child safety harnesses, reflective armbands, waist straps and buoyancy aids) are always standard-rated.

(6) **Play outfits**

HMRC accept as clothing

- play outfits (eg cowboy suits or nurses' outfits) made of standard materials, and
- play hats of normal millinery materials

as they serve the purpose of clothing.

Novelty hats, costumes made of flimsy materials or 'play shoes' (rigid plastic sandals for dressing-up purposes) are not regarded as clothing (and, if included in a play outfit, would give rise to a mixed supply).

(7) **Ethnic clothing**

To distinguish items which are of a 'wrap-around' nature (eg saris and lungis) from mere lengths of cloth, HMRC insist that to be clothing, such items must have permanently sewn hems (and maximum measurements, see 13.5 below).

(8) **Incomplete articles**

An unfinished article may be considered to be clothing if it has been processed to such an extent that it could not reasonably be used for any other purpose (eg cut-out parts of a garment or pleated skirt lengths). See *Ali Baba Tex Ltd* above.

(VAT Notice 714, paras 2.1–2.3; Internal Guidance V1–7, Chapter 14 paras 2.1, 2.2).

13.4 Items made of fur

Clothing does not included any articles made wholly or partly of 'fur skin' apart from

- headgear,
- gloves,
- buttons, belts and buckles; and
- any garment merely trimmed with fur skin unless the trimming has an area greater than one-fifth of the area of the outside material or, in the case of a new garment, represents a cost to the manufacturer greater than the cost of the other components.

'*Fur skin*' means any skin with fur, hair or wool attached except

- rabbit skin;
- woolled sheep or lamb skin; and
- the skin, if neither tanned nor dressed, of bovine cattle (including buffalo), equine animals, goats or kids (other than Yemen, Mongolian and Tibetan goats or kids), swine (including peccary), chamois, gazelles, deer or dogs.

[*VATA 1994, Sch 8 Group 16 Notes 2 and 3*].

These provisions are designed to exclude zero-rating for children's clothing made from luxury furs. Subject to satisfying the other tests in 13.2 above, zero-rating can be applied to

- articles made using artificial fur;
- fur footwear; and
- fur lined boots.

(VAT Notice 714, para 3.1; Internal Guidance V1–7, Chapter 14 para 3.1).

13.5 Items designed for young children

Although sizes and measurements are not referred to in the legislation, it has been agreed with the industry working party that they represent a fair reflection of the interpretation of the law.

(1) **Clothing**

HMRC in general accept that garments are designed for young children provided they are up to the tabled measurements below. These measurements are based on those for children up to the eve of their 14th birthday (as set out in the relevant British Standard). The garments should be measured on a flat surface, with creases smoothed out, buttons (or equivalent) fastened and any intended overlap in place. Chest measurements should normally be taken 2.5

cms below the base of the armhole and multiplied by two. Similarly, waist measurements should be taken from one side of the fastened waistband to the other and multiplied by two.

Maximum garment sizes	*Boys*		*Girls*	
	Chest	Waist	Chest	Waist
Shirts	104cm	—	105cm	—
Knitwear	104cm	—	105cm	—
Jackets/waistcoats	109cm	—	110cm	—
Top coats/outerwear	114cm	—	115cm	—
Dresses	—	—	98cm	—
Skirts*	—	—	—	71cm
Trousers/shorts*	—	72cm	—	71cm
Underwear/swimwear	88cm	72cm	89cm	71cm
Nightwear	105cm	73cm	106cm	72cm

* Garments with elasticated waistbands should be measured at their full stretch. Those that have no fastening may be zero-rated up to a maximum stretched waist of 85 cms for boys and 90 cms for girls.

Some products are normally judged by different criteria or measurements. The following garments are also accepted as being designed for young children.

Maximum garment sizes — other garments
Lifejackets — Max body weight 52kg
Leotards/body stockings/swimsuits — Shoulder to crotch 70cm
Saris — 442cm × 104cm
Lungis — 156cm × 94cm
Socks (by shoe size) — Boys 6.5; Girls/unisex 5.5
Tights — Waist-crotch-waist measurement 51cm for lightweight and 56cm for heavyweight
Teen bras — Size 34B

Style considerations. In a minority of cases, it may be necessary to consider factors inherent in the garment as making it suitable for older persons. If this applies, a garment within the maximum measurements above could still fail the 'design' test and be standard-rated. See, for example, *Walter Stewart Ltd (VTD 83) (TVC 12.10)* where a leather coat which did not exceed the maximum measurements failed the test because it was a relatively high-cost fashion garment more likely to appeal to adults and because a three-inch bust dart had been inserted.

Larger sizes. If the above measurements are exceeded, HMRC will still accept that garments are designed for young children if *either* of the following conditions can be satisfied.

(*a*) If it can be shown that

- the garment has been designed for a person under 14,
- it is only suitable for young children (see 13.6 below); and
- the body measurements used are at or below those in the table below.

Body size	*Boys*	*Girls*
Height	163cms	161cms
Chest	84cms	85cms
Waist	70cms	69cms
Hips	85cms	90cms
Arm (shoulder to wrist)	59cms	57cms
Inside leg	77cms	76cms

(*b*) The clothing is restricted by some other design feature to those under 14. HMRC must be satisfied that the body sizes used are appropriate to the under 14s and the garments produced are only suitable for that age group. They must be given the specifications and reasoning and must have given written agreement before zero-rating can be applied in such cases.

One-size and stretch garments. Zero-rating cannot be applied to articles of clothing which are sold in one size only and that are suitable for both children and adults. Articles that stretch to fit, such as some sportswear, can be zero-rated provided the garment is designed to fit a body size in accordance with the second table above or at its maximum stretch does not exceed the measurements for maximum garment sizes in the first table above. See also *Jeffrey Green & Co Ltd (VTD 69) (TVC 12.9).*

(2) **Footwear**

HMRC accept that footwear is designed for young children up to the following measurements.

- Boys' shoes — up to and including UK size 6.5 or American size 7 (unless 7.5 is marked as equal to UK 6.5) or Continental size 40
- Girls' court shoes (ie low cut shoes without straps or other fastenings) — up to and including UK size 3 or American size 4.5 or Continental size 35.5 (or 35 if no half sizes)
- Other girls' shoes — as for court shoes but where the heel height does not exceed the sole depth by more than 4 cms, up to UK size 5.5 or American size 7 or Continental size 38.5 (38 if no half sizes)

See also *Brays of Glastonbury Ltd (VTD 650) (TVC 12.12)* and *Gura (t/a Vincent Footwear) (VTD 18416) (TVC 12.13).*

Larger sizes. It may still be possible to zero-rate larger sizes if HMRC are satisfied that

- the product has been designed exclusively for children under 14; and
- it is only suitable for young children (see 13.6 below)

but HMRC must be given the specifications and reasoning and must have given written agreement before zero-rating can be applied in such cases.

Unisex footwear. Most lines of footwear are designed for one sex or the other and should be zero-rated according to the rules relating to girls' or boys' footwear as appropriate. True 'unisex' footwear can only be zero-rated up to and including size 5.5 (the maximum size for girls' footwear).

Feet of differing sizes. Where a child has one foot significantly larger than the other, or requires an unusually high heel for one foot, the pair of shoes can be zero-rated if the smaller shoe qualifies for the relief.

(3) **Hats and other headgear**

Hats. Many children's hats fit adults. It is still possible to zero-rate hats (including caps and other items of headgear) which are suitable by design only for young children (eg babies' bonnets, school hats) or which are clearly held out for sale for young children. Where there is no specific style differentiation between childrens' and adults' hats, it is likely that only the very smallest sizes of headwear are likely to pass the 'design' test.

In *Benrose Ltd (t/a Multi-Stock Company) (VTD 15783) (TVC 12.22)* which concerned knitted acrylic hats bearing logos of famous football teams, the tribunal held that, although it was physically possible for an adult to wear the hats, they were too close-fitting for comfortable wear over an extended period. Also, as they were intended as cheap imitations of official football club hats, supporters over 14 would want the official hats. This decision stresses the point that size is not always the crucial test and that design or style must be considered.

HMRC have accepted the following items as falling within the relief.

- Protective helmets (such as those for skateboarding or ice hockey) up to a maximum size of 59 cms as long as they are designed and marketed exclusively for children (13.6 below).
- Riding hats up to and including size 6.75 (jockey skulls up to size 1) even if they are not held out for sale for children. Sales of larger riding hats specifically for young children can be zero-rated as long as they are fitted, adapted or otherwise appropriate only for young children (eg by being less sophisticated in terms of design and appearance) but HMRC's written approval must be received before zero-rating larger sizes.

All cycle helmets are zero-rated irrespective of size or how they are held out for sale (see 13.9 below).

(3) **Belts, braces and other items**

HMRC accept belts, braces, neckties, gloves, garters, scarves, ruffs, collars and shirt frills as traditional items of clothing and they may be zero-rated irrespective of size as long as they are held out for sale for young children only (see 13.6 below).

(VAT Notice 714, paras 4.1–4.3; Internal Guidance V1–7, Chapter 14 paras 4.1.9, 4.1.11).

13.6 Items suitable only for young children

The final test that must be satisfied if an item is to be zero-rated (see 13.2 above) is that it must only be suitable for young children, ie not suitable for older persons. This can be met by ensuring that it is 'held out for sale' for young children.

'*Held out for sale*' means the way in which an article is labelled, packaged, displayed, invoiced or advertised. It includes any promotional items and the heading under which an article is listed in a catalogue, web page or price list.

13.7 Clothing and Footwear

Articles cannot necessarily be zero-rated on sale simply because they were zero-rated when purchased. How they are held out for sale affects their VAT liability. Goods, which may qualify at the design stage, fail the suitability test if they are labeled

- to fit sizes larger than those in 13.5 above;
- as suitable for age '13/14' and above; or
- by the ladies sizing system (8, 10, 12, and so on).

In particular:

- *Manufacturers* must be able to show that items qualify for zero-rating from product specification or other documentation and must identify them appropriately on any labelling and packaging, and in any promotional material and on invoices.
- *Wholesalers and distributors* must clearly identify the article as being only suitable for children on invoices and price lists. If the goods are on display they must clearly be identified and segregated. Any catalogue should identify the articles as being for young children, preferably in a separate children's section and the identical product must not appear in both adults' and children's sections.
- *Retailers* can zero-rate clothing for young children only if it is clear from labels, signs, packaging, advertising, etc that it is intended for young children and they either

  (i) sell it from a shop, a separate department in a shop, or a separate section of a catalogue which caters exclusively for children; or

  (ii) keep it apart from adult garments by selling it from separate shelves, racks, etc which are clearly marked up as 'boys', 'girls' or 'children's'.

  The extent to which this is possible will vary depending upon the size and type of retail outlet but any retailer should be able to show that it has as good a system as is practical in the circumstances. The potential purchaser should not be left in any doubt that the retailer is selling items for young children.
- *Mail order and internet suppliers* must clearly identify the goods as being for young children in any price list, page, catalogue or other promotional material, preferably using a discrete children's section. The potential purchaser should be in no doubt that the goods they are looking at are for young children and the identical goods must not appear in both adults' and children's sections.

(VAT Notice 714, paras 5.1–5.6).

13.7 Treatment in particular cases

(1) School uniforms

There is no specific relief for items of school uniform which are subject to the normal rules for children's clothes. But, by concession, if garments are supplied under a specific agreement with a school catering exclusively for pupils under 14 years of age, it is possible to apply the zero rate beyond the garment measurements in 13.5 above provided the garments are

- unique to that school by design, such as a prominent badge or piping in school colours, and
- held out for sale as being for that school only.

In particular HMRC allow zero-rating, irrespective of size, for

- short school trousers if sold exclusively for wear by primary or prep school children up to the age of 13;
- long socks with turn-down tops if they bear a mark identifying them to a primary or prep school; and
- school sweatshirts bearing a prominent identifying logo if they are sold exclusively to pupils of a primary or prep school who are under 12 years (and specifically not sold to staff, PTA members, etc).

Where a school also caters for pupils of 14 and over, the normal rules apply and obtaining a declaration that the relevant garment is intended for a pupil under the age of 14 is not sufficient for zero-rating to apply (*Smart Alec Ltd (VTD 17832) (TVC 12.19)*).

(VAT Notice 714, para 6.1; Internal Guidance V1–7, Chapter 14 para 9.2).

(2) **Youth organisations**

By concession, garments worn only by members of groups or organisations which cater exclusively for under-14 year olds qualify for zero-rating, irrespective of size, even though they may fit older persons. The concession relates only to garments intended for the children's wear and not to garments intended for sale to the general public (eg sweatshirts sold for fund-raising purposes). HMRC apply the following rules.

- Brownie T-shirts, sweatshirts (hooded and ordinary), polo shirts, leather belts, yellow neckerchiefs, and caps can be zero-rated, primarily because they bear a prominent logo identifying them to the organisation.
- Identifiable items of Beaver uniform can be zero-rated.
- Cub scout uniform cannot be zero-rated as it consists of similar items of uniform to Scouts.
- As very few Girl Guides remain in the organisation after the age of 14, by special concession sweatshirts (hooded and ordinary), T-shirts, polo shirts, and caps may be zero-rated because they bear a prominent logo. For other items of Girl Guide uniform, normal size criteria apply.
- For Scouts, there are no special rules and normal size criteria apply, as membership continues to 16 years and over.
- Girls Brigade soft forage hats can be zero-rated as they are clearly identifiable to an organisation whose membership is comprised of young children.
- Hats for cadets of the St John's Ambulance Brigade can be zero-rated as a special concession as they are clearly identifiable to members of the organisation. These may reach a maximum of 15 years, but are predominantly young children.

Other articles specifically designed for youth organisations can be zero-rated, irrespective of size provided they are designed exclusively for the organisation, worn only by under-14s, and clearly identifiable to the organisation.

(VAT Notice 714, para 6.1; Internal Guidance V1–7, paras 4.1.1, 9.2).

(3) **Cloth kits**

Packaged kits for making children's clothes can be zero-rated provided

- the clothes themselves would be zero-rated;
- the material is already cut to the pattern or the pattern is indelibly printed on the material; and
- it is clear from the labelling or other promotional material that the made-up garment is only suitable for young children.

(VAT Notice 714, para 7.1).

(4) **Multiple supplies**

Where an article consists of both zero-rated clothing and *incidental* standard-rated items at an inclusive price (eg a cowboy suit with a toy gun or a policeman's uniform with toy handcuffs), HMRC consider this a single supply of children's clothing and the whole price can be zero-rated.

Where the standard-rated element is not incidental (eg a baby's gift set comprising of a bib and feeding cup) there is a multiple supply which must be apportioned between the zero-rated and standard-rated elements. See 47.3 OUTPUT TAX.

(VAT Notice 714, para 8.1).

(5) **Hire or loan of children's clothing and footwear**

The hire or loan of any item of children's clothing or footwear is zero-rated if the item would itself be zero-rated. [*VATA 1994, Sch 8 Group 16 Note 5*]. This covers, for example, hire of bridesmaids' and page boys' outfits, fancy dress costumes, and nappy hire services where the nappies are collected for laundering and replaced with fresh ones.

The separate supply of ice-skates, roller skates, ten-pin bowling shoes, etc is also eligible for zero-rating in accordance with the size criteria for footwear in 13.5 above. But a single price for admission that also includes the loan of footwear is a multiple supply which must be apportioned between the zero-rated and standard-rated elements. See 47.3 OUTPUT TAX.

(6) **Supplies of services**

(*a*) *Cut, make and trim.* Making up young children's clothing from cloth owned by someone else can be zero-rated. Other processes may also be eligible for zero-rating if, after the work is finished, the processed article clearly becomes a child's garment which itself is normally zero-rated or the processed goods can only be incorporated in such an item. This is because such work is treated as a supply of services and zero-rated under *VATA 1994, s 30(2A)* as the application of a process to another person's goods which produces goods which are themselves zero-rated.

(*b*) *Alteration, repair, embroidery and similar services.* These services do not qualify for zero-rating as they are applied to goods that maintain their essential nature. For example, a blazer that has its sleeve length altered, its collar repaired, or a school badge embroidered on its pocket, is not sufficiently changed by that process to produce a new item. However, if the blazer were changed into a waistcoat by the process, the service would have produced a new item and, if this waistcoat meets the criteria for zero-rating, the process would also be zero-rated.

(VAT Notice 714, paras 9.1–9.3).

13.8 PROTECTIVE BOOTS AND HELMETS FOR INDUSTRIAL USE

The supply to a person for use otherwise than by employees of his of protective boots and helmets for industrial use is zero-rated. [*VATA 1994, Sch 8 Group 16 Item 2*]. In addition to outright sales, zero-rating also applies to a supply of services where the articles are hired or loaned or where they are put to private use provided that, in each case, the articles are for use otherwise than by the employees of the person to whom the services are supplied. [*VATA 1994, Sch 8 Group 16 Note 5; SI 2000/1517*].

The following conditions apply.

(*a*) The articles must be protective boots or helmets. The British Standards Institution (BSI) defines a boot as having a minimum leg height of 90mm measured vertically from the insole at the back. The European Standard gives the minimum height of the upper (measured vertically from the insole at the back) of 103mm for a size 36 (UK 3) and below, through to a minimum height of the upper of 121mm for a size 45 (UK 11) and above. (The British Standard specifications will eventually be withdrawn and the definition of a boot will then be based on the European specification. In the meantime, HMRC accept both Standard measurements.)

Protective shoes that fall outside these specifications are not eligible for zero-rating, even if they meet the remaining requirements.

(VAT Notice 701/23/02, para 2.2).

(*b*) The articles must be for industrial use. HMRC apply a strict normal day-to-day meaning to the words 'industrial use'. They do not see the phrase as covering, for example, jockey skullcaps or motorcycle boots. (VAT Notice 701/23/02, para 2.6; Internal Guidance V1–7, Chapter 29 para 2.8).

(*c*) The articles concerned must

- be manufactured to standards approved by the British Standards Institution and bear a mark indicating conformity with those standards; or
- be manufactured to standards which satisfy requirements imposed (whether under UK law or that of another EC country) to give effect to *EC Council Directive 89/686/EEC as amended* and bear any mark of conformity required to that effect.

[*VATA 1994, Sch 8 Group 16 Note 4; SI 2000/1517; SI 2001/732*].

Approved markings include the appropriate European Standard (EN) or British Standard (BS) numbers and the EC 'CE' mark (indicating conformity with the EC Directive) and/or the British Standard 'kitemark'. The EN for boots and helmets sourced in other EC countries may be prefixed by another country code such as 'NF' for a French manufactured product or 'DS' for one of Danish manufacture.

In some instances, particular boots and helmets may have been manufactured to a different specification to those laid down in the harmonised European Standards. These alternative specifications must satisfy the requirements of the Directive and be approved by a 'notified body', which in turn has been approved and appointed by the authorities of an EC country. These boots and helmets will still carry the 'CE' mark, but also the notified body number.

(VAT Notice 701/23/02, paras 2.3–2.5).

(*d*) The articles must not be supplied to a person for use by his employees. Supplies from a manufacturer to a wholesaler who in turn supplies them to a retailer, and supplies from an employer to an employee, can be zero-rated subject to the above conditions. But otherwise, before zero-rating a supply, the supplier should establish that the customer is not an employer purchasing the boots or helmets for use by employees by asking himself does

- the customer's trading style suggest the customer is an employer;
- the quantity ordered suggest a bulk purchase by an employer for use of employees; and
- the nature of the contract indicate a trade order, eg a number of pairs of boots paid for by one customer for delivery to individuals.

(VAT Notice 701/23/02, para 2.7).

Zero-rating covers accessories (eg visors and ear protectors) fitted as an integral part of a qualifying helmet but not accessories supplied on their own. (VAT Notice 701/23/02, para 2.8).

13.9 **PROTECTIVE HELMETS**

The supply of protective helmets for wear by a person driving or riding a motor bicycle or riding a pedal cycle is zero-rated provided the helmets are

- of a type that on 30 June 2000 was prescribed by regulations made under *Road Traffic Act 1988, s 17* (types of helmet recommended as affording protection to persons on or in motor cycles from injury in the event of accident), see the *Motor Cycles* (*Protective Helmets*) *Regulations 1988* (*SI 1988/1807*); or
- manufactured to a standard which satisfies requirements imposed (whether under UK law or the law of another EC country) to give effect to *EC Council Directive 89/686/EEC as amended* and bear any mark of conformity required to that effect.

In addition to outright sales, zero-rating also applies to a supply of services where the articles are hired or loaned or where they are put to private use.

[*VATA 1994, Sch 8 Group 16 Item 3, Notes 4A, 5; SI 2000/1517; SI 2001/732*].

Motor cycle helmets. To qualify for zero-rating, motor cycle helmets must comply with the appropriate British Standard (in which case it will be marked with a British Standard 'kitemark') or European Standard (in which case it will be marked with a UN 'E' mark).

Zero-rating covers accessories (eg visors, ear protectors or communication systems) fitted as an integral part of a qualifying helmet but not accessories supplied on their own.

(VAT Notice 701/23/02, paras 3.1–3.3).

Pedal cycle helmets. Approved markings include the appropriate European Standard (EN) number and the EC 'CE' mark (indicating conformity with the EC Directive). The EN for helmets sourced in other EC countries may be prefixed by another country code such as 'NF' for a French manufactured product or 'DS' for one of Danish manufacture.

Some cycle helmets may have been manufactured to a different specification to those laid down in the harmonised European Standards. These alternative specifications must satisfy the requirements of the Directive and be approved by a 'notified body', which in turn has been approved and appointed by the authorities of an EC country. These helmets will still carry the 'CE' mark, but also the notified body number.

Zero-rating covers accessories (eg visors or ear protectors) fitted as an integral part of a qualifying helmet but not accessories supplied on their own.

(VAT Notice 701/23/02, paras 4.1–4.5).

14 Clubs and Associations

Cross-references. See 9.6 BUSINESS ENTERTAINMENT for free entertainment of members; 11.9 CATERING for franchised catering in clubs; and 20.19 EDUCATION for the provision of youth club facilities.

De Voil Indirect Tax Service. See V2.112.

The contents of this chapter are as follows.

14.1 INTRODUCTION

Under *EC 6th Directive, Art 13A*, countries must exempt certain activities in the public interest. Those relating to clubs and associations are covered by *Art 13A*(*l*) (see 22.17(*l*) EUROPEAN COMMUNITY LEGISLATION). The provisions have been incorporated into UK legislation in two ways.

First, under *VATA 1994, Sch 9 Group 9*, if the organisation is a non-profit making trade union, professional or representative body, supplies to members referable to its aims and available without payment other than a membership subscription are exempt. Exemption also applies to such supplies made by a non-profit making body with objects which are in the public domain and are of a political, religious, patriotic, philosophical or philanthropic nature. [*VATA 1994, s 94*(*3*)*; FA 1999, s 20; SI 1999/2769*]. See 14.7 below.

Secondly, subject to the above, if a 'club, association or organisation' provides facilities or advantages to its members in return for a 'subscription or other consideration', it is deemed to be carrying on a business activity. [*VATA 1994, s 94*(*2*)(*a*)]. Such a body must therefore register for VAT (subject to the registration limit) and account for VAT on its subscription income (but see 14.2 below for apportionment of subscriptions).

Particular types of clubs and associations. The provisions of *VATA 1994, s 94*(*2*)(*a*) have been held to be applicable in *C & E Commrs v British Field Sports Society, CA [1998] STC 315 (TVC 13.10)* (campaigning on behalf of stag and deer hunting), *Eastbourne Town Radio Cars Association v C & E Commrs, HL [2001] STC 606 (TVC 60.31)* (association of taxi-drivers) and *Manor Forstal Residents Society Ltd (VTD 245) (TVC 13.1)* (association of local residents); and not applicable in *New Ash Green Village Association (VTD 245) (TVC 13.11)* (village development association), *Nottingham Fire Service Messing Club (VTD 348) (TVC 13.12)* (canteen at fire station) and *Friends of the Ironbridge Gorge Museum (VTD 5639) (TVC 13.14)* (fund-raising association for a museum).

14.2 SUBSCRIPTIONS

Single and multiple supplies. The same person may be supplied, at the same time, with a number of different goods or services or both. If the individual elements are all liable to VAT at the same rate, VAT can be calculated in the normal way but if they are not, it is necessary to decide whether a single or multiple supply is being made.

- In a single supply where one element of the supply is the principal element to which all the other elements are ancillary, integral or incidental, the whole transaction is treated as having the VAT liability of the principal element. See below, however, for a concession in the case of non-profit making bodies.
- In a multiple supply, each element is distinct and independent and takes its own VAT liability.

See 64.6 SUPPLY for more detailed coverage of single and multiple supplies.

Treatment of subscriptions for VAT purposes. Where members pay a subscription to obtain or gain entitlement to any 'substantive' benefits of membership, VAT due is calculated on the total amount of the subscription. '*Substantive benefits*' include

- magazines, periodicals or handbooks;
- priority booking rights;
- guaranteed seats;
- discounts on admission charges; and
- items with a resale value.

These benefits are considered to be substantive regardless of whether there is any cost to the organisation in supplying them and what that cost might be. Benefits that have a nominal value can be ignored (eg simple acknowledgements of support in the form of membership badges, flags or stickers, and listing of names in a programme or on a theatre seat or entrance).

The VAT liability of subscriptions depends on the liability of the membership benefits supplied in return. In most cases clubs supply a package of benefits so that the supply will have more than one element. If there is a multiple supply (see above) and the separate elements have different VAT liabilities, the subscription charge must be apportioned. The most common need for apportionment arises from the supply of zero-rated magazines, periodicals or handbooks supplied to members.

Subscriptions which are voluntary payments or donations. If the whole of the subscription is an entirely voluntary payment and secures nothing or only nominal benefits in return, it is all a donation and must be treated as being outside the scope of VAT.

Subscriptions which may include a voluntary payment or donation. It is only possible to treat part of a subscription as a voluntary payment or donation if the organisation is a charity or a body which has objects that are both in the public domain and of a philanthropic nature (see 14.7(*e*) below) and either

- all the substantive benefits (ie ignoring any nominal benefits) provided are available to non-members at no charge or more cheaply than the subscription; or
- some or all of the substantive benefits are exclusive to members and the organisation can demonstrate that the amount paid is higher than the amount that the subscriber would normally have to pay for similar goods or services.

If these requirements are met, see below for how to apportion the subscription.

Exempt subscriptions. The supply of benefits to members by trade unions and political, religious, patriotic, philosophical, philanthropic or civic bodies may qualify for exemption. See 14.8 below. See also 57.9 RECREATION AND SPORT for certain membership subscriptions of non-profit making bodies providing sport and physical education services.

Additional joining fees. Any additional joining fee of a *general* nature should be treated in the same way as a subscription, applying the same apportionment, if any. Where an additional fee is charged for obtaining a *particular* facility, VAT must be accounted for based on the liability of the particular service or goods provided.

Life membership fees. These must be treated in the same way as annual subscriptions, unless life members are supplied with additional benefits not available to ordinary members.

Charges for being placed on a waiting list for membership. Such a fee is exempt if it is

- deducted from the new member's first subscription or entrance fee and the subscription or fee itself will qualify for exemption; and
- refundable in the event that the candidate fails to become a member for any reason, including voluntary withdrawal.

In all other circumstances, the fee is consideration for the right to be on the waiting list and is standard-rated.

Payment by instalments. Where members can pay annual subscriptions by instalments over the subscription period and the total instalments exceed the single annual payment subscription, the additional amount is exempt from VAT as interest on a grant of credit.

Apportionment of subscriptions. If the subscription is consideration for a multiple supply (see above) and the separate elements have different liabilities, the subscription must be apportioned.

In most cases there is one principal benefit or reason for joining. In these circumstances, the subscription is consideration for a single supply (see above) and its liability is determined by the liability of the main benefit. No apportionment can normally be made. However, by concession, *non-profit making bodies* who charge their members a subscription that entitles them to a package of benefits, may apportion the subscription between the various elements as if there had been a multiple supply, even if under the general rules there is a single supply. The concession does not work in reverse, ie non-profit making bodies cannot treat their multiple supplies as single supplies. It is up to the organisation to decided whether it wishes to take advantage of the concession. If it does (eg because of zero-rated printed matter), it must apportion all types and elements of subscriptions – it cannot 'pick and choose'.

The fact that subscriptions are used to purchase zero-rated or exempt supplies from a third party will not, in itself, entitle an organisation to apportion the value of subscriptions.

How to apportion. There are no specific rules for making an apportionment. See 47.3 OUTPUT TAX for general guidance on apportionment. HMRC generally accept apportionment of the total subscription income to reflect the relative cost of providing the different supplies to members. The calculations for the current financial year can be based on the accounts for the previous financial year, provided this method is adopted consistently. Calculations must be kept for inspection by HMRC. If the organisation wishes to use any other method of apportionment, it should write to HMRC, setting out the proposed method and supporting it with copies of the annual accounts and other relevant documents.

Where a subscription includes a donation (see above), if the organisation calculates the value of any standard-rated, zero-rated and exempt supplies, it can treat the balance of the subscription as a donation and outside the scope of VAT. It should calculate the value of the substantive benefits (ie ignoring nominal benefits), using the price at which they are available to non-members or the amount the subscriber would normally have to pay for similar goods or services. The difference between the amount of the subscription and the total value of the benefits is the donation.

Subscriptions from overseas members. Overseas subscriptions normally follow the same VAT liability as subscriptions paid by UK members but are treated differently where overseas members

- receive different benefits from UK members in return for their subscription to a UK club; or
- receive the same benefits as UK members, but the VAT rules require a different treatment.

In these circumstances, the apportionment of the overseas subscription must be carried out separately.

The different treatment of benefits for overseas members is as follows.

- *Services*. In certain situations, some supplies of services are treated as made where the customer belongs, and therefore fall outside the scope of UK VAT. See 64.26 SUPPLY.
- *Goods sent to members outside the EC* are zero-rated as exports.
- *Goods sent to VAT-registered members in other EC countries for use in their business* are zero-rated subject to certain conditions.
- *Goods sent to non VAT-registered members in other EC countries*. VAT is due on the goods in the UK until the value of such supplies exceeds a threshold set by the EC country to which the goods are sent. Once this threshold is exceeded, VAT is due in that EC country and the organisation may need to register for VAT there to fulfil its obligations. See 23.10 EUROPEAN COMMUNITY: SINGLE MARKET.

(VAT Notice 701/5/02, paras 4.2–4.6, 5.1–5.13; VAT Notice 48, ESC 3.35).

Payment by deed of covenant. Where a member pays a subscription under a deed of covenant (to allow the club or association to reclaim a sum of money that is related to the basic rate of income tax from the Inland Revenue)

- if the member still pays the same amount in money as a non-covenanting member, the value of the supply is the monetary charge only (because the payer gains no advantage by completing the covenant); and
- if the member pays less in money than a non-covenanting subscriber, the covenant is regarded as non-monetary consideration given in return for the reduction in charge. The value of this non-monetary consideration is equal to the amount by which the subscription charge has been reduced. The full value of the subscription for VAT purposes is therefore the amount actually paid plus the reduction in charge.

(Internal Guidance V1–12, para 7.4.14).

14.3 REGISTRATION

Any club or association with business activities and a turnover from standard-rated, reduced-rated and zero-rated supplies (including subscriptions) above the current registration limits must register for VAT and account for VAT on its taxable supplies. Business activities include

- providing benefits to members in return for membership subscriptions (for members' racing clubs where subscriptions finance the purchase of racehorses, see 63.33 SPECIAL SCHEMES);
- providing benefits to members in return for a separate charge;
- making supplies to non-members for a charge;
- admission to any premises for a charge; and
- providing catering, social and other facilities to non-members in return for a charge.

(VAT Notice 701/5/02, paras 2.1, 2.2).

For the requirements relating to registration see 59 REGISTRATION. Even if a club, etc is not required to register under the general requirements based on taxable supplies in the UK, it may be liable to register for VAT where it makes certain acquisitions of goods from other EC countries in excess of an annual threshold. See 59.18 REGISTRATION.

A club, etc may be registered in the name of that club and in determining whether goods and services are supplied to or by it, or whether goods are acquired by it from another EC country, no account is taken of any change in its members. HMRC are empowered to make provisions to determine what persons are responsible for carrying out the requirements of the VAT legislation where a club, etc is managed by its members or a committee. Under these powers HMRC have regulated that the necessary requirements are the joint and several responsibility of

- every member holding office as president, chairman, treasurer, secretary or any similar office; or in default of any thereof,
- every member holding office as a member of a committee; or in default of any thereof,
- every member.

[*VATA 1994, s 46(2)(3); SI 1995/2518, Reg 8*].

14.4 Clubs in sections and multi-tiered bodies

There are no set rules for determining whether a section or branch has its own separate legal status, independent of its parent organisation, or whether that section or branch should register separately for VAT purposes. Unless the section or branch concerned can demonstrate that it has both constitutional and financial independence from its parent organisation, its supplies should be included with those of the parent organisation when accounting for VAT.

(VAT Notice 701/5/02, para 2.4).

14.5 COMMON TRANSACTIONS OTHER THAN SUBSCRIPTIONS

The following is a list of some of the more common transactions made by clubs and associations.

(1) **Admission charges**

Admission charges are standard-rated in most cases but admission charges to

- museums, galleries, art exhibitions and zoos; and

- theatrical, musical and choreographic performances of a cultural nature

supplied by public authorities and by certain other eligible bodies may qualify for exemption.

See 57.6 RECREATION AND SPORT.

(2) **Bar sales, catering and teas**

Food and drink is always standard-rated if it is supplied in the course of catering. This includes hot take-away food and food and drink supplied for consumption on the premises. See 11 CATERING. The argument that there is no 'supply' because, in law, drinks obtained by members are not sold to them has been dismissed. (*Carlton Lodge Club v C & E Commrs, QB [1974] STC 507 (TVC 13.29)*).

(3) **Bingo**

The VAT treatment of bingo depends on whether cash bingo or prize bingo is played and whether the premises are licensed or registered under Part II of the Gaming Act. See 57.2 RECREATION AND SPORT. Admission charges are standard-rated with an exception for certain one-off fund-raising events (see below).

(4) **Competition entry fees**

Competition entry fees are normally standard-rated but may be exempt in the case of certain competitions in sport or physical recreation (see 57.5 RECREATION AND SPORT).

(5) **Discos, dances, socials and similar events**

Admission charges are standard-rated (but see below for certain one-off fund-raising events).

VAT must be accounted for on the gross amount of taxable supplies (eg admission, catering, etc) and not on the net amounts after band, floor shows, etc expenses are paid.

(6) **Fixture cards**

Fixture cards are standard-rated if any portion for completion occupies more than 25% of total area, otherwise they are generally zero-rated. See also 54.5 PRINTED MATTER, ETC.

(7) **Fund-raising events**

Admission charges to qualifying events held by charities for charitable purposes and by non-profit making qualifying bodies exclusively for their own benefit may be exempt. See 12.10 CHARITIES.

(8) **Gaming and amusement machines**

All receipts from gaming and amusement machines are standard-rated. See 57.3 RECREATION AND SPORT.

(9) **Gaming club subscriptions**

Subscriptions to gaming, bingo, bridge, etc clubs, in return for which members have the right to place bets or play games of chance for no further payment, are standard-rated. See 57.1 RECREATION AND SPORT.

(10) **Hire of rooms, halls and facilities**

The hire of a room or a hall is exempt from VAT provided that

- the person to whom the room or hall is hired has exclusive occupation of it during the period of hire;
- the room or hall is not designed or equipped for sport or physical recreation, which excludes such places as gyms, sports halls; and
- the organisation has not opted to tax the building in which the room or hall is situated.

Exemption includes

- facilities such as a kitchen or bar area within the room or next to it; and
- those fixtures and fittings that form a part of the hire (eg lighting and sound equipment if the room is used as a discotheque).

(11) **Insurance supplied with goods or other services**

Depending on the circumstances, where a charge is made for insurance, that charge could be exempt where it is the member's own risk which is insured (rather than the club's risk). See 37.17 INSURANCE.

(12) **Jumble sales**

Unless they qualify as fund-raising events (see above)

- any charge for admission is standard-rated; and
- the goods sold are liable to VAT at the rate applicable to such goods.

(13) **Levies**

These are normally demanded from existing members when a body requires additional funds. Where a levy is raised and members' benefits remain unaltered, the levy is liable to VAT as if it was an additional subscription. However, if the levy entitles the member to different benefits, VAT must be accounted for, where appropriate, based on the liability of those benefits.

(14) **Lotteries**

Income from lotteries (including raffles, totes, instant bingo tickets, etc) is exempt (see 57.4 RECREATION AND SPORT).

(15) **Loans from members**

Clubs often raise capital to finance the renewal or development of facilities by means of loans from members.

Compulsory interest-free loans. VAT must be accounted for on the notional interest on the loans. This is determined by establishing the amount of interest free loans and calculating the notional interest using the London Clearing Bank's Base Lending Rate in force either on the first day of the month in which the subscriptions are due to be paid or the first day of the club's financial year if more convenient. VAT liability is calculated by applying the same VAT liability to the notional interest as the subscription and using the appropriate VAT fraction to calculate the VAT due.

Obtaining loans at a significantly lower interest rate than from the bank. If the interest rate charged to members is significantly lower than the bank would have charged, VAT liability is determined by

- calculating the notional interest as for compulsory interest-free loans above;
- deducting the amount of interest actually paid, including any on returned loans, from the notional interest; and
- applying the same VAT liability to the remainder as applies to the subscriptions and using the appropriate VAT fraction to calculate the VAT due.

Additional loan repayments to members who are leaving. Members are often required to lend a specified sum which is only repaid on cessation of membership. It is often also a requirement that the member will find a new member to take over the loan or to make an equivalent loan. On cessation the ex-member receives a sum, frequently based on the rate of inflation. VAT liability is determined by

- calculating the notional interest as for compulsory interest-free loans above;
- deducting the amount of interest actually paid (if any);
- deducting the additional payment; and
- applying the same VAT liability to the remainder as applies to the subscriptions and using the appropriate VAT fraction to calculate the VAT due.

Reducing or waiving a member's subscription in return for an interest-free loan or purchase of a share or debenture. Where this is done, VAT must be accounted for, at the time the subscriptions are due, on the amount of subscription payable by a member who has not made any such payment.

Compulsory loans where members decide unconditionally to waive entitlement to repayment. The loan can be regarded as having been converted into an outside the scope donation and the club will no longer be required to account for VAT from the date of waiver on the notional interest.

See also *Exeter Golf and Country Club Ltd v C & E Commrs, CA [1981] STC 211 (TVC 13.32)* and *Dyrham Park Country Club Ltd (VTD 700)(TVC 13.31).*

(16) **Payphone charges**

See 47.8(16) OUTPUT TAX.

(17) **Prizes**

Special rules apply to prizes in betting, gaming and lotteries. See 57.1–57.4 RECREATION AND SPORT. Otherwise prizes awarded to competitors in sports and games competitions are always treated in the same way, regardless of whether the entry fees for the competition are exempt or taxable.

- Where the prize is goods, VAT must be accounted for based on the cost of the goods unless the cost of the individual prize to the organisation was £50 or less (excluding VAT).

- Where the prize is in the form of services (eg a holiday), if input tax has been claimed on the purchase of services given away as prizes, an equal sum of output tax is due at the time the prize is awarded. If no input tax is incurred no output tax is due.
- Cash prizes are outside the scope of VAT. However, it is important to distinguish between prize money and payments made by sponsors to event organisers which are called prize money but are, in fact, payments for taxable supplies.
- A trophy which remains the property of the competition organiser is outside the scope of VAT.

For prize money from horseracing see 63.31 SPECIAL SCHEMES.

(18) **Shares and debentures**

These are used by clubs to raise extra finance from members or prospective members. It is necessary to consider:

- Whether or not there is a single supply (and, if so, whether it is of an exempt security or standard-rated subscriptions).
- If there is a mixed supply, can either element be disregarded on minimal grounds.
- Whether the standard-rated benefits are only being granted as an inducement to persuade people to acquire the exempt supply. See *Hinckley Golf Club Ltd (VTD 9527) (TVC 13.15)* where the tribunal held that the offer of free membership to certain shareholders was simply an inducement to invest and the only supply to those shareholders was an exempt supply of shares in consideration for the purchase price of those shares. See also *Rugby Football Union (VTD 18075) (TVC 26.42)* where the whole of the amount paid by the purchasers of 75-year non-interest-bearing debentures was held to relate to the exempt supply of the debentures and no part to the right given to them to purchase tickets for rugby matches at Twickenham for ten years.

Where any part of the consideration for a share or debenture is to be treated as an additional payment for the advantages of membership, it should be treated as a levy or, for non-monetary consideration, as an interest-free loan (see above).

Shares and debentures with a right to nominate a member. Clubs sometimes sell the right to nominate a person to membership of the club with a share, bond or debenture. (Normally it will be the purchaser of the security that is expected to nominate himself for membership.) In those cases where the purchase price represents monetary consideration for the exempt security and a standard-rated 'nomination right', it is necessary to apportion the overall value between the exempt and standard-rated elements.

- Where security holders pay a lower membership subscription than non-shareholders or do not have to pay a joining fee like the latter, this price differential may be taken as representing the part of the purchase price attributable to the standard-rated right.
- In other cases where there is no joining fee, it is difficult to apply one of the normal apportionment methods based on cost or market value (see 47.3 OUTPUT TAX) because the nomination rights have negligible costs and no recognised market value. HMRC have, in some cases, calculated

the value for the right by reference to a 'notional joining fee' as follows (although this general formula may have to be adapted according to the facts of the individual case).

(1) Calculate a joining fee by considering what a joining fee for a similar club would be and adapting this for any special factors (eg increasing it for any facility offered that is unique to this club and decreasing it where something is not offered that other similar clubs supply).

(2) Calculate a 'multiplier'. This can be based upon the potential 'joinings' attached to the nomination right. The first holder of the security can be treated as 1 'joining' and there will be at least 1 subsequent further 'joining' upon transfer of the security to his immediate purchaser. If the first holder is entitled to nominate a relative as an associate or social member with less benefits than full members, a fractional 'joining' of, say 0.5, should then be added on. A further fractional 'joining' may also be added to cover later holders of the right after the first holder and his immediate purchaser, say 0.25. This will give a total multiplier (in this example 2.75).

(3) Multiply the adapted joining fee in (1) by the 'multiplier' in (2). This gives the element of the total purchase price attributable to the 'nomination right'.

(4) The VAT liability is found by multiplying the figure in (3) above by the VAT fraction.

(19) **Sponsorship rights**

Output tax is due not only on the money received from the sponsor but also on any payments made by the sponsor to third parties. This includes expenses of staging a competition or event and the value of any prizes given under the terms of the sponsorship agreement. See 57.18 RECREATION AND SPORT.

(20) **Sport and physical recreation facilities**

Use of such facilities (including billiards, pool and snooker, tennis courts, bowling greens, etc) are normally exempt when made by an eligible body and standard-rated in other cases. Where a grant of facilities for playing any sport or participation in any physical recreation amounts to a grant of land or property, it may qualify for exemption under the '24 hour' rule or the 'series of lets' provisions. See 57.7–57.13 RECREATION AND SPORT.

When payments are linked to the operation of lighting eg squash courts or snooker tables, the full amount payable by players is standard-rated as the charge is for the right to use the facilities and does not relate to the supply of electricity. See *St Anne's-on-Sea Lawn Tennis Club Ltd (VTD 434) (TVC 28.4)*.

(21) **Swipe cards, vouchers and other types of payment credits**

If an organisation arranges for its members to maintain credit balances in order to make payment for goods and services (eg when using the bar facilities), it must consider the following points to determine when it must account for VAT.

(*a*) Where a member makes a payment that creates or contributes to a credit balance, (whether as a compulsory or voluntary levy) on either

- the issue, renewal or topping up of a card; or

- the purchase of vouchers

the organisation need not account for VAT until the credit is used to make taxable purchases, even if the payment is not refundable.

The payment must not be treated as part of the subscription for VAT purposes.

(*b*) Where an unused credit balance is repayable to the member, the credit and refund have no VAT consequences.

(*c*) Where unused balances or unredeemed vouchers revert to the organisation, it must account for VAT at the time of reversion as if they were part of the member's subscription.

(22) **Tours organised by clubs, etc**

Where a club buys hotel accommodation and travel, for example, from a third party, and sells them on as principal, the club must use the TOUR OPERATORS' MARGIN SCHEME (66).

(VAT Notice 701/5/02, paras 6.1–6.7, 7.1, 8, 9.1–9.4, 10.1–10.3; Internal Guidance V1–12, para 7.4.2).

14.6 NON-BUSINESS ACTIVITIES

A club or association may have non-business activities. These are mainly activities for which no payment is required or, where there is a payment, no benefit is provided in return. Examples include

- free admission to premises for non-members;
- spreading political beliefs or lobbying for a public or charitable good cause (but not lobbying on behalf of members which is a business activity);
- providing free literature to non-members; and
- the receipt of freely given donations, where no benefit is supplied in return (see 14.2 above for more information on subscriptions and donations).

See 8 BUSINESS generally for what constitutes a business for VAT purposes.

Any VAT incurred on goods or services used wholly for the purpose of a non-business activity is not input tax and cannot be reclaimed.

If goods or services are purchased partly for business and partly for non-business purposes, the VAT incurred must be apportioned to reflect the amount attributable to business activities. Only this amount can be reclaimed. Alternatively, in the case of goods (but not services) purchased partly for business and partly for non-business purposes, the full amount of tax can be reclaimed as input tax provided output tax is accounted for on the non-business use in each VAT period. See 35.7 INPUT TAX for fuller details.

(VAT Notice 701/5/02, paras 2.3, 3.2).

14.7 TRADE UNIONS, PROFESSIONAL AND OTHER PUBLIC INTEREST BODIES

Subscriptions. The provision of facilities and advantages to members of clubs, associations and other organisations is normally standard-rated (see 14.1 above) but their provision by certain professional, learned or representational associations can be exempt. See 22.17(*l*) and (*o*) EUROPEAN COMMUNITY LEGISLATION for the provisions of the *EC 6th Directive*.

The eligible organisations are those 'non-profit making' bodies falling into one of the following categories.

(*a*) **Trade unions and other organisations** whose main objectives are to negotiate the terms and conditions of employment of their members.

'*Trade union*' is an organisation (whether permanent or temporary) which consists wholly or mainly of

- workers of one or more descriptions; or
- constituent or affiliated organisations; or
- representatives of such constituent or affiliated organisations. The principal purposes of the organisation must include the regulation of relations between workers and employers or employers' associations.

[*VATA 1994, Sch 9 Group 9 Item 1*(*a*); *Trade Union and Labour* (*Consolidation*) *Act 1992, s 1*].

EC 6th Directive, Art 13(*A*)(*l*) (in English translation) refers to 'organisations with aims of a ... trade-union ... nature'. The CJEC has held this to mean 'an organisation whose main aim is to defend the collective interests of its members—whether they are workers, employers, independent professionals or traders carrying on a particular economic activity—and to represent them vis-à-vis the appropriate third parties, including the public authorities' provided those objects were put into practice. (*Institute of the Motor Industry v C & E Commrs, CJEC [1998] STC 1219 (TVC 21.211)*).

(*b*) **Professional associations,** membership of which are 'wholly or mainly' restricted to individuals who have or are seeking a qualification appropriate to the practice of the profession concerned. [*VATA 1994, Sch 9 Group 9 Item 1*(*b*)].

Membership of the association should be obligatory, or at least customary, for those pursuing a career in that profession.

'*Wholly or mainly*' is regarded as 75% or more.

The qualifications held or sought must relate to what is a recognised profession. They should be obligatory or customary to enable the profession to be undertaken and should be awarded by the association of which the holder is a member.

'Profession' is not defined but HMRC regard it as restricted to those occupations which would be generally understood to be professions. Indications which point towards this are

- the status of the occupation and those engaged in it;
- whether or not persons within the occupation require a qualification;
- whether the persons within the occupation are governed by a code of conduct;
- a distinctive and broad base of knowledge from which a person may subsequently diversify into more specialised areas;
- the association's aims and objectives; and

- the actual activities carried out by it.

However, these are not fixed criteria and some occupations which are not currently regarded as professions may acquire that status in the future.

(VAT Notice 701/5/02, paras 11.6, 11.8).

Bookmaking (*The Bookmakers' Protection Association (Southern Area) Ltd (VTD 849) (TVC 62.9)*), driving a taxi-cab (*City Cabs (Edinburgh) Ltd (VTD 928) (TVC 60.10)*) and the practice of reflexology (*The Association of Reflexologists (VTD 13078) (TVC 62.22)*) have been held not to be professions but the teaching of dance has been so held (*Allied Dancing Association Ltd (VTD 10777) (TVC 62.1)*). See also *Institute of Leisure and Amenity Management v C & E Commrs, QB [1988] STC 602 (TVC 62.14)*. For a fuller list of associations which have been held to fall within or, as the case may be, outside these provisions, see the chapter *Trade Unions, Professional and Public Interest Bodies* in Tolley's VAT Cases.

(*c*) **Learned societies,** ie any association, the 'primary purpose' of which is the advancement of a particular 'branch of knowledge' or the fostering of professional expertise, connected with the past or present professions or employments of its members. Membership must be restricted 'wholly or mainly' to individuals whose present or previous professions or employments are directly connected with the purposes of the association. [*VATA 1994, Sch 9 Group 9 Item 1*(*c*)].

'*Primary purpose*'. An association can have only one primary purpose (although it does not have to be the sole purpose) which should be clear from

- the objects and objectives set out in the memorandum and articles of association or constitution;
- the powers and actual activities of the association;
- what the association itself and the members consider its primary purpose to be.

The '*branch of knowledge*' must be a recognised branch of science or the arts and should therefore be more academic than practical in content. Normally it would be included in a degree course or equivalent. Knowledge relating to the confined area of a specific job does not constitute a branch of knowledge.

See (*b*) above for a consideration of 'profession'. Professional expertise is construed accordingly.

'*Wholly or mainly*' is regarded as 75% or more.

(VAT Notice 701/5/02, paras 11.11–11.14).

See *Royal Photographic Society (VTD 647) (TVC 62.8)* (where lack of the restriction on membership disqualified the Society from exemption) and *Institute of Leisure and Amenity Management v C & E Commrs, QB [1988] STC 602 (TVC 62.14)*.

(*d*) **Representational trade associations,** ie any association, the 'primary purpose' of which is to make representations to the Government on legislation and other public matters which affect the business or professional interests of its members. Membership must be restricted 'wholly or mainly' to individuals or corporate bodies whose business or professional interests are directly connected with its aims. [*VATA 1994, Sch 9 Group 9 Item 1*(*d*)].

See (*c*) above for the primary purpose test. The representations should be to the UK government.

'*Wholly or mainly*' is regarded as 75% or more.

(VAT Notice 701/5/02, para 11.15).

(*e*) **Bodies of a political, religious, patriotic, philosophical, philanthropic or civic nature which have objects in the public domain.** [*VATA 1994, Sch 9 Group 9 Item 1(e); FA 1999, s 20; SI 1999/2834*]. These bodies have objects which are directed outside the particular organisation and beyond the members themselves to the general community. Bodies which are not registered charities may qualify. Major political or religious bodies will also often satisfy this requirement because the public will have a general interest in their activities.

There are no legal definitions of the various bodies included but HMRC suggest that the following describes their everyday meaning.

- A political body is one that campaigns for or against legislative and constitutional changes or campaigns in local and central government elections.
- A religious body includes all denominations, creeds, old and new, that command a following.
- A patriotic body does good work for the benefit of a nation state or for those who have served their country and their dependants.
- A philosophical body is one whose primary purpose is the advancement of a particular way of thinking but which is not of a political or religious nature. It is very similar to a learned society as described in (*c*) above in that they are both of an academic nature.
- A philanthropic body does good work for the direct benefit of the general community or a particular section of the community or is designed to promote the wellbeing of mankind.
- A civic body is one which has objects which promote rights and duties of citizens in matters of public interest and public affairs, and whose objects do not solely or mainly benefit its members.

(VAT Notice 701/5/02, paras 12.1, 12.2).

See also *The English-Speaking Union of the Commonwealth (VTD 1023) (TVC 13.5)*.

(*f*) An organisation or association, the membership of which consists wholly or mainly of constituent or affiliated associations which as individual associations would be within (*a*) to (*d*) above. [*VATA 1994, Sch 9 Group 9 Note (3)*].

'*Non-profit making*'. HMRC consider, when judging whether an organisation is non-profit making, the objects for which an organisation has been established, as distinct from the financial policy being pursued. Although the organisation may generate income surpluses from various activities, they will not refuse recognition as a non-profit making organisation simply because these surpluses subsidise other activities. If a body has a constitution or articles of association that bars it from distributing surpluses of income over expenditure to its members, shareholders or any other party, other than in the event of a liquidation or cessation of activities, HMRC normally accept it as non-profit making for the purposes of this exemption. However, the existence of any provision barring distribution will not necessarily be the sole factor in determining whether an organisation is non-profit making. (VAT Notice 701/5/02, para 11.3).

Fund-raising events. The supply of goods and services by a non-profit making body within (*a*)–(*f*) above in connection with an event whose primary purpose is the raising of money and which is promoted as such is exempt from VAT where

- the event is organised exclusively for its own benefit; or
- the event is organised, jointly by one or more charities and the non-profit making body, exclusively for charitable purposes or that body's own benefit or a combination of those purposes.

See 12.10 CHARITIES for full details.

De Voil Indirect Tax Service. See V4.156.

14.8 Exempt supplies

Supplies of services, and related goods, by a non profit-making body within 14.7(*a*)-(*f*) above to its members are exempt provided

- they are made available without payment (other than a membership subscription); and
- they are referable only to the aims of the organisation.

[*VATA 1994, Sch 9 Group 9 Item 1*].

Exemption does not apply to

(*a*) supplies that do not relate to the body's aims as set out in its rules, articles of association, constitution, etc. (although see 14.9 below for provision of hospitality to members);

(*b*) the supply of any right of admission to any premises, event or performance (eg for a conference) for which non-members have to pay [*VATA 1994, Sch 9 Group 9 Note (1)*];

(*c*) any supplies which are not provided automatically as part of the membership benefits and for which an additional sum is charged; and

(*d*) supplies to non-members.

Supplies within (*a*)–(*d*) above are taxable unless exempt under any other provision. These might include training under *VATA 1994, Sch 9 Group 6* (see 20.7 EDUCATION), fund-raising events organised by charities and non-profit making bodies under *VATA 1994, 9 Sch Group 12* (see 12.10 CHARITIES) and sporting events under *VATA 1994, Sch 9 Group 10* (see 57.9 RECREATION AND SPORT).

Where any clearly identifiable zero-rated benefits (such as a year book) are provided in return for members' subscriptions, such supplies can be treated as zero-rated and any related input tax can be recovered, subject to the normal rules.

Value of exempt supply. The value of the exempt supply is normally the full amount of the subscriptions. Where, however, subscriptions also cover taxable supplies (including zero-rated supplies) the subscriptions must be apportioned. See 14.2 above.

Discounted admission charges and exclusive right of attendance. Exemption does not cover any supplies that are not automatically supplied in return for the subscription and for which there is an additional charge (see above). Where events are held for which an additional charge is made to members for admission:

- If the event is intended to be self-financing and not subsidised by subscription income, no element of the subscription can be for the right of admission. In which case an element of the subscription may either be for the right to attend the event (if for members only) or for the right to a discount (where members pay less than non-members). As these rights are 'available without payment other than the membership subscription' they qualify for exemption, as long as all the other criteria are met.
- If the event is subsidised by subscriptions, there is an element of the subscription that can be linked to the right of admission. As admission is not gained without further payment, it fails to qualify for the exemption.

Example

A trade union which satisfies all the other criteria for exemption under *VATA 1994, Sch 9 Group 9* organises a Christmas meal and dance and an annual conference.

Christmas meal and dance

(1) *Admission confined to members who pay no charge to attend.* Part of the subscription represents consideration for the right of admission to the event. This supply is not 'referable' to the union's aims and an appropriate element of the subscription should be standard-rated.

(2) *Admission confined to members, who may each bring a guest. Neither the members nor their guests pay any charges to attend.* Part of the subscription represents consideration for the right of admission to the event. There is also an additional entitlement to bring a guest. The supply is not 'referable' to the union's aims. The presence of guests does not prevent this being a supply to the members because the members have specifically been given the right to bring guests and the event was not open to non-members. An appropriate element of the subscription should be standard-rated.

(3) *Admission is available to members and non-members. Non-members pay for admission but members do not.* The free admission for members is a benefit supplied in return for their subscription but is excluded from exemption by (*b*) above. Also it is not a benefit which is 'referable' to the union's aims, but it is one for which the only payment is an appropriate part of the subscription. An appropriate element of the subscription should be standard-rated. Non-member admission payments are also standard-rated.

(4) *Admission is available to members and non-members. Members are admitted for half the charge to non-members.* If the event is intended to be self-financing without any subsidy from members' subscriptions, the benefit the members receive for their subscription is the right to a discount. However, if the subscriptions do go towards the cost of the event, an element is for part payment of admission. In either case, the benefit is not 'referable' to the union's aims, and so an appropriate element of the subscription should be standard-rated. The additional admission payments received from members and non-members are also standard-rated.

(5) *Members and non-members pay the same charge for admission.* There is no benefit to the members, therefore the admission aspect can be ignored when any apportionment of the subscription is made. Admission payments received from the members and non-members are standard-rated.

Annual conference

(1) *Admission is confined to members, who pay no charge to attend.* Part of the subscription represents the consideration for the supply of admission. It is 'referable' to the union's aims and there is no charge above the relevant subscription element. An appropriate element of the subscription can be treated as exempt.

(2) *Admission is confined to members, who may bring a guest, and selected 'honorary invitees'. In practice, members seldom bring guests. No admission charge is made to members, guests or 'honoraries'.* The presence of a few selected non-members does not prevent this being a supply to the members. The supply is 'referable' to the union's aims, there is no charge other than the subscription and there is no admission payment from non-members. An appropriate element of the subscription can be treated as exempt.

(3) *Admission is confined to members but they have to pay a separate charge to attend.* Members receive a benefit in return for their subscriptions in that non-members cannot attend the conference. The conference is 'referable' to the union's aims and there are no non-members being charged for admittance. If the event is self-financing, the element of the subscription that relates to the event is exempt. However, where the separate charge is subsidised by subscriptions, the element of the subscription acts as a prepayment for admission and fails to satisfy the criterion that there should be no charge in addition to the subscription. The admission charges paid by members to attend the conference are standard-rated.

(4) *Admission is free to members, but non-members have to pay an admission charge.* The free admission for members is a benefit supplied in return for the subscription. The conference is 'referable' to the union's aims but there is an admission charge to non-members rendered taxable under (*b*) above. The charges received from non-members and an appropriate element of the subscription are standard-rated.

(5) *There is a charge for non-members and a lower one for members.* If the event is self-financing then the benefit supplied in return for the subscription is the right to a discount. The event is 'referable' to the union's aims, and there is no additional charge to the members for this particular right enabling an appropriate element of the subscription to be exempt. However, if the members' charge for admission is subsidised by subscriptions, then the appropriate element of the subscription is part payment for admission. The admission is not available without further payment and so exemption does not apply. Charges made to members and non-members are standard-rated.

(VAT Notice 701/5/02, paras 13.1–13.3; Internal Guidance V1–7, Chapter 24 para 2.3).

14.9 **Other supplies**

Registration fees. In certain professions, persons cannot practice unless they are registered with a statutory body and have paid fees which are prescribed by law. Such registration fees are normally outside the scope of VAT because, in carrying out these statutory functions, the organisation is not supplying a service in the course of its business. Where, however, there is no such statutory requirement, the liability is as follows.

- *Registration in return for a subscription payment*. Where no additional fee is charged and the member is automatically registered on payment of the subscription, the service of registration is standard-rated unless referable to the aims of the association in which case it qualifies for exemption under 14.8 above.
- *Registration for a separate fee*. As the registration is in return for a payment 'other than a membership subscription' it cannot qualify for exemption under 14.8 above and is standard-rated.

If the registration is accompanied by other clearly identifiable supplies of goods or services, the fee must be apportioned accordingly.

Collection charges for union subscriptions. Charges raised by employers for deducting union subscriptions from employees' pay are exempt under *VATA 1994, Sch 9 Group 5*. See 27.9(5) FINANCIAL SERVICES.

Provision of hospitality. Where meals, hotel accommodation, etc. are provided to members without charge, then unless directly connected with the organisation's aims (eg at the annual conference), the supply is standard-rated and the subscription must be apportioned. Such hospitality is not business entertainment (because the membership in general is paying for it in the subscription) and input tax incurred can therefore be deducted, subject to the normal rules. The business entertaining provisions do apply to free hospitality to non-members and input tax cannot be deducted.

The provision of hospitality for a charge to members or non-members is standard-rated.

(VAT Notice 701/5/02, paras 13.5–13.7).

15 Customs: Administration

The contents of this chapter are as follows.

15.1 RESPONSIBILITY FOR VAT

The collection and management of VAT is the responsibility of the Commissioners for Her Majesty's Revenue and Customs ('HMRC') (previously the Commissioners of Customs and Excise). [*VATA 1994, s 96(1), Sch 11 para 1; CRCA 2005, Sch 4 para 56*].

The Central Unit at Alexander House, 21 Victoria Avenue, Southend-on-Sea SS99 1AA (Tel: 01702 348944; Fax: 01702 366687) keeps registration records, despatches return forms and reminders, receives completed forms and VAT payments, and repays VAT.

VAT offices deal with the administration of VAT in their area but not the issue of return forms or the receipt of VAT which is dealt with by VAT Central Unit. All VAT offices are linked to the central VAT computer.

15.2 CUSTOMS CHARTER

The Customs Charter explains the standards of service which can be expected from Customs when

- a person contacts them (eg in writing, by telephone or by e-mail);
- they contact a person (eg by visit or by replying to a letter or e-mail);
- they deal with a person's documents and activities (eg when a person makes an application or request, sends a form or records to them, or imports or exports goods); and
- a person complains or appeals.

Customs will

- treat a person's affairs in strict confidence, within the law;
- want a person to pay or receive only the right amount of tax (or duty) due;
- provide a good quality service;
- handle a person's affairs promptly and accurately;
- be accessible in ways that are convenient;
- try to keep a person's costs to the minimum necessary;
- take reasonable steps to meet special needs; and
- be courteous and professional.

Specific standards set by Customs are as follows.

(*a*) **Dealing with correspondence**. Customs aim to reply to 93% of correspondence within 10 working days. Where they take longer (eg because the answer is complex or needs a Ministerial decision) they aim to send an interim reply within 10 days indicating the reason for the delay, the person to contact with any questions or further information, and when a full reply can be expected.

(*b*) **Visitors**. Customs aim to see 99% of visitors with an appointment within 10 minutes and, in offices with a public counter, to see 95% of visitors without an appointment within 15 minutes. Customs will ensure that visitors with an appointment will

- get an answer to any question or, if Customs cannot answer the question on the spot, be told when an answer can be expected; and
- have reasonable access to a telephone.

(*c*) **Telephone calls**. Customs aim to answer 80% of calls to the National Advice Service, national help-lines and dedicated enquiry offices within 20 seconds. They aim to return 95% of calls to help-line and enquiry point answer-phones within three working hours.

Staff will give their names and advice should be clear and easy to understand. If any question cannot be answered, it will be re-routed promptly to the appropriate office or else the caller will be given the telephone number of the office he needs to speak to.

(*d*) **VAT registration**. Provided they receive accurate and complete information, Customs aim to process a VAT registration within 15 working days. They will offer new businesses a choice of options to learn about how VAT works (a videotape, seminar or one-to-one meeting with a member of the Business Education Team) and deliver the choice within three months of a request.

(*e*) **VAT repayments**. Provided they receive accurate and complete details, Customs aim to pay claims for repayment within 30 days of the receipt of the claim and, if they delay authorising a claim beyond 30 days, they will pay a supplement.

(*f*) **Damage to goods**. If Customs examine goods, they will take care of them, but if they do damage them, they will explain what happened and how compensation can be claimed; and they aim to resolve all compensation claims within 20 working days.

(*g*) **Visits by Customs officers**. See 17.12 CUSTOMS: POWERS.

(*h*) **Making complaints**. See 15.6 below.

(Customs Notice 400).

15.3 PUBLICATIONS

Customs issue

- **Notices** and (formerly) **leaflets**, which are numbered booklets explaining various aspects of VAT. See 16.1 CUSTOMS: NOTICES, ETC. for those currently in issue. Most of the notices and leaflets are available from the National Advice Service (tel: 0845 010 9000).

- **VAT Notes** to bring to the notice of all registered persons details of information available from VAT offices. They are sent out with VAT return forms.
- **News releases** and **business briefs** are issued as informative news items. They are numbered and dated.
- **VAT information sheets** on items of particular interest.

Publicity by Customs of changes in policy and interpretation of VAT law and the correction of errors arising.

(*a*) *Changes in policy.* Generally, a change in Customs' policy is not applied retrospectively. Most changes are announced in a Business Brief and in VAT Notes issued to all registered traders. They will be applied either from a current date or from some future date in order to give businesses time to prepare for the change. Alternatively, Customs may provide for a transitional period so that businesses have an opportunity, for example, to benefit from an existing policy before a less beneficial policy is introduced.

(*b*) *Changes in interpretation of the law.* Customs apply what they consider to be the correct interpretation of the law relating to VAT. Significant changes in their interpretation of the law will be announced in a Business Brief and in VAT Notes issued to all registered traders. But a change in interpretation of the law, which will usually take place as a result of litigation, means that, in Custom's view, the relevant legislative provision should always have been applied in accordance with the revised interpretation. Changes in their interpretation of the law are, therefore, essentially retrospective.

Where past declaration errors were made on returns on the basis of Customs' interpretation of the law, there are three general principles that they will apply in correcting matters. These principles also reflect the view that businesses cannot take the benefit of a change in interpretation of the law without the burden.

(1) Customs will not expect or require businesses to correct past declaration errors, which were made on the basis of Customs' interpretation of the law. Businesses will only be required to apply the new interpretation of the law from a current or future date, which they will announce. Where the new interpretation means that additional VAT is due, this date will normally be after every registered trader has been informed of the change via VAT Notes.

(2) If, following an announcement of a new interpretation of the law, a business chooses to correct historical errors, Customs will accept the corrections provided the neutrality of the VAT is respected (ie the business is no better off and the Exchequer is no worse off than they would have been if the mistaken interpretation had not been made).

(3) Where Customs exercise a discretion not to collect arrears of VAT due (including circumstances covered by the existing misdirection class concession, see 17.13 CUSTOMS: POWERS), Customs will do so in a manner consistent with the above principles.

(Business Brief 28/04). See the Business Brief for examples illustrating how these general principles apply in particular circumstances.

15.4 CONTACTING CUSTOMS

National Advice Service. The National Advice Service deals with all general telephone enquiries from both businesses and the public on 0845 010 9000. A textphone service, for customers with hearing difficulties, is available on 0845 000 0200 and a Welsh speaking service is available on 0845 010 0300. All services are available from 8.00am to 8.00pm on Mondays to Fridays.

The service is for all general enquiries about Customs' taxes and duties, including VAT, Excise, Customs, Insurance Premium Tax, Landfill Tax, Aggregates Tax, Air Passenger Duty, Climate Change Levy and Mineral Oils. The service should be used in particular for

- queries on Customs rules and procedures;
- rates of VAT chargeable on particular goods;
- requests for publications (eg forms and notices); and
- requests for duplicate VAT returns.

Where a question cannot be answered, it will be re-routed to the appropriate office or the caller will be given the phone number of the office required.

General written enquiries. A registered person who has a general enquiry about VAT and wishes to write to Customs about it should address the enquiry to the nearest written enquiry team. The latest available details at the time of writing are reproduced below. Customs frequently amend this list and the reader is referred to the HMRC website at

www.hmrc.gov.uk

for the latest available list. A reply to an enquiry may come from a different Customs address to the one advertised for a particular postcode.

Written enquiry team	*Postcode for business*
Cardiff Portcullis House, 21 Cowbridge Road East, Cardiff, South Glamorgan CF11 9SR	BA1–BA7, BS, CF, CH4–CH8, CH99, EX, GL, LD, LL, NP, PL, SA, SN10–SN16, SY1–SY13, SY15–SY25, TA, TF, TQ, TR, WR12, WR78, WR99
Cheadle Boundary House, Cheadle Point, Cheadle, Cheshire SK8 2JZ	B1–B22, B72, B74, BB, BL, CH1–CH3, CH41–CH49, CH60–CH66, CW1–CW2, CW4–CW12, DN1–DN9, DN11, DN12, DN14, FY, L, LA1–4, LE16, M, NN, OL1–OL13, OL15–OL16, OL95, OX10, OX17, PE8, PR, R, RG1–RG9, RG13–RG20, RG30, RG31, RG41, S1–S14, S17, S19–S20, S25, S26, S30, S31, S35, S36, S49, S60–S68, S70–S75, SK1–SK12, SK14–SK16, SY14, WA, WN
City Thomas Paine House, Angel Square, Torrens Street, London EC1V 1TA	BR, CR0, CR2, CR4–CR5, CR7, CR8, DA5–DA8, E, E1W, EC, EN1–EN5, HA, IG1–IG6, IG8, IG11, KT1–KT6, KT9, N, NW, RM1–RM3, RM5–RM14, SE, SM1–SM6, SW, TW1–TW14, UB, W, WC

15.4 Customs: Administration

Written enquiry team	*Postcode for business*
Glasgow Portcullis House, 21 India Street, Glasgow G2 4PZ	AB, B23–B71, B76–B78, B80, B91–B98, CV1–CV12, CV21–CV47, DD, DG, DY8, DY9, DY12, EH, FK, G, GU34, HR, IV, KA, KW, KY, ML, PA, PH, SO1–SO40, SO45, SO50–SO53, SP1, SP2, SP4, SP9–SP11, TD1–TD11, TD13, TD14, WR1–WR11, WR13–WR15, WS1–WS6, WS9, WS10, WV, ZE
Newcastle upon Tyne Dobson House, Regent Centre, Gosforth, Newcastle upon Tyne NE3 3PF	BD, BT, CA, CT1–CT21, DA1–DA4, DA14–DA18, DH, DL, DN13, DN15–DN21, DN31–DN41, DE55, GU1–GU4, GU7–GU25, GU46, GU47, GU51, GU52, HD, HG, HP5–HP22, HP27, HS, HU, HX, KT7–KT19, KT21–KT24, LA5–LA23, LS, ME1–ME20, MK1–MK19, MK46, NE1Z, OL14, OX1–OX9, OX11–OX16, OX18, OX20, OX25–OX29, OX33, OX39, OX44, OX49, PE10–PE12, PE20–PE25, RG10–RG12, RG21–RG29, RG40, RG42, RG45, SL, SM7, SN1–SN9, SN17, SN25–SN26, SN38, SN42, SN99, SR, TD12, TD15, TN9–TN12, TN15, TN23–TN25, TN27, TS, TW15–TW20, WF, YO
Southend-on-Sea 12th Floor Alexander House, Victoria Avenue, Southend, Essex SS99 1BD	AL, BA8–BA10, BH, BN, CB, CM, CO, CR3, CR6, CV13–CV20, CW3, DE, DN10, DN22, DT, DY1–DY7, DY10, DY11, DY13, DY14, EN6–EN11, GU5, GU6, GU26–GU33, GU35, HP1–HP4, HP23, IG7, IG9, IG10, IP, KT20, LE (except LE16), LN, LU, MK40–45, MK98, NG, NR, PE1–PE7, PE9, PE13–PE19, PE26–PE38, PO, RH, RM4, RM15–RM20, S18, S21, S32, S33, S40–S45, S80, S81, SG, SK13, SK17, SK22, SK23, SO41–SO43, SP3, SP5–SP8, SS, ST, TN1–TN8, TN13, TN14, TN16–TN22, TN26, TN28–TN40, WD, WS7–WS8, WS11–WS15,

E-mail enquiries. A registered person who has a general enquiry about VAT and wishes to contact Customs by e-mail should address the enquiry to the nearest e-mail address as follows.

Belfast	enquiries.ni@hmrc.gsi.gov.uk
Birmingham	enquiries.wm@hmrc.gsi.gov.uk
Cardiff	enquiries.wales@hmrc.gsi.gov.uk
Glasgow	enquiries.sco@hmrc.gsi.gov.uk

Hove	enquiries.se@hmrc.gsi.gov.uk
London	enquiries.lon@hmrc.gsi.gov.uk
Newcastle upon Tyne	enquiries.yhne@hmrc.gsi.gov.uk
North West England	enquiries.nw@hmrc.gsi.gov.uk
Poole	enquiries.estn@hmrc.gsi.gov.uk
Reading	enquiries.sec@hmrc.gsi.gov.uk
Southend-on-Sea	enquiries.estn@hmrc.gsi.gov.uk

Note. This is a facility for forwarding general enquiries. It is not a secure route for sending personal/commercial information.

Personal visits. The National Advice Service can make appointments for one-to-one consultations on any VAT matter at a mutually convenient venue.

VAT registration, change in registration details and deregistration. Contact should be made directly with the appropriate registration or deregistration office. See 59.38 REGISTRATION.

VAT registration of overseas traders with no UK establishment, tax representative or agent. Contact should be made directly with:

H M Revenue and Customs, Custom House, 28 Guild Street, Aberdeen, AB11 6GY
Tel: 01224 844653 (from outside the UK +44 1224 844653)
Fax: 01224 844611 (from outside the UK +44 1224 844611)

Payment problems. Where a business has problems in clearing an existing VAT debt, it should contact the National Advice Service (0845 010 9000) and will be put in touch with the appropriate Regional Debt Management Unit.

National Insolvency Helpdesk. Telephone 0151 703 8450.

Tax advisers should address written queries about specific client's affairs to the client's VAT office. Factual queries which are not specific to a particular client should be by telephone to the National Telephone Advice Service (see above) or in writing to the tax adviser's own VAT office. Approach should only be made to Customs Headquarters if enquiries are being made on behalf of an entire industry or if lobbying or otherwise acting as a member of a representative or consultative body concerned with the effect of present or proposed legislation.

15.5 CUSTOMS' RULINGS

Most VAT enquiries can be dealt with by a telephone call to Customs National Advice Service or, in the case of more detailed questions, in writing to one of the written enquiries teams. See 15.4 above.

It is also possible to write to Customs to ask for their view on how a particular transaction that has occurred, or is due to occur shortly, should be treated for VAT purposes. Normally, the supplier should ask for a ruling on the liability to VAT of goods or services and a customer should apply for a ruling on a question of VAT recovery.

Applying for a ruling. When requesting a ruling on VAT, the following information should be provided.

- Business name and VAT registration number. (VAT advisers should give these details for the business on whose behalf they are writing.)

- The full facts and context concerning the transactions or issues in question (see below).
- The intended use of the decision.
- A statement that, to the best of the taxpayer's knowledge and belief, the facts given are correct and that the full facts and relevant information have been disclosed.

Information to be given to Customs. For a ruling to be binding, Customs must be given the full facts and context of the transaction or issues in question by the taxpayer and/or his adviser at the time when the ruling is sought. It is the responsibility of the taxpayer/adviser to ensure that this happens. The information required will depend on the circumstances of the individual case but, where there is any doubt about whether particular details are relevant, they should be disclosed. Customs advise taxpayers/advisers to include the following.

- A clear explanation of the precise point(s) about which they are unclear of the VAT consequences.
- Where a taxpayer has received professional advice in respect of the query being raised, the reason for uncertainty.
- Where possible alternative VAT treatments have been considered, a brief indication of them.
- If the point at issue concerns a transaction which has yet to take place, a copy of the final draft contract, where appropriate, and full details of the other parties involved, to the extent that this is possible. (Where a ruling is sought before contracts are finalised, a ruling may still be given, but will not be binding if a contract is produced later and the facts vary significantly from those disclosed.)
- Copies of all of the relevant documents with the relevant areas clearly highlighted (or otherwise drawn attention to).
- An estimate of the money associated with the decision (eg the annual value of sales of an item in respect of which a ruling on the liability to VAT is sought).
- Any transactions (proposed or actual) related to, consequent upon, or forming part of a series with the transaction in respect of which a ruling is sought, whether or not these transactions are certain to take place.

Circumstances where Customs do not give rulings. Customs do not give

- general rulings and, unless clearly stated otherwise, will only be bound in respect of the taxpayer who sought the ruling;
- rulings on hypothetical transactions or answer 'what if?' questions;
- tax planning advice and, in particular, they do not 'approve' tax planning arrangements and will refuse to give rulings if they suspect that the transactions are part of a tax avoidance scheme;
- advance rulings on transactions unless reasonably satisfied that the transaction, as described, will take place;
- rulings in response to applications that do not involve genuine points of doubt or difficulty to taxpayers or their professional advisers; and

- rulings where they believe that the point is covered by their Notices or other published guidance (in which case they will refer the applicant to the relevant publications).

Time limit for response. Customs aim to resolve most enquiries within ten days but in complex cases they will acknowledge the enquiry and let the applicant know when a full reply can be expected. They will attempt to respond in the timescale that the business circumstances require but sufficient time should be allowed for the query to be properly considered.

Disagreeing with a ruling. A taxpayer or adviser who disagrees with a ruling given by Customs can ask for the ruling to be reconsidered. There is no general right of appeal to a VAT tribunal against a Customs ruling although some rulings are appealable matters (eg the VAT liability of a particular supply).

Reliance on rulings by others. Normally, only the taxpayer requesting the ruling can rely upon it. This does not, however, apply where

- Customs agree rulings with trade bodies;
- Customs' correspondence clearly states otherwise; or
- the ruling is about a particular type of product or activity.

Where a taxpayer wishes to pass on the decision to other businesses or a trade association, this should be made clear in the application so that Customs can explain how far it has a general application.

Where a taxpayer subsequently wishes to use a ruling given to an associated company carrying on an identical activity or operation, a simplified procedure can be used. The associate can send a copy of the existing ruling to Customs, and explain either that it operates in precisely the same way or explain how its procedures differ from that of the original company. In some such circumstances, Customs may need to ask for further information before confirming that the same ruling can be used.

Rulings ceasing to apply. Any ruling given ceases to apply in the following circumstances.

- When the law changes.
- When a court or tribunal ruling indicates that it is wrong.
- When Customs' policy changes (eg with regard to the interpretation of an aspect of law or as a result of the withdrawal or introduction of a concession) in which case Customs will publicise the change and the date from which it is to be applied.
- When the details of a planned transaction change with a material impact on the transaction as a whole.

Consequently, if a significant period of time elapses following a Customs ruling, a taxpayer should, for his own protection, seek a further ruling. If the facts have not changed, a simple letter asking for confirmation that Customs' view has not changed since the original ruling was given should normally be sufficient.

Binding nature of rulings on Customs. A ruling is normally only binding on Customs for the particular transaction(s) for which, and taxpayer to whom, it was given. Customs do not consider themselves bound by a ruling if

- the nature of the transaction changes in technical detail with a material impact on the transaction as a whole; or

- the information given to Customs, at the time of the request or later, was either incorrect or incomplete or both.

Incorrect rulings. Where Customs have, when in possession of the full facts (see above),

- given a clear and unequivocal written ruling which turns out to be wrong, or
- misled a trader to his detriment,

any assessment of VAT due will be based on the correct ruling from the date the error is brought to the taxpayer's attention. (VAT Notice 48, ESC 3.5). Once discovered, the incorrect VAT treatment must not continue although, depending on the circumstances, Customs will normally allow a short period of grace for systems changes, etc to be made.

Where a taxpayer has benefited from an incorrect ruling given to him individually in the past, Customs will not allow other taxpayers to claim similar benefits unless they have also received the same ruling.

(VAT Notice 700/6/03).

15.6 MAKING COMPLAINTS ABOUT CUSTOMS

The following remedies are available to a person who has a complaint against Customs.

(*a*) **Complaints to Customs**. If a person has a complaint against Customs, and is unable to resolve it on the spot with the officer concerned, he should contact one of the Regional Complaints Units listed below. Complaints may be made

- by speaking directly to a Customs officer;
- by phone; or
- in writing, by letter, e-mail, or fax.

It should be made clear that the problem is to be treated as a complaint.

Central	Haven House, 17 Lower Brook Street, Ipswich IP4 1DN (tel 01473 235831; fax 01473 235702; e-mail complaints.cen@hmrc.gov.uk)
London	Dorset House, Stamford Street, London SE1 9PY (tel 020 8929 6731; fax 020 8929 6788; e-mail complaints.slt@hmrc.gov.uk)
North	Peter Bennett House, Redvers Close, West Park Ring Road, Leeds LS16 6RQ (tel 0113 389 4222; fax 0113 389 4482; e-mail complaints.nth@hmrc.gov.uk)
Northern Ireland	Custom House, Custom House Square, Belfast BT1 3ET (tel 028 9056 2618; fax 028 9056 2970; e-mail complaints.ni@hmrc.gov.uk)
Scotland	44 York Place, Edinburgh EH1 3JW (tel 0131 469 7347; fax 0131 469 7341; e-mail complaints.sco@hmrc.gov.uk)

South	Compass House, Ordnance Survey Site, Romsey Road, Southampton SO16 4HP (tel 023 8079 7013; fax 023 8079 7018; e-mail complaints.sth@hmrc.gov.uk)
Wales	Portcullis House, 21 Cowbridge Road East, Cardiff CF11 9SS (tel 029 2038 6423; fax 029 2038 6440; e-mail complaints.wwb@hmrc.gov.uk)
Investigation/Intelligence	Custom House, Lower Thames Street, London EC3R 6EE (tel 0870 785 7798; fax 0870 785 6549; e-mail complaints.nis@hmrc.gov.uk)

As much background information as possible should be given, eg VAT registration number and date of visit or correspondence if appropriate. The appropriate local manager will carry out a thorough investigation of the complaint and will send a full reply, normally within ten working days of receipt. If this is not possible, he will indicate when a full reply will be sent.

If unhappy with the response to the complaint, a person can ask for it to be reconsidered on behalf of the Regional or Business Head. If still not satisfied with the decision reached by Customs, the independent Adjudicator can be asked to look into the case (see (*b*) below).

Reimbursement of costs. If, as a direct result of mistake or unreasonable delay by Customs, a person is left out of pocket, Customs will consider reimbursing reasonable costs. These might include the costs of postage, phone calls, travelling expenses, professional fees or financial charges. Customs will not compensate for the time spent by the complainant unless he can show lost earnings as a direct result. They may ask for evidence in support of the claim.

Compensation for worry and distress. Mistakes by Customs can, in some circumstances, cause considerable worry and distress. If so, they may be able to make a payment in addition to any direct costs they reimburse to acknowledge any distress suffered. Similarly, they may also make a payment if they handle a complaint badly or take an unreasonable time to deal with it. Customs consider each case on its own merits. These payments are not intended to put a value on the distress which might have been suffered and will typically range from £25 to £500.

(Customs Notice 1000).

(*b*) **Complaint to the independent Adjudicator**. The Adjudicator for the Inland Revenue also deals with unresolved complaints about Customs. The Adjudicator will consider (amongst other things) complaints about delay, rudeness, mistakes, harassment during a VAT investigation, application of extra-statutory concessions, requests for time to pay and refusal of information under the Open Government provisions. The Adjudicator will not examine cases which are appealable to a VAT tribunal nor intervene once a matter is before the criminal courts.

The address of the Adjudicator is

The Adjudicator's Office
Haymarket House
28 Haymarket
London SW1Y 4SP

Tel: 020 7930 2292
Fax: 020 7930 2298
e-mail: adjudicators@gtnet.gov.uk

(*c*) **Complaint to a Member of Parliament**. A person can complain to his local MP. If appropriate, the MP can deal with the complaint

- personally (eg by direct correspondence with Customs or by asking a Parliamentary question); or
- with the person's consent, by forwarding the complaint to the Parliamentary Commissioner for Administration (PCA) normally known as the 'Ombudsman'.

The PCA can only act on written complaints forwarded by an MP alleging maladministration and has no power to enforce a remedy.

The postal address for MPs is (Name of MP), House of Commons, London SW1A 1AA or, as the case may be, The Scottish Parliament, Edinburgh EH99 1SP, The National Assembly for Wales/Cynulliad Cenedlaethol Cymru, Cathays Park, Cardiff CF10 3NQ, or The Northern Ireland Assembly, Parliament Buildings, Belfast BT4 3XX.

(*d*) **Appeal to a VAT tribunal**. An appeal to a VAT tribunal can only be made against a decision of Customs falling within one of the categories in *VATA 1994, s 83* (see 5.3 APPEALS). Although some of these categories relate to administrative decisions, in general a VAT tribunal does not have supervisory jurisdiction over administrative decisions taken by Customs. Tribunals do have jurisdiction to hear appeals against decisions which, although not falling within *VATA 1994, s 83*, result in a decision (eg an assessment) which does. [*VATA 1994, s 84(10)*].

(*e*) **Judicial review**. Where a tribunal does not have power to review an administrative decision, a taxpayer can apply to the High Court for a judicial review. Applications are heard by the Queen's Bench Division.

De Voil Indirect Tax Service. See V1.280–V1.285.

15.7 DISCLOSURE OF INFORMATION BY HMRC OFFICIALS

Subject to 15.8 below, 'Revenue and Customs officials' may not disclose information which is held by HMRC in connection with a function of it. '*Revenue and Customs officials*' is a reference to any person who is or was

- a Commissioner of HMRC;
- an HMRC officer;
- a person acting on behalf of the Commissioners or an officer; or
- a member of a committee established by the Commissioners.

[*CRCA 2005, s 18(1)(4)*].

15.8 Authorised disclosure

The general provisions in 15.7 above do not apply, and disclosure of information is allowed, in the following circumstances. But it should be noted that this does not authorise the making of a disclosure which

- contravenes the *Data Protection Act 1998*; or

- is prohibited by *Regulation of Investigatory Powers Act 2000, Part 1.*

[*CRCA 2005, s 22*].

(*a*) **Functions of HMRC**. Disclosure of information is permitted where it is made for the purposes of a function of HMRC and does not contravene any restriction imposed by the Commissioners. [*CRCA 2005, s 18*(*2*)(*a*)].

(*b*) **Public interest disclosure** is permitted where

- it is of a kind listed below or as specified in regulations made by the Treasury, and
- it is made on the instructions of the Commissioners (which may be general or specific) and the Commissioners are satisfied that it is in the public interest.

The listed categories are as follows.

(i) Disclosure made to a person exercising public functions (whether or not within the UK) for the purposes of the prevention or detection of crime, and in order to comply with an obligation of the UK government under an agreement relating to the movement of persons, goods or services.

(ii) Disclosure to a body which has responsibility for the regulation of a profession and which relates to misconduct on the part of a member of the profession relating to a function of HMRC.

(iii) Disclosure to a constable where either the constable is exercising functions which relate to the movement of persons or goods into or out of the UK or the disclosure is made for the purposes of the prevention or detection of crime.

(iv) Disclosure to the National Criminal Intelligence Service for a purpose connected with its functions under *Police Act 1997, s 2*(*2*) (criminal intelligence).

(v) Disclosure to a person exercising public functions in relation to public safety or public health and for the purposes of those functions.

(vi) Disclosure to the Police Information Technology Organisation for the purpose of enabling information to be entered in a computerised database, and which relates to a person suspected of or arrested for an offence, the results of an investigation, or anything seized.

[*CRCA 2005, ss 18*(*2*)(*b*), *20*].

(*c*) **Disclosure to a 'prosecuting authority'** is permitted if made for the purpose of enabling the authority

- to consider whether to institute criminal proceedings in respect of a matter considered in the course of an investigation conducted by or on behalf of HMRC, or
- to give advice in connection with a criminal investigation or criminal proceedings.

'*Prosecuting authority*' means the Director of Revenue and Customs Prosecutions, in Scotland, the Lord Advocate or a procurator fiscal and, in Northern Ireland, the Director of Public Prosecutions for Northern Ireland.

It is an offence to disclose further any information disclosed to a prosecuting authority under these provisions except for a purpose connected with the exercise of the prosecuting authority's functions or with the consent of the Commissioners (which may be general or specific).

[*CRCA 2005, ss 18(2)(b), 21*].

(*d*) **Civil and criminal proceedings, etc**. Disclosure of information is permitted if made for the purposes of civil proceedings, criminal investigation or criminal proceedings (in each case whether or not within the UK) relating to a matter in respect of which HMRC have functions. [*CRCA 2005, s 18(2)(c)(d)*].

(*e*) **Court orders**. Disclosure of information is permitted if made in pursuance of an order of a court. [*CRCA 2005, s 18(2)(e)*].

(*f*) **Her Majesty's Inspectors of Constabulary, etc**. Disclosure of information is permitted if made to Her Majesty's Inspectors of Constabulary, the Scottish inspectors or the Northern Ireland inspectors for the purpose of an inspection by virtue of *CRCA 2005, s 27*. [*CRCA 2005, s 18(2)(f)*].

(*g*) **Independent Police Complaints Commission**. Disclosure of information is permitted if made to the Independent Police Complaints Commission, or a person acting on its behalf, for the purpose of the exercise of a function by virtue of *CRCA 2005, s 28*. [*CRCA 2005, s 18(2)(g)*].

(*h*) **With agreement of parties**. Disclosure of information is permitted if made with the consent of each person to whom the information relates. [*CRCA 2005, s 18(2)(h)*].

(*i*) **Inland Revenue** (before the merger with Customs to form HMRC). Customs were authorised to disclose information to the Commissioners of Inland Revenue (or an authorised officer of the Commissioners) to assist them in the performance of their duties. Information could also be disclosed for the purposes of any proceedings connected with the duties performed. [*FA 1972, s 127 repealed by CRCA 2005, Sch 4 para 16*]. In practice, exchanges of information took place at local level with particular emphasis on combating large cases of suspected tax evasion. (C & E News Release 12/88, 8 March 1988).

Following the formation of HMRC, information acquired by HMRC in connection with a function may be used by them in connection with any other function (subject to any provision which restricts or prohibits the use of information and which is contained in any *Act* (other than of the Scottish Parliament or NI Assembly) or international or other agreement of which the UK is a party). [*CRCA 2005, s 17(1)(2)*].

(*j*) **Department of Works and Pensions**. HMRC may disclose information to the Department for the purposes of preventing, detecting, investigating and prosecuting offences relating to social security and for maintaining and improving the accuracy of social security information. [*Social Security Administration (Fraud) Act 1997, s 1; SI 1997/1577*].

(*k*) **Charity Commissioners**. HMRC may disclose to the Charity Commissioners the name and address of any institution which they have treated as established for charitable purposes; information on the purposes of an institution (and the trusts under which it is established or regulated) in order to determine whether that institution should be treated as established for charitable purposes; and information about an institution which has been so treated but which HMRC believe has carried on activities which are not charitable or has applied funds for non-charitable purposes. [*Charities Act 1993, s 10*].

(*l*) **Office for National Statistics or the Departments of Trade and Industry**. For statistical purposes, HMRC are authorised to disclose VAT registration numbers allocated to persons and reference numbers for members of a group; the names, trading styles and addresses of persons so registered or of members of groups and status and trade classifications of businesses; and actual or estimated value of supplies. The information disclosed may be further disclosed only to another government department for similar purposes. Otherwise it may only be disclosed with the consent of the registered person or in such a form that individual particulars cannot be identified. [*VATA 1994, s 91; SI 1996/273*].

(*m*) **Isle of Man Customs** may be given information for the purpose of facilitating the proper administration of common duties and the enforcement of prohibitions or restrictions on imports or exports between the IOM and the UK. [*IMA 1979, s 10*].

(*n*) **Tax authorities of other EC countries**. No obligation as to secrecy (imposed by statute or otherwise) precludes HMRC from disclosing to the competent authority of another EC country any information required to be so disclosed under the *Mutual Assistance Directive No 77/799/EEC* (as amended). Before disclosing any information, they must be satisfied that the competent authority is bound by, or has undertaken to observe, rules of confidentiality not less strict than in the UK and that it will use the information for tax purposes or to facilitate legal proceedings for failure to observe the tax laws of the receiving country. [*FA 2003, s 197*]. *Before 10 July 2003*, similar provisions applied under *FA 1978, s 77* and *FA 1980, s 17*.

Under *EC Directive 77/799/EEC* and *79/1070/EEC* information may be exchanged

(*a*) on the request of an EC country (although the other country need not comply if the requesting country has not exhausted its own usual sources of information) [*Article 2*];

(*b*) regularly in certain determined categories of cases [*Article 3*]; and

(*c*) spontaneously where

(i) there may be a loss of tax in the other EC country;

(ii) a person liable to VAT obtains a reduction in, or an exemption from, VAT in the one EC country which would give rise to an increase in VAT, or to liability to VAT, in the other EC country;

(iii) business dealings between a person liable to VAT in an EC country and a person liable to VAT in another EC country are conducted through one or more countries in such a way that a saving in VAT may result in either or both countries;

(iv) the competent authority of an EC country has grounds for supposing that a saving of VAT may result from artificial transfers of profits within groups of enterprises; and

(v) information forwarded to one EC country by the competent authority of another EC country has enabled information to be obtained which may be relevant in assessing liability to VAT in the latter EC country.

[*Article 4*].

Compounded settlements. Although not specifically covered in legislation, Customs have powers under *CEMA 1979 s 152* to compound any offence (whether or not proceedings have been instituted in respect of it) and compound proceedings, ie offer an alleged offender the option of paying a penalty out of court rather than be prosecuted. See 52.2 PENALTIES. Customs will disclose details of any settlement reached to

- other Government Departments whose statutory responsibilities are directly affected;
- the courts for sentencing purposes after conviction, in cases where there has been an earlier compounded settlement for a similar matter within the five-year time limit specified for offences by the *Rehabilitation of Offenders Act*;
- employers when it is apparent that
  - (i) the nature of the employment has facilitated the offence; or
  - (ii) where drugs offences or indications of serious alcohol abuse are involved, the nature of the employment or duties requires a high degree of unimpaired judgment or faculties; and
- in response to enquiries from Parliament or the media about cases which have excited public attention, if disclosure is considered to be in the public interest.

In all cases, persons considering an offer to compound for an alleged offence will be warned when the offer is made that details of the settlement may be disclosed in the above circumstances.

(Hansard Vol 151, cols 562, 563, 26 April 1989; Customs Notice 12, para 1.6).

De Voil Indirect Tax Service. See V1.270.

15.9 **Wrongful disclosure**

A person commits an offence if he contravenes the provisions of 15.7 above by disclosing 'revenue and customs information relating to a person' whose identity is specified in the disclosure or can be deduced from it.

'*Revenue and customs information relating to a person*' means information about, acquired as a result of, or held in connection with, the exercise of a function of HMRC in respect of the person; but it does not include information about internal administrative arrangements of HMRC (whether relating to Commissioners, officers or others).

It is a defence for a person charged with an offence under these provisions to prove that he reasonably believed that

- the disclosure was lawful, or
- the information had already and lawfully been made available to the public.

A person guilty of an offence under these provisions is liable, on conviction on indictment, to imprisonment for a term not exceeding two years or to a fine or to both and, on summary conviction, to imprisonment for a term not exceeding 12 months (six months in Scotland and NI) or to a fine not exceeding the 'statutory maximum' or to both. The '*statutory maximum*' is currently £5,000.

[*CRCA 2005, s 19*].

Before the merger of the Inland Revenue and Customs, the offence for wrongful disclosure was contained in *FA 1989, s 182*. The provisions, which also apply to VAT tribunals (and the General and Special Commissioners), have not been repealed and therefore continue to apply to Revenue and Customs officers. Under those provisions, a person who discloses any information which he holds or has held in the exercise of 'tax functions' is guilty of an offence if it is information about any matters relevant, for the purposes of those functions, to VAT in the case of any 'identifiable person'.

'*Tax functions*' means, *inter alia*, functions relating to VAT of HMRC and its officers and persons carrying out the administration work of any VAT tribunal, together with any other person providing, or employed in the provision of, services to any such officer or person.

'*Identifiable person*' means a person whose identity is specified in the disclosure or can be deduced from it.

The provisions do not apply to any disclosure of information with 'lawful authority'; with the consent of any person in whose case the information is about a matter relevant to VAT; or which has been lawfully made available to the public before the disclosure is made. A disclosure of information is made with '*lawful authority*' if, and only if, it is made

- by a Crown servant in accordance with his official duty,
- by any other person for the purposes of the function in the exercise of which he holds the information and without contravening any restriction duly imposed by the '*person responsible*' ie the Commissioners,
- to, or in accordance with an authorisation duly given by, the person responsible,
- in pursuance of any enactment or of any order of a court, or
- in connection with the institution of, or otherwise for the purposes of, any proceedings relating to any matter within the general responsibility of HMRC.

It is a defence for a person charged under these provisions to prove that, at the time of the alleged offence, he believed that he had lawful authority to make the disclosure and had no reasonable cause to believe otherwise *or* he believed that the information had previously been lawfully made available to the public and had no reasonable cause to believe otherwise.

A person guilty of an offence under these provisions is liable, on conviction on indictment, to imprisonment for a term not exceeding two years or a fine or both, and on summary conviction, to imprisonment for a term not exceeding six months or a fine not exceeding the statutory maximum or both.

[*FA 1989, s 182; CRCA 2005, Sch 4 para 39*].

15.10 DISCLOSURE OF INFORMATION TO HMRC

The following are authorised to disclose information to HMRC.

- **Department of Works and Pensions**. The Department are authorised to pass information to the Commissioners (or any person by whom services are being provided to the Commissioners) for use in the prevention, detection, investigation or prosecution of offences which it is the function of HMRC to prevent, etc. The information may also be used in connection with the assessment or determination of non-criminal penalties and to check the accuracy of information held by HMRC. [*FA 1997, s 110; Tax Credits Act 2002, Sch 5 para 13; SI 1997/1603*].

- **Charity Commissioners**. The Charity Commissioners may disclose to HMRC any information received by them, under or for the purposes of any Act or statutory instrument, where the disclosure is made for any purpose connected with the discharge of their functions and to enable or assist HMRC to discharge any of its functions. Where any information has been disclosed to the Charity Commissioners under *Charities Act 1993, s 10* (which also applies to other government departments, etc) subject to any express restriction on the disclosure of the information by the Charity Commissioners, their power of disclosure to HMRC (and other government departments, etc) under these provisions is exercisable subject to any such restriction. [*Charities Act 1993, s 10*].

Before the merger with Customs to form HMRC, the Inland Revenue were authorised to disclose information to the Commissioners of Customs and Excise (or an authorised officer of the Commissioners) to assist them in the performance of their duties. Information could also be disclosed for the purposes of any proceedings connected with the duties performed. [*FA 1972, s 127 repealed by CRCA 2005, Sch 4 para 16*]. In practice, exchanges of information took place at local level with particular emphasis on combating large cases of suspected tax evasion. (C & E News Release 12/88, 8 March 1988). *Following the formation of HMRC*, information acquired by HMRC in connection with a function may be used by them in connection with any other function (subject to any provision which restricts or prohibits the use of information and which is contained in any Act (other than of the Scottish Parliament or NI Assembly) or international or other agreement of which the UK is a party). [*CRCA 2005, s 17(1)(2)*].

15.11 CUSTOMS ACCESS TO CORRESPONDENCE, ETC BETWEEN BUSINESSES AND THEIR TAX ADVISERS

Information relating to goods and services, etc. Customs need access to information relating to goods and services and to their supply, acquisition or importation, to enable them to check the amounts of VAT payable or recoverable by a business and to ensure that liabilities are correctly accounted for. They have statutory powers of access in this respect.

Confidential advice by tax advisers. As part of their services to clients, tax advisers communicate with clients or other tax advisers to give or obtain opinions or advise about client's past and future affairs. Such communications may include notes of meetings and telephone calls, internal memoranda, letters and faxes. Customs will not normally request a tax adviser or trader to produce such a communication relating to confidential opinions or advice. Auditors' working papers and management letters also fall into this category unless containing information relating to goods and services, etc.

Mixed information. Where a document (eg working papers or a management letter) contains both information relating to goods and services (eg details about the origins of figures in accounts, returns and other information submitted to Customs, or the relationship of those figures with the books and records of the business) and confidential advice, Customs will normally accept an extract from the document. This should be supported by a written statement from the tax adviser or auditor that in his opinion Customs do not have the power to see the other part or parts of the document.

(VAT Leaflet 700/47/93).

15.12 DIRECT CORRESPONDENCE BETWEEN CUSTOMS AND TAX ADVISERS

Customs cannot reveal confidential information it holds on individual taxpayers unless statutory provisions allow (see 15.8 above).

As many taxpayers instruct their tax advisers to assist in their VAT affairs, Customs have produced the following standard wording so that they can disclose confidential information to them. The signed letter should be sent to the appropriate written enquiry office (see 15.4 above).

Example letter from a taxpayer to HMRC authorising disclosure of confidential information to a third party

> [Date]
>
> I [name and VAT registration number] authorise HM Revenue and Customs to disclose VAT information held about my business affairs to [name and address of nominee], who is acting on my behalf. This authorisation covers all VAT matters within the responsibility of HM Revenue and Customs and includes approaches which may be made to obtain information from all sections of the department, such as the National Advice Service, Debt Management Units, National Registration Service and Complaints Units. This authority will remain in force until I give you written notice to the contrary.
>
> I do not wish the following information to be disclosed*
>
> I undertake to inform HM Revenue and Customs of any change to the above authorisation.
>
> (Signed)
>
> *To be included if applicable.

16 Customs: Notices, Etc.

16.1 NOTICE AND LEAFLETS

48	Extra-statutory concessions (2002 with Updates 1 to 3)
60	The Intrastat general guide (2004)
400	H M Customs and Excise Charter (2002)
700	The VAT guide (2002 with Updates 1 and 2)
700/1/02	Should I be registered for VAT? (with Correction Slip, Updates 1 to 3, and Supplement to Notices 700/1 and 700/11)
700/2/05	Group and divisional registration
700/6/03	VAT rulings
700/7/02	Business promotion schemes (with Update 1)
700/8/04	Disclosure of VAT avoidance schemes
700/9/02	Transfer of a business as a going concern (with Update 1)
700/11/02	Cancelling your registration (with Update 1 and Supplement to Notices 700/1 and 700/11)
700/12/02	Filling in your VAT return (with Update 1)
700/14/04	Video cassette films: rental and part-exchange
700/15/02	The ins and outs of VAT
700/17/02	Funded pension schemes
700/18/02	Relief from VAT on bad debts
700/21/02	Keeping records and accounts (with Update 1)
700/24/03	Postage and delivery charges
700/25/02	Taxis and hire cars
700/34/05	Staff
700/35/97	Business gifts and samples
700/41/02	Late registration penalty
700/42/02	Misdeclaration penalty and repeated misdeclaration penalty
700/43/03	Default interest
700/44/02	Barristers and advocates
700/45/02	How to correct VAT errors and make adjustments or claims (with Update 1)
700/46/02	Agricultural flat rate scheme
700/47/93	Confidentiality in VAT matters (tax adviser) – statement of practice
700/50/04	Default surcharge
700/52/05	Notice of requirement to give security to Customs and Excise
700/56/02	Insolvency
700/57/04	Administrative agreements entered into with trade bodies (with Update 1)
700/58/02	Treatment of VAT repayment returns and VAT repayment supplement (with Update 1)
700/60/03	Payments on account

700/62/03	Self-billing
700/63/03	Electronic invoicing
700/64/02	Motoring expenses (with Updates 1 and 2)
700/65/02	Business entertainment
700/67/02	Registration scheme for racehorse owners
701/1/04	Charities (with Update 1)
701/2/04	Welfare
701/5/02	Clubs and associations (with update 1)
701/6/03	Charity-funded equipment for medical, veterinary, etc uses (with Supplement issued in 1997)
701/7/02	VAT reliefs for disabled people
701/8/03	Postage stamps and philatelic supplies
701/9/02	Derivatives and terminal markets
701/10/03	Zero-rating of books, etc
701/12/02	Disposals of antiques, works of art etc from historic houses
701/13/04	Gaming and amusement machines
701/14/02	Food
701/15/05	Animals and animal food
701/16/02	Water and sewerage services (with Update 1)
701/18/02	Women's sanitary protection products
701/19/02	Fuel and power (with Update 1)
701/20/04	Caravans and houseboats
701/21/02	Gold
701/21A/05	Investment gold coins
701/22/02	Tools for the manufacture of goods for export
701/23/02	Protective equipment
701/26/04	Betting and gaming
701/27/02	Bingo
701/28/03	Lotteries
701/30/02	Education and vocational training (with Updates 1 and 2)
701/31/02	Health and care institutions
701/32/03	Burial, cremation and the commemoration of the dead
701/35/04	Youth clubs
701/36/02	Insurance (with Update 1)
701/38/03	Seeds and plants
701/39/04	VAT liability law
701/40/02	Food processing services
701/41/02	Sponsorship
701/45/02	Sport
701/47/03	Culture (with Update 1)
701/48/02	Corporate purchasing cards (with Update 1)

16.1 Customs: Notices, Etc.

701/49/02	Finance and securities (2002)
701/57/02	Health professionals
701/58/02	Charity advertising and goods connected with collecting donations (with Update 1)
701/59/02	Motor vehicles for disabled people
702	Imports (2004 with Updates 1 and 2)
702/7/04	Import VAT relief for goods supplied onward to another country in the European community
702/9/98	Warehouses and free zones (temporarily suspended with effect from 25 November 2003)
703	Exports and removals of goods from the UK (2005)
703/1/04	Supply of freight containers for export or removal from the United Kingdom (with Updates 1 and 2)
703/2/02	Sailaway boats supplied for export outside the EC (with Update 1)
703/3/02	Sailaway boat scheme (with Update 1)
704	VAT Retail exports (2004)
704/1/04	Tax free shopping: VAT refunds for travellers departing from the European Community
705	Buyer's guide to personal export of new motor vehicles to destinations outside the EC (2004)
705A	VAT: supplies of vehicles under the Personal Export Scheme for removal from the EC (2004)
706	Partial exemption (2004)
706/2/02	Capital goods scheme
708	Buildings and construction (2002)
708/6/02	Energy-saving materials
709/1/02	Catering and take-away food
709/3/02	Hotels and holiday accommodation (with Update 1)
709/5/04	Tour operators' margin scheme
709/6/02	Travel agents and tour operators
714	Zero-rating young children's clothing and footwear (2002)
718	Margin scheme for second-hand goods, works of art, antiques and collectors' items (2003 with Updates 1 and 2)
719	VAT refunds for 'do-it-yourself' builders and converters (2002 with Update 1)
723	Refunds of VAT in the European community for EC and non-EC businesses (2003)
725	The single market (2002 with Update 1)
726	Joint and several liability in the supply of specific goods (2003)
727	Retail schemes (2002)
727/2/02	Bespoke retail schemes
727/3/02	Retail schemes: how to work the point of sale scheme (with Update 1)
727/4/02	Retail schemes: how to work the apportionment schemes (with Update 1)
727/5/02	Retail schemes: how to work the direct calculation schemes (with Update 1)

728	New means of transport (2003 with Update 1)
730	Civil penalty investigations: statement of practice (2004)
731	Cash accounting (2004)
732	Annual accounting (2003 with Update 1)
733	Flat rate scheme for small businesses (2004 with Update 1)
741	Place of supply of services (2002 with Update 1)
742	Land and property (2002 with Updates 1 and 2)
742A	Option to tax land and buildings (2002 with Updates 1 to 3)
742/3/02	Scottish land law terms
744A	Passenger transport (2002)
744B	Freight transport and associated services (2002)
744C	Ships, aircraft and associated services (1997)
744D	International services: zero-rating (2002)
747	VAT notices having the force of law (2003)
749	Local authorities and similar bodies (2002)
915	Assessments and time limits: statement of practice (2002)
920	The single currency (1999)
930	What if I don't pay? (2002)
989	Visits by Customs officers (2002)
998	VAT refund scheme for National museums and galleries (2003 with Update 1)
999	Catalogue of publications (2005)
1000	Complaints and putting things right (2002)
–	VAT: Appeals and applications to the tribunals (1995)
CWL4	Fund-raising events: exemption for charities and other qualifying bodies (2001)

16.2 VAT INFORMATION SHEETS

The following information sheets relating to VAT had been issued and not withdrawn or superceded at the time of publication.

5/95	VAT: changes to the tour operators' margin scheme from 1 January 1996
6/95	NHS dispensing doctors
1/96	Filling in your EC Sales List
3/96	Tour operators' margin scheme: practical implementation of the 'airline charter option' following the changes which came into effect on 1 January 1996
4/96	Tour operators' margin scheme: practical implementation of the 'agency option' following the changes which came into effect on 1 January 1996
1/97	Tour operators' margin scheme: practical implementation of the 'trader to trader (wholesale) option' following the changes which came into effect on 1 January 1996
6/97	Drugs, medicines and aids for the handicapped: liability with effect from 1 January 1998
3/98	Local authorities and NHS joint stores depots

16.2 Customs: Notices, Etc.

5/98	Local authorities: supplies to new unitary authorities under local government reorganisation (transitional arrangements)
6/98	Local authority pension funds: VAT treatment and administrative concessions
8/98	Charities: supply, repair and maintenance of relevant goods (including adapted motor vehicles) (with correction)
2/99	Local authorities: agreement of section 33 recovery methods
3/99	VAT: New Deal Programme
6/99	Charities: liability of routine domestic tasks
8/99	Opticians: apportionment of charges for supplies of spectacles and dispensing
9/99	Imported works of art, antiques and collectors' pieces: changes to the reduced rate of VAT
10/99	Financial exemptions: changes brought about by the 1999 Finance Order
12/99	VAT on business cars: changes to take effect on 1 December 1999
2/00	Exports and removals: conditions for zero-rating
3/00	Supplies through undisclosed agents: revised VAT treatment
2/01	Single or multiple supplies — how to decide
6/01	Changes to the VAT second-hand margin scheme
1/02	VAT civil evasion cases: a new approach to investigations: statement of practice
4/02	Budget 2002: VAT: partial exemption – standard method over-ride
1/03	Electronically supplied services and broadcasting services: new EU place of supply rules
2/03	Clarification of VAT treatment of services by financial advisers
3/03	Modernisation of face value vouchers
4/03	Electronically supplied services: a guide to interpretation
5/03	Electronically supplied services: evidence of customer location and status
6/03	Tribunal decision on VAT treatment of repossessed and voluntarily returned cars
7/03	Electronically supplied services: special scheme for non-EU businesses
10/03	Electronically supplied services: supplementary information on the special scheme for non-EU businesses
11/03	Electronic point of sale (EPOS) systems
12/03	Face value vouchers
13/03	Electronically supplied services: VAT on e-services special scheme for non-EU businesses – currency exchange rates for the reporting period ending 30 September 2003
14/03	New time of supply rules for on-going supplies
15/03	The VAT treatment of share registration services
16/03	VAT invoicing changes
17/03	Changes to the VAT flat-rate scheme
1/04	Electronically supplied services: special scheme for non-EU businesses – currency exchange rates for reporting period ending 31 December 2003
3/04	Electronically supplied services: EU enlargement
4/04	Electronically supplied services: special scheme for non-EU businesses – currency exchange rates for reporting period ending 31 March 2004

5/04	Claims made in the light of GMAC High Court decision: VAT treatment of returned cars and other goods
6/04	Electronically supplied services: special scheme for non-EU businesses – currency exchange rates for reporting period ending 30 June 2004
7/04	Eligibility rules for VAT grouping
8/04	Electronically supplied services: special scheme for non-EU businesses – currency exchange rates for reporting period ending 30 September 2004
9/04	Partial exemption; fair recovery of VAT on costs of incidental financial supplies
10/04	Changes to the place of supply of natural gas and electricity
11/04	Electronically supplied services: special scheme for non-EU businesses – currency exchange rates for reporting period ending 31 December 2004
1/05	E-supplied services: special scheme for non-EU businesses – exchange rates
2/05	Electronically supplied services: changes to Greece VAT rate

17 Customs: Powers

Cross-references. See 6.1 ASSESSMENTS for powers of HMRC to raise assessments and to assess an over-repayment and 6.3 ASSESSMENTS for assessments of penalties, interest and surcharges; 8.5 BUSINESS for powers to make a direction treating two or more persons as one taxable person; 15.7 CUSTOMS: ADMINISTRATION for the power to disclose or exchange information with other authorities and government departments; 31.5 GROUPS OF COMPANIES for powers re groups; 51.5 PAYMENT OF VAT for power to withhold a repayment of VAT due where returns are outstanding; 52.2–52.4 PENALTIES for powers of arrest; 52.22 PENALTIES for power of mitigation; 56.1 RECORDS for the power to require records to be kept; and 59.10 REGISTRATION for powers to enforce compulsory deregistration.

The contents of this chapter are as follows.

17.1 POWER TO REQUIRE SECURITY AND PRODUCTION OF EVIDENCE

HMRC have the following powers relating to the production of evidence and the requirement for security.

(*a*) HMRC can, as a condition of allowing or repaying any input tax to any person, require the production of such evidence relating to VAT as they may specify (before 10 April 2003, require the production of such documents relating to VAT as may have been supplied to that person). [*VATA 1994, Sch 11 para 4*(*1*); *FA 2003, s 17*(*3*)].

(*b*) If they think it necessary for the protection of the revenue, HMRC can require, as a condition of making any VAT credit, the giving of such security for the amount of the payment as appears appropriate to them. [*VATA 1994, Sch 11 para 4*(*1A*); *FA 2003, s 17*(*3*)].

HMRC may issue a Notice of Requirement under this provision where a business makes a large or unusual VAT claim which they need time to verify. They may also do so in other circumstances (eg where a business has been, or is about to be, notified that it may be jointly and severally liable for unpaid VAT, see 17.3 below).The amount of security will be no more than the VAT credit that HMRC are due to make or are considering making. HMRC will usually accept security in the form of a bank or building society guarantee or a joint bank or building society account, but in either case any guarantee must be with a financial institution approved by them. If any security required is not provided, any VAT claim covered by the Notice of Requirement will be withheld until it is verified (or until any notices of joint and several liability for unpaid VAT are paid or withdrawn). The security will be returned once the claim is verified (or any notices of joint and several liability for unpaid VAT are paid or withdrawn). If all or part of the repayment claim is disallowed, HMRC may offset the security to recover any credit already paid. They may also offset the security against any unpaid notices of joint and several liability. (VAT Notice 700/52/05, paras 2.1–2.8).

(*c*) If they think it necessary for the protection of the revenue, HMRC may require a taxable person, as a condition of his supplying (or after 9 April 2003 being supplied with) goods and services under a taxable supply, to give security (or further security) for the payment of any VAT that is or may become due from the taxable person. The security can be of such amount, and must be given in such a manner, as HMRC determine.

[*VATA 1994, s 48(7), Sch 11 para 4(2)(4)(5); FA 2003, s 17(4)*].

This provision allows HMRC to require an amount of security from a business if they consider there is a risk of VAT being unpaid by the business. They may issue a Notice of Requirement if, for example

- a person in his previous or current business has failed to comply with his VAT obligations;
- a business is run by disqualified directors or by undischarged bankrupts;
- a person has previously been prosecuted or penalised for a VAT offence; or
- other persons concerned in the current registration of a business are connected with past failures to pay VAT due.

Where they have strong grounds to suspect that revenue is at risk, HMRC may require security without warning. Factors which may be taken into account in determining the amount of security include

- VAT declared on VAT returns from the current and any previous business;
- VAT declared on VAT returns from businesses of a similar size, with similar customers and in the same trade class; and
- taxable turnover.

HMRC may also add any outstanding VAT from the current registered business. Where quarterly returns are submitted, HMRC will require an amount of security based on the VAT they estimate the business would have to pay over six months (four months if monthly returns are made). There is no rule to prevent security being required in excess of estimated liabilities (*Labelwise Ltd (VTD 1499) (TVC 14.43)*).

HMRC normally accept security by way of

- cash or bankers draft;
- bank or building society guarantee; or
- a joint bank or building society account

but they will only accept a guarantee from a financial institution approved by them.

It is a criminal offence to continue to trade without providing the security. On conviction, a penalty of up to £5,000 may be charged for each taxable supply made without providing the security. If a business does not provide the security, HMRC may prosecute for the whole period of trading from the date the Notice of Requirement was issued. Where the business is a company, both the company and individuals involved may be prosecuted and individuals may be liable for paying any fines and compensation awarded by the court.

HMRC will regularly review the requirement for security and will return it when they consider there is no longer a risk to the collection of VAT. At the very least, they will review the requirement within twelve months of it being provided in the case of monthly returns and two years in the case of quarterly returns.

If the business falls behind with payments of VAT, HMRC may offset the security against the VAT due and may then ask the business to provide a further amount of security.

(VAT Notice 700/52/05, paras 3.1–3.10).

(*d*) After 9 April 2003, if they think it necessary for the protection of the revenue, HMRC may require a taxable person, as a condition of his supplying or being supplied with goods and services under a taxable supply, to give security (or further security) for the payment of any VAT that is or may become due from any person by or to whom goods or services supplied by or to the taxable person are supplied. The security can be of such amount, and must be given in such a manner, as HMRC determine.

[*VATA 1994, s 48(7), Sch 11 para 4(2)–(5); FA 2003, s 17(4)*].

This provision allows HMRC to require an amount of security from a business if there is a risk of VAT being unpaid by other businesses or individuals in a supply chain in which the business trades. They may issue a Notice of Requirement if, for example

- a business has previously been engaged in one or more supply chains involving businesses or individuals who evade substantial VAT payments by
  - (i) deliberately using VAT registration numbers belonging to other businesses without their knowledge;
  - (ii) going missing; or
  - (iii) becoming insolvent owing VAT;
  - (iv) deliberately deciding not to pay VAT; or
  - (v) participating in business transactions structured so that it is not possible for the VAT owing to be paid; and
- a business is unable to show that it has taken reasonable steps to establish the business credentials of its suppliers and customers.

HMRC will not issue a Notice of Requirement under these provisions without prior warning. When they consider that a business has been involved in a supply chain where VAT has been evaded, HMRC will alert the business to the steps it can take to help it to avoid dealing with high risk businesses or individuals in the future.

The amount of security required will be based on HMRC's estimate of the VAT that will go unpaid if a business or individual in the supply chain evades payment of any VAT due. They may also add any outstanding VAT of the business on whom the Notice of Requirement is served.

The same provisions as to acceptable forms of security and offences for failure to supply security apply as under (*c*) above.

HMRC will regularly review the requirement for security and will return it when they consider there is no longer a risk to the collection of VAT. At the very least, they will review the requirement within twelve months of it being provided.

If the business falls behind with payments of VAT, or a business or individual in the supply chain leaves VAT unpaid, HMRC may offset the security against any VAT unpaid and may then ask the business to provide a further amount of security.

(VAT Notice 700/52/05, paras 4.1–4.10).

(*e*) Where a person fails to appoint a VAT representative when required to do so (see 3.8 AGENTS), HMRC may require him to provide security, or further security, as they think appropriate for the payment of any VAT which is or may become due from him. [*VATA 1994, s 48*(*7*)].

Reconsiderations and appeals. Where a business has been issued with a Notice of Requirement under (*b*)–(*e*) above, they can ask HMRC to review the requirement or appeal against the decision to a VAT tribunal (see 5.3(*l*) APPEALS).

Where an appeal is brought against a requirement for security under (*d*) above, the tribunal must allow the appeal unless HMRC satisfy the tribunal that

- there has been an evasion of, or an attempt to evade, VAT in relation to goods or services supplied to or by that person, or
- it is likely, or without the requirement for security it is likely, that VAT in relation to such goods or services will be evaded

and for these purposes evading VAT includes obtaining a VAT credit that is not due or a VAT credit in excess of what is due.

[*VATA 1994, s 84*(*4E*)(*4F*); *FA 2003, s 17*(*7*)].

Subject to this, when considering HMRC's requirement for security, the tribunal's jurisdiction is appellate rather than merely supervisory. The tribunal should consider whether HMRC acted reasonably and took account of all relevant material, but has no power to substitute its own decision for one reached on an incorrect basis (except that it can dismiss an appeal where it is shown that, even if additional material had been taken into account, the decision would *inevitably* have been the same). The tribunal should consider whether HMRC acted in a way in which no reasonable panel of Commissioners could have acted or whether they took into account some irrelevant matter or disregarded something to which they should have given weight. However, the tribunal cannot exercise a fresh discretion since the protection of the revenue is not a responsibility of the tribunal or of a court (*C & E Commrs v John Dee Ltd, CA [1995] STC 941 (TVC 14.28)*). In that case, the tribunal found that HMRC had failed to enquire into the company's financial status and that, if it had done, the result would not have inevitably been the same.

In *C & E Commrs v Peachtree Enterprises Ltd, QB [1994] STC 747 (TVC 14.54)* Dyson J observed that the tribunal must limit itself to considering facts and matter which existed at the time the challenge to the decision was taken and should not, for example, take into account the fact that the person concerned had subsequently made all returns and paid the VAT due on time.

De Voil Indirect Tax Service. See V5.186.

17.2 **RECOVERY OF VAT**

Where an invoice shows a supply of goods or services with VAT chargeable on it, the person issuing the invoice is liable for the amount of VAT shown (or the amount of VAT included if not shown separately) whether or not

(*a*) the invoice has been correctly prepared as required by the legislation (see 40 INVOICES);

(*b*) the supply actually takes, or has taken, place;

(*c*) the amount shown as VAT, or any amount of VAT, is or was chargeable on the supply; or

(*d*) the person issuing the invoice is a taxable person.

[*VATA 1994, Sch 11 para 5(1)–(3)*].

If any of the conditions in (*b*)-(*d*) above are not met, the sum recoverable is not VAT due under *VATA 1994* but is a debt due to the Crown. The practical effect of this is that normal assessment procedures cannot be used. The recovery of the incorrectly shown VAT is effected by means of a formal demand letter.

Penalties for unauthorised issue of invoices (see 52.12 PENALTIES) and interest on late paid VAT (see 51.14 PAYMENT OF VAT) may also be due.

Concessionary reliefs. Where the amount shown on an invoice is not actually VAT, the person issuing the invoice has no legal entitlement to treat the VAT incurred on his own related purchases as input tax. Equally, the person receiving the invoice has no legal entitlement to claim the VAT shown on the invoice as input tax. However, by concession, HMRC may allow

- VAT incurred on purchases directly related to the invoiced supplies to be treated as input tax and deducted from the amount due provided
  - (i) a supply has taken place;
  - (ii) there is satisfactory evidence of the VAT incurred;
  - (iii) there is positive evidence of costing the supply on the VAT-exclusive cost of the trader's purchases;
  - (iv) the input tax does not exceed the amount recoverable from the supplier under *VATA 1994, Sch 11 para 5* above; and
  - (v) the claim does not include VAT on capital goods or petrol; and
- the customer, if he acted in good faith, to retain the amount of input tax deducted.

(VAT Notice 48, ESC 3.9; Internal Guidance V1–24A, para 2.43).

Partnerships. See also 50.4 PARTNERSHIPS AND JOINT VENTURES for recovery of VAT from individual partners.

VAT due to other EC countries. Where recovery of a debt in any EC country proves unsuccessful, that country can request another EC country to attempt recovery where it appears that the debtor now resides, or has assets, there. The provisions of the Mutual Assistance Recovery Directive (*Council Directive 76/308/EEC*, as amended) are enacted in the UK as *FA 2002, s 134* and *Sch 39* (and supporting regulations) in relation to the recovery in the UK of amounts in respect of which a request for enforcement has been made by the tax authorities of another EC country. Such proceedings may be taken by, or on behalf of, HMRC to enforce the foreign claim (by way of legal proceedings, distress, diligence or otherwise) as might be taken to enforce a corresponding UK claim.

Unless otherwise permitted, no proceedings can be taken against any person if he shows that proceedings relevant to his liability on the foreign claim are pending, or about to be instituted, in the other EC country concerned but proceedings may be taken in the UK if the proceedings in that other country are not prosecuted or instituted with reasonable expedition. If the person shows that a final decision on the foreign claim has been given in his favour in the other EC country, no proceedings can be taken in the UK under these provisions.

De Voil Indirect Tax Service. See V1.271; V5.171.

17.3 **Joint and several liability for unpaid VAT**

Note. The question of whether the following statutory provisions contravene *EC 6th Directive, Arts 21(3), 22(8)* has been referred to the CJEC in *R (oao Federation of Technological Industries & Others) v C & E Commrs, QB [2004] STC 1008 (TVC 2.282)*.

With effect from 10 April 2003, where

(*a*) a taxable person receives a taxable supply of 'relevant goods and services',

(*b*) at the time of the supply he knew, or had 'reasonable grounds to suspect', that some or all of the 'VAT payable' on that supply, or on any previous or subsequent supply of those goods or services, would go unpaid to HMRC, and

(*c*) HMRC have served on him a notice of liability under these provisions

he may be held jointly and severally liable to HMRC for the 'net VAT unpaid' on those goods or services.

> *Example*
>
> A business buys 100 mobile phones from a supplier who bought them as part of an order for 1000 mobile phones.
>
> It may be held liable, under joint and several liability, for any unpaid VAT on the 100 phones it has bought (but not the remaining 900 phones which its supplier has bought).

Relevant goods and services. At present, these provisions only apply where there is a supply of goods or services that are subject to widespread Missing Trader Intra-Community (MTIC) VAT fraud although the Treasury are given powers to include different goods and services. '*Relevant goods and services*' are currently

- telephones and any other equipment, including parts and accessories, made or adapted for use in connection with telephones or telecommunication; and
- computers and any other equipment, including parts, accessories and software, made or adapted for use in connection with computers or computer systems.

Parts and accessories include computer chips, telephone chargers and memory cards but not, for example, screws or wires used in the manufacture of general items. (VAT Notice 726, para 1.4).

'Reasonable grounds to suspect'. Without prejudice to any other way of establishing reasonable grounds for suspicion, a person is presumed to have reasonable grounds for suspecting some or all of any VAT payable has not been paid if the price payable by him for the goods or services in question was less than the

- lowest price that might reasonably be expected to be payable for them on the open market, or
- price payable on any previous supply of those goods.

This presumption is, however, rebuttable on proof that the low price payable for the goods was due to circumstances unconnected with failure to pay VAT.

Businesses within a particular trade sector should be generally aware of the market price day-to-day. In most cases of MTIC fraud, transactions for goods take place at such a substantially lower rate than any plausible current market rate that it is transparent that they are part of a fraudulent activity. If goods are being offered for sale at a lower price than is prevalent within the current market, a business should ascertain the reason for the low price. (VAT Notice 726, para 3.2). See below for suggested checks to ascertain the integrity of a supply, supplier and/or customer.

'VAT payable'. The amount of VAT that is payable in respect of a supply is the lesser of

- the amount chargeable on the supply, and
- the amount shown as due on the supplier's return for the VAT period in question (if he has made one), together with any amount assessed as due from him for that period (subject to any appeal by him). The latter includes any amount assessed by HMRC even where it is not notified to the supplier because it is impracticable to do so.

'Net VAT unpaid' means the VAT charged on the goods or services in question less any input tax incurred on their purchase by the person who has not paid the VAT. (VAT Notice 726, para 2.2). An amount of VAT counts as unpaid only to the extent that it exceeds the amount of any refund due.

Reconsiderations and appeals. Where a business has been issued with a notice of liability under these provisions, it can ask HMRC to reconsider its decision, particularly if there are facts which should have been taken into account. An appeal can also be made to a VAT tribunal against any liability arising as a result of a such a notice. See 5.1 APPEALS for further details on reconsiderations and 5.3 APPEALS.

[*VATA 1994, s 77A; FA 2003, s 18*].

Exceptions. HMRC will not apply these provisions on the supply of specified goods and services where

- VAT goes unpaid as a result of genuine bad debts or genuine business failure;
- goods are bought by a business for its own use, rather than onward sale;
- a business can demonstrate that the low purchase price paid for the goods was due to circumstances unconnected with the failure to pay VAT;
- there is a legitimate reason for the price paid by the customer to be lower than the price paid by the supplier; or

- a business has genuinely done everything it can to check the integrity of the supply chain (and can demonstrate it has done so), has taken notice of any indications that VAT may go unpaid, and has no other reason to suspect VAT would go unpaid.

HMRC will use this measure to combat MTIC fraud. As this fraud generally involves wholesale of the relevant goods and their dispatch from the UK, it is highly unlikely that manufacturers or retail suppliers of the relevant goods will be affected by these provisions.

(VAT Notice 726, paras 2.4, 4.9).

How HMRC will apply the provisions. HMRC will send a notification letter to a business if

- the business has bought and/or sold relevant goods or services;
- they believe they can show that the transactions carried out through a particular supplier took place within a supply chain where VAT would go unpaid;
- they believe they can show that the business knew, or had reasonable grounds to suspect, that VAT would go unpaid; and
- they are satisfied that supplies are made by way of an economic activity.

Before the issue of a notification letter, each case will be independently reviewed and authorised by a central team within HMRC to ensure that the case is an appropriate one for the joint and several liability provisions and that there is sufficient evidence, on balance of probabilities, to show the requisite knowledge.

A notification letter will be sent to each known business in the chain of supply. Each business will have 21 days in which to provide evidence of its reasons and explanations why it should not be held jointly and severally liable under these provisions, including any steps it has taken to verify the integrity of its supply chain (see below). Any factors a business wishes to bring to HMRC's attention will be independently reviewed after consideration by the officer who issued the letter.

If, after a period of 21 days, a business has not responded or has not provided satisfactory evidence or explanation, HMRC will issue it with a notice of liability for the net tax unpaid. This will demand payment of the amount of VAT for which HMRC consider it is jointly and severally liable.

(VAT Notice 726, paras 4.1–4.3).

Checking the integrity of the supply chain. HMRC advise that a business should carry out checks to establish the legitimacy of its supplier in order to avoid being caught up in a supply chain where VAT would go unpaid. They do not expect it to go beyond what is reasonable and a business is not necessarily expected to know its supplier's supplier or the full range of selling prices throughout its supply chain. However, they do expect a business to make a judgement on the integrity of its supply chain and recommend that a business should undertake reasonable commercial checks to

- consider the legitimacy of customers or suppliers (eg their history in the trade; whether normal commercial arrangements are in place for the financing of the goods; whether the goods are adequately insured; and what recourse there is if the goods are not as described);
- ensure the commercial viability of the transaction (eg whether the goods are superseded or outdated models; whether it is commercially viable for the price

of the goods to increase within the short duration of the supply chain; whether normal commercial practices have been adopted in negotiating prices; and if there a commercial reason for any third party payments); and

- ensure the goods will be as described by the supplier (eg whether the goods exist, are in good condition and not damaged; and whether similar goods have been previously supplied to the business).

Examples of specific checks which could be carried out before dealing with a supplier or customer include

- obtaining copies of the certificate of incorporation and VAT registration certificate;
- verifying VAT registration details with HMRC;
- obtaining letters of introduction on headed paper;
- obtaining some form of trade reference, either written or verbal;
- obtaining credit checks or other background checks from an independent third party;
- insisting on personal contact with a senior officer of the prospective supplier and making an initial visit to their premises whenever possible;
- obtaining the prospective supplier's bank details, to check whether payments would be made to a third party or that, in the case of imports, the supplier and their bank shared the same country of residence; and
- checking details provided against other sources (eg websites, letterheads, BT landline records).

HMRC also recommend that any paperwork received in addition to invoices (eg purchase orders, pro-forma invoices, delivery notes, CMRs (Convention Merchandises Routiers) or airway bills, allocation notifications, and inspection reports, etc) should be kept as evidence of a transaction's legitimacy.

If the checks carried out by a business indicate that there may be a fraud, it should consider whether it wishes to continue with the transaction and may also wish to inform HMRC Confidential on 0800 595 000.

(VAT Notice 726, paras 4.5, 4.7, 8.1, 8.2).

17.4 DISTRESS (NOT SCOTLAND)

Where, following a written demand, a person neglects or refuses to pay any VAT due (or any amount recoverable as if it were VAT) a Revenue and HMRC officer may levy distress on that person's goods and chattels. He may also direct, by warrant, any authorised person to levy such distress in which case distress must be levied by or under the direction of, and in the presence of, that authorised person.

Goods and chattels subject to levy. Distress may be levied on any goods and chattels located in any place (including on the public highway) except for the following.

- Any of the under-mentioned goods and chattels which are located in a dwelling house and which are reasonably required for domestic needs of any person residing in that house:

Beds and bedding; household linen; chairs and settees; tables; food; lights and lighting fittings; heating appliances; curtains; floor coverings; furniture, equipment and utensils for cooking, storing or eating food; refrigerators; articles used for cleaning, mending or pressing clothes; articles used for cleaning the home; furniture used for storing clothing, bedding, household linen, articles for cleaning the home and utensils for cooking or eating food; articles used for safety in the home; toys for the use of a child within the household; and medical aids and medical equipment.

- Any of the under-mentioned goods and chattels which are located in premises used for any profession, trade or business:

  Fire-fighting equipment for use on the premises; and medical aids and medical equipment for use on the premises.

Perishable goods which cannot be restored to the debtor in the same condition as when distress is levied are exempt from distress (*Morley v Pincombe, ExD 1848, 2 ExD 101*). Tools of the trade are only exempt from distress for rent and not for tax (*MacGregor v Clamp & Sons, KB [1914] 1 KB 288*).

Time limits. Where the VAT is due under *VATA 1994, s 73(9)* (see 6.1(*a*)-(*f*) ASSESSMENTS) distress cannot be levied during the period in which an appeal against the assessment can be raised (ie 30 days from the date of the assessment or such longer period as HMRC allow for an appeal against it). The fact that distress has been correctly levied does not prevent a late appeal being entertained by a VAT tribunal (*PJ Davies (VTD 791) (TVC 2.182)*).

A levy of distress must commence between 8 am and 8 pm but may continue outside that period until the levying is complete. Where, however, a business is carried on partly or wholly outside these hours, a levy of distress may commence at any time during its business hours.

Costs. The owner of the goods and chattels is liable to pay the Revenue and HMRC officer or authorised person for costs in connection with the levying of distress, including scale charges for levying distress and taking possession of the goods, reasonable costs for appraising, removing and storing goods and advertising their sale, and scale charges for selling the goods based on the sum realised. An authorised person can retain costs out of the net proceeds but only after accounting for the VAT due to HMRC. If there is any dispute with regard to costs, the amount must be taxed by a county court judge.

Sale. The goods and chattels taken must be kept for five days to allow the person in default time to settle the outstanding VAT and costs. Otherwise, the goods, etc may be sold. Any surplus remaining, after retaining the VAT due and costs, must be restored to the owner of the goods.

[*FA 1997, s 51; SI 1997/1431*].

De Voil Indirect Tax Service. See V5.173.

17.5 DILIGENCE (SCOTLAND)

Where any VAT (or any sum recoverable as if it were VAT) is due and has not been paid, the sheriff, on an application by HMRC accompanied by a certificate by them, must grant a summary warrant in a form prescribed by Act of Sederunt authorising the recovery of the amount remaining due and unpaid by means of

- an earnings arrestment; or

- an arrestment and action of forthcoming or sale.

The certificate issued by HMRC must state that none of the persons specified in the application has paid the VAT or other sum due from him; state that payment of the amount due from each such person has been demanded from him; and specify the amount due from and unpaid by each such person.

No fee must be charged by the sheriff to the debtor for collecting, and accounting to HMRC for, sums paid to him by the debtor. Subject to this, the sheriff officer's fees, together with the outlays necessarily incurred, in connection with the execution of a summary warrant are chargeable against the debtor.

Both the application to the sheriff and the certificate may be made on behalf of HMRC by a Revenue and HMRC officer of rank not below that of Job Band 7 (as defined). Such person is also authorised to do any of the acts which HMRC are entitled to do as a creditor during the course of the poinding or sale (other than the exercise of the power under *Debtors (Scotland) Act 1987, Sch 5 para 18(3)*).

[*FA 1997, s 52, Sch 18; Abolition of Poindings and Warrant Sales Act 2001, s 3 and Sch; SI 1995/2518, Reg 213; SI 1996/2098; SI 1997/1432*].

De Voil Indirect Tax Service. See V5.173.

17.6 FURNISHING OF INFORMATION AND PRODUCTION OF DOCUMENTS

Furnishing of information. In order to maintain their records, HMRC have powers to make regulations requiring taxable persons to notify them of any changes in personal or business circumstances. In addition, every person

(*a*) who is concerned (in whatever capacity) in the supply of goods or services in the course or furtherance of a business, or

(*b*) to whom a supply within (*a*) above is made, or

(*c*) who is concerned (in whatever capacity) in the acquisition of goods from another EC country, or

(*d*) who is concerned (in whatever capacity) in the importation of goods from a place outside the EC in the course or furtherance of business

must furnish HMRC, within such time and in such form as they may reasonably require, such information relating to the goods or services or to the supply, acquisition or importation as HMRC may reasonably specify.

A person to whom the right to receive the whole or part of the consideration for a supply of goods or services has been assigned is treated as a person concerned in the supply.

[*VATA 1994, Sch 11 para 7(1)(2)(9); FA 1999, s 15*].

The above does not entitle HMRC to send an officer to put oral questions to a taxable person and demand oral answers on the spot (*C & E Commrs v Harz & Power, HL 1966, [1967] 1 All ER 177 (TVC 14.77)*). See also *EMI Records Ltd v Spillane and Others, CD [1986] STC 374 (TVC 14.79)*.

Production of documents. In addition, any person who is connected (in whatever capacity) with the activities in (*a*)–(*d*) above must, upon demand by a person acting under the authority of HMRC (an '*authorised person*') produce for inspection by that person any 'document' relating to the goods or services or to the supply, acquisition or importation. The document must be produced at the principal place of business (or at such other place as may be reasonably required) at such time as may be reasonably required. The authorised person also has power to require the production of the documents concerned from any other person who appears to be in possession of them (but without prejudice to any right of lien). He may take copies or make extracts of any document and may, at a reasonable time and for a reasonable period, remove any document, giving a receipt if requested. Where any document removed is reasonably required for the proper conduct of the business, a copy must be provided free of charge as soon as practicable. If any documents removed are lost or damaged, reasonable compensation must be paid. [*VATA 1994, Sch 11 para 7(2)(3)(5)–(8)*].

'*Document*' means anything in which information of any description is recorded and '*copy*', in relation to a document, means anything onto which information recorded has been copied, by whatever means and whether directly or indirectly. [*VATA 1994, s 96(1); Civil Evidence Act 1995, Sch 1 para 20*]. Any profit and loss account or balance sheet, relating to the business in the course of which the goods or services are supplied or the goods are imported, is included. In the case of an acquisition from another EC country, any profit and loss account or balance sheet relating to any business or other activity of the person by whom the goods are acquired is included. [*VATA 1994, Sch 11 para 7(4)*].

In addition to any profit and loss and balance sheet, HMRC may also ask to inspect

- management accounts, auditor's report and working papers, etc (but where these documents also contain non-financial or confidential information, see 15.11 CUSTOMS: ADMINISTRATION); and
- bank statements, bank paying-in slips, etc insofar as they relate to supplies of goods and services or the acquisitions or importation of goods.

HMRC will generally examine the documents at the principal place of business even where they are kept elsewhere (eg at a computer bureau).

Failure to produce documents. Where a business fails to produce the documents required even though its obligation to do so has been pointed out to it, HMRC's policy is as follows.

- Issue a formal warning letter to the business explaining the penalties for failure to meet its obligation to produce records.
- Put a stop on any repayments claimed.
- Arrange a follow up visit to see if the warning has had the desired effect.
- Where failure continues, serve a formal Notice of Demand to produce the documents, normally at the principal place of business, at a specified date giving not less than 14 days notice.
- Where failure still continues, consider civil penalty action. See 52.14 PENALTIES.
- Where failure continues following a civil penalty, consider imposing a further civil penalty at the higher rate or applying for a High Court Order (or Petition in Scotland) to secure production of the records.

Lien over documents held by third parties. Where an accountant or solicitor has a lien under common law upon a client's books as security for payment for work done, the duty to produce the records for VAT purposes prevails over the lien. If, however, HMRC remove the books, they must ensure that the lien is not undermined, eg by returning the books to the client rather than the accountant or solicitor.

Removal of documents. HMRC will normally only remove documents when absolutely necessary (eg if there is a complicated assessment to be calculated or the physical conditions of the business premises are such that they present a safety hazard to the visiting officer) and even then only with permission. In the event of a refusal to allow removal, HMRC will

- draw attention to their powers of removal;
- if refusal continues, write to the business confirming the legal provisions and warning of the penalties for failure to comply with them;
- arrange a further visit to remove the records; and
- if refusal still continues, consider civil penalty action under 52.14 PENALTIES.

(Internal Guidance V1–24B, paras 3.7–3.9, 3.11, 3.13, 3.17, 3.18 and Tables 6 and 8).

De Voil Indirect Tax Service. See V5.234; V5.235.

17.7 POWER TO TAKE SAMPLES

A person acting under the authority of HMRC may at any time, if he deems necessary on the grounds of fraud or mistake, take samples from the goods in the possession of

- any person who supplies goods or acquires them from another EC country, or
- a fiscal warehousekeeper

in order to determine how the goods, or the materials of which they are made, should be treated for VAT purposes. Any sample may be disposed of and accounted for as HMRC may direct but where it is not returned in a reasonable time (not defined) and in good condition, HMRC must pay compensation of the cost of the sample or any greater amount as they determine. [*VATA 1994, Sch 11 para 8; FA 1996, Sch 3 para 16*].

De Voil Indirect Tax Service. See V5.240.

17.8 OPENING OF GAMING MACHINES

A person acting under the authority of HMRC may at any reasonable time require a person supplying services by means of gaming machines (or any person acting on his behalf) to open any gaming machine and to carry out any other operation which may be necessary in order to ascertain the value of taxable supplies. [*VATA 1994, Sch 11 para 9*]. See 57.3 RECREATION AND SPORT for the definition of 'gaming machine'. The provisions do not apply to amusement machines.

De Voil Indirect Tax Service. See V5.238.

17.9 ENTRY AND SEARCH OF PREMISES

A person acting under the authority of HMRC (an '*authorised person*') may at any reasonable time

(*a*) enter premises used in connection with the carrying on of a business;

(*b*) enter and inspect any premises and any goods found on them if he has reasonable cause to believe those premises are used as a fiscal warehouse or in connection with

(i) the supply of goods under taxable supplies,

(ii) the acquisition of goods under taxable acquisitions from other EC countries, or

(iii) supplies of investment gold within 30.2(*a*) or (*b*) GOLD AND PRECIOUS METALS

and that goods to be so supplied or acquired are on those premises.

[*VATA 1994, Sch 11 para 10(1)(2); FA 1996, Sch 3 para 17; SI 1995/2518, Reg 31C; SI 1999/3114*].

Officers are invariably authorised in writing and instructed to produce the authority on request. Entry will normally be by prior appointment, eg under (*a*) for an audit visit (see 17.12 below). There is no requirement that the supplier is registered for VAT purposes and the provisions are sufficiently wide to include domestic premises from which a business is conducted. See 52.7 PENALTIES for obstruction of officers in the performance of their duties.

Invigilation. Invigilation is a method of checking sales as they take place to establish the level, quantity and description of sales in a given place in a given period of time. Although there is no express provision in the law to invigilate, HMRC has been advised that it is lawful to do so using implied powers under (*b*) above and/or under (*a*) above in conjunction with their powers of assessment under *VATA 1994, s* 73. As a matter of policy, Revenue and HMRC officers should always obtain the traders' consent, preferably in writing, before invigilating. (Internal Guidance V1–24B, para 2.5).

Use of warrants. A justice of the peace (justice in Scotland) may issue a written *warrant* authorising entry and search of premises, if necessary by force, if satisfied, on information under oath, that there are reasonable grounds for suspecting a 'fraud offence' which appears to be of a serious nature has been, is being or is about to be, committed or that evidence of such an offence is to be found there. The entry and search must be carried out within one month of the issue of the warrant. Any persons entering the premises under the authority of the warrant may, where there are reasonable grounds, seize and remove documents, etc required as evidence in proceedings and search any person on the premises who may be in possession of documents, etc. No woman or girl may be searched except by a woman.

'*Fraud offence*' means any offence within *VATA 1994, s 72(1)–(8)*. See 52.2–52.4 PENALTIES.

Search warrants may specify the maximum number of authorised persons who may carry out the search and the times at which it may be exercised and may provide that a constable in uniform should be present. A copy of the warrant must be supplied to the occupier or person in charge of the premises or, failing this, must be left in a prominent place.

[*VATA 1994, Sch 11 para 10(3)–(6); Criminal Procedure (Consequential Provisions) (Scotland) Act 1995, Sch 4 para 91*].

See also 17.10 below for procedure where documents are removed.

For matters relating to issues of warrants generally, see *CIR and Another v Rossminster Ltd and Others, HL 1979, 52 TC 106, [1980] STC 42.*

De Voil Indirect Tax Service. See V5.231–233.

17.10 **ORDER FOR ACCESS TO RECORDED INFORMATION**

On application, a justice of the peace (justice in Scotland) may make an order permitting a person acting under the authority of HMRC (an '*authorised person*') to have access to, copy or make extracts from, or remove recorded information reasonably required. Where the recorded information consists of data stored in electronic form, the information must be produced in a visible and legible form (or from which it can be produced in a visible and legible form) and, if required, in a form which can be removed. The justice must be satisfied that there are reasonable grounds for believing that a VAT offence has, is being, or is about to be committed and that the information in the possession of the person named in the order may be required as evidence. The order must be acted upon within seven days of issue (or such longer period as the order specifies).

For the conditions for making an order, see *R v Epsom Justices (ex p Bell and Another), QB 1988, [1989] STC 169 (TVC 14.87)* and *R v City of London Magistrates (ex p Asif and Others), QB [1996] STC 611 (TVC 14.88).*

Procedure where documents are removed. Where an authorised person removes any documents under 17.9 above or recorded information under the above provisions, he must, on request and within a reasonable time, provide a record of what has been removed. The officer in overall charge of the investigation (ie the person whose name is endorsed on the order) must, on request, allow access to such documents etc and allow them to be copied or photographed unless he has reasonable grounds for believing that to do so would prejudice any investigation or criminal proceedings. Where a person acting on behalf of HMRC has failed to comply with these requirements, an application may be made to a magistrate's court (sheriff in Scotland and court of summary jurisdiction in Northern Ireland) which may order that person to comply.

[*VATA 1994, Sch 11 paras 11–13; Criminal Procedure* (*Consequential Provisions*) (*Scotland*) *Act 1995, Sch 4 para 91; Criminal Justice and Police Act 2001, Sch 2 para 13*].

De Voil Indirect Tax Service. See V5.236.

17.11 **POWER TO INSPECT COMPUTERS**

A person authorised by HMRC is entitled, at any reasonable time, to have access to, and to inspect and check the operation of, any computer (and any associated apparatus or material) used in connection with any document which a person is required to

(i) produce, furnish or deliver (or cause to be produced, etc) to HMRC; or

(ii) permit HMRC to inspect, copy or make extracts from, or remove.

The authorised person may also require the person by whom, or on whose behalf, the computer is used, or any person concerned in the operation of the computer, to give such assistance as is necessary for those purposes.

For these purposes, any provision of any Act which requires a person to comply with (i) or (ii) above has effect as if

- any reference to a document were a reference to anything in which information of any description is recorded; and
- any reference to a copy of a document were a reference to anything onto which information recorded in a document has been copied, by whatever means and whether directly or indirectly.

Note that these provisions allow computer records to be copied and removed but the computer itself may not be removed.

Any person who obstructs an authorised person or who fails to assist him without reasonable excuse within a reasonable time, is liable, on summary conviction, to a penalty of level 4 on the standard scale laid down in *Criminal Justice Act 1982, s 75*.

[*FA 1985, s 10; Civil Evidence Act 1995, Sch 1 para 11*].

Electronic tills. HMRC have been advised that an electronic till with a constant memory and processing function can be considered to be a 'computer' for the above purposes and their powers extend to reprogramming if there is no other way to retrieve the data held on the machine. (Internal Guidance V1–24B, para 2.7).

De Voil Indirect Tax Service. See V5.237.

17.12 VISITS BY HMRC OFFICERS

A Revenue and HMRC officer will examine the business records, methods and premises and give guidance. HMRC emphasise that it is the taxpayer's responsibility to account for VAT correctly. It cannot be assumed that this is so simply because a Revenue and HMRC officer does not find any errors. The interval between visits will vary depending on the size and complexity of the business and past compliance. Businesses which send in late or incorrect declarations and payments are visited more often. For a small business, a visit may only take a few hours; for a large or complex business it can last two or more days. A visit will normally take place at the main place of business. If records are kept elsewhere, HMRC should be informed when the appointment is made. The person in charge of VAT affairs should be present. A professional adviser can also be there.

Before the visit, HMRC will

- confirm who they will want to see;
- agree a mutually convenient appointment date and time;
- advise the name and contact number of the officer conducting the visit;
- indicate the records and relevant periods required;
- indicate the likely length of the visit;
- give the business the opportunity to indicate any matters of concern so that the officer can be better prepared; and
- give the business the option to have the above details confirmed in writing.

If it is necessary to postpone a visit, HMRC should be given as much notice as possible.

On occasions, HMRC will call without an appointment. One reason for this may be to see the day-to-day operation of the business. At this time, HMRC will indicate what records are required for inspection.

During a visit, HMRC will

- identify themselves by name on arrival, and if requested, produce an identity card;
- explain the main purpose of the visit;

- discuss the various aspects of the business at the outset so as to keep claims on staff's time to a minimum (although new points may arise as they look at the records);
- examine the records of the business and, where appropriate, inspect the premises and goods thereon;
- where appropriate, take details of supplies made to/by the business to check the correct VAT treatment in the records of the business's suppliers/customers. (Occasionally, this will be the main purpose for the visit but HMRC will explain this at the time they make the appointment.);
- deal with VAT affairs confidentially;
- advise of overpayments as well as underpayments;
- where possible, endeavour to resolve matters during the visit.

At the end of the visit, HMRC will

- review the main work done;
- explain any areas of concern in relation to that work, discuss them and agree any future action that needs to be taken; and
- illustrate as fully as possible the size and the reason for any adjustment to the VAT payable, describe how the adjustment will be made, agree the adjustment whenever possible, and inform the business of how it may seek review or appeal of the decision if it disagrees.

After the visit, HMRC will

- where requested, or where they feel it is necessary, put in writing a summary of the visit, any rulings, agreements or recommendations; and
- where matters are unresolved, give the business a reasonable time within which to provide further information or comment.

(VAT Notice 700, para 2.2; Customs Notice 989).

De Voil Indirect Tax Service. See V5.221–224.

17.13 ESTOPPEL

Where, following a visit or otherwise, a Revenue and HMRC officer makes representations which are later shown to be incorrect, a taxpayer may seek to claim that the doctrine of estoppel should be applied. This doctrine prevents a person from acting inconsistently with a representation which he has made to another party, in reliance upon which that other party has acted to his detriment. The representation may be by words, conduct or silence, but it must be a representation of existing fact and not a representation of law or of intention.

In *Société Internationale de Télécommunications Aeronatiques (No 2) (VTD 17991) (TVC 2.105)* a Belgian company (S) operated a telecommunications network for aircraft. In 1973, HMRC issued a ruling that its supplies should be standard-rated but a tribunal allowed an appeal by S that its supplies should be treated as zero-rated *(VTD 19) (TVC 64.35)*. In 1997 HMRC issued a further ruling that the supplies were standard-rated. S appealed contending, amongst other things, that HMRC were bound by the earlier tribunal decision. The tribunal rejected this and held that the 1973 decision did not give rise to any estoppel, observing that the public policy behind the general application of issue estoppel is to ensure the finality of litigation. In taxation cases, however, that aspect of public policy has been overridden by a different element of public policy. Where recurring business transactions, which fall to be assessed period by period, are involved (as is the case of supplies of a VAT-registered trader), administrative flexibility is needed to enable the even-handed management of the revenue. To impose on a trader the unalterable privilege or disadvantage of a particular tax treatment of his supplies as the result of a decision of a tribunal or court might lead to inequity as between him and other traders making similar supplies the liability of which had been determined at a later date. The principle of public policy that applies in that situation is that of ensuring that the tax operates uniformly.

It has been held that there is no question of estoppel against HMRC (*Cupboard Love Ltd (VTD 267) (TVC 2.92)*), the Crown (*T Wood (VTD 6992) (TVC 2.97)*) or the mandatory provisions of a taxing statute (*Medlam (VTD 545) (TVC 2.94)*). More specifically, there is no claim if the element of detriment or prejudice is lacking eg where on advice VAT has been incorrectly calculated but the taxpayer has had the benefit of the cash he should have accounted for at the time and there is no evidence that he has charged lower prices because of the advice (*Ribbans (VTD 346) (TVC 2.93)*). It has also been held that an inspection of a trader's records and a general assurance that they are in order is insufficient to form the basis of an estoppel (*GUS Merchandise Corporation Ltd (VTD 553) (TVC 2.95)*).

In Scotland, the equivalent of estoppel is a plea of personal bar. It has been held that such a plea, at all events in matters of taxation, does not operate against the Crown, following *Lord Advocate v Meiklam, (1860) 22 D 1427* and other authorities (*Milne and Mackintosh t/a Jack and Jill (VTD 1063) (TVC 2.102)*).

HMRC's practice where taxpayer misled by an officer. HMRC have indicated that where an officer, with the full facts before him, has given a clear and unequivocal ruling on VAT in writing or, knowing the full facts, has misled a trader to his detriment, they will only raise an assessment based on the correct ruling from the date the error was brought to the attention of the registered person concerned (VAT Notice 48, ESC 3.5). This concession applies not only to incorrect rulings in writing but also to incorrect oral rulings, including those given by telephone. (*Hansard, 20 November 2002, col 189*). This practice is not, however, binding and should not be relied upon in all cases. It is not clear whether a tribunal has the jurisdiction to hear an appeal on whether circumstances fall within the statement of practice although a tribunal has found that a taxpayer was misled to such an extent that the statement was operative (*C & G Developments Ltd (VTD 2384) (TVC 2.99)*).

See also *F & I Services Ltd v C & E Commrs, CA [2001] STC 939 (TVC 2.284)* where a local officer ruled that no tax was chargeable on certain sales of vouchers but subsequently HMRC withdrew this ruling and ruled that the sales were chargeable. Carnwath J observed that, applying *dicta* of Lord Browne-Wilkinson in *R v CIR (ex p. Matrix Securities Ltd), HL [1994] STC 272*, the test is one of fairness to the taxpayer, HMRC and the general body of taxpayers. The legitimate expectation is not that the clearance will be treated as binding come what may, but that, if there is a change in the understanding of the legal position, it will not be treated as retrospective. The CA upheld this decision.

De Voil Indirect Tax Service. See V1.286; V1.287.

17.14 EVIDENCE BY CERTIFICATE, ETC

A certificate of HMRC of any of the following is sufficient evidence of that fact until proved to the contrary.

- A person was, or was not, at any date, registered.

- Any return required has not been made or had not been made at any date.
- Any EC sales list (see 2.19 ACCOUNTING PERIODS AND RETURNS) has not been submitted or had not been submitted by any given date.
- Notification of liability on an acquisition of exciseable goods or a new means of transport (see 23.9 and 23.35 EUROPEAN COMMUNITY: SINGLE MARKET) has not been given or had not been given by any date.
- Any VAT shown as due in any return or assessment has not been paid.
- A person was or was not, at any date, taxable in another EC country.
- Any VAT payable under the law of another EC country has or has not been paid.

A photograph of any document furnished to HMRC, certified by them, is admissible in any civil or criminal proceeding to the same extent as the document itself.

Any document purporting to be a certificate under the above provisions is deemed to be such a certificate until the contrary is proved.

[*VATA 1994, s 92(5), Sch 11 para 14*].

18 Customs: Standard Forms

De Voil Indirect Tax Service. See V16.1.

18.1 The following is a list of the more common forms issued by HMRC for VAT use and which can be downloaded from the HM Revenue and Customs website (apart from Form VAT 100) at

www.hmrc.gov.uk/home.htm

SIVA 1	Application for simplified VAT accounting (SIVA)
SIVA 2	Deferment schedule — SIVA reduced security
VAT 1	Value Added Tax: Application for registration (see 59.5 REGISTRATION)
VAT 1A	Application for registration: Distance selling (see 59.13 REGISTRATION)
VAT 1B	Application for registration: acquisitions (see 59.20 REGISTRATION)
VAT 1C	VAT registration notification (see 59.28 REGISTRATION)
VAT 1TR	Appointment of tax representative (see 3.11 AGENTS)
VAT 2	Value Added Tax: Partnership details (see 59.5 REGISTRATION)
VAT 7	Application to cancel your VAT registration (see 59.32 REGISTRATION)
VAT 50	Application for VAT group treatment (see 31.3 GROUPS OF COMPANIES)
VAT 51	Application for VAT group treatment – company details (see 31.3 GROUPS OF COMPANIES)
VAT 56	Application to change the representative member of a VAT group (see 31.3 GROUPS OF COMPANIES)
VAT 65	Application by a business person established in the Community for refund of VAT
VAT 65A	Application by a business person not established in the Community for refund of VAT
VAT 68	Request for transfer of a registration number (see 59.36 REGISTRATION)
VAT 98	Flat rate scheme for agriculture (see 63.27 SPECIAL SCHEMES)
VAT 100	VAT return (see 2.5 ACCOUNTING PERIODS AND RETURNS)
VAT 101	EC sales list notes on completion and forms (see 2.20 ACCOUNTING PERIODS AND RETURNS)
VAT 101A	EC sales list continuation sheet notes on completion and forms
VAT 101B	EC sales list correction sheet notes on completion and forms (see 2.20 ACCOUNTING PERIODS AND RETURNS)
VAT 162	Notice of assessment of surcharge liability notice extension (yellow)
VAT 411	New means of transport (see 23.32 EUROPEAN COMMUNITY: SINGLE MARKET)
VAT 414	Vehicles brought into the United Kingdom from within the European community

18.1 Customs: Standard Forms

VAT 415	New means of transport: Notification of acquisition
VAT 426	Insolvent traders: Claim for input tax after deregistration (see 36.13 INSOLVENCY)
VAT 427	Claims for input tax/relief from VAT on goods and services supplied before/after cancellation of registration
VAT 431	VAT refunds for DIY builders — Parts 1, 2A, 2B, 3, 3 continuation sheet, 4, 4 continuation sheet (see 42.34 LAND AND BUILDINGS)
VAT 487	Request for guidance in completing a return form
VAT 600 AA	Annual accounting application (see 63.10 SPECIAL SCHEMES)
VAT 600 AA/FRS	Application to join the annual accounting scheme and the flat rate scheme
VAT 600 FRS	Application to join the flat rate scheme
VAT 622	Standing order/BACS authority
VAT 623	Instructions to your bank or building society to pay direct debits
VAT 652	Voluntary disclosure of errors on VAT returns (see 56.11 RECORDS)
VAT 769	Notification of insolvency details (see 36.2 INSOLVENCY)
VAT 833	Statement of Value Added Tax on goods sold in satisfaction of debt
VAT 1614	Option to tax land and buildings – notification form

See also 5.7 APPEALS for standard forms for use in connection with appeals and applications to VAT and Duties Tribunal.

19 Death and Incapacity

The contents of this chapter are as follows.

19.1 VAT CONSEQUENCES OF DEATH

Assets passing to personal representatives. Where the control of a deceased person's assets passes to a personal representative or person otherwise acting in a representative capacity, that person must comply with the VAT requirements relating to accounting, payment and records. However, any requirement to pay VAT is limited to the assets over which he has control in his capacity as personal representative. [*SI 1995/2518, Reg 30*]. HMRC may therefore require the personal representative to account for any outstanding returns or VAT which was due on the date of death.

If the deceased's estate has not been finalised within a year from death, HMRC are likely to consider seeking to register the personal representative in his own right as the taxable person carrying on the business. (Internal Guidance V1–28, para 69.1.5).

Carrying on a business. Where a taxable person dies, HMRC may, from the date of death until some other person is registered in respect of the taxable supplies made (or intended to be made) by a business, treat any person carrying on the business as a taxable person. The person carrying on the business must, within 21 days of commencing to do so, inform HMRC in writing of the date of death and the fact that the business is being continued. [*VATA 1994, s 46(4); SI 1995/2518, Reg 9*]. The person carrying on the business is responsible for ensuring that all the VAT obligations are complied with and must account for any VAT due on supplies made by the business whilst he controls the business as if he were the taxable person.

Executor *de son tort*. An executor *de son tort* is a person, neither appointed by the deceased or the court to administer the deceased's property, who nevertheless 'interferes' with the deceased's property, eg by carrying on the business activities.

Where an executor has been appointed (whether by the deceased or by the court) and there is also an executor *de son tort* who is running the business on a day-to-day basis, HMRC will regard the executor *de son tort* as both the 'person otherwise acting in a representative capacity' within *SI 1995/2518, Reg 30* and as the 'person carrying on that business' within *SI 1995/2518, Reg 9*. This means that the liability for any debts arising from the business activities of the deceased, whether pre-death or post-death, can be treated as being the liability of the executor *de son tort* and the appointed executor will be ignored as far as the VAT debts of the business are concerned.

(Internal Guidance V1–28, paras 69.1.6, 69.2.3).

Death of a partner. Under *Partnership Act 1890, s 33(1)*, subject to any agreement between the partners, every partnership is dissolved as regards all the partners by the death of any partner. Until the death is notified to HMRC in writing, the registration and VAT liability of the partnership continues unchanged. See 50.3 PARTNERSHIPS AND JOINT VENTURES. On the death of a partner

- where the business of the partnership is to continue only for the purposes of winding up the partnership affairs, HMRC will consider using powers under *SI 1995/2518, Reg 9* rather than require the business to be re-registered for VAT purposes;
- where two or more partners remain after the death and continue to trade
  (i) if the partnership is registered in the name of the firm, HMRC will simply strike off the name of the deceased partner from the Form VAT 2; and
  (ii) if the partnership is registered in the names of the individual partners, it will amend the trader's name on the register (using Form VAT 12) and strike off the name of the deceased partner from the Form VAT 2; and
- where only one surviving partner remains after the death
  (i) if he intends to continue trading on his own as a sole proprietor, HMRC will deregister the partnership and register the sole proprietor under a new VAT number (using Form VAT 1). The surviving partner may, however, apply for the transfer of the existing registration under the procedure in 59.36 REGISTRATION, in which case he must sign the Form VAT 68 both on behalf of the partnership and on his own behalf as a sole proprietor;
  (ii) if he intends to find a replacement for the deceased partner and the new partner takes up his position in the partnership more or less immediately, HMRC will amend the trader's name (if the partnership is registered in the names of the individual partners), and ask the new partner to sign a Form VAT 2; and
  (iii) if he intends to find a replacement for the deceased partner but it appears that there may be some delay before this happens, HMRC will register the remaining partner as a sole proprietor either by de-registering the partnership and registering the sole proprietor or, on request, transferring the existing registration under the procedure in 59.36 REGISTRATION.

(Internal Guidance V1–28, para 69.3).

Death of a sole proprietor. Normally, on the death of a sole proprietor, HMRC will seek to re-register the person carrying on the business in his own right, regardless of the official status of that person. This may mean deregistration followed by re-registration or the transfer of registration under the procedure in 59.36 REGISTRATION (with the executor signing a Form VAT 68 on behalf of the deceased's estate in favour of the person carrying on the business). If the executor or administrator of the estate carries on the business, he will not be registered in his official capacity but as the individual and the 'taxable person' who is carrying on the business.

HMRC will only generally invoke the *SI 1995/2518, Reg 9* procedure above where it is clear that the business will be transferred to the beneficiary or sold on as a going concern within the near future. Once the estate is settled and the business is in the hands of the new owner, HMRC will then register the new taxable person, either by deregistration followed by re-registration or the transfer of registration under the procedure in 59.36 REGISTRATION.

(Internal Guidance V1–28, para 69.4.1).

Appeals to VAT tribunals. Where a person who is in the course of applying or appealing to a VAT tribunal dies and his liability or interest passes to another person (the 'successor'), the tribunal may direct, on the application of HMRC or the successor, that the successor is substituted for the original applicant or appellant. Written consent is required from the successor. Where this is not received within two months of being requested by the tribunal, the tribunal may, of its own motion or on application by HMRC, and after having given written notice to the successor, dismiss the application or appeal. It may similarly dismiss any application or appeal where it is satisfied that there is no person interested in it in succession to the original applicant or appellant. [*SI 1986/590, Rule 13; SI 1994/2617*].

19.2 VAT CONSEQUENCES OF INCAPACITY

Assets passing to another person. Where a person becomes 'incapacitated' and control of his assets passes to another person, that person must comply with the VAT requirements relating to accounting, payment and records. However, any requirement to pay VAT is limited to the assets of the incapacitated person over which he has control. [*SI 1995/2518, Reg 30*]. HMRC may therefore require that person to account for any outstanding returns or VAT which was due when incapacity commenced.

HMRC consider a person to be '*incapacitated*' if, as the result of some physical affliction or disability or of some mental disorder, he is, either temporarily or permanently, incapable of controlling and managing his property and business affairs and, consequently, incapable of meeting his obligations under the VAT legislation. They will only treat a person as being mentally incapacitated in those cases where a medical determination has been made that a person has a mental disorder within the meaning of the *Mental Health Act 1983*. The question of whether a physical incapacity constitutes incapacity for these purposes will depend on the facts of the particular case. (Internal Guidance V1–28, para 69.1.9).

Carrying on a business. Where a taxable person becomes incapacitated (see above), HMRC may, from the date of incapacitation until some other person is registered in respect of the taxable supplies made (or intended to be made) by a business, treat any person carrying on the business as a taxable person. The person carrying on the business must, within 21 days of commencing to do so, inform HMRC in writing of the date of incapacity and the fact that the business is being continued. [*VATA 1994, s 46(4); SI 1995/2518, Reg 9*]. The person carrying on the business is responsible for ensuring that all the VAT obligations are complied with and must account for any VAT due on supplies made by the business whilst he controls the business as if he were the taxable person.

Incapacity of a partner. A partnership is not automatically dissolved in the event that one of the partners becomes incapacitated although a partner may apply to the court for a dissolution of the partnership if he can show that one of the partners is 'lunatic' or 'of permanently unsound mind'. [*Partnership Act 1890, s 35*]. On the incapacity of a partner,

- where the incapacity of a partner is likely to be temporary and there are two or more partners continuing to trade, HMRC will allow the partnership to continue accounting for VAT under its existing registration (in accordance with *VATA 1994, s 45(1)*, see 50.2 PARTNERSHIPS AND JOINT VENTURES) and make no amendments to the registration details;
- where a court orders the dissolution of the partnership or the incapacitated partner resigns but, in either case, two or more partners remain and continue to trade

(i) if the partnership is registered in the name of the firm, HMRC will simply strike off the name of the incapacitated partner from the Form VAT 2; and

(ii) if the partnership is registered in the names of the individual partners, it will amend the trader's name on the register (using Form VAT 12) and strike off the name of the incapacitated partner from the Form VAT 2; and

- where a court orders the dissolution of the partnership or the incapacitated partner resigns but, in either case, only one partner remains, HMRC will either

(i) deregister the partnership and register the sole proprietor under a new VAT number (using Form VAT 1); or

(ii) at the request of the remaining partner, transfer the existing registration under the procedure in 59.36 REGISTRATION, in which case he must sign Form VAT 68 both on behalf of the partnership and on his own behalf as a sole proprietor.

(Internal Guidance V1–28, para 69.6).

Incapacity of a sole proprietor. On the incapacity of a sole proprietor,

- where there is strong evidence that the incapacity is only likely to be short-term, HMRC may treat the person carrying on the business as the taxable person under *SI 1995/2518, Reg 9* above until the proprietor is capable of taking over the business again. The trader's name on the register will be amended to read 'X carrying on the business of Y';
- where the incapacity is likely to be long-term or permanent and another person carries on the business, HMRC will register that person in his own right as the taxable person; and
- where the incapacity is likely to be long-term or permanent and the business ceases altogether, the business will be deregistered with effect from the date on which trading ceased.

(Internal Guidance V1–28, para 69.7).

19.3 RELIEF FOR IMPORTATIONS OF GOODS ACQUIRED BY INHERITANCE

Certain persons who have become entitled as legatees to property situated outside the EC may import that property without payment of VAT (and duty). See 34.15(13) IMPORTS.

19.4 RELIEF FOR IMPORTATIONS RE WAR GRAVES, FUNERALS

Certain goods can be imported without payment of VAT (and duty). These comprise goods for the upkeep of war graves, memorials, etc; coffins and urns containing human remains; and flowers, wreaths, etc with no commercial intent. See 34.15(12) IMPORTS.

19.5 AMERICAN WAR GRAVES

In order to place inland purchases on the same footing as imported goods, VAT is remitted on the supply of goods and services to the American Battle Monuments Commission for the maintenance of the American Military Cemetery and Memorial at Maddingley, Cambridge and Brookwood, Surrey. (VAT Notice 48, ESC 2.5).

19.6 BURIAL AND CREMATION

The *EC Sixth Directive, Art 28(3)(b)* allows EC countries to continue to exempt certain services listed in *Annex F*. These include services supplied by undertakers and cremation services, together with goods related thereto. Under this provision, UK law exempts

- the disposal of the remains of the dead, and
- the making of arrangements for, or in connection with, the disposal of the remains of the dead.

[*VATA 1994, Sch 9 Group 8*].

Certain other services, such as the right to a grave space and the right to place an urn in a niche, are exempt under *VATA 1994, Sch 9 Group 1* (see 19.7 below).

HMRC has always regarded the EC and UK law in *Group 8* as applying only to the *essential* goods and services that an undertaker or crematorium has to supply in order to dispose of the remains of the dead. This follows the opinion of the tribunal in *UFD Ltd (VTD 1172) (TVC 16.1)* which considered that the normal meaning of the words 'disposal of the remains of the dead' were to be construed to mean, and to be confined to, the services supplied by undertakers *as such* and cremation services. This allows undertakers and crematoria to exempt their services of burial (including burial at sea) and cremation, and the arrangements that have to be made to provide those services. Although there is no definitive list of such arrangements, they will involve the custody or care of the deceased.

The supply of goods which are incidental and closely related to these services is also exempt. But supplies of, for example, wreaths and headstones which are traditionally associated with funerals but are not sufficiently related to the actual disposal of the remains of the dead do not fall within the exemption (see further below).

(1) **Supplies by undertakers**

Although an undertaker does not directly dispose of the remains of the dead, he arranges for this to take place as part of his supply of a funeral. To qualify as the supply of an exempt funeral, the undertaker's service should contain

(*a*) the supply of a coffin; and

(*b*) the carriage of the deceased to a cemetery or crematorium.

Related services. Exempt services fall broadly into three categories.

(i) The supply of the services of embalming and the digging, preparation and refilling of graves are always exempt supplies.

(ii) If an undertaker supplies an exempt funeral (see above), he may also exempt the arrangements he has to make in order to provide the funeral. These will normally include

- the provision of bearers;
- the transport of mourners (following cars);
- use of a chapel of rest; and
- bell tolling and music at the funeral service.

(iii) If an undertaker is involved in arrangements which are directly connected to the disposal of a body, the supply is exempt even if a coffin is not provided (eg where a body is brought from a different part of the UK by another undertaker or repatriated from abroad).

The supply of services not falling within (i)–(iii) above by an undertaker who is not involved in the disposal of the body is standard-rated.

Related goods. Goods which are incidental, and closely related, to an exempt funeral may be included in the exempt supply. These will normally include such items as

- the cover and fittings for the coffin;
- the casket or urn; and
- a shroud or robe.

A supply of goods which is not part of an exempt funeral is standard-rated (eg where the bereaved carry out a 'do-it-yourself' funeral, but need to buy a coffin from an undertaker beforehand).

Use of subcontractors. If an undertaker employs a subcontractor to provide some of the services involved in a funeral, the subcontractor's supply is normally standard-rated unless it amounts to the supply of an exempt funeral. Where, for example, two undertakers are contracted by the bereaved because the body has to be moved from the place of death to a crematorium or burial ground and these are in different parts of the UK, both supplies are exempt as both undertakers have made arrangements for, or in connection, with the disposal of the remains of the dead. However, an undertaker who is subcontracted to provide additional limousines for the transport of the bereaved must standard rate his supply as he is simply hiring out vehicles.

(2) **Supplies by cemeteries and crematoria**

Cemeteries and crematoria are directly engaged in the business of disposing of the remains of the dead, and their principal supplies of burial and cremation are always exempt. Any other goods or services they provide are exempt only if they are closely related to the making of that principal supply. These include

- burial or cremation in a cemetery or crematorium;
- the digging, preparation and refilling (but not the brick-lining or walling) of a grave;
- the supply of an urn or casket in connection with a particular funeral; and
- the provision of music during a particular funeral.

Standard-rated supplies include

- the supply of a coffin and shroud by a local authority where they do not also provide the funeral; and
- any charge to a monumental mason for the right to operate in the cemetery or crematorium (eg the right to operate a showroom or to erect, work on or repair monuments).

See also 19.7 below.

Local authorities. In *Rhondda Cynon Taff County Borough Council (VTD 16496) (TVC 21.99)* the tribunal held that the provision and maintenance of *cemeteries* by a local authority was not a business activity for VAT purposes as the activities had been carried out under a special legal regime applicable to public authorities. The tribunal also concluded that, as there are so few privately-owned cemeteries, the non-business ruling would not distort competition. Following this decision, HMRC take the view that:

- The decision only applies to the provision and maintenance of local authority cemeteries. Non-business activities include the grant of a right to an exclusive burial, the right to place and maintain a tombstone, the keeping and storage of the plans and records of burials, general maintenance, and any actions intended to remove dangerous obstructions, eg collapsed vaults or broken headstones. Other services offered for which a charge is made (eg the provision of books of remembrance and the erection of headstones) remain business activities as the provision of these services is not covered by the special legal regime applicable to cemeteries.
- Although crematoria are governed by special legal provisions similar to those which apply to cemeteries, the higher incidence of privately-owned crematoria means that a distortion of competition would result if local authorities were allowed to treat these activities as non-business.
- Where local authorities operate sites which contain both cemeteries and crematoria and they have exceeded the partial exemption *de minimis* limits, a business/non-business apportionment must be made between the activities.

(3) **Miscellaneous supplies**

(*a*) *Non-essential items.* Goods and services that cannot be regarded as essential to a funeral are not covered by the exemption. These include

- flowers and wreaths;
- newspaper announcements and announcement cards;
- orders of service (zero-rated as printed matter); and
- refreshments.

(*b*) *The hire or letting out of a room or hall* for a funeral reception is normally exempt unless the option to tax has been exercised (see 42.8 LAND AND BUILDINGS). The letting of a room in a hotel or similar establishment where catering is also provided is standard-rated (see 33.1 HOTELS AND HOLIDAY ACCOMMODATION).

(*c*) *Memorials and commemoration.* Supplies of goods or services which are concerned with the commemoration, as opposed to the burial or cremation, of the dead are standard-rated. These include

- the supply, erection, inscription, repair and maintenance of headstones and memorials; and
- the supply of memorial plaques and vases, trees and bushes, memorial seats, recordium panels and books of remembrance, and any entry or inscription on them.

The removal, refixing and incidental cleaning of a memorial, where a grave is disturbed to allow for a further burial, is exempt as it forms part of the arrangements made in connection with that burial. But VAT must be charged for adding another inscription to the memorial.

(*d*) *Transport of bodies.* The transport of a body as part of the supply of a funeral is exempt. Thus, if undertaker A transports the body to the family home or a chapel of rest and then undertaker B transports the body to the cemetery, both supplies of transport are exempt. But the transport of a body

- to a hospital for an autopsy, or
- from the scene of an accident to a mortuary

is standard-rated.

If a university or other eligible body is responsible for the collection of a body for research, the supply of transport may be exempt under *VATA 1994, Sch 9 Group 6* (see 20 EDUCATION). When the body is later taken for burial or cremation, the transport becomes part of the exempt arrangements for the disposal of the remains of the dead.

The transport of a body between the UK and a place outside the EC is zero-rated to the extent that it takes place in the UK and otherwise outside the scope of UK VAT. The transport of a body from the UK to another EC country is standard-rated unless the customer is registered for VAT in another EC country, in which case there is no need to charge VAT and the customer must account for the VAT due in the other EC country under the 'reverse charge' procedure.

Where a coffin containing a body or an urn containing ashes is brought into the UK from abroad, no import VAT or acquisition tax is due. (The same also applies to flowers and wreathes accompanying the coffin or urn.)

(*e*) *Exhumation and reburial.* The exhumation of human remains is standard-rated. The subsequent service of reburial is exempt unless carried out as part of a contract for the single supply of exhumation and reburial, in which case it is standard-rated.

(*f*) *Fees and certificates.* The fees payable to

- churches and clergy in connection with funerals, and
- Registrars for certified copies of death certificates

are outside the scope of VAT.

Fees charged by a doctor for a certificate issued before a body can be cremated are exempt.

(*g*) *Funerals for pets* are standard-rated.

(4) **Mixed supplies and disbursements**

Apportionment. Where exempt supplies (including those relating to land under 19.7 below) and standard-rated commemorative items are provided as a single price package, a suitable apportionment must be made for VAT purposes. There is no special method of apportionment but the result must be fair and justifiable. See 47.3 OUTPUT TAX for various methods of apportionment.

Disbursements. Funeral packages frequently contain 'bought in' supplies. For example, undertakers may pay third parties for wreaths, refreshments, newspaper advertisements or statutory fees as part of their services as agents of their client. If the payments meet the relevant conditions set out in 3.7 AGENTS, they may be treated as disbursements and can be excluded when calculating any VAT due on the main supply.

(5) **Prepayment schemes**

Where an individual prepays for his or her funeral (ie in order to safeguard their estate from the effects of inflation, pays an undertaker, either by lump sum or in instalments, for a funeral of a given standard at some future date but at current prices) the supply is an exempt supply. Where an agent is involved, any payment which the agent receives for recommending the prepayment plan and making the necessary arrangements is standard-rated (as the agent is not personally making arrangements for the disposal of the remains of the dead). Note that where a whole life insurance policy is used as a 'funeral expenses insurance', any commission received by an agent for arranging the policy qualifies for exemption under the *VATA 1994, Sch 9 Group 2 Item 4* provided the necessary conditions in that *Group* are met. See 37.13 INSURANCE.

(VAT Notice 701/32/03; Internal Guidance V1–7, Chapter 23; Business Brief 4/2000).

De Voil Indirect Tax Service. See V4.151.

19.7 **Grants re land**

The grant or an interest in, right over or licence to occupy land is exempt under *VATA 1994, Sch 9 Group 1*. See 42.2 LAND AND BUILDINGS. Services which are exempt under this *Group* do not have to rely on a connection with a particular funeral. Examples include the right to

- a grave space;
- bury ashes in a specified plot;
- construct a vault (the actual construction would be standard-rated);
- place an urn in any type of niche (rockery, columbaria, etc) (the supply of the urn and any sealing tablet would also be exempt).

(VAT Notice 701/32/03, paras 4.1, 4.2; Internal Guidance V1–7, Chapter 23 para 3.2).

The grantor, however, has the option to tax any such supply at the standard rate (see 42.8 LAND AND BUILDINGS).

20 Education

Cross-references. See 22.17 EUROPEAN COMMUNITY LEGISLATION for the provisions of the *EC 6th Directive*; 29.8 FUEL AND POWER for supplies of fuel and power to charitable schools; 32.11 HEALTH AND WELFARE for supplies by registered nurseries and playgroups.

De Voil Indirect Tax Service. See V4.141.

The contents of this chapter are as follows.

20.1 EXEMPT SUPPLIES

VAT exemption for education, research and training is largely dependent on

- whether the body is in business for VAT purposes (see 20.2 below); and
- if so, whether it is an eligible body (see 20.3 below).

Having established that the activities are business

(*a*) supplies of education and vocational training by an eligible body are exempt (see 20.4 and 20.7 below respectively);

(*b*) supplies of research by an eligible body to another eligible body are exempt (see 20.6 below); and

(*c*) supplies of certain goods and services related to exempt supplies within (*a*) and (*b*) above are also exempt (see 20.8 below).

Where the business is not an eligible body, exemption may also apply, subject to conditions, to

- private tuition (see 20.9 below);
- examination services (see 20.10 below); and
- government approved training schemes (see 20.14 below).

20.2 Business

For VAT purposes, business has a wide meaning and includes any continuing activity which is mainly concerned with making supplies to other persons for any form of payment or consideration. For a general consideration of the meaning of business, see 8.1 to 8.3 BUSINESS.

A supply of education takes place for VAT purposes where it is provided by way of business and in return for a consideration. If there is no payment, the education is not a supply and is a non-business activity outside the scope of VAT.

Education is normally funded in one of three ways.

(1) **By making a charge**. In such cases, there is a business activity whoever pays the charges (eg a student, an employer or a local authority) and whether charges raised are sufficient to meet full costs or are subsidised (eg by central government grant, bursaries or scholarships).

Establishments which normally provide education in return for fees and are therefore in business include

- independent fee paying schools, including non-maintained special schools;
- universities; and
- institutions teaching English as a foreign language.

(2) **By direct funding from local or central government**. Education funded in this way is not a business activity and the supply is outside the scope of VAT. This normally applies to

- community schools;
- foundation schools;
- voluntary aided schools, including former special agreement schools;
- voluntary controlled schools;
- community special schools;
- foundation special schools;
- grant maintained (integrated) schools (Northern Ireland);
- self-governing schools (Scotland);
- city technology colleges; and
- city academies.

Where such schools charge for additional tuition (eg music or sport instruction), this is a business activity.

(3) **By a combination of government grants and charges**. In such cases, there is a supply for VAT purposes. The government funding is an outside the scope contribution to a business activity. Institutions which *may* require payment include

- sixth form colleges;
- tertiary colleges; and
- colleges of further education.

These institutions normally provide education for no charge to students who are 19 or under (18 or under in Scotland) at the start of their courses (non-business) but charge for older students and foreign nationals (business). The important factor is always whether they require payment, not the age or identity of the student.

(VAT Notice 701/30/02, paras 2.1–2.8, 3.1–3.4).

20.3 **Eligible bodies**

An '*eligible body*' for the purposes of providing exempt education comprises any of the following.

(*a*) A school within the meaning of *Education Act 1996*, *Education* (*Scotland*) *Act 1980*, *Education and Libraries* (*Northern Ireland*) *Order 1986* (*SI 1986/594*) or *Education Reform* (*Northern Ireland*) *Order 1989* (*SI 1989/2406*) which is

(i) provisionally or finally registered (or deemed to be registered) as a school within the meaning of that legislation in a register of independent schools;

(ii) a school in respect of which grants are made by the Secretary of State to the proprietor or managers;

(iii) a community, foundation or voluntary school within the meaning of the *School Standards and Framework Act 1998*, a special school within the meaning of *Education Act 1996, s 337* or a maintained school within the meaning of *Education and Libraries* (*Northern Ireland*) *Order 1986*;

(iv) (before 31 December 2004) a public school within the meaning of *Education* (*Scotland*) *Act 1980, s 135*(*1*);

(v) a self-governing school within the meaning of *Self-Governing Schools* (*Scotland*) *Act 1989*; or

(vi) a grant-maintained integrated school within the meaning of *Education Reform* (*Northern Ireland*) *Order 1989, Art 65.*

This covers all of the schools listed in 20.2 above. Many of these schools (notably community, foundation and voluntary schools and their counterparts in Scotland and NI) do not generally make a charge for the education they provide and this education is, for the most part, non-business and outside the scope of VAT (see 20.2 above). However, under limited circumstances, they can make a charge (eg music or sport tuition or mature students filling sixth form places) and, because they are eligible bodies, such charges are exempt.

Schools not covered by (i)–(vi) above may be covered by the eligible body criteria in (*e*) below.

(*b*) A UK university, and any college, institution, school or hall of such a university. *Not included* are subsidiary companies that universities and colleges set up to pursue commercial business.

A company providing degree-level education to overseas students and where successful students were awarded degrees from the University of Lincolnshire and Humberside was held to be a college of a university in *C & E Commrs v School of Finance and Management (London) Ltd, Ch D [2001] STC 1690 (TVC 20.10)*. The court concluded that the level of affiliation between the school and the university was sufficiently close to make the school a college of the university. HMRC have accepted the decision on the facts but, in general, consider that the *Education* (*Recognised Bodies*) (*England*) *Order 2000* (which lists colleges, halls and schools of universities) determines whether a particular college is a college of a university.

A Students Union was held not to be an integral part of the University and therefore not part of an eligible body in *C & E Commrs v University of Leicester Students Union, CA 2001, [2002] STC 147 (TVC 20.15)*.

The UK campus of a foreign university is not covered but it is likely to be an eligible body under (*e*) below.

(*c*) An institution

(i) falling within *Further and Higher Education Act 1992, s 91*(*3*)(*a*) or (*b*) or *s 91*(*5*)(*b*) or (*c*);

(ii) which is a designated institution as defined in *Further and Higher Education* (*Scotland*) *Act 1992, s 44*(*2*);

(iii) managed by a board of management as defined in *Further and Higher Education* (*Scotland*) *Act 1992, s 36*(*1*); or

(iv) to which grants are paid by the Department of Education for Northern Ireland under *Education and Libraries* (*Northern Ireland*) *Order 1986, Art 66*(*2*).

This includes all further education colleges or organisations defined or designated as such under the various *Education Acts* (including the Workers' Educational Association (WEA)), together with higher educational institutions defined in the *Education Acts* but not covered by (*b*) above.

(*d*) A government department or local authority (or a body which acts for public purposes and not for its own profit and performs functions similar to those of a government department or local authority). *Included* are executive agencies and Health Authorities.

(*e*) A body which

(i) is precluded from distributing and does not distribute any profit it makes; and

(ii) applies *any* profits made from exempt supplies of education, research or vocational training to the continuance or improvement of such supplies.

Most such bodies will be charities, professional bodies or companies limited by guarantee. However, provided they satisfy the conditions in (i) and (ii) above, *ad hoc* groups organising specific conferences or training events are eligible. The UK campuses of foreign universities are also eligible bodies but non-profit making organisations that belong overseas do not qualify as eligible.

(*f*) A body not falling within (*a*)–(*e*) above which provides the teaching of English as a foreign language (see 20.11 below).

[*VATA 1994, Sch 9 Group 6 Note 1; SI 1994/2969; Education Act 1996, Sch 37 Part 1 para 125; School Standards and Framework Act 1998, Sch 30*].

Eligible bodies do not include bodies such as tutorial colleges, computer training organisations, secretarial schools and correspondence colleges which operate with a view to making and distributing a profit.

(VAT Notice 701/30/02, paras 4.1–4.5).

20.4 **Education**

The provision of 'education' is exempt

(*a*) when provided by an '*eligible body*' (see 20.3 above); or

(*b*) to the extent that the consideration payable is ultimately a charge to funds provided by the Learning and Skills Council for England or the National Council for Education and Training for Wales under *Learning and Skills Act 2000, Parts I or II*. *Included* is the supply of any goods or services essential to the education provided directly to the person receiving the education by the person providing the education.

[*VATA 1994, Sch 9 Group 6 Items 1*(*a*)*, 5A; Learning and Skills Act 2000, Sch 9 para 47*].

'*Education*' is not defined in the legislation. HMRC regard education as meaning a course, class or lesson of instruction or study in any subject, whether or not normally taught in schools, colleges or universities and regardless of where and when it takes place. Examples are courses of instruction in dance, physical training, sports, flower arranging, and arts and crafts. Education includes lectures, educational seminars, conferences and symposia, together with holiday, sporting and recreational courses. It also includes distance learning (see 20.5 below) and associated materials, if the student is subject to assessment by the teaching institution. Any separate charge for registration is part of the supply of education.

In the sports sector, education includes classes that are led and directed rather than merely supervised. For example

- in a gymnasium, the supply of instruction in the use of equipment and warming-up techniques and the assessment of a person when he or she first enrols is the supply of education; but a charge to use the gym in a separate session where no instruction takes place is a charge for admission; and
- in a swimming pool, if the staff are on hand primarily to coach, any charge is the supply of education; but if staff are on hand primarily to satisfy health and safety and insurance requirements, any charge is for admission.

(VAT Notice 701/30/02, paras 5.1, 5.2).

See 20.10 below for the teaching of English as a foreign language.

Pre-school education, nurseries, playgroups, etc. The provision of pre-school education without charge is non-business. Breakfast clubs and after-school child-minding/homework clubs are also non-business in the LEA sector even when a charge is made provided the school offers the service strictly to its own pupils and that the fee charged is designed to do no more than cover overhead costs.

The provision of a day-nursery is a business activity. If the provider is registered with OFSTED (normally the case) the supplies are an exempt supply of welfare services in a state-regulated institution under *VATA 1994, Sch 9 Group 7 Item 9* (see 32.14 HEALTH AND WELFARE). Otherwise, the supplies will normally be standard-rated unless the supplier is an eligible body (see 20.3 above) and there is *clear* evidence that the supplies follow an educational curriculum, in which case they may be exempt supplies of education.

Where exemption applies, it also extends to the supply of meals and drinks for the children, plus other sundry items provided as part of the children's care (eg picture books, crayons and toys). It does not extend to

- children's parties or day trips where the supply is advertised as a separate and identifiable package; or
- meals and drinks to staff and visitors.

Where a local authority provides nursery services to children in care under obligations imposed by the *Children Act 1989*, this is considered to be non-business.

(Internal Guidance V1–7,Chapter 21 para 4.6).

20.5 *Distance learning*

Distance learning covers home study or correspondence courses from suppliers that range from commercial businesses to colleges of further education and universities and in subjects that range from leisure pursuits to those leading to full academic qualifications.

The VAT liability of the supply depends upon the exact nature of what is being supplied. This may be

- an exempt supply of education by an eligible body;
- a standard-rated supply of education by a business which is not an eligible body;
- a single supply of zero-rated printed matter; or
- a multiple supply of printed matter and education, in which case an apportionment is necessary.

Place of supply rules. Under *SI 1992/3121, Art 15* (see 64.23 SUPPLY) educational services are treated as supplied where physically carried out. HMRC, however, take this as referring only to supplies consisting of classroom or other face-to-face tuition, ie where physical performance is a determining factor. They do not regard a supply consisting purely of distance learning elements as covered by this rule. For these supplies, they take the view that it is necessary to consider whether there is a supply of services falling under *VATA 1994, Sch 5* (for which, depending upon the circumstances, the place of supply may be where the recipient belongs or the supplier belongs, see 64.26 SUPPLY) or a supply of goods (in which case the normal place of supply rules for goods apply, see 64.8 *et seq.* SUPPLY).

Where the place of supply is outside the UK, there is no need to consider UK VAT liability law.

Calculation of VAT liability. The following procedure should be use to calculate the VAT liability.

(1) *Establish what is being supplied.* For example, does the course include written material (in printed or electronic form), access to tutorial support, student assignments (in which case what feedback is involved), classroom training, and any examination or accreditation services. The relative weighting of tutorial support to printed or other matter offered as part of a course should be considered.

(2) *Determine whether there is a single or multiply supply.* The criteria set out by the CJEC in *Card Protection Plan Ltd v C & E Commrs, CJEC [1999] STC 270 (TVC 21.223)* must be used to determine whether there is a single or multiple supply. See 64.6 SUPPLY.

(*a*) If there is a multiple supply of standard-rated/exempt education and zero-rated printed matter, the value of each supply must be calculated in order to arrive at any output tax due. Any calculation of the apportionment of the total price must be fair and reasonable. See 47.3 OUTPUT TAX.

(*b*) If there is a single supply, consideration must be given as to whether that supply is of education or printed matter (or electronic equivalent). The principles in *Card Protection Plan* above should be used to consider which elements predominates, with the other being ancillary.

HMRC regard the following as being indicators to a supply of education.

- Successful completion of the course leads to a recognised qualification.
- The course is based on a recognised syllabus.
- The tutor/support service element is integral and significant.
- Assignments contribute to the successful completion of the course.
- The supplier is recognised as an education provider.

HMRC regard the following as being indicators to a supply of printed matter.

- Tutor involvement is not integral to the supply.
- The supplier does not author the course.
- The supplier is a publisher rather than an educator.
- The course does not lead to a qualification.

In *The College of Estate Management v C & E Commrs, CA [2004] STC 1471 (TVC 5.8)* although both the tribunal and High Court held that there was single exempt supply of education, the Court of Appeal ruled that there was a separate supply of printed material from which the students were to study and prepare assignments. The writing, preparation and distribution of the books formed a substantial part of the undertaking of the College so that the supply of the written material was a distinct and separate supply which was not ancillary to the supply of educational services. HMRC have appealed against this decision to the House of Lords.

See also *The Rapid Results College Ltd (VTD 48) (TVC 5.2)* where fees for correspondence courses were held to be apportionable between the supply of books and tuition but compare *International News Syndicate Ltd (VTD 14425) (TVC 5.3)* where the small element of external tuition was held to be incidental and the whole supply treated as zero-rated. However, these decisions pre-dated the decision in *Card Protection Plan* above and must be read in the light of the criteria set out in that case.

(Internal Guidance V1–7, Chapter 21 para 4.5).

20.6 **Research**

Note. In *EC Commission v Federal Republic of Germany, CJEC [2002] STC 982 (TVC 21.209)* the CJEC held that remunerated research activities of State universities were not closely related to university education and did not fall within the scope of the exemption. While such projects might be of assistance to university education, they were not essential to the objective of teaching students to enable them to carry out a profession and many universities achieved that aim without carrying out research projects for consideration. The exemption of research under UK law and the following provisions of this paragraph must be read in the light of that decision.

The provision of research supplied *by* an 'eligible body' *to* an eligible body is exempt. [*VATA 1994, Sch 9 Group 6 Item 1(b)*]. See 20.3 above for '*eligible body*'.

'*Research*' is not defined in the legislation. HMRC regard research as meaning 'original investigation undertaken in order to gain knowledge and understanding'. It is the intention at the beginning of a project that determines whether a supply qualifies as research. If the intention is to advance knowledge and understanding, the supply is one of research. By contrast, merely confirming existing knowledge and understanding is not research. The fact that a project may have a specific commercial application does not necessarily mean that it cannot also be research.

The following are examples of work which HMRC do not regard as being research.

- Consultancy and business efficiency advice.
- Collection and recording statistics, without also collating, analysing or interpreting of them.
- Market research and opinion polling.
- Writing computer programs.
- Routine testing and analysis of materials, components and processes.

But some of these activities do qualify if supplied as an integral part of a research project (eg where a specialised software program must be devised before the provider can embark upon the main body of the project).

(VAT Notice 701/30/02, para 5.6; Internal Guidance V1–7, Chapter 21 para 5.3).

If either of the parties to a supply of research is not an eligible body (eg a commercial organisation) the supply will normally be standard-rated (but see below for supplies to overseas bodies). Note, however, that the recipient of the supply does not have to be involved in the field of education, research or vocational training. If the recipient is a non-profit making body satisfying the criteria in 20.3(*e*)(i) above, but making no supplies of education, etc, the criteria of 20.3(*e*)(ii) above have no relevance and it is an eligible body. Supplies of research to that body are exempt. The supplier must determine the status of the customer and, if not satisfied that the customer is an eligible body, must standard-rate the supply.

Supplies to overseas bodies. Where a supply of research falls within *VATA 1994, Sch 5 para 3* (see 64.27(3) SUPPLY) then if the recipient either

- belongs outside the EC, or
- belongs in another EC country and the services are supplied for business purposes

the place of supply of the services is where the recipient belongs and the supply is outside the scope of UK VAT (see 64.26 SUPPLY). The supplier of the research can recover any attributed input tax as the supplies would have been taxable if made in the UK (see 35.3 INPUT TAX).

European Commission Framework 5 and 6 research programmes. If a research provider carried out research under these programmes, payments received are consideration for a supply. VAT should not be charged to the Commission as it is recognised as an international organisation by its host country, Belgium, and the supply is therefore exempt under *EC Sixth Directive, Art 15(10)*, see 22.21(*g*) EUROPEAN

COMMUNITY LEGISLATION. The provider can recover input tax directly attributable to the exempt supply. All other funding of research by the Commission must be considered under the normal rules described above. (VAT Notice 701/30/02, para 5.8; Internal Guidance V1–7, Chapter 21 para 5.6).

20.7 Vocational training

The provision of 'vocational training' by an 'eligible body' is exempt. [*VATA 1994, Sch 9 Group 6 Item 1*(*c*)]. See 20.3 above for '*eligible body*'.

'*Vocational training*' means training, re-training or the provision of work experience for

- any trade, profession or employment; or
- any voluntary work connected with education, health, safety or welfare or with the carrying out of activities of a charitable nature.

[*VATA 1994, Sch 9 Group 6 Note 3; SI 1994/2969*].

Vocational training includes courses, conferences, lectures, workshops and seminars designed to prepare those attending for future employment or to add to their knowledge in order to improve their performance in their current work. *Not included* are

- services such as counselling, business advice and consultancy, which are designed to improve the working practices and efficiency of an organisation as a whole rather than to enhance the ability of individuals (although these services might still qualify for exemption if provided as part of a comprehensive training package or supplied to one-person businesses); and
- conferences and other activities, the main object of which is to expound various aspects of Government, industry or company policies.

Secretarial and computer training organisations usually operate on a commercial basis and are unlikely to be eligible bodies. Training courses provided by such bodies are unlikely to qualify for exemption.

Supplies by persons other than eligible bodies. Although falling outside the above provisions, such supplies may be exempt if

- the business contracts or subcontracts to provide vocational training under one of the government's approved vocational training schemes and its services are ultimately funded by the Learning and Skills Council, the National Council for Education and Training for Wales, a Local Enterprise Company or the European Social Fund (under a scheme approved by the Department for Education and Skills), see 20.14 below; or
- provided by a sole proprietor or partnership and also qualifying as private tuition within 20.8 below.

(VAT Notice 701/30/02, paras 5.3–5.5; Internal Guidance V1–7, Chapter 21 paras 6.2, 6.3).

20.8 Related goods and services

Exemption also applies to the supply of any goods or services (other than examination services within 20.10 below) which are 'closely related' to an exempt supply within 20.4 to 20.7 above (the 'principal supply') provided (*a*) the supply is made *by* or *to* the 'eligible body' making the principal exempt supply;

(*b*) the goods or services are for the direct use of the pupil, student or trainee (as the case may be) receiving the principal supply; and

(*c*) where the supply is *to* the eligible body making the principal supply, it is made by another eligible body.

[*VATA 1994, Sch 9 Group 6 Item 4*].

See 20.3 above for '*eligible body*'.

Meaning of closely related. '*Closely related*' limits the provisions to goods and services that are necessary for delivering the education to the pupil, student or trainee. An eligible body may treat as closely related any accommodation, catering, transport, school trips and field trips it provides (subject to the rules below for selling goods to pupils).

HMRC give the following examples of goods and services that are not closely related to supplies of education and are taxable, in principle, unless relief is available elsewhere. (This is subject to the overriding principle that supplies of catering by an eligible body to its pupils, students or trainees may be treated as closely related.)

- Supplies to staff (including tutors on summer schools) and to other non-students.
- Sales of goods from school shops, campus shops and student bars.
- Sales from vending machines.
- Sales of goods that are not needed for regular use in class.
- Separately charged laundry and other personal services.
- Sales of school uniforms and sports clothing.
- Admission charges (other than for taking part in sports activities), eg admissions to plays, concerts, dances, sporting venues, exhibitions, museums, zoos.
- Administration and management services.
- Commission for allowing sales by outside organisations at an educational establishment.
- Sales by a sole proprietor or partnership in connection with private tuition.

Where closely related supplies are eligible for exemption and zero-rating (eg books and other printed matter and transport) either liability may be applied. Supplies of goods and services which are not closely related to education are taxable unless relief is available elsewhere.

Closely related goods and services sold to pupils by an eligible body providing education, etc. The provisions relating to closely related supplies only apply where the principal supply is an *exempt* supply. They do not apply where the principal supply is outside the scope of VAT as a non-business supply. As a result where education, research or vocational training is supplied by an eligible body

- in the course or furtherance of business (an exempt supply), closely related goods or services sold to pupils are also exempt; and

- for no charge (outside the scope of VAT), closely related goods or services sold to pupils are non-business and outside the scope of VAT provided they are sold at or below cost (otherwise they assume their normal VAT liability).

If the goods and services sold to pupils are not closely related to the education, etc provided, they are standard-rated unless relief is available elsewhere.

Closely related goods and services sold to pupils of other eligible bodies. The VAT liability can found by working though the following steps.

(1) Are the supplies *direct* to pupils or students of an educational institution (school, college, university) or LEA?

If Yes, go to (2). If No, go to (3).

(2) Is the supplier an educational institution or LEA?

If Yes, the supplies are not liable to VAT.

If No, the supplies are standard-rated unless relief is available elsewhere.

(3) Are the supplies to a body supplying education by way of business (ie charging fees)?

If Yes, the supplies are not liable to VAT.

If No, the supplies are standard-rated unless relief is available elsewhere.

(VAT Notice 701/30/02, paras 8.1–8.7).

Supplies of staff between eligible bodies. The following rules apply.

- The supply of teaching staff qualifies as a supply of education in its own right and is exempt. This includes the supply of classroom assistants.
- The supply of staff for the purposes of catering and accommodation qualifies as closely related to the education and is exempt where the recipient eligible body provides education for a charge.
- The supply of staff for administration and other services not qualifying as closely related (eg ground maintenance) is standard-rated.

(Internal Guidance V1–7, Chapter 21 para 9.8).

20.9 Private tuition

The supply of private tuition is an exempt supply provided it is

(*a*) in a subject ordinarily taught in a school or university; and

(*b*) given by an individual teacher acting independently of an employer.

[*VATA 1994, Sch 9 Group 6 Item 2*].

See, however, *Empowerment Enterprises Ltd (VTD 18963) (TVC 21.210A)* where the tribunal held that the wording in (*b*) above was not authorised by *EC Sixth Directive, Art 13A1(j)* and entitlement to exemption should not depend upon the legal form in which the taxable person carries out the activity.

A reasonable test for 'ordinarily' is whether the subject is taught in a number of schools and/or universities on a regular basis.

Following the tribunal decision in *C & E Clarke; A & H Clarke (VTD 15201) (TVC 20.32)* HMRC have accepted that private tuition is exempt when supplied by a sole proprietor, a partnership or any member of a partnership. However, because of the wording in (*b*) above (subject to the decision in *Empowerment Enterprises* above), exemption does not extend to instruction delivered by anyone employed (even if the teacher concerned is the sole shareholder of a company). Where a sole proprietor or partnership also employs teachers, supplies can be apportioned between exempt and taxable elements using and fair and reasonable method. If this is impractical, all supplies of tuition can be treated as standard-rated regardless of who actually delivers them. Employing someone in a non-teaching capacity has no effect on the VAT liability of tuition supplied.

A supply of private tuition services is exempt whether the individual teacher

- delivers the instruction to one person or a group;
- contracts with an individual or with an organisation (which then makes an onward supply of the services); or
- works under a franchise agreement allowing the use of the teaching methods of another person or organisation, or the use of their name or trading style.

Private tuition includes instruction or coaching in sporting or recreational activities provided the necessary conditions are met. Motor cycling lessons are potentially covered by the exemption (see *TK Phillips (t/a Bristol Motorcycle Training Centre) (VTD 7444) (TVC 20.25)*) but HMRC currently hold that car driving lessons, carried out on public highways, are not a subject ordinarily taught in a school or university.

Supplies of any goods and services in connection with the supply of tuition, even if closely linked, are standard-rated unless relief is available elsewhere (eg books may be zero-rated).

(VAT Notice 701/30/02, paras 6.1–6.3; Internal Guidance V1–7, Chapter 21 paras 7.3, 7.5).

20.10 Examination services

The provision of 'examination services'

(*a*) by or to an 'eligible body', or

(*b*) to a person receiving education or vocational training which is

  (i) exempt under 20.4, 20.7 or 20.9 above or 20.14 below, or

  (ii) provided otherwise than in the course or furtherance of a business

is an exempt supply.

'*Examination services*' include

- the setting and marking of examinations;
- the setting of educational or training standards;
- the making of assessments; and
- other services provided with a view to ensuring educational and training standards are maintained.

[*VATA 1994, Sch 9 Group 6 Item 3* and *Note 4; Learning and Skills Act 2000, Sch 9 para 47*].

See 20.3 above for '*eligible body*'.

Examples of activities treated as examination services are services connected with GCSE examinations, etc, National Vocational Qualification (NVQ) assessments, course accreditation services, validation, certification, assessment and registration of candidates. *Not included* are

- services of printers, graphic designers, and typesetters; and
- non-specialist secretarial, advertising or promotional services (unless provided as part of a broader package of predominantly examination services by the same person who provides those services).

Supplies direct to pupils. Included under (*b*) above is the supply of examination services *directly* to

- pupils of independent fee paying schools;
- pupils of community, foundation or voluntary schools;
- students of further education colleges;
- trainees of government approved training schemes; and
- employees receiving in-house training from their employers.

Examination boards normally provide GCSE examinations direct to school pupils. Schools can usually treat as disbursements the payments they receive from and on behalf of pupils for these examinations. See 3.7 AGENTS for the treatment of disbursements.

School inspections. School inspections are in principle within the scope of exemption for examination services. However, because of the way in which the inspection system operates in the state sector, with greater use of private contractors, HMRC have been reviewing the VAT treatment of school inspections. While this review is in progress, they accept that the supply of school inspection services by the contractors to OFSTED are standard-rated. The contractors are therefore entitled to recover as input tax any VAT incurred on goods and services used in connection with supplying school inspection services to OFSTED.

All other school inspection services are exempt. This includes inspections supplied direct to a school in the state sector (eg some schools request pre-inspection visits and the school pays the contractor directly for such a service). School inspections and similar services commissioned by independent fee-paying schools are always exempt.

(VAT Notice 701/30/02, paras 7.1–7.5; Internal Guidance V1-7, Chapter 21 para 8.7).

20.11 English as a foreign language (EFL)

Exemption applies to tuition in EFL by *any* body (see 20.3(*f*) above). Where, however, the body does not also qualify as an eligible body under another category within 20.3(*a*)–(*e*) above, exemption does not extend to any other supplies which the body makes apart from the 'teaching of English as a foreign language'. [*VATA 1994, Sch 9 Group 6 Note 2; SI 1994/2969*].

HMRC interpret this as meaning that exemption does not extend to other education, research or vocational training (eg tuition in a language other than English or training in the teaching of EFL) supplied by a commercial provider of EFL who is not within 20.3(*a*)–(*e*) above.

Following the decision in *Pilgrims Languages Courses Ltd v C & E Commrs, CA [1999] STC 874 (TVC 20.16)* HMRC accept that all elements integral to the supply of any course in the teaching of EFL by a commercial provider are covered by the exemption (eg sports, recreational, sightseeing or social activities aimed at promoting fluency in the use of the English language). In addition, any separate supplies of closely related goods and services are also exempt provided they meet the conditions set out in 20.7 above.

Where courses are supplied in modular form, comprising some tuition in EFL plus broader coverage of other subjects, the supply can be apportioned to reflect the exempt element using any fair and reasonable method. If this is inconvenient or impractical, the whole supply can be standard-rated.

(VAT Notice 701/30/02, paras 9.1–9.3).

20.12 EDUCATION SUPPLIED BY LOCAL AUTHORITIES

Any education or vocational training provided by local authorities for no charge, or which they provide acting as a public authority, is a non-business activity. Local authorities are, however, eligible bodies (see 20.3(*d*) above) and all other educational or vocational training courses that they provide for any form of charge or payment are generally exempt business supplies, irrespective of any subsidy they may receive. See *City of London Corporation (VTD 17892) (TVC 21.101)* where the tribunal held that, on the facts, the Corporation was not carrying on a business activity in respect of three schools, even though it charged fees to most of the parents. The schools had been established under special legal provisions and the Corporation was required to maintain them.

Most schools in the state sector belong to one of three categories of 'maintained school', namely community, foundation or voluntary. All such schools are maintained by a Local Education Authority (LEA) and receive funding from it. The governing body of each school acts as agent of the LEA for goods and services it pays for either out of the school's delegated budget from the LEA or from amounts given to the school from LEA central funds for specific purposes. The local authority can recover VAT incurred on such purchases under *VATA 1994, s 33* (see 43.7 LOCAL AUTHORITIES AND PUBLIC BODIES).

Private funds of LEA schools. LEA maintained schools (including voluntary aided schools) are funded largely via the local authority but they can also generate income independently (eg through vending machines or charges for the use of the premises outside normal hours). Such 'private fund' income is generally kept in a separate bank account and is not part of the local authority for VAT purposes but a separate entity. The private fund might be held in the name of the governing body, the head teacher (acting as agent of the governing body) or some other entity (eg a Parent Teacher Association). Subject to the normal threshold, a school (in the guise of its private fund) must register for VAT separately if it makes taxable supplies that generate income which does not belong to the LEA and which it uses purely to augment its own funds.

Input tax recovery on purchases using private funds. If the private fund is separately registered for VAT, it can recover input tax subject to the normal rules and the local authority cannot recover the VAT incurred on any private fund purchases.

Alternatively, where a private fund has obtained income other than via the local authority, it can opt to donate the money to the local authority for them to buy goods and services on the private fund's behalf. The local authority can then recover the VAT incurred provided it

- makes the purchase itself (ie places the order, receives the supply and a VAT invoice addressed to it, and makes the payment);
- retains ownership of the purchase and uses it for its own non-business activities; and
- keeps sufficient records of the purchase and the purpose for which it is made.

This donational route is not, however, available in respect of

- certain direct grants from the Department for Education and Skills (DfES) to the governing bodies of foundation schools; and
- income, including direct grants from the DfES, used to fund works which are the responsibility of the governors of a voluntary aided school.

Where the LEA owns the buildings, any income a maintained school obtains from letting its premises normally goes to the LEA unless it agrees that the school may use this income. If so, the income can be treated in the same way as budget share funds when the school uses it to buy goods and services (ie the school is deemed to be acting as agent of the LEA in spending the money and the LEA is entitled to recover VAT incurred on the purchases). This does not apply in the case of foundation and voluntary aided schools (where the LEA is not the owner of the buildings).

Sales of 'closely related' supplies made by a local authority to its own pupils and students. Local authorities are 'eligible bodies' so that any education they provide for a charge (eg adult education classes) is an exempt business activity. Any closely related goods and services they supply in connection with this education are also exempt (see 20.8 above). However, most of the education that local authorities provide is not for a charge and is therefore a non-business activity and outside the scope of VAT. This includes the education provided through LEA maintained schools to pupils of compulsory school age and those on 'A' level courses in the sixth forms of these schools. Because LEA maintained schools do not supply education in the course or furtherance of business, it follows that any goods and services they provide to their pupils for a charge in connection with this education are not exempt, even though they might be closely related. As a concession, LEA maintained schools can treat the closely related goods and services they supply to pupils as non-business, provided it complies with the following rules which have been agreed with CIPFA.

- The goods and services must be closely linked to the education provided (ie for the direct use of the student and necessary for delivering the education to the student).
- The pupil must receive education from the LEA in either an LEA maintained school or in connection with some other LEA run educational activity (eg an orchestra).
- The goods and services required must be purchased from the LEA.
- Payment for the goods must be made either to the LEA or to the school (and, if the latter, it must be paid into official funds).
- Some evidence (eg an order form) must be kept to show that the recipient of the goods and services has been receiving education from the LEA, and that what has been supplied was essential to that education.
- The price of the goods and services supplied must be at or below cost. 'Cost' means the overhead-inclusive price of supplying the goods or services to the pupil.

Where any goods are leased, the same conditions apply as for sales.

In practice, regardless of the precise nature of the activity, any school trips that a school organises for the benefit of its pupils can be treated as part of its non-business provision of education.

Supplies of food and drink in LEA schools. Sales of food and drink by an LEA in its maintained schools to its pupils are non-business and therefore outside the scope of VAT if made at or below cost (see above). The 'at or below cost' criterion can be determined in one of two ways.

- A school can look at all the LEA catering outlets on its premises (eg canteen, refectory, tuck shop, kiosk, trolley, vending machine. etc). Provided the total sales are at or below cost, the school can treat all its sales of food as non-business. HMRC, exceptionally, allow a school to apply the 'at or below cost' criterion for each catering outlet. Output tax would then only be due in relation to the outlets where cost is exceeded.
- An LEA can analyse all its school catering outlets together. This will produce a single set of figures, from which the LEA can determine whether catering is provided at or below cost across its whole school portfolio.

This treatment applies only to sales of food and drink by a local authority school to its pupils and from outlets operated by either the local authority itself or the governing body. If the supply of food and drink is by a catering contractor, see 11.8 CATERING.

If staff and visitors are free to use any of the catering outlets provided by the school, an apportionment by any fair and reasonable means must be applied to determine the level of taxable business sales.

Closely related supplies made by a local authority other than to its own pupils and students. By concession, LEA maintained schools may treat as non-business any closely related goods and services they supply direct to the *pupils* of other schools and to the students or trainees of eligible bodies (eg FE colleges and universities). They cannot exempt any closely related goods and services they supply to *other eligible bodies* unless they also supply the education or training itself.

Grant assistance for students on training courses. Where a local authority provides a grant to a student attending further education establishments (eg to cover tuition, board, and other necessary expenses), regardless of whether the grant is paid to the training establishment or the student, it does not represent payment for any supplies made to the local authority. As the supplies are made to the student and not the local authority, there is no entitlement to input tax recovery by the local authority. This remains the case even where the local authority is billed direct for any of the supplies made.

Adult education. Where local authorities are not under a statutory obligation to provide adult education, the provision of courses is a business activity carried out in direct competition with other suppliers of further education. Any charge for such a course, whether subsidised or not, is an exempt supply of education.

Community education. Local authorities must ensure that certain forms of community education are available in their area although they are not obliged to supply it themselves. If they choose to do so, they compete with a broad range of education providers offering similar services in different parts of the country. This is a business activity.

School photographs. See 20.18 below.

Fuel and power. See 29.8(1) FUEL AND POWER.

(VAT Notice 701/30/02, paras 10.1–10.9; VAT Notice 749, para 5.8; Internal Guidance V1–14, paras 12.1, 12.2; Business Brief 14/95).

20.13 EDUCATION ACTION ZONES ('EAZS')

EAZs consist of local clusters of maintained schools working in partnership with the local Education Authorities ('LEAs'), local parents, businesses, Training and Enterprise Councils and others. A major aim of the EAZ initiative is to raise education standards in certain deprived areas. Under the scheme, the governing bodies of participating schools can delegate their powers to the Education Action Forum which runs the EAZ. Membership of the Forum is drawn from the above groups. EAZs receive Government funding each year and are expected to raise further funding from the private sector. They are not, however, part of the local authority and are not entitled to make use of the refunds scheme for non-business activities under *VATA 1994, s 33* (see 43.7 LOCAL AUTHORITIES AND PUBLIC BODIES).

Recovery of VAT by an EAZ. If a statutory EAZ buys goods and services

- using funds delegated to it by an LEA via the governors of participating schools, the LEA can recover any VAT incurred (as the EAZ is acting as agent to the LEA in the purchase);
- using funds that it has obtained from other sources, the LEA cannot recover any VAT incurred (as the EAZ is not acting as its agent);
- via the governors of participating schools using funds it has obtained from non-LEA sources, the LEA cannot recover any VAT incurred (as the governors are not acting as its agent);
- and incurs VAT that the LEA cannot recover, the VAT sticks with the EAZ as a real cost (as the EAZ makes no taxable supplies of its own and so is not registrable for VAT); and
- from an LEA using funding channelled to it by the LEA via the governors of participating schools, the transaction is outside the scope of VAT (as the EAZ is acting as agent of the LEA and no supply takes place).

If an LEA supplies teaching staff to an EAZ for purposes of instruction, the LEA should not charge VAT (as both the LEA and the EAZ are eligible bodies and the supply is exempt).

If an EAZ is non-statutory (ie one not established under the *School Standards and Framework Act 1998*), then the LEA can recover VAT on goods and services supplied to the EAZ (as the EAZ is acting as agent of the LEA in the purchase).

(VAT Notice 701/30/02, paras 11.1–11.3).

20.14 GOVERNMENT APPROVED VOCATIONAL TRAINING SCHEMES

The provision of 'vocational training' is exempt to the extent that the consideration payable is ultimately a charge to funds provided

- pursuant to arrangements made under *Employment and Training Act 1973, s 2*, *Employment and Training Act* (*Northern Ireland*) *1950, s 1A* or *Enterprises and New Towns* (*Scotland*) *Act 1990, s 2*; or

- by the Learning and Skills Council for England or the National Council for Education and training for Wales under *Learning and Skills Act 2000, Parts I or II.*

Included is the supply of any goods or services essential to the vocational training provided directly to the trainee by the person providing the training. [*VATA 1994, Sch 9 Group 6 Item 5 and Note 5; Learning and Skills Act 2000, Sch 9 para 47; SI 1994/2969*].

The provisions exempt the supply of vocational training under government approved vocational training schemes by suppliers who are not 'eligible bodies' within 20.3 above. Supplies of vocation training by eligible bodies are exempt under the wider provisions in 20.7 above, which see for a general consideration of 'vocational training'.

This exemption covers supplies of

- vocational training, including work experience, and
- any goods and services supplied directly to trainees that are essential to the training

to the extent that they are ultimately funded by schemes approved by the Department for Education and Skills, the Jobcentre Plus (part of the Department for Work and Pensions), Government Offices for the regions and their national counterparts in Wales, Scotland and Northern Ireland. The schemes usually provide vocational training to young and unemployed people but also cover other forms of training (eg training workplace assessors in connection with National Vocational Qualifications and training aimed at providing additional skills for use in the workplace such as to Health and Safety and First Aid Officers). The schemes are administered and funded by the Learning and Skills Council (LSC), the National Council for Education and Training for Wales, Local Enterprise Companies (LECs) in Scotland and the Training and Employment Agency in Northern Ireland. In most cases, the LSC, etc do not provide training themselves but instead contract with a training provider (which in turn may further sub-contract all or part of the training). Approved schemes also include schemes that are paid for using funds derived from the European Social Fund and training administered by further education colleges and funded by any of the bodies listed above.

Exemption does not cover

- counselling and careers guidance services (unless a compulsory part of a vocational training package); or
- accreditation or assessment services (although these might qualify for exemption as examination services (see 20.10 above).

Supplies by training providers. Where a training provider contracts to supply vocational training under one of the government's approved schemes, its supply is exempt to the extent that the consideration payable is ultimately a charge to funds from one of the approved schemes. But the following should be taken into account.

(*a*) If the contract allows for a separate supply of management services, these are not covered by the exemption and must be standard-rated.

(*b*) If the trainee or an employer pays part of the cost of the training from their own resources, that part of the supply is not covered by the special exemption. The training provider should apportion between the exempt and standard-rated elements (unless it is an eligible body, see 20.3 above).

(*c*) Where the training provider's contract is with a further education college, it must find out what proportion of the payment by the college derives from approved funds within these provisions as, similarly, only this proportion qualifies automatically for exemption (unless the training provider is an eligible body). In determining the proportion, the college may opt to apply a global formula rather than perform a separate calculation each time it buys in a supply of vocational training, ie it may express its annual funding allocation as a percentage of its total income for the year and apply this percentage to each purchase of vocational training made in the subsequent year in order to arrive at the proportion that qualifies for exemption.

Where a training provider is given a training credit voucher by a trainee to redeem with the local office of the LSC, the income received from the voucher is part of the consideration for the exempt supply.

Supplies by subcontractors. Exemption also extends to a subcontractor's supplies to the extent that the training provider pays for the supplies using government funding obtained within these provisions. It may be difficult to establish the extent to which exemption applies. The subcontractor should ask the training provider for, and keep, evidence that all or part of the supplies are ultimately funded under the scheme. The subcontractor can then exempt supplies to the extent of the funding. If not fully funded, HMRC should accept any apportionment which seems reasonable on the available information. Otherwise, unless the subcontractor is an eligible body within 20.3 above, it should account for VAT on its supplies if the training provider does not confirm that the supplies are ultimately funded under an approved scheme.

Any funding received which must be passed on to trainees or students (eg statutory living allowances, travel costs and lodging expenses) is outside the scope of VAT and does not form part of the supply of vocational training.

Work placement providers. Where a work placement provider supplies work experience to a trainee who is its own employee, any payments made to the trainee as wages or allowances are outside the scope of VAT. Where it supplies work experience to

- a trainee or employee of another business, or
- a college student under one of the government's approved vocational training schemes,

any charge for the services of the employee by the business, or the trainee by the college, are standard-rated. This is separate from the supply of exempt vocational training by the work provider to the trainee or student.

Unemployed trainees qualify for a statutory living allowance and, in some cases, expenses. If the work provider funds any such allowances or expenses from its own resources, the amount paid is consideration for a standard-rated supply of the trainee's services by the training provider or college. This applies even if no actual payment is made to the training provider or college.

(VAT Notice 701/30/02, paras 13.1–13.5; Business Brief 13/96).

20.15 NEW DEAL PROGRAMME

New Deal is a programme designed primarily to help young people aged 18–24 who have been unemployed for six months or more to obtain long-term employment by providing opportunities for education, vocational training and work experience. The intention is to encourage employers to recruit these people, in return for which they are paid a subsidy. The unemployed are given opportunities to study towards accredited qualifications whilst continuing to claim an allowance equivalent to Jobseeker's Allowance. Although aimed primarily at the 18–24 age group (see 20.16 below), there is also provision for the over 25s (see 20.17 below).

The Jobcentre Plus (JP) leads and co-ordinates the delivery of New Deal. This is done via partnerships with other agencies and organisations including employers, local authorities, local Learning and Skills Councils and Local Enterprise Companies (LECs), the Connexions Service, further education colleges, voluntary and environmental organisations, disability groups and others. In some areas the lead delivery partner will be the JP, in others it will be a private company or public agency. The partners may choose to ask the JP to undertake the contracting on their behalf. Another possibility is for partners to form a consortium or joint venture to deliver the whole or large parts of the scheme under contract to the JP.

(VAT Information Sheet 3/99, paras 1, 3; Internal Guidance V1–7, Chapter 21 paras 17.1, 17.2).

20.16 Components of New Deal for 18–24 age group

For 18–24 year olds the package is made up of the following components.

(*a*) *Gateway*. This lasts for a maximum of four months and offers an intensive period of counselling, advice and guidance, including extensive help from the Jobcentre Plus (JP). Other organisations (the 'partners' in the scheme) provide specialist help where needed (eg professional careers advice or debt, homelessness or dependency counselling). Where necessary, short courses in basic skills and brief 'tasters' of the various options available are included in order to decide which is best suited to the individual.

VAT liabilities

- Statutory living and travel allowances are outside the scope of VAT when paid by the Department of Work and Pensions/JP to the partners and in turn by the partners on to the unemployed person.
- The provision of careers guidance and other advice by the JP itself is outside the scope of VAT.
- If partners contract with the JP to supply specific services of counselling, careers advice and other forms of guidance, the supply is to the JP and is standard-rated (unless provided as part of a vocational training package, in which case it is exempt).
- Separately identifiable short courses and 'tasters' covered by such contracts qualify as exempt training and work experience under 20.14 above. However, these elements can be treated as standard-rated if it is impractical to separately identify them.
- If partners use the money they have obtained from the JP to buy in supplies of vocational training and work experience, the supplies made to them are exempt under 20.14 above but supplies of careers advice and other guidance are standard-rated (unless provided as part of a vocational training package, in which case it is exempt).

(*b*) *Options*. After entering the Gateway, and assuming that they have not already been successful in securing unsubsidised employment, 18–24 year olds are obliged to take up one of five options, all of which include an element of education or vocational training.

(1) *Employment option*. Under this option, employers receive a subsidy of £60 per week for up to six months in return for offering young people a job with training. Up to £750 is available towards the cost of vocational training. Young people are paid a wage from the employer and have full employee status with normal conditions of employment.

VAT liabilities

- Payments by the JP to employers of £60 per week wage subsidies and lump sum payments towards the cost of vocational training are outside the scope of VAT.
- If employers use this money to buy in vocational training or work experience, the supply to them is exempt under 20.14 above.

(2) *Voluntary sector option*. This option offers work with training within the voluntary sector for six months. Up to £750 is available towards the cost of training for an approved qualification, in addition to the fee paid to the job provider. Young people on this option receive an allowance equivalent to Jobseeker's Allowance benefit, plus a grant of up to £400 paid in instalments. Voluntary bodies taking part in the scheme are encouraged to take on participants as employees if they prefer and pay them a wage.

VAT liabilities

- Payments by the JP to work placement providers for non-employed trainees are consideration for exempt supplies of work experience and vocational training under 20.14 above.
- If placement providers use this money to buy in vocational training and work experience, the supply made to them is exempt under 20.14 above.
- Any separately identifiable payments for careers guidance, counselling, job search, etc are consideration for standard-rated supplies by partners to the JP.
- If placement providers employ the participants, the payments they receive from the JP are outside the scope subsidies towards wage costs.
- Living and travel allowances, and grants of up to £400, passed on to the unemployed person, are also outside the scope of VAT.

(3) *Environmental task force option*. The option offers work with training on an environmental task force for six months. Payments both to providers and trainees are on the same basis as (2) above.

VAT liabilities. As (2) above.

(4) *Full-time education and training*. This option, aimed primarily at young people without NVQ level 2 qualifications or the equivalent, lasts up to twelve months. The education and training is available through a variety of local sources (eg further education colleges and private training providers). Allowances are paid that are equivalent to benefit, and access is provided to a discretionary fund for help with general living expenses.

VAT liabilities

- Supplies of vocational training and work experience are exempt under 20.14 above.
- Living and travel allowances paid by the JP to partners, and by partners on to unemployed persons, are outside the scope of VAT.

(5) *Employment option* (*self-employment*). Participants normally enter the self-employment route after three months in Gateway. At this stage, they benefit from a special package of counselling, advice and support carried out by a training provider, including a basic awareness and information session. A second stage involves a period of one-to-one counselling or, alternatively, a short course spread over four weeks. At the final stage (self-employment proper), participants receive further training and support from a training provider and the opportunity to set up and run a business on a trial basis whilst receiving a training/trading allowance for up to 26 weeks.

VAT liabilities

- At the first stage, the JP pays the training provider £25 for each participant who attends an awareness session. This is consideration for a standard-rated supply by the provider to the JP.
- At the second stage, the JP pays the training provider £200 for each participant who successfully completes the short course and produces an approved business plan. This is consideration for a supply of vocational training by the provider to the JP which is exempt under 20.14 above. If the provider is paid the £200 for any participant who has successfully produced a business plan without undergoing a training course, payment is consideration for a standard-rated supply of counselling. Sometimes the provider receives an additional sum of £100 for any participant going straight from Gateway into independent self-employment or unsubsidised work with an employer. This payment is further consideration for the standard-rated supply of general Gateway services by the training provider to the JP.
- At the final stage, the JP pays the training provider £1,500 for each participant in three stages, the first two of 25% each and the final of 50% when the training provider confirms to the JP that the participant is still in self-employment or in a job with an employer 13 weeks after leaving the option. All payments are consideration for the exempt supply of vocational training by the training provider to the JP. It follows that, where training providers subcontract for any of these final stage services, supplies by the subcontractors to them are also exempt under 20.14 above to the extent that payments are ultimately derived from JP funding.
- Living and travelling allowances paid to participants are outside the scope of VAT if separately identifiable.

(*c*) *Follow-through*. This is designed to meet the needs of young people who return to unemployment after completing their option. It involves further intensive help from the JP to get them into work.

VAT liabilities

- If partners contract with the JP to supply specific services of careers advice, guidance and mentoring (including access to jobclubs), the supply is to the JP and is standard-rated.
- The supply of work experience (including trial placements) and key skills training is exempt under 20.14 above.
- If partners use money they have obtained from the JP to buy in vocational training or work experience, the supply to them is also exempt under 20.14 above.
- Other services are exempt or standard-rated depending on precisely what is offered and the balance between training and guidance elements.

General principles. The above analysis is based on the premise that, under all the possible arrangements between the JP and partners/contractors (see 20.15 above), the JP is the recipient of a supply of services by the partners/contractors. Where this is the case, the following general principles apply.

- That supply is standard-rated counselling, advice and careers guidance unless it consists of vocational training, in which case it is exempt under 20.14 above.
- Where a single supply comprises elements of both vocational training and careers advice, etc the vocational training element may be exempted where separately identifiable. If this is impractical, the supply is standard-rated. Alternatively, if the supply is predominantly one of vocational training, any standard-rated elements can be disregarded if it is impractical to separately identify them. At the Gateway and Follow-through stages, elements are predominantly standard-rated. At the Options stage, elements are predominantly exempt.
- Consideration for the supply is the total payment made by the JP to the partner less any element that the partner is obliged to pass on to the unemployed by way of living allowances and travel expenses. (This is subject to the proviso that all payments made by the JP in respect of employed trainees can be treated as outside the scope subsidies towards wage costs.)
- If one partner subcontracts work to another, or to an unrelated third party, in return for payment, that payment is consideration for a supply of services.
- Under consortium and joint venture arrangements, no supply is made to a lead partner or administrator when these merely disburse the JP funding to another partner. The supply is by that partner to the JP.
- Any charge made by the lead partner or administrator to other partners in return for disbursing the JP payments is consideration for the standard-rated supply of a management service.

(VAT Information Sheet 3/99, paras 2, 4; Internal Guidance, V1–7 Chapter 21 paras 17.3, 17.4).

20.17 **New Deal for job seekers aged 25 and over**

Main 25+ scheme. Jobseekers aged 25 and over who have been unemployed for two years or more are covered by an Employment Option under which employers are encouraged to offer jobs, for which they receive a subsidy equal to £75 per week for up to six months. These payments from Jobcentre Plus (JP) are outside the scope of VAT, together with any contribution towards the cost of vocational training.

Jobseekers may also take up an Education and Training Option under which they receive, for example, basic literacy and numeracy training at a further education college. Payments to the college by the JP are consideration for exempt supplies of education or training.

25+ pilot New Deal schemes. A number of pilot schemes have been introduced which aim to extend to unemployed persons as a whole, the principles of the New Deal that applies to the young unemployed (see 20.16 above). The broad objective of the scheme is to allow the individual to benefit from a package of advice and counselling, vocational training, work experience and jobsearch activities to enhance prospects of long-term employment. The schemes have the following components.

(*a*) *Gateway*. This is a period usually lasting a maximum of 13 weeks with a series of advisory interviews with a personal adviser. Contractors must be able to provide access to a formal training needs assessment, together with basic skills and pre-vocational training for those who need it.

(*b*) *Intense Activity*. For participants not successful in finding a job as a direct result of (*a*) above, an Intensive Activity period (usually lasting for 13 weeks or until the unemployed person leaves Jobseeker's Allowance) comprises continuing and concentrated jobsearch. If this still does not result in full-time subsidised or unsubsidised work with an employer, participants are entitled to a tailored package which may include work experience, training, advice on self-employment, and further help with jobsearch. Throughout this period, in addition to their full entitlement to Jobseeker's Allowance, participants also qualify for a top-up grant of up to £200, together with an employer subsidy of £75 per week for six months. Both the grant and subsidy paid to employers are outside the scope of VAT.

(*c*) *Follow-through*. There is provision in the scheme for assistance in the form of advice and training to be extended into a further period known as Follow-through, where the help can either be provided by the JP itself or by the contractor in conjunction with the JP.

(*d*) *Follow-up*. For those who find employment, New Deal contractors must be able to offer additional help to both the participant and the employer, aimed at ensuring wherever possible that the individual remains in that employment. This period of sustained assistance in employment is known as Follow-up.

Funding levels. The JP pay contractors an average of £1,300 per participant. This payment by the JP is consideration for the supply of New Deal services by the contractor to the JP, with the liability of the supply depending on exactly what is provided and the extent to which it can be separately identified. In the absence of appropriate evidence to the contrary, the funding from the JP should be treated as consideration for the standard-rated supply of placement services.

(VAT Information Sheet 3/99, para 5; Internal Guidance V1–7, Chapter 21 para 17.5).

20.18 SCHOOL PHOTOGRAPHERS

The photographer may supply the photographs

- direct to the pupils, in which case the school or LEA makes a separate supply of the use of premises, facilities and other services to the photographer in return for the commission or discount they receive; or
- to the school or Local Education Authority (LEA), in which case the school or LEA sells the photos on to the pupils.

Sales of photographs by the photographer directly to pupils. The photographer must account for VAT on the final selling price of the photographs to the pupils.

The position of the school depends upon whether it is independent or LEA maintained and, if the latter, also upon whether it acts for the LEA or for the governing body in supplying the use of its facilities to the photographer, the type of school and whether it is VAT-registered.

(*a*) In the case of

- community and voluntary controlled schools in England and Wales,
- public schools in Scotland (as defined in *Education* (*Scotland*) *Act 1980, s 135*), and
- 'controlled' schools in Northern Ireland,

the school (normally in the person of the head teacher) may act an agent for the LEA when contracting with the photographer. If so, the LEA must account for VAT on the commission or discount the school receives.

Alternatively, following the tribunal decision in *Lancashire County Council (VTD 14655) (TVC 60.333)* HMRC accept that, where the school has full control over the funding it receives from non-LEA sources and acts as agent for the governing body, the governing body must account for VAT on the supply of the facilities to the photographer where its taxable turnover (including income from the photographer) exceeds the VAT registration threshold or where it has voluntarily registered.

To decide the correct VAT treatment of the discount or commission they give, school photographers should confirm which situation applies for each contract they enter into.

(*b*) In the case of

- foundation and voluntary aided schools in England and Wales,
- self-governing schools in Scotland, and
- voluntary-maintained, voluntary grammar and grant-maintained integrated schools in Northern Ireland

the head teacher is an employee of the governing body of the school and acts on its behalf. The governing body must account for VAT on the supply of the facilities to the photographer where its taxable turnover (including income from the photographer) exceeds the VAT registration threshold or where it has voluntarily registered.

(*c*) In the case of independent schools, the school must account for VAT on the supply of the facilities to the photographer where its taxable turnover (including income from the photographer) exceeds the VAT registration threshold or where it has voluntarily registered.

Sales of photographs by the photographer to LEA's, schools and other bodies. Where the contractual arrangements provide that the supply of photographs is to the LEA, school or other body,

- *if the LEA, etc is registered for VAT*, the photographer must account for VAT on the price actually charged. The LEA, etc can recover the VAT as input tax subject to the normal rules and must account for output tax on the full value of the supply to the pupils.
- *if the LEA, etc is not registered for VAT*, the photographer should contact HMRC and, pending their advice, account for VAT on the amount actually charged to the LEA, etc. HMRC may subsequently issue a Notice of Direction under *VATA 1994, Sch 6 para 2* requiring the photographer to account for VAT on the final selling price charged by the unregistered school to the pupils.

(VAT Notice 701/30/02, paras 12.1–12.5; Internal Guidance V1-7, Chapter 21 paras 15.1–15.5).

20.19 Youth clubs

The provision of 'facilities' is exempt if supplied by

- a 'youth club' or an 'association of youth clubs' to its members; or
- an association of youth clubs to members of a youth club which is a member of that association.

A club is a '*youth club*' if

(*a*) it is established to promote the social, physical, educational or spiritual development of its members;

(*b*) its members are mainly under 21 years of age;

(*c*) it is precluded from distributing and does not distribute any profit it makes; and

(*d*) it applies any profits made from exempt supplies to the continuance or improvement of such supplies (ie it must not use any of its income to subsidise any outside activity).

[*VATA 1994, Sch 9 Group 6 Item 6 and Note 6*].

An '*association of youth clubs*' is an organisation, the members of which are youth clubs.

In addition to (*a*)–(*d*) above, HMRC expect a club to meet the following conditions in order to qualify as a youth club.

- It should provide a range of activities. A single activity club (eg a swimming club) is not regarded as a youth club even if its members are mainly under 21 years of age.
- It should have its own constitution. HMRC do not regard youth sections of organisations such as sports clubs, cultural societies and environmental groups as youth clubs unless separately constituted. See also *Haggs Castle Golf Club (VTD 13653) (TVC 20.42)*.
- It should be able to produce its own accounts.

Exemption covers

- in the case of a youth club, any facilities which the club supplies to members in return for their subscriptions or, if the facilities are directly related to the club's ordinary activities, for an additional payment; and
- in the case of an association of youth clubs, any facilities which the association supplies to
  - (i) youth clubs that are members of the association in return for subscriptions, affiliation fees or similar payment; and
  - (ii) members of individual youth clubs which are part of the association of youth clubs where the facilities are of a type that would be exempt if provided by a youth club.

Not exempt under these provisions are

- supplies to non-members; and
- supplies not commonly provided by a youth club to its members, eg
  - — sales of foods and drink;
  - — overnight accommodation similar to the type provided by a hotel;
  - — purely recreational holidays; and
  - — fund-raising events where tickets are sold to the public (although certain fund-raising events may be exempt under *VATA 1994, Sch 9 Group 12*, see 12.10 CHARITIES).

'*Facilities*'. HMRC takes 'facilities' to mean the provision of an amenity or service that enables an activity to be carried out. Facilities therefore include

- a shop (but not selling items from the shop);
- a fitness centre (but not aerobics classes);
- an internet café (but not surfing the web);
- a library (but not the hire of videos or use of photocopier); and
- access to student union bar through payments of union subscriptions (but not the purchase of alcohol and food from the bar).

(VAT Notice 701/35/04; Internal Guidance V1–7, Chapter 27 para 3.3).

21 European Community: General

The contents of this chapter are as follows.

21.1 EC INSTITUTIONS

The three European Communities are the European Coal and Steel Community ('ECSC'), the European Community ('EC') (previously the European Economic Community but renamed by the Maastricht Treaty) and the European Atomic Energy Community ('EAEC' or 'Euratom').

The EC is the body principally concerned with VAT. It was set up by *The First Treaty of Rome* ('*EC Treaty*') with effect from 1 January 1958 and was entered into initially by Belgium, Federal Republic of Germany, France, Italy, Luxembourg and The Netherlands (who were also the initial members of ECSC and EAEC). By *The Treaty of Accession*, the UK, Ireland and Denmark entered the Communities with effect from 1 January 1973. The relevant UK legislation is *European Communities Act 1972*. Greece joined with effect from 1 January 1981, Spain and Portugal with effect from 1 January 1986 and Austria, Finland and Sweden with effect from 1 January 1995. Cyprus, Czech Republic, Estonia, Hungary, Latvia, Lithuania, Malta, Poland, Slovak Republic and Slovenia joined with effect from 1 May 2004, raising the total number of EC countries to 25.

21.2 European Community: General

The *EC Treaty* is widely drafted and there is an emphasis on provisions for the free movement of persons, goods, services and capital as well as powers for the implementation of common policies in many areas of economic and social life. It provides for a *Council of Ministers* which is composed of representatives of the governments of the member countries and effectively has the power to make decisions.

The *European Commission* is the executive constitution of the EEC and also formulates the policy acted upon by the Council.

The *European Parliament* has, primarily, only supervisory and consultative powers.

The *European Court of Justice* is empowered to ensure that in the interpretation and application of the *EC Treaty* the law is observed. In this connection it is the ultimate court of appeal.

All the above bodies are common to both ECSC and EAEC.

The *European Council,* consisting of Heads of State of the member countries, is not recognised as such by the *EC Treaty*, although this body has become an important focus of attention.

21.2 **VAT TERRITORY OF THE EC**

The VAT territory of the EC consists of

- Austria
- Belgium
- Cyprus (from 1.5.04)*
- Czech Republic (from 1.5.04)
- Denmark (not the Faroe Islands and Greenland)
- Estonia (from 1.5.04)
- Finland (not the Aland Islands)
- France (including Monaco but not including Martinique, French Guiana, Guadeloupe, Reunion and St Pierre and Miquelon)
- Germany (not Busingen and the Isle of Heligoland)
- Greece (not Mount Athos (Agion Poros))
- Hungary (from 1.5.04)
- Ireland
- Italy (not the communes of Livigno and Campione d'Italia and the Italian waters of Lake Lugano)
- Latvia (from 1.5.04)
- Lithuania (from 1.5.04)
- Luxembourg
- Malta (from 1.5.04)
- The Netherlands
- Poland (from 1.5.04)

- Portugal (including the Azores and Madeira)
- Slovak Republic (from 1.5.04)
- Slovenia (from 1.5.04)
- Spain (including the Balearic Islands but not Canary Islands, Ceuta or Melilla)
- Sweden
- United Kingdom (including the Isle of Man and, from 1.5.04, UK Sovereign Base Areas of Akrotiri and Dhekelia (Cyprus) but not the Channel Islands or Gibraltar)

[*VATA 1994, s 93; SI 1995/2518, Regs 136, 137, 139; SI 2004/1082, Reg 6*].

*The European Commission has advised that whilst the entire island of Cyprus joined the EC on 1 May 2004, as the situation stands at present, the application of the EC *aquis communautaire* (ie the body of common rights and obligations which bind all the countries together within the EC) is suspended in those areas of Cyprus in which the Government of the Republic of Cyprus does not exercise effective control.

De Voil Indirect Tax Service. See V1.213–218.

21.3 CUSTOMS TERRITORY OF THE EC

The customs territory of the EC consists of the VAT territory (see 21.2 above) plus

- Andorra
- The Aland Islands
- Channel Islands
- San Marino
- The Canary Islands
- The overseas departments of the French Republic (Guadeloupe, Martinique, Reunion and French Guiana)
- Mount Athos (Agion Poros)

21.4 EXCISE TERRITORY OF THE EC

The excise territory of the EC consists of the VAT territory (see 21.2 above) plus

- San Marino

21.5 TRADE STATISTICS TERRITORY OF THE EC

EC countries and their associated or dependent territories for Intrastat purposes are as follows.

Austria (including Jungholz and Mittelberg)
Belgium (excluding all dependent/associated territories)
Cyprus
Czech Republic

Denmark (excluding the Faroe Islands)

Estonia

Finland (including the Aland Islands)

France (including Monaco but excluding all French Overseas Departments and territories (see note below))

Germany (including Heligoland but excluding Busingen)

Greece (including Mount Athos)

Hungary

Ireland

Italy (excluding Livigno, Campione d'Italia, San Marino, the Italian Waters of Lake Lugano, and The Vatican)

Latvia

Lithuania

Luxembourg

Malta

Netherlands (excluding all dependent/associated territories)

Poland

Portugal (including the Azores and Madeira)

Slovakia

Slovenia

Spain (including the Balearic Islands but excluding Ceuta, Melilla, and the Canary Islands (see note below))

Sweden

United Kingdom (including the Channel Islands and the Isle of Man but excluding Cyprus Sovereign Base and Gibraltar)

Note. The French territories of French Guiana, Guadeloupe, Martinique and Reunion are now part of the statistical territories of France and the Canary Islands are now part of the statistical territory of Spain. However, as customs documentation (the SAD) is still required for trade with these territories for the purpose of trade facilitation, and to avoid any danger of duplication, trade statistics between the UK and both the French territories and the Canary Islands continue to be collected from the SAD.

Although the entire island of Cyprus joined the EC on 1 May 2004, the application of the EC *aquis communautaire* (ie the body of common rights and obligations which bind all the countries together within the EC) will be suspended in those areas of Cyprus in which the Government of the Republic of Cyprus does not exercise effective control.

(Customs Notice 60, Appendix B).

21.6 **TRADE WITH TERRITORIES WITH WHICH THE EC HAS SPECIAL RELATIONS**

The following rules apply.

- For trade with such territories outside the VAT, customs, excise *and* trade statistics territories (see 21.2 to 21.5 above), the same procedures apply as before the introduction of the single market. Such territories are treated in the same way as any other non-EC country.
- For trade with the Azores, the Balearic Islands, Madeira and Monaco (which are within the VAT, customs, excise *and* trade statistics territories, see 21.2 to 21.5 above), the same procedures apply as for trade with other EC countries. This also applies to trade between the Isle of Man and EC countries other than the UK.
- Where goods are imported into the EC from any of the additional territories within the Customs territory (see 21.3 above), there is no liability to customs duty but VAT may be payable. (There are special schemes for goods such as cut flowers which enter the UK from the Channel Islands.) Excise duty may also be payable but not on goods imported from San Marino (which is inside the Excise territory).

21.7 **AUSTRIA**

What is VAT called? Mehrwertsteuer (Mwst). Umstatzsteuer (Umst)

Address for general information on VAT system. Finanzamt Graz-Stadt, Referat fürausländische Unternehmer, Conrad von Hötzendorfstrasse 14–18, 8018 GRAZ

Tel: (+43) (316) 8810

Fax: (+43) (316) 817608

Country code. AT

VAT registration numbers. An Austrian VAT registration number consists of the letter 'U' followed immediately by eight digits, all in one block (eg U12345678)

(VAT Notice 725, paras 1.15, 12.16, 12.17, 16).

21.8 **BELGIUM**

What is VAT called? (French): Taxe sur la Valeur Ajoutée (TVA). (Dutch): Belasting over de Toegevoegde Waarde (BTW)

Address for general information on VAT system. Central BTW – kantoor voor buitenlandse belastingplichtigen – information Controle Zaveltoren – 24ste verdieping, Stevenstraat 7, 1000 BRUSSEL

Tel: (+32) (2) 5525933 or 5525934

Fax: (+32) (2) 5525541

Country code. BE

VAT registration numbers. A Belgian VAT registration number (numèro TVA (N° TVA) or BTW-Nummer (BTW-Nr)) consists of nine digits (eg 123456789)

(VAT Notice 725, paras 1.15, 12.16, 12.17, 16).

21.9 **CYPRUS**

Address for general information on VAT system. Ministry of Finance, VAT Service-Headquarters, Corner of Karaoli and Afxentiou, 1096, Nicosia, Cyprus

Fax: +357–22660484

e-mail: headquarters@vat.mof.gov.cy

website: http://www.mof.gov.cy/ce

Country code. CY

VAT registration numbers. A Cypriot VAT registration number consists of 9 characters of which the last is an alpha character (eg 12345678X)

21.10 **CZECH REPUBLIC**

Address for general information on VAT system. Ministry of Finance, Central Financial and Tax Directorate, Department of Indirect Taxes, Letenská 15, 115 00 Praha 1, Czech Republic

Tel: +420 257 041 111

Fax: +420 257 042 788

e-mail: podatelna@mfcr.cz

website: http://cds.mfcr.cz/

Country code. CZ

VAT registration numbers. A Czech VAT registration number consists of either 8, 9 or 10 digits (eg 12345678, 123456789 or 1234567890). Where 11, 12 or 13 digit numbers are quoted, delete the first three digits (as these are a tax code).

21.11 **DENMARK**

What is VAT called? Omsaetningafgift

Address for general information on VAT system. Told-og Skattestyrelsen, Hermodsgade 8, 200 KØBENHAVEN

Tel: (+45) 35 87 73 00

Fax: (+45) 31 85 90 94

Country code. DK

VAT registration numbers. A Danish VAT registration number (varemodtagers moms-nr (SE-nr)) consists of eight digits (eg 12345678)

(VAT Notice 725, paras 1.15, 12.16, 12.17, 16).

21.12 **ESTONIA**

Address for general information on VAT system. Estonian Tax Board, Narva mnt 9a, Tallinn 15176, Estonia

Tel: +372 1811

Fax: +373 683 5709

e-mail: maksuamet@ma.ee

website: http://www.ma.ee

Country code. EE

VAT registration numbers. An Estonian VAT registration number consists of 9 digits (eg 123456789)

21.13 FINLAND

What is VAT called? Arvonlisavero (ALV)

Address for general information on VAT system. Uudenmaan verovirasto, Yritsverotoimisto, PL.32, 00052 VEROTUS

Tel: (+358) (9) 73114327

Fax: (+358) (9) 73 114700

Country code. FI

VAT registration numbers. A Finnish VAT registration number consists of eight digits (eg 12345678)

(VAT Notice 725, paras 1.15, 12.16, 12.17, 16).

21.14 FRANCE

What is VAT called? Taxe sur la Valeur Ajoutée (TVA)

Address for general information on VAT system. Direction Générale Des Impôts, Bureau de gestion de la fiscalité professionelle, 86–92 Alle de Bercy, Teledoc 971, 75574 PARIS CEDEX 12

Tel: (+33) (1) 53181113

Fax: (+33) (1) 53189501

Country code. FR

VAT registration numbers. A French VAT registration number (numéro d'identification) always consists of 11 characters, normally 11 digits but in some cases (mostly local authorities and government departments) the first, second or first and second characters are alpha characters. All alpha characters except I and O are valid

(VAT Notice 725, paras 1.15, 12.16, 12.17, 16).

21.15 GERMANY

What is VAT called? Mehrwertsteuer (Mwst). Umstatzsteuer (Umst)

Address for general information on VAT system. Bundesamt für Finanzen, Friedhofstrasse 1, 53225 BONN

Tel: (+49) 228 4060

Fax: (+49) 228 4062661

Country code. DE

VAT registration numbers. A German VAT registration number (Umsatzsteuer-Identifikationsnummer (USt-IdNr)) consists of nine digits (eg 123456789)

(VAT Notice 725, paras 1.15, 12.16, 12.17, 16).

21.16 **GREECE**

What is VAT called? Arithmos Forologikou Mitroou (FPA)

Address for general information on VAT system. Ministry of Finance, 14th Directorate of VAT and Indirect Taxes, Sina 2–4, 10672 Athens

Tel: (+30) 1 36 472 03

Fax: (+30) 1 36 454 13

Country code. EL

VAT registration numbers. A Greek VAT registration number consists of nine digits commencing with a zero (eg 012345678)

(VAT Notice 725, paras 1.15, 12.16, 12.17, 16).

21.17 **HUNGARY**

Country code. HU

VAT registration numbers. A Hungarian VAT registration number consists of eight digits (eg 12345678)

21.18 **IRELAND**

What is VAT called? Value added tax (VAT).

Address for general information on VAT system. Taxes Central Registration Office, Arus Brugha, 9/15 Upper O'Connell Street, Dublin 1

Tel: (+353) 1 87 46 821

Fax: (+353) 1 87 46 078

Country code. IE

VAT registration numbers. An Irish VAT registration number consists of eight characters including one or two alpha characters either last or second and last (eg 1234567X or 1X34567X)

(VAT Notice 725, paras 1.15, 12.16, 12.17, 16).

21.19 **ITALY**

What is VAT called? Imposta sul valore Aggiunto (IVA)

Address for general information on VAT system. Ministero Delle Finanze, Segretariato Generale, Ufficio Relazoni Internazionali, Viale dell' Aeronautica. 122, 00149 ROMA

Tel: (+39) 06 5912983

Fax: (+39) 06 5912971

Country code. IT

VAT registration numbers. An Italian VAT registration number (codice IVA or numero di partita IVA (P.IVA)) consists of eleven digits (eg 12345678901)

(VAT Notice 725, paras 1.15, 12.16, 12.17, 16).

21.20 **LATVIA**

Address for general information on VAT system. State Revenue Service, National Tax Board, 1 Smilsu Stree, Riga, LV–1878, Latvia

Fax: +371 7028814

website: http://www.vid.gov.lv

Country code. LV

VAT registration numbers. A Latvian VAT registration number consists of eleven digits (eg 12345678901)

21.21 **LITHUANIA**

Address for general information on VAT system. State Tax Inspectorate under the Ministry of Finance, Vasaria 16–osios str. 15, LT 2600 Vilnius

Tel: +370 5 268 78 00

Fax: +370 5 212 56 04

e-mail: vimi@vmi.lt

website: www.vmi.lt

Country code. LT

VAT registration numbers. A Lithuanian VAT registration number consists of nine or twelve digits (eg 123456789 or 123456789012)

21.22 **LUXEMBOURG**

What is VAT called? Taxe sul la Valeur Ajoutée (TVA)

Address for general information on VAT system. Administration de l'Enregistrement et des Domaines, Bureau d'imposition 10, 7 Rue de Plébiscite, BP 31, 2010 Luxembourg

Tel: (+352) 4490 51(switch board); (+352) 44905451 (Bureau 10)

Fax: (+352) 291193 (Bureau 10)

Country code. LU

VAT registration numbers. A Luxembourg VAT registration number (numéro d'identification) for EC trade purposes consists of eight digits (eg 12345678)

(VAT Notice 725, paras 1.15, 12.16, 12.17, 16).

21.23 **MALTA**

Address for general information on VAT system. VAT Department, Centre Point Building, Ta' Paris Road, Birkirkara BKR 13, Malta

Tel: +356–21.49.47.84 or +356–22.79.92.30

Fax: +356–21.49.93.65

e-mail: vat@gov.mt

website: http://www.vat.gov.mt

Country code. MT

VAT registration numbers. A Maltese VAT registration number consists of eight digits (eg 12345678)

21.24 **NETHERLANDS**

What is VAT called? Omzetbelasting (OB). Belasting over de Toegevoegde Waarde (BTW)

Address for general information on VAT system. Belasting dienst Particulieren, Ondernemingen Buitenland, Postbus 2865, 6401 D J Heerlen

Tel: (+31) (45) 573 6666

Fax: (+31) (45) 573 6684

Country code. NL

VAT registration numbers. A Dutch VAT registration number (Omzetbelasting-nummer (OB nummer)) consists of nine digits followed by a three character suffix in the range B01–B99 (eg 123456789B01)

(VAT Notice 725, paras 1.15, 12.16, 12.17, 16).

21.25 **POLAND**

Country code. PL

VAT registration numbers. A Polish VAT registration number consists of ten digits (eg 1234567890)

21.26 **PORTUGAL**

What is VAT called? Imposto sobre o Valor Acrescentado (IVA)

Address for general information on VAT system. Serviço de Administraçáo do IVA, Ava. João XXI 76, 1000 Lisboa

Tel: (351–1) 793 6673

Fax: (351–1) 793 65 28

Country code. PT

VAT registration numbers. A Portuguese VAT number (numero de identifiaçao fiscal (NIPC)) consists of nine digits (eg 123456789)

(VAT Notice 725, paras 1.15, 12.16, 12.17, 16).

21.27 **SLOVAK REPUBLIC**

Address for general information on VAT system. Tax Office Bratislava 1, Radlinského 37, PO Box 89, 817 89 Bratislava 15, Slovakia

Tel: +421 2 5737 8111

Fax: +421 2 5244 2181

website: http://www.finance.gov.sk

Country code. SK

VAT registration numbers. A Slovak VAT registration number consists of nine or ten digits (eg 123456789 or 1234567890)

21.28 **SLOVENIA**

Address for general information on VAT system. Tax Administration of the Republic of Slovenia, Tax Division, Šmartinska 55, Ljubljana, Slovenia

Tel: +386 1 478 27 84

Fax: +386 1 478 27 43

website: http://www.gov.si/durs

Country code. SI

VAT registration numbers. A Slovenian VAT registration number consists of eight digits (eg 12345678)

21.29 **SPAIN**

What is VAT called? Impuesto sobre el Valor Añadido (IVA)

Address for general information on VAT system. Subdirección General de Informacion y Assistencia, Agencia Estatal de La Admistracion Tributaria (AEAT), C/Infanta Mercedes No. 37, 28071 Madrid

Tel: (+34) (91) 583 8976

Fax: (34) (91) 583 8808

Subdirección General de Impuestos Sobre el Consumo, Dirección General de Tributos, C/. Alcala 5, 28014 MADRID

Tel: (+34) (91) 5958000 (ask for 'IVA')

Fax: (34) (91) 5958454

Country code. ES

VAT registration numbers. A Spanish VAT registration number (numero de identificacion fiscal (NIF)) consists of nine characters including one or two alpha characters either first, last or first and last (eg X12345678 or X1234567X)

(VAT Notice 725, paras 1.15, 12.16, 12.17, 16).

21.30 **SWEDEN**

What is VAT called? Mervärdeskatt (MOMS)

Address for general information on VAT system. Skattemyndigheten I, Stockholms Län, Skattekantor riks, 106 61 Stockholm, Sweden

Tel: (+46) 8 6941000

Fax: (+46) 8 6435230

Country code. SE

VAT registration numbers. A Swedish VAT registration number consists of 12 digits (eg 123456789012)

(VAT Notice 725, paras 1.15, 12.16, 12.17, 16).

21.31 **REFUND OF VAT TO PERSONS ESTABLISHED IN OTHER EC COUNTRIES**

When a business registered for VAT in one EC country buys goods or services in another EC country, it may have to pay VAT there. If goods are bought for removal from that EC country, there is usually no problem as such dispatches are normally VAT-free. But if the goods or services bought in that EC country are also used there (eg at a trade fair), the business cannot treat any VAT incurred as input tax on a VAT return in its own country.

To avoid this, subject to conditions being met, the *EC 8th Directive* sets up a scheme which allows a business to reclaim certain VAT suffered in another EC country. Broadly, if a business is registered for VAT in any EC country, it can use the scheme to reclaim VAT paid in any other EC country provided that it

- is not registered or liable to be registered there (in which case that country's domestic VAT legislation would apply);
- has no place of business or other residence there; and
- does not make any supplies there other than
  - (i) transport (and related) services carried out in connection with the international carriage of goods; or
  - (ii) services where VAT on the supply is payable by the person to whom they are supplied. (These may vary slightly between EC countries but broadly correspond to those listed in *VATA 1994, Sch 5*, see 64.27 SUPPLY.)

See 22.48 EUROPEAN COMMUNITY LEGISLATION for a more detailed summary of the provisions of the *EC 8th Directive*.

The business must comply with the following conditions.

(*a*) *Claim form.* The business must complete a special claim form. The form is available in all the official languages of the EC and must be completed in the official language and currency of the EC country where the VAT was paid. It must be sent to the authorities there with proof of the VAT paid (see (*b*) below). A certificate of status may also have to be sent (see (*c*) below).

(*b*) *Proof of VAT.* A claim form must be supported by correctly completed invoices, vouchers or receipts from suppliers showing

- an identifying number;
- supplier's name, address and VAT registration number;
- claimant's name and address;
- details of the goods or services supplied;
- the date of supply;
- the cost of the goods or services (excluding VAT);
- the rate of VAT; and
- the amount of VAT charged.

If the goods have been imported, the VAT copy of the import entry or other Customs document showing the amount of VAT paid is also required.

Only originals of documents are acceptable.

(*c*) *Certificates of status*. When making its first claim in any EC country, a business must also include the original of a certificate from its own tax authority showing that it is registered for VAT there. When applying for the certificate, it must ask for all the information that the authorities will need to process the claim to be shown (eg if the invoices are made out in a company's trading name, the certificate must show this, as well as the name under which it is registered).

A separate certificate is required for each EC country where a claim is to be made. Each certificate is valid for twelve months from the date of issue and will cover any claims made in that country in the year. Once the certificate has expired, a new one must be sent with the next claim.

A UK business wishing to make a claim in another EC country can obtain a certificate (Form VAT 66) by writing to the

National Registration Service
VAT 66 Section
Deansgate
62–70 Tettenhall Road
Wolverhampton WV1 4TZ

by fax to: 01902 392202
or by e-mail to: VAT66@hmrc.gsi.gov.uk.

(*d*) *Time limit*. The claim must be made no later than six months from the end of the calendar year in which the VAT was incurred. A claim must cover any VAT being claimed over a period of at least three months (unless less than three months of a calendar year remains) but not more than a full calendar year. Items missed on earlier claims can be included as long as they relate to VAT charged in the year of the claim.

(VAT Notice 723, paras 2.1, 2.2, 2.6, 3.1–3.6).

De Voil Indirect Tax Service. See V5.151.

21.32 Applications to other EC countries by UK taxable persons

The domestic VAT legislation of EC countries other than the UK is outside the scope of this book. As such provisions will have a significant bearing on the making of an application for recovery of VAT suffered, professional advice may need to be sought. See 21.33 to 21.56 below for details of where to obtain forms, non-refundable VAT, minimum claims in different EC countries, use of agents, appeals, etc.

The scheme cannot be used to reclaim VAT on

- dispatches of goods (but these will be VAT-free provided the supplier has the necessary evidence), or
- goods and services (eg hotel accommodation) which have been bought for resale and which are for the direct benefit of travellers

but otherwise it can be used to reclaim VAT on any supplies used by the business, subject to the normal rules for claiming input tax in that EC country.

There is no maximum amount that can be claimed but each EC country has set a minimum amount that can be refunded in any one claim. The authority responsible for payment must pay a refund within six months of receiving satisfactory evidence.

(VAT Notice 723, paras 2.3, 2.5, 4.1).

Flat-rate scheme for farmers. Where a VAT-registered person in the UK acquires goods from a farmer in another EC country who charges the flat-rate addition (see 63.25 SPECIAL SCHEMES for the equivalent scheme for UK farmers), the addition must be reclaimed from the VAT authority in the supplier's country (not Customs via the VAT return). (VAT Notice 700/46/02, para 6.2).

21.33 *Austria*

VAT refunds can only be applied for by using form number U5 obtainable from

Finanzamt Graz-Stadt
Referat für ausländische Unternehmer
Conrad von Hötzendorfstrasse 14–18
8018 GRAZ
Austria

Tel: +43 316 88 10 34

Fax: +43 316 81 76 08

The form must be completed in German.

Non-refundable VAT. In addition to the supplies listed in 21.32 above, refunds cannot be claimed on entertainment expenses, car hire and petrol.

Minimum claim. The minimum amount refundable is €36 for a one year period and €360 for a quarter or another period of less than one year.

Time limit. The Austrian tax authorities are bound by law to refuse claims which exceed the time limit specified in 21.31 above.

Method of repayment. Repayment will be made by credit transfer to the bank account of the business.

Using an agent. If a business wishes to appoint somebody to either represent it as a tax adviser or to receive refunds, a specific mandate must be given to that person.

Appeals against rejection of claims. After a claim has been checked, the cancelled invoices will be returned with notification of details of any refund. This notification is a formal notice of assessment against which an appeal can be lodged within one month of the notice of assessment. The German term for this appeal is *Berufung.*

(VAT Notice 723, para 5.1).

21.34 *Belgium*

Forms and other information are obtainable from

(French):

Bureau Central de TVA pour assujettis etrangers
Remboursement
Tour Sablon 25ème étage,
Rue Joseph Stevens, 7
B–1000 BRUXELLES

(Dutch):

Centraal BTW kantoor voor buitenlandse belasting-plichtigen
Terruggaven,

Zaveltoren 25ste verdieping
Stevensstraat, 7
B–1000 BRUSSEL

Tel: +32 2 5525977 or 5525982

Fax: +32 2 5525542

The form must be completed in French or Dutch, using block capitals and in triplicate.

Non-refundable VAT. In addition to the supplies listed in 21.32 above, refunds cannot be claimed on manufactured tobacco; alcoholic drinks (unless intended for resale or to be provided as part of a supply of services); entertainment expenses; or accommodation and food and drink for on-the-spot consumption (unless the cost is incurred by staff supplying goods or services away from business premises or a taxable person who supplies it on for a consideration).

In addition, only 50% of VAT incurred can be reclaimed on a motor vehicle used wholly or partly for passenger transport and on any supplies related to the vehicle.

Minimum claim. If a claim is for a year, it cannot be less than €25. If a claim is for less than a year, it must not be less than €200.

Method of repayment. A business can choose to be paid by

- credit transfer to a postal account kept in Belgium or abroad by it or its agent; or
- transfer to a bank or other financial institution established in Belgium, which must be
  - (i) an institution specified in Article 1(2)(1) or Royal Decree No 185 dated 9 July 1935, on banking supervision and the system of security issues; or
  - (ii) an undertaking specified in Article 1(2)(3) of the same Royal Decree; or
  - (iii) a credit association authorised by the Caisse Nationale de Credit Professional; or
  - (iv) a 'caisse de credit' authorised by the Institut national de Credit Agricole.

If none of these methods of repayment is suitable, a business will be paid by postal order or international money order.

Using an agent. If using an agent, a Power of Attorney must be attached to the application. If the power of attorney is

- in a form established in a state bound by the Hague Convention of 5 October 1981, it must be annotated as required by that convention;
- in the form of a private agreement established in Belgium, signatures must be certified by the authorities of the commune or authenticated by a Belgian notary; or
- in any other form, it must be authenticated by the UK diplomatic or consular agent and the Belgian Ministry of Foreign Affairs.

Appeals against rejection of claims. Any appeal must be made within two years of the date of the decision to refuse the claim. Appeal proceedings are begun by serving a writ on the Belgian authority by a 'process server'. Appeals are heard by the ordinary civil courts under usual civil procedures. Alternatively, a request for the decision to be reconsidered can be made in writing to the authority explaining why it is believed the refund should be paid. This action will not prevent a formal appeal being made at a later date but will not suspend the two year limit for making such an appeal and so will reduce the time left for making a formal appeal.

(VAT Notice 723, para 5.2).

21.35 *Cyprus*

Forms and other information are obtainable from

VAT Service
Dep. Of Customs and Excise
Corner of M.Karaoli and G.Afxentiou
1096 NICOSIA
Postal address: VAT Service, 1471 Nicosia

Tel: +357 22601834
Fax: +357 22660484

Minimum claim. If a claim is for a year, it cannot be less than €25.52. If a claim is for less than a year, it must not be less than €204.18.

21.36 *Czech Republic*

Forms and other information are obtainable from

Finaní úad pro Prahu 1
Štpánská 28,
112 33 PRAHA 1

Tel. : + 420 2 2404 2153 or (1154)
Fax : + 420 2 2404 1920

Minimum claim. If a claim is for a year, it cannot be less than 1,000 CZK. If a claim is for less than a year, it must not be less than 7,000 CZK.

21.37 *Denmark*

The appropriate form (Form R 86 1) and other information are obtainable from

Told-og Skatteregion Sønderborg
Hilmar Finsens Gade 18
DK6400 SØNDERBORG
Denmark

Tel: +45 72 37 50 00

Fax: +45 72 37 50 03

The form must be completed in Danish, using block capitals. An instruction booklet (VAV 27) is available in English, German and French.

Non-refundable VAT. In addition to the supplies listed in 21.32 above, refunds cannot be claimed on entertainment expenses, hotel expenses or car rental. Only VAT which a Danish firm could include in its input tax calculations can be reclaimed.

Minimum claim. If for less than a year, a claim must be for at least DKr1,500 (unless it is for the final period of the year). No claim can be for less than DKr200.

Method of repayment. Repayment will be made by credit transfer to the bank account or postal giro account of the business. The business must pay the charges for any transfer to an account outside Denmark.

Using an agent. An agent must have specific authority to act.

Appeals against rejection of claims. An appeal against a decision by the regional office in Sønderborg can be made to the Central Customs and Tax Administration (Told-og Skattestyrelsen) in Copenhagen.

(VAT Notice 723, para 5.3).

21.38 *Estonia*

Forms and other information are obtainable from

Northern Regional Tax Center
Endla 8,
15177 TALLINN

Tel: +372 6934194
Fax: +372 6934111

Minimum claim. If for less than a year, a claim must be for at least 3,000 EEK (unless it is for the final period of the year). No claim can be for less than 400 EEK.

21.39 *Finland*

Forms and other information are obtainable from

Uudenmaan verovirasto
Yritsverotoimisto
PL 34 00521 VEROTUS

Tel: + 358 9 731 120
Fax: + 358 9 7311 4392

The form must be completed in Finnish or Swedish, using block capitals.

Non-refundable VAT. In addition to the supplies listed in 21.32 above, refunds cannot be claimed on business entertainment; car hire, fuel and car repairs; and motor cycles, caravans, private aircraft and all related supplies.

Minimum claim. The minimum amount refundable is €25 for a one year period or the last three months of a year; and €200 for a quarter or another period less than a year.

Method of repayment. Repayment will be made by credit transfer to the bank or postal account of the business in Finland, or to its bank account abroad.

Using an agent. If using an agent, a letter of authority must be attached to the claim stating that the agent is authorised to sign the refund application and/or to receive the repayment.

Appeals against rejection of claims. An appeal may be made to the Provincial Court of Uusimaa in writing. Petitioners, or their legally authorised representatives, must submit the appeal petition to the Provincial Tax Office within three years of the end of the calendar year of the period concerned by the decision.

(VAT Notice 723, para 5.4).

21.40 *France*

Forms and other information are obtainable from

Direction Générale des Impôts
Service de remboursements de la TVA aux assujettis établis e l'étranger
Centre des Non-Résidents
10, Rue d'Uzès
75080 PARIS Cedex 02

Tel: +33 1 44822540 or 44822541

Fax: +33 1 40410536

The form must be completed in French, using block capitals.

Non-refundable VAT. In addition to the supplies listed in 21.32 above, refunds cannot be claimed on housing, hotel accommodation, lodging, entertainment and restaurant expenses; passenger transport and any incidental activities; motor fuel (except diesel fuel on which a proportion can be claimed provided it is used solely for business purposes); goods and services supplied free or at much less than the normal price (except for goods of a very low value); and services relating to non-deductible goods such as repairs to cars.

Minimum claim. If a claim is for a year, it must not be less than €25. If a claim is for a three-month period, it must not be less than €200.

Method of repayment. Repayment will be made by bank or postal order. If a business wants the payment to be made to in its own country but has no facilities for bank transfer, it must state on its claim form whether it wants to be paid by cash or banker's draft. If repaid in its own country, a business will have to pay the bank charges or costs and should mark Box 7 of its claim form 'Frais a la charge du beneficiare' ('Costs to be charged to the payee').

Using an agent. An agent must have specific authority to act.

Appeals against rejection of claims. Detailed instructions on French appeals procedures can be obtained from the address above.

(VAT Notice 723, para 5.5).

21.41 *Germany*

Forms and other information are obtainable from

Bundesamt für Finanzen
Friedhofstrasse 1
53225 BONN
Germany

Tel: +49 228 4060

Fax: +49 228 406 2661

The form must be completed in German, using block capitals.

Non-refundable VAT. In addition to the supplies listed in 21.32 above, refunds cannot be claimed on food and accommodation expenses or costs incurred in respect of the travel element for staff vehicles. VAT can only be reclaimed on 50% of expenses related to means of transport which are not used exclusively for the business and 80% of VAT related to business entertainment. Full details must be provided for business entertainment claims. If proof of the amount of hospitality expenditure, or the fact that it was for business purposes, cannot be provided, no VAT will be refunded.

Minimum claim. If a claim is for less than a year, it must not be less than €200 (unless it is for the final period of the year). No claim can be less than €25.

Method of repayment. Repayment will be made by credit transfer to the bank or postal account of the business, in Germany or abroad.

Using an agent. An agent must have authority to act.

Appeals against rejection of claims. A review of the decision can be requested in writing. Alternatively, a statement of appeal can be put on official record. Any appeal must be made to the office that gave the decision within one month of receiving written notification of their reasons for refusing repayment. Where no written explanation of the refusal is given, an appeal can be made up to a year after the refusal.

(VAT Notice 723, para 5.6).

21.42 *Greece*

Forms and other information are available from

Ministry of Finance
14th Directorate of VAT and Indirect Taxes
Sina 2–4
10672 ATHENS
Greece

Tel: +30 1 0364 72 03

Fax: +30 1 0364 54 13

Forms must be completed in Greek, using block capitals.

Non-refundable VAT. In addition to the supplies listed in 21.32 above, refunds cannot be claimed on non-business supplies; food; drink and tobacco products; hotel and other accommodation; entertainment, hospitality or amusements; acquisition, leasing or hire, modification, repair or maintenance of passenger motor vehicles, pleasure boats and private aircraft; and transport of taxable persons or of members of their staff.

Minimum claim. If a claim is for a three-month period, it must not be less than €200. For November and December only, the minimum claim is €25. The minimum claim for a full calendar year is also €25.

Method of repayment. The refund may be made either by credit to the applicant's bank account or by direct payment. Refunds may be made to duly authorised persons.

Using an agent. An agent must submit a Power of Attorney or letter of authority stating that they can make claims and accept monies on behalf of their principal.

Appeals against rejection of claims. The Greek authorities reserve the right to refuse all or part of a claim and will duly state the reasons for the refusal to the applicant. Claimants may appeal against a rejected claim. Detailed instructions on Greek appeals procedure can be obtained from the above address.

(VAT Notice 723, para 5.7).

21.43 *Hungary*

Forms and other information are obtainable from

APEH szak-budapesti Igazgatósága
Külföldiek gyeit Intéz Fosztály
Postacím: H–1387 Budapest, Pf. 45

Minimum claim. If a claim is for a year, it must not be less than €25 (7,000 HUF). If a claim is for a three-month period, it must not be less than €200 (51,000 HUF). Where the amount exceeds 300,000 HUF the claimant can apply for a refund immediately.

21.44 *Ireland*

Forms and other information are obtainable from

The Revenue Commissioners
VAT Repayment Section
Government Buildings
ENNIS
County Clare
Republic of Ireland

Tel: +353 65 68412 00

Fax: +353 65 68 49248

The form must be completed in English, using block capitals.

Non-refundable VAT. In addition to the supplies listed in 21.32 above, refunds cannot be claimed on food and drink; hotel and other accommodation; personal services; entertainment expenses; purchase and hire of passenger motor vehicles; petrol; goods or services used for the purpose of an exempt activity; and goods for supply in Ireland or for hiring out for use there.

Minimum claim. If a claim is for a year, it must not be less than €200. If it is for a three-month period, it must not be less than €25.

Method of repayment. Repayment will be made by payable order (cheque) sent to the claimant by post.

Using an agent. An agent must have authority to act.

Appeals against rejection of claims. An appeal can be made to the Revenue Commissioners and the courts. The Commissioners must be given written notice of the intention to appeal within 21 days of the notification of the refusal. The appeal itself takes the form of a hearing between the appellant (or its legal representative) and a representative of the Commissioners. If either the appellant or the Revenue Commissioners disagree with the appeal decision, they can make a further appeal to the ordinary courts.

(VAT Notice 723, para 5.8).

21.45 *Italy*

Forms and other information are obtainable from

Agenzia delle Entrate
Centro Operativo di Pescara
Team rimborsi IVA ai non residenti

Via Rio Sparto No 21
65100 Pescara
Italy

Tel: +3985 577 2359 or 2318 or 2380

Fax: +3985 577 2325

E-mail: centrooperativo.pescara.ivanonresidenti@agenziaentrate.it

The form must be completed in Italian, using capital letters.

Non-refundable VAT. In addition to the supplies listed in 21.32 above, refunds cannot be claimed on hotel accommodation; food and drink; travel; the acquisition or hire of passenger motor vehicles, aeroplanes, pleasure boats and motorcycles; petrol, diesel or other fuels for the above transport; and luxury goods such as furs, sparkling wines and oriental carpets.

Minimum claim. If a claim is for a year, it must not be less than €200. If a claim is for a three-month period, it must not be less than €25.

Method of repayment. Repayments will only be made in lire to an account in the name of the business at an Italian bank or post office.

Using an agent. An agent must have authority to act.

Appeals against rejection of claims. Refusal to make a refund by the Refund Office can be contested before the Taxation Commission according to the provisions relating to tax disputes. For this purpose, it is necessary for the Refund Office to issue an order giving grounds which contains all the particulars of the formal order of refusal document.

(VAT Notice 723, para 5.9).

21.46 *Latvia*

Forms and other information are obtainable from

Valsts ienemumu dienesta Lielo nodoklu maksataju parvalde
(Large Taxpayers Board of the State Revenue Service),
Smilsu Street 12,
RIGA, LV–1050

Tel: +371 70 28 803

21.47 *Lithuania*

Forms and other information are obtainable from

Vilniaus apskrities valstybine mokesciu inspekcija,
Sermukonio g. 4, 2600 VILNIUS

Tel: +370 5 261 66 35
Fax: +370 5 268 76 89

21.48 *Luxembourg*

Forms and other information are obtainable from

Administration de l'Enregistrement et des Domaines
Bureau d'Imposition XI

67–69, rue Verte
BP 31
2010 LUXEMBOURG

Tel: +352 44 905 455 (Bureau XI) or +352 44 9051 (switchboard)
Fax: +352 25 07 96

Forms must be completed in French, using block capitals.

Non-refundable VAT. In addition to the supplies listed in 21.32 above, refunds cannot be claimed on recreation or entertainment expenses.

Minimum claim. If a claim is for less than a year, it must not be less than €200 (unless it is for the final period of the year). No claim can be less than €25.

Method of repayment. A business can choose to be paid (either in Luxembourg or in its own country) by credit transfer, cheque or money order.

Using an agent. An agent must have authority to act.

Appeals against rejection of claims. It is possible to either make a statement of appeal to the tax authorities or institute judicial appeal proceedings in the civil courts. In the latter case, notice of the proceedings must be served on the Director of the Administration de l'Enregistrement et des Domaines within three months of the date of the notification of refusal.

(VAT Notice 723, para 5.10).

21.49 *Malta*

Forms and other information are obtainable from

VAT Department
Centre Point Building, Ta' Paris Road,
Birkirkara BKR 13, MALTE

Tel: +356 21 49 47 84 or +356 22 79 92 30
Fax: +356 21 49 93 6521.50

Netherlands

Forms and other information are obtainable from

Belastingdienst Limburg/Kantoor Buitenland
Postbus 2865
6401 DJ HEERLEN

Tel: +31 45 577 9500
Fax: +31 45 577 9634

The form must be completed in Dutch (although, in practice, claim forms completed in English, French or German are also accepted by the tax authorities), using block capitals.

Non-refundable VAT. In addition to supplies listed in 21.32 above, refunds cannot be claimed on food and drink for on-the-spot consumption in hotels, cafes, restaurants, boarding houses and similar establishments supplied to persons staying only a short time; goods and services used to maintain a certain status, such as luxuries, amusements or entertainment; goods or services to be used as business or other gifts to people who would not be able to deduct all or most of the turnover tax on them if it had been charged to them; and goods or services to be used to make supplies to staff of housing, wages in kind, sport and recreational facilities, private transport and any other supplies for their personal use (except for food and drink).

Minimum claim. If a claim is for less than a year, it must not be less than €200 (unless it is for the final period of the year). No claim can be less than €25.

Method of repayment. Repayment will be made by credit transfer to the claimant's bank (in the Netherlands or abroad) or, on request, by postal order.

Using an agent. An agent must have authority to act.

Appeals against rejection of claims. If a claim is refused, there is a right to lodge an appeal to the VAT authorities within six weeks after the decision. In the event of an unfavourable decision by the tax office, an appeal may be made within six weeks to the Tax Chamber of the District Court of Appeal.

(VAT Notice 723, para 5.11).

21.51 *Poland*

Forms and other information are available from

Drugi Urzad Skarbowy Warsawa – Srodmiescie
Second Tax Office for Warsawa – Srodmiescie,
ul.Lindleya 14, 02–013 WARSZAWA SRODMIESCIE

Tel: +48 22 6217249
Fax: +48 22 6255006

21.52 *Portugal*

Forms and other information are available from

Direcçâo-Geral das Contribuiçôes e Impostos
Direccão de Serviços de Reembolsos do. IVA
Avenida Joâo XXI
Apartado 8220
1802 LISBOA Codex

Tel: +351 217 610582/3/5
Fax: +351 21 793 8133

Forms are also available from specialist stationers' shops, bookshops of the National Press and offices of the Public Treasury. They must be completed in Portuguese, using block capitals.

Non-refundable VAT. In addition to the supplies listed in 21.32 above, refunds cannot be claimed on the supply, manufacture, importation or hire of a private vehicle; the purchase of petrol (gas oil is allowed at 50% of the tax paid); transport, business trips, and tolls; accommodation, food, drinks, tobacco or entertainment; and amusements or luxuries.

Minimum claim. If a claim is for less than a year, it must not be less than €159.62 (unlcss it is for the final period of the year). No claim can be less than €19.95.

Method of repayment. Repayment will be made by payable order to the applicant or, where the claimant completes Section 6 on the form, by transfer to an account of a bank in Portugal. In cases where the refund entails charges for the transfer of funds, these will be deducted from the amount to be refunded.

Using an agent. An agent must have authority to act.

Appeals against rejection of claims. Decisions relating to the refusal of a refund will state the reasons for the refusal, and be notified to the applicant. Information about the appeals procedure can be obtained from the address above.

(VAT Notice 723, para 5.12).

21.53 *Slovak Republic*

Forms and other information are obtainable from

Daoví úrad Bratislava I, Radlinského 37, P.O. Box 89
817 89 BRATISLAVA 15,

Tel: +421 2 57 37 83 52

Fax: +421 2 57 37 89 00

Minimum claim. If a claim is for less than a year, it must not be less than 8,000 SKK (unless it is for the final period of the year). No claim can be less than 1,000 SKK.

21.54 *Slovenia*

Forms and other information are obtainable from

Davcni Urad Ljubljana, Tax Office Ljubljana
Dunajska c.22,
1000 LJUBLJANA

Tel: +386 1 474 46 02 or +386 1 474 42 97
Fax: +386 1 474 43 71

Minimum claim. If a claim is for less than a year, it must not be less than 50,000 SIT (unless it is for the final period of the year). No claim can be less than 12,000 SIT.

21.55 *Spain*

Forms and other information are obtainable from

Delegación Especial de Madrid de la Agencia Estatal de Administración Tributaria
Dependencia Regional de Gestión Sección de Regimenes Especiales
C/ Guzmán el Bueno, 139, Planta 1a
28071 MADRID

Tel: + 34–91 582 67 39

Fax: +34–91 582 67 57

The form must be completed in Spanish, using block capitals.

Non-refundable VAT. In addition to the supplies listed in 21.32 above, VAT cannot be reclaimed on accommodation, meals and travel expenses (unless deductible for personal or corporate income tax purposes); entertainment expenses; and car hire and fuel (unless used exclusively for business activities).

Minimum claim. If a claim is for a three-month period, it must not be less than €201.34. No claim can be less than €25.34.

Method of repayment. Repayment will be made by cheque or money order.

Using an agent. An agent must have authority to act.

Appeals against rejection of claims. Detailed instructions on Spanish appeals procedure can be obtained from the above address.

(VAT Notice 723, para 5.13).

21.56 *Sweden*

Forms and information are obtainable from

Särskilda Skattekontoret
77183 LUDVIKA
Sweden

Tel: +46 240 870 00

Fax: +46 240 103 40

Forms and instructions are also obtainable from the Swedish Embassy in London. Forms must be completed in Swedish or English, using block capitals.

Non-refundable VAT. In addition to the supplies listed in 21.32 above, VAT cannot be reclaimed on entertainment expenses; transport (unless used exclusively for business activities); and car hire (50% of VAT can be recovered if used exclusively for business).

Minimum claim. If the claim covers a period of three months, the minimum claim is SEK 2,000. If it is for a year, the claim must be not be less than SEK 250.

Method of repayment. Repayment will be made by either postal giro in Sweden, to a bank account in Sweden or abroad, or to the claimant in Sweden or abroad.

Using an agent. An agent must have authority to act.

Appeals against rejection of claims. Appeals against rejected claims should be lodged with the tax authorities at the above address within two months of receipt of its decision.

(VAT Notice 723, para 5.14).

21.57 **Applications to the UK by persons established in other EC countries**

Persons to whom the provisions apply. The provisions apply to any business carried on in an EC country other than the UK but do not apply to such a business if, in the period of claim, it

(*a*) was established in the UK; or

(*b*) made supplies in the UK of goods and services other than

(i) transport of freight outside the UK or to or from a place outside the UK (and ancillary services); and

(ii) services where the VAT on the supply is payable solely by the person to whom they are supplied under the reverse charge provisions (see 39.4 INTERNATIONAL SERVICES); and

(iii) goods where the VAT on the supply is payable solely by the persons to whom they are supplied under *VATA 1994, s 9A* (gas and electricity supplies, see 29.9 FUEL AND POWER) or *VATA 1994, s 14* (triangulation, and installed and assembled goods, see 23.22 and 23.29 EUROPEAN COMMUNITY: SINGLE MARKET).

For these purposes a business is treated as established in a country if

- it has an establishment there from which business transactions and effected; or
- it has no such establishment (there or elsewhere) but its usual place of residence is there. The usual place of residence of a company is where it is legally constituted. A person carrying on business through a branch or agency in any country is treated as having a business establishment there.

Method of claiming. Claim forms are obtainable from the National Advice Service (0845 010 9000) or from

HM Revenue and Customs
VAT Overseas Repayment Unit
Custom House
PO Box 34
LONDONDERRY
BT48 7AE
Northern Ireland

Tel: +44 (0) 2871 376200

Fax: +44 (0) 2871 372520

E-mail: enq.oru.ni@hmrc.gsi.gov.uk

Main exhibition centres also hold stocks of forms.

Forms must be completed in English, using block capitals, and must be sent to the above address, together with the supporting documentation and, if appropriate, a certificate of status (see 21.31 above).

Non-refundable VAT. Refunds cannot be claimed on VAT incurred on

- non-business supplies (if a supply covers both business and non-business use, VAT can be reclaimed on the business element of the supply);
- a supply or importation of goods or a supply of services used (or intended to be used) by the claimant for the purpose of any supply by him in the UK;
- a supply or importation of goods which the claimant has removed (or intends to remove) to another EC country or which he has exported (or intends to export) outside the EC;
- a supply or importation where input tax recovery is restricted in the UK (eg most motor cars, business entertainment, and second-hand goods for which no VAT invoice is issued);
- goods and services which have been bought for resale and which are for the direct benefit of travellers (eg hotel accommodation bought in by tour operators, travel agents, etc to make up package holidays).

Minimum claim and time limit. If the claim is for less than a year, it must be for at least £130 (unless it is for the final part of the calendar year). No claim can be for less than £16.

The claim must be made not later than six months after the end of the calendar year in which the VAT claimed was charged. It must be for a period of not less than three months (except where that period represents the final part of a calendar year) and not more than one calendar year.

Methods of repayment. Payments can be made by any of the following methods.

- Directly to the claimant's own bank through SWIFT (Society for Worldwide Inter-Bank Financial Telecommunications). The claimant must provide full bank account details (bank name, address and identification code; account name and number; and currency of account) and a copy of a bank credit slip with the claim form.
- To any UK bank.
- By payable order in sterling directly to the claimant or an appointed agent.

Where any repayment is made to a claimant in the country in which he is established, HMRC may reduce the repayment by the amount of any bank charges or costs incurred.

Agents. If the claimant appoints an agent to act on his behalf, the agent must submit to HMRC a power of attorney or letter of authority stating that it can make claims and accept monies on the claimant's behalf. The following is an example of the format of a letter of authority acceptable to HMRC.

> I [name and address of claimant] hereby appoint [name and address of agent] to act on my behalf in connection with any claims I make to Her Britannic Majesty's Commissioners of Revenue and Customs under the Value Added Tax Regulations 1995 as from time to time amended or replaced. Any repayment of VAT to which I am entitled pursuant to such claim made on my behalf by my above named agent shall be paid to [name and address of payee].
>
> Date..............................Signed..............................[by the claimant]

Appeals. An appeal may be made to an independent VAT tribunal against a refusal by HMRC to allow all or part of a repayment. A Notice of Appeal must be served at the VAT tribunal within 30 days of the date of the letter notifying the refusal. Alternatively, the applicant may first ask HMRC to reconsider their decision and extend the time for service of a Notice of Appeal. If HMRC allow an extension but do not change their decision, the applicant then has a further 21 days from the date of the letter upholding the decision to serve a Notice of Appeal.

Importations. The above provisions also allow repayment of VAT charged on the importation of goods into the UK from places outside the EC but only if no other relief is available.

[*VATA 1994, s 39; SI 1995/2518, Regs 173–184*]. (VAT Notice 723, para 5.15).

Isle of Man. For VAT purposes, the Isle of Man is treated as part of the UK. VAT is chargeable in the Isle of Man under Manx legislation, which is broadly similar to UK legislation. The above scheme applies equally to refunds of VAT incurred in the Isle of Man and any references above to the UK are to be taken to include the Isle of Man. (VAT Notice 723, para 1.3).

22 European Community Legislation

De Voil Indirect Tax Service. See V1.220–233.

The contents of this chapter are as follows.

22.1 LEGAL INSTRUMENTS OF THE EC

Statements of the European Council and European Commission are graded under the *EC Treaty* as follows.

- **Regulations** are binding in their entirety and have general effect to all EC countries. They are directly applicable in the legal systems of EC countries.

- **Directives** are binding as to result and their general effect is specific to named EC countries. The form and methods of compliance are left to the addressees.

- **Decisions** are binding in their entirety and are specific to an EC country, commercial enterprise or private individual.

- **Recommendations and Opinions** are not binding and are directed to specific subjects on which the Council's or Commission's advice has been sought.

De Voil Indirect Tax Service. See V1.223–229.

22.2 **EC LEGISLATION AS PART OF UK LEGISLATION**

EC law is made effective for UK legislation. [*European Communities Act 1972, s 2*]. The basis for VAT as the common EC turnover tax derives from *EC Treaty, Art 88EC* and Council and Commission statements thereunder. The effects of EC law as regards UK VAT legislation can be summarised as follows.

(*a*) **Direct effect**. Although *EC Treaty, Article 249EC* does not specifically allow for direct effect in an EC country, the Court of Justice has held 'wherever the provisions of a directive appear ... to be unconditional and sufficiently precise, those provisions may ... be relied upon as against any national provision which is incompatible with the directive insofar as the provisions define rights which individuals are able to assert against the state' (*Becker v Finanzamt Münster-Innenstadt, CJEC [1982] ECR 53; [1982] 1 CMLR 499 (TVC 21.240)*). See also *Staatssecretaris van Financien v Cooperatieve Verenigning Cooperatieve Aardappelenbewaarplaats GA, CJEC [1981] ECR 445; [1981] 3 CMLR 337 (TVC 21.53)* which case was considered in *UFD Ltd (VTD 1172) (TVC 16.1)* in which it was said 'in all appeals involving issues of liability, the tribunal should consider the relevant provisions of the Council directives to ensure that the provisions of the UK legislation are consistent therewith'. See also *Yoga for Health Foundation v C & E Commrs, QB [1984] STC 630 (TVC 21.200)* where exemption from VAT was allowed for certain welfare services under *EC 6th Directive* although there was no corresponding provision in the UK legislation.

(*b*) **Primacy of EC Directives over national legislation**. A national court which is called upon, within the limits of its jurisdiction, to apply provisions of Community law, is under a duty to give full effect to those provisions, if necessary refusing of its own motion to apply any conflicting provision of national legislation, even if adopted subsequently, and it is not necessary for the court to request or await the prior setting aside of such provisions by legislative or other constitutional means (*Amministrazione delle Finanze dello Stato v Simmenthal SpA, CJEC [1978] ECR 629; [1978] 3 CMLR 263 (TVC 21.21)*).

In *EC Commission v United Kingdom, CJEC [1988] STC 456 (TVC 21.327)* the CJEC ruled that the UK had contravened the provisions of *EC 6th Directive* by zero-rating certain supplies of sewerage and water, news services, supplies of fuel and power and the construction of commercial buildings. In the earlier decision *EC Commission v United Kingdom, [1988] STC 251 (TVC 21.189)* the CJEC had similarly ruled in relation to the exempting of supplies of spectacles, contact lenses and hearing aids. As a result of each decision, the UK law was amended.

In *Direct Cosmetics v C & E Commrs, CJEC [1985] STC 479 (TVC 21.320)* it was held that an amendment to UK legislation, which had been previously enacted under the derogation powers in *EC 6th Directive, Art 27* (see 22.30 below), was itself a 'special measure' requiring derogation to be authorised by the European Commission. As this had not been obtained, the whole provisions failed and could not be relied on against the taxpayer.

(*c*) **Interpretation of UK law**. If the domestic VAT legislation of the UK is unclear or ambiguous, tribunals are 'entitled to have regard to the provisions of the *Sixth Directive* in order to assist in resolving any ambiguity in the construction of the provisions under consideration' (*English-Speaking Union of the Commonwealth (VTD 1023) (TVC 13.5)*). If EC law appears unclear it may be interpreted by referring to the legislative history ('*travaux preparatoires*') but such evidence has been held to be admissible only by reference to tests in *Fothergill v Monarch Airlines Ltd, [1981] AC 251* (*The Open University (VTD 1196) (TVC 20.3)*). This decision is open to doubt. See, for example, *EC Commission v The Kingdom of Belgium, CJEC [1984] ECR 1861, [1985] 1CMLR 364 (TVC 21.322)* where the Belgium government used minutes of a Council meeting held prior to the adoption of the *EC 6th Directive* in evidence.

(*d*) **State liability to pay damages for failure to implement Directive**. In an Italian case, the CJEC held that the Italian government was liable to pay compensation to employees of an insolvent company, who had suffered financial loss through Italy's failure to implement a directive guaranteeing such employees their arrears of wages (*Francovich v Italian State, CJEC Case C–6/90; [1991] 1 ECR 5357; [1993] 2 CMLR 66 (TVC 21.27)*). The principles laid down in *Francovich* were applied in two subsequent cases in which national legislation was held to be contrary to EC law. The CJEC ruled that 'the principle that Member States are obliged to make good damage caused to individuals by breaches of Community law attributable to the state is applicable where the national legislature was responsible for the breach in question' (*Brasserie du Pêcheur SA v Federal Republic of Germany; R v Secretary of State for Transport (ex p. Factortame Ltd & Others) (No 3), CJEC Cases C–46/93, C–48/93; [1996] 1 ECR 1029; [1996] 1 CMLR 889; [1996] 2 WLR 506; [1996] AEECR 301 (TVC 21.28)*) See also *R v Secretary of State for Employment (ex p. Equal Opportunities Commission), HL [1994] 1 All ER 910 (TVC 21.33)* where Lord Keith of Kinkel observed that 'if there is any individual who believes that he or she has a good claim to compensation under the *Francovich* principle, it is the Attorney-General who would be defendant in any proceedings directed to enforcing it'.

Judgments in the European Court of Justice also have supremacy over domestic decisions even if the proceedings commenced in another EC country.

De Voil Indirect Tax Service. See V1.235.

22.3 **VAT HARMONISATION DIRECTIVES**

A directive must be read as a whole. The preamble, which sets out the purpose of the legislation, is an essential part of it. Moreover, as distinct from UK law, it is acceptable when determining the purpose of the legislation to consider the discussions, decisions, etc ('*travaux preparatoires*') which led to the legislation being drafted in its final form.

The principal directives issued by the EC Council on the harmonisation of legislation of EC countries concerning turnover taxes, and which are still current and relevant in the UK, are as follows.

- *1st Directive*. [*67/227/EEC*]. This provides for a common VAT system to be operated by EC countries.
- *6th Directive*. [*77/388/EEC*]. This is the so-called 'harmonisation directive' and clarifies many of the definitions of basic terms used in the legislation of individual EC countries. See 22.4 *et seq* below.
- *7th Directive*. [*94/5/EEC*]. This provides for special arrangements applicable to second-hand goods, works of art, collectors' items and antiques. See SECOND-HAND GOODS (61).

- *8th Directive*. [*79/1072/EEC*]. This provides for the refund of VAT suffered by Community traders in those EC countries where they do not have a business establishment. See 22.48 below.
- *10th Directive*. [*84/386/EEC*]. This amends and clarifies the provisions of the *6th Directive* in connection with the hiring out of movable tangible property.
- *13th Directive*. [*86/560/EEC*]. This provides for refund of VAT to taxable persons not established in the EC. See 22.49 below.
- *18th Directive*. [*89/465/EEC*]. This abolishes a number of derogations provided for in *6th Directive*.

A number of subsidiary directives have also been made.

De Voil Indirect Tax Service. See V1.227; V1.228.

22.4 SIXTH DIRECTIVE

Many of the *Articles* of the *EC 6th Directive* are similar to the provisions of the *VATA 1994*. Where they are unconditional and precise (eg as evidenced by the use of the word 'must' in the text below) their wording takes preference to that in the *VATA 1994*. Where *Articles* are discretionary (eg as evidenced by the use of the words 'countries may' in the text below) the UK may apply the provisions or not as it wishes. However, where they are applied, the provisions once adopted must be applied precisely.

22.5 Scope

VAT applies to

- the supply of goods or services (see 22.7 and 22.8 below) effected for consideration within the territory of the country by a taxable person (see 22.6 below) acting as such; and
- the 'importation of goods'.

'*Importation of goods*' means

(i) the entry of goods into the EC which do not satisfy the conditions laid down in *EC Treaty, Arts 23EC, 24EC* or, where the goods are covered by the *Treaty establishing the European Coal and Steel Community*, are not in free circulation; and

(ii) the entry into the Community of goods from a 'third territory', other than goods covered by (i) above. '*Third territory*' means any territory other than those defined as the territory of an EC country in 21.2 EUROPEAN COMMUNITY: GENERAL.

[*EC 6th Directive, Arts 2, 7*(*1*)].

'Effected for consideration'. It follows from the above that there is no supply for VAT purposes where there is no consideration. See *Staatssecretaris van Financiën v Cooperatieve Vereniging 'Cooperatieve Aardappelenbewaarplaats GA', CJEC Case 154/80; [1981] ECR 445; [1981] 3 CMLR 337 (TVC 21.53)*. Similarly, in *Staatssecretaris van Financiën v Hong Kong Trade Development Council, CJEC Case 89/81; [1982] ECR 1277; [1983] 1 CMLR 73 (TVC 21.54)* the CJEC held that the provision of services for no consideration could not be subject to VAT and, where no other activity was involved, the provider of the services could not be regarded as a taxable person.

In *Apple & Pear Development Council v C & E Commrs, CJEC Case 102/86; [1988] STC 221 (TVC 21.55)* the CJEC held that, for a supply of services to be for consideration within the above provisions, there must be a direct link between the service provided and the consideration received. On the evidence in that case, there was no relationship between the level of the benefits which individual fruit growers obtained from the Council's services and the amount of the mandatory charges which they were obliged to pay. Accordingly, the compulsory annual charges did not constitute 'consideration' and the Council was not making supplies of services for consideration.

In *Tolsma v Inspecteur der Omzetbelasting Leeuwarden, CJEC [1994] STC 509 (TVC 21.59)* an individual who played a barrel organ on the public highway and invited donations from the public was held not to be supplying services for a consideration. There was no agreement between the parties and also 'no necessary link between the musical service and the payment to which it gave rise'.

Lawful and unlawful transactions. The principle of fiscal neutrality precludes a generalised differentiation between lawful and unlawful transactions except where, because of the special characteristics of certain products, all competition between a lawful economic sector and an unlawful sector is precluded. Thus the illegal sale of drugs is not a supply for VAT purposes (*Mol v Inspecteur der InVoerrechten Accijinzen, CJEC [1988] ECR 3627, [1989] BVC 205 (TVC 21.56)*) but the supply of counterfeit perfume is. See *R v Goodwin and Unstead, CA [1997] STC 22, CJEC [1998] STC 699 (TVC 21.57)*. The prohibition on such products stems from the fact that they infringe intellectual property rights and is conditional not absolute (as in the case of drugs and counterfeit money). There is scope for competition between counterfeit perfumes and perfumes which are traded lawfully and although supply of the former is unlawful, such perfume is not liable to seizure in the hands of the final customer. The unlawful operation of a form of roulette was similarly held to be a supply for VAT purposes in *Fischer v Finanzamt Donaueschingen, CJEC [1998] STC 708 (TVC 21.248)*. However, although the unlawful playing of a game of chance is a supply, it is not taxable where the corresponding activity is exempt when carried on lawfully by a licensed casino.

'Effected by a taxable person acting as such'. In *Finanzamt Ülzen v Armbrecht, CJEC Case C–291/92; [1995] STC 997; [1995] 1 ECR 2775; [1995] AEECR 882 (TVC 21.64)*, a hotelier sold a guesthouse, part of which had been used for private rather than business purposes. The CJEC ruled that where a taxable person sold property, part of which he had chosen to reserve for private use, the sale of that part was outside the scope of the above provisions. This should be compared to the decision in *Bakcsi v Finanzamt Fürstenfeldbruck, CJEC Case C–415/98; [2002] STC 802; [2002] 2 WLR 1188 (TVC 21.65)* where a trader purchased a car and used it mainly for business purposes but partly for private purposes. The CJEC held that where a taxable person used a capital item for both business and private purposes, and had incorporated that item wholly into his business assets, the sale of that item was wholly subject to VAT. The CJEC also observed that a taxable person who acquired a capital item for mixed purposes 'may retain it wholly within his private assets and thereby exclude it entirely' from the VAT system.

22.6 **Taxable persons**

'Taxable person' means any person who 'independently' carries out in any place any 'economic activity' whatever the purpose or result of that activity.

Economic activity. This comprises all activities of producers, traders and persons supplying services including mining and agricultural activities and activities of professions. Included is the exploitation of tangible and intangible property for the purposes of obtaining income on a continuing basis.

In *Rompelman v Minister van Financien, CJEC [1985] 3 CMLR 202; [1985] ECR 655 (TVC 21.71)* the acquisition of a future right of joint ownership in property under construction with a view to letting that property in due course was held to be an economic activity although objective evidence (eg proposed contracts, planning permission) that arrangements have been made to begin making taxable supplies should be produced. The first investment expenditure incurred for the purpose of a business can be regarded as an economic activity even if it does not give rise to any taxable transactions. See *Intercommunale voor Zeewaterontzilting (in liquidation) v Belgian State, CJEC [1996] STC 569 (TVC 21.77)* where VAT was held to be deductible under *Art 17* (see 22.23 below) on a profitability study although, as a result of the study, the company did not move to the operational phase. See also *WM van Tiem v Staatssecretaris van Financien, CJEC 1990, [1993] STC 91 (TVC 21.76)* and *Finanzamt Goslar v Breitsohl, CJEC [2001] STC 355 (TVC 21.84)*. In the latter case it was held that the right to deduct the VAT paid on transactions carried out with the view to a realisation of a planned economic activity still existed even where the tax authorities were aware, from the time of the first tax assessment, that the economic activity envisaged, which was to give rise to taxable transactions, would not be taken up (although, in such cases, the input tax recovery might be subject to later adjustment under *Art 20*, see 22.24 below).

The holding of shares does not amount to an economic activity if the shareholder is not involved in the management of the companies whose shares it holds. Neither is it the exploitation of assets for the purposes of obtaining income because any dividend received arises from the ownership of the shares, not from an economic activity (*Polysar Investments Netherlands BV v Inspecteur der Invoerrechten en Accijnzen, Arnhem, CJEC [1993] STC 222 (TVC 21.73)*). See also *Harnas & Helm CV v Staatssecretaris van Financien, CJEC [1997] STC 364 (TVC 21.79)*. The purchase and sale of shares by trustees in the course of the management of a charitable trust does not amount to an economic activity (*The Wellcome Trust Ltd v C & E Commrs, CJEC [1996] STC 945 (TVC 21.78)*).

See 8.1 BUSINESS for the meaning of 'business' under UK legislation.

'Independently'. The hiring out of intangible property with a view to obtaining income therefrom on a continuing basis is an economic activity even where a person's sole economic activity consists in the letting such an item to a company or partnership of which he is a member (*Staatssecretaris van Financiën v Heerma, CJEC Case C–23/98, [2001] STC 1437 (TVC 21.75)*).

The use of the word 'independently' excludes employed and other persons from VAT in so far as they are bound to an employer by a contract of employment or by any other legal ties creating the relationship of employer and employee as regards working conditions, remuneration and employer's liability.

Occasional transactions. Countries may also treat as taxable persons anyone who carries out, on an occasional basis, a transaction relating to an economic activity and in particular

- the supply before first occupation of buildings (or part) and the land on which they stand. Countries may apply criteria other than first occupation eg the period elapsing between the date of completion of the building and the date of first supply (not exceeding five years) or the period elapsing between the date of first occupation and the date of subsequent supply (not exceeding two years); and
- the supply of building land.

Single taxable person. Each country may treat different persons established in their territory as a single taxable person where those persons, although legally independent, are closely bound to one another by financial, economic and organisational links. See 8.5 BUSINESS for UK provisions.

Local authorities, etc. States, regional and local government authorities and other bodies governed by public law are not considered taxable persons in respect of the activities or transactions in which they engage as public authorities unless treatment as non-taxable persons would lead to significant distortions of competition. In any case, provided they are not carried out on such a small scale as to be negligible, these bodies are considered taxable persons in relation to the activities of telecommunications; the supply of water, gas, electricity and steam; the transport of goods; port and airport services; passenger transport; supply of new goods manufactured for sale; agricultural intervention agencies; the running of trade fairs and exhibitions; warehousing; the activities of commercial publicity bodies and travel agents; the running of staff shops, cooperatives and industrial canteens and similar institutions; and public radio and television bodies of a commercial nature. For a general consideration of these provisions see *Ufficio Distrettuale delle Imposte Dirette di Fiorenzuola d'Arda v Comune di Carpaneto Piacentino* and *Ufficio Provinciale Imposta sul Valore Aggiunto di Piacenza v Comune di Rivergaro and Others, CJEC 1989, [1991] STC 205 (TVC 21.89).*

Countries may also treat activities of these bodies which are exempt under 22.17 to 22.19 and 22.31 below as activities they engage in as public authorities. This applies even if the body acted in a similar manner to a private trader (*Finanzamt Augsburg-Stadt v Marktgemeinde Welden, CJEC [1997] STC 531 (TVC 21.92)*).

[*EC 6th Directive, Art 4*].

See 43 LOCAL AUTHORITIES AND PUBLIC BODIES for UK provisions.

De Voil Indirect Tax Service. See V2.101; V2.108.

22.7 Supply of goods

Supply of goods means the transfer of the right to dispose of 'tangible property'.

'*Tangible property*' includes electric current, gas, heat, refrigeration and the like. Countries may consider it to include certain interests in movable property; rights *in rem* giving the holder a right of user over immovable property (see *WM van Tiem v Staatssecretaris van Financien, CJEC 1990, [1993] STC 91 (TVC 21.76)*); and shares, etc giving the holder *de jure* or *de facto* rights of ownership or possession over immovable property.

A supply of goods includes

(*a*) the transfer, by order made by or in the name of a public authority or in pursuance of the law, of the ownership of property against payment of compensation;

(*b*) the actual handing over of goods under a contract for the hire of goods for a certain period or for the sale of goods on deferred terms, where the contract provides that in the normal course of events ownership must pass at the latest upon payment of the final instalment;

(*c*) the transfer of goods pursuant to a contract under which commission is payable on purchase or sale;

(*d*) the application by a taxable person of business assets for his private use or that of his staff;

(*e*) the disposal of business assets free of charge;

(*f*) the application of business assets other than for business purposes;

and, at the consideration of the country, may include

(*g*) the handing over of certain works of construction;

(*h*) the application by a taxable person for the purposes of his business of goods produced, constructed, extracted, processed, purchased or imported in the course of the business, where the VAT on the goods would not be wholly deductible had the goods been acquired from another taxable person; and

(*j*) the application of goods for a non-taxable transaction or the retention of goods by a taxable person or his successors where VAT was wholly or partly deductible on acquisition or upon application under (*h*) above.

Under (*d*) to (*f*) above, the supply is only treated as a supply of goods for a consideration if VAT on the goods in question or the component parts thereof was wholly deductible and the supply is not the giving of samples or the making of gifts of small value for the purposes of the business.

See 64.3 SUPPLY for UK provisions.

Transfers of businesses, etc. In the event of a transfer of all the assets (or part thereof) countries may consider that no supply of goods takes place. In that event the recipient must be treated as the successor to the transferor. Countries may take the necessary measures to prevent distortion of competition where the recipient is not wholly liable to VAT. See 8.10 BUSINESS for UK provisions.

[*EC 6th Directive, Art 5*].

22.8 **Supply of services**

Supply of services means any transaction which does not constitute a supply of goods (see 22.7 above). Included is

(*a*) the assignment of intangible property;

(*b*) an obligation to refrain from an act or to tolerate an act or situation;

(*c*) the performance of services in pursuance of an order by or in the name of a public authority or in pursuance of the law;

(*d*) the use of business assets for the private use of the taxable person or his staff or generally for non-business purposes where VAT on such goods is wholly or partly deductible;

(*e*) the supply of services carried out free of charge by the taxable person for his own private use or that of his staff or generally for non-business purposes.

Countries may derogate from the provisions of (*d*) and (*e*) above provided that this does not lead to distortion of competition. However, this power to derogate from the obligation to charge tax on private use of business assets does not allow them to impose tax where VAT on the original purchase was not wholly or partly deductible (*Kühne v Finanzamt München III, CJEC Case 50/88; [1989] ECR 1925; [1990] STC 749; [1990] 3 CMLR 287 (TVC 21.123)*).

Where a taxable person acting in his own name but on behalf of another person takes part in the supply of services, he must be considered to have received and supplied the services himself.

Self-supply of services. To prevent distortion of competition, countries may treat the supply by a taxable person of services for the purposes of his undertaking as a supply of services for a consideration provided the VAT on the service would not have been wholly deductible had it been supplied by another taxable person.

[*EC 6th Directive, Art 6*].

See 64.4 SUPPLY for the UK provisions.

22.9 **Place of supply of goods**

The place of supply of goods is deemed to be as follows. See, however, 22.36 below for transitional provisions applying to trade between EC countries until a definitive VAT system, based on the principle of taxation of goods in the EC country of origin, can be decided upon.

(*a*) *In the case of goods dispatched or transported*, the place where the goods are at the time when dispatch or transport to the person to whom they are supplied begins. Where the goods are installed or assembled by or on behalf of the supplier, the place of supply is deemed to be the place where the goods are installed or assembled. If this is a different EC country to that of the supplier, the country within which the installation or assembly is carried out must take necessary steps to avoid double taxation in that country.

By way of derogation, where the place of departure of the consignment or transport of the goods is in a country outside the EC, the place of supply by the importer and the place of any subsequent supplies is deemed to be within the EC country of import of the goods.

(*b*) *In the case of goods not dispatched or transported*, the place where the goods are when the supply takes place.

(*c*) *In the case of goods supplied on board ships, aircraft or trains during the part of a transport of passengers effected in the EC* at the point of the departure of the transport of passengers.

[*EC 6th Directive, Art 8*].

Imports. The place of supply of imports is the EC country within the territory of which the goods are when they enter the EC except that where goods are, on entry into the EC, placed under one of the arrangements referred to in 22.22(*b*)(i)–(iv) below, under arrangements for temporary importation with total exemption from import duty or under external transit arrangements, the place of import is the EC country within the territory of which they cease to be covered by those arrangements.

See 64.8 SUPPLY for the UK provisions.

22.10 **Place of supply of services**

General rule. Subject to below, services are deemed to be supplied in the place where the supplier has established his business or has a fixed establishment from which the service is supplied or, in the absence of any such place of business or establishment, the place where he has his permanent address or usually resides. See, however, 22.39 below for transitional provisions applying to services rendered by intermediaries until a definitive VAT system, based on the principle of taxation of services in the EC country of origin, can be decided upon.

For a consideration of 'fixed establishment', see *Berkholz v Finanzamt Hamburg-Mitte-Altstadt, CJEC Case 168/84; [1985] ECR 2251; [1985] 3 CMLR 667 (TVC*

21.134) and *ARO Lease BV v Inspecteur der Belastingdienst Grote Ondernemingen Amsterdam, CJEC Case C–190/95; [1997] STC 1272 (TVC 21.135).*

The general rule above is overridden in the following circumstances.

(*a*) The place of supply of services connected with immovable property, including the services of estate agents and experts, and services for preparing and co-ordinating construction services (eg architects and on-site supervisors) is the place where the property is situated.

(*b*) The place of supply of transport services is where the transport takes place, having regard to the distance covered. See, however, 22.37 below for transitional provisions applying until a definitive VAT system, based on the principle of taxation of services in the EC country of origin, can be decided upon.

(*c*) The place of supply of services relating to

(i) cultural, artistic, sporting, scientific, educational, entertainment or similar activities, including the activities of the organisers of such activities, and where appropriate the supply of ancillary services,

(ii) ancillary transport activities such as loading, unloading, handling, and similar activities, and

(iii) valuation of, and work on, movable tangible property,

is the place where those services are physically carried out.

See, however, 22.38 and 22.39 below for transitional provisions applying to services under (ii) and (iii) above respectively until a definitive VAT system, based on the principle of taxation of services in the EC country of origin, can be decided upon.

(*d*) The place where the following services are supplied when performed for customers established outside the EC, or for taxable persons established in the EC but not in the same country as the supplier, is the place where the customer has established his business or has a fixed establishment to which the service is supplied or, in the absence of such a place, the place where he has a permanent address or usually resides. The services in question are

(i) transfers and assignments of copyrights, patents, licences, trade marks and similar rights;

(ii) advertising services (see *EC Commission v French Republic, CJEC 1993, [1997] STC 684 (TVC 21.147)*);

(iii) services of consultants, engineers, consultancy bureaux, lawyers, accountants and other similar services, as well as data processing and the supply of information;

(iv) obligations to refrain from pursuing or exercising, in whole or in part, a business activity or a right within this list;

(v) banking, financial and insurance transactions including reinsurance, with the exception of the hire of safes;

(vi) the supply of staff;

(vii) the services of agents who act in the name and for the account of another, when they procure for their principals the services referred to within this list;

(viii) the hiring out of movable tangible property with the exception of all forms of transport;

(ix) telecommunications services;

(x) radio and television broadcasting services; and

(xi) for a three year period commencing 1 July 2003, electronically supplied services, including *inter alia* website supply, web-hosting, distance maintenance of programmes and equipment and supply of

- software and updating thereof;
- images, text and information, and making databases available;
- music, film and games, including games of chance and gambling games, and political, cultural, artistic, sporting, scientific and entertainment broadcasts and events; and
- distance teaching.

Where the supplier of a service and his customer communicate via electronic mail, this does not of itself mean that the service performed is an electronic service under these provisions.

The place where the services referred to in (xi) above are supplied when performed

- for non-taxable persons who are established, have their permanent address or usually reside in an EC country
- by a taxable person who has established his business or has a fixed establishment from which the service is supplied outside the EC or, in the absence of such a place of business or fixed establishment, has his permanent address or usually resides outside the EC,

is the place where the non-taxable person is established, has his permanent address or usually resides.

In order to avoid double taxation, non-taxation or the distortion of competition, a country *may*, in relation to services under (*d*) above (other than services under (xi) above when supplied to non-taxable persons and the hiring out of forms of transport), treat the place of supply of services

(i) which would otherwise be within that country as being outside the EC where the effective use and enjoyment of the services takes place outside the EC; and

(ii) which would otherwise be outside the EC as being within that country where the effective use and enjoyment of the services takes place within that country.

A country *must* adopt the place of supply rules under (ii) above in relation to

- telecommunications services within (*d*)(ix) above; and
- radio and television broadcasting services under (*d*)(x) above when performed for non-taxable persons who are established, have their permanent address or usually reside in an EC country by a taxable person who has established his business or has a fixed establishment from which the service is supplied outside the EC or, in the absence of such a place of business or fixed establishment, has his permanent address or usually resides outside the EC.

[*EC 6th Directive, Art 9, Annex L*].

See 64.18 SUPPLY for the UK provisions.

22.11 **Time of supply**

A chargeable event occurs and VAT becomes chargeable when goods are delivered or services performed. Deliveries of goods (other than those in 22.7(*c*) above) and supplies of services which give rise to successive statements of account or payments are regarded as being completed at the time when the periods, to which such statements of account or payments pertain, expire. Countries may, however, in certain cases provide that continuous supplies of goods and services which take place over a period of time shall be regarded as being completed at least at intervals of one year.

Where a payment is made on account before the goods are delivered or the services performed, VAT becomes chargeable on receipt of the payment and on the amount received.

By way of derogation from the above, countries may provide that VAT becomes chargeable, for certain transactions or for certain categories of taxable person, either

(*a*) no later than the issue of the invoice; or

(*b*) no later than receipt of the price; or

(*c*) where an invoice is not issued, or is issued late, within a specified period from the date of the chargeable event.

See 64.32 SUPPLY for the UK provisions.

Imported goods. The chargeable event occurs and the VAT becomes chargeable when the goods are imported. Where, on entry, goods are placed under

- one of the arrangements referred to in 22.22(*b*) below, or
- arrangements for temporary importation with total exemption from import duty, or
- external transit arrangements

the chargeable event occurs and the VAT becomes chargeable only when the goods cease to be covered by those arrangements.

Where, however, imported goods are subject to customs duties or agricultural levies or similar charges, the chargeable event occurs and the VAT becomes chargeable at the same time.

See 34.2 IMPORTS for the UK provisions.

[*EC 6th Directive, Art 10*].

22.12 **Taxable amount: supplies within a country**

Subject to the exceptions below, the taxable amount in respect of supplies of goods or services is everything which constitutes the consideration which has been or will be obtained by the supplier from the purchaser, the customer or a third party for such supplies, including 'subsidies directly linked to the price' of the supplies. The exceptions are as follows.

- In respect of supplies within 22.7(*d*)(*e*)(*f*)(*h*) and (*j*) above, the taxable amount is the purchase price of the goods or of similar goods or, in the absence of a purchase price, the cost price, determined at the time of supply.

- In respect of supplies within 22.8(*d*) and (*e*) above, the full cost to the taxable person of providing the services.
- In respect of the self-supply of services under 22.8 above, the open market value of the services supplied.

Included in the taxable amount are

(*a*) taxes duties, levies and charges, excluding VAT itself;

(*b*) incidental expenses eg commission, packing, transport and insurance costs charged by the supplier;

but excluded are

(*c*) price reductions by way of discount for early payment;

(*d*) price discounts and rebates allowed to the customer and accounted for at the time of supply; and

(*e*) the amounts received by a taxable person from his purchaser or customer as repayment for expenses paid out in the name and for the account of the latter and which are entered in his books in a suspense account. The taxable person must furnish proof of the actual amount of this expenditure and cannot deduct any VAT which may have been charged on these transactions.

[*EC 6th Directive, Art 11*].

'*Subsidies directly linked to the price*' must be interpreted as covering only subsidies which constitute the whole or part of the consideration for a supply of goods or services and which are paid by a third party to the seller or supplier (*Office des Produits Wallons ASBL v Belgium, CJEC 2001, [2003] STC 1100 (TVC 21.172)*).

See 69 VALUATION for UK provisions.

22.13 Taxable amount: imports

The taxable amount is the value for customs purposes as determined in accordance with EC provisions in force.

The taxable amount includes taxes etc as in 22.12(*a*) above due outside the importing EC country and those due by reason of importation, excluding the VAT to be levied; and incidental expenses as in 22.12(*b*) above incurred up to the 'first place of destination' within the territory of the importing country. It must not include 22.12(*c*) and (*d*) above.

'*First place of destination*' is the place mentioned on the consignment note, etc or, in the absence of any such indication, the place of first transfer of cargo in the importing EC country.

The incidental expenses referred to above must also be included in the taxable amount where they result from transport to another place of destination within the EC provided that place is known when the chargeable event occurs.

Where goods have been temporarily exported from the EC and are re-imported after having undergone repair, processing or adaptation, or after having been made up or reworked, outside the EC, countries must take steps to ensure that the treatment of goods for VAT purposes is the same as that which would have applied to the goods in question had the operations been carried out within the territory of the country.

[*EC 6th Directive, Art 11*].

See 69.15 VALUATION for UK provisions.

22.14 **Miscellaneous provisions**

(*a*) In case of *cancellation, refusal or total or partial non-payment*, or where the price is reduced after the supply takes place, the taxable amount must be reduced accordingly under conditions determined by each EC country although, in the case of total or partial non-payment, countries may derogate from this rule.

(*b*) Where information for determining the taxable amount is expressed in *foreign currency*,

- for importations, the exchange rate must be determined in accordance with EC provisions governing the calculation of the value for customs purposes (see *EC Council Regulation 1224/80/EEC*); and
- the exchange rate applicable for transactions other than importations is the latest selling rate recorded, at the time the VAT becomes chargeable, on the most representative exchange market or markets of the EC country concerned.

See 69.18 VALUATION for the UK provisions.

(*c*) As regards *returnable packing costs*, countries may either

- exclude them from the taxable amount and take the necessary measures to see that this amount is adjusted if the packing is not returned; or
- include them in the taxable amount and take the necessary measures to see that this amount is adjusted where the packaging is returned.

[*EC 6th Directive, Art 11*].

22.15 **Rates**

The rate applicable to taxable transactions is that in force at the time of the chargeable event. However, where a payment is made on account before the goods are delivered or the EC country has derogated under 22.11(*a*) to (*c*) above, the rate to be used is that in force when the VAT becomes chargeable.

Importation of goods. The rate applicable on the importation of goods is that applied to the supply of like goods within the country at the time the VAT on the importation becomes chargeable.

Standard rate. A standard rate of VAT must be applied which cannot be less than 15%.

Reduced rates. Countries may also apply either one or two reduced rates (which cannot be less than 5%) to the following.

(*a*) Goods or services listed in *Annex H*. These include foodstuffs, water supplies, pharmaceutical products and medical equipment, aids for the handicapped, passenger transport, books and printed matter, admissions to shows and sporting events and use of sporting facilities, housing supplies as part of a social policy, holiday accommodation, certain charitable supplies, undertakers' and cremation services, and medical and dental care.

(*b*) With the approval of the EC Commission to any two (in exceptional circumstances three) of the following categories of services.

- Small services of repairing bicycles, shoe and leather goods, and clothing and household linen.
- Renovation and repairing of private dwellings (excluding materials which form a significant part of the value of the supply).
- Window cleaning and cleaning in private households.
- Domestic care services (eg home help and care of young, elderly, sick or disabled).
- Hairdressing.

The services concerned must be labour-intensive, provided largely to final consumers, be mainly local and not likely to create distortions of competition. There must be a close link between the lower prices resulting from the rate reduction and the foreseeable increase in demand and employment.

(*c*) Supplies of natural gas and electricity (provided that no risk of distortion of competition exists) and imports of works of art, collectors' items and antiques.

During a transitional period until a definite VAT system is decided upon, exemptions with refund of VAT paid at the preceding stage (ie zero-rating in the UK) may be maintained provided they were in force on 1 January 1991 and were in accordance with Community law.

[*EC 6th Directive, Arts 12, 28(2)(6)*].

22.16 **Exemptions**

EC countries must exempt certain activities under conditions that they lay down for the purpose of ensuring the correct and straightforward application of such exemptions and of preventing any possible evasion, avoidance or abuse. These are divided into exemptions for certain activities in the public interest (see 22.17 below), other exemptions (see 22.18 below), exemptions on importation (see 22.20 below) and exemption of exports and like transactions and international transport (see 22.21 below).

22.17 *Exemptions for certain activities in the public interest*

The following activities should be exempt.

(*a*) The supply by the public postal service of services other than passenger transport and telecommunications services, and the supply of goods incidental thereto.

(*b*) Hospital and medical care and closely related activities undertaken by bodies governed by public law or, under social conditions comparable to those applicable to bodies governed by public law, by hospitals, centres for medical treatment or diagnosis and other duly recognised establishments of a similar nature.

(*c*) The provision of medical care in the exercise of the medical or paramedical professions as defined by the country concerned.

(*d*) Supplies of human organs, blood and milk.

(*e*) Services supplied by dental technicians in their professional capacity and dental prostheses supplied by dentists and dental technicians.

(*f*) Services supplied by independent groups of persons whose activities are exempt from or not subject to VAT, for the purpose of rendering their members the services directly necessary for the exercise of their activity, where these groups merely claim from their members exact reimbursement of their share of joint expenses, provided that such exemption is not likely to produce distortion of competition.

(*g*) The supply of services and of goods closely linked to welfare and social security work, including those supplied by old people's homes, by bodies governed by public law or by other organisations recognised as charitable by the country concerned. The expression 'social welfare' means the well-being (whether in the physical, mental or material sense) of individuals as members of society. The provision of benefits which tends directly to improve the health or conditions of life of individuals comes *prima facie* within the expression 'social welfare' (*Yoga for Health Foundation v C & E Commrs, QB [1984] STC 630 (TVC 21.200)*). 'Spiritual welfare' is also included (*International Bible Students' Association v C & E Commrs, QB 1987, [1988] STC 412 (TVC 21.201)*).

In *Bulthuis-Griffioen v Inspector der Omzetbelasting, CJEC Case C–453/93; [1995] STC 954 (TVC 21.204)* the CJEC held that this exemption was only available to 'bodies governed by public law or other organisations' and did not apply to sole proprietors. This decision was not followed in *J & M Gregg v C & E Commrs, CJEC Case C–216/97, [1999] STC 935 (TVC 21.205)* where the CJEC held that the provisions were sufficiently broad to include natural persons as well.

(*h*) The supply of services and of goods closely linked to the protection of children and young persons by bodies governed by public law or by other organisations recognised as charitable by the country concerned.

(*i*) Children's or young people's education, school or university education, vocational training or retraining, including the supply of services and of goods closely related thereto, provided by bodies governed by public law having such as their aim or by other organisations defined by the country concerned as having similar objects. Exemption does not extend to the undertaking by State universities of research projects for consideration as this cannot be regarded as an activity closely related to university education (*EC Commission v Federal Republic of Germany, CJEC Case C–287/00, [2002] STC 982 (TVC 21.209)*).

(*j*) Tuition given privately by teachers and covering school or university education.

(*k*) Certain supplies of staff by religious or philosophical institutions for the purposes of (*b*), (*g*), (*h*) or (*i*) above and with a view to spiritual welfare.

(*l*) Supply of services and goods closely linked thereto for the benefit of their members in return for a subscription fixed in accordance with their rules by non-profit-making organisations with aims of a political, trade union, religious, patriotic, philosophical, philanthropic or civic nature, provided that this exemption is not likely to cause distortion of competition.

(*m*) Certain services closely linked to sport or physical education supplied by non-profit-making organisations to persons taking part in sport or physical education.

(*n*) Certain cultural services and goods closely linked thereto supplied by bodies governed by public law or by other cultural bodies recognised by the country concerned. The expression 'other cultural bodies' does not exclude soloists performing individually (*Hoffmann, CJEC Case C–144/00, [2004] STC 740 (TVC 21.218)*).

(*o*) The supply of services and goods by organisations whose activities are exempt under (*b*), (*g*), (*h*), (*i*), (*l*), (*m*) and (*n*) above in connection with fund-raising events organised exclusively for their own benefit provided that exemption is not likely to cause distortion of competition. Countries may introduce any necessary restrictions in particular as regards the number of events or the amount of receipts which give entitlement to exemption.

(*p*) The supply of transport services for sick or injured persons in vehicles specially designed for the purpose by duly authorised bodies.

(*q*) Activities of public radio and television bodies other than those of a commercial nature.

The supply of goods and services under (*b*), (*g*), (*h*), (*i*), (*l*), (*m*) and (*n*) above is not exempt if

- it is not essential to the transaction exempted; or
- its basic purpose is to obtain additional income for the organisation by carrying out transactions which are in direct competition with those of commercial enterprises liable for VAT.

Countries may make the granting to bodies other than those governed by public law of exemption under (*b*), (*g*), (*h*), (*i*), (*l*), (*m*) and (*n*) above subject to one or more of the following conditions.

(i) They do not systematically aim to make profit. Any profits arising must not be distributed but assigned to the continuance or improvement of the services supplied.

(ii) They must be managed and administered on an essentially voluntary basis by persons who have no direct or indirect interest in the results of the activities concerned. See *C & E Commrs v Zoological Society of London, CJEC [2002] STC 521 (TVC 21.220)*.

(iii) They charge prices approved by the public authorities or which do not exceed such approved prices or, in respect of those services not subject to approval, prices lower than those charged for similar services by commercial enterprises subject to VAT.

(iv) Exemption of the service concerned must not be likely to create distortions of competition such as to place at a disadvantage commercial enterprises liable to VAT.

[*EC 6th Directive, Art 13A*].

22.18 *Other exemptions*

The following activities should be exempt.

(*a*) Insurance and reinsurance transactions, including related services performed by insurance brokers and agents.

(*b*) The leasing or letting of immovable property other than

- the provision of accommodation in the hotel or similar sectors, including holiday camps and camping sites;
- the letting of premises and sites for parking vehicles;
- letting of permanently installed equipment and machinery; and

- hire of safes.

The letting of a building constructed from prefabricated components fixed to or in the ground in such a way that they cannot be either dismantled or easily moved constitutes a letting of immovable property, even if the building was to be removed at the end of the lease and reused on another site (*Maierhofer v Finanzamt Augsburg-Land, CJEC [2003] STC 564 (TVC 21.232)*).

(*c*) The granting and the negotiation of credit and the management of credit by the person granting it.

(*d*) The negotiation of, or any dealings in, credit guarantees or any other security for money and the management of credit guarantees by the person who is granting the credit.

(*e*) Transactions, including negotiations, concerning deposit and current accounts, payments, transfers, debts, cheques and other negotiable instruments, but excluding debt collecting and factoring.

(*f*) Transactions, including negotiations, concerning currency, bank notes and coins used as legal tender, with the exception of collectors' items.

(*g*) Transactions, including negotiations but excluding management and safekeeping, in shares, interests in companies or associations, debentures and other securities, excluding

- documents establishing title to goods;
- rights *in rem* giving the holder thereof a right of user over immovable property; and
- shares or interests equivalent to shares giving the holder thereof *de jure* or *de facto* rights of ownership or possession over immovable property or part thereof.

(*h*) Management of special investment funds as defined by countries.

(*i*) The supply at face value of postage stamps valid for use for postal services within the territory of the country, fiscal stamps and similar stamps.

(*j*) Betting, lottery and other forms of gambling, subject to conditions and limitations laid down by each country.

(*k*) The supply of buildings or parts thereof, and of land on which they stand, other than the supply before first occupation.

(*l*) The supply of land which has not been built on other than building land as defined by each country.

(*m*) Supplies of goods

- used wholly for an activity exempted under (*a*) to (*l*) above or under 22.17 above or by an EC country under a derogation when these goods have not given rise to the right to deduction; or
- on the acquisition or production of which VAT did not become deductible.

[*EC 6th Directive, Art 13B*].

For a consideration of the scope of (*e*) and (*f*) above see *Sparekassernes Datacenter (SDC) v Skatteministeriet, CJEC [1997] STC 932 (TVC 21.243).*

22.19 *Options*

Countries may allow taxpayers a right of option to tax in cases of

- letting and leasing of immovable property; and
- the transactions under 22.18(*c*)–(*g*), (*k*) and (*l*) above.

[*EC 6th Directive, Art 13C*].

22.20 *Exemptions on importation*

Countries must exempt the following.

(*a*) Final importation of goods of which the supply by a taxable person would in all circumstances be exempted within the country.

(*b*) Final importation of goods qualifying for exemption from customs duties other than as provided for in the Common Customs Tariff. Countries have the option of not granting exemption if this might have a serious effect on conditions of competition.

(*c*) Reimportation by the person who exported them of goods in the same state as which they were exported, where they qualify for exemption from customs duties.

(*d*) Importation of goods under diplomatic and consular arrangements, etc which qualify for exemption from customs duties; by international organisations; and into the territory of EC countries which are parties of the North Atlantic Treaty by the armed forces of other states which are parties to the treaty.

(*e*) Importation into ports by sea fishing undertakings of their catches, unprocessed (except for preservation) but before being supplied.

(*f*) The supply of services in connection with the importation of goods where those services are included in the taxable amount (see 22.13 above).

(*g*) Importations of gold by central banks.

[*EC 6th Directive, Art 14*].

22.21 *Exemption of exports from the EC and like transactions and international transport*

Countries must exempt the following.

(*a*) The supply of goods dispatched or transported to a destination outside the EC

(i) by or on behalf of the vendor, or

(ii) by or on behalf of a purchaser not established in the country (except for goods transported by the purchaser himself for equipping, fuelling, etc pleasure boats and private aircraft or any other means of transport for private use). In the case of a supply of goods to be carried in the personal luggage of travellers, this exemption applies on condition that the traveller does not hold an EC passport; the goods are transported to a destination outside the EC before the end of the third month following that in which the supply takes place; and the total value of the supply (including VAT) is more than the equivalent of 175 euro in national currency (countries may exempt supplies with lower values).

(*b*) The supply of services consisting of work on movable property acquired or imported for the purpose of undergoing such work in the EC and dispatched or transported out of the EC by the person providing the services *or* by his customer if established outside the country *or* on behalf of either of them.

(*c*) The supply of goods for the fuelling and provisioning of vessels

(i) used for navigation at sea and carrying passengers for reward or used for the purposes of commercial, industrial or fishing activities;

(ii) used for rescue or assistance at sea;

(iii) of war leaving the country and bound for foreign ports or anchorages.

(*d*) The supply, modification, repair, maintenance, chartering and hiring of sea-going vessels within (*c*)(i) and (ii) above or aircraft used by airlines operating for reward chiefly on international routes and the supply, hiring, repair and maintenance of equipment (including fishing equipment) incorporated or used therein.

(*e*) The supply of goods for the fuelling and provisioning of aircraft within (*d*) above.

(*f*) The supply of services other than those referred to in (*d*) above to meet the direct needs of sea-going vessels or aircraft referred to in (*d*) above or of their cargoes.

(*g*) Supplies of goods and services

(i) under diplomatic and consular arrangements, etc;

(ii) to international organisations;

(iii) effected within an EC country which is a party to the North Atlantic Treaty and intended for use by the forces of other states which are party to the treaty or the civilian staff accompanying them, or for supplying their messes and canteens when such forces take part in the common defence effort; and

(iv) to another EC country and intended for the forces of any EC country which is a party to the North Atlantic Treaty, other than the country of destination itself, for the use of those forces, etc as under (iii) above.

(*h*) Supplies of gold to Central Banks.

(*i*) Goods supplied to approved bodies which export them from the EC as part of their humanitarian, charitable or teaching activities outside the EC.

(*j*) The supply of services including transport and ancillary operations (but excluding the supply of services exempted under 22.17 to 22.19 above) where these are directly linked with

(i) the export of goods;

(ii) the import of goods placed under one of the arrangements in 22.22(*b*)(i)–(iv) below under arrangements for temporary importation with total exemption from import duty or under external transit arrangements; or

(iii) the import of goods intended to be placed under warehousing arrangements other than customs.

(*k*) Services supplied by brokers and other intermediaries, acting in the name and for the account of another person, where they form part of transactions within this *Article* or of transactions carried out outside the EC. This exemption does not apply to travel agents who supply in the name and for the account of the traveller services which are supplied in other EC countries.

[*EC 6th Directive, Art 15*].

22.22 *Special exemptions linked to international goods traffic*

Countries may take special measures designed to relieve the following transactions from VAT, provided that they are not aimed at final use or consumption and that the amount of VAT charged at entry for home use corresponds to the VAT which should have been charged had the transaction been taxed on import or within the country.

(*a*) imports of goods which are intended to be placed under warehousing arrangements other than customs;

(*b*) supplies of goods which are intended to be

(i) produced to customs and, where applicable, placed in temporary storage;

(ii) placed in a free zone or in a free warehouse;

(iii) placed under customs warehousing arrangements or inward processing arrangements;

(iv) admitted into territorial waters either to be incorporated in, or for the purposes of repair of, drilling or production platforms or for the fuelling and provisioning of such platforms;

(v) placed under warehousing arrangements other than customs;

(*c*) supplies of services relating to supplies of goods under (*b*) above;

(*d*) supplies of goods and services carried out in the places listed in (*b*) and still subject to one of the arrangements specified therein; and

(*e*) supplies of goods

(i) still subject to arrangements for temporary importation with total exemption from import duty or to external transit arrangements; or

(ii) imported from a territory within 21.2 EUROPEAN COMMUNITY: GENERAL and still subject to the internal Community transit procedure under 22.32 below.

Re-exportations. Countries may also opt to exempt imports for, and supplies of goods to, a taxable person intending to export them as they are or after processing, as well as supplies of services linked with the export business, up to a maximum equal to the value of his exports during the preceding 12 months. See, however, 22.44 below for transitional provisions.

[*EC 6th Directive, Art 16*].

22.23 **Deductions**

The right to deduct input tax arises when the deductible VAT becomes chargeable.

Where goods and services are used for the purposes of his taxable transactions, a taxable person is entitled to deduct from the VAT which he is liable to pay (*a*) VAT due or paid in respect of goods or services supplied or to be supplied to him by another taxable person;

(*b*) VAT due or paid in respect of imported goods; and

(*c*) VAT due under 22.7(*h*) above or the self-supply rules under 22.8 above.

Included is VAT in so far as the goods and services are used for the purposes of

(i) transactions relating to economic activities carried out in another country which would be eligible for deduction if carried out in that country;

(ii) transactions within 22.20(*f*), 22.21 and 22.22(*b*) to (*d*) and re-exportations; and

(iii) any of the transactions exempted under 22.18(*a*)(*c*)–(*g*) when the customer is established outside the EC or when the transactions are directly linked with goods intended to be exported to a country outside the EC.

See 35.1-35.3 INPUT TAX for the UK provisions.

Where goods and services are used by the taxable person both for transactions covered by (*a*) and (*b*) above and for transactions in respect of which VAT is not deductible, the proportion deductible is given by the fraction

$$\frac{A}{B}$$

where

A = the total amount, exclusive of VAT, of turnover per year attributable to transactions in respect of which VAT is deductible; and

B = the total amount, exclusive of VAT, of turnover per year attributable to all transactions.

The proportions must be determined on an annual basis, fixed as a percentage and rounded up to a figure not exceeding the next unit. By derogation, EC countries may exclude supplies of capital goods, incidental transactions within 22.18(*c*)–(*h*) and incidental real estate and financial transactions.

Countries may, however, authorise or compel the taxable person to determine a proportion for each sector of his business and keep separate accounts for each sector or to make deductions on the basis of the use of the goods and services. Countries may also provide that where non-deductible VAT is insignificant it is treated as nil.

See 49 PARTIAL EXEMPTION for the UK provisions.

[*EC 6th Directive, Arts 17, 19*].

22.24 *Adjustments of deductions*

The initial deduction must be adjusted, according to the procedures laid down by the EC country where, for example, that deduction was higher or lower than that to which the taxable person was entitled or after the return is made changes occur in the factors used to determine the amount to be deducted. [*EC 6th Directive, Art 20*].

22.25 *Capital goods*

In the case of capital goods, adjustments must be spread over five years including that in which the goods were acquired or manufactured. By derogation the period may commence from the time the goods are first used. The annual adjustment must be made only in respect of one-fifth of the VAT imposed on the goods and must be made on the basis of the variations in the deduction entitlement in subsequent years in relation to that for the year in which the goods were acquired or manufactured.

In the case of immovable property, the adjustment period may be extended to up to 20 years.

Where capital goods are supplied during the period of adjustment, they are treated as if they had still been applied for business use by the taxable person until the expiry of the period of adjustment. Such business activities are presumed to be fully taxed in cases where the supply of the goods is taxed and fully exempt where the supply is exempt. The adjustment is made only once for the whole period of adjustment still to be covered.

[*EC 6th Directive, Art 20*].

See CAPITAL GOODS SCHEME (10) for UK provisions.

22.26 *Exercising the right to deduct*

To exercise his right to deduct, the taxable person must

(*a*) in respect of deductions under 22.23(*a*) hold a proper VAT invoice;

(*b*) in respect of deductions under 22.23(*b*) hold an import document specifying him as consignee or importer and stating or permitting the calculation of the amount of VAT due;

(*c*) in respect of deductions under 22.23(*c*) comply with the formalities laid down by each EC country; and

(*d*) when he is required to pay VAT as a customer or purchaser under 22.27(*a*)-(*c*) below, comply with the formalities laid down by the EC country.

He then effects the deduction by subtracting from the total amount of VAT due for a given tax period the total amount of the VAT in respect of which, in the same VAT period, the right to deduct has arisen.

Countries may require that, for taxable persons who carry out occasional transactions, the right to deduct can be exercised only at the time of the supply.

Where for a given VAT period the amount of authorised deductions exceeds the amount of VAT due, the EC country may either make a refund or carry the excess forward to the following period according to conditions which they determine.

[*EC 6th Directive, Art 18*].

22.27 Persons liable to pay the VAT

The person liable to pay the VAT is as follows.

(*a*) The taxable person carrying out the taxable supply of goods or of services, except for the cases referred to in (*b*) or (*c*) below.

Where the taxable transaction is carried out by a taxable person not established within the territory of a country, that country may, under conditions it determines, lay down that the person liable to pay VAT is the person for whom the taxable supply of goods or services is carried out.

(*b*) A taxable person to whom services within 22.10(*d*) above (and, during a transitional period until a definite VAT system can be agreed upon, 22.37, 22.38

or 22.39 below) are supplied if the services are carried out by a taxable person not established within the territory of the country.

(*c*) The person to whom the supply of goods is made where

- the taxable transaction is a supply of goods falling within 22.44(*c*) below;
- the person to whom the supply is made is another taxable person or a non-taxable legal person identified for VAT purposes within the EC country; and
- the invoice issued by the taxable person not established in the EC country in question conforms to the requirements in 22.28(*c*) below.

A country may, however, provide for a derogation from this obligation where the non-established taxable person has appointed a tax representative in that country.

(*d*) Any person who mentions VAT on an invoice or other document serving as an invoice.

(*e*) During a transitional period until a definite VAT system can be agreed upon, any person effecting a taxable intra-EC acquisition of goods.

(*f*) By way of derogation from the above provisions

- where the person liable to pay the VAT is a taxable person not established within an EC country, that country may, subject to such conditions and procedures as it lays down, allow him to appoint a tax representative as the person liable to pay the VAT; and
- where the taxable transaction is effected by a taxable person who is not established within the territory of a country and no legal instrument exists with the country where he is established relating to mutual assistance in the field of indirect taxation, that country may provide that the person liable for the payment of the VAT shall be a tax representative appointed by the non-established person.

(*g*) In any of the situations within (*a*)-(*f*) above, a country may provide that someone other than the person liable for payment of the VAT is jointly and severally liable for the VAT.

(*h*) On importation, the person liable is the person designated or accepted as being liable by the EC country into which the goods are imported.

[*EC 6th Directive, Arts 21, 28g*].

22.28 **Obligations of taxable persons and EC countries**

Taxable persons and EC countries have the following obligations. Many of the obligations arise only during a transitional period until a definitive VAT system, based on the principle of taxation of services in the EC country of origin, can be decided upon.

(*a*) Every taxable person must state when his activity as a taxable person commences, changes or ceases. From 1 July 2003, EC countries must, subject to conditions which they lay down, allow the taxable person to make such statements by electronic means, and may also require that electronic means are used.

During the transitional period

- without prejudice to the above, every taxable person within 22.34(*a*)(i)–(iii) below must state that he is effecting intra-EC acquisitions of goods when the conditions for application of the derogation are not fulfilled; and
- with certain exceptions, EC countries must take measures to identify, by means of an individual number, every taxable person who effects supplies of goods and services, or intra-EC acquisitions, within the territory of the country and every taxable person within 22.34(*a*)(i)–(iii) below or who exercises the option for the derogation not to apply.

(*b*) Every taxable person must keep accounts in sufficient detail for VAT to be applied and inspected by the tax authority.

(*c*) Every taxable person must issue an invoice in respect of

(i) goods and services supplied by him to another taxable person or, during the transitional period, to a non-taxable legal person,

(ii) during the transitional period, supplies of goods within 22.36 below and goods supplied under the conditions within 22.40(*a*) below, and

(iii) payments on account made to him before any supply of goods within (i) or (ii) above or made to him by another taxable person or by a non-taxable legal person before the provision of services is completed

and must keep copies thereof. The invoice must clearly state the price exclusive of VAT and the relevant VAT at each rate as well as any exemptions.

During the transitional period, the invoice must also show

- for transactions falling within 22.37 to 22.39 below, the number by which the taxable person is identified in the territory of the country and the number by which the customer is identified and under which the service has been rendered to him;
- for transactions falling within 22.40(*a*) below, the number by which the taxable person is identified in the territory of the country and the number by which the person acquiring the goods is identified in another EC country; and
- in the case of the supply of a new means of transport, the necessary particulars to show that the vehicle, etc falls within those provisions.

Countries must lay down the criteria for deciding whether a document may be considered an invoice.

(*d*) Every taxable person must submit a return within an interval after the end of the VAT period (not more than two months) to be determined by each EC country. From 1 July 2003, EC countries must, subject to conditions which they lay down, allow the taxable person to make such returns by electronic means, and may also require that electronic means are used. The return must set out

(i) all information needed to calculate the VAT that has become chargeable and the deduction to be made;

(ii) where appropriate, the total value of transactions relative to the VAT and deductions within (i) above and the value of any exempt transactions;

(iii) during the transitional period, the total value, less VAT, of supplies of goods within 22.40(*a*) below on which VAT has become chargeable in the period;

(iv) during the transitional period, the total value, less VAT, of the supplies of installed or assembled goods and goods within 22.36 above effected within the territory of another EC country for which VAT has become chargeable in the return period where the place of departure of the dispatch or transport of the goods is situated in the territory of the country;

(v) during the transitional period, the total value, less VAT, of intra-EC acquisitions within 22.34(*a*) below effected within the territory of the country on which VAT has become chargeable; and

(vi) during the transitional period, the total value, less VAT, of supplies as in (iv) above effected within the territory of the country where the place of departure of the dispatch or transport of the goods is situated in the territory of another EC country.

Every taxable person must pay the net amount of VAT when submitting the return although countries may fix a different date or may demand an interim payment.

(*e*) Countries may require a taxable person to submit a statement, including all the particulars within (*d*) above, concerning all transactions carried out in the preceding year. EC countries must, subject to conditions which they lay down, allow the taxable person to make such returns by electronic means, and may also require that electronic means are used.

(*f*) During the transitional period, every taxable person identified for VAT purposes must submit a recapitulative statement for every quarter of the acquirers identified for VAT purposes to whom he has supplied goods under the conditions in 22.40(*a*) and (*d*) below. EC countries must, subject to conditions which they lay down, allow the taxable person to make such returns by electronic means, and may also require that electronic means are used. The statement must show

(i) the VAT registration number of the taxable person;

(ii) the VAT registration number of his customer in another EC country, together with a country identifier; and

(iii) the aggregate value of goods and associated services supplied to that customer.

The Council may authorise a country to allow any taxable person to file such recapitulative statements annually where his supplies do not exceed specified limits and a taxable person who already prepares annual VAT returns to prepare the recapitulative statement for the same period where his supplies do not exceed a (higher) specified limit.

(*g*) During the transitional period, where supplies of new means of transport are effected under the conditions in 22.40(*b*) below by a taxable person identified for VAT purposes to a purchaser not identified for VAT purposes (or by a person regarded as a taxable person for these purposes under 22.40 above), countries must take the measures necessary to ensure that the vendor supplies all the necessary information to the tax authorities.

(*h*) Countries may impose other obligations which they deem necessary for the correct collection of VAT and the prevention of evasion, subject to the requirement of equal treatment for domestic transactions and transactions carried out between member states.

[*EC 6th Directive, Arts 22, 28h*].

Imports. Countries must lay down the detailed rules for the making of the declarations and payments and may provide that VAT need not be paid at the time of importation. [*EC 6th Directive, Art 23*].

22.29 **Special schemes**

(*a*) **Small undertakings.** Countries may apply simplified procedures to small undertakings for charging and collecting VAT and may grant an exemption from VAT to taxable persons whose annual turnover is below a certain limit.

(*b*) **Common flat-rate scheme for farmers.** Countries may apply such a scheme to farmers where the application of the normal VAT scheme, or the simplified rules for small undertakings above, would give rise to difficulties. See 63.25 SPECIAL SCHEMES for UK provisions.

(*c*) **Special schemes for travel agents.** Where a travel agent (including a tour operator) deals with customers in his own name and uses supplies and services of other taxable persons in the provision of travel services, all transactions performed by him in respect of a journey are treated as a single service supplied by him to the traveller. The supply is taxable in the EC country in which the travel agent has established his business or has a fixed establishment from which he has provided the services. The taxable amount, and the price exclusive of VAT under 22.28(*c*) above, is the travel agent's margin, ie the difference between the total amount to be paid by the traveller, exclusive of VAT, and the actual cost to the travel agent of supplies and services provided by other taxable persons where these transactions are for the direct benefit of the traveller. See *Independent Coach Travel (Wholesaling) Ltd (VTD 11037) (TVC 61.3)* where the tribunal held that 'customers' should be construed as a reference to 'travellers' and that these provisions only apply to travel agents dealing with travellers and not those who act as wholesalers making supplies to retailers.

Where transactions carried out by other taxable persons on behalf of the travel agent are performed outside the EC, the travel agent's services are treated as an exempt intermediary transaction under 22.21(*k*) above.

VAT charged to the travel agent by other taxable persons on the transactions which are for the direct benefit of the traveller is not eligible for deduction or refund in the EC.

The above provisions do not apply to travel agents who are acting only as intermediaries and accounting for VAT under 22.12(*e*) above.

The fact that the travel agent provides accommodation only, and not transport, does not exclude such a service from the ambit of these provisions (*Beheersmaatschappij Van Ginkel Waddinxveen BV and Others v Inspecteur der Omzetbelasting, Utrecht, CJEC 1992, [1996] STC 825 (TVC 21.312)*).

See 66 TOUR OPERATORS' MARGIN SCHEME for UK provisions.

(*d*) **Second-hand goods, works of art, collectors' items and antiques.** All countries must apply special arrangements for taxing the profit margin made by a taxable dealer in respect of supplies by him of second-hand goods, works of art, collectors' items and antiques where those goods were supplied to him by

- a non-taxable person;
- another taxable person insofar as the supply of goods by that other person is exempt under 22.18(*m*) above;
- another taxable person insofar as the supply of goods by that other person qualifies for exemption under (*a*) above and involves capital assets; or
- another taxable dealer insofar as the supply of goods by that other dealer was subject to VAT under these special arrangements.

The taxable amount is the profit margin (ie the difference between the selling price and the buying price) made by the taxable dealer, less the VAT relating to it.

Countries must also allow taxable dealers to opt to use the scheme for supplies of works of art, collectors' items and antiques which they have imported and works of art supplied by their creators (or their successors in title).

Where supplies are made under the scheme, any input tax incurred on the purchase of the goods cannot be deducted.

To simplify the procedure for charging VAT, countries may provide that, for certain transactions or certain categories of dealer, the taxable amount of supplies of goods under the scheme is to be determined for each VAT period as a whole (rather than for each individual transaction).

Countries may make special arrangements for sales by public auctions.

See 61 SECOND-HAND GOODS for UK provisions.

(*e*) **Special scheme for investment gold**. All countries must exempt the supply, acquisition and importation of 'investment gold', including investment gold represented by certificates for allocated or unallocated gold or traded on gold accounts and including, in particular, gold loans and swaps, involving a right of ownership or claim in respect of investment gold, as well as transactions concerning investment gold involving futures and forward contracts leading to a transfer of right of ownership or claim in respect of investment gold. Countries must also exempt services of agents acting in the supply of investment gold for their principals.

'*Investment gold*' comprises bars and wafers of very high purity as traded in the bullion markets and gold coins the value of which primarily reflects their gold price. Such coins are not, for these purposes, considered to be bought for numismatic interest. Each country must before 1 July each year inform the EC Commission of coins meeting the specified criteria which are traded in that country.

Option to tax. Countries must allow taxable persons who produce investment gold, or transform any gold into investment gold, a right to opt to tax supplies of investment gold to another taxable person. They may also allow taxable persons who supply gold for industrial use to opt to tax the supply to another taxable person of investment gold in the form of bars and wafers (but not coins). Where the supplier has exercised such an option, a country may allow any agent acting for that supplier to opt to tax his services. It may also designate the purchaser as the person liable to pay the tax under the reverse charge procedure.

Transactions on the regulated gold bullion market. An EC country may disapply the exemption for investment gold in respect of specific transactions, other than intra-EC supplies or exports, concerning investment gold taking place in that country

(*a*) between taxable persons who are members of a regulated bullion market; and

(*b*) where the transaction is between a member of a regulated bullion market and another taxable person who is not such a member.

Under such circumstances, the transactions are taxable.

Input tax. Taxable persons are entitled to deduct VAT due or paid in respect of

- investment gold supplied to them by a person who has exercised the option to tax as above or under the procedure for regulated bullion markets as above,
- the supply to them, or intra-EC acquisition or importation by them, of gold other than investment gold which is subsequently transformed by them (or on their behalf) into investment gold, and
- services supplied to them consisting of change of form, weight or purity of gold including investment gold,

if their subsequent supply of the gold is exempt under these provisions.

Taxable persons who produce investment gold, or transform any gold into investment gold, are entitled to deduct VAT due or paid in respect of supplies, intra-EC acquisitions, importations or services linked to the production or transformation of that gold as if their subsequent supply of the gold exempted under these provisions were taxable.

(*f*) **Special scheme for non-established taxable persons supplying electronic services to non-taxable persons.** EC countries must permit a 'non-established taxable person' (NETP) supplying 'electronic services' to a non-taxable person who is established or has his permanent address or usually resides in an EC country to use a special scheme in accordance with the following provisions. The special scheme must apply to all those supplies within the EC. A '*non-established taxable person*' means a taxable person who has neither established his business nor has a fixed establishment within the territory of the EC and who is not otherwise required to be identified for VAT purposes under 22.28 above. '*Electronic services*' mean those referred to in 22.10(*d*) above.

The NETP must state to the '*EC country of identification*' (ie the EC country which he chooses to contact to state when his activity as a taxable person within the EC commences in accordance with these provisions) when his activity as a taxable person commences, ceases or changes to the extent that he no longer qualifies for the special scheme. Such a statement must be made electronically.

The information from the NETP to the EC country of identification when his taxable activities commence must contain details of name; postal address; electronic addresses, including websites; national tax number, if any; and a statement that the person is not identified for VAT purposes within the EC. The NETP must notify the EC country of identification of any changes in the submitted information. The EC country of identification must identify the NETP by means of an individual number and must notify him of the number allocated by electronic means. Based on the information used for this identification, *EC countries of consumption* (ie the EC country in which the supply of the electronic services is deemed to take place under 22.10 above) may keep their own identification systems.

The EC country of identification must exclude the NETP from the identification register if

- he notifies that he no longer supplies electronic services;
- it otherwise can be assumed that his taxable activities have ended;
- he no longer fulfils the requirements necessary to be allowed to use the special scheme; or
- he persistently fails to comply with the rules concerning the special scheme.

The NETP must submit a VAT return by electronic means, whether or not electronic services have been supplied, to the EC country of identification for each calendar quarter within 20 days following the end of the period. The VAT return must set out the identification number and, for each EC country of consumption where tax has become due, the total value, less VAT, of supplies of electronic services for the reporting period and total amount of the corresponding VAT. The applicable VAT rates and the total VAT due must also be indicated. The VAT return must be made in euro. EC countries which have not adopted the euro may require the VAT return to be made in their national currencies. If the supplies have been made in other currencies, they must be converted using the exchange rates published by the European Central Bank for the last date of the reporting period or, if there is no publication on that day, on the next day of publication.

The NETP must pay the VAT when submitting the return to a bank account designated by the EC country of identification.

A NETP making use of this special scheme must, instead of making deductions for input tax under 22.23 above, be granted a refund under the *EC 13th Directive* (see 22.49 below).

The NETP must keep records of the transactions covered by this special scheme in sufficient detail to enable the tax administration of the EC country of consumption to determine that the VAT return referred to above is correct. These records should be made available electronically on request to the EC countries of identification and consumption. They must be maintained for a period of ten years from the end of the year when the transaction was carried out.

[*EC 6th Directive, Arts 24–26(c)*].

22.30 Derogations

The Council may authorise any EC country to introduce special measures for derogation from the provisions of the *6th Directive* in order to simplify the procedure for charging VAT (without affecting the amount of VAT due at the final consumption stage except to a negligible extent) or to prevent certain types of tax evasion or avoidance. In addition, countries were allowed to retain special measures which were in force on 1 January 1977 provided that they notified the Commission of them before 1 January 1978 (when the *6th Directive* was implemented).

The derogations granted to the UK government are in connection with the following.

- Special RETAIL SCHEMES (60).
- Exemption from registration where, although taxable supplies exceed the registration limit, all supplies are, or would be, zero-rated if the taxable person was registered. See 59.6 REGISTRATION.
- Valuation for VAT purposes where certain companies, for example, in the field of cosmetics, sell products to individuals who are outside the tax net for resale to the final customer. See 22.2(*b*) above and 69.23 VALUATION.
- Operation of UK TERMINAL MARKETS (65).
- Long stays in hotels. See 33.2 HOTELS AND HOLIDAY ACCOMMODATION.
- Treatment of goods in warehouse.
- Voluntary accounting scheme for transactions in GOLD AND PRECIOUS METALS (30).
- Fuel expenditure for company cars. See 45.16 MOTOR CARS.
- Cash accounting scheme. See 63.2 SPECIAL SCHEMES.
- Transfer of assets to a partly exempt group. See 31.7 GROUPS OF COMPANIES.
- Direction to use open market value for exempt supplies to connected persons (see 69.19 VALUATION) and acquisitions of goods from connected persons (see 69.12 VALUATION).
- Taxation of self-supplies of land and buildings to be based on open market value. This derogation has not been introduced.
- Preparation of annual EC sales lists by persons with low turnover and by persons who prepare annual VAT returns. See 2.21 ACCOUNTING PERIODS AND RETURNS.
- Transport services directly linked to an intra-EC transport of goods. See 68.26 TRANSPORT AND FREIGHT.
- Restricting to 50% the right of the hirer or lessee to deduct input tax on car hire or leasing transactions where the car is used for private purposes and waiving VAT payable on the private use of the car in question. See 45.11 MOTOR CARS.
- The place of supply of telecommunications services. See 64.28 SUPPLY.

[*EC 6th Directive, Art 27*].

22.31 Transitional provisions

For a transitional period, countries are allowed to

- continue to tax certain items set out in *Annex E* to the *Directive* which are otherwise exempted under the provisions of 22.17, 22.18 and 22.21 above; and
- continue to exempt certain items set out in *Annex F* to the *Directive* which are otherwise taxable.

The *18th Directive* phased out most of these provisions over the period from 1 January 1990 to 1 January 1993.

[*EC 6th Directive, Art 28*].

22.32 Trade with countries in the customs territory of the EC

Goods entering the EC from, or as the case may be dispatched from the EC to, a territory which forms part of the customs territory of the EC but which is considered a third country for VAT purposes (see 21.3 EUROPEAN COMMUNITY: GENERAL) are subject to special provisions. The formalities relating to the entry into the EC/(export from the EC) of such goods are the same as those in force for the import of goods into/(export of goods from) the customs territory of the EC.

[*EC 6th Directive, Art 33a*].

22.33 SIXTH DIRECTIVE — TRANSITIONAL ARRANGEMENTS FOR THE TAXATION OF TRADE BETWEEN EC COUNTRIES

The transitional arrangements in 22.34 to 22.47 below modify or extend the provisions in 22.5 to 22.32 above. They will apply until a definitive system, based upon the taxation of goods and services in the EC country of origin, can be decided on and enter into force. [*EC 6th Directive, Art 28l*].

22.34 Scope

(*a*) **Intra-EC acquisitions of goods.** Subject to the derogation below, 'intra-EC acquisitions of goods' for a consideration within the territory of a country by a taxable person or a non-taxable legal person are subject to VAT where the vendor is a registered taxable person who is not covered by the arrangements for installed or assembled goods (see 22.9(*a*) above) or the derogation in 22.36 below.

By way of derogation, VAT is not chargeable on intra-EC acquisitions of goods (other than new means of transport and products subject to excise duty) effected by

(i) a taxable person eligible for a flat-rate scheme for farmers (see 22.29 above),

(ii) a taxable person who only supplies goods or services that are not deductible, or

(iii) a non-taxable legal person

for a total amount not exceeding, during the current calendar year, a threshold to be determined by each EC country (but which must not be less than the national equivalent of 10,000 euro). To qualify in any calendar year, the total of intra-EC acquisitions effected by that person in the previous calendar year must not have exceeded the threshold set by that country.

Intra-EC acquisitions of goods includes the use by a taxable person for the purposes of his undertaking in an EC country of goods dispatched from another EC country where they were produced, purchased, acquired or imported by him within the framework of his undertaking.

(*b*) **Intra-EC acquisitions of new means of transport.** Such acquisitions (as defined) are subject to VAT when effected for a consideration within the country by taxable persons, non-taxable legal persons qualifying for the derogation in (*a*) above or any other non-taxable person.

(*c*) **Intra-EC acquisitions of goods subject to excise duty.** Such goods are subject to VAT when effected for a consideration within the country by taxable persons or non-taxable legal persons qualifying for the derogation in (*a*) above.

'*Intra-EC acquisitions of goods*' means acquisition of the right to dispose as owner of movable tangible property dispatched or transported to the person acquiring the goods to an EC country other than that from which the goods are dispatched or transported.

Where goods acquired by a non-taxable legal person are dispatched or transported from a country outside the EC and imported by that person into an EC country other than the country of arrival of the goods, the goods are deemed to have been dispatched, etc from the EC country of import.

A person who from time to time supplies a new means of transport under the conditions laid down in 22.40 below must be regarded as a taxable person. EC countries must lay down detailed rules allowing the taxable person the right of deduction of the VAT, at the time of supply, included in the purchase, acquisition or importation price not exceeding the VAT for which he would be liable if the supply were not exempt.

Goods effected for a consideration include the transfer by a taxable person of goods from his undertaking to another EC country (subject to exceptions).

[*EC 6th Directive, Art 28a*].

22.35 **Place of intra-EC acquisition of goods**

Subject to below, the place of the intra-EC acquisition of goods is deemed to be the place where the goods are at the time when dispatch or transport to the person acquiring them ends.

Without prejudice to the above, the place of intra-EC acquisition of goods within 22.34(*a*) above is deemed to be within the EC country which issued the VAT identification number under which the person acquiring the goods made the acquisition (unless the person acquiring the goods establishes that that acquisition has been subject to VAT in accordance with the above general rule).

[*EC 6th Directive, Art 28b*(*A*)].

22.36 **Place of supply of goods**

Derogation. Subject to the exception below, by way of derogation from 22.9(*a*), the place of supply of goods dispatched or transported from an EC country other than that of arrival of the dispatch or transport is deemed to be the place where the goods are when dispatch or transport to the purchaser ends provided

(*a*) the supply is effected for a taxable person eligible for the derogation under 22.34(*a*) above, a non-taxable legal person eligible for the same derogation or for any other non-taxable person; and

(*b*) the supply is of goods other than new means of transport and other than goods supplied after assembly or installation by or on behalf of the supplier.

Where the goods thus supplied are dispatched or transported from a country outside the EC and imported by the supplier into an EC country other than that of arrival of the goods, they are to be regarded as having been dispatched or transported from the EC country of import.

Exception to the derogation. Where the supply is of goods other than products subject to excise duty, the above provisions do not apply to supplies of goods dispatched or transported to the same EC country of arrival where

- the total value of such supplies, less VAT, does not in one calendar year exceed the equivalent of 100,000 euro; and
- the total value, less VAT, of supplies of goods other than products subject to excise duty effected under those provisions in the previous calendar year did not exceed the equivalent of 100,000 euro.

Countries have the option of restricting the figure of 100,000 euro above to 35,000 euro if it would otherwise lead to the distortion of conditions of competition.

Countries within the territory of which the goods are at the time of departure of the dispatch or transport must grant those taxable persons who effect supplies of goods eligible for the exception the right to choose that the place of such supplies shall be determined under the derogation above.

[*EC 6th Directive, Art 28b*(*B*)].

22.37 **Place of supply of services in the intra-EC transport of goods**

By way of derogation from 22.10(*b*) above, the place of supply of services in the 'intra-EC transport of goods' is to be determined as follows.

(*a*) Subject to (*b*) below, the place of supply of services in the intra-EC transport of goods is the place of departure.

(*b*) The place of supply of such services rendered to customers identified for VAT purposes in a country other than that of the departure of the transport is deemed to be within the EC country which issued the customer with the VAT identification number under which the service was rendered to him.

(*c*) Countries need not apply VAT to that part of the transport corresponding to journeys made over waters which do not form part of the territories of the EC.

The '*intra-EC transport of goods*' means transport where the place of departure and place of arrival are in two different EC countries. The transport of goods where the place of departure and arrival are in the same country is treated as intra-EC transport of goods where such transport is closely linked to transport of goods where the place of departure and arrival are in different EC countries.

[*EC 6th Directive, Art 28b*(*C*)].

22.38 **Place of supply of services ancillary to the intra-EC transport of goods**

By way of derogation from 22.10(*c*)(ii) above, the place of supply of services involving activities ancillary to the intra-EC transport of goods, rendered to customers identified for VAT purposes in an EC country other than that within which the services are physically performed, is deemed to be within the EC country which issued the customer with the VAT identification number under which the service was rendered to him.

[*EC 6th Directive, Art 28b*(*D*)].

22.39 **Place of supply of services — other provisions**

Services rendered by intermediaries. By way of derogation from the general rule in 22.10 above, the place of supply of services rendered by intermediaries acting in the name and for the account of other persons is, subject to below,

(*a*) where the services form part of the supply of services in the intra-EC transport of goods, the place of departure of the goods;

(*b*) where the services form part of the supply of services the purpose of which is activities ancillary to the intra-Community transport of goods, the place where the ancillary services are physically performed; and

(*c*) where such services form part of a transaction not falling within (*a*) or (*b*) above or 22.10(*d*) above, the place where those transactions are carried out.

Where, however, the customer for whom the services under (*a*) to (*c*) above are rendered by the intermediary is identified for VAT purposes in an EC country other than the place of supply under those provisions, the place of supply is deemed to be within the EC country which issued the customer with the VAT identification number under which the services were rendered to him by the intermediary.

[*EC 6th Directive, Art 28b*(*E*)].

Valuation of or work on movable tangible property. By way of derogation from 22.10(*c*)(iii) above, the place of supply of services involving valuations or work on movable tangible property, provided to customers identified for VAT purposes in an EC country other than that in which the services are physically carried out, is deemed to be within the EC country which issued the customer with the VAT identification number under which the service was carried out for him. This derogation does not apply where the goods are not dispatched or transported out of the EC country where the services were physically carried out.

[*EC 6th Directive, Art 28c*(*F*)].

22.40 **Exempt supplies of goods**

Without prejudice to other EC provisions and subject to such conditions as they stipulate, countries must exempt the following supplies.

(*a*) Supplies of goods (as defined in 22.7 above) dispatched or transported out of the territory but within the EC, effected for another taxable person or a non-taxable legal person in an EC country other than that of the departure of the dispatch or transport of the goods except for

- supplies of goods by taxable persons exempt from registration; and
- supplies of goods effected for taxable persons or non-taxable legal persons who qualify for derogation under 22.34(*a*) above.

(*b*) Supplies of new means of transport, dispatched or transported to the purchaser out of the territory but within the EC, effected for taxable persons, non-taxable legal persons who qualify for the derogation under 22.34(*a*) above or any other non-taxable person.

(*c*) Supplies of goods subject to excise duty dispatched or transported to the purchaser outside the territory but inside the EC and effected for taxable persons or non-taxable legal persons who qualify for the derogation under 22.34(*a*) above. This does not, however, apply to supplies of goods subject to excise duty effected by taxable persons who benefit from the exemption from VAT set out in *Art 24* (special schemes for small undertakings).

(*d*) The transfer, under certain circumstances, by a taxable person of goods from his undertaking to another EC country (deemed to be a supply of goods under 22.34 above) if such a supply would qualify for exemption under (*a*)–(*c*) above if carried out for another taxable person.

[*EC 6th Directive, Art 28c*(*A*)].

22.41 **Exempt intra-EC acquisitions of goods**

Without prejudice to other EC provisions and subject to such conditions as they stipulate, countries must exempt the intra-EC acquisition of goods

(*a*) the supply of which by taxable persons would in all circumstances be exempt within the territory of the country;

(*b*) the importation of which in all circumstances would be exempt under 22.20 above; and

(*c*) where, under 22.23(i)–(iii) above, the person acquiring the goods would in all circumstances be entitled to full reimbursement of the VAT due under 22.34(*a*) above.

[*EC 6th Directive, Art 28c*(*B*)].

22.42 **Exempt transport services**

Countries must exempt the supply of intra-EC transport services involved in the dispatch or transport of goods to and from the Azores and Madeira as well as the dispatch or transport of goods between those islands. [*EC 6th Directive, Art 28c*(*C*)].

22.43 **Exempt importation of goods**

Where goods dispatched or transported from a country outside the EC are imported into an EC country other than that of arrival of the dispatch or transport, countries must exempt such imports where the supply of such goods by the importer is exempt under 22.40 above. [*EC 6th Directive, Art 28c*(*D*)].

22.44 **Other exemptions**

(*a*) Where countries adopt the special measures under 22.22 above, they must take necessary measures to ensure that intra-EC acquisitions of goods intended to be placed under one of the arrangements, etc under 22.22(*b*) above benefit from the same provisions as supplies of goods effected within the territory of the country under the same conditions.

(*b*) The provisions in 22.22 above under the heading *Re-exportation* are extended to intra-EC acquisitions of goods made by a taxable person. The goods must be exported outside the EC.

(*c*) An EC country must take specific measures to ensure that VAT is not charged on the intra-EC acquisition of goods effected within that country where

(i) the acquisition is effected by a taxable person (A) who is not established in that country but is identified for VAT purposes in another EC country;

(ii) the acquisition is effected for the purposes of a subsequent supply of the goods made by a taxable person (B) in the EC country in question;

(iii) the goods acquired by B are directly dispatched or transported from another EC country than that in which he is identified for VAT purposes and destined for the person for whom he effects the subsequent supply (C);

(iv) C is a taxable person or a non-taxable legal person who is identified for VAT in the EC country in question; and

(v) C has been designated in accordance with 22.27(*c*) above as the person liable for the VAT due on the supplies effected by A.

[*EC 6th Directive, Art 28c*(*E*)].

22.45 **Chargeable event and chargeability of VAT**

The chargeable event occurs when the intra-EC acquisition of goods is effected ie when the supply of similar goods is regarded as being effected within the territory of the country.

VAT becomes chargeable on intra-EC acquisitions of goods, and supplies of goods effected under the conditions in 22.40 above, on the 15th day of the month following that during which the chargeable event occurs or on the issue of the invoice (or document serving as an invoice) if earlier.

[*EC 6th Directive, Art 28d*].

22.46 **Taxable amount and rate applicable**

For intra-EC acquisitions of goods, the taxable amount must be established on the same basis as those used under 22.12 above to determine the taxable amount for supply of the same goods within the territory of the country. The rate of VAT is that in force when the VAT becomes chargeable on the supply of like goods within the territory of the country. [*EC 6th Directive, Art 28e*].

22.47 **Right of deduction**

The right to deduct input tax is extended to cover VAT due on intra-EC acquisitions under 22.34(*a*) above and goods or services used for the purposes of transactions which are exempt under 22.40 above.

To exercise the right to deduct VAT on intra-EC acquisitions, the taxable person must keep records of all the information needed for the amount of that VAT to be calculated and hold a proper invoice.

[*EC 6th Directive, Art 28f*].

22.48 **EIGHTH DIRECTIVE: REFUNDS OF VAT TO PERSONS ESTABLISHED IN OTHER EC COUNTRIES**

The *8th Directive* enables a taxable person to recover VAT suffered in another EC country provided he is not already registered in that country (in which case that country's domestic VAT legislation would apply).

Subject to the conditions below, an EC country must refund to 'a taxable person who is not established in that country' (but *is* established in another EC country) any VAT charged in respect of

- services or movable property supplied to him by other taxable persons within that EC country, or
- the importation of goods into that country

to the extent that such goods and services are used for the purposes of

(*a*) transactions relating to economic activities carried out in another country which would have been deductible if performed within that country;

(*b*) transactions related to imports and exports and the international goods traffic; and

(*c*) supplies of services where the VAT on the supply is accounted for solely by the person to whom they are supplied. (These may differ slightly between EC countries but broadly correspond to those listed in *VATA 1994, Sch 5* (see 64.27 SUPPLY).)

[*EC 8th Directive, Art 2*].

The effect of (*a*) above is that a taxable person who carries out taxable and exempt transactions in his own country (and so is partially exempt there) only has a right of partial refund under the *EC 8th Directive* in the other EC country. The refundable amount should be calculated, first, by determining which transactions gave rise to a right of deduction in the country of establishment and, second, by taking account solely of the transactions which would also have given rise to a right of deduction in the EC country of refund if they has been carried out there and of the expenses giving rise to a right to deduction in the later country (*Ministre du Budget and another v Société Monte Dei Paschi Di Siena, CJEC 2000, [2001] STC 1029 (TVC 21.345)*).

'*A taxable person who is not established in that country*' means a person carrying out an economic activity within *EC Sixth Directive, Art 4* who, during the period of the claim,

- has had neither the seat of his economic activity nor a fixed establishment from which business transactions are effected in that country;
- if no such seat or fixed establishment exists, has not had his domicile or normal place of residence in that country, and
- has supplied no goods or services deemed to have been supplied in that country except for *either* transport (and related) services carried out in connection with the international carriage of goods *or* services within (*c*) above.

[*EC 8th Directive, Art 1*].

To qualify for a refund, the taxable person must

- submit to the competent authority of the relevant country a prescribed application form *completed in block capitals in the language of that country* attaching originals of invoices or import documents (but see *Société Générale des Grandes Sources d'Eaux Minérales Françaises v Bundesamt für Finanzen, CJEC [1998] STC 981 (TVC 21.348)* where it was held that a country *could* accept duplicate or photocopied invoices where the originals had been lost through no fault of the taxpayer and there was no risk of a further application for a refund. Moreover, if that country accepted internal claims for input tax in similar circumstances, the principle of non-discrimination in the preamble to the *8th Directive* required it to extend the same possibility to persons established in other EC countries);
- produce a certificate of status (valid for one year) issued by the official authority of the country in which he is registered stating that he is a taxable person (see *Debouche v Inspecteur der Invoerrechten en Accijnzen, CJEC [1996] STC 1406 (TVC 21.347)*);
- give a written declaration that no goods or services have been supplied in the EC country (except as above); and
- undertake to repay any sum recovered in error.

[*EC 8th Directive, Arts 3, 4*].

VAT is not refundable if it would be disallowed for credit if incurred by a person registered in the EC country. Similarly, exempt supplies of goods are outside the provisions. However, the country must not impose any condition as to recoverability outside the *Directive's* provisions otherwise than to justify an application. [*EC 8th Directive, Arts 5, 6*].

Applications must relate to invoiced supplies or imports made during a period of not less than three months or not more than one calendar year. Applications may, however, relate to a period of less than three months where the period represents the remainder of a calendar year. An application may relate to invoices, etc not covered by previous applications although applicable to charges incurred during the calendar year in question, but applications must otherwise be submitted within six months of the end of the calendar year in which the VAT became chargeable. Provision is made for the exclusion of small claims, the prevention of invoices being used more than once and the return of documents to the claimant within one month. A decision whether or not to grant an application must be made by the relevant authority within six months of submission. Payment must be made within the same period either in the relevant country or in the country in which the applicant is registered, in which case any bank charges must be borne by the applicant. Refusal to grant an application must give grounds for the decision and appeals must be allowed to be made on the same basis as domestic cases. A competent authority is given powers to reclaim amounts paid under fraudulent applications for a period of two years from the date of the fraudulent application. [*EC 8th Directive, Art 7*].

See 21.32–21.56 and 21.57 EUROPEAN COMMUNITY: GENERAL for applications to other EC countries by UK taxable persons and applications to the UK by persons established in other EC countries respectively.

22.49 THIRTEENTH DIRECTIVE: REFUNDS OF VAT TO PERSONS ESTABLISHED OUTSIDE THE EC

The *13th Directive* requires each EC country to introduce a scheme to enable a taxable person established outside the EC to recover VAT suffered in that country provided he is not already registered there.

The taxable person must not make supplies of goods or services in the particular EC country other than

- supplies of transport (and related) services carried out in connection with the international carriage of goods; or
- services where the VAT on the supply is accounted for solely by the person to whom they are supplied.

Countries may make the refunds conditional upon the granting of comparable advantages regarding turnover tax by the territory where the taxable person is established. [*EC 13th Directive, Arts 1, 2*].

Administrative arrangements and conditions for submitting applications, time limits and periods covered, minimum amounts claimable and methods of repayment are left to the individual countries. Refunds cannot be granted on terms more favourable than those applied to EC taxable persons. Countries may provide for the exclusion of certain expenditure. [*EC 13th Directive, Arts 3, 4*].

See 48.5 OVERSEAS TRADERS below for the scheme introduced in the UK.

23 European Community: Single Market

Cross-references. See 2.19 ACCOUNTING PERIODS AND RETURNS for EC sales statements; 2.27 ACCOUNTING PERIODS AND RETURNS for Intrastat; 21.2 EUROPEAN COMMUNITY: GENERAL for the VAT territory of the EC; 40.5 INVOICES for particulars required on VAT invoices issued to persons in other EC countries; 56 RECORDS generally; 59.11 *et seq* REGISTRATION for the liability to register in the UK in respect of distance sales from another EC country; 59.18 *et seq* REGISTRATION for the liability to register in the UK in respect of acquisitions from other EC countries; 64.8 SUPPLY for the place of supply of goods; 68.26 and 68.28 TRANSPORT AND FREIGHT for special provisions applying to intra-EC freight transport and ancillary services; 69.11–69.14 VALUATION for the valuation rules applying to acquisitions from other EC countries; 70 WAREHOUSED GOODS AND FREE ZONES for movement of goods in warehouse and free zones to and from EC countries.

The contents of this chapter are as follows.

23.1 INTRODUCTION

With the completion of the Single Market on 1 January 1993, and the removal of fiscal frontier controls between EC countries, fundamental changes took place in the way VAT is charged and accounted for on goods moving within the EC. See 21.2 EUROPEAN COMMUNITY: GENERAL for a list of the territories which make up the VAT territories of the EC.

The concepts of 'imports' and 'exports' of goods now apply only to transactions with countries outside the EC. For intra-EC movements of goods, goods coming into the UK from other EC countries are referred to as 'acquisitions' and goods leaving the UK to go to other EC countries are referred to as 'despatches' or 'removals'.

The rules are complex and were only intended to be transitional until a definitive system for the taxation of trade between EC countries was introduced, based on the principle of taxing goods and services in the EC country of origin. However, there seems little possibility that such a system will be introduced in the near future.

De Voil Indirect Tax Service. See V1.210.

23.2 MOVEMENTS OF GOODS BETWEEN EC COUNTRIES: GENERAL PROVISIONS

Transfers of goods to be treated as supplies. Unless specifically overridden by other provisions, where goods forming part of the assets of a business are

- removed from any EC country, by or under the directions of the person carrying on the business, and
- so removed in the course or furtherance of the business for the purpose of being taken to another EC country

then whether or not the removal is, or is in connection with, a transaction for a consideration, there is a supply of goods by that person. [*VATA 1994, Sch 4 para 6*(*1*)]. Specifically excluded, from 1 January 2005, is the removal of gas through the natural gas distribution network or electricity. [*SI 2004/3150*]. The supply is treated as taking place in the EC country from which the goods are removed. [*VATA 1994, s 7*(*7*)].

There is no supply under the above provisions where

- the goods are removed from an EC country in the course of their removal from one part of that country to another part of the same country (eg goods removed from England to Northern Ireland via Ireland); or
- the goods have been removed from a place outside the EC for entry into the territory of the EC and are removed from an EC country before the time when any EC customs duty on their entry into the EC would be incurred. See 34.18 IMPORTS.

[*VATA 1994, Sch 4 para 6*(*2*)].

The effect of the above provisions is, in addition to normal commercial transactions, certain transfers by a business of its own goods to another EC country are also treated as supplies of goods (see 23.23–23.27 below).

Charging and accounting for VAT. Subject to special rules in the cases listed below

- *for transactions between VAT-registered traders*, the supplier in one EC country need not charge VAT on dispatch of goods to a customer in another EC country.

Any VAT due is payable on acquisition of the goods by the customer who must account for it on their normal VAT return at the rate in force in the country of destination of the goods; and

- *where the customer in another EC country is unregistered or a private individual*, VAT is normally charged and accounted for by the supplier in the EC country from which the goods are dispatched.

See 23.3 *et seq* below for acquisitions of goods in the UK from other EC countries and 23.11 *et seq* below for supplies from the UK to other EC countries.

Special rules apply to the following.

- Certain transfers of own goods between EC countries. See 23.23–23.27 below.
- The supply of goods to be installed or assembled at a customer's premises in another EC country. See 23.29 below.
- Distance sales (ie sales to non-taxable persons in another EC country where the supplier is responsible for delivery) above certain limits. See 23.10 below for distance selling to the UK and 23.18 for distance selling from the UK.
- Acquisitions by non-VAT-registered businesses and non-taxable organisations in excess of an annual threshold. See 59.18 REGISTRATION for the liability to register for VAT in the UK in respect of acquisitions where there is no liability to be registered in respect of UK supplies.
- The supply of goods subject to excise duty purchased by non-taxable persons. See 23.9 below for acquisitions in the UK and 23.17 below for supplies to other EC countries.
- New means of transport. See 23.31 *et seq* below.
- Supplies to diplomats, international organisations, NATO forces and other entitled persons and bodies in other EC countries which may in certain circumstances be relieved from VAT. See 23.21(1) below.

Returns. In addition to the appropriate entries on the VAT return, a business trading with other EC countries may also have to complete

- an EC sales list (a list of supplies made to VAT-registered traders in other EC countries, see 2.19–2.26 ACCOUNTING PERIODS AND RETURNS); and
- an Intrastat supplementary declaration (for use, together with VAT returns, in the compilation of statistics on the trade in goods between EC countries, see 2.27 ACCOUNTING PERIODS AND RETURNS).

(VAT Notice 725, paras 1.9, 1.10, 2.2, 2.3).

De Voil Indirect Tax Service. See V3.213.

23.3 ACQUISITIONS OF GOODS IN THE UK FROM OTHER EC COUNTRIES

It is not necessary to make an import declaration on an acquisition of goods from another EC country (with certain exceptions) or pay VAT at the frontier. Instead, where a business registered for VAT in the UK receives goods from another EC country supplied by a business registered for VAT in that country, it must account for VAT in the UK on the acquisition of the goods. [*VATA 1994, s 1(1)*]. The rate of VAT due is that applicable to the supply of identical goods in the UK. No VAT will therefore be due on the acquisition of goods which are currently zero-rated in the UK.

Any VAT due must be accounted for on the VAT return for the period in which the tax point occurs and, subject to the normal rules, the business may recover the VAT as input tax on the same VAT return.

(VAT Notice 725, paras 4.1, 4.2, 4.4).

These provisions are considered in more detail in 23.4 to 23.10 below.

De Voil Indirect Tax Service. See V3.361–V3.364; V3.389.

23.4 Meaning of 'acquisition of goods from another EC country'

An '*acquisition of goods from another EC country*' is any acquisition of goods under a transaction where both of the following conditions are satisfied.

(*a*) The transaction is, or is treated for the purposes of *VATA 1994* as, a supply of goods.

(*b*) The transaction involves the movement of goods from another EC country.

For these purposes, it is immaterial whether the removal of the goods is undertaken by or on behalf of the supplier, the customer or some other person.

Where the person with the property in the goods does not change in consequence of anything treated as a supply under *VATA 1994*, that supply is to be treated as a transaction under which there is an acquisition of goods by the person making it. The transfer of a business's own goods to another EC country therefore leads to an acquisition of goods by it in that country. See 23.23 below.

The Treasury may provide, by order, that, in relation to any type of transaction, the acquisition of goods under such a transaction is not to be treated as an acquisition of goods from another EC country. See, for example, 30.7 GOLD AND PRECIOUS METALS for gold supplied to a Central Bank by a supplier in another EC country and 61.7 SECOND-HAND GOODS for goods bought from a registered business in another EC country where VAT on the supply is accounted for in that EC country by reference to the profit margin.

[*VATA 1994, s 11*].

De Voil Indirect Tax Service. See V3.363.

23.5 Scope of VAT on acquisitions

Subject to *zero-rating* and *VAT relief* below, VAT is charged in the UK on any acquisition from another EC country where the following conditions are satisfied.

(*a*) The acquisition is a 'taxable acquisition' and takes place in the UK (see 23.6 below).

An acquisition from another EC country is a '*taxable acquisition*' if

- the goods are acquired by
  - (i) a person in the course or furtherance of a business carried on by him, or
  - (ii) by a body corporate, club, association, organisation or other unincorporated body in the course or furtherance of any activities carried on by it otherwise than by way of business, and

and the supplier is taxable in another EC country at the time of the relevant transaction and is acting in the course or furtherance of a business carried on by him, or

- the goods are a new means of transport (see 23.31 below)

and provided that in either case the acquisition is not an '*exempt acquisition*' ie an acquisition where the goods are acquired in pursuance of an exempt supply falling within *VATA 1994, Sch 9* (see 24 EXEMPT SUPPLIES).

(*b*) The acquisition is not in pursuance of a taxable supply in the UK (see, for example, 23.28 below for installed and assembled goods).

(*c*) Either

(i) the person making the acquisition is a '*taxable person*' ie a person who is, or is required to be, registered; or

(ii) the goods are subject to excise duty (see 23.9 below); or

(iii) the goods are a new means of transport (see 23.31 below).

[*VATA 1994, ss 10, 31*(*1*)].

See 59.18 REGISTRATION for the requirement to register by persons within (*a*)(ii) above who make acquisitions above an annual threshold and who would not otherwise be liable for registration in respect of supplies made.

Liability for VAT. The VAT on any acquisition is a liability of the person who acquires the goods and, subject to provisions about accounting and payment, becomes due at the time of acquisition (see 23.7 below). [*VATA 1994, s 1*(*3*)].

Zero-rating. Where the goods acquired fall within *VATA 1994, Sch 8*, no VAT is chargeable on their acquisition, except as otherwise provided in that *Schedule*. [*VATA 1994, s 30*(*3*)].

VAT relief. Certain goods imported into the UK from outside the EC are subject to relief from import VAT under *SI 1984/746*. With effect from 15 August 2002, these goods are also subject to relief when coming into the UK from other EC countries

- if supplied by a taxable person in another EC country to a taxable person in the UK; or
- where there is a deemed supply on the transfer of a taxable person's own goods from another EC country to the UK (see 23.23 below).

See 34.15(1)–(12) IMPORTS for details of the qualifying goods.

[*VATA 1994, s 36A; FA 2002, s 25; SI 2002/1935*].

De Voil Indirect Tax Service. See V3.366–371.

23.6 Place of acquisition

VAT on an acquisition is due in the country where the acquisition is deemed to take place. Subject to below, the following provisions apply for determining whether goods acquired from another EC country are acquired in the UK.

(*a*) Goods are treated as acquired in the UK if the transaction involves their removal to the UK and does not involve their removal from the UK (ic the transport of the goods ends in the UK). The goods are otherwise, subject to the following provisions, to be treated as acquired outside the UK.

(*b*) Goods are treated as acquired in the UK where a business uses a UK VAT registration number in order to acquire the goods (whether or not the goods are to be transported to the UK) unless it can establish to HMRC that VAT fell to be paid, and has been paid, in another EC country on the acquisition of those goods there under provisions corresponding to the UK provisions in (*a*) above.

The above is subject to the special provisions applying to warehoused goods (see 70.6 WAREHOUSED GOODS AND FREE ZONES). See also 23.22 below for modification of the rules where there are three parties involved in the transaction (triangulation) and 23.28 below for special treatment for installed or assembled goods.

[*VATA 1994, s 13; FA 1996, Sch 3 para 4*].

Under the above rules, VAT on an acquisition will, in most cases, be due only in the country where the goods are received.

Example

A UK business acquires goods from a supplier in Germany for delivery to the UK and quotes its VAT registration number.

The place of supply is the UK under both (*a*) and (*b*) above.

If, however, a UK business quotes its UK VAT registration number to a supplier in Germany but the goods are delivered to France, there is an acquisition in France (under French rules similar to (*a*) above) and an acquisition in the UK under (*b*) above. In such circumstances

- the business will be liable to account for acquisition VAT in the UK unless it can demonstrate that VAT has already been paid in the EC country to which the goods were sent (France); and
- if it has accounted for acquisition VAT in the UK and is later required to pay VAT on the acquisition in France, it can obtain a refund of the VAT paid in the UK but only where it has not claimed, or not been able to claim, full input tax credit in respect of the acquisition (see 23.8 below).

(VAT Notice 725, paras 4.8–4.10).

De Voil Indirect Tax Service. See V3.376; V3.377.

23.7 **Time of acquisition**

Any VAT on an acquisition becomes due in the VAT period when the tax point (time of acquisition) occurs. Subject to below, the time of acquisition of goods from another EC country (which is the same time as the corresponding supply of goods in the EC country of dispatch, see 23.16 below) is the earlier of

(*a*) the 15th day of the month following that in which the *first* removal of the goods involved in the transaction forming the basis of the acquisition occurred; and

(*b*) the date of issue of an invoice in respect of the transaction containing such details as HMRC require. For this purpose, the invoice is one which is issued by the supplier or, with effect from 1 January 2004, the customer under the provisions of the law of the EC country from where the goods were despatched corresponding to the provisions in *SI 1995/2518, Regs 13, 13A, 14* relating to invoices for supplies in the UK. See 40 INVOICES.

Note that, unlike the rules for supplies in the UK, part or full payment for the goods does not create a tax point for acquisitions. However, the receipt of a payment on account does make the supplier liable to raise an invoice which will in turn trigger a tax point under (*b*) above.

HMRC may, by regulations, make provisions in specific cases in relation to the time at which an acquisition is treated as taking place where the whole or part of any consideration is determined or payable periodically, or from time to time, or at the end of a period. Under these powers, where any water, gas or any form of power, heat, refrigeration or ventilation within 64.46 SUPPLY is acquired from another EC country on such terms, the goods are treated as separately and successively acquired on each occasion that an invoice within (*b*) above is issued.

See also 70.6 WAREHOUSED GOODS AND FREE ZONES for special rules for warehoused goods.

[*VATA 1994, s 12; FA 1996, Sch 3 para 3; SI 1995/2518, Regs 83, 87; SI 2003/3220, Regs 12, 14*]. (VAT Notice 725, paras 4.3, 4.5, 4.6).

De Voil Indirect Tax Service. See V3.388.

23.8 **Recording and accounting for VAT due on acquisitions**

In addition to the normal VAT records, a UK-registered business which acquires goods from businesses registered for VAT in other EC countries must

(*a*) keep VAT invoices issued to it and any other documents relating to the goods it acquires from other EC countries;

(*b*) calculate the VAT due on the acquisition of these goods and enter it on the 'VAT payable' side of its VAT account; and

(*c*) subject to the normal rules for allowable input tax, deduct the VAT due on the acquisition as input tax on the 'VAT allowable' side of the VAT account.

Where the time of acquisition of any goods from another EC country is determined under 23.7(*b*) above by reference to the issue of an invoice, VAT must be accounted for and paid in respect of the acquisition only on so much of its value as is shown on the invoice. [*SI 1995/2518, Reg 26*].

The amount of VAT due on an acquisition is the tax value multiplied by the VAT rate. See 69.11–69.14 VALUATION for the valuation rules applying to acquisitions from other EC countries.

VAT return. VAT due under (*b*) above should be entered in Box 2 of the VAT return for the VAT period in which the time of acquisition occurs (see 23.7 above) and the input tax under (*c*) above in Box 4 on the same return. The invoice or contract value must be included in Boxes 7 and 9.

Supplementary declarations. Details of an acquisition may have to be disclosed on a supplementary declaration as an arrival. See 2.27 ACCOUNTING PERIODS AND RETURNS.

(VAT Notice 725, paras 4.11, 12.4, 12.7).

23.9 **Acquisition of goods subject to excise duty**

All taxable acquisitions (ie acquisitions for business purposes and acquisitions for non-business purposes by clubs, associations, etc from registered businesses in other EC countries, see 23.5 above) of exciseable goods are taxed in the EC country of destination.

Acquisitions by VAT-registered businesses. Where the business that acquires the exciseable goods from a supplier in another EC country is UK VAT-registered, it must account for VAT in the same way as for any other acquisition.

Acquisitions by non-registered persons. Where the person making the taxable acquisition is not registered for UK VAT (because turnover is under the registration limit or because activities are not business activities), VAT cannot be accounted for by means of a VAT return. In order to avoid the need to register all persons making such acquisitions, HMRC are empowered to introduce a special mechanism to collect the VAT due.

Under these provisions, where

(*a*) a taxable acquisition of goods subject to excise duty takes place in the UK,

(*b*) the acquisition is not in pursuance of a taxable supply, and

(*c*) the person acquiring the goods is not a taxable person at the time of the acquisition,

the person acquiring such goods must notify HMRC of the acquisition at the time of the acquisition or the arrival of the goods in the UK, whichever is the later. The notification must be in writing in English and contain the following particulars.

- The name and current address of the person acquiring the goods.
- The time of acquisition.
- The date when the goods arrived in the UK.
- The value of the goods including any excise duty payable.
- The VAT due on the acquisition.

The notification must include a signed declaration that all the information given is true and complete.

The VAT due is payable at the time of notification and, in any event, not later than the last date on which the person is required to make such notification as above. Where the person required to make the notification dies or becomes incapacitated, the liability to notify passes to the personal representative, trustee in bankruptcy, liquidator, etc, as does the liability to pay the VAT (although only to the extent of assets passing to that person).

Note. The effect of (*b*) above is that the provisions are only necessary where the person acquiring the goods arranges for their delivery. If the supplier arranges delivery, the distance selling provisions in 23.10 below apply and the supplier must register for VAT in the UK, whatever his level of sales in this country.

[*VATA 1994, Sch 11 para 2*(*4*)(*5*); *SI 1995/2518, Regs 31*(*3*), *36*].

De Voil Indirect Tax Service. See V5.126.

23.10 Distance selling to the UK from other EC countries

Distance selling occurs when a taxable supplier in one EC country supplies goods, and is responsible for their delivery, to a customer in another EC country who is not registered for VAT. This may include not only private individuals but public bodies, charities and businesses too small to register or with activities that are entirely exempt. The most common examples of distance sales are mail order and goods ordered over the internet.

Such distance sales to non VAT-registered customers in the UK from another EC country are normally subject to VAT in that other country. However, once the value of such distance sales to the UK exceeds an annual threshold

- the supplier is automatically liable to register for VAT in the UK (see 59.11 REGISTRATION);
- the UK becomes the place of supply (see 64.11 SUPPLY); and
- VAT on any further sales is taxed in the UK.

Each EC country has the option of applying a distance selling threshold of €35,000 or €100,000 per calendar year (or its own currency equivalent). The UK has adopted a threshold of €100,000 euro, set at £70,000.

The supplier may, if he wishes, opt to make the UK the place of supply before reaching the annual threshold. See 59.14 REGISTRATION.

Goods subject to excise duty. Distance sales of such goods to non VAT-registered customers in the UK are always taxed (for excise duty and VAT purposes) in the UK whatever the level of sales and the EC supplier is required to register in the UK.

VAT returns. For distance sales to the UK over the distance selling threshold (or where the seller has voluntarily registered in the UK), output tax must be included in Box 1 and the invoice or contract value in Box 6.

Supplementary declarations. Details may have to be disclosed on a supplementary declaration as an arrival. See 2.27 ACCOUNTING PERIODS AND RETURNS.

(VAT Notice 725, paras 15.1, 15.12, 15.13).

23.11 SUPPLIES OF GOODS FROM THE UK TO OTHER EC COUNTRIES

Supplies of goods to other EC countries can be zero-rated provided the following conditions are satisfied.

(*a*) The supply involves the removal of the goods from the UK to another EC country.

(*b*) The goods are acquired by a customer who is registered for VAT in another EC country.

(*c*) The supplier obtains his customer's VAT registration number and shows this (including the 2-letter country code prefix) on his VAT invoice. See 23.12 below for checking a customer's VAT registration number and 40.1 and 40.5 INVOICES for the obligation to provide a VAT invoice and the particulars to be included thereon.

(*d*) The supplier obtains and keeps valid commercial documentary evidence that the goods have been removed from the UK

- within three months of the time of supply (see 23.16 below) for direct and indirect removals and goods involved in groupage or consolidation prior to removal; and
- within six months of the time of supply for goods involved in processing or incorporation prior to removal.

See 23.13–23.15 below for evidence of removal.

(*e*) The goods must not be second-hand goods or works of art, etc which the supplier has opted to tax on the profit margin. See 61.12 SECOND-HAND GOODS.

[*VATA 1994, s 30(8); SI 1995/2518, Reg 134*]. (VAT Notice 703, para 8.4 and VAT Notice 725, para 3.1 which have the force of law; VAT Information Sheet 2/00).

If all of the above conditions cannot be met, the UK supplier must charge VAT at the same rate applicable to a supply of the goods in the UK. The standard UK time of supply rules will then apply (see 64.39 SUPPLY). A supply from the UK to a customer in another EC country cannot be zero-rated under the above provisions where

- the supply is to a non-registered customer in another EC country (in which case, if the supplier is responsible for delivery of the goods, the distance selling provisions apply, see 23.18 below);
- the supply is to a UK VAT-registered business;
- the supplier delivers to, or allow the goods to be collected by, a UK customer at a UK address; or
- the supplier allows the goods to be used in the UK in the period between supply and removal (except where specifically authorised elsewhere).

(VAT Notice 725, paras, 18.5, 18.7).

Supplies of goods. See 64.3 SUPPLY for a general consideration of what is a supply of goods (as opposed to a supply of services).

Reporting requirements. The following table summarises the reporting requirements for supplies of goods to customers in other EC countries.

Type of supply	*VAT return*	*EC sales list*
Supplies of goods to VAT-registered customers in other EC countries where the conditions above are satisfied	Enter the value in Boxes 6 and 8	Yes
Supplies of goods to customers in other EC countries where the conditions above are not satisfied	Enter the VAT due in Box 1 and the value in Box 6	No

(VAT Notice 725, para 3.15).

Invoicing requirements. See 40.5 INVOICES.

Failure to receive evidence of removal. Where a supply is initially zero-rated on the assumption that the necessary evidence of removal will be received within the time limit but this is not the case, the supplier must account for VAT on the supply at the standard rate (unless the goods are zero-rated in their own right). VAT records must be amended and VAT accounted for on the taxable proportion of the invoiced amount or consideration received, ie 7/47ths of the total for a VAT rate of 17.5%. This amount must be entered on the VAT payable side of the VAT account and included in Box 1 of the VAT return for the period in which the time limit expires. If the supplier subsequently receives the evidence of removal of the goods, he can then zero-rate the supply and adjust the VAT account for the period in which the conditions were met.

(VAT Notice 725, para 18.18).

Effect of failure to comply with conditions. Where the supply of any goods has been zero-rated under the above provisions and either any of the above conditions is not complied with or the goods are found in the UK after the date of alleged removal, the goods are liable to *forfeiture*. Any VAT which would have been due but for zero-rating is payable forthwith by the person to whom the goods were supplied or by any other person in whose possession the goods are found in the UK. HMRC may waive payment of the VAT in whole or in part. [*VATA 1994, s 30*(*10*)].

De Voil Indirect Tax Service. See V4.341–366.

23.12 Checking VAT registration numbers

HMRC recommend that UK businesses

- write to customers in other EC countries asking for VAT registration numbers which have been allocated for intra-EC trade (to ensure that they do not provide an internal tax or fiscal number used only in their own country); and
- keep a record of these VAT registration numbers and retain the accompanying letters or advices.

Where a business has a doubt as to whether a particular registration number is valid, it should check that it follows the format for the appropriate country (see 21.7–21.30 EUROPEAN COMMUNITY: GENERAL) and contact the National Advice Service who can normally check and confirm whether this is the case and whether the number is correctly associated with a specific name or address.

A business will not be liable to account for VAT where a registration number, obtained from a customer and quoted on an invoice, subsequently turns out to be false provided all reasonable steps have been taken to ensure that the customer is registered for VAT in the EC country of acquisition and all other conditions for zero-rating have been complied with. HMRC do not regard reasonable steps as having been taken if a VAT number is used

- which does not conform to the published format for the customer's country (see 21.7–21.30 EUROPEAN COMMUNITY: GENERAL);
- after HMRC advise that it is invalid; or
- which is known not to belong to the customer.

(VAT Notice 725, paras 3.3–3.8).

23.13 Evidence of removal of goods

A combination of the documents shown below must be used to provide clear evidence that a sale has taken place and that the goods have been removed from the UK.

- Customer's order (including customer's name, VAT number and delivery address for the goods).

- Inter-company correspondence.
- Copy sales invoice (including a description of the goods, an invoice number and customer's EC VAT number etc).
- Advice note.
- Packing list.
- Commercial transport document(s) from the carrier responsible for removing the goods from the UK.
- Details of insurance or freight charges.
- Bank statements as evidence of payment.
- Receipted copy of the consignment note as evidence of receipt of goods abroad.
- Any other documents relevant to the removal of the goods in question which would normally be obtained in the course of intra-EC business.

Documents used as proof of removal must clearly identify the following. (These requirements have the force of law.)

- The supplier.
- The consignor (where different from the supplier).
- The customer.
- The goods.
- An accurate value.
- The mode of transport and route of movement of the goods.
- The EC destination.

Vague descriptions of goods, quantities or values are not acceptable (eg 'various electrical goods' must not be used when the correct description is '2000 mobile phones Make ABC and Model Number XYZ2000').

Goods delivered personally by the supplier. In addition to the examples of acceptable documentary evidence listed above, travel tickets can also be used to demonstrate that an intra-EC journey took place for the purpose of removing the goods from the UK.

(VAT Notice 725, paras 18.8–18.10).

23.14 *Goods collected in the UK by the customer*

If the EC customer collects or arranges the collection of the goods and their removal from the UK, it can be difficult for the supplier to obtain adequate proof of removal as the carrier is contracted to the customer. As a result, for this type of transaction the standard of evidence required to substantiate VAT zero-rating is high. The supplier should seek confirmation of how the goods are to be removed from the UK and what proof of removal will be sent. He should also consider taking a deposit from the customer equal to the amount of VAT, in case satisfactory evidence of removal is not received.

Evidence must show that the goods supplied have left the UK. Copies of transport documents alone are not sufficient and information held must identify the date and route of the movement of goods and the method of transport involved. It should include the following.

- A written order from the customer which shows their name, address and EC VAT number, and the address where the goods are to be delivered.
- Copy sales invoice showing customer's name, EC VAT number, a description of the goods and an invoice number.
- Delivery address for the goods.
- Date of departure of goods from the supplier's premises and from the UK.
- Name and address of the haulier collecting the goods.
- Registration number of the vehicle collecting the goods and the name and signature of the driver.
- Name and address of the haulier, signature for the goods and registration number of the vehicle where the goods are to be taken out of the UK by an alternative haulier or vehicle.
- Route (eg Channel Tunnel, port of exit).
- Copy of travel tickets.
- Name of ferry or shipping company and date of sailing or airway number and airport.

The information held should also include (where applicable):

- Trailer number.
- Full container number.
- Name and address for consolidation, groupage, or processing.

(VAT Notice 725, paras 3.10, 18.11).

23.15 *Postal services and couriers, etc*

See VAT Notice 725, paras 18.14, 18.15 for details of acceptable evidence for goods sent by Parcel Force or courier and fast parcel operators, including details of what action is required by the supplier in each case.

23.16 Time of supply

Zero-rated supplies to taxable persons in another EC country. Where any supply of goods involves both

- the removal of the goods from the UK, and
- their acquisition in another EC country by a person who is liable for VAT on the acquisition under the provisions of that country corresponding to those in 23.3 above,

the time of supply (tax point) is the earlier of

- the 15th day of the month following that in which the goods are removed (ie sent to the customer or, as the case may be, taken away by the customer); and

- the day of the issue of a VAT invoice or other prescribed invoice in respect of the supply.

Unlike a UK domestic supply, the receipt of payment before the issue of an invoice does not create a tax point. However, it does make the supplier liable to issue an invoice for the amount paid (see 40.1 INVOICES) which in turn will create a tax point in respect of the amount invoiced.

Where a series of invoices are issued relating to the same supply of goods, the three-month time limit for obtaining valid evidence of removal (see 23.11(*d*) above) begins from the date of the final invoice.

The tax point should be used as the reference date for including these supplies on the VAT return and EC sales list.

Supplies to non-taxable persons in another EC country. These are taxable in the UK and the tax point is determined under the normal rules. See 64.32 *et seq* SUPPLY.

[*VATA 1994, s 6(7)(8)*]. (VAT Notice 725, paras 3.11–3.14).

23.17 **Supplies of exciseable goods to other EC countries**

VAT-registered customers. Supplies of exciseable goods to a VAT-registered customer in another EC country where the supplies are used for business purposes are taxable on the customer in that country. The customer will account for the VAT on his tax return as an acquisition.

Non-registered persons for non-private purposes. There are special arrangements for supplies of exciseable goods to non-registered persons in other EC countries when the purchases are made for *non-private* purposes. This applies to purchases by businesses which are below the registration threshold in their country or by non-registered legal persons (associations and unincorporated bodies, etc) whose activities are not business activities for VAT purposes. Such supplies can be zero-rated provided the following conditions are met.

(*a*) The goods must be removed from the UK to a destination in another EC country and the place of supply must not, by virtue of the place of supply rules in 64.12 SUPPLY, be treated as outside the UK. This effectively means that the goods must be removed by or on behalf of the customer as if the supplier arranges for the delivery of excise goods to a non VAT-registered person in another EC country, he is liable to register in that country under the distance selling arrangements (see 23.18 below).

(*b*) All goods must travel with an accompanying document.

- If the goods are moving under authorised duty suspension arrangements (eg from an excise warehouse), the consignor must complete an Administrative Accompanying Document (AAD). In these cases there must be a financial guarantee to cover all excise duty liabilities during the movement.
- If UK excise duty has already been paid on the goods, they should travel with a Simplified Administrative Accompanying Document (SAAD). The customer must also provide evidence that the excise duty in the EC country of destination has been paid or secured to the satisfaction of the fiscal authorities there, *before* the supplier despatches the goods.

(*c*) Within 15 days of the end of the month in which the goods are removed, the supplier must obtain and keep a receipted copy 3 of the accompanying document certified by the consignee or fiscal authority of the EC country of destination.

(*d*) The movement of the goods must be completed as soon as possible and the certificate of receipt for the goods must be issued within four months of the date of despatch.

(*e*) The goods must not be second-hand goods or works of art, etc which the supplier has opted to tax on the profit margin. See 61.12 SECOND-HAND GOODS.

If the above conditions are met, the customer then pays the VAT (and excise duty) in the EC country of destination.

[*SI 1995/2518, Reg 135*]. (VAT Notice 725, paras 10.9–10.11).

De Voil Indirect Tax Service. See V4.352.

23.18 DISTANCE SELLING FROM THE UK TO OTHER EC COUNTRIES

Distance selling occurs when a VAT-registered business in one EC country supplies goods, and is responsible for their delivery, to a customer in another EC country who is not registered or liable to be registered for VAT. Such customers are known as non-taxable persons and may include not only private individuals but public bodies, charities and businesses too small to register or with activities that are entirely exempt. The most common examples of distance sales are mail order or goods ordered over the internet.

VAT on such distance sales by a UK business to customers in another EC country are subject to UK VAT until the value of supplies to any particular EC country exceeds an annual threshold set by that country for distance selling. Then

- the supplier is automatically liable to register for VAT in that country;
- that country becomes the place of supply (see 64.12 SUPPLY); and
- VAT on any further sales is taxed in the EC country of destination of the goods.

Each EC country has the option of applying a distance selling threshold of €35,000 or €100,000 per calendar year (or its own currency equivalent). The latest available thresholds are as follows.

Country	*Euro*	*National currency*
Austria	€100,000	
Belgium	€35,000	
Cyprus	€34,220	CYP 20,000
Czech Republic	€35,000	CZK 1,131,200
Denmark	€37,528	Dkr 280,000
Estonia	€35,151	EEK 550,000
Finland	€35,000	
France	€100,000	

Country	*Euro*	*National currency*
Germany	€100,000	
Greece	€35,000	
Hungary	€35,000	HUF 9,144,100
Ireland	€35,000	
Italy	€27,889*	
Latvia	€36,952	LVL 24,000
Lithuania	€36,207	LTL 125,000
Luxembourg	€100,000	
Malta	€35,000	MTL 14,900
Netherlands	€100,000	
Poland	€35,000	
Portugal	€31,424*	
Slovakia	€35,000	SKK 248,450
Slovenia	€35,000	SIT 248,450
Spain	€35,000	
Sweden	€35,809	Skr 320,000
UK	€109,598	£70,000

* Euro equivalent of the national currency limits set before the introduction of the euro.

Goods subject to excise duty. Distance sales of such goods to non-VAT-registered customers in another EC country are always taxed (for excise duty and VAT purposes) in the country of destination whatever the level of sales and a UK supplier is required to register in that country.

Records. A UK business must keep a separate record of its distance sales to each EC country to allow it to determine whether a liability to register for VAT in that country arises.

Compulsory registration. UK businesses that are required to register for VAT in another EC country must notify the tax authority in that country, allowing sufficient time to become registered by the appropriate date in accordance with the rules of that country.

Tax representatives. It may be possible for a UK business to appoint a tax representative to act on its behalf in the other EC country. This is a matter for the fiscal authority in the appropriate country.

Voluntary registration. A UK business may, if it wishes, opt to make the EC country of destination the place of supply of goods *before* reaching the distance selling threshold as above. If it does so, it must

- notify its local VAT Business Advice Centre in writing of the exercise of the option, not less than 30 days before the date of the first supply to which the option relates, informing HMRC of the name of the country/countries involved;

- notify the EC country/countries involved, at least 30 days before making the first supply, of its exercise of the option, providing written evidence that it has informed the UK authorities;
- register for VAT in country/countries concerned from the date of the first supply and comply with the VAT rules there; and
- within 30 days of the first supply after the option, provide HMRC with documentary evidence that it has notified the tax authority in the other EC country/countries.

Where a business has exercised such an option, it can be withdrawn (and the place of supply moved back to the UK) by further written notice to HMRC but not earlier than

- 1 January which is, or next follows, the second anniversary of the date of the first supply following the option (ie until at least two full *calendar* years have elapsed); and
- 30 days after the receipt by HMRC of notification of withdrawal;

and not later than 30 days before the date of the first supply the business intends to make after the withdrawal.

[*SI 1995/2518, Reg 98*].

VAT groups. UK VAT groups are not recognised outside the UK and each individual group member must monitor the value of its own distance sales to each EC country to determine whether it is liable to register for VAT in that country in its own right. A group member can exercise the option to account for VAT on its distance sales before it reaches an EC country's threshold.

Reporting requirements. The following table summarises the reporting requirements for supplies of goods to customers in other EC countries.

Type of supply	*VAT return*	*EC sales list*
Distance sales from the UK below the distance selling threshold to another EC country	Enter the VAT due in Box 1 and the value in Box 6	No
Distance sales from the UK on or over the distance selling threshold to another EC country (or where the business has voluntarily registered there)	Enter the value in Boxes 6 and 8	No

(VAT Notice 725, paras 15.1–15.11, 15.13).

23.19 Goods lost, destroyed or stolen in transit

VAT must be accounted for on goods sent to other EC countries which have been accidentally lost, destroyed or stolen *en route* as follows.

- **If lost, etc before supplied,** no VAT is due.
- **If lost, etc in transit and the supplier is responsible for transport,**
  - (i) if the supplier has valid proof of removal from the UK *and* the VAT registration number of the customer, zero-rating may stand; and

(ii) where (i) does not apply, VAT is due in the UK unless the supplier holds evidence of loss, etc (eg an insurance claim, police investigation, etc).

- **If lost, etc in transit and the customer is responsible for transport,**

  (i) if the supplier has valid proof of removal from the UK *and* the VAT registration number of the customer, zero-rating may stand but as an acquisition has taken place in the EC country where the goods have disappeared, the customer may be liable to account for VAT in that country; and

  (ii) if the goods are lost, etc in the UK, VAT is due in the UK (because the goods have been delivered in, but not removed from, the UK) unless the customer has provided evidence of loss, etc (eg an insurance claim, police investigation, etc).

It should also be noted that if any goods are lost, etc *en route* to the customer, but in an EC country other than that of destination, there may be a VAT liability both in the country where the loss, etc takes place and as an acquisition in the country of destination.

(VAT Notice 725, para 10.13).

23.20 **Tax-free shops**

With effect from 1 July 1999, VAT and duty-free sales to travellers on 'intra-EC journeys' have been abolished. '*Intra-EC journeys*' are those commencing in one EC country and ending in another EC country without calling at any country or territory outside the EC. It is irrelevant whether or not the journey passes through international seas or airspace. See, however, 34.17 IMPORTS for transitional provisions for certain countries joining the EC from 1 May 2004.

As a result, subject to those transitional arrangements

(*a*) *sales from a shop at a port or airport situated in the UK* to persons travelling on intra-EC journeys are subject to UK VAT (and duties) at rates applicable to other retail sales in the UK; and

(*b*) *sales on board a ship or aircraft on an intra-EC journey* are subject to VAT at the rate applicable in the EC country of departure (ie the first passenger point of embarkation in the EC) provided

- the goods are to be taken away at the end of the journey (see below for onboard consumption); and
- the sales take place either on a wholly intra-EC journey or a leg of a journey from the first point of passenger embarkation of the ship or aircraft in the EC until the final point of passenger disembarkation in the EC.

Examples

1. Goods sold on a Dover to Calais ferry are subject to UK VAT. On the return Calais-Dover leg they are subject to French VAT.

2. Goods sold on an aircraft flying from London to Paris and then on to Rome are subject to UK VAT throughout the journey.

3. Goods sold on a flight from London to New York are outside the scope of UK/EC VAT.

4. A flight from London to New York makes a stop-over in Paris. If passengers disembark at Paris, the London to Paris leg is an intra-EC journey and UK VAT is due on goods sold during the leg; the Paris to New York leg is an international journey and sales of goods are outside the scope of UK/EC VAT. If passengers do not disembark at Paris, the whole flight is an international journey and sales of goods on board are outside the scope of UK/EC VAT.

5. A flight from New York to Frankfurt makes a stop-over at London. If passengers embark at London, the London to Frankfurt leg is an intra-EC journey and any goods sold are subject to UK VAT. If there is no passenger embarkation in London, the sale of goods throughout the journey is outside the scope of UK/EC VAT.

6. A flight from New York to Vienna makes stop-overs at London and Frankfurt with passengers embarking in London. The New York to London leg is an international journey outside the scope of UK/EC VAT. The first place of passenger embarkation in the EC is at London and therefore UK VAT is due on goods sold on board during the entire journey from London to Frankfurt to Vienna. The Frankfurt to Vienna journey is not a separate leg for VAT purposes.

As VAT is due in the EC country of departure, airline and ferry operators may be liable to register for VAT in more than one EC country.

'*On board consumption*'. Goods (eg foods, drink and tobacco) sold for consumption

- on board ships and aircraft are free of VAT and excise duty; and
- on trains are free of VAT (but not excise duty).

All sales of these commodities from an on-board bar or restaurant are treated as being for immediate consumption although sales of alcohol and tobacco are subject to certain conditions and restrictions. For example, alcohol must be sold by the glass or, in the case of wine, from opened bottles and there are set maximum quantities for tobacco products on ferries. (As smoking is not permitted in aircraft, no sales of tobacco qualify for consumption on board.)

For VAT purposes, food, confectionery and soft drinks sold anywhere on board a ship or aircraft are treated as goods consumed on board and relieved of VAT, provided it is self-evident that these products are of a type that are more suitable for on-board consumption than gift purchase or home use. Products that, by virtue of their packaging, are clearly not suitable to be treated as consumed on board (eg boxes of chocolates or tins of biscuits) are subject to VAT in the normal way, even if actually consumed on board the ship or the aircraft.

Cruises. HMRC accept that food, drink, tobacco and most toiletries sold on an intra-EC cruise ship are normally consumed on board. Sales of these goods continue to be relieved from VAT provided the quantities sold indicate that the passengers are unlikely to take them away at the end of the cruise. Such goods bought with the intention of taking them away at the final port of disembarkation are subject to VAT at the rate applicable in the country of departure (see (*b*) above). Where a cruise which starts and ends in the UK calls at a non-EC country (eg Malta) or a place outside the EC fiscal territory (eg the Channel Islands) VAT-free sales to passengers for take-away are allowed provided the passengers have the opportunity to disembark and make purchases in that country or territory.

(VAT Information Sheet: Excise duty and VAT arrangements following the withdrawal of duty free sales of goods to intra-Community travellers; Business Brief 17/04).

De Voil Indirect Tax Service. See V4.285.

23.21 **Miscellaneous**

(1) **Embassies, Consulates, international organisations, NATO forces, etc in other EC countries**

Supplies to diplomatic missions, 'international organisations', visiting NATO forces and their personnel based in other EC countries may be zero-rated under special provisions provided all the following conditions are met. The scope of the relief, and the restrictions and any conditions attached, are determined by the host authority for the entitled person or body. If the customer has any doubts regarding these arrangements, it should contact its host taxation authorities.

- The goods (or services) must be for either the personal use of entitled persons or the official use of entitled bodies.
- The goods are not new means of transport (which may be zero-rated but under the different rules in 23.32 below).
- The supplier must obtain documentation from the customer, as laid down by the host authority, for claiming exemption under *EC Sixth Directive, Art 15(10)*. If the supplier has any doubts about the documentation received, he should contact the National Advice Service.
- Any goods supplied must be removed from the UK.
- The supplier must obtain and keep proof of the removal of the goods within three months of the supply.

For these purposes, an 'international organisation' means an organisation established by a treaty between sovereign states or governments. A body formed by agreement between non-governmental bodies (eg bodies representing a trade, limited companies, or charities) is not an 'international organisation' in this sense. Nor is a body set up by a single state or government (eg a government department). Well-known international organisations include the institutions of the European Union, the United Nations and its various subsidiary organisations, and the North Atlantic Treaty Organisation (NATO).

Distance sales. In general, transactions zero-rated under these provisions are not regarded as distance sales and do not count towards the distance selling threshold. However, in the case of supplies to customers based in Germany, the supplier should check with the German authorities whether registration in Germany is required.

EC sales lists. Entries on EC sales lists are not required for these supplies.

(VAT Notice 725, paras 10.16–10.21; VAT Notice 48, ESC 8.2).

(2) **Freight containers**

The removal of a container to another EC country can be zero-rated provided

(i) the supplier obtains the customer's VAT registration number (with a two digit country code prefix) and shows this on the VAT invoice;

(ii) the container is sent from the UK to a destination in another EC country; and

(iii) within three months of the date of supply, the supplier obtains and keeps valid commercial evidence that the container has been removed from the UK.

See 25.7 EXPORTS for the definition of a 'container'.

Where the customer collects or arranges collection of the container and its removal from the UK, the supplier should confirm with the customer how the container is to be removed and what evidence of this will be available.

If the customer is not registered for VAT in another EC country, or all the above conditions are not met, the supply is standard-rated.

(VAT Notice 703/1/04, para 2.3 which has the force of law).

Leasing or hiring of containers. Where a container is leased/hired to a customer in business in another EC country, the supply is treated as made in that other country. No UK VAT is due and the customer will normally have to account for VAT there under the reverse charge procedure.

Incidental charges which under the terms of the lease agreement are charged to the lessee are regarded as part of the consideration for the leasing of the container and have the same VAT liability. Included are repair, delivery, regulator and handling charges, extra rental and any charge for the option to terminate the lease at an earlier date.

(VAT Notice 703/1/04, paras 2.7, 2.10).

Temporary movements of containers. The temporary movement of a container from the UK to another EC country (whether involved in transporting goods or where the container is on lease/hire) is not treated as a removal from the UK with acquisition in the destination country. See 23.24 below. Details of the movement must be entered in a register of temporary movements. See 23.28 below. (VAT Notice 703/1/04, para 2.9).

(3) **Samples**

Industrial and commercial samples

- sent to an actual or potential customer in another EC country;
- for which no charge is made; and
- which are in a form not normally available to the public

are disregarded for intra-EC supply and acquisition purposes.

No entries are required on the VAT return, EC sales list or supplementary declaration.

(VAT Notice 725, para 13.3).

(4) **Ships and aircraft stores**

The arrangements under 25.3 EXPORTS continue to apply to all ships, etc leaving the UK. There is no need to obtain the VAT registration number of the customer if goods are supplied as stores at UK airports and ports. The goods do not have to be entered on the EC sales lists.

Additionally, UK suppliers can zero-rate the supply of spares and provisions to other EC countries for loading on a ship or aircraft there on a non-private journey to *any* destination (inside or outside the EC) provided the supplier

(i) receives a written statement from the agent or master of the vessel placing the order that the supply is exempt under *EC 6th Directive, Art 15.4–15.7* (see 22.21(*c*)–(*e*) EUROPEAN COMMUNITY LEGISLATION);

(ii) makes a similar statement on the delivery note and sales invoice; and

(iii) within three months of the supply, obtains and keeps commercial evidence that the goods have been removed from the UK and delivered directly to the vessel or aircraft, and a receipt for the goods from the master, commander or other responsible officer of the vessel or aircraft.

(Internal Guidance V1–16, Chapter 2 para 3.7; VAT Information Sheet 2/00).

(5) **Tools for the manufacture of goods for export**

Machine tools are goods used in the manufacture of other goods (eg jigs, patterns, templates, dies, moulds, punches and similar tools). The supply of machine tools, that remain in the UK, are normally standard-rated. However, the supply of a tool can be zero-rated if

- the customer specifically asks the supplier to make it, or buy it, for him;
- the supplier uses the machine tool to manufacture goods for the same customer and makes a specific charge to him for the supply of the tool;
- the tool is an integral part of the contract, or series of contracts, to supply goods to a VAT-registered customer in another EC country and title to the tool passes to the customer;
- the supplier obtains and shows the customer's VAT registration number (with its two digit country code prefix) on the VAT sales invoice;
- the manufactured goods are sent or transported out of the UK to a destination in another EC country; and
- the supplier holds commercial documentary evidence that the goods have been removed from the UK.

(VAT Notice 701/22/02, paras 1.2–1.4, 3.1).

23.22 TRIANGULATION

General background. This is the term used to describe a chain of supplies of goods involving three or more parties where, instead of the goods physically passing from one party to the next, they are delivered directly from the first party to the last party in the chain. This may occur, for example, when goods are moved directly from a supplier in one EC country to the final customer in another EC country on the instruction of an intermediate party located in yet another EC country.

> *Example*
>
> An original supplier (A) invoices an intermediate supplier (B) who in turn invoices the customer (C) in the EC country of destination. The goods are delivered directly by A to C.

Normal procedure. If the simplified arrangements below are not adopted, such supplies are treated for VAT purposes as follows.

- The supply by A to B involves the removal of goods from one EC country to another (even though this is not to the country where B is established). A can therefore zero-rate the supply of goods to B, subject to meeting the normal conditions in 23.11 above.
- The supply by B to C, however, does not involve the movement of goods from the country where B belongs. B is treated as making an acquisition of the goods in the EC country of destination (see 23.6(*a*) above) and an onward supply of the goods there. B should therefore register for VAT in the country of destination and account for tax there on its acquisition and onward supply.
- C need do nothing.

(VAT Notice 725, paras 9.1–9.4).

Simplified procedure. To avoid imposing this burden of registration on B, all EC countries have agreed to a simplified procedure. As a result, businesses registered for VAT in one EC country may no longer be required to register for VAT in another EC country purely because of triangular transactions. Instead, based on the above example, provided B is not registered or otherwise required to be registered in the country of destination, and C is registered there, B can opt to have his C account for the VAT due in the country of destination on his behalf. If B does so opt, C *must* account for the VAT on the supply of goods made to him (ie the simplification procedure is compulsory if B so opts) and the acquisition of the goods by B is disregarded both in the country where he belongs and the country of destination. A still treats his transaction in the same way as any other intra-EC supply, ie he may zero-rate the supply subject to the usual conditions in 23.11 above and should record the supply on an EC sales list in the normal way. (VAT Notice 725, paras 9.5, 9.6).

UK provisions. UK provisions specifically cover the two positions where either the customer C or the intermediate supplier B is registered in the UK.

(*a*) *Customers registered in the UK*. Where

- the original supplier A makes a supply of goods to B who 'belongs in another EC country',
- that supply involves the removal of the goods from another EC country and their removal to the UK but does not involve the removal of goods from the UK,

- both that supply, and the removal of the goods to the UK, are for the purposes of a supply by B to a UK VAT-registered customer,
- neither of those supplies involves the removal of the goods from an EC country in which B is taxable at the time of the removal without also involving the previous removal of the goods to that country, and
- there would be a taxable acquisition by C in the UK if the supply to him involved the removal of goods from another EC country to the UK,

then, provided B complies with requirements laid down by HMRC, the supply by A to B is disregarded for the purposes of *VATA 1994*, and the supply by B to C is treated, other than for the purposes of *VATA 1994, Sch 3* (registration in respect of acquisitions from another EC country), as a taxable acquisition. The taxable acquisition is treated as taking place on the date of the issue of the invoice for the transaction.

A person '*belongs in another EC country*' if

(i) he has no business establishment or other fixed establishment in the UK and does not have his usual place of residence in the UK;

(ii) he is neither registered nor required to be registered under *VATA 1994* (ignoring supplies disregarded under these provisions);

(iii) he does not have, and is not for the time being required to appoint, a VAT representative; and

(iv) he is taxable in another EC country.

[*VATA 1994, s 14(1)(3)(4)(5)*].

Notification. Where an intermediate supplier B wishes to take advantage of the simplified procedure, he must notify HMRC and the customer C in writing of his intention to do so. The notification must include

- B's name and address;
- B's VAT registration number (including alphabetical code, see 40.5 INVOICES) used for the purposes of the supply to him by the original supplier (A);
- the date upon which the goods are first delivered; and
- the name, address and VAT registration number of C to whom the goods are supplied (and who will account for the VAT).

Notification to HMRC must be direct to Business Advice Centre 050, Custom House, 28 Guild Street, Aberdeen, AB9 2DY.

B's notification must be made no later than the provision of the first invoice in relation to the supply (see below). It must be made separately in relation to each customer to whom B intends to make supplies under these provisions but, once made in relation to the first supply to any customer, is deemed to apply to all subsequent supplies to that customer as long as B continues to belong in another EC country.

[*SI 1995/2518, Reg 11*].

Invoices. B must issue an invoice to C which complies with the requirements of the EC country that issued the VAT registration number used for the purposes of the supply to him by the original supplier A. In addition, it must also be endorsed 'VAT: EC ARTICLE 28 SIMPLIFICATION INVOICE'. The invoice must be issued no later than 15 days after, and must relate to a supply of at least the same extent as would have been required under, the normal time of supply rules if these provisions had not applied. Such an invoice is then treated as if it were an invoice for the purposes of 23.7(*b*) above. [*SI 1995/2518, Reg 18*].

EC sales list. The intermediate supplier B must record the supply on his EC sales list in the country where he is registered.

Recording and accounting for VAT. The UK customer C must account for the VAT on the goods supplied to him as an acquisition. See 23.8 above.

(VAT Notice 725, paras 9.9–9.11).

(*b*) *Intermediate suppliers registered in the UK.* If the simplified procedure is used in a triangular transaction where the intermediate supplier B in the example above is registered in the UK and the goods are removed to another EC country of destination, the supply of those goods by the original supplier A to B and the supply of those goods by B to the customer C are both disregarded for the purposes of *VATA 1994* but without prejudice to the power of HMRC to require production of records and accounts and furnishing of information. [*VATA 1994, s 14(6)*]. In order to use the simplified procedure, B must

- use his UK VAT registration number to allow A to zero-rate the supply of the goods in the EC country of despatch;
- issue C with a VAT invoice which must contain all the details normally required for intra-EC supplies (see 40.5 INVOICES) together with an endorsement 'VAT: EC ARTICLE 28 SIMPLIFICATION INVOICE'. [*SI 1995/2518, Reg 17*];
- not enter details of triangular transactions involving either A or C on his VAT returns or supplementary returns; and
- include triangular transactions separately on his EC sales lists
  - (i) quoting the VAT number of C in the country of destination of the goods;
  - (ii) entering the total value of the triangular transactions to each EC customer on a single line separately from the total of other intra-EC supplies to that customer; and
  - (iii) identifying triangular transactions by the figure '2' entered in the indicator box.

B should contact the National Advice Service who will arrange for EC sales lists to be sent to him automatically.

(VAT Notice 725, para 9.7).

De Voil Indirect Tax Service. See V3.380.

23.23 TRANSFER OF OWN GOODS TO ANOTHER EC COUNTRY

Subject to the exceptions in 23.24–23.26 below, and unless specifically overridden by other provisions, the transfer of goods within the same legal entity from one EC country to another (eg between branches of the same company) is deemed to be a supply of goods for VAT purposes under the general provisions of *VATA 1994, Sch 4 para 6* (see 23.2 above) and is liable to VAT under the normal arrangements for intra-EC supplies. (Specifically excluded, from 1 January 2005, is the removal of gas through the natural gas distribution network or electricity [*SI 2004/3150*].) Therefore, where a UK business transfers its own goods from the UK to another EC country in the course of its business (eg to sell them on from that country or to use them there), it is liable to account for VAT in that EC country on the acquisition of the goods. It may need to register for VAT in that EC country both to meet its obligations there and to use an overseas VAT registration number to support zero-rating of the deemed supply when the goods leave the UK. Otherwise the business must account for VAT in the UK on the goods (and cannot recover this as input tax in the other EC country).

Where a UK business is not VAT-registered in the EC country of arrival of the goods at the time the goods are transferred, it may subsequently become registered there retrospectively to include the time when the goods were transferred. When this registration is obtained, the deemed supply of goods from the UK can be zero-rated quoting the VAT registration number in the EC country of arrival of the goods (subject to the normal conditions). Some EC countries may not allow retrospective VAT registration. In these circumstances, the business should obtain confirmation from the tax authorities in that EC country that they will not allow retrospective registration. When this has been obtained (and subject to the normal conditions), HMRC may allow the deemed supplies to be zero-rated.

Similarly, where a business transfers its own goods from another EC country to the UK in the course of its business, VAT must be accounted for on the acquisition of the goods in the UK under the normal rules. See 23.5 above for VAT relief on certain transfers.

Reporting requirements. The following table summarises the reporting requirements for transfers of own goods to other EC countries.

Type of supply	*VAT return*	*EC sales list*
Transfers of own goods from the UK to other EC countries	Enter the value in Boxes 6 and 8 based on the cost of the goods	Enter value based on cost of the goods
Transfers of own goods from another EC country to the UK	Enter acquisition VAT (for positive-rated goods) in Box 2 and input tax (subject to the normal rules) in Box 4. Enter the value of goods based on cost included in Boxes 7 and 9	No

(VAT Notice 725, paras 6.1–6.9; Internal Guidance V1–16, Chapter 2 para 2.2).

Consignment stock. This is a term used to describe goods which a business moves from one EC country to another to create a stock from which supplies will subsequently be made by or on its behalf in that country.

- Where a UK business moves goods to another EC country to be held as consignment stocks, the movement of goods is treated as a transfer of own goods under the above arrangements.
- Where a UK-registered business brings its own goods into the UK to be held as consignment stock, it must account for VAT on acquisition of the goods and on the subsequent supply here.

- Where a business registered in another EC country but not in the UK transfers its own goods to the UK to be held as consignment stock, it may be liable to register for VAT here. Alternatively, the business may be able to avoid registering in the UK by engaging the services of a VAT-registered agent and using the procedure in *VATA 1994, s 47(2)* (see 3.4 AGENTS). The goods can then be treated as supplied to, and acquired by, the agent in the UK and supplied on by the agent when a customer is eventually found. The business can zero-rate the supply in its own EC country by quoting the agent's UK VAT registration number (subject to the normal rules).
- Where any of the consignment stock is later returned to the EC country of origin, there is a further transfer of own goods if the business is registered in the EC country in which the goods have been held. If the procedure in *VATA 1994, s 47(2)* has been used, there is an intra-EC supply by the agent from the UK to the business in the EC country to which the goods are returned.

Reporting requirements. The following table summarises the reporting requirements for consignment stock moving between EC countries.

Type of supply	*VAT return*	*EC sales list*
Consignment stocks transferred from the UK to other EC countries	Enter the value in Boxes 6 and 8 based on the cost of the goods	Enter value based on cost of the goods
Consignment stocks transferred to the UK from other EC countries	Enter acquisition VAT (for positive-rated goods) in Box 2 and input tax (subject to the normal rules) in Box 4. Enter the value of goods based on cost included in Boxes 7 and 9	No

(VAT Notice 725, paras 10.6–10.8; Internal Guidance V1–16, Chapter 2 para 2.25).

23.24 Temporary movements of own goods

The following temporary movements of own goods between EC countries are not treated as supplies for VAT purposes and no VAT is due in the VAT period in which the removal takes place.

(*a*) Where

(i) the owner is established in the EC country of dispatch but not that of arrival;

(ii) the goods are removed for the sole purpose of being used by the owner in the course of a supply of services to be made by him;

(iii) at the time of their removal, there is a legally binding obligation to make that supply of services (ie a specific contract to fulfill); and

(iv) the owner intends to remove the goods back to the EC country of dispatch when he has ceased to use them in making the supply (and does in fact do so).

This could apply, for example, to tools and equipment and goods intended for loan, hire or leasing.

The removal back to the EC country of dispatch under (iv) is also not treated as a supply for VAT purposes.

(*b*) Where goods are removed to another EC country for temporary use there and

(i) temporary importation relief would have been given if the goods had been imported from outside the EC; and

(ii) the owner intends to export the goods outside the EC or remove them to an EC country other than the country to which the goods have been removed, in either case not later than two years after the day upon which the goods were removed (and he does in fact do so).

See 34.26 IMPORTS for goods eligible for temporary import relief.

The export or removal under (ii) is also not treated as a supply for VAT purposes.

If the circumstances of the transfer under (*a*) or (*b*) above change and the movement no longer qualifies for treatment under these temporary movement provisions (eg the goods are sold or are to remain in the other EC country for more than two years), the original movement should be treated, belatedly, as a deemed supply and acquisition under 23.23 above. The owner must account for VAT in the VAT period in which the condition is not complied with.

[*SI 1992/3111, Arts 4(f)(g)(h), 5; SI 1995/2518, Reg 42*]. (VAT Notice 725, paras 7.1–7.5).

Although the above transfers are not treated as supplies for VAT purposes, commercial documentary evidence should be held to prove that the goods have left the UK and have later returned. (VAT Notice 725, para 7.6).

See 23.28 below for the requirement to keep a register of such movements of goods.

Reporting requirements. The following table summarises the reporting requirements for temporary movements of own goods between EC countries.

Type of supply	*VAT return*	*EC sales list*
Goods sent from the UK on loan, hire, or lease for less than two years	No entry required but details must be recorded in a register of temporary movement of goods (see 23.28 below)	No
Goods sent from the UK on loan, hire or lease for two years or more	No entry required but details must be recorded in a register of temporary movement of goods (see 23.28 below)	No
Goods sent from the UK to be used in making a supply of services in another EC country (eg tools and equipment)	No entry required but details must be recorded in a register of temporary movement of goods (see 23.28 below)	No

Type of supply	*VAT return*	*EC sales list*
Temporary transfers of goods to other EC countries for less than two years, where the goods would be eligible for temporary importation relief if imported from outside the EC	No entry required but details must be recorded in a register of temporary movement of goods (see 23.28 below)	No

(VAT Notice 725, para 7.7).

23.25 *Goods sent for treatment, processing, valuation or repair work, etc*

A supply of goods is not treated as taking place in the following circumstances.

(*a*) Where the owner, who is registered in the EC country of dispatch but is not registered in the EC country of arrival,

(i) sends the goods to another person in another EC country for treatment or processing; and

(ii) intends that the goods produced will be returned to him in the EC country of dispatch upon completion.

It is a condition for the dispatch of the goods not to be treated as a supply of goods that the intention of the owner under (ii) above is fulfilled. Where it is not, the original movement of goods must be belatedly treated as a deemed intra-EC supply and acquisition and the owner must account for VAT in the VAT period in which the condition is not complied with.

(*b*) Where the owner

(i) sends the goods to another person in another EC country who is to value the goods or to carry out any work on them; and

(ii) the supply made by the person to whom the goods are sent is or will be a supply of services treated as having been made in that EC country.

This covers movement of goods between EC countries for repair or minor alteration.

The return of the goods to the original EC country is also not treated as a supply of goods.

[*SI 1992/3111, Art 4*(*d*)(*e*)(*h*)(*i*), *Art 5; SI 1995/2518, Reg 42*].

See 23.28 below for the requirement to keep a register of movement of the goods.

23.26 *VAT treatment of the work carried out on the goods*

Special place of supply rules apply to the *services* of treatment, processing, valuation or repair work, etc. See 64.25 SUPPLY for full details. The effect of these rules, in conjunction with the provisions under 23.25 above relating to the underlying goods, are as follows.

(*a*) *UK supplier providing such services within the EC to a customer registered for VAT in another EC country.* The place of supply of the services is where they are physically performed unless the customer

- is VAT-registered in an EC country which is different to the one in which the service is performed: and
- gives the UK supplier his VAT registration number.

Where these two conditions are satisfied:

- If the goods subsequently leave the country in which the services were performed, the place of supply moves to the EC country where the customer is registered. The UK supplier should not charge VAT although the invoice or contract value of the work should be entered in Box 6 of the VAT return. The customer is required to account for VAT under the 'reverse charge' procedure in his own country.
- If the goods do not subsequently leave the country in which the services were performed, the place of supply remains in the country of performance. This will normally be the UK and the UK supplier must charge and account for VAT in the normal way. But if the place of supply is another EC country, the UK supplier may be liable to register for VAT in that country and account for any VAT due there.

Movement of goods. No entry is required on the VAT return in relation to the goods either when they are received in the UK from the EC customer or subsequently returned to him but details must be recorded in a register of temporary movement of goods (see 23.28 below). Commercial evidence must be held that the goods have been removed from the UK after the work has been carried out.

The movement of goods is not required to be shown on EC sales lists but must be shown as an arrival and despatch on any supplementary declaration.

(*b*) *UK supplier providing such services within the EC to a customer not registered for VAT in any EC country.* The place of supply of the services is the country where the service is physically performed. This will normally be the UK and the supplier must charge and account for VAT in the normal way. But if the place of supply is another EC country, the UK supplier may be liable to register for VAT in that country and account for any VAT due there.

Movement of goods. No entry is required on the VAT return in relation to the goods either when they are received in the UK from the EC customer or subsequently returned to him but details must be recorded in a register of temporary movement of goods (see 23.28 below). Commercial evidence must be held that the goods have been removed from the UK after the work has been carried out.

The movement of goods is not required to be shown on EC sales lists but may be required to be shown as an arrival and despatch on any supplementary declaration.

(*c*) *UK supplier providing such services to a customer registered for VAT in the UK.*

(i) Where the services are performed in the UK, the place of supply is the UK whether or not the goods subsequently leave the UK. The supplier must account for any UK VAT in the normal way.

(ii) Where the services are performed in an EC country other than the UK

- if the goods subsequently leave the country where the services are physically performed, the place of supply is where the customer is registered (ie the UK) although as this is also the place where the supplier is registered, the supplier must account for any UK VAT in the normal way; and

- if the goods do not subsequently leave the country where the services are physically performed, the place of supply remains in that country. The UK supplier may be liable to register for VAT and account for any VAT due there. The UK VAT-registered customer may be eligible to make a claim for a refund of the overseas VAT under the *EC 8th Directive* refund procedure.

Movement of goods. No entry is required on the VAT return in relation to any movement of the goods into or from the UK but commercial evidence must be held of any such movement. Details must also be recorded in a register of temporary movement of goods (see 23.28 below).

Any movement of goods is not required to be shown on EC sales lists but must be shown as an arrival or despatch on any supplementary declaration.

(*d*) *UK supplier providing such services outside the EC.* If a UK supplier physically performs these services outside the EC, the supply is outside the scope of UK and EC VAT. This applies irrespective of the location and VAT registration status of the customer.

(*e*) *UK supplier sending goods for processing, etc to another EC country.* Where such services are performed in the EC for a UK VAT-registered customer

- by a supplier who is established outside the UK (including outside the EC), and

- the goods do not remain in the country where the work has been performed,

provided the UK customer gives the supplier his VAT registration number, the place of supply is the UK and the UK customer must account for any UK VAT due under the 'reverse charge' procedure.

The place of supply remains in the EC country of physical performance if either

- the goods are not subsequently removed from that country (in which case a UK VAT-registered customer may be eligible to make a claim under the *EC 8th Directive*); or

- the UK customer is not registered for VAT (in which case the supplier must charge and account for any VAT).

(*f*) *UK customer buying goods in another EC country for processing there before return to the UK.* In these circumstances, the provisions in 23.25 above do not apply (because the goods are not physically sent to another EC country for processing). The UK customer must account for VAT on the goods as an acquisition and account for VAT on the value of the processing work under the reverse charge procedure. The movement of goods must be shown as an arrival on a supplementary declaration where applicable.

(VAT Notice 725, paras 11.1–11.3, 13.4).

23.27 *Goods sold on sale or return, approval or similar terms*

Goods sent to a customer in another EC country on sale or return, approval or similar terms are treated as intra-EC transfers of own goods under 23.23 above. As a result:

(*a*) Where a UK business supplies goods on such terms to a customer in another EC country

- it initially makes an acquisition of the goods in that country; and
- it makes a supply of goods there if and when the goods are eventually adopted by the customer.

The business may need to register for VAT in that EC country both to account for any VAT due on the acquisition and supply of the goods and in order to use an overseas VAT registration number to support zero-rating of the deemed supply when the goods leave the UK.

(*b*) Where a business in another EC country supplies goods on such terms to a UK customer

- it will be liable to account for VAT on the acquisition of the goods in the UK; and
- it will also be liable to account for VAT on the earlier of
  - (i) the date when the goods are eventually adopted by the customer;
  - (ii) twelve months after their time of removal to the UK; or
  - (iii) the time of issue a VAT invoice in respect of the goods

under the normal UK rules for sale or return goods in the UK (see 64.43 SUPPLY).

Reporting requirements. The following table summarises the UK reporting requirements for goods sold on sale or return, approval or similar terms.

Type of supply	*VAT return*	*EC sales list*
Goods supplied to registered customers in other EC countries	Enter the value in Boxes 6 and 8 based on the cost of the goods	Enter value based on cost of the goods
Goods received in the UK from suppliers in other EC countries — *supplier's* reporting requirements	Enter acquisition VAT (for positive-rated goods) in Box 2 and input tax (subject to the normal rules) in Box 4. Enter the value of goods based on cost included in Boxes 7 and 9	No

(VAT Notice 725, paras 10.14, 10.15).

23.28 **REGISTER OF TEMPORARY MOVEMENT OF GOODS**

Every taxable person must keep and maintain a register of goods moved to, and goods received from, other EC countries on a temporary basis. The register need not be kept in any particular format but it must be readily available for all goods temporarily moved to and from the UK.

The register *must* include the following information for all goods moved between the UK and other EC countries if they are to be returned within a period of two years after their first removal or receipt. (It would be advisable also to include any goods where the date of return is not certain.)

- The date of removal of goods to another EC country and the date of receipt of those goods when they are returned from that or another EC country.
- The date of receipt of goods from another EC country and the date of removal of those goods when they are returned to that or another EC country.
- A description of the goods sufficient to identify them.
- A description of any process, work or other operation carried out on the goods either in the UK or in another EC country.
- The consideration for the supply of the goods.
- The consideration for the supply of any processing, work or other operation carried out on the goods either in the UK or another EC country.

[*SI 1995/2518, Reg 33*]. (VAT Notice 725, paras 12.8–12.10).

De Voil Indirect Tax Service. See V5.212.

23.29 INSTALLED AND ASSEMBLED GOODS

A supply of installed or assembled goods occurs where the supplier of the goods has a contractual obligation to install or assemble them (eg a supplier of studio recording equipment could have a contractual obligation to not only supply the equipment, but also install it in the customer's studio). (VAT Notice 725, para 8.1).

General rule. Where the supply of goods involves their installation or assembly, they are treated as supplied in the country where they are installed or assembled. [*VATA 1994, s 7(3)*].

Reporting requirements. Unless the simplification procedure below is applied, the reporting requirements for installed or assembled goods are as follows.

- Where a UK business supplies goods which it is to install or assemble in another EC country, its supply takes place in that country and it is liable for any VAT there. The business may need to register there in order to account for the VAT due. As regards its reporting UK requirements, the invoice/contract value should be included in Box 6 on the VAT return and the value based on the cost of the goods at the time of dispatch should be entered in Box 8. No entries are required on an EC sales list but an entry is required on any supplementary declaration as a dispatch based on the cost of the goods.
- Where a business supplies goods from another EC country to be installed or assembled in the UK, the supply is liable to UK VAT and the business may have to register in the UK. If the business is registered in the UK, it must include output tax in Box 1 of its VAT return and the invoice or contract value in Box 6. No entries are required on an EC sales list but an entry is required on any supplementary declaration as an arrival based on the cost of the goods.

(VAT Notice 725, paras 8.6, 8.7).

Simplification procedure. To avoid imposing the burden of registration in another EC country on the supplier of installed or assembled goods, simplified procedure has been agreed by *some* EC countries. Where it applies, instead of registering in that other

EC country, the supplier can opt to have his customer account for the VAT due there on his behalf provided the customer is registered in that EC country. If the supplier so opts, the customer *must* account for the VAT (ie the simplification procedure is compulsory if the supplier opts).

The operation of this simplified procedure is a matter for each EC country to decide. Any business needs to contact the tax authority in the EC country where it is proposing to make a supply to find out if they are operating a simplified procedure. The contact addresses can be found in 21.7–21.30 EUROPEAN COMMUNITY: GENERAL. In the absence of simplification arrangements, the general rules above apply and a business may be required to register for VAT in that EC country.

Installation or assembly in the UK. Where

(*a*) a person belonging in another EC country makes a supply of goods to a UK VAT-registered person and the supply involves their installation or assembly at a place in the UK to which they are removed; and

(*b*) there would be a taxable acquisition by the UK-registered person if, instead of treating that supply as a taxable supply in the UK (under the general rule above), it was treated as involving the removal of the goods from another EC country to the UK,

then, provided the supplier complies with requirements laid down by HMRC, the supply is treated, other than for the purposes of *VATA 1994, Sch 3* (registration in respect of acquisitions from another EC country), as a taxable acquisition. The taxable acquisition is treated as taking place on the date of the issue of the invoice for the transaction.

For these purposes, a person is treated as '*belonging in another EC country*' if

- he has no business establishment or other fixed establishment in the UK and does not have his usual place of residence in the UK;
- he is neither registered nor required to be registered under *VATA 1994* (ignoring supplies disregarded under these provisions);
- he does not have, and is not for the time being required to appoint, a VAT representative; and
- he is taxable in another EC country.

[*VATA 1994, s 14(2)–(5)*].

Notification. If the EC supplier wishes to take advantage of the simplification provisions and avoid registering for VAT in the UK, he must notify HMRC and the registered person in writing of his intention to do so. The notification must include

- the name and address of the EC supplier;
- the VAT registration number (including alphabetical code, see 40.5 INVOICES) by which that person is identified for VAT in the EC country in which he belongs;
- the date upon which the installation or assembly of the goods commences; and
- the name, address and VAT registration number of the UK VAT-registered customer.

Notification to HMRC must be direct to VAT Business Advice Centre 050, Custom House, 28 Guild Street, Aberdeen, AB9 2DY.

The notification must be made no later than the provision of the first invoice in relation to the supply (see below). It must be made separately in relation to each registered person to whom it is intended to make supplies under these provisions but, once made in relation to the first supply to any registered person, is deemed to apply to all subsequent supplies to that registered person as long as the person making the supply continues to belong in another EC country.

[*SI 1995/2518, Reg 12*].

Invoices. The EC supplier must issue an invoice to the UK VAT-registered customer which complies with the requirements of that EC country and bears the legend 'SECTION 14(2) VATA INVOICE'. The invoice must be provided no later than 15 days after what would have been the normal time of supply if these provisions had not applied. It must relate to a supply of at least the same extent as would have been required under the normal time of supply rules if these provisions had not applied. Such an invoice is then treated as if it were an invoice for the purposes of 23.7(*b*) above. [*SI 1995/2518, Reg 19*].

Reporting requirements. The UK customer must account for VAT on the acquisition. The VAT must be recorded on the VAT payable side of his VAT account and included in Box 2 of his VAT return. (VAT is not due on goods which are zero-rated in the UK.) The net value of the supply must also be included in Box 9 of the return. He can also deduct this VAT as input tax on the same return (subject to the normal rules). The VAT must be recorded on the VAT deductible side of his VAT account and included in Box 4 of his VAT return. The net value of the acquisition must be included in Box 7 of the return. (VAT Notice 725, para 8.14).

No entry is required on an EC sales list but an entry is required on any supplementary declaration as an arrival based on the cost of the goods if known (otherwise the open market value).

De Voil Indirect Tax Service. See V3.381.

23.30 'CALL-OFF' STOCKS

'*Call-off stock*' applies where a business transfer goods from one EC country to another for 'call-off', ie for use and payment by its customers as they need the goods. Goods delivered to storage facilities operated by the supplier in another EC country can be dealt with as call-off stock provided the customer is aware of the details of deliveries into storage. Otherwise, the goods should be dealt with as consignment stock (see 23.23 above).

The VAT treatment of call-off stock is as follows.

(*a*) If a UK business send goods to another EC country so that its customer can maintain a stock for 'call off', the supply is in the UK and can be treated under the normal arrangements for intra-EC movements. The goods can therefore be zero-rated when sent from the UK subject to the normal requirements. However, it should be noted that not all EC countries interpret a 'call-off' transaction in the same way as HMRC and a UK supplier may be required to register for VAT in the country to which the goods have been sent and account for VAT on supplies made there. Businesses are advised to contact the appropriate overseas tax authority for advice. (Internal Guidance V1–16, Chapter 2 para 2.24). The contact addresses can be found in 21.7–21.30 EUROPEAN COMMUNITY: GENERAL.

(*b*) If a UK business receives 'call-off' stocks in the UK from a supplier in another EC country, it must account for VAT on the acquisition on the basis of the movement of the goods even though title may not pass until it calls-off the goods. However, these arrangements only apply when the goods are intended for use solely by the UK customer (whether in the business or to make onward supplies to own customers). Stocks sent to the UK by an EC supplier for, or for call-off by, more than one customer they should be treated as consignment stock (see 23.23 above).

Reporting requirements. The following table summarises the UK reporting requirements for call-off stocks.

Type of supply	*VAT return*	*EC sales list*
Goods supplied to VAT-registered customers in other EC countries	Enter the value in Boxes 6 and 8 based on the cost of the goods	Enter value based on cost of the goods
Goods received in the UK from VAT-registered suppliers in other EC	Enter acquisition VAT (for positive-rated goods) in Box 2 and input tax (subject to the normal rules) in Box 4. Enter the value of goods based on cost included in Boxes 7 and 9	No

(VAT Notice 725, paras 10.2–10.5).

23.31 NEW MEANS OF TRANSPORT

The following are regarded as new means of transport (NMT) for the purposes of 23.32–23.36 below, provided that, in each case, it is intended for the transport of persons or goods.

(*a*) Any ship, including a hovercraft, exceeding 7.5 metres in length (overall) provided that three months or less have elapsed since its first entry into service or, since that time, it has travelled under its own power for 100 hours or less. A ship is treated as having first entered into service

- when it is delivered from its manufacturer to its first purchaser or owner or is first made available to that person (whichever is the earlier); or
- if applicable, when its manufacturer first takes it into use for demonstration purposes.

(*b*) Any aircraft the take-off weight of which exceeds 1,550 kilograms provided that three months or less have elapsed since its first entry into service or, since that time, it has travelled under its own power for 40 hours or less. An aircraft is treated as having first entered into service

- when it is delivered from its manufacturer to its first purchaser or owner or is first made available to that person (whichever is the earlier); or
- if applicable, when its manufacturer first takes it into use for demonstration purposes.

(*c*) Any motorised land vehicle which

- has an engine with a displacement or a cylinder capacity exceeding 48 cc; or

- is constructed or adapted to be electrically propelled using more than 7.2 kilowatts

provided that six months or less have elapsed since its first entry into service or, since that time, it has travelled under its own power for 6,000 kilometres or less. A motorised land vehicle is treated as having first entered into service

(i) on its first registration for road use in the EC country of its manufacturer or when a liability to register for road use is first incurred there (whichever is the earlier); or

(ii) where (i) does not apply, its removal by its first purchaser or owner, its first delivery or its being made available to its first purchaser (whichever is the earlier); or

(iii) if applicable, when its manufacturer first takes it into use for demonstration purposes.

Where the time of first entry into use under (*a*)–(*c*) above cannot be established to the satisfaction of HMRC, a means of transport is to be treated as having first entered into service on the issue of an invoice relating to its first supply.

[*VATA 1994, s 95; SI 1994/3128; SI 1995/2518, Reg 147*].

De Voil Indirect Tax Service. See V1.294.

23.32 **Supplies by persons registered in the UK to non-registered persons in other EC countries**

A non-registered person who buys a NMT in the UK to take to another EC country must pay any taxes due on it in the EC country of destination under the laws of that country. To avoid double taxation, a UK-registered supplier can zero-rate the supply of a NMT to such a person provided the following conditions are met (which have the force of law).

(*a*) The means of transport qualifies as 'new' under 23.31 above.

(*b*) The purchaser (or his authorised chauffeur, pilot or skipper) personally takes delivery of the NMT and removes it from the UK to the EC country of destination within two months of the date of supply.

(*c*) The supplier and the customer make a joint declaration on Form VAT 411.

Form VAT 411 is a declaration by the customer that he will take the NMT to another EC country within two months and pay the VAT there. It is also a declaration by the supplier that he has supplied a NMT to the customer for removal from the UK.

Copies of Form VAT 411 are obtainable from the National Advice Service (tel: 0845 010 9000). It comprises an original (or top sheet) and three copies. When the form has been fully completed, the supplier must send the original to

HM Revenue and Customs
Central Processing Unit
Postal Depot
Charlton Green
Dover
Kent CT16 1EH

within six weeks of the end of the calendar quarter in which the supply is made.

The first copy of Form VAT 411 should be given to the customer. The second copy is retained by the supplier and, where the NMT is a vehicle, the third copy is used to register it for road use if it is to be driven out of the UK (see below).

Sales subject to a finance agreement. Where a non-registered person funds the purchase of the NMT using a hire purchase or similar agreement, the dealer makes a standard-rated supply to the finance house and the finance house makes a zero-rated supply of the NMT to the non-registered person. The dealer should ensure that the VAT 411 clearly shows that it is the finance house supplying the vehicle and must send the second copy of the Form VAT 411 to the finance house to support the zero-rating of the supply. The other copies of the form should be distributed in the normal manner. (Internal Guidance V1–17, para 3.10).

Using a new vehicle on UK roads. Any new vehicle cannot be used on UK roads before its removal to another EC country unless it is licensed, registered and properly insured against third party liability. If the vehicle is not already licensed at the time of purchase, the supplier will obtain the registration number (a special 'VAT-free' series which allows the vehicle to be identified as tax free whilst it remains in the UK prior to removal) by presenting the third copy of the completed Form VAT 411, attached to the application for registration, to one of the following DVLA local offices.

Scotland	
Aberdeen	Greyfriars House, Gallowgate, Aberdeen AB10 1WG Tel: 01224 648216
Dundee	Caledonian House, Greenmarket, Dundee DD1 4QP Tel: 01382 225765
Edinburgh	Department of Transport, Saughton House, Broomhouse Drive, Edinburgh EH11 3XE Tel: 0130 455 7919
Glasgow	46 West Campbell Street, Glasgow, G2 6TT Tel: 0141 226 4161
Inverness	Longman House, 28 Longman Road, Inverness IV1 1SF Tel: 01463 239321/2
North England	
Beverley	Crosskill House, Mill Lane, Beverley HU17 9JB Tel: 01482 887884
Carlisle	Ground Floor, 3 Merchants Drive, Parkhouse CA3 0JW Tel: 01228 539401/2
Chester	Norroy House, Nuns Road, Chester CH1 2ND Tel: 01244 348195
Leeds	Ist Floor, 42 Eastgate, Leeds LS2 7DQ Tel: 0113 244 3035
Manchester	Trafford House, Chester Road, Manchester M32 0SL Tel: 0870 241 2146
Newcastle upon Tyne	Eagle Star House, Regent Farm Road, Newcastle upon Tyne NE3 3QF Tel: 0191 284 1026
Preston	Buckingham House, Glovers Court, Preston PR1 4DQ Tel: 01772 823911

Sheffield	Bank House, 100 Queen Street, Sheffield S1 1JX Tel: 0114 272 236
Stockton	St Marks House, St Marks Court, Thornaby, Stockton on Tees TS17 6QR Tel: 01642 796600
Midlands	
Birmingham	2nd Floor, Edward House, Edward Street, Birmingham B1 2RF Tel: 0121 212 0155
Northampton	Wootton Hall Park, Northampton NN4 0GA Tel: 01604 762131
Nottingham	Block 6, Government Buildings, Chalfont Drive, Nottingham NG8 3RA Tel: 0115 929 9924
Shrewsbury	Whitehall, Monkmoor Road, Shrewsbury SY2 5DR Tel: 01743 366422/350511
Worcester	Clerkenleap Barn, Broomhall, Kempsey WR5 3HR Tel: 01905 821720
Eastern England	
Chelmsford	2nd Floor, Parkway House, 49 Baddow Road, Chelmsford CM2 0XJ Tel: 0870 241 2147
Ipswich	Podium Level, St Clare House, Greyfriars, Ipswich IP1 1UT Tel: 01473 258451
Lincoln	Firth House, Firth Court, Lincoln LN5 7WD Tel: 01522 543681
Luton	2 Dunstable Road, Luton LU1 1EB Tel: 01582 412143
Norwich	11 Prince of Wales Road, Norwich NR1 1UP Tel: 01603 616411
Peterborough	88 Lincoln Road, Peterborough PE1 2ST Tel: 01733 551671
London and Southern England	
Bournemouth	Tregonwell Court, 118 Commercial Road, Bournemouth BH2 5LN Tel: 01202 5585531
Brighton	4th Floor, Mocatta House, Trafalgar Place, Brighton BN1 4UE Tel: 01273 692271
Maidstone	Coronet House, 11 Queen Anne Road, Maidstone ME14 1XB Tel: 01622 675432
Oxford	Ground Floor, 3 Cambridge Terrace, Oxford, OX1 1RW Tel: 01865 724056

Portsmouth	5th Floor, Baltic House, Kensington Crescent, North End, Portsmouth PO2 8AH Tel: 02392 639421
Reading	77–81 Basingstoke Road, Reading RG2 0ER Tel: 0870 241 5161
Sidcup	12–18 Station Road, Sidcup DA15 7EQ Tel: 020 8302 2134
Stanmore	Government Buildings, Canon Park, Honeypot Lane, Stanmore HA7 1BD Tel: 0870 241 1269
Wimbledon	Ground Floor, Connect House, 133–137 Alexandra Road, Wimbledon SW19 7JY Tel: 0870 600 6767
West of England	
Bristol	Northleigh House, Lime Kiln Close, Stoke Gifford, Bristol BS34 8SR Tel: 0117 969 2211
Exeter	Hanover House, Manaton Close, Matford Business Park, Marsh Barton Trading Estate, Exeter EX2 8EF Tel: 01392 824330
Truro	Pydar House, Pydar Street, Truro TR1 2TG Tel: 01872 278635
Wales	
Bangor	Penrhos Road, Penrhosgarnedd, Bangor LL57 2JF Tel: 01248 351822
Cardiff	Archway House, 77 Ty Glas Avenue, Llanishen CF14 5DX Tel: 0292 075 3355
Swansea	Hoel Pentrefelin, Swansea SA6 7HG Tel: 01792 783900
Northern Ireland	
Coleraine	Vehicle Licensing Central Office, County Hall, Castlerock Road, Coleraine, Co. Londonderry BT51 3HS Tel: 01265 44133

Failure to remove the NMT from the UK within the time allowed. If, in exceptional circumstances, the customer is unable to remove the NMT from the UK, he must inform HMRC immediately in writing at HM Revenue and Customs, Personal Transport Unit, PO Box 242, Dover, Kent CT17 9GP. HMRC will then calculate the VAT due and issue a demand for immediate payment. If the NMT is not removed from the UK within the time allowed and HMRC have not been informed, the vehicle may be liable to forfeiture.

'Type approval'. This is the official recognition that the vehicle has satisfied certain international safety standards. A vehicle cannot be licensed and registered in the UK unless it is type approved or otherwise exempt. For type approval purposes a motor vehicle is

- a passenger vehicle with four or more wheels, or three wheels if it has a maximum gross weight of more than 1,000 kilograms, intended to carry no more than eight passengers, excluding the driver; or
- a three-wheeled passenger vehicle with a maximum gross weight of under 1,000 kilograms, if it has either a maximum speed of more than 50 kilometres per hour or an engine capacity of more than 50 cubic centimetres; or
- a goods vehicle.

Further information on type approval can be found from The Vehicle Certification Agency, 1 The Eastgate Office Centre, Eastgate Road, Bristol BS5 6XX (Tel: 01272 524125).

NMT vehicles supplied in the UK are exempted from UK-type approval requirements for as long as they are relieved from VAT whilst awaiting removal from the UK. If the vehicle is not removed, and as a consequence becomes liable to UK VAT, the exemption from type approval is withdrawn. The absence of type approval may affect the customer's ability to register the vehicle in the UK for permanent use on UK roads.

[*SI 1995/2518, Regs 22(6), 155*]. (VAT Notice 728, paras 6.1–6.7, 8.8, 8.11, 8.12, 9.2, 9.5, 9.7, 9.9, 9.10, 10).

De Voil Indirect Tax Service. See V5.272.

23.33 Supplies by persons registered in the UK to persons registered in other EC countries

A supplier who is registered for VAT in the UK should zero-rate the supply of a NMT to a VAT-registered person from another EC country provided

(*a*) the means of transport qualifies as 'new' under 23.31 above;

(*b*) the customer's VAT registration number (with two digit code prefix) is shown on the invoice;

(*c*) the NMT is dispatched or transported from the UK to another EC country within two months of the date of issue of the invoice for the supply; and

(*d*) the supplier holds valid commercial documentary evidence that the NMT has been removed from the UK (see 23.13 above).

The customer must account for any VAT due on the acquisition in the EC country of destination under the laws of that country.

Using a new vehicle on UK roads. If any new unregistered vehicle is to be used in the UK before its removal to another EC country, it must be licensed, registered and insured against third-party liabilities before delivery. The supplier and the customer must complete and sign a declaration on Form VAT 411A obtainable from the National Advice Service (tel: 0845 010 9000). This form must be sent or produced to one of the DVLA local offices listed in 23.32 above who will allocate a registration mark in the tax-free series.

If the customer's plans change and he decides to keep the vehicle in the UK permanently, he cannot retain the tax-free registration mark and should contact HMRC at HM Revenue and Customs, Personal Transport Unit, PO Box 242, Dover, Kent CT17 9GP.

Failure to remove the NMT from the UK within the time allowed. If the customer does not remove the NMT from the UK in the time allowed, he will be liable to pay UK VAT.

'Type approval'. See 23.32 above.

EC sales lists. An entry is required in any EC sales list. See 2.19 *et seq* ACCOUNTING PERIODS AND RETURNS.

(VAT Notice 728, paras 8.8. 8.10, 8.14, 9.3–9.5).

23.34 Supplies by non-registered persons: recovery of VAT

Where a non-taxable person supplies a NMT which involves its removal to another EC country, HMRC must, on a claim, refund to him the VAT which he paid on the supply to him (or acquisition or importation by him, as the case may be) but not exceeding the amount of VAT which would have been payable on the supply by him involving removal if it had been a taxable supply by a taxable person and had not been zero-rated. [*VATA 1994, s 40*].

The claim must be in writing and be made no earlier than one month, and no later than 14 days, before the making of the supply by virtue of which the claim arises. It must include a signed declaration that all the information entered in, or accompanying it, is true and complete and must be sent to HM Revenue and Customs, Personal Transport Unit, PO Box 242, Dover, Kent CT17 9GP. It must contain the following information. (A form for the purpose is reproduced in VAT Notice 728, section 11.)

- The name, current address and telephone number of the claimant.
- The place where the NMT is kept and the times when it may be inspected. (HMRC may need to inspect the NMT before it is sold to confirm its eligibility for refund.)
- The name and address of the person who supplied the NMT to the claimant.
- The price paid by the claimant for the supply of the NMT to him, excluding VAT.
- The amount of any VAT on that supply.
- The amount of any VAT paid by the claimant on the acquisition or importation of the NMT by him.
- The name and address of the proposed purchaser, the EC country to which the NMT is to be removed and the date of the proposed purchase.
- The price to be paid by the proposed purchaser.
- A full description of the NMT (make, model, colour, registration number, engine number and chassis/hull/airframe number) including, in the case of a motorised land vehicle, its mileage since first entry into service and, in the case of a ship or aircraft, its hours of use since that time. See 23.31 above for the time of first entry into service.
- Details (as the case may be) of
  - (i) the ship's length in metres
  - (ii) the aircraft's take-off weight in kilograms; or

(iii) the motorised land vehicle's displacement or cylinder capacity in cubic centimetres (if powered by a combustion engine) or maximum power output in kilowatts (if an electrically propelled vehicle).

- The amount of the refund being claimed.

HMRC will advise the claimant if they wish to examine the NMT before it is sold to confirm its eligibility for refund.

Before any refund is received, HMRC will also need to see

- proof of original purchase (normally the invoice or import entry);
- evidence that the VAT has been paid on the original purchase;
- proof of sale (normally the bill of sale and evidence that payment has been received); and
- evidence that the NMT has been removed to another EC country.

[*SI 1995/2518, Regs 146, 149–154*]. (VAT Notice 728, paras 7.1–7.5).

23.35 **Acquisitions by non-registered persons in the UK from other EC countries**

An acquisition of a NMT is taxed in the EC country of destination. In order to avoid the need to register persons making such acquisitions in the UK who would not otherwise be liable to be registered, HMRC are empowered to introduce a special mechanism to collect the VAT due. [*VATA 1994, Sch 11 para 2(4)(5)*].

Under these powers, where a non-taxable person makes a taxable acquisition of a NMT in the UK, he must notify HMRC within seven days of its acquisition or its arrival in the UK, whichever is the later.

The notification should be in writing in English on Form VAT 415 which is available from the National Advice Service (tel: 0845 010 9000) and DVLA local offices or it can be down-loaded from HMRC website at:

www.hmrc.gov.uk

The completed form should be sent by post to HM Revenue and Customs, Personal Transport Unit, PO Box 242, Dover, Kent CT17 9GP or can be handed to the DVLA local office when the vehicle is licensed and registered. See 23.32 above for a list of DVLA local offices. (Note that the Personal Transport Unit only accepts postal notifications and has no public enquiry counters and if the notification is made via a DVLA local office, it will send the necessary documents to HMRC.)

HMRC will also need to see the final purchase invoice showing the chassis number and price paid and any invoices for accessories purchased with the vehicle. They can process the notification more quickly if it is accompanied by these documents.

Foreign currency conversion. If the invoice for the NMT is in currency other than sterling, the Personal Transport Unit will convert it into sterling using the rate of exchange current at time of acquisition. This will automatically be done using the HMRC period rate of exchange which closely reflects the UK market rate. However, the purchaser may make a specific request in writing at the time of notification to use the actual market rate applicable on the date of acquisition. The rates published in national newspapers will be acceptable as evidence of the rate at the relevant time.

Calculation of VAT due. VAT is calculated on the total amount paid for the NMT, including any extras fitted to it at the time it was supplied, plus any delivery or incidental charges made by the supplier.

Payment of VAT. HMRC will calculate the VAT due and send a written demand which must be paid within 30 days of issue.

Disabled persons. Where the NMT is a vehicle constructed or adapted for a disabled person, see 32.34 HEALTH AND WELFARE.

Return of faulty vehicles. Where a manufacturer has agreed to replace a faulty NMT vehicle acquired from another EC country, acquisition VAT will only be due where

- the vehicle supplied, as a replacement, is of a higher specification due to lack of availability of the original model; or
- the customer has asked for a higher specification vehicle.

Acquisition VAT will then be due on the difference between the original vehicle's value and the replacement vehicles value provided

- the vehicle is returned to the EC country of supply;
- the acquirer notifies the Personal Transport Unit in writing of the return of the faulty vehicle, advising the UK registration mark and vehicle identification number; and
- a replacement invoice for the new vehicle with a copy of the original vehicle invoice is sent to the Personal Transport Unit, with a Form VAT 415 for the new vehicle, so that any additional VAT can be assessed.

(Internal Guidance V1–17, para 4.9).

Records. The person acquiring the NMT must keep his copy of the purchase invoice, and proof that he has paid the VAT, for six years. If the NMT is sold within this period, these records should be passed on to the new owner so that he can demonstrate its VAT status. [*VATA 1994, Sch 11 para 6(1); SI 1995/2518, Reg 31(3)*].

[*SI 1995/2518, Reg 148*]. (VAT Notice 728, paras 3.1–3.15).

Penalties. The provisions of *VATA 1994, s 67* (failure to notify) are extended to impose a penalty where an unregistered person fails to notify an acquisition of a new means of transport. See 52.12 PENALTIES.

23.36 **Acquisitions by persons registered in the UK from other EC countries**

Where a VAT-registered person in the UK acquires a NMT free of VAT from a registered person in another EC country, he should

- provide the supplier or vendor with his UK VAT registration number to enable them to zero-rate the supply of the vehicle;
- account for the VAT due on his normal VAT return for the period in which he acquires the NMT.

If the NMT is a vehicle, it must be licensed and registered before it is used on public roads. When a person applies to register a vehicle on his own behalf, or on behalf of a customer, the DVLA local office (see 23.32 above) will ask for completion of Form VAT 414 declaring the VAT-free status of the vehicle and the VAT registration number used to make the acquisition into the UK. See also 23.32 above for 'type approval' requirements.

Onward supply. Where a VAT-registered person acquires and makes an onward supply of a NMT, he must still account for acquisition VAT on the vehicle. If it forms part of his stock in trade, he can recover input tax equal to the amount of acquisition VAT declared. Output tax must be charged on the onward supply.

(VAT Notice 728, paras 8.1–8.4).

23.37 SALES AND PURCHASES OF SECOND-HAND GOODS

The liability of sales and purchase of second-hand goods within the EC is as follows.

- **Sale by UK-registered person to a person registered in another EC country**.

  Such a sale under the Margin Scheme is taxable in the UK with no further liability to pay VAT on acquisition in another EC country. If the sale is excluded from the Margin Scheme, it may be zero-rated subject to the normal conditions but the customer will not be able to include the goods in a second-hand scheme in his own country.
- **Sale by UK-registered person to a private individual in another EC country**. Such a sale is taxable in the UK. VAT is calculated on the margin for eligible goods sold under one of the schemes for SECOND-HAND GOODS (61).
- **Acquisition by UK-registered person from a person registered in another EC country**. Such an acquisition from a seller who deals with the goods under a second-hand scheme is subject to VAT in the other EC country with no liability to acquisition VAT on entry into the UK. Eligible goods may be sold under one of the schemes for SECOND-HAND GOODS (61) as the invoice will not show VAT as a separate item. If the sale is not dealt with under a second-hand scheme in the other EC country it will be zero-rated subject to the normal conditions and the UK buyer must account for any VAT due on the acquisition. The UK buyer cannot deal with the goods under the Margin Scheme.
- **Acquisition by UK-registered person from a private individual in another EC country**. No VAT is due when the goods are brought into the UK and the goods can therefore be sold under one of the special schemes for SECOND-HAND GOODS (61).
- **Acquisition by a private individual in the UK from a registered person in another EC country**. Such an acquisition is subject to VAT in the other EC country.

23.38 GOODS OBTAINED IN THE EC BY TRAVELLERS RETURNING TO THE UK VIA A NON-EC COUNTRY

Where travellers return to the UK through non-EC countries (including the Channel Islands) carrying goods purchased for their personal use duty and VAT paid in another EC country, no further duty will be payable in the UK on production, if requested, of evidence of payment of that duty and VAT (eg an invoice). (C & E News Release 57/93, 20 August 1993).

24 Exempt Supplies

The contents of this chapter are as follows.

24.1 EXEMPT SUPPLIES

A supply of goods or services is an exempt supply if it is of a description for the time being specified as such under various Group headings in *VATA 1994, Sch 9*. [*VATA 1994, s 31(1)*]. A person who makes exempt supplies but no taxable supplies is not a taxable person and cannot be registered. [*VATA 1994, s 3(1), s 4(2)*]. Output tax is not chargeable on exempt supplies or recoverable on related input tax. Where both exempt and taxable supplies are made, the rules as to PARTIAL EXEMPTION (49) are applied and only part of the input tax may be reclaimable.

The general categories of exemption are

Group 1	Land (see 42.2 LAND AND BUILDINGS)
Group 2	Insurance (see 37 INSURANCE)
Group 3	Postal services (see 24.2 below)
Group 4	Betting, gaming and lotteries (see 57.1–57.4 RECREATION AND SPORT)
Group 5	Finance (see 27 FINANCIAL SERVICES)
Group 6	Education (see 20 EDUCATION)
Group 7	Health and welfare (see 32.1 HEALTH AND WELFARE; 12.11 CHARITIES; 43.12 LOCAL AUTHORITIES AND PUBLIC BODIES and 24.3 below)
Group 8	Burial and cremation (see 19.6 DEATH AND INCAPACITY)
Group 9	Subscriptions to trade unions, professional and other public interest bodies (see 14.7 CLUBS AND ASSOCIATIONS)
Group 10	Sport, sports competitions and physical education (see 57.5 and 57.9 RECREATION AND SPORT)
Group 11	Works of art, etc — certain disposals exempted from capital taxes (see 71.1 WORKS OF ART, ETC)
Group 12	Fund-raising events by charities and other qualifying bodies (see 12.10 CHARITIES)
Group 13	Cultural services, etc — admission to museums, exhibitions, zoos and performances of a cultural nature supplied by public bodies and eligible bodies (see 57.6 RECREATION AND SPORT)
Group 14	Supplies of goods where input tax cannot be recovered (see 24.4 below)
Group 15	Investment gold (see 30.2 GOLD AND PRECIOUS METALS)

[*VATA 1994, Sch 9*].

The descriptions of the Groups above are for ease of reference only and do not affect the interpretation or the description of items within them. [*VATA 1994, s 96(10)*]. The

Treasury may vary the Groups (and notes contained therein which form an integral part) by adding, deleting or amending any description of supply for the time being specified. The *Schedule* may also be varied so as to describe a supply of goods by reference to the use which has been made of them or to other matters unrelated to the characteristics of the goods themselves. [*VATA 1994, s 31(2), s 96(9)*].

Where a supply of goods falls within one of the above Groups but is also covered by the provisions relating to ZERO-RATED SUPPLIES (72), the latter take priority. [*VATA 1994, s 30(1)*].

De Voil Indirect Tax Service. See V4.101–103.

24.2 POSTAL SERVICES

EC legislation. See 22.17(*a*) and 22.18(*i*) EUROPEAN COMMUNITY LEGISLATION.

UK legislation. The following are exempt from VAT.

- The conveyance by the *Post Office Company* (or any of its wholly-owned subsidiaries) of any postal packets ie letters, postcards, reply postcards, newspapers, printed packets, sample packets, parcels and every packet or article transmissible by post (but not telegrams).
- The supply by the *Post Office Company* (or any of its wholly-owned subsidiaries) of any services (except the letting on hire of goods) in connection with the conveyance of postal packets.

[*VATA 1994, Sch 9 Group 3; Postal Services Act 2000, Sch 8 para 22*]. (VAT Notice 48, ESC 3.33).

The cost of postage charged by a supplier in addition to the cost of goods is not within the exemption, see 47.8(18) OUTPUT TAX.

Stamps. Unused current or valid UK and Isle of Man postage stamps are not chargeable with VAT if supplied at or below face value. *First day covers* are taxable at the standard rate on their full value whether supplied by the Post Office Philatelic Bureau or stamp dealers. For stamps generally, see 57.19 RECREATION AND SPORT.

De Voil Indirect Tax Service. See V4.126.

24.3 RELIGIOUS COMMUNITIES

The supply, 'otherwise than for a profit', of goods and services incidental to the provision of 'spiritual welfare' by a religious community (eg a nunnery or monastery) is exempt when supplied to a resident member of that community in return for a subscription or other consideration paid as a condition of membership. [*VATA 1994, Sch 9 Group 7 Item 10*].

'Otherwise than for a profit'. Following the decision in *C & E Commrs v Bell Concord Educational Trust Ltd, CA 1988, [1989] STC 264 (TVC 20.8)*, HMRC accept that supplies are made 'otherwise than for a profit' if they are made by charities in circumstances where any surpluses are applied solely to the furtherance of the activity which generated the surplus. Where, however, a charity pursues more than one activity, the welfare services will not be supplied otherwise than for a profit if surpluses from welfare services are applied to the maintenance or furtherance of the other activities, even though charitable.

'Spiritual welfare' can include

- spiritual counselling to an individual;

- guided exploration of spiritual needs and development; and
- discussion, meditation and prayer or worship sessions

but does not include

- conferences or retreats when the spiritual welfare element is incidental, and not the predominant purpose of the supply;
- educational courses in theology, or similar subjects, where the predominant purpose is to expand knowledge of spiritual matters rather than to provide spiritual welfare services; or
- meetings to discuss theology or aspects of Church doctrine.

(VAT Notice 701/3/04, para 2.9).

24.4 SUPPLIES OF GOODS WHERE INPUT TAX CANNOT BE RECOVERED

A supply of goods is an exempt supply where each of the following conditions is satisfied.

(*a*) The person making the supply (the '*relevant supplier*'), or any 'predecessor' of his, has incurred (or will incur) input tax on obtaining

- the goods supplied; or
- any other goods used in the process of producing the goods supplied so as to be incorporated in them.

For this purpose, input tax is deemed to include VAT incurred by the person concerned when he was not a taxable person (ie when he was not registered or liable to be registered).

In the particular case where the supply is the grant of a 'major interest' in land (see 42.1(9) LAND AND BUILDINGS), other than one excluded under (*c*) below, the input tax must be incurred on either

- acquiring a major interest in the land concerned; or
- goods used in the construction of a building or civil engineering work so as to become part of the land.

(*b*) All of the input tax referred to in (*a*) above is 'non-deductible input tax'.

'*Non-deductible input tax*', subject to below, comprises the following.

(i) Input tax on goods used to make exempt supplies. No part of the input tax may be deductible as attributable to supplies giving a right to input tax deduction, whether the right to deduction arises before or after the supply of goods under consideration. However, an input tax entitlement arising only from the operation of the partial exemption *de minimis* rules (see 49.7 PARTIAL EXEMPTION) is ignored.

(ii) Input tax which is solely excluded from credit under the provisions relating to

- BUSINESS ENTERTAINMENT (9);
- non-building materials incorporated in a building or its site (see 42.15 LAND AND BUILDINGS); or
- motor cars (see 45.3 MOTOR CARS).

(iii) VAT incurred by the person concerned when he was not a taxable person (ie when he was not registered or liable to be registered).

Specifically excluded from non-deductible input tax is any VAT which has been, or will be, recovered under *VATA 1994, s 33* (see 43.7 LOCAL AUTHORITIES AND PUBLIC BODIES), *VATA 1994, s 33A* (museums and galleries, see 35.13(16A) INPUT TAX), *VATA 1994, s 39* (repayments of VAT to overseas traders, see 48.5 OVERSEAS TRADERS) or *VATA 1994, s 41* (refunds to government departments, see 43.11 LOCAL AUTHORITIES AND PUBLIC BODIES). This ensures that exemption under these provisions cannot apply in such cases.

(*c*) The supply made by the relevant supplier is not a supply which would be exempt under *VATA 1994, Sch 9 Group 1 Item 1* (see 42.2 LAND AND BUILDINGS) but for the option to tax having been exercised (see 42.8 LAND AND BUILDINGS).

Self-supplies. Input tax arising on any supply, acquisition or importation of goods is disregarded for the purposes of (*a*) and (*b*) above if, after that supply, etc and before the supply by the relevant supplier, the relevant supplier or any predecessor of his is treated as having self-supplied the goods to himself under any provision of *VATA 1994*. This ensures that, in cases of self-supplies (eg the self-supply of a motor car, on which input tax was initially recovered, following a change of use) exemption under these provisions can still apply.

A person (A) is the '*predecessor*' of another (B) if the goods (or anything comprised in the goods)

- are transferred from A to B as part of a transfer of a going concern which was treated as neither a supply of goods nor a supply of services (see 8.10 *et seq.* BUSINESS); or
- formed part of the assets of A when it became a member of a VAT group of which B was the representative member;
- formed part of the assets of A, or any other company which was a member of the same VAT group as A, when the representative member of the VAT group changed from A to B; or
- formed part of the assets of B when it ceased to be a member of a VAT group of which A was the representative member.

A person's predecessors include the predecessors of his predecessor through any number of transactions.

[*VATA 1994, Sch 9 Group 14; FA 2001, s 98(9); SI 1999/2833*].

Examples where the above provisions apply

- Business cars (see 45.3 MOTOR CARS).
- Goods used for business entertainment (see 9.7 BUSINESS ENTERTAINMENT).
- Fixtures and fittings incorporated by developers in new homes (see 42.15 LAND AND BUILDINGS).
- Goods used by charities for exempt and non-business activities, provided VAT has been incurred on the goods and has not been recovered.

Examples where the above provisions do not apply

- Goods on which any part of the input tax has been or will be recovered, either on purchase or later as a result of partial exemption or capital goods scheme adjustments.
- Goods eligible for the second-hand margin scheme.
- Goods on which no VAT is incurred.
- The resale of services of any type (eg copyrights).

25 Exports

De Voil Indirect Tax Service. See V4.301–339.

The contents of this chapter are as follows.

GENERAL NOTES

(*a*) **Trade with other EC countries**. The provisions of this chapter only apply to goods which are exported outside the EC. See 21.2 EUROPEAN COMMUNITY: GENERAL for the VAT territory of the EC. For the provisions relating to supplies of goods from the UK to other EC countries, see 23.11 EUROPEAN COMMUNITY: SINGLE MARKET.

Cyprus. The European Commission has advised that the application of the *EC 6th Directive* is to be suspended in those areas of Cyprus in which the Government of the Republic of Cyprus does not exercise control. From 1 May 2004, goods sent to these destinations continue to be eligible for treatment as exports.

(*b*) **The Isle of Man**, although not part of the UK, is treated as part of the UK for VAT purposes. All references in this chapter to the UK apply equally to the Isle of Man. Under no circumstances can goods sent to the Isle of Man be treated as exports and VAT must be charged at the appropriate rate. (VAT Notice 703, para 2.7).

(*c*) **The Channel Islands** are part of the EC for customs purposes but *outside* the EC for VAT purposes. Supplies of goods sent to the Channel Islands are therefore regarded as exports. (VAT Notice 703, para 2.7).

25.1 CONDITIONS FOR ZERO-RATING

To zero-rate supplies for export, an 'exporter' must comply with all the following conditions (which have the force of law). If all the conditions cannot be met, the supply cannot be zero-rated as an export and VAT must be accounted for at the appropriate UK rate.

(*a*) The exporter must ensure that the goods are exported from the UK within a specified time limit. For 'direct exports' and 'indirect exports' the time limit is three months from the time of supply.

In most cases, the time of supply is the earlier of

- the date on which the goods are sent to the customer or the customer takes them away, and
- the date full payment is received for the goods.

Any deposit or progress payment received is an advance part payment towards the total cost of the supply and has the same VAT liability as the final supply. If the final supply is to be zero-rated as an export, these payments can also be zero-rated. But if the goods are not eventually exported (or the supplier fails to obtain valid evidence of export), he must account for VAT on the total value of the supply, including any deposit or progress payments.

'*Direct exports*' are where the supplier sends the goods to his customer outside the EC and is responsible either for arranging the transport himself or appointing an agent (see below). The goods may be exported in own baggage or transport, by rail, by post or courier service, by a shipping line or airline, or by an agent employed by the supplier (but not by an agent acting on behalf of an overseas person).

'*Indirect exports*' are where the customer or his agent collects, or arranges for the collection of, the goods from the supplier in the UK and then takes them outside the EC.

(*b*) The exporter must obtain and keep valid commercial evidence or official evidence of export. See 25.24 *et seq* below for acceptable proof of export. The time limit for obtaining this evidence is, for direct exports and indirect exports, three months from the time of supply.

(*c*) In the case of direct exports, the supplier must not

- deliver or post the goods to a UK customer's address in the UK; or
- allow the goods to be collected by or on behalf of a UK customer even if it is claimed that they are for subsequent export. See 25.9 below for details of deliveries made to another UK trader for consolidation, processing or incorporation prior to export.

(*d*) In the case of indirect exports, the supplier must not supply goods to

- a private customer who is resident in the UK; or
- an overseas business that has a place of business in the UK from which taxable supplies are made.

(*e*) The exporter must keep supplementary evidence of the export transaction (see 25.24 *et seq* below).

(*f*) The exporter must comply with the conditions specified in the legislation and in VAT Notice 703 which for this purpose has the force of law. As to whether the conditions laid down by HMRC are reasonable or complied with, see *Henry Moss of London Ltd and Another v C & E Commrs, CA 1980, [1981] STC 139 (TVC 24.1)*.

An '*exporter*' is the person who, for VAT purposes,

- supplies and controls the export of the goods,
- supplies the goods directly to a person who resides outside the EC; or
- where there is no such supply (see 25.23 below), is the owner of the goods exported.

(VAT Notice 703, paras 2.3, 2.10, 2.11, 2.13, 3.3, 3.4, 11.4).

Effect of failure to comply with conditions. Where the supply of any goods has been zero-rated as an export and either

- any of the above conditions (or any other specific conditions relating to a particular type of export) is not complied with, or
- the goods are found in the UK after the date of alleged exportation,

the goods are liable to *forfeiture*. Any VAT which would have been due but for zero-rating is payable forthwith by the person to whom the goods were supplied or by any other person in whose possession the goods are found in the UK. HMRC may waive payment of the VAT in whole or part. [*VATA 1994, s 30*(*10*)].

Appointment of an agent. A supplier (or for indirect exports an overseas customer) can appoint a freight forwarder, shipping company, airline or other person to handle the export transactions and produce the necessary declarations to customs on their behalf. The agent must be provided with a full description of the goods, including value, quantity and weight, together with export invoices, packing lists and technical details to enable the export declaration and transport documents to be completed accurately. The agent must then

- take reasonable steps to ensure that the goods are as described by the exporter;
- ensure the customs formalities are complied with;
- ensure the goods exported within the time limits;
- keep records of each export transaction;
- obtain and provide valid evidence of export and send it to the exporter once the goods have been exported; and
- notify the HMRC Export Officer if the export is aborted after lodgement of the export documentation.

If the agent fails to fulfil its obligations, the supplier or overseas customer is responsible for accounting for any VAT which becomes chargeable.

(VAT Notice 703, paras 2.4, 2.5).

De Voil Indirect Tax Service. See V4.305, V4.307, V4.309.

25.2 **CATEGORIES OF ZERO-RATED EXPORTS**

Subject to meeting the general conditions in 25.1 above and any specific conditions in the appropriate paragraph of this chapter, the following categories of exports are zero-rated.

- **Direct exports**. [*VATA 1994, s 30(6)*]. See 25.1(*a*) above.
- **Stores for ships, aircraft, etc** [*VATA 1984, s 30(6)*]. See 25.3 below.
- **Certain supplies in connection with the management of defence projects**. [*VATA 1994, Sch 8 Group 13 Item 2*]. See 25.4 below.
- **Tools for the manufacture of goods for export**. [*VATA 1994, Sch 8 Group 13 Item 3*]. See 25.5 below.
- **Goods exported by a charity** (whatever the nature of the goods). [*VATA 1994, Sch 8 Group 15 Item* 3]. See 12.6 CHARITIES.
- **Exports of freight containers**. [*SI 1995/2518, Reg 128*]. See 25.7 below.
- **Supplies to overseas persons**. [*SI 1995/2518, Reg 129*]. See 25.8 and 25.9 below.
- **Supplies to persons departing from the EC – retail export scheme**. [*SI 1995/2518, Regs 130, 131*]. See 25.11 to 25.15 below.
- **Exports of motor vehicles**. [*SI 1995/2518, Regs 132, 133*]. See 25.16 to 25.18 below.
- **Sailaway boats supplied for export**. See 25.19 below.
- **Supplies to the FCO and other government departments**. See 25.20 below.
- **Supplies to regimental shops**. See 25.21 below.
- **Supplies intended for continental shelf installations**. See 25.22 below.
- **Supplies at tax-free shops**. Where goods which are liable to VAT are supplied to persons leaving on flights to destinations outside the EC at tax-free shops approved by HMRC, the supplier may be regarded as the exporter and zero-rate the supply of those goods which are exported. See VAT Notice 48, ESC 8.1.

25.3 **Stores for use in ships, aircraft or hovercraft**

Stores are goods for use in a ship, aircraft or hovercraft and include

- fuel;
- goods for running repairs or maintenance (eg lubricants, spare and replacement parts);
- goods for general use on board by the crew; and
- goods for sale by retail to persons carried on voyages or flights who intend to use the stores on board only.

A supplier can zero-rate supplies of stores for the fuelling and provisioning of vessels and aircraft provided

- they are for use on a voyage or flight with a non-private purpose and with an eventual destination outside the UK (see below for an extra-statutory concession covering supplies of marine fuel to vessels for voyages in home waters);
- they are shipped from the UK within three months of supply; and
- the conditions outlined in (*b*) below are met.

A VAT-registered shipping line or airline operator can choose either of the following options for supplies made to it.

(*a*) It can have all supplies, including those intended for stores, delivered to its premises and charged to VAT at the appropriate rate. If so, input tax can be deducted (subject to the normal rules) and the subsequent transfer of the goods from the premises to the ship or aircraft is a non-supply.

(*b*) It can have supplies of eligible stores made direct to the foreign-going craft. Such supplies can then be zero-rated provided the following conditions are met.

(i) The person to whom the goods are supplied is the end user (eg the master of the vessel).

(ii) The goods are for use as stores on a voyage or flight which is to be made for a non-private purpose and the person to whom the goods are to be supplied declares this in writing.

(iii) The stores are to be shipped from the UK within three months of supply.

(iv) The supplier obtains and keeps a written order or confirmation given by the master or duly authorised agent. This must contain a declaration that the goods are solely for use as stores on a named ship or aircraft that is entitled to duty-free stores for the voyage or flight in question ie to an eventual destination outside the UK. Aircraft making through international flights are eligible to receive VAT-free stores even if the aircraft makes one or more stops in the UK in the course of such a flight.

(v) The goods must be sent either direct to the ship or aircraft or through freight forwarders for consolidation and delivery direct to the ship or aircraft or addressed and delivered to the master c/o the shipping company or agent.

(vi) The supplier must obtain and keep a receipt confirming delivery of the goods on board the ship or aircraft signed by the master, commander or other responsible officer of the ship or aircraft. The supplier can accept such a receipt signed by a responsible official of the airline concerned but airlines using this facility must obtain prior written agreement from HMRC. The airline must confirm that the signatory is in a position to provide the receipt based on personal knowledge of flight details and that the airline will maintain documentation enabling HMRC staff to verify entitlement to relief.

(vii) Where supplies are made direct from a warehouse not operated or owned by the supplier to an eligible vessel or aircraft, the supplier must hold a signed and dated certificate of export from the warehousekeeper. The advice note issued by the warehousekeeper normally serves this purpose.

Where goods are supplied to a shore-side storage tank, the supplier may not zero-rate the supply unless he holds the necessary evidence that his customer is the exporter of the goods.

Goods for sale. These provisions also apply to goods supplied for sale in ships' shops and on board aircraft even though there may be no taxable supply at the time of shipment (eg transfer of own goods, supply on sale or return terms). Where goods have been shipped on a foreign-going ship or aircraft, any later sale of the goods is a supply outside the UK and there is no further liability to VAT unless they are re-landed (see below). VAT is charged on goods sold on board a vessel on a coastwise journey or aircraft on an internal flight.

Relanded stores. Stores supplied under the above provisions and re-landed are treated as IMPORTS (34).

Marine fuel. By concession, vessels engaged on commercial voyages within UK territorial waters (or within the limits of a port) may receive certain types of fuel VAT-free. The supplier can zero-rate the supply provided

- a written declaration is obtained from the person to whom the marine fuel is supplied that the goods are for use as stores on a non-private voyage;
- a written order or confirmation is obtained from the master, owner or duly authorised agent of the vessel declaring that the fuel is solely for use on a named ship;
- the fuel is sent direct to the ship or addressed and delivered to the master of a named vessel c/o the shipping agent or line; and
- a receipt confirming delivery of the fuel on board, signed by the master or other responsible officer, is held.

The concession extends only to those supplies of fuel which were zero-rated before 1 July 1990. It does not cover petrol, ultra low sulphur diesel (ULSD) or lubricating oil.

Mess and canteen stores. Goods can be zero-rated where supplied for use as mess and canteen stores on HM ships about to leave for a foreign port or a voyage outside UK territorial waters of more than 15 days' duration. The goods must be ordered for the general use on board by the ship's company. Orders must be certified by the Commanding Officer and goods delivered direct to the ship. A receipt must be obtained and kept.

Duty-free goods supplied on sale or return to messes in HM ships cannot be zero-rated when sent out to the ship. The taxable supply occurs only when the goods are adopted, ie

- when the customer pays for the goods or otherwise indicates his wish to keep them; or
- at the end of twelve months or any shorter period agreed for the goods to be bought or returned.

The supplier is responsible for ensuring that the messes inform him promptly of when the adoption of the goods took place. If adoption occurs when the vessel is in UK territorial waters, the supply is taxable; if outside, there is no supply for VAT purposes. Commanders of HM ships will provide suppliers with this information.

[*VATA 1994, s 30(6)*]. (VAT Notice 703, paras 8.2, 10.1–10.7; VAT Notice 48, ESC 9.2).

De Voil Indirect Tax Service. See V4.321; V4.322.

25.4 **International collaboration defence arrangements (ICDAs)**

The supply to, or by, an 'overseas authority', 'overseas body' or 'overseas trader', charged with the management of any defence project which is the subject of an 'international collaboration arrangement' (or under direct contract with any government or government-sponsored international body participating in defence projects under such an arrangement) of goods or services made for the purpose of fulfilling contracts is zero-rated. The zero-rating only applies to a limited number of projects and traders who are concerned with them are notified individually by HMRC.

'*Overseas authority*' means any country other than the UK or any part of, or place in, such a country or the government of such a country, part or place.

'*Overseas body*' means a body established outside the UK.

'*Overseas trader*' means a person who carries on a business and has a principal place of business outside the UK.

An '*international collaboration arrangement*' is any arrangement made between the UK government and the government of one or more other countries (or any government-sponsored international body, eg NATO) for collaboration in a joint project of research, development or production. The arrangement must specifically provide for participating governments to relieve the cost of the project from taxation.

[*VATA 1994, Sch 8 Group 13 Item 2*].

Under an ICDA, the responsibility for project definition, direction, control and funding rests with the participating governments (with the Ministry of Defence (MOD) representing the UK). The participants usually use a single body as a project management organisation (PMO). This may be an agency of one of the governments (eg the MOD Procurement Executive) or a multi-national body which may be set up specifically for the purpose (eg the NATO Multi-Role Combat Aircraft Management Agency). A PMO is funded by the participants and acts as contracting authority to procure the work required. It will be responsible to the participants and will employ one or more prime contractors which it will pay with funds provided by the participants. Any UK PMO will be registered for VAT. Participants' funding of the PMO is consideration for supplies by the PMO to the extent that the supplies come within the scope of UK VAT. Prime contractors will be appointed by the PMO (or the individual participants if there is not a PMO) from different countries to carry out specific technical responsibilities. Each prime contractor may engage first level subcontractors who may in turn engage second level subcontractors and so on. Zero-rating under *VATA 1994, Sch 8 Group 13 Item 2* cannot apply below the first level of transactions between a prime contractor and a first level subcontractor.

The agreement reached by the different governments involved in the project is recorded in a Memorandum of Understanding (MOU). This document determines whether the project is approved as an ICDA for the purposes of *Item 2*. If so, the MOD will notify HMRC and give details of the participants, PMO (if any) and prime contractor(s) for the individual projects. Zero-rating then applies to any supply by or to any of these bodies where one or other of them belongs overseas and the supply is in a chain that leads to the delivery to the participants of services or equipment in accordance with the objectives of the arrangement.

All supplies made in the UK between the MOD and UK contractors follow the normal VAT rules as relief under *Item 2* applies only to supplies made to or by an overseas body charged with the management of an ICDA. Goods forming part of an ICDA may be delivered from one participating contractor to another within the UK for process or assembly.

Following discussions with the MOD, HMRC accept that relief under *Item 2* includes the supply of the finished product (ie the final supply) of a collaborative project.

Own variant products from ICDAs which, whilst researched, developed or produced jointly, include features specific to the requirements of an individual country, qualify for relief under *Item 2* provided they are funded by the ICDA.

(Internal Guidance V1–7, Chapter 13 paras 3.1, 3.2, 4.1, 4.3, 4.5, 4.6). See Internal Guidance V1–7 Chapter 13 generally for further information.

De Voil Indirect Tax Service. See V4.283.

25.5 **Tools for the manufacture of goods for export**

The supply to an 'overseas authority', 'overseas body' or 'overseas trader' (see 25.4 above) of jigs, patterns, templates, dies, moulds, punches and similar machine tools used in the UK solely for the manufacture of goods for export is zero-rated. The overseas authority, etc must not be

- a taxable person,
- another EC country,
- any part of or place in another EC country,
- the government of any such country, part or place,
- a body established in another EC country, or
- a person who carries on business, or has a place of business, in another EC country,

otherwise the supply is taxable in the normal way.

[*VATA 1994, Sch 8 Group 13 Item 3*].

A machine tool is supplied for these purposes where the customer specifically asks the supplier to make it, or buy it, for him and the supplier

- uses the machine tool to manufacture goods for the same customer; and
- makes a specific charge to the customer for the supply of the tool.

In addition to holding normal commercial proof of export, the supplier must obtain a signed statement (or other similar definite evidence) from the customer that they are neither registered nor required to be registered in the UK and are not an authority, body or trader in another EC country.

(VAT Notice 701/22/02, paras 1.4, 2.1).

25.6 **Export houses**

An 'export house' is any person registered for VAT in the UK who, in the course of business in the UK, arranges or finances the export of goods from the UK to a place outside the EC.

Supplies by export houses. Export houses can zero-rate supplies to overseas customers as exports subject to the normal conditions.

Supplies to export houses. Supplies to export houses are treated in the same way as any other supplies made to UK customers.

De Voil Indirect Tax Service. See V4.324.

25.7 **Freight containers supplied for export**

Subject to such conditions as HMRC impose, the supply of a 'container' is zero-rated where HMRC are satisfied that it is to be exported.

For these purposes, a '*container*' is defined as an article of transport equipment (lift-van, movable tank or similar structure)

- fully or partially enclosed to constitute a compartment for goods;
- of a permanent character strong enough for repeated use;
- designed to facilitate the carriage of goods, by one or more modes of transport, without intermediate reloading;
- designed for ready handling and to be easy to fill and empty; and
- having an internal volume of one cubic metre or more.

It includes accessories and equipment as appropriate but excludes vehicles, spares for vehicles and packaging.

[*SI 1995/2518, Regs 117(2), 128*].

Although not strictly within the definition, 'flats' or 'Lancashire flats' (ie bases with or without head and tail boards which are designed to carry goods and have the floor area of a 20 ft or 40 ft container) are included, as are air transport containers whatever their internal volume. Pallets, road vehicles and trailers including tanks on wheels are not included. (VAT Notice 703/1/04, para 2.1).

Direct export. The supply of a container for direct export may be zero-rated provided the container is actually exported and the normal conditions for export are complied with. (VAT Notice 703/1/04, para 2.2).

Indirect export. The supply of a freight container for indirect export may be zero-rated provided the supplier obtains a written undertaking from the customer that

(*a*) the container will be exported from the EC;

(*b*) the container will not be used in the EC except for

  (i) a single domestic journey before export (on which inland freight may be carried) on a reasonably direct route between the point of supply and the place where the container is to be loaded with the export cargo or exported; and

  (ii) international movement of goods (which may include a journey within the UK for the purpose of loading or unloading the goods);

(*c*) the customer will keep records sufficient to satisfy HMRC that

  (i) the container has not been used in the EC (except as allowed under (*b*) above); and

  (ii) the container has either been exported or has been sold/leased to someone else who has given a similar written undertaking.

(VAT Notice 703/1/04, paras 2.4, 2.5 which have the force of law).

Lease or hire of containers. *Where the supplier and the customer both belong in the UK*, the supply is treated as made in the UK and VAT must be charged on the supply.

However, if the customer is to export the container from the EC, the leasing/hiring may be zero-rated provided the supplier obtains a written undertaking from the customer as for indirect exports above.

Where the supplier belongs in the UK but the customer belongs outside the EC, the supply is treated as being made in the customer's country and no UK VAT is due.

Incidental charges which under the terms of the lease agreement are charged to the lessee are regarded as part of the consideration for the leasing of the container and have the same VAT liability. Included are repair, delivery, regulator and handling charges, extra rental and any charge for the option to terminate the lease at an earlier date.

(VAT Notice 703/1/04, paras 2.7, 2.10).

De Voil Indirect Tax Service. See V4.323.

25.8 Supplies to overseas persons

Where HMRC are satisfied that goods intended for export have been supplied to an 'overseas person' who is not a taxable person, the supply is zero-rated. For export of motor vehicles generally, see 25.16 to 25.18 below.

'*Overseas person*' is

- a person not resident in the UK;
- a trader who has no business establishment in the UK from which taxable supplies are made; or
- an overseas authority (ie any country other than the UK or any part or place in such a country or the government of any such country, part or place). This includes goods ordered through embassies, High Commissions and purchasing agents of foreign governments in the UK.

For supplies made before 1 July 2003, the above provisions did not apply to supplies to a member of a crew of any ship or aircraft departing from the UK. Instead the retail export scheme could be used (see 25.11 below).

[*SI 1995/2518, Regs 117(7), 129; SI 1996/210; SI 2003/1485*].

Supplies to overseas persons generally are indirect exports and must meet the normal conditions for zero-rating of such supplies (see 25.1 above). In addition, in the case of supplies to overseas authorities which are ordered through their embassies, High Commissions or purchasing agents in the UK, HMRC require the following conditions to be satisfied before the supply can be zero-rated.

- The supplier must keep a separate record of each transaction, including evidence that the supply has been to an overseas authority (eg the order for the goods, sales invoice made out to the overseas authority, evidence of payment from the overseas authority, etc).
- The goods must not be used between the time of leaving the supplier's premises and export, either for their normal purpose or for display, exhibition or copying.

(VAT Notice 703, paras 3.4, 4.11).

De Voil Indirect Tax Service. See V4.326.

25.9 *Supplies to overseas persons for export after consolidation, processing or incorporation*

Goods supplied for export to an overseas person but delivered to a third person in the UK who is also making a taxable supply to that overseas person are zero-rated provided

(*a*) the goods are only being delivered and not supplied to the third person in the UK;

(*b*) no use is made of the goods other than for processing or incorporation into other goods, or consolidation with other goods, for export;

(*c*) the goods are exported from the EC within six months of the time of supply and proof of export is obtained within the same time limit.

(*d*) the supplier's records show the

- name and address of the overseas person,
- invoice number and date,
- description, quantity and value of goods,
- name and address of the third person in the UK to whom the goods were delivered,
- date by which the goods must be exported and proof of export obtained, and
- date of actual exportation.

In cases where the third party is not the UK but in another EC country, the same conditions will generally apply to allow the supply to be zero-rated.

(VAT Notice 703, para 3.6).

Racehorses. Where a racehorse is supplied to an overseas person but is to remain in the UK for breaking, conditioning, training or covering before export, under an agreement between HMRC, the British Horseracing Board and the Thoroughbred Breeders Association the vendor can ask HMRC to extend the time limit in (*c*) above from six months to twelve months from the date of purchase. The extension is subject to the conditions that

- the horse must not be raced in the UK before export; and
- the relief cannot be transferred to another overseas person.

(VAT Notice 700/57/04).

25.10 Multiple transactions leading to a single movement of goods

Where a single movement of goods is supported by two or more transactions, only the final transaction can be zero-rated.

Example

A (outside the EC) orders goods from B (in the UK). B purchases the goods from C (also in the UK) but instead of taking delivery of the goods, agrees with C that it will send the goods directly to A.

The supply of goods from C to B is a UK supply and VAT must be charged at the appropriate rate. The supply of goods by B to A is zero-rated as an export if the necessary conditions are met.

(VAT Notice 703, para 4.1).

Retail export scheme

25.11 The VAT retail export scheme allows

- overseas visitors (see 25.12(*a*) below) to receive a refund of VAT paid on goods exported to destinations outside the EC subject to the conditions in 25.12 below being met; and
- retailers to zero-rate goods sold to overseas visitors when they have the necessary evidence of export and have refunded the VAT to the customer.

See 21.2 EUROPEAN COMMUNITY: GENERAL for the VAT territory of the EC.

It is a voluntary scheme and retailers do not have to operate it. Where it is operated, retailers

- need not operate it for all lines of goods; and
- can set a minimum sales value below which they will not operate the scheme.

A simplified Notice aimed specifically at travellers, VAT Notice 704/1 *Tax Free Shopping: VAT Refunds for travellers departing from the European Community* (*EC*), highlights the main aspects of the scheme. It is available, in various languages, from the National Advice Service (tele: 0845 010 9000). Copies can be usefully given to customers using the scheme.

(VAT Notice 704, paras 1.5, 2.1, 2.2, 2.7).

Various changes were made to the scheme with effect from 1 July 2003 including withdrawal of the scheme for goods exported as freight, special arrangements for cruise operators and the amalgamation of certain procedures and forms. See Tolley's VAT 2003 First Edition and earlier editions for full details of the earlier rules.

Conditions for using the scheme

25.12 Retailers and refund companies can only operate the scheme when the following conditions (which have the force of law) are met.

(*a*) The customer must be an 'overseas visitor'. For these purposes, an '*overseas visitor*' is one of the following.

(i) A traveller (including a member of the crew of a ship or aircraft) who is not established in the EC. This means a person

- whose domicile or habitual residence is not situated within the EC. For this purpose, a person's domicile or habitual residence is the place entered as such on their valid passport, identity card or other acceptable document such as a driving licence (which must be produced to the retailer to prove eligibility);

- who intends to leave the UK for a final destination outside the EC, with the goods, by the last day of the third month following that in which the goods were purchased; and
- who exports the goods having produced them, their receipts and the VAT refund document to an HMRC officer at the point of departure from the EC.

Student or migrant workers entering the UK from outside the EC are classed as overseas visitors but to avoid abuse of the system (by reclaiming VAT under the scheme prior to returning home and then bringing the goods back to the UK within a short period of time), with effect from 1 October 2004, such persons additionally

- are only entitled to purchase goods under the scheme during the last four months of their stay in the UK; and
- having left the EC must remain outside the EC for a minimum period of 12 months.

Such a visitor will have been issued with a pre-entry visa and, in the case of work periods of six months or more, a separate work permit document by the UK authorities. The visa is contained in the passport and shows the start and end date for the study or work period authorised. Retailers should ask to see the visa or work permit before selling goods under the scheme.

(ii) For the purposes of this scheme only, a traveller established in the EC who

- intends to leave the UK with the goods by the last day of the third month following that in which the goods were purchased for an immediate destination outside the EC;
- remains outside the EC for a period of at least 12 months (which must be proved to the retailer typically by evidence such as an overseas work permit, approved visa application or residency permit); and
- exports the goods having produced them, their receipts and the VAT refund document to an HMRC officer at the point of departure from the EC.

(*b*) The goods must be eligible to be purchased under the scheme. Any standard-rated and lower-rated goods can be sold under the scheme except for the following.

- New and second-hand motor vehicles for personal export (see 25.16 below).
- Sailaway boats (see 25.19 below).
- Goods over £600 in value (excluding VAT) exported for the customer's business purposes.
- Goods that will be exported as freight or unaccompanied baggage.
- Goods requiring an export licence (apart from antiques). Antiques may be exported only on production of a valid export licence to HMRC at the point of departure from the UK. Further advice can be obtained from

The Department of Culture, Media and Sport
2–4 Cockspur Street
London SW1Y 5DH

A retailer selling goods treated as antiques should explain this to customers as they will probably need assistance to obtain an export licence.

- Unmounted gemstones.
- Bullion (over 125g, 2.75 troy ounces or 10 Tolas).
- Goods for consumption in the EC. (No certification of export will be given for used consumable items (eg perfumes) which are wholly or partly consumed in the EC.)
- Goods purchased by mail order including those purchased over the internet. However, a mail order company or an internet retailer with a retail outlet can use the scheme for goods sold from that outlet provided all the conditions of the scheme are complied with.

The scheme cannot be used for

- zero-rated goods (eg books and children's clothing); or
- supplies of services (eg hotel accommodation, meals and car hire). This applies even where services are sold with the goods (eg labour costs for fitting spare parts to a motor vehicle). Where a vehicle brought into the UK for the use of the overseas visitor requires repairs, the sale of the spare parts only and not the cost of fitting can be included in the scheme. Extended warranty work cannot be zero-rated under the retail export scheme.

(*c*) The customer must make the purchase in person and complete the form in full at the retailer's premises at the time of sale (although a third party may pay for the goods). It is not possible for a representative to attend in place of the customer at the time of sale.

(*d*) The goods must be exported from the EC by the last day of the third month following that in which the goods are purchased (eg goods bought on 3 February must be exported by 31 May). This time limit cannot be extended. Goods exported after the time limit must not be zero-rated even if the VAT refund document has been stamped in error by a UK or other EC Customs officer.

(*e*) The customer must send the retailer or refund company evidence of export stamped by HMRC on an official version of Form VAT 407, an approved version of Form VAT 407 or an officially approved invoice. See 25.13 below.

(*f*) The retailer or refund company must not zero-rate the supply until the VAT has been refunded to the customer (see 25.15 below).

[*SI 1995/2518, Regs 117(7A)–(7D), 131; SI 1995/3147; SI 1999/438, Reg 10; SI 2003/1485*]. (VAT Notice 704, paras 2.3, 2.4, 2.6, 2.8, 2.9, 3.1, 6.5).

De Voil Indirect Tax Service. See V4.331.

Procedure

25.13 *At the time of sale*, a retailer should:

- Check that the customer is entitled to use the scheme (see 25.12(*a*) above).

- Check that the goods are eligible for the scheme (see 25.12(*b*) above).
- Check the eligible customer is present to buy the goods (see 25.12(*c*) above).
- Check that the customer intends to leave the EC with the goods for a final destination outside the EC by the last day of the third month following that in which the goods were purchased.
- Fill in a VAT refund document (see below). A responsible member of staff should ensure all sections are fully completed, unused lines are ruled through and the customer and retailer declarations are signed at the time of the sale.

  By concession, HMRC allow completion of the refund form on production of receipts for past purchases provided the retailer can satisfy HMRC that it has adequate security procedures in place to prevent abuse of the scheme. This includes

  (i) stamping till receipts to show that the goods have been purchased under the retail export scheme (eg 'VAT Export');

  (ii) a till system allowing the retailer to check that the receipts produced are genuine and can only appear once on a VAT 407 refund document; and

  (iii) a system allowing the retailer to check whether a refund for returned goods has already been made for a receipt produced or a VAT 407 refund document has been issued for goods where a refund for returned goods is sought.

  Where a retailer cannot show that it has adequate security procedures in place, it must only complete VAT refund documents at the time of the sale.

  Where a retailer does have adequate safeguards in place and a customer asks for a refund document to cover a series of purchases over a period of time, the retailer must include only those goods that will be exported by the last day of the third month following that in which the goods were purchased. The purchase date entered on the refund document must be the date of the earliest purchase.
- Give the customer a copy of VAT Notice 704/1 *Tax-free shopping: VAT refunds for travellers departing from the EC*.
- Agree with the customer how the refund will be made.
- Explain any administrative or handling fees to be deducted from the VAT refund to avoid any subsequent misunderstanding.
- Mark the customer's sales receipt to indicate that the goods have been included on a VAT refund document (eg 'VAT Export').
- Explain that no refund will be made on items (eg perfume) wholly or partly consumed in the EC.
- Advise the customer that any items not exported from the UK should be clearly deleted from the refund document before it is presented to a UK or EC Customs officer for stamping and that it is an offence to make a false declaration.
- Advise the customer that he must produce the refund document (together with the goods and receipts, if required) to the Customs officer for stamping at the point of departure from the EC and explain that failure to do so will mean that a VAT refund will not be made.

- Advise the customer to allow plenty of time in which to produce the goods and refund form prior to departure. (This is particularly important if they are exporting goods in hold baggage as they may need to allow up to two hours in addition to the advised check in time.)
- Advise the customer to carry items of high value (eg jewellery, furs, cameras, watches, silverware, lap top computers and small antiques) in hand baggage.

The VAT refund document can be either of the following.

(*a*) Form VAT 407, in which case it can be either

- Form VAT 407 issued by HMRC and available free of charge from the National Advice Service; or
- the retailer's or refund company's own version of Form VAT 407 containing the same information as HMRC's version and approved beforehand by HMRC.

Part A of the form must be completed in full by the customer at the time of sale.

Part B, which is for completion by the retailer, must include a full and accurate description of the goods quoting identification numbers, serial numbers or other identifying marks (eg hallmarks) together with the quantity (and weight in the case of jewellery) of goods sold. Descriptions such as stock numbers, 'See invoice attached', 'Jewellery' or 'Designer goods' are not acceptable. The description must be clear enough to allow the UK or EC Customs officer to readily identify the goods. Any unused lines on the form should be crossed through. Each of the following must be shown.

- The total amount payable (including VAT) in both words and figures.
- The VAT included in the price.
- The amount of any administration fee that will be deducted from the refund.
- The amount of refund to be paid to the customer.

Part C is the retailer's declaration. It must show

- the retailer's full business name, address and VAT number; and
- the date the goods were sold to the customer;

and must be signed by a responsible person.

Part D is for official use and will be stamped by the Customs officer at the point of departure from the EC to validate the export. (Whilst desirable, it is not essential the Customs officer signs the form.) Customs officers may refuse to stamp refund forms completed incorrectly or not completed in full. For example, forms showing inadequate descriptions of goods may be rejected.

(*b*) A sales invoice approved beforehand by HMRC. It must closely follow the design of Form VAT 407, and ideally be A4 size or A5 size.

It must include the data protection statement shown on the face of the form and the information shown on the reverse side of the HMRC version of Form VAT 407. This includes

- the heading 'Retail Export Scheme';

- providing spaces for the retailer's and the customer's declarations as stipulated on the Form VAT 407, including details of the customer's passport/identity number and country of issue, date of arrival in the EC, intended date of departure from the EC; and
- a separate box not less than 5cm by 3.5cm for official stamping by a Customs officer at the customer's point of departure from the EC.

The total amount payable must be shown in words as well as figures. The invoice must also show the amount of any administrative charge and the net refund due to the customer.

In addition, any officially approved invoice must also meet the requirements of invoicing legislation generally. See 40.7 INVOICES for requirements of a retailer's less detailed invoice where the consideration does not exceed £250 and, where the customer agrees, a modified invoice. Otherwise the invoice must comply with the full requirements of an invoice under 40.4 INVOICES.

Whilst a single refund document is acceptable, it is recommended that retailers issue separate VAT refund documents (but make only one administrative charge) for customers intending to carry some goods in hand baggage and other goods in hold baggage. This is particularly important for customers leaving on a through (transit) flight via another EC airport because the goods in hold baggage must be declared before check in, whilst the goods in hand baggage must be declared at the final point of departure from the EC.

On completion of the refund document, the customer should be given

- the refund document;
- a reply-paid envelope addressed to the retailer or, as the case may be, the refund company administering the refund (alternatively, the retailer should make it clear that it is the customer's responsibility to provide the envelope and pay the correct postage); and
- a copy of VAT Notice 704/1

and advised to produce the refund document (together with the goods and receipts if required) to the Customs officer at the point of departure from the EC.

Control of blank or partly completed VAT refund documents. Whichever form of refund document is used, retailers must keep stocks of the blank documents secure and not issue blank or partly completed forms to any person outside the business.

Goods returned for refund or exchange. If a customer wishes to return goods that have been sold under the scheme (either for a full refund or for exchange) he must take the receipt and the VAT refund document back to the retailer. The retailer should delete the entry for the returned goods (or cancel the VAT refund document and issue a new one) as appropriate.

Action required by the customer on leaving the UK. If the customer decides to leave any goods bought under the scheme in the EC, he must clearly delete those items from the VAT refund document before presenting it, and the remaining goods, to HMRC for examination and stamping.

Action required for goods which are taken outside the EC depends upon how the customer is leaving the EC.

- If leaving for an immediate destination outside the EC, the VAT refund document must be presented to HMRC at the port/airport of departure from the UK. The goods and receipts must be available for inspection if required. (If leaving by air, goods too large or too heavy to be carried on board an aircraft can be packed in hold baggage but, in this case, the VAT refund document should be presented to HMRC before checking in. But high value items including jewellery, furs, cameras, expensive watches, silverware, laptop computers and small antiques, should be carried in hand baggage.)

- If leaving the EC via another EC country, the goods and the refund form must be presented to the Customs authorities of that country.
- If leaving the EC on a through (transit) flight via another EC airport,
  - (i) goods carried as hand baggage must be produced, with the refund form, to Customs in the last EC airport before leaving the EC; and
  - (ii) goods carried as hold baggage must be produced, with the refund form, to HMRC before checking in baggage.

Where a HMRC officer cannot be located to stamp the refund document (eg because there is no 24-hour HMRC presence) there will either be a telephone to speak to HMRC or a clearly marked post box to deposit the refund document and a reply-paid envelope.

There is no facility to have a refund document stamped in the country of destination outside the EC.

If satisfied, HMRC will certify the VAT refund document and return it to the customer. The customer must then (depending on whichever method was agreed with the retailer)

- post the refund document back to the retailer to arrange payment of the refund;
- post the refund document to a VAT refund company to arrange payment of the refund; or
- hand the refund document to a cash refund booth operated by the refund company at the airport of departure from the UK which will arrange immediate payment. (Not all airports or refund companies offer this facility.)

Receipt of evidence by the retailer. On receipt of a refund document stamped by UK or other EC Customs, the retailer or refund company must check that all goods have been exported from the EC by the last day of the third month following that in which the goods were purchased and, if so, make the refund to the customer by the method agreed at the time of sale. If a refund document is sent back unstamped, the retailer cannot zero-rate the supply because export of the goods from the EC has not been certified as required by the scheme.

Loss of VAT refund documents. If a customer loses the refund document *before* leaving the EC, the retailer may provide a duplicate clearly marked as such. When issuing the document, the retailer should

- make sure the original document has not been received and already processed;
- be satisfied that a sale took place by the production of till receipts or other information; and
- advise the customer that, if he subsequently finds the original refund document, it is to be cancelled.

If the customer loses the refund document *after* certification by HMRC, a duplicate may only be issued where a photocopy of the stamped original is produced. The duplicate and photocopy must then be sent to the HMRC officer who stamped the original document for certification of the duplicate. Only then should the refund be made.

(VAT Notice 704, paras 3.1–3.7, 4.1–4.4, 4.7, 4.8, 4.10, 4.11, 6.1, 6.4, 7.5–7.7).

Special arrangements for intra-EC cruises

25.14 Non-EC passengers on wholly intra-EC cruises may not have access to their luggage and to any purchases made under the retail export scheme from disembarkation until they arrive at their final non-EC destination. They cannot, therefore, produce the goods and VAT refund document to the Customs officer for stamping at their point of final departure from the EC. The special arrangements outlined below apply to wholly intra-EC cruises

- which start in the UK; and
- where the final port of disembarkation is also within the UK.

(*a*) *Individual purchases below £1,000*

Cruise operators may produce an omnibus bulk refund document for all eligible goods below £1,000 per item purchased on board by entitled individual passengers. This document must accompany the passengers' luggage to the airport of departure. If satisfied, the Customs officer will stamp the bulk refund form and return it to the cruise operator. On receipt of the certified form, the cruise operator must account for the sales in their VAT records as under 25.15 below.

The format of the bulk refund document must be approved beforehand by HMRC. It must be clearly headed 'Retail Export Scheme' and must only include those goods that

- were sold on board the vessel;
- are supplied to entitled customers (see 25.12(*a*) above); and
- are eligible to be supplied under the retail export scheme (see 25.12(*b*) above).

It must also give the following details.

- Cruise operator's name, address and VAT registration number.
- Customers' name and usual address.
- Customers' passport number and country of issue.
- A description which clearly identifies the goods and the quantity involved.
- The amount payable per item. (Where this includes VAT, the amount payable inclusive of VAT and the amount of VAT included in the total price should be shown.)

In addition, the refund document must include a retailer declaration as stipulated on Form VAT 407 which must be signed by a responsible ship's officer, and a separate box (at least 5 cm by 3.5 cm) for official certification by Customs.

The cruise operator must account for VAT on any goods on the bulk refund form that are not exported from the EC within the prescribed limits.

(*b*) *Individual purchases over £1,000*

The normal VAT 407 form or equivalent (see 25.13 above) must be completed for individual purchases over £1,000 per item. The customer must produce the goods and the form for certification to the Customs officer at the point of final departure from the EC.

(VAT Notice 704, paras 8.1, 8.2).

Accounting for VAT

25.15 At the point of sale, any standard-rated and lower-rated goods sold under the scheme must be treated as liable to VAT. It is therefore in the interest of the retailer to initially charge VAT to the customer. A sale can only be zero-rated when

- the stamped refund document has been received; and
- the refund of VAT has been made to the customer by the agreed method.

The stamped refund document must be retained together with evidence of the refund made to the customer to support zero-rating.

If the certified VAT refund document is received after VAT has been accounted for, the VAT can be refunded and the sale can be zero-rated by reducing output tax by the relevant amount in Box 1 of the VAT return.

Suppliers also using a special retail scheme. See 60.9 RETAIL SCHEMES.

Retailers not using a retail scheme. Such retailers must keep a record of all sales including VAT under the retail export scheme. When a stamped VAT refund document is received and the VAT has been refunded, the sale can be zero-rated in the records.

Refund companies. Where a retailer contracts with a refund company to administer the refund on its behalf, the refund company normally provides an officially approved VAT refund document of its own design for use by the retailer. In such circumstances, the retailer must still account for the VAT as explained above and must retain the certified VAT refund documents and evidence that the VAT has been refunded in its records to support any zero-rating claimed.

Concession shops. Where a larger store operates concessions for other retailers within its own store:

- If the sale is rung through the main store tills, it is acceptable for the VAT refund document to be issued by the host store (typically at the main customer service desk). The host store is then responsible for complying with the conditions of the scheme and accounting for the VAT.
- If the concession operates its own tills and issues receipts showing its own name and VAT number, any VAT refund documents must be issued by the concession and not the host store. The concession is then responsible for complying with the conditions of the scheme and accounting for the VAT.

Direct reclaim system. This involves two distinct transactions: a retailer sells goods to a refund company who immediately sells them on to an eligible traveller. The accounting procedure is as follows.

- The retailer must invoice the sale to the refund company as this is a business-to-business supply (not a retail sale) and must account for VAT on the supply. It may, however, include the sale in its daily gross takings for retail scheme purposes if it wishes.

- The refund company may use the retailer's invoice to reclaim input tax on the purchase. It must also account for VAT on the sale to the traveller. It may subsequently zero-rate the supply but only where all the conditions of the scheme are met.

Sales under the margin scheme for second-hand goods. The margin scheme for second-hand goods and the retail export scheme can both be used for the same transaction but as the amount of VAT charged cannot be shown separately on a valid invoice under the margin scheme, the VAT refund document should be adapted as follows.

- Head the document 'Second-hand goods – this document is adapted in accordance with Notice 704, para 5.8'.
- Leave the line 'Amount of VAT included in the price' blank.
- Complete the refund due box.

Sales by auctioneers. If an auctioneer sells goods on behalf of a retailer to a person entitled to use the retail export scheme and a VAT refund document is completed, the retailer can zero-rate the sale when the stamped refund document is returned and the refund has been made to the customer. Note, however, that the scheme cannot be used for goods exported as freight.

If the auctioneers are registered for VAT and sell goods in their own name to someone who is entitled to use the scheme then, for VAT purposes, they may be treated as both receiving and making a supply of goods. They can zero-rate the sale provided they hold a certified VAT refund document and have refunded the VAT to the customer.

Administration or handling fees. If an amount is deducted from the VAT refund due to cover administrative or handling expenses, the amount deducted is consideration for the supply of services to the customer in connection with the export of goods to a destination outside the EC, and is zero-rated under *VATA 1994, Sch 8 Group 7 Item 2(a)*.

(VAT Notice 704, paras 5.1–5.10).

25.16 Motor vehicles

Direct exports. Any motor vehicle, new or second-hand, supplied for direct export may be zero-rated provided it is exported from the EC and the conditions in 25.1(*a*) above are satisfied. Evidence of exportation must be obtained and retained.

Indirect exports. The supply of a new or second-hand motor vehicle can be zero-rated under the conditions in 25.17 below. A motor vehicle can also be zero-rated under the Personal Export Scheme in 25.18 below.

De Voil Indirect Tax Service. See V4.334.

25.17 *Vehicles delivered in the UK for subsequent export by or on behalf of the purchaser*

The supply to an overseas person (see 25.8 above) of any motor vehicle (new or second-hand) can be zero-rated provided

- the supplier keeps supplementary evidence of the export (see 25.25 below);
- the vehicle is exported within three months of the supply; and
- the supplier obtains proof of export within three months of the time of supply.

25.18 *Vehicles delivered in the UK for temporary use and subsequent export by the purchaser (the 'Personal Export Scheme')*

The Personal Export Scheme allows new and used motor vehicles (including motor cycles and motor caravans but not pedal cycles and trailer caravans) to be purchased free of VAT provided certain conditions (which have the force of law) are met. It should be noted that

- it is not possible to get a refund of VAT on a motor vehicle purchased VAT-paid even if it is later exported and would have qualified under the scheme; and
- it can be very difficult to import motor vehicles into some countries and it is advisable to check with the relevant Embassy or High Commission in the UK before ordering a vehicle under the scheme.

The conditions are as follows.

(*a*) The vehicle must be purchased from a VAT-registered business which operates the Personal Export Scheme.

(*b*) Only the purchaser who applies to use the scheme may take delivery of the vehicle in the UK without the written authority of the Personal Transport Unit (see below for contact details).

(*c*) The purchaser must intend to leave the EC within

- 15 months or less if an 'overseas visitor'; or
- 9 months or less in any other case.

See 21.2 EUROPEAN COMMUNITY:GENERAL for the VAT territory of the EC.

An '*overseas visitor*' for these purposes is a person who has not been in the EC for more than either 365 days in the two years immediately before the date of application or 1,095 days in the six years immediately before that date.

(*d*) The purchaser must export the vehicle within

- 12 months of the date of delivery if an overseas visitor (see (*c*) above); or
- 6 months of the date of delivery in any other case.

For new vehicles, the final date for exportation is shown in the registration document. *For second-hand vehicles*, the final date of export is shown on the Form VAT 410 (see below).

(*e*) The purchaser (whether or not an overseas visitor) must intend to leave and remain outside the EC with the vehicle for a period of at least six months.

(*f*) The vehicle may be driven in the UK in the period before exportation but only by

- the purchaser or their spouse;
- a chauffeur; or
- provided the purchaser is still in the UK, any other person who has his permission to use it and who intends to leave the EC.

(*g*) The purchaser must not attempt to dispose of the vehicle in the UK (or elsewhere in the EC) by hire, pledge as security, sale, gift or any other means.

If any of the above conditions are broken, the vehicle is liable to forfeiture and may be seized. VAT is then payable on the value of the vehicle when purchased. Even if the vehicle cannot be exported for unavoidable reasons (eg theft or accident write-off) the VAT must still be paid.

(1) *Procedure at time of sale*

If the supplier is satisfied that the applicant is entitled to use the scheme, he should

- give the applicant a copy of *Notice 705 Buyer's guide to personal exports of motor vehicles to destinations outside the EC* and an application form VAT 410 (both obtainable from the National Advice Service on 0845 010 9000);
- explain the conditions of the scheme; and
- advise the applicant that it is an offence to give incorrect information on the form and that, if they do so, they may be liable to prosecution.

The applicant must complete the form and sign the declaration. In doing so, the applicant declares that they have received, read and understood Notice 705 and will comply with all the conditions of the scheme.

The form VAT 410 is carbonated and incorporates 4 copies:

Part 1 (blue) – Customs copy

Part 2 (green) – Purchaser's copy

Part 3 (pink) – Supplier's copy

Part 4 (yellow) – DVLA local office copy.

Completed application forms must be serially numbered by the supplier in the top right hand corner. (Each separate franchise at the same location requires a separate series of numbers.) Part 1 must be submitted, at least two weeks before date of delivery of the vehicle, to

HM Revenue and Customs
Personal Transport Unit
PO Box 242
Dover
Kent
CT17 9PG

Tel: 01304 664556/7

Fax: 01304 664567

An incomplete or incorrect application form will be returned to the supplier for correction and this may delay the delivery of the vehicle.

(2) *Cancellation of order before delivery*

If, after the application is approved, the order for the vehicle is cancelled by the applicant before delivery, the supplier must immediately notify the PTU at the above address, quoting

- name of applicant,
- make/model of vehicle;
- serial number of the application; and

- in the case of second-hand vehicles, the vehicle registration number.

(3) *Invoicing*

The supplier must supply and invoice a VAT-free vehicle direct to the applicant. Factory fitted extras can only be supplied VAT-free if they are included on the initial invoice for the supply of the vehicle at the time of purchase.

(4) *Registration and licensing with the Driver and Licensing Agency (DVLA)*

New vehicles. To register a new vehicle, the supplier must complete an application form V55 headed prominently in block letters 'PERSONAL EXPORT (VAT FREE) VEHICLE', attach it to the DVLA copy (Part 4) of form VAT 410, and send it to the DVLA local office in either Beverley, Birmingham, Bristol, Chelmsford, Glasgow, Leeds, Luton, Lincoln, Maidstone, Manchester, Northampton, Norwich, Oxford or Stockton (see 23.32 EUROPEAN COMMUNITY: SINGLE MARKET for addresses).

Second-hand vehicles. As a second-hand vehicle will already have been registered, the supplier must notify the DVLA local office of the change of keeper and apply for a special tax disc. This is done by submitting

(i) the completed V5 Registration Document,

(ii) form V10 (vehicle licence application form),

(iii) the DVLA copy (Part 4) of form VAT 410, and

(iv) form VX304 if the purchaser is entitled to claim exemption from payment of vehicle excise duty

to the DVLA local office in either Beverley, Birmingham, Bristol, Chelmsford, Glasgow, Leeds, Luton, Lincoln, Maidstone, Manchester, Northampton, Norwich, Oxford or Stockton (see 23.32 EUROPEAN COMMUNITY: SINGLE MARKET for addresses).

A second-hand vehicle must not be supplied with any pre-existing tax disc. If a disc is already in force, it should be surrendered separately to the DVLA local office for a refund.

(5) *Insuring the vehicle*

The purchaser should insure the vehicle for its full VAT-inclusive value because

- it must be insured before it is used; and
- if the purchaser is unable to export the vehicle (eg because it has been stolen or involved in an accident and written-off), the VAT amount not paid at the time of purchase becomes due.

(6) *Delivering the vehicle*

Before delivering a new vehicle, the supplier must complete the details required on pages 5 and 8 of the pink registration book, showing the amount of VAT remitted, the date of delivery, and the final date for export (see (*c*) above).

The vehicle must be delivered to the applicant in the UK (see (*b*) above). On delivery, the supplier must obtain a dated certificate of receipt for the vehicle signed by the applicant. This must be kept with the other records.

(7) *Urgent delivery procedure*

Where an overseas visitor intends to leave the UK within one month of their application to use the scheme, the supplier must complete a Certificate for Urgent Delivery authorised by a sole proprietor, partner, director, company secretary or a duly authorised person at a responsible level. At least three working days before the date of delivery of the vehicle to the applicant, the supplier must then fax to the Personal Transport Unit

- a copy of the Certificate for Urgent Delivery;
- a copy of the VAT 410 form; and
- for new vehicles, the V55 Form.

The original papers should then be posted to the Personal Transport Unit.

This procedure must not be used if the initial application by the customer has been rejected or returned for amendment.

(8) *Supplier's records*

For a new vehicle, in addition to the normal VAT records and his copy of the form VAT 410, the supplier must keep a separate record of each vehicle supplied under the scheme showing

- date of delivery;
- applicant's name and UK address;
- particulars of the vehicle including type, chassis number and registration number;
- amount of VAT remitted on the delivery price (including any accessories or extras and any delivery charges, less any discount allowed); and
- a certificate of receipt of the vehicle, detailing chassis number and registration number, which must be signed and dated by the applicant.

For a second-hand vehicle, the supplier should already have a record of it in his second-hand stock book under the margin scheme for second-hand goods. When he sells a second-hand vehicle under the Personal Export Scheme, he must close this stock book entry and include a cross-reference to the serial number of the form VAT 410, inserting 'zero-rate' in the VAT rate column of his stock book and 'Nil' in the VAT due column. He must then record the sale separately and include the same details as required for sales of new vehicles above. He can, if he wishes, include his second-hand sales with his records of new vehicle sales (if any).

(9) *Use of vehicle before exportation from the EC*

The vehicle can be used in the UK before exportation provided it is insured, exported by the final due date (see (*d*) above) and only used by an approved person (see (*f*) above).

It may also be used to make a temporary visit to another EC country. If so, it can be brought back to the UK without any Customs formalities provided it is returned to the UK before the final due date for exportation (see (*d*) above) and the customer still intends to export and depart with the vehicle from the EC by that date. The purchaser is advised to check with the relevant VAT authority of the other EC country to establish whether, because the vehicle has been supplied free of VAT, it is necessary to comply with any Customs requirements on entry into that country.

It is not normally advisable to make a temporary visit to a non-EC country prior to the final date for export (see (*d*) above). When the vehicle is re-imported into either the UK or another EC country, the VAT amount not paid at the time of purchase will become due (unless qualifying for relief under the re-importation rules (see below).

(10) *Change of plans by purchaser before exportation from EC*

If the purchaser changes his plans before the vehicle is removed from the UK and can no longer comply with the conditions in (*c*) or (*d*) above, he must notify the Personal Transport Unit immediately and pay the full amount of VAT not paid when the vehicle was bought. If the vehicle is in another EC country, the purchaser should contact the fiscal authorities of that country (and pay VAT and any other local taxes due).

(11) *Procedure on exportation*

For new vehicles, the final date for exportation is shown on the pink registration document. The tear-off section of the document must be completed and returned to the DVLA local office as shown on the document.

For second-hand vehicles, the final date of exportation is shown on the customer's copy (Part 1) of form VAT 410. The customer must complete the relevant section of the V5 registration document and send the entire document to the DVLA local office as shown on the document. The DVLA will issue an export certificate to enable the vehicle to be re-registered in the country of destination. If the purchaser intends to leave the UK within 14 days of acquiring the vehicle, he should tell the dealer before purchase so that the dealer can arrange for the DVLA to issue an export certificate straightaway.

Shipping arrangements must be made in good time to ensure that the vehicle is exported by the final date.

(12) *Reimportation*

If the vehicle is brought back into the UK after the date shown for export, taxes must be paid on importation unless the person is eligible for relief from VAT and duty (see Customs Notice 3 *Bringing your belongings and private motor vehicle to the UK from outside the European Community*) in which case no VAT will be charged. Where the purchaser is not eligible for relief,

- if the vehicle is re-imported six months or more after the date for export (or the owner can show that he and the vehicle have remained outside the EC for at least six consecutive months), the VAT payable will be based on the value of the vehicle at the time of re-importation; and
- in all other cases, the VAT payable will be that which was not charged on purchase.

The vehicle must also be registered and licensed on return to the UK unless it is not to be used or kept on the public roads. The owner should contact the nearest DVLA local office and produce proof of payment of, or exemption from, VAT in order to re-license or re-register the vehicle.

If the vehicle is re-imported into another EC country after it was exported from the EC, the owner should contact the VAT authority in that country and pay the VAT (and any other local taxes) due.

[*SI 1995/2518, Regs 117(8), 132, 133; SI 1999/438, Reg 10; SI 2000/258, Reg 6*]. (VAT Notice 705; VAT Notice 705A).

25.19 **Sailaway boats supplied for export**

Under the conditions outlined below (which have the force of law) it is possible to zero-rate the supply of a '*sailaway boat*', ie a boat to be

- delivered to the purchaser or their authorised skipper within the EC; and
- to be exported under its own power to a destination outside the VAT territory of the European Community (see 21.2 EUROPEAN COMMUNITY: GENERAL).

As the supply can only be zero-rated after receipt of evidence that the boat has been exported in the time limit allowed, it is advisable to treat any sale under the scheme as liable to VAT until this evidence is received. It is recommended, therefore, that a deposit is taken equal to the amount of VAT, to be refunded when the required evidence of export is received.

Who is entitled to use the scheme. The scheme can only be used for the private purchase of a boat by

- an 'overseas visitor' who intends to export the boat under its own power to a destination outside the EC within six months of the 'date of delivery'; or
- an 'EC resident' (or emigrant) who intends to export the boat under its own power to a destination outside the EC within two months of the date of delivery. The boat must be kept outside the EC for a continuous period of at least twelve months.

The scheme must not be used for commercial purchases.

An '*overseas visitor*' is someone who normally lives outside the EC and has not been in the EC for more than 365 days in the two years before the date of purchase.

An '*EC resident*' is a person (including an overseas student or worker) who has lived in the EC for more than 365 days in the two years before the date of purchase.

'*Date of delivery*' is normally the date the boat leaves the supplier's premises.

The scheme cannot be used

- where the supplier arranges delivery of the boat (either on a trailer or by using a skipper employed by the supplier) to a destination outside the EC (see 25.1(*a*) above for the conditions for zero-rating direct exports);
- a boat supplied for private use for removal from the UK to another EC country (see 23.32 EUROPEAN COMMUNITY: SINGLE MARKET for the conditions for zero-rating such a sale); or
- parts or accessories (which may be supplied under the retail export scheme (see 25.11 above)).

Forms. The supplier needs to prove that the boat has been removed from the EC before zero-rating the sale in his records. The forms needed for this purpose are

- **Form VAT 436** – Notification of VAT-free purchase of a sailaway boat, and customers declaration. This form is in four parts.

Copy 1	copy for certification
Copy 2	Customs copy
Copy 3	customer's copy
Copy 4	supplier's copy

- **Form C88** (Single Administrative Document). This form is in three parts.

Copy 1	Community transit copy where applicable
Copy 2	UK Customs copy
Copy 3	For certification when the boat finally leaves the EC

- **Form C1331** – to advise departure from the UK.

The use of the forms vary according to whether a boat departs to a destination outside the EC directly from the UK or via another EC country.

Action required by the supplier. The supplier must

- check that the customer is entitled to use the scheme (see above);
- ensure that the customer intends to export the boat from the EC under its own power within the permitted time limit;
- in the case of a customer who is an EC resident, ensure that he intends to keep the boat outside the EC for a continuous period of at least twelve months;
- explain the conditions of the scheme to the customer and give the customer a copy of VAT Notice 703/3. (In completing the Form VAT 436, applicants declare that they have received and read the Notice, and that they will abide by the conditions relating to the scheme.);
- ensure that the customer knows that he must not dispose, or attempt to dispose, of the boat in the EC by hire, pledge as security (other than as part of the financing arrangement for the purchase of the boat itself), sale, gift or any other means;
- agree how any refund of deposited VAT will be paid;
- ensure that Form VAT 436 is fully completed and, at least two weeks before due delivery of the boat, that Copy 2 is submitted to HM Revenue and Customs (MSO), National Unit for Personal Transport (PTU), PO Box 242, Dover, Kent, CT17 9GP (Tel: 01304 224556; Fax: 01304 224567). All forms should be serially numbered in the top right hand corner. Forms which are incorrect or incomplete will be returned for correction and this may delay the delivery of the boat. If, after the form is processed, the order for the boat is cancelled by the customer before delivery, the supplier must immediately notify the PTU of the customer's name, details of the boat, and the serial number of the form;
- keep a separate record for the sale; and
- advise the customer what action must be taken at the time of exportation.

Export procedure

- *If the customer is leaving the UK directly for a destination outside the EC*, the customer must
  - (i) complete Form C1331 Notice of Intended Departure;
  - (ii) make the boat available for inspection by HMRC at exportation (where possible this should be arranged in advance);
  - (iii) take the Form VAT 436 completed with the supplier and the Form C1331 to the UK HMRC nearest the place of departure. HMRC will retain Form C1331, sign and stamp Form VAT 436 to show that the boat has been declared for exportation, and return the Form VAT 436 to the customer; and

(iv) return the certified Form VAT 436 to the supplier.

- If the customer is calling into another EC country before finally exporting the boat from the EC, the customer must
  (i) take the completed Forms C88 (copies 2 and 3) and VAT 436 to the UK HMRC office nearest the place of departure from the UK. HMRC will keep copy 2 of Form C88 and return copy 3 with Form VAT 436 to the customer;
  (ii) export the boat from the EC within the specified time limit;
  (iii) take copy 3 of Form C88 and VAT 436 to the Customs office at the place of final departure from the EC for certification; and
  (iv) return the certified Form C88 and VAT 436 to the supplier.

Accounting arrangements. A separate record must be kept of all boats sold under the scheme. The sales invoice must clearly show that the supply of the boat was made under the sailaway boat scheme.

If evidence of export is not obtained and held within one month of the date of export, VAT must be accounted for. Any deposit taken of the VAT due should be brought to account. Where no deposit has been taken, the VAT records must be amended and VAT accounted for on the taxable proportion of the invoiced amount or consideration received (ie where the rate of VAT is 17.5%, the VAT element is 7/47ths). The amendment should be made in the VAT account and VAT return for the period in which the time limit expires.

If evidence of export within the permitted time limit is subsequently received, the supply can be zero-rated and any deposit refunded. The VAT account can be adjusted for the period in which evidence is received.

Re-importation of VAT-free boats. If a boat that was supplied VAT free at purchase is brought back to the EC, it must be declared to Customs in the EC country of importation. The supplier should ensure that the customer is fully aware of the need to make an import declaration. VAT will be payable unless some other relief is available.

The Channel Islands. The Channel Islands are outside the EC VAT area and therefore qualify as a final destination for boats supplied under the sailaway boat scheme. EC residents who register VAT-free boats in the Channel Islands cannot claim VAT-free temporary importation of such boats into an EC country. VAT is payable on these importations. Private persons resident in the Channel Islands may be entitled to import their own boats temporarily into the VAT territory of the EC for their own personal use for up to 18 months, without payment of import VAT.

(VAT Notice 703/2/02; VAT Notice 48, ESC 8.1).

25.20 Supplies to the FCO and other government departments

Foreign and Commonwealth Office (FCO). Goods ordered by British Embassies, High Commissions and diplomats abroad which are delivered to FCO for export via diplomatic channels can be zero-rated provided a certificate of receipt for the goods is obtained from the FCO within three months of the time of supply of the goods. See VAT Notice 703, para 12.1 for an example of the certificate. The certificate may be on a copy of the sales invoice or itemised list and must be retained. To show that the supply was to an overseas person, the supplier must also retain documents (eg the order) to identify the destination of the goods.The supply of goods ordered by and delivered to the FCO for general distribution cannot be zero-rated.

Ministry of Defence (MOD). The MOD is registered for VAT in the UK and all supplies to them or to any military establishment in the UK on their behalf should include VAT at the appropriate rate. Direct exports to overseas military and similar installations may be zero-rated provided the supplier holds valid proof of export.

Other government departments. The supply of goods to other government departments can only be zero-rated if supplied by direct export to a destination outside the EC. Goods for export delivered to government departments in the UK must not be zero-rated even if the goods are ordered for or by an overseas establishment.

(VAT Notice 703, paras 4.8, 4.10, 7.10).

25.21 **Supplies to regimental shops**

Supplies to regimental shops are normally taxable. However, where the regiment (or equivalent military unit) is about to be posted to a location outside the UK, supplies of goods (except new and second-hand motor vehicles) to a regimental shop can be zero-rated provided the following conditions are satisfied.

(*a*) Each written order received from the President of the Regimental Institute (PRI) states that the regiment is about to take up an overseas posting and that the goods ordered will be exported from the UK.

(*b*) The goods are delivered to the PRI ready packed for shipment no more than 48 hours before the regiment is due to depart for the overseas posting.

(*c*) The goods are exported outside the UK.

(*d*) The supplier retains a certificate of receipt signed by the PRI which clearly identifies the goods, gives full shipment details and states the date on which they were exported from the UK.

The PRI will keep a full record of such transactions for reference purposes for a period of not less than six years.

(VAT Notice 703, para 4.9).

25.22 **Supplies intended for continental shelf installations**

The following provisions apply to the export of goods to structures such as oil rigs, dwelling units, accommodation platforms and similar oil or gas exploration/exploitation structures. It also applies to mobile floating structures such as drill ships, tankers, jack-up rigs, semi-submersible rigs and Floating Production Storage and Offloading (FPSO) vessels which are often stationed at fixed locations.

Exports to installations outside EC territorial waters.

- *Goods supplied and exported by a supplier to an installation which he does not own.* Such supplies are zero-rated as direct exports provided proof of export is obtained within three months of the supply.
- *Goods sent to an installation owned by the supplier or goods sent to replenish own stocks on an installation not owned by the supplier.* This is a transfer of own goods and not a taxable supply (see 25.23 below). Valid proof of export must still be held to demonstrate how the goods have been disposed of.

Goods supplied for sale on installations situated outside UK territorial waters. Such supplies can be zero-rated provided

(*a*) a written order for the goods is obtained from a responsible person on the installation to which the goods are to be sent;

(*b*) the goods are supplied either direct to the installation or through an agent for consolidation followed by direct delivery to the installation; and

(*c*) a receipt for the goods, signed by a responsible person on the installation, is obtained within three months of the time of supply.

(VAT Notice 703, para 4.7).

Goods supplied and delivered within the UK (including territorial waters). If such goods are

- supplied to an overseas person (see 25.8 above) for export by that person as an indirect export and the necessary conditions in 25.1 above are met, or
- supplied to an overseas person but delivered to a third person in the UK for processing, etc and subsequent export and the conditions in 25.9 above are met,

the supply can be zero-rated.

Otherwise, VAT must be charged at the appropriate rate.

25.23 EXPORTS WHERE THERE IS NO TAXABLE SUPPLY

There is no need to account for VAT in the following circumstances.

- The supply and export of goods which the supplier is to install outside the EC for his customer (as the supply takes place in the country where the goods are installed).
- The temporary export of goods for exhibition or processing.
- The export of goods on sale or return where the goods remain the property of the supplier until they are sold.
- The transfer of own goods to a place outside the EC by a UK business. Such transactions should be treated as direct exports and the appropriate time limits and accounting procedures applied. Any related input tax can be deducted (subject to the normal rules) but the value of any transferred goods should not be included in Box 6 of the VAT return.

The supplier must still hold valid proof of export to demonstrate to HMRC how the goods were disposed of. He must also declare any goods returned to the UK.

(VAT Notice 703, paras 2.14, 2.15).

25.24 PROOF OF EXPORT

A supplier must ensure that he has proof of export readily available for HMRC. This must be obtained within the appropriate time limit (see 25.1(*a*) above) and retained for six years.

Proof of export consists of:

- *Official evidence* — this is produced by HMRC (eg Goods Departed Messages (GDM) generated by the New Export System (NES)). Alternatively it may be in the form of a Single Administrative Document (SAD) endorsed by HMRC at the point of exit from the EC.
- *Commercial evidence* — eg authenticated sea-waybills or air-waybills; PIM/PIEX International consignment notes; master air-waybills or bills of lading; certificates of shipment containing the full details of the consignment and how it left the UK; or International Consignment Note/Lettre de Voiture International (CMR) fully completed by the consignor, the haulier and the receiving consignee, or Freight Transport Association (FTA) own account transport documents fully completed and signed by the receiving customer.

Equal weight is put on official and commercial evidence but both must be supported by supplementary evidence.

Supplementary evidence. A supplier must hold sufficient evidence to prove that a transaction has taken place and that the transaction relates to the goods physically exported. Accounting records are likely to include the following (although it will probably not be necessary to hold all the items listed.

- Customer's order.
- Sales contract.
- Inter-company correspondence.
- Copy of export sales invoice.
- Advice note.
- Consignment note.
- Packing list.
- Insurance and freight charges documentation.
- Evidence of payment.
- Evidence of the receipt of the goods abroad.

Evidence of export. The evidence obtained as proof of export, whether official or commercial, or supporting must clearly identify the following. (These requirements have the force of law.)

- The supplier.
- The consignor (where different from the supplier).
- The customer.
- The goods.
- An accurate value.
- The export destination.
- The mode of transport and route of the export movement.

Vague descriptions of goods, quantities or values are not acceptable (eg 'various electrical goods' must not be used when the correct description is '2000 mobile phones make ABC and model number XYZ2000').

Lost or mislaid export evidence. If an exporter has lost or mislaid the official or commercial evidence of export supplied by the ship owner or carrier, duplicate evidence of export may be obtained. The replacement evidence of export must be clearly marked 'DUPLICATE EVIDENCE OF EXPORT' and be authenticated and dated by an official of the issuing company.

Photocopies. Photocopy certificates of shipment are not normally acceptable as evidence of export, nor are photocopy bills of lading, sea waybills or air waybills (unless authenticated by the shipping or air line).

(VAT Notice 703, paras 6.1–6.4, 6.10).

25.25 Evidence where the supplier does not arrange shipment

If the overseas customer collects or arranges the collection of the goods and their removal from the UK, it can be difficult for the supplier to obtain adequate proof of export as the carrier is contracted to the customer. As a result, for this type of transaction the standard of evidence required to substantiate VAT zero-rating is high. The supplier should seek confirmation of what evidence of export will be provided. He should also consider taking a deposit from the customer equal to the amount of VAT, in case satisfactory evidence of export is not received.

Evidence must show that the goods supplied have left the UK. Copies of transport documents alone are not sufficient and information held must identify the date and route of the movement of goods and the method of transport involved. It should include the following.

- A written order from the customer which shows their name, address and the address where the goods are to be delivered.
- Copy sales invoice showing invoice number, customer's name, and a description of the goods.
- Delivery address for the goods.
- Name and address of the haulier collecting the goods, registration number of the vehicle collecting the goods and the name and signature of the driver.
- Where the goods are to be taken out of the UK by an alternative haulier or vehicle, the name and address of that haulier, the registration number of the vehicle and a signature for the goods.
- Route (eg Channel Tunnel, port of exit).
- Copy of travel tickets.
- Name of ferry or shipping company and date of sailing or airway number and airport.

The information held should also include (where applicable):

- Trailer number.
- Full container number.
- Name and address for consolidation, groupage, or processing.

(VAT Notice 703, para 6.5).

25.26 **Evidence in specific circumstances**

See VAT Notice 703 as indicated below for specific evidence of export that must be obtained according to the method of export used. In all cases the official or commercial transport evidence obtained must be supported by the supplementary evidence in 25.24 above to show that the transaction has taken place.

Air and sea freight	Para 7.1
Road freight	Para 7.2
Merchandise in Baggage (MIB)	Para 7.3
Groupage or consolidation transactions	Para 7.4
Postal exports (including Royal Mail Parcel Force and courier and fast parcel services	Para 7.5
Exports by rail	Para 7.6
Exports through packers	Para 7.7
Exports from Customs, Excise and/or fiscal warehouses	Para 7.9

25.27 **Exports through auctioneers**

Auctioneers not acting in their own name. A supplier who sells goods through auctioneers who

- are not acting in their own name; and
- export the goods

may zero-rate the supply provided a certificate of export is obtained from the auctioneers within three months of the time of supply (see VAT Notice 703, paras 12.2 and 12.3 for the format of the certificates). The auctioneer must hold valid evidence of export for the goods.

Auctioneers acting in their own name. If a supplier sells goods through auctioneers who act in their own name, the goods are treated as being supplied to the auctioneer and must not be zero-rated by the supplier as an export. The auctioneer will be able to zero-rate the onward supply subject to the normal rules.

(VAT Notice 703, para 7.8).

25.28 **Exports to the Channel Islands**

Evidence of export for goods sent to the Channel Islands is one of the following (as appropriate).

- Official proof of export produced by NES.
- For goods shipped by air — an authenticated master air-waybill or house air-waybill.
- For goods carried as Merchandise in Baggage — a Customs' certified copy 3 of the SAD (Form C88).
- For goods shipped through a freight forwarder — a certificate of shipment issued by the freight forwarder or an authenticated copy of the Consignment Note and Customs Declarations (CNCD).
- For goods shipped through a fast parcel or courier service — evidence as per VAT Notice 703, para 7.5.

- For goods shipped directly by the south coast ferry companies — an authenticated copy of the CNCD.

(VAT Notice 703, para 7.11).

25.29 **Exports via EC countries**

Where goods are exported outside the EC but via other EC countries, official or commercial documentary evidence is required that the goods have left the EC.

Official evidence of export will normally be copy 3 of the export SAD (Form C88) or NES equivalent endorsed at the customs office of exit from the EC. The office of exit will vary depending on the type of transport used and the nature of the supply.

Where goods subject to excise duty are moving under duty suspension arrangements, the customs office of exit from the EC will certify the accompanying document (an 'attestation' in EC terms) and return it to the consignor as evidence of exportation from the EC. The standard time limits for obtaining the evidence of export apply.

(VAT Notice 703, para 7.12).

25.30 **RECORDS AND RETURNS**

Where goods are exported (or supplied as ships' stores), the normal rules for record keeping still apply (see 56 RECORDS). In addition, evidence of export must be retained as set out in 25.24 to 25.26 above.

Exports can be zero-rated in the records at the time of supply to the customer. But if the supplier does not ensure the goods have been exported and obtain and hold the required evidence of export within the relevant time limit for the supply, he must account for VAT at the appropriate rate on a supply of the goods in the UK.

VAT must be accounted for on the taxable proportion of the invoiced amount or consideration received (ie for a VAT rate of 17.5% the VAT element would be calculated at 7/47). This VAT must be included in Box 1 of the VAT return for the period in which the relevant time limit expires.

If the goods are subsequently exported and/or evidence of export is obtained, the supply can then be zero-rated and the VAT account adjusted for the period in which the evidence is obtained.

Retail schemes. See 60.9 RETAIL SCHEMES for treatment of exports where a retail scheme is used.

Goods returned damaged. Where export goods are damaged after shipment and relanded in the UK, they must be declared to customs. If the supplier, or a member of a salvage association, subsequently sell the goods, the seller must account for VAT at the appropriate UK rate on the sale price.

(VAT Notice 703, paras 11.1–11.3).

26 Extra-Statutory Concessions

The contents of this chapter are as follows.

26.1 EXTRA-STATUTORY CONCESSIONS

The following is a summary of all VAT concessions in force as published by HMRC in Notice 48 (March 2002).

International field

2.1 **Visiting forces, NATO and US and Canadian government expenditure**. VAT (and duty including all import and excise duties) are remitted or refunded on

(*a*) goods and services imported by or supplied to visiting forces and their instrumentalities, for the official use of the force, or their instrumentalities;

(*b*) goods and services imported by or supplied to NATO military headquarters, organisations or agencies, for their official use;

(*c*) US and Canadian government expenditure on mutual defence or mutual aid contracts; and

(*d*) temporary importations of equipment required by contractors for fulfilling NATO infrastructure contracts or in connection with the provision and maintenance of US forces defence facilities in the UK.

2.2 **UK-manufactured alcoholic liquor and tobacco products purchased by diplomats**. VAT (and duty) are remitted on alcoholic liquor and tobacco products of UK manufacture imported by, or supplied to, diplomatic representatives of foreign states in the UK who are entitled to similar privileges in respect of imported products of foreign manufacture under *Diplomatic Privileges Act 1964*.

2.3 **United States Air Force**. Relief from VAT (and/or excise duty) is allowed, in accordance with certain conditions agreed with the US Air Force, on

(*a*) charges for admission to air shows and open days; and

(*b*) goods sold by US forces organisations during air shows and open days to persons not entitled to receive/consume them unless customs charges have been paid.

2.4 **Gifts by US forces**. VAT (and duty) are remitted on gifts (whether imported or purchased in the UK) from US forces to charitable organisations.

2.5 **American war graves**. See 19.5 DEATH.

2.7 **Aircraft ground and security equipment**. See 34.22 IMPORTS.

Concessions designed to remove inequities or anomalies in administration

3.1 **Purchases of road fuel.** *VATA 1994, s 56* requires payment of a scale charge if road fuel purchased by a business is used for private journeys. However, where input tax is not claimed on *any* road fuel used by the business, whether for business or private journeys, the VAT scale charge will not apply. See 45.16 MOTOR CARS.

3.2 **Group supplies using an overseas member: anticipation of legislative changes.** A charge to VAT arises where supplies of a type within *VATA 1994, Sch 5* are purchased by an overseas group member and used for making supplies within *Sch 5* to a UK group member. The amount of the VAT charge is calculated by reference to the value of the supply by the overseas member to the UK member but may be reduced to the value of the *Sch 5* services purchased by the overseas member provided certain conditions are met. See 31.6 GROUPS OF COMPANIES.

This concession cannot be used for tax avoidance purposes.

3.3 **Zero-rating of supplies of certain goods used in connection with collection of monetary donations by charities.** With effect from 1 April 2000, the supply to a charity of certain goods may be treated as if it were a zero-rated supply. See 12.7 CHARITIES.

3.4 **Misunderstanding by a VAT trader.** Where certain conditions are fulfilled, VAT undercharged by a registered trader as a result of a *bona fide* misunderstanding may be remitted. See 47.1 OUTPUT TAX.

3.5 **Misdirection.** If a Revenue and Customs officer, with the full facts before him, has given a clear and unequivocal ruling on VAT in writing or, knowing the full facts, has misled a registered person to his detriment, any assessment of VAT due will be based on the correct ruling from the date the error was brought to the registered person's attention. See 15.5 CUSTOMS: ADMINISTRATION and 17.13 CUSTOMS: POWERS.

3.6 **Coin-operated machines.** As an accounting convenience, operators may delay accounting for VAT until the takings are removed from the machine. See 57.3 RECREATION AND SPORT and 64.56 SUPPLY.

3.7 **VAT on minor promotional items supplied in linked supply schemes.** These are schemes in which a minor article is linked with a main article and sold at a single price. Provided the cost of the minor article is within certain limits, it can be treated as taxable at the same rate as the main article. See 67.5 TRADE PROMOTION SCHEMES.

3.8 **Use of margin scheme for vehicle sales when incomplete records have been kept.** Where a dealer has the required information on the purchase or sale of a car but not both, subject to conditions VAT may be accounted for on the purchase price or half the selling price. See 61.35 SECOND-HAND GOODS.

3.9 **Recoveries of VAT under *VATA 1994, Sch 11 para 5* (VAT charged by unregistered persons).** Where an amount is shown or represented as VAT on an invoice issued by a person who is neither registered nor required to be registered for VAT at the time the invoice is issued, HMRC may require that person to pay an equivalent amount to them. By concession, the person may be permitted to deduct any VAT incurred on supplies to him that were directly attributable to the invoiced supplies. Also by concession, if the recipient of the supplies is a taxable person HMRC may allow the recipient to treat the amount shown or represented as VAT as input tax. See 17.2 CUSTOMS: POWERS.

3.10 **VAT on necessary meals and accommodation provided by recognised representative sporting bodies to amateur sports persons chosen to**

represent that body in a competition. In such circumstances, the input tax incurred may be deductible as input tax and not treated as business entertainment. See 9.6 BUSINESS ENTERTAINMENT.

3.11 **Incorrect customer declaration**. Where a customer provides an incorrect declaration claiming eligibility for zero-rating under *VATA 1994* and the supplier, despite having taken all reasonable steps to check the validity of the declaration, fails to identify the inaccuracy and, in good faith, zero-rates the supply, HMRC will not seek to recover the VAT due from the supplier. See 12.7 CHARITIES, 29.2 FUEL AND POWER, 32.35 HEALTH AND WELFARE, 42.32 LAND AND BUILDINGS, 47.1 OUTPUT TAX, 68.13 TRANSPORT AND FREIGHT and 72.2 ZERO-RATED SUPPLIES.

3.12 **Buses with special facilities for carrying disabled persons**. Where a vehicle has less than ten seats because it is equipped with facilities for carrying persons in wheelchairs, it can be treated, for VAT purposes, as if it had at least ten seats. See 45.1 MOTOR CARS and 68.16 TRANSPORT AND FREIGHT.

3.13 **Repayment of import VAT to shipping agents and freight forwarders**. Under certain conditions, import VAT may be repaid directly to shipping agents and freight forwarders where importers go into insolvency or receivership leaving the agents unable to recover VAT paid on their behalf. See 34.8 IMPORTS.

3.14 **Zero-rating of certain supplies of free zone goods**. The supply of goods subject to import VAT which are free zone goods in the UK may be zero-rated on condition that there is an agreement between the supplier and the customer that the customer will clear the goods for removal from the zone and will take responsibility for payment of the import VAT. See 70.23 WAREHOUSED GOODS AND FREE ZONES.

3.15 **Printed matter published in instalments**. Individual component parts of loose-leaf books may be zero-rated. See 54.3 PRINTED MATTER, ETC

3.16 **Connection to gas and electricity mains supply**. The first time connection to the gas or electricity mains supply of a qualifying building, residential caravan or houseboat may be zero-rated. See 29.7 FUEL AND POWER.

3.17 **Zero-rating of supplies of training for foreign governments**. Zero-rating applies to training services supplied to a foreign government in furtherance of its sovereign activities. See 39.6 INTERNATIONAL SERVICES.

3.18 **Exemption of all domestic service charges**. All mandatory service charges paid by occupants of residential property towards the upkeep of the property and the provision of caretakers are exempt. See 42.4 LAND AND BUILDINGS.

3.19 **Supplies of 'relevant goods' to charities**. Zero-rating may be applied to supplies of 'relevant goods' to a charity either whose sole or main purpose is to provide a range of care services to meet the personal needs of handicapped people or which provides transport services predominantly for handicapped people. See 12.8 CHARITIES.

3.20 **Bad debt relief: repayment of input tax by purchaser: insolvency**. Where certain conditions are met, an insolvency practitioner need not repay input tax under *VATA 1994, s 36(4A)* where, after an insolvency procedure has commenced, the practitioner receives notice of a claim to VAT bad debt relief from a supplier in respect of a pre-insolvency transaction. See 7.13 BAD DEBT RELIEF and 35.4 INPUT TAX.

3.21 **Sale of poor quality donated goods**. The supply by a charity of goods which have been donated to it for sale can be zero-rated where the goods, although of a kind normally zero-rated by being made available to the general public for purchase, are by reason of their poor quality not fit to be so made available. See 12.6 CHARITIES.

3.22 **Valuation of the refurbishment or fitting out of a building for the purposes of the capital goods scheme**. Where it is difficult to identify goods affixed to a building for the purposes of *SI 1995/2518, Reg 113*(*h*), subject to conditions, goods which have not been affixed may be included in the value of capital expenditure. See 10.2 CAPITAL GOODS SCHEME.

3.23 **Supplies by Financial Ombudsman Services Ltd to ombudsman authorities**. Payments of any amount by the

- Office of the Building Societies Ombudsman (OBSO)
- Office of the Banking Ombudsman (OBO)
- Insurance Ombudsman Bureau (IOB)
- Personal Assurance Arbitration Service (PASS)
- PIA Ombudsman Bureau (PIAOB)
- Office of the Investment Ombudsman Bureau (OIOB)
- SFA Complaints Bureau and Arbitration Service (SFACBAS)
- FSA Independent Investigator (FSAII)

to Financial Ombudsman Services Ltd (FOS) for the supply of services by FOS in connection with the ombudsman and complaint handing scheme duties by OBSO, OBO, IOB, PAAS, PIAOB, OIOB, SFACBAS and FSAII (as the case may be) between 1 April 2000 and 1 October 2000 are not treated as consideration for any supply in the course of any business carried on by FOS.

3.24 **Charities providing care in an institution and also supplying goods to disabled persons resident in their own and other institutions**. Where conditions are met, zero-rating can be applied to supplies by a charity at or below cost of certain goods designed solely for use by a visually handicapped person even though the recipient of the supply is a resident, or is attending the premises of, the charity's own institution. See 32.17 HEALTH AND WELFARE.

3.25 **Resuscitation training models supplied to charities and other eligible bodies for use in first aid training**. These can be treated as relevant goods for the purposes of *VATA 1994, Sch 8 Group 15 Note* (*3*) and their supply zero-rated in certain cases. See 12.8 CHARITIES.

3.26 **Works of art, antiques and collectors' items**. Where certain works of art, collector's items and antiques are imported for exhibition with a view to possible sale, any sale of those items by auction when still subject to temporary importation arrangements is treated as neither a supply of goods nor a supply of services. See 71.4 WORKS OF ART, ETC.

3.27 **Use of the auctioneers' scheme for sales of goods at auction on behalf of non-taxable persons**. An auctioneer selling, on behalf of a third party vendor who is a non-taxable person, goods which have been grown, made or produced (including bloodstock or livestock reared from birth) by that person, may enter the goods into the auctioneers' scheme provided he holds an appropriate certificate from the vendor. See 61.54 SECOND-HAND GOODS.

3.28 **Supplies by Financial Services Authority to self-regulating organisations.** The payment of any amount at any time by

- the Investment Management Regulatory Organisation (IMRO),
- the Personal Investment Authority (PIA) or
- the Securities and Futures Authority (SFA)

to the Financial Services Authority (FSA) for the supply by the FSA in the carrying out of the regulatory functions of IMRO, PIA or SFA (as the case may be) between 1 April 1998 and 1 October 2000, and similar payments by

- the Registrar of Friendly Societies (RFS), and
- the Insurance Directorate of HM Treasury (ID)

(as the case may be) between 1 January 1999 and 1 October 2000

are not treated as consideration for any supply in the course or furtherance of any business carried on by FSA.

3.29 **Charitable buildings.** Where a building is used for business and non-business purposes, business use can be disregarded if less than 10%. See 42.1(13) LAND AND BUILDINGS.

3.30 **Retail pharmacists.** In applying a retail scheme, certain goods which are standard-rated when dispensed to individuals for personal use whilst an inpatient or resident of, or attending, a hospital or nursing home may be treated as zero-rated. See 60.19 RETAIL SCHEMES.

3.31 **Supplies by the Financial Services Compensation Scheme Ltd (FSCS) to compensation scheme authorities.** The payment of any amount at any time by the Investors Compensation Scheme (ICS), the Deposit Protection Scheme (DPS), the Building Societies Investor Protection Scheme (BSIPS), the Policyholders Protection Scheme (PPS), the Friendly Societies Protection Scheme (FSPS), and the Section 43 Scheme (S43S) for the supply of services by FSCS in carrying out the compensatory scheme functions of ICS, DPS, BSIPS, PPS, FSPS, and S43S (as the case may be) between 1 February 2001 and the coming into effect of the *Financial Services and Markets Act 2000* shall not be treated as consideration for any supply in the course of any business carried on by FSCS.

3.32 **Electronic face value vouchers.** Under *VATA 1994, Sch 6 para 5*, where a right to receive goods or services for an amount stated on any token, stamp or voucher is granted for a consideration, the consideration is disregarded except to the extent (if any) that it exceeds that amount. Although before 9 April 2003 the law only had application in relation to face value vouchers, etc which had a physical form, such as paper vouchers, from 8 March 2001 it was extended to face value vouchers, etc in electronic form provided that they operated in the same way as their physical counterparts. See 67.11 TRADE PROMOTION SCHEMES. *Note.* With effect from 9 April 2003, electronic face value vouchers are covered by legislation.

3.33 **Supplies previously made by the Post Office.** The *Postal Services Act 2000* replaced each reference to 'the Post Office' within VAT legislation with a reference to the Post Office Company. This concession maintains the scope of existing VAT reliefs following a restructuring of the Post Office corporation immediately prior to the transfer of the property, rights and liabilities of the corporation to the Post Office Company.

This concession extends the reference to the 'the Post Office Company' to include a reference to any wholly owned subsidiary of the Post Office Company providing the public postal service, for the purposes of

(*a*) the VAT exemption provided for postal services in *VATA 1994, Sch 9 Group 3, Items 1 and 2*; and

(*b*) the zero-rating of transport services provided for in *VATA 1994, Sch 8, Group 8, Item 4*(*b*); and

(*c*) the interpretation of 'datapost packet' provided for in *SI 1995/2518, Reg 2*(*1*).

Any reference in this concession to a wholly owned subsidiary shall be construed in accordance with *Companies Act 1985, s 736.*

3.34 **VAT reclaimed by museums and galleries covered by *VATA 1994, s 33A*.** Museums and galleries specified in an *Order* made under *VATA 1994, s 33A*(*9*) are not required to repay input tax, properly recovered at the time, on goods and services used in connection with taxable supplies of admitting the public for payment, solely on account of the move to free admission. See 35.13(16A) INPUT TAX.

3.35 **Apportionment of certain membership subscriptions to non-profit making bodies.** Bodies that are non-profit making and supply a mixture of zero-rated, exempt and/or standard-rated benefits to their members in return for their subscriptions may apportion such subscriptions to reflect the value and VAT liability of those individual benefits, without regard to whether there is one principal benefit. See 14.2 CLUBS AND ASSOCIATIONS.

3.36 **Imported works of art, antiques etc.** In case of works of art, antiques, etc falling within *VATA 1994, s 21*(*5*) with effect from 1 November 2001, *VATA 1994, s 21*(*6D*) ceases to have effect except in cases where conditions have been created artificially for obtaining the advantage of the reduced rate of VAT on importation. See 71.3 WORKS OF ART, ETC.

3.37 **Exemption for supplies of welfare services by private welfare agencies pending registration.** Where certain conditions are met, the exemption provided by statute for supplies of welfare services by private agencies with effect from 3 January 2003 applies to such supplies where the agency intends to be, but has not yet been, registered under the appropriate health care legislation. See 32.14 HEALTH AND WELFARE.

Facilitation of exports

8.1 **Sailaway boats.** Where a boat is supplied to a UK resident who intends to export it under its own power within two months of delivery and keep the boat outside the VAT territory of the EC for a continuous period of at least twelve months, the supplier may, subject to conditions, zero-rate the supply of the boat. See 25.19 EXPORTS.

Non-commercial transactions

9.1 **VAT on goods supplied at duty-free and tax-free shops.** Where goods liable to VAT are supplied to intending passengers at duty-free and tax-free shops approved by HMRC, the supplier may be regarded as the exporter and zero-rate the supply of those goods which are exported. See 25.2 EXPORTS.

9.2 **Marine fuel**. Certain supplies of marine fuel may be received free of VAT. See 25.3 EXPORTS.

9.3 **Personal reliefs for goods permanently imported from third countries**. Property purchased by diplomats, members of certain international organisations and NATO forces which otherwise qualifies for relief on the transfer of normal residence from outside the EC will not be refused relief solely because HMRC cannot satisfy themselves that the goods have borne all duties and taxes normally applicable in their country of origin. See 34.15(13) IMPORTS.

9.4 **Personal reliefs for goods permanently imported from third countries**. Property purchased outside the EC by UK forces which otherwise qualifies for relief on the transfer of normal residence from outside the EC will not be refused relief solely because HMRC cannot satisfy themselves that the goods have borne all duties and taxes normally applicable in their country of origin. See 34.15(13) IMPORTS.

9.5 **Personal reliefs for goods permanently imported from third countries**. Property purchased under a UK export scheme by members of the UK diplomatic service, members of UK forces and members of International Organisations and which otherwise qualifies for relief on the transfer of normal residence from outside the EC will not be refused relief solely because HMRC cannot satisfy themselves that the goods have borne all duties and taxes normally applicable in their country of origin. See 34.15(13) IMPORTS.

9.6 **Personal reliefs for goods permanently imported from third countries**. Personal belongings otherwise qualifying for relief on the transfer of normal residence from outside the EC may still be granted relief from VAT on importation if failing to qualify only because they have not been possessed and used for the specified period. See 34.15(13) IMPORTS.

9.7 **Personal reliefs for goods permanently imported from third countries**. Personal belongings otherwise qualifying for relief on the transfer of normal residence from outside the EC may still be granted relief from VAT on importation if failing to qualify only because the property is declared for relief outside the specific periods. See 34.15(13) IMPORTS.

De Voil Indirect Tax Service. See V1.239.

26.2 AGREEMENTS WITH TRADE BODIES

HMRC have entered into a number of agreements with trade bodies which permit their members to use procedures to meet their obligation under VAT law and which take into account their individual circumstances.

The agreements apply only to areas where HMRC can exercise discretion and they convey no direct financial advantage or relief from the legal requirements. Some of the agreements might usefully be applied to other businesses but note that any special method based on these arrangements can only be adopted with the approval of HMRC.

Agreements entered into at the time of publication are as follows. For full details, see VAT Notice 700/57/04.

- London Bullion Market Association (supplies of bullion).

- Brewers' Society (deduction of input tax in respect of brewers' tenanted estate).
- Association of British Factors and Discounters (partial exemption).
- Finance Houses Association Ltd (partial exemption).
- Association of British Insurers (recovery of input tax incurred in the UK in connection with supplies by branches outside the EC).
- Association of Investment Trust Companies (partial exemption).
- British Printing Industries Federation (apportionment of subsidy publishing supplies).
- Marine, aviation and transport insurance underwriters who are members of an (unnamed) trade organisation (claims-related input tax and associated imported services).
- Association of British Insurers, Lloyd's of London, the Institute of London Underwriters and the British Insurance and Investment Association (coding supplies of marine, aviation and transport insurance services).
- National Caravan Council Limited and the British Holiday and Home Park Association Limited (method of valuing removable contents sold with zero-rated caravans).
- Association of Unit Trust and Investment Managers (VAT liability of charges made in connection with personal equity plans).
- British Bankers' Association (VAT liability of electronic banking/cash management services).
- British Vehicle Rental and Leasing Association (car leasing and repairs and maintenance services).
- Society of Motor Manufacturers and Traders (output tax on the self-supply of a motor vehicle).
- Gaming Board for Great Britain and the British Casino Association (competitions in card rooms).
- British Phonographic Industry (VAT liability of promotional items given free of charge).
- Thoroughbred Breeders Association (arrangements under which racehorse owners may register for VAT).
- British Horseracing Board (revised arrangements under which racehorse owners may register for VAT).
- British Horseracing Board and Thoroughbred Breeders Association (racehorses applied permanently to personal or other non-business use).
- British Horseracing Board and Thoroughbred Breeders Association (keeping of stallions at stud).
- British Horseracing Board and Thoroughbred Breeders Association (racehorses and time limits for exportation).
- Meat and Livestock Commission (VAT treatment of levies collected (invoiced) from 1 October 1990 by the Commission from operators of slaughterhouses and exporters of live animals).

26.2 Extra-Statutory Concessions

- Society of Motor Manufacturers and Traders Ltd (how the one tonne payload test will be applied in practice to double cab pick-ups).
- Society of Motor Manufacturers and Traders Ltd (simplified method by which motor manufacturers, importers and wholesale distributors may calculate the VAT due on the private use of stock in trade cars provided to directors and employees free of charge).
- Retail Motor Industry Federation (simplified method by which retail motor dealers may calculate the VAT due on the private use of demonstrator cars provided to directors and employees free of charge).
- British Vehicle Rental and Leasing Association (simplified method which daily rental companies may use to calculate the VAT due on the incidental private use of their hire fleets).

27 Financial Services

Cross-reference. See 22.18 EUROPEAN COMMUNITY LEGISLATION for the provisions of the *EC 6th Directive*.

De Voil Indirect Tax Service. See V4.136.

The contents of this chapter are as follows.

27.1 INTRODUCTION

Before considering the question of the VAT liability of financial services, there are other relevant related areas of VAT law which affect financial services and which need to be taken into account.

27.2 Place of supply of financial services

Special place of supply rules apply to services falling within *VATA 1994, Sch 5 paras 1–8*. This includes financial services (*Sch 5 para 5*) and services rendered by one person to another in procuring such services for the other (*Sch 5 para 8*).

The place of supply of such services is treated as being

(*a*) where the *recipient* belongs if

- he belongs outside the EC; or
- he belongs in an EC country other than that of the supplier and the services are supplied to him for his business purposes; and

(*b*) where the *supplier* belongs in all other cases, ie where the recipient

- belongs in the UK or Isle of Man; or
- belongs in an EC country but not in the same country as the supplier and receives the supply other than for business purposes.

[*VATA 1994, s 7(10)(11); SI 1992/3121, Art 16*].

These provisions are considered in more detail in 64.26 and 64.27 SUPPLY. See 64.19 SUPPLY for the place of belonging. For the countries making up the EC, see 21.2 EUROPEAN COMMUNITY: GENERAL.

In the case of a UK supplier, supplies within (*a*) above are outside the scope of UK VAT and supplies within (*b*) above are exempt or taxable in the UK (depending on the nature of the supply).

Special 'easement' rule for sales of securities. When (and only when) the identity (and hence the place of belonging) of a purchaser of securities is not known to a UK supplier, the supplier may either treat the supply as taking place in the UK or may determine the place of supply as follows.

(i) *If the place of the transaction* (*ie relevant security exchange*) *is known*

- a sale transacted in the UK is treated as made to a person belonging in the UK (ie within (*b*) above);
- a sale transacted elsewhere in the EC is treated as made to a taxable person belonging in another EC country (ie within (*a*) above); and
- a sale transacted outside the EC is treated as made to a person belonging outside the EC (ie with (*a*) above).

(ii) *If the place of the transaction is not known*, the place of supply can be deemed to be where the security is listed.

(iii) *If the place of the transaction is not known and the security is not listed* (*or is listed on both an EC and non-EC exchange*), then a sale can be deemed to be transacted where the final broker belongs.

(VAT Notice 701/49/02, para 9.2).

27.3 Input tax recovery

Subject to the normal rules, input tax may be recovered which relates to

- taxable supplies of financial services (ie supplies with a place of supply in the UK other than exempt supplies);
- supplies of financial services with a place of supply outside the UK but which would be taxable supplies if made in the UK;
- supplies of financial services which

  (i) are supplied to a person who belongs outside the EC; or

  (ii) are directly linked to the export of goods to a place outside the EC; or

  (iii) consist of the provision of intermediary services (see 27.25 below) in relation to any transaction within (i) or (ii) above

  provided the supply is exempt or would have been exempt if made in the UK.

[*VATA 1994, s 26(1)(2); SI 1999/3121*].

27.4 Reverse charge on financial services from abroad

Where a business belonging in the UK

- receives financial services for the purpose of its business from a person who belongs abroad, and
- those services would be taxable financial services within *VATA 1994, Sch 5* (see 64.26 SUPPLY) if supplied in the UK,

the same consequences apply as if the business had itself supplied those services in the UK. [*VATA 1994, s 8(1)(2)*]. It must account for output tax, calculated on the full value of the supply received, in Box 1 of its VAT return and, subject to the normal rules, can include the VAT as input tax in Box 4 on the same return.

This 'reverse charge' procedure does not apply to services provided by an overseas head office or branch which is the same legal entity as the business (unless it simply pays for such a service received by the UK business). But it does apply to certain services received within a VAT group, which are bought in by an overseas group member and supplied on either in their own right or as a component in a larger supply, to the UK members of the group. See 31.6 GROUPS OF COMPANIES.

27.5 Partial exemption

As will be seen later in this chapter, most suppliers of financial services are likely to be either wholly exempt (and can recover none of their input tax) or partly exempt (because their input tax relates to both taxable and exempt supplies). In the latter case, they may not be able to reclaim all of their input tax and will have to use a partial exemption method to calculate the proportion which can be claimed. See 49 PARTIAL EXEMPTION.

27.6 Single or multiple supply

Certain financial services (eg intermediary services and outsourcing) can constitute a number of component services which, if supplied separately, may have different VAT liabilities. In order to establish the correct liability of such packaged services, certain tests must be applied to determine the overall VAT liability. See 64.6 SUPPLY.

27.7 OVERVIEW OF THE LAW ON THE LIABILITY OF FINANCIAL SERVICES

EC legislation. Certain financial services are exempt from VAT under *EC Sixth Directive, Art 13B(d)*. See 22.18(*c*)–(*h*) EUROPEAN COMMUNITY LEGISLATION.

UK law. The equivalent UK provisions are in *VATA 1994, Sch 9 Group 5*. This lists a number of *Items* which provide for exemption for the following categories (subject to qualifications and definitions which are dealt with in the appropriate part of the chapter).

(1) The issue, transfer or receipt of, or any dealing with, money, any security for money or any note or order for the payment of money. See 27.8 below.

(2) The making of any advance or the granting of any credit. See 27.11 below.

(2A) The management of credit by the person granting it. See 27.11 below.

(3) The provision of the facility of instalment credit finance in a hire purchase, conditional sale or credit sale agreement for which facility a separate charge is made and disclosed to the recipient of the supply of goods. See 27.11 below.

(4) The provision of administrative arrangements and documentation and the transfer of title to the goods in connection with the supply described in Item (3) if the total consideration therefor is specified in the agreement and does not exceed £10. See 27.11 below.

(5) The provision of intermediary services in relation to any transaction comprised in Items (1), (2), (3), (4) or (6) (whether or not any such transaction is finally concluded) by a person acting in an intermediary capacity. See 27.25 below.

(5A) The underwriting of an issue within Item (1) or any transaction within Item (6). See 27.23 below.

(6) The issue, transfer or receipt of, or any dealing with, any security or secondary security. See 27.17 below.

(7) (Deleted).

(8) The operation of any current, deposit or savings account. See 27.24 below.

(9) The management of an authorised unit trust scheme or of a trust based scheme. See 27.20 below.

(10) The management of the scheme property of an open-ended investment company. See 27.21 below.

Many services which are associated with finance are not covered by the exemption. In addition to services covered in the text generally when dealing with exemptions, see 27.32 below for a list of some of the more common finance-rated supplies which are standard-rated.

It is common for businesses in the finance sector to sub-contract some of their work to a third party. This is usually known as 'outsourcing' and the VAT position is considered in 27.30 below.

27.8 DEALINGS WITH MONEY AND SECURITIES FOR MONEY

Exemption applies to the issue, transfer or receipt of, and any dealings with

- money,
- any security for money; or
- any note or order for the payment of money

but excludes the following.

- All services falling within 27.17 below (which are exempt under those provisions).
- A supply of services which is preparatory to the carrying out of such a transaction (eg the preparation and delivery of data such as a wages roll, which is then put into effect by someone else). Preparatory services carried out by an intermediary as part of their overall exempt supply are exempt (see 27.25 below).
- The supply of coins or banknotes (whether legal tender or not) as collectors' pieces or investment articles. This includes items of numismatic interest (including proof coins and Maundy money) which are normally taxable on the full selling price, whether or not they are sold for more than their face value. See, however, 61.3 SECOND-HAND GOODS for the use of the second-hand

scheme for supplies of collectors' pieces. Sales of some gold coins are exempt as investment gold. See 30 GOLD AND PRECIOUS METALS.

[*VATA 1994, Sch 9 Group 5 Item 1 and Notes 1, 1A, 2; SI 1999/594*]. (VAT Notice 701/49/02, paras 2.4, 2.6).

Issue. The issue of *money* can only be by a bank or similar financial institution. A coin or banknote can only be issued once (the first time) and this can only be done by a bank with a statutory entitlement to do so (eg the Bank of England). The above exemption is normally superseded by *VATA 1994, Sch 8 Group 11 Item 1* which zero-rates the issue by a bank of a note payable to the bearer on demand (see 72.4 ZERO-RATED SUPPLIES). But see *Royal Bank of Scotland Group plc v C & E Commrs, CS [2002] STC 575 (TVC 26.3)* where the bank was authorised to issue its own bank notes, which it did from automated cash machines. The court held that the 'reciprocity fees' which the bank received from other banks whose customers had used its machines to withdraw cash were not consideration for a zero-rated supply of bank notes but for an exempt supply of the provision of the facilities to obtain money.

Transfer. For the purposes of *EC Sixth Directive, Art 13B(d)(3)* a 'transfer' has been defined as a ' transaction consisting of the execution of an order for the transfer of a sum of money from one bank account to another. It is characterized in particular by the fact that it involves a change in the legal and financial situation existing between the person giving the order and the recipient and between those parties and their respective banks.' (*Sparekassernes Datacenter (SDC) v Skatteministeriet, CJEC [1997] STC 932 (TVC 21.243)*).

Money. '*Money*' includes currencies other than sterling [*VATA 1994, s 96(1)*] and comprises currency, coins or banknotes, in sterling or any other currency, when supplied as legal tender in a financial transaction. (VAT Notice 701/49/02, para 2.1).

Security for money. A 'security for money' has been defined as a document under seal or under hand at a consideration containing a covenant, promise or undertaking to pay a sum of money (*Dyrham Park Country Club Ltd (VTD 700) (TVC 13.31)*). Examples include bills of exchange, promissory notes, travellers' cheques and postal orders.

For the purposes of *Item 1* above, securities do not include stocks, shares, bonds and other similar securities for which exemption is covered by *VATA 1994, Sch 9 Group 5 Item 6* (see 27.17 below). It is often difficult to decide whether securities for money fall within *Item 1* or *Item 6*. If the security only gives to a person a right of money it will probably fall within *Item 1* whereas if it gives a right to shares, legal entities, etc (which rights may themselves give rise to the payment of money (eg debentures)) it will fall within *Item 6*. Although both supplies are exempt, the distinction is important as, if intermediaries are involved in an *Item 1* supply, they must carry out some preparatory work in order for their supplies to be exempt. There is no such requirement for intermediaries involved in *Item 6* supplies. See 27.25 below.

The value of the exempt supply is the charge made (which may not necessarily be the face value of the security). The redemption of a security for money is outside the scope of VAT.

(VAT Notice 701/49/02, para 3.1; Internal Guidance V1–7, Chapter 20 para 2.3.2).

Note or order for the payment of money. A note for the payment of money is a banknote. An order can include postal orders, giros and cheques, etc but can be as informal as an 'IOU'. An example of an exempt transaction is where a building society charges its customer a fee for withdrawing funds by cheque.

The actual price paid is the consideration for a supply and amounts payable on redemption remain outside the scope of VAT.

(Internal Guidance V1–7, Chapter 20 para 2.3.3).

Dealing with money. A supply of services involving dealing with money is exempt provided:

- The services deal with money as money and not as goods. It is important to distinguish between money (and other financial instruments) being dealt 'in' as physical goods (eg a numismatic dealer or a security company stocking up ATMs) and money being dealt 'with' as a service (eg a bank's over-the-counter foreign exchange service).
- A financial transaction is carried out.

The more obvious dealings with money are the routine financial transactions carried out by banks, building societies, bureaux de change and similar institutions, eg

- the acceptance of deposits of money on current account or otherwise;
- money transfer services; and
- exchange of legal tender.

(VAT Notice 701/49/02, para 2.1; Internal Guidance V1–7, Chapter 20 para 2.3.5).

27.9 Related transactions

Listed below are examples of common transactions connected with supplies within 27.8 above and their VAT liability.

(1) **Automatic teller machines (ATMs)**

The supply of

- an ATM or the software required to run it (whether or not the consideration is based on the ATM's use), and
- ATM replenishment services

are taxable supplies.

ATM providers sometimes make charges described as convenience fees, interchange fees or reciprocity fees. These are charges to banks by other banks when those other bank's customers use their ATM facilities. Where the charge is for

- the facility to obtain money,
- the provision of money,
- transaction processing, or
- the operation of accounts

the supply is exempt.

The provision of a site for an ATM is an exempt licence to occupy land (subject to the option to tax being exercised by the site owner).

(VAT Notice 701/49/02, para 2.9).

See also *Royal Bank of Scotland Group plc v C & E Commrs, CS [2002] STC 575 (TVC 26.3)*.

(2) **Cash collection services and sorting and counting money**

Services of carriage of cash, re-stocking cash machines, sorting and counting money are, when supplied on their own, taxable. This is because the services being applied to the cash are the same as that which could be applied to any type of goods. For the exemption to apply the service must deal with money as money and not purely as goods. See *Williams & Glyn's Bank Ltd (VTD 118) (TVC 26.1)* and *Nationwide Anglia Building Society (VTD 11826) (TVC 26.2)*.

Services that have the effect of making payments or transfers between bank accounts where there is no further intervention by the bank are exempt. Where a supply has a mixture of taxable and exempt elements, its overall character will determine the liability.

(VAT Notice 701/49/02, para 2.2).

(3) **Compensation payments for dishonoured cheques**

Any compensation sought from customers to cover bank charges incurred because they have failed to honour their cheques or direct debit payments is outside the scope of VAT. (VAT Notice 701/49/02, para 2.11).

(4) **Currency swaps**

These may arise where, for example, a British firm needs to buy American dollars and an American firm needs to buy sterling. As the firms may be able to borrow funds more cheaply in their own countries, they agree to borrow their own currency and contract to charge each other the interest payments on the principal amounts.

Where there is no transfer of the principal sum, a currency swap is an exempt supply, the value of which is the net amount received by either party on the payment date. Where there is an actual transfer of a principal sum, the supply is also exempt but the value of the supply is the gross amount received by each party, excluding the amount of the principal sum.

(5) **Deductions from pay**

Charges made by an employer for deductions from pay of employees for items such as insurance premiums, mortgage repayments or union subscriptions are exempt.

Any charges made for deductions from the pay in compliance with an attachment of earnings order are seen as reimbursement for expenses incurred in carrying out a statutory duty and are outside the scope of VAT.

(VAT Notice 701/49/02, para 2.12).

(6) **Derivatives**

Derivatives are used to protect against risk. They are known as 'derivatives' because their price is derived from an underlying asset, sometimes known as the 'underlying'. The most common types of derivatives are related to an underlying commodity, financial instrument or currency. To establish the VAT liability of the derivative, in most cases, it is necessary to know what the 'underlying' is.

(*a*) *Commodity futures, options and other derivatives.* A commodity is a raw material such as grain, coffee, metal or oil and is traded on a commodity market. This can be based in the country of the commodity's origin or on a 'terminal market' (a commodity market in a trading centre, such as

London). As commodity prices fluctuate widely, commodity exchanges assist in enabling producers and users of the commodity to hedge the price risk with outside speculators and investors.

See 65 TERMINAL MARKETS for the zero-rating of transactions traded on certain terminal markets by or with a member of that market or by a person acting as an agent or broker between a member of the market and another person.

For transactions not traded on one of those terminal markets:

- Commodity futures and actuals follow the liability of the underlying commodity.
- The premium paid for a commodity option is separate from the price of underlying commodity and is payable whether or not the buyer exercises the option. The payment for the right to buy a commodity, rather than a contract to buy it, is a standard-rated supply of services. If the option is exercised, there will be a separate supply of the commodity itself.

(*b*) *Financial futures*. Financial futures are exempt from VAT and for VAT purposes are divided into two categories, cash settled contracts and non-cash settled contracts. Although both are exempt, which category the supply falls into is important because it may affect whether the supply by an agent or intermediary arranging the transaction is exempt or taxable. See 27.29(3) below.

(i) *Cash settled contracts* (*Item 1* contracts), ie contracts where there are no underlying deliverable securities. These include short-term interest rate futures, FT-SE 100 and other stock index futures.

The supply of cash settled contracts for a consideration as principal is exempt from VAT. Where a futures contract runs to maturity, there is no further supply for VAT purposes. Cash settlements under these contracts are not consideration for a supply and must be excluded from partial exemption calculations and VAT returns.

(ii) *Non-cash settled contracts* (*Item 6* contracts), ie contracts where there are underlying deliverable securities. These include gilts, T-bonds and other securities (not being securities for money).

The supply of a non-cash settled contract is exempt. Where the contract specification does not provide for delivery of the underlying security (ie they are cash settled), it should be treated as a cash settled contract (under (i) above). If a contract runs to maturity there is a separate exempt supply of the underlying security. Transactions on exchanges are treated as being made between either the member and the client or the member and the relevant clearing house. The value of the supply of the securities is the price that was agreed when the contract was made.

Exchange trading in financial futures falls into three categories:

- *Member-to-client and member-to-member transactions*. Members of certain exchanges deal as principals and the 'turn' (or commission) charged by the member to a client for transacting a financial futures contract represents the value of the member's supply. A member may charge for each leg, or for a 'round trip' in a closed-out transaction. The full value of each charge is the measure of the supply for VAT purposes. The 'turn' (or commission) is consideration for an exempt supply of financial futures.

There is no supply for VAT purposes when members trade on their own account with other members or when members close out their position.

- *Client-to-member transactions.* There is no supply by a client to a member in a closed-out financial futures transaction.
- *Members acting for another member.* Where a member acts for another member in executing a transaction, he is a principal and the 'turn' (or commission) charged is exempt. The value of the supply is the amount charged to the member. Clearing fees charged by a clearing member to a non-clearing member are also consideration for an exempt supply.

(*c*) *Financial options.* There are three main types of financial options contracts:

- *Options based on financial futures contracts.* Options on short-term interest rate futures, index-based futures and cash-settled futures are exempt from VAT. (These are options on cash settled contracts under (*b*)(i) above.) There is no further supply when an option is exercised to obtain or supply the underlying futures contracts.
- *Equity options.* These options have equities, rather than financial futures contracts, as the underlying instrument and are exempt from VAT. (These are options on non-cash settled contracts under (*b*)(ii) above.) If such an option is exercised there will be a further exempt supply of equities.
- *Index-based options.* Unlike equity options, index-based options do not provide for delivery but are cash settled. This type of option is exempt (as an option on a cash settled contract under (*b*)(i) above).

Although both are exempt, whether the option is on a cash settled or non-cash settled contract is important because it may affect whether the supply of an agent or intermediary arranging the transaction is exempt or taxable. See 27.29(3) below.

(*d*) *Contracts for differences* (CFDs). Contracts offer speculators the opportunity to buy or sell the performance of a share, equity, etc without the need to own the underlying asset. A CFD is exempt from VAT as a financial derivative. The CFD is treated as a cash settled contract for the purposes of defining the VAT liability of an intermediary's supply (see 27.29(3) below).

(VAT Notice 701/9/02, paras 2.2–2.4).

(7) **Face value vouchers**

Face value vouchers that give a right to goods or services are not seen as securities for money. However, where a voucher gives a guarantee that the bearer will be reimbursed in money to the amount stated on the voucher, this is a security for money and is exempt. (VAT Notice 701/49/02, para 3.1). See 67 TRADE PROMOTION SCHEMES.

(8) **Financial spread bets**

This is betting on financial instruments and involves speculating by placing a bet on an index of commodity prices or the FT-SE 100 index. In the same way as sports betting, financial spread betting is exempt from VAT under the *VATA 1994, Sch 9, Group 4*. (Internal Guidance V1–7, Chapter 20 para 2.10.3).

(9) **Foreign exchange transactions**

Foreign exchange transactions are exempt supplies. Where a person acts as principal, the consideration is any fees or commission charged. Following the decision in *C & E Commrs v First National Bank of Chicago, CJEC [1998] STC 850 (TVC 21.62)* HMRC accept that where no specific commission or fee is charged on particular transactions (eg where services are paid for by the spread between the bid and offer rates), those transactions are nevertheless supplies for VAT purposes, the consideration being 'the net result of the transactions of the supplier of the service over a given period of time', ie the net profit on the transactions. In most cases it will be appropriate to isolate the input tax incurred on foreign exchange transactions and deal with VAT separately within the partial exemption method used. (Business Brief 16/98).

(10) **Guarantees and surety bonds**

The VAT liability of these types of products depends on the precise nature of the arrangements. They must be financial instruments which are securities for money as defined above. Exemption will not apply to the supply of warranties or contracts for the supply, repair or maintenance of goods even though they are sometimes referred to as guarantees. (VAT Notice 701/49/02, para 3.1).

(11) **Interest rate swaps**

Interest rate swaps are a form of dealing between banks and other financial institutions in which borrowers exchange fixed interest rates on their debts for floating interest rates, or vice versa. For VAT purposes, during the term of the swap there is a continuous supply of services and, to the extent that any money changes hands, there is an exempt supply. The party making the net payment is regarded as making a supply for no consideration (therefore, no supply for VAT purposes). (Internal Guidance V1–7, Chapter 20 para 2.10.1).

(12) **Internet payment services (IPS)**

With the growth of shopping on the internet, the question of secure payment methods have become a priority for retailers and customers. Many retailers use IPS providers whose sole aim is to offer a payment service and deal with the collection and distribution of customers' payments. Typically:

- The customer accesses the site of an e-retailer and purchases goods. When deciding to pay, he is taken from the e-retailer's site to the site of the IPS provider where he will complete an on-screen form with his name, address and payment details.
- The IPS provider requests payment from the customer. This payment is transferred into the IPS provider's bank account where it remains for a specified time. The IPS provider then transfers the money, less commission, to the e-retailer.
- At no time does the IPS provider deal with the goods.

In such circumstances, the IPS provider's services are exempt. If, instead, the IPS provider instructs the customer to issue payment to directly to the e-retailer, although there is no 'dealing with money' in this case, the services may still be exempt as it is affecting 'transfers' of money.

(Internal Guidance V1–7, Chapter 20 para 2.5.8).

(13) **Payment services for household bills**

Several organisations offer over-the-counter bill payment services, either directly or through a corner shop network. The public presents utility, council tax and other bills, with payment, at the counter. Payments are accepted, collated and passed to the utility company, etc. Such services can be funded by a charge to the utility company or a charge to the member of the public using the service. In either case the supply is exempt.

Payments made by a collecting organisation to retailers in the corner shop network are also exempt. They are payment for exempt supplies of services by the retailer to the collecting organisation.

(Internal Guidance V1–7, Chapter 20 para 2.5.5).

(14) **Travellers' cheques**

The issue or encashment of travellers' cheques is exempt. Unissued or unsigned travellers' cheques are neither securities for money nor notes for the payment of money, and their supply to, or importation by, the issuing bank is taxable on their value as stationery.

(VAT Notice 701/49/02, para 3.1).

27.10 DEBT ASSIGNMENT, FACTORING AND DISCOUNTING

Businesses may sell their debts and/or sell the underlying title to the goods represented by the debts. Such transactions include the following.

(1) **Debt assignment**

Instead of waiting for payment of a debt and carrying the risk of late settlement or default, a business may sell the debt to someone else. The assignment of a debt for a consideration is exempt under *VATA 1994, Sch 9 Group 5 Item 1* (see 27.8 above). The value of the supply is the gross amount that the assignee pays for the debt. (VAT Notice 701/49/02, para 4.1).

(2) **Factoring**

Factors may make a number of supplies. They purchase a client's debts, payable at an agreed future date, but may also provide pre-payment finance facilities and an administration service made up of a sales ledger and credit management function. The VAT treatment of these services may vary.

Recourse and non-recourse agreements.

- A recourse agreement allows the factor to take sole responsibility for debtor account management. The factor normally provides an advance of money to the supplier (creditor) with monies owed by the debtors accepted as collateral. The normal requirement is for the management of the debt to revert back to the supplier if certain conditions, specified in the agreement, have not been satisfied (eg if a customer fails to pay a debt within a certain period of time or a legal dispute arises concerning the goods or services supplied).

- A non-recourse agreement is a simpler form of agreement where the factor buys the debt even if the suppliers' customer does not pay. If the debt is legally assigned to the factor, the factor will be able to sue in its own name in the event of default. However, if the assignment is an equitable one, the assignee can only sue the debtor if it does so jointly with the assignor who has no recourse in the event of non-payment by the debtor.

Exempt supplies. The elements which make up an exempt factoring service are:

- The sale of certain rights in a debt to a factor (including the right to receive payment).
- The advance of money charged for by interest (sometimes known as a 'discount fee').
- The payment facility made by electronic transfer by the factor for a debt, usually charged for by a fee.

Administration services provided by a factor are taxable and usually include all or some of the following.

- Credit approval of clients' customers
- Despatch of clients' invoices
- Sales ledger and credit management facilities
- Sending out monthly statements to customers
- Collecting payments from customers of clients
- Pursuing late payers including issuing court proceedings
- Providing reports on collections
- Providing accounting information (such as statistics and debt analysis)
- Service charges imposed by a factor in a recourse or non-recourse agreement

Cash accounting scheme. See 63.6 SPECIAL SCHEMES for accounting for VAT where the cash accounting scheme is used.

Bad debts relief. See 7.1 BAD DEBT RELIEF.

(VAT Notice 701/49/02, para 4.2).

(3) **Invoice discounting**

Invoice discounters usually provide financial facilities but with little or no administration. Agreements often require clients to collect their own outstanding debts. The provision of finance is generally exempt under *VATA 1994, Sch 9 Group 5 Item 2* (see 27.11 below), whilst the supply of separate administration services is taxable.

(4) **Block discounting**

Under block discounting, a retailer normally enters into a contract with a customer for the hire of goods and then assigns the interest in the goods, including the right to receive rental payments, to a finance house in return for a capital sum. The finance house benefits from the difference between the lump sum paid and the total rent it will receive over the life of the arrangements.

- Where the title of the goods passes from the dealer to the finance house (but not under hire purchase or conditional sale agreements), the transaction is subject to VAT at the same rate as the supply of the goods. The finance house becomes the lessor for the period of the block discount and accounts for output tax on the rentals received. The retailer continues to collect all the rental payments under the original contract, remitting them to the finance house which, in turn, invoices the retailer for the total monthly sum. The finance house has no direct dealings with the customer.
- Where there is no transfer of title in the goods, the transaction is an exempt assignment of debts (see (1) above). The retailer is responsible for accounting for VAT on the rental receipts.

(Internal Guidance V1–7, Chapter 20 para 4.5).

27.11 PROVISION OF CREDIT

The following supplies of financial services in the UK are exempt from VAT.

(*a*) The making of any advance or the granting of any credit. *Included* is the supply of credit by a person, in connection with the supply of goods or services by him, for which a separate charge is made and disclosed to the recipient of the supply of goods or services. [*VATA 1994, Sch 9 Group 5 Item 2 and Note 3*].

Item 2 covers most of the normal types of credit transactions, eg loans, overdrafts and other forms of advances. The value of the exempt supply is normally the gross interest but there is sometimes an arrangement fee or other type of fee charged. All these represent consideration for the supply of the advance or credit and are exempt.

Interest paid on deposits with a bank or building society is also consideration for the making of an advance – the advance being made by the customer.

Where a business takes out a commercial mortgage, even though the loan is often secured against the asset purchased, this still represents free-standing credit because the money is lent as finance. The mortgage company is making an exempt supply of credit to the mortgagor and the consideration is the interest charged for that loan.

(Internal Guidance V1–7, Chapter 20 para 5.3).

(*b*) *With effect from 1 August 2003*, the management of credit by the person granting it. [*VATA 1994, Sch 9 Group 5 Item 2A; SI 2003/1569*].

A supply of credit management could typically include the following transactions:

(i) Credit checking (includes debt profiling, assessing credit worthiness, electoral roll checks and obtaining references).

(ii) Valuation (of assets such as property, land, vehicles).

(iii) Authorisation services (beyond just checking the applicant's signature or agreeing credit or payment limits).

(iv) Taking decisions on credit applications.

(v) Creating and maintaining records in order to fulfil legal obligations.

(vi) Monitoring a creditor's payment record or dealing with overdue payments.

After 9 March 1999 and before 1 August 2003, a supply of services comprising the 'management of credit', other than such a supply made by the person granting the credit, was specifically excluded from exemption and was standard-rated. For these purposes, a person made a supply of services comprising the '*management of credit*' if he performed any one or more of the transactions in (i)–(vi) above in relation to the operation of a credit, a credit card, a chargecard or a similar payment card.

These provisions were introduced following the tribunal decision in *FDR Ltd (VTD 16040) (TVC 26.4)*. The company provided various credit card transaction processing services to banks which could broadly be described as 'clearing house' services for card transactions. The tribunal held that the services should be treated as transfers of money and exempt from VAT. The Court of Appeal upheld the tribunal decision (*FDR Ltd v C & E Commrs, CA [2000] STC 672 (TVC 26.4)*). In his judgment, Laws LJ also indicated that the supplies in question fell within *EC Sixth Directive, Art 13B(d)(3)* and as such, despite the change in UK legislation, would still be exempt under EC law. As a result, HMRC confirmed that where a business supplying outsourced services was able to show that it was making a single supply, and a transfer between accounts was at the core of that supply (or was the predominant element) then it was entitled to exemption. (Business Brief 10/01).

The removal of this exclusion means that, from 1 August 2003, a relevant supply of financial services is taxed or exempted according to its overall character instead of by reference to the presence or absence of any of the services listed above.

(*c*) The provision of the facility of instalment credit in a hire purchase, conditional sale or credit sale agreement for which a separate charge is made and disclosed to the recipient of the goods. [*VATA 1994, Sch 9 Group 5 Item 3 and Note 3*]. The value of the exempt supply is the interest paid with each repayment. See 27.12 to 27.15 below for hire purchase, conditional sale and credit sale agreements generally.

(*d*) The provision of administrative arrangements and documentation and the transfer of title to the goods in connection with the supply within (*c*) above if the total consideration is specified in the agreement and does not exceed £10. [*VATA 1994, Sch 9 Group 5 Item 4*]. The value of the exempt supply is the fee for the administrative arrangements, etc.

See, however, *Wagon Finance Ltd (VTD 16288) (TVC 26.13)* where the tribunal held that administrative fees in connection with credit transactions were exempt from VAT irrespective of the £10 limit as the company had provided customers with the facility of instalment credit within (*c*) above. Customs decided not to appeal against this decision and accept that exemption applies to any connected credit ancillary charge unless the contract explicitly states that the charge relates, wholly or partially, to the supply of goods. Such exempt charges are likely to be shown as administration, documentation or acceptance fees. Fees related to the goods (eg option fees or fees for transfer of title) are taxable unless within the £10 limit. (Business Brief 27/99).

27.12 **Hire purchase, etc**

If the possession of goods is transferred under agreements which expressly contemplate that the property also will pass at some time in the future (determined by, or ascertainable from, the agreements but in any case not later than when the goods are fully paid for) a supply of goods takes place. [*VATA 1994, Sch 4 para 1*(*2*)(*b*)].

The most common methods of supplying goods with credit are:

(*a*) **Hire purchase agreements**. Legally, under such agreements goods are hired for periodic payments and the hirer has the option to purchase. However, the VAT supply position is the same as for conditional sale (see below) because it is intended that ownership is to be transferred.

(*b*) **Conditional sale agreements**. These are agreements for the sale of goods where the price is payable by instalments and the goods remain the property of the seller until the full price is paid or another condition is met by the customer. The full amount of VAT on the goods is normally payable with the first instalment.

(*c*) **Credit sale agreements**. These are agreements for the sale of goods which immediately become the property of the customer but where the price is payable by instalments.

Supplies not involving finance companies. If an agreement is made to supply goods under (*a*)–(*c*) above without involving a finance company (self-financed credit), any charge for credit disclosed as a separate charge to the customer is exempt. The consideration for the taxable supply of goods is the cash price stated in the agreement, before any deposit is paid.

If the goods are supplied on interest-free credit, allowing the customer to pay for the goods over a set period without charging interest, the supply of the goods is taxed according to their liability. As there is no charge for credit, there is no exempt supply for VAT purposes.

Any connected credit ancillary charges are exempt unless the contract explicitly states that the charge relates, wholly or partially, to the supply of goods. If the supply relates to the credit, normally shown as administration, documentation or acceptance fees, it is exempt. Fees that relate to the goods (eg option fees or fees for transfer of title) are not exempt unless the charge for them is £10 or less (see 27.11(*d*) above).

Finance companies. If the finance company becomes the owner of goods (eg when a purchase is financed by a hire-purchase agreement) the supply of goods is by the supplier to the finance company, not the customer, and is taxable. The finance company in turn, makes a supply of goods and a supply of credit. The supply of credit is exempt if the credit charge is disclosed to the customer in writing.

If the finance company does not become owner of the goods (eg when a purchase is financed by a loan agreement) the supply of goods is to the customer, not the finance company, even though that company may make the payment direct to the supplier. The supply is taxable and VAT is due on the selling price to the customer even if a lesser amount is received from the finance company. See *C & E Commrs v Primback Ltd, CJEC [2001] STC 803 (TVC 21.168)*. The finance company, in a separate transaction, makes a supply of credit facilities to the customer.

(VAT Notice 700, para 8.4).

Time of supply. VAT is due on the full value of the *goods* at the time of supply (see 64.32 SUPPLY). The tax point for the exempt supply of the *services* is treated as taking place each time a payment is received unless HMRC has approved a written application for an earlier date to be used. (VAT Notice 700, para 15.11). For administrative reasons, application is often made to treat the supply of goods and exempt services as taking place together.

27.13 *Transfers of agreements*

(*a*) **By the owner**. If the owner of the goods assigns his rights, interests and ownership under a hire-purchase or conditional sale agreement to

- *a bank or finance company* (for example, under a block discounting arrangement) the transfer is outside the scope of VAT. [*SI 1995/1268, Art 5(4)*]; or
- *a dealer* (for example, under a recourse agreement) the transfer is a single supply of goods and is taxable in the normal way.

(*b*) **By the customer**. If a customer buys goods under a hire purchase or conditional sale agreement and subsequently transfers his rights and obligations to another customer, he is making a standard-rated supply of services to the new customer. There is no supply for VAT purposes from the owner to the new customer. VAT must be accounted for on the open market value of the supply, ie the total amount payable by the new customer to the owner to complete the agreement plus any amount he pays to the original customer to secure the transfer. See also *Phillip Drakard Trading Ltd v C & E Commrs, QB [1992] STC 568 (TVC 60.94)*.

27.14 *Repossession of goods*

Where goods are supplied under a hire purchase or conditional sale agreement, including a reservation of title (Romalpa) agreement, all VAT due under the agreement on the goods is payable at the outset. See 27.12 above. If the goods are subsequently repossessed or returned, there is no supply of goods since title has not yet passed and the goods return to their legal owner. Neither is there a supply of services as there is no consideration. On repossession of goods not fully paid for, the supplier cannot issue a credit note for the amount invoiced and substitute a new invoice for hire charges for the period of use (*Mannesmann Demag Hamilton Ltd (VTD 1437) (TVC 38.75)*).

The supplier can claim bad debt relief on the unpaid amount. See 7.8 BAD DEBT RELIEF.

27.15 *Sale of repossessed assets*

The sale of goods by

- a person (including a finance company) who repossessed them under the terms of a finance agreement, or
- an insurer or mortgagee who has taken possession of them in settlement of a claim under a policy of insurance or terms of mortgage

is a supply and VAT must normally be paid on the full selling price. However, sales of

(i) boats and aircraft by a mortgagee after he has taken possession of them under the terms of a marine or aircraft mortgage, or

(ii) works of art, antiques and collectors' items (see 71.3 WORKS OF ART, ETC), and second-hand goods by a person who has repossessed them under the terms of a finance agreement or by an insurer in settlement of a claim under an insurance policy

are outside the scope of VAT if the following conditions are met.

(*a*) The goods so disposed are in the same condition at the time of disposal as when they were repossessed or taken into possession. The condition of goods has been changed if any improvements, repairs, replacement parts or the generally making good of any damage has been carried out. The cleaning of goods generally does not affect the condition nor does the inclusion of instruction manuals if they are otherwise missing. (Business Brief 19/01).

(*b*) For goods other than motor cars,

(i) if the goods had been supplied in the UK by the person from whom they were obtained, that supply would not have been chargeable with VAT or would have been chargeable on less than full value (eg because the defaulting customer had not acquired the goods for business purposes or they were margin scheme supplies);

(ii) if the goods have been imported into the UK, they must have borne VAT which has neither been reclaimed nor refunded; and

(iii) the goods must not have been reimported having previously been exported from the UK free of VAT by reason of zero-rating.

(*c*) In the case of motor cars, the VAT on any previous supply, acquisition or importation must have been wholly excluded from credit.

[*SI 1992/3122, Arts 2, 4; SI 1995/1268, Arts 2, 4; SI 1995/1269; SI 1995/1385; SI 1995/1667; SI 1999/3118; SI 1999/3120; SI 2001/3649, Art 432; SI 2004/3084; SI 2004/3085*].

Where the above conditions are not satisfied, VAT is normally chargeable on the full amount realised on the sale (not the original cost of the asset, see *Darlington Finance Ltd (VTD 1337) (TVC 42.75)*). Where, however, the goods in question were second-hand at the time when a finance agreement was entered into, the repossessed goods can be sold under the margin scheme. The purchase price for the purpose of calculating the margin is then the original price paid by the finance company to the dealer.

Following the decision in *C & E Commrs v General Motors Acceptance Corporation (UK) plc, Ch D [2004] STC 577 (TVC 42.49)* HMRC accept that, in the case of a finance company, 'repossessed goods' can mean goods

- voluntarily returned under an HP agreement;
- repossessed under the terms of a finance agreement; or
- returned by a customer under the *Consumer Credit Act* once they have made 50% of the total payments due.

(VAT Notice 718, para 24.13).

De Voil Indirect Tax Service. See V3.117.

27.16 Transactions related to the provision of credit

(1) Check trading companies

Check trading is a means of buying goods on credit whereby a check trading company sells a trading check for a specified amount to a customer who pays for the check on credit terms over a period of time. The customer then uses the check to purchase goods from the participating retailer.

Charges made by check trading companies to participating retailers are treated as exempt. (C & E Press Notice 1045, 21 October 1985).

(2) **Credit, debit and charge cards**

Any supply by a person carrying on a credit card, charge card or similar card operation is exempt when made in connection with that operation to a person who accepts the card used in the operation when presented to him in payment for goods or services. [*VATA 1994, Sch 9 Group 5 Note (4)*]. The consideration for these supplies usually takes the form of a discount on the amount reimbursed to the retailer, etc. See *C & E Commrs v Diners Club Ltd and Another, CA [1989] STC 407 (TVC 26.16)*.

Credit, debit and charge cards include MasterCard, Visa, American Express, Diner's Club, Connect and Switch. Banks and financial services institutions issue these cards under the umbrella of these organisations. In addition, certain companies provide in-house card schemes for retailers or retail outlets.

Accounting for VAT on retail credit, debit and charge card sales. Retailers must account for VAT at the time of supply on the full price charged to the customer for the goods/services supplied. If the retailer charges for accepting payment by one of the above cards, the charge is further consideration for the supply of goods/services. VAT is chargeable at the same rate as the goods or services supplied.

Liability of various associated services. Cardholders can either pay their outstanding balance on the receipt of their statement or pay on an instalment basis, interest being charged on the outstanding amount. The following list of charges are normally consideration for exempt supplies:

- Interest charged on the outstanding balance on a card account.
- Annual membership, joining and subscription charges or charges made by card companies to the cardholder for the issue of the card.
- The charge made to merchants (retailers) by credit card companies. This charge usually takes the form of discounts from the amounts the card companies reimburse the merchant.
- Joining fees charged to merchants by card companies.
- Interchange fees.
- Imprinter/terminal rental charges when provided as an ancillary part of other exempt card services.

The following charges are consideration for taxable supplies:

- Imprinter/terminal rental charges when an optional or additional service by card company to retailer.
- The consideration for a sale of goods (eg imprinters/terminals in connection with any card scheme).

(VAT Notice 701/49/02, para 5.3).

Charges made to customers paying by credit card. See above for charges by retailers or other persons supplying the goods. However, if the charge is made by an agent acting for the supplier of the goods or services (eg a travel agent acting on behalf of a tour company), HMRC consider that the charge is for a separate supply of exempt services, ie accepting payment in the form of a credit card. (Business Brief 17/98).

(3) **Deferred payment**

The expression 'the granting of credit' in 27.11(*a*) above is wide enough to encompass credit provided by a supplier of goods in the form of deferment of payment for the goods. The wording does not require exemption to be confined to credit granted by banks and financial institutions (*Muys en De Winters's Bouw-en Aannemingsbedriff BV v Staatssecretaris van Financiën, CJEC 1993, [1997] STC 665 (TVC 21.242)*).

Where customers are allowed to defer payment but for an extra charge, if the charge relates to

- periods before and up to the time of the supply, it is not a charge for credit but further consideration for the supply of the goods or services; and
- periods beyond the time of supply, such a charge is consideration for an exempt supply of credit.

(VAT Notice 701/49/02, para 5.2).

(4) **Discount for prompt payment**

Where goods are supplied for a consideration in money and on terms allowing a discount for prompt payment, the consideration is to be taken as reduced 'by the discount', whether or not payment in made in accordance with those terms. [*VATA 1994, Sch 6 para 4*].

In *Saga Holidays Ltd (VTD 18591)(VTD 65.93)* S sold holidays and offered customers discounts for prompt payment. It failed to take account of such discounts and submitted a repayment claim. Customs agreed to refund the amounts which S had overpaid where customers actually received discounts but rejected the claim where discount had been offered but the customers had not actually taken advantage of it. The tribunal agreed with this treatment, observing that the legislation provided that the consideration should be taken as reduced 'by the discount' and holding that these words could more readily be interpreted as a reference to a discount that has actually come into existence than to one that was available but may never come into existence. Therefore, *Sch 6 para 4(1)* should be construed as meaning that the consideration is only reduced where the discount is achieved.

This does not appear to be the interpretation which HMRC state in their published material. In VAT Notice 700, para 7.3 and VAT Notice 701/49/02, para 5.2 they indicated that the value for VAT is the discounted amount 'whether of not the customer takes up the offer' and even more emphatically in Internal Guidance V1–12, para 5.14 they state that it is the discounted amount 'whether or not the purchaser has made his payment within the specified time limit'.

(5) **Fuel card schemes**

See 45.14 MOTOR CARS.

(6) **Late payment penalties**

It is common for hire-purchase companies, credit card companies and similar institutions to impose a penalty for late payment. Where a customer is not explicitly allowed to defer payment and a late payment penalty is imposed because payment is not made by the due date, the penalty is not consideration for a supply and is outside the scope of VAT. (VAT Notice 701/49/02, para 5.2).

(7) **Loan arrangements and execution services**

In *C & E Commrs v Electronic Data Systems Ltd, CA [2003] STC 688 (TVC 21.245)* a bank (L) arranged for a company (E) to operate a call centre on its behalf. E received and processed loan applications, gathered and verified information about applicants, signed loan agreements on behalf of L, and released L's funds to borrowers. The Court of Appeal held that the supplies qualified for exemption under *EC 6th Directive, Art 13B(d)*. Following that decision, HMRC accept that supplies of loan arrangements and execution services where the payment or transfer of funds is central to the supply are exempt. To qualify for exemption, HMRC take the view that a business making a supply that consists of services to a loan provider prior to and after the granting of a loan must be undertaking all of the following functions as a central part of the supply.

- The operation of bank accounts on behalf of the credit provider.
- Arranging the transfer of funds of the borrower.
- The processing of loan repayments (and any additional charges or fees) received by direct debit or cheque.

(Business Brief 4/04).

(8) **Pawnbrokers**

Redeemed pledges. There is no supply for VAT purposes if a person redeems a pledge within the agreed redemption period.

Unredeemed pledges. The following rules apply. The relevant law is in *Consumer Credit Act 1974, ss 120, 121.*

(*a*) *Loans not exceeding £75 with a six month redemption period.* Ownership of the pledge passes to the pawnbroker if the goods are not redeemed within the six months statutory redemption period. A disposal of the goods to a third party after that time is a taxable supply.

Where, however, the goods are restored by the pawnbroker to their original owner within three months following the end of the redemption period, the transaction is treated as a redeemed pledge and there is no supply for VAT purposes. [*SI 1986/896*]. The pawnbroker must record the redemption in his pledge stock records and stamp the 'Credit Agreement and Pawn Receipt' with the date of redemption and keep it for inspection by HMRC. If the pawnbroker and pledgor have agreed to extend the original agreement by one or more further six month periods, the three month 'grace period' starts when the extension expires.

The restoration of an unredeemed pledge more than three months after the redemption period is a taxable supply.

(*b*) *Other loans*. For loans over £75 or where the redemption period has been agreed for a period other than six months, ownership of the pledge does not pass to the pawnbroker at the end of the redemption period. The onward supply to a third party is not, therefore, a taxable supply by the pawnbroker. It is, however, a taxable supply by the pledgor if he is a taxable person and the pledge is something he has acquired in the course of his business. The pawnbroker (or auctioneer if the goods are sold by auction) must follow the procedure in 2.18 ACCOUNTING PERIODS AND RETURNS.

Other charges.

- *Interest payments* received under credit agreements are exempt from VAT.
- *Valuation fees* relating to the pledged goods are regarded as part of the charge for the loan and are exempt.
- *Charges for selling unredeemed pledges*, provision for which is made in the loan contract, are exempt as a further charge for the granting of credit. Included is an element for cleaning and repairing the goods before they are put on display.

Second-hand goods scheme. Pawnbrokers may use the scheme for SECOND-HAND GOODS (61) for sales of unredeemed pawns within (*a*) above provided they have taken title to the goods and the normal scheme conditions are met. The purchase price is the amount of the loan plus the initial six months interest payable, less any payment received. The interest relating to the three month period of grace and other items such as cleaning, repair charges, storage and overhead expenses must not be added to the purchase price.

Pawnbrokers may, if they wish, use the credit agreement and pawn receipt as the purchase invoice provided

- the contract number is entered in the stock record and is cross-referred to the agreement; and
- a copy of the interest calculations and total purchase value for margin scheme purposes is attached to the document if it differs from the amount shown.

(VAT Notice 718, paras 23.1–23.3).

Pawnbrokers selling at auction. A pawnbroker may use the auctioneers' scheme for the sale of eligible second-hand goods (see 61.61 SECOND-HAND GOODS) provided the pawn value is greater than £75 and the pledgor is not VAT-registered. If the pledgor is VAT-registered, VAT must be accounted for on the full selling price. (VAT Notice 718, para 7.10).

(9) **Solicitors investing clients' money**

It is customary for solicitors in practice to receive and hold money on behalf of their clients. Such money must be paid into a bank account and kept separate from the practice's own bank account. The account may be either designated for a particular client or a general, undesignated client account.

Where the money belonging to a particular client is deposited in a separate designated account, that client is usually entitled to the interest. When the interest is passed from the solicitor to the client, this is not consideration for any supply and outside the scope of VAT.

Where client's money is held in a general account, it is usual for the solicitor to keep any interest earned from the bank although a solicitor may occasionally pass to the client a sum equivalent to the interest that would have been earned if the money had been in a separate designated account.

Any interest earned, either by the solicitor or if it is passed to the client, is regarded as consideration for an exempt supply of services to the bank under *VATA 1994, Sch 9 Group 5, item 2*. The gross interest received is the amount of the exempt output and may affect the partial exemption calculations of whoever keeps it.

Occasionally solicitors may also hold money for non-clients. In this situation, the rules in respect of interest payments are the same as for their own clients, ie it depends upon whether or not there is a designated account.

(Internal Guidance V1–3, para 4.13).

See also *Hedges and Mercer (VTD 271) (TVC 26.15)*.

27.17 SECURITIES

The issue, transfer or receipt of, or any dealing with, any security or secondary security in the UK is exempt from VAT. For these purposes, a security or secondary security comprises

- shares, stock, bonds, notes (other than promissory notes), debentures, debenture stock or shares in an oil royalty;
- any document relating to money, in any currency, which has been deposited with the issuer or some other person, being a document which recognises an obligation to pay a stated amount to bearer or to order, with or without interest, and being a document by the delivery of which, with or without endorsement, the right to receive that stated amount, with or without interest, is transferable;
- any bill, note or other obligation of the Treasury or of a Government in any part of the world, being a document by the delivery of which, with or without endorsement, title is transferable, and not being an obligation which is or has been legal tender in any part of the world;
- any letter of allotment or rights, any warrant conferring an option to acquire a security included in these provisions, any renounceable or scrip certificates, rights coupons, coupons representing dividends or interest on such a security, bond mandates or other documents conferring or containing evidence of title to or rights in respect of such a security;
- units or other documents conferring rights under any trust established for the purpose, or having the effect of providing, for persons having funds available for investment, facilities for the participation by them as beneficiaries under the trust, in any profits or income arising from the acquisition, holding, management or disposal of any property whatsoever.

[*VATA 1994, Sch 9 Group 5 Item 6*].

Securities transactions. Transactions by a principal concerning the issue, sale, transfer or holding of securities are exempt supplies. The main consideration for such a supply is the amount received from the sale. In addition, some securities yield interest and others dividends. Receipt of interest by the security holder is consideration for an exempt supply. However, dividends are outside the scope, because they do not represent consideration for any supply of goods or services by the holder of the security.

Redemption of securities at maturity does not give rise to any exempt output and is outside the scope, as there is no supply of goods or services by the holder.

Exempt supplies of securities also include

- securities traded for profit or investment;
- securities that underpin arbitrage dealings on international financial exchanges;
- securities that involve capital raising operations by companies, governments or other organisations; and
- transactions involving share placings and rights issues.

(VAT Notice 701/49/02, para 8.4).

International transactions. See 27.2 above for the place of supply of services within these provisions, including the special rule for the place of supply of securities sold where the identity of the purchaser is not known. The place of supply affects both the VAT liability of a financial service and whether the supplier can reclaim related input tax. See 27.3 above.

27.18 Stock lending

Stock lending describes a situation where one business obtains securities from another in order to complete a stock transaction to which the first business is committed. The borrower agrees to return an equivalent number of the same securities at a later date.

For VAT purposes, there is an exempt supply under 27.17 above by the lender to the borrower. The exempt supply is that of the temporary transfer of stock to the borrower, the consideration being the fee charged to the borrower. The borrower should not account for the value of securities returned to the lender. Any dividends which the borrower receives whilst the stocks are loaned are not consideration for a supply.

Such deals commonly involve secondary supplies of interest. These occur where the borrower puts up collateral (eg cash, interest bearing securities, certificates of deposit (CDs)) as default security. If the lender temporarily invests the cash collateral on interest-earning deposits or interest-bearing securities, there is an additional exempt supply. Similarly, the receipts of interest on interest-bearing securities or CDs used as collateral constitutes the consideration for further exempt supplies.

If the borrower defaults and the lender retains all or part of the cash collateral, that retention is compensation and outside the scope of VAT. Any part of the collateral returned to a defaulted borrower is also outside the scope of VAT, as the payment is not consideration for any supply.

(VAT Notice 701/49/02, para 8.5; Internal Guidance V1–7, Chapter 20 para 3.13).

27.19 Transactions related to securities

(1) Clearing and settlement services

The services provided by organisations in the securities market that involve

- matching parties to share deals,
- identifying payments for transactions,
- balancing accounts for the principals, and
- notifying final liabilities to the parties for settlement purposes

are exempt under *VATA 1994, Sch 9 Group 5 Item 5* (see 27.25 below) as intermediary's services provided the necessary conditions are fulfilled.

(Internal Guidance V1–7, Chapter 20 para 3.16.3).

(2) **Custody services**

Safe custody services are standard-rated. This includes the provision of the purely physical service of safekeeping (safe deposit facilities) and applies irrespective of where the recipient belongs and irrespective of whether the securities are stored in the UK, at an overseas branch of the business or elsewhere. This is because such services are expressly excluded from services within *VATA 1994, Sch 5 para 5* and therefore the place of supply is, under the basic rule, where the supplier belongs.

Where a specific site is hired to a client (rather than the service of secure storage within the supplier's own premises), the supply is in the UK if the site is in the UK, but outside the scope of UK VAT if the site is overseas. There may, however, be a liability to account for VAT in another EC country if the place of supply is elsewhere in the EC.

Global custody services involve a package of services that may include safe custody, collection of dividends/interest on securities held, dealing with scrip/rights issues, and payment against the delivery or receipt of stock. In such a case, the supply of the whole service, including the safe custody element, is exempt.

(VAT Notice 701/49/02, para 8.8).

(3) **Dealing systems and data services**

The supply of a dealing system which allows

- a user to insert bid and offer quotes for securities,
- another user to insert acceptance, and
- for the system to match buy and sell deals,

is exempt.

Electronic data services which simply provide subscribers with a message facility or an information service (eg on share price movements or financial news) are taxable.

(VAT Notice 701/49/02, para 10.3).

(4) **Investment/portfolio management**

The management of a client's holding of securities is taxable. The purpose and substance of the service is to make available the professional skill needed to buy, hold and sell securities in the way that best meets the investment needs of a client. Any broking or dealing charges incurred are cost components of the taxable service provided.

In other investment management situations, it may be that the arrangements between manager and client involve both management services and broking services. This depends upon whether the manager is acting as an intermediary and meets the conditions set out in 27.25 below.

Examples

- A contract provides for investment management for a periodic fee. This is taxable. Broking services are commissioned for the client who must bear the separate transaction charges of the broker. The fund manager passes on to the client the exact amount of broking charges incurred on the client's behalf. The onward charge for broking services is outside the scope of VAT provided the conditions set out in 3.7 AGENTS are met.
- A contract provides for investment management for a periodic fee. This is taxable. The manager also makes a separate charge for arranging a securities deal. Provided the charge is specific to an actual securities transaction undertaken by the manager for the client, the supply is exempt.

(VAT Notice 701/49/02, para 12.1).

(5) **Nominee services**

The services of acting as nominal holder of securities on behalf of the beneficial owner are exempt. (VAT Notice 701/49/02, para 8.7).

(6) **Share registration services**

Share registration services may include some or all of the following (the list is not exhaustive).

- All aspects of operating company share registers.
- Administration of scrip schemes, share option schemes, profit-sharing schemes and dividend reinvestment plans.
- Arrangements for advertising the closure of a share offer.
- Attending shareholders' meetings and organising polls at such meetings.
- Arranging 'break out' for bulk nominee accounts.
- Capital gains enquiries and other correspondence and enquiries.
- Conversion of loan stock.
- Preparation, designation and despatch of certificates, correction of errors on certificates, and issuing of duplicated documents.
- Administrative services in relation to mergers, placings, rights issues, reorganisations and acquisitions.
- Processing forms of proxy.
- Registration of grants of probate.
- Regular reports on share movements.
- Administrative services in relation to savings plan schemes.

These services are treated as supplied where the supplier belongs under the basic rule for the supply of services (see 64.20 SUPPLY). They are standard-rated if supplied in the UK unless provided as one element of a single composite supply featuring other services with a different VAT liability, in which case the liability may change. See 64.6 SUPPLY for single and multiple supplies.

Although VAT Notice 701/49/02, para 10.5 clearly states that share registration services are standard-rated, the British Bankers' Association (BBA) Blue Book (detailing the VAT treatment of a majority of services conducted by banks and financial institutions) current at December 2003 incorrectly specified that share registration services were supplied where the customer belonged, with the service qualifying for exemption from VAT when supplied in the UK. It has been accepted that this was incorrect but, in order to allow for adjustment of accounting systems, Customs did not require businesses affected to apply the correct liability and place of supply until 1 April 2004. HMRC are not seeking to recover VAT underdeclared as the result of relying on the incorrect information contained in the BBA Blue Book.

Statutory fees charged for inspection of the register and for production of lists of shareholders in accordance with companies' legislation are disbursements (and subject to the rules in 3.7 AGENTS).

(VAT Notice 701/49/02, para 10.5; VAT Information Sheet 15/03).

(7) **Valuation, research and advisory services**

The supply of services such as

- the valuation of assets, or
- assessing the direct tax liabilities of such a holding,

are taxable unless they form an ancillary part of an exempt service (eg a broking service).

Also taxable are services which may help a client make decisions on the buying, holding or selling of securities but do not in themselves have the characteristics of an intermediary service. These include

- investment analysis;
- market sector research;
- share consultancy; and
- general financial or investment advice.

(VAT Notice 701/49/02, para 10.4).

27.20 Unit trusts

A unit trust is a pooled fund, held by trustees on behalf of investors, used to buy assets, normally securities or property.

Supplies of units in a unit trust are securities for the purposes of 27.17 above and their issue *by the manager* of the trust is exempt. The value of the exempt supply by the manager is the total price paid for the units by the investor.

A unit trust itself will hold and carry out transactions in securities within 27.17 above. The sale of these underlying securities is also an exempt supply by the trust.

Management of authorised unit trusts. Investment management services are normally taxable (see 27.19(4) above). However, there is an exception to this rule for authorised unit trusts.

The management of an 'authorised unit trust scheme' or of a 'trust based scheme' is exempt.

'*Authorised unit trust scheme*' has the meanings given in *Financial Services and Markets Act 2000, s 237(2)(3)*, ie a unit trust scheme which is authorised for the purposes of that *Act* by an authorisation order in force under *FSMA 200, s 243*.

'*Trust based scheme*' means a scheme the purpose or effect of which is to enable persons taking part in the scheme, by becoming beneficiaries under a trust, to participate in or receive profits or income arising from the acquisition, holding, management or disposal of property of a kind described in *Financial Services and Markets Act 2000, s 239(3)(a)* or sums paid out of such profits or income.

[*VATA 1994, Sch 9 Group 5 Item 9 and Note 6; SI 2001/3649, Art 348; SI 2003/1569*].

Before 1 August 2003, exemption only applied to the management of a scheme by the operator of the scheme. But despite that wording, until 24 March 1997, HMRC's policy had been to extend exemption to services provided by a third party to the operator. From that date, this relaxation was withdrawn, subject to a gradual relief for contracts existing at that date. (C & E News Release 12/97, 13 March 1997). However, from 16 January 2001, exemption was again extended following the tribunal decision in *Prudential Assurance Co Ltd (VTD 17030) (TVC 26.47)* where it was held that the restriction of exemption to management by the operator of the scheme was not in accordance with *EC Sixth Directive, Art 13B(d)(6)*. This exempts 'management of special investments funds as defined by Member States', ie exemption is not limited in any way as to function or its provider.

'*Management*'. The management service is made up of a number elements including monitoring the performance of the scheme property, making investment decisions, dealing with paperwork and bookkeeping, offering advice on the growth of the portfolio, and contracting with dealers to buy and sell assets on behalf of their clients.

Where the whole management service is sub-contracted out to a third party or a sub-fund manager who makes a single supply of management to the operator, the supply is exempt. But if the sub-contracted manager only provides particular elements, the VAT liability may vary (eg advice, advertising and data processing would be standard-rated).

(Internal Guidance V1–7, Chapter 20 para 3.9.2).

Management of an unauthorised unit trust is liable to VAT at the standard rate.

27.21 **Open-ended investment companies('OEICs')**

OEICs are a form of collective investment scheme similar to a unit trust except that investors buy shares in a company whose sole purpose is investing in transferable securities. The capital of an OEIC increases and decreases as shares in the OEIC are created and cancelled. An OEIC is governed by a board. Each company has an authorised corporate director (ACD) whose functions include managing the company's investments, selling the OEIC shares and buying back the OEIC shares from shareholders on demand.

Issue of new shares. Issues of shares in an OEIC are exempt under 27.17 above. The OIEC will also hold and deal in securities within 27.17 above and the sale of these underlying securities is an exempt supply by the OEIC. (VAT Notice 701/49/02, para 12.2).

Management of an OEIC. Investment management services are normally taxable (see 27.19(4) above). However, there is an exception to this rule for OEICs.

The management of the scheme property of an OEIC is exempt. For these purposes, an OEIC's scheme property is the property subject to the collective investment scheme constituted by that company. See *Financial Services and Markets Act 2000, s 235* and *s 236* respectively for the meaning of 'collective investment scheme' and 'open-ended investment company'. [*VATA 1994, Sch 9 Group 5 Item 10 and Notes 8 and 10; SI 2003/1569*].

Before 1 August 2003, exemption only applied to the services of the 'authorised corporate director' of an OEIC so far as they consisted in managing the company's scheme property. A person was an '*authorised corporate director*' of an OEIC if for the time being that person was a director of the company and had responsibility for the management of (and was managing) the company's scheme property. However, from 19 December 2001, following the tribunal decision in *Abbey National plc (VTD 17506) (TVC 26.48)* where it was held that the UK provisions were not in accordance with *EC Sixth Directive, Art 13B(d)(6)*, exemption could be applied to fund management services provided by third-party managers to authorised corporate directors.

Management. See under 27.22 above for the interpretation of 'management' which applies equally to the management of an OEIC by its authorised corporate director or by a contracted-out third party.

27.22 **Individual savings accounts (ISAs) and personal equity plans (PEPS)**

ISAs. ISAs, launched on 6 April 1999 as a replacement to the PEP (see below), are composed of cash, insurance, stocks and shares or a mix of these components. ISAs allowing for more than one component are referred to as 'maxi ISAs'.

- **Cash mini ISAs**. There are usually no charges connected with cash ISAs. The ISA manager's service to the investor is exempt as the operation of a bank account. But where the ISA is based on cash unit trusts, it is treated as a stocks and shares mini ISA for VAT purposes and management charges are taxable.
- **Insurance mini ISAs**. An insurance ISA comprises a life insurance policy insuring the life of the ISA holder. Charges made by the ISA manager to the investor are exempt as insurance-related services.
- **Stocks and shares mini ISAs**. Stocks and shares mini ISAs are generally intended for savers who do not need immediate access to their savings. See VAT Notice 701/49/02, para 12.5 for details of the VAT liabilities associated with stocks and shares ISAs as agreed between HMRC and the Association of Unit Trust and Investment Funds.
- **Maxi ISAs**. These can comprise a mixture of cash, insurance and stocks and shares components but most tend to consist solely of stocks and shares. Where a maxi ISA consists of multiple components, each component, although packaged together for tax purposes, is usually managed and charged for separately. The VAT liability of supplies made in respect of the stocks and shares component of a maxi ISA is the same as that for a stocks and shares mini ISA.

PEPs. After 5 April 1999, no new subscriptions can be made to PEPs but savers holding PEPs at that date can continue to hold them (without affecting the amount which can be subscribed to an ISA).

PEPs are treated the same as stocks and shares ISAs for VAT purposes (see above).

See VAT Notice 700/57/04 for an agreement between HMRC and the Association of Unit Trust and Investment Managers about the VAT liability of charges made in connection with PEPs.

(VAT Notice 701/49/02, para 12.3).

27.23 UNDERWRITING

The underwriting of an issue within *VATA 1994, Sch 9 Group 5 Item 1* (see 27.8 above) or any transaction within *VATA 1994, Sch 9 Group 5 Item 6* (see 27.17 above) is exempt. [*VATA 1994, Sch 9 Group 5 Item 5A; SI 1999/594, Art 3*].

Where, for a fee, an underwriter's services provide that

- a securities issue or sale will be subscribed for or purchased; and
- the issuer will receive a certain amount of capital,

that supply is exempt.

An underwriter may underwrite an issue by agreeing to purchase the whole block of securities offered by the issuer, instead of guaranteeing that buyers will be found. In this case, exemption applies under 27.17 above. There is an exempt supply of securities by the issuer to the underwriter and a subsequent exempt supply of securities by the underwriter.

Where an underwriter's charge for services is adjusted to reflect the entitlement to purchase his allotted securities at a special price, the value of the discount must be regarded as part of the consideration for his exempt supply of underwriting services. The supply by the issuer of the right to acquire the securities at a special price is exempt under 27.17 above, the value being the discount allowed. However, where an underwriter is obliged to buy further securities which remain unsold and the underwriting agreement allows him to buy these unsold securities at a price lower than the offer price, this reduction is not regarded as consideration for the underwriting service and is outside the scope of VAT.

Sub-underwriters. Exemption also applies to the supply made by a sub-underwriter who agrees to underwrite a proportion of the issue or sale. Depending upon the contractual arrangements, a sub-underwriter's client may be the underwriter or the issuer. Where the underwriting has international aspects, this will affect the VAT position. For example, if a sub-underwriter's supply is to a lead underwriter belonging in the UK, the supply is exempt with no input tax recovery (even though the issuer belongs outside the EC). If, on the other hand, the sub-underwriter's supply was to the issuer belonging outside the EC, the supply would be outside the scope of UK VAT (see 27.2 above) with input tax credit (see 27.3 above), even though the lead underwriter belongs in the UK.
(VAT Notice 701/49/02, para 8.6).

27.24 BANKS AND BUILDING SOCIETIES

The operation of any current, deposit or savings account is exempt. [*VATA 1994, Sch 9 Group 5 Item 8*]. This covers charges made by a bank or similar organisation.

Banks and similar financial institutions are not exempt just because of their status. Exempt services include mortgage lending, personal loans and credit cards under 27.11 above and taxable services include

- accounting services;
- equipment leasing;
- investment management; and

- taxation advice.

Other activities with which they will be involved include dealing with money (see 27.8 above), intermediary services (see 27.25 below) and outsourcing (see 27.30 below).

Other banking charges. Banks may carry out other services and functions for which they make a charge to the customer. If so, it is necessary to establish whether they are supplies in their own right or ancillary to the exempt banking service. See 64.6 SUPPLY for the distinction between single and multiple supplies.

Charges for additional or special printing of cheque and credit books is seen as further consideration for an exempt supply of banking services. (Internal Guidance V1–7, Chapter 20 para 7.4).

Electronic banking and cash management services. See VAT Notice 700/57/02 *Administrative agreements entered into with trade bodies* for an agreement between HMRC and the British Bankers' Association setting out the liability to VAT on these services.

27.25 INTERMEDIARY SERVICES

The *EC Sixth Directive, Art 13B*(*d*) exempts the 'negotiation' of many financial services. See 22.18(*c*)–(*g*) EUROPEAN COMMUNITY LEGISLATION.

Under UK legislation, the provision of 'intermediary services' in relation to a transaction within

(*a*) *VATA 1994, Sch 9 Group 5 Item 1* (the issue, transfer or receipt of, and any dealings with money or securities for money, see 27.8 above),

(*b*) *VATA 1994, Sch 9 Group 5 Item 2* (the making or an advance or the granting of credit, see 27.11(*a*) above),

(*c*) *VATA 1994, Sch 9 Group 5 Item 3* (the provision of instalment credit finance by hire purchases, etc, see 27.11(*c*) above),

(*d*) *VATA 1994, Sch 9 Group 5 Item 4* (the provision of administrative arrangements, etc in connection with a supply under *Item 3* where the consideration does not exceed £10, see 27.11(*d*) above), or

(*e*) *VATA 1994, Sch 9 Group 5 Item 6* (the issue, transfer or receipt of, or dealings with certain securities and secondary securities, see 27.17 above)

by a person 'acting in an intermediary capacity' is exempt. This applies whether or not any such transaction is finally concluded so that where qualifying intermediary services are performed but the deal falls through and there is no financial transaction, the intermediary service is still exempt.

'*Intermediary services*' for these purposes consist of

- 'bringing together' persons who are or may be seeking to receive financial services and persons providing such services, with a view to the provision of such services; *together with*
- in the case of financial services falling within (*a*)–(*d*) above (but *not* (*e*) above) the performance of 'work preparatory to the conclusion of contracts' for the provision of those financial services

but do not include the supply of any market research, product design, advertising, promotional or similar services or the collection, collation and provision of information in connection with such activities.

A person is '*acting in an intermediary capacity*' where he is acting as an intermediary (or one of the intermediaries) between

- a person providing financial services; and
- a person who is or may be seeking to receive such services

unless, before 1 August 2003, the financial service in question was the grant of credit and he was also making supplies of services comprising the 'management of credit' (see 27.11(*b*) above) to the grantor (or prospective grantor) of the credit.

[*VATA 1994, Sch 9 Group 5 Item 5 and Notes 5, 5A, 5B; SI 1999/594; SI 2003/1569*].

'*Bringing together*' in most cases will mean introducing them to each other for the first time (eg a mortgage broker bringing together a housebuyer and a mortgage company). There are situations, however, where an intermediary is approached by parties who already know and plan to deal with each other (eg he may be asked to put together a transaction which is already envisaged). Provided the other criteria are met, his services are exempt. But an intermediary should be independent of the parties entering into a financial services contract and not carrying out sub-contracted services for one of the parties. In *CSC Financial Services Ltd (aka Continuum (Europe) Ltd) v C & E Commrs, CJEC 2001, [2002] STC 57 (TVC 21.244)*, CSC supplied services to Sun Alliance, which issued personal equity plans. It dealt with telephone enquires, sent application forms to potential customers and checked completed application forms. But the customers had already been approached by Sun Alliance and the parties were not brought together by CSC, who acted not in an intermediary capacity but as a sub-contractor for Sun Alliance in processing applications. The CJEC confirmed that CSC was not an intermediary because it was standing in the shoes of Sun Alliance while taking calls and receiving forms, and also because CSC's activities were clerical activities which would normally have been done by Sun Alliance.

'*Work preparatory to the conclusion of contracts*' could include completing or assisting with the completion of application forms; checking completed applications and forwarding forms to the provider of financial services; making representations on behalf of one party to the other; and acting as a go-between generally. Note that the legislation provides that, in relation to a transaction falling within (*e*) above, preparatory work is not necessary and exemption can apply to the mere introduction of a person seeking to buy or sell securities to a person effecting transactions in securities.

Intermediary services may contain more than one component. Services which include market research, product design or similar services excluded above may still be exempt provided that this is a minor and ancillary part of the overall intermediary service. See also 27.31 below for where financial advisers provide mixed supplies of advice and intermediary services.

(VAT Notice 701/49/02, para 6.1; VAT Information Sheet, 10/99; Internal Guidance V1–7, Chapter 20 para 6.3.2).

27.26 Mortgage/money brokerage services

The intermediary services of mortgage and money brokers in arranging for any advance of money, or granting any credit, are exempt unless, after 9 March 1999 and before 1 August 2003, they are performed as part of a supply of the 'management of credit' (see 27.11 above). The mere introduction of a client to a broker or lender, without any preparatory work (eg assistance with the completion of, and checking, forms and their submission to the lender) does not qualify for exemption. Car dealers and furnishing and electrical retailers, for example, who for a commission introduce customers to finance houses who provide credit finance, are not providing exempt services unless they undertake some 'work preparatory to the conclusion of contracts' (see 27.25 above).

(VAT Information Sheet 10/99).

27.27 Securities broking services

The introductory service of bringing together a person who wishes to buy securities to a person selling securities is exempt if made in the UK, even if the intended securities transaction later falls through (see 27.25(*e*) above). The exemption covers

- any stock or share broking services (see below); and
- arranging issues or placements of securities whether as offers for sale, rights issues, cash offers, vendor placings or bids with underwritten cash alternatives, including the service of co-ordinating an issue when a number of participants are involved in the share or other placing. But see 27.28 below which covers corporate finance services.

Exemption does not apply to professional services supplied in connection with share issues, acquisitions or disposals, which do not secure the connection between buyer and seller. Accountancy services, tax and legal advice, supplying a draft prospectus, or preparing advice on a take-over bid are therefore all standard-rated.

Broking services. Where a broker acts as an 'execution only' broker, buying or selling securities on client's instructions, but does not offer advice on securities, his supply is exempt. Where a broker acts as an advisory broker, arranging transactions and offering investment advice to the client,

- if the advice is made as a separate supply and for an identifiable charge it is taxable; but
- if his contract with the client is for arranging transactions in securities, and he raises charges only in relation to transactions executed, with advice being simply incidental to that service, a single exempt supply is made for VAT purposes.

Where a broker arranging a securities transaction splits the contract note to show as separate items the basic charge for broking services and any compliance or regulatory charges made to cover the cost of meeting regulatory requirements, the additional charges are still part of the consideration for his exempt broking service. This does not, however, apply to any statutory levies (eg stamp duty) which are a liability of the client. These are outside the scope of VAT.

International transactions. The services of arranging a sale or disposal of securities in the UK is exempt. However, the VAT position is also affected by the place of belonging of the recipient of the brokerage services and, sometimes, by the place of belonging of the buyer of securities. The following table summarises the liability of supplies of brokerage in the most common transactions.

Commission charged to supplier belonging in	*VAT*	*Sells to*	*Commission charged to recipient belonging in*	*VAT*
UK or other EC (private)	E		UK or other EC (private)	E
UK or other EC (private)	E		Other EC (business)	OS

Commission charged to supplier belonging in	*VAT*	*Sells to*	*Commission charged to recipient belonging in*	*VAT*
UK or other EC (private)	E(R)		Non-EC	OS(R)
Other EC (business)	OS		UK or other EC (private)	E
Other EC (business)	OS		Other EC (business)	OS
Other EC (business)	OS(R)		Non-EC	OS(R)
Non-EC	OS(R)		UK or other EC (private)	E
Non-EC	OS(R)		Other EC (business)	OS
Non-EC	OS(R)		Non-EC	OS(R)

Key
E = Exempt
E(R) = Exempt but with refund of related input tax
OS = Outside the scope of UK VAT with no refund of related input tax
OS(R) = Outside the scope of UK VAT with refund of related input tax

(VAT Notice 701/49/02, paras 9.1, 10.1, 10.2).

27.28 **Corporate finance services**

Corporate finance services provided by corporate finance departments might include

- general advice on raising capital where no specific transaction is contemplated;
- advice on defending take-over bids; and
- services of arranging and underwriting particular share issues.

Although advisory services are taxable, where these lead to, or are associated with, a transaction in securities by the client which is an exempt supply, then the services may themselves be exempt as the provision of intermediary services for a transaction in securities. There is no clearly defined line dividing exempt from taxable services in this area. The features of each contract must be taken into account in determining the appropriate VAT treatment. The terms of an engagement letter between bank and client and any other documentary evidence available may help in determining the correct VAT liability provided that they are consistent with the services actually performed.

Corporate financing is often a two-stage process. First, the sponsor seeks information from a variety of professional sources and, having obtained it, prepares a prospectus detailing the proposal. Normally, the services performed by advisers or other professionals in providing information and advice at this first stage is taxable. The advice given may result in a second stage, ie financing the business. Services performed during this stage, the actual transaction in securities, may qualify for exemption.

Exemption only applies to the services provided by the party (or parties if more than one person is engaged) who actually negotiates or co-ordinates components of the transaction and helps conclude it. Typically this might include

- bringing together sellers/issuers and purchasers/investors;
- carrying out/co-ordinating the necessary negotiations essential to the conclusion of the whole deal;
- instructing/organising and co-ordinating the work of other parties involved, such as lawyers and accountants;
- carrying out the necessary consultations with appropriate regulatory authorities; and
- acting as a central point of contact and execution between the party intending to effect a transaction in securities and their other advisers.

Other professional services (eg legal advice or document printing) are separate taxable supplies, even if supplied in connection with the second stage.

Examples of corporate finance arrangements that may involve exempt transactions include the following.

- *Clear or specific mandate agreements.* Where an engagement makes it clear from the outset that the client has an objective comprising the issue, sale or purchase of securities, the services are exempt. If the mandate is on the same basis but the objective is the acquisition or disposal of assets and no share issue or sale is involved, services will be taxable.
- *Open mandates.* Where the terms of engagement do not specifically envisage any transaction in securities being effected, and the client is billed for services which are of a general nature, such services are taxable. If the client subsequently decides to effect a transaction involving the issue or sale of securities, services will be exempt apart from any identifiable charge for the advisory element.
- *Aborted projects.* Where a clear or specific mandate agreement (see above) is aborted, the services provided are regarded as exempt if there is consideration. In the case of an open mandate agreement (see above), the liability of the services provided up to the time the decision is taken to abort depends on the nature of the services provided. If they are essentially advisory and provided for consideration, the services are taxable. If the services have been supplied for a consideration and have the character of negotiation, it may be possible to treat them as exempt. Evidence to support exemption, such as letter of confirmation and instructions to produce a prospectus, must be available to support the claim.
- *Takeovers.* Services supplied to a client defending a hostile take-over bid are taxable if the defence does not involve intermediary services in respect of the issue or sale of shares or securities (eg through a de-merger or sale of a subsidiary). Where such services are rendered, they may consist of both taxable and exempt elements. The VAT treatment will depend on exactly what is supplied. The terms of any consideration might help determine the liability of the supplies. In normal circumstances where a bid is contested, it is unlikely that there will be any supply of intermediary services for securities transactions, except where it is decided that a break-up defence is to be followed.

  Where services are supplied to a company in connection with an agreed bid, these may involve the adviser in giving only taxable advice. However, if the adviser becomes involved in the detailed aspects of the proposal (eg by setting the terms and conditions for the final deal), services can be exempt.
- *Flotation.* Advice on bringing a company to market are taxable. Where, at the same time as the listing, there is an equity-raising exercise, then a listing fee is

taxable whilst the fee for the equity-raising exercise is exempt. Where an instruction is obtained on the basis of an intended flotation which involves the issue/placement of shares, then it is likely that the whole fee will be exempt.

(VAT Notice 701/49/02, paras 11.1, 11.2).

27.29 **Other intermediary services**

(1) **Affinity credit card schemes**

These schemes typically involve a charity or interest group endorsing a credit card and recommending its use to their members or supporters. The charity or interest group receive a commission or similar income, usually linked to the taking out and subsequent usage of the card.

Charities have been granted a special concession which recognises a 'donational' element in the affinity card scheme. See 12.5(3) CHARITIES.

Non-charity organisations operating affinity credit card schemes are subject to the normal VAT rules. In *BAA plc v C & E Commrs, CA 2002, [2003] STC 35 (TVC 26.19)* a company, in return for a commission, provided a bank with information concerning potential credit card customers. It targeted suitable applicants, issued applications, assisted in the completion of the forms and screened and processed them on return. In *Institute of Directors v C & E Commrs, CA 2002, [2003] STC 35 (TVC 26.20)*, which case was heard in the Court of Appeal with *BAA plc*, the IoD similarly provided a list of suitable members, encouraged members to apply, and assisted them with their applications and validated completed forms. The Court of Appeal held that, in both cases, the activities carried out were within the definition of 'negotiation of credit' for the purposes of *EC 6th Directive, Art 13B(d)* and exempt from VAT in the UK as intermediary services.

As a result of these judgments, HMRC take the view that a body that introduces its members, supporters or customers to a credit card provider and undertakes work preparatory to the provision of the credit card is providing exempt negotiation or intermediary services. It is not necessary for the introducer to be capable of affecting the terms of the principal financial service for the exemption to apply. Exemption, therefore, applies where an intermediary

- stands between the parties to a contract in the performance of a distinct act of mediation;
- brings the two parties to the contract together; and
- undertakes 'work preparatory' such as completing or assisting with the completion of application forms, forwarding forms to the credit card company, and making representations on behalf of either party.

HMRC do not view marketing and promotional services supplied in isolation, nor the performing of clerical functions (eg providing a list of names or access to a database) as exempt intermediary services.

(Business Brief 18/03).

(2) **Debt negotiation services**

In *Debt Management Associates Ltd (VTD 17880) (TVC 26.31)* the tribunal held that a creditor who granted his debtor some indulgence in repayments was granting him credit (even if it was additional credit) and that a company providing the debt negotiation services was providing exempt intermediary services.

Following the tribunal decision, HMRC now accept that a business will be providing exempt intermediary services of debt negotiation where it attempts to mediate a change to the payment terms between a debtor and creditor, and does all that is necessary for them to enter into a contract but without having any interest of its own in the terms of the contract. Debt negotiation services may include

- summarising details of income and expenditure, creditors and the amounts outstanding, and preparing and presenting a payment plan to the creditor;
- agreeing to act on behalf of the debtor with the creditor in negotiating the payment plan; and
- agreeing to receive payments from the debtor and passing these payments on to the creditors (with or without first deducting commission charges).

However, a business which merely

- issues letters to the debtor on behalf of the creditor demanding payment;
- seeks to locate a debtor on behalf of the creditor; or
- provides accounting services to the creditor (ie monitors the debtor's payment account and notifies the creditor of any defaulted payments)

will not be providing debt negotiation services. Where both debt negotiation services and one or more of these services are provided, it is necessary to determine which element predominates.

(Business Brief 30/03).

(3) **Derivatives**

Services of a person acting as an agent, broker or other intermediary for supplies of *financial* derivatives may be exempt from VAT. The rules are different depending on the type of financial service which is provided.

(*a*) *Cash settled contracts* (see 27.9(6) above). The supply is exempt if the intermediary

(i) acts between a person selling and a person buying a cash settled financial derivative;

(ii) brings those parties together; and

(iii) carries out some form of preparatory work to the conclusion of contracts.

(*b*) *Non-cash settled contracts* (see 27.9(6) above). The supply is exempt if the intermediary

(i) acts between a person selling and a person buying non-cash settled financial derivatives; and

(ii) brings those parties together.

An intermediary's supply is *not* exempt from VAT if acting between

- principals trading in *commodity* derivatives;
- principals trading on one of the terminal markets listed in 65.2 TERMINAL MARKETS; or
- members of the London Bullion Market Association trading investment gold.

(VAT Notice 701/9/02, para 2.5).

27.30 OUTSOURCING

Financial institutions often buy-in or sub-contract services that once would have been provided in-house. This is sometimes known as 'outsourcing'. It can include such services as data processing, telephone help lines and general administration. Outsourcing is a contentious area because financial institutions seek exemption wherever possible in order to keep overheads down.

The key decision on outsourcing is *Sparekassernes Datacenter (SDC) v Skatteministeriet, CJEC [1997] STC 932 (TVC 21.243)*. A company (SDC) carried out a variety of operations on behalf of Danish savings banks which each bank would have otherwise had to carry out for itself. These included the execution of transfers of funds by electronic means between the various banks and between those banks and their clients, the provisions of advice on and trade in securities, and the management of deposits, purchase contracts and loans. The CJEC held that exemption is not restricted to transactions effected by financial institutions or any particular type of legal person. Nor does it matter that the supply is carried out wholly or partly by electronic means or manually. It is not necessary for the services to be provided by an institution which has a legal relationship with the end customer and the fact that the services are provided by a third party does not prevent those services from falling within the exemption. Transactions concerning transfers and payments, and services consisting of the management of deposits, purchase contracts and loans included operations carried out by a data-handling centre if those operations were distinct in character and were specific to, and essential for, the exempt transactions. However, services which merely consisted of making information available to banks and other users did not qualify for exemption.

Liability therefore depends on the nature of the supply itself, not whether it is supplied to someone who is making exempt supplies. The exact nature of the supply must be determined and, to be exempt, the sub-contracted service must be of a description which itself falls within the exemption. HMRC regard the test for this as being that the service provided has the effect of making changes to the legal and financial situation, ie a change in the ownership of money or in the financial obligations between the parties. For example, if the services provided involve making account entries that have the effect of transferring funds, the supply is exempt. However, if the services only assist another person who is making the account entries, the supply is taxable. Where a mixture of these services are provided, the liability will depend on the essential nature of the supply(ies) made.

Most processing services are standard-rated. In addition, services preparatory to transactions in money, any security for money or any note or order for the payment of money (eg data preparation work for transferring funds between bank accounts) are specifically excluded from exemption. See 27.8 above.

(VAT Notice 701/49/02, paras 4.1, 4.2, 7.1, 7.2; VAT Information Sheet 10/99).

In *CSC Financial Services Ltd (aka Continuum (Europe) Ltd) v C & E Commrs, CJEC 2001, [2002] STC 57 (TVC 21.244)* a company supplied services to a group of companies which issued personal equity plans. It dealt with telephone enquiries and with replies to advertisements placed by the group and sent application forms to potential customers and checked completed application forms. The CJEC held that exemption under *EC 6th Directive, Art 13B(d)(5)* for 'transactions including negotiation' did not extend to services limited to providing information about a financial product and, as the case may be, receiving and processing applications for subscriptions, without issuing them.

27.31 FINANCIAL ADVISERS

(1) Mixed supplies of advice and intermediary services

A financial adviser may be approached by a customer seeking

- advice only (taxable);
- intermediary services only (normally exempt under 27.25 above); or
- a mixture of both.

Often, customers will initially seek advice which leads to their purchasing a financial product. In these cases, it is necessary to establish which of the two elements predominates. Where advice directly results in a customer taking out a financial product, and all the criteria for intermediary services are met, HMRC regard the whole of the services (including the advice element) as exempt from VAT. The advice is seen as ancillary to an overall exempt supply of intermediary services. If the financial adviser also receives commission from the finance product provider, it is consideration for a separate exempt supply of intermediary services.

Occasionally, the advice given far outweighs the work done to arrange a contract (eg where a customer is given a general financial review and then only buys a minor product requiring minimal intermediary services). In these circumstances, the intermediary services are seen as ancillary to the advice, and VAT is due on the whole service.

Which is the predominant service in any supply is a question of fact.

If supplies of advice and intermediary services are supplied distinctly and separately (eg where advice is given under a fixed contract that runs its course and the financial adviser then makes intermediary supplies under a further and separate contract), each contract has its own VAT liability.

(VAT Information Sheet 2/03).

(2) Treatment of services supplied by independent financial adviser networks

Independent financial adviser (IFA) firms, authorised to carry out regulated activities under the *FSMA 2000*, frequently operate as networks for non-authorised financial advisers. Under these arrangements, the authorised IFA firm takes regulatory responsibility for non-regulated advisers, known as appointed representatives (ARs), enabling the ARs to carry out 'regulated activities' without the need to be authorised directly by the Financial Services Authority (FSA). '*Regulated activities*' means the selling of investment products, selling of mortgages (from 31 October 2004) and general insurance sales (from January 2005).These network arrangements are permitted under *FSMA 2000, s 39* but are subject to strict regulatory rules (see the Supervision Manual of the FSA Handbook, Chapter 12). In particular:

- The network appoints the ARs and trains them to operate in accordance with FSA requirements.
- In all dealings with the client, the ARs make it clear, both orally and on any paperwork, that they are acting on behalf of the network.
- The network has the contractual relationship with the financial product providers and at all times the AR acts on the network's behalf.
- The network maintains a high level of control over the ARs, carrying out regular checks and audits and imposing sanctions where appropriate.
- The network accepts responsibility for the actions of the ARs and handles all customer complaints made against the AR.
- The network meets the regulatory requirement relating to professional indemnity insurance to cover any claims resulting from the activities of the ARs and is legally liable for any sanctions imposed under the *FSMA 2000*.
- All fees or commissions for regulated activities are paid by the clients or product providers to the network and these form part of the income of the network for accounting and direct tax purposes.

When networks operate in this way, a 'sub-agency' or 'sub-contract' arrangement in effect exists between the network and the ARs. The network acts as principal, making supplies of financial intermediary services to the financial product providers and supplies of advice and/or financial intermediary services to the clients. The networks effectively sub-contract their functions to the ARs who interact directly with the client and the product providers in the provision of individual supplies on behalf of the network.

The VAT treatment of such arrangements is as follows.

- All payments (whether by fees or commissions) received by the network from the product providers or clients for the supplies of regulated financial *intermediary services* provided via the ARs is the network's VAT exempt income. The onward payment made to the ARs is consideration for the AR's VAT exempt intermediary services supplied to the network.
- Fees, whether paid directly to the network or via the ARs, in respect of regulated *advice only* services which fall outside the exemption for intermediary services are standard-rated income of the network. Any onward payment made by the network to the ARs is consideration for the provision of those services by the ARs to the network on which VAT is due if the AR is registered or required to be registered for VAT.
- Any optional services supplied by the network to the ARs for additional consideration (eg specific compliance or IT services) are separate supplies and the relevant VAT liability will apply.
- Any non-regulated services provided by ARs may fall outside the network arrangements altogether. If so, they are made directly by the ARs to the client/product provider.

A different VAT treatment applies to supplies made by networks that do not operate in the way outlined above (eg firms which on first appearance look like networks but are set up to provide marketing and/or compliance support services to directly authorised IFA firms). In the event of any doubt, businesses are advised to contact HMRC.

(Business Brief 26/04).

27.32 **STANDARD-RATED SUPPLIES**

There are various services which,, although associated with finance, are not covered by the exemption. These include:

- Debt collection and credit control
- Accounting and bookkeeping services
- Equipment leasing
- Executor and trustee services and the administration of estates
- Investment, finance and taxation advice
- Management consultancy
- Management of investment trusts
- Management of unauthorised unit trusts
- Merger and take-over advice
- Portfolio management (see 27.19(4) above)
- Registrar services (see 27.19(6) above)
- Safe custody (safe keeping rather than global custody) services (see 27.19(2) above) and safe transportation services
- Service companies' activities, eg administration, payment of salaries and wages

(VAT Notice 701/49/02, para 1.4).

28 Food

Cross-references. See also CATERING (11) for supplies in the course of catering and take-away food; 47.8(15) OUTPUT TAX for packaging of food products.

De Voil Indirect Tax Service. See V4.221; V4.226.

The contents of this chapter are as follows.

28.1 ZERO-RATING GENERALLY

The supply of food (including drink) comprised in the following *General items*, is zero-rated.

1. Food of a kind used for human consumption (see 28.2 to 28.14 below).
2. Animal feeding stuffs (see 28.15 and 28.19 below).
3. Seeds or other means of propagation of plants within 1. or 2. above (see 28.20 below).
4. Live animals of a kind generally used as, or yielding or producing, food for human consumption (see 28.21 to 28.23 below).

There are, however, a number of *Excepted items* (which are standard-rated) and *Overriding items* (which are zero-rated because they override the *Excepted items*).

Catering. Specifically excluded from zero-rating is any supply in the course of catering which includes

- any supply of food for consumption on the premises where it is supplied; and
- any supply of hot food for consumption off those premises.

See 11 CATERING for full details.

[*VATA 1994, Sch 8 Group 1 General Items 1–4*].

In applying zero-rating, the law is primarily concerned with the nature of the product itself rather than with its end use. For example, the sale of fish, such as mackerel, fit for human consumption is covered by *General Item 1* above (and not covered by any of the *Excepted items*) and can therefore be zero-rated. No consideration need be given to the use to which it will be put even, for example, if it is sold as bait. Similarly, salt of a culinary type is zero-rated because it is of a kind used for human consumption even though it may be put to other uses. However, in some cases, the wording of the law requires a distinction to be made. For example, some products can be used both as animal feeding stuffs (zero-rated) and as pet food (standard-rated). It then becomes important to determine how a product is 'held out for sale' taking into account packaging, labelling, advertising and any notices or displays.

(Internal Guidance V1–7, Chapter 1 para 1.7).

28.2 FOOD FOR HUMAN CONSUMPTION

The supply of food of a kind used for human consumption is zero-rated. Food includes drink. [*VATA 1994, Sch 8 Group 1 General Item 1*].

Meaning of 'food'. The law does not include a definition of 'food' and the word should therefore be given its ordinary and everyday meaning (applying *Brutus v Cozens, [1972] 2 All ER 1297*).

A product is considered to be 'food' if the average person would consider it so. HMRC regard the term as including products eaten as part of a meal or snack. However, many products are sold in a form in which they are not fit to be consumed without some preparation by the user and the words 'of a kind used for' are included to reflect this fact (*C & E Commrs v Macphie & Co (Glenbervie) Ltd, CS [1992] STC 886 (TVC 27.77)*). Products, therefore, like flour which, although not eaten by themselves, are generally recognised as food ingredients are included. 'Food' would not normally include

- medicines and medicated preparations (but see 32.15 HEALTH AND WELFARE for zero-rating of certain medicines),
- dietary supplements (see 28.11 below), or
- food additives and similar products (see 28.12 below)

which, although edible, are not generally regarded as 'food'.

Palatability and other matters may be taken into account (*Marfleet Refining Co Ltd (VTD 129) (TVC 27.85)*) and also nutritive value (*Soni (VTD 897) (TVC 27.72)*).

Waste and contaminated food products (including used cooking oil) are not allowed zero-rating because, although they could be described as 'food', they are not 'of a kind used for human consumption'. (They may, however, qualify for zero-rating as animal feeding stuffs, see 28.15 below.)

(VAT Notice 701/14/02, para 2.3).

Exceptions. Food of a kind used for human consumption is generally zero-rated under *General Item 1* above. There are, however, a number of categories of *Excepted items* (including ice cream and similar products, confectionery, alcoholic and other beverages, crisps, roasted and salted nuts) which are standard-rated and *Overriding items* (including tea and coffee) which override the *Excepted items* and remain zero-rated.

For a consideration of food for human consumption generally, see 28.3 to 28.14 below.

Catering. For food supplied in the course of catering and take-away food generally, see CATERING (11).

Asian food products and additives. For a useful list of such products and their VAT liabilities, see Internal Guidance V1–7, Chapter 1 paras 13.1, 13.2.

28.3 Basic foodstuffs

All supplies of unprocessed foodstuffs such as raw meat and fish, vegetables and fruit, nuts and pulses and fresh culinary herbs are zero-rated provided they are of a quality fit for human consumption. This applies whether the produce is supplied direct to the public or for use as ingredients in the manufacture of processed foods. (If not fit for human consumption, it may still be eligible for zero-rating as animal feeding stuffs, see 28.15 below.)

Meat and poultry. Zero-rating applies whether sold as a complete carcass or butchered and extends to more exotic meats such as ostrich, crocodile, kangaroo, horsemeat, etc. (The rules are different for sale of live animals where zero-rating only applies if the animal is of a species generally used for consumption in the UK so that, for example, the sale of a live horse is standard-rated, see 28.21 below.)

Fish. The same rules apply as for meat above. Provided the species is one generally used for human consumption in the UK, it is zero-rated whether supplied live, whole or filleted.

Vegetables, fruit and culinary herbs are zero-rated when sold unprocessed provided they are fit for human consumption (eg ornamental cabbages are standard-rated). See 28.20 below for supplies of growing plants and seeds. Zero-rating only applies to culinary herbs not medicinal ones (unless in the form of herbal teas). See 28.12 below for a list of herbs accepted by HMRC as culinary.

Fruit and vegetable pulps are zero-rated but most juices and juice concentrates are standard-rated as beverages (see 28.8 below).

Cereals (wheat, barley, maize, etc) of a kind fit for human consumption are zero-rated whether supplied as a growing crop, in bulk, or cleaned and packaged for retail sale. (Cereals unfit for human consumption may be eligible for zero-rating as animal feeding stuffs, see 28.15 below.)

See 28.14 below for processing other people's cereal crop.

Nuts and pulses. Raw and unprocessed nuts and pulses fit for human consumption are zero-rated, as are nuts roasted or salted in their shells. This applies whether they are sold in bulk or in small retail packs. Nuts which are shelled and either roasted or salted are standard-rated (see 28.9 below).

Bakery products. *Bread and bread products* (eg rolls, baps, pitta bread) are zero-rated unless supplied as part of a hot take-away meal (eg a bun containing a hot hamburger). For hot take-away food, see 11 CATERING. *Cakes* and *biscuits* (other than chocolate covered biscuits) are normally zero-rated (see 28.6 below) but other confectionery is normally standard-rated (see 28.5 below).

Freshly baked products. Many bakery products (eg pies, pasties and other savouries) are baked on the premises and sold while hot. See 11.1 CATERING for the distinction between freshly baked food (zero-rated) and hot take-away food (standard-rated).

Processed food. *Canned* and *frozen foods* take the liability of the equivalent unprocessed product. Ice creams, etc are standard-rated (see 28.4 below).

Ready meals. Sales of convenience foods and prepared meals which require further preparation (eg reheating) at home are zero-rated; but where premises and/or facilities for eating the food are provided or hot take-away food is supplied, there could be a supply of standard-rated catering. See 11 CATERING.

Sandwiches supplied pre-packed as part of a general range of prepared grocery items are usually zero-rated. However, if supplied as part of a buffet or party service, or if premises are provided for their consumption, there could be a supply of standard-rated catering. See 11 CATERING.

(VAT Notice 701/14/02, paras 3.1, 3.3, 3.4).

28.4 **Ice cream, etc**

The supply of ice cream, ice lollies, frozen yoghurt, water ices and similar frozen products, and prepared mixes and powders for making such products, are standard-rated. [*VATA 1994, Sch 8 Group 1 Excepted Item 1*]. Yoghurt unsuitable for immediate consumption when frozen is zero-rated. [*VATA 1994, Sch 8 Group 1 Overriding Item 1*]. The use of the expression 'similar frozen products' assumes that the adjective 'frozen' applies to any of the former, specifically enumerated items. What those items have in common is that they are supplied for consumption at a temperature below the freezing point of water. They do not have in common any particular degree of viscosity or solidity. See *Meschia's Frozen Foods v C & E Commrs, Ch D 2000, [2001] STC 1 (TVC 27.114)* where the court held that frozen yoghurt in the context of *Excepted Item 1* meant yoghurt reduced to a temperature below the freezing point of water.

Standard-rated items include

- sorbets and granitas
- ice cream gateaux and cakes, including arctic rolls
- fruit syrups sold in plastic tubes for home freezing as ice lollies

Zero-rated items include

- products which are supplied frozen but which have to be cooked (eg baked alaska) or thawed completely (cream gateaux, mousse) before eating
- desserts which can be eaten either straight from the freezer or left to thaw (unless primarily designed for eating while frozen and made substantially of ice cream or any of the other excepted items)
- toppings, sauces and syrups for serving with ice cream (unless sold on the ice cream)

Wafers, cones, etc sold complete with ice cream are standard-rated as part of that ice cream. If sold separately, they are treated as biscuits (see 28.6 below).

(VAT Notice 701/14/02, para 3.5).

28.5 **Confectionery**

'Confectionery' is standard-rated. '*Confectionery*' includes chocolates; sweets; biscuits wholly or partly covered with chocolate or with some product similar in taste and appearance; drained, glacé or crystallised fruits (but not drained cherries or candied peel which are zero-rated); and any item of sweetened prepared food which is normally eaten with the fingers. [*VATA 1994, Sch 8 Group 1 Excepted Item 2; Overriding Items 2 and 3* and *Note* (*5*)].

In *Popcorn House Ltd, [1968] 4 All ER 782* (a purchase tax case) 'confectionery' was described as any form of food normally eaten with the fingers and made by a cooking process, other than baking, which contains a substantial amount of sweetening matter.

In *C & E Commrs v Ferrero UK Ltd, CA [1997] STC 881 (TVC 27.125)*, the Court confirmed (and HMRC have accepted) the following principles adopted by the tribunal as the correct approach to take when deciding whether a product is confectionery or a cake or biscuit.

- The words in the law must be given their ordinary meaning.
- What is relevant is the view of the ordinary man in the street.
- VAT treatment of other products is not relevant.
- If a product has characteristics of two categories, it can be placed in the category in which it has sufficient characteristics to qualify.
- Factors that should also taken into account include appearance, size and ingredients, manufacturing process, taste and texture, time and place of eating, and packaging. Marketing may also be of varying degrees of relevance.

(Internal Guidance V1–7, Chapter 1 para 8.2).

Confectionery items must be both sweetened *and* have some sweetness in the taste. Standard-rating applies to products falling within the general definition of confectionery even if intended to meet special nutritional needs (eg chocolate for diabetics and slimmers' meal replacements in biscuit form with a chocolate or similar coating).

Standard-rated items include

- chocolates, chocolate bars (including those containing nuts, fruit, toffee, biscuit or any other ingredient), liqueur chocolates
- boiled sweets, lollipops and candyfloss
- fruit pastilles and gums and similar jelly sweets
- turkish delight
- sherbet
- marshmallows, 'snowballs', fondants and similar confectionery
- chewing and bubble gum
- nuts or fruit with a coating, eg of chocolate, yoghurt or sugar
- crystallised or sugared ginger (but ginger preserved in syrup, drained ginger or dusted ginger can be zero-rated as long as not held out for sale as confectionery)
- compressed fruit bars, consisting mainly of fruit and nuts, with added sweetening matter
- bars consisting mainly of sesame seeds and sugar or other sweetening matter (but halva is zero-rated unless coated with chocolate or chocolate substitute or held out for sale as confectionery)
- marrons glacé
- sweetened popcorn (*C & E Commrs v Clark's Cereal Products Ltd, QB 1965, [1968] 3 All ER 778 (TVC 27.130)* – a purchase tax case)
- sweetened dried fruit, eg banana chips, pineapple and papaya (unless sold as suitable for confectionery/snacking *and* home cooking (see 28.12 below) when zero-rated irrespective of bag size)

- cereal bars, whether or not coated with chocolate (except for bars qualifying as cakes)
- florentines
- coconut ice

Zero-rated items include

- Angelica, 'glacé' cherries, and cocktail or maraschino cherries
- cakes (see 28.6 below)
- biscuits not covered with chocolate or a similar product (see 28.6 below)
- chocolate spread
- liquid chocolate icing
- toffee apples (*Candy Maid Confections Ltd & Others v C & E Commrs, Ch D [1968] 3 All ER 773 (TVC 27.116)* – a purchase tax case) and other apples on a stick covered with chocolate, nuts, etc.
- traditional Indian and Pakistani delicacies, eg barfis, halvas, jelabi, laddoos (but not petha which is crystallised fruit)
- traditional Japanese delicacies
- chocolate cups

See 28.6 below for edible and inedible cake decorations and 28.13 below for mixtures and assortments.

(VAT Notice 701/14/02, paras 3.4, 3.6).

28.6 Cakes and biscuits

Cakes and biscuits (other than biscuits wholly or partly covered with chocolate or some product similar in taste and appearance) are zero-rated. [*VATA 1994, Sch 8 Group 1 Excepted Item 2*].

Cakes include (whether or not they are covered with chocolate)

- sponges and fruitcakes
- meringues
- slab gingerbread (gingerbread men are treated as biscuits)
- flapjacks (but not flapjack-type products containing cereals other than oats, which are confectionery, see 28.5 above)
- marshmallow teacakes (despite the fact that they comprise a combination of chocolate coated biscuit and marshmallow, both of which are regarded as standard-rated confectionery) but not 'snowballs' which are confectionery, see 28.5 above
- 'crunch cakes' consisting of corn flakes or other breakfast cereal products coated in chocolate or carob and pressed into flat cakes (see *Doves Farm Foods Ltd (VTD 17805)*)
- caramel or 'millionaire's' shortcake (*Marks & Spencer plc (VTD 4510) (TVC 27.122)*)

- lebkuchen
- jaffa cakes (see *United Biscuits (UK) Ltd (VTD 6344) (TVC 27.123)*)

Cakes provided as part of a supply of catering are standard-rated as part of that supply. See 11 CATERING. However, if a commemorative cake is provided to a caterer or individual, the supply can be zero-rated provided the supplier

- takes no further part in the provision of catering; and
- does not take the cake to the premises to set it up/supervise its disposal.

Cake decorations. *Inedible* cake decorations are standard-rated where sold on their own. If supplied as part of a cake, an inedible decoration can be zero-rated unless it is clearly a separate item in its own right (eg a toy with a child's birthday cake intended to be used after the cake is eaten although, even then, if the linked goods concession can be applied, the supply can be treated as a single supply, see 28.13 below).

Edible cake decorations are zero-rated when sold as part of a cake. They are also zero-rated when sold separately unless standard-rated as confectionery (see 28.5 above) or roasted nuts (see 28.9 below).

Zero-rated cake decorations include

- chocolate couverture
- chocolate chips
- hundreds and thousands, vermicelli and sugar strands
- chocolate leaves, scrolls, etc, jelly shapes, and sugar flowers, leaves, etc (provided designed specifically for cake decorations)
- royal icing
- toasted coconut and toasted almonds held out specifically for baking use
- cherries used in baking ('glacé')

Standard-rated cake decorations include

- chocolate buttons
- chocolate flakes (except where supplied within the bakery and ice cream industries when they may be zero-rated if sold in packs of 144 or more and clearly labelled 'for use as cake decorations only: not for retail sale')
- any other items sold in the same form as confectionery

Biscuits. HMRC regard 'biscuit' as generally referring to a product made from wheat flour, fat and sugar in a fairly stiff (rather than runny) dough which is generally cut or rolled for baking, with low moisture content giving a crisp consistency. It has a long shelf life of several months and goes soft when stale. The main borderline problem between confectionery and biscuits has been with products which contain an element of biscuit together with other ingredients, and on this question the tribunals have not generally been concerned with the technical details of biscuit manufacture. (Internal Guidance V1–7, Chapter 1 para 8.7).

Biscuits covered or partly covered in chocolate (or some other product similar in taste and appearance) are standard-rated. Other biscuits are zero-rated.

Standard-rated biscuits include

- chocolate shortbread
- gingerbread men decorated with chocolate (unless only dots for eyes)
- ice cream wafers partly covered in chocolate, eg chocolate oysters (but see *Marcantonio Foods Ltd (VTD 15486) (TVC 27.119)* for waffle cones)

Zero-rated biscuits include

- chocolate chip biscuits where the chips are either included in the dough or pressed into the surface before cooking
- bourbon and other biscuits whether the chocolate or similar product only forms a sandwich layer
- biscuits coated with caramel or some other product that does not resemble chocolate in taste and appearance

See also *C & E Commrs v Ferrero UK Ltd, CA [1997] STC 881 (TVC 27.125).*

Mixtures and assortments. See 28.13 below.

(VAT Notice 701/14/02, para 3.4).

28.7 **Alcoholic drinks**

Beverages chargeable with any excise duty specifically charged on spirits, beer, wine or made-wine and preparations thereof are standard-rated. [*VATA 1994, Sch 8 Group 1 Excepted Item 3*].

All supplies of drinks containing alcohol are standard-rated, whether sold for consumption on or off the premises. This includes

- beer, cider and perry (including black beer and shandy)
- wine (including made-wine and fermented communion wine)
- spirits and liqueurs

Food products, other than beverages, containing alcohol follow the normal liability rules, eg fruit preserved in alcohol is zero-rated as any other preserved fruit and rum babas are zero-rated as cakes. Liqueur chocolates are standard-rated.

(VAT Notice 701/14/02, para 3.7).

28.8 **Non-alcoholic drinks**

Supplies of 'beverages' not within 28.7 above (including fruit juices and bottled waters) and syrups, concentrates, essences, powders, crystals or other products for the preparation of beverages are standard-rated, subject to the following overriding exceptions which are zero-rated.

(*a*) Tea, maté, herbal teas and similar products, and preparations and extractions thereof.

(*b*) Cocoa, coffee and chicory and other roasted coffee substitutes, and preparations and extractions thereof.

(*c*) Milk and preparations and extracts thereof.

(*d*) Preparations and extracts of meat, yeast or eggs.

[*VATA 1994, Sch 8 Group 1 Excepted Item 4, Overriding Items 4–7; FA 1999, s 14*].

All hot beverages, and beverages sold for consumption on the premises, are standard-rated.

'*Beverage*' must be given its ordinary meaning and covers drinks and liquids that are commonly consumed. Liquids that are commonly consumed are those that are characteristically taken to increase bodily liquid levels, to slake thirst and to fortify or give pleasure (*Bioconcepts Ltd (VTD 11287) (TVC 27.146)*). HMRC have accepted this definition.

Following the tribunal decision in *McCormick (UK) plc (VTD 15202) (TVC 27.149)* HMRC accept that mulling spices, whiskey todd mixtures, spiced cider mixtures, etc are not 'products for the preparation of beverages' and are zero-rated.

Standard-rated beverages include

- carbonated drinks such as lemonade, cola and mixers such as tonic and soda
- fruit cordials and squashes
- mineral, table and spa waters held out for sale as beverages
- alcohol-free beer and wines
- fruit and vegetable juices (but lemon juice for culinary use is not a beverage)
- ginger, glucose, honey, peppermint and barley water drinks
- flavourings for milk shakes (except preparations and extracts of cocoa or coffee, which are zero-rated)
- purgative and laxative 'teas', such as senna, and similar medicinal teas
- soft drinks containing tea as only one of several ingredients, eg fruit flavoured 'iced tea', see *Snapple Beverage Corporation (VTD 13690) (TVC 27.150)*

Following the decision in *Dr X Hua (VTD 13811) (TVC 27.74)* where the tribunal held that herbal teas sold at a homeopathic clinic were substantially the same as herbal teas sold commercially, HMRC accept that supplies of herbal teas are zero-rated even when they are prescribed for a medical reason. (Internal Guidance V1–7, Chapter 1 para 3.2.3).

Khat (or Chat) is standard-rated as HMRC do not regard it as a food product. (Business Brief 25/97).

Drinks which are not beverages. Some drinks do not fall within the definition of 'beverage'. Such drinks, and mixes, etc for making them, can therefore be zero-rated. These include

- plain soya or rice milk (unflavoured and unsweetened)
- coconut milk
- meal replacement drinks for slimmers or invalids
- unfermented fruit juice specifically for sacramental purposes (see 28.11 below)
- angostura bitters

(VAT Notice 701/14/02, para 3.7).

Milk based drinks. Zero-rating under (*c*) above applies to

- drinks which are substantially based on milk (eg milk shakes, Ovaltine, Horlicks and Complan);
- edible products made from milk such as coffee whiteners and creamers, lactose, whey, edible casein, caseinate, and lactalbumin; and
- flavoured milk powder which when mixed with water gives a complete milk shake. (If it is merely a flavouring, it is standard-rated unless it is a preparation of cocoa or coffee when it is zero-rated.)

The liability of beverages which comprise a mixture of milk extracts (eg yoghurt) and other ingredients such as fruit juice can only be decided on a basis of fact and impression. HMRC regard them as zero-rated when they have the texture and nature of a milky drink or where the predominant ingredient is a milk extract such as whey or lactoserum. However, they would be standard-rated as beverages where the milk or milk extract content is not predominant and their nature is that of, for example, a fruit drink. In *Rivella (UK) Ltd (VTD 16382) (TVC 27.152)* the company manufactured a canned sparkling drink called 'Rivella'. Lactoserum comprised 35% of the drink but on a dry analysis of the ingredients (ie excluding water) the lactoserum was over 50% of the contents. The tribunal noted that the relative weight of the four factors considered in the *Snapple* case above (ie ingredients, manufacturing process, appearance and taste, and marketing and packaging) would vary on a case by case basis but, in this case, it found that the first two were predominant and decisive, supported by the marketing process which has been successful in linking in the minds of the potential consumers the principal source of the products as extracts of milk. The appearance and taste test had little or no value because the lactoserum did not possess the 'milkiness' of milk or preparations of milk. The tribunal concluded that Rivella was zero-rated.

(Internal Guidance V1–7, Chapter 1 para 9.9).

28.9 Savoury snacks

The following are standard-rated.

(*a*) Potato crisps, sticks or puffs and similar products made from potato, potato flour or potato starch when packaged for human consumption without further preparation.

(*b*) Savoury food products made by swelling cereals or cereal products when packaged for human consumption without further preparation.

(*c*) Salted or roasted nuts other than nuts in shell.

[*VATA 1994, Sch 8 Group 1 Excepted Item 5*].

'Without further preparation' effectively means that the items are sold in retail packs for eating out of the packet with the fingers. *Excepted Item 5* does therefore not cover products which would otherwise meet the descriptions within it but which are sold for use in cooking or products which need other preparation before being ready to eat (eg breakfast cereals). (Internal Guidance V1–7, Chapter 1 para 10.2).

Standard-rated products include

- savoury popcorn (but not corn for popping, eg 'microwave' popcorn)
- prawn crackers sold in retail packs if made from potato, etc and falling within (*a*) above or made by swelling cereals, etc and falling within (*b*) above. Those made

from tapioca (which is made from a root crop) are zero-rated as are unpackaged prawn crackers (eg those supplied in unsealed bags as part of a take-away meal)

- rice cakes (but not unflavoured rice cakes intended for consumption with cheese or other toppings)
- 'light' extruded products where air is introduced under pressure into the cereal flour or starch paste during manufacture to produce an expanded, aerated product

Zero-rated products include

- tortilla chips
- corn chips
- bagel chips
- breadsticks, mini-garlic breads and other bread-based snacks
- twiglets
- cocktail cheese savouries
- Japanese rice crackers
- 'microwave' popcorn
- toasted coconut, almonds and chopped nuts held out for sale in retail packs specifically for home baking

(VAT Notice 701/14/02, para 3.8).

In *Procter & Gamble UK (VTD 18381) (TVC 27.154)* the tribunal accepted that 'dipping chips', including 38% potato flour and intended to be eaten with a sauce or dip, were not (i) intended for human consumption without further preparation; (ii) a 'similar product' under (*a*) above; or (iii) made from potato flour. Standard-rating under (*a*) above only applied to products which are almost entirely made from potato. (The full tribunal decision contains a detailed list of a number of competing products, some of which HMRC treat as standard-rated and some of which they accept as zero-rated.)

See 28.13 below for mixtures containing standard and zero-rated items (eg Bombay mix).

28.10 Ingredients for domestic beer and wine making

Goods otherwise qualifying as food for human consumption, animal feeding stuffs (see 28.15 below) or seeds (see 28.20 below) but which are canned, bottled, packaged or prepared for use in domestic

- brewing of beer,
- making of cider or perry, or
- production of wine or made-wine

are standard-rated. [*VATA 1994, Sch 8 Group 1 Excepted Item 7*].

Included are

- kits for home-brewing, wine-making, etc

- retail packs of hopped malt extract, malted barley, roasted barley and hops
- special wine and brewer's yeast
- grape concentrates
- retail packs of foods which are specialised to home wine-making, eg dried elderberries or sloes

Any general food product that is held out for sale specifically for home wine making or brewing must also be standard-rated. In this context, goods are held out for sale for home brewing and wine making if

(*a*) sold in a retail outlet (or department or section of a general outlet) specialising in home brewing and wine making;

(*b*) labelled, advertised or otherwise displayed as materials for home brewing or wine making; or

(*c*) provided or packaged with any brewing or wine making recipes or instructions for using them in the making of beer or wine.

(VAT Notice 701/14/02, para 3.7).

28.11 **Specialised products**

The liability of such products depends upon whether they fall within the normal meaning of 'food' (see 28.2 above). If they do, then they are treated under the normal rules and are zero-rated unless falling within one of the *Excepted items*.

(*a*) **Food supplements**. Dietary supplements of a kind not normally purchased and used as food are standard-rated. This includes

- vitamin and mineral supplements of all kinds
- royal jelly products but not regular products such as honey which have royal jelly added (see *Grosvenor Commodities Ltd (VTD 7221) (TVC 27.87)*)
- tablets, pills and capsules containing, for example, wheatgerm, iron, calcium, fibre, yeast, garlic, pollen, propolis, seaweed, evening primrose, guarana or other similar herbal preparations, and powders of these other than garlic and yeast. See *Nature's Balance Ltd (VTD 12295) (TVC 27.88)* and *Hunter Ridgeley Ltd (VTD 13662) (TVC 27.89)* for algae tablets and *National Safety Associates of America (UK) Ltd (VTD 14241) (TVC 27.90)* for fruit and vegetable tablets. A high protein powder marketed as a dietary supplement and intended to be mixed with water and drunk was held to qualify as food in *Arthro Vite Ltd (VTD 14836) (TVC 27.79)*
- charcoal biscuits
- cod liver oil and other fish oils held out for sale as dietary supplements (see *Marfleet Refining Co Ltd (VTD 129) (TVC 27.85)*)
- elixirs and tonics, including mixtures of cider vinegar and honey sold as a dietary supplement
- malt extract with cod liver oil (but the supply of plain malt extract, with or without added vitamins, is zero-rated unless held out for sale for home brewing, etc)

(*b*) **Medicated foods.** The liability of a medicated food depends on whether the main purpose of eating the product is nutrition (zero-rated as food) or the therapeutic effects of its medicinal ingredient (standard-rated as medicine). Most zero-rated medicated foods are complete diets designed to meet the special nutritional needs of people with particular medical conditions, to which medicinal substances (eg antibiotics) have been added. Standard-rated items include medicated pastilles (for sore throats etc), syrups and linctuses. (Internal Guidance V1–7, Chapter 1 para 3.3). See also Internal Guidance V1–7, Chapter 1 para 3.7 for the liability of a range of medicated foods and non-foods.

(*c*) **Enteral nutrition** products are treated as food for VAT purposes and zero-rated. (Internal Guidance V1–7, Chapter 1 para 3.5).

(*d*) **Parenteral nutrition** (PN). The liability of PN products is judged by the same criteria as 'normal' food. Those that provide sufficient nutritional value to be considered the equivalent of a meal are zero-rated; those which simply provide a vitamin or mineral supplement are treated in the same way as vitamin and mineral supplements taken orally and standard-rated. To be treated as 'food' a PN solution would have to contain

- amino acids (either alone or with vitamins and minerals);
- amino acids together with carbohydrates;
- carbohydrate (eg glucose); or
- lipids.

Supplementary products consisting of single vitamins and/or vitamin-mineral mixes are standard-rated.

Most intravenous glucose solutions are eligible for zero-rating as PN products. But low level glucose solutions (eg 5%–10%) are generally not administered for their nutritional content but are carriers for antibiotics etc. These 'carrier' solutions are standard-rated.

(Internal Guidance V1–7, Chapter 1 para 3.6).

(*e*) **Invalid foods**. These products, including parenteral products given intravenously, can be zero-rated (subject to the normal rules) provided they are designed to meet the nutritional needs of the consumer and not to provide treatment for any medical condition. See *Ridal (C149) (TVC 27.81)* (a customs duty case) where the tribunal held that NuTriVeneD powder, an anti-oxidant specially formulated for Down's Syndrome sufferers and taken mixed with a fruit puree at each meal, was exempt from customs duty and VAT on importation from the USA as being within the definition of food. Foods intended to build patients up which are sold in liquid form are zero-rated as food since they fall outside the definition of a beverage (see 28.8 above).

(*f*) **Diabetic and hypoallergenic products**. Specialised foods designed for diabetics or allergy sufferers are zero-rated (eg sugar-free preserves or gluten-free flour and cakes) unless falling within any of the *Excepted items* (eg sugar-free confectionery or gluten-free chocolate biscuits) in which case they are standard-rated.

(*g*) **Slimmers' foods**. Low calorie foods for slimmers are treated in the same way as their mainstream food equivalent. Slimmers' meal replacement products (including drinks) are zero-rated unless in the form of confectionery (see 28.5 above).

Appetite suppressants in whatever form are not food and must be standard-rated. Genuine slimmers' food products containing appetite suppressants (eg soups containing cellulose) can be zero-rated provided the product is obviously food and is meant to take the place of a 'normal' food equivalent in the slimmers' daily food intake.

(*h*) **Sports products**. HMRC express the following opinion on the VAT liability of sports products.

- *Sports/energy drinks*. These are standard-rated beverages (see 28.8 above) unless a product meets all the following conditions in which case it is zero-rated. The conditions are

  (i) it is aimed at supplying energy to enhance performance and/or accelerate recovery after exercise and both the packaging and advertising of the product reflect this;

  (ii) it is not primarily marketed for consumption as a soft drink;

  (iii) its primary purpose is the provision of energy or creatine or to build bulk and not rehydration;

  (iv) it is in the form of powder, syrup, concentrate, essence, crystal or gel or is the equivalent of these with water added; and

  (v) it has as its main ingredient(s), other than water, *either* carbohydrate (the majority of which is not sugar) *or* creatine *or* protein *or* a mixture of each.

  Drinks that are preparations of milk, meat, yeast or egg are zero-rated in their own right.

  See also *SIS (Science in Sport) Ltd (VTD 16555) (TVC 27.80)* where the tribunal held that zero-rating applied to products consisting primarily of carbohydrate or creatine, in powder form, which were designed to be mixed with water and drunk. They were consumed for nutritional purposes and therefore within the normal meaning of 'food'.
- *Tablets* are standard-rated with the exception of glucose, dextrose and Horlicks tablets which are zero-rated.
- *Creatine*. With the exception of sports/energy drinks (see above), items made up wholly or mainly of creatine are standard-rated. Where it is clear that the main benefit of the product is not the creatine but carbohydrate, protein or fat, then it is treated as a food, and is zero-rated unless falling within one of the excepted items.
- *Cereal/fruit bars*. Standard-rating applies to any product falling within the general definition of confectionery even when that product is intended to meet the special nutritional needs of athletes. See 28.5 above.

(*i*) **Food and drink for religious and sacramental use**. Religious laws requiring certain foods to be prepared in particular ways (eg kosher or halal) does not affect the liability of the final product. However, by concession, zero-rating has been agreed for the following food products which have exclusive sacramental use.

- Communion wafers used in the celebration of the Christian Communion, Mass or Eucharist

- Unfermented communion wine (fermented wine is standard-rated)
- Unfermented grape juice for use at the Jewish seder or kaddish provided it is marked prominently in English 'for sacramental use only'

(VAT Notice 701/14/02, paras 4.1–4.7).

28.12 **Ingredients and additives**

Home cooking. Most ingredients used in home cooking and baking (eg flour and sugar) are clearly foodstuffs in their own right. As a general principle, products sold for use as an ingredient in home cooking or baking can be zero-rated if

- it has some measurable nutritional content;
- it is used solely or predominantly, in the particular form in which it is supplied, in the manufacture of food; and
- it does not fall within any *Excepted item*.

Pre-mixes. Prepared cake, soup, sauce and other mixes sold for making up in the home kitchen are zero-rated except for mixes for ice creams and similar frozen products within 28.4 above.

Cooking oils. Maize (corn) oil, rapeseed oil, groundnut (arachis) oil, olive oil (including olive oil BP), almond oil (but not bitter almond oil), sesame seed oil, sunflower seed oil, palm kernel oil, walnut oil, soya oil and blends of any of these oils can be zero-rated provided

- they are of a type suitable for culinary use; and
- they do not contain any substance, such as perfume, that would make them unsuitable for culinary use.

If they meet these conditions, such oils may be zero-rated even if held out for sale for other purposes (eg massage or cosmetic oils).

Linseed oil and essential oils are always standard-rated. Waste and used oils for recycling are ineligible for relief as 'food for human consumption' but may be eligible for relief as animal feeding stuffs (see 28.15 below).

Starch and gelatine are zero-rated if edible but standard-rated if inedible or unsuitable for human consumption (eg starch for stiffening collars and 'photographic' gelatine).

Salt for culinary use is zero-rated. This includes fine salt (undried vacuum and pure dried vacuum), dendritic salt, and rock and sea salt in retail packs for culinary use (12.5 kilo packs or less). Non-culinary salt is standard-rated. This includes compacted, granular and soiled salt, and salt of any type specifically held out for use in dishwashers or for other non-food use.

Sweeteners. Natural products used as sweeteners (eg sugar and honey) are food products in their own right and zero-rated. Artificial sweeteners (eg saccharin, aspartame and sorbitol) can also be zero-rated.

Sweetened dried fruit sold as suitable for home baking *and* snacking can be zero-rated irrespective of the bag size. If sold purely as confectionery, it is standard-rated under 28.5 above. (Business Brief 18/98).

Herbs. See 28.20 below.

Other flavourings and flavour enhancers. Zero-rating applies to

- natural flavouring essences (eg vanilla, peppermint and culinary rosewater)
- synthetic flavourings if designed specifically for food use
- flavouring mixes (eg dusting powders or blended seasonings) whether made or natural or synthetic components
- mixes for marinating meat, fish or poultry before cooking
- mulling spices, whiskey todd mixtures, spiced cider mixtures, etc (see *McCormick (UK) plc (VTD 15202) (TVC 27.149)*)

Unflavoured brining mixes (wet or dry) and flavour enhancers (eg monosodium glutamate) which do not contribute flavour themselves are standard-rated.

Other additives. By concession, zero-rating applies to baking powder, cream of tartar and rennet. Pectin is zero-rated if supplied in retail packs for culinary use.

Bicarbonate of soda is always standard-rated, as are saltpetre and other single chemicals that may be sold for use in the brining or other processing of meats or fish.

(VAT Notice 701/14/02, para 3.2).

Commercial food manufacture. Many substances are used in the preparation of commercially produced foodstuffs which would not be used in the domestic kitchen. The distinction between standard and zero-rated products is largely the distinction between zero-rated ingredients (which are included for their nutritional content and are food products in their own right) and standard-rated additives (which are included for other than strictly nutritional reasons and are not themselves food).

Ingredients. Most ingredients in commercial food production are the same as those used in home cooking and baking and clearly foodstuffs in their own right. As a general principle, any edible product supplied for incorporation as ingredients in foodstuffs be zero-rated if

(*a*) it has some measurable nutritional content;

(*b*) it is used solely or predominantly, in the particular form in which it is supplied, in the manufacture of food; and

(*c*) it is not one of the *excepted items*.

Products which do not meet these criteria are standard-rated as food additives with the exception of flavourings (natural and synthetic) which may be zero-rated provided they meet the criteria in (*b*) and (*c*) above. This includes sausage skins (see *Devro Ltd (VTD 7570) (TVC 27.78)*).

Additives. Products supplied for incorporation in foodstuffs which do not meet the requirements in (*a*)-(*c*) above are treated as additives and standard-rated. They are generally included for commercial reasons (eg to prolong shelf life) and do not fall within the everyday meaning of the word 'food' (see 28.2 above). This includes

- preservatives including unflavoured wet and dry brine mixes and cures for curing or salting meats
- anti-oxidants including vitamins A and E
- vitamin supplements (including those required by law to fortify flour before it can be put on the market)
- stabilisers and thickening agents (eg agar, carageenan, guar gum, gum arabic, gum tragacanth and xanthan gum, but not corn starch)

- fillers and bulking agents other than flour and starch
- colourants other than naturally-derived colourings which are also culinary spices in their own right (eg caramel, cocoa, saffron, turmeric and cochineal)
- flavour enhancers (eg monosodium glutamate), ribonucleotides and hydrolysed vegetable protein
- flour improvers and bleaching agents

Some commercial additives are accepted for VAT purposes as food in their own right. These are

- food grade, naturally derived emulsifiers and stabilisers (eg lecithin) specifically tailored and mixed for food purposes which are essential to the production of that food and cannot be used for any other purpose
- artificial sweeteners and artificial flavourings

(VAT Notice 701/14/02, paras 5.1–5.3).

28.13 Mixed supplies and assortments

There is a mixed supply if standard and zero-rated food items, or zero-rated food items and standard-rated non-food items) are supplied together for a single price. Examples of mixed supplies containing foodstuffs include

- food hampers
- special gift or presentation packs containing linked items (eg coffee supplied with a mug, tea with a pack of chocolate biscuits)
- linked goods promotions
- food supplied in or with re-usable storage containers

Normally, the total price must be apportioned in order to arrive at the output tax due. See 47.3 OUTPUT TAX for the general rules on the treatment of mixed supplies and various methods of apportionment.

Linked goods concession. Where, however, a *minor* standard-rated item is supplied with a main zero-rated item, the supply can be treated as a single supply of the main zero-rated item provided the standard-rated item

- is not charged at a separate price;
- costs no more than 20% of the total cost of the supply; and
- costs no more than £1 (excluding VAT).

Once these conditions have been met, the linked goods are treated as a single zero-rated supply throughout the distribution chain. A wholesaler or retailer receiving goods already linked, and who is unsure whether the conditions have been met, should refer to the supplier's supporting documentation and, if still in doubt, check with the supplier.

Mixtures and assortments Some food contains mixtures which are both zero-rated and standard-rated when supplied separately. Generally, the tax value of each part must be ascertained to calculate VAT due. See 47.3 OUTPUT TAX. However, the following products, containing only small quantities of standard-rated items, may, by concession, be treated as a single zero-rated supply.

- Assortments of biscuits where the weight of standard-rated chocolate biscuits (see 28.6 above) does not exceed 15% of total net weight.
- Fruit and nut mixes (including Bombay and similar savoury mixes) where the weight of standard-rated items (eg sweetened fruit, chocolate pieces or roasted nuts) does not exceed 25% of total net weight.
- Petits fours where the net weight of chocolate biscuits and sweets does not exceed 15% of total net weight (25% where sweets only are included).

The concession only applies to mixtures and assortments supplied in a single pack, not to 'variety' selections of individual packs.

If any of the above assortments fail to meet the conditions, they can still be treated as a single zero-rated supply if they satisfy the linked goods concession above.

(VAT Notice 701/14/02, paras 6.1, 6.2; VAT Notice 48, ESC 2.7).

For mixtures involving food packaging (eg containers, storage jars), see 47.8(15) OUTPUT TAX.

28.14 Food processing

Any work done on another person's goods is a supply of services. The supply of a treatment or process to another person's goods can be zero-rated, if by doing so, zero-rated goods are produced. [*VATA 1994, s 30(2A); FA 1996, s 29(2)(5)*]. Processing which results in the production of a new zero-rated food product may therefore be zero-rated. Processing which does not result in the production of a new food product, or which results in the production of a standard-rated food product, is a standard-rated supply.

New goods are produced when a process alters the essential characteristics of the goods. This may include size and shape, appearance, composition, use and, specifically for food items, readiness to use or eat. For example, the process of smoking salmon is zero-rated because the new product, the smoked salmon, is a new zero-rated food item. The smoked salmon is immediately edible and thus distinct and different following the process of smoking. The process of smoking cod, on the other hand, is standard-rated as it does not produce a new zero-rated food item (because the smoked cod is not immediately edible) and the essential characteristics have not changed following the smoking.

Zero-rated processes

Meat and fish processing

- butchering carcasses including boning and jointing meat
- brining or curing pork into ham
- processing meat into sausages
- smoking trout and salmon

Fruit and vegetable processing

- drying, cleaning and coating seeds or grain to make it marketable as seed for sowing
- milling grain into flour, meal or semolina
- cooking, canning or otherwise preserving fruit and vegetables

- drying fruit
- roasting and/or grinding coffee beans
- grinding granulated sugar into caster or icing sugar

Other services

- refining crude oil into edible oil
- processing used or contaminated oil into edible oil
- processing of liquid milk into dried milk
- kneading blocks of frozen butter, adding salt and water and packing

Standard-rated processes

Meat and fish processing

- slaughtering animals without further process (see 28.24 below)
- smoking herring to make kippers
- smoking cod and haddock
- shelling shrimps, prawns or other shellfish
- skinning fish

Fruit and vegetable processing

- cleaning and conditioning grain
- drying grain
- harvesting crops
- malting barley
- blending tea
- roasting or salting peanuts or other nuts

Other services

- sorting, grading or packaging any product
- maturing cheese or any other product (effectively a process of storage during which a natural change occurs)
- pasteurisation or sterilisation
- supervision of foodstuffs to ensure that manufactured and prepared foods meet religious dietary regulations

(VAT Notice 701/40/02, paras 1.1–1.4, 2.1, 2.2).

28.15 **ANIMAL FEEDING STUFFS**

The supply of 'animal' feeding stuffs is zero-rated. '*Animal*' includes bird, fish, crustacean and mollusc. [*VATA 1994, Sch 8 Group 1 General Item 2*].

Most commodities recognised as animal feeds are zero-rated unless

- sold for non-food purposes (eg bedding, packaging, thatching, fertiliser); or

- 'held out for sale' (see 28.1 above) as pet food or food for wild birds (see 28.19 below).

Zero-rated items (subject to the above) include the following.

- Cereal and cereal by-products including bran, sharps and similar residues
- Compound feeds consisting of a number of different ingredients (including major minerals, trace elements, vitamins and other additives), mixed and blended in appropriate proportions to provide properly balanced diets for all types of livestock at every stage of growth and development
- Feed blocks
- Fish meal and fish residue meal
- Forage crops
- Ground oyster shell
- Hay and straw unless held out for sale for non-feed purposes (eg bedding). In the case of straw holding out for sale for non-food use includes supplies to customers known to be market gardeners or other horticultural concerns and industrial packers or other non-agricultural businesses
- Molasses
- Oils and fats (including tallow) suitable for use in animal feeding stuffs unless *either* they require further processing before becoming suitable for inclusion in animal feeds *or* are held out for sale for non-feed purposes. Waste oil from fish and chip shops, etc normally requires processing and is therefore standard-rated (a need for sieving, decanting or heating does not disqualify the oil from zero-rating)
- Oilseed residue (except castor oil)
- Peanuts
- Protein concentrates, ie products specifically designed for further mixing (at an inclusion rate of 5% or more) with planned proportions of cereals and other feeding stuffs. They consist of appropriate blends of animal or vegetable protein (or both), plus other essential nutrients, eg vitamins, minerals, etc.
- Rabbit food
- Specialised diets formulated for laboratory animals
- Specialised diets formulated for racing greyhounds. To be zero-rated (as opposed to standard-rated as pet food) (i) the product must be a complete feed providing all the required elements for a balanced diet for a dog without having to be mixed with any other food (apart from water); (ii) the product must be specifically held out for sale for racing greyhounds; and (iii) the supplier must be able to demonstrate that the product is designed specifically to meet the nutritional requirements of racing greyhounds (for a retailer, this information will normally be provided to him by the manufacturer on the packaging or in the accompanying literature)
- Straights, ie single feeding stuffs of animal or vegetable origin which may have undergone some form of processing. Examples include wheat, barley, flaked maize, field beans, groundnut cake and meal, soya bean meal, fish meal, meat meal and meat and bone meal

- Supplements, ie products designed for adding to other feed in a proportion of less than 5% of the whole (see also protein concentrates above) to supply planned proportions of vitamins, trace minerals, one or more non-nutrient additives and other special ingredients. Normally, the active ingredients are combined with an inert 'carrier' (eg cereal) to make for easier mixing by the purchaser. They may be supplied to manufacturers or to farmers for making feed on the farm. Their liability will depend on whether they are for medicinal or nutritional purposes (see 28.18 below for the borderline), but most are nutritional and so zero-rated. Zero-rated nutritional supplements (whether intended to be added to normal feed or given separately, eg in pill or capsule form) include grit (soluble and insoluble) for poultry and game; and mineral blocks, mixes and licks. Supplements designed for pet species, and held out for sale for pets, are standard-rated

Standard-rated items include the following.

- Additives (ie substances added to either compound feeds or protein concentrates – see above – in the course of manufacture for some specific purpose other than as a direct source of nourishment) supplied on their own. This would include antibiotics and other medicinal products, anti-oxidants, colouring agents, binders, flavourings, etc. Once additives have been incorporated into a feed, the liability of the final product will depend on its nature (see 28.18 below) although normally, it will still be primarily a feeding compound and so zero-rated
- Bait (eg lugworms, maggots) except for fish of a kind and quality suitable for human consumption which may be zero-rated. See also *Fluff Ltd (t/a Mag-It) v C & E Commrs, QB 2000, [2001] STC 674 (TVC 27.96)*
- Castor oil seed residue
- Single chemicals and minerals, other than salt (even when fed direct to animals)
- Thatching material (eg Norfolk reed, wheat reed or straw reed)
- Urea (unless specifically held out for sale for animal feeding purposes)

(VAT Notice 701/15/05, paras 5.1, 5.3, 5.4, 9.3, 9.5, 9.7, 9.8; Internal Guidance V1–7, Chapter 1 para 19.6).

28.16 Keep of animals and grazing rights, etc

Keep of animals. The supply of the keep of animals is standard-rated. Even if animal feed is supplied as part of the service of keeping animals, the full consideration for the service provided is standard-rated, ie the feed cannot be treated as a separate zero-rated supply.

Grazing rights. The granting of grazing rights (ie the right to allow someone else's animal(s) to graze on your land, also known as grass keep letting) is zero-rated as a supply of animal feeding stuffs (ie grass). However, if an element of 'care' for the animal(s) is included, then the supply becomes that of the keep of animals and the whole consideration is standard-rated as above. In this context 'care' includes turning the animals out to graze, feeding, mucking out, spreading straw or other bedding, exercising, and taking on behalf of the owner any responsibility for the welfare of the animal(s) beyond a minimal 'seen daily' or 'twice daily' arrangement.

Stabling services. Where a business rents stabling to a horse owner then, provided the owner is allowed exclusive use of the stabling (ie is allocated all or an identifiable part of the stabling for the sole use of their horse), there is a supply of a right over land. This is an exempt supply unless the business has exercised the option to tax (see 42.8 LAND AND BUILDINGS). Where the business does not make a supply of a right over land, the supply is standard-rated.

Where, in conjunction with a supply of stabling, the owner is also supplied with feed (either as general animal feed or in the form of grazing rights) this can be treated as a separate zero-rated supply of animal feeding stuffs *provided* that there is no element of care. If any elements of care are present, then there is a single supply of the keep of animals, and the whole supply is standard-rated (see above).

Livery services are services provided for horses in a stable that go beyond the right to occupy the stable. They may include feeding and watering, mucking out, turning out, worming, clipping, plaiting, exercising, cleaning tack, grooming, breaking in, schooling and arranging for vets (but not clearly identifiable separate supplies such as vets' services).

With effect from 1 January 2002, following the tribunal decision in *Window (VTD 17186) (TVC 39.16)* HMRC accept that where livery services are supplied in conjunction with stabling, the stabling is the principal element of the supply and the livery services are ancillary to it. There is therefore a single exempt supply. Previously HMRC's policy was that the supply of livery services in conjunction with the supply of stabling was a single standard-rated supply. Application for refunds can be made to HMRC for VAT charged on such supplies before 1 January 2002. Any refund is subject to the 3-year cap and the unjust enrichment provisions and any claim must be adjusted to take account of any input tax previously reclaimed. (The decision in *Window* above does not affect the liability of the supplies made by racehorse trainers and stud farm owners or stables that specialise, for example, in breaking in and schooling. The principal supply in these circumstances is not the supply of the right to occupy a stable.)

D-I-Y livery is a supply of stabling only (see above).

(VAT Notice 701/15/05, paras 10.1–10.3; Business Brief 21/01).

28.17 Products which may be used both as animal feed and for other purposes

Many products sold as animal feed ingredients have other uses. In deciding the VAT liability of these products, it is necessary to determine whether the trader is supplying the product as zero-rated animal feed or some other standard-rated supply.

- Where products are produced in different grades for feed and non-feed use, regulations require all products sold for animal feed to be accompanied by a 'statutory declaration' identifying the product and giving details of its composition and purpose. In most cases, therefore, identification of animal feed will not be difficult.
- Organic products (eg blood, bonemeal, fishmeal and other meat and fish by-products) which may be used either as animal feeding stuffs (usually as an ingredient in a compound feed) or as a fertiliser similarly require a form of statutory declaration when used for fertiliser.
- Where there is no physical difference between feed and non-feed products, liability will depend on how the product is 'held out for sale' (see 28.1 above).

Silage enhancers are products, usually derived from molasses or other sugars, which are added to silage to increase fermentation and absorb and retain the liquid effluent which would otherwise escape during the process and be lost. Most silage enhancers, including all bacterial products, are not fed directly to animals and are therefore standard-rated. Non-bacterial products which are marketed as having an alternative direct-feed use may be zero-rated.

(Internal Guidance V1–7, Chapter 1 paras 20.1–20.4).

28.18 **The borderline between feed and medicine**

Medicines are often administered to farm animals in feed. The products may be provided as medicines to be added by the farmer, or pre-mixed into a specialised feed, eg a normal compound feed may include an anti-parasitic compound.

Medicines. Purely medicinal products are always standard-rated. They can normally be readily identified by the packaging or accompanying documentation which will carry dosage instructions and identify the condition the product is intended to cure or guard against.

Feed products containing medicines. Feeds containing medicines may be zero-rated or standard-rated according to whether they are used primarily as a feed (ie taken for purposes of nutrition) or a medicine (taken to cure or prevent a specific medical condition). HMRC's policy is to follow that of the Department for Environment, Food and Rural Affairs and class a product as 'medicinal' (and therefore standard-rated) if it requires a marketing authorisation issued by that Department.

Growth promoters (ie antibiotics for incorporation into animal feed to prevent a low-level infection retarding normal development) are standard-rated. Feed containing growth promoters should be judged according to the principles of feed products containing medicines above.

Probiotics increase the efficiency of the digestive tract, improving the animal's resistance to disease and countering the detrimental effects of stress. They are not considered to be medicinal products by DEFRA but equally, as they are not a source of direct nourishment in their own right, they are not considered to be foodstuffs and are standard-rated for VAT purposes.

Vitamin supplements are regarded as essential ingredients of manufactured feed included for nutritional rather than therapeutic reasons. They are therefore zero-rated for VAT purposes both as single vitamins and supplement mixtures. (Compare the VAT treatment of vitamin supplements for humans which are not considered to be 'food of a kind used for human consumption' and are standard-rated.)

(VAT Notice 701/15/05, paras 5.2, 9.4; Internal Guidance V1–7, Chapter 1 paras 20.5–20.9).

28.19 **Pet food**

The following items are standard-rated.

(*a*) **Pet food which is canned, 'packaged' or 'prepared'.** [*VATA 1994, Sch 8 Group 1 Excepted Item 6*].

Meaning of 'pet'. There is no definition of 'pet' in *VATA 1994*. In *Popes Lane Pet Food Supplies (VTD 2186) (TVC 27.157)* the tribunal suggested that a pet was 'an animal (tamed if it was originally wild) which is kept primarily as an object of affection [including] an animal kept primarily for ornament.' On this basis, HMRC regard the following animal species as 'pet species' in that the great majority of that species are kept and reared as objects of affection.

- Cage birds.

- Cats.
- Dogs (but see below for working dogs and racing greyhounds).
- Ferrets.
- Goldfish, aquarium fish and pond fish.
- Guinea pigs.
- Hamsters, gerbils, rats and mice (except rats and mice bred specifically for the laboratory).

Other species (including most farm animals) can be as clearly identified as 'non-pets'.

Between these extremes are species which HMRC regard as 'mixed' species, ie animals which are sometimes kept as pets, and sometimes as food or working animals, or simply left in the wild. Included are rabbits and most of the 'exotics'. Tribunals have also treated dogs as within this category, distinguishing between pet dogs and working dogs (eg sheep dogs, police dogs, guard dogs, gun dogs and packs of hounds). See *Popes Lane Pet Food Supplies* above, *LJ & H Norgate (t/a Dog's Dinner) (VTD 5241) (TVC 27.159)* and *Peters & Riddles (t/a Mill Lane Farm Shop) (VTD 12937) (TVC 27.160)*.

Pet food is any product that is supplied for consumption by pet animals which would include both 'pet species' and individual pets of 'non-pet' or 'mixed' species (see above). Animal foods products are not necessarily pet food because they are sold in pet shops or because a company name or trading name refers to pets. For VAT purposes, pet food is animal feed which is

(i) 'held out for sale' as pet food (see 28.1 above);

(ii) formulated specially for a 'pet species' of animal; or

(iii) otherwise specialised for the pet food market by undergoing any one of certain processes. These are the addition of colouring, flavouring, preservative, binder or gelling agents; the mixing or blending of ingredients to meet the specific nutritional requirements of a pet species within (ii) above; the cooking of meats and meat products; and the mixing or blending of four or more meat and/or fish products.

Having established that a product is a pet food, it is then necessary to decide whether it is canned, packaged *or* prepared before it is ruled standard-rated.

'*Packaged*' means pre-packed for retail sale in a sealed bag, carton or other container of 12.5 kilograms or less. Putting a loose product in a plain paper or polythene bags at the point of sale (whether after purchase by the customer or in anticipation of sales) is not considered packaging. See *B Beresford (VTD 9673) (TVC 27.162)*.

'*Prepared*' means having undergone any of the following (or similar) processes.

(1) Products, other than food for working dogs (see below) and food for human consumption, which have undergone any of the following processes are pet food and are standard-rated however they are held out for sale.

   (i) The addition of colouring, flavouring, preservative or gelling agents (eg sodium metabisulphite).

(ii) The mixing or blending of ingredients to meet specific nutritional requirements of a pet species (eg blending a mix of cereal products specifically for hamsters).

(iii) The cooking of meats or meat products.

(iv) The mixing or blending of four or more meats, fish or fish and meat products.

(2) Products which have undergone any of the following processes are animal food but are standard-rated only if they are packaged or held out for sale as pet food

(i) Mixing or blending of different ingredients (other than those described in (1) above).

(ii) Washing or polishing.

(iii) Cooking (except meat or meat products, see (1) above).

(iv) Mincing, dicing and similar processes (except meat for dogs, see below).

(v) Inclusion of additives.

Meat and fish products for dogs. As tribunals have decided that not all dogs are pets (see above), such products cannot be classed as pet food simply because they are for feeding to dogs. Meat and fish products for dogs (or dogs *and* cats) are standard-rated if they have undergone any process which would specialise them for the pet food market (see above). However, HMRC regard supplies of fresh, frozen or chilled meat and fish (including offal) for dogs (or dogs *and* cats), whether or not packaged, as zero-rated (even if minced or diced) provided it has not undergone any further preparation and it is not held out for sale as pet food. See *Popes Lane Pet Food Supplies* and *LJ & H Norgate* (*t/a Dog's Dinner*) above and *Norman Riding Poultry Farm Ltd (VTD 3726) (TVC 27.158).*

Food for racing greyhounds. Diets formulated specifically for racing greyhounds can be zero-rated provided

- the product is a genuinely complete feed providing *all* the required elements for a balanced diet for the dog without having to be mixed with any other foods (other than water);
- the product is specifically held out for sale for racing greyhounds; and
- the person selling it can demonstrate that the product is designed specifically to meet the nutritional requirements of racing greyhounds. In the case of retailers, this information will normally be provided to them by the manufacturer.

Food for working dogs. Canned, packaged or prepared food can be zero-rated provided

- it is specifically formulated and held out for sale for working dogs;
- there is no indication on the packaging that it is equally suitable for all breeds, size and age of dog (in which case it remains standard-rated pet food); and
- it is not biscuits or meal (see (*c*) below).

Food for fish. The VAT liability of food for fish follows the normal rules, according to whether the fish species involved is a 'pet', 'non-pet' or 'mixed' species (see above). Dry compounded diets blended specifically for pet fish (usually in granular or flake form) are therefore standard-rated, while those blended for farmed fish are zero-rated. Live food (other than Artemia) is supplied virtually exclusively for ornamentals, and is therefore pet food. However, it is only standard-rated if 'canned, packaged or prepared' which, given the nature of the product, is unlikely. Live Artemia are fed to farmed fish, in the early stages of rearing, as well as to pet fish, and therefore are not considered to be 'pet food'. Frozen or freeze-dried Artemia, daphnia, etc are 'prepared' pet food and standard-rated.

Day-old chicks, rats, mice, etc sold as food for 'exotics'. Because exotic species (eg snakes) are not 'pet' species (see above), such food is treated in the same way as any other food for a 'mixed' species, ie zero-rated unless they are specifically held out for sale as pet food *and* canned, packaged or prepared. The initial killing of the creatures does not constitute 'preparation' for VAT purposes. See 28.21 below for sales of live animals.

(*b*) **Bird food**. Packaged foods (not being pet food) for birds other than poultry (see 28.22 below) and game is standard-rated. [*VATA 1994, Sch 8 Group 1 Excepted Item 6*].

Cage birds. Cage birds (eg budgerigars, finches, parrots, etc) are treated as a 'pet species' (see (*a*) above). Food for such birds is therefore treated as pet food. Prepared foods include mixes specifically designed for cage bird species and seeds compressed into blocks, millet sprays or seeds and sunflower seed. Packaged foods include packaged seeds.

Wild bird food. Food for wild birds (other than poultry or game) is standard-rated if packaged and held out for sale for feeding to wild birds. HMRC regard 'packaged' in this context as meaning supplied in a retail or mail order pack and includes bags, boxes, nets and bird feeders. It does not include bags over 12.5 kg weight which are usually sold wholesale and broken down into smaller quantities for retail sale. Food which is sold loose and simply put into bags at the point of retail sale is not regarded as packaged. Single products (eg peanuts) are standard-rated if they are advertised, etc as being for wild birds. HMRC consider a mixture specifically aimed at a particular species of wild bird as being held out for sale for feeding to that type of bird, regardless of the way it is advertised, etc If it is also packaged it is standard-rated.

Other birds. Zero-rating can be applied to

- food for game birds;
- pigeon food (unless containing canary, millet or sunflower seed when standard-rated); and
- pigeon grit, whether soluble or insoluble poultry food.

(*c*) **Biscuits and meal for cats and dogs**. [*VATA 1994, Sch 8 Group 1 Excepted Item 6*]. Biscuits and meal for cats and dogs is standard-rated whether or not for pet animals and whether or not sold packaged or loose. HMRC regard the terms 'biscuit' and 'meal' as meaning dry products either

- coarsely ground basic commodities; or
- baked products consisting predominantly of cereal and fat and not providing all the nutrients required by the animal.

(VAT Notice 701/15/05, paras 6.1–6.5, 7.2, 8.1–8.5, 9.2; Internal Guidance V1–7, Chapter 1 paras 21.2–21.7, 22.2).

28.20 SEEDS AND PLANTS

Plants grown as food for human consumption or animal feeding stuffs are zero-rated under *VATA 1994, Sch 8 Group 1 General Items 1 and 2*. See 28.2 *et seq* and 28.15 *et seq* above. Any crop that generally produces items that are not fed to humans or animals (ie for 'industrial' purposes) is always standard-rated.

Seeds or other means of propagation of plants used for human consumption or animal feeding stuffs are also zero-rated. [*VATA 1994, Sch 8 Group 1 General Item 3*].

Examples of zero-rated plants and seeds

- Seeds, seedlings, crowns, spores, tubers and bulbs of edible vegetables and fruit.
- Mushroom spawn.
- Cucumber and tomato 'rootstock'.

Examples of standard-rated plants and seeds

- Plants that are primarily grown for their ornamental effect (eg ornamental nursery stock including trees, shrubs, herbaceous plants, alpines and pot plants).
- Seeds, tubers, bulbs, corms, crowns, rhizomes, cuttings, etc of flowers (but see (5) below for seeds producing edible flowers).
- Cut flowers which are bought for their ornamental effect.
- Plants, seeds and fruit of a kind used for the production of perfumes, pharmaceutical products, insecticides, fungicides and other non-food uses (eg evening primrose which is grown for the extraction of its oils and Norfolk reed which is grown for thatching material).
- Any produce which is 'held out for sale' as pet food or packaged as food for birds other than poultry or game (see 28.19 above).
- Any produce which is 'held out for sale' for non-food purposes.
- Rootstock (plants, usually the common thorn, used in the horticultural industry for grafting purposes) irrespective of whether they are used in the growing of zero-rated or standard-rated plants and trees (but not cucumber and tomato rootstocks which are zero-rated).

'*Held out for sale*' means the way a product is labelled, packaged, displayed, invoiced, advertised or promoted and the heading under which the product is listed in any catalogue, web page or price list.

In addition to the general provisions above, HMRC give the following information.

(1) **Trees and fruit bearing shrubs**

Plants, bushes and trees normally used in this country for the production of edible fruit (including nuts) are zero-rated. (Strictly the law zero-rates only plants which *themselves* are food of a kind used for human consumption but HMRC extend this to plants *producing* food because it was considered reasonable and sensible to do so.)

HMRC regard the following as the *definitive* list of fruit-producing plants which may be zero-rated.

Almond (not 'flowering almond')	Apple	Apricot
Blackberry	Blackcurrant	Blueberry
Boysenberry	Bullace	Cherry (not 'flowering cherry')
Citrus trees (not ornamental varieties)	Cobnut	Common quince (not chaenomeles)
Cowberry	Crab (only fruiting varieties)	Cranberry
Damson	Fig	Filbert
Gages	Gooseberry	Grapevines
Hazel	Huckleberry	Loganberry
Medlar	Mulberry	Nectarine
Peach	Pear	Raspberry plum (not 'flowering plum')
Redcurrant	Strawberry	Sweet chestnut
Tayberry	Walnut	Whitecurrant
Wineberry	Worcesterberry	

(2) **Oilseed rape**

Some varieties of oilseed rape are not suitable for human consumption. The liability of those that are not suitable will depend on the purpose for which they are supplied.

(*a*) *'OO' type*. Most oilseed rape is of this type and the oilseed yields oil fit for human consumption as well as meal for animals. These 'OO' varieties of oilseed rape, including the actual seeds and edible meal by-products, are zero-rated.

(*b*) *'HEAR' varieties*. These varieties of oilseed rape give a high erucic acid content in the oil and this is regarded as nutritionally undesirable in food for human consumption. The pressed oil is primarily used as an anti-corrosion agent and lubricant in mineral oil extraction and is standard-rated. The residual meal can be used to feed ruminant livestock and it is zero-rated when supplied for feeding purposes. The actual seeds of the HEAR varieties are used to plant for subsequent crops and as an animal feed and are zero-rated.

(3) **Linseed and flax**

Varieties of the crop are grown for its seeds and subsequent oil and residual meal, or for its flax fibre. As the predominant use of linseed oil is for industrial purposes (eg paint, varnish, linoleum), it is standard rated. The residual meal is largely used for incorporating into animal feed and can be zero-rated. Zero-rating also applies to the actual seed when used as animal feed or for sowing.

Where flax varieties are grown for the resulting fibre, both the stems (processed into linen) and the left over woody portion (used for making paper) are standard-rated. The small yield of seeds are zero-rated when used as animal feed.

(4) **Herbs**

Culinary herbs. Plants of species which are generally accepted as reared primarily for culinary use are zero-rated irrespective of how they are held out for sale. These comprise the following.

Angelica	Anise	Anise hyssop
Basil	Borage	Caraway
Cardamom	Cardoon	Celery wild
Celery wild alpine	Chervil	Chicory
Chives	Coriander	Cumin
Curry leaf	Dandelion	Dill
Fennel	Fenugreek	Garlic
Ginger	Good King Henry	Horseradish
Lemon grass	Liquorice	Lovage
Marjoram	Mint	Onion
Orache	Oregano	Parsley
Pennyroyal	Rocket	Rosemary
Saffron	Sage	Salad burnet
Savory	Skirret	Sorrel
Tarragon	Thyme	Watercress

Ornamental herbs sometimes used for culinary purposes. Plants which, although not species supplied predominantly as culinary herbs, do have recognised culinary uses, may be zero-rated provided

(*a*) they have been raised according to the conditions required by *Food and Environment Protection Act 1985* (evidence of which may be required);

(*b*) they have been held out for sale (see above) as culinary herbs and, where appropriate, displayed apart from ornamentals with other culinary herbs;

(*c*) they are supplied in individual pots (not bedding strips) of a size less than two litres; and

(*d*) in the case of bay plants, they do not exceed 50cm in height and have not been clipped, shaped or topiarized in such a way as to specialise them as ornamentals.

Provided the above conditions are satisfied, the following herbs can also be zero-rated.

Alecost	Alexanders	Allspice
Asafoetida	Bay	Bergamot
Bistort	Catmint	Chamomile

Comfrey	Clove pink	Clover
Cowslip	Curry plant	Elder
Feverfew	Hop	Hyssop
Juniper	Landcress	Lavender
Lemon balm	Lemon verbena	Marigold, pot
Melilot	Nasturtium, salad	Pelarqonium (scented)
Purslane	Rue	Sweet Cecily
Tansy	Violet (sweet)	Woodruff

Medicinal herbs. Herbs supplied for medical rather than culinary use are not eligible for zero-rating as 'food' and are standard-rated, even if they have been raised under the same conditions as culinary herbs. This includes plants used in the preparation of food supplements (eg evening primrose and ginseng).

(5) **Seeds**

All seeds that produce food of a kind for human consumption or animal feeding stuffs can be zero-rated. Included are

- vegetable seeds;
- seeds for producing culinary herbs; and
- wheat, barley and other agricultural seeds grown to produce food for human or animal consumption.

But any seed that generally produces items that are not fed to humans or animals is always standard-rated. This applies to

- seeds or bulbs for growing flowers (but see edible flowers below);
- plants and trees mainly for ornamental effect; and
- agricultural crops for industrial/non-feed use.

Seeds producing edible flowers. The seed varieties listed below are zero-rated where it can be demonstrated that they are held out for sale as food of a kind used for human consumption. For these purposes, seeds would be so held out for sale if

- the variety is indicated as edible in a catalogue (or, where no catalogue is produced, in information at the point of sale);
- further details of food usage can be supplied on a customer's request; and
- food-based information is available on seed packets (eg recipe ideas).

Bergamot	Clove pink	Lavender
Nasturtium	Pelargonium	Pink
Poppy	Pot Marigold	Sunflower
Violets		

Grass seed. Most grass seed is zero-rated because of the extensive use of grass as animal feed. This includes supplies to and by garden centres, local authorities and grass seed to be grown on set aside land. Pre-germinated grass seed and turf are not used for the propagation of animal feed and are therefore standard-rated. See 28.15 above for supplies of hay and straw and 28.16 above for grazing rights.

Seeds that undergo a treatment or process. See 28.14 above.

Seeds sold with a book. See (7) below.

(6) **Plant-growing kits**

Plant-growing kits typically include seeds, growing medium, fertilizer, a container, and an instruction leaflet. Such kits are generally standard-rated but may be zero-rated if the seeds are zero-rated and either

- the standard-rated element (eg growing medium, fertiliser and pot) accounts for less than 10% of the total cost; or
- the planting medium, which is impregnated with edible vegetable or fruit seeds, is no more than a means of simplifying the planting of the seeds (eg peat cubes of less than 125cc impregnated with seeds, or thin layers of tissue incorporating seeds).

Mushroom growing kits. VAT treatment depends upon the container. If the kit is supplied in a non-reusable container, HMRC take the view that the whole supply can be zero-rated as the container is seen as normal and necessary packaging.

If the kit is supplied in a plastic bucket or similar reusable container, there may be a mixed supply, the spawn and growing medium being zero-rated and the container standard-rated. Each case needs to be judged on its own merits after consideration of general principles in *Card Protection Plan* (see 64.6 SUPPLY). See also the decisions in *Kimberly-Clark Ltd v C & E Commrs, Ch D [2004] STC 473* (which related to nappies sold in a plastic reusable box) and *Cheshire Mushroom Farm (VTD 71) (TVC 27.107)* (although the latter case preceded the judgment in *Card Protection Plan*).

(7) **Seeds/growing kits sold with books**

Where a zero-rated book on a generalised gardening theme is sold with a standard-rated packet of seeds or plant-growing kit, the selling price must normally be apportioned. However, by concession, if the minor article

- is not charged separately to the customer,
- costs the supplier no more than 20% of the total cost of the combined supply (excluding VAT), and
- costs the supplier no more than £1 (excluding VAT) if included with the goods intended for retail sale or £5 (excluding VAT) otherwise,

the supplier may account for VAT on the minor article at the same rate as the main article so that no apportionment is necessary.

An apportionment is not permitted where the 'book' element is merely a specialised instruction leaflet. In such a case, the liability follows that of the seeds, etc.

(VAT Notice 701/38/03; Internal Guidance V1-7, Chapter 1 paras 23.6, 25.6.1, 25.7, 25.8).

28.21 LIVE ANIMALS

The 'supply' of 'animals' of a kind generally used as, or yielding or producing, food for human consumption is zero-rated. '*Supply*' includes sale, hire or loan and supply of a part interest (a share) as '*animals*' include birds, fish, crustacea and molluscs. [*VATA 1994, Sch 8 Group 1 General Item 4*]. HMRC interpret this zero-rating as being limited to live animals which are widely used or bred as food *in the UK*. It does not cover animals which are used as food outside the UK unless they have become widely available, or are being reared primarily for food, within the UK, as is the case, for example, with ostriches. (Internal Guidance V1–7, Chapter 1 para 26.1).

Examples of zero-rated animals are

- meat animals;
- dairy animals;
- poultry (see 28.22 below) including those for egg production;
- honey bees; and
- fish (except ornamental breeds and coarse fish), including those for production of edible roes (see 28.23 below).

Examples of standard-rated animals are

- bumble bees;
- ornamental birds and fish;
- racing pigeons; and
- horses.

The test is whether the animal is of a kind generally used as, or yielding or producing, food for human consumption. Subject to this, the actual use does not matter. For example:

- Kangaroo steak may be sold as food in shops but kangaroos are not animals of a kind generally reared for food in the UK so that live kangaroos are standard-rated.
- Rabbits, other than ornamental breeds, are animals of a kind that is normally used for human food production and are therefore always zero-rated even if kept as pets.
- Sheep kept mainly for their wool, or bulls used for breeding, are zero-rated because they are animals of a kind normally producing food for human consumption.

Animals which are removed from the human food chain because they are no longer fit for human consumption (eg because of disease) are standard-rated.

Embryos, eggs and semen for breeding. Embryos of species which are normally used for human food may be zero-rated if they are to be used for breeding. Anything below the embryo stage is standard-rated. Eggs and fish roes which are normally used for food for human consumption and are fit for such use are always zero-rated.

(VAT Notice 701/15/05, paras 2.1–2.8).

28.22 **Birds**

Most breeds of chicken are zero-rated, as are game birds and ostriches. Ornamental breeds of birds are standard-rated.

The following breeds of ducks, geese and turkeys are zero-rated.

- Ducks (Aylesbury, Campbell (Khaki Campbell), Indian Runner, Muscovy, Pekin and derivatives and crossbreeds of these).
- Geese (Brecon Buff, Chinese Commercial, Embdem, Roman, Toulouse and derivatives and crossbreeds of these).
- Turkeys (Beltsville White, British White, Broadbreasted White, Bronze (Broadbreasted Bronze), Norfolk Black and derivatives and crossbreeds of these).

(VAT Notice 701/15/05, para 3.1).

28.23 **Fish**

The VAT liability of fish is as follows.

(*a*) *Freshwater fish*. Eels, salmon and trout and others recognised as food for human consumption are zero-rated. Bream, perch, pike, carp and tench are standard-rated.

(*b*) *Shellfish*. Oysters, mussels, whelks, etc are zero-rated but non-food species are standard-rated.

(*c*) *Fish for aquaria* are standard-rated.

(*d*) *Fish used as* bait. Fish of a kind used for, and fit for, human consumption are zero-rated. All other supplies are standard-rated.

(*e*) *Ornamental fish* are standard-rated. See *JR Chalmers (VTD 1433) (TVC 27.108)* for koi carp.

(VAT Notice 701/15/05, para 3.2).

28.24 **ABATTOIRS**

Processing generally. Any work done on another person's goods is a supply of services. The supply of a treatment or process to another person's goods can be zero-rated, if by doing so, zero-rated goods are produced. [*VATA 1994, s 30(2A); FA 1996, s 29(2)(5)*]. Processing which results in the production of a new zero-rated food product may therefore be zero-rated. Processing which does not result in the production of a new food product, or which results in the production of a standard-rated food product, is a standard-rated supply. New goods are produced when a process alters the essential characteristics of the goods. This may include size and shape, appearance, composition, use and, specifically for food items, readiness to use or eat.

Slaughtering and dressing. The service of slaughtering animals without applying further processes is standard-rated (see *Darlington Borough Council (VTD 961) (TVC 27.84)*). If other processes are applied at the same time to produce new zero-rated goods, for example, dressing the carcass, then the whole supply is zero-rated. Not all services of slaughtering and dressing produce new zero-rated goods. The liability of some of the goods produced by abattoirs is considered below.

Goods produced in abattoirs are standard-rated if

- held out for sale for a non-feeding purpose, eg blood for fertiliser (normally recognisable by declaration of nitrogen/phosphoric acid content);
- used for a non-feeding purpose, eg hair, hides, horns, hoofs, manure, pelts, skins and wool;
- held out for sale without further process as canned, packaged or prepared pet food (see 28.19 above);
- they have undergone some further preparation beyond mincing and dicing, which would specialise the products to the pet food market (see 28.19 above); or
- used exclusively in the preparation of pharmaceutical products, eg gall bags, glands, ovaries, placenta.

Greaves supplied in pieces of a size suitable for feeding to pets are also standard-rated.

Goods produced in abattoirs are zero-rated if

- they are fit for human consumption; or
- they are animal materials, used in the manufacture of food for animals or pets, and

  (*a*) the *Animal By Products Order 1992* permits the use of the materials, and

  (*b*) the animal materials are used in premises approved by that *Order*.

Examples of zero-rated goods from cattle, sheep, goats and pigs are

- *Organs* including bladders, hearts, kidneys, livers, lungs or lites, manifolds, pancreas glands, rede, stomach, and sweetbreads (pancreas only in cattle);
- *Body parts* including bones, feet, paddywacks, runners (except cattle), tails, udders and weasand; and
- *Fluids and tissue* including blood, dripping, fat (provided it is not attached to specific risk material), and meat.

Other zero-rated parts commonly produced from cattle include melts (from calves under six months), tripe and vells.

Incidental supplies. Where the services of slaughtering and then processing the carcass produce new standard-rated and zero-rated goods (eg standard-rated skins and zero-rated foodstuffs)

- if the standard-rated goods are incidental to the main zero-rated supply back to the owner of the animal, the whole supply is zero-rated; and
- if the new standard-rated goods are the main element of the supply to the owner of the animal, and the zero-rated goods are incidental, then the whole supply is standard-rated.

Ancillary services supplied by abattoirs. Supplies of separate ancillary services are normally standard-rated, for example

- cold storage;
- pennage;
- carriage; and
- porterage.

If specific stalls or pens are allocated for the exclusive use of a customer, the supply is exempt from VAT (subject to the option to tax being exercised, see 42.8 LAND AND BUILDINGS).

Meat and Livestock Commission (MLC) levies. There are two levies on slaughterers and food producers to cover a range of benefits received from the MLC, ie

- a general levy absorbed 50% by the slaughterers and 50% by the producers; and
- a promotional levy wholly on the producers.

The levies are subject to VAT at the standard rate.

A slaughterer is charged the whole amount of both levies by the MLC, and must then recharge the producer 50% of the general levy, and the whole of the promotional levy. The MLC provide one invoice to the slaughterer confirming the amount of each levy and the output and input tax due. The slaughterer can recover the VAT charged on his 50% of the general levy as input tax, subject to the normal rules. As he acts as agent for the MLC in recharging the levies to the producer, he must also account for VAT as follows.

- The input tax incurred on the rechargeable elements of the levies may be recovered in full.
- He must charge, and account for in the same period, a corresponding amount of output tax to the producer.

A producer can recover the VAT charged to him by the slaughterer as input tax, subject to the normal rules.

An exporter of live animals must follow the above procedures to account for VAT on levies incurred and recharged.

(VAT Notice 700/57/04; VAT Notice 701/40/02; VAT Notice 701/15/05, para 9.1).

29 Fuel and Power

Cross-reference. See 25.3 EXPORTS for stores for use in ships, aircraft and hovercraft; 64.46 SUPPLY for the time of supply rules; 72.2 ZERO-RATED SUPPLIES for supplies of hot water and steam.

De Voil Indirect Tax Service. See V4.406.

The contents of this chapter are as follows.

29.1 INTRODUCTION AND RATES OF VAT

The supply of any form of power, heat, refrigeration or ventilation is a supply of goods (and not a supply of services). [*VATA 1994, Sch 4 para 3*].

The rates of VAT on supplies of fuel and power are as follows.

1.9.97 onwards	5% for 'qualifying use' 17.5% for all other supplies
1.4.94–31.8.97	8% for 'qualifying use' 17.5% for all other supplies
1.7.90–31.3.94	Zero-rated for 'qualifying use' 17.5% for all other supplies
Before 1.7.90	Zero-rated for all supplies

The reduced rates applying from 1 April 1994 also apply to acquisitions from other EC countries and importations from outside the EC.

[*VATA 1994, ss 2(1A)–(1C), 29A(1)(2); FA 1995, s 21; F(No 2)A 1997, s 6; FA 2001, s 99*].

29.2 QUALIFYING USE

'*Qualifying use*' means domestic use or use by a charity otherwise than in the course or furtherance of a business.

The following *de minimis* supplies are always supplies for domestic use, even when supplied to a business.

(*a*) A supply of not more than one tonne of coal or coke held out for sale as domestic fuel. The weight limit of one tonne applies to the total delivered weight of all types of such coal or coke supplied at any one time, not to the weight of supplies of individual products (eg lignite, anthracite, etc).

(*b*) A supply of wood, peat or charcoal not intended for sale by the recipient (regardless of the amount supplied).

(*c*) A supply to a person at any premises of '*piped gas*' (ie gas within 29.4 below, or petroleum gas in a gaseous state, provided through pipes) where the gas (together with any other piped gas provided to him at the premises by the same supplier) was not provided at a rate exceeding 150 therms a month or, if the supplier charges for gas by reference to the number of kilowatt hours supplied, 4397 kilowatt hours a month. (This limit applies whether the bill is based on a meter reading or on an estimate.)

(*d*) A supply of petroleum gas in a liquid state where the gas is supplied in cylinders the net weight of each of which is less than 50 kilogrammes and either the number of cylinders supplied is 20 or fewer or the gas is not intended for sale by the recipient.

(*e*) A supply of petroleum gas in a liquid state, otherwise than in cylinders, to a person at any premises at which he is not able to store more than two tonnes of such gas.

(*f*) A supply of not more than 2,300 litres of fuel oil, gas oil or kerosene. HMRC regard a supply for this purpose as comprising all deliveries to the same customer at the same site on the same day. This is the case even if separate delivery notes or invoices are issued. Deliveries that take place on different days or to different sites are regarded as separate supplies, even if a single invoice is raised for more than one delivery. Supplies of different products (eg fuel oil and gas oil) are always regarded as separate supplies. But supplies of different types of the same product (eg different grades of kerosene) must not be broken down into each type when considering whether the *de minimis* limit has been exceeded.

(*g*) A supply of electricity to a person at any premises where the electricity (together with any other electricity provided to him at the premises by the same supplier) was not provided at a rate exceeding 1,000 kilowatt hours a month. (This limit applies whether the bill is based on a meter reading or on an estimate.)

Supplies not within (*a*)–(*g*) above are supplies for domestic use if, and only if, the goods supplied are supplied for use in

(i) a building, or part of a building, which consists of a dwelling or number of dwellings or which is used for a 'relevant residential purpose';

(ii) self-catering holiday accommodation (including any accommodation advertised or held out as such);

(iii) a caravan; or

(iv) a 'houseboat' ie a boat or other floating decked structure designed or adapted for use solely as a place of permanent habitation and not having means of, or capable of being readily adapted for, self-propulsion.

Use for a '*relevant residential purpose*' means use as a home or other institution providing residential accommodation either for children or with personal care for persons in need of such care by reason of old age, disablement, past or present dependence on alcohol or drugs or past or present mental disorder; a hospice; residential accommodation for students or school pupils or members of any of the armed forces; a monastery, nunnery or similar establishment; or an institution which is the sole or main residence of at least 90% of its residents. *Excluded* is use as a hospital, a prison or similar institution or an hotel or inn or similar establishment.

[*VATA 1994, Sch 7A Group 1, Notes 3, 5, 6, 7; FA 1995, s 21; FA 2001, Sch 31 para 1*]. (VAT Notice 701/19/02, paras 6.1, 7.1; Business Brief 18/01).

The following are treated as a part of the same residential unit.

- Buildings such as garages used with houses.
- Subsidiary buildings situated a short distance away (eg a garage in a block located away from the house).
- Corridors, lifts, hallways and stairways in a residential unit.

(VAT Notice 701/19/02, para 3.2).

Part qualifying use. Where a supply of fuel or power is partly for qualifying use and partly not, then provided at least 60% is supplied for qualifying use, the whole supply is to be treated as a supply for qualifying use. In any other case, an apportionment must be made. [*VATA 1994, Sch 7A Group 1, Note 4; FA 2001 Sch 31 para 1*].

Certificates. If in doubt about the liability of the supply under (i)–(iv) above, the supplier should get a certificate from the customer declaring what percentage of the fuel or power supplied for use at each premises is for qualifying use. A certificate is not required if the supply falls within (*a*)–(*g*) above. The following information should be shown on the certificate.

- Supplier's name and address.
- Customer's name, address and, if applicable, VAT registration number.
- Address of the premises to which the supply relates.
- Amount of qualifying use expressed as a percentage of the total use. A precise percentage should always be given. Do not say 'over 60%' or use any similar form of words.
- A declaration given by a responsible officer or official of the customer as to the truth and accuracy of the facts given. This should include
  - (i) the signature, name, and position of the person giving the declaration;
  - (ii) the date on which it is made; and
  - (iii) an endorsement that the customer has read and understood the guidance, and that they know they must notify the supplier if there is a change in the qualifying use.

If any supply is incorrectly charged at the reduced rate, the supplier may have to pay any VAT undercharged unless he holds a valid certificate *and* has good reason to believe that the fuel or power supplied to the customer is for qualifying use. It is the supplier's responsibility to take reasonable steps to satisfy himself that the customer is entitled to be charged at the reduced rate and the declaration is correct. Where, however, despite taking all reasonable steps, the supplier fails to identify the inaccuracy and in good faith makes the supplies concerned at the reduced rate, HMRC will not seek to recover the VAT due from the supplier. (VAT Notice 48, ESC 3.11).

(VAT Notice 701/19/02, para 3.5).

See 52.17 PENALTIES for the penalty for giving an incorrect certificate.

29.3 SOLID FUELS

Supplies of coal, coke and other solid substances are taxable at the reduced rate provided they are held out for sale solely as fuel and are supplied for qualifying use (see 29.2 above). Included are combustible materials put up for sale for kindling fires but not matches. [*VATA 1994, Sch 7A Group 1 Item 1(a) and Note 1; FA 2001, Sch 31 para 1*]. All other supplies of solid fuels are standard-rated.

To be taxable at the reduced rate, the fuel must be offered in a form and at a price that is compatible with it being sold as fuel.

'*Held out for sale*' as fuel means that the supplier advertises and otherwise describes the product at its point of sale as fuel or firewood, and that this is consistent with the packaging and wrapping in which it is supplied.

Reduced-rate supplies. Provided the conditions for qualifying use are met, the reduced rate can be applied to the following solid fuels.

- Coal (including anthracite and lignite)
- Coal dust
- Coal briquettes
- Coke (eg Coalite, Thermabrite, Coalite Nuts, Beacon Beans, Sunbrite small nuts, Blazeglow)
- Pulverised coal
- Smokeless fuel
- Wood logs
- Other firewood (including offcuts, chips, shavings, scrap or damaged wood and compresses or agglutinated sawdust)
- Barbecue fuels
- Briquettes of straw and recycled waste or other combustible materials
- Charcoal
- Firelighters
- Peat blocks, sods or briquettes
- Solid methaldehyde (solid meths)

Standard-rated supplies. The following items are always standard-rated.

- Any product not consumed in the lighting process (eg pumice blocks, pottery, etc soaked in paraffin, gas pokers, electric hot-air igniters)
- Artists' charcoal
- Binding agents used to convert coal dust or sawdust in blocks
- Coke for use in manufacturing
- 'DIY' offcuts and remnants
- Filtration charcoal or coke
- Forestry thinnings for fencing or staking
- Laboratory charcoal blocks
- Peat for use in horticulture or as cattle litter
- Sawdust, chips or shavings for pet litter

- Standing trees
- Wood for pulping

(VAT Notice 701/19/02, para 7.1).

Barbecue food flavour enhancers (eg hickory chips) which are absorbed into the food by burning are not fuel (or food for human consumption) and are standard-rated. (VAT Notes 1992 No 1).

29.4 **GASES**

Coal gas, water gas, producer gas and similar gases and petroleum gases, and other gaseous hydrocarbons, whether in a gaseous or liquid state, are taxable at the reduced rate provided they are supplied for qualifying use (see 29.2 above). Excluded is any road fuel gas (within the meaning of the *Hydrocarbon Oil Duties Act 1979*) on which excise duty has been or is chargeable. [*VATA 1994, Sch 7A Group 1 Items 1(b)(c) and Note 1; FA 2001, Sch 31 para 1*].

Reduced rate supplies. Provided the conditions for qualifying use are met, the reduced rate can be applied to liquefied petroleum gas (eg propane or butane), acetylene, butylene, methane, natural gas and propylene. Minor impurities in a hydrocarbon gas can be ignored but otherwise any such gas that does not consist entirely of carbon and hydrogen is standard-rated.

Standard-rated supplies. Supplies of all other gases (eg carbon dioxide, hydrogen, oxygen, ammonia, chlorine, nitrogen and refrigeration and aerosol gases) are standard-rated although certain gases for medical care (eg anaesthetics and oxygen) may be zero-rated under *VATA 1994, Sch 8 Group 12* or exempt under *VATA 1994, Sch 9 Group 7*.

(VAT Notice 701/19/02, paras 4.1, 4.3).

Standing charges. Gas bills include a variable consumption charge and a fixed standing charge. The standing charge represents the upkeep of the pipes required to deliver gas. For VAT purposes it is regarded as part of the charge for a supply of gas even though shown separately on bills. If the supply of gas is for qualifying use (see 29.2 above) the whole bill, including the standing charge, is taxable at the reduced rate.

Where standing charges for gas are made by a third party (eg a local authority) rather than the fuel supplier, they do not form part of the supply of gas and are standard-rated, regardless of the customer.

(VAT Notice 701/19/02, para 10.10).

Charges made by fuel and power suppliers. See 29.7 below.

VAT treatment in particular cases. See 29.8 below.

Special rules for place of supply and supplies by persons outside the UK. See 29.9 below.

Gas sold in cylinders and similar containers

Disposable cartridges. When gas is supplied in disposable cartridges at an inclusive price covering both gas and cartridge, the supply is standard-rated throughout the supply chain until the point of final sale. A supply of disposable cartridges at the point of final sale is taxable at the reduced rate.

Charged refillable cylinders. On the first sale of a refillable cylinder containing gas taxable at the reduced rate, the price must be apportioned and VAT accounted for on the standard-rated cylinder which becomes the property of the buyer. (The price of the cylinder should be taken as the difference between the VAT-exclusive price of the filled cylinder and the charge for refilling a customer's own cylinder.)

When a filled container is exchanged for an empty one of the same size owned by the customer, the refill charge is treated as being wholly for the supply of gas and any nominal charge for inspection and maintenance can be ignored.

Rented cylinders. On the first supply of gas in a rented cylinder, VAT must be accounted for at the standard rate on the hire charge. When an empty cylinder is exchanged for a full one of the same size, any refill charge, including any nominal charge for inspection or maintenance, can be taxed at the reduced rate (subject to qualifying use of the gas). Any charge made for a lost or damaged cylinder (such as the loss of a deposit) is outside the scope of VAT. But if a separate charge is made for the retention of a cylinder this is standard-rated.

Bulk storage tanks installed on customers' premises normally remain the property of the supplier. Charges for gas consumed are at the reduced rate (subject to qualifying use) but any charge specifically for repair, maintenance etc of equipment is standard-rated.

(VAT Notice 701/19/02, paras 4.5–4.8). See *Calor Gas Ltd (VTD 47) (TVC 28.1).*

Gases used as road fuel. Supplies of gases for use as road fuel are standard-rated. VAT is due on the total value including the excise duty chargeable. (VAT Notice 701/19/02, para 4.4).

29.5 OILS

'Fuel oil', 'gas oil' and 'kerosene' are taxable at the reduced rate provided they are supplied for qualifying use (see 29.2 above). Excluded is hydrocarbon oil on which a duty of excise has been or is to be charged without relief from, or rebate of, such duty by virtue of the provisions of the *Hydrocarbon Oil Duties Act 1979.* All other supplies of oil are standard-rated.

'*Fuel oil*' means heavy oil containing in solution an amount of asphaltenes of not less than 0.5 per cent or which contains less than 0.5 per cent but not less than 0.1 per cent of asphaltenes and has a closed flash point not exceeding 150°C.

'*Gas oil*' means 'heavy oil' of which not more than 50 per cent by volume distils at a temperature not exceeding 240°C and of which more than 50 per cent by volume distils at a temperature not exceeding 340°C.

'*Kerosene*' means heavy oil of which more than 50 per cent by volume distils at a temperature not exceeding 240°C.

'*Heavy oil*' has the same meaning as in the *Hydrocarbon Oil Duties Act 1979.*

Fuel oil, gas oil and kerosene chargeable with excise duty at a full (unrebated) rate, together with other heavy hydrocarbon oils, light hydrocarbon oils, lubricating oils and lubricants, are standard-rated.

[*VATA 1994, Sch 7A Group 1 Item 1(d) and Notes 1, 2; FA 2001, Sch 31 para 1*].

The effect of the above is that fuel oil, gas oil or kerosene (which includes paraffin) within the above definitions are taxed at the reduced rate provided they are supplied for qualifying use, are not supplied as road fuel and are either chargeable with excise duty at a rebated rate or are relieved from excise duty.

Standard-rated supplies include any heavy oil for use as road fuel; aviation spirit; avgas; creosote; crude oil; derv; kerosene, paint thinners or white spirit; liquid lighter fuel; waste oil; bitumen; black varnish; coal tar; lubricating oils and greases; methylated spirit; other articles which contain hydrocarbon oil but are not themselves wholly hydrocarbon oil; petrol substitutes; and petrol and other light oils (eg benzene, toluene and naphtha).

(VAT Notice 701/19/02, paras 6.1, 6.2).

Marine fuel. Supplies of fuel to foreign-going vessels is zero-rated provided certain conditions are met. By concession, commercial vehicles engaged on voyages within UK territorial waters may also receive certain types of fuel VAT-free. See 25.3 EXPORTS.

29.6 ELECTRICITY, HEAT AND AIR CONDITIONING

Supplies of electricity, heat and air conditioning are taxable at the reduced rate provided they are supplied for qualifying use (see 29.2 above). [*VATA 1994, Sch 7A Group 1 Item 1(e); FA 2001, Sch 31 para 1*]. All other supplies of electricity, etc are standard-rated.

Electricity supplied by mobile generator. Where electricity is supplied through the use of a mobile generator, the liability of the supply depends upon whether the supplier is supplying the electricity or hiring out the machine.

- If the supplier operates the equipment and charges for power supplied for a qualifying use, the total charge is at the reduced rate.
- If the supplier charges for the hire of the generator to the customer, the supply is standard-rated.

Batteries. Supplies of batteries on hire, recharging of batteries or exchanging charged batteries for discharged ones are standard-rated.

Standing charges. Electricity bills include a variable consumption charge and a fixed standing charge. The standing charge represents the upkeep of the wires required to deliver electricity. For VAT purposes it is regarded as part of the charge for a supply of electricity even though shown separately on bills. If the supply of electricity is for qualifying use (see 29.2 above) the whole bill, including the standing charge, is taxable at the reduced rate.

Where standing charges for electricity are made by a third party (eg a local authority) rather than the fuel supplier, they do not form part of the supply of electricity and are standard-rated, regardless of the customer.

(VAT Notice 701/19/02, para 10.10).

Charges made by fuel and power suppliers. See 29.7 below.

VAT treatment in particular cases. See 29.8 below.

Special rules for place of supply and supplies by persons outside the UK. See 29.9 below.

Use of system, transmission and other charges. Where a price includes a charge for electricity and standing and/or other charges, the whole supply is taxed at the reduced rate (even if the supplier has incurred costs in making that supply that were taxed at the standard rate).

If a supplier makes a charge to allow the use of transmission or distribution lines, transformers, meters, or makes other similar supplies of services, without any supply of electricity, such supplies are always standard-rated.

New electricity trading arrangements (NETA). These arrangements have replaced the pool system. Generators, suppliers, and non-physical traders now negotiate bilateral and multilateral contracts 'over-the-counter'. These contracts are for wholesale supplies of electricity and are standard-rated. The arrangements provide a mechanism for the settlement of imbalances between physical and contractual positions. The following elements arising from the balancing mechanism are standard-rated.

- Balancing mechanism unit cash flow
- Non-delivery charges
- Energy imbalance cash flow
- Residual element cash flow

The information imbalance charges are outside the scope of VAT.

(VAT Notice 701/19/02, paras 5.4–5.7).

Steam and heated water. Supplies of steam and heated water are not eligible for the zero-rating applicable to water (see 72.2 ZERO-RATED SUPPLIES). Instead they are, for VAT purposes, a form of heat.

Supplies of steam and heated water for qualifying use (see 29.2 above) are taxed at the reduced rate. For these purposes

- water that has been heated as part of a treatment process but is supplied at the temperature at which it was before it was heated (ie after it has cooled down) is not heated water;
- water that is hot because it is drawn from a hot spring is not treated as heated water; and
- water that has been deliberately heated by geo-thermal, solar or other natural heat or energy sources is treated as heated.

(VAT Notice 701/19/02, para 8.1).

Ventilation, air-conditioning and refrigeration. Supplies of air-conditioning, refrigeration and quick-freezing for a qualifying use (see 29.2 above) are taxed at the reduced rate. Supplies of ventilation, air-conditioning or refrigeration provided from a central plant are taxable at the reduced rate when supplied for a qualifying use.

Where premises are in multiple occupation, any charges to tenants in addition to the rent which are made in respect of the common parts or areas, are treated as further payment for the right to occupy and have the same liability as the main supply. See 42.4(6) LAND AND BUILDINGS.

(VAT Notice 701/19/02, para 9).

29.7 **CHARGES MADE BY FUEL AND POWER SUPPLIERS**

Reduced rate supplies. Any of the charges listed below are treated as part of the payment for a reduced rate supply of fuel and power provided the charges are

(*a*) made by a person who supplies the fuel and power to the consumer (up to and including the meter),

(*b*) made to that consumer, and

(*c*) inseparable from a supply of fuel or power to that consumer

and the supply of fuel and power is for a qualifying purpose;

- Disconnection and re-connection of the supply and special meter readings at the instigation of the supplier
- Installation by a supplier of liquefied petroleum gas of a bulk gas tank regarded as essential to the supply of liquefied petroleum gas
- Installation of check meters
- Installation or replacement of lines and switchgear belonging to the electricity supplier
- Installation tests and re-tests where required by the supplier to protect their equipment
- Maximum demand and minimum guarantee charges
- Removal of damaged coins from meters
- Rental charges for meters, including secondary meters used by landlords to apportion charges between their tenants
- Rental of a bulk gas tank in conjunction with the supply of liquid petroleum gas to that tank
- Repair, maintenance or replacement of equipment and gas pipes or electric cables belonging to the supplier up to and including the consumer's meter. (Where the supplier's conduits are within the fabric of a building, reduced rate supplies by the supplier are limited to work essential for getting at the conduits, and making good. All consequential work is standard-rated. Contractors' supplies to the supplier are standard-rated.)
- Replacing a credit meter with a pre-payment meter under the supplier's Code of Practice, or replacing or re-siting by a supplier of their meter at their instigation
- Replacement of mains fuses and provisions of earthing terminals
- Standing charges (see also 29.4 and 29.6 above).

Any of the above supplies are standard-rated when supplied

- by a contractor other than the supplier of fuel and power (even if a fuel and power supplier instructs a contractor to send a bill direct to a consumer for work that would have been at the reduced rate if invoiced by the supplier); and
- by a subcontractor to a fuel and power supplier.

Standard-rated supplies. The following supplies are always standard-rated.

- Repairs, maintenance and replacement of pipes not belonging to the fuel or power supplier (normally those on the consumer's side of the meter)

- Servicing contracts (other than supplies of insurance)
- Sale of meters to commercial, industrial and domestic consumers for their own use
- Altering coin mechanisms of secondary meters
- Services in connection with tests carried out, for example, at the request of estate agents or prospective purchasers of premises
- Replacement of meters not under the supplier's Code of Practice and re-siting meters at the request of the consumer
- Diverting mains to meet local authority requirements (these supplies are zero-rated when work is carried out in the course of construction of new dwellings)
- Raising or lowering of overhead power lines in connection with the movement of abnormal loads, including escorting the loads (these supplies are zero-rated when work is carried out in the course of construction of new dwellings)
- Supply, repair and maintenance of public lighting circuits to local authorities
- Temporary floodlighting, emergency or decorative lighting
- Charges for playing games such as squash, tennis, billiards and snooker collected by means of a coin-operated lighting meter (ie a time switch controlling the availability of light for a fixed period of time (may be exempt in certain circumstances, see 57.9 RECREATION AND SPORT)
- Blast freezing

Outside the scope supplies. The following charges are outside the scope of VAT.

- Replacement by the gas or electricity supplier of dangerous, obsolete or inefficient appliances or parts, after the meter, under statutory contractual obligation (This covers only the limited circumstances of work undertaken by gas and electricity utilities to comply with their statutory contractual obligations to supply fuel and power. It does not cover modification works to gas water heater flues in caravans.)
- Charges by a gas or electricity supplier for repairs to its own property following damage

Zero-rating. Supplies of civil engineering services in the course of construction, alteration or conversion of a building may be zero-rated in certain circumstances. See 42.18 to 42.21 LAND AND BUILDINGS. This includes the first time provision of gas and electricity from the building up to the nearest existing supply.

In addition, by concession, customer contribution to a first time connection to the gas or electricity mains supply which would have been zero-rated before 1 April 1994 may continue to be zero-rated after that date provided it is the connection to the mains of

- a building, or part of a building, which consists of a dwelling or number of dwellings;
- a building, or part of a building, used solely for a 'relevant residential purpose' (see 42.1(15) LAND AND BUILDINGS);
- a residential caravan (ie a caravan on a site in respect of which there is no covenant, statutory planning consent or similar permission precluding occupation throughout the year);

- a houseboat; or
- a building, or part of a building, used by a charity for its non-business activities

and provided that the person receiving the supply does not do so for the purposes of any business carried on by him.(VAT Notice 48, ESC 3.16).

(VAT Notice 701/19/02, paras 2.2–2.4, 2.6).

29.8 **VAT TREATMENT IN PARTICULAR CASES**

(1) **Supplies to schools and other educational institutions**

Supplies of fuel and power to educational institutions are taxed at the reduced rate in the following circumstances.

(*a*) *The institution has charitable status and is receiving the supply for non-business use.* If the charity does not make a charge, its activities are generally non-business. Independent and other schools which are charities but which do charge fees are in business for VAT purposes and supplies of fuel and power to them are generally standard-rated (but see (*b*) below).

Voluntary aided schools automatically meet this criterion (but not community and controlled schools which are not deemed to have charitable status). Reduced rating applies regardless of whether the supply is made to the school itself (the governing body or headmaster) or to the LEA and regardless of whether the governors are deemed to be acting as agent to the LEA under the provisions of the *School Standards and Framework Act 1998*.

(*b*) *The fuel and power is supplied to separate residential premises for the accommodation of pupils and students.* Where the residential quarters form part of the main building, the supply partly qualifies for the reduced rate and must be apportioned (subject to the 60% rule, see 29.2 above) unless the school, etc also qualifies under (*a*) above.

(VAT Notice 701/19/02, para 10.1; Internal Guidance V1–14, para 12.2).

(2) **Supplies by wholesalers to retailers**

Supplies of fuel and power by wholesalers to retailers are standard-rated unless supplied in small *de minimis* amounts (see 29.2 above). This applies even if it is known that the goods will eventually be supplied for qualifying use. (VAT Notice 701/19/02, para 10.2).

(3) **Supplies by shops and other retailers**

There are no special rules for supplies by retailers. In practice, most supplies of fuel and power by retail (eg coal supplied in bags) will be taxed at the reduced rate because the amount supplied will be below the *de minimis* limits for that fuel (see 29.2 above). (VAT Notice 701/19/02, para 10.3).

(4) **Supplies to landlords, managing agents, caravan park owners and residents' associations**

Such supplies are taxable at the reduced rate provided the fuel or power is used for qualifying purposes. The charge should be apportioned if only part of the premises to which the supply relates is used for qualifying purposes (eg on-site accommodation for employees or proprietors). In all other cases supplies of fuel and power to landlords, etc are standard-rated. (VAT Notice 701/19/02, para 10.4).

(5) **Supplies by landlords (other than local authorities)**

(*a*) *Heated, air-conditioned or refrigerated accommodation.* Where a landlord supplies fuel and power to tenants in the form of heated, air-conditioned or refrigerated accommodation, this will usually be a single supply of accommodation. This accommodation can be used for any purpose (domestic, charitable or business). In practice, heated and air-conditioned accommodation is usually used for residential or office purposes and cold stores are used for storing perishable goods. Storage with no specific right over land is normally standard-rated. If the landlord grants the user of a cold store a right over land, then the supply is exempt (subject to the option to tax, see 42.8 LAND AND BUILDINGS).

- Where a landlord and tenant contract for a single supply of heated, air-conditioned or cooled accommodation, it is a single supply of accommodation and is taxed as such. If the landlord makes a fixed charge for supplies of gas or electricity or includes an amount in the rent to cover them, the payment is normally treated as part of the rent and liable to VAT at the same rate as the supply of accommodation.
- Where a landlord and tenant contract for two separate supplies, one of heat, air-conditioning or cooling, and the other of accommodation, each supply is dealt with separately. If tenants have coin-operated gas or electricity meters, the money placed in the coin box is payment for a supply of gas or electricity and is taxed at the reduced rate when made for qualifying use. This applies whether the gas or electricity is supplied at cost or with a mark-up. If the landlord rents or owns a secondary credit meter, supplies of gas or electricity are liable to VAT at the reduced rate when made for a qualifying use.

(*b*) *Service charges for common areas*

Mandatory charges for fuel and power used in common areas (eg corridors and stairwells in blocks of flats) that are included in the service charge made to owners of flats and/or freehold property, form part of the payment for the overall supply. See 42.4(6) LAND AND BUILDINGS.

(VAT Notice 701/19/02, paras 10.6, 10.7).

(6) **Supplies by local authorities**

(*a*) *Domestic tenants – single supplies of heated accommodation.* The supply of accommodation by a local authority is a non-business activity for VAT purposes. The VAT liability of any supplies of fuel and power made by local authorities to their domestic tenants as part of the single supply of heated accommodation follows that of the main supply which is one of accommodation. The fuel and power element of the supply is therefore outside the scope of VAT.

(*b*) *Separate supplies of fuel and power.* Separate supplies for domestic use is liable to VAT at the reduced rate. Where a local authority continues to supply fuel and power to accommodation it previously owned, it is a business activity and the supply is taxed at the reduced rate if it is for a qualifying use (see 29.2 above).

(*c*) *Mandatory service charges* raised by a local authority to leasehold owners are non-business and outside the scope of VAT.

(VAT Notice 701/19/02, paras 10.5, 10.7).

(7) **Heating contracts**

If a contractor, under a heating contract, supplies both the fuel and the staff required to operate and maintain a customer's heating system, the whole supply is taxable at the reduced rate (subject to qualifying use of the heat). But maintenance or repairs or replacement of the plant alone can only be taxable at the reduced rate if

- covered by an overall contract for the supply of heat; and
- directly related to and essential for maintaining that supply of heat.

Where a contract is for labour only for the operation and routine maintenance of a customer's boiler and distribution system, and the customer obtains fuel from another source, the supply is always standard-rated.

(VAT Notice 701/19/02, para 10.8).

(8) **Facilities requiring fuel and power**

The use of washing machines, hot showers and all other facilities (including those for playing sport) which depend on temporary power or light and which are charged for by meter, are *not* supplies of fuel and power. They are supplies of the particular facility concerned and liable to VAT at the appropriate rate. (VAT Notice 701/19/02, para 10.9). See *Mander Laundries Ltd (VTD 31) (TVC 67.1)* and *St Anne's-on-Sea Lawn Tennis Club Ltd (VTD 434) (TVC 28.4)*.

See also *Showtry Ltd (VTD 10028) (TVC 28.11)* where the supply of fuel for use in hired agricultural machinery was held to be part of a composite standard-rated supply under the hire contract.

(9) **Gas and electricity suppliers: bad debt relief on transferred debts**

Subject to meeting certain conditions, a business can recover some or all of the VAT it has paid to HMRC on supplies made where a customer has failed to pay. See 7 BAD DEBT RELIEF. One of the conditions is that the person who makes the supply is the only person entitled to claim relief.

With effect from 2 August 2004, by concession, a supplier of gas and/or electricity can obtain relief from VAT on debts owed by a domestic customer where the supplier has accepted the transfer of that customer and his debt from another supply company. The detailed provisions of the concession are as follows.

Where a contract for the supply of 'gas' or electricity is substituted by a new contract ('novation') as a result of a 'domestic consumer' transferring from one supplier to another, then, by concession, the new supplier may claim bad debt relief on a supply of gas or electricity made by the former supplier to that consumer, provided that

- the whole or any part of the consideration for the supply is outstanding at the time of the novation;

- the whole of the debt is transferred to the new supplier;
- at the time of the novation, the former supplier (if he has not already done so) accounts for VAT on the supply at the appropriate rate or, if he has already received a refund upon a claim for bad debt relief in relation to that supply, repays to HMRC the amount of that refund;
- the claim is not made until six months after payment for the novation and takes account of any payments made by the customer after the date of the novation;
- both the former supplier and the new supplier have evidence of
  - (i) the value of the debt (including the VAT amount) that has been transferred, and
  - (ii) the date of payment for the novation; and
- the new supplier has a copy of the document issued by him to the consumer to recover the debt (not required if a pre-payment meter is in use).

'*Gas*' means gas that is conveyed through pipes to premises by a person authorised to do so under *Gas Act 1986, s 7*.

'*Domestic consumer*' means a person to whom fuel or power is supplied for domestic use (see 29.2 above).

This concession does not apply in circumstances where its application would give rise to tax avoidance.

(Business Brief 20/04).

(10) **Free coal for miners**. Miners, ex-miners and their widows may be entitled to supplies of free coal or its cash equivalent from private companies supplying coal. Such supplies are subject to the normal rules for gifts of goods (see 47.6 OUTPUT TAX). Where the cost to the company of providing the coal is more than £50 per year, there is a deemed supply of goods and VAT is payable at the reduced rate on their open market value. Any cash payments received by the miners and their dependents are not liable to VAT. (Internal Guidance V1–7, Chapter 5 para 4.3).

29.9 SPECIAL RULES FOR GAS AND ELECTRICITY SUPPLIES

With effect from 1 January 2005, there are special rules for supplies of '*relevant goods*' ie gas supplied through the natural gas distribution network, and electricity.

Place of supply. The place of supply of relevant goods is determined as follows.

(*a*) Relevant goods supplied to a 'dealer' are treated as supplied at

- the place where that dealer has established his business or has a fixed establishment to which the relevant goods are supplied, or
- in the absence of such a place of business or fixed establishment, the place where he has his permanent address or usually resides.

'*Dealer*' means a person whose principal activity in respect of receiving supplies of relevant goods is the re-selling of those goods and whose own consumption of those goods is negligible. Re-selling does not include

- re-sale as part of a single composite supply of other goods or services, or
- re-sale as a supply that falls to be disregarded as a supply to another member of the same VAT group where relevant goods are to be effectively used and consumed by a member of the VAT group.

(*b*) Supplies of relevant goods not falling within (*a*) above are treated as supplied at

(i) the place where the recipient of the supply has effective use and consumption of the goods or

(ii) in relation to any part of the goods not consumed,

- the place where the recipient of the supply has established his business or has a fixed establishment to which the goods are supplied, or
- in the absence of such place of business or fixed establishment, the place where he has his permanent address or usually resides.

For the purposes of (i) above effective use and consumption includes a supply of the goods

- by the recipient as part of a single composite supply of other goods or services; and
- to a member of a VAT group, where the goods are effectively used and consumed by a member of that group.

[*SI 2004/3148, Arts 9–13*].

Reverse charge on supplies by persons outside the UK. The reverse charge procedure applies where a person who is outside the UK supplies 'relevant goods' to a person who is registered under *VATA 1994* for the purposes of any business carried on by the recipient. The recipient is treated as if he had himself supplied the relevant goods in the course or furtherance of his business and as if that supply were a taxable supply. He must therefore account for output tax on the full value of the supply received. He can, however, subject to the normal rules, include the VAT as input tax on the same VAT return. Supplies which are treated as made by the recipient under these rules are not taken into account when calculating any entitlement to input tax under the PARTIAL EXEMPTION (49) rules.

[*VATA 1994, s 9A; FA 2004, s 21*].

For these purposes a person is outside the UK if

- he has established his business or has a fixed establishment outside the UK; or
- in the absence of such a place of business or fixed establishment, the place where he has his permanent address or usually resides is outside the UK.

[*SI 2004/3148, Art 14*].

The reverse charge also applies to the provision of access to, and of transport or transmission through, natural gas and electricity distribution systems and the provision of other directly linked services. See 64.27(5A) SUPPLY.

Time of supply. Goods which are treated as supplied by a person under *VATA 1994, s 9A* above are treated as being supplied when the goods are paid for or, if the consideration is not in money, on the last day of the VAT accounting period in which the goods are removed or made available. [*SI 1995/2518, Reg 82A; SI 2004/3140, Reg 4*].

Valuation of supply. In relation to supplies made after 16 March 2005, where any goods are treated as made by a UK VAT-registered recipient under *VATA 1994, s 9A* above, the value of the supply is taken to be

- where the consideration for the supply was in money, the amount of that consideration; and
- where the consideration did not consist, or not wholly consist, of money, such amount in money as is the equivalent to that consideration.

[*VATA 1994, Sch 6 para 8; F(No 2)A 2005, s 5*].

30 Gold and Precious Metals

Cross-reference. See 65 TERMINAL MARKETS for zero-rating of certain transactions in gold on the London Gold Market.

De Voil Indirect Tax Service. See V4.277.

The contents of this chapter are as follows.

30.1 SPECIAL SCHEME FOR INVESTMENT GOLD

A special scheme applies for investment gold. It puts investment in gold on a similar footing with other financial investments, eg shares, by making it exempt from VAT (see 30.2 below). Businesses are generally unable to reclaim input tax directly attributable to an exempt supply. Unlike shares, however, gold may be purchased from a variety of taxable sources before being transformed into investment gold. If the normal rules applied, the input tax incurred on these costs would not be reclaimable and the seller would either have to absorb the VAT cost or pass it on to the investor (which would make investing in the gold less attractive). The scheme for investment gold therefore has three special features.

- Certain persons may opt to tax specified transactions, so enabling them to reclaim all of their input tax (subject to the normal rules). See 30.3 below.
- Taxable persons can reclaim the input tax incurred on purchases of gold and on the costs of transforming any gold into investment gold. See 30.4 below.
- Taxable persons who are producers and transformers of investment gold can reclaim the input tax they incur on certain costs linked to the production or transformation process. See 30.4 below.

The special scheme for investment gold also allows special procedures for transactions on the London Bullion Market. See 65.3 TERMINAL MARKETS.

30.2 EXEMPT SUPPLIES OF INVESTMENT GOLD

The following supplies are exempt.

(*a*) The supply of 'investment gold'.

(*b*) The grant, assignment or surrender of any right, interest, or claim in, over or to investment gold if the right, interest or claim is or confers a right to the transfer of possession of investment gold. *Not included* is

- the grant of an option; or
- the assignment or surrender of a right under an option at a time before the option is exercised.

A supply of this description includes supplies of unallocated investment gold (ie gold which is an unidentifiable part of a larger stock held by the supplier), loans, swaps, and forward and future contracts concerning investment gold. (VAT Notice 701/21/02, para 2.2).

(*c*) The supply, by a person acting as an agent for a disclosed principal, of services consisting of

- effecting a supply within (*a*) or (*b*) above that is made by or to his principal; or
- attempting to effect such a supply which is not in fact made.

The effect of this is that if an agent (including an auctioneer) sells and invoices the goods in the name of their principal, the supply of investment gold is made by the principal (and exempt under (*a*) or (*b*) above). The agent supplies only his services which are exempt under this provision. The agent may opt to tax the services if the principal also opts to tax his onward supply (see 30.3(*c*) below).

Where an agent acts in his own name (ie for an undisclosed principal), the goods are treated for VAT purposes as supplies both to and by the agent. See 3.4 AGENTS. The special scheme for investment gold applies to the agent in the same way as it would apply to a principal and the agent's supply is exempt unless he can opt to tax under 30.3 below. However, when an agent or auctioneer is acting in their own name their supply of services to either the buyer or the seller is taxable.

(VAT Notice 701/21/02, para 7.3 which has the force of law).

Excluded is a supply

- between members of the London Bullion Market Association; or
- by a member of that association to a taxable person who is not a member; or
- by a taxable person who is not a member to a member of that association.

'*Investment gold*' means any of the following.

(i) Gold of a purity not less than 995 thousandths in the form of a bar or wafer of a weight accepted by the bullion markets. See VAT Notice 701/21/02, para 15 for list of the weights in which bars and wafers are commonly traded.

(ii) A gold coin minted after 1800 that

- is of a purity of not less than 900 thousandths;
- is, or has been, legal tender in its country of origin; and
- is of a 'type' that is 'normally sold' at a price that does not exceed 180% of the open market value of the gold contained in the coin.

(iii) A gold coin of a 'description' laid down in VAT Notice 701/21A/05, Section 3 which for these purposes has the force of law. The list, comprising over 500 gold coins from around the world, is produced by the EC Commission and is updated annually. It applies in all EC countries.

All gold coins falling within (ii) or (iii) above that have the same denomination (face value), size and gold fineness constitute a single 'type' or 'description' for the purposes of these provisions. Thus a gold coin type may be a single issue for one year or may have been produced for many years (eg a British sovereign). (VAT Notice 701/21A/05, para 2.2).

HMRC regard the price at which a coin is 'normally sold' as the price that can most usually be demanded for that particular type of coin. It does not matter that an individual coin is of special interest to collectors; if the usual value of the coin type does not exceed 180% of the value of the gold contained therein, all coins of that type are exempt. Similarly, if a coin type is usually valued at more than 180% of the gold value (because of interest to collectors), any coin of that type is taxable even if a particular coin is in such poor condition that it is worth less than 180% of its gold value. The normal selling price of coins is affected by the finish. Investment gold coins fall into two broad classes. First, relatively older issues made to circulate as currency and normally worn from circulation. Secondly, generally more recent issues primarily produced as a store of wealth. The second type may have been issued in a number of finishes (eg 'brilliant uncirculated' or 'proof') and if the majority of a type of coin are, for example, of brilliant uncirculated quality, then the brilliant uncirculated value normally reflects the normal selling price. If a trader is uncertain whether the normal selling value falls within the 180% criterion, he should contact HMRC. (VAT Notice 701/21A/05, paras 2.4, 2.5).

[*VATA 1994, Sch 9 Group 15; SI 1999/3116, Reg 2*].

30.3 **Option to tax investment gold**

The special scheme for investment gold allows some businesses to opt to tax certain otherwise exempt transactions provided they meet conditions laid down by HMRC (which have the force of law).

(*a*) **Producers and transformers of gold**. Where a taxable person supplies investment gold which he has produced or transformed *to another taxable person* and the supply would otherwise fall within 30.2(*a*) or (*b*) above, the supplier can elect to waive exemption and opt to tax the supply. The business must notify HMRC if it intends to make use of this provision who will send an acknowledgement. If this is not received within 28 days, it is the responsibility of the business to check that HMRC have received the notification.

(*b*) **Other taxable persons**. HMRC may permit a taxable person, who in the normal course of his business makes supplies of gold for industrial purposes, to opt to tax the supply of investment gold described in 30.2(i) above if made to another taxable person. Prior permission must be obtained by writing to HMRC, giving the VAT registration number and confirming that the business normally trades in gold for industrial purposes. If permission is given, HMRC will send a letter of approval within 28 days setting out the conditions of permission. Once authorisation is received, the business may opt to tax supplies of investment gold bars or wafers made to other taxable persons. It cannot opt to tax supplies of investment gold coins or sales to non-taxable persons. HMRC may withdraw authorisation for the protection of the revenue. In such a case, the election ceases to have effect from the date specified in the notification.

(*c*) **Agents**. Where an agent acts on behalf of a named principal and that principal has made an election under (*a*) or (*b*) above as supplier, then the agent may also opt to tax any supply of services which would otherwise fall to be exempt under 30.2(*c*) above and which is directly linked to the relevant supply. The agent must notify HMRC that he intends to opt to tax his services. HMRC will send an acknowledgement. If this is not received within 28 days, it is the agent's responsibility to check that HMRC have received the notification.

Any such election made by the supplier or his agent is subject to any conditions laid down by HMRC and

- applies in respect of an individual supply;
- has effect on or after the day from which the election is made;
- is irrevocable.

How to opt. Once the conditions outlined above have been fulfilled, to opt to tax a particular transaction it is simply necessary to include the following statement on the sales invoice.

'We have opted to tax this transaction.'

Special accounting arrangements for opted transactions. By opting to tax a transaction in investment gold, the transaction becomes subject to the special accounting scheme under which the responsibility to account for and pay the output tax falls to the purchaser. See 30.9 below.

Invoicing requirements. A taxable person selling investment gold which he has opted to tax must comply with all the normal invoicing requirements for taxable transactions (see 40 INVOICES) and the requirements of the special accounting scheme for gold (see 30.9 below).

[*SI 1999/3116, Reg 3*]. (VAT Notice 701/21/02, paras 4.3–4.7 which have the force of law).

30.4 Deduction of input tax

Where a business opts to tax a particular supply of investment gold (see 30.3 above) it can reclaim all the related input tax as it is making a taxable supply of investment gold. To reclaim all input tax, it must be able to show that none of its input tax relates to any exempt supplies of investment gold.

As a general rule, input tax incurred on goods or services which are used to make exempt supplies cannot be reclaimed. Exceptionally, where a taxable person makes exempt supplies of investment gold within 30.2(*a*) or (*b*) above

(*a*) input tax incurred in any VAT period in respect of such supplies is allowable as being attributable to those supplies to the extent that it is incurred on

(i) the purchase of investment gold which would have fallen to be exempt within 30.2(*a*) or (*b*) above but for

- an option to tax having been exercised under 30.3 above; or
- the supply having been excluded from exemption because it was between a member of the London Bullion Market Association and a taxable person who was not a member;

(ii) the acquisition of investment gold from another EC country;

(iii) a supply to him, or an acquisition or importation by him, of gold other than investment gold which is to be transformed by him (or on his behalf) into investment gold; and

(iv) services supplied to him comprising a change of form, weight or purity of gold; and (*b*) if he produces investment gold or transforms any gold into investment gold, he is also entitled to credit for input tax incurred on any goods or services supplied to him, or goods acquired or imported by him, to the extent that they are linked to the production or transformation of that gold into investment gold. This includes, for example, in addition to the gold itself

- tools, tooling and equipment;
- machinery, plant and fittings;
- fuel and power;
- crucibles and furnace linings;
- buildings and maintenance of buildings;
- laboratory instruments and equipment; and
- fume abatement and effluent treatment

but not, for example, a computer used to record exempt sales because the input tax is not directly linked to the production or transformation process.

If a building is to be used for the production of investment gold which will be sold exempt from VAT and an area of the building is set aside for the sale of that investment gold, the input tax on the building must be apportioned to reflect the fact that only a part of it is linked to the *production* of the investment gold.

Input tax partly attributable to exempt supplies of investment gold. Where input tax has been incurred on goods or services which are used or to be used in making supplies of investment gold within 30.2(*a*) or (*b*) above and other supplies, the proportion attributable to the investment gold must first be established (by being expressed as a proportion of the whole use or intended use) and the rules in (*a*) and (*b*) above must then be applied to the proportion attributable to the investment gold.

Examples

1. A business makes exempt supplies of investment gold but is not a producer or transformer of gold and does not buy in transformation services. It receives a mixed supply, part of which is investment gold that it intends to supply partly as exempt investment gold and partly as other goods or services.

   The business can only deduct VAT incurred on the investment gold itself. It must first work out the extent to which the input tax on the mixed supply received is attributable to the various supplies to be made. For the element attributable to the exempt supply of investment gold, it must then work out how much of that input tax relates to the gold itself. It cannot, for example, deduct any input tax incurred on a separate delivery service of that gold.

2. A business makes exempt supplies of investment gold and is not a producer or transformer of gold. However, it does buy in transformation services.

   The business can deduct VAT incurred on the investment gold itself (or other gold) and the VAT incurred on any out-sourced transformation services. If it incurs any input tax which is partly attributable to supplies of exempt investment gold and party attributable to other supplies, it must first work out the extent to which the input tax incurred is attributable to its various supplies. Then, for the element attributable to the exempt supply of investment gold, it must work out the extent to which it relates to the gold itself and to the transformation services.

3. A business makes exempt supplies of investment gold and is also a producer and/or transformer of gold.

   The business can deduct the VAT incurred on any related gold and also any VAT incurred on production and/or transformation costs. If it incurs any input tax which is partly attributable to its supplies of exempt investment gold and partly attributable to other supplies, it must first work out the extent to which that input tax is attributable to its various supplies and then, for the element attributable to the exempt supply of investment gold, it must work out the extent to which it relates only to the gold and production/transformation.

[*SI 1995/2518, Reg 103A; SI 1999/3114*]. (VAT Notice 701/21/02, paras 5.1–5.4).

30.5 Accounting and record keeping requirements

There are special accounting and record keeping requirements for persons who trade in exempt investment gold. The requirements apply to exempt sales of investment gold where the gold is delivered, or otherwise made available, to the customer. The requirements apply whether or not the supplier is registered or liable to be registered for VAT. [*SI 1995/2518, Regs 31A, 31B; SI 1999/3114*]. (VAT Notice 701/21/02, para 6.1). See 52.20 PENALTIES for penalties for failure to comply with the record-keeping requirements.

Notification. On the first occasion that a person makes an exempt supply of investment gold which exceeds £5,000 in value, or when the value of his supplies of investment gold to any one customer exceeds £10,000 in any twelve month period, he must notify HMRC at the following address.

The Gold Team
HM Revenue and Customs
Thomas Paine House
Angel Square
Torrens Street
LONDON EC1V 1TA

If, at the time of notification, the person is not VAT-registered, he must also provide the following information.

1. Name of company, partnership or sole proprietor.
2. Company number or details of partners.
3. Address(es).
4. Telephone number.
5. Contact name.
6. Accountant name, address and telephone.
7. Any associated VAT registration numbers.

HMRC will send acknowledgement. If this is not received within 28 days, it is the person's responsibility to check that HMRC have received the notification.

It is not necessary to notify HMRC of subsequent supplies.

(VAT Notice 701/21/02, para 3.1 which has the force of law). See VAT Notice 701/21/02, para 3.2 for a standard letter which may be used.

Invoicing requirements. *Where an invoice is issued for the sale of exempt investment gold which is over £5,000 or the total value of sales of exempt investment gold to that customer have exceeded £10,000 in the last year*, the invoice must contain the following details if appropriate.

(i) A unique identifying number.

(ii) Name and address of seller and name and address of person raising invoice (if different to the seller, eg an agent).

(iii) Name and address of the purchaser, delivery address (if different) and unique customer reference (see under *Customer record* below).

(iv) Date of invoice and delivery date.

(v) Type of supply (for example, sale).

(vi) If the seller, agent or the customer is registered for VAT, the VAT registration number of the seller and agent.

(vii) A description of the gold supplied.

(viii) For bars and wafers: the form, weight and purity and any other identifying feature (including any proprietary mark, hallmark and serial number where applicable).

(ix) For investment gold coins: the coin type, country of origin and whether or not the coin is included on the list of gold coins reproduced in VAT Notice 701/21A/05, Section 3.

(x) The number of items.

(xi) The total amount payable.

Where a business sells investment gold on which it has charged VAT (eg because it has opted to tax), the invoice must comply with the normal invoicing requirements (see 40 INVOICES) and the requirements for the special accounting scheme for gold (see 30.9 below).

(VAT Notice 701/21/02, paras 6.2, 6.4 which have the force of law).

Where taxable items (including gold) and exempt investment gold are supplied together, all the items may be included on the same invoice, provided the invoice contains all the appropriate details.

(VAT Notice 701/21/02, para 6.6).

Purchasing investment gold from persons not trading in investment gold. Where a person purchases exempt investment gold from a person who does not trade in investment gold and

- the value of the purchase is more than £5,000, or
- if more than one purchase has been made from the same customer, the total value of purchases from that customer has exceeded £10,000 in the last year,

the purchaser must issue an invoice on behalf of the seller containing all the relevant details specified in (i)–(xi) above.

In addition, the invoice must bear the following declaration which must be signed by the seller.

'I declare that to the best of my knowledge the details shown on this invoice are correct.' (signature and name).

The purchaser must keep and maintain a copy of the invoices so issued with his purchase records.

(VAT Notice 701/21/02, para 6.3 which has the force of law).

Special records. Subject to below, any person (whether or not registered for VAT) who sells exempt investment gold which is delivered or available to be taken away by the customer must keep and maintain a record showing the following information as part of the business records.

(A) *Accounting records* showing

(i) invoice number;

(ii) invoice date;

(iii) customer reference number;

(iv) customer's VAT registration number (if applicable);

(v) description of the gold (form, quantity and purity);

(vi) name and address of the agent (if applicable);

(vii) name and address of the purchaser; and

(viii) transaction value.

(B) *Customer record* identifying customers who purchase exempt investment gold. This record must have a unique reference number and contain details of the purchaser's

(i) name;

(ii) date of birth;

(iii) current address; and

(iv) telephone number if available.

The seller must take reasonable steps to ensure that the customer has given correct information. In order to do this, the seller must ask for and examine at least one document from *each* of the following lists.

List 1
Passport
Full driving licence
National Insurance card
Birth certificate
National identity card

List 2
Telephone bill
Other utility bill

Deeds
Tenancy lease
Council tax bill
Hotel key card (for non-UK residents only)

Alternative satisfactory evidence may be agreed with HMRC.

If possible, copies should be kept of the documents seen. The seller should write on each copy 'certified as original document' and must sign and date this declaration. If it is not possible to keep a copy of any document seen, the seller must record, as part of your customer record, sufficient details to enable HMRC to obtain a copy if they so require. As a minimum the seller should record

- the name of the document;
- the reference number; and
- the name and address of the issuing authority.

The seller must insist that the customer produces the original document.

Internet and mail order sales. If investment gold is sold over the internet or by mail order, the seller may as an alternative to the customer record under (B) above keep and maintain the following record.

- If the supply is paid for by credit card and the delivery address is also the card holder's address, a record of the customer's name, the credit card issuer and the card number.
- If the supply is paid for by cheque, a record of the customer's name, the name of the bank and the customer's account number.

Whether payment is by credit card or cheque, the seller must also keep proof of despatch of the investment gold to the customer's address.

Sales to other VAT-registered businesses. If investment gold is sold to another VAT-registered business, the seller may, as an alternative to the customer record under (B) above, ask the customer for their VAT registration number. The seller must, however, check with HMRC that the VAT registration number provided is authentic.

Banks and other financial service businesses. If the seller is a bank or other financial service business which, for the purposes of the *Money Laundering Regulations 1993* (*SI 1993/1933*) is a 'relevant financial business' it may, as an alternative to the customer record set out in (B) above, keep and maintain the records specified in those *Regulations.* Relevant financial businesses to whom this applies must conduct the appropriate identification procedures and keep the required records in the case of all transactions in investment gold where

- the value of a one-off transaction exceeds 15,000 euro, or
- two or more one-off transactions appear linked and their value together exceeds 15,000 euro.

For these purposes, the exchange rate between the euro and the UK £ is the rate published in the Official Journal of the Communities.

(VAT Notice 701/21/02, paras 7.1, 7.2, 7.4, 7.6 which have the force of law).

Additional special record for taxable persons. If the seller is registered for VAT and is

- authorised to opt to tax supplies of investment gold (see 30.3 above), or

- a producer or transformer of investment gold,

he must keep and maintain with his VAT account, in addition to the records set out above, a record of any supply of investment gold made to another taxable person where the seller has delivered or otherwise made the gold available to that person, and on which the seller has *not* opted to tax.

(VAT Notice 701/21/02, para 7.5 which has the force of law).

Records of exports and dispatches. A seller is not required to keep any of the records described above for supplies of investment gold physically exported outside the EC or despatched to a business in another EC country. (VAT Notice 701/21/02, para 7.1). See 30.8 below.

Retention of records. The seller must retain all the documents and records specified above for a minimum of six years from the date of the transaction. In the case of regular customers, he must keep the customer record under (B) above for six years following the most recent supply of investment gold.

Any person who purchases investment gold must keep the purchase invoice for a minimum of six years from the date of the transaction.

(VAT Notice 701/21/02, para 7.7 which has the force of law).

30.6 SUPPLIES OF GOLD OTHER THAN INVESTMENT GOLD

Zero-rated supplies of gold involving Central Banks. The supply of gold (including gold coins) held in the UK by

- a Central Bank to either another Central Bank or a member of the London Bullion Market, or
- a member of the London Bullion Market to a Central Bank

is zero-rated. Included is the granting of a right to acquire gold and the supply of a part interest in gold. [*VATA 1994, Sch 8 Group 10*].

Other supplies. The VAT liability of a supply of gold which is not

- zero-rated under the above provisions,
- investment gold within the meaning in 30.2 above, or
- eligible for relief under the provisions relating to TERMINAL MARKETS (65)

generally falls into one of the following categories.

(*a*) **'Allocated gold'**. The supply of allocated gold held

(i) outside the UK is outside the scope of UK VAT; and

(ii) in the UK is standard-rated (unless zero-rated because the gold is physically exported under the normal rules for the export of goods).

'*Allocated gold*' is gold set apart and designated as belonging to or reserved for specific persons or purposes. If gold, etc is delivered, it is of necessity allocated.

(*b*) **'Unallocated gold' supplied by UK traders**. The supply is

(i) standard-rated if the customer belongs in the UK;

(ii) outside the scope of UK VAT (but with input tax credit) if made to a customer who belongs outside the EC;

(iii) outside the scope of UK VAT (but with input tax credit) if the customer is a business in another EC country; and

(iv) standard-rated if made to a customer in another EC country not fulfilling the conditions in (iii).

'*Unallocated gold*' is gold or gold coins forming an unidentifiable part of a large stock held by a supplier. The supply of unallocated gold or gold coins is a supply of a service for VAT purposes which is a financial service for the purposes of *VATA 1994, Sch 5* (see 64.27 SUPPLY). As a result, under (ii) and (iii) above, the place of supply of services is treated as made where the recipient belongs under *SI 1992/3121, Art 16* but under (i) and (iv) is made where the supplier belongs under the general rule for place of supply of services.

(*c*) **Unallocated gold—supplies received in the UK from suppliers belonging abroad.** Such a supply of 'unallocated gold' (see (*b*) above) is

- standard-rated as the importation of a financial service if received by a taxable person, the UK customer accounting for the VAT under the reverse charge procedure (see 39.4(*a*) INTERNATIONAL SERVICES and 64.27(5) SUPPLY); and
- outside the scope of UK VAT if received by a private or non-taxable person.

See 21.2 EUROPEAN COMMUNITY: GENERAL for the VAT territory of the EC.

(VAT Notice 701/21/02, paras 10.2, 16).

30.7 IMPORTATIONS AND ACQUISITIONS OF GOLD

Importations. VAT is not chargeable on

- the importation of gold (including gold coin) from outside the EC by a Central Bank [*SI 1992/3124*]; or
- the importation of investment gold (see 30.2 above) from outside the EC [*SI 1999/3115*]. The investment gold must be entered to Customs Procedure Code (CPC) 40 00 73 in order to gain the exemption.

Other importations of gold are chargeable to VAT at the standard rate. But see 71.3 WORKS OF ART, ETC for special valuation provisions applying to the importation of gold coins which are collectors' pieces.

Acquisitions. Acquisitions of gold in the UK from another EC country are subject to the normal rules, ie the rate of VAT is the same as would be applicable if the gold in question was the subject of a supply in the UK (see 23.3 EUROPEAN COMMUNITY: SINGLE MARKET). The effect of this is that the acquisition of investment gold is exempt from VAT but the acquisition of other gold is standard-rated.

Central banks. Where gold is supplied to a Central Bank by a supplier in another EC country and the transaction involves the removal of the gold from that or some other EC country to the UK, the taking possession of the gold by the Central Bank concerned is not treated as an acquisition of goods from another EC country. [*SI 1992/3132*]. Consequently, VAT does not become chargeable on the receipt of such gold by the Central Bank concerned.

(VAT Notice 701/21/02, paras 8.1, 10.7).

30.8 EXPORTS AND REMOVALS

- **Investment gold**. The supply of investment gold which is physically exported to a place outside the EC or despatched to a business in another EC country does not attract UK VAT. It is not necessary to keep the special records in 30.5 above but the normal evidence of the export or despatch is required. See 25.24 EXPORTS and 23.13 EUROPEAN COMMUNITY: SINGLE MARKET.

  EC sales lists/intrastat. There is no need to complete ESLs for exempt sales of investment gold to businesses in other EC countries but any required intratstat declaration must be completed.

  (VAT Notice 701/21/02, paras 8.2, 8.3).

- **Other gold**. The supply of gold, other than investment gold which is physically exported to a place outside the EC or despatched to another business in another EC country is zero-rated with input tax recovery (subject to the normal rules).

  (VAT Notice 701/21/02, para 10.8).

For the liability of sales to overseas customers where the gold is not physically removed from the UK, see 30.6 above.

30.9 SPECIAL ACCOUNTING SCHEME FOR GOLD TRANSACTIONS

A special accounting scheme for gold must be used for certain transactions between VAT-registered traders. Where it applies, it transfers the responsibility for paying the VAT due to HMRC from the seller to the buyer. The detailed provisions are set out below.

The scheme must be applied in relation to 'supplies of gold', where

(*a*) the seller and buyer are both registered for VAT or liable to be registered as a consequence of the transaction (see below),

(*b*) the supply by the seller is by way of business, and

(*c*) the buyer is making the purchase in connection with any business carried on by him.

In determining liability for registration under (*a*) above for the purposes of *VATA 1994, Sch 1*, a standard-rated supply of gold (but not a zero-rated supply) is treated as a taxable supply by the buyer in the course or furtherance of his business (as well as a taxable supply by the seller). The supply by the purchaser cannot be disregarded on the grounds that it is a supply of capital assets for his business. In such a case, if the purchaser is not entitled to register or is exempted from registration, he must account for output tax on the purchase directly to HMRC.

'*Supplies of gold*' within the scheme are as follows.

(i) Supplies of fine gold of a purity of 995 parts per thousand or greater. *Excluded* are supplies of dental gold, gold slugs and gold targets.

(ii) Supplies of gold grain of any purity.

(iii) Supplies of gold coins of any purity. Gold coins, if they are collectors' items of numismatic interest, may be accounted for under the margin scheme for SECOND-HAND GOODS (61). However, gold coins may not be sold under the margin scheme if they are investment gold coins or if they were purchased under the special accounting scheme.

(iv) Supplies of goods containing gold where the amount paid or payable for the supply (apart from the VAT) does not exceed, or exceeds by no more than a negligible amount, the 'open market value' of the gold contained in the goods. This includes supplies of scrap (including live scrap, ie scrapped jewellery, broken jewellery, watch cases, cigarette cases, etc) and sweepings. The '*open market value*' of the gold is the 'fix price' of the gold at the time of supply. This is the price set twice a day in London by members of the London Bullion Market Association.

(v) The supply of the services of treating or processing goods to make fine gold, gold grain or gold coins.

(vi) The supply of investment gold which would otherwise fall to be exempt under 30.2(*a*) or (*b*) above but which is standard-rated because the seller has exercised the option to tax under 30.3 above. [*SI 1999/3116, Reg 4*].

(vii) A supply of investment gold by

- a member of the London Bullion Market Association (LBMA) to a taxable person who is not a LBMA member, or
- a taxable person who is not a LBMA member to a LBMA member.

Such a transaction is not zero-rated, is specifically excluded from the exemption applying under 30.2 above and as a result is standard-rated. The special accounting scheme applies to these transactions regardless of whether the supply is classed as a supply of goods or a supply of services.

However, where the non-member who makes or receives the supply is only liable to be registered for VAT under *VATA 1994, Sch 1* or *Sch 3* solely by virtue of that supply or acquisition, the non-member is not required to notify liability for registration and the LBMA member must, on the non-member's behalf, keep a record of the transaction and pay the VAT due to HMRC.

[*SI 1973/173, Arts 5-7; SI 1999/3117*].

Operation of the scheme. If a VAT-registered person supplies goods within (i)–(vii) above, the goods must be sold to another VAT-registered person in order for the scheme to apply. The seller may therefore wish to ask his customer to provide a purchase order detailing the name, address and VAT registration number appropriate to the business.

Under the special scheme, the purchaser of the gold pays the seller the VAT-exclusive price of the gold and must declare the VAT due to HMRC on his VAT return. At the same time the purchaser can deduct, as input VAT, the amount of VAT shown on the seller's invoice (subject to normal rules).

If a VAT-registered person purchases manufactured goods containing gold which are held out for sale as such, and pays over VAT to the seller, the purchaser may be required to prove that the purchase did not fall within the provisions of the special accounting scheme for gold. If he cannot prove this, he may be treated as if he purchased gold and will be required to account for the output tax due under the special accounting scheme.

Issue of VAT invoices. For supplies under the special scheme, the seller must issue a VAT invoice to the buyer showing all the information normally required on a VAT invoice (see 40.4 INVOICES) and, for investment gold, the information required under 30.5 above. The time of supply is ordinarily the date of delivery of the gold or when the gold is made available for removal by the purchaser. The description of the goods must include the weight and purity of the gold; the number of individual items where possible; and the fix price of the gold on the day of delivery.

The invoice must also include a form of words to the effect that the output tax shown on the invoice is payable to HMRC by the purchaser of the gold. The suggested form of words is:

'£.....output tax on this supply of gold to be accounted for to HM Revenue and Customs by the buyer.'

Completion of the VAT return

Box 1. Include VAT due on any purchases of gold under the special scheme in the period covered by the return. VAT on any sales of gold under the scheme should *not* be shown in this box.

Box 2. Include acquisition VAT on gold acquired from other EC countries.

Box 4. Include the VAT due on purchases of gold under the special scheme (subject to the normal rules).

Box 6. Include the VAT-exclusive value of sales under the special scheme and purchases under the scheme (which are treated as deemed supplies).

Box 7. Include the value of gold purchased under the special scheme.

Sales of gold to non-registered persons. Where gold that falls within the scheme is sold to a person who is not registered or liable to be registered for VAT, the seller should charge and account for VAT in the normal way. The purchaser should pay the full amount due including VAT.

Antique items containing gold may fall outside the scheme (because the value of the goods substantially exceeds the open market value of the gold in them or because VAT due on the supply of the item may be treated under the second-hand scheme). However, antique gold coins cannot be sold under the second-hand scheme if they are investment gold or if they were purchased under the special accounting and payment scheme.

Smuggled gold. All smuggled gold is liable to forfeiture even if the gold is found in the hands of an innocent purchaser. It is therefore important that a purchaser of gold looks at the evidence of origin of the gold before agreeing to buy it. See VAT Notice 701/21/02, para 14.1 for guidance for dealers who may be invited to purchase gold so that they can satisfy themselves as to the origin of the gold on offer.

[*VATA 1994, s 55; FA 1996, ss 29(3)(5), 32*]. (VAT Notice 701/21/02, paras 11.1–11.6, 12.14).

De Voil Indirect Tax Service. See V5.143.

30.10 MANUFACTURED GOLD JEWELLERY

For a consideration of the basis of the valuation of a supply for VAT purposes where gold jewellery is made for customers wholly or partly by refashioning gold supplied by the customer, see *C & E Commrs v SAI Jewellers, QB [1996] STC 269 (TVC 65.72)*.

30.11 OTHER PRECIOUS METALS

The provisions in 30.6(*b*) and (*c*) above relating to supplies of unallocated gold also apply to supplies of unallocated silver, platinum, palladium, rhodium, ruthenium, osmium and iridium. (Business Brief 20/94).

31 Groups of Companies

Cross-references. See 7.11 BAD DEBT RELIEF; 23.18 EUROPEAN COMMUNITY: SINGLE MARKET for distance selling from the UK by VAT groups; 42.8 LAND AND BUILDINGS for election to waive exemption.

The contents of this chapter are as follows.

31.1 VAT GROUP TREATMENT

EC legislation allows countries to treat independent legal persons as a single taxable person provided such legal persons are closely bound to one another by financial, economic and organisational links and are established within the confines of the particular country. [*EC 6th Directive, Art 4(4)*].

UK legislation applicable to the registration of groups of companies is considered in 31.2 to 31.4 below. It should be noted that the term 'group' in this context is used for VAT purposes only.

VAT group registration reduces the burden on businesses by allowing two or more associated companies to account for VAT as a single taxable person. It may be administratively convenient where a group accounting function is centralised. Also, because supplies between group members are normally disregarded for VAT purposes, VAT invoices need not be issued for such supplies. On the other hand, because a single VAT return is submitted for the whole group, there may be practical problems in gathering together the information necessary to complete the return on time.

31.2 Eligibility for group treatment

Two or more 'bodies corporate' (see (1) below) are eligible to be treated as members of a group if

- each of the bodies is 'established' (see (3) below) or has a 'fixed establishment' (see (4) below) in the UK;
- they satisfy the control test, ie
  - (*a*) one of them 'controls' (see (2) below) each of the others,
  - (*b*) one person (whether a body corporate or an individual) controls all of them, or
  - (*c*) two or more individuals carrying on a business in partnership control all of them; and
- where applicable, they satisfy the anti-avoidance provisions below.

However, with effect from 22 July 2004, a body corporate cannot be treated as a member of more than one group at a time and a body which is a member of one group is not eligible by virtue of the above provisions to be treated as a member of another group.

[*VATA 1994, ss 43A(1), 43D(1)(2); FA 1999, Sch 2 para 2; FA 2004, s 20(2)*].

HMRC have no discretion to accept group registration where these requirements are not met (*E Du Vergier & Co Ltd (VTD 4) (TVC 30.1)*).

Anti-avoidance provisions. With effect from 1 August 2004, special provisions apply in order to stop abusive arrangements whereby a jointly-owned entity would otherwise be able to join a VAT group, even though it was run by and for the benefit of an external third party which exercised control over it in practice. Additional conditions prevent certain suppliers from being in the same VAT group as their customers where third parties control the suppliers or receive most of the benefits of their activities.

Specifically, a body corporate that is a 'specified body' (see (5) below) is only eligible to be treated as a member of a group if

- it satisfies the control test above; *and*
- it satisfies both the 'benefits condition' (see (6) below) and the 'consolidated accounts condition' (see (7) below).

[*SI 2004/1931, Art 2*].

A specified body which was a member of a VAT group at 1 August 2004 but failed either the benefits condition or consolidated accounts provision at that date is no longer eligible to be a member of a VAT group. It must leave the group from a date agreed with, or determined by, HMRC. (VAT Notice 700/2/04, para 3.2).

Definitions for the above purposes.

(1) *Body corporate*

A body corporate is a form of corporation where a number of persons are united and consolidated together so as to be considered as one person in law. There are several ways in which a body might be incorporated.

- *Companies Act 1985* provides five ways in which a body may be incorporated (public limited companies limited by shares or by guarantee with a share capital; private companies limited by shares; private companies limited by guarantee with a share capital; private companies limited by guarantee; and unlimited companies).
- Bodies may also be incorporated by Act of Parliament, Royal Charter or company law of another country.

(VAT Notice 700/2/04, paras 6.1–6.3).

(2) *Control*

A body corporate is taken to control another body corporate in two sets of circumstances.

- If it is 'empowered by statute' to control the company's activities. '*Empowered by statute*' means empowered by a provision contained in an Act of Parliament (*British Airways Pension Fund Trustees Ltd (VTD 846) (TVC 30.2)*).

- If it is the company's 'holding company' within the meaning of *Companies Act 1985, s 736*.

An individual or individuals shall be taken to control a body corporate if he or they, were he or they a company, would be that body's holding company.

[*VATA 1994, s 43A(2)(3); FA 1999, Sch 2 para 2*].

A company is a subsidiary of another company, its '*holding company*', if

- that other company holds a majority of the voting rights in it;
- that other company is a member of it and has the right to appoint or remove a majority of its board of directors;
- that other company is a member of it and controls alone, pursuant to an agreement with other shareholders or members, a majority of the voting rights in it; or
- it is a subsidiary of a company which is itself a subsidiary of that other company.

[*CA 1985, s 736; CA 1989, s 144*].

(3) *Established*

A company is established in the UK if it has its principal place of business or registered office in the UK, which means if

- the central management and control of the company are carried on in the UK; or
- its headquarters or head office are in the UK.

A company will normally be established in only one country.

(VAT Notice 700/2/04, para 6.4).

(4) *Fixed establishment*

A company has a fixed establishment in the UK for VAT group purposes if it has a real and permanent trading presence in the UK. This would apply, for example, if it has

- a permanent place of business with the necessary human and technical resources to carry on its business activities; or
- a branch or office in the UK with its own staff and equipment.

For VAT group purposes, a company does not have a fixed establishment in the UK purely by virtue of the fact that

- it is incorporated and has its registered office in the UK;
- it has a simple brass plate presence in the UK; or
- it has a UK-based branch.

(VAT Notice 700/2/04, para 6.4).

(5) *Specified body*

A body corporate or limited liability partnership which is in, or applying to join, a VAT group is a specified body if all of the following conditions are satisfied.

(*a*) It carries on a relevant business activity (see (6) below). A dormant company cannot therefore be a specified body.

(*b*) The value of the group's supplies in the year then ending has exceeded £10 million or there are reasonable grounds for believing that it will exceed £10 million in the year then beginning.

Turnover is the value of all supplies made by the VAT group to persons outside the group whether (ie it excludes intra-group supplies) whether or not the place of supply is in the UK. This is the same as the definition for Box 6 of the VAT return. The expected turnover for the coming year should be determined on the assumption that the specified body applying to join the group is included in the group. If the body corporate is the sole general partner of a limited partnership, then the limited partnership's turnover is included. (VAT Notice 700/2/04, para 3.3).

(*c*) At any time when the relevant business activity is being carried on the body corporate concerned is

- not a 'wholly-owned subsidiary' of a person who controls all of the other members of the group (or, where the body corporate is or will be a member of the group, all of the other members apart from himself);
- managed, directly or indirectly, in respect of the business activity concerned, by a third party (see (9) below) in the course or furtherance of a business carried on by him; or
- the sole general partner of a limited partnership.

A body corporate is a '*wholly-owned subsidiary*' of a person if it has no members except that other person and that other person's wholly-owned subsidiaries or persons acting on behalf of that other person or his wholly-owned subsidiaries. In determining whether a body corporate is a wholly-owned subsidiary of a person, the membership of

- any employee or director of the body, or
- where the body is a limited liability partnership, any member of the body

is disregarded.

(*d*) The body corporate is not

- a body corporate that controls all of the members of the VAT group (or, where it is a member of the group, all of the members apart from itself);
- a body corporate whose activities another body corporate is empowered by statute to control;
- a body corporate whose only activity is acting as the trustee of an occupational pension scheme (as defined by *Pension Schemes Act 1993, s 1*) established under a trust; or
- a charity.

[*SI 2004/1931, Arts 3, 7(3)*].

(6) *Relevant business activity*

A relevant business activity is one where

(*a*) the business activity involves making one or more supplies of goods or services to one or more members of the VAT group;

(*b*) those supplies are not 'incidental' to the business activity;

(*c*) at least one of those supplies is chargeable to VAT at a rate other than the zero rate (or would be if the body corporate was not in the VAT group); and

(*d*) the representative member is not entitled to credit for the whole of the VAT on supplies falling within (*c*) above as input tax (or would not be able to do so if the body corporate was not in the VAT group).

When applying this criteria to a body corporate which is already a member of the VAT group, it is deemed not to be a member.

[*SI 2004/1931, Art 4*].

'*Incidental*' has its normal meaning. In general, intra-group supplies are incidental to a business activity if

- they are occasional or minor supplies made in connection with the activity;
- they do not employ a substantial proportion of the resources devoted to the activity; and
- they are not sufficiently separate from the main business activity to constitute a business activity in their own right.

HMRC give the example of occasional intra-group supplies made by a retailer whose business is mainly selling to the public.

(VAT Notice 700/2/04, para 3.4).

(7) *Benefits condition*

The benefits condition is satisfied unless 50% of the benefits of the relevant business activity (see (6) above) 'accrue', directly or indirectly, to one or more third parties (see (9) below).

The following are benefits of a business activity for these purposes.

(*a*) Profits (whether or not distributed).

(*b*) Charges for managing the business activity (including charges for providing staff to manage it).

(*c*) The amounts, if any, by which any other charges made to the body exceed the open market value of the goods or services concerned.

If there are no such benefits, any business activity is deemed to generate profits of £100.

Benefits that accrue to a person in his capacity as a member of a body corporate which controls all of the other members of the group (or, where the body is or will be a member of the group, all of the other members apart from itself) are not to be regarded as accruing to a third party.

If the specified body is the sole general partner of a limited partnership, then the benefits concerned are those arising from the limited partnership's business activity.

[*SI 2004/1931, Arts 5, 7(1)*].

Benefits do not include

- cost savings made by being a customer of the body corporate (eg price reductions, discounts or rebates); and
- under (*b*) above remuneration or bonuses paid to directors or employees of the body.

As regards (*c*) above, HMRC do not expect traders in normal commercial relationships to undertake extra work to verify that transactions are at open market value.

'*Accrue*'. Technically the benefits condition applies at a given time but profits, etc are normally determined for a period (usually a year). They can be taken to accrue evenly over that period. Profits accrue to the persons who are expected to get the benefit in practice (eg side agreements between shareholders or expectations that profits are to be gifted to a particular person should be taken into account). If ownership of a company changes during the year, profits up to the point of change will normally accrue to the former owner (whether or not distributed to him).

(VAT Notice 700/2/04, para 3.5).

(8) *Consolidated accounts condition*

The consolidated accounts condition is satisfied if

(*a*) consolidated accounts prepared for the person who controls all of the other members of the group (or, where the person is or will be a member of the group, all of the other members apart from himself) would be required by 'generally accepted accounting practice' to include accounts for the specified body as his subsidiary; and

(*b*) consolidated accounts prepared for a third party (see (9) below) would not be required by generally accepted accounting practice to include accounts for the specified body as his subsidiary.

Where the specific body is the general partner of a limited liability partnership, then the consolidation condition applies to the limited partnership (eg the limited partnership must be consolidated as a subsidiary in the consolidated group accounts).

In applying this test at any particular time

- the reference to consolidated accounts is a reference to consolidated accounts for a period including that time and insofar as they relate to that time;
- any principle of generally accepted accounting practice that permits accounts of a subsidiary undertaking to be excluded from a consolidation as being immaterial are disregarded; and

- the reference to consolidated accounts prepared for a person is a reference to consolidated accounts of a kind that could be prepared for him in accordance with generally accepted accounting practice; and for this purpose it does not matter

  (i) whether accounts are actually prepared for him (whether for a particular period or at all), or

  (ii) in particular, whether he is required to prepare accounts.

  This covers the rare situations where a person controlling a VAT group with a turnover of over £10 million does not have to prepare consolidated accounts (eg where the only person controlling the VAT group is an individual or partnership).

'*Generally accepted accounting practice*' has the meaning given by *FA 2004, s 50(1)* or, in relation to any time when that section does not have effect, has the meaning given by *ICTA 1988, s 836A*. It is normal accounting practice in the UK. It means that the accounts should comply with UK Financial Reporting Standards (FRSs), in particular UK FRS 2 (Subsidiary undertakings), FRS 5 (Reporting the substance of transactions) and FRS 9 (Associates and joint ventures). From 1 January 2005, GAAP also includes consolidated accounts prepared to International Accounting Standards (IASs), eg IAS 27 (Consolidated and separate financial statements), IAS 28 (Investment in associates) and IAS 31 (Investment in joint ventures).

If more than one person controls the VAT group (eg there is a series of holding companies), condition (*a*) above only has to be satisfied by one of them.

The consolidated accounts provision has to be applied at a current date for which consolidated accounts will not yet have been prepared. In most cases, whether the condition is satisfied will be obvious from the most recent consolidated accounts unless there has been some significant change in the specified body since then. Where the position is not clear, HMRC will normally accept a professional accountant or auditor's statement that the specified body will be consolidated as a subsidiary in the accounts for the current period.

[*SI 2004/1931, Art 6*]. (VAT Notice 700/2/04, para 3.6).

(9) *Third party*

For the purposes of (5), (7) and (8) above, a third party is any person or partnership except

(*a*) anyone who controls the body corporate and all of the other members of the group (ie the direct holding company and indirect holding companies up to the ultimate holding company);

(*b*) anyone controlled by a person in (*a*) above (which therefore includes all fellow subsidiaries);

(*c*) an individual who is an employee or director of the body corporate; and

(*d*) where the body corporate is a limited liability partnership, any individual who is a partner in the partnership.

Broadly speaking, therefore, any person outside the corporate group that includes the VAT group is a third party, except individuals working for the body corporate itself.

[*SI 2004/1931, Art 7(3)*]. (VAT Notice 700/2/04, para 3.3).

Transitional provisions at 27 July 1999. A company treated as a member of a VAT group under the eligibility rules applying before 27 July 1999 (see Tolley's VAT 2002 and earlier editions) continues to be treated as a member under the current rules even if no longer eligible (because it is not established or does not have a fixed establishment in the UK) until HMRC give notice terminating its treatment as a member of the group (see 31.3 below).

Group treatment and divisional registration under 59.37 REGISTRATION are mutually exclusive. A corporate body which is registered for VAT in the names of its divisions cannot have one of its divisions included in a VAT group. Similarly, a company that is a member of a VAT group will not be allowed to register one of its divisions separately outside the group. (VAT Notice 700/2/04, para 1.13).

De Voil Indirect Tax Service. See V2.190.

31.3 Applications re group treatment and termination of membership

Applications. An application can be made to HMRC for

(*a*) two or more eligible bodies corporate (see 31.2 above) to be treated as members of a group;

(*b*) another eligible body corporate to be treated as a member of an existing group;

(*c*) a body corporate to cease to be treated as a member of an existing group;

(*d*) a member to be substituted as the group's representative member (see 31.4 below); or

(*e*) the bodies corporate forming an existing group no longer to be treated as members of a group.

An application is taken to be granted with effect from the day on which the application is received by HMRC or such earlier or later time as HMRC allow. In practice, a grouping application is given immediate provisional effect from the date it is received (although HMRC then have 90 days in which to make enquiries and refuse it, see below). HMRC aim to respond within 15 working days of receipt to confirm the application has been approved and give the new VAT registration number. They will also confirm that the application has been successful or advise that further enquiries need to be made. HMRC should be contacted immediately if a new VAT registration number has not been received within 15 working days.

[*VATA 1994, s 43B(1)-(4); FA 1999, Sch 2 para 2, para 6(3)(5); FA 2004, s 20(4)*]. (VAT Notice 700/2/04, paras 2.6, 2.7, 2.12).

Making the application. The application must be to the National Registration Service (see 59.38 REGISTRATION) using the following forms.

Under (*a*) above	Form VAT 1 signed by the representative member Form VAT 50 (signed by either the applicant company or the person controlling the group) Form VAT 51 for each company applying to join the group (signed by the same person as the Form VAT 50)

Under (*b*) and (*c*) above	Form VAT 50 and a Form VAT 51 for each company joining or leaving the group
Under (*d*) above	Form VAT 56 (and Forms VAT 50 and VAT 51 if the new representative member is not already a member of the group)
Under (*e*) above	Form VAT 50 and a Form VAT 51 for each member of the group to be excluded

Existing VAT registration numbers already held are cancelled in respect of new members forming a group. The group itself is allocated a new registration number (in the name of the representative member) which identifies the group as a taxable person. This number remains unchanged even if the membership is varied or the representative member changes. On the termination of the group treatment, the group registration number is cancelled. Any member still liable to be registered, or wishing to register voluntarily, is allocated a new number.

(VAT Notice 700/2/04, paras 1.8, 2.4, 2.5, 7.3, 7.4).

Retrospective effect. The wording of the legislation permits retrospective group registration but only within the discretion of HMRC and not a tribunal (*C & E Commrs v Save and Prosper Group Ltd, QB 1978, [1979] STC 205 (TVC 30.3)*). HMRC may give retrospective effect to an application to form a new group or amend an existing one by up to 30 days before the date on which the application is received by HMRC or, if later

- the beginning of the current VAT period of an existing group; or
- the beginning of the current VAT period of any of the companies applying to form, join or leave the VAT group.

Applications for retrospective group registration for periods longer than 30 days will only be allowed if

- HMRC lose an application and the applicant can supply details of its original application and attempts to follow it up; or
- if the delay was caused by lack of action on HMRC's part.

(VAT Notice 700/2/04, paras 2.13, 2.14).

Companies already members of another VAT group. With effect from 22 July 2004,

- where an application is made under (*a*) above and at the time of the application one or more of bodies corporate is already a member of another VAT group, the application has effect but with the exclusion of that body or those bodies;
- where an application is made under (*b*) above and the applicant body is already a member of another VAT group, the application has no effect; and
- where a body is subject to two applications under (*a*) or (*b*) above that have not been granted or refused, the applications have no effect.

[*VATA 1994, s 43D(3); FA 2004, s 20(2)*].

Refusal of application. HMRC may refuse an application within 90 days of receipt

- under (*a*) above if the bodies corporate are not eligible to be treated as members of a group under the criteria in 31.2 above;

- under (*b*) above if the proposed additional member is not eligible to be treated as a member of the group under the criteria in 31.2 above; or
- under any of (*a*)-(*e*) above if necessary for the protection of the revenue.

[*VATA 1994, s 43B*(*5*)(*6*)*; FA 1999, Sch 2 para 2; FA 2004, s 20*(*4*)].

HMRC have given the following as broad examples of where an application for group treatment may be refused, but the list should not be taken as exhaustive.

- The proposed group members have poor compliance records which might pose a threat to HMRC's ability to collect VAT.
- HMRC have reason to believe that the applicants intend to use the grouping facilities to operate a VAT avoidance scheme.
- Group treatment would create a distortion in the VAT liability of the group's supplies (eg where exempt supplies would become taxable with consequent increase in input tax recovery or where entitlement to recover previously irrecoverable input tax is increased).

(Business Brief 31/97).

Where application is refused, it will be treated as if it had never been made in the first place. As a result:

- If any of the proposed members were registered for VAT before applying for group treatment, the previous registration will be reinstated with effect from the date on which it was cancelled.
- If, during the period that a company was provisionally treated as a member of a VAT group, it would have been required to notify its liability to register for VAT, it will have 30 days after the date of the letter of refusal to register.
- If a company was not liable to register at the time it applied for grouping and it would not have become liable during the period when it was provisionally treated as a member of a VAT group, it can apply for voluntary registration after group membership has been annulled.
- If, while the application to join a VAT group was being considered, the group submitted a VAT return which included supplies made and received by any 'group' company, the representative member must correct the error by adjusting the return following HMRC's decision (if below £2,000) or by submitting a voluntary disclosure.

(VAT Notice 700/2/04, para 2.10).

'Protection of the revenue'. The protection in question may be against any loss of revenue which is not *de minimis* whether or not it follows from the normal operations of grouping. It certainly covers an artificial avoidance scheme but it also covers a straightforward case which would not be characterised as avoidance or abusive. The phrase must be considered in its totality and involves a balancing exercise in which HMRC must weigh the effect of refusal on the applicant (eg higher administrative costs) against the loss of revenue likely to result from grouping (*National Westminster Bank plc (VTD 15514)*). HMRC will not normally use their protective powers when they consider that the revenue loss follows from the normal operating of the group, ie because VAT is eliminated on supplies between group members. This includes any loss arising from supplies between group members being disregarded where the recipient would not normally be able to deduct that VAT because it makes exempt supplies.

If HMRC have concerns that the revenue loss goes beyond the accepted consequences of VAT grouping, they will ask for

- relevant information about the administrative savings that grouping brings in the particular circumstances, and
- an estimate of the revenue impact of grouping.

They will also normally ask for comment on the impact on the business of any refusal to allow grouping or removal of a company from the VAT group.

HMRC will make a judgement based on the information provided, and any other information that they have. If a business fails to provide the information requested, although HMRC will endeavour to come to a balanced decision based on the information that they have, some factors may not be taken into account and this may affect the outcome of their considerations. Consistent failure to provide information or records reasonably requested in the course of enquiries may be treated as sufficient grounds for exercising the revenue protection powers.

(VAT Notice 700/2/04, paras 4.1–4.4).

Appeals against HMRC's refusal. An appeal may be made against HMRC's refusal of an application under (*a*)-(*e*) above. See 5.3(*k*) APPEALS. Where the refusal of the application is on the grounds of protection of the revenue, the tribunal's jurisdiction is supervisory in that it cannot allow the appeal unless it considers that HMRC could not reasonably have been satisfied that there were grounds for refusing the application. Any refusal has effect pending the determination of the appeal but, if the appeal is allowed, the refusal is deemed not to have occurred. [*VATA 1994, s 84(4A); FA 1999, Sch 2 para 4*].

Ceasing to satisfy eligibility criteria. If any member of a VAT group ceases to satisfy the criteria for group treatment under 31.2 above (eg by ceasing to be a subsidiary or ceasing to be established, or have a fixed establishment, in the UK) HMRC must be notified within 30 days of the change in circumstances. [*SI 1995/2518, Reg 5(2); SI 2000/794*]. This is effectively done in the application to HMRC for the company in question to cease to be a member of the VAT group. The application is taken to be granted with effect from the day on which it is received by HMRC or such earlier or later time as HMRC allow (see above). This means that, if the application is made *after* the company leaves the group, HMRC are not obliged to exclude the company as soon as it ceases to be a member. This was confirmed in *C & E Commrs v Barclays Bank plc, CA [2001] STC 1558* where Customs were able to prevent the company leaving the VAT group before the introduction of the anti-avoidance provisions in 31.5 below. HMRC have confirmed that, as this could cause commercial difficulties, in practice their policy will be to agree the date requested by the selling group. They will set a later date only if VAT avoidance is involved or is otherwise likely to arise. (Business Brief 30/02).

Termination of membership by HMRC. Where a body corporate is treated as a member of a group and it appears to HMRC that the body is not, or is no longer, eligible to be so treated under the criteria in 31.2 above, they must give notice to that body terminating its treatment as a member of the group from a date specified in the notice. [*VATA 1994, s 43C(3); FA 1999, Sch 2 para 2; FA 2004, s 20(4)*]. The date specified can be earlier than the date the notice is given but cannot be *earlier* than the date on which, in HMRC's opinion, the body became ineligible to be treated as a member of the group. [*VATA 1994, s 43C(4); FA 1999, Sch 2 para 2*].

HMRC may also give notice to a body terminating its treatment as a member of a group from a specified date if it appears necessary for the 'protection of the revenue' (see above). The date specified can be the date the notice is given or any later date. [*VATA 1994, s 43C(1)(2); FA 1999, Sch 2 para 2*].

Appeals. An appeal may be made against any notice by HMRC terminating membership of a group. See 5.3(*ka*) APPEALS. Where the appeal is against

- notice of termination of membership due to ineligibility and the grounds for the appeal relate (wholly or partly) to the date specified in the notice, or
- notice of termination of membership on the grounds of protection of the revenue,

the tribunal's jurisdiction is supervisory in that it cannot allow the appeal unless it considers that HMRC could not reasonably have been satisfied that date was appropriate or, as the case may be, there were grounds for giving the notice.

In either case, the notice has effect pending the determination of the appeal but, if the appeal is allowed, the notice is deemed never to have had effect.

[*VATA 1994, s 84(4B)-(4D); FA 1999, Sch 2 para 4*].

De Voil Indirect Tax Service. See V2.190.

31.4 Consequences of group treatment

Group registration is a facilitation method which allows two or more corporate bodies to be treated as a single taxable person. One of the companies applying for group treatment is nominated as the representative member (see 31.3 above) and the registration is then made in the name of that member (VAT Notice 700/2/04, paras 1.3, 1.4).

The consequences of group treatment include the following.

(*a*) Any business carried on by a member of the group is treated as though carried on by the representative member.

(*b*) Subject to the anti-avoidance provisions in 31.5 below and the provisions relating to group supplies using an overseas member in 31.6 below, any supply of goods or services by a member of the group to another member of the group is disregarded for VAT purposes. This means that VAT need not be accounted for on these supplies and no VAT invoices must be issued in respect of them.

(*c*) Any supply not disregarded under (*b*) above which is a supply of goods (including a SELF-SUPPLY (62)) or services (including deemed supply) by or to a group member is treated as a supply by or to the representative member.

(*d*) Any VAT paid or payable by a group member on the acquisition of goods from an EC country or on the importation of goods from outside the EC is treated as paid or payable by the representative member and the goods are treated as having been acquired or imported by the representative member.

(*e*) Input tax recovery is determined in accordance with the use of the VAT group as a whole of the goods and services received by each individual member.

> *Example*
>
> Group member A buys in computer equipment and leases it to group member B, who uses the equipment to make exempt supplies to third parties outside the group.

> The input tax is attributable to exempt supplies and restricted (subject to the normal *de minimis* limits).

Input tax incurred by all the group members can be deducted to the extent that it is attributable to supplies made to persons outside the group which carry the right to deduct input tax.

(*f*) All members of the group are jointly and severally liable for any VAT due from the representative member. If the representative member is unable to meet a debt of the group, each member will be held liable for the amount of the debt until it is discharged. A former member is also liable for VAT due during its period of membership.

For liability of members when the representative member goes into liquidation, see 36.14 INSOLVENCY, and where a corporate pension trustee is a member, see 53.3 PENSION SCHEMES.

(*g*) Assessments can be validly raised on the representative member where relating to earlier periods when it was not the representative member and even if it was not a member of the group at that time (*Thorn plc (VTD 15283) (TVC 30.16)*). Also, under the anti-avoidance provisions in 31.5 below, current members of a VAT group may be held liable for assessments relating to periods when they were not members of the group.

(*h*) Most of the PARTIAL EXEMPTION (49) rules apply to a VAT group in the same way as they would to a stand-alone business. Therefore

- the *de minimis* limits apply to the group as a whole and not the members individually; and
- any change in the group members may have a significant effect on an agreed special method which may need revising.

Special care should be taken over a prospective member which makes any exempt supplies to ensure that the group as a whole does not suffer the loss of input tax through the partial exemption rules.

See also 31.7 below for special provisions where a partly exempt group acquires a business as a going concern.

(*i*) The limit for voluntary disclosures of errors on past returns applies to the group as a whole. See 56.11 RECORDS. The representative member must be informed of any misdeclarations made by any other members of the group since joining it, and either

- enter the amount to the group's VAT account; or
- if necessary, make a single voluntary disclosure on behalf of the whole group.

(*j*) The cash accounting limits apply to the group as a whole and not to the members individually. See 63.2 AND 63.7 SPECIAL SCHEMES.

(*k*) The payment on account limits (see 51.4 PAYMENT OF VAT) apply to the group as a whole and not to the members individually.

(*l*) Special provisions also apply under the capital goods scheme when a VAT group is formed or disbanded or there is a change in membership. See CAPITAL GOODS (10).

(*m*) In *J & W Waste Management Ltd; J & W Plant & Tool Hire Ltd (VTD 18069) (TVC 30.8)* the tribunal held that VAT group membership does not imply abandonment of any right to appeal against demands for VAT. It specifically disapproved of the earlier decision in *Davis Advertising Service Ltd (VTD 5) (TVC 2.67)* that only the representative member has *locus standi* to bring an appeal.

The representative member is therefore responsible for

- accounting for any VAT due on supplies made by the group to third parties outside the group;
- completing a single VAT return and paying/reclaiming VAT on behalf of the whole group.

This is particularly helpful if accounting is centralised but group members will need to make sure that the representative member has all the necessary information to submit a VAT return for the group by the due date.

No taxable supplies outside the VAT group. The fact that no taxable supplies are made outside the VAT group does not prevent a group being formed provided one of the members is making taxable supplies which would make it liable or eligible for registration in its own right. However, as taxable supplies between group members are ignored, a group will not be able to recover any input tax unless it makes

- UK taxable supplies outside the group;
- supplies outside the UK that would be taxable supplies if made in the UK; or
- exempt financial/insurance supplies to customers outside the EC.

See 35.3 INPUT TAX for fuller details.

'Special status' companies. The VAT liability of certain supplies, acquisitions and importations is dependent on the status of the person by or to whom the supply, etc is made (eg education, water and certain supplies involving charities). In such cases, the VAT liability is decided by looking at the status of the person actually making/receiving the supply, even though for other VAT purposes the representative member is treated as making/receiving the supply.

[*VATA 1994, s 43(1)(1AA)(1AB); FA 1995, s 25; FA 1997, s 40(1)(3); FA 1999, Sch 2 para 1; FA 2004, s 20(4)*]. (VAT Notice 700/2/04, paras 1.5–1.7, 5.1, 5.5, 5.7–5.9, 5.12).

De Voil Indirect Tax Service. See V2.190.

31.5 Anti-avoidance provisions

HMRC may direct that

- separately registered companies eligible to be treated as members of a VAT group are to be treated as grouped from a specified date;
- a company within a group is removed from that group from a specified date; or
- a supply within a VAT group initially treated as a disregarded supply is to be subjected to VAT.

The provisions are designed for use only against certain categories of avoidance scheme which rely on the existence of the group registration provisions in *VATA 1994, ss 43-43C*. Features common to such avoidance schemes are that input tax deduction is taken against standard-rated supplies, but output tax does not fall on the full value of those supplies because they are treated to some extent as being made between members of the same VAT group and so are disregarded for VAT. The simplest means of bringing the disregard into play is by moving a company into or out of a VAT group at a critical moment. But a similar result could be secured by entering into some other transaction, such as the transfer of assets or the assignment of an agreement to or from a group member.

The detailed provisions are outlined below. HMRC have issued a Statement of Practice (SP) dated June 1996 setting out how they will seek to apply the provisions. Extracts are included in the text where appropriate.

Power to give directions. HMRC may give a direction if certain conditions are met. [*VATA 1994, Sch 9A para 1(1); FA 1996, Sch 1*]. Taken together, the conditions require that a relevant event causes a situation where standard-rated supplies, which have given rise to an input tax credit by any person, are not taxed on their full value, so leading to a tax advantage. The conditions are as follows.

(*a*) A '*relevant event*' has occurred, ie a company has either

(i) joined or ceased to be a member of a group, or

(ii) entered into any 'transaction'

after that date. [*VATA 1994, Sch 9A para 1(2), para 4(2); FA 1996, Sch 1*].

The word '*transaction*' is capable of a very wide meaning but, in the context of this provision, the key to its interpretation is that a relevant event occurs when a taxpayer *enters into* a transaction. Generally, HMRC will take this to mean when the taxpayer enters into a contract or other disposition, such as a gift. For example, HMRC will regard entering into a lease or the assignment, variation or surrender of a lease as a transaction which might potentially bring a company within the provisions. The performance of obligations under the lease (eg carrying out repairs or paying rent) would not normally be caught unless, exceptionally, such obligation constituted the entering into of a separate contract. (SP, para 3.5).

(*b*) There has been (or will or may be) a taxable supply on which VAT has been (or will or may be) charged otherwise than by reference to its full value due to the supply in question being disregarded under 31.4(*b*) above. [*VATA 1994, Sch 9A para 1(3)(a)(9); FA 1996, Sch 1*]. Supplies which, although not disregarded under 31.4(*b*) above, are less than full value for other reasons are not covered. HMRC could not, for example, compulsorily group the parties to a lease and leaseback agreement under arrangements that had nothing to do with the operation of an intra-group disregard. (SP, para 3.6).

(*c*) At least part of the supply in (*b*) above is not (or would not be) zero-rated. [*VATA 1994, Sch 9A para 1(3)(b); FA 1996, Sch 1*].

(*d*) The charging of VAT on the supply in (*b*) above otherwise than by reference to full value gives rise (or would give rise) to a tax advantage because a person has become entitled to

(i) credit for input tax as attributable to that supply (or part of it); or

(ii) a repayment of VAT under the provisions in 21.57 EUROPEAN COMMUNITY: GENERAL or 48.5 OVERSEAS TRADERS (refunds of VAT to persons in business abroad).

[*VATA 1994, Sch 9A para 1(3)(c)(4)(5); FA 1996, Sch 1*].

It is not essential that the right to credit or repayment should be that of the supplier of the undercharged supply. The legislation specifically provides that the condition is also fulfilled where the supplier acquires the goods and/or services VAT free under the provisions relating to the transfer of a business as a going concern, and the transferor (or some previous owner) of the business has been entitled to an input tax credit. [*VATA 1994, Sch 9A para 1(6)(7); FA 1996, Sch 1*].

(*e*) The requirements in (*b*)-(*d*) above would not be fulfilled apart from the occurrence of the relevant event.

(*f*) Where the relevant event is a transaction within (*a*)(ii) above, the supply on which VAT is undercharged must not be the only supply by reference to which the case falls within (*a*)-(*e*) above.

To pre-empt avoidance of the provisions, in determining whether the input tax credit is used to make an undercharged supply, separate rights to goods or services (including options or priorities in connection with goods or services), and the goods or services themselves are treated as a single supply. [*VATA 1994, Sch 9A para 1(8)(10); FA 1996, Sch 1*].

HMRC must not give a direction if satisfied that the main purpose, or each of the main purposes, of the relevant event was a genuine commercial purpose unconnected with the consequences in (*b*)-(*d*) above. This does not apply where the relevant event is the termination of a body corporate's treatment as a member of a group by HMRC under *VATA 1994, s 43C* (see 31.3 above). [*VATA 1994, Sch 9A para 2; FA 1999, Sch 2 para 5*]. This recognises the fact that, in the vast majority of cases, businesses are moved into and out of groups for reasons which have no avoidance motive whatsoever. However, it is important to realise that where, in addition to acceptable commercial purpose, HMRC also identify other main purposes indicating VAT avoidance, they will seek to use their powers to nullify that advantage. (SP, paras 3.11–3.13, Annexes 1–3).

Form of directions. A direction may take the following forms.

(i) That a supply of goods or services, in whole or part, from one company to another does not fall within 31.4(*b*) above (where it otherwise would).

(ii) That for such periods as may be described in the directions a company is not to be treated as a member of a group (where it otherwise would). To the extent that the direction applies to VAT periods after the direction is issued, *all* supplies between that company and other group members are treated as taxable supplies. For events prior to the issue of the direction, see under the heading *Assessments* below.

(iii) That for such periods as may be described in the directions, a company is to be treated as a member of a group (where it otherwise would not). Such a direction may also identify the company which is assumed to be the representative member of the group for those periods.

Subject to the time limits below, the periods under (ii) or (iii) above may comprise times before the giving of the direction or times afterwards or both.

Where a direction requires any assumptions to be made, *VATA 1994* has effect from the date of the direction in accordance with those assumptions. (For periods before the date of the direction, the assumptions are given effect by HMRC raising an assessment for unpaid VAT, see below.)

The fact that HMRC have accepted or refused an application for a company to join a group does not prejudice their powers to make a direction to the opposite effect.

[*VATA 1994, Sch 9A para 3(1)-(6)(8); FA 1996, Sch 1; FA 1999, Sch 2 para 5*].

Withdrawal of direction. HMRC may withdraw a direction at any time by notice in writing to the person to whom it was given. [*VATA 1994, Sch 9A para 3(7); FA 1996, Sch 1*].

Time limits. A direction cannot be given more than six years after the later of

- the occurrence of the relevant event; and
- the time when the entitlement to input tax under (*d*)(i) or (*d*)(ii) above arose.

However, where a direction is appropriate, it can require assumptions to be made about transactions made before either of those times without any limit. [*VATA 1994, Sch 9A para 4(1)(3); FA 1996, Sch 1*].

HMRC will not, however, seek application of any direction from a date earlier than that required to nullify the tax advantage derived from the relevant event. Usually, this will be the first day of the VAT period in which the scheme commences or the relevant event occurs (whichever is earlier). (SP, para 3.18).

Method of giving directions. A direction relating to a supply under (i) above may be given to the person who made the supply and a direction relating to a company under (ii) or (iii) above may be given to that company. In either case, the direction may also be given to the representative member of the group. Any direction must be in writing and must specify the relevant event by reference to which it is given. [*VATA 1994, Sch 9A para 5; FA 1996, Sch 1*].

Assessments. Where a direction is given and there is an amount of unpaid VAT for which a 'relevant person' would have been liable based on the assumptions specified in the direction, HMRC may, to the best of their judgment, assess the amount of unpaid VAT as VAT due from a relevant person and notify their assessment to that person. The assessment may be incorporated in the direction. See 6.1 ASSESSMENTS for interpretation of 'to the best of HMRC's judgment'. Where, however, HMRC are satisfied that the actual revenue loss is less than the unpaid VAT the amount assessed must not exceed the revenue loss (calculated to the best of their judgment). [*VATA 1994, Sch 9A para 6(1)-(5); FA 1996, Sch 1*].

'*Relevant person*' means the person to whom the direction is given, the representative member of the group to which that person was treated as being a member, or any company which, under the direction, is treated as being the representative member of such a group. [*VATA 1994, Sch 9A para 6(11); FA 1996, Sch 1*].

Calculation of VAT charge.

- Where a direction is made under (i) above, VAT will become payable according to its value (adjusted as appropriate to take account of any direction issued under *VATA 1994, Sch 6 para 1* — supplies between connected persons, see 69.19 VALUATION). A credit will be allowed for that part of the VAT which would have been deductible according to the partial exemption method of the VAT group registration.

- Where a direction is made under (ii) above, in relation to events prior to the issue of the direction, only those transactions relevant to the tax advantage will be affected. Input tax that would have been deductible on the basis of the assumptions in the direction can be taken into account in appropriate cases. All other supplies made by the parties involved will be unaffected so there will be no need for any retrospective VAT accounting adjustment in their regard.
- Where a direction is made under (iii) above, the purpose of the direction will normally be to enable HMRC to recoup any excess claim to input tax. In such cases, the amount of VAT to be charged will be the amount of input tax recovered less the amount which would otherwise have been recoverable in accordance with the partial exemption method of the appropriate VAT group registration. A credit will also be allowed in connection with any output tax charged between the parties which would not have been due according to the assumptions specified in the directive.

(SP, paras 3.18, 5.1–5.3).

The amount assessed and notified to a person is, subject to appeal, deemed to be an amount of VAT due and is recoverable, from that person or the representative member of the group, unless the assessment is subsequently withdrawn or reduced. To the extent that more than one person is liable for the same unpaid VAT under any assessment, they are each jointly and severally liable for the full amount. [*VATA 1994, Sch 9A para 6(7)(8); FA 1996, Sch 1*].

Time limit. An assessment under these provisions cannot be made more than one year after the date of the direction or in the case of any direction which has been withdrawn. [*VATA 1994, Sch 9A para 6(6); FA 1996, Sch 1*].

Supplementary assessments. Where it appears to HMRC that the amount which ought to have been assessed exceeds the amount actually assessed, a supplementary assessment of the amount of the excess may be made and notified under the same provisions and within the same time limit as the original assessment. [*VATA 1994, Sch 9A para 6(9); FA 1996, Sch 1*].

Interest payable. The provisions of *VATA 1994, s 74* on interest (see 51.14 PAYMENT OF VAT) also apply to assessments under the above provisions, except that interest runs from the date on which the assessment is notified rather than the reckonable date. The period for interest is confined to the two years ending with the time when the assessment to interest is made. [*VATA 1994, Sch 9A para 6(9)(10); FA 1996, Sch 1*].

Appeals against directions by HMRC. An appeal may be made against a direction by HMRC under the above provisions. See 5.3(*wa*) APPEALS. The tribunal must allow the appeal if satisfied that

- the conditions for making the direction were not fulfilled; or
- the main purpose, or each of the main purposes, of the relevant event was a genuine commercial purpose unconnected with the consequences in (*b*) above.

[*VATA 1994, s 84(7A); FA 1996, s 31*].

Following correction of a tax advantage to the satisfaction of HMRC, they will consider any subsequent application to join or leave a group subject to their normal powers of discretion. (SP, para 3.20).

De Voil Indirect Tax Service. See V2.190B.

31.6 Group supplies using an overseas member

A supply between a member of a VAT group (*'the supplier'*) and another member of the group (*'the UK member'*) is not disregarded under 31.4(*b*) above if the following conditions are satisfied.

(*a*) If there were no group, the supply would be a supply of services falling within *VATA 1995, Sch 5* to a person belonging in the UK.

(*b*) Those services are not within any of the descriptions specified in *VATA 1994, Sch 9* (exempt supplies).

(*c*) The supplier has been supplied (whether or not by a person belonging in the UK) with any services falling within *VATA 1994, Sch 5 paras 1-8* (see 64.27 SUPPLY) which are not within any of the descriptions specified in *VATA 1994, Sch 9* (exempt supplies).

(*d*) The supplier belonged outside the UK when it was supplied with the services in (*c*) above.

(*e*) Those services have been used by the supplier for making the onward supply to the UK member.

The provisions apply even if the bought-in supply only forms a cost component of the onward supply to the UK group member but generally HMRC will treat bought-in supplies as *de minimis* if their value is less than 5% of the value of the onward supply. However, HMRC will not apply this rule rigidly (eg where they suspect that supplies or values have been manipulated to meet the 5% test or where, despite the fact that the 5% test is not met, the charge would be insignificant). The extent to which VAT on the charge could be recovered under the group's partial exemption method, along with the amount of the charge in the context of the group's size, will also be considered when deciding whether a potential charge is *de minimis*. (Business Brief 11/97).

Where the condition are met, the following consequences apply.

(1) The supply is treated as a taxable supply in the UK by the representative member to itself.

(2) Except as allowed by HMRC, the deemed supply by the representative member cannot be taken into account when determining its allowable input tax.

(3) The deemed supply is treated as a supply between connected persons for the purposes of any direction by HMRC as to open market value under *VATA 1994, Sch 6 para 1* (see 69.19 VALUATION).

(4) Subject to (3) above, the deemed supply has the normal value rules for supplies subject to the reverse charge (see 39.4 INTERNATIONAL SERVICES), ie it is calculated on the value of the supply by the overseas member to the UK member. However, by concession, the value may be reduced to the value of the services *purchased* by the overseas group member where

(i) evidence of this valuation can be produced in the UK;

(ii) those services have not been undervalued; and

(iii) the concession is not used for tax avoidance purposes.

(VAT Notice 48, ESC 3.2).

Under (i) above, where a service is bought in by an overseas group member for the exclusive use of a UK group member, copies of invoices from the external supplier are acceptable evidence. Alternatively, businesses may be able to agree with their VAT office that different evidence is adequate (eg evidence that the overseas group member buys in services and applies a fixed mark-up would normally be satisfactory evidence that the value of the bought-in service was equal to the value of the onward supply less the mark-up). Where services are not bought in for exclusive use or mark-ups vary, a fair and reasonable value must be calculated. HMRC have indicated that, in most cases, the evidence required to support the reduced value consists of a summary statement of the overseas member's costs; an outline of the basis on which the overseas member calculates its charge; and a record of the method for reducing the charge to an amount based on the bought-in supplies. (Business Brief 11/97).

Transfers of going concerns. Where a business or part of a business is transferred as a going concern and is treated as neither a supply of goods nor services under 8.10 BUSINESS (or would be so treated if made in the UK), if the transferor satisfied conditions (*c*) and (*d*) above before the transfer and the services in question are used by the transferee to make the supply within (*e*) above, the services are deemed to have been supplied to the transferee at a time when the transferee belonged outside the UK (so that the above conditions are deemed to have been met). The conditions are also deemed to be met in cases involving successive business transfers.

[*VATA 1994, s 43(2A)-(2E); FA 1997, s 41*].

Interim payments. Where interim payments are made in respect of supplies subject to these provisions, VAT must be accounted for on each payment. If the group cannot calculate the reduced value of the charge by the time it has to account for VAT, it should account for VAT from month to month on a best estimate, making an appropriate adjustment at the end of the year.

Misdeclaration penalties. Failure to comply with the provisions may incur a misdeclaration penalty, subject to normal rules. See 52.10 PENALTIES.

(Business Brief 11/97).

De Voil Indirect Tax Service. See V3.267.

31.7 ACQUISITION OF A BUSINESS AS A GOING CONCERN BY A PARTLY EXEMPT VAT GROUP

Where a business, or part of a business, carried on by a taxable person is transferred as a going concern to any member of a VAT group and the transfer of any 'chargeable assets' involved is treated as neither a supply of goods nor a supply of services (see 8.10 BUSINESS), then, subject to below, the chargeable assets are treated (at the time of the transfer) as being supplied to the representative member of the group for the purpose of its business and supplied by that member in the course or furtherance of its business. The supply is at the 'open market value' of the chargeable assets.

Assets are '*chargeable assets*' if their supply in the UK by a taxable person in the course or furtherance of his business would be a taxable supply (and not a zero-rated supply).

'*Open market value*' is the price that would be paid on a sale (on which no VAT was payable) between a buyer and seller who are not in such a relationship as to affect the price.

The above provisions do not apply if

(*a*) the representative member is entitled to credit for the whole of the input tax on supplies to it and acquisitions and importations by it during the VAT period in which the assets are transferred *and* any longer accounting period over which input tax is attributed under the partial exemption provisions;

(*b*) HMRC are satisfied that the assets were assets of the taxable person transferring them more than three years before the day on which they are transferred; or

(*c*) the chargeable assets consist of certain computers, computer equipment, land or buildings covered by the capital goods scheme (see 10.2 CAPITAL GOODS).

A supply treated as made by the representative member under these provisions is not taken into account when determining the allowance of input tax for the group under the partial exemption provisions.

HMRC may reduce the VAT chargeable under these provisions if they are satisfied that the person transferring the chargeable assets has not received credit for the full amount of input tax arising on the supply to him, or acquisition or importation by him, of the chargeable assets.

[*VATA 1994, s 44*].

If the transferor of the assets is unconnected with the VAT group, the consideration paid for the chargeable assets will normally be accepted as the open market value. If VAT is not due on some of the assets, the consideration must be apportioned fairly between the standard-rated and other assets.

In a case where the transferor's partial exemption recovery rate (during the partial exemption tax year in which the assets were purchased) is equal to or less than the transferee's recovery rate (during the partial exemption tax year in which the assets were acquired), the VAT charge will be reduced to nil, although no VAT will be refunded.

(VAT Notice 700/9/02, paras 5.2–5.4).

De Voil Indirect Tax Service. See V3.246.

31.8 SURRENDER OF CORPORATION TAX LOSSES

Under *ICTA 1988, s 402*, companies within a *corporation tax* group may surrender the benefit of corporation tax losses from one to another under certain circumstances. The company receiving the benefit usually makes a payment for the use of the losses. See Tolley's Corporation Tax. Where the two companies involved are also within the same VAT group the surrender has no VAT effect following 31.4 above. Where the two companies are not in the same VAT group HMRC have stated that group relief payments in themselves do not usually give rise to taxable supplies (CCAB Statement TR 344 June 1979). See, however, 44.3 MANAGEMENT SERVICES AND SUPPLIES OF STAFF.

31.9 SUPPLIES THROUGH SUBSIDIARY COMPANIES WITHOUT ASSETS ('SHELL' COMPANIES)

A principal company with one or more trading subsidiaries may transfer the business, assets, and liabilities of those subsidiaries to itself. The principal company therefore becomes the main trading company, and both makes and receives supplies which were formerly made or received by the subsidiaries. The subsidiaries become empty 'shells' and make no trading supplies. Sometimes a subsidiary may continue to employ staff and supply their services to the principal company. In this situation, the principal company must account for VAT on sales to third parties using one of the options below but the subsidiary is still making taxable supplies to the principal company and must account for VAT on these (unless under the VAT registration limit and/or in a group registration with the principal company).

The principal company must account for VAT on supplies to third parties in one of the following ways.

- The principal invoices its customers direct. The shell companies must then deregister unless they supply services to the principal as indicated above.
- The principal applies for a group registration to cover both itself and the shell companies (see 31.2-31.4 above).
- The principal company uses the shell companies as agents and adopts the provisions of *VATA 1994, s 47(3)* (see 3.4 AGENTS). The principal company issues VAT invoices to the shell companies. The shell companies reclaim input tax and, in the same VAT period, issue VAT invoices to the same value to the third parties. Shell companies thus make nil returns unless they supply services to the principal company as indicated above.

(Internal Guidance V1–5, Chapter 3 paras 3.47–3.49).

31.10 HOLDING COMPANIES

The basic functions of a holding company are to acquire and hold shares in subsidiaries from which it may receive dividends; defend itself and its subsidiaries from takeovers; and make disposals. From time to time it may invest, deposit or lend money, and issue or sell shares. Some of these activities are outside the scope of VAT while others are exempt. A holding company which has no other activities is not eligible to register for VAT and is not able to recover any VAT on its purchases.

Registration. Holding companies are liable to register for VAT where they have taxable trading activities, supply management services to subsidiaries or are included in a VAT group with trading subsidiaries.

If 'management services' are the only supplies which a holding company appears to make, HMRC are likely to examine these carefully to ensure that an actual supply has taken place. If a supply has not taken place, the holding company will not be able to register for VAT. HMRC regard the following factors as indications that no supply by the holding company has taken place.

- No staff are employed by the holding company.
- The directors are common to both the holding company and the recipient of the services.
- The holding company has no business premises or assets.
- There is no visible or documentary evidence of supplies other than the invoice and/or book-keeping entry.
- The business is unable to specify what supplies are covered by the charge.

(Internal Guidance V1–3, para 10.5).

In *Cibo Participations SA v Directeur régional des impôts du Nord-Pas-de-Calais, CJEC [2002] STC 460 (TVC 21.80)* the CJEC held that the management of subsidiary companies could qualify as an economic activity if it was accompanied by activities such as the performance of administrative, financial, commercial or technical services.

See also *Polysar Investments Netherlands BV v Inspecteur der Invoerrechten en Accijnzen, CJEC [1993] STC 222 (TVC 21.73)* and *Newmir plc (VTD 10102) (TVC 7.111)*.

Input tax deduction. Subject to below, deduction of input tax for holding companies is calculated on the following basis.

- Input tax on supplies to the holding company must be attributed to taxable, exempt or other non-taxable outputs to the greatest possible extent, and the normal rules applied.
- Any residual input tax which cannot be directly attributed will be accepted as a general overhead of the taxable person.
- The amount of the residual input tax which can be recovered will be determined in accordance with the partial exemption rules.

Most costs related to acquisitions and defence against takeovers fall into the 'overhead' category.

However, where a VAT-registered holding company is not

- an active trading company in its own right, or
- grouped with active trading subsidiaries making taxable supplies outside the group, or
- providing genuine management services to separate trading subsidiaries,

it will not be able to recover input tax on costs incurred in acquiring another company, disposing of a subsidiary, restructuring the group or any subsidiary, or holding investments. This is because HMRC do not regard such costs as relating to any taxable supply. This change follows the decision in *Polysar Investments Netherlands BV v Inspecteur der Invoerrechten en Accijnzen, CJEC [1993] STC 222 (TVC 21.73)* which held that the basic activities of a holding company are not business activities and there is no right to deduct the VAT incurred in carrying out such activities.

(C & E News Release 59/93, 10 September 1993).

In *Empresa de Desenvolvimento Mineiro SGPS v Fazenda Publica, CJEC Case C–77/01, [2005] STC 65 (TVC 21.294)* the CJEC held that the simple sale of securities (eg holdings in investment funds) did not constitute economic activities and that placement in investment funds did not constitute supplies of services effected for a consideration. As a result, turnover relating to such transactions should be excluded from any partial exemption calculation. However, the annual granting by a holding company of interest-bearing loans to companies in which it had shareholdings and placements by that holding company in bank deposits or in securities (eg Treasury notes or certificate of deposit) constituted economic activities carried out by a taxable person acting as such (and where exempt from VAT under *EC Sixth Directive, Art 13B(d)*). In any partial exemption calculation, such transactions were to be regarded as 'incidental transactions' insofar as they involved 'only very limited use of assets or services subject to VAT' and it was for the national court to establish whether this was the case.

See also *BLP Group plc v C & E Commrs, CJEC [1995] STC 424 (TVC 21.279)* where input tax on professional fees incurred in connection with the disposal of shares in a subsidiary company to pay debts was held as being not recoverable as relating to the exempt sale of shares (rather than recoverable as relating to the payment of debts derived from taxable transactions effected by the company).

Dividends and interest. Dividends received by a holding company from subsidiaries where there is no involvement in the management are to be excluded from total income in making any proportionate calculations (*Satam SA v Minister Responsible for the Budget, CJEC 1993, [1997] STC 226 (TVC 21.291)*). This was confirmed in *Floridienne SA v Belgian State; Berginvest SA v Belgian State, CJEC [2000] STC 1044 (TVC 21.293)* where the court also held that interest paid on loans to subsidiaries should be similarly excluded where the relevant loans did not constitute an economic activity of the holding company within *EC Sixth Directive, Art 4(2)*. Whether the loans were within the charge to VAT was for the national courts to decide.

32 Health and Welfare

Cross-references. See 12.8 CHARITIES for charity funded equipment for medical and veterinary use; 34.15(15) IMPORTS for relief from VAT on the importation of various health-related goods.

De Voil Indirect Tax Service. See V4.146.

The contents of this chapter are as follows.

32.1 EXEMPT HEALTH SUPPLIES

EC legislation. See 22.17(*b*)–(*e*), (*g*), (*k*), (*o*) and (*p*) EUROPEAN COMMUNITY LEGISLATION.

UK legislation. Supplies within 32.2 to 32.14 below are exempt. This includes supplies by '*health professionals*' ie the following professionals when they are enrolled or registered on the appropriate statutory register.

- Medical practitioners (see 32.2 below).
- Ophthalmic and dispensing opticians (see 32.3 below).
- Professionals registered under the *Professions Supplementary to Medicine Act 1960* (see 32.4 below).
- Osteopaths (see 32.4 below).
- Chiropractors (see 32.4 below).
- Nurses, midwives and health visitors (see 32.5 below).
- Hearing aid dispensers (see 32.6 below).
- Dentists; dental auxiliaries and dental chemists (see 32.8 below).
- Pharmacists (see 32.10 below).

Services of health professionals (whether provided direct to the patient or to a third party such as an employer or an insurer) are exempt provided (*a*) the services consist of care, diagnosis, treatment or assessment of a patient;

(*b*) the services are within the discipline in which the health professional is registered to practise; and

(*c*) performance of the services require application of the knowledge, skills and judgement acquired in the course of professional training.

Examples of exempt supplies of services that meet the above conditions when provided by the appropriate health professional include

- medical or dental examination, assessment, diagnosis or treatment of a patient;
- certain medical or dental reports (but see the decision in *d'Ambrumenil* under 32.2(4) below);
- certification of medical sickness or fitness (but again see the decision in *d'Ambrumenil* under 32.2(4) below);
- personal or nursing care provided in a patient's own home; and
- pharmaceutical advice.

Examples of services that are not exempt from VAT

- Services not performed by an appropriately qualified and registered health professional, except when either directly supervised by such a person (see 32.9 below) or provided within a hospital or similar institution (see 32.11 below).
- Any service, the performance of which does not require application of professional knowledge, skills or judgement by a health professional. This includes any service not related to health or medical care.
- Services not aimed at the prevention, diagnosis, treatment or cure of a disease or health disorder. Examples include paternity testing or the writing of articles for journals.
- Services directly supervised by a pharmacist.
- Services that are predominantly medico-legal services (see 32.2 below).
- General administrative services such as countersigning passport applications, providing character references and photocopying medical records.

Clinical trials. Whether such work is exempt depends upon the extent to which the trial requires the medical assessment, diagnosis or treatment of patients. If analytical testing services are provided that involve little contact, or no contact at all, with patients, this service is standard-rated.

Where a health professional is required in the course of a clinical trial to administer drugs to a patient, or to monitor or assess a patient's condition, the supply is exempt from VAT provided that the conditions outlined above are met.

(VAT Notice 701/57/02, paras 2.1–2.3, 2.6).

32.2 **Doctors**

The supply of services by a person registered or enrolled on the register of medical practitioners, or the register of medical practitioners with limited registration, is exempt. [*VATA 1994, Sch 9 Group 7 Item 1*(*a*)].

See 32.1 above for an overview of the conditions for exemption.

HMRC regard exemption as extending to supplies of goods which are a minor and inseparable part of the service of medical care, eg bandages, drugs, medicines. (VAT Notice 701/57/02, para 2.4).

The following is a list of the principal activities undertaken by doctors and their VAT liabilities.

(1) **NHS work**

Most GPs performing NHS work do so as independent contractors rather than as NHS employees. This means that individual GPs and partnerships are making business supplies to the NHS. NHS allowance payments or reimbursements in respect of the following activities (calculated in accordance with the 'Statement of Fees and Allowances') are always exempt when received by a GP.

- Asthma or diabetes management.
- Basic practice allowance.
- Cervical cytology targets.
- Child health surveillance.
- Contraceptive services.
- Deprivation payments.
- Emergency treatment.
- Health promotion.
- Minor surgery.
- Maternity medical services.
- Night visits.
- Payments in respect of temporary residents.
- Registration fees.
- Rural practice payments.
- Standard capitation fees.
- Vaccinations and immunisations.

(VAT Notice 701/57/02, paras 4.1, 4.4).

(2) **Payments for dispensing**

Payments for NHS dispensing of drugs can, in certain circumstances, be zero-rated under *VATA 1994, Sch 8 Group 12 Item 1A* (see 32.15 below). Fees for private dispensing are always standard-rated.

(3) **Payments for personally administering drugs**

All GPs can administer drugs at the time of treatment (whether or not they are also NHS dispensing GPs). HMRC have always taken the view that drugs and other items (eg vaccines, anaesthetics, injections, diagnostic reagents, intra-uterine, contraceptive caps and diaphragms, and pessaries) personally administered ('immediately administered' in Scotland) to the patient by the doctor at the time of treatment are an inseparable part of the exemption for medical care under *VATA 1994, Sch 9 Group 7 Item 1(a)* above. This has now been confirmed in *C & E Commrs v Dr Beynon & Partners, HL 2004, [2005] STC 55 (TVC 19.6)*. Reversing the earlier tribunal decision in *Drs Woodings, Rees, Crossthwaite & Jones (VTD 16175) (TVC 19.5)* and applying the principles laid down in *Card Protection Plan Ltd v C & E Commrs, CJEC [1999] STC 270 (TVC 21.223)*, the court held that, where drugs are administered at the time of treatment, there is a single supply of exempt services, the transaction being the patient's visit to the doctors which should not be split into smaller units.

(4) **Private treatment of patients**

In *d'Ambrumenil v C & E Commrs; Dispute Resolution Services Ltd v C & E Commrs, CJEC 2003, [2005] STC 650 (TVC 21.196)* the court held that exemption (under *EC Sixth Directive, Art 13A1(c)*) applies to

- medical examinations of individuals for employers or insurance companies;
- the taking of blood or other bodily samples to test for the presence of viruses, infections or other diseases on behalf of employers or insurers; and
- the certification of medical fitness (eg as to fitness to travel) where those services are intended principally to protect the health of the person concerned;

but does not apply to

- giving certificates as to a person's medical condition for purposes such as entitlement to war pension (see also *Unterpertinger v Pensionversicherungsanstalt der Arbeiter, CJEC 20 November 2003 unreported (TVC 21.195)* where the services of a doctor in making an expert report on a person's health in order to support a claim for disability pension was held to be subject to VAT);
- medical examinations conducted with a view to preparing medical reports regarding
  - (i) issues of liability and the quantification of damages for individuals contemplating personal injury litigation; or
  - (ii) professional medical negligence for individuals contemplating litigation; or
- the preparation of medical reports, either following such examinations or based on medical notes without conducting a medical examination.

HMRC are taking legal advice and are in contact with the British Medical Association to establish which medical services would be affected by the decision in *d'Ambrumenil*. But in the meantime, doctors and other health professionals are not required to take any action to register for VAT or charge VAT on these services. Any changes will be implemented from a future date and there will be no compulsory back-dating of VAT registration. (Business Brief 29/03).

See also *D v W, CJEC 2000, [2002] STC 1200 (TVC 21.193)* where the court ruled that exemption applies to the provision of medical care and that this does not include medical interventions carried out for a purpose other than that of diagnosing, treating and, if possible, curing diseases and health disorders.

Services not having such a therapeutic aim are therefore subject to VAT and exemption does not apply to services of establishing the genetic affinity of individuals through biological tests. In that particular case, fees of a medical expert instructed by a court to establish on the basis of a genetic test whether the claimant in the proceedings could be the child of the defendant were held to be subject to VAT.

Subject to the above, see Internal Guidance V1–7, Chapter 22 para 7.4 for a list of services provided by doctors and HMRC's view of their liabilities.

(5) **Fees for medico-legal services**

These are services that consist of both medical and legal elements. Examples of medico-legal services that might be carried out by a doctor include

- negotiation or advocacy;
- arbitration, mediation or conciliation;
- investigation of the validity of an insurance or negligence claim;
- consideration of medical reports and other evidence with a view to resolving disputes; and
- any work carried out for lawyers and insurers.

Subject to further consideration of the decision in *d'Ambrumenil* (see (4) above), HMRC treat these services as standard-rated where the predominant element is legal. Services that are predominantly medical are exempt, even when performed in the course of a legal or insurance case or on behalf of an insurance company or employer.

(VAT Notice 701/57/02, para 2.5).

(6) **Fundholding management allowance**

The payment of the 'management allowance' to a fundholding GP does not represent the consideration for any supply but simply the reimbursement to the GP of costs incurred for being a fundholder. These payments are outside the scope of VAT. (Internal Guidance V1–7, Chapter 22 para 2.5.5).

(7) **Miscellaneous services**

Services provided by GPs that are standard-rated include

- administrative services such as the signing of passport applications;
- clinical trials or market research services for drug companies that do not involve the care or assessment of a patient; and
- paternity testing.

(VAT Notice 701/57/02, para 4.3).

Deputising services to doctors. The provision of a deputy for a person registered in the register of medical practitioners or the register of medical practitioners with limited registration is exempt. [*VATA 1994, Sch 9 Group 7 Item 5*].

A deputising service is an arrangement under which a substitute doctor (the deputy) is made available when the patient's own doctor is not available. Typically, a number of GPs subscribe to a deputising company. They receive a package consisting of deputising cover provided by other GPs (who may themselves be fellow subscribers) and a range of accompanying administrative and support services.

Item 5 is intended to cover more than the services of the deputy (as these would be exempt under *VATA 1994, Sch 9 Group 7 Item 1*(*a*) by virtue of him being a registered medical practitioner). HMRC regard *Item 5* as exempting the organisation of providing a deputy so that exemption can apply to a range of accompanying administrative and support services, including

- agency registration and administration fees,
- charges for transport,
- telephone and stationery costs, and
- any other charges integral to the supply of a deputy medical practitioner's services

provided the following conditions are met.

- The back-up services must be provided by the same body that makes the deputising services of the GP available (ie where a deputising company buys in the services of administrative staff, hire of transport, etc in order to provide its services, the company can exempt its supply but the third party is making a separate supply of services to the company which is not covered by the exemption).
- The back-up services must be integral to the provision of a deputy for a medical practitioner. Where, for example, a doctor engages the services of someone who in his absence merely takes calls and messages and passes them onto him when he next returns, HMRC do not regard this supply as integral to the provision of a deputy but as a separate supply of taxable administrative services.

The charges made by a deputising company to a subscribing GP may include the following, all of which represent the consideration for the company's exempt supply of deputising services.

- A registration or joining fee.
- A fixed fee per call answered by the deputy (which may or may not include an additional charge for drugs used).
- A fixed fee per night/weekend/month sometimes with an additional fee if the number of calls dealt with exceeds a stipulated or minimum number.
- An additional charge for telephone services (exempt only where they are integral as indicated above).

The charge made by the deputy and usually paid by the company is exempt under *VATA 1994, Sch 9 Group 7 Item 1*(*a*).

(VAT Notice 701/57/02, paras 6.1, 6.2; Internal Guidance V1–7, Chapter 22 paras 2.5.8–2.5.10).

Visiting EC practitioners. Included in the exemption under *VATA 1994, Sch 9 Group 7 Item 1*(*a*) is the supply of services in an urgent case as mentioned in the *Medical Act 1983, s 18*(*3*) by a person who is not registered in the visiting EC practitioners list in the register of medical practitioners at the time he performs the services but who is entitled to be registered in accordance with that *section*. [*VATA 1994, Sch 9 Group 7 Note 4*].

32.3 **Opticians**

Overview. The supply of services by a qualified optician is exempt (see below). Exemption can also extend to the services of unqualified staff if they are directly supervised by a qualified optician (see 32.9 below). But the supply of spectacles and contact lenses is standard-rated (see below). As the charge for spectacles or contact lenses normally includes an element for services, an apportionment is required.

Supplies of services. The supply of services by persons registered in either of the registers of ophthalmic opticians or the register of dispensing opticians kept under the *Opticians Act 1989* or either of the lists under *section 9* of that *Act* of bodies corporate carrying on business as ophthalmic opticians or as dispensing opticians is exempt. [*VATA 1994, Sch 9 Group 7 Item 1(b)*].

See 32.1 above for an overview of the conditions for exemption.

Opticians can be divided into the following categories.

(*a*) *Ophthalmic opticians* (also called optometrists) are qualified to perform eye tests and write prescriptions. They can dispense both spectacles and contact lenses. Their supplies of eye testing, medical care and dispensing are exempt.

(*b*) *Dispensing opticians* are not qualified to perform eye tests or write prescriptions, but are qualified to dispense spectacles. Some hold an additional qualification which permits them to dispense contact lenses and, if necessary, modify a prescription where contact lenses are required. In the event that contact lenses are required, a second check of the eye can be performed by a dispensing optician with the additional qualification. Such an optician can also provide certain other medical services such as a glaucoma test and a slit lamp examination. Any supplies of dispensing, plus other medical services supplied in relation to contact lens medical care, are exempt.

(*c*) *Ophthalmologists* are registered medical practitioners and their services are exempt under 32.2 above. While they often carry out eye tests, they rarely supply goods.

(*d*) *Unregistered dispensers* can dispense sight correcting spectacles (but not contact lenses) from a prescription, but not to children under 16 or to blind or partially-sighted people. A registered optician must be on the premises before they can dispense spectacles. In order to exempt their supplies, they must demonstrate that the dispensing is carried out by that registered optician or directly supervised for VAT purposes by that registered optician, according to the guidelines for the direct supervision of unqualified staff in 32.9 below.

(*e*) *Other suppliers*. The provision of spectacles is de-regulated. Anyone can sell ready-made reading spectacles provided the spectacles conform to the requisite British Standards and are not supplied to children under 16 or the partially sighted. Such suppliers cannot dispense and so their supplies are standard-rated.

Exempt supplies include medical tests (eye testing, slit lamp examination of cornea, keratometry measurement of corneal curvature, measurement of visible iris diameter, and glaucoma testing). Any charge made for professional advice is also exempt.

Standard-rated supplies include services which do not amount to care or treatment (eg repairs, repolishing and cleaning contact lenses) are standard-rated.

(Internal Guidance V1–7, Chapter 22 paras 2.6.3, 8.3, 8.5).

Supplies of spectacles. Supplies of spectacles are standard-rated unless the goods are certain specialised appliances designed solely for use by the handicapped (eg artificial eyes and certain low vision aids), in which case they are zero-rated (see 32.23 below). Supplies of ancillary goods (eg cases, cleaning solution) are also standard-rated.

In *C & E Commrs v Leightons Ltd, QB [1995] STC 458 (TVC 31.7)*, the court held that the price paid for spectacles includes two separate supplies – a standard-rated supply of goods (the spectacles) and an exempt supply of opticians' services. Although this decision pre-dated the criteria for single/multiple supplies set out by the CJEC in *Card Protection Plan Ltd v C & E Commrs, CJEC [1999] STC 270 (TVC 21.223)* (see 64.6 SUPPLY) a tribunal has subsequently accepted that the decision in *Leightons* was correct in law and that payments should be apportioned (*Leightons (No 2); Eye-Tech Opticians (No 3) (VTD 17498) (TVC 31.8)*). The tribunal held that it was implicit in the *Card Protection Plan* decision that there could be separate exempt supplies of medical care together with standard-rated supplies of goods. The VAT system would be distorted if the supply of corrected spectacles were to be treated as a single standard-rated supply, as this would not give effect to the exemption in the *EC Sixth Directive* which is mandatory.

As a result of these decisions, it is necessary to adopt the following approach when determining the liability of the supplies of spectacles.

(i) Determine whether the establishment supplying the spectacles qualifies for exemption in its own right (by being registered as a body corporate under the *Opticians Act 1989*) or whether the supply is by an optician who is a sole proprietor with the necessary qualifications to carry out all the dispensing work. If so, an element of the charge made for spectacles is exempt (and it is not necessary to consider (ii) below).

(ii) Determine whether dispensing is carried out by, or directly supervised by, an optician qualified as set out in (*a*)–(*e*) above. Two situations commonly occur. First, an establishment run by a partnership or other corporate body may mostly employ unqualified staff but may also have qualified staff present on a permanent basis (eg as employees or because a partner or director has the necessary qualifications). Secondly, an establishment may have no permanent qualified staff, but may bring in qualified opticians for specified periods as locums.

    If either of these situations apply, the role that the qualified individual performs must be determined. If he only carries out eye tests, supplies of spectacles made by the unqualified optical establishment must be wholly standard-rated (although the eye test will be exempt whether the qualified optician or shop charges the patient for it). For exemption to apply to an element of the supply of spectacles, the optical practice must be able to show that the qualified optician either carries out dispensing or directly supervises the unqualified dispensing staff.

(iii) If the conditions in (i) or (ii) above are satisfied, the total charge for a pair of spectacles should be divided into its standard-rated and exempt elements.

(Internal Guidance V1–7, Chapter 22 para 2.6.5).

There are no set methods of apportionment of spectacle sales between exempt and standard-rated elements. If practicable, opticians should calculate VAT by separating the standard-rated and exempt elements at the point of sale. If this is not possible, an individual method must be agreed with HMRC which gives a fair and reasonable valuation of VAT payable without placing an undue burden on the optician.

Suggested method of apportionment based on full cost apportionment.

(1) *Establish the cost of goods.* This is made up of the following.

(*a*) Cost of purchase of bought-in frames.

(*b*) Cost of purchase of bought-in lenses. (Where, rather than buying in lenses cut to individual patients' prescriptions, a business purchases blank lenses and glazes them in-house, establish the cost of glazing and the directly attributable expenses incurred on consumables. Indirect costs such as depreciation of equipment should not be included.)

(*c*) Cost of delivery if the business has frames/lenses delivered from a central point of distribution to a chain of outlets. (The cost must be apportioned where the delivery charge also relates to other goods such as cases, chains, contact lens fluids, etc.)

These costs should include any VAT.

(2) *Establish the cost of services.* This is made up of the following.

(*a*) 'Direct costs' of any ophthalmic optician (OO) relating to spectacle sales. An OO is allowed to carry out sight tests as well as dispense spectacles. Eye tests have always been exempt and opticians need to determine what proportion of the cost of an OO is attributable to the exempt eye test and what proportion is to be attributed to the exempt dispensing service element of spectacle sales. In some practices, the OO may also perform various administrative activities. If the actual costs attributable to each activity are not identifiable, the total costs will need to be apportioned, possibly using the formula

$$\frac{\text{Income from spectacles}}{\text{Income from spectacles} + \text{contact lenses} + \text{sight tests}} \times \text{direct cost of OO}$$

This formula may not be appropriate for all opticians and alternatives may be agreed with HMRC. For example, if an OO spends half his time providing eye examinations and the other half dispensing, it would be more appropriate simply to use half the costs for the purposes of the apportionment calculation. An optician who considers that factors other than time should be taken into account in the apportionment should identify those factors and submit an appropriate apportionment method for HMRC's approval.

In general, HMRC are prepared to accept that an element of an OO's time is spent on dispensing activity. The actual level of dispensing activity should be demonstrated and agreed with HMRC.

(*b*) 'Direct costs' of any dispensing optician (DO). The direct labour costs to the practice of the time that any DO spends in the dispensing of spectacles must be calculated.

(*c*) 'Direct costs' of directly supervised persons. A proportion of the direct labour costs of those unqualified employees providing a dispensing service, and who either work as part of a qualifying body corporate or who are directly supervised by a registered optician (see 32.9 below) may also be included in the calculation. The actual percentage of these costs relating to dispensing duties must be agreed between the trader and HMRC.

'*Direct costs*' should be calculated using conventional accounting procedures. In calculating the direct cost of OOs, DOs and directly supervised persons, the following principal costs should be included (although this is not necessarily an exhaustive list).

- Salary
- Employers' national insurance contributions
- Pension contributions by employer
- Cost of provision of vehicle to OOs and DOs involved in dispensing of spectacles
- Optical training of opticians and supervised persons
- Professional body subscriptions incurred by the practice (only in respect of services received, not goods)
- Professional indemnity costs incurred by the practice
- Recruitment costs

These costs should include any VAT.

(3) *Calculation of percentage of income from spectacle sales attributable to taxable supplies.* Once the above costs of goods and services have been calculated, it is necessary to establish the average cost of each supply. This is achieved by dividing the costs of the goods and services by the number of spectacles (new and reglazed) dispensed in the period.

The taxable element of the sale is then calculated using the formula

$$\text{VAT due on sale} = \frac{\text{Cost of goods}}{\text{Cost of goods and services}} \times \text{spectacles income} \times \frac{7}{47}$$

Having established the percentage applicable to taxable sales, this percentage should be used as the basis of the optician's VAT return. As businesses change over time, the percentage should be recalculated whenever a major change takes place in the optician's business, and in any case at three-yearly intervals. HMRC consider a 'major change' as constituting anything which significantly alters the costs of the supplies including

- opening an additional branch or closing an existing one;
- increasing or decreasing the number of OOs, DOs or supervised staff employed;
- restructuring the practice (eg where an OO who has previously performed both eye examinations and dispensing services exclusively performs eye examinations); and
- changing from buying in lenses to glazing in-house (or vice versa).

New business. When a new practice opens, it is not possible to immediately perform an accurate apportionment of the charges made for spectacles and dispensing, particularly if the apportionment method is based on costs. New practices should therefore agree a provisional basis of apportionment with HMRC and revise the apportionment in the light of actual costs at the end of the first year's trading.

(VAT Information Sheet 8/99).

Contact lenses. As with spectacles, the supply of contact lenses is a mixed supply of goods and services in which the services element extends to all types of professional services, including measuring and fitting.

It is necessary to consider the same three stages as in (i)–(iii) under the heading *Spectacles* above to determine the liability of supplies of contact lens.

The following table shows the most common elements involved in the supply of contact lenses and their VAT liabilities.

	Standard-rated	*Exempt*
Eye tests		Medical tests (see under the heading *Supplies of services* above)
Consideration for contact lenses (to be apportioned)	Lenses	Fitting tests (includes assessment of fit using magnification, assessment of vision with contact lenses, over-refraction with contact lenses)
	Supply of disposable or replacement lenses where this does not involve new check ups or refitting	Further professional advice (includes instructions on insertion or removal, instruction on cleaning and maintenance, discussion of wearing schedule, advice on type of lens material, advice on brand of lens, advice on coatings, tints etc, and final decision on best wearing schedule)
	Repolishing and cleaning contact lenses	Follow up action (including checking of fit and comfort, review of insertion and removal procedures on follow up visits, lens assessment and trial of different types and altering power or shape of lenses)
	Lipo treatment to soft lenses	Producing a report on the condition of a patient's eye(s)
	Accessories (eg lens fluids and cases)	

The following table shows the costs which should be allocated to standard and exempt elements respectively.

Standard-rated supplies	*Exempt supplies*
Cost of lenses and accessories and other consumables	Sight test equipment
Delivery of lenses to sales premises	Prescription forms
Insurance of lenses	Optician's remuneration directly attributable to dispensing
Storage costs	

Costs of manufacture (where a business makes the lenses itself) – includes materials, labour, storage, manufacturing equipment, delivery charges to place of manufacture, equipment maintenance costs and equipment overheads Display equipment	

Any method of apportionment can be used (including one of those in 47.4 OUTPUT TAX) provided it gives a fair and reasonable result and can be supported by valid calculations.

(Internal Guidance V1–7, Chapter 22 paras 2.6.6, 2.6.7, 8.5, 8.6).

Replacement/aftercare schemes. These usually involve the wearer, when purchasing the lens, paying an additional fixed fee which entitles him to a range of benefits. These vary from supplier to supplier but might include either regular check ups and sight test examinations, maintenance of the lenses and discounts on replacement lenses or new supplies of disposable lenses at regular intervals throughout a given period.

If the replacement scheme entitles the wearer to no more than the replacement of lenses or supplies of disposable lenses with no sight tests or check ups, the whole supply is standard-rated. For other schemes, HMRC accept that traders can apportion their supplies between standard-rated and exempt elements. As with supplies of spectacles and contact lenses, exemption cannot apply unless the dispensing or fitting elements are carried out or directly supervised by, a registered or enrolled optician. The following table lists some typical benefits available under these schemes and indicates whether they are standard-rated or exempt.

Standard-rated benefits	*Exempt benefits*
Polishing and deproteinising of lenses	Periodic check ups
Lipo treatment to soft lenses	Examinations connected with the above
Replacement lenses or uprating of power, shape, etc	Sight test examinations
Supply of lens case	Lens assessment and trial of different types
Discount on lenses	
Discounts on contact lens solutions and accessories	
Discounts on spare contact lenses	
Credit for existing lenses when upgrading to a higher type	

(Internal Guidance V1–7, Chapter 22 para 8.7).

Free eye tests. Some opticians offer free eye tests to attract business.

- If the patient can leave an optician offering a free eye test, with either a clean bill of health or with a prescription which he is able to take elsewhere, then there is no consideration and no supply for VAT purposes. Any costs relating to the free supply should not be included when the optician apportions supplies of spectacles or contact lenses.

- If the 'free' test is conditional on the purchase of spectacles or contact lenses, there is a supply for consideration and the optician must apportion the charge made for spectacles or contact lenses.

(Internal Guidance V1–7, Chapter 22 para 2.6.13).

NHS vouchers (available to children, full-time students under 19, people on low income and those requiring complex lenses) have a face value and are part payment for the supply of exempt services and standard-rated goods. They are treated in the same way as cheques for VAT purposes. (Internal Guidance V1–7, Chapter 22 para 2.6.15).

Hospital optical dispensing. HMRC do not accept that an optician who happens to operate from a hospital premises can make wholly exempt supplies of spectacles or contact lenses under *VATA 1994, Sch 9 Group 7 Item 4* (see 32.11 below). They take the view that *Item 4* allows exemption for the provision of care or medical or surgical treatment in a hospital. As opticians do not provide this, the goods that they dispense cannot benefit from that exemption. This view was supported by the tribunal in *Coleman (VTD 10215) (TVC 31.40)* (which related to hearing aid dispensers in hospitals). HMRC do, however, accept that in specialist eye hospitals, any optical goods supplied to patients are incidental to that hospital's supply of medical care to its patients and are thus exempt under *Item 4* as goods 'in connection with' the supply of services. (Internal Guidance V1–7, Chapter 22 para 2.6.17).

32.4 **Supplementary professions, osteopaths and chiropractors**

The supply of services by persons on the following registers is exempt. See 32.1 above for an overview on the conditions for exemption.

(*a*) Any register kept under the *Health Professions Order 2001* (*SI 2002/254*). [*VATA 1994, Sch 9 Group 7 Items 1*(*c*); *SI 2002/254*]. These professionals are

arts therapists;

chiropodists;

clinical scientists;

dieticians;

medical laboratory scientific officers;

occupational therapists;

orthoptists;

paramedics;

physiotherapists;

prosthetists and orthotists;

radiographers; and

speech and language therapists.

(VAT Notice 710/57/02, para 2.1).

Any drugs, appliances etc which are administered by the above practitioners at the time of treatment are considered a minor and inseparable part of their professional service and also exempt. Standard-rating applies to

- supplies of goods which are not minor and inseparable; and

- supplies by practitioners who are not registered under the *Health Professions Order 2001* (eg acupuncturists, psychologists, psychotherapists and psychoanalysts). (Psychiatrists are qualified medical practitioners and are exempt under 32.2 above.)

(*b*) The register of osteopaths maintained in accordance with the provisions of the *Osteopaths Act 1993*. [*VATA 1994, Sch 9 Group 7 Items 1*(*ca*)*; SI 1998/1294*].

An applicant who successfully applies to be entered on the register administered by the General Osteopathic Council (GOC) receives a letter to Customs confirming that the named osteopath is on the register. This letter should be sent to Customs with any application to deregister for VAT purposes as evidence of entry on the register of osteopaths. (Internal Guidance V1–7, Chapter 22 para 2.10.2).

(*c*) The register of chiropractors maintained in accordance with the provisions of the *Chiropractors Act 1994*. [*VATA 1994, Sch 9 Group 7 Items 1*(*cb*)*; SI 1999/1575*].

An applicant who successfully applies to be entered on the register administered by the General Chiropractic Council (GCC) receives a letter of confirmation, giving the registration number and effective date of registration. This letter can be sent to Customs with any application to deregister for VAT purposes as evidence of entry on the register of chiropractors. Some applicants may be given a 'conditional' registration where detailed conditions must be complied with if registration is to continue. For VAT purposes, a chiropractor with conditional registration qualifies for exemption but, should this lapse, exemption no longer applies. (Internal Guidance V1–7, Chapter 22 para 2.10.3).

32.5 Nurses, midwives and health visitors

The supply of services by a person registered in the register of qualified nurses, midwives and health visitors kept under *Nurses, Midwives and Health Visitors Act 1997, s 7* is exempt. [*VATA 1994, Sch 9 Group 7 Item 1*(*d*)*; Nurses, Midwives and Health Visitors Act 1997, Sch 4*].

See 32.1 above for an overview of the conditions for exemption.

Exemption only applies to the professional services for which the nurse, etc has been trained. HMRC do not accept that, for example, a nurse can exempt supplies of acupuncture or osteopathy under this provision.

Qualified personnel. The supply of services by registered nurses, midwives and health visitors are exempt under *Item 1*(*d*) above wherever they are performed (in the UK).

Unqualified personnel. The supply of services by a nursing auxiliary (or other similar unqualified nursing personnel) is not exempt under *Item 1*(*d*) above. As a result, where unqualified personnel

- supply services to individuals in their own homes or in establishments which are not approved, licensed, etc, in the rare occasions that their income exceeds the VAT registration threshold, they must register for VAT and charge VAT at the standard rate on their supplies; and
- supply services to hospitals or state-regulated institutions, their services are exempt under 32.11 below provided they form part of the care made to patients. (This includes supplies made to NHS hospitals even though their provision of care to patients is non-business and outside the scope.)

Nursing agencies. Nurses frequently register with agencies who find them work in hospitals, nursing homes and similar establishments, and homes of individual patients. Some of these agencies may act as agent and others may act as principal in their supply of nursing personnel. See 3.13 AGENTS for the treatment of employment bureau generally.

Where a nursing agency acts as principal in the supply of nurses or auxiliaries, the agency makes one supply to the client. This supply is exempt in the following circumstances.

- The supply is one of the services of a person registered under *Item 1*(*d*) above. This is because *VATA 1994, Sch 9 Group 7 Note 2* exempts a supply by a person who is not so registered (ie the agency) where the services are wholly performed by a person who is so registered.
- The supply is one of the services of an unqualified nurse and either
  - (i) that person will be 'directly supervised' by a qualified person (see 32.9 below); or
  - (ii) those services are supplied to a hospital (NHS or private) or similar institution and form part of the care made to the patient (see 32.11 below).

Where the above criteria are not met, the supply is standard-rated (eg where it takes place in a private home, and is not performed or directly supervised by a medically registered person).

Where the nursing agency acts as agent, the supply of nursing services is made by the nurse or auxiliary. In the rare occasion where income exceeds the VAT registration limit, an auxiliary must register and account for VAT at the standard rate. A qualified nurse, etc. will not have to register in respect of exempt supplies. The agency must account for VAT on its supply of agency services, regardless of to whom the supply is made and whether it is in relation to a nurse or auxiliary.

(Internal Guidance V1–7, Chapter 22 para 2.11).

32.6 **Hearing aid dispensers**

A supply of services by a person registered in

- the register of dispensers of hearing aids, or
- the register of persons employing such dispensers maintained under the *Hearing Aid Council Act 1968, s 2*

is exempt. [*VATA 1994, Sch 9 Group 7 Item 1*(*e*)].

See 32.1 above for an overview of the conditions for exemption.

Services covered by the exemption include

- the examination of a patient;
- testing a patient's hearing (including an audiogram test carried out by a dispenser for a doctor or an employer as well as a test carried out for a private patient); and
- providing professional advice (eg choice of device, instruction in use, cleaning, etc).

Liability of supply of hearing aids, etc. Most hearing aids are dispensed free by the NHS as part of its provision of healthcare. Such supplies are outside the scope of VAT. Otherwise supplies of hearing aids and their repair, batteries, accessories and spare parts are standard-rated (apart from hearing aids designed for the auditory training of deaf children which are zero-rated, see 32.23(6) below).

Apportionment of value of supply. Where a supply includes an element for dispensing services and the hearing aid, the criteria set out by the CJEC in *Card Protection Plan Ltd v C & E Commrs, CJEC [1999] STC 270 (TVC 21.223)* (see 64.6 SUPPLY) must be applied to determine whether there is a single or multiple supply.

Where a multiple supply is established, a fair proportion of the total payment must be allocated to the standard-rated supply of the hearing aid, etc. and the exempt supply of services. No set method is laid down. See 47.4 OUTPUT TAX for various methods of apportionment. HMRC suggest that *Example 3* in that paragraph is likely to be the most appropriate and easily operable method for hearing aid dispensers provided the level of uplift adopted is consistent with the trader's level of profitability.

Hospital dispensing. Hearing dispensers who operate from hospital premises cannot exempt their supplies of hearing aids under 32.11 below as their activities are not the provision of care or medical or surgical treatment (see *Coleman (VTD 10215) (TVC 31.40)*). HMRC do accept, however, that specialist hospitals for hearing disorders can exempt any goods supplied in connection with their supply of medical care (as the patients usually have complex medical problems and do not require the services of a 'normal' commercial hearing aid dispenser).

(Internal Guidance V1–7, Chapter 22 para 2.12).

32.7 Hire of equipment

The letting on hire of goods in connection with a supply of other services within *VATA 1994, Sch 9 Group 7 Item 1* (see 32.2 to 32.6 above) is exempt. [*VATA 1994, Sch 9 Group 7 Note 1*].

Increasingly, companies are purchasing specialised equipment and offering the use of it to NHS and private hospitals. The effect of *Note 1* above is that

- if goods are let on hire without attendant staff, or the attendant staff are not qualified under *Item 1*, the supply is taxable; and
- if the equipment is supplied as part of a package,
  (i) where the principal supply is the hire of equipment and the provision of *Item 1* services is subsidiary to that supply, the whole supply is standard-rated; and
  (ii) where the principal supply is the provision of *Item 1* services and the hire of the equipment is subsidiary to that supply, the whole supply is exempt under *Item 1*.

  See *Aslan Imaging Ltd (VTD 3286) (TVC 31.15)* where the tribunal held that the principal supply was the standard-rated hiring of a radiological scanner and the services supplied by the radiographer who accompanied it were subsidiary and *Cleary & Cleary (t/a Mobile X-rays) (VTD 7305) (TVC 31.1)* where the tribunal held that the principal supply was an exempt mobile chest X-ray service and the equipment hiring was secondary.

HMRC give the following guidance to help in determining the VAT liability of letting on hire.

Factor	*Indications of standard-rated supply of goods*	*Indications of single supply of exempt services*
Training	Supplier/manufacturer sends a representative to train hospital staff for a significant period (2 or 3 weeks)	No training given to the hospital staff by supplier/manufacturer
Medical personnel	Hospital supplies qualified medical personnel (eg consultant radiologists or qualified radiographers). Equipment supplier/manufacturer supplies personnel to a lesser extent	No medically qualified personnel from the hospital are present; all medically qualified personnel are supplied by the supplier/manufacturer
Who carries out the diagnostic function?	Qualified medical personnel from the hospital decide what use is to be made of the equipment in relation to each patient (eg in the case of a scanner, how many images are to be taken, of what part of the body and at what angles). Personnel of the supplier/manufacturer have no say in this	Staff of the supplier/manufacturer decide what procedures are required, process the results (eg by developing the films) and send these back to the hospital
Degree of control	Hospital's medical personnel in charge throughout	Medical personnel of supplier/manufacturer have absolute control
Why are personnel of the supplier/ manufacturer present?	To ensure that the machine is used properly and that no harm comes to anyone. Not to operate the machine, although they may occasionally be consulted or asked for technical advice	To perform all the procedures
Charge	Annual flat rate plus a unit charge	Set fee per examination
Location	On hospital premises (eg in car park or similar), so as to be close to readily available medical personnel who are trained to use the equipment	Outside the hospital premises, (eg on the premises of the supplier/manufacturer)

(Internal Guidance, V1–7, Chapter 22 paras 2.16, 13).

32.8 Dentists, etc

The supply of any services or dental prostheses by

(*a*) a person registered in the dentists' register,

(*b*) a person enrolled in any roll of dental auxiliaries having effect under *Dentists Act 1984, s 45*, or

(*c*) a dental technician

is exempt. [*VATA 1994, Sch 9 Group 7 Item 2*].

Dental prostheses. These are not defined in the legislation but mean artificial replacements for parts of the body. HMRC take exemption as applying to

- partial and full dentures;
- fixed and removable bridges;
- crowns and inlays;
- orthodontic appliances;
- obturators, splints and other specially designed appliances;
- dental palates;
- individual artificial teeth; and
- gold when supplied as part of the above

but not to

- high-speed grinders and other dental machinery;
- acrylic dust;
- sales of toothpaste, toothbrushes, dental floss, etc, and
- display, demonstration, or wholesale supplies.

(Internal Guidance, V1–7, Chapter 22 para 2.13.2).

Dental services. The exemption extends to any services supplied by dentists provided they are acting in their professional capacity (eg professional advice on dental matters). Supplies within (*c*) above are exempt, irrespective of whether the supply is made directly to the patient or to a dentist.

Exemption also covers the supply of consumables used or administered in the course of treatment. As dentists are not allowed to dispense drugs, the administration of anaesthetics, etc during the course of treatment forms part of their exempt supply.

(VAT Notice 701/57/02, para 8.1; Internal Guidance, V1–7, Chapter 22 para 2.13.4).

Supplies between dentists in the same practice. Under model agreements issued by the British Dental Association (BDA), there are four main types of arrangement by which dentists may co-operate in a practice.

(1) *Employer/employee*

A dentist may employ another dentist as an assistant. The provision of goods or services by the employer to the assistant to enable him to carry out his contract of employment does not constitute supplies for VAT purposes.

(2) *Partnership*

A partnership is a single business for VAT purposes and supplies of each of the partners are supplies of the business. Any supplies of goods or services between the partners are disregarded for VAT purposes.

(3) *Associateship agreements*

It is common for one dentist to be the practice owner (sometimes referred to as the 'principal') and then make facilities available to other dentists (the 'associates'). The associate dentists are not in partnership with the practice owner; each being self-employed with their own patients and a separate business for VAT purposes. They do not act as agent or subcontractor for the practice owner.

Such an arrangement usually involves the supply of goods and services by the practice owner to the associate dentists (eg the use of a fully equipped surgery, the supply of materials and consumables necessary in the provision of treatment, the services of a chair-side assistant, the introduction of patients, laboratory services, the use of reception, accounting and other common services). The practice owner may also agree to provide professional help and guidance to the associate. In return, the associate dentist undertakes to pay to the practice owner a percentage of his fee income. This is normally collected directly by the practice owner by deducting the agreed percentage from income received (usually referred to as 'retained fees') and passing the balance to the associate. These retained fees are exempt provided that they relate to services or facilities which are

- predominantly medical in nature; and
- necessary to allow the recipient to perform dentistry.

Exemption does not apply to

- any supplies made by a dentist who has ceased to practise,
- any supplies by a practice owner who is not a dentist (although exemption will apply where the practice owner does not practise dentistry in the practice itself but does so elsewhere, for example, in another practice or a dental hospital);
- supplies of goods (other than dental prostheses) such as toothpaste and toothbrushes from one dentist to another; or
- any sales of dental equipment by a practice owner (to an associate or anyone else).

(4) *Expense sharing agreements*

Typically, these involve a number of independent dentists who agree to share the common expenses of the practice (eg insurance, lighting and heating, staff and other office expenses) but each remains an independent practitioner and is equal in status.

The VAT implications of shared expenses depend on the facts of each case but, broadly, where one party pays initially for the supplies and charges the other parties a proportion as their agreed share, there is a supply from one dentist to the other. If the amounts paid are the consideration for supplies of dental services or facilities as in (3) above, the supply is exempt.

Where the agreement provides for common ownership of goods, any payment from one of the parties in respect of their share in the items commonly owned is not the consideration for the supply of goods and outside the scope of VAT. But where one dentist initially buys equipment and another takes exclusive ownership of it, the amount paid is consideration for a supply of goods and taxable in the normal way.

Where an expense-sharing arrangement is in existence and a dentist sells his share in the premises, goodwill, and assets to another dentist, the sale of part of the business can be a transfer of part of a going concern (see 8.10 BUSINESS).

(VAT Notice 701/57/02, para 8.2; Internal Guidance V1–7, Chapter 22 paras 2.13.6, 10).

32.9 **Supervised services**

Supplies of services made by a person who is not registered or enrolled in any of the registers or rolls specified in 32.2 to 32.5 or 32.8(*a*) or (*b*) above are exempt where the services are 'wholly performed' or 'directly supervised' by a person who is so registered or enrolled. [*VATA 1994, Sch 9 Group 7 Note 2*].

See 32.1 above for limitations on the services which are exempt.

'Wholly performed'. This covers the situation where a company (which is not a 'person registered or enrolled') makes the supply but uses the services of its medically qualified personnel (eg a company employing registered chiropodists). (Internal Guidance V1–7, Chapter 22 paras 2.15.3, 12.1, 12.2, 12.4). Although *Note 2* above only refers to 32.8(*a*) or (*b*) and not 32.8(*c*) (dental technicians), HMRC accept that supplies made by dental technicians through a company can also be exempt. (Internal Guidance V1–7, Chapter 22 para 2.13.1).

'Directly supervised'. Following consultation with professional bodies and others, HMRC have produced guidelines for various professions on their requirements for services to be treated as directly supervised. The guidelines are not law and the facts in each case must be taken into account. HMRC require all the conditions to be satisfied.

(*a*) *Guidelines for the direct supervision of unqualified homecare staff*

(1) The supervisor must be a person who is registered in

- the register of medical practitioners or the register of medical practitioners with limited registration;
- the register of qualified nurses, midwives and health visitors kept under *Nurses, Midwives and Health Visitors Act 1997, s 7*;
- the register of physiotherapists kept under the *Health Professions Order 2001*; or
- the register of occupational therapists kept under the *Health Professions Order 2001*.

(2) Supervision cannot take place via a third party (ie the supervisor must always be in a direct relationship with the unqualified staff).

(3) The presence of the appropriately qualified supervisor must be required in the process, and he or she must be responsible, contractually, for supervising the unqualified staff. In particular, HMRC will not accept that direct supervision exists where a supervisor is introduced primarily to gain VAT exemption and in practice carries out little or no supervision.

(4) The services performed by the unqualified staff must require supervision. HMRC will not accept exemption for services performed by unqualified staff for which no supervision is required (eg cleaning, shopping or cooking). These services can be only be exempt from VAT if they are supplied as part of a package of care provided by the organisation.

(5) The supervisor must be readily available for the whole of the time that the unqualified staff are working. The supervisor need not always be the same individual (eg a team of supervisors, all of whom are qualified as above, can rotate the supervision of particular staff amongst themselves to fit in with their other commitments; or a 'locum' qualified supervisor may be brought in to cover the normal supervisor during holiday periods or similar).

(6) The supervisor must see the client at the outset of treatment. If, in an emergency, unqualified staff are sent to provide care before contact between client and supervisor can be made, the supervisor must make arrangements to see the patient as soon as is practically possible afterwards.

(7) The supervisor must have a say in the level of care to be provided.

(8) The supervisor must be able to demonstrate that they monitor the services of the unqualified carers. This should be done by checking on the level and standard of the care provided with both the carer and the client. Consequently, after treatment has commenced, but not necessarily at the same time, the supervisor must have a face to face meeting with the client and the carer at least every six months, and other contact (eg by telephone) at least every four weeks.

(9) The supervisor must be responsible for supervising no more than 2,000 hours per week of unqualified staff time (or 2,000 hours per supervisor for supervisory teams). For the purposes of this calculation, the actual hours worked by unqualified staff whose services are provided on an hourly or nightly basis will be used, but unqualified staff who 'live in' will be deemed to have been supplied for 10 hours per day.

(*b*) *Guidelines for the direct supervision of unqualified optical staff*

(1) The supervisor must be a person who is registered under

- the register of ophthalmic opticians kept under the *Opticians Act 1989*; or
- the register of dispensing opticians kept under the *Opticians Act 1989*.

(2) Supervision cannot take place via a third party (ie the supervisor must always be in a direct relationship with the unqualified staff).

(3) The presence of the appropriately qualified supervisor must be required at appropriate times during the process and he or she must be responsible, contractually, for supervising the unqualified staff. HMRC will not accept that direct supervision exists where a supervisor is introduced primarily to gain VAT exemption and in practice carries out little or no supervision.

(4) The services performed by the unqualified staff must require supervision. If neither sight testing, nor the fitting and supply of contact lenses, nor

the dispensing of spectacle prescriptions take place on the premises, HMRC will not accept that there is a legitimate need for direct supervision by a registered optician.

(5) The supervisor must be readily available for the whole of the time that the unqualified staff are working, and must be able to take appropriate action in an emergency. The supervisor need not always be the same individual (eg a number of registered opticians working within an establishment can supervise different unqualified staff as demand dictates; or registered locum opticians may be brought in to cover periods of holiday or similar).

(6) The supervisor must see the client at the outset of treatment and at the outset of any new treatment required thereafter.

(7) The supervisor must decide the treatment to be provided by the unqualified staff.

(8) The supervisor must be able to demonstrate that they monitor the services of the unqualified staff. This could be done by checking the records of patients treated by the unqualified staff and by observing the standard of service provided.

(9) The ratio of registered opticians to unqualified staff must be such that it enables (5) above to be fulfilled.

(*c*) *Guidelines for the direct supervision of unqualified staff: general*

(1) The supervisor must be an appropriately registered person.

(2) Supervision cannot take place via a third party (ie the supervisor must always be in a direct relationship with the unqualified staff).

(3) The presence of the appropriately qualified supervisor must be required at appropriate times during the process and he or she must be responsible, contractually, for supervising the unqualified staff. HMRC will not accept that direct supervision exists where a supervisor is introduced primarily to gain VAT exemption and in practice carries out little or no supervision.

(4) The services performed by the unqualified staff must require supervision. HMRC will not accept exemption for services performed by unqualified staff for which no supervision is required and will not accept that services which are not broadly of a medical or caring nature can gain exemption simply by the use of a qualified individual in a supervisory or managerial role.

(5) The supervisor must be readily available for the whole of the time that the unqualified staff are working, and must be able to take appropriate action in an emergency. The supervisor need not always be the same individual (eg a number of registered professionals working within an establishment can supervise different unqualified staff as demand dictates; registered locums may be brought in to cover periods of holiday or similar; or a team of supervisors, all of whom are qualified as above, can rotate the supervision of particular staff amongst themselves to fit in with their other commitments).

(6) The supervisor must see the client at the outset of treatment and at the outset of any new treatment required thereafter.

(7) The supervisor must decide the treatment to be provided by the unqualified staff.

(8) The supervisor must be able to demonstrate that they monitor the services of the unqualified staff.

(9) The ratio of registered professionals to unqualified staff must be such that it enables (5) above to be fulfilled.

Where all the above conditions are not met, HMRC regard the services are standard-rated, even when performed to meet the medical or personal care needs of a client.

(VAT Notice 701/57/02, para 3.2; Internal Guidance V1–7, Chapter 22 para 2.15.5).

The above guidelines were considered in detail in *Land (VTD 15547) (TVC 31.6)* where the tribunal held that an unqualified dispenser of spectacles, and his unqualified staff, were directly supervised by an ophthalmic medical practitioner who performed eye tests in the shop on five half-days a fortnight. On the evidence, the tribunal held that the supplies were supervised even though, as required by HMRC (see condition (3), there was no explicit contract requiring the supervisor to undertake this task. The tribunal observed that, although a contract may be valuable evidence of responsibility, its absence did not prove that there was no responsibility. On the evidence, supervision was an implicit term of the relationship.

See also *A & S Services (VTD 16025) (TVC 31.21)*.

Supervision does not necessarily require the supervisor continually to observe the unqualified person or necessarily be on the same premises provided there is a check as often as the circumstances require and a system for that person to contact the supervisor. Supervision is 'direct' if carried out on a one-to-one basis without an intermediary. (*Elder Home Care Ltd (VTD 11185) (TVC 31.4)*). See also *M G Parkinson (VTD 6017) (TVC 31.3)*.

HMRC do not accept that *Note 2* above exempts services of complementary practitioners, who do not appear on any statutory register, to whom patients are referred by consultants or medical practitioners. Neither the act of referral nor the relationship between the two parties (who are invariably from two distinct areas of medicine/treatment and thus, have different skills) constitute any degree of supervision. This was confirmed in *Pittam (VTD 13268) (TVC 31.22)* which related to patients referred to a chiropractor. (Note that the services of a registered chiropractor are now exempt (see 32.4 above) but the principle involved still applies.)

32.10 **Pharmaceutical chemists**

The supply of any services (but not the letting on hire of goods) by

- a person registered in the register of pharmaceutical chemists kept under the *Pharmacy Act 1954* or the *Pharmacy* (*Northern Ireland*) *Order 1976*, or
- by a person who is not so registered (eg a company or partnership) but where the services are performed by a person who is so registered

is exempt. [*VATA 1994, Sch 9 Group 7 Item 3 and Notes 2A and 3; SI 1996/2949*].

See 32.1 above for limitations on the services which are exempt.

The main activity undertaken by pharmacists is the dispensing of drugs in accordance with a doctor's prescription. This activity is zero-rated under 32.15 below. *Item 3* above exempts professional services for which a pharmacist has been trained and is required to exercise professional judgement. This includes

- carrying out pregnancy testing; and

- acting as a locum in a dispensary.

It also applies to certain payments received from the NHS such as

- rota service payments (for opening after hours, on early closing days and bank holidays etc);
- rural dispensing payments (in areas where access to the next pharmacy is difficult); and
- urgent fees (where a prescription is dispensed outside both normal hours and the late-night rota hours).

(Internal Guidance V1–7, Chapter 22 para 2.14).

32.11 Hospitals and care institutions

Exemption applies to the provision of

- 'care' or medical or surgical treatment, and
- in connection with it, the supply of any goods,

in any hospital or other institution approved, licensed or registered (or exempted from registration) by any Minister or other authority pursuant to a provision of a public general Act of Parliament or the Scottish Parliament (or equivalent NI legislation) other than a provision that is capable of being brought into effect at different times in relation to different local authority areas. [*VATA 1994, Sch 9 Group 7 Item 4 and Note 8*].

Qualifying institutions. HMRC list the following as '*qualifying institutions*' under these provisions provided they are approved, licensed or registered under the relevant social legislation or exempted from obtaining such an approval or registration by the relevant legislation.

- A hospital or hospice.
- A nursing home.
- A children's home.
- A residential home for disabled, elderly or infirm residents.
- A residential home for people with a past or present dependence on alcohol or drugs, or a past or present mental disorder.
- A nursery, crèche or playgroup.
- An after-school club or similar provider of non-residential care for children (see further below).

Supplies made by a qualifying institution are exempt whether supplied direct to the beneficiary or to a third party such as a local authority. An institution may be qualifying regardless of whether its activities are carried out on a charitable or commercial basis.

(VAT Notice 701/31/02, paras 2.1, 2.2).

Meaning of care. '*Care*', in the opinion of HMRC, includes the protection, control or guidance of an individual, when this is provided to meet medical, physical, personal or domestic needs. This will usually involve some personal contact between the provider of the care or treatment and the beneficiary. Examples of care or treatment supplied by a qualifying institution include

- general assistance with everyday tasks provided to residents of a home for disabled, elderly or infirm people;
- meals and accommodation provided to in-patients, residents or other care beneficiaries;
- nursing of sick or injured patients in a hospital, hospice or nursing home;
- looking after and supervising children in a day nursery or an after school club; and
- entertainment, leisure and other organised activities within a qualifying institution, where these are not separable from the main supply of care or treatment.

(VAT Notice 701/31/02, para 2.3).

Psychological services and vocational training provided at residential children's homes were held to be within the definition of 'care' in *Catholic Care Consortium Ltd (VTD 17315) (TVC 31.50)*.

HMRC have always maintained that the supply of care by all providers is exempt regardless of their status provided they are registered under the relevant legislation. (Business Brief 1/97). This was confirmed in *J & M Gregg v C & E Commrs, CJEC [1999] STC 935 (TVC 21.205)* although in the case of *C & E Commrs v Kingscrest Associates Ltd & Montecello Ltd (t/a Kingscrest Residential Care Homes), Ch D [2002] STC 490 (TVC 31.49)* the tribunal declined to follow the earlier decision. It held that supplies by a partnership operating residential care homes for people with learning disabilities did not constitute the provision of exempt care within *Item 4* which connotes care connected with medical or surgical treatment. The tribunal did confirm that care provided in nursing and convalescent homes was medical in nature and exempt under *Item 4*. The High Court supported the tribunal's decision. To remove any doubt about the liability for commercially provided care (other than nursing and medical care), the provisions of *VATA 1994, Sch 9 Group 7 Item 9* (see 32.14 below) were amended with effect from 21 March 2002 to provide exemption under that *Item* for welfare services provided by state-regulated welfare institutions.

Services supplied by qualifying institutions which are not exempt. Supplies which are not exempt under these provisions include:

- Any service that is not provided under the terms of an approval, license, registration or exemption from registration, granted under the appropriate social legislation (but see under *School clubs, etc* below for special rules applying to certain care services provided to children over the age of eight).
- Any service provided to a person other than an in-patient, resident or other beneficiary of care or treatment. This includes any supply made to visitors. Special rules apply to the supply of meals and accommodation to parents staying with a sick child in hospital (see below).
- Any goods or services that are separable from care or treatment provided within the institution. Examples include day excursions and other activities that take place at a location other than the institution's premises, and charges made for the use of public telephones.

(VAT Notice 701/31/02, para 2.4).

Drugs and other items supplied to patients in a hospital or nursing home. Drugs, medicines, bandages, plasters or ointments provided by a qualifying institution in the course of care or treatment are exempt when provided to

(*a*) an in-patient or resident of a hospital or nursing home;

(*b*) any person attending the premises of a hospital or nursing home for care or treatment; or

(*c*) any other person or establishment where the item is for use by, or in connection with, either of the above.

Supplies of drugs or medicines to any of the above people other than by a qualifying institution are usually standard-rated (even when the items are dispensed on the prescription of a medical practitioner). However, by concession, HMRC allow pharmacists (including in-house or independent pharmacists operating from hospital premises) to zero-rate drugs, medicines and other qualifying goods that are supplied to any person within (*a*) or (*b*) above if all of the following conditions are met.

- The items dispensed are goods designed or adapted for use in connection with medical or surgical treatment.
- The items are dispensed by a pharmacist in the normal way on the prescription of a medical practitioner who is providing primary health care services.
- The items are intended for self-administration by the person named on the prescription.
- The items are supplied separately from, and do not form any part of, any medical services, treatment or care provided in the hospital or nursing home.
- In the case of NHS prescriptions, the pharmacist is acting under the appropriate NHS Pharmaceutical regulations, and is reimbursed for the dispensed items by one of the NHS bodies that pay for community pharmacy services.

The application of this concession must not give rise to any abuse of the VAT system and HMRC may withdraw or restrict the application of this concession if they have reasonable cause to believe that it is being used for VAT avoidance purposes.

(VAT Notice 701/31/02, para 2.7).

Goods supplied as part of a package of care and treatment in a qualifying institution. Most goods supplied by a qualifying institution as part of a package of care or treatment are exempt. Examples include

- incontinence products; drugs and medicines; bandages; plasters and ointments supplied to residents or patients of a nursing home or hospital;
- meals and refreshments provided to in-patients, residents or other beneficiaries of care or treatment;
- accommodation and meals provided to relatives staying with a sick child in hospital (see *Nuffield Nursing Homes Trust (VTD 3327) (TVC 31.33)* where the provision of accommodation and catering to a parent of a child patient was held to be a supply of care to the patient). No other supplies to visitors, relatives or carers qualify for exemption;
- transport provided that forms an integral part of an exempt supply of care or treatment;

- toiletry products provided to in-patients, residents or other beneficiaries of care or treatment for which no additional charge is made; and
- items provided to children by playgroups or nurseries, such as picture books, crayons and toys when these are provided in connection with care.

Items that are separable from the care and treatment provided by the qualifying institution are not exempt. Examples include cigarettes, toiletries provided to in-patients for an additional charge, pet food, newspapers, merchandise such as commemorative T shirts, and goods provided to any person other than the beneficiary of the care or treatment. The liability of such goods should be determined in accordance with the normal liability rules.

(VAT Notice 701/31/02, paras 2.5, 2.6, 2.10).

Goods and services supplied on the premises of a qualifying institution. Some qualifying institutions allow outside businesses or practitioners to operate from their premises, for example

- retail outlets or independent health professionals that occupy areas within a hospital building;
- self-employed hairdressers who provide services in a residential home; and
- employment businesses that supply staff to work in a qualifying institution.

For a supply made by such a business to qualify for exemption, all of the following conditions must be met.

- The goods or services supplied must form part of the care or treatment provided within the qualifying institution.
- The goods or services supplied must be of a type commonly provided to beneficiaries of care services.
- The supply must not consist of drugs, medicines, incontinence products, bandages, plasters, ointments or any other items that are integral to the care or treatment provided in the qualifying institution.
- The supply must involve direct contact between the provider and the beneficiary, and must contribute directly to the welfare of the beneficiary.
- The supply must not take place in a qualifying institution for reasons of geographical convenience only. This means that the supply must not be of a type that might equally be provided at a location other than the premises of a qualifying institution.

There are very few supplies made by outside businesses from the premises of a qualifying institution that meet all of the above conditions but examples include services supplied by

- nursing auxiliaries and other carers; and
- outside contractors providing renal dialysis services in hospitals.

(VAT Notice 701/31/02, para 3.3).

After-school clubs, holiday clubs and other non-residential care for children. After-school clubs and other providers of non-residential care for children are only required to register under the appropriate social legislation if they provide a designated number of hours of care to children under the age of eight. A qualifying institution that

- provides care on a commercial basis to children who are younger than eight years old as well as to older children,
- operates identical hours of opening for all age groups, and
- provides activities for over eights that are comparable with those provided for younger children,

can choose to regard the care provided to over eights as VAT exempt, in addition to the care provided to younger children.

(VAT Notice 701/31/02, para 4.1).

32.12 Human blood, organs and tissue

The supply of

- human blood,
- products for therapeutic purposes derived from human blood, and
- human (including foetal) organs or tissue for diagnostic or therapeutic purposes or medical research

is exempt. [*VATA 1994, Sch 9 Group 7 Items 6–8*].

The importation of these items is also exempt from VAT. See 34.15(5) IMPORTS.

Teaching exhibits, skeletons and curiosities such as shrunken heads are not covered by the exemption and are standard-rated.

Drugs and therapeutic substances contain one or more 'active' ingredients and may also contain 'non-active' ingredients. Exemption does apply under this provisions to a product which contains

- two or more active ingredients, only one of which is derived from human blood; or
- one active ingredient which is not derived from human blood, even if the product contains a blood product as a non-active ingredient.

Examples of blood products which are covered by the exemption when supplied as the active ingredient are blood plasma (fresh or dried); plasma protein fraction; haemoglobin; globulin; albumin (fresh or dried); human Factor VIII fraction; human factor IX fraction (partial and total prothrombin complexes); fibrinogen; thrombin; normal and specific immunoglobulins; plasmin; and plasminogen.

(Internal Guidance V1–7, Chapter 22 para 4.4).

Recombinant factor VIII (as opposed to plasma-derived human factor VIII) is outside the exemption as it is not derived from human blood. (HC Written Answer, Vol 267 col 837, 30 November 1995; *Baxter Healthcare Ltd (VTD 14670) (TVC 31.51)*).

32.13 Transport of sick and injured

The supply of transport services for sick or injured persons in vehicles specially designed for that purpose is exempt. [*VATA 1994, Sch 9 Group 7 Item 11*].

HMRC require three conditions to be satisfied before exemption can apply.

(1) The passengers transported must be sick or injured persons. They interpret 'sick or injured persons' in this context as meaning persons in need of, or having just received, medical care or treatment.

(2) The transport must form part of a journey to or from a place of medical treatment (although it should be noted that there is no reference to this requirement in the legislation). The journey need not be an emergency. Where the transport supplied forms part of a journey to or from a place of medical treatment, but does not itself begin or end at the place of treatment (eg transporting a person injured at sea by a helicopter only so far as a conventional ambulance to complete the journey to hospital by road) the exemption applies if all other conditions are met.

(3) The vehicle must be 'specially designed' for the purpose. HMRC take this to mean that the vehicle must

- have the facility to secure a recumbent person on a stretcher, or
- be fitted with a ramp or a lift and clamps sufficient to enable a person in a wheelchair to be safely wheeled on, transported in, and wheeled off the vehicle.

HMRC accept that where a vehicle has been adapted to be suitable for carrying sick or injured persons in one of these ways, it can be treated as 'specifically designed' for the purposes even though the vehicle did not qualify from inception.

(Internal Guidance V1–7, Chapter 22 para 5.4).

32.14 Welfare services

EC Sixth Directive, Art 13A directs countries to exempt 'the supply of services and goods closely linked to welfare and social security works'. In *Yoga for Health Foundation v C & E Commrs, QB [1984] STC 630 (TVC 21.200)*, it was held that the word 'welfare' was not confined to services connected with the relief of poverty or provision of purely material benefits.

Under UK legislation, the supply by a

(*a*) charity,

(*b*) 'public body',

(*c*) 'state-regulated' welfare institution (eg a residential care home), or

(*d*) with effect from 31 January 2003 (see transitional arrangements below), 'state-regulated private welfare agency'

of 'welfare services', and of goods supplied in connection with those welfare services, is exempt.

The supply of accommodation or catering is excluded unless ancillary to the provision of care, treatment or instruction. The supply of catering to elderly people in sheltered housing accommodation was held to be ancillary in *Viewpoint Housing Association Ltd (VTD 13148) (TVC 31.53)* and the supply of hotel accommodation and catering to cancer patients and their families was held to be ancillary in *Trustees for the Macmillan Cancer Trust (VTD 15603) (TVC 31.58)*.

See 12.1 CHARITIES for bodies qualifying as charities. It should be noted that not all welfare services provided by charities are business. If such services are provided consistently below cost to distressed people for the relief of their distress, they are non-business supplies. See 12.5(21) CHARITIES.

'*Public body*' means

- a government department,
- a local authority, or
- any other body which acts under any enactment or instrument for public purposes and not for its own profit and which performs functions similar to those of a government department or local authority (eg most NHS trusts).

'*State-regulated*' means approved, licensed, registered or exempted from registration by any Minister or other authority pursuant to a provision of a public general Act of Parliament or the Scottish Parliament (or equivalent NI legislation) other than a provision that is capable of being brought into effect at different times in relation to different local authority areas.

[*VATA 1994, Sch 9 Group 7 Item 9 and Notes 5, 7 and 8; SI 2002/762; SI 2003/24*].

State-regulated private welfare institution or agency A state-regulated private welfare institution or agency means an institution or agency that is registered with and/or regulated by

- the National Care Standards Commission;
- the Scottish Commission for the Regulation of Care;
- the Care Standards Inspectorate for Wales;
- the Northern Ireland Health and Personal Social Services Regulation and Improvement Authority;
- the Office for Standards in Education; or
- any other similar regulatory body.

It can include a domiciliary care agency, an independent fostering agency, a voluntary adoption agency, and a nursing agency.

(VAT Notice 701/2/04, para 2.4).

Welfare services. Welfare services mean services directly connected with (1)–(3) below. In the case of services supplied by a state-regulated private welfare institution under (*c*) above, it only includes those services in respect of which the institution is so regulated.

(1) The provision of care, treatment or instruction designed to promote the physical or mental welfare of elderly, sick, distressed or disabled persons. [*VATA 1994, Sch 9 Group 7 Note 6(a); SI 2002/762*].

In *Watford & District Old People's Housing Association Ltd (t/a Watford Help In The Home Service) (VTD 15660) (TVC 31.54)* the tribunal held that domestic help services such as cleaning, cooking and shopping could constitute 'care' when supplied to people for whom there is either current or imminent substantial risk to the health and welfare of the person, and who are unable to provide even basic self care or who have major difficulty in safely carrying out some key daily living tasks. The tribunal stressed the significance of the high level of recipients' needs which, in that case, had been identified by Social Services assessments.

Following that case, HMRC reviewed their interpretation of 'care'. They regard care or treatment as including 'the protection, control or guidance of an individual, when this is provided to meet medical, physical, personal or domestic needs' and give the following as examples of care that is a welfare service when provided to an elderly, sick, disabled or distressed person.

- Personal or nursing care (including assistance with bathing, dressing, toileting and other personal hygiene).
- General assistance and support with everyday tasks such as form-filling, letter reading/writing, bill-paying.
- Certain routine domestic tasks (such as housework, simple odd jobs, shopping and collecting a prescription or pension) provided all of the following conditions are met.
  (i) An assessment of the recipients' health condition, medical needs and ability to perform each task has been carried out by an appropriately trained person (eg a medical or health professional or any person with relevant training or experience in social work or social care).
  (ii) This assessment has shown that the recipient is unable to carry out the tasks safely (because performance involves a likelihood of physical harm or injury) or properly or effectively (eg an elderly or disabled person who has mobility problems may be unable to shop regularly enough to meet their nutritional needs) or without 'significant' pain or discomfort and that this inability presents a risk to their health or welfare. 'Significant' is used to distinguish between low levels of pain or discomfort (experienced by many people in carrying out routine domestic tasks) and a significant level of pain or discomfort (that restricts ability to carry out such tasks).
  (iii) A record of each assessment is maintained by the supplier of the service.
  (iv) The service provided is a routine domestic task that the majority of the population would expect to carry out for themselves and which is required to keep a household going. This would exclude specialist services (eg non-essential gardening, decorating and other house maintenance including re-roofing, plumbing and electrical services).
- Counselling.
- Looking after or supervising vulnerable people.
- Support or instruction designed to develop or sustain a person's capacity to live independently in the community.
- Protection, control, guidance or companionship that is required to meet an individual's personal or domestic needs.
- Residential care, including accommodation, board and other services provided to residents as part of a care package.

(VAT Notice 701/2/04, para 2.7).

(2) *The care or protection of children and young persons*. [*VATA 1994, Sch 9 Group 7 Note 6*(*b*)*; SI 2002/762*].

HMRC regard this as applying to services directly connected with the care and protection of specific children, rather than children in general. Examples include

- care provided in a children's home;
- day care services such as those provided by a nursery, playgroup or after school club (but not activity-based clubs such as dance classes, etc);
- payments or allowances received by agencies for the placement of children with foster carers;
- other payments for the care, support and protection of looked-after children; and
- training and assessment of prospective adopters by an adoption agency.

Some welfare providers, such as independent fostering agencies, receive fees for services that, although concerned with the overall welfare of one or more child, are not primarily and directly connected with the care or protection of a specific child. HMRC do not usually regard these services as exempt unless they are provided as part of an exempt composite supply of care and protection. Examples include fees received

- for training of carers, or potential carers, where this is not linked to the needs of a specific child;
- for assessment of potential foster carers suitability to look after children, where this is not linked to the needs of a specific child;
- by activity-based clubs not required to be registered with OFSTED such as football clubs and dancing lessons;
- for consultancy or research services; and
- for education of children.

See, however, 20 EDUCATION for exemption for certain education and training services provided by eligible bodies.

(VAT Notice 701/2/04, para 2.8).

(3) *The provision of spiritual welfare by a religious institution as part of a course of instruction or a retreat, not being a course or retreat designed primarily to provide recreation or a holiday.* [*VATA 1994, Sch 9 Group 7 Note 6*(*c*)*; SI 2002/762*].

Examples include

- spiritual counselling to an individual;
- guided exploration of spiritual needs and development; and
- discussion, meditation and prayer or worship sessions

but does not include

- conferences or retreats when the spiritual welfare element is incidental, and not the predominant purpose of the supply;
- educational courses in theology, or similar subjects, where the predominant purpose is to expand knowledge of spiritual matters rather than to provide spiritual welfare services; and

- meetings to discuss theology or aspects of Church doctrine.

(VAT Notice 701/2/04, para 2.9).

Goods provided in connection with welfare services. Goods provided as part of, or in connection with, an exempt supply of welfare services are also exempt. Examples include

- meals and refreshments provided to beneficiaries of welfare services in the course of care or spiritual welfare services; and
- bandages, plasters or ointments supplied in the course of a supply of care and treatment in the recipient's home.

Any goods that are separable from an exempt welfare service, or are not provided in connection with such a service, are not exempt.

(VAT Notice 701/2/04, para 2.6).

Transitional arrangements for state-regulated private welfare agencies at 31 January 2003. For state-regulated private welfare agencies within (*d*) above which were already registered with, and/or regulated by, the appropriate regulatory body on 31 January 2003, exemption automatically applied from that date. For other agencies, *statutory* exemption takes effect from the first date on which they are so registered, etc. However, by concession, any private welfare agency within (*d*) above can exempt supplies within these provisions from 31 January 2003 if

- in the case of an agency in England and Wales, it is required to register under the *Care Standards Act 2002*;
- in the case of an agency in Scotland, it is required to register under the *Regulation of Care (Scotland) Act 2001*;
- in the case of an agency in Northern Ireland, it has a reasonable expectation of being required to register under the *Health and Personal Social Services (Quality, Improvement and Regulation) (Northern Ireland) Order 2003*;
- the agency is not registered owing to the fact that either
  - (i) the regulations providing for the mechanics of such registration and the keeping of registers are not yet in force;
  - (ii) they are in force but the agency's application for registration is being processed; or
  - (iii) the date by which it must apply for registration has not yet passed;
- the agency applies the exemption to all supplies of welfare services (as defined above) which it makes; and
- the agency applies for registration under the appropriate *Act* or *Order* in accordance with the provisions of the relevant regulations no later than the date specified as the date by which an agency must so apply.

The concession ceases to apply once an agency is registered under the appropriate *Act* or *Order* (when exemption applies by law) or where an agency has its application for registration refused. HMRC may withdraw or restrict the application of the concession if they have reasonable cause to believe that it is being abused.

Use of the concession is voluntary and, until it registers with the appropriate regulatory body, a commercial provider of welfare services may choose to continue taxing its supplies. However, once a business registers with the regulatory body, and thereby becomes a state-regulated private welfare agency, all of the welfare services it provides are exempt.

(VAT Notice 48, ESC 3.37).

De Voil Indirect Tax Service. See V4.146.

32.15 ZERO-RATED DISPENSING OF DRUGS, ETC

The supply of goods can be zero-rated in the following circumstances.

(1) **Pharmacists**

The supply (including the letting on hire) of any 'qualifying goods' dispensed to an individual for his 'personal use' where the dispensing is by a registered pharmacist (as defined) on the 'prescription' (NHS or private) of a person registered in

- the register of medical practitioners,
- the register of medical practitioners with limited registration, or
- the dentists' register.

For these purposes, a person who is not registered in the visiting EEC practitioners lists in the register of medical practitioners at the time he performs services in an urgent case (as mentioned in *Medical Act 1983, s 18(3)*) is treated as being so registered where he is entitled to be registered under that section.

[*VATA 1994, Sch 8 Group 12 Item 1 and Notes 2, 5; SI 1997/2744*].

'*Qualifying goods*' means any goods designed or adapted for use in connection with any medical or surgical treatment except hearing aids, dentures, spectacles and contact lenses [*VATA 1994, Sch 8 Group 12 Note 2A*].

Where the goods are prescribed (or dispensed under (*b*) below) under the NHS, if the NHS agrees to the prescribing and dispensing of the goods in question, then HMRC accept that they are qualifying goods. Doctors or dentists may privately prescribe anything which they feel will benefit their patient. Provided the goods are listed in the Drugs Tariff, or are of a type comparable to those listed in the Drugs Tariff, HMRC accept that they are qualifying goods. (Internal Guidance V1–7, Chapter 22 para 6.2).

'*Personal use*' is not defined but see 32.17 below for a general consideration of the term. Specifically, however, it does not include use by an individual while being provided with medical or surgical treatment, or any form of care, as an in-patient or resident of, or whilst attending, a hospital, nursing home or other institution which is approved, licensed or registered (or exempted by legislation from any requirement to be so approved, etc). [*VATA 1994, Sch 8 Group 12 Notes 5A, 5I; SI 1997/2744*].

In the following specific circumstances, however, HMRC accept that there is personal use of qualifying goods prescribed by a GP or a general dental practitioner (GDP) even though the patient is an in-patient, a resident or attending the premises of a hospital or nursing home.

(i) For NHS prescriptions, HMRC accept that prescribed qualifying goods are dispensed for an individual's personal use when

- the goods are ordered from a community pharmacist by a GP or GDP in the usual way;
- the goods are dispensed in accordance with the NHS regulations governing community pharmacists; and
- the pharmacist is reimbursed by one of the NHS authorities that pay for community pharmacy services.

(ii) For private prescriptions, HMRC accept that qualifying goods dispensed by a retail pharmacist to an individual patient on the private prescription of a GP or GDP are for the individual's personal use when the goods do not form part of the care provided by a hospital or nursing home, and are part of that GP's or GDP's primary health care. This means that private prescriptions written in similar circumstances to those in (i) above are treated in the same way.

(Internal Guidance V1–7, Chapter 22 para 6.2).

A '*prescription*' is an order or authorisation written by a doctor or a dentist to enable a patient to obtain the required drugs or medicines from a pharmacist. The NHS requires doctors and pharmacists to use a particular form for NHS prescriptions. There is no set form for a private prescription, but it must contain at least

- the name and address of the practitioner issuing it;
- the date;
- an indication as to whether the practitioner is a doctor or dentist;
- the name and address of the patient; and
- the item(s) to be dispensed.

(Internal Guidance V1–7, Chapter 22 para 6.2).

Acquisitions and imports. Goods prescribed as above which are acquired in the UK from another EC country or imported from a place outside the EC are not zero-rated on acquisition or importation. [*VATA 1994, Sch 8 Group 12 Note 1*].

Scope and effect of the above provisions.

(*a*) *'High street' pharmacies.* Most dispensing in a high street retail pharmacy is zero-rated under *VATA 1994, Sch 8 Group 12 Item 1* above. Supplies to hospitals or nursing homes which do not have their own pharmacy (eg a cottage hospital or a specialist clinic) will normally be standard-rated but may be zero-rated if the goods are for an individual named patient and the pharmacist is satisfied that either

- the goods will not be used while the patient is within the institution; or
- one of the concessions in (i) or (ii) above applies.

Where a pharmacist is asked to supply prescription-only medicines in an emergency, the zero rate will apply if these emergency supplies are made on the direction of a doctor and provided the doctor provides a prescription within 72 hours. Where a request for an emergency supply is made by a patient, then the conditions of *Item 1* are not met (because the goods are not supplied on the prescription of a doctor) and the supply cannot be zero-rated.

(*b*) *Hospital pharmacies.* Where an NHS hospital pharmacy supplies qualifying goods to out-patients or discharged patients as part of the NHS's statutory obligation of care, this is not a business supply for VAT purposes. Otherwise, hospital pharmacies can zero-rate dispensing of qualifying goods to out-patients or discharged patients for their personal use, including dispensing by

- pharmacies in private hospitals;
- independent pharmacies situated in NHS hospitals (eg where the pharmacy is run by a private company); or
- NHS hospital pharmacies dispensing to private patients.

(Internal Guidance V1–7, Chapter 22 para 6.3).

(2) **Dispensing doctors**

The supply (including the letting on hire) of any 'qualifying goods' by a person registered in

- the register of medical practitioners, or
- the register of medical practitioners with limited registration

in accordance with a requirement or authorisation under NHS regulations.

[*VATA 1994, Sch 8 Group 12 Item 1A and Note 5; SI 1995/652; SI 1997/2744*].

Under such regulations dispensing doctors can be required or authorised by the NHS to provide pharmacy services to particular patients. The usual qualification is that the patient lives more than one mile from the nearest pharmacy (although there are others). Dispensing doctors cannot dispense drugs to their other patients and other doctors are not authorised to dispense drugs to any of their patients.

See under (*a*) above for '*qualifying goods*'.

Acquisitions and imports. Goods dispensed as above which are acquired in the UK from another EC country or imported from a place outside the EC are not zero-rated on acquisition or importation. [*VATA 1994, Sch 8 Group 12 Note 1; SI 1995/652*].

Registration. GPs providing NHS pharmacy services may register for VAT and reclaim the VAT on their purchases of drugs and a proportion of overheads relating to the NHS pharmacy services. Alternatively, if their zero-rated supplies exceed the registration threshold but they do not wish to register, they can apply for exemption from registration (see 59.6 REGISTRATION). (VAT Information Sheet 6/95).

Administration of drugs at the time of treatment. This must be distinguished from the dispensing of drugs and is an exempt supply. See 32.2 above. As a result, zero-rating under *VATA 1994, Sch 8 Group 12 Item 1A* above only applies to dispensing of 'take-away' goods which the patient will self-administer.

(Internal Guidance V1–7, Chapter 22 para 6.4).

Private prescriptions. The dispensing of goods on private prescription (eg drugs, vitamin supplements and homeopathic preparations) by a doctor is always standard-rated.

De Voil Indirect Tax Service. See V4.281.

32.16 ZERO-RATED SUPPLIES TO DISABLED PERSONS AND CHARITIES

The legislation zero-rates certain supplies of specialised goods and services when needed by '*handicapped*' persons. As the term 'handicapped' is not now in general usage, in line with HMRC's practice, in the following paragraphs the term 'disabled' is used instead.

Meaning of 'disabled'. '*Handicapped*' in the context of zero-rating is defined as 'chronically sick or disabled' [*VATA 1994, Sch 8 Group 12 Note 3*] but there is no further definition of 'chronically sick' and 'disabled' in the legislation.

The Shorter Oxford English dictionary defines 'chronic' as 'lasting a long time, lingering, inveterate' or 'constant, also bad'. The opposite of chronic is 'acute' which is defined as 'coming sharply to a crisis, not chronic'.

HMRC regard a person as 'chronically sick or disabled' if he/she

- has a physical or mental impairment which has a long-term (as opposed to acute or short-term) and substantial adverse effect upon his/her ability to carry out everyday activities,
- has a condition which the medical profession treats as a chronic sickness (eg diabetes), or
- is terminally ill

but do *not* regard the term as extending to

- a frail elderly person who is otherwise able-bodied (see also *C & E Commrs v Help the Aged, QB [1997] STC 406 (TVC 11.15)*); or
- any person who is only temporarily disabled or incapacitated (eg where suffering from a broken limb).

Tribunals have similarly held that a person is not chronically sick or disabled where suffering from a slipped disc (*Aquakraft Ltd (VTD 2215) (TVC 19.7)*) or neck and back pain *(Posturite (UK) Ltd (VTD 7848) (TVC 19.40))*.

See *Tempur Pedic (UK) Ltd (VTD 13744) (TVC 19.21)* for a consideration of the meaning of the words 'chronically sick'.

'Disabled' includes

- mental disability;
- blindness or visual impairment; and
- acute hearing loss.

Despite the tribunal decisions in *The Dyslexia Institute Ltd (VTD 12654) (TVC 11.20)* and *GD Searle & Co Ltd (VTD 13439) (TVC 19.46)*, HMRC have concluded that where a person's dyslexia or asthma has a *substantial long-term adverse effect* on his/her ability to carry out normal day-to-day activities, then he/she should be treated as being disabled for VAT purposes.

(VAT Notice 701/7/02, para 3.2; Internal Guidance V1–7, Chapter 12 paras 4.2, 4.3).

Parents, spouses, etc. If a parent, spouse or guardian acts on behalf of a disabled person, the supply is treated as being made to that disabled person. (VAT Notice 701/7/02, para 3.2).

Conditions for zero-rating. For zero-rating to apply, it is essential that both

- the goods or services qualify; and
- the recipient qualifies.

The relief is not intended to cover all supplies of goods and services to disabled persons (or charities providing facilities for the disabled), nor does it mean that eligible goods and services can be zero-rated when supplied to people who are not disabled. For example, supplies to a nursing home would not be zero-rated under these provisions even if all the residents were disabled. See *Conroy (VTD 1916) (TVC 19.78)*.

The supplier is responsible for correctly accounting for VAT and ensuring that all the conditions for zero-rating are met. Therefore where relief depends on the designer's intention and the supplier has not designed or manufactured the goods himself (eg a retailer), he should seek written confirmation from the manufacturer (or importer) that the goods are eligible for VAT relief (see below and also 32.23 below). HMRC recommend that suppliers obtain written declarations from each customer claiming entitlement to VAT relief. See 32.35 below.

Liability rulings by HMRC. Following discussions with representatives of trade bodies and disability groups, it has been agreed that, except in the minority of cases, HMRC will only give liability rulings on goods for the purposes of *VATA 1994, Sch 8 Group 12* to the manufacturer or importer of the goods concerned.

Retailers. The initial line of enquiry for retailers should be to their supplier or the manufacturer, and not to their local VAT office. If the manufacturer is not prepared to state that the goods are designed solely for use by a disabled person, that will normally be the end of the matter. But if the manufacturer indicates that the goods should, or might qualify for relief, but is unwilling to take up the VAT liability with his local VAT office, retailers or purchasers may ask for a ruling to be issued to them.

Where a retailer relies on a written statement from the manufacturer that HMRC have accepted their claim that the goods are designed solely for use by a disabled person, if the statement turns out to be incorrect, HMRC would not seek to recover VAT from a retailer who, acting in good faith, zero-rated the final supply. Any such written statement must clearly and accurately specify the products/models to which it relates.

Third party requests. In the exceptional cases where HMRC are prepared to consider giving a ruling to a retailer (see above) or a purchaser, the person requesting the ruling should produce whatever details of the product (brochures, literature etc) he may have, plus any other available evidence of the manufacturer's design intention and any correspondence with the manufacturer or supplier.

(VAT Notice 701/7/02, para 2.3; Internal Guidance, V1–7, Chapter 12 paras 2.5–2.8).

De Voil Indirect Tax Service. See V4.281.

32.17 **Supplies of goods**

Subject to the exclusions below, zero-rating applies to the supply (including the letting on hire) to

- a disabled person for 'domestic or personal use', or

- a charity for making available, by sale or otherwise, to disabled persons for domestic or personal use

of any of the goods within 32.18 to 32.25 below. [*VATA 1994, Sch 8 Group 12, Item 2* and *Note 5*].

See 32.16 above for the interpretation of 'disabled'.

Domestic or personal use. This phrase is not defined in the legislation (apart from the specific exclusion below). Domestic use means use in the disabled person's private residence. This includes circumstances where an eligible charity makes goods available for the use of one or more disabled residents in a residential home. See also *Attorney General v Milliwatt Ltd, KB [1948] All ER 332* where Cassels J stated that domestic in the context of that case (which concerned electric pads and blankets) meant the house or the home.

In *Aquakraft Ltd (VTD 2215) (TVC 19.7)* the tribunal held that 'personal use' meant 'private or exclusive' use. HMRC therefore take the view that the goods must be used specifically by an eligible individual (or series of eligible individuals, eg where a wheelchair is loaned to successive disabled persons) so that zero-rating will not apply under these provisions to

- goods and services used for business purposes; or
- supplies made widely available for a whole group of people to use as they wish, even if all such users are disabled (see *Portland College (VTD 9815) (TVC 19.41)*). For example, a stair lift in a charity building for the use or convenience of all disabled persons who might use the building would not qualify for relief. This is because the charity is making the lift available for the general use of all those people who might require it, rather than for the personal use of specified individuals.

(VAT Notice 701/7/02, para 3.5; Internal Guidance V1–7, Chapter 12 paras 5.2, 5.3).

Exclusions. Subject to the extra-statutory concession below, zero-rating is restricted in the following circumstances.

(1) '*Domestic or personal use*' does not include any use by the disabled person in question while being provided (whether or not by the person making the supply) with medical or surgical treatment or any form of care

- as an in-patient or resident of a 'relevant institution', or
- whilst attending at the premises of a relevant institution

in respect of

(*a*) supplies to a disabled person by

(i) a Strategic Health Authority or Special Health Authority in England; a Health Authority, Special Health Authority or Local Health Authority in Wales; a Health Board or Special Health Board in Scotland; a Health and Social Services Board in Northern Ireland; the Common Services Agency for the Scottish Health Service, the Northern Ireland Central Services Agency for Health and Social Services and the Isle of Man Health Services Board; a National Health Service trust established under *National Health Service and Community Care Act 1990, Part I* or the *National Health Service (Scotland) Act 1978*; an NHS Foundation Trust; a Primary Care Trust established under *National Health Service Act 1977, s 16A*; or a Health and Social Services trust established under *Health and Personal Social Services (Northern Ireland) Order 1991, Art 10*, or

(ii) any person not falling within (i) above who is engaged in the carrying on of any activity in respect of which a relevant institution is required to be approved, licensed or registered or as the case may be, would be so required if not exempt

other than the supply of a wheelchair or invalid carriage or any parts or accessories designed solely for use therein; and

(*b*) supplies to a disabled person by any other person not within (*a*) above of

- medical or surgical appliances within 32.18 below and parts and accessories designed solely for use with such goods; and
- incontinence products and wound dressings.

Supplies to charities are not affected by this restriction.

(2) Zero-rating does not apply to

(*a*) a supply made in accordance with an agreement, arrangement or understanding to which any of the persons mentioned in (1)(*a*)(i) or (ii) above is or has been a party otherwise than as the supplier, or

(*b*) a supply where all or any part of the consideration has been provided (directly or indirectly) by any such person

but in the case of a supply of an invalid wheelchair or invalid carriage to a disabled person only if *either* a person within (1)(*a*)(ii) is involved *or* the *whole* of the consideration has been provided by a person within (1)(*a*)(i) above.

For the purposes of (1) and (2) above, references to an invalid wheelchair and invalid carriage do not include references to any mechanically propelled vehicle intended or adapted for use on roads.

A '*relevant institution*' is any institution (whether a hospital, nursing home or other institution) which provides care or medical or surgical treatment and is *either* approved, licensed or registered *or* specifically exempt from any such requirement.

By concession, the above exclusions do not apply (and a supply of goods can be treated as if it were zero-rated) where

- the goods fall within 32.23 below and are supplied by a charity at or below cost;
- the goods are goods other than spectacles or contact lenses, and are designed solely for use by a visually disabled person;
- the recipient of the supply is a resident, or is attending the premises of, a relevant institution; and
- the charity is not actively engaged in supplying such goods solely to disabled persons who are resident in or attending the premises of a relevant institution operated, managed or controlled by the charity.

(VAT Notice 48, ESC 3.24).

[*VATA 1994, Sch 8 Group 12 Notes 5B–5I; Health and Social Carer (Community Health and Standards) Act 2003, Sch 4 para 96; SI 1997/2744; SI 2000/503; SI 2002/2813*].

The effect of the above exclusions is that it prevents institutions such as private hospitals, nursing homes and residential homes from recovering VAT charged on the purchase of supplies for disabled persons which are used in their supply to in-patients and residents. It also prevents them, and the NHS, from making arrangements for third parties to make VAT-free supplies (eg incontinence products and wound dressings) on the institution's behalf to patients who live in their own homes and for which the institution pays. Instead, such supplies are supplied by the institution as part of its exempt care. Supplies of incontinence products, etc direct to the disabled person by independent suppliers and for which the disabled person pays are not affected. (VAT Information Sheet 6/97).

32.18 *Medical and surgical appliances*

Provided the conditions in 32.17 above are met, zero-rating applies to medical or surgical 'appliances' designed solely for the relief of a 'severe abnormality' or 'severe injury'.

Excluded are hearing aids (unless designed for auditory training of deaf children, see 32.23 below); dentures (but these are usually exempt under 32.8 above); and spectacles and contact lenses (but see 32.23 below for certain low vision aids).

Included are

- clothing (eg mastectomy bras and swimwear), footwear and wigs (which are often supplied during illness to mask hair loss); and
- renal haemodialysis units, oxygen concentrators, artificial respirators and other similar apparatus.

[*VATA 1994, Sch 8 Group 12, Item 2*(*a*) *and Note 4*].

An '*appliance*' is a device or piece of equipment with a specific function. It can be designed for use outside or inside the body.

The words 'severe abnormality' and 'severe injury' are not defined but among the disabilities falling within this category are amputation, rheumatoid or severe osteo-arthritis, severe disfigurement, congenital deformities, organic nervous diseases, learning disabilities and blindness.

Examples of zero-rated appliances, in addition to those specified in the legislation above, include

- artificial joints;
- artificial limbs;
- heart pacemakers;
- leg braces; and
- neck collars.

Examples of appliances that are not zero-rated, in addition to those specified in the legislation above, include

- plates or pins for use in repairing broken bones, bandages, plasters or other wound dressings as they are not appliances; and
- medical or surgical appliances that are not designed solely for the relief of a severe abnormality or severe injury, particularly those used in cosmetic surgery, such as breast implants.

(VAT Notice 701/7/02, para 4.2).

32.19 *Adjustable beds*

Provided the conditions in 32.17 above are met, zero-rating applies to electrically or mechanically adjustable beds designed for invalids. [*VATA 1994, Sch 8 Group 12, Item 2*(*b*)].

A distinction must be made between a bed and a mattress (*Back In Health Ltd (VTD 10003) (TVC 19.42)*). The same tribunal also considered what makes a bed 'electrically or mechanically adjustable' and held that the key factor was whether it was adjustable for height, drop and angle, so as to enable a person to slide from a wheelchair to a bed at a lower level.

Beds must clearly stand out as being something specialised for the use of invalids. As well as being electrically or mechanically adjustable, they should additionally have specific design features which distinguish them from a standard bed. (VAT Notice 701/7/02, para 4.3).

See also *Niagara Holdings Ltd (VTD 11400) (TVC 19.11)* and *Hulsta Furniture (UK) Ltd (VTD 16289) (TVC 19.12)*.

32.20 *Sanitary devices*

Provided the conditions in 32.17 above are met, zero-rating applies to

- commode chairs and stools,
- devices incorporating a bidet jet and warm air drier, and
- frames or other devices for sitting over or rising from sanitary appliances.

[*VATA 1994, Sch 8 Group 12, Item 2*(*c*)].

The toilet will also be eligible for zero-rating if part of a single supply with the qualifying attachments.

Products not eligible for zero-rating include bed pans and bed pan washers.

(Internal Guidance V1–7, Chapter 12 paras 33.1, 33.2).

32.21 *Chair lifts and stair lifts*

Provided the conditions in 32.17 above are met, zero-rating applies to 'chair lifts' and 'stair lifts' designed for use in connection with invalid wheelchairs. [*VATA 1994, Sch 8 Group 12, Item 2*(*d*)].

A '*chair lift*' is a platform conveyed along a rail up or down the stairs.

A '*stair lift*' conveys the individual between floors, often to a wheelchair at either end. For zero-rating to apply, it must be designed so as to be able to transfer the individual easily from the wheelchair to the lift. It is not the same as the shaft lifts that operate in offices or tower blocks.

(Internal Guidance V1–7, Chapter 12 paras 13.2, 13.3).

Although the lift must be capable of conveying a wheelchair-bound disabled person up and down stairs or from one level to another, the legislation does not require the disabled person to be seated in the wheelchair when using the lift. (VAT Notice 701/7/02, para 4.3).

See also 32.31 below for zero-rating of ordinary vertical lifts for disabled people who are not wheelchair-bound.

32.22 *Hoists and lifters*

Provided the conditions in 32.17 above are met, zero-rating applies to hoists and lifters designed for use by invalids. [*VATA 1994, Sch 8 Group 12, Item 2*(*e*)].

Included are

- hoists for lifting wheelchairs into motor vehicles and invalids in/out of a bed/bath or on/off the lavatory;
- lifting chairs and seats which, often operated by automatic button, enable disabled people who need assistance to move from a seated to a standing position;
- recliner chairs which have a seat raising and lowering feature capable of raising a person from a seated position to a standing position (and *vice versa*).

(Internal Guidance V1–7, Chapter 12 paras 13.2–13.4).

32.23 *Equipment designed solely for the disabled*

Provided the conditions in 32.17 above are met, zero-rating applies to 'equipment and appliances' not falling within 32.18 to 32 22 above but which is 'designed solely for use by a disabled person'. *Specifically included* are invalid wheelchairs and carriages (other than mechanically propelled vehicles intended or adapted for use on roads) and hearing aids designed for the auditory training of deaf children. *Excluded* are other types of hearing aids, dentures (but these are usually exempt under 32.8 above); and spectacles and contact lenses (but see (10) below for certain low vision aids). [*VATA 1994, Sch 8 Group 12, Item 2*(*g*) and *Notes 4, 5G*].

'*Equipment and appliances*' should be construed in the context of *Item 2* as a whole. Articles such as sprays, chemicals, etc are more in the nature of substances than equipment and so do not qualify for zero-rating, even though they may be of benefit to some disabled people. (Internal Guidance V1–7, Chapter 12 para 38.2).

It is not sufficient that the equipment or appliance is merely intended for use by a disabled person, or is mainly purchased by disabled persons. General purpose equipment (eg ordinary or orthopaedic beds, orthopaedic or reclining chairs, etc) may benefit disabled people but is designed for general use or for use by disabled and able-bodied people alike. Such products are not, therefore, eligible for relief. On the other hand, equipment designed solely for use by disabled people will remain eligible for relief when supplied to a disabled person or charity, even though available to be purchased by able-bodied people. (VAT Notice 701/7/02, para 4.5.1).

'*Designed solely for use by a disabled person*'. In the opinion of HMRC, this means that the original intention of the designer was to produce equipment or an appliance designed solely to meet the needs of persons with one or more disabilities (see also, for example, *Tempur Pedic (UK) Ltd (VTD 13744) (TVC 19.21)*). The design must succeed in that the product does, in fact, meet the needs of disabled persons. There are a number of conditions which may, but do not invariably, result in disability (eg asthma, psoriasis and dyslexia). Equipment which meets the needs of people with such conditions only qualifies for zero-rating if designed solely for the purpose of meeting the needs of *disabled* sufferers of the condition. (VAT Notice 701/7/02, para 4.5.2).

Determination of zero-rating. Only the designer or manufacturer can determine whether the goods qualify for zero-rating. The designer, manufacturer or importer of the goods must retain evidence which demonstrates that the goods in question fulfil the conditions for relief including

- marketing literature (eg brochures and catalogues);
- design specifications detailing the disability that needs to be addressed;
- the product specification for meeting those needs;
- results of tests demonstrating that the product meets the design intention; or
- patents or patent applications.

If necessary, the manufacturer or importer should seek liability rulings from HMRC.

Any other person, who thinks that the equipment or appliances he is selling have been designed solely for use by a disabled person, should seek confirmation from the manufacturer or importer. (Their advertising literature may contain a statement to this effect.) Local Business Advice Centres have been asked to refuse requests for liability rulings from retailers.

(VAT Notice 701/7/02, para 4.5.3; Internal Guidance V1–7, Chapter 12 para 3.1).

VAT liability of specific equipment and appliances. The following is a list of equipment and appliances which have been considered (either by HMRC, a tribunal or the courts) for inclusion within *VATA 1994, Sch 8 Group 12, Item 2(g)*.

(1) *Air conditioning*

Air-conditioning and similar general purpose equipment does not qualify for relief. Oxygen concentrators, artificial respirators and 'similar apparatus' specifically designed for providing artificial ventilation for patients are included under 32.18 above. (Internal Guidance V1–7, Chapter 12 paras 7.1, 7.2).

See also *Simmons (VTD 6622) (TVC 19.38)* where two air-conditioning units, purchased by a person suffering from multiple sclerosis, and which helped considerably in coping with the condition, were held to have been designed for general purpose use and not for use by a disabled person. The fact that the design would have been the same whether the equipment was to be used by a disabled person or for the general purposes did not bring the equipment within the scope of *Item 2(g)*. Air-conditioning units could also not be regarded as 'similar apparatus' (see above) and therefore fall within 32.18 above.

(2) *Asthma, hay fever and allergy products*

Supplies of all vacuum cleaners, air purification products and similar allergy relief products are standard-rated irrespective of to whom they are supplied. (Business Briefs 16/96, 17/96, and 20/97; Internal Guidance V1–7, Chapter 12 para 9.1).

See also *GD Searle & Co Ltd (VTD 13439) (TVC 19.46)* which concerned aerosol pesticide sprays, designed to kill dust mites and supplied to pharmacists for sale to asthmatics or sufferers from eczema. The tribunal held that, as not all sufferers from asthma could be described as 'chronically sick or disabled', the sprays were not 'designed solely for use by a handicapped person', and thus failed to qualify for zero-rating.

(3) *Carpets*

In *The David Lewis Centre, QB [1995] STC 485 (TVC 19.24)* woollen carpets, purchased to protect patients from scorching when falling as a result of an epileptic seizure, were held not to qualify for zero-rating since the carpets were not specifically designed for the use of the disabled.

Similarly, in *Vassall Centre Trust (VTD 17891) (TVC 19.28)* carpets, adapted by having a light coloured strip along both edges up to the doorway or access point to assist the partially sighted in moving about the building, were held not to be designed solely for use by disabled persons.

(4) *Computer equipment*

Computer systems are increasingly being used to aid disabled people. They are generally made up of both standard-rated, general use items of hardware and software, together with other items designed solely for use by a disabled person and which are therefore eligible for zero-rating. To simplify the application of VAT for such computer systems sold as a complete package, suppliers may use either or both of the following concessions provided

- the computer system is a tool to aid the disabled person to overcome communication problems; and
- the computer system is for the personal or domestic use of a disabled person.

The arrangements apply only to complete packages. Replacement units or upgrading items are subject to VAT at the standard rate unless they are designed solely for use by disabled people.

(*a*) *Concession 1 – zero-rating of central processor.* A central processor may be zero-rated if

- it is sold as part of a computer system; and
- it has software installed which enables a disabled person to use the computer system or other software effectively, or to carry out tasks effectively when otherwise they could not.

No other general purpose hardware may be zero-rated under this or any other concession.

(*b*) *Concession 2 – composite rate of VAT for computer systems.* Traders supplying disabled people with complete computer systems that contain significant specialist items for use by disabled customers may use a composite VAT rate for such supplies. This rate is based on supplies of such packages made by that supplier over a recent representative period. In addition to the items of equipment designed solely for the use of a disabled person, the suppliers may include the values of the following elements of the package in the zero-rated portion.

- The central processor described in (*a*) above; and
- costs charged to the customer for the installation of the equipment and for the training in its use.

Example

Z Ltd supplies five different qualifying packages of computer equipment in a representative period of three months. In package

A, the zero-rated element (central processor, speech synthesiser, Braille embosser, specialist software, installation and training) is £1,500 at sales value and the standard-rated element (printer, keyboard, VDU and standard software) is £500 plus £87.50 VAT. The total cost of the package is £2,087.50 of which £87.50 is VAT. The composite rate is the rate which needs to be applied to the total VAT-exclusive sale value (£2,000) to ensure the correct VAT is declared, ie

87.50 ÷ 2,000 × 100 = 4.375% (rounded up to 4.4%)

The composite rates and value of sales for each of the five packages offered in the representative period are as follows.

Package	*Composite rate*	*Sales value*	*VAT*
		£	£
A	4.4%	50,000	2,200
B	6%	20,000	1,200
C	3%	10,000	300
D	3.8%	10,000	380
E	4.1%	10,000	410
		£100,000	£4,490

The overall composite rate is

4,490 ÷ 100,000 × 100 = 4.49% (rounded to 4.5%)

Z Ltd can apply a composite rate of 4.5% to all sales of qualifying packages. The overall composite rate should be recalculated every twelve months.

(VAT Notice 701/7/02, paras 4.5, 9.1–9.5).

(5) *Golf buggies*

In *Foxer Industries (VTD 13817) (TVC 19.47)* single-seat golf buggies, marketed for sale to elderly golfers, were held not to have been designed solely for the use of disabled persons. (In a subsequent appeal (*Foxer Industries (VTD 14469) (TVC 19.59)*) the partnership claimed that work done in adapting a number of buggies for specific customers should be treated as qualifying for zero-rating. The tribunal held that, in one case, the modifications to the basic design were so fundamental that the entire buggy should be treated as zero-rated under *Item 2(g)*. In the other eight cases, an appropriate proportion of the price was treated as zero-rated under 32.27 below.)

See also *C F Leisure Mobility Ltd (VTD 16790) (TVC 19.48)*.

(6) *Hearing aids and induction loop systems*

Certain specialist equipment designed for people with severely defective hearing, which do not constitute 'hearing aids' (specifically excluded, see above) as the term is generally used, may be zero-rated. These include the following.

- Hearing aids designed for the auditory training of deaf children. [*VATA 1994, Sch 8 Group 12 Note 4*].

- TV hearing aids (an amplifier and earpiece connected to a TV set, radio, etc to enable a near-deaf person to hear sound without turning up the volume).
- Tinnitus maskers (an earpiece which generates a constant noise to mask the effect of ringing in the ears).
- Induction loop equipment (a system that allows a hearing aid user or anyone wearing an induction loop receiver to listen to a sound source (eg a television or radio) without the interference of airborne background noise).

NHS hearing aids supplied on free loan to NHS patients are not supplies in the course or furtherance of a business activity and are outside the scope of the VAT. Supplies to health authorities are standard-rated.

HMRC have also indicated that vibrating pillows for deaf or hard of hearing people qualify for zero-rating.

(VAT Notice 701/7/02, paras 4.5, 4.6; Internal Guidance V1–7, Chapter 12 paras 18.3–18.5).

(7) *Hydrotherapy pools*

Following the decisions in *The David Lewis Centre (VTD 10860) (TVC 19.26)* and *Boys' and Girls' Welfare Society (VTD 15274) (TVC 19.24)*, although it remains their general policy that swimming pools are not equipment that has been designed solely for the use of disabled persons, HMRC now accept that a hydrotherapy pool qualifies for zero-rating provided it at least

- is sited indoors;
- has a uniform or a very gradual change in depth of water;
- has water heated to at least 32 degrees centigrade;
- has fixed means of access to the pool either by way of ramps, shallow rising steps with railings or a fixed hoist; and
- incorporates safety features to prevent accidents.

(Internal Guidance V1–7, Chapter 12 paras 20.1, 20.3).

(8) *Incontinence products*

HMRC have always accepted that incontinence products are goods of a kind which qualifying for zero-rating but their supply can only be zero-rated in certain circumstances.

- *Retail sales.* People who are incontinent and live in their own homes are entitled to buy incontinence products at the zero rate. Eligible incontinence products (eg disposable and washable incontinence pads, waterproof or leak-proof underwear and collecting devices) can be zero-rated on the shelf.
- *Internet and mail order sales* also qualify for zero-rating provided they are made to individuals and not institutions.

Zero-rating does not apply to incontinence products supplied to a disabled person (whether by a Health Authority, hospital or any other person) whilst that person is an in-patient or receiving residential care (see under 32.18 below).

Bulk sales. In practice, there is no requirement for a retail customer to provide a written eligibility declaration under 32.35 below to the retailer confirming the incontinence products are eligible for VAT relief. However, HMRC will expect retailers, internet and mail order suppliers to have a signed declaration, or other supporting evidence that the supply is to an incontinent individual (and not to an institution such as a nursing home) for customers who buy more than

— 200 disposable pads;

— 50 washable pads;

— 5 collecting devices; or

— 10 pairs of waterproof or leak-proof underwear.

(VAT Notice 701/7/02, para 4.5; Internal Guidance V1–7, Chapter 12 paras 21.2–21.4).

(9) *Kitchens*

Kitchen furniture fitted into a kitchen during the construction of a new dwelling may be zero-rated under *VATA 1994, Sch 8 Group 5 Item 4* (see 42.26 LAND AND BUILDINGS).

For existing kitchens, equipment designed solely for use by a disabled person (eg specially adapted taps with long handles), together with the services of installation (see 32.29 below) and the services of adapting goods to suit the condition of a disabled person (see 32.27 below) can also be zero-rated.

See also *Softley Ltd (t/a Softley Kitchens) (VTD 15034) (TVC 19.20)* where it was held that certain items of kitchen equipment could be zero-rated when made to the individual specifications of a disabled person. HMRC take the decision as meaning that suppliers who design, supply and install kitchens to meet the specific needs of a disabled person must charge VAT on appliances such as cookers and refrigerators, standard kitchen cabinet units and work surfaces but can zero-rate specially designed equipment such as cupboards which are accessible to wheelchair users. In such cases, design or installation charges must be apportioned between their standard-rated and zero-rated elements.

Suppliers of mass production kitchen equipment cannot benefit from zero-rating, even if that equipment might be of more use to disabled people than others.

(Internal Guidance V1–7, Chapter 12 paras 23.3, 23.4).

(10) *Low vision aids and other aids for the blind*

Although spectacles and contact lenses are specifically excluded (see above), zero-rating can be applied to other types of low vision aids. This equipment tends to fall into two categories.

- Spectacle-mounted low vision aids which are custom made to the prescription of a qualified optician where the prescription identifies the appliance as a low vision aid.

- Other low vision aids, including technical aids for reading and writing, which are designed exclusively for visually impaired people (eg closed circuit video magnification equipment capable of magnifying text and images).

HMRC also list the following as examples of equipment qualifying for relief.

- Braille embossers.
- Whistling cups for blind people.
- White canes for blind people.

(VAT Notice 701/7/02, paras 4.5, 4.7; Internal Guidance V1–7, Chapter 12 paras 26.2, 26.3).

(11) *Over bed tables*

This type of equipment is designed for use by hospital patients in general and not just those who are chronically sick or disabled. They therefore cannot be said to be 'designed solely for use by a handicapped person' and do not qualify for relief. See *Princess Louise Scottish Hospital (VTD 1412) (TVC 19.29).*

(12) *Pain relief equipment*

Following the tribunal decision in *Neen Design Ltd (VTD 11782) (TVC 19.8)* TENS (Transcutaneous Electrical Nerve Stimulators) machines are taken as designed solely for use by disabled persons (ie sufferers of chronic pain) even though frequently used by sufferers of acute (short-term) pain (eg sports injuries and labour pains). Neither the latter, nor the fact that the product was subsequently marketed for use by sufferers of chronic *and* acute pain, outweighed the original design intention. As a result, TENS machines can be zero-rated when meeting the conditions in 32.17 above. TENS machines supplied for use by people suffering short-term pain are taxable at the standard rate. (Internal Guidance V1–7,Chapter 12 para 31.10).

(13) *Radiators*

In *The David Lewis Centre (VTD 10860) (TVC 19.24)* low surface temperature radiators, designed so that their surface would not burn the skin of a disabled person who fell against them, were held to be zero-rated because the heating system in its entirety had been designed specifically for the charity. HMRC regard this decision as one made on the facts of the case and will only apply it in identical circumstances. They do not treat it an authority for zero-rating supplies of low surface temperature radiators to eligible charities or disabled people. (Internal Guidance V1–7, Chapter 12 para 25.1).

In *Boys and Girls Welfare Society (VTD 15274) (TVC 19.74)* the tribunal held that low surface temperature radiators did not qualify for zero-rating under *Item 2(g)* since they were not 'designed solely for use by a handicapped person', but that they qualified for zero-rating under 32.30 below where they were installed in bathrooms, washrooms or lavatories.

In *Joulesave EMES Ltd (VTD 17115) (TVC 19.23)* the tribunal held that radiator and pipe covers had been designed solely for use by disabled people and were eligible for zero-rating when meeting the conditions in 32.17 above.

(14) *Soft games rooms and observation windows*

The design, supply and equipping of soft games rooms, and observation windows, used by disabled persons were held to be standard-rated supplies of construction services in *C & E Commrs v The David Lewis Centre, QB [1995] STC 485 (TVC 11.7).*

(15) *Spa baths*

In *Aquakraft Ltd (VTD 2214) (TVC 19.8)* the tribunal held that a spa bath supplied to hospitals and nursing homes, even though it had special features such as handrails, provision for the fitting of a hoist and recessed taps for safety, was not subject to relief under *Item 2(g)* because all kinds of hospital patients could be expected to use it.

A spa bath might be eligible for zero-rating under 32.30 below (as a supply of goods in connection with extending or adapting a bathroom in a disabled person's private residence).

(16) *Walkways*

A walkway is

- a structure over a path providing shelter from the elements; or
- a covered bridge above the ground linking buildings and providing shelter from the elements.

Although beneficial to disabled people, walkways do not incorporate any special features that render them 'designed solely for use by a disabled person' and so are not eligible for zero-rating under *Item 2(g)*. See *Portland College (VTD 9815) (TVC 19.41)*.

(Internal Guidance V1–7, Chapter 12 paras 36.1, 36.2).

(17) *Wheelchairs*

Invalid wheelchairs and carriages (other than mechanically propelled vehicles intended or adapted for use on the roads) are specifically included in *VATA 1994, Sch 8 Group 12 Item 2* by *Notes 4(b)* and *5G*.

An '*invalid carriage*' is defined by *The Chronically Sick and Disabled Persons Act 1970, s 20* as a vehicle, whether mechanically propelled or not, constructed or adapted for the carriage of one person, being a person suffering from some physical defect or disability.

(18) *Writing boards*

Zero-rating does not apply to a general purpose item that is marketed for use by disabled people, even if some changes are made to the design to make it useful for them. An objective test must be applied to see if the item has been designed solely for use by a disabled person. The design intention must be met for zero-rating to be achieved. See *Posturite (UK) Ltd (VTD 7848) (TVC 19.40)*.

32.24 *Parts and accessories*

Provided the conditions in 32.17 above are met, zero-rating applies to 'parts' and 'accessories' designed solely for use in or with goods described in 32.18 to 32.23 above and 32.26(*a*) below. [*VATA 1994, Sch 8 Group 12, Item 2(h)*].

'*Parts*' means integral components without which the equipment is incomplete.

'*Accessories*' means optional extras which can be used to improve the operation of the equipment, or enable it to be used, or to be used to better effect, in particular circumstances.

Zero-rating does not apply to general use items even if purchased to be used with a zero-rated item. See *Poole Shopmobility (VTD 16290) (TVC 19.58)* (standard batteries) and *Mills (VTD 1893) (TVC 19.56)* (portable generator). If, however, batteries were designed solely to operate within a zero-rated item, they would be eligible for zero-rating. (VAT Notice 701/7/02, para 4.8). See also *The Princess Louise Scottish Hospital (VTD 1412) (TVC 19.26)* where overbeds were held not to qualify as accessories to a zero-rated bed within 32.19 above, even though designed by the same designer, as they could be used on other beds.

Parts and accessories for boats. Although the legislation specifically refers to parts and accessories for goods within 32.18 to 32.23 above, HMRC consider this to be a drafting error and accept the provisions should also apply to 32.25 below. (Internal Guidance V1–7, Chapter 12 para 39.5).

32.25 *Boats*

Provided the conditions in 32.17 above are met, zero-rating applies to boats designed, or substantially and permanently adapted, for use by disabled persons. [*VATA 1994, Sch 8 Group 12, Item 2*(*i*)].

To qualify for relief, the boat should include all or most of the following features.

- A ramp for wheelchairs.
- Lifts and level non-cambered surfaces to accommodate wheelchair movements.
- Specialised washing and lavatory facilities accessible to disabled people.
- Specially equipped galley and sleeping areas and steering facilities designed for use by disabled people.
- Handrails.
- Wheelchair clamps.

(VAT Notice 701/7/02, para 4.4).

A boat would not necessarily have to contain all of the above features to qualify for zero-rating (eg a boat providing day trips would require only those needed for its intended use). If the special features are present when initially supplied, the whole boat is 'designed solely' and so can be zero-rated. If the boat contains none or insufficient features at that time, the initial supply of the boat would be standard-rated. Zero-rating could then apply to any subsequent qualifying adaptations under 32.27 below. (Internal Guidance V1–7, Chapter 10 para 10.2).

Although the legislation in 32.24 above does not refer to parts and accessories for boats within this item, HMRC consider this to be a drafting error and allow zero-rating where a person supplies parts and accessories which meet all the other criteria of 32.24 above. (Internal Guidance V1–7, Chapter 12 para 39.5).

32.26 **Motor vehicles**

Zero-rating applies to the supply of a motor vehicle in the following circumstances.

(*a*) The supply (including the letting on hire) to

- a disabled person for 'domestic or personal use', or
- a charity for making available, by sale or otherwise, to disabled persons for domestic or personal use

of a motor vehicle designed or substantially and permanently adapted for the carriage of a disabled person in a wheelchair or on a stretcher and of no more than eleven other persons.

See 32.17 above for the interpretation of '*domestic and personal use*'.

[*VATA 1994, Sch 8 Group 12, Item 2(f); SI 2001/754*].

(*b*) The supply (including the letting on hire) of a 'qualifying motor vehicle' to

- a disabled person, who usually uses a wheelchair or is usually carried on a stretcher, for domestic or his personal use; or
- a charity for making available to such a disabled person, by sale or otherwise, for domestic or his personal use.

A '*qualifying motor vehicle*' is a motor vehicle (other than one capable of carrying 12 or more persons including the driver) that

- is designed or substantially and permanently adapted to enable a disabled person, who usually uses a wheelchair or who is usually carried on a stretcher, to enter, and drive or otherwise be carried in, the motor vehicle; or
- by reason of its design, or being substantially or permanently adapted, includes features whose design is such that their sole purpose is to a allow a wheelchair used by a disabled person to be carried in or on the motor vehicle.

[*VATA 1994, Sch 8 Group 12 Item 2A and Notes 5, 5L; SI 2001/754*].

HMRC give the following advice and interpretations on the above.

(1) A wheelchair user can choose to remain in the wheelchair or use any of the seats.

(2) A '*wheelchair*' is a chair for invalids on wheels which is manually or mechanically propelled. A mobility scooter (ie a scooter which is mechanically propelled, has a central steering column, has a maximum speed of four miles per hour for pavement use, and is generally only used outside the home) is not a wheelchair for VAT purposes.

(3) A '*wheelchair user*' is anyone who has to use a wheelchair (electrically powered or otherwise) in order to be mobile. A disabled person with a degenerative condition, such as multiple sclerosis, who does not need to use a wheelchair all the time, but only when the condition requires it, also qualifies as a wheelchair user. A person who only occasionally uses a wheelchair (eg when visiting a shopping centre or gardens) or temporarily (eg because he has a broken leg) is not considered normally to use a wheelchair and is not eligible for the relief.

(4) A '*stretcher user*' for these purposes is anyone who has to use a stretcher in order to be transported.

(5) '*Domestic or personal use*'. To qualify for zero-rating the adapted vehicle must be for the domestic or personal use of the disabled wheelchair/stretcher user. This may also include vehicles that are used by the disabled wheelchair/stretcher user in his work capacity provided this is incidental to the vehicle's main use as a private vehicle. Zero-rating does not apply to vehicles supplied to businesses regardless of who uses them or how they have been adapted (eg it is not possible to zero-rate an adapted vehicle that will be used as a taxi).

(6) *Adapted motor vehicles*. An eligible adapted motor vehicle is one adapted to meet the specific needs of a disabled wheelchair/stretcher user where the adaptation

- allows him to enter and travel in the vehicle whilst seated in the wheelchair or on the stretcher;

- allows him to enter, travel in or leave the vehicle;
- enables him to drive the vehicle; or
- allows a wheelchair to be carried on, or in, the vehicle.

A '*permanent*' adaptation is one that can be used for as long as the disabled person requires it. Generally the adaptation would require welding or bolting to the vehicle.

A '*substantial*' adaptation enables a wheelchair/stretcher user to use a vehicle which he could not use before it was adapted. For example, a spinner device, such as a knob on a steering wheel, may not seem substantial to an able-bodied person but it would be substantial for a disabled wheelchair user who could not otherwise drive the vehicle.

Included are

- a swivel seat;
- a hoist to lift a wheelchair into or onto the vehicle;
- a box for the wheelchair, which is fitted to the top or the back of the vehicle;
- adaptations that enable a wheelchair user to drive the vehicle, such as a push/pull brake and accelerator, hand controls or other aids that operate the primary driving controls; and
- an infra-red control unit that operates the secondary controls.

Not included are

- the fitting of a roof rack or standard roof box,
- the attachment of a trailer to the back of a vehicle, or
- the fitting of automatic transmission

because they are for general use and not specifically designed for disabled people.

Second-hand adapted motor vehicles can be zero-rated if the above conditions are met. (Although second-hand cars are usually sold under the second-hand margin scheme, an eligible vehicle can be sold outside that scheme and invoiced in the normal way.)

A family member can purchase the adapted vehicle provided that it is purchased for the personal use of the disabled wheelchair/stretcher user.

(VAT Notice 701/59/02, paras 2.2–2.5, 2.7, 3.2–3.6, 4.1).

Motability scheme. See also 32.33 below for zero-rating of motor vehicles under this scheme.

Time of adaptation. If, before the vehicle is supplied, it is adapted by

- the supplier, or
- a specialist converter who supplies his services to the supplier,

then the vehicle and any necessary conversion work can be zero-rated provided the supplier receives one payment to cover the cost of both the vehicle and the conversion.

If a vehicle is adapted to meet the criteria for zero-rating after the initial supply, only the chargeable conversion is eligible for zero-rating under 32.27 below.

Parts and accessories. A supplier can zero-rate *any* parts or accessories with the first supply of an adapted vehicle. Supplies after this first sale only qualify for zero-rating under 32.24 above if those goods themselves qualify as having been designed solely for use by a disabled person (eg a replacement wheelchair hoist).

(Internal Guidance V1–7, Chapter 12 paras 29.5–29.7).

32.27 **Adaptation of goods**

Zero-rating applies to the supply

- to a disabled person of services of adapting general purpose goods to suit his or her condition, and
- to a charity of services of adapting general purpose goods to suit the condition of a disabled person to whom the goods are to be made available, by sale or otherwise, by the charity,

and to any goods necessarily supplied in connection with the services of adaptation.

Zero-rating applies only to the adaptation services (and incidental goods). It does not apply to the goods themselves being adapted. Therefore, where the supplier of the services also supplies the goods, and has adapted them prior to the supply of adaptation services, he must apportion the value of the supply between the unadapted standard-rated goods and the zero-rated service of adaptation.

[*VATA 1994, Sch 8 Group 12 Items 3, 4, 6 and Note 8*].

Separate rules apply to the sale of substantially and permanently adapted motor vehicles. See 32.26 above.

Buildings. Apart from the first grant of a major interest in a building which is deemed to be a supply of goods by virtue of the *VATA 1994, Sch 4 para 4*, buildings are not 'goods' and therefore the adaptation of a building to suit the condition of a disabled person does not fall within the above provisions. See *Arthritis Care (VTD 13974) (TVC 19.49)*. The only reliefs which apply to adaptations of buildings are those in 32.30 and 32.31 below.

Apportionment. See 47.4 OUTPUT TAX for various methods of apportionment. It may not be valid to look merely at the price difference between the adapted model and a standard factory model. Any initial research and development costs related to the adaptation should be costed as zero-rated in addition to the basic extra cost passed on to the customer (see *Foxer Industries (VTD 14469) (TVC 19.47)*). HMRC accept this provided that, overall, the method used produces a fair and reasonable result.

(Internal Guidance V1–7, Chapter 12 paras 43.3, 43.4).

32.28 **Repair and maintenance**

Zero-rating applies to the supply to a disabled person or charity of a service of repair or maintenance of

- any goods which were zero-rated on supply under 32.17 to 32.26 above,
- any goods supplied in connection with adaptation services under 32.27 above or repair and maintenance services under these provisions,

- any goods supplied in connection with the installation of a lift under 32.31 below, and
- any alarm call system zero-rated under 32.32 below

together with a supply of any goods 'in connection with those repair and maintenance services'.

[*VATA 1994, Sch 8 Group 12 Items 5 and 6; SI 2001/754*].

The supply of any goods 'in connection with those repair and maintenance services' applies only to goods which are ancillary to the service of the repair and maintenance and not to the goods which are themselves the subject of the repair and maintenance.

See also 32.30 below under the heading *Goods supplied in connection with construction services.*

(Internal Guidance V1–7, Chapter 12 para 41.3).

32.29 **Installation of goods**

Zero-rating applies to the supply to a disabled person or to a charity of services necessarily performed in the installation of equipment or appliances (including parts and accessories for them) which are zero-rated under 32.17 to 32.25 above. [*VATA 1994, Sch 8 Group 12 Item 7*].

Examples of services of installation which can be zero-rated under these provisions are

- plumbing in a sanitary appliance;
- wiring up an electrically adjustable bed; and
- installing a chair lift.

(VAT Notice 701/7/02, para 5.1).

Where parts and accessories are used, these are eligible for zero-rating under this provision provided they are part of the single supply of installation services. Parts and accessories supplied separately are eligible for relief under 32.24 above.

32.30 **Building alterations**

Zero-rating applies to the following supplies.

(*a*) The supply to a disabled person of a service of constructing ramps or widening doorways or passages (but not constructing new doorways or passages) for the purposes of facilitating his entry to, or movement within, his private residence. [*VATA 1994, Sch 8 Group 12 Item 8*].

Construction of a ramp includes

- the raising of a floor level to match that of another existing floor level so as to remove a step or steps;
- the reduction of the angle of an incline; or
- the creation of a slope.

A passage can be outdoors as well as indoors. Widening a passage includes

- the widening of a room through which a disabled person passes to gain access to another room, eg a bedroom which has an en suite facility (see *Cannings-Knight (VTD 11291) (TVC 19.66)*); or

- the widening of an existing path across a disabled person's garden (but not the construction of a new path).

(VAT Notice 701/7/02, para 6.2).

(*b*) The supply to a charity of services within (*a*) above for the purpose of facilitating a disabled person's entry to, or movement within, *any* building (not just a private residence). [*VATA 1994, Sch 8 Group 12 Item 9*].

(*c*) The supply to a disabled person of a service of providing, extending or adapting a bathroom, 'washroom' or lavatory in that person's private residence where such provision, extension or adaptation is necessary by reason of his condition. [*VATA 1994, Sch 8 Group 12 Item 10*].

(*d*) The supply to a charity of a service of providing, extending or adapting a bathroom, 'washroom' or lavatory for use by disabled persons

(i) in a residential home or self-contained living accommodation, in either case provided as a residence (whether on a permanent or temporary basis or both) for handicapped persons (but not including an inn, hotel, boarding house or similar establishment or accommodation in any such type of establishment), or

(ii) in a day-centre where at least 20% of the individuals using the centre are handicapped persons

where such provision, extension or adaptation is necessary by reason of the condition of the disabled persons.

[*VATA 1994, Sch 8 Group 12 Item 11* and *Note 5J; SI 2000/805*].

Zero-rating applies even if the residential home, etc is not managed or used by the charity to which the supply is made. Care, however, should be taken when supplies are made to residential homes as many such homes are not operated by charities, in which case supplies to them do not qualify for zero-rating under these provisions. (VAT Notice 701/7/02, para 6.3).

(*e*) The supply to a charity of a service of providing, extending or adapting a 'washroom' or lavatory for use by disabled persons in a building (or part of a building) used principally by a charity for charitable purposes (eg a church hall, day centre or village hall) where such provision, etc is necessary to facilitate the use of the washroom or lavatory by disabled persons. [*VATA 1994, Sch 8 Group 12 Item 12*].

(*f*) The supply of goods in connection with the supply of services within (*a*)–(*e*) above. [*VATA 1994, Sch 8 Group 12 Item 13*].

Building materials and other goods can be zero-rated under this provision when supplied by

- the building contractor in connection with the zero-rated services (see above), or
- a builders merchant, etc to the disabled person or charity themselves for use by their building contractor (see *Flather (VTD 11960) (TVC 19.67)*) provided the builders merchant is happy that the actual building work will qualify for zero-rating and can demonstrate this subsequently to any visiting HMRC officer

but not when the materials are bought by a disabled person or charity in connection with building works which will be performed free of charge by a friend or relative, or in a do-it-yourself capacity by the disabled person or charity themselves (because there is no subsequent supply of zero-rated construction services to which these materials can be connected).

(VAT Notice 701/7/02, para 6.9).

For the purposes of (*c*)–(*e*) above

- '*washroom*' means a room that contains a lavatory or washbasin (or both) but does not contain a bath or a shower or cooking, sleeping or laundry facilities [*VATA 1994, Sch 8 Group 12 Notes 5K; SI 2000/805*];
- bathroom includes a shower room (VAT Notice 701/7/02, para 6.3); and
- lavatory is a room containing a toilet and possibly, but not always, a washbasin (VAT Notice 701/7/02, para 6.3).

Private residence. This means where a person lives by virtue of a personal rather than a public or general right. The word 'private' does not require ownership or sole occupation (eg the fact that a property is occupied by a family does not prevent it being the 'private residence' of each of the occupants). But it cannot mean a communal residence, such as a nursing home.

Zero-rating need not be confined solely to work on a single building, but can be extended to linked or associated buildings, courtyards or gardens. Qualifying work can, for example, be zero-rated when related to

- 'granny annexes' whether attached to or integral with the main dwelling house or in a separate building within the curtilage of the main dwelling house;
- a detached outside toilet of a house;
- the construction of a ramp or the widening of a path across the garden of the disabled person's house;
- the lowering of a pavement outside a disabled person's private residence to facilitate his or her access to that residence; and
- qualifying work relating to the detached garage of a house, even where that garage is located down the road, provided the garage is within reasonable proximity of the house and both properties have the same landlord and tenant.

(Internal Guidance V1–7, Chapter 12 para 11.5).

Preparatory work and necessary restoration work can also be zero-rated provided the supply is made to the disabled person or charity concerned, as the case may be. This would include, eg

- when widening a doorway, the removal of bricks and mortar and restoration of the immediate décor; and
- when providing a bathroom, the preparation of footings, including ground levelling, work for the provision of water, gas, electricity and drainage as necessary, and restoration of the immediate décor.

Professional services. Services of an architect, surveyor or any person acting as a consultant or in a supervisory capacity, even when supplied in connection with a supply of qualifying building services, are standard-rated in all circumstances.

Additional construction work in the course of a zero-rated supply. Where economy and feasibility dictate that a bathroom, washroom or lavatory has to be constructed in, or extended into, a space occupied by an existing room (eg a bedroom or kitchen), the restoration of that room to its original size can be regarded as part of the work essential to the provision of the bathroom, etc and can be zero-rated provided the supply is also made to the disabled person. Where, on the other hand, a builder constructs, extends or adapts a bathroom, washroom or lavatory and at the same time constructs additional accommodation (eg an adjoining new bedroom/day room), the supply must be apportioned between the zero-rated and standard-rated parts.

(VAT Notice 701/7/02, paras 6.5, 6.7, 6.8).

Supplies to other persons on behalf of a disabled person. Where, strictly, the supply should be to the disabled person, zero-rating will normally still be permitted if

- the disabled person is a minor or a dependent relative living with the householder so that the supply may technically be to the householder;
- a relative commissions work before a disabled person moves into the residence and the disabled person subsequently dies before moving in; or
- a local authority takes over a grant assigned to a disabled person and carries out the work (but not if the local authority commissions and pays for the work and the disabled person is merely a passive recipient).

Tenants cannot normally authorise substantial alterations to be made to buildings which they rent. In practice, the services will be supplied to the landlord regardless of who pays for them.

(Internal Guidance V1–7, Chapter 12 para 11.4).

32.31 **Lift installation**

The following supplies are zero-rated.

(*a*) The supply to a disabled person of services necessarily performed in the installation of a lift for the purpose of facilitating his or her movement between floors within that person's own private residence. [*VATA 1994, Sch 8 Group 12 Item 16*].

This provision overlaps with 32.21 above (zero-rating of chair and stair lifts) but extends relief to lifts which, although not specially designed for use by disabled people, help them to move between floors within their home.

HMRC allow zero-rating for an external lift at a disabled person's private residence where the only means of access to the disabled person's accommodation on an upper floor is by an external staircase. (Internal Guidance V1–7, Chapter 12 para 24.2).

(*b*) The supply to a charity providing a permanent or temporary residence or day centre for disabled persons of services necessarily performed in the installation of a lift for the purpose of facilitating movement of disabled persons between floors in that building. [*VATA 1994, Sch 8 Group 12 Item 17*].

If the building is a permanent or temporary residence, then there is no requirement for that residence to be exclusively for disabled persons. A supply can be zero-rated if there is at least one disabled person occupying the residence.

Similarly, to qualify as a day centre, the building need not have been set up principally or exclusively for disabled persons but it must be capable of being regarded as a day centre in the ordinary sense of the term. This probably means that the disabled persons receive some form of care. See *Union of Students of the University of Warwick (VTD 13821) (TVC 19.80)* and *Aspex Visual Arts Trust (VTD 16419) (TVC 19.81)* where a lift in a students union building and an art gallery respectively failed to qualify for zero-rating.

Educational institutions. As a consequence of comments made by the High Court in *C & E Commrs v Help the Aged, QB [1997] STC 406 (TVC 11.15)* HMRC initially formed the view that charitable educational institutions (eg grant-maintained schools and universities) could be regarded as day centres providing care for disabled people and therefore the installation of lifts in their *non-residential* buildings could be zero-rated under the above provisions (providing all other conditions were met). They subsequently decided that this view was incorrect. As a transitional measure, where a contract for the installation of a lift in a non-residential building was entered into before 31 March 2005, HMRC accept that the supply can be zero-rated providing all other conditions have been met. Where the installation of a lift has been zero-rated under these arrangements, subsequent supplies of repair and maintenance of that lift can also be zero-rated. Where a contract for the installation of a lift in a non-residential building is entered into after that date, the supply of installation services (and any subsequent supplies of repair and maintenance) is standard-rated. (Business Brief 3/05). This does not apply to lift installations in those buildings where an educational institution provides permanent or temporary residence, which remains zero-rated, provided all other conditions are met.

(Internal Guidance V1–7, Chapter 12 para 24.3).

(*c*) The supply of goods in connection with the supply of services within (*a*) or (*b*) above. [*VATA 1994, Sch 8 Group 12 Item 18*].

Building materials and other goods can be zero-rated under this provision when supplied

- by the building contractor in connection with the zero-rated services (see above), or
- by a builders merchant, etc to the disabled person or charity themselves for use by their building contractor (see *Flather (VTD 11960) (TVC 19.67)*) provided the builders merchant is happy that the actual building work will qualify for zero-rating and can demonstrate this subsequently to any visiting HMRC officer

but not when the materials are bought by a disabled person or charity in connection with building works which will be performed free of charge by a friend or relative, or in a do-it-yourself capacity by the disabled person or charity themselves (because there is no subsequent supply of zero-rated construction services to which these materials can be connected).

(VAT Notice 701/7/02, para 6.9).

Preparatory work and necessary restoration work can also be zero-rated provided the supply is made to the disabled person or charity concerned, as the case may be.

Professional services. Services of an architect, surveyor or any person acting as a consultant or in a supervisory capacity, even when supplied in connection with a supply of qualifying building services, are standard-rated in all circumstances.

(VAT Notice 701/7/02, paras 6.7, 6.8).

Repair and maintenance of any qualifying goods is zero-rated under 32.28 above.

32.32 **Alarm call systems**

The following supplies are zero-rated.

(*a*) The supply to

- a disabled person for his 'domestic or personal use', or
- a charity for making available to disabled persons, by sale or otherwise, for domestic or their personal use

of an alarm system designed to be capable of operation by a disabled person, and to enable him to alert directly a 'specified person or a control centre'.

(*b*) The supply of services necessarily performed by a control centre in receiving and responding to calls from an alarm system within (*a*) above.

A '*specified person or control centre*' is a person or centre who or which is appointed to receive directly calls activated by the alarm system; and who or which retains information about the disabled person to assist that person in the event of illness, injury or similar emergency.

[*VATA 1994, Sch 8 Group 12 Items 19, 20* and *Note 9*].

See 32.17 above for HMRC's interpretation of '*domestic or personal use*'.

To qualify for zero-rating, the alarm system must have some special operational feature specific to the needs of the disabled person (eg a pendant worn around the neck, with a button that can be pressed as an emergency buzzer). A specified person could be a relative, friend or neighbour.

Not included is

- the installation of ordinary telephone lines or the supply of ordinary telephones, internal communication systems, and intruder alarm systems which activate bells, lights or sirens; or
- specialist emergency services for the general public, even if they may benefit a disabled person.

(VAT Notice 701/7/02, para 7.1; Internal Guidance V1–7, Chapter 12 para 8.2).

Repair and maintenance of any qualifying item is zero-rated under 32.28 above.

32.33 **Motability scheme**

Zero-rating applies to the letting on hire of *any* motor vehicle (ie whether or not specially designed/adapted for a disabled person) to a disabled person in receipt of a disability living allowance by virtue of entitlement to the mobility component or of mobility supplement (as defined) provided

- the lessor's business consists predominantly of the provision of motor vehicles to such persons;
- the vehicle is unused at the commencement of the period of letting;
- the letting is for a period of not less than three years; and
- the consideration for the letting consists wholly or partly of sums paid to the lessor, directly by the Department for Works and Pensions or the Ministry of

Defence on behalf of the lessee, in respect of mobility allowance or mobility supplement to which the lessee is entitled.

[*VATA 1994, Sch 8 Group 12 Item 14*].

In practice, only vehicles leased under the Motability scheme meet the above conditions. Further information on the scheme is available from Motability Operations, City Gate House, 22 Southwark Bridge Road, London SE1 9HB (Tel: 0845 456 4566) or from their website at

www.motability.co.uk

Excess mileage. Motability excess mileage is further consideration for the zero-rated lease. (Internal Guidance V1–7, Chapter 12 para 28.3).

Sale of ex-lease vehicles. The sale of the motor vehicle which has been let on hire under the above conditions is also zero-rated provided the sale constitutes the first supply after the period of letting. [*VATA 1994, Sch 8 Group 12 Item 15*]. In practice, Motability only sells the vehicle back to the car dealer from whom it was originally purchased. Following the tribunal decisions in *Peugeot Motor Co plc (VTD 15314) (TVC 42.63)*, HMRC accept that the subsequent sale by the dealer of these motor vehicles is within the margin scheme.

See also 32.26 above for letting on hire of other vehicles.

32.34 **Imports, acquisitions, exports and removals**

Imports into the UK. Where goods within 32.17 to 32.33 above are imported from outside the EC by

- a disabled person for domestic or his personal use, or
- a charity for making available to disabled persons (by sale or otherwise),

they can be relieved of the VAT due on importation under the same conditions as for zero-rating the supply of such goods in the UK. [*VATA 1994, Sch 8 Group 12 Note 1*].

The disabled person or charity (as the case may be) must make a declaration in the appropriate form (see 32.35 below) and lodge it with the import entry declaration made to HMRC at the port, airport or postal depot of importation.

A supplier importing goods does not qualify for relief in this way. He must pay any VAT due on importation but can reclaim it as input tax, subject to the normal rules.

(VAT Notice 701/7/02, para 8.1).

Acquisitions from other EC countries. VAT-registered traders acquiring goods from other EC countries are not normally required to pay VAT at the place of importation but must account for any VAT due (and, subject to the normal rules, claim it back as input tax) on their next VAT return. A *VAT-registered* charity which acquires qualifying goods within 32.17 to 32.33 above from another EC country for disabled persons can account for VAT at the zero rate on its acquisition of such goods.

Persons who are not registered for VAT (including disabled persons and non-registered charities) do not have this facility.

- If they buy goods in another EC country, they may be required to pay tax on those goods in that EC country at the prevailing rate there. Any tax payable cannot be refunded in the UK by HMRC. Each EC country has its own rules about the extent of VAT relief on goods for disabled persons and the reliefs set out in 32.17 to 32.33 above do not apply to supplies made in other EC countries.

- If they buy goods in another EC country but the supplier arranges delivery, special 'distance selling' rules apply (see 23.10 EUROPEAN COMMUNITY: SINGLE MARKET) and the VAT treatment will depend upon whether the supply is treated as taking place in that other EC country or the UK.

Motor vehicles for disabled wheelchair/stretcher users. If the vehicle acquired qualifies as a new means of transport (see 23.31 EUROPEAN COMMUNITY: SINGLE MARKET), VAT is not due in the country in which the vehicle is purchased, but is due in the UK at the time of acquisition. VAT relief on the acquisition will apply, provided the same conditions are met to enable the supply of the adapted vehicle to a disabled person to be zero-rated (see 32.26 above) if it had been supplied in the UK. If the vehicle does not qualify as a new means of transport, VAT is due at the rate applicable in the EC country where the vehicle is purchased.

(VAT Notice 701/7/02, para 8.2; VAT Notice 701/59/02, para 6.2).

Exports and removals of goods from the UK. Goods or services supplied to disabled people from other countries, who are visiting the UK, can be zero-rated under the conditions set out in 32.17 to 32.33 above. If the goods do not qualify for this VAT relief, it may still be possible to zero-rate the supply, subject to certain conditions, under the retail export scheme (see 25.11 EXPORTS) which applies to persons resident outside the EC who are exporting the goods to a place outside the EC. VAT must be charged on all other retail sales of standard-rated goods. (VAT Notice 701/7/02, para 8.3).

The eligibility declaration regime (see 32.35 below) applies to these exports and removals in exactly the same way as it does to internal UK sales.

Where the value of a UK supplier's sales to citizens (whether disabled or not) of any single EC country exceeds that country's threshold for distance selling, then

- the other country becomes the place of supply; and
- VAT on any sales to that country becomes due there at the rate applicable in that country.

See 23.18 EUROPEAN COMMUNITY: SINGLE MARKET for further details.

32.35 Eligibility declarations by disabled persons and charities

HMRC recommend that a supplier obtains a written declaration from each customer claiming entitlement to VAT relief for goods and services under 32.17 to 32.33 above. Such a declaration should contain sufficient information to demonstrate that a customer fulfils all the criteria for eligibility. It should be separate, or clearly distinguishable from, any order form or invoice against which the goods or services are supplied. A customer signing an order should not automatically be signing a declaration of eligibility for VAT relief.

Suggested forms of declaration are reproduced in VAT Notice 701/7. The supplier should keep this declaration for production to any VAT officer.

Electronic declarations (eg received over the internet or by fax) are acceptable. Not all electronic declarations will have the means to incorporate a signature. In these circumstances, it is important that the supplier retains evidence of the origin of the document, such as the e-mail message incorporating the sender's address. As with paper declarations, electronic ones should be distinguishable from an order form or invoice.

Where a disabled person is unable to sign a declaration, the signature of a parent, guardian, doctor or another responsible person is acceptable.

A declaration only confirms the customer's status as a person eligible to receive zero-rated goods and services and the use to which he will put them. It does not mean that the goods and services themselves fulfil all the conditions for zero-rating. It is still the supplier's responsibility to take reasonable steps to satisfy himself that the goods or services being supplied qualify for zero-rating, the customer is entitled to zero-rating and the declaration is correct. If he believes an eligibility declaration to be inaccurate or untrue, he must not zero-rate the supply. The supplier should also take care that procedures, forms and literature do not encourage or lead customers to make such a declaration. HMRC will not, however, seek to recover VAT due from a supplier where a customer provided an incorrect declaration and the supplier, having taken all reasonable steps to check the validity of the declaration, fails to identify the inaccuracy and, in good faith, makes the supply at the zero rate. (VAT Notice 48, ESC 3.11).

(VAT Notice 701/7/02, paras 3.7–3.10, 10.1–10.4; VAT Notice 701/59/02, paras 13, 14).

Disabled students' allowance. This is a scheme operated by the Department for Education and Skills to make grants to assist disabled students. Payment to purchase goods may be made directly to the student or to the local authority but, in either case, the purchaser of the relevant goods or services is the disabled person.

Provided the supplier can show that

- the goods purchased were designed solely for use by a disabled person; and
- the purchase was funded by DSA

HMRC will accept, without a formal declaration from the purchaser, that

- the purchaser of the goods is a disabled person; and
- the goods are for that person's domestic or personal use.

(Internal Guidance V1–7, Chapter 12 paras 47.1–47.3).

32.36 **'Talking books' for the blind**

'Talking books' for the blind and severely handicapped are zero-rated when supplied to the Royal National Institute for the Blind, the National Listening Library and other similar charities. Included is certain apparatus and tapes designed or specially adapted for such use and non-specialist sound recording equipment. Also zero-rated are wireless receiving sets and non-specialist sound recording equipment supplied to a charity for free loan to the blind. See 12.7(*a*) and (*b*) CHARITIES for full details.

33 Hotels and Holiday Accommodation

Cross-reference. See 66 TOUR OPERATORS' MARGIN SCHEME.

De Voil Indirect Tax Service. See V4.113.

The contents of this chapter are as follows.

33.1 HOTELS, INNS AND BOARDING HOUSES

Supplies of accommodation. The provision in a hotel, inn, boarding house or 'similar establishment' of

(*a*) sleeping accommodation;

(*b*) accommodation in rooms which are provided in conjunction therewith (eg private bathrooms and sitting-rooms in suites); and

(*c*) accommodation for the purpose of a supply of catering

is standard-rated.

'*Similar establishment*' includes premises in which there is provided furnished sleeping accommodation (with or without board or facilities for the preparation of food) and which are used by or held out as being suitable for use by visitors or travellers.

[*VATA 1994, Sch 9 Group 1 Item 1*(*d*)].

Accommodation in motels, guest houses, bed and breakfast establishments, private residential clubs and hostels is included as are serviced flats for use by guests other than as a permanent place of residence. In most cases such establishments will provide one or more meals, possibly at an inclusive price, but board, or the facilities for the preparation of food, is *not* necessary for an establishment to be regarded as a hotel, etc. (VAT Notice 709/3/02, para 2.1). Possible characteristics of an hotel, inn or boarding house are:

- They provide accommodation as their main purpose. In some student accommodation, the provision of a communal or corporate atmosphere is considered important which is not a normal characteristic of a hotel, etc. See *International Student House (VTD 14420) (TVC 39.82)* where buildings were not held to be 'similar establishments' and fees for accommodation were held to be exempt because the charity was providing the accommodation to help overseas students and improve international relations. But compare *Acorn Management Services Ltd (VTD 17338) (VTD 39.83)* where accommodation for US students was held to be standard-rated.
- They provide accommodation for a transient class of people or people who are temporarily homeless. See *Namecourt Ltd (VTD 1560) (TVC 39.85)* where the tribunal held that *Item 1*(*d*) above was directed at the sort of establishment

which provided accommodation for a transient or floating class of resident. It could be long-term (see also *McGrath v C & E Commrs, QB [1992] STC 371) (TVC 39.91)*) or short-term but it was accommodation which a person would go to with a view to moving on from in due course.

- They usually provide breakfast (although this is no longer always the case).
- In some premises (eg serviced flats) simple cooking facilities are provided in rooms.
- Sleeping accommodation is provided with a range of services and facilities (eg room service, laundry, cleaning of rooms, bed making, TV rooms, telephone services, receptionist, etc.) which will vary according to the type of establishment.
- Residents will normally enjoy a degree of privacy by being provided with their own lockable rooms.
- There will normally be a resident manager, proprietor or member of staff on the premises at all times.
- There is normally a booking service.
- The establishment is run with a view to making a profit.

Other aspects to be taken into account include

- any rules imposed (eg whether additional overnight guests can stay free of charge which is not a normal feature of a hotel, etc);
- whether any formal tenancy agreement is entered into (which would indicate a supply of domestic accommodation);
- treatment for rating purposes;
- whether the physical appearance of the building is consistent with it being a hotel, etc; and
- whether the establishment is in competition with hotels, etc.

(Internal Guidance V1–8, paras 10.2, 10.3).

A lodge used to provide supervised residential accommodation for people with mental health problems was held not to be a 'similar establishment' in *Dinaro Ltd (t/a Fairway Lodge) (VTD 17148) (TVC 39.87)*.

Accommodation used for catering. Where accommodation is supplied in a hotel, etc for the purpose of a supply of catering *by the person supplying the room*, the supply is standard-rated under (*c*) above whatever the length of the let. Thus, wedding receptions, private parties and other functions held in hotels, etc are fully taxed. See *Willerby Manor Hotels Ltd (VTD 16673) (TVC 39.97)* where the tribunal held that, following the decision in *Card Protection Plan Ltd v C & E Commrs, CJEC [1999] STC 270 (TVC 21.223)*, the hire of a function room for an evening reception was a supply ancillary to those of wedding reception facilities and the company had made a composite supply of standard-rated wedding reception facilities, the main ingredient of which was a supply of catering.

If the rooms are let without catering (or the catering is supplied by another person) the letting of the room is normally exempt. This is the case even though people using the room may eat in the dining room, paying for their meal separately.

(VAT Notice 709/3/02, para 4.1; Internal Guidance V1–8, para 10.5).

Other accommodation and services. Other supplies of accommodation (eg hiring a room for a meeting or letting of shops and display cases) are generally exempt, subject to the option to tax under 42.8 LAND AND BUILDINGS). Where an exempt supply, such as providing a room for a meeting or a conference, is made and minimal refreshments (eg tea, coffee and biscuits) are served, the room and the incidental catering are treated as a single exempt supply. But where substantial refreshments, such as a meal or buffet, are served, the catering should be treated as a separate taxable supply and VAT accounted for based on the normal charges for such catering.

Where a single inclusive 24 hour conference rate is charged then the whole supply will be taxable.

Any goods or services provided such as restaurants, car parking, use of equipment, licensed bars, commissions from taxi firms, or goods or services charged for separately, are standard-rated.

(VAT Notice 709/3/02, para 4.3).

33.2 Stays over four weeks

For the first four weeks of any stay VAT is due on the full amount payable in the normal way.

Where accommodation within 33.1 above is provided to an *individual* for a period exceeding four weeks, from the 29th day of the stay (or letting) VAT is only due on

(*a*) meals, drinks and service charges; and

(*b*) facilities provided apart from the right to occupy the accommodation (ie the value of the accommodation is excluded from the VAT calculation).

The value of the facilities subject to VAT under (*b*) above must not be less than 20% of the total amount due for those facilities and the accommodation.

Throughout the period the accommodation must be provided *for the use of the individual* either alone or with one or more other persons who occupy the accommodation with him but not either directly or indirectly at their own expense.

[*VATA 1994, Sch 6 para 9*].

As the rule only applies where the supply of the accommodation is made to the individual who will occupy it, HMRC take the view that the rule does not apply

- where the supply of accommodation for homeless people is made to a local authority or
- to accommodation supplied to a business for use by its employees (eg accommodation arranged by airlines for crew stopovers). Where, however, the supply of the accommodation is made to an individual who receives reimbursement from an employer, this can be treated under the rule as long as the use of the accommodation by the individual exceeds 28 days.

(VAT Notice 709/3/02, para 3.3).

Example

Weekly terms for accommodation, facilities and meals are £235 (£200 plus £35 VAT) of which £94 (£80 + £14 VAT) represents the charge for meals. For the first 4 weeks, the VAT charge is the full £35 but thereafter a reduced VAT value may be calculated in one of the following ways. The proportion for meals has been taken to be 40% but this will not always be so.

(*a*) *If charges are expressed in VAT-exclusive terms*

	£	£
Total VAT-exclusive weekly charge	200.00	
VAT-exclusive charge for meals	80.00	14.00
	£120.00	
VAT-exclusive value of facilities (20% minimum)	24.00	4.20
VAT due		£18.20

Weekly terms are therefore £200.00 + £18.20 VAT.

(*b*) *If charges are expressed in VAT-inclusive terms and the total amount charged to the guest is reduced to take account of the reduced element of VAT*

VAT is as under (*a*) above but the calculation is

	£	£
Total VAT-inclusive charge	235.00	
VAT-inclusive charge for meals	94.00	14.00
VAT-inclusive charge for facilities and accommodation	141.00	
VAT included 7/47 × £141	21.00	
Balance (exclusive of VAT)	£120.00	
VAT-exclusive value of facilities (20% minimum)	24.00	4.20
VAT due		£18.20

The weekly terms are £200 + £18.20 VAT.

(*c*) *If charges are expressed in VAT-inclusive terms but the total amount charged to the guest is not reduced to take account of the reduced element of VAT*

	£	£
Total VAT inclusive charge	235.00	
VAT-inclusive charge for meals	94.00	14.00
VAT-inclusive charge for facilities and accommodation	141.00	
VAT included 7/207* × £141	4.76	4.76
VAT-exclusive charge for facilities and accommodation	£136.24	
Total VAT		£18.76

The weekly terms are not reduced (ie £235 including £18.76 VAT).

* = (17.5 × facilities element %) ÷ (100 + [17.5 × facilities element %])

= 7/207 where the facilities element is 20%

Although VAT is only due on the reduced amount, the full VAT-exclusive amount (£200.00 in (*a*) and (*b*) and £216.24 in (*c*)) must be included in Box 6 of the VAT return. This is because the accommodation element of the total charge continues to be the consideration for a standard-rated supply even though the value for the purposes of calculating the VAT becomes nil after the first four weeks.

Breaks in stays. Normally, the reduced value rules above cannot be used unless the guest stays for a continuous period of more than four weeks. For example, stays of three weeks in every month are subject to VAT in full. Similarly, if a guest stays for five weeks, is away for a week and then returns for five weeks, each stay is treated separately and the reduced value basis can only be used for the fifth week of each stay. There are exceptions to this. A period of absence is not treated as ending a stay if the guest

- is a long-term resident and leaves for an occasional weekend or holiday; or
- is a student who leaves during the vacation but returns to the same accommodation for the next term; or
- pays a retaining fee.

In such cases, the stay is treated as continuous and VAT need only be charged in full for the first four weeks of the overall stay. A guest need not necessarily occupy the same room for his stay to be treated as continuous.

If a retaining fee is paid for a period of absence during the first four weeks of a stay, VAT is due on it at the standard rate. If paid for a period of absence after that period, then the reduced value rules above apply. Provided the fee is no more than the amount treated as payment for accommodation, no VAT is due. Otherwise the fee must be treated as payment for both accommodation and facilities using the rules outlined above.

(VAT Notice 709/3/02, paras 3.2, 3.3, 7.4).

33.3 Accommodation and catering supplied by employers to employees

The value of accommodation and catering in a hotel, etc supplied to its employees is to be taken to be nil unless made for a consideration wholly or partly in money in which case the value is determined without regard to any consideration other than money. [*VATA 1994, Sch 6 para 10*(*1*)(*b*)]. Any payments (eg in cash or by a deduction from wages not provided for in the contract of employment) are treated as VAT-inclusive. The reduced value provisions in 33.2 above may apply to accommodation. Where employees are paid a minimum wage under a *Wages Order* for an industry and that *Order* allows for appropriate reductions to be made for catering and accommodation, these calculations are steps in arriving at the amount of the weekly wage to be paid and are *not* monetary consideration on which the employer is liable to VAT (*RW & MJ Goodfellow (VTD 2107) (TVC 60.13)*). (VAT Notice 709/3/02, para 4.2).

33.4 Deposits, cancellation charges, booking fees and retention fees

Most deposits are advance payments on which VAT must be accounted for in the return period in which they are received. If a deposit has to be refunded, any VAT accounted for can be reclaimed.

If a cancellation charge is made when a customer cancels a booking, no VAT is due on the charge (because it is not a payment in respect of a supply). If the customer has to forfeit a deposit, any VAT accounted for on the deposit can be reclaimed.

If a business provides a guarantee or insurance against a customer having to pay a cancellation charge, VAT is due on any charge made to the customer. However, if the business arranges for insurance to be provided to the customer along with the goods or services supplied and, under the policy, it is the individual customer's risk which is insured, the supply by the business of arranging the insurance may be exempt providing certain disclosure requirements are met. See 37.17 INSURANCE.

Booking fees charged by a person supplying accommodation are treated as deposits above. Booking fees charged by agents who arrange a supply on behalf of someone else are the consideration for a taxable supply and VAT is due whether or not the accommodation is taken up.

Retention fees paid to reserve accommodation for future use are standard-rated (but see 33.2 above for retention fees paid for a period of absence after the first 28 days).

(VAT Notice 700, para 8.13; VAT Notice 709/3/02, paras 7.1–7.4).

Charges levied on customers who make 'guaranteed reservations' of hotel accommodation but do not take up that accommodation are subject to VAT (*C & E Commrs v Bass plc, QB 1992, [1993] STC 42 (TVC 60.81)*).

33.5 HOLIDAY ACCOMMODATION, ETC IN THE UK

The grant of any interest in or right over or licence to occupy 'holiday accommodation' is standard-rated. *Included* is

- the grant of an interest in, or in any part of, a building designed as a dwelling or number of dwellings or the site of such a building if
  - (i) the interest granted is such that the grantee is not entitled to reside in the building, or part, throughout the year; or
  - (ii) residence there throughout the year, or the use of the building or part as the grantee's principal private residence, is prevented by the terms of a covenant, statutory planning consent or similar permission; and
- any supply made pursuant to a tenancy, lease or licence under which the grantee is or has been permitted to erect and occupy holiday accommodation.

Excluded (and therefore exempt) is the grant of the fee simple, or a tenancy, lease or licence to the extent it is granted for consideration in the form of a premium, in a building or part which is not a 'new building'. A '*new building*' is one completed less than three years before the grant.

'*Holiday accommodation*' includes any accommodation in a building, hut (including a beach hut or chalet), caravan, houseboat or tent which is advertised or held out as holiday accommodation or as suitable for holiday or leisure use, but excludes any accommodation within 33.1 above. Residential accommodation that happens to be situated in a holiday resort is not necessarily holiday accommodation.

See 42.1(7) LAND AND BUILDINGS for the meaning of '*interest in or right over*' and 42.1(8) LAND AND BUILDINGS '*licence to occupy*'.

[*VATA 1994, Sch 9 Group 1 Item 1(e), Notes 11–13*].

The effect of the above is that the sale or lease of a house, flat or other accommodation is generally standard-rated as holiday accommodation if the property is new and the purchaser cannot reside there throughout the year or use it as his principal private residence. VAT must be accounted for on the initial charge and on any periodic charges such as ground rent and service or other charges. If the accommodation is no longer new, any payment for the freehold or premium under the lease is exempt but any periodic charges, including rent and service charges, are standard-rated. However, following the tribunal decision in *Ashworth (Mrs B) (VTD 12924) (TVC 39.106)*, the sale or lease of a flat or house which can be used as a person's principal private residence but which cannot be occupied throughout the year due to a time-related restriction on occupancy (in *Ashworth* the lessees were unable to occupy the property for the month of February each year) is exempt provided the development on which the property is situated is not a holiday development and is not advertised or held out as such. This also applies to any periodic charges such as rent and service charges.

The provision of a site for holiday accommodation under a tenancy, lease or licence is standard-rated even if the person to whom the site is provided is responsible for erecting the accommodation on it.

(VAT Notice 709/3/02, paras 5.1, 5.3, 5.4).

See *RW and B Sheppard (VTD 481) (TVC 39.100)* for a case concerning short letting of furnished flats treated as holiday accommodation in which the above tests were considered.

Even where a property has been 'held out' as holiday accommodation, where there is no causative nexus between the publication of the advertisement of holiday accommodation and the letting of the whole building for some different purpose, there is no provision of holiday accommodation. See *Cooper and Chapman (Builders) Ltd v C & E Commrs, QB 1992, [1993] STC 1 (TVC 44.150)*.

Options to purchase interests or rights. The grant of any right to call for or to be granted an interest or right which would be standard-rated under the provisions above is also standard-rated. *Included* is an equitable right, a right under an option or right of pre-emption and, in relation to Scotland, a personal right. [*VATA 1994, Sch 9 Group 1 Item 1*(*n*)].

Value for VAT purposes. VAT is payable on the full amount due for the holiday accommodation, including incidental services, irrespective of the length of the stay. (See 33.2 above for long stay arrangements in hotels, etc.) (VAT Notice 709/3/02, para 5.7).

Deposits, cancellation charges and booking fees. See 33.4 above.

33.6 Off-season letting

Holiday accommodation let during the off-season can be treated as exempt from VAT provided

- it is let to a person as residential accommodation;
- it is let for more than 28 days; and
- holiday trade in the area is clearly seasonal.

A copy of the tenancy agreement or similar evidence should be kept to show that the accommodation was occupied for residential purposes only. In such cases the whole of the let, including the first 28 days, can be treated as an exempt supply.

The holiday season normally lasts from Easter to the end of September, though some areas such as London are not regarded as having a seasonal holiday trade.

(VAT Notice 709/3/02, para 5.5).

See, however, 42.8 LAND AND BUILDINGS for the option to tax such lettings.

33.7 **Time-share and multi-ownership schemes**

A supply of holiday accommodation in a house, flat, chalet, etc under a time-share or multi-ownership scheme is standard-rated if the supply is of 'new' accommodation. The supply of a timeshare, etc in a property that is not new is exempt to the extent that the grant is made for a consideration in the form of a premium. A property is '*new*' if completed less than three years before the grant. Rent payments made after the initial lump sum, and any annual management fees and service charges, are standard-rated in all cases. (VAT Notice 709/3/02, para 5.6).

See *American Real Estate (Scotland) Ltd (VTD 947) (TVC 39.102)*. Time-shares, etc cannot be zero-rated as tenancies for a term certain exceeding 21 years (or Scottish equivalent) within the definition of 'major interest'. [*VATA 1994, Sch 8 Group 5 Item 1 and Note 13; SI 1995/280*]. See also *Cottage Holiday Associates Ltd v C & E Commrs, QB 1982, [1983] STC 278 (TVC 15.104)* and *Mr & Mrs Cretney (VTD 1503) (TVC 39.103)* where an option to purchase freehold reversion was also offered.

For time-sharing of a yacht based abroad, see *Oathplan Ltd (VTD 1299) (TVC 39.105)*.

33.8 **Construction of holiday accommodation**

A builder can zero-rate the supply of services in the course of construction of a dwelling even though it will be used to supply holiday accommodation. The word 'dwelling' takes on its normal everyday meaning.

33.9 **Caravans and camping**

Holiday accommodation provided in any type of caravan already sited on a pitch is standard-rated. (The provision of *other* accommodation in such a caravan is exempt.)

[*VATA 1994, Sch 8 Group 9 Item 3; Sch 9 Group 1 Item 1*(*e*)]. (VAT Notice 709/3/02, para 6.2).

Caravan pitches. See 42.3(*e*) LAND AND BUILDINGS for caravan pitches.

Camping. The provision of holiday accommodation in a tent is standard-rated. [*VATA 1994, Sch 9 Group 1 Item* (*e*)]. Any associated facilities are also standard-rated. See 42.3(*e*) LAND AND BUILDINGS for tent pitches.

34 Imports

Cross-references. See 30.7 GOLD for importations of gold; 39.4 INTERNATIONAL SERVICES for imported services; 52.23–52.26 PENALTIES for penalties for evasion of, and non-compliance with, import VAT; 69.15 VALUATION for valuation of imports; 70 WAREHOUSED GOODS AND FREE ZONES; 71.3, 71.4 and 71.5 WORKS OF ART, ETC for importations and reimportations.

De Voil Indirect Tax Service. See V3.301–358.

The contents of this chapter are as follows.

34.1 GENERAL NOTES

Trade with other EC countries. The provisions of this chapter only apply to importations of goods from outside the EC. See 21.2 EUROPEAN COMMUNITY: GENERAL for the VAT territory of the EC. For the provisions relating to acquisitions of goods from other EC countries, see 23.3 EUROPEAN COMMUNITY: SINGLE MARKET.

EC enlargement. 10 new countries (ie Cyprus, Czech Republic, Estonia, Hungary, Latvia, Lithuania, Malta, Poland, Slovak Republic, and Slovenia) joined the EC with effect from 1 May 2004. As a result,

- with effect from that date, goods moving from one of those countries to the UK are treated as acquisitions, rather than importations, of goods; and
- if a consignment of goods was despatched from one of those countries prior to 1 May 2004 but arrived at its UK destination on or after that date, a customs import declaration was required and the goods were liable to import VAT.

As regards Cyprus, the European Commission has advised that the application of the *EC 6th Directive* is to be suspended in those areas of Cyprus in which the Government of the Republic of Cyprus does not exercise control. From 1 May 2004, goods from these areas continue to be treated as imports.

The Isle of Man, although not part of the UK, is treated as part of the UK for VAT purposes. VAT is chargeable in the Isle of Man under Manx law which generally parallels UK legislation. Goods removed from the Isle of Man to the UK are not normally treated as imports provided any VAT has been accounted for in the Isle of Man or, if the goods were relieved of VAT in the Isle of Man, the conditions of that relief have not been broken. However, where goods are removed from the Isle of Man into the UK and were charged to VAT in the Isle of Man at a different rate to that applicable in the UK (or were relieved from VAT subject to a condition which was not subsequently complied with) the difference in the tax will be charged in the UK. [*SI 1982/1067, Art 3*]. (VAT Notice 702, para 1.7).

The Channel Islands are part of the Customs territory of the EC but not part of the VAT territory. Any goods received from the Channel Islands are therefore regarded as imports. (VAT Notice 702, para 1.8).

Trader's Unique Reference Number (TURN). Any VAT-registered person who imports goods from outside the EC needs a TURN. Without this, it may not be possible to get the evidence needed to reclaim the VAT paid on imports. TURNs are obtained by writing (stating full name, address and VAT registration number) to

TURN Team
HM Revenue and Customs
Ty Myrddin
Old Station Road
Carmarthen
SA31 1BT

Tel: 01267 244054/244049

De Voil Indirect Tax Service. See V3.302.

34.2 THE CHARGE TO VAT

VAT is charged and payable on the importation of goods into the UK (which for VAT purposes includes the territorial sea of the UK ie waters within twelve nautical miles of the coastline) as if it were a duty of customs. The rate of VAT is the same as if the goods had been supplied in the UK (whether or not the person importing the goods is registered for VAT). The VAT is chargeable in addition to any customs and/or excise duty or other charges due and is calculated on the value which includes such charges. See 69.15 VALUATION.

CEMA 1979 and other UK legislation relating to customs or excise duties charged on importation into the UK and any Community legislation relating to customs duties charged on goods entering the EC, apply in modified form so as to relate to VAT on importations.

Goods are treated as imported from a place outside the EC where

(*a*) they arrive in the UK directly from outside the EC and are entered for home use in the UK (or customs duty otherwise becomes payable on them); or

(*b*) they have been placed, in another EC country or in the UK, under one of the customs arrangements listed below and are entered for removal to home use in the UK (or customs duty otherwise becomes payable on them).

[*VATA 1994, s 1(1)(4), s 2(1), s 15, s 16, s 96(11)*].

The customs arrangements referred to in (*b*) above are as follows.

(i) Temporary storage (not strictly a customs arrangement but all goods arriving from outside the EC have the status of goods in temporary storage until they are entered and cleared for home use or another procedure).

(ii) Free zones.

(iii) Customs warehousing.

(iv) Inward processing relief (duty suspension system).

(v) Temporary importation (including means of transport) with total relief from customs duty.

(vi) External Community Transit (T1) arrangements.

(vii) Internal Community Transit (T2) arrangements (applies to some trade with special territories inside the EC customs area but outside the EC for VAT purposes).

(viii) Goods admitted into territorial waters in order to be incorporated into drilling or production platforms for purposes of the construction, repair, maintenance or alteration or fitting-out of such platforms, or to link such drilling or production platforms to the mainland.

(ix) Goods admitted into territorial waters for the fuelling and provisioning of drilling or production platforms.

(VAT Notice 702, paras 1.1, 10).

VAT is also payable on imported goods removed from HMRC warehouses and free zones. See 70 WAREHOUSED GOODS AND FREE ZONES.

The time of importation of any goods is

- where brought by sea, when the ship carrying them comes within the limits of a port;
- where brought by air, when the aircraft carrying them lands in the UK or when the goods are unloaded in the UK, whichever is the earlier;
- where brought by land, when the goods are brought across the boundary into Northern Ireland;
- where brought by pipeline, when the goods are brought within the limits of a port or brought across the boundary into Northern Ireland.

[*CEMA 1979, s 5(2)(6)*].

In short, the time of importation for VAT purposes is the moment when customs duty is due on the goods.

Supplies between the time of arrival in the UK and before delivery of import entry. If imported goods are supplied between the time of their arrival in the UK and the time when an import entry is delivered to Customs, the supply can be zero-rated provided, by arrangement, the purchaser is required to make the import entry. [*VATA 1994, Sch 8 Group 13 Item 1*].

De Voil Indirect Tax Service. See V3.302; V3.312; V3.313.

34.3 **IMPORT ENTRY PROCEDURE**

Goods are declared to Customs using the Single Administrative Document (SAD) (Form C88). Import VAT is dealt with in the same way as customs duty.

The import declaration must normally be accompanied by a declaration of value on Form C105, C105A, C105B or C109 as appropriate.

Unless the goods are placed under excise warehousing or one of the customs arrangements listed in 34.2 (i)–(ix) above, any VAT due must normally either be paid at the time of importation or be deferred with any duty if the importer or his agent are approved for deferment.

Amendment of entries. Where amendment of an entry is made after the goods have been cleared out of official charge and this results in less VAT being payable than was originally declared and paid, the higher amount of VAT should generally be reclaimed in the normal way. Exceptionally, the procedure for reclaiming VAT overpaid in 34.6 below can be used. Where amendment of an entry after clearance results in more VAT being payable, a completed Form C18 must be submitted together with the additional amount of VAT due. The additional payment will appear on the import VAT certificate as evidence for input tax deduction (see 34.11 below).

Postal imports

- *Consignments* (*other than Datapost packets*) *not exceeding £2,000.* A VAT-registered person importing goods for business purposes does not have to pay VAT immediately on importation. Instead, he may account for the VAT due in Box 1 of the VAT return covering the period of importation. Input tax deduction can be claimed on the same return (subject to the normal rules). A customs declaration must accompany the goods showing the consignee's VAT registration number and the nature, quantity and value of the goods. If the VAT number is not clearly shown, VAT may be charged. A cash refund will not be made so the charge label, postal wrapper and any customs declaration attached to the package must be kept to support the claim to input tax. [*SI 1995/2518, Reg 122*].

- *Datapost packets not exceeding £2,000 in value.* For such imports, the Post Office require payment of the VAT when the package is delivered. The charge label attached must be kept to support any claim to input tax. It is not possible to defer payment of import charges.

- *Consignments over £2,000 in value.* For these imports, an entry (which will be sent to the consignee) must be made and returned to HMRC together with an invoice or other acceptable evidence of value. VAT and other charges due at importation are payable immediately unless the consignee is approved to use the deferment scheme. After payment, HMRC send the consignee a copy of the entry to support any claim to input tax.

Goods received from outside the EC and consigned to another EC country. Where a person receives goods from outside the EC and consigns them to a destination in another EC country, he must normally either

(*a*) put the goods in free circulation in the UK, paying any customs duty and/or import VAT due; or

(*b*) place the goods under the external Community Transit (T1) arrangements, in which case any duty and/or VAT is payable in the EC country of destination.

See, however, 34.18 below for VAT relief for goods imported and put into free circulation in the UK in the course of a zero-rated supply of those goods to a taxable person in another EC country.

(VAT Notice 702, paras 2.2, 4.1–4.4).

De Voil Indirect Tax Service. See V3.318.

34.4 PAYMENT OF VAT

Payment of VAT on imported goods is due at the time of importation (or removal from warehouse) unless the importer or his agent is approved for deferment. [*CEMA 1979, s 43(1), s 44(1), s 45, s 93(1)(2); VATA 1994, s 38*].

De Voil Indirect Tax Service. See V5.115–122.

34.5 Deferment of VAT

A business, approved by HMRC and holding a Deferment Approval Number (DAN), can defer paying charges due on importation or removal of goods from a customs or an excise warehouse or from a free zone. An agent (including a warehousekeeper) who enters goods for an importer or owner may also use the scheme.

The charges which can be deferred are:

- *Where payable on imported goods at the time of import or on removal from Customs warehouses or free zones*: import VAT; customs duties; excise duties (including tobacco products duty); levies imposed under the Common Agricultural Policy (CAP) of the EC; positive Monetary Compensatory Amounts under the CAP; anti-dumping or countervailing duties imposed by the EC; compensatory interest on IPR goods diverted to free circulation; temporary import interest on TI goods diverted to free circulation; and interest charged on Customs debts.
- *Where payable on removal from excise warehouse*: VAT and excise duty on the following home-produced or home-manufactured goods, namely spirits and liqueurs (including perfume and composite goods containing excisable spirit); wine and made-wine fortified or rendered sparkling in the warehouse; cider and perry; beer and other alcoholic beverages.
- *Where payable on hydrocarbon oils on removal from warehouse*: Excise duty and VAT.

Deposits for the above charges may also be deferred.

Period of deferment. Except for excise duties, charges deferred during a calendar month (‘*the accounting period*’) must be paid as a total sum on the 15th of the next month or, if that is not a ‘working day’, on the next working day *after* it. For excise duty, the accounting period runs from the 15th of one month to the 14th of the next month and payment must be made on the 29th of the latter month (28th February in non-leap years) or, if that is not a working day, on the working day *before* it. ‘*Working day*’ is any day on which the Bank of England in London is open for business.

Payment. Payment must be made by the BACS system of direct debit (although HMRC may require special arrangements if an emergency prevents them collecting that way). No other method of payment is accepted for the deferment scheme. A business wishing to pay by other means must pay each time its goods are cleared.

If a direct debit fails, the business will be expected to settle immediately. Failure to do so may result in the duty deferment facility being stopped or even withdrawn. Other customs facilities that are dependent upon duty deferment may also be affected and interest charges may also arise.

An agent (see below) acting in his own name but on behalf of an importer is jointly and severally liable for any customs debt that may arise.

It is not currently possible to make BACS direct debit payments in euro.

Guarantees. A guarantee on Form C1201 is required from an approved bank, insurance company or building society. The form is obtainable from the Central Deferment Office, (see below under *Approval*) although some guarantors hold their own supplies. The guarantor agrees to cover all amounts deferred up to an overall maximum amount in any calendar month (the '*deferment limit*') which must be enough to cover all deferrable liabilities (but see below for import VAT under SIVA).

If the guarantee level/deferment limit is exceeded in any calendar month, it is not possible to defer any more charges for the remainder of that month (and all further import charges would need to be paid immediately by another payment method until either the guarantee level/deferment limit is increased or a new calendar month begins). The guarantee can be varied by replacement with a bigger (or smaller) amount or by giving a supplementary guarantee to cover extra liabilities in peak periods.

Guarantees can be cancelled by contacting the guarantor or by advising the Central Deferment Office directly in writing. A period of notice of termination of no less than seven days must be given.

Simplified import VAT accounting (*SIVA*). From 1 December 2003, a trader who holds a live deferment account (or who intends to apply for one) can apply to reduce the level of financial guarantee required to operate it *for VAT purposes only*. Customs duties and excise duties must still be fully secured. Applicants must satisfy the following criteria.

- They must have been VAT-registered for three years or more.
- They must have a good VAT compliance history. This will be assessed against the number of errors made on VAT returns, the timeliness of rendering VAT returns, the number of assessments raised on VAT returns, the number and value of VAT underdeclarations, and the number and reasons for any default surcharges.
- Debtor history. Traders in debt to HMRC within the three months prior to application will not qualify.
- Sufficient financial means are required to meet any amount deferred under SIVA. All traders whose businesses are in administration, liquidation, insolvency, bankruptcy, receivership or in financial difficulties (time to pay arrangements, etc) may not be eligible for SIVA.
- A good HMRC offence record is necessary (serious offences will result in automatic expulsion).
- Payment history. The Departmental payment record of the business in connection with duty deferment will be reviewed. A business which has defaulted on deferment payments more than once in the twelve-month period prior to application will be refused approval. VAT payment history (VAT returns, surcharges and underdeclarations, debts) will also be assessed to ensure timely payment is rendered.

- Additional checks. Traders may also be subject to external credit checking where there is a perceived revenue risk (eg non-deferment holders who are applying for an import VAT only account and not, therefore, providing any form of financial guarantee may be subject to such a check). Additionally, non-deferment holders will be required to have a compliant, twelve-month international trade operating history prior to being granted SIVA.

The SIVA application form (SIVA 1) can be downloaded from HMRC's website:

www.hmrc.gov.uk

Application forms should be completed and returned to SIVA Approvals Team, HM Revenue and Customs, 6th Floor North, Portcullis House, 27 Victoria Avenue, Southend-on-Sea, Essex SS2 6AL.

If approval is granted, businesses will then have to arrange any subsequent changes to their guarantee amount with their guarantor and then with HMRC. The deferment account will have two limits.

- A deferment account limit which must be sufficient to cover all deferred charges.
- A deferment guarantee level which must be backed up by a deferment guarantee and sufficient to cover all deferred customs and excise duties.

Approval. Application forms for deferral can be downloaded from HMRC's website (see above) and are also available from HM Revenue and Customs, A&CGs Branch 6, Central Deferment Office, 10th Floor South East, Alexander House, 21 Victoria Avenue, Southend-on-Sea, Essex SS99 1AA (Tel: 01702 367425/29/31/50; Fax: 01702 366091). A set of forms comprises

Form C1200	Application for approval of deferment arrangements
Form C1201	Guarantee for payment of sums due to HMRC
Form C1202	Duty deferment – instruction to bank or building society to pay by direct debit
Form C1207N	Standing authority for agent/freight forwarder to request duty deferment of duty payment against importer's DAN (see below)

If satisfied with the application, guarantee given and payment arrangements, HMRC will issue a Certificate of Approval showing a deferment approval number (DAN). This must be quoted on each request for deferment and in any correspondence with HMRC (including correspondence from the guarantor).

Approval covers the business to the limit of its guarantee (or deferment account limit if SIVA is approved, see above) for deferment of all eligible charges and can be used at any port, airport, warehouse, etc in the UK. Companies which are members of the same group registration for VAT can apply for group approval.

The CDO must be notified immediately if the business

- changes its name, address or VAT registration number;
- ceases to trade (including where the business is carried on by another legal entity); or
- wishes to cancel its duty deferment account.

A new direct debit mandate on Form C1202 must be sent at least 10 days before the next payment is due if the bank account is transferred to another bank.

Approval can be revoked at any time for reasonable cause. The direct debit mandate must not be cancelled until all deferred payments have been made.

Procedure. *At importation*, deferment is requested on the import entry by entering the DAN and the correct payment code in the boxes provided. Charges may be deferred against the importer's DAN or an agent's DAN (see below). Deferment cannot be requested on importations for which no entry is required (unless an entry is made for them) or on postal importations (except those with a value exceeding £2,000 and entered on Form C88A).

On removal from an approved customs and excise warehouse, deferment is requested on the entry or warrant for removal. This also applies under scheduling or other approved simplified arrangements where the entry is presented after the removal of the goods. Charges due on deficiencies in warehouse or in transit cannot be deferred.

On removal from a free zone, deferment is requested on the entry presented when the goods are removed from the zone.

Where, after having allowed deferment, it is found that more or less was payable on the entry, HMRC will normally adjust the deferment account accordingly. Where this is not possible, if more was payable, the balance is payable immediately and if less was payable, the amount overdeclared will be repaid on, or as soon as possible after, the direct debit day on which it is paid. However, repayments of VAT are not normally made to VAT-registered traders who are expected to recover the amount on their next VAT return.

Agents. An agent making an entry can request deferment against his principal's approval number provided he is authorised to do so. This can be done in two ways.

- On Form C1207N, at the time of seeking approval for deferment (see above) or subsequently. This is a standing authority which allows the agent to use his principal's approval number whenever or wherever entering goods on his behalf.
- On Form C1207S which is a 'one-off' authority in respect of a specific consignment or removal of goods. The form is available on the HMRC website (see above). The completed form must be given to the agent to present with the entry.
- In emergencies (eg when goods are diverted to another port at short notice) HMRC will accept:

  (*a*) A fax on company-headed paper authorising the agent to act. It must be signed by a responsible officer and sent to the agent to present with the entry. The fax should be worded:

> *To HM Revenue and Customs at* (*insert name of port/airport*)
>
> 1. I am/we are (insert name of business)
> 2. My/our telephone number is (insert number)
> 3. I/we hereby authorise (insert name of agent) to use my/our deferment approval number (insert number) when requesting deferment of the charges on the goods imported by

me/us on the attached entry.

(*b*) A fax copy of a completed Form C1207S signed by a responsible officer. It must be sent to the agent to present with the entry.

(*c*) A fax copy of a completed form C1207N sent to the Central Deferment Office.

(*d*) An e-mail from the importer, sent to the port of entry, giving specific authority and providing a contact name and telephone number for the importer, along with all other importer and agent's details. Customs at the port of entry should be contacted for the appropriate e-mail address.

If an agent appoints a sub-agent (eg because he has no office at a particular port)

- where the sub-agent is shown as declarant on the entry, he can request deferment against his own DAN or the importer's DAN if authorised under the above procedure; and
- where the main agent is shown as the declarant on the entry and the sub-agent signs the declaration as a representative of the main agent, the sub-agent can request deferment against the importer's DAN (if that importer has authorised the main agent) or against the main agent's DAN.

An agent making a bulked entry of goods consigned to several importers may use his own account to defer the charges payable but cannot defer the charges against individual importer's accounts.

Statements. HMRC send out 'periodic deferment statements' at approximately weekly intervals summarising details of deferments at each of their accounting centres and showing the total amount deferred so far in that particular month. Any queries should be taken up immediately with the accounting centre concerned. 'Nil' statements are not normally sent.

Deferment statements cannot be used as evidence for input tax deduction. See 34.11 below for evidence required.

The Duty Deferment Electronic Statements (DDES) service offers a facility to obtain copies of periodic deferment statements electronically via the internet. In order to use DDES a business must register, enrol and activate the service through a central registration process within the Government Gateway. Once registered, DDES can be accessed via the HMRC website and selecting the 'Electronic services' and 'DDES' links. More information on electronic services is provided on the Government Gateway website at

www.governmentgateway.gov.uk

[*SI 1976/1223; SI 1978/1725*]. (Customs Notice 101).

De Voil Indirect Tax Service. See V3.306.

34.6 Reclaiming VAT overpaid

General. Import VAT can only be reclaimed as input tax by a VAT-registered importer. However, amounts overpaid as import VAT (eg because of misclassification) are generally repayable to the person who paid the amount to HMRC, subject to certain conditions.

Repayments to VAT-registered traders. A VAT-registered trader who has overpaid import VAT can apply for the payment to be adjusted. The importer or his agent must complete Form C285 and the importer must support the request with the signed written declaration:

'I am expecting direct repayment/partial repayment to be made, and no claim to input tax deduction has been or will be made by me on the basis of the document as originally issued.'

If the request is accepted, HMRC will make the repayment. Any such repayment will be processed through the duty adjustment system. VAT repayments are not given special priority, and consideration should therefore be given as to whether the money could be recovered more quickly through the normal input tax deduction system.

A claim for immediate repayment may also be made if VAT has been wrongly charged because an incorrect Deferment Approval Number (DAN) has been quoted or keyed. Any claim should be submitted to the relevant Entry Processing Unit.

Repayments to agents. See 34.8 below for the normal rules. However, an agent who has overpaid import VAT (eg because goods have been misclassified) may be able to reclaim the amount overpaid if he can provide evidence that he has not been, and will not be, reimbursed by his importer.

(VAT Notice 702, para 2.6).

34.7 **Goods lost or destroyed before clearance**

In such an event, application can be made to Customs at the place where the import entry was presented for repayment or remission of the VAT due using Form C285 (see above under *Reclaiming VAT overpaid*). (VAT Notice 702, para 2.9).

34.8 **Repayment of import VAT to shipping and forwarding agents by HMRC if the importer fails to pay them**

If an importer fails to pay a shipping or forwarding agent any VAT paid by the agent on his behalf, in normal circumstances the agent's only recourse is to the importer. However, by concession, if an importer becomes insolvent without reimbursing the agent for VAT paid or deferred, HMRC will repay the import VAT to the agent provided all the following conditions are satisfied.

(*a*) Either

- the importer has gone into liquidation; or
- an administrator or administrative receiver has been appointed who certifies that in his opinion the assets of the insolvent importer are insufficient to cover payment of *any* dividend to the unsecured creditors.

(*b*) The interval between the date of import entry for the goods and the date of insolvency is no more than six months.

(*c*) The agent entered the goods in accordance with instructions from the importer.

(*d*) The goods have been re-exported from the UK in the same state as they were imported and, during the time they were in the UK, the goods were under the control of the agent and were not used.

(*e*) The agent must write to the Entry Processing Unit (EPU) where the goods were entered and VAT paid enclosing

- evidence that the input tax has been paid to HMRC;
- a certificate from the liquidator, etc that the VAT has not been, and will not be, reclaimed as input tax;
- confirmation from the liquidator, etc of (*b*) above;
- a declaration that he will not recover the relevant VAT in whole or in part from the insolvency; and
- evidence to satisfy HMRC of (*c*) above.

(VAT Notice 702, para 2.5; VAT Notice 48, ESC 3.13).

De Voil Indirect Tax Service. See V5.160.

34.9 **Unregistered persons**

Where goods are imported for business purposes, the same procedures apply for entry of goods on importation and payment or deferment of VAT as for registered traders except that an unregistered person does not require an import VAT certificate (C79) and is not entitled to claim import VAT and does not therefore receive a copy of the import VAT certificate. He may reclaim VAT paid on imported goods only when VAT was overpaid (by using Form C285) or the goods were not in accordance with contract (see 34.20 below). See also 34.19 below for relief for re-importations by unregistered persons. (VAT Notice 702, para 6.1).

34.10 **INPUT TAX DEDUCTION**

VAT paid on the importation of goods can be claimed as input tax subject to the normal rules.

34.11 **Evidence for input tax deduction**

The normal evidence of the payment of import VAT is the Import VAT Certificate (Form C79) which is issued monthly. This certificate is sent, normally around the 12th day of the following month, to the VAT-registered person whose VAT registration number, plus a three digit suffix, is shown on the import entry. The whole number is known as the Trader Unique Reference Number (TURN). The date when the VAT shown on the certificate may be treated as input tax is normally the accounting date alongside each item, not the date when the certificate is issued.

The certificate may be copied for internal purposes and a copy is allowed as an accounting document for input tax deduction provided the original is made available for inspection by the control officer on demand.

If a monthly certificate is lost, replacements can be obtained (for up to six years) from HM Revenua and Customs, VAT Central Unit, Section 4B, 1st Floor Alexander House, Victoria Avenue, Southend-on-Sea, SS99 1AU. Applications should be in writing quoting VAT registration number and the month(s) for which replacement is required.

There are still, however, some types of importation which do not appear on Form C79. The following list summarises the various methods of import procedures and the acceptable evidence of payment.

Import procedure	Evidence for input tax deduction
Air/maritime imports	
Single Administration Document (SAD) – manually processed	Monthly VAT certificate
SAD – trader input/computer processed	Monthly VAT certificate
SAD – Customs input/computer processed	Monthly VAT certificate
Registered consignees	Customs authenticated invoices
Period entry	Trader produced computer schedule
SAD (simplified)	PE 33 (not authenticated by Customs)
Period entry – Adjustment schedules only	Monthly VAT certificate
Transit Shed Register – imports not exceeding £600 (non DTI)	Customs authenticated commercial invoice or locally produced forms certified by Customs. The concession allowing use of copies of agents' disbursement invoices in certain circumstances will continue
Postal imports	
Exceeding £2,000 – SAD	Authenticated copy 8 SAD
Not exceeding £2,000 – Customs declaration (Form CI (Green Label) or Form C2/CPU)	No input tax evidence issued
Post entry correction	Monthly VAT certificates
Removals from warehouse	
Customs warehouse	Monthly VAT certificates
Excise or HMRC warehouse	Monthly VAT certificates
Hydrocarbon oils	Monthly VAT certificates

(VAT Notice 702, paras 8.1, 8.6, 8.7, 8.13, 8.18, 8.19).

34.12 **Shipping and forwarding agents**

Where a shipping or forwarding agent acts for an importer and pays the VAT on his behalf (or defers it under his own deferment guarantee), this is only a commercial arrangement. The agent cannot claim the VAT as input tax as the goods are not imported for the purpose of his business. Only the importer has the legal right to reclaim the VAT paid on the imported goods as input tax, subject to the normal rules. (VAT Notice 702, para 2.4). See, however, 34.8 above for concessional repayment of import VAT to agents in certain cases where the importer fails to pay him.

34.13 **Goods lost or destroyed after clearance**

In such an event, the VAT paid can be deducted as input tax (subject to the normal rules) provided the goods were to be used for business purposes. There is no need to account for output tax unless the goods were supplied to someone else before the loss or destruction. (VAT Notice 702, para 2.9).

34.14 RELIEFS FROM CHARGE

There are a number of reliefs available as a result of which import VAT is not due on specific goods.

- Aircraft ground and security equipment (see 34.22 below).
- Capital goods and equipment on transfer of activities from abroad (see 34.15(2) below).
- Certain imports by and for charities (see 34.15(6) below).
- Decorations and awards (see 34.15(9) and 34.15(13) below).
- Electricity and natural gas (see 34.23 below).
- Fuel, animal fodder and feed, and packing necessary during transportation (see 34.15(11) below).
- Funerals, war graves, etc (see 34.15(12) below).
- Goods for examination, analysis or test purposes (see 34.15(4) below).
- Goods imported for sale to another EC country (see 34.18 below).
- Health, including animals and biological or chemical substances for research, blood and human organs, blood-grouping and tissue-typing re-agents, and equipment for medical research funded by charities and voluntary contributions (see 34.15(5) below).
- Inherited goods (see 34.15(13) below).
- Miscellaneous items including, with exceptions, any consignment not exceeding £18 in value (see 34.15(8) below).
- Personal belongings (see 34.15(13) below).
- Printed matter (see 34.15(3) and 34.15(7) below).
- Promotion of trade (see 34.15(3) below).
- Reimported goods (see 34.19 below).
- Rejected goods (see 34.20 below).
- Small non-commercial consignments (see 34.16 below).
- Temporary importations (see 34.25 below).
- Travellers' allowances (see 34.17 below).
- United Nations visual and auditory materials (see 34.15(1) below).
- Visiting forces (see 34.21 below).
- Works of art and collectors' pieces. See 34.15(10), 34.24 and 34.26 below and 71.3 and 71.4 WORKS OF ART, ETC
- Zero-rated goods under *VATA 1994, Sch 8* (with some exceptions). See 72.1 ZERO-RATED SUPPLIES. [*VATA 1994, s 30(3)*].

34.15 **Imports relieved under EC Council Directive 83/181/EEC and equivalent UK provisions**

The following provisions describe goods that can be imported into the UK free of VAT from

- outside the customs territory of the EC (see 21.3 EUROPEAN COMMUNITY: GENERAL); and
- the 'special territories' or countries having a customs union with the EC.

The 'special territories' are the Aland Islands, the Canary Islands, the Channel Islands, French Guiana, Guadeloupe, Martinique, Mount Athos and Reunion. These countries or areas are part of the customs territory of the EC but not part of the VAT territory. VAT is therefore due on imports from these territories unless any of the reliefs detailed below are applicable and claimed.

The customs territory of the EC has customs unions with Turkey, San Marino and Andorra. These enable most goods in free circulation to move freely between them without the need to claim duty relief, subject to the production of any necessary preference or Community Transit documentation. (In the case of Andorra, the union only covers goods in Chapters 25–97 of the Tariff.) VAT is still due on imports from Turkey, San Marino and Andorra, however, unless any of the reliefs detailed below are applicable and claimed.

General condition for relief. Where relief is available under any of the provisions listed below by reference to a use or purpose of the goods, the goods must be put to that use or purpose in the UK.

(1) **United Nations visual and auditory materials**

No VAT is charged on the importation, for whatever purpose, of the following goods produced by the United Nations or by a United Nations organisation.

- Holograms for laser projection.
- Multi-media kits.
- Materials for programmed instructions, including materials in kit form, with the corresponding printed materials.
- Films and film strips of an educational, scientific or cultural character.
- Newsreels (with or without soundtrack) depicting events of current news value (limited to two copies of each for copying) and archival film material (with or without soundtrack) for use with newsreel films.
- Microcards or other information storage media required in computerised information and documentation services of an educational, scientific or cultural character.
- Recordings of an educational, scientific or cultural nature.
- Wall charts, patterns and models of an educational, scientific or cultural character designed solely for demonstration and education purposes.
- Mock-ups or visualisations of abstract concepts such as molecular structures or mathematical formulae.

[*SI 1984/746, Art 4, Sch 1; SI 1987/2108; EC Council Directive 83/181/EEC, Art 79, Annex*].

(2) **Capital goods and equipment on transfer of activities from abroad**

No VAT is charged on 'capital goods and equipment' imported by a person for the purposes of a business

- he has ceased to carry on *either* outside the customs territory of the EC *or* in the 'special territories' *or* in countries having a customs union with the EC (see above);
- which he notifies HMRC is to be carried on by him in the UK; and
- which is concerned exclusively with making taxable supplies.

For these purposes, a person is not to be treated as intending to carry on a business in the UK if such business is to be merged with, or absorbed by, another business already carried on there, unless a new activity is to be set up.

The goods must

(*a*) have been used in the business for at least twelve months before it ceased to be carried on abroad;

(*b*) be imported within twelve months of the business ceasing to be carried on abroad; and

(*c*) be appropriate both to the nature and size of the business to be carried on in the UK.

HMRC can waive the conditions under (*a*) and (*b*) above in special circumstances (eg if political upheaval in the country where the business was located prevented twelve months use or the import within twelve months of cessation). (Customs Notice 343, para 2.4).

'*Capital goods and equipment*' includes livestock where the business transferred is an agricultural holding (but not livestock in the possession of a dealer) but not food for human consumption or animal feeding stuffs, fuel, stocks of raw materials or finished or semi-finished products or any motor vehicle ineligible for deduction of input tax (see 45.3 MOTOR CARS). Examples of items included are office and shop equipment or machinery, and other tools of trade; means of transport used for the purposes of production or for providing a service; and computer and other technical equipment needed to run the business. (Customs Notice 343, para 2.2).

[*SI 1984/746, Sch 2 Group 1; SI 1992/3120; EC Council Directive 83/181/EEC, Arts 24–28*].

It is not necessary to obtain prior authorisation from the DTI or to present a DTI approval letter to HMRC at the time of import. Instead, HMRC will consider eligibility for relief from duty and VAT at the time the goods are imported and grant relief if appropriate.

(3) **Promotion of trade**

No VAT is charged on the following imports.

(*a*) Articles of no intrinsic commercial value sent free of charge by suppliers of goods and services for the sole purpose of advertising.

(*b*) Samples of negligible value of a kind and in quantities capable of being used solely for soliciting orders for goods of the same kind. Where

HMRC require, the goods must be rendered permanently unusable, except as samples, by being torn, perforated, clearly and indelibly marked, or by any other process.

Relief is not available for goods not presented as samples at import but subsequently to be made into samples (eg unaltered rolls of fabric imported to be cut up and made into swatch books). (Customs Notice 367, para 2.4).

(*c*) Printed advertising matter, including catalogues, price lists, directions for use or brochures, which relates to goods for sale or hire by a person established outside the EC or to transport, commercial insurance or banking services offered by a person established outside the EC. The material must clearly display the name of the person established outside the EC by whom the goods or services are offered. Subject to below, relief does not apply to consignments containing two or more copies of different documents or to consignments containing two or more copies of the same document (unless the total gross weight of the consignment does not exceed one kilogram). Any goods which are the subject of grouped consignments from the same consignor to the same consignee are also excluded. These restrictions on relief do not apply in the case of imported printed matter intended for free distribution and relating to either goods for sale or hire.

(*d*) Goods to be distributed free of charge at an 'event' as small 'representative samples' for use or consumption by the public (excluding fuels, alcoholic beverages and tobacco products).

(*e*) Goods imported solely for the purpose of being demonstrated at, or used in the demonstration of any machine or apparatus displayed at, an 'event' (excluding fuels, alcoholic beverages and tobacco products).

(*f*) Paints, varnishes, wallpaper and other low value materials to be used in the fitting out or decoration of a temporary stand at an 'event'.

(*g*) Catalogues, prospectuses, price lists, advertising posters, calendars, unframed photographs and other printed matter or articles advertising goods displayed at an 'event', supplied without charge for distribution free of charge to the public at such event.

'*Event*' comprises

- any trade, industrial, agricultural or craft exhibition, fair or similar show or display which is not being organised for private purposes in a shop or on business premises with a view to the sale of the goods displayed;
- any exhibition or meeting primarily organised for charitable purposes or to promote *either* friendship between peoples *or* religious knowledge or worship *or* any branch of learning, art, craft, sport or scientific, technical, educational, cultural or trade union activity or tourism;
- any meeting of representatives of international organisations and ceremonies of an official or commemorative character; and
- any representative meeting or ceremony of an official or commemorative character.

'*Representative samples*' means goods which are

- imported free of charge or obtained at such event from goods imported in bulk;
- identifiable as advertising samples of low value;
- not easily marketable and, where appropriate, packaged in quantities which are less than the lowest quantity of the same goods as marketed; and
- intended to be consumed at such event, where the goods comprise foodstuffs or beverages not so packaged.

Relief under (*d*)–(*g*) above only applies where the aggregate value and quantity of the goods is appropriate to the nature of the event, number of visitors and extent of the exhibitor's participation. Where relief is available under (*e*) or (*f*) above in respect of goods for demonstration or use, the goods must be consumed, destroyed or rendered incapable of being used again for the same purpose either in the course of, or as a result of, such demonstration or use.

[*SI 1984/746, Art 6(2), Sch 2 Group 3; SI 1988/2212; SI 1992/3120; EC Council Directive 83/181/EEC, Arts 61–69*].

(4) **Goods for examination, analysis or test purposes, etc**

No VAT is charged on goods imported for examination, analysis or testing

- to determine their composition, quality or their technical characteristics;
- to provide information; or
- for industrial or commercial research.

To qualify for relief

- the quantities imported must not exceed the amounts necessary for their purpose;
- the examination, etc itself must not constitute a sales promotion;
- the examination, etc must be completed within such time as HMRC require; and
- any goods not completely used up or destroyed in the course of (or as a result of) the examination, etc, and any products resulting from the examination, etc, must be destroyed or rendered commercially worthless or exported (see further below).

[*SI 1984/746, Art 6(3), Sch 2 Group 4; EC Council Directive 83/181/EEC, Arts 70–76*].

Testing must normally be completed by the date stated on the SAD or postal form. If this is not possible, a letter of explanation with a request for an extension of time should be sent, before the stated time is reached, to

National Import Reliefs Unit
HM Revenue and Customs
Custom House
Killyhevlin Industrial Estate
Enniskillen
County Fermanagh, Northern Ireland
BT74 4EJ

Tel: 028 6632 2298
Fax: 028 6632 4018

If the goods are transferred, prior notice must be given to NIRU stating to whom and where the goods are to be transferred.

When testing is completed, NIRU must be informed in writing of

- place of importation or postal depot;
- number and date of the customs entry or postal docket;
- quantity, value and description of the goods and date of receipt;
- details of the tests, including the address(es) where the testing took place and where records are available for inspection;
- the date on which testing was completed; and
- details of any materials remaining and proposals for their disposal.

Any materials remaining (including goods not used, or not completely used up in the test and goods resulting from the test, including waste and scrap) may

- have VAT (and duty) paid on them; or
- with HMRC's permission, be destroyed, free of duty and VAT; or
- with HMRC's permission, be converted into waste or scrap and released on payment of any VAT (and duty) which may be due.

NIRU will consider applications to export goods remaining after the testing is over on satisfactory explanation of why the goods cannot be destroyed or converted into waste or scrap and have to be exported.

(Customs Notice 374, paras 4.2–4.5).

(5) **Health**

Certain goods can be zero-rated on supply in the UK to disabled persons or to charities for making available to disabled persons. Such goods can also be relieved of any VAT payable on importation. See 32.16 to 32.35 HEALTH AND WELFARE.

In addition, the following importations are free of VAT.

(*a*) Animals specially prepared for laboratory use and sent free of charge to a 'relevant establishment'.

'*Relevant establishment*' means

- a public establishment, or a department of such, principally engaged in education or scientific research (eg a university, NHS or teaching hospital, mobile health laboratory, research laboratory of a government department, or laboratory of a research council); or
- a private establishment so engaged, which is approved by the Home Office.

A private establishment must apply for a letter from the Home Office confirming that it is a designated establishment under the terms of the

Animals (Scientific Procedures) Act 1986. (Customs Notice 365, para 2.1). Also see Customs Notice 365 for import prohibitions and restrictions and animal welfare provisions.

[*SI 1984/746, Sch 2 Group 5 item 1; EC Council Directive 83/181/EEC, Art 35*].

(*b*) Approved biological or chemical substances (see Customs Notice 366, para 4) sent to a 'relevant establishment' (see (*a*) above) from outside the EC.

A private establishment must apply to the National Import Reliefs Unit (at the address under (4) above) for authorisation to claim relief. The application must be made in advance of importation and detail the research project for which the imported substance will be used. If the application is successful, NIRU will issue an approval letter. (Customs Notice 366, para 3.1).

[*SI 1984/746, Sch 2 Group 5 item 3; SI 1992/3120; EC Council Directive 83/181/EEC, Art 35*].

(*c*) Any of the following goods, namely

- human blood
- products for therapeutic purposes derived from human blood (whole human blood, dried human plasma, human albumin and fixed solutions of human plasmic protein, human immunoglobulin and human fibrinogen);
- human (including foetal) organs or tissue for diagnostic or therapeutic purposes or medical research;
- 'Blood-grouping re-agents' and 'tissue-typing re-agents' imported by 'approved institutions or laboratories' for use exclusively for non-commercial medical or scientific purposes.

Relief also applies to any special packaging essential for transport of the goods and any solvents or accessories necessary for their use.

'*Blood-grouping reagents*' means all re-agents (whether of human, animal, plant or other origin) used for blood-type grouping and for the detection of blood grouping incompatibilities.

'*Tissue-typing reagents*' means all re-agents (whether of human, animal, plant or other origin) used for the determination of human blood types or in determining human tissue types.

'*Approved institutions and laboratories*' include

- a public establishment or laboratory (eg Regional and District Health Authorities, Health Boards in Scotland, Health and Social Service Boards in Northern Ireland, public health laboratories, research laboratories of government departments, research councils and similar bodies, all blood transfusion services, schools of pharmacy and medical schools); and
- a private establishment which has been authorised by the Department of Health to receive such goods VAT (and duty) free.

A private establishment must apply in advance of importation to the Department of Health Public Health Group, PH6.6, Room 631B, Skipton House, 80 London Road, London SE1 6TE (tel: 020 7972 5142) indicating

- the status of the establishment;
- the nature of activities (eg medical research); and
- the type of goods to be imported.

If the application is successful, the DoH will issue a letter of authorisation. (Customs Notice 369, para 3.1).

[*SI 1984/746, Sch 2 Group 5 items 4–8; EC Council Directive 83/181/EEC, Arts 36–38*].

(*d*) Pharmaceutical products by or on behalf of persons or animals for their use while visiting the UK to participate in an international sporting event.

[*SI 1984/746, Sch 2 Group 5 item 9; EC Council Directive 83/181/EEC, Art 39*].

(*e*) Samples of reference substances approved by the World Health Organisation for the quality control of materials used in the manufacture of medicinal products provided the samples are addressed to consignees authorised to receive them free of VAT.

[*SI 1984/746, Sch 2 Group 5 item 10; SI 1988/2212; EC Council Directive 83/181/EEC, Art 38c*].

(6) **Charities, etc**

Certain goods which can be zero-rated on supply to or for charities in the UK can also be relieved of any VAT payable on importation. See 12.7 and 12.8 CHARITIES.

In addition, no VAT is payable on the importation of the following goods.

(*a*) Basic necessities (ie food, medicines, clothing, blankets, orthopaedic equipment and crutches, required to meet a person's immediate needs) obtained without charge for distribution free of charge to the needy by a 'relevant organisation'. *Excluded* are alcoholic beverages, tobacco products, coffee, tea and motor vehicles other than ambulances.

(*b*) Goods donated by a person established outside the EC to a 'relevant organisation' for use to raise funds at occasional charity events for the benefit of the needy. There must be no commercial intent on the part of the donor. *Excluded* are alcoholic beverages, etc as in (*a*) above. HMRC treat an occasional charity event as one held not more than four times a year by any one organisation.

(*c*) Equipment and office material donated by a person established outside the EC to a 'relevant organisation' for meeting its operating needs and carrying out its charitable aims. There must be no commercial intent on the part of the donor. *Excluded* are alcoholic beverages, etc as in (*a*) above.

(*d*) Goods imported by a 'relevant organisation' for distribution or loan, free of charge, to victims of, or for meeting its operating needs in the relief of, a disaster affecting the territory of one or more EC countries. This relief only applies where the EC Commission has made a decision authorising the importation of the goods.

(*e*) Articles donated to and imported by an approved organisation principally engaged in the education of, or the provision of assistance to, blind or other physically or mentally handicapped persons for loan, hiring out or transfer other than on a profit-making basis (and whether for consideration or free of charge) to such persons and specially designed for their education, employment or social advancement. There must be no commercial intent on the part of the donor.

(*f*) Spare parts, components or accessories for any article within (*e*) above, including tools for its maintenance, checking, calibration or repair. The goods must be imported with an article within (*e*) above to which they relate or, if imported subsequently, must be identifiable as being intended for such an article.

The above reliefs are conditional on

- any guarantee, declaration, undertaking, document or other details being given to HMRC as required;
- the goods being put to the use or purpose specified; and
- unless specifically allowed above, the goods not being lent, hired out or transferred unless to an organisation which would itself be entitled to the relief if importing the goods on that date. In the latter case, prior notification in writing must be received from HMRC and the goods must be used solely in accordance with the relieving provisions.

Where any condition ceases to be satisfied and written notice of this fact is given to HMRC, VAT becomes payable as if the goods had been imported on that date and VAT is calculated accordingly. The VAT must not, however, exceed the VAT relieved in the first place.

'*Relevant organisation*' means a State organisation or other approved charitable or philanthropic organisation. HMRC have given general approval to the following charitable and philanthropic organisations.

- Organisations registered with the Charity Commissioners.
- State organisations which are devoted to welfare.
- Any of the following organisations provided they are non-profit making and their objective is the welfare of the needy, *viz* hospitals; youth organisations; clubs, homes and hostels for the aged; orphanages and children's homes; organisations set up for the relief of distress caused by particular disasters in the EC; and organisations concerned with the relief of distress generally (such as the British Red Cross and the Salvation Army).

[*SI 1984/746, Art 6(1), Art 7, Art 8, Sch 2 Group 6; SI 1992/3120; EC Council Directive 83/181/EEC, Arts 41–55*]. (Customs Notice 317, para 2.1).

(7) **Printed matter, etc**

The following printed matter may be imported free of VAT from a country outside the EC.

- Documents sent free of charge to public services in the UK.
- Publications of foreign governments or official international organisations for free distribution.
- Ballot papers for elections organised by bodies outside the EC.
- Specimen signatures and circulars concerning signatures forming part of exchanges of information between banks and public services.
- Official printed matter sent to a Central Bank in the UK.
- Documents from a company incorporated outside the EC to holders of its issued securities.
- Files and other documents for use at international meetings, etc and reports of such gatherings.
- Plans, drawings, traced designs and other documents sent by any person for participating in a competition in the UK or to obtain or fulfil an order executed outside the EC.
- Documents to be used in examinations held in the UK on behalf of institutions established outside the EC.
- Printed forms to be used as official documents in the international movement of vehicles or goods pursuant to international conventions.
- Printed forms, labels, tickets and similar documents sent to travel agents (including airlines, national railway undertakings, ferry operators and similar organisations) in the UK by transport and tourist undertakings outside the EC.
- Used commercial documents.
- Official printed forms from national or international authorities.
- Printed matter conforming to international standards for distribution by an association in the UK and sent by a corresponding association outside the EC.
- Documents (leaflets, brochures, books, magazines, guidebooks, posters (whether or not framed), unframed photographs and photographic enlargements, maps (whether or not illustrated) window transparencies, and illustrated calendars for free distribution to encourage persons to visit foreign countries, in particular to attend cultural, tourist, sporting, religious, trade or professional meetings or events (provided the goods do not contain more than 25% of private commercial advertising)).
- Free distribution copies of hotel lists and yearbooks published by or on behalf of official tourist agencies and timetables for foreign transport services (provided the goods do not contain more than 25% of private commercial advertising).
- Yearbooks, lists of telephone and telex numbers, hotel lists, catalogues for fairs, specimens of craft goods of negligible value and literature on museums, universities, spas or similar establishments, supplied as reference material to accredited representatives or correspondents appointed by official national tourist agencies and not intended for distribution.

- Official publications issued under the authority of the country of exportation, international institutions, regional or local authorities and bodies governed by public law established in the country of exportation (provided VAT or any other tax has been paid on the publication or printed matter in the third country from which it has been exported and the publication, etc has not benefited from any relief from payment by virtue of exportation).
- Printed matter distributed by officially recognised political organisations, established outside the EC on the occasion of European Parliament or national elections in the country in which the printed matter originates (provided VAT or any other tax has been paid on the publication or printed matter in the third country from which it has been exported and the publication, etc has not benefited from any relief from payment by virtue of exportation).

[*SI 1984/746, Art 2(5), Sch 2 Group 7; SI 1988/2212; SI 1992/3120; EC Council Directive 83/181/EEC, Arts 78, 79*].

(8) **Articles sent for miscellaneous purposes**

No VAT is charged on the following imports.

- Materials relating to trademarks, patterns or designs and supporting documents and applications for patents imported for submission to competent bodies to deal with protection of copyright or industrial or commercial patent rights.
- Objects imported for submission as evidence, or for a like purpose, to a court or other official body in the EC.
- Photographs, slides and stereotype mats for photographs sent to press agencies and publishers of newspapers or magazines.
- Recorded media, including punched cards, sound recordings and microfilm, sent free of charge for the transmission of information.
- Goods (other than alcoholic beverages or tobacco products) sent on an occasional basis as a gift of friendship or goodwill between bodies, public authorities or groups carrying on an activity in the public interest. The goods must not be of a commercial character.
- Any consignment of goods (other than alcoholic beverages, tobacco products, perfumes or toilet waters) not exceeding £18 in value.

[*SI 1984/746, Sch 2 Group 8 Items 1–4, 7, 8; SI 1988/2212; SI 1995/3222; EC Council Directive 83/181/EEC, Arts 22, 57–59, 77, 79*].

(9) **Decorations and awards**

No VAT is charged on the following imports.

- Any honorary decoration conferred by a government or Head of State outside the EC on a person resident in the UK and imported on his behalf.
- Any cup, medal or similar article of an essentially symbolic nature, intended as a tribute to activities in the arts, sciences, sport or public service, or in recognition of merit at a particular event. It must be donated by an authority or person established outside the EC for the purpose of

being presented in the UK or awarded outside the EC to a person resident in the UK and imported on his behalf.

- Awards, trophies and souvenirs of a symbolic nature and of limited value intended for free distribution at business conferences or similar international events to persons normally resident in a country other than the UK.

The awards, etc must not be of a commercial character.

[*SI 1984/746, Sch 2 Group 8 Items 5, 6, 9; SI 1988/2212; SI 1992/3120; EC Council Directive 83/181/EEC, Art 56*].

A person is resident where he spends at least 185 days in a period of 12 months because of personal ties and occupational ties (if any) but if personal ties are in one country and occupational ties in another, HMRC treat a person as resident in the country of his personal ties if

- his stay in the country of his occupational ties is in order to carry out a task of definite duration; or
- he returns regularly to the country of his personal ties.

Not eligible for relief are

- watches, cameras, cars;
- long service awards made to employees by employers or colleagues;
- prizes won in unimportant competitions such as deck games and card games;
- articles purchased with prize money;
- gifts or prizes given in lieu of payment;
- gifts where the donor appears to be motivated largely by commercial considerations;
- any consumables, eg alcoholic drinks, tobacco products, foods; and
- souvenirs distributed which are not in keeping with the nature of the event.

VAT relief may be claimed by the recipient or the person who is to present the award, etc. As proof that relief is due, HMRC will normally be satisfied with any certificate or press publicity material relating to the decoration or award, or a letter or statement from the donor or organiser of the event.

(Customs Notice 364, paras 2.1, 2.3–2.5).

(10) **Works of art and collectors' pieces for exhibition**

Works of art and collectors' pieces imported by approved museums, galleries or other institutions for a purpose other than sale can be imported free of VAT provided the following conditions are met.

- The institution must be approved by the National Import Reliefs Unit. It should apply for approval in writing to NIRU as far in advance of the first anticipated importation as possible, detailing the scope and nature of the exhibits or specimens. If successful, NIRU will issue a letter of approval against which HMRC will allow relief.

- The exhibits must be of an educational, scientific or cultural character.
- The exhibit must be dispatched directly to the approved establishment and must be used exclusively as exhibits or specimens under its control.
- Records of the imported exhibits must be kept.
- The exhibits must be imported either free of charge, or, if for a consideration, must not be supplied to the importer in the course or furtherance of any business.

The exhibits may be lent, hired out or transferred to other institutions which are approved under this procedure provided prior permission is obtained from NIRU.

[*SI 1984/746, Sch 2 Group 9; EC Council Directive 83/181/EEC 3, Art 79*]. (Customs Notice 361, paras 2.1, 3.1).

See also 71.3 and 71.4 WORKS OF ART, ETC for an effective reduced rate of VAT of 5% on the importation of works of art including any antique more than 100 years old.

(11) **Fuel, animal fodder and feeding stuffs, and packing for use during transportation**

No VAT is charged on the following imports.

- Fuel contained in the standard tanks (as defined) of a motor road vehicle or of a 'special container', for use exclusively by such vehicle or such special container. '*Special container*' means any container fitted with specially designed apparatus for refrigeration, oxygenation, thermal insulation and other systems.
- Fuel, not exceeding 10 litres for each vehicle, contained in portable tanks carried by a motor road vehicle, for use exclusively by such vehicle. This does not apply to a special purpose vehicle or one which, by its construction and equipment, is designed for and capable of transporting goods or more than nine persons including the driver.
- Lubricants contained in a motor road vehicle, for use exclusively by such vehicle and necessary for its normal operation during the journey.
- Litter, fodder and feeding stuffs contained in any means of transport carrying animals, for the use of such animals during their journey.
- Disposable packings for the stowage and protection (including heat protection) of goods during their transportation to the UK and where the cost is included in the consideration for the goods transported.

[*SI 1984/746, Sch 2 Group 10; SI 1988/2212, Art 8; EC Council Directive 83/181/EEC 3, Arts 80–86*].

(12) **Funerals, war graves, etc**

The following goods are relieved from VAT on importation from a country outside the EC.

- Goods imported by an approved organisation for use in the construction, upkeep or ornamentation of cemeteries, tombs and memorials in the UK which commemorate war victims of other countries.

- Coffins containing human remains and urns containing human ashes, together with accompanying flowers, wreaths or other ornamental objects.
- Flowers, wreaths or other ornamental objects imported without commercial intent by a person resident outside the EC for use at a funeral or to decorate a grave.

[*SI 1984/746, Art 2, Sch 2 Group 11; SI 1992/3120; EC Council Directive 83/181/EEC, Arts 87, 88*].

(13) **Personal belongings, etc**

Personal property can be imported without VAT liability in the circumstances set out in (*a*)–(*e*) below. See also 34.19(1) below for belongings returned to the UK after previously being exported.

In addition to any specific conditions, relief is only due if the following general conditions are met.

- The goods are declared for relief to the proper officer on importation. Where any goods are declared before the date on which a person becomes normally resident in the UK or, if he intends to become so resident on the occasion of his marriage, before such marriage has taken place, relief is subject to such security as HMRC require being furnished.
- Where relief is given otherwise than under (*c*) or (*d*) below, the goods must not, unless indicated otherwise below, be lent, hired-out, given as security or transferred in the UK without authorisation from HMRC within a period of 12 months from the relief being given. Where HMRC do give authorisation, they may discharge the relief and require payment of the VAT at the rate then in force (or, if lower, the rate at the time of importation).
- Any conditions for receiving relief (including the intention of becoming normally resident and the use to which the goods are put) must be complied with. If not, the VAT becomes payable forthwith (unless HMRC see fit to waive payment or part) and the goods are liable to forfeiture.

[*SI 1992/3193, Arts 6–10*].

(*a*) **Relief for persons transferring their normal residence from outside the EC.** A person entering the UK is not required to pay VAT (or duty) chargeable on 'property' imported into the UK provided

- he has been 'normally resident' outside the EC for a continuous period of at least twelve months;
- he intends to become normally resident in the UK;
- the property has been in his possession and used by him in the country where he has been normally resident for at least six months before its importation;
- the property is intended for his personal or household use in the UK;
- the property is declared for relief not earlier than six months before the date of becoming normally resident in the UK (or earlier where HMRC are satisfied that a person has given up normal residence

outside the EC but is prevented by occupational ties from becoming normally resident in the UK) and not later than twelve months after that date; and

- HMRC are satisfied that the property has borne (and not been exempted from, or had refunded, because of exportation) all duties and taxes normally applicable in its country of origin or exportation.

'*Property*' means any personal property intended for personal use or meeting household needs, including household effects, provisions and pets; riding animals, cycles, motor vehicles, caravans, pleasure boats and private aircraft; but excluding any goods which, by their nature or quantity, indicate they are being imported for a commercial purpose. Specifically excluded are

- alcoholic beverages and tobacco products;
- any motor vehicle designed for or capable of transporting more than nine persons including the driver, or goods;
- any special purpose vehicle or mobile workshop; and
- any articles for use in a trade or profession, other than portable instruments of the applied or liberal arts.

'*Normally resident*'. A person is treated as normally resident in a country where he usually lives

(i) for a period, or aggregate of periods, of at least 185 days in a period of twelve months; and

(ii) because of his 'occupational ties'; and

(iii) because of his 'personal ties'.

Where a person has no occupational ties, he is treated as normally resident in a country on the basis of (i) and (iii) above only, provided his personal ties show close links with that country.

Where a person has occupational ties and personal ties in different countries, he is treated as normally resident in the country where he has personal ties provided

- the stay in the country where he has occupational ties is to carry out a task of a definite duration; or
- he returns regularly to the country with personal ties.

However, a UK citizen with personal ties in the UK but with occupational ties outside the EC may be treated as normally resident in the country of his occupational ties provided that he satisfies the condition in (i) above in the country with occupational ties.

'*Occupational ties*' do not include attendance by a pupil or student at a school, college or university.

'*Personal ties*' mean family or social ties to which a person devotes most of his time not devoted to occupational ties.

[*SI 1992/3193, Arts 2, 3, 11, 12; EC Council Directive 83/181/EEC, Arts 2–10*].

See also *Rigsadvokaten v N C Ryborg, CJEC [1993] STC 680.*

By concession, relief may still be granted where personal belongings fail to qualify only because they have not been possessed and used for the specified period or have been declared for relief outside the specified time limit. In addition, property (including motor vehicles) purchased

- by diplomats, members of certain international organisations and NATO forces,
- by UK forces (or civilian staff accompanying them) outside the EC, and
- under a UK export scheme by members of the UK diplomatic service, members of UK forces and members of certain international organisations

which otherwise qualifies for relief will not be refused relief solely because HMRC cannot satisfy themselves that the goods have borne all duties and taxes normally applicable in their country of origin.

(VAT Notice 48, ESCs 9.3–9.7).

(*b*) **Relief on marriage**. A person entering the UK is not required to pay VAT (or duty) on 'property' imported into the UK provided

- he has been 'normally resident' outside the EC for a continuous period of at least 12 months;
- he intends to become normally resident in the UK on the occasion of his marriage; and
- declared for relief not earlier than two months before the date fixed for the marriage (in which case security for the VAT and duty will be required which will be discharged on subsequent submission of the marriage certificate to HMRC) and not later than four months after the marriage.

'*Property*' for these purposes is limited to household effects and trousseaux, other than tobacco products and alcoholic beverages (ie it does not extend to motor vehicles and their trailers, caravans, mobile homes, pleasure boats and aircraft although some of these may alternatively qualify for relief under (*a*) above).

In addition, such a person is not required to pay VAT (or duty) on any wedding gift (meaning any property, other than tobacco products or alcoholic beverages, customarily given on the occasion of a marriage) not exceeding £800 in value imported into the UK by him or on his behalf provided the gift is

- given or intended to be given to him on the occasion of his marriage by a person normally resident outside the EC; and
- declared for relief not earlier than two months before the date fixed for the marriage (in which case security for the VAT and duty will be required which will be discharged on subsequent submission of the marriage certificate to HMRC) and not later than four months after the marriage.

See (*a*) above for the definition of '*normally resident*'.

[*SI 1992/3193, Arts 13–15; EC Council Directive 83/181/EEC, Arts 11–15*].

(*c*) **Pupils and students**. A person is not required to pay VAT (or duty) in respect of 'scholastic equipment' imported in to the UK provided

- he is a pupil or student normally resident outside the EC who has been accepted to attend a full-time course at a school, college or university in the UK; and
- the equipment belongs to him and is intended for his personal use during the period of his studies.

'*Scholastic equipment*' means household effects representing the normal furnishings for the room of the pupil or student, clothing, uniforms, and articles or instruments normally used by pupils or students for their studies, including calculators and typewriters.

[*SI 1992/3193, Art 16; EC Council Directive 83/181/EEC, Arts 20, 21*].

(*d*) **Honorary decorations, awards and goodwill gifts**. No VAT (or duty) is chargeable on the importation into the UK

- by a person normally resident in the UK of any honorary decoration confirmed on him by a government outside the EC or any cup, medal or similar article of an essentially symbolic nature awarded to him outside the EC as a tribute to his activities in the arts, sciences, sport or public service or in recognition of merit at a particular event;
- by a person normally resident in the UK, returning from an official visit outside the EC, of goods not intended for a commercial purpose given to him on his visit by the host authorities; or
- by a person normally resident outside the EC paying an official visit to the UK of goods not intended for a commercial purpose which are in the nature of an occasional gift he intends to offer to the host authorities during his visit.

Imports of tobacco products and alcoholic beverages are excluded.

[*SI 1992/3193, Arts 17–20*].

(*e*) **Personal property acquired by inheritance**. A person who is either

- 'normally resident' in the UK or Isle of Man,
- a 'secondary resident' who is not normally resident outside the EC, or
- a body incorporated in the UK or Isle of Man solely concerned with carrying on a non-profit making activity

and who has become entitled as legatee to 'property' situated outside the EC is not liable to pay any VAT (or duty) on importation of the property into the UK provided

- the property is imported not later than two years after the date of entitlement as legatee is finally determined (unless HMRC allow otherwise); and

- the person produces the property to the proper officer for examination and furnishes proof of his entitlement as legatee.

'*Property*' means any personal property intended for personal use or meeting household needs, including household effects, provisions and pets; riding animals, cycles, motor vehicles, caravans, pleasure boats and private aircraft; but excluding any goods which, by their nature or quantity, indicate they are being imported for a commercial purpose. Specifically excluded are

- alcoholic beverages and tobacco products;
- any motor vehicle designed for or capable of transporting more than nine persons, including the driver, or goods;
- any special purpose vehicle or mobile workshop;
- articles (other than portable instruments of the applied or liberal arts) used in the exercise of a trade or profession before his death by the person from whom the legatee has acquired them;
- stocks of raw materials and finished or semi-finished products; and
- livestock and agricultural products exceeding the quantities for normal family requirements.

See (*a*) above for the meaning of '*normally resident*'.

A '*secondary resident*' is a person who, without being normally resident in the UK or Isle of Man, has a home there which he owns or is renting for at least twelve months.

[*Customs and Excise Duties* (*General Reliefs*) *Act 1979, s 7; SI 1992/3193, Art 21; EC Council Directive 83/181/EEC, Arts 16–19*].

The following must be provided as proof of inheritance.

- A copy of the will (or other legal documents if the deceased died intestate) proving entitlement to the relief and identifying the goods, certified by the executors of the estate or other persons responsible for winding up the deceased's estate.
- If the goods are not precisely specified in the will, etc (eg where they formed part of the residue) a list of the goods and their approximate value prepared by the executors, etc and confirmation from them that title to the goods passed to the legatee.
- A signed declaration on Form C1421 (claim for relief).

(Customs Notice 368, paras 3.1, 4).

34.16 Small non-commercial consignments

No VAT is charged on the importation of a small non-commercial consignment, not forming part of a larger consignment, provided

- the consignment is of an occasional nature;
- the value for customs purposes does not exceed £36 (45 euro);
- it is consigned by one private individual to another;

- it is not imported for any consideration in money or money's worth; and
- it is intended solely for personal use of the consignee, or of his family, and not for any commercial purpose.

Any of the following goods included in the consignment must be below the permitted quantities shown. Otherwise no relief is given for any goods of that description in the consignment.

Tobacco	50 cigarettes *or* 25 cigarillos *or* 10 cigars *or* 50g of smoking tobacco
Alcoholic beverages	1 litre of spirits, etc with an alcoholic strength exceeding 22% by volume *or* 1 litre of spirits, aperitifs, etc with an alcoholic strength of 22% by volume or less, fortified wines and sparkling wines *or* 2 litres of still wines
Perfume and toilet water	50g of perfume *or* 250cc/ml of toilet water

This relief does not apply to goods contained in the baggage of, or carried with, a person entering the UK (for which see 34.17 below).

[*SI 1986/939; SI 1992/3118; EC Council Directive 78/1035/EEC*].

34.17 Travellers' allowances

A person who has travelled from a country outside the VAT territory of the EC (see 21.2 EUROPEAN COMMUNITY: GENERAL) is relieved from payment of VAT (and duty) on goods of up to the values listed below which he has obtained outside the VAT territory of the EC (or in a duty free shop in the EC on an outward journey) and which are contained in his personal luggage. The goods must not be imported or used for commercial purposes otherwise they are liable to forfeiture.

Tobacco	200 cigarettes *or* 100 cigarillos *or* 50 cigars *or* 250g of smoking tobacco
Alcoholic beverages	1 litre with an alcoholic strength of more than 22% by volume *or* 2 litres with an alcoholic strength of 22% by volume or less, fortified wines and sparkling wines *and* 2 litres of still wines
Perfume	60cc/ml
Toilet water	250cc/ml
Other goods (including gifts, souvenirs, beer and cider)	£145

No one under the age of 17 is entitled to relief for tobacco or alcoholic beverages.

Transitional provisions. Although the following countries joined the EC with effect from 1 May 2004, the above provisions continue to apply to the specified items until the dates shown.

Czech Republic	200 cigarettes	31 December 2007
	50 cigars, 100 cigarillos or 250 grammes of smoking tobacco	31 December 2006
Estonia	200 cigarettes or 250 grammes of smoking tobacco	31 December 2009
Hungary	200 cigarettes	31 December 2008
Latvia	200 cigarettes	31 December 2009
Lithuania	200 cigarettes	31 December 2009
Poland	200 cigarettes	31 December 2008
Slovakia	200 cigarettes	31 December 2008
Slovenia	200 cigarettes	31 December 2007

[*SI 1994/955; SI 1995/3044; SI 2004/1002*].

34.18 Goods imported for sale to another EC country

Subject to such conditions as HMRC impose, the VAT charged on the importation of goods from outside the EC is not payable where

- a taxable person imports goods in the course of an onward zero-rated supply of those goods by him to a taxable person in another EC country; and
- HMRC are satisfied that he intends to remove the goods to another EC country and he does in fact so remove the goods within one month of the date of importation (ie the date the goods enter free circulation). HMRC may approve a longer period.

HMRC may require the deposit of security up to the amount of the VAT chargeable on the importation.

[*SI 1995/2518, Reg 123*].

In the above circumstances, no import VAT is due in the UK or the EC country of destination but VAT on the supply/acquisition is accounted for by the purchaser in the EC country of destination.

Relief under these provisions cannot be claimed for goods imported for process and supply to a customer in another EC country.

The relief can be used by freight/forwarding agents provided they will be making a zero-rated supply of the imported goods, not merely dispatching them, to a taxable person in another EC country.

Records. As the onward supply is to a consignee in another EC country who will account for tax on the acquisition, the normal procedures must be adopted. In particular a VAT invoice must be issued and details recorded on an EC sales list and, where appropriate, a Supplementary Declaration.

(VAT Leaflet 702/7/04).

34.19 Reimported goods

Goods which have previously been exported can be reimported without payment of VAT in the following circumstances.

(1) **Reimportations by non-taxable persons**. Subject to any conditions that HMRC impose, VAT chargeable on the importation of goods which have been previously exported from the EC is not payable if HMRC are satisfied that

- the importer is not a taxable person or, if he is, the goods are not imported in the course of his business;
- the goods were last exported from the EC by him or on his behalf;
- *either* the goods were supplied in, acquired in or imported into the EC before export and VAT or other tax due was paid and has not been and will not be refunded *or* the goods are imported by the person who made them;
- the goods were not exported free of VAT under the zero-rating provisions in *VATA 1994, s 30(6)–(8)* or equivalent provisions elsewhere in the EC;
- the goods have not been subject to process or repair outside the EC other than necessary running repairs which did not increase their value; and
- the goods either
  - (i) were, at the time of exportation, intended to be reimported; or
  - (ii) have been returned for repair or replacement, after rejection by a customer outside the EC, or because it was not possible to deliver them; or
  - (iii) were, prior to the time of exportation, in private use and possession in the EC.

[*SI 1995/2518, Reg 124*].

(2) **Reimportations by taxable persons**. Subject to any conditions that HMRC impose, VAT chargeable on the importation of goods which have been previously exported from the EC is not payable if HMRC are satisfied that

- the importer is a taxable person importing the goods in the course of his business;
- the goods were last exported from the EC by him or on his behalf;
- the goods have not been subject to process or repair outside the EC other than necessary running repairs which did not increase their value;
- the goods either
  - (i) were owned by him at the time of exportation and have remained his property;
  - (ii) have been returned from the continental shelf; or
  - (iii) were owned by him at the time of exportation and have been returned after rejection by a customer outside the EC or because it was not possible to deliver the goods to such a customer; and
- if the goods were supplied in, acquired in or imported into the EC before their export, any VAT chargeable on that supply, acquisition or importation was paid and neither has been or will be refunded. Refunded does not mean deducted as input tax.

[*SI 1995/2518, Reg 125*].

As an alternative to claiming this relief, a taxable person may choose to pay or defer the VAT due on reimportation and, subject to the normal rules, deduct it as input tax on the next VAT return.

(3) **Reimportation after exportation for treatment or process.** Subject to any conditions that HMRC may impose, VAT chargeable on the importation of goods which have been temporarily exported outside the EC and are reimported

- after repair, process or adaptation outside the EC, or
- after having been made up or reworked outside the EC

is payable as if such treatment or process had been carried out in the UK, provided HMRC are satisfied that

- at the time of exportation the goods were intended to be reimported after completion of the treatment or process; and
- the ownership in the goods was not transferred to any other person at exportation or at any time the goods were abroad.

[*SI 1995/2518, Reg 126*].

The effect of this is that goods so reimported bear VAT only on the value of the treatment or process *plus* any freight and insurance if not already included *plus* any customs or excise duty or other import charges payable in the UK. No VAT is due on reimportation if the process has been carried out for no charge (eg because the goods were under warranty or guarantee) or where the goods processed are zero-rated in the UK. (VAT Notice 702, para 5.3).

See also CustomsNotice 236 *Returned goods free of duty and tax*.

34.20 **Repayment or remission of VAT on rejected goods**

(1) **Goods not in accordance with contract.** Repayment or remission of VAT can be claimed on goods imported if the goods

- are rejected because, at the time of declaring them to Customs, they
  - (i) are defective;
  - (ii) do not comply with the terms of the contract under which they were imported; or
  - (iii) were damaged before being cleared by Customs;
- are those declared to Customs;
- have not been used more than was necessary to establish that they were defective or did not comply with contract;
- have not been sold after they have been found to be defective or not to comply with the contract; and
- are disposed of by
  - (i) exportation;
  - (ii) destruction at the expense of the importer;
  - (iii) destruction by order of a public authority; or

(iv) placing in a customs warehouse or a free zone (in which case the goods are treated as non-Community goods and can be subsequently re-entered to free circulation or another customs procedure or re-exported).

HMRC must be notified on Form 1179 at least 48 hours before the intended disposal and disposal must take place under Customs control. Any waste or scrap resulting from authorised destruction of the goods is liable to VAT (and duty) unless exported from the EC.

Claims must be made within 12 months of the date Customs charges became due and for an amount exceeding 10 euros.

A fully taxable VAT-registered person importing goods for business purposes should normally be able to deduct the VAT due on importation on his next VAT return. However, a direct repayment can be claimed under the above provisions. If so, he must surrender the import VAT certificate relating to the goods and make a signed declaration that he will not make a corresponding claim for input tax deduction on a VAT return.

A partly exempt person whose method of apportionment does not allow him to recover all the relevant input tax, a non-registered person or a taxable person importing goods for non-business purposes should submit a claim for direct repayment.

See Customs Notice 266 for details of how to make the claim.

(2) **Goods in special situations**. Repayment or remission of VAT can be claimed on imported goods in a number of special situations provided the goods have not been used or sold after import and the claim (which must be for an amount exceeding 10 euros) is made within 12 months of the date Customs charges became due. Each case will be decided on its merits but examples include where the goods are

- in a means of transport which it is impossible to open on arrival at its destination after the goods have been released for free circulation (provided the goods are immediately re-exported);
- forbidden to be marketed by a judicial body and are re-exported from the EC or destroyed under customs supervision (provided the goods have not been used in the UK);
- entered by a declarant empowered to do so on their own initiative and which, through no fault of the declarant, cannot be delivered to the consignee;
- addressed to the consignee in error, eg wrongly labelled, not ordered by the consignee, or received in excess of the quantity ordered (provided the goods are re-exported to the original supplier or to an address specified by them and, in the case of excess goods, the consignee refused the goods immediately the excess was discovered);
- found to be unsuitable because of an obvious error in the consignee's order (eg wrong goods received due to quoting an incorrect reference number);
- found not to have complied, at the time of entry into free circulation, with the rules in force concerning their use or marketing and cannot therefore be used as the consignee intended;

- unable to be used because of official measures taken after the date of entry for free circulation (eg new safety or hygiene laws);
- delivered to a consignee after a fixed delivery date (eg because of shipping delays); and
- found to be unsaleable in the EC and are to be donated to charity, in which case the goods must either be
  - (i) exported and given free of charge to a charity operating outside the EC, provided that the charity is also represented in the EC; or
  - (ii) delivered free of charge to a charity operating in the EC, provided the charity is eligible to import similar goods free of VAT and duty under 34.15(6) above, 12.7, 12.8 CHARITIES or 32.34 HEALTH AND WELFARE.

(Customs Notice 266, paras 3.1, 3.2).

34.21 Visiting forces

No VAT is required where

- an 'entitled person' imports any goods, or
- a gift of goods, other than tobacco products or alcoholic beverages, is made to an entitled person by dispatching them to him from outside the EC

subject to the following conditions.

(*a*) The goods must not be lent, hired-out, given as security or transferred in the UK without the prior authorisation in writing by HMRC. Where HMRC do authorise such disposal, the entitled person must then pay the VAT relieved at the lower of the rate in force at the time of relief and the rate at the time of disposal.

(*b*) The goods must be used exclusively by the entitled person or a member of his family forming part of his household.

(*c*) In the case of a motor vehicle,

- no relief is available if the entitled person has previously been afforded relief in respect of any other motor vehicle unless he has disposed of all such vehicles (or all but one if his spouse is present in the UK) and paid any duty or tax required by HMRC as under (*a*) above; and
- the entitled person must deliver, or cause to be delivered, four copies of a completed Form C941, each signed by the entitled person and his commanding officer. One copy is to be delivered to the visiting forces, and three copies to the proper officer.

An '*entitled person*' means a person who is

- a serving member of a visiting force, other than the UK, which is a member of NATO or a person recognised by the Secretary of State as a member of the civilian component of such a force; or
- a person who is a military or civilian member of NATO International Military Headquarters

who is neither a UK national nor a permanent resident of the UK.

Where any conditions are not complied with, the VAT becomes payable forthwith (unless HMRC sanction non-compliance in writing) and the goods are liable to forfeiture. Any VAT due is the liability of the entitled person or any person in possession of the goods at that time.

[*SI 1992/3156*].

34.22 **Aircraft ground and security equipment**

By concession, no VAT or duty is chargeable on the importation of the following ground and security equipment for aircraft by an airline of another contracting state of the Convention on International Civil Aviation (Chicago Convention).

- All repair, maintenance and servicing equipment; material for airframes, engines and instruments; specialised aircraft repair kits; starter batteries and carts; maintenance platforms and steps; test equipment for aircraft, aircraft engines and aircraft instruments; aircraft engine heaters and coolers; ground radio equipment.
- Passenger-handling equipment: passenger-loading steps; specialised passenger-weighing devices; specialised catering equipment.
- Cargo-loading equipment: vehicles for moving or loading baggage, cargo, equipment and supplies; specialised cargo-loading devices; specialised cargo-weighing devices.
- Component parts for incorporation into ground equipment including the items listed above.
- Security equipment: weapon-detecting devices; explosives-detecting devices; intrusion detecting devices.
- Component parts for incorporation into security equipment.

Claims for relief under this concession should be addressed to the Customs Entry Processing Unit where the goods are to be cleared.

(Customs Notice 48, ESC 2.6).

Electricity and natural gas

34.23 *With effect from 1 January 2005*, VAT is not payable on the importation of

- gas through the natural gas distribution network; or
- electricity.

[*SI 2004/3147*].

This forms part of the implementation of *EC Council Directive 2003/92/EC*.

34.24 **GOODS IMPORTED UNDER CUSTOMS SUSPENSIVE ARRANGEMENTS**

Any goods imported from outside the EC and placed under one of the following customs suspension arrangements do not constitute imports for VAT purposes. No import VAT is therefore normally due unless, or until, the goods are removed from those arrangements.

(*a*) *Temporary storage* (not strictly a customs arrangement but all goods arriving from outside the EC have the status of goods in temporary storage until they are entered and cleared for home use or another procedure).

(*b*) *Free zones.* It is possible to import goods into a free zone without payment of customs duty and import VAT and to process them there. Exports from the zones and movements from zone to zone are free of VAT. By concession, the supply of free zone goods which were originally imported into the UK may be zero-rated if the supplier and customer agree that the customer will clear the goods for removal from the free zone to home use and will take responsibility for the import VAT. See 70.21 WAREHOUSED GOODS AND FREE ZONES for further details.

(*c*) *Customs warehousing.* Import VAT and duties are suspended whilst the goods remain in the warehousing regime. On removal from the warehouse, the deferment system may be used. The main purpose of customs warehousing is storage and only minor handling is allowed. Processing is not normally permitted but where it is, the processing is treated as a supply of services which is relieved from VAT. See 70.2 WAREHOUSED GOODS AND FREE ZONES for further details.

(*d*) *Inward processing relief* (duty suspension system). See 34.30 below.

(*e*) *Temporary importation* (including means of transport) with total relief from customs duty. See 34.25 below.

(*f*) *External Community Transit* (*T1*) *arrangements.*

(*g*) *Internal Community Transit* (*T2*) *arrangements* (applies to some trade with special territories inside the EC customs area but outside the EC for VAT purposes).

(*h*) *Goods admitted into territorial waters*

- in order to be incorporated into drilling or production platforms for purposes of the construction, repair, maintenance or alteration or fitting-out of such platforms, or to link such drilling or production platforms to the mainland; or
- for the fuelling and provisioning of drilling or production platforms.

Transfers of goods. Goods can be moved from one suspensive regime to another, for example, from customs warehousing to IPR suspension, without payment of import VAT.

Acquisitions of goods under suspensive arrangements. VAT-registered traders who acquire goods held in one of the arrangements listed in (*a*)–(*h*) above from a taxable person in another EC country, must normally account for VAT on the acquisition in accordance with the normal rules, even though the import VAT remains suspended.

Supplies of goods under suspensive arrangements. Supplies of goods held under suspensive arrangements are chargeable with VAT in the normal way. This is subject to the following special rules.

(i) *Goods in temporary storage under* (*a*) *above.* Where there is a supply of imported goods between the time of their arrival in the UK and the time when an import entry is delivered to HMRC and, by arrangement, the purchaser is required to make the import entry, then the seller may zero-rate the supply.

(ii) *Goods under temporary import arrangements under* (*e*) *above supplied to persons established outside the EC.* Where goods held under temporary import arrangements are supplied, that supply is treated as neither a supply of goods nor a supply of services provided that

- the goods remain eligible for temporary importation arrangements; and
- the supply is to a person established outside the EC.

[*SI 1992/3130*].

(iii) *Second-hand goods and works of art under temporary import arrangements under* (*e*) *above*. Where

- second-hand goods are imported with a view to their sale by auction, or
- 'works of art' are imported for exhibition with a view to possible sale,

any sale of the second-hand goods (provided it is by auction) or the works of art at a time when the goods are still subject to temporary importation arrangements with total exemption from import duty is treated as neither a supply of goods nor a supply of services and can be disregarded for VAT purposes.

The provision of any services relating to such supplies (eg auctioneers' charges) may similarly be disregarded (but must be included in the value for VAT at importation).

'*Works of art*' mean any such items falling within the definition in *VATA 1994, s 21* (see 71.3(*a*) WORKS OF ART, ETC).

[*SI 1995/958; SI 1999/3119*].

Removal of goods for home use. Import VAT is normally due when the goods are removed for home use in the UK.

(VAT Notice 702, paras 2.10, 5.2).

34.25 Relief for temporary importations (TI relief)

Persons who temporarily import goods may either

- take advantage of the TI relief provisions, pay no VAT (or duty) at the time of importation but deposit any security required by HMRC for VAT (and duty) which would become due if the conditions for temporary importation are not met; or
- if they are taxable persons importing the goods for business purposes, pay the VAT at the time of temporary importation (or defer it under the provisions relating to deferment of VAT, see 34.5 above) and reclaim the VAT paid as input tax subject to the normal rules. If this is done, there is no limit on the length of time that the goods may be held in the UK before re-exportation (although the relevant controls and time limits for any duty remain).

Subject to meeting certain conditions, it is possible to obtain total relief from import duties and VAT on a range of goods imported from outside the EC if they are intended for re-export within a specified time (usually a maximum of two years). See 34.26 below for eligible goods. In most cases, application for authorisation to use TI relief can be made at the time of importation. There are, however, other types of authorisations available. See Customs Notice 200, sections 2 and 3 for the various types of authorisation and how to apply for them, and the documentary evidence which must be presented to HMRC to use the relief.

For most importations, it is necessary to provide security (either by cash deposit or bank guarantee) equal to the full amount of duty and import VAT potentially due. This may be reclaimed when the goods have been re-exported and satisfactory documentary evidence can be provided. See 34.27 below.

34.26 *Goods eligible for TI relief*

The various TI reliefs that provide for total relief from duties and VAT on importation are as listed below. The following general conditions apply.

- Unless otherwise stated, goods imported under TI provisions may remain in the EC for a maximum of two years. Application can be made in writing, before expiry of the original TI period, for a longer period. If TI goods are transferred to another Customs suspensive arrangement (eg IPR or customs warehousing) only the remaining balance of the TI period will be available to those goods if they are re-entered to TI at a later date.
- Goods must remain in the same state. Repairs and maintenance, including overhaul and adjustments or measures to preserve the goods or to ensure their compliance with the technical requirements for their use under the arrangements are admissible.

[*EC Commission Regulation No 2454/93, Arts 553, 554*].

(1) **Pallets**. [*EC Commission Regulation No 2454/93, Art 556*].

(2) **Containers** which have been durably marked in an appropriate and clearly visible place with the following information.

- The identity of the owner or operator shown by either full name or an established identification (symbols such as emblems or flags being excluded).
- (With certain exceptions), the identification marks and numbers of the container, given by the owner or operator; its tare weight, including all its permanently fixed equipment.
- Apart from containers used for transport by air, the country to which the container belongs.

Containers may be used once in the UK before being re-exported for transporting goods loaded and intended to be unloaded within the UK where the containers would otherwise have to make an unloaded journey.

[*EC Commission Regulation No 2454/93, Art 557*]. See also Customs Notice 306.

(3) **Means of transport**. Means of road, rail, air, sea and inland waterway transport where

- they are registered outside the EC in the name of a person established outside the EC (or, if the means of transport are not registered, they are owned by a person established outside the EC);
- they are used by a person established outside the EC; and
- in the case of commercial use and with the exception of means of rail transport, are used exclusively for transport which begins or ends outside the EC except that they may be used in internal traffic where the provisions in force in the field of transport, in particular those concerning admission and operations, so provide.

Where the means of transport referred to above are re-hired by a professional hire service established in the EC to a person established outside the EC, they must be re-exported within eight days of entry into force of the contract.

Persons established in the EC benefit from total relief from VAT and import duties where

- means of rail transport are put at their disposal under an agreement whereby each network may use the rolling stock of the other networks as its own;
- a trailer is coupled to a means of road transport registered in the EC;
- means of transport are used in connection with an emergency situation and their use does not exceed five days; or
- means of transport are used by a professional hire firm for the purpose of re-exportation within a period not exceeding five days.

Natural persons established in the EC benefit from total relief from VAT and import duties

- where they privately use means of transport occasionally, on the instructions of the registration holder, this holder being in the EC at the time of use; and
- for the occasional private use of means of transport, hired under a written contract, to

  (i) return to their place of residence in the EC, or

  (ii) leave the EC.

  The means of transport must be re-exported or returned to the hire service established in the EC within five days of the entry into force of the contract under (i) above and re-exported within two days of the entry into force of the contract under (*b*) above.

Total relief from VAT and import duties is also granted where

- means of transport are to be registered under a temporary series in the EC, with a view to re-exportation, *either* in the name of a person established outside the EC *or* in the name of a natural person established inside the EC where that person is preparing to transfer normal residence to a place outside the EC (in which case the means of transport must be exported);
- means of transport are used commercially or privately by a natural person established in the EC and employed by the owner of the means of transport established outside the EC or otherwise authorised by the owner. Private use must have been provided for in the contract of employment; and
- (in exceptional cases) means of transport are commercially used for a limited period by persons established in the EC.

Period of discharge. Without prejudice to other special provisions, the periods for discharge are as follows.

- For means of rail transport: 12 months.

- For commercially used means of transport other than rail transport: the time required for carrying out the transport operations.
- For means of road transport privately used by students: the period the student stays in the EC for the sole purpose of pursuing their studies.
- For means of road transport privately used by persons fulfilling assignments of a specified duration: the period this person stays in the EC for the sole purpose of fulfilling their assignment.
- For means of road transport privately used in other cases, including saddle or draught animals and the vehicles drawn by them: six months.
- For privately used means of air transport: six months.
- For privately used means of sea and inland waterway transport: 18 months.

[*EC Commission Regulation No 2454/93, Art 558–562*].

(4) **Personal effects and goods for sports purposes** imported by a traveller from outside the EC. [*EC Commission Regulation No 2454/93, Art 563*].

Personal effects. TI relief can be claimed for personal effects reasonably required for a journey (eg clothing, toiletries, personal jewellery and other articles clearly of a personal nature, including pets). Relief can be claimed for the period of stay in the EC up to a maximum of 24 months. Sporting firearms and ammunition are also eligible for relief but a full TI authorisation is needed and this requires prior approval from HMRC on Form 1331 at least one month before the intended import.

Students coming to stay in the EC for the purpose of full-time study do not need to use the TI procedures for clothing and household linen, items to be used in their studies (eg PCs), and household effects for furnishing their student's room.

Private motor vehicles. TI relief can be claimed on a vehicle temporarily imported for private use (including any accompanying spare parts, accessories and equipment) if

- it is registered outside the EC or, if not registered, belongs to the visitor, etc or someone else who has their normal home outside the EC;
- the vehicle is not sold, lent or hired out or otherwise disposed of in the EC; and
- it is re-exported from the EC within six months except that, in the case of a student or someone on an assignment of a specific duration, the vehicle can remain in the EC for the period of studies or until the end of the assignment.

Extending the period of a visit or deciding to live permanently in the EC. The period allowed under TI relief can, in exceptional circumstances, be extended within reasonable limits. Written application, giving reasons for the extension, must be made to National Import Reliefs Unit (NIRU), Custom House, Killyhevlin Industrial Estate, Enniskillen, County Fermanagh, Northern Ireland BT74 4EJ (Tel: 028 6632 2298; Fax: 028 6632 4018) or by e-mail to

enquiries.niru.rbs@hmrc.gsi.gov.uk

If a visitor decides to live permanently in the EC, any personal effects and vehicle may qualify for other reliefs in this chapter. The visitor should write to NIRU advising them of the decision and giving details of the personal effects and vehicle.

(Customs Notice 3, paras 4.1, 4.3, 4.6).

Goods for sports purposes include track and field equipment (eg hurdles, javelins, discuses, poles, shots, hammers); ball game equipment (eg balls of any kind, rackets, mallets, clubs, sticks and the like; nets of any kind, goal posts); winter sports equipment (eg skis and sticks, skates, bobsleighs, curling equipment); sports wear, shoes, gloves, headgear, etc of any kind; water sports equipment (eg canoes and kayaks, sail and row boats, sails, oars and paddles, surf boards and sails); motor vehicles and craft (eg cars, motor bicycles, motor boats); equipment for miscellaneous events (eg sports arms and ammunition, non-motorised bicycles, archer's bows and arrows, fencing equipment, gymnastics equipment, compasses, wrestling mats and tatamis, weight-lifting equipment, riding equipment, sulkies, hang-gliders, delta wings, windsurfers, climbing equipment, music cassettes to accompany the performance; and auxiliary equipment (eg measuring and score display equipment, blood and urine test apparatus). (Customs Notice 200, Appendix C).

(5) **Welfare materials for seafarers** where they are

- used on a vessel engaged in international maritime traffic;
- unloaded from such a vessel and temporarily used ashore by the crew; or
- used by the crew of such a vessel in cultural or social establishments managed by non-profit-making organisations or in places of worship where services for seafarers are regularly held.

[*EC Commission Regulation No 2454/93, Art 564*].

Included are reading material (eg books of any kind, correspondence courses, newspapers, journals and periodicals, pamphlets on welfare facilities in ports); audio-visual material (eg sound and image reproducing instruments, tape-recorders, radio sets, television sets, cinematographic and other projectors, recordings on tapes or discs of language courses, radio programmes, greetings, music and entertainment, films, exposed and developed, film slides, videotapes); sports gear (eg sports wear, balls, rackets and nets, deck games, athletic equipment, gymnastic equipment); hobby material (eg indoor games, musical instruments, material for amateur dramatics, materials for painting, sculpture, woodwork and metalwork, carpet making, etc); equipment for religious activities; and parts and accessories for welfare material. (Customs Notice 200, Appendix C).

(6) **Disaster relief material** where it is used in connection with measures taken to counter the effects of disasters or similar situations within the EC and intended for state bodies or bodies approved by the competent authorities. [*EC Commission Regulation No 2454/93, Art 565*].

(7) **Medical, surgical and laboratory equipment** where it is dispatched on loan at the request of a hospital or other medical institution which has urgent need of such equipment to make up for the inadequacy of its own facilities and where it is intended for diagnostic or therapeutic purposes. [*EC Commission Regulation No 2454/93, Art 566*].

(8) **Animals owned by a person established outside the EC**. [*EC Commission Regulation No 2454/93, Art 567*].

(9) **Goods for use in frontier zones,** ie

- equipment owned by a person established in the frontier zone adjacent to the frontier zone of temporary importation and used by a person established in that adjacent frontier zone, and
- goods used for the building, repair or maintenance of infrastructure in such a frontier zone under the responsibility of public authorities.

[*EC Commission Regulation No 2454/93, Art 567*].

(10) **Sound, image or data carrying media** for processing information for the purpose of presentation prior to commercialisation, or free of charge, or for provision with a sound track, dubbing or copying. [*EC Commission Regulation No 2454/93, Art 568*]. *Included* are documentary films, records, tape recordings and other sound recordings intended for use in performances at which no charge is made, but excluding those whose subjects lend themselves to commercial advertising and those which are on general sale in the EC country of temporary importation. (Customs Notice 200, Appendix C).

(11) **Publicity material**. [*EC Commission Regulation No 2454/93, Art 568*]. *Included* is material for display in the offices of the accredited representatives or correspondents appointed by the official national tourist agencies or in other places approved by the customs authorities of the EC country of temporary importation, pictures and drawings, framed photographs and photographic enlargements, art books, paintings, engravings or lithographs, sculptures and tapestries and other similar works of art; materials intended for display in show-cases, stands and similar articles, including electrical and mechanical equipment required for operating such display; a reasonable number of flags; dioramas, scale models, lantern-slides, printing blocks, photographic negatives, specimens, in reasonable numbers, of articles of national handicrafts, local costumes and similar articles of folklore. (Customs Notice 200, Appendix C).

(12) **Professional equipment**

- owned by a person established outside the EC;
- imported either by a person established outside the EC or by an employee of the owner (the employee may be established in the EC); and
- used by the importer, or under their supervision, except in cases of audiovisual co-productions.

Relief does not apply to equipment to be used for the industrial manufacture or packaging of goods or, except in the case of hand tools, for the exploitation of natural resources, for the construction, repair or maintenance of buildings or for earth moving and like projects.

[*EC Commission Regulation No 2454/93, Art 569*].

Included is

- Equipment for the press.
- Sound broadcasting, television broadcasting and cinematographic equipment and vehicles designed or specially adapted for use with such equipment.

- Other equipment for erection, testing, commissioning, checking, control, maintenance or repair of machinery, plant, means of transport, etc.
- Equipment necessary for: businessmen, business efficiency consultants, productivity experts, accountants and members of similar professions; experts undertaking topographical surveys or geophysical prospecting work; experts combating pollution; doctors, surgeons, veterinary surgeons, midwives and members of similar professions; archaeologists, palaeontologists, geographers, zoologists and other scientists; entertainers, theatre companies and orchestras; lecturers to illustrate their lectures; photography trips; and vehicles designed or specially adapted for these purposes (eg mobile inspection units, travelling workshops and travelling laboratories).

(Customs Notice 200, Appendix C).

(13) **Educational material and scientific equipment**

- owned by a person established outside the EC;
- imported by public or private scientific, teaching or vocational training establishments which are essentially non-profit making and exclusively used in teaching, vocational training or scientific research under their responsibility;
- imported in reasonable numbers, having regard to the purpose of the importation; and
- not used for purely commercial purposes.

[*EC Commission Regulation No 2454/93, Art 570*].

Included is

- sound or image recorders or reproducers;
- sound and image media;
- specialised material (eg bibliographic equipment and audio-visual material for libraries, mobile libraries, language laboratories, simultaneous interpretation equipment, programmed teaching machines, mechanical or electronic, material specially designed for the educational or vocational training of handicapped persons);
- other material (eg wall charts, models, graphs, maps, plans, photographs and drawings, instruments, apparatus and models designed for demonstration purposes, collections of items with visual or audio educational information, prepared for the teaching of a subject, instruments, apparatus, tools and machine-tools for learning a trade or craft equipment, including specially adapted or designed vehicles for use in relief operations, which is imported for the training of persons involved in relief operations); and
- other goods imported in connection with educational, scientific or cultural activities (eg costumes and scenery items sent on loan free of charge to dramatic societies or theatres, music scores sent on loan free of charge to music theatres or orchestras).

(Customs Notice 200, Appendix C).

(14) **Packings** where

- if imported filled, is intended for re-exportation whether empty or filled; and
- if imported empty, is intended for re-exportation filled.

Packings are not to be used in internal traffic, except with a view to the export of goods. In the case of packings imported filled, this condition only applies from the time that they are emptied of their contents.

[*EC Commission Regulation No 2454/93, Art 571*].

(15) **Moulds, dies, etc.** Moulds, dies, blocks, drawings, sketches, measuring, checking and testing instruments and other similar articles

- owned by a person established outside the EC, and
- used in manufacturing by a person established in the EC

provided at least 75% of the production resulting from their use is exported.

[*EC Commission Regulation No 2454/93, Art 572(1)*].

(16) **Special tools.** Special tools and instruments where the goods are

- owned by a person established outside the EC, and
- made available free of charge to a person established in the EC for the manufacture of goods which are to be exported in their entirety.

[*EC Commission Regulation No 2454/93, Art 572(2)*].

(17) **Goods for testing, etc.** Relief applies to

(*a*) goods subjected to tests, experiments or demonstrations;

(*b*) goods subject to satisfactory acceptance tests that are imported in connection with a sales contract containing the provisions of the satisfactory acceptance tests and subjected to those tests; and

(*c*) goods used to carry out tests, experiments or demonstrations without financial gain.

The period for re-export of goods under (*b*) above is six months.

[*EC Commission Regulation No 2454/93, Art 573*].

(18) **Samples** imported in reasonable quantities and solely used for being shown or demonstrated in the EC. [*EC Commission Regulation No 2454/93, Art 574*].

(19) **Replacement means of production** temporarily made available to a customer by a supplier or repairer, pending the delivery or repair of similar goods. The period for re-export is six months. [*EC Commission Regulation No 2454/93, Art 575*].

(20) **Goods to be exhibited or used at a public event** not purely organised for the commercial sale of the goods, or obtained at such events from goods placed under TI arrangements. [*EC Commission Regulation No 2454/93, Art 576(1)*].

(21) **Goods for approval** where they cannot be imported as samples and the consignor wishes to sell the goods and the consignee may decide to purchase them after inspection. The period for re-export is two months. [*EC Commission Regulation No 2454/93, Art 576(2)*].

(22) **Works of art, collectors' items and antiques** imported for the purposes of exhibition, with a view to possible sale. [*EC Commission Regulation No 2454/93, Art 576(3)(a)*].

(23) **Second-hand goods** imported with a view to their sale by auction. [*EC Commission Regulation No 2454/93, Art 576(3)(b)*].

(24) **Spare parts, accessories and equipment** used for repair and maintenance, including overhaul, adjustments and preservation of goods entered for the arrangements. [*EC Commission Regulation No 2454/93, Art 577*].

(25) **Miscellaneous goods.** Goods

- not falling within other than those listed in (1)–(24) above, or
- falling within (1)–(24) above but not complying with the relevant conditions

which are imported

- occasionally and for a period not exceeding three months; or
- in particular situations having no economic effect.

[*EC Commission Regulation No 2454/93, Art 578*].

34.27 *Security and guarantees*

Security is required on most temporary importations to cover the full amount of charges (including VAT and duty) that could become due if the goods are not ultimately re-exported. Any security required must be provided by a cash deposit or banker's guarantee. Regular importers may be able to lodge a single guarantee which HMRC will adjust accordingly as goods subject to TI relief (or any other procedure requiring a security) are imported. Cash deposits can be taken from a deferment account.

The need to provide security on importation can be avoided, as well as covering the Customs declarations needed

- in the EC,
- where the goods are based, and
- for transit between different locations,

by using an ATA carnet. These are issued by the relevant authority in the country where the goods are permanently based. For further information on the ATA Carnet system contact the Customs National Advice Service for a copy of Notice 104.

To re-claim any security or guarantee, the importer must show that he has

- re-exported the goods (providing the certified export declaration or acceptable commercial evidence);
- transferred the goods to another authorised trader (evidence will depend upon the method of transfer used and type of authorisation held);
- diverted the goods to free circulation (attaching a copy of the Customs entry); or
- transferred the goods to another Customs suspensive procedure.

For goods imported for a specific purpose, evidence will also be required to show that conditions attached to their import have been met.

(Customs Notice 200, paras 7.1, 7.2).

34.28 *Record keeping requirements*

Detailed records of the receipt, use and disposal of any goods imported must be kept showing

- the goods entered, ie the commercial or technical description of the goods sufficient to identify them;
- that security (where required) has been provided;
- when and where goods were entered including details of any transfer of TI goods;
- where the TI goods are held at any time including any movement of goods to or between users specified in the authorisation;
- locations where the goods will be used;
- how goods entered to TI relief are identified, eg manufacturer's marks or serial numbers, illustrations or technical descriptions; and
- when and where goods are exported including documents relating to their disposal.

Where computerised records are to be kept, HMRC must be advised when applying for authorisation to ensure that these records meet their requirements.

All records must be kept for four years after disposal of the goods.

(Customs Notice 200, para 2.17).

34.29 *Discharging TI arrangements*

TI is completed or discharged as follows.

- The goods are exported from the EC (directly or via another EC country).
- The goods are transferred to another Customs suspensive arrangement or to another operator authorised to use one of those procedures.
- The goods are transferred to another EC country to be entered to another Customs suspensive procedure in that country.
- The goods are transferred to another TI authorisation holder in the UK or another EC country.
- The goods are diverted to free circulation.
- In respect of goods imported to be exhibited or used at a public event not organised for commercial sale of the goods, if they are consumed, destroyed or distributed free of charge to the public at the event, provided the quantity of goods corresponds to the nature of the event, the number of visitors and the authorisation holder's participation in the event. (This does not apply to alcoholic beverages, tobacco goods or fuels.)
- In respect of moulds, dies, blocks, drawings, sketches, measures, checking and testing instruments and other similar articles, when they have been used in manufacturing and at least 75% of products resulting from their use are exported. Records that the manufactured products have been exported must be kept.

- In respect of special tools and instruments made available free of charge for the manufacture of goods, when they are re-exported and all products resulting from their use are exported. Records that the manufactured products have been exported must be kept.
- The goods are destroyed under Customs supervision. If goods are found on or after entry, to be defective, contaminated, obsolete or otherwise unusable, they may be destroyed, without payment of the VAT and duty, with prior agreement of HMRC. VAT and duty will be charged if any waste and scrap resulting from destruction has a commercial value.

(Customs Notice 200, paras 5.1, 5.7).

34.30 **Inward processing relief (IPR)**

Duty is relieved on imports of non-EC goods which are processed in the EC and re-exported (or transferred to another IPR authorisation holder in the UK or another EC country) provided the trade does not harm the essential interests of EC producers of similar goods. Processing can be anything from re-packing or sorting goods to the most complicated manufacturing.

There are two methods of duty relief.

- **Suspension**. Customs duties are suspended when the goods are first entered to IPR in the EC. Import VAT is not due unless the goods are released to the EC market. See Customs Notice 221, para 27.2 for goods which must be entered to suspension. These include agricultural goods, some licensable goods (mostly textiles) and any goods intended to be processed under IPR in a Customs warehouse or free zone. See Customs Notice 221, section 28 for the conditions for using suspension.
- **Drawback**. Customs duties and import VAT are paid when the goods are entered to IPR. Duty can only be reclaimed if the goods are exported, transferred to an IPR suspension authorisation holder or disposed of in an approved way. Import VAT can be reclaimed as input tax. See Customs Notice 221, section 27 for the conditions and restrictions for using drawback.

In either case there must be an intention to re-export goods from the EC and an authorisation to enter goods to IPR will be required. Goods must be processed within a certain period and records kept for all operations carried out. Under the suspension method, returns detailing receipts and disposals must be submitted.

(Customs Notice 221, paras 1.2, 1.4–1.6).

34.31 *Records*

Records must be kept of all goods entered to IPR showing

- details of the quantities of goods entered to IPR. If authorisation restricts the quantity or value of goods on which IPR can be claimed, records must be sufficient to allow this to be monitored;
- what goods are entered, ie the commercial or technical description of the goods sufficient to identify them;
- when and where goods were entered to IPR, including transfers received and documents relating to their entry;

- where all goods and compensating products held under the authorisation are held at any time including any movement of goods and compensating products to or between operators specified in the authorisation;
- what processing is carried out on the goods;
- locations where processing takes place;
- how goods entered to IPR are identified in the products produced;
- production data that establishes the rate of yield achieved, ie how many products are produced including any secondary compensating products (by-products); and
- when and where goods were exported or disposed of including documents relating to their disposal.

Where computerised records are to be kept, HMRC must be advised when applying for authorisation to ensure that these records meet their requirements.

All records must be kept for four years after disposal of the goods.

(Customs Notice 221, para 3.12).

34.32 *Discharging IPR*

Duty and VAT can be reclaimed on drawback goods or IPR liability can be discharged on suspension goods if the goods are disposed of in one of the following ways.

- Export from the EC directly or via another EC country.
- Transfer either to another Customs procedure or to another operator authorised to use one of those procedures.
- Transfer to another EC country to be entered to another Customs procedure in that country.
- Transfer to a Customs approved use such as export shops, armed forces, NAAFI, embassies, ships stores or bunkers or use as commissary stores and use in tray type meals.
- Disposal of aircraft or aircraft parts and using goods in satellite construction.
- Use of aviation fuel for third country or intra-EC flights.
- Export to the Continental Shelf (outside territorial waters).
- Sale to customers who take goods abroad in their baggage.
- Diversion to the EC market with payment of duty, import VAT and compensatory interest (suspension goods).
- In exceptional circumstances, diversion of goods that are eligible for End Use relief with payment of duty, import VAT and compensatory interest (suspension goods) at the End Use rate of duty.
- Destruction of the goods under customs supervision (suspension goods only).

For suspension goods it is necessary to complete a return of receipts and disposals to account for the goods periodically. For drawback goods a return must be completed detailing the receipt and disposal of goods on which repayment of duty is sought.

(Customs Notice 221, para 15.2).

34.33 **IMPORTING COMPUTER SOFTWARE**

Imported computer software may be classified as goods and/or services.

Goods are the tangible carrier medium on which the software resides.

- If the tangible carrier medium is magnetic tape, disk, diskette compact disk (CD) and read only CD videos, the VAT treatment depends on whether, at the time of importation, the items are 'normalised' (off the shelf) or 'specific' (custom made) products as explained below.
- If the information resides on semiconductors, integrated circuits or similar devices or articles incorporating such circuits or devices, VAT must be paid on the whole value at importation.

Services may comprise the data, program and/or instructions (but not sound, cinematographic or video recordings). The VAT treatment of services received from outside the EC depends on whether they are 'normalised' (off the shelf) or 'specific' (custom made) software as explained below.

The transmission and provision of information by satellite, telephone, telex, facsimile, etc is treated as a service. See 39.9 INTERNATIONAL SERVICES.

'Normalised' comprises mass-produced items which are freely available to all customers and usable by them independently, after installation and limited training, in a standard form to carry out the same applications or functions. They are made up of a coherent set of programs and support material and often include the service of installation, training and maintenance. *Included are* personal and home computer software, game packages, etc and standard packages adapted at the supplier's instigation to include security or similar devices.

Importations of normalised items are regarded as importations of both goods (made up of the carrier medium, see above) and services (the data and/or the instructions).

- Where the goods and services are not identified separately, the whole importation is treated as an importation of goods.
- Where the goods and services are identified separately, a UK taxable person may pay VAT on importation only on the cost or value of the carrier medium. Normal valuation rules apply (see 69.15 VALUATION). The supply of services falls within *VATA 1994, Sch 5 para 3* and VAT on these must be accounted for under the 'reverse charge' procedure (see 39.4 INTERNATIONAL SERVICES).

'Specific' software products are

- items made to customers' special requirements (either as unique programs or adaptations from standard programs);
- inter-company information data and accounts;
- enhancements and updates of existing specific programs; and
- enhancements and updates of existing normalised programs supplied under contractual obligation to customers who have bought the original program.

The importation of a specific item of software is made up of an importation of goods (the carrier medium, see above) and a supply of services (the data and/or the instructions) but to simplify import procedures, the carrier medium is treated as a supply of services. No import VAT is charged on the carrier medium at importation.

34.33 Imports

The supply of services falls within *VATA 1994, Sch 5 para 3* and a UK business must account for VAT on the supply under the 'reverse charge' procedure. See 39.4 INTERNATIONAL SERVICES. No VAT is payable for specific items imported free of charge.

(VAT Notice 702, paras 7.1–7.13).

35 Input Tax

Cross-references. See 9 BUSINESS ENTERTAINMENT for disallowed input tax; 10 CAPITAL GOODS SCHEME; 21.32 EUROPEAN COMMUNITY: GENERAL for recovery of input tax suffered in another EC country; 31.10 GROUPS OF COMPANIES for recovery of input tax by holding companies; 34 IMPORTS; 42.33 LAND AND BUILDINGS for refund of VAT to do-it-yourself housebuilders; 43.7 LOCAL AUTHORITIES AND PUBLIC BODIES for refund of input tax for non-business purposes; 45 MOTOR CARS for disallowed input tax on cars, accessories and petrol, etc; 49 PARTIAL EXEMPTION for restriction on recovery of input tax where exempt supplies are made; 53.2 PENSION SCHEMES.

The contents of this chapter are as follows.

35.1 INTRODUCTION

EC legislation. See 22.23 EUROPEAN COMMUNITY LEGISLATION for the provisions of the *EC Sixth Directive*.

UK legislation. Input tax, in relation to a taxable person, comprises VAT

(*a*) on goods and services supplied to him;

(*b*) on the acquisition of any goods by him from another EC country; and

(*c*) paid or payable by him on the importation of goods from outside the EC

provided the goods or services are used, or to be used, for the purpose of business carried on, or to be carried on, by him.

[*VATA 1994, s 24*(*1*)].

VAT paid does not, however, become input tax simply because it has been incurred. It becomes input tax when it satisfies various criteria in 35.2 below arising out of the above definition and other legal requirements.

35.2 CRITERIA FOR VAT INCURRED TO BE TREATED AS DEDUCTIBLE INPUT TAX

Before any VAT paid can be deducted as input tax, the following criteria must be met.

(*a*) The recipient of the supply, or the person acquiring or importing the goods, must be a taxable person (ie registered or required to be registered under *VATA 1994*) at the time the VAT was incurred. See, however, 35.10 and 35.11 below for pre-registration and post-deregistration VAT.

(*b*) The VAT must relate to an actual supply, acquisition or importation. Where payments are made in advance but the goods are never physically supplied, input tax cannot be reclaimed as no supply has taken place. See *Weldons (West*

One) Ltd (VTD 984) (TVC 34.520), Theotrue Holdings Ltd (VTD 1358) (TVC 34.522) and *C & E Commrs v Pennystar Ltd, QB 1995, [1996] STC 163 (TVC 34.527)*.

(*c*) The amount to be claimed is the VAT properly chargeable and not the VAT actually charged where this is different. See *Podium Investments Ltd (VTD 314) (TVC 34.552)* and *Genius Holding BV v Staatssecretaris van Financien, CJEC 1989, [1991] STC 239 (TVC 21.275)*. This gives rise to a number of consequences.

(i) If the supplier is not a taxable person but shows VAT on the invoice, the VAT is not input tax and there is no automatic right of deduction. However, by concession, HMRC may allow a claim in these circumstances where they are satisfied that

- the recipient of the supply is neither involved in nor has close knowledge of the supplier's business;
- it was reasonable for the recipient to consider that he had been lawfully charged VAT; and
- the claim is made in respect of goods and services genuinely supplied at the stated value.

(ii) If the supplier is a taxable person but has failed to register for VAT, any VAT charged is recoverable as input tax (subject to meeting the other conditions for recovery) even though there can be no valid VAT invoice because, *inter alia*, the supplier has no registration number (see *Ellen Garage (Oldham) Ltd (VTD 12407) (TVC 38.10)*).

(iii) VAT wrongly charged on a supply, etc which is outside the scope of VAT, exempt or zero-rated is not input tax. See *Da Conti International Ltd (VTD 6215) (TVC 34.559)*).

(*d*) The goods or services on which the VAT was charged must have been supplied to, or acquired or imported by, the person seeking to claim the input tax. See 35.5 below.

(*e*) The supplies must have been incurred for the purpose of the business. See 35.6 below.

(*f*) The supplies received must not be subject to input tax restriction either in the form of a Treasury 'blocking order' or otherwise. See 35.8 below.

(*g*) The supplies must normally be received in the accounting period in which the claim is to be made. See 35.9 below.

(*h*) The person seeking to claim input tax must hold a valid invoice or other document. See 56.7 RECORDS.

See, however, *Croydon Hotel & Leisure Co Ltd (VTD 14920) (TVC 34.540)* where it was held that a person is entitled to reclaim input tax even where a VAT invoice has not been issued, the right to deduct not being limited to cases were output tax has been paid but extending to cases where it is payable. In that case, the tribunal held that a payment of £2 million by the company was VAT-inclusive even though an earlier tribunal (*Holiday Inns (UK) Ltd (VTD 10609) (TVC 60.124)*) had (incorrectly in the second tribunal's opinion) held that in the hands of the recipient the payment did not represent consideration for a taxable supply.

(VAT Notice 48, ESC 3.9; Internal Guidance V1–13, paras 1.3, 2.2, 2.3, 8.14).

De Voil Indirect Tax Service. See V3.402.

35.3 **AMOUNT OF ALLOWABLE INPUT TAX**

The amount of allowable input tax is so much of the input tax on supplies, acquisitions and importations in the period as is allowable as being attributable to the following supplies made, or to be made, by the taxable person in the course or furtherance of his business.

(*a*) '*Taxable supplies*', ie supplies of goods or services made in the UK other than exempt supplies.

(*b*) Supplies outside the UK which would be taxable supplies if made in the UK.

(*c*) Supplies of services which

(i) are supplied to a person who belongs outside the EC, or

(ii) are directly linked to the export of goods to a place outside the EC, or

(iii) consist of the provision of intermediary services in relation to any transaction within (i) or (ii) above

provided that the supply is exempt (or would have been exempt if made in the UK) by virtue of *VATA 1994, Sch 9 Group 2* (insurance) or *VATA 1994, Sch 9 Group 5 Items 1–8* (finance).

(*d*) Supplies made either in or outside the UK which fall, or would fall, within *VATA 1994, Sch 9 Group 15 item 1* or *2* (investment gold, see 30.2 GOLD AND PRECIOUS METALS).

HMRC must make regulations for securing a fair and reasonable attribution of input tax to the supplies within (*a*) to (*c*) above.

[*VATA 1994, ss 4(2), 26; SI 1992/3123; SI 1999/3121*].

See 22.23 EUROPEAN COMMUNITY LEGISLATION for the provisions of the *EC Sixth Directive*.

The effect of the above is that VAT cannot be reclaimed on goods and services which are not used for business purposes (see 35.6 below) and, where exempt supplies are made, it may not be possible to recover all input tax incurred. See PARTIAL EXEMPTION (49).

If input tax can be reclaimed in full, the amount to reclaim is normally that shown on the VAT invoice received from the supplier (but see 35.2(*c*) above where VAT is incorrectly charged). In the case of a less detailed tax invoice (see 40.7 INVOICES) which does not show VAT separately, input tax is found by applying the VAT fraction (see 47.2 OUTPUT TAX) to the total amount charged.

No taxable supplies. Where a person has made no taxable supplies in the period concerned or any previous period, any refunds of input tax are subject to such conditions as HMRC think fit to impose, including conditions as to repayment in specified circumstances. [*VATA 1994, s 25(6)*]. This could arise, for example, where a person has recently registered and is incurring expenditure but has yet to make any supplies. See, however, *D A Rompelman v Minister van Financien, CJEC [1985] 3 CMLR 202 (TVC 21.71)* for when input tax credit becomes deductible.

De Voil Indirect Tax Service. See V3.418.

35.4 **REPAYMENT OF INPUT TAX WHERE CONSIDERATION NOT PAID**

In relation to a supply made on or after 1 January 2003, where a person has

- claimed deduction of the whole or part of the VAT on the supply as input tax, and
- not paid the whole or any part of the consideration for that supply by the '*relevant date*' ie within six months of
  - (i) the date of the supply, or
  - (ii) if later, the date on which the consideration for the supply, or (as the case may be) the unpaid part of it, became payable

then, subject to below, he must make a negative entry in the VAT allowable portion of his VAT account for the VAT period in which the end of the relevant six-month period falls. The amount of this negative entry is calculated by formula

$$I \times \frac{U}{C}$$

where

I = the input tax claimed on the supply

U = the amount of the consideration for the supply which has not been paid before the end of the relevant six-month period; and

C = the total consideration for the supply.

The above provisions

- do not apply where the cash accounting scheme is used and the operative date for the recovery of input tax is the date of payment (see 63.6 SPECIAL SCHEMES); and
- are not to be regarded as giving rise to any application of the voluntary disclosure requirements for correction or errors (see 56.11 RECORDS).

> *Example 1*
>
> B purchases goods for £1,175 (£1,000.00 plus £175.00 VAT) and reclaims the full amount of VAT. By the relevant date, it has only paid £500.00 (leaving £675 unpaid).
>
> It must make a repayment of input tax to HMRC of
>
> 175 × (675 ÷ 1,175) = £100.53

For the purposes of (ii) above, HMRC will accept the date of invoice as the due date for payment. This means that, normally, the date on which input tax becomes repayable is six months after the date of invoice (unless the supplier allows time to pay, for example, 30 or 60 days, in which case repayment of input tax is not required until six months from this later date). The only exception is, on the rare occasions, where the invoice is not issued within 14 days of the date of supply and where the due date for payment falls before the date on which the invoice is issued. In such a case, the input tax will become repayable six months after the date of supply or, if later, the date when the payment was due. (VAT Notice 700/18/02, para 4.3).

Where a customer is in dispute with the supplier, and the supplier agrees to extend the due date for payment of the amount in dispute, repayment is not required until six months after the agreed extended date for payment. (VAT Notice 700/18/02, para 4.4).

Insolvency. By concession, an insolvency practitioner need not repay input tax under the above provisions where the supply was made prior to the insolvency procedure commencing but the requirement to repay input tax occurs after that date provided

- HMRC have been properly notified of the insolvency (see 36.2 INSOLVENCY); and
- the application of the concession does not give rise to tax avoidance.

The concession applies whether or not the business of the insolvent person is carried on.

The '*insolvency procedures*' to which the concession applies are bankruptcies, compulsory liquidations, creditors' and members' voluntary liquidations, administrative receiverships, administration orders, individual and company voluntary arrangements, Scottish trust deeds, deeds of arrangement, partnership voluntary arrangements and liquidations, partnership administration orders, sequestrations, county court administration orders, schemes of arrangement, and deceased persons' administration orders.

The effective date for the application of the concession is the date of HMRC's claim in the insolvency (ie the relevant date of the insolvency and the date of the insolvency meeting if applicable or, in the case of an administration order, the date of that order). The concession only applies to a provisional liquidation if it is followed by a permanent liquidation although, in such a case, the concession takes effect from the date of the provisional liquidation.

If an insolvency arrangement fails, the requirement to account for clawback is reinstated.

(VAT Notice 48, ESC 3.20; VAT Notice 700/18/02, para 4.9).

Restoration of an entitlement to credit for input tax. Where a person

- has made an entry in his VAT account in accordance with the above provisions ('*the input tax repayment*'),
- has made the return for the VAT period concerned, and has paid any VAT payable by him in respect of that period, and
- after the end of the relevant period, has paid the whole or part of the consideration for the supply in relation to which the input tax repayment was made,

then, subject to below, he may make a positive entry in the VAT allowable portion of his VAT account for the VAT period in which payment of the whole or part of the consideration is made. The amount of this positive entry is calculated by the formula

$$R \times P \div C$$

where

R = the amount of the input tax repayment;

P = the whole or part of the consideration for the supply in relation to which the input tax repayment was made and which is subsequently paid; and

C = the consideration for the supply which was not paid before the end of the relevant period.

> *Example 2*
>
> The facts are the same as in *Example 1* above. After making the repayment of £100.53 to HMRC, B subsequently makes a further payment of £300.
>
> B can now reclaim VAT from HMRC of
>
> 100.53 × (300 ÷ 675) = £44.68

The above provisions are not to be regarded as giving rise to any application of the voluntary disclosure requirements for correction or errors (see 56.11 RECORDS).

Attribution of payments. The rules on the attribution of payments in 7.6 and 7.8(*a*) BAD DEBT RELIEF apply for determining whether anything paid is to be taken as paid by way of consideration for a particular supply.

[*VATA 1994, s 26A; FA 2002, s 22; SI 1995/2518, Regs 172F–172J; SI 2002/3027, Reg 8; SI 2002/3028; SI 2003/532*].

In relation to a supply made before 1 January 2003, similar rules applied but repayment was only required where the supplier made a valid claim for bad debt relief and gave notification of the claim to the customer. See 7.13 BAD DEBT RELIEF.

35.5 WHO CAN CLAIM INPUT TAX

Subject to below, for an input tax claim to be valid, the claim must be made by the person to whom the supply was made. This is a fundamental principle and overrides the question of who may have paid for the supply or who may have possession of the relevant invoice or other evidence.

Where a third party pays for goods or services which are supplied to another person, the third party does not have the right to deduct input tax. This applies whether the payment was made due to a legal requirement or is simply a normal commercial practice. Examples of where this is likely to occur include

- payment of legal costs awarded against the unsuccessful party in litigation (see 35.13 below);
- payment of a landlord's costs by a tenant for the drawing up of a lease (see 42.4 LAND AND BUILDINGS); and
- payment by a business of the costs of a viability study undertaken by a bank in respect of the business's activities (see 36.11 INSOLVENCY).

For a consideration of whether a supply has been made to a taxable person, even though it is physically delivered to a third party (eg in a tripartite arrangement) see *Leesportfeuille 'Intiem' CV v Staatssecretaris van Financien, CJEC [1989] 2 CMLR 856 (TVC 21.268)* (petrol supplied to employees) and *C & E Commrs v Redrow Group plc, HL 1998, [1999] STC 161 (TVC 34.66)* (estate agents' fees for sales of existing homes paid for by builder on purchase of one of its new houses). See also the Input Tax chapter in Tolley's VAT Cases under the heading *Whether supplies made to the appellant*.

(Internal Guidance V1–13, paras 7.1, 7.2).

Supplies to employees. HMRC accept that, in certain circumstances, a supply which is *prima facie* to an employee, can be treated as made to the employer provided the employer meets the full cost and the supply is legitimately financed by the employer for the purposes of the business. Examples include

- subsistence costs (see 35.13(21) below);
- removal expenses arising from company relocations or transfer of staff (see 35.13(18) below); and
- sundry items such as small tools, materials, etc purchased 'on site'.

Self-employed labourers and contractors. In addition to supplies to employees, HMRC accept that VAT can be treated as input tax where a business reimburses subsistence, road fuel and other motoring costs incurred by self-employed persons working for the business where the following conditions are met.

- The individual is 'employed' on the same basis as an employee, ie is paid on a fixed rate basis, being unassociated with the trading profits of the business.
- The individual incurs the expenditure only in respect of 'employment' by the business. Where the individual represents a number of firms at the same time (eg a self-employed salesman) any subsistence does not relate to one 'employer' and none of those firms can treat the VAT incurred as input tax.
- The individual receives no payment from the end customer.
- The business reimburses the individual at cost, including VAT, dealing with the expense in the normal business accounts.

The above treatment also applies to actors, extras and other casual workers engaged in film, TV or similar productions.

Where the self-employed individual is VAT-registered, the VAT should normally be treated as incurred by the individual for the purpose of their business although, exceptionally, HMRC may allow recovery by the 'employer' if satisfied that the individual has not recovered VAT under their own registration.

If a self-employed labourer or contractor buys tools or materials to use for a specific job for a business, HMRC may accept that the VAT incurred is input tax of the business provided additionally, in the case of tools, they become the property of the business and, in the case of materials, they are incorporated into and become a cost component of the supply by the business to the end customer.

(Internal Guidance V1–13, paras 7.4, 7.5).

Commercial and agricultural premises leased in the name of a partner or director. It is common for a landlord to grant a lease to a partner (rather than to the partnership of which he is a member) or a director (rather than the incorporated company) as it is easier for the landlord to take effective action should the rent not be paid. In such circumstances, HMRC accept that the partnership/company is entitled to treat the VAT as input tax provided

- the individual is not VAT-registered in his own right and simply passes the rent invoice over to the business for payment to the landlord; and

- the business uses the whole of the premises for the purposes of its business and shows the expenditure in full in its accounts.

(Internal Guidance V1–13, para 7.7).

35.6 USE FOR BUSINESS PURPOSES

There is no definition of whether goods or services have been supplied for the 'purposes of the business'. Where the connection between the expenditure and the business is not clear, the following tests can be applied.

(*a*) Determine the intention of the person at the time of incurring the expenditure. This is a subjective test and where there is no obvious association between the business and the expenditure concerned, the court should approach any assertion that it is for the business with circumspection and care (*Ian Flockton Developments Ltd v C & E Commrs, QB [1987] STC 394 (TVC 34.263)*).

(*b*) Establish whether or not there is a clear connection between the actual or intended use of the goods or services and the activities business. This is an objective test of the use to which the goods or services are put.

Expenditure, even if for the benefit of the business, is not necessarily for the purpose of the business. See, for example, *C & E Commrs v Rosner, QB 1993, [1994] STC 228 (TVC 34.157)* and *Wallman Foods Ltd (VTD 1411) (TVC 34.163)* where VAT on legal costs incurred in defending a sole trader/director against criminal charges was held to be non-deductible under this principle. Compare, however, *P & O European Ferries (Dover) Ltd (VTD 7846) (TVC 34.154)* where VAT on legal costs in defending the company and certain of its employees charged with manslaughter following the sinking of a ferry was held to be deductible as it had clearly been incurred for the purpose of the business even though it also had the effect of benefiting individual employees.

Where goods or services supplied are not used for business purposes, any VAT suffered is not input tax and cannot be reclaimed. This includes

- expenditure related to domestic accommodation (see 35.13(7) below);
- pursuit of personal interests such as sporting and leisure activities (see also 35.13(20) below);
- expenditure for the benefit of company directors, proprietors, etc;
- supplies to a business used in connection with a non-business activity (see 35.7 below for apportionment where used for both a business and non-business activity);
- supplies for another person's business; and
- supplies to another person, even if the taxable person pays for them (see 35.5 above).

(Internal Guidance V1–13, paras 4.2, 4.3).

Tribunal and court decisions. There have been a large number of court and tribunal cases concerned with whether supplies are used for the purpose of the business, in particular in relation to legal costs, premises costs of sole traders and partnerships, sporting activities (horse racing, show jumping, powerboat racing, motor racing and rallying, yachting, etc) and personalised number plates. See the chapter Input Tax in Tolley's VAT Cases under the heading *Whether supplies used for the purposes of the business.*

De Voil Indirect Tax Service. See V3.406.

35.7 **Goods and services only partly used for business purposes**

Where

- goods or services supplied to a taxable person,
- goods acquired by a taxable person from another EC country, or
- goods imported by a taxable person from a place outside the EC

are used or to be used *partly* for the purposes of a business carried on or to be carried on and *partly* for other purposes, VAT paid must be apportioned so that only so much as is referable to business purposes is counted as input tax. [*VATA 1994, s 24(5)*].

Businesses generally apportion the VAT that they have paid on goods and services at the outset with the proportion attributable to business use being treated as input tax. See, however, under (3) below for an alternative treatment which may be available under the Lennartz mechanism. This allows all the input tax to be recovered initially with output tax being accounted for on any subsequent private or non-business use.

(1) **Apportionment for private use**

Common examples of goods and services which are part business/part private are telephone, light and heat, repairs and maintenance, etc where a business is conducted from home or the taxpayer lives above a shop.

> *Example*
>
> VAT of £100 is paid on an item and one quarter of its use is for business purposes.
>
> Input tax is £100 × 1/4 = £25

(2) **Apportionment for non-business use**

Where both business and non-business activities are undertaken (eg by a charity) it is unlikely that all the VAT incurred can be treated as input tax. The following procedure should be adopted.

- Identify as far as possible VAT which relates to goods or services obtained solely for the purposes of the business activity. This is input tax and can be recovered subject to the normal rules.
- Identify as far as possible VAT which relates solely to the non-business activity. This is not input tax and cannot be recovered.
- VAT which relates to both business and non-business activities (eg VAT incurred on overhead costs) should be apportioned in order to identify the proportion which is input tax. Alternatively, in certain circumstance, the Lennartz mechanism can be adopted (see (3) below).

Methods of apportionment. The VAT legislation does not specify any particular method of apportionment. Any method used must be fair and reasonable taking into account the various activities and the purposes for which the expenditure is incurred. In practice, there is likely to be a range of acceptable methods of apportionment in any particular case and HMRC officers are instructed only to challenge an apportionment if it is completely outside what they perceive to be this range. It may be that a single apportionment of all overhead VAT does not achieve a 'fair and reasonable' result and that a range of apportionments for different items of overhead expenditure is required. The following are example methods of how VAT could be apportioned.

(*a*) *Fixed percentage.* The simplest method is to adopt a fixed percentage figure and apply this to the total non-attributable VAT incurred. This can be an acceptable approach where the balance between business and non-business activities does not fluctuate.

(*b*) *Income methods.* These are probably the most common methods of apportionment and usually work by defining income received from business supplies as business income and the income from outside the scope sources (eg grants) as non-business income. The apportionment is calculated each quarter by dividing the total of business income by total income.

> *Example*
>
> A taxable person pays £1,000 VAT on purchases which are used for both business and non-business purposes. Income from business activities (taxable and exempt supplies) amounts to £20,000 in the VAT period. Total income from all sources, including business activities, grants and donations, amounts to £50,000. Input tax is calculated as follows.
>
> Proportion of income which is business income =
>
> £20,000 ÷ £50,000 = 40%
>
> VAT to be provisionally treated as input tax = £1,000 × 40% = £400

Income methods have the advantage of simplicity in that they rely on accounting information that is normally readily available. However, they will not give a fair and reasonable result where

- the balance of business/non-business activities does not reflect the balance of funding (eg where the majority of time and resources is devoted to non-business activities but the majority of income arises from business supplies); or
- commercial activities are partially subsidised by the receipt of grants (eg where a heavily subsidised transport operator also runs free community projects).

It is sometimes possible to adapt income methods so that distortive income is removed from the calculation or alternatively the calculation is weighted in some way.

(*c*) *Expenditure-based methods.* These are similar in calculation to the income-based methods except that the ratio of business/non-business expenditure is applied to the unattributable VAT. Such methods are only appropriate if

- the majority of expenditure can be attributed to distinct business/non-business categories; and
- this ratio is a fair reflection of business/non-business activities (eg an expenditure-based method would not be appropriate where a charity with overwhelmingly non-business expenditure purchased a computer system principally to make taxable business supplies).

(*d*) *Time-based methods.* Where detailed records are kept of the amount of time that staff spend on business and non-business activities, these can provide the basis for a method of apportionment if the business/non-business ratio of staff time reflects the extent of business use of non-attributable expenditure. Such methods would not be appropriate where non-business activities are staff intensive but business activities are goods and services intensive.

A time-based method can also be applied by keeping records of the use made of an object (eg a yacht or aircraft).

(*e*) *Transaction-based methods.* A method can be based upon a record of transactions (eg paid admissions to a museum or books loaned out for a charge by a library). A common difficulty with such a method is that non-business activities often do not involve recordable transactions. HMRC officers are advised not to automatically dismiss transaction-based methods but to take extra care to ensure that they are founded on a valid indicator of business and non-business activity.

(*f*) *Area-based methods.* These, for example, involve calculating within a building the extent to which the floor areas are used for business and non-business purposes.

Whatever method of apportionment is used, provisional input tax is reclaimed at the end of each VAT period, subject to the normal rules. At the end of each VAT year, an adjustment is made by applying the same calculation to total figures for the year. Where quarterly returns are made, the VAT year ends on 31 March, 30 April or 31 May depending on the VAT periods allocated. Where monthly returns are made, the VAT year ends on 31 March.

Waiver of apportionment. Where the non-business element is regarded as insignificant, HMRC officers may use their discretion to allow a waiver of apportionment. There is no recommended *de minimis* level in terms of a monetary or percentage figure, the decision being left to the judgement of the officer concerned as to whether the benefit in terms of revenue is outweighed by the cost to both the business and HMRC in carrying out and checking the apportionment. Where an officer allows a waiver of apportionment, the business will be advised that the concession applies only for as long as the existing rate of non-business activity prevails.

Change in method of apportionment. If any method used is considered no longer suitable, details of a proposed new method should be submitted to HMRC. A retrospective change will only be agreed if the business can show that

- the former method did not produce a fair and reasonable result; and
- the proposed method does achieve this objective.

See *Victoria & Albert Museum Trustees v C & E Commrs, QB [1996] STC 1016 (TVC 11.45).* Although the income-based method of apportionment outlined in (*b*) above previously used by the Museum was criticised in *Whitechapel Art*

Gallery v C & E Commrs, QB [1986] STC 156 (TVC 11.35) on the grounds that grants and donations received should not be included in the calculation, that method was still held to be a fair and reasonable method of apportionment and its adoption, even if disadvantageous, did not constitute an 'error' which could be subsequently corrected.

(3) **The Lennartz mechanism**

Lennartz v Finanzamt Munchen III, CJEC 1991,[1995] STC 514 (TVC 21.297) concerned business/private use of a car although the mechanism was seen as applicable to supplies of goods in general. The Court ruled that where goods are acquired *solely* for a private or non-business purpose, VAT incurred is not recoverable, even if the goods in question are later put to a deductible business use (because the right to deduct VAT arises, and is exercisable, at the time when the VAT is incurred). However, a taxable person who acquires goods and used them partly for business purposes and partly for private or non-business purposes has a right to total and immediate input tax deduction (unless the goods are subject to input tax restriction under 35.8 below). Where the goods are later used for private or non-business purposes, that use is to be treated as a taxable supply of services and VAT must be accounted for under *VATA 1994, Sch 4 para 5(4)* (see 47.7 OUTPUT TAX) in each VAT period in which private or non-business use of the asset occurs. Records must be kept showing how the relevant asset has been used.

HMRC initially took the view that the Lennartz mechanism did not apply to VAT on services so that where there was business and non-business/private use, apportionment was mandatory. However, in *Seeling v Finanzamt Starnberg, CJEC [2003] STC 805 (TVC 21.126)* in which a German businessman constructed a house both as his home and for use in his business, the Court made it clear that all the construction costs could be dealt with through the Lennartz mechanism. It therefore accepted that VAT on construction *services* that result in the construction of a building can be dealt with under the mechanism. Following the judgment *in Seeling*, HMRC apply the Lennartz mechanism as follows.

- While there is a potential argument that the Lennartz mechanism should be seen as a narrow 'private use' mechanism rather than one that is available for wider 'non-business' use, HMRC continue their policy of not drawing such a distinction.
- The Lennartz mechanism can apply in respect of purchases of services where those services are incorporated into goods used in the business and significantly increase the value of the goods to the business.
- The Lennartz mechanism is not available for land, buildings or civil engineering works (or services related to them such as construction services) where no entitlement for any qualifying input tax arose prior to 9 April 2003 (see below).
- The Lennartz mechanism is available for other types of goods (eg computers, motor caravans, yachts and aircraft). Services which improve these goods (eg a substantial refurbishment) would also qualify. HMRC will normally require the output tax charge under the Lennartz mechanism to be calculated over a maximum five-year period based on straight-line depreciation (see the *Example* below).
- VAT on services that are consumed in relation to day-to-day activity (eg repair and maintenance) must continue to be apportioned. However, if

businesses consider that they should be entitled to use the mechanism for a particular service (eg the major restoration of a business vehicle), they should contact HMRC National Advice Service on 0845 010 9000 with details.

- In all cases where the Lennartz mechanism is available for use by a business, the business does not have to use that mechanism and can instead apportion the VAT paid, treating as input tax the proportion attributable to business use (see (1) and (2) above).

Land, buildings and civil engineering works. After 9 April 2003, as an anti-avoidance measure, for the purposes of private/non-business use, supplies of

- a major interest in land,
- any building or part of a building,
- any civil engineering work or part of such a work, or
- any goods incorporated, or to be incorporated, in a building or civil engineering work (whether by being installed as fixtures or fittings or otherwise)

are treated as supplies of services rather than goods and it is not possible to apply the Lennartz approach to such assets. See 47.7 OUTPUT TAX.

Buildings, civil engineering works and related services — pre-9 April 2003. HMRC now accept that the Lennartz mechanism can be applied to construction services which result in the construction of a new building or civil engineering work, or a major refurbishment or extension of an existing building, provided at least part of the input tax on those services was incurred before 9 April 2003. This means that, where the building works had started and an entitlement to input tax had been established prior to 9 April 2003, the Lennartz mechanism can be applied to any input tax incurred on the services connected with that project after that date. Output tax will then have to be accounted for on private/non-business use of the building. The Lennartz mechanism is not available for projects where no entitlement to input tax on the services arose prior to 9 April 2003 and all input VAT must be apportioned between taxable and private/non-business use. Taxpayers who have incurred input tax after 9 April 2003 but think that they may be entitled to use the Lennartz mechanism under these transitional arrangements should contact HMRC National Advice Service on 0845 010 9000.

The calculation of the Lennartz charge for private use of a building poses particular problems in arriving at a reasonable value for the annual cost of the private or non-business use. Following the *Seeling* case, HMRC have decided that, when applying the Lennartz mechanism to immovable property, the output tax charge should be calculated over a maximum 20-year period based on straight-line depreciation, unless a shorter period is indicated (eg where a taxpayer's leasehold interest in the building has under 20 years to run).

Back-dated claims for services. Taxpayers who wish to make claims for input tax on construction services incurred before 9 April 2003 or past claims for other services may do so by making a voluntary disclosure to their local VAT office (subject to the three-year time limit). Any claims must take into account the output tax due under the mechanism.

> *Example*
>
> B purchases a yacht for business and private use for £1,000,000 plus £175,000 VAT. He makes no exempt supplies and chooses to claim the whole £175,000 as input tax on the VAT return for the period in which the yacht was purchased. Over a five-year period, the baseline figure each year is £200,000, ie £50,000 per quarterly VAT period.
>
> In the first VAT return period, 50% of B's use of the yacht is for private purposes. Output tax is due on £25,000 in that period (ie 50% × £50,000).
>
> In the second VAT return period, non-business use increases to 75%. VAT is due on £37,500 (ie 75% × £50,000) in that period.
>
> Output tax is payable in each VAT return period in which non-business use occurs over the remaining 17 quarterly tax periods.
>
> If the yacht remains in the business after the end of the five-year chargeable period and it continues to be used for non-business purposes, it is no longer necessary to account for output tax. The effect is, therefore, that the non-business use is treated as consumption and taxed over the five-year period. See below for the consequences of selling the yacht before the end of the five-year period.

Partial exemption. Where exempt supplies are made, this may also affect the amount of input tax reclaimable. In such a case:

- Where initial apportionment is used, the apportionment of VAT incurred between business and private/non-business use must be made first. Only then should any apportionment of input tax be made because of the partial exemption rules.
- Where the Lennartz mechanism is used, if the current partial exemption method does not facilitate the Lennartz mechanism, HMRC will consider proposals for a revised partial exemption method. The revised method must result in a fair and reasonable attribution of input tax to taxable supplies for all the trading activities within the VAT registration. Methods that give a good result for the Lennartz sector but do not achieve a fair and reasonable result overall will not be approved.

Treatment of goods at sale or deregistration. Under the Lennartz mechanism, goods, including land and property, are treated as wholly business assets. This means that, on sale of the goods or deregistration of the business (other than in connection with a transfer as a going concern) VAT is due on the full selling price of the goods. However, where apportionment is applied at the time of purchase, VAT need only be accounted for on sale or deregistration on the proportion treated as business. The Lennartz mechanism may not, therefore, always be advantageous to taxpayers, particularly where the goods are likely to appreciate in value.

(VAT Notice 700, paras 33.1–33.7; Internal Guidance V1–6, paras 5.2, 5.4–5.8, 5.10; Business Brief 22/03).

De Voil Indirect Tax Service. See V3.408; V3.409.

35.8 **NON-DEDUCTIBLE INPUT TAX**

Input tax cannot usually be reclaimed on the following.

- Goods to be sold under one of the margin schemes for SECOND-HAND GOODS (61).
- Goods or services to be used for the purpose of BUSINESS ENTERTAINMENT (9).
- Motor cars other than taxis unless purchased for one of the qualifying uses (see 45.3 MOTOR CARS).
- Certain accessories installed in motor cars (see 45.13 MOTOR CARS).
- Purchases which fall within the TOUR OPERATORS' MARGIN SCHEME (66).
- Certain articles to be installed in new dwellings (see 42.15 LAND AND BUILDINGS).
- Assets acquired under the transfer of a business as a going concern (see 8.10 BUSINESS).
- Domestic accommodation for its directors or proprietors (see 35.13(7) below).
- Goods imported by a taxable person where
  - (i) at the time of importation the goods belong wholly or partly to another person, and
  - (ii) the purposes for which they are to be used include private purposes either of himself or of the other person.

  In such a case, the VAT due on import is not available for deduction as input tax, but a separate claim for repayment may be made to HMRC if a double charge to VAT would arise. The repayment of VAT to the taxable person will be made only to the extent necessary to avoid a double charge and HMRC will have regard to the circumstances of the importation and, as far as appears relevant, things done with, or occurring in relation to, the goods at any subsequent time.

  [*VATA 1994, s 27*].

De Voil Indirect Tax Service. See V3.416; V5.153.

35.9 **WHEN TO CLAIM INPUT TAX**

A '*taxable person*' (ie a person who is, or is required to be, registered under *VATA 1994*) is entitled, at the end of each VAT period, to credit for so much of his input tax as is allowable. [*VATA 1994, s 3(1), s 25(2)*].

Input tax should be claimed on the VAT return for the period in which the VAT became chargeable, ie the period covering

- for supplies of goods and services, the supplier's tax point;
- for goods acquired from another EC country, the date of acquisition;
- for imported goods, the date of the importation; and
- for goods removed from a customs and/or excise warehouse, the date of removal.

[*SI 1995/2518, Reg 29(1); SI 1997/1086, Reg 4*].

Late claims for input tax. The method of claiming the input tax depends upon the reason for the late claim.

(*a*) *Lack of proper evidence*. If a business is unable to claim input tax in the correct period as above because it has not received the proper evidence (normally a VAT invoice), it can claim the input tax on receipt of that evidence (subject to the time limit below). This can be done either by including the VAT in Box 4 of the return for a later period or by making a voluntary disclosure (see 56.11 RECORDS). If proper evidence is not available, a business can ask HMRC for permission to make a claim based on alternative evidence. HMRC may then allow it to claim input tax based on the alternative evidence if it is suitable, but this is discretionary and again subject to the time limit below.

(*b*) *Error*. If a business has the necessary evidence to claim input tax in the correct period but fails to do so, this is an error. It must make a voluntary disclosure (see 56.11 RECORDS), subject to the time limit below.

If a business has ceased to be registered for VAT, it may use Form VAT 427 to claim input tax on goods or services supplied to it for business purposes while it was registered but which it had not claimed because of (*a*) or (*b*) above. Such a claim is also subject to the time limit below. Invoices must be provided confirming that the goods or services were supplied before cancellation of registration.

(VAT Notice 700/45/02, paras 6.1–6.3, 11.4–11.7).

Time limit for late claims. Input tax cannot be claimed more than three years after the date by which the return for the period in which the VAT was chargeable is required to be made. [*SI 1995/2518, Reg 29(1A)*; *SI 1997/1086, Reg 4*]. The validity of this three-year time limit was confirmed in *Local Authorities Mutual Investment Trust v C & E Commrs, Ch D 2003, [2004] STC 246 (TVC 46.5)*. The Court held that *Reg 29(1A)* was authorised by *EC Sixth Directive, Art 18(3)* which allowed countries to determine the 'conditions and procedures' under which input tax was deductible. This expression included time limits in fiscal claims (in order to establish the fundamental principle of legal certainty) and time limits were valid provided, *inter alia*, that (i) they did not make it impossible to exercise the underlying rights (the equivalence principle); and (ii) they went no further than was necessary in order to attain their objectives (the principle of proportionality). There was no evidence that any of these rights had been breached. Neither was there any infringement of *Human Rights Act 1998, Sch 1 Part II, Art 1*.

Cash accounting. Certain small businesses are allowed to account for VAT on the basis of cash paid and received. See 63.2 SPECIAL SCHEMES. Where the cash accounting scheme is used, a taxable person must not reclaim input tax until the necessary evidence is received and the supply has been paid for.

Claims for early payment. HMRC may authorise a claim for early payment of input tax (ie before the end of the normal VAT period) but only in cases where serious delay has occurred as a result of HMRC's action (eg such as undue delay in processing an application for registration). All such requests must be submitted in writing. (Internal Guidance V1–13, para 6.16).

35.10 Pre-registration VAT

Although VAT incurred before registration is not input tax, it can be treated as such subject to certain conditions. The VAT should be claimed on the first VAT return required to be made following registration. HMRC may allow the claim to be made on a later return but cannot allow a claim to be made more than three years after the date the first return was required. Any claim must be supported by invoices and such other evidence as HMRC require.

VAT on goods. HMRC may allow a taxable person to treat as input tax any VAT on goods supplied to him before the date on which he was (or was required to be) registered or paid by him on the acquisition or importation of goods before that date provided the following conditions are satisfied.

- The goods are for the purpose of a business which either was carried on or was to be carried on by him at the time of the supply or payment.
- The goods have not been supplied *by* or (unless HMRC otherwise allow) consumed by the taxable person before the date with effect from which he was (or was required to be) registered (see *Schemepanel Trading Co Ltd v C & E Commrs, QB [1996] STC 871 (TVC 34.513)*). HMRC deem this condition to be satisfied if the goods have been used to make other goods which are still held at that date. (VAT Notice 700, para 11.2).
- The goods must not have been supplied to, or imported or acquired by, the taxable person more than three years before the date with effect from which he was (or was required to be) registered.
- All the normal rules allow the input tax to be reclaimed.
- A stock account is compiled (and preserved for such a period as HMRC require) showing separately quantities purchased, quantities used in the making of other goods, date of purchase and date and manner of subsequent disposals of both such quantities.

VAT on services. HMRC may allow a taxable person to treat as input tax any VAT on services supplied to him before the date on which he was (or was required to be) registered provided the following conditions are satisfied.

- The services are for the purpose of a business which either was carried on or was to be carried on by him at the time of such supply.
- The services have not been supplied *by* the taxable person before the date with effect from which he was (or was required to be) registered.
- The services have not been performed on
  - (i) goods which have been supplied *by* or (unless HMRC otherwise allow) consumed by the taxable person before the date with effect from which he was (or was required to be) registered (eg repairs to a machine sold before registration); or
  - (ii) goods which have been supplied to, or imported or acquired by, the taxable person more than three years before that date.
- The services have not been supplied to the taxable person more than six months before the date with effect from which he was, or was required to be, registered. There is no discretion to allow VAT recovery on services received more than six months before registration. The only way that this can be done is by backdating the registration.
- All the normal rules allow the input tax to be reclaimed.
- A list showing the description, date of purchase and date of disposal (if any) of the services is compiled and preserved for such period as HMRC require.

VAT on supplies before incorporation. HMRC may allow a body corporate (including a company, charity or association) to treat as input tax any VAT on goods obtained for it before its incorporation, or on the supply of services before that time for its benefit or in connection with its incorporation, provided the following conditions are satisfied.

- The person to whom the supply was made or who paid VAT on the importation or acquisition
  - (i) became a member, officer or employee of the body and was reimbursed (or has received an undertaking to be reimbursed) by the body for the whole amount of the price paid for the goods or services;
  - (ii) was not at the time of supply, acquisition or importation a taxable person; and
  - (iii) imported, acquired or was supplied with the goods or received the services for the purpose of a business to be carried on by the body and has not used them for any purpose other than such business.
- The conditions for recovery of input tax on goods or, as the case may be, services as detailed above are satisfied. In the case of pre-incorporation supplies, the references in those conditions to supplies, etc of goods and services to and by the taxable person before registration are to be taken as references to such supplies to and by the person who obtained the supplies for the company before registration.

[*SI 1995 No 2518, Reg 111*(*1*)-(*4*); *SI 1997/1086, Reg 7*].

Partial exemption. The provisions in *Reg 111* above do not specify how pre-registration VAT of a partly exempt business should be treated. HMRC take the view that it is only allowable to the extent that, at the time the VAT was incurred, the relevant goods and services were used, or to be used, to make taxable supplies, ie they apply direct attribution. This approach was upheld by the tribunal in *T Douros (t/a Olympic Financial Services) (VTD 12454) (TVC 44.165)* and *GN Byrd (t/a GN Byrd and Co) (VTD 12675) (TVC 44.167)*. (Internal Guidance V1–13, para 6.8).

VAT groups. If an unregistered company joins a VAT group, the representative member may recover VAT incurred by the new member prior to its entry into the group subject to the normal rules above. (Internal Guidance V1–13, para 6.13).

De Voil Indirect Tax Service. See V3.431; V3.432.

35.11 POST-DEREGISTRATION VAT

As a general rule, input tax cannot be claimed on supplies received after the date of deregistration. However, on a claim, HMRC may refund to a person any VAT on *services* supplied to him after the date from which he ceased to be (or to be required to be) registered and which relate to taxable supplies of the business carried on by him before deregistration. No such claim can be made more than three years after the date on which the supply of services was made. [*SI 1995/2518, Reg 111*(*5*)-(*7*); *SI 1997/1086, Reg 7*].

This covers, for example, solicitors' and accountants' services which cannot be claimed on the final returns as the invoices are not received in time. Claims should be made as soon as possible after cancellation of registration on Form VAT 427. The relevant invoices must be submitted. (VAT Notice 700/11/02, paras 8.2, 8.5).

Insolvencies. For the procedure for claiming post-deregistration input tax in insolvencies, see 36.13 INSOLVENCY.

Partial exemption. Where the business made exempt supplies whilst registered for VAT, direct attribution of VAT must be used when submitting the claim. There is no *de minimis* limit following deregistration so that no VAT incurred which relates to the making of exempt supplies can be claimed. With regard to non-attributable input tax, the recoverable proportion applicable immediately prior to deregistration should be used. (Internal Guidance V1–13, para 6.12).

VAT groups. If a member leaves a VAT group and does not register in its own right, the representative member may recover VAT incurred by the departed company after the date of its leaving, subject to the normal rules above. (Internal Guidance V1–13, para 6.13).

De Voil Indirect Tax Service. See V3.431A; V5.165.

35.12 APPEALS IN RESPECT OF INPUT TAX

An appeal may be made to a VAT tribunal in connection with the amount of input tax that may be credited and the proportion of input tax allowable under *VATA 1994, s 26*. See 5.3(*c*)(*e*) APPEALS.

Luxuries, amusements and entertainment. In any appeal relating to input tax where

(*a*) the appeal relates, in whole or in part, to a determination by HMRC

   (i) as to the purposes for which any goods or services were, or were to be, used by any person, or

   (ii) as to whether and to what extent input tax was attributable to matters other than the making of supplies within 35.3(*a*)–(*c*) above, and

(*b*) the input tax for which, following the determination, there is no entitlement to credit relates to a supply, acquisition or importation or something in the nature of a luxury, amusement or entertainment,

the tribunal cannot allow the appeal so far as it relates to that determination unless it considers that it was unreasonable to make that determination. In reaching this conclusion, the tribunal may take into consideration information brought to their attention which could not have been made available to HMRC at the time.

[*VATA 1994, s 84(4)(11)*].

The effect of the above provisions is that in cases involving expenditure on luxuries, amusements and entertainment, a tribunal cannot apply a decision of its own to the case but is restricted to considering whether HMRC's decision was reasonable. Even though it might not have arrived at the same decision, the tribunal must uphold HMRC's decision unless it considers that they acted unreasonably.

35.13 TREATMENT OF INPUT TAX IN PARTICULAR CASES

(1) Accountancy fees

Accountancy fees of a sole trader or a partnership normally relate to a number of services, eg general accountancy advice, VAT advice and income tax advice. Although it is arguable that income tax is the responsibility of the sole trader or partner as an individual and is not strictly a business matter, to avoid lengthy disputes, HMRC's policy is that such fees should usually be allowable in full, subject to the normal rules. The only exception to this treatment is where the accountant's fees clearly relate to taxation matters which are not related to the VAT-registered business (eg significant costs relating to inheritance tax).

The position is similar in the case of companies paying corporation tax. The exception in this case would cover, for example, advice relating to a director's inheritance tax liabilities.

(Internal Guidance V1–13, para 13.10).

(2) **Bad debt relief**

See 7.13 BAD DEBT RELIEF for repayment of input tax by the purchaser on supplies made before 1 January 2003 where a valid claim for bad debt relief has been made by the supplier.

(3) **Barristers in chambers**

Barristers may share chambers, office equipment and services, etc and periodically apportion costs between them on an agreed basis. Invoices for the supply of common goods or services may be made out to the head of chambers, a nominated member or the barristers' clerk (if the clerk is not a registered person).

Three special accounting methods have been agreed. The choice of method is up to the barristers, but whichever method is chosen the conditions relating to it must be complied with.

Method 1

The nominated member to whom invoices are addressed treats the full amount of VAT as input tax. Output tax is accounted for on the shares charged out to all the other members of chambers. Registered members are entitled to deduct the VAT charged as input tax. By concession, VAT invoices need not be issued by the nominated member. Each member's record must be cross-referenced to

- output tax charged by the nominated member;
- the input tax deducted by other members; and
- the original VAT invoice.

The records of all members of chambers must be available during a visit to any one of them.

Method 2

The nominated member to whom invoices are addressed does not charge output tax on the member's contributions. The input tax is apportioned so that registered members may deduct it on the basis of their own contributions. Records must be kept of the apportionment of input tax between the members of chambers. Each member's records should cross-reference the input tax deducted to the VAT invoice to ensure that no more than the total VAT stated on the invoice has been deducted. The records of all members of chambers must be available during a visit to any one of them.

Method 3

The nominated member to whom invoices are addressed deducts the whole amount of input tax but also pays an equal amount into the common fund. This method may only be used when all members of chambers are registered for VAT.

(Internal Guidance V1–13, para 8.15).

(4) **Capital goods**

See 10 CAPITAL GOODS SCHEME for possible adjustment in subsequent years to the initial input tax recovery on certain items of computer equipment, land and buildings and civil engineering works used for non-taxable purposes.

(5) **Churches and cathedrals**

Cathedrals and churches exist primarily for non-business purposes but frequently derive significant income from their status as tourist attractions. Informal agreement has been reached between HMRC and The Churches Main Committee on the recovery of input tax which is not directly attributable to a business or non-business activity, notably repairs and maintenance, etc to the cathedral or church itself and all associated buildings within its curtilage except domestic accommodation. A *cathedral* is allocated to one of the following bands for rate of recovery of input tax.

- Band A (90%) — to apply where there are significant admission charges to all main areas (eg St Paul's Cathedral, Ely Cathedral).
- Band B (65%) — to apply where there is no admission charge into the Cathedral, but there are high numbers of visitors and significant taxable income (eg from admission charges to other areas such as crypt, museum, tower, etc; lettings for concerts, etc).
- Band C (45%) — to apply where is no admission charge into the Cathedral, insignificant taxable income from admission charges for other areas, but a reasonable number of visitors generating income from other sources (eg the book/souvenir shop).
- Band D (25%) — to apply where there are no admission charges or only a few small charges and small numbers of visitors and little taxable income.

Where any exempt supplies are made, a separate partial exemption calculation must be made based on the total of input tax attributable to business activities and the proportion of residual input tax as calculated above.

Churches such as Bath Abbey, Beverley Minster, etc are considerable tourist attractions and make significant taxable supplies. Where a church is in this position it can be allowed to use the 'Cathedral' banding system above. The vast majority of churches, however, have only minimal business activities, ie the sale of books, magazines, postcards, etc (often on an 'honesty' basis from a table near the church door) and in these cases the normal apportionment provisions should apply.

Domestic accommodation is outside the banding system. HMRC consider input tax recovery to be dependent upon the occupants' terms of employment and duties and whether they are engaged on business or non-business activities. For persons engaged by the Church for religious purposes HMRC consider none of the tax is input tax. For lay persons engaged on some business activities an apportionment of VAT may be agreed. See *The Dean and Chapter of Hereford Cathedral (VTD 11737) (TVC 34.244)*, concerning VAT incurred on renovation work to accommodation lived in by vergers. On the facts, the tribunal allowed 50% of the VAT to be treated as input tax although each case will need to be decided on its own merits. (Only 25% of the VAT on refurbishing houses occupied by the Dean and three Canons was allowed in *Dean and Chapter of Bristol Cathedral (VTD 14591) (TVC 34.460).*)

(Internal Guidance V1–13, paras 11.2–11.7).

(6) **Clothing**

Subject to the special cases below, the provision of clothing is normally a personal responsibility. VAT on clothing purchased 'to cultivate a professional image' in order to attract business was disallowed in *BJ Brown (VTD 6552) (TVC 34.115)* as was VAT on suits worn while working in *JK Hill and SJ Mansell (t/a JK Hill & Co), [1988] STC 424 (TVC 34.116)*. VAT on a fur coat purchased by an author was held to be partly input tax in *RA Sisson (VTD 1056) (TVC 34.114)* although an appeal in such a case would now be restricted under 35.12 above. The following special cases are recognised.

(*a*) *Uniforms and protective clothing.* VAT incurred by a business person on uniforms or protective clothing worn by the proprietors or their employees in the performance of their duties is input tax.

(*b*) *Employees.* Perks are an accepted business expense therefore if employers decide to provide their employees with clothing (not falling within (*a*) above) the VAT incurred is input tax. However, a supply of goods has also taken place and the normal business gifts rules apply. See 47.6 OUTPUT TAX.

(*c*) *Barristers.* The wig, gown and bands that a barrister is required to wear in court are considered to be a uniform and the VAT incurred is input tax. It is also a court requirement that barristers wear dark clothing. For example, male barristers may wear striped trousers, a black jacket and a waistcoat with a white wing-collar, and for a female barrister a dark (black, navy or grey) suit and a white blouse. If barristers claim that this clothing would not have been purchased if they did not have to attend court, the VAT may be deducted as input tax. See also *EM Alexander (VTD 251) (TVC 34.113)*.

(*d*) *Entertainers.* The VAT on clothing used solely as stage costumes is input tax. Ordinary clothing worn by an entertainer or TV personality will usually be worn privately as well, in which case HMRC regard the provisions of 35.7 above for part business/private use as applying. See, however, *J Pearce (VTD 7860) (TVC 34.119)* where the tribunal allowed full input tax recovery on clothing such as dress suits worn by a actor where it had not been worn privately. See also *JM Collie (VTD 6144) (TVC 34.121)* where input tax was allowed in full on a wig purchased by a professional musician to maintain his image.

(Internal Guidance V1–13, para 23.3).

(6A) **Debt enforcement services provided by Under Sheriffs and Sheriffs' Officers**

HMRC are prepared to treat debt enforcement services provided by Under Sheriffs and Sheriffs' Officers in enforcing High Court judgment debts, and those of the County Court transferred to the High Court for enforcement, as supplies by Under Sheriffs to creditors. As a result, where such creditors are registered for VAT, they can recover VAT charged on the services, subject to the normal rules. Where Under Sheriffs and Sheriffs' Officers collect fees for their enforcement services from debtors, they must only issue VAT invoices to creditors. Any documents issued to debtors must make it clear that they are not VAT invoices.

(Business Brief 6/00).

(7) **Domestic accommodation**

As a general principle, the provision of domestic accommodation is regarded as a personal rather than a business responsibility and in most cases the VAT incurred is not input tax. However, the fact that a business is operated from home does not prevent VAT that is genuinely incurred for business purposes being deducted as input tax.

(*a*) **Sole proprietors and partners**. If a sole proprietor or partner carries on a business from home and uses a particular room or area specifically for business (eg an office or workshop), VAT incurred on costs which can be identified specifically to that area can be treated wholly as input tax. This would apply mainly to fixtures and fittings and decorating costs. VAT on any items used purely for domestic purposes (eg a bedroom suite) is not deductible. Where expenditure relates to both domestic and business use (eg fuel and power, security systems and general maintenance), the procedure in 35.7 above should be followed. (Internal Guidance V1–13, para 14.3). See also under (*d*) below for farmhouses.

(*b*) **Directors**. Where a company purchases, acquires or imports goods or services which are used or to be used in connection with the provision of domestic accommodation by the company for a 'director' of the company or a person connected with a director of the company, those goods and services are not treated as used or to be used for the company's business and any input tax is not recoverable.

'*Director*' means

- where the company is managed by a board of directors or similar body, a member of that board or body;
- where it is managed by a single director or similar person, that director or person; and
- where it is managed by the members, a member of the company.

A person is connected with a director if that person is the director's wife or husband, or is a relative (or the wife or husband of a relative) of the director or of the director's wife or husband.

[*VATA 1994, s 24*(*3*)(*7*)].

The provisions cover repairs, maintenance, refurbishments, furnishing and legal and estate agents' fees. They apply whether or not the accommodation is a main residence, whether or not it is provided for a consideration and even if the business owns the accommodation.

Where a domestic room or rooms is put to business use HMRC may agree to an apportionment using an objective test of the extent to which the room is put to business use.

(VAT Notice 700, para 12.2; Internal Guidance V1–13, paras 14.6, 14.7).

For apportionment on the purchase of time share accommodation used by the directors for business and domestic purposes, see *Suregrove Ltd (VTD 10740) (TVC 34.256)*. See also *Giffenbond Ltd (VTD 13481) (TVC 34.261)* for apportionment where a garage was constructed at a director's home on land transferred to the company.

(*c*) **Employees**. Where a business has to provide domestic accommodation to its employees in order to facilitate the running of the business, the expenditure is regarded as having been incurred wholly for a business purpose. The most frequent instances of employers providing accommodation for staff are in the farming and hotel industries where it is essential to have staff available at all times of the day and where there is very little or no suitable accommodation available within reasonable distance of the business premises.

If an employer pays for

- goods which become the property of its employees
- the domestic fuel and power of its employees, or
- the private telephone calls of employees

the VAT incurred is treated as the employer's input tax, but the business must account for output tax as a supply of goods or services as appropriate (see 47.7 OUTPUT TAX).

(Internal Guidance V1–13, para 14.4).

(*d*) **Repairs, renovations, etc to farmhouses**. The following guidelines have been agreed with the National Farmers Union as regards input tax claims by sole proprietors and partnerships. Where the occupant of the farmhouse is a director of a limited company, or a person connected with the director of the company, the provisions under (*a*) above apply. The guidelines do not give an automatic entitlement to recover VAT and businesses should continue to consider their own particular circumstances, and use the guidelines to assess the proportion of input tax that is claimable.

- Where VAT is incurred on repairs, maintenance and renovations, 70% of that VAT may be recovered as input tax provided the farm is a normal working farm and the VAT-registered person is actively engaged full-time in running it. Where farming is not a full-time occupation and business for the VAT-registered person (ie income is received from either full-time employment or other sources) input tax claimable is likely to be between 10%-30% on the grounds that the dominant purpose is a personal one.
- Where the building work is more associated with an alteration (eg building an extension) the amount that may be recovered will depend on the purpose for the construction. If the dominant purpose is a business one then 70% can be claimed. If the dominant purpose is a personal one HMRC would expect the claim to be 40% or less, and in some cases, depending on the facts, none of the VAT incurred would be recoverable.

(Business Brief 18/96 which also see for retrospective claims).

De Voil Indirect Tax Service. See V3.410.

(7A) **Employee benefits and perks**

(a) **General**. Businesses commonly provide their employees with certain benefits and rewards. These may take the form of either goods or services. Such benefits are a legitimate business expense and are provided for the purposes of the business (mainly to reward or motivate staff). The VAT incurred on their provision is consequently all input tax and no apportionment under 35.7 above is necessary although a charge to output tax may be necessary under 47.7 OUTPUT TAX. Even if a charge to output tax is due, HMRC do not generally apply such a charge to benefits or facilities which are provided to all employees. However, 'perks' which are provided to specific individuals within a business should generally be subject to an output tax charge.

(*b*) **Retraining prior to redundancy**. VAT incurred on the provision of such programmes is incurred for the purposes of the employer's business and is input tax. It is not HMRC's policy to apply a charge to output tax on the free supply of services to the employees. (Internal Guidance V1–13, para 5.24.1).

(*c*) **Relocation expenses**. See (18) below.

(*d*) **Information technology supplied for homeworking**. If computers are not put to any business use, the VAT incurred on the machines is not input tax. If there is an intention that *some* home business use will occur, then the VAT will all be input tax and no apportionment is required.

If the equipment is provided for a charge, then even if the machine will not be used for business use, the VAT incurred is input tax as it relates to the business activity of hiring out computers. The hire is a taxable supply and output tax should be accounted for on the value of this supply.

(Internal Guidance V1–13, para 5.24.3).

(*e*) **Mobile telephones**. See (15A) below.

(*f*) **Domestic accommodation**. See (7) above.

(*g*) **Sports, canteen and recreational facilities available to staff in general**. Where such facilities are provided by a business and are available to all employees, whether or not for a charge, the VAT incurred in the provision of these facilities can be treated as input tax. It is not HMRC's policy to apply a charge to output tax on the free supply of services to the employees.

If a business is unable to provide suitable facilities within its own organisation and chooses to provide membership for their employees at external establishments, input tax can be recovered (and no output tax charge applies) as long as all employees are provided with the facilities. Where such facilities (eg membership of a golf or health club, etc) are provided as a 'perk' to specific employees, there is an onward supply of services under 47.7 OUTPUT TAX.

(Internal Guidance V1–13, para 5.24.6).

(8) **Entertainment**

See 9.1–9.6 BUSINESS ENTERTAINMENT.

(9) **Financial services**

See 27.3 FINANCIAL SERVICES for input tax recovery in respect of financial services.

(10) **Holding companies**

See 31.10 GROUPS OF COMPANIES.

(11) **Imports**

See 34.10–34.13 IMPORTS.

(12) **Insurance**

See 37.3 INSURANCE for input tax recovery in respect of insurance services and 37.10 INSURANCE for input tax re insurance claims.

(13) **Land and buildings**

See 42.11 LAND AND BUILDINGS for input tax recovery where the option to tax has been exercised; 42.15 LAND AND BUILDINGS for deduction of input tax by developers; and 42.33 LAND AND BUILDINGS for deduction of input tax by do-it-yourself housebuilders.

(14) **Legal costs**

For VAT on legal costs to be recoverable as input tax, the legal services should be supplied for the purpose of the business rather than for the trader, directors or employees in a personal capacity. The extent to which the substance of an action does relate to the activities of a business is a matter of judgement.

Criminal cases. VAT on legal costs has been disallowed in *Wallman Foods Ltd (VTD 1411) (TVC 34.163)* (handling stolen property); *Britwood Toys Ltd (VTD 2263) (TVC 34.164)* (successfully defending a charge of corruption in relation to acquisition of stock); *LHA Ltd (VTD 11911) (TVC 34.166)* (personal assault); *C & E Commrs v Rosner, QB 1993, [1994] STC 228 (TVC 34.157)* (conspiracy to defraud); and *RN Scott (VTD 2302) (TVC 34.160)* (motoring offences). VAT has been held to be deductible in *P & O European Ferries (Dover) Ltd (VTD 7846) (TVC 34.154)* (employees charged with manslaughter). In *SR Brooks (VTD 12754) (TVC 34.156)* VAT on legal costs of successfully defending charges in connection with evasion of Customs duties on gold transactions was held to be allowable although the tribunal indicated that this might not have been the case if the defendant had been charged with a smuggling offence.

Civil cases. VAT on legal costs has been disallowed in *JG & MV Potton (VTD 2882) (TVC 34.38)* (freeholder's costs paid by lessees in a breach of covenant case); *Ingram (t/a Ingram & Co) (VTD 4605) (TVC 34.48)*, *C Mills (VTD 4864) (TVC 34.133)*, *B Stone (VTD 12442) (TVC 34.51)* and *K Lister (VTD 13044) (TVC 34.134)* (partnership disputes); *G A Swinbank (VTD 18192) (TVC 34.143)* (defending claim by former wife over assets including business assets); *Brucegate Ltd (VTD 4903) (TVC 34.45)* and *Ash Fibre Processors Ltd (VTD 12201) (TVC 34.135)* (transfer of share capital); *Morgan Automation Ltd (VTD 5539) (TVC 34.144)* (director's dispute with previous company); and *HD Marks (VTD 11381) (TVC 34.147)* and *P Oldfield (VTD 12233) (TVC 34.148)* (action against former employer).

Payment of another party's legal costs. Where

- following completion of litigation (or arbitration), one party is ordered to pay the other party's costs, or

- a party to a transaction undertakes to pay the other party's costs, and the matter does not proceed to completion, so the costs are 'abortive'

the liability of the paying party is one of indemnity only and thus in itself outside the scope of VAT. Where payment is on an indemnity basis, the following general principles apply.

(*a*) The solicitor whose costs are to be paid should deliver a VAT invoice to his own client. (If the client is not VAT-registered, it is permissible to deliver a VAT-inclusive bill without distinguishing the VAT element, although this would not be common practice.)

(*b*) If the solicitor's client is a VAT-registered fully taxable person, and the supply of legal services is obtained for the purpose of the client's business, the client is entitled to full input tax credit. The indemnifying party need only pay the VAT-exclusive costs.

(*c*) If the solicitor's client is not registered for VAT and cannot therefore obtain input tax credit, the indemnifying party is liable to pay the VAT-inclusive costs but cannot recover the VAT as the legal services were not supplied to him.

(*d*) If the solicitor's client is a VAT-registered but partly-exempt, (*b*) above applies only to the extent that the client can obtain credit for input tax and (*c*) above applies to the balance.

In no circumstances may a VAT invoice be issued by the client's solicitor to the paying party who is not entitled to deduct the input tax credit as the services have not been rendered to him. The paying party should therefore receive a note of the other party's costs in such terms that the note cannot be mistaken for a VAT invoice issued to the paying party.

See also *NO Turner (t/a Turner Agricultural) v C & E Commrs, QB [1992] STC 621 (TVC 34.39).*

There are other circumstances where the payment of costs by a third party is regarded as consideration for the supply for VAT purposes. See, for example, 42.4 LAND AND BUILDINGS under the heading *Indemnity payments under lease agreements*.

(Internal Guidance V1–3, paras 17.3, 18).

Debt collection agencies. See 3.16 AGENTS.

(15) **Local authorities**

See 43.6 LOCAL AUTHORITIES AND PUBLIC BODIES.

(15A) **Mobile phones provided to employees**

HMRC have agreed the following treatment where a business provides its employees with mobile phones.

(*a*) *Purchase and connection.* If the phones are provided for business use, the business can treat as input tax all VAT incurred on purchasing the phone and on standing charges for keeping it connected to the network (whether or not it allows private use of the phone). See, however, (*e*) below.

(*b*) *Calls where business use only.* If the business does not allow employees to make private calls, all VAT incurred on calls is input tax. HMRC will accept that this is the case where a business has imposed clear rules prohibiting private use and enforces them. Under such circumstances, a small amount of private use will be treated as insignificant and will not prevent all VAT incurred being treated as input tax.

(*c*) *Charges by business for private use*. If a business charges its employees for any private calls, it may treat all VAT incurred on calls as input tax but must account for output tax on the amount it charges.

(*d*) *Free private calls*. If a business allows its employees to make private calls without charge, it must apportion the VAT incurred on the call charges by a method which produces a fair and reasonable result. For example, it could analyse a sample of bills taken over a reasonable period of time and use the ratio for future VAT recovery.

(*e*) *Fixed monthly charges*. Where the phone package allows the business to make a certain quantity of calls for a fixed monthly payment and there is no separate standing charge, it must apportion the VAT on the total charge for the package. Similarly, where the contract is for the purchase of the phone and the advance purchase of a set amount of call time for a single charge, apportionment applies to the whole charge.

(VAT Notice 700, paras 12A.1–12A.3).

(16) **Motor cars and motoring expenses**

See in particular 45.3 MOTOR CARS for purchases of cars, 45.7 MOTOR CARS for car dealers, 45.11 MOTOR CARS for leasing or hiring motor cars, 45.12 MOTOR CARS for repairs and maintenance, 45.13 MOTOR CARS for accessories and 45.14 and 45.15 MOTOR CARS for motor fuel.

(16A) **Museums and galleries**

Museums and galleries that offer free admission to the public are not regarded as being engaged in any business in relation to this activity. Ordinarily, it is not possible to recover the VAT incurred on goods and services purchased to support non-business activities and VAT incurred in connection with the free admission of the public would be irrecoverable. However, the Government reimburses this otherwise irrecoverable VAT to certain national museums and galleries under a special VAT refund scheme. The detailed provisions are set out below. (VAT Notice 998, paras 1.1, 1.5).

Where

- VAT is chargeable on the supply of goods or services to, or the acquisition or importation of goods by, a specified 'body',
- the supply, acquisition or importation is attributable to the provision by the body of free rights of admission to a 'relevant museum or gallery',
- the supply is made, or the acquisition or importation takes place, after 31 March 2001, and
- the VAT is not excluded from credit under *VATA 1994, s 25(7)* (see, for example, 9 BUSINESS ENTERTAINMENT and 45.3 MOTOR CARS),

HMRC must, on a claim being made in the appropriate form, refund to the body the amount of VAT so chargeable. The claim must be made within the period of three years beginning with the day on which the supply is made or the acquisition or importation takes place (or such shorter period as HMRC determine).

Where the goods or services in question cannot conveniently be distinguished from goods or services supplied to, or acquired or imported by, the body that are not attributable to free admissions, the refund is the amount remaining after deducting from the whole of the VAT to which the claim relates such proportion as HMRC consider to be attributable otherwise than to free admissions.

'*Bodies*' and their '*relevant museums and galleries*'. The Treasury has specified the following bodies and their relevant museums and galleries from 1 April 2001 or such later date as indicated.

Body	*Relevant museums and galleries*	*Date*
British Museum	British Museum, Great Russell Street, London WC1B 3DG	
Imperial War Museum	Imperial War Museum, Lambeth Road, London SE1 6HZ	1.12.01
	IWM North, Trafford Wharf Road, Trafford Park, Manchester M17 ITZ	1.4.02
The National Gallery	The National Gallery, Trafalgar Square, London WC2N 5ND	
National Maritime Museum	National Maritime Museum, Romney Road, London SE10 9NF	1.12.01
National Museums and Galleries on Merseyside	Walker Art Gallery, William Brown Street, Liverpool L3 8EL	1.12.01
	Liverpool Museum, William Brown Street, Liverpool L3 8EN	1.12.01
	Merseyside Maritime Museum, Albert Dock, Liverpool L3 4AQ	1.12.01
	Museum of Liverpool Life, Pier Head, Liverpool L3 1PZ	1.12.01
	The Lady Lever Art Gallery, Port Sunlight Village, Bebington, Wirral, Merseyside L62 4XE	1.12.01
	Sudley House, Mossley Hill Road, Liverpool L18 8BX	1.12.01
	The Conservation Centre, Whitechapel, Liverpool L1 6HZ	1.12.01
	HM Revenue and Customs National Museum, Merseyside Maritime Museum, Albert Dock, Liverpool L3 4AQ	1.12.01
National Portrait Gallery	National Portrait Gallery, St Martin's Place, London WC2H OHE	

Natural History Museum	Natural History Museum, Cromwell Road, London SW7 5BD	1.12.01
	Natural History Museum Zoological Museum, Akeman Street, Tring, Herts HP23 6AD	1.12.01
Royal Armouries	The Royal Armouries, Armouries Drive, Leeds, West Yorkshire LS10 ILT	1.12.01
	Royal Armouries at Fort Nelson, Fort Nelson, Down End Road, Fareham, Hants PO17 6AD	1.12.01
Science Museum	Science Museum, South Kensington, London SW7 2DD	1.12.01
	National Museum of Photography, Film and Television, Bradford, West Yorkshire BD1 ILQ	
	National Railway Museum, Leeman Road, York YO26 4XJ	1.12.01
	Science Museum, Wroughton Airfield, Swindon Wilts SN4 9NS	
	National Coal Mining Museum for England, Caphouse Colliery, New Road, Overton, Wakefield, West Yorkshire WF4 4RH	1.4.02
	Locomotion, the National Railway Museum at Shildon, Shildon, County Durham DL4 1PQ	10.2.03
Tate Gallery	Tate Britain, Millbank, London SW1P 4RG	
	Tate Modern, Bankside, London SE1 9TG	
	Tate Liverpool, Albert Dock, Liverpool L3 4BB	
Victoria and Albert Museum	Victoria and Albert Museum, Cromwell Road, London SW7 2RL	22.11.01
	Bethnal Green Museum of Childhood, Cambridge Heath Road, London E2 9PA	
	Theatre Museum: National Museum of Performing Arts, Russell Street, Covent Garden, London WC2 7PR	22.11.01
	Wellington Museum, Apsley House, 149 Piccadilly, Hyde Park Corner, London W1J 7NT	22.11.01
The Wallace Collection	The Wallace Collection, Hertford House, Manchester Square, London W1U 3BN	

The Greater Manchester Museum of Science and Industry	Museum of Science and Industry in Manchester, Liverpool Road, Castlefield, Manchester M3 4FP	1.12.01
Sir John Soane's Museum	Sir John Soane's Museum, 13 Lincoln's Inn Fields, London WC2A 3BP	
Museum of London	Museum of London, London Wall, London EC2Y 5NH	1.12.01
	Museum of London Archaeological Service, Mortimer Wheeler House, 46 Eagle Wharf Road, London N1	1.12.02
Geffrye Museum	Geffrye Museum, Kingsland Road, London E2 8EA	
Horniman Museum	Horniman Museum, 100 London Road, Forest Hill, London SE23 3PQ	
British Library*	British Library, 96 Euston Road, London NW1 2DB	
The National Army Museum	The National Army Museum, Royal Hospital Road, Chelsea, London SW3 4HT	
The Royal Air Force Museum	The Royal Air Force Museum, Hendon, London NW9 5LL	1.12.01
National Museums & Galleries of Wales	National Museum & Gallery, Cathays Park, Cardiff CF10 3NP	
	National Museums of Welsh History:	
	Roman Legionary Museum, High Street, Caerleon NP6 1AE	
	Segontium Roman Fort Museum, Beddgelert Road, Caernarfon, Gwynedd LL55 2LN	
	Museum of Welsh Life St Fagans, Cardiff CF5 6XB	
	National Museums of Welsh Industry:	
	Welsh Slate Museum, Llanberis, Gwynedd LL55 4TY	
	Big Pit, National Mining Museum of Wales, Blaenafon Torfaen NP4 9XP	
	Museum of the Welsh Woollen Industry, Drefach Felindre, Llandysul SA44 5UP	

	Collections Centre, Nantgarw, Trefforest Industrial Estate, Pontypridd CF15 7QT National Waterfront Museum Swansea, Museum Square, Maritime Quarter, Victoria Road, Swansea SA1 1SN *National Museum of Art:* Turner House, Plymouth Road, Penarth, South Glamorgan CF64 3DM	18.10.01
The National Library of Wales*	The National Library of Wales, Aberystwyth, Ceredigion SY23 3BU	
National Museums and Galleries of Northern Ireland	Ulster Museum, Botanic Gardens, Belfast BT9 5AB Armagh County Museum, The Mall East, Armagh	
National Museums of Scotland	Royal Scottish Museum, Chambers Street, Edinburgh EH1 1JF Museum of Scotland, Chambers Street, Edinburgh EH1 1JF National War Museum of Scotland, Edinburgh Castle, Edinburgh	
National Galleries of Scotland	National Gallery of Scotland, The Mound, Edinburgh EH2 2EL Scottish National Portrait Gallery, Queen Street, Edinburgh EH2 1JD Scottish National Gallery of Modern Art, Belford Road, Edinburgh EH4 3DR Dean Gallery, Belford Road, Edinburgh EH4 3DR	
National Library of Scotland*	George IV Bridge, Edinburgh EH1 1EW 33 Salisbury Place, Edinburgh	

* In respect of the historical collections in its galleries, temporary exhibitions and other related public programmes and events.

[*VATA 1994, s 33A; FA 2001, s 98*(2); *SI 2001/2879*].

Input tax refundable under the scheme. Refunds of VAT can be claimed on goods and services purchased in order to make the principal collections in the museum or gallery available and accessible to the public free of any charges. The museum must place the order, receive the supply, receive a VAT invoice addressed to it, and pay from its own funds (including funds awarded to it, eg lottery funds). Provided these conditions are met, VAT incurred can be reclaimed on

- items and collections on display provided they have borne VAT (eg buying, acquiring or importing the items and collections);
- goods and services necessary for their upkeep (eg cleaning and restoring the displayed items);
- upkeep of the part of the building (including common areas) in which the items are housed (eg making secure, cleaning, repairs and maintenance);
- provision of free information in relation to the items on display (eg advertising and other promotional material; 'virtual' access to, and information about items via a free website provided it is not a business activity; free lectures);
- building a new wing to house items; and
- costs related to those areas, such as office space, that are not themselves open to the public but which are used for administration purposes in connection with free admissions.

Provided the public has free access to the principal collections on display, it does not matter that the public are occasionally charged to see special exhibitions, etc. However, any VAT incurred in relation to such a special exhibition is subject to the normal rules of input tax deduction.

VAT cannot be reclaimed under the scheme on

- non-business activities other than providing free admission to the public (eg grant-funded research); or
- any business activities (eg shops, catering outlets, commercial sponsorship (including commercially sponsored websites), or educational courses provided for consideration).

(VAT Notice 998, paras 2.3, 2.5–2.8).

Recovering the VAT.

- *VAT-registered museums* should claim a refund in Box 4 of the VAT return (in addition to any input tax incurred in making taxable business supplies). The net value of total purchases should be included in Box 7.
- *Non-VAT-registered museums* must make a claim in writing to Banking/GABS, HM Revenue and Customs, 7th Floor SW, Alexander House, 21 Victoria Avenue, Southend-on-Sea SS99 1AU. Any claim must relate to a period of at least one calendar month or, if it is for less than £100, at least twelve months. The period chosen must end on the last day of a calendar month.

  There is no special form to apply for the repayment and a declaration can be made along the following lines

> I am claiming a refund of £ for the period to to cover VAT charged on goods and services bought for (name of body) in connection with the provision of free admission to the public.

Signed
For (name of body)
Address
Contact name
Contact telephone number

The basis of calculation should be explained and the museum should keep invoices and other records to support its claims for six years unless HMRC agrees in writing to a shorter period.

(VAT Notice 998, paras 3.2, 3.5, 4.3–4.5).

VAT groups. Bodies within these provisions can group for VAT purposes if they meet the requirements for VAT group treatment in 31.2 GROUPS OF COMPANIES. (VAT Notice 998, para 1.10).

Extra-statutory concession. A qualifying museum or gallery can recover the VAT attributable to the free right of admission from the date specified in the above list. The scheme is not retrospective and does not, therefore, extend to goods or services acquired before the admission date (and used in connection with the taxable business activity of charging admissions) but subsequently used in connection with the non-business activity of admitting the public free of charge.

By concession, HMRC will apply the following provisions (unless used for VAT avoidance) to ensure that a museum or gallery is not required to repay input tax, properly recovered at the time, solely on account of the move to free admission. The concession takes effect from 1 April 2001 (or such later date specified for the qualifying museum or gallery in the above table), whether or not that date was before the date of publication of the concession.

- A qualifying museum or gallery need not account for output tax on goods and services which, after purchase, are subsequently put to a non-business use. Such transactions, which would otherwise be taxable (see 47.7 OUTPUT TAX), are treated as neither a supply of goods nor a supply of services, provided the change in use of the goods and services arose solely as a direct result of the body using them for the purpose of offering free rights of admission to their relevant museum or gallery.
- A qualifying museum or gallery need not make adjustments in the case of goods within the CAPITAL GOODS SCHEME (10) where input tax has been recovered, insofar as a change in use of a capital item relates to free admission with related refunds under the scheme. Where this applies, the museum, etc should, in each subsequent interval, adjust the total input tax on the capital item and the extent of its taxable use as follows.
  - (i) The total input tax on the capital item is deemed to be the proportion that would have been input tax if admissions, which have subsequently become free, had been free at the time the VAT was incurred.
  - (ii) The extent of taxable use of the capital item, at the time the original entitlement to deduction was determined, is deemed to be

the extent of taxable use at that time if admissions which have subsequently become free had been free at that time.

Where free admission is introduced part way through a capital goods scheme interval (eg a museum with a VAT year ending 31 March charges for admission until 31 December, then gave free admission from 1 January onwards), the CGS adjustment comprises two calculations. In the example given, three-quarters of the input tax should be adjusted under normal rules and one quarter of the input tax should be adjusted using the concession. Where free admission is phased in, gradual variations can be covered by looking at the year as a whole. Significant variations should be handled with more than one calculation.

(VAT Notice 48, ESC 3.34; VAT Notice 998, paras 5.1–5.3, 6.4, 6.5).

(17) **Pension schemes**

See 53.2 PENSION SCHEMES for input tax deductible by employers.

(18) **Removal/relocation expenses**

Employers may provide assistance to employees or future employees in relocating nearer their new job. Assistance may take many forms, including

- the payment of estate agent's fees,
- payment for a removal firm when moving house,
- the provision of maintenance/gardening for an employee's former property awaiting sale, and
- short-term accommodation in a hotel, etc.

Providing such expenditure is linked to the actual relocation, it can be treated as being the employer's input tax. It is not HMRC's policy to apply a charge to output tax on the free supply of services to the employees.

If, however, the expenditure is not linked specifically to the relocation, but forms part of the ongoing living expenses at the new property, then it is not input tax. For example, the provision of new, bespoke curtains or carpets for a new house is acceptable as it is a normal expense of moving house; but the provision of a new stereo system would not be acceptable as it is an expenditure unrelated to the relocation.

(Internal Guidance V1–13, para 5.24.2).

(19) **Second-hand goods**

See 61.2 SECOND-HAND GOODS for disallowance of input tax on goods sold under the scheme.

(20) **Sporting, recreational and sponsorship activities**

There can be considerable difficulties in establishing to what extent, if any, there is entitlement to deduct input tax in respect of sporting, recreational and sponsorship activities. HMRC's policy in this area is to ensure that the legitimate costs of a taxable person in promoting his business or providing facilities to his staff are allowed, whilst not providing, in effect, a tax subsidy to persons who control businesses in respect of their own favoured sporting or recreational activities.

(*a*) *Provisions for staff.* Where sports and recreational facilities are available to all employees, whether or not for a charge, any VAT incurred can be treated as input tax. This equally applies where smaller businesses are unable to provide suitable facilities within their own organisation and provide membership for their employees at external establishments.

Where such facilities (eg membership of a golf or health club, etc) are provided as a 'perk' to specific employees, the provisions relating to private use of services in 47.7 OUTPUT TAX may apply.

(*b*) *Provisions for sole proprietors, partners and company directors.* Where the sporting or recreational facilities provided (eg membership of a golf or country club) are available only to the proprietor, partners, or directors of a company (and the relatives and friends of these persons), it is unlikely that this expenditure can be treated as being for the purpose of the business and the VAT incurred does not therefore qualify as input tax. Even if membership does result in business contacts, following the decision in *C & E Commrs v Rosner, QB 1993, [1994] STC 228 (TVC 34.157)*, the expenditure is probably not sufficiently connected to the purpose of the business.

(*c*) *Sponsorship, advertising and business promotion.* In certain cases, there is undoubtedly widespread exposure gained by the sponsoring business (eg 'Dunhill' golf masters, FA Barclays Premiership, etc) so that no difficulty arises in allowing input tax deduction. In the case of sponsorship of sporting events by smaller businesses, there is, however, more likelihood that the 'sponsorship' is actually conducted for a private purpose (eg a trader may 'sponsor' a local amateur football club because of a personal connection with the team).

Similarly, participation in various sporting or recreational events may be claimed to be for business purposes in the form of advertising or promotion.

HMRC approach such cases by applying the 'business purpose' test in 35.6 above. If, at the time the VAT is incurred, the business purpose tests are met, the VAT is input tax. It is irrelevant whether the business's intentions are misconceived or that the envisaged benefits do not materialise, and the fact that the participant enjoys the activity is not sufficient reason in itself to deny input tax.

HMRC officers may consider the following questions in reaching any decision as to the deductibility of VAT incurred as input tax.

1. Does the sole proprietor, partner or director actively participate in the sport?
2. If the trader cannot take part because of injury, business commitments, etc is another (independent) person employed to drive, etc?
3. Does a member of the trader's family actively take part in the sport?
4. Is there a connection between the sport and the business?
5. Where does the sporting activity take place?
6. Is there supplementary advertising at the racing venue or in programmes?

7. Is there related advertising or promotional material?
8. Does the business name appear on the sporting vehicle, transporter, clothing, etc?
9. For companies and partnerships is there a record of a decision to use sporting facilities for advertising?
10. Can the business produce any evidence of research into the benefits to be obtained by the advertising?
11. Are the benefits of the advertising monitored?
12. Is the car, boat, etc an asset of the business?
13. What other forms of advertising are there?
14. Has the Inland Revenue given a ruling?
15. If the intention of the alleged advertising or promotion is the expansion of trade, could the business cope with an expansion of trade?

(Internal Guidance V1–13, paras 12.1–12.4, 12.10).

(21) **Subsistence expenses**

Where an employee is paid a flat rate for subsistence expenses, no VAT can be claimed as input tax. If the business pays the actual cost of the supplies, input tax incurred can be reclaimed as below. If the business pays a proportion of the actual costs, it can reclaim as input tax the VAT fraction (see 47.2 OUTPUT TAX) of the amount it pays.

Meals. If the business provides canteen facilities, all input tax incurred in providing these facilities can be recovered subject to the normal rules (even on meals for a sole proprietor, partner or director). Any VAT incurred on meals for employees can be treated as input tax. In the case of a sole proprietor, partner or director, the VAT must be incurred on meals taken away from the normal place of work on a business trip.

Hotel accommodation. All VAT incurred on accommodation for employers and employees when away from the normal place of work on business trips can be treated as input tax. See, however, *Co-operative Insurance Society Ltd (VTD 14862) (TVC 34.17)* where input tax was disallowed on hotel accommodation reserved by employees and only deductible if reserved by the company.

Where, occasionally, an employee uses overnight accommodation near the normal work place, VAT incurred is input tax and deductible if the employer requires the employee to stay in the accommodation and the expense is fully borne by the business and recorded as such in the accounting records. For other persons, whether VAT is deductible on such accommodation depends on the facts of the particular case. For example, if a partner stays at an hotel near to the normal work-place because there is a rail strike which will make it difficult to get to work and the business bears the cost, this is accepted as being for the purpose of the business.

(VAT Notice 700, para 12.1; Internal Guidance V1–13, para 23.1).

See also *British Broadcasting Corporation (VTD 73) (TVC 34.230)* and *Ledamaster Ltd (VTD 344) (TVC 34.235)*. See 9 BUSINESS ENTERTAINMENT where accommodation, meals etc are provided for persons other than employees.

(22) Tour operators' margin scheme

See 66.14 TOUR OPERATORS' MARGIN SCHEME for disallowance of input tax on goods or services acquired for re-supply as margin scheme supplies.

(23) Transfers of going concerns

See 8.15 BUSINESS for deduction of related input tax.

(24) Viability studies by accountants

See 36.11 INSOLVENCY.

36 Insolvency

Cross-references. See 5.7 APPEALS by persons becoming insolvent; 6.9 ASSESSMENTS for assessments on persons representing insolvent persons.

The contents of this chapter are as follows.

36.1 INTRODUCTION

Insolvency occurs when businesses do not have sufficient assets to cover their debts, or are unable to pay their debts when they become due. HMRC refer to the official receiver, or to the insolvency practitioner appointed over an insolvent business's affairs, as the 'office holder'. Office holders are liable to account for VAT in the normal way following their appointment (see below).

Types of insolvency. There are various types of insolvency procedure into which a VAT-registered business may enter. HMRC distinguish between 'formal' insolvencies (which are dealt with by The Insolvency Branch of the Legal Recovery Unit in Liverpool) and 'informal' insolvencies (which are dealt with by staff at local insolvency units). There are also certain receiverships which HMRC do not treat procedurally as insolvencies.

Formal insolvencies

- *Administrative receivership.* An administrative receiver may be appointed to manage the affairs of a company by a secured creditor who holds a debenture agreement containing floating, or fixed and floating, charges over the whole, or substantially the whole, of a company's assets. Upon the appointment of the administrative receiver, the floating charges crystallise. The administrative receiver must treat the business assets covered by the charges in such a way as to recover the money due to the secured creditor. If the administrative receiver deems it to be in the best interests of the secured creditor, the business may continue to trade. Preferential creditors rank above floating charge holders.

- *Bankruptcy.* A bankrupt is an individual against whom a bankruptcy order has been made by the court. The court can declare a person bankrupt on petition from the individual, one or more creditors, or the supervisor of an individual voluntary arrangement. The order indicates that the person is unable to pay his debts and, subject to certain exceptions, deprives him of his property, which can then be sold in order to pay creditors.

  The bankruptcy process of an individual or partnership (firm) in Scotland is known as sequestration.

- *Creditors' voluntary liquidation.* A creditors' voluntary liquidation usually relates to an insolvent company and is commenced by a resolution of the shareholders.

A creditors' meeting is called so that the creditors of the company may, if they wish, appoint another insolvency practitioner in place of the shareholders' appointee.

- *Members' voluntary liquidation.* A members' voluntary liquidation is preceded by the directors of a company, or the majority of its directors, making a Declaration of Solvency. The declaration must be made within the five weeks immediately preceding the date of the passing of the resolution for winding up. Liquidation takes place when the resolution is passed.
- *Compulsory winding up.* A compulsory winding up is ordered by the court as the result of the presentation of a petition by the company, its creditors, its directors, one or more of its shareholders, or the Secretary of State.
- *Partnership winding up.* A compulsory winding up is ordered by the court as a result of the presentation of a petition by the members of the partnership or by a creditor.
- *Provisional liquidation.* A provisional liquidator may be appointed by the court after the presentation of a petition for a winding up in order to protect the assets of a company before a winding up order is made. Where a provisional liquidator has been appointed, HMRC do not treat the case as an insolvency until a winding up order is made and a 'permanent' liquidator appointed.

Informal insolvencies

- *Administration.* An administrator is appointed by a court order following an application by either the company, its directors or one or more of its creditors, which is intended to allow
  - (*a*) the survival of the company and the whole or part of its undertaking as a going concern;
  - (*b*) the approval of a voluntary arrangement;
  - (*c*) the approval of a scheme under *Companies Act 1985, s 425*; and
  - (*d*) a better realisation of the company's assets than would be obtained from winding up the company.
- *Partnership administration.* An administrator is appointed by a court order following an application by the members of the partnership or by a creditor, which is intended to allow
  - (*a*) the partnership, or part of it, to survive in a restructured form;
  - (*b*) the approval of a partnership voluntary arrangement; and
  - (*c*) a better realisation of the partnership's assets than would be obtained from winding up the partnership.
- *County court administration.* The court makes an order for regular payments to be made over a period of time in settlement of debts. The court administers the scheme. The scheme is only available to individuals and there is no provision for preferential creditors.
- *Administration of a deceased person's estate.*
- *Deed of arrangement.* This is a method by which an individual can arrange terms with creditors.

- *Scheme of arrangement*. This term is normally used to describe a compromise or arrangement between a company and its creditors or members (or any class of them) which may involve a scheme for the reconstruction of the company.
- *Scottish trust deeds*. A debtor grants a deed in favour of the trustee which transfers their assets to the trustee for the benefit of creditors.
- *Voluntary arrangements*. A voluntary arrangement provides an alternative to bankruptcy or liquidation. The debtor makes proposals through a licensed insolvency practitioner which are presented at a meeting of creditors. Creditors must be given 14 clear days notice of such a meeting. The proposals usually entail delayed and/or reduced payment of debts, and can be advantageous to both the debtor and the creditors. A Supervisor is appointed to monitor the scheme for its duration, although the business usually continues to be responsible for its own business activities.

  In individual voluntary arrangements, the court makes an interim order which prevents certain recovery actions in order to grant a breathing space (a moratorium). This interim order remains in force until the creditors meet to decide whether to approve the arrangement. There is no equivalent procedure for companies.
- *Partnership voluntary arrangements*. These are similar to *Voluntary arrangements* above but have no moratorium.

Procedures not treated as insolvencies by HMRC

- *Agricultural charge receivership*. A secured creditor can appoint a receiver under the *Agricultural Credits Act 1928* over the assets of a farm estate.
- *Fixed charge receivership*. A receiver, or receiver and manager, is appointed by a secured creditor who holds a fixed charge over specific assets which belong to a business. The assets are used for the benefit of the secured creditor. If a secured creditor possesses a valid registered debenture agreement containing a valid fixed charge on book or other debts, then HMRC will repay pre-appointment VAT credits to the office holder providing they are satisfied that there would be an overall shortfall to the debenture holder if they did not do so.
- *Law of Property Act receivership*. A lender, such as a bank, can appoint a receiver over a mortgaged property under the *Law of Property Act 1925* to recover money advanced. The receiver usually tries to arrange for the property to be sold or is responsible for collecting rents for the mortgagee. The business may continue to trade independently of the receiver's appointment.

(VAT Notice 700/56/02, paras 2.1–2.5).

Person carrying on the business. If a taxable person becomes 'bankrupt or incapacitated', HMRC may treat any person carrying on the business as a taxable person from the date of the bankruptcy or incapacity until either some other person is registered in respect of the taxable supplies made (or intended to be made) by that taxable person or the incapacity ceases. Any person carrying on the business must notify HMRC in writing within 21 days of

- the nature of any incapacity and the date on which it began; and
- the date of any bankruptcy order.

The VAT provisions apply to any person treated as carrying on the business as though he were a registered person.

[*VATA 1994, s 46(4); SI 1995/2518, Reg 9; SI 1996/1250, Reg 5*].

See 36.2 and 36.3 below.

Where any person becomes bankrupt or incapacitated and control of his assets passes to another person, that other person must, if HMRC require and so long as he has control, comply with the general accounting, record and payment requirements of VAT. However, any requirement to pay VAT only applies to the extent of the assets of the incapacitated person over which he has control so that he is treated to that extent as if he were the incapacitated person himself. [*SI 1995/2518, Reg 30*].

If no person carries on the business (ie taxable supplies cease to be made) the normal procedures for cancellation of registration apply (see 59.33 REGISTRATION).

Companies in receivership and liquidation. In relation to a company which is a taxable person, the references above to a taxable person becoming 'bankrupt or incapacitated' are to be construed as references to its going into liquidation or receivership or to administration. [*SI 1995/2518, Reg 9; SI 2003/2096, Art 56*].

36.2 NOTIFICATION OF INSOLVENCY

Subject to below, a person appointed

- office holder over the affairs of an insolvent VAT-registered trader, or
- liquidator in a members' voluntary liquidation

must notify HMRC within 21 days of appointment (or, in the case only of an office holder appointed after an official receiver and who has difficulty in obtaining the necessary information, within 21 days of becoming aware of the required information). This must be done on Form VAT 769, supplies of which are available from the National Advice Service (tel: 0845 010 9000).

Form VAT 769 should not be used in the following circumstances and notification should simply be made in writing to the VAT Business Advice Centre which controls the area of the principal place of business of the insolvent business.

- Notification of a proposed creditors meeting for either voluntary arrangements or creditors' voluntary liquidations.
- The appointment of a receiver under *Law of Property Act*.
- The appointment of a receiver or manager under a fixed charge only.
- The appointment of a receiver under the *Agricultural Credits Act 1928* over assets of a farm estate.
- The appointment of a provisional liquidator (as such a person has no status with regard to the trader's VAT registration).

Where a liquidator is appointed after the appointment of an administrative receiver, it is not necessary to complete a second Form VAT 769. HMRC will, however, need extra information (eg who is in control of the assets and who will be responsible for completing VAT returns). This information, together with the name, address and date of appointment of the liquidator, should be sent to HM Revenue and Customs, Insolvency Branch, Legal Recovery Unit, Queens Dock, Liverpool L74 4AA quoting the VAT registration number.

(VAT Notice 700/56/02, paras 3.1–3.6).

36.3 **CLAIMS BY HMRC**

On notification of an insolvency, HMRC will calculate its claim based on the amount outstanding at the 'relevant date'.

'*Relevant date*' is

- in relation to a company which is being wound up
  - (i) where the company is being wound up by a court and the winding-up order was made immediately upon the discharge of an administration order, the date of the making of the administration order;
  - (ii) in a case not within (i) above where the company is being wound up by the court and had not commenced to be wound up voluntarily before the date of the making of the winding-up order, the date of appointment (or first appointment) of a provisional liquidator or, if no such appointment has been made, the date of the making of the winding-up order; and
  - (iii) in any other case not within (i) or (ii) above, the date of the passing of the resolution for the winding up of the company;
- in relation to a company in receivership, the date of appointment of the receiver; and
- in relation to a bankrupt
  - (i) where at the time the bankruptcy order was made there was an interim receiver of the debtor's estate appointed under *Insolvency Act 1986, s 286*, the date on which the interim receiver was first appointed after the presentation of the bankruptcy petition; and
  - (ii) in any other case, the date of making the bankruptcy order.

[*Insolvency Act 1986, Sch 6*].

The claim details notified to the office holder show totals of the preferential and non-preferential debts due to HMRC (see 36.4 and 36.5 below). A more detailed breakdown of the claim is available on request.

Where the business continues to trade, the office holder has responsibility for the VAT affairs of the business from the relevant date onwards with the exception of bankrupts continuing to trade, *Law of Property Act* receiverships, fixed charge receiverships, voluntary arrangements, deeds and schemes of arrangement, and county court administration orders (see 36.1 above for these terms).

(VAT Notice 700/56/02, paras 4.1, 4.2).

De Voil Indirect Tax Service. See V5.187.

36.4 **Preferential claim**

With effect from 15 September 2003 (but not where the relevant insolvency commenced before that date), HMRC's preferential claim in an insolvency is abolished under *Enterprise Act 2002, s 251*.

Before 15 September 2003, any VAT which was referable to the period of six months next before the relevant date was a preferential debt in the insolvency.

Where the whole of a VAT period fell within the six-month period, the whole of the VAT for that period was referable to the relevant period. In any other case, the VAT liability for the accounting period was apportioned between the non-preferential claim and the preferential claim according to the number of days within the accounting period. (The normal VAT period in which the relevant date occurred was in any case divided into two periods, see 2.2(*e*) ACCOUNTING PERIODS AND RETURNS.)

[*Insolvency Act 1986, Sch 6*].

36.5 Non-preferential claim

The non-preferential claim comprises the following.

- Any amount of outstanding VAT not treated as preferential under 36.4 above.
- The amount of any penalty, default surcharge or default interest assessed in respect of any period before the relevant date ie even if relating to the six months before the relevant date. This is because the penalty, etc is recoverable 'as if it were' VAT and is not VAT as such.
- Import duties, including import VAT.

(VAT Notice 700/56/02, paras 4.4, 4.8).

36.6 Assessments

Where a return has not been submitted for any VAT period prior to the relevant date, HMRC will raise an assessment and initially base their claim upon the amount so assessed. Where the office holder submits an acceptable VAT return for the period in question, the assessment will be withdrawn.

Where an assessment is raised following a VAT inspection or voluntary disclosure before the relevant date, any additional VAT due is related directly to the original accounting period in determining whether it is preferential or non-preferential.

(VAT Notice 700/56/02, para 4.7).

36.7 Set-off of credits

As a general rule, under *VATA 1994, s 81(3)(3A)* any amount due from HMRC to any person ('the credit') must be set against any sum due from that person by way of VAT, penalty, interest or surcharge ('the debit') and to the extent of the set-off, the obligations of both HMRC and that person are discharged. See 51.6 PAYMENT OF VAT for full details.

However, this general rule does not apply where

(*a*) an 'insolvency procedure' has been applied to the person entitled to the credit;

(*b*) the credit became due after that procedure was so applied; and

(*c*) the liability to pay the debit either

(i) arose before that procedure was so applied; or

(ii) (having arisen afterwards) relates to, or to matters occurring in the course of, the carrying on of any business at times before the procedure was so applied.

For these purposes, the time when an '*insolvency procedure*' is to be taken to be applied to any person is when

(i) a bankruptcy order is made in relation to that person (unless any of (vii)–(ix) below already applies to that person);

(ii) a winding up order is made in relation to that person (unless any of (iv)–(ix) already applies to that person);

(iii) an award of sequestration is made in relation to that person (unless any of (vii)–(ix) already applies to that person);

(iv) an administration order is made in relation to that person (unless any of (v) or (vii)–(ix) already applies to that person);

(v) that person is put into administrative receivership;

(vi) that person, being a corporation, passes a resolution for voluntary winding up;

(vii) any approved voluntary arrangement comes into force in relation to that person;

(viii) a registered deed of arrangement takes effect in relation to that person; or

(ix) that person's estate becomes vested in any other person as that person's trustee under a trust deed.

[*VATA 1994, s 81(4A)–(4D)(5), Sch 13 para 21; FA 1995, s 27; SI 1994/1253; SI 2003/2096, Art 26*].

De Voil Indirect Tax Service. See V5.172.

36.8 Crown set-off

HMRC can offer credits arising from insolvent traders' VAT repayment claims accruing before the relevant date to other government departments. [*IA 1986, s 323; SI 1986/1925, Rule 4.90*]. See also *Re Cushla v C & E Commrs, Ch D [1979] STC 615 (TVC 14.95)* and *Re DH Curtis (Builders) Ltd, [1978] 2 All ER 183 (TVC 14.95)*.

HMRC currently only operate the Crown set-off procedure for repayments which exceed £500 and offer credits to the Inland Revenue, the Department of Works and Pensions, the Department of Trade and Industry and the Ministry of Defence. Any VAT repayments due falling below the limit are automatically repaid to the office holder (or to the trader in the case of voluntary arrangements, deeds or schemes of arrangement and County Court administration orders).

Crown set-off takes place after all pre-relevant date returns have been received and/or assessments raised and offset.

If a creditor is secured by a fixed charge on book or other debts of the business, Crown set-off does not apply to any VAT credit due from HMRC. See also 36.11(2A) below.

(VAT Notice 700/56/02, paras 13.1, 13.2).

36.9 Dividends

If the office holder declares a dividend from an insolvent estate, cheques should be made payable to HM Revenue and Customs and sent to Southend (see 15.1 CUSTOMS: ADMINISTRATION). Receipts and payments accounts should be sent to Insolvency Branch, Legal Recovery Unit, Queens Dock, Liverpool L74 4AA, with a copy to the local VAT Business Advice Centre.

Dividends for businesses subject to

- any form of administration orders, should be sent to the Insolvency Branch, Legal Recovery Unit in Liverpool;
- Scottish trust deeds and deeds or schemes of arrangement, should be sent to the trader's local informal insolvency unit; and
- voluntary arrangements should be sent to the Voluntary Arrangement Service, Durrington Bridge House, Barrington Road, Worthing, West Sussex BN12 4SE.

(VAT Notice 700/56/02, paras 8.1, 8.2).

36.10 **RETURNS**

All returns completed by the office holder for pre- and post-insolvency periods must be sent to VAT Central Unit in Southend in the normal way.

Pre-insolvency returns. The insolvent business is responsible for submitting pre-insolvency returns. However, the office holder may submit a return for any pre-relevant date period for which the business has not rendered a return. Such a return should be unsigned but carry the legend, 'completed from the books and records of the company/trader'.

The final pre-insolvency return covering the period up to the relevant date is issued automatically to the office holder and is not subject to default surcharge.

Split period return covering the relevant date. Where the relevant date (see 36.3 above) falls within a VAT period, that period is divided into two periods. The first period ends on the day prior to the relevant date. The return for that period is issued directly to the person in charge of the insolvency and must be submitted by the last day of the following month. Default surcharge is not applicable to this return. The second period begins on the relevant date and ends (and all subsequent periods end) on the normal last day for the VAT periods of the insolvent trader. [*SI 1995/2518, Reg 25*(*3*)].

Post-insolvency returns are the legal responsibility of the office holder (except for *Law of Property Act* receiverships, fixed charge receiverships, voluntary arrangements, deeds and schemes of arrangement, and county court administration orders (see 36.1 above for these terms). Returns are issued automatically to the office holder. The returns must be submitted, and any VAT paid, by the normal due date (see 51.1 PAYMENT OF VAT).

Repayments due are, subject to below, repaid in the name of the insolvent business, c/o the office holder. The repayment should be made by HMRC within 30 days of receipt of the return but may be delayed by any inaccuracies on the Form VAT 769 or failure to notify HMRC of the appointment of an insolvency practitioner or official receiver.

Repayments for businesses in voluntary arrangements, deeds and schemes of arrangement or county court administration orders (see 36.1 above for these terms) are sent to the address of the registered business unless the trader has given written permission for the payment to be sent to the insolvency practitioner.

Repayment supplement is added if the normal conditions are satisfied (see 51.15 PAYMENT OF VAT).

Penalties, default surcharge and default interest are currently not applied to post-insolvency VAT returns. They are, however, applied in the case of administration orders, partnership administration orders, deceased persons administration orders, deeds and schemes of arrangement, Scottish trust deeds, county court administration orders; and voluntary arrangements (see 36.1 above for these terms).

Compliance. HMRC have the right to check the accuracy of all returns submitted and to require that the books and records of the business are made available for inspection. In certain circumstances, where it can be shown that an office holder has consistently not complied with regulations, a report may be made to the appropriate licensing authority.

(VAT Notice 700/56/02, paras 5.1–5.8).

36.11 MISCELLANEOUS VAT PROCEDURES

(1) Bad debt relief

BAD DEBT RELIEF (7) can be claimed in insolvencies subject to the normal rules. Claims can be made on the normal VAT return where the VAT registration remains open and on Form VAT 426 where registration has been cancelled. A letter scheduling the claim, together with copies of the relevant invoices, must be submitted to Insolvency Branch, Legal Recovery Unit for approval. HMRC need to know the periods in which the supplies subject to the claim were made, whether returns have been submitted for those periods and whether the VAT due for each period has been paid. In cases where the VAT for the period in question has been paid in full and the declared output tax exceeds the bad debt relief claim, relief may be allowed. (VAT Notice 700/56/02, paras 10.1, 10.2). See also 7.13 BAD DEBT RELIEF for a concession concerning the repayment of input tax where an insolvency practitioner receives notice of a claim for bad debt relief on a pre-insolvency transaction.

(2) Cash accounting

The cash accounting scheme allows VAT-registered businesses to account for VAT on the basis of payments received and made rather than on VAT invoices issued and received. See 63.2 SPECIAL SCHEMES. The office holder responsible for the business may use the scheme in the post relevant date period if the insolvent business was eligible to use the scheme pre-insolvency and continues to be eligible to do so. This may be appropriate in cases where trading has continued after the relevant date.

The office holder must also, within two months of the date of insolvency, account for VAT due on all supplies made or received up to the date of the insolvency which have not previously been accounted for. [*SI 1995/2518, Reg 62*]. The VAT due should be entered on to the VAT return for the period immediately preceding the relevant date, and is treated as a liability arising before the insolvency.

(VAT Notice 700/56/02, paras 11.1–11.3).

(2A) Charges over book debts

HMRC and Redundancy Payments Service have agreed a joint approach to the question of fixed charges over book debts following the decision of the Privy Council in *Re Brumark Investments Ltd [2000] 1 BCLC 353* on 5 June 2001 casting new light on the distinction between fixed and floating charges. This will impact on the distribution of book debt proceeds in insolvent cases.

A fixed charge is a form of mortgage debenture on specified property, including uncollected book debts. In insolvency cases, lenders holding a fixed charge are paid ahead of all other creditors, including preferential creditors. The decision in *Brumark* states that a charge that allows the collection and free use of the proceeds of a book debt by the company is not a fixed charge. A fixed charge requires the collected proceeds to be paid into a blocked account (ie an account to which the company does not have unfettered access and cannot draw on the proceeds without the specific consent of the chargeholder). It is not enough for a debenture to provide for a blocked account: such an account must actually be operated.

The ruling means that, for distributions made with effect from 5 June 2001, the Crown Departments will monitor the distribution of book debt proceeds in insolvency cases and reserve the right to challenge distributions made to fixed chargeholders if they believe the charge in question was actually a floating charge. In addition, pre-insolvency VAT credits will be paid to companies subject to insolvency procedures in preference to other Crown creditors only in cases where a debenture is provided showing a fixed charge over book debts that HMRC are satisfied is a valid fixed charge.

(Business Brief 5/02).

(3) **Credit notes**

Where the office holder issues or receives a credit note for supplies made in a pre-insolvency VAT period, the VAT adjustment is related back to the period in which the original supply took place and HMRC's claim in the insolvency will be reduced or increased accordingly. To enable HMRC to make the necessary adjustments to the trader's VAT account, such credit notes should not be declared on a VAT return. Instead, they should be declared to the local insolvency unit, either by letter or by means of a voluntary disclosure, giving details of the VAT element and the date of the original supply.

Note that because of the introduction of the three-year time limit for VAT adjustments, a credit note adjustment cannot take effect if the credit note is issued more than three years after the end of the VAT accounting period in which the original supply took place.

(VAT Notice 700/56/02, paras 12.1–12.3).

(4) **Partial exemption**

The provisions relating to PARTIAL EXEMPTION (49) apply to all VAT-registered businesses including those which are insolvent. The person in charge must comply with these requirements in respect of returns completed for pre- and post-relevant date VAT periods. An insolvent business can apply to change the method of calculating entitlement to input tax recovery if there has been a substantial change in circumstances although such changes cannot be applied retrospectively.

Where a business is already partly exempt, the annual adjustment should be made at the end of the business's partial exemption year. Approval may be sought from HMRC to allow the annual adjustment to be made in the VAT period which ends with the relevant date.

(VAT Notice 700/56/02, paras 15.1, 15.2).

(5) **VAT on insolvency practitioners' fees**

As the practitioner's services do not relate to any specific supply, fees are a general overhead of the business concerned.

(a) Insolvent businesses which continue to trade.

- Where the business remains fully taxable it can deduct input tax on the practitioner's fees.
- Where the business remains or becomes partly exempt, deduction of input tax is subject to restriction in accordance with the partial exemption method in place.

(*b*) *Insolvent businesses which cease to trade but which remain registered.* The principal activity will be the sale of assets. As anything done in connection with the termination or intended termination of a business is done in the course or furtherance of that business, input tax incurred on the practitioner's fees should be considered in the light of the taxable status of the business prior to the insolvency. Where the business was previously fully taxable, the input tax on these fees is fully deductible. Where the business was previously partially exempt, the business should continue to use the method in place in the normal way.

A change of partial exemption method should be requested from HMRC if, in the light of changing circumstances, the method in place no longer produces a fair and reasonable attribution of input tax to taxable supplies. Any change of method cannot be applied retrospectively.

Where the practitioner's fees include costs charged by third parties, these should be separately identified and deducted to the extent that they are used to make taxable supplies.

(VAT Notice 700/56/02, para 15.3; Internal Guidance V1–15, para 20.4).

(6) **Distress/diligence**

HMRC may levy distress (do diligence in Scotland). See 17.4 and 17.5 CUSTOMS: POWERS respectively. In the case of

- a bankruptcy order or compulsory winding up order, any distress action which has not been completed (ie where the goods which have been distrained upon have not been sold) is abandoned. If distress has been completed within the three months immediately preceding the date of a bankruptcy order, the proceeds of the distress may be payable to the trustee in bankruptcy if the bankrupt is unable to pay the preferential creditors in full. In Scotland, distress action will not be taken against a trader who has been sequestrated within the preceding three years; and
- a creditors' or members' voluntary winding up or an administrative receivership, if distress has been levied (goods have been poinded) before the appointment of a liquidator or administrative receiver, then the distress/poinding remains valid and will be maintained and/or completed.

Any money received by HMRC for the sale of distrained goods will be set against the earliest pre-insolvency liability and HMRC's claim amended accordingly.

Where a floating charge crystallises on insolvency, the distress will be maintained if HMRC have already levied on goods which are subject to the floating charge.

(VAT Notice 700/56/02, paras 14.1–14.5).

(7) **Retention of records**

The liquidator of an insolvent company may destroy the books, papers and records, including the VAT records, one year after the date of dissolution of the company. [*SI 1994/2507, Reg 16*]. By concession, official receivers may also, on request, destroy the books and records of a company after one year. Normal rules for retention of records apply to other insolvencies, ie records should normally be retained for six years. (VAT Notice 700/56/02, para 19.1).

(8) **Viability studies by accountants**

Accountants engaged to conduct viability studies are treated as making supplies of their services to the person who has commissioned the work, instructed them and who receives the end product. The effect of this is as follows.

- Where either the company or the bank commission the work, the accountants should issue any invoices to the company or bank (as the case may be). The supply is then received for business purposes and input tax is deductible subject to the normal rules. The supply is not necessarily made to the person paying for the services. The fact that the other party, or a third party, receives a copy of the report is not relevant.
- Where the bank receives one report and the company another, the accountant is making two separate supplies and should issue separate invoices to allow recovery of input tax subject to the normal rules.
- Where the company and bank issue joint instructions and receive copies of the same report, the accountant should issue invoices for 50% of the cost to each party.
- Where the company commissions the work but does not receive a copy of the report, the accountant's supply is to the company but is not used for business purposes. Therefore neither the company nor the bank can recover any input tax.

(Internal Guidance V1–3, para 17.4; Business Brief 6/95).

See also *Eagle Trust plc (VTD 12871) (TVC 34.93)*.

36.12 DEREGISTRATION

Deregistration should be applied for as soon as trading has ceased and VAT on remaining taxable stocks and assets would be £250 or less.

The deregistration process depends on the type of insolvency.

- In a bankruptcy, sequestration, compulsory liquidation, partners' liquidation or creditors' or members' voluntary liquidation, HMRC issue Form VAT 167 (a deregistration questionnaire) at the same time as lodging their claim. They subsequently issue a warning letter (Form VAT 168) five weeks after Form VAT 167 advising that, unless a reply is received within seven days, deregistration will be automatically effected on the eighth day without notification. If at any time after the issue of Form VAT 167 and within seven days of issue of Form VAT 168, the office holder contacts HMRC to say that deregistration is not appropriate, the deregistration process will be suspended until agreed with HMRC. Once deregistration has been agreed, a final VAT return (Form VAT 193) is issued for completion.
- In an administrative receivership, HMRC issue Form VAT 167 (a deregistration questionnaire) at the same time as lodging their claim but deregistration is not

effected until the office holder confirms that it is appropriate. Once deregistration has been agreed, a final VAT return (Form VAT 193) is issued for completion.

- In voluntary arrangements, deeds and schemes of arrangement, county court administration orders, Scottish trust deeds, administration orders, partnership administration orders, and deceased persons' administration orders, the normal rules for deregistration and submission of VAT returns apply.

(VAT Notice 700/56/02, paras 6.1–6.4).

36.13 POST-DEREGISTRATION

Output tax. Any output tax arising after the date of deregistration should be accounted for on Form VAT 833.

- In deeds and schemes of arrangement, county court administration orders, Scottish trust deeds and deceased persons' administration orders (see 36.1 above for these terms), Form VAT 833 should be obtained from the National Advice Service (tel: 0845 010 9000) and submitted to the VAT Central Unit at Southend.
- In all other insolvencies, Form VAT 833 can be requested from Legal Recovery Unit, Liverpool, and must be returned there with full payment of any VAT due.

See 36.16 below for how *Law of Property Act* receivers should account for output tax.

Input tax – Form VAT 426 procedure. A special scheme for claiming post-deregistration input tax on Form VAT 426 (available from the National Advice Service (tel: 0845 010 9000)) can be used by a trustee in bankruptcy, a trustee in sequestration (in Scotland), an official receiver, an official assignee (in Northern Ireland), a liquidator or an administrative receiver. The scheme is *not* available for use by solvent deregistered traders, office holders in informal insolvencies (see 36.1 above) and other incapacitated traders. These categories include supervisors in voluntary arrangements, administrators in administration orders, a trustee appointed under a trust deed (in Scotland), a receiver appointed under the *Law of Property Act 1925*, a receiver appointed in a partnership dispute, a receiver appointed by a court, a receiver appointed under the *Agricultural Credits Act 1928*, an office holder appointed for a scheme of arrangement, an administrator appointed for a deceased persons' administration order, and a liquidator in a members' voluntary liquidation.

Subject to the normal rules, the form can be used to claim VAT on

- services supplied after deregistration but relating to business carried on before deregistration;
- goods and services supplied and invoiced before deregistration that has not already been claimed on a VAT return;
- the services of agents (eg solicitors, estate agents, stockbrokers) unless relating to exempt supplies; and
- realisation fees.

The form can also be used to claim bad debt relief. It cannot be used to claim VAT relating to a petitioning creditor's costs.

The completed form should be sent to VAT 426 Claims Section, Insolvency Branch, Legal Recovery Unit, Queens Dock, Liverpool L74 4AA. It is not necessary to send supporting invoices with the claim unless felt necessary to clarify any transaction. The claim should be processed and paid within 30 working days. HMRC select some claims for verification, in which case a VAT officer will make arrangements to visit the office holder within 30 working days of receipt of the claim. Most verification visits will be made after HMRC have authorised the repayment claim. Because of the possibility of verification, all invoices supporting the claim must be retained with the relevant books and records.

Input tax - Form VAT 427 procedure. The normal procedure for reclaiming post-deregistration VAT on Form VAT 427 (see 35.11 INPUT TAX) should be used where a liquidator has been appointed in

- members' voluntary liquidations and all administration orders (in which case the Form VAT 427 should be sent to the VAT 426 Claims section in Liverpool, see above);
- Scottish trust deeds and deeds or schemes of arrangement (in which case the Form VAT 427 should be sent to the trader's appropriate deregistration unit); and
- voluntary arrangements (in which case the Form VAT 427 should be sent to the Voluntary Arrangement Service, Durrington Bridge House, Barrington Road, Worthing, West Sussex BN12 4SE).

(VAT Notice 700/56/02, paras 7.1–7.9).

36.14 GROUPS

In a VAT group of companies, the claim for preferential debts extends to a non-representative member because under *VATA 1994, s 43(1)* such a member is jointly and severally liable for VAT due from the representative member (*Re Nadler Enterprises Ltd, Ch D [1980] STC 457 (TVC 30.9)*). See 31 GROUPS OF COMPANIES.

Where the representative member of a group becomes insolvent, HMRC regard the group treatment as ceasing to have effect from the relevant date. All the members of the group are automatically deregistered and each solvent member which continues to trade is automatically re-registered. Any insolvent member can also apply to be re-registered provided the company continues to trade. Continuation of group treatment may be allowed on request, however, but this will require prompt action to avoid automatic deregistration.

If the representative member of a group remains solvent but another group member becomes insolvent, HMRC will not automatically exclude that member from the group.

36.15 PARTNERSHIPS

Where a partnership becomes insolvent, HMRC may pursue any of the partners for any liability due.

If all partners are insolvent, HMRC will lodge one claim with the office holder in the name of the partnership. This claim should stand in the joint estate and separate estates of all the insolvent partners. HMRC should therefore be included in any dividend declared in any of the insolvent estates.

If one or more partners remain solvent, responsibility for rendering returns and paying VAT remains with the solvent partner(s). HMRC may lodge a claim with the office holder of the estate of the insolvent partner(s) for any debts accrued up to the date of insolvency. An office holder who has VAT to account for on the administration of the insolvent estate must not account for it on a solvent partner's return. HMRC will issue forms to the office holder on request so that the VAT can be accounted for direct to HMRC.

If a partnership is wound up but individual partners remain solvent, the office holder is treated as the taxable person with effect from the date of the winding up and will be responsible for rendering returns and paying any VAT due on returns for the period after the date of winding up. A claim will be lodged with the office holder in the name of the insolvent partnership for any liabilities due to HMRC up to the date of winding up.

Where insolvent partners have different relevant dates, HMRC will lodge individual claims in the individual estates of the partners calculated from their respective relevant dates.

(VAT Notice 700/56/02, paras 16.1–16.5).

36.16 RECEIVERS APPOINTED UNDER THE LAW OF PROPERTY ACT 1925

A receiver appointed under the *Law of Property Act* is unlikely to be allowed to register separately for VAT. This is because the receiver is appointed under a legal charge and is deemed to be the agent of the company. The trader/directors retain responsibility for their own VAT registration and all taxable supplies made by either the trader or the receiver must normally be accounted for on the trader's registration. See *Sargent v C & E Commrs, CA [1995] STC 399 (TVC 14.92)* where it was held that 'incapacitated' in *SI 1995/2518, Reg 9* should be construed as 'incapable of carrying on business'. This would only result from administrative receivership, liquidation or administration and not from the partial incapacity resulting from the appointment of a receiver of specific properties.

If a *Law of Property Act* receiver makes continuing supplies such as renting or leasing, then any VAT due should be accounted for through the trader's VAT account and the trader's VAT registration number should be used on any invoices issued. If the VAT-registered person does not agree to this, the receiver may account for output tax separately via a Form VAT 833.

If assets are sold, then the VAT due must be accounted for and paid to HMRC using Form VAT 833 (obtainable from the National Advice Service (tel: 0845 010 9000)). The trader's VAT registration number should be used on sales invoices or quoted on the Form VAT 833.

Law of Property Act receivers cannot make a separate claim for the input tax which should properly be claimed via the trader's VAT return.

(VAT Notice 700/56/02, paras 17.1, 17.2).

36.17 BANKRUPT CONTINUING TO TRADE

Where trading continues after bankruptcy, the bankrupt retains responsibility for the submission of VAT returns and payment of VAT covering post-bankruptcy periods. HMRC will establish the pre-bankruptcy position so that they can lodge a claim with, or make a repayment to, the office holder, or operate Crown set-off (see 36.8 above) as appropriate.

If the office holder has VAT to account for in respect of the period of administration, he must not include this VAT on the business's post-bankruptcy returns. HMRC will issue forms on request so that VAT can be accounted for direct to them.

(VAT Notice 700/56/02, paras 9.1, 9.2).

37 Insurance

De Voil Indirect Tax Service. See V4.121.

The contents of this chapter are as follows.

37.1 INTRODUCTION

Characteristics of insurance. There is no legal definition of insurance. In *Medical Defence Union Ltd v Department of Trade [1979] 2 All ER 421* the judge held that there must be three specific elements present in any contract of insurance.

- The contract must provide that the insured will become entitled to money or money's worth on the occurrence of some event. The reference to 'money or money's worth' means that a claim can be settled through the provision of a service or replacement goods.
- The event must be one which involves some element of uncertainty. If the element of uncertainty is absent, any 'premiums' paid would more closely resemble contributions to a savings plan. (It could be argued that there is no uncertainty involved with life insurance. However, the timing of claims is the uncertain factor.)
- The insured must have an insurable interest in the subject matter of the contract. This means that if the insured risk occurs, the person who is insured stands to suffer some loss.

Generally, HMRC regard something as insurance for VAT purposes if it is an activity that requires the provider to be authorised as an insurer under the provisions of the *Financial Services and Markets Act 2000* (*FSMA*).

In addition to this, they accept that

- certain funeral plan contracts are insurance (and therefore exempt from VAT) even though they are not regulated as such under the *FSMA* insurance regulatory provisions (see 37.6(3) below); and
- vehicle breakdown insurance is insurance even though providers are given a specific exclusion under the *FSMA* from the requirement to be authorised (see 37.6(11) below).

The regulation of insurance. The *Financial Services and Markets Act 2000* is the law under which financial services, including insurance, are regulated in the UK. The FSMA came into force on 1 December 2001 and replaced the previous law regulating insurance, the *Insurance Companies Act 1982*.

The provisions of the *FSMA* make it illegal for UK businesses to effect contracts of insurance without being authorised to do so (with the exception of certain bodies specifically granted exemption from the need for authorisation). The regulation of companies and unincorporated bodies under *FSMA, s 19* is carried out by the Financial Services Authority (FSA).

(VAT Notice 701/36/02, paras 2.2, 2.3; Internal Guidance V1–7, Chapter 17 para 2.3).

37.2 PLACE OF SUPPLY OF INSURANCE SERVICES

Although no VAT is payable on insurance wherever it is supplied, the place of supply is important for VAT purposes because it determines whether or not VAT can be recovered on any costs incurred in making that supply.

Special place of supply rules apply to services falling within *VATA 1994, Sch 5 paras 1–8*. These include insurance services (*Sch 5 para 5*) and services rendered by one person to another in procuring such services for the other (*Sch 5 para 8*).

The place of supply of such services is treated as being

(*a*) where the *recipient* belongs if the recipient

- belongs in a country, other than the Isle of Man, which is not an EC country; or
- belongs in an EC country other than that of the supplier and the insurance services are supplied to the recipient for business purposes; and

(*b*) where the *supplier* belongs in all other cases, ie where the recipient

- belongs in the UK or Isle of Man; or
- belongs in an EC country but not in the same country as the supplier and receives the supply other than for business purposes.

[*VATA 1994, s 7(10)(11); SI 1992/3121, Art 16*].

See 64.19 SUPPLY for the place of belonging and 21.2 EUROPEAN COMMUNITY: GENERAL for the countries comprising the EC.

The place of supply rules for insurance above, also apply to reinsurance. Supplies of reinsurance are made to the principal insurer and not to the parties insured under the policy. The VAT treatment of a supply of reinsurance, therefore, is determined by the place of belonging of the insurer to whom the reinsurance is supplied.

Multiple insured parties. Some policies name more than one party as being insured under the contract. The customer's place of belonging in such instances should be determined by reference to the principal insured. Where there is no one principal insured and insured parties are based both inside and outside the EC, the supply of insurance should be treated as being received where the majority of the insured parties belong or, where applicable, where the party belongs that has been most directly involved in entering into the contract and/or stands to be the main beneficiary.

(VAT Notice 701/36/02, paras 6.1, 6.3, 6.4).

37.3 **INPUT TAX RECOVERY IN RESPECT OF INSURANCE SERVICES**

Subject to the normal rules, input tax may be recovered which relates to

(*a*) taxable supplies of insurance services (ie supplies with a place of supply in the UK other than exempt supplies);

(*b*) supplies of insurance services with a place of supply outside the UK which would be taxable if made in the UK; and

(*c*) supplies of insurance services which

(i) are supplied to a person who belongs outside the EC; or

(ii) are directly linked to the export of goods to a place outside the EC; or

(iii) consist of the provision of intermediary services in relation to any transaction within (i) or (ii) above

where that supply is exempt or would have been exempt if made in the UK.

See 64.19 SUPPLY for the place of belonging and 21.2 EUROPEAN COMMUNITY: GENERAL for the countries comprising the EC.

Apart from the special cases in (*c*) above, input tax which relates to exempt supplies of insurance services cannot be recovered.

[*VATA 1994, s 26(1)(2); SI 1992/3123; SI 1999/3121*].

HMRC regard the entitlement to input tax under (*c*)(ii) above as only applying where

- the goods are being exported by the recipient of the insurance;
- the insurance is directly linked to the specific goods being exported; and
- the insurance covers the risks of the person who owns the goods or is responsible for their export.

(VAT Notice 701/36/02, para 6.6).

37.4 **SUPPLIES OF INSURANCE AND REINSURANCE**

EC legislation. See 22.18(*a*) EUROPEAN COMMUNITY LEGISLATION.

With effect from1 January 2005, exemption applies to all insurance and reinsurance transactions [*VATA 1994, Sch 9 Group 2, Item 1; SI 2004/3083*] and no longer depends upon the status of the provider.

This change in the legislation follows the decision in *Card Protection Plan Ltd v C & E Commrs, CJEC [1999] STC 270 (TVC 21.223)* where the CJEC held that under EC law the UK could not restrict the scope of exemption for insurance transactions exclusively to supplies by insurers who were permitted by national law to pursue the activity of an insurer. The House of Lords subsequently held that, in the light of the CJEC ruling, the company was making exempt supplies of insurance (*HL [2001] STC 174 (TVC 36.32)*).

Although this means that insurance supplied by an unauthorised insurer is exempt from VAT, such a business could be liable to prosecution under the *Financial Services and Markets Act 2000* and HMRC may refer cases that come to their attention to the Financial Services Authority. Businesses are therefore advised to clarify their regulatory position with the Financial Services Authority (Authorisation Enquiries Department, 25 The North Colonnade, Canary Wharf, London E14 5HS: tel 020 7676 1000).

As a result of the UK legislation, the place of supply rules in 37.2 above, and the input tax recovery rules in 37.3 above, the VAT position of insurance and reinsurance in the UK can be summarised as follows.

	Insured belonging in			
	UK	*EC (non-business)*	*EC (business)*	*Non-EC*
Insurance directly related to the export of goods to a place outside the EC	E(R)	E(R)	OS(R)	OS(R)
All other classes of insurance	E	E	OS	OS(R))

Key

E = Exempt (no input tax recovery)

E(R) = Exempt but with refund of related input tax

OS = Outside the scope of UK VAT with no refund of related input tax

OS(R)= Outside the scope of UK VAT with refund of related input tax

(VAT Notice 701/36/02, para 6.6).

In *Winterthur Life UK Ltd (VTD 14935) (TVC 36.9)* the operation of personal pension schemes by a group of companies was held to be an exempt supply of insurance services. On the facts, the services were not simply trust administration but embodied insurance contracts and were 'part and parcel' of the provision of insurance.

Before 1 January 2005, UK VAT legislation restricted VAT exemption for insurance or reinsurance to supplies in the course of insurance business (ie business which consisted of effecting and carrying out 'contract' of insurance') as set out in (*a*)–(*f*) below. However, following the decision in *Card Protection Plan* above, HMRC accepted that a business providing insurance without permission was entitled to exemption and that consequently, to all intents and purposes, (*a*)–(*f*) below were redundant. But the same comments applied as above regarding insurance supplied by an unauthorised insurer.

(*a*) A person who has permission under *Financial Services and Markets Act 2000, Part 4* to effect or carry out contracts of insurance (*before 1 December 2001*, a person who was authorised under *Insurance Companies Act 1982, ss 3, 4*).

(*b*) A person who is exempt in respect of effecting or carrying out contracts of insurance by reason of an order under *Financial Services and Markets Act 2000, s 38* and accordingly may effect or carry out contracts of insurance without contravening the general prohibition (*before 1 December 2001*, a person exempt under *Insurance Companies Act 1982, s 2* from the requirement to be authorised).

(*c*) A person who carries on an 'insurance market activity' within the meaning given in *Financial Services and Markets Act 2000, s 316*(*3*).

(*d*) A person (not falling within (*a*) above) who would require permission to effect or carry out

(i) a contract of insurance under which the benefits provided by that person are exclusively or primarily benefits in kind in the event of accident to or breakdown of a vehicle, or

(ii) a contract in the course of a 'Community co-insurance operation',

but for the identity of the person carrying on that activity.

'*Community co-insurance operation*' has the same meaning as in *EC Council Directive 78/472/EEC* of 30 May 1978 on the co-ordination of laws, regulations and administrative provisions relating to Community co-insurance.

(*e*) An insurer or reinsurer who belongs outside the UK where the insurance or reinsurances relates to any of the risks or other things described in the Annex to *EC Council Directive 73/239/EEC* of 24 July 1973 (the 'first non-life insurance directive') or the Annex to EC Council Directive 79/267/EEC of 5 March 1979 (the 'first life insurance directive') (*before 1 December 2001*, any of the risks or other things described in *Insurance Companies Act 1982, Sch 1, Sch 2*).

(*f*) The Export Credits Guarantee Department.

'*Contracts of insurance*' and the effecting and carrying out of such contracts must be read with *Financial Services and Markets Act 2000, s 2* (and any relevant order made under it) and *Sch 2*.

[*VATA 1994, Sch 9 Group 2 Items 1–3, Notes (A1),(B1),(C1); SI 2001/3649, Art 347 before amendment*].

37.5 **Reinsurance**

Reinsurance contracts are those under which an original insurer is indemnified by a reinsurer for a risk undertaken by the original insurer. (VAT Notice 701/36/20, para 2.2). Unless specifically stated otherwise, references to insurance in this chapter are to be taken to include reinsurance.

Abatement of costs. A reinsurer frequently reimburses the insurer for part of the cost of obtaining the original insurance. The technical term given to this arrangement is an abatement of costs although it may be described as commission. There is no supply to the reinsurer in respect of this deduction and the payment is outside the scope of VAT.

Right to deduct input tax. The right to deduct input tax relating to supplies of reinsurance is determined by where the insurance company receiving the reinsurance belongs, and not by where the recipient of the underlying insurance belongs. Only where the recipient is outside the EC is there an entitlement to recover related input tax. It is not possible to 'look through' the reinsurance transaction to base the liability on the underlying primary insurance.

Example A UK company provides reinsurance to an insurer based in the EC. It may not reclaim input tax in respect of the supply, even if the parties who received the initial supply of insurance belong outside the EC.

If the EC insurer in the above example has an entitlement to input tax recovery because the insurance is directly linked to the export of goods outside the EC, the entitlement to input tax recovery does not extend to the reinsurer.

(Internal Guidance V1–7, Chapter 17 paras 3.4, 6.6).

37.6 **Particular supplies of insurance**

(1) **Block insurance policies**

The key characteristics of a block policy are that

- there is a contract between the block policyholder and the insurer which allows the block policyholder to effect insurance cover subject to certain conditions;
- the block policyholder, acting in its own name, procures insurance cover for third parties from the insurer;
- there is a contractual relationship between the block policyholder and third parties under which the insurance is procured; and
- the block policyholder stands in place of the insurer in effecting the supply of insurance to the third parties.

Following the decision in *Card Protection Plan Ltd v C & E Commrs, CJEC [1999] STC 270 (TVC 21.223)* HMRC regard supplies made by block policyholders as being insurance transactions for the purposes of the VAT exemption, even though they would not be seen as insurance for regulatory purposes. This means that block policyholders are acting as principals when they are effecting insurance transactions rather than as intermediaries arranging supplies of insurance.

This type of policy is often taken out by a supplier of goods or services to cover a number of small transactions over a set period, eg

- a removal company may take out a block policy to provide its customers with insurance against the risk of damage to their belongings during the house move; or
- a pony club may arrange insurance under a block policy to provide its members with cover against the risk of injury or liability for another's injury whilst taking part in equestrian events.

Sometimes a block policy will cover the risks of the block policyholder as well as those of their customers (eg the removal company's policy may also cover its own risk of damaging its customers' property).

Block policyholders supply VAT-exempt insurance transactions as principals rather than insurance-related services as intermediaries. As a result, the whole consideration received by a block policyholder (ie in respect of own services and the purchase of the insurance cover for customers) is income of the business. This could have implications for the calculation of recoverable input tax under the partial exemption method used.

(VAT Notice 701/36/02, para 2.5).

(2) **Supplies by Friendly Societies**

Friendly Societies are organisations registered under the *Financial Services and Markets Act 2000*. Their main purpose is to provide insurance against distress in the event of accident, sickness, old age and widowhood. Their insurance capital is provided by subscriptions from members.

Where these subscriptions relate solely to the provision of insurance, they are exempt from VAT. If the subscription also covers other goods and services, the part of the subscription relating to those other supplies is not exempt as insurance but may qualify for VAT relief elsewhere (eg under the exemption which covers certain supplies relating to health and welfare).

(VAT Notice 701/36/02, para 3.2).

(3) **Funeral plans**

Some funeral plans are written under contracts of insurance, so that on death a life insurance policy pays out the cost of the funeral. These types of funeral plan are treated as insurance for VAT purposes, and therefore exempt, even though they are not regulated as such.

Where a funeral plan represents pre-payment for a funeral it will not be exempt as insurance but will probably be eligible for exemption as the provision of a funeral (see 19.6 DEATH AND INCAPACITY).

Management charges for funeral plans which are not insurance and are not prepayments (for example, where the client's money is placed in a trust to be spent on a funeral on his death) are standard-rated.

(VAT Notice 701/36/02, para 3.5).

(4) **Guarantees and warranties**

Retailers often sell guarantees and warranties with certain goods, such as domestic electrical equipment and cars.

Under a '*guarantee or warranty arrangement*', the purchase price of the goods includes an amount in consideration of which the manufacturer or retailer undertakes to replace or repair defective goods within a specified period.

Under an '*extended warranty arrangement*' the provider enters into a distinct contract under which it undertakes, for a consideration, to be subject to the same (and possibly some additional) obligations as covered in the original warranty. The provider of an extended warranty could be the retailer or manufacturer of the goods (or possibly a company within the same group as either of them), or be an independent third party company completely unconnected to the original supply of the goods.

Guarantees and warranties that are written under contracts of insurance (that is, those which are recognised as insurance by the Financial Services Authority (FSA)) will, in principle, fall within the VAT exemption for insurance (but see 37.7 below for insurance supplied with other goods and services).

The supply of a non-insurance warranty by a UK business is standard-rated. Guarantees and warranties provided by the manufacturer or retailer of the goods are very unlikely to be seen as insurance by the FSA because

- when provided by the retailer, the guarantee or warranty is seen as an automatic (often statutory) consequence of the contract of sale, not the provision of insurance cover; and
- in the case of the manufacturer's warranty, the risk of product failure lies within the control of the manufacturer and contracts under which the occurrence of an uncertain event lie within the control of either the provider or the recipient are unlikely to be regarded as insurance.

Some extended warranties may not be seen as insurance by the FSA regardless of who provides them (eg because the provider undertakes to maintain or repair goods at least partly at the recipient's expense or because the contract contains both insurance and non-insurance elements, such as regular servicing, and on balance the provider's obligation is not seen as being one to insure).

Where a business takes out an insurance policy to protect against the risk of there being a shortfall in the fund used to pay for any repairs covered by a warranty, there is no contract of insurance between the insurer and the customer taking out the warranty. The supply of the insurance and the supply of the warranty are two separate supplies, one exempt and one taxable.

(VAT Notice 701/36/02, para 3.7).

(5) **Insurance directly linked to exports of goods outside the EC**

There is specific provision for input tax to be recovered if it is incurred in respect of supplies of insurance which are *directly linked* to exports of goods to a place outside the EC. See 37.3(*c*) above.

Types of cover under a policy qualifying as 'directly linked' could include delay of delivery of, and loss or theft of, or damage to, goods. Not included, for example, is fire insurance cover for a warehouse used for storing goods in the UK prior to their eventual export.

A particular policy may not only cover risks associated with a trader's exports of goods but also his imports of goods and/or dispatches of goods to other EC countries. In such a case, an apportionment must be made to identify the appropriate export element. If the insurer is unable to establish this from information held, the trader should treat such supplies as exempt with no entitlement to input tax recovery.

(Internal Guidance V1–7, Chapter 17 para 6.8).

(6) **Marine Aviation and Transport (MAT) insurance**

The classes of risk covered by MAT insurance are

- accident (in connection with MAT risks only);
- railway rolling stock;
- aircraft;
- ships;
- goods in transit;
- aircraft liability; and
- liability of ships

but not

- motor and land vehicles;
- oil and gas rigs permanently fixed to the sea bed;
- specific policies for ships laid-up or aircraft grounded;
- specific policies for ships and aircraft under repair; and

- port and airport owners and operators' liability and manufacturers' liability.

Due to the nature of MAT insurance, HMRC have agreed guidelines with trade representatives for determining and recording where MAT insurance is supplied for VAT purposes. The trade agreement, summarised below, only applies to supplies of MAT insurance, it does not extend to supplies of other types of insurance or to MAT reinsurance.

Coding MAT insurance. There are three codes that should be used to identify the VAT status of supplies of MAT insurance.

X	to indicate that the supply of insurance was not directly related to an export of goods from inside to outside the EC and was made to a customer belonging within the EC and therefore carries with it no entitlement to input tax recovery.
Z	to indicate that the insurance was supplied to a customer belonging outside the EC or directly related to an export of goods from inside to outside the EC and therefore carries with it an entitlement to input tax recovery.
M	only if the insurance does not directly relate to the export of goods from inside to outside the EC and the policy has no clear principal insured and at least one, but not all, of the insured parties belongs outside the EC. The M (mixed) code gives an entitlement to treat 50% of input tax incurred on related goods and services as recoverable and 50% as non-recoverable.

Determining the place of supply for MAT insurance. The following rules should be used to determine whether the X or the Z code is appropriate, based on the location of the insured party/ies.

(*a*) *Single insured*. The insurer's address shown on the broker's slip (or equivalent document) is to be taken as the place of belonging of the insured. If no address is shown, the address should be determined by asking the broker or other intermediary who arranged the supply.

Where the insured has more than one address, the address on the slip or equivalent document should be used unless it is clear that this is simply an administrative address for payment or other purposes.

(*b*) *Multiple insureds*. Certain types of insurance (eg hull) often have multiple insureds identified on the slip, including the owner, managers, operators, the manning or crew agents, time charterers and mortgagors. Where possible, the principal insured should be identified and their place of belonging used to decide the VAT code as with a single assured under (*a*) above. The principal insured may be the only named insured (as distinct from others shown as additional insured) or may be the first-named on the policy. Where the principal insured cannot be identified, the places of belonging of all the insureds should be ascertained (if practicable) and the business coded according to whether the insured parties are all based in the EC, or all outside the EC or some inside and some outside.

(*c*) *Unidentified insured*(*s*). Where the place(s) of belonging of the insured(s) cannot otherwise be determined, VAT coding should be decided by reference to

- the country of origin of the business;
- the address of the originating broker/cover holder;
- the address of the overseas agent (where applicable) and
- any additional information on the slip.

In the case of conflict between indicators, best judgement should be used.

Where it is not possible to determine whether the X or Z code is appropriate using the above guidelines, then specific transactions may be coded M. The M code should only be used as a last resort where it is not possible to determine the place of belonging of the insured party or where an insurance contract provides cover for insured parties belonging both inside the EC and outside the EC and it is not possible to identify the principal insured party.

(VAT Notice 701/36/02, para 6.7; VAT Notice 700/57/04).

Also see VAT Notice 700/57/04 for details of an arrangement allowed to MAT insurance underwriters who are members of a particular trade association in respect of claims-related input tax and associated imported services.

(7) **Supplies by Medical and Welfare funds**

Subscriptions to such funds which, although not friendly societies, provide *specified* benefits in the event of illness, accident, etc are exempt from VAT as insurance.

Where the benefits are *not specified* and the amounts paid out are at the discretion of persons controlling the fund, the subscriptions may qualify as donations and be outside the scope of VAT.

(VAT Notice 701/36/02, para 3.3).

(8) **Protection and indemnity (P & I) clubs**

A P & I club is normally a mutual association of ship owners established to insure its members and specialising mainly in third party liability cover and insurance of the balance of collision risks not covered by the company or London market. P & I clubs are non-profit making and operate on a system of payments (usually based on the previous year's costs) with supplementary payments (termed 'calls') to settle claims and rebates to balance underwriting years. The club is deemed to be making a supply of insurance, the liabilities of which are determined as in the table in 37.4 above.

(VAT Notice 701/36/02, para 3.4).

(9) **Run-off business**

Where an insurer has ceased to underwrite insurance (or a particular class) but a liability remains to deal with claims under contracts already underwritten, such contracts are said to be 'running-off'. Any additional premiums receivable under existing contracts follow the liability of the original supply of insurance.

An insurer will often appoint third parties to administer the run-off of contracts on their behalf. Where a third party takes over responsibility for an insurer's run-off business, (including handling and settling claims and dealing with premium adjustments), the services supplied are not exempt as insurance transactions (ie as supplies of insurance). This is because the third party does not have a contractual relationship with the insured party and is not taking on the risk attached to the insurance which remains with the original insurer. It is possible, however, that some or all of the run-off services supplied by the third party will qualify for exemption as insurance-related services (see 37.15 below).

(VAT Notice 701/36/02, para 3.8).

(10) **Sale of part paid endowment policies**

The sale of part-paid endowment policies is not exempt under the insurance exemption because the risk covered by the underlying insurance remains that of the original policyholder. There is, however, a financial transaction taking place and the consideration received is exempt as finance.

(VAT Notice 701/36/02, para 3.9).

(11) **Vehicle breakdown services**

Subscriptions to motoring organisations usually include an element for assistance in the event of a breakdown provided under a contract of insurance. With this kind of insurance the benefits to the insured party (the member) are given in kind rather than in monetary form (that is, roadside repairs and recovery services).

Where vehicle breakdown insurance is provided as an independent supply, the element of the subscription that is attributable to it will be exempt from VAT. See 37.7 below for information on the VAT treatment of goods and/or services supplied together.

(VAT Notice 701/36/02, para 3.6).

37.7 Insurance supplied with other goods or services

Where exempt insurance is supplied with goods or services that are liable to VAT, it is necessary to determine the correct VAT treatment of the supplies. See 64.6 SUPPLY for the tests laid down in *Card Protection Plan Ltd v C & E Commrs, CJEC [1999] STC 270 (TVC 21.223)*. These involve:

(1) Identifying the essential features of a transaction to determine what the customer is actually receiving (ie is the customer receiving two or more supplies each distinct and independent from the other or is the customer receiving one supply made up of a number of component parts).

(2) If (1) above does not identify separate supplies, it is necessary to consider whether any of the parts can properly be regarded as a principal supply to which the other goods or services are ancillary (ie they do not constitute an aim in themselves but rather a means of better enjoying the principal supply).

Applying these tests to

- where there are two or more distinct supplies each independent of the other, the part of the consideration received which relates to insurance is exempt from VAT and the rest of the consideration is liable to VAT at the appropriate rate; and

- where there is one principal supply to which the other goods or services are ancillary, the whole transaction will take the VAT treatment of the principal supply. As a result,

  (i) where the insurance is the principal supply, the whole consideration received for both the insurance and the taxable goods or services is VAT-exempt; and

  (ii) where the insurance is ancillary to a supply of taxable goods or services, the whole consideration received is liable to VAT at the appropriate rate.

Each case has to be considered on its own merit but factors that could indicate separate rather than composite supplies include

- whether the customers can choose to have the goods or services without the insurance and (where appropriate) vice versa;
- whether both the insurance and the goods or services have their own price and this is reflected in the amount customers pay should they choose to have one without the other (ie the overall amount customers pay is reduced by the cost of the insurance should they decide to buy your goods or services without insurance); and
- whether customers are fully aware they are receiving more that one supply, as evidenced by the invoicing and contractual arrangements in place.

(VAT Notice 701/36/02, paras 4.1–4.3).

In *Peugeot Motor Co plc and Another v C & E Commrs, Ch D [2003] STC 1438 (TVC 46.17)*, the appellants sold cars to the public (end-users) either through dealers within the same VAT group (direct sales) or through independent franchised dealers or finance houses (indirect sales). In both categories, the appellants used various promotion schemes in which the end-user received motor insurance from an insurance company for no additional payment, the insurance company being paid by the appellants. The court held that the appellants made an insurance-related supply in respect of both direct and indirect sales but that, first, this formed part of a single supply with the motor car and, secondly, the insurance element of the supply was ancillary to the supply of the car. The full price paid for the car by the end-user (in the case of direct sales) or by the independent dealer or finance house (in the case of indirect sales) was taxable at the standard rate.

37.8 *Add-on services*

Add-on services are additional services supplied as part of a package with the main supply of insurance (eg helplines). They may be supplied under the contract of insurance itself or under a separate contract. They may also be provided by

- companies (which may or may not be insurers) other than the insurance company or companies underwriting a particular contract of insurance; or
- one or more of the underwriting insurers themselves.

The VAT treatment of these services depends upon the contractual arrangements in place between the parties and the nature of the services being supplied.

Add-on services supplied by third party to insurers. Where the add-on service being supplied to an insurer for incorporation into an insurance contract is

- itself insurance provided by one insurer (the 'add-on insurer') to another insurer (the 'direct insurer') who has a contract with a policyholder, the premium received by the add-on insurer from the direct insurer is exempt from VAT; and
- not insurance, and the service does not fall within another exemption or zero rate, VAT is chargeable on the supply by the third party to the insurer.

Some add-on services may qualify for VAT exemption as insurance-related services.

Add-on services supplied to policyholders. Where the add-on service is insurance, the entire supply is exempt. Each insurer is treated as making an exempt supply, the value of which is the part of the premium they have underwritten.

Where the add-on service is not insurance but is supplied by the insurer under the same contract as the insurance, there may be a liability to VAT on the consideration received by the insurer in respect of the add-on service. This depends on the liability of the add-on service and the nature of the package being supplied by the insurer (see 37.7 above).

Where the add-on service is not insurance and is supplied under a separate contract from that under which the insurance is supplied, there may be a liability to VAT on the consideration received in respect of the add-on service. In this instance, the add-on service is less likely to be ancillary to the supply of insurance and more likely to be a separate supply in its own right, but consideration should still be given to the guidance on single and composite supplies in 37.7 above.

(VAT Notice 701/36/02, para 4.4).

37.9 *Engineering insurance and inspection services*

Engineering insurance provides cover for large items of capital plant, machinery or structures on land such as industrial boilers, cranes and lifts. It is intended to protect the insured against the risk of the plant or equipment going wrong.

Insurers providing such insurance may also contract with customers to provide inspection services in connection with the insurance, perhaps to identify ways to reduce cover or prevent the need for a claim. Inspection services supplied on their own are subject to VAT at the standard rate. Therefore, an insurer supplying inspection services with insurance will need to determine the correct VAT treatment for its supplies under the rules in 37.7 above.

(VAT Notice 701/36/02, para 4.5).

37.10 Insurance claims

Establishing who is receiving supplies made in connection with, or in settlement of, insurance claims is important because this will determine who could have the right to recover any VAT charged on those supplies as input tax.

Supplies made to the insured party. Where supplies of claims-related goods or services are made to the insured party and the claim relates to their VAT-registered business, any VAT incurred on those supplies may be deducted as input tax subject to normal rules. Where the insured party can recover the VAT from HMRC, the insurer need normally only pay the net amount due (less any excess payable by the insured party) under the insurance claim.

Supplies made to the insurer. Where supplies of claims-related goods and services are made to the insurer, the amount of VAT recoverable depends on the insurer's partial exemption method.

Where an insurer incurs costs in respect of an individual claim (eg legal costs where the insurer is in dispute with the policyholder), any VAT on those costs is directly attributable to the associated supply of insurance and the recoverability of any VAT charged will depend upon whether or not the relevant supply of insurance gives a right to input tax deduction (see 37.3 above). See also *C & E Commrs v Deutsche Ruck Reinsurance Co Ltd, QB 1994, [1995] STC 495 (TVC 44.4)*.

Goods supplied to the insurer for transfer to the insured party. The insurer may choose to recover the VAT charged on the goods as input tax and account for output tax on the cost price when the goods are handed over. Alternatively, the insurer may refrain from claiming the VAT charged and, therefore, not be liable to account for output tax when the goods are transferred to the insured party.

Legal costs. Where an insurer obtains legal services in connection with, for example, policy interpretation or in relation to a dispute with a policyholder, the supply of the legal services is to the insurer. In the case of subrogated claims (ie claims where the insurer exercises its right to pursue or defend a claim against a third party in the name of the insured party) supplies of legal services in connection with those claims are made to the insured party and not to the insurer.

Loss adjusters, etc. Loss adjusters are normally contracted to act on behalf of the insurer and the supply of their services is therefore made to the insurer rather than the insured party. Loss assessors, on the other hand, are normally appointed by, and act in the interest of, the insured party and the supply of their services is therefore made to the insured party rather than to the insurer.

Indemnification by way of replacement goods or services. Where settlement of a claim is made by way of replacement goods or services, the supply position depends upon the terms of the contractual arrangements between the parties concerned. The supply of these replacement goods or services by a third party supplier is normally seen as being made to the insured party, although in some instances, the facts, including the terms of the insurance contract, may mean that the supply is made to the insurer.

Financial indemnification. If an insurer settles an insurance claim by paying money by way of financial indemnification to the insured party, there is no supply for VAT purposes. The money paid by the insurer in settlement of the claim is outside the scope of VAT.

(VAT Notice 701/36/02, paras 5.1–5.5).

37.11 *Surrender of goods following an insurance claim*

The disposal of

- works of art, antiques and collectors' items (see 71.3 WORKS OF ART, ETC), and
- second-hand goods (ie tangible movable property that is suitable for further use either as it is or after repair)

by an insurer who has taken possession of them in settlement of a claim under an insurance policy (eg salvaged goods damaged by fire or water or stolen goods recovered after a claim has been paid) is outside the scope of VAT provided the following conditions are met.

(*a*) The goods are in the same condition at the time of disposal as when they were taken into the insurer's possession.

(*b*) For goods other than motor cars

(i) if the goods had been supplied in the UK by the policyholder, that supply would not have been chargeable with VAT or would have been chargeable on less than full value;

(ii) if the goods have been imported into the UK, they must have borne VAT which has neither been reclaimed nor refunded; and

(iii) the goods must not have been reimported having previously been exported from the UK free of VAT by reason of zero-rating.

(*c*) In the case of motor cars, the VAT on any previous supply, acquisition or importation must have been wholly excluded from credit.

[*SI 1992/3122, Arts 2, 4; SI 1995/1268, Arts 2, 4; SI 1995/1269; SI 1995/1385; SI 1995/1667; SI 1999/3118; SI 1999/3120; SI 2001/3649, Art 432; SI 2004/3084; SI 2004/3085*].

Where the above conditions are not satisfied, VAT is chargeable on the full amount realised on the sale (not the original cost of the asset, see *Darlington Finance Ltd (VTD 1337) (TVC 42.75)*).

The insurer will therefore need to know the VAT status of the policyholder and be able to cross reference this information to the disposal of each item in order to decide whether VAT must be accounted for.

Motor vehicles received by an insurer as scrap metal are treated as tangible movable property rather than motor cars. Insurers are not required to account for VAT on the disposal of the scrap unless the policyholder would have charged VAT.

(VAT Notice 701/36/02, para 5.6).

37.12 Accounting for VAT on insurance transactions

Recovery of input tax. See 37.3 above for the rules on input tax recovery. Where input tax is recoverable relating to insurance within 37.3(*c*)(i) or (ii), HMRC will expect to see appropriate documentation in support of the claim, such as

- policy documents;
- cover notes;
- credit/debit notes;
- broker's slips; and
- any relevant correspondence.

Recovery of input tax incurred on supplies made by overseas branches. UK insurers can recover VAT incurred in the UK in connection with supplies made by overseas branches belonging outside the EC. As insurance companies may have difficulty identifying this input tax, HMRC have agreed with the Association of British Insurers (ABI) methods by which the amount of recoverable input tax can be arrived at. See VAT Notice 700/57/04.

Contact and representative offices of overseas insurers. Such offices are established for public relations purposes generally. They are not permitted to accept insurance business in the UK and do not normally make supplies in the UK.

A contact office can apply for voluntary registration in the UK if it incurs input tax in connection with supplies of insurance made outside the EC by the overseas insurer. Input tax reclaimed should be based on the proportion of supplies made by the overseas supplier as a result of contacts made by the contact office. It can only recover input tax on supplies on which VAT would have been recoverable had they been supplied in the UK.

Where the overseas insurer is unable to provide a breakdown of actual supplies made to policyholders, the notional liability of its supplies can be determined as follows.

- If the head office/branch is in the EC, it is treated as if it makes all supplies within the EC with no entitlement to recovery of related input tax.
- If the head office/branch is outside the EC, it is treated as if it makes all its supplies outside the EC with entitlement to recovery of input tax.
- If some establishments to which the contact office supplies services are inside, and some outside, the EC, the proportion of its input tax which may be reclaimed can be arrived at using the ratio of the number of non-EC establishments to the total number of establishments.

The contact office may apply for an alternative method. The agreement referred to above for recovery of input tax incurred in connection with supplies made by overseas branches also applies to overseas insurers with branches in the UK.

Tax point (time of supply). Although, as a general rule, supplies of insurance are exempt, the time of supply may be important for partial exemption purposes, eg to determine the recoverable proportion of non-attributable output tax where an outputs-based method is used.

The tax points for supplies of insurance covering one-off (short-term) risks are

- basic tax point – this occurs on completion of cover (ie when the insurance contract is finalised and signed); and
- actual tax point — this may arise when some or all of the premium is received in advance of the basic tax point.

Renewable policies covering long-term risks will normally represent continuous supplies of services, in which case the only tax point is the date of receipt of the premium.

Value of supplies. The value of supplies of insurance is the total gross premiums due under the contract without deducting any commission due to brokers and agents.

Accounting for VAT on run-off business. Where an insurer has contracts in run-off (see 37.6(9) above, and uses a partial exemption method based on the ratio of supplies which attract input tax recovery to total supplies, it should exclude return premiums from its calculations for run-off business only. This is to prevent the return premiums that are attributable to earlier VAT years/periods distorting the ratios of the current VAT year/period. Alternatively, to avoid complex calculations it may apply in writing to HMRC to use a method whereby a flat-rate recovery percentage is applied to its gross input tax based on the premium income for the last three years of active underwriting.

Accounting arrangements for the Lloyd's insurance market. HMRC have agreed special VAT accounting arrangements for the Lloyd's insurance market.

- *Syndicates with two or more members*. Where a syndicate has two or more members, it is the syndicate rather than the member that is registered for VAT as the taxable person for all syndicate transactions. Where there is a syndicate registration, a Lloyd's member, whether corporate or natural, can also have its own registration in relation to non-syndicate activities. Syndicate activities cannot, however, be dealt with through that registration.

- *Syndicates with only one member.* Where syndicate has only one member (which in practice only occurs with a corporate member) the syndicate cannot itself be registered. The corporate member must be registered and all syndicate business accounted for under its registration. Where the corporate member is covered by a group VAT registration, the group registration is used.
- *Managing agents.* Managing agents administer syndicates on behalf of members but are not themselves insurers. They may be VAT-registered, and their supplies are those of an insurance agent (see 37.13 below). The VAT treatment follows that of the insurance underwritten by the syndicate or syndicates that they manage.

Each Lloyd's syndicate, member or managing agent that registers for VAT and makes taxable and/or specified supplies in addition to exempt supplies, must agree a special partial exemption method with HMRC.

(VAT Notice 701/36/02, paras 7.1–7.7).

37.13 INSURANCE-RELATED SERVICES SUPPLIED BY INSURANCE BROKERS, AGENTS AND OTHER INTERMEDIARIES

Note. In *Staatssecretaris van Financiën v Arthur Andersen & Co, CJEC Case C–472/03; [2005] STC 508 (TVC 21.225A)* (a Netherlands case) the CJEC held that *EC Sixth Directive Art 13B(a)* must be interpreted as meaning that 'back office' activities, consisting in rendering services, for payment, to an insurance company do not constitute the performance of services relating to insurance transactions carried out by an insurance broker or an insurance agent within the meaning of that provision and do not qualify for exemption. The activities carried out by Andersen Consulting Management Consultants (ACMC) included the issuing, management and cancellation of policies, the management of claims and, in most cases, taking decisions that bound the insurer to enter into insurance contracts. To qualify for exemption, ACMC had to qualify as either insurance brokers or insurance agents. The CJEC held that the essential characteristic of insurance brokers was that they had complete freedom as to choice of insurer for their clients and that, although insurance agents were tied to a particular insurer, their essential characteristic was that they introduced prospective customers to that insurer. As ACMC did not qualify on either count, its services were taxable at the standard rate. Following this decision, HMRC's view is that UK VAT exemption for insurance-related services in *VATA 1994, Sch 9 Group 2* is too wide and must be amended. The CJEC judgment is binding on the UK but no action will be taken to change UK law or policy until a formal consultation is complete. In the meantime, there will be no change in the scope of the UK VAT exemption for insurance-related services as it is currently explained in HMRC guidance and notices. Businesses affected may, however, apply the revised VAT liability to their services from a current date or make an adjustment retrospectively. (Business Brief 11/05).

Subject to the above and the exceptions in 37.14 below, the provision by an insurance broker or an insurance agent of any of the 'services of an insurance intermediary' is exempt from VAT where those services are

(*a*) related to an insurance transaction or a reinsurance transaction (before 1 January 2005, related to the provision of exempt insurance or reinsurance within 37.4 above) (whether or not a contract of insurance or reinsurance is finally concluded); and (*b*) provided by the broker or agent in the course of acting in an '*intermediary capacity*' ie acting as an intermediary (or one of the intermediaries) between a person providing insurance or reinsurance (before 1 January 2005 a person providing exempt insurance under 37.4 above) and a person who is seeking insurance or reinsurance or is an insured person.

'*Services of an insurance intermediary*' consist of any of the following.

(i) Bringing together, with a view to the insurance or reinsurance of risks, of persons seeking and persons providing insurance and reinsurance.

It is sometimes difficult to distinguish between exempt introductory services under this heading and advertising services which are excluded from exemption (see 37.14(*a*) below). In such cases, HMRC accept that there is a single exempt supply of insurance-related introductory services where

- the intermediary is targeting its own customer base;
- the intermediary is paid per successful take-up of an insurance policy; and
- the product or the insurer is endorsed by the intermediary.

> *Example*
>
> A finance company is an agent for an insurer providing loan protection insurance. It recommends this insurance to all its customers. Those customers that take out a policy when taking out a loan complete a proposal form included with the loan agreement papers and returning this to the finance company. The finance company forwards it to the insurer and receives commission.
>
> There is an argument that the finance company is providing an advertising service. However, as the finance company is targeting its own customers; is recommending the product; and is being paid per successful take up, the commission it receives is treated as consideration for an exempt supply of introductory insurance services.

(VAT Notice 701/36/02, para 8.3).

(ii) Carrying out work preparatory to the conclusion of a contract of insurance or reinsurance.

(iii) Assistance in the administration and performance of such contracts, including claims handling.

Assistance in the administration. HMRC regard assisting in the administration and performance of contracts as covering the services that insurance intermediaries perform in connection with the day-to-day administration of policies, eg

- maintaining up-to-date details of policyholders; and
- dealing with requests from policyholders for changes to cover.

UK courts have found that the definition of assisting in the administration and performance of contracts of insurance goes wider than the examples above and include the following.

- Pension review services carried out as a result of the Financial Services Authority inspired review of possible pension mis-selling (see *Century Life plc v C & E Commrs, CA 2000, [2001] STC 38 (TVC 36.11)*). Following that decision, HMRC accept that mis-selling review services carried out on behalf of insurers are exempt when the supplier is required to be involved in the decision-making process (ie assessing whether, and how much, loss has occurred and/or the amount and appropriate form of redress) and acts as an insurance intermediary, having contact with insured persons on behalf of insurers.

  See also *Winterthur Life UK Ltd (No 3) (VTD 17572) (TVC 36.12)* where a company provided services to another company concerning the management of a self-administered personal pension scheme.

- Certain kinds of helpline services. See *C & V (Advice Line) Services Ltd (VTD 17310) (TVC 36.16)* where a company providing a telephone helpline service to an insurance company's customers was held to be acting as an insurance intermediary so that its supplies qualified for exemption.

  HMRC accept that where telephone helplines provide assistance to insured parties on matters such as variations of contract and the making of claims, these services are directly related to the supply of insurance and, where a third party supplies them to the insurer, their supplies will be exempt. Where such helpline services are only incidental to the supply of insurance (eg where a legal helpline gives advice to insured parties on legal matters generally but does not advise on matters specific to the contract of insurance itself, such as scope of cover or claims procedures) the supply to the insurer is taxable.

Claims handling. The term 'claims handling' is used to describe a number of services that may be provided by an intermediary following the making of a claim by a policyholder, including

- checking that documents are correctly completed;
- ensuring that the claim falls within the terms of a policy;
- processing the claim;
- ensuring that insurers are advised of their exposure;
- agreeing the validity and/or quantum of the claim and
- arranging for settlement to be made.

The supply of claims handling may also include a number of elements of an advisory, investigative, or administrative nature that would be subject to VAT if supplied in isolation. Where these elements form a minor and ancillary part of a single composite supply of claims handling, however, the entire supply will be exempt from VAT. See also 37.16 below for the VAT treatment of claims handling services supplied by loss adjusters and other experts in connection with the assessment of a claim.

(VAT Notice 701/36/02, paras 8.4, 8.5, 10.3, 10.4; Business Brief 3/01).

(iv) The collection of premiums.

An insurance intermediary may collect insurance premiums as part of another supply (eg exempt insurance introductory or administration services) but where a separate charge is made for these services, it will be exempt under this heading.

If the premium collection services are not supplied in connection with other insurance intermediary services, they may be liable to VAT (eg the services of a debt-collector collecting overdue premiums for an insurer).

Where an employer, who did not arrange the original insurance, allows an insurer to use its payroll system to collect premiums from its employees by deductions from their pay, the consideration received by the employer falls within the exemption for finance rather than insurance.

(VAT Notice 701/36/02, para 8.6).

[*VATA 1994, Sch 9 Group 2 Item 4, Notes* (*1*), (*2*)*; FA 1997, s 38; SI 2001/3649, Art 347; SI 2004/3083*].

In *Re Försäkringsaktiebolaget Skandia, CJEC [2001] STC 754 (TVC 21.224)* (a Swedish case) an insurance company (S) undertook to run the insurance business of one of its subsidiary companies including the sale of insurance and the settlement of claims. The CJEC held that the undertaking did not qualify as an 'insurance transaction' so that the supply was one of management services on which VAT was chargeable. The decision was reached on the basis that the third party service provider did not have any relationship with the insured. The Court did not examine whether the services could have been exempt 'insurance-related services', because the terms of Skandia's licence under Swedish insurance regulations prevented it from acting as an agent or broker. As a result, the decision is expected to have limited impact in the UK, where services provided to an insurer on an outsourced basis would normally fall within the 'insurance-related services' definition.

Brokers and agents. For VAT purposes, brokers and agents are defined in terms of what they do rather than what they are and, as well as insurance brokers and agents by profession, it can apply to other intermediaries making supplies of 'related services'. (VAT Notice 701/36/02, para 9.1).

Members' agents for Lloyd's underwriters. In *SOC Private Capital Ltd (VTD 17747) (TVC 36.13)* the tribunal held that supplies of insurance were made by underwriting members (rather than the syndicates) and therefore a company acting as a members' agent for Lloyds' underwriters was an insurance agent within *VATA 1994, Sch 9 Group 2 Item 4* above and its supplies qualified for exemption.

Insurance involving more than one broker or agent. Where more than one party is involved in procuring a specific supply of insurance, each agent or broker in the chain may claim exemption for their supplies provided the criteria set out above are met in relation to each supply. (Internal Guidance V1–7, Chapter 17 para 5.6).

37.14 Supplies not regarded as services of an insurance intermediary

Supplies of the following services are specifically excluded from exemption under 37.17 above.

(*a*) Market research, product design, advertising, promotional or similar services (or the collection, collation and provision of information for use in connection with such activities).

> *Example*
>
> A firm of actuaries designs a new life insurance product. A life insurance company takes up the product, and agrees to pay the actuaries a commission in respect of each policy sold. The actuaries do not take any part in selling the product to customers.
>
> The actuaries make a taxable supply of product design services as product design is not an insurance related service and is not provided in an intermediary capacity.

(Internal Guidance V1–7, Chapter 17 section 5.15).

(*b*) Valuation or inspection services. See also 37.9 above for inspection services and engineering insurance.

(*c*) Services by loss adjusters, average adjusters, motor assessors, surveyors or other experts unless

(i) the services consist of claims handling under a contract of insurance or reinsurance; and

(ii) the person handling the claim is authorised to act on behalf of the insurer or reinsurer and has written authority to accept or reject the claim, and to settle any amount agreed to be paid.

See also 37.16 below.

(*d*) Services supplied in pursuance of a contract of insurance or reinsurance (or any arrangements in connection with such a contract) either instead of any financial indemnity which the insurer is contractually obliged to provide or for the purpose of satisfying any claim under that contract (in whole or part). This applies, for example, where a plumber's services are supplied free of charge to the insured to mend a burst pipe and the insurer meets the plumber's fee. The fee is excluded from exemption. (VAT Notice 701/36/02, para 8.2).

[*VATA 1994, Sch 9 Group 2 Notes (7)–(10); FA 1997, s 38*].

Where one of the above excluded supplies is provided as a minor and ancillary part of a single composite supply of exempt insurance-related services provided in an intermediary capacity, the entire supply is treated as exempt. (VAT Notice 701/36/02, para 8.2). See also 27.31 FINANCIAL SERVICES for mixed supplies of advice and financial services by a financial adviser. These provisions equally apply to mixed supplies of advice and insurance-related intermediary services.

37.15 Particular supplies of insurance-related services

See the Note at 37.13 above.

(1) Broker-managed funds offered by life assurance companies

Life assurance backed broker-managed funds are provided under contracts between the life company which operates the fund, the policyholder and the broker who arranges the policy (usually referred to as the 'Broker Fund Adviser'). The Broker Fund Adviser, with authorisation from the policy holder/investor, provides investment advice to the life assurance company, recommending the switching of money invested between the various funds operated by the assurance company or, where permitted, directly into other forms of investment (eg shares or gilts).

Commission paid to the Broker Fund Adviser for arranging the life insurance policy is exempt under 37.13 above. Any other fees for services (including investment advisory services and any 'performance fee' based on the increased value of investments) are standard-rated.

(VAT Notice 701/36/02, para 10.7).

(2) **Internet services**

There are any number of ways in which the internet can be used in connection with insurance and the liability of supplies of internet services to insurers (or possibly to insured or prospective insured parties) need to be considered on their own merits using the guidance laid out in 37.13 above. Factors indicating that a supply of Internet services is exempt as a supply of insurance-related services include:

- acting between insurers and insured (or prospective insured) parties;
- requirement for some specific insurance input rather than just pure facilitation; and
- direct connection to contracts of insurance either by bringing them about initially, or administering them, or handling claims made under them.

(VAT Notice 701/36/02, para 10.5).

(3) **Protection and Indemnity (P & I) Club managers and agents**

See 37.6(8) above for what is meant by a P & I Club.

P & I Club managers are required to be separately VAT-registered from the clubs they manage. Services which they carry out include the day-to-day running of the club, employing staff, and assessing the level and weighting of contributions. They may also supply premises and facilities. If P & I Club managers are empowered to accept risks on behalf of the club, HMRC accept that they are intermediaries making supplies of related services that are exempt from VAT when supplied in the UK.

A P & I Club agent acts for a P & I Club manager when the manager has no presence in the UK. They make supplies of management services to the manager that would be taxable if supplied in the UK. These services are usually the kind of intangible services that are supplied where the recipient of the supply belongs. Where these services are supplied to P & I Club managers belonging outside the UK, therefore, they are outside the scope of VAT with input tax recovery. Management services that do not qualify as intangible services, however, will be liable to UK VAT regardless of where the recipient belongs.

(VAT Notice 701/36/02, para 10.2).

(4) **Run-off services**

See 37.6(9) above for run-off business generally. An insurer will often appoint a third party to administer the run-off of insurance contracts on its behalf. The sort of services supplied could include

- responsibility for accountancy and legal work in connection with the business in run-off;
- services of handling and settling claims; and
- dealing with additional or return premium adjustments.

A composite supply of such run-off services falls within the VAT exemption as insurance-related services. Separate supplies of administrative services (such as accountancy, supplies of staff and management of invested premiums) do not qualify for exemption and are liable to VAT when supplied in the UK.

(VAT Notice 701/36/02, para 10.6).

(5) **Telephone sales services**

In *Teletech UK Ltd (VTD 18080) (TVC 36.14)* the company acted on behalf of an insurance company, cold-selling health insurance policies by telephone using contact lists provided by the insurer. The tribunal held that the company's services were exempt on the grounds that it was selling (or trying to sell) insurance policies as agents. The decisive factor was that, where calls led to sales, the company was able to put the insurer on risk and the customer on cover. The Tribunal Chairman also observed that the manner of remuneration, ie whether by flat fee (as in this case) or commission, had no bearing on the VAT treatment.

As a result of this decision, HMRC now accept that supplies of telephone sales services to insurers are exempt when the call centre is able to put the insurer 'on risk' and the customer 'on cover' at the point of sale. This applies regardless of whether the call centre provider is remunerated by way of commission or flat-rate fee.

(VAT Notice 701/36/02, para 10.4; Business Brief 7/03).

37.16 **Loss adjusters and similar 'experts'**

See the Note at 37.13 above.

Services of loss adjusters, average adjusters, motor assessors, surveyors or 'other experts' (eg assessing damage or investigating potential fraud) are normally standard-rated. If they also provide insurance claims handling services, however, their services will be exempt when acting as the agent of the insurer when supplying those services. But services qualify for exemption where all of the following conditions are met.

- The services consist in the handling of a claim under a contract of insurance or reinsurance;
- The person handling the claim is authorised when doing so to act on behalf of the insurer or reinsurer.
- That person holds the insurer's written authority (see below) to determine whether to accept or reject a claim.
- Where the claim is accepted in whole or in part, that person has the insurer's written authority to settle the amount to be paid on the claim.

[*VATA 1994, Sch 9 Group 2 Note* (*9*); *FA 1997, s 38*].

'*Other experts*' means anybody who is contracted by insurers to assess or value insurance claims because of their expertise in a particular field and could include

- solicitors assessing loss in personal injury claims cases;
- jewellers valuing items of stolen jewellery; or
- antiques experts assessing damage to antique furniture.

The term 'other expert' does not apply to specialist claims handling organisations. Where an insurer contracts a supply of claims handling services from a business, not because of that business's expertise in a particular field, but because of its expertise in claims handling generally, the services of the business are exempt under 37.13(iii) above and the above provisions do not apply.

Insurer's written authority. If an insurer gives written authority to another person (such as a broker) who in turn issues written authority to a loss adjuster, the loss adjuster's services will still be exempt provided that the original authority from the insurer gave the original recipient power to delegate the authority in this way.

The written authority must allow the loss adjuster, etc to investigate claims, perform any service necessary for the claim to be settled and agree the amount of a claim or cost of repairs or replacement without reference to the insurer. The authority may also include avoiding or repudiating claims. In all circumstances it must bind the insurance company to pay the amount of a claim or meet the cost of repair or replacement as determined by the loss adjuster.

Claims handling supplied with valuation/assessment services. Where a loss adjuster, etc supplies exempt claims handling services with taxable claims valuation and/or assessment services, the VAT treatment of the services depends upon whether they are provided as two separate supplies or as one composite supply with the claims handling services ancillary to the taxable services or vice versa. Where taxable valuation and/or assessment services are ancillary to a principal supply of claims handling, the whole supply is exempt from VAT.

(VAT Notice 701/36/02, para 9.3).

37.17 Insurance-related services supplied with other goods or services

See the Note at 37.13 above.

Insurance is frequently arranged by businesses in connection with other services or goods they are supplying as their main business activity, eg

- mechanical breakdown insurance (MBI) with cars and domestic appliances;
- travel insurance with holidays;
- insurance with removal services;
- insurance with rented property; and
- insurance with car hire.

Where this insurance is provided under a block insurance policy with the supplier of the goods or services being the policyholder, the appropriate VAT treatment is given in 37.6(1) above.

In other instances not involving block policies, there will be a separate supply of exempt insurance by the insurer to the customer buying the goods or services where

- the cover being supplied is genuine insurance which qualifies for exemption under 37.4 above; and

- it is the customer's own risk which is being insured and not the risk of the supplier of the goods or services.

A supplier of the goods or services who arranges cover for customers may be able to treat the insurance premiums received from the customers or onward payment to the insurer as a disbursement. See 37.19 below.

Treatment of arrangement fees and commission charged by suppliers of goods and services. Where

(i) a person supplies goods or services to a customer,

(ii) those goods or services are liable to VAT (and not zero-rated),

(iii) a transaction under which insurance is to be, or may be, arranged for the customer is entered into in connection with that supply,

(iv) insurance-related services are provided by the supplier of the goods or services (or a person 'connected' with that person (see 69.19 VALUATION) who deals directly with the customer in connection with the insurance), and

(v) the insurance-related services are not claims handling services (which are exempt under 37.13(iii) above without considering these requirements),

any amount charged by the supplier to the customer (eg an arrangement fee or commission) in addition to the premium is not exempt under 37.13 above unless

- a document containing details of the amount of the premium, and also any fees charged in addition to the premium, is prepared;
- those matters are disclosed to the customer at or before the time when the insurance transaction is entered into; and
- the supplier complies with any published requirements of HMRC as to the preparation and form of the document, the manner of disclosing those matters to the customer and delivery of a copy of the document to the customer.

If these conditions are not met, there is still no VAT chargeable on the amount collected by the supplier and passed on to the insurer for the supply of insurance. But any fees or commission received by the supplier for arranging the insurance is liable to VAT at the same rate as the goods or services themselves.

HMRC have published specific requirements in the following circumstances (which have the force of law).

(1) *Transactions by telephone or electronic communication.* The disclosure conditions may create a problem in such cases as the customer and supplier are not physically together when the sale takes place. To overcome this, if the insurance-related services are to be exempt, HMRC require a supplier selling taxable goods by such means to

  - make full disclosure of the premium at the time of the transaction (eg a trader selling holidays over the telephone must orally inform the customer of the amount of the premium and any fee charged over and above the premium in relation to the insurance);
  - have in place a system whereby the sales staff must annotate a document (even if this only involves ticking a box) at the time they make the oral or electronic disclosure to customers to indicate that they have done so;

- prepare, and issue to the customer, a document with the information required as above (albeit after the time the insurance transaction has been entered into); and
- retain a copy of these records as they would their normal VAT records.

(2) *Second-hand schemes.* Where a person supplies goods or services under one of the second-hand schemes, the disclosure must be made on the relevant VAT invoice issued by that person.

Subject to these requirements, it was held in *Smith Glaziers (Dunfermline) Ltd v C & E Commrs, HL [2003] STC 419 (TVC 36.21)* that the above provisions are concerned with identifying the information which the document must disclose rather than specifying any particular form. All that is necessary is that the allocation is unequivocally stated in the document, even if this requires some knowledge of arithmetic.

[*VATA 1994, Sch 9 Group 2 Notes (3)–(6); FA 1997, s 38*]. (VAT Notice 701/36/02, paras 11.1–11.3).

37.18 Insurance-related services supplied outside the UK

See the Note at 37.13 above.

Place of supply. Although no VAT is payable on qualifying insurance-related services regardless of where those services are supplied, the place where insurance-related services are supplied for VAT purposes is important because it helps to determine whether VAT on any costs incurred making that supply can be recovered. See 37.2 above for determining the place of supply of insurance services.

Determining who the customer is for services related to insurance and reinsurance. An insurance intermediary could be supplying insurance-related services to either the insured party (or the party seeking insurance) or to the insurer supplying the insurance. He could also be acting as a sub-agent and be supplying his services to another agent in the chain of supply of the insurance. It is, therefore, important to determine precisely who the customer is when one or more of the parties in the supply chain belongs outside the UK. This will be clear-cut in some cases (based on the contractual, financial and practical arrangements in place at the time) but in other instances, it is not so easily determined. HMRC will normally see the supply of intermediary services as being made to the insured party unless there are clear indications to the contrary. In the case of reinsurance, unless there are clear indications otherwise, services related to reinsurance are assumed to be made to the ceding insurer.

Input tax recovery. See 37.3 above. The following table summarises the position in relation to supplies of intermediary services by UK businesses.

	VAT treatment where place of supply is		
	UK	*Elsewhere in EC*	*Outside EC*
Services related to insurance directly linked to the export of specific goods from the EC to outside the EC	E(R)	OS(R)	OS(R)

	VAT treatment where place of supply is		
	UK	*Elsewhere in EC*	*Outside EC*
Other insurance-related services when insured party belongs in the UK or elsewhere in the EC	E	OS	OS(R)
Other insurance-related services when the insured party belongs outside the EC	E(R)	OS(R)	OS(R)

Key

E = Exempt (no input tax recovery)

E(R)= Exempt but with refund of related input tax

OS = Outside the scope of UK VAT with no refund of related input tax

OS(R)= Outside the scope of UK VAT with refund of related input tax

(VAT Notice 701/36/02, paras 12.1–12.3).

Claims handling services supplied to non-UK customers. The recipient of claims handling services is usually the insurer and not the insured. In order to determine the liability of claims handling services supplied outside the UK, it is necessary to establish the place of belonging of

- the insurance company;
- the claimant (the insured party); and
- the person providing the claims handling service.

The supply to an insurer of claims handling services that fall within the insurance exemption will be

- exempt if the insurer belongs in the UK;
- outside the scope of VAT with no input tax recovery if the insurer belongs in the EC; and
- outside the scope of VAT with input tax recovery if the insurer belongs outside the EC.

However, where the insurer belongs in the UK or elsewhere in the EC, there is a right of input tax recovery where the insured party belongs outside the EC.

If a supply of claims handling services does not qualify for exemption as an insurance-related service, it is liable to VAT at the standard rate when supplied in the UK and outside the scope with input tax recovery when supplied elsewhere.

(VAT Notice 701/36/02, para 12.4).

37.19 **Accounting for VAT on insurance-related services**

Input tax recovery. See 37.3 above for the rules on input tax recovery.

Tax points (time of supply). The time of supply for insurance-related services follows the normal tax point rules (see 64.49 *et seq* SUPPLY). The actual tax point occurs when a debit note or (where appropriate) VAT invoice is issued to the customer to collect the premium or separate fee (if one is charged) or the date on which payment is received, whichever happens first.

Value of supplies of related services. The value of a supply of insurance-related services is the amount of consideration received in respect of gross commission, flat-rate fee and/or recharge of costs incurred, whichever payment method applies to the particular transaction. In the case of commission, no deduction should be made for any commission payable in turn to other intermediaries employed. It is the gross commission, not the net retained or earned commission, that is the value for VAT purposes.

The amount of any premium collected to be passed back to the insurer in respect of the supply of insurance itself should not be included in the value of the supplies of related services.

Mechanical breakdown insurance (MBI). There are special rules for determining the value attributable to MBI when it is sold with a used vehicle for a single selling price. See 61.31 SECOND-HAND GOODS.

Disbursements. If a business makes supplies of goods or services and arranges insurance cover for its customers in connection with those goods or services, any premium collected from the customer to be passed on to the insurer for the supply of insurance may, in certain circumstances, be treated as a disbursement and therefore outside the scope of VAT. This applies only to the amount due from the customer to the insurer. It does not cover any amount retained by the business in respect of commission for insurance-related services or costs incurred in making the supplies (eg travel, subsistence and overhead costs passed on).

For the premium due to an insurer to qualify as a disbursement, all of the following conditions must be met.

- The customer must have specifically requested that the insurance cover is obtained on his behalf.
- It must be the customer's own risks which are insured under the policy.
- The supplier must recover only the exact amount of net premium from the customer.
- The amount paid by the customer must be in respect of cover for the customer alone.
- The exact amount of the net premium must be separately itemised on any invoice issued by the supplier to the customer.

Accounting procedures for company groups. Where a holding company arranges insurance cover for the group as a whole, any amount charged to each company for arranging the insurance are exempt as insurance-related services (subject to the conditions 37.17 above if the insurance is supplied with other goods or services). Where the exact insurance premium is charged to an associated or subsidiary company, this may be treated as a disbursement if the conditions under the heading *Disbursements* above are satisfied.

37.19 Insurance

If the companies are all part of the same VAT group (see 31 GROUPS OF COMPANIES), any charges between the members are not supplies for VAT purposes.

(VAT Notice 701/36/02, paras 13.1–13.5).

38 Interaction with Other Taxes

The contents of this chapter are as follows.

38.1 DIRECT TAXES

Direct taxes which are likely to interact with VAT are income tax, corporation tax and capital gains tax. In general such taxes are imposed on profits or gains or some other measure of monies receivable less monies payable. VAT as an indirect tax is charged on the *supply* of goods and services in the course or furtherance of a business [*VATA 1994, s 4*], so it is immaterial for the charging of VAT whether there is any money payment and whether any profit is made on the supply. For information regarding direct taxes see Tolley's Income Tax, Tolley's Corporation Tax and Tolley's Capital Gains Tax.

38.2 Business profits

Taxable persons making wholly taxable supplies. In general, a taxable person making wholly taxable supplies should treat the receipt for income tax or corporation tax purposes as being exclusive of any VAT charged. Similarly, expenditure for income tax, etc purposes (including capital items) should be treated as being exclusive of VAT if input VAT is able to be reclaimed on the related supply. If credit for input tax is specifically denied (eg most supplies of motor cars and business entertainment) the expenditure inclusive of VAT should be taken into account for income tax purposes. Any allowance made for bad debts for income tax purposes is inclusive of the VAT which has been accounted for on the related supply. (VAT on bad debts may be reclaimed from HMRC in certain circumstances, see 7 BAD DEBT RELIEF. It follows that if VAT is recoverable from HMRC it cannot be claimed for income tax purposes or alternatively a recovery of VAT should be treated as a taxable income receipt if a VAT-inclusive bad debt has previously been allowed.)

Taxable persons making both exempt and taxable supplies. A taxable person who makes both exempt and taxable supplies should treat income tax receipts as above. However, as under the partial exemption rules such a person will only be able to obtain credit for part of the input VAT applicable to expense etc payments made, it is necessary to allocate the VAT ultimately suffered to the various expense payments made. Inspectors of taxes are prepared to consider any reasonable arrangements made to carry out this apportionment. Where credit for VAT input is specifically denied, the related expenditure is VAT-inclusive for income tax purposes as explained above.

Non-taxable persons. A person who is *not* a taxable person (eg making wholly exempt supplies or below the registration limit) should treat all expenses, etc as being VAT-inclusive for income tax, etc purposes (including capital allowances).

(Inland Revenue Statement of Practice SP B1 7 May 1973).

38.3 Stock

Individuals, partnerships and companies, who are taxable persons for VAT should treat the cost of purchases, and hence the value of stock, as being VAT-exclusive. A taxable person who makes both taxable and exempt supplies is unable to obtain credit for input tax attributable to exempt supplies and accordingly the cost of purchases and value of trading stock should be inclusive of the VAT unable to be credited. (Inland Revenue Statement of Practice SP B2 3 December 1974).

38.4 **Tax on employment income**

Returns of expenses incurred by employees, etc and subsequently reimbursed by the employer (Forms P9D and P11D) should include any amounts of VAT suffered in connection with the expenses, whether or not the employer may subsequently obtain credit for the relevant input tax. Similar observations apply to returns of employee pecuniary liabilities met by the employer and to expenditure incurred by the employer in providing a benefit (including the use of an asset) for an employee. (Inland Revenue Statements of Practice SP A6 29 March 1973 and SP A7 17 July 1974).

Entertainers' expenses. Where agents' fees paid by actors, musicians, etc are deductible for employment income purposes, any additional VAT payable is also deductible. [*ITEPA 2003, s 352*].

38.5 **Subcontractors in the construction industry**

A subcontractor who is a taxable person for VAT should account for VAT on the total consideration which he charges for his services. Where the appropriate valid tax exemption certificate is not held or not presented, the person paying the consideration is obliged to make a deduction at a specified rate from the part of the payment representing labour and profit on materials. VAT and cost of materials are excluded. [*ICTA 1988, s 559(4)*]. (Inland Revenue Pamphlet IR 14/15).

38.6 **Capital gains tax**

If VAT is payable in respect of the acquisition of an asset but is available for credit by a taxable person, then the cost of the asset for capital gains tax purposes is the cost exclusive of VAT. Where no VAT credit is available the cost is inclusive of VAT ultimately suffered.

Where an asset is disposed of, any VAT on the supply of the asset is disregarded in computing the disposal consideration for capital gains tax purposes. It appears that a taxable person making both taxable and exempt supplies should treat as part of the capital gains tax cost of an asset the input VAT that was not available for credit in respect of the acquisition (see under 38.2 above). (Inland Revenue Statement of Practice SP D7 7 June 1973).

38.7 **Capital allowances**

Where the CAPITAL GOODS SCHEME (10) applies adjustments to the original input tax reclaimed may be necessary for a period of up to 10 years. Any additional VAT liability under the scheme is to be treated as extra qualifying capital expenditure incurred at the time when the VAT is paid. Similarly, any additional VAT rebate is to be taken into account in the capital allowances computation for the period in which it is repaid by HMRC. Earlier capital allowances computations are not disturbed. [*FA 1991, s 59, Sch 14*].

38.8 **VAT penalties, surcharge and interest**

No deduction is allowed in computing any income, profit or loss for tax purposes in respect of

- default surcharge under *VATA 1994, s 59* (see 52.15 PENALTIES);
- a penalty under *VATA 1994, ss 60–70* (see 52.9–52.14, 52.17–52.20 PENALTIES); or
- interest under *VATA 1994, s 74* (see 51.14 PAYMENT OF VAT).

Repayment supplement for VAT under *VATA 1994, s 79* is disregarded for income tax and corporation tax purposes.

[*ICTA 1988, s 827; VATA 1994, Sch 14 para 10; IT(TOI)A 2005, ss 54(1)–(3), 869(3)–(5)*].

38.9 INDIRECT TAXES

In valuing imported goods for VAT purposes, indirect taxes (eg customs duty) levied (whether abroad or in the UK) are specifically taken into account if not already included in a price in money. See 69.15 VALUATION.

39 International Services

Cross-references. See 37.4 and 37.18 INSURANCE for the supply of international insurance services; 41 ISLE OF MAN; 68 TRANSPORT AND FREIGHT for certain international movements of passengers and freight.

De Voil Indirect Tax Service. See V4.246.

The contents of this chapter are as follows.

39.1 INTRODUCTION

Certain services *received by* UK persons from outside the UK are deemed to be *supplied by* those persons who must account for VAT on them if required to be registered. See 39.4 below.

In addition, certain supplies of international services *made by* UK taxable persons are zero-rated or outside the scope of UK VAT. See 39.5 *et seq.* below.

39.2 TERRITORIAL EXTENT OF UK

The UK consists of Great Britain, Northern Ireland and the territorial sea of the UK (ie waters within 12 nautical miles of the coast line). [*VATA 1994, s 96(11)*].

For VAT purposes the Isle of Man is treated as part of the UK and VAT is chargeable there under Manx law which generally parallels UK legislation. See 41 ISLE OF MAN. *References in this chapter to the UK apply also to the Isle of Man unless otherwise indicated.*

De Voil Indirect Tax Service. See V1.215.

39.3 PLACE OF SUPPLY OF SERVICES

See 64.18 *et seq.* SUPPLY for a detailed consideration of the place of supply of services.

39.4 REVERSE CHARGE ON SERVICES RECEIVED FROM ABROAD

Normally, the supplier of a service is the person who must account to the tax authorities for any VAT due on the supply. However, in certain situations, the position is reversed and it is the customer who must account for any VAT due. This is known as the '*reverse charge*' procedure.

Situations in which the reverse charge procedure applies in the UK. There are three different situations in which the procedures can apply.

(*a*) *Services within VATA 1994, Sch 5 paras 1-8.* The reverse charge procedure applies where a person who belongs outside the UK supplies '*relevant services*' (ie services within *VATA 1994, Sch 5 paras 1-8*, see 64.27 SUPPLY) to a *person* who belongs in the UK for the purposes of any business carried on by him and the place of supply of those services is in the UK. [*VATA 1994, s 8(1)(2)*].

See 64.19 SUPPLY for the place of belonging.

The consequence of the provisions applying to a *person* rather than a *taxable person* is that anyone carrying on a business in the UK will become liable to be registered for VAT if the total value of reverse charge services within these provisions and turnover from any taxable business supplies made in the UK exceed the registration limit. (VAT Notice 741, para 15.12).

Where services within *VATA 1994, Sch 5 paras 1-8* (except exempt services) are purchased by an overseas member of a UK VAT group and provided to a UK member of that VAT group, its representative member is required to account for any UK VAT due under the intra-group reverse charge provisions. See 31.6 GROUPS OF COMPANIES.

(*b*) *Services with an EC simplification.* The place of supply of certain services made in the EC can be further adjusted if the customer gives a VAT registration number from a different EC country. As a result, the reverse charge provisions apply to the following services where a UK recipient receives a supply for business purposes from a supplier belonging outside the UK and gives the supplier his UK VAT registration number.

- Valuation of, or work carried out on, any goods. See 64.25 SUPPLY.
- Intra-EC freight transport services and related ancillary services. See 64.29 SUPPLY and 68.26 and 68.28 TRANSPORT AND FREIGHT.
- Arranging intra-EC freight transport services and related ancillary services. See 64.29 SUPPLY and 68.30 TRANSPORT AND FREIGHT.
- Most intermediary services supplied in the EC. See 64.31 SUPPLY.

The reverse charge cannot apply to these services if the recipient is not already VAT-registered in the UK. Such supplies do not count as taxable supplies for the purposes of determining liability to registration.

Where the conditions are not met (eg because the supplies are used for non-business purposes or the UK recipient is not VAT-registered) the supplier must account for the VAT due in the appropriate EC country.

(VAT Notice 741, para 15.12).

(*c*) *Extension to other services supplied within the UK.* The reverse charge procedure applies to all services not falling within (*a*) above where the place of supply is the UK, the supplier belongs outside the UK and the recipient is a UK VAT-registered person who uses the services for business purposes. [*VATA 1994, s 8(1)(2), Sch 5 para 9; SI 1997/1523, Reg 3*].

This covers the following services.

- Services relating to land. See 64.21 SUPPLY.
- Services supplied where physically carried out. See 64.22-64.25 SUPPLY.
- Passenger transport services. See 64.29 SUPPLY.
- Freight transport services not covered by (*b*) above. See 64.29 SUPPLY.
- Hire of means of transport. See 64.30 SUPPLY.

The reverse charge cannot apply to these services if the recipient is not already VAT-registered in the UK. Such supplies do not count as taxable supplies for the purposes of determining liability to registration.

Where the conditions are not met (eg because the supplies are used for non-business purposes or the UK recipient is not VAT-registered or does not provide a VAT registration number) the supplier must account for the VAT due. If not already registered in the UK, the supplier may be liable to register (subject to the registration limit).

The existence of the reverse charge procedure for these services does not prevent overseas suppliers from registering for VAT in the UK under the normal rules. If they do register, they must invoice UK VAT in the normal way and the recipient is not then required to account for VAT under the reverse charge procedure.

(VAT Notice 741, para 15.13).

The reverse charge procedure does not apply to

- services where the supplier belongs in the UK;
- services which, under the place of supply rules, are supplied in another country which, by definition, are outside the scope of UK VAT and are subject to VAT, if any, in that other country; or
- services provided by an overseas establishment within the same legal entity since this is not a supply for VAT purposes.

(VAT Notice 741, paras 15.8, 15.9).

Accounting for VAT and recovery of input tax. Where the reverse charge procedure applies, the recipient of the services must act as both the supplier and the recipient of the services. On the same VAT return, the recipient must

- account for output tax, calculated on the full value of the supply received, in Box 1;
- (subject to the normal rules) include the VAT as input tax in Box 4; and
- include the full value of the supply in both Boxes 6 and 7.

Exempt and zero-rated supplies. The reverse charge does not apply to exempt services. [*VATA 1994, s 8(2)*]. In the case of zero-rated services, although there is no output tax due and no input tax to recover, Boxes 6 and 7 of the VAT return should be completed.

Partial exemption rules. Supplies which are treated as made by the recipient under these rules are not to be taken into account as output for the purpose of calculating entitlement to input tax deduction under the PARTIAL EXEMPTION (49) rules. [*VATA 1994, s 8(3)*].

The effect of the provisions is that the reverse charge has no net cost to the recipient if he can attribute the input tax to taxable supplies and can therefore reclaim it in full. If he cannot, the effect is to put him in the same position as if had received the supply from a UK supplier rather than from one outside the UK.

UK VAT incurred by the overseas supplier. The overseas supplier whose customer accounts for VAT under the reverse charge procedure may be able to reclaim VAT incurred in the UK on supplies made to it through the mechanism of the *8th* or *13th*

Directive. See 21.31 EUROPEAN COMMUNITY: GENERAL and 48.5 OVERSEAS TRADERS for applications to the UK for refunds of VAT by persons established in other EC countries and outside the EC respectively.

(VAT Notice 741, paras 15.4, 15.5, 15.10–15.13).

Value of supply. The value of the deemed supply is to be taken to be the consideration in money for which the services were in fact supplied or, where the consideration did not consist or not wholly consist of money, such amount in money as is equivalent to that consideration. [*VATA 1994, Sch 6 para 8*]. The consideration payable to the overseas supplier for the services excludes UK VAT but includes any taxes levied abroad. (VAT Notice 741, para 15.6).

Time of supply. The time of supply of such services is the date the supplies are paid for or, if the consideration is not in money, the last day of the VAT period in which the services are performed. [*VATA 1994, s 8(4); SI 1995/2518, Reg 82*].

De Voil Indirect Tax Service. See V3.231.

39.5 VAT LIABILITY OF INTERNATIONAL SERVICES

The liability of a supply of international services depends on the rules for the place of supply of services. These are considered in detail in 64.18 *et seq.* SUPPLY. Where the place of supply is deemed to be outside the UK, the services are outside the scope of UK VAT. Where the place of supply is deemed to be in the UK, the services are subject to the normal UK provisions. Apart from the specific categories of zero-rating for international services in 39.6–39.8 below, international services deemed to be supplied in the UK are therefore standard-rated unless they can be treated as ZERO-RATED SUPPLIES (72) or EXEMPT SUPPLIES (24) under the general rules.

See 35.3 INPUT TAX for the position regarding the right to deduct input tax in respect of most (but not all) international services deemed to be made outside the UK.

39.6 Training supplied to overseas Governments

By concession, zero-rating applies to training services (other than exempt training within 20.7 EDUCATION) supplied in the UK to overseas Governments for the purpose of their sovereign activities (and not their business activities). The supplier must retain a statement in writing from the Government concerned (or its accredited representative) certifying that the trainees are employed in the furtherance of its sovereign activities. *Included* is the training of Government officials, public servants and members of organisations such as the armed forces, police, emergency services and similar bodies answerable to the Government concerned. *Excluded* is training of personnel from Government-owned businesses or sponsored commercial organisations such as state airlines or nationalised industries. Relief does not extend to any associated services supplied *separately* (eg accommodation or transport). (VAT Notice 48, ESC 3.17; VAT Notice 744D, paras 4.1–4.5).

39.7 Work on goods obtained, acquired or temporarily imported for that purpose and subsequent export

EC legislation. See 22.21(*b*) EUROPEAN COMMUNITY LEGISLATION.

Note. The following provisions do *not* apply where the work is carried out for a VAT-registered customer in another EC country, the goods physically leave the EC country where the work has been carried out, and the customer gives a valid VAT registration number. In such a case, the place of supply moves to the country where the customer belongs and the customer must account for VAT under the reverse charge procedure. See 64.25 SUPPLY.

The supply of services of work carried out on goods which, for that purpose, have been obtained or acquired in, or imported into, any EC country is zero-rated provided the goods are intended to be (and are) subsequently exported to a place outside the EC. The goods must be exported by (or on behalf of) the supplier or, where the recipient of the services belongs outside the EC, by (or on behalf of) the recipient. *Excluded* are any services of a description falling within *VATA 1994, Sch 9 Group 2* (insurance) or *Group 5* (finance). [*VATA 1994, Sch 8 Group 7 Item 1*].

See 64.19 SUPPLY for the concept of belonging. The goods must be exported within a reasonable time after the work on them has been carried out. The goods must not be used in the UK between the time of leaving the supplier's premises and exportation. Normal rules apply for proof of export of the goods (see 25.24 EXPORTS). If, in anticipation of export, the supply is zero-rated but, in the event, the goods are either used before export or export does not take place, it will be necessary to reconsider both the place of supply of the services and, if it is in the UK, the appropriate VAT rate.

Any goods used in conjunction with the work performed (eg spare parts, paint, etc) should be treated as part of the supply of services.

Included are

- alterations and repairs, calibrations, cleaning, insulating, lacquering, painting, polishing, resetting (jewellery), cutting (of precious stones), sharpening, varnishing and waterproofing;
- the repair of freight containers;
- services directly related to the 'covering' of a mare provided the mare is exported before the birth of the foal;
- the gelding and/or breaking in of a young horse (eg training yearling racehorses to the stage where they can be ridden safely in races) but note that actual racing is not accepted as training and if any horse is acquired or temporarily imported with the intention of racing it in the EC before re-export, zero-rating under this provision will not be allowed; and
- the restoration of classic cars.

Not included is

- work which is not physical work carried out on the goods themselves (eg mere inspection or testing and analysis);
- repair or other work which becomes necessary after acquisition or importation of goods (eg incidental running repairs while the goods are being used); and
- valuation services.

(VAT Notice 744D, paras 2.1–2.8).

De Voil Indirect Tax Service. See V4.246.

39.8 Services of intermediaries

There are special place of supply rules for services of intermediaries, the place of supply depending upon both the nature of the main goods or services whose supply is being arranged and the location of the customer. See 64.31 SUPPLY. Where the supply of an intermediary's services is within the scope of UK VAT, it is zero-rated if consisting of the making of arrangements for

- the export of any goods to a place outside the EC;
- a supply of services of the description specified in *VATA 1994, Sch 8 Group 7 Item 1* (see 39.7 above); or
- any supply of services which is made outside the EC.

Excluded are any services of a description falling within *VATA 1994, Sch 9 Group 2* (insurance) or *Group 5* (finance).

[*VATA 1994, Sch 8 Group 7 Item 2*].

The intermediary's services can be supplied to the supplier (in finding a customer) or the customer (in finding a supplier) or even to both.

(VAT Notice 744D, paras 3.1–3.7).

39.9 TELECOMMUNICATION SERVICES

There are special rules for relevant telecommunications services. See 64.27(7A) SUPPLY for the definition of telecommunication services.

Place of supply rules and summary of UK VAT position. See 64.26-64.28 SUPPLY.

Reverse charge on services received from abroad. Where the reverse charge procedure on services received from abroad applies to relevant telecommunication services, the normal value and time of supply rules are applied (see 39.4 above) but only to the extent that the services are not chargeable to VAT in another EC country.

[*SI 1997/1523, Regs 4, 7, 10*].

Continuous supplies of telecommunications services. Special time of supply rules apply to continuous supplies of any services. See 64.50 SUPPLY.

Rights to relevant telecommunications services. A 'right' to relevant telecommunications services is treated as supplied in the same place as the supply of the services to which the right relates (whether or not the right is exercised).

A 'right' includes any right, option or priority with respect to the supply of services and the supply of an interest deriving from any right or services.

[*SI 1992/3121, Art 21; SI 1997/1524, Art 5*].

39.10 BROADCASTING AND ELECTRONICALLY SUPPLIED SERVICES

With effect from 1 July 2003, the place of supply of radio and TV broadcasting services and electronically supplied services is normally in the country where the customer belongs subject, in certain circumstances, to where the services are effectively used and enjoyed. See 64.26–64.28 SUPPLY for further details of the place of supply rules.

Under the rules in force until 1 July 2003, radio and TV broadcasting services, and most electronically supplied services, were subject to VAT in the country where the supplier belonged under the basic place of supply rule. This meant UK businesses were required to charge UK VAT on those services to all their customers, irrespective of their customer's location. Similarly, businesses in other EC countries were required to charge VAT at their local rate. However, non-EC businesses were not required to charge EC VAT on supplies to EC customers. Special place of supply rules for these services were introduced with effect from 1 July 2003 to remove this distortion of competition so that EC and non-EC businesses are taxed in a similar way.

Supplies spanning 1 July 2003. Businesses must account for VAT on broadcasting and electronic services supplied in the UK to the extent which provides a fair and reasonable reflection of the services performed in the UK on or after 1 July 2003. Where, however, a business receives services from a business in another EC country which span the implementation date, UK VAT is not required provided the recipient can demonstrate that it has paid VAT in another EC country. (VAT Information Sheet 1/03, para 9.4).

Special scheme for non-EC suppliers of electronically supplied services. See 63.34 SPECIAL SCHEMES.

40 Invoices

Cross-references. See 52.12 PENALTIES for improper use of invoices; 56.3 and 56.10 RECORDS for obligations to retain invoices and adjustments of errors in invoices; 63.30 SPECIAL SCHEMES for invoices raised by flat-rate farmers; 69.24 VALUATION for discounts on invoices.

De Voil Indirect Tax Service. See V3.511–529.

The contents of this chapter are as follows.

40.1 OBLIGATION TO PROVIDE A VAT INVOICE

With certain exceptions or unless HMRC allow otherwise, a registered person *must* provide the customer with an invoice showing specified particulars including VAT (a '*VAT invoice*') in the following circumstances.

(*a*) He makes a supply of goods or services in the UK (other than an exempt supply) to a taxable person.

(*b*) He makes a supply of goods or services (other than an exempt supply) to a person in another EC country. This covers

(i) standard-rated supplies to a person registered in another EC country;

(ii) zero-rated supplies for acquisition by a person registered in another EC country; and

(iii) standard-rated supplies to a non-taxable person (eg a public body, charity or an unregistered business) in another EC country;

(iv) distance sales of goods (eg by mail order) to unregistered persons in other EC countries; and

(v) the supply of a new means of transport (see 23.31 EUROPEAN COMMUNITY: SINGLE MARKET) to a person in another EC country.

(*c*) He receives a payment on account from a person in another EC country in respect of a supply he has made or intends to make.

A VAT invoice is important as it is normally essential evidence to support a customer's claim for deduction of input tax. The supplier must keep the copy and the original should be retained by the recipient.

[*VATA 1994, Sch 11 para 2A; FA 2002, s 24; SI 1995/2518, Reg 13*(*1*)].

Exceptions. The above provisions do not apply to the following supplies.

- Exempt supplies.
- Zero-rated supplies (other than supplies for acquisition by a person registered in another EC country, see (*b*)(ii) above). [*SI 1995/2518, Reg 20*(*a*)].
- Supplies where the VAT charged is excluded from credit under *VATA 1994, s 25*(*7*) (eg business entertaining and certain motor cars) [*SI 1995/2518, Reg 20*(*b*)] although a VAT invoice may be issued in such cases.
- Supplies on which VAT is charged but which are not made for a consideration. [*SI 1995/2518, Reg 20*(*c*)]. This includes gifts and private use of goods. See, however, 40.2 below under the heading *Business gifts* for 'tax certificates' issued in connection with business gifts to support a deduction of input tax.
- Sales of second-hand goods under one of the special schemes. [*SI 1995/2518, Reg 20*(*d*)]. Invoices for such sales must not show any VAT. See 61.11 and 61.45 SECOND-HAND GOODS for the special invoices required.
- Supplies that fall within the TOUR OPERATORS' MARGIN SCHEME (66). VAT invoices must not be issued for such supplies.
- Supplies where the customer operates a self-billing arrangement. See 40.6 below.
- Supplies by retailers unless the customer requests a VAT invoice.
- Supplies by one member to another in the same VAT group.
- Transactions between one division and another of a company registered in the names of its divisions. See 59.37 REGISTRATION.
- Supplies where the taxable person is entitled to issue, and does issue, invoices relating to services performed in fiscal and other warehousing regimes. [*SI 1995/2518, Reg 13*(*1*); *SI 1996/1250, Reg 6*]. See 70.19 WAREHOUSED GOODS AND FREE ZONES.

Continuous supplies of services. In *Europhone International Ltd v Frontier Communications Ltd, Ch D [2001] STC 1399 (TVC 60.428)* F agreed to provide E with telecommunications services. E fell into arrears with its payments. F continued to provide the relevant services but did not issue invoices (which would have obliged it to account for output tax). E went into receivership and the receivers claimed that F was obliged to issue a VAT invoice. The court held that *SI 1995/2518, Reg 13*(*1*) above imposed a requirement to provide a VAT invoice upon a person who made a taxable supply. The making of the taxable supply must, therefore, precede or be contemporaneous with the arising of the obligation. Under the rules for continuous supplies of services (see 64.50 SUPPLY for full details), F only made a taxable supply to E when it received payment or it issued a VAT invoice. As there was no question of E making a payment in respect of the services supplied by F, *Reg 13* was ineffective to impose an obligation on F to issue a VAT invoice.

De Voil Indirect Tax Service. See V3.513.

40.2 DOCUMENTS TREATED AS VAT INVOICES

Although not strictly VAT invoices, certain documents listed in (1)–(5) below are treated as VAT invoices either under the legislation or by HMRC.

(1) **Self-billing invoices**

Self-billing is an arrangement between a supplier and a customer in which the customer prepares the supplier's invoice and forwards it to him, normally with the payment. See 40.6 below.

(2) **Copy purchase invoices used as sales invoices**

A business may use photocopies of purchase invoices to serve as sales invoices (eg for onward supplies to associated companies at cost) provided the photocopy is adapted to meet the full requirements of a VAT invoice (see 40.4 below). In particular the adapted invoice must show

- the new supplier's name and address;
- the new customer's name and address;
- the new date of supply (if applicable); and
- a unique reference number.

(Internal Guidance V1–24A, para 2.27).

(3) **Sales by auctioneer, bailiff, etc.**

Where goods (including land) forming part of the assets of a business carried on by a taxable person are, under any power exercisable by another person, sold by that person in or towards satisfaction of a debt owed by the taxable person, the goods are deemed to be supplied by the taxable person in the course or furtherance of his business.

The particulars of the VAT chargeable on the supply must be provided on a sale by auction by the auctioneer and where the sale is otherwise than by auction by the person selling the goods. The document issued to the buyer is treated as a VAT invoice. [*VATA 1994, Sch 4 paras 7, 9; SI 1995/2518, Reg 13(2)*]. See 2.18 ACCOUNTING PERIODS AND RETURNS.

(4) **Authenticated receipts in the construction industry**. See 42.31(1) LAND AND BUILDINGS.

(5) **Business gifts**

Where a business makes a gift of goods on which VAT is due (see 47.6 OUTPUT TAX), and the recipient uses the goods for business purposes, that person can recover the VAT as input tax (subject to the normal rules). The donor cannot issue a VAT invoice (because there is no consideration) but instead may provide the recipient with a 'tax certificate' which can be used as evidence to support a deduction of input tax. The tax certificate may be on normal invoicing documentation overwritten with the statement:

> *Tax certificate*
>
> No payment is necessary for these goods. Output tax has been accounted for on the supply.

Full details of the goods must be shown on the documentation and the amount of VAT shown must be the amount of output tax accounted for to HMRC.

(VAT Notice 700/35/97, para 1.4).

The following are not to be regarded as VAT invoices (even if showing all the details required of a VAT invoice) provided they are clearly marked 'This is not a VAT invoice'.

- Any consignment note, delivery note or similar document (or any copy thereof) issued by the supplier before the time of supply where
  - (i) goods are removed before it is known whether a supply will take place (eg goods on approval or sale or return), or
  - (ii) the tax point is treated as taking place at the time an invoice is issued under the 14 day rule (see 64.39 SUPPLY).
- Any pro-forma invoice used to offer goods or services to a potential customer.

[*SI 1995/2518, Reg 14*(*3*)]. (VAT Notice 700, para 17.3).

40.3 INVOICING REQUIREMENTS AND PARTICULARS

A VAT invoice must contain certain basic information. See 40.4 below. In addition, special rules apply to

- VAT invoices issued to persons in other EC countries (see 40.5 below);
- self-billing invoices (see 40.6 below);
- retailers' invoices (see 40.7 below);
- invoices issued by cash and carry wholesalers (see 40.8 below);
- arrangements for particular businesses (see 40.9 below); and
- electronic invoicing (see 40.10 below);
- invoices using corporate purchasing cards (see 40.11 below).

40.4 VAT invoices generally

Unless HMRC allow otherwise, a VAT invoice must show the following particulars.

(*a*) An identifying number.

(*b*) The time of the supply, ie tax point.

Where it is a trader's practice to show only the tax point date on a VAT invoice and no other date appears, this date need not be identified as the tax point. Where more than one date appears, the tax point must be separately identified. (Internal Guidance V1–24A, para 2.7).

(*c*) The date of issue of the document.

(*d*) The name, address and registration number of the supplier.

(*e*) The name and address of the person to whom the goods or services are supplied.

(*f*) *Before 1 January 2004*, the type of supply by reference to the following categories:

- by sale,
- on hire purchase or any similar transaction,
- by loan,

- by way of exchange,
- on hire, lease or rental,
- of goods made from customer's materials,
- by sale on commission,
- on sale or return or similar terms, or
- any other type of supply which HMRC may at any time by notice specify.

With effect from 1 January 2004, this information is optional.

(*g*) A description sufficient to identify the goods or services supplied.

Where services are supplied, a description of the services may be taken as sufficient to describe also the type of supply under (*f*) above and their extent under (*h*) below. For professional services, a description such as 'professional services rendered' is acceptable.

See 40.8 below for use of coded descriptions by cash and carry wholesalers. Coded descriptions may also be accepted in other circumstances (eg builders' merchants) where businesses whose trade is restricted to a large number of specialised parts or fittings issue illustrated catalogues to customers.

(Internal Guidance V1–24A, paras 2.7, 2.8).

(*h*) For each description, the quantity of the goods or extent of the services, the rate of VAT and amount payable, excluding VAT, expressed in any currency (before 1 January 2004, in sterling).

(*i*) With effect from 1 January 2004, the unit price.

This applies to 'countable' goods and services. For services, the countable element might be, for example, an hourly rate or a price paid for standard services. If the supply cannot be broken down into countable elements, the total VAT-exclusive price is the unit price. Additionally, the unit price may not need to be shown at all if it is not normally provided in a particular business sector *and* is not required by the customer. (VAT Notice 700, para 16.3).

(*j*) The gross amount payable, excluding VAT, expressed in any currency (before 1 January 2004, in sterling).

(*k*) The rate of any cash discount offered.

(*l*) *Before 1 January 2004*, each rate of VAT chargeable and the amount of VAT chargeable, expressed in sterling, at each rate. *With effect from 1 January 2004*, this information is optional.

(*m*) The total amount of VAT chargeable express in sterling.

Exempt or zero-rated supplies. Invoices do not have to be raised for exempt or zero-rated transactions when supplied in the UK. But if such supplies are included on invoices with taxable supplies, the exempt and zero-rated supplies must be totalled separately and the invoice must show clearly that there is no VAT payable on them.

VAT invoices where person supplied accounts for the VAT. Where a registered person provides a VAT invoice relating in whole or part to a supply in respect of which the person supplied must account for and pay the VAT due on the supplier's behalf, the supplier must state that fact, and the amount of the VAT to be accounted for, on the VAT invoice.

Leasing of motor cars. Where an invoice relates wholly or partly to the letting on hire of a motor car other than for self-drive, the invoice must state whether the car is a qualifying vehicle (see 45.11 MOTOR CARS).

[*VATA 1994, Sch 11 para 2A; FA 1996, s 38; FA 2002, s 24; SI 1995/2518, Reg 14(1)(4)(5)(6); SI 1995/3147; SI 1996/1250, Reg 7; SI 2003/3220, Reg 7*].

De Voil Indirect Tax Service. See V3.514.

Example of a VAT invoice

ABC plc

26 Green Road, South Croydon, CR2 5ZX

VAT Reg. No. 987 6543 21

Sales invoice No 15,618

AN Other Ltd

9 North Street

London N8 5QQ

Time of supply 31/01/05 **Date of Issue** 3/02/05

Quantity	Description and price	Amount excluding VAT £	VAT rate %	VAT £
12	Purple kingsize quilt covers @ £15	180.00		
20	Pillows at £12.50	250.00		
50	Purple pillow cases at £8.50 per pair	212.50		
		642.50	17½	106.82
	Delivery (strictly net)	12.00	17½	2.10
Terms: Cash discount of 5% if paid within 30 days		654.50		108.92
	VAT	108.92		
	Total	£763.42		

40.5 **VAT invoices to persons in other EC countries**

Unless HMRC allow otherwise, where a registered person provides a person in another EC country with

- a VAT invoice or,
- with effect from 1 January 2004, any document that refers to a VAT invoice and is intended to amend it (eg a credit note)

it must show the following particulars.

(*a*) An identifying number.

(*b*) The time of the supply, ie tax point.

Where it is a trader's practice to show only the tax point date on a VAT invoice and no other date appears, this date need not be identified as the tax point. Where more than one date appears, the tax point must be separately identified. (Internal Guidance V1–24A, para 2.7).

(*c*) The date of issue of the document.

(*d*) The name, address and registration number of the supplier. The letters 'GB' must be shown as a prefix to the registration number.

(*e*) The name and address of the person to whom the goods or services are supplied.

(*f*) The registration number, if any, of the recipient of the supply of goods or services containing the alphabetical code of the EC country in which the recipient is registered, namely

Austria—AT
Belgium—BE
Cyprus—CY
Czech Republic—CZ
Denmark—DK
Estonia—EE
Finland—FI
France—FR
Germany—DE
Greece—EL
Hungary—HU
Ireland—IE
Italy—IT
Latvia—LV
Lithuania—LT
Luxembourg—LU
Malta—MT
Netherlands—NL
Poland—PL
Portugal—PT
Slovak Republic—SK
Slovenia—SI
Spain—ES
Sweden—SE

Enquiry letters in a number of foreign languages to request the correct VAT registration number from an EC customer are available on the HMRC website.

(*g*) *Before 1 January 2004*, the type of supply by reference to the following categories:

- by sale,
- on hire purchase or any similar transaction,
- by loan,
- by way of exchange,

- on hire, lease or rental,
- of goods made from customer's materials,
- by sale on commission,
- on sale or return or similar terms, or
- any other type of supply which HMRC may at any time by notice specify.

With effect from 1 January 2004, this information is optional.

(*h*) A description sufficient to identify the goods or services supplied. Where the supply is of a new means of transport (see 23.31 EUROPEAN COMMUNITY: SINGLE MARKET) a description sufficient to identify it as such.

Where services are supplied, a description of the services may be taken as sufficient to describe also the type of supply under (*g*) above. For professional services, a description such as 'professional services rendered' is acceptable.

(Internal Guidance V1–24, Part A para 2.7).

(*i*) For each description, the quantity of the goods or the extent of the services, and where a positive rate of VAT is chargeable, the rate of VAT and the amount payable, excluding VAT, expressed in sterling.

(*j*) With effect from 1 January 2004, the unit price.

This applies to 'countable' goods and services. For services, the countable element might be, for example, an hourly rate or a price paid for standard services. If the supply cannot be broken down into countable elements, the total VAT-exclusive price is the unit price. Additionally, the unit price may not need to be shown at all if it is not normally provided in a particular business sector *and* is not required by the customer. (VAT Notice 700, para 16.3).

(*k*) The gross amount payable, excluding VAT.

(*l*) The rate of any cash discount offered.

(*m*) *Before 1 January 2004*, where the supply of goods was a taxable supply, each rate of VAT chargeable and the amount of VAT chargeable, expressed in sterling, at each rate. *With effect from 1 January 2004*, this information is optional.

(*n*) Where the supply of goods is a taxable supply, the total amount of VAT chargeable expressed in sterling.

[*VATA 1994, Sch 11 para 2A; FA 1996, s 38; FA 2002, s 24; SI 1995/2518, Regs 2, 14(2); SI 1996/1250, Reg 7; SI 2003/3220, Reg 8; SI 2004/1082, Reg 3*].

Note that there is no requirement for the gross amount payable (excluding VAT) to be in sterling. Where, therefore, a VAT invoice is issued in respect of a zero-rated supply for acquisition by a customer registered in another EC country and their registration number is quoted on the invoice, the invoice may be in any currency. Where UK VAT is chargeable (eg on distance sales) this must always be expressed in sterling.

De Voil Indirect Tax Service. See V3.515.

Example of a VAT invoice

ABC plc
26 Green Road, South Croydon, CR2 5ZX
VAT Reg. No. GB987 6543 21

Sales invoice No 15,618
Eine Andere AG
9 Nord Straße
Berlin
VAT Reg. No. DE 123456789

Time of supply 31/01/05 **Date of Issue** 3/02/05

Quantity	Description and price	Amount excluding VAT £	VAT rate %	VAT £
12	Purple kingsize quilt covers @ £15	180.00		
20	Pillows at £12.50	250.00		
50	Purple pillow cases at £8.50 per pair	212.50		
		642.50	0	0
	Delivery	35.00	0	0
Terms: Cash discount of 5% if paid within 30 days		677.50		
	VAT	0.00		
	Total	£677.50		

40.6 **Self-billing**

Self-billing is an established practice under which the customer prepares a VAT invoice in the name of, and on behalf of, the supplier and then sends it to the supplier, normally with the payment.

Prior approval from HMRC is no longer required but all businesses wishing to use the scheme need to meet conditions set out in *SI 1995/2518, Reg 13* and VAT Notice 700/62. HMRC may also impose further conditions in particular cases.

The detailed provisions are as follows.

Where a registered person (the '*customer*') provides a document to himself (a '*self-billed invoice*') that purports to be a VAT invoice in respect of a supply of goods or services to him by another registered person (the '*supplier*'), that document is treated as the VAT invoice required to be provided by the supplier provided certain conditions are met.

(*a*) The self-billed invoice must have been provided under an agreement (a '*self-billing agreement*') entered into between the supplier and the customer.

(*b*) The self-billed invoice must contain the particulars required under 40.4(*a*)–(*m*) above or, as the case may be, 40.5(*a*)–(*n*) above.

(*c*) The self-billed invoice must relate to a supply or supplies made by a supplier who is a taxable person. If not, any amount claimed as input tax will be disallowed, see *MJ Gleeson Group plc (VTD 13332) (TVC 38.46)*.

(*d*) The self-billed invoice must be clearly marked

'THE VAT SHOWN IS YOUR OUTPUT TAX DUE TO REVENUE & CUSTOMS'

(*e*) The customer must keep the names, addresses and VAT registration numbers of all the suppliers who have agreed to self-billing, and be able to produce them for inspection by HMRC if required.

(*f*) The customer must raise self-billed invoices for all transactions with the supplier during the currency of the agreement.

If all the conditions are not met, any self-billed invoices issued are not proper VAT invoices. As such, they cannot be used as evidence of entitlement to input tax by the customer and the supplier will have to issue his own invoices.

Self-billing agreements. A self-billed invoice can only be issued under an agreement between the customer and supplier (see (*a*) above).

A self-billing agreement must:

- Authorise the customer to produce self-billed invoices in respect of supplies made by the supplier for a specified period ending not later than either

  (i) the end of a period of 12 months, or

  (ii) the end of the period of any contract between the customer and the supplier for the supply of the particular goods or services to which the self-billing agreement relates.

  Most self-billing agreements will therefore normally last for twelve months and must then be renewed. However, where the customer has a business contract with its supplier, the self-billing agreement can be incorporated in the contract, in which case the self-billing agreement lasts until the end date of the contract.

- Specify that the supplier will not issue VAT invoices in respect of supplies covered by the agreement.
- Specify that the supplier will accept each self-billed invoice created by the customer in respect of supplies made to him by the supplier.
- Specify that the supplier will notify the customer if he ceases to be a taxable person, changes his registration number or transfers his business as a going concern. (A new agreement must be set up if the supplier changes his VAT registration number or if he transfers his business as a going concern and the new supplier wants to continue operating self-billing.)
- Be in writing (either on paper or in electronic form).
- Be produced to HMRC on request (by the customer or supplier).

It is also helpful for the agreement to make it clear if the customer intends to outsource responsibility for issuing the self-billed invoices to a third party (eg an accounting bureau), although it should be noted that in such a case the customer still remains responsible for ensuring that all the conditions of the scheme are met.

An example of a self-billing agreement acceptable to HMRC is reproduced below. It is not necessary to follow the exact wording provided the agreement used contains all the relevant information.

Self-Billing Agreement

This is an agreement to a self-billing procedure between

Customer name	VAT number
Supplier name	VAT number

The self-biller (the customer) agrees:

1. To issue self-billed invoices for all supplies made to them by the self-billee (the supplier) until.../.../... (insert either an end date for the agreement or the date the contract ends).

2. To complete self-billed invoices showing the supplier's name, address and VAT registration number, together with all the other details which constitute a full VAT invoice.

3. To make a new self-billing agreement in the event that their VAT registration number changes.

4. To inform the supplier if the issue of self-billed invoices will be outsourced to a third party.

The self-billee agrees:

1. To accept invoices raised by the self-biller on their behalf until .../.../... (insert either an end date for the agreement or the date the contract ends).

2. Not to raise sales invoices for the transactions covered by the agreement.

3. To notify the customer immediately if they
   - change their VAT registration number
   - cease to be VAT-registered; or
   - sell their business, or part of their business.

Signed by	Signed by
On behalf of	On behalf of
Date	Date

Customers in other countries. Self-billing is not restricted to domestic supplies and self-billing agreements can be made with businesses in other EC countries and in countries outside the EC. However, it should be borne in mind that EC countries set their own conditions for self-billing agreements and any such agreement negotiated must meet the conditions and procedures in place in the EC country in whose territory the goods or services are supplied. Points to bear in mind include:

- Where a customer in another EC country provides a document to himself in respect of a supply to him by a UK-registered person,

(i) the document must comply with the conditions set out in (*a*)–(*c*) above and, in the case of an electronic self-billed document, must be one which the UK supplier's accounting system can accept; and

(ii) in the case of a supply of goods, the UK supplier must still be able to meet all the conditions in 23.11 EUROPEAN COMMUNITY: SINGLE MARKET in order to have evidence for zero-rating.

- Where a UK customer raises a self-billed invoice on behalf of his supplier in another EC country,

  (i) that invoice may, with effect from 1 January 2004, establish the time of acquisition in the same way as an invoice issued by the supplier (see 23.7 EUROPEAN COMMUNITY: SINGLE MARKET); and

  (ii) in the case of an electronic self-billed invoice, the supplier may have problems with the format of the invoice if the electronic method used is neither advanced electronic signature nor electronic data interchange (EDI). This is because some tax authorities do not accept all the electronic methods of raising invoices that are permissible in the UK.

- Where a customer outside the EC provides a document to himself in respect of a supply of goods to him by a UK-registered person, the UK supplier must still be able to meet all the requirements for documentary evidence of export (see 25.24 EXPORTS).

- Where a UK customer raises a self-billed invoice on behalf of a supplier of goods from outside the EC, the customer may need to check what information the supplier will need to be included on the invoice raised on his behalf so that it is acceptable to his own tax authorities as evidence of export.

- For supplies of services to and from all non-UK businesses, the UK customer/supplier must be familiar with the place of supply rules (see 64.18–64.31 SUPPLY) and agree the correct VAT treatment of the supply with the other party from the outset.

Tax points for self-billed supplies. See 64.35 SUPPLY.

Self-billed debit notes. Where a self-billing arrangement is in operation, a customer cannot reduce the value of the supply on a subsequent self-billed invoice. He must issue a debit note showing the amount of the adjustment to the value of the supply.

[*SI 1995/2518, Reg 13(3)(3A)–(3F); SI 2003/3220, Reg 4*]. (VAT Notice 700/62/03, paras 3.1, 3.3, 3.4, 4.1, 4.2, 4.4, 4.6, 7.1–7.4, 8).

Understated VAT. If the self-billed invoice understates the VAT chargeable on the supply, HMRC may, by notice served on the recipient and the supplier, elect that the amount of VAT understated by the document is VAT due from the recipient and not the supplier. [*VATA 1994, s 29*].

40.7 Retailers' invoices

Where the registered taxable person is a retailer, he is not required to provide a VAT invoice unless a customer requests it. Where an invoice is requested, one of the following options may be available.

(*a*) **Less detailed VAT invoices**. Provided the consideration does not exceed £250 (£100 before 1 January 2004) and provided the supply is not to a person in another EC country, the VAT invoice need only contain particulars of

- the name, address and registration number of the retailer;
- the time of supply;
- a description sufficient to identify the goods or services supplied;
- the total amount payable including VAT; and
- for each rate of VAT chargeable, the gross amount payable including VAT, and the VAT rate applicable.

The effect of the above is that where an EC customer requests an invoice a full VAT invoice must be issued.

The invoice must not contain any reference to any exempt supply.

[*SI 1995/2518, Reg 16; SI 2003/3220, Reg 10*].

See below for VAT invoices for petrol and derv.

Where *credit cards* are accepted, the sales voucher given to the cardholder at the time of sale may be adapted to serve as a less detailed VAT invoice by including all the above information. Where an invoice is issued as well as the credit card voucher, only one of the documents must be in the form of a VAT invoice.

To calculate the amount of VAT in a VAT-inclusive price, the VAT fraction (currently 7/47) must be applied to the total invoice amount.

(*b*) **Modified VAT invoices**. Provided the customer agrees, an invoice can be issued showing the *VAT-inclusive* value of each standard-rated or reduced rate supply (instead of the VAT-exclusive value — see 40.4(*h*) above). At the foot of the invoice, there must be shown separately

- the total VAT-inclusive value of standard-rated or reduced rate supplies;
- the total VAT payable on those supplies shown in sterling;
- the total value, excluding VAT, of those supplies;
- the total value of any zero-rated supplies included on the invoice; and
- the total value of any exempt supplies included on the invoice.

In all other respects the invoice should show the details required for a full VAT invoice (see 40.4 above).

Where options (*a*) or (*b*) are not available, a full VAT invoice under 40.4 above must be supplied. (VAT Notice 700, para 16.6).

Petrol and diesel oil (derv). Where the VAT-inclusive amount is £250 or less (£100 or less before 1 January 2004), a less detailed VAT invoice may be issued (see (*a*) above). Where the VAT-inclusive amount is more than £250 (£100 before 1 January 2004) the particulars required on a full VAT invoice are modified so that the vehicle registration number and not the customer's name and address is shown on the VAT invoice. The type of supply and the number of gallons/litres need not be shown. (VAT Notice 700, para 17.1).

Foreign currency invoices. If a VAT invoice is issued in a foreign currency, all values required to be entered for VAT purposes under (*a*) and (*b*) above must be converted into sterling. See 69.18 VALUATION.

De Voil Indirect Tax Service. See V3.555.

40.8 **Cash and carry wholesalers**

Cash and carry wholesalers pose special problems because, although in many respects they resemble normal retailers, they sell mainly to registered customers and have to provide VAT invoices. Under the special arrangements detailed below, they may adapt their till rolls to meet the VAT invoice requirements. Official approval is not required to operate the arrangements but all the conditions must be fully complied with. If not, HMRC may require normal VAT invoices to be issued.

The essential features of the arrangements are as follows.

(*a*) The arrangements can only be used for sales of goods and not for services.

(*b*) A product code is used which identifies the different classes of goods sold. The coding system should be devised by the wholesaler using a number of at least two digits and probably three or more digits where the range of products sold is wide. As far as possible, codes should identify classes of goods to limit the use for re-coding in the event of a change of rate affecting part of a group. Groups of products under the same code number should be of a similar type, but goods subject to different rates of VAT must not be described under the same code number. Codes should not normally be allocated to groups which cover individual products that have widely differing mark-ups (eg a single code should not be allocated to beers, wine and spirits).

(*c*) Product code lists are prepared and provided to all VAT-registered customers who must retain them for VAT inspection. Suppliers must issue new code lists, showing the operative date, whenever the coding is changed. These should preferably be sent to all VAT-registered customers but it is essential that all VAT-registered customers have up-to-date code lists.

(*d*) The till roll must provide all the following details to satisfy VAT invoice requirements.

- *Identifying number and date.*
- *Time of supply* (if earlier than invoice date).
- *Supplier's name, address and registration number.*
- *Customer's name* (*or trading name*) *and address.* This may be indicated by a reference number allocated by the wholesaler provided the wholesaler keeps a record of numbers allocated and advises customers of their number in writing. If the wholesaler issues 'buying cards' to customers, the card number may be used but HMRC prefer the number to be the customer's VAT registration number where possible.
- *Type of supply.* As the majority of supplies are by 'sale' it is not necessary for the description 'sale' or 'cash sale' to appear on the till roll.
- *Description sufficient to identify the goods.* See (*b*) and (*c*) above for use of product codes and product code lists.
- *Quantity and price for each line.* Each entry must represent a single item or single unit pack unless there is a specific indication to the contrary.
- *Rates and amount of VAT charged.* Where, for technical reasons, the rate cannot be shown as a percentage, a code may be used but if so it must be explained in the product code list (see (*c*) above). If invoices contain a mixture of positive-rated and zero-rated goods, each line must be marked with the appropriate rate indicator.

- *Total of VAT and goods at each positive rate of VAT.*
- *Total amount of VAT charged.*

(*e*) Copy till rolls and product code lists must be kept for six years or such shorter period as HMRC may allow.

Credits to customer. Where credits are returned to customers through the cash register, the item must be marked as a credit. If there are sales items as well as credits on the same invoice, the total of goods and VAT may be shown net of credits. The wholesaler must ensure that the deduction is made within the correct VAT category.

(VAT Notice 700, para 17.2; Internal Guidance V1–24A, paras 4.8–4.15).

De Voil Indirect Tax Service. See V3.525.

40.9 **Arrangements for particular businesses**

(*a*) **Authenticated receipts in the construction industry**. See 42.31(2) LAND AND BUILDINGS.

(*b*) **Banks**. It has been agreed with the British Bankers' Association that a bank may modify the details required on a full VAT invoice in the following ways.

- The customer's account number may be used instead of the address on VAT invoices for services provided by the bank.
- Identifying numbers may be omitted from such invoices.
- The bank branch or department issuing invoices may use their sorting code number in place of the bank address.

(Internal Guidance V1–24A, para 4.7).

(*c*) **Cash and carry wholesalers**. See 40.8 above.

(*d*) **Retailers**. See 40.7 above.

(*e*) **Solicitors.** For reasons of confidentiality, many solicitors invoice clients with a two-part document, usually consisting of

- a bill section in the upper part showing separate charges for professional services and expenses; and
- a tear-off VAT invoice in the lower part for production to HMRC.

The bill section must not be capable of being mistaken for a VAT invoice. In particular it should not show the supplier's VAT registration number and should preferably contain a statement such as 'This is not a VAT invoice'. If VAT is shown as a separate amount, the rate should not be specified and a clear reference to the accompanying VAT invoice should be made.

The VAT invoice section should contain a description of the supply sufficient to identify it as solicitor's professional services.

(Internal Guidance V1–24A, para 4.41).

(*f*) **Stockbrokers.** Contract notes are frequently the only transaction records issued by stockbrokers who adapt them for use as VAT invoices. As contract notes often show only an abbreviated address for the client (or show no address at all), HMRC have agreed with the Stock Exchange Council that computerised unique code reference numbers will be accepted in lieu of addresses on contract notes used as VAT invoices provided

- clients are formally advised of their code reference numbers and asked to retain the advice for production to HMRC when required; and
- the record of code reference numbers is available for similar inspection at the offices of the stockbroker.

HMRC reserve the right to insist on full addresses being shown if considered necessary in any particular case.

(Internal Guidance V1–24A, para 4.42).

40.10 Electronic invoicing

Revised rules on electronic invoicing apply in the UK with effect from 1 January 2004. These implement the provisions of the *EC VAT Invoicing Directive* which amended *EC Sixth Directive, Art 22.*

A business which intends to begin invoicing electronically on or after 1 January 2004 must advise HMRC within 30 days of beginning to do so. This can be done by contacting the National Advice Service or in writing. See 15.4 CUSTOMS: ADMINISTRATION. (Businesses which were invoicing electronically before 1 January 2004, and had previously received authorisation from HMRC, did not have to notify them again.)

'*Electronic invoicing*' is the transmission and storage of invoices, without the delivery of paper documents, by electronic means. Electronic equipment employing wires, radio transmission, optical technologies or other electromagnetic means is used for the processing (including digital compression) and storage of data.

Conditions for electronic transmission of invoices. Where, in respect of a supply of goods of services, a registered business provides a document that purports to be a VAT invoice by electronic transmission, the document can only be treated as a VAT invoice if certain conditions are satisfied.

(*a*) *Contents of the invoice*. Electronic invoices must contain the same information as paper invoices. See 40.4 and, in respect of invoices to other EC countries, 40.5 above.

Batches of invoices. Where a business provides invoices in batches to the same recipient by electronic transmission, details common to each invoice need only be stated once for each batch file (rather than once per invoice). For example, instead of repeating the full name and address of the customer on every invoice in the batch, a business could include the full information on the batch header and use an abridged or coded version of that information within each individual invoice message.

Credit notes. See 40.15 below for details required on credit notes raised for UK supplies. From 1 January 2004, where a business provides a person in another EC country with a document which amends a VAT invoice (eg a credit note) that document must contain all the information required to be included on an invoice (see 40.5 above).

(*b*) *Authenticity of the origin and integrity of the invoice data*. Both the supplier and the customer must be able to guarantee the authenticity of the origin and integrity of the contents of the invoice data. The *EC VAT Invoicing Directive* requires all EC countries to allow electronic invoicing using an advance electronic signature or Electronic Data Interchange (see (i) and (ii) below) but they can also accept other means of e-invoicing for supplies on their own country. HMRC accept the following means.

(i) An '*advanced electronic signature*', ie an 'electronic signature' which is

- uniquely linked to the 'signatory';
- capable of identifying the signatory;
- created using means that the signatory can maintain under his sole control; and
- linked to the data to which it relates in such a manner that any subsequent change of the data is detectable.

'*Electronic signature*' means data in electronic form which are attached to or logically associated with other electronic data and which serve as a method of authentication.

'*Signatory*' means a person who holds a signature-creation device and acts either on his own behalf or on behalf of the natural or legal person or entity he represents.

An electronic invoicing system that meets these requirements can be used without HMRC authorisation and can be used for both UK domestic electronic invoicing and electronic invoicing to other EC countries.

(ii) '*Electronic data interchange*' ('EDI'), ie the computer-to-computer exchange of structured data that permits automatic processing by the recipient. It is traditionally more commonly used for high-volume data transfers between businesses, using agreed standards (eg UN/EDIFACT) to structure the data. There should be an interchange agreement between the EDI trading partners making provision for the use of procedures that guarantee the authenticity of the origin and integrity of the data. Examples of such procedures include

- use of secure networks;
- controls over access to networks (eg checking 'trading relationships');
- syntax checking of data in accordance with the rules of the transmission standard; and
- summary file control reporting.

An electronic invoicing system that meets these requirements can be used without HMRC authorisation and can be used for both UK domestic electronic invoicing and electronic invoicing to other EC countries.

(iii) *Such other electronic means as may be approved by HMRC where the document relates to supplies of goods or services made in the UK* provided the supplier (or, in the case of self-billed electronic invoices, the customer) is able to

- impose a satisfactory level of control over the authenticity and integrity of the invoice data (eg security of networks/ communication links, access controls, and message transfer protocols (such as http-s)); and

- meet all the other conditions for electronic invoicing.

Examples of allowable systems are

- Internet-based systems (including EDI via Internet) such as XML/XSL messages transmitted using http; EDI files sent under FTP or as attachments to e-mail; and free format or structured text messages sent by Internet e-mail;
- intermediary service providers; and
- bill presentment where invoices are 'presented' on websites, hosted either by suppliers or their agents, and customers simply access these websites to view their invoices.

Tax authorities in some other EC countries may not accept invoicing using these means. If so, potential customers in those countries would not be able to use a supplier's invoices as evidence of a taxable supply to them and may not be willing to do business with that supplier.

Where a business wishes to invoice electronically but its system is not covered by (i) or (ii) above and it is not sure whether its system meets the requirements of (iii) above, it should write to the National Advice Service with, if possible,

- an indication of the standard under which the invoice message has been drafted;
- a formatted 'dump' of an example invoice; and
- an overview of the main system concepts, including control over authenticity and integrity of data.

HMRC will then comment on the acceptability of the invoice message. If it is not acceptable, they will advise on what further information is required and how this may be accommodated.

(*c*) *Controls over the transmission of invoices.* Businesses must transmit invoices in a secure environment, using industry-accepted security technologies on

- the messages themselves; or
- communication links/networks over which the invoices are transferred.

Examples of these include http-s, SSL, S-MIME and FTP. Other procedural means that offer similar assurances may also be used.

(*d*) *Protecting the authenticity and integrity of invoices.* Businesses must be able to ensure the authenticity and integrity of their invoice data during the transfer between trading partners. HMRC will not be over-prescriptive in specifying the detailed forms that control may take but a business must be able to demonstrate that it has control over

- completeness and accuracy of the invoice data;
- timeliness of processing;
- prevention of, or detection of, possible corruption of data during transmission;
- prevention of duplication of processing (by the recipient); and

- prevention of the automatic processing, by the recipient, of certain types of invoice on which VAT may not be recoverable (eg margin scheme invoices).

A business must also be able to demonstrate that it has a recovery plan in case of a system failure or loss of data and maintain an audit trail between its electronic invoicing system(s) and the internal application system(s) that are used to process the electronic invoices.

Supplies to other EC countries. Where a UK business issues electronic invoices for supplies to other EC countries, it must meet the UK conditions for electronic invoicing. But it should also check whether the customer's system can accept invoices in the format used before he agrees to receive them electronically. The tax authorities of certain other EC countries, although accepting the use of advance electronic signature and EDI, do not accept all the electronic methods of raising invoices that are permissible in the UK.

Conditions for electronic storage. A business (whether supplier or customer) must:

- Guarantee the authenticity and integrity of its invoice data during and after application processing (see (*d*) above) and throughout the storage period by electronic or procedural means, and store all the data related to its invoices.
- Store its invoices in a readable format and be able to readily recreate the invoice information as at the time of its original transmission.
- Keep history files so that it can find the appropriate details from any particular time in the past if asked to do so by an HMRC officer.
- Keep copies of all electronic invoices issued or received for six years (although if this causes serious storage problems or undue expense, HMRC may agree to a shorter period for some records).

Ordinarily, if invoices are sent electronically they should be stored electronically. If a business wishes to store its electronic invoices in a paper-based system, it must write to HMRC for approval to do so.

Storage abroad. Electronic invoices can be stored in another EC country provided they can be produced to HMRC when required in a readable form, and within a reasonable period of time, at a mutually agreed place. HMRC recommend that a business maintains on-line access to its records if it stores them outside the UK. Electronic invoices can also be stored outside the EC provided that, additionally, the country where they are stored respects European Data Protection principles regarding the storage of personal data (names, addresses, etc).

Outsourcing electronic invoices. A business may outsource the physical responsibility for the issuing of its electronic sales invoices to a third party, although all the legal obligations relating to the contents, storage and production of the invoices raised remain with the business.

Inability to meet the e-invoicing conditions. If a business

- is unable to meet all the conditions for transmission and storage of electronic invoicing set out above, it must issue paper invoices;
- has issued and stored invoices electronically, but failed to meet the conditions, it must issue paper invoices until HMRC are satisfied that its system is acceptable; and
- persistently fails to meet the conditions, it may be liable to a penalty.

Use of paper and electronic VAT invoicing at the same time. In normal circumstances, it is only possible for a business to run a dual system (ie raising both electronic and paper invoices for the same supplies or with the same trading partners) when running a controlled trial of an electronic invoicing system. Once the trial is over, the business must stop running the dual system and the electronic invoice becomes the legal document for VAT purposes. However, where a business has a specific need to run a dual system, it should contact the National Advice Service who will decide whether an exception can be made.

Customs' access to electronic systems. In order to check electronic systems, HMRC may request access to

- the operations of any computer systems which produce or receive VAT invoices or documents, and to the data stored on them;
- supporting documentation including file structures etc, audit trail, controls, safe keeping, and information on how the accounting system is organised; and
- advice on interrogation facilities available on the system.

HMRC must be able to take copies of information from the system, if required. A business may be able to meet its obligations as regards production of records by giving HMRC

- physical access to systems at its premises;
- indirect access (by providing information on electronic media or possibly via remote access);
- a resident audit programme installed at the request of the visiting HMRC officer; or
- any other reasonable method agreed with HMRC.

See also 17.11 CUSTOMS: POWERS for powers of HMRC to inspect computers generally.

[*SI 1995/2518, Regs A13, 13A; 14(6); SI 2003/3220, Regs 3, 5, 9*]. (VAT Notice 700/63/03; VAT Information Sheet 16/03, para 5.3).

De Voil Indirect Tax Service. See V3.516.

40.11 Corporate purchasing (procurement) cards

Such cards are designed to eliminate much of the paperwork in the purchasing process. Where a purchase is made, the supplier normally transmits the invoice information to the appropriate card company or bank (the 'transmission date'). At agreed intervals, the purchaser receives a VAT invoice report from the card company or bank. Some purchasing cards offer two levels of invoice detail, the level of detail received by the cardholder being dependent upon the capability of the supplier's accounting system. *The provisions in both* (*a*) *and* (*b*) *below have the force of law.*

(*a*) *Line Item Detail* (*LID*) *invoices.* These provide detailed, itemised information on a line-by-line basis. HMRC have agreed to waive the requirement to show the date of issue of the document under 40.4(*c*) above. The invoice report issued to the purchaser will show the transmission date for each transaction and is acceptable as evidence for input tax recovery (subject to the normal rules) from that date.

(*b*) *Summary VAT invoices.* Where a supplier's system cannot transmit LID invoices, HMRC generally do not require a supplier to issue an invoice to the customer. Instead they accept a Summary VAT invoice report issued by the card company or bank in support of an input tax claim provided no single transaction has a value of more than £5,000 and the report contains the following information.

- Value of the supply.
- VAT amount charged.
- VAT rate.
- Time of supply.
- Description of the goods.
- Supplier's name, address and VAT registration number.
- Customer's name and address.

A supplier must issue a VAT invoice if the value of a 'single transaction' exceeds £5,000 or if specifically requested by the customer. In the latter case, the invoice must be clearly endorsed 'Paid by Purchasing Card – Supplementary VAT invoice'. A '*single transaction*' is the total value of purchases made using a card at any one time, eg one 'swipe' of the card.

In all cases, the supplier must continue to generate contemporaneous VAT invoices for output tax accounting purposes for all purchasing card transactions.

(VAT Notice 701/48/02, paras 3.1–3.4).

De Voil Indirect Tax Service. See V3.527.

40.12 ROUNDING OF VAT ON INVOICES

Invoice traders. By concession, invoice traders (as opposed to retailers) may round *down* the total VAT payable on all goods and services shown on a VAT invoice to a whole penny (ie they may ignore any fraction of a penny). The concession is applicable only where the VAT charged to customers and the VAT paid to HMRC is the same.

Calculations of VAT based on lines of goods or services included with other goods or services in the same invoice must either be made by

(*a*) rounding down to the nearest 0.1p; or

(*b*) rounding to the nearest 1p or 0.5p.

For example, 86.76p and 86.74p would both be rounded down to 86.7p under (*a*) but rounded up to 87p and down to 86.50p respectively under method (*b*).

Whichever method is used must be adopted consistently. The final amount of VAT payable may be rounded down to the nearest whole penny.

Calculations of VAT based on VAT per unit or per article, eg for price lists, must be either

(i) to four decimal places and then rounded down to three places (eg £0.0024 rounded down to £0.002 (0.2p)); or

(ii) to the nearest 1p or 0.5p (but not to 'nil' on any unit or article, ie a minimum of 0.5p per article or unit).

Calculation of VAT at retailers. Retailers who do not use a retail scheme but use till technology to identify the VAT due on each transaction and issue an invoice, calculating VAT at line level or invoice level, must not round the VAT figure down. They may, however, round (up and down) each VAT calculation. Retailers using a retail scheme to account for VAT are not affected by these provisions.

(VAT Notice 700, paras 17.5, 17.6).

40.13 TIME LIMITS FOR ISSUING INVOICES

A VAT invoice or a document treated as VAT invoice under 40.2 above must be provided within 30 days after the time when the supply is treated as taking place (see 64.32 *et seq.* SUPPLY) or within such longer period after that time as HMRC allow in general or special directions. [*VATA 1994, Sch 11 para 2A; FA 2002, s 24; SI 1995/2518, Reg 13(5)*]. Extension of this time limit is permitted *without application* where

- an extension has been allowed for tax point purposes under the 14 day rule (see 64.39 and 64.49 SUPPLY);
- special accounting arrangements have been approved; or
- where a newly registered business has not been notified of its VAT registration number (in which case the VAT invoice must be issued within 30 days from the date of advice of that number).

In all other cases, application must be made, in writing, to HMRC for an extension of the time limit.

(VAT Notice 700, para 16.2).

De Voil Indirect Tax Service. See V3.517.

40.14 TRANSMISSION OF INVOICES

As an alternative to sending VAT invoices by post, they may be sent to customers by fax or e-mail. The normal rules regarding VAT invoices apply. Invoices received in either of these ways are acceptable as evidence for input tax deduction (subject to the normal rules). However, where transmission is by fax, if the customer has a thermal-paper fax machine, the invoice may not be permanent and the customer may not be able to fulfil the obligation to preserve the invoice for six years. It is suggested that the supplier warns the customer of this possibility, preferably on the VAT invoice itself.

See also 40.10 above for electronic transmission of invoices, including the use of 'outsourcing' for the issue of invoices.

(VAT Notice 700, para 17.8).

40.15 CREDIT AND DEBIT NOTES

Where credit or contingent discount (eg discount on condition that the customer buys more goods at a later date) is allowed to a customer who can reclaim all the VAT on the supply as input tax, there is no obligation to adjust the original VAT charge provided both parties agree not to do so (although records of outputs and inputs will still need to be adjusted). Otherwise an adjustment should be made to the original VAT charge in the appropriate period. See 56.6 RECORDS. A credit note should be issued to the customer and a copy retained. Alternatively, if both parties agree, the customer can issue a VAT debit note. A valid debit note places the same legal obligations on both parties as a valid credit note and must fulfil the same conditions.

To be valid for VAT purposes, a credit or debit note must reflect a genuine mistake or overcharge or an agreed reduction in the value of the supply and be issued within one month of this being discovered or agreed. It must give value to the customer, ie represent a genuine entitlement or claim on the part of the customer for the amount overcharged to be either refunded or offset against the value of future supplies. It should be headed 'credit note' or 'debit note' as appropriate and show

(*a*) identifying number and date of issue;

(*b*) supplier's and customer's name and address;

(*c*) supplier's registration number;

(*d*) description identifying goods or services for which credit is given;

(*e*) quantity and amount credited for each description and reason for credit, eg 'returned goods';

(*f*) total amount credited excluding VAT;

(*g*) rate and amount of VAT credited;

(*h*) number and date of the original VAT invoice. If not possible, HMRC will need to be satisfied that VAT has been accounted for on the original supply.

Where a credit note includes credits for zero-rated or exempt supplies, each must be totalled separately and the credit note must show clearly that no credit for VAT has been given for them.

Credit notes issued without VAT adjustment should state 'This is not a credit note for VAT'. It will still be necessary to adjust records of outputs and inputs in order to complete the VAT returns.

Credit notes to persons in other EC countries. With effect from 1 January 2004, a credit note issued to a person in another EC country must contain the same particulars as the VAT invoice(s) that it is intended to amend. See 40.5 above. Before 1 January 2004, there were no separate rules for such credit notes and the general rules as set out above applied.

Accounting for credit or debit notes. Where an adjustment has to be made for a credit or debit note, the following procedure should be followed.

- *If a credit note is issued or a debit note is received*, deduct the amount of the VAT credit/debit from the amount of VAT payable in the VAT account. Include the value of that adjustment in the current VAT return. If the amount of the VAT credit/debit exceeds the total VAT charged on sales in the current VAT period, write the figure in brackets (paper return) or insert a minus sign (electronic return) in Box 1 of the VAT return.

- *If a credit note is received or a debit note is issued*, deduct the amount of the VAT credit/debit from the amount of VAT deductible in the VAT account. Include the value of that adjustment in the current VAT return. If the amount of the VAT credit/debit exceeds the total VAT reclaimed on purchases in the current VAT period, write the figure in brackets (paper return) or insert a minus sign (electronic return) in Box 4 of the VAT return.

No VAT adjustment may be made in this way more than three years after the end of the VAT period in which the original supply took place. The three-year time limit was upheld in *Valley Chemical Co Ltd (VTD 17989) (TVC 57.27)* but in *General Motors Acceptance Corporation (UK) plc (VTD 17990) (TVC 42.49)* the tribunal held that this requirement infringed a person's basic right to be taxed on the consideration received and was incompatible with *EC Sixth Directive, Art 11* (see 22.14 EUROPEAN COMMUNITY LEGISLATION). The time limit should not prevent adjustment before the first opportunity to make it arose. HMRC have accepted this. (VAT Information Sheet 6/03).

Bankruptcy, insolvent liquidation and administrative receivership. The tax point for credit or debit notes issued by or on behalf of insolvent traders is the date on which the supply was originally made or received.

Cancelled registrations. The tax point for any credit or debit note issued or received after the date of cancellation of registration is the date of the original supply. If this happens after the final VAT return has been submitted, HMRC should be contacted.

VAT rate. The rate of VAT to be used for a credit or debit note is the one in force at the tax point of the original supply.

Returned or replaced goods. Where such goods are replaced with similar goods, the original VAT charge may stand or be cancelled (by issuing a credit note if a VAT invoice has previously been issued) and VAT charged on the replacement. If the original VAT charge is allowed to stand, VAT need not be accounted for on the replacement goods provided they are supplied free of charge. If supplied at a *lower* price, the VAT charged may be reduced by a credit note. If supplied at a *higher* price, additional VAT must be accounted for.

[*SI 1995/2518, Reg 38; SI 1997/1086, Reg 6*]. (VAT Notice 700, paras 18.2, 18.3; VAT Notice 700/45/02, paras 9.2–9.10).

Bad debts. Output tax paid on an invoice which proves to be a bad debt cannot subsequently be reclaimed by issuing a credit note for the unpaid amount. See 7 BAD DEBT RELIEF.

De Voil Indirect Tax Service. See V3.519; V3.520.

40.16 **Correction of VAT invoices following a change in the VAT rate**

Under *VATA 1994, s 88*, a trader may elect to override certain of the normal tax point rules which determine whether a particular supply is taxable at the old or new rate when there is a change in the rate of VAT or in the descriptions of exempt, zero-rated or reduced-rate supplies. The trader is allowed to account for VAT at the old rates on supplies actually 'made' before the date of change but for which the invoice and payment tax points would have occurred later. See 55.6 RATES OF VAT for full details.

Where under the above circumstances a VAT invoice is issued before the election, the supplier must within 14 days provide the customer with a credit note headed 'Credit note – change of VAT rate' showing the information required in 40.15 (*a*)–(*d*), (*g*) and (*h*) above. [*SI 1995/2518, Reg 15; SI 2003/1485*]. See 56.6 and 56.9 RECORDS for the recording of credit notes.

40.17 FOREIGN LANGUAGE INVOICES

Where a person in the UK receives a VAT invoice (or part of a VAT invoice) in a language other than English, HMRC may, by notice in writing, require that person to provide them with an English translation of the invoice within 30 days of the date of the notice. [*SI 1995/2518, Reg 13B; SI 2003/3220, Reg 6*]. This will be done on an exceptional basis and any requests will be targeted at selective invoices only. (VAT Information Sheet 16/03, para 7.1).

41 Isle of Man

De Voil Indirect Tax Service. See V1.216; V1.217.

The contents of this chapter are as follows.

41.1 ADMINISTRATION

The Isle of Man (IOM) is not part of the UK and the common tax area between the two countries results from an administrative agreement between the UK and the IOM governments contained in the *Customs and Excise Agreement 1979* (as amended). In the UK, the agreement was implemented by the *Isle of Man Act 1979*. *Section 6* of that Act relates to VAT.

VAT is administered and collected in the IOM by the Manx Customs and Excise Service under the *Value Added Tax Act 1996* (of Tynwald).

The spirit of the agreement between the UK and IOM is that IOM legislation parallels UK legislation and procedures, with certain exceptions, but so that VAT is not charged twice on the same transaction. [*IMA 1979, s 6; SI 1982/1067; SI 1982/1068*]. Differences include

- legislation relating to VAT on gaming machines under *VATA 1994, s 23* (see 57.3 RECREATION AND SPORT) does not have an equivalent in the IOM [*IMA 1979, s 1(d)*];
- legislation relating to refund of VAT on the construction of new homes by do-it-yourself housebuilders under *VATA 1994, s 35* (see 42.33 LAND AND BUILDINGS) does not have an equivalent in the IOM [*SI 1982/1067, Art 9*]; and
- the rate of VAT on accommodation in hotels and similar establishments in the IOM, including the provision of holiday accommodation and the letting of camp sites, is 5%.

41.2 REGISTRATION

Separate VAT registers are maintained in the IOM and the UK. There are special provisions for determining, or enabling HMRC to determine, where a person is to be registered who would otherwise be liable to be registered in both places.

A person who is *liable to be registered* in the UK under *VATA 1994, Sch 1 para 1* (see 59.3 REGISTRATION) and who

(*a*) has 'an establishment' both in the UK and the IOM, or

(*b*) does not have an establishment in either country

will be registered in the UK or IOM as HMRC determine; but unless or until they determine that he should be registered in the IOM, he is required to be registered in the UK. HMRC may, however, at any time determine that a person within (*a*) or (*b*) above

- who is registered in the UK, is instead to be registered in the IOM, in which case he ceases to be, or required to be, registered in the UK from such date as they determine (although still remaining liable for payment of VAT on business assets held on the last day of registration, see 59.34 REGISTRATION); and

- who is registered in the IOM, is instead to be registered in the UK from such date as they determine, in which case any amount of VAT required to be paid in the IOM is deemed to have been an amount of VAT due in the UK.

Where a person is registered, or required to be registered, in the IOM, the provisions of *VATA 1994, Sch 1 para 5* (notification of liability for, and date of registration in, the UK, see 59.4 REGISTRATION) and *VATA 1994, Sch 1 para 9* (entitlement to be registered, see 59.2 REGISTRATION) do not apply to that person. HMRC may, however, determine that any person to whom those provisions do apply shall be registered in the IOM.

A person registered in the UK who has no establishment in the IOM, or is the representative member of a VAT group (see 31.2 GROUPS OF COMPANIES) no member of which has an establishment there, must notify HMRC if such an establishment is subsequently acquired. Such notification may be treated as an event requiring the cancellation of the person's, or that group's, registration.

'*An establishment*' in a country is where there is a place from which a person carries on a business in that country or carries on business through a branch or agent in that country. For this purpose an agent is a person who has the authority or capacity to create legal relations between his principal and a third party. [*SI 1982/1067, Arts 11, 12*].

Liability to be registered. When determining whether a person is liable to be registered for VAT the value (or estimated value) of taxable supplies, distance sales, relevant acquisitions and certain supplies of assets made in both the UK and the IOM must be taken into account. (Internal Guidance V1–28, para 71.3).

Divisional and group registration. Where registration of a company in the names of its divisions is requested and allowed (see 59.37 REGISTRATION) all the divisions must be registered in the same country. Where group registration is requested for a group which has establishments in both countries, HMRC (in consultation with the IOM Customs) have powers to determine who will be the representative member of the group. This will be a company established in the country of registration. (Internal Guidance V1–28, para 71.5).

De Voil Indirect Tax Service. See V2.127; V2.140; V2.156.

41.3 IMPORTS, EXPORTS AND REMOVALS

Within the common tax area of the UK and the IOM, a registered business accounts for VAT in the country in which it is registered. For example, an IOM business, making taxable supplies in the UK accounts for the VAT in the IOM. If the business imports goods into the common tax area, the import VAT can be paid (or deferred) and reclaimed as input tax in the IOM subject to the normal rules for input tax deduction.

Movements of goods from the UK to the IOM and vice versa are not normally treated as exports or imports provided that, for goods removed from the IOM to the UK

- any VAT due has been accounted for in the IOM, or
- if the goods are relieved of VAT in the IOM, the conditions of that relief have not been broken.

42 Land and Buildings

Cross-references. See 7.11 BAD DEBT RELIEF for sales of repossessed properties by lenders; CAPITAL GOODS SCHEME (10) for the deduction, and adjustment of deduction, of input tax on certain land and buildings by partly exempt businesses; 59.33 REGISTRATION for land and buildings in hand in cancellation of registration; 64.21 SUPPLY for the place of supply of services relating to land outside the UK and the Isle of Man; 64.44 SUPPLY for the time of supply of land and property.

The contents of this chapter are as follows.

PART I DEFINITIONS, ETC.

42.1 DEFINITIONS AND MEANINGS OF TERMS

The following general definitions and terms apply for the purposes of this chapter.

(1) **'Approved alteration'**

An approved alteration means any of the following.

(*a*) In the case of a '*protected building*' (see (12) below) which is an ecclesiastical building excluded from the planning consent requirements by

Planning (*Listed Buildings and Conservation Areas*) *Act 1990, s 60*, any works of alteration. A building used or available for use by a minister of religion wholly or mainly as a residence from which to perform the duties of his office is not to be treated as an ecclesiastical building for these purposes. [*VATA 1994, Sch 8 Group 6, Note* (*6*)].

In England and Wales, the religious denominations which have been granted exclusion are the Church of England, the Church in Wales, the Roman Catholic Church, the Methodist Church, the Baptist Union of Great Britain and the Baptist Union of Wales, and the United Reformed Church.

In Scotland and Northern Ireland, all listed (or their equivalent in Northern Ireland) places of worship are excluded from planning consent requirements for the purposes of VAT relief on alterations.

The churches, however, operate their own controls that follow a Government Code of Practice (eg the Church of England has a system called 'faculty jurisdiction' under which the Diocesan Chancellor decides the faculty application taking advice from the Diocesan Advisory Committee).

Any alteration, which is not work of repair or maintenance (see below), to the fabric of a listed place of worship that has ecclesiastical exemption is an approved alteration. The Church should keep a copy of the 'faculty' (or other documentation) in its records.

(VAT Notice 708, para 9.4).

Alterations to ecclesiastical buildings which require planning consent fall within (*b*) below.

(*b*) In any other case, works of alteration which cannot be carried out unless authorised under *Planning* (*Listed Buildings and Conservation Areas*) *Act 1990*, *Planning* (*Listed Buildings and Conservation Areas*) (*Scotland*) *Act 1997*, *Planning* (*Northern Ireland*) *Order 1991* or *Ancient Monuments and Archaeological Areas Act 1979* and for which consent has been obtained under the appropriate legislation. [*VATA 1994, Sch 8 Group 6, Note* (*6*)].

'Crown' and 'Duchy' interest buildings. Listed building consent may not be needed for alterations to buildings on Crown or Duchy land even though it would be needed for similar alterations to listed buildings elsewhere. In such a case, an alteration to the fabric of the building which would otherwise have required consent and which is not work of repair or maintenance (see below) is an approved alteration. [*VATA 1994, Sch 8 Group 6, Note* (*6*)].

Scheduled monuments. All work affecting scheduled monuments requires scheduled monument consent from the Secretary of State. Approved alterations are those works of alteration for which consent has been obtained. It is possible for a building to be both scheduled and listed. If so, only scheduled monument procedures apply and it should be treated as a scheduled monument for VAT purposes.

Listed building consent. In most cases, an approved alteration falls within (*b*) above and is an alteration for which listed building consent is both needed and has been obtained from the appropriate planning authority (or, in some circumstances, the Secretary of State) prior to the commencement of the work. A supplier will need to find out from his customer (or their architect or surveyor) to what extent the work he is contracted to do has both required and received listed building consent. Listed building consent is not the same as planning permission. In general terms, listed building consent is needed for work on a listed building which would affect its character as a building of special architectural or historic interest. The construction of an extension, or alterations following partial demolition, would certainly require consent but it is difficult to generalise about less radical work, especially as regards internal alterations. It is an offence to carry out work to a listed building without obtaining any required listed building consent. Where this happens, the planning authority cannot issue retrospective listed building consent for the work, although they may permit the unauthorised works to be retained. Such works are *not* then approved alterations (because consent has not been granted at the time the work is carried out) and are standard-rated. Where works to a listed building are carried out without listed building consent being obtained or where work carried out does not comply with a condition in the consent, the local planning authority may issue a 'listed building enforcement notice' for the carrying out of further work. An alteration, which is not work of repair or maintenance (see below), to the fabric of the building under the terms of an enforcement notice is an approved alteration.

(VAT Notice 708, para 9.4).

Alteration or repair and maintenance? HMRC regard a building as being altered when its fabric, such as its walls, roof, internal surfaces, floors, stairs, windows, doors, plumbing and wiring is changed in a meaningful way. Works of repair or maintenance, or any incidental alteration resulting from works of repair or maintenance, are standard-rated, even if the work has been included in the listed building consent.

See *C & E Commrs v Viva Gas Appliances, HL [1983] STC 819 (TVC 54.7)* where Lord Diplock stated that alteration of a building should be construed as any work on the fabric of the building except that which is so slight or trivial as to attract the application of the *de minimis* rule (although it should be noted that in *The Vicar and Parochial Church Council of St Petroc Minor (VTD 16450) (TVC 53.44)* the tribunal specifically declined to apply this *dicta* on the basis that the context in which 'alteration' was used in that case no longer appears in *VATA 1994*).

Works of repair or maintenance are those tasks designed to minimise, for as long as possible, the need for, and future scale and cost of, further attention to the fabric of the building. Changes to the physical features of the building are not zero-rated alterations if, in the exercise of proper repair and maintenance of the building, they are either

- trifling or insignificant, or
- dictated by the nature and use of modern building materials.

Similarly, if the amount of work or cost is significant, that does not make the work a zero-rated alteration if the inherent character of the work is repair and maintenance.

Examples

Work	*VAT treatment*
Extensions	Alteration
Opening/closing doorways	Alteration
Replacement of rotten wooden windows with UPVC double glazing	Repair or maintenance
Installing a window where one did not exist before	Alteration
Re-felt and batten roof	Repair or maintenance
Replacement of a flat roof with a pitched roof	Alteration
Replacement of straw thatch with reeds; and changes to the ridge detail of a thatched roof	Repair or maintenance when carried out as part of the normal renewal programme.
Damp proofing	Repair or maintenance
Making good	Follows the liability of the main work
Re-decorating	Repair or maintenance
Re-pointing	Repair or maintenance
Re-wiring	Repair or maintenance
Extending wiring and plumbing systems	Alteration
Replacing boilers at the same time as extending plumbing systems	Alteration when replaced as a direct consequence of deciding to extend the plumbing system. But repair or maintenance when the decision to extend the plumbing system is made following the need to replace a boiler.
Flood lighting	Alteration when installed on the building. But neither an alteration nor repair or maintenance (and therefore standard-rated) when installed within the grounds of a building – there is no work to the fabric of the building.

(VAT Notice 708, para 9.3).

Only mains electrical wiring and lighting systems that are either on, or in, the structure of the building itself will be considered to be part of the fabric of the building. Those parts which extend beyond the structure into the grounds (eg wiring to floodlights) will not. Electrical appliances which are attached to, and serviced by, the mains supply are not considered to be part of the mains wiring system. (Business Brief 7/2000).

The construction of a building 'separate' from, but in the curtilage (see (3) below) of, a protected building does not constitute an alteration of the protected building and cannot be zero-rated as an approved alteration, even if the work has listed building consent. [*VATA 1994, Sch 8 Group 6 Item 2* and *Notes (6)–(8), (10); SI 1995/283*]. Zero-rating may, however, be available under the rules for construction of new buildings under 42.18 below (ie if it is (i) the construction of a completely new self-contained dwelling (including a garage built at the same time for use with it) where there are no restrictions on disposal; or (ii) a completely new self-contained building for use solely for a '*relevant residential purpose*' or a '*relevant charitable purpose*' (see (15) and (13) below respectively)). (VAT Notice 708, para 9.3).

See *C & E Commrs v Arbib, QB [1995] STC 490 (TVC 53.39)* for a consideration of the meaning of 'separate'. In that case, a swimming pool connected to a listed farmhouse by a covered walkway and a brick wall was held not to be a separate building so that the building work on it fell to be zero-rated.

(2) **'Construction of a building'**

There is no definition in the legislation of the '*construction of a building*' for zero-rating purposes, other than it does not include

- the conversion, reconstruction or alteration of an existing building;
- any enlargement of, or extension to, an existing building except to the extent that this creates an additional dwelling or dwellings; or
- the construction of an annexe to an existing building unless
  - (i) the whole or a part of the annexe is intended solely for use for a '*relevant charitable purpose*' (see (13) below);
  - (ii) it is capable of functioning independently from the existing building; and
  - (iii) the only access (or main access where more than one) to the annexe is *not* via the existing building and *vice versa*.

  The significance of the amendment in (i) above with effect from 1 June 2002 is that, in conjunction with *VATA 1994, Sch 8 Group 5 Note 10* which provides for apportionment between zero-rated and standard-rated supplies, zero-rating can be applied to supplies made in connection with a part of an annexe which is to be used *solely* for relevant charitable purposes. Where an annexe, or part of an annexe (including common areas such as entrance lobbies) will be used for a mixture of relevant charitable and other purposes, it (or that part) is not used solely for a relevant charitable purpose and is standard-rated. By concession, minor non-qualifying use can be ignored (see (13) below).

For these purposes, a building only ceases to be an existing building when

- it is demolished completely to ground level; or
- the part remaining above ground level consists of no more than a single façade (double façade where a corner site), the retention of which is a condition or requirement of statutory planning consent or similar permission.

[*VATA 1994, Sch 8 Group 5 Notes (16)–(18); SI 1995/280; SI 2002/1101*].

Examples of the construction of a zero-rated building

HMRC give the following guidance to help decide if a zero-rated building is being constructed.

- It is built from scratch, and, before work starts, any pre-existing building is demolished completely to ground level (cellars, basements and the 'slab' at ground level may be retained).
- The new building makes use of no more than a single facade (or a double facade on a corner site) of a pre-existing building, the pre-existing building is demolished completely (other than the retained facade) before work on the new building is started *and* the facade is retained as an explicit condition or requirement of statutory planning consent.
- A semi-detached building is built.
- An existing building is enlarged or extended and the enlargement or extension creates an additional dwelling or dwellings which is/are wholly within the enlargement or extension. So, for example, a new eligible flat built on top of an existing building can qualify for zero-rating. If the new dwelling is partly or wholly contained within the existing building, the work does not qualify for zero-rating, although it may qualify for reduced-rating as a 'changed number of dwellings conversion' under 42.23 below.
- *Relevant charitable purpose annexes.* The construction of a building intended for use solely for a '*relevant charitable purpose*' (see (15) below) is zero-rated, with additions to an existing building normally being standard-rated. However, an addition can qualify as the construction of a building (and be zero-rated subject to the normal conditions) when all the following conditions are met.

  (i) An 'annexe' is constructed, rather than an extension or enlargement. An '*annexe*' is a structure which has only a minimal physical connection with the existing building (eg it could be linked to the existing building by means of an enclosed walkway, or abut the existing building along one wall with a connecting door). It should be easily recognisable as a structure that would be a separate building were it not for the physical connection. In contrast, 'enlargements' and 'extensions' are physically connected in a major way with the existing building. Typically, they dovetail in with, merge with, are built on top of, or have several interconnecting access points with the existing building.

  (ii) The whole annexe, or a part of it, is intended for use solely for a relevant charitable purpose. The activities carried on in the annexe need not be similar to, or associated with, the activities in the existing building. For example, the annexe need not be an annexe to a building used solely for a relevant charitable purpose. What is important is that the annexe itself is intended for use solely for a relevant charitable purpose.

  (iii) The whole annexe must be capable of functioning independently from the existing building, even if only part of it is used solely for a relevant charitable purpose. An annexe is capable of functioning independently when the activities in the annexe can be carried on without reliance on the existing building, ignoring the existence of building services (electricity and water supplies, etc) that are shared with the existing building.

(iv) The annexe and the existing building each has its own independent main access. So, even if the annexe has its own entrance, the main access to the annexe must not be through the existing building and the annexe must not create the main access to the existing building.

The demolition and reconstruction of part of an existing building, such as the wing of a building, cannot be the construction of an annexe.

- *Infilling*. The building of a new house within an existing terrace of houses on the site of a house that has been totally demolished ('*infilling*') apart from

  (i) party walls at the end of the infill site forming part of a neighbouring property that is not being developed; and

  (ii) any facade which is retained as an explicit condition or requirement of statutory planning consent.

  Where neighbouring houses in a terrace are being re-developed, the party wall between those houses will also need to be demolished if the works are to qualify as 'constructing a building' for VAT purposes.

- A garage is built, or a building is converted into a garage; and the construction or conversion takes place at the same time as, and the building is intended to be occupied with, a building 'designed as a dwelling or number of dwellings' (see (4) below.
- A building is built that is one of a number of buildings constructed at the same time on the same site and it is intended to be used together with those other buildings as a unit solely for a 'relevant residential purpose' (see (15) below).

Examples not qualifying as the construction of a zero-rated building

HMRC give the following as examples of construction work that cannot be zero-rated.

- A 'granny' annexe which cannot be used, or disposed of, separately from a main house. This is because the annexe is not 'designed as a dwelling' (see (4) below) in its own right.
- A detached, enclosed swimming pool in the grounds of a new house. This is because the building being constructed is not 'designed as a dwelling' (see (4) below).
- A detached building in the grounds of an existing care home which extends the facilities of the home. This is because the building being constructed will not be used for a 'relevant residential purpose' (see (15) below) in its own right and it was not constructed at the same time as the rest of the home.

(VAT Notice 708, para 3.2).

(3) **'Curtilage'**

In VAT Notice 708 (August 1997 Edition) HMRC defined curtilage as a reasonable amount of land, surrounding the building, which may include other buildings. What constitutes a reasonable amount of land will depend on the type of building and its setting. Although this definition is not reproduced in the latest edition of VAT Notice 708, there is no reason to suppose that their interpretation of the term has changed.

(4) **'Designed as a dwelling'**

There is no definition in the legislation of 'dwelling' but see *Calam Vale* and *Amicus Group* considered in (10) below.

For the purposes of zero-rating, a building is designed as a dwelling or number of dwellings where the following conditions are satisfied in relation to each dwelling.

(*a*) The dwelling consists of self-contained living accommodation.

(*b*) There is no provision for direct internal access from the dwelling to any other dwelling or part of a dwelling.

(*c*) The separate use, letting or disposal of the dwelling is not prohibited by the terms of any covenant, statutory planning consent or similar provision. Occupancy restrictions (eg working in agriculture or forestry or being over a specified age) are not prohibitions on separate use or disposal and do not affect whether a building is designed as a dwelling or number of dwellings. (VAT Notice 708, para 14.2).

(*d*) Statutory planning consent has been granted in respect of that dwelling and its construction or conversion has been carried out in accordance with that consent.

[*VATA 1994, Sch 8 Group 5 Note (2); SI 1995/280*].

See *University of Bath (VTD 14235) (TVC 15.45)* (students' accommodation) and *A J White (VTD 15388) (TVC 63.81)* (living accommodation over public houses) where in each case cooking and toilet facilities were shared.

For cases where (*c*) above was in point, see *Sherwin & Green (VTD 16396) (TVC 15.35)*, *P Thompson, (VTD 15834) (TVC 15.37)* and *PH Wiseman (VTD 17374) (TVC 15.41)* and for a case where (*d*) was in point, see *AI Davison (VTD 17130) (TVC 15.44)*.

In *Oldrings Development Kingsclere Ltd (VTD 17769) (TVC 15.33)* a single storey, self-contained building was constructed in the grounds of a large house. It comprised one large room, plus a small room with a WC and washbasin, and had its own central heating system, hot water and electricity supply. The tribunal held that it was 'designed as a dwelling' and qualified for zero-rating, even though it was primarily used as an artist's studio, as it was capable of being used as a studio flat.

(5) **'Grant'**

Grant includes assignment or surrender. [*VATA 1994, Sch 8 Group 5 Note 2; SI 1995/280*].

A grant is a sale of a freehold or other interest, or a lease or letting of land. An assignment is the transfer of a lease by the existing tenant to a new tenant. A surrender is the giving up of an 'interest in or right over' land (see (7) below) to the grantor. (VAT Notice 742, para 2.2).

The grant of any interest frequently gives rise to a number of further supplies at later times. For example, a supply is made each time that a payment is received for rent. In such cases, the liability of each subsequent supply is determined at the time when that supply is made rather than by reference to the time of the original grant. [*VATA 1994, s 96(10A); FA 1997, s 35(1)*].

(6) **'In the course of construction'**

Services supplied 'in the course of the construction' comprise

(*a*) work on the building itself prior to its 'completion'; and

(*b*) any other service closely connected to the construction of the building.

For examples of services included, and not included, see 42.25 below.

'*Completion*' takes place at a given moment in time. That point in time is determined by weighing up the relevant factors of the project, such as

- when a Certificate of Completion is issued;
- the intention of the developer;
- the scope of the planning consent and variations to it;
- when the building is sold; and
- when the building is occupied.

Generally, once a building has been completed, any further work to the building is standard-rated. But see 42.25 below.

Examples

(1) A developer is in the process of constructing a house for sale. The buyer, would like to include an attached conservatory and so contracts with a conservatory specialist to supply and install it prior moving in. The developer refuses the conservatory supplier access to the site until after he has finished his work and the house has been conveyed to the buyer.

In such circumstances, the supply of the conservatory is not work in the course of the construction of the house but work to an existing building and cannot be zero-rated.

(2) A developer constructs and sells 'shell' loft apartments for fitting out by the buyer. When the developer sells the lofts, their construction is not 'complete'.

Future work to fit them out can be zero-rated until such time as they are 'complete'. Typically, this would be when the buyer moves in.

(3) A non-fee-paying school obtains planning permission to construct a building that will be used solely for a relevant charitable purpose. Due to limited funds, the extent of the work is scaled down and a smaller building is constructed instead. Funds are later obtained to extend and enlarge the building to produce a building of the same capacity as originally planned.

> In such circumstances, the building would be 'complete' at the end of the first set of works and the later works are standard-rated.
>
> See also *C & E Commrs v St Mary's Roman Catholic High School, QB [1996] STC 1091 (TVC 15.136)* where work began on the building of a new secondary school in 1979 and the school opened to pupils in 1981, although some of its original buildings were not completed until 1983. Under the original plans, the school was to have been equipped with two playgrounds but these were not completed until 1994. The QB held that, on the evidence, the interval between the completion of the building work on the school and the construction of the playgrounds was far too long to establish the necessary temporal link. Accordingly, the building of the playgrounds failed to qualify for zero-rating.

(VAT Notice 708, para 3.3).

A building has been held to be in the course of construction until the main structure is completed, the windows glazed and all essential services and fittings, such as plumbing and electricity, have been installed. Thereafter the building ceases to be in course of construction and the phase of fitting out and furnishing is ready to begin (*University of Hull (VTD 180) (TVC 15.132)*). See also *JM Associates (VTD 18624) (TVC 15.133)* where the supply and construction of conservatories for newly-built houses was held to be standard-rated as the work of construction only took place after the house was completed.

(7) **'Interest in or right over'**

An interest in land can be

- a *legal interest*, ie the formal ownership of an interest in or right over land such as a freehold or leasehold interest in it; or
- a *beneficial* (*or equitable*) *interest*, ie the right to receive the benefit of supplies of it (eg the sales proceeds or rental income).

A beneficial interest may be held and transferred separately from the legal interest.

Rights over land include

- *rights of entry* which allow an authorised person or authority to enter land (eg they might allow someone to come onto land to perform a specific task);
- *easements* which grant the owner of neighbouring land a right to make their property better or more convenient, such as a right of way or right of light;
- *wayleaves*, ie a right of way to transport minerals extracted from land over another's land, or to lay pipes or cables over or under another's land; and
- *profits a prendre*, ie rights to take produce from another's land, such as to extract minerals.

(VAT Notice 742, para 2.4).

(8) **'Licence to occupy'**

A licence is an authority to do something that would otherwise be a trespass. HMRC regard a licence to occupy land as being created when the following criteria are met.

(*a*) The licence should be granted in return for a consideration paid by the licensee.

(*b*) The licence to occupy must be of a specified piece of land, even if the licence allows the licensor to change the exact area occupied (eg to move the licensee from the third floor to the fourth floor).

(*c*) The licence is for occupation of the land by the licensee.

(*d*) Another person's right to enter the specified land does not impinge upon the occupational rights of the licensee; and either

 (i) the licence allows the licensee to physically enjoy the land for the purposes of the grant (eg to hold a party in a hall); or

 (ii) the licence allows the licensee to exploit economically the land for the purposes of its business (eg to run a nightclub).

(VAT Notice 742, para 2.5).

See also *Abbotsley Golf and Squash Club Ltd (VTD 15042) (TVC 39.139)* where, applying dicta of Lord Templeman in *Street v Mountford, HL [1985] 2 All ER 289 (TVC 39.139)*, the tribunal held that exclusivity of occupation was an essential condition of a tenancy but not of a licence to occupy.

Examples of licences to occupy land

- The provision of office accommodation (eg a specified bay, room or floor together with the rights to use shared areas such as reception, lifts, restaurant, rest rooms, leisure facilities, etc).
- The provision of a serviced office which includes use of telephones, computer system, photocopier, fax machine, etc.
- Granting a concession to operate a shop within a shop where the concessionaires are granted an area from which to sell their goods or services.
- Granting space to erect advertising hoardings.
- Granting space to place a fixed kiosk on a specific site (eg sweet/newspaper kiosks, flower stands at railway stations).
- Hiring out a hall or other accommodation for meetings, parties, etc including use of a kitchen area, lighting, furniture, etc.
- Granting a catering concession, where the caterer is granted a licence to occupy specific kitchens and restaurant areas, even if the grant includes the use of kitchen or catering equipment.
- Granting traders a pitch in a market or at a car boot sale (even if only for one day, see *Tameside Metropolitan Borough Council (VTD 733) (TVC 39.5)*).

Not included as licences to occupy land (*and therefore standard-rated*)

- Sharing business premises where more than one business has use of the same parts of the premises without having their own specified areas.

- Providing another person with access to office premises to make use of the facilities (eg remote sales staff away from home base having access to telephones, fax machines, etc at another office).
- Allowing the public to tip rubbish on land.
- Storing someone else's goods in a warehouse without allocating any specified area for them.
- Granting an ambulatory concession (eg ice-cream vans on the sea front, hamburger vans at sporting events).
- Allowing the public admission to premises or events (see 57.6 RECREATION AND SPORT but note that admission to certain one-off fund-raising events by charities may be exempt).
- Any grant of land clearly incidental to the use of the facilities on it, such as hiring out safes to store valuables, the right to use facilities in a hairdressing salon or granting someone the right to place a free-standing or wall-mounted vending or gambling machine on premises.

  As regards hairdressers' chairs in open-plan salons, see *Price (N & J) (VTD 1443) (TVC 39.67)*; *Field & Field (t/a Paul Field Hair and Beauty Salon (VTD 2047) (TVC 39.68)*; *Genc (VTD 2595) (TVC 39.69)* and *Winder (t/a Anthony and Patricia) (VTD 11784) (TVC 39.73)* although in other cases the tribunal has held that a licence to occupy land existed (see *Quaife (VTD 1394) (TVC 39.64)* and *Daniels & Daniels (t/a Group Montage) (VTD 12014) (TVC 39.66)*). Subsequent, however, to these decisions, in *Simon Harris Hair Design Ltd (VTD 13939) (TVC 39.75)* the tribunal held that there was a single standard-rated supply by the owner to the stylists even though each stylist had (and was separately charged for) an allocated space within the salon. A licence to occupy that space was economically useless without the right to use other facilities such as junior staff, basins and dryers.

  HMRC's view regarding vending/gambling machines follows the decision in *Sinclair Collis Ltd v C & E Commrs, CJEC [2003] STC 898 (TVC 21.235)*. Before that decision, they took the view that such a supply was a licence to occupy land and therefore exempt. Standard-rating must be applied to such supplies from 1 January 2004 although site owners could apply the change earlier if they wished (Business Brief 18/2003).

(VAT Notice 742, paras 2.6, 2.7).

See also *Altman Blane & Co (VTD 12381) (TVC 39.8)* where payments for non-exclusive use of a room were held to be exempt.

(9) **'Major interest'**

In relation to England, Wales and Northern Ireland, a major interest in relation to land means the 'fee simple' or a tenancy for a term certain exceeding 21 years.

In relation to Scotland, following the abolition of feudal tenure, it will mean the interest of the owner or the lessee's interest under a lease for a period of not less than 20 years. Until the abolition, it is

(*a*) the estate or interest of the proprietor of the *dominium utile*, or (*b*) in the case of land not held under feudal tenure, the estate or interest of the owner, or the lessee's interest under a lease for a period of not less than 20 years.

'Fee simple'

- in relation to England and Wales means the freehold;
- in relation to Scotland means the interest of the owner (and, until the abolition of feudal tenure, the estate or interest of the proprietor of the *dominium utile*); and
- in relation to Northern Ireland, includes the estate of a person who holds land under a fee farm grant.

[*VATA 1994, s 96(1); FA 1998, s 24; Abolition of Feudal Tenure etc (Scotland) Act 2000, Sch 12 para 57*].

(10) **'Non-residential'**

A building or part of a building is 'non-residential' if

(*a*) it is neither

(i) designed nor adapted for 'use as a dwelling' or number of dwellings (see (4) above); nor

(ii) designed nor adapted for use for a '*relevant residential purpose*' (see (15) below), or

(*b*) it is designed or adapted for use within (*a*)(i) or (ii) above but

(i) where 42.13(*c*) below applies (grant of major interest by a developer), it was constructed more than ten years before the grant of the major interest and no part of it has been used as a dwelling or for a relevant residential purpose in the period of ten years immediately preceding the grant;

(ii) where 42.20 below applies (conversion services supplied to housing associations), it was constructed more than ten years before the commencement of the conversion work, no part of it has been used as a dwelling or for a relevant residential purpose in the period of ten years immediately preceding the commencement of those works, and no part of it is being so used; and

(iii) where 42.33(*a*)(iii) below applies (D-I-Y housebuilders), it was constructed more than ten years before the commencement of the conversion work and no part of it has been used as a dwelling or for a relevant residential purpose in the period of ten years immediately preceding the commencement of those works.

Before 1 August 2001, a building or part of a building was non-residential if it was designed or adapted for use within (*a*)(i) or (ii) above but was constructed before 1 April 1973 and not used for such purposes at any time since that date.

References to a non-residential building or a non-residential part of a building do not include a reference to a garage occupied together with a dwelling.

[*VATA 1994, Sch 8 Group 5 Notes (7)(7A)(8); SI 1995/280; SI 2001/2305*].

For a building to be have been in '*use as a dwelling*' under (*a*)(i) above, HMRC state that the living accommodation need not have been self-contained or to modern standards. Buildings, therefore, that have been in use as a dwelling include

- public houses and shops where any private living accommodation for the landlord, owner, manager or staff is not self-contained – normally because part of the living accommodation, such as the kitchen, is contained within the commercial areas rather than the private areas;
- bed-sit accommodation; and
- crofts.

As a result, where these types of property are converted into a building '*designed as a dwelling or number of dwellings*' (see (4) above) or intended for use solely for a '*relevant residential purpose*', (see (15) below) then, unless the 10-year rule applies, the sale of, or long lease in, the property cannot be zero-rated under 42.13(*c*) below and the supply of conversion services to housing associations cannot be zero-rated under 42.20 below.

The case law in this area has been confusing. In *Temple House Developments Ltd (VTD 15583) (TVC 15.86)* the tribunal held that living accommodation over a public house did not satisfy the test of 'designed as a dwelling' as the cooking and toilet facilities were shared with the public house below. In particular, it read (*a*)(i) above in terms of the test for dwellings in *VATA 1994, Sch 8 Group 5, Note (2)* which requires that a dwelling consists of self-contained living accommodation (see (4) above). In *Look Ahead Housing Association (VTD 16816) (TVC 15.158)* the tribunal similarly held that bedsits were non-residential. Although it concluded that (*a*) above should *not* be read in terms of *Note* (*2*), it followed the tribunal decision in *University of Bath (VTD 14235) (TVC 15.45)*. To be a dwelling in the ordinary sense, each of the bedsits would have to have contained within it all the major activities of life, particularly sleeping, cooking and feeding, and toilet facilities. As they had shared bathroom and kitchen facilities, they were not 'dwellings' and qualified as 'non-residential'.

However, in *Calam Vale Ltd (VTD 16869) (TVC 15.87)* the tribunal, although following *Look Ahead Housing Association* in concluding that (*a*) above should *not* be read in terms of *Note* (*2*), decided that living accommodation which had shared a kitchen with a downstairs public house was, in common usage of the term, a dwelling because the landlord and his family had lived there. Subsequently, in *Amicus Group Ltd (VTD 17693) (TVC 15.159)* where a housing association converted two properties from bedsits into self-contained flats, the tribunal specifically disapproved of the decision in *Look Ahead Housing Association*. Applying the *dicta* of Lord Irvine in *Uratemp Ventures Ltd v Collins, HL, [2002] 1 All ER 46* (a non-VAT case) a 'dwelling' should be interpreted as 'a place where one lives, regarding and treating it as a home'. It was no less a person's home because he did not cook there. Therefore, the bedsit accommodation had qualified as 'dwellings' and did not qualify as 'non-residential'. These later cases are more in line with HMRC's views. See also *Agudas Israel Housing Association Ltd (VTD 18798) (TVC 15.34)* where, again applying *Uratemp Ventures* above, the tribunal held that premises with their own front door, en suite bathing facilities and the ability to cook with a microwave cooker and a kettle were self-contained living accommodation.

See also *C & E Commrs v Lady Blom-Cooper, CA [2003] STC 669 (TVC15.85)* where a claim for refund under the D-I-Y builders scheme was made for work on converting a former public house into a single family dwelling. Customs rejected the claim on the basis that the first and second floors had previously been used by the publican as residential accommodation, so that it was not a 'non-residential building' as defined above and the work was therefore not a residential conversion as defined by *VATA 1994, s 35(1D)*. The CA upheld Customs' rejection of the claim, holding that the effect of *VATA 1994, Sch 8, Group 5, Note 9* (conversion of a non-residential part of a building which already contains a residential part is not zero-rated unless the result of the conversion is to create an *additional* dwelling or dwellings) was that no refund was due. *VATA 1994, s 35(4)* plainly required that that same restricted meaning also applied for the purposes of *VATA 1994, s 35(1D)*.

Unoccupied for ten years. It is the responsibility of the developer, contractor or D-I-Y converter (as the case may be) to hold evidence that, on balance, the property has not been lived in for the relevant ten-year period under (*b*) above. Evidence can include electoral roll and council tax data, information from utilities companies, evidence from empty property officers in local authorities, or information from other reliable sources. If a developer, etc holds a letter from an empty property officer certifying that a property has not been lived in for ten years, no other evidence is needed. If an empty property officer is unsure about when a property was last lived in, he should write with his best estimate and HMRC may then call for other supporting evidence.

When considering when a dwelling was last lived in, any

- illegal occupation by squatters, and
- use that is not residential in nature, such as storage for a business

can be ignored.

If the dwelling has been lived in on an occasional basis (eg because it was a second home) in the ten-year period, it does not qualify as 'non-residential'.

(VAT Notice 708, paras 5.3, 6.3).

(11) **'Person constructing a building'**

A person is a 'person constructing' a building if, in relation to that building, he is, or has at any point in the past

- acted as a developer (ie physically constructed, or commissioned another person to physically construct, the building, in whole or in part, on land that he owns or has an interest in); or
- acted as a contractor or subcontractor (ie provided construction services to the developer or another contractor for the construction of the building, sub-contracting work as necessary).

More than one person can enjoy 'person constructing' status but such status is not transferred when the property is transferred. Each person must meet the conditions specified above. For example, where a developer takes over and finishes a partly completed building, both the first and second developer has 'person constructing' status because they have both been involved in physically constructing the building.

VAT groups. Although for VAT purposes, any business carried on by a member of a VAT group is treated as carried on by the representative member, when determining whether a supply can be zero-rated, 'person constructing' status is only considered from the perspective of the group member who, in reality, makes the supply (which may not be the representative member).

> *Examples*
>
> (1) A VAT group includes a holding company as the representative member and a development company as a member. The development company constructs and sells houses to the public.
>
> The development company has 'person constructing' status and so the sales can be zero-rated.
>
> (2) A VAT group includes a development company as representative member and an investment company as a member. The development company constructs a block of flats and sells it to the investment company, who in turn leases the flats to the public on long leases.
>
> The investment company does not have 'person constructing' status. Even though the representative member does, the leases cannot be zero-rated and are exempt.

Beneficial interests. Where the beneficial owner of a property must register for VAT instead of the legal owner (see 42.5 below), the beneficial owner must have 'person constructing' status before the sale or long lease of the property can be zero-rated.

(VAT Notice 708, para 4.5).

In *C & E Commrs v Link Housing Association Ltd, CS [1992] STC 718 (TVC 15.1)*, the court held that the phrase 'a person constructing' should be read as meaning 'a person who has constructed' and the original builder is therefore entitled to zero-rate his supply of a dwelling, however long after construction that might be. (In the case of *Link* the houses had been constructed before the introduction of VAT in 1973.) It held that the phrase is purely descriptive and designed only to ensure that it was the person who was constructing or had constructed the building who was entitled to zero-rating. HMRC have taken the narrow view that the decision applies only in relation to input tax on disposal costs. (Business Brief 15/92).

(12) **'Protected building'**

A protected building means any building which is

- a listed building (within the meaning of *Planning* (*Listed Buildings and Conservation Areas*) *Act 1990* or *Planning* (*Listed Buildings and Conservation Areas*) (*Scotland*) *Act 1997* or *Planning* (*Northern Ireland*) *Order 1991*), or
- a scheduled monument (within the meaning of *Ancient Monuments and Archaeological Areas Act 1979* or *Historic Monuments and Archaeological Objects* (*Northern Ireland*) *Order 1995*)

and which satisfies one of the following conditions.

(*a*) It is designed to remain as or become a dwelling or number of dwellings. This condition is satisfied where, in relation to each dwelling

- the dwelling consists of self-contained living accommodation; and
- there is no provision for direct internal access from the dwelling to any other dwelling or part of a dwelling; and
- the separate use or disposal of the dwelling is not prohibited by the terms of any covenant, statutory planning consent or similar provision. Occupancy restrictions (eg working in agriculture or forestry or being over a specified age) are not prohibitions on separate use or disposal for these purposes. (VAT Notice 708, para 14.3).

Included is a garage (occupied together with the dwelling) either constructed at the same time as the building or, where the building has been substantially reconstructed, at the same time as that reconstruction. Following the decision in *Grange Builders (Quainton) Ltd, LON/02/982 (VTD 18905) (TVC 53.4B)* HMRC accept that, provided a garage is in use as a garage before any alteration or reconstruction takes place and continues to be used as one afterwards, it is not necessary for the garage to have been constructed as a garage. It can also have been constructed as something different (eg, as in this instance, as a barn). (Business Brief 11/05).

(*b*) It is intended for use solely for a '*relevant residential purpose*' or a '*relevant charitable purpose*' (see (15) and (12) below respectively) after the reconstruction or alteration.

[*VATA 1994, Sch 8 Group 6 Notes* (*1*) and (*2*); *SI 1995/283; SI 1995/1625*].

Listed buildings. A listed building is one included in a statutory list of buildings of special architectural or historic interest compiled by the Secretary of State for National Heritage in England and by the Secretaries of State for Scotland, Wales and Northern Ireland. In England and Wales there are three categories of listed building, Grade I, Grade II*, and Grade II. In Scotland the equivalent categories are Grade A, Grade B and Grade C(S). There is no statutory grading of listed buildings in Northern Ireland, although the Environment and Heritage Service: Built Heritage (an agency within the Department of Environment for Northern Ireland) operates an internal grading system for administrative purposes. Unlisted buildings in conservation areas, or buildings included in a local authority's non-statutory list of buildings of local interest, which used to be known as Grade III buildings, are not 'protected' buildings for VAT purposes.

Under *Planning* (*Listed Buildings and Conservation Areas*) *Act 1990, s 1*(*5*), a listed building also includes

(i) any object or structure fixed to the building; and

(ii) any object or structure within the curtilage of the building which, although not fixed to the building, forms part of the land and has done so since before 1 July 1948 (the date listed building control began in its present form).

For VAT purposes, any approved alteration carried out to buildings within (ii) above can only be zero-rated if the building being altered falls within (*a*) or (*b*) above. It must therefore either be a qualifying garage (see (*a*) above) or an outbuilding, etc which is itself designed to remain as or become a dwelling within (*a*) above or is intended solely for relevant residential or charitable purposes under (*b*) above. This view has been upheld in *C & E Commrs v Zielinski Baker & Partners Ltd, HL [2004] STC 456 (TVC 53.7)*. In that case, the owners of a protected building arranged for the conversion of an outbuilding into changing rooms and a games room. Both the protected building and the outbuilding had been built in 1830 but the outbuilding, which was accepted as being within the curtilage of the protected building, had only been used for residential purposes for about twelve months in 1945. The court held that the outbuilding was not designed to remain as or become a dwelling house. As it was only the outbuilding, not the house, that was altered and it was the house, not the outbuilding, that had been listed, the outbuilding was not within the definition of a 'protected building' and the work on it failed to qualify for zero-rating.

(VAT Notice 708, para 9.2).

(13) **'Relevant charitable purpose'**

This means use by a charity in either or both of the following ways.

(*a*) *Otherwise than in the course or furtherance of a business*. It is essential that all or part of the building is used for non-business purposes. The term 'business' is a widely drawn concept. See 8 BUSINESS. See also *Newtownbutler Playgroup Ltd (VTD 13741) (TVC 15.60)*.

Activities that do not make a profit, or activities where any profit is only used to further the aims and objectives of the charity, can still be business activities.

Examples of qualifying buildings include

- places of worship; and
- offices used by charities for administering non-business activity, such as the collection of donations.

Examples of non-qualifying buildings include

- youth group huts where the organisation charges a membership fee (although the building may qualify under (*b*) below as a building similar to a village hall if it is used and run by people who are not connected with the youth group);
- child nurseries where a fee is charged;
- school buildings where a fee is charged for the provision of education; and
- offices used by charities for administering business activities, such as fund-raising events where an entrance fee is charged.

Concession for small business use. By concession, and subject to any necessary HMRC approval where a building is used by a charity for business and non-business purposes, business use can be disregarded if

(i) the entire building will be used solely for non-business activity for more than 90% of the total time it is available for use;

(ii) in the case of an identifiable part of a building, that part will be used solely for non-business activity for more than 90% of the total time that part of the building is available for use;

(iii) 90% or more of the floor space of the entire building will be used for non-business activity; or

(iv) 90% or more of the people using the entire building (on a head count basis) will be engaged solely on non-business activity.

For any one building, only one of the four methods can be used. Once a method is chosen, it cannot be changed, even if circumstances change. Methods (iii) and (iv) can only be applied to the whole building. The concession must be calculated and applied at the time a relevant supply is made and must be applied in a way which ensures a result which is fair and reasonable to both the taxpayer and HMRC. It is a condition of the relief that the building continues to be used for qualifying non-business purposes for ten years after completion. If during that ten years the building (or part) is put to business use that exceeds the terms of the concession, VAT must be accounted for on the deemed self-supply that arises under 42.12 below.

Permission must be sought from HMRC to use methods (ii)–(iv). Written application should be made to HMRC with

- a full description of how the building (or the part on which zero-rating or reduced-rating is sought) will be used, including the non-qualifying use;
- when applying to use the floor space method, details of the total floor space and qualifying floor space in the building, and supporting plans that clearly identify the qualifying parts;
- when applying to use the head count method, a full list of the normal occupants of the building, a description of their role in the organisation, and confirmation as to whether they take part in the non-qualifying use of the building;
- the representative period over which it is intended to monitor the use of the building (or part); and
- if the building (or part) is also to be occupied by another person, how that person will use their part of the building and copies of any lease arrangements with that person.

HMRC will not approve use of a method that produces an unfair or unreasonable result, uses a combination of methods or is used for tax avoidance purposes. They may also withdraw or restrict the concession once in force if they consider that it is being used to avoid tax.

The construction of a garage, within the curtilage of a church building, for cars used for pastoral work has been held to be for a relevant charitable purpose, any private use being *de minimis* and disregarded (*St Dunstan's Roman Catholic Church Southborough (VTD 15472) (TVC 15.64)*).

(*b*) *As a village hall or similarly in providing social or recreational facilities for a local community*. In the opinion of HMRC, in order to qualify, the building must satisfy the following requirements.

- It is owned, organised and administered by the community for the benefit of the community. This contention was accepted in *C & E Commrs v Jubilee Hall Recreation Centre Ltd, CA 1998, [1999] STC 381 (TVC 53.11)* in which a charity used premises to run a sports and fitness centre. The charity contended that work on a substantial refurbishment should be zero-rated on the basis that the building was intended for use solely for a 'relevant charitable purpose'. The CA rejected this contention. On the evidence, the use of the building was not 'similar to the use of a village hall in providing social or recreational facilities for a local community'. The relevant conditions were only satisfied 'where a local community is the final consumer in respect of the supply of the services … in the sense that the local community is the user of the services (through a body of trustees or a management committee acting on its behalf) and in which the only economic activity is one in which they participate directly'. *Jubilee Hall* was heard together with *C & E Commrs v St Dunstan's Educational Foundation, CA 1998, [1999] STC 381 (TVC 15.69)* in which a charity arranged for the construction of a sports hall, which was intended to be used by an independent fee-paying school, and to be made available for community use at specified times. The Court similarly held that the building was not intended for use 'in providing … recreational facilities for a local community', since the community use was secondary to the use by the school. Insofar as pupils at the school benefited from that facility, they did so not as members of the local community, but as pupils on whose behalf fees were paid to the school. See also *Ormiston Charitable Trust (VTD 13187) (TVC 15.67)*.

- The facilities on offer are multi-purpose.
- The facilities are available for use by a local community at large rather than just particular sections of it.
- The facilities are available for use for a variety of public and private purposes.

Examples of non-qualifying buildings include buildings that are dedicated for use as a

- sport centre or swimming pool;
- theatre (but see *Ledbury Amateur Dramatic Society (VTD 16845) (TVC 15.58)* where a theatre was held to be used similarly to a village hall);
- membership club; or
- child nursery.

[*VATA 1994, Sch 8 Group 5 Note 6; SI 1995/280*]. (VAT Notice 48, ESC 3.29; VAT Notice 708, paras 14.6, 17.1–17.6).

(14) **'Relevant housing association'**

A relevant housing association is

- in England and Wales, a registered social landlord within the meaning of *Housing Act 1996, Part I*;
- in Scotland, a Scottish registered housing association within the meaning of *Housing Associations Act 1985*; and

- in Northern Ireland, a Northern Irish registered housing association within the meaning of *Housing (Northern Ireland) Order 1992 (SI 1992/1725), Part II.*

[*VATA 1994, Sch 8 Group 5 Note (21), Sch 10 para 3(8); SI 1997/50; SI 1997/51*].

(15) **'Relevant residential purpose'**

Use for a relevant residential purpose means use as

- a home or other institution providing residential accommodation for children;
- a home or other institution providing residential accommodation with personal care for persons in need of such care by reason of old age, disablement, past or present dependence on alcohol or drugs or past or present mental disorder;
- a hospice;
- residential accommodation for students or school pupils;
- residential accommodation for members of any of the armed forces;
- a monastery, nunnery or similar establishment; or
- an institution which is the sole or main residence of at least 90% of its residents.

Excluded is the use as a hospital, prison or similar institution or an hotel, inn or similar establishment.

Where a number of buildings are constructed at the same time and on the same site and are intended to be used together as a unit solely for a relevant residential purpose, each of those buildings (to the extent that they would not otherwise be so regarded) are to be treated as intended for use solely for a relevant residential purpose.

[*VATA 1994, Sch 8 Group 5 Notes (4) and (5); SI 1995/280*].

'*Home*' and '*institution*'. To determine if a building (or group of buildings) is used as a home or institution, all relevant factors need to be considered including

- the use to which the building is put;
- whether the building is used in conjunction with other buildings nearby;
- whether there is common ownership, financial control, management or administration;
- how the use of the building is promoted in advertising, etc; and
- how the use of the building is licensed by any controlling authority.

For example, a bedroom block constructed in the grounds of a registered care home cannot be zero-rated as the construction of a building intended for use solely for a relevant residential purpose because it is not, in itself, a home or institution but part of a larger home or institution.

A rehabilitation home for people who have suffered brain injuries has been held to be a 'home or other institution providing residential accommodation' rather than a 'hospital or similar institution' (*General Healthcare Group Ltd (VTD 17129) (TVC 15.50)*).

'*Residential accommodation*' means lodging, sleeping or overnight accommodation and does not suggest the need for such accommodation to be for any fixed or minimum period. See *Urdd Gobaith Cymru (VTD 14881) (TVC 15.47)*. For example, accommodation for students attending a residential training course is residential accommodation. A building containing living accommodation is not residential accommodation unless the building contains sleeping accommodation. For example, if the only living accommodation in a building is a dining hall then that is not residential accommodation. But if a building contains both bedrooms and a dining hall then both parts are residential accommodation.

(VAT Notice 708, para 14.7).

De Voil Indirect Tax Service. See V4.232.

PART II LAND AND PROPERTY TRANSACTIONS

42.2 EXEMPT SUPPLIES

See 22.18(*b*) and (*l*) EUROPEAN COMMUNITY LEGISLATION for the provisions of the *EC Sixth Directive.*

The 'grant' of any

- 'interest in or right over' land,
- 'licence to occupy' land, or
- in relation to Scotland, any 'personal right' to call for or be granted any such interest or right (see below)

is, subject to certain exceptions, an exempt supply. [*VATA 1994, Sch 9 Group 1*].

See 42.1(5) above for the meaning of '*grant*', 42.1(7) above for '*interest in or right over*' and 42.1(8) above for '*licence to occupy*'.

'*Land*' includes buildings, civil engineering works, walls, trees, plants and other structures and natural objects in, under or over it as long as they remain attached to it. (VAT Notice 742, para 2.1). Where fixtures are included with a building or land, they are not treated as supplies for VAT purposes and their liability is the same as that for the land or buildings with which they are being supplied. (VAT Notice 742, para 7.9).

A '*personal right*' in Scotland is a contractual right, as opposed to a real right (which is a right secured over the property itself). Such personal rights are exempt in the rest of the UK as equitable interests in land. (VAT Notice 742/3/02).

Under *EC Sixth Directive, Art 13B*(*h*) countries must exempt the supply of land which has not been built upon other than '*building land*' ie any unimproved or improved land defined as such by the individual country. In *Norbury Developments Ltd v C & E Commrs, CJEC [1999] STC 511 (TVC 21.331)* the tribunal held that building land should therefore be taxable rather than exempt unless the exemption was authorised by *Art 28*(*3*)(*b*) (which allows countries to continue to exempt certain supplies, including building land, for a transitional period). The tribunal referred the case to the CJEC which held that the UK was entitled to exempt the supply under *Art 28*(*3*)(*b*).

Anti-avoidance provisions. After 8 April 2003, where any grant of a fee simple (freehold) is exempt under the above provisions (and not standard-rated under the provisions in 42.3 below), those standard-rating provisions do not prevent the exemption of a supply arising from the prior exempt grant. This is designed to block avoidance schemes involving the sale of vacant land and the subsequent construction of a commercial building. [*VATA 1994, s 96(10B); FA 2003, s 20*].

Exceptions include

- the first grant of a major interest in a 'qualifying building' ie

  (i) a dwelling or building intended for use for a relevant residential or charitable purpose,

  (ii) a dwelling converted from a non-residential building, or

  (iii) a substantially reconstructed protected building

  by the person constructing, converting or, as the case may be, reconstructing it (which is zero-rated, see 42.13 and 42.14 below);
- the sale of the freehold interest in a new or uncompleted non-qualifying building or civil engineering work (which is standard-rated, see 42.3(*a*) below);
- supplies falling within one of the categories in 42.3(*b*)-(*k*) below which are specifically excluded from exemption and standard-rated;
- any supply which would otherwise be exempt but in respect of which an election to waive exemption ('option to tax') has been exercised (see 42.8 below); and
- certain supplies which form part of the transfer of a business as a going concern (which are outside the scope of VAT, see 8.10 BUSINESS).

Options to purchase/sell or lease land. A person granted an option to purchase an interest in land and buildings (a 'call option') acquires the right to buy it at a future date for a specified price. That right is an interest in land and therefore the grant of the option is exempt if the purchase of the property would be exempt at the time of the grant. If the purchase would be taxable at that time, the grant of the option is taxable (see 42.3(*k*) below).

A person granted the right to require someone to purchase his interest in land or buildings at a fixed price at a future date (a 'put' option) does not receive an interest in land and the grant of such an option is generally standard-rated.

(VAT Notice 742, para 7.4).

De Voil Indirect Tax Service. See V4.111; V4.112.

42.3 STANDARD-RATED SUPPLIES

The supplies of within (*a*)-(*k*) below are excluded from the general VAT exemption for land under 42.2 above and are standard-rated.

(*a*) **New and uncompleted non-qualifying buildings and civil engineering works.**

The 'grant' or assignment of the fee simple (freehold interest) in

- a building which has not been 'completed' and which is not a '*qualifying building*' (ie is neither designed as a 'dwelling' or number of dwellings nor intended for use for solely a 'relevant residential purpose' or a 'relevant charitable purpose'),
- a 'new' building which is not to be used as a qualifying building after the grant,
- a civil engineering work which has not been completed, or
- a new civil engineering work

is standard-rated. (Supplies of qualifying buildings are exempt unless zero-rated under the provisions in 42.13 or 42.14 below.)

A building/civil engineering work is to be taken as '*completed*' when an architect/engineer issues a certificate of practical completion in relation to it or it is fully occupied/used, whichever happens first. It is to be taken as '*new*' if it was completed less than three years before the grant.

See 42.1(5) above for the meaning of '*grant*', 42.1(15) above for '*relevant residential purpose*' and 42.1(13) above for '*relevant charitable purpose*'.

Issue of certificates. A grant or assignment cannot be taken as relating to a building (or part) intended for use solely for a relevant residential or charitable purpose as above unless

- it is made to a person who intends to use the building (or part) for such a purpose; and
- before it is made, that person has given the grantor a certificate stating that the grant relates to such a building.

See 42.32 below for further details on the issue and form of certificates.

Part-qualifying buildings. Where part of a building is designed as a dwelling or number of dwellings or intended for relevant use as above and part is not (eg shop premises with a flat over them) an apportionment is necessary if the grant does not relate exclusively to one part or the other.

[*VATA 1994, Sch 9 Group 1 Item 1*(*a*) and *Notes 1 to 6*].

Anti-avoidance provisions. After 8 April 2003:

- Where any grant is standard-rated under these provisions, any subsequent supply arising from that grant is also standard-rated. This is designed to block avoidance schemes that deliberately made the price uncertain in order to take advantage of the provisions of *SI 1995/2518, Reg 84*(*2*) allowing VAT to be declared when the payment is received rather than at the date of sale. See 64.44 SUPPLY.
- Where any grant of a fee simple (freehold) is exempt under 42.2 above (and not standard-rated under these provisions), these provisions do not prevent the exemption of a supply arising from the prior exempt grant. This is designed to block avoidance schemes involving the sale of vacant land and the subsequent construction of a commercial building.

[*VATA 1994, s 96(10B); FA 2003, s 20*].

Options, etc to purchase. See (*k*) below.

Mixed supplies of land and civil engineering work. Where the freehold interest in bare land is sold but that land is ancillary to new or part completed civil engineering works (eg an airfield or oil refinery) there is a single standard-rated supply.

The sale of freehold of land containing new civil engineering works which are a minor part of the supply (eg building land on which roads have been built or pipes laid for connection to mains services) is a mixed supply of exempt land (unless the option to tax has been exercised, see 42.8 below) and standard-rated civil engineering works. The charge must be fairly and reasonably apportioned between the two supplies. (VAT Notice 742, para 3.3).

De Voil Indirect Tax Service. See V4.113.

(*b*) **Gaming and fishing rights**

The 'grant' of any interest, right or licence to take game or fish is standard-rated unless, at the time of the grant, the grantor grants to the grantee the fee simple of the land over which the right to take game or fish is exercisable. Where a grant of an interest in or right over land or a licence to occupy land includes a valuable right to take game or fish, an apportionment must be made to determine the exempt and standard-rated parts. [*VATA 1994, Sch 9 Group 1 Item 1*(*c*) and *Note 8*]. See 57.14 RECREATION AND SPORT for further details.

Options, etc to purchase. See (*k*) below.

(*c*) **Hotel accommodation**

The provision in an hotel, inn, boarding house or 'similar establishment' of sleeping accommodation or of accommodation in rooms which are provided in conjunction with sleeping accommodation or for the purposes of a supply of catering is standard-rated. '*Similar establishment*' includes premises in which there is provided furnished sleeping accommodation, whether with or without the provision of board or facilities for the preparation of food, which are used by, or held out as being suitable for use by, visitors or travellers. [*VATA 1994, Sch 9 Group 1 Item 1*(*d*) and *Note 9*].

Where guests stay for a continuous period of four weeks or more, VAT is chargeable on a reduced value from the 29th day.

See 33.1 to 33.4 HOTELS AND HOLIDAY ACCOMMODATION for further details.

Options, etc to purchase. See (*k*) below.

(*d*) **Holiday accommodation**

The grant of any interest in or right over or licence to occupy holiday accommodation (including any accommodation in a building, hut, chalet, caravan, houseboat or tent which is advertised or held out as holiday accommodation or as suitable for holiday or leisure use) is standard-rated. *Excluded* is the grant of the fee simple, or a lease, etc for a premium, in a building which is not a 'new building'. [*VATA 1994, Sch 9 Group 1 Item 1*(*e*) and *Notes 12* and *13*]. See 33.5 to 33.9 HOTELS AND HOLIDAY ACCOMMODATION for further details.

Options, etc to purchase. See (*k*) bclow.

(*e*) **Caravan and tent pitches and camping facilities**

The provision of 'seasonal pitches' for caravans, and the grant or assignment of facilities at caravan parks to persons for whom such pitches are provided, are standard-rated. The provision of pitches for tents or of camping facilities is also standard-rated.

A 'seasonal pitch' is

(i) any pitch which is provided for a period of less than a year; and

(ii) a pitch provided for a year or more but which the person to whom it is provided is prevented by the terms of any covenant, statutory planning consent or similar permission from occupying by living in a caravan at all times throughout the period for which the pitch is provided.

[*VATA 1994, Sch 9 Group 1 Items 1(f)(g)* and *Note 14*].

Following the tribunal decision in *Ashworth (Mrs B) (VTD 12924) (TVC 39.110)*, HMRC accept that a pitch is only regarded as seasonal under (ii) above if it is on a site, or part of a site, which is advertised or held out for holiday use. (VAT Notice 701/20/96, para 3).

The effect of the above is that exemption applies to the provision of pitches at

- permanent residential caravan parks;
- sites for travellers; and
- seasonal sites provided
  - (i) the site is not advertised or held out for holiday use; and
  - (ii) the caravan can be used as a principal private residence. (This applies even if it cannot be occupied throughout the year due to a time-related restriction or occupancy imposed by the site owner.)

(VAT Notice 791/20/04, para 4.1).

The supply of rented accommodation in any caravan or mobile home is exempt unless the accommodation is holiday accommodation which is always standard-rated under (*d*) above.

See also 42.36 below for caravans generally.

Options, etc to purchase. See (*k*) below.

De Voil Indirect Tax Service. See V4.113.

(*f*) **Parking facilities**

The grant or assignment of facilities for parking a vehicle is standard-rated. [*VATA 1994, Sch 9 Group 1 Item 1(h)*].

There is normally a standard-rated supply of parking facilities if a specific grant is made and the facilities are designed for, or provided specifically for the purpose of, parking vehicles.

Standard-rated supplies include the following.

- The letting or licensing of garages (even if used for other purposes, eg storage of goods) or designated parking bays or spaces. See *C & E Commrs v Trinity Factoring Services Ltd, CS [1994] STC 504 (TVC 39.123)* where the court held that the lease of a lock-up garage was standard-rated even though the lessor and lessee had agreed in advance that the garage would be used for the storage of goods. *Prima facie* facilities had been granted for parking a vehicle and the terms of the lease did not preclude such usage.

The letting of a garage or parking space *separately* from the letting of a dwelling is standard-rated. This scenario commonly occurs when a local authority tenant renting a dwelling and garage then decides to purchase the dwelling. The local authority retains the garage and continues to lease it to their former tenant. As the local authority is only supplying a garage, and not domestic accommodation, the supply is standard-rated. See (viii) below for the letting of a garage in conjunction with the letting of a dwelling.

- The provision of rights to park vehicles (and accompanying trailers) in, for example, car parks and commercial garages.
- The letting or licensing of land specifically for the construction of a garage or for use solely for the parking of a vehicle.
- The letting or licensing of a purpose-built car park (eg to a car park operator).
- The letting of taxi ranks.
- The provision of storage for bicycles or touring caravans.
- The freehold sale of a 'new' or partly completed garage, car park or car parking facilities other than in conjunction with the sale of a new dwelling. See (*a*) above for the meaning of '*new*'. (The sale of a garage or parking space together with a new dwelling by the person constructing it is normally zero-rated under 42.13 below unless the dwelling is standard-rated holiday accommodation under (*d*) above.)

Exempt supplies. The following supplies are not regarded by HMRC as supplies of parking facilities and are therefore exempt under the general provisions in 42.2 above (subject to the exercise of an option to tax under 42.8 below).

(i) The letting of land or buildings (other than garages) where the conveyance or contract makes no specific reference to use for parking facilities.

(ii) The letting of land or buildings where any reference to parking a vehicle is incidental to the main use.

(iii) The letting of land or buildings to a motor dealer for storing stock-in-trade.

(iv) The letting of land or buildings to a vehicle transportation firm, a vehicle distributor or a vehicle auctioneer for business use.

(v) The letting of land (including land used at other times as a car park) for purposes such as a market or car boot sale.

(vi) The letting of land for the exhibition of vehicles.

(vii) The letting of land to a travelling fair or circus (and the incidental parking of vehicles).

(viii) The letting of a garage or parking space in conjunction with the *letting* of a dwelling for permanent residential use provided it is reasonably near to the dwelling and the letting is by the same landlord to the same tenant (whether under a single or separate agreement). See also *Skatteministeriet v Henriksen, CJEC 1989, [1990] STC 768 (TVC 21.227)*. (If the dwelling is owned freehold, the letting of the garage is standard-rated, see above.)

(ix) The freehold sale of garages, car parks or parking facilities which are not 'new'. See (*a*) above for the meaning of '*new*'.

The supply of garage or other parking facilities provided in conjunction with the letting of *commercial* premises is treated as a single supply provided both lettings are by the same landlord to the same tenant and *either* the facilities are on or reasonably near the property *or* the facilities are with a complex. The supply may therefore be exempt or, where the option to tax under 42.8 below has been exercised, standard-rated. In any other circumstances, the provision of parking facilities with commercial property is standard-rated. See also *Skatteministeriet v Henriksen, CJEC 1989, [1990] STC 768 (TVC 21.227)*.

(VAT Notice 742, paras 4.2–4.5).

Local authorities. See 43.4 LOCAL AUTHORITIES AND PUBLIC BODIES.

Caravans and houseboats. See 42.36 and 42.37 below for parking facilities for caravans and houseboats.

Options, etc to purchase. See (*k*) below.

De Voil Indirect Tax Service. See V4.113.

(*g*) **Timber rights**

The grant or assignment of any right to fell and remove standing timber is standard-rated. [*VATA 1994, Sch 9 Group 1 Item 1*(*j*)].

The grant must be separate and specific. If land is sold which happens to contain standing timber which the buyer will be able to fell, the whole supply is exempt with the option to tax under 42.8 below. (VAT Notice 742, para 3.1).

Options, etc to purchase. See (*k*) below.

(*h*) **Storage, mooring of aircraft, ships, etc.**

The grant or assignment of facilities for housing, or storage of, an aircraft or for 'mooring', or storage of, a ship, boat or other vessel is standard-rated. '*Mooring*' includes anchoring or berthing. [*VATA 1994, Sch 9 Group 1 Item 1*(*k*) *and Note 15*].

Even if a person is merely granted permission to lay down his own mooring and owns the ground tackle, the grant is considered to be excluded from exemption and is standard-rated whether or not there is a formal lease or licence. (C & E Press Notice 355, 25 June 1975). See also *J W Fisher (VTD 179) (TVC 39.129)* and *Strand Ship Building Co Ltd (VTD 1651) (TVC 39.130)*.

See, however, 68.9 TRANSPORT AND FREIGHT for facilities zero-rated when supplied in ports or customs airports and 42.37 below for exempt mooring of qualifying houseboats.

Options, etc to purchase. See (*k*) below.

(*i*) **Boxes, seats, etc.**

The grant or assignment of any right to occupy a box, seat or other accommodation at a sports ground, theatre, concert hall or other place of entertainment is standard-rated. [*VATA 1994, Sch 9 Group 1 Item 1*(*l*)]. Included is any kind of accommodation which is intended for use by individuals or groups for viewing a match, race, show or other form of entertainment, regardless of whether the entertainment is actually in progress when the accommodation is used. (VAT Notice 742, para 3.4).

Options, etc to purchase. See (*k*) below.

(*j*) **Sports facilities**

The grant or assignment of facilities for playing any sport or participating in any physical recreation is standard-rated. [*VATA 1994, Sch 9 Group 1 Item 1*(*m*)].

Exemption is, however, retained where the facilities are to be used for more than 24 hours or, provided certain conditions are met, a series of at least ten shorter periods. See 57.8 RECREATION AND SPORT. See also 57.9 RECREATION AND SPORT for certain sporting services provided by non-profit making bodies.

(*k*) **Options, etc to purchase interests or rights within (*a*) to (*j*) above**

The grant of any right, including

- an equitable right,
- a right under an option or right of pre-emption, or
- in relation to land in Scotland, a 'personal right',

to call for or to be granted an interest or right which would fall to be standard-rated under (*a*) to (*j*) above is also standard-rated.

A '*personal right*' in Scotland is a contractual right, as opposed to a real right (which is a right secured over the property itself). (VAT Notice 742/3/02).

[*VATA 1994, Sch 9 Group 1 Item 1*(*n*)].

42.4 SUPPLIES BETWEEN LANDLORDS AND TENANTS

(1) **Lease payments**

- *Inducements* (*reverse premiums*). Following representations from, and detailed discussions with, various bodies, HMRC now accept that lease obligations, to which tenants are normally bound, do not constitute supplies for which inducement payments on entering leases are consideration. As a result, they believe that the majority of such inducements are likely to be outside the scope of VAT, being no more than inducements to tenants to take leases and to observe the obligations in them. There will be a taxable supply only where a payment is linked to benefits a tenant provides outside normal lease terms. This change of policy effectively puts inducement payments on a similar VAT footing to rent free periods (see below) in being mainly outside the scope of VAT and only a taxable consideration where directly linked to a specific benefit supplied by a tenant to a landlord.

  Examples of taxable benefits by tenants that may be supplied in return for such inducements are

  - carrying out building works to improve the property by undertaking necessary repairs or upgrading the property (undertakings to use improved materials as part of continuous repairs under a tenant repairing lease would not constitute a taxable benefit to the landlord);

- carrying out fitting-out or refurbishment works which the landlord has responsibility for and is paying the tenant to undertake; and
- acting as anchor tenant (publicity indicating that Company X is to take a lease in a development does not, in itself, determine that the company is an anchor tenant).

Past transactions. Tenants who have wrongly declared output tax on inducements received are not obliged to adjust their VAT position. However, if they choose to, then, subject to the three-year capping provisions,

- where both the tenant and the landlord are registered for VAT, and provided they both agree, the tenant may raise a credit note and both parties would then adjust their VAT account; or
- where the landlord is not registered for VAT, the tenant may make a claim under *VATA 1994, s 80* for overpaid tax (see 51.8 PAYMENT OF VAT). Any such claim would be also be subject to the unjust enrichment defence.

In all cases where a tenant chooses to correct past transactions, it will be necessary for the tenant to review the attribution of any input tax incurred on costs and rework partial exemption calculations. A VAT-registered landlord will also have to reduce input tax deductions in respect of the inducements which could also require partial exemption calculations to be revised.

(Business Brief 12/05).

Previously, HMRC regarded an inducement paid by

- a landlord to a prospective tenant for the latter to enter into a lease, or
- a tenant to a third party to accept the assignment of a lease or the grant of a sub-lease

as consideration for a standard-rated supply of services by the tenant/assignee following the decision in *Mirror Group plc v C & E Commrs, CJEC [2001] STC 1453 (TVC 21.230)*.

- *Grant of a lease.* The grant of a lease is, subject to certain exceptions, exempt from VAT. See 42.2 above.
- *Subsequent supplies under a lease.* The granting of a lease usually gives rise to a number of further supplies at later times. For example, a supply is made each time that lease is surrendered or assigned. In such cases, the liability of each subsequent supply is determined at the time when that supply is made rather than by reference to the time of the original grant. [*VATA 1994, s 96(10A)*; *FA 1997, s 35(1)*].
- *Variations of leases.* Sometimes a lease is varied either to alter its terms (eg so that it can be used for different purposes), to extend the length of the tenancy or to alter the demised premises (eg by renting additional floor space). Under English land law, the effect of such a variation is that the old lease is deemed to be surrendered (see below) and a new lease granted in its place. Where there is no consideration, no supply is seen as taking place. (VAT Notice 742, para 10.5).

- *Surrender of lease*. The grant of an 'interest in or right over' land or a 'licence to occupy' land includes a surrender of that interest, etc [*VATA 1994, Sch 9 Group 1 and Note* (*1*)*; SI 1995/282*].

  The general provisions relating to grants in 42.2 above therefore also apply to surrenders, ie they are exempt subject to certain exceptions. Similarly, the assignment of any interest, etc back to the lessor or licensor, by the lessee or licensee, is generally exempt. However, a surrender of an interest falling within the exclusions from exemption in 42.3 above remains standard-rated and where a tenant has, prior to the surrender, opted to tax the property in question under 42.8 below, the surrender is covered by the election and therefore taxable. (VAT Notice 742, para 10.3).

- *Reverse surrenders and assignments*. Normally, when a lease is surrendered, consideration is paid by the landlord to the tenant. A '*reverse surrender*' occurs where a tenant surrenders an onerous lease to the landlord before the term of the lease has expired and pays the landlord to accept the surrender.

  The grant of an interest in or right over land, or of any licence to occupy land, includes the supply made by the person to whom an interest is surrendered when there is a reverse surrender. [*VATA 1994, Sch 9 Group 1 and Notes* (*1*) *and* (*1A*)]. The general provisions relating to grants in 42.2 above therefore also apply to reverse surrenders, ie they are exempt subject to certain exceptions. Where the person making the supply (ie the landlord) has opted to tax the property, the supply is standard-rated. (VAT Notice 742, para 10.4).

- *Dilapidation payments*. A lease may provide for the landlord to recover from a tenant, at or near the end of the lease, an amount to cover the cost of restoring the property to its original condition. Such dilapidation payments represent a claim for damages by the landlord against the tenant. The payment is not consideration for a supply for VAT purposes and is outside the scope of VAT. (VAT Notice 742, para 10.10).

- *Indemnity payments under lease agreements*. In general any payment made by a prospective tenant to obtain the grant of a lease or licence, including any disbursement or indemnification of the costs incurred by the landlord, is part of the consideration for that grant.

  Many leases provide that an existing tenant reimburses the landlord for legal or other advisory costs incurred by the landlord as a result of the tenant exercising rights already granted under the lease. For example, the tenant may be able to assign the lease, sublet or make alterations provided the tenant first obtains the landlord's consent. Such reimbursements by the tenant to the landlord are consideration for the principal supply of the lease.

  If a tenant makes a payment to the landlord to obtain an *additional* right, it is consideration for the variation of the lease (see above).

  (VAT Notice 742, para 10.8).

(2) **Mesne profits**

These are damages for the profits lost by a landlord by reason of wrongful occupation of his property and can only be recovered in respect of continued occupation of property after that right of occupation has expired. As such, an award of mesne profits is not consideration for a supply and is outside the scope of VAT. Where a landlord on the cash accounting system has opted to tax and, in addition to a claim for mesne profits, arrears of rent accrue, payment received following litigation should be treated firstly as relating to rent arrears and only then as relating to mesne profits to the extent that the total received exceeds the outstanding rents. (If the landlord is not on the cash accounting basis, the tax points for the periods in respect of which he is claiming rent arrears will have already been determined under the normal rules.) (Law Society's Gazette, 14 October 1992, p 16).

(3) **Rental payments**

Rent is the periodic payment made by a tenant to a landlord and is normally the subject of a written agreement. Rent payments can be non-monetary, and can include costs incurred by the landlord under the agreement which are recharged to the tenant. This may include items such as service charges and rates where the landlord is the rateable person.

Rental income is generally exempt from VAT although the landlord may opt to tax rents from non-domestic property (see 42.8 below).

- *Rent adjustments when buildings are sold or leases assigned.* Rent adjustments between landlords on the sale of tenanted property and between tenants on the assignment of a lease are outside the scope of VAT. For VAT purposes the consideration for the sale of the building or the assignment of the lease is the full value of the supply before any rent adjustment is made. (VAT Notice 742, para 10.9).

- *Recovery of rent from a third party.* There are two common ways in which a landlord can recover rent from a third party. Where such payments are received, the landlord should still address any related VAT invoice to the tenant to whom the premises have been leased or let. The supply is still to the tenant, not the third party.

  (i) If a tenant sub-lets land or buildings to a third party and the tenant defaults on payment of rent to the landlord, the landlord can issue a notice under the *Law of Distress Amendment Act* and collect the rent arrears from the third party. In turn, the third party can reduce his rent payable to the tenant by the amount he has paid to the landlord. If this happens the supply chain remains the same. There is a supply of the land or building from the landlord to the tenant and from the tenant to the third party. If the landlord has opted to tax, any VAT invoice must be issued to the tenant.

  (ii) A surety or guarantor is normally party to any agreement between the landlord and the tenant. If the tenant is unable to meet the agreed periodic rental payments to the landlord, the surety or guarantor will make the payments on the tenant's behalf. There is no supply by the landlord to the surety or guarantor who will not be able to recover any VAT paid.

  (VAT Notice 742, para 7.5).

- *Rent-free periods.* The grant by a landlord of a rent-free period is not a supply for VAT purposes except where the rent-free period is given in exchange for something which the tenant agrees to do (eg carry out works for the benefit of the landlord). In the latter case, VAT is due on the amount of the rent foregone. (VAT Notice 742, para 4.10). See *Neville Russell (VTD 2484) (TVC 60.110)* where a rent-free period was held not to be consideration for a supply but compensation for the fact that the landlord had failed to finish the fitting out before occupation of the building by the tenant; and *Port Erin Hotels v The Isle of Man Treasury (VTD 5045) (TVC 60.113)* and *Ridgeons Bulk Ltd v C & E Commrs, QB [1994] STC 427 (TVC 60.114)* where waiver of rent was held to be consideration for building work carried out by the tenant and therefore subject to VAT.

- *Rent paid while premises unoccupied.* In *Harper Collins Publishers Ltd (VTD 12040) (TVC 44.47)*, the company, following reorganisation, moved out of two floors of its leased business premises but was unable to sublet immediately. The landlords in the meantime exercised the option to tax (see 42.8 below). The tribunal held that, although unoccupied, the two floors were still retained by the company for business purposes, the original purpose in taking the leases not having changed. Input tax suffered on the rents paid could be recovered (in this instance in part only by inclusion in the residual input tax on general overheads under the company's partial exemption computations).

(4) **Restricted covenants**

Restrictive covenants may be placed on land to control its use. The lifting of such a restricted covenant (eg to permit development which was previously forbidden) is exempt from VAT (unless the person receiving the payment has opted to tax). (VAT Notice 742, para 10.6).

(5) **Service charges, etc.**

The VAT treatment of service charges and other payments relating to premises depends upon the nature of the property and the terms of the arrangements.

- *General services for tenants of leasehold non-domestic property provided by the landlord.* Leases often stipulate that the landlord will provide, and the tenants pay for, the services required for the upkeep of the building as a whole. The lease may provide for an inclusive rental or it may require the tenants to contribute by means of an additional charge to the basic rent, generally referred to as a service or maintenance charge. This service charge assumes the same VAT liability as the premium or rent payable under the lease or licence provided

  (*a*) it is connected with the external fabric or the common parts of the building, etc as opposed to the demised areas of the property of the individual occupants; and

  (*b*) it is paid for by all the occupants through a common service charge.

  The service charge is therefore generally exempt unless the landlord has opted to tax the property (see 42.8 below) or the underlying lease is standard-rated, eg holiday or time share accommodation (see 33.5 HOTELS AND HOLIDAY ACCOMMODATION).

  (VAT Notice 742, paras 11.1, 11.2, 11.4).

- *Specific services for tenants of leasehold non-domestic property provided by the landlord.* A payment made by a tenant to the landlord may be (*a*) further payment for the main supply of accommodation and therefore exempt or, if the option to tax has been exercised, standard-rated,

(*b*) for supplies other than accommodation (normally standard-rated), or

(*c*) disbursements and therefore outside the scope of VAT (see 3.7 AGENTS).

The following are typical examples.

(i) *Insurance and rates.* If the landlord is the policyholder or rateable person, any payment for insurance or rates from the tenant is part payment for the main supply. If the tenants are the policyholders or rateable persons, any payments on their behalf by the landlord should be treated as disbursements. See also 37.17 INSURANCE for insurance supplied with other goods and services.

(ii) *Telephones.* If the telephone account is in the name of the landlord, any charge to the tenants (including calls, installation and rental) is standard-rated. If the account is in the name of the tenant but the landlord pays the bill, any recovery from the tenant is a disbursement.

(iii) *Reception and switchboard.* A charge by the landlord under the terms of the lease for use of such facilities which form a common part of the premises is further consideration for the main supply.

(iv) *Office services.* A separate charge for such services (eg typing and photocopying) is a separate standard-rated supply. If, however, under the terms of the lease, one inclusive charge is made for office services and accommodation, and the tenant is expected to pay for the services whether used or not, the liability for the services follows that of the main supply.

(v) *Fixtures and fittings.* These are regarded as part of the overall supply of the property and any charges for them are normally included in the rent. Where a separate charge is made by the landlord, the supply is standard-rated.

(vi) *Electricity, light and heat.* If the landlord makes a separate charge for un-metered supplies of gas and electricity used by tenants, it should be treated as further payment for the main supply of accommodation. However, where a landlord operates secondary credit meters, the charges to the tenants for the gas and electricity they use are consideration for separate supplies of fuel and power. These supplies will be standard-rated. See 29.8 FUEL AND POWER for further details. See, however, *Suffolk Heritage Housing Association Ltd (VTD 13713) (TVC 28.9)* where the tribunal held that the association's long standing practice of recovering heating costs as a separate charge from the rent should be treated as a separate supply for VAT purposes.

(vii) *Management charges.* Charges by landlords for managing a development as a whole and administering the collection of service charges is additional consideration for the main supply.

(viii) *Recreational facilities.* If the charges for the use of recreational facilities are compulsory, irrespective of whether the tenant uses the facilities, then the liability follows the main supply of accommodation.

(VAT Notice 742, para 11.7).

- *Services for occupants of leasehold non-domestic property provided by third parties.* Where a person is responsible for providing services to occupants of property but has no interest in that property (eg a managing agent) the supply of services is always standard-rated as they are not part of the supply of the accommodation itself. (VAT Notice 742, para 11.5).
- *Services supplied to freehold occupants of non-domestic property.* Service charges raised where the property has been sold freehold are a separate standard-rated supply as there is no continuing supply of accommodation to the occupant by the provider of the services. (VAT Notice 742, para 11.3).
- *Shared premises.* Where the owner or tenant of premises does not grant other occupants an exempt licence to occupy, any service charge must be standard-rated. This applies even if the owner/tenant is simply passing on appropriate shares of costs (eg electricity, gas, telephone and staff wages). The only exception is where a bill is paid which is entirely the liability of another occupant (eg a telephone bill or insurance premium in the other occupant's name) which can be treated as a disbursement. (VAT Notice 742, para 11.8).
- *Service charges on domestic accommodation.*

  Common areas. Service charges relating to the upkeep of common areas of an estate of dwellings, or the common areas of a multi-occupied dwelling, are exempt from VAT so long as they are required to be paid by the leaseholder or tenant to the landlord under the terms of the lease or tenancy agreement. This is because the service charge is treated as ancillary to the main supply of exempt domestic accommodation.

  Services provided to freehold owners of dwellings are taxable because there is no supply of domestic accommodation to link those services to. However, by concession, all *mandatory* service charges paid by occupants of dwellings toward the

  (*a*) upkeep of the common areas of a housing estate (eg such as paths, driveways and communal gardens),

  (*b*) upkeep of the common areas of a block of flats (eg lift maintenance, corridors, stairwells and general lounges),

  (*c*) general maintenance of the exterior of the block of flats or individual dwellings (eg painting) if the residents cannot refuse this, and

  (*d*) provision of an estate warden, house manager or caretaker,

  can be treated as exempt from VAT. (VAT Notice 48, ESC 3.18).

  In *Devine (VTD 15312) (TVC 39.53)* the leaseholders were obliged to keep their properties in good repair with the landlords reserving the right to appoint a factor to ensure this was done. The landlords subsequently appointed a factor and imposed VAT on the service charge. The tribunal held that the charges did not qualify for exemption (because they were not part of the original supply of land) and noted that they did not fall within ESC 3.18 because they were not mandatory in the sense required by the concession, drawing a distinction between the obligations to maintain the property (which were mandatory) and the methods by which the proprietors chose to implement those obligations (which were not).

Electricity, light and heat. If the landlord makes a separate charge for *un-metered* supplies of gas and electricity used by occupants, it should be treated as further payment for the main supply of exempt domestic accommodation. However, if the landlord operates a secondary credit meter, the charges to the occupants for the gas and electricity they use are separate supplies of fuel and power subject to VAT at the reduced rate. See, however, *Suffolk Heritage Housing Association Ltd (VTD 13713) (TVC 28.9)* where the tribunal held that the association's long standing practice of recovering heating costs as a separate charge from the rent should be treated as a separate supply for VAT purposes.

Optional services supplied personally to occupants (eg shopping, carpet cleaning or painting a private flat) are standard-rated.

Managing agents. A managing agent acting on behalf of a landlord can treat the mandatory service charges to occupants as exempt, providing the agent invoices and collects the service charges directly from the occupants. Any management fee collected from the occupants is standard-rated because it relates to the managing agent's supply to the landlord.

Tenant-controlled management companies. Occupants of an estate may form a tenant-controlled management company which sometimes purchases the freehold of the estate and engages a service provider to maintain the common areas and provide any necessary warden or housekeepers. Providing the company is bound by the terms of the lease to maintain the common areas of the estate (or provide a warden), and the occupants are invoiced by, and pay the service charges directly to, the service provider, the service charges may still be treated as exempt. However, any management fee collected from the occupants is standard-rated because it relates to the service provider's supply to the tenant-controlled management company.

(VAT Notice 742, paras 12.1–12.5).

(6) Statutory compensation

Statutory compensation paid by a landlord to a tenant under the terms of the *Landlord and Tenant Act 1954* or the *Agricultural Tenancies Act 1995* is outside the scope of VAT. This applies even if, for example, an agricultural tenant has issued a 'notice to quit' having decided to retire from farming. Examples of items for which statutory compensation is given on a tenant quitting property are milk quotas left behind, manurial values and standing crops.

Where the landlord and tenant agree that the tenant will leave in return for additional payments, these payments are consideration for the tenant surrendering the lease and are exempt unless the tenant has opted to tax.

(VAT Notice 742, para 10.7).

De Voil Indirect Tax Service. See V4.111.

42.5 JOINT OWNERSHIP OF LAND AND BENEFICIAL INTERESTS

Joint owners. Where more than one person owns land or buildings or receives the benefit of the consideration from the grant of an interest in land or buildings, (eg tenants in common), those persons are treated as a single person. If they are required to register for VAT purposes, they must register as if they were a partnership even if no legal partnership exists. (VAT Notice 742, para 7.2).

Beneficial interests. Where the benefit of the consideration for a grant, etc accrues to the beneficial owner but that person is not the person making the grant (the legal owner) the beneficial owner is deemed to be the legal owner for VAT purposes and any input tax entitlement attributable to the grant is also transferred to the beneficial owner. [*VATA 1994, Sch 10 para 8*(*1*)]. For example, where property is held on bare trusts, although the trustees are the legal owners, if the benefit of the income accruing from the property passes to beneficiaries it is they who are treated as the person making the grant and who may need to register for VAT and, if so, can, subject to the normal rules, claim any input tax arising. (VAT Notice 742, para 7.1).

Benefit accruing to trustees. Where the benefit of the consideration for a grant, etc accrues directly to trustees, it is the trustees who should, if required, register for VAT. (VAT Notice 742, para 7.1).

42.6 COMMONHOLD

The *Commonhold and Leasehold Reform Act 2002* recognises a third form of property ownership in addition to freehold and leasehold. This is known as commonhold and is available for residential, commercial or mixed use developments. It confers upon owners ('unit-holders') of parts of a building occupied in common, freehold interests in their respective parts (units) of the property. The freehold interest in the property's communal area and often its structure (the common parts) is owned by a commonhold association whose membership comprises the owners of the units. The commonhold association is responsible for the upkeep of the common parts and provides an estimate of annual expenditure (the commonhold assessment).

A commonhold unit is a freehold in a property that follows the normal VAT accounting rules. Some of the more common situations where a VAT liability may arise are considered below.

(1) **Supplies of qualifying buildings (eg residential property)**

Where the normal conditions for zero-rating are met (see 42.13 below), the developer of a '*qualifying building*' (ie a building designed as a dwelling or number of dwellings or intended for use solely for a relevant residential or a relevant charitable purpose) can zero-rate

- the first sale of the freehold units in a commonhold to prospective unit-holders; and
- the transfer by operation of law of the freehold of the common parts in the commonhold to the commonhold association, on the registration of the commonhold.

Any subsequent supplies of the units are exempt.

(2) **Supplies of non-qualifying buildings (eg commercial property)**

Such supplies are exempt from VAT unless the supply is either the sale of

- a commonhold unit or freehold of a new building (ie one that is less than three years old) or a partly-completed 'non-qualifying' building; or
- a commonhold unit or freehold of a commercial property where the option to tax has been exercised (and not disapplied), see 42.8 and 42.9 below),

in which case it is standard-rated.

(3) **Setting up of a commonhold by a developer following construction of a new building**

In the case of commercial property, the first supply of each unit is standard-rated provided it is made before the property is three years old or, if not, the developer has opted to tax (subject to the disapplication rules).

In the case of residential property, the supply is zero-rated.

For both residential and commercial property, the freehold interest in the common parts is vested in the commonhold association. Although there is normally no consideration attributed to this disposal, it may be a supply for VAT purposes with a requirement to charge VAT. See 42.7(4) below.

(4) **A number of freeholds are converted into a single commonhold**

This may occur where freeholders apply for commonhold status because they have communal facilities (eg shared roadways, paths or services, etc) and may involve some of the existing freeholders giving up title to areas of their land which are to become the common parts. It is likely that any payment made to a former freeholder will be seen as consideration for the surrender of the freehold interest with the VAT liability being

- in the case of commercial property, exempt (standard-rated where the property is less than three years old or an option to tax has been made (and not disapplied)); and
- in the case of residential property, exempt (zero-rated where a major interest has not been previously granted in the property, eg because the freeholder was also the person who constructed the building for his own occupation).

(5) **A leasehold is converted into commonhold**

On registration as commonhold, all pre-existing leases are extinguished.

Where the former leaseholder gains ownership of a commonhold unit in the same property as under the lease, the only supply is that of the freehold. The lease ceases to have legal effect and there is no supply of it for VAT purposes.

However, where the lease is extinguished and the freehold is transferred to some other person, or the freehold units have different boundaries from the previous leasehold premises, for VAT purposes there is a supply of a surrender of an interest in the property by the former leaseholder with the VAT liability being

- in the case of commercial property, exempt (standard-rated if the lessee has opted to tax the supply (subject to the disapplication rules); and
- in the case of residential property, exempt.

Where the leaseholder pays a consideration for the freehold interest in the unit he acquires, the liability for

- commercial property is exempt (unless the property is less than three years old or the option to tax has been exercised), and
- residential property is exempt (unless it is the first supply of a major interest in which case it is zero-rated).

(6) **Sale of a commonhold unit by a unit holder**

The disposal of a unit in a commercial property is exempt unless the property is less than three years old or an option to tax has been made (and not disapplied) in which case the supply is standard-rated.

The disposal of a unit in a residential property is exempt.

On purchase of a commonhold unit, the purchaser will also acquire membership of the commonhold association and an interest in the common parts. Normally, there will be no consideration attributed to the transfer of interest but it is a supply for VAT purposes and VAT must be charged if the conditions in 42.7(4) below apply.

(7) **The termination of a commonhold**

A commonhold can be terminated in the following circumstances.

- *Voluntary winding up*. The commonhold association must specify proposals for the transfer of the commonhold land and explain how the assets of the association are to be distributed. Any payment received by either the commonhold association or by the unit-holders is consideration for a freehold interest and the liability is in accordance with the normal rules as above.
- *Winding up by court*. Where a commonhold association becomes insolvent, a successor commonhold association may be registered as the proprietor of the freehold estate in the common parts. Normally, there will be no consideration attributed to the disposal but it is a supply for VAT purposes and VAT must be charged if the conditions in 42.7(4) below apply.

(8) **Treatment of the commonhold assessment**

Charges ('commonhold assessments') will normally be levied by the commonhold association to pay for the upkeep of common parts. These charges are treated in the same way as service charges to a long leaseholder or a non-commonhold freeholder. See 42.4(5) above.

(VAT Notice 742, paras 13.1–13.8).

42.7 OTHER LAND TRANSACTIONS

(1) **Compulsory purchase**

The disposal of land under a compulsory purchase order is an exempt supply unless standard-rated because it is a new building or civil engineering work within 42.3(*a*) above, holiday accommodation less than three years old (see 42.3(*d*) above) or the option to tax has been exercised (see 42.8 below). If the full amount of compensation is not known at what would otherwise be the time of supply under the normal rules, there is a tax point each time any compensation payment is received. (*SI 1995/2518, Reg 84(1)*; VAT Notice 742, para 7.3). See, however, *L Landau (VTD 13644) (TVC 55.91)* where the tribunal chairman gave the opinion that VAT generally became chargeable on the transfer of the right to dispose of the land and the taxable amount included consideration to be obtained later. Where consideration was not quantified, there was no reason why VAT should not be accounted for on an estimated amount.

(2) **Dedications of roads and sewers, transactions under planning agreements, etc.**

If a developer

(*a*) dedicates, for no monetary consideration, a new road to a local authority (under *Highways Act 1980* or *Roads (Scotland) Act 1984*) or a new sewer or ancillary works to a sewerage undertaker (under *Water Industries Act 1991* or *Sewerage (Scotland) Act 1968*),

(*b*) provides goods or services free, or at a purely nominal charge, to a local or other authority (under *Town and Country Planning Acts* or other similar agreements which may loosely be described as 'planning gain agreements'), or

(*c*) transfers (usually for a nominal consideration) the *basic* amenities of estate roads, footpaths, communal parking and open space of a private housing or industrial estate to a management company which maintains them,

this does not constitute a taxable supply by the developer and no VAT is chargeable.

Included under (*b*) are buildings such as community centres or schools, amenity land or civil engineering works or an agreement to construct something on land already owned by a local authority or third party.

Any input tax incurred on such work is, however, attributable to the supply (or self-supply) of the main development (ie houses, shops, community centre, factory units, etc) and recoverable or not depending upon whether that supply is taxable or exempt.

Any sums of money which have to be paid by the developer to the local authority, etc (eg for the future maintenance of the building or land or as a contribution towards improvement of the infrastructure) are not consideration for a taxable supply to the developer by the local authority, etc.

(3) **Agreements with the Highways Agency**. When a development is undertaken, there may need to be road improvements. These will normally be undertaken in one of the following ways

- *Works carried out by the Highways Agency*. The Highways Agency will arrange for the works to be carried out and may then, under *Highways Act 1980, s 278*, recover from the developer the costs of certain road improvements. These costs normally include irrecoverable VAT that has been charged to the Highways Agency by a contractor. As there is no supply between the Highways Agency and the developer, merely a reimbursement of VAT-inclusive costs, the developer is not entitled to recover the VAT element as input tax.
- *Works carried out by the developer*. If the developer is permitted by the Highways Agency to carry out the works at his own cost, then there is no supply by the developer of the works to the Highways Agency (because the developer does not receive any consideration for the works from the Highways Agency). However, the developer may recover the input tax as

attributable to his own ultimate supply of land and buildings from the development if the development is a taxable supply.

(VAT Notice 742, paras 8.1–8.5).

(4) **Free supplies of land and buildings**

The normal rules for business gifts and private use of property apply. Where

(*a*) land or buildings forming part of the assets of a business are transferred or disposed of free of charge, or

(*b*) such land or buildings are made available for anyone else to use, free of charge or for a private or non-business purpose

the business must account for output tax on such supplies if

- it was charged VAT on the purchase, construction, reconstruction or refurbishment of the land or buildings;
- it treated all that VAT as input tax and did not apportion it between business and non-business use;
- it was eligible to treat all or part of the input tax as deductible; and
- the supply is standard-rated (see below).

Any such transfer or disposal of land or buildings is taxable if it is standard-rated in its own right or the business has opted to tax (and the option is not disapplied). The value is the market value at the time of its disposal.

Making a building available free of charge, or for private or non-business use, is always taxable. The amount of the charge is equal to that part of the input VAT deducted on the building that is fairly attributable to this use. Where no VAT was incurred on the building before 9 April 2003, then this charge only arises if the intended use of the building is changed after incurring the VAT (as a single output tax charge at the time of the change of use). If the free of charge, private or non-business use is intended at the time the VAT is incurred, the business must apportion the VAT incurred at that point and there will be no further charge when the free of charge, private or non-business use actually happens.

(VAT Notice 742, para 7.6).

See 47.6 and 47.7 OUTPUT TAX for full details.

(5) **Mortgages**

The mortgaging of a property, as security for borrowing money, is not regarded as a supply of the property for VAT purposes.

Sales of repossessed property.

- *Sales under a power of sale.* Where a financial institution or any other lender sells land or buildings under a power of sale in satisfaction of a debt owed to it, there is a supply of the property by the *borrower*. If VAT is due on that supply, the *lender* or other person selling the property is responsible for accounting for that VAT using the procedure set out in 2.18 ACCOUNTING PERIODS AND RETURNS.
- *Foreclosures.* If, instead of selling property under a power of sale, a lender obtains a Court Order and forecloses on land or buildings belonging to the borrower, there is a supply by the borrower to the lender of the land

or building unless it is treated as an asset of a business transferred as a going concern (see 8.10 BUSINESS). If the land or building is subsequently sold, this is a supply by the lender foreclosing, who may, if he wishes, opt to tax the property.

Renting out of repossessed property. If a lender

- repossesses land or buildings, or
- appoints a *Law of Property Act* receiver without foreclosing

and rents the property out to tenants, the borrower makes a supply to the tenant if the rental income received by the lender is used to reduce the debt owed or to service interest payments due in respect of that debt. If the supply is a standard-rated supply, the lender or LPA receiver should account for VAT using the procedure set out in 2.18 ACCOUNTING PERIODS AND RETURNS.

(VAT Notice 742, paras 9.1–9.4).

See also 7.11 BAD DEBT RELIEF for recovery of VAT on costs incurred by mortgage lenders.

(6) **Transfer of a business as a going concern**

See 8.10 BUSINESS.

42.8 OPTION TO TAX

The 'option to tax' provisions (also known as the 'election to waive exemption' provisions) allow certain supplies of land, which would otherwise be exempt under *VATA 1994, Sch 9 Group 1* (see 42.2 above) to be standard-rated. [*VATA 1994, Sch 10 para 2*(*1*); *SI 1994/3013*]. The purpose of the option is to allow the recovery of input tax (see 42.11 below) which would otherwise be lost under the partial exemption rules.

For these purposes, '*land*' includes any buildings or structures permanently affixed to it. A business does not need to own the land in order to opt to tax it. (VAT Notice 742A, para 1.2).

Effect of opting to tax. Once a business has opted to tax any property, it must charge VAT on *all* future supplies it makes in relation to that property which would otherwise be exempt (normal tax point rules applying, see below) unless

- the supply falls within 42.9 below, or
- the option has been revoked (see 42.10 below).

It is not possible, for example, for a business to opt to tax rents but then not tax a subsequent sale of the property. The option remains effective even if the business

- sells the property and subsequently re-acquires it; or
- ceases to be registered for VAT due to a fall in turnover but subsequently has to register again.

Only supplies which the business makes are affected. Its option to tax will not affect supplies made by anyone else. For example, if it is selling an opted building, the purchaser has the choice of whether to opt to tax or not. Similarly, if a tenant of the business is sub-letting, they too have this same choice. For this reason, it is advisable to inform any tenant of the decision to opt at the earliest opportunity so that they may safeguard their right to recover input tax by opting to tax, if they should so wish. (VAT Notice 742A, para 4.4).

Effect on existing leases. Unless the lease specifically provides otherwise, the lessor or licensor has a right to add VAT to the rent agreed under the lease following an option to tax. [*VATA 1994, s 89*]. If an election has been made but, under the terms of the lease, VAT cannot be added, any rent received should be treated as VAT-inclusive and the VAT element calculated by multiplying the rent received by the appropriate VAT fraction.

Scope of the option. When opting to tax, a business can specify an area of land or a building.

(*a*) *Land*. An option to tax land has effect in relation to any land specified, or of a description specified, in the election. [*VATA 1994, Sch 10 para 3(2)*]. When a business makes the option in respect specified land

- (*a*) it covers all the land, and any buildings or civil engineering works which are part of the land;
- (*b*) it does not affect any adjoining land; and
- (*c*) if the business later constructs a building on land that it has opted to tax, that building will not be covered by the option.

(VAT Notice 742A, para 2.4).

(*b*) *Buildings*. Where an election is made in relation to, or to part of, a building (or planned building) it has effect in relation to the whole of the building and the land within its curtilage (see further below). For these purposes, the following are taken to be a single building.

- Buildings linked internally or by a covered walkway.

  HMRC regard a link as an internal access or a covered walkway between buildings the purpose of which is to allow movement of goods and people. It does not include a car park (above or below ground), a public thoroughfare or a statutory requirement, such as a fire escape.

- Complexes consisting of a number of units grouped around a fully enclosed concourse (eg a shopping mall).

HMRC also make the following comments.

- The option to tax covers the whole of the building and the land under and immediately around that building (eg forecourts and yards). If the business's interest in the building is restricted to one floor, the option to tax will still cover the remaining floors of the building.
- If the building stands in a large area of land, how far the option to tax extends over the land depends on how far the services of the building can be utilised. For example, a racecourse grandstand may provide electricity and shelter for stalls, or other facilities, within its peripheral area. An option to tax on the grandstand would extend over the whole area of land that uses the benefits.
- If the building is demolished or destroyed, the option to tax will *not* apply to the land on which the building stood. If the business later constructs another building on that land, it will not be covered by the option to tax.
- If a business makes changes to a building after it has opted to tax, it will need to consider whether the option covers those changes. The most common changes, and HMRC's views on those changes are as follows.

(i) *Extensions*. The option to tax will apply to any later extension (whether upwards, downwards or sideways).

(ii) *Linked buildings*. If a building subject to the option to tax is subsequently linked to another building, the option will not flow through with the link unless a single building is created (see above).

(iii) *Forming a complex*. Where a group of units that have been treated as separate buildings for the option to tax and subsequently enclosed, the option to tax will not spread to the un-opted units.

[*VATA 1994, Sch 10 para 3(3); SI 1995/279*]. (VAT Notice 742A, paras 2.2–2.5).

Groups of companies. Where a company has opted to tax land or buildings and subsequently joins a VAT group (see 31.2 GROUPS OF COMPANIES), any supply made of those land or buildings by any member of the VAT group is taxable. Similarly, if a company is a member of a VAT group, and any member of that group has opted to tax any land or buildings, the company is bound by that option. This is the case even if the option to tax was made before it joined the VAT group. Where a company leaves a group but retains an interest in a property on which the group would have charged VAT, the company must standard-rate any supplies of that property which it subsequently makes. [*VATA 1994, Sch 10 para 2(1), para 3(7)*]. (VAT Notice 742A, para 6.3).

Time of supply (tax point). The normal tax point rules apply to all supplies of land or buildings. See 64.44 SUPPLY. In a tenanted building, a tax point might not occur until after payment is received. In these circumstances, where a business opts to tax after the rent becomes due but before it is paid, it must account for output tax on the rental receipt. This is the case even if the payment covers a period before the option to tax took effect. (VAT Notice 742A, para 10.3).

Transfer of a business as a going concern. See 8.12 BUSINESS for the transfer of land or buildings as part of a transfer of a going concern and 8.15 BUSINESS for the deduction of related input tax.

De Voil Indirect Tax Service. See V4.115.

42.9 Supplies not affected by an option

There are some supplies which an option to tax does not affect and which remain exempt even though the option has been exercised on the property in question. These are as follows.

(*a*) **Dwellings, etc.** Any supply in relation to a building (or part of a building) intended for use as a dwelling or a number of dwellings or solely for a '*relevant residential purpose*' (see 42.1(15) above).

However, this restriction does not apply and an option to tax can still be applied where

- the person making the grant and the person to whom it is made agree in writing, at or before the time of the grant, that the option to tax is to apply; and
- at the time the supply is made, the person purchasing the property intends to convert it from a non-residential building to residential use for the purpose of making a supply which is zero-rated under 42.13(*c*) below.

A supply of a building (or part of a building) cannot be taken as intended for use for a relevant residential purpose unless, before it is made, the person to whom the supply is made gives the supplier a certificate to that effect. See 42.32 below.

In *PJG Developments Ltd; Red Developments (London) Ltd (VTD 19097) (TVC 6.2A)* a company owned a disused public house which it had opted to tax. It sold the property to another company, which intended to convert the building into residential units, and charged output tax on the sale. The purchaser appealed and the tribunal held that VAT should not have been charged since the building was intended for use as a 'dwelling or a number of dwellings'. Compare the earlier decision in *SEH Holdings Ltd (VTD 16771) (TVC 6.2)* where the circumstances were similar except that the immediate purchaser resold the property on the same day and contracted with the new purchasers to build residential units on the site. The tribunal concluded that the option to tax did apply as the seller only had to consider the intended use of the building by the immediate purchaser since this provided certainty for him. As a result of this decision, HMRC have confirmed that a vendor who has opted to tax a property must account for output tax on the sale if the immediate purchaser does not intend to use the building himself as a dwelling nor to convert it into dwellings. (Business Brief 8/01).

(*b*) **Charitable use**. A supply in relation to a building (or part of a building) intended for use solely for a '*relevant charitable purpose*' (see 42.1(13) above) other than as an office.

(*c*) **Residential caravans**. A supply of a pitch for a residential caravan. For this purpose, a caravan is not a residential caravan if residence in it throughout the year is prevented by the terms of a covenant, statutory planning consent or similar permission (ie the caravan cannot lawfully be occupied as a permanent residence).

(*d*) **Residential houseboats**. A supply of facilities for the mooring (including anchoring or berthing) of a residential houseboat. For this purpose, a houseboat is a boat or other floating structure designed or adapted for use solely as a place of permanent habitation and not having means of, or capable of being readily adapted for, self-propulsion. A houseboat is not a residential houseboat if residence in it throughout the year is prevented by the terms of a covenant, statutory planning consent or similar permission (ie the houseboat cannot lawfully be occupied as a permanent residence).

(*e*) **Housing associations**. A supply to a 'relevant housing association' which has given the supplier a certificate stating that the land is to be used (after any necessary demolition work) for the construction of a building or buildings for use as a dwelling or a number of dwellings or solely for a 'relevant residential purpose'. See 42.1(14) above for the meaning of '*relevant housing association*', and 42.1(15) above for '*relevant residential purpose*'.

(*f*) **DIY builders**. A supply of land to an individual where the land is to be used for the construction, otherwise than in the course or furtherance of a business carried on by him, of a building intended for use by him as a dwelling.

(*g*) **Certain supplies affected by anti-avoidance measures**. Certain businesses, which are not entitled to recover all of the input tax they incur on the purchase of land or buildings or on major construction projects, enter into arrangements designed to either increase the amount of input tax they can claim or to spread the VAT cost of the purchase or construction over a number of years. To counter this avoidance, HMRC have introduced a test which is applied each time a grant is made. If the test is met, the option to tax will not have effect (it will be 'disapplied') in respect of the supplies that arise from that particular grant. A business that normally receives credit for most of the input tax it incurs is unlikely to be affected by these anti-avoidance measures.

The test is that, if at the time of the 'grant' of land and buildings (the development)

(i) the development is either

- a capital item for the purposes of the capital goods scheme (see 10.2 CAPITAL GOODS SCHEME) owned by the 'grantor', or
- property which the grantor or a 'person responsible for financing the grantor's development' intends or expects to be treated as a capital item owned by either the grantor or any person to whom it is to be transferred for the purposes of the capital goods scheme,

(ii) the grant is made during the period of adjustment of input tax for the capital item under the capital goods scheme (see 10.3 CAPITAL GOODS SCHEME),

(iii) the grantor or a 'person responsible for financing the grantor's development' intends or expects that the property will, at any time during that period of adjustment, be occupied, or continue to be occupied by

- the grantor,
- a person responsible for financing the grantor's development, or
- a person connected with either such person under *ICTA 1988, s 839*, see 69.19 VALUATION, and

(iv) that occupation will be other than wholly or mainly for 'eligible purposes'

then the option to tax will not have effect in respect of supplies that arise from that particular grant (eg sale premium and rental income received).

Additionally, in relation to supplies made after 17 March 2004, where someone other than the person who made the grant makes a supply of land that arises from that grant, for the purposes of the above test that person is treated as making that grant at the time of their first supply arising from it. Thus, any person making supplies under a lease (but who did not make the initial grant) must apply the above test as though they had made a new grant. In such circumstances, where the only reason that the new grant fails otherwise to satisfy the disapplication test is that it occurs after the period of adjustment of input tax for the capital item, the new grant is to be treated as satisfying that test.

'*Grant*' refers to the act that transfers the land or building, such as a freehold sale of land or a building, the leasing or licensing of land or a building, or the assignment or surrender of that lease or licence. (VAT Notice 742A, para 13.4).

'*Grantor*' is the person who sells, leases or lets any of the land or buildings and can be anywhere in the chain of people who have an interest in the land or buildings concerned. For example, where a freeholder sells land to another party who constructs a new commercial building on the land and lets it to another business for occupation for its own use, there are two grantors: the seller of the land and the business which constructs and leases the new commercial building.

If the occupying business sub-lets part of the building to another business, there would then be three grantors. The test should be applied to each grant made. (VAT Notice 742A, para 13.4).

A '*person responsible for financing the grantor's development*' is a person who has

- provided finance for the grantor's development of the land; or
- entered into any agreement, arrangement or understanding (whether or not legally enforceable) to provide finance for the grantor's development of the land.

Providing funds is widely defined. It includes directly or indirectly providing funds *either* to meet the whole (or part) of the cost of the grantor's development of the land *or* to discharge the whole (or part) of any liability incurred in raising funds to meet that cost. It also includes directly or indirectly procuring the provision of funds by another person for either of those purposes. The ways the funds can be provided include

- making a loan of funds to be used for that purpose;
- providing a guarantee or other security in relation to such a loan;
- providing any of the consideration for the issue of shares or securities issued wholly or partly for raising those funds;
- in relation to supplies made after 17 March 2004, providing any consideration for the acquisition by any person of shares or securities issued wholly or partly for raising those funds; and
- any other transfer of assets or value as a consequence of which any of the funds are made available.

See also *Winterthur Life UK Ltd (No 2) (VTD) (TVC 6.5)*.

'*Eligible purposes*'. Occupation for eligible purposes means one of the following.

- Occupation by a taxable person for the purpose of making supplies which are in the course or furtherance of a business carried on by him and of such a description that he is entitled to credit for any wholly attributable input tax. HMRC accept that a business is in occupation of the development for eligible purposes if it occupies them for the purpose of making *mainly* taxable supplies or for other supplies which entitle them to credit for their input tax. 'Mainly' means substantially more than half. (VAT Notice 742A, para 13.10).
- Occupation by a specified body within *VATA 1994, s 33* (see 43.2 LOCAL AUTHORITIES AND PUBLIC BODIES) to the extent that the body occupies the land for non-business purposes.
- Occupation by a government department.

For these purposes

- where occupation is by a person who is not a taxable person but whose supplies are treated for the purposes of *VATA 1994* as made by another person who is a taxable person, those two persons are to be regarded as a single taxable person; and

- a person is taken to be in occupation of any land whether he occupies it alone or together with one or more other persons and whether he occupies all of that land or only part of it.

Intentions and expectations. HMRC will consider commercial documents and other evidence such as minutes of meetings, business plans and finance requests to establish the intention and expectation of the businesses that are involved in the particular development. There does not have to be an intention to avoid VAT for the grant to be caught by the test. (VAT Notice 742A, para 13.5).

Where a grant within (*a*) to (*f*) above gives rise to supplies at different times after the making of the grant (eg rent), the liability of each of those supplies is determined at the time when the supply is made rather than by reference to the time of the original grant.

Supplies partially affected by an option. Where a business has opted to tax a property but the option cannot have effect in relation to part of that property (eg a shop with a flat to be used as a dwelling over it), the consideration for any supply must be apportioned between the standard-rated element and the exempt or zero-rated part. [*VATA 1994, Sch 8 Group 5 Note 10, Sch 10 para 9; SI 1995/279; SI 1995/280*]. The business can choose the method of apportionment but it must provide a fair and reasonable result. (VAT Notice 742A, para 3.10).

[*VATA 1994, s 96(10A), Sch 10 para 2(2)(2A)(2B)(3)(3AA)(3AAA)(3B), para 3(7A)(8), para 3A, para 9; FA 1997, ss 35–37; SI 1994/3013; SI 1995/279; SI 1997/51; SI 1999/593; SI 2004/778*].

42.10 **Making and revoking the option**

There are two stages in opting to tax.

- Making the decision to opt which may take place at a board meeting or similar, or less formally. However reached, HMRC recommend that a written record is kept showing clear details of the land or buildings to be covered by the option and the date the decision is made.
- Notifying HMRC of the decision (see below).

Requirement for permission where previous exempt supply. Where, after 31 July 1989 and before the date the option is to take effect (see below), an exempt supply of a property has been (or will be) made, a business cannot opt to tax that property unless either of the following applies.

(*a*) Any of the following conditions for automatic permission specified in VAT Notice 742A, para 5.2 (which have the force of law) are met.

(1) It is a mixed-use development and the only exempt supplies have been in relation to the dwellings.

(2) The business does not wish to recover any input tax in relation to the land or building incurred before the option to tax has effect; *and*

- the consideration for exempt supplies has, up to the date when the option to tax is to take effect, been solely by way of rents or service charges and excludes any premiums or payments in respect of occupation after the date on which the option takes effect. Regular rental and/or service charge payments can be ignored for the purposes of this condition. Payments are considered regular where the intervals between them are no more than a year and where each represents a commercial or genuine arms length value; and

- the only input tax relating to the land or building that the business expects to recover after the option to tax takes effect will be on overheads, such as regular rental payments, service charges, repairs and maintenance costs. If it expects to claim input tax in relation to refurbishment or redevelopment of the building, it will not meet this condition.

In deciding whether this condition is met, a business should disregard

- (with effect from 2 March 2005), any VAT refundable to a local authority or similar body under *VATA 1994, s 32(2)(b)* (see 43.8 LOCAL AUTHORITIES AND SIMILAR BODIES);
- any input tax it can otherwise recover by virtue of the partial exemption *de minimis* rules; and
- any input tax it is entitled to recover on general business overheads not specifically related to the land or building, such as audit fees.

(3) The only input tax the business wishes to recover in relation to the land or building incurred before the option to tax takes effect relates solely to VAT charged by a tenant or tenants upon surrender of a lease; *and*

- the building or relevant part of the building has been unoccupied between the date of the surrender and the date the option to tax is to take effect;
- there will be no further exempt supplies of the land or building; and
- the business does not intend or expect that it will occupy the land or building other than for taxable purposes.

(4) The exempt supplies have been incidental to the main use of the land or building. For example, where the business has occupied a building for taxable purposes, the following would be seen as incidental to the main use and this condition would be met.

- Allowing an advertising hoarding to be displayed.
- Granting space for the erection of a radio mast.
- Receiving income from an electricity sub-station.

The letting of space to an occupying tenant, however minor, is not incidental.

If any one of the above conditions is met, the business must still write to HMRC to notify the option (see below). The notification should state that, although the business has made previous exempt supplies of the land or building, it satisfies the conditions for automatic permission.

(*b*) The business has obtained prior written permission to opt from the Option to Tax National Unit, HM Revenue and Customs, Portcullis House, 21 India Street, Glasgow, G2 4PZ. Note that the application should be made to this address even if the business is not VAT-registered but an option to tax would result in it needing to do so. The letter to HMRC seeking permission should give details of the date from which it would like the option to have effect (a future date allowing HMRC at least one month to consider the request) together with the following information.

- A brief description of future plans for the land or building if permission is granted.
- Details of any input tax incurred in the 10 years before opting to tax that the business wishes to recover. HMRC need details of the amount of input tax claimed, how this has been calculated, what the input tax relates to and when it was incurred. The business must also give details of any input tax that it expects to incur in the period between the request for permission and the date it wishes the option to tax to take effect.
- The value of input tax the business expects to incur in the future if HMRC grant permission to opt to tax, and what this input tax will relate to (eg rents, premiums, surrenders or refurbishments).
- The total value of exempt supplies of the land or building in the 10 years before the request for permission. The business also needs to give details of the value of any supplies it expects to make between the date of request for permission and the date the option is to be effective. HMRC need details of any grants that have been made for a premium or prepayment of rent, including the dates they were made, their values and the period to which they relate.
- The expected value of the taxable supplies the business intends to make in the foreseeable future after the date of the option to tax, should HMRC grant permission. Where these taxable supplies are the result of the granting of standard-rated leases, the business should advise how long the leases already in place are expected to run, and if it has any reason to suspect they will not run their full course. It should indicate whether it is likely to make any exempt grants after the option to tax takes effect, for example, supplies where the option to tax will not apply for any reason.
- Whether the business, or anyone who has helped to fund the land or building, or anyone connected to the business or the financier, is occupying or intending to occupy any part of the land or buildings (see 42.9(*g*) above).

HMRC cannot grant permission to opt to tax until all the information detailed above is provided together with any additional information that they ask for. Occasionally, HMRC will refuse permission if they are not satisfied that granting permission would result in a fair and reasonable attribution of input tax. However, if they are satisfied, HMRC will advise the business in writing and ask it to confirm that it wishes to put the option into effect. The business must then formally notify HMRC (see below).

HMRC cannot grant retrospective permission. Therefore, if a business fails to ask for permission

- any VAT charged in error is not output tax and, unless it is refunded, HMRC will collect it as a debt due to them; and
- any input tax claimed in error is exempt input tax and is not allowable. If HMRC grant permission and the business opts to tax from a later date, they will need to take account of any exempt supplies incorrectly treated as taxable when agreeing an apportionment of pre-option input tax.

[*VATA 1994, Sch 10 para 3*(9)]. (VAT Notice 742A, paras 5.1–5.8).

Written notification. Whether or not permission is required as above, to have legal effect, written notification of the option to tax must be given to HMRC, together with such other information as they require, within 30 days of the date of election (or such longer period as HMRC allow). (Note that where an election made before 1 March 1995 did not require to be notified to HMRC because the total value for all supplies of the property covered by the election were expected to be less than £20,000 in the following twelve months, such an election remains valid after 1 March 1995 and does not require written notification after that date.) [*VATA 1994, Sch 10 para 3*(6)*; SI 1995/279*].

The written notification must state clearly what land or buildings is covered by the option to tax and the date from which the option has effect. HMRC suggest that Notification Form VAT 1614 is used (obtainable from the National Advice Service). If a business is opting to tax discrete areas of land, HMRC suggests that it sends a map or plan clearly showing the opted land with the notification. Similarly, if opting to tax a building, the full post address, including postal code, should be included.

It is important that an appropriate person signs the notification, and any accompanying list or schedule (see further below).

For businesses already VAT-registered, all notifications of, and queries relating to, the option to tax should be made

- in writing to the Option To Tax National Unit, HM Revenue and Customs, Portcullis House, 21 India Street, Glasgow, G2 4PZ;
- by fax to 0141 308 3367; or
- by e-mail to optiontotaxnationalunit@hmrc.gsi.gov.uk

Where a business becomes liable to be registered for VAT purposes as a result of the option to tax, the application to register for VAT *and* the notification of the option to tax should be submitted together to the appropriate VAT Registration Unit (see 59.38 REGISTRATION).

(VAT Notice 742A, para 4.2).

Responsibility for opting to tax. The person responsible for making the decision and notifying the option to tax depends on the type of legal entity holding (or intending to hold) the interest in the land or building, and who within that entity has the authority to make decisions concerning VAT. Following the tribunal decision in *Blythe Limited Partnership (VTD 16011) (TVC 6.29)* where written notification of an option made by solicitors acting for the partnership was held to be inaccurate and not binding, HMRC have issued guidance on notifying an option to tax. HMRC recommend that the letter notifying an option (and any accompanying list or schedule of properties) is signed (as appropriate) by a director, two or more partners (or trustees), an authorised administrator or by a sole proprietor. If a business authorises a third party to notify an option on its behalf, HMRC require confirmation that the third party is authorised to do so. They would also like to be notified if the business withdraws that authority. Other more unusual situations are

- *Beneficial owners.* Where there is a beneficial owner and a legal owner of land or buildings (eg a bare trust), for VAT purposes it is the beneficial owner who is making the supply of the land or building and who should opt to tax. Where, however, there are numerous beneficiaries (eg unit trusts and pension funds) the person making the supply is the trustee who holds the legal interest and receives the immediate benefit of the consideration.

- *Joint owners* should together notify a single option to tax if they want supplies of the jointly-owned land or building to be standard-rated.
- *Limited partnerships*. The general partner(s) should opt to tax. Where title to the land or building is held jointly in the names of the general partner(s) and the limited partner(s), only the titleholders can make any supplies of that land or building together. That suggests that the limited partner(s) is/are involved in the management and running of the partnership and, as such, HMRC treat them as general partners. If the partnership decides to opt to tax, one or more of the partners should sign the notification.
- *Limited liability partnerships*. A limited liability partnership is a corporate body and is liable to register for VAT, subject to the normal registration rules. If the partnership decides to opt to tax, one or more members must sign the notification.

(VAT Notice 742A, paras 7.1–7.5).

Effective date of option to tax. An option to tax has effect from the date on which it is made (or such later date specified in the election). Where the election was made before 1 November 1989, it had effect from 1 August 1989 (or such later date specified in the election). [*VATA 1994, Sch 10 para 3(1)*]. It should be borne in mind that HMRC must be notified of the option within 30 days of making your decision (see above). If a business fails to do this it should contact HMRC immediately. In no circumstances can an option to tax have effect from a date before a business makes the decision to opt. (VAT Notice 742A, para 4.3).

Revoking the option to tax. Once made, the option to tax can only be revoked in the following limited circumstances.

- It can be revoked with effect from the date on which it has effect provided
  - (*a*) written consent of HMRC is obtained within three months from that date;
  - (*b*) no VAT has become chargeable and no credit for input tax has been claimed by virtue of the election (disregarding any input tax that would have been recovered under normal partial exemption rules); and
  - (*c*) the property has not been sold together with a business (or part of a business) as a transfer of a going concern (see 8.10 BUSINESS).
- The option to tax may be revoked where more than 20 years have elapsed since the date on which it had effect. Revocation takes effect from the date on which written consent is given by HMRC or such later date as they specify in their written consent.

[*VATA 1994, Sch 10 para 3(4)(5); SI 1995/279*].

42.11 Recovery of input tax

Input tax incurred on or after the date of the option to tax. Once the option to tax has been made, a business can recover input tax on any related expenditure subject to the normal rules.

- Where taxable supplies of the land or buildings are made, any input tax relating to those supplies can be recovered.

- Where wholly exempt supplies of the land or building are made (because the supplies are not affected by the option, see 42.9 above), any input tax relating to those supplies cannot be recovered.
- Where supplies that are both taxable and exempt are made (eg where an opted building is to be used for both commercial and residential purposes), the input tax relating to the taxable supplies can be recovered using the partial exemption rules.

Input tax incurred before the date of the option to tax. There are four situations in which input tax incurred before the date of the option to tax can be recovered.

(*a*) Where the supply of land or buildings is taxable in its own right (eg a freehold sale of a commercial building within three years of its completion is always standard-rated).

(*b*) Where there have been no exempt supplies in relation to the land and buildings after 31 July 1989 and prior to such supplies being made, the intention of the business to make exempt supplies changes to an intention to make taxable supplies. In such circumstances, the business may be able to recover previously exempt input tax incurred after 31 July 1989 under the partial exemption 'payback' rule. See 49.10 PARTIAL EXEMPTION. If the change of intention is not accompanied by an option to tax, the business will need to retain suitable evidence of its new intention (see (*d*) below).

(*c*) Where an exempt supply of the land or buildings has been made after 31 July 1989 and permission to exercise the option has been received (see 42.10 above), application can be made to HMRC to recover a fair and reasonable proportion of the VAT incurred in the period from 1 August 1989 to the date the option has effect, taking into account the exempt use of the property and the intended taxable use. (In practice, where written permission is required from HMRC, the application should include a suggested attribution of input tax between exempt and taxable use, see 42.10 above.)

(*d*) Input tax relating to future supplies can be recoverable where there is a clear intention, at the time the costs are incurred, that the supplies of the buildings or land will be taxable. An option to tax is the best evidence of an intention to make taxable supplies for land and property transactions. But where, exceptionally, a business wishes to delay making the option until a future date, it may still be able to recover the input tax if it can produce unequivocal documentary evidence that, at the time it seeks to reclaim the input tax, it intends the supplies to be taxable.

HMRC give the following as examples of the types of documents that may contain evidence of intention.

- A signed agreement/contract that specifies that the vendor will opt to tax prior to the sale.
- An investment appraisal or business plan accepted by a bank that confirms that supplies will be treated as taxable.
- Marketing literature that has been distributed to the public and where the scale and type of distribution, together with the nature of the advertisement itself, makes it clear that taxable supplies will be made.
- Instructions or advice from professional advisers that specifies the VAT treatment, together with confirmation of acceptance of the advice by the business.

- Any other similar document that shows that the intention is to make taxable supplies.

The list is not intended to be exhaustive and whether a particular document provides the evidence depends largely upon its content. It is unlikely that any single document alone will provide sufficient evidence and businesses are advised to hold a number of separate documents to prove its intention. HMRC will normally consider evidence as satisfactory where it involves third parties and shows a firm commitment to the making of taxable supplies. A document that merely sets out an option or number of options will not be acceptable.

Where input tax relating to future taxable supplies has been recovered, a business must retain any documents used as evidence of intention and make them available to HMRC on request. If there is any change in the intention to make taxable supplies, HMRC must be informed as soon as possible and a record must be kept of the date these changes occurred, together with appropriate evidence. VAT previously deducted before the intention changed may need to be adjusted and repaid to HMRC.

An option to tax must be made and notified to Customs prior to any supplies of the land or buildings being made.

[*VATA 1994, Sch 10 para 2(4)–(9); SI 1995/279*]. (VAT Notice 742A, paras 9.1, 9.2).

Input tax on speculative and abortive costs. See 42.15 below.

Pre-registration input VAT. A business may become registered for VAT as a result of option to tax. Special rules apply to all newly-registered businesses under which they may be entitled to claim relief on VAT incurred on supplies obtained before registration. See 35.10 INPUT TAX. The amount claimable is restricted which may lead to inequitable treatment compared with a business carrying out similar activities but which was already VAT-registered when the input tax was incurred. If a business has suffered because of this, it should write to the Option to Tax National Unit, HM Revenue and Customs, Portcullis House, 21 India Street, Glasgow, G2 4PZ and explain the circumstances. (VAT Notice 742A, para 9.4).

Brewers' tenanted properties. Agreement has been reached between HMRC and the Brewers' Society on the deduction of input tax in respect of tied tenanted licensed houses containing a residential element where the brewer has elected to waive exemption on the rents from all its tenanted properties. See VAT Notice 700/57/04 for full details.

42.12 RESIDENTIAL AND CHARITABLE BUILDINGS: CHANGE OF USE

Disposal, part disposal or letting. Where

(*a*) a person receives a grant or other supply of a building (or part) intended solely for use for a 'relevant residential purpose' or a 'relevant charitable purpose' which is zero-rated under *VATA 1994, Sch 8 Group 5* (see 42.13 below), and

(*b*) within the period of ten years beginning with the day on which the building was 'completed', that person grants an 'interest in or right over' or 'licence to occupy' the building (or part) so that it is no longer intended for such a relevant purpose,

the grant is treated as a business supply taxable at the standard rate. An apportionment can be made where as a result of the grant, only part of the building originally zero-rated ceases to be used for a relevant purpose.

See 42.1(15) above for the meaning of '*relevant residential purpose*', 42.1(13) above for '*relevant charitable purpose*', 42.1(7) above for '*interest in or right over*' and 42.1(8) above for '*licence to occupy*' a building.

For these purposes, a building is '*completed*' when an architect issues a certificate of practical completion in relation to it, or it is first fully used, whichever happens first.

The VAT due must be accounted for on the VAT return for the VAT period in which the supply is made.

Change of use without disposal. Where

- (*a*) above applies; and
- within the period of ten years beginning with the day on which the building is 'completed' (see above), that person uses the building (or part) for a purpose which is neither a relevant residential purpose nor a relevant charitable purpose,

he is treated as having made, at that time, a standard-rated self-supply in the course or furtherance of a business.

The value of the supply is calculated by the formula

$A \times (10 - B) \div 10$

where

A = the amount such that the VAT chargeable on it is equal to the VAT that would have been chargeable on the initial relevant zero-rated supply (or, where there was more than one supply, the aggregate amount which would have been chargeable on them) if the building (or part) no longer used for a qualifying purpose had not been zero-rated at that (or those) earlier times (ie the value of the supply is not adjusted to current market value and changes in VAT rates are ignored); and

B = the number of whole years since the day the building was completed for which the building (or part concerned) has been used for a relevant residential purpose or a relevant charitable purpose.

The VAT due on the deemed self-supply must be accounted for as output tax on the VAT return for the period in which the use is changed. The VAT can be deducted as input tax on the same return to the extent that it relates to any other taxable supplies made. It may be necessary to make subsequent adjustments to the amount of input tax deducted under the CAPITAL GOODS SCHEME (10) where

- the 'tax-exclusive amount' equivalent to the output tax due is £250,000 or more, and
- the building is used to make exempt supplies.

The '*tax-exclusive amount*' is the amount such that, when applying the standard rate of VAT in force at the time of the change in use of the building, it equals the output tax due.

[*VATA 1994, Sch 10 para 1; SI 2002/1102*]. (VAT Notice 708, paras 19.5, 19.7).

Example

On 1 March 2000 a charity paid £1 million for a new zero-rated building for its non-business use. On 1 August 2002 it changes the use of the entire building to business use.

The VAT that would have been payable if the initial supply had been standard-rated is

£1m × 17.5% = £175,000

The amount due to HMRC is £175,000 × 80% = £140,000.

Limitation of above provisions. The affect of (*a*) above only applying to zero-rating under *VATA 1994, Sch 8 Group 5* means that the rules only apply where the original grant or supply was

- zero-rated as the construction of a new building;
- zero-rated as the sale of, or long lease in, a new building;
- zero-rated as the sale of, or long lease in, a non-residential building; or
- zero-rated as the conversion of a non-residential building for a relevant housing association.

The rules do not apply to the extent that the original grant or supply was

- zero-rated as approved alterations to a protected building;
- zero-rated as the sale or long lease in a substantially reconstructed protected building;
- reduced-rated; or
- an interest in a building that was exempt from VAT

or where a refund was received under the D-I-Y builders scheme.

VAT registration. The charges and deemed self-supplies described above are included in taxable turnover when deciding whether VAT registration is required.

(VAT Notice 708, paras 19.1, 19.6, 19.8).

De Voil Indirect Tax Service. See V3.248.

PART III PROPERTY DEVELOPERS

42.13 ZERO-RATED SUPPLIES OF QUALIFYING BUILDINGS

The following supplies are zero-rated.

(*a*) **New dwellings**. The first 'grant' of a 'major interest' in, or in any part of, a building, dwelling or its site by a 'person constructing a building' 'designed as a dwelling' or number of dwellings unless either

(i) the interest granted is such that the grantee is not entitled to reside in the building, or part, throughout the year (eg a time-share); or

(ii) residence there throughout the year or the use of the building or part as the grantee's principal private residence, is prevented by the terms of a covenant, statutory planning consent or similar permission (ie accommodation which cannot lawfully be occupied as a permanent residence).

[*VATA 1994, Sch 8 Group 5 Item 1*(*a*) and *Note* (*13*)*; SI 1995/280*].

See 42.1(5) above for the definition of '*grant*', 42.1(9) above for '*major interest*', 42.1(11) above for '*person constructing a building*' and 42.1(4) above for '*designed as a dwelling*'.

First sale or long lease. The above provisions only zero-rate the first sale of, or grant of a long lease in, a building but zero-rating is not affected by

- the length of time between completion of construction and sale of, or grant of a long lease in, the building;
- any sale of, or grant of a long lease in, the building made by other people (even if they also have 'person constructing' status or have made their own zero-rated supply in the building);
- any short leases that may have been made (although this is likely to affect input tax recovery); or
- any sales of, or grant of long leases in, other parts of the building that the same person may have made (eg the developer of a block of flats can zero-rate his first long lease in each flat).

A grantor cannot zero-rate any second or subsequent long lease in the building (or sell the building after leasing it on a long lease).

Land included. In addition to the dwelling, zero-rating also applies to

- the land on which the building stands (the 'foot print'); and
- a reasonable plot of land surrounding it. This will depend on the size, nature and situation of the building and the nature of the surrounding land.

Partly-constructed buildings. Provided the other conditions above are met, zero-rating also applies to the sale of, or grant of a long lease in, land that will form the site of a building provided a building is clearly under construction (ie it has progressed beyond the foundation stage).

Apportionment for part-qualifying buildings.

(1) *General.* Where part of a building qualifies for zero-rating under the above provisions and part does not (eg shop premises with a flat over them), a grant or supply relating only to the part within these provisions is to be treated as relating to a zero-rated building and, similarly, a grant or supply relating only to the part outside those provisions is not to be so treated. In the case of any other grant or supply, an apportionment must be made to determine the extent to which it is to be so treated. [*VATA 1994, Sch 8 Group 5 Note (10); SI 1995/280*].

    Building work that relates to the fabric of the building affecting both qualifying and non-qualifying parts of the building must be apportioned, such as work to

    - roofs,
    - foundations,
    - lifts, and
    - building services that supply the whole building (eg wiring and plumbing).

(2) *Facilities for tenants in blocks of flats.* Work to build facilities shared by the tenants of a block of flats (eg a swimming pool, gym or laundry room) is standard-rated.

(3) *Live-work units.* In a live-work unit (ie a property that combines, within a single unit, a dwelling and commercial or industrial working space as a requirement or condition of planning permission), zero-rating is only available to the extent that the unit comprises the dwelling (provided it meets the other conditions for zero-rating above). Dwellings that contain a home office are not live-work units and no apportionment is needed.

Units where the work area is shown as a discrete area of floor space, whether an office or workshop, must be apportioned to reflect the presence of the commercial element. Where planning permission requires that a minimum amount of the unit (eg 20%) must be used for commercial or industrial purposes, the remaining amount (ie 80%) can be treated as being the dwelling element for VAT purposes.

However, where a unit has neither

- an area that must, as a requirement or condition of planning permission, be used for commercial or industrial purposes, nor
- planning permission requiring a certain percentage of the floor space be used for commercial or industrial purposes;

it may be treated for VAT purposes as if it were entirely a dwelling and no apportionment is required.

Apportionment for mixed sites. Where a person sells, or grants a long lease in, a qualifying dwelling at the same time as a non-qualifying building or land that does not form part of the site (see under *Land included* above), an apportionment must be made between them on a fair and reasonable basis.

Shared ownership schemes. These involve the sharing of equity in a dwelling between, typically, an occupier and a housing association. The occupier purchases a dwelling at a proportion of its value and then pays rent to cover the share in the retained equity. Occupiers have the option of increasing their share of the equity by making additional payments, acquiring a further share related to the current value of the property ('staircasing'). The rent is then reduced accordingly. The initial payment by the occupier for his share of the equity can be zero-rated but the subsequent rental payments and any additional 'staircase' payments are not zero-rated but exempt.

Holiday homes. The restrictions under (i) and (ii) above typically prevent holiday homes from qualifying for zero-rating.

(VAT Notice 708, paras 4.3, 4.4, 4.6, 4.7, 15.1–15.4).

(*b*) **New residential and charitable buildings** The first 'grant' of a 'major interest' in, or in any part of, a building, dwelling or its site by a 'person constructing a building' intended for use solely for a 'relevant residential purpose' or a 'relevant charitable purpose'. [*VATA 1994, Sch 8 Group 5 Item 1(a); SI 1995/280*].

See 42.1(5) above for definition of '*grant*', 42.1(9) above for '*major interest*', 42.1(11) above for '*person constructing a building*', 42.1(15) above for '*relevant residential purpose*' and 42.1(13) above for '*relevant charitable purpose*'.

The provisions within (*a*) above under the headings *First sale or long lease*, *Land included*, *Partly constructed buildings*, *Apportionment for part-qualifying buildings* and *Apportionment for mixed sites* also apply for these purposes.

In addition, where the supply is in connection with a building intended for use as

- residential accommodation for students or school pupils, or
- residential accommodation for members of any of the armed forces

the supply can only be zero-rated to the extent that it relates to the residential accommodation. An apportionment need not be made for supplies in connection with a building intended for use for any other relevant residential purpose (eg a care home). Instead, areas such as administrative areas within the building can also be zero-rated.

(VAT Notice 708, paras 4.6, 4.7, 15.1–15.5).

Issue of certificates. Where all, or any part of, a building is intended for use solely for a relevant residential purpose or relevant charitable purpose, the grant of a major interest cannot be zero-rated under this provision unless, before the grant is made, the grantee has given the grantor a certificate to that effect. See 42.32 below.

(*c*) **Conversion of non-residential buildings**. The first 'grant' of a 'major interest' in, or in any part of, a building, dwelling or its site by a 'person converting'

(i) a 'non-residential' building, or

(ii) a non-residential part of a building

into a building 'designed as a dwelling' or number of dwellings or a building intended for use solely for a 'relevant residential purpose' unless either

(A) the interest granted is such that the grantee is not entitled to reside in the building, or part, throughout the year (eg a time share); or

(B) residence there throughout the year or the use of the building or part as the grantee's principal private residence, is prevented by the terms of a covenant, statutory planning consent or similar permission (ie accommodation which cannot lawfully be occupied as a permanent residence).

Where (ii) applies and the building already contains a residential part, then for zero-rating to apply, the conversion must either be to a building for use for a relevant residential purpose or must create an additional dwelling or dwellings.

[*VATA 1994, Sch 8 Group 5 Item 1*(*b*) and *Note* (*9*)*; SI 1995/280*].

See 42.1(5) above for the definition of '*grant*', 42.1(9) above for '*major interest*', 42.1(10) above for '*non-residential*', 42.1(4) above for '*designed as a dwelling*', and 42.1(15) above for '*relevant residential purpose*'.

'*Person converting*' a building has the same meaning as 'person constructing' a building in 42.1(11) above substituting references to converting/conversion for constructing/construction throughout.

Examples of a non-residential conversion include the conversion of

- a commercial building (such as an office, warehouse, shop, etc),

- an agricultural building (such as a barn), or
- a redundant school or church

into a building designed as a dwelling or number of dwellings.

The provisions within (*a*) above under the headings *First sale or long lease* and *Land included* apply in the same way for these purposes.

Holiday homes. The restrictions under (A) and (B) above typically prevent holiday homes from qualifying for zero-rating.

Amalgamating non-residential parts of a building with other parts. To qualify for zero-rating, the conversion must only use non-residential parts of the building. If the conversion uses a mixture of non-residential parts of the building and other parts, then the sale of, or long lease in, the property cannot be zero-rated. For example, where

- a two-storey public house containing bar areas downstairs and private living areas upstairs (and so in part being used as a dwelling, although see the case law uncertainty on this point in 42.1(10) above) is converted into a single house, or
- the same property is converted by splitting it vertically into a pair of semi-detached houses, each of which use part of what was the living accommodation,

the onward sale or long lease is not zero-rated and the charge cannot be apportioned.

Partly converted buildings. Subject to satisfying the other conditions, zero-rating can be applied to the sale of, or grant of a long lease in, a building where a real and meaningful start on the conversion has been made. This means that the work must have been more than securing or maintaining the existing structure.

Apportionment.

(1) *Apportionment for converted parts of buildings*. It is only possible to zero-rate the sale of, or grant of a long lease in, a building (or part of a building) when the new qualifying residential accommodation is created wholly from a non-residential building or part of a building. Where a mixture of qualifying and non-qualifying conversions in a building is carried out, the charge can be apportioned and zero-rating applied to the sale of, or grant of a long lease in, the qualifying parts. For example

- A shop is converted into a flat and existing flats above the shop, that have been lived in within the last ten years, are refurbished. Zero-rating applies to the sale of, or grant of a long lease in, the converted shop but not the refurbished flats.
- A two-storey public house containing private living areas and bar areas is converted into a pair of flats. The living areas have been 'used as a dwelling' (although see the case law uncertainty on this point in 42.1(10) above) and so the sale of, or long lease in, those parts cannot be zero-rated. The sale of, or grant of a long lease in, the converted bar areas can be zero-rated provided that the new flat is created solely from the non-residential areas.

(2) *Apportionment for mixed sites*. Where a development site, containing a mixture of buildings that qualify for zero-rating as the conversion of a

non-residential building (or part of a building) and other buildings, is sold or long-leased, the supplies must be apportioned on a fair and reasonable basis.

(VAT Notice 708, paras 5.3–5.7).

Issue of certificates. Where all, or any part of, a building is intended for use solely for a relevant residential purpose, the grant of a major interest cannot be zero-rated under these provisions unless, before the grant is made, the grantee has given the grantor a certificate to that effect. See 42.32 below.

Garages. The construction of a building under (*a*) above or the conversion of a non-residential building under (*c*) above includes the construction of, or conversion of a non-residential building to, a garage provided

- the dwelling and the garage are constructed or converted at the same time; and
- the garage is intended for occupation with the dwelling or one of the dwellings.

[*VATA 1994, Sch 8 Group 5 Note* (*3*)*; SI 1995/280*].

Tenancies and leases. Where the major interest granted under (*a*)–(*c*) above is a tenancy or lease, zero-rating only applies to the premium payable on the grant or, if no premium is payable, the first payment of rent due under the tenancy or lease. [*VATA 1994, Sch 8 Group 5 Note* (*14*)*; SI 1995/280*]. Ongoing payments, such as further rents, ground rent or service charges cannot be zero-rated.

Change of use of relevant residential or charitable buildings. Where the grant of a major interest in a building is zero-rated under these provisions because the grantee certifies that the building will be used for a relevant residential purpose or a relevant charitable purpose, the grantee will be treated as making a standard-rated supply of the property if, within ten years of its completion, he either sells, lets or uses the building for any other purpose. See 42.12 above for full details.

Groups of companies. In the rare situation when a group member makes more than one grant of a major interest in a building, the first of which is to another group member, HMRC do not consider that first grant to be the 'first grant of a major interest' in the building for the purpose of zero-rating. In effect, this means that the first grant of a major interest to a person outside the group can be zero-rated, regardless of the previous activity within the VAT group, so long as the group member making the grant is a person constructing (or converting) the building and it meets all the other criteria. (Business Brief 11/03).

Joint ownership and beneficial interests. See 42.5 above.

De Voil Indirect Tax Service. See V4.233; V4.234.

42.14 SUBSTANTIAL RECONSTRUCTIONS OF PROTECTED BUILDINGS

The first 'grant' by a person 'substantially reconstructing' a 'protected building' of a 'major interest' in, or in any part of, the building or its site is zero-rated. [*VATA 1994, Sch 8 Group 6 Item 1; SI 1995/283*].

See 42.1(5) above for the definition of '*grant*', 42.1(12) above for '*protected building*' and 42.1(9) above for '*major interest*'.

The grant of an interest in a building 'designed as a dwelling' (see 42.1(4) above) or number of dwellings (or the site of such a building) is *not* zero-rated under these provisions if either

(i) the interest granted is such that the grantee is not entitled to reside in the building throughout the year (eg a time-share); or

(ii) residence there throughout the year, or use of the building as the grantee's principal private residence, is prevented by the terms of a covenant, statutory planning consent or similar permission (ie accommodation which cannot lawfully be occupied as a permanent residence).

[*VATA 1994, Sch 8 Group 5 Note* (*13*)*, Group 6 Note* (*3*)*; SI 1995/283*].

The restrictions under (i) and (ii) above typically prevent holiday homes from qualifying for zero-rating. (VAT Notice 708, para 10.5).

'Substantially reconstructing'. A protected building is substantially reconstructed when major work takes place to its fabric, including the replacement of much of the internal or external structure. (VAT Notice 708, para 10.3). In addition, a protected building is not to be regarded as substantially reconstructed unless one or both of the following conditions are fulfilled when the reconstruction is completed.

- At least 60% of the cost of the reconstruction work would, if supplied by a taxable person, qualify for zero-rating as the supply of services in the course of approved alterations under 42.21 below or building materials and other items to carry out those works under 42.26 or 42.27 below. When determining if at least 60% of the work could be zero-rated as 'approved alterations', all of the work to the building should be considered, even if only part will be used for qualifying purposes. But only those alterations to the qualifying parts can count towards the zero-rated element.
- The reconstructed building incorporates no more of the original building before reconstruction began than the external walls, together with other external features of architectural or historic interest.

[*VATA 1994, Sch 8 Group 6 Note* (*4*)*; SI 1995/283*].

Tenancies and leases. Where the major interest is a tenancy or lease, zero-rating only applies to the premium payable on the grant or, if no premium is payable, the first payment of rent due under the tenancy or lease. [*VATA 1994, Sch 8 Group 5 Note* (*14*)*; Group 6 Note* (*3*)*; SI 1995/283*]. (The effect of this is that zero-rating only covers the sum payable when the lease is granted and subsequent payments such as ground rent or service charges cannot be zero-rated.)

Part-qualifying buildings.

(1) *General.* Where part of a protected building qualifies for zero-rating under the above provisions and part does not (eg shop premises with a flat over them), a grant or supply relating only to the part within these provisions is to be treated as relating to a zero-rated building and, similarly, a grant or supply relating only to the part outside those provisions is not to be so treated. In the case of any other grant or supply, an apportionment must be made to determine the extent to which it is to be so treated. [*VATA 1994, Sch 8 Group 6 Note* (*5*)*; SI 1995/283*].

Building work that relates to the fabric of the building affecting both qualifying and non-qualifying parts of the building must be apportioned, such as work to

- roofs,
- foundations,
- lifts, and

- building services that supply the whole building (eg wiring and plumbing).

(2) *Facilities for tenants in blocks of flats.* Work to build facilities shared by the tenants of a block of flats (eg a swimming pool, gym or laundry room) is standard-rated.

(3) *Live-work units.* In a live-work unit (ie a property that combines, within a single unit, a dwelling and commercial or industrial working space as a requirement or condition of planning permission) zero-rating is only available to the extent that the unit comprises the dwelling (provided it meets the other conditions for zero-rating above). Dwellings that contain a home office are not live-work units and no apportionment is needed.

Units where the work area is shown as a discrete area of floor space, whether an office or workshop, must be apportioned to reflect the presence of the commercial element. Where planning permission requires that a minimum amount of the unit (eg 20%) must be used for commercial or industrial purposes, the remaining amount (ie 80%) can be treated as being the dwelling element for VAT purposes.

However, where a unit has neither

- an area that must, as a requirement or condition of planning permission, be used for commercial or industrial purposes, nor
- planning permission requiring a certain percentage of the floor space be used for commercial or industrial purposes;

it may be treated for VAT purposes as if it were entirely a dwelling and no apportionment is required.

Apportionment for mixed sites. Where a person sells, or grants a long lease in, a development site containing buildings that qualify for zero-rating as substantially reconstructed protected buildings (or parts of buildings) and other buildings, he must apportion the charge between them on a fair and reasonable basis.

Issue of certificates. Where all or any part of the substantially reconstructed building is intended for use solely for a relevant residential or charitable purpose, the grant of a major interest cannot be zero-rated under these provisions unless, before the grant is made, the grantee has given the grantor a certificate to that effect. See 42.32 below.

'Person substantially reconstructing' status. A person is a 'person substantially reconstructing' a protected building if, in relation to that building, he is, or has at any point in the past

- acted as a developer (ie physically substantially reconstructed, or commissioned another person to physically substantially reconstruct, the building that he owns or has an interest in); or
- acted as a contractor or subcontractor (ie provided reconstruction services to the developer or another contractor for the substantial reconstruction of the building, sub-contracting work as necessary).

More than one person can enjoy 'person substantially reconstructing' status but such status is not transferred when the property is transferred. Each person must meet the conditions specified above. For example, where a developer takes over and finishes a partly reconstructed building, both the first and second developer has 'person substantially reconstructing' status because they have both been involved in physically reconstructing the building.

VAT groups. Although for VAT purposes, any business carried on by a member of a VAT group is treated as carried on by the representative member, when determining whether a supply can be zero-rated, 'person substantially reconstructing' status is only considered from the perspective of the group member who, in reality, makes the supply (which may not be the representative member). For example

(1) A VAT group includes a holding company as the representative member and a development company as a member.

The development company substantially reconstructs and sells a protected building. It has 'person substantially reconstructing' status and so the sales can be zero-rated.

(2) A VAT group includes a development company as representative member and an investment company as a member. The development company substantially reconstructs a block of flats and sells it to the investment company, who in turn leases the flats to the public on long leases.

The investment company does not have 'person substantially reconstructing' status. Even though the representative member does, the leases cannot be zero-rated and are exempt.

Beneficial interests. Where the beneficial owner of a property must register for VAT instead of the legal owner (see 42.5 above), the beneficial owner must have 'person substantially reconstructing' status before the sale or long lease of the property can be zero-rated.

First sale or long lease. The above provisions only zero-rate the first sale of, or long lease in, a building (or part of a building) but zero-rating is not affected by

- the length of time between completion of the reconstruction and sale of, or long lease in, the building;
- any sale of, or long lease in, the building made by other people (even if they also have 'person reconstructing' status or have made their own zero-rated supply in the building);
- any short leases that may have been made (although this is likely to affect input tax recovery); or
- any sales of, or long leases in, other parts of the building that the same person may have made (eg if the developer of a block of flats can zero-rate his first long lease in each flat).

A grantor cannot zero-rate any second or subsequent long lease in the building (or sell the building after leasing it on a long lease).

Land included. In addition to the protected buildings, zero-rating also applies to

- the land on which the building stands (the 'foot print'); and
- a reasonable plot of land surrounding it. This will depend on the size, nature and situation of the building and the nature of the surrounding land.

Garages. Where a grant of a major interest in a substantially reconstructed dwelling is zero-rated under these provisions, zero-rating extends to a garage constructed, or converted from a non-residential building, provided that

- the dwelling and the garage are constructed or converted at the same time; and
- the garage is intended to be occupied with the dwelling or one of the dwellings.

Extensions. A protected building is not 'substantially reconstructed' where the only major alteration is the addition of an extension. However, as work to extend a protected building could be zero-rated as an 'approved alteration' if supplied by a builder, provided other major works are carried out to reconstruct the building, the construction of the extension can count towards the 60% substantial reconstruction calculations (see above).

Joint owners and beneficial interests. See 42.5 above.

Exempt supplies. Other supplies of protected buildings not within the above provisions are normally exempt, eg where

- the building has not been substantially reconstructed;
- the interest granted is not a major interest;
- a major interest is granted by a person other than someone with 'person substantially reconstructing' status (see above);
- the building is not used as a dwelling or for a qualifying purpose.

See, however, 42.8 above for the option to tax under certain circumstances.

(VAT Notice 708, paras 10.3, 10.6–10.8).

De Voil Indirect Tax Service. See V4.235.

42.15 DEDUCTION OF INPUT TAX

Speculative and abortive costs. Developers must normally attribute input tax to either taxable or exempt supplies, depending on the supplies they intend to make, using the partial exemption rules. However, they may investigate many potential projects and incur costs (eg finders' fees in looking for sites, options to purchase lands, oil tests, general feasibility, viability and research studies, consultants and other professional fees, etc) without knowing what, if any, supplies they will eventually make. Such '*speculative supplies*' may not be followed through, in which case they are '*abortive supplies*'.

- Where a developer has a clear intention of what supplies he intends to make, he must attribute the input tax incurred to the liability of the intended supply. So, for example, if the intention is only to build and sell new houses, input tax on speculative costs is attributable to the intended taxable (zero-rated) supplies. See also *Beaverbank Properties Ltd (VTD 18099) (TVC 34.466)*.
- Where a developer has no firm intention of what supplies he will make, VAT incurred on speculative costs is input tax (because investigating potential projects is a business activity) but the input tax is 'residual' for partial exemption purposes.

If potential projects are not followed through and no supplies are actually made, where, up to the time of aborting the project, there is no firm intention regarding the liability of the supplies to be made (and as a result it is not possible to attribute the input tax to the liability of the intended supply), the related input tax should be left as residual.

If, on the other hand, the developer decides to proceed with a project, he will have a clear intention as to what supplies will be made and hence what the VAT liability of those supplies will be. (It is normally at this point that the developer decides whether to opt to tax for land and property supplies.) If the developer has not attributed the input tax previously, he should then adjust the input tax accordingly under the 'payback' and 'clawback' rules (see 49.10 PARTIAL EXEMPTION). Input tax on the ongoing costs should be attributed to the expected taxable or exempt supplies.

(VAT Notice 742A, para 9.3).

Goods incorporated into the building or its site. Where a taxable person constructing a building or effecting any works to a building, in either case for the purpose of granting a major interest in the building (or any part of it) or its site, incorporates goods other than building materials in any part of the building or its site, input tax on the supply, acquisition or importation of the goods is excluded from credit. [*SI 1992/3222, Art 6; SI 1995/281*].

See 42.26 and 42.27 below for examples of zero-rated building materials and zero-rated electrical goods and 42.28 below for a list of standard-rated goods on which VAT is not recoverable under these provisions.

Input tax on related services of installing the goods can be reclaimed provided the services are separately identified and VAT is correctly charged by the person supplying them.

Goods not incorporated into the building. Input tax can be recovered on goods which are not incorporated into the building or its site (eg free-standing items). A separate supply takes place when these goods are sold with the building on which output tax must be accounted for at their normal rate.

Showhouses. VAT cannot be reclaimed on standard-rated goods within 42.28 below incorporated into a showhouse if they are to be included in the sale of the house. No output tax is due when these goods are sold with the house.

Removing and disposing of goods on which input tax has been blocked. Where goods to which 'blocking' applies are removed from a property and sold independently (eg where the customer prefers a different model appliance), the developer is blocked from deducting input tax on both the original item and any replacement. The disposal of the original item is exempt from VAT.

(VAT Notice 708, paras 12.1–12.4).

Supplies of goods on which input tax blocked. With effect from 1 March 2000, where, under the above provisions, input tax has been blocked on goods incorporated in a building, any onward supply of those goods is an exempt supply. See 24.4 EXEMPT SUPPLIES. This includes items incorporated in showhouses where these sales are not treated as part of the supply of the building.

De Voil Indirect Tax Service. See V3.444.

PART IV SUPPLIES IN THE CONSTRUCTION INDUSTRY

42.16 INTRODUCTION

The construction of a new building and work to an existing building is normally standard-rated. There are, however, various exceptions to this.

- Certain supplies of construction services may qualify for zero-rating. See 42.17 below.

- Other construction services may be taxable at the reduced rate of 5%. See 42.22 below.

All work that is not specifically zero-rated or taxable at the reduced rate is standard-rated.

Rate of VAT chargeable. The lowest rate applicable to a supply should be charged. For example, where an approved alteration to an empty listed dwelling qualifies for zero-rating under 42.21 below (as an approved alteration to a protected building) and for reduced-rating under 42.24 below (as an alteration of an empty dwelling), zero-rating should be applied.

Retention payments. The same VAT rate applies to retention payments as applied to previous payments made under the contract.

(VAT Notice 708, para 2.1).

De Voil Indirect Tax Service. See V4.237–V4.242.

42.17 ZERO-RATED SUPPLIES

Zero-rating applies to the following.

- Services supplied in the course of construction of new qualifying dwellings and certain other residential properties and charitable buildings. See 42.18 below.
- Services supplied in the course of construction of civil engineering work for the development of a new permanent residential caravan park. See 42.19 below.
- Services supplied to housing associations in the course of converting non-residential buildings into residential buildings. See 42.20 below.
- Approved alterations to protected buildings. See 42.21 below.
- Building materials and certain electrical goods incorporated into a building by a builder who is also supplying any of the above zero-rated services. See 42.26 to 42.28 below.
- Certain goods and services supplied to disabled persons. See 32.16 *et seq* HEALTH AND WELFARE.
- The first time connection to the gas or electricity mains of dwellings and certain other residential buildings. See 29.7 FUEL AND POWER.

42.18 Construction services

Services supplied 'in the course of construction' of a building

(*a*) 'designed as a dwelling' or number of dwellings, or

(*b*) intended for use solely for a 'relevant residential purpose' or 'relevant charitable purpose'

and which relate to the construction, are zero-rated. Specifically excluded (and therefore standard-rated) are

- the separate supply of architectural, surveying, consultancy or supervisory services. See 42.31(1) below for where a supply of such services takes place under different forms of building contract;

- the hire of goods on their own (eg plant and machinery without an operator, scaffolding without erection/dismantling, security fencing and mobile office); and
- the private use of goods.

[*VATA 1994, Sch 8 Group 5 Item 2*(*a*) and *Note* (*20*); *SI 1995/280*]. (VAT Notice 708, para 3.4).

Building materials and certain electrical goods, supplied by the person providing the above services and incorporated into the building in question, are also zero-rated. See 42.26 to 42.28 below.

See 42.1(6) above for the definition of '*in the course of construction*', 42.1(4) above for '*designed as a dwelling*', 42.1(15) above for '*relevant residential purpose*', and 42.1(13) above for '*relevant charitable purpose*'.

With certain exceptions, '*constructing a building*' specifically excludes converting, reconstructing, altering, enlarging and extending an existing building or constructing an annexe to an existing building. See 42.1(2) above for full details.

See 42.25 below for examples of services zero-rated under these provisions and other services not regarded as within these provisions and therefore standard-rated.

Garages. The construction of a building designed as a dwelling or number of dwellings includes the construction of a garage provided that

- the dwelling and the garage are constructed at the same time; and
- the garage is intended to be occupied with the dwelling or one of the dwellings.

[*VATA 1994, Sch 8 Group 5 Note* (*3*); *SI 1995/280*].

Apportionment for part-qualifying buildings.

(1) *General.* Where part of a building qualifies under the above provisions and part does not (eg shop premises with a flat over them), a supply of services relating only to the qualifying part of the building is zero-rated and, similarly, a supply of services relating only to the non-qualifying part is standard-rated. In the case of any other supply, an apportionment must be made to determine the extent to which the supply is zero-rated. [*VATA 1994, Sch 8 Group 5 Note* (*10*); *SI 1995/280*].

Building work that relates to the fabric of the building affecting both qualifying and non-qualifying parts of the building must be apportioned, such as work to

- roofs,
- foundations,
- lifts, and
- building services that supply the whole building (eg wiring and plumbing).

(2) *Treatment of communal areas in blocks of flats.* Where a new building (typically a block of flats) contains both individual dwellings and areas for the use of all residents (such as a lounge, laundry and refuse area)

- if the communal areas are only used by residents and their guests, HMRC accept that the construction of the whole building is zero-rated; and

- if the communal areas are partly used by others (eg if they contain leisure or gym facilities, whether or not for a charge) then the construction of the communal areas is standard-rated.

(Business Brief 11/03).

(3) *Live-work units.* In a live-work unit (ie a property that combines, within a single unit, a dwelling and commercial or industrial working space as a requirement or condition of planning permission) zero-rating is only available to the extent that the unit comprises the dwelling (provided it meets the other conditions for zero-rating above). Dwellings that contain a home office are not live-work units and no apportionment is needed.

Units where the work area is shown as a discrete area of floor space, whether an office or workshop, must be apportioned to reflect the presence of the commercial element. Where planning permission requires that a minimum amount of the unit (eg 20%) must be used for commercial or industrial purposes, the remaining amount (ie 80%) can be treated as being the dwelling element for VAT purposes.

However, where a unit has neither

- an area that must, as a requirement or condition of planning permission, be used for commercial or industrial purposes, nor
- planning permission requiring a certain percentage of the floor space be used for commercial or industrial purposes;

it may be treated for VAT purposes as if it were entirely a dwelling and no apportionment is required.

(4) *Relevant residential purpose buildings.* Where the supply is in connection with a building intended for use as

- residential accommodation for students or school pupils, or
- residential accommodation for members of any of the armed forces

the supply can only be zero-rated to the extent that it relates to the residential accommodation. An apportionment need not be made for supplies in connection with a building intended for use for any other relevant residential purpose (eg a care home). Instead, areas such as administrative areas within the building can also be zero-rated.

(VAT Notice 708, paras 3.5, 15.1–15.5).

Apportionment for mixed sites. Where a service falling within the above provisions is supplied in part in relation to the construction of a building and in part for other purposes (eg a mixed site development including new dwellings and shops), an apportionment may be made to determine the extent to which the supply is to be treated as falling within the above provisions.

[*VATA 1994, Sch 8 Group 5 Note* (*11*); *SI 1995/280*].

Buildings for relevant residential/charitable purposes. The following additional provisions apply where all or part of a building is intended for use solely for a relevant residential or relevant charitable purpose.

- *Subcontractors' supplies, etc.* No supply of services relating to a building (or part of it) can be taken for the above purposes as relating to a building intended for such use unless it is made to a person who intends to use the building (or part) for such a purpose. [*VATA 1994, Sch 8 Group 5 Note* (*12*); *SI 1995/280*]. The main effect of this is that, although the main contractor can zero-rate the construction of such a building, a subcontractor must standard-rate all supplies to the main contractor on such building projects.

- *Issue of certificates*. Where all or part of a building is intended for use solely for a relevant residential or relevant charitable purpose, a supplier of services within these provisions cannot zero-rate the supply until the customer has given him a certificate to that effect. See 42.32 below.

42.19 **Civil engineering work for residential caravan parks**

Services supplied 'in the course of construction' of any civil engineering work necessary for the development of a permanent park for 'residential caravans', and which relate to the construction, are zero-rated. Specifically excluded (and therefore standard-rated) are

- the separate supply of architectural, surveying, consultancy or supervisory services. See 42.31(1) below for where a supply of these services takes place under different forms of building contract;
- the hire of goods on their own (eg plant and machinery without an operator, scaffolding without erection/dismantling, security fencing and mobile office); and
- the private use of goods.

Building materials, supplied by the person providing the above services and incorporated into the site in question, are also zero-rated. See 42.26 below.

See 42.1(6) above for the meaning of '*in the course of construction*'. The construction of a civil engineering work does not include the conversion, reconstruction, alteration or enlargement of a work.

'*Residential caravan*'. A caravan is not a residential caravan if residence in it throughout the year is prevented by the terms of a covenant, statutory planning consent or similar permission. The development of a holiday park of fixed caravans, or parks for touring caravans, is, therefore, normally standard-rated. (VAT Notice 708, para 20.2).

[*VATA 1994, Sch 8 Group 5 Item 2*(*b*) and *Notes* (*15*), (*19*) and (*20*); *SI 1995/280*].

Examples of zero-rated civil engineering work

- Laying new roads, drives, parking bays and paths
- Laying new pitches or bases for the caravans
- Installing water, electricity and gas supplies
- Installing drainage and sewerage

Examples of civil engineering work that is unnecessary (and standard-rated)

- Construction of playgrounds
- Hard landscaping

Examples of work that is not civil engineering work (and standard-rated)

- Indoor swimming pools
- Social centres
- Shops
- Fitness clubs
- A doctor's surgery
- A manager's house (although the work may be zero-rated under 42.18 above)

Alterations to existing works. The reconstruction, alteration or improvement of an existing work (eg widening or upgrading an existing road) cannot be zero-rated.

Apportionment.

(1) *Zero-rated and standard-rated work.* Where both zero-rated and standard-rated civil engineering work is supplied, an apportionment must be made to reflect the differing liabilities.

(2) *Mixed site developments.* Where a service is supplied in part in relation to necessary civil engineering work and in part for other purposes, an apportionment may be made to determine the extent to which the supply is treated as being zero-rated. If the supplier decides not to make an apportionment, then none of the work can be zero-rated.

(VAT Notice 708, paras 20.1, 20.3–20.5).

42.20 **Conversion services supplied to housing associations**

Zero-rating applies to services supplied to a 'relevant housing association' 'in the course of conversion' of

(*a*) a 'non-residential' building, or

(*b*) a non-residential part of a building

into a building (or part of a building) which is

(i) 'designed as a dwelling' or number of dwellings, or

(ii) intended solely for use for a 'relevant residential purpose'

and where the services relate to the conversion.

Specifically excluded (and therefore standard-rated) are

- the separate supply of architectural, surveying, consultancy or supervisory services. See 42.31(1) below for where a supply of such services takes place under different forms of building contract;
- the hire of goods on their own (eg plant and machinery without an operator, scaffolding without erection/dismantling, security fencing and mobile office); and
- the private use of goods.

Building materials and certain electrical goods, supplied by the person providing the above services and incorporated into the building in question, are also zero-rated. See 42.26 to 42.28 below.

Where (*b*) above applies and the building already contains a residential part, for zero-rating to apply the conversion must either be to a building for use for a relevant residential purpose or must create an additional dwelling or dwellings.

See 42.1(14) above for the definition of '*relevant housing association*', 42.1(10) above for '*non-residential*', 42.1(4) above for '*designed as a dwelling*', and 42.1(15) above for '*relevant residential purpose*'.

[*VATA 1994, Sch 8 Group 5 Item 3* and *Notes* (*9*), (*20*) and (*21*); *SI 1995/280; SI 1997/50*].

Garages. The conversion of a non-residential building to a building designed as a dwelling or number of dwellings includes the conversion of a non-residential building to a garage, provided that

- the dwelling and the garage are converted at the same time; and
- the garage is intended to be occupied with the dwelling or one of the dwellings.

[*VATA 1994, Sch 8 Group 5 Note* (*3*); *SI 1995/280*].

Examples of a non-residential conversion include the conversion of

- a commercial building (such as an office, warehouse, shop, etc),
- an agricultural building (such as a barn), or
- a redundant school or church,

into a building designed as a dwelling or number of dwellings.

See 42.25 below for examples of services zero-rated under these provisions and other services not regarded as within these provisions and therefore standard-rated.

Evidence and certificates. A supplier must hold evidence to show that his customer is a relevant housing association (eg a copy of their registration certificate). In addition, a supplier who is converting the building into a building intended for use solely for a relevant residential purpose must also hold a certificate confirming the intended use of the building. See 42.32 below.

Subcontractors. Subcontractors' services are not made directly to a relevant housing association and are, therefore, standard-rated.

Amalgamating non-residential parts of a building with other parts. To qualify for zero-rating, the conversion must only use non-residential parts of the building. If the conversion uses a mixture of non-residential parts of the building and other parts, then the services cannot be zero-rated. For example, where

- a two-storey public house containing bar areas downstairs and private living areas upstairs (and so in part being used as a dwelling, although see the case law uncertainty on this point in 42.1(10) above) is converted into a single house, or
- the same property is converted by splitting it vertically into a pair of semi-detached houses, each of which use part of what was the living accommodation,

none of the work is zero-rated and the charge cannot be apportioned.

Apportionment.

(1) *Part qualifying buildings.* Where part of a building qualifies under the above provisions and part does not (eg shop premises with a flat over them), a supply of services relating only to the qualifying part of the building is zero-rated and,

similarly, a supply of services relating only to the non-qualifying part is standard-rated. In the case of any other supply, an apportionment must be made to determine the extent to which the supply is zero-rated. [*VATA 1994, Sch 8 Group 5 Note* (*10*)*; SI 1995/280*]. For example, if a shop is converted into a flat and at the same time an existing flat above the shop (that has been lived in within the last ten years) is refurbished, zero-rating applies to the work to convert the shop but not the refurbishment of the flat.

(2) *Mixed sites.* Where a service falling within the above provisions is supplied in part in relation to the conversion of a building and in part for other purposes (eg a mixed site development including new dwellings and shops), an apportionment may be made to determine the extent to which the supply is to be treated as falling within the above provisions. [*VATA 1994, Sch 8 Group 5 Note* (*11*)*; SI 1995/280*]. For example, a road that serves a building being converted and a neighbouring house (eg a barn and a farm house) is upgraded as part of the conversion. As the road serves both buildings, the work carried out relates, in part, to the conversion and, in part, for other purposes. The liability of upgrading the road may be apportioned on a fair and reasonable basis. If the supplier decides not to make an apportionment, then none of his work can be zero-rated.

(VAT Notice 708, paras 6.2, 6.3, 6.5, 6.6).

42.21 Approved alterations of protected buildings

The supply of services in the course of an 'approved alteration' of a 'protected building' is zero-rated. Specifically excluded (and therefore standard-rated) are:

- The separate supply of architectural, surveying, consultancy or supervisory services. See 42.31(1) below for where a supply of such services takes place under different forms of building contract.
- The hire of goods on their own (eg plant and machinery without an operator, scaffolding without erection/dismantling, security fencing and mobile office).
- The private use of goods.

Building materials and certain electrical goods, supplied by the person providing the above services and incorporated into the building in question, are also zero-rated. See 42.26 to 42.28 below.

See 42.1(1) above for the definition of '*approved alteration*' and 42.1(12) above for '*protected building*'.

[*VATA 1994, Sch 8 Group 6 Item 2* and *Note* (*11*)*; SI 1995/283*]. (VAT Notice 708, para 9.6).

Provided the necessary conditions are satisfied, this provision can be used to zero-rate services supplied in carrying out an approved alteration to

- a protected building which is a dwelling, relevant residential building or relevant charitable building; and
- any other protected building in order to convert it into a dwelling, relevant residential building or relevant charitable building.

Services 'in the course of an approved alteration'. A business supplies services in the course of an approved alteration of a protected building when it

(*a*) physically carries out the approved alteration; or

(*b*) provides any other service closely connected to the alteration (see 42.25 below).

The effect of (*b*) above is that, even if the work did not require approval, it can still be zero-rated provided it is closely connected to an approved alteration. Examples include

- preparation work for an approved alteration; or
- the carrying out of remedial work resulting from an approved alteration.

(VAT Notice 708, para 9.5).

Issue of certificate by recipient of services. Where all or part of a protected building is intended for use solely for a relevant residential or relevant charitable purpose, a supplier of approved alterations to the building within these provisions cannot zero-rate the supply until the customer has given him a certificate to that effect. See 42.32 below.

Apportionment.

(1) *Part qualifying work*. In cases where a service is supplied partly in relation to an approved alteration and partly for other purposes (eg repairs and maintenance), an apportionment must be made to determine the part zero-rated. [*VATA 1994, Sch 8 Group 6 Note* (*9*); *SI 1995/283*].

(2) *Part qualifying buildings*. Where only part of a building is a protected building, zero-rating can be applied to the work to the qualifying parts. For example, if alterations are carried out to a listed building used by a charity, it may be that only part of the building will be used solely for a relevant charitable purpose. If so, only the approved alterations to that part of the building can be zero-rated.

(3) *Mixed site developments*. Where a service (eg carrying out civil engineering work) is supplied in part in relation to an approved alteration and in part for other purposes, a fair and reasonable apportionment may be made to determine the extent to which the supply is treated as falling within these provisions.

If the supplier decides not to make an apportionment, then none of his work can be zero-rated.

(VAT Notice 708, para 9.7).

Repairs to listed places of worship. Unless qualifying as part of an approved alteration under the above provisions, any repair and maintenance work is standard-rated and the UK is not permitted under current EC legislation to tax such supplies at a reduced rate. However, a special non-discretionary grant scheme (the 'Listed Place of Worship Grant Scheme') has been introduced for all works of repair and maintenance to listed buildings throughout the UK that are principally used as places of worship. For eligible works carried out after 31 March 2001 and before 1 April 2004 the scheme used the difference between the VAT paid (normally 17.5%) and 5% to calculate the grant due. For eligible work carried out after 31 March 2004, the scheme returns the full amount of VAT paid. Listed places of worship of all religions are eligible and the scheme also applies to places of worship owned or vested in a number of specified organisations which look after redundant churches. Applications are only accepted in arrears. The scheme is currently due to continue until 31 March 2006 unless a permanent reduced rate in achieved earlier. (The government has made proposals to the European Commission for a reduced rate of 5% for repairs and maintenance to listed places of worship.) Documentation relating to the scheme can be obtained

- via the internet at www.lpwscheme.org.uk;

- by telephoning 0845 601 5945; or
- by writing to Listed Places of Worship Grant Scheme, PO Box 609, Newport NP10 8QD.

42.22 REDUCED RATE SUPPLIES

VAT is charged at the reduced rate of 5% on

(*a*) qualifying services supplied in the course of certain residential conversions (see 42.23 below);

(*b*) qualifying services supplied in the course of renovating and altering certain buildings that have been empty for three or more years (see 42.24 below);

(*c*) building materials and certain electrical goods incorporated into a building by a builder who is also supplying services within (*a*) or (*b*) above (see 42.26 to 42.28 below); and

(*d*) installation of energy-saving materials and the grant-funded installation of heating equipment or security goods or connection of a gas supply. See 58.2 and 58.3 REDUCED RATE SUPPLIES.

42.23 Residential conversions

Overview. The VAT liability of conversion work generally is summarised in the following table.

Before conversion	*After conversion*		
	Single household dwelling(s)	Multiple occupancy dwelling(s)	Relevant residential purpose building
Single household dwelling(s)	Normally standard-rated unless the number of dwellings changes when reduced-rated	Reduced-rated	Reduced-rated
Multiple occupancy dwelling(s)	Reduced-rated	Standard-rated	Reduced-rated
Relevant residential purpose building	Reduced-rated	Reduced-rated	Standard-rated

Any building not listed above (eg a building which has never been lived in)	Reduced-rated	Reduced-rated	Reduced-rated

Detailed provisions. 'Qualifying services' supplied in the course of a 'qualifying conversion' and which are related to the conversion are subject to a reduced rate of VAT of 5%.

Building materials and certain electrical goods, supplied by the person providing the above services and incorporated into the building in question or its immediate site, are also subject to the reduced rate. See 42.26 to 42.28 below.

The reduced rate also applies to the acquisition from another EC country, or the importation from outside the EC, of goods the supply of which would be subject to the reduced rate.

[*VATA 1994, s 29A(1)(2), Sch 7A Group 6 Items 1* and *2; FA 2001, ss 97, 99, Sch 31*].

'Qualifying conversion'. A '*qualifying conversion*' means one of the following three types of conversion provided, in each case, any statutory planning consent needed and any statutory building control approval needed for the conversion has been granted. [*VATA 1994, Sch 7A Group 6 Note (10); FA 2001, Sch 31*].

(1) **Conversions into 'single household dwellings'**, ie the conversion of premises consisting of a building or part of a building where

(i) after the conversion the premises being converted contain a number of single household dwellings that is different from the number (if any) that the premises contain before the conversion, and greater than, or equal to, one; and

(ii) there is no part of the premises being converted that is a part that, after the conversion, contains the same number of single household dwellings (whether zero, one or two or more) as before the conversion.

[*VATA 1994, Sch 7A Group 6 Note (3); FA 2001, Sch 31*].

This covers the following scenarios.

Building before conversion	*Building after conversion*
One single household dwelling	Two or more single house dwellings
A number of single house dwellings	A different number of single house dwellings (more or less)
Non-residential	One or more single house dwellings
One or more houses in multiple occupation	One or more single house dwellings

Building before conversion	*Building after conversion*
Relevant residential property	One or more single house dwellings

The provisions also cover the conversion of a building which may have been lived in but which does not qualify as a single household dwelling (such as a public house with staff accommodation) into one or more single household dwellings. (VAT Notice 708, para 7.3).

(2) **Conversions into 'multiple occupation dwellings'**, ie the conversion of premises consisting of a building or part of a building where the following conditions are satisfied.

(i) Before the conversion the premises being converted do not contain any multiple occupancy dwellings.

(ii) After the conversion those premises contain only a 'multiple occupancy dwelling' or two or more such dwellings.

(iii) The use to which those premises are intended to be put after the conversion is not to any extent use for a 'relevant residential purpose'.

[*VATA 1994, Sch 7A Group 6 Note* (*5*)*; FA 2001, Sch 31; SI 2002/1100*].

A qualifying conversion includes the conversion into a multiple occupancy dwelling of

- a single household dwelling;
- a building used for a relevant residential purpose, such as a care home; and
- a property that has never been lived in.

It does not include, for example, the creation of additional bedrooms at a dwelling consisting of bed-sits.

(VAT Notice 708, para 7.4).

(3) **Conversions into premises for use for a 'relevant residential purpose'**, ie a conversion of premises consisting of one or more buildings or one or more parts of buildings (or any combination of buildings and parts of buildings) where the following conditions are satisfied.

(i) The use to which the premises being converted were last put before the conversion was not to any extent use for a relevant residential purpose and those premises are intended to be used solely for a relevant residential purpose after the conversion.

(ii) Where the relevant residential purpose for which the premises are intended to be used is an 'institutional purpose', the premises being converted must be intended to form, after the conversion, the entirety of an institution used for that purpose.

For such a conversion to be subject to the reduced rate

- it must be made to the person who intends to use the premises being converted for the relevant residential purpose; and
- before it is made, that person must give the supplier a certificate of intended use. See 42.32 below.

[*VATA 1994, Sch 7A Group 6 Notes* (*7*)(*8*); *FA 2001, Sch 31; SI 2002/1100*].

A qualifying conversion includes the conversion of

- a single household dwelling,
- a multiple occupancy dwelling, and
- a property that has never been lived in

into premises that will be used solely for a relevant residential purpose.

It does not include

- the remodelling of an existing relevant residential purpose building; or
- any conversion where a new qualifying residential home or institution is not created in its entirety, such as the conversion of outbuildings into additional bedrooms for an existing care home.

'Single household dwelling'. A single household dwelling means a dwelling that

- is designed for occupation by a single household either because
  - (i) it was originally designed on construction for occupation for that purpose and has not been subsequently adapted for occupation of any other kind; or
  - (ii) it is so designed as a result of adaptation;
- consists of self-contained living accommodation;
- has no provision for direct internal access to any other dwelling or part of a dwelling; and
- is not prohibited from separate use or separate disposal by the terms of any covenant, statutory planning consent or similar provision. Occupancy restrictions (eg working in agriculture or forestry or being over a specified age) are not prohibitions on separate use or disposal and do not affect whether a building is designed as a dwelling or number of dwellings. (VAT Notice 708, para 14.4).

[*VATA 1994, Sch 7A Group 6 Note* (*4*); *FA 2001, Sch 31*].

'Multiple occupancy dwelling'. A multiple occupancy dwelling means a dwelling that

- is designed for occupation by persons not forming a single household either because
  - (i) it was originally designed on construction for occupation for that purpose and has not been subsequently adapted for occupation of any other kind; or
  - (ii) it is so designed as a result of adaptation;
- is not to any extent used for a relevant residential purpose;
- consists of self-contained living accommodation;

- has no provision for direct internal access to any other dwelling or part of a dwelling; and
- is not prohibited from separate use or separate disposal by the terms of any covenant, statutory planning consent or similar provision. Occupancy restrictions (eg working in agriculture or forestry or being over a specified age) are not prohibitions on separate use or disposal and do not affect whether a building is designed as a dwelling or number of dwellings. (VAT Notice 708, para 14.5).

[*VATA 1994, Sch 7A Group 6 Note* (*4*)*; FA 2001, Sch 31; SI 2002/1100*].

A multiple occupancy dwelling is normally a dwelling consisting of a number of bed-sits. it does not include

- single household dwellings with accommodation for au pairs, family guests or 'live-in' lodgers; or
- hotels, guest houses, and similar establishments providing accommodation for holiday makers, travellers and similar temporary guests.

(VAT Notice 708, para 14.5).

Use for a relevant residential purpose. '*Use for a relevant residential purpose*' means use as

(*a*) a home or other institution providing residential accommodation for children;

(*b*) a home or other institution providing residential accommodation with personal care for persons in need of such care by reason of old age, disablement, past or present dependence on alcohol or drugs or past or present mental disorder;

(*c*) a hospice;

(*d*) residential accommodation for students or school pupils;

(*e*) residential accommodation for members of any of the armed forces;

(*f*) a monastery, nunnery or similar establishment; or

(*g*) an institution which is the sole or main residence of at least 90% of its residents.

except use as a hospital, prison or similar institution or an hotel, inn or similar establishment.

Use for an '*institutional purpose*' means a purpose under (*a*)–(*c*), (*f*) or (*g*) above.

[*VATA 1994, Sch 7A Group 6 Notes* (6)(*7*)*; FA 2001, Sch 31*].

Qualifying services. Qualifying services mean either of the following.

- Carrying out work to the fabric of the building/part of the building being converted (excluding the incorporation, or installation as fittings, in the building/part of any goods that are not building materials).
- Carrying out work within the immediate site of the building in connection with
  - (i) the means of providing water, power, heat or access to the building/part,
  - (ii) the means of providing drainage or security for the building/part, or
  - (iii) the provision of means of waste disposal for the building/part.

[*VATA 1994, Sch 7A Group 6 Note* (*11*)*; FA 2001, Sch 31*].

This includes all works of repair, maintenance (eg decoration) or improvement (eg the construction of an extension or the installation of double glazing) to the fabric of the building where the work forms an intrinsic part of changing the number of dwellings.

Example 1

A block of flats consists of four floors, each with four flats. A lift is installed and work is carried out throughout the whole building. On the ground, first and second floors the footprint of each flat is changed to take account of the new lift. This results in the internal configuration of each flat being changed. On the third floor three penthouse flats are created from the original four.

Although the overall number of dwellings in the building has changed (there has been a reduction by one unit) only the work to convert the top floor will be eligible for the reduced rate because it is only in this part of the building that the number of dwellings has changed.

Example 2

The facts are as in *Example 1* except that the reduction in the number of flats on the third floor happens by combining two of the original flats together, the other two being refurbished.

The reduced rate will only apply to the work to merge the two flats together.

Example 3

The facts are as in *Example 1* above except that, as well as the changes to the top floor, the number of flats on the ground floor is changed to five smaller units.

Although the overall number of dwellings in the building has not changed (there are 16 units both before and after the work) as the number of dwellings has changed on both the ground floor and the third floor, the reduced rate can apply to the conversion work done on these floors.

All other services are standard-rated. For example

- the installation of goods that are not building materials, such as carpets and fitted bedroom furniture;
- the hire of goods;
- landscaping; and
- the provision of professional services, such as those provided by architects, surveyors, consultants and supervisors.

(VAT Notice 708, paras 7.3, 7.6).

Part-qualifying services. Where part of a supply of services qualifies under these provisions and part does not, the supply can be apportioned to determine the extent to which the reduced rate can be applied. [*VATA 1994, Sch 7A Group 6 Note (1); FA 2001, Sch 31*].

Garages. A qualifying conversion within (1)–(3) above includes the construction of a garage or the conversion of a 'non-residential' building (or of a non-residential part of a building) that results in a garage provided

- the garage works are carried out at the same time as the conversion; and
- the resulting garage is intended to be occupied
  - (i) where (1) above applies, with a single household dwelling that will after the conversion be contained in the building, or part of a building, being converted;
  - (ii) where (2) above applies, with a multiple occupancy dwelling that will after the conversion be contained in the building, or part of a building, being converted; or
  - (iii) where (3) above applies, with the institution or other accommodation resulting from the conversion.

'*Non-residential*' means neither designed, nor adapted, for use as a dwelling or two or more dwellings, or for a relevant residential purpose.

[*VATA 1994, Sch 7A Group 6 Note* (*9*)*; FA 2001, Sch 31*].

Provided the above conditions are satisfied, the construction of a drive serving the garage can also be zero-rated. (VAT Notice 708, para 7.6).

Subcontractors who carry out some or all of the qualifying renovation or conversion work can apply the reduced rate to their services *unless* the work is the conversion into a relevant residential property.

Dwellings adapted for non-residential use and subsequently converted back into a dwelling. If a property was originally a dwelling but then adapted for non-residential use, on conversion back to a dwelling the reduced rate would apply where the whole building had been used for a non-residential purpose as the conversion is of a non-residential building into a single household dwelling. It is the use of the building at the time of conversion that is relevant and not any earlier use.

Example 1

A building originally designed as a dwelling has been adapted for use as a dental surgery. No part of the building after adaptation has been used as living accommodation.

The reduced rate applies to the work of converting the building back into a dwelling as there has been a change in the number of single household dwellings from none to one.

Example 2

A building originally designed as a dwelling is adapted for use as a dental surgery on the ground floor with a self-contained flat on the first floor.

The reduced rate does not apply to the conversion of the whole building back into a single dwelling as the building is a single household dwelling before and after conversion.

Example 3

A room in a building designed as a single dwelling is used as an office. The rest of the house is used as living accommodation.

The conversion of the room used as an office back into use as part of the existing house does not qualify for the reduced rate as there is single household dwelling

> before and after conversion. However, if the area used as the office is converted to create a self-contained dwelling, there would be a change in the number of single household dwellings (from one to two) the work would then qualify for the reduced rate.

De Voil Indirect Tax Service. See V4.411.

42.24 **Residential renovations and alterations**

VAT is charged at the reduced rate of 5% on the renovation or alteration of a single household dwelling that has not been lived in for three years or more and a building to be used solely for a relevant residential purpose (eg a care home) or a multiple occupancy dwelling (eg bed-sits), again provided the premises have not been lived in for at least three years. Included are works in connection with garages. The detailed provisions are considered below.

'Qualifying services' supplied in the course of the renovation or alteration (including extension) of 'qualifying residential premises', and which are related to the renovation or alteration, are subject to a reduced rate of VAT of 5% provided the following conditions are satisfied.

- Empty home condition (1) below is satisfied or, if the premises are a 'single household dwelling' either empty home condition (1) or (2) below is satisfied.
- Any statutory planning consent needed for the renovation or alteration has been granted.
- Any statutory building control approval needed for the renovation or alteration has been granted.
- Where the premises in question are a building, or part of a building, which, when it was last lived in, was used for a relevant residential purpose,
  - (i) the building or part must be intended to be used solely for such a purpose after the renovation or alteration, and
  - (ii) before the supply is made, the person to whom it is made must give the supplier a certificate stating that intention. See 42.32 below.

  Where a number of buildings on the same site are renovated or altered at the same time and intended to be used together as a unit solely for a relevant residential purpose, then each of those buildings, to the extent that it would not be so regarded otherwise, is to be treated as intended for use solely for a relevant residential purpose.

Building materials and certain electrical goods, supplied by the person providing the above services and incorporated into the qualifying residential premises in question or their immediate site, are also subject to the reduced rate. See 42.26 to 42.28 below.

The reduced rate also applies to the acquisition from another EC country, or the importation from outside the EC, of goods the supply of which would be subject to the reduced rate.

[*VATA 1994, s 29A(1)(2), Sch 7A Group 7 Items 1, 2* and *Notes (3)(4)(4A); FA 2001, s 99, Sch 31; SI 2002/1100*].

'*Qualifying residential premises*' means

- a 'single household dwelling',
- a 'multiple occupancy dwelling', or
- a building, or part of a building, which, when it was last lived in, was used for a 'relevant residential purpose'. Where a building, when it was last lived in, formed part of a 'relevant residential unit' then, to the extent that it would not be so regarded otherwise, the building is to be treated as having been used for a relevant residential purpose. For these purposes, a building forms part of a relevant residential unit at any time when

  (i) it is one of a number of buildings on the same site, and

  (ii) the buildings are used together as a unit for a relevant residential purpose.

The expressions '*multiple occupancy dwelling*', '*single household dwelling*', and '*use for a relevant residential purpose*' have the same meaning as in 42.23 above.

[*VATA 1994, Sch 7A Group 7 Note* (2); *FA 2001, Sch 31; SI 2002/1100*].

Empty home conditions. The empty home conditions are as follows.

(1) Neither

  (*a*) the premises concerned, nor

  (*b*) where those premises are a building, or part of a building, which, when it was last lived in, formed part of a 'relevant residential unit' (see above), any of the other buildings that formed part of the unit,

  have been lived in during the period of three years ending with the commencement of the 'relevant works'.

(2) To cover the situation where a dwelling is occupied whilst the work is being carried on, the reduced rate can also be applied where

  (i) the dwelling was not lived in during a period of at least three years;

  (ii) the person, or one of the persons, whose beginning to live in the dwelling brought that period to an end was a person who (whether alone or jointly with another or others) acquired the dwelling at a time

  - no later than the end of that period, and
  - when the dwelling had been not lived in for at least three years;

  (iii) no works by way of renovation or alteration were carried out to the dwelling during the period of three years ending with the acquisition (although HMRC are prepared to ignore any minor works that were necessary to keep the dwelling dry and secure, see VAT Notice 708, para 8.3);

  (iv) the supply is made to a person who is

  - the person, or one of the persons, whose beginning to live in the property brought to an end the period in (i), and
  - the person, or one of the persons, who acquired the dwelling as mentioned in (ii); and

  (v) the 'relevant works' are carried out during the period of one year beginning with the day of the acquisition.

For the purposes of (1) and (2) above, the '*relevant works*' means

- where the supply is qualifying services within these provisions, the works that constitute the services supplied; and
- where the supply is building materials supplied with those services, the works by which the materials concerned are incorporated in the premises concerned or their immediate site.

References in (2) above to a person acquiring a dwelling are to that person having a major interest in the dwelling granted, or assigned, to him for a consideration.

[*VATA 1994, Sch 7A Group 7 Note (3); FA 2001, Sch 31; SI 2002/1100*].

To reduce-rate his supply, a supplier must hold evidence that, on balance, shows the premises have not been lived in during the three years immediately before his work starts. The evidence can include the electoral roll and council tax data, information from empty property officers in local authorities and other sources of reliable information. If a contractor holds a letter from an empty property officer certifying that a property has not been lived in for three years (or will have been when the work starts), no other evidence is needed. If an empty property officer is unsure about when a property was last lived in, he should write with his best estimate. HMRC may then call for other supporting evidence.

In determining whether a property has been lived in, any

- illegal occupation by squatters, and
- non-residential use, such as storage for a business

can be ignored but if the dwelling has been lived in on an occasional basis (eg as a second home) in the three years immediately before work starts, the supply cannot be reduced-rated.

(VAT Notice 708, para 8.3).

Qualifying services. Qualifying services means either of the following.

- Carrying out work to the fabric of the premises (excluding the incorporation, or installation as fittings, in the premises of any goods that are not building materials).
- Carrying out work within the immediate site of the premises in connection with
  - (i) the means of providing water, power, heat or access to the premises;
  - (ii) the means of providing drainage or security for the premises; or
  - (iii) the provision of means of waste disposal for the premises.

[*VATA 1994, Sch 7A Group 7 Note (5); FA 2001, Sch 31; SI 2002/1100*].

This includes any work of repair, maintenance (eg redecoration) or improvement (eg an extension or the installation of double glazing) carried out to the fabric of the premises.

All other services are standard-rated, including

- the installation of goods that are not building materials, such as carpets or fitted bedroom furniture;
- the hire of goods;

- landscaping; and
- the provision of professional services, such as those provided by architects, surveyors, consultants and supervisors.

(VAT Notice 708, para 8.4).

Part-qualifying services. Where part of a supply of services qualifies under these provisions and part does not, the supply can be apportioned to determine the extent to which the reduced rate can be applied. [*VATA 1994, Sch 7A Group 7 Note (1); FA 2001, Sch 31*].

Related garage work. For the above purposes, a renovation or alteration of any premises includes any 'garage works' related to the renovation or alteration. '*Garage works*' means

- the construction of a garage,
- the conversion of a building, or of a part of a building, that results in a garage, or
- the renovation or alteration of a garage

and garage works are related to a renovation or alteration if

- they are carried out at the same time as the renovation or alteration of the premises concerned, and
- the garage is intended to be occupied with the premises.

[*VATA 1994, Sch 7A Group 7 Note (3A); FA 2001, Sch 31; SI 2002/1100*].

Subcontractors who carry out some or all of the qualifying renovation or conversion work can apply the reduced rate to their services unless the work is the renovation of an empty single household dwelling where the owner is in residence (as only a person making supplies to the occupier can apply the reduced rate, see above).

De Voil Indirect Tax Service. See V4.413.

42.25 CONSTRUCTION SERVICES — EXAMPLES

Zero-rated services

The services which can be zero-rated under 42.18 to 42.21 above include the following where supplied in the course of construction.

(*a*) *Work on the building itself* (including applying any usual decorative features) prior to 'completion' of the building (see 42.1(6) above).

'*Snagging*' (or the correction of faults) is often carried out after the building has been completed. The work can be zero-rated if provided by the supplier who carried out the initial building work and the snagging forms part of that building contract. If, however, the work is carried out as a separate supply (eg a builder may be contracted to correct work performed by another person) and it is performed after the building has been completed, then the work is to an existing building and cannot be zero-rated under these provisions.

(*b*) *Work closely connected to the construction of the building*. Subject to (*c*) below, work is closely connected to the construction of the building when it either

(i) allows the construction of the building to take place, for example

- demolishing existing buildings and structures immediately prior to the commencement of construction work;
- providing or improving an access point to a building site to allow deliveries to be made;
- carrying out ground works (including the levelling and drainage of land); and
- providing site clearance or 'builders' clean' services; or

(ii) produces works that allow the building to be used, such as works in connection with

- the means of providing water and power to the building (this can extend to the work required to make the connection to the nearest existing supply);
- the means of providing, within the development site, access to the building (eg roads, footpaths, parking areas, drives and patios);
- the means of providing security (such as walls, fences and gates – but note that most electrical appliances are always standard-rated, see 42.27 below); or
- the provision of soft landscaping (ie the application of top-soil, the laying of grass, planting of trees, shrubs, etc as opposed to the construction of fencing, paths, etc) within the site of a building to the extent that it is detailed on a landscaping scheme approved by a planning authority under the terms of a planning consent condition. It does not include work outside the plot (eg screening planted along roadside verges) or the replacement of trees and shrubs that die, or become damaged or diseased. See *Rialto Homes plc (VTD 16340) (TVC 15.197)*.

The lists are not exhaustive.

(*c*) *Services carried out before or after the construction of the building*. Services closely connected to the construction of the building, and carried out either before or after the physical construction of the building takes place, may only be zero-rated if it can be shown that there is a close connection between when they are performed and when the physical construction of the building takes place. Where there is a time delay, both the reason for, and the length of, any delay must be considered.

Services described in (*b*) above may be zero-rated (subject to the normal conditions) where, for example

- soft landscaping work is carried out after the building has been completed because the work has been delayed due to seasonal weather conditions

but are standard-rated where, for example

- site investigation or demolition work is carried out prior to the letting of a building contract;
- the services for a building (water, electricity, etc) are installed on land which is to be sold as building land; or
- the work is delayed until after the building is complete owing to an insufficiency of funds.

(*d*) *Connecting utilities to existing buildings.* The connection of utilities to an existing building is normally standard-rated as work to an existing building. However, as a concession, the first time connection of gas or electricity supplies can sometimes be zero-rated. See 29.7 FUEL AND POWER.

Standard-rated services

Examples of work that cannot be zero-rated include

- the provision of on-site catering;
- the cleaning of site offices;
- landscaping, including the construction of fish ponds, rockeries and other ornamental works, except to the extent zero-rated above;
- the provision of outdoor leisure facilities for a dwelling such as tennis courts and swimming pools (although the provision of a playground at a school would qualify as it is needed for the school to be used);
- works outside the site of the building (other than those zero-rated above), including where that work is carried out under a 'planning gain' agreement with a planning authority; and
- the granting of a right to remove materials.

(VAT Notice 708, para 3.3; Business Brief 7/2000).

42.26 **BUILDING MATERIALS AND OTHER GOODS**

Subject to the exceptions in 42.28 below, where a person supplies

- zero-rated construction services within 42.18 to 42.21 above, or
- reduced rate construction services within 42.23 or 42.24 above,

building materials, supplied by the person providing those services and incorporated into the building in question or its immediate site, are also zero-rated or, as the case may be, subject to the reduced rate.

'*Building materials*' in relation to a particular building, mean goods 'ordinarily' incorporated or installed as fittings by builders in a building of that description (or its site) but do not include any of the supplies within 42.28(*a*)–(*c*) below.

[*VATA 1994, Sch 7A Group 6 Note* (*12*), *Sch 7A Group 7 Note* (*6*), *Sch 8 Group 5 Item 4* and *Notes* (*22*) and (*23*), *Sch 8 Group 6 Item 3* and *Note* (*3*)*; FA 2001, s 97, Sch 31 para 1; SI 1995/280; SI 1995/283*].

The effect of the above is that building materials can be zero-rated or reduced-rated, as the case may be, along with the supply of building services where all of the following conditions are met.

1. **The articles are 'incorporated' in the building or its site.**

   HMRC regard an article as 'incorporated' in a building (or its site) when it is fixed in such a way that its fixing or removal would either

   - require the use of tools; or
   - result in either the need for remedial work to the fabric of the building (or its site), or substantial damage to the goods themselves.

Examples of articles incorporated in a building (or its site) include

- built-in and fitted furniture (although only built-in or fitted *kitchen* furniture are building materials, see 42.28(*a*) below);
- built-in, wired-in or plumbed-in appliances such as boilers or wired-in storage heaters (although only certain gas and electrical appliances are building materials, see 42.27 below, and most are normally standard-rated, see 42.28(*b*) below);
- flooring (although carpets are not building materials, see 42.28(*c*) below); and
- trees and plants (although the service of incorporating trees and plants in the site of a building is only zero-rated in certain circumstances, see 42.25 above, and is never reduced-rated).

Examples of goods that are not incorporated in a building (or its site) include

- free-standing appliances that are merely plugged in; and
- free-standing furniture such as sofas, tables and chairs, etc.

2. **The articles are 'ordinarily' incorporated by builders in that type of building.**

HMRC take the view that an article is '*ordinarily*' incorporated in a building or its site when, in the ordinary course of events, it would normally be incorporated in a building of that generic type, such as a dwelling, church, or school. They do not split generic types of buildings into sub-categories so no distinction is drawn between large detached houses and small terraced houses. HMRC also take the same approach when determining if the goods themselves are the 'norm' for that type of building (eg a tap would be regarded as being ordinarily incorporated whether it is chromium or gold-plated). The range of items considered to be ordinarily incorporated is likely to change over time in line with trends and consumer expectations. Goods which need to be installed in defined areas of the country (eg sound-proofing near airports) can still qualify (*British Airports Authority (No 5) (VTD 447) (TVC 15.183)*).

Examples of articles ordinarily incorporated in a dwelling

- Air conditioning
- Bathroom accessories, such as fixed towel rails, toilet roll holders, soap dishes, etc.
- Builders' hardware
- Burglar alarms
- Curtain poles and rails
- Decorating materials
- Doors
- Dust extractors and filters (including built-in vacuum cleaners)
- Fencing permanently erected around the boundary of the dwelling
- Fireplaces and surrounds
- Fire alarms

- Fitted furniture (although only kitchen furniture is building materials, see 42.28(*a*) below)
- Flooring materials (although carpets are not building materials, see 42.28(*c*) below)
- Gas and electrical appliances when wired-in or plumbed-in (although only certain gas and electrical appliances are building materials, see 42.27 below)
- Guttering
- Heating systems (including radiators and controls, ducted warm-air systems, storage heaters and other wired in heating appliances, gas fires and solar powered heating)
- Immersion heaters, boilers, hot and cold water tanks
- Kitchen sinks, work surfaces and fitted cupboards
- Letter boxes
- Lifts and hoists
- Light fittings (including chandeliers and outside lights)
- Plumbing installations, including electric showers and 'in line' water softeners
- Power points (including combination shaver points)
- Sanitary ware
- Saunas
- Shower units
- Smoke detectors
- Solar panels
- Solid fuel cookers and oil-fired boilers
- Swimming pools inside the house, including water heaters and filters but not diving boards and other specialist equipment
- Turf, plants and trees (although the incorporation of trees and plants in the site of a building is only supplied in the course of the work being carried out in certain circumstances, see 42.25 above)
- TV aerials
- Ventilation equipment (including cooker hoods)
- Warden call systems
- Window frames and glazing
- Wiring (including power circuits and computer, telephone and TV cabling)

Examples of articles ordinarily incorporated in buildings used for a relevant residential purpose

- Mirrors

Examples of articles ordinarily incorporated in buildings used for a relevant charitable purpose

- Blinds and shutters
- Lighting systems
- Mirrors

Examples of articles ordinarily incorporated in schools

- Blackboards fixed to or forming part of the wall
- Gymnasium wall bars
- Notice and display boards
- Mirrors and barres (in ballet schools)

Examples of articles ordinarily incorporated in churches

- Altars
- Amplification equipment
- Church bells
- Fonts
- Humidifying plant
- Lecterns
- Pews (when bolted to the fabric of the church) (although pews are furniture and therefore not building materials, see 42.28(*a*) below)
- Pipe organs
- Pulpits

3. **Other than kitchen furniture, the articles are not finished or prefabricated furniture, or materials for the construction of fitted furniture.** See 42.28(*a*) below.
4. **With certain exceptions, the articles are not electrical or gas appliances.** See 42.27 and 42.28(*b*) below.
5. **The articles are not carpets or carpeting material.** See 42.28(*c*) below.

(VAT Notice 708, paras 13.2–13.4, 13.8).

42.27 **Electrical and gas appliances**

Most electrical and gas appliances are not building materials for VAT purposes, even if they are required to be incorporated in a building as a requirement of *Building Regulations*. They are, therefore, standard-rated (see 42.28(*b*) below). The following can, however, be zero-rated when supplied with zero-rated construction services within 42.18 to 42.21 above or charged at the reduced rate when supplied with reduced rate construction services within 42.23 and 42.24 above.

(*a*) An appliance designed to heat space or water (or both) or designed to provide ventilation, air cooling, air purification or dust extraction.

(*b*) A door-entry system, waste disposal unit or machine for compacting waste but only if in each case it is intended for use in a building designed as a number of dwellings (eg a block of flats).

(*c*) A burglar alarm, fire alarm or fire safety equipment designed solely for the purpose of enabling aid to be summoned in an emergency.

(*d*) A lift or hoist.

[*VATA 1994, Sch 7A Group 6 Note* (*12*), *Sch 7A Group 7 Note* (*6*), *Sch 8 Group 5 Note* (*22*), *Group 6 Note* (*3*); *FA 2001, s 97, Sch 31 para 1; SI 1995/280; SI 1995/283*].

Cookers which are designed to have the dual purpose of heating the room or the building's water are included under (*a*) above but telephones or electric gates and barriers are not included under (*c*) above. Fixed amplification equipment in churches may also be zero-rated.

Appliances powered by other fuels (eg solid fuel or oil-fired cookers) are building materials when they are ordinarily incorporated in the building.

(VAT Notice 708, para 13.6).

42.28 **Standard-rated goods**

The following goods are specifically excluded from the definition of building materials and their supply is always standard-rated.

(*a*) **Finished or prefabricated 'furniture' (other than furniture designed to be fitted in kitchens) and materials for the construction of 'fitted furniture' (other than kitchen furniture).**

'*Furniture*' is not defined in law and whether an item is furniture is very much a matter of impression (see *C & E Commrs v McLean Homes Midland Ltd, QB [1993] STC 335 (TVC 15.168)*).

HMRC give the following as examples of articles which are *not* furniture and are building materials for VAT purposes. They therefore qualify for zero-rating or reduced-rating, subject to meeting the conditions in 42.26 above.

- Basic storage facilities formed by becoming part of the fabric of the building, such as airing cupboards and under-stair storage cupboards.
- Items that provide storage capacity as an incidental result of their primary function, such as shelves formed as a result of constructing simple box work over pipes, and basin supports which contain a simple cupboard beneath.
- Basic wardrobes installed on their own with *all* the following characteristics.
  - (i) The wardrobe encloses a space bordered by the walls, ceiling and floor. But units whose design includes, for example, an element to bridge over a bed or create a dressing table are furniture and are not building materials.
  - (ii) The side and back use three walls of the room (such as across the end of a wall), or two walls and a stub wall. But wardrobes installed in the corner of a room where one side is a closing end panel are furniture and are not building materials.

(iii) On opening the wardrobe the walls of the building can be seen. These would normally be either bare plaster or painted plaster. Wardrobes that contain internal panelling, typically as part of a modular or carcass system, are furniture and are not building materials.

(iv) The wardrobe should feature no more than a single shelf running the full length of the wardrobe, a rail for hanging clothes and a closing door or doors. Wardrobes with internal divisions, drawers, shoe racks or other features are furniture and are not building materials.

All other finished or prefabricated furniture, and materials for the construction of fitted furniture, are not building materials for VAT purposes and cannot be zero-rated or reduced-rated as the case may be. These include

- wardrobes (other than the basic wardrobes described above) including basic wardrobes installed as part of a larger installation of furniture in the room;
- elaborate vanity units;
- wall units, such as bathroom cabinets;
- laboratory work benches; and
- pews, choir and clergy stalls.

(*b*) **Electrical or gas appliances** except for those specifically covered in 42.27 above. Standard-rated items include refrigerators; cookers (including split-level cookers); washing and dish-washing machines; tumble dryers; and waste disposal units and entry phone systems (except in buildings designed as a number of dwellings, eg blocks of flats, see 42.27 above).

(*c*) **Carpets or carpeting material**. Carpets, carpet tiles and underlay are not building materials for VAT purposes. Other forms of flooring or floor covering, such as linoleum, ceramic tiles, parquet and wooden floor systems are building materials.

[*VATA 1994, Sch 7A Group 6 Note* (*12*), *Sch 7A Group 7 Note* (*6*), *Sch 8 Group 5 Note* (*22*), *Group 6 Note* (*3*); *FA 2001, s 97, Sch 31 para 1; SI 1995/280; SI 1995/283*]. (VAT Notice 708, paras 13.5, 13.7).

42.29 TIME OF SUPPLY

(1) Single payment contracts

Single payment contracts are subject to the normal tax point rules (see 64.49 SUPPLY) including the creation of a basic tax point when the work has been completed. (VAT Notice 708, para 23.1).

Retention payments. Building contracts frequently include retention clauses which allow customers to hold back a proportion of the contract price on completion of the work pending confirmation that the supplier has done the work properly and has rectified any immediate faults that might be found.

There are special tax point rules that apply to retention payments generally *other than those for stage or interim payment contracts under* (*2*) *below*. The tax point for the retention element of the contract is the earlier of

- the time when a payment in respect of any part of the retention is received by the supplier; or
- the date that the supplier issues a VAT invoice relating to the retention.

[*SI 1995/2518, Reg 89; SI 1997/2887, Reg 3; SI 2003/3220, Reg 16*]. (VAT Notice 708, para 23.1).

(2) **Stage or interim payment contracts**

Where services, or services together with goods, are supplied in the course of the construction, alteration, demolition, repair or maintenance of a building or of any civil engineering work under a contract which provides for payment for such supplies to be made periodically or from time to time (often referred to as 'stage' or 'interim' payment contracts), those services (or goods and services) are normally treated as separately and successively supplied at the earliest of the following times.

(*a*) Each time a payment is received by the supplier.

(*b*) Each time the supplier issues a VAT invoice.

There is, therefore, no basic tax point when the work is completed unless the contract is covered by the following special anti-avoidance rules that can apply in some cases.

Special anti-avoidance rules. If a VAT invoice is not issued, the tax point (and therefore VAT payment) can be delayed. The special anti-avoidance rule counters the VAT effect of contracts where payment does not become due for many years after the completion of the work. The rules are complex but, briefly, do *not* apply if

- whoever will be occupying the works can recover at least 80% of the VAT charged by the main contractor in respect of those works; or
- the supplier is unconnected with the proposed occupiers *and* can be sure that neither he, nor any of his subcontractors, is receiving any form of finance from the proposed occupiers, nor anyone connected with them. In this connection, finance does not include interim payments for construction work, on which VAT is accounted for.

(VAT Notice 708, para 24.2).

In more detail, where services are 'relevant services' which have not already been treated as supplied under (*a*) or (*b*) above, there is an additional tax point on the day on which the services are performed.

Services are '*relevant services*' if, at the time they are performed, either of the following conditions is satisfied.

(*a*) The supplier or a 'person responsible for financing the supplier's costs' intends or expects that the land on which the building or civil engineering work in question is situated will be occupied (whether immediately or eventually) or will continue to be occupied (for a period at least) by

- the supplier,
- a person responsible for financing the supplier's costs, or
- a person connected with either such person under *ICTA 1988, s 839* (see 69.19 VALUATION)

other than wholly or mainly (see under the heading *The 80% test* below) for 'eligible purposes'.

Occupation for '*eligible purposes*' means

- occupation by a taxable person for the purpose of making supplies which are in the course of furtherance of a business and are supplies of such a description that any input tax wholly attributable to those supplies would be input tax for which he would be entitled to credit, or
- occupation by a specified body within *VATA 1994, s 33* (see 43.2 LOCAL AUTHORITIES AND PUBLIC BODIES) to the extent that the body occupies the land for non-business purposes, or
- occupation by a government department

and for these purposes, where occupation is by a person who is not a taxable person but whose supplies are treated for the purposes of *VATA 1994* as made by another person who is a taxable person, those two persons are to be regarded as a single taxable person.

(*b*) The supplier has received (and used in making his supply) from a subcontractor any supply of services, or services together with goods, the time of supply of which was determined under these anti-avoidance provisions (or would have been but for the issue by that subcontractor of a VAT invoice other than one which has been paid in full).

Thus a main contractor is affected by the anti-avoidance rules if any of his subcontractors are affected by it. If, for example, a bank gives a loan to a subcontractor specifically to do work on one of its banks, the subcontractor would be affected by the anti-avoidance rule, and so would the contractor. However, HMRC will not be seeking to catch a contractor out on a technicality in this area, and if it does come to their attention that a contractor is inadvertently affected by the rule because of his subcontractors, they will look at his case sympathetically. (VAT Notice 708, para 24.8).

A '*person responsible for financing the supplier's costs*' is a person who has

- provided finance for the supplier's costs; or
- entered into an agreement or understanding (whether or not legally enforceable) to provide finance for the supplier's costs.

Providing funds is widely defined. It includes directly or indirectly providing funds *either* to meet the whole or part of the supplier's costs *or* to discharge the whole or part of any liability incurred in raising funds to meet those costs. It also includes directly or indirectly procuring the provision of funds by another person for either of those purposes. The funds may be provided by way of loan, guarantee or other security, consideration for a share issue used to raise the funds or any other transfer of assets or value as a consequence of which the funds are made available. Providing funds does not include making interim payments for construction work on which VAT is accounted for.

A '*supplier's costs*' are his costs of supplying the services, or services together with goods, and comprise

- amounts payable by the supplier for supplies to him of goods and services used in making his supply; and

- the supplier's staff and other internal costs of making his supply.

[*SI 1995 No 2518, Reg 93; SI 1997/2887, Reg 5; SI 1999/1374*].

HMRC give the following decision table to show the questions a supplier must ask himself to determine whether the anti-avoidance provisions apply to him.

1. Do you know who will occupy the works?

   If 'yes', go to step 3.

   If 'no', go to step 2.

2. Do any of your subcontractors know who will occupy the works?

   If 'yes', go to step 4.

   If 'no', you do not have to account for VAT when you complete your work and you can follow the normal rules for stage and interim payment contracts.

3. Will you, or someone connected with you, occupy the works?

   If 'yes', go to step 7.

   If 'no', go to step 4.

4. Will one of your subcontractors, or someone connected with one of your subcontractors, occupy the works?

   If 'yes', go to step 7.

   If 'no', go to step 5.

5. Will someone who gave you finance to pay for the costs of your work, or someone connected with your financer, occupy the works?

   If 'yes', go to step 7.

   If 'no', go to step 6.

6. Will someone who gave your subcontractor finance to pay the costs of his work, or someone connected with his financer, occupy the works?

   If 'yes', go to step 7.

   If 'no', you do not have to account for VAT when you complete your work and you can follow the normal rules for stage and interim payment contracts.

7. Will the occupier be able to reclaim at least 80% of their VAT on the works?

   If 'yes', you do not have to account for VAT when you complete your work and you can follow the normal rules for stage and interim payment contracts.

   If 'no', you must account for VAT no later than when you complete your work.

(VAT Notice 708, para 24.3).

The 80% test. HMRC take the view that a building is used 'wholly or mainly' for eligible purposes if the occupier can recover 80% or more of the VAT relating to that building. It does not matter whether their overall ability to recover VAT is greater or less than 80%. Buildings that *will not* normally attract VAT recovery of 80% or more include those used

- as a bank, or the headquarters of a banking group;
- as an insurance broker's office, or the office of an insurance company;
- as a school, college or university;
- as an office for a charity (but the special anti-avoidance rules do not apply if the work for a charity is zero-rated);
- as a private hospital, or the head office of a private healthcare business; or
- for any purpose if the occupier is not registered for VAT (but the special anti-avoidance rules do not apply if the work is zero-rated, such as constructing a house).

Buildings that *will* normally attract VAT recovery of 80% or more include those used as the head office of a fully taxable business or

- as a retail shop,
- as a wholesale outlet,
- as a factory or workshop,
- as an importer's office or warehouse, or
- as a charity shop

provided that the retailer, etc is registered for VAT.

(VAT Notice 708, para 24.7).

When services are performed. HMRC treat services as performed when the work is completed. See 42.1(6) above for a general consideration of the meaning of 'completion'. (VAT Notice 708, paras 24.3, 24.9).

Accounting for VAT. Where the anti-avoidance rules apply, VAT must be accounted for on the full value of the contract, less any amounts on which VAT has already become due because a payment has been received or a VAT invoice issued. The full value of the contract includes retentions and disputed amounts.

Where there is a dispute, or where it is not possible to know the exact value of the contract for any other reason, a reasonable estimate of the value must be made. In cases of dispute, a supplier need not account for VAT on the full amount he is claiming from the customer if he feels that he will most likely be forced in the end to settle for a lower amount. He should account for VAT on his best estimate of the amount that will eventually be agreed. (HMRC recommend that the supplier documents the basis of his estimate, so that he can later show that it was reasonable.) Subsequently, when the value of the contract is finalised, the supplier may need to make an adjustment to the VAT paid.

(VAT Notice 708, para 24.10).

Public/Private Partnership (formerly Private Finance Initiative). If a PPP or PFI arrangement relates to a building that will be occupied exclusively by a government department (including an NHS hospital), the anti-avoidance rules do not apply. However, some PPP and PFI arrangements relate to buildings that will be occupied by private sector businesses as well as government departments.

In such cases, the part of the building occupied by the private sector business may be caught by the special anti-avoidance rules. If so, there is no need to account for VAT on the entire building on completion, only on a proportion of the overall price that fairly reflects the part of the building that will be occupied by private companies. (VAT Notice 708, para 24.7).

(3) **Self-billing**

Under a self-billing arrangement, the customer makes out VAT invoices on behalf of the VAT-registered supplier (eg a main contractor makes out VAT invoices on behalf of its registered subcontractor) and sends a copy of the invoice to the supplier with the payment. See 40.6 INVOICES for conditions of self-billing and 64.35 SUPPLY for the time of supply and a notional tax point for input tax deduction purposes.

(4) **Goods supplied without services**

Where materials, etc are not supplied in connection with the supply of services (eg a supply by a builders' merchant to a builder), the time of supply is that under the normal rules for supplies of goods. See 64.39 SUPPLY.

(5) **Insolvency**

There are no concessions for tax points in the construction industry when a business becomes insolvent. The normal tax point rules as in (1)–(4) above apply equally to transactions before and after the appointment of an insolvency practitioner. (Business Brief 4/96).

42.30 SELF-SUPPLY OF CONSTRUCTION SERVICES

Where a person, in the course or furtherance of a business carried on by him, and for the purpose of that business and otherwise than for a consideration, performs any services in connection with

(*a*) the construction of a building,

(*b*) the extension or alteration of, or the construction of an annexe to, any building such that additional floor area of not less than 10% of the floor area of the original building is created,

(*c*) the construction of any civil engineering work, or

(*d*) the carrying out of any demolition work at the same time as, or in preparation for, any of the services in (*a*) to (*c*) above

those services are treated as both supplied to him for the purpose of that business and supplied by him in the course or furtherance of it (ie self-supplied) unless

- the open market value of the services performed is less than £100,000, or
- such services would, if supplied for a consideration in the course or furtherance of a business by a taxable person, be zero-rated.

VAT must be accounted for on the open market value of the services performed (subject to the *de minimis* limit of £100,000) in the VAT return for the period in which the services are performed. This output tax on the self-supply can be recovered as input tax in the same period to the extent that it is attributable to taxable supplies under the normal rules, ie to the extent that the building in question is used or to be used for making taxable supplies. Therefore

- where the building or work is occupied or used for a taxable business activity, or is sold or let after the exercise of an option to tax, the self-supply VAT should be fully recoverable;
- where the building or work is used wholly for exempt purposes or let without the option to tax being exercised, the self-supply VAT is not recoverable; and
- where the building or work is used partly for exempt and partly for taxable business purposes, VAT on the self-supply charge is recoverable according to the partial exemption method used.

Where the value of the self-supply exceeds £250,000, adjustments may be required in future years under the CAPITAL GOODS SCHEME (10).

Input tax incurred on goods and services for such building works are treated as relating to the taxable self-supply and can be deducted in full (subject to the normal rules).

In relation to GROUPS OF COMPANIES (31), for these purposes all companies within a VAT group are treated as one person but anything done which would fall to be treated under these provisions as services supplied to and by that person are to be treated as supplied to and by the representative member (see 31.4 GROUPS OF COMPANIES).

Registration. Where a person not registered for VAT makes a self-supply falling within these provisions, the value of the self-supply will make him liable for registration.

[*SI 1989/472*]. (VAT Notice 708, paras 25.3, 25.4).

De Voil Indirect Tax Service. See V3.244.

42.31 TREATMENT IN PARTICULAR CIRCUMSTANCES

(1) Architects, surveyors, consultants and supervisors

The separate supply of architectural, surveying, consultancy and supervisory services is always standard-rated. However, these services can be procured in a number of ways.

Design and build. The building client engages a contractor to carry out both the design and construction elements of the project. Where the design, workmanship and materials are supplied under a 'design and build' lump sum contract, the VAT liability of the design element follows that of the building work. This also applies where the part of the sum for the design element is shown separately solely for internal analysis purposes. But separate supplies of design or similar professional services are always standard-rated.

Project management. The building client engages a project manager (usually a construction company) to plan, manage and co-ordinate the whole project, including establishing competitive bids for all elements of the work. The successful contractors are employed directly by the building client. Management fees paid by the building client to the project manager are standard-rated.

Management contracting. This system can take various forms but normally the building client first appoints a professional design team and engages a management contractor to advise them. If the project goes ahead, the management contractor acts as the main contractor for the work (engaging 'works contractors' to carry out work to him as necessary). His preliminary advisory services are then treated in the same way as his main construction services. If the project does not go ahead, his preliminary advisory services are standard-rated.

(VAT Notice 708, para 3.4).

(2) **Authenticated receipts**

The authenticated receipt procedure (not to be confused with self-billing, see 40.6 INVOICES) allows a supplier to issue an authenticated receipt for payment instead of a normal VAT invoice.

The procedure works by the customer preparing a receipt for a supply received and forwarding it to the supplier with payment. The receipt is only valid for VAT purposes when the supplier has authenticated it. The time limits for the issue of an authenticated receipt is the same as for a VAT invoice (see 40.13 INVOICES).

The procedure can only be used when all of the following conditions are satisfied.

- The customer and the supplier mutually agree to operate the procedure.
- Services, or services together with goods, are supplied in the course of the construction, alteration, demolition, repair or maintenance of a building or of any civil engineering work.
- The contract provides for payments for such services to be made periodically, or from time to time ('stage' or 'interim payment' contracts). The procedure should not therefore be used for supplies made under single payment contracts.
- The receipt contains all the particulars required on a VAT invoice (see 40.4 INVOICES).
- No VAT invoice or similar document is issued.

An authenticated receipt is not a VAT invoice and its issue does not create a tax point. The tax point for the supply is therefore solely determined by the receipt of payment by the supplier or, where the special anti-avoidance rules described in 42.29(2) above apply, the date the work is completed.

An authenticated receipt is, however, acceptable as evidence for input tax purposes. The customer may claim input tax in the VAT period in which the supplier receives the stage payment, without waiting for an authenticated receipt. But he must obtain and keep a copy of the authenticated receipt. Suppliers cannot authenticate a receipt and return it to the customer until they have received the payment.

If a customer experiences difficulty in obtaining an authenticated receipt from a supplier, he should contact HMRC in writing on the third successive occasion that this happens. A claim to input tax may still be allowed if satisfactory alternative evidence is available, or the customer can show that reasonable efforts were made to secure an authenticated receipt and the claim is otherwise correct.

[*SI 1995/2518, Reg 13*(*4*)]. (VAT Notice 708, para 23.3).

(3) **CITB levy**

Any agreed deduction in respect of the Construction Industry Training Board levy can be deducted from the gross amount for the purposes of calculating VAT due, and the value of the supply is treated as reduced by any such levy. (VAT Notice 708, para 22.2).

(4) **Income tax deductions**

Where a contractor is required to make a deduction on account of income tax from a payment to a subcontractor who is not exempt from such deduction, the value of the subcontractor's services for VAT purposes is the gross amount before income tax is deducted. (VAT Notice 708, para 22.1).

(5) **Liquidated damages**

Liquidated damages are agreed pre-estimated sums to be paid in the event of a breach of contract by one of the parties. The amount is either a set figure or determined by a formula.

- Liquidated damages received are not payment for a supply made and no VAT is due on the amount received.
- Where a person is due to make a payment for liquidated damages and also due to receive from the other party a payment for a supply, he cannot reduce the value of his supply (and therefore cannot reduce the amount of VAT chargeable), even if he sets the amounts off against each other.

(VAT Notice 708, para 22.3).

PART V CERTIFICATES

42.32 CERTIFICATES FOR RELEVANT RESIDENTIAL/CHARITABLE PURPOSES

Where a zero-rated or reduced-rated supply is made in connection with all or part of a building which is intended for use solely for a '*relevant residential purpose*' or a '*relevant charitable purpose*' (see 42.1(15) and 42.1(13) above respectively), the grant or other supply cannot be taken as relating to the building (or part) intended for such use unless

(*a*) it is made to the person who intends to use the building (or part) for such purposes (the 'customer'); and

(*b*) before it is made, the customer has given to the grantor or supplier a certificate, in such form as is prescribed by HMRC, stating that the grant or other supply relates to such a building (or part).

[*VATA 1994, Sch 7A Group 6 Note* (*8*), *Group 7 Note* (*4A*), *Sch 8 Group 5 Note* (*12*), *Group 6 Note* (*3*); *SI 1995/280*].

The effect of the above is that, before a developer or builder can zero-rate or reduce-rate certain grants and other supplies, he must obtain a certificate from the customer. A certificate must be used for any of the following supplies.

(1) The first grant of a major interest in a building (or part of a building) for use solely for a relevant residential purpose or a relevant charitable purpose (see 42.13 above).

(2) The first grant of a major interest in a building (or part of a building) for use solely for a relevant residential purpose by the person who has converted it (see 42.13 above).

(3) The first grant of a major interest by a person substantially reconstructing a protected building where the building is to be used solely for a relevant residential purpose or a relevant charitable purpose (see 42.14 above).

(4) The supply of goods and services in the course of construction of a new building intended solely for a relevant residential purpose or a relevant charitable purpose (see 42.18 above).

(5) The supply to a relevant housing association of goods and services in the course of conversion of a non-residential building (or a non-residential part of a building) into a building (or part of a building) intended for use solely for a relevant residential purpose (see 42.20 above).

(6) The supply of goods and services in the course of an approved alteration to a protected building intended solely for use for a relevant residential purpose or a relevant charitable purpose (see 42.21 above).

(7) The supply of qualifying services in the course of a qualifying conversion into premises for use for a relevant residential purpose (see 42.23 above).

(8) The supply of qualifying services in the course of the renovation or alteration of a qualifying residential property last used for a relevant residential purpose (see 42.24 above).

Possession of a valid certificate does not mean that a supplier can automatically zero-rate or reduce-rate his charge. He must still meet all of the conditions for zero-rating or reduced-rating. The supplier must also take all reasonable steps to check the validity of the certificate, including corresponding with his customer to confirm the details of the use of the building. Such correspondence should be retained within his records. Where, however, despite taking all reasonable steps to check the validity of the certificate, a supplier fails to identify the inaccuracy and, in good faith, zero-rates or reduce-rates the supply, HMRC will not seek to recover VAT due from the supplier.

Subcontractors working for a main contractor should not be issued with a certificate and so should always standard-rate their supplies.

Issue of certificates. The customer issues the certificate. He can either copy the certificate from VAT Notice 708 or create his own certificate provided it contains the same information and declaration. It must be issued before the supplier makes his supply. However, as a concession, HMRC will allow a supplier to adjust his VAT charge on receipt of a belated certificate (subject to the three-year cap) provided that

- the customer can demonstrate to the supplier that, at the time of supply, he intended that the building would be used in the way being certified; and
- all other conditions for zero-rating or reduced-rating are met.

The two available certificates confirm that the customer is eligible to receive either

- zero-rated or reduced-rated building work; or
- a zero-rated sale or long lease.

Penalties for incorrect certificates. See 52.17 PENALTIES.

Form of certificate. The two certificates prescribed by HMRC (which have the force of law) are as follows.

Certificate for zero-rated and reduced-rated building work
1. Address of the building:

2. Name and address of organisation receiving the building works: VAT Registration number (if registered): Charity registration (if registered):
3. Date of completion (or estimated date of completion) of the work: Value (or estimated value) of the supply: £ Name, address and VAT registration number of building contractor:
4. I have read the relevant parts of Notice 708 *Buildings and construction* and certify that this organisation (in conjunction with any other organisation where applicable) will use the building, or the part of the building, for which zero-rating is being sought solely for (tick box as appropriate): • a relevant charitable purpose, namely by a charity in either or both of the following ways: (a) otherwise than in the course or furtherance of business,☐ or (b) as a village hall or similarly in providing social or recreational facilities for a local community.☐ • a relevant residential purpose, namely as: (a) a home or other institution providing residential accommodation for children,☐ (b) a home or other institution providing residential accommodation with personal care for persons in need of personal care by reason of old age, disablement, past or present dependence on alcohol or drugs or past or present mental disorder,☐ (c) a hospice,☐ (d) residential accommodation for students or school pupils,☐ (e) residential accommodation for members of any of the armed forces,☐ (f) a monastery, nunnery or similar establishment,☐ or (g) an institution which is the sole or main residence of at least 90 per cent of its residents;☐ and will not be used as a hospital, prison or similar institution or an hotel, inn or similar establishment.
5. I certify that: • the information given is complete and accurate; and • if the building, or a part of the building, for which zero-rated supplies have been obtained, is let or otherwise used for a purpose which is not solely for a relevant residential purpose or relevant charitable purpose within a period of 10 years from the date of its completion, a taxable supply will have been made, and this organisation will account for tax at the standard rate. Name (print): Position held:

Signed:	Date:

General warning

1. Customs reserves the right to alter the format of the certificate through the publication of a new notice. You must ensure that the certificate used is current at the time of issue.

Warnings for the issuer

2. You may be liable to a penalty if you issue a false certificate.

3. You are responsible for the information provided on the completed certificate.

Warnings for the developer

4. You must take all reasonable steps to check the validity of the declaration given to you on this certificate.

5. You must check that you meet all the conditions for zero-rating or reduced-rating your supply – see Notice 708 *Buildings and construction*.

Certificate for sales and long leases of zero-rated buildings

1. Address of the building:

2. Name and address of organisation buying, or entering into a long lease on, the building (or part of the building):

VAT Registration number (if registered):

Charity registration (if registered):

3. Date (or estimated date) of purchase or commencement of the lease:

Value (or estimated value) of the supply: £

Name, address and VAT registration number of the developer:

4. I have read the relevant parts of Notice 708 *Buildings and construction* and certify that the building, or the part of the building, for which zero-rating is being sought will be used solely for (tick box as appropriate):

- a relevant charitable purpose, namely by a charity in either or both of the following ways:
  - (a) otherwise than in the course or furtherance of business,☐ or
  - (b) as a village hall or similarly in providing social or recreational facilities for a local community.☐
- a relevant residential purpose, namely as:
  - (a) a home or other institution providing residential accommodation for children,☐
  - (b) a home or other institution providing residential accommodation with personal care for persons in need of personal care by reason of old age, disablement, past or present dependence on alcohol or drugs or past or present mental disorder,☐

(c)	a hospice,☐
(d)	residential accommodation for students or school pupils,☐
(e)	residential accommodation for members of any of the armed forces,☐
(f)	a monastery, nunnery or similar establishment,☐ or
(g)	an institution which is the sole or main residence of at least 90 per cent of its residents;☐

and will not be used as a hospital, prison or similar institution or an hotel, inn or similar establishment.

5. I certify that:

- the information given is complete and accurate; and
- if the building, or a part of the building, for which zero-rated supplies have been obtained, is let or otherwise used for a purpose which is not solely for a relevant residential purpose or relevant charitable purpose within a period of 10 years from the date of its completion, a taxable supply will have been made, and this organisation will account for tax at the standard rate.

Name (print):	Position held:
Signed:	Date:

General warning

1. Customs reserves the right to alter the format of the certificate through the publication of a new notice. You must ensure that the certificate used is current at the time of issue.

Warnings for the issuer

2. You may be liable to a penalty if you issue a false certificate.

3. You are responsible for the information provided on the completed certificate.

Warnings for the developer

4. You must take all reasonable steps to check the validity of the declaration given to you on this certificate.

5. You must also check that you meet all the conditions for zero-rating your supply—see Notice 708 *Buildings and construction.*

Student accommodation. Provided a new building is clearly intended primarily for use as student accommodation for ten years from the date of its completion, HMRC have agreed that higher education institutions may issue a certificate for the construction or acquisition of such a building as a relevant residential building despite any letting of the accommodation for holiday use or for non-educational conferences, etc during vacations. (Concordat between HMRC, University Vice-Chancellors and Principals, para 37a). See also *R v C & E Commrs (oao Greenwich Property Ltd), Ch D [2001] STC 618 (TVC 2.77).*

(VAT Notice 48, ESC 3.11; VAT Notice 708, paras 16.1–16.7, 18.1, 18.2).

PART VI D-I-Y HOUSEBUILDERS

42.33 D-I-Y HOUSEBUILDERS

A special VAT Refund Scheme puts D-I-Y builders and converters in a broadly similar position to a developer selling a zero-rated property, by refunding them the VAT on their main construction or conversion costs.

Under the scheme, HMRC must refund any VAT chargeable on the supply, acquisition or importation of any goods used in connection with construction or conversion work where the following conditions are satisfied.

(*a*) The work must comprise

- (i) the 'construction of a building' 'designed as a dwelling' or number of dwellings;
- (ii) the constructing of a building for use solely for a 'relevant residential purpose' or for a 'relevant charitable purpose'; or
- (iii) a '*residential conversion*', ie the conversion of a 'non-residential' building or the non-residential part of a building into *either* a building designed as a dwelling or number of dwellings *or* a building intended solely for a relevant residential purpose *or* anything which would fall into either of those categories if different parts of a building were treated as separate buildings.

(*b*) The work is carried out lawfully and otherwise than in the course or furtherance of any business.

(*c*) The goods are building materials which, in the course of the works, are incorporated in the building in question or its site. See 42.26 to 42.28 above for goods which do and do not qualify. Refunds can be claimed on the building materials which would be zero-rated when supplied with the zero-rated work but *not* on those which would be standard-rated.

(*d*) The claim is made within such time and in such form and manner, contains such information, and is accompanied by such documents as HMRC require. See 42.34 below.

See 42.1(2) above for the definition of '*construction of a building*', 42.1(4) above for '*designed as a dwelling*', 42.1(15) above for '*relevant residential purpose*', 42.1(13) above for '*relevant charitable purpose*' and 42.1(10) above for '*non-residential*'.

Refund also covers VAT chargeable on a supply of any goods under the law of another EC country.

Conversions using contractors, etc. Where a person carries out a residential conversion and arranges for the work to be done by someone else ('a contractor'), then provided

- (i) the person's carrying out of the residential conversion is lawful and otherwise than in the course or furtherance of any business, and
- (ii) the contractor is not acting as an architect, surveyor or consultant or in a supervisory capacity,

HMRC must, on a claim, refund any VAT chargeable on any services consisting of work done by the contractor.

Garages. The construction of, or the conversion of a non-residential building to, a building designed as a dwelling or number of dwellings includes the construction of, or conversion to, a garage. The dwelling and the garage must be constructed or converted at the same time and the garage must be intended for occupation with the dwelling or one of the dwellings.

[*VATA 1994, s 35; FA 1995, s 33; FA 1996, s 30; SI 2001/2305*].

The scheme can therefore be used to reclaim VAT on

- eligible goods used to construct a new qualifying dwelling, communal residential building or charity building; and
- eligible goods and services used to convert a non-residential building into a qualifying dwelling or communal residential building.

The buildings must not be intended to be used for business purposes and cannot therefore be used by, for example, speculative developers, landlords, bed and breakfast operators, care home operators who make a charge (even if not for profit) to their residents, and membership clubs and associations.

Examples of works that are not included

Dwellings

- 'Granny' annexes that cannot be used, or disposed of, separately from a main house.
- Detached workshops, playrooms or enclosed swimming pools in the grounds of a new dwelling.

Relevant residential buildings

- 'Relevant residential purpose' buildings that are used for a business purpose (eg where a charge is made to the residents for staying at a home).
- A detached building in the grounds of an existing care home that extends the facilities of the home.
- Hospital ward blocks.
- Day care units at hospices.

Charitable buildings

- Child nurseries where a fee is charged.
- School buildings where a fee is charged for the provision of education.
- Offices used by charities for administering business activities, such as fund-raising events where an entrance fee is charged.
- Sport centres and swimming pools.
- Theatres.
- Facilities for membership clubs.

Specialist help may be employed and it is not necessary for claimants to do any of the work themselves. They can claim for eligible goods bought and given to a builder to incorporate into the building (or its site) provided that the work is done before the date of completion.

Partly completed buildings. VAT can be claimed on qualifying goods and services bought to complete the construction or conversion of a building which a developer has not finished (eg a building bought as a 'shell' and fitted out). Relief cannot, however, be claimed for extra work done on a completed building bought from a builder or developer (eg adding a conservatory, patio, double-glazing, tiling, or a garage).

Claiming VAT on goods. Retailers and builder's merchants charge VAT at the standard-rate on most items they sell and this can be recovered under the scheme if the conditions are met.

Builders, however, charge VAT on building materials that they supply and incorporate in a building (or its site) at the same rate as for their work. Thus, if their work is zero-rated or reduced-rated, then so are the building materials. (This does not apply to certain building materials on which VAT cannot be claimed which remain standard-rated.) The scheme can only be used reclaim VAT that has been correctly charged. If VAT is incorrectly charged in error, any refund must be sought from the builder who may be able to obtain a VAT refund from HMRC by adjusting his account with them.

See 42.26 to 42.28 above for goods that do and do not qualify as building materials.

Building land and buildings for conversion. The vendor should not charge VAT on

- land upon which a dwelling is to be constructed, or
- a building which is intended (following conversion) for use as a dwelling or solely for a relevant residential purpose

provided the purchaser declares his intention before purchase (in the case of a building to be used solely for a relevant residential purpose in writing in a specified form). If the vendor does not know what the purchaser's intentions are, VAT may be charged on the sale price. If the purchaser pays VAT to a vendor who was entitled to charge it, neither the purchaser nor the vendor can claim it back from HMRC.

Claiming VAT on services. Builder's services in connection with the construction a new building should be zero-rated. For conversions, a builder can sometimes charge VAT at the reduced rate of 5%. It is important to ensure that the correct amount of VAT is charged as only VAT that has been correctly charged can be reclaimed under the scheme. A claimant should not wait until the project is finished to ensure this, especially on larger projects, as a VAT-registered supplier can only correct the amount of VAT charged within three years of the time of supply.

In general, VAT cannot be reclaimed on services whether constructing or converting a building. For example, VAT cannot be claimed on

- professional and supervisory services, including the fees of architects and surveyors, and any other fees for management, consultancy, design and planning; and
- the hire of goods on their own (eg plant and machinery such as generators without an operator, scaffolding without erection/dismantling, skips and temporary fencing).

VAT can, however, be claimed on building services relating to the conversion of a non-residential building (see above).

Other work. Provided they are incorporated in the building or its site before the construction or conversion is completed, claims can be made for goods used to produce works that allow the building to be used, including works such as

- drainage,

- main paths on the site,
- driveways,
- retaining walls, and
- boundary walls and fences.

Refunds cannot be claimed on

- outdoor leisure facilities such as tennis courts and swimming pools,
- fish ponds, rockeries and other ornamental works,
- work outside the site of the building.

A building is normally complete when it has been finished according to the original plans. In cases of doubt, a building can be regarded as still under construction up until the date when a certificate of completion is issued by the local planning authority.

(VAT Notice 719, paras 3.1–3.3, 4.3, 5.3, 6.4, 8.2, 8.6, 9.1, 9.2, 10.3).

De Voil Indirect Tax Service. See V5.164.

42.34 **Making the claim**

A claim pack consisting of the following forms is available from our National Advice Service (Tel: 0845 010 9000).

- VAT 431 part 1 – Claim form
- VAT 431 part 2A – Description of building and quantities of goods and materials used
- VAT 431 part 2B – Description of services for DIY conversions
- VAT 431 part 3 – Goods, materials and services claimed for which the invoices show VAT separately
- VAT 431 part 3 continuation sheet
- VAT 431 part 4 – Goods, materials and services claimed for invoices not showing VAT separately
- VAT 431 part 4 continuation sheet

Alternatively the forms can be printed from the HMRC website at:

www.hmrc.gov.uk

Part 1 must be completed. The information for parts 2, 3 and 4 can be listed on plain paper or a computer spreadsheet provided it is given in the same format. In any case, the 'total' boxes on parts 3 and 4 must be completed.

A claimant who has bought a prefabricated house kit does not need to list individual items in the kit. He need only send with his claim the supplier's specification listing all the items in the kit, together with a list of any other items used.

Only one claim can be made for each building. The completed claim form and supporting evidence (see below) must be sent to HMRC no later than three months after the completion of the construction or conversion. If this is not possible for any reason, HMRC should be informed. The claim will be acknowledged within ten working days and, if there are no further enquiries, refunds will normally be made within 30 working days.

With effect from 1 April 2004, all claims must be submitted to

HM Revenue and Customs
2 Broadway
Broad Street
Five Ways
Birmingham
West Midlands
B15 1BG

Tel: 0121 697 4000
Fax: 0121 697 4002

Unless HMRC agree otherwise, the following documentation must be sent with the claim forms.

- A certificate of completion from the local authority, for Building Regulation purposes or otherwise, or such other evidence of completion as is satisfactory to HMRC.

  HMRC have indicated that they will also accept

  (i) a habitation certificate or letter from the local authority (or, in Scotland, a temporary certificate of habitation);

  (ii) a valuation rating or council tax assessment; and

  (iii) a certificate from a bank or building society stating 'This is to certify that the .... Bank/Society* released on ....(insert date) the last instalment of its loan secured on the dwelling/building* at ....(insert address) because it then regarded that building as complete.'

  * Delete as applicable

- Invoices and other documents for all eligible goods (and, for conversion, any services) supplied to the claimant for which a claim is being made. The invoices must show

  (i) the supplier's VAT registration number;

  (ii) quantity and description of the goods and/or services;

  (iii) the price of each item; and

  (iv) if the value of the goods is over £100 (including VAT) the name and address of the claimant.

  The invoices must be originals. Any adjustments made by a supplier for returned goods, credits or discounts must be reflected in the claim.

- In respect of eligible goods imported from outside the EC, proof of importation (eg originals of any shipping or transit documents) and evidence of the VAT paid.

- In respect of acquisitions from other EC countries, invoices for the goods with the VAT converted to sterling.

- Documentary evidence that planning permission for the building has been granted. The plans should also be included.
- A certificate signed by a quantity surveyor or architect that the goods shown in the claim were or, in his judgment, were likely to have been, incorporated in the building or its site. (HMRC do not include this as a requirement in their published Notice.)
- If the claim is in respect of a building to be used for a relevant charitable purpose, a declaration as to whether the charity is using (or seeking approval to use) the 'minor non-qualifying use' concession.

Receiving the refund. HMRC will acknowledge receipt of a claim by letter within ten working days. In that letter, if there are no queries concerning the claim, HMRC will give a date by which the refund should be received.

[*SI 1995/2518, Regs 200, 201*]. (VAT Notice 719, paras 10.1, 10.2, 11.1–11.6, 12.5, 12.6).

Appeals. If a claim for a refund is refused or HMRC disagree with the amount of the refund, an appeal may be made to a VAT tribunal. See 5.3(*g*) APPEALS.

PART VII CARAVANS AND HOUSEBOATS

42.35 ZERO-RATED SUPPLIES

Supplies of the following are zero-rated.

(*a*) **Caravans** exceeding the limits of size currently in force for trailers which may be towed on roads by a motor vehicle having an unladen weight of less than 2,030 kilogrammes. *Excluded* are certain removable contents, see 42.36 below. [*VATA 1994, Sch 8 Group 9 Item 1 and Note* (*a*)].

At present the limits referred to above are 7 metres long and 2.3 metres wide (excluding towing bars and similar apparatus used solely for the purpose of attaching the caravan to a vehicle). Consequently, the supply of a caravan which exceeds either of these dimensions is zero-rated. The supply of any other caravan is standard-rated.

The term 'caravan' is not defined in the VAT legislation. In practice, HMRC follow the definition in *The Caravan Sites and Control of Development Act 1960*, ie 'any structure designed or adapted for human habitation that is capable of being moved from one place to another (whether being towed, or by being transported on a motor vehicle so designed or adapted)'. In the case of a twin unit caravan, HMRC follow the definition in *The Caravans Sites Act 1968*, ie a structure 'composed of not more than two sections separately constructed and designed to be assembled on site by means of bolts, clamps or other devices'.

HMRC see the term 'caravan' as including mobile homes, residentials, statics, etc.

(VAT Notice 701/20/04, paras 2.1, 2.2).

(*b*) **Houseboats**, ie boats or other floating decked structures designed or adapted for use solely as places of permanent habitation and not having means of, or capable of being readily adapted for, self-propulsion. *Excluded* are certain removable contents. [*VATA 1994, Sch 8 Group 9 Item 2 and Note* (*a*)].

The term '*self-propulsion*' refers to any vessel that is either

- independently propelled; or
- not independently propelled but could readily be adapted to be capable of self-propulsion (eg by installing an engine, propeller or mast).

It is unlikely, therefore, that a vessel such as a barge or a yacht would be regarded as a houseboat.

(VAT Notice 700/20/04, para 7.2).

(*c*) **Caravans or houseboats** qualifying under (*a*) or (*b*) above which are let or loaned or, if business assets, are put to any private use or are used, or made available to any person for use, for non-business purposes, subject to the overriding exception for accommodation below. [*VATA 1994, Sch 8 Group 9 Item 3*].

The supply of *accommodation* is excluded. [*VATA 1994, Sch 8 Group 9 Note* (*b*)].

De Voil Indirect Tax Service. See V4.275.

42.36 SUPPLIES ASSOCIATED WITH CARAVANS

For a general consideration of the recovery of input tax in relation to caravan parks, see *Stonecliff Caravan Park (VTD 11097) (TVC 15.108)* and *Harpcombe Ltd, QB [1996] STC 726 (TVC 44.22)*.

(1) **Accommodation**

Holiday accommodation. The provision of accommodation in a caravan

- sited on a park advertised or held out for holiday use; and
- let to a person as holiday accommodation

is standard-rated.

Off-season letting. The provision of accommodation in a caravan during the off-season can be treated as exempt provided

- it is let to a person as residential accommodation;
- it is let for more than 28 days; and
- holiday trade in the area is clearly seasonal.

The supplier should keep a copy of his tenancy agreement or similar evidence to show that the caravan was occupied for residential purposes only. In such cases the whole of the let, including the first 28 days, should be treated as an exempt supply.

The holiday season normally lasts from Easter to the end of September although some areas (eg London) are not regarded as having a seasonal holiday trade.

Residential accommodation. The provision of accommodation in a caravan is exempt where it is

- on a site designated by the local authority as for permanent residential use; and
- let to a person as residential accommodation.

(VAT Notice 701/20/04, paras 5.1–5.3).

(2) **Brick skirting**

The provision of brick skirting is generally integral to the agreement to supply a caravan and its liability follows the liability of that supply.

The input tax that is attributable to these supplies should be determined accordingly.

(VAT Notice 701/20/04, para 3.6).

(3) **Car parking/garage fees**

The supply of a garage or parking space in conjunction with the supply of a permanent residential caravan pitch is exempt providing

- the supplier retains ownership of the land on which the garage or parking space is sited; and
- the garage or parking space is reasonably close to the caravan pitch.

In all other circumstances supplies of garages and parking are standard-rated.

(VAT Notice 701/20/04, para 6.1).

(4) **Caravan pitches**

Pitches. See 42.3(*e*) above for the liability of pitch fees and rents received for the granting of the right to caravan owners to keep their caravans on pitches.

Pitch agreements generally impose certain obligations upon site owners such as the construction of pitches, bases and the park infrastructure. Any one-off charge raised which is directly related to these obligations follows the liability of the supply of the pitch.

Reservation fees or premiums charged by a park owner are part of the consideration for the pitch and follow the liability of the pitch fee or rent.

(VAT Notice 700/20/04, paras 4.1, 4.7, 4.8).

(5) **Commission received**

Park owners' commission on sales of second-hand sited caravans. The 'commission' which a park owner is entitled to receive under the *Mobile Homes Acts* and/or Code of Practice when a caravan owner sells a caravan 'on site' at his park follows the liability of the pitch fee or rent.

Any additional charge to the seller in connection with the sale (eg for agency services) is standard-rated.

Charges made to dealers, allowing them to place caravans which have been sold on an owner's site, are standard-rated. Where the charge is passed on to the caravan purchaser it is treated as part of the dealer's costs and forms part of the consideration for the caravan. The VAT treatment will follow the liability of the caravan.

Fees received by park owners from third parties. Any commission from a caravan manufacturer/dealer for the sale of a caravan is standard-rated.

(VAT Notice 700/20/04, paras 3.4, 3.5).

(6) **Delivery, unloading and positioning charges**

Such charges made by the supplier of the caravan at the same time as that supply, provided they are reasonable, follow the liability of the 'delivered' caravan. This applies whether the supply is made by the manufacturer, dealer or site owner. Any delivery service provided which is unconnected with the supply of the caravan is standard-rated.

(VAT Notice 700/20/04, para 3.3).

(7) **Electricity, gas, water and sewerage charges**

Connection to mains services. Where a park owner makes a charge to a caravan owners to connect their caravan to the mains services (gas, electricity, water and sewerage) available at their pitch:

- If the charge is for a first and one-off connection fee, it forms part of the consideration for the supply of the caravan and its liability follows that of the caravan. (The connection fee does not include general maintenance or the provision of the infrastructure which supplies the utilities to the pitch itself.)
- In all other cases connection fees are to be treated as standard-rated.

Electricity and gas. Supplies of electricity and gas to a caravan are liable at the reduced rate provided the users actual consumption can be identified (ie it is metered). Otherwise, the liability of the supply follows that of the main supply of the pitch rental.

Where, for touring caravans and motor homes, an optional hook-up charge is made and the caravan owner chooses to have electricity supplied to the pitch, the supply is subject to VAT at the reduced rate. Any non-optional charge forms part of the overall pitch fee which is standard-rated.

Water and sewerage charges. Charges by a park owner to individual caravan owners for these utilities may be zero-rated if they cover supplies received by the park owner which are supplied on to the caravan owners. The supplies received by the park owner must be apportioned on a fair and reasonable basis and consumption by the communal buildings, other common parts of the park and caravans owned by the park owner must be excluded in calculating the zero-rated charges to individual caravan owners. As an apportionment method, it would normally be acceptable to use the rateable value of that part of the site attributable to the individually owned caravans.

Where, for touring caravans and motor homes, an optional hook-up charge is made, the supply is zero-rated. Any non-optional charge forms part of the overall pitch fee which is standard-rated.

(VAT Notice 700/20/04, paras 3.2, 4.2, 4.3).

(8) **Fixtures, fittings and removable contents**

Where the supply of a caravan is zero-rated, then zero-rating also applies to those goods which a builder would ordinarily incorporate into a new house (eg sinks, baths, WCs, fixed partitions and water heaters). See 42.26 and 42.27 above for further details. Other fixtures and any removable contents supplied with the caravan (eg tables, chairs, mattresses, seat cushions, fridges, carpets, washing machines) are standard-rated even where they are sold together on a 'take-it-or-leave-it' basis (see *Talacre Beach Caravan Sales Ltd v C & E Commrs, Ch D [2004]STC 817 (TVC 67.8)*).

If a caravan and its removable contents are advertised at separate prices and the customer is entirely free to purchase the caravan at the lower price without the removable contents, then, provided the breakdown between the two figures is not a sham, the charges for the removable contents may be treated as a separate taxable supply. Otherwise, and in all cases where there is a single consideration, an apportionment is required. Methods for arriving at the value of the removable contents in new and used caravans are described below. These methods do not have to be used but any different method must give a fair and reasonable result.

New caravans. Standard-rated removable contents included in the price of a new caravan can be calculated by reference to the costs incurred.

> *Example*
>
> A caravan is purchased from a manufacturer for resale. Its cost is £20,000 plus £150 VAT giving a total cost of £20,150. It is sold for £30,000 including VAT.
>
> The VAT on sale must be the same proportion of the sale price as it was of the total cost.
>
> VAT due = sale price × VAT on purchase ÷ total cost
> = £30,000 × 150 ÷ £20,150 = £223.32

If further removable contents are added to those provided by the manufacturer (or some provided are taken out) before sale, these costs must be added/subtracted as appropriate before making the above calculations.

Used caravans. Standard-rated removable contents included in the price of used caravans can be calculated using either of the following methods. Whichever method is adopted, it must be applied consistently and a supplier must not alternate between methods when calculating the VAT due on each of his supplies.

- *Actual values.* Calculate a precise value for each of the standard-rated removable contents. Adequate documentary evidence must be produced to support each valuation if required.

- *Standard apportionment of values.* This is a standard method of apportionment that has been agreed with the National Caravan Council Ltd and the British Holiday and Home Parks Association Ltd. The value of the standard-rated removable contents is taken as 10% of the VAT-exclusive selling price of the complete caravan. If a caravan is sold at a VAT-inclusive price, the VAT element in that price is currently 7/407ths.

  If the margin scheme for SECOND-HAND GOODS (61) is used for sale of the caravan, then the 10% apportionment is applied to the margin rather than the full selling price. The margin is always be VAT-inclusive, so the VAT is calculated as follows:

  Margin on the sale of caravan × 10% × 7/47

Other charges included in the selling price. Charges made at the time of supply of the caravan for delivery, unloading and positioning (see (6) above) and for connections to mains services (see (7) above) are regarded as part of a single supply of the caravan, and form part of its price. If any of the above methods of apportionment are used, the calculation should be made on the total of all such amounts. Other charges, such as reservation fees or premiums, pitch fees or commissions should be excluded from the calculations.

(VAT Notice 700/20/04, paras 3.1, 8.1–8.6; VAT Notice 700/57/04; Internal Guidance V1–12, para 7.3).

(9) **Insurance**

Insurance premiums paid by a park owner to cover general liability or risks are exempt. If the park owner recovers this cost by making a separate charge to caravan owners, the charge is treated as part of the overall consideration for the supply of the pitch and has the same VAT liability as the pitch fee or rent.

Where a park owner is asked by a caravan owner to arrange insurance cover for the caravan owner's risks, any charge made, or any commission earned, for arranging the insurance is exempt provided the caravan owner is the recipient of the supply of insurance made by the insurer.

Any payments received in relation to the renewal of existing insurance policies follow the liability of the original supplies as above.

(VAT Notice 700/20/04, para 4.6).

(10) **Local authority charges**

For seasonal or holiday parks, the park owner must pay non-domestic rates on the whole site. If the park owner attributes a proportion of the rates to individual caravan owners using the official apportionment made by the local valuation officer (under Regulation 4 notice), any charge is outside the scope of VAT.

Any onward charge of the rates element for the communal buildings, general facilities, etc or any caravans owned by the site owner, is part of the pitch fee or rental and is standard-rated.

For permanent caravan parks, caravans not owned by the site owner attract non-domestic rates and are subject to council tax for which the resident or owner is liable.

(VAT Notice 700/20/04, para 4.4).

(11) **Maintenance of common areas**

Any costs relating to the development or maintenance of the common areas of the park (eg installation of street lighting, resurfacing of roads, planting of trees and erection of fences) relate exclusively to the supply of the pitches. Recovery of the input tax depends on whether the site is a residential or holiday site.

(VAT Notice 700/20/04, para 6.3).

(12) **Miscellaneous charges**

Other charges made to individual caravan owners by the park owner are standard-rated. These include:

- Holiday booking services
- Off-season storage and security (on-pitch or off-pitch). Storage of touring caravans is always standard-rated (whether or not a specific area of

land is granted to the caravan owner and including contracts where the period of storage is in excess of one year).

- Club membership.
- Repair and maintenance of caravans.
- Drainage of water-systems.

(VAT Notice 700/20/04, paras 6.2, 6.4).

(13) **Service charges**

Service charges to individual caravan owners for general upkeep and maintenance of the park as a whole (its common areas) follow the liability of the pitch fee or rent. Specific services provided to particular residents are normally standard-rated.

(VAT Notice 700/20/04, para 4.5).

42.37 **HOUSEBOATS**

Accommodation; Delivery, unloading and positioning charges; Connection to mains services; and **Fixtures, fittings and removable contents.** The same provisions apply as for caravans in 42.36 above.

Mooring rights for a houseboat are exempt. See 42.3(*h*) above for moorings generally.

Garages and parking spaces. The supply of a garage or parking space to the owner of a houseboat is exempt provided it is

- supplied by the person who is supplying the mooring; and
- reasonably close to the mooring.

(VAT Notice 701/20/04, paras 7.4–7.8).

43 Local Authorities and Public Bodies

Cross-references. See 8.1 BUSINESS for the meaning of 'business'; 20.12 EDUCATION; 51.15 PAYMENT OF VAT for repayment supplement; 52.10 and 52.11 PENALTIES for serious misdeclaration or neglect resulting in understatements or overclaims; 53.4 PENSION SCHEMES.

The contents of this chapter are as follows.

43.1 EC PROVISIONS: 'BODIES GOVERNED BY PUBLIC LAW'

For a transaction to be within the scope of VAT, it must, amongst other conditions, be made by a taxable person. Certain 'bodies governed by public law' are given special treatment under EC legislation. They are not treated as being taxable persons when they engage in certain transactions which, if engaged in by other persons, would result in them being considered taxable persons.

Although the term '*bodies governed by public law*' is used in the *EC 6th Directive*, the phrase is not used in UK law. In *EC Council Directive 93/36* it is interpreted as any body

- established for the specific purpose of meeting needs in the general interest, not having an industrial or commercial character;
- having legal personality; and
- financed, for the most part, by the State, or regional or local authorities, or other bodies governed by public law, or subject to management supervision by those bodies, or having an administrative, managerial or supervisory board, more than half of whose members are appointed by the State, regional or local authorities or by other bodies governed by public law.

Treatment as non-taxable persons. Specifically, state, regional and local government authorities and other bodies governed by public law are not considered taxable persons in respect of activities or transactions where the following conditions are met. This applies even where they collect dues, fees, contributions or payments in connection with these activities or transactions.

(*a*) *The body is engaged in the activity or transaction 'as a public authority'.*

There is nothing in EC legislation specifying those activities in which bodies engage as public authorities and it does not follow that just because a body is a public authority that all activities it undertakes are non-taxable activities (or 'non-business' as such activities are more commonly referred to in the UK).

In *Comune di Carpaneto Piacentino and Others v Ufficio Provinciale Imposta sul Valore Aggiunto di Piacenza, CJEC [1990] 3 CMLR 153 (TVC 21.90)* the CJEC held that activities pursued as 'public authorities' were those engaged in by bodies governed by public law under the special legal regime applicable to them, but did not include activities pursued by them under the same legal conditions as those applying to private traders.

For example, a body would be acting as a public authority where the law gives it

- the right to make people or organisations pay for a service provided but without giving them any say in what is, or how it is provided; and
- powers to impose penalties where people do not comply.

In *Norwich City Council (VTD 11822) (TVC 40.8)* it was accepted that the Council was a body governed by public law. The Council granted advertising facilities to commercial sponsors of various campaigns which it organised but did not account for VAT on the sponsorship payments. The tribunal held that although the Council was using the sponsorship payments in support of its statutory functions, the sponsorship deals were not in themselves part of the statutory functions of the Council and were carried out under the same legal provisions as applied to private traders.

In *Arts Council of Great Britain (VTD 11991) (TVC 7.81)* the Council's main activity was the distribution of an annual Parliamentary grant. The tribunal held that this was not an economic activity. Although the Council was not a specified body within *VATA 1994, s 33(3)* (see 43.2 below), it was 'a public body, performing a public function, whose costs were paid out of public funds'.

See also *Royal Academy of Music (VTD 11871) (TVC 53.10)* where the tribunal held that the Academy was not a public authority body and was not governed by public law so that its activities fell outside the scope of *EC 6th Directive, Art 4.5.*

(*b*) *Treatment as a non-taxable person does not lead to a significant distortion of competition.*

There is no definition in UK law to quantify the term 'significant' in relation to distortion of competition. In *Comune di Carpaneto Piacentino* above the CJEC considered the matter but did no more than decide that individual EC countries should determine whether distortion of competition was significant and that they were not required to lay down precise quantitative limits.

HMRC take the view that significant distortions of competition occurs when non-business treatment

- places private traders at a commercial disadvantage compared to the body; or
- deters private traders from starting up businesses supplying similar goods or services in competition with the body.

Significant distortion *can* result if a body

- does not charge VAT on a supply, while its competitors making similar supplies have to; or
- recovers the VAT attributable to an exempt supply or a non-business activity, while the VAT incurred by its competitors in making similar supplies effectively sticks with them as a real cost.

See *Metropolitan Borough of Wirral (VTD 14674) (TVC 40.9)* where a district council operated an information service, collecting and distributing information relating to the county in which it was located, in accordance with a statutory requirement. The tribunal held that the work in question could have been undertaken by a private organisation and that to treat the council as a non-taxable person would be unfair on private organisations.

If a body has no local competitor, an activity can be treated as non-business provided no other person could carry out the activity in the same way, and in similar conditions, as the body has to carry it out, and thereby achieving the results as the body has to achieve. HMRC regard this as normally applying where

- the body's clients could not equally well obtain the goods or services from some other supplier;
- the activity is not carried on generally by suppliers outside the public authority sector, unless on such a small scale as to be negligible; and
- non-business treatment would not act as a disincentive to a private trader capable of going into business in direct local competition with the body.

The question of the extent of competition was considered in *The Lord Mayor and Citizens of the City of Westminster (VTD 3367) (TVC 21.88)*. The city council managed a hostel providing accommodation to homeless men. The tribunal held that the accommodation provided was of such a type that the council was clearly not supplying services in competition with proprietors of commercial hotels, inns or boarding houses and therefore no distortion of competition arose from the supply being treated as non-business.

In most cases it should be clear whether treating a particular activity as non-business would lead to significant distortion of competition. In cases of doubt, the body should contact HMRC.

Many of the activities which local authorities have a statutory obligation to provide are now subject to contracting out and competitive tendering (eg domestic refuse collection). In these cases, whilst the tenderers are in competition to supply the service to the responsible local authority, there is no competition to provide the service to third parties. Such services provided under a statutory obligation to a third party using an outside body acting as agent are non-business provided there is no competition between the local authority and others to supply the services to the third party.

(*c*) Unless carried out on such a scale as to be negligible, the activity does not relate to

- telecommunications;
- the supply of water, gas, electricity and steam;
- the transport of goods;
- port and airport services;
- passenger transport;
- supply of new goods manufactured for sale;
- the transactions of agricultural intervention agencies in respect of agricultural products carried out pursuant to Regulations on the common organisation of the market in these products;
- the running of trade fairs and exhibitions;

- warehousing;
- the activities of commercial publicity bodies;
- the activities of travel agencies;
- the running of staff shops, co-operatives and industrial canteens and similar institutions; and
- transactions of radio and television bodies of a commercial nature.

[*EC 6th Directive, Art 4*(*5*)]. (VAT Notice 749, paras 5.4–5.7; Internal Guidance V1–14, paras 3.1, 3.7, 4.2, 4.3).

Exempt activities. EC countries *may* consider activities of bodies governed by public law which are exempt under *EC 6th Directive, Art 13* (see 22.17–22.19 EUROPEAN COMMUNITY LEGISLATION) or *Art 28* (see 22.31 EUROPEAN COMMUNITY LEGISLATION) as activities which they engage in as public authorities. [*EC 6th Directive, Art 4*(*5*)].

43.2 **UK PROVISIONS**

UK law does not specifically refer to 'bodies governed by public law' (see 43.1 above). However, it does provide special treatment for 'specified bodies'. The combined effect of the EC and UK provisions is as follows.

(1) All 'bodies governed by public law', which phrase includes but is not restricted to 'specified bodies', can treat certain of their activities as non-taxable activities (or 'non-business' activities as they are more commonly referred to in the UK). See 43.3 below for a consideration of business and non-business activities.

Any such body that is registered, or liable to be registered, for VAT (see 43.5 below) must charge and account for VAT on all its business activities, subject to the normal rules. This applies whether the customer is a private individual, trader, government department or another public body. It must not charge VAT on non-business activities.

(2) As a general rule, it is only possible to recover VAT incurred if registered for VAT and if the VAT can be attributed to taxable business activities. Where VAT relates to non-business or (subject to certain *de minimis* limits) exempt activities, any VAT incurred 'sticks' as a real cost. To minimise this sticking VAT, a special scheme allows 'specified bodies', whether or not registered for VAT, to

- reclaim the VAT suffered on non-business activities (see 43.7 below); and
- recover any VAT attributed to exempt business activities where HMRC consider it an insignificant proportion of the total VAT incurred (see 43.8 below).

It should be noted that 'bodies governed by public law' which are not 'specified bodies', although not benefiting from the special scheme under (2) above, are still able to treat certain otherwise taxable business supplies as non-business.

The '*specified bodies*' are as follows.

(*a*) A '*local authority*', ie

- the council of a county, county borough, district, London borough, parish or group of parishes (or, in Wales, community or group of communities),
- the Common Council of the City of London,

- the Council of the Isles of Scilly,
- any joint committee or joint board established by two or more of the foregoing, and
- in relation to Scotland, a regional, islands or district council within the meaning of the *Local Government* (*Scotland*) *Act 1973*, any combination and any joint committee or joint board established by two or more of the foregoing, and any joint board to which *section 226* of that *Act* applies.

There are many bodies closely associated with local authorities, receiving funding from them or having local authority members on their boards, which are not themselves a local authority for these purposes. Local authorities may discharge certain of their functions through committees and they have an interest in other committees (eg those responsible for the day-to-day management of community centres, youth clubs and sports halls). Only those committees which are discharging a local authority function may be treated as a local authority and it is therefore necessary to determine whether a particular committee is in fact doing so. For a committee to be considered as discharging a local authority function it must

(i) be established by a local authority, or two or more authorities, under *Local Government Act 1972, s 101*(*2*) or be preserved under *Local Government Act 1972, s 101*(*9*) (or be a sub-committee of any such committee); and

(ii) have voting rights restricted to local authority members, unless exception to this requirement is provided by *SI 1990/1553, Regs 4* or *5*.

HMRC do not consider the following bodies to be local authorities.

- Joint boards/committees set up by bodies other than local authorities, even where they include local authorities as members or participants, eg boards established by order of a Minister of the Crown.
- Bodies which merely receive financial assistance from local authorities.
- Committees set up under *Local Government Act 1972, s 102*(*4*). These are committees whose role is advisory only and which do not carry out local authority functions.
- Community Councils in England or Scotland.
- Community Associations.
- Parish meetings.
- Parochial church councils.
- Village hall management committees.
- Charities.

(*b*) A river purification board established under *Local Government* (*Scotland*) *Act 1973, s 135* and a water development board within the meaning of the *Water* (*Scotland*) *Act 1980, s 109*.

(*c*) An internal drainage board.

(*d*) A passenger transport authority or executive established under *Transport Act 1968, Part II*.

(*e*) A port health authority within the meaning of *Public Health* (*Control of Disease*) *Act 1984*, and a port local authority and joint port local authority constituted under *Public Health* (*Scotland*) *Act 1897, Part X*.

(*f*) A police authority.

(*g*) A development corporation within the *New Towns Act 1981* or the *New Towns* (*Scotland*) *Act 1968*; a new town commission within the *New Towns Act* (*Northern Ireland*) *1965* and the Commission for the New Towns.

(*h*) A general lighthouse authority within the meaning of *Merchant Shipping Act 1995, Part VIII* (except that no VAT refund is made which HMRC consider is attributable to activities other than the provision, maintenance or management of lights or other navigational aids).

(*i*) The British Broadcasting Corporation.

(*j*) The appointed news provider referred to in *Communications Act 2003, s 280* (except that no VAT refund is made which HMRC consider is attributable to activities other than the provision of news programmes for broadcasting by holders of regional Channel 3 licences within the meaning of *Broadcasting Act 1990, Part 1*).

(*k*) Any body specified by an order made by the Treasury. Currently, these comprise

- the Commissions for Local Administration in England, Wales, and Scotland; and the Commission for Local Authority Accounts in Scotland [*SI 1976/2028*];
- the Inner London Education Authority, the Inner London Interim Education Authority; The Northumbria Interim Police Authority; the London Fire and Civil Defence Authority; the London Residuary Body; a metropolitan county Police Authority, Fire and Civil Defence Authority, Passenger Transport Authority or Residuary Body [*SI 1985/1101*];
- a probation committee constituted by the *Powers of Criminal Courts Act 1973, s 47, Sch 3 para 2* (now replaced by local probation boards under *Criminal Justice and Courts Act 2000*); a magistrates' courts committee established under *Justice of the Peace Act 1979, s 19*; and the charter trustees constituted by *Local Government Act 1972, s 246*(*4*) or (*5*) [*SI 1986/336*];
- authorities established under *Local Government Act 1985, s 10* (waste regulation and disposal authorities) [*SI 1986/532*];
- National Rivers Authority [*SI 1989/1217*];
- the Environment Agency [*SI 1995/1978*];
- a National Park authority (within the meaning of *Environment Act 1995, s 63*) [*SI 1995/2999*];
- a fire authority constituted by a combination scheme made under *Fire Service Act 1947, s 6* [*SI 1995/2999*];
- charter trustees established under *Local Government Act 1992, s 17* or any other statutory instrument made under *Part II* of that Act [*SI 1997/2558*];
- the Broads Authority [*SI 1999/2076*];

- the Greater London Authority [*SI 2000/1046*];
- the London Fire and Emergency Planning Authority [*SI 2000/1515*];
- Transport for London (the body established under *Greater London Act 1999, s 154*) [*SI 2000/1672*]; and
- the Greater London Magistrates' Courts Authority [*SI 2001/3453*].

[*VATA 1994, ss 33(3)–(5), 96(4); Merchant Shipping Act 1995, Sch 13; Communications Act 2003, Sch 17 para 129; SI 1995/1510, Art 2*]. (VAT Notice 749, paras 2.2, 4.1, 4.2; Internal Guidance V1–14, paras 3.6, 5.5).

43.3 BUSINESS AND NON-BUSINESS ACTIVITIES

Because of the special provisions which apply to them, it is important for 'bodies governed by public law' (see 43.1 above), which include the 'specified bodies' listed in UK law (see 43.2 above), to distinguish between their business and non-business activities. The business/non-business test applied should not be confused with the business/non-business test applied to the activities of normal traders and the following steps should be considered in reaching a decision.

(*a*) Is the body making the supply a 'body governed by public law' (see 43.1 above)?

If Yes, go to (*b*).

If No, the activity is business.

(*b*) Is the body engaged in the activity 'as a public body' (see 43.1(*a*) above)?

If Yes, go to (*c*).

If No, the activity is business.

(*c*) Would non-business treatment lead to a significant distortion of competition (see 43.1(*b*) above)?

If Yes, the activity is business.

If No, go to (*d*).

(*d*) Is the activity one of those specified in the list in 43.1(*c*) above?

If Yes, go to (*e*) below.

If No, go to (*f*) below.

(*e*) Is the activity carried out on a negligible scale?

If Yes, go to (*f*) below.

If No, the activity is business.

(*f*) Is the body a Government Department or Health Authority (see 43.11 below)?

If Yes, go to (*g*) below.

If No, the activity is non-business.

(*g*) Is the activity subject to a Treasury direction (see 43.11 below)?

If Yes, the activity is business.

If No, the activity is non-business.

The restriction on non-business treatment for the activities under (*d*) above has little practical effect on most specified bodies as

- they do not generally engage in these activities as 'public authorities' and therefore fail the test under (*b*) above; and
- where the activities are carried out as 'public authorities', they are generally also provided by private bodies and non-business treatment would lead to a significant distortion of competition so that the test under (*c*) above would be failed.

(VAT Notice 749, para 5.1; Internal Guidance V1–14, paras 4.4, 4.5).

De Voil Indirect Tax Service. See V2.108.

43.4 **Common activities of local authorities and police authorities**

Specified bodies within 43.2 above which are registered for VAT can claim a refund of the VAT they incur on both their business and their non-business activities (see 43.7 below) and do not have to separate the VAT incurred on the two types of activity. It is, however, important to distinguish between business and non-business activities for output tax and partial exemption purposes. It is also important to distinguish between such activities when dealing with non VAT-registered bodies who may incorrectly treat business activities as non-business and consequently not register for VAT at the correct time.

This paragraph considers a number of activities in relation to specified bodies.

(1) **Bailiffs**

If local authorities are unsuccessful in obtaining payment of council tax from defaulters, they may contract with bailiffs to collect the arrears plus any statutory charges for the enforcement of the debt. Bailiffs supply their services to, and should therefore invoice, the local authority for their statutory charges and any agreed commission based on the amount of the arrears due or collected. VAT is chargeable on the full value of these services and not the lesser amount received from the local authority where payments from debtors are retained and netted-off against the total charge. The local authority can recover the VAT it is charged because it relates to its non-business activity of collecting the council tax. (Internal Guidance V1–14, para 7.2).

(1A) **Beach huts**

Under *Public Health Act 1936, s 232* local authorities may provide huts or other conveniences for bathing on any land belonging to them or under their control, and may make charges for their use. The law neither requires local authorities to provide beach huts nor states that they must do so in a particular way. Consequently, provision of beach huts by a local authority is a standard-rated business activity. See also *Shearing (VTD 16723) (TVC 7.25)* and *Poole Borough Council (VTD 7180) (TVC 39.109)*. (Internal Guidance V1–14, para 7.3).

(2) **Car parking charges**

Where a public authority imposes charges (including excess parking charges) for parking at meter bays on the public highway, it does so under statutory powers that nobody other than a public authority can exercise. This activity is non-business.

As regards off-street parking in garages, buildings and open spaces, in *C & E Commrs v Isle of Wight Council, Ch D 2004 [2005] STC 257 (TVC 21.94A)* the tribunal held that the Council was not engaged in a business activity when providing off-street parking as the provision of those spaces was subject to the *Road Traffic Regulation Act 1984*. It also held that the UK had not properly implemented *EC Sixth Directive, Art 4(5)*, thereby preventing HMRC from arguing that to treat off-street parking as non-business would distort competition. On appeal, the High Court held that *Art 4(5)* was properly implemented in UK law and remitted the case to the tribunal to consider the substantive issue of whether treating the council's receipts as non-taxable would lead to 'significant distortions of competition'. In the meantime, HMRC take the view that to treat off-street parking as non-business would be a distortion of competition. See Business Brief 3/05.

HMRC have always accepted that penalty charges imposed by local authorities operating off-street parking under the *Road Traffic Act 1991* are outside the scope of VAT. In addition, following the decision in *Bristol City Council (VTD 17665) (TVC 60.197)* they also accept that excess charges levied in local authority off-street car parks under the *Road Traffic Regulation Act 1984* are statutory penalties of which warning is given on the car park signs. Accordingly, the excess charges are not consideration for a supply of parking and are also outside the scope of VAT.

(VAT Notice 749, para 5.8; Business Brief 19/2002).

(3) **Care and welfare**

Most local authorities are required to provide a wide range of services to people of all ages, ranging from children and young persons to the provision of accommodation and domiciliary care for elderly persons. They may be entitled to make a charge to recover all or part of the costs they incur in providing these services.

- Where an authority is acting under a special legal regime applicable to it and not under the same legal conditions as those that apply to private traders, these activities are non-business.
- Where an authority merely provides residential accommodation, for example, because someone has chosen it in preference to similar facilities available from a charity or commercial provider, if such accommodation is not provided under a statutory function the supply of accommodation by the authority is a business activity. Similarly, the supply of services such as creches and playgroups, and recreational holidays for elderly people not in statutory care is a business activity.

(VAT Notice 749, para 5.8).

(4) **Cemeteries and crematoria**

The provision and maintenance of cemeteries by a local authority is a non-business activity but the provision of crematoria is primarily a business activity. (VAT Notice 749, para 5.8). See also 19.6 DEATH.

(5) **Coastal defence contributions**

Local authorities which border the sea are required to obtain contributions, usually from those who derive most benefit, towards the cost of maintaining coastal defence facilities (eg sea walls). HMRC take the view that these contributions are not consideration for a supply of services but outside the scope of VAT. (Internal Guidance V1–14, para 6.17).

(6) **Disposal of goods under special legal provisions**

The police have statutory powers to dispose of goods the owners of which cannot be traced (eg property handed into police stations and recovered after the detection of a crime, abandoned vehicles, goods found in local authority property, etc). The statutory powers relate only to the circumstances of acquisition and disposal and not to the supply of the goods. As the goods disposed of are second-hand goods commonly supplied in the private sector, their supply is a business activity. (Internal Guidance V1–14, para 15.6).

(7) **Education**

See 20.12 EDUCATION.

(7A) **Groundwork trusts**

See 8.4(13) BUSINESS.

(8) **Housing and property improvements**

Local authorities have wide statutory obligations and powers in relation to housing.

(*a*) **The provision and operation of social housing.**

(i) *Bed and breakfast accommodation*. Where, due to a shortage of its homes for letting, a local authority has to place homeless people in bed and breakfast accommodation, it is carrying out a non-business activity. The local authority does not have to account for output tax on any contributions it receives towards the cost of providing such accommodation (eg housing benefit paid directly to it by the Department of Work and Pensions).

The supply of the accommodation is to the local authority, not to the homeless, so the reduced VAT rate for long-term residents cannot be applied.

(ii) *Home improvements and tenants contributions*. Most local authorities have a rolling programme to maintain or improve the quality of their housing stock. Where a tenant has no choice in the matter, any permanently increased rent is a charge for the overall supply of the right to occupy the accommodation which is a non-business activity.

Where improvements are carried out only at the tenants request, the local authority may seek a contribution from the tenant towards the costs of the improvement work. These contributions may take the form of a lump sum payment or instalments paid with the rent. Lump sum payments, or instalments paid with the rent but over a limited period only, are generally standard-rated (but see 32.16 *et seq* HEALTH AND WELFARE for zero-rating of certain supplies to disabled persons). Any permanently increased rent is a charge for the overall supply of the right to occupy the accommodation which is a non-business activity.

(iii) *Third party management of local authority housing stock*. Many local authorities delegate the management and maintenance of their housing stock to a tenant management company either in the form of a Tenant Management Co-operative (TMC) or a Tenant Management Organisation (TMO).

A TMC enters into a standard agreement with the local authority under which repairs and maintenance are the delegated responsibility of the TMC. It acts as principal in purchasing materials and carrying out the work or engaging contractors to carry it out on its behalf. The TMC receives the supplies of goods or services and receives a management and maintenance allowance from the local authority. The local authority cannot recover input tax on the supplies of goods and services. But, if the TMC is VAT-registered, as the delegated maintenance relates to the non-business activity of providing housing, the local authority can recover any VAT charged to it by the TMC under 43.7 below.

A TMO takes on varying degrees of management responsibility and receives payments from the local authority for a range of services it may undertake. It can also administer and collect rents. Most supplies received by the TMO, whose costs are reimbursed by the local authority, are supplies to an agent acting in its own name. The only supplies a TMO normally makes as principal relate to its management charges to the local authority. If the TMO is VAT-registered, this can be recovered by the local authority under 43.7 below as relating to its non-business activity.

(iv) *Local authority garage rentals.* The letting of garages is normally standard-rated but, subject to certain conditions, where it is let in conjunction with a dwelling it can take on the same liability as the dwelling. See 42.3(*f*) LAND AND BUILDINGS for further details. As the letting of houses and flats by a local authority is a non-business activity, where it lets garages/parking spaces to a housing tenant and the necessary conditions are met, the supply is non-business.

Under 'right to buy' legislation, council tenants can buy, rather than rent, their homes. Where they have continued to rent a garage, the liability of the garage rental depends on whether the main property has been sold freehold or leasehold. Following a freehold sale, the rental of the garage becomes a taxable supply because the local authority is no longer the landlord for the dwelling. But following a leasehold sale, where the tenant continues to pay ground rent to the local authority, the local authority remains the landlord (albeit only the ground landlord). In these circumstances, where a tenant pays ground rent for both the dwelling and the garage, or pays ground rent for the dwelling and rents the garage, the provision of the parking facility is a non-business activity.

(v) *Repair and maintenance of dwellings.* Any repairs to its housing stock which a local authority is responsible for and which it carries out without charge are considered to be part of the non-business activity of providing public sector housing.

Any charge made to a tenant still in residence is a standard-rated supply of services to the tenant. Any charge for repairs and making good to a tenant who has vacated premises and left them in an unfit condition are regarded as compensation and outside the scope of VAT. Similarly, charges made to third parties to recover the costs of repairing damage to council dwellings are also regarded as compensation.

Any VAT incurred in carrying out repairs to dwellings can be recovered, either as input tax or under the refund scheme in 43.7 below.

(vi) *Refugees*. The provision of housing (and lighting, heating, food, etc) for refugees by a local authority is a non-business activity.

(*b*) **Property improvements, including grant funding**.

(i) *Care and Repair scheme*. This is designed to provide help to elderly and disabled homeowners to enable them to improve their property. Any grant from a local authority or the Office of the Deputy Prime Minister is outside the scope of VAT. The scheme is administered by a limited company but is carried out by a care and repair agency which may be a charity or housing association but is usually a local authority. The agency makes all arrangements for the work to be carried out and makes all payments on behalf of the homeowner, charging a percentage of the cost of the building works as its fee.

The services of the agency are a business activity when carried out by a local authority although the supplies are exempt under *VATA 1994, Sch 9 Group 7, Item 9* (see 32.14 HEALTH AND WELFARE).

As actual contracts for the work are between the homeowner and the building contractor, the local authority cannot recover VAT charged by the builder to the homeowner.

(ii) *Default works*. A local authority may issue an enforcement notice to a person who has failed to maintain their property in a satisfactory state of repair.

Where the recipient of the notice agrees to the work being carried out and arranges for either the local authority or some other contractor to undertake it, the contractor's service are supplies to the recipient of the notice. If the local authority arranges the contractor's supplies on behalf of the recipient, it may treat the supply as being made both to it and by it under *VATA 1994, s 47(3)* (see 3.4 AGENTS).

Where the recipient of the notice refuses to comply, the local authority may exercise its statutory powers to have the work carried out and recover the cost from the recipient. As only a local authority can issue the default notice and exercise these statutory powers, this is a non-business activity. See also *Glasgow City Council (VTD 15491) (TVC 40.16)* where the tribunal held that works in default and the subsequent recovery of costs under *Housing (Scotland) Act 1987, ss 108, 109* were not supplies for VAT purposes.

When the supply of the work is to the local authority, it can recover the VAT charged by the contractor. If it makes an onward taxable supply of the work in the course or furtherance of business, it can recover the VAT incurred as input tax. If it does not make a taxable supply but imposes the work under its statutory powers, it can recover the VAT under the refund scheme in 43.7 below.

(iii) *Property improvement grants*. For a consideration of grants generally, see 69.9(2) VALUATION. The most important points to consider are to whom is the supply made, who actually owns the grants, and what happens to any contributions made by third parties.

The most common situations are those where a local authority funds part of the cost of a householder's planned improvements work by means of a grant. There are normally two ways in which grant-funded improvements are carried out.

The first method is where the homeowner has arranged directly with a builder to carry out some works and a grant is paid by the local authority for that work to be done. The local authority payment is a third party consideration which does not entitle it to recovery under the scheme in 43.7 below. See *Doncaster Borough Council (VTD 12458) (TVC 40.2)*.

The second method is where the homeowner has arranged with the local authority for it to act as his agent in organising the building work. The local authority's contributions are still third party consideration and it is not entitled to recovery under the scheme in 43.7 below. If the local authority charges for its agency services to the homeowner, then that fee is standard-rated. This follows the decision in *Ashfield District Council v C & E Commrs, Ch D [2001] STC 1706 (TVC 40.3)*.

(iv) *Group repair schemes and block improvement grants.* Local authorities in England and Wales have powers under *Housing Grants, Construction and Regeneration Act 1996, s 65* to carry out improvements to the exterior of blocks and terraces of private sector housing with the permission of the properties' owners ('group repair schemes'). Normally, the local authority receives a grant from central government and a compulsory contribution from the property owner towards the costs of the work. The contribution by the property owner and any grant received direct from central government are also outside the scope of VAT. However, where the owner asks the local authority to provide additional works for a separate payment, this is a business supply.

The local authority can recover any VAT incurred in carrying out non-business activities under the provisions in 43.7 below but any VAT incurred in making business supplies must be recovered under the normal rules.

(*c*) **Building inspection fees.**

(i) *Planning, building notice, inspection and reversion fees. In England and Wales*, competition exists across the whole range of building control work and such services provided by local authorities are business. *In Scotland and Northern Ireland*, the supply of building control services is the monopoly of local authorities and classed as non-business for VAT purposes.

Local authorities retain their statutory monopoly over planning applications and reversions and the fees they charge for this work is non-business.

(ii) *Regularisation fees.* Where a local authority issues a regularisation certificate because building work has been carried out without its prior approval, as approved inspectors in the private sector do not have the legal power to carry out this function, this is a non-business activity.

(*d*) **The provision and maintenance of community projects, including village halls.**

(i) *Village halls owned by the local authority.* Where the local authority uses its own funds to carry out work to the hall, it is not making a supply for VAT purposes. Where it receives funds from another body (eg a village hall management committee) the funds are most likely to be consideration for its use of the hall. Alternatively, the funds may be a donation and outside the scope of VAT.

Whether the local authority can recover the VAT incurred on the work depends on the use to which the hall is put. If it is used for the local authority's own non-business activities, the VAT is recoverable under 43.7 below. If it is used to make a business supply (eg use in return for a payment), the normal VAT rules will apply. If the local authority uses donated funds to make a purchase it can recover the VAT incurred under 43.7 below provided it makes the purchase itself (ie places the order, receives the supply and a VAT invoice addressed to it and makes payment), retains ownership of the purchase and uses it or makes it available for its own non-business purposes, and keeps sufficient records for the purchase (and the purpose for which it is made) to be easily identified.

(ii) *Village halls not owned by the local authority.* If the local authority uses its own funds to carry out work to such a hall, and it then gives this work away to the owners (eg a voluntary group), this is not a supply for VAT purposes provided that it receives nothing in return. Any VAT incurred is recoverable under the scheme in 43.7 below. If it does receive something in return (including non-monetary consideration such as use the hall) it is likely to be consideration for the taxable business supply of the works.

If the hall is owned by a voluntary group and they, or a third party, pass funds to the local authority which arranges work to the hall, then these funds are likely to be the consideration for the supply of the work to the voluntary group. The local authority may act as a 'main contractor' (receiving supplies and making an onward business supply to the voluntary group, the consideration for which is the funding received) or may act as the agent of the voluntary group in arranging the work on its behalf.

(*e*) **Shared ownership schemes.**

Such arrangements usually involve the sharing of equity in a dwelling between an occupier and a housing association. The occupier purchases a dwelling at a proportion of its value and then pays rent to cover the share in the equity retained by the housing association. Under these circumstances, the rent paid by the occupier is consideration for a supply in the course of business by the housing association. Where local authorities enter into similar shared ownership schemes and receive payment of rents, the activity is also business.

(*f*) **Sales and letting of land.**

Where a local authority sells and lets land and property, it is in direct competition with the private sector. These are normally business transactions. However, by concession, where a local authority provides domestic accommodation to people seeking housing (normally on a list maintained by the authority) or disposes of properties under the 'right to buy' legislation, it is non-business, regardless of the circumstances and whether or not they are acting under any special legal regime applicable to them.

(*g*) **Housing stock transfers.**

In order to bring their housing stock up to the Government's 'decent homes standard', many local authorities have transferred their stock to registered social landlords (RSLs) once residents have been balloted and agreed to proposals.

Such transfers can take one of two forms with differing VAT consequences.

Under the first method, the RSL agrees to purchase the housing stock in its existing condition, and any refurbishment works that may be required is paid for by the purchasing RSL. Any VAT that the purchasing RSL incurs on the refurbishment works cannot be recovered as it is wholly attributable to the letting activities of the RSL. This was confirmed in *South Liverpool Housing Ltd (VTD 18750) (TVC 40.17)*.

Under the second method, the RSL agrees to purchase the housing stock, but as a condition of purchase (normally a contractual requirement) requires the local authority to improve the properties. As sometimes thousands of properties are involved, and it would be impractical for the parties to enter into a piecemeal arrangement whereby a housing unit only passed to the RSL once the local authority had upgraded it, normally the house stock passes to the RSL before it has been upgraded, but the local authority enters into a binding obligation to ensure that the necessary works of maintenance are undertaken at its expense. The local authority can recover the VAT incurred on these works under the scheme in 43.7 below (even though most of the work actually takes place after the housing has been transferred) provided the following conditions are satisfied.

- The transfer contract must contain a clear obligation on the part of the local authority to carry out the works (or there must be a suitable addendum or other document detailing this obligation).
- The scope and quantum of the works must have been agreed prior to the transfer, and this information should form part of the contract.
- The scope of the works should only relate to local authority tenants, common areas, and the outside fabric for right-to-buy leaseholders or freeholders.
- The works in question must be supplied to the local authority (ie the local authority must have entered into one or more contracts for the works to be done and paid consideration for the works).
- From time to time the local authority will be expected to substantiate any VAT claims by providing a clear audit trail which links the VAT to the works required under the transfer contract.

It does not matter that the parties have agreed for the RSL to undertake the works as building contractor and charge the local authority accordingly. The local authority is not allowed to recover VAT on works that are the responsibility of the RSL after the transfer has taken place (eg day-to-day repairs and maintenance).

(VAT Notice 749, para 5.8; Internal Guidance V1–14, paras 9.1, 11.2–11.5; Business Brief 19/98).

(9) **Local authority and NHS joint stores depots**

Operation. Some joint store depots are operated by a local authority and others by NHS bodies. The organisation which operates and maintains a depot must charge VAT on the income received as payment for the services it supplies (eg salary costs and fuel and power). This charge is often made as a supplement to charge for stock or as a periodic charge. A local authority recipient of these services is able to reclaim this VAT (subject to the normal rules). An NHS body recipient may currently claim it as a refund under the contracted-out service regime.

Stock purchase. Only one participant in a joint stores' arrangement is responsible for accounting for an item of stock within its books. It is this participant that is to incur any VAT charged when the goods are taken into stock. When stock is ordered, arrangements should be made to ensure that the purchase invoice provided by the supplier to the operator is made out to the participant with accounting responsibility for the item in question. However, HMRC are willing to grant prior approval for an alternative to cover the few occasions where this may cause difficulty (eg the inability to use bulk purchase facilities). This allows the store operator

(i) to initially purchase the stock;

(ii) to sell on those items for which the other party has accounting responsibility; and

(iii) for the items referred to at (ii) to reclaim the equivalent VAT on the supplier's invoice as input tax, having invoiced the other party and charged VAT as output tax.

VAT reclaims on stock items are available only by a local authority recipient and only when it has accounting responsibility (subject to the normal rules).

Hire of stock. Where the participant with responsibility for accounting for an item of stock within its books 'lends' or hires it to the other (ie to cover temporary shortages) VAT should not be levied on any charge made because this is not seen to be a business activity for VAT purposes. Where items are hired in from outside contractors, VAT reclaims are available only to a local authority recipient and only when it has accounting responsibility (subject to the normal rules)

(Internal Guidance V1–14, para 8.10).

(10) **Local authority purchasing consortia**

Under *Local Authorities* (*Goods and Services*) *Act 1970* a number of authorities may get together to form a joint committee which acts as a central purchasing organisation known as a Local Authority Purchasing Consortia (LAPC).

Following the decision in *Comune di Carpaneto Piacentino and Others v Ufficio Provinciale Imposta sul Valore Aggiunto di Piacenza, CJEC [1990] 3 CMLR 153*

(TVC 21.90) HMRC have concluded that LAPCs are not acting under any special legal regime and that their supplies do not fall to be treated as non-taxable under *EC 6th Directive, Art 4.5*. They are not, therefore, entitled to use the refund scheme under 43.7 below.

(Internal Guidance V1–14, para 7.28).

(11) **Mayoral/chairman's expenses**

A mayor or chairman, although elected, is treated in the same way as an employee when carrying out official duties. Any input tax incurred in the course of official duties can be recovered provided

- the local authority accepts responsibility for the actual expenses incurred and enters them in its normal accounts;
- the goods/services are ordered in the name of the authority and invoices are addressed to it, and
- adequate records are kept.

If a car is used to transport the mayor between home and civic events, the related motoring expenses can be recovered if the above conditions are met. If a car is made available for a mayor's private use, VAT recovery on its purchase is blocked.

Input tax cannot be recovered on any flat-rate allowance given in the form of money placed freely at the disposal of the mayor/chairman.

(Internal Guidance V1–14, para 7.21).

(12) **Meals on wheels**

Local authorities may use the services of their own staff to provide the meals or may buy them in from outside contractors. Alternatively, they may use the services of voluntary organisations who act as their agent in preparing and/or delivering the meals. The provision of meals to the elderly for a charge is a non-business activity of the local authority if provided as a part of a package of care (see 43.12 below). Otherwise the supply is liable to VAT at the standard rate. Any charge made to the local authority by the voluntary body or other organisation for implementing the service is also taxable, regardless of whether the supply is below cost or whether it includes an incidental element of care provided to the recipient of the meal. However, the local authority can recover the VAT charged under 43.7 below.

Facilities for home cooking. Instead of making arrangements for a daily delivery of meals on wheels, some local authorities make periodic deliveries of frozen meals. To support this activity, they supply cost price mini freezers, microwaves and steamers to the recipients of the food. Equipment sold in this way to facilitate a package of non-business welfare is itself a non-business supply. Any equipment that is sold for a profit, or which does not form part of a package of care, is subject to normal VAT liabilities.

(Internal Guidance V1–14, para 9.4).

(13) **Motor mileage allowances and fuel scale charges**

Where a local authority or other 'specified body' within 43.2 above pays its employees mileage allowances to reimburse them for the cost of road fuel incurred on business activities, the body can recover the input tax under the same conditions as apply to other businesses. See 45.15 MOTOR CARS. By concession, a statutory body can recover the VAT it incurs on mileage allowances paid to all persons engaged on its official activities, including its non-business activities. The concession extends not only to employees but also to councillors, JPs and voluntary workers acting as agents of the authority (eg the WRVS delivering meals on wheels). It also covers mileage rates paid to police doctors and to parents taking their children to school where the local authority would otherwise be obliged to provide transport (eg in rural areas). HMRC require that

- the individual receiving the mileage allowance is not a taxable person;
- there is a contract (written or oral) between the body and the individual covering the activities in question;
- the individual carries out the activity on a regular basis; and
- the body is obliged to undertake the activity on which the road fuel costs are incurred (or would be if the recipient of the mileage allowance did not do so).

Alternatively, where a specified body provides an employee or other person with road fuel or reimburse them for fuel used, VAT must be accounted for using the scale charges in 45.17 MOTOR CARS if the car is used for the *business* activities of the body and the latter funds any private motoring.

(Internal Guidance V1–14, Chapter 2 paras 7.23, 7.30).

(14) **Open government**

Normally, the provision of information is a standard-rated supply, unless it can be zero-rated as printed matter. But under the *Freedom of Information Act 2000* public authorities (including all local authorities, police authorities and Government departments) must provide certain information if requested. Any charge made is non-business. This non-business treatment also extends to information that they are not obliged to provide (because the cost of provision is too high) but which they choose to provide for a charge.

There is no obligation for authorities to provide information that is available from other sources, even if the enquirer cannot readily access those other sources (eg because they do not have internet access). Information provided in these circumstances is a business activity.

(Internal Guidance V1–14, para 7.27).

(15) **Police authorities**

(i) *The escort and transportation of prisoners.* Following the increasing tendency for the majority of such services to be supplied by private security firms, this is now regarded as a business activity. In a few instances, there is still a legal requirement for police authorities, or other similar official bodies, to carry out prisoner escort duties. Such services remain non-business activities.

(ii) *Police attendance at sporting events.* Local authorities are required by the *Safety of Sports Grounds Act 1975* to issue safety certificates on such terms and conditions as they consider necessary to designated stadia in their area. Where such a certificate includes conditions which make it obligatory on the holder to request the provision of police officers prior to each event, this creates a statutory monopoly for the police authority and therefore the provision of the police is a non-business activity. If, however, the holder of the certificate is not under an obligation to request the presence of the police but can instead have the event 'policed' by a private sector security firm, there is no statutory monopoly. Provision of police in these circumstances is in competition with the private sector and is a business activity.

Policing outside a stadium is non-business as this is policing in a public place. Policing in off-street shopping centres is commonly a business supply when a charge is made because many of these sites are privately owned, and the police patrol at the request of the centre managers. The supply is standard-rated as private security firms can also provide such a service.

(iii) *Contracted out vehicle removal.* See 47.8(13) OUTPUT TAX.

(Internal Guidance V1–14, paras 15.7, 15.14).

See also Internal Guidance V1–14, para 16 for examples of police activities and their VAT liabilities.

(16) **Recycling credits**

Under *Environmental Protection Act 1990, s 52(1)* waste disposal authorities must pay waste collection authorities when they divert waste from the household waste stream for recycling. Where waste is collected and sent for recycling by third parties (eg local scout groups or existing recycling companies) then both disposal and collection authorities have powers, under *Environmental Protection Act 1990, s 52(3)(4)* to pay credits to the third parties.

The payment of these recycling credits is not the consideration for a supply and is therefore outside of the scope of VAT. However, in some cases, although credits may be due to a third party, they may be retained by a local authority as consideration for a supply made to that third party (eg the granting of a licence to occupy a site for a bottle bank). In these circumstances, the credits retained by the local authority are not outside the scope of VAT but follow the liability of the supply for which they are being treated as consideration.

(Internal Guidance V1–14, para 7.29).

(17) **Returning officers' and other election expenses**

Parliamentary and European elections. Council officers frequently act as returning officers in Parliamentary and European elections. However, they are not acting as an officer of the council but in a different capacity. The Office of the Deputy Prime Minister (ODPM) makes a payment to the local authority for the provision of a returning officer to compensate it for one of its staff being diverted from local authority functions. As a local authority has to provide a returning officer by law, this payment is not subject to VAT. Similarly, where a local authority is required by law to provide polling places (eg schools) and other services, any reimbursement by the ODPM is not subject to VAT. The transport of ballot boxes is not done under any statutory obligation and is standard rated.

Where local authorities have to provide certain facilities by law, any VAT incurred on their provision will be recoverable under 43.7 below. But where the returning officer has bought goods or services from sources other than the local authority, any VAT incurred is not recoverable by the local authority and should be included in any reimbursement received from the ODPM.

The ODPM also provides funding for the purchase of such election requirements as polling booth screens and ballot boxes. Often these will be bought for the returning officer by the local authority. If the items will be used in a local election (see below) as well as other elections, the local authority can recover the VAT in full. If, however, they are bought exclusively for Parliamentary or European elections, the local authority can only recover VAT to the extent that it recharges it to the returning officer as his buying agent. Such VAT recharged to the returning officer should form part of his funding from the ODPM.

Local elections. The local authority is under a statutory obligation to provide the returning officer and it can recover any VAT it incurs in connection with local elections under the refunds scheme in 43.7 below.

(Internal Guidance V1–14, para 7.12).

(17A) **Social services activities**

See Internal Guidance V1–14, para 10.1 for a list of the duties and VAT status of various social services activities in relation to children, the elderly, and the disabled.

(18) **Sports and leisure**

If a local authority charges members of the public for sporting or recreational facilities, it is not acting in its capacity as a public authority and the activity is business.

(i) *Supplies of sporting services.* Most sporting services are exempted from VAT. See 57.9 RECREATION AND SPORT. However, local authorities are specifically excluded from the exemption and sporting services provided by them remain taxable. If the services include an element of educational training or instruction, they may qualify as exempt supplies of education. See 20.4 EDUCATION.

(ii) *Operation of leisure centres.* Local authorities may deliver leisure services by means of a

- direct service organisation (DSO) within the local authority's own leisure services department;
- non-profit distributing organisation (NPDO) such as a trust or industrial and provident society, in which the local authority may have a degree of representation; or
- a wholly independent 'for profit' leisure management contractor.

In the case of a DSO, it is the local authority itself that makes all supplies. Otherwise, the various arrangements that flow from the contracting-out process can give rise to a number of potential supplies for VAT purposes. The precise nature of these supplies and the VAT treatment of them is set out in a Memorandum of Understanding jointly agreed by HMRC and the Chartered Institute of Public Finance and Accountancy.

Leisure service membership schemes. Many local authorities offer leisure schemes where a customer can make periodic payments, normally monthly or annually, to receive free or discounted use of the authority's leisure facilities. This scheme membership is a standard-rated charge for the right to use the facilities unless the membership is exclusively for exempt activities when the charge is exempt. If the membership is used for a variety of taxable and exempt activities the charge is not to be apportioned, but is treated as wholly standard-rated. A tax point arises every time that the member pays an instalment of the fee. If the total charge for paying by instalments is greater than that for a one-off fee, then the extra charge is for an exempt supply of finance.

(VAT Notice 749, para 5.8; Internal Guidance V1–14, paras 13.1–13.3). See Internal Guidance V1–14, para 14 for the Memorandum of Understanding referred to above.

(19) **Statutory licences, etc.**

Public authorities charge for various forms of licensing and approval in a broad range of public activities taking place in their area (eg approving premises for civil marriages, registering childminders, issuing fire certificates, and licensing and registering firearms). In doing so, they are empowered to act under special legal provisions that private traders cannot call upon. This is a non-business activity. (VAT Notice 749, para 5.8).

(20) **Supplies between local authorities**

(i) *Supplies of goods*. Following the decision in *Comune di Carpaneto Piacentino and Others v Ufficio Provinciale Imposta sul Valore Aggiunto di Piacenza, CJEC [1990] 3 CMLR 153 (TVC 21.90)* HMRC have concluded that supplies of goods between local authorities are not made under any special legal regime and that the supplies do not fall to be treated as non-taxable under *EC 6th Directive, Art 4.5*. They are not, therefore, eligible for the refund scheme under 43.7 below.

(ii) *Supplies of services*. Supplies of services which include a supply of goods should be treated as business and taxable according to the normal rules. Services supplied between local authorities are non-business where they are made under a statutory obligation or where they are not in competition with the private sector. Otherwise supplies of services are business supplies.

(VAT Notice 749, para 5.2; Internal Guidance V1–14, para 7.32; Business Brief 9/95).

(21) **Supplies of staff**

Following the decision in *Comune di Carpaneto Piacentino and Others v Ufficio Provinciale Imposta sul Valore Aggiunto di Piacenza, CJEC [1990] 3 CMLR 153 (TVC 21.90)*, if a specified body within 43.2 above supplies the services of its staff

- under the same legal conditions as those applying to private businesses, it is not acting in its capacity as a public body and the supply is in the course or furtherance of a taxable business activity; and
- under a special legal regime applicable to it, the body is acting in its capacity as a public body. It can treat the supplies of staff it makes as non-business providing that such treatment would not lead to a significant distortion of competition with other bodies. See 43.1(*b*) above.

Taxable business activities include secondments of staff by

- one police authority to another for purely administrative purposes;
- a police authority to outside organisations to advise, for example, about security matters;

- a local fire service to an outside organisation to advise on fire safety matters;
- a local authority Direct Labour Organisation (DLO) to boost the management team of another DLO; or
- an LEA to an examination board to advise on methods of assessment.

Non-business activities include

- a police authority providing normal policing assistance to another force (eg in connection with an ongoing investigation) or seconding officers to the National Crime Squad or the National Criminal Intelligence Service;
- local authority fire brigades seconding experienced serving officers to the Fire Service College to act as instructors in advanced safety and rescue techniques (as no other organisations have the necessary expertise to offer an equivalent service to the college); and
- agreements to release, rather than supply, staff (eg where teachers undertake GCE and GCSE exam work or where staff are seconded to other government departments or commercial companies for career development purposes). Where staff are seconded in these circumstances and have two discrete contracts, then the authority is not considered to be making a taxable supply of the services of staff. Any reimbursement of salary is not liable to output tax. However, if the authority makes a charge for administration, this is consideration for the supply of a payroll service, and it must account for output tax on the supply.

(VAT Notice 749, para 5.8; Internal Guidance V1–14, para 7.33).

(22) **Voucher schemes**

Local authorities operate a number of different voucher schemes to enable them to fulfil their statutory obligations (eg for clothing/school uniform, decorating materials, etc). The schemes involve the issue of vouchers by the local authority which the holder can exchange for specific goods or services at nominated suppliers. The supplier forwards the redeemed vouchers to the local authority which then refunds the supplier up to the value of the vouchers redeemed.

There are no output tax implications for the authority when the vouchers are issued (providing it receives no consideration). It can only recover input tax on goods/services supplied under the various schemes where the supply is to the local authority which then makes an onward supply to the recipient. These conditions are met if the local authority

- holds a proper VAT invoice addressed to it from the supplier;
- has entered the purchase in its normal accounts; and
- holds the redeemed vouchers submitted to it by the supplier of the goods.

The local authority can only recover input tax on the value of the voucher or, if less, the value of the goods or services supplied.

(Internal Guidance V1–14, para 7.34).

(23) **Weighing instruments**

The *evaluation* and *surveillance* of non-automatic weighing instruments, to meet EC requirements, is a service that any trader with the necessary expertise can supply commercially. If a local authority carries it out, the activity is business. On the other hand, where a local authority charges to *verify* such instruments, it does so in its capacity as a public authority, using legal powers that no private contractor is entitled to exercise. Such verification is a non-business activity. (VAT Notice 749, para 5.8).

(24) **Youth centres**

There are two types of youth centre.

- *A youth centre which is part of the local authority.* HMRC accept that any purchase it makes from its own funds is actually made by the local authority which can reclaim any VAT incurred (subject to the normal rules). If income from taxable activities of the youth centre accrues to the local authority, it must also account for output tax.
- *Youth centres with charitable status.* These are independent of the local authority which is not normally entitled to recover VAT on any of the costs incurred.

However, in some cases, independent youth centres may donate funds to the local authority for a specific purpose. Where this occurs, the local authority is eligible for VAT refund if it

(i) makes the purchase (ie places the order, etc);

(ii) retains ownership;

(iii) uses the items purchased for its own non-business purposes; and

(iv) keeps sufficient records of the purchase and the purpose for which it was made to enable it to be easily identified.

If these conditions are not met, the normal VAT rules apply. The money given represents consideration for a supply by the local authority to the independent youth centre and the local authority must account for VAT.

VAT recovery. Common areas of expenditure incurred by youth centres include the following.

(*a*) *Utility costs* (eg gas and electricity). The VAT incurred is only recoverable by the local authority under 43.7 below if the youth centre is part of the local authority (and not if the centre is independent of the local authority but donates money to it to cover utility costs).

(*b*) *Repairs and maintenance to buildings.* The treatment is broadly similar to that under (*a*) above. However, if the local authority holds the freehold or lease on the premises and does not charge the independent youth centre for use of the premises, the authority is normally entitled to recover any VAT incurred.

(*c*) *Minibuses.* Where an individual youth centre purchases a minibus, the VAT treatment is as under (*a*) above. Where the purchase is by a local authority using donated funds, the local authority can recover the VAT if it satisfies (i)–(iv) above. Alternatively, HMRC may accept that the local authority can recover VAT on the purchase if

  - use of the minibus is pooled, ie it is available for use by more than one youth centre;
  - the minibus carries the local authority logo;

- the local authority treats it as part of its assets, covering repair and maintenance costs; and
- the local authority does not charge the centres for use of the minibus.

Where this applies, however, the local authority must account for output tax when the vehicle is sold.

Where an independent youth centre buys a minibus using grants provided by the local authority, the authority cannot recover the VAT.

(*d*) *Fixtures and fittings*. A local authority can recover VAT it incurs on fixtures and fittings, including sports equipment, at its own youth centres. If it uses donated funds to make the purchase, it can recover VAT if it satisfies (i)–(iv) above. This means that the items must become assets of the local authority and be available for use by other youth centres. A local authority may also recover the VAT it incurs on purchases made from its own funds and then freely given away to independent youth centres.

(*e*) *Private fund income*. Some local authority youth centres may undertake activities independently of the local authority. Any income arising as a result is 'private fund' income, normally paid to a separate account, and does not form part of local authority funds. The private fund is a separate entity for VAT purposes and the local authority cannot recover the VAT incurred on any of its purchases and need not account for output tax on supplies made by the fund.

Liability of income of local authority youth clubs. Because local authority youth centres are provided under the *Education Act 1996*, and this is a special legal regime, membership fees and subscriptions are non-business. Separately charged for activities and events will also generally be non-business.

- *Social evenings, outings and similar events*. Where such activities are arranged by the youth service for the members of the club, this income is non-business. This does not apply to events organised by other parties (eg where the youth service merely arranges for its members to be able to buy discounted tickets from an event organiser which remains a business supply by the event organiser to the individuals who take up the offer). Neither does it apply to events and activities attended by other people unless the numbers of such people are minimal (eg family outings where youth club members will not be in the significant majority are not non-business).
- *Coin operated machines*. The provision of games, amusements and entertainment machines form part of the youth service and any income derived from them is non-business.
- *Tuck shops and cafes*. Provided that sales within club premises to club members are made at or below their overhead-inclusive cost, they can be treated as non-business.

(Internal Guidance V1–14, para 7.36).

(25) Youth offending teams (YOTs)

YOTs are set up by local authorities, in partnership with police authorities, probation committees and health authorities, to establish a local structure of teams and services to deal with young offenders. Each YOT must contain at least a social worker, probation officer, police officer, a person nominated by a health authority in the local authority area, and a person nominated by the local authority's Chief Education Officer. The local authority receives funding from the Home Office for the project and the partners (who may or may not receive Home Office funding) are responsible for their share of staff and any associated costs.

Local authorities and police authorities can recover any costs under the refund scheme in 43.7 below. The only bodies unable to benefit from the refund scheme are health authorities and probation committees, although they are able to recover VAT on certain contracted out services under *VATA 1994, s 41* (see 43.11 below).

Because of the possibility of double claims by different bodies, HMRC suggest that YOT committees should 'appoint' the local authority as the claiming body for the purposes of 43.7 below (although they have no objections to the police being appointed). Any staff provided by the members would be outside the scope of VAT (as they are not being supplied to the local authority but to the scheme) and any funds that may be given would be considered outside the scope contributions.

In certain cases, local authorities may form joint YOTs. In such cases, HMRC recommended that one authority takes the lead for refund purposes, with the other simply making outside the scope contributions.

(Internal Guidance V1–14, para 7.37).

43.5 REGISTRATION

Public bodies other than local authorities. The normal registration rules apply to public bodies other than local authorities, including those specified bodies listed in 43.2 above, ie they are required to be registered only if their taxable supplies exceed the registration limit (see 59.3 REGISTRATION) but they may apply for voluntary registration under 59.2 REGISTRATION. Exemption from registration can be sought in cases where the majority of supplies are zero-rated and if registered, they would normally be in a repayment situation. See 59.6 REGISTRATION.

Local authorities. Every local authority which makes taxable supplies (including zero-rated supplies) in the course or furtherance of its business is required to be registered *whatever the value of its supplies*. [*VATA 1994, s 42*]. Despite this, HMRC do not actively encourage registration where it is expected to produce output tax of less than £1,000 a year (eg parish councils whose only taxable supplies are the occasional sale of assets).

Joint boards and joint committees. Similar rules apply to joint committees/boards which qualify as local authorities (see 43.2 above). Normally separate VAT registration is required but such bodies may, as a concession, apply to account for VAT under the VAT registration of one of the member authorities. Applications requesting such treatment are generally sought in cases where one authority has responsibility for all the accounting records or where separate registration would result in the partial exemption *de minimis* limits being exceeded. Any such application must be made to HMRC, in writing, giving reasons for wishing to do so. Permission will not generally be withheld unless there is evidence of a tax advantage to the authority which is to account for the VAT as a result of the arrangement.

Bodies having close links with a local authority (other than a joint board or committee) but which are legally separate from it and not eligible for the refund scheme (e.g housing trusts and enterprise agencies) must normally register if the value of their taxable supplies exceeds the registration limit (see 59.3 REGISTRATION).

Group registration. Specified bodies within 43.2 above, including local authorities and their joint committees, cannot normally meet the control requirements for group registration. However, where group registration is requested and all requirements for group treatment are met, claims on non-business activities are restricted to those of the specified body only not the group as a whole. Group registrations are not accorded the special treatment under 43.8 below and the group as a whole is subject to the normal partial exemption rules.

(VAT Notice 749, paras 3.1–3.3; Internal Guidance V1–14, paras 6.1–6.4).

Acquisitions of goods from other EC countries. Even if a local authority or other statutory body is not required to register under the general requirements based on taxable supplies in the UK, it may be liable to register for VAT where it makes certain acquisitions of goods from other EC countries in excess of an annual threshold. See 59.18 REGISTRATION.

43.6 RECLAIMING VAT

Where bodies within 43.2 above incur VAT in connection with taxable business activities, they can recover the VAT as input tax subject to the normal rules.

However, many of the activities of such bodies are non-business activities for VAT purposes and outside the scope of VAT. As a general rule, it is only possible to recover any VAT incurred if registered for VAT and if the VAT can be attributed to taxable business activities. Any VAT that relates to non-business or (subject to certain limits) exempt activities is not recoverable. To minimise this 'sticking' VAT for such bodies, a special scheme allows them to

- reclaim the VAT suffered on non-business activities (see 43.7 below); and
- recover any VAT attributed to exempt business activities where HMRC consider it an insignificant proportion of the total VAT incurred (see 43.8 below).

43.7 REFUND SCHEME FOR NON-BUSINESS ACTIVITIES

Generally, there is no entitlement to recovery of VAT incurred for the purposes of non-business activities. However, a special refund scheme permits a specified body within 43.2 above to reclaim the VAT chargeable on supplies of goods or services to it, acquisitions of goods by it from other EC countries and imports of goods by it from outside the EC if

- the supply, acquisition or importation is not for the purposes of a business activity carried on by the body concerned; and
- the VAT is not excluded from credit in relation to business activities (see under *Non-recoverable VAT* below).

[*VATA 1994, s 33(1)(6)*].

The scheme applies whether or not the body is registered for VAT or makes taxable supplies but non VAT-registered bodies, who cannot quote a VAT registration number when purchasing from other EC countries, will be charged VAT at source on such purchases. Any VAT charged by other EC countries is not recoverable under the scheme and refunds to non VAT-registered bodies are therefore restricted to VAT incurred on supplies and importations only.

The purpose of the scheme is to prevent VAT being a burden on local authority funding. A body can claim refunds on goods and services supplied, etc to it for non-business purposes provided the following conditions are met.

- It places the order.
- It receives the supply.
- It receives a VAT invoice addressed to it. In the case of local authorities invoices are sometimes made out in the name of a particular local authority institution (eg a school) or even an employee (eg a head teacher). Provided that the purchase meets all the other conditions for inclusion in the scheme then the VAT on such invoices may be recovered.
- It makes payment from its own funds or certain donated funds or trust funds (see below).

(VAT Notice 749, para 7.1, Internal Guidance V1–14, para 5.6).

The scheme extends to the following.

(*a*) Goods and services bought using funds given to a body for specified purposes provided

(i) the person who gives the money does not do so on condition that the body gives something or does something in return or that other persons benefit as a direct result of the payment;

(ii) the person who has given the money does not in fact receive anything in return;

(iii) the body buys the goods or services itself (ie places the order, receives the supply and a VAT invoice addressed to it and makes payment);

(iv) the body remains the owner of the goods or services and uses them, or makes them available, for its own non-business purposes; and

(v) the body keeps sufficient records for HMRC to identify the goods and services bought and the reason for buying them.

Examples of supplies which are likely meet these conditions are those used

- in local education authority maintained schools and paid for with donations from parent/teacher associations and school funds;
- in local authority welfare establishments and paid for with donations from amenity funds;
- by local authority homes and schools for the disabled and paid for with donations from voluntary bodies (eg mini-buses and TV sets, etc); and
- in local authority owned halls (or halls where the local authority is sole trustee) and paid for with donations from management or fund-raising committees.

(*b*) Purchases made from funds of a trust but only if

- the body acts as sole managing trustee (not just custodian trustee) without payment;
- the activities of the trust relate so closely to the functions of the body that they cannot be easily distinguished (eg the upkeep of a village hall);

- the claim relates to the non-business activities of the trust; and
- purchases made from the funds of a trust must not be on such a scale that they are distortive of competition.

(VAT Notice 749, paras 7.3, 7.5; Internal Guidance V1–14, paras 5.10, 5.11).

Where such non-business supplies, acquisitions or importations cannot be conveniently distinguished from business supplies, etc the refund is the amount remaining after deducting from the whole of the VAT chargeable such proportion as HMRC consider to be attributable to business purposes. [*VATA 1994, s 33(2)*].

Non-recoverable VAT. VAT which is specifically excluded from credit by the Treasury under *VATA 1994, s 25(7)* in relation to business activities is also excluded from credit by bodies in respect of their non-business activities. See, for example, 9 BUSINESS ENTERTAINMENT and 45.3 MOTOR CARS.

43.8 INPUT TAX ATTRIBUTABLE TO EXEMPT BUSINESS ACTIVITIES

A specified body within 43.2 above can recover input tax incurred directly attributable to its exempt business activities where HMRC consider it to be an 'insignificant' proportion of the total VAT incurred. [*VATA 1994, s 33(2)(b)*].

Where a special partial exemption method for specified bodies within *Sec 33* is used, '*insignificant*' means

- not more than £625 per month on average (ie not more than £7,500 p.a.); or
- less than 5% of the total VAT incurred on all goods and services purchased in a year. This total includes goods and services for business and non-business activities but excludes those on which input tax cannot be reclaimed, see 35.8 INPUT TAX.

If the input tax attributable to exempt supplies exceeds both of the above limits, then none of it may be recovered.

Where a body chooses not to adopt a special partial exemption method for specified bodies within *Sec 33*, it can use any alternative method of partial exemption calculation (see 49 PARTIAL EXEMPTION) but in that case the normal *de minimis* limits in 49.7 PARTIAL EXEMPTION apply.

(VAT Notice 749, paras 8.2–8.4).

See also 53.4 PENSION SCHEMES for concessional treatment for certain local authority pension funds.

Where any partial exemption method is used, the body must do a calculation at the end of each period, followed by an annual adjustment at the end of each financial year. This adjustment should be included in the VAT return for the next period.

Partial exemption methods. All bodies must have a partial exemption method in place that has been agreed with HMRC and continue using it until it is either withdrawn by HMRC or a new method is agreed. If a body has not agreed a special method with HMRC, it must either use the *special method for specified bodies within Sec 33* outlined below or the standard partial exemption method (see 49.4 PARTIAL EXEMPTION) but in the latter case it must then separate business and non-business activities.

A body wishing to opt for a special partial exemption method must

- contact HMRC before the start of the financial year in order to obtain advice on using a special method;
- by the start of the financial year, agree with HMRC the broad principles of the method intended to be used;
- by three months before the end of the financial year, complete discussions with HMRC and have the final method agreed in writing; and
- by 31 October following the end of the financial year include all annual calculations on a return and submit it to HMRC.

If a special method has not been agreed before the end of a financial year, it cannot be applied to that year. Under these circumstances

- a body can only begin using a special method from the start of the next tax year; and
- in the meantime, it should use the model special partial exemption method outlined below.

(VAT Notice 749, paras 8.5–8.7).

Special partial exemption method for specified bodies within *Sec 33*. This method, which is based on the budget structure, takes a worst case scenario. It assumes that where a budget heading contains an exempt activity, than all taxable expenditure within that heading is attributable to that exempt activity. If this approach shows that a body's exempt input tax is insignificant, there is no requirement to refine the calculations.

Step 1	*Identifying exempt activities.* List, within committee, all budget headings/cost centres that contain any element of exempt activity.
Step 2	*Identifying taxable expenditure.* Within each budget heading/cost centre identified under Step 1, record all expenditure (net of VAT) for both capital and revenue that would normally carry VAT.
Step 3	*Recharges.* For recharges to budget headings/cost centres that contain any element of exempt activity, record all expenditure that would normally carry VAT.
Step 4	*Calculate the percentage of exempt-related input tax.* Add up the standard-rated expenditure identified in Steps 2 and 3 and calculate the VAT on it by multiplying by 17.5%.

If the total at Step 4 is insignificant (see above), no further calculations are required. If it is not, a progressively detailed analysis must be made of the amount of expenditure which is put to exempt use. If, at any stage, a result is achieved showing that the VAT is insignificant, no further action is required. There is no set method of allocation or apportionment. A body may adopt a different method for each particular area or activity based on the information available (eg number of staff, amount of income, floor area used, number of sessions, or time, etc) provided it can demonstrate that any method used is fair and equitable. Where, despite detailed analysis of the amount of expenditure put to exempt use, the VAT identified still exceeds the 'insignificant' limit, none of the VAT relating to exempt supplies is recoverable.

(VAT Notice 749, paras 9.1–9.5).

Change of intention. Where a specified body within 43.2 above incurs VAT which it intends to use to make taxable or exempt supplies or to carry on a non-business activity, but changes that intention before it actually makes those supplies or undertakes that activity, it must review the original attribution and make any appropriate adjustment.

- *Change from taxable or non-business to exempt use*

  (1) Identify the VAT attributable to the relevant activity.

  (2) The VAT identified under (1) must be added to the total exempt input tax already determined by the refund calculation for the year in which that VAT was originally incurred. The revised result using the same method should be noted.

  (3) If the revised result can still be treated as *de minimis* or 'insignificant' (see above) for the year in which the VAT was originally incurred, no further action is required.

  (4) If the revised result exceeds, or still exceeds, the *de minimis* limit/insignificant amount for the year in which the VAT was originally incurred, then the VAT identified under (1) above must be repaid to HMRC on the next VAT return. Note that it is only the VAT refunded in respect of which there has been a change of intention that needs to be repaid. No adjustment need be made in respect of any other VAT included in the original refund calculation.

- *Changes from exempt to taxable or non-business use*

  (1) If, in the year in which the VAT was originally incurred, the body was within its *de minimis* limit, no further adjustment is required.

  (2) Otherwise, identify the VAT attributable to the relevant activity.

  (3) The VAT identified under (2) should be deducted from the exempt input tax already identified for the year in which the VAT was originally incurred.

  (4) If the new total can be treated as *de minimis*/insignificant, the VAT identified under (2) above may be reclaimed from HMRC. Note that it is only that VAT which has been identified under (2) above that may be reclaimed from HMRC. No adjustment can be made in respect of any other VAT included in the original refund calculation.

Error in attribution. If, in a subsequent year, it transpires that there has been an error in attributing VAT incurred to taxable or exempt supplies or non-business activities, the body must rework the refund calculation for the year in which the VAT was originally attributed and amend its calculation accordingly.

- If the body was *de minimis* for the year in question but, as a result of the amendment to the calculation, exempt input tax is increased so that the *de minimis* level is exceeded, the body should repay all the exempt input tax.
- If the body had already exceeded the *de minimis* level for the year in question and, as a result of the amendment to the calculation, the amount of exempt input tax increases, the authority should repay that additional exempt input tax.
- If the body had exceeded its *de minimis* level for the year in question but, as a result of the amendment to the calculation, the amount of exempt input tax decreases so that on the basis of the revised calculation the body is now within its *de minimis* limit, the body should reclaim all the exempt input tax it repaid because of previously exceeding its *de minimis* limit.

- If the authority had exceeded its *de minimis* level for the year in question and, as a result of the amendment to the calculation, the amount of exempt input tax decreases but on the basis of the revised calculation the authority still exceeds its *de minimis* limit, the authority should reclaim the amount by which its exempt input tax has been reduced.

Any adjustments required should be made in accordance with normal procedure for correcting errors (see 56.11 RECORDS).

Capital goods items adjustments. The CAPITAL GOODS SCHEME (10) cannot be applied to specified bodies within 43.2 above because the regulations refer to goods being used for business purposes rather than a mixture of business and non-business. However, it is still necessary to recognise that capital items are used over a period of time and have the ability to deal with any change of use. For this reason, the special partial exemption method includes a capital goods adjustment.

Where a specified body has a capital item as defined in 10.2 CAPITAL GOODS SCHEME and the extent to which that item is used in making exempt supplies changes, the body must carry out an appropriate adjustment to the amount of VAT which it reclaimed on the initial acquisition. For the purpose of the special method

- non-business use is treated as if it were taxable use; and
- if a body's exempt input tax is insignificant, no adjustments are required.

Otherwise, accounting adjustments should be carried out in accordance with the guidance as given in 10 CAPITAL GOODS SCHEME.

(*a*) *Change from taxable to exempt use*.

  - The amount of the adjustment should be calculated. It must not be treated as exempt input tax for the purposes of the refund calculation for the year in question and does not count towards the body's *de minimis* limit.
  - If, at the end of the year, the body remains within its *de minimis* limit, no further action is needed in respect of the capital items scheme adjustment. However, should the authority exceed its *de minimis* limit and become partly exempt, the amount calculated as needing to be adjusted must be repaid to HMRC at the same time as the exempt input tax is repaid.

(*b*) *Change from exempt to taxable use*.

  - The amount of the adjustment should be calculated. It must not be treated as input tax for the purposes of the refund calculation for the year in question and does not count towards the body's *de minimis* limit.
  - If the VAT incurred on the initial acquisition of the item was recovered in full because, in that year, the body remained below its *de minimis* limit, no further action is required in respect of the capital items scheme adjustment as the VAT was not originally restricted. But if some or all of the VAT on the initial acquisition was restricted because the body exceeded its *de minimis* limit in that year, the amount of the adjustment can be reclaimed in line with other adjustments following the refund calculation.

Bodies should keep a record of relevant capital items and the amount of VAT initially incurred and claimed as, although they may originally be *de minimis*, an adjustment may be required several years later when the *de minimis* limit is exceeded.

(*c*) *Change in VAT liability*. Where a local authority incurs VAT and attributes it to

(i) an intended taxable supply or non-business activity, or

(ii) an intended exempt supply

but, before that activity or supply takes place there is a change in the VAT liability of that supply such that it becomes exempt from VAT or taxable/non-business as the case may be, there will be no requirement retrospectively to change the treatment of the VAT previously incurred or revisit the refund calculation for the year in which the VAT was originally incurred. Where (i) above applies, it will remain recoverable in full and where (ii) above applies, it will remain exempt input tax.

(VAT Notice 749, paras 10.1–10.5: Internal Guidance V1–14, para 18.2).

43.9 CLAIMING THE REFUND

VAT-registered bodies make the claim by including the amount refundable in Box 4 of the VAT return.

Unregistered bodies. The first claim for a refund made by a non-registered body must be in writing. The claim must relate to a period of at least one month and, if for under £100, must cover a period of at least twelve months. The period chosen should always end on the last day of a calendar month. The claim should be set out as follows.

> Banking/GABS
> HM Revenue and Customs
> 7th Floor SW
> Alexander House
> 21 Victoria Street
> Southend-on-Sea
> SS99 1AU
>
> I am claiming a refund of £ for the period to to cover VAT charged on goods and services bought for [insert name of body] non-business activities. *The tax claimed includes VAT incurred for exempt business activities which can be reclaimed under Notice 749 *Local authorities and similar bodies*.
>
> Signed
>
> For [insert name of authority]
>
> Address
>
> Contact name
>
> Contact telephone number
>
> * Delete as appropriate

Second and subsequent claims are made on Form VAT 126 which is sent out with each repayment.

Time limits for claims. VAT refund claims under *VATA 1994, s 33* are subject to the three-year time limit.

- For VAT-registered bodies, the time limit is three years after the due date for the return for the VAT period in which the VAT became chargeable.
- For bodies which are not registered for VAT, the time limit is three years after the end of the month in which the body received the supply, acquisition or importation.

(VAT Notice 749, paras 8.8, 12.3–12.5).

Repayment supplement, interest and penalties.

(1) *VAT-registered bodies.* Where the repayment of a claim is delayed, repayment supplement may be due. See 51.15 PAYMENT OF VAT. Any supplement due is calculated on the full amount of the claim, including both business and non-business activities.

Where any VAT has been overpaid or underclaimed under *VATA 1994, s 78*, statutory interest may be payable. See 51.16 PAYMENT OF VAT.

Any interest or penalties due as a result of errors made on VAT returns or late submission/payment of returns is calculated on the full amount of VAT involved, including VAT attributable to both business and non-business activities.

(2) *Non-VAT-registered bodies.* Claims by such bodies are subject to neither repayment supplement nor interest/penalties. Statutory interest, may be due in certain circumstances.

De Voil Indirect Tax Service. See V5.162.

43.10 ESTIMATED RETURNS BY LOCAL AUTHORITIES

A local authority, because of the wide range of its activities, is not always able to process all its purchase invoices in time to include them on the appropriate VAT return. It may therefore apply to HMRC for permission to estimate input tax and *VATA 1994, s 33* refunds due. If approved, the local authority must calculate the average time lag for the processing of invoices, ie the time from receipt of an invoice to the date of payment. Although any appropriate method may be used, HMRC suggest the following method.

- Carry out a sampling exercise on a fully representative basis in each spending department so as to produce information on the typical time lag experienced. Samples should exclude any transactions not involving VAT.
- Calculate the overall time lag for all departments using a weighting to take into account the relative amounts spent by the various departments.

The estimate for any return period is then calculated using the formula

$I \times P \div C$

where

I = Input tax and *VATA 1994, s 33* refunds on payments made during the period

P = Number of weeks taken to process invoices

C = Number of weeks covered by the claim

The estimate is then added to the normal claim on payments made in the period. In the following and successive VAT periods, the estimate added in the previous month is deducted and the new estimate based on the current period included.

To take account of any changes in the time lag, a similar sampling exercise should be undertaken every two years and also when there is a fundamental change to the accounting system or payment policy.

(Internal Guidance V1–24A, para 5.8 and Appendix D).

43.11 GOVERNMENT DEPARTMENTS

EC law. Government departments and health authorities are 'bodies governed by public law' and, as such, are covered by *EC 6th Directive, Art 4(5)* and treated as non-taxable persons when satisfying the conditions in 43.1 above.

UK law. *VATA 1994* applies in relation to taxable supplies made by the Crown as it applies to taxable supplies by taxable persons. [*VATA 1994, s 41(1)*].

(*a*) **Supplies by government departments**. Where a 'Government department' supplies goods or services which do not amount to the carrying on of a business but it appears to the Treasury that similar supplies are, or might be, supplied by taxable persons in the course of furtherance of any business, then the Treasury may direct that the supplies by that department are treated as supplies in the course or furtherance of a business carried on by it.

'*Government department*' includes the Scottish Administration, the National Assembly for Wales, a NI department, a Northern Ireland health and social services body, any body of persons exercising functions on behalf of a Minister of the Crown (including a health service body, a National Health Service trust, an NHS foundation trust, a Primary Care Trust and a Local Health Board) and any part of such a department designated for these purposes by the Treasury.

[*VATA 1994, s 41(2)(6)–(8); Government of Wales Act 1998, Sch 12 para 35; Scotland Act 1998, Sch 8 para 30; Health Act 1999, Sch 8 para 86; National Health Service Reform and Health Care Professions Act 2002, Sch 5 para 40, Health and Social Care (Community Health and Standards) Act 2003, s 33(3)*].

The Treasury from time to time issues a direction listing, for each Government department, those supplies which are treated as supplied in the course or furtherance of a business when supplied by that department. The latest such direction was dated 3 March 1993 and has been subsequently amended by directions on 3 March 1994, 9 March 1995, 6 March 1996, 3 March 1997 and 16 March 1998.

For supplies by government departments of welfare services otherwise than for a profit, see 32.14 HEALTH AND WELFARE.

(*b*) **Supplies to government departments**. Where VAT is chargeable on

- the supply of goods or services to a 'Government department' (see above),
- the acquisition of goods by a Government department from another EC country, or

- the importation of any goods by a Government department from outside the EC

and the supply, acquisition or importation is not for the purpose of any business carried on by the department (or any supply treated as such under the above provisions) then, on a claim, the VAT may still be refunded if the Treasury so directs. The claim must be in such form and manner as HMRC determine and any refund is conditional on the department complying with requirements as to the keeping, preservation and production of records relating to the supply.

[*VATA 1994, s 41*(*3*)(*4*)].

The Treasury periodically issues a direction with a list of eligible government departments and a list of eligible goods and services on which VAT will be refunded provided the supply of those goods and services is not for the purposes of either any business carried on by the department or any supply by the department treated as a supply in the course or furtherance of a business. The latest such direction was reproduced in The London, Edinburgh and Belfast Gazettes on 10 January 2003. In practice, the only activities where such a direction is issued are those services which have been 'contracted out' to private contractors and on which the private contractor then charges VAT. See also Business Brief 18/03 for HMRC's views on the VAT position of two PFI (Private Finance Initiative) arrangements, ie 'Composite Trade' ('Contract Debtor') and 'NHS LIFT'.

Registration. Government departments and health authorities are subject to the normal VAT registration requirements. They must notify their liability to registration once their taxable turnover exceeds the registration limits (see 59.3 REGISTRATION). Alternatively, they may seek voluntary registration if their taxable turnover is below the registration threshold (see 59.2 REGISTRATION).

Accounting for VAT by government departments to the Consolidated Fund. Where a government department makes taxable supplies of goods or services and its receipts include amounts paid to it in respect of those supplies, the Treasury may allow the department to deduct any or all of the output tax due to HMRC on those supplies from the gross receipts due to the Consolidated Fund. [*FA 1999, s 21*]. In practice, such procedures have generally been adopted since the introduction of VAT.

De Voil Indirect Tax Service. See V5.161.

43.12 WELFARE SERVICES

EC legislation. See 22.17(*g*) EUROPEAN COMMUNITY LEGISLATION.

The supply by a public body of welfare services and of goods supplied in connection therewith is exempt. [*VATA 1994, Sch 9 Group 7 Item 9*].

The identical provisions apply to such supplies made by charities, state-regulated private welfare institutions (from 21 March 2002) and state-regulated private welfare agencies (from 31 January 2003). See 32.14 HEALTH AND WELFARE for full details.

Transport services. The supply of transport services for sick or injured persons in vehicles specially designed for that purpose is exempt. [*VATA 1994, Sch 9 Group 7 Item 11*].

43.13 **ADMISSION CHARGES**

Subject to certain restrictions, admission charges by public bodies to

- a museum, gallery, art exhibition or zoo, or
- a theatrical, musical or choreographic performance of a cultural nature

are exempt. See 57.6 RECREATION AND SPORT for full details.

44 Management Services and Supplies of Staff

The contents of this chapter are as follows.

44.1 MANAGEMENT SERVICES

Management services commonly arise where several traders who are separately registered for VAT, but are associated in some way, decide that one of them should purchase overhead items required by the various businesses, pay all the bills, and then recover an agreed proportion of the costs from the other traders participating in the scheme. Such an arrangement is common where the same office facilities and/or staff are shared. The 'management charges' or 'service charges' normally contain elements of staff salaries, office equipment, rent, rates, heating and lighting, stationery, telephone and postage, etc. Although such arrangements are 'domestic' and may not involve any element of profit, there may nevertheless be a taxable supply for VAT purposes, as under *VATA 1994, s 5(2)(b)* anything which is not a supply of goods but is done for a consideration is a supply of services.

However, there is no taxable supply if the persons involved are part of the same legal entity or if facilities are provided between businesses covered by a single VAT registration, eg businesses run by the same legal partnership or business included in a VAT group registration (see 31 GROUPS OF COMPANIES). Additionally, a payment described as a management charge or management services will only be a consideration if something is done by the recipient of the payment. Accounting entries or invoices are not sufficient evidence on their own of a supply having taken place. To establish whether a management charge is actually consideration for a supply for VAT purposes, HMRC consider the following questions.

- Do the supplies exist? Does the value given represent any actual supplies or is it just a book figure?
- Who is making the supply and what supply is being made? For example, if consultancy services are provided by a director who is a director of both companies, then no supply has occurred because his services are provided in the capacity of director of the second company, see *Newmir plc (VTD 10102) (TVC 7.111)*.
- How are the supplies costed? Do the values expressed have any relation to the supplies they are supposed to be for?

(Internal Guidance V1–3, para 10.5).

See *Smith & Williamson; Smith & Williamson Securities (VTD 281) (TVC 41.13)* and *C & E Commrs v Tilling Management Services Ltd* at 44.3 below. For decisions as to whether such supplies are made in the course or furtherance of a business or are domestic arrangements not in the course of any business, see *Cumbrae Properties (1963) Ltd v C & E Commrs, QB [1981] STC 799 (TVC 60.23)*, *Durham Aged Mineworkers' Homes Association v C & E Commrs, QB [1994] STC 553 (TVC 60.40)* and *Processed Vegetable Growers Association Ltd (VTD 25) (TVC 60.37)*. For the position where charges are raised between companies for use of capital, see *Laurence Scott Ltd (VTD 2004) (TVC 38.81)*.

44.2 **Sharing of premises**

The VAT treatment of any costs recovered relating to premises shared with other persons depends upon the precise terms of the arrangements. See 42.4 LAND AND BUILDINGS for a general consideration of service charges and joint occupation of premises.

44.3 **Management services and group relief**

HMRC have expressed the following views.

(*a*) If Company A incurs a tax loss and surrenders it to Company B under *ICTA 1988, s 402* without any payment, HMRC do not see any taxable supply of goods or services for VAT purposes.

(*b*) If Company A incurs a tax loss and surrenders it to Company B under *ICTA 1988, s 402* with a payment or credit to current account for the surrender of the tax loss, again HMRC do not see any taxable supply of goods or services.

(*c*) It is possible in cases (*a*) and (*b*) above, that Company A might render management services to Company B without a separate charge being made for those services. The position here depends on whether there is any arrangement linking the provision of management services to, say, the procurement or making of group relief payments. If there is, then HMRC would see a non-monetary consideration for the management services which would have to be valued to determine the amount of VAT due. If there is no such arrangement, then if the management services are provided free of charge there is no taxable supply.

(*d*) Again, Company A may render management services to Company B and make a charge for those services, at the same time surrendering group relief, with or without payment. In such a case there is clearly a taxable supply of management services, but what has to be determined is whether the money charge is the full consideration for the supply. If there is an arrangement linking the supply of management services to the procurement or making of group relief payments, then once again there would be a non-monetary consideration which would have to be valued. In such circumstances VAT would be due on the full consideration, ie on the sum of the monetary and non-monetary considerations. However, if there is no link between the management services and the group relief payments, then VAT will be due only on the charge actually made for the management services.

HMRC have also confirmed that where services are rendered between companies within the same VAT group registration then no liability to VAT arises.

(CCAB Statement TR344 June 1979).

See also *C & E v Tilling Management Services Ltd, QB 1978, [1979] STC 365 (TVC 41.1)*.

44.4 **SUPPLIES OF STAFF**

Definition. A supply of staff (which includes directors and other office holders) is made for VAT purposes if the use of an individual who is contractually employed by the supplier is provided to another person for consideration. This applies whether the terms of the individual's employment are set out in a formal contract or letter of appointment, or are on a less formal basis. The determining factor is that the staff are not contractually employed by the recipient but come under its direction. Where staff are supplied to another person but continue to operate under the direction of the supplier, this is not a supply of staff, but is a supply of those services. (The distinction is significant where the services may be zero-rated or exempt, or when determining whether or not the supply is made in the UK.)

Liability. A supply of staff is normally regarded as being made in the course or furtherance of a business and VAT must be accounted for at the standard rate. This is subject to the following exceptions.

- Certain supplies of staff are not always made in the course or furtherance of business and thus may be outside the scope of VAT. These include
  - (i) secondments between and by government departments,
  - (ii) secondments between National Health bodies, and
  - (iii) some secondments between local authorities and by local authorities where they have a statutory obligation or monopoly.
- The supply of staff to a person who belongs outside the EC or to a business belonging in another EC country is outside the scope of UK VAT.

Where supplies of staff are received from a person who belongs outside the UK, VAT must be accounted for on those supplies at the standard rate under the 'reverse charge' procedure (see 39.4 INTERNATIONAL SERVICES).

Value of supply. VAT must be charged on the full amount of the consideration for the supply of staff (whether full-time or part-time). As well as any fee, this includes recovery of staff costs from the recipient (eg salary, NICs and pension contributions). Even if the arrangements do not involve the recipient paying these staff costs to the supplier (eg because the salary is paid directly to the individual or the NICs directly to the DSS) these amounts are still part of the consideration for the taxable supply of staff. See below for limited concessions in certain cases where the recipient of the staff pays their salaries directly to the employees and/or meets the employer's obligations for PAYE, NICs, pension contributions, etc. Even where a concession applies, VAT must still be accounted for on any payments that the recipient makes direct to the employer.

Similar rules apply to the value of supplies received from outside the UK under the reverse charge procedure.

(VAT Notice 700/34/05, paras 1.1, 2.1–2.3).

(1) *Concession for hire of staff by employment businesses*

This concession will continue in force until HMRC have completed their review of the impact on employment businesses of the *Conduct of Employment Agencies and Employment Businesses Regulations 2003* made by the DTI and which came into effect on 6 July 2004. The review will commence 18 months after that date. (Business Brief 2/04).

Where an employment business within the meaning of the *Employment Agencies Act 1973* supplies a member of its staff (the employee) to another business which

(*a*) is responsible for paying the employee's remuneration directly to the employee, and/or (*b*) discharges the obligations of the employment business to pay to any third party PAYE, NICs, pension contributions and similar payments relating to the employee,

then, to the extent that any such payments form the consideration (or part) for the supply of the employee to the other business, they are disregarded in determining the value of the supply of the employee. HMRC accept that the condition in (*a*) above is satisfied where the client has a contract with a payroll company (which may be owned by, but be separate from, the employment business).

(2) *Concession for secondment of staff by businesses other than employment businesses*

Where an employer (other than an employment business within the meaning of the *Employment Agencies Act 1973*) seconds a member of its staff (the employee) to another business which

(*a*) exercises exclusive control over the allocation and performance of the employee's duties during the period of secondment; and

(*b*) is responsible for paying the employee's remuneration directly to the employee and/or discharges the employer's obligations to pay to any third party PAYE, NICs, pension contributions and similar payments relating to the employee,

then, to the extent that any payments within (*b*) above form the consideration (or part) for the secondment of the employee to the other business, they are disregarded in determining the value of seconding the employee. For these purposes, an employer is not to be treated as seconding an employee to another business if the placing of the employee with that other business is done with a view to the employer (or any person associated with him) deriving any financial gain from

- the placing of the employee with the other business, or
- any other arrangements or understandings (whether or not contractually binding and whether or not for any consideration) between the employer (or any person associated with him) and the other business (or any person associated with it) with which the employee is placed.

(3) *Concession for placement of disabled workers under the Sheltered Placement Scheme (or any similar scheme)*

Where the sponsor of a disabled worker places the worker with a host company under the Sheltered Placement Scheme (or any similar scheme) and the host company

- is responsible for paying the worker's remuneration directly to the worker; and/or
- discharges the sponsor's obligations to pay to any third party PAYE, NICs, pension contributions and similar payments relating to the worker,

then, to the extent that any such payments form the consideration (or part) for the placing of the worker with the host company, they are disregarded in determining the value of placing the worker with the host company.

(VAT Notice 700/34/05, para 4).

Employment agencies and bureaux. See 3.13 AGENTS.

Charities. See 12.5(19) CHARITIES.

44.5 Temporary suspension of an employment contract

Where an employee takes up a temporary post with another employer, there is no supply of staff provided that

(*a*) the temporary post is organised on the employee's own initiative; and

(*b*) the second employer issues the employee with a new contract or letter of appointment, temporarily suspending the employee's contract with the first employer.

To avoid doubt, a temporary suspension should normally be supported by evidence that

- there is an agreement with the first employer that the employee is to be transferred for a fixed or open-ended period, often with an entitlement to return;
- there are new conditions of employment with the second employer;
- the second employer has control over the terms and conditions of employment; or
- the second employer fixes the salary.

(VAT Notice 700/34/05, para 3.1).

44.6 Joint employment

In cases of joint employment, there is no supply of staff for VAT purposes between the joint employers.

Staff are regarded as jointly employed if their contracts of employment or letters of appointment make it clear that they have more than one employer. The contract must specify who the employers are (eg 'Company A, Company B and Company C' or 'Company A and its subsidiaries').

Staff are not regarded as jointly employed (and the provisions of 44.4 above apply) if their contract is with a single company or person, even if it

- lays down that the employee's duties include assisting other companies;
- lays down that the employee will work full-time for another company; or
- shows by the job title that the employee works for a group of associated companies (eg group accountant).

(VAT Notice 700/34/05, para 3.2).

44.7 Paymaster services for associated companies

Paymaster services commonly arise in two situations.

- Where staff are jointly employed, one of the joint employers may undertake to pay all salaries, National Insurance and pension contributions which are then recovered from the other employers.
- Where a number of associated companies each employs its own staff, one company may pay all salaries, etc on behalf of the others, each associate then paying its share of the costs to the paymaster.

In either case, the recovery of monies paid out by the paymaster is not subject to VAT and is treated as a disbursement (see 3.7 AGENTS).

VAT must be accounted for on any charge made for paymaster services over and above the reimbursement of the costs paid out unless

- the recipient belongs outside the EC or is a business which belongs in another EC country (in which case the supply is outside the scope of UK VAT); or
- the supply is between companies within the same VAT group registration (in which case it is disregarded).

(VAT Notice 700/34/05, para 3.3).

44.8 **Appointments to directorships and other offices**

The appointments of an individual as a director or other paid office holder (eg secretary, treasurer) can give rise to a VAT liability as a supply of staff in the following circumstances.

(1) **Sole proprietors and partnerships providing professional services**

A sole proprietor providing professional services (eg a solicitor or accountant) or a partner in a firm providing such services who takes up a professional appointment as a director or other office holder must account for VAT on any payment received if

(i) the appointment results from the professional expertise exercised in the business or partnership business,

(ii) the duties as a director or other office holder involve, at least in part, the use of that expertise, and

(iii) in the case of a partnership, the payments received accrue to the partnership and are not retained by the partner personally.

See *Birketts (VTD 17515) (TVC 60.152)* concerning various offices held by partners in the firm. The tribunal held that the tests to be applied were 'did one or more of the solicitors accept the offices in the course of furtherance of their profession' and 'did one or more of the solicitors accept the offices in the course or furtherance of the partnership business'.

See also *Oglethorpe Sturton & Gillibrand (VTD 17491) (TVC 60.151).*

Where, however, under the terms of an appointment as an office holder, the person concerned is treated as an employee, any fees or payments made to the sole proprietor or partner personally are outside the scope of VAT.

(2) **Employees and directors**

(*a*) *Request made to a company for the supply of a director.* If a company allows an employee or director to serve as a director of a second company, following an approach from that company, it must account for VAT on any payment it receives for agreeing to the appointment.

(*b*) *Common directors.* An individual involved in a number of companies may be a director of each. In general, where, for convenience, his total emoluments from all the businesses are paid by one company which recovers appropriate proportions from the others, any services to which the charges relate (eg attending meetings or approving expenditure) can only be the director's supplies to the companies of which he is a director.

As these services are supplied directly to the relevant businesses by the individual and not across from one company to another, there is no supply from one company to another and no VAT is due on the share of money recovered from each company.

(*c*) *Voluntary personal appointment of a director.* Where an individual director or employee personally arranges to be appointed to the directorship of a second company and receives payment from that company in return, the first company is not required to account for VAT on any payments to the appointee. The appointment must be a purely personal one and not a means for the first company to deliver its service (eg consultancy services).

(*d*) *Right of a company to appoint a director.* Where a company exercises a legal or contractual right to appoint a director to the board of another company (eg a company in which it is investing) and that director does not give expert advice or take an active part in the running of the company, there is no supply for VAT purposes and any remuneration is outside the scope of VAT. Normally, however, in such circumstances the director is appointed because of his specialist knowledge and to give expert advice to the other company. In such a case, any fee charged by the company appointing the director for such advice and for taking an active part in the running of the other company is a supply for which the remuneration is taxable.

(*e*) *Banks, etc.* Where a bank or similar institution appoints a director to the board of a UK investee company as the condition of a loan, any charges for the director's services are part of the consideration for the loan and treated as an exempt supply. (Hansard 3 February 1993, Cols 185, 186).

(VAT Notice 700/34/05, paras 3.4–3.8).

45 Motor Cars

Cross-references. See 23.34 EUROPEAN COMMUNITY: SINGLE MARKET for the refund of VAT on the supply of a new motor car by a non-taxable person to another EC country; 23.35 EUROPEAN COMMUNITY: SINGLE MARKET for the acquisition of a new motor car from another EC country by a non-taxable person; 25.16 EXPORTS for sale of vehicles outside the EC; 34.15(13) IMPORTS; 61 SECOND-HAND GOODS for the second-hand scheme for motor cars and 62 SELF-SUPPLY for explanation of such deemed supplies.

The contents of this chapter are as follows.

45.1 DEFINITION OF A MOTOR CAR

For VAT purposes a motor car is any motor vehicle of a kind normally used on public roads which has three or more wheels and either

(*a*) is constructed or adapted solely or mainly for the carriage of passengers; or

(*b*) has to the rear of the driver's seat roofed accommodation which is fitted with side windows or which is constructed or adapted for the fitting of side windows.

It does not include the following.

(i) Vehicles capable of accommodating only one person.

(ii) Vehicles capable of carrying twelve or more seated persons and which meet the requirements of *Road Vehicles* (*Construction of Use*) *Regulations 1986*, *Sch 6* (road safety regulations).

(iii) Vehicles of not less than three tonnes unladen weight (as defined in *Road Vehicles* (*Construction of Use*) *Regulations 1986*).

(iv) Vehicles constructed to carry a 'payload' of one tonne or more. '*Payload*' is the difference between a vehicle's kerb weight and its maximum gross weight, both terms as defined in *Road Vehicles* (*Construction of Use*) *Regulations 1986*. This change means that certain dual purpose vehicles, commonly called twin cab or double cab pick-ups, are no longer cars for VAT purposes. A few double cabs carry a payload of under one tonne. Customs Centre of Operational Expertise for the Motor Trade (COPE) maintains a schedule of double cab pick-up vehicles and their ex-works payloads. Agreement has been reached with the Society of Motor Manufacturers and Traders about the treatment of optional accessories which dealers or others may add to a double cab potentially converting it into a car (by increasing the kerb weight and decreasing the payload). (See Internal Guidance V1–13, para 25.1 and VAT Notice 700/57/04).

(v) Caravans, ambulances and prison vans.

(vi) Vehicles constructed for a special purpose other than the carriage of persons and having no other accommodation for carrying persons than such as is incidental to that purpose.

[*SI 1992/3122, Art 2; SI 1995/1268, Art 2; SI 1999/2831; SI 1999/2832*].

In a case concerning provisions in *Car Tax Act 1983* similar to *SI 1992/3122, Art 2*, it was held that in (*b*) above 'accommodation' means only accommodation for passengers and, if the space is unsuitable for this purpose, the vehicle is not within the definition even if there are side windows (*R v C & E Commrs (ex p Nissan UK Ltd), CA [1988] BTC 8003 (TVC 42.39)*).

Vehicles regarded as motor cars (subject to (iv) above)

- *Imported versions of saloon cars* even where they are 'normally used on public roads' which are outside the UK (*Withers of Winsford Ltd v C & E Commrs, QB [1988] STC 431 (TVC 42.3)*).
- An *estate car* with the rear seat removed (*County Telecommunications Systems Ltd (VTD 10224) (TVC 42.8)*); used for business purposes by a builder (*Gardner (MC) (VTD 588) (TVC 42.6)*); and licensed as a goods vehicle and used by a garage and grocery store (*Howarth (VTD 632) (TVC 42.7)*).
- A Chevrolet K10 Blazer (*Yarlett (VTD 1490) (TVC 42.9)*).
- A Citroen van modified by fitting windows behind the driver's seat (*Browsers Bookshop (VTD 2837) (TVC 42.23)*).
- A Daihatsu Fourtrak Estate (*Specialised Cars Ltd (VTD 11123) (TVC 42.25)*).
- A Datsun pick-up truck, modified by the addition of a detachable hard top superstructure with two side windows and a hatchback to the rear of the driver's seat but no seating accommodation (*HKS Coachworks Ltd (VTD 1124) (TVC 42.16)* but see *R v C & E Commrs* (*ex p Nissan UK Ltd*) above).
- A Ford Escort, the rear seats of which could be folded away (*RC Lucia (VTD 5776) (TVC 42.4)*).
- An Isuzu pick-up (*BC Kunz (t/a Wharfdale Finance Co) (VTD 13514) (TVC 42.29)*).
- A Land Rover converted into a 'motor car' by being fitted with a hard top body with side windows and upholstered seats (*Chartcliff Ltd (VTD 262) (TVC 42.1)*); or by being modified by the addition of a metal canopy with side windows (*Wigley (VTD 7300) (TVC 42.2)*).
- A Range Rover even though first registered, and taxed, as a heavy goods vehicle and not used for domestic purposes (*C & E Commrs v Jeynes t/a Midland International (Hire) Caterers, QB 1983, [1984] STC 30 (TVC 42.18)*).
- A Suzuki jeep modified by the fitting of a rear seat although it had no rear windows (*S Compton (t/a Stan Compton Electrical Engineers & Contractors) (VTD 10259) (TVC 42.21)*); and a Suzuki Vitara Sport *(W McAdam (VTD 13286) (TVC 42.27)*).

- A Toyota Hiace van fitted with side windows (*Knapp (VTD 778) (TVC 42.11)*); a Toyota Hilux (*Western Waste Management Ltd (VTD 17428) (TVC 42.15)*); a Toyota Previa with the middle and rear rows of seats removed for delivery purposes (*Gorringe Pine (VTD 14036) (TVC 42.12)*); and a Toyota Space-cruiser with the rear seats removed and a hanging rail for transporting clothes installed (*Mr & Mrs M Gohil (t/a Gohil Fashions) (VTD 15435) (TVC 42.14)*).

- A Volkswagen tipping truck with, in addition to the driver's cab with room for one other passenger, a second roofed cab behind the driver's cab with room for three more passengers (*Weatherproof Flat Roofing (Plymouth) Ltd (VTD 1240) (TVC 42.5)*); a Volkswagen pick-up truck with roofed accommodation fitted with side windows to the rear of the driver's seat (*Readings & Headley (VTD 1535) (TVC 42.10)*); and a Volkswagen Caravelle with removable rear seats (*Intercraft UK Romania (VTD 13707) (TVC 42.32)*).

Vehicles not regarded as motor cars

- Ice cream vans, mobile shops and offices, hearses (see also *KP Davies (VTD 831) (TVC 42.36)*) and bullion vans (which are all regarded as falling under (v) above). (VAT Notice 700/64/02, para 2.2).

- Vehicles originally suitable for carrying twelve or more persons but with seating capacity reduced below twelve because of the provision of wheelchair space for disabled passengers. (VAT Notice 48, ESC 3.12). To benefit from this concession, the owner must make a written request to HMRC giving details of the vehicle and with a declaration that it conforms with recognised standards of construction and is equipped with approved fittings and means of access for disabled travellers. (HC Official Report, 21 March 1991, vol 188 cols 506, 507).

- Motor caravans provided they conform with criteria agreed with the Society of Motor Manufacturers and Traders (SMMT). The agreement specifies that, to be treated as a motor caravan, the vehicle must incorporate a permanently installed sink and cooking facilities; seating arrangements to enable diners to sit at the meal table; at least one bed with a minimum length of 1.82 metres; and a permanently installed fresh water tank with a minimum capacity of 10 litres. (Internal Guidance V1–13, para 17.6).

- A pick-up truck with an attached, removable canopy (*K M Batty (VTD 2199) (TVC 42.37)*).

- A Daihatsu Fourtrak Commercial Hard Top with two folding rear seats (*AL Yeoman Ltd (VTD 4470) (TVC 42.43)*).

- A Ford van fitted with wooden benches but no side windows (*Chartcliff Ltd (VTD 262) (TVC 42.35)*); and a Ford Transit van adapted by inserting rear seats of heavy duty plastic but with no rear windows, handrails or seat belts (*Chichester Plant Contractors Ltd (VTD 6575) (TVC 42.41)*).

- A Land Rover with two folding seats in the rear (*Bolinge Hill Farm (VTD 4217) (TVC 42.42)*); a 12-seat Land Rover with the rear bench seats removed (*P Oddonetto (VTD 5208) (TVC 42.44)*); and a Land Rover modified by a half-sized window in the nearside rear panel (*TH Sheppard (VTD 13815) (TVC 42.45)*).

- A Peugeot van modified by adding a window on each side behind the driver's seat for safety reasons (*John Beharrell Ltd (VTD 6530) (TVC 42.46)*).

Car-derived vans. A number of manufacturer's models start life as a motor car but are subsequently altered. On the exterior, these vehicles look like a motor car but their interior has been altered to give the appearance and functionality of a van. The rear seats and seat belts along with their mountings have been completely removed and the rear area of the shell is fitted with a new floor panel to create a load area. In addition, the side windows to the rear of the driver's seat are fitted with immovable opaque panels. HMRC do not view such a car-derived vehicle as a motor car for VAT purposes if:

- The technical criteria specified in HMRC guidance are met by the manufacturer. The criteria relate to how any alterations to the vehicle have been effected.
- The adaptations give the vehicle the functionality of a commercial vehicle. (The removal of a bench seat or similar from what is essentially a two-seater car would not automatically satisfy HMRC's requirements.)
- The space that remains behind the front row of seats is highly unsuitable for carrying passengers.

HMRC, in partnership with the manufacturers, are developing a list of car-derived vans on which VAT can be deducted (subject to the normal rules). In the meantime, if businesses are in any doubt, they should obtain confirmation in writing from the vendor that the vehicle meets the technical criteria.

(Business Brief 16/04).

Combination vans. Whilst these vehicles have the appearance of vans, they are designed to be fitted with or include additional seats behind the front row of seats to enable the carriage of passengers. Such vehicles are motor cars for VAT purposes except in the case of:

- Larger vehicles which have a payload of more than one tonne (see (iv) above).
- Those vehicles where the dedicated load area (ie that load area which is completely unaffected by the additional seating) is of a sufficient size compared to the passenger area to make the carriage of goods the predominant use of the vehicle.

Where a business has bought a combination van which does not fall within the above exceptions, it is a motor car under VAT legislation. If it has recovered the VAT incurred on the purchase, it must make an adjustment to correct this overclaim.

(Business Brief 16/04).

De Voil Indirect Tax Service. See V1.293.

45.2 TRANSACTIONS INVOLVING MOTOR CARS

The Treasury may, by order, provide that VAT charged on specified supplies, acquisitions and importations is excluded from credit for input tax against output tax. [*VATA 1994,s 25(7)*]. Provisions relating to motor cars have been made under *The Value Added Tax (Cars) Order 1992 (SI 1992/3122)* and the *Value Added Tax (Input Tax) Order 1992 (SI 1992/3222)* as amended. With certain exceptions, a taxable person cannot reclaim input tax on the purchase of a car (see 45.3 below) and no VAT is chargeable when the car is sold unless the selling price exceeds the purchase price (see 45.4 below). Certain transactions are not treated as taxable supplies (see 45.5 below) and special rules apply to self-supplies (see 45.6 below). For the position of car dealers see 45.7 below.

The validity of the UK input tax blocking order was upheld in *Royscot Leasing Ltd and others v C & E Commrs, CJEC [1999] STC 998 (TVC 21.282)*.

Fleet buyer bonuses and dealer demonstration bonuses. A fleet buyer bonus is given by a manufacturer or sole concessionaire to a customer who makes a bulk purchase of vehicles. A dealer demonstrator bonus is a payment made, or credit allowed, by a manufacturer or sole concessionaire to a dealer who agrees to adopt a car as a demonstration vehicle. HMRC now accept that such bonuses are normally to be treated as discounts by the manufacturer or sole concessionaires which reduce the value of their supplies. (Business Brief 16/97).

Fleet leasing bonuses. A fleet leasing bonus is given by a car manufacturer or dealer to a business which has leased a number of vehicles previously sold by the manufacturer or dealer to intermediaries. HMRC now accept that such bonuses are normally to be treated as discounts by the manufacturer or dealer which reduce the value of their supplies (rather than consideration for a supply of services by the customer). (Business Brief 1/98).

45.3 **Purchase of a car**

Apart from the special cases listed below, VAT cannot be reclaimed on the purchase (including acquisition or importation) of a motor car as defined in 45.1 above. Purchase means not only outright purchase but also any purchase under a hire purchase agreement or any other agreement whereby property in the car eventually passes eg a lease-purchase agreement. See 45.11 below for input tax on cars leased or hired.

VAT on supplies integral with the supply of a motor car is only deductible where input tax on the motor car is deductible. This includes manufacturer's warranty (although VAT on the purchase of an extension of the period of warranty is deductible). It has been held to include manufacturer's delivery charges passed on by dealers to customers. See *Wimpey Construction UK Ltd (VTD 808) (TVC 42.91)* and *C & E Commrs v British Telecommunications plc, HL [1999] STC 758 (TVC 42.92)*.

See 45.13 below for fitted optional extras and accessories.

Special cases. VAT may be reclaimed on the purchase, acquisition or importation of a motor car in the following special circumstances.

(*a*) **Exclusive business use.** The motor car is a 'qualifying' motor car (see below) supplied to, or acquired or imported by, a taxable person who intends to use the motor car exclusively for business purposes. This condition is *not* satisfied if the taxable person intends to

(i) let it on hire to any person either for no consideration or consideration less than would be payable in an arm's length commercial transaction; or

(ii) make it available, otherwise than by letting on hire, to any person (including, where the taxable person is an individual, himself or, where the taxable person is a partnership, a partner) for private use (whether or not for a consideration).

HMRC regard a car as being used exclusively for a business purpose if it is used only for business journeys *and* it is not available for private use, a car being treated as available for private use when there is nothing preventing the owner or an employee from using the car for private use. HMRC do accept that

- VAT can be recovered on the purchase of a pool car provided it is

(1) normally kept at the principal place of business;

(2) not allocated to an individual; and

(3) not kept at an employee's home;

- cars bought or imported for the purpose of sale and lease back will not be treated as available for private use provided output tax is accounted for on the resale to the leasing company in the same VAT period as input tax is recovered on the purchase; and
- VAT can be recovered on cars bought for in-house leasing provided the amounts charged to the lessee are not less than those for a commercial arm's length letting.

(VAT Notice 700/64/02, paras 3.5–3.9).

Court decisions. In *Upton (t/a Fagomatic) v C & E Commrs, CA [2002] STC 640 (TVC 42.102)* a trader, who lived in Central London, reclaimed input tax on the purchase of a Lamborghini. The tribunal allowed the trader's appeal, as all the shops which the trader visited were within walking distance of his home and he always used taxis to attend social engagements. The High Court, however, reversed this decision holding that, on the evidence, the trader had made the car available for private use. The fact that the tribunal had accepted the trader's evidence that he did not need to use the car privately was not conclusive. The only cars which could be held to be used exclusively for business purposes were

- those which were not physically available for private use (eg cars used for leasing);
- cars which it would not be realistically possible to put to a private use (eg marked police cars and emergency vehicles); and
- cars which were insulated from the possibility of private use through the way in which they were allocated to staff (eg business cars held in a pool and not allocated to any individual).

The Court of Appeal upheld this decision. The 'intention to use' is not synonymous with the 'intention to make available'. Where an individual trader acquires a car, the very fact of his deliberate acquisition of the car, whereby he makes himself the owner of the car and controller of it, means that he must intend to make it available to himself for private use, even if he never intends to use it privately.

The decision in *Upton* was approved in *C & E Commrs v Skellett (CH) (t/a Vidcom Computer Services), CS 2003, [2004] STC 201 (TVC 42.103)*. It was held that the effect of (i) and (ii) above was that where a motor vehicle is acquired by a sole trader, the vehicle will have been made available to that person for private use unless effective steps are taken to render the vehicle *incapable* of such use by that person. In that case, input tax deduction was not allowed on the purchase of a Mitsubishi Shogun even though the appellant claimed that it was used solely for business purposes (having been equipped as a mobile office and workshop with computer and e-mail facilities) and he used another car owned by his fiancée for private motoring.

However, in *C & E Commrs v Elm Milk Ltd, Ch D [2005] STC 776) (TVC 42.127)* a claim for input tax recovery on the purchase of a Mercedes was allowed where the company had minuted a resolution that it was for business use only and that it would be breach of the employee's terms of employment to use it for private use.

Tribunal decisions. There have been a significant number of tribunal cases where the appellant was unsuccessful. In *Martinez (VTD 16320) (TVC 42.101)* the tribunal rejected a claim by a second-hand car dealer that a four-wheel drive Nissan, used to pull a trailer for collection and delivery of vehicles, had been purchased exclusively for business purposes, even though the appellant maintained that the trailer was kept permanently attached to the car. As the appellant's only other private car was not purchased until two months after the Nissan, the tribunal concluded that, at the time of acquiring the Nissan, the appellant could not have been sure of having another car available at all times for private use (despite being able to use any of the business stock of cars) and therefore had probably not intended the Nissan to have exclusive business use. See also *GDG Jones (VTD 14535) (TVC 42.98)* and *PC & AM Wood (VTD 14804)*. In the latter case, the tribunal observed, applying *dicta* of the Advocate-General in *Enkler v Finanzamt Homburg, CJEC [1996] STC 1316 (TVC 21.81)*, that 'the important point is that the consumer always has the opportunity to use the asset whenever he finds it necessary or desirable to do so'. If circumstances change and the car is subsequently made available for private use, output tax must be accounted for at the time of change on the full current value of the car. HMRC have indicated that they will look closely at all cases of purported change of intention and, in the case of incorrect claims, will charge interest and penalties where appropriate.

Appellants have been successful in some tribunal cases although these should now be considered in the light of the court decisions above. In *Neil MacLeod (Prints & Enterprises) Ltd (VTD 17144) (TVC 42.114)* the tribunal accepted exclusive business use where a car had been issued to the company's sales representative who already had a private car and had been instructed not to use the company car for private motoring. In *Lowe (VTD 15124) (TVC 42.116)* the tribunal accepted that a large four-wheel drive vehicle had been purchased exclusively for business use as the trader already owned two other vehicles, including a saloon car used for private journeys. In *Thompson (VTD 14777) (TVC 42.115)* the appellant successfully contended that four cars which he purchased were used exclusively for business purposes as he had insured them for business use only so that they would be uninsured if used for any private purpose. But subsequently the same appellant's appeal was dismissed in *Thompson (t/a HAS Thompson & Co) v C & E Commrs (No 2) [2005] All ER(D) 202 (Mar) (TVC 42.105)* where the tribunal held, applying *Upton* above, that six cars purchased were available for private use, even though he already owned other cars which he could use privately. In *Squibb & Davies (Demolition) Ltd (VTD 17829) (TVC 42.125)* the tribunal, distinguishing *Upton* above, accepted exclusive business use of a Range Rover (equipped with a fax machine and designed as a mobile office for overnight work on railway sites) and a Jaguar (purchased to transport important clients and which was not available for private motoring and had only travelled 10,000 miles in 18 months with each journey being recorded in a notebook).

(*b*) **Mini-cabs, self-drive hire, driving instruction**. The motor car is a 'qualifying' motor car supplied to, or acquired or imported by, a taxable person who intends to use the motor car primarily

(i) to provide it on hire with the services of a driver for the purposes of carrying passengers;

(ii) to provide it for 'self-drive hire'; or

(iii) as a vehicle in which instruction in driving of a motor car is to be given by him.

'*Self-drive hire*' means hire where the hirer is the person normally expected to drive the motor car and the period of hire to each hirer (together with the period of hire of any other motor car expected to be hired to him by the taxable person) will normally be less than both 30 consecutive days and 90 days in any twelve month period.

(*c*) **Motor dealers and manufacturers**. The motor car forms part of the 'stock in trade' of a 'motor manufacturer' or a 'motor dealer'.

'*Stock in trade*' means new or second-hand motor cars (other than second-hand motor cars which are not qualifying motor cars as defined below) which are

- produced by a motor manufacturer for the purpose of resale and intended to be sold by that manufacturer within 12 months of their production, or
- supplied to, or acquired from another EC country or imported by, a motor dealer for the purpose of resale and intended to be sold by that motor dealer within 12 months of their supply, acquisition or importation.

Such motor cars do not cease to be stock in trade where they are temporarily put to a use in the motor manufacturer's or motor dealer's business which involves making them available for private use. Where a car does cease to be stock in trade and no longer qualifies for input tax recovery, a self-supply arises under 45.6 below.

'*Motor manufacturer*' means a person whose business consists (in whole or part) of producing motor cars including producing a motor car by conversion of a vehicle (whether a motor car or not).

'*Motor dealer*' means a person whose business consists (in whole or in part) of obtaining supplies of, or acquiring from another EC country or importing, new or second-hand motor cars for resale with a view to making an overall profit on the sale of them (whether or not a profit is made on each sale).

(*d*) **Motability Scheme**. The motor car is unused and is supplied to a taxable person whose only taxable supplies are concerned with the letting of motor cars on hire to another taxable person whose business consists predominantly of making supplies within *VATA 1994, Sch 8 Group 12 Item 14* (see 32.33 HEALTH AND WELFARE).

'Qualifying' motor cars. A 'qualifying' motor car for the purposes of (*a*)-(*c*) above is generally one which has never been supplied, acquired or imported in circumstances where VAT was wholly excluded from credit as input tax. Under normal circumstances, therefore, a qualifying car will be a new car or a used car where the previous owners were able to recover VAT on their purchase in full (eg cars disposed of by a leasing company with a registration letter of 'N' or later are likely to be qualifying cars).

This is subject to two qualifications.

(1) Specifically excluded from qualifying is a motor car which is supplied, etc to a taxable person on or after 1 August 1995 and which has been supplied on a letting on hire by him before that date. However, HMRC are, by concession, prepared to accept a car as 'qualifying' (despite any prepayment of leasing charges made before 1 August 1995) provided the car is first registered and the

lease is first invoiced on or after 1 August 1995; the invoice identifies the car as 'qualifying'; and both the lessor and lessee follow the tax rules applying to qualifying vehicles (which includes applying the 50% block to the lessee's deduction of VAT on the prepayment, see 45.11 below). (Business Brief 21/95).

(2) As a transitional measure, a taxable person may elect to treat a motor car as a qualifying motor car if it was supplied, etc to him before 1 August 1995 in circumstances where VAT was wholly excluded from credit as input tax; it is first registered on or after 1 August 1995; and it was not supplied on a letting on hire by him before that date. Where such an election is made and the motor car meets all the necessary conditions for 100% input tax relief, input tax may be recovered in the first VAT period commencing on or after 1 August 1995.

[*SI 1992/3222, Art 7; SI 1995/281; SI 1995/1666; SI 1999/2930*].

Fleet buyer bonuses. See 45.2 above.

De Voil Indirect Tax Service. See V3.443.

45.4 Disposal of a motor car used in a business

Where input tax was wholly excluded from credit on the purchase of the car. Following the decision in *EC Commission v Italian Republic, CJEC [1997] STC 1062 (TVC 21.238)*, the onward sale of a motor car on which input tax was blocked on purchase is an exempt supply under *VATA 1994, Sch 9 Group 14*, regardless of whether it is sold at a profit or loss. See 24.4 EXEMPT SUPPLIES. Any input tax incurred in making the sale (eg valeting fees, auction fees) is exempt input tax and not recoverable. (VAT Notice 700/64/02, para 7.2).

Where any input tax was deductible on the purchase of the car, output tax must be accounted for on the full selling price. A VAT invoice must be issued to a VAT-registered buyer who requests one. Such a car cannot be sold under the margin scheme for SECOND-HAND GOODS (61). (VAT Notice 700/64/02, para 7.1).

Where VAT was not charged on the purchase of the car (eg a purchase from a private individual or from a dealer who sold it under the VAT second-hand margin scheme) VAT need not be accounted for on the full selling price. The second-hand margin scheme can be used to account for VAT only on any profit made on the sale. See 61 SECOND-HAND GOODS. (VAT Notice 700/64/02, para 7.3).

45.5 Transactions not treated as taxable supplies

The following transactions relating to motor cars have been designated as outside the scope of VAT so as to be neither a supply of goods nor a supply of services.

(*a*) The disposal by a person who repossessed it under the terms of a 'finance agreement' of a used motor car in the same condition as it was when it was so repossessed. This does not apply unless the VAT on any previous supply, acquisition or importation was wholly excluded from credit under 45.3 above.

'*Finance agreement*' means any agreement for the sale of goods whereby the property in those goods is not to be transferred until the whole of the price has been paid and the seller retains the right to repossess the goods.

As a finance company that repossesses a motor car may have some practical difficulty in establishing whether or not input tax has previously been blocked, HMRC have agreed with the trade that where

- an 'N' or later registration prefix car has been supplied under the terms of a finance agreement to a leasing company or car dealer, or
- a 'K' or later registration prefix car has been similarly supplied to a taxi, driving school or daily rental business

the finance company should treat the repossessed car as input tax relieved by the purchaser (unless it has evidence to the contrary) and therefore account for VAT on its sale. (Internal Guidance V1–9, para 18.21).

(*b*) The disposal of a used motor car by an 'insurer' who has taken it in settlement of a claim under a policy of insurance where the car is disposed of in the same condition as it was when it was so acquired. This does not apply unless the VAT on any previous supply, acquisition or importation was wholly excluded from credit under 45.3 above.

Before 1 January 2005, '*insurer*' was restricted to either

- a person who has permission under *Financial Services and Markets Act 2000, Part 4* to effect and carry out contracts of insurance against risks arising from loss of or damage to goods; or
- an EEA firm of the kind mentioned in *Financial Services and Markets Act 2000, Sch 3 para 5*(*d*) which has permission under *para 15* of that *Schedule* to effect and carry out in the UK contracts of insurance against risks arising from loss of or damage to goods.

(*c*) The disposal of a motor car for no consideration (eg scrap). This does not apply unless the VAT on any previous supply, acquisition or importation was wholly excluded from credit under 45.3 above.

(*d*) Services in connection with a supply of a used motor car provided by an agent acting in his own name to the purchaser of the motor car, the consideration for which is taken into account in calculating the price at which the agent sold the car. See 61.26 SECOND-HAND GOODS.

(*e*) Services in connection with the sale of a used motor car provided by an auctioneer acting in his own name to the vendor or purchaser of the motor car, the consideration for which is taken into account in calculating the price at which the agent obtained (or, as the case may be, sold) the car. See 61.53 SECOND-HAND GOODS.

(*f*) Where a taxable person has purchased or has let on hire a motor car

(i) the letting on hire of that motor car by the taxable person to any person for no consideration or consideration less than would be payable in an arm's length commercial transaction, or

(ii) the making available of that motor car (otherwise than by letting on hire) by the taxable person to any person for private use (whether or not for a consideration)

provided that VAT on any previous supply, acquisition, importation or letting on hire of the motor car was wholly excluded from credit under 45.3 above or partly excluded from credit under 45.11 below.

Where the taxable person is an individual or partnership, included under (ii) above is the making available of the motor car to the individual himself or a partner.

The effect of this is that most charges to employees for the private use of a car are not taxable. See 45.18 below.

[*VATA 1994, s 5(3); SI 1992/3122, Arts 2, 4; SI 1995/1269; SI 1995/1667; SI 2001/3649, Art 432; SI 2004/3084*].

45.6 Self-supply

Where a person has obtained input tax credit on a motor car, and has put it to a use that would not qualify for such credit, special 'self-supply' provisions require him to account for VAT on the motor car. The detailed provisions are as follows.

A motor car is treated as self-supplied where

(*a*) it is produced by a taxable person otherwise than by conversion of a vehicle obtained by him,

(*b*) it is produced by a taxable person by the conversion of another vehicle (whether a motor car or not) and VAT on the supply to, or acquisition or importation by, the taxable person of that vehicle was not wholly excluded from credit, or

(*c*) it is supplied to, or acquired from another EC country or imported by, a taxable person and input tax on that supply, acquisition or importation was not wholly excluded from credit,

and that motor car has not been supplied by the taxable person in the course or furtherance of any business carried on by him but is used by him such that, had the motor car been supplied to, or acquired or imported by, him at that time, any input tax would have been wholly excluded from credit under 45.3 above.

A motor car is also treated as self-supplied where

(i) it was transferred to a taxable person under a transaction relating to the transfer of a business as a going concern (TOGC) which was treated as neither a supply of goods nor a supply of services (see 8.10 *et seq* BUSINESS);

(ii) in the hands of the transferor or any 'predecessor' of his the self-supply provisions applied by virtue of (*a*), (*b*) or (*c*) above; and

(iii) the motor car has not been treated as self-supplied under these provisions by the transferor or any of his predecessors.

For this purpose, a person is the '*predecessor*' of the transferor where the transferor acquired the motor car from him under a TOGC which was treated as neither a supply of goods nor a supply of services; and a transferor's predecessors include the predecessors or his predecessor through any number of transactions.

Where a group registration is in operation, self-supplies by group members are deemed to be made by the representative member.

[*VATA 1994, s 5(5), s 43(2); SI 1992/3122, Arts 5, 7; SI 1995/1269; SI 1995/1667; SI 1999/2832*].

Value of self-supply. *If the car is new*, the value of the self-supply by a UK manufacturer is the full cost of manufacturing the vehicle including related production overheads. For volume manufacturers, this can be taken to be ⅔rds of the current retail list price. Non-volume manufacturers may also use this approximation with the agreement of HMRC. For non-manufacturing traders, the self-supply cost should include the purchase price plus any cost of incorporated parts of UK manufacture and delivery charge. Discounts received after the time of supply should be disregarded unless contractually agreed before that time. Where delivery charges cannot be determined, a fixed charge of £50 per vehicle may be used. (VAT Notice 700/57/04).

If the car is used, the value of the self-supply is the current purchase price of a vehicle *identical* in every respect (including age and condition and, where appropriate, any accessories fitted) to the car concerned or, if that is not available, the price for the purchase of a *similar* car. Failing this, it is the current production cost [*VATA 1994, Sch 6 para 6; SI 1992/1867*] or two thirds of the current list price approximation of a new vehicle. (VAT Notice 700/57/04).

Time of self-supply. The time of supply is treated as taking place when the motor car is appropriated to the use giving rise to the self-supply. [*VATA 1994, s 6(11)*].

Appropriation for this purpose cannot normally be said to have taken place until at least the occurrence of some overt, unconditional event that can be said to show appropriation to the use that gives rise to the supply, eg use of the vehicle in the business as a demonstration model. The tax point is then the date when, by any positive and recorded action, the car is transferred from new car sales stock. A mere intention to appropriate the motor car is not normally sufficient to create a tax point in these circumstances. (VAT Notice 700, para 15.2; Internal Guidance V1–11, para 29.2).

See 45.8 below if the vehicle has been converted and then applied for business use.

See also *A & B Motors (Newton-le-Willows) Ltd (VTD 1024) (TVC 42.51).*

De Voil Indirect Tax Service. See V3.242.

45.7 Motor dealers

(1) **Purchase of 'stock in trade' motor cars**

A motor dealer can reclaim input tax charged on used and unused cars purchased as stock in trade for resale even where there is temporary private use (see 45.3 above).

(2) **Private use of stock in trade cars**. Dealers must account for VAT on the private use by employees or similar persons of cars which form part of the stock in trade. They are not obliged to account for VAT on the private use of cars which they have loaned to third parties (eg cars loaned to potential customers) for business purposes.

As the normal rules are complex, HMRC's policy is to allow dealers maximum flexibility within the law to achieve a fair and reasonable result. There are currently three choices.

(*a*) *The 'normal rules'.*

Under *VATA 1994, Sch 4 para 5(4)* (see 47.7 OUTPUT TAX), where a manufacturer or dealer allows a demonstration car to be made available for private use, whether or not for a consideration, this is a deemed supply of services. Where there is no consideration, the value of the deemed supply is the full cost to the manufacturer or dealer. [*VATA 1994, Sch 6 para 7*]. Where there is consideration, subject to the anti-avoidance provisions below, the value of the supply is that consideration.

Businesses that opt for the normal rules must keep records to show, in relation to each stock in trade car which has been used for private purposes in the period

- what cost elements should be included in the charge;
- what value to put upon the total cost of those elements over the period in question; and
- what proportion of private use to apply to that value.

Anti-avoidance provisions. Under the above rules, where a nominal consideration is charged (say £1 per year) for the use of a motor car, VAT is only due on that nominal amount rather than the full cost of providing the motor car. The following anti-avoidance rules apply with effect from 1 January 2005 and allow HMRC to direct that VAT is accounted for on an open market valuation of supplies of such motor cars to employees.

In relation to any use, or availability of use, of a motor car on or after a date to be appointed, where

- the value of a supply made by a taxable person for a consideration is (apart from these provisions) less than its open market value,
- the taxable person is a 'motor manufacturer' or 'motor dealer',
- the person to whom the supply is made is *either* an employee of the taxable person *or* a person who, under the terms of his employment, provides services to the taxable person *or* a relative (ie husband, wife, brother, sister, ancestor or lineal descendant) of such a person,
- the supply is a supply of services by virtue of *VATA 1994, Sch 4 para 5(4)* (see above),
- the supply relates to a motor car (whether or not any particular motor car) that forms part of the 'stock in trade' of the taxable person, and
- the supply does not fall within the general rules for transactions between connected persons in *VATA 1994, Sch 6 para 1* (see 69.19 VALUATION)

HMRC may direct that the value of the supply (and any further supplies satisfying these conditions) is to be taken to be its open market value. Any such direction must be given by notice in writing to the motor manufacturer or dealer but no direction may be given more than three years after the time of the supply.

See 45.1 above for the definition of '*motor car*' and 45.3(*c*) above for the definitions of '*motor manufacturer*', '*motor dealer*' and '*stock in trade*'.

[*VATA 1994, Sch 6 para 1A; FA 2004, s 22(2)*].

(*b*) *An individual simplified method.*

In view of the burdens posed by the normal rules, HMRC allow a business to agree a simplification provided that

- the method is compatible with the normal rules (ie it is a simplification within the normal rules and not an entirely different method such as a scale charge); and
- the resulting output tax charge fairly and reasonably taxes the actual private use of those cars in comparison to the normal rules.

HMRC do not accept the contentions that

- because a car which has been put to private use is sold for more than its cost to the dealer, the value of the deemed supply is 'nil'; ie there has been no depreciation of the asset. They argue that there is still a cost, which in these circumstances is probably best measured in terms of the loss in net realisable value; ie the loss of the car's market value; and
- because the residual value of a demonstration car that has not been used for private journeys is virtually the same as one which has, the value of the deemed supply is 'nil' or minimal. They argue that precedent in this area is quite clear that the value of the deemed supply is the full cost of providing the asset for private use, not the marginal cost (see *Enkler v Finanzamt Homburg, CJEC [1996] STC 1316 (TVC 21.81)*).

(*c*) *A standard simplified method.*

Alternatively, businesses may use, without further question, a standard simplification method. HMRC agreed such a method with the Retail Motor Industry Federation (RMI) which could be applied from 1 December 1999 and subsequently a revised method with effect from 1 July 2000. A similar agreement was reached with the Society of Motor Manufacturers and Traders Ltd (SMMT) with effect from 1 July 2000. Although the original RMI method is effectively cancelled as a formal agreement, HMRC have agreed that a dealer may choose to continue to use it without seeking prior approval. The three methods are as follows. Dealers who choose to use a simplified method must use it for all their cars that are put to private use.

RMI agreement with effect from 1 July 2000. For each individual who has used a stock in trade car for private journeys in a VAT period, the trader must identify the list price of the car he has typically used and include the relevant amount from the following table as output tax in the VAT return.

List price band range	*Average price*	*VAT due on annual return*	*VAT due on quarterly return*	*VAT due on monthly return*
£	£	£	£	£
0–9,000	7,500	80.00	20.00	6.67
9,001–12,000	10,300	106.00	26.50	8.83
12,001–16,000	14,200	142.00	35.50	11.83
16,001–21,000	18,650	184.00	46.00	15.33
21,001–26,000	23,400	228.00	57.00	19.00
Over 26,000	see below			

Dealers with non-standard VAT periods should apply the appropriate proportion to the annual VAT due amount.

For cars with list prices in excess of £26,000, the annual VAT due is calculated by

(1) applying 25% annual depreciation to the cost price of the car or a locally agreed average;

(2) adding a standard £250 for repairs and maintenance to the depreciation;

(3) applying a 25% private use proportion to depreciation plus repairs and maintenance to arrive at the full cost of providing the car for private use ('the value for private use'); and

(4) applying the current VAT rate to the value for private use.

The resulting figure (rounded down to the nearest pound) is the annual VAT due.

SMMT agreement with effect from 1 July 2000. For each individual who has used a stock in trade car for private journeys in a VAT period, the trader must identify the list price of the car he has typically used and include the relevant amount from the following table as output tax in the VAT return.

List price band range	*Average price*	*VAT due on annual return*	*VAT due on quarterly return*	*VAT due on monthly return*
£	£	£	£	£
0–9,000	7,500	72.00	18.00	6.00
9,001–12,000	10,300	95.00	23.75	7.92
12,001–16,000	14,200	127.00	31.75	10.58
16,001–21,000	18,650	163.00	40.75	13.58
21,001–26,000	23,400	202.00	50.50	16.83
Over 26,000		see below		

Dealers with non-standard VAT periods should apply the appropriate proportion to the annual VAT due amount.

For cars with list prices in excess of £26,000, the annual VAT due is calculated as under the RMI agreement above.

(VAT Notice 700/57/04; Internal Guidance V1–13, paras 18.27, 25.2, 25.3).

(3) Disposals of cars on which input tax was recovered

VAT must be charged on the full selling price. See also 45.6 above for self-supply, eg where an unused car on which VAT has been reclaimed is transferred from sales stock to use in the business that would not qualify for input tax recovery.

(4) 'Bumping'

A car dealer may accept a second-hand car in part-exchange and then make arrangements with a finance company for the sale of the replacement car to the customer, treating the part-exchange value as the deposit required by the finance company. As the finance company normally requires a minimum deposit, it is common practice to inflate the part-exchange value and the sales price of the replacement car by a similar amount so that the minimum deposit can be met without resort to a cash payment from the customer (a practice known as 'bumping'). In such cases, the car dealer must account for VAT on the inflated price of the car as shown on the HP agreement (*North Anderson Cars Ltd v C & E Commrs, CS [1999] STC 902 (TVC 42.140)*).

(5) **Premium, 'nearly new' and 'personal import' cars**

Franchised dealers are not permitted by the terms of their franchise to sell a new car to another dealer. Therefore, non-franchised dealers must secure regular supplies by other means, eg by employing an agent to purchase a car from a franchised dealer. Similarly, 'personal import' cars are sometimes acquired by VAT-registered dealers from private importers immediately following their importation.

The normal rules for supplying goods through buying agents apply (see 3.6 AGENTS). Non-franchised dealers are only able to recover input tax on the purchase of a motor car if it is purchased

- directly from a manufacturer or another dealer;
- through an agent acting in the name of the non-franchised dealer; or
- through an 'undisclosed agent' acting in his own name if the agent is registered for VAT and has issued a proper VAT invoice. However, to be registered, such an agent must be in business for VAT purposes and, given the nature of the tests which must be applied to establish this (see 8.2 BUSINESS), it is unlikely that HMRC will regard the intention to sell a single car as constituting 'business'. Even if registered, an undisclosed agent will suffer a block on input tax recovery on the purchase of a car if it is made available for private use. This may apply if there is a gap between the purchase of the car and the supply to the non-franchised dealer.

(Business Brief 4/98).

(6) **Damaged or stolen cars**

The following rules apply.

- *Insurance compensation.* All compensation payments received from insurers are outside the scope of VAT.
- *Damage to unused cars in transit.* Where a car is damaged whilst in transit to dealer's premises, the carriers may only recover VAT paid on car repairs if the supply of repairs is to them. If manufacturers or dealers arrange for the repairs, the VAT is their input tax (even if the carrier is liable for the cost of the repair).
- *Damage to unused cars at dealer's premises.* If an unused car is held on sale or return and is damaged beyond repair, the dealer may adopt the car in order to sell it as a write-off. VAT incurred on the supply of damaged cars to the dealer is deductible but the dealer must account for output tax on the price at which the car is sold.

  If a damaged car is adopted for use in the dealer's business, the input tax is not deductible.

Any VAT incurred by the dealer in carrying out repairs is input tax, whether the damaged car is to be sold or used in the business.

- *Cars stolen in transit.* A car stolen from the carriers in transit has not been supplied and therefore no output tax is due from the manufacturer, dealer or carrier.

(Internal Guidance V1–13, para 18.18).

(7) **Dealer demonstration bonuses**

See 45.2 above.

45.8 **Conversion of a vehicle into a motor car and vice versa**

Conversion of a commercial vehicle into a car. A commercial vehicle can be converted into a car for VAT purposes. Where VAT is recovered on the purchase of the vehicle, output tax must be accounted for when the conversion is completed. The value for VAT purposes is the value of the vehicle at the time the conversion is completed, including the cost of the conversion. VAT incurred on any parts bought for the conversion are recoverable.

Examples of the conversion of a vehicle into a motor car are:

- The fitting of a side window or windows into a van to the rear of the driver's seat.
- The fitting of a rear seat or seats to a van, even without the insertion of side windows.
- The removal of seats from a twelve-seater vehicle.

(VAT Notice 700/64/02, para 2.4).

See, however, *Bolinge Hill Farm (VTD 4217) (TVC 42.42)*; *P Oddonetto (VTD 5208) (TVC 42.44)*; *John Beharrell Ltd (VTD 6530) (TVC 42.46)* and *Chichester Plant Contractors Ltd (VTD 6575) (TVC 42.41)*.

Conversion of a car into a commercial vehicle. This can be done, for example, by removing rear seats and windows or by adding additional seats so that the vehicle can legally seat twelve or more people. VAT can only be recovered on the car if it was bought specifically for this conversion and not used as a car. (VAT Notice 700/64/02, para 2.5).

45.9 **Car kits**

Where a car is made from a kit or separately purchased parts, any VAT charged as input tax may be reclaimed subject to the normal rules. If the finished car is used in the business for a purpose that would not qualify for input tax recovery, VAT must be accounted for under the self-supply rules (see 45.6 above). The tax value must be based on the VAT-exclusive cost of the parts and the cost of construction. The VAT cannot be reclaimed. If the finished car is sold, VAT must be accounted for on the full selling price in the normal way. (VAT Notice 700/64/02, para 2.6).

45.10 **MOTOR EXPENSES**

Provided the vehicle is used in the business, VAT on leasing or hiring a vehicle, road fuel (whether bought by the business or reimbursed to employees) and repair and maintenance charges can be treated as input tax. This applies even if the vehicle is used partly for private motoring. Private usage may, however, create a liability to output tax.

The provisions are considered in more detail in 45.11 to 45.19 below. For these purposes it is important to understand the difference between 'business' and 'private' motoring.

A '*business*' journey is one made by an employer or employee for the purpose of the business.

A '*private*' journey is any journey not for the purpose of the business.

Travel between a person's home and normal workplace is private motoring. Travel from home to any other place for business purposes is a business journey.

45.11 Leasing or hiring a motor car

The following provisions apply to motor cars that are hired or leased for business purposes. The provisions do not apply to hire purchase or lease-purchase agreements, for which see 45.3 above.

If a motor car as defined in 45.1 above is leased or hired, only 50% of the input VAT on the rental charges is available for the credit except in the following circumstances when 100% relief is available.

(*a*) The motor car is a 'qualifying' motor car let on hire to a taxable person who intends to use the motor car exclusively for business purposes. This condition is *not* satisfied if the taxable person intends to

- let it on hire to any person either for no consideration or consideration less than would be payable in an arm's length commercial transaction; or
- make it available, otherwise than by letting on hire, to any person (including, where the taxable person is an individual, himself or, where the taxable person is a partnership, a partner) for private use (whether or not for a consideration).

(*b*) The motor car is a 'qualifying' motor car let on hire to a taxable person who intends to use the motor car primarily

- to provide it on hire with the services of a driver for the purposes of carrying passengers;
- to provide it for 'self-drive hire'; or
- as a vehicle in which instruction in driving of a motor car is to be given by him.

'*Self-drive hire*' means hire where the hirer is the person normally expected to drive the motor car and the period of hire to each hirer (together with the period of hire of any other motor car expected to be hired to him by the taxable person) will normally be less than both 30 consecutive days and 90 days in any twelve-month period.

(*c*) The motor car is not a 'qualifying' motor car. However, following the decision in *C & E Commrs v BRS Automotive Ltd, CA [1998] STC 1210 (TVC 42.97)* (where a tax avoidance scheme was used to exploit the change to the VAT treatment of business cars which took effect from 1 August 1995) this does not apply to leasing charges after 12 November 1998 to a lessee if the only reason that the motor car is not a qualifying motor car is that it was let on hire to that same lessee before 1 August 1995. For further details of the effect of the anti-avoidance provisions, see Business Brief 25/98.

(*d*) The motor car is unused and is let on hire to a taxable person whose business consists predominantly of making supplies within *VATA 1994, Sch 8 Group 12 Item 14* (see 32.33 HEALTH AND WELFARE) by a taxable person whose only taxable supplies are concerned with the letting on hire of motor cars to such taxable persons.

See 45.3 above for the definition of a '*qualifying*' motor car.

[*SI 1992/3222, Art 7; SI 1995/281; SI 1995/1666; SI 1998/2767*].

Identifying qualifying cars on leasing invoices. HMRC have agreed with a main leasing trade organisation a recommended form of invoice for leasing companies to adopt for lettings. The invoice must clearly identify whether or not the car is a qualifying car (a legal requirement, see 40.4 INVOICES) and, if it is, the amount of VAT which is potentially subject to the 50% input tax restriction (depending upon the customer's use). Where the leasing company has not indicated whether the car is a qualifying car or not, the lessee can assume that a car with an 'M' registration or earlier prefix is non-qualifying and recover VAT in full subject to the normal rules. A car with an 'N' or later registration prefix should normally be treated as a qualifying car and the 50% restriction applied (unless the usage qualifies for 100% deduction under (*a*) or (*b*) above). Full input tax relief may, however, be claimed on rental charges on 'N' registration cars if the hirer incurred any VAT on rental on it before 1 August 1995.

The requirement to identify whether or not a car is a qualifying car does not apply to self-drive hire cars (see below). Unless there is evidence to the contrary, any self-drive hire car should be treated as a qualifying car if it has a 'K' registration or later prefix.

Charges subject to the 50% restriction. There are frequently two distinct elements of the rental: basic rental for the provision of the car (including depreciation, funding cost, VED and a proportion of overheads/profit) and an optional additional charge (covering repairs, maintenance and roadside assistance and a proportion of overheads/profit). The optional charges are also subject to the 50% restriction unless they are separately described in the contract hire agreement and periodic invoices and are genuinely optional, in which case they are recoverable in full subject to the normal rules. VAT on an excess mileage charge should similarly be separated into two distinct elements on a basis identical to the split of the rental. For full details, see the agreement between the British Vehicle Rental and Leasing Association and HMRC reproduced in VAT Notice 700/57/04.

Rental rebates. Where a lessor sells a car at the end of a lease and uses the proceeds to rebate the monthly rental payments made to the lessee, a lessee who incurred a 50% input tax restriction on the rental charges on the car need only adjust for 50% of the VAT on the credit note issued by the lessor for rebate of rentals.

Early lease termination. Where a lease is terminated early, the leasing company may treat both the termination payment and any rental rebate as taxable or treat both as outside the scope of VAT. If it chooses to tax, it will normally set off the termination payment against any rebate and issue a VAT invoice for the difference.

- Where the termination payment exceeds the rebate, any VAT is not subject to the 50% restriction.

- Where any rebate exceeds the termination payment, the leasing company must issue a credit note for the balance. A lessee who incurred a 50% input tax restriction on the rental charges need only adjust for 50% of the VAT on the credit note.

Self-drive hire (daily rental). The 50% restriction applies to self-drive hire as well as leasing on a longer-term basis. If the car is hired simply to replace an off-the-road ordinary company car, the 50% block applies from the first day of hire. By concession, HMRC accept that in other cases (eg where the business does not have a company car) the 50% block does not apply if a car is hired for not more than 10 days (before 1 January 2002, 5 days) to use specifically for business purposes.

Interaction with other apportionments. Where the 50% input tax restriction applies and there are both business and non-business activities and/or exempt supplies, the order for carrying out the various apportionments is

- VAT incurred between business and non-business activities (see 35.7 INPUT TAX)
- 50% input tax restriction on the VAT amount which relates to business activities
- any necessary PARTIAL EXEMPTION (49) calculation.

(VAT Notice 700/64/02, paras 4.4–4.10; VAT Information Sheet 12/95; Business Brief 15/95).

VAT due by daily rental companies on incidental private use of their hire fleet. Under the normal rules, where assets are used for private purposes a supply of services takes place. Where the services are provided for no consideration, the value of those services is the cost to the employer of providing those services. The calculation of this value would involve, in each VAT period, reference to

- the depreciation of the capital cost of the car;
- the value (excluding VAT) of repairs, maintenance and other running costs (excluding road fuel) on which VAT had been recovered; and
- the actual proportion of business and private use.

As these calculations might be complex, HMRC and the British Vehicle Rental and Leasing Association have agreed that daily rental companies may choose to apply a simplified method of establishing the output tax due. Daily rental companies who choose to use the simplified method must do so for all their daily rental cars which are put to private use. Daily rental companies who choose not to adopt the simplified method must either apply the normal rules or apply to HMRC to use an individual simplified method. For each VAT period, the daily rental company must calculate output VAT on the private use of the daily rental cars as follows.

- Identify staff that use a daily rental car for private journeys in the period.
- For each person, identify the cc band of car they have typically used in the period.
- For each person, include the VAT amount as per the following table as output tax due in the VAT account for the period.

Price band	*Engine size cc*	*VAT due on annual return*	*VAT due on quarterly return*	*VAT due on monthly return*
1	Up to 1200	51.06	12.76	4.25
2	Up to 1400	61.69	15.42	5.14
3	Up to 1800	75.95	18.98	6.32
4	Over 1800	91.19	22.80	7.60

Daily rental companies with non-standard VAT periods should apply the appropriate proportion to the annual amount.

(VAT Notice 700/57/04).

Fleet leasing bonuses. See 45.2 above. Receipt of such a bonus reduces the VAT recoverable by the customer (if any) on the lease payments. For example, where 50% of the VAT incurred on lease payments can be recovered, VAT due on the bonus payment is

7/47 × 50% × gross bonus payment

(Business Brief 1/98).

45.12 **Repairs and maintenance**

If a vehicle is used for business purposes, VAT on repairs and maintenance can be treated as input tax provided the work done is paid for by the business. This applies even if the vehicle is used for private motoring and even if no VAT is reclaimed on any road fuel in order to avoid use of the scale charges, see 45.16 below. VAT on repairs, etc relating to a vehicle used by a sole trader or partner for private motoring only cannot be treated as input tax. (VAT Notice 700/64/02, para 5.1).

If an employer agrees to pay the full cost of repair and maintenance of employees' private cars, the VAT incurred may be treated as input tax provided the costs are recorded in the trader's accounts. (Internal Guidance V1–13, para 20.1).

45.13 **Accessories**

Where a car is purchased on which input tax is blocked, VAT charged on accessories fitted to a car when purchased cannot be reclaimed even if optional and separately itemised on the sales invoice. See *Turmeau (VTD 1135) (TVC 42.93)*.

VAT on accessories subsequently purchased can only be treated as input tax if

- the vehicle is owned by the business or used in the business but not owned by it (eg an employee's or director's own car); and
- the accessory has a business use.

(VAT Notice 700/64/02, paras 5.2, 5.3).

Input tax on personalised number plates has been disallowed in a considerable number of cases including *Ava Knit Ltd (VTD 1461) (TVC 34.393)* and *E N Jones (VTD 5023) (TVC 34.403)* but allowed in *MW Alexander (VTD 7208) (TVC 34.386)*; *Sunner & Sons (VTD 8857) (TVC 34.388)* and *Hamlet's (Radio & TV) Ltd (VTD 12716) (TVC 34.389)*. See Tolley's VAT Cases.

45.14 Fuel bought by the business

Where a business pays for road fuel, if the fuel is used for business motoring only, subject to the normal rules it can claim all of the VAT because 100% is used for business purposes. Where the fuel purchased is used both for business and private motoring, the business has three options.

(*a*) It can claim all VAT charged and apply the fuel scale charge (see 45.16 below).

(*b*) It can use detailed mileage records to separate business mileage from private mileage. This avoids using the scale charge. Records must be kept of total mileage, split between business and private mileage, and total fuel costs.

> *Example*
>
> Total business mileage is 4,290 of which 3,165 relates to business mileage. The total cost of fuel is £250.
>
> The cost of the business mileage is
>
> £250 × 3,165 ÷ 4,290 = £184.44
>
> Input tax is £184.44 × 7/47 = £27.46

(*c*) It can neither claim input tax on any road fuel purchased nor apply the scale charge (see 45.16 below).

(VAT Notice 700/64/02, paras 8.1–8.5).

Non-business activities. VAT on non-business journeys (eg journeys in connection with charitable activities of charities) is not reclaimable. Where fuel is used for both business and non-business activities, the total cost should be apportioned.

Fuel card schemes. Fuel cards allow companies who own fleets of vehicles to purchase fuel, and other motor-related goods and services, from garages by means of a card. The schemes are designed contractually to provide that, where a card is used to buy fuel, the fuel is supplied from the garage to the card company and then by the card company to the cardholders. With a normal credit card transaction, the garage supplies goods and services direct to the cardholders, the credit card being used simply as a means of payment. Whether the schemes work depends upon the precise terms of the contractual arrangements between the parties.

Five schemes were considered in a test case by the VAT tribunal in *Harpur Group Ltd (VTD 12001) (TVC 26.21)*. In its decision, the tribunal found that ownership in the fuel passes at the pump. In respect of the two 'standard' schemes (see below) it was held to be crucial that the cardholder indicated, before the supply commenced, that it was to be made against a Harpur contract. Otherwise, property in the goods passed direct to the only other known party to the supply, ie the cardholder. Subsequent production of the card could not alter this legal position and its use then simply was to discharge the holder's obligation to pay for the fuel. Although the 'Bunkerfuel' and 'Pre-purchase' schemes (see below) differed in detail, a common factor was that stock owned by Harpur was mixed with the merchant's stock. On the basis that, in common law, when stock is mixed both parties are co-owners as tenants in common, the tribunal decided that the agreements provided for the appropriation of Harpur's stock. This was then a supply from Harpur to the cardholder direct. In the final scheme, 'OFIS' (see below), the supplies were not of fuel but of other goods and services such as repairs, tyres etc. The tribunal decided that the contractual arrangements succeeded in directing the supply via Harpur to the cardholders. Crucially, the arrangements in this case required the cardholder to produce the OFIS card before the supply commenced.

In the light of *Harpur*, HMRC agreed that fuel card companies could alter their standard arrangements to follow the lines sanctioned by the tribunal.

Where the arrangements succeed in creating a supply via the card company this means that

- a company operating a large fleets of vehicles can receive a single, monthly itemised VAT invoice from the fuel card company with details of all the fuel and other motor-related purchases made by its employees. This reduces the administrative burden of ensuring that employees render all their receipts to the company's accounting section; and
- by selling the fuel to its cardholders, the fuel card company is fully taxable and avoids partial exemption problems. (If it was not supplying goods to the cardholders, it would be seen as operating a credit card service which would be an exempt financial service.)

The standard schemes. For the scheme to work

- the garage and cardholder agreements should state that the cardholder must present his card to the garage prior to the commencement of any transaction. This identifies, in advance, that the transaction is to be made under the terms of a contract which directs the supply via the card company;
- there should be a clause in the agreement stating that, on production of the card, the fuel is supplied to the fuel card company by the garage; and
- as the fuel card company cannot physically make the supply of fuel at the pump, there should also be a clause indicating that the garage is acting as agent of the card company in effecting the supply.

However, provided the contractual and other circumstances indicate that the supply is via the card company and officers have no reason for suspicion, HMRC do not expect its officers to actively police the requirement to show the card before purchase.

'Bunkerfuel' and 'pre-purchase' schemes. Under a Bunkerfuel scheme, the card company buys stocks of fuel that it then delivers to a garage. The pre-purchase scheme involves the fuel card company pre-purchasing stock from the garage. In both cases, its fuel is stored with that of the garage in common tanks. Although not essential, both types of agreement usually contain a clause authorising the garage to act as the card company's agent for the purposes of selling the card company's fuel to its cardholders. There is also usually some acknowledgement that the garage is principal when supplying from its own stock.

'OFIS' and similar schemes. These schemes are used mainly for supplies of goods and services such as repairs, maintenance, parts, tyres. etc. They are very similar contractually to the standard schemes above. The terms of these schemes have always required the cardholder to produce the card before the services or goods are supplied, with the other contractual clauses being designed to direct the supply via the card company.

(Internal Guidance V1–3, para 17.7).

See, however, *Auto Lease Holland BV v Bundesamt fur Finanzen, CJEC Case C–185/01, [2005] STC 598 (TVC 21.106)* where a Netherlands company (H) leased a number of motor vehicles and gave the lessees the use of a credit card to purchase fuel. It contended that it should be treated as having received the fuel from the retail companies and as having made an onward supply to the lessees. The Court held that, in the circumstances of the case, the lessor of a vehicle did not make any supply of fuel to the lessee even if the vehicle was filled up in the name and at the expense of that lessor.

45.15 Fuel bought by employees

Note. The CJEC have confirmed in *EC Commission v United Kingdom (No 4), CJEC Case C–33/03 [2005] STC 582 (TVC 21.270)* that in allowing an employer to deduct VAT in respect of certain supplies of road fuel to its employees, the UK was in breach of *EC Sixth Directive, Arts 17, 18*. However, HMRC have confirmed that taxpayers will have the right to rely on UK legislation until it is amended and there is no question of any change being retrospective. (Business Brief 21/99).

Road fuel bought by an employee (or any other non-taxable person) is treated as having been supplied to a business for business purposes provided one of the following methods of reimbursement is adopted.

(*a*) The employee is reimbursed for the actual cost of the fuel.

(*b*) The employee is paid an amount determined by reference to the total distance travelled by the vehicle (whether or not including private or non-business mileage) and the cylinder capacity of the vehicle.

Normally, this will take the form of a mileage allowance which may also cover reimbursement of other costs. If so, input tax on road fuel is calculated by multiplying the fuel element of the mileage allowance by the VAT fraction.

HMRC require the business to keep a record for each employee showing

- mileage travelled
- whether journeys are both business and private
- the cylinder capacity of the vehicle
- the rate of the mileage allowance
- the amount of input tax claimed.

(*c*) From 28 January 2002, the Inland Revenue has published advisory fuel only mileage rates for company cars based on the engine capacity of the car and the type of fuel used as follows.

Engine Size	*Petrol*	*Diesel*	*LPG*
1400cc or less	10p	9p	6p
1401cc to 2000cc	12p	9p	7p
Over 2000cc	14p	12p	9p

It is understood that HMRC will also accept these figures as the basis for reimbursing an employee for fuel bought for business purposes.

Reimbursement by either method can also cover fuel bought for private use although in such a case the business must then account for output tax on the private use using the scale charges (see 45.16 and 45.17 below).

[*SI 1991/2306*]. (VAT Notice 700/64/02, paras 8.6–8.8).

De Voil Indirect Tax Service. See V3.436.

45.16 Fuel for private motoring

Where in any VAT period a taxable person supplies 'fuel for private motoring' to an individual, VAT must be accounted for using the scale charges in 45.17 below which represent the VAT-inclusive value of the fuel in respect of any one vehicle.

'*Fuel for private motoring*' is fuel which is (or has previously been) supplied to, acquired from another EC country by, imported from outside the EC by, or manufactured by, a taxable person in the course of his business and which is

- provided or to be provided by the taxable person to an individual by reason of his employment or office for private use in his 'own vehicle' or a vehicle allocated to him;
- where the taxable person is an individual, appropriated or to be appropriated by him for private use in his own vehicle; or
- where the taxable person is a partnership, provided or to be provided to any of the individual partners for private use in his own vehicle.

Fuel is not regarded as provided to any person for his private use if it is supplied at a price not less than that at which it was supplied to or imported by the taxable person, or in the case of manufactured fuel, at a price not less than the aggregate of costs of raw materials and of manufacturing together with any excise duty thereon. See below for the VAT treatment where fuel is charged at such a price.

'*Business travel*' is that which an individual is necessarily obliged to do in the performance of the duties of his employment, the partnership, or in the case of the taxable person himself, his business.

'*Own vehicle*' includes any vehicle of which for the time being the individual has the use (other than a vehicle 'allocated to' him).

'*Vehicle*' means any mechanically propelled road vehicle other than a motor cycle or an invalid carriage. HMRC have, however, confirmed that the scale rate charges will apply only to cars (see below).

A vehicle is at any time '*allocated to*' an individual if at that time it is made available (without any transfer of property in it) either to the individual himself or to any other person, and is so made available by reason of the individual's employment and for private use. However, a vehicle is not regarded as allocated to an individual by reason of his employment if, in any VAT period, it is a pooled car ie

- it was made available to, and actually used by, more than one of the employees or one or more (of the) employers and, in the case of each of them, it was made available to him by reason of his employment but was not in the period ordinarily used by any one of them to the exclusion of the others;
- in the case of each of the employees, any private use of the vehicle made by him was merely incidental to his other use of it in that period; and
- it was not normally kept overnight on or in the vicinity of any residential premises where any of the employees was residing, except while being kept overnight on premises occupied by the person making the vehicle available to them.

The provision of fuel is treated as a supply in the course or furtherance of a business by the taxable person at the time when fuel for private use is put into the fuel tank of the individual's own vehicle or a vehicle allocated to him. An appropriation by a taxable person to his own private use is treated as a supply to himself in his private capacity. A provision of fuel by a member of a group within *VATA 1994, s 43* (see 31 GROUPS OF COMPANIES) is treated as provision by the representative member.

Input tax. VAT on the supply, acquisition or importation of fuel for private use is to be treated as input tax subject to the normal rules notwithstanding that the fuel is not used or to be used for business purposes.

Changing vehicles. Where an individual is supplied with fuel for private use for one vehicle in respect of part of a VAT period and another vehicle for another part of the same period, then, provided that at the end of the period one of the vehicles neither belongs to him nor is allocated to him, supplies made to the individual are treated as made in respect of one vehicle only. Where each vehicle falls within the same category in the above tables, the table is applied as if fuel had been supplied for one vehicle only throughout the period. Otherwise the figures are rateably apportioned depending on the period for which fuel for private use was supplied for each vehicle.

[*VATA 1994, ss 56, 57*].

Records. Where scale charges apply, records must be kept showing the number of vehicles for which free or below cost fuel is supplied; the cylinder capacity of each vehicle; and whether the car is diesel or petrol driven. If a vehicle is changed, the date of change, fuel category and the engine capacity of the replacement vehicle must also be shown. (VAT Notice 700/64/02, para 9.8).

Concession not to pay scale charges. If fuel is supplied for private motoring free or for less than the amount paid for it, the only way to avoid accounting for VAT using the scale charge is by not reclaiming input tax on *any* fuel purchased whether used for business or private motoring in cars or commercial vehicles. (VAT Notice 748, ESC 3.1). If this method is adopted, HMRC must be advised before the start of the period in which it is to take effect and they will then treat the decision as remaining in force until told otherwise.

Partly exempt traders. Where a partly exempt business is unable to separate business and private motoring, all input tax on fuel (including that for private motoring) must be apportioned in the partial exemption calculations. To compensate for this, the scale charge for private motoring may be reduced to equal the percentage of input tax recovered under the partial exemption method. For example, if only 80% of the input tax is recovered, only 80% of the appropriate scale charge is to be paid. Where an annual adjustment is carried out, the scale charge must also be adjusted. (Internal Guidance V1–15, para 19.5).

Accounting for VAT. The VAT due per the scale charge table in 45.17 below should be included in the total output tax figure on the return. The net amount (ie the scale charge for the fuel less the VAT due) should be included in the total value of outputs on the return.

Example

L Ltd provides its employees with cars and pays all day-to-day running expenses, including the cost of any petrol used for private motoring. Each employee submits a monthly return showing opening and closing mileage, together with fuel and servicing receipts for the period.

T, the sales director, has a 2,000cc car and puts in a monthly claim for July 2005. He supports this with petrol bills totalling £97.80 and a service invoice for £94.00 (£80.00 plus VAT £14.00). The company prepares monthly VAT returns.

The company should code the expenses claim as follows.

Debit		£
Servicing		80.00
Fuel £97.80 × 40/47	83.23	
Scale charge — see 45.17 below	15.34	
		98.57
Input VAT — on service	14.00	
— on petrol £97.80 × 7/47	14.57	
		28.57
		£207.14
Credit		
Expenses reimbursed to T		
£97.80 + £94.00		191.80
Output VAT		15.34
		£207.14

De Voil Indirect Tax Service. See V3.266.

45.17 Fuel for private motoring — scale charges

Proposed future changes. The Treasury have powers to change the basis of charge from the engine size and fuel type to one based on carbon dioxide emissions. [*VATA 1994, s 57(4A)–(4G)(9)(10); F(No 2)A 2005, s 2*]. This would align the VAT system with that operated for income tax purposes. The proposal is subject to the UK obtaining a derogation from the EC Commission.

VAT periods beginning after 30.4.05

Cylinder capacity	*Annual VAT returns*		*Quarterly VAT returns*		*Monthly VAT Returns*	
	Scale charge £	VAT due per vehicle £	Scale charge £	VAT due per vehicle £	Scale charge £	VAT due per vehicle £
Diesel engine						
2,000 or less	945	140.74	236	35.15	78	11.62
More than 2,000	1,200	178.72	300	44.68	100	14.89
Other engines						
1,400 or less	985	146.70	246	36.64	82	12.21
1,400 to 2,000	1,245	185.43	311	46.32	103	15.34
More than 2,000	1,830	272.55	457	68.06	152	22.64

[*SI 2005/722*].

VAT periods beginning after 30.4.04 and before 1.5.05

Cylinder capacity	*Annual VAT returns*		*Quarterly VAT returns*		*Monthly VAT Returns*	
	Scale charge £	VAT due per vehicle £	Scale charge £	VAT due per vehicle £	Scale charge £	VAT due per vehicle £
Diesel engine						
2,000 or less	865	128.82	216	32.17	72	10.72
More than 2,000	1,095	163.08	273	40.65	91	13.55
Other engines						
1,400 or less	930	138.51	232	34.55	77	11.46
1,400 to 2,000	1,175	175.00	293	43.63	97	14.44
More than 2,000	1,730	257.65	432	64.34	144	21.44

[*SI 2004/776*].

VAT periods beginning after 30.4.03 and before 1.5.04

	Annual VAT returns		*Quarterly VAT returns*		*Monthly VAT Returns*	
Cylinder capacity	Scale charge	VAT due per vehicle	Scale charge	VAT due per vehicle	Scale charge	VAT due per vehicle
	£	£	£	£	£	£
Diesel engine						
2,000 or less	900	134.04	225	33.51	75	11.17
More than 2,000	1,135	169.04	283	42.14	94	14.00
Other engines						
1,400 or less	950	141.48	237	35.29	79	11.76
1,400 to 2,000	1,200	178.72	300	44.68	100	14.89
More than 2,000	1,770	263.61	442	65.82	147	21.89

[*SI 2003/1057*]

VAT periods beginning after 30.4.02 and before 1.5.03

	Annual VAT returns		*Quarterly VAT returns*		*Monthly VAT returns*	
Cylinder capacity	Scale charge	VAT due per vehicle	Scale charge	VAT due per vehicle	Scale charge	VAT due per vehicle
	£	£	£	£	£	£
Diesel engine						
2,000 or less	850	126.59	212	31.57	70	10.42
More than 2,000	1,075	160.10	268	39.91	89	13.25
Other engines						
1,400 or less	905	134.78	226	33.65	75	11.17
1,400 to 2,000	1,145	170.53	286	42.59	95	14.14
More than 2,000	1,690	251.70	422	62.85	140	20.85

[*SI 2002/1099*].

45.18 **Private motoring – charge for use of a vehicle**

Charge for use. Certain charges for the private use of a motor car are treated as neither a supply of goods or services. See 45.5(*f*) above. The effect of this is that a taxable person must account for VAT on any charge for the use of a vehicle unless, *in the case of a motor car*,

(i) the car is owned by the taxable person and input VAT on it was wholly excluded from credit on the supply to, or acquisition or importation by, that taxable person (see 45.3 above); or

(ii) the car was bought under the second-hand margin scheme; or

(iii) the car is leased by the taxable person and the 50% input tax restriction applies to the leasing charges incurred (see 45.11 above); or

(iv) the car is leased by the taxable person and input VAT on the car was wholly excluded from credit on the supply to, or acquisition or importation by, the leasing company. Leasing companies should identify these cars on their invoices as 'non-qualifying' cars. In practice, any car leased with an 'M' or earlier registration prefix falls into this category.

Health authorities. By a Treasury direction under *VATA 1994, s 41*, health authorities which lease cars are not subject to the 50% block on VAT incurred. This means that any charges made to an employee are subject to VAT unless the health authority gives the employee a choice between

- a particular rate of wages, salary or employment, and
- a lower rate and, in addition, the right to the private use of the car

in which case the salary sacrifice element of any charge is excluded from VAT. Contributions for cars leased prior to 1 August 1995 are not subject to VAT. [*SI 1992/630*]. (Internal Guidance V1–13, para 18.23).

Salary sacrifice. Where an employer gives an employee a choice between

(*a*) a particular rate of wages, salary or emoluments, or

(*b*) in the alternative a lower rate of wages, etc and, in addition, the right to the private use of a motor car provided by the employer,

and the employee chooses (*b*) above, then the provision to the employee of the right to use the motor car privately is not liable to VAT to the extent that the consideration is the difference between the wages, etc available to him under (*a*) and (*b*) above. [*SI 1992/630*].

Trading down. Where a business allows employees to trade down to a cheaper model with a smaller salary sacrificed, HMRC accept that no VAT is due and the above provisions can be applied.

Trading up. Where a business allows employees to trade up to a more expensive model than they are entitled to, and a charge is made for the use of the car, the charge made is consideration for a supply.

Sacrificing benefits. There is a general move in industry towards providing a package of benefits for staff as part of the remuneration package (eg enhanced termination arrangements, longer holidays, payment of non-pensionable allowances, and private health insurance). Rather than simply sacrificing salary, employees may also effectively sacrifice other routine benefits and entitlements. However, as long as no specific charge is made for the use of the car, HMRC do not regard the sacrificing of routine benefits rather than salary as consideration for a supply.

(Business Brief 9/92).

(VAT Notice 700/64/02, paras 6.1–6.3).

See 45.7 above for private use of stock in trade cars of motor dealers.

45.19 **Private motoring — vehicle used for no payment**

Where a charge for use would be taxable under 45.18 above but no charge is made, VAT must be accounted for on the cost of making the vehicle available. Over any period of time, this includes depreciation, repairs and other running costs (excluding any VAT recovered as input tax) but excludes fuel costs (VAT on which must be accounted for separately, see 45.16 above) and costs which were not subject to VAT (eg road tax and insurance). The costs incurred should be multiplied by the proportion that private mileage bears to total mileage.

(VAT Notice 700/64/02, para 6.4).

45.20 **SECOND-HAND SCHEME FOR MOTOR CARS**

In general, VAT is charged on the full value of any goods, including second-hand motor cars, sold by a taxable person. The Treasury may, however, by order, provide for a taxable person to opt to charge VAT on the profit margin (instead of full value). [*VATA 1994, ss 32, 50A: FA 1995, s 24*]. An order under these provisions has been made by *SI 1995/1268* which covers all second-hand goods. The effect of the provisions is that, provided all the conditions are met, the margin scheme may be used to account for VAT only on the amount by which the selling price exceeds the purchase price. The gross margin includes the VAT to be accounted for.

For full details of the margin scheme, see 61 SECOND-HAND GOODS.

46 Northern Ireland

46.1 The provisions of the *VATA 1994* apply to Northern Ireland [*VATA 1994, s 101*(*3*)] but not the Republic of Ireland.

Refund of VAT to Government of Northern Ireland. HMRC must refund to the NI Government any VAT charged on

- the supply of goods or services to that Government,
- the acquisition of goods by that Government from another EC country, or
- the importation of any goods by that Government from a place outside the EC

after deducting an amount (agreed between HMRC and the Department of Finance and Personnel for NI) attributable to supplies, acquisitions and importations for the purposes of a business carried on by that Government.

[*VATA 1994, s 99*].

See also 43.11 LOCAL AUTHORITIES AND PUBLIC BODIES for supplies by 'government departments', including those in NI.

47 Output Tax

Cross-references. See 2.18 ACCOUNTING PERIODS AND RETURNS for goods sold in satisfaction of a debt by a person selling under a power of sale; 7 BAD DEBT RELIEF; 24 EXEMPT SUPPLIES; 27.12 FINANCIAL SERVICES for output tax under hire purchase, conditional sale and credit sale agreements; 55.3–55.17 RATES OF VAT for changes in the rate of tax; 59.34 REGISTRATION for output tax on the deemed supply of business assets when a trader is deregistered; 60 RETAIL SCHEMES for special schemes for retailers; 61 SECOND-HAND GOODS for special schemes in operation for such goods; 62.2 SELF-SUPPLY for output tax on stationery produced and used by partly exempt traders; 69.24 VALUATION for calculation of output tax where discounts are allowed; 72 ZERO-RATED SUPPLIES.

De Voil Indirect Tax Service. See V3.5.

The contents of this chapter are as follows.

47.1 GENERAL

Output tax in relation to a 'taxable person' means VAT on

- supplies which he makes; and
- acquisitions of goods by him from another EC country (including VAT which is also counted as input tax under 35.1(*b*) INPUT TAX).

A '*taxable person*' is a person who is, or is required to be, registered under *VATA 1994*.

[*VATA 1994, s 3(1), s 24(2)*].

Output tax on supplies. A taxable person must charge VAT on any taxable supply of goods or services made in the UK in the course or furtherance of any business carried on by him.

A '*taxable supply*' is a supply of goods or services made in the UK other than an exempt supply. [*VATA 1994, s 4*]. See 8.1 BUSINESS for the meaning of 'business'. For VAT purposes the UK includes the territorial sea of the UK (ie waters within twelve nautical miles of the coast-line).

The output tax is normally the liability of the person making the supply. [*VATA 1994, s 1(2)*]. As a general rule, the determination of the liability of VAT is the responsibility of the supplier. In certain special cases, a supply can be zero-rated where a customer gives the supplier a declaration claiming eligibility for such treatment. Under these circumstances, if the supplier, despite having taken all reasonable steps to check the validity of the declaration, fails to identify any inaccuracy and, in good faith, makes the supply at the zero rate, HMRC will not seek to recover the VAT due from the supplier. (VAT Notice 48, ESC 3.11).

The VAT becomes due at the time of supply [*VATA 1994, s 1(2)*] but in practice is accounted for and paid by reference to tax returns completed for VAT accounting periods. See 2 ACCOUNTING PERIODS AND RETURNS and 51 PAYMENT OF VAT.

Certain small businesses are allowed to account for VAT on the basis of cash received and/or by means of only one VAT return a year. See 63 SPECIAL SCHEMES.

Output tax on acquisitions. See 23.3 EUROPEAN COMMUNITY: SINGLE MARKET for tax on acquisitions from other EC countries.

Rates of output tax. There are currently three main rates of output tax, standard rate (17.5%), reduced rate (5%) and zero rate (nil). See 72 ZERO-RATED SUPPLIES for the effects of zero-rating and the categories of goods and services to which it applies. See 58 REDUCED RATE SUPPLIES for a 5% reduced rate applying to a limited number of supplies.

Misunderstanding. VAT undercharged by a registered trader on account of a *bona fide* misunderstanding may be remitted provided all the following conditions are fulfilled.

(*a*) There is no reason to believe that the VAT has been knowingly evaded.

(*b*) There is no evidence of negligence.

(*c*) The misunderstanding does not concern an aspect of VAT clearly covered in general guidance published by HMRC or in specific instructions to the trader concerned.

(*d*) The VAT due was not charged, could not now reasonably be expected to be charged to customers, and will not be charged.

Where at the time the misunderstanding comes to light there are unfulfilled firm orders from customers, for which the price quoted has been based mistakenly on the assumption that no VAT, or less VAT than properly due, would be chargeable, VAT undercharged may be remitted in respect of such orders provided the conditions above are met. (VAT Notice 48, ESC 3.4).

De Voil Indirect Tax Service. See V3.501; V3.502.

47.2 VAT FRACTION

Normally, VAT is calculated at the appropriate percentage of a price which has first been decided without VAT and the VAT invoice shows these separate amounts. Sometimes, however, VAT has to be calculated from a price in which it is already included (eg in a less detailed tax invoice). To do this, the VAT fraction is required.

$$\text{VAT fraction} = \frac{\text{rate of VAT}}{100 + \text{rate of VAT}}$$

Rate of VAT	VAT fraction
17.5%	7/47
5%	1/21

Example

M refills his car with petrol and receives a less detailed invoice totalling £36.78.

The VAT included is £36.78 × 7/47 = £5.48

47.3 APPORTIONMENT OF MONETARY CONSIDERATION

A single monetary consideration may be the payment for two or more supplies of different liabilities. In such a situation, the business must allocate a fair proportion of the total payment to each of the supplies. [*VATA 1994, s 19(4)*]. The legislation prescribes no set method by which this is to be achieved. The commonest methods are based upon the costs incurred in making the supplies or the normal selling prices of the supplies. Various methods of apportionment are considered in 47.4 below.

Apportionment is only necessary where the price charged is the only consideration for the supplies. If the consideration is not wholly in money, VAT must be accounted for as explained in 69.5 VALUATION.

However, before an apportionment calculation is carried out, the following four questions should be considered in order to determine whether an apportionment is appropriate and, if it is, what supplies it relates to.

(*a*) **Is there more than one supply?** It is important to distinguish between a single (composite) supply and a multiple (mixed) supply. In a single supply (eg air travel and catering during the flight), there is only one overall type of supply and one VAT liability with no scope for apportionment. In a multiple supply, a single inclusive price is charged for a number of separate supplies of goods or services each with their own VAT liability. See 64.6 SUPPLY for further details.

(*b*) **Is there a single consideration?** Apportionment can only be applied to a single consideration that is given in return for more than one supply. If each supply has its own consideration, then there is no power under the *VATA 1994* to reapportion the value between them, although it is possible that the arrangement can be challenged if it is purely a 'sham'. See, for example, *Charlesworth (t/a Centurions) (VTD 9015) (TVC 36.24)* regarding the apportionment of profits between a second-hand car and an additional charge for a warranty.

In practice it is not always simple to distinguish between a payment that is a single consideration and a payment that is made up of several considerations that appear to be one because they are made simultaneously. There is no definitive test as to whether there are one or more considerations in any given case but it is likely that the customer has to know the charge for each particular supply before it can be accepted that there is more than one consideration. See *Thorn EMI plc; Granada plc (VTD 9782) (TVC 36.7)*.

(*c*) **Can any part of the payment be treated as outside the scope of VAT?** A common argument (frequently used by a charitable or other non-profit making organisation seeking to raise funds for a particular cause from the general public) is that part of the payment for a supply or group of supplies should be treated as an 'outside the scope' donation because the supplies are not 'worth' the money that has been given for them. Such an argument is flawed in three material respects. First, for VAT purposes, the consideration is the amount of payment that results in a supply being made and it is irrelevant that in other situations the consideration given may have been higher or lower. Secondly, the reason why a business charges a particular amount for a supply, or the recipient is prepared to pay that amount, is irrelevant in determining whether or not the amount constitutes consideration. Thirdly, as a donation is a freely given payment in return for which nothing is supplied at all and a consideration is payment for a supply, by definition no part of a consideration can be a donation. As *VATA 1994, s 19(4)* only operates to apportion the value of a consideration, it cannot be used to attempt to identify part of that consideration as a donation. See *C & E Commrs v Tron Theatre Ltd, CS 1993, [1994] STC 177 (TVC 65.107)*.

There are, however, two circumstances in which HMRC recognise an element of donation upon an informal concessionary basis.

- In some circumstances HMRC are prepared to regard a supply as so minimal that it can be disregarded on a *de minimis* basis. This has been done with sponsorship schemes where the 'sponsor' receives nothing more than a simple acknowledgement of their support. Consequently, the payment is not treated as consideration and valuation is not necessary.
- Subscriptions to certain types of organisation can occasionally be viewed as partly donational and outside the scope of VAT if certain conditions are met. See 14.2 CLUBS AND ASSOCIATIONS.

(*d*) **What are the liabilities of the supplies in question?** All the supplies to which a consideration relates must be identified and their respective liabilities established. Where all supplies are liable to VAT at the same rate, output tax due is calculated in the normal way and no apportionment is necessary. Otherwise the tax value of each supply must be calculated in order to arrive at the total output tax due.

(Internal Guidance V1–12, paras 3.1, 3.3–3.7).

47.4 Methods of apportionment

Although *VATA 1994, s 19(4)* provides for apportionment of consideration, it does not stipulate how this has to be done, simply that the values attributed to the various supplies are 'properly attributable', ie on a fair and reasonable basis. There are two basic apportionment methods that, with appropriate adaptations, can be used in most circumstances. One of these uses the costs attributable to the different supplies being made, the other is based upon the normal selling prices. However, a business is not obliged to use these methods and can propose any method of apportionment. HMRC have no power to insist that any particular method must be used unless a business refuses to make an apportionment calculation or declines to change a method that produces an unfair result.

Cost-based method of apportionment where costs of all supplies can be identified. In many cases, it is possible to identify costs directly attributable to all of the supplies that are being made. The proportion of these costs attributable to supplies at each liability is then calculated and applied to the total selling price. The calculation can be applied to either VAT-inclusive or VAT-exclusive selling prices. The following points should be noted.

- Most businesses incur some costs that are not readily attributable to any of the supplies being made by them, eg rental of premises, heating, lighting, telephone bills and staff costs. Where such costs cannot be directly attributed, they can either be excluded from the calculation completely or split in the same proportions as the costs that are directly attributable. For example, if the directly attributable costs result in 20% being attributed to zero-rated supplies and 80% to standard-rated supplies, the 'general costs' should be allocated in the same ratio.
- Under this method of apportionment HMRC officers are advised to check that
  - the costs have been directly attributed to the fullest possible extent;

— all of the supplies being made and all of the costs incurred have been taken into account in the first instance (complete omission of a supply or of a particular cost can result in a distorted valuation);

— costs which have been directly attributed to a supply have been attributed to the correct supply;

— figures are accurate by reference to the accounts of the business or other commercial records; and

— the business can support the allocation of value on the chosen basis of attribution where a particular cost is being attributed on some unusual basis (eg staff costs by reference to time spent by the member of staff in producing various supplies).

Example 1: Apportionment based on cost of both supplies: VAT-inclusive price

A VAT-inclusive price of £140 is charged for a supply of zero-rated goods which cost £23 and standard-rated goods which cost £40 (excluding VAT).

Proportion of the total cost represented by standard-rated goods =
(40 + VAT) ÷ ([40 + VAT] + 23) = 47/70

VAT-inclusive price of standard-rated goods = 47/70 × £140 =	£94
VAT included = £94 × VAT fraction = £94 × 7/47 =	£14
Tax value of zero-rated supply = £140 – £94 =	£46

Total price is therefore apportioned

Value of standard-rated supply	80
VAT on standard-rated supply	14
Value of zero-rated supply	46
	£140

Example 2: Apportionment based on cost of both supplies: VAT-exclusive price

A VAT-exclusive price of £126 is charged for a supply of zero-rated goods which cost £23 and standard-rated goods which cost £40 (excluding VAT).

Proportion of the total cost represented by standard-rated goods =
40/63

VAT-exclusive value of standard-rated goods = 40/63 × £126 =	£80
VAT on standard-rated goods = £80 × 17.5% =	£14
Tax value of zero-rated supplies = £126 – £80 =	£46

Total price is therefore	
Value of standard-rated supply	80
Value of zero-rated supply	46
	126
VAT on £80 at 17.5%	14
	£140

Costs-based method of apportionment where the costs of only one supply can be identified. Difficulties are more likely to be met where it is only possible to directly attribute costs to one of the supplies involved. This is particularly the case if the supply to which a direct attribution of costs is not possible is a significant element of the outputs. Two methods of apportionment have been approved by VAT tribunals in such cases.

In *IC Thomas (VTD 1862) (TVC 65.122)* admission to a greyhound stadium (standard-rated) included the provision of a programme (zero-rated) and it was not possible to directly attribute any costs to the supply of admission. The tribunal approved an apportionment which applied a 'mark-up' to the costs that could be directly attributed, deducted this figure from the total selling price and treated the remainder as the value of the other supply. If appropriate, the figures derived from a sampling exercise in this way can be expressed as a percentage and applied to total relevant income over a period. (Note that, following the decision in *Card Protection Plan v C & E Commrs, CJEC [1999] STC 270 (TVC 21.223)* HMRC now expect that, in the majority of cases such as this, there is a single supply of standard-rated admission, the programme being an ancillary item.)

In *BH Bright (VTD 4577) (TVC 65.123)* which was concerned with membership fees of a dating agency, the approved method of apportionment similarly applied a 'mark-up' to the costs that could be directly attributed (annual cost of zero-rated literature). It then calculated the uplifted figure as a percentage of the total costs for the year, arriving at a proportion of costs attributable to zero-rated supplies and, by deduction, the proportion attributable to standard-rated supplies. The latter proportion was then applied to subscription income for the year to arrive at the consideration for standard-rated supplies and consequently the output tax due.

The tribunal applied a 50% mark-up in *Thomas* and a 100% mark-up in *Bright*, although neither gave any reason for the percentages used. The mark-up applied must be acceptable in the light of the circumstances of the business. It is not HMRC policy to impose a range of acceptable uplifts but HMRC officers are advised to take the following points into consideration.

- If widely discrepant levels of profit are being claimed for the different supplies, the business should be asked to provide a full explanation for the difference of treatment. The 'weighting' of value in favour of supplies of favourable liability is a fairly common means by which VAT can be manipulated.
- The overall profits being generated by a business may be an indication of what would be a suitable uplift.
- Where the business makes other supplies that have the same liability as the supply in relation to which the costs are being uplifted, the level of profit on those supplies may give an indication of a suitable uplift.

- The business may be part of a particular trade within which the profit levels generally fall within a range that constitutes a 'norm'. However, specific factors may have to be taken into account for an individual business (eg the degree of competition locally) that could explain a departure from that established norm.

Arguments that standard-rated items are supplied at cost and all profits are derived from exempt or zero-rated supplies are likely to be rejected. See *Waterhouse Coaches Ltd (VTD 1417) (TVC 65.120)* and *Tynewydd Labour Working Men's Club and Institute Ltd v C & E Commrs, QB [1979] STC 570 (TVC 23.8).*

Example 3; Apportionment based on the cost of one supply only

A VAT-inclusive price of £142 is charged for a supply of zero-rated goods which cost £26 and standard-rated services, the cost of which cannot be identified. A fair and reasonable uplift on the zero-rated goods, consistent with actual profit margins of the business, is 50%.

Value of zero-rated supplies = £26 + 50% =	£39.00
VAT-inclusive price of standard-rated goods = £142 – £39 =	£103.00
VAT on standard-rated goods = £103 × 7/47 =	£15.34

The total price is therefore apportioned

Value of zero-rated supply	39.00
Value of standard-rated supply	87.66
	126.66
VAT on £87.66 at 17.5%	15.34
	£142.00

Example 4; Apportionment based on the cost of one supply only—annual calculation using the method approved in Thomas

Assume that the figures in Example 3 above are representative of similar transactions and the total VAT-inclusive income from such transactions in the year is £25,000.

Zero-rated percentage = 39/142 × 100 =	27.465%
Value of zero-rated supplies in year = £25,000 × 27.465%	£6,866
Consideration for standard-rated supplies in year =	
£25,000 – £6,866 =	£18,134
Output tax due = £18,134 × 7/47 =	£2,700.81

Example 5; Apportionment based on the cost of one supply only—annual calculation using the method approved in Bright

VAT-inclusive subscription income of £400,000 is received in a year in respect of supplies of zero-rated literature with direct costs of £42,000 and standard-rated services, the direct cost of which cannot be identified. The total costs of the business (excluding depreciation) amount to £250,000 in the year. A fair and reasonable uplift to the direct costs of the zero-rated literature to allow for indirect costs is 100%.

Direct cost of zero-rated supplies	42,000
Uplift of 100%	42,000
Full cost of providing zero-rated supplies	£84,000

Proportion of costs attributable to zero-rated supplies =	
84,000/250,000 × 100 =	33.6%
Proportion of costs attributable to standard-rated supplies =	66.4%
Consideration for standard-rated supplies =	
£400,000 × 66.4% =	£265,600.00
Output tax = £265,600.00 × 7/47 =	£39,557.45

Apportionment based upon normal selling prices (market values). This method is based on the prices the particular business normally charges for supplies, when made for separate considerations, and uses these amounts to apportion a single consideration given in return for comparable supplies.

Example 6; Apportionment based on normal selling-prices: VAT-inclusive price

A VAT-inclusive price of £200 is charged for a zero-rated supply (which would separately be charged at £50) and a standard-rated supply (which would separately be charged at £200 including VAT).

Proportion of the total normal price represented by standard-rated goods =	
200 ÷ (200 + 50) = 4/5	
VAT-inclusive price of standard-rated goods = 4/5 × £200 =	£160.00
VAT included = £160 × VAT fraction = £160 × 7/47 =	£23.83
Tax value of zero-rated supply = £200 – £160	£40.00

The total price is therefore apportioned

Value of standard-rated supply (£160 – £23.83)	136.17
VAT on standard-rated supply	23.83
VAT on zero-rated supply	40.00
	£200.00

(VAT Notice 700, paras 8.1, 32.1, 32.2; Internal Guidance V1–12, paras 3.2, 3.8–3.13).

47.5 Retrospective apportionment

Whether HMRC will allow a business to apply an apportionment retrospectively depends on the circumstances of the individual case. Set out below are the situations in which a request for retrospective apportionment is most likely to arise and how HMRC consider they should be treated.

(1) **No apportionment operated in the past and all supplies wholly standard-rated: business unaware that apportionment was available.** The business can make an apportionment in respect of the past for clearly identifiable zero-rated or exempt supplies that have been made. Overpaid VAT can be claimed under *VATA 1994, s 80* for up to three years. See 51.7 PAYMENT OF VAT.

(2) **No apportionment operated in the past and all supplies wholly standard-rated: business aware that apportionment was available but chose not to apply it.** The business is still entitled to perform an apportionment retrospectively at a later date, even if HMRC have specifically advised of the possibility and the business has chosen not to act on that advice.

(3) **Apportionment operated correctly in the past but business requests retrospective use of a different method.** This is the most problematic scenario. The only requirement under *VATA 1994, s 19(4)* is that an apportionment must achieve a 'proper attribution' of values. The end result must therefore be fair and supportable. However, in many cases, it is possible to apply one of several apportionment methods to a given mixture of supplies, each of which is likely to produce a different attribution of values without any one method being right or wrong. In such cases, therefore, HMRC will expect the business to provide convincing evidence that the previous method was unfair or, at the very least, that the end result achieved by the proposed new method produces a substantially more accurate attribution of values than the old method. Whatever the position, the proposed new method can be allowed from a current date.

(4) **Apportionment operated correctly in the past but discovery of an error not directly connected to the method of apportionment leads to the business requesting retrospective use of a different method.** This might arise, for example, where a supply that should have been exempt was incorrectly treated as standard-rated and, as a result, the business proposes a different apportionment method when the error is discovered. VAT liability for the past periods could be recalculated either by applying the old method to the corrected liabilities or using a new method. HMRC's treatment is as for (3) above.

(5) **Acceptable method of apportionment operated in the past but applied incorrectly: business requests retrospective use of a different method.** In such a case (eg where costs have been attributed to zero-rated supplies that were properly attributable to standard-rated supplies), HMRC would normally expect a recalculation for the past periods to be performed using the old method with the correct operation. Any new method would only be accepted from a current date unless the business can demonstrate that the old method, when operated correctly, produced an unfair result or was significantly inaccurate compared to the new one.

(6) **Past agreed apportionment method inherently defective: business requests retrospective use of a different method.** In this case, there has not been a 'proper attribution' of values as required by *VATA 1994, s 19(4)* and retrospection should be allowed in this situation if the proposed new method is acceptable to HMRC.

If HMRC consider that a business has been applying a method of apportionment that has not resulted in a 'proper attribution' of values, then

- if the business has correctly adopted one of the suggested apportionment methods in VAT Notice 700, Part 32 (see *Examples 1, 2, 3* and *6* in 47.4 above) but HMRC subsequently consider that the end result is not fair, it will normally only seek change from a current date; and
- if the operation of the chosen method was flawed (eg the business was attributing costs to zero-rated supplies that were properly attributable to standard-rated supplies), then HMRC may issue an assessment in respect of the past period.

(Internal Guidance V1–12, para 3.14).

47.6 BUSINESS GIFTS

For VAT purposes, an article is a gift where the donor is not obliged to give it and the recipient is not obliged to do or give anything in return. (VAT Notice 700, para 8.9). Business gifts cover a wide range of items including

- brochures, posters and advertising matter;
- 'executive presents';
- long service awards (see *RHM Bakeries (Northern) Ltd v C & E Commrs, QB 1978, [1979] STC 72 (TVC 60.9)*);
- retirement gifts;
- goods supplied to employees under attendance or safety at work schemes;
- items distributed to trade customers;
- prizes dispensed from amusement and gaming machines (see 57.3 RECREATION AND SPORT); and
- prizes of goods in betting and gaming and free lotteries (see 57.1 RECREATION AND SPORT).

(VAT Notice 700/35/97, para 1.1).

Gifts of goods. A gift of business assets (including land) is a supply of goods [*VATA 1994, Sch 4 paras 5(1), 9*] and is taxable as such subject to certain exceptions and special rules, including the following.

(*a*) There is no supply (and no VAT liability arises) unless the donor (or any of his 'predecessors') has or will become entitled to

  (i) credit for the whole or any part of the input tax on the supply, acquisition or importation of the goods or of anything comprised in them; or

  (ii) a refund of VAT on the supply or importation of those goods (or anything comprised in them) under the *EC 8th Directive* (refunds of VAT to persons established in other EC countries, see 21.57 EUROPEAN COMMUNITY GENERAL) or the *EC 13th Directive* (refunds of VAT to persons established outside the EC, see 48.5 OVERSEAS TRADERS).

  For this purpose, a person is the '*predecessor*' of the donor where the donor acquired the goods from him under a transaction relating to the transfer of a business as a going concern which was treated as neither a supply of goods nor a supply or services (see 8.10 *et seq* BUSINESS). The donor's predecessors include the predecessors of his predecessor through any number of transactions. The effect of this is that, for no VAT liability to arise, no entitlement to input tax on the goods must have arisen through any number of such going concern transactions.

[*VATA 1994, Sch 4 para 5(5)(5A); FA 1998, s 21; FA 2000, s 136(9)*].

The wording in (i) above is derived from *EC 6th Directive, Art 5(6)*. This was considered in *Finanzamt Burgdorf v Fischer, CJEC [2001] STC 1356 (TVC 21.111)* where a car dealer who had not reclaimed input tax on the initial purchase of a vintage car subsequently did so on substantial repairs to it. On ceasing to trade he retained the car as a private asset. The CJEC held that the effect of *Art 5(6)* was that VAT was payable on 'component parts' in respect of which input tax had been deducted (but not on the whole value of the car, since input tax had not been reclaimable on its initial purchase). The taxable amount for this purpose should be determined by reference to the price, at the time of the allocation, of the goods incorporated in the vehicle which constitute component parts of the goods allocated. Furthermore, where input tax had been reclaimed but there was no output tax liability under *Article 5(6)* (eg on extensive bodywork repairs which did not involve the addition of component parts), the input tax deducted had to be adjusted under *EC 6th Directive, Art 20(1)* where the value of the work in question had not been entirely consumed in the context of the business activity of the taxable person before the vehicle was allocated to his private assets.

(*b*) *After 30 September 2003*, there is no supply (and no VAT liability arises) on a gift of goods made in the course or furtherance of a business where 'the cost to the donor of acquiring or producing the goods', together with the cost of any other such business gifts made to the same person in 'the same year', was not more than £50. '*The same year*' means any period of twelve months that includes the day on which the gift is made.

In determining the '*cost to the donor of acquiring or producing the goods*', where the donor acquired the goods under a transaction relating to the transfer of a business as a going concern which was treated as neither a supply of goods nor a supply or services (see 8.10 *et seq* BUSINESS), the donor and his 'predecessors' are treated as if they were the same person. For this purpose, a '*predecessor*' is the transferor under such a transaction and a person's predecessors include the predecessors of his predecessor through any number of transactions. The effect of this is that the cost of the goods gifted remains unchanged by the transfer of a business as a going concern through any number of such transfers.

[*VATA 1994, Sch 4 para 5(2)(2A); FA 1996, s 33; FA 1998, s 21; FA 2003, s 21; SI 2001/735*].

Before 1 October 2003, there was no supply (and no VAT liability arose) on a gift of goods made in the course or furtherance of a business, not forming part of a series or succession of gifts to the same person, where the 'cost to the donor of acquiring or producing the goods' (see above) was £50 or less (£15 or less before 8 March 2001).

Where gifts were made to the same person on more than one occasion, this was a series or succession of gifts and VAT was due on all the goods regardless of cost. However, if it was simply by chance that the same person received a gift more than once, then HMRC did not regard this as a series or succession of gifts, ie it was the intention of the donor that was important. Examples of gifts which may not have formed part of a series or succession included

- annual gifts (such as at Christmas);
- gifts distributed on a random basis, eg where a salesman gave small personal items to trade contacts;
- small items given away to trade customers, eg ashtrays and beer mats given away by brewers; and
- advertising posters handed out for display at the premises of trade customers.

(VAT Notice 700/35/97, para 1.3).

Free prospectuses issued by a college to local residents on a regular basis were held to form part of a series or succession of gifts in *C & E Commrs v West Herts College, Ch D [2001] STC 1245 (TVC 60.101)*.

(*c*) Samples (see 47.8(23) below).

(*d*) No VAT is due on free meals or drinks to employees by way of catering (see 11.4 CATERING) or the provision of accommodation for employees in a hotel, etc (see 33.3 HOTELS AND HOLIDAY ACCOMMODATION). [*VATA 1994, Sch 6 para 10*].

(*e*) No further VAT may be due where additional goods or services are offered with normal taxable supplies as part of a business promotion (see 67 TRADE PROMOTION SCHEMES).

(*f*) Prizes donated for competitions in newspapers and magazines (for which special rules apply, see 57.18 RECREATION AND SPORT).

(*g*) Free fuel to employees for private motoring (for which special rules apply, see 45.16 MOTOR CARS).

(*h*) Free meals or drinks to non-employees is not normally a supply and no VAT is due (but see 9 BUSINESS ENTERTAINMENT for non-deductible input tax).

(*i*) A gift of goods for sale, export or letting by a charity (or a taxable person who is a profits-to-charity person) is zero-rated. See 12.7 CHARITIES.

(*j*) Where a business consists of promoting a sporting, entertainment or similar activity and

- the business does no more than organise an event at which trophies are given away,
- there is no other associated competition/event, and
- a charge is made for admission to see the presentation

part of the admission charge is regarded as being payment for the trophies and no further VAT is due on the 'gift' of the trophies.

(VAT Notice 700/35/97, para 1.1).

Input tax on goods purchased for business gifts is deductible. If the recipient of the goods also uses them for business purposes, that person can recover any VAT charged on the gift as input tax (subject to the normal rules). The donor cannot issue a VAT invoice (because there is no consideration) but see 40.2 INVOICES for the form of a VAT certificate which can be issued instead.

Value of the supply. Where a gift of goods is a taxable supply, the value of the goods on which VAT must be accounted for is the price the person would have to pay (excluding VAT), at the time of the supply, to purchase goods *identical* in every respect (including age and condition) to the goods concerned. Where that value cannot be ascertained, the price for the purchase of goods *similar* to, and of the same age and condition as, the goods concerned must be used. If that value is also not possible to ascertain, the cost of producing the goods concerned at that time is to be used. [*VATA 1994, Sch 6 para 6*].

A gift of services where the recipient is not required to do or give anything in return is generally not a taxable supply. See, however, 47.7 below where bought-in services are used by any person outside the business free of charge.

Inducements, etc. Goods or services supplied on condition that a purchase is made or some action is performed of benefit are not true gifts but constitute supplies in return for non-monetary consideration. This includes articles supplied under 'self-introduction' or 'introduce-a-friend' schemes by retail mail order companies where the introducer has a contractual right to receive the chosen articles. See 69.5 VALUATION and *GUS Merchandise Corporation Ltd v C & E Commrs, CA [1981] STC 569 (TVC 56.1)* and *Empire Stores Ltd v C & E Commrs, CJEC [1994] STC 623 (TVC 21.160)*. See also *C & E Commrs v Westmorland Motorway Services Ltd, CA [1998] STC 431 (TVC 65.144)* where free meals given to coach drivers as an inducement to stop at a motorway service station were held to be valued at the normal retail price of the meals.

47.7 PRIVATE OR NON-BUSINESS USE

Goods. Where by, or under the direction of, a person carrying on a business, goods held or used for the purpose of the business are

- put to any private use, or
- used, or made available to any person for use, for any non-business purpose

a supply of service is treated as taking place (whether or not there is any consideration for the supply).

Exceptions. These provisions do not apply in the following circumstances.

(*a*) Where no consideration is received, there is no supply (and no VAT liability arises) unless the person carrying on the business (or any of his 'predecessors') has or will become entitled to credit for the whole or any part of the VAT on the supply, acquisition or importation of the goods.

For this purpose, a person is a '*predecessor*' of the person carrying on the business where that person acquired the goods from the predecessor under a transaction relating to the transfer of a business as a going concern which was treated as neither a supply of goods nor a supply or services (see 8.10 *et seq.* BUSINESS). A person's predecessors include the predecessors of his predecessor through any number of transactions. The effect of this is that, for no VAT liability to arise, no entitlement to input tax on the goods must have arisen through any number of such going concern transactions.

(*b*) With effect from 9 April 2003, the provisions do not apply to

- any interest in land,
- any building or part of a building,
- any civil engineering work or part of such a work, or

- any goods incorporated or to be incorporated in a building or civil engineering work (whether by being installed as fixtures or fittings or otherwise)

unless the person carrying on the business or any of his predecessors (see (*a*) above) became entitled to credit for the whole or any part of the VAT on the supply, acquisition or importation of the asset in question before that date.

The effect of this change, in conjunction with the change to the provisions relating to services (see below) is that such assets are treated as services rather than goods for the purposes of private/non-business use and it is not possible to apply the 'Lennartz approach' (see 35.7 INPUT TAX) to the initial input tax deduction.

Value of the supply where no consideration is given. Except in the cases covered by 69.27 VALUATION (supplies of accommodation and catering by employers to employees) output tax is due on the 'full cost' to the taxable person of providing the services. Following the decision in *Finanzamt München III v Mohsche, CJEC 1993, [1997] STC 195 (TVC 21.125) 'full cost'* does not include cost of services in respect of which the owner of the goods has not been able to deduct input tax, ie it only covers full taxable costs and not exempt costs (eg insurance) or costs outside the scope of VAT (eg vehicle excise duty).

Over a period of time, full taxable costs are the amount of depreciation of the goods (where the item being depreciated was itself a taxable supply) plus any other taxable costs related to the goods and the value on which VAT is due is

$$\text{Full taxable costs} \times \frac{\text{period of non-business use}}{\text{period of total use}}$$

No account should be taken in the calculation of any periods when the goods were not in use at all. See *Enkler v Finanzamt Homburg, CJEC [1996] STC 1316 (TVC 21.81).* For example, if there were 51 days' private use and 69 days' business use over a year, the proportion of full taxable costs to be taken is 51/120 and not 51/365.

(VAT Notice 700, para 9.3; Internal Guidance V1–12, para 5.19).

[*VATA 1994, Sch 4 para 5(4)(4A)(5)(5A), para 9, Sch 6 para 7; FA 1995, s 33(3); FA 1998, s 21; FA 2003, s 22*].

Special rules apply to private use of road fuel and motor cars. See 45.16 and 45.18 MOTOR CARS respectively.

See 64.54 SUPPLY for the time of supply of the private use of goods.

Free loan of business assets in the course of business. The above provisions do not apply where assets of the business are freely lent in the course of the lender's business. Such loans are outside the scope of VAT provided there is no obligation on the lender to make any payment in money or in kind and the assets loaned are not for the lender's private use (marginal private use being ignored). The expectation that commercial goodwill will be encouraged by the loan does not preclude it from being accepted as free. The following are typical examples of free loans for the lender's business purposes which are outside the scope of VAT.

- Vans and other equipment lent by a trader to a subcontractor for use in connection with work under the subcontract.
- Goods lent free of charge to a customer as a temporary replacement while the customers goods are being serviced or repaired.

- Equipment lent free of charge by an employer to an employee (eg protective clothing) for use in connection with the employee's work.
- Machinery lent by a manufacturer free of charge to a user in connection with development work. The user must have a liability to return the machinery to the manufacturer if the latter so requires, even though it may be understood that the person to whom the goods are lent will keep them in use until they have reached the end of their useful life.
- Bar equipment lent by a brewer to licensees.
- Storage and dispensing equipment lent by an oil company to garages.
- Signboards and other equipment lent by manufacturers to garages.
- Sacks lent by a wholesaler to farmers for potatoes.
- Coffee making and similar machines lent by suppliers of tea, coffee and the like to regular trade customers for their product, provided there is no variation in the price charged for the beverage to take account of the free loan.
- Trophy and challenge cups given temporarily (eg for a year) to the winner of a race or competition.

(Internal Guidance V1–3, para 6.2).

Services. Where a person carrying on a business puts services which have been supplied to him to any private or non-business use, he is treated as having supplied those services in the course or furtherance of the business (except for the purposes of determining whether VAT on the supply of any services to him after 9 April 2003 is allowable input tax). Private use includes use outside the business by any person and own personal use where a business is carried on by an individual. After 9 April 2003, services supplied to a person include supplies of

- a major interest in land,
- any building or part of a building,
- any civil engineering work or part of such a work, or
- any goods incorporated, or to be incorporated, in a building or civil engineering work (whether by being installed as fixtures or fittings or otherwise)

and where these provisions apply to such supplies, the person is treated as supplying a service of making the goods available. The effect of this change, in conjunction with the change to the provisions relating to goods (see above) is that such assets are treated as services rather than goods for the purposes of private/non-business use and it is not possible to apply the 'Lennartz approach' (see 35.7 INPUT TAX) to the initial input tax deduction.

Exceptions. The provisions do not apply, however,

- where the services are used, or made available for use, for a consideration;
- where no input tax has been deducted or will become deductible on the supply to him;
- where any part of the input tax on the supply to him was not counted as input tax because of an apportionment under *VATA 1994, s 24(5)*, see 35.7 INPUT TAX (ie the provisions do not apply where an apportionment has been made between business and non-business use at the time of supply);

- where the services supplied consist of
  - (i) the provision in the course of catering of food or beverages to employees; or
  - (ii) the provision of accommodation for employees in a hotel, inn, boarding house or similar establishment; or
- where the services supplied consist of the letting on hire of a motor car and 50% of the input tax has already been excluded from credit (see 45.11 MOTOR CARS).

Value of supply. The value of the supply is that part of the value of the supply of services to him as fairly and reasonably represents the cost to him of providing the services. The total VAT charged (cumulative where the services are supplied on more than one occasion) cannot exceed the amount of input tax which has been deducted or will become deductible.

Anti-avoidance re business transfers. Where the transfer of the assets of a business as a going concern is treated as neither a supply of goods nor a supply of services (see 8.10 *et seq.* BUSINESS) the liability of the transferee to tax under these provisions is determined as if the transferor and the transferee were the same person. Where the business has been transferred VAT-free as a going concern more than once, the transferee is treated as if he and all the previous transferors were the same person.

[*SI 1993/1507; SI 1995/1668; SI 1998/762; SI 2003/1055*].

The above provisions relating to private use of services are concerned with major changes of use which continue over time or are permanent. Minor or occasional private or non-business use will be treated as *de minimis* and will not give rise to a liability to VAT. The type of services affected include computer software, building construction and refurbishment, particularly to domestic premises, and sporting rights.

Calculating the VAT due. There are no set rules for calculating the VAT due. If use of services permanently changes from business to non-business use, the accounting convention normally adopted for depreciating business assets may be used to calculate the VAT due, ie the value on which VAT is due is

$$\text{Cost of services} \times \frac{\text{Projected period of non-business use}}{\text{Period over which comparable assets are depreciated}}$$

Alternatively, any other fair and reasonable basis can be used. VAT should not be accounted for beyond the point at which

- the asset is fully depreciated, or
- the accumulated VAT accounted for equals the amount of input tax on the service which has proved to be not attributable to business use,

whichever is the earlier.

(Business Brief 17/94).

De Voil Indirect Tax Service. See V3.212; V3.216.

47.8 TREATMENT OF OUTPUT TAX IN PARTICULAR CASES

(1) Accommodation

See 33.1-33.4 HOTELS AND HOLIDAY ACCOMMODATION for supplies of accommodation in hotels, boarding houses, etc and 33.5-33.9 HOTELS AND HOLIDAY

ACCOMMODATION for the provision of holiday accommodation in the UK, including time share, caravans and camping.

(1A) **Adoption services**

Charities. Services provided by a charitable adoption agency in connection with domestic adoptions are exempt from VAT where the supply is made 'otherwise than for profit' (see 12.11 CHARITIES). This includes the provision of pre-adoption training, advice and guidance; the assessment of prospective adopters; as well as the actual placement of a child.

Any charge made by a charitable adoption agency for a home study assessment in connection with an inter-country adoption application is also exempt from VAT, provided that the assessment is supplied on an 'otherwise than for profit' basis. Previously, these assessments had been subject to VAT at the standard rate.

Local authorities. Services provided by a local authority in connection with adoption are non-business activities. They are not subject to VAT when carried out as part of the local authority's statutory responsibility.

Other suppliers. All supplies in connection with any adoption that are not made by a charity on an 'otherwise than for profit' basis or by a local authority are standard-rated.

(Business Brief 21/01).

(2) **Agricultural grant schemes**

VAT is not to be applied to payments under the following grant schemes.

DEFRA

Farm Woodland Scheme
Set Aside Scheme
Agricultural Act 1986, s 18 (Environmentally Sensitive Areas)
Outgoers under the *Milk (Cessation of Production) Act 1985*

Department of the Environment

Nature Conservancy Council management agreements
Countryside Premium Scheme for Set Aside Land
Countryside Commission Community Forests Scheme

Forestry Commission

Woodland Grant Scheme
Farm Woodland Scheme

(C & E Press Release 58/89, 9 August 1989).

EC grants. Grants paid by the Intervention Board to processors of dried animal fodder are within the scope of VAT although, to the extent that supplies of animal fodder are zero-rated, no VAT is due. Processors who supply dried fodder must include the value of grants received in the total value of sales in Box 6 of the VAT return. Where the grant relates to fodder for the processors' own use, there is no VAT supply and grants should continue to be treated as outside the scope of VAT.

Other EC grants are generally outside the scope of VAT.

(Business Brief 28/99).

(3) **Change in rate of VAT**

See 55.6 *et seq.* RATES OF VAT for the effects on the calculation of output tax where there is a change in either the rate of VAT or the VAT liability of a particular supply.

(4) **Compensation payments**

Compensation payments for damage or loss are normally outside the scope of VAT as they are not consideration for a supply. This is because the payments are made either as a result of a Court Order or through an agreement between the two parties involved to compensate one party for suffering some inconvenience, loss or damage.

Early termination of contracts. Two conflicting tribunal decisions on exactly the same facts show the difficulties in determining the VAT position of payments arising out of early contract termination. In *Holiday Inns (UK) Ltd (VTD 10609) (TVC 60.124)* a company (C) owned a hotel which was managed by another company (H) under a management agreement. As the agreement did not allow for early termination, the parties entered into a separate termination agreement under which C paid H £2m as compensation. C wished to reduce the cost of the settlement by treating part of the payment as VAT (which it recovered as input tax) on the basis the H had made a supply of granting C the right to terminate. The tribunal held that, although drawn up years apart, the termination agreement constituted a part of the original management agreement, effectively inserting a termination clause into the latter. As this meant C already had the right to terminate, it could not have purchased the right from H and therefore there had been no supply for VAT purposes.

As a result of this decision, HMRC sought to obtain repayment of the input tax that C had claimed and C appealed (*Croydon Hotel & Leisure Company Ltd (VTD 14920) (TVC 34.540)*). The tribunal, with the same facts as the earlier hearing, held that the termination agreement and £2m payment did represent a supply for VAT purposes, following the CJEC's subsequent decision in *Lubbock Fine & Co, CJEC Case C–63/92, [1994] STC 101 (TVC 21.228)*.

In *Lloyds Bank plc (VTD 14181) (TVC 60.125)* the bank decided to vacate a property it leased. The lease did not provide for early cancellation. Lloyds and its landlord therefore agreed a variation to the lease, setting out terms for early termination and the bank paid £597,220 as compensation. Because the parties effected the early termination on the same day as agreeing the variation, the tribunal held that there had been a supply by the landlord of granting and exercising an option to terminate the lease in return for a payment by Lloyds and its vacating the premises.

On the basis of these tribunal decisions, HMRC take the view that

- there is no supply for VAT purposes of 'the right to terminate' or other such services where a contract originally contains a clause allowing the parties to terminate early in lieu of compensation for perceived losses arising from the termination; but
- there will be supplies where no such right exists and agreements have separately to be reached properly to terminate the contracts. This is so even if these agreements refer to monetary 'compensation'.

It is also possible that a supply takes place even when there is a right to terminate but a period of notice of the termination is required. In such circumstances, one party may seek the right to waive the period of notice, producing a result similar to those in the *Croydon Hotel* and *Lloyds* cases.

Liquidated damages. Agreements that allow for early termination will invariably include related clauses that provide a formula for payment of compensation in the event of such termination. These amounts are generally to compensate for loss of earnings and are often referred to as liquidated damages. They are not consideration for supplies and are outside the scope of VAT.

Leases for goods. Lease agreements for movable goods frequently include clauses that allow lessees to terminate early on payment of liquidated damages. Such sums are not liable to VAT. However, an agreement with the leasing industry allows lessors to treat lease terminations generally as taxable supplies if they wish (although they cannot be required to do so).

Breach of contract. Leases and other agreements may terminate early if a particular event occurs (eg the customer breaches the terms or the lessee calls in receivers). The contract deems that such events cancel its terms or effectively allow the lessor to terminate as though there had been a breach. Again, any moneys deemed to be due as a result are damages and outside the scope of VAT. See *Financial & General Print Ltd (VTD 13795) (TVC 34.539)*.

Settlement of disputes. Where disputes involve an argument over price or poor standard of workmanship, any settlement paid by the customer is consideration for the goods or services previously supplied and the value of the supply is the agreed amount of settlement (either following a Court Order or an out of court agreement). If an 'interest' payment is also due under the settlement, this is not consideration for any supply and is a form of damages to compensate the supplier for being paid late.

Where disputes involve damages (eg a suit for slander, libel or unauthorised use of a trade name, etc) any settlement is normally outside the scope of VAT. If, however, a payment is made in addition to the damages for the past offence (eg for future authorised use of a trade name or copyright) that element of the payment constitutes consideration for a taxable supply.

See *Whites Metal Co (VTD 2400) (TVC 34.536)*, *Cooper Chasney Ltd (VTD 4898) (TVC 60.120)* and *Hurley Robinson Partnership (VTD 750) (TVC 60.118)*. See also Internal Guidance V1–3, para 8 for agreed minutes on a meeting between HMRC and the Law Society on the settlement of disputes generally.

Land and property payments. See 42.4 LAND AND BUILDINGS for dilapidation payments and statutory compensation from landlords to tenants.

Compensation for damaged goods held in trust or on hire. Where goods held in trust (eg left for repair) or supplied on hire are lost or destroyed while out of the custody of the owner,

- replacement of the goods with similar goods, or
- payments to cover the cost of repair or replacement

by the person to whom the goods were entrusted is not a supply for consideration. Such payments are outside the scope of VAT.

Manufacturers' and retailers' warranties. See 69.9 VALUATION.

(Internal Guidance V1–3, paras 7.8, 7.9, 10.14).

Surrender of firearms. Compensation payments made by the Home Office to VAT-registered firearms dealers required to surrender certain calibre handguns are taxable supplies under *EC Sixth Directive, Art 5(4)(a)* (see 22.7(*a*) EUROPEAN COMMUNITY LEGISLATION) where the surrendered firearms were business stock. The compensation payments therefore include a VAT element. Under powers contained in *SI 1995/2518, Reg 25(5)*, HMRC are prepared to allow any VAT due to be accounted for on the VAT return for the period in which the payment of compensation is received. (Business Brief 27/97). See also *Parker Hale Ltd v C & E Commrs, QB [2000] STC 388 (TVC 60.127)*.

Compensation payments generally. For cases concerning whether compensation was in respect of a taxable supply or outside the scope of VAT, see *F Penny (t/a FMS Management Services) (VTD 10398) (TVC 60.123)* (compensation payment for loss of consultancy); *Galaxy Equipment (Europe) Ltd (VTD 11415) (TVC 38.44)* (compensation for faulty goods); and *Hometex Trading Ltd (VTD 13012) (TVC 34.537)* (compensation payments made by order of court). Compensation under *EC Council Regulation 1336/86* for discontinuing milk production is not subject to VAT (*Mohr v Finanzamt Bad Segeberg, CJEC [1996] STC 328 (TVC 21.120)*).

See also 69.9(1) VALUATION for fines and penalty charges.

(5) **Energy-saving materials and grant-funded installation of heating equipment or security goods, etc.**

Supplies of certain energy-saving materials and other qualifying goods and their installation are subject to VAT at the reduced rate of 5%. See 58.2 and 58.3 REDUCED RATE SUPPLIES.

(6) **Exempt supplies**

Output tax is not chargeable on exempt supplies. See 24 EXEMPT SUPPLIES for a list of the categories of exemption and cross-references to supporting chapters.

(7) **Gifts**

See 47.6 above.

(8) **Goods obtained by fraud**

Where the agreement for the supply of goods has been rescinded, no supply has taken place and the supplier can adjust the output tax he has paid provided he gets authorisation before doing so. Adjustment is specifically to the VAT account and credit notes should not be issued. In order to get authorisation, the trader must apply to HMRC enclosing evidence of fraud and a copy of the invoice. The evidence required by HMRC is

- evidence that the trader has been victim of the fraud proved in the courts or, where the person who committed the fraud goes missing, confirmation from the police that they are satisfied that a fraud has actually taken place;
- evidence that the trader has made a statement to the police for use in the prosecution; and
- a verifiable description of the goods involved.

Suitable evidence might take the form of police letters and press reports describing the injured party and the goods.

If the person who committed the fraud is convicted, any part payment made in the course of the fraud (eg by paying some cash and the balance by fraudulent cheque) cannot be the consideration for a supply and is outside the scope of the tax. If the person who committed the fraud is ordered to make restitution, that is compensation and outside the scope of the VAT.

If payment is made after conviction and output tax has been adjusted, there is a new contract or agreement and any supply would be considered on its own merits.

Where rescission of the supply is blocked because

- the supplier affirms the agreement by pursuing the person who committed the fraud for payment rather than the return of goods,
- the supplier unduly delays in rescinding the contract after discovering the fraud, or
- the goods have been supplied on to a third party,

by concession, the supplier is allowed to recover the VAT declared if the fraud is reported to the police and HMRC are satisfied that the business has been defrauded.

(Internal Guidance V1–3, paras 21.4, 21.5).

See also *Harry B Litherland & Co Ltd (VTD 701) (TVC 60.154)*.

De Voil Indirect Tax Service. See V5.158.

(9) **Lost, stolen or destroyed goods**

HMRC may require a taxable person from time to time to account for goods supplied to, or acquired or imported by, him in the course or furtherance of his business (including any goods transferred from another EC country). If such goods have been lost or destroyed, HMRC may assess him on the VAT which would have been chargeable in respect of the supply of the goods if he is unable to prove such loss or destruction. [*VATA 1994, s 73*(*7*)].

Where, therefore, a taxable person can prove that his goods have been lost, stolen or destroyed, output tax is only chargeable if the goods have been supplied. Where goods are *lost, etc in transit* to the customer, then

- if, under the contract, the customer is responsible for any loss before delivery, output tax is due; and
- if, under the contract, the supplier is responsible for any such loss, output tax is due where a VAT invoice has been issued. If a VAT invoice has not been issued, no output tax is due because there has not been a supply.

See also 23.19 EUROPEAN COMMUNITY: SINGLE MARKET for goods lost, etc in transit to other EC countries.

(VAT Notice 700, para 8.10).

(10) **Management services**

See 44.1-44.3 MANAGEMENT SERVICES AND SUPPLIES OF STAFF.

(11) **Milk quotas**

The VAT liability of the supply or transfer of a milk quota to another farmer depends upon whether it is supplied with or without land.

- Where the supply or transfer of a milk quota is linked with the supply of land under one agreement, there is a single supply and VAT liability follows that of the land. This applies whether the land is sold freehold or leasehold and even if separate identifiable sums are shown on the invoice and paid for the land and quota.
- The supply or transfer of a milk quota without land is a standard-rated supply of services.
- Where a milk quota is transferred with a grazing licence, there are two separate supplies, a zero-rated supply of animal feeding stuffs through the grazing licence and a standard-rated supply of the milk quota.

(Business Brief 17/94).

For further information, see Internal Guidance V1–7, Chapter 1 paras 27.1–27.8.

See (2) above for surrender of a milk quota in return for a DEFRA grant.

(12) **Motor cars**

See 45.4 MOTOR CARS for disposal of a motor car used in a business and 45.16 MOTOR CARS for VAT on fuel supplied for private motoring.

(13) **Motor vehicles — statutory fees, etc.**

MOT tests. The charge for an MOT test provided direct by a test centre to its customers is outside the scope of VAT, provided it does not exceed the statutory maximum. Any discount given by a test centre to an unapproved garage is treated as a normal trade discount and not seen as consideration for a taxable supply by the unapproved garage to the test centre.

Where an unapproved garage shows the exact amount charged by the test centre separately on the invoice to its customer, and meets the other conditions for disbursements in VAT Notice 700, para 25.1 (see 3.7 AGENTS), it may treat this element as a disbursement and also outside the scope of VAT. Any amount charged over and above the amount charged by the test centre is consideration for its own service of arranging the test on behalf of its customer and is taxable at the standard rate. If the unapproved garage chooses not to treat the amount charged by the test centre as a disbursement, or otherwise does not satisfy all the conditions for disbursements, it must account for VAT on the full invoiced amount.

(VAT Notice 700, para 25.4; Business Brief 21/96).

Driving tests. Fees charged by the Department of Transport (and training bodies appointed by them) for Part 1 of the *motorcycle* driving test are liable to VAT at the standard rate. The Department of Transport supplies Part 2 of that test and *other motor vehicle* driving tests as part of its statutory obligation and the fees involved are outside the scope of VAT. (C & E Press Notice 909, 27 April 1984).

Removal/recovery services. Statutory fees for removal and storage of vehicles are outside the scope of VAT when levied by the police on the motorist or owner of the vehicle. If the police contract out this service, such fees collected by the contractor on behalf of the police are not consideration for any supply by the contractor to the motorist and are also outside the scope of VAT. Where, however, in such circumstances the contractor retains some or all of the amounts collected, the retained amount represents consideration for the supply of services from the contractor to the police authority and is liable to VAT at the standard rate. (Business Brief 9/99).

Vehicle clamping and towaway fees. Where landowners use parking enforcement contractors to enforce parking restrictions on their premises, fees payable to the contractor, as agent for the landowner, are outside the scope of VAT, being damages or compensation for the trespass suffered by the landowner. Where, however, under the terms of the agreement with the landowner, the contractor retains some or all of the amount collected, the retained amount represents consideration for the supply of services by the contractor to the landowner and is liable to VAT at the standard rate. VAT is also due on any management charge to the landowner. (Business Brief 7/00).

(14) **Non-existent goods**

A supply of goods is made only when they are passed to someone. Therefore, where goods do not exist and do not later come into existence, no supply can occur, no output tax is chargeable and no input tax is claimable. (Internal Guidance V1–3, para 21.2). See also *P Howard (VTD 1106) (TVC 34.530)*, *Theotrue Holdings Ltd (VTD 1358) (TVC 34.522)* and *MS Munn (VTD 3296) (TVC 34.531)*.

(15) **Packaging**

General. Normal and necessary packaging, including ordinary tins, bottles and jars, is treated as part of the goods which it contains so that if the goods are zero-rated, zero-rating also applies to the packaging. However,

- where the packaging is more than normal or necessary, there may be a multiple supply. The consideration must then be apportioned if the goods are not standard-rated and VAT is due on the packaging (see 47.3 above). This could apply to storage containers and other types of packaging which could be sold separately;
- where an additional charge is made with a supply of goods for their container to ensure that it is safely returned and the additional charge is to be refunded on its safe return, this additional charge is not subject to VAT; and
- where an additional charge is raised to cover the loan, hire or use of a container, then the charge is standard-rated.

(VAT Notice 700, para 8.2).

Food packaging. Where the purpose of the packaging is simply to contain, protect and promote the food it contains, HMRC consider it as part of the supply of the food inside, rather than a supply in its own right, and it takes the same liability as its contents. This is so even if the packaging is more than the minimum strictly necessary. This follows the decision in *C & E Commrs v United Biscuits (UK) Ltd t/a Simmers, CS [1992] STC 325 (TVC 27.75)* where it was held that decorative biscuit tins amounting to 55% of the total production cost (as opposed to 28% for ordinary cardboard packaging) were normal packaging for biscuits. The court held that the tin was integral to the biscuits, not merely in the sense that it was the container in which they were packaged, but further in that it prolonged their shelf-life and kept the biscuits in better condition once consumption had begun.

Where packaging is clearly designed to be 'extra' to the food, there is a multiple supply of food and packaging and normally the total price must be apportioned in order to arrive at the output tax due (see 47.3 above). Subject to the linked goods concession below, this applies to the following types of containers.

- Any container specifically advertised or held out for sale as having a value in its own right (eg by advertising the product as 'with a free storage tin').
- Any container with a clear and obviously intended after-use (eg tumblers containing coffee, honey or preserves in ceramic serving bowls).
- Storage jars obviously intended for use in storing future supplies of the product.
- Biscuit tins containing built-in hydroscopic crystals.
- Tea caddies (but not simple tins bearing the supplier's name and details of the weight and variety of tea where it is the supplier's practice to sell tea in this way).
- Ceramic pâté pots and other ceramic containers which are clearly suitable for future decorative use. See, however, *Paterson Arran Ltd (VTD 15041) (TVC 27.76)* where, following *United Biscuits Ltd* above, zero-rating was applied to the sale of quality biscuits in a ceramic jar aimed at the Christmas market, even though the jar represented 70% of the total cost.
- Hampers and picnic baskets (other than simple cardboard cartons).

Outer cases and boxes, etc and seasonal packaging (although frequently more elaborate than supplied during the rest of the year) are not normally considered separate supplies unless falling within one of the above categories.

Linked goods concession. Where, however, standard-rated packaging is supplied with zero-rated food, the supply can be treated as a single supply of zero-rated food provided the packaging

- is not charged at a separate price;
- costs no more than 20% of the total cost of the supply; and
- costs no more than £1 (excluding VAT).

(VAT Notice 701/14/02, para 6.3).

(16) **Payphones**

Telephones. Where a payphone is rented from British Telecom or another supplier, the person renting the machine makes the supplies to the users and VAT is due on these supplies. Output tax is calculated by applying the VAT fraction to the money removed.

With some installations it is possible to switch from payphone mode to domestic mode and make calls without inserting money. If the domestic mode is used to make non-business calls, all VAT charged by British Telecom cannot be treated as input tax.

Phonecards. See 60.9(3) RETAIL SCHEMES.

(VAT Notice 700, para 8.12).

(17) **Personal service companies**

A service company may be set up to provide the services of a single worker to a client in circumstances where, without the service company, the worker would be an employee of the client. The use of a service company in this way allows the client to make payments to the company, rather than the individual, without deducting PAYE or NICs. The worker could then take the money from the service company in the form of dividends rather than salary, again avoiding NICs. In order to counter such avoidance, the Inland Revenue, under IR35 rules, can treat the payments made by the service company to the worker as chargeable to income tax under Schedule E and subject to NICs. This 'IR35' Schedule E status in respect of income ascribed to the worker does not affect the VAT position on supplies by the service company to the client. This is because the company, not the worker, contracts to provide the services to the client and it is, subject to registration requirements, liable to account for VAT on these supplies. (Internal Guidance V1–3, para 17.6).

(18) **Postage and delivery charges**

A supply of goods may involve delivery to the customer. The way any delivery charge is treated for VAT purposes depends on the circumstances in which the goods are supplied.

- **Where goods are delivered to a customer with no additional charge.** If delivery is free, or the cost is built into the normal price, VAT is accounted for on the goods in the normal way based on the liability of the goods themselves. This applies whether or not delivery is required under the contract.

- **Where delivery is required under the sales contract and a charge is made.** If, under the terms of the contract, the seller has to deliver the goods to a place specified by the customer (eg the address of the customer, his friends or relatives or his own customers), the seller is making a single supply of delivered goods for which the VAT liability is based on the liability of the goods being delivered. The position is not affected by whether the charge made for delivery is separately itemised or invoiced to the customer. For example, any element of the price attributed to the doorstep delivery of milk and newspapers will also be zero-rated. On the other hand, any element attributed to the delivery of standard-rated mail order goods will be standard-rated.

  See also *C & E Commrs v Plantiflor Ltd, HL [2002] STC 1132 (TVC 23.2)*.

- **Where delivery is not required under the contract or someone else's goods are delivered.** Delivery services are normally treated as a separate supply of services where

  (i) goods are supplied under a contract that does not require delivery but where, nevertheless, the seller agrees to deliver the goods and make a separate charge; or

  (ii) a business provides a service of delivering somebody else's goods (see also below for direct mailing services).

  In such cases, the liability of the delivery charge is not affected by the liability of the goods being delivered and there is a separate supply of delivery services which is normally standard-rated (although special rules apply if the delivery forms part of the movement of goods to or from a place outside the UK, see 68.24 TRANSPORT AND FREIGHT). For example, the charge for the distribution of a publisher's zero-rated newspapers is a standard-rated supplies of services. Similarly, where the seller arranges for goods to be delivered by post, the supply of delivery services is taxable even though the charges are identical to the exempt supply to him by the Post Office.

Direct mailing services. Where a supplier provides the service of posting client's mail (eg publicity or advertising material or promotional goods), the supplier may treat the charges by the Royal Mail (which for these purposes includes other operators licensed by Postcomm) as a disbursement for VAT purposes provided

(*a*) the general conditions for treatment as a disbursement are satisfied (see 3.7(*a*)–(*h*) AGENTS);

(*b*) the client specifies who to send the mail to or has access to the mailing list before the mail is sent out;

(*c*) the supplier's responsibility for the mail ceases when it is accepted for safe delivery by Royal Mail; and

(*d*) the supplier passes on any Royal Mail discount or rebate to the client in full or, if the supplier obtains any discount or rebate from posting various clients' mail at the same time, it is apportioned fairly between them.

If conditions (*a*)–(*d*) are not met, the full amount of postal charges must be included in the value of the direct mailing service. This is normally standard-rated if the mail is sent to addresses in the UK. Special rules, however, apply if the delivery is, or forms part of, the movement of goods to or from a place outside the UK, see 68.24 TRANSPORT AND FREIGHT.

Freepost. Freepost is an arrangement whereby the recipient (ie the advertiser) of a returned mailshot pays the postage costs on behalf of the sender (eg a member of the public). Commonly a PO box number will also be used. The supply by Royal Mail of the Freepost and PO Box licences, plus any handling service for which an additional fee is charged, is made to the licence holder. This may be the recipient (advertiser) or an agent handling the mail on the recipient's behalf. However, the supply of postage is made to the sender of the mail, although the recipient (advertiser) or the agent meets the cost. This means that where an agent is employed to handle the Freepost

- any recovery of the postage costs by the agent from the recipient (advertiser) is not liable to VAT; and
- where the licence is taken out by the agent in the name of the recipient (advertiser), the costs may be disbursed to the recipient, subject to the normal rules referred to above.

Retail schemes. For supplies of *delivered goods*,

- under the Point of Sale scheme, include the full amount charged in daily gross takings;
- under Apportionment Scheme 1, include the full amount charged in daily gross takings and do not adjust the record of purchases; and

- under Apportionment Scheme 2 and the Direct Calculation schemes, include the full amount charged in daily gross takings and also allow for the delivery charge element in the calculation of expected selling prices.

If delivery services are provided for an extra charge,

- under the Point of Sale scheme and the Apportionment schemes, account for VAT due on the delivery services outside the scheme used; and

- under the Direct Calculation schemes,
  - (i) where minority goods are zero-rated, include delivery charges in daily gross takings; and
  - (ii) where minority goods are standard-rated, the delivery charges will not be included in the expected selling prices calculation and can be added back as part of the standard-rated sales figure. Otherwise, account for VAT due on delivery services outside the scheme.

Packing services. A separate supply of packing services will normally be standard-rated. Special rules, however, apply if the delivery forms part of the movement of goods to or from a place outside the UK, see 68.24 TRANSPORT AND FREIGHT.

(VAT Notice 700, para 8.3; VAT Notice 700/24/03; VAT Notice 727/3/02, para 6.10; VAT Notice 727/4/02, para 7.11; VAT Notice 727/5/02, para 6.10).

(19) **Postage stamps and philatelic supplies**

See 57.19 RECREATION AND SPORT.

(20) **Private or non-business use of goods**

See 47.7 above.

(21) **Promotion schemes**

See 67 TRADE PROMOTION SCHEMES.

(21A) **Reduced rate supplies**

VAT is chargeable on certain supplies at a reduced rate (currently 5%). See 58 REDUCED RATE SUPPLIES.

(21B) **Payments to a retail consortium**

Retailers may join together to form a purchasing consortium for the purposes of negotiating lower prices for the goods they purchase. Any payments made by a manufacturer or supplier to the consortium are regarded as the consideration for a taxable supply of services by the consortium of introducing the manufacturer/supplier to a larger customer base. The purchasing consortium must account for VAT at the standard rate on all such receipts. See *Landmark Cash and Carry Group Ltd (VTD 883) (TVC 60.172)*. (Business Brief 12/93).

(22) **Royalty and licence fees**

Where a customer is recharged with payments made for royalty or licence fees incurred in making the supply to him, these charges are not disbursements for VAT purposes. The recharge is part of the consideration for the supply to the customer and VAT must be accounted for on the full value including the recharge. (VAT Notes (No 2) 1985/86).

(23) **Samples**

A gift to any person of a sample of any goods is not a taxable supply except that, where a number of identical samples (or samples not differing in any material respect) are given to the same person (whether on one or different occasions), only one of those samples is deemed not to be a supply. [*VATA 1994, Sch 4 para 5(2)(3)*].

Samples for testing. No VAT is due on samples given free of charge to someone for testing. The limit of one sample per person (see above) may be exceeded if it can be shown that the items are given for quality assurance testing either on behalf of the supplier or a potential customer.

Samples given to the general public via an intermediary (eg samples supplied by a manufacturer to a retailer for giving away as samples to the retailer's customers). No VAT is due provided the following conditions are met.

- Neither the supplier nor the intermediary charge for the goods.
- The samples are supplied for genuine business purposes and are given as an illustrative example of the product.
- The samples remain the property of the supplier until they are given to the final customer.
- Any samples not used are returned to the supplier or destroyed.

Sale of samples. If a person sells goods given to him as samples, VAT is due on the sale.

(VAT Notice 700/35/97, paras 3.1–3.4).

(24) **School photographers**

See 20.18 EDUCATION.

(25) **Second-hand goods**

See 61 SECOND-HAND GOODS.

(26) **Solicitors**

Oath fees. Under *Solicitors Act 1974, s 81* every solicitor holding a practising certificate may exercise the powers of a commissioner for oaths. Oath fees are regarded as deriving from the personal qualification of a solicitor, such that the solicitor who administers oaths receives the fees in a personal capacity. Whether or not VAT is due will depend upon the circumstances of the individual solicitor concerned.

(*a*) *Sole practitioners and partners*. Fees received in respect of oaths administered by a solicitor in sole practice or a partner in a firm of solicitors are regarded as consideration for services supplied in the course of the business. If the practice/partnership is registered for VAT, VAT is due. Fees received in a VAT period should be treated as VAT-inclusive.

(*b*) *Assistant solicitors*. VAT treatment depends upon whether or not the assistant solicitor accounts to the firm for oath fees received.

- Where fees are accounted for to the firm, they are part of the firm's business receipts and VAT must be accounted for as under (*a*) above.

- Where the firm allows the assistant solicitor to retain fees personally, the fees will not be subject to VAT unless the assistant solicitor is individually registered for VAT by virtue of other activities (or required to be registered taking into account the level of oath fees received).

(*c*) *Solicitors employed otherwise than in practice or retired solicitors.* Any fees received will not be subject to VAT unless the individual is registered for VAT by virtue of other activities (or required to be registered taking into account the level of oath fees received).

(Law Society's Gazette, 8 June 1994).

(27) **Sponsorship income**

See 57.18 RECREATION AND SPORT.

(28) **Sport and physical recreation facilities**

See 57.7 RECREATION AND SPORT.

(29) **Supplies of staff**

See 44.4–44.8 MANAGEMENT SERVICES AND SUPPLIES OF STAFF.

(29A) **Toll charges**

In *EC Commission v UK, CJEC [2000] STC 777 (TVC 21.93)* the court ruled that, in certain circumstances, central and local government bodies act as public authorities when they operate tolled bridges, tunnels and roads. Tolls in this category are outside the scope of VAT. This applies to

- Cleddau Bridge
- Dartford Crossing
- Erskine Bridge
- Forth Road Bridge
- Humber Bridge
- Itchen Bridge
- Mersey Tunnel
- Tamar Bridge
- Tay Bridge
- Tyne Tunnel

But the court held that, in any other circumstances, a toll charge is consideration for a standard-rated supply. The decision was implemented in the UK with effect from 1 February 2003. As a result, from that date:

- Tolls payable to private sector operators for use of roads, road bridges and road tunnels are subject to VAT. As this becomes a business activity, toll operators affected can recover input tax on many of their costs. Arrangements have been put in place by the Department of Transport and the Scottish Executive to manage the impact of these changes.
- VAT-registered businesses can recover the VAT charged on tolls if they are entitled to do so under the normal rules. It is not necessary to obtain a

VAT invoice to support a claim for input tax on a toll paid at a toll booth for a single or return journey costing up to £25. Otherwise a VAT invoice or other proof of payment must be obtained as appropriate. Businesses are advised to enquire about the VAT status of toll charges when they pay them.

(Business Brief 3/03).

(30) **Vending machines**

Where customers are provided with 'free' use of vending or similar machines then, provided the customer pays the same price for the products dispensed (coffee, tea, etc) as other customers who simply buy the product, no VAT is due on the hire of the machines. If, however, a higher amount is charged, VAT must be accounted for at the standard rate on the price difference. (VAT Notice 700/7/02, para 6.9). For supplies in the course of catering, see 11.1 CATERING.

(31) **Video/DVD films and games**

Rental of a video/DVD, where the customer must normally return it by a given date and the film/game remains the property of the supplier, is a supply of services. The value for VAT purposes is the amount paid for the use of the film/game over the rental period.

In a **part-exchange transaction**, the customer's film/game is accepted as payment (or part payment) for another film/game which then becomes the customer's property. Part-exchange is a supply of goods the value of which is the amount the customer would have had to pay for the film/game if there were no part-exchange. See *C & E Commrs v Bugeja, CA [2001] STC 1568 (TVC 65.82)*. In that case, a trader (B) sold videos for, say, £20 but where a customer offered a video previously purchased from B in part-exchange, B only charged the customer £10 for the new video. The Court of Appeal held that the consideration for such a sale was £20 (rejecting both the contention of the appellant that he should only be required to account for output tax on the £10 cash payment and the High Court decision (*QB 1999, [2000] STC 1*) that consideration for the sale was the £10 paid in cash plus the value of the second-hand video which, on the evidence, could not be more than £2 to £3).

Output tax using one of the special RETAIL SCHEMES (60).

Rental. All rental payments and membership fees (see below) can be included in gross takings under

- the Point of Sale scheme; and
- Direct Calculation Schemes 1 and 2 (provided the minority goods under the scheme are zero-rated or taxable at the reduced rate).

Under any other scheme, such receipts must be excluded from gross takings and dealt with outside the scheme. The value of any videos/DVDs bought for rental must also be excluded from the scheme calculations.

Part-exchange. Whichever scheme is used, the full normal retail selling price, including VAT, must be included in gross takings without deduction for the value of films/games taken in part-exchange. Where videos/DVDs taken in part-exchange are subsequently resold, it may be possible to use the margin scheme for SECOND-HAND GOODS (61). If not, they can be included in the retail scheme calculations.

Other charges.

Membership fees are taxable on the full amount charged even if refunded when the customer gives up membership.

Deposits. A refundable deposit for the safe return of a rental film/game is not taxable even if retained because the film/game is lost or damaged.

Overdue films/games. A charge for an overdue film/game is further payment for the use of the film/game and liable to VAT.

(VAT Notice 700/14/04).

(32) **Zero-rated supplies**

Output tax is not chargeable on zero-rated supplies. See 72 ZERO-RATED SUPPLIES for a list of the categories of zero-rating and cross-references to supporting chapters.

48 Overseas Traders

Cross-references. See 3.8 AGENTS for tax representatives and agents employed by overseas traders; 39 INTERNATIONAL SERVICES for services generally made to or by overseas traders.

De Voil Indirect Tax Service. See V2.106.

The contents of this chapter are as follows.

48.1 DEFINITION OF OVERSEAS TRADERS

An '*overseas trader*' (also referred to as a '*non-established taxable person*') is any person who

- is not normally resident in the UK;
- does not have a 'business establishment' in the UK; and
- if a company, is not incorporated in the UK.

A '*business establishment*' is usually premises from which trading activities directly related to the business are carried out. Where a business provides book-keeping, accountancy or invoicing services at its premises for an overseas trader who does not actually make supplies in the UK, HMRC do not consider the premises to be a business establishment.

An overseas business which has a business establishment in the UK is not an overseas trader and must be registered for VAT in the UK at the address of its principal UK place of business. It must keep its VAT records and accounts at this address which must be available for HMRC to inspect. Someone responsible for VAT affairs should be available at the address. If that person is an employee, he must have written authority to act on behalf of the business A suggested form of words for this authority is at 48.3 below under the appointmen of an agent. A separate authority will not be required if

- the name of the person concerned has been notified to the Registrar of Companies under the *Companies Act 1985, Part XXIII* as a UK resident authorised to accept service of process on behalf of the company; or
- for a partnership the person concerned is a partner, resident in the UK.

(VAT Notice 700/1/02, paras 8.1, 8.2, 9.3).

48.2 REGISTRATION OF OVERSEAS TRADERS

An overseas trader *must* register for VAT in the UK if

- he makes taxable supplies of goods and services in the UK in the course of furtherance of his business (see 47.1 OUTPUT TAX) and the total value of those supplies exceeds the VAT registration threshold (see 59.3 REGISTRATION);
- the business is registered for VAT in another EC country, he sells and delivers goods in the UK to customers who are not VAT-registered ('distance sales') and the value of those distance sales exceeds the relevant threshold (see 59.12 REGISTRATION);

- he acquires goods in the UK directly from a VAT-registered supplier in another EC country (see 23.3 EUROPEAN COMMUNITY: SINGLE MARKET) and the total value of the acquisitions exceeds the acquisitions threshold (see 59.19 REGISTRATION); or
- he makes a claim under the *EC 8th Directive* or *EC 13th Directive* and subsequently supplies, or intends to supply, the relevant goods in the UK (see 59.27 REGISTRATION).

For VAT purposes, the UK includes the territorial sea of the UK (ie waters within twelve nautical miles of the coastline).

There is no need to register if the only UK supplies are supplies of services on which the customer is liable to account for any VAT due under the 'reverse charge' procedure. See 39.4 INTERNATIONAL SERVICES.

An overseas trader *may* also be registered if

- he has started in business but is not yet making taxable supplies, provided he can show the intention of making taxable supplies in the future as part of his business; or
- his turnover is below the threshold, provided he can prove to HMRC that he is carrying on a business for VAT purposes and making taxable supplies.

See 59.2 REGISTRATION.

Consequences of registration. An overseas trader who is registered or required to be registered for VAT in the UK must account for VAT in respect of those supplies and acquisitions taking place in the UK. He is also liable to VAT on importations of any goods into the UK (see 34 IMPORTS) and on the acquisition in the UK of exciseable goods or of new means of transport from another EC country whether or not he is required to be registered (see 23.9 and 23.35 EUROPEAN COMMUNITY: SINGLE MARKET respectively).

[*VATA 1994, ss 1, 3, 4, 10, 96(11)*]. (VAT Notice 700/1/02, paras 8.3–8.5).

See 64.8 SUPPLY for the place of supply of goods and 64.18 SUPPLY for the place of supply of services.

48.3 Registration options available

An overseas trader who is required or entitled to be registered in the UK can normally choose between three registration options.

1. He may appoint a VAT representative who will be jointly and severally liable for any VAT debts. The overseas trader must still complete a VAT registration form. In addition to this, both the overseas trader and the VAT representative must complete a Form VAT 1TR. See 3.8 AGENTS for further details on VAT representatives. It is understood that, in practice, very few businesses are prepared to provide the services of a VAT representative because they are unwilling to become liable for any VAT debts of the overseas trader.
2. He may appoint an agent to deal with the VAT affairs. The agent cannot be held responsible to HMRC for any VAT debts and HMRC reserve the right not to deal with any particular agent. The overseas trader must still complete a VAT registration form. In addition, HMRC will need a letter of authority. A suggested letter of authority approved by HMRC is:

..(Name of principal) of..(Address of principal) hereby appoints..(Name of UK agent or employee) of..(Address of UK agent or employee) to act as agent for the purpose of dealing with all their legal obligations in respect of Value Added Tax. This letter authorises the above-named agent to sign VAT return forms 100 and any other document needed for the purpose of enabling the agent or employee to comply with the VAT obligations of the principal.

Signed ... (Signature of principal)
Date

3. He may deal with all the VAT obligations (including registration, returns and record-keeping) personally. To register, the overseas trader should contact the Aberdeen VAT office at 28 Guild Street, Aberdeen AB9 2DY (Tel: 01224 844653/4/5).

The appropriate VAT registration application form is

- Form VAT 1 if in respect of taxable supplies;
- Form VAT 1A if in respect of distance sales; or
- Form VAT 1B if in respect of acquisitions.

(VAT Notice 700/1/02, paras 10.1–10.6).

48.4 Alternatives to registration

Accounting for VAT through customers. *VATA 1994, s 14* implements the VAT simplification procedures for triangular trade between EC countries and the UK. The provisions allow UK customers to be designated as liable to account for the VAT that would otherwise be due to be accounted for by intermediate suppliers in other EC countries. See 23.22 EUROPEAN COMMUNITY: SINGLE MARKET for fuller details.

Import agents. An overseas trader not registered for VAT in the UK who

- imports goods for onward supply in the UK, and
- does not supply any other goods or services within the UK to a total value exceeding the current registration limit,

can arrange for a UK-resident agent registered for VAT to import and supply the goods on his behalf. The agent is treated as importing and supplying the goods as principal. He must make any necessary Customs entries as the importer, pay or defer the VAT and take delivery of the goods. He can reclaim any import VAT as input tax (subject to the normal rules) but must issue proper VAT invoices for the supplies of the goods and charge and account for VAT on the onward sale in the normal way. See 3.4 AGENTS for the treatment of commission. (VAT Notice 702, para 2.7).

48.5 APPLICATIONS TO THE UK FOR REFUNDS OF VAT BY PERSONS ESTABLISHED OUTSIDE THE EC

When a trader registered for business purposes in a country outside the EC buys goods or services in the UK, he may have to pay UK VAT. If goods are bought for export, there is usually no problem as the supply will be zero-rated. But if the goods or services bought in the UK are also used here (eg at a trade fair), the trader cannot treat the VAT incurred as input tax because he is not registered here.

To avoid this, the *EC 13th Directive* has set up a scheme which allows overseas traders, subject to conditions being met, to reclaim VAT charged on imports into the UK or purchases of goods and services used in the UK. See 22.49 EUROPEAN COMMUNITY

LEGISLATION for a summary of the provisions of the *EC 13th Directive*. The provisions have been implemented in the UK as set out below.

Persons to whom the provisions apply. The provisions apply to any trader carrying on a business established in a '*third country*' (ie a country outside the EC) provided that in the period of claim

(*a*) he was not registered or liable to be registered for VAT in the UK;

(*b*) he was not established in any EC country;

(*c*) he made no supplies of goods and services in the UK other than

 (i) transport of freight outside the UK or to or from a place outside the UK (and ancillary services);

 (ii) services where the VAT on the supply is payable solely by the person to whom they are supplied under the reverse charge provisions (see 39.4 INTERNATIONAL SERVICES); or

 (iii) goods where the VAT on the supply is payable solely by the person to whom they are supplied; and

(*d*) where the trader is established in a third country having a comparable system of turnover taxes, unless HMRC allow otherwise, that country provides reciprocal arrangements for refunds to be made to taxable persons established in the UK.

For these purposes a person is treated as established in a country if

- he has a business establishment there; or
- he has no business establishment (there or elsewhere) but his permanent address or usual place of residence is there. The usual place of residence of a company is where it is legally constituted.

A person carrying on business through a branch or agency in any country is treated as having a business establishment there.

Refundable/non-refundable VAT. A person to whom the provisions apply is entitled to be repaid VAT charged on

- goods imported by him into the UK in respect of which no other relief is available; and
- supplies made to him in the UK if that VAT would be input tax of his were he a taxable person in the UK.

Refunds cannot be claimed on VAT incurred on

- non-business supplies (if a supply covers both business and non-business use, VAT can be reclaimed on the business element of the supply);
- any supply or importation which the trader has used, or intends to use, for the purpose of any supply by him in the UK;
- any supply or importation which has been exported, or is intended for exportation, from the UK by or on behalf of the trader;
- a supply or importation where input tax recovery is restricted in the UK (eg most motor cars, business entertainment and second-hand goods for which no VAT invoice is issued, see 35.8 INPUT TAX);

- VAT charged on a supply to a travel agent, tour operators, etc which is for the direct benefit of a traveller other than the travel agent or his employee; and
- in relation to VAT charged after 2 December 2004, VAT on a supply used (or to be used) in making supplies of insurance and financial services within 35.3(*c*) INPUT TAX.

Method of claiming. Claim forms (VAT 65A) are obtainable from the National Advice Service (tel: 0845 010 9000) or

HM Revenue and Customs
VAT Overseas Repayments
Custom House
PO Box 34
Londonderry
BT48 7AE
Northern Ireland

Tel: +44 (0) 2871 376200

Fax: +44 (0) 2871 372520

E-mail: enq.oru.ni@hmrc.gsi.gov.uk

Forms must be completed in English, using block capitals, and must be sent to the above address, together with proof of the VAT paid and, if appropriate, a certificate of status.

Proof of VAT paid. A claim form must be supported by correctly completed invoices, vouchers or receipts from suppliers showing

- supplier's name, address and VAT registration number;
- the date of supply;
- details of goods or services supplied;
- the cost of the goods or services (including VAT); and
- the rate of VAT

and additionally if the value of the supply is over £100 (including VAT)

- an identifying number;
- the claimant's name and address; and
- the amount of VAT charged.

If the goods have been imported, the VAT copy of the import entry or other Customs document showing the amount of VAT paid is also required.

Only originals of documents are acceptable. HMRC will refuse to accept any supporting documentation if it already bears an official stamp indicating that it has been furnished in support of an earlier claim.

Certificate of status. When making the first claim in the UK, a trader must also include a certificate from the official authority in his own country showing that he is registered for business purposes there. When applying for the certificate, it is important to make sure that it shows all thc information that the UK authorities will need to process the claim (eg if the invoices are made out in a company's trading name, the certificate must show this, as well as the name under which it is registered).

The certificate must be an original (not a photocopy) and contain

- the name, address and official stamp of the authorising body;
- the claimant's name and address;
- the nature of the claimant's business; and
- the claimant's business registration number.

Each certificate is valid for twelve months from its date of issue and will cover any claims made during that year. Once the certificate has expired, the trader must send a new one with his next claim.

Time limit. The claim must be made not later than six months after the end of the 'prescribed year' in which the VAT is incurred. The '*prescribed year*' is the year ended 30 June.

Period of claim. Any claim must be for a period of not less than three months (unless less than three months of the prescribed year remains) and not more than one year. Items missed on earlier claims can be included as long as they related to VAT charged in the year of the claim.

Minimum claim. If the claim is for less than one year, it must be for at least £130 (unless it is for the final part of the prescribed year). No claim can be for less than £16.

Repayment. The refund will be made within six months of receiving a satisfactory claim. Payments can be made by any of the following methods.

- Directly to the claimant's own bank through SWIFT (Society for Worldwide Inter-Bank Financial Telecommunications). The claimant must provide full bank account details (bank name, address and identification code; account name and number; and currency of account) and a copy of a bank credit slip with the claim form.
- To any UK bank.
- By payable order in sterling directly to the claimant or an appointed agent.

Where any repayment is made to a claimant in the country in which he is established, HMRC may reduce the repayment by the amount of any bank charges or costs incurred.

Use of agents. An overseas trader can prepare and send in his own claim or have this done by an agent. Any agent will need either a Power of Attorney or letter of authority before HMRC will accept that he is acting for, and can receive money on behalf of, the trader.

The following is an example of the format of a letter of authority acceptable to HMRC.

> I [name and address of claimant] hereby appoint [name and address of agent] to act on my behalf in connection with any claim I make to Her Britannic Majesty's Commissioners of Revenue and Customs under the Value Added Tax Regulations 1995 as from time to time amended or replaced. Any repayment of VAT to which I am entitled pursuant to any such claim made on my behalf by my above named agent shall be paid to [name and address of payee].
>
> Date Signed [by the claimant]

Appeals. An appeal may be made to an independent VAT tribunal against a refusal by HMRC to allow all or part of a repayment. A Notice of Appeal must be served at the VAT tribunal within 30 days of the date of the letter notifying the refusal. Alternatively, the applicant may first ask HMRC to reconsider their decision and extend the time for service of a Notice of Appeal. If HMRC allow an extension but do not change their decision, the applicant then has a further 21 days from the date of the letter upholding the decision to serve a Notice of Appeal.

Isle of Man. For VAT purposes, the Isle of Man is treated as part of the UK. VAT is chargeable in the Isle of Man under Manx legislation, which is broadly similar to UK legislation. The above scheme applies equally to refunds of VAT incurred in the Isle of Man and any references above to the UK are to be taken to include the Isle of Man.

[*VATA 1994, s 39; SI 1995/2518, Regs 185–197; SI 2004/3140, Reg 15*]. (VAT Notice 723, paras 1.3, 6.1, 6.3, 6.5, 6.6, 7.1–7.5, 8.1–8.3).

Retail export scheme. A VAT retail export scheme allows non-EC visitors a refund of VAT on certain goods that they buy in the EC. See 25.11 EXPORTS.

Special scheme for electronically supplied services. There is a special scheme for overseas businesses which provide electronically supplied services to non-business customers in the EC. See 63.34 SPECIAL SCHEMES. The special scheme provides only for payment of the VAT due on sales to EC customers without any deductions of EC VAT incurred on purchases. However, a business in the scheme can reclaim VAT charged on

- goods it imports into the UK; and
- supplies it makes in the UK

in connection with making qualifying supplies while it is a participant in the special scheme. The provisions outlined above apply with the omission of conditions (*c*) and (*d*) above.

[*VATA 1994, Sch 3B para 22; FA 2003, Sch 2 para 4*].

De Voil Indirect Tax Service. See V5.152.*

49 Partial Exemption

Cross-references. See 10 CAPITAL GOODS SCHEME for deduction, and adjustment of deduction, of input tax on capital items by partly exempt businesses; 31.10 GROUPS OF COMPANIES for input tax incurred by holding companies; 22.23, 22.24 EUROPEAN COMMUNITY LEGISLATION; 24 EXEMPT SUPPLIES.

De Voil Indirect Tax Service. See V3.461–467.

The contents of this chapter are as follows.

49.1 INTRODUCTION

A registered business which makes both taxable and exempt supplies cannot charge VAT on the exempt supplies and equally cannot normally reclaim the VAT incurred on the purchases used to make those supplies. Where input tax cannot be claimed because it relates to an exempt supply, it is known as *exempt input tax* and the registered business is known as *partly exempt*. See 24 EXEMPT SUPPLIES and supporting chapters for details of goods and services the supplies of which are exempt.

A partly exempt business will normally have to use an approved partial exemption method (see 49.3-49.6 below) to work out how much of its input tax can be reclaimed. This would usually be the standard method (see 49.4 below) unless it feels that this would not give a fair or reasonable result, in which case it can apply to HMRC for a special method (see 49.6 below). All methods should provide for direct attribution and apportionment of the input tax incurred. Direct attribution involves identifying VAT on goods and services which are used exclusively to make taxable supplies or exempt supplies: the former is deductible, the latter is not. Apportionment is required for the remaining input tax (eg on overheads) which cannot be directly attributed.

Where a partly exempt business prepares VAT returns and deducts input tax on a quarterly or monthly basis, the input tax deduction is provisional. The business also has a longer period at the end of which it is required to review the extent of its allowable input tax and revise its deduction accordingly. In general, the longer period ends on the last day of the quarter ending March, April or May and the adjustment is known as the annual adjustment. Newly registered traders have a longer period known as a registration period. See 49.9 below.

Even if a partial exemption method has to be used, the *de minimis* limits in 49.7 below may allow all input tax to be recovered (subject to the normal rules).

Where a business has deducted VAT based on its intention to use the relevant goods and services to make taxable supplies and at any time within six years, not having made the intended supply, it changes its mind and uses, or forms the intention to use, the goods and services to make an exempt supply, it must adjust its original claim. Conversely, rules permit a claim where VAT was restricted because the business's original intention was to make exempt supplies but in the event a taxable supply is either subsequently intended or made. See 49.10 below.

Capital goods scheme. The capital goods scheme covers input tax incurred in respect of land and property or computers above certain values. Under the scheme, the owner of the capital item must review the extent to which the item is used to make taxable supplies over a period of time (five or ten years) and make an adjustment where appropriate. See 10 CAPITAL GOODS SCHEME.

Non-business activities. Any VAT incurred relating to non-business activities is not input tax for these purposes. Where a business also carries on non-business activities, it must normally first determine the proportion of VAT incurred relating to those activities and disregard any such VAT before applying the rules in this chapter. Alternatively, it can apply the *Lennartz* mechanism to certain supplies. It then treats the supplies as business supplies for input tax purposes but must account for output tax on subsequent non-business use. See 35.7 INPUT TAX for the calculation of VAT of non-business activities and the *Lennartz* mechanism.

49.2 GENERAL PROVISIONS RELATING TO ALLOWABLE INPUT TAX

The amount of allowable input tax for which a taxable person is entitled to credit at the end of any period is so much of the input tax on supplies, acquisitions and importations in the period as is allowable as being attributable to the following supplies made, or to be made, by the taxable person in the course or furtherance of his business.

(*a*) '*Taxable supplies*', ie supplies of goods and services made in the UK other than exempt supplies.

(*b*) Supplies outside the UK which would be taxable supplies if made in the UK.

(*c*) Supplies of services which

- (i) are supplied to a person who belongs outside the EC, or
- (ii) are directly linked to the export of goods to a place outside the EC, or
- (iii) consist of the provision of intermediary services in relation to any transaction within (i) or (ii) above

provided that the supply is exempt (or would have been exempt if made in the UK) by virtue of *VATA 1994, Sch 9 Group 2* (insurance) or *VATA 1994, Sch 9 Group 5 Items 1–8* (finance).

(*d*) Supplies made either in or outside the UK which fall, or would fall, within *VATA 1994, Sch 9 Group 15 item 1 or 2* (investment gold, see 30.2 GOLD AND PRECIOUS METALS).

HMRC must make regulations for securing a fair and reasonable attribution of input tax to the supplies within (*a*) to (*c*) above.

[*VATA 1994, ss 4(2), 26; SI 1992/3123; SI 1999/3121*].

Regulations made are considered in 49.3 to 49.10 below. In those paragraphs:

- '*Exempt input tax*' means input tax incurred by a taxable person on
  - (i) goods or services supplied to, or goods imported or acquired by, him insofar as they are used by him, or a 'successor' of his, in making exempt supplies, or
  - (ii) supplies outside the UK which would be exempt if made in the UK,

other than input tax which is allowable under *SI 1995/2518, Reg 103* (see 49.8(1) below), *Reg 103A* (input tax attributable to exempt supplies of investment gold, see 30.4 GOLD AND PRECIOUS METALS) or *Reg 103B* (incidental financial services, see 49.8(2) below).

See 49.5 below for the meaning of '*successor*'.

Before 18 April 2002 (when the standard method over-ride was introduced as an anti-avoidance provision, see 49.5 below), exempt input tax meant input tax, or a proportion of input tax, which was attributable to

(i) exempt supplies under the partial exemption method used;

(ii) supplies outside the UK which would be exempt if made in the UK (other than those supplies falling within (*c*) above); and

(iii) with effect from 1 January 2000, exempt supplies of investment gold to the extent that the input tax was not allowable under the special provisions for investment gold in 30.4 GOLD AND PRECIOUS METALS.

- Nothing is to be construed as allowing a taxable person to deduct the whole or any part of the VAT on the importation or acquisition by him of goods or the supply to him of goods or services where those goods or services are not used or to be used by him in making supplies in the course or furtherance of a business carried on by him.

[*SI 1995/2518, Regs 99*(*1*)(*a*), *100; SI 1999/3114; SI 2004/3140, Reg 9*].

49.3 CALCULATION OF RECLAIMABLE INPUT TAX

If a business is not fully taxable, subject to the *de minimis* limit in 49.7 below, it cannot recover all its input tax. It is therefore necessary to determine how much of the input tax incurred can be reclaimed. This must be done in accordance with the following rules.

(*a*) Identify goods imported or acquired by, and goods or services supplied to, the business in the VAT period which are used

- *exclusively* in making taxable supplies; and
- *exclusively* in making exempt supplies.

This process is known as *direct attribution.*

(*b*) Input tax is reclaimable on such of those goods and services as are used, or are to be used, *exclusively* in making taxable supplies or other supplies which carry the right to deduct.

(*c*) No part of the input tax can be reclaimed on such of those goods or services as are used, or are to be used, in making exempt supplies or other supplies in respect of which input tax is non-deductible.

[*SI 1995/2518, Reg 101*(*2*)].

In most partly-exempt businesses, however, there will still be further input tax which cannot be directly attributed under (*a*)-(*c*) above because it relates to

- goods and services used, or intended to be used, for making both taxable and exempt supplies; or
- general overheads of the business (eg accountancy costs, telephone bills).

Input tax on these costs which cannot be directly attributed is normally referred to as 'non-attributable' or 'residual' input tax. A partial exemption method must then be used to apportion this residual input tax to determine how much of it is reclaimable. A business should normally use the standard method in 49.4 below to calculate provisionally how much residual input tax can be reclaimed but in certain circumstances it may be possible to apply a special method, subject to prior approval of HMRC. See 49.6 below.

Unless the *de minimis* limit in 49.7 below applies (in which case all input tax is recoverable subject to the normal rules), the total VAT reclaimable in the VAT period is then the directly attributable input tax under (*b*) above plus the reclaimable portion of residual input tax. The provisional amount reclaimed in the VAT period may then need to be adjusted at the end of a 'longer period', normally twelve months. See 49.9 below.

Both the provisional attribution and the annual adjustment must be made on the basis of facts as they existed at the time when the input tax was incurred, not on the changed facts as they existed at the time the claim was made. See *C & E Commrs v University of Wales College Cardiff, QB [1995] STC 611 (TVC 44.160)* where apportionment was based on income received in the relevant periods rather than subsequent use.

49.4 **The standard method**

Under the standard method (use of which does not require HMRC approval), the percentage of residual input tax (see 49.3 above) which can be reclaimed is calculated as follows.

$$\text{Claimable \%} = \frac{\text{Value of taxable supplies in the period (excluding VAT)}}{\text{Value of all supplies in the period (excluding VAT)}} \times 100$$

If the resulting percentage is not a whole number, it should be rounded *up* to the next whole number except that, for VAT periods beginning on or after 1 April 2005, where the residual input tax to which the fraction is applied is £400,000 per month on average or greater, it should be rounded up to two decimal places.

In making the calculation, the value of all the following supplies must be excluded.

(*a*) Any sum receivable in respect of a supply of capital goods used for the purposes of the business. There is no statutory definition of capital goods but the term is wider than simply goods within the CAPITAL GOODS SCHEME (10). In *C & E Commrs v JDL Ltd, Ch D 2001, [2002] STC 1 (TVC 44.80)* motor cars were held to be capital goods as they were of substantial durability and value as compared to other articles used in the management and day-to-day running of the business.

(*b*) Any sum receivable in respect of any of the following descriptions of supplies made where such supplies are incidental to one or more of the business activities.

- Any supply falling within *VATA 1994, Sch 8 Group 5 Item 1* or *Group 6 Item 1* (see 42.13 and 42.14 LAND AND BUILDINGS).
- Any exempt grant which falls within *VATA 1994, Sch 9 Group 1 Item 1* (see 42.2 LAND AND BUILDINGS).
- Any standard-rated grant which falls within *VATA 1994, Sch 9 Group 1 Item 1*(*a*) (see 42.3(*a*) LAND AND BUILDINGS).

- Any grant which would be an exempt grant but for an election having been made to opt to tax under *VATA 1994, Sch 10 para 2* (see 42.8 LAND AND BUILDINGS).
- Any supply which falls within *VATA 1994, Sch 9 Group 5* (finance).

What constitutes an 'incidental' supply can be viewed in two ways. First, it can be a one-off situation (eg the sale of a factory by a fully taxable manufacturing company) where there is activity but not sufficient to be regarded as a business. Secondly, it could be regular income (eg interest from bank deposits which are received passively, incurring no related input tax) where, in reality, there is no activity at all. In *C H Beazer (Holdings) plc (VTD 3283) (TVC 44.81)* the tribunal considered incidental to mean 'occurring or liable to occur in fortuitous or subordinate conjunction with'. HMRC's policy is to identify all the business activities and then consider whether the supply in question is incidental to *any* of these business activities (not just the *main* activities). It is possible that a supply might be distortive but not incidental. In such a case, it is open to the trader to apply for, or HMRC to direct, a special method. (Internal Guidance V1–15, para 4.4).

(*c*) That part of the value of any supply of goods on which output tax is not chargeable by virtue of a Treasury order under *VATA 1994, s 25(7)* unless the business has imported, acquired or been supplied with the goods for the purpose of selling them.

(*d*) The value of any supply which, under or by virtue of any provision of *VATA 1994*, the business makes to itself.

[*SI 1995/2518, Reg 101; SI 2004/3140, Reg 10; SI 2005/762*].

(*e*) The value of any goods or services provided as a business transaction which is neither a taxable nor an exempt supply (eg the transfer of a business as a going concern).

(*f*) The value of certain imported services specified in *VATA 1994, Sch 5* subject to the reverse charge under *VATA 1994, s 8(1)* (see 39.4 INTERNATIONAL SERVICES).

(VAT Notice 706, para 4.4).

Annual adjustments. The claimable proportion of residual input tax for a tax period as calculated is only provisional and subject to adjustment at the end of the 'longer period'. See 49.9 below.

Outside the scope supplies. In *C & E Commrs v Liverpool Institute for Performing Arts, HL [2001] STC 891 (TVC 44.128)*, the court confirmed HMRC's view that two separate regimes exist for determining the amount of VAT that a business can deduct: *SI 1995/2518, Reg 101* (the standard method above) which determines the deduction of VAT relating to supplies made within the UK; and *SI 1995/2518, Reg 103(1)* which determines the deduction of VAT relating to '*foreign supplies*' and '*specified exempt supplies*' made outside the UK (see 49.8(1) below).

Where a business makes

- taxable and exempt supplies in the UK for which it uses the standard method above, and
- foreign and/or specified exempt supplies within 49.8(1) below,

then both the standard method and the provisions in 49.8(1) below need to be applied. The latter provisions must always be applied first.

'*Non-specified exempt supplies*' (ie those supplies made outside of the UK that would be exempt if they were made within the UK but which do not fall within the definition of 'specified exempt supplies') should be given a similar treatment to exempt supplies made in the UK. Whilst the VAT incurred in making these supplies cannot be deducted, their value must be included within the standard method calculation. See also *Liverpool Institute of Performing Arts* above.

The following procedure should therefore be adopted.

(1) Determine the amount of VAT incurred that relates to foreign and specified exempt supplies on the basis of use in accordance with 49.8(1) below. This VAT may be deducted.

(2) The remaining VAT incurred that relates to taxable and exempt UK supplies and 'non-specified' exempt supplies is dealt with under the standard method. The proportion that can be deducted equals the value of taxable supplies divided by the total value of taxable and exempt UK supplies and non-specified exempt supplies (subject to the requirement to exclude the values of certain distorting supplies). The values of foreign and specified exempt supplies dealt with in (1) above must not be included.

(Business Brief 12/01).

See *Easyjet plc (VTD 18230) (TVC 44.129)*.

Example

In its tax year beginning on 1 April 2004, X Ltd makes the following supplies.

	Total (excl VAT)	Standard-rated (excl VAT)	Exempt
	£	£	£
First quarter	442,004	392,286	49,718
Second quarter	310,929	266,712	44,217
Third quarter	505,867	493,614	12,253
Fourth quarter	897,135	876,387	20,748
	£2,155,935	£2,028,999	£126,936

Input tax for the year is analysed as follows

	Attributable to taxable supplies	Attributable to exempt supplies	Remaining input tax	Total input tax
	£	£	£	£
First quarter	36,409	4,847	11,751	53,007
Second quarter	20,245	311	5,212	25,768
Third quarter	34,698	1,195	10,963	46,856
Fourth quarter	69,707	5,975	9,357	85,039
	£161,059	£12,328	£37,283	£210,670

First quarter

	£	£
Input tax attributable to taxable supplies	36,409	
Proportion of residual input tax deductible = 392,286/442,004 = 88.75%		
£11,751 × 89% =	10,458	
		46,867

Second quarter

Input tax attributable to taxable supplies	20,245	
Proportion of residual input tax deductible = 266,712/310,929 = 85.78%		
£5,212 × 86% =	4,482	
	£24,727	

The value of exempt input tax is £1,041 (311 + [5,212 – 4,482]). As this is not more than £625 per month on average and is less than 50% of all input tax in the quarter, all input tax in the quarter is recoverable.

Deductible input tax		25,768

Third quarter

Input tax attributable to taxable supplies	34,698	
Proportion of residual input tax deductible = 493,614/505,867 = 97.58%		
£10,963 × 98% =	10,744	
	£45,442	

The value of exempt input tax is £1,414 (1,195 + [10,963 – 10,744]). As this is not more than £625 per month on average and is less than 50% of all input tax in the quarter, all input tax in the quarter is recoverable.

Deductible input tax		46,856

Fourth quarter

Input tax attributable to taxable supplies	69,707	
Proportion of residual input tax deductible = 876,387/897,135 = 97.69%		
£9,357 × 98% =	9,170	
		78,877
		£198,368

For the annual adjustment required, see Example 1 in 49.9 below.

De Voil Indirect Tax Service. See V3.461.

49.5 *Standard method over-ride*

The standard method is a simple way of calculating how residual input tax can be attributed to taxable supplies and deducted. In the vast majority of cases, it provides for a fair and reasonable apportionment. But a number of larger businesses have aggressively exploited the standard method to deduct large amounts of input tax on purchases used to make exempt supplies. Also, in a few other cases not involving abuse, businesses have been able to either deduct large amounts of input tax on purchases used in making exempt supplies or unable to deduct input tax on purchases used to make taxable supplies. The over-ride provisions below were introduced with effect from 18 April 2002 to address these difficulties. They apply to VAT incurred on or after that date. Except in cases of deliberate abuse, HMRC believe that the provisions will rarely apply. In any case, the provisions do not apply to businesses using a special method.

The over-ride can apply in the two situations in (*a*) and (*b*) below. Normally, it applies, if at all, under (*b*) at the end of a tax year and any over-ride adjustment is made and accounted for in the same period as the annual adjustment (or longer period adjustment). However, where a business does not carry out an annual adjustment (because it first becomes partly exempt in the last period of a tax year) any over-ride adjustment must be accounted for under (*a*) on the next VAT return.

(*a*) Where

- for a VAT period, a taxable person has used the standard method to attribute a proportion of the residual input tax to taxable supplies using the formula in 49.4 above,
- that VAT period does not form part of a longer period (see 49.9 below),
- the attribution differs substantially from one which represents the extent to which the goods or services are used by him, or are to be used by him, or a 'successor' of his, in making taxable supplies, and
- residual input tax incurred in the VAT period is more than £50,000 p.a. (£25,000 p.a. for group undertakings (as defined in *Companies Act 1985, s 259*) which are not members of the same VAT group), adjusted *pro rata* for the length of the VAT period in question,

the taxable person must calculate the difference and account for it on the return for the VAT period next following the VAT period in question (unless HMRC allow otherwise). If his registration has been cancelled at or before the end of that VAT period, he must account for any adjustment on his final return.

[*SI 1995/2518, Regs 107A, 107E; SI 2002/1074*].

(*b*) Where

- a taxable person has determined for a longer period (see 49.9 below) the input tax attributable to that period under the standard method,
- the attribution differs substantially from one which represents the extent to which the goods or services are used by him, or are to be used by him, or a 'successor' of his, in making taxable supplies, and
- residual input tax incurred in the longer period is more than £50,000 p.a. (£25,000 p.a. for group undertakings (as defined in *Companies Act 1985, s 259*) which are not members of the same VAT group), adjusted *pro rata* for a period which is not 12 months,

the taxable person must calculate the difference and, in addition to any amount required to be included as over-deducted or under-deducted in respect of the normal annual adjustment, account for the amount so calculated on the return for the VAT period next following the longer period (unless HMRC allow otherwise). If his registration has been cancelled at or before the end of that VAT period, he must account for any adjustment on his final return.

[*SI 1995/2518, Regs 107B, 107E; SI 2002/1074*].

For the above purposes, a difference is substantial if it exceeds

- £50,000; or
- 50% of the residual input tax incurred in the VAT period or longer period, as the case may be, and £25,000.

A person is the '*successor*' of another if he is a person to whom that other person has transferred assets of his business by means of a transfer as a going concern which is treated as neither a supply of goods nor a supply of services (see 8.10 *et seq* BUSINESS). Successor in this context includes a reference to a successor's successor through any number of transfers.

[*SI 1995/2518, Regs 107C, 107D; SI 2002/1074*].

The over-ride only applies where the standard method fails to provide a fair and reasonable deduction of input tax given the extent to which purchases are used, or to be used, to make taxable supplies. This can happen where

- purchases are incurred in one tax year but used in a different tax year in which the proportion of deductible VAT is very different (eg purchases are made in one VAT period or tax year in setting up a new line of business which will significantly affect the relative values of taxable and exempt supplies in future tax years when the purchases are to be used);
- purchases are not used in proportion to the values of taxable and exempt supplies made (eg *either* exceptionally high value transactions are undertaken which do not consume inputs to an extent significantly greater than transactions of lower value *or* the pattern of business is such that inputs are not consumed in proportion to the values of outputs); or
- the value of outputs may give a distortive pattern for the residual percentage.

Calculating the extent of use. Any calculation is acceptable if it produces a fair and reasonable attribution of input tax according to the use, or intended use, of purchases in making taxable supplies. The easiest way to prepare a fair and reasonable calculation is to consider why the standard method breaks down and to correct for it. Provided residual costs (those relating to both taxable and exempt supplies) are used in proportion to the values of taxable and exempt supplies made in the period in which they are incurred, the standard method will give a deduction that reflects use. Any costs that are not used in proportion to the values of supplies made can be dealt with separately from the standard method calculation.

The existing *de minimis* provisions (see 49.7 below) continue to apply. If, after an over-ride adjustment, the input tax attributed to exempt supplies is within the current *de minimis* limits, then all input tax for that period can be deducted. However, if a business has deducted all its input tax under the *de minimis* rules, but after applying the over-ride it is not entitled to do so, it must make an adjustment and pay back the amount of input tax originally deducted.

Rounding. The over-ride is not triggered by the rounding provision in the standard method. But if the over-ride creates a substantial difference, merely because of rounding, then there is a need to consider whether the standard method is fair and reasonable.

Capital goods scheme. If a business incurs input tax on an item subject to the CAPITAL GOODS SCHEME (10) within a period covered by the over-ride, it must include that input tax in considering whether the over-ride applies and, if so, consider the use or intended use of the capital item in determining if there is a substantial difference.

Capital goods scheme adjustments must not be counted as input tax when determining whether the over-ride applies. However, the basis of adjustments in subsequent intervals will be affected where the over-ride applies to the tax year or longer period that is a subsequent CGS interval, where the standard method is used as the basis of adjustment for the subsequent interval.

Periods spanning 18 April 2002. The over-ride only applies to input tax incurred on or after 18 April 2002. For the tax year or longer period that spans this date, a business should:

- Calculate the annual adjustment for the whole tax year or longer period in the normal way.
- Determine the amount of residual input tax incurred between 18 April 2002 and the end of the tax year.
- Compare this to the over-ride threshold of £50,000 (£25,000 for group undertakings) per annum, *pro rata* for the period 18 April 2002 to the end of the tax year.
- If this residual input tax exceeds the threshold, compare the standard method attribution of this tax (using the percentage applied by the annual adjustment calculation) with an attribution based on use.
- If the difference is substantial, include both the annual adjustment amount for the whole period, and the over-ride amount for the period from 18 April 2002, in the VAT account and VAT return for the annual adjustment period.

Where no longer period applies, the over-ride threshold should be applied *pro rata* to the residual input tax incurred between 18 April 2002 and the end of the VAT period.

If there is a substantial difference between the attribution of this tax using the standard method and one based on use, this is to be entered as an over-ride adjustment on the return for the next VAT period.

(VAT Notice 706, paras 5.3, 5.5, 5.7, 5.8, 5.10, 5.11, 5.14). See also VAT Information Sheet 4/2002 for examples of how HMRC see the over-ride provisions applying in practice.

De Voil Indirect Tax Service. See V3.461A.

49.6 **Special methods**

HMRC may approve or direct the use of another method other than the standard method in 49.4 above except that

(*a*) where use of the method was allowed before 1 August 1989, there must not be included in the calculation (if the method would otherwise allow it)

(i) the value of any supply which, under or by virtue of any provision of *VATA 1994*, the business makes to itself; and

(ii) the input tax on such a supply; and

(*b*) despite any provision to the contrary effect in the method approved, in calculating the proportion of any input tax on goods or services used or to be used by the business in making both taxable and exempt supplies which is to be treated as attributable to taxable supplies, the value of any supply within 49.4(*a*)–(*d*) above must be excluded (ie those supplies which must be excluded from the standard method of calculation must also be excluded from any special method).

Application and approval. A business may apply to HMRC to use a special method if it considers that the standard method does not provide a fair and reasonable result. HMRC require precise details of how the proposed method will work in practice and are prepared to discuss proposals before a formal application is submitted. HMRC will normally approve a special method provided it is fair and reasonable.

With effect from 1 April 2005, any approval or direction by HMRC only has effect if it is in writing in the form of a document which identifies itself as being such an approval or direction. This is intended to give clarity to both businesses and HMRC. Previously, either HMRC or a business often argued that a special method had been given *de facto* approval. In *Wellington Private Hospital (VTD 10627) (TVC 44.99)* the tribunal found that the criteria for *de facto* approval were that the taxpayer must have knowingly adopted or sought to adopt a special method and HMRC must have been aware what the taxpayer was doing or seeking to do. But such *de facto* agreements often lead to confusion and from 1 April 2005 any further such agreements are not possible. Pre-existing *de facto* agreements will be updated in due course. (Business Brief 7/05).

'Gaps' in special methods. A special method has a 'gap' if it fails to specify how to deal with an amount of residual input tax. This may arise because the method is poorly drawn up or the circumstances of the business have changed after the method has been approved. With effect from 1 April 2005, where a business using a special method which has been approved or directed by HMRC incurs input tax

- the attribution of which to taxable supplies is not prescribed in whole or in part by that special method' and
- which does not fall to be attributed to taxable or other supplies under 49.8(1) or (2) below or 30.4 GOLD AND PRECIOUS METALS

the input tax is to be attributed to taxable supplies to the extent that the goods or services are used in making taxable supplies, expressed as a proportion of the whole use or intended use. Where the input tax is only in part not prescribed by the method (ie only part if the input tax falls into the gap), only that part not covered by the method falls within these provisions.

These provisions do not mean that gaps in methods are acceptable. They simply set out how to cope with any gaps that arise. Once a gap has arisen, HMRC will expect that, in due course, the business will make suitable proposals for a new or revised method that takes the gaps into account. (Business Brief 7/05).

Changing a special method. A business using a special method approved or directed by HMRC must continue to use it until HMRC approve or direct the termination of its use (but see below under the heading *Special method over-ride*). Any direction for the use, or termination of use, of a special method takes effect from the date of the direction or such later date as HMRC specify. Retrospective changes of method are not allowed. However, HMRC may approve a change of method with effect from the start of the tax year in which the written application is received (although there is no statutory basis for this).

[*SI 1995/2518, Reg 102; SI 2004/3140, Reg 11; SI 2005/762*]. (VAT Notice 706, paras 6.10, 6.11; Internal Guidance V1–15, para 7.5).

Possible methods. A special method can be any method agreed by HMRC and devised to suit the needs of the particular business, eg one based on any of the following ratios.

- *Outputs-based apportionment*, ie apportioning between supplies in the same ratio as the value of taxable supplies bears to the value of all supplies. This is the default measure of use, being the mechanism used for the standard method. It is most likely to give a fair and reasonable result where the supplies are made in the same VAT year as the costs are incurred, and where the input tax-bearing costs used in making a supply increase in proportion to the value of a supply (eg where a £1,000 supply will use about ten times the costs of a £100 supply).

- *Transaction-based apportionment*, ie apportioning between supplies in the same ratio as the number of taxable transactions made bears to all transactions made. This usually involves counting the number of supplies made, rather than the value of those supplies. However, other 'numbers of things' might also be appropriate to count (eg when considering residual input tax in respect of a landlord, the number of buildings where a taxable rental is charged divided by total number of buildings rented out).

  Transaction counts can be weighted (eg if supply A uses four times the input tax-bearing costs of supply B, each occurrence of supply A counts as 4 transactions, and each supply B counts as 1 transaction).

- *Staff time and headcount apportionment*. Staff time apportionment is where the apportionment is made in the same ratio as the staff time spent making taxable supplies bears to all staff time. Such methods are only appropriate where the staff record their time for purposes other than partial exemption calculations and the liability of the supplies they are working on can be identified (eg solicitors and accountants record time regularly on time sheets for fee accuracy, but most other businesses will not). For these reasons, staff time is rarely a 'fair and reasonable' method of attributing input tax, often being both difficult to operate and impossible to verify.

A headcount method has a similar effect to the using of staff time except that it can be used by a business that does not keep time sheets.

- *Input tax and inputs-based apportionment.* These are calculations where the apportionment is made in the same ratio as the input tax directly attributable to taxable supplies bears to all directly attributable input tax. Such calculations are most commonly used where costs involved in making supplies are normally incurred in a different VAT year than the year the supplies are made. To be able to produce a fair and reasonable result

  (i) there must be directly attributable input tax incurred relating to both taxable and exempt supplies;

  (ii) a significant proportion of the input tax must be directly attributable; and

  (iii) the directly attributable input tax must be incurred in about the same proportion as the residual input tax is used to make taxable and exempt supplies.

- *Floor space apportionment.* This is apportionment in the same ratio as the floor space occupied by income-generating staff involved exclusively in making taxable supplies bears to the total floor space of income-generating staff. It is most likely to produce a fair and reasonable result where the main residual input tax-bearing costs relate to buildings (eg taxable rent incurred, heating, lighting, fixtures and fittings). In order to reflect use, it requires that specific areas be used for supplies of a particular liability and that these represent a significant proportion of the floor area. Methods based on floor area are, therefore, seldom fair and reasonable for retailers and unlikely to be accepted by HMRC. See *Optika Ltd (VTD 18627) (TVC 44.111)* and Business Brief 34/04).

A special method may also be based on separate calculations for different sectors of the business or, in the case of a group registration, different businesses or groups of businesses within the VAT group.

The percentage recovery rate produced by a special method should be calculated to two decimal places. The only exception to this is a special method based on a single outputs calculation and agreed with HMRC before 1 April 2005, in which case the recovery rate can be rounded up to the next whole number percentage (because the method closely resembles the standard method which allowed rounding up). But for all new special methods approved or directed on or after 1 April 2005 (and when any pre-existing special method is reviewed or updated), HMRC will only allow rounding to two or more decimal places. (Business Brief 7/05).

Annual adjustments. The claimable proportion of residual input tax for a tax period as calculated is only provisional and subject to adjustment at the end of the 'longer period'. See 49.9 below.

Changes in circumstances. HMRC should be informed of any change in the business, or in group membership if in a VAT group, which has a substantial effect on the amount of input tax claimable. The special method will then be reviewed by HMRC and if no longer suitable, a direction to stop using the method will be issued. The taxable person must then either use the standard method or propose an alternative special method. But see also under the heading *Special method over-ride* below.

(VAT Notice 706, paras 6.1–6.9; Internal Guidance V1–15, paras 12.1–12.5).

Agreements with trade bodies. HMRC have agreed special methods with the Association of British Factors and Discounters, the Finance Houses Association Ltd, the Association of British Insurers and the Association of Investment Trust Companies. See VAT Notice 700/57/04 for full details.

Outside the scope supplies. In *C & E Commrs v Liverpool Institute for Performing Arts, HL [2001] STC 891 (TVC 44.128)*, the court confirmed Customs' view that two separate regimes exist for determining the amount of VAT that a business can deduct: *SI 1995/2518, Reg 101* (the standard method, see 49.4 above) which determines the deduction of VAT relating to supplies made within the UK; and *SI 1995/2518, Reg 103(1)* which determines the deduction of VAT relating to '*foreign supplies*' and '*specified exempt supplies*' made outside the UK (see 49.8(1) below). Where a business uses a special method instead of the standard method, if that method has been approved by HMRC and already deals with foreign supplies and specified exempt supplies, no further action is needed following the House of Lords' decision. Where a special method does not deal with these supplies, then the business must deal with them under the provisions in 49.8(1) below before applying the special method. (Business Brief 12/01).

Example

The facts are the same as in the example in 49.4 above except that HMRC allow X Ltd to use a special method and calculate the proportion of residual input tax attributable to taxable supplies by the formula

$$\text{Residual input tax} \times \frac{\text{Input tax attributable to taxable supplies}}{\text{Total input tax}}$$

	£	£
First quarter		
Input tax attributable to taxable supplies	36,409	
Proportion of residual input tax deductible =		
£11,751 × 36,409/53,007 =	8,071	
		44,480
Second quarter		
Input tax attributable to taxable supplies	20,245	
Proportion of residual input tax deductible =		
£5,212 × 20,245/25,768 =	4,095	
	£24,340	

The value of exempt input tax is £1,428 (311 + [5,212 – 4,095]). As this is not more than £625 per month on average and is less than 50% of all input tax in the quarter, all input tax in the quarter is recoverable.

Deductible input tax		25,768

Third quarter		
Input tax attributable to taxable supplies	34,698	
Proportion of residual input tax deductible =		
£10,963 × 34,698/46,856 =	8,118	
		42,816
Fourth quarter		
Input tax attributable to taxable supplies	69,707	
Proportion of residual input tax deductible =		
£9,357 × 69,707/85,039 =	7,670	
		77,377
		£190,441

For the annual adjustment required at the end of the tax year, see Example 2 in 49.9 below.

Special method over-ride. Particularly when business circumstances change, a special method agreed with HMRC might no longer produce a fair and reasonable result and a new method must be found. As this can take time, and because a new method cannot normally be backdated, HMRC or the business can suffer as a result. Special rules allow either HMRC or the business concerned to introduce an over-ride with immediate effect and correct the unfair method to ensure that VAT deducted fairly and reasonably reflects the principle of use. This will continue until a replacement method is implemented. It is, however, only a temporary measure and HMRC expect its use to be rare. The detailed provisions are as follows.

In relation to input tax incurred on goods imported or acquired by, or goods or services supplied to, a taxable person after 31 December 2003, where that person is using a special method which does not fairly and reasonably represent the extent to which goods or services are used by him (or are to be used by him) in making taxable supplies

- HMRC may serve a notice on him to that effect, setting out their reasons in support of that notification and stating the effect of the notice, and
- subject to any such notice, the taxable person may serve a notice on HMRC to that effect, setting out his reasons in support of that notification.

Where such a notice is served by HMRC (or served by the taxable person and approved by HMRC), then in relation to

- VAT periods commencing on or after the date of the notice (or such later date as may be specified in the notice), and
- longer periods (see 49.9 below) to the extent of that part of the longer period falls on or after the date of the notice (or such later date as may be specified in the notice)

the taxable person must calculate the difference between

(*a*) the amount of deductible VAT using the current special scheme, and (*b*) the amount of deductible VAT calculated in accordance with the principle of use

and account for the difference on the return for that VAT period or on the return on which that longer period adjustment is required to be made. HMRC may allow another return to be used for this purpose.

This procedure then continues until HMRC either approve or direct the termination of the special method currently being adopted.

[*SI 1995/2518, Regs 102A–102C; SI 2003/3220, Reg 21*].

HMRC will only serve or approve a notice where

- they have clear evidence that the current special method does not fairly and reasonably reflect the principle of use; and
- they are satisfied that preparing a replacement method will not conclude quickly and that they, or the business, would otherwise lose out

and additionally will only serve a notice when

- (for VAT periods beginning before 1 April 2005), they have attempted, unsuccessfully, to persuade the business to comply, and have the evidence to show this; and
- they have decided that direction of a special method is not appropriate.

Serving and approving a notice. A notice must specify that it is a special method over-ride notice and state the current or future date from which it takes effect. It must also give the reasons why the current special method does not produce a fair result.

When HMRC approve a notice served by a business, they will do so in writing as soon as possible, ideally within 30 days of receipt.

Complying with a notice. In most cases the reasons given by HMRC or the business in the notice will provide a basis for determining the notice correction. However, a business must still consider its whole method and determine whether there are any other aspects that would otherwise give an unfair result. The notice correction must therefore ensure that each time a VAT return is prepared, the amount of VAT deducted fairly and reasonably reflects the extent that costs and purchases are used (or will be used) in making taxable supplies (the principle of use). If a business does not make corrections to the amount of VAT deducted, and HMRC conclude that a notice correction should have been made, they will make the correction by way of VAT assessment.

Right of appeal. A business can appeal to a VAT tribunal against

- HMRC's decision to serve a notice;
- HMRC's decision not to approve a notice; and
- any VAT assessments made under a notice.

(VAT Notice 706, paras 7.1–7.8; Business Brief 27/03).

De Voil Indirect Tax Service. See V3.462.

49.7 De minimis limit

Normal de minimis rules. Subject to special provisions below, where 'relevant input tax'

- in any VAT period, or
- in any longer period, see 49.9 below (taken together, where appropriate, with the amount of any adjustment under 49.5(*b*) above)

is not more than

(*a*) £625 per month 'on average', and

(*b*) one half of all input tax for the period concerned,

all such input tax in that period is treated as attributable to taxable supplies.

When applying these provisions to a longer period,

- any treatment of relevant input tax as attributable to taxable supplies in any VAT period is disregarded, and
- no account is to be taken of any amount or amounts which may be deductible or payable under the CAPITAL GOODS SCHEME (10).

'*Relevant input tax*' is input tax attributed to exempt supplies or to supplies outside the UK which would be exempt if made in the UK (not being supplies falling within 49.2(*c*) above) under

- the standard method (see 49.4 above),
- a special method (see 49.6 above),
- the rules for foreign and specified supplies (see 49.8(1) below),
- the rules for incidental financial supplies (see 49.8(2) below),
- the rules for attribution to exempt supplies of investment gold, see 30.4 GOLD AND PRECIOUS METALS), and
- where appropriate, the annual adjustment (see 49.9 below).

[*SI 1995/2518, Reg 106; SI 2002/1074, Reg 4; SI 2004/3140, Reg 12*].

'*On average*' means the average over the relevant VAT period or, as the case may be, longer period. For group registrations, the rules apply to the group as a whole. (VAT Notice 706, para 9.3).

Special provisions where the standard method over-ride applies. Where, taken together with the amount of any over-ride adjustment under 49.5(*a*) above, input tax attributed to exempt supplies or to supplies outside the UK which would be exempt if made in the UK (not being supplies falling within 49.2(*c*) above) under

- the standard method (see 49.4 above),
- the rules for foreign and specified supplies (see 49.8(1) below),
- the rules for incidental financial supplies (see 49.8(2) below), and
- the rules for attribution to exempt supplies of investment gold, see 30.4 GOLD AND PRECIOUS METALS),

is not more than

(*a*) £625 per month 'on average', and

(*b*) one half of all input tax for the period concerned,

all such input tax in that period is treated as attributable to taxable supplies.

Where this applies to a taxable person, he must calculate the difference between

- the total amount of input tax for that VAT period, and
- the amount of input tax deducted in that VAT period, taken together with the amount of any adjustment under 49.5(*a*) above

and include this difference as an under-deduction in the return for the first VAT period next following that in which the substantial difference arose under the provisions in 49.5(*a*) above (unless HMRC allow otherwise). If his registration has been cancelled by then, the adjustment must be made on his final VAT return.

Where, on the other hand, a taxable person has treated input tax as attributable to taxable supplies under the normal *de minimis* rules but is not entitled to do so because of the special provisions above, he must include the amount so treated as an over-deduction in the return for the first VAT period next following that in which the substantial difference arose under the provisions in 49.5(*a*) (unless HMRC allow otherwise). If his registration has been cancelled by then, the adjustment must be made on his final VAT return.

[*SI 1995/2518, Reg 106A; SI 2002/1074, Reg 4; SI 2004/3140, Reg 13*].

De Voil Indirect Tax Service. See V3.465.

49.8 ATTRIBUTION OF INPUT TAX

Direct and immediate link. In *C & E Commrs v Midland Bank plc, CJEC [2000] STC 501 (TVC 21.265)* the CJEC held that input tax can only be attributed to a supply if there is a 'direct and immediate link' between a particular input transaction and a particular output transaction. The full amount of input tax cannot be deducted where the supply in question is used, not for the purpose of carrying out a deductible transaction, but in the context of activities which are no more than the consequence of making such a transaction, unless the taxpayer can show, by means of objective evidence, that the expenditure involved was part of the various cost components of the output transaction.

The national court should apply this 'direct and immediate link' test to the facts of each particular case. The point in question in the *Midland Bank* case was whether VAT on legal costs incurred defending a claim alleging negligent misrepresentation was wholly attributable to the zero-rated supplies made to the client or whether it should be apportioned between taxable and exempt supplies.

In *C & E Commrs v Southern Primary Housing Ltd, CA 2003, [2004] STC 209 (TVC 44.24)* a company purchased some land and paid VAT on the price (because the vendor had elected to waive exemption in respect of the land). It then sold the land to a housing association, under a contract whereby it agreed to build flats on the land for the association. The company considered that the VAT incurred on the purchase of the land was partly attributable to taxable supplies of building work. The Court of Appeal held that the input tax on the cost of buying the land was not a 'cost component' of the contract for the development of the land. There was nothing about the development contract as such which made the land purchase and sale essential. If the housing association had already owned the land or had bought it from some third party, the inputs of the development contract would have been just the costs of carrying it out. The fact that there were commercially linked land transactions did not mean that those transactions were directly linked to the costs of the development contract.

Ultimate purpose of transactions. It is not possible to deduct input tax used for making an exempt supply even if the ultimate purpose of the transaction is the carrying out of a taxable transaction (*BLP Group plc v C & E Commrs, CJEC [1995] STC 424 (TVC 21.264)*). In that case, the company incurred input tax on professional fees in connection with the disposal of shares in a subsidiary company in order to pay debts. The court held that the input tax was not recoverable as it related to the exempt sales of shares, even though the ultimate purpose of this exempt supply was to enable the business to continue to make taxable supplies.

Attribution of input tax in particular cases is considered below.

(1) **Foreign and specified supplies**

Where input tax is incurred by a business in any VAT period on goods or services which are used (or to be used) in whole or part in making

(*a*) '*foreign supplies*', ie supplies outside the UK which would be taxable supplies if made in the UK; or

(*b*) '*specified exempt supplies*', ie supplies of services which

(i) are supplied to a person who belongs outside the EC, or

(ii) are directly linked to the export of goods to a place outside the EC, or

(iii) consist of the provision of intermediary services in relation to any transaction within (i) or (ii) above

and where the supply would have been exempt if made in the UK under *VATA 1994, Sch 9 Group 2* (insurance) or *VATA 1994, Sch 9 Group 5 items 1–8* (finance)

the input tax must be attributed to taxable supplies to the extent that the goods or services are so used (or to be used). The attribution must be expressed as a proportion of the whole use (or intended use). It is up to the business to decide how this can be achieved.

[*SI 1995/2518, Reg 103*(*1*)].

Any method of calculation is acceptable to HMRC provided the result is both fair and reasonable. If it is not, HMRC can raise an assessment to rectify the position.

Where a business makes

- taxable and exempt supplies in the UK for which it uses the standard method (see 49.4 above), and
- foreign and/or specified exempt supplies within (*a*) and (*b*) above,

then both the standard method and the provisions above need to be applied. The provisions above must always be applied first. See 49.4 above.

'*Non-specified exempt supplies*' (ie those supplies made outside of the UK that would be exempt if they were made within the UK but which do not fall within (*b*) above) should be given a similar treatment to exempt supplies made in the UK. Whilst the VAT incurred in making these supplies cannot be deducted, their value must be included within the standard method calculation (see 49.4 above). See also *C & E Commrs v Liverpool Institute for Performing Arts, HL [2001] STC 891 (TVC 44.128)*.

(Business Brief 12/01).

In relation to input tax incurred before 3 December 2004, where input tax falling within the above provisions was incurred on goods or services used or to be used in making both

- financial services within *VATA 1994, Sch 9 Group 5 Items 1* or *6* (see 27.8 and 27.17 FINANCIAL SERVICES) which were incidental to one or more of the taxable person's main business activities; and
- any other supply

input tax had to be attributed as above despite any provision to the contrary effect in any method required or approved by HMRC.

[*SI 1995/2518, Reg 103*(*2*)*; SI 1999/3114*].

In relation to input tax incurred after 2 December 2004, similar provisions apply but under the more general provisions applying to all incidental financial supplies under (2) below.

(2) **Services and related goods used partly to make incidental financial supplies**

In relation to input tax incurred after 2 December 2004, where

- a business incurs input tax in any VAT period on supplies to it of any of the services listed below and of any related goods,
- those services and related goods are used or to be used by the business in making both
  - (i) a '*relevant supply*' (ie a supply of financial services within *VATA 1994, Sch 9 Group 5 Items 1* or *6* (see 27.8 and 27.17 FINANCIAL SERVICES) or a supply of the same description which is made in another EC country); *and*
  - (ii) any other supply, and
- the relevant supply is incidental to one or more of its business activities,

that input tax must be attributed to taxable supplies (including supplies falling within (1) above) to the extent that the services or related goods are so used (or to be used). The attribution must be expressed as a proportion of the whole use (or intended use). This applies despite any provision of any input tax attribution method that the business is required or allowed to use which purports to have the contrary effect.

The services in question are those supplied by

- accountants;
- advertising agencies;
- bodies which provide listing and registration services;
- financial advisers;
- lawyers;
- marketing consultants;
- persons who prepare and design documentation; and

- any person or body which provides similar services to those listed above.

[*SI 1995/2518, Reg 103B; SI 2004/3140, Reg 8*].

Incidental supplies are those which are subordinate to the main activities of the business. They tend to consume little by way of general overheads but may incur significant direct costs. Incidental financial supplies will usually be issues of new shares, bonds and similar securities and sales of existing shares in subsidiaries where these are made on an occasional basis and do not represent a business activity.

General business overheads (eg a company's annual audit) are not covered and, if the company is otherwise partly exempt, fall to be dealt with under the normal partial exemption method.

The effect of the above provisions is that input tax incurred on the services listed above must be divided into four categories:

(1) Input tax used to make financial services within the EC (non-recoverable).

(2) Input tax used to make financial supplies to individuals and businesses outside the EC (recoverable).

(3) Input tax used to make taxable supplies (recoverable).

(4) Input tax used to make other exempt transactions (non-recoverable).

HMRC will accept any calculation to determine extent of use if it provides a fair and reasonable attribution of input tax according to use (or intended use) of the relevant costs. For example, where professional services are incurred in connection with a share issue and shares are issued to subscribers in the UK and Japan, apportionment could be based on the number of subscribers, the number of shares issued or the value of the shares issued, provided the method used gives a fair and reasonable result.

(VAT Information Sheet 9/04).

In relation to input tax incurred before 3 December 2004, where a business incurred costs that related partly to an incidental financial supply

- if that supply was to an individual or body based outside the EC, the business similarly had to apportion the related VAT on the basis of use (but under the provisions in *SI 1985/2518, Reg 103(2)*, see (1) above); and

- if that supply took place in the UK or another EC country, the business had to apportion the related VAT under its partial exemption method.

(2A) **Share issues, etc**

In *Kretztechnik AG v Finanzamt Linz, CJEC Case C–465/03; 24 February 2005 unreported (TVC 21.63A)*, an Austrian company issued shares and reclaimed input tax on the related costs. The tax authority rejected the claim (on the grounds that the issue of shares was an exempt supply) but the CJEC held that the issue of shares by a public limited company is not a supply within *EC Sixth Directive, Art 2(1)* and that input tax on services acquired for the purposes of such a share issue may be deducted to the extent that the company charges VAT on its output transactions.

HMRC accept this decision applies to companies making first issues of shares in circumstances that are the same as those in *Kretztechnik*. Therefore, companies with wholly taxable outputs are entitled to recover all of the relevant input tax, while those with both exempt and taxable outputs can recover a proportion in accordance with their partial exemption method. Claims for input tax in respect of past share issues can be made subject to the three-year 'capping' rules.

Previously, HMRC's view, based on the decision in *Trinity Mirror plc (aka Mirror Group Newspapers Ltd) v C & E Commrs, CA [2001] STC 192 (TVC 26.37)*, was that where a company issued its own shares, input tax incurred exclusively on related costs was deductible according to the liability of the issue. If the issue was wholly exempt, the input tax is not recoverable (subject to the *de minimis* limit). If all the shares were sold to persons outside the EC, the input tax was claimable in full. But where some only of the shares were sold to persons outside the EC, a proportion of the input tax on the share costs was claimable. This could normally be calculated most accurately by using the ratio of the number of shares sold outside the EC to the total number of shares sold. But if this method did not provide a fair and reasonable result, an alternative calculation could be used.

There are other situations in which a company may issue shares where the circumstances are different from those in *Kretztechnik* (eg a share issue may take place as part of a company merger, demerger or other restructuring). Businesses may also raise capital through the issue of financial instruments or securities other than shares (eg bonds, debentures or loan notes). The CJEC did not comment upon the extent to which the same principles would apply to other types of issues. HMRC are obtaining legal advice on whether the decision in *Kretztechnik* applies in this broader context.

(Business Brief 12/05).

In *Water Hall Group plc (VTD 18007) (TVC 34.565)* the company made an issue of shares. 70.3% of the purchasers were located outside the EC but, of that percentage, 36.6% were issued to a UK nominee company which therefore held legal title to the shares. Water Hall argued that input tax was deductible as the holders of the beneficial title were outside the EC. The tribunal held that input tax was not recoverable in respect of these shares as, in the case of nominees, the VAT legislation did not permit 'looking through' to the underlying beneficial owner. HMRC are also reviewing their policy in the light of the decision in *Water Hall*. (Business Brief 2/05).

(3) **Costs of Stock Exchange listing**

A Stock Exchange listing that takes place *without* an issue of shares is not a supply for VAT purposes. Related costs are treated as general overheads of the business. VAT on overhead costs is residual input tax and may be deducted in part according to the partial exemption method in place.

Where a Stock Exchange listing takes place in conjunction with a share issue, costs incurred on the listing are normally treated as wholly related to a share issue and dealt with as under (2) above. This is because, at the time of the listing or afterwards, there is an intention to issue shares to raise capital. This is established HMRC policy and was supported by the tribunal decision in *Actinic plc (VTD 18044) (TVC 26.40)*. However, in *Halladale Group plc (VTD 18218) (TVC 44.38)* the tribunal held that an AIM listing was, in part, for general business purposes and was not an essential element of the issue of shares, so that the expenditure had a dual purpose.

Following the decision in *Halladale*, HMRC accept that, on some occasions, costs in connection with Stock Exchange listings can be treated as residual if the number of shares issued is small and this is not done in order to raise capital (although some capital may be raised as a result). For example,

- a business applying for existing shares to be issued on the London Stock Exchange is required to issue additional shares merely to comply with Stock Exchange rules; or
- a close company applying for listing on the Alternative Investment Market issues further shares in order to create a market price for its existing shares.

HMRC will consider each case on its facts but state that it is likely the costs will be considered general overheads if, for example,

- the number of shares issued is small compared to the number listed; and
- the capital raised by the issue is minor compared with the costs incurred.

Supplies of services related to the issue *and* listing must not be artificially aggregated or split to distort VAT deduction. Where a contract for professional services comprises a number of different supplies, each supply must be considered in its own right when determining whether the VAT relates to the share issue or is residual. This was confirmed in *Actinic plc* above.

(VAT Notice 706, para 8.8; Business Brief 30/03).

(4) **Self-supplies**

Where under or by virtue of any provision of *VATA 1994* a person makes a supply to himself, the input tax on that supply must not be allowable as attributable to that supply. [*SI 1995/2518, Reg 104*].

(7) **Acquiring a business as a going concern**

Following the decision in *C & E Commrs v UBAF Bank Ltd, CA [1996] STC 372 (TVC 44.6)*, HMRC have confirmed that where a business acquires assets by way of the transfer of a going concern, and the assets are used exclusively to make taxable supplies, the VAT incurred on the cost of acquiring those assets should be attributed to those taxable supplies and can be recovered in full. Conversely, if the assets of the acquired business are to be used exclusively to make exempt supplies, none of the input tax on the cost of acquiring those assets can be recovered. However, if the assets are to be used in making both taxable and exempt supplies, any input tax incurred is non-attributable and must be apportioned in accordance with the agreed VAT partial exemption method. In *UBAF Bank Ltd* the court held that input tax on professional fees incurred in connection with the acquisition of shares was on supplies wholly used, or to be used, by the bank in making taxable supplies of equipment leasing and recoverable in full. Before that decision, HMRC had treated such costs as general business overhead costs. (Business Brief 7/96).

See, however, the decision in *RAP Group v C & E Commrs, Ch D [2000] STC 980 (TVC 44.36)* which also related to professional services incurred in connection with the acquisition of the issued share capital of another company. The court held that the important question was whether the services were used for an exempt transaction (the issue of shares in RAP) in which case the input tax was not allowable or whether they were used for that and some other taxable supply (in which case apportionment would apply). The tribunal had applied the 'direct and immediate link' test in *Midland Bank plc* above and, on the facts, held that no such link existed between the professional services supplied and the taxable supplies to be made by acquired company. As a result, the VAT on the professional services must relate to the exempt issue of shares and was not recoverable. As this was a question of fact, the court would not disturb the decision (although it did allow the appeal in part on the grounds that the legal services provided related to more general matters than the issue of the shares so that the tribunal should have allowed apportionment).

De Voil Indirect Tax Service. See V3.464.

49.9 ANNUAL ADJUSTMENTS

The deductions of input tax for each VAT period are provisional whether the standard or a special method is adopted. This is because the amount deductible in some such periods may be unfairly affected, eg by seasonal variations. It is normally necessary, therefore, to recalculate the amount of input tax reclaimable over a 'longer period'. If a special method is used, the letter of approval will state whether an annual adjustment is required.

Where a business incurs exempt input tax during any 'tax year', its '*longer period*' corresponds with that tax year unless it did not incur exempt input tax during its immediately preceding tax year or 'registration period' in which case its longer period begins on the first day of the first VAT period in which it incurs exempt input tax and ends on the last day of that tax year. Where, however, the only exempt input tax of the business is incurred in the last VAT period of its tax year, no longer accounting period is applied in respect of that tax year.

There are also rules to deal with special circumstances where the longer period is not a period of twelve months.

- *Newly-registered businesses*. Where a business incurs exempt input tax during its registration period, its longer period begins on the first day on which it incurs exempt input tax and ends on the day before the commencement of its first tax year.
- *Belated registration*. Where a business is registered retrospectively, its first VAT return may cover a period longer than a tax year. In such a case, the period must be broken down and a longer period adjustment made in respect of the registration period and each subsequent tax year.
- *Deregistration*. In the case of a business ceasing to be taxable during a longer period, that period ends on the day it ceases to be taxable.

'*Tax year*' is the twelve months ending on 31 March, 30 April or 31 May according to the VAT periods allocated. HMRC may approve or direct that a tax year be for a period other than twelve months. These powers are mostly exercised where businesses ask to change their VAT return dates (in order to bring their tax year end into line with the end of their financial year) or change their tax year to end with a different existing return date (eg from 31 March to 31 December to coincide with its financial year end).

The '*registration period*' of a taxable person means the period commencing on his effective date of registration and ending on the day before the commencement of his first tax year.

[*SI 1995/2518, Reg 99; SI 2000/794*]. (VAT Notice 706, paras 10.3, 10.7–10.9; Internal Guidance V1–15, paras 17.3–17.5).

Calculation of annual adjustments. Unless HMRC dispense with the requirements, a taxable person must calculate the reclaimable proportion of any residual input tax not directly attributed on the same basis as in each of the VAT periods but using the figures for the longer period.

Any difference between the amount of reclaimable input tax recalculated at the end of the longer period and the total amount provisionally deducted during the VAT periods is an over or under declaration of VAT and must be entered on the VAT return for the first VAT period after the end of the longer period (unless HMRC allow otherwise). Where registration has been cancelled, the annual adjustment should be entered on the VAT return for the final period ending on the effective date of deregistration.

If the recalculation shows that the exempt input tax is below the *de minimis* limits in 49.7 above, any input tax not already reclaimed is an under deduction of VAT and should be entered on the next VAT return.

Annual adjustments which have been correctly carried out are not errors and do not have to be disclosed under the voluntary disclosure procedure (see 56.11 RECORDS). Where, however, an error is made in the partial exemption calculation for a VAT period (eg input tax is incorrectly treated as exempt when the goods or services were used to make taxable supplies) this should not be 'corrected' by the annual adjustment but should be notified separately under the voluntary disclosure procedure.

[*SI 1995/2518, Reg 107; SI 1999/599; SI 2002/1074*]. (VAT Notice 706, paras 10.4, 10.6).

Example 1

At the end of the tax year, X Ltd in the example in 49.4 above must carry out the following annual adjustment.

	£
Input tax attributable to taxable supplies	161,059
Proportion of residual input tax deductible =	
2,028,999/2,155,935 = 94.11%	
£37,283 × 95% =	35,419
Deductible input tax for year	196,478
Deducted over the four quarters	198,368
Under declaration to be paid to HMRC	£1,890

Example 2

At the end of the tax year, X Ltd in the example in 49.6 above must carry out the following annual adjustment.

	£
Input tax attributable to taxable supplies	161,059
Proportion of residual input tax deductible =	
£37,283 × 161,059/210,670 =	28,503
Deductible input tax for year	189,562
Deducted over the four quarters	190,441
Under declaration to be paid to HMRC	£879

De Voil Indirect Tax Service. See V3.466.

49.10 ADJUSTMENTS FOR CHANGE IN USE OF GOODS AND SERVICES

Attribution of input tax should be initially carried out on the basis of the use made, or intended to be made, of the goods or services (see 49.3 above). However, there may be occasions when the intended or actual use of those goods or services changes. Where a business either

- changes its intention before using the goods or services, or
- actually uses the goods or services for a different purpose,

the following 'clawback' or 'payback' provisions apply.

(*a*) **'Clawback' provisions** apply where a taxable person has deducted an amount of input tax which has been attributed to taxable supplies because he intended to use the goods or services in making either

(i) 'taxable supplies', or

(ii) both taxable and 'exempt supplies',

and during a period of six years commencing on the first day of the VAT period in which the attribution was determined and before that intention is fulfilled, he uses or forms an intention to use the goods or services in making exempt supplies (or where (i) above applies, in making both taxable and exempt supplies).

Subject to below, under such circumstances, unless HMRC allow otherwise, the taxable person must account for an amount equal to the input tax which has ceased to be attributable to taxable supplies in accordance with the method he was required to use when the input tax was first attributed. This should be done on the return for the VAT period in which the use occurs or the revised intention is formed. (VAT Notice 706, paras 11.7, 11.8).

In *Belgium v Ghent Coal Terminal NV, CJEC [1998] STC 260 (TVC 21.272)*, a company purchased some land, had work carried out on it and reclaimed the input tax on these supplies. Subsequently the local council required the company to exchange the land before it had been used for any taxable purpose. The CJEC held that the right to deduction was exercisable immediately the inputs were incurred and, once it had arisen, remained acquired even if, by reason of circumstances beyond its control, the taxable person never used the goods or services in question for the purposes of taxable transactions. This would not apply in cases of fraud or abuse and such a supply might give rise to a subsequent adjustment under the CAPITAL GOODS SCHEME (10).

In *C & E Commrs v Briararch Ltd; C & E Commrs v Curtis Henderson Ltd, QB [1992] STC 732 (TVC 43.155, TVC 44.157)* the court held that apportionment of input tax applied under this provision where a property is, or is intended to be, the subject of sequential supplies at different VAT liabilities. In the cases involved, the companies had reclaimed input tax in full on the basis that the properties concerned would be the subject of taxable supplies but, when the building work was completed, they were obliged to obtain temporary rental income on short leases which was an exempt supply. In circumstances such as these, where goods or services are put to an interim use different to that originally intended, provided the original intention is still retained, the input tax must be apportioned on a fair and reasonable basis. In *Briararch Ltd* the company let the property on a 4-year exempt lease whilst still intending to make a taxable supply of a 25-year lease. The court held that 25/29 of the input tax related to the intended taxable supply and that the clawback provisions applied to 4/29 of the original claim.

See also *Cooper and Chapman (Builders) Ltd v C & E Commrs, QB [1993] STC 1 (TVC 44.150)* where a building was converted into flats with the intention that they would all be let as holiday accommodation (standard-rated) but, after some flats had been so let, the company granted a one-year lease of the whole building (an exempt supply).

(*b*) **'Payback' provisions** apply where a taxable person has incurred input tax which has not been attributed to taxable supplies because he intended to use the goods or services in making either

(i) 'exempt supplies', or

(ii) both 'taxable' and exempt supplies

and during a period of six years commencing on the first day of the VAT period in which the attribution was determined and before that intention is fulfilled, he uses or forms an intention to use the goods or services in making taxable supplies (or where (i) above applies, in making both taxable and exempt supplies).

Subject to below, under such circumstances, HMRC must, on application by the taxable person in such form as HMRC require, repay to him an amount equal to the input tax which has become attributable to taxable supplies in accordance with the method he was required to use when the input tax was first attributed.

In practice, the taxable person should write to HMRC and, when they have confirmed the amount to be repaid, enter the amount due in the VAT account as an underclaim and include it in the next VAT return. (VAT Notice 706, paras 11.9, 11.10).

In *Royal & Sun Alliance Insurance Group plc v C & E Commrs, HL [2003] STC 832(TVC 44.161)* a company decided that certain properties were no longer needed for its exempt insurance business. It decided to sublet the properties and opted to tax them. It initially treated the input tax incurred on rents and service charges during the periods the properties were vacant prior to the exercise of the option as attributable to exempt supplies. Subsequently, it claimed a repayment of this input tax. The HL (by a 3 to 2 majority, reversing the decisions of the Ch D and CA and restoring the decision of the tribunal) held that to come within the payback provisions, the company must first have had an intention to use the inputs in supplying exempt sub-leases and then used them, or formed the intention to use them, in supplying taxable sub-leases. As the company had not opted to tax at the relevant time, it did not satisfy the second condition and the payback provisions could not apply.

Any question as to the liability of a supply under (*a*) or (*b*) above is to be determined in accordance with the legislation in force at the time that the supply was received. Thus, if a business recovers input tax based upon an intention to make taxable supplies but, before those supplies are made, the liability changes and those intended supplies become exempt, no clawback is due under (*a*) above. In the reverse situation where liability changes from exempt to taxable, no payback can be claimed under (*b*) above. (Internal Guidance V1–15, para 18.3).

Where (*a*) or (*b*) above applies, subject to the provisions relating to foreign supplies in 49.8(1) above and incidental financial supplies in 49.8(2) above, if

- the use to which the goods or services are put (or to which they are intended to be put) includes the making of supplies outside the UK, and
- at the time when the taxable person was first required to attribute the input tax he was not required to use a method approved or directed under 49.6 above (or he was required to use such a method but that method did not expressly provide for the attribution of input tax attributable to supplies outside the UK)

then the relevant amount under (*a*) or (*b*) above is to be calculated by reference to the extent to which the goods or services concerned are used (or intended to be used) in making taxable supplies, expressed as a proportion of the whole use (or intended use).

'*Exempt supplies*' includes supplies outside the UK which would be exempt supplies if made in the UK (other than those supplies falling within 49.2(*c*) above). With effect from 1 January 2000, it also includes supplies of investment gold but only to the extent that there is, or would be, no credit for input tax on goods and services under *SI 1995/2518, Reg 103A* (see 30.4 GOLD AND PRECIOUS METALS).

'*Taxable supplies*' includes supplies within 49.2(*b*) or (*c*) above. With effect from 1 January 2000, it also includes supplies of investment gold but only to the extent that there is, or would be, credit for input tax on goods and services under *SI 1995/2518, Reg 103A* (see 30.4 GOLD AND PRECIOUS METALS).

[*SI 1995/2518, Regs 108-110; SI 1999/3114; SI 2004/3140, Reg 14*].

De Voil Indirect Tax Service. See V3.467.

49.11 TREATMENT IN SPECIAL CIRCUMSTANCES

(1) **Abortive supplies**. There may be occasions where a business incurs VAT in connection with intended supplies that are never actually made.

- If the goods or services are used to make an alternative supply of a different liability, then the adjustment provisions in 49.10 above apply.
- If the initial intention is frustrated and the goods or services are not used to make any supply (eg architect's fees on an aborted building project), following the decision of the CJEC in *Belgium v Ghent Coal Terminal NV, CJEC [1998] STC 260 (TVC 21.272)*, no adjustment to the initial claim of input tax is required. Previously, Customs' policy was to treat such abortive supplies as part of the general overhead costs of the business so that the input tax formed part of the residual input tax to be apportioned under the partial exemption method used. (VAT Notice 706, para 11.14).

See also 42.15 LAND AND BUILDINGS for abortive supplies by speculative developers.

(2) **Holding companies**. See 31.10 GROUPS OF COMPANIES.

(3) **Professional fees on share acquisitions**. In *Southampton Leisure Holdings plc (VTD 17716) (TVC 44.37)* the tribunal held that whilst certain professional services connected with the acquisition of share capital in a company (eg public relations) had been exclusively used in making an exempt transaction (the share issue), other professional services had been used partly for the exempt transaction and partly for the general purposes of the business, so that the relevant input tax fell to be treated as residual input tax.

Following the tribunal's decision, HMRC now accept that any taxed supplies of professional services, which include, in the circumstances of a merger and acquisition or management buy-out,

- acting as financial adviser,
- the drafting of service contracts for the directors,
- the due diligence review of the target company's affairs,
- the investigation of title and/ or the valuation of that company's property; and
- coordinating the transaction

has to some extent a direct and immediate link with the whole of the taxpayer's business. The VAT incurred is residual input tax and is attributable to taxable supplies by reference to the partial exemption method used. However, where a taxed supply of professional services is partly used in making an issue of shares to a person belonging outside the EC, then the deductible proportion of tax is to be determined on a 'use' basis under *SI 1995/2518, Reg 103B* (see 49.8(2) above).

HMRC take the view that the decision has no application where shares are issued for subscription (eg an initial public offer or rights issue). In these instances, the taxed professional services relating to the offer are used exclusively for the purposes of the exempt supply of an issue of shares. But HMRC do accept that any services providing general advice on the means of raising capital (provided it is just that) is part of the business' overheads and that the VAT incurred on any such services should be treated as residual input tax.

HMRC will, subject to the normal capping rules, accept claims for overpaid tax.

(Business Brief 23/02).

(4) **Share issues**. See 49.8(2A) above.

(5) **Transfers of going concerns** (TOGCs). See 49.8(5) above for the position of the transferee and 8.15 BUSINESS for the position of the transferor.

See also 31.7 GROUPS OF COMPANIES for acquisitions of TOGCs by partly-exempt groups.

(6) **Research and development**. Input tax on research and development work is normally not directly attributable to any supply by the business. Input tax recovery is, therefore, determined by the liability of the activities which the research and development supports. Where research and development work is of a more general nature which cannot be said to lead directly to identifiable

supplies, provided that it does not relate to any non-business activities, the input tax can be treated as part of the business's non-attributable input tax. (Internal Guidance V1–15, para 19.2).

(7) **Free supplies of catering for employees**. Where employees are provided with food or drink free of charge, the employer is making a taxable supply, albeit for a nil consideration. See 11.4 CATERING. Any input tax attributable to the supply is fully recoverable. (Internal Guidance V1–15, para 19.3).

(8) **Costs of settling insurance claims**. See 37.10 INSURANCE.

(9) **Credit notes**. For credit notes generally, see 40.15 INVOICES. The following rules apply to the partial exemption calculations.

Credit notes received.

- If received in the same VAT period as the original supply, the VAT return should be prepared on the basis of the adjusted input tax taking into account both the credit note and the original invoice.
- If received in a subsequent VAT period but in the same tax year, no adjustment is due in the subsequent VAT period. The amended input tax value should be substituted for the original input tax value in the annual adjustment and the adjustment calculated in the normal way.
- If received in a subsequent VAT period not in the same tax year, the annual adjustment covering the original VAT period should be reconsidered to see what effect the revised value has on that annual adjustment. Any resulting amendment should be included in the VAT period covering the date of the credit note and is an adjustment outside the partial exemption calculations of that VAT period.

Credit notes issued.

- If issued in the same VAT period as the original supply, the amended value should be used in any partial exemption calculation used to determine the recoverable proportion of non-attributable input tax.
- If issued in a subsequent VAT period but in the same tax year, no adjustment is necessary in the subsequent VAT period. The amended value should be used in any partial exemption calculation under the annual adjustment.
- If issued in a subsequent VAT period but not in the same tax year, the annual adjustment covering the original output should be reconsidered. Any resulting amendment should be included in the VAT period covering the date of the credit note and is an adjustment outside the partial exemption calculations of that VAT period.

(Internal Guidance V1–15, para 1.14).

(10) **Petrol scale charges**. See 45.16 MOTOR CARS.

(11) **VAT on insolvency practitioners' fees**. See 36.11 INSOLVENCY.

(12) **MOT testing**. VAT incurred by an approved garage in relation to the annual testing of motor vehicles on behalf of the Department of Transport is for the purpose of its business and can be claimed in full. Where the business is partly exempt, the business should isolate any VAT incurred in respect of MOT

testing and recover this in full. Any remaining input tax should be recovered according to the normal partial exemption rules. (Internal Guidance V1–15, para 20.3).

(13) **Reverse charge on services from abroad.** VAT must be accounted for on certain services received from abroad. See 39.4 INTERNATIONAL SERVICES. The VAT can also be treated as input tax. However, for partial exemption purposes these services are not regarded as supplies and input tax on these imported services can only be claimed in full if the services are used wholly for the making of taxable supplies. If used partly for taxable supplies, the input tax must be included in the non-attributable input tax and apportioned according to the partial exemption method used.

The value of imported services must be excluded from the calculation to apportion residual input tax where either the standard method under 49.4 above is used or a special method under 49.6 above is used which is based on output values.

Exempt input tax on imported services should be included with other exempt input tax when applying the *de minimis* rules in 49.7 above.

(VAT Notice 706, para 12.6).

(14) **Self-supplies.** Before 1 June 2002, where a business could not be treated as fully taxable and produced *stationery or similar material* for its own use to a value above the VAT registration limit, it had to account for VAT on those self-supplies. See 62.2 SELF-SUPPLIES for VAT treatment generally including the deduction of related input tax.

In certain circumstances a business may similarly be required to account for VAT on self-supplies of construction services. See 42.30 LAND AND BUILDINGS.

(15) **Late adjustments and the capping provisions.**

Belated claims to input tax within the last three years. Where a partly exempt business makes a belated claim for input tax incurred in the last three years, it can only recover the input tax to the extent that it would have been recoverable had it been claimed in the VAT period in which it was incurred. The business must therefore work out its recoverable input tax using the rules in force when it was incurred. It must also consider what effect such a claim has on other input tax deducted in that period and the relevant longer period calculation. For example, if a business is using a method based upon input tax, then a revision to either its taxable or total input tax values alters the amount of residual input tax deductible. The business must also reconsider its *de minimis* position for the initial VAT period and longer period in the light of the revised values for exempt input tax following the amended calculation.

Any resulting claim due is proper to the VAT period covering the time that the claim is made even though the amount allowed is dependent upon the VAT period covering the tax point of the supply in question. Any such claim is outside the partial exemption calculations and *de minimis* measurement for the VAT period when the claim is actually made.

(Internal Guidance V1–15, para 14.6).

Effect of the capping provisions. In certain circumstances, a three-year time limit applies to HMRC's powers to raise assessments for errors (see 6.2 ASSESSMENTS) and a business's right to recover underclaimed input tax (see 51.8 and 51.11 PAYMENT OF VAT). This is known as capping.

Where the capping rules apply in the context of a partial exemption calculation, the calculation should be carried out in the normal way (ignoring the capping) as if all the input tax were being reclaimed. Only then should the capping time limit be identified and any VAT relating to a VAT period more than three years old should not be adjusted.

Where the period in which the annual adjustment is due is not capped, but the earlier periods making up the longer period are themselves capped,

- the annual adjustment can be used to take account of a change of use during the longer period (because the annual adjustment is properly used to reconsider any direct attribution made during the year and make adjustments to reflect the use of goods or services in the longer period);
- the annual adjustment can be used to apply the *de minimis* limits to the longer period provided the business has correctly applied the *de minimis* limits to each of the capped periods in the longer period. Where the business was entitled to apply the *de minimis* limits to such a capped period but failed to do so, any affected input tax in that period is not recoverable in the annual adjustment because the business failed to exercise the right to deduct within the three-year period; and
- if an error has been made in a period which is capped, the annual adjustment cannot be used to correct that error but when recalculating the annual adjustment, the corrected figures for the earlier periods should be used (although the input tax relating to those earlier periods cannot be reclaimed).

(VAT Notice 706, paras 11.18–11.20; Business Brief 8/99).

(16) **Divisional registration**. A corporate body may apply to be registered in the names of its separate divisions. See 59.37 REGISTRATION. HMRC will not allow divisional registration if the exempt input tax of the body as a whole exceeds the *de minimis* limit in 49.7 above. If, at any time, a body corporate registered in divisions exceeds the *de minimis* limit, it should advise its local VAT Business Centre immediately and a decision will be made as to whether the divisional registration should be allowed to continue. If the divisional registration is cancelled for the corporate body as a whole, then, if it is still liable to be registered, the single VAT registration must cover all the taxable business activities of the body corporate as a whole. (VAT Notice 706, para 12.3).

(17) **Group registration**. The normal rules for group registration apply (see 31 GROUPS OF COMPANIES). Input tax recovery by a VAT group must be considered in terms of the use by the VAT group as a whole of the goods and services received by each individual member. All intra-group supplies are disregarded. Thus, input tax on advice received by company A used to provide advice intra-group to company B is exempt input tax if company B uses the advice it receives to make supplies with no right to deduct. Company A may therefore incur exempt input tax on behalf of the VAT group even if it only makes taxable supplies itself.

A VAT group can only have one partial exemption method as there is only one taxable person and the *de minimis* limit must also be applied to the group as a whole. However, in deciding whether a VAT group can treat property or financial transactions as incidental for the purposes of the standard method calculation (see 49.4 above) the business activities carried on by the members of a VAT group arc considered separately.

(VAT Notice 706, para 12.1; Internal Guidance V1–15, para 20.3).

(18 **Local authorities**. See 43.8 LOCAL AUTHORITIES AND PUBLIC BODIES.

(19) **Land and property**.

(*a*) *Input tax and the option to tax*. See 42.11 LAND AND BUILDINGS.

(*b*) *Part-exchange houses*. Where a builder takes a customer's existing house in part-exchange for the new home, HMRC generally accept that input tax incurred on legal fees, valuation and structural reports, and sundry costs (eg checking and closing down the gas, electricity or water systems) is used in making both the zero-rated supply of the new house and the ultimate exempt sale of the part-exchange house. As a result, the input tax incurred on these items can properly be treated as residual input tax to be apportioned by means of the builder's agreed partial exemption method. On the other hand, they regard any input tax on estate agents fees and remedial costs (ie repair or maintenance costs) known about at the time of purchase to be attributable exclusively to the intended exempt sale and therefore restricted in full, subject to the *de minimis* limit.

Where the builder is using the standard method for partial exemption under 49.4 above, whether the proceeds for the exempt sale of the part exchange house can be considered an 'incidental' supply depends on the facts of each individual case. In the view of HMRC, if the builder advertises that it will take existing houses in part-exchange for new houses, this would suggest that the sales of the existing houses are either part of the trader's main house building business or else a separate business of selling used houses. They would not then be incidental real estate transactions. Conversely, where a builder does not normally accept existing houses in part-exchange but does so exceptionally in order to dispose of a new house that has proved hard to sell, the sale of the existing house would be incidental to its main business.

Where a builder uses a special partial exemption method, the 'incidental' criterion may not arise, but the method should fairly apportion non-attributable input tax to reflect the use of the builder's general overheads in dealing with the sale of part-exchange houses. On some occasions the supply of part-exchange houses may well be distortive even if they are not incidental.

(Internal Guidance V1–15, para 20.6).

(*c*) *Input tax and speculative builders*. See 42.15 LAND AND BUILDINGS.

49.12 RECORDS AND ACCOUNTS

See 56 RECORDS for records and accounts which every registered person is required by law to keep. In addition, for partial exemption purposes records must also enable a business to work out the amount of input tax it can recover in each VAT period and in each VAT year. Any other records that are used in calculating its recoverable input tax must also be kept.

(VAT Notice 706, para 2.7).

50 Partnerships and Joint Ventures

Cross-references. See 8.5 BUSINESS for deemed partnerships.

De Voil Indirect Tax Service. See V2.110.

The contents of this chapter are as follows.

50.1 PARTNERSHIPS

In English law a partnership, or firm, is not a legal entity but is defined as 'the relation which subsists between persons carrying on business in common with a view to profit'. [*Partnership Act 1890, s 1(1)*].

In Scottish law a partnership is a legal person distinct from the partners who compose it.

Despite this, in general VAT legislation applies similarly under English and Scottish law so that the partnership itself is treated as a taxable person.

Normally the essential elements of a partnership are that

- there are two or more parties in business together with a view to making a profit;
- those parties share any net profits and losses arising from the business activities; and
- those parties individually have the power, by their words or actions, to legally bind the other members of the firm in relation to transactions with third parties.

A formal, written agreement is not a necessary prerequisite and even if such a document exists, it is not, of itself, conclusive evidence that the relationship between two or more parties constitutes a partnership.

(Internal Guidance V1–28, para 3.4.4).

See also *Leighton-Jones and Craig (t/a Saddletramps) (VTD 597) (TVC 45.15)* approving *dicta* in *Weiner v Harris [1910] 1 KB 285*.

For alleged husband and wife partnerships see *Cooper (VTD 1218) (TVC 45.45)*, *Jackson (RD & Mrs SL) (VTD 1959) (TVC 45.42)* and *Britton (VJ) (VTD 2173) (TVC 45.45)* and for an alleged partnership with infant children see *Bridgeman (VTD 1206) (TVC 45.50)*.

For whether joint venture agreements amount to a partnership, see *Strathearn Gordon Associates Ltd (VTD 1884) (TVC 45.52)*, *Keydon Estates Ltd (VTD 4471) (TVC 45.53)* and *Fivegrange Ltd (VTD 5338) (TVC 45.54)*.

Salaried partners. Whether a salaried partner is a full partner or an employee depends upon the facts of the particular case.

- A salaried partner should be treated as an employee (and not included in the registration of the firm) if, despite being held out as a partner, he is paid either by a fixed salary or a share of the profits but is denied the rights and duties normally accorded to a full partner, ie the obligation to contribute capital and to share losses and the right to fully participate in the management of the firm.

- If a person who is called a salaried partner enjoys a share of the profits and an interest in the partnership capital, he should be treated as a full partner and included in the registration of the firm.

If a salaried partner is included as a partner on the VAT registration forms, in the absence of any evidence to the contrary, HMRC take him to be a full partner on the basis that he is holding himself out as such (see 50.4 below).

(Internal Guidance V1–28, para 3.4.10).

Limited partnerships. A limited partnership is a partnership which consists of

- one or more partners called 'general partners' who are liable for all debts and obligations of the firm, and
- one or more persons called 'limited partners' who
  (i) at the time of entering into the partnership contribute a sum as capital and are not liable for debts and obligations of the firm beyond the amount contributed; and
  (ii) cannot take part in the management of the partnership business and do not have power to bind it.

  If a limited partner should take part in the management of the partnership business, he is liable for all the debts, etc incurred while he so took part as if he were a general partner.

A limited partnership must be registered as such with the Registrar of Companies, otherwise all the partners are treated as general partners.

(Internal Guidance V1–28, para 3.5.1).

50.2 Registration

VAT registration of persons carrying on business in partnership, or carrying on in partnership any other activities in the course or furtherance of which they acquire goods from another EC country, may be in the name of the firm. In such a case, no account is to be taken of any change in the partnership in determining for the purposes of *VATA 1994* whether goods or services are supplied to or by such persons or are acquired by such persons from another EC country. [*VATA 1994, s 45(1)*].

An application to be registered (Form VAT 1) for a partnership must also be accompanied by Form VAT 2. [*SI 1995/2518, Reg 5(1); SI 2000/794*]. Form VAT 1 must be signed by one of the partners and Form VAT 2 should normally be signed by all the partners. Where large firms have offices all over the country, or even all over the world, it may be impractical for the office of the firm dealing with the application to gather together quickly the Forms VAT 2 with the details of all the partners in the firm. Where the firm only has offices in the UK, it might be worth suggesting that each office send its own Form VAT 2 signed by all the partners in that office. However, where the firm has offices abroad, HMRC accept a list of the details of all the partners, with the partners' signatures, produced on the firm's headed letter paper. For example, a firm with offices in London, Paris and New York could send a VAT 2 with the details of the partners in the London office and ask that the offices in Paris and New York send a list of the partners in that office, giving their names, addresses and phone numbers (ie all the information required on the Form VAT 2) with each partner's signature under his or her respective details. In practice, HMRC may process a VAT 1 on the basis of a notarised list of the partners' names, but this would be on the understanding that the partnership provides a full list of partners' details in due course. (Internal Guidance V1–28, Chapter 2 para 2.19).

In England and Wales, where separate businesses are carried on by the same individuals in partnership only one registration applies (*C & E Commrs v Glassborow and Another, QB [1974] STC 142 (TVC 55.1)*).

In Scotland, because a partnership is a legal person, each separate business carried on by the same partners may have a separate registration. For example, if A and B have six retail outlets and treat them as six different partnerships, each can be registered individually even though A and B are the only partners in each partnership. In practice, HMRC will only allow separate registration where it can be shown that there is a separate partnership agreement for each of the businesses. (Internal Guidance V1–28, para 3.4.17).

Limited partnerships are registered in the names of the general partners and those treated as general partners (see 50.1 above). The normal procedures for the registration of partnerships is followed except

- where there is only one general partner, the registration will be raised in the name of that sole general partner;
- where a sole general partner is already registered for VAT, the business activities of the limited partnership should be accounted for under the existing registration;
- where two or more persons are registered for VAT as a partnership and those same persons are all the general partners in a limited partnership, the business activities of the limited partnership should be accounted for under the existing registration of the partnership;
- where the general partner is an incorporated company and a member of a VAT group, the business activities of the limited partnership are part of that group and must be accounted for under the existing group registration;
- where two individuals carry on two businesses in partnership, each being a general partner in one business and a limited partner in the other, separate registration applies (*Saunders and Sorrell (VTD 913) (TVC 45.13)*); and
- where land is held jointly in the names of all the general and limited partners, it may be necessary to register all those partners as a normal partnership, separately from any existing registration the limited partnership may have. A Form VAT 2 must be signed by all the general and limited partners.

(Internal Guidance V1–28, para 3.5.3, 3.5.5).

50.3 Ceasing to be a partner

Without prejudice to *Partnership Act 1890, s 36*, a person who has ceased to be a partner continues to be regarded as a partner for VAT purposes (in particular for the purposes of any VAT liability) until the date on which the change is notified to HMRC. [*VATA 1994, s 45(2)*]. (*Partnership Act 1890, s 36* provides, *inter alia*, that a person who deals with a firm after a change in its constitution is entitled to treat all apparent members of the old firm as still being members of the firm until he has notice of the change.)

Where a person ceases to be a partner in a VAT period, (or is treated as doing so under *VATA 1994, s 45(2)* above) any notice, whether of assessment or otherwise, which is served on the partnership and relates to that period or an earlier period during the whole or part of which he was a partner is treated as served on him. [*VATA 1994, s 45(2)(3)*].

50.4 **Liability for VAT**

Subject to below

- **in England and Wales,**
  - (*a*) all the partners in a firm are liable jointly for all the debts and jointly and severally for the obligations of the firm which arise while they are members of that firm; and
  - (*b*) after death, a partner's estate is severally liable for such debts so far as they remain unsatisfied but subject to the prior payment of his separate debts; and
- **in Scotland**, because a partnership is a legal person distinct from the persons of whom it is composed, it is the partnership which is liable for debts. The partners themselves only become liable for any debts if the partnership has insufficient assets to meet those debts. Where the partners do become liable, they are liable jointly and severally.

Where a person is a partner during part only of a VAT period his liability for VAT on the supply of goods or services during that period, or on the acquisition during that period of any goods from another EC country, is limited to such proportion of the firm's liability as may be just. [*VATA 1994, s 45(5)*].

However,

- a partner's liability does not end automatically on leaving a partnership (see 50.3 above); and
- limited partners (see 50.1 above) are not liable for any debts or obligations of the limited partnership over and above the capital which they contributed.

Holding out. Anyone who by spoken word, writing or conduct represents himself, or allows himself to be represented, as a partner in a particular firm, is liable as a partner to anyone who has on the faith of any such representation 'given credit' to the firm. [*Partnership Act 1890, s 14*]. This is known as 'holding out'. HMRC consider that the phrase '*given credit*' should not be construed in a technical or restrictive sense but as describing any transaction with the firm. On this basis

- anyone who holds himself out as a partner in a firm will be liable for the debts and obligations of the partnership as if he were a partner;
- where two or more persons hold themselves out as a partnership in an application for registration, HMRC will treat those persons as partners (with joint liability for all debts); and
- where two or more persons hold themselves out to other traders and third parties as a partnership, HMRC will also treat them as if they were a *bona fide* partnership so that they are not put at a disadvantage in their relationship with that business as against third parties.

(Internal Guidance V1–28, para 3.4.6).

50.5 Notices to and by partnerships

Notices to partnerships. Any notice (whether an assessment or otherwise) addressed to the partnership by the name in which it is registered and validly served under *VATA 1994* will be regarded as served on the partnership (including any former partners as in 50.3 above). This is without prejudice to *Partnership Act 1890, s 16* which provides that notice to any partner who habitually acts in the partnership business operates as notice to the firm generally, except in cases of fraud involving that particular partner. [*VATA 1994, s 45(4)*].

Notices by partnerships. Where any notice is required to be given for VAT purposes, it is the joint and several liability of all the partners to give it, but it is sufficient if it is given by one partner. *In Scotland*, any authorised person, whether a partner or not, may give the required notice as specified by *Partnership Act 1890, s 6*. [*VATA 1994, Sch 11 para 7; SI 1995/2518, Reg 7*]. Notice of appeal may be made in the partnership name (see 5.7 APPEALS).

50.6 Partners holding office

Where a person (including partners of a firm), in the course or furtherance of a trade, profession or vocation, accepts any office, services supplied by him as the holder of that office are treated as supplied in the course or furtherance of the trade etc [*VATA 1994, s 94(4)*]. This point will obviously be of importance if the recipient of a supply suffers restriction of input tax or, as regards the supplier, the consideration for the supply was fixed with no contemplation that VAT was applicable. See *Lean & Rose (VTD 54) (TVC 60.326)* where, on the facts, a solicitor who was a partner in a private practice was held to have a personal contract as a part-time salaried solicitor of a borough council and, accordingly, was not making taxable supplies.

See also 44.8 MANAGEMENT SERVICES AND SUPPLIES OF STAFF.

50.7 Contributions to partnerships

In *KapHag Renditefonds v Finanzamt Charlottenburg, CJEC Case C–442/01, [2003] All ER(D) 362(Jun) (TVC 21.63)* a German partnership admitted a new partner, who made a payment of 38 million marks to the partnership. The partnership reclaimed input tax on legal fees relating to this. The tax authority rejected the claim on the basis that the fees related to an exempt supply of services. The partnership appealed and the case was referred to the CJEC, which ruled that no supply was being made under *EC Sixth Directive, Art 2(1)* by either the individual partners or the partnership to the incoming partner in return for the capital contribution.

Although in the *KapHag* case the incoming partner was contributing cash in return for admission into the partnership, contributions are frequently made in the form of other assets. The CJEC decision tacitly accepted the Advocate-General's Opinion that the same principles would apply whether the contribution consisted of cash or other assets. Whatever the nature of the assets comprising the contribution, there is no reciprocal supply from the partnership. However, where the assets are not cash, the making of the partnership contribution may have other VAT consequences.

Following the CJEC decision, HMRC have issued the following guidance on the implications of the decision.

(1) **Contribution to partnership comprising services.** This could be, for example, a trademark or trading logo or the use of an asset the ownership of which is retained by the incoming partner. A supply can arise under *VATA 1994, Sch 4 para 5(4)* in certain circumstances where a taxable person applies

business goods to private use or makes them available for purposes other than those of his business. Similarly, *SI 1993/1507* provides that a supply arises where a taxable person applies bought-in services to private or non-business use for no consideration where he has been entitled to input tax credit. See 47.7 OUTPUT TAX for fuller details.

Where either of the above circumstances apply, a VAT-registered incoming partner must account for VAT on the supply of services that he is regarded as making in the disposal of the services from his existing business. The partnership may be able to recover this as its input tax where the contributed services are to be used for its business (see (5) below).

(2) **Contribution to partnership comprising goods other than land.** If a partnership contribution comprises goods other than land that the transferor held as assets, then a deemed supply arises under *VATA 1994, Sch 4 para 5(1)*. See 47.6 OUTPUT TAX. Where such a deemed supply arises, the incoming partner must account for VAT. The partnership may be able to recover this as its input tax where the contributed assets are to be used for its business (see (5) below).

(3) **Contribution to partnership comprising land or interests in land.** The VAT treatment of land or interests in land depends upon whether the incoming partner, or his predecessor, was entitled to deduct input tax in relation to the contributed property. For example, if he had opted to tax the property, or it was taxable as new freehold commercial property, there may be a deemed supply as described at (2) above. The incoming partner must then account for VAT on this supply. As with other contributed goods, the partnership may be entitled to recover this as input tax where the property is to be used for the partnership's business (see (5) below).

(4) **Transfers of going concerns.** It is possible that assets transferred by way of a partnership contribution could qualify to be treated as a transfer of a going concern. If so, no VAT is due from the transferor. See 8.10 BUSINESS.

(5) **Recovery by the partnership of output tax accounted for by an incoming partner on his contribution as its input tax.** If an incoming partner contributes goods and/or services (on which VAT is due as described above) and the partnership uses them for its business purposes, the partnership can recover the VAT as input tax subject to the normal rules. The incoming partner cannot issue a VAT invoice, but in order to provide the partnership with acceptable evidence to support a claim for recovery of input tax, he may use his normal invoicing documentation overwritten with the following statement.

> 'Certificate for VAT on partnership contribution
>
> No payment is necessary for these goods/services. Output tax has been accounted for on the supply.'

The incoming partner must show full details of the goods and/or services on the documentation and the amount of VAT shown must be the amount of output tax accounted for to HMRC.

(6) **Capital goods scheme consequences.** Where the capital contribution is in the form of an interest in land or a computer, it may be an existing capital item

of the incoming partner under the capital goods scheme. If the transfer to the partnership constitutes a supply which is a disposal of an existing capital goods scheme item, a disposal adjustment may be due. If the transfer also constitutes a TOGC, then this ends the current interval for the incoming partner and the partnership becomes responsible for making adjustments for any remaining intervals. See 10 CAPITAL GOODS SCHEME for full details of the scheme.

(7) **Transfer of assets out of a partnership**. *KapHag* was only concerned with assets moving into a partnership in the form of a partnership contribution. It did not cover the reverse situation, where partnership assets are paid out to an outgoing partner or otherwise disposed of by the partnership for no consideration. Where a transfer of assets out of a partnership for no consideration occurs, one of the following sets of circumstances applies.

(*a*) If the incoming partner accounted for output tax when he contributed the assets to the partnership and the partnership was entitled to recover all or part of this as its input tax, there is a subsequent supply by the partnership when the same assets are transferred out (unless the transfer out satisfies the TOGC rules).

(*b*) If no output tax was accounted for when the assets were contributed to the partnership because they constituted a TOGC, the transfer out of the same assets is a deemed supply upon which the partnership must account for VAT (unless the transfer out satisfies the TOGC rules).

(*c*) If the partnership is transferring out more assets than those originally contributed to it, although the original contribution to the partnership may not have been a TOGC, the subsequent transfer out may satisfy the TOGC rules. If so, no VAT is due from the partnership.

(*d*) If the original contribution to the partnership was a TOGC but the partnership is transferring out less of the assets than were originally contributed, then unless the assets being transferred out still meet the TOGC rules in their own right, there may be a deemed supply upon which the partnership must account for VAT.

(Business Brief 21/04).

Disposal of a share in a partnership

50.8 *KapHag* (see 50.7 above) established that a partnership or the existing partners make no supply when a new partner is admitted in return for making a capital contribution. This paragraph considers whether the disposal by a partner of his share in the partnership is a supply for VAT purposes. It should be noted that this 'share' is distinct from the assets that were contributed by the partner on joining the partnership. As a result, even if the selling price of the share is determined by the value of those assets, they are not the subject of the later sale which has its own liability for VAT purposes.

Although the CJEC has not considered the disposal of shares in a partnership, it has considered transactions involving shares in companies. These cases have established that the mere acquisition and holding of shares in a company is not to be regarded as an economic activity, although transactions in shares or interests in companies and associations may constitute economic activity in three situations.

- Where the transactions constitute the direct, permanent and necessary extension of an economic activity.

- Where the transactions are effected in order to secure a direct or indirect involvement in the management of a company in which the holding is acquired.
- Where the transactions are effected as part of a commercial share-dealing activity.

HMRC considers that the same principles apply to transactions involving partnership shares and give the following as common examples.

Circumstances in which the disposal of a partnership share will not constitute a supply

- *The share is disposed of for no consideration*. A share in a partnership comprises services rather than goods. When services are transferred, assigned or otherwise disposed of for no consideration, they do not constitute any supply for VAT purposes.
- *The share being sold was acquired simply as an investment*. Where a partner has acquired his share merely to secure a share in any future profits and has had no involvement in running the partnership, the subsequent sale or assignment of that share for consideration will not constitute a supply for VAT purposes.

Circumstances in which the disposal of a partnership share will constitute a supply

- *Where the partnership share was acquired and disposed of as a direct extension of the partner's economic activities*. Where a partner is a taxable person in his own right, the partnership share may have been acquired in the course or furtherance of his own economic activities. If so, the subsequent transfer or assignment of that share for a consideration will also be an economic activity (eg a partner may have a business asset for sale and, rather than selling it directly, may have contributed the asset into a partnership and sold the resultant partnership share instead).
- *Where the partnership share was acquired in order to obtain an active role in the business of the partnership*. Where a partner is a taxable person in his own right and had acquired the partnership share in order to actively participate in, or control, the business of the partnership, then the sale of that share can be economic activity on the part of the partner. The sale of the share will constitute a supply for VAT purposes.
- *Where the partnership share was acquired as part of a commercial partnership share-dealing activity*. A partner who is a taxable person may have a business of dealing in partnership shares. This will be an economic activity on the part of the partner. Sales or assignments of the partnership shares that were acquired in the course of this activity and that are sold for a consideration constitute supplies for VAT purposes.

Where the disposal of a partnership share is a supply, the supply is exempt as the supply of a financial service.

VAT on associated purchases. Where the disposal of a partnership share is not a supply, the VAT incurred in connection with the disposal is normally not input tax. Where the disposal is a supply, the related VAT is input tax, but, subject to the *de minimis* provisions, recovery is normally fully restricted under the partial exemption rules.

Application to past transactions. HMRC will apply the above principles to transactions on or after 19 November 2004. Where an earlier transaction has been treated differently and resulted in an underdeclaration, HMRC will take no further action. If a past transaction has been treated differently and resulted in an overdeclaration, a business may use the voluntary disclosure procedure to reclaim the VAT (subject to the three-year capping rules).

(Business Brief 30/04).

50.9 JOINT VENTURES

Where two or more parties join together for a specific business venture, it is necessary to determine whether

- the venture itself has made a supply, or
- the venturers are supplying each other prior to one of them carrying out the final transaction.

If a partnership exists, the partnership is a legal entity eligible to register for VAT (see 50.2 above). Supplies are made to and from the partnership and, where they trade independently and are not acting in their partnership capacity, can be made to and from partners. Supplies are not made within the partnership and therefore the financing of a partnership by the partners and the distribution of partnership profits are not the consideration for any supply.

If a partnership does not exist, treatment depends upon whether the supply in question is one of goods or services. There are very few instances where it is possible for goods to be jointly purchased and supplied (eg shares in horses, boats, or planes) for which see 64.4 SUPPLY. In most cases, the title to goods rests with one person (the 'leading venturer') who initially purchases the goods and other venturers later buy in to the purchase. It is, however, possible for two or more parties to jointly make a supply of services, provided that they are equal participants in a joint venture.

(*a*) *Joint supplies of goods for resale.* Two methods of accounting for VAT are possible.

(i) *The normal procedure*

- The leading venturer reclaims input tax on the initial purchase of the goods.
- The contribution of a 'share' in the goods by another venturer in hope of the profit on resale is not consideration for a supply of goods or services and is outside the scope of VAT. Invoices or other documents relating to these contributions must bear a statement indicating the name, address and VAT registration number of the venturer who is accounting for VAT on the goods as a whole.
- The resale of the goods is a supply by the leading venturer who must account for output tax in the normal way.
- The subsequent distribution of sale proceeds to the other venturers is outside the scope of VAT as a profit share.

If any venturer supplies a service (eg repair or maintenance) in respect of the goods to the joint venture, that is a separate supply which should be invoiced to the leading venturer who can deduct any input tax which has been charged.

(ii) *The alternative procedure*

- The goods are supplied and invoiced initially to one VAT-registered venturer who claims input tax.
- Payments received from other venturers for their 'shares' in the goods are regarded as consideration for supplies of services. The venturer who claimed input tax must account for output tax on those supplies of services and input tax is recoverable by the other venturers subject to the normal rules.
- When the goods are resold, they can be treated as supplied by any one of the venturers and output tax charged if it is VAT-registered.
- The payments made from the proceeds of sale to other venturers are consideration for a supply of services by each of them (ie the sale of their 'share' to the seller). Each venturer must account for output tax, if registered for VAT, and input tax may be claimed by the seller.

HMRC only allow use of the alternative procedure if satisfied that there is no revenue risk involved and are likely to insist on the normal accounting procedure where

- a registered business reclaims input tax but attempts to make the sale through a non-registered business; and
- a venture exists between two businesses, one fully taxable and one partly exempt, and there is an attempt to route the purchase and sale through the partly exempt business in order to increase its recovery rate, even though the taxable business takes title to the goods.

(*b*) *Joint purchase of an article for use by the joint owners* (eg a farm machine bought by a group of farmers). The correct accounting procedure is as follows.

- The goods are supplied to one VAT-registered member or to the group if separately registered (eg as a syndicate). The member/group may reclaim input tax subject to the normal rules.
- Payments made by other members to that member/group, whether for the initial purchase or repairs and maintenance, etc are consideration for the right to use the goods. This is a supply of services and output tax must be accounted for by the member/group.
- If the goods are eventually resold, any output tax is due from whoever originally received the article, ie the member/group.
- Payments made by the member/group to the other members in order to pass on the proceeds of the sale are outside the scope of VAT as a profit share.

(*c*) *Joint supplies of services.* Where two or more venturers come together to make supplies of services, for reasons of administrative convenience, it is normal to create an accounting chain so that the supply is invoiced by one venturer only. HMRC allow this if satisfied that there is no revenue loss.

The alternative is for each venturer to be responsible for the supply according to the level of output which the venture stipulates it makes. If all venturers are registered for VAT, they must declare output tax on the value of their proceeds from the venture under their individual registrations but if one or more venturer is not registered (and the proceeds of the venture are not sufficient to cause registration), the proceeds accruing to that venturer escape VAT. Because of associated revenue risks, HMRC only allow this alternative if the parties specifically request it and HMRC are satisfied that the parties are truly equal participants in the venture, ie the agreed obligations and resources put into the venture by each venturer are reflected in the level of benefit which they each receive when the profits of the venture are shared. Profits need not necessarily be split 50/50 but, for example, if one venturer contributes 70% of the cost, HMRC would expect it to receive a 70% share of the eventual profits.

(Internal Guidance V1–5, Chapter 2 paras 2.19–2.23).

Joint ventures in property. Where parties come together to refurbish a property and then sell it on, it can be difficult to decide whether one party has supplied refurbishment services to the other, who has then sold the property, or whether the two parties have sold the property jointly. For relevant tribunal cases, see *Strathearn Gordon Associates Ltd (VTD 1884) (TVC 45.52)*, *Keydon Estates Ltd (VTD 4471) (TVC 45.53)* and *Fivegrange Ltd (VTD 5338) (TVC 45.54)*. These cases support HMRC's view that a true joint venture cannot exist where only one party owns the property in question and is in a dominant and controlling position over the other parties. In such cases, HMRC will not register the joint venture and supplies are made

- by the controlling venturer to outside bodies; and
- within the venture, from one venturer to another.

The effect of this is that a standard-rated supply of services of refurbishment to the property owner results in 'sticking' input tax if the property owner makes an exempt supply of the property.

(Internal Guidance V1–8, para 4.4).

50.10 LIMITED LIABILITY PARTNERSHIPS

Limited liability partnerships (LLPs) can be formed with effect from 6 April 2001. An LLP has a legal status distinct from its members and can enter into contracts in its own right. Individual members of the LLP are protected from debts or liabilities arising from negligence and wrongful acts or misconduct of another member, employee or agent of the LLP.

An LLP is a corporate body and it, rather than the members, is the legal entity for VAT purposes so that the LLP itself becomes liable for VAT registration (subject to the normal registration rules).

Where an existing partnership changes to an LLP, as the legal entity has changed from that of a partnership to a corporate body, the LLP may have to apply for VAT registration (subject to the normal rules). The normal rules for the transfer of a business as a going concern will apply (see 8.10 BUSINESS). If the general partnership ceases to exist, it may be possible for the VAT number to be transferred to the LLP (see 59.36 REGISTRATION).

VAT groups. An LLP can join a VAT group provided it meets the control conditions in *VATA 1994, s 43A* (see 31.2 GROUPS OF COMPANIES). Where the control conditions are satisfied, a VAT group could be formed by, for example

- an LLP with a number of subsidiary companies; or
- two or more eligible companies and an LLP in which those companies are controlling partners.

(Business Brief 3/01).

51 Payment of VAT

Cross-references. See 2.18 ACCOUNTING PERIODS AND RETURNS for payments by persons selling under a power of sale; 5.4 APPEALS for payment of VAT as a condition of appeal; 6.1 ASSESSMENTS for repayments of VAT made in error; 17.1–17.5 CUSTOMS: POWERS for power to require security or production of evidence before making repayments, power to recover VAT and power to distraint for payment and diligence (Scotland); 34 IMPORTS for VAT payable on importation; and 36.3 INSOLVENCY for priority of payment in insolvency.

The contents of this chapter are as follows.

51.1 PAYMENT OF VAT

Subject to the provisions in 51.3 and 51.4 below, VAT due for a VAT period is payable to the Controller at VAT Central Unit, Southend-on-Sea not later than the last day on which the return for that period must be submitted ie

- for Form VAT 100 (the normal return) not later than one month after the end of the VAT period; and
- for Form VAT 193 (final return) not later than one month after the effective date for cancellation of registration (or, in the case of a taxable person not registered, one month after the date when liability to be registered ceases).

[*SI 1995/2518, Reg 25(1)(4), Reg 40(2); SI 1996/1250, Reg 9; SI 2000/258, Reg 3*].

Where the amount of VAT due to HMRC is under £1, no payment need be made. [*VATA 1994, Sch 11 para 2(13)*]. Such amount should not be carried forward to the next return. (VAT Notice 700, para 21.5).

De Voil Indirect Tax Service. See V5.109.

51.2 Method of payment

VAT can be paid by

- cheque/postal order crossed 'A/c payee' and made payable to 'HM Revenue and Customs' and with a line through any spaces on the 'pay' line; or
- electronically by Bank Giro Credit transfer, Bankers Automated Clearing Systems (BACS) or Clearing House Automated Payment System (CHAPS). If paying by BACS or CHAPS the payer's bank must quote the VAT registration number as the payer's reference and make the payment to

Bank of England
Threadneedle Street
London EC2R 8AH

Account Name: HMRC VAT
Sort Code 10 00 00

Account No 52055000

(VAT Notice 700, para 21.3).

If paying by Bank Giro, the payer should contact HMRC on 01702 366 376 or 01702 366 314 to order a book of paying-in slips and counterfoils, one of which will need to be completed each time a payment is made.

Electronic returns. Where a return is made using HMRC's eVAT return service (see 2.1 ACCOUNTING PERIODS AND RETURNS) it is a condition of the scheme that any relevant payment must be made solely by electronic means acceptable to HMRC for that purpose. [*SI 1995/2518, Reg 40(2A); SI 2000/258*]. HMRC accept payment by BACS, CHAPS or Bank Giro Credit transfer (see above).

As payments have to be made electronically, the provisions for extending the due date of payment in 51.3 below apply.

Payments in euros. UK businesses can pay VAT (and other duties) in euros, although banks are not making BACS euro direct debit available. All declarations must continue to be made in sterling. Exchange rates are likely to fluctuate between the time payment is initiated and the time the payment is cleared. Businesses will be credited with the sterling value received by HMRC and any over/under payments will be dealt with using existing debt management practices. Costs incurred by HMRC in converting euro payments into sterling will not be passed on to businesses and will be borne by HMRC. (Business Brief 1/99).

Non-payment. If the taxpayer is unable to pay all the VAT due, he should still send in the VAT return by the due date and write to HMRC explaining why he cannot pay. HMRC may be able to help businesses experiencing short-term difficulty by agreeing a brief period in which to pay a VAT debt. Post-dated cheques should *not* be sent. If sent and dated after the due date for payment, the taxpayer will automatically be in default under 52.15 PENALTIES below. Where a compromise solution cannot be agreed or no response is received to a request for payment, HMRC may take action to recover the VAT due. This may include the issue of a distress warrant (diligence warrant in Scotland) under which assets may be removed and sold (see 17.4 and 17.5 CUSTOMS: POWERS) or requesting the court to make a bankruptcy or winding up order (see 36 INSOLVENCY). (VAT Notice 930).

Unpaid cheques. Due to the cost involved, HMRC do not re-present cheques to banks which have previously been returned unpaid through lack of funds. The onus is on the taxpayer to cancel and replace any such cheques. (VAT Notes No 4 1996).

51.3 Extending the due date

A business which makes use of electronic means of payment (BACS direct credit, bank giro credit transfer or CHAPS but not payments via Girobank) will automatically receive a seven-day extension for the submission and payment of VAT returns. Payments must be in HMRC's bank account on or before the 7th calendar day from the standard due date. If the 7th day falls on a weekend, the payment must be received by the previous Friday. If the 7th day falls on a bank holiday, payment must be received by the last working day beforehand (but see *Avonwave Ltd (t/a Gatewood Joinery)*

(VTD 17509) (TVC 18.504)). A business is free to change the method of payment on a return-by-return basis (unless submitting electronic returns) without notifying HMRC but if it changes back to payment by cheque for any return, the seven-day extension does not apply to that return.

The concession cannot be used

- by businesses required to make payments on account unless it makes monthly returns (see 51.4 below);
- by businesses using the annual accounting scheme; or
- to make VAT payments other than VAT return payments (eg assessments).

(VAT Notice 700, para 21.3).

Note that 'nil' or 'claim' returns do not receive the seven-day extension even if the business would normally submit payment returns and pay the VAT by electronic means.

In *Wood Auto Supplies Ltd (VTD 17356) (TVC 18.503)* the company consistently initiated payment on the penultimate day of the seven-day extension. HMRC imposed a default surcharge when two consecutive payments were not received until the eighth day but the tribunal held that since the company's account had been debited within the seven-day period it had a reasonable excuse for believing that it had made the payments within the extended time limit.

51.4 Payments on account

The Treasury may, if they consider it is desirable to do so in the interests of national economy, provide by SI that certain taxable persons must make payments on account of their VAT liability for a VAT period. [*VATA 1994, s 28; FA 1996, s 34; FA 1997, s 43*]. Under these provisions, every VAT-registered business with an annual VAT liability of more than £2 million is required to be in the Payments on Account (POA) scheme. Once in the scheme each business must make interim payments at the end of the second and third months of each VAT quarter as POAs of the quarterly VAT liability. A balancing payment for the quarter is then made with the VAT return. All POAs and balancing payments must be made by electronic transfer. The detailed provisions of the POA scheme are set out below.

When the scheme must be used. POAs are required to be made, in respect of each VAT period exceeding one month beginning after 31 March each year, by

(*a*) a taxable person whose total liability for VAT for the VAT periods ending in the period of one year up to the last day of his VAT period ending next before the previous 1 December (ie normally the year ending the previous 30 September, 31 October or 30 November) exceeded £2 million; and

(*b*) a taxable person whose total liability for VAT did not exceed £2 million in the period specified in (*a*) above but did exceed that amount in the VAT periods ending in any subsequent period of one year.

The period of one year referred to under (*a*) or (*b*) above is known as the '*basis period*'.

VAT liability is calculated by adding together the VAT due to be declared on returns (including assessments or voluntary disclosures) and, if applicable, the VAT due on imports and goods ex warehouse. If liability exceeds £2 million, HMRC will notify the business that it is in the scheme.

Timing of payments. POAs must be sent so as to clear Customs' account not later than the last working day of the second and third months of every VAT quarterly period (with the exception of the first period in the scheme when only one payment is required at the end of the third month). Quarterly balancing payments must also be cleared by the last working day of the month following the return period. Where non-standard period end dates have been agreed with HMRC, payments must be cleared to Customs' account by the due date for those returns (or the last working date before the due date if that date is not a working date).

Set POAs. Unless one of the alternatives below is used, set POAs must be made.

The initial level of POAs are determined by the VAT liability in the period in which the £2 million threshold was exceeded under (*a*) or (*b*) above. The amount of each POA is one twenty-fourth of the total amount of VAT (excluding VAT on imports from outside the EC and goods ex warehouse) for that period. If the business has been in operation for less than twelve months, the payments will be calculated on a proportionate basis.

HMRC must notify the business of the amounts it is required to pay and how these amounts have been calculated.

From the beginning of the next annual cycle for POAs, the amount of the POAs is one twenty-fourth of the total amount of VAT (excluding VAT on imports from outside the EC and goods ex warehouse) which the business was liable to pay in its reference year determined as follows.

VAT return periods: quarters ending	Reference year	Annual cycle begins
30 Mar, 30 Jun, 30 Sept, 31 Dec	Y/ended 30 Sept	1 Apr
30 Apr, 31 July, 31 Oct, 31 Jan	Y/ended 31 Oct	1 May
31 May, 31 Aug, 30 Nov, 28/29 Feb	Y/ended 30 Nov	1 June

Alternatives to set POAs. The following alternatives are available to set POAs.

- *Monthly VAT returns.* A business can contact HMRC and change to monthly VAT returns. It will be expected to continue making such returns for a reasonable period, normally at least twelve months. If monthly returns are prepared and payment made by electronic means (see below) or credit transfer, a further seven days beyond the due date may be allowed to render returns and make payments. This is the only circumstance in which a business liable to be in the POA scheme may be granted such an extension.
- *Payments based on actual liabilities.* A business may elect to pay its actual VAT liability for the preceding month instead of the set POAs but without rendering a monthly VAT return. Such an election must be made in writing to HMRC stating the date on which it is to take effect (which must not be less than 30 days after the date of notification). Such an election then continues to have effect until a date notified in writing to HMRC. An election cannot be withdrawn earlier than the first anniversary of the date on which it took effect and, where an election is withdrawn, a further election cannot be made within twelve months of the date of withdrawal. HMRC may at any time give written notice that an election is to cease with effect from a specified date where they are not satisfied that the correct amounts are being paid. An appeal may be made against any such notice.

Payments based on actual liabilities may be beneficial where there are seasonal variations in the VAT liability. However, where the business is in credit in any month, no immediate repayment is made. Neither can a credit in respect of the first month of an accounting period be netted off against a liability for the second month to reduce the POA for that month. The business must wait to bring the credit forward to the VAT return as normal. Where immediate repayments are required, the business should consider changing to monthly returns.

Method of payment. Payment must be made by electronic transfer direct to HMRC's account. The VAT registration number should be quoted as a reference when making payments. Acceptable methods of payment are

- Clearing House Automated Payment System (CHAPS);
- Bankers Automated Clearing System (BACS);
- bank giro credit using official HMRC bank giro slips (available by contacting ASD 2C, Alexander House, 21 Victoria Avenue, Southend on Sea, Essex, SS99 1AA; tel: 01702 366376 or the National Advice Centre; tel: 0845 000 0200);
- (exceptionally) bank giro credit using non-official slips; and
- standing order.

In all cases the business must make the necessary arrangements to ensure the payment is received on time. The seven days period of grace allowed for payment by electronic means (see 51.3 above) does *not* apply to payments under the POA scheme. Whichever payment method is used, the same method must also be used to make any balancing payments due in respect of VAT returns.

HMRC's bank details for making the payments are

Bank	Bank of England
Bank Account Number	52055000
Sort Code	
- CHAPs, BACS, SO	10–00-00
- official giro credits	10–70-90
- non-official giro credits	10–70-50

Failure to pay. Where a business fails to make a POA by the due date, the payment is recoverable as if it were VAT due. The business is also liable to the default surcharge. See 52.15 PENALTIES.

Completion of VAT return. VAT returns should be completed and submitted in the normal way. The figures must not be adjusted to take account of POAs made. The amount to be paid is the net liability shown on the return less any payments on account already made in respect of that period.

Overpayments. Where the payments made on account for a VAT period exceed the total due in that period, the excess must be repaid by HMRC (if not liable to set-off under *VATA 1994, s 81*, see 51.6 below). If the return is a repayment return, the repayment will be made in the normal way and the POAs made in the quarter will also be repaid.

Removal from scheme. Where VAT liability in a reference year (see above) falls below £2 million, a business will be removed from the POA scheme six months later.

For example, if the liability in the year to 30 September 2001 is below £2 million, the last payment on account will be due in March 2002. HMRC will notify the business of its withdrawal from the scheme and the effective date of withdrawal.

If the total VAT liability in any completed year ending after a reference year is less than £1.6 million, written application may be made to cease making POAs to HMRC at Large Payers Unit, 3rd Floor North, Queen's Dock, Liverpool L74 4AA. The requirement to make such payments then ceases with effect from the date of written approval by HMRC.

Reduction in payments on account. If

- the total VAT liability (excluding VAT on imports from outside the EC and goods ex warehouse) in any completed year ending after the year on which current payments are based is less than 80% of the liability for that year, or
- HMRC are satisfied that the total VAT liability (excluding VAT on imports from outside the EC and goods ex warehouse) in any year which has commenced but not yet ended will be less than 80% of that liability

written application can be made to HMRC at the Large Payers Unit (see above) to have the POAs reduce to reflect the current liability. Further payments on account will then be based on one twenty-fourth of the reduced amount with effect from the date of written approval by HMRC.

Increase in payments on account. HMRC may increase the POAs due where the total VAT liability (excluding VAT on imports from outside the EC and goods ex warehouse) in any year ending after the year on which current POAs are based exceeds by 20% or more the total liability for that year. Where they do so, further payments on account will be based on one twenty-fourth of the increased amount. There are similar provisions as above to reduce the payments on account where VAT liability in any subsequent year falls below 80% of the increased amount.

Businesses carried on in divisions. Where a company is registered for VAT in the names of divisions, each division is regarded as a separate business for the POA scheme, ie the £2 million test is applied to each division (and not the company as a whole). Any overpayment by a division is not liable to set-off against a liability of the company or another division.

Groups of companies. The POA scheme applies to a VAT group as if all the companies in the group were one taxable person. The representative member is responsible for the POA but, in default, all members are jointly and severally liable.

Deregistration. A business should continue to make POAs until such time as deregistration is confirmed in writing in order to avoid the risk of incurring default surcharge. However, as an alternative to POAs, a business can opt to pay the actual monthly amount due. (VAT Notice 700/11/02, para 6.10).

[*SI 1993/2001; SI 1995/291; SI 1995 No 2518, Regs 40A, 44–48; SI 1996 No 1196; SI 1996 No 1198; SI 1997/2542*]. (VAT Notice 700/60/96).

De Voil Indirect Tax Service. See V5.110.

51.5 REPAYMENT OF VAT

If, at the end of a VAT accounting period, allowable credits exceed any output tax due, HMRC automatically make the appropriate repayment unless the amount of VAT due from HMRC is under £1, in which case no repayment is made. If, however, the business has failed to submit any return for an earlier period, HMRC may withhold payment until it has complied with those requirements. [*VATA 1994, s 25(3)(5), Sch 11 para 2(13)*]. See also the right of set-off under 51.6 below.

Method of repayment. HMRC make repayments by the Bankers Automated Clearing System (BACS). In order to receive repayment by this method, the National Registration Service must be advised of the bank account details in writing. (This is a requirement on the application for VAT registration.) In exceptional circumstances when bank account details are not known, HMRC may make repayment by payable order. (VAT Notice 700, para 21.4).

51.6 RIGHT OF SET-OFF

Subject to special provisions for insolvent traders (see 36.7 INSOLVENCY) where

(*a*) any amount is due from HMRC to any person under *VATA 1994*; and

(*b*) that person is liable to pay any sum by way of VAT, penalty, interest or surcharge,

the amount in (*a*) can be set against the sum in (*b*) and, to the extent of the set-off, the obligations of HMRC and the person concerned are discharged. Any interest payable by HMRC to a person on a sum due to him under or by virtue of any provision of *VATA 1994* is treated (except for the purposes of determining entitlement to, or the amount of, that interest) as an amount due by way of credit under *VATA 1994, s 25(3)* and can therefore be taken into account under (*a*) above.

[*VATA 1994, s 81(1)-(3)*].

The effect of the above provisions is to permit both HMRC and the person concerned to adopt commercial practice and strike a balance between all types of debits and credits within the taxpayer's account. For example:

- A taxpayer may offset any payment of interest or a VAT refund owed by HMRC against debts owed to HMRC. Usually this would be done by the taxpayer rendering a VAT return with a reduced payment, the reduction being equal to the refund that is due. It should be noted, however, that HMRC do not consider that a taxpayer can set-off an amount owed to it until HMRC have written to the taxpayer confirming that the claimed refund is due. Where a taxpayer makes a set-off without receiving this clearance, HMRC are likely to commence debt recovery action for the balance. (Internal Guidance V1–33, para 10.1).
- Where any interest is payable by HMRC, it can be set off against any output tax due or payment may be withheld where outstanding returns are due for earlier periods.

HMRC can also set off a refund due to a business which is to be reimbursed to customers under the scheme in 51.9 below against a liability of the business to HMRC. (Internal Guidance V1–33, para 5.7).

The set-off provisions and VAT refund claims. Where

- HMRC are liable to pay or repay any amount to a person because of a mistake previously made about the VAT due, and
- because of the mistake, a liability of that person to pay a sum by way of VAT, penalties, interest or surcharges was not assessed,

the normal time limits for enabling recovery (eg by assessment) are disregarded in determining the amount under (*b*) above to set off against the amount under (*a*) above. [*VATA 1994, s 81(3A); FA 1997, s 48*].

Effectively, this means that where a taxpayer has overpaid VAT (eg because exempt supplies have been treated as taxable) and seeks a refund, any refund can take into account input tax which the taxpayer should not have recovered even if HMRC are out-of-time to issue an assessment for that input tax (eg because of lengthy litigation).

51.7 CLAIMS FOR VAT CREDITS AND REFUNDS

A business may be entitled to a credit for, or refund of, VAT for a number of reasons, eg

- output tax may have been incorrectly charged because of a mathematical error, a misunderstanding of the law (eg charging VAT on a zero-rated supply) or because HMRC incorrectly instructed the business to charge VAT;
- input tax may have been underclaimed in earlier periods; or
- bad debt relief may be available to recover output tax previously paid.

VATA 1994, s 80 contains special provisions covering some, but not all, of the situations where credit or refund is due. Certain conditions must be satisfied. In particular, any credit must not unjustly enrich the claimant and the claim must be made within a set time limit. These provisions are considered in 51.8–51.10 below.

Where *VATA 1994, s 80* does not apply, there can be no defence of unjust enrichment by HMRC and the method of, and time limit for, claiming is different. These provisions are considered in 51.11 below.

See also 51.12 below for a summary of the various scenarios and particular problem areas in relation to claims generally.

51.8 Credit for, or repayment of, overstated or overpaid VAT

Provisions applying to claims made after 25 May 2005

In relation to claims made after 25 May 2005 (whenever the event occurred in respect to which the claim is made),

(*a*) where a person

   (i) has accounted to HMRC for VAT for a VAT period (whenever ended), and

   (ii) in doing so, has brought into account as output tax an amount that was not output tax due,

   HMRC are liable to credit the person with that amount;

(*b*) where HMRC

   (i) have assessed a person to VAT for a VAT period (whenever ended), and

   (i) in doing so, have brought into account as output tax an amount that was not output tax due,

   they are liable to credit the person with that amount; and

(*c*) where a person has for a VAT period (whenever ended) paid to HMRC an amount by way of VAT that was not VAT due to them, otherwise than as a result of

(i) an amount that was not output tax due being brought into account as output tax (which is covered by (*a*) above), or

(ii) an amount of input tax allowable not being brought into account

HMRC are liable to repay to that person the amount so paid. This would cover the situation, for example, where a tax liability has been paid twice.

[*VATA 1994, s 80(1)(1A)(1B); F(No 2)A 2005, s 3(2)*].

HMRC are only liable to credit or repay an amount under these provisions if the following conditions are satisfied.

(1) *A valid claim is made.* To be valid,

- a claim must be in writing, state the amount of the claim, and explain the method used to calculate it; and
- the claimant must possess sufficient documentary evidence to substantiate the claim.

[*VATA 1994, s 80(2)(6); SI 1995/2518, Reg 37; F(No 2) A 2005, s 3(3)*].

In theory, this means that any claims not complying with these provisions can be rejected. However, in practice, many claims are not submitted strictly in accordance with these provisions and HMRC accept claims via the 'voluntary disclosure' route where net overpayments do not exceed £2,000 (see 56.11 RECORDS). However, if a claim is submitted primarily to recover a sum within these provisions, it should be noted that the time limits under 51.10 below apply rather than those under the voluntary disclosure provisions (see 51.11 below). (Internal Guidance V1–33, para 2.5).

The only party entitled to submit a claim is the person who actually accounted for the VAT to HMRC. There is no mechanism that allows the recipient of a supply to submit refund claims. See *Aberdeen Estates Ltd (VTD 13622) (TVC 46.11)*.

(2) *Unjust enrichment.* In relation to any claim under (*a*) or (*b*) above, the crediting of any amount to the claimant must not unjustly enrich it. [*VATA 1994, s 80(3); F(No 2)A 2005, s 3(5)*]. See 51.9 below for further detail on what is meant by unjust enrichment and for arrangements for reimbursing customers where a claimant accepts that, by receiving a credit, it would be unjustly enriched.

(3) *Time limit.* The claim must be made within the appropriate time limit (see 51.10 below).

Where, as a result of a claim under (*a*) or (*b*) above, HMRC accept that credit is due, they are only liable to pay (or repay) the amount due net of any VAT liabilities of the person concerned. [*VATA 1994, s 80(2A); F(No 2)A 2005, s 3(4)*].

Assessment of excess credits. See 6.5 ASSESSMENTS for HMRC's power to make a recovery assessment when a person has been overcredited following a claim under (*a*) or (*b*) above.

Provisions applying to claims made before 26 May 2005

Where a person *paid* an amount to HMRC by way of VAT which was not VAT due to them, HMRC were liable to repay that VAT [*VATA 1994, s 80(1)*] provided the following conditions were satisfied.

(1) *A valid claim was made.* To be valid,

- a claim had to be in writing, state the amount of the claim, and explain the method used to calculate the refund; and
- the claimant had to possess sufficient documentary evidence to substantiate the claim.

[*VATA 1994, s 80(2)(6)* (*as originally enacted*)*; SI 1995/2518, Reg 37*].

In theory this meant that any claims not complying with these provisions could be rejected. However, in practice, many claims were not submitted strictly in accordance with these provisions and HMRC accepted claims via the 'voluntary disclosure' route where net overpayments did not exceed £2,000 (see 56.11 RECORDS). However, if a claim was submitted primarily to recover a sum overpaid as VAT, the time limits under *VATA 1994, s 80(4)* applied (see 51.10 below) rather than those under the voluntary disclosure provisions (see 51.11 below). (Internal Guidance V1–33, para 2.5).

The only party entitled to submit a refund claim was the person who actually accounted for the VAT to HMRC. There was no mechanism that allowed the recipient of a supply to submit refund claims. See *Aberdeen Estates Ltd (VTD 13622) (TVC 46.11)*.

(2) *Unjust enrichment*. The repayment of any amount to the claimant could not unjustly enrich it. [*VATA 1994, s 80(3)*]. See 51.9 below for further detail on what was meant by unjust enrichment and for arrangements for reimbursing customers where a claimant accepted that, by receiving a credit, it would be unjustly enriched.

(3) The claim had to be made within the appropriate time limit (see 51.10 below).

The significance of the word 'paid' in *VATA 1994, s 80(1)* (as then enacted) was that the provisions only applied where a business had made an actual payment to HMRC and was claiming some or all of that payment was not due. Additionally, in its judgment in *C & E Commrs v University of Sussex , CA 2003, [2004] STC 1 (TVC 46.2)* the Court of Appeal held that *VATA 1994, s 80* only applied to amounts of output tax overdeclared and overpaid pursuant to payment returns and that all late claims to input tax fall within the scope of *SI 1995/2518, Reg 29* (see 51.11 below).

Assessment of overpaid repayment. See 6.5 ASSESSMENTS for HMRC's power to assess for recovery of repayments made under the above provisions in excess of the repayment liability.

51.9 *Unjust enrichment*

A basic principle under EC law is that when taxes/duties have been paid contrary to EC law they should be refunded. However, it has been accepted by the CJEC that money need not be refunded if the claimant would be unjustly enriched (see *Société Comateb & others v Directeur Général des Douanes et droits indirects, CJEC [1997] STC 1006 (TVC 21.360)*).

HMRC take the term 'unjust enrichment' to apply where, by meeting a claimant's VAT refund claim, the claimant would be put in a better economic position than if it had not mistakenly accounted for the VAT, ie it would receive a 'windfall' profit.

HMRC can only successfully invoke the defence of unjust enrichment if they can show that someone other than the claimant effectively bore the burden of the VAT, ie that the claimant passed the VAT claimed on to its customers. (Note that it is for HMRC to prove this and not for the claimant to show that it would not be unjustly enriched if the claim were to be paid.) If HMRC can successfully show this, it is then for the claimant to produce evidence that it suffered loss or damage. If it can, the claim will be paid in part or total depending on the extent of that loss or damage. Such loss or damage cannot exceed the amount claimed, even where the actual loss and damage suffered does. [*VATA 1994, s 80(3A)–(3C); FA 1997, s 46(1)(4); F(No 2)A 2005, s 3(6)(7)*].

It cannot be assumed that any VAT charged has been passed on to customers because VAT is meant to be a tax borne by the final consumer or because it is shown on an invoice. The claimant may have absorbed the VAT by accepting a reduced margin. See Internal Guidance V1–33, para 4.4 for factors taken into account by HMRC officers in deciding whether VAT has been passed on to customers.

Arrangements for reimbursing customers. Where a claimant accepts that, by receiving a refund of overpaid VAT, it would be unjustly enriched, HMRC will only make the refund if, on or before the time of making the claim, the claimant signs a written undertaking confirming the following.

(*a*) At the date of the undertaking it is able to identify the names and addresses of the customers it has reimbursed or intends to reimburse.

(*b*) The reimbursements will be completed by no later than 90 days after the repayment by HMRC.

(*c*) No deduction will be made from the 'relevant amount' by way of fee or charge (however expressed or effected). If an administration fee is charged, HMRC can recover this amount by assessment (see below).

(*d*) Reimbursement will be made only in cash or by cheque.

(*e*) Any part of the relevant amount that is not reimbursed within the time limit in (*b*) above will be repaid to HMRC.

(*f*) Any interest paid by HMRC on the relevant amount will be treated in the same way as the relevant amount falls to be treated under (*b*) and (*c*). (The provisions do not, however, specify how the interest is to be apportioned where some customers paid earlier than others.)

(*g*) The claimant will keep records of the names and addresses of those customers that it has reimbursed or intends to reimburse; the total amount reimbursed to each such customer; the total amount of interest included in each total amount reimbursed to each customer; and the date that each reimbursement is made.

(*h*) The records in (*g*) above will be produced to HMRC on receipt of written notice to that effect from a HMRC officer. The notice must state the place and time at which the records are to be produced and may be given before or after HMRC have made the repayment to the claimant.

See VAT Notice 700/45/02, para 16 for the format of the undertaking.

The '*relevant amount*' means that part (which may be the whole) of the claim which the claimant has reimbursed or intends to reimburse to customers.

The claimant must, without prior demand, make any repayments due to HMRC under (*e*) or (*f*) above within 14 days of the end of the 90-day period referred to in (*b*) above. Where it is not possible to make some of the refunds within 90 days (eg because customers have moved) HMRC may agree to an extension but not an open-ended one. If, after any extension, the claimant has still been unable to locate any customers, it should be assumed that they are not interested in getting a refund and the appropriate amount repaid to HMRC. (Internal Guidance V1–33, para 5.12).

[*VATA 1994, s 80A; FA 1997, s 46(2); F(No 2)A 2005, s 4(3); SI 1995/2518, Regs 43A–43H; SI 1998/59; SI 1999/438*].

Where HMRC accept that a claimant has not been unjustly enriched, the reimbursement arrangements above do not apply and no undertaking will be required. (Business Brief 4/98). The arrangements do apply to partial reimbursements. For example, if a business submits a claim for £50,000 and it is agreed that £30,000 should be passed on to customers but the remaining £20,000 can be retained, the £30,000 is subject to the scheme.

To ensure that the terms of reimbursement agreements are complied with, HMRC have powers to assess businesses which fail to reimburse their customers in the manner agreed. See 6.5 ASSESSMENTS.

51.10 *Time limit for claims*

Provisions applying to claims made after 25 May 2005. HMRC are not liable to credit an amount to a claimant under 51.8(*a*) or (*b*) above or repay an amount to a claimant under 51.8(*c*) above if the claim is made more than three years after the 'relevant date'.

The 'relevant date' is

(*a*) in the case of a claim under 51.8(*a*) above, the end of the VAT period there mentioned (unless (*b*) below applies);

(*b*) in the case of a claim under 51.8(*a*) above in respect of an 'erroneous voluntary disclosure', the end of the VAT period in which the disclosure was made;

(*c*) in the case of a claim under 51.8(*b*) above in respect of an assessment issued on the basis of an 'erroneous voluntary disclosure', the end of the VAT period in which the disclosure was made;

(*d*) in the case of a claim under 51.8(*b*) above in any other case, the end of the VAT period in which the assessment was made; and

(*e*) in the case of a claim under 51.8(*c*) above, the date on which the payment was made.

Where a claimant has ceased to be registered for VAT, any reference in (*b*) to (*d*) above to a VAT period includes a reference to a period that would have been a VAT period had the person continued to be registered.

For the above purposes, an '*erroneous voluntary disclosure*' occurs where

- a person discloses to HMRC that he has not brought into account for a VAT period (whenever ended) an amount of output tax due for the period;
- the disclosure is made in a later VAT period (whenever ended); and
- some or all of the amount is not output tax due.

[*VATA 1994, s 80(4)(4ZA)(4ZB); F(No 2)A 2005, s 3(8)*].

Provisions applying to claims made before 26 May 2005. HMRC were not liable to repay any amount 'paid' to them more than three years before the making of a claim for a refund under 51.8 above. [*VATA 1994, s 80(4) before amendment*]. HMRC treated the '*paid*' date as the date they received a cheque at VAT Central Unit, Southend or received a direct electronic transfer payment. (Internal Guidance V1–33, para 6.1.5).

When is a claim made? Generally, HMRC accept that a claim takes effect from the date on the claim, rather than the date it is received. But if it arrived (say) two weeks after it is dated, they are more likely to use the post mark as the date of the claim. (Internal Guidance V1–33, para 6.1.7).

Protective claims. Legally there is no such thing as a 'protective' claim. However, HMRC accept that, with a three-year time limit for making claims, it is important for businesses to protect their positions when submitting claims subject to litigation. HMRC will hold the claim on file and reconsider it in light of any judgment that subsequently supports the validity of the claim. In the event that the judgment does go in the taxpayer's favour, the date on which the 'protective claim' was originally submitted will be treated as the effective date for the purposes of applying the three-year cap. If the claim is rejected, the taxpayer will have 21 days to appeal to a VAT tribunal.

HMRC will not follow this course of action in all cases. For example, they will reject speculative claims submitted on the basis that future litigation of benefit to their claim may be undertaken by an unconnected party, ie for a claim to be valid either the claimant must be prepared to defend the basis of the claim before a tribunal or there must already be on-going litigation.

(Internal Guidance V1–33, para 2.7).

51.11 Claims for refunds not falling within VATA 1994, s 80

The provisions of *VATA 1994, s 80* described in 51.8 to 51.10 above do not cover all situations where VAT has been overpaid. Where those provisions do not apply, refund claims must be made under one of the following procedures and within the time limits as indicated in the text.

- Late claims for input tax under *SI 1995/2518, Reg 29* (see 35.9 INPUT TAX).
- Voluntary disclosure of errors under *SI 1995/2518, Regs 34, 35* (see 56.11 RECORDS).
- Adjustments to take account of increases and decreases in consideration (eg following the issue of a credit/debit note) under *SI 1995/2518, Reg 38* (see 40.15 INVOICES).
- Pre-registration expenses and post-deregistration expenses under *SI 1995/2518, Reg 111* (see 35.10 INPUT TAX and 35.11 INPUT TAX respectively).
- Adjustments under the capital goods scheme under *SI 1995/2518, Reg 115* (see 10.10 CAPITAL GOODS SCHEME).
- Claims for bad debt relief under *SI 1985/2818, Reg 165A* (see 7.3 BAD DEBT RELIEF).

There is no three-year limit in the following instances.

- Claims or adjustments which cover VAT appearing on both sides of a VAT return and which therefore cancel each other out (eg those in respect of acquisition VAT or the reverse charge).
- Correction of tax point errors.
- (Before 1 July 2005) simple duplications of output tax.

- Returns following *compulsory* backdated registration for VAT. Where a business is registered for VAT with retrospective effect, it can claim input tax on its first return even if the VAT was incurred more than three years previously.
- Claims by DIY housebuilders.
- Penalties paid which are subsequently shown not to be due.
- Where VAT invoices are received from suppliers for supplies made more than three years previously. This most commonly arises in two situations.

  (i) Late registration cases where a trader's registration is backdated more than three years and he issues VAT invoices in the hope that past customers will pay the VAT element of the supplies.

  (ii) Where a trader has mistakenly zero-rated a standard-rated supply and as a consequence HMRC have issued an assessment.

  In such cases, although strictly the time limit for late claims for input tax under *SI 1995/2518, Reg 29* applies, by concession, HMRC will treat the three-year time limit as running from the date of receipt of the VAT invoice. They will allow input tax to be recovered by the trader's customers, subject to the normal rules, if satisfied that the trader has paid the VAT due to HMRC and the customer has paid the VAT invoice.

  The concession does not apply where a standard-rated supply was made but the customer did not receive a VAT invoice or mislaid it, and therefore failed to recover input tax. In such cases, HMRC take the view that the customer could have asked them to exercise their discretion and allow alternative evidence to recover the input tax.

(C & E News Release No 10 (Budget), 26 November 1996; Business Brief 9/97; Internal Guidance V1–33, para 7.1.5).

51.12 Summary: scenarios and particular problem areas

In summary, there are four different scenarios for claims against HMRC.

- A claim for underclaimed input tax comes under *SI 1995/2518, Reg 29* (see 35.9 INPUT TAX) whether it

  (i) reduces the amount payable to HMRC in respect of an earlier payment return;

  (ii) increases the amount to which the taxpayer is entitled on an earlier repayment return; or

  (iii) exceeds the amount paid with an earlier return and turns it from a payment to a repayment return.

- A claim for overdeclared output tax in respect of an earlier payment return (reducing the amount payable to HMRC) comes under *VATA 1994, s 80* (see 51.8 above).
- A claim for overdeclared output tax in respect of an earlier repayment return (increasing the amount to which the taxpayer is entitled)

  (i) for claims made after 25 May 2005 comes under *VATA 1994, s 80* (see 51.8 above); and

  (ii) for earlier claims came under *SI 1995/2518, Regs 34, 35* (see 56.11 RECORDS).

- A claim for overdeclared output tax in respect of an earlier payment return where the amount claimed exceeds the amount paid with the earlier return (and turns it from a payment to a repayment return)
  (i) for claims made after 25 May 2005 comes under *VATA 1994, s 80* (see 51.8 above); and
  (ii) for earlier claims, the amount of the claim that was equal to the amount paid with the return came within the scope of *VATA 1994, s 80* (see 51.8 above) and the remainder came under *SI 1995/2518, Regs 34, 35* (see 56.11 RECORDS).

Particular problem areas

(1) **Partial exemption**

See 49.11(15) PARTIAL EXEMPTION.

(2) **Single long period returns and belated notifications of registration**

Single long period returns tend to arise when a business has failed to register for VAT. Since no VAT has been accounted for or paid to HMRC, *VATA 1994, s 80* cannot apply.

- Where a business decides to voluntarily register, HMRC limits retrospective registration to a date no earlier than three years before the date of application (see 59.2 REGISTRATION). See 35.10 INPUT TAX for the time limit on claiming pre-registration input tax on goods and services.
- Where a business has failed to register and its registration is compulsorily backdated, the three-year capping rule does not apply and input tax should be recovered and output tax accounted for the full period (up to 20 years).

(Internal Guidance V1–33, para 6.2.3).

(3) **Annual accounting**

It is possible for a business using the annual accounting scheme to recover overpaid VAT for more than four years as it is not until the annual return is submitted and 'paid' that the time limit provisions can be applied.

> *Example*
>
> A business with a turnover of more than £100,000 has an annual accounting period from 1 April 2004 to 31 March 2005. It made nine interim payments from July 2004 to March 2005 and submitted the annual return on 31 May 2005. The business has until 30 May 2008 to submit a refund claim for the period 1 April 2004 to 31 March 2005, ie 4 years 2 months after the start of the period.

(Internal Guidance V1–33, para 6.2.4).

(4) **Payments on account (POA)**

Payments on account made under *VATA 1994, s 28* (see 51.4 above) should be treated for the purposes of the three-year time limit as if they were paid on the due date for the relevant VAT return provided they are actually paid by the due date for that return. Normally, therefore, HMRC will treat a business in the POA scheme which makes

- its two monthly payments on account as required at the end of months 2 and 3 of the VAT period, and
- its correct balancing payment with the return on or before the due date,

as having paid the full VAT return liability on due date.

(Internal Guidance V1–33, para 6.2.5).

51.13 INTEREST, ETC.

Amounts due to HMRC. Where a business fails to submit a return and/or pay the VAT shown by the due date, it may be liable to penalty under the default surcharge provisions. See 52.15 PENALTIES. In addition, where HMRC raise an assessment for VAT undeclared or overclaimed, they may charge interest. See 51.14 below.

Amounts due from HMRC. A business is entitled to repayment supplement where HMRC do not make any repayment due within a specified time. See 51.15 below. In other cases where, due to an error by HMRC, a business overpays output tax or underclaims input tax, HMRC must pay interest to the date of repayment. See 51.16 below.

Award of interest by a tribunal. A VAT tribunal may award interest to the appellant or to HMRC in certain cases. See 51.17 below.

51.14 Interest payable to HMRC (default interest)

Circumstances in which interest may be charged. A taxable person may be charged interest in the following circumstances.

(*a*) Where HMRC raise an assessment for a VAT period to recover any VAT which has been underdeclared or overclaimed on a VAT return.

(*b*) Where HMRC raise an assessment for a VAT period in respect of which an earlier assessment has already been notified (ie where HMRC issue an assessment following the failure to submit a VAT return but a further assessment is necessary as the original assessment is later found to be too low).

(*c*) Where HMRC raise an assessment relating to a VAT period which exceeds three months and begins on the date with effect from which the person concerned was, or was required to be, registered.

(*d*) Where HMRC raise an assessment relating to a VAT period at the beginning of which the person concerned was, but should no longer have been, exempted from registration under *VATA 1994, Sch 1 para 14(1)* (see 59.6 REGISTRATION), *VATA 1994, Sch 3 para 8* (see 59.22 REGISTRATION) or *VATA 1994, Sch 3A para 7* (see 59.29 REGISTRATION).

(*e*) Where, before an assessment is made under (*a*)-(*d*) above, the VAT due or other amount concerned is paid by voluntary disclosure (so that no assessment is necessary). Interest is only charged on voluntary disclosures where the net value of errors exceeds £2,000 (ie it will not be charged where the taxable person could have adjusted the errors in his current VAT return but chose instead to make voluntary disclosure direct to HMRC).

[*VATA 1994, s 74(1)(2); FA 1996, s 197; FA 2000, s 136(5)*].

In general, however, HMRC only charge interest where they consider it represents '*commercial restitution*', ie compensation for the loss of use of any underdeclared or overclaimed VAT. They normally only charge interest if they have been deprived of this VAT for a period of time. They would not, for example, generally charge interest if an amount of VAT is underdeclared which would have been immediately reclaimable as input tax by a third party.

HMRC use the following decision making processes to determine if the charging of interest will represent commercial restitution

(*a*) **Overclaimed input tax.**

(1) Is the input tax properly claimed by another registered person?

If Yes, go to (2). If No, go to (3).

(2) Is the other registered person partly exempt?

If Yes or Don't know, interest will be charged.

If No, interest will not be charged unless the input tax has been claimed more than once.

(3) Is there any other reason why interest should not be charged?

If Yes, interest may not be charged.

If No, interest will be charged.

Overclaimed input tax generally occurs where evidence of entitlement is not held, claims are made too early, errors are made within the accounting system or claims are made for a non-deductible charge.

(*b*) **Output tax underdeclared**

(1) Is the underdeclaration an additional assessment (ie where HMRC have assessed for a period in the absence of a return and the true liability is later found to exceed the assessment)?

If Yes, interest will be charged.

If No, go to (2).

(2) Is the error wholly within an accounting system (eg arithmetical and accounting errors, retail scheme errors, assessments based on comparison with annual accounts, cash reconciliation and mark-up exercises)?

If Yes, interest will be charged.

If No, go to (3).

(3) Is the customer unregistered for VAT (eg underdeclarations arising from retail transactions where goods are wrongly zero-rated)?

If Yes, interest will be charged.

If No, go to (4).

(4) Is the customer partly exempt?

If Yes, some commercial restitution will be required and interest will be charged on an agreed basis.

If No, interest may not be charged but it will be due if

- VAT has been charged to the customer; or
- VAT has been undercharged (eg by incorrectly zero-rating) and the customer cannot immediately reclaim the VAT in full).

Any differences in VAT period groups between the person in default and his customer or supplier will normally be ignored when considering the need for commercial restitution.

(VAT Notice 700/43/03, paras 2.1–2.3).

Circumstances in which interest will not be charged. HMRC will not charge interest if the net value of errors discovered on previous VAT returns is £2,000 or less (see (*e*) above). In addition, interest will not be charged on the following.

- VAT declared on returns but unpaid.
- Assessments raised because a VAT return has not been rendered on time (but see (*b*) above for follow-up assessments).
- Penalties and interest.
- Amendments made to VAT returns before they are fully processed.

(VAT Notice 700/43/03, para 2.4).

Calculation of interest. Interest runs on the amount assessed or paid from the 'reckonable date' (even if not a business day) until the date of payment. In practice, however, interest runs to the date shown on the Notice of Assessment (Form VAT 655) or the Notice of Voluntary Disclosure (Form VAT 657). If any interest-bearing VAT shown on the Notice is not paid within 30 days, a further liability to interest arises. Interest will continue to be charged on a monthly basis and notified on Form VAT 658 or VAT 659 until all the interest-bearing VAT charged on the original assessment or voluntary disclosure is paid. However, interest is limited to a maximum of three years prior to the date of calculation shown on the Notice of Assessment or Notice of Voluntary Disclosure. In practice, interest will be charged where appropriate on the net amount of underdeclarations liable to interest, less any overdeclarations, for each VAT period.

The '*reckonable date*' is the latest date on which a return is required for the VAT period to which the amount assessed or paid relates (ie one month after the end of the period) except that

- where the amount assessed or paid is an incorrect repayment of VAT or a payment in respect of excess credits, the reckonable date is the seventh day after HMRC authorised the repayment; and
- where an assessment is made under *VATA 1994, s 73*(*7*) in respect of goods which cannot be accounted for (see 6.1(*e*) ASSESSMENTS), the sum assessed is to be taken to relate to the period for which the assessment was made.

[*VATA 1994, ss 74*(*1*)-(*3*)(*5*), *76*(*1*)(*7*)(*8*), *Sch 13 para 18*]. (VAT Notice 700/43/03, paras 2.5, 2.6, 2.8).

Rate of interest. The rate of interest is adjusted automatically from the 6th of each month by reference to changes in the average of base lending rates of certain clearing banks. Rates of interest are:

6 July 1998 – 5 January 1998	9.5%	[*SI 1998/1461*]
6 January 1999 – 5 March 1999	8.5%	
6 March 1999 – 5 February 2000	7.5%	
6 February 2000 – 5 May 2001	8.5%	
6 May 2001 – 5 November 2001	7.5%	
6 November 2001 – 5 September 2003	6.5%	
6 September 2003 – 5 December 2003	5.5%	
6 December 2003 – 5 September 2004	6.5%	
6 September 2004 –	7.5%	

Invoices issued by unauthorised persons. Where an 'unauthorised person' issues an invoice showing an amount as being or including VAT, interest runs on the appropriate amount from the date of the invoice to the date of payment.

'*Unauthorised person*' means anyone other than

- a person registered for VAT; or
- a body corporate within a group registration; or
- a person treated as carrying on the business of a taxable person who has died or become bankrupt or incapacitated; or
- a person selling business assets of a taxable person towards satisfaction of a debt owed by that taxable person (eg sale of assets seized by a bailiff); or
- a person acting on behalf of the Crown.

[*VATA 1994, s 74(4)*].

Appeals, etc. If a taxpayer disagrees with the imposition of interest or with the amount of interest charged, he may ask HMRC to reconsider the matter. This will be done by an officer not involved in the original decision.

If still not satisfied with the amount of the interest charged, the taxpayer may appeal to a VAT tribunal (see 5.3(*q*) APPEALS). There is no right of appeal against the rate of, or liability to, interest. A tribunal can only vary the amount of interest assessed insofar as it is necessary to reduce it to an amount which is appropriate under the above provisions. [*VATA 1994, s 84(6)*].

De Voil Indirect Tax Service. See V5.361–365.

51.15 Repayment supplement

Where

- a person is entitled to a repayment of VAT credits under *VATA 1994, s 25(3)*,
- a registered statutory body is entitled to a refund under *VATA 1994, s 33* (see 43.7 LOCAL AUTHORITIES AND PUBLIC BODIES), or
- a registered body is entitled to a refund under *VATA 1994, s 33A* (museums and galleries, see 35.13(16A) INPUT TAX)

the payment due is increased by a supplement of 5% of that amount or £50, whichever is the greater, provided

(*a*) the return or claim is received by HMRC not later than the last day on which it is required to be made;

(*b*) HMRC do not issue a written instruction directing the making of the payment or refund due within the 'relevant period'; and

(*c*) the amount shown as due on the return or claim does not exceed the amount in fact due by more than 5% of that amount or £250, whichever is the greater.

The '*relevant period*' is the period of 30 days beginning with

- the date of receipt of the return or claim by HMRC; or
- the day after the last day of the VAT period to which the return or claim relates, if later.

Any supplement paid is treated (except for the purposes of determining the amount of the supplement) as an amount due by way of credit under *VATA 1994, s 25(3)* or an amount due by way of refund under *VATA 1994, s 33* or *VATA 1994, s 33A* as the case may be. Where the repayment, therefore, is not due in whole or in part and is recoverable by assessment, interest may be due on the repayment supplement as well as the VAT. See 51.14 above.

In calculating the period of 30 days referred to above, periods relating to the following are left out of account.

- The raising and answering of any reasonable inquiry relating to the return or claim in question. This period begins with the date on which HMRC first consider it necessary to make such an inquiry and ends with the date on which HMRC either satisfy themselves that they have received a complete answer to their inquiry or determine not to make the inquiry or, if they have already made it, not to pursue it further.
- The correction by HMRC of any errors or omissions in the return or claim. The period begins on the date when the error or omission first came to their notice and ends on the date when it is corrected by them.
- In a case where a person is entitled to a repayment of VAT credits, the continuing failure to submit returns in respect of an earlier VAT period. The period is determined in accordance with a certificate of HMRC issued to that effect under *VATA 1994, Sch 11 para 14(1)(b)*.
- In a case where a person is entitled to a repayment of VAT credits, failure to produce documents or give security as a condition of repayment of VAT under *VATA 1994, Sch 11 para 4(1)*. The period begins on the date of the service of the written notice of HMRC requiring the production of documents or giving of security and ends on the date when they received the required documents or the required security.

[*VATA 1994, s 79; FA 1999, s 19; FA 2001, s 98(4)-(7); SI 1995/2518, Regs 198, 199*].

For a general consideration of how VAT repayment claims are received and internally processed by HMRC and the their code of practice for dealing with repayment returns, see VAT Notice 700/58/02 *Treatment of VAT repayment returns and VAT repayment supplement*.

Repayment supplement will not be paid on

- refunds paid to EC traders;
- refunds to do-it-yourself housebuilders;
- claims relating to services received after deregistration;
- amounts notified by HMRC as overdeclared (including those resulting from voluntary disclosures made in writing to HMRC); or
- claims for interest as a result of official error.

(VAT Notice 700, para 21.6).

De Voil Indirect Tax Service. See V5.191; V5.192.

51.16 **Interest payable by HMRC in cases of official error**

Where, due to an error by HMRC, a person has

(*a*) accounted to HMRC for output tax which was not due to them and, as a result, they are liable to pay (or repay) an amount to him, or

(*b*) failed to claim credit for input tax to which he was entitled and which HMRC are in consequence liable to pay to him, or

(*c*) otherwise than under (*a*) or (*b*) paid to HMRC any VAT not due (eg import VAT) and which they are in consequence liable to repay, or

(*d*) suffered delay in receiving payment of an amount due from HMRC in connection with VAT (including, for example, a refund under the DIY builder's scheme or under (*a*) to (*c*) above but excluding any interest due under this provision),

then, if they would not otherwise be liable to do so, HMRC must pay interest to him for the 'applicable period' at the following rates.

1.4.97– 5.1.99	6%	[*SI 1997/1016; SI 1998/1461*]
6.1.99 – 5.3.99	5%	
6.3.99 – 5.2.00	4%	
6.2.00 – 5.5.01	5%	
6.5.01 – 5.11.01	4%	
6.11.01 – 5.9.03	3%	
6.9.03 – 5.12.03	2%	
6.12.03 – 5.9.04	3%	
6.9.04 –	4%	

The rate of interest is adjusted automatically from the 6th of each month by reference to changes in the average of base lending rates of certain clearing banks.

Although not specified in the legislation, interest is calculated on a simple rather than compound basis. See *National Council for YMCAs Inc (VTD 10537) (TVC 46.97)*.

These provisions do not require HMRC to pay interest on any amount on which repayment supplement is due under 51.15 above (see *THI Leisure Two Partnership (VTD 16876) (TVC 46.61)*), or on the amount of that repayment supplement. Additionally, where a claim for any payment or repayment has to be made, interest is only due on the amount of the claim which HMRC are required to satisfy or have satisfied (ie interest is limited to the period for which VAT is refundable under *VATA 1994, s 80*).

Interest is not due under these provisions where penalties, surcharge or default interest have been charged in error and repayment is made by HMRC. However, repayment of penalties, etc will normally be accompanied by an *ex gratia* payment as compensation using the same interest rates as above. (Internal Guidance V1–33, para 11.2).

Claims. Interest is only due if a claim is made in writing for that purpose. Any claim must be made within three years after the end of the applicable period to which it relates.

Period of interest. The '*applicable period*' is the period beginning with the date that HMRC

- under (*a*) or (*b*) above received payment, or as the case may be authorised a repayment or set off, for the return period to which the output tax or input tax related;
- under (*c*) above, received the payment; or
- under (*d*) above, might reasonably have been expected to authorise the payment or set-off in question

and ending with the date on which HMRC authorised payment of the amount on which the interest is payable. References to HMRC 'authorising' a payment of any amount include references to their discharging liability to pay that amount by way of set-off against VAT due to them. Broadly, statutory interest is therefore payable on the net amount repayable by HMRC at any particular time.

In calculating the applicable period, any period by which HMRC's authorisation of the payment of interest is delayed by the claimant's conduct is left out of account. This includes, in particular, any period referable to the following.

- Unreasonable delay in making the claim for interest or the claim for payment or repayment of the amount on which interest is claimed. A business should not use HMRC as a bank. Once a business knows that a claim could be made, HMRC's general view is that, if the claim is not complicated, two months is not an unreasonable time for a claim to be made. What is 'complicated' depends upon the individual circumstances of the business but HMRC generally seek to apply an upper limit of six months for the most difficult refund claims. (Internal Guidance V1–33, para 11.12).
- A failure by the claimant or his representative to provide HMRC with all the information they require to determine the amount of the payment or repayment due and the interest thereon (whether at or before the time of making the claim or subsequently in response to a request by HMRC). For these purposes, there is to be taken as referable to a person's failure to provide information in response to a request by HMRC any period beginning with the date on which HMRC reasonably require the person to provide it and ending with the earliest date they could reasonably conclude that the information required has been supplied or is no longer necessary.
- The making of a claim (as part of or in association with the claim for payment or repayment or interest) to anything to which the claimant was not entitled. HMRC regard this as applying where a claim is submitted and although the majority of it is agreed a small area needs clarification. If the business unreasonably delays providing the information in relation to that area, the interest clock

will stop for the whole of the claim (not just the part being checked). It also applies where the business has included items in its claim which it is not entitled to include and HMRC consider that the inclusion of these items is in effect a delaying tactic to get more interest. Again, HMRC can stop the interest clock on the whole amount. (Internal Guidance V1–33, para 11.12).

Appeals. An appeal may be made to a VAT tribunal against a decision of HMRC not to pay interest under these provisions (see 5.3 APPEALS).

[*VATA 1994, s 78; FA 1996, s 197; FA 1997, s 44; F(No 2)A 2005, s 4(2)*].

A claim for interest was upheld where HMRC incorrectly advised that input tax had to be apportioned because some of the company's income was outside the scope of VAT. This ruling (although pre-dating it) was inconsistent with the decision in *Lennartz v Finanzamt Munchen III* (see 35.7 INPUT TAX) and led to the company failing to claim credit for input tax to which it was entitled (*North East Media Development Trust Ltd (VTD 13104) (TVC 46.91)*. Following the decision, the company claimed interest on the whole of the input tax which HMRC had wrongly refused to repay. However, the tribunal upheld HMRC's contention that interest should be computed upon an amount equal to the net overpayment of VAT (*North East Media Development Trust Ltd (VTD 13425) (TVC 46.99)*).

A claim for interest was also upheld where the organisation contended that a HMRC leaflet had not been updated and that it had been misled by a VAT officer (*Wydale Hall (VTD 14273) (TVC 46.94)*).

Assessment of overpaid interest. See 6.5 ASSESSMENTS for HMRC's power to assess for interest that has been overpaid to a claimant under the above provisions.

De Voil Indirect Tax Service. See V5.196.

51.17 Award of interest by a tribunal

Where a tribunal decides that any 'VAT paid or deposited' should be repaid to the appellant or any amount of input tax should be paid to him, it may direct that the amount is repaid with interest at such rate as it may specify. Similarly, where an appeal has been entertained despite the fact that VAT determined by HMRC has not been paid or deposited (see 5.21 APPEALS) and it is found on the appeal that the amount is due, such amount must be paid with interest at such rate as the tribunal may specify. [*VATA 1994, s 84(8)*].

'*Tax paid or deposited*' includes paying VAT charged on a supply 'without prejudice' should the VAT be found not to be payable (*WJM Mahoney (VTD 258) (TVC 2.419)*).

Although the award of interest is mandatory the rate has been subject to a variety of treatments by tribunals.

52 Penalties

Cross-references. See 5.2 APPEALS for penalty for failure to comply with a direction of a tribunal.

De Voil Indirect Tax Service. See V5.3.

The contents of this chapter are as follows.

52.1 CRIMINAL OFFENCES AND PENALTIES

Criminal proceedings may be brought under the offences in 52.2 to 52.7 below. Most VAT defaults are, however, dealt with by civil penalties and only serious cases of fraudulent VAT evasion are investigated as criminal matters. The proceedings may only be instituted by HMRC or a law officer of the Crown.

Except as otherwise provided in the Customs *Acts*,

- proceedings for an indictable offence must be commenced within 20 years of the date when the offence was committed; and
- proceedings for a summary offence must be commenced within three years of that date but, subject to that, may be commenced at any time within six months from the date on which sufficient evidence to warrant the proceedings came to the knowledge of the prosecuting authority. For these purposes, a certificate of the prosecuting authority as to the date on which the evidence came to its knowledge is conclusive evidence of the fact.

There are further detailed provisions relating to service of process, place of trial, non-payment of penalties, application of penalties, proof of certain documents and other procedural matters. [*CEMA 1979, ss 145–151, 153–155; VATA 1994, s 72(12)*].

False statements to the prejudice of the Crown and public revenue are indictable as a criminal offence (*R v Hudson, CCA 1956, 36 TC 561*). False statements may also involve liability to imprisonment for up to two years, under the *Perjury Act 1911, s 5*, for 'knowingly and wilfully' making materially false statements, etc for VAT purposes.

De Voil Indirect Tax Service. See V5.301–308.

52.2 **Fraudulent evasion of VAT**

A person who is knowingly concerned in, or in taking steps with a view to, the fraudulent 'evasion of VAT' by him or any other person, is liable

- on summary conviction, to a penalty of the 'statutory maximum' or three times the 'amount of VAT', whichever is the greater, *or* imprisonment for a term not exceeding six months *or* to both; or
- on conviction on indictment, to a penalty of any amount *or* to imprisonment for a term not exceeding seven years *or* to both.

'*Evasion of VAT*' includes obtaining

(i) a payment of a VAT credit;

(ii) a refund under *VATA 1994, s 35* (do-it-yourself housebuilders), *VATA 1994, s 36* or *VATA 1983, s 22* (bad debts) or *VATA 1994, s 40* (new means of transport supplied to another EC country by a non-taxable person);

(iii) a refund under regulations made by virtue of *VATA 1994, s 13(5)* (VAT paid in the UK on an acquisition from another EC country where VAT has already been paid in that other country); or

(iv) a repayment under *VATA 1994, s 39* (repayment of VAT to those in business overseas).

'*Amount of VAT*' in relation to a payment within (i) above is the aggregate of the amount (if any) falsely claimed as input tax and the amount (if any) by which output tax was falsely understated. In relation to a refund or repayment within (ii) to (iv) above, it is the amount falsely claimed.

A person acting under the authority of HMRC may arrest anyone whom he has reasonable grounds for suspecting to be guilty of an offence.
[*VATA 1994, s 72(1)(2)(9)*].

'*Statutory maximum*' is currently £5,000.

Nothing in the above denies the right for an assessment to be made in respect of the VAT actually evaded.

'Evasion' includes deliberate non-payment of VAT and it is not necessary to show any permanent intention to deprive (*R v Dealy, CA Criminal Division 1994, [1995] STC 217 (TVC 47.10)*).

'*Taking of steps*' to evade VAT need not necessarily be confined to the taking of positive steps (*R v McCarthy, CA Criminal Division [1981] STC 298 (TVC 47.1)*).

The existence of the above provisions does not rule out the possibility of conviction under the common law offence of cheating the public revenue. This offence is preserved by the *Theft Act 1968, s 32(1)* and can include any form of fraudulent conduct which results in diverting money from the public revenue and in depriving the public revenue of money to which it is entitled. In practice, the common law charge is reserved for serious cases and the penalties, including imprisonment, are unlimited. No positive act of deception is required. An omission to do an act is sufficient. See *R v Mavji, CA [1986] STC 508 (TVC 47.15)* and *R v Redford, CA [1988] STC 845 (TVC 47.16)*.

Most cases of VAT evasion are dealt with under the civil provisions (see 52.9 below) which are more cost-effective. HMRC's aim is to focus criminal investigation and prosecution activity on the most serious cases of VAT evasion. Prosecution will normally be considered where a strong deterrent message is required and the civil option may not achieve this and where one or more of the following circumstances apply.

- The evasion involves a registration of one or more businesses whose activities are solely or primarily bogus or undertaken as a systematic fraud against the tax.
- There is, during the course of investigation of a civil offence, a deliberate intent to deceive.
- The evasion is perpetrated by lawyers, accountants or others who advise businesses in respect of VAT matters, by current or former tax officials, or by a person who occupies a prominent position in the field of law or government.
- The evasion is executed together with other criminal activities, eg excise evasion or where the case is being investigated criminally by the Inland Revenue.
- There has been a previous VAT or Customs offence resulting in the imposition of a penalty, the compounding of proceedings or a criminal conviction.
- There is a conspiracy to evade VAT other than by persons with the same legal entity.
- Where the evasion is perpetrated by an undischarged bankrupt.
- Where HMRC have directed that a security should be given under *VATA 1994, Sch 11 para 4(2)* (see 17.1 CUSTOMS: POWERS) and taxable supplies take place without the security being given.

There is no upper or lower limit of revenue evaded which triggers criminal investigation.

Compounding. Under *CEMA 1979, s 152*, HMRC may accept a financial settlement (a '*compound settlement*') in lieu of criminal proceedings. This saves time and money for both the taxpayer and HMRC by avoiding the need for legal proceedings. HMRC do not offer a compound settlement in all cases and will normally prosecute where a HMRC officer has been assaulted or obstructed or the taxpayer is subject to a suspended prison sentence, on parole, an undischarged bankrupt (in liquidation if a limited company), a persistent offender or is being investigated for other related offences (whether by HMRC, the police or other government departments).

Each case is considered on its merits but HMRC will take into account the seriousness of the offence; the penalty that a court might impose; the nature and value of the goods and the amount of tax/duty involved; the costs of investigating the offence; any aggravating circumstances; and the ability of the taxpayer to pay.

HMRC may disclose details of a compound settlement to the courts (if prosecuted for a similar offence in the next five years); an employer; other government departments whose statutory responsibilities are directly affected by the actions involved; and Parliament or the media (if in the public interest).

(VAT Notice 700, para 27.4; Customs Notice 12).

De Voil Indirect Tax Service. See V5.311.

52.3 **False documents and statements**

Any person who

(*a*) produces, furnishes, sends or otherwise makes use of, for the purposes of VAT, any document which is false in a material particular with the intent to deceive or secure that a machine will respond to the document as if it were a true document; or

(*b*) causes a document to be produced, etc as in (*a*) above; or

(*c*) makes any statement in furnishing information for the purposes of VAT which he knows to be false in a material particular *or* who recklessly makes a statement which is false in a material particular,

is liable

- on summary conviction, to a penalty of the 'statutory maximum' (see 52.2 above) *or* to imprisonment for a term not exceeding six months *or* to both. Where the document referred to is a return *or* a refund or repayment under 52.2(ii)–(iv) above *or* the information under (*c*) above is contained in or relevant to such a document, an alternative penalty of three times the amount falsely claimed is, if greater, substituted for the statutory maximum; or
- on conviction on indictment, to a penalty of any amount *or* to imprisonment for a term not exceeding seven years *or* to both.

A person acting under the authority of HMRC may arrest anyone whom he has reasonable grounds for suspecting to be guilty of an offence.

[*VATA 1994, s 72(3)–(7)(9)*].

De Voil Indirect Tax Service. See V5.312; V5.313.

52.4 **Conduct which must have involved an offence**

Where a person's conduct during any specified period must have involved the commission by him of one or more offences under 52.2 or 52.3 above, then, whether or not the particulars of the offence are known, he is guilty of an offence and liable

- on summary conviction, to a penalty of the greater of the 'statutory maximum' (see 52.2 above) and three times the amount of any VAT that was, or was intended to be, evaded by his conduct *or* to imprisonment for a term not exceeding six months *or* to both; or
- on conviction on indictment, to a penalty of any amount *or* to imprisonment for a term not exceeding seven years *or* to both.

See 52.2 above for 'evasion of VAT'.

A person acting under the authority of HMRC may arrest anyone whom he has reasonable grounds for suspecting to be guilty of an offence.

[*VATA 1994, s 72(8)(9)*].

De Voil Indirect Tax Service. See V5.314.

52.5 **Knowledge that evasion intended**

A person who acquires possession of, or deals with, any goods or accepts the supply of services, having reason to believe that VAT on the supply, acquisition or importation has been or will be evaded, is liable to a penalty on summary conviction of the greater of level 5 on the 'standard scale' or three times the amount of the VAT evaded. [*VATA 1994, s 72(10)*].

'*Standard scale*' can be altered by statutory instrument and level 5 is currently £5,000.

De Voil Indirect Tax Service. See V5.316.

52.6 **Failure to provide security**

A person who supplies, or after 9 April 2003 is supplied with, goods or services in contravention of a requirement to give security under *VATA 1994, Sch 11 para 4(2)* (see 17.1(*c*) CUSTOMS: POWERS) is liable to a penalty of level 5 on the standard scale (see 52.5 above). [*VATA 1994, s 72(11); FA 2003, s 17(5)*].

De Voil Indirect Tax Service. See V5.317.

52.7 **Obstruction of officers**

A person commits an offence if, without reasonable excuse, he obstructs an HMRC officer or a person acting on behalf of or assisting an HMRC officer. Any person found guilty of such an offence is liable, on summary conviction, to imprisonment for up to 51 weeks or a fine up to level three on the 'standard scale' or both. The standard scale can be altered by statutory instrument and level 3 is currently £1,000. [*CRCA 2005, s 31*].

Before the merger of the Inland Revenue and Customs, any person who obstructed, hindered, molested, or assaulted a Customs officer or did anything which was likely to impede any search or production of evidence was liable, on summary conviction, to a penalty of £2,500 or imprisonment for a term not exceeding three months or to both, or, on conviction on indictment, to a penalty of any amount or to imprisonment for a term not exceeding two years or to both. [*CEMA 1979, s 16 repealed by CRCA 2005, Sch 4 para 21*].

52.8 **CIVIL PENALTIES**

In addition to the criminal penalties under 52.1 to 52.7 above, there are also civil penalties and surcharges. These are detailed in 52.9 to 52.20 below.

Reasonable excuse for conduct. No penalty or surcharge arises under 52.10 to 52.15 and 52.17 to 52.21 below if the person concerned can satisfy HMRC, or on appeal a tribunal, that there is a reasonable excuse for his conduct. Although 'reasonable excuse' is not defined (and, therefore, to be determined by HMRC or a tribunal) the following are not to be taken as a reasonable excuse.

- An insufficiency of funds to pay any VAT due.
- Where reliance is placed on 'any other person' to perform any task, the fact of that reliance or any other dilatoriness or inaccuracy on the part of the person relied upon. See *C & E Commrs v Harris and Another, QB [1989] STC 907 (TVC 49.83)*. '*Any other person*' is not restricted to outside advisers and includes a company's accountant (*Profile Security Services (South) Ltd v C & E Commrs, QB [1996] STC 808 (TVC 18.551)*).

[*VATA 1994, s 71(1)*].

It is necessary to distinguish between the reason and the excuse. Although insufficiency of funds by itself is not a reasonable excuse, where the shortfall is totally unforeseen and not due to the normal hazards of trade (eg the dishonesty of a former employee) the defence of reasonable excuse may possibly be invoked (*C & E Commrs v Salevon Ltd, QB [1989] STC 907 (TVC 18.304)*). See also *C & E Commrs v Steptoe, CA [1992] STC 757 (TVC 18.320)* where it was held that there was reasonable excuse where the taxpayer was unable to pay the VAT due because the customer for whom he worked almost exclusively was persistently late in paying invoices. The correct test is whether, given the exercise of reasonable foresight, due diligence and a proper regard for the fact that the VAT will become due on a particular date, the lack of funds which led to the default was reasonably avoidable.

HMRC have indicated the following *guidelines* on the interpretation of 'reasonable excuse' although any decision will be judged by HMRC or a VAT tribunal on the circumstances of the individual case.

(*a*) **Reasonable excuse for late registration**

- *Compassionate circumstances* where an individual is totally responsible for running a small business and he, or a member of his immediate family, was seriously ill or recovering from such an illness at the time notification was required.
- *Transfer of a business as a going concern* where such a business is taken over with little or no break in the trading and returns have been submitted and VAT paid on time under the registration number of the previous owner.
- *Doubt about liabilities of supplies* where there is written evidence of an enquiry to HMRC about the liability of supplies and liability has remained in doubt.
- *Uncertainty about employment status* where there are genuine doubts as to whether a person is employed or self-employed or where correspondence with the Revenue can be produced about these doubts.

(VAT Notice 700/41/02, para 3.1).

(*b*) **Reasonable excuse for not sending in return or paying VAT on time**

- *Computer breakdown* where the essential records are held on computer and it breaks down either just before or during the preparation of the return. Reasonable steps to correct the fault must be taken.
- *Illness* of the person normally responsible for preparing the return provided it can be shown that no-one else was capable of completing the return. If the illness is prolonged, reasonable steps to get someone else to complete the return must be taken.
- *Loss of key personnel* responsible for preparing the return at short notice where there is no-one else to complete it on time.
- *Unexpected cash crisis* where funds are unavailable to pay VAT because of the sudden reduction or withdrawal of overdraft facilities, sudden non-payment by a normally reliable customer, insolvency of a large customer, fraud, burglary or act of God such as fire.
- *Loss of records.* The excuse only applies if records for the current VAT period are stolen or destroyed. If records relating to a future VAT return are lost, HMRC must be notified immediately. If the records are elsewhere (eg with accountants or the Revenue) it is the taxpayer's responsibility to get them, or copies of them, back.

HMRC will take into account whether the circumstances could have been foreseen and, if so, what steps were taken to make alternative arrangements; whether HMRC was contacted for help or advice; whether sufficient priority was given to completing the VAT return; and whether the VAT (or a reasonable estimate) was paid by the due date.

(VAT Notice 700/50/02, paras 3.2, 3.3).

There have been numerous tribunal decisions as to whether, on the facts of a particular case, there is a reasonable excuse against the assessment of a penalty. For a summary of these see the chapters DEFAULT SURCHARGE, PENALTIES: FAILURE TO NOTIFY, ETC, PENALTIES: MISDECLARATION and PENALTIES: REGULATORY PROVISIONS in Tolley's VAT Cases.

Mitigation. See 52.22 below.

Right of set-off. See 51.6 PAYMENT OF VAT.

De Voil Indirect Tax Service. See V5.335.

52.9 VAT evasion: conduct involving dishonesty

Most cases of VAT evasion are dealt with under the following civil provisions but, for aggravated or serious offences, the matter may be investigated for criminal proceedings. See 52.2 above for criminal proceedings and an indication of where cases are likely to be dealt with as such.

Where

(*a*) for the purpose of 'evading VAT', a person does any act or omits to take any action; and

(*b*) his conduct involves dishonesty (whether or not it is such as to give rise to criminal liability),

he is liable to a penalty equal to 'the amount of the VAT evaded' (or sought to be evaded). However, where he is convicted of a criminal offence by reason of conduct within (*a*) and (*b*) above, he is not also liable to a penalty under these provisions.

'*Evading VAT*' includes dishonestly obtaining a VAT credit; a refund under *VATA 1994, s 35* (do-it-yourself builders), *VATA 1994, s 36* or *VATA 1983, s 22* (bad debts) or *VATA 1994, s 40* (new means of transport supplied to another EC country by a non-taxable person); a refund under regulations made by virtue of *VATA 1994, s 13*(*5*) (VAT paid in the UK on an acquisition from another EC country where VAT has already been paid in that other country on the acquisition); and a repayment under *VATA 1994, s 39* (repayment of VAT to those in business overseas).

'*The amount of VAT evaded*' is the amount falsely claimed by way of credit for input tax (including any amount claimed as a deduction from VAT due) or the amount by which output tax is falsely understated *or* the amount falsely claimed by way of refund or repayment.

In any criminal proceedings against the person concerned in respect of any offence in connection with VAT or in any proceedings against him for recovery of any sum due, statements made or documents produced on his behalf are not inadmissible on the grounds that he was (or may have been) induced to make or produce them after it had been brought to his attention that

(i) HMRC might assess a civil penalty rather than bring criminal proceedings against him if he made a full confession of any dishonest conduct and gave full facilities for investigation; or

(ii) the penalties might be mitigated.

[*VATA 1994, ss 60, 71(2)*].

For a consideration of the test of 'dishonesty' see *dicta* of Lord Lane in *R v Ghosh, CA [1982] 3 WLR 110 (TVC 48.27)*. It is dishonest if a company officer signs a return containing a mis-statement and he has no honest belief in the truth of the statement he has made, and in particular if he makes the statement recklessly, not caring whether it is true or false. See *Adam Geoffrey & Co (Management) Ltd (VTD 16074) (TVC 3.99)* where the accountant had not declared a sale of a property on a company's return and the controlling director had signed the return without checking its contents and ensuring that they were complete and correct.

The penalty can be applied in cases of non-registration and is not restricted to cases where there has been a fraudulent understatement of output tax or overstatement of input tax (*CS Stevenson v C & E Commrs, CA [1996] STC 1096 (TVC 48.1)*).

Customs' approach to civil evasion investigations and mitigation of the penalty. See 52.22 below for mitigation generally.

Full civil evasion procedure. Where HMRC investigate the VAT affairs of a business under their civil evasion penalty (CEP) procedure, an investigating officer will set up an interview, explain the CEP procedure, and ask for co-operation in establishing the true VAT liability. The officer will explain why it is felt that any underdeclaration arises from dishonest conduct, but will listen to any explanations that the business, or its advisers, wish to give. If there is a satisfactory explanation for the discrepancy, a CEP will not apply. Although the officer starts with a penalty figure of 100% of the VAT alleged (or agreed) to be underdeclared, this can be reduced significantly. At interview, an early and truthful admission of the extent of the arrears *and* why they arose will attract a considerable reduction. A further major reduction can be received by co-operation in supplying information promptly, attending interviews, answering questions honestly and accurately, and giving the relevant facts to establish the true liability. On the other hand, no penalty reduction may be given at all where there is a total lack of co-operation or the course of the investigation is generally obstructed. Reductions from the 100% penalty figure will normally be made for three reasons, to the maximum percentages specified, as follows.

- An early and truthful explanation as to why the arrears arose and the true extent of them — up to 40%.
- Co-operation in substantiating the true amounts of arrears — up to 25%.
- Attending interviews and producing records and information as required — up to 10%.

The maximum reduction obtainable is normally therefore 75% of the VAT underdeclared although in exceptional cases (eg where a full and unprompted voluntary disclosure has been made) consideration will be given to a further reduction.

(VAT Notice 730).

New approach to civil evasion investigation. At an initial meeting, which may be held at HMRC or the business's offices, HMRC will explain their new approach to civil evasion investigation, the aim of which is to reach an agreement on the nature, extent and reason for VAT irregularities. This entails full co-operation from the business an early stage and subsequent preparation of a report by the business detailing the nature of, and quantifying, the irregularities. At the meeting, the business will be given the option of participating in the new approach. If it does not wish to do so, HMRC will undertake its investigation using the full civil evasion procedure above.

If the business decides to proceed, a responsible person will be asked to respond 'yes' or 'no' to four formal questions.

- Have any transactions been omitted from, or incorrectly recorded, in the books and records of (name of legal entity) with which you are (responsible status)?
- Are the books and records you are required to keep by HMRC for (name of legal entity) with which you are (responsible status), correct and complete to the best of your knowledge and belief?
- Are all the VAT returns of the (name of legal entity) which you are (responsible status) correct and complete to the best of your knowledge and belief?
- Were you aware that any of the VAT returns were incorrect or incomplete at the time they were submitted?

HMRC do not necessarily expect precise quantification of any inaccuracies at the initial meeting although they will ask for a general explanation of any irregularities.

If the business indicates that there are no matters to be disclosed, HMRC will normally undertake an investigation under the full civil evasion procedure outlined above.

If there are matters to be disclosed, HMRC will invite the business to provide a disclosure report which will normally include

- a brief history of the business (approximately half a page);
- a description of the nature of the irregularities and how those arose (approximately one page);
- a description of the extent of the irregularities including any accounting assumptions and steps taken to verify amounts;
- a summary of the irregularities; and
- a detailed schedule by VAT period of the irregularities.

A time scale for producing the report will be agreed at the meeting.

HMRC expect the business to demonstrate a willingness to agree realistic proposals to make early payment of arrears. They offer the business the chance to make payments on account towards any additional VAT they think is due, both at the initial meeting, and throughout the enquiry. A summary of the main issues discussed at the meeting will be sent to the business to agree, or amend, then sign and return.

HMRC may well ask for further meetings and, if they are not satisfied with the progress being made, reserve the right to carry out the investigation themselves.

Once the business is satisfied that the report is a complete account, it should be signed by a responsible person as representing a full disclosure of irregularities, and sent to HMRC within the agreed timescale. A person who produces a report contains a statement known to be false may be prosecuted.

Once the signed report has been received, HMRC may undertake selective checks on the information supplied. If they disagree with any aspect of the report, a further meeting may be necessary.

Once the nature and extent of the irregularities have been agreed, HMRC will inform the business of the VAT, interest and penalty due. HMRC start with a penalty figure of 100% of the agreed irregularities of VAT. That figure is reduced by an amount which depends on whether the business has fully disclosed full details of its true VAT liability, and by the extent of its co-operation during the whole enquiry. Reductions from the 100% penalty figure will normally be made, to the maximum percentages specified, as follows.

- An early and truthful explanation as to why the arrears arose and the true extent of them — up to 40%.
- Fully embracing and meeting responsibilities under this procedure (eg by supplying information promptly, including full written disclosure, attending meetings and answering questions) — up to 40%.

The maximum reduction obtainable is normally therefore 80% of the VAT underdeclared although in exceptional cases (eg where a full and unprompted voluntary disclosure has been made) consideration will be given to a further reduction.

(VAT Information Sheet 1/02).

Standard of proof. In a civil action, the plaintiff has to establish its case on the 'balance of probabilities' whereas in a criminal action the standard of proof required by the prosecution is 'beyond reasonable doubt'. In *First Indian Cavalry Club Ltd v C & E Commrs, CS 1997, [1998] STC 293 (TVC 48.62)* it was held that Parliament had clearly intended the standard of proof for penalties under *VATA 1994, s 60* to be the normal civil standard of the balance of probabilities. See now, however, *C & E Commrs v Han & Yau (and related appeals), CA [2001] STC 1188 (TVC 32.5)*. The tribunal applied the guidelines in *Engel v Netherlands, ECHR 1980, 1 EHRR 647*, namely that in deciding whether a penalty was civil or criminal, the criteria to be considered were the classification of the proceedings in domestic law, the nature of the offence, and the severity of the penalty which may be imposed. On this basis, the tribunal held that the penalties were 'criminal charges' within *European Convention of Human Rights, Art 6*. The Court of Appeal, by a majority, upheld this decision but made it clear that not all civil penalties would be so categorised. The effect of this decision is that statements made with a view to reducing the civil penalty under any 'offence' under *VATA 1994, s 60* may not be admissible because the makers of such statements were induced to do so by statements from HMRC that co-operation would reduce the penalty imposed. However, the Court of Appeal indicated that, if matters were made clear to the taxpayer at the time when the nature and effect of the inducement procedure were also made clear to him, it is difficult to see that there would be any breach of *Article 6*. Even if the *Police and Criminal Evidence Act* were applicable, it was most unlikely that a court or tribunal would rule inadmissible any statements made or documents produced as a result.

See also *Georgiou and another (t/a Marios Chippery) v UK, ECHR 2000, [2001] STC 80 (TVC 32.1)*.

Liability of directors, etc. Where the conduct of a body corporate gives rise to a penalty under the above provisions and it appears to HMRC that that conduct, in whole or part, is attributable to the dishonesty of a person who is (or at the material time was) a director or 'managing officer' (the named officer) of the body corporate, HMRC may serve a notice on the named officer proposing to recover all or part of the penalty from him. The portion specified is then assessable and recoverable as if the named officer were personally liable to that part of the penalty. The body corporate is then only assessed on the balance, if any, and is discharged from liability on the amount assessed on the named officer.

The body corporate may appeal against HMRC's decision as to its liability to the penalty and against the amount of the full penalty as if it were specified in an assessment. The named officer may appeal against the decision that the conduct of the body corporate is, in whole or part, attributable to his dishonesty and against the portion of the penalty which HMRC propose to recover from him. Otherwise, there are no grounds for appeal.

'*Managing officer*' means any manager, secretary or other similar officer of the body corporate and any person purporting to act in any such capacity or as a director. Where the affairs of a body corporate are managed by its members, the provisions apply in relation to the conduct of a member in connection with his functions of management as if he were a director of the body corporate.

[*VATA 1994, s 61*].

The notification of liability to a director, etc must show both the amount of the basic penalty and the portion of it which HMRC propose to recover from that director (*MK & ME Nazif (VTD 13616) (TVC 48.4)*). See *C & E Commrs v Bassimeh, CA 1996, [1997] STC 33 (TVC 48.2)* for apportionment of penalties where there is more than one culpable director.

De Voil Indirect Tax Service. See V5.341.

52.10 Misdeclaration or neglect resulting in VAT loss

Subject to below, a person is liable to a penalty where

(*a*) a return is made understating liability to VAT or overstating entitlement to a repayment of VAT credits, or

(*b*) an assessment is made understating liability to VAT and, within 30 days from the date of the assessment, the taxpayer has not taken all such steps as are reasonable to draw the understatement to the attention of HMRC

and the 'VAT which would have been lost' for the period concerned if the inaccuracy had not been discovered equals or exceeds the lesser of

- where (*a*) above applies, £1 million and 30% of the 'gross amount of VAT'; and
- where (*b*) above applies, £1 million and 30% of the 'true amount of VAT for the period'.

The penalty is 15% of the VAT which would have been lost.

Where supplementary assessments are raised, any penalty is calculated at the percentage rate in force at the time of the original assessment. A penalty is assessed on the date of the decision to make the assessment and the calculation of the amount due, not the date of the notice of assessment if different (*Dart (VTD 9066) (TVC 3.67)*).

'*VAT which would have been lost*'. This is the amount of the understatement of liability or, as the case may be, overstatement of entitlement to repayment for the VAT period in question.

'*Gross amount of VAT*' is the total of the amount of input tax and output tax which should have been stated in the return for that period. Input tax for this purpose includes any refunds or repayments due in the period which may be aggregated with input tax on the return.

'*True amount of VAT*' means the VAT due from the person concerned or, as the case may be, the amount of the payment to which he is entitled in the period.

For the purposes of ascertaining the '*VAT which would have been lost*', the '*gross amount of VAT*' and the '*true amount of VAT*' where any under or over statement is correspondingly adjusted in a subsequent return, each of those returns is assumed to be a correct statement (so far as not inaccurate in any other respect) for the VAT period to which it relates.

A person is not liable to a penalty under these provisions

(A) if he is convicted of a criminal offence or assessed to a penalty under 52.9 above by reason of conduct within (*a*) or (*b*) above; or

(B) where he satisfies HMRC, or on appeal a tribunal, that there is 'reasonable excuse' for the conduct (see 52.8 above); or

(C) if, at a time when he had no reason to believe that HMRC were enquiring into his affairs, he furnished them with full information with respect to the inaccuracy concerned.

Additionally, HMRC have indicated that such a penalty *will not normally be imposed*

(D) if the penalty amount would be less than £300;

(E) during a 'period of grace' from the end of the VAT period in which the misdeclaration is made to the date for furnishing the VAT return for the following accounting period;

(F) when a misdeclaration has been corrected by a compensating misdeclaration in respect of the same transaction for the following accounting period with no overall loss of VAT; or

(G) where the misdeclaration has been disclosed

- *before HMRC begin to make enquiries* (ie normally when an appointment is made to visit and inspect the records); or
- *after a visit has been arranged* (unless HMRC believe that the errors were discovered earlier and only disclosed because of the proposed visit); or
- *during or after a visit* (unless they believe the disclosure was prompted by an enquiry into the trader's affairs).

In such cases, the disclosure will be treated as a voluntary disclosure, see 56.11 RECORDS.

See 52.22 below for mitigation of penalties.

Local authorities and similar bodies. The provisions above and in 52.11 below apply to LOCAL AUTHORITIES AND PUBLIC BODIES (43) as if

- any reference to VAT credit included a reference to a refund under *VATA 1994, s 33*; and
- any reference to a credit for input tax to include a reference to VAT chargeable on supplies, acquisitions or importations which were not for the purpose of any business carried on by the body.

Museums and galleries. After 31 August 2001, the provisions above apply to museums and galleries to which *VATA 1994, s 33A* applies (see 35.13(16A) INPUT TAX) as if

- any reference to VAT credit included a reference to a refund under those provisions; and

- any reference to a credit for input tax included a reference to VAT chargeable on supplies, acquisitions or importations which were attributable to the provision by the body of free rights to admission to a relevant museum or gallery.

[*VATA 1994, ss 63, 71(2), Sch 13 para 15; FA 2001, s 98(3)*]. See also VAT Notice 700/42/02.

De Voil Indirect Tax Service. See V5.343; V5.343A.

52.11 Repeated misdeclarations

A person is liable to a repeated misdeclaration penalty where the following circumstances apply.

(i) He makes a 'material inaccuracy' in respect of any VAT period. Subject to below, a 'material inaccuracy' arises where a return is made which understates liability to VAT or overstates entitlement to a repayment of VAT credits and the 'VAT which would have been lost' for that period if the inaccuracy had not been discovered equals or exceeds whichever is the lesser of £500,000 and 10% of the 'gross amount of VAT' for that period. See 52.10 above for the meaning of 'VAT which would have been lost' and 'gross amount of VAT'.

(ii) HMRC serve a penalty liability notice on the person concerned before the end of the five consecutive VAT periods beginning with the period in respect of which there was the material inaccuracy.

(iii) The penalty liability notice specifies a penalty period of eight consecutive VAT periods beginning with the period in which the date of the notice falls.

(iv) He makes at least two further material inaccuracies in VAT periods within the penalty period.

No liability arises in respect of the first further material inaccuracy under (iv) above but for the second and any subsequent material inaccuracy the person concerned is liable to a penalty of 15% of the VAT which would have been lost for that VAT period if the inaccuracy had not been discovered.

HMRC have indicated that a penalty will not normally be imposed if either the penalty amount would be less than £30 or the circumstances in 52.10(E)-(G) above apply.

An inaccuracy is not regarded as material in the following circumstances.

(*a*) The person concerned satisfies HMRC, or on appeal a tribunal, that there is a reasonable excuse for the inaccuracy (see 52.8 above).

(*b*) At a time when he had no reason to believe that HMRC were enquiring into his affairs, he furnished them with full information with respect to the inaccuracy.

(*c*) By reason of conduct falling within (i) above, the person is convicted of an offence or assessed to a penalty under 52.9 or 52.10 above in respect of that inaccuracy. This, however, does not prevent an inaccuracy resulting in the assessment of a penalty under 52.10 above from being regarded as

- a material inaccuracy in respect of which HMRC may serve a penalty liability notice under (ii) above; or
- the first further material inaccuracy under (iv) above.

Where under (*a*)–(*c*) above an inaccuracy is not regarded as material for the purposes of serving a penalty liability notice, any such notice served in respect of that inaccuracy is deemed not to have been served.

[*VATA 1994, s 64, Sch 13 para 16; FA 1996, s 36*].

See also 52.22 below for mitigation of penalties.

De Voil Indirect Tax Service. See V5.344.

52.12 **Failures to notify and unauthorised issue of invoices**

Failure to notify. Where a person fails to comply with

(*a*) *VATA 1994, Sch 1 para 5* (duty to notify liability for registration on the basis of supplies in the previous year under 59.3(*a*) REGISTRATION) or *VATA 1994, Sch 1 para 6* (duty to notify liability for registration on the basis of supplies in the next 30 days under 59.3(*b*) REGISTRATION),

(*b*) *VATA 1994, Sch 1 para 7* (duty to notify liability for registration on the transfer of a going concern under 59.3(*c*) REGISTRATION),

(*c*) *VATA 1994, Sch 1 para 14(2)(3)* (change in nature of suppliers, etc by a person exempted from registration, see 59.6 REGISTRATION),

(*d*) *VATA 1994, Sch 2 para 3* (duty to notify liability for registration in respect of supplies from other EC countries, see 59.13 REGISTRATION),

(*e*) *VATA 1994, Sch 3 para 3* (duty to notify liability for registration in respect of acquisitions from other EC countries, see 59.20 REGISTRATION),

(*f*) *VATA 1994, Sch 3 para 8(2)* (duty to notify change in nature of supplies by a person exempt from registration in respect of acquisitions from other EC countries, see 59.22 REGISTRATION),

(*g*) *VATA 1994, Sch 3A paras 3, 4* (duty to notify liability for registration by overseas traders in respect of disposal of assets for which a VAT repayment claimed, see 59.28 REGISTRATION),

(*h*) *VATA 1994, Sch 3A para 7(2)(3)* (duty to notify change in nature of supplies by an overseas trader exempt from registration in respect of disposal of assets for which a VAT repayment claimed, see 59.29 REGISTRATION), or

(*j*) regulations under *VATA 1994, Sch 11 para 2(4)* (notification of acquisition of excise duty goods or new means of transport, see 23.9 and 23.35 EUROPEAN COMMUNITY: SINGLE MARKET respectively)

he is, subject to below, liable to a penalty of the greater of £50 and

- 5% of the 'relevant VAT' where HMRC are notified or become aware of the failure no more than nine months late (three months late where (*j*) above applies);
- 10% of the relevant VAT where notification, etc is over nine months late but not more than 18 months late (over three months but no more than six months where (*j*) above applies); and
- 15% of the relevant VAT in any other case.

Where supplementary assessments are raised, any penalty is calculated at the percentage rate in force at the time of the original assessment (if different).

'*Relevant VAT*' is

(i) subject to below, where (*a*), (*d*), (*e*) or (*g*) above applies, the VAT for which the person would be liable for the period beginning on the date he was required to be registered and ending on the date on which HMRC received notification, or otherwise became fully aware, of his liability to be registered;

(ii) subject to below, where (*b*) above applies, the VAT for which the person would be liable for the period beginning on the date he was required to be registered (or, if later 1 January 1996) and ending on the date on which HMRC received notification, or otherwise became fully aware, of his liability to be registered;

(iii) where (*c*), (*f*) or (*h*) above applies, the VAT for which the person would be liable for the period beginning on the date on which the change in the nature of the supplies, etc occurred and ending on the date on which HMRC received notification, or otherwise became fully aware, of that change; and

(iv) where (*j*) above applies, the VAT on the acquisition to which the failure relates.

Where the relevant VAT under (i) or (ii) above includes VAT on the acquisition of goods from another EC country and HMRC are satisfied that VAT has been paid under the law of another EC country on the supply in question (either to a supplier or directly to the fiscal authority), an allowance is to be made for the VAT so paid (not exceeding the amount of the VAT due).

A person is not liable to a penalty under these provisions where by reason of conduct falling within (*a*)–(*j*) above, he is convicted of an offence or assessed to a penalty under 52.9 above. Conduct falling within the provisions does not give rise to a penalty if the person concerned satisfies HMRC, or on appeal a tribunal, that there is a 'reasonable excuse' for his conduct. See 52.8 above for '*reasonable excuse*'. See also 52.22 for mitigation.

From 10 April 2003 until 30 September 2003, as a one-off exercise, businesses trading over the VAT registration threshold but which fail to register for VAT can notify their liability to register outside the statutory time limits without incurring a late notification penalty providing they pay any arrears of VAT in full and furnish all returns and payments on time for the twelve months after registration. (C & E Budget Notice 23/03).

Unauthorised issue of invoices. Where an 'unauthorised person' issues one or more invoices showing an amount as being, or including, VAT he is, subject to below, liable to a penalty of the greater of £50 and a percentage of the 'relevant VAT' as follows.

Penalty assessed	*% of relevant VAT*
Before 1.1.95	30%
1.1.95 onwards	15%

Where supplementary assessments are raised, any penalty is calculated at the percentage rate in force at the time of the original assessment.

'*Relevant VAT*' is the amount which is, or is the aggregate of, the amounts which are

- shown on the invoice or invoices as VAT; or
- to be taken as representing VAT.

'*Unauthorised person*' means anyone other than

- a person registered for VAT; or
- a body corporate within a group registration; or

- a person treated as carrying on the business of a taxable person who has died or become bankrupt or incapacitated; or
- a person selling business assets of a taxable person towards satisfaction of a debt owed by that taxable person (eg sale of assets seized by a bailiff); or
- a person acting on behalf of the Crown.

It includes any person who issues an invoice showing a fixed flat rate compensation percentage under the special scheme for farmers when not authorised to do so (see 63.25 SPECIAL SCHEMES).

A person is not liable to a penalty under these provisions where by reason of his conduct, he is convicted of an offence or assessed to a penalty under 52.9 above. Conduct falling within the provisions does not give rise to a penalty if the person concerned satisfies HMRC, or on appeal a tribunal, that there is a 'reasonable excuse' for his conduct. See 52.8 above for '*reasonable excuse*'. See also 52.22 below for mitigation.

[*VATA 1994, s 67; FA 1995, s 32; FA 1996, s 37; FA 2000, s 136(2)*].

De Voil Indirect Tax Service. See V5.347–350.

52.13 Breaches of walking possession agreements

The following provisions apply where distress is authorised to be levied on the goods and chattels of a person in default who has refused or neglected to pay any VAT due (or any amount recoverable as if it were VAT due) and the person levying the distress and the person in default have entered into a 'walking possession agreement'. See 17.4 CUSTOMS: POWERS for levying of distress.

If the person in default breaches the undertakings contained in that agreement, he is liable to a penalty equal to half of the VAT due or amount recoverable unless he satisfies HMRC, or on appeal a tribunal, that there is a 'reasonable excuse' for the breach in question. See 52.8 above for '*reasonable excuse*'.

'*Walking possession agreement*' is an agreement under which the property distrained is allowed to remain in the possession of the person in default and its sale delayed in return for

- an acknowledgement that the property is under distraint, and
- an undertaking not to remove or allow removal of the property from the premises named in the agreement without the consent of HMRC and subject to such conditions as they impose.

These provisions do not apply in Scotland.

[*VATA 1994, s 68; FA 1997, s 53(7)*].

De Voil Indirect Tax Service. See V5.351.

52.14 Breaches of regulatory provisions

Penalties are payable under the circumstances in (*a*) and (*b*) below but if the person in default is, by reason of his conduct within those circumstances, convicted of an offence or assessed for a penalty under 52.9 or 52.10 above or a surcharge under 52.15 or 52.16 below, he is not also liable to a penalty under these provisions. Additionally, no liability to a penalty arises under the following provisions if the person concerned satisfies HMRC, or on appeal a tribunal, that there is a 'reasonable excuse' for the failure. See 52.8 above for '*reasonable excuse*'.

(*a*) If any person fails to comply with a requirement to preserve records under *VATA 1994, Sch 11 para 6*(*3*) (see 56.3 RECORDS) he is liable to a penalty of £500.

(*b*) A person is liable to a penalty where he fails to comply with any requirement imposed under

(i) *VATA 1994, Sch 1 para 11* or *12* (notification of end of liability or entitlement to be registered, see 59.9 REGISTRATION);

(ii) *VATA 1994, Sch 2 para 5* (notification of matters affecting the continuation of registration in respect of supplies from other EC countries, see 59.16 REGISTRATION);

(iii) *VATA 1994, Sch 3 para 5* (notification of matters affecting the continuation of registration in respect of acquisitions from other EC countries, see 59.24 REGISTRATION);

(iv) *VATA 1994, Sch 3A para 5* (notification of matters affecting the continuation of registration by overseas traders in respect of disposals of assets for which a VAT repayment is claimed, see 59.31 REGISTRATION);

(v) any regulations made under *VATA 1994, s 48* requiring a VAT representative, for the purposes of registration, to notify HMRC that his appointment has taken effect or ceased to have effect, see 3.11 AGENTS;

(vi) *VATA 1994, Sch 11 para 6*(*1*) (duty to keep records, see 56.1 RECORDS);

(vii) *VATA 1994, Sch 11 para 7* (furnishing of information and production of documents, see 17.6 CUSTOMS: POWERS);

(viii) any regulations or rules made under that *Act* (other than procedural rules for tribunals);

(ix) any Treasury order made under that *Act*;

(x) any regulations made under the *European Communities Act 1972* and relating to VAT; or

(xi) *VATA 1994, s 18A* (conditions imposed by HMRC in connection with fiscal warehousing, see 70.12 WAREHOUSED GOODS AND FREE ZONES).

No penalty can be assessed under (vi) to (x) above unless, within the two years preceding the assessment, HMRC have issued a written warning of the consequences of a continuing failure to comply with the requirements.

The daily rate of penalty is £5 if there has been no previous occasion in the two-year period preceding the beginning of the failure in question on which the person concerned has failed to comply with that requirement. If there has been one such occasion in that period, the daily rate is £10 and in any other case, the daily rate is £15. The maximum penalty payable is 100 days at the appropriate rate and the minimum penalty is £50.

Where a person's failure to comply with any VAT regulation consists of not paying VAT or failing to make a return in the required time, for the daily penalties above, there is substituted, if greater, a daily penalty of 1/6th, 1/3rd or 1/2 of one per cent of the 'VAT due' in respect of that period. '*VAT due*' is, if a return has been furnished, the amount shown on the return; otherwise, it is the amount assessed by HMRC.

For the purposes of calculating the penalty

- a failure is disregarded if, as a result, the person becomes liable to a surcharge under 52.15 or 52.16 below;
- a continuing failure is regarded as one occasion of failure occurring on the date on which it began;
- if the same omission gives rise to a failure to comply with more than one such requirement, it is regarded as the occasion of only one failure;
- if the failure is to comply with the requirements concerning furnishing of returns or payment of VAT, a previous failure to comply with either requirement is regarded as a failure to comply with the requirement in question; and
- any earlier failure is disregarded where HMRC, or on appeal a tribunal, have been satisfied that there is a 'reasonable excuse' for the failure. See 52.8 above for '*reasonable excuse*'.

Where HMRC issue a notice of assessment specifying a date (not later than the date of the notice) to which the penalty is calculated, if the person liable pays the penalty within the period notified by HMRC in the assessment, then the penalty is treated as paid on the specified date (and no further penalty accrues after that date). If the penalty is not paid within the notified period, a further assessment may be made to recover additional penalties.

The Treasury may, by statutory instrument, adjust any of the monetary sums above but not so as to apply to a failure which began before the date on which the order comes into force.

[*VATA 1994, s 69, s 76(2)(7)(8); FA 1996, s 35(6), Sch 3 para 9; FA 2000, s 136(3)*].

De Voil Indirect Tax Service. See V5.352–354.

52.15 **Default surcharge**

Unless the provisions in 52.16 below apply, if, by the last day on which a taxable person is required to 'furnish' a return for a VAT period, HMRC have not 'received' that return (or have received the return but not the amount of VAT shown on the return as payable) the taxable person is in default for the purposes of these provisions. See below for the interpretation of '*furnish*' and '*received*'.

Subject to below, a taxable person is liable to a surcharge under these provisions where

(*a*) he is in default in respect of a VAT period;

(*b*) HMRC serve on him either

- a *surcharge liability notice* specifying a surcharge period from the date of the notice to the first anniversary of the last day of the VAT period under (*a*) above; or
- where that last day occurs during an existing surcharge period, a *surcharge liability notice extension* extending the existing surcharge period to the first anniversary of the last day of the VAT period under (*a*) above;

(*c*) he is again in default in respect of another VAT period which ends within the surcharge period specified in (or extended by) that notice; and

(*d*) he has 'outstanding VAT' for the VAT period in (*c*). (There is, therefore, no *liability* to surcharge if a nil or repayment return is submitted late or the VAT due is paid on time but the return is submitted late. HMRC will, however, record the default and issue a surcharge liability extension notice.)

The surcharge is the greater of £30 and the 'specified percentage' of his outstanding VAT for the VAT period under (*d*) above.

The 'specified percentage' is determined by reference to the number of VAT periods in respect of which he is in default in the surcharge period and for which he has outstanding VAT.

	Specified percentage
In relation to the first such period	2%
In relation to the second such period	5%
In relation to the third such period	10%
In relation to each such period after the third	15%

A person has '*outstanding VAT*' for a VAT period if some or all of the VAT due for that period has not been paid by the last day on which he is required to make a return for that period.

Where a liability to surcharge is established, HMRC will not issue a surcharge assessment at the 2% or 5% rates for an amount of less than £400 (£200 before January 2002). In these circumstances a default will be recorded, a surcharge liability extension notice will be issued, and the rate of surcharge will increase if there are any further defaults in the surcharge period. (VAT Notice 700, para 21.2).

A person is not liable to a surcharge and not to be treated as having been in default in respect of the VAT period in question if he satisfies HMRC, or on appeal a tribunal, that in the case of a default which is 'material to the surcharge' either of the following applies.

(i) The return or, as the case may be, the VAT shown on it, was despatched at such time and in such manner that it was reasonable to expect that it would be received by HMRC within the appropriate time limit. The despatch of a cheque within reasonable time cannot be equated with the despatch of the VAT where the cheque proves to be worthless (*C & E Commrs v Palco Industry Co Ltd, QB [1990] STC 594 (TVC 18.404)*). See also below under the heading *Meaning of 'furnish' and 'received'*.

(ii) There is a 'reasonable excuse' for the return or VAT not having been despatched. See 52.8 above for '*reasonable excuse*'.

A default is '*material to the surcharge*' if it is *either* the default which gave rise to the surcharge *or* is a default taken into account in the service of the surcharge liability notice upon which the surcharge depends and the person concerned has not been previously liable to a surcharge in respect of a VAT period ending within the surcharge period specified in, or extended by, the notice.

Where a person is treated as not having been in default under (i) or (ii) above, any surcharge liability notice the service of which depended on that default is deemed not to have been served.

A default is also to be left out of account for the above purposes if the conduct giving rise to the default falls within 52.14(*b*) above and the person is assessed to a penalty under those provisions.

[*VATA 1994, s 59, Sch 13 para 14; FA 1996, s 35(4)*].

Surcharge liability notices. For non-receipt of a surcharge liability notice, see *C & E Commrs v Medway Draughting & Technical Services Ltd; C & E Commrs v Adplates Offset Ltd, QB [1989] STC 346 (TVC 18.1, 18.2)*. Where a surcharge liability notice has not been received, subsequent extension notices are not effective as valid surcharge liability notices as they only specify the end of the surcharge period and not the date on which it began; any surcharge assessments must therefore be discharged (*Dow Engineering (VTD 5771) (TVC 18.12)*). A surcharge liability notice which incorrectly stated that a return had not been received (when it had been received late) has been held to be invalid (*Coleman Machines Ltd (VTD 3196) (TVC 18.7)*).

Appeals. A person who thinks he has grounds for appeal against a default surcharge should write to HMRC within 30 days of the date of issue of the *surcharge liability notice extension* and ask them to reconsider the case. They will either confirm the original decision and give 21 days in which to lodge an appeal with a VAT tribunal or send a revised decision and give 30 days in which to lodge such an appeal. Alternatively a person can appeal directly to a VAT tribunal without contacting HMRC in which case he must do so within 30 days of the issue of the *surcharge liability notice extension*. A VAT tribunal cannot hear an appeal until a surcharge liability notice extension has been issued (see *Expert Systems Design Ltd (VTD 7974) (TVC 2.32)*). At this stage an appeal can be made against any or all of the defaults which led to the person becoming liable to the surcharge. This is the only time that the VAT tribunal can be asked to hear an appeal against these defaults. If the person later becomes liable to a further surcharge because he has defaulted again, he will be outside the time limit for appealing against the earlier defaults. It is not necessary to pay the surcharge before appealing to a VAT tribunal but all outstanding returns and VAT must be paid.

Meaning of 'furnish' and 'received'. 'Furnish' means putting the return into the possession of HMRC. The current VAT return states 'You could be liable to a financial penalty if your completed return and all the VAT payable are not received by the due date'. Given this, and the use of the word 'received', a clear distinction should be drawn for those purposes between 'received' and 'despatched'. 'Received' should be taken to mean actual receipt by HMRC. Earlier decisions (see *Aikman v White, CS 1985, [1986] STC 1 (TVC 57.7)* and *Hayman v Griffiths and Another; Walker v Hanby, QB [1987] STC 649 (TVC 57.8)*), that HMRC adopted the Post Office as their agents by requesting the use of prepaid envelopes and that a return is furnished when complete and posted, should no longer therefore be relied upon for these purposes (*C & E Commrs v W Timms & Son (Builders) Ltd' QB [1992] STC 374 (TVC 57.9)*).

HMRC have indicated that a return will be accepted as posted on time if posted at least one working day before the due date (assuming it has been sent in the official envelope or by first class post). At the same time they also indicated that where the due date falls on a weekend or bank holiday, the return and the VAT due will be accepted as received in time if received on the next following working day (but see below for electronic payments). (STI 1991, p 389 quoting from The Tax Journal, 21 March 1991, p 2). Despite this apparent assurance, tribunals have continued to uphold default surcharge assessments where returns have been posted one day before the due date. In *La Reine (Limoges Porcelain) Ltd (VTD 10468) (TVC 18.44)* the tribunal held that a return due on a Sunday and posted at 7 pm on the previous Friday had not been posted early enough that it was reasonable to expect that it would be received by

HMRC on or before the Sunday. This decision was not followed, and was implicitly disapproved of, in *Halstead Motor Company (VTD 13373) (TVC 18.46)*. In that case the tribunal held that, by posting a return before the last collection on Friday, the company had dispatched the return in a manner such that it was reasonable to expect that it would be delivered on Saturday and be received by HMRC within the appropriate time limit. Treatment otherwise by HMRC would be inconsistent with their statement reproduced at STI 1991, p 389.

A business which uses electronic means of payment will automatically receive a seven-day extension for the submission of the return and the payment of VAT due. In this connection, HMRC expect payments to be in their bank account on or before the 7th calendar day so that if the 7th day falls on a weekend or bank holiday, payment must be in their bank account by the last working day beforehand (see 51.3 PAYMENT OF VAT). Thus, where, say, the 7th day is a Saturday, payment of the VAT on the previous Friday by bank giro credit would not be sufficient (although, following the decision in *Halstead* above, posting the return on the Friday presumably would be sufficient).

De Voil Indirect Tax Service. See V5.371–380.

52.16 *Default surcharge: payments on account*

A taxable person is in default in respect of any VAT period for which he is required to make payments on account (see 51.4 PAYMENT OF VAT) if

(i) HMRC have not received in full any payment on account by the due date; or

(ii) he would be in default in respect of that period under 52.15 above (but for the fact that periods in respect of which payments on account are required are specifically excluded from those provisions).

Subject to below, a taxable person is liable to a surcharge under these provisions where

(*a*) he is in default in respect of a VAT period;

(*b*) HMRC serve on him either

- a *surcharge liability notice* specifying a surcharge period from the date of the notice to the first anniversary of the last day of the VAT period under (*a*) above; or
- where that last day occurs during an existing surcharge period, a *surcharge liability notice extension* extending the existing surcharge period to the first anniversary of the last day of the VAT period under (*a*) above;

(*c*) he is again in default in respect of another VAT period which ends within the surcharge period specified in (or extended by) that notice; and

(*d*) the 'aggregate value of defaults' for that VAT period is more than nil. The '*aggregate value of defaults*' is the total value of

- any payment or payments on account (or part payment or payments) not received by HMRC by the due date for such payments; and
- any outstanding VAT due for the period not paid by the last day on which he is required to make a return for that period (less the amount of unpaid payments on account).

The surcharge is the greater of £30 and the 'specified percentage' of the aggregate value of defaults for the VAT period under (*d*) above.

The '*specified percentage*' is determined by reference to the number of VAT periods in respect of which he is in default in the surcharge period and for which the value of his defaults is more than nil.

	Specified percentage
In relation to the first such period	2%
In relation to the second such period	5%
In relation to the third such period	10%
In relation to each such period after the third	15%

A person is not liable to a surcharge and not to be treated as having been in default in respect of the VAT period in question if he satisfies HMRC, or on appeal a tribunal, that in the case of a default which is 'material to the surcharge' either of the following applies.

(A) The payment on account (where (i) above applies) or the return or VAT shown on it (where (ii) above applies) was despatched at such time and in such manner that it was reasonable to expect that it would be received by HMRC by the due date.

A payment on account is not to be taken as received by the due date unless, by the last day for payment, all the transactions can be completed that need to be completed before the whole of the payment becomes available to HMRC.

The despatch of a cheque within reasonable time cannot be equated with the despatch of the VAT where the cheque proves to be worthless (*C & E Commrs v Palco Industry Co Ltd, QB [1990] STC 594 (TVC 18.404)*). See also 52.15 above under the heading *Meaning of 'furnish' and 'received'*.

(B) There is a 'reasonable excuse' for the payment on account (where (i) above applies) or the return or VAT (where (ii) above applies) not having been despatched. See 52.8 above for '*reasonable excuse*'.

A default is '*material to the surcharge*' if it is either the default which gave rise to the surcharge or is a default taken into account in the service of the surcharge liability notice upon which the surcharge depends and the person concerned has not been previously liable to a surcharge in respect of a VAT period ending within the surcharge period specified in, or extended by, the notice.

Where a person is treated as not having been in default under (A) or (B) above, any surcharge liability notice the service of which depended on that default is deemed not to have been served.

A default is also to be left out of account for the above purposes if the conduct giving rise to the default falls within 52.14(*b*) above and the person is assessed to a penalty under those provisions.

[*VATA 1994, s 59A; FA 1996, s 35(2)*].

See *VATA 1994, s 59B* for deeming provisions where a VAT period in respect of which payments on account are required ends within a surcharge period begun or extended by the service of a surcharge liability notice under 52.15 above; and a VAT period for which payments on account are not required ends within a surcharge period begun or extended by the service of a surcharge liability notice under the above provisions.

See also 52.15 above under the headings *Surcharge liability notices* and *Appeals*, which provisions also apply to default surcharges in relation to payments on account.

De Voil Indirect Tax Service. See V5.381.

52.17 Incorrect certificates as to zero-rating, etc.

Subject to below, where

(*a*) a customer gives to a supplier a certificate

- that the supply or supplies made or to be made fall wholly or partly within *VATA 1994, Sch 8 Group 5* or *6* or *VATA 1994, Sch 9 Group 1* (see 42.32 LAND AND BUILDINGS), or
- in connection with fiscal warehousing as required by *VATA 1994, s 18B* or *18C* (see 70.15 and 70.19 WAREHOUSED GOODS AND FREE ZONES), or
- that the supply or supplies made or to be made are reduced rate supplies falling wholly or partly within any of the Groups of *VATA 1994, Sch 7A* (see 58.1 REDUCED RATE SUPPLIES), or

(*b*) a person acquiring goods from another EC country prepares a certificate for the purposes of *VATA 1994, s 18B* (see 70.15 WAREHOUSED GOODS AND FREE ZONES),

and the certificate is incorrect, the person giving or preparing the certificate is liable to a penalty. The amount of the penalty is, where (*a*) above applies, the difference between the VAT which should have been charged and the VAT actually charged and, where (*b*) above applies, the VAT actually chargeable on the acquisition.

A person is not liable to a penalty under these provisions if

(i) he satisfies HMRC or, on appeal, a VAT tribunal, that there is a reasonable excuse for his having given or prepared the certificate; or

(ii) by reason of his having given or prepared it, he is convicted of an offence.

[*VATA 1994, s 62; FA 1996, Sch 3 para 8; FA 1999, s 17; FA 2001, Sch 31 para 3*].

De Voil Indirect Tax Service. See V5.342.

52.18 Inaccuracies in EC sales lists (ESLs)

Where

(*a*) a person has submitted an ESL (see 2.19 ACCOUNTING PERIODS AND RETURNS) containing a 'material inaccuracy' to HMRC;

(*b*) within six months of discovering that inaccuracy, HMRC have issued him with a written warning identifying the statement and stating that future inaccuracies might result in the service of a notice under these provisions;

(*c*) the person submits a second ESL containing a material inaccuracy to HMRC and the 'submission date' is within the period of two years beginning with the day after the warning was issued;

(*d*) HMRC have, within six months of discovering the second inaccuracy served on him a notice identifying the ESL and stating that future inaccuracies will attract a penalty under these provisions; and (*e*) the person submits yet another ESL containing a material inaccuracy to HMRC the submission date of which is not more than two years after

- the service of the notice under (*d*) above; or
- the date on which any previous ESL attracting a penalty was submitted,

that person is liable to a penalty of £100 in respect of the statement under (*e*) above.

An ESL contains a '*material inaccuracy*' if, having regard to the matters to be included, the inclusion or omission of any information is misleading in any material respect.

'*Submission date*' means the last date for submission of the ESL or the day on which it was actually submitted, whichever is the earlier.

An inaccuracy is not regarded as material for these purposes if

(i) the person submitting the ESL satisfies HMRC, or on appeal a VAT tribunal, that there is a 'reasonable excuse' for the inaccuracy (see 52.8 above);

(ii) at a time when he had no reason to believe that HMRC were enquiring into his affairs, he furnished them with full information with respect to the inaccuracy; or

(iii) he is convicted of an offence by reason of the submission of the ESL containing the material inaccuracy.

Where the only ESL identified in a warning under (*b*) above or a notice under (*d*) above is one which is regarded as containing no material inaccuracies (whether by virtue of (i) to (iii) above or otherwise) that warning or notice is deemed not to have been issued or served.

[*VATA 1994, s 65*].

De Voil Indirect Tax Service. See V5.346.

52.19 **Failure to submit EC sales lists (ESLs)**

If by the last day on which a person is required to submit an ESL (see 2.19 ACCOUNTING PERIODS AND RETURNS) for any period, HMRC has not received the statement, that person is regarded for the purposes of these provisions as being in default in relation to that statement until such time as it is delivered.

Where any person is in default in respect of any ESL, HMRC may serve a notice on him stating that he is in default but that no action will be taken if the default is remedied within 14 days of the notice, otherwise he will become liable to a penalty as calculated below. The notice may also state that the person will become liable, without further notice, to penalties if he commits any more defaults before a period of twelve months has elapsed without his being in default.

Where such a notice is served, the person will become liable

(*a*) in respect of the ESL to which the notice relates to a penalty of the greater of £50 *or* £5 for each day the default continues after the 14-day period (up to a maximum of 100 days); and

(*b*) in respect of any other ESL in relation to which he is in default, the last day for submission of which is after the service and before the expiry of the notice, to a penalty of the greater of £50 *or*, as the case may be, £5, £10 or £15 for each day the default continues up to a maximum of 100 days. The daily fine is £5, £10 or £15 depending upon whether the ESL in question is the first, second, or third or subsequent ESL (including, where applicable, the ESL within (*a*) above) in respect of which the person has become liable to a penalty while the notice is in force.

For the purposes of (*b*) above, the notice continues in force for twelve months from the date of service but, where at any time in that twelve-month period the person defaults in submitting an ESL other than one in relation to which he was in default when the notice was served, the notice continues until a period of twelve months has elapsed without that person becoming liable to a penalty under these provisions in respect of any ESL.

A person is not treated as being in default in relation to an ESL under these provisions if he satisfies HMRC, or on appeal a tribunal, that

- the ESL has been submitted at such time and in such manner that it was reasonable to expect that it would be received by HMRC within the appropriate time limit; or
- there is a 'reasonable excuse' for the ESL not having been dispatched (see 52.8 above).

In such a case, he is not liable to a penalty in respect of that ESL and any notice served on him exclusively in relation to the failure to submit that ESL has no effect for the purposes of these provisions.

[*VATA 1994, s 66*].

De Voil Indirect Tax Service. See V5.355.

52.20 **Breach of record-keeping requirements, etc in relation to transactions in gold**

A person who fails to comply with the accounting and record-keeping requirements relating to investment gold in *SI 1995/2518, Regs 31A, 31B* and VAT Notice 701/21 (see 30.5 GOLD AND PRECIOUS METALS) is liable to a penalty not exceeding 17.5% of the value of the transaction to which the failure relates. HMRC must determine the value of any transaction to the best of their judgement and notify the person liable.

A person is not liable to a penalty under these provisions

- if he is convicted of a criminal offence or assessed to a penalty under 52.9 above by reason of conduct which would otherwise give rise to a penalty under these provisions; or
- where he satisfies HMRC or, on appeal, a tribunal that there is 'reasonable excuse' for the failure (see 52.8 above).

See also 52.22 below for mitigation of penalties.

Where a person is liable for a penalty under these provisions, the provisions under 52.14 above do not apply.

[*VATA 1994, s 69A(1)–(3)(6)(7); FA 2000, s 137(2)*].

52.21 **Failure to notify use of certain avoidance schemes**

Subject to below, a person who fails to comply with the provisions of *VATA 1994, Sch 11A para 6* (duty to notify HMRC of certain avoidance schemes, see 4.5 and 4.9 ANTI-AVOIDANCE) is liable to a penalty of

(*a*) £5,000 for failing to disclose a hallmarked scheme; or (*b*) 15% of the 'VAT saving' for failing to disclose a listed scheme.

For the purposes of (*b*) above, the '*VAT saving*' is

(i) where a return gives rise to a requirement to notify, the difference between

- the amount of VAT shown on the returns submitted for the VAT periods beginning with that in respect of which the duty to notify first arose and ending with that in which the taxable person duly notified HMRC or, if earlier, the VAT period immediately preceding the notification by HMRC of the penalty assessment; and
- the amount of VAT which, but for the scheme, would have been shown on those returns;

(ii) where a repayment claim for earlier VAT periods in respect of which returns have been submitted gives rise to a requirement to notify, the difference between the amount claimed and the amount which, but for the scheme, would have been claimed; or

(iii) where an amount of non-deductible tax gives rise to the requirement to notify, the excess amount claimed (to the extent that it is not included in the tax saving under (i) or (ii) above).

A person is not liable to a penalty under these provisions

- if he satisfies HMRC or, on appeal, a tribunal that there is a 'reasonable excuse' (see 52.8 above) for the failure to notify; or
- where, by reason of the failure to notify, he is convicted of a criminal offence (whether under *VATA 1994* or otherwise) or assessed to a penalty under *VATA 1994, s 60* (VAT evasion: conduct involving dishonesty, see 52.9 above).

See also 52.22 below for mitigation.

[*VATA 1994, Sch 11A paras 10, 11; FA 2004, Sch 2 para 2; F(No 2)A 2005, Sch 1 para 7*].

52.22 MITIGATION OF CIVIL PENALTIES

Mitigation by HMRC. In relation to penalties assessed under 52.9 to 52.12, 52.20 and 52.21 above, HMRC may reduce the penalty to such amount (including nil) as they think proper but, in doing so, must not take into account

- insufficiency of funds available to any person to pay VAT due or the penalty;
- the fact that there has been no significant loss of VAT; or
- the fact that the person liable to the penalty or a person acting on his behalf has acted in good faith.

HMRC have no powers to mitigate a penalty under 52.13 to 52.19 above.

HMRC will consider the possibility of mitigation where a trader does not have a reasonable excuse for non-compliance (see 52.8 above). Reasonable excuse concentrates on the behaviour that led to the error, whereas mitigation also allows subsequent behaviour to be taken into account.

In deciding how much mitigation to allow, HMRC officers have discretion but each mitigating factor has a suggested range expressed as a percentage (see the mitigation framework table below). If more than one factor applies, then they can be aggregated.

It may be necessary to reduce the amount of mitigation to take account of negative factors (eg obstructive or unco-operative behaviour). Once all individual factors have been taken into account, officers are advised to consider the case as a whole and decide if the overall percentage level of mitigation is reasonable. All the facts of the case should be taken into account including size and maturity of the business and whether or not a professional adviser (eg accountant) is used. Although the law allows HMRC to reduce a penalty to nil, 100% mitigation is rare and officers are advised that where the total amount of mitigation earned according to the framework amounts to or exceeds 100%, consideration should be given as to whether or not it is an appropriate result.

Mitigation framework table	
(1) *How the infringement occurred*	Maximum of 50%
Compassionate grounds (where the circumstances are insufficient to warrant a reasonable excuse), eg — unforeseen serious illness of the person responsible for completing the VAT returns (including third party such as professional adviser); and — death of a close relative of the person responsible for completing the VAT returns.	20%–50%
Other unforeseen and relevant events (which are considered not to provide a reasonable excuse in their own right) supported by evidence, eg — computer or software errors; — flood, fire or other damage to premises; — theft or break in; — pressure of work, ie exceptional and significant increase in workloads not in keeping with normal work fluctuations; — staff problems, ie where the person responsible for completing the VAT return leaves at short notice; and — clerical errors particularly in complex circumstances where management controls are in place but have failed to spot the error.	10%–50%
Complexity of liability in relation to the size of the business and frequency of transaction.	10%–50%
(2) *Degree of co-operation in disclosing and quantifying arrears (belated notification)*	Maximum of 50%
A voluntary disclosure of a belated notification of a liability to be registered, or the acquisition of a new means of transport,	
— accompanied by full quantification of the arrears	Up to 50%
— not accompanied by quantification of the arrears.	Up to 25%
Full quantification of arrears within X number of days of identification of the belated notification of a liability to be registered, or the acquisition of a new means of transport.	Up to 25%
(3) *Degree of co-operation in identifying and quantifying the error (misdeclarations)*	Maximum of 50%

Full co-operation and quantification.	Up to 50%
Partial co-operation and quantification.	Up to 25%
Alleged full quantification that later turns out to be partial but where the reason was unintentional.	Up to 10%
Supplying information promptly and answering questions accurately to allow officers to quantify the underdeclaration.	Up to 10%
Other actions which result in a saving of HMRC's time and resources.	Up to 10%
(4) *Other factors*	Maximum of 50%
Published guidance is unclear or not up-to-date.	Up to 40%
Evidence of efforts made to seek advice.	Up to 10%
Evidence of steps taken to correct systems in order to prevent similar errors in future.	5%–25%
Compliance history of trader over the last three registered years has been good	Up to 25%

Example: late registration

	Mitigation
Voluntary disclosure (late registration through own volition by trader) accompanied by full quantification of arrears	50%
Evidence of efforts made to seek advice	10%
Total mitigation calculated	60%
Penalty on arrears of (say) £15,000 at 5%	£750
Mitigation of 60% reduces penalty to	£300

Internal Guidance V1–27, section 15).

See 52.9 above for HMRC's policy with regard to mitigation of VAT evasion penalties.

Mitigation by a tribunal. An appeal may be made to a tribunal against any liability to a penalty or surcharge under 52.9 to 52.20 above or the amount of any such penalty or surcharge in an assessment. See 5.3(*n*)(*q*) APPEALS. The tribunal has similar powers of mitigation as HMRC above. In addition, where a penalty has been mitigated by HMRC, a VAT tribunal may, on an appeal relating to the penalty, cancel the reduction in whole or in part.

Subject to the above, a tribunal may not vary the amount assessed by way of penalty or surcharge other than to reduce it to the amount which is appropriate under the relevant provisions.

[*VATA 1994, ss 70, 84*(*6*)*, Sch 13 para 17; FA 2000, s 137*(*3*)*; FA 2004, Sch 2 para 3*].

De Voil Indirect Tax Service. See V5.334.

52.23 IMPORT VAT: EVASION AND NON-COMPLIANCE

With effect from 27 November 2003, penalties are imposed where a person engages in any conduct

- for the purpose of evading import VAT (see 52.24 below); or
- by which he contravenes a duty, obligation, requirement or condition imposed by or under relevant rules relating to import VAT (see 52.25 below).

The penalties also apply to customs duty, Community export duty, Community import duty and customs duty of a preferential tariff country, but these provisions are outside the scope of this book.

[*FA 2003, s 24; SI 2003/2985*].

52.24 **Penalty for evasion**

Where

- a person engages in any conduct for the purpose of 'evading import VAT', and
- his conduct involves dishonesty (whether or not such as to give rise to any criminal liability),

he is liable to a penalty equal to 'the amount import VAT evaded' (or sought to be evaded). However, where by reason of such conduct he is

- convicted of a criminal offence,
- given (and has not had withdrawn) a demand notice in respect of a penalty to which he is liable under 52.25 below, or
- liable to a penalty imposed upon him under any other provision of the law relating to import VAT

that conduct does not also give rise to a liability to a penalty under these provisions.

'*Evading import VAT*' includes wrongly obtaining or securing

(i) any repayment, relief or exemption from, or any allowance against, import VAT, or

(ii) any deferral or other postponement of his liability to pay any import VAT.

It also includes evading the cancellation of any entitlement to, or the withdrawal of, any such repayment, relief, exemption or allowance.

'*The amount of import VAT evaded*' is, as the case may be, the amount of

- the repayment;
- the relief, exemption or allowance; or
- the payment which, or the liability to make which, is deferred or otherwise postponed.

[*FA 2003, s 25*].

Liability of officers of a body corporate. Where the conduct of a body corporate gives rise to a penalty under the above provisions and it appears to HMRC that that conduct, in whole or in part, is attributable to the dishonesty of a person who is (or at the material time was) a director or 'managing officer' (the 'relevant officer') of the body corporate, HMRC may give a notice to the body corporate (or its representative) and to the relevant officer (or his representative) stating

- the full amount of the penalty; and

- that they propose to recover a specified portion (which may be the whole) of that penalty from the relevant officer.

The relevant officer is then treated as if he were personally liable under the above provisions to a penalty corresponding to that specified portion. The body corporate is then only liable to the balance (if any) of the full penalty and is discharged from liability on the amount recoverable from the relevant officer.

'*Managing officer*' means a manager, secretary or other similar officer of the body corporate, and any person purporting to act in any such capacity or as a director. Where the affairs of a body corporate are managed by its members, the provisions apply in relation to the conduct of a member in connection with his functions of management as if he were a director of the body corporate.

[*FA 2003, s 28*].

Reduction of the amount of a penalty. Where a person is liable to a penalty under the above provisions

- HMRC or, on appeal, a tribunal may reduce the penalty to such amount (including nil) as they think proper; and
- HMRC (on a review) or a tribunal (on an appeal) may cancel the whole or any part of the reduction previously made by HMRC

but in doing so neither HMRC or the tribunal must take into account

- insufficiency of the funds available to any person to pay the import VAT or the penalty;
- the fact that there has been no significant loss of import VAT; or
- the fact that the person liable to the penalty, or a person acting on his behalf, has acted in good faith.

[*FA 2003, s 29*].

52.25 **Penalty for contravention of relevant rules**

The Treasury may make an order to the effect that a person is liable to a penalty of up to £2,500 if he engages in any conduct by which he contravenes a duty, obligation, requirement or condition relating to import VAT imposed by or under any of the following.

- *CEMA 1979* any other Act or any statutory instrument.
- Community customs rules (as laid down in *EC Council Regulation 2913/92/EEC* of 12 October 1992 and including provisions adopted at Community level or nationally to implement them).
- Any directly applicable EC legislation.
- Any relevant international agreements having effect as part of the law of any part of the UK by virtue of any Act or statutory instrument or any directly applicable EC legislation.

Exceptions. A person is not liable to a penalty under these provisions in the following circumstances.

(*a*) If he satisfies HMRC, or on appeal a tribunal, that there is a reasonable excuse for his conduct. Although 'reasonable excuse' is not defined (and therefore to be determined by HMRC or a tribunal) the following are not to be taken as a reasonable excuse.

- An insufficiency of funds available to any person for paying any import VAT or any penalty due.
- That reliance was placed by any person on another to perform any task.
- That the contravention is attributable, in whole or in part, to the conduct of a person on whom reliance to perform any task was so placed.

(*b*) If, by reason of conduct relating to import VAT, that person is

- prosecuted for an offence;
- given (and has not had withdrawn) a demand notice in respect of a penalty to which he is liable under 52.24 above;
- liable to a penalty imposed upon him under any other provision of the law relating to import VAT; or
- liable to a penalty under 52.10 to 52.14 or 52.17 to 52.20 above (or would be so liable except that, by reason of his conduct, he is convicted of an offence or liable to a different penalty under those provisions).

[*FA 2003, ss 26, 27*].

Reduction of the amount of a penalty. The same provisions apply as under 52.24 above. [*FA 2003, s 29*].

52.26 **Administration, etc of the penalties**

Demand notices. Where a person is liable to a penalty under 52.24 or 52.25 above, HMRC may give him (or his representative) a notice in writing demanding payment of the penalty due. Any amount so demanded is recoverable as if it were due from him (or the representative) as an amount of customs duty but subject to

- any appeal to a tribunal (see below);
- the demand being subsequently withdrawn; or
- the amount of the penalty being reduced.

Time limits. A demand notice cannot be given

- in the case of a penalty under 52.24 above,
  - (i) more than 20 years after the conduct giving rise to the penalty ceased;
  - (ii) more than two years after evidence of facts, sufficient in the opinion of HMRC to justify the giving of the demand notice, comes to their knowledge; or
  - (ii) where a deceased person was liable to such a penalty before his death, more than three years after his death; and
- in the case of a penalty under 52.25 above
  - (i) more than three years after the conduct giving rise to the penalty ceased; or

(ii) more than two years after evidence of facts, sufficient in the opinion of HMRC to justify the giving of the demand notice, comes to their knowledge.

Consequences of issue on criminal proceedings. Once a demand notice is given for payment of a penalty under 52.25 above in respect of any conduct of a person, no proceedings may be brought against that person for any offence constituted by that conduct (whether or not the demand notice is subsequently withdrawn).

[*FA 2003, ss 30–32*].

Review by HMRC. HMRC can be asked to review their decision in the following circumstances.

(*a*) Where HMRC give a person (or his representative) a notice informing him that, in their opinion, he is liable to a penalty under 52.25 above but that they do not propose to give a demand notice, the person (or his representative) may give written notice to HMRC requiring them to review their decision that liability to a penalty exists.

(*b*) Except where (*c*) below applies, where HMRC give a demand notice to a person (or his representative), the person (or his representative) may by written notice require HMRC to review their decision

- that the person is liable to a penalty under 52.24 or 52.25 above; or
- as to the amount of the penalty.

(*c*) In the case of a penalty under 52.24 above where HMRC give a demand notice to a body corporate and an officer

(i) the officer (or his representative) may by written notice require HMRC to review their decision

- that the conduct of the body corporate is, in whole or in part, attributable to the relevant officer's dishonesty, or
- as to the portion of the full penalty which HMRC are seeking to recover from the officer (or his representative); and

(ii) the body corporate (or its representative) may by written notice require HMRC to review their decision

- that the body corporate is liable to a penalty; or
- as to amount of the full penalty as if it were the amount specified in the demand notice.

Time limit. HMRC need not review any decision under the above provisions unless the required notice is given to them within 45 days of the date which they gave the relevant notice under (*a*)–(*c*) above. But this does not prevent HMRC from agreeing to review a decision in a case where the notice required is not given within the permitted period.

Right to further review. A person can only give notice under the above provisions requiring a decision to be reviewed a second or subsequent time

- on the grounds that HMRC did not, on any previous review, have the opportunity to consider any particular facts or matters; and

- provided he does not, on the further review, require HMRC to consider any facts or matters which were considered on a previous review of the decision (unless they are relevant to any issue to which the facts or matters not previously considered relate).

Powers of HMRC on a review. Where HMRC are required to review a decision or agree to do so outside the time limit, they may

- confirm the decision; or
- withdraw or vary the decision, in which case they may also take such further steps (if any) in consequence of the withdrawal or variation as they consider appropriate.

If HMRC do not give notice of their determination on the review within 45 days beginning with the day on which the review

- is required by the person (or his representative), or
- is agreed to by HMRC,

they are to be taken as having confirmed the decision.

[*FA 2003, ss 33–35*].

Appeals. An appeal can be made to a tribunal against any decision by HMRC on a review (including a case where they fail to review their decision within 45 days and it is assumed that their original decision is confirmed). The appellant must be

- the person who required the review in question;
- where the person who required that review did so as representative of another person, that other person, or
- a representative of a person falling within either of the previous two categories.

The tribunal may quash or vary a decision and may substitute its own decision for any decision so quashed.

The burden of proof as to whether a liability arises under 52.24 or 52.25 above lies with HMRC but it is for the appellant to show that the grounds on which any such appeal is brought have been established.

The provisions of *VATA 1994, s 85* (settling an appeal by agreement) and *VATA 1994, s 87* (enforcement of decisions) also apply for these purposes with the appropriate modifications. See 5.14 and 5.27 APPEALS. Any costs awarded against an appellant on an appeal are recoverable as if they were an amount of customs duty which the appellant is required to pay.

[*FA 2003, ss 36, 37*].

Admissibility of certain statements and documents in criminal proceedings. Statements made or documents produced by, or on behalf of, a person are not inadmissible in

- any criminal proceedings against that person in respect of any offence in connection with import VAT, or
- any proceedings against that person for the recovery of any sum due from him in connection with import VAT

by reason only that any of the following matters have been drawn to his attention and that he was, or may have been, induced as a result to make the statements or produce the documents.

- HMRC have power, in relation to import VAT, to issue a demand notice by way of a civil evasion penalty rather than begin criminal proceedings.
- HMRC's practice is to take into account, in deciding whether or not to issue a demand notice, that a person has made a full confession of any dishonest conduct and has fully co-operated in an investigation.
- HMRC or, on appeal, a tribunal have power to reduce an evasion penalty and that, in deciding the extent of such a reduction, HMRC or a tribunal will have regard to the extent of the person's co-operation during the investigation.

[*FA 2003, s 38*].

Service of notices. Any notice to be given to any person for the above purposes or for the purposes of 52.24 or 52.25 above may be given by sending it by post in a letter addressed to that person (or his representative) at the last or usual residence or place of business of that person (or representative). [*FA 2003, s 39*].

Representatives. Representative, in relation to any person, means

- his personal representative'
- his trustee in bankruptcy or interim or permanent trustee, and
- any receiver or liquidator appointed in relation to that person or any or his property,

together with any other person acting in a representative capacity in relation to that person.

[*FA 2003, s 24*].

53 Pension Schemes

The contents of this chapter are as follows.

53.1 FUNDED PENSION SCHEMES

A funded pension scheme is a pension scheme in which the employers' and employees' contributions are vested in separate trustees, who may be individuals or corporate bodies. The pension scheme is normally separate and distinct from the employer's business. The VAT provisions in 53.2 and 53.3 below apply to such schemes but not to

(*a*) schemes where the employer makes provision for the payment of pensions by a segregated reserve fund in the balance sheet, represented by specific assets;

(*b*) unfunded pension schemes where the employer does not set aside funds for this purpose; or

(*c*) insurance-based schemes where retirement benefits are secured through insurance policies.

The normal VAT rules apply to schemes within (*a*)-(*c*) above.

(VAT Notice 700/17/02, paras 1.2, 1.4).

53.2 Employers

Input tax deductible. The *management* of a pension fund for own employees (but not normally the business activities of the pension fund) is part of an employer's business. A VAT-registered employer can therefore deduct input tax incurred in setting up the fund and on its day-to-day management. This applies even where the responsibility for the general management of the scheme rests with the trustees or the trustees pay for the services provided. HMRC give the following examples of expenses on which input tax may be reclaimed.

- Making of arrangements for setting up the pension fund
- Management of the scheme (ie collection of contributions and payment of pensions)
- Advice on a review of the scheme and implementing any changes
- Accountancy and audit services relating to the management of the scheme (eg preparation of annual accounts)
- Actuarial valuations of the assets of the fund
- Actuarial advice in connection with the fund's administration
- Providing general statistics in connection with the performance of the fund's investments, properties, etc.
- Legal instructions and general legal advice including drafting of Trust deeds insofar as they relate to the management of the scheme

To claim input tax, the employer must hold a VAT invoice made out in his name. Where the supplies are paid for by the trustees on behalf of the employer, the employer should arrange for the invoice to be issued in his name.

Input tax not deductible. Except where the employer is the sole trustee of his pension scheme (see below), the pension fund itself is not part of the employer's business activities. Any VAT incurred on supplies relating to the *investment* activities carried on by the trustees (eg making investments, acquiring property and collecting rents) is not input tax of the employer even if he pays for such expenses. HMRC give the following examples of services on which employers cannot claim input tax.

- Advice in connection with making investments
- Brokerage charges
- Rent and service charge collection for property holdings
- Producing records and accounts in connection with property purchases, lettings and disposals, investments, etc.
- Trustees services (ie services of a profession trustee in managing the assets of the fund)
- Legal fees paid on behalf of representative beneficiaries in connection with changes in pension fund arrangements
- Custodian charges

For cases concerning the recoverability of input tax by employers, see *Linotype & Machinery Ltd (VTD 594) (TVC 52.2)*, *Manchester Ship Canal Co v C & E Commrs, QB [1982] STC 351 (TVC 52.6)* and *Ultimate Advisory Services Ltd (VTD 9523) (TVC 39.44)*.

Sole trustees. Where an employer is the sole trustee of a pension fund for his own employees, any activities carried on, or supplies made by the fund, are made by the employer. The employer is entitled to treat all input tax incurred on supplies received in connection with the fund as input tax. See *C & E Commrs v British Railways Board (No 1), CA [1976] STC 359 (TVC 52.1)*. However, if either the business or the pension fund makes exempt supplies, the amount of input tax deductible may be restricted. See 49 PARTIAL EXEMPTION.

Management of the pension scheme.

(*a*) *Services performed by the employer*. Where an employer uses own staff to manage the pension fund and these services are provided free of charge, there is no supply for VAT purposes. See *National Coal Board v C & E Commrs, QB [1982] STC 863 (TVC 52.9)*. The employer's entitlement to claim input tax on office overhead expenses is not affected.

If an employer is reimbursed by the trustees (or specifically charges them) for costs incurred in managing the pension scheme and the services fall within those on which input tax is deductible (see above), there is no need to account for output tax on the supply to the trustees. However, if such arrangements apply to services for investment advice or other services connected with the pension fund's own business activities, the employer is making a taxable supply to the trustees and must account for output tax.

(*b*) *Services performed by third parties*. Where a third party (eg a fund manager, property manager or professional trustee) is used to manage a pension scheme and their charges cover both general management (input tax deductible) and investment services (input tax non-deductible) the input tax must be apportioned. Normally this apportionment will be made by the supplier. If, however, the supplier only issues one invoice for a composite supply, 30% of the input tax shown may be treated as deductible unless the employer provides a detailed breakdown to support a different figure.

Pensions provided for employees of more than one company. Where a pension fund covers pension arrangements for employees of several companies which are not in the same VAT group registration, each employer may treat as input tax only that proportion of VAT incurred on the management of the fund that is attributable to his own employees. Where the person supplying the management services to the fund issues a single invoice, one of the participating employers (or, in the case of entirely separate employers, the trustees) may act in the capacity of paymaster and claim all the VAT incurred for the eligible services, issuing a VAT invoice to each of the other employers for their share of the costs and VAT thereon. The other employers can then treat that VAT as their input tax.

Cessation of business by employer. If an employer ceases business, the trustees of any continuing pension scheme who are VAT-registered may treat VAT incurred on services connected with the management of the scheme as their input tax (subject to the normal rules). If this situation arises, the trustees should inform HMRC.

(VAT Notice 700/17/02, paras 2.1–2.10).

53.3 Trustees

Where the trustees of a pension fund make taxable supplies, they may be required to register for VAT. See 59 REGISTRATION for details. If registered, the trustees can treat VAT on goods and services used for the purposes of their business activities as input tax. However, except where the employer has ceased to be in business (see 53.2 above) VAT on supplies for the purposes of the management of the pension scheme is not input tax since these supplies are regarded as the responsibility of the employer. Recovery of input tax may also be restricted under the PARTIAL EXEMPTION (49) rules.

Corporate trustee in a VAT group registration. Where the sole trustee of a pension fund is a corporate body, it may be possible for that trustee to form part of a VAT group registration with the employer. See 31.2 and 31.3 GROUPS OF COMPANIES for eligibility and application for group treatment. If a corporate trustee becomes such a member, the representative member of the group is entitled to treat the VAT incurred on supplies to the trustee as input tax. Subject to the normal rules, this means that the representative member can deduct as input tax VAT incurred on both the *management* and *business* activities of the pension fund. See *BOC International Ltd (VTD 1248) (TVC 52.7)*.

Where the fund provides pensions for employees of companies outside the VAT group registration, any VAT incurred in respect of the *management* of the scheme for those companies is not for the purposes of the representative member's business and not allowable. VAT must therefore be apportioned between that attributable to employees within the VAT group (allowable) and outside the group (non-allowable). Alternatively, the representative member may elect to use the paymaster arrangements. See 53.2 above under *Pensions provided for employees of more than one company*.

All members of a group registration are jointly and severally liable for VAT due from the representative member and in the event of that member being unable to meet the VAT debt of the group, as a general rule each member will be liable for the amount of the debt arising during the period that it was a member of the group. However, where corporate trustees are included in a group registration, HMRC have been advised that this liability does not extend to the assets of any trust (eg a pension fund) of which the corporate trustee is the trustee, except to the extent that the group VAT debt is attributable in whole or part to the administration of the trust.

Any supplies made by the corporate trustee in a VAT group (including dealing in the assets of the fund) are treated as made by the representative member. Therefore any exempt supplies made must be taken into account in the partial exemption position of the VAT group.

Fund managers, property managers, professional trustees, etc may provide

- supplies to the employer in connection with the management of the scheme; and
- supplies to the trustees in connection with their business activities.

It is important to distinguish between the various kinds of services supplied so that separate VAT invoices can be issued to the employer and the trustees for input tax recovery purposes. If services cannot be segregated, HMRC are prepared to allow the total value of services to be divided in the ratio of 30% to the employer and 70% to the trustees. Any other apportionment will only be agreed to by HMRC if detailed information in support of the split is provided.

(VAT Notice 700/17/02, paras 3.1–3.3, 4.1–4.3).

53.4 LOCAL AUTHORITY PENSION FUNDS

Unlike other employers, local authorities may be prevented by legislation from setting up a separate Trust to administer their pension fund. Local authority pension funds are usually therefore similar to sole trustee schemes (see 53.2 above). The assets of the fund are vested in the authority and the funds' activities cannot be separated from the other activities of the authority. Consequently any exempt input tax incurred, such as that relating to investments, is included when the authority calculates whether it has exceeded the 5% *de minimis* limit above which it loses all its exempt input tax. See 43.7 LOCAL AUTHORITIES AND PUBLIC BODIES.

Administration expenses. Recovery of these expenses by local authorities should be broadly in line with that of other pension scheme providers.

- If the authority administers the scheme free of charge, then this is a non-business activity of the authority and it may recover the VAT under *VATA 1994, s 33*.
- If the scheme includes employees of other local authorities (scheduled bodies) who are obliged to remain within the scheme, any charge for the administration to those other authorities is a non-business activity of the authority. The VAT incurred is recoverable under *VATA 1994, s 33*.
- If the scheme includes employees of non-authority bodies (admitted bodies) for whom it is not obliged to provide a pension scheme, any charge for the administration of the scheme is a business activity of the authority and is standard-rated. If no charge is made but the level of contribution is adjusted to reflect a charge, this is viewed as consideration for the supply of administration services.

Investment expenses. HMRC's general view is that the investment activities undertaken by pension funds are carried out in the course or furtherance of a business (although they will consider representations from any local authority which believes that it can demonstrate that it has some non-business investment activities). Most of the VAT incurred on these investment activities is exempt input tax. If the authority remains within its *de minimis* limit it can recover this VAT. However, if the level of exempt input tax incurred pushes the authority over its *de minimis* limit it loses *all* its exempt input tax.

Administrative concession. By concession, when the percentage of exempt input tax is calculated for the purposes of the *VATA 1994, s 33* recovery method, the expenses relating to employees for whom the authority is obliged by law to provide a pension scheme may be excluded from the calculation (from both the numerator and denominator). The following conditions must be satisfied.

(*a*) The local authority must be prevented by legislation from setting up separate trustees for its pension fund.

(*b*) When VAT relating to the expenses of the pension fund is incurred, it must be reclaimed in accordance with the guidance set out above for administration and investment expenses.

(*c*) Prior written agreement must be obtained from HMRC. The concession will form part of the authority's *Sec 33* recovery method and should be agreed at the same time as the method.

(*d*) VAT relating to those persons for whom the authority is not obliged to provide a pension fund, such as admitted bodies, must be included in the *Sec 33* calculation.

(*e*) All VAT relating to those persons for whom the authority is obliged to provide pensions must be excluded from the *Sec 33* calculation. This includes the VAT incurred in respect of the non-business and taxable activities, whether administration or investment activities.

(*f*) Sufficient records must be kept to enable the pension fund expenses to be easily identified.

(*g*) The concession must operate for at least one year and coincide with a complete tax year.

Any abuse or misapplication of its provisions may result in the withdrawal of the concession in particular cases.

If, having excluded the pension fund expenses under the concession, the authority remains *de minimis*, it will be entitled to recover all its VAT including that relating to the exempt pension fund activities. If, however, the authority exceeds the *de minimis* limit even with these pension fund activities excluded, it will not be entitled to recover the VAT incurred on any of its exempt activities, including that relating to the pension fund. If exempt input tax has been recovered prior to the authority exceeding its *de minimis* levels, the authority will be required to repay this VAT to HMRC.

(Internal Guidance V1–14, paras 18.3.2, 18.3.3).

54 Printed Matter, etc

Cross-references. See 34.15(7) IMPORTS for certain printed matter which may be imported free of VAT from a country outside the EC.

De Voil Indirect Tax Service. See V4.273.

The contents of this chapter are as follows.

54.1 INTRODUCTION

To determine the liability for any supply involving printed or similar matter, it is helpful to consider the following questions.

(*a*) Is a complete item of printed or similar matter being supplied?

(*b*) Is the printed matter being supplied in its own right?

If satisfied that the answers to both of these questions are 'yes', then see 54.2 to 54.13 below for categories of printed matter which can be zero-rated. Other items are normally standard-rated (see 54.14 below).

If the answer to (*a*) is 'no' (or if unsure), consider 54.19 to 54.25 below for guidance on the processes leading to the production of printed matter.

If the answer to (*b*) is 'no' (or if unsure), see 54.15 to 54.18 below for printed matter supplied with other services and goods.

54.2 ZERO-RATED PRINTED MATTER

Supplies of the following are zero-rated.

- Books and booklets (see 54.3 below).
- Brochures and pamphlets (see 54.4 below).
- Leaflets (see 54.5 below).
- Newspapers (see 54.6 below).

- Journals and periodicals (see 54.7 below).
- Children's picture books and painting books (see 54.8 below).
- Music (printed, duplicated or manuscript) (see 54.9 below).
- Maps, charts and topographical plans (see 54.10 below).
- Covers, cases and other articles supplied with any of the above items and not separately accounted for (see 54.11 below).

Included is the letting on hire or loan of, or the supply of a part interest in, any of the above items. See 54.12 below.

Not included are plans or drawings for industrial, architectural, engineering, commercial or similar purposes.

[*VATA 1994, Sch 8 Group 3*].

The legislation does not define any of the above items. In the absence of any legal definition, HMRC do not seek to impose their own formal definition but instead use the following guiding principles.

(*a*) *Ordinary and everyday meaning*. The words in *Group 3* are used in their ordinary, everyday sense. This means they are restricted to goods produced on paper and similar materials such as card (but see 54.4 below). Most items qualifying for the zero-rating will be products of the printing industry (including items printed in Braille), but goods which are photocopied, typed or hand-written may, in some cases, also qualify.

Goods containing text in other formats (eg audio or video cassettes or CD Rom) are standard-rated. This includes the storage and distribution of text by fax, e-mail, microfiche, or any similar process. Transcripts or print-outs made of such information are zero-rated if they are supplied in the form of books, booklets, brochures, pamphlets or leaflets within *Group 3*.

(*b*) *Physical characteristics and function*. When judging whether an item meets the 'ordinary and everyday' meaning, HMRC look first to physical characteristics. The function of an item is a secondary question, and is only important if it is so far removed from the normal function of an item as to prevent it qualifying as a book, leaflet, etc in the ordinary meaning of those words.

(*c*) *The item is to be judged, not the method of production*. The provisions cover 'printed and similar matter'. Although printing is the traditional way of producing books, brochures, newspapers etc, documents produced by other means may still qualify (eg handwritten documents, photocopies, and even faxes). The test to apply is whether the document has the characteristics of any item in *Group 3*, not how that document was produced, or what that document is a copy of.

(*d*) *Is the supply in question one of goods or services*? Printed matter is frequently used as a medium in the course of a supply of services and it is therefore necessary to determine exactly what is being supplied (eg expert or professional information that has been produced to the specific directions of the customer or printed matter which is just the 'mechanical' production of information).

The supply of text by electronic transmission, via the internet, or similar means is also standard-rated. Such supplies are of services, not of goods, and different VAT rules apply.

54.2 Printed Matter, etc

Examples of common zero-rated items. The following is a list of items which HMRC commonly regard as qualifying for zero-rating. A list of items they would normally treat as standard-rated is reproduced at 54.14 below. However, liability of any specific item should not be determined from these lists only and reference should be made to the appropriate paragraph of the text.

Accounts (fully printed)
Advertising leaflets
Agendas (fully printed)
Almanacs
Amendments (loose leaf)
Annuals
Antique books and maps
Articles of association (complete in booklet form)
Astronomical charts
Atlases
Autograph books (completed)
Bibliographies
Bills of quantity (completed)
Booklets
Books
Brochures
Bulletins
Catalogues
Charts (geographical or topographical)
Circulars
Colouring books (children's)
Comics
Company accounts and reports
Crossword books
Diaries (completed)
Dictionaries
Directories (completed)
Election addresses
Encyclopaedias
Football programmes
Geological maps
Handbills
Holiday and tourist guides
Hydrographical charts
Hymn books
Instruction manuals
Journals
Leaflets
Magazines
Mail order catalogues
Manuals
Maps
Memorandum of association (complete in booklet form)
Missals
Monographs
Music
Music scores
Newspapers
Orders of service

Painting books (children's)
Pamphlets
Periodicals
Picture books
Poster magazines (see 54.7 below)
Prayer books
Price lists (fully printed leaflets or brochures)
Programmes
Rag books (children's)
Recipe books
Road maps
Scrap books (completed)
Ships' logs (completed)
Sports programmes
Staff journals
Text books
Theses
Timetables (in book or leaflet form)
Topographical plans
Tracts
Trade catalogues
Trade directories
Travel brochures

(VAT Notice 701/10/03, paras 2, 8; Internal Guidance V1–7, Chapter 3 para 2.3).

54.3 Books and booklets

The supply of books and booklets is zero-rated. [*VATA 1994, Sch 8 Group 3 Item 1*].

Whether a particular item falls within the scope of 'books and booklets' depends mainly on its physical characteristics and function but also, to a lesser extent, on its content.

Physical characteristics. To qualify for zero-rating as a complete book or booklet, HMRC usually require an item to have the following physical characteristics.

- It must have several pages.
- It must have a cover that is stiffer than the pages. (Items which fail this test may still be eligible for zero-rating under 54.4 below.)
- It must either be bound or adapted for inclusion in a ring-binder.

  HMRC consider that it is the act of binding that makes a collection of papers into a complete book. This can take place either by traditional book-binding or by the issue of a ring-bound book. They therefore allow zero-rating for

  (i) complete sets of loose leaves, adapted for inclusion in a binder of the customer's choice;

  (ii) a binder (titled or untitled) which is supplied in conjunction with the complete loose leaf pages of a book; and

  (iii) a binder bearing the exact title of the book it is intended to contain (a company name alone is not enough) but supplied independently of the book itself. In such a case, the book must be complete when the binder is issued, loose-leaved, and incapable of existence without its binder. See *A E Walker Ltd (VTD 3) (TVC 5.1)* and *Marshall Cavendish Ltd (VTD 16) (TVC 5.26)*.

Parts of books and unbound pages are standard-rated.

A book or booklet may be printed in any language or characters (eg Braille or shorthand), photocopied, typed or hand-written. Zero-rated items include literary works, reference books, directories and catalogues, antique books, and collections of letters or documents permanently bound in covers.

Books published in instalments. In continuity or part-work publishing, a product is supplied in parts over varying periods but builds up into a greater whole (ie a loose-leaf book). The parts may be issued *either* in magazine format with the pages stapled together *or* as a collection of loose pages, possibly wrapped in clear plastic or lightly gummed together, which are often not consecutive but designed to be separated and placed in the appropriate section of a binder. Unless a loose-leaf, when viewed independently, is a book at the time of supply, it is not strictly entitled to zero-rating. By concession, if at that time an instalment is part of a larger finite work which itself would fall to be zero-rated as a book, then the individual component parts may also be zero-rated where they are supplied either direct by the publisher or through a distribution chain to the final consumer. (VAT Notice 48, ESC 3.15).

Card-based publications. By way of further concession, card-based boxed publications, even though not bound or held together other than in or by their container, are treated for VAT purposes as a book provided they have all the other characteristics of a book. (VAT Notice 48, ESC 3.15).

Amendments to zero-rated loose-leaf publications may be zero-rated, even if issued separately.

The function test. Items which have the physical characteristics of books may nevertheless be standard-rated if their main function is not that of a book. These fall into two main categories.

(i) *Items which do not convey information by means of text*. Since children's picture books are specifically zero-rated (see 54.8 below), HMRC take the view that adults' picture books would have also been specifically relieved if that was the intention of the law. They therefore expect items that are intended for adults to convey information by means of text in order to be eligible for zero-rating. This text may be in any language or in Braille. Items which ordinarily fail this test (and are standard-rated) include

- albums containing collections of picture cards or stamps unless they contain a substantial amount of reading matter which is complete in itself *and* no more than 25% of the album is set aside for the mounting of cards and stamps;
- photograph collections such as wedding albums;
- books of postcards;
- books of posters or frameable prints; and
- books giving samples of types of carpet, paint, paper, etc.

Such items may still qualify for zero-rating if containing text with value in its own right rather than being merely incidental to the pictures, stamps, samples, etc.

Books of plans or drawings for industrial, architectural, engineering, commercial or similar purposes are specifically excluded from zero-rating by *VATA 1994, Sch 8 Group 3, Note* (*a*).

Items which consist mainly of music may qualify under 54.9 below and items which convey information by means of geographical representations may be eligible for zero-rating as maps under 54.10 below.

(ii) *Items whose main significance lies in parts to be completed or detached.* Such items include the following.

- Accounts books and exercise books are standard-rated.
- Diaries and address books. HMRC regard address books and unused diaries as standard-rated and completed diaries as zero-rated. This view was upheld in *C & E Commrs v Colour Offset Ltd, QB 1994, [1995] STC 85 (TVC 5.37)* which confirmed that 'book' should be given its ordinary meaning ie as having the minimum characteristics of something to be read or looked at. A filled-in diary of historic or literary interest might be a book but a blank diary was not a book in the ordinary sense. Neither was an address book simply because its name included the word 'book'. Compare, however, *Scholastic Publications Ltd (VTD 14213) (TVC 5.13)* where a children's publication containing a year planner and address section was held to be zero-rated as the remaining pages (more than 50% overall) were quizzes and jokes 'designed to be read as entertainment'.
- School work books, etc. Where these are in question and answer format, HMRC's policy is that the spaces provided for the insertion of answers are purely incidental to the essential character of the publication. They may thus qualify for zero-rating if they have the physical characteristics of books or booklets. This policy extends to examination papers in question and answer format (eg multiple choice) and to crossword and other puzzle books. However, where the main value of a school work book, etc is in the parts to be completed, that item is standard-rated.

For tribunal decisions involving articles with more than one function, see *WF Graham (Northampton) Ltd (VTD 908) (TVC 5.11)*, *The Book People (VTD 18240) (TVC 5.12)*, and *Scholastic Publications Ltd (VTD 14213) (TVC 5.13)* (children's cut-out books) and *London Cyrenians Housing (VTD14426) (TVC 5.17)* (book and calendar).

(VAT Notice 701/10/03, paras 3.1, 4.4; Internal Guidance V1–7, Chapter 3 paras 3.1–3.4).

54.4 Brochures and pamphlets

The supply of brochures and pamphlets is zero-rated. [*VATA 1994, Sch 8 Group 3 Item 1*].

Whether a particular item falls within the scope of 'brochures and pamphlets' is a matter of fact and impression and depends mainly on its physical characteristics and function but also, to a lesser extent, on its content.

Physical characteristics. To qualify for zero-rating as a brochure or pamphlet, HMRC usually require the item to satisfy the following physical characteristics.

- A brochure usually consists of several sheets of reading matter fastened or folded together (although not necessarily bound in a cover). It usually contains advertising material in the form of text or illustrations.

- A pamphlet is similar but usually comprises material of a political, social or intellectual nature.

See also the definition given by the chairman in *Schusman (VTD 11835) (TVC 5.52)*.

The function test. An item which has the physical characteristics of a brochure or pamphlet may nevertheless be standard-rated if it fails to satisfy the function test by falling into one of the following categories.

(*a*) *An item whose main significance lies in parts to be completed or detached.* An item which might otherwise be considered a brochure or pamphlet may not be zero-rated if it is primarily intended for completion or detachment. This distinguishes a brochure or pamphlet from a standard-rated form. HMRC accept that items are *not* primarily intended for completion or detachment if 25% or less of their total area consists of

- areas which are blank and available for completion; or
- parts to be detached and returned.

Where there is both an area for completion and a part to be detached and returned, then the two together should not exceed 25% of the total area of the publication. However, there is no basis in law for this and the '25% test' is no more than a rule of thumb.

Where an item has areas for completion or detachment which exceed 25%, but it is considered that it is nevertheless not primarily a form, it is advisable to obtain a written ruling from the National Advice Service before zero-rating the item.

Whatever the area for completion, a publication which is designed to be returned whole after completion is always standard-rated.

See also *Full Force Marketing Ltd; Framesouth Ltd (VTD 15270) (TVC 5.79)* where the sale of an A4 document incorporating a 'discount card' entitling the holder to obtain free meals was essentially a supply of standard-rated services rather than a zero-rated brochure.

(*b*) *Items which do not convey information by means of text.* As a brochure is normally an advertising vehicle, it will often contain numerous illustrations. However, there must be some thematic text to link these illustrations in order for zero-rating to be accepted (eg a collection of paint samples with only the names and numbers of the particular shades is not a brochure, although it might possess the right physical characteristics).

Single sheet and 'wallet' type brochures. A brochure designed with a flap may be zero-rated provided it

- conveys information;
- contains a substantial amount of text, with some indication of contents or the issuing organisation;
- is not primarily designed to hold other items; and
- is supplied complete.

A wallet containing zero-rated reading material does not become a brochure with the folder acting as an outer cover. In these circumstances, HMRC view the wallet as a means of creating a package of printed matter. See 54.16 below.

(VAT Notice 701/10/03, paras 3.2, 3.4; Internal Guidance V1–7, Chapter 3 paras 4.1–4.4).

54.5 Leaflets

The supply of leaflets is zero-rated. [*VATA 1994, Sch 8 Group 3 Item 1*].

There is no definition of a 'leaflet' and whether a particular item is a leaflet is a matter of fact and impression and depends mainly on its physical characteristics and function but also, to a lesser extent, on its content.

Physical characteristics. HMRC look for certain physical characteristics if an item is to qualify as a leaflet.

(*a*) It must be limp. In *Panini Publishing Ltd (VTD 3876) (TVC 5.69)* the tribunal held that a leaflet must be limp and generally, if not inevitably, on unlaminated paper. However, in *Multiform Printing Ltd (VTD 13931) (TVC 5.48)* it was held that there is no need for a leaflet to be flimsy. HMRC do not therefore regard items printed on stiff paper as automatically excluded from the definition of leaflets. However, they do regard the use of stiff paper and card as an indicator that an item has a function which *would* exclude it.

(*b*) It must be designed to be held in the hand for reading by individuals rather than for hanging up or general display. See *Arbroath Herald Ltd (VTD 182) (TVC 5.62)* (car stickers), *Pace Group (Communications) Ltd (VTD 510) (TVC 5.65)* (window banners and door stickers); and *Cronsvale Ltd (VTD 1552) (TVC 5.47)* (advertisements for public meetings).

(*c*) It should consist of a single sheet of paper not greater than A4 size (although larger publications up to A2 size can be zero-rated provided they are printed on both sides, folded down to A4 or smaller, and meet the other conditions). See *Cronsvale Ltd* above where the tribunal held a leaflet to mean a small-sized leaf of paper or a sheet folded into leaves (but not stitched) and containing printed matter, chiefly for gratuitous distribution.

(*d*) It should be complete in itself (and not part of a larger work, see *Odhams Leisure Group Ltd v C & E Commrs, QB [1992] STC 332 (TVC 5.71)*).

(*e*) It should be widely distributed (ie intended to reach an audience of at least 50) either free or for a nominal consideration. This rules out

- very small productions; and
- letters with an individual's name or address added (which thereby restrict the letter to an audience of one). The supply of uncompleted 'stock' or basic letters is zero-rated if the portion for completion consists of no more than the recipient's name and address, a reference number and a signature.

(*f*) It should convey information by means of text. Items that are principally photographs with no significant or thematic text to support those photographs cannot be zero-rated.

The function test. An item which has the physical characteristics of a leaflet may nevertheless be standard-rated if it fails to satisfy the function test by falling into one of the following categories.

(i) *Items whose main function is not to convey information.* (eg all types of tickets, coupons, vouchers, labels and fragrance samples).

(ii) *Items primarily intended for completion or detachment*. An item which might otherwise be considered a leaflet may not be zero-rated if it is primarily intended for completion or detachment. This distinguishes a leaflet from a standard-rated form. HMRC accept that items are *not* primarily intended for completion or detachment if 25% or less of their total area consists of

- areas which are blank and available for completion; or
- parts to be detached and returned.

Where there is both an area for completion and a part to be detached and returned, then the two together should not exceed 25% of the total area of the publication. However, there is no basis in law for this and the '25% test' is no more than a rule of thumb.

Where an item has areas for completion or detachment which exceed 25%, but it is considered that it is nevertheless not primarily a form, it is advisable to obtain a written ruling from the National Advice Service before zero-rating the item.

Whatever the area for completion, a publication which is designed to be returned whole after completion is always standard-rated.

(iii) It should be

- of an ephemeral nature (designed to be read a few times and then thrown away rather than kept); or
- designed to accompany some other product or service (eg an instruction leaflet) rather than used for a specific purpose in its own right.

Examples of items that HMRC would not regard as being leaflets would be those designed

- as a calendar;
- to obtain admission to premises;
- to obtain a discount on goods or services; or
- as reference material.

HMRC also consider that items printed on laminated paper are designed to be kept and therefore are not leaflets. On the other hand, orders of service are not normally designed to be kept and may be zero-rated.

(VAT Notice 701/10/03, paras 3.3, 3.4, 4.3; Internal Guidance V1–7, Chapter 3 paras 5.1–5.4).

54.6 Newspapers

The supply of newspapers is zero-rated. [*VATA 1994, Sch 8 Group 3 Item 2*].

There is no definition of a 'newspaper' and whether a particular item is a newspaper is a matter of fact and impression and depends mainly on its physical characteristics and function but also, to a lesser extent, on its content.

Physical characteristics. To qualify for zero-rating as a newspaper, HMRC usually require an item to satisfy the following conditions.

- It should usually consist of several large sheets folded rather than bound together.

- It must be published at regular intervals (usually daily but at least weekly) in a continuous series under the same title. Each issue should usually be dated and/or serially numbered. The intervals between publication should be determined by the wishes of the publisher, not prompted by some external event.

Included are occasional 'souvenir' issues of established newspapers (eg those commemorating a royal marriage or the results of a general election). *Not included* are theatre or sporting programmes even if issued in the format of a newspaper.

The function test. To qualify as a newspaper, a publication must be predominantly devoted to the dissemination of 'news' in the broad sense of the word (ie information about recent or imminent events of a local, national or international interest). It may also carry 'non-news' articles (eg readers' letters, the weather forecast, crosswords and features on fashion, gardening, etc) but these should be an incidental feature.

Publications which do not carry a substantial amount of news are not newspapers (eg a publication which takes a newspaper format but consist almost entirely of advertisements is not a newspaper although it may qualify as a periodical under 54.7 below).

For a general consideration of the requirements of a newspaper, see *Evans and Marland Ltd (t/a Greyform Publications) (VTD 3158) (TVC 5.83)*.

Delivery and handling charges. Charges for delivered newspapers are normally zero-rated (see 47.8(18) OUTPUT TAX). This should be distinguished from handling charges which a magazine publisher pays a newspaper proprietor for agreeing to distribute a free magazine in conjunction with a newspaper and which the newspaper will, in turn, pay its newsagents for its insertion and delivery to householders. HMRC view both payments as standard-rated, regardless of the liability of the printed matter involved.

(VAT Notice 701/10/03, para 3.5; Internal Guidance V1–7, Chapter 3 paras 6.1–6.3).

54.7 Journals and periodicals

The supply of journals and periodicals is zero-rated. [*VATA 1994, Sch 8 Group 3 Item 2*].

There is no definition of a 'journal' or 'periodical' and whether a particular item qualifies is a matter of fact and impression and depends mainly on its physical characteristics and function but also, to a lesser extent, on its content.

Physical characteristics. To qualify for zero-rating as a journal or periodical, HMRC usually require an item to satisfy the following conditions.

- It should either be in newspaper format or a paper-bound publication.
- It must be published in a series at regular intervals (more frequently than once a year). The intervals between publication should be determined by the wishes of the publisher, not prompted by some external event. (For this reason, HMRC do not regard theatre or sporting programmes as qualifying since these are only published to support a particular event. Even if that event takes place regularly, it is the event which dictates the frequency of publication of the programme.)

The function test. To qualify as a journal or periodical, an item should meet the following functional requirements.

- It must be designed for reading and not for use as stationery packaged in journal or periodical format (eg forms for completion or primarily spaces for note taking).

- Its main purpose must be to convey information, not to act as a vehicle for self-promotion. Journals or periodicals may contain a wide variety of information. They may contain information of a specialised nature (eg legal, medical, financial, commercial, fashion or sporting) or be of more general interest (eg popular fiction magazines). They may also consist almost entirely of advertisements providing that these originate from a number of sources. However, publications which serve primarily to promote the proprietor's own business, either by way of written articles or advertisements, do not qualify as periodicals (although they may qualify as brochures, see 54.4 above). See *Snushall Dalby & Robinson v C & E Commrs, QB [1992] STC 537 (TVC 5.82)* where the tribunal held that a monthly property guide, consisting almost entirely of advertisements for houses but with one or two articles on the housing market, could not be regarded as a journal as it contained no news and could not be regarded as a periodical as it was not sold to the public.

HMRC used to take the view that an item had to convey information by way of text to qualify as a journal or periodical. They have now withdrawn this view following the decision in *EMAP Consumer Magazines Ltd (VTD 13322) (VTC 5.84)* where a magazine consisting mainly of posters was held to be a periodical even though some could not be viewed without removing the staples. The tribunal chairman held that the word 'periodical' should be given its ordinary natural meaning and a publication consisting mainly of pictorial matter is capable of being a periodical.

(VAT Notice 701/10/03, para 3.6; Internal Guidance V1–7, Chapter 3 paras 7.1, 7.2).

54.8 Children's picture books and painting books

The supply of children's picture books and painting books is zero-rated. [*VATA 1994, Sch 8 Group 3 Item 3*]. This provision does not cover books for older children where the text is the main component, even if supported by pictures. Such books should be considered for zero-rating under 54.3 above.

Physical characteristics. To qualify for zero-rating under this heading, HMRC usually require an item to satisfy the following conditions.

- It must have several pages.
- It must be either bound, fastened, or folded in a 'concertina' fashion.
- It must be printed on paper, cardboard, textiles (eg rag books) or waterproof plastic (in the case of 'bath-time books').

The function test. Many children's picture or painting books also involve other elements more akin to toys or stationery. It is therefore necessary to establish the main function of an item. Zero-rating will only apply if it is that of a picture or painting book.

(*a*) *Children's picture books*. *Included* are books where the reader is invited first to read and then to cut out an item from the story. *Not included* are:

- Books consisting wholly or mainly of pictures or models for cutting out, following which there is little left that could be considered a book. HMRC suggest that such books with at least 25% text (other than assembly instructions) related to the material for cutting out can be zero-rated. However, there is no basis in law for this and the '25% test' is no more than a rule of thumb. See also *Scholastic Publications Ltd (VTD 14213) (TVC 5.13)* and *The Book People Ltd (VTD 18240) (TVC 5.12)*.
- Books where the 'pages' are boards for games.

For a general consideration of children's reading books and picture books, see *W F Graham (Northampton) Ltd (VTD 908) (TVC 5.11)*.

(*b*) *Children's painting books*. HMRC interpret 'painting books' as including most types of books which are designed to exercise a child's mind other than by way of a traditional 'story'. *Included* are:

- Children's painting books and drawing books with sample pictures for copying, or outlines of pictures for colouring, painting or drawing.
- Similar books with 'invisible' outlines to colour which can be made visible by rubbing with a pencil or applying water with a paint brush.
- Painting books in which the small amounts of water colour required for colouring are contained in the book (eg in the form of a palette).
- Activity books which combine pages of colouring with pages of puzzles, quizzes and the like.
- Books which feature pictures onto which stickers are stuck or transfers are superimposed.

Not included are:

- Items which include puzzles, pictures for colouring, etc but which are primarily cut-out toys or board games.
- Items which allow a drawing to be made outside the book itself by means of stencils.
- Items which are primarily stationery for children to write in.

(VAT Notice 701/10/03, paras 3.7, 3.8; Internal Guidance V1–7, Chapter 3 paras 8.1–8.4).

54.9 Music

The supply of music (printed, duplicated or manuscript) is zero-rated. [*VATA 1994, Sch 8 Group 3 Item 4*].

Any complete music which is presented on paper is zero-rated whether

- instrumental or vocal;
- printed or hand-written;
- bound or on loose sheets;
- illustrated or not; or
- in any system of notation, including numerical symbols or Braille.

Not included are

- music rolls;
- blank manuscript paper;
- a piece of music commissioned from a composer (see 54.17 below); and
- items which are primarily educational aids for the teaching of music (eg pictures of how to play chords on the guitar) although these items may qualify for relief as a book or booklet under 54.3 above depending upon their physical character-

istics. See also *Flip Cards (Marine) Ltd (VTD 14483) (TVC 5.98)* where 'music' was defined as 'the written or printed score or set of parts of a musical composition' and held not to include cards containing questions and answers about music.

(VAT Notice 701/10/03, para 3.9; Internal Guidance V1–7, Chapter 3 para 9.1).

54.10 **Maps, charts and topographical plans**

The supply of maps, charts and topographical plans is zero-rated. [*VATA 1994, Sch 8 Group 3 Item 5*].

Physical characteristics. To qualify for zero-rating as a map, chart or topographical plan, HMRC require an item to satisfy the following physical characteristics.

- The map, etc may be printed on paper or other material (eg cloth) and in the form of a single or folded sheets or a collection of such sheets bound together in book form (eg an atlas).
- It must be two-dimensional. Traditional maps and charts, and even business cards, may qualify but globes, other three-dimensional items and 'novelty maps' printed onto items such as mugs are excluded.
- It must provide a geographical representation of an area of land, sea or the heavens. It must be more than an aerial photograph but the representation need not be strictly accurate or to scale. It may cover only a minor area of the printed matter, the remainder of which is devoted to supporting pictures or text.

  The restriction of relief for charts to geographical representations is supported by the decision in *Brooks Histograph Ltd (VTD 1570) (TVC 5.99)* where the tribunal held that the word 'chart' must be construed in the context in which it appears. Since it appears between the words 'maps' and 'topographical plans' it refers to an area of land, sea or the skies and not to an historical chart.

The function test. To qualify for zero-rating under this heading, the primary function of the item must be for use as a map, chart, or topographical plan. HMRC do not regard the following as satisfying the test.

- Plans or drawings for industrial, architectural, engineering, commercial or similar purposes (which are excluded from zero-rating by *VATA 1994, Sch 8 Group 3, Note* (*a*)).
- Framed maps which are primarily decorative items. Zero-rating can be applied where a map remains functional rather than decorative even after framing (eg where laminated and mounted onto wood or soft board to allow the use of marker pens and/or to enable pins to be inserted).
- Posters.
- Pictorial wall charts.
- Aerial photographs.
- Decorative maps printed or woven into textile items (eg scarves, handkerchiefs, tea-towels, tapestries, rugs).

(VAT Notice 701/10/03, para 3.10; Internal Guidance V1–7, Chapter 3 paras 10.1, 10.2).

54.11 Incidental items supplied with zero-rated printed matter and binders

Covers, cases and other articles supplied with items within 54.3 to 54.10 above, and not separately accounted for, are zero-rated. [*VATA 1994, Sch 8 Group 3 Item 6*].

Minor accessories (eg dust covers, clasps, book marks and presentation cases) supplied with any zero-rated item are usually regarded as forming part of the zero-rated item (but see 54.15 below).

Certain booksellers specialise in providing public libraries with books fitted with plastic dust-jackets, ticket-pockets and similar accessories. In these limited circumstances, provided the accessory is firmly fitted to the book itself so as to form an integral part of it, the fact that invoices normally show separate charges for books and for the fitting of the jackets, etc does not preclude zero-rating simply because these items are 'separately accounted for'.

HMRC do not accept that zero-rating under this heading applies to

- covers which are a means of packaging a multiplicity of items (eg plastic envelopes enclosing direct mail packs or children's activity packs); and
- printed folders into which other printed matter items are inserted.

for which see 54.16 below.

Most folders and wallets are standard-rated but if they convey information themselves they may qualify as brochures (see 54.4 above).

Binders. For the treatment of loose-leaf binders, see 54.3 above. All other binders or files for general or office use are standard-rated. This includes binders for part works, journals and periodicals (whether specifically titled or not).

Small order surcharges. A surcharge imposed for handling a small order is treated as part of the price of the goods and is zero-rated if the goods are zero-rated.

(VAT Notice 701/10/03, paras 5.1, 5.2, 5.5; Internal Guidance V1–7, Chapter 3 paras 11.1, 11.2).

54.12 Loans, hire and shares

The transfer of any undivided share in, or the possession of, any item zero-rated under 54.3 to 54.11 above is zero-rated. [*VATA 1994, Sch 8 Group 3 Note* (*b*)].

This provision allows zero-rating to apply to

(*a*) the lending or hiring out of any item, or

(*b*) the sale of a share or part interest in any item

which is zero-rated under 54.3 to 54.11 above.

Libraries which charge for the loan of books therefore make zero-rated supplies. This also applies to

- reference libraries which charge for the use of their books on their own premises; and
- the hire of collections of books (particularly technical manuals) to educational institutions by wholesalers or publishers.

(VAT Notice 701/10/03, para 5.3; Internal Guidance V1–7, Chapter 3 para 17.1).

54.13 **Supplies of printed advertising to charities**

Zero-rating applies to supplies of all charity advertisements in all media, ie there ceases to be any restriction on either the type of media or the purpose of the advertising. [*VATA 1994, Sch 8 Group 15 items 8–8C; SI 2000/805*]. These more general provisions are considered in 12.7 CHARITIES.

54.14 **STANDARD-RATED PRINTED MATTER**

Examples of common standard-rated items. The following is a list of items which HMRC commonly regard as being standard-rated. A list of items they would normally treat as zero-rated is reproduced at 54.2 above. However, it should not be assumed that any item is zero-rated simply because it is not included in the list below and the liability of any specific item should be determined by reference to the appropriate paragraph of the text.

Acceptance cards
Account books
Address books
Albums
Amendment slips
Announcement cards
Appointment cards
Autograph albums (uncompleted)
Badges
Bags (paper)
Ballot papers
Bankers' drafts
Billheads
Bills of lading
Bills of quantity (blank)
Binders (but see 54.3 above)
Bingo cards
Biorhythm charts
Blotters
Book covers
Book marks
Book tokens
Bookmakers' tickets
Business cards
Calendars
Certificates
Cheques and cheque books
Cigarette cards
Cloakroom tickets
Colour cards
Compliment slips
Copy books
Correspondence cards
Coupon books
Coupons
Credit cards
Delivery notes
Diaries (unused)
Dividend warrants

Dressmaking patterns
Engineers' plans
Envelopes
Exercise books
Fashion drawings
Flash cards
Folders
Football pool coupons
Form letters (but see 54.5 above)
Forms
Framed decorative maps
Games
Globes
Graph paper
Greetings cards
Index cards
Inlay cards for cassettes, CDs or videos
Insurance cover notes
Invitation cards
Invoices
Labels
Letter headings
Letters (handwritten)
Log books (blank)
Lottery tickets and cards
Manuscript paper
Manuscripts
Medical records
Membership cards
Memo pads
Menu cards
Microfiche
Microfilm
Microform copies
Music rolls
Note books, pads and paper
Order books and forms
Paper (unprinted)
Parts of books (see 54.3 above)
Pattern cards
Photograph albums
Photographs
Plans (but see 54.10 above)
Playing cards
Poll cards
Pools coupons
Postcards (whether completed or not)
Posters
Price cards and tags
Printed pictures
Questionnaires
Receipt books and forms
Record books and labels
Record books

Record labels
Record sleeves
Registers
Rent books
Reply-paid coupons and envelopes
Reproductions of paintings
Score cards
Scrap books (blank)
Scrolls (hand-written)
Seals
Shade cards (unless containing substantial printed text)
Share certificates
Stamp albums (whether completed or not)
Stationery
Stationery books
Stickers
Swatch books
Swatch cards
Sweepstake tickets
Tags
Temperature charts
Tickets
Time cards and sheets
Tokens (but see book tokens below)
Toys
Transcripts
Transfers
Transparencies
Visiting cards
Vouchers
Wall charts
Waste paper
Wills
Winding cards
Wrapping paper
Wreath cards

Posters. Sheets intended for public display are standard-rated but see 54.7 above for 'poster-magazines'.

Stationery. Stationery items (eg account books and exercise books) are standard-rated. Some items which are standard-rated stationery when new and unused can be zero-rated if sold after they have been completed, provided that they then have the physical characteristics of a book or other zero-rated item (eg completed diaries or ships' logs but not completed stamp albums).

Letters. Individual manuscript or typed letters are standard-rated as are collections of such letters which are unbound or loosely bound. Permanently bound collections are zero-rated. See 54.5 above for printed stocks of standard letters.

Photocopies. Photocopies of zero-rated items are always standard-rated unless the copies can be properly described as books, booklets, brochures, pamphlets, leaflets, etc and meet all the criteria for zero-rating such items. A bundle of photocopies does not constitute a book unless it includes copies of all the pages of the book and is in permanent binding. Photocopies of parts of books, extracts from periodicals, etc cannot be zero-rated unless complete in themselves and having the characteristics of zero-rated items. Where a business provides 'instant' photocopying or duplicating services and cannot determine the VAT liability of the copies supplied, it should charge VAT at the standard rate.

Book tokens. Printing of book tokens is standard-rated. On the sale of a book token to the general public

- for its face value or less, no VAT is due; and
- for more than its face value, VAT is due on the difference between the selling price and its face value.

Any separate charge for a greetings card is standard-rated.

(VAT Notice 701/10/03, paras 4.1–4.3, 4.5, 5.4, 8).

54.15 SINGLE AND MULTIPLE SUPPLIES

Goods which would normally be zero-rated or standard-rated as printed matter may be supplied in conjunction with other goods and/or services. A single inclusive price may, or may not, be charged. If the individual elements are all liable to VAT at the same rate, VAT due can be calculated in the normal way. But if the individual supplies are not liable to VAT at the same rate, the criteria set out by the CJEC in *Card Protection Plan Ltd v C & E Commrs, CJEC [1999] STC 270 (TVC 21.223)* must be used to determine whether there is a single or multiple supply.

- A single supply occurs where one element of the supply is the principal or significant element to which all the other elements are ancillary, integral or incidental. In such a case, the whole transaction must be treated as having the VAT liability of the principal element.
- A multiple supply occurs where more than one element is distinct and independent. In such a case, each element will take its own liability and, where a single, inclusive price is charged for the transaction, the price must be apportioned.

There is more detailed coverage of single and multiple supplies in 64.6 SUPPLY.

However, there are two exceptions to the normal rules for

- packages consisting entirely of items printed on paper or card (see 54.16 below); and
- certain cover mounted items on magazines (see 54.18 below).

54.16 Packages of zero-rated and standard-rated printed matter

Where a business makes a multiple supply of a 'package' consisting *entirely* of standard-rated and zero-rated printed matter, it can account for VAT by apportionment between the standard-rated and zero-rated elements. Alternatively, by concession, it can apply the package test so that

- if the package contains more zero-rated than standard-rated items, the package as a whole can be zero-rated;
- if there are more standard-rated items, the package as a whole is standard-rated; and
- where there are equal numbers of zero-rated and standard-rated items, the liability of the package is decided by the costs of the goods. If the zero-rated elements of the package cost more, the whole package is zero-rated and vice

versa. In the unlikely event that the standard and zero-rated elements cost exactly the same amount, apportionment should be applied.

For these purpose, a '*package*' is a collection of items printed on paper or card usually enclosed in some sort of wrapper. The articles must physically form a package and have a common link in that they are intended to be used together. Examples include

- packages contained in an outer polythene or paper envelope (eg a package sent to a shareholder which includes company reports, circulars, a proxy voting form and a reply-paid envelope);
- cardboard folders with pockets into which are inserted a variety of forms, leaflets, etc; and
- advertising packages often from financial institutions.

The outer envelope in which the package items are enclosed is *not* taken into account when counting the number of standard/zero-rated items but a reply-paid envelope counts as a standard-rated item.

If any item in the package is not printed on paper or card the package test cannot be applied.

(VAT Notice 701/10/03, para 6.5).

The package test for charities. By concession, supplies of certain goods to a charity for use in connection with collecting monetary donations can be treated as if they were zero-rated. See 12.7(*g*) CHARITIES. *From 1 August 2003*, where a package of printed matter is supplied to a charity some items connected with collecting monetary donations can be treated as zero-rated for the purposes of the package test provided they meet the criteria set out in 12.7(*g*) CHARITIES.

Item	*Treatment for the package test*
Letter appealing for donations	Zero-rated
Printed envelopes for use with appeal letters	Zero-rated
Money collecting envelopes	Zero-rated
Stickers	Standard-rated
Money collecting boxes made of card	Zero-rated
Any item not made of paper or card	Package test cannot be used

(VAT Notice 701/10/03, para 6.6).

54.17 Printed matter supplied with other services

The following are common situations where printed matter is supplied with other services.

(1) **Services of an original or specialist nature**

The supply of services such as original writing or composition or those involving a specialism are standard-rated. Any goods supplied with those services are incidental products and must be standard-rated even if they would be zero-rated printed matter. Examples include

- the manuscript of a book supplied by an author;

- a piece of music commissioned from a composer;
- a report commissioned from a consultant;
- a translation;
- a shorthand transcription; and
- a typing service.

Extra copies of such items may be zero-rated provided they are

- in a format which qualifies for zero-rating; and
- supplied at a price which covers only the cost of producing the extra copies and a reasonable mark-up.

(VAT Notice 701/10/03, para 7.2).

(2) **Printed matter used to supply discount facilities**

Where a publication contains a number of discount vouchers and details of establishments where the vouchers may be used, the important point to establish is where the value of the publication lies. If it has some value as printed matter in its own right, some allowance must be made for this element which may be zero-rated under the normal requirements in 54.2 *et seq.* above. However, if a person would only really buy the publication for the discounts which it contains, there is one standard-rated supply of discount services to which the printed matter is incidental.

HMRC consider the following in reaching a decision in any particular case.

- Is it possible to physically separate the vouchers from the guide, and if so, are the two parts ever offered for sale separately?
- How is the guide promoted – is the 'discount' aspect stressed?
- Does the price increase if more vouchers are supplied?
- What is the historical background – has the guide ever been supplied independently with no vouchers or is this an entirely new venture?

(Internal Guidance V1–7, Chapter 3 para 13.3).

See also *Status Cards Ltd (VTD 128) (TVC 5.9)*, *Graham Leisure Ltd (VTD 1304) (TVC 5.30)* and *Interleisure Club Ltd (VTD 7458) (TVC 5.31)*.

(3) **Printed matter supplied with correspondence courses**

Correspondence courses often involve a mixture of tuition in class and home study through course manuals or booklets. The liability of the supply will depend upon what exactly is being supplied. This may be a single supply of education by an eligible body (exempt) or a non-eligible body (standard-rated), a single supply of printed matter (zero-rated) or a multiple supply of education and printed matter (in which case apportionment is required). See 47.3 OUTPUT TAX for methods of apportionment.

The criteria set out by the CJEC in *Card Protection Plan Ltd v C & E Commrs, CJEC [1999] STC 270 (TVC 21.223)* must be used to determine whether there is a single or multiple supply. Where it is established that there is a single supply, consideration must be given as to whether either of the two elements, education and printed matter, is the principal supply with the other being ancillary. If so, the whole supply takes on the liability of the principal supply. HMRC regard the following as being indicators to a supply of education.

- Successful completion of the course leads to a recognised qualification.
- The course is based on a recognised syllabus.
- The tutor/support service element is integral and significant.
- Assignments contributed to the successful completion of the course.
- The supplier is recognised as an education provider.

HMRC regard the following as being indicators to a supply of printed matter.

- Tutor involvement is not integral to the supply.
- The supplier does not author the course.
- The supplier is a publisher rather than an educator.
- The course does not lead to a qualification.

(Internal Guidance V1–7, Chapter 21 para 4.5).

Fees for correspondence and residential courses have been held to be apportionable between the supply of books (zero-rated) and tuition (standard-rated) in *The Rapid Results College Ltd (VTD 48) (TVC 5.2)*, *LSA (Full Time Courses) Ltd (VTD 1507) (TVC 5.6)* and *Force One Training Ltd (VTD 13619) (TVC 5.7)*. Compare, however, *EW (Computer Training) Ltd (VTD 5453) (TVC 5.32)* where manuals were held to form part of a single supply of standard-rated tuition and *International News Syndicate Ltd (VTD 14425) (TVC 5.3)* where the small element of external tuition was held to be incidental and the whole supply treated as zero-rated. However, all these decisions pre-dated the decision in *Card Protection Plan* above and must be read in the light of the criteria set out in that case. In the subsequent case of *The College of Estate Management v C & E Commrs, CA [2004] STC 1471 (TVC 5.8)* although both the tribunal and High Court held that there was single exempt supply of education, the Court of Appeal ruled that there was a separate supply of printed material from which the students were to study and prepare assignments. The writing, preparation and distribution of the books formed a substantial part of the undertaking of the College so that the supply of the written material was a distinct and separate supply which was not ancillary to the supply of educational services. HMRC have appealed against this decision to the House of Lords.

(4) Printed matter supplied in return for a subscription

Membership subscriptions. See also 14.2 CLUBS AND ASSOCIATIONS.

Magazine subscriptions. Where magazines are supplied on an annual subscription basis, the whole supply may be zero-rated provided only the magazine is being supplied. However, where the subscription confers other rights (eg the right to buy goods at discounted rates or the right to participate in selling schemes and thereby earn commission) the subscription should be apportioned to reflect the zero-rated element relating to the magazine. (Internal Guidance V1–7, Chapter 3 para 13.5).

(5) Programmes supplied as part of an admission fee

It is common practice for admission to events to include the provision of a programme. Following the judgment of the CJEC in *Card Protection Plan Ltd v C & E Commrs, CJEC [1999] STC 270 (TVC 21.223)* HMRC now accept that in the majority of such cases there is a single supply of admission, the programme being an ancillary item.

(Internal Guidance V1–7, Chapter 3 para 13.6).

(6) **Subsidy or vanity publishing**

An author who is unable to have a work published through the usual commercial channels may sometimes pay for it to be published. This is known as either 'subsidy' publishing or 'vanity' publishing.

Where the publisher, in return for a payment from the author, produces a quantity of books which are *all* delivered to the author, the payment by the author to the publisher is a consideration for a supply of books and is zero-rated.

More usually, however, the author is supplied only with a small number of copies of the book. The publisher retains the bulk of the print run, selling the books in the normal manner and paying the author a royalty on copies sold. In such cases, payment by the author to the publisher is partly the consideration for the zero-rated supply of books to the author and partly consideration for standard-rated publishing services (eg marketing the remaining books, providing statutory copies to the British Library, etc). The following simplified method of calculation of the zero-rated and standard-rated supplies has been agreed between HMRC and the British Printing Industries Federation.

Step A	Calculate non-variable costs of initial print run.
Step B	Calculate variable costs of initial print run.
Step C	Divide total at Step B by number of copies in initial print run and multiply by number of copies issued to author.
Step D	Add totals at Step A and Step C to calculate cost of the zero-rated element of the supply.
Step E	Add the costs of initial print run and run-on charges to establish full cost of supply.
Step F	Divide total at Step D by total at Step E to calculate zero-rated percentage of cost of supply.
Step G	Apply percentage in Step F to the net sales charge to establish the zero-rated element of the supply made.

A business which does not wish to calculate an apportionment for each individual supply may calculate an apportionment on the basis of an average resulting from the application of the above to a number of representative supplies made. The method is subject to review by HMRC to ensure it produces a fair result and should also be regularly reviewed by the business to take account of changing circumstances.

(Internal Guidance V1–7, Chapter 3 para 13.7; VAT Notice 700/57/02; VAT Notice 701/10/03, para 5.7).

54.18 Printed matter supplied with other goods

See 54.16 above for supplies of zero-rated and standard-rated printed matter.

Cover-mounted items. Where a cover-mounted item (eg a sachet of perfume or a CD) is linked to a magazine, it can, by concession, be zero-rated if the following conditions are met.

- No separate charge is made for it.
- The issue is sold at the same price as other issues without a cover-mounted item.
- The cost of the item included with any individual issue does not exceed either £1 (excluding VAT) or 20% of the total cost of the combined supply (excluding VAT).

Magazines often pass through a number of traders before they are retailed to the end-customer. In determining whether the concession can apply, it is necessary to identify the first trader in the chain responsible for linking the items and then apply the above conditions to that trader. If, at the point of linkage, the supply satisfies the terms of the concession, it becomes a single zero-rated supply and continues as such throughout the chain. If the supply does not satisfy the terms of the concession, the normal rules must be considered to determine whether it is a single or multiple supply.

(VAT Notice 701/10/03, para 6.7; VAT Notice 48, ESC 3.7).

See also *Keesing (UK) Ltd (VTD 16840) (TVC 5.92)* where the company's magazine was distributed by another company which paid Keesing 55% of the cover price of the magazine. The tribunal held that 'total cost' for the purposes of the concession was the 55% which Keesing received, rather than the full cover price, and on that basis the conditions of the concession were not satisfied.

Books and CDs/tapes. HMRC regard a single supply as taking place in the following circumstances.

(*a*) Where children's books are packaged with a tape or CD and there is 'audible interaction' between the operation of the tape/CD and the book, there would be a single zero-rated supply. Examples of audible interaction are

- a noise to indicate the turning of a page;
- an instruction to operate the tape/CD on specific pages of the book; or
- exercises on the tape/CD which require the book to proceed.

(*b*) Where educational books are packaged with a tape/CD and there is clear interaction between the book and the tape/CD, there would be a single zero-rated supply. The tape/CD must

- be clearly subservient to the written material;
- have negligible independent use without the book; and
- not be available for sale separately.

(*c*) Where an educational tape/CD incorporates a booklet and the booklet is simply an instructional manual explaining how to use the tape/CD, there would be a single standard-rated supply.

(Business Brief 20/03).

54.19 PRODUCTION PROCESS OF PRINTED MATTER

Any article of printed matter goes through a production process, beginning with the original idea and ending with a complete article of printed matter. For the purposes of VAT liability, this process can be divided into five stages.

- Preliminary services (see 54.20 below).
- Preparatory work (see 54.21 below).
- The production of goods (see 54.22 below).
- Post-production services (see 54.23 below).
- Alterations (see 54.24 below).

See also 54.25 below where subcontractors are used.

(Internal Guidance V1–7, Chapter 3 para 12.1).

54.20 **Preliminary services**

This stage covers the drawing together of the basic contents of a work which will later become an article of printed matter. Preliminary services may be supplied in two ways.

- A business may supply an article while it is still at the preliminary service stage (eg an author writing and supplying a manuscript or the copy for a pamphlet or leaflet). This supply is always standard-rated. The customer is paying for the thoughts of the author to which any printed matter is incidental.
- A business may be contracted to provide a continuous process, starting with preliminary services and culminating in the issue, on a wide scale, of an article of printed matter (eg a contract to research the information for a catalogue, and then arrange the production and printing). In such a case, provided there is no separate supply of the preliminary services, they can be treated as an integral part of the supply of the printed matter.

(Internal Guidance V1–7, Chapter 3 para 12.2).

54.21 **Preparatory work**

Preparatory work includes

- graphic design,
- typesetting, and
- printing of large sheets containing several individual pages or leaflets.

It may be supplied in two ways.

- If the business has a contract to supply zero-rated printed matter, preparatory work may be zero-rated as part of the same supply.
- If the business does not supply zero-rated printed matter, any supply of preparatory work must be standard-rated.

See *AP Carpenter (VTD 15253) (TVC 5.53)* (whether a graphic designer was responsible for the production of a brochure) and 54.22 below to establish whether the business has supplied zero-rated goods.

Abortive fees. If work is aborted before intended zero-rated printed matter is produced, any 'abortive work fee' charged is standard-rated as the preparatory work did not result in the production of printed matter.

(Internal Guidance V1–7, Chapter 3 para 12.3).

54.22 **Production of goods**

At some stage in the production process, goods are given the essential characteristics of a zero-rated article of printed matter. This stage will vary according to the article concerned. HMRC give the following examples although a flexible approach should be adopted.

- *Book production* – when sheets are bound into a cover. See also *GUS Catalogue Order Ltd (VTD 2958) (TVC 5.10)* where catalogues covered with a temporary cardboard cover were held to be recognisable as books and the remaining work of permanently covering was post-production services (see 54.23 below).
- *Loose-leaf book* – when a complete set of sheets are hole-punched.
- *Pamphlets* – when pages are stapled together or saddle-stitched.
- *Leaflets* – when large sheets are cut into single sheets of leaflets.

It is important to identify the stage at which zero-rated goods are produced for the following reasons.

- If a business undertakes this stage of the production process, it may always zero-rate its supply. For example, a business which binds the pages of a book into a cover (even if the pages have been printed, cut and collated elsewhere) has produced a book and may zero-rate its supply.
- If a business has a contract to supply zero-rated printed matter, HMRC regard both the preparatory work (see 54.21 above) and any post-production services (see 54.23 below) as part of that supply. Those stages may therefore also be zero-rated.

Amendments and self-contained instalments. Both amendments to complete ring-bound books and self-contained instalments of books are normally zero-rated (see 54.3 above). A business responsible for the production stage at which the zero-rated goods are produced can zero-rate its supply.

Part works. 'Part works' which do not form a self-contained instalment cannot strictly be zero-rated as books, booklets or brochures in their own right although, by concession, HMRC allow such part works to be zero-rated provided the completed work would itself be zero-rated as a book (see 54.3 above). However, this concession applies only to retail or mail order sales. A business which produces these part works has not produced goods which are eligible for zero-rating according to a strict interpretation of the law and cannot therefore zero-rate its supply to the retailer or mail order house.

(Internal Guidance V1–7, Chapter 3 para 12.4).

Incomplete publications. Component parts of books, journals (eg covers, unbound pages, illustrations) in the course of production are standard-rated as they have not been assembled into completed books (*Butler & Tanner Ltd (VTD 68) (TVC 5.28)*). (VAT Notice 701/10/03, para 4.4).

54.23 **Post-production services**

Even when goods are already recognisable as zero-rated books, booklets, leaflets, etc, further services may be required (eg packing books for delivery, packaging and wrapping loose-leafs for delivery, inserting pamphlets in envelopes, folding and trimming leaflets).

If a business has supplied zero-rated printed matter (see 54.22 above), post-production services may be zero-rated as part of the same supply. Otherwise, any supply of post-production services must be standard-rated.

(Internal Guidance V1–7, Chapter 3 para 12.5).

54.24 Alterations and work on other people's goods

Alterations. If an article of zero-rated printed matter is produced and then altered at a later stage, such alterations are always standard-rated as they do not produce new zero-rated goods. However, if the goods which result from the alteration are then sold on to a third party, that sale can be zero-rated.

(Internal Guidance V1–7, Chapter 3 para 12.7).

Work on other people's goods. Where a treatment or process is applied to someone else's goods which produces new goods, the liability of the service follows that of the goods produced. If these new goods would qualify for zero-rating, then the services provided are zero-rated.

54.25 Use of subcontractors

A printer with a contract to the final customer to supply zero-rated printed matter may zero-rate any preparatory work (see 54.21 above) or post-production services (see 54.23 above) charged to the customer, even if subcontractors have been employed to perform some parts of the production process. However, a subcontractor can only zero-rate preparatory or post-production work when these services are supplied in conjunction with zero-rated printed matter.

Example

An author produces a manuscript for a booklet and sells it to a publisher. The publisher agrees to supply 10,000 copies of the booklet to a retailer and employs three separate subcontractors who

(1) type-set the manuscript;

(2) print, cut, collate and stitch together the booklets; and

(3) package and deliver the booklets.

The supply by the author to the publisher is a standard-rated supply of preliminary services. The services of subcontractor (1) are standard-rated as preparatory work. The stitching carried out by subcontractor (2) is a zero-rated supply because it produces zero-rated goods. The printing, cutting and collating can also therefore be zero-rated as they are supplied in conjunction with zero-rated printed matter. The services of subcontractor (3) are standard-rated as the supply of post-production services in isolation. The whole charge by the publishing house to the retailer can be zero-rated as a supply of booklets.

(Internal Guidance V1–7, Chapter 3 para 12.6).

55 Rates of VAT

Cross-references. See 22.15 EUROPEAN COMMUNITY: LEGISLATION for rates allowed under the EC Sixth Directive; 64.32–64.57 SUPPLY for the rules relating to the tax point of supply.

De Voil Indirect Tax Service. See V1.111-V1.131.

The contents of this chapter are as follows.

55.1 INTRODUCTION

VAT is levied on the supply of goods and services, the acquisition of goods from another EC country and the importation of goods from a place outside the EC. The Treasury may, by Order, vary the standard rate of VAT for the time being in force by a percentage of the current rate not exceeding 25% but any Order ceases to have effect one year from the date on which it takes effect unless continued by a further Order. [*VATA 1994, s 2; FA 2001, Sch 31 para 2*].

55.2 RATES

Apart from certain EXEMPT SUPPLIES (24) and ZERO-RATED SUPPLIES (72) on which no VAT is chargeable, there are currently two rates of VAT.

Standard rate		
1.4.73–28.7.74	10%	[*FA 1972, s 9(1)*]
29.7.74–17.6.79	8%	[*SI 1974/1224*]
18.6.79–31.3.91	15%	[*F(No 2)A 1979, s 1*]
1.4.91–	17.5%	[*FA 1991, s 13*]
Reduced rate		
1.4.94–31.8.97	8%	[*FA 1995, s 21*]
1.9.97–	5%	[*F(No 2)A 1997, s 6*]

See 58 REDUCED RATE SUPPLIES for the supplies subject to the reduced rate.

55.3 CHANGE IN VAT RATES

The provisions in 55.4 to 55.17 below apply when there is a change in the VAT rate (ie the standard rate is changed or a new rate is introduced) or where there is a change in the VAT liability of particular supplies (eg a supply previously standard-rated becomes zero-rated through a change in the law or its interpretation). Any such change is effective from a specific date and VAT is due at the new rate on supplies made on or after that date. The date on which supplies of goods and services are treated as taking place for the purposes of charging VAT is governed by the tax point rules (see 64.32–64.57 SUPPLY). Normally no change of rate can apply to any supply with a tax point before the effective date of change (but see 55.6 below and the special rules for warehoused goods in 55.17 below). See 60.7 RETAIL SCHEMES for the effects of a change in VAT rates or VAT liabilities where one or more of the special retail schemes are in operation but see also 55.6 below. (VAT Notice 700, paras 30.2–30.4).

55.4 **VAT returns**

VAT must be accounted for in the period in which the normal tax point occurs. This applies even if one the special rules in this chapter is adopted for deciding the rate of VAT to charge. Amounts shown on the return should not be split between the old and new rates. (VAT Notice 700, para 30.7).

55.5 **Reclaiming input tax**

Input tax following a change in VAT rate or VAT liability must be reclaimed at the rate charged by the supplier. Where the amount of VAT is not separately shown (eg on a less detailed VAT invoice — see 40.7 INVOICES), VAT is calculated by applying the VAT fraction which was appropriate at the tax point (see 64.32–64.57 SUPPLY). See also 55.9 below for continuous supplies of services invoiced ahead of the supply. (VAT Notice 700, para 30.6).

55.6 **Output tax – general principles**

When there is a change in the VAT rate or a VAT liability, VAT is chargeable according to the normal tax point rules (see 64.32–64.57 SUPPLY) unless the taxpayer elects for the special change of rate provisions below. It is not possible to avoid the consequences of an announced increase in VAT by preparing invoices which, although agreed by the customer, are not issued (ie physically sent or given to him) before the date of change. See *C & E Commrs v Woolfold Motor Co Ltd, QB [1983] STC 715 (TVC 60.374).* In any case, an invoice issued for a zero-rated supply does not create a tax point.

Special change of rate provisions.

(*a*) On an election, *the rate at which VAT is chargeable on a supply, or any question whether the supply is zero-rated or exempt or a reduced rate supply*, is determined by the *basic tax point* only ie the date on which goods are removed or made available or on which services are performed. Election may be made for all affected supplies or only some of them but an election may not be made where VAT invoices are issued under a self-billing arrangement (see 40.6 INVOICES) or when goods are sold from the assets of a business in satisfaction of a debt. [*VATA 1994, s 88(2)(6); FA 2001, Sch 31 para 4; FA 2002, s 24*]. The effect of the election is that, where the VAT rate increases, VAT may be charged at the old rate on goods removed or services performed before the date of change even though the tax point would normally be established by the issue of a VAT invoice after the change. Similarly, where the VAT rate goes down, VAT may be charged at the new rate on goods removed or services performed after the date of change, even though payment has been received or a VAT invoice issued before that date.

(VAT Notice 700, para 30.8).

(*b*) On an election, *the rate at which VAT is chargeable on an acquisition of goods from another EC country, or any question as to whether it is zero-rated or exempt or a reduced rate acquisition*, is determined by reference to the time of the first removal of the goods involved in the transaction (or, in the case of goods on sale or return, such later time when it becomes certain that they have been acquired). [*VATA 1994, s 88*(*4*)(*7*); *FA 2001, Sch 31 para 4*].

55.7 Credit notes

Where an invoice has already been issued showing VAT at the old rate, it must be corrected with a credit note issued within 14 days of the change. See 40.16 INVOICES for details. (VAT Notice 700, para 30.8).

55.8 Supplies of services

Output tax may be charged at the old rate on the part completed before the date of a change in the VAT rate and at the new rate on the part completed on or after that date provided the supply can be apportioned on a basis of measurable work or in accordance with a supplier's normal costing or pricing system. Where VAT is reduced in this way and a VAT invoice was issued or payment was received before the date of VAT change, a credit note must be provided (see 55.7 above). (VAT Notice 700, para 30.9).

55.9 Continuous supplies of goods and services

Where there is a continuous supply of goods or services (including hire, lease and rental of goods) VAT is normally chargeable at the rate applying at each tax point. See 64.50 SUPPLY for services and 64.46 SUPPLY for a continuous supply of goods in the form of water, gas and electricity. Any VAT invoice issued up to one year ahead, giving the amounts and dates when payments are due, is invalid in respect of payments due after the change (and not received before it). [*SI 1995/2518, Reg 90*(*3*)]. A new invoice, referring to and cancelling the superseded part of the original invoice, must be issued. The customer cannot use the original invoice to support a claim for input tax after the change and must make the necessary adjustments on receipt of the new invoice.

Where a continuous supply spans a change in the VAT rate, VAT may be accounted for at the *old* rate on that part of the supply made before the change even though the normal tax point would occur after the change (eg where a payment is received in arrears of the supply). Conversely, VAT may be accounted for at the *new* rate on that part of the supply made after the change even though the normal tax point occurred before the change (eg where a payment is received in advance of the supply). In each case, VAT should be accounted for on the basis of the value of goods actually supplied or services actually performed before or after the change as appropriate. Where VAT liability is reduced on a supply for which a VAT invoice has been issued at a higher rate, a credit note must be issued (see 55.7 above). (VAT Notice 700, para 30.10).

55.10 Facilities provided by clubs, associations, etc.

Clubs, associations, etc supplying facilities in return for a member's subscription must normally account for VAT at the rate applying when the subscription is received or a VAT invoice is issued, whichever happens first. Where payment is made by instalments or separate invoices are issued, the procedure for continuous supply of services should be followed (see 55.9 above). (VAT Notice 700, para 30.11).

55.11 Hire purchase, conditional and credit sales

Under any of these agreements, there is a single supply of goods and the normal tax point is the earliest of

(*a*) the date of removal of the goods;

(*b*) the date of issue of the agreement (provided the agreement is in the form of a VAT invoice); and

(*c*) the date of the issue of a separate VAT invoice.

See 64.42 SUPPLY.

The signing of an agreement, or its date, does not constitute a tax point. Where there is a change in the VAT rate, the tax point will be whichever of (*a*) to (*c*) above results in the lower rate of VAT being charged. (VAT Notice 700, para 30.12).

55.12 Deposits and payments in advance of the basic tax point

Where full or part payment is made, or a VAT invoice issued, before the basic tax point (see above), VAT will normally be due on the amount paid or invoiced at the rate in force at that date. Where full payment is made in advance but the money is loaned back to the customer on the understanding that it will be repaid as the work proceeds, the transaction has been held to be genuine and not to fall foul of the decision in *W T Ramsay Ltd v IRC* even if the scheme is designed purely to save VAT. A similar decision has been reached where monies are paid into deposit accounts of the builders but only released against architects' certificates (*C & E Commrs v Faith Construction Ltd and related appeals, CA [1989] STC 539 (TVC 60.386)*). If there is a change in the VAT rate before the supply is actually made, VAT may be charged at the rate applicable when the supply is made and a credit note issued (see above) to amend the VAT invoice. These provisions do not apply to deposits taken as security (eg to ensure safe return of goods hired out) which are refundable or subject to forfeiture *or* if the deposit does not relate to a particular supply or contract (eg money paid into a client's account). (VAT Notice 700, para 30.13).

55.13 Credit and contingent discounts

Where a credit note (not arising from the change in rate) is issued to adjust an original invoice, VAT should be credited at the rate in force at the tax point of the original supply. Where contingent discount is allowed and the original VAT charge is adjusted, VAT should be credited at the rate in force at the time of each supply qualifying for the discount. (VAT Notice 700, para 30.14).

55.14 Price escalation clauses and other adjustments

Where an additional payment is required after a change in the VAT rate and after the tax point for the original supply determined under the normal rules, VAT is chargeable on the further payment at the old rate. Where VAT was not determined under the normal rules on the original supply, the tax point for the additional payment is the earlier of the date of receipt of a further payment or the issue of a VAT invoice and VAT is chargeable at the rate then in force. (VAT Notice 700, para 30.15).

55.15 Existing contracts

Where, after the making of a contract for the supply of goods or services and before those goods or services are supplied, there is a change in the VAT charged, then, unless the contract provides otherwise, the consideration for the supply is increased or decreased by an amount equal to the change. These provisions apply in relation to a tenancy or lease as they apply in relation to a contract.

A landlord is able to add VAT to the rent where

- he makes an election to charge VAT on rents at the standard rate under the option to tax provisions (see 42.8 LAND AND BUILDINGS); or
- there is an increase in the rate of VAT

unless the terms of the lease specifically prevent him from passing on VAT to his tenants.

[*VATA 1994, s 89*].

HMRC do not advise on contracts. (VAT Notice 700, para 30.16).

55.16 **Second-hand goods**

VAT chargeable on the sale of a second-hand article under the Margin Scheme for SECOND-HAND GOODS (61) is calculated by applying the appropriate VAT fraction at the tax point to the VAT-inclusive amount. The tax point is the earlier of the date of removal of the goods and the receipt of payment. If there is a change in the VAT rate before the goods are removed, VAT may be accounted for at the rate in force when the goods are removed even if payment has already been received. (*Note*. A VAT invoice must not be issued for goods supplied under a second-hand scheme). (VAT Notice 700, para 30.17).

55.17 **Warehoused goods**

Imported goods. When imported goods are removed from bonded warehouse for home use, the rate of VAT chargeable is that in force at the time of removal.

Home-produced goods subject to excise duty which have been supplied whilst in warehouse. The rate of VAT chargeable is that in force when the excise duty is paid. For goods relieved of excise duty, the rate of VAT chargeable is that applicable at the time of their removal from warehouse.

(VAT Notice 700, para 30.18).

56 Records

Cross-references. See 17.6 CUSTOMS: POWERS for the production of documents; 40 INVOICES for details to be recorded on sales invoices; 63.5 SPECIAL SCHEMES for records under the cash accounting scheme; 63.21 SPECIAL SCHEMES for records under the flat-rate scheme for small businesses; 63.29 and 63.30 SPECIAL SCHEMES for records and invoices under the flat-rate scheme for farmers.

The contents of this chapter are as follows.

56.1 GENERAL REQUIREMENTS FOR RECORDS BY TAXABLE PERSONS

Every taxable person must keep such records as HMRC may require. [*VATA 1994, Sch 11 para 6(1)*].

Specifically, every taxable person must, for the purposes of accounting for VAT, keep the following records.

- His business and accounting records.
- His VAT account.
- Copies of all VAT invoices issued by him.
- VAT invoices received by him.
- Certificates issued under provisions relating to fiscal or other warehouse regimes.
- Documentation received by him relating to acquisitions of any goods from other EC countries.
- Copy documentation issued by him, and documentation received by him, relating to the transfer, dispatch or transportation of goods by him to other EC countries.
- Documentation relating to importations and exportations by him.
- All credit notes, debit notes and other documents which evidence an increase or decrease in consideration that are received, and copies of all such documents that are issued by him.
- A copy of any self-billing agreement to which he is a party (see 40.6 INVOICES).
- Where he is a customer, party to a self-billing agreement, the name, address and VAT registration number of each supplier with whom he has entered into a self-billing agreement (see 40.6 INVOICES).

[*SI 1995/2518, Reg 31*(*1*); *SI 1996/1250, Reg 8*; *SI 2003/3220, Reg 11*].

Additionally, HMRC may supplement the above provisions by a Notice published by them for that purpose. [*SI 1995/2518, Reg 31*(*2*)]. These requirements, which are contained in VAT Notice 700, Section 19, are considered below in this chapter. They supplement the statutory requirements and *have legal force*.

Business records include, in addition to specific items listed above, orders and delivery notes, relevant business correspondence, purchases and sales books, cash books and other account books, records of daily takings such as till rolls, annual accounts, including trading and profit and loss accounts and bank statements and paying-in slips.

Unless the business mainly involves the supply of goods and services direct to the public and less detailed VAT invoices are issued (see 40.7 INVOICES), all VAT invoices must also be retained. *Cash and carry wholesalers* must keep all till rolls and product code lists.

Records must be kept of all taxable goods and services received or supplied in the course of business (standard and zero-rated), together with any exempt supplies, gifts or loans of goods, taxable self-supplies and any goods acquired or produced in the course of business which are put to private or other non-business use.

All records must be kept up to date and be in sufficient detail to allow calculation of VAT. They do not have to be kept in any set way but must be in a form which will enable HMRC officers to check easily the figures on the VAT return. Records must be readily available to HMRC officers on request. If a taxable person has more than one place of business, a list of all branches must be kept at the principal place of business.

(VAT Notice 700, paras 19.2, 19.4).

Special records. In addition to the above general requirements, special records are necessary where the taxable person is operating the cash accounting scheme (see 63.5 SPECIAL SCHEMES), the flat-rate scheme for farmers (see 63.29 SPECIAL SCHEMES), one of the RETAIL SCHEMES (60) or one of the schemes for SECOND-HAND GOODS (61). These requirements are dealt with in the appropriate chapter. See also 23.28 EUROPEAN COMMUNITY: SINGLE MARKET for the requirement to keep a register of temporary movement of goods to and from other EC countries.

Failure to keep records. Where a business has failed to keep the required records, HMRC's policy is as follows.

- Point out the deficiencies and remind the business of its obligations to keep records under the above provisions.
- Arrange a return visit, giving the business a reasonable amount of time in which to set up the required records.
- Where failure continues and further action is thought necessary, issue a formal warning letter, specifying the deficiencies and explaining the penalties for failure to comply. (HMRC may also, at the same time, put a stop on any VAT repayments until the records are improved.)
- Where, following a further visit, there is still no improvement, serve a formal Notice of Requirement to keep specified records.
- If, after 60 days from the date of issue of the Notice of Requirement, failure continues, issue a Notice of Demand to produce the records on a specified date (unless HMRC already have firm evidence that the records have not been kept, in which case they will proceed to the next stage).

- Where failure still continues, consider civil penalty action. See 52.14 PENALTIES.

(Internal Guidance V1–24B, para 3.3 and Table 3).

De Voil Indirect Tax Service. See V5.201.

56.2 RECORDS BY NON-TAXABLE PERSONS

Non-taxable persons are generally outside the scope of VAT and are not therefore required to keep any records for VAT purposes. However, any person who, at a time when he is not a taxable person, acquires in the UK from another EC country any goods which are subject to excise duty or which consist of a new means of transport must keep such records of the acquisition as HMRC specify in any Notice published by them. [*SI 1995/2518, Reg 31*(*3*)]. See 23.9 and 23.35 EUROPEAN COMMUNITY: SINGLE MARKET.

56.3 PRESERVATION OF RECORDS

Every taxable person must keep and preserve such records as are required for a period of six years or such lessor period as HMRC allow. [*VATA 1994, Sch 11 para 6*(*3*)]. If this causes storage problems or involves undue expense, HMRC should be consulted. They will be able to advise whether some records can be retained for a shorter period. Agreement of HMRC must be obtained before any business records are destroyed within six years. (VAT Notice 700, para 19.2).

HMRC are unlikely to agree to a shorter retention period than

- one year for copies of orders, delivery notes, dispatch notes, goods returned notes, invoices for expenses incurred by employees, production records, stock records (except those for second-hand schemes), job cards, appointment books, diaries, and business letters;
- three years for import, export and delivery from warehouse documents, day books, ledgers, cash books, and second-hand scheme stock books;
- four years for purchase invoices, copy sales invoices, credit notes, debit notes, authenticated receipts, daily gross takings records, records related to retail scheme calculations, and catering estimates; and
- five years for bank statements and paying in books, management accounts, and annual accounts.

Any records containing the VAT account must always be kept for the full six years.

(Internal Guidance V1–24A, para 1.11).

De Voil Indirect Tax Service. See V5.202.

56.4 Forms in which records may be preserved

The duty to preserve records may be discharged by the preservation of the information contained in them by such means as HMRC may approve. [*VATA 1994, Sch 11 para 6*(*4*)]. In addition to the preservation of the full original records, HMRC have approved the use of the following.

- **Microfilm and microfiche** provided that the copies can readily be produced and that there are adequate facilities for HMRC to view when required. Clearance must be obtained in advance from HMRC before any transfer to microfilm or microfiche. HMRC may require the old and new systems to be operated side by side for a limited time.

- **Computer records** provided the storage media eg magnetic tape, disc, etc can readily be converted into a legible form on request by HMRC. Where records are kept on a computer, HMRC can have access to it and can check its operation and the information stored. They can also ask for help from anyone concerned with the operation of the computer or its software. See 17.11 CUSTOMS: POWERS. Where the records are kept by a computer bureau, the taxable person is responsible for arranging for the bureau to make the records available to HMRC when required. Normally this will be at the principal place of business. Where a taxable person decides to use a computer or the services of a bureau for VAT accounting after registration, HMRC should be notified (at the systems design stage or earlier for in-house computers).

(VAT Notice 700, para 19.2).

As a condition of approval HMRC may impose such reasonable requirements as appear to them necessary for securing that the information will be readily available to them as if the original records had been kept. [*VATA 1994, Sch 11 para 6*(*5*)]. HMRC may refuse or withdraw approval for the use of microfilm, etc or computer media in any individual case if their requirements cannot be met.

De Voil Indirect Tax Service. See V5.206; V5.207.

56.5 **RECORDS OF OUTPUT TAX**

Note. The following does not apply to supplies dealt with under one of the special schemes for retailers. For records required in these cases, see 60 RETAIL SCHEMES.

Records must be kept of all supplies made in the course of business including goods sent out on sale or return, approval or similar terms. Information recorded must contain all the information required on VAT invoices. See 40.3 INVOICES. Where fully detailed invoices are issued and filed so as to be readily available, the record required is a summary (in the same order as copy invoices) enabling separate totals to be produced for each VAT period of

(*a*) the amount of VAT chargeable on supplies and acquisitions. The VAT on adjustment for credits allowed (see 56.6 below) should be deducted from the amount of VAT payable in the VAT account (see 56.12 below);

(*b*) the VAT-exclusive value of standard-rated and zero-rated supplies and acquisitions;

(*c*) the value of any exempt supplies and acquisitions; and

(*d*) the amount of VAT due on goods imported by post (other than Datapost) with a value not exceeding £2,000 (see 34.3 IMPORTS) and on certain services received from abroad (see 39.4 INTERNATIONAL SERVICES). These amounts should also be carried to the VAT payable portion of the VAT account (see 56.12 below).

Under (*b*) and (*c*) above, no deduction should be made for *cash* discounts allowed but any credits allowed (see 56.6 below) should be deducted.

Goods given away or put to private or other non-business use. If acquired or produced in the course of business, VAT is due and a record must be kept showing date of transaction, description and quantity of the goods, VAT-exclusive cost and rate and amount of VAT chargeable. See 47.6 and 47.7 OUTPUT TAX for the value of the supply.

Self-supplies. See 45.6 MOTOR CARS for motor cars used by motor manufacturers or dealers who have produced or acquired them in the course of business. Records must show the tax point, value on which VAT is chargeable and the rate and amount of VAT. See 62.2 SELF-SUPPLY for records to be kept by a partly exempt trader who self-supplies certain printed matter.

(VAT Notice 700, para 19.5).

56.6 RECORDS OF CREDITS ALLOWED TO CUSTOMERS

Note. Where a RETAIL SCHEME (60) is used, the following only applies where the credit involves a VAT invoice.

Records must be kept of all credits allowed for taxable (including zero-rated) and exempt supplies and acquisitions. A record of a credit relating to

- **a VAT invoice** must contain the information required on VAT invoices (see 40.3 INVOICES) or indicate (eg by cross-reference to filed copies of credit notes) where the details can be found; and
- **zero-rated or exempt supplies** must show the date and amount of the credit and indicate whether an export is a zero-rated supply in the UK or an exempt supply.

For VAT purposes, where filed copies of credit notes are complete and accessible no separate record need be kept.

(VAT Notice 700, para 19.6).

56.7 RECORDS OF INPUT TAX

EC legislation. See 22.26 EUROPEAN COMMUNITY LEGISLATION.

UK legislation. Records must be kept of all standard-rated, reduced-rated and zero-rated supplies received for business purposes. They must be kept in such a way that, given the invoice date and the supplier's name, they can be easily produced to HMRC.

At the time of claiming input tax deduction, one of the items listed in (*a*)–(*d*) below (as appropriate) must normally be held to support a claim to input tax. HMRC *may*, however, direct that a claimant can hold or provide other evidence (before 16 April 2003, other *documentary* evidence) of the VAT charged. Such a direction may be made generally or in relation to particular cases or classes of cases.

(*a*) **A supplier's invoice**. Subject to below, where the supply is from another UK VAT-registered business, the claimant must hold a 'valid VAT invoice' or a document treated as such (see 40.2 INVOICES). See also 63.30 SPECIAL SCHEMES for invoices from flat-rate farmers. An invoice marked 'pro forma' or 'this is not a VAT invoice' is not acceptable for the purposes of reclaiming VAT.

Exceptions. No VAT invoice is required where total expenditure for each taxable supply is £25 or less (including VAT) and relates to

- telephone calls from public or private telephones;
- purchases through coin-operated machines;
- car park charges (on-street parking meters are not subject to VAT); or

- (from 1 February 2003) a single or return standard-rated toll charge (see 47.8(29A) OUTPUT TAX) paid at the tollbooth. But a VAT invoice is required, irrespective of the price of each individual toll, if
  - (i) a book of toll tickets is purchased; or
  - (ii) a tolled road, bridge or crossing is used under an arrangement where either payment is made in advance (eg where an electronic tag is used) or an invoice is raised in arrears (eg an account customer).

A '*valid VAT invoice*' is one that meets the full requirements in 40.4(*a*)–(*m*) INVOICES or, as the case may be, the reduced requirements in 40.7 to 40.9 INVOICES.

An '*invalid VAT invoice*' is one that does not meet those full requirements. Even if an invoice contains all the information required, it is still invalid if, for example, it relates to a business other than the one making the supply or the details shown relate to a company in liquidation. Some invalidities may be easy to detect (eg whether the goods or services are correctly described) but it may be more difficult to detect a false name, address or VAT number. HMRC have established a team who can confirm that any given VAT registration details are current, valid and match information held by them (tel: 01737 734 516/577/612/761) but this cannot be viewed as authorisation of a transaction with that VAT registration by the supplier in question. The claimant should be able to demonstrate that the person shown as making the supply is the same person who actually made the supply.

A claimant holding an invalid VAT invoice should, wherever possible, ask the supplier to issue a valid VAT invoice. HMRC expect that only a very small number of businesses will be unable to obtain a valid VAT invoice in this way.

Where a valid VAT invoice cannot be obtained, HMRC may apply their discretion and still allow recovery. With effect from 16 April 2003:

(i) For supplies of goods comprising

- computers and any other equipment, including parts, accessories and software, made or adapted for use in connection with computers or computer systems,
- telephones and any other equipment, including parts and accessories, made or adapted for use in connection with telephones or telecommunications,
- alcoholic liquors liable to excise duty which are defined by *Alcoholic Liquor Duties Act 1979, s 1* or in any regulations made under that *Act* (eg spirits, wines and fortified wines, made-wines, beer, cider and perry), and
- oils that are held out for sale as road fuel

claimants will need to be able to answer satisfactorily *all or nearly all* of questions (1)–(6) below (plus any additional questions HMRC ask in individual circumstances, in particular questions to test whether they took reasonable care in respect of transactions to ensure that their supplier and the supply were 'bona fide').

(ii) For supplies of goods falling within (i) above, claimants will need to be able to answer satisfactorily *most* of questions (1)–(6) below. In most cases, this will be little more than providing alternative evidence to show that the supply of goods or services has been made. (This has always been HMRC's policy.)

The questions to determine whether there is a right to deduct in the absence of a valid VAT invoice are as follows.

(1) Does the claimant have alternative documentary evidence other than an invoice (eg a supplier's statement)?

(2) Does the claimant have evidence of receipt of a taxable supply on which VAT has been charged?

(3) Does the claimant have evidence of payment?

(4) Does the claimant have evidence of how the goods/services have been consumed within the business or their onward supply?

(5) How did the claimant know that the supplier existed?

(6) How was the claimant's relationship with the supplier established? For example:

- How was contact made?
- Does the claimant know where the supplier operates from (and has he been there)?
- How does the claimant contact the supplier?
- How does the claimant know the supplier can supply the goods or services?
- If goods, how does the claimant know the goods are not stolen?
- How can faulty supplies be returned?

Incomplete invoices. Normally the invoice or other document should contain the full particulars required for a valid VAT invoice (see above). However, HMRC may accept as satisfactory evidence an invoice complete except for

- an identifying number;
- the customer's name and address; and
- the tax point (provided there is a date which can be taken to be the tax point)

provided the supplies in question are clearly for business purposes.

Originals normally required. VAT invoices held to substantiate claims to input tax should be originals. Copies are not normally accepted.

Where, however, the accounting arrangements require the original VAT invoice to be sent to a destination within the business which is different from the registered address for VAT (eg a branch), HMRC may accept a photocopy of the original as evidence in support of input tax claims provided

- each photocopy is certified by a responsible officer as being a true copy of the original; and
- the original invoice is produced for inspection by HMRC on formal request.

All requirements of a VAT invoice apply to the photocopy. HMRC will notify the business in writing of the conditions and the business must give a written acceptance.

Invoices sent by fax or e-mail. HMRC now accept that, as an alternative to sending VAT invoices by post, they may be sent to customers by fax or e-mail. See 40.14 INVOICES. If the invoice is received via fax and the recipient has a thermal-paper fax machine, the invoice may not be permanent and the recipient may not be able to fulfil the obligation to preserve the invoice for six years.

Cash and carry wholesalers' invoices. If the invoice is only in the form of a till roll with goods represented by product code numbers, an up-to-date copy of the wholesaler's product code list must be kept with the till rolls.

Invoices in name of employees. Certain invoices made out in the name of employees can be accepted as evidence for input tax purposes. See 35.5 INPUT TAX.

Court and tribunal decisions. A claim for input tax has been allowed where invoices were destroyed accidentally (*JJ Newman (VTD 781, VTD 903) (TVC 38.52)*) and where invoices were lost on a change of residence but had previously been checked by the firm's accountants (*Read and Smith (VTD 1188) (TVC 38.54)*). See *Chavda (t/a Hare Wines) (VTD 9895) (TVC 38.9)* where the tribunal held that HMRC had not acted reasonably by refusing to exercise their discretion to accept other documentary evidence (delivery notes) of the input tax incurred by the appellant. However, in the vast majority of tribunal and court decisions, claims for input tax without supporting invoices have been rejected and it has been ruled that *EC 6th Directive, Art 22(3)* confers on countries the power to require production of original invoices (*Reisdorf v Finanzamt Köln-West, CJEC [1997] STC 180 (TVC 21.304)*). Where HMRC refuse to use their discretion to allow credit, tribunals only have a supervisory jurisdiction, the burden of proof being on the appellant to show that HMRC acted unreasonably. See *Kohanzad v C & E Commrs, QB [1994] STC 967 (TVC 38.61)* and the Invoices and Credit Notes chapter in Tolley's VAT Cases.

(*b*) **Evidence of VAT on goods imported or removed from bonded warehouse.** On importation of goods, the claimant must hold a document showing him as importer, consignee or owner and showing an amount of VAT charged on the goods and authenticated or issued by the proper officer. For goods which have been removed from warehouse, the claimant must hold a document authenticated or issued by the proper officer showing the claimant's particulars and the amount of the VAT charged on the goods. See 34.11 IMPORTS for the official evidence (or other acceptable evidence) required which serves the same purpose as a VAT invoice from a registered UK supplier.

(*c*) **Evidence of VAT on goods acquired from another EC country**. On the acquisition of goods from another EC country, the claimant must hold a document required to be issued by the authority in that other country showing the claimant's VAT registration number (including the prefix 'GB'), the registration number of the supplier (including alphabetical code), the consideration for the supply exclusive of VAT, the date of issue of the document and a description of the goods supplied sufficient to identify them. Where the goods are a new means of transport (see 23.31 EUROPEAN COMMUNITY: SINGLE MARKET) the description must be sufficient to identify the acquisition as a new means of transport.

(*d*) **Evidence of services received from abroad**. Where any of the services listed in *VATA 1994, Sch 5* are received from abroad (see 39.4 INTERNATIONAL SERVICES) the relevant invoice from the person supplying the services should be held.

[*SI 1995/2518, Reg 29(2); SI 2003/1114*]. (VAT Notice 700, para 19.7; Internal Guidance V1–13, paras 8.7, 8.8; C & E Statement of Practice (VAT strategy: input tax deduction without a valid invoice), paras 8–3, 17, 18, Appendices 2, 3).

Non-deductible items. VAT is not reclaimable on certain supplies received for the business eg motor cars and entertainment expenses (see 35.8 INPUT TAX for details). However, a record must be kept of such supplies received even though the VAT charged is not to be included in the total carried to the VAT account.

De Voil Indirect Tax Service. See V3.415; V3.421; V3.425–427.

56.8 **Form of records**

Where fully detailed invoices are received and filed so as to be readily available, the record required is a summary (in the same order as the invoices are filed) enabling a separate total to be produced for each VAT period of

(*a*) the amount of VAT charged on goods and services received including any VAT paid at import or on removal from bonded warehouse. Where adjustment is required for credit received from suppliers in the period (see 56.9 below) this should be deducted;

(*b*) the amount of VAT due on any goods imported by post (other than Datapost) with a value of £2,000 or less and on certain services received from abroad (see 39.4 INTERNATIONAL SERVICES);

(*c*) the VAT-exclusive value of all supplies received, including all such goods and services within (*b*) above.

Subject to the normal rules, the total amount of deductible input tax ((*a*) plus (*b*)) should be carried to the VAT allowable portion of the VAT account (see 56.12 below).

Under (*c*) above no deduction for *cash* discounts should be made but all credits received from suppliers should be deducted.

An add-list is an acceptable summary if it shows VAT and values separately itemised in the order in which the VAT invoices are batched or filed. Alternatively, **cashbook accounting for inputs** may be used where it is the normal accounting practice to claim input tax when suppliers are paid. In practice, the cash book payments record is adapted to serve as a record of inputs. On a change in basis of accounting to this method, VAT already claimed on a previous return should be excluded. See also 63.2 SPECIAL SCHEMES.

Note. If any of the RETAIL SCHEMES (60) is used, the cash book can also be used to work out the value of goods received for resale provided amounts owed to suppliers at the beginning of the period are subtracted and amounts owed at the end of the period are added.

(VAT Notice 700, para 19.8).

56.9 RECORDS OF CREDITS RECEIVED FROM SUPPLIERS

Records must be kept of all credits received for taxable (including zero-rated) inputs. A record of a credit relating to

- **a VAT invoice** must contain the information listed in 40.3 *et seq.* INVOICES, or indicate (eg by cross-reference to filed credit notes) where the details can be found; and

- **zero-rated supplies** need only indicate the date and amount of the credit.

For VAT purposes, where filed credit notes are complete and easily accessible, no separate record need be kept.

VAT adjustments. Where a credit is received relating to deductible input tax (see 40.15 INVOICES) and a VAT adjustment has to be made, records of supplies received and input tax must be adjusted. Whatever method is used to do this, the nature of the adjustment and reason for it must be clear from the accounts and supporting documents. At the end of each VAT period the deductible input tax entered in the VAT account and the VAT return entries must be the net amount, ie after deducting any VAT credits received in the period. If VAT credits received from suppliers exceed VAT charged on purchases in any VAT period, a minus figure (shown in brackets) should be entered in the input tax box on the VAT return. Where debit notes are issued to suppliers from whom credit is due and the commercial records are then adjusted, the VAT record may also be adjusted at that time. If later credit notes are received from suppliers, any errors should be corrected but the debit and credit notes should not be both used as accounting documents.

Provided both parties to the transaction agree, the *original* VAT charged need not be adjusted on a debit note issued by a fully taxable person.

(VAT Notice 700, para 19.8).

56.10 ADJUSTMENTS WHERE WRONG AMOUNT OF VAT SHOWN ON VAT INVOICES

Note. This paragraph does *not* apply where there has been a change in the consideration for the supply, ie if the price has changed and consequently the amount of VAT. In these circumstances, see 40.15 INVOICES for the provisions relating to credit and debit notes.

This paragraph explains how to correct an error if the wrong amount of VAT was shown on an invoice, eg where

- an arithmetical mistake is made in calculating the VAT value and/or the VAT element of the supply; or

- VAT is charged on a supply where no VAT was due.

Unless both the supplier and customer agree to adjust their VAT accounts (see below):

(*a*) *If the VAT shown on the invoice is too high,*

- the supplier must account for the higher amount in his records; and

- the customer must only include the amount which should have been charged in his records.

(*b*) *If the VAT shown on the invoice is too low,*

- the supplier must account for the amount which should have charged; and

- the customer must only include the lower amount.

Where the supplier is unwilling or unable to recover the whole of the balance due from the customer, a VAT adjustment, calculated from the total VAT-inclusive amount actually charged, should be made.

Example

	£
Value of goods on VAT invoice	500.00
VAT due = £500 × 17.5% = £87.50 but incorrectly stated as	55.00
Invoiced amount	£555.00
Adjusted VAT due	
£555 × 7/47 (VAT fraction)	82.66
Deduct VAT charged	55.00
Balance payable	£27.66

If both the supplier and the customer agree to adjust their VAT accounts and ensure that adjustment works its way through to the VAT returns, then, provided the error occurred in a VAT period ending in the last three years, either

- the original invoice can be cancelled and the supplier can issued a replacement showing the proper amount of VAT due, if any;
- the supplier can issue a credit note or supplementary VAT invoice to the customer; or
- the customer can issue a debit note to the supplier.

The adjustment should be reflected in an adjusted total of VAT due from or to the business for the VAT period in which the adjustment is made in the accounts. Any document issued by the supplier or customer by way of correction should have a reference to the number and date of the erroneous invoice and show clearly both the correct and incorrect amounts of VAT.

(VAT Notice 700, para 19.10; VAT Notice 700/45/02, paras 3.1–3.4).

De Voil Indirect Tax Service. See V3.518; V3.519.

56.11 VOLUNTARY DISCLOSURE OF ERRORS IN PREVIOUS VAT RETURNS

Consequences of non-disclosure. Errors on returns discovered by HMRC may give rise to a misdeclaration penalty (see 52.10 PENALTIES). To avoid this, any errors discovered should be voluntarily disclosed before HMRC begin to make enquiries (ie normally before an appointment is made to visit and inspect the records). However, a misdeclaration penalty will not normally be imposed where voluntary disclosure is made

- after a visit has been arranged (unless HMRC believe that the errors were discovered earlier and only disclosed because of the proposed visit); or

- during or after a visit (unless HMRC believe that disclosure was prompted by the enquiry).

In addition, deliberate failure to correct an underdeclaration of VAT may give rise to a civil penalty for dishonest evasion (see 52.9 PENALTIES) or criminal prosecution (see 52.2 PENALTIES).

(VAT Notice 700/45/02, para 2.4).

Recording of errors. Any error should be recorded as soon as it is discovered. It may be useful to keep a separate record of errors showing

- the date the error was discovered;
- the period in which it occurred;
- whether it related to output tax or input tax; and
- where the supporting documentation can be found.

Such a record will help decide which is the appropriate method to use when correcting errors (see below).

(VAT Notice 700/45/02, para 4.9).

Method of disclosure. There are two methods of voluntary disclosure. Before deciding which to use, it is necessary to calculate the net value of all errors discovered on previous returns. This is the difference between the total amount of VAT due to HMRC (if any) and the total amount of VAT due from HMRC (if any).

(*a*) **Method 1: for errors not exceeding £2,000**. Where the net value of errors discovered does not exceed £2,000, the VAT account for the period can be adjusted (see 56.12 below) and the value of that adjustment included in the current VAT return. Where errors are adjusted in this way, no default interest will be charged.

(*b*) **Method 2: for errors of any size**. Disclosure can be made on Form VAT 652 or Welsh version Form VAT 652(W) (obtainable from the National Advice Centre (tele: 0845 010 9000)) or by simply writing to the appropriate regional Voluntary Disclosure Team depending upon the postcode of the business. See 56.14 below.

In either case, full details of the errors must be given including

- how each error arose;
- the VAT period in which it occurred;
- if it was an input tax or output tax error;
- the VAT underdeclared or overdeclared in each VAT period;
- how the VAT underdeclared or overdeclared has been calculated;
- whether any of the errors resulted in the business *paying* HMRC an amount of VAT that was not due (in which case see 51.8 PAYMENT OF VAT); and
- the total amount to be adjusted.

Where any error was an amount underdeclared, sufficient detail should be given, on a separate sheet if necessary, to enable HMRC to decide whether interest should be charged.

Interest *may* be charged on underdeclarations made by this method but only where the net value of the errors exceeds £2,000.

Where a voluntary disclosure is made using Method 2, details will be passed to the VAT Central Unit. VAT Central Unit will amend the records of the business and will normally, within 21 days, issue a 'Notice of Voluntary Disclosure' (confirming the amount of the correction and any interest calculated on it) and a 'Statement of Account' (showing the current balance payable to, or repayable by, HMRC. Where, however, the correction generated a repayment which is subject to the unjust enrichment provisions (see 51.9 PAYMENT OF VAT) the business will be notified by letter and will not receive these documents.

Where payment is due to HMRC, full payment should be sent to The Controller, VAT Central Unit, Alexander House, 21 Victoria Avenue, Southend-on-Sea SS9 1AT. Further interest may be charged if the amount due is not paid in full within 30 days from the calculation date shown on the Notice of Voluntary Disclosure. Payment can be made by any of the methods in 51.2 PAYMENT OF VAT. Where repayment is due from HMRC, they will use it to reduce any outstanding balance due to them (if any) and repay the remainder either by BACS or payable order (again subject to the unjust enrichment provisions).

Normally, it is best to wait until the end of the current VAT period before deciding whether Method 1 or Method 2 applies. However, if an individual error is so large that the £2,000 limit will inevitably be breached, a voluntary disclosure using Method 2 can be made immediately.

[*SI 1995/2518, Regs 34, 35; SI 1997/1086, Reg 5*]. (VAT Notice 700/45/02, paras 4.2–4.4, 4.9, 7.1–7.4).

Time limit for corrections. Generally, errors cannot be corrected using Method 1 or 2 above more than three years after the VAT period in which they arose, except that there is no time limit for correcting

- tax point errors (ie where an amount of VAT has been declared on the return which immediately precedes or follows the return for which the amount was due); or
- (before 1 July 2005 only) errors arising from simple duplication of output tax.

[*SI 1995/2518, Reg 34(1A); SI 1997/1086, Reg 5*]. (VAT Notice 700/45/02, para 4.5; Business Brief 27/04).

Voluntary disclosures are not required for adjustments which are not errors but which must be made as part of the normal operation of VAT. These include

- retail scheme annual adjustments or other adjustments required when ceasing to use a particular retail scheme;
- adjustments under the CAPITAL GOODS SCHEME (10);
- use of an approved estimation procedure;
- partial exemption annual adjustments (see 49.9 PARTIAL EXEMPTION);
- partial exemption clawback and payback adjustments (see 49.10 PARTIAL EXEMPTION);

- exports and intra-EC supplies of goods where the necessary evidence of export is not received within the specified time limits (see 25.28 EXPORTS and 23.11 EUROPEAN COMMUNITY: SINGLE MARKET);
- issuing or receiving credit and debit notes (see 40.15 INVOICES);
- claims for BAD DEBT RELIEF (7); and
- adjustments where the wrong amount of VAT has been shown on a VAT invoice (see 56.10 above).

(VAT Notice 700/45/02, para 4.8).

De Voil Indirect Tax Service. See V3.419; V3.506; V5.144.

56.12 VAT ACCOUNT

Every taxable person must keep and maintain an account to be known as the VAT account. It must be divided into separate parts relating to the VAT periods of the taxable person and each part must be divided into two portions known as 'the VAT payable portion' and 'the VAT allowable portion'.

The **VAT payable portion** comprises the following.

- Output tax due from the taxable person for that VAT period.
- Output tax due on acquisitions from other EC countries by the taxable person for that VAT period.
- Corrections to the VAT payable portion of a previous return which may be corrected on the current return (see 56.11 above).
- Subject to the time limit below, a positive/negative entry where there is an increase/decrease in the taxable consideration due on a supply *made* in a previous accounting period. The entry must be made in the return for the period in which the adjustment is given effect in the business accounts (unless the taxable person is insolvent in which case the entry must be made in the return for the period in which the supply was made).

  No adjustment must be made where that increase/decrease occurs more than three years after the end of the VAT period in which the original supply took place. The three-year time limit was upheld in *Valley Chemical Co Ltd (VTD 17989) (TVC 57.27)* but in *General Motors Acceptance Corporation (UK) plc (VTD 17990) (TVC 42.49)* the tribunal held that this requirement infringed a person's basic right to be taxed on the consideration received and was incompatible with *EC Sixth Directive, Art 11* (see 22.14 EUROPEAN COMMUNITY LEGISLATION). The time limit should not prevent adjustments before the first opportunity to make it arose. HMRC have accepted this. (VAT Information Sheet 6/03).

  It is essential that a credit note or debit note is prepared to support the adjustment (see 40.15 INVOICES). It is not possible to adjust the consideration on the original invoice without such a document (*British Telecommunications plc (VTD 14669) (TVC 38.97)*).
- Adjustments to the amount of VAT payable by the taxable person for that VAT period which are required, or allowed, by or under any VAT *Regulations*.

The **VAT allowable portion** comprises the following.

- Input tax allowable to the taxable person for that VAT period.

- Input tax allowable in respect of acquisitions from other EC countries by the taxable person for that VAT period.
- Corrections of the VAT allowable portion of a previous return which may be corrected on the current return (see 56.11 above).
- Subject to the time limit below, a positive/negative entry where there is an increase/decrease in the taxable consideration due on a supply *received* in a previous accounting period. The entry must be made in the return for the period in which the adjustment is given effect in the business accounts (unless the taxable person is insolvent in which case the entry must be made in the return for the period in which the supply was received).

  No adjustment must be made where that increase/decrease occurs more than three years after the end of the VAT period in which the original supply took place.

  It is essential that a credit note or debit note is prepared to support the adjustment (see 40.15 INVOICES).
- Adjustments to the amount of input tax allowable to the taxable person for that VAT period which are required, or allowed, by or under any VAT *Regulations*.

[*SI 1995/2518, Regs 32, 38; SI 1997/1086, Reg 6*].

De Voil Indirect Tax Service. See V5.211.

56.13 AUDIT OF VAT RECORDS

Where a business is subject to an independent audit, the audit will normally cover the VAT account and other records relating to VAT. However, as an auditor's responsibilities normally arise under statute, this does not mean that the auditor must make a specific reference to the VAT records in his report. (VAT Notice 700, para 19.2).

De Voil Indirect Tax Service. See V5.203.

56.14 APPENDIX: ADDRESSES OF REGIONAL VOLUNTARY DISCLOSURE TEAMS

Region	Postcode of business
Central Region Voluntary Disclosure Team, HM Revenue and Customs, Bowman House 100, 102 Talbot Street, Nottingham NG1 5NF Tel: 0115 971 2287	AL, B, CB, CM, CO, CV, CW3, DE, DN10, DN21, DN22, DN36, DN38, DY, EN6–11, HP1–4, HP23, HR, IG7, IG9, IG10, IP, LE, LN, LU, MK40–45, NG, NN, NR, OX17, PE, RM4, RM15–20, S18, S21, S32, S33, S40–45, S80, S81, SG, SK13, SK17, SK22, SK23, SS, ST, SY1–9, SY11–13, TF, WD, WR1–11, WR13–15, WR78, WR99, WS, WV
London Region Voluntary Disclosure Team, HM Revenue and Customs, 365 High Road, Wembley, Middlesex HA9 6AY Tel: 0208 929 1328	BR1–7, CR0, CR2, CR4, CR5, CR, CR9, DA5–8, DA14–18, E, EC, EN1–5, HA, IG1–6, IG8, IG11, KT1–6, KT9, N, NW, RM1–3, RM5–14, SE, SM1–6, SW, TW1–14, UB, W, WC

North Region Voluntary Disclosure Team, HM Revenue and Customs, Peter Bennett House, Redvers Close, Leeds LS16 6RQ Tel: 0113 389 4432	BB, BD, BL, CA, CH1–3, CG41–49, CH60–66, CW1, CW2, CW4–12, DH, DL, DN1–9, DN11–20, DN23–35, DN37, DN39–41, FY, HD, HG, HU, HX, L, LA, LS, M, NE, OL, PR, S1–14, S17, S19–20, S25, S26, S30–31, S35–36, SK1–12, SK14–16, SR, SY14, TD12, TD15, TS, WA, WF, YO
North Wales Voluntary Disclosure Team, HM Revenue and Customs, Eden House, Lakeside, Chester Business Park, Wrexham Road, Chester CH4 9QY Tel: 01244 684248	CH4–8, CH88, CH89, CH99, LD, LL, SY10, SY15–25
Northern Ireland Voluntary Disclosure Team, HM Revenue and Customs, Custom House, Custom House Square, Belfast, Northern Ireland BT1 3ET Tel: 028 90562844/850	BT
Scotland Region Voluntary Disclosure Team, HM Revenue and Customs, 44 York Place, Edinburgh EH1 3JW Tel: 0131 469 7357	AB, DD, DG, EH, FK, G, HS, IV, KA, KW, KY, ML, PA, PH, TD1–11, TD13, TD14, ZE
South Region Voluntary Disclosure Team, HM Revenue and Customs, Merrywalks House, 2 The Hill, Stroud, Glos GL5 1QD Tel: 1453 847785	BA, BH, BN, BR8, BS, CR3, CR6, CT, DA1–4, DA9–13, DT, EX, GL, GU, HP5–22, HP27, KT7, KT8, KT10–24, ME, MK1–19, MK46, OX1–16, OX18, OX20, OX25–OX29, OX33, OX39, OX44, OX49, PL, PO, RG, RH, SL, SM7, SN, SO, SP, TA, TN, TQ, TR, TW15–20, WR12
South Wales Voluntary Disclosure Team, HM Revenue and Customs, Ty Nant, 180 High St, Swansea SA1 5AP Tel: 01792 657349/350	CF, NP, SA

57 Recreation and Sport

Cross-references. See 22.17(*m*) and (*o*) EUROPEAN COMMUNITY LEGISLATION for exemption of certain sporting services supplied by non-profit-making organisations; 35.13(20) INPUT TAX for entitlement to deduct input tax in respect of sporting, recreational and sponsorship activities.

The contents of this chapter are as follows.

57.1 BETTING AND GAMING

EC legislation. See 22.18(*j*) EUROPEAN COMMUNITY LEGISLATION.

UK legislation. The provision of any facilities for the placing of bets or the playing of any 'game of chance' is exempt. There are, however, four important exceptions which are standard-rated.

(*a*) Admission to any premises where betting and gaming takes place.

(*b*) Charges levied under *Gaming Act 1968, s 14* or the *Betting, Gaming, Lotteries and Amusements (NI) Order 1985*.

This covers session and participation charges levied at premises that are either licensed (eg casinos) or registered (eg smaller scale organisations such as social and sports clubs and miner's welfare institutes where betting and gaming is normally confined to members) under *Gaming Act 1968, Part II*.

There are two aspects to participation/session charges.

- Games against the 'house' (eg roulette, blackjack, etc) in which the player pays an amount for the right to take part in betting and gaming. The payment also covers the use of facilities (eg roulette wheel, card tables, etc) for playing the game.
- Games organised by the 'house' where casinos, etc provide facilities for customers to play against each other (eg poker and backgammon). Such games may be held in the form of competitions or tournaments.

Each player is charged an amount to take part that may be described as 'table money', 'session charges or fees' or 'competition fees'. Charges may also be made retrospectively according to time spent at the table. These charges are standard-rated even if the charges make no contribution to casino profits and the money is used wholly or partly to top up the stakes to enhance the prize money/winnings for successful players. See *Rum Runner Casino Ltd (VTD*

1036) (TVC 23.10). HMRC also regard 'buy-ins' (ie where players have lost all their starting chips and have the option under competition rules to purchase further chips in order to continue in the game) as participation fees.

Competitions in card rooms. See VAT Notice 700/57/04 for an agreement between HMRC, the Gaming Board for Great Britain and the British Casino Association regarding competitions in card rooms (including poker and backgammon). Competitions conducted in strict compliance with the agreed guidelines are outside the scope of VAT.

(*c*) Club subscriptions (including those to gaming, bingo and bridge clubs, etc).

(*d*) Gaming machine takings (see 57.3 below).

[*VATA 1994, Sch 9 Group 4 Item 1 and Note* (*1*)]. (VAT Leaflet 701/26/95, paras 3, 6, 10; Internal Guidance V1–7, Chapter 19 Part 1para 3.5).

Games of chance. '*Game of chance*' has the same meaning as in the *Gaming Act 1968, s 52*(*1*) (or the NI equivalent, see (*b*) above). This states that 'game of chance' does not include any athletic game or sport but does include a game of chance and skill combined and a pretend game of chance or of chance and skill combined. For the purposes of determining whether a game, which is played otherwise than against one or more other players, is a game of skill and chance combined, the possibility of superlative skill eliminating the element of chance is to be disregarded.

Basically, therefore, a game of chance is either

- a game of pure chance (eg dice or roulette) where the result cannot be influenced by the player; or
- a game of chance and skill combined (eg whist or rubber bridge) where the player either cannot eliminate chance or can only do so by exercising superlative skill.

See also *W & D Grantham (VTD 853) (TVC 23.12)*.

Included is pool betting and bingo (see 57.2 below). *Not included* are any athletic games or sport or games of skill (eg duplicate bridge and chess).

Spot the ball competition pool betting. If a spot the ball competition is to determine as nearly as possible the actual position of the ball in an original photograph, it is pool betting. A competition decided, however, by reference to the decision of a panel of judges is a game of skill.

(VAT Notice 701/26/04, paras 2.1, 3.1; Internal Guidance V1–7, Chapter 19 Part 1 paras 2.1, 2.2).

Value of the exempt supply. The value of the exempt output is the full amount of stakes or takings less only any money paid out as winnings or, if prizes are goods, their cost (including VAT) to the supplier. Betting or gaming duty is not deductible. (VAT Notice 701/26/04, para 2.3).

Session or participating charges are standard-rated if falling within (*b*) above but otherwise are exempt.

Stake money (ie the amount paid by each player which they risk in the game and is returned in winning to the winning player) is outside the scope of VAT. (Internal Guidance V1–7, Chapter 19 Part 1 para 3.6).

Composite charges covering admission charges, stake money and payments for the provision of facilities for placing bets must be apportioned. (Internal Guidance V1–7, Chapter 19 Part 1 para 3.7).

Small scale gaming. *Gaming Act 1968, s 40* allows small scale gaming at certain clubs and institutes. The maximum participation charge is laid down. Such charges are exempt unless made by a club registered or licensed under *Gaming Act 1968, Part II* when standard-rated (see (*b*) above). (VAT Notice 701/26/04, para 2.4).

Gaming for fund-raising purposes. *Gaming Act 1968, s 41* allows small scale gaming (including bingo, bridge and whist) other than on licensed or registered premises within (*b*) above, but only for fund-raising purposes. The maximum payment to play and the maximum prize money are specified. Any charge to take part in such a game is exempt (apart from admission charges which are always standard-rated). (VAT Notice 701/26/04, para 2.5).

Unlawful gaming. It is unlawful under the *Gaming Act 1968* for gaming to take place unless the organisation providing it is licensed or registered under *Gaming Act 1968, Part II* or comes within the descriptions set out in *Gaming Act 1968, ss 40 or 41* (see above). However, payments connected with gaming that is unlawful under the *Gaming Act* are not unlawful under VAT law. This means that admission charges and subscriptions are always standard-rated and stake money is always outside the scope of VAT. The treatment of session/participation charges depends, however, upon the particular circumstances.

- Where a club is licensed or registered under *Gaming Act 1968, Part II*, the whole of the session/participation fee is excluded from exemption under (*b*) above and standard-rated. HMRC take this view even where the amounts charged exceed the maximum permitted under the *Act* and are therefore illegal.
- Where a gaming club is operating illegally under the *Act* but its session/participation fees satisfy the conditions for exemption under *VATA 1994*, HMRC have been advised that although the fees are unlawful under *Gaming Act 1968*, the charges are exempt under *VATA 1994*.

(Internal Guidance V1–7, Chapter 19 Part 1 paras 5.1, 5.2).

Agent's services. Services of football pools agents, concessionaires and collectors are covered by the exemption for betting and gaming and therefore no VAT is payable on their commission charges. The services of bookmakers who act as agents for other bookmakers or for the Tote in accepting bets, and the services of bookmakers' agents, are also exempt. (VAT Notice 701/26/04, para 2.7; Internal Guidance V1–7, Chapter 19 Part 1 para 1.3).

Use of call centres for telephone betting. In *United Utilities plc v C & E Commrs, CA [2004] STC 727 (TVC 23.19)* the court held that supplies by a company providing call centre services relating to the receipt of telephone bets on behalf of Littlewoods did not qualify for exemption as the provision of betting. The company was providing essentially administrative services for Littlewoods' betting services and in doing so, was not providing them with any facilities for the placing of bets.

Prizes. The following treatment applies.

- Cash prizes are outside the scope of VAT.
- Prizes of goods in free lotteries and as bonus prizes in cash bingo are gifts and VAT is due if the current purchase price exceeds £50 (£15 before 8 March 2001). Prizes of services are outside the scope of VAT. See 47.6 OUTPUT TAX.

- Prizes of goods or services in exempt betting and gaming should be treated as part of the exempt supply. Output tax is not due but the input tax on purchase is not deductible (subject to the partial exemption *de minimis* limits).
- Where prizes of goods or services are given in taxable competitions (eg spot the ball) no further VAT is due.

(VAT Notice 701/26/04, para 4.1).

Payments made by bookmakers attending greyhound and horse racecourses.

(*a*) *Badge money*. This is an admission charge paid by on-course bookmakers attending greyhound racetracks and horse racecourses which entitles them to stand and take bets at the track. Under *Betting, Gaming and Lotteries Act 1963, s 18*(*1*) the amount must not exceed five times the normal charge made to the public for their admittance to that part of the stadium. Badge fees paid at greyhound tracks are normally standard-rated because the bookmaker is not granted a specific site on which to stand. However, at horse racecourses a bookmaker is normally granted the right to occupy a specific site in an enclosure in return for the payment. In such cases, the payment is exempt as the grant of a licence to occupy land (subject to the option to tax being exercised).

(*b*) *Tober money*. This is an amount of money paid by bookmakers which is in excess of the maximum amount under (*a*) above and is normally allocated to prize money by the course management. As the payments would be illegal if they were part of the admission charge, HMRC accept that they can be treated as voluntary donations and outside the scope of VAT, provided

- the payments are entirely voluntary and at the discretion of the bookmaker as to the amount and frequency: and
- the bookmaker does not receive any publicity or other advantage in return for the payment.

HMRC have agreed with the National Greyhound Racing Club that a statement in the programme such as 'The … Stadium on-course bookmakers have contributed the whole/part of the prize money for this meeting' would not be regarded as publicity. However, the mention of an individual bookmaker's name would be regarded as publicity and would make the payments standard-rated.

(Internal Guidance V1–7, Chapter 19 Part 1 para 6.5).

Betting and gaming duties. For information, see the following Customs Notices available from Excise offices: pool betting duty (147); general betting duty (off course) (451); gaming licence duty (453); general betting duty (on course) (455).

De Voil Indirect Tax Service. See V4.131.

57.2 **Bingo**

Stake money (ie the amount risked by a player in the game, all of which is returned as winnings to the winning player(s)) is outside the scope of VAT and no VAT is due on the amount received.

Prize bingo. This can be played on any premises. Prizes are generally not in cash but the following monetary limits apply.

- The maximum individual stake per person is 50p.

- The total value of all prizes must not exceed £120 per game.
- Cash prizes must not exceed a maximum of £15 per game.

Session and participating charges (ie charges for the right to take part in the game) are exempt. [*VATA 1994, Sch 9 Group 4 Item 1*]. This applies even if the charges exceed the maximum permitted under law. Prizes given are not a separate supply for VAT purposes and are part of the exempt supply. VAT need not be accounted for on goods given as prizes.

The value of the exempt supply of session and participation charges is the total amount charged to play bingo less the VAT-inclusive cost of the goods given as prizes. The following calculation should be used for each VAT period.

Step 1	Add up gross session and participation charges including any prize vouchers used to pay for further games of bingo. Do not deduct any bingo duty payable	A
Step 2	Calculate	
	The VAT-inclusive cost of goods and vouchers given as prizes (where vouchers are redeemed against goods, the value of the goods should be used not the face value of the vouchers)	B
	The value of any cash prizes. Do not include any participation charges used as additional prize money	C
	Payments made to retailers who redeem prize vouchers for goods	D

Exempt output = A – (B + C + D)

Admission charges are standard-rated. See 57.6 below.

Cash bingo.

Session and participating charges (ie charges for the right to take part in the game). The VAT liability depends on the premises.

(*a*) Where cash bingo is played for cash prizes on premises licensed or registered under *Gaming Act 1968, Part II* (or *Betting, Gaming, Lotteries and Amusements* (*Northern Ireland*) *Order 1985, Chapter III*), any session and participating charges are excluded from exemption by *VATA 1994, Sch 9 Group 4 Note* (*1*) and are standard-rated.

(*b*) Where small scale cash bingo is played on premises not licensed or registered as under (*a*) above, there is a maximum participation charge of 60p per day which is exempt from VAT.

The value of the session and participation charges for each VAT period is calculated as follows.

Step 1	Add up total value of charges made for session and participation charges and stake. Do not deduct any bingo duty	A
Step 2	Add up the value of stake money given back to players as prizes. This is the value of stake money received. Do not include any participation charges used as additional prize money	B

Value of session and participation charges = A – B

Admission charges are standard-rated. See 57.6 below.

Bonus prizes in games of cash bingo are gifts and VAT must be accounted for on the current purchase price where this is more than £50 (£15 before 8 March 2001) excluding VAT.

Fund-raising bingo. This is bingo played at functions (eg fêtes, dances, etc) where all proceeds are devoted to purposes other than private gain.

Session and participating charges are exempt. The following monetary limits apply.

- One payment of entrance fee or stake of not more than £4 is made by each player.
- The total value of prizes must not exceed £400 for a one day event or £700 for events covering more than one day.

Composite bingo charges. Where a single charge is made to each player covering stake money, session and participation charges and possibly admission fee, the total charge must be apportioned and the correct VAT liability applied to each part. The value of any amount due for admission (standard-rated) must be calculated first and then the session and participation charges must be worked out using the appropriate method detailed above.

It may be difficult to determine whether a component part of the charge is stake money or a participation fee subsequently used to top-up prizes to the winning players. (The distinction is important because if a charge is liable to VAT as a participation fee it may also become liable to bingo duty when returned as additional prize money that exceeds the stakes risked in the game.) See the conflicting tribunal decisions in *Fakenham Conservative Association Bingo Club (VTD 76) (TVC 23.7)* and *WMT Entertainments Ltd (VTD 9385) (TVC 23.9)*.

Multiple and linked bingo is where two or more clubs join together with others to play for collective stakes of members in a telephone link to play a single simultaneous game. Each club must account for VAT on admission and session and participation charges at its own premises in the normal way. The money sent to the organiser for prize money is treated as stake money and is outside the scope of VAT.

Instant, parti and mechanised bingo. These may be played as an interval game and become operative when a coin is inserted. The participating charges retained by the club, etc follows the normal VAT liability of the bingo game being played. The balance which is then paid out in prizes is treated as stake money and is outside the scope of VAT.

(VAT Notice 701/27/02).

Unlawful bingo. Services supplied in connection with bingo that are unlawful under the *Gaming Act 1968* or the *Betting, Gaming, Lotteries and Amusements* (*Northern Ireland*) *Order 1985* should be treated for VAT purposes as if they were legal. Stake money is always outside the scope of VAT and admission charges and subscriptions are always standard-rated. The treatment of session and participation charges depends, however, upon the particular circumstances.

- Where premises are licensed or registered under *Gaming Act 1968, Part II* or *NI Order, Chapter III* but amounts charged are illegal as exceeding the maximum allowed under those provisions, the whole of the session/participation fee is treated in the same way as if it were legal, ie standard-rated as under (*a*) above.
- Where premises should be licensed or registered under those provisions but are not, session/participation charges are exempt (whereas they would have been excluded from exemption and standard-rated if the premises had been legally licensed or registered).

(Internal Guidance V1–7, Chapter 19 Part 3 paras 3.1–3.3).

57.3 Gaming and amusement machines

The provision of a 'gaming machine' is specifically excluded from the general exemption from VAT applying to betting and the playing of games of chance (see 57.1 above). The takings from gaming machines (and 'amusement machines' generally) are therefore standard-rated. Note that the provisions of *VATA 1994, s 23* below do not apply to the Isle of Man. [*IMA 1979, s 1(d)*]. Where gaming machine takings would also qualify for exemption by satisfying the requirements for being a lottery under 57.4 below, it has been held that to exempt the supply would defeat the legislative intent (*McCann (t/a Ulster Video Amusements) (VTD 2401) (TVC 23.14)*).

Definition of a gaming machine. '*Gaming machine*' means a machine which satisfies each of the following criteria.

- It is 'constructed or adapted' for playing a game of chance by means of it. See 57.1 above for the definition of game of chance. The most common example of games that are solely of chance are those played on 'one-armed bandits' or 'fruit machines'. 'Constructed or adapted' means originally constructed or subsequently altered. See *Backer v Secretary of State for the Environment [1983] 2 All ER 1021.*
- A player pays to play the machine (except where he has an opportunity to play payment-free as the result of having previously played successfully) either by inserting a coin or token into the machine or in some other way. 'In some other way' includes giving cash to the machine operator who 'clocks up' credits on the machine or the player using a card similar to a credit or phone card.
- The element of chance must be provided by means of the machine.

Gaming machines include 'amusement with prizes' machines, jackpot machines, crane grab machines, pin tables and 'penny fall' machines. It should be noted that, if a machine satisfies the above requirements, it is a gaming machine whether or not any winnings are obtainable from it.

[*VATA 1994, s 23(4), Sch 9 Group 4 Note (3)*]. (VAT Notice 701/13/04, para 2.1; Internal Guidance V1–7, Chapter 19 Part 2 paras 3.3, 3.4, 3.6, 3.7).

Meaning of an amusement machine. An '*amusement machine*' can be either of the following.

- A machine on which there is no prize in any circumstances. Such a machine may not only be an amusement machine but also a gaming machine. A machine within this category would be one that provides a player with a game of chance but which gives no reward to successful players, eg a pinball machine that did nothing more than record highest scores.
- A 'skill with prizes' machine, ie a machine where the prize depends on the skill or knowledge of the player and is not dependent on chance (eg a general knowledge quiz).

'Entertainment only' machines, including juke boxes, pool tables and video games (other than video poker games) are amusement machines for VAT purposes.

(VAT Notice 701/13/04, para 2.2; Internal Guidance V1–7, Chapter 19 Part 2 Annex A).

Place of supply. Supplies of services consisting of enabling the public to use gaming machines in amusement arcades are regarded as entertainment or similar activities within *EC Sixth Directive, Art 9(2)(c)*, so that the place of supply is where the services are physically carried out (*RAL (Channel Islands) Ltd v C & E Commrs (and related appeals), CJEC Case C–452/03, [2005] All ER(D) 171 (May) (TVC 21.145A)*). The equivalent UK provisions are in *SI 1992/3121, Art 15* (see 64.23 SUPPLY).

Hiring of machines. Hire charges, whether for a fixed rental or a share of the profits, are standard-rated. (VAT Notice 701/13/04, para 3.2).

Site rentals. Charges for siting machines are standard-rated. (VAT Notice 701/13/04, para 3.2). This follows the decision in *Sinclair Collis Ltd v C & E Commrs, CJEC [2003] STC 898 (TVC 21.235)* where the court held that the grant by the owner of premises to the owner of a cigarette vending machine

- of the right to install the machine and to operate and maintain it on the premises
- in a place nominated by the owner of the premises
- in return for a percentage of the gross profits on the sales of cigarettes
- but with no rights of possession or control being granted to the machine owner other than those expressly set out in the agreement between the parties

did not amount to the letting of immovable property and was therefore standard-rated. Before the decision in *Sinclair Collis*, Customs took the view that such rentals were exempt under *VATA 1994, Sch 9 Group 1* as a supply of a licence to occupy land (see 42.2 LAND AND BUILDINGS) although the supplier could opt to tax the supply (see 42.8 LAND AND BUILDINGS). Standard-rating must in all cases be applied to such supplies from 1 January 2004 although site owners could apply the change earlier if they wished. (Business Brief 18/03).

Accounting for VAT on machine takings. VAT on the takings must be accounted for by the person who supplies the use of the machine to the public. This is normally the person who exercises day-to-day control over the operation of the machine and is entitled to the takings, ie the person who controls the premises on which the machine is sited, allows access to the public and has the right to refuse to allow any person to play any particular machine.

(*a*) *In respect of gaming machines*, this is

- for licensed commercial gaming premises, the holder of the licence issued under *Gaming Act 1968, Part II* or that person's employee;
- for registered clubs or miners' institutes, any officer or member of the club or institute, or any person employed by them;
- for travelling pleasure fairs, the showman who owns or operates the fair;
- for public houses, cafes, amusement arcades, etc, the person named on the permit issued under *Gaming Act 1968, Part III*; and
- for an unlicensed gaming machine, normally the person who controls its operation, but the supply will depend on the particular arrangements in each case. See also *R v Ryan & Others, CA [1994] STC 446 (TVC 47.18)* where, in a criminal prosecution, the machine owners were held to be liable to account for VAT on the unlawful operation of unlawful credit gaming machines.

(*b*) *In respect of amusement machines*, this is

- the site operator (if the machine is purchased, hired or rented by the occupier of the premises on which it is sited); or
- the owner of the machine (where the owner pays a rent to the occupier of the premises on which the machine is sited).

If the machine is operated on a profit-sharing basis, the supplier of its use to the public is the person who controls its operation.

(VAT Notice 701/13/04, para 4.1; Internal Guidance V1–7, Chapter 19 Part 2 para 5.1).

Examples of supplies between machine owners and site occupiers

	Supply/accounting for VAT
Gaming/amusement machine supplied to a brewery with a managed pub	Machine owner makes a standard-rated supply of hire of the machine to the brewery and accounts for VAT on the hire charge Brewery makes a standard-rated supply of use of the machine to the public and accounts for VAT on the machine takings
Gaming/amusement machine is supplied to the tenant of a brewery-owned pub	Machine owner makes a standard-rated supply of hire of the machine to the tenant and accounts for VAT on the hire charge Tenant makes a standard-rated supply of use of the machine to the public and accounts for VAT on the machine takings Brewery makes a standard-rated supply of a licence to trade to the tenant to site the machine on its premises and accounts for VAT on the charge for siting the machine
Owner of a gaming/amusement machine pays rent (eg a fixed sum or share of the profits) to a brewery with a managed or tenanted pub	The brewery makes a standard-rated supply of a licence to trade to the machine owner in allowing the machine to be sited on its premises and accounts for VAT on the charge for siting the machine The machine owner makes a standard-rated supply of the use of the machine to the public and accounts for VAT on the machine takings

Calculation of VAT due. The tax point for supplies made from coin-operated machines is the date the machine is used. However, as an administrative convenience, operators may delay accounting for VAT until the takings are removed from the machine. (VAT Notice 48, ESC 3.6). For all other purposes, the normal tax point rules apply. Therefore, in the event of a theft of takings from a machine, VAT must still be accounted for in full on any supplies that have been made from the machine. (VAT Notice 701/13/04, para 4.7).

Taxable take of a gaming machine. Whenever cash or tokens are removed from the machine, the 'taxable take' must be calculated and recorded. '*Taxable take*' is the amount paid by persons to play the game less the amount (if any) received by persons playing successfully (other than the person making the supply and persons acting on his behalf). [*VATA 1994, s 23(1)(2)*]. Included is any money in the 'tubes' in excess of the float. Any foreign coins, fakes or facsimiles inserted may be disregarded. In practice, when the machine is opened, the float should be restored to its original level with cash and tokens taken from the machine. The balance of coins and tokens remaining in the machine is then the taxable take upon which VAT is due. VAT is calculated by applying the VAT fraction (currently 7/47) to this amount. No deduction must be made for hire or rental charges to the machine owner; any share of profits or other charge due to another person; any payments made out of the takings such as those under maintenance contracts; or gaming machine licence duty. See also *HJ Glawe Spiel-und Unterhaltungsgeräte Aufstellungsgesellschaft mbH & Co KG v Finanzamt Hamburg-Barmbek-Uhlenhorst, CJEC [1994] STC 543 (TVC 21.165)* where it was held that the taxable amount did not include the prescribed proportion of the coins inserted which had, by statute, to be paid out as winnings.

Usually the taxable take should be calculated for each individual machine. However, in the case of an amusement arcade with large numbers of machines, HMRC may give approval to the calculation on a site-wide basis.

(VAT Notice 701/13/04, paras 4.2, 4.4, 7).

Taxable take for amusement machines. The provisions of *VATA 1994, s 23* above do not apply to an amusement machine unless it is also a gaming machine. For an amusement machine which falls outside those provisions, VAT is normally due on a gross basis, ie all the money put into the machine by players. However, in the case of a 'skill with prizes' machine, HMRC permit a business to account for output tax on a 'net take' basis as if *VATA 1994, s 23* did apply in order to ensure parity of treatment with gaming machine operators. (Internal Guidance V1–7, Chapter 19 Part 2 para 1.1, Annex A).

Negative machine takings and top-ups by traders. It is possible that a sequence of large payouts may exhaust a gaming machine's float and a player's prize has to be 'topped-up' with cash from other sources. In such an event

- cash given to the player should not be deducted from the source from which it has been obtained (eg if a player is given £50 from the bar takings, these should not be reduced by the £50);
- a record should be kept of any sums paid out as prizes and, when the machine is opened, it is permissible for the cash takings within the machine to be reduced by the total of manual pay-outs made; and
- if the amount paid out manually, together with the amount needed to refill the float, equals or exceeds the reservoir of cash within the machine, the trader is entitled to a credit because of the overall negative take position that has arisen.

HMRC are, however, likely to look closely at any recurrence of a loss takings position.

(Internal Guidance V1–7, Chapter 19 Part 2 para 6.4).

See also *Feehan v C & E Commrs, QB 1994, [1995] STC 75 (TVC 23.16)*. The wording of the legislation contemplates payment for playing by insertion of a token 'into the machine' but there is no such restriction on the receipt of winning being 'from a machine'. In that case, the court therefore upheld the tribunal's decision that the value of the supply was the net amount of receipts after deducting winnings paid to players by the publican.

Tokens. The insertion of a token into a machine should be treated as the payment of an amount equal to that for which the token can be obtained. [*VATA 1994, s 23*(*3*)].

Replayable tokens. The receipt of a replayable token (ie those that can be used to play the machine) by a person playing successfully is treated as the receipt of an amount equal to its cash value. [*VATA 1994, s 23*(*3*)]. This value can be established by reference to the charge for playing the machine. For example, if a machine can be operated by the insertion of 20p cash or a token to obtain a single game, then that token would have a value of 20p. In calculating the taxable take, it is simplest, therefore, to regard replayable tokens as if they were coins of a particular denomination. Where, however, a machine has a facility for the site occupier or machine owner to insert tokens to refill the float without opening the machine, any tokens inserted in this fashion are outside the scope of VAT and can be omitted from the total when the taxable take is calculated.

Where replayable tokens are exchanged for prize goods, this exchange transaction is a separate supply for VAT purposes and should be treated as a supply of the goods by way of normal retail sale. If the business also sells the goods to the public, the value of the supply is its normal retail selling price of the goods; if it does not, the value is the equivalent cash value of the tokens that is taken in exchange. Input tax incurred on the purchase of the prize goods is deductible (subject to the normal rules).

(VAT Notice 701/13/04, para 4.3; Internal Guidance V1–7, Chapter 19 Part 2 paras 7.1–7.3).

Non-replayable tokens. These are tokens that are awarded by machines but which cannot be used to play them. Their treatment for VAT purposes depends upon whether or not they have a recognised cash value.

- Where non-replayable tokens have a recognised cash value (ie they can be exchanged for cash or goods that the business also sells) they should be treated in the same way as replayable tokens. [*VATA 1994, s 23*(*3*)].
- Where non-replayable tokens have no recognised cash value (ie they are only exchangeable for goods not sold by the business) the machine's taxable take is determined solely by its cash takings. If the machine only awards non-replayable tokens, the taxable take is all the cash that players have put into the machine; if it awards both cash and non-replayable tokens, the taxable take is determined by applying the taxable take rules above to the cash take only. No deduction should be made from machine takings for tokens awarded by the machine, tokens used to restore the machine's float or prizes given in exchange for the tokens. When these tokens are exchanged for goods, however, the business is not required to account for VAT upon the exchange transaction (as it has already effectively been accounted for on the value of the goods because there has been no reduction of the machine's taxable take to allow for this).

(VAT Notice 701/13/04, para 4.3; Internal Guidance V1–7, Chapter 19 Part 2 paras 7.4–7.6).

Retail schemes. Treatment of gaming and amusement machine takings depends on the scheme used.

- Under the Point of Sale scheme, taxable take of the machine should be added to standard-rated daily gross takings on the day the cash and/or tokens are removed.
- Under an apportionment scheme, takings should be excluded from daily gross takings and VAT calculated outside the scheme as explained above.

- Under a direct calculation scheme,
  - (i) where minority goods are zero-rated or reduced rate goods, taxable take of the machine should be added to daily gross takings on the day the cash and/or tokens are removed; and
  - (ii) where minority goods are standard-rated or lower-rated, takings should be excluded from daily gross takings and VAT calculated outside the scheme as explained above.

  (VAT Notice 701/13/04, para 4.6).

Prizes. Machine prizes (eg from a crane grab machine) are treated as business gifts and VAT need not be accounted for on the value if costing £50 or less (£15 or less before 8 March 2001). (VAT Notice 701/13/04, para 4.5). See 47.6 OUTPUT TAX. See above for the VAT treatment of prize goods exchanged for tokens.

Amusement machine licence duty. This is outside the scope of VAT if either the licence is obtained by the occupier of the premises where the machine is sited or the machine owner obtains the licence on behalf of the site occupier and itemises its cost separately on the invoice for the machine. However, if the gaming machine supplier charges for the supply of a licensed machine, the cost of obtaining the licence is part of a single supply of a gaming machine, and the whole amount is standard-rated. (VAT Notice 701/13/04, para 4.8).

For details of amusement machine licence duty, see Customs Notice 454.

De Voil Indirect Tax Service. See V4.131.

57.4 LOTTERIES

EC legislation. See 22.18(*j*) EUROPEAN COMMUNITY LEGISLATION.

UK legislation. The granting of a right to take part in a lottery is exempt. [*VATA 1994, Sch 9 Group 4 Item 2*]. Exemption essentially covers the sale of the lottery tickets to the public as these acknowledge that a right to participate has been granted to the participants. If the lottery is free to enter, there is no exempt supply (but see below for prizes given in free lotteries).

The value of the exempt supply is the gross proceeds from ticket sales *less* the cash prizes given or the cost (inclusive of VAT) of the goods given as prizes.

There is no statutory definition of 'lottery'. In *Readers Digest Association Ltd v Williams, [1976] 1 WLR 1109* it was defined as 'the distribution of prizes by chance where the persons taking part in the operation, or a substantial number of them, make a payment or consideration in return for obtaining their chance of a prize'. This includes the playing of on-line interactive lottery games. If any merit or skill plays a part in determining the outcome, the event is not a lottery but a competition.

Types of lawful lotteries. The promotion of lotteries is only lawful in the specified circumstances set out in the *Lotteries and Amusement Act 1976* or, for local authorities, the *Lotteries Regulations 1977*.

(*a*) Under the *Lotteries and Amusement Act 1976* lotteries can be run by, or on behalf of, societies that are established wholly or mainly for

- charitable purposes;
- participation in support of athletic sports or games or cultural activities; or

- other purposes which are neither for private gain nor a commercial undertaking.

The society must nominate and authorise in writing an individual member to be the promoter of the lottery (although the exempt supply is still treated as having been made by the society).

If the society sets up a separate development association or other organisation to promote its lottery, it is that association which makes the exempt supply. The payment of the net proceeds of the lottery by that association to the society is outside the scope of VAT and any expenses relating to the lottery, where these are deductible, cannot be reclaimed by the society as its input tax.

See below for the use of a separate lottery management company.

(*b*) Local authorities can promote lotteries under the *Lotteries Regulations 1977*. Such lotteries are treated in the same way as those run by societies and thus in the course of their business activities. A local authority proposing to run a lottery should contact the National Advice Service (0845 010 9000) to discuss the circumstances, with particular regard to the amount of input tax that the authority will be entitled to deduct.

(*c*) Private lotteries which are promoted by and on behalf of people who all work or live together at the same place.

(*d*) Small lotteries, with prizes in kind, which are run incidental to entertainments such as bazaars, dances or fêtes.

(*e*) The National Lottery is regulated by the National Lottery Commission and is the only lottery of its kind that may legally be run in the United Kingdom.

Lottery duty. Most lotteries falling within (*a*)–(*d*) above (but not the National Lottery under (*e*) above) are exempt from lottery duty. See Customs Notice 458 *Lottery duty* for further information.

Lottery management companies. A '*lottery management company*' is an individual, partnership or limited company that supplies lottery management services to the promoter (ie a society, development association or local authority). This service is usually comprehensive and may include arranging for printing of tickets, organising publicity, arranging ticket sales and paying out prizes. A lottery management company cannot promote a lottery.

The supply of lottery management services is standard-rated and VAT must be accounted for on

- any fee or commission paid by the lottery promoter, *plus*
- any additional amounts retained from gross ticket sales to cover the cost of running the lottery, *plus*
- any commission received and retained by selling agents used by the lottery management company

less the amount paid out in cash prizes by the management company (or the VAT-inclusive cost of goods given as prizes).

However, if a lottery management company also sells tickets itself using its own outlets and employees (rather than merely arranging for their sale by independent sellers), it can exempt this direct selling service like any other ticket seller (see below). If the company does not specify a separate charge for its own selling service, it must apportion its global charge to the promoter between exempt and standard-rated supplies. The exempt element must be shown separately on the VAT invoice. See 47.3 OUTPUT TAX for apportionment of consideration.

Where a lottery is run on behalf of a charity, it may be possible to argue that part of the charge represents zero-rated advertising supplied to the charity provided

- there is a clearly identifiable and severable supply of advertising to the charity; and
- this separate advertising supply satisfies the criteria for zero-rating (see 12.7 CHARITIES).

Lottery ticket sellers. The service of selling lottery tickets is an exempt supply but it is important to know in what capacity a person is selling the tickets in order to establish who is to be attributed with the receipt of the income from the ticket sales.

- *If the seller is an employee of a lottery management company*, that company is supplying the exempt service and can apportion that part of its charges to the promoter which can be attributed to this exempt service (see above).
- *If the seller is an independent selling agent*, the seller's exempt output is the fee or commission the seller receives plus any other amounts which the seller is entitled to deduct or retain from the ticket sales. Where this service is provided to a lottery management company, these retained commissions are still to be included as part of the value of the company's standard-rated management service.

  If a ticket seller is a retailer using one of the retail schemes, the exempt outputs must be excluded from scheme calculations. Also, any money taken from ticket sales and included in daily gross takings must be excluded before making the scheme calculations.
- *If the seller is acting as a principal* (eg where a retailer buys tickets from the lottery management company or promoter and sells them on to the public at a higher price), the ticket seller's exempt income is the money received from sales of tickets less any prizes he pays. In such circumstances, the lottery management company need not treat the monies retained by the ticket seller as part of the value of its taxable management services and the moneys received by it from the ticket seller are exempt output of the company.

The status of the ticket seller will depend upon the contract or other written agreement made between the ticket seller and the lottery management company or promoter.

Treatment of prizes. Prizes given in lotteries where participants have paid to enter are regarded as an integral part of the supply of the right to participate in a lottery. No output VAT is due on their award. See below, however, for free lotteries. Any VAT incurred on purchasing prizes can be deducted as input tax subject to the normal partial exemption rules.

No VAT is due on prizes of services.

Free lotteries. If a lottery is free to enter, there is no exempt supply. Any goods given as prizes should be treated as business gifts and VAT must be accounted for on the VAT-exclusive cost if the prize exceeds £50 (£15 before 8 March 2001) (see 47.6 OUTPUT TAX). Input tax is then deductible in the normal manner. However, it should be noted that

- VAT incurred on holidays provided as prizes cannot be reclaimed (under the business entertainment provisions); and
- where a motor car is given away as a prize,
  - (i) input tax can only be reclaimed if the car is not made available for private use before it is given away; and
  - (ii) if VAT can be reclaimed on the purchase, output tax must be declared on the VAT-exclusive cost of the car when it is given away.

  Any input tax claimed will be subject to the partial exemption rules.

(VAT Notice 701/28/03; Internal Guidance V1–7 Chapter 19 Part 4 paras 2.1, 2.4, 3.2, 4.2).

De Voil Indirect Tax Service. See V4.131.

57.5 SPORTS AND PHYSICAL RECREATION COMPETITIONS

EC Legislation. See 22.17(*m*) EUROPEAN COMMUNITY LEGISLATION.

Entry fees. An entry fee for the right to enter a 'competition' is normally standard-rated. However, the grant of a right to enter a competition in 'sport or physical recreation' is exempt in the following circumstances.

(*a*) Where the entry fee is money which is allocated *wholly* towards the provision of a prize or prizes awarded in that competition. [*VATA 1994, Sch 9 Group 10 Item 1; SI 1999/1994*]. This exemption applies whatever the status of the entity granting the right of entry. If all or any of the entry fees are carried forward as prizes in other competitions, the entry fee for the original competition is outside the scope of the exemption and standard-rated. The introduction of other income to the entry fees of later competitions does not, of itself, prevent those later fees from being exempt.

(*b*) Where the grant is made by an 'eligible body' established for the purposes of sport or physical recreation. [*VATA 1994, Sch 9 Group 10 Item 2; SI 1999/1994*]. See 57.9 below for the definitions of '*eligible body*'. Exemption does not, however, apply to competitions organised by local authorities because providing such competitions is not the sole basis of their existence and they are therefore not *established* for that purpose.

Entry fees to horse races governed by the Jockey Club rules are outside the scope of VAT, although 'entry receiving fees' are standard-rated as the supply of administrative services by the Jockey Club.

HMRC define '*competition*' as meaning 'a structured and organised contest, tournament or race where prizes or titles are awarded. The prizes may consist of money, goods, a cup or a trophy.' This definition was supported by the tribunal in *Wimborne Rugby Football Club (VTD 4547) (TVC 23.20).*

'*Sports or physical recreation*' is not defined in the legislation but includes all the activities listed in 57.11 below. Physical recreation activities such as greyhound/pigeon racing, clay pigeon shooting and darts are also included. *Not included* are activities such as chess, card games, dominoes, and spot the ball and other newspaper competitions. Where animals are involved, it is important to distinguish between animal shows (which are outside the exemption) and activities which qualify as sport or physical recreation, such as a competition where the animals are assessed wholly or partially upon their sporting abilities, eg jumping and racing. Where an entry fee covers both (eg pony shows involving examining the animals and jumping classes) the fee can be apportioned.

Value of the exempt supply. This is normally the full amount of entry fees (without deduction for amounts returned as prizes). However, it is only the supply of the right to enter the competition that is exempt. Where the 'entry fee' includes elements that are standard or zero-rated supplies, it is necessary to decide whether a single or multiple supply is being made. See 64.6 SUPPLY. HMRC appear to accept the latter and to allow apportionment where non-essential standard-rated goods and services (eg buffet lunches during a golf competition) are supplied and where zero-rated supplies are provided.

Prizes. The VAT position of prizes awarded to competitors is the same whether the entry fees are exempt or standard-rated.

- *Prizes in the form of goods* (eg sports equipment, trophies that are owned permanently by the winner). These are treated as business gifts. No VAT is due on individual prizes costing £50 or less. Where the goods cost more than that amount, VAT must be accounted for on the cost of the goods (and input tax incurred on the purchase can be deducted). See 47.6 OUTPUT TAX.
- *Prizes in the form of services* (eg holidays). Where input tax has been claimed on the purchase of the services given away as prizes, an equal sum of output tax is due at the time the prize is awarded. If no input tax is incurred, no output tax is due.
- *Prizes in the form of cash*. Cash prizes for being successful in a particular competition are outside the scope of VAT. The fact that an individual makes a living from prize money does not affect the position. However, prize money must be distinguished from guaranteed prize money and appearance money (see below).
- *Loans of challenge cups, shields and other perpetual trophies* which remain the property of the organisation or club mounting the competition is a supply of services but, because there is no consideration, the supply is outside the scope of VAT. The outright gift of cups, etc is generally a prize in the form of goods (see above). See also, however, *C & E Commrs v Professional Footballers' Association (Enterprises) Ltd, HL [1993] STC 86 (TVC 65.9)* where it was held that the consideration for trophies presented at a dinner were included in the price of the tickets on which the company had accounted for VAT.

Guaranteed payments and appearance money. Where competitors are paid by the promoter or organiser to take part in an event, the payment is the consideration for the standard-rated supply of the individual's services. Where individuals are guaranteed a participation payment or they negotiate individually a guaranteed amount (even if this depends on the degree of success), such payments must be treated as appearance money.

Input tax. The entitlement to deduct input tax on purchases in connection with the running of competitions is subject to the normal rules, including those for partial exemption. See *Manx International Rally Ltd v Isle of Man Treasury (VTD 6711) (TVC 44.64)* where the company received income from sponsorship (standard-rated) as well as entries fees (exempt). The tribunal held that the rally was the subject of a supply to the sponsors as well as the competitors and the appropriate proportion of the input tax was therefore deductible. HMRC believe that this decision was unique to the facts and does not set a precedent in similar cases.

(VAT Notice 701/5/02, para 9.1; VAT Notice 701/45/02, paras 6.1–6.6; Internal Guidance V1–7, Chapter 25 paras 4.1, 5.1, 5.3–5.5, 5.7, 6.1, 7).

De Voil Indirect Tax Service. See V4.161.

57.6 ADMISSION CHARGES TO ENTERTAINMENT, CULTURAL ACTIVITIES, SPORT, ETC.

The VAT liability of admission charges depends upon the nature of the event and the person promoting the event.

(1) Standard-rated admission charges

Unless falling within (2)–(6) below, the full amount of any admission charges are normally standard-rated. *Included* are admissions to cinemas, theatres, swimming pools, amusement arcades and fun fairs, dances, sports events, museums and galleries, parks and gardens, historic houses, areas of the countryside for general recreational purposes, zoos and safari parks, and air shows.

(2) Exempt admission charges by public bodies

Admission charges by a 'public body' to

(*a*) a 'museum, gallery, art exhibition or zoo', or

(*b*) a 'theatrical, musical or choreographic performance of a cultural nature'

are exempt unless this would be likely to create 'distortions of competition' such as to place a commercial enterprise carried on by a taxable business at a disadvantage.

The performance under (*b*) above must be provided exclusively by one or more public bodies, one or more eligible bodies (see (3) below) or any combination of public bodies and eligible bodies. Exemption does not apply where, for example, a local authority acts as ticket broker for a commercial promoter or has a profit/income sharing arrangement with that promoter for a qualifying performance. (VAT Notice 701/47/03, para 3.2).

A '*public body*' means

- a local authority;
- a government department within the meaning of *VATA 1994, s 41*(*6*) (see 43.11 LOCAL AUTHORITIES AND PUBLIC BODIES); or
- a non-departmental public body which is listed in the 1995 edition of the publication prepared by the Office of Public Service and known as 'Public Bodies'. (Copies of this document may be obtained from HMSO Publication Centre, PO Box 276, London, SW8 5DT.)

[*VATA 1994, Sch 9 Group 13, Item 1, Notes* (*1*)(*3*)(*4*)*; SI 1996/1256*].

What is a '*museum, gallery, art exhibition or zoo*' has to be judged by reference to the normal everyday meaning of the words, taking into account indicative evidence such as the nature of the collections, objects, artefacts, site and exhibits on show. However, for the avoidance of doubt, a botanical garden does not qualify for exemption.

Similarly, whether an event is a '*theatrical, musical or choreographic performance of a cultural nature*' must be judged on the individual merits of the event.

However, HMRC will generally accept a live performance of any form of stage play, dance or music as cultural for the purposes of this exemption.

(VAT Notice 701/47/03, paras 2.3, 2.4)

'*Distortions of competition*'. A public body must take steps to notify all identifiable commercial suppliers of similar facilities or performances (eg a local authority should identify any such supplier within its geographical area of authority from its business rating, planning, taxation and other records). But it only needs to look at (*a*) and (*b*) above in isolation (eg if it wishes to exempt admission charges to a museum, it must demonstrate that it would not disadvantage commercial museums, galleries, art exhibitions and zoos within its geographical area, but would not have to take account of commercial theatrical, musical and choreographical performances).

Notice must be in writing but can be by individual letter or public notice in the local press for its geographical area. The notice must specify a date by which objections to exemption must be lodged. If no objections are received, the body can then start to exempt supplies but must retain copies of relevant correspondence and advertisements for future examination. If any objection is received, HMRC should be asked for a ruling (see 15.5 CUSTOMS: ADMINISTRATION) and in the meantime supplies should not be exempt. Once exemption is in place, it is not necessary to check on competition for each performance under (*b*) above or to make periodic checks for a new commercial supplier. It is for that supplier to approach HMRC.

Even if a public body is unable to identify any commercial supplier of similar services, it is HMRC's policy to allow the body to tax admissions of a qualifying nature if it wishes although this policy remains subject to review.

(VAT Notice 701/47/03, paras 3.3–3.10).

(3) **Exempt admission charges by eligible bodies**

Admission charges by an 'eligible body' to

(*a*) a 'museum, gallery, art exhibition or zoo', or

(*b*) a 'theatrical, musical or choreographic performance of a cultural nature'

are exempt. [*VATA 1994, Sch 9 Group 13, Item 2; SI 1996/1256*].

See (2) above for HMRC's interpretation of '*museum, gallery, art exhibition or zoo*' and '*theatrical, musical or choreographic performance of a cultural nature*'.

An '*eligible body*' means any body (other than a public body, see (2) above) which satisfies the following conditions.

(i) It is precluded from distributing, and does not distribute, any profit it makes. [*VATA 1994, Sch 9 Group 13 Note* (2); *SI 1996/1256*].

HMRC will normally accept a body as having satisfied this condition if

- its constitution or articles of association preclude it from distributing surpluses of income over expenditure to its members, shareholders, parent or associated companies, or any other party (other than in the event of a liquidation or cessation of activities), and
- it does not, as a matter of fact, distribute any profit.

For these purposes, distribution of profit does not include grants or donations made by charities in pursuit of their wider charitable objectives. (VAT Notice 701/47/03, para 4.5).

(ii) It applies any profits made from admission charges exempt under this provision to the continuance or improvement of the facilities made available by means of the supplies. [*VATA 1994, Sch 9 Group 13 Note* (*2*); *SI 1996/1256*]. HMRC regard this as being satisfied if the body applies profits in the making of related cultural supplies (eg research or conservation projects). But if profits are applied to any other activities of the body, the body is not eligible for exemption. (VAT Notice 701/47/03, paras 4.4, 4.6).

(iii) It is 'managed and administered on a voluntary basis' by persons who have no direct or indirect financial interest in its activities. [*VATA 1994, Sch 9 Group 13 Note* (2); *SI 1996/1256*].

HMRC's policy from 1 June 2004. In *Glastonbury Abbey (VTD 14579) (TVC 23.36)* the tribunal disagreed with HMRC's earlier view (see below) and stated that the UK law should read 'managed and administered on an *essentially* voluntary basis' as set out in *EC Sixth Directive, Art 13A*(*2*)(*a*) (see 22.17 EUROPEAN COMMUNITY LEGISLATION). Subsequently, in *C & E Commrs v The Zoological Society of London, CJEC [2002] STC 521 (TVC 21.220)* the Court held that the aim of the condition in *Art 13A*(*2*)(*a*) was to reserve the VAT exemption for bodies with no commercial purpose by requiring that the persons who participate in the management and administration of such bodies have 'no financial interest of their own in their results, by means of remuneration, distribution of profits or any other financial interest'. Therefore, the condition refers only to

- members of that body who are designated to direct it at the highest level; and
- other persons who, without being so designated, in fact direct inasmuch as they take the decisions of last resort concerning the policy of the body, especially in the financial area, and carry out the higher supervisory tasks.

HMRC have accepted this decision and also that 'voluntary' in UK law means 'essentially voluntary'.

Persons who are remunerated for carrying out purely executory tasks (ie those who implement, rather than take high level decisions) will not cause the cultural body to fail this condition.

HMRC regard a person as having a 'direct or indirect financial interest' in the activities of a body in the following circumstances.

- He receives or has a right to remuneration. 'Remuneration' means a commercial rate of pay (ie comparable to payment levels for similar jobs at a similar-sized cultural activity). HMRC accept that a token payment only, or payment solely to reimburse out-of-pocket expenses, would not disqualify a body from exemption provided all other conditions are met.

  If a person has a right to a remuneration but opts not to take it, this 'right' disqualifies the body from exemption because that person still has a direct financial interest in the activities of the body.

- He takes up an 'as of rights' provision. Such a provision gives a trustee the right to charge and be paid reasonable remuneration for (typically) professional services within the scope of the authority. The right does not depend on the charity or its trustees entering into a contract with the trustee affected. 'As of rights' provisions are often not exercised for long periods or are used intermittently. The presence of such a clause in itself (ie where it has not been exercised) will therefore not disqualify a body from exemption. It is only as and when remuneration is paid under this clause that the potential arises for it to cause disqualification from exemption. However, this will depend on the frequency, number and size of any payments made (see below).
- He is in any other way rewarded directly or indirectly by the body.
- He has any other financial interest in the body.

In determining whether a body is '*essentially voluntary*'

- the fact that remunerated staff take part occasionally or peripherally in the adoption of the decision of last resort will not, in itself, disqualify a body from exemption;
- if any person identified as managing and administering the body at the highest level receives remuneration, then the body will not qualify for exemption; and
- in the case of 'as of rights' provisions (see above), the issue is one of degree, ie the frequency, number and size of any payments made. Each case will depend on its own facts and HMRC recommend that if a body considers that its continued eligibility for exemption turns on payments made under an 'as of rights' provision, it should seek a ruling from its local VAT Office.

(VAT Notice 701/47/03, paras 4.8–4.13; Internal Guidance V1–7, Chapter 28 para 2.3).

Transitional relief for major building projects in progress at 1 June 2004. By concession, where a body had a 'major building project' in progress at 1 June 2004 which has been costed and funded on the basis that any input tax incurred will be recoverable, from 1 June 2004 to 31 May 2007 it may deduct input tax incurred on such a project, which cannot otherwise be deducted, as if its admission charges were still treated as taxable. This is subject to the following conditions.

- Any such deduction can only be claimed to the extent that it exceeds any net claim made (or to be made) and/or any benefit obtained (or to be obtained) resulting from the application of exemption for any periods which end prior to 1 June 2004 or span that date (see below under the heading *Before 1 June 2004*). In view of this, any claim (or claims) for relief under the concession should only be submitted after all back claims have been made.
- If any of the input tax deducted is also subsequently recoverable as a result of a body's longer period adjustment for partial exemption, it must make a further adjustment to cancel this out, on the same VAT return as the longer period adjustment. This is to prevent a double deduction.

- As this concession allows additional input tax recovery for certain construction services over and above the actual taxable use of the asset, where a claim is made under the concession, adjustments for subsequent intervals 2 to 10 under the capital goods scheme (see 10.6 CAPITAL GOODS SCHEME) can only be made if the actual use made of the asset is outside the range between the percentage which was initially correctly reclaimable under the partial exemption rules and the percentage which has been effectively recovered including all adjustments under this concession. Where an adjustment falls to be made because the usage in any subsequent interval is outside the range defined above, it can only be made to the extent that the usage falls outside this range.

Before recovering any input tax under this concession, a body must submit calculations to its local VAT office and obtain their written approval. Full details of all partial exemption calculations, irrecoverable building-related input tax and previous claims relating to the exemption should be provided. HMRC may also request further supporting evidence (eg contracts/invoices) in support of the claim.

For the purposes of this concession, a '*major building project*' means any building project covered by the CAPITAL GOODS SCHEME (12). However, consideration will also be given to similar smaller projects which would have qualified for treatment under that scheme had their total value exceeded £250,000 VAT-bearing value.

A building project is 'in progress' at 1 June 2004 where

- construction services have been contracted for before 10 December 2003; or
- grant-funding has been formally approved before 10 December 2003; or
- there is documentary evidence that negotiations were at an advanced stage before 10 December 2003 and construction work has commenced as at 1 June 2004.

HMRC may withdraw or restrict the application of this concession if they have reasonable cause to believe that it is being abused.

(VAT Notice 701/47/03, paras 10.4, 11).

HMRC's policy before 1 June 2004, HMRC's policy is that in order to be 'managed and administered on a voluntary basis' an eligible body must not make *any* payment for managerial or administrative services, including those carried out on a day-to-day basis by an employee or contractor. (VAT Notice 701/47/03, para 4.2).

Organisations in a position to take advantage of the revised policy applying from 1 June 2004 (see above) from an earlier date are free to do so. But once a decision to apply exemption has been taken, it must be applied consistently to all subsequent periods. If the net value of any adjustment is £2,000 or less, bodies my amend their VAT account and include the adjustment on their current VAT return. Otherwise, a separate claim for payment must be submitted to the local VAT Office. All adjustments or claims must take into account any over-claimed input tax (because input tax previously claimed is now attributable to exempt supplies) and are subject to the three-year cap and the usual unjust enrichment rules (see 51.8–51.10 PAYMENT OF VAT). A body must be able to produce suitable evidence (eg its constitution, minutes, annual accounts) to show that it satisfies all the conditions for eligible body status (see above) and must be able to substantiate the amount of any claim made. (VAT Notice 701/47/03, paras 9.1, 9.2).

(4) **Fund-raising events**

Certain admission charges are exempt under more general provisions applying to fund-raising events by charities and other qualifying bodies (including eligible bodies within (3) above). See 12.10 CHARITIES for full details.

(5) **Donations in lieu of admission**

True donations are outside the scope of VAT. Where there is no admission charge and the public are asked for a donation instead, then this money is outside the scope of VAT. However, to qualify as a donation the payment must be entirely voluntary and secure nothing in return for the donor, and the actual amount to be given must be entirely at the donor's discretion. It must also be clear to the donor that admission can be gained whether a payment is made or not. If the person has to pay, or is made to think they have to pay, to get in then it is not a true donation but a standard-rated admission charge (unless otherwise exempt). (Internal Guidance V1–6, para 9.2).

For donations in addition to charging admission at charitable functions, see 12.5(1) CHARITIES.

(6) **Admission by programme only**

It is common practice for admission to events to include the provision of a programme. Following the decision by the CJEC in *Card Protection Plan Ltd v C & E Commrs, CJEC [1999] STC 270 (TVC 21.223)* HMRC now accept that in the majority of cases there is a single supply of admission, the programme being an ancillary item. In any case, a programme does not qualify for zero-rating if it is no more than an elaborate ticket which has to be bought to get into the event, etc. Payment for such a programme is the consideration for admission even if payment cannot be legally enforced.

Boxes, seats, etc. See 42.3(i) LAND AND BUILDINGS.

Recovery of input tax. Admission for a charge is always a business activity for VAT purposes and related input tax incurred will normally be deductible unless the admission charges are exempt (see above) in which case the partial exemption rules may apply.

If the public is admitted free of charge to any premises there is no business activity and VAT incurred is not input tax. If the premises are also used for business purposes, input tax may be apportioned, see 35.7 INPUT TAX.

De Voil Indirect Tax Service. See V4.176.

57.7 SPORT AND PHYSICAL RECREATION FACILITIES

Subject to the exemptions in 57.8 and 57.9–57.13 below, the granting of facilities for playing any sport or participating in any physical recreation is standard-rated. The grant of any right to call for or be granted facilities which would be standard-rated under this provision is also standard-rated. Included is an equitable right, a right under an option or right to pre-emption and, in relation to Scotland, a personal right.

[*VATA 1994, Sch 9 Group 1 Item 1*(*m*)(*n*)].

Standard-rating has been applied to the supply of a football ground for international matches, the presence of ticket-paying spectators not preventing the facilities granted being those for playing sport rather than a licence to occupy land (*Queens Park Football Club Ltd (VTD 2776) (TVC 39.136)*). HMRC accept that this decision applies to supplies by other sporting stadia, both indoors and outdoors. (C & E News Release 72/88, 20 September 1988). Standard-rating has also been applied to the use of a practice range at a golf club (*L H Johnson (VTD 14955) (TVC 39.138)*).

57.8 Letting of facilities

The letting of facilities designed or adapted for playing any sport or taking part in physical recreation is normally standard-rated. However, the letting of such facilities may be exempt if the letting is for over 24 hours or there is a series of lettings to the same person over a period of time. Exemption will also apply if certain general purpose facilities are hired for sporting use or if sports facilities are hired out for non-sporting purposes. See below for further details.

24 hour rule. Where the facilities are provided for a continuous period of use exceeding 24 hours, the grant is exempt. The person to whom the facilities are let must have exclusive control of them throughout the period of letting.

Series of lets. Also exempt is the granting of such facilities for a series of ten or more periods (whether or not exceeding 24 hours) to a school, club, association or an organisation representing affiliated clubs or constituent associations where

(i) each period is in respect of the same activity carried on at the same place;

(ii) the interval between each period is not less than one day and not more than fourteen days;

(iii) consideration is payable by reference to the whole series and is evidenced by written agreement; and

(iv) the grantee has exclusive use of the facilities.

[*VATA 1994, Sch 9 Group 1 Note 16*].

Under (i) above, a different pitch, court or lane at the same sports ground or premises would count as the same place.

Under (ii) above the duration of the sessions may be varied but there is no exception for intervals greater than 14 days through the closure of the facility for any reason.

Under (iii) above, there must be evidence that payment is to be made in full, whether or not the right to use the facility for any specific session is actually exercised. Provision for a refund given by the provider in the event of the unforeseen non-availability of their facility would not affect this condition.

Premises are sports facilities if they are designed or adapted for playing any sport or taking part in any physical recreation (eg swimming pools, football pitches, dance studios and skating rinks). Each court or pitch (or lane in the case of bowling alley, curling rink or swimming pool) is a separate sports facility.

(VAT Notice 742, paras 5.1–5.4).

Option to tax. A supplier may be able to choose to standard-rate some of the above supplies which would otherwise be exempt. See 42.8 LAND AND BUILDINGS.

57.9 **Sporting services provided by eligible/non-profit making bodies**

VAT exemption applies to the supply of services closely linked with and essential to sport or physical recreation supplied to individuals taking part in the activity where the supplies are made by

- an 'eligible body' (before 1 January 2000 a 'non-profit making body') having a membership scheme to those of its members who are granted membership for a period of three months or more; and
- an 'eligible body' (before 1 January 2000 a 'non-profit making body') which does not run a membership scheme (eg a charity).

Specifically excluded are

- the supply of any services of residential accommodation, catering or transport;
- supplies by local authorities;
- supplies by government departments within the meaning of *VATA 1994, s 41(6)* (see 43.11 LOCAL AUTHORITIES AND PUBLIC BODIES); and
- supplies by non-departmental public bodies (such as Sports Councils) which are listed in the 1993 edition of the publication prepared by the Office of Public Service and Science and known as Public Bodies.

Eligible body. Subject to the specific exclusions above, an eligible body means a non-profit making body which

- cannot distribute any profit it makes otherwise than to another non-profit making body or its own members on winding up or dissolution;
- (except on winding up or dissolution) applies any profits it makes from supplies exempted by these provisions *either* to maintain or improve the facilities made available in connection with those supplies *or* for the purposes of a non-profit making body; and
- is not subject to 'commercial influence'.

To decide whether a body is non-profit making, it is necessary to look at its constitution, its activities and its use of funds to determine whether it was established with a purpose, intention or motive which excluded profit making. A non-distribution clause in the constitution of an organisation does not, in itself, answer this question.

If the organisation is a company limited by shares, HMRC have accepted that

(*a*) the non-distribution condition will be satisfied by the passing of a resolution to

- delete, if appropriate *Table A, Arts 102–108* (dividend arrangements) and *Art 110* (capitalisation of profits); and
- adopt a new Article preventing distributions by way of dividend, bonus and any other means; and

(*b*) adoption of *Art 117* on winding up fulfills the winding-up criterion.

(VAT Notice 701/45/02, paras 4.2, 4.3).

'*Commercial influence*'. A body is considered to be subject to commercial influence in relation to any supply which would otherwise be exempt under these provisions (the '*sports supply*') if (and only if), there is a time in 'the relevant period' when

- a person 'associated with the body' made a 'relevant supply' to it; or

- a person 'associated with the body' received an emolument from it determined at least in part by reference to the body's profits or gross income; or
- an arrangement existed for a relevant supply to be made or emolument to be received after the end of the relevant period.

The following definitions apply for the purposes of 'commercial influence'.

(1) '*The relevant period*' for a sports supply made before 1 January 2003 is the period from 14 January 1999 to the time of the sports supply. For a sports supply made after 31 December 2002, the relevant period is the three years before the sports supply.

(2) Subject to below, a person is '*associated with the body*' at the time, as the case may be, of the relevant supply, receipt of emolument or arrangement, if at any time in the relevant period the person concerned was an 'officer' or 'shadow officer' of the body or an 'intermediary for supplies' to that body or was connected to any such person. '*Officer*' includes director of a body corporate and any committee member or trustee concerned in the general control and management of the administration of the body. '*Shadow officer*' means a person in accordance with whose directions the members or officers of the body are accustomed to act. An '*intermediary for supplies*' is anyone who acts between the body and an officer in making the relevant supply. A person is treated as connected with another under the provisions of *ICTA 1988, s 839* (see 69.19 VALUATION). A person is *not* treated as associated with the body at the time of the relevant supply, etc if the only times when that person, or the person connected with him, was an officer or shadow officer of the body occurred before 1 January 2000 *unless* that body would be treated as subject to commercial influence as a result of an agreement entered into after 13 January 1999 and before 1 January 2000.

(3) '*Emoluments*' include all salaries, fees, wages, perquisites and profits calculated or varied wholly or partly by reference to

- the profits from some or all of the activities of the body paying the emolument; or
- the level of that body's gross income from some or all of its activities.

Perquisites ('perks') are allowances paid, or goods and services provided, over and above a settled wage.

Payment of honoraria to a club secretary or treasurer will not disqualify a club from exemption, unless the amount is calculated by reference to profits or gross income.

(VAT Notice 701/45/02, paras 5.5, 5.7).

(4) A '*relevant supply*' is, subject to below,

(*a*) the grant of any interest in, right over or licence to occupy land (or, in the case of land in Scotland, any personal right to call for or be granted any such interest or right) which at any time in the relevant period was or was expected to become 'sports land';

(*b*) a supply arising from a grant falling within (*a*) above made after 31 March 1996 (eg rent payable for the use of sports land under a lease);

(*c*) the supply of any services of managing or administering of any facilities provided by the body, and (*d*) the supply of any goods or services for a consideration in excess of what would have been agreed between parties entering into a commercial transaction at arm's length.

Where a club uses a committee member's firm to perform routine bookkeeping, accounting or legal services, HMRC do not treat supplies of such services as management and administration within (*c*) above and this will not therefore disqualify the club from exemption. (VAT Notice 701/45/02, para 5.7).

Included is any such supply between VAT group members which would otherwise be disregarded but specifically excluded is any such supply which is

- by a person to a body whose principal purpose at the time of the sports supply is to provide sports and physical recreation facilities for use by the employees of that person;
- by a charity or local authority;
- a gift of sports land or of the use of sports land;
- sports land supplied for a nominal amount; or
- the use of sports land supplied for a nominal amount provided the original grant of land was also for a nominal amount.

In normal circumstances, HMRC will treat any payment below £1,000 as nominal and will give consideration to claims for higher amounts to be so treated. Bodies wishing to be sure that HMRC will treat a payment as nominal before exempting supplies are advised to write to HMRC setting out the full facts. (VAT Notice 701/45/02, para 5.4).

(5) '*Sports land*' is land used, or held to be used, by the body for or in connection with sport and/or physical recreation.

[*VATA 1994, Sch 9 Group 10 Item 3 and Notes 1–17; SI 1999/1994*].

'*Non-profit making body*'. A body whose constitution or articles of association preclude it from distributing surpluses of income over expenditure to its members, shareholders or any other party (other than in the event of a liquidation or cessation of activities) is normally accepted as non-profit making for these purposes. However, the lack of any provision precluding distribution is not necessarily the sole factor in determining whether an organisation is non-profit making. The term is given its natural meaning applying the principles in *C & E Commrs v Bell Concord Educational Trust Ltd, CA 1988, [1989] STC 264 (TVC 20.8)*. For example, in view of the ruling in that case that 'the words "otherwise than for profit" refer to the objects for which the organisation is established and not the budget policy being pursued', sporting services are not excluded from exemption simply because profits on certain activities are used to subsidise other activities (eg profits on the bar are used to subsidise subscriptions). (VAT Notice 701/45/94 (now superseded), paras 6–8).

De Voil Indirect Tax Service. See V4.161.

57.10 *Individuals qualifying as members of a membership body*

Where a body has a membership scheme, exemption applies to services supplied to a *playing* 'individual' granted membership for a period of three months or more (including life membership). Where an individual becomes a member less than three months before the end of the club's subscription period and pays less than three months' subscription, the subscription can still be exempt provided the grant of membership is for not less than three months.

It is usually clear from the literature, rules, regulations and constitution of the body whether it is operating a membership scheme, eg by references to

- arrangements for application for membership;
- membership categories and subscriptions;
- benefits available to members (including voting rights at AGMs);
- conduct of members; and
- members' involvement in running the club.

For the purposes of this exemption, an '*individual*' is a person who actually takes part in the sporting or physical education activity and this includes

- family groups; and
- informal groups, where one individual makes a booking on behalf of a group of users of the sporting facilities.

Supplies to individuals do not include supplies

- by a club to one of its sections where the individual section has a separate and independent constitution, eg the squash section of a multiple-sports club; or
- to travel agents or tour operators, which have agreements with a sports club to supply use of sporting facilities to individuals, groups or corporate bodies. This includes, for example, supplies to individuals who are identified through having booked through a travel agent.

(VAT Notice 701/45/02, para 3.4).

'Privilege cards', issued in conjunction with a monthly or three-monthly season ticket and entitling cardholders to free admission to a sports centre run by an eligible body (before 1 January 2000 a non-profit making body), do not make the holders 'members' thereby resulting in the standard-rating of facilities used by other 'non-members' (*Basingstoke and District Sports Trust Ltd (VTD 13347) (TVC 23.21)*).

Following this decision, HMRC issued the following clarification.

(i) Where a body does not operate a full membership scheme (eg where members do not have voting rights or any form of control over the management of the centre), sporting and physical education services provided are exempt from VAT subject to the normal conditions. This applies irrespective of whether users are called 'members' for the purpose of obtaining discount on use of the facilities.

(ii) Where a body operates a full membership scheme but limits its application to selected activities or locations, exemption of qualifying services is limited to supplies to members even if other activities are not within the membership scheme. For example, where a body provides a swimming pool and squash courts and the membership scheme is only for squash players, supplies to all users of the pool, other than squash members, is standard-rated even though there is no membership scheme for the swimming pool.

(Business Brief 3/96).

57.11 Sports qualifying for exemption

The following sports, etc qualify for exemption.

Aikido	American football	Angling
Archery	Arm wrestling	Association football
Athletics	Badminton	Ballooning
Baseball	Basketball	Baton twirling
Biathlon	Bicycle polo	Billiards
Bobsleigh	Boccia	Bowls
Boxing	Camogie	Canoeing
Caving	Chinese martial arts	Cricket
Croquet	Crossbow	Curling
Cycling	Dragon boat racing	Equestrian
Exercise and fitness	Fencing	Field sports
Fives	Flying*	Gaelic football
Gliding	Golf	Gymnastics
Handball	Hang/paragliding	Highland games
Hockey	Horse racing	Hovering
Hurling	Ice hockey	Ice skating
Jet skiing	Ju jitsu	Judo
Kabaddi	Karate	Kendo
Korfball	Lacrosse	Lawn tennis
Life saving	Luge	Modern pentathlon
Motor cycling	Motor sports	Mountaineering
Movement and dance	Netball	Octopush
Orienteering	Parachuting	Petanque
Polo	Pony Trekking	Pool
Quoits	Racketball	Rackets
Racquetball	Rambling	Real tennis
Roller hockey	Roller skating	Rounders
Rowing	Rugby league	Rugby union
Sailing/yachting	Sand and land yachting	Shinty
Shooting	Skateboarding	Skiing
Skipping	Snooker	Snowboarding
Softball	Sombo wrestling	Squash
Stoolball	Street hockey	Sub-aqua
Surf life saving	Surfing	Swimming
Table tennis	Taekwondo	Tang soo do
Tchoukball	Tenpin bowling**	Trampolining

Triathlon	Tug of war	Unihoc
Volleyball	Water skiing	Weightlifting
Wrestling	Yoga	

* Includes those model flying activities, success in which is dependent on physical skill or fitness.

** Includes skittles.

Application may be made to HMRC to include other activities. HMRC will then consult with the Department of Culture, Media and Sport and other representative bodies and give a decision in writing. If exemption is refused, an appeal can be made to a VAT tribunal.

(VAT Notice 701/45/02, para 3.2).

Pigeon racing does not qualify for exemption (*Royal Pigeon Racing Association (VTD 14006) (TVC 23.33)*).

57.12 *Services qualifying for exemption*

Services qualifying for exemption where supplied by a membership body to its qualifying members or, where applicable, by a non-membership body (eg a sports centre) to individuals include the following.

- Use of changing rooms, showers and playing equipment, trolley and locker hire and storage of equipment essential to sport.
- Provision of playing area (eg court, pitch or green fees).
- Use of multi-sport playing facilities.
- Refereeing, umpiring and judging services. Supplies by a self-employed referee registered for VAT are not exempt from VAT because he is not an eligible body.
- Coaching, training and physical education services. Sports coaching by professionals is not within the exemption as it is not supplied by an eligible body (although it may qualify for the exemption for education, see 20.9 EDUCATION).
- Membership subscriptions covering active participation in sport (including life subscriptions entitling the member to playing services for life where the annual subscription is exempt).

  Clubs and associations often supply a number of different benefits in return for their subscriptions and must decide whether their subscriptions are consideration for a single supply or a multiple supply. If there is one principal benefit or reason for joining, with other benefits supplied being less important, the subscription is consideration for a single supply and its liability is determined by the liability of the main benefit. There is an exception, however, for non-profit making bodies which supply a mixture of benefits with different VAT liabilities. As a concession, these bodies *may* apportion their subscriptions to reflect the value and VAT liability of each individual benefit, even if they are consideration for a single supply. If the subscription is consideration for a multiple supply and the separate elements have different liabilities, the subscription must be apportioned. See 14.2 CLUBS AND ASSOCIATIONS for further details.

- Joining fees where the benefits supplied in return are the same as for the subscription and the subscription is itself exempt. If the joining fee entitles the member to different benefits, VAT must be accounted for, where appropriate, on the liability of those benefits.
- Fees for remaining on the waiting list for membership but only if
  - (i) they are deducted from the new member's first subscription or entrance fee and this itself qualifies for exemption; and
  - (ii) they are refundable in the event that the candidate fails to become a member for any reason including voluntary withdrawal.

  Otherwise the fee is standard-rated.
- Match fees for the use of playing facilities/pitch hire. Match fees also covering the cost of catering and transport may need to be apportioned.
- Mooring, hangarage, use of workshops (excluding use of parts or services of an engineer).

Services not qualifying for exemption include

- sporting services supplied to
  - (i) corporate members;
  - (ii) members' guests (irrespective of who pays the guests' fees);
  - (iii) temporary members (those granted membership for less than three months); and
  - (iv) visitors from other members' clubs and societies;
- social or non-playing membership subscriptions;
- admission charges for spectators;
- use of residential accommodation;
- use of transport;
- catering, bars, gaming machines and social functions; and
- parking.

(VAT Notice 701/45/02, paras 3.3–3.5).

See *Royal Thames Yacht Club (VTD 14046) (TVC 23.31)* where the subscriptions of ordinary members were apportioned between exempt sporting facilities and standard-rated clubhouse facilities which were capable of being enjoyed to the exclusion of the sporting facilities.

57.13 *Subscriptions to sports governing bodies*

A non-profit making sports governing body can exempt its affiliation fees insofar as they can be attributed to 'services closely linked and essential to sport' which are supplied to individuals either direct or via sports clubs. Where affiliation to a governing body is restricted to groups of individuals such as members' clubs, the governing body may still exempt the supply of playing services to clubs provided

- the affiliation fee is calculated on a basis which can be related to an individual (eg per person or directly linked to the number of club members); and

- the services are closely linked to active participation in the sport.

However, where the principal benefit is of priority purchase rights for international match or tournament admission tickets, the fee is standard-rated.

Treatment as disbursements. A club can treat the onward charge of the affiliation fees charged by a governing body to its members or customers as disbursements for VAT purposes (and outside the scope of VAT) provided

- the affiliation fee charged by the governing body qualifies for exemption;
- the principal beneficiary of the services supplied by the governing body is the individual sports person;
- the club itemises the fee separately from its subscription or charge to the individual member or customer on the VAT invoice; and
- the amount charged by the club to the individual member or customer does not exceed the fee charged by the governing body.

(VAT Notice 701/45/02, para 3.6).

57.14 SPORTING RIGHTS

The grant of any interest, right or licence to take game or fish is standard-rated subject to the exceptions in 57.15 to 57.17 below where sporting rights and land are sold or leased together. The grant of any right to call for or be granted an interest or right which would be standard-rated under this provision is also standard-rated. Included is an equitable right, a right under an option or right to pre-emption and, in relation to Scotland, a personal right. [*VATA 1994, Sch 9 Group 1 Item 1*(*c*)(*n*)].

De Voil Indirect Tax Service. See V4.113.

57.15 Sporting rights and land

Where, at the time of the grant of the rights

- the grantor grants the grantee the fee simple (broadly freehold in England and Wales and *dominium directum* or *dominium utile* in Scotland) of the land over which the right to take game or fish is exercisable, or
- the sporting rights are leased together with that land and the sporting rights represent no more than 10% of the value of the whole supply,

the total consideration is taken to be for the supply of the land alone and is exempt (unless the grantor has opted to tax the supply, see 42.8 LAND AND BUILDINGS, in which case the whole of the supply is standard-rated).

Where the sporting rights are leased with the land and represent more than 10% of the value of the whole supply, an apportionment must be made between the standard-rated rights and the exempt supply of land (unless the option to tax has been exercised).

[*VATA 1994, Sch 9 Group 1 Item 1*(*c*)]. (VAT Notice 742, para 6.2).

57.16 Shooting rights only

Standard-rating applies to a grant over land owned by the grantor or over which he has the shooting rights. The provisions cover both freehold sales of rights and leasing or letting for any length of time.

Shooting in hand. If a landowner keeps control of the shooting over his land and makes all the arrangements to stock the land with game ('shooting in hand') and invites others to join him in shooting, there is no business activity (and no input tax can therefore be recovered) if the individuals are asked to contribute towards the costs of maintaining the shoot provided

(*a*) only friends and relatives are permitted to shoot;

(*b*) the availability of the shoot is not advertised to the public;

(*c*) the shooting accounts show an annual loss equivalent to, at least, the usual contribution made a 'gun' over a year; and

(*d*) the loss is borne by the landowner personally rather than by the estate or farm business.

Syndicates. A group of individuals set up solely to share the expenses of a shoot is not normally in business and therefore not regarded as making supplies to the individual members. However, if the syndicate regularly supplies shooting facilities to non-members, or makes taxable supplies of other goods or services, it is regarded as being in business and all its activities, including the supply of shooting facilities to its members, are business activities.

If a landowner or tenant grants shooting rights for less than their normal value to a syndicate of whom he is a member, he must account for VAT on the open market value of those rights. If he supplies other goods or services (eg the services of a gamekeeper or beater), VAT should be charged in the normal way.

(VAT Notice 742, para 6.3).

See also *C & E Commrs v Lord Fisher, QB [1981] STC 238 (TVC 7.6)* where, on the facts, shooting was not held to constitute a business and *J O Williams (VTD 14240) (TVC 60.132)* where a farmer was treated as carrying on a business for VAT purposes even though the Inland Revenue treated the shooting as 'hobby farming' giving rise to neither a profit or a loss.

57.17 **Fishing only**

Standard-rating applies to the grant of rights to take fish either from the grantor's own waters or from waters over which he has fishing rights. The provisions apply to both freehold sales of the rights and letting or leasing for any length of time.

Still-water fisheries. Any charges made to fishermen are standard-rated even if both fishing rights and fish are supplied. However, if the grantor allows a person freely to choose whether to take away fish caught or to throw them back, and makes a separate charge solely for those fish taken away, that charge is accepted to be the consideration for the zero-rated supply of fish (provided they are of a species generally used as food in the UK).

Rod licences. Rod licences issued by the National Rivers Authority or similar bodies which do not themselves give specific rights to fish are outside the scope of VAT.

Salmon fishing in Scotland. The sale of salmon fishing rights in Scotland (whether or not the rights are sold with land) involves the grant of a separate heritable interest in land and is registrable in the General Register of Sasines. The supply is standard-rated unless the heritable right is expressly conveyed together with the *dominium directum* or *dominium utile* of the land (similar to freehold elsewhere in the UK) over which the right is exercisable, in which case the supply is exempt (with the option to tax).

Time-share of fishing rights. A time-share in fishing rights is standard-rated. However, in Scotland, where there is a supply of fishing rights restricted to, say, one week a year together with a *pro indiviso* share of land over which the rights are exercisable, the supply is exempt (with the option to tax). This is because a purchaser of a *pro indiviso* share of land acquires full title to the land in joint ownership with other purchasers; ie he is granted a fee simple of the land.

Lakes. Where a lake that is empty of fish is let to a person who will stock it with fish, there is an exempt supply of land (subject to the option to tax) rather than a standard-rated right to take those fish.

(VAT Notice 742, para 6.4; Internal Guidance V1–8, paras 9.2–9.4).

57.18 SPONSORSHIP INCOME

Sponsorship is a common feature of artistic, sporting, educational and charitable activities. However, it is not restricted to these areas and it can involve payment in the form of goods and services as well as money. The payments may also be described as something else, for example, as a donation.

A person who receives sponsorship, or some other form of support, will normally be making taxable supplies if, in return, he is obliged to provide the sponsor with a significant benefit. This might include

- naming an event after the sponsor;
- displaying the sponsor's company logo or trading name;
- participating in the sponsor's promotional or advertising activities;
- allowing the sponsor to use the name or logo of the person being sponsored;
- giving free or reduced price tickets;
- allowing access to special events such as premieres or gala evenings;
- providing entertainment or hospitality facilities; or
- giving the sponsor exclusive or priority booking rights.

This list is not exhaustive and there are many other situations in which a sponsor may be receiving tangible benefits. What matters is that the agreement or understanding with the sponsor requires the person being sponsored to do something in return.

In *C & E Commrs v Tron Theatre Ltd, CS 1993, [1994] STC 177 (TVC 65.107)* sponsors were entitled, amongst other things, to priority bookings. It was held that the theatre would not have provided the goods and services it did for less than the consideration which the sponsors paid. As a result, the whole of the sponsorship received was consideration in money and subject to VAT.

Donations. Financial or other support might also be received in the form of donations or gifts. Where the sponsor's support is freely given and secures nothing in return, the recipient does not make a taxable supply and the sponsorship (whether in the form of money, goods or services) can be treated as a donation outside the scope of VAT. A taxable supply is not created where the sponsor provides an insignificant benefit such as a minor acknowledgement of the source of the support. Examples of this can include any of the following.

- Giving a flag or sticker.
- Naming the donor in a list of supporters in a programme or on a notice.

- Naming a building or university chair after the donor.
- Putting the donor's name on the back of a seat in a theatre.

In *C & E Commrs v EMAP MacLaren Ltd, QB [1997] STC 490 (TVC 65.109)* a company published a scientific periodical and organised cash awards to scientists. The costs of the awards was met by sponsors who received publicity in the periodical and tickets to attend the annual award. It was held that the sponsorship payments were not consideration obtained in return for the supply of benefits to sponsors.

Mixed sponsorship and donation. Provided it is entirely separate from the sponsorship agreement, a person is not required to account for VAT on any donation or gift (of the kind described above) received from a sponsor in addition to the sponsorship. However, it must be clear that any benefits the sponsor receives are not conditional on the making of the donation or gift.

Provision of goods and/or services by the sponsor rather than money. In such a case, if the sponsor provides

- goods and/or services to somebody who, in return, is making a taxable supply, he is making a taxable supply of those goods and/or services;
- goods to somebody as a gift or donation, he may be liable to account for VAT under the business gift rules (see 47.6 OUTPUT TAX); and
- services to somebody as a gift or donation, no VAT is due.

Accounting for VAT. VAT must normally be accounted for on everything received under the sponsorship agreement. A VAT invoice must be issued to any VAT-registered sponsor. The sponsor can then reclaim the VAT as input tax subject to the normal rules. Where the amount of the sponsorship is agreed without reference to VAT, it must be treated as VAT-inclusive. A sponsor who provides sponsorship in the form of taxable supplies of goods and/or services is also required to issue a VAT invoice.

Where a charity makes supplies to sponsors as part of a fund-raising event, the supplies may be exempt. See 12.10 CHARITIES.

Where supplies of advertising services and publicity are made to overseas sponsors, the services may be outside the scope of UK VAT. See 64.26 SUPPLY.

(VAT Notice 701/41/02, paras 1.2, 2.1–2.4, 3.1, 3.4).

See *Bird Racing (Management) Ltd (VTD 11630) (TVC 7.94)* where a company incorporated with the aim of attracting sponsorship for a motor racing driver was held, on the facts, to be predominantly concerned with the making of taxable supplies to sponsors for a consideration and therefore carrying on a business and entitled to be registered for VAT.

57.19 POSTAGE STAMPS AND PHILATELIC SUPPLIES

Stamps which are valid for postage in the UK. 'Valid postage stamps' are the payment for a postal service that is exempt from VAT.

No VAT is chargeable on the sale of UK or Isle of Man stamps which are valid postage stamps and which are sold at or below face value. If such stamps are sold above face value, VAT must be accounted for at the standard rate on the amount by which the price exceeds that value.

'*Valid postage stamps*' are unused postage stamps of the present monarch's reign on which the value is

- £1 or a multiple of £1;
- in decimal currency, or
- designated for 1st or 2nd class postage.

All other stamps. Sales of other stamps, including

- all used stamps,
- all foreign stamps (even if valid for postage abroad), and
- UK and Isle of Man stamps of earlier reigns or which have a value expressed in pre-decimal currency

are standard-rated. It may be possible to treat such stamps as collector's items so that VAT can be accounted for on the difference between the purchase and selling price under the margin scheme for SECOND-HAND GOODS (61). If the conditions of the scheme are not met, VAT is due on the full selling price.

Combinations of valid and other stamps. Where philatelic items are sold which consist of, or contain, valid postage stamps (see above), VAT must be accounted for on the full amount charged less the face value of the valid stamps.

First day covers. A first day cover is an envelope bearing postage stamps with a postmark of the first day of their issue.

- If an envelope with unfranked stamps (whether the stamps are fixed to the envelope or not) is sold for customers to post themselves, the face value of the unused stamps can be disregarded and VAT accounted for on the rest of the charge only.
- If an envelope with the new stamps is posted to the customer on the first day of issue, VAT must be accounted for at the standard rate on the full selling price of the first day cover (without deduction for the face value of the stamps).
- First day covers sold after the first day of issue are standard-rated. However, it may be possible to treat them as collector's items so that VAT can be accounted for on the difference between the purchase and selling price under the margin scheme for SECOND-HAND GOODS (61).

Stamped stationery. Stamped stationery which is unused and valid for postage in the UK or Isle of Man is standard-rated on the amount charged less the face value of the stamps. This applies whether the stamps are printed on the stationery or are ordinary postage stamps that have been stuck on.

Imported collector's items. Some items of philatelic interest are eligible for a reduced valuation at importation which gives an effective VAT rate of 5%. See 71.3 WORKS OF ART, ETC.

Postage and packing. If delivery is included in the contract with the customer, there is a single supply of delivered goods (in the case of philatelic supplies) or services (in the case of valid postage stamps). The liability of the delivery or postage and packing charge follows that of the items being delivered, ie standard-rated in the case of philatelic supplies or exempt in the case of valid postage stamps. For postage charges generally, see 47.8(18) OUTPUT TAX.

(VAT Notice 701/8/03).

58 Reduced Rate Supplies

The contents of this chapter are as follows.

58.1 INTRODUCTION

VAT is levied on the supply of goods and services, the acquisition of goods from another EC country and the importation of goods from a place outside the EC. The standard rate of VAT is currently 17.5% but VAT charged on certain supplies of goods and services is chargeable at a reduced rate, currently 5%. The reduced rate also applies to the acquisition from another EC country, or the importation from outside the EC, of goods the supply of which would be subject to the reduced rate. [*VATA 1994, ss 2(1A)–(1C), 29A(1)(2); FA 1995, s 21; F(No 2)A 1997, s 6; FA 2001, s 99*].

The categories of goods and services to which the reduced rate applies as specified in *VATA 1994, Sch 7A* are as follows.

Group 1	Supplies of domestic fuel or power (see 29 FUEL AND POWER)
Group 2	Installation of energy-saving materials (see 58.2 below)
Group 3	Grant-funded installation of heating equipment or security goods or connection of gas supply (see 58.3 below)
Group 4	Women's sanitary products (see 58.4 below)
Group 5	Children's car seats (see 58.5 below)
Group 6	Residential conversions (see 42.23 LAND AND BUILDINGS)
Group 7	Residential renovations and alterations (see 42.24 LAND AND BUILDINGS)

The Treasury may vary the Groups (and notes contained therein which form an integral part) by adding, deleting or varying any description of supply for the time being specified. The *Schedule* may also be varied so as to describe a supply of goods or services by reference to matters unrelated to the characteristics of the goods or services themselves including, in the case of a supply of goods, the use that has been made of those goods. [*VATA 1994, ss 2(1A)-(1C), 29A(3)(4), s 96(9); FA 2001, s 99, Sch 31 para 5*].

58.2 INSTALLATION OF ENERGY-SAVING MATERIALS

The supplies listed below are subject to a reduced rate of VAT. It should be noted that

- the reduced rate only applies to supplies made by installers of energy-saving materials and does not apply to purchases of energy-saving materials by businesses or to purchases for DIY use;
- relief does not apply to the installation of double glazing and similar products (eg low-emissivity glass) or the supply of energy-efficient domestic appliances; and

- energy-saving materials which are incorporated by a builder in a new dwelling are zero-rated (see 42.26 LAND AND BUILDINGS).

The following supplies are subject to a reduced rate of VAT of 5%.

(*a*) Supplies of services of 'installing' 'energy-saving materials' in 'residential accommodation' or in a building intended for 'use solely for a relevant charitable purpose'.

(*b*) Supplies of 'energy-saving materials' by a person who installs those materials in 'residential accommodation' or in a building intended for 'use solely for a relevant charitable purpose'.

'*Energy-saving materials*' means any of the following.

(i) Insulation for walls, floors, ceilings, roofs or lofts or for water tanks, pipes or other plumbing fittings. '*Insulation*' means materials designed and installed because of their insulating. *Not included* are essentially decorative products or treatments (eg curtains and carpets).

Walkways, walkboards and ladders that are permanently fixed as part of the installation of roof insulation can be charged at the reduced rate. (Internal Guidance V1–7, Chapter 6 para 3.3).

(ii) Draught stripping for windows and doors. These are strips fixed around interior and exterior doors, windows and loft hatches.

(iii) Central heating system controls (including thermostatic radiator valves) and hot water system controls. *Included* are manual or electronic timers, thermostats, and mechanical or electronic valves.

(iv) Solar panels. *Included* are all systems installed in, or on the site of, a building which are

- solar collectors such as evacuated tube or flat plate systems, together with associated pipework and equipment (eg circulation systems, pump, storage cylinder, control panel and heat exchanger); or
- photovoltaic (PV) panels with cabling, control panel and AC/DC inverter.

(v) Wind turbines (including mounting poles, electrical cables, battery banks and voltage controllers).

(vi) Water turbines (including electrical cables, battery banks and voltage controllers).

(vii) Ground source heat pumps (from 1 June 2004).

(viii) Air source heat pumps (from 7 April 2005).

(ix) Micro combined heat and power units (from 7 April 2005).

'*Residential accommodation*' means

- a building, or part of a building, that consists of a dwelling or a number of dwellings (owner-occupied homes, homes rented from private landlords, local authorities and housing associations);
- a building, or part of a building, used for a '*relevant residential purpose*' (see 42.1(15) LAND AND BUILDINGS);

- a caravan used as a place of permanent habitation (ie a residential caravan sited at a permanent caravan park and exceeding the limits of size currently in force for trailers which may be towed on roads, see 42.36 LAND AND BUILDINGS); or
- a houseboat (ie a boat designed or adapted for permanent habitation and having no means of self-propulsion *or* a boat used as a person's sole or main residence such as a canal boat on which the owner pays Council Tax or domestic rates).

'*Use for a relevant charitable purpose*' means use by a charity in either or both of the following ways, namely

- otherwise than in the course or furtherance of a business; or
- as a village hall or similarly in providing social or recreational facilities for a local community.

For further interpretation of these uses, see 42.1(13) LAND AND BUILDINGS.

[*VATA 1994, Sch 7A Group 2; FA 2000, s 135, Sch 35; FA 2001, Sch 31 para 1; SI 1998/1375; SI 2004/777; SI 2005/726*]. (VAT Notice 708/6/02, paras 2.2, 2.5).

'Installing'. The reduced rate is only available where the goods and materials are provided *and* installed by a VAT-registered business. The supply of energy saving-materials without installing them is standard-rated. Installation means putting in place energy-saving materials. This involves some process by which the materials are permanently fixed in place, although loft insulation may simply need to be unrolled and positioned in place to be installed.

Any incidental work undertaken as part of the installation process is eligible for the reduced rate. This includes minor building work (eg planing doors or windows, enlarging loft hatches and painting/plastering to make good). But if the installation of energy-saving materials is incidental to another supply (eg the building of an extension or the replacement of a roof) there is a single supply of construction services.

(VAT Notice 708/6/02, para 2.1).

De Voil Indirect Tax Service. See V4.409.

58.3 GRANT-FUNDED INSTALLATION OF HEATING EQUIPMENT OR SECURITY GOODS OR CONNECTION OF A GAS SUPPLY

The following supplies are subject to a reduced rate of VAT of 5%.

(*a*) Supplies to a 'qualifying person' of

- services of 'installing' 'heating appliances' in the qualifying person's sole or main residence, and
- 'heating appliances' by the person installing those appliances in the qualifying person's sole or main residence

to the extent that the consideration for the supply is, or is to be, funded by a grant made under a 'relevant scheme'.

'*Heating appliances*' means any of the following.

- Gas-fired room heaters that are fitted with thermostatic controls
- Electric storage heaters
- Closed solid fuel fire cassettes

- Electric dual immersion water heaters with factory-insulated hot water tanks
- Gas-fired boilers
- Oil-fired boilers
- Radiators

(*b*) Supplies to a 'qualifying person' of

- services of connecting, or reconnecting, a mains gas supply to the qualifying person's sole or main residence, and
- goods by the person connecting, or reconnecting, that gas supply where the installation of those goods is necessary for the connection, or reconnection, of the gas supply

to the extent that the consideration for the supply is, or is to be, funded by a grant made under a 'relevant scheme'.

(*c*) Supplies to a 'qualifying person' of

- services of 'installing', maintaining or repairing a central heating system (including a system which generates electricity) in the qualifying person's sole or main residence, and
- goods by the person installing, maintaining or repairing that central heating system where installation of those goods is necessary for the installation, maintenance or repair of the central heating system

to the extent that the consideration for the supply is, or is to be, funded by a grant made under a 'relevant scheme'.

Included are

- installation of a boiler, radiators, pipework and controls forming a central heating system; and
- the repair/replacement of a boiler, radiators, pipework and controls forming a central heating system (whether or not the system was originally installed under a relevant grant-funded scheme).

(*d*) Supplies consisting in the leasing of goods that form the whole or part of a central heating system (including a system which generates electricity) installed in the sole or main residence of a 'qualifying person' to the extent that the consideration for the supply is, or is to be, funded by a grant made under a 'relevant scheme'.

Under this type of arrangement, the installer installs the central heating system as usual but then sells the equipment to a leasing company (standard-rated) which makes an annual 'lease' charge to the householder which is paid for by grant-funding (reduced-rated).

(*e*) Supplies of goods that form the whole or part of a central heating system (including a system which generates electricity) installed in the sole or main residence of a 'qualifying person' where, immediately before being supplied, the goods were leased under arrangements such that the consideration for the leasing of the goods was, in whole or in part, funded by a grant made under a 'relevant scheme'.

Supplies only fall within this provision to the extent that the consideration for the supply of goods is either

- funded by a grant made under a relevant scheme; or
- a payment becoming due only by reason of the termination (whether by the passage of time or otherwise) of the leasing of the goods in question. This covers the termination fee paid if the householder sells his home before the end of the lease term and the end of the lease payment.

(*f*) Supplies to a 'qualifying person' of

- services of installing, maintaining or repairing a 'renewable source heating system' in the qualifying person's sole or main residence, and
- goods by the person installing, maintaining or repairing that renewable source heating system where the goods are necessary for the installation, maintenance or repair of the system

to the extent that the consideration for the supply is, or is to be, funded by a grant made under a 'relevant scheme'.

A '*renewable source heating system*' means a space or water heating system which uses energy from renewable sources (including solar, wind and hydroelectric power) or near renewable resources (including ground and air heat).

(*g*) Supplies to a 'qualifying person' of

- services of 'installing' 'qualifying security goods' in the qualifying person's sole or main residence, and
- qualifying security goods by a person who installs those goods in the qualifying person's sole or main residence

to the extent that the consideration for the supply is, or is to be, funded by a grant made under a 'relevant scheme'.

'*Qualifying security goods*' means any of the following.

- Locks or bolts for windows
- Locks, bolts or security chains for doors
- Spy holes
- Smoke alarms

A '*qualifying person*' is a person who, at the time of the supply, is aged 60 or over or is in receipt of one or more of the following benefits.

- Council tax benefit
- Disability living allowance
- Any element of child tax credit other than the family element
- Working tax credit
- Housing benefit
- Income support
- An income-based jobseeker's allowance

- Industrial injuries disablement pension payable at the increased rate to include constant attendance allowance
- War disablement pension payable at the increased rate to include constant attendance allowance or mobility supplement

Where there are qualifying and non-qualifying persons living in the same dwelling, relief applies if the supply is to a qualifying person. In practice, for a supply to be to a qualifying person, that person must be responsible for ordering the work to be done.

A '*relevant scheme*' is a scheme which

- has as one of its objects the funding of the installation of energy-saving materials in the homes of qualifying persons; and
- disburses grants (directly or indirectly) in whole or part out of funds made available to it for that objective by the Secretary of State, the Scottish Ministers, the National Assembly for Wales, a Minister or a Northern Ireland Department, the EC, a local authority or under an arrangement approved by the Gas and Electricity Markets Authority or the Director General of Electricity Supply for Northern Ireland.

This means schemes such as the Home Energy Efficiency Scheme (HEES), the Domestic Energy Efficiency Scheme (DEES) in Northern Ireland and similar schemes in Scotland and Wales; certain local authority schemes; and other schemes operated by utility companies which involve disbursing grants under schemes authorised by the Office of Gas and Electricity Markets (OFGEM). (Internal Guidance V1–7, Chapter 6 para 4.6).

[*VATA 1994, Sch 7A Group 3; FA 2000, s 135, Sch 35; FA 2001, Sch 31 para 1; Tax Credits Act 2002, Sch 3 para 48; SI 1998/1375; SI 2002/1100*]. (VAT Notice 708/6/02, paras 3.2, 3.3).

'Installing'. The reduced rate is only available where the goods and materials are provided *and* installed by a VAT-registered business. The supply of goods and materials without installing them is standard-rated. Installation means putting in place the goods in question. This involves some process by which the materials are permanently fixed in place.

Any incidental work undertaken as part of the installation process is eligible for the reduced rate.

(VAT Notice 708/6/02, para 2.1).

Apportionment where grants received. Where a grant is made to fund supplies within (*a*) to (*g*) above (relevant supplies) and other supplies (non-relevant supplies), the charge must be apportioned. The proportion of the grant attributed to the relevant supplies is

$G \times A \div B$

where

G = the full grant received

A = the consideration reasonably attributable to the relevant supplies (excluding VAT)

B = the total consideration for relevant and non-relevant supplies (excluding VAT)

[*VATA 1994, Sch 7A Group 3, Note 3; FA 2001, Sch 31 para 1; SI 1998/1375; SI 2002/1100*].

Example 1: Full grant received covering all work

A builder installs relevant supplies to a value of £300 and carries out other building work to a value of £700 (both excluding VAT) for C in his main residence. A grant is received to cover the full cost of work.

	£	£
Value of relevant supplies	300.00	
VAT thereon (5%)	15.00	
		315.00
Value of non-relevant supplies	700.00	
VAT thereon (17.5%)	122.50	
		822.50
Total cost covered by grant		£1,137.50

Example 2: Partial grant received which the grant-awarding body allocates to the installation of relevant supplies

The facts are as in *Example 1* above except that C receives a grant of £200 towards the installation of the relevant supplies and pays for the rest of the work himself.

	£	£
Value of relevant supplies which are grant-funded	200.00	
VAT thereon (5%)	10.00	
		210.00
Value of other supplies	800.00	
VAT thereon (17.5%)	140.00	
		940.00
Total cost including VAT		1,150.00
Grant received		200.00
Contribution from C		£950.00

Example 3: Partial grant received which the grant-awarding body does not allocate

The facts are as in *Example 1* above except that C receives a grant of £200 towards the total cost and pays for the rest of the work himself.

Proportion of total grant allocated to relevant supplies

£200 × 300/1000 = £60

	£	£
Value of relevant supplies which are grant-funded	60.00	
VAT thereon (5%)	3.00	
		63.00
Value of other supplies	940.00	
VAT thereon (17.5%)	164.50	
		1,104.00
Total cost including VAT		1,167.50
Grant received		200.00
Contribution from C		£967.50

De Voil Indirect Tax Service. See V4.407; V4.408; V4.416.

58.4 WOMEN'S SANITARY PRODUCTS

Supplies of 'women's sanitary products' are subject to a reduced rate of VAT of 5% (previously standard-rated).

'*Women's sanitary products*' means any of the following.

- Products that are designed, and marketed, as being solely for use for absorbing, or otherwise collecting, lochia (discharge from the womb after childbirth) or menstrual flow. *Excluded* are protective briefs or any other form of clothing.

  This includes sanitary towels, sanitary pads, tampons, keepers and maternity pads.

- Panty liners, other than panty liners that are designed as being primarily for use as incontinence products.

  Panty liners designed for sanitary protection, but marketed as also suitable for protection against light incontinence or light feminine discharges, are eligible for supply at the reduced rate. Panty liners designed primarily as incontinence products are not eligible for the reduced rate, but may qualify for a separate VAT relief (see below).

- Sanitary belts (for use with looped towels or pads).

The reduced rate does not apply to

- complementary products such as feminine wipes and sprays;

- incontinence products (which are specifically excluded because zero-rating may be available for such products bought by incontinent people living in their own homes, see 32.23 HEALTH AND WELFARE);
- clothing or sanitary accessories (eg disposable or protective pants or briefs that either hold sanitary protection in place or protect the wearer from leakage). Certain items of children's clothing may be zero-rated under a separate relief, see 13 CLOTHING AND FOOTWEAR; and
- dual-purpose products designed to protect against both menstrual flow and incontinence.

[*VATA 1994, Sch 7A Group 4; FA 2001, Sch 31 para 1; SI 2000/2954*]. (VAT Notice 701/18/02, paras 2.1–2.5).

De Voil Indirect Tax Service. See V4.417.

58.5 CHILDREN'S CAR SEATS

The supply, acquisition or importation of 'children's car seats' is subject to VAT at the reduced rate of 5% (previously standard-rated).

A '*children's car seat*' is any of the following.

(*a*) A '*safety seat*', ie a seat

- designed to be sat in by a child in a road vehicle;
- designed so that, when in use in a road vehicle, it can be restrained
  - (i) by a seat belt fitted in the vehicle,
  - (ii) by belts, or anchorages, that form part of the seat being attached to the vehicle, or
  - (iii) in either of those ways, and
- incorporating an integral harness, or integral impact shield, for restraining a child seated in it.

(*b*) A children's travel system comprising a combination of a safety seat (see (*a*) above) and a '*related wheeled framework*'. For these purposes a wheeled framework is 'related' to a safety seat if the framework and the seat are each designed so that

- when the seat is not in use in a road vehicle it can be attached to the framework, and
- when the seat is so attached, the combination of the seat and the framework can be used as a child's pushchair.

(*c*) A '*booster seat*', ie a seat designed

- to be sat in by a child in a road vehicle, and
- so that, when in use in a road vehicle, it and a child seated in it can be restrained by a seat belt fitted in the vehicle.

(*d*) A '*booster cushion*', ie a cushion designed

- to be sat on by a child in a road vehicle, and

- so that a child seated on it can be restrained by a seat belt fitted in the vehicle.

For the above purposes, a '*child*' means a person aged under 14 years.

[*VATA 1994, ss 2(1A)–(1C), 29A, Sch 7A Group 5; FA 2001, s 96, Sch 31 para 1*].

Reduced-rating is not tied to any manufacturing standards but children's car seats approved to the latest European Standard will be marked with a UN 'E' mark.

A carrycot with restraint straps is not reduced-rated under the above provisions.

Children's travel systems. There are currently two types of travel system.

- A safety seat within (*a*) above and a pram/pushchair that can be fitted together and where both of the elements can be used independently of each other.

  In such a case, the safety seat is reduced-rated and the pram/pushchair element is standard-rated.

- A safety seat within (*a*) above, a related wheeled framework as in (*b*) above and a pram/pushchair seat. Any combination of the three elements may be supplied together but either the safety seat or the pram/pushchair seat can be attached to the framework for use as a pram. The framework is only of use when one of the other two elements is attached.

  In such a case

  (i) when supplied separately, a safety seat is reduced-rated, a wheeled framework is standard-rated and a pram seat is standard-rated;

  (ii) the supply of just a safety seat and a wheeled framework is wholly reduced-rated;

  (iii) the supply of just a pram seat and a wheeled framework is wholly standard-rated; and

  (iv) when all three elements are supplied together, the pram seat is standard-rated and the other two elements are reduced-rated.

Cars supplied with a fitted children's car seat. Where a car is supplied with a fitted children's car seat, whether as an integral part or as an optional extra, the supply is wholly standard-rated.

(VAT Notice 701/23/02, paras 5.1–5.5).

De Voil Indirect Tax Service. See V4.418.

59 Registration

Cross-references. See 8.5 BUSINESS for anti-avoidance measures to combat business splitting and the conditions for the separation of a previously single business into independent parts for registration purposes; 8.10 BUSINESS for sale or transfer of a business as a going concern; 12.3 CHARITIES for registration by charities; 14.3–14.4 CLUBS AND ASSOCIATIONS for registration by clubs, etc; 31 GROUPS OF COMPANIES for group registration; 35.10 INPUT TAX for VAT paid on goods and services obtained before registration; 36 INSOLVENCY for the effect of individuals becoming bankrupt or companies entering receivership or liquidation; 41 ISLE OF MAN; 43.5 LOCAL AUTHORITIES AND PUBLIC BODIES; 48.1–48.4 OVERSEAS TRADERS; 50.2 PARTNERSHIPS AND JOINT VENTURES for partnership registration; 53.3 PENSION SCHEMES.

De Voil Indirect Tax Service. See V2.1.

The contents of this chapter are as follows.

59.1 REGISTRATION IN RESPECT OF UK SUPPLIES

A 'person' who is in business and either makes or intends to make 'taxable supplies' of goods or services in the course or furtherance of that business may be liable or entitled to register for VAT.

Person includes a body of persons corporate or unincorporate. [*Interpretation Act 1978, Sch 1*]. In effect there are two types of persons.

(*a*) *Legal persons*. A legal person is an entity or body which has an existence separate and distinct from the 'persons' (legal or natural) comprising that entity or body. This includes

- bodies corporate;
- corporations sole;
- Scottish partnerships; and
- European Economic Interest Groupings.

(*b*) *Natural persons*. A sole proprietor is clearly a natural person but so are partnerships and unincorporated associations. In the case of partnerships and associations, it is the sum of the members that are the 'person'. This can be up to 20 in the case of a partnership (although some types of professional partnerships have no limit on their membership), or perhaps many hundreds in the case of an association.

(Internal Guidance V1–28, para 2.3).

It is the 'person' who is required to register, not the business or businesses carried on. Thus, where a person is operating more than one business, even though they are dissimilar, *all* the person's business activities must be covered by one registration (*C & E Commrs v Glassborow and Another QB, [1974] STC 142 (TVC 55.1)*). This applies even if one or more of the businesses would be under the registration limit if carried out alone.

Taxable supplies are the supplies of goods or services made in the UK other than EXEMPT SUPPLIES (24). [*VATA 1994, s 4(2)*].

De Voil Indirect Tax Service. See V2.101–103.

59.2 Entitlement to be registered

Persons making or intending the make taxable supplies. Where a person who is not registered or liable to be registered in the UK satisfies HMRC that he

(i) makes taxable supplies; or

(ii) is carrying on a business and intends to make such supplies in the course or furtherance of that business,

HMRC must, if he so requests, register him from the day on which the request is made or from such earlier date as may be agreed between the person and HMRC. [*VATA 1994, Sch 1 para 9*]. See 8.1 BUSINESS for the test of whether an activity is to be treated as a business.

Retrospective registration. The provisions allow a person to negotiate registration from a date prior to the date of application provided this is done at the time of initial application and not subsequently after registration. HMRC's view (confirmed by the Solicitor's Office) is that the provisions must be read as a whole so that the condition 'or from such earlier date as may be agreed' would only operate if the person is 'not liable to be registered and is not already so registered' at the time of seeking the earlier date. (Internal Guidance V1–28, para 7.2.2). See also *C & E Commrs v Eastwood Care Homes (Ilkeston) Ltd and Others, CA [2001] STC 1629 (TVC 30.6)*. In any case application cannot be made to backdate registration any earlier than three years before the date of application. (VAT Notice 700/1/02, para 2.4).

'*Intending traders*'. The provisions under (ii) above allow registration for a person who is carrying on a business, is not yet making taxable supplies at the time of applying but who intends to do so in the future. Intending traders normally seek registration from a current date in order to reclaim input tax incurred in the setting up and development of the business. In some cases the amounts involved may be substantial and cover long periods. HMRC must therefore be satisfied that there is a firm intention to make taxable supplies before allowing registration as an intending trader.

(Internal Guidance V1–28, para 3.3.3).

Persons only making exempt or certain outside the scope supplies. Where a person who is not registered or liable to be registered in the UK satisfies HMRC that

(*a*) he has a 'business establishment' (including a branch or agency) in the UK or his 'usual place or residence' is in the UK,

(*b*) he does not make or intend to make taxable supplies in the UK, and

(*c*) he either

  (i) makes supplies

  - outside the UK which would be taxable supplies if made in the UK, or
  - falling within 35.3(*c*) INPUT TAX (mainly exempt financial services), or

  (ii) he is carrying on a business and intends to make such supplies in the course or furtherance of that business,

HMRC must, on request, register that person from the day on which the request is made or from such earlier date as is mutually agreed.

The '*usual place of residence*' of a company means the place where it is legally constituted.

[*VATA 1994, Sch 1 para 10; FA 1997, s 32*].

For these purposes a '*business establishment*' includes the registered office of an overseas company. Where a business provides accountancy services at its premises for a non-established taxable person who does not make supplies in the UK, HMRC do not consider these premises to be a business establishment.

An overseas business has a branch in the UK if it maintains a permanent office at which staff are employed. It has an agency in the UK if it has a permanent UK agent which enters into contracts for the purchase of goods and services or for the import of goods in its name on a regular basis. An agent who merely acts as an intermediary in bringing together customer and supplier but is not directly involved in the supply chain does not constitute an agency.

(Internal Guidance V1–28, para 7.7.2).

These provisions allow a UK business to register where it does not make taxable supplies in the UK but makes supplies within (*c*)(i) above. It also means that an overseas business with a business establishment, but no taxable supplies, in the UK can register in the UK and, because of (*b*) above, can recover input tax on taxable supplies it receives from UK VAT-registered businesses or on goods it imports into the UK (subject to the normal rules). See 35.3(*b*) INPUT TAX. An overseas business with no business establishment, and no taxable supplies, in the UK can only recover UK VAT under the *EC 8th Directive* (if established in another EC country, see 22.48 EUROPEAN

COMMUNITY LEGISLATION) or the *EC 13th Directive* (if in business outside the EC, see 22.49 EUROPEAN COMMUNITY LEGISLATION).

De Voil Indirect Tax Service. See V2.120; V2.121; V2.144; V2.146.

59.3 Compulsory registration

Subject to the exception below, a person who makes taxable supplies but is not registered under *VATA 1994* becomes liable to be registered under these provisions as follows.

(*a*) At the end of any month if the value of his taxable supplies in the period of one year then ending has exceeded the limit in Table A below. (If taxable supplies have been made for a period of less than 12 months, the value of all taxable supplies to the end of the month in question must be compared to the limit in Table A below, see *Mr & Mrs Norton (VTD 151) (TVC 55.13)*.)

(*b*) At any time, if there are reasonable grounds for believing that the value of his taxable supplies in the period of 30 days then beginning will exceed the limit in Table A below.

(*c*) Where a business carried on by a taxable person is transferred to another person as a going concern and the transferee is not registered under *VATA 1994* at the time of the transfer, the transferee becomes liable to be registered under these provisions at that time if

   (i) the value of his taxable supplies in the period of one year ending at the time of the transfer has exceeded the limit in Table A below; or

   (ii) there are reasonable grounds for believing that the value of his taxable supplies in the period of 30 days beginning at the time of the transfer will exceed the limit in Table A below.

   For these purposes, the transferee is treated as having carried on the business before as well as after the transfer, ie under (i) above the transferor's taxable supplies in the one year to the date of transfer must also be taken into account.

Table A

Effective date	*Limit*
1.4.05	£60,000
1.4.04–31.3.05	£58,000
10.4.03–31.3.04	£56,000
25.4.02–9.4.03	£55,000
1.4.01–24.4.02	£54,000
1.4.00–31.3.01	£52,000
1.4.99–31.3.00	£51,000

[*VATA 1994, s 49(1)(a), Sch 1 para 1(1)(2); SI 1999/595; SI 2000/804; SI 2001/640; SI 2002/1098; SI 2003/1058; SI 2004/775; SI 2005/727*].

A person is treated as having become liable to be registered at any time when he would have become so liable under the above provisions but for any existing registration which is subsequently cancelled under 59.10(3), 59.17(*b*), 59.25(*c*) or 59.32(*b*) below. [*VATA 1994, Sch 1 para 1*(*5*); *FA 2000, s 132*(*6*)].

Exception. A person does not become liable to be registered under (*a*) or (*c*)(i) above if HMRC are satisfied that the value of his taxable supplies in the period of one year beginning at the time at which he would become liable to be registered will not exceed the limit in Table B below.

Table B

Effective date	*Limit*
1.4.05	£58,000
1.4.04–31.3.05	£56,000
10.4.03–31.3.04	£54,000
25.4.02–9.4.03	£53,000
1.4.01–24.4.02	£52,000
1.4.00–31.3.01	£50,000
1.4.99–31.3.00	£49,000

[*VATA 1994, s 49*(*1*)(*a*), *Sch 1 para 1*(*3*); *SI 1999/595; SI 2000/804; SI 2001/640; SI 2002/1098; SI 2003/1058; SI 2004/775; SI 2005/727*].

This gives HMRC discretion to allow requests for retrospective exception. Exception is generally granted on the basis of the value of taxable supplies made and future anticipated supplies, at the time when the application is made. It should, however, be noted that, if HMRC grant exception, taxable supplies must still be monitored on a monthly basis in order to determine whether a further liability to registration arises. If, for example, a person is granted exception but one month later the value of his supplies render him liable to registration under (*a*) above, then he must either register for VAT or again satisfy HMRC that his expected turnover for the forthcoming 12 months will not exceed the limit in Table B above. (Internal Guidance V1–28, paras 6.5.3, 6.5.4).

See, however, *dicta* of Lord Granchester in *WF Shephard (VTD 2232) (TVC 49.52)*. Where a trader has not applied to HMRC at the right time to consider the relevant circumstances, this exception can only be relied upon by a trader if he establishes that, at the right time, HMRC could not reasonably have come to any conclusion other than that taxable supplies in the year would not exceed the relevant amount. These *dicta* were followed in *RJ & J Nash (VTD 14944) (TVC 55.22)* where, although it was accepted that turnover had fallen below the registration limit following a transfer of a going concern, there were no grounds on which HMRC could have been expected, at the date of the transfer, to have believed that this would be the case. See also *Gray (t/a William Gray and Son) v C & E Commrs, Ch D [2000] STC 880 (TVC 55.26)*.

Taxable supplies. A taxable supply is a supply of goods or services made in the UK other than an exempt supply. [*VATA 1994, s 4*(*2*)]. In determining whether the registration limits in Tables A and B above have been exceeded, it is therefore necessary to take into account the VAT-exclusive value of all standard and zero-rated supplies of goods and services, including

- the value of 'reverse charge' services received from abroad (see 39.4 INTERNATIONAL SERVICES); and

- the value of any SELF-SUPPLIES (62).

The following special rules, however, apply.

- *Capital assets*. Supplies of goods or services that are capital assets of the business in the course or furtherance of which they are supplied are to be disregarded. Specifically, however, any standard-rated supply of an interest in, right over, or licence to occupy land is not to be regarded as a capital asset and does form part of the person's taxable supplies for registration purposes. [*VATA 1994, Sch 1 para 1*(*7*)(*8*)].

  Capital assets may be tangible or intangible and include premises, plant, machinery, office machinery, computers, office furniture, used company cars, patent rights which have been exploited and which are sold outright, and goodwill. Capital goods have been defined as 'goods used for the purposes of some business activity and distinguishable by their durable nature and their value and such that the acquisition costs are not normally treated as current expenditure but written off over several years' (*Verbond van Nederlandse Ondernemingen v Inspecteur der Invoerrechten en Accijnzen, CJEC [1977] 1 CMLR 413 (TVC 21.284)*). In *The Trustees of the Mellerstain Trust (VTD 4256) (TVC 7.104)* the tribunal followed this definition and held that paintings sold from an historic house open to the public were capital assets which had been used to make taxable supplies, and as such did not render the trust liable to register for VAT. It would appear, however, that HMRC have successfully argued (in a case not brought before a tribunal) that where a company sold various paintings which it owned as investment assets, the paintings were not capital assets but part of the stock of the company, on the grounds that they were not utilised in the making of taxable supplies. (Internal Guidance V1–28, para 2.8).

- *Distance sales*. Supplies can be disregarded if they are only taxable supplies in the UK because an overseas business makes distance sales to non-taxable persons in the UK and is required to register under *VATA 1994, Sch 2* (see 59.11 *et seq* below). [*VATA 1994, Sch 1 para 1*(*7*)].

  The value of any distance sales where the place of supply is considered to be in another EC country must also be excluded when calculating taxable turnover. (Internal Guidance V1–28, para 2.7).

- *Previous registration*. For the purposes of (*a*) and (*c*)(i) above, supplies made at a time when the person was previously registered under *VATA 1994* can be disregarded if his registration was cancelled otherwise than under 59.10(3), 59.17(*b*), 59.25(*c*) or 59.32(*b*) below and HMRC are satisfied that before his registration was cancelled he had given them all the information they needed in order to determine whether to cancel his registration. [*VATA 1994, Sch 1 para 1*(*4*)*; FA 2000, s 136*(*6*)].

- *Fiscal warehousing*. Supplies to which *VATA 1994, s 18B*(*4*) (last acquisition or supply before removal from fiscal warehousing) applies and supplies treated as made under *VATA 1994, s 18C*(*3*) (self-supply of services on removal of goods from warehousing) can be disregarded. See 70.17 and 70.20 WAREHOUSED GOODS AND FREE ZONES respectively. [*VATA 1994, Sch 1 para 1*(*9*)*; FA 1996, Sch 3 para 13*].

- *Margin schemes*. Under the schemes for SECOND-HAND GOODS (61), the taxable supplies are the full selling prices of the goods. Under the TOUR OPERATORS' MARGIN SCHEME (66), taxable supplies are the total margin (ie difference between buying prices and the selling prices) on margin scheme supplies plus the full value of any other taxable supplies (including all in-house supplies).

- *Supplies of long-term accommodation.* The value of certain supplies of long-term accommodation can be excluded when calculating taxable turnover. See 33.2 HOTELS AND HOLIDAY ACCOMMODATION.

De Voil Indirect Tax Service. See V2.135–137.

59.4 Notification and date of registration

Where a person becomes liable to be registered by virtue of

(*a*) 59.3(*a*) above, he must notify HMRC of the liability within 30 days of the end of the relevant month. HMRC must then register him (whether or not he so notifies them) with effect from the end of the month following the relevant month or from such earlier date as is mutually agreed;

> *Example*
>
> On 22 May, W determines that his supplies in the past twelve months have exceeded the registration threshold.
>
> W becomes liable to be registered on 30 May. He must notify HMRC of his liability to be registered by 30 June. Unless mutually agreed otherwise, HMRC will register him with effect from 1 July.

(*b*) 59.3(*b*) above, he must notify HMRC of the liability before the end of the period by reference to which the liability arises. HMRC must then register him (whether or not he so notifies them) with effect from the beginning of that period;

> *Example*
>
> On 20 January, Y expects that his supplies in the next 30 days will exceed the registration threshold.
>
> Y becomes liable to be registered on 20 January. He must notify HMRC of his liability to be registered by 20 February. HMRC will register him with effect from 20 January.

(*c*) 59.3(*c*) above, he must notify HMRC of the liability within 30 days of the time when the business is transferred. HMRC must then register any such person (whether or not he so notifies them) with effect from the time when the business is transferred; and

(*d*) 59.3(*a*) above *and* 59.3(*b*) or 59.3(*c*) above at the same time, HMRC must register him under (*b*) or (*c*) above, as the case may be, rather than under (*a*) above.

[*VATA 1994, Sch 1 paras 5–8*].

Failure to notify. Failure to notify a liability to register may incur a penalty. See 52.12 PENALTIES. Late notification of a liability to register will result in the backdating of the registration, HMRC having no discretion in the matter (*SJ Whitehead (VTD 202) (TVC 55.70)*) and VAT must be accounted for from the correct date whether or not it has been charged (*JR Atkinson (VTD 309) (TVC 55.73)*).

De Voil Indirect Tax Service. See V2.126; V2.128.

59.5 **Application for registration**

Application for registration under 59.2 and 59.3 above must be made in such form and containing such particulars as HMRC may by regulation prescribe. Application must currently be made on Form VAT 1 (or Welsh version Form VAT 1(W)) and must include a signed declaration that all information entered in it, or accompanying it, is true and complete. VAT Notice 700/1 *Should I be Registered for VAT?* has extensive notes on how to complete the form. A partnership applying for registration must also complete Form VAT 2 (or Welsh version Form VAT 2(W)). [*VATA 1994, Sch 1 para 17; SI 1995/2518, Reg 5*(*1*); *SI 2000/794*]. See also 50.2 PARTNERSHIPS AND JOINT VENTURES.

When submitting the above VAT application form, details to support an application for VAT periods to correspond with the financial year of the business (see 2.2(*d*) ACCOUNTING PERIODS AND RETURNS) should be sent if appropriate.

The completed application forms, with any extra information requested by HMRC, should be sent to the appropriate VAT Registration Office (see 59.38 below for addresses). When HMRC have checked the details on the application form, they send a certificate of registration (Form VAT 4) showing the effective date of registration, the registration number, the date on which the first VAT period ends and the length of future VAT periods (ie three-monthly or monthly). If a reply is not received from HMRC within three weeks of submitting Form VAT 1, it is advisable to contact them to make sure that the application was received. (VAT Notice 700/1/02, para 3.5).

HMRC may amend a certificate of registration issued with the wrong date and issue assessments for any earlier periods then coming within the scope of VAT (*Maidstone Sailing Club (per DG Oliver) (VTD 511) (TVC 55.82)*). The certificate is no more than a notification of the registration date and number. Other matters shown on the certificate, including the dates on which returns are to be made, are entered as matters of administrative convenience and therefore are not appealable matters within *VATA 1994, s 83*(*a*) (*Punchwell Ltd (VTD 1085) (TVC 57.2)*). Further, the allocation of registration numbers is within the administrative discretion of HMRC (see *L Reich & Sons Ltd (VTD 97) (TVC 55.186)* where HMRC refused to reallocate the registration number of a company to a newly formed subsidiary which took over the trade previously carried on by the parent company).

A business must start keeping records and charging VAT to its customers from the date it knows it has to be registered. It can charge VAT before it is actually registered but, until it has received a registration number, it must not show VAT as a separate item on any invoice issued. It should change its prices to include VAT and explain to any VAT-registered customers that it will be sending them VAT invoices at a later date. Once the business has its registration number, it should send the necessary invoices showing VAT within 30 days.

Where a business has asked for voluntary registration (see 59.2 above), it should start keeping records and charging VAT from the date it is registered, ie normally the date requested on the application form.

(VAT Notice 700/1/02, para 4.1).

Electronic application. A business not yet registered for VAT can use HMRC's eVAT service to register instead of completing the paper version of Form VAT 1. An agent, authorised by the business, may also fill out the online form on its behalf. The business must first be authorised to use the eVAT service. This can be done via Online services on the HMRC website.

At the end of the application process, a business will receive an online acknowledgment and a unique reference number. The date and time shown on this will be the time the notification was made for legal purposes. It is therefore recommended that a copy of the acknowledgement is taken for record purposes. If an electronic acknowledgment is not received, it should be presumed that the request has not been received by HMRC.

All electronic applications are processed in strict date order. HMRC aim to process an application within 15 working days of receiving the online application although it may take longer if additional information is requested. For security reasons, VAT registration numbers are only notified in writing and by post to the address confirmed as the principal place of business. If a VAT registration number has not been received within 15 working days, the business should contact the National Advice Service on 0845 010 9000 and quote the acknowledgment reference number. Similarly, the National Advice Service should be contacted if an error is discovered in the original application or the business wishes to cancel the application.

[*SI 1995/2518, Reg 5(4)–(14); SI 2004/1675*].

59.6 **Exemption from registration**

Where a person who makes or intends to make taxable supplies satisfies HMRC that 'any such supply' is zero-rated (or would be so if he were a taxable person) they may, if he so requests and they think fit, grant exemption from registration under the above provisions. On a material change in the nature of the supplies made, the person exempted must notify HMRC of the change within 30 days of the end of the day on which it occurred or, if no particular day is so identifiable, within 30 days of the end of the particular quarter in which it occurred. On a material alteration in any quarter in the proportion of taxable supplies of such a person that are zero-rated, he must notify HMRC of the alteration within 30 days of the end of that quarter. Exemption applies until it appears to HMRC that the request should no longer be acted upon or the request is withdrawn by the trader. [*VATA 1994, Sch 1 para 14*].

'*Any such supply*' has its ordinary meaning and HMRC therefore have discretion in applying the provisions where not all of the supplies are zero-rated (*Fong (VTD 590) (TVC 55.139)*). HMRC will therefore exempt a person from registration if only a small proportion of his taxable supplies is standard-rated provided that, if registered, input tax would normally exceed output tax.

HMRC will consider applications from unregistered persons who have reached the registration threshold and from persons who are already registered. Unregistered applicants are still required to complete form VAT 1.

(VAT Notice 700/1/02, para 2.7; Internal Guidance V1–28, para 6.6.5).

A material alteration affecting exemption from registration would arise where, if the person was registered, output tax would exceed input tax in any twelve-month period. (VAT Notice 700, para 26.12).

Exemption saves a person the trouble and expense of having to keep proper records and accounts for VAT purposes and rendering returns but it does mean that input tax paid on purchases of goods or services for the business is not reclaimable.

De Voil Indirect Tax Service. See V2.147.

59.7 **Changes in circumstances**

Except where other time limits are specified, a registered person must notify HMRC, within 30 days and with full written particulars of any change in the name, constitution or ownership of the business or any other event which may necessitate the variation of the register or cancellation of registration. [*SI 1995/2518, Reg 5(2); SI 2000/794*].

The appropriate VAT registration office should be advised of the changes (see 59.38 below). Registration number and date of change should be given in any correspondence.

Electronic notification. A business can also use HMRC's eVAT service to notify changes in registration details. The business must first be authorised to use the service. This can be done via Online services on the HMRC website. This method of notification can only be used to make changes to an existing and continuing registration. Changes involving deregistration (see below) or transfer of a registration number to a new business must continue to be made by post, as must the appointment of, or changes to, an appointed VAT representative.

Following notification, the business will receive an online acknowledgment and a unique reference number. The date and time shown on this will be the time the notification was made for legal purposes. It is therefore recommended that a copy of the acknowledgement is taken for record purposes. If an electronic acknowledgment is not received, it should be presumed that the request has not been received by HMRC.

[*SI 1995/2558, Reg 5(4)(11); SI 2004/1675*].

Changes not involving deregistration. Registration details must be amended for changes in any of the following.

- The names of the proprietors of, or partners in, the business.
- The name, business name or trading style of the business.
- The name of an incorporated company.
- The composition of a partnership where one or more of the former partners remains in the partnership.
- The name and/or address of the UK agent for VAT purposes appointed by an overseas company or resident.
- The address of the principal place of business.
- The registered office of an incorporated company.
- The main business activity.
- A limited company is re-registered as an unlimited company, or vice versa.
- A private company is re-registered as a public limited company, or vice versa.

- Bank or National Giro account number or bank sorting code. If the annual accounting scheme is used, the registered person must notify the bank and VAT Central Unit Annual Accounting Section immediately.
- Certain changes affecting group treatment. See 31.3 GROUPS OF COMPANIES.

Changes involving deregistration. The following changes will require deregistration.

- Sale of the business.
- Death, insolvency or incapacity of a taxable person. See 19.1 DEATH AND INCAPACITY and 36.1 INSOLVENCY.
- Conversion of a business into an incorporated company.
- Conversion of an incorporated company into a partnership or a sole proprietorship.
- A sole proprietor takes one or more persons into partnership.
- A partnership ceases to exist but one of the former partners becomes the sole proprietor of the business.
- Changes in the name or status of an unincorporated company.
- The transfer of business from one incorporated company to another.
- The business ceases to supply taxable goods or services.
- There is a complete change in the composition of a partnership at any one time.
- The business is otherwise disposed of.

(VAT Notice 700, para 26.3; Internal Guidance V1–28, paras 12.7, 12.8).

59.8 **Cessation of liability to be registered**

A person who has become liable to be registered under 59.3 above only ceases to be liable to be registered in the following circumstances.

- At any time if HMRC are satisfied that
  - (i) he has ceased to make taxable supplies; or
  - (ii) he is not at that time a person in relation to whom any of the conditions in 59.3(*a*)–(*c*) above is satisfied.
- If HMRC are satisfied that the value of his taxable supplies in the period of one year then beginning will not exceed the following specified limits.

Effective date	*Limit*
1 April 2005	£58,000
1 April 2004	£56,000
10 April 2003	£54,000
25 April 2002	£53,000
1 April 2001	£52,000
1 April 2000	£50,000

Effective date	*Limit*
1 April 1999	£49,000

However, that person does not cease to be liable to be registered under these provisions if HMRC are satisfied that the reason the value of his taxable supplies will not exceed the above limit is that in the period in question he will cease making taxable supplies or will suspend making them for a period of 30 days or more.

Taxable supplies. In determining the value of a person's supplies for the above purposes, supplies of goods or services that are 'capital assets' of the business in the course or furtherance of which they are supplied are disregarded. However, this is not to include the taxable supply of an interest in, right over or licence to occupy any land which is not zero-rated. See 59.3 above for the definition of '*capital assets*'.

Any supplies which are taxable supplies only because an overseas trader making distance sales in the UK is required to register under *VATA 1994, Sch 2* (see 59.11 *et seq* below) can also be disregarded in determining the value of his supplies for the above purposes.

Taxable supplies for the above purposes are determined on the basis that no VAT is chargeable on the supply (ie VAT-exclusive).

[*VATA 1994, Sch 1 paras 3, 4, 15, 16; SI 1999/595; SI 2000/804; SI 2001/640; SI 2002/1098; SI 2003/1058; SI 2004/775; SI 2005/727*].

59.9 Notification of end of liability or entitlement to registration

A person

- voluntarily registered under *VATA 1994, Sch 1 para 9* (persons making or intending to make taxable supplies, see 59.2 above) or compulsorily registered under 59.3 above who ceases to make or have the intention of making taxable supplies, or
- voluntarily registered under *VATA 1994, Sch 1 para 10* (persons only making exempt or certain outside the scope supplies, see 59.2 above) who ceases to satisfy either of the conditions in 59.2(*b*) or (*c*) above

must notify HMRC of that fact within 30 days of the date on which he does so unless he would, when he so ceases, be otherwise liable or entitled to be registered under 59.11 *et seq* or 59.18 *et seq* below. [*VATA 1994, Sch 1 paras 11, 12*]. The notification must be in writing and state the date on which the registered person ceased to make or have the intention of making taxable supplies. [*SI 1995/2518, Reg 5*(3);*SI 2000/794*]. See 59.38 below for the VAT office which should be notified and 52.14 PENALTIES for failure to notify within 30 days.

59.10 Cancellation of registration

In the situations outlined in (*a*) and (*b*) below, the registration of a business making taxable supplies must or, as the case may be, can be cancelled. However, it should be remembered that where a business also makes

- distance sales from another EC country (see 59.11 below),

- acquisitions of goods from another EC country (see 59.18 below), and
- in the case of an overseas trader, disposals of assets for which a VAT repayment is claimed (see 59.26 below)

it cannot apply to deregister until it has either ceased to make those supplies or its combined taxable turnover from taxable supplies and *all* those supplies falls below the deregistration limit.

The provisions are also subject to *VATA 1994, Sch 3B para 18* (cancellation of registration under these provisions where a non-EC business intends to apply for registration under the special scheme for electronically supplied services in the EC, see 63.39 SPECIAL SCHEMES).

(*a*) A business *must* cancel its registration if any of the following occur.

(i) It ceases to make taxable supplies (see 59.9 above).

(ii) It sells its business (unless the new owner wishes to retain the VAT registration number, see 59.36 below).

(iii) Its legal status changes (eg a sole proprietor takes in one or more partners, a partnership is dissolved and the business run by a sole proprietor, a company is incorporated to take over the business previously carried on by a sole proprietor or partnership, or a company is wound up and replaced by a sole proprietor or partnership). In such a case, the business will normally cancel its existing registration (by completing Form VAT 7) and apply for a new registration number by completing an application Form VAT 1. It may, however, ask to retain its previous registration number, in which case it must complete an application form as well as Form VAT 68. If the new legal entity is a partnership, it must also complete Form VAT 2.

(iv) It is the representative member of a VAT group (see 31 GROUPS OF COMPANIES) and wishes to disband the group. In such circumstances, the registered person ceases to exist and the business will therefore need to cancel its registration. If any member of the disbanded group is continuing to trade, it must determine whether it will need to be registered in its own right.

Where a member of a VAT group other than the representative member leaves the group, there is no need to cancel its registration unless the group only consists of the representative member and that one other member.

(v) It wishes to join a VAT group. Its existing registration must be cancelled as it is not possible to have two active registrations.

(vi) It wishes to join the agricultural flat-rate scheme (see 63.25 SPECIAL SCHEMES).

(vii) It was allowed registration on the basis that it intended to make taxable supplies and no longer intends to do so (see 59.9 above).

(viii) It was allowed registration on the basis that it made, or intended to make, supplies outside the UK which would have been taxable supplies if made in the UK and it has stopped making, or intending to make, those supplies.

(ix) It was allowed registration on the basis that it made, or intended to make, supplies of warehoused goods which were permitted to be disregarded for VAT and it has stopped making, or intending to make, those supplies.

(*b*) A business *may* ask for voluntary deregistration if any of the following occur.

(i) It satisfies HMRC that its taxable turnover in the next 12 months will not exceed the deregistration limit.

(ii) It closes down part of its business and satisfies HMRC that its taxable turnover for the remainder will not exceed the deregistration limit.

(iii) Its VAT-exclusive turnover in the past 12 months has been below the current registration threshold.

(iv) Its turnover exceeds the registration limits but it satisfies the conditions for exemption under 59.6 above.

(VAT Notice 700, para 26.2; VAT Notice 700/11/02, paras 1.2, 1.4–1.8, 2.1, 2.2).

Date of deregistration.

(1) Where a registered person satisfies HMRC he is no longer liable to be registered, HMRC must cancel his registration with effect from the day on which the request is made from such later date as is mutually agreed (provided they are satisfied that he would not be required to be registered on that date).

(2) Where HMRC are satisfied that a registered person has ceased to be 'registrable', they may cancel his registration with effect from the day on which he so ceased or from such later date as is mutually agreed (provided they are satisfied that he would not be required to be, or entitled to be, registered on that date).

(3) Where HMRC are satisfied that on the day on which a registered person was registered he was not registrable, they may cancel his registration with effect from that day.

'*Registrable*' means liable to be registered or entitled to be registered.

[*VATA 1994, Sch 1 paras 13, 18; FA 2003, Sch 2 para 3*].

Under (1) and (2) above, there is no provision to allow deregistration from an earlier date (see *S Moloney (VTD 14873) (TVC 55.114)*) but, on application, HMRC may agree to defer deregistration by up to six months if considered necessary for either

- the disposal of capital assets for which VAT invoices may need to be issued, or
- to allow input tax to be reclaimed on VAT invoices for supplies attributable to the business but which are not received until after the business has ceased to be a taxable person.

(Internal Guidance V1–28, para 13.13).

De Voil Indirect Tax Service. See V2.151–153.

59.11 REGISTRATION IN RESPECT OF SUPPLIES FROM ANOTHER EC COUNTRY ('DISTANCE SELLING')

Additional registration requirements may apply in respect of 'distance selling'. This occurs when a supplier in one EC country supplies goods, and is responsible for their delivery, to any person in another EC country who is not registered for VAT. This may include supplies not only to private individuals but to public bodies, charities and businesses too small to register or with activities that are entirely exempt. The most obvious example of this type of supply is mail order. VAT on sales to non-VAT registered customers in another EC country are in principle charged and accounted for by the supplier in the country from which the goods are dispatched. However, once the value of distance sales to any particular EC country has exceeded an annual threshold, further sales are subject to VAT in the EC country of destination and the supplier is liable to register for VAT in that country or appoint a VAT representative (see 3.8 AGENTS) who will be responsible for accounting for VAT there on his behalf.

The provisions outlined in 59.12 to 59.17 below relate to the registration of suppliers from other EC countries not already registered for VAT in the UK.

Registration by UK suppliers in other EC countries. See 23.18 EUROPEAN COMMUNITY: SINGLE MARKET.

De Voil Indirect Tax Service. See V2.171–177.

59.12 Liability to be registered

A 'person' who is not registered under *VATA 1994*, and is not liable to be registered under 59.3 above, becomes liable to be registered under these provisions on any day if, in the period beginning with 1 January in that year, he has made 'relevant supplies' whose value exceeds £70,000.

In addition, a person who is not registered or liable to be registered as above becomes liable to be registered under these provisions (whatever the value of supplies) in the following circumstances.

(*a*) He has exercised an option, under the laws of another EC country where he is taxable, to treat relevant supplies made by him as taking place outside that country and

- the supplies to which the option relates involve the removal of the goods from that country;
- if the option had not been exercised, under the law of that country the supplies would have been treated as taking place in that country; and
- he makes any relevant supply in the UK at a time when the option is in force.

(*b*) He makes a supply of goods subject to duty of excise where

- the supply involves the removal of the goods to the UK by, or under the directions of, the person making the supply;
- the supply is a transaction under which goods are acquired in the UK from another EC country by a person who is not a taxable person;
- the supply is made in the course or furtherance of a business carried on by the supplier and is not treated as a supply only by virtue of *VATA 1994, Sch 4 para 5*(*1*) or (*6*) (transfers of goods forming part of the assets of the business).

'*Person*' includes a sole proprietor, partnership, limited company, club, association or charity. It is the person who is required to register, not the business or businesses carried on. The registration covers all the businesses of the registered person in the UK.

A supply of goods is a '*relevant supply*' where

(i) the supply involves the removal of the goods to the UK by, or under the directions of, the person making the supply;

(ii) the supply does not involve the installation or assembly of goods at a place in the UK;

(iii) the supply is a transaction under which goods are acquired in the UK from another EC country by a person who is not a taxable person; and

(iv) the supply is made in the course or furtherance of a business carried on by the supplier and is not

- an exempt supply;
- a supply of goods subject to a duty of excise;
- a new means of transport (see 23.31 EUROPEAN COMMUNITY: SINGLE MARKET); or
- treated as a supply only by virtue of *VATA 1994, Sch 4 para 5(1)* or *(6)* (transfers of goods forming part of the assets of the business).

A person is treated as having become liable to be registered under the above provisions at any time when he would have become so liable but for any registration which is subsequently cancelled under 59.10(3) above or 59.17(*b*), 59.25(*c*) or 59.32(*b*) below.

In determining the value of relevant supplies for the above purposes, any part of the consideration representing a VAT liability of the supplier under the law of another EC country is disregarded. Also disregarded are supplies to which *VATA 1994, s 18B(4)* (last acquisition or supply of goods before removal from fiscal warehousing) applies. See 70.17 WAREHOUSED GOODS AND FREE ZONES.

[*VATA 1994, Sch 2 paras 1, 10; FA 1996, Sch 3 para 14; FA 2000, s 136(6)*].

Persons already registered in the UK. If a person making relevant supplies of distance sales is already registered for VAT in the UK under 59.3 above in respect of taxable supplies, he does not need also to register under these provisions but must account for VAT in the UK on distance sales even where the threshold above is not reached. (VAT Notice 700/1/02, para 5.4).

59.13 Notification of liability and registration

A person who becomes liable to registration under 59.12 above must notify HMRC of the fact within 30 days after that day.

HMRC must then register him (whether or not he so notifies them) with effect from the day on which the liability to register arose or from such earlier time as is agreed between them.

[*VATA 1994, Sch 2 paras 3, 9*].

Notification must be in such form and contain such particulars as HMRC prescribe. Application must currently be made on Form VAT 1A (or Welsh version Form VAT1A(W)) which include a signed declaration that all the information entered on the form, and accompanying it, is correct and complete. See VAT Notice 700/1 *Should I Be Registered for VAT?* for notes on how to complete the form. Where the person being registered is a partnership, Form VAT 2 must also be completed. [*SI 1995/2518, Reg 5(1);SI 2000/794*].

59.14 **Request to be registered**

A person who is not liable to be registered under *VATA 1994* and is not already so registered may request to be registered under these provisions. Provided he can satisfy HMRC that he intends

(*a*) to exercise an option referred to in 59.12(*a*) above and, from a specified date, to make relevant supplies to which the option relates, or

(*b*) from a specified date to make relevant supplies in relation to any such option which has already been exercised, or

(*c*) from a specified date to make supplies satisfying the conditions in 59.12(*b*) above,

HMRC may then, subject to such conditions as they think fit, register him from such date as is agreed between them. Any person who decides to opt to tax under this provision before reaching the threshold must notify HMRC at least 30 days before the date of the first supply to which the option is intended to apply. Application should be made using Form VAT 1A (and also Form VAT 1TR if a VAT representative is being appointed). Written evidence should be enclosed showing that firm arrangements have been made to make distance sales.

Where a person who requests registration under the above provisions is also entitled to be registered under 59.2 above, he must be registered under those provisions.

[*VATA 1994, Sch 2 para 4*].

59.15 **Cessation of liability**

A person who has become liable to be registered under 59.12 above ceases to be liable if at any time

(*a*) his relevant supplies in the year ended 31 December last before that time did not exceed £70,000 and did not include any dutiable supply falling within 59.12 above;

(*b*) HMRC are satisfied that the value of his relevant supplies in the year immediately following that year will not exceed £70,000 and will not include any such dutiable supply; and

(*c*) no such option as is mentioned in 59.12(*a*) above is in force in relation to him.

[*VATA 1994, Sch 2 para 2*].

59.16 **Notification of matters affecting registration**

A person must notify the following matters to HMRC in writing within 30 days.

(*a*) Where he is registered under these provisions and 'ceases to be registrable under *VATA 1994*'. Notification must state the date on which he ceased to be registrable.

(*b*) Where he is registered under 59.14 above, the exercise of any option or, as the case may be, the first occasion after registration when he makes a supply.

(*c*) Where he has exercised an option under 59.12(*a*) above, and the option ceases to have effect (as a consequence of its revocation or otherwise) in relation to any relevant supplies by him.

A person '***ceases to be registrable under VATA 1994***' where

- he ceases to be a person who would be liable or entitled to be registered under that *Act* if his registration were disregarded; or
- he has been registered under 59.14 above and ceases to have any intention to exercise an option or make supplies as there mentioned.

Notification must be in such form and contain such particulars as HMRC prescribe.

[*VATA 1994, Sch 2 paras 5, 9; SI 1995/2518, Reg 5(3); SI 2000/794*].

Changes in circumstances. A person registered under these provisions must notify HMRC, within 30 days and with full written particulars, of any change in the name, constitution or ownership of the business or any other event which may necessitate the variation of the register or cancellation of registration. [*SI 1995/2518, Reg 5(2); SI 2000/794*].

59.17 **Cancellation of registration**

Subject to below, the registration of a person registered under these provisions must, or as the case may be, can be cancelled in the following circumstances.

(*a*) Where a person registered under these provisions satisfies HMRC that he is not liable to be so registered, they *must*, on request, cancel his registration with effect from the day on which the request is made or such later date as is mutually agreed. HMRC must be satisfied that, at the date of the proposed cancellation, the person would not be liable to be registered under any other provision of *VATA 1994*.

(*b*) Where HMRC are satisfied that, on the day on which a person was registered under these provisions, he was not liable to be registered (or, where he was registered under 59.14 above, did not have the intention by reference to which he was registered), they may cancel his registration with effect from that day.

(*c*) Where HMRC are satisfied that a person who has been registered under 59.14 above and is not for the time being liable to be registered under 59.12 above

(i) has not, by the date specified in his request to be registered, carried out the intentions by reference to which he was registered; or

(ii) has contravened any condition of his registration,

they may cancel his registration from the date so specified or, as the case may be, the date of the contravention (or such later date as may be agreed between them). HMRC must be satisfied that, at the date of the proposed cancellation, the person would not be liable or entitled to be registered under any other provision of *VATA 1994*.

The registration of a person who has exercised an option with 59.12(*a*) above cannot be cancelled unless it has been in force for two complete calendar years.

[*VATA 1994, Sch 2 paras 6, 7*].

59.18 **REGISTRATION IN RESPECT OF ACQUISITIONS OF GOODS FROM OTHER EC COUNTRIES**

VAT on goods purchased from other EC countries is no longer paid when the goods enter the UK. Instead, for most transactions between registered persons, VAT becomes due on the acquisition of the goods by the customer and is accounted for on the normal VAT return. Where a person is not registered for VAT in the UK, any goods purchased from a registered supplier in another EC country bear VAT at origin.

59.19 Registration

To avoid distortions of VAT, additional registration requirements apply in respect of certain acquisitions from other EC countries by persons who acquire goods in excess of an annual threshold but who are not registered, or required to be registered, under the provisions in 59.1 *et seq* or 59.11 *et seq* above. The provisions apply to any person not currently registered (including public bodies, charities and even private individuals if they are not acting in a purely personal capacity).

De Voil Indirect Tax Service. See V2.181–188.

59.19 **Liability to be registered**

A 'person' who is not registered under *VATA 1994*, and is not liable to be registered under 59.3 or 59.12 above, becomes liable to be registered under these provisions if

(*a*) at the end of any month, in the period beginning with 1 January in that year, he has made 'relevant acquisitions' whose value exceeds, or

(*b*) there are reasonable grounds for believing that the value of his relevant acquisitions in the period of 30 days then beginning will exceed,

the following limits.

Effective date	*Limit*
1.4.05	£60,000
1.4.04–31.3.05	£58,000
10.4.03–31.3.04	£56,000
25.4.02–9.4.03	£55,000
1.4.01–24.4.02	£54,000
1.4.00–31.3.01	£52,000
1.4.99–31.3.00	£51,000

'*Person*' includes a sole proprietor, partnership, limited company, club, association or charity. It is the person who is required to register, not the business or businesses carried on. The registration covers all the businesses of the registered person in the UK.

For a transaction to be an acquisition it must, under *VATA 1994, s 11*,

- be a supply of goods (including anything treated for the purposes of *VATA 1994* as a supply of goods); and
- involve the removal of the goods from another EC country.

For the purposes of determining a person's entitlement or requirement to be registered under these provisions, however, only certain acquisitions are taken into account. These are called '*relevant acquisitions*' which are acquisitions which meet all of the following conditions.

- The goods are acquired in the course or furtherance of
  - (i) a business carried on by any person; or
  - (ii) any activities carried on otherwise than by way of business by any body corporate or by any club, association, organisation or other unincorporated body.

- The person who carries on that business or, as the case may be, those activities acquires the goods.
- The supplier is taxable in another EC country at the time of the transaction and the transaction is in the course or furtherance of his business.
- The goods are not acquired in pursuance of an exempt supply.
- The goods are not subject to excise duty (see 23.9 EUROPEAN COMMUNITY: SINGLE MARKET).
- The goods do not consist of a new means of transport (see 23.35 EUROPEAN COMMUNITY: SINGLE MARKET).
- The acquisition is treated as taking place in the UK.

An acquisition is not, however, a relevant acquisition where, although the goods are transported to the UK, they are deemed to be supplied in the UK (eg installed goods).

A person is treated as having become liable to be registered under the above provisions at any time when he would have become so liable but for any registration which is subsequently cancelled under 59.10(3) or 59.17(*b*) above or 59.25(*c*) or 59.32(*b*) below.

In determining the value of relevant acquisitions for the above purposes, any part of the consideration representing a VAT liability of the supplier under the law of another EC country is disregarded. Also disregarded are supplies to which *VATA 1994, s 18B*(*4*) (last acquisition or supply of goods before removal from fiscal warehousing) applies. See 70.17 WAREHOUSED GOODS AND FREE ZONES.

[*VATA 1994, s 31*(*1*), *Sch 3 paras 1, 10, 11; FA 1996, Sch 3 para 15; FA 2000, s 136*(*7*); *SI 1999/595; SI 2000/804; SI 2001/640; SI 2002/1098; SI 2003/1058; SI 2004/775; SI 2005/727*].

59.20 Notification of liability and registration

A person who becomes liable to registration under 59.19 above must notify HMRC of that fact as follows.

(*a*) Where 59.19(*a*) above applies, within 30 days of the end of the relevant month.

HMRC must then register him (whether or not he so notifies them) with effect from the end of the month following the relevant month or from such earlier date as is agreed between them.

> *Example*
>
> On 22 May, W who is not registered for VAT, calculates that, since the previous 1 January, he has made relevant acquisitions exceeding the registration threshold.
>
> W becomes liable to register on 31 May. He must notify HMRC of his liability to register in respect of acquisitions by 30 June. Unless mutually agreed otherwise, HMRC will register him with effect from 1 July.

(*b*) Where 59.19(*b*) above applies, before the end of the period by reference to which the liability arises.

HMRC must then register him (whether or not he so notifies them) with effect from the beginning of that period.

> *Example*
>
> On 22 May, W who is not registered for VAT, estimates that the value of his relevant acquisitions in the next 30 days will exceed the registration threshold.
>
> W becomes liable to register on 22 May. He must notify HMRC of his liability to register in respect of acquisitions by 20 June. HMRC will register him with effect from 22 May.

[*VATA 1994, Sch 3 paras 3, 10*].

Notification must be in such form and contain such particulars as HMRC prescribe. Application must currently be made on Form VAT 1B (or Welsh version Form VAT 1B(W)) which includes a signed declaration that all the information entered on the form, and accompanying it, is correct and complete. See VAT Notice 700/1 *Should I Be Registered for VAT?* for notes on how to complete the form. Where the person being registered is a partnership, Form VAT 2 must also be completed. [*SI 1995/2518, Reg 5(1); SI 2000/794*]. Completed application forms, with any extra information requested by HMRC, should be sent to the appropriate VAT registration office (see 59.38 below). Once registered, in addition to accounting for VAT on acquisitions, VAT must be accounted for on any taxable supplies made.

59.21 Entitlement to be registered

Where a person who is not liable to be registered under *VATA 1994* and is not already so registered satisfies HMRC that

(*a*) he makes relevant acquisitions, or

(*b*) he intends to make relevant acquisitions from a specified date,

HMRC must, if he so requests, register him from the day on which the request is made or such earlier date as is mutually agreed. Any person who decides to register voluntarily under this provision before reaching the threshold must notify HMRC at least 30 days before the date from which registration is to be effective. Application should be made on Form VAT 1B and where (*b*) above applies evidence should be enclosed showing that firm arrangements have been made to make acquisitions.

Where a person who requests registration under the above provisions is also entitled to be registered under 59.2 above, he must be registered under those provisions.

[*VATA 1994, Sch 3 para 4*].

59.22 Exemption from registration

Where a person who makes or intends to make relevant acquisitions satisfies HMRC that any such acquisitions would be zero-rated if they were taxable supplies by a taxable person, HMRC may, if the person so requests and they think fit, grant exemption from registration under these provisions (although Form VAT 1B must still be completed).

Where a person exempted under these provisions makes a relevant acquisition which would not be zero-rated if it were a taxable supply by a taxable person, he must notify HMRC within 30 days of the date of acquisition.

The exemption remains in force until it appears to HMRC that the request should no longer be acted upon or until it is withdrawn.

[*VATA 1994, Sch 3 para 8*].

59.23 Cessation of liability to be registered

A person who has become liable to be registered under 59.19 above ceases to be liable if at any time

(*a*) his relevant acquisitions in the year ended 31 December last before that time did not exceed, and

(*b*) HMRC are satisfied that the value of his relevant acquisitions in the year immediately following that year will not exceed

the following limits.

Effective date	*Limit*
1.4.05	£60,000
1.4.04–31.3.05	£58,000
10.4.03–31.3.04	£56,000
25.4.02–9.4.03	£55,000
1.4.01–24.4.02	£54,000
1.4.00–31.3.01	£52,000
1.4.99–31.3.00	£51,000

However, that person does not cease to be liable to be registered under these provisions at any time if there are reasonable grounds for believing that the value of his relevant acquisitions in the period of 30 days then beginning will exceed that limit.

[*VATA 1994, Sch 3 para 2; SI 1999/595; SI 2000/804; SI 2001/640; SI 2002/1098; SI 2003/1058; SI 2004/775; SI 2005/727*].

59.24 Notification of matters affecting registration

A person must notify the following matters to HMRC in writing within 30 days.

(*a*) Where he is registered under these provisions and 'ceases to be registrable under *VATA 1994*'. Notification must state the date on which he ceased to be registrable.

(*b*) Where he is registered under 59.21(*b*) above, the first occasion after registration when he makes a relevant acquisition.

A person '*ceases to be registrable under VATA 1994*' where

- he ceases to be a person who would be liable or entitled to be registered under that *Act* if his registration were disregarded; or
- he has been registered under 59.21(*b*) above and ceases to have any intention of making relevant acquisitions.

[*VATA 1994, Sch 3 paras 5, 10; SI 1995/2518, Reg 5(3); SI 2000/794*].

See 59.38 below for the VAT office which should be notified.

Changes in circumstances. A person registered under these provisions must notify HMRC, within 30 days and with full written particulars, of any change in the name, constitution or ownership of the business or any other event which may necessitate the variation of the register or cancellation of registration. [*SI 1995/2518, Reg 5(2); SI 2000/794*]. The appropriate VAT registration office should be advised of the changes (see 59.38 below).

59.25 Cancellation of registration

The registration of a person registered under these provisions must, or as the case may be, can be cancelled in the following circumstances.

(*a*) Subject to below, where a person registered under these provisions satisfies HMRC that he is not liable to be so registered, they *must*, on request, cancel his registration with effect from the day on which the request is made or such later date as is mutually agreed. HMRC must be satisfied that, at the date of the proposed cancellation, the person would not be liable to be registered under any other provision of *VATA 1994*.

(*b*) Subject to below, where HMRC are satisfied that a person registered under these provisions has, since his registration, ceased to be 'registrable' under these provisions, they may cancel his registration with effect from the day on which he so ceased or such later day as is mutually agreed. HMRC must also be satisfied that, at the date of the proposed cancellation, the person would not be liable or entitled to be registered under any other provision of *VATA 1994*.

(*c*) Where HMRC are satisfied that, on the day on which a person was registered under these provisions

(i) he was not registrable under these provisions, or

(ii) where he was registered under 59.21(*b*) above, he did not have the intention by reference to which he was registered,

they may cancel his registration with effect from that day.

(*d*) Where HMRC are satisfied that a person who has been registered under 59.21(*b*) above and is not for the time being liable to be registered under 59.19 above

(i) has not, by the date specified in his request to be registered, begun to make relevant supplies, or

(ii) has contravened any condition of his registration,

they may cancel his registration from the date so specified or, as the case may be, the date of the contravention (or such later date as may be mutually agreed). HMRC must also be satisfied that, at the date of the proposed cancellation, the person would not be liable or entitled to be registered under any other provision of *VATA 1994*.

A person is '*registrable*' under these provisions at any time when he is liable to be registered under these provisions or makes relevant acquisitions.

The registration of a person

- who is registered under 59.21 above, or

- who would not be liable or entitled to be registered under any provision of *VATA 1994* except 59.21 above if he were not registered,

cannot be cancelled under (*a*) or (*b*) above unless it has been in force for two complete calendar years.

[*VATA 1994, Sch 3 paras 6, 7*].

59.26 REGISTRATION BY OVERSEAS TRADERS IN RESPECT OF DISPOSALS OF ASSETS FOR WHICH A VAT REPAYMENT IS CLAIMED

The provisions detailed in 59.27 to 59.32 below require overseas traders (also referred to as non-established taxable persons) to be registered for VAT in the UK if they make claims under the *EC 8th Directive* or *EC 13th Directive* and subsequently supply, or intend to supply, the relevant goods in the UK. The provisions apply regardless of the value of the relevant supplies, ie there is no registration threshold. Once registered for VAT, the business must account for VAT on all its taxable supplies and can recover input tax in the normal way. The business will no longer be entitled to claim refunds under the *EC 8th Directive* or *EC 13th Directive*.

De Voil Indirect Tax Service. See V2.189-V2.189D.

59.27 Liability to be registered

A person who is not registered under *VATA 1994* and is not liable to be registered under 59.3, 59.12 or 59.19 above becomes liable to be registered under these provisions at any time if

(*a*) he makes 'relevant supplies'; or

(*b*) there are reasonable grounds for believing that he will make relevant supplies within the period of 30 days then beginning.

Relevant supplies. A supply is a '*relevant supply*' where

- the supply is a taxable supply;
- the goods are assets of the business in the course or furtherance of which they are supplied; and
- the person by whom they are supplied, or a 'predecessor' of his, has received or claimed, or is intending to claim, a VAT repayment on the supply to him, or the importation by him, of the goods (or of anything comprised in them) under the *EC 8th Directive* (refunds of VAT to persons established in other EC countries, see 21.57 EUROPEAN COMMUNITY GENERAL) or the *EC 13th Directive* (refunds of VAT to persons established outside the EC (48.5 OVERSEAS TRADERS).

For these purposes, a '*predecessor*' is someone who has transferred the goods in question to the registrable person under the provisions allowing relief from VAT on the transfer of a business, or part of a business, as a going concern (see 8.10 BUSINESS). A person's predecessors include the predecessors of his predecessor through any number of transactions.

A person is treated as having become liable to be registered under these provisions at any time when he would have become so liable but for any registration which is subsequently cancelled under 59.10(3), 59.17(*b*) or 59.25(*c*) above or 59.32(*b*) below.

[*VATA 1994, Sch 3A paras 1, 9; FA 2000, s 136(8)(10), Sch 36*].

59.28 NOTIFICATION OF LIABILITY AND REGISTRATION

A person who becomes liable to registration under 59.27 above must notify HMRC of that fact as follows.

(*a*) Where 59.27(*a*) above applies, within 30 days of the date on which liability arises. HMRC must then register that person (whether or not he so notifies them) with effect from the beginning of the day on which liability arises.

(*b*) Where 59.27(*b*) above applies, before the end of the period by reference to which the liability arises. HMRC must then register that person (whether or not he so notifies them) with effect from the beginning of that period.

[*VATA 1994, Sch 3A paras 3, 4; FA 2000, Sch 36*].

Notification must be in such form and contain such particulars as HMRC prescribe. Application must currently be made on Form VAT1C which includes a signed declaration that the information entered on the form and contained in any accompanying document is true and complete. [*SI 1995/2518, Reg 5(1); SI 2000/794*]. The form is available from the Non-Established Taxable Persons Unit (NETPU), HM Revenue and Customs, Customs House, 28 Guild Street, Aberdeen AB11 6GY (Tel: 01224 844844). See VAT Notice 700/1 *Should I Be Registered for VAT?* for notes on how to complete the form. Where the person being registered is a partnership, Form VAT 2 must also be completed.

Businesses may appoint a tax representative to act on their behalf (see 48.3 OVERSEAS TRADERS).

59.29 Exemption from registration

Where a person who makes or intends to make relevant supplies satisfies HMRC that any such supply would be zero-rated if he were a taxable person, HMRC may, if the person so requests and they think fit, grant exemption from registration under these provisions. Application should be made to Non-Established Taxable Persons Unit (NETPU), HM Revenue and Customs, Customs House, 28 Guild Street, Aberdeen AB11 6GY giving full details. A completed Form VAT1C should also be forwarded.

On a material change in the nature of the supplies made, the person exempted must notify HMRC within 30 days of the date on which the change occurred or, if no particular date is so identifiable, within 30 days of the end of the quarter in which it occurred. On a material alteration in any quarter in the proportion of relevant supplies of such a person that are zero-rated, he must notify HMRC of the alteration within 30 days of the end of the quarter.

Exemption applies until the date it appears to HMRC that the request should no longer be acted upon or until the date the request is withdrawn. HMRC must then register the person with effect from that date.

[*VATA 1994, Sch 3A para 7; FA 2000, Sch 36*].

59.30 Cessation of liability to be registered

A person who has become liable to be registered under 59.27 above ceases to be liable to be registered if at any time HMRC are satisfied that he has ceased to make relevant supplies. [*VATA 1994, Sch 3A para 2; FA 2000, Sch 36*].

59.31 NOTIFICATION OF MATTERS AFFECTING REGISTRATION

Change in circumstances. A person registered under these provisions must notify HMRC, within 30 days and with full written particulars, of any change in the name, constitution or ownership of the business or any other event which may necessitate the variation of the register or cancellation of registration. [*SI 1995/2518, Reg 5(2); SI 2000/794*].

End of liability to be registered. A person registered under these provisions who ceases to make, or have the intention of making, relevant supplies must notify HMRC of that fact within 30 days of the day on which he does so. Notification is not required if the person would, when he so ceases, be liable or entitled to be registered under any other provision of *VATA 1994*. [*VATA 1994, Sch 3A para 5; FA 2000, Sch 36*]. The notification must be in writing and must state the date on which the registered person ceased to make, or have the intention of making, relevant supplies. [*SI 1995/2518, Reg 5(3); SI 2000/794*].

59.32 Cancellation of registration

The registration of a person under these provisions may be cancelled in the following circumstances.

(*a*) Where HMRC are satisfied that a registered person has ceased to be liable to be registered under these provisions, they may cancel his registration with effect from the day on which he so ceased or such later date as is mutually agreed. However, HMRC must not cancel a person's registration with effect from any time unless they are satisfied that the person would not be liable or entitled to be registered under any other provision of *VATA 1994*.

(*b*) Where HMRC are satisfied that on the day on which a registered person was registered he was not registrable, they may cancel his registration with effect from that day.

[*VATA 1994, Sch 3A para 6; FA 2000, Sch 36*].

An application to have registration cancelled should be made on Form VAT 7 (or Welsh version Form 7(W)) obtainable from NETPU at the address in 59.28 above.

59.33 CONSEQUENCES OF DEREGISTRATION

Notice of cancellation and final return. When the date of cancellation of registration has been arranged, either a formal notice of cancellation (Form VAT 35) or a formal notice of exemption from registration (Form VAT 8) is sent. Unless the registration number has been re-allocated to a person who is taking over the business as a going concern (see 8.10 BUSINESS), a final return Form VAT 193 or VAT 197 (Welsh version) is issued. See 2.2 and 2.3 ACCOUNTING PERIODS AND RETURNS. (VAT Notice 700/11/02, paras 7.1, 7.2).

VAT invoices must not normally be issued or VAT charged as from the date of cancellation (although where a deregistered person has undercharged VAT on a supply made before deregistration, HMRC may agree to a VAT invoice being raised to the customer concerned so that the trader does not have to account for any additional VAT due from his own resources). The previous VAT registration number must not be shown on any invoices issued. HMRC should be consulted before using an existing stock of invoices and crossing out the registration number. If a self-billing arrangement (see 40.6 INVOICES) or the authenticated receipt procedure for the construction industry (see 42.31(2) LAND AND BUILDINGS) are in operation customers must be notified immediately of the deregistration and informed that VAT must not be charged. (VAT Notice 700/11/02, para 7.3; Internal Guidance V1–24A, para 2.15).

Input tax cannot be claimed on purchases made from the date of deregistration except for VAT on the supply of certain services after deregistration made for the purposes of the business carried on before that time. See 35.11 INPUT TAX.

Partial exemption. Where partial exemption applies to the business, a final adjustment in accordance with the normal partial exemption method must be made on the final return. The period for the final adjustment normally runs from the beginning of the tax year to the date of registration. However, where no exempt input tax was incurred in the previous tax year or, as the case may be, the registration period (see 49.9 PARTIAL EXEMPTION for definitions) the period for final adjustment runs from the first day of the VAT period in the final tax year in which exempt input tax is incurred and ends on the date of deregistration. (VAT Notice 700/11/02, para 6.7).

Capital goods scheme. A final adjustment may be required in respect of items still within the adjustment period. See 10.7 CAPITAL GOODS SCHEME.

Records. All VAT records including a list of all business assets on hand, together with their values, should be kept *whether or not they are liable to VAT*. See also 56.1 RECORDS for preservation of records generally.

Payments on account scheme. A business in the scheme (see 51.4 PAYMENT OF VAT) should continue to make POAs until such time as deregistration is confirmed in writing in order to avoid the risk of incurring default surcharge. However, as an alternative to POAs, a business can opt to pay the actual monthly amount due. (VAT Notice 700/11/02, para 6.10).

59.34 Payment of VAT on business assets

VAT must be accounted for on the final return of any 'goods' forming part of the business assets which are on hand at the close of business or on the last day of registration as if they were supplied in the course or furtherance of the business unless

(*a*) the business is transferred as a going concern to another taxable person (see 8.10 BUSINESS);

(*b*) the taxable person has died, become bankrupt or incapacitated and the business is carried on by another person who under *VATA 1994, s 46*(*4*) is treated as a taxable person (see 19.1 DEATH AND INCAPACITY and 36.1 INSOLVENCY); or

(*c*) the VAT on the deemed supply would not be more than £1,000 (£250 before 1 April 2000).

'*Goods*' for these purposes means tangible goods (eg unsold stock, plant, furniture, commercial vehicles, computer, etc) and intangible goods such as patents, copyrights and goodwill can be disregarded. (VAT Notice 700/11/02, para 6.1). It includes goods purchased where title has not yet passed to the business but where input tax on the purchase has been allowed (eg goods on hire purchase or lease purchase and goods subject to reservation of title). Land forming part of the business assets is treated as if it were goods.

The provisions do not apply to any goods where the taxable person can show to the satisfaction of HMRC that

(i) no credit for input tax has been allowed to him in respect of the supply of goods, their acquisition from another EC country or their importation from a place outside the EC; *and*

(ii) the goods did not become his as part of the assets of a business transferred as a going concern from another taxable person (see 8.10 BUSINESS); *and*

(iii) he has not obtained rebate of purchase tax or revenue duty under *FA 1973, s 4* which was allowed when VAT was introduced.

The provisions also do not apply where a person ceased to be a taxable person in consequence of being certified to join the flat-rate scheme for farmers (see 63.25 SPECIAL SCHEMES).

[*VATA 1994, Sch 4 paras 8 and 9; SI 2000/266*].

The following are excluded from the charge to VAT.

- Goods bought from unregistered businesses.
- Motor cars (except qualifying cars on which input tax has been claimed).
- Goods bought under the provisions of one of the second-hand schemes.
- Goods used wholly for business entertainment.
- Goods that have been directly attributed to an exempt business activity (unless the input tax was reclaimable through the partial exemption rules).
- Goods not bought for business purposes.
- Land or buildings which were purchased under an exempt supply even though
  - (i) the option to tax has been exercised and subsequently standard-rated supplies have been made and/or input tax recovered on the refurbishment of the building; or
  - (ii) without the option to tax they have otherwise been used to make standard-rated supplies (eg holiday accommodation).
- Land or buildings which were purchased under a supply on which VAT was recovered (eg where a fully taxable business buys a new commercial property) if at the time of deregistration the sale would be exempt (because the business has not opted to tax the property which is then over three years old). In such circumstances, VAT due on the supply of the property would be nil and so not exceed the £250 limit in (*c*) above.

Where a business has standard-rated land or buildings on hand at the time of deregistration on which it claimed input tax deduction, the property is deemed to be supplied on deregistration. To avoid the cash flow problem that this might create, the business could defer the cancellation of registration until the property is sold so that it would then be required to account for output tax on the actual sale of the property. HMRC are prepared to consider, if necessary, deferring the cancellation of registration longer than the normal six months, until after the property is sold.

(VAT Notice 700/11/02, para 6.2; Internal Guidance V1–3, Chapter 2A para 5.6).

Value of the supply. The value of the goods on which VAT must be accounted for is the price the person would have to pay (excluding VAT), at the time of the supply, to purchase goods *identical* in every respect (including age and condition) to the goods concerned. Where that value cannot be ascertained, the price for the purchase of goods *similar* to, and of the same age and condition as, the goods concerned must be used. If that value is also not possible to ascertain, the cost of producing the goods concerned at that time is to be used. [*VATA 1994, Sch 6 para 6*].

De Voil Indirect Tax Service. See V3.261.

59.35 **Retail schemes**

Whichever retail scheme is used, the provisions under 59.34 above apply.

Where a retail business is sold as a going concern, any retail schemes previously operated must be wound up at the date of deregistration and cannot be transferred to the buyer. But if the transfer of the business is the result of a simple change in legal entity (eg if a sole proprietor takes one or more persons into partnership) and trade continues as before without a break, then the trader must continue to use the same scheme as before. (VAT Notice 700/11/02, para 6.8). See also 60.6 RETAIL SCHEMES for rules to be followed when ceasing to use a retail scheme.

59.36 **TRANSFER OF REGISTRATION**

Where a business is transferred as a going concern (see 8.10 BUSINESS) then provided

(*a*) the transferor's registration under *VATA 1994, Sch 1* has not already been cancelled; and

(*b*) on the transfer of the business the registration of the transferor is to be cancelled *and* the transferee either becomes liable or entitled to be registered under that *Schedule*,

HMRC may, under powers given to them in *VATA 1994, s 49*, cancel the transferor's registration and, from the date of the transfer, register the transferee with the registration number previously allocated to the transferor. An application must be made on Form VAT 68 (or Welsh version Form VAT 68(W)) by, or on behalf of, both parties. The application constitutes notice by the transferor of end of liability or entitlement to registration (see 59.9 above) but must be submitted within 30 days of the transfer to avoid any penalty for late notification. [*SI 1995/2518, Reg 6*(*1*)(*2*)].

Consequences of transfer of registration number. Where a registration number has been re-allocated as above then both the previous and new owners must agree to the following consequences.

- Any liability of the transferor at the transfer date to submit a return or to account for or pay VAT becomes the liability of the transferee (see *WH & AJ Ponsonby v C & E Commrs, QB 1987, [1988] STC 28 (TVC 63.99)* and *Bjellica (t/a Eddy's Domestic Appliance) v C & E Commrs, CA [1995] STC 329 (TVC 55.78)* where the previous owner should have registered twelve years before he actually did and the firm to which he transferred the business was held liable for the VAT).

- Any right of the transferor, whether or not existing at the date of the transfer, to credit for or to repayment of input tax becomes the right of the transferee (eg VAT recoverable on any services supplied to the previous owner for his business before the transfer but which are invoiced afterwards).

- Any right of either the transferor, whether or not existing at the date of transfer, or the transferee to payment by HMRC for recoverable input tax under *VATA 1994, s 25*(*3*) is satisfied by payment to either of them.

- Any right of the transferor, whether or not existing at the date of the transfer, to a claim for bad debt relief becomes the right of the transferee but, equally, any liability of the transferor to make repayments of input tax where bad debt relief has been claimed and the transferor was the debtor also becomes the liability of the transferee.

- Where the transferee has been registered with the registration number of the transferor during a VAT period subsequent to that in which the transfer of the business took place but with effect from the date of the transfer of the business, any return made, VAT accounted for or paid or right to credit for input tax claimed, is treated as having been done by the transferee (whether in fact done by, or in the name of, the transferee or transferor).

[*SI 1995/2518, Reg 6(3)(4); SI 1997/1086, Reg 3*].

The transferee therefore takes over responsibility for any debits or credits before and after the transfer (although he is not liable to any penalty for actions by the transferor). Once reallocation has been granted, HMRC cannot take enforcement action against the transferor. (Internal Guidance V1–28, paras 10.6.5, 10.6.6).

Additional conditions to be met. Apart from the conditions specified in the *Regulations* as detailed above, HMRC require the following conditions to be met before allowing the reallocation of a VAT registration number.

- No VAT group registration must be involved.
- Where the transferor was a company, it must not have been dissolved before the VAT 68 is signed.
- The transferor must not be the subject of a direction in respect of disaggregation of business activities (see 8.5 BUSINESS).
- Any centrally raised assessment notified to the transferor covering periods after the date of transfer must be paid.
- Any default surcharge incurred by the transferor for periods prior to the date of transfer must have been paid with no indication of an appeal.
- No civil penalty has been or is to be imposed on the transferor under *VATA 1994, s 60* (VAT evasion, see 52.9 PENALTIES), *VATA 1994, s 68* (breach of walking possession agreements, see 52.13 PENALTIES) or *VATA 1994, s 69* (breaches of regulatory provisions, see 52.14 PENALTIES). In the case of a *VATA 1994, s 67* penalty (failure to notify and unauthorised issue of invoices, see 52.12 PENALTIES), reallocation may be allowed if the penalty has been paid.

(Internal Guidance V1–28, para 10.6.7).

Belated notification of a transfer of going concern (TOGC). If a TOGC is belatedly notified to HMRC and the transferee has been accounting for VAT under the transferor's registration number, an application may be made for retrospective reallocation of the registration number. (Internal Guidance V1–28, para 10.7).

Special arrangements relating to the transferor's registration. If the transferor had any special arrangements (eg annual accounting, use of a retail or flat-rate scheme), these cease from the date of transfer and a fresh application must be made by the transferee. (Internal Guidance V1–28, para 10.9).

Preservation of records. Business records normally have to be retained for six years. Any of the transferor's records relating to the business which are required to be preserved for any period after the transfer must be preserved by the transferee instead of the transferor unless HMRC, at the request of the transferor, allow otherwise. [*VATA 1994, s 49(1)(b)*]. This has more significance where large businesses are involved with ongoing orders. HMRC normally allow records to be retained by the transferor as it is accepted that they are needed for Revenue purposes. A condition of retention is that the records of the pre-transfer period are made available if required and that any change in location is advised by the transferor (Internal Guidance V1–28, paras 10.12.1, 10.12.2).

De Voil Indirect Tax Service. See V2.131.

59.37 **DIVISIONAL REGISTRATION**

A 'body corporate' carrying on its 'business' in several divisions may, if it requests and HMRC see fit, register in the names of those divisions. For these purposes, 'business' includes any other activities in the course or furtherance of which the body corporate acquires goods from another EC country. [*VATA 1994, s 46(1)(6)*]. See 31.2 GROUPS OF COMPANIES for the meaning of '*body corporate*'.

Divisional registration is a facility which allows a corporate body carrying on business through a number of self-accounting units to register each of those units or divisions separately for VAT. Each division is given a separate VAT registration number and makes its own VAT return. However, the corporate body is still a single taxable person and it remains liable for the VAT debts of all the divisions.

Conditions for divisional registration. HMRC will only approve divisional registration if all the following conditions are satisfied.

(*a*) It is satisfied that there would be real difficulties in submitting a single VAT return for the corporate body as a whole within 30 days of the end of the VAT period.

(*b*) All the divisions must be registered, even those whose turnover is under the registration limit (see 59.3 above).

(*c*) All divisions must be independent units with their own accounting systems and must be

- operating from different geographical locations;
- supplying different commodities; or
- carrying out different functions (eg manufacture, wholesale, retail, export, etc).

(*d*) The corporate body as a whole must be, or be treated as being, fully taxable (ie where any exempt supplies are made, input tax attributable to those exempt supplies must be less than the *de minimis* limits in 49.7 PARTIAL EXEMPTION. The *de minimis* limits apply to the whole corporate body and not to each division).

(*e*) All divisions must complete VAT returns for the same VAT periods. These will normally be allocated by HMRC although an application for non-standard VAT periods can be made. Where the corporate body as a whole expects to receive regular repayments of VAT, monthly returns may be allowed but, in such a case, all of the divisions must make monthly returns.

If, once registered in divisions, a body corporate no longer satisfies any of the above conditions, it must notify HMRC in writing within 30 days. HMRC will then decide whether to allow the divisional registration to continue.

Applications must be made by letter and sent to the National Registration Service (see 59.38 below) explaining why it is difficult to submit a single VAT return for the whole body corporate. A Form VAT 1 must be completed for each division with the name of the body corporate entered in Box 1 and the name of the division followed by the name of the corporate body in Box 2 (eg Textile division of ABC Ltd). Copies of incorporation certificates and charters and copies of any Acts of Parliament under which the body was incorporated (other than the *Companies Acts*) or any other proof of incorporation should also be included.

Effective date of commencement. Approval of an application for divisional registration normally takes effect from a current date unless there are exceptional circumstances. Consequently, if the company is already registered, it should continue to account for VAT under the existing registration until the divisional registration is formally approved and processed. HMRC have no objection to an application being effected retrospectively, provided that the company can show that all the conditions (especially (*d*) above) were met throughout the period for which the company is seeking retrospective divisional registration.

Adding and removing divisions. Applications to add any new divisions should be made following the same procedure as above. Where an existing division is sold off or closed down, the National Registration Service must be advised in writing and that division will then be removed from the divisional registration of the corporate body.

Overseas bodies. A corporate body constituted outside the UK may apply for divisional registration provided it has at least two self-accounting units in the UK and it can comply with the above conditions. One of the UK divisions is deemed to cover the activities of those divisions or sites which are outside the UK so that, if any of those overseas divisions, etc starts to make taxable supplies in the UK, VAT is accounted for on those supplies by the UK-based division covering for them.

Divisional registration and group treatment under 31.1 GROUPS OF COMPANIES are mutually exclusive. Where a company which is a member of a VAT group wishes to register some of its divisions separately, it must first apply to leave the VAT group. Conversely, a corporate body with divisional registration which wishes to form or join a VAT group must first apply to cancel the registration of all of its divisions.

Accounting for VAT. VAT invoices must not be issued for transactions made between divisions of the same corporate body. These are not considered to be supplies for VAT purposes.

(VAT Notice 700/2/04, paras 1.10–1.13, 9.3–9.13; Internal Guidance V1–28, paras 70.15, 70.16).

De Voil Indirect Tax Service. See V2.190A.

59.38 APPENDIX: HMRC REGISTRATION AND DEREGISTRATION OFFICES

Postcode of business	Registration	Changes in details	Cancellation of registration/ deregistration
AB	Grimsby	Grimsby	Grimsby
AL	Grimsby	Grimsby	Grimsby
B	Wolverhampton	Wolverhampton	Wolverhampton
BA1–7, 10–16	Carmarthen	Carmarthen	Carmarthen
BA8–9, 20–22	Wolverhampton	Carmarthen	Carmarthen
BB	Wolverhampton	Wolverhampton	Wolverhampton

Postcode of business	Registration	Changes in details	Cancellation of registration/ deregistration
BD	Grimsby	Grimsby	Grimsby
BH	Wolverhampton	Wolverhampton	Wolverhampton
BL	Wolverhampton	Wolverhampton	Wolverhampton
BN	Wolverhampton	Wolverhampton	Wolverhampton
BR	Newry	Newry	Newry
BS	Carmarthen	Carmarthen	Carmarthen
BT	Newry	Newry	Newry
CA	Grimsby	Grimsby	Grimsby
CB	Wolverhampton	Wolverhampton	Wolverhampton
CF	Carmarthen	Carmarthen	Carmarthen
CH1–3, 41–66	Wolverhampton	Wolverhampton	Wolverhampton
CH4–8, 88, 99	Carmarthen	Wolverhampton	Wolverhampton
CM0–20, 22, 24	Newry	Grimsby	Grimsby
CM21, 23	Grimsby	Grimsby	Grimsby
CO	Newry	Newry	Newry
CR0–2, 4–5, 7–9	Newry	Carmarthen	Carmarthen
CR3, 6	Carmarthen	Carmarthen	Carmarthen
CT	Wolverhampton	Wolverhampton	Wolverhampton
CV	Wolverhampton	Wolverhampton	Wolverhampton
CW	Wolverhampton	Wolverhampton	Wolverhampton
DA1–4, 11–13	Wolverhampton	Wolverhampton	Wolverhampton
DA5–10, 14–18	Newry	Wolverhampton	Wolverhampton
DD	Grimsby	Grimsby	Grimsby
DE1–11, 15–73, 75–99	Grimsby	Wolverhampton	Wolverhampton
DE12–14, 74	Wolverhampton	Wolverhampton	Wolverhampton
DG	Grimsby	Grimsby	Grimsby
DH	Grimsby	Grimsby	Grimsby
DL	Grimsby	Grimsby	Grimsby
DN	Grimsby	Grimsby	Grimsby
DT	Wolverhampton	Wolverhampton	Wolverhampton
DY	Wolverhampton	Wolverhampton	Wolverhampton
E	Newry	Newry	Newry
EC	Newry	Newry	Newry
EH	Grimsby	Grimsby	Grimsby

Postcode of business	Registration	Changes in details	Cancellation of registration/ deregistration
EN1–5, 9	Newry	Grimsby	Grimsby
EN6–8, 10–11	Grimsby	Grimsby	Grimsby
EX1–15, 17–24	Wolverhampton	Wolverhampton	Wolverhampton
EX16, 31–39	Carmarthen	Wolverhampton	Wolverhampton
FK	Grimsby	Grimsby	Grimsby
FY	Wolverhampton	Wolverhampton	Wolverhampton
G	Grimsby	Grimsby	Grimsby
GL	Carmarthen	Carmarthen	Wolverhampton
GU1–10, 12, 18, 21–24	Carmarthen	Carmarthen	Carmarthen
GU11, 13–17, 19–20, 25–35, 46–51	Wolverhampton	Carmarthen	Carmarthen
HA	Newry	Newry	Newry
HD	Grimsby	Grimsby	Grimsby
HG	Grimsby	Grimsby	Grimsby
HP1–4, 23	Grimsby	Grimsby	Grimsby
HP5–22, 27	Wolverhampton	Grimsby	Grimsby
HR	Wolverhampton	Wolverhampton	Wolverhampton
HS	Grimsby	Grimsby	Grimsby
HU	Grimsby	Grimsby	Grimsby
HX	Grimsby	Grimsby	Grimsby
IG	Newry	Newry	Newry
IP	Wolverhampton	Wolverhampton	Wolverhampton
IV	Grimsby	Grimsby	Grimsby
KA	Grimsby	Grimsby	Grimsby
KT1–13, 15–17, 19–24	Wolverhampton	Wolverhampton	Wolverhampton
KT14, 18	Carmarthen	Wolverhampton	Wolverhampton
KW	Grimsby	Grimsby	Grimsby
KY	Grimsby	Grimsby	Grimsby
L	Wolverhampton	Wolverhampton	Wolverhampton
LA1–4	Wolverhampton	Grimsby	Grimsby
LA5–23	Grimsby	Grimsby	Grimsby
LD	Carmarthen	Carmarthen	Carmarthen

Postcode of business	Registration	Changes in details	Cancellation of registration/ deregistration
LE	Wolverhampton	Wolverhampton	Wolverhampton
LL	Carmarthen	Carmarthen	Carmarthen
LN	Grimsby	Grimsby	Grimsby
LS	Grimsby	Grimsby	Grimsby
LU	Grimsby	Grimsby	Grimsby
M	Wolverhampton	Wolverhampton	Wolverhampton
ME	Wolverhampton	Wolverhampton	Wolverhampton
MK1–19, 46–98	Wolverhampton	Wolverhampton	Wolverhampton
MK20–45	Grimsby	Wolverhampton	Wolverhampton
ML	Grimsby	Grimsby	Grimsby
N	Newry	Newry	Newry
NE	Grimsby	Grimsby	Grimsby
NG	Grimsby	Grimsby	Grimsby
NN	Wolverhampton	Wolverhampton	Wolverhampton
NP	Carmarthen	Carmarthen	Carmarthen
NR	Wolverhampton	Wolverhampton	Wolverhampton
NW	Newry	Newry	Newry
OL	Wolverhampton	Wolverhampton	Wolverhampton
OX	Wolverhampton	Wolverhampton	Wolverhampton
PA	Grimsby	Grimsby	Grimsby
PE1–8, 13–16, 18–19, 26–38	Wolverhampton	Grimsby	Grimsby
PE9–12, 17, 20–25	Grimsby	Grimsby	Grimsby
PH	Grimsby	Grimsby	Grimsby
PL	Wolverhampton	Wolverhampton	Wolverhampton
PO	Wolverhampton	Wolverhampton	Wolverhampton
PR	Wolverhampton	Wolverhampton	Wolverhampton
RG	Wolverhampton	Wolverhampton	Wolverhampton
RH1–12, 18–19	Carmarthen	Carmarthen	Carmarthen
RH13–17, 20	Wolverhampton	Carmarthen	Carmarthen
RM	Newry	Newry	Newry
S	Grimsby	Grimsby	Grimsby
SA	Carmarthen	Carmarthen	Carmarthen
SE	Newry	Newry	Newry

Postcode of business	Registration	Changes in details	Cancellation of registration/ deregistration
SG	Grimsby	Grimsby	Grimsby
SK	Wolverhampton	Wolverhampton	Wolverhampton
SL	Wolverhampton	Wolverhampton	Wolverhampton
SM1, 3–6	Newry	Wolverhampton	Wolverhampton
SM2, 7	Wolverhampton	Wolverhampton	Wolverhampton
SN1–6, 9, 17–99	Wolverhampton	Carmarthen	Carmarthen
SN7–8, 10–16	Carmarthen	Carmarthen	Carmarthen
SO	Wolverhampton	Wolverhampton	Wolverhampton
SP	Wolverhampton	Wolverhampton	Wolverhampton
SR	Grimsby	Grimsby	Grimsby
SS	Newry	Newry	Newry
ST	Wolverhampton	Wolverhampton	Wolverhampton
SW	Newry	Newry	Newry
SY1–9, 11–14	Wolverhampton	Carmarthen	Carmarthen
SY10, 15–25	Carmarthen	Carmarthen	Carmarthen
TA1–11, 21–24	Carmarthen	Carmarthen	Carmarthen
TA12–20	Wolverhampton	Carmarthen	Carmarthen
TD	Grimsby	Grimsby	Grimsby
TF	Wolverhampton	Wolverhampton	Wolverhampton
TN1–22, 26, 28–40	Carmarthen	Carmarthen	Carmarthen
TN23–25, 27	Wolverhampton	Carmarthen	Carmarthen
TQ	Wolverhampton	Wolverhampton	Wolverhampton
TR	Wolverhampton	Wolverhampton	Wolverhampton
TS	Grimsby	Grimsby	Grimsby
TW1, 6, 9–11	Newry	Wolverhampton	Wolverhampton
TW2–5, 7–8, 12–20	Wolverhampton	Wolverhampton	Wolverhampton
UB	Newry	Newry	Newry
W	Newry	Newry	Newry
WA	Wolverhampton	Wolverhampton	Wolverhampton
WC	Newry	Newry	Newry
WD	Grimsby	Grimsby	Grimsby
WF	Grimsby	Grimsby	Grimsby
WN	Wolverhampton	Wolverhampton	Wolverhampton
WR1–15	Wolverhampton	Wolverhampton	Wolverhampton
WR78–99	Carmarthen	Wolverhampton	Wolverhampton

Postcode of business	Registration	Changes in details	Cancellation of registration/ deregistration
WS	Wolverhampton	Wolverhampton	Wolverhampton
WV	Wolverhampton	Wolverhampton	Wolverhampton
YO	Grimsby	Grimsby	Grimsby
ZE	Grimsby	Grimsby	Grimsby

Carmarthen Registration & Deregistration Unit, HM Revenue and Customs, Ty-Myrddin, Old Station Road, Carmarthen SA31 1BT
Tel: 0845 758 5831

Grimsby Registration Unit, HM Revenue and Customs, Imperial House, 77 Victoria Street, Grimsby DN31 1DB
Tel: 0845 039 0279

Newry Registration & Deregistration Unit, HM Revenue and Customs, PO Box 40, Carnbane Way, Damolly, Newry Co Down, BT35 6PJ
Tel: 0845 711 2114

Wolverhampton Registration & Deregistration Unit, HM Revenue and Customs, Deansgate, 62–70 Tettenhall Road, Wolverhampton WV1 4TZ
Tel: 0845 039 0129

These offices deal with registration and deregistration according to the post code of the business. For further details contact the National Advice Service on 0845 010 9000 or go to the HMRC website at

www.hmrc.gov.uk

click on the Contact Us button at the top of the page and follow the link for matters relating to VAT dealt with by post.

60 Retail Schemes

Cross-references. See 11.3 CATERING for accounting for supplies of catering when take-away food is also sold; 47.8(31) OUTPUT TAX for video cassettes; 56 RECORDS; 63.13 SPECIAL SCHEMES for the annual accounting scheme; and 67 TRADE PROMOTION SCHEMES where such schemes are operated under a retail scheme.

De Voil Indirect Tax Service. See V3.551–577.

The contents of this chapter are as follows.

60.1 INTRODUCTION

VAT retail schemes were introduced at the start of VAT in 1973 because it was recognised that many businesses dealing directly with the public (primarily shopkeepers) and making supplies at different rates of VAT would be unable to keep records of every sale in order to calculate the VAT due in the normal way. The retail schemes are therefore methods for arriving at the value of taxable retail supplies and determining what proportion of those sales are taxable at different rates of VAT.

HMRC's powers. Under *VATA 1994, Sch 11 para 2(6)* and *SI 1995 No 2518, Regs 67, 68*, HMRC are empowered to permit the value of supplies by a retailer which are taxable at other than the zero rate to be determined by a method

- described in a notice published by them, or
- agreed with the retailer.

They may refuse to permit a retailer to use a particular scheme in the following circumstances.

(*a*) If the use of any particular scheme does not produce a fair and reasonable valuation during any period.

(*b*) It is necessary to do so for the protection of the revenue.

(*c*) The retailer could reasonably be expected to account for VAT in the normal way.

Since the introduction of VAT, there has been a revolution in information technology available to, and used by, retailers (eg use of bar codes and sophisticated till technology). HMRC consider that these changes mean that the original need for retail schemes, which only provide an approximation of the VAT due, is greatly diminished. They are, therefore, examining every retailer's need to continue using a retail scheme and will only permit the use of a scheme where the retailer cannot reasonably be expected to account for VAT in the normal way, ie by identifying each individual supply, its value and the rate of VAT. (VAT Information Sheet 7/96).

Where both retail and non-retail sales are made, a retail scheme can only be used for the retail sales and VAT on the non-retail sales must be accounted for outside the scheme in the normal way. (VAT Notice 727, paras 2.1, 2.2 which have the force of law). See *The Oxford, Swindon and Gloucester Co-operative Society v C & E Commrs, QB [1995] STC 583 (TVC 56.9)*.

Sales to other VAT-registered businesses. These must normally not be included in a retail scheme. However, by exception, *occasional* cash sales (eg a garage supplying petrol to a VAT-registered customer or a retail DIY store supplying building materials to a VAT-registered builder) may be included within a retail scheme. (VAT Notice 727, para 2.4 which has the force of law).

Flat-rate scheme for small businesses. No retailer may use a retail scheme at the same time as the flat-rate scheme for small businesses (see 63.15 SPECIAL SCHEMES). [*SI 1995/2518, Reg 69A; SI 2002/1142*].

60.2 SUMMARY OF SCHEMES

A retail business with an annual VAT-exclusive turnover over £100 million and which needs to use a retail scheme is only eligible to do so if it agrees a bespoke scheme with HMRC. See 60.13 below.

Apart from such bespoke schemes, there are five published standard schemes.

(*a*) **Point of Sale scheme**. VAT due is calculated by identifying the correct VAT liability of supplies at the time of sale, eg by using electronic tills. See 60.14 below.

(*b*) **Apportionment Scheme 1**. This is the simpler apportionment scheme designed for smaller businesses with an annual VAT-exclusive turnover not exceeding £1 million. Each VAT period, the retailer must work out the value of purchases for resale at different rates of VAT and apply the proportions of those purchase values to sales. For example, if 82% of the value of goods purchased for retail sale are standard-rated, it is assumed that 82% of takings are from standard-rated sales. Once a year, a similar calculation is made based on purchases for the year and any over or under payment adjusted. See 60.15 below.

(*c*) **Apportionment Scheme 2**. Under this scheme, a retailer must calculate the expected selling prices (ESPs) of standard-rated and reduced rate goods received for retail sale. He must then work out the ratio of these to the expected selling prices of all goods received for retail sale and apply this ratio to takings. For example, if 82% of the ESPs of goods received for retail sale are standard-rated and 18% are zero-rated, then 82% of takings are treated as standard-rated and 18% zero-rated. See 60.16 below.

(*d*) **Direct Calculation Scheme 1**. This is available to businesses with an annual VAT-exclusive turnover not exceeding £1 million. To work the scheme, a retailer must calculate expected selling prices (ESPs) of goods for retail sale at one or more rates of VAT so that the proportion of takings on which VAT is due can be calculated. ESPs are, as a general rule, calculated for minority goods, ie those goods at the rate of VAT which forms the smallest proportion of retail supplies. For example, if 82% of sales are standard-rated and 18% are zero-rated, the minority goods are zero-rated. Expected selling prices of the zero-rated goods received, made or grown for retail sale are calculated and deducted from takings to arrive at a figure for standard-rated takings. However, a retailer may mark up the majority goods if this would be a simpler option. See 60.17 below.

(*e*) **Direct Calculation Scheme 2**. This scheme works in exactly the same way as Direct Calculation Scheme 1 but requires an annual stock-take adjustment. See 60.18 below.

(VAT Notice 727, paras 3.4–3.13).

Adaptations to the standard schemes. HMRC may approve an adaptation of any of the above standard schemes provided

- a written request is received from the retailer;
- the retailer is unable (rather than unwilling) to use a standard scheme or an acceptable mixture of them within 60.4 below;
- the proposed adaptation produces a fair and reasonable valuation of standard-rated, and where applicable reduced rate, supplies and there is no risk to the revenue in allowing it; and
- the retailer will not gain any undue tax or competitive advantage through use of the adaptation.

See under the details of the various schemes for adaptations allowed by HMRC.

(Internal Guidance V1–23, Chapter 10 paras 7.2, 7.3).

60.3 CHOOSING A SCHEME

A retailer can chose to use any of the published schemes provided

- he meets the conditions for use of the scheme in question; and
- HMRC have not refused to let him use the scheme (see 60.1 above).

The following general comparisons can be made of the different schemes.

Point of Sale scheme

- Only available scheme if all supplies are standard-rated or all supplies are taxable at the reduced rate. (VAT Notice 727, para 3.4 which has the force of law).
- Turnover limit of £100 million.
- Can be used for services, catering supplies, self-made and self-grown goods.
- Does not involve stock-taking or working out expected selling prices.
- No annual adjustment required.
- The scheme is potentially both the simplest and most accurate but electronic tills are expensive and staff must be able to operate the system correctly at all times.

60.3 Retail Schemes

Apportionment Scheme 1

- Cannot be used for services, catering supplies, self-made or self-grown goods.
- Turnover limit of £1 million.
- Does not involve stock-taking or working out expected selling prices.
- Annual adjustment required.
- The scheme is relatively simple. However, if on average a higher mark-up is achieved for zero-rated goods than standard-rated or reduced rate goods, more VAT could be payable under this scheme than another available alternative scheme.

Apportionment Scheme 2

- Cannot be used for services or catering supplies but can be used for self-made or self-grown goods.
- Turnover limit of £100 million.
- Stock-taking required at the start of using the scheme, but not thereafter.
- Expected selling prices must be worked out.
- No annual adjustment required but a rolling calculation used.
- The scheme can be complex to operate but if worked properly it will provide a more accurate valuation of supplies over a period of time.

Direct Calculation Scheme 1

- Services can only be included if they are liable at a different rate from the minority goods.
- Cannot be used for catering supplies but can be used for self-made or self-grown goods.
- Turnover limit of £1 million.
- Expected selling prices must be worked out. The scheme can produce inaccuracies if expected selling prices are not calculated accurately. In addition, where expected selling prices are set for standard-rated goods and stock of these goods has a slow turnover, the scheme may not be the most appropriate as VAT is paid in the period in which the goods are received and not necessarily when they are sold.
- Does not involve stock-taking.
- No annual adjustment required.
- The scheme can be relatively simple where goods are sold at two rates of VAT and there is a small proportion of supplies at one of those rates.
- The scheme can be complex to work where goods are sold at three rates of VAT although it may be possible to account for a small number of goods at a third rate outside the scheme.

Direct Calculation Scheme 2

- Services can only be included if they are liable at a different rate from the minority goods.
- Cannot be used for catering supplies but can be used for self-made or self-grown goods.
- Turnover limit of £100 million.
- Expected selling prices must be worked out. The scheme can produce inaccuracies if expected selling prices are not calculated accurately. In addition, where expected selling prices are set for standard-rated goods and stock of these goods has a slow turnover, the scheme may not be the most appropriate as VAT is paid in the period in which the goods are received and not necessarily when they are sold.
- Stock-taking required at the start of using the scheme and annually thereafter.
- Annual adjustment required.

(VAT Notice 727, paras 3.4–3.13, 11).

60.4 MIXTURE OF SCHEMES AND SEPARATE ACCOUNTING BY DIFFERENT PARTS OF THE BUSINESS

A retailer cannot use more than one scheme at any one time except as indicated in any notice published by HMRC or as specifically allowed by them. [*SI 1995 No 2518, Reg 69*]. Currently HMRC allow the following mixtures of schemes. (Note that it is always possible to use the normal method of accounting with any scheme or any allowable mixture of schemes.)

Mixtures of schemes. It may be necessary to use different schemes in different parts of the business. Provided the retailer is eligible to use the relevant schemes, the Point of Sale scheme can be mixed with either Direct Calculation Scheme 1 or 2 or Apportionment Scheme 1 or 2. It is also possible to use any individual scheme, or any acceptable mixture of schemes, with normal accounting. It is not possible to mix

- Apportionment Scheme 1 and 2;
- Direct Calculation Scheme 1 and 2; or
- Apportionment Scheme 1 or 2 with Direct Calculation Scheme 1 or 2.

(VAT Notice 727, para 4.1 which has the force of law).

Using the same scheme in different parts of a business. The same scheme can be used separately at a number of distinct business locations. If so, under any scheme other than the Point of Sale scheme, it may be necessary to make adjustments to account for transfers between the different parts of the business. Details of such adjustments must be agreed with HMRC. (VAT Notice 727, para 4.1 which has the force of law).

60.5 CHANGING SCHEMES

Compulsory change of scheme. A retailer must cease to use a particular scheme if he becomes ineligible to use it. From the start of the next VAT accounting period, he must then change to another scheme (or a mixture of schemes if permitted, see 60.4 above) or to the normal method of accounting.

Voluntary change of scheme. Unless HMRC allow otherwise, a retailer using a retail scheme must, so long as he remains a taxable person, continue to use that scheme for a period of not less than one year from its adoption and any change from one scheme to another must be made at the end of a complete year reckoned from the beginning of the VAT period in which he first adopted the scheme. This does not apply where a retailer ceases to use a retail scheme and joins the flat-rate scheme for small businesses (see 63.15 SPECIAL SCHEMES). [*SI 1995/2518, Reg 71; SI 2002/1142*]. If, for exceptional reasons, a change is required at any other time, written agreement from HMRC is required.

Where the annual accounting scheme is used, a retail scheme can only be changed at the end of the annual accounting year.

Retrospective changes. Retrospective changes to a retail scheme are not normally allowed. See *Summerfield (VTD 108) (TVC 56.11)* and *RJ Vulgar (VTD 304) (TVC 56.12)* where Customs' decision not to exercise discretion to allow retrospective changes in the scheme was upheld by the tribunal. In A & *C Wadlewski (VTD 13340) (TVC 56.22)* the tribunal held that Customs' refusal was unreasonable because of the high proportion of additional VAT payable but this decision was not followed in *L & J Lewis (VTD 14085) (TVC 56.18)* or *L & P Fryer (VTD 14265) (TVC 56.19)*.

HMRC may, in exceptional cases, allow retrospective change. The only clear examples of exceptional circumstances are

- where the business has been misdirected (by omission or commission) by a HMRC officer; or
- where the business can clearly demonstrate that the scheme which it is proposed to use retrospectively would produce a more accurate liability *and* the difference in VAT due is a very high proportion of the business's profit. In *Wadlewski* above, the tribunal allowed retrospection where the difference in liability amounted to 40% of the business's profit.

Application should be made in writing to HMRC giving as much detail as possible. The maximum period of recalculation is three years. The retailer must have been eligible to use the new scheme during the full period of recalculation.

Where HMRC allow a retrospective change of scheme, the difference between the output tax declared under the original scheme and that falling due under the new scheme is liable to be repaid under *VATA 1994, s 80* subject to a claim being made and any defence HMRC may have on the grounds of unjust enrichment if the claim is met (see 51.7 PAYMENT OF VAT). Interest under *VATA 1994, s 78* (see 51.11 PAYMENT OF VAT) is not normally payable where a retailer changes schemes retrospectively.

(VAT Notice 727, paras 4.2, 4.3; VAT Notice 727/3/02, paras 2.5, 2.6; VAT Notice 727/4/02, paras 2.5, 2.6; VAT Notice 727/5/02, paras 2.5, 2.6; Internal Guidance V1–23, Chapter 10 paras 3.11, 3.13).

60.6 CEASING TO USE A SCHEME

A retailer must notify HMRC before ceasing to account for VAT under a retail scheme. He may then be required to pay VAT on such proportion as HMRC consider fair and reasonable of any sums due to him at the end of the VAT period in which he last used the scheme. [*SI 1995 No 2518, Reg 72*].

See under the individual scheme rules for adjustments which may be necessary on ceasing to use a particular scheme. Apart from these special rules, HMRC may require additional adjustments where unusual patterns of trade prevent the chosen scheme from producing a fair and reasonable result.

The following points should also be noted.

- Only goods sold by retail can be included in the retail scheme. If a retailer ceases to use a scheme because he sells all or part of his business as a going concern, the value of stock transferred must be excluded from the retail scheme.
- On ceasing to trade, VAT may become due on the value of stocks and assets. See 59.34 REGISTRATION.

(VAT Notice 727, paras 6.1, 6.2 which have the force of law).

60.7 CHANGE IN VAT RATE AND VAT LIABILITIES

A change in the VAT rate means that a rate of VAT has been changed or a new rate has been introduced. A change in VAT liability occurs when a supply which is either exempt or zero-rated becomes taxable at a positive rate or vice versa. Either change may affect the particular scheme used and a retailer must then take the necessary steps relating to his chosen scheme as directed in VAT Notices or as agreed with HMRC. [*SI 1995 No 2518, Reg 75*].

If the change of rate falls halfway through a VAT period, the retailer must make two calculations: one using the old VAT rate and one using the new rate. This will reflect supplies made before and after the rate change. These amounts must then be added together to give the VAT liability for the period.

(VAT Notice 727, paras 7.1–7.5).

Effect on gross takings. Any change in the rate of VAT or liability is effective from a specified date. VAT is due at the new rate on all amounts charged for supplies made on or after the date of change, except that the special provisions in 55.3 *et seq.* RATES OF VAT can be applied to individual transactions provided they are dealt with outside the retail scheme.

60.8 GROSS TAKINGS

All retail schemes work by applying the appropriate VAT fraction(s) to positive-rated daily gross takings in order to establish the amount of VAT due. It is therefore necessary to keep a record of daily gross takings. This term can be misleading because, for retail scheme purposes, daily gross takings is not simply a record of payments received or cash in hand on any particular day but is a record of supplies made that day. The record of daily gross takings can be a listing made from copies of sales vouchers but will normally be a till roll.

Inclusions in daily gross takings. The following must be included in daily gross takings, *the provisions having the force of law*.

- All payments as they are received from cash customers. This includes payment by notes and coins, cheques, debit or credit card vouchers, Switch, Delta or similar electronic transactions, and electronic cash.
- The full value, including VAT, of credit sales (excluding any disclosed exempt charge for credit) on the day the supply is made.
- The value of any goods taken out of the business for own use. See also 60.9(24) below.
- The cash value of any payment in kind for retail sales.

- The face value of gift, book and record vouchers, etc taken in place of cash (but see also 67.12 TRADE PROMOTION SCHEMES where the business supplies the voucher at a discount).
- Any other payments for retail sales.

But where turnover is less than £1 million and customers do not pay for goods when received (eg milkmen, newsagents) it may be possible to agree an adaptation to eliminate opening and closing debtors in the scheme calculation (see 60.9(10) below).

Adjustments to daily gross takings. There are a number of required and allowable adjustments to be made to arrive at the final daily gross takings figure for retail scheme purposes. These are to reflect the fact that daily gross takings should, as far as possible, reflect the supplies made by the retailer and the consideration received for those supplies. Thus, where goods are stolen from a retailer, there has been no supply: no VAT is due and nothing should be included in daily gross takings. Where cash is stolen, there has been a supply on which VAT remains due: the value of the supply should be reflected in daily gross takings.

Daily gross takings may be reduced for the following.

- Receipts recorded for exempt supplies.
- Receipts for goods or services which are to be accounted for outside the scheme.
- Refunds given to customers in respect of taxable supplies to cover accidental overcharges or where goods are unsuitable or faulty.
- Instalments in respect of credit sales.
- Void transactions (where an incorrect transaction has not been voided at the time of the error).
- Illegible credit card transactions (where a customer's account details are not legible on the credit card voucher and therefore cannot be presented at the bank).
- Unsigned or dishonoured cheques from cash customers (but not from credit customers).
- Counterfeit notes.
- Where a cheque guarantee card is incorrectly accepted as a credit card.
- Acceptance of out-of-date coupons which have previously been included in daily gross takings but which are not honoured by the promoters.
- Supervisor's float discrepancies.
- Till breakdowns (where incorrect till readings are recorded due to mechanical faults, eg till programming error, false reading and till reset by an engineer).
- Use of training tills (where the till used by staff for training has been returned to the sales floor without the zeroing of figures).
- Customer overspends using Shopacheck.
- Inadvertent acceptance of foreign currency where discovered at a later time (eg when cashing up) unless reimbursed by the bank.

A record of any adjustments to the daily gross taking should always be kept.

If any adjustment is made for which a payment is subsequently received, the amount received must be included in daily gross takings.

See also 60.9 below generally for special transactions which may require adjustments to be made to figures for daily gross takings.

(VAT Notice 727, para 4.4; VAT Notice 727/3/02, paras 5.1–5.5; VAT Notice 727/4/02, paras 6.1–6.5; VAT Notice 727/5/02, paras 5.1–5.5, all of which have the force of law).

Till shortages and excesses (unders and overs). Most retailers reconcile their till rolls with payments received. Even after making the required and allowable adjustments above, they often discover that value of sales recorded on the till roll is greater than the money in the till (a till shortage or 'under') or there is more money in the till than the value of sales on the till roll (a till excess or 'over'). The general principle is that the till operator is a servant of the retailer. Any errors or dishonesty by the till operator are therefore the responsibility of the retailer. In such circumstances, daily gross takings must reflect the consideration actually received. See, however, below where there is collusion between the till operator and customer.

In the case of unders, the VAT liability is established by the till record unless the retailer can persuade HMRC that the actual amount of cash is more accurate. The burden of proof falls on the retailer. However, where HMRC are satisfied that the discrepancy arises from genuine operator error (as opposed to theft of cash), they may agree a set percentage of adjustments for till errors on the basis of a sampling exercise. If this is done, HMRC will wish to check that the size and frequency of the sample ensure a reasonable level of accuracy.

In the case of overs, this may be evidence of unrecorded sales arising from operator error or suppression.

The following table lists common causes of discrepancy between a retailer's record of daily gross takings and the actual cash in the till, together with the effect this has on the daily gross takings. The table deals with cases of genuine error. See below where there is collusion between the till operator and the customer.

Type of discrepancy/example of error	*Consideration/effect*
(1) Over ringing Goods value £1. Customer hands over £1. Cashier rings £10 into till. £10 recorded in DGT	Consideration £1. DGT should reflect consideration. Adjustment allowed if error is evidenced.
(2) Under ringing Goods value £10. Customer hands over £10. Cashier rings £1 into till. £1 recorded in DGT	Consideration £10. DGT should be increased to reflect consideration
(3) Over changing Goods value £10. Customer hands over £10. Cashier rings £10 into till but gives customer £5 change in error. £10 recorded in DGT	Consideration £10. DGT should reflect consideration. No adjustment for cash shortfall

Type of discrepancy/example of error	*Consideration/effect*
(4) Under changing Goods value £10. Customer hands over £20 in error. Cashier rings £10 or £20 into till. Same amount recorded in DGT	Consideration £10. DGT should reflect consideration. In theory the customer could return to the shop and ask for the extra £10 back
(5) Under charging Goods with shelf price £10. Customer hands over £1. Cashier accepts this in error, but records sale of £10 in DGT	Consideration £1. In principle, this is an allowable reduction but unless the error can be evidenced £10 should be included in DGT
(6) Over charging Goods shelf price £1. Customer hands over £10 in error and this is recorded as a sale of £10	Consideration £1. In principle, the DGT may be adjusted to reflect the lower amount. Any adjustment must be evidenced

Collusion. This occurs where a till operator and customer conspire so that the customer obtains goods without having paid the full price. Where the till operator puts some money in the till, that payment represents consideration received by the retailer for their supplies. However, where the till operator simply pockets the money given by the customer, there may be an exception to the general principle outlined above. If the retailer can demonstrate to the satisfaction of HMRC that there has been collusion to deprive the retailer of consideration, HMRC accept that this can amount to a theft of goods from the retailer so that no supply has taken place. See also *WH Smith Ltd (VTD 16505) (TVC 56.39)* which concerned VAT in respect of sales by a retailer in circumstances where staff receive payment for goods at the till but steal the money and do not record the sale so that the proceeds are not reflected in daily gross takings or declared outputs. The tribunal concluded that an adjustment should be made, where necessary, to daily gross takings for sales not recorded by dishonest staff and that how this was to be done should be expressly covered in the Retail Scheme Notices. At the time of writing, HMRC have not amended their notices to cover this point.

(Internal Guidance V1–23, Chapter 10 paras 5.3, 6).

Weekly summary of daily gross takings. Branches of some multiple retailers make weekly 'returns', calculated from daily gross takings, to their head office. These returns are then collated to arrive at the total takings for the business so that head office is only keeping a weekly summary of the returns made by its branches. HMRC may allow this arrangement subject to the following conditions.

- Each branch must keep a record of its own daily gross takings and must be able, if required, to support the information on its weekly return to head office by reference to the daily records.
- Branches must make returns covering part weeks, and the head office must collate and account for those returns in their retail scheme if the end of a VAT period occurs in the middle of a week or a change in the rate of VAT or liability is made in the middle of a week.

(Internal Guidance V1–23, Chapter 10 para 5.5).

De Voil Indirect Tax Service. See V3.556–558.

60.9 SPECIAL TRANSACTIONS

The following is a list of the more common transactions which might have to be taken into account in using a retail scheme and/or calculating gross takings.

(1) **Acquisitions from other EC countries.** Suppliers from elsewhere in the EC do not charge VAT on their sales and the retailer must account for VAT at the rate applicable to the goods in the UK. See 23.3 *et seq.* EUROPEAN COMMUNITY: SINGLE MARKET for further details.

For retail scheme purposes, references to zero-rated goods apply only to goods which are zero-rated in the UK. Goods which are zero-rated on acquisition from other EC countries, but standard-rated in the UK, must be treated as standard-rated goods in the retail scheme calculations.

See (22) below for goods imported from outside the EC.

(2) **Amusement and gaming machine takings.** See 57.3 RECREATION AND SPORT.

(3) **BT phonecards.** See 67.11 and 67.12 TRADE PROMOTION SCHEMES.

(4) **Business entertainment/gifts.** *If goods are purchased specifically to be consumed in the course of business entertainment or to supply as gifts,*

- under the Point of Sale scheme, any VAT due must be accounted for by adding the value of the goods to daily gross takings at the relevant time; and
- under the Apportionment Schemes 1 and 2 and Direct Calculation Schemes 1 and 2, any VAT due on the supply must be accounted for outside the scheme.

See 47.6 OUTPUT TAX for VAT due on gifts.

If goods from normal stock are used for business entertainment or supplied as gifts,

- under the Point of Sale scheme, any VAT due must be accounted for by adding the value of the goods to daily gross takings at the relevant time;
- under Apportionment Scheme 1, the full value of the goods should be included in daily gross takings;
- under Apportionment Scheme 2, the full value of the goods should be included in daily gross takings and the necessary adjustment should be made to expected selling prices;
- under Direct Calculation Schemes 1 and 2, VAT can be accounted for under the scheme as follows:

  (i) if the goods are standard-rated or reduced rate goods and the minority goods are zero-rated, by adding the value of the supply to daily gross takings; and

  (ii) if the minority goods are standard-rated or reduced rate goods, no addition to the daily gross takings is necessary but the expected selling prices must be adjusted to reflect the value to be accounted for.

(5) **Business overheads**. Any purchases of goods and services which are not for resale should be excluded from the scheme calculations.

(6) **Business promotion schemes**. See 67 TRADE PROMOTION SCHEMES.

(7) **Cash discounts**. If goods are offered on cash discount or early settlement terms, the discounted value should be included in daily gross takings at the time of supply.

(8) **Catering supplies**. Apportionment Schemes 1 and 2 and Direct Calculation Schemes 1 and 2 all assume that goods bought at one rate of VAT will be sold at the same rate. Food bought at the zero rate often becomes standard-rated when supplied in the course of catering and therefore the Point of Sale scheme must normally be used for such supplies. See, however, 11.3 CATERING for a catering adaptation which may be used.

(9) **Credit card transactions**. Retailers are allowed to charge different prices to customers using a credit card. The different prices charged may either take the form of discounts to cash customers (see (7) above) or a surcharge being made to those paying by credit card.

- If the charge for payment by credit card is made by the supplier of the goods/services being bought, HMRC regard this as a further payment for the purchase, VAT being payable at the same rate as on the goods/services.
- If the charge is made by an agent acting for the supplier of the goods/services (eg a travel agent acting on behalf of a tour operator) HMRC consider that the charge is for a separate supply of exempt services (ie accepting payment in the form of a credit card).

Card-handling fees. Many high street retailers operate a scheme whereby, when customers pay for goods by credit or debit card, small print on the receipt asks them to agree to pay a 'card-handling fee' (typically 2.5%), even though the price is exactly the same as it would be for a cash sale. The fee is then claimed as an exempt supply so that VAT is only paid on 97.5% of the price of the goods. In *Debenhams Retail plc v C & E Commrs, Ch D [2004] STC 1132 (TVC 26.8)* the tribunal had held that this treatment was incorrect and that the whole amount paid was consideration for a taxable supply of goods. However, the High Court overturned that decision thereby allowing the so-called 'card-handling fees' to be free of VAT. HMRC have indicated that they will appeal this decision to the Court of Appeal and will also work immediately with other EC countries to amend EC VAT law to put this matter beyond doubt.

(C & E News Release 29/04, 30 June 2004).

(10) **Credit transactions**. The full value of the goods must be included in daily gross takings at the time of supply. Do not wait until payment is received and do not include instalments as they are received. Additional rules apply depending upon the way credit sales are financed.

(*a*) Where *credit for customers is arranged through a finance house, etc* which takes ownership of the goods, the transaction should be treated as a cash sale to the finance house and the full amount payable by the customer should by included in daily gross takings at the time of supply.

In *C & E Commrs v Primback Ltd, CJEC [2001] STC 803 (TVC 21.168)* Primback sold furniture on interest free credit. Credit was provided by a separate finance company introduced to the customer by Primback. The finance company did not charge interest and title in the goods passed directly from Primback to the customer. The customer then paid the full price of the goods in instalments to the finance company. The finance company did not pay Primback the full price charged to the customer but a net amount after retaining a 'discount' equivalent to the amount that the finance company would have charged the customer for a loan at a commercial rate. At issue was whether VAT was due on the full amount paid by the customer, or on the lower amount received by Primback. The CJEC held that where a retailer sells goods in return for payment of the advertised price which he invoices to the purchaser and which does not vary according to whether the customer pays in cash or by way of credit, the taxable amount is the full amount payable by the purchaser.

(*b*) *Where credit transactions are financed from own resources*, any separate credit charge (additional to the cash price) is exempt from VAT provided that it is disclosed to the customer (see 27.11 FINANCIAL SERVICES). If so, it should be excluded from daily gross takings.

Adaptations for newsagents/small retailers. In principle, the above requirements apply to all businesses. However, HMRC recognise that this may cause administrative difficulties for small businesses with turnover of less than £1 million (eg milkmen/newsagents who make doorstep deliveries of largely zero-rated goods and small retailers such as corner shops who may provide goods 'on tick'). In such cases, retailers can take account of opening and closing debtors for a VAT period in their scheme calculations. (VAT Notice 727, para 4.5; Internal Guidance V1–23, Chapter 10 para 5.8).

(11) **Delivery charges**. See 47.8(18) OUTPUT TAX.

(12) **Deposits**. Deposits which are advance payments must be included in daily gross takings. Other deposits (eg those taken as security for the safe return of goods hired out) must be excluded (regardless of whether the deposit is eventually refunded or forfeited for loss or damage).

(13) **Dishonoured cheques and counterfeit bank notes**. Unsigned or dishonoured cheques from cash customers (but not credit customers) and counterfeit notes received may be deducted from daily gross takings.

(14) **Disposal of business assets**. VAT must be accounted for outside the retail scheme.

(15) **Exempt supplies**. These must always be dealt with outside the scheme, whichever scheme is used.

(16) **Exports (to countries outside the EC).**

Retail exports. Where goods are supplied for retail export under the retail export scheme, including supplies to entitled EC residents and ships' crews going abroad (see 25.11 to 25.15 EXPORTS) the supplies must be allowed for in the scheme calculations as follows.

(*a*) Under the Point of Sale scheme, Apportionment Schemes 1 and 2 and, if the minority goods are zero-rated, Direct Calculation Schemes 1 and 2, follow the normal scheme rules but

(i) include all takings, including VAT, for goods sold for retail export in daily gross takings. (Do not deduct the refunds which are expected to be made to the customer.);

(ii) at the end of each period, add up the takings for standard-rated goods actually exported. (This is the total of amounts shown on the officially certified forms returned during the period.);

(iii) calculate notional VAT on the takings at (ii) above, using the VAT fraction that applied at the time the sale was included in gross takings; and

(iv) subtract the notional VAT at (iii) from the scheme output tax.

(*b*) Under Direct Calculation Schemes 1 and 2 where the minority goods are standard-rated, follow the normal scheme rules but at the end of each VAT period

(i) add up the original expected selling prices, including VAT, of the standard-rated goods which have actually been exported. (These will be the goods shown on the officially certified forms returned during the period.);

(ii) calculate notional VAT on the total at (i) above using the VAT fraction that applied when the amounts were included in the scheme calculations; and

(iii) subtract the notional VAT at (ii) from the scheme output tax.

Direct and indirect exports. Where goods are directly exported or supplied in the UK to an overseas trader for subsequent export,

- under the Point of Sale scheme, the supplies must be dealt with outside the scheme;
- under Apportionment Schemes 1 and 2 and, if the minority goods are zero-rated, Direct Calculation Schemes 1 and 2, the procedure is similar to that for retail exports in (*a*) above except that the calculations relate to goods sent for export and the comments in brackets do not apply. If proof of export is not received within three months of the date of supply, the notional VAT calculated under (*a*)(iii) above must be included as an addition on the VAT payable side of the VAT account for the current VAT period; and
- under Direct Calculation Schemes 1 and 2 where the minority goods are standard-rated, the procedure is similar to that for retail exports in (*b*) above except that the calculations relate to goods sent for export and the comment in brackets does not apply. If proof of export is not received within three months of the date of supply, the notional VAT calculated under (*b*)(ii) above must be included as an addition on the VAT payable side of the VAT account for the current VAT period.

See (28) below for retail sales to persons from other EC countries.

(17) **Foreign currency transactions**. Many retailers accept foreign currency in order to encourage spending by tourists to the UK. No reduction to the daily gross takings can be made for commission payable to the bank, etc for converting the currency. The total sterling equivalent of the value charged on the day the supply is made must be included in the daily gross takings (see 69.18 VALUATION). Note that this is not necessarily the same as the sterling sale price of the goods and depends on the exchange rate applicable at the time of supply.

If the retailer also charges the customer a 'premium' for accepting payment in foreign currency, this is additional consideration for the supply of goods (or services) and must be included in the daily gross takings.

See 60.8 above for inadvertent acceptance of foreign currency.

(18) **Gift, book, and record vouchers**. See 67.11 and 67.12 TRADE PROMOTION SCHEMES.

(19) **Goods bought at one rate and sold at another**. For some goods, the rate of VAT depends upon how they are held out for sale, eg meat held out for sale for human consumption is zero-rated but the same meat held out for sale for pet food is standard-rated.

For the provisions applying to chemists, see 60.19 below and for a special scheme for take-away food, see 11.3 CATERING.

All other goods bought at one rate and sold at another must be treated as follows.

Point of Sale scheme. No action is required because takings are separated into each rate of VAT at the point of sale.

Apportionment Schemes 1 and 2 and Direct Calculation Schemes 1 and 2.

- Where separate stocks are kept of goods that are held out for sale at the different VAT rates, on receipt such goods must be entered in the records of goods for resale at the VAT rate that will apply when they are sold.
- Where common stocks are kept of those goods that are drawn on to sell at different VAT rates, such goods must initially be entered in the scheme records at cost or expected selling price (depending on the scheme used) at the rate of VAT that applied when the goods were received. But when the goods are put up or held out for sale at the other VAT rate, it is necessary to deduct the appropriate amounts from the scheme records at the VAT rate that applied when the goods were received and enter the corresponding amounts in the scheme records at the VAT rate that applies when the goods are sold.

(20) **Goods bought from unregistered suppliers**. Where goods for retail sale are bought from unregistered suppliers,

- under Apportionment Schemes 1 and 2, such goods must be included in the retail scheme calculation at the appropriate rate; and
- under Direct Calculation Schemes 1 and 2, only such goods which are taxable at the minority rate must be included in expected selling price calculations.

(21) **Goods sold on sale or return or similar terms**. A separate record must be kept of goods supplied on a sale or return basis. Such goods should only be included in daily gross takings when the customer adopts the goods. See (12) above if the customer pays a deposit.

(22) **Imports (from countries outside the EC)**. The normal scheme rules apply, as for other purchases, under all schemes.

See (1) above for goods acquired from other EC countries.

(23) **Part-exchange**. Where goods or services are accepted in part-exchange, the full retail selling price, including VAT, of the goods supplied must be included in daily gross takings.

Where any goods taken in part-exchange are subsequently resold, it may be possible to sell them under the margin scheme for SECOND-HAND GOODS (61). If not, they can be included in the retail scheme calculations.

(23A) **Phonecards**. See 67.11 and 67.12 TRADE PROMOTION SCHEMES.

(24) **Private or personal use of goods**. VAT is normally due on any goods purchased for resale that are taken out of the business for personal or private use. See 47.7 OUTPUT TAX.

- Under the Point of Sale scheme, the value of any positive-rated goods taken for private or personal use must be included in daily gross takings.
- Under Apportionment Scheme 1, the value of such goods must be included in daily gross takings.
- Under Apportionment Scheme 2, the value of such goods must be included in daily gross takings and the necessary adjustments must be made to expected selling prices.
- Under the Direct Calculation Schemes 1 and 2,

  (i) if the minority goods are zero-rated, the value of any positive-rated goods taken for private or personal use must be included in daily gross takings; and

  (ii) if minority goods are standard-rated or reduced rate goods, the value of any positive-rated goods taken for private or personal use should be added to expected selling prices and daily gross takings.

(25) **Recall of goods by manufacturers**. If a manufacturer recalls contaminated or otherwise faulty goods,

- under Apportionment Scheme 1, purchase records must be adjusted;
- under Apportionment Scheme 2 and Direct Calculation Schemes 1 and 2, expected selling price records must be adjusted.

(26) **Refunds to customers**. Amounts refunded or credited to customers can be deducted from daily gross takings to a maximum of the amount originally charged.

(27) **Rented payphones**. If a payphone is rented from British Telecom or another supplier, the retailer makes a supply of services to the user of the telephone. VAT is due on the money removed from the payphone which should be dealt with as follows.

- Under the Point of Sale scheme, include the money in standard-rated daily gross takings.
- Under Apportionment Schemes 1 and 2, deal with the supply outside the scheme.
- Under Direct Calculation schemes 1 and 2

  (i) where minority goods are zero-rated or reduced rate goods, include the money in daily gross takings; and

(ii) where the minority goods are standard-rated, deal with the supply outside the scheme.

See also 47.8(16) OUTPUT TAX.

(28) **Retail sales to persons from other EC countries**. Any retail sale made in the UK to a person from another EC country should be accounted for as a normal domestic retail sale. Special arrangements apply to distance selling, ie where goods are sold to persons in other EC countries who are not registered for VAT and the supplier is responsible for delivery to the customer. See 23.18 EUROPEAN COMMUNITY: SINGLE MARKET.

See (16) above for exports to countries outside the EC.

(29) **Road fuel**. If road fuel is used for private motoring, VAT due must be accounted for outside the scheme. See 45.16 MOTOR CARS.

(30) **Sale of discount vouchers (or discount cards)**. The VAT consequences of selling vouchers or cards entitling the holder to discounts on purchases depend upon where the vouchers or cards can be used.

(*a*) If vouchers or cards can only be used for purchases from the retailer selling them, he should include the payment received in daily gross takings. Under the Point of Sale scheme, if, for example, the card can only be used for purchases of zero-rated goods, the amount charged for the card should be added to zero-rated takings.

(*b*) If vouchers or cards can be used at several traders, this is a standard-rated supply of services. See *C & E Commrs v Granton Marketing Ltd; C & E Commrs v Wentwalk Ltd, CA [1996] STC 1049 (TVC 65.62).*

- Under the Point of Sale scheme, payments received should be added to standard-rated daily gross takings.
- Under Apportionment Schemes 1 and 2 and Direct Calculation Schemes 1 and 2, payments received must be dealt with outside the scheme used.

(31) **Sale or assignment of debts**. Where debts due from customers are sold or assigned, no further action is required as the correct amount will have already been included in daily gross takings at the time of supply.

(32) **Saving stamps, travel cards and pools coupons**. If a retailer

- buys and sells travel cards and/or savings stamps for gas, electricity, television licences, etc, or
- receives commission from distributing and collecting pools coupons

these must be dealt with outside the retail scheme and not be included in daily gross takings. This follows the decision in *TE, M & IJ Parr (VTD 1967) (TVC 56.6).*

(33) **Second-hand goods**. VAT on second-hand goods sold, may be accounted for

- within the retail scheme in the same way as new goods; or
- under the margin scheme for SECOND-HAND GOODS (61).

(34) **Theft, shrinkage, leakage and stock losses**. Where there are unexplained accounting discrepancies between stock and sales, to the extent that this is attributable to unrecorded sales, such as theft, shrinkage, etc, the value must be

added back to the records of daily gross takings. Where possible, these adjustments should be allocated to the specific VAT period in which they took place. Otherwise such stock losses should be apportioned across relevant VAT periods on a fair and reasonable basis. Unless there is evidence of the liability of the unaccounted supplies, adjustments must be made in line with the usual proportion of standard against zero-rated supplies. Depending upon the scheme used, it may also be necessary to consider whether the shrinkage for which the daily gross takings has been adjusted requires further adjustment to expected selling prices.

(VAT Notice 727/3/02, paras 6.1–6.31; VAT Notice 727/4/02, paras 7.1–7.34; VAT Notice 727/5/02, paras 6.1–6.33, all of which have the force of law).

60.10 EXPECTED SELLING PRICES ('ESPS')

Under certain of the retail schemes, a retailer must

- calculate ESPs; and
- make adjustments to those ESPs to reflect factors which prevent him from achieving them.

ESPs are used to calculate the expected value of retail sales at different rates. The way ESPs are calculated has, therefore, a direct effect on the VAT paid and must be done as accurately as possible. For this reason, calculations should never include

- goods sold by wholesale;
- goods bought for private use; or
- disposals of stocks resulting from a sale of all or part of the business.

(VAT Notice 727/4/02, para 5.3; VAT Notice 727/5/02, para 4.3, which have the force of law).

60.11 Calculating ESPs

ESPs can be calculated in any way which produces a fair and reasonable result. The same method must always be used (but see below for mixtures) and, whatever method is used, the adjustments described below must also be made. The most common methods of calculation are as follows.

(*a*) *Mark up each line of goods* (the most accurate).

(*b*) *Mark up classes of goods* (eg vegetables or confectionery). This method can only be used if

- it is not possible to mark up each line (as in (*a*) above);
- the variation in mark up within the group is no more than 10% (20% under the old scheme calculations);
- the mark up is reviewed each quarter; and
- the class of goods has a commercial basis and is not constructed artificially.

(*c*) *Use recommended retail prices*. This method can only be used if

- recommended retail prices can be recorded on receipt of the goods; and

- purchases invoices or other supplier documentation (i) shows the VAT-inclusive recommended retail price of each separate line of goods; (ii) distinguishes standard-rated, reduced rate and zero-rated items; and (iii) totals goods at each rate of VAT.

(VAT Notice 727/4/02, para 5.3; VAT Notice 727/5/902, para 4.3, which have the force of law).

Example

In a particular class of zero-rated goods, a retailer purchases the following lines at the actual mark-ups shown.

Line of goods	*Purchase price*	*Actual mark-up*	*Expected selling price*
	£		£
A	150	7%	160.50
B	70	5%	73.50
C	50	16%	58.00
D	30	19%	35.70
E	70	10%	77.00
F	30	6%	31.80
	£400		£436.50

Using the actual mark-up for each line of goods, expected selling prices are £436.50.

If, however, it was not possible to break down the total purchase price of £400 between the various lines, the average mark-up basis could be used.

Average mark-up = (7 + 5 + 16 + 19 + 10 + 6) ÷ 6 = 10.5%

Expected selling prices are £442 (£400 × 1.105).

Mixtures. HMRC will normally expect only one method of setting ESPs to be used but recognise that a mixture of schemes may be used provided

- the same mix is used consistently;
- the conditions for each method used as set out above are satisfied; and
- the overall result is fair and reasonable.

(Internal Guidance V1–23, Chapter 10 para 5.13).

60.12 Adjustment to ESPs

As ESPs will rarely be fully achieved, adjustments must be made at the end of each VAT period to take account of factors which affect the selling price. These include (ie the list is not exhaustive)

- price changes (increases and decreases), eg sell by date reductions;

- special offers and promotion schemes;
- wastage;
- freezer breakdowns;
- breakages;
- shrinkage (ie pilferage and loss of stock); and
- bad debts that have been written off in the period.

How such adjustments are made is up to the individual retailer but a consistent method must be used (both within each period and from one period to the next). Records of adjustments and working papers must be kept with the retail scheme calculations.

If it proves difficult to make such adjustments, it may be more appropriate to use another scheme. Alternatively, HMRC may agree to a method of sampling where reductions cannot be established accurately or the omission of certain adjustments where the effect does not distort the retail scheme.

(VAT Notice 727/4/02, para 5.3; VAT Notice 727/5/02, para 4.3, which have the force of law).

60.13 BESPOKE RETAIL SCHEMES

If VAT-exclusive taxable retail supplies in the previous twelve months have exceeded £100 million, a retailer cannot continue to use a published retail scheme (VAT Notice 727, para 5.1, which has the force of law) and must then do one of the following.

(*a*) **Account for VAT in the normal way**. This does not require the issue of a VAT invoice to unregistered customers. However, it does require the VAT-exclusive value and VAT to be identified for each supply and periodic total of those amounts to be produced.

(*b*) **Agree a bespoke scheme with HMRC**. HMRC will only agree to a bespoke scheme if

- the retailer cannot be expected to account for VAT normally under (*a*) above;
- the method produces a fair and reasonable result;
- the method reflects commercial reality and does not unnecessarily complicate the accounting system of the business or HMRC's ability to audit the VAT declarations; and
- they do not consider it necessary to withhold agreement for the protection of the revenue.

A bespoke scheme must be used for all periods during which the business is ineligible to use a published scheme. Retailers with annual turnover approaching £100 million are therefore advised to contact HMRC well in advance so that the details and conditions of any bespoke scheme can be agreed.

A bespoke scheme will normally be based on a published scheme (or a mixture of published schemes) but it can be based on any method which meets the conditions set by HMRC under (*b*) above. HMRC are unlikely to agree a bespoke scheme based on a scheme with a threshold cap of £1 million (ie currently Apportionment Scheme 1 or Direct Calculation Scheme 1).

Key elements of a bespoke scheme. Any bespoke scheme will be agreed in writing and include the following provisions.

- The start date and review date of the agreement.
- Details of which supplies will be accounted for within the scheme and which, if any, will be accounted for in the normal way.
- Full details of the method of valuing retail supplies.

  Under a scheme based on the Point of Sale scheme, this should cover product VAT coding (including adjustments for errors and mixed-rate products), unscanned products, non-EPOS departments and tills, till breakdowns, refunds, special offers, vouchers, multisaves, staff discount, etc. HMRC have produced detailed notes on *VAT guidance for EPOS* systems. See VAT Information Sheet 11/03.

  Under a scheme based on expected selling prices (ESPs), it should cover the basis of setting and adjusting ESPs, product VAT coding (including adjustments for errors and mixed-rate products), direct deliveries to customers, treatment of services, trading patterns, the level of calculation (business, store, department), etc.

  See VAT Notice 727/2/02, paras 5.1, 5.2, 6.1–6.3 for further details but even these checklists are only a guide and any special circumstances should also be covered.
- Full details of the method of valuing daily gross takings including use of tills, till breakdowns, deliveries direct to customers, adjustments for special transactions (see 60.9 above), etc. See VAT Notice 727/2/02, paras 4.1, 4.2 for further details but even this checklist is only a guide and any special transactions should also be covered.
- Name, status and signature of an HMRC officer and an authorised signatory of the retailer.

The agreement is based on full disclosure of the current business structure and trading patterns. If these change to such an extent that the agreed method ceases to produce a fair and reasonable result, HMRC must be informed immediately in writing.

Any changes to the scheme will normally be made with mutual consent although HMRC may withdraw their agreement and refuse the use of the scheme if it ceases to meet any of the conditions under (*b*) above.

Retrospective changes may be appropriate where there is a fundamental flaw in the scheme.

(VAT Notice 727/2/02, paras 2.1–2.12, 3.1, 3.2).

60.14 POINT OF SALE SCHEME

The Point of Sale scheme can be used if

- taxable turnover does not exceed £100 million (if so a bespoke scheme must be agreed, see 60.13 above); and
- either

  (i) all supplies are made at one positive rate (ie all at the reduced rate or all standard-rated) — if so the Point of Sale scheme is the *only* retail scheme which can be used; or

(ii) supplies are made at two or more rates and the correct liability of supplies can be identified at the time of sale. This, increasingly, means an electronic point of sale system (EPOS) utilising bar-code scanners to identify the items being sold and calculate the appropriate VAT amounts. HMRC have produced detailed notes on *VAT guidance for EPOS*. See VAT Information Sheet 11/03. Alternatively, separate tills can be used for different rates.

How to calculate output tax. For each VAT period (quarterly or monthly)

Step 1	Add up daily gross takings from standard-rated supplies =	A
Step 2	Add up daily gross takings from reduced rate supplies =	B
Step 3	To calculate output tax, add the total at Step 1 multiplied by the VAT fraction for standard-rated goods to the total at Step 2 multiplied by the VAT fraction for reduced rate goods	

In algebraic form output tax is

Sales after 31.8.97 (VAT at 5% on reduced rate goods)

$(A \times 7/47) + (B \times 1/21)$

Sales before 1.9.97 (VAT at 8% on reduced rate goods)

$(A \times 7/47) + (B \times 2/27)$

Gross takings. See 60.8 and 60.9 above for gross takings together with adjustments and special transactions which have to be taken into account.

Records. In addition to the normal records required, a record of daily gross takings must be kept.

Annual accounting scheme. If this scheme is also used, see 63.13 SPECIAL SCHEMES.

Change in VAT rate. See 60.7 above.

Cancellation of registration. VAT is due on business assets, including stock in hand. See 59.34 and 59.35 REGISTRATION.

(VAT Notice 727/3/02, paras 3.2, 3.4, 4.2 which have the force of law).

Adaptations. Retailers who wish to treat minor levels of zero-rated or reduced rate sales as standard-rated may do so. The advantages of such treatment (mainly simplification of VAT records and accounting) must be compared with the disadvantage of paying VAT which is not being charged to customers. (Internal Guidance V1–23, Chapter 10 para 7.4).

Example

N Ltd is a garden centre selling plants and gardening equipment. It also sells gardening books and magazines and barbecue supplies. Due to the product mix, the company splits takings at the time of sale using multi-button tills. At the end of its VAT period, standard-rated takings totalled £125,639.34, zero-rated sales of books, etc totalled £1,549.28 and reduced rate sales of barbecue fuels totalled £194.32.

Output tax for the period is

(£125,639.34 × 7/47) + (£194.32 × 1/21) = £18,721.49

60.15 **APPORTIONMENT SCHEME 1**

In order to use the scheme

- supplies must be made at two different rates of VAT;
- total VAT-exclusive retail sales must be less than £1 million per year. The limit applies to the whole business, eg the scheme cannot be applied to one shop if total turnover of two or more shops owned exceeds the limit; and
- any supplies of services, grown or self-made goods or supplies of catering must be dealt with outside the scheme.

How to calculate output tax. For each VAT period (whether quarterly or monthly)

Step 1	Add up daily gross takings =	A
Step 2	Add up the cost, including VAT, of all goods received for resale at the standard rate =	B
Step 3	Add up the cost, including VAT, of all goods received for resale at the reduced rate =	C
Step 4	Add up the cost, including VAT, of all goods received for resale at standard, reduced and zero rates =	D
Step 5	Calculate the proportion of daily gross takings from sales at the standard rate by dividing the total at Step 2 by the total at Step 4 and multiplying by the total in Step 1	
Step 6	Calculate the proportion of daily gross takings from sales at the reduced rate by dividing the total at Step 3 by the total at Step 4 and multiplying by the total in Step 1	
Step 7	To calculate output tax, add the total at Step 5 multiplied by the VAT fraction for standard-rated goods to the total at Step 6 multiplied by the VAT fraction for reduced rate goods	

In algebraic form output tax is

Sales after 31.8.97 (VAT at 5% on reduced rate goods)

(B ÷ D × A × 7/47) + (C ÷ D × A × 1/21)

Sales before 1.9.97 (VAT at 8% on reduced rate goods)

(B ÷ D × A × 7/47) + (C ÷ D × A × 2/27)

Annual adjustment. An annual adjustment has to be made to cover any under or overpayment of VAT. The adjustment must be made on

- 31 March — for retailers with three-monthly VAT periods ending on 30 June, 30 September, 31 December and 31 March and all retailers with monthly VAT periods;

- 30 April — for retailers with three-monthly VAT periods ending on 31 July, 31 October, 31 January and 30 April; and
- 31 May — for retailers with three-monthly VAT periods ending on 31 August, 30 November, 28/29 February and 31 May.

If, at the first appropriate date for the annual adjustment, the scheme has been operated for one VAT period or less, no adjustment is required until the following year. The first adjustment must include all VAT periods from first use of the scheme. For all later adjustments, only VAT periods since the previous adjustment are included. The adjustment is calculated as follows.

Step A	Calculate the VAT due by following the procedure as in Steps 1 to 7 above but using takings and cost figures for the period since the last adjustments (or, as the case may be, from the start of using the scheme) =	D
Step B	Add together the output tax already accounted for under the scheme in the year =	E

If D is less than E, too much VAT has been paid and the difference should be included in the VAT deductible side of the VAT return for the period covering the adjustment. If D is greater than E, too little VAT has been paid and the difference must be included in the VAT payable side of the VAT return for that period.

Gross takings. See 60.8 and 60.9 above for gross takings together with adjustments and special transactions which must be taken into account.

Imports and acquisitions. The cost of goods received for resale under Steps 2 to 4 above include

- any imports from outside the EC at the full price paid (including customs duty and VAT), and
- any goods acquired from another EC country at the full price paid (including excise duty and with the addition of VAT at the appropriate UK rate).

Opening stock. Goods in stock when the scheme is started are not normally treated as goods received in the period. However, if there are any stock items which are to be sold but not replenished, these may be included in the calculations unless already allowed for in a previous scheme.

Records. In addition to the normal records required, records must be kept of daily gross takings.

Annual accounting scheme. If this scheme is also used, see 63.13 SPECIAL SCHEMES.

Ceasing to use the scheme. The annual adjustment as explained above must be carried out for the period from the last adjustment to the date of ceasing to use the scheme. This applies even if leaving the scheme before the anniversary of starting to use the scheme.

Cancellation of registration. VAT is due on business assets, including stock in hand. See 59.34 and 59.35 REGISTRATION.

(VAT Notice 727/4/02, paras 3.3, 3.5, 3.6, 4.2, 4.3 which have the force of law).

Adaptations. HMRC may allow an adaptation to bring the annual adjustment in line with the financial year end. They will, however, consider the effect on the first such annual adjustment and authorise a period longer than twelve months where necessary to ensure any distortions are avoided. (Internal Guidance V1–23, Chapter 10 para 7.5).

Example

B Ltd has figures for the four quarterly periods in a VAT year as follows.

	Cost of standard-rated goods for resale (incl VAT)	*Cost of reduced rate goods for resale (incl VAT)*	*Total cost of goods for resale (incl VAT)*	*Gross takings*
	£	£	£	£
First quarter	9,429	78	15,701	21,714.55
Second quarter	10,418	124	17,840	24,316.51
Third quarter	9,972	312	15,919	21,899.29
Fourth quarter	7,076	25	11,293	16,149.61
	£36,895	£539	£60,753	£84,079.96

First quarter

Standard-rated sales are

9,429 ÷ 15,701 × £21,714.55 = £13,040.35

Reduced rate sales are

78 ÷ 15,701 × £21,714.55 = £107.87

Output tax = (£13,040.35 × 7/47) + (£107.87 × 1/21) =	1,947.32
By similar calculations output tax in the remaining quarters is	
Second quarter	2,122.96
Third quarter	2,063.57
Fourth quarter	1,508.80
	£7,642.65

Annual adjustment

Standard-rated sales for the year are

36,895 ÷ 60,753 × £84,079.96 = £51,061.35

Reduced rate sales for the year are

539 ÷ 60,753 × £84,079.96 = £745.96

Output tax = (£51,061.35 × 7/47) + (£745.96 × 1/21) = £7,640.40

£2.25 must be included in the VAT deductible side of the VAT return.

60.16 APPORTIONMENT SCHEME 2

In order to use the scheme

- taxable turnover must be less than £100 million (if above a bespoke scheme must be used, see 60.13 above);
- supplies must be made at two different rates of VAT;
- it must be possible to calculate expected selling prices of goods in stock when the scheme is started; and
- any supplies of services or catering must be dealt with outside the scheme.

How to calculate output tax.

For the first three quarterly VAT periods or the first eleven monthly VAT periods

Step 1	Calculate the expected selling price, including VAT, of standard-rated goods for retail sale in stock at the commencement of using the scheme =	A
Step 2	Calculate the expected selling price, including VAT, of reduced rate goods in stock for retail sale at the commencement of using the scheme =	B
Step 3	Calculate the expected selling price, including VAT, of *all* goods in stock for retail sale at the commencement of using the scheme =	C
Step 4	Add up daily gross takings for the VAT period =	D
Step 5	Add up expected selling prices, including VAT, of standard-rated goods (i) received, made or grown for retail sale since starting to use the scheme; and (ii) acquired from other EC countries since starting to use the scheme =	E
Step 6	Add the total in Step 5 to the total in Step 1	
Step 7	Add up expected selling prices, including VAT, of reduced rate goods (i) received, made or grown for retail sale since starting to use the scheme; and (ii) acquired from other EC countries since starting to use the scheme =	F
Step 8	Add the total in Step 7 to the total in Step 2	
Step 9	Add up expected selling prices, including VAT, of *all* goods (standard-rated, reduced rate and zero-rated) (i) received, made or grown for retail sale since starting to use the scheme; and	

	(ii) acquired from other EC countries since starting to use the scheme =	G
Step 10	Add the total in Step 9 to the total in Step 3	
Step 11	Calculate the proportion of gross takings from sales at the standard rate by dividing the total at Step 6 by the total at Step 10 and multiplying by the total at Step 4	
Step 12	Calculate the proportion of gross takings from sales at the reduced rate by dividing the total at Step 8 by the total at Step 10 and multiplying by the total at Step 4	
Step 13	To calculate output tax, add the total at Step 11 multiplied by the VAT fraction for standard-rated goods to the total at Step 12 multiplied by the VAT fraction for reduced rate goods	

In algebraic form, output tax is

Sales after 31.8.97 (VAT at 5% on reduced rate goods)

$$[(A + E) \div (C + G) \times D \times 7/47] + [(B + F) \div (C + G) \times D \times 1/21]$$

Sales before 1.9.97 (VAT at 8% on reduced rate goods)

$$[(A + E) \div (C + G) \times D \times 7/47] + [(B + F) \div (C + G) \times D \times 2/27]$$

For the fourth and all later quarterly VAT periods or the twelfth and all later monthly VAT periods

Step A	Add up daily gross takings for the VAT period =	H
Step B	Add up expected selling prices, including VAT, of standard-rated goods (i) received, made or grown for retail sale; and (ii) acquired from other EC countries in the current VAT period and the previous three quarterly (or eleven monthly) VAT periods =	J
Step C	Add up expected selling prices, including VAT, of reduced rate goods (i) received, made or grown for retail sale; and (ii) acquired from other EC countries in the current VAT period and the previous three quarterly (or eleven monthly) VAT periods =	K
Step D	Add up expected selling prices, including VAT, of *all* goods (standard-rated, reduced rate and zero-rated) (i) received, made or grown for retail sale; and (ii) acquired from other EC countries in the current VAT period and the previous three quarterly (or eleven monthly) VAT periods =	L
Step E	Calculate the proportion of gross takings from sales at the standard rate by dividing the total at Step B by the total at Step D and multiplying by the total in Step A	

Step F	Calculate the proportion of gross takings from sales at the reduced rate by dividing the total at Step C by the total at Step D and multiplying by the total at Step A
Step G	To calculate output tax, add the total at Step E multiplied by the VAT fraction for standard-rated goods to the total at Step F multiplied by the VAT fraction for reduced rate goods

In algebraic form output tax is

Sales after 31.8.97 (VAT at 5% on reduced rate goods)

$(J \div L \times H \times 7/47) + (K \div L \times H \times 1/21)$

Sales before 1.9.97 (VAT at 8% on reduced rate goods)

$(J \div L \times H \times 7/47) + (K \div L \times H \times 2/27)$

Opening stock. If it is not possible to perform a physical stocktake on the date of starting to use the scheme, the ESP values of goods received for resale in the previous three months may be used.

Gross takings. See 60.8 and 60.9 above for gross takings together with adjustments and special transactions which must be taken into account.

Expected selling prices. See 60.10 to 60.12 above for calculation of expected selling prices.

Records. In addition to the normal records required, records must be kept of daily gross takings and expected selling prices.

Annual accounting scheme. If this scheme is also used, see 63.13 SPECIAL SCHEMES.

Ceasing to use the scheme. No adjustment is normally necessary unless ceasing to use the scheme in part only of the business. In such a case, the rolling calculation for that part still using the scheme must not include stock and expected selling prices of the part no longer using the scheme.

Cancellation of registration. VAT is due on business assets, including stock in hand. See 59.34 and 59.35 REGISTRATION.

(VAT Notice 727/4/02, paras 3.3, 3.5, 3.6, 5.2, 5.4 which have the force of law).

Adaptations.

(1) *Opening stock*. If it is not possible to perform a physical stocktake on the date of starting to use the scheme, the expected selling price values of goods received for resale in the previous three months may be used. Alternatively, where even this is impossible or impractical, HMRC may also approve

- updating the most recent stocktake to take account of goods received for retail sale and supplied since the stocktaking took place;
- allowing a stocktaking to be carried out during the first period of use of the scheme and adjusting this to take account of goods received for retail sale and supplied from the start of using the scheme to the date of the stocktaking; or

- use of stock records produced by management accounts where these are used consistently and considered by the retailer to be of such accuracy that they are relied upon for commercial stock management and statutory accounts.

(2) *Using periodic stock adjustments rather than a rolling calculation.* HMRC are likely to accept an adaptation using quarterly stock adjustments. They may also accept an adaptation using an annual stock adjustment in which case HMRC will also consider bringing the annual adjustment in line with the financial year end.

(3) *Adjusting historical purchase data to reflect changes in the mix of goods.* Where a retailer's mix of goods to be sold under the scheme has changed from the first period under the rolling calculation, HMRC may approve an adaptation under which

- where VAT on supplies made by a particular department or for a specific class of goods is no longer to be accounted for under this rolling calculation scheme (eg because a different scheme is to be used), the historic purchase/expected selling price data is excluded from the calculation; and
- similarly when new departments/classes of goods are brought into the scheme, the historic purchase/expected selling price data is also included in the rolling calculation.

(Internal Guidance V1–23, Chapter 10 para 7.5).

Example

Z Ltd owns a store and can analyse all purchases of stock for resale. It decides to use Apportionment Scheme 2 and calculates that the expected selling price, including VAT, of stock for retail sale at the commencement of using the scheme is £818,703, of which £331,379 represents standard-rated lines. Trading figures for the first four quarters under the scheme are

	ESP of standard-rated goods received for resale (incl VAT)	*Total ESP of goods received for resale (incl VAT)*	*Gross takings*
	£	£	£
First quarter	393,741	1,009,199	835,265
Second quarter	400,829	891,685	829,524
Third quarter	314,227	905,859	1,018,784
Fourth quarter	493,207	1,235,087	1,486,381

Output tax is calculated as follows

First quarter		
Opening stock	331,379	818,703
First quarter	393,741	1,009,199
	£725,120	£1,827,902

Standard-rated sales = 725,120 ÷ 1,827,902 × £835,265 = £331,345

Output tax = £331,345 × 7/47			£49,349.25
Second quarter			
Opening stock	331,379	818,703	
First quarter	393,741	1,009,199	
Second quarter	400,829	891,685	
	£1,125,949	£2,719,587	

Standard-rated sales = 1,125,949 ÷ 2,719,587 × £829,524 = £343,435

Output tax = £343,435 × 7/47 =			£51,149.89
Third quarter			
Opening stock	331,379	818,703	
First quarter	393,741	1,009,199	
Second quarter	400,829	891,685	
Third quarter	314,227	905,859	
	£1,440,176	£3,625,446	

Standard-rated sales = 1,440,176 ÷ 3,625,446 × £1,018,784 = £404,702

Output tax = £404,702 × 7/47			£60,274.76
Fourth quarter			
First quarter	393,741	1,009,199	
Second quarter	400,829	891,685	
Third quarter	314,227	905,859	
Fourth quarter	493,207	1,235,087	
	£1,602,004	£4,041,830	

Standard-rated sales = 1,602,004 ÷ 4,041,830 × £1,486,381 = £589,136

Output tax = £589,136 × 7/47 =	£87,743.66

60.17 **DIRECT CALCULATION SCHEME 1**

In order to use the scheme

- total VAT-exclusive retail sales must be less than £1 million per year. The limit applies to the whole business, eg the scheme cannot be applied to one shop if total turnover of two or more shops owned exceeds the limit;
- any supplies of services with the same VAT liability as the minority goods must be dealt with outside the scheme; and
- any supplies of catering must be dealt with outside the scheme.

The scheme works by calculating expected selling prices (ESPs) of goods for retail sale. ESPs are normally only calculated for minority goods, ie those goods at the rate of VAT which

- where goods are supplied at two rates of VAT, forms the smallest proportion of retail supplies; or
- where goods are supplied at three rates of VAT, forms the two smaller proportions of retail supplies.

See, however, under the heading *Adaptations* below.

How to calculate output tax. For each VAT period (quarterly or monthly)

Where the minority goods are zero-rated and/or reduced rate goods (*ie main goods are standard-rated*).

Step 1	Add up daily gross takings =	A
Step 2	Add up ESPs of zero-rated goods received, made or grown for retail sale =	B
Step 3	Add up ESPs of reduced rate goods received, made or grown for retail sale =	C
Step 4	Calculate the standard-rated element of takings by deducting the totals at Step 2 and Step 3 from the total at Step 1	
Step 5	To calculate output tax, add the total in Step 4 multiplied by the VAT fraction for standard-rated goods to the total in Step 3 multiplied by the VAT fraction for reduced rate goods	

In algebraic form, output tax is

Sales after 31.8.97 (VAT at 5% on reduced rate goods)

$((A - B - C) \times 7/47) + (C \times 1/21)$

Sales before 1.9.97 (VAT at 8% on reduced rate goods)

$((A - B - C) \times 7/47) + (C \times 2/27)$

Where the minority goods are standard-rated and/or reduced rate goods (*ie main goods are zero-rated*).

Step 1	Add up daily gross takings. (Although this figure is not used in the calculation, it is still a requirement of operating the scheme and is also used in completing the VAT return.)	
Step 2	Add up ESPs of standard-rated goods received, made or grown for retail sale =	D
Step 3	Add up ESPs of reduced rate goods received, made or grown for retail sale =	E
Step 4	To calculate output tax, add the total in Step 2 multiplied by the VAT fraction for standard-rated goods to the total in Step 3 multiplied by the VAT fraction for reduced rate goods	

In algebraic form, output tax is

Sales after 31.8.97 (VAT at 5% on reduced rate goods)

(D × 7/47) + (E × 1/21)

Sales before 1.9.98 (VAT at 8% on reduced rate goods)

(D × 7/47) + (E × 2/27)

Gross takings. See 60.8 and 60.9 above for gross takings together with adjustments and special transactions which must be taken into account.

Expected selling prices. See 60.10 to 60.12 above for calculation of expected selling prices.

Opening stock. Goods in stock when the scheme is started are not normally treated as goods received in the period. However, if there are any stock items which are to be sold but not replenished, these may be included in the calculations unless already allowed for in a previous scheme.

Records. In addition to the normal records required, records must be kept of daily gross takings and expected selling prices.

Annual accounting scheme. If this scheme is also used, see 63.13 SPECIAL SCHEMES.

Cancellation of registration. VAT is due on business assets, including stock in hand. See 59.34 and 59.35 REGISTRATION.

(VAT Notice 727/5/02, paras 3.1, 3.6, 3.7, 4.2, 4.4 which have the force of law).

Adaptations. If marking up the 'majority' rather than the 'minority' goods would be more straightforward, retailers may do so. For example, newsagents may find it easier to set estimated selling prices for their majority sales of newspapers and magazines as there are likely to be fewer purchase records than for minority standard-rated sales of tobacco, confectionery, etc (Internal Guidance V1–23, Chapter 10 para 7.6).

Example

K runs a typical corner shop selling newspapers and magazines (zero-rated), confectionery and tobacco (standard-rated), a limited range of food items (zero-rated) and barbecue fuels (reduced rate goods). At the end of a VAT period, gross takings are £18,714.55. The expected selling prices of purchases in the period are £11,236.19 for standard-rated goods, £8,154.27 for zero-rated goods and £157.93 for reduced rate goods.

The minority goods are zero-rated and reduced rate goods. Output tax is calculated as follows.

	£	£
Gross takings		18,714.55
Expected selling prices of zero-rated goods	8,154.27	
Expected selling prices of reduced rate goods	157.93	
		8,312.20
Standard-rated element of takings		£10,402.35

Output tax = (£10,402.35 × 7/47) + (£157.93 × 1/21) =	£1,556.81

60.18 DIRECT CALCULATION SCHEME 2'

In order to use the scheme

- taxable turnover must be less than £100 million (if above a bespoke scheme must be used, see 60.13 above);
- it must be possible to calculate expected selling prices of minority goods in stock when the scheme is started and annually thereafter;
- any supplies of services with the same VAT liability as the minority goods must be dealt with outside the scheme; and
- any supplies of catering must be dealt with outside the scheme.

The scheme works by calculating expected selling prices (ESPs) of goods for retail sale. ESPs are only calculated for '*minority goods*', ie those goods at the rate of VAT which

- where goods are supplied at two rates of VAT, forms the smallest proportion of retail supplies; or
- where goods are supplied at three rates of VAT, forms the two smaller proportions of retail supplies.

How to calculate output tax. For each VAT period, the same rules apply as for Direct Calculation Scheme 1, see 60.17 above.

Annual adjustment. This scheme is based on retail trade over a full year which runs from the beginning of the first VAT period in which the scheme was used. An annual adjustment is required after making the output tax calculation for the fourth quarter (twelfth month) and any difference is accounted for on the return for that period. The adjustment must take into account any disposals since the last adjustment which were not by way of retail sale. This is done by excluding, from the figures used in the calculation, the value of any goods which were previously part of the scheme calculation (or included in the opening stock figure) but have not been sold by way of retail sale. The adjustment is also required if part of the business leaves the scheme.

Where the minority goods are zero-rated and/or reduced rate goods (ie main goods are standard-rated).

Step 1	Add up daily gross takings for the year =	A
Step 2	For zero-rated goods for retail sale calculate:	
	ESPs of such goods in stock at the beginning of the year	
	plus	
	ESPs of such goods received, made or grown for retail in the year	
	less	
	ESPs of such goods in stock at the end of the year =	B
Step 3	For reduced rate goods for retail sale calculate:	
	ESPs of such goods in stock at the beginning of the year	

	plus	
	ESPs of such goods received, made or grown for retail in the year	
	less	
	ESPs of such goods in stock at the end of the year =	C
Step 4	Calculate the standard-rated element of takings for the year by deducting the totals at Step 2 and Step 3 from the total at Step 1	
Step 5	To calculate output tax, add the total in Step 4 multiplied by the VAT fraction for standard-rated goods to the total in Step 3 multiplied by the VAT fraction for reduced rate goods	

In algebraic form, output tax is

Sales after 31.8.97 (VAT at 5% on reduced rate goods)

$((A - B - C) \times 7/47) + (C \times 1/21)$

Sales before 1.9.97 (VAT at 8% on reduced rate goods)

$((A - B - C) \times 7/47) + (C \times 2/27)$

This gives the correct total for output tax due for the year. If the total is less than that calculated under the scheme in the four quarters (twelve months), the difference should be included in the VAT deductible side of the VAT account for the fourth quarter (twelfth month). Similarly, if the total is more, the difference should be included in the VAT payable side of the VAT account for that period.

Where the minority goods are standard-rated and/or reduced rate goods (*ie main goods are zero-rated*).

Step 1	For standard-rated goods for retail sale calculate:	
	ESPs of such goods in stock at the beginning of the year	
	plus	
	ESPs of such goods received, made or grown for retail in the year	
	less	
	ESPs of such goods in stock at the end of the year =	D
Step 2	For reduced rate goods for retail sale calculate:	
	ESPs of such goods in stock at the beginning of the year	
	plus	
	ESPs of such goods received, made or grown for retail in the year	
	less	
	ESPs of such goods in stock at the end of the year =	E

Step 3	To calculate output tax, add the total at Step 1 multiplied by the VAT fraction for standard-rated goods to the total at Step 2 multiplied by the VAT fraction for reduced rate goods

In algebraic form, output tax is

Sales after 31.8.97 (VAT at 5% on reduced rate goods)

(D × 7/47) + (E × 1/21)

Sales before 1.9.97 (VAT at 8% on reduced rate goods)

(D × 7/47) + (E × 2/27)

This gives the correct total for output tax due for the year. If the total is less than that calculated under the scheme in the four quarters (twelve months), the difference should be included in the VAT deductible side of the VAT account for the fourth quarter (twelfth month). Similarly, if the total is more, the difference should be included in the VAT payable side of the VAT account for that period.

Gross takings. See 60.8 and 60.9 above for gross takings together with adjustments and special transactions which must be taken into account.

Expected selling prices. See 60.10 to 60.12 above for calculation of expected selling prices.

Opening stock. Goods in stock when the scheme is started are not normally treated as goods received in the period. However, if there are any stock items which are to be sold but not replenished, these may be included in the calculations unless already allowed for in a previous scheme.

Records. In addition to the normal records required, records must be kept of daily gross takings and expected selling prices.

Annual accounting scheme. If this scheme is also used, see 63.13 SPECIAL SCHEMES.

Ceasing to use the scheme. The annual adjustment as explained above must be carried out for the period from the last adjustment to the date of ceasing to use the scheme. This applies even if leaving the scheme before the anniversary of starting to use the scheme. An adjustment must also be made if part of the business ceases to use the scheme.

Cancellation of registration. VAT is due on business assets, including stock in hand. See 59.34 and 59.35 REGISTRATION.

(VAT Notice 727/5/02, paras 3.1, 3.4, 3.6, 3.7, 4.2, 4.4, 4.5 which have the force of law).

Adaptations.

(1) *Using expected selling prices of non-minority goods.* An adaptation which uses estimated selling prices for goods which do *not* form the minority sales will be considered where it is not only simpler for the retailer but also easier for HMRC to audit (eg a newsagent whose major portion of sales is newspapers and magazines).

(2) *Valuing stock.* If a physical stocktake at the start of the scheme year is impossible or impractical, HMRC may also approve

- updating the most recent stocktake to take account of goods received for retail sale and supplied since the stocktaking took place;
- allowing a stocktaking to be carried out during the first period of use of the scheme and adjusting this to take account of goods received for retail sale and supplied from the start of using the scheme to the date of the stocktaking; or
- use of stock records produced by management accounts where these are used consistently and considered by the retailer to be of such accuracy that they are relied upon for commercial stock management and statutory accounts.

(3) *Annual adjustment*. HMRC may allow an adaptation to bring the annual adjustment in line with the financial year end. They will, however, consider the effect on the first such annual adjustment and authorise a period longer than twelve months where necessary to ensure any distortions are avoided.

(Internal Guidance V1–23, Chapter 10 para 7.6).

Example

K decides to use Direct Calculation Scheme 2. When he starts to use the scheme, his opening stock, valued at expected selling prices, is

	£
Standard-rated goods	3,145.91
Zero-rated goods	2,250.34
Reduced rate goods	142.51

For the first four quarters, his relevant details are

	ESP of standard-rated goods purchased	*ESP of zero-rated goods purchased*	*ESP of reduced rate goods purchased*	*Gross takings*
	£	£	£	£
First quarter	11,236.19	8,154.27	157.93	18,714.55
Second quarter	9,075.02	11,667.67	259.32	20,726.40
Third quarter	9,872.90	10,124.75	137.54	20,855.88
Fourth quarter	11,431.39	11,008.62	21.43	22,649.04
	£41,615.50	£40,955.31	£576.22	£82,945.87

At the end of the fourth quarter, his closing stock, valued at expected selling prices, is

	£
Standard-rated goods	4,217.22
Zero-rated goods	3,151.44

Reduced rate goods	119.19	

First quarter

The minority goods are zero-rated and reduced rate goods. Output tax is calculated as follows.

	£	£
Gross takings		18,714.55
ESP of zero-rated goods	8,154.27	
ESP of reduced rate goods	157.93	
		8,312.20
Standard-rated element of takings		£10,402.35

Output tax = (£10,402.35 × 7/47) + (£157.93 × 1/21) = £1,556.81

Second quarter

The minority goods are standard-rated and reduced rate goods. Output tax is calculated as follows.

(£9,075.02 × 7/47) + (£259.32 × 1/21) = £1,363.95

Third quarter

The minority goods are standard-rated and reduced rate goods. Output tax is calculated as follows.

(£9,872.90 × 7/47) + (£137.54 × 1/21) = £1,476.98

Fourth quarter

The minority goods are zero-rated and reduced rate goods. Output tax is calculated as follows.

	£	£
Gross takings		22,649.04
ESP of zero-rated goods	11,008.62	
ESP of reduced rate goods	21.43	
		11,030.05
Standard-rated element of takings		£11,618.99

Output tax = (£11,618.99 × 7/47) + (£21.43 × 1/21) = £1,731.51

The annual adjustment is as follows

The minority goods are zero-rated and reduced rate goods. Output tax is calculated as follows

	£	£
Gross takings		82,945.87
Less zero-rated goods		
opening stock:	2,250.34	
ESP of goods purchased	40,955.31	
	43,205.65	
closing stock	3,151.44	
		40,054.21
		42,891.66
Less reduced rate goods		
opening stock:	142.51	
ESP of goods purchased	576.22	
	718.73	
closing stock	119.19	
		599.54
Standard-rated element of takings		£42,292.12
Output tax = (£42,292.12 × 7/47) + (£599.54 × 1/21) =		6,327.38
Output tax already calculated		
£1,556.81 + £1,363.95 + £1,476.98 + £1,731.51		6,129.25
Additional VAT payable with return for fourth quarter		£198.13

60.19 RETAIL CHEMISTS

Many of the goods that a retail chemist buys at the standard rate may subsequently be either sold over the counter (at the standard rate) or dispensed on prescription (normally at the zero rate but at the standard rate where dispensed for a patient being cared for in a nursing home or hospital, see 32.15 HEALTH AND WELFARE). There is thus no direct relationship between the proportions of goods bought and sold at the different rates of VAT.

HMRC give the following guidance on how the standard schemes need to be adjusted to take account of this fact.

Point of Sale scheme. Under this scheme the correct rate of VAT is identified at the time of supply and no adjustment is therefore necessary. (VAT Notice 727, para 9.3).

Apportionment Scheme 1 and Direct Calculation Schemes 1 and 2. The following adjustments are required at the end of each VAT period.

Step 1	Calculate output tax under the normal scheme rules — daily gross takings to include the total amount from prescription charges and NHS cheque (less the value of any exempt supplies such as rota payments) =	A
Step 2	Add up payments *received* in the period for all *Group 12* goods, even if not supplied in the period. (Any exempt or standard-rated supplies in the NHS cheque must be excluded.) =	B
Step 3	Estimate the value of goods included in Step 2 that were zero-rated on receipt. (This must be based on a sample of actual purchases for a representative period, taking account of seasonal fluctuations, etc. A new estimation must be made each VAT period.) =	C
Step 4	Subtract the total at Step 3 from the total at Step 2	
Step 5	Work out the VAT included in Step 1 from *Group 12* goods by multiplying the total at Step 4 by the VAT fraction	
Step 6	Calculate output tax by deducting the total at Step 5 from the total at Step 1	

In algebraic form, output tax is

$$A - ((B - C) \times 7/47)$$

Where a Direct Calculation scheme is used, a retail chemist must normally calculate expected selling prices for minority goods (see 60.17 and 60.18 above). If the minority goods are standard-rated when sold but the minority of purchases are zero-rated, the chemist may calculate expected selling prices on the basis of the zero-rated goods received for resale.

Apportionment Scheme 2. The retail chemist adjustment cannot be made with this scheme.

(VAT Notice 727, paras 9.4, 9.5 which have the force of law).

By concession, where

- goods supplied are dispensed to an individual for his/her personal use whilst an inpatient or resident, or whilst attending, a hospital or nursing home,
- the goods are ordered and dispensed in accordance with NHS regulations, and
- the person dispensing the goods is paid for doing so by the Prescription Pricing Authority, the Prescription Information and Pricing Services Division of the Welsh Health Common Services Authority, the Pharmacy Practice Division of the Common Services Agency, or the Central Services Agency,

for the purposes of the retail scheme calculations, the supply may be treated as if it were a zero-rated supply. (VAT Notice 48, ESC 3.30).

60.20 RETAIL FLORISTS

The following provisions apply to florists and other retailers who are members of organisations such as Interflora, Teleflorist and Flowergram which facilitate the purchase and delivery of flowers. The provisions have the force of law under *SI 1995/2518, Reg 67.*

The adjustments to be made depend upon the retail scheme used and whether the florist is the '*sending member*' (ie the member receiving payment direct from the customer) or the '*executing member*' (ie the member delivering the flowers and receiving payment from the organisation).

The documentation received from the agency may show output tax payable to HMRC. This is 'self-billed' output tax as the agency issues the invoice for supplies made by the florist. The florist should check the agency documentation and, if correct, add the self-billed output tax to any VAT calculated in accordance with its own retail scheme.

Point of Sale scheme.

- *Sending member*. No adjustment is required by a sending member. Payments received should be included in daily gross takings at the time of the order.
- *Executing member.* Do not include payments received from the agency in daily gross takings and account for any VAT due outside the retail scheme.

Apportionment schemes.

- *Sending member*. Identify from agency documentation the value of supplies made as a sending member and account for any VAT due outside the retail scheme. Do not include payments for those supplies in daily gross takings under the retail scheme calculations.
- *Executing member*. Do not include payments received from the agency in daily gross takings and account for any VAT due outside the retail scheme on the basis of agency documentation.

  If Apportionment Scheme 1 is used, exclude the value of flowers sent as an executing member from purchase records.

  If Apportionment Scheme 2 is used, adjust expected selling prices for the value of flowers sent as an executing member and accounted for outside the retail scheme.

Direct calculation schemes.

- *Sending member*. Identify from agency documentation the value of supplies made as a sending member and account for any VAT due outside the retail scheme. Do not include payments for those supplies in daily gross takings under the retail scheme calculations.
- *Executing member*. Do not include payments received from the agency in daily gross takings and account for any VAT due outside the retail scheme on the basis of agency documentation. Adjust expected selling prices for the value of flowers sent as an executing member and accounted for outside the retail scheme.

(VAT Notice 727, paras 10.1–10.4).

60.21 SPECIAL ARRANGEMENTS FOR CERTAIN RETAILERS

(1) Caterers

See 11.3 CATERING for a special adaptation.

Goods taken out of another part of the business for use in the catering business. Where, for example, a bakery or delicatessen makes catering supplies or a supermarket uses stock in a staff canteen, if an apportionment or direct calculation retail scheme is being used in that other part of the business, adjustments must be made to the expected selling prices to reflect the effective transfer of stock between the different parts of the business. If it is difficult to do this precisely, a fair and reasonable estimate as to the proportion of purchases which are subsequently used in the catering business must be made. This could be done based on usage and the pattern of trading in previous periods. That proportion must then be excluded from the purchase records under Apportionment Scheme 1 or the record of expected selling prices under Apportionment Scheme 2 and Direct Calculation Schemes 1 and 2. (Internal Guidance V1–23, Chapter 10 para 9.1).

(2) **Chemists**

See 60.19 above.

(3) **Concessions/shops within shops**

Department stores frequently contain various 'shops within shops' where part of the premises are operated as 'concessions' by other retailers. The VAT treatment depends upon the terms of the agreement between the store and the concessionaire.

(*a*) Where the concessionaire makes its supplies directly to the customer, it is liable to account for VAT on its sales. Its stock, goods received for retail sale and daily gross takings should not be included in the host store's retail scheme calculations, even where the retailer operating the concession uses the host store's staff and services. The host store must account for VAT on the commission received from the concessionaire.

(*b*) Where the host store makes the supply to the customer (and therefore the concessionaire only makes supplies to the host store), the host store is accountable for the output tax due on the retail supply to shoppers and the concessionaire is effectively making wholesale supplies to the host store which cannot be accounted for within the concessionaire's retail scheme.

Where (*a*) above applies, difficulties that may arise include

- the host store recognising such sales and ensuring that they are not included in its daily gross takings;
- the concessionaire ensuring that it is advised of its sales figures by the host store in time to account correctly for VAT;
- dealing with retail exports of the concessionaire's goods;
- dealing with discounts given across the store; and
- dealing with bad debts and bounced cheques, etc where the debt relates to, or the cheque was given as payment for, both the host's and the concessionaire's goods.

Promotional discounts. Where (*a*) above applies and the host retailer funds promotional discounts on sales by the concessionaire, the value of the retail sale to be included in the concessionaire's daily gross takings is the amount charged to the customer less the discount. The payment by the host retailer to the concessionaire is consideration for a supply of services and should therefore be accounted for outside the concessionaire's retail scheme. See *JE Beale plc (VTD 15920) (TVC 34.70)*. This would arise, for example, where a 10% discount is offered on all first purchases made using a host retailer's store card, including sales made by any concessionaires. If the host retailer agrees to fund the discount by paying the 10% to the concessionaire, such payment is consideration for a supply of services and not part of the consideration for the supply of the goods to the customer.

(Internal Guidance V1–23, Chapter 10 para 9.3).

(4) **Florists**

See 60.20 above.

(5) **Hampers (eg Christmas Clubs)**

Some businesses may run a separate operation retailing hampers whereby they receive periodic payments over the course of a year with the hamper actually being supplied once all payments have been received. The periodic payments are normally advance payments for the supply of the hamper and therefore create a tax point. As such they should be included in the daily gross takings at the time of receipt. Where, during the early course of the year, the business only makes a few purchases of goods to be included in the hamper, this may cause problems in using a retail scheme which will produce a fair and reasonable result. One option may be to use the previous year's (or season's) catalogue to agree an overall standard-rated percentage to be applied on a provisional basis to the current year's catalogue hamper sales. At the year end, the actual standard-rated split of the hampers supplied can be calculated and any VAT adjustment made. (Internal Guidance V1–23, Chapter 10 para 9.6).

(6) **Mail order businesses**

Mail order businesses may use a retail scheme if they cannot account for VAT in the normal way. HMRC prefer the use of the Point of Sale scheme. Otherwise a modified apportionment scheme using the expected selling prices of goods despatched to customers less goods returned from customers is likely to produce a fair and reasonable valuation of taxable supplies made. Under such a scheme, a distortive effect could be caused by goods sent to agents but lost in transit if the original goods and replacements are both included in despatches. An adjustment for this should be included in the retail scheme agreement with HMRC.

Agent's own purchases (*AOPs*). Agents normally receive

(i) commission on sales to other customers; and

(ii) commission on purchases for own personal use (including goods purchased for use as gifts).

Commission under (i) above does not reduce the value of the supply for VAT purposes (even if passed on to customers by the agent). Commission under (ii) above on AOPs is seen as a genuine discount and the value of the supply may be reduced at the appropriate time.

If the mail order business cannot distinguish between AOPs and other sales on an item by item basis, HMRC may agree to a sampling method to establish an agreed percentage of AOPs or to the use of a fixed percentage. Whatever method is agreed, it must satisfy the 'fair and reasonable' test and can only be used for the period specified in the letter of agreement with HMRC. Once made, the agreement cannot be unilaterally be resiled by the mail order business

(*GUS Merchandise Corporation Ltd (No 2) v C & E Commrs, CA 1994 [1995] STC 279 (TVC 56.50)*) or by HMRC (*Tesco plc (VTD 12740) (TVC 56.56)*).

Timing of AOP discount. The value of the commissions earned by an agent is normally posted to a separate commission account (on the basis of payments received rather than sales made) and held in abeyance until 'credited' to the agent when claimed either

- as a reduction against the agent's balance;
- as a monetary payment; or
- to pay for further goods.

Not all agent's commision is claimed. Following the decision in *Freemans plc v C & E Commrs, CJEC [2001] STC 960 (TVC 21.177)* a mail order business can only claim credit for the discounts given to agents for their own purchases at the time the agents use their accumulated commission in one of the three ways detailed above (and not when the discounts are posted to the agents' commission accounts).

Time of supply. Mail order businesses normally supply goods on approval terms. This delays the basic tax point until the time when the goods are adopted by the customer or twelve months from the date the goods were originally despatched if later. See 64.43 SUPPLY. Most mail order businesses have a minimum 14-day approval period and the goods are deemed to have been adopted at the end of that period if not returned earlier. Adoption can also be earlier if the customer either expressly or impliedly (eg by paying) adopts the goods before that time. Note that in *Littlewoods Organisation plc (VTD 14977) (TVC 60.357)* the tribunal held that the company's terms of trading did not amount to the goods in question being on approval. HMRC did not appeal against the decision because it turned on the particular circumstances of the case and it remains their view that mail order businesses normally supply goods on approval.

Bad debts. HMRC have agreed a relaxation to the normal requirements for claiming bad debt relief and accept that it is not necessary for mail order businesses to identify the precise supply to which the claim relates. An apportionment can be applied to the figure of outstanding debts over six months old to reflect the ratio of standard to zero rate supplies. In agreeing the appropriate method of apportionment, HMRC may consider a rolling calculation because the standard/zero split at the time the debt is written off for the purposes of the relief may be significantly different to the split at the time the supply actually took place and the VAT was accounted for. To establish that a period of six months has elapsed from the time when payment was due or, if later, the time of supply, an average period of time for debts entering the default account should be agreed with HMRC.

Bad debt relief cannot be claimed where customers have paid an agent but the agent has defaulted (as payments to an agent constitute payments to the business). It is therefore necessary to analyse unpaid agency accounts to distinguish defaults by the agent and by the customers. If this is not possible, HMRC may allow the use of a fixed percentage adjustment to the bad debt calculation.

(Internal Guidance V1–23, Chapter 10 paras 10.2–10.5).

(7) **Petrol stations**

Fuel cards. Many petrol stations accept fuel cards. See 45.14 MOTOR CARS for details of the schemes. Where the supply of petrol, etc to the motorist is made by the card company, the site operator merely acts as an agent for the card company in providing the fuel to the card company's customer. Such transactions are not retail sales by the site operator and must be excluded from any retail scheme calculations. The supply by the site operator to the card company must be accounted for outside the side operator's retail scheme.

Customers leaving without payment. Where a motorist drives off without paying for petrol already taken, there is no supply for VAT purposes and the daily gross takings can be adjusted provided the retailer has satisfactory records.

Use of pump readings. Subject to the implications on use of fuel cards (see above), the use of daily meter readings to record the daily gross takings for petrol supplies is allowable at the discretion of HMRC if it results in a accurate valuation of retail sales and is carried out at least daily. Sales to other VAT-registered businesses, other than occasional cash sales, must be dealt with outside the retail scheme. The retailer must use the full VAT-inclusive retail selling price for each grade of fuel. If a discount is given for bulk sales, the daily gross takings calculation must be adjusted accordingly.

Alternatively, storage tank dipstick readings may be used to assess opening and closing stock in each VAT period; or meter readings may be used to calculate delivered quantities on a quarterly basis, provided HMRC are satisfied that this gives an accurate result.

(Internal Guidance V1–23, Chapter 10 para 9.8).

(8) **Sub-post offices**

Supplies made by sub-post offices are actually made by the Post Office, the sub postmaster being treated as employed by the Post Office. Where a sub-post office operates under the same management as a normal retail outlet, the takings from the Post Office section should be segregated from the retail takings. Post Office supplies are not retail supplies for the purposes of the retail schemes and can be disregarded for turnover purposes. (Internal Guidance V1–23, Chapter 10 para 9.9).

(9) **Women's Royal Voluntary Service (WRVS) hospital units**

In many hospitals WRVS units operate a canteen, hospital shop, ward trolley service, etc. The sale of the following items to inpatients and outpatients (but not staff and visitors) are regarded as exempt under *VATA 1994, Sch 9 Group 7 item 4* as coming within the provision of 'care' (see 32.11 HEALTH AND WELFARE).

- All beverages which may be sold without an excise licence (eg tea, coffee, fruit juices and soft drinks but not intoxicating liquors).
- Food such as cakes, biscuits, sandwiches or fruit.
- Ice cream or similar frozen products.
- Chocolate or other confectionery.
- Potato crisps or similar snack products.
- Nuts.

Exemption does not extend to stationery, toiletries or other items which are not edible as food or beverages.

Output tax is usually calculated by apportioning daily gross takings on the basis of the cost of purchases but because zero or standard-rated purchases can become exempt supplies, this alone gives an incorrect result. WRVS units can therefore operate the special adaptation below if it is unable to operate one of the published schemes and keeps the appropriate records. As they make exempt supplies, most WRVS units are partly exempt and can recover input tax only to the extent that it relates to their taxable supplies (unless their exempt input tax is within the partial exemption *de minimis* limits). Guidance on how they can work out their recoverable input tax is also shown below. Authorisation to use the adaptation or partial exemption method must be in writing.

Records required. The following records must be kept by any unit opting to use the special adaptation.

- Purchases of standard-rated non-catering goods (Date/Invoice No/VAT-inclusive purchase price/VAT-exclusive purchase price/VAT/Expected selling price)
- Purchases of zero-rated non-catering goods (Date/Invoice No/Purchase price/Expected selling price)
- Purchases of catering goods (Date/Invoice No/VAT-inclusive purchase price/VAT-exclusive purchase price/VAT)
- Expense items (Date/Invoice No/VAT-inclusive purchase price/ VAT-exclusive purchase price/VAT)
- Sales (Date/daily gross takings)

If necessary, HMRC may also require the WRVS unit to keep invoices in the order in which they are entered into the purchase records and to record the daily gross takings in the cash book so that, at the end of each quarter, the actual amount for the sale of goods can be easily calculated.

How to calculate output tax. For each VAT period

Step 1	Add up the daily gross takings =	A
Step 2	Add up the expected selling prices of standard-rated non-catering supplies =	B
Step 3	Add up the expected selling prices of zero-rated non-catering supplies =	C
Step 4	Add the total at Step 2 to the total at Step 3	
Step 5	Calculate how much of the daily gross takings is for catering supplies = (Total at Step 1) – (Total at Step 4)	
Step 6	Calculate standard-rated catering sales (ie sales to people who are not patients) = (Total at Step 5) × z% (see below)	
Step 7	Calculate standard-rated sales for the period = (Total at Step 2) + (Total at Step 6)	
Step 8	Calculate output tax = (Total at Step 7) × VAT fraction for standard-rated goods (7/47)	

In algebraic form, output tax is

[B + (A – B – C) × z%] × 7/47

Recoverable input tax is the total of (*a*)-(*c*) below.

(*a*) All input tax incurred on non-catering standard-rated purchases for resale.

(*b*) A proportion of input tax incurred on catering purchases, equivalent to the percentage of sales to non-patients agreed with HMRC, ie

Total catering input tax × z% (see below)

(*c*) A percentage of the input tax incurred on expenses calculated as follows.

Step 1	Add up daily gross takings	£___
Step 2	Add up the expected selling prices of standard-rated non-catering supplies	£___
Step 3	Add up the expected selling prices of zero-rated non-catering supplies	£___
Step 4	(Total at Step 2) + (Total at Step 3)	£___
Step 5	Calculate total catering sales = (Total at Step 1) – (Total at Step 4)	£___
Step 6	Calculate standard-rated catering sales (ie sales to people who are not patients) = (Total at Step 5) × z% (see below)	£___
Step 7	Calculate total standard-rated sales = (Total at Step 2) + (Total at Step 6)	£___
Step 8	Calculate total VAT-exclusive standard-rated sales = (Total at Step 7) × 40/47	£___
Step 9	Calculate total taxable sales (standard and zero-rated) = (Total at Step 3) + (Total at Step 8)	£___
Step 10	Calculate total sales (taxable and exempt) = (Total at Step 5) – (Total at Step 6) + (Total at Step 9)	£___
Step 11	Calculate the percentage of input tax deductible on expense items, ie $\frac{\text{Total at Step 9}}{\text{Total at Step 10}} \times 100$ If this percentage is not a whole number, round up to the nearest whole number =	x%
Step 12	Add up VAT shown in the record of expense items	£___
Step 13	Calculate input tax allowable on expense items = (Total at Step 12) × (% at Step 11)	£___

z% = the agreed percentage of catering supplies which are standard-rated (ie solely to non-patients). This must be estimated by the WRVS and agreed by HMRC. The percentage must be reviewed at regular intervals.

(Internal Guidance V1–23, Chapter 10 paras 9.11, 9.12, Annex 7A).

61 Second-Hand Goods

Cross-references. See 7.9 BAD DEBT RELIEF; 27.16(8) FINANCE for sales by pawnbrokers; 34.24 IMPORTS for the sale of temporarily imported second-hand goods by auction; 37.17 INSURANCE for insurance supplied in a package with second-hand goods; 55.16 RATES OF VAT for the effect of a change in the rate of VAT between payment and removal of goods.

De Voil Indirect Tax Service. See V3.531–538.

The contents of this chapter are as follows.

61.1 INTRODUCTION

In general, VAT is charged on the full value of any goods, including second-hand goods, sold by a business. The Treasury may, however, by statutory instrument, provide for a business to opt to charge VAT on the profit margin (instead of their value) on supplies of

- works of art, antiques or collectors' items;
- motor vehicles;
- second-hand goods; and
- goods through a person who acts as an agent, but in his own name, in relation to the supply.

The purpose of this is to avoid double taxation on goods which have previously borne VAT when sold as new. [*VATA 1994, s 50A; FA 1995, s 24*].

The Margin Scheme covers virtually all second-hand goods. See 61.2 to 61.38 below for details. A similar scheme is available throughout the EC and goods sold under the scheme anywhere in the EC are taxable in the country of origin rather than that of destination. They are not therefore subject to the normal distance selling rules and are not subject to acquisition VAT when taken into another EC country.

There is also a Global Accounting Scheme in the UK because of the low value, bulk volume goods some dealers handle and the impracticality of keeping detailed records of purchases and sales. Under the scheme, VAT is accounted for on the difference between the total purchases and sales of eligible goods in each VAT period rather than on an item by item basis. See 61.39 to 61.52 below for full details.

De Voil Indirect Tax Service. See V3.531; V3.532.

61.2 **THE MARGIN SCHEME**

VAT is normally due on the full value of goods sold. The margin scheme allows a VAT-registered person who meets all the conditions in 61.4 below to calculate VAT on the 'profit margin' ie the difference (or margin) between the price at which the goods were obtained and their selling price. If no profit is made (because the purchase price exceeds the selling price) then no VAT is payable. [*VATA 1994, s 50A(4); FA 1995, s 24*]. The seller's margin is not revealed to the buyer.

The scheme is not compulsory and goods eligible for the scheme can still be sold outside the scheme in the normal way, even if bought under the scheme. In that case, there is no input tax to deduct on the purchase and VAT must be charged on the full selling price. Similarly, if an eligible item is sold but all the conditions of the scheme cannot be met (eg record-keeping, invoicing and accounting requirements) the margin scheme cannot be used and the sale must be dealt with outside the scheme in the normal way, accounting for VAT on the full selling price.

Although VAT is charged on the profit margin only, taxable turnover for registration purposes includes the total VAT-exclusive value of any goods sold under the scheme.

(VAT Notice 718, paras 2.1, 2.4, 2.5).

Disallowance of input tax. Any input tax charged on the supply to, or acquisition or importation by, a business of eligible goods is excluded from credit where

(*a*) VAT on the supply was chargeable on the profit margin under the UK margin scheme or corresponding provision of the law of another EC country;

(*b*) in the case of a motor car, VAT was charged on the margin on a supply before 1 March 2000 because of an earlier input tax restriction; or

(*c*) the goods are

(i) a work of art, antique or collectors' item within 61.3(*b*)–(*d*) below and the business imported the goods itself, or

(ii) a work of art within 61.3(*b*) below and were supplied to the business by, or acquired from another EC country by the business from, its creator or his successor in title

and the business has opted to account for VAT chargeable on its supplies of such goods on the profit margin and not elected to account for VAT by reference to value.

[*SI 1992/3222, Art 4; SI 1995/1267; SI 1995/1666; SI 1999/2930; SI 1999/3118*].

61.3 **Eligible goods**

The following goods are eligible for the margin scheme.

(*a*) **Second-hand goods** ie tangible movable property that is suitable for further use (as it is or after repair) other than

(i) the items within (*b*)–(*d*) below;

(ii) precious metals (which includes any goods containing precious metals where the consideration for the supply (excluding VAT) does not exceed the open market value of the metal contained in the goods); and

(iii) precious stones of any age which are not mounted, set or strung. For this purpose, precious stones are diamonds, rubies, sapphires and emeralds.

(VAT Notice 718, para 25.1).

(*b*) **Works of art** falling within the definition in *VATA 1994, s 21* (see 71.3(*a*) WORKS OF ART, ETC).

(*c*) **Collectors' items,** ie any collection or collector's piece falling within the definition in *VATA 1994, s 25(5)* (see 71.3(*c*) WORKS OF ART, ETC) but, with effect from 1 January 2000, excluding investment gold coins, ie

- any gold coin minted after 1800 with a purity value of 900 thousandths or more which is, or has been, legal tender in its country of origin and which is of a type normally sold at a price which does not exceed 180% of the open market value of the gold contained in the coin; and
- any other gold coin specified in VAT Notice 701/21A/05, Section 3.

Where gold coins falling within the definition of investment gold coins have been mistakenly included as purchases in the margin scheme records, the records should be adjusted and the entry closed and noted accordingly. (VAT Notice 701/21A/05, para 2.6).

(*d*) **Antiques** ie objects not falling within (*b*) or (*c*) above which are more than 100 years old.

[*SI 1992/3222, Art 2; SI 1995/1268, Art 2; SI 1999/3118; SI 1999/3120; SI 2001/3649, Art 500*].

Goods on hand at 1 January 1995 (when the current provisions were introduced), which were not eligible for the scheme when purchased, can be sold under the scheme provided they qualify as eligible goods with effect from that date; the conditions of the margin scheme are met; and evidence of the purchase price is held. (VAT Notice 718 (1995 edition), para 4).

61.4 **Conditions of the scheme**

A business may opt to use the margin scheme and account for VAT on the profit margin on any eligible goods within 61.3 above provided the following conditions are met.

(*a*) It took possession of the goods by any of the following means.

(i) On a supply on which no VAT was chargeable. This includes purchases from private individuals and unregistered businesses but also includes a zero-rated supply (*Peugeot Motor Co plc (VTD 15314) (TVC 42.63)*).

(ii) On a supply on which VAT was chargeable on the profit margin under the UK margin scheme or under the corresponding provisions in the Isle of Man or another EC country.

(iii) Under a transaction treated as neither a supply of goods nor a supply of services (other than a transaction within (iv) below).

(iv) Under a transaction treated as neither a supply of goods nor a supply of services where the transaction in question was

(1) the transfer of assets of a business as a going concern (see 8.10 BUSINESS), or

(2) on or after 1 July 2002, the assignment of the rights in hire purchase or conditional sales agreements to a bank or other financial institution

and the business has a 'relevant predecessor'. For this purpose, a '*relevant predecessor*' is the person from whom the business took possession of the motor car or goods and who himself took possession of the motor car or goods in circumstances that qualified for use of the margin scheme (otherwise than under (1) or (2) above). Where the motor car or goods have been the subject of a succession of two or more transactions within (1) or (2) above (or both), culminating in the transaction in question, the relevant predecessor is the first person in the chain who took possession of the motor car or goods in circumstances that qualified for use of the margin scheme.

(v) If the goods are a work of art, on a supply, or acquisition from another EC country, from the creator or his successor in title (whether or not the purchase invoice shows VAT separately). See 61.38 below.

(vi) If the goods are a work of art, collectors' item or antique, by importing the goods himself. See 61.38 below.

(vii) If the goods are a motor car, on a supply received before 1 March 2000 on which VAT was charged on the margin because of an earlier input tax restriction.

Any item which was purchased on a VAT invoice on which input tax is recoverable is not eligible to be sold under the scheme.

(*b*) The supply by the business is not a letting on hire.

(*c*) The goods are not sold by the business on a VAT invoice or similar document showing an amount as being VAT or as being attributable to VAT.

(*d*) If the supply is of an airgun, the business is registered for the purposes of the *Firearms Act 1968*.

(*e*) If the supply by the business is the sale of repossessed assets within 27.15 FINANCIAL SERVICES but the supply does not satisfy the conditions for treatment as outside the scope of VAT as there stated.

(*f*) If the supply by the business is a motor car which the business produced itself, the car must have previously been supplied by the business in the course or furtherance of its business or treated as self-supplied under 45.6 MOTOR CARS.

(*g*) The business keeps such records and accounts as HMRC specify.

[*SI 1992/3122, Art 8(1)–(3)(8)(9); SI 1995/1268, Art 12(1)–(4)(8)(10)(11); SI 1995/1269; SI 1997/1615; SI 1997/1616; SI 1999/2832; SI 2002/1502; SI 2002/1503*].

61.5 **Reclaiming VAT on expenses**

Subject to the normal rules, a taxable person may reclaim VAT charged on business overheads, repairs, parts and accessories, etc but must not add these costs to the purchase price of the goods sold under the scheme.

(VAT Notice 718, para 2.6).

61.6 **Purchases**

The following provisions have the force of law.

On a purchase from a private person or an unregistered dealer who does not provide an invoice, the buyer must check that the goods are eligible for the scheme and, if so, make out a purchase invoice showing

- seller's name and address;
- own name and address;
- stock book number;
- invoice number;
- date of transaction;
- description of the goods including any unique identification (eg registration number, make/model, hallmark, type, class, chassis number, etc); and
- total price (no other costs may be added to this amount).

On purchase from an unregistered dealer who provides an invoice, the buyer must ensure that the invoice contains all the necessary details as above.

On purchase from another VAT-registered dealer, that dealer will make out the invoice which must include a declaration that 'Input tax deduction has not been and will not be claimed in respect of the goods on this invoice'. See 61.11 below.

Stock book. Details of the purchase must be entered in the stock book (see 61.23 below).

(VAT Notice 718, paras 3.4, 3.5).

Invoices in foreign currency. If an invoice is in a foreign currency, it must be converted into sterling using one of the methods in 69.18 VALUATION or, in the case of acquisitions from another EC country, 69.14 VALUATION. Where a number of items are bought for an inclusive price which are not to be sold as one lot, the price must be converted into sterling and then apportioned between the various items. The sterling amounts on an item by item basis must be entered in the stock records. (VAT Notice 718, para 3.9).

61.7 *Acquisitions from other EC countries*

The margin scheme is available throughout the EC. Eligible goods sold under the scheme in any EC country are taxable in the country of origin rather than of destination and are not subject to the normal distance selling rules.

- *Goods purchased from a private individual in another EC country*. No VAT is due when the goods are brought into the UK and the goods can therefore be sold under the margin scheme or global accounting scheme.

- *Goods purchased from a registered business in another EC country under the margin scheme or global accounting scheme*. Goods purchased from a dealer in another EC country can only be sold under the scheme if the goods are supplied by that dealer under a margin scheme.

  It is important, therefore, to check that the goods are being supplied under a margin scheme. With effect from 1 January 2004 (following the implementation of the *EC Invoicing Directive*), all margin scheme invoices *must* include a reference to *EC Sixth Directive, Art 26* or *26a* or another declaration to indicate that the goods have been sold under the margin scheme. Before 1 January 2004, most EC countries specified declarations for use on sales invoices so as to identify the transaction as a margin scheme sale, but not all were mandatory. The following list contains declarations that were used by various countries before 1 January 2004, some of which may be retained. The updated mandatory list, including declarations for new EC countries, will be included here when available.

  Austria: 'Differenzbesteuert gemäß §24 UStG 1994' (Margin Scheme supply per §24 UStG 1994) and/or 'Berechtigt nicht zum Vorsteuerabzug' (Input tax may not be deducted).

  Belgium: 'Livraison soumise au regime particulier d'imposition de la marge beneficiaire – TVA non deductible'. (Supply subject to the special arrangements for taxation of the profit margin – VAT non-deductible).

  Denmark: Either, 'Varerne saelges efter de saerlige regler for brugte varer m.v.' (Goods are sold in accordance with the special VAT scheme for second-hand goods) or 'Prisen er en samlet pris, inkl. moms' (The price is a total price including VAT) or 'Momsbelobet, der er indeholdt i prisen, kan ikke fradrages som kobsmoms' (The purchaser cannot deduct the input tax).

  Finland: 'Marginaaliverotus, ei sisalla vahennettavaa veroa' (Margin scheme, does not include deductible tax).

  France: Either 'TVA incluse' (VAT included) or 'Prix TTC' (Price inclusive of all taxes) or 'Livraison effectuee dans le cadre de la 7eme directive' (Supply made under the terms of the 7th Directive).

  Greece: Supply under the scheme of Article 36a of Law No 1642/86. (Contact HMRC for an example of the Greek text).

  Ireland: 'Margin Scheme – this invoice does not give the right to an input credit of VAT'.

Italy: Either 'Operazione soggetta al regime del margine ai sensi dell'art. 36 del DL 23 febbraio 1995 No 41' (Transaction subject to the margin scheme under the terms of Art. 36 of decree law 23.2.95 No 41) or 'Operazione soggetta al regime del margine, ai sense dell'art. 36 del DL 41/95' (Transaction subject to the margin scheme, under the terms of Art. 36 of decree law 41/95) or 'IVA inclusa' (VAT included).

Luxembourg: 'Regime particulier d'imposition de la marge beneficiare' (Special arrangements for taxation of the profit margin).

Netherlands: 'Verkocht on der marge regeling' (Sold under the margin scheme).

Portugal: Either 'IVA-bens em segunda mao' (VAT – second-hand goods) or 'IVA – Objectos de Arte' (VAT – works of art).

Spain: 'Entrega con arreglo a lo dispuesto en la directiva 94/5/CE – IVA incluido' (Supply in accordance with the provisions of Directive 94/5/EC – VAT included).

Sweden: Either 'Begagnade varor' (second-hand goods) or 'Vinstmarginalbeskattning' (Margin scheme).

In addition, it should be noted that, as from 1 January 2004, some EC countries require invoices for supplies made in their country to include the customer's VAT registration number. This means that a UK dealer may receive an invoice for a supply from another EC country which includes a margin scheme declaration but also a VAT registration number. Provided the dealer is sure that the supply has been made under the margin scheme, he can enter the details in his stock records. If in any doubt about how the supply has been treated, the dealer should contact his supplier.

(VAT Notice 718, paras 15.1, 16.1).

New means of transport are always liable to VAT on the EC country of destination. See 23.31 EUROPEAN COMMUNITY: SINGLE MARKET. This means that any new means of transport acquired from another EC country is not eligible for the margin scheme. (VAT Notice 718, para 15.4).

61.8 *Imports from outside the EC*

VAT is normally due on importation of second-hand goods and the margin scheme cannot be used to sell the goods. On sale, VAT must be charged on the full selling price, the VAT paid at importation being deductible subject to the normal rules. This general rule is subject to the following exceptions.

- Certain works of art, antiques, collections and collectors' pieces are entitled to a reduced valuation at importation (see 71.3 WORKS OF ART, ETC). Where any of the works of art, etc listed there are imported, the purchaser may either use the margin scheme or import and resell the goods under the normal VAT rules. See 61.38 below.

- Second-hand cars. See 61.29 below.

(VAT Notice 718, para 17.1).

61.9 *Bulk purchases*

Where a number of eligible goods are bought at an inclusive price with the intention of reselling them separately, the price paid must be apportioned. There is no set way of doing this but the method used must be fair and reasonable and the price allocated to each must be as accurate as possible. The separate figures must be shown in the stock book (see 61.23 below). (VAT Notice 718, para 3.4).

Alternatively, the global accounting scheme may be used for low-value bulk purchases. See 61.39 to 61.52 below.

61.10 *Purchases of repossessed goods*

Sales of eligible goods by an insurance company which has taken possession of them in settlement of an insurance claim or by a finance company which has repossessed them are outside the scope of VAT provided certain conditions are met. See 27.15 FINANCIAL SERVICES. As no VAT is charged on the supply of the goods, they can be purchased for sale under the margin scheme provided the necessary scheme conditions in 61.4 are satisfied. (VAT Notice 718, para 24.2).

61.11 Sales

Note. The following provisions have the force of law.

On the sale of eligible goods, the seller must check that the rules in 61.6 above were applied on purchase and, if so, make out a sales invoice showing

- own name and address and VAT registration number;
- buyer's name and address;
- stock book number;
- invoice number;
- date of sale;
- particulars of the goods including any unique reference number (eg registration number, make/model, hallmark, type, class, chassis number, etc);
- total price, including VAT. Where more than one item is sold on the same invoice, a separate price must be shown for each item; and
- a declaration that: 'Input tax deduction has not been and will not be claimed by me in respect of goods sold on this invoice'.

The invoice must not show VAT as a separate item.

If any insurance product is being sold with the goods, the full price of this must be disclosed separately on the invoice, plus any fees charged for the product outside the contract of insurance. See 37.17 INSURANCE.

The seller must then give the invoice to his customer, keep a copy for his own records and enter details of the sale in the stock book (see 61.23 below).

(VAT Notice 718, paras 3.6, 3.7).

Invoices in foreign currency. If an invoice is issued in a foreign currency, it must also show the sterling equivalent of the value of the goods. Normally, where a number of items are sold on the same invoice, the foreign currency and sterling price must be shown for each item and the sterling amounts entered in the stock records. If, however, the sales invoice is for one lot of goods which were also bought as one lot, it is only necessary to show a total foreign currency and sterling value for that lot. The foreign currency value must be converted into sterling using one of the methods in 69.18 VALUATION. (VAT Notice 718, para 3.9).

61.12 *Sales to other EC countries*

The margin scheme is available throughout the EC. Eligible goods sold under the scheme in any EC country are taxable in the country of origin rather than of destination and are not subject to the normal distance selling rules.

- *Sales by UK dealers to dealers in other EC countries.*

  Sales made under the margin scheme are taxable in the same way as sales within the UK and the normal margin scheme sales invoice must be issued. There is no requirement to obtain the dealer's registration number. No further VAT is due from the buyer when the goods are taken into the other EC country. Alternatively, the goods can be sold outside the margin scheme in which case the sale can be zero-rated subject to the normal conditions for supplies of goods to VAT-registered customers in other EC countries (see 23.11 EUROPEAN COMMUNITY: SINGLE MARKET). The buyer must then account for VAT in his own country and cannot sell the goods under the margin scheme.

- *Sales by UK dealers to private individuals in other EC countries.* Such sales are taxable in the UK on the margin.

(VAT Notice 718, para 15.2).

New means of transport are always liable to VAT in the EC country of destination. See 23.31 EUROPEAN COMMUNITY: SINGLE MARKET. This means that any new means of transport sold to another EC country is not eligible for the margin scheme. (VAT Notice 718, para 15.4).

61.13 *Exports outside the EC*

Where eligible goods are sold for direct export, the sale is zero-rated provided appropriate evidence of exportation is held. See 25.24 EXPORTS. The retail export scheme can also be used to zero-rate the indirect export of certain second-hand goods. See 25.15 EXPORTS. 'Nil' should be entered in the VAT due column of the stock book.

However, it is not normally possible to zero-rate an export of eligible goods if the goods are sold through an auctioneer or dealer who acts as an agent in his own name. This is because, under the special rules for agents who act in their own name, the sale of the goods must be treated as a supply to the agent and a supply by the agent. Thus, the sale by the dealer has to be treated as a supply to the agent, rather than as a supply to the final purchaser, and cannot be treated as a zero-rated export unless the agent is located outside the EC.

(VAT Notice 718, para 17.2).

Where a vehicle is supplied to an overseas person for export, the transaction may be zero-rated provided the vehicle is only used in the UK for the trip to the place of departure from the EC. See 25.17 EXPORTS.

The Personal Export Scheme can also be used to zero-rate sales of second-hand cars exported outside the EC. See 25.18 EXPORTS.

See also 25.19 EXPORTS for special provisions relating to sailaway boats.

61.14 *Transfers of own goods to another EC country*

The transfer of goods within the same legal entity from one EC country to another is deemed to be a supply for VAT purposes. See 23.23 EUROPEAN COMMUNITY: SINGLE MARKET. Where goods are transferred under the margin scheme from the UK to another EC country (eg for sale, or use in the business, in that country) there is no liability to UK VAT on the goods provided that they are transferred from the UK at the price for which they were obtained. There should be no liability to account for acquisition VAT in the other EC country. (VAT Notice 718, para 15.3).

61.15 *Part exchange*

If a dealer sells eligible goods and takes other goods in part exchange, his selling price includes the amount allowed for the other goods as well as the amount received in cash from the buyer.

> *Example*
>
> A car is sold for £2,000 cash plus a car for which £1,000 is allowed in part exchange.
>
> A selling price of £3,000 must be entered in the stock book. As the article taken in exchange is an eligible article which is to be resold under the scheme, the rules in 61.6 above must be followed. The amount allowed in part exchange (£1,000) is the purchase price. The purchase must also be recorded in the stock book (see 61.23 below).

A dealer must obtain a purchase invoice for part-exchanged goods bought from another VAT-registered dealer. However, if he buys from a private person or an unregistered dealer, he may include details of part-exchange items on his sales invoice provided all the requirements of 61.6 above are met.

(VAT Notice 718, para 24.11).

In *Lex Services plc v C & E Commrs, HL 2003, [2004] STC 73 (TVC 42.80)* the company accepted second-hand cars in part exchange. The documentation showed a vehicle price (say £20,000) and an agreed price for the part exchange car (say £2,000) which was used to arrive at the amount actually payable by the customer (£18,000). In most cases, however, in order to secure the sale the part exchange price was higher than the 'trade value' for the car (say £1,500). The relevant transaction could be cancelled by the customer within 30 days and the documentation stipulated that if the part exchange car had previously been sold, the customer was only entitled to a refund of the lower 'trade value' which was also disclosed in the documentation. The Court held that the taxable amount for VAT purposes was the cash received (£18,000) plus the value of the non-monetary consideration agreed with the customer (£2,000).

Lex Services above was, however, distinguished in *Hartwell plc v C & E Commrs, CA [2003] STC 396 (TVC 42.81)* where the company issued 'purchase plus vouchers' to customers in order to encourage sales without having to overvalue the part-exchanged car. Where, for example, the price of the replacement vehicle was £20,000 but the correct 'trade-value' of the used car was £1,500, if the customer was unwilling to pay £18,500 the company might issue a purchase plus voucher for £500. The court held that the consideration the dealer received for the supply of the £500 voucher was the agreement of the purchaser to the sale and that its non-monetary value was nil. The voucher did not form part of the consideration for the part-exchanged car. The taxable amount for VAT purposes was the cash received (£18,000) plus the trade in value of the used car (£1,500).

61.16 *Hire purchase sales*

Note. The following provisions have the force of law.

Eligible goods sold under a hire purchase agreement are sold to the finance company which in turn sells them to the customer. The sale should be treated as a cash sale and the cash price of the goods (as shown on the HP agreement) should be entered in the stock book as the selling price. No VAT is charged on the finance charges if itemised separately. In some circumstances the dealer may issue his own sales invoice to the customer. He must attach a copy of the completed HP agreement to the customer's sales invoice or include a cross-reference to the agreement in his sales records. If the HP agreement is held by the finance company and the dealer does not receive a copy for his records, he should keep a copy of the agreed quotation or agreed proposal documents in his sales records, together with the name of the finance company, date and reference number of the final agreement.

A copy of the HP agreement can be treated as the sales invoice provided

- it shows all the identifying details required; and
- the cash price is shown as the gross price payable ie the amount borrowed plus cash paid, plus any amount allowed for part exchange (see 61.15 above).

VAT must not be shown separately on the HP agreement or any invoice.

(VAT Notice 718, para 24.10).

See 27.15 FINANCIAL SERVICES for the sale of repossessed goods.

61.17 *Gifts*

If a taxable person sells an article received as a gift, he must charge VAT on its full selling price and not use the margin scheme.

No VAT is chargeable on eligible goods which could have been sold under the scheme but which are given away but full details of the person to whom the goods are given must be included in the stock book.

(VAT Notice 718, para 24.4).

61.18 *Private sales*

The private sale of goods which are not assets of the business is usually outside the scope of VAT.

Where a sole proprietor transfers eligible goods from a private holding to the business, VAT may be accounted for under the margin scheme provided evidence can be produced of the purchase price when originally bought for private use. If not, VAT must be accounted for on the full selling price.

(VAT Notice 718, para 24.5).

61.19 *Sales from historic houses*

If owners of historic houses admit members of the public for a charge, any works of art, etc owned and displayed to the public are treated as business assets and their disposal is normally subject to VAT. There is, however, special VAT relief in certain cases. See 71.6 WORKS OF ART, ETC.

See also 71.1 WORKS OF ART, ETC for exemption from VAT on certain disposals to approved bodies, and property accepted in satisfaction of inheritance tax.

61.20 *Shares in eligible goods*

If a share in an eligible article held in stock is sold, no output tax is due on the sale of the share and a VAT invoice must not be issued to the purchaser.

When an item in which other people own shares is sold under the margin scheme, the full amount of VAT due must be accounted for (not just VAT on the taxable person's share of the proceeds). The purchase price is the full purchase price (not just the taxable person's share) and statements must be issued to the other shareholders showing their share of the sale proceeds, excluding VAT. See also 61.21 below.

(VAT Notice 718, para 14.1).

61.21 **Joint purchases and sales**

The following procedure (which has the force of law) should be used where dealers jointly buy an eligible article for resale.

(*a*) **On purchase**, one of the joint buyers (JB1) must keep the purchase invoice with the details set out under 61.6 above and must invoice the other joint buyer(s) for the agreed contribution towards the cost, excluding VAT. Each invoice must be endorsed 'This payment is your contribution towards the purchase of the above article. I shall be accounting for the full amount of VAT due under the scheme when it is sold.' Copies of the invoice(s) must be retained.

JB1 must record the full purchase details in his stock book, together with details of the sales invoices to the other joint buyer(s).

(*b*) **On resale by the original buyer,** JB1 must issue (and keep a copy of) a sales invoice showing all the details in 61.11 above and enter the sales and accounting details in his stock book. The selling price is the full joint selling price (not just JB1's share of the proceeds).

JB1 must then issue a statement to the other joint buyer(s) showing their share of the proceeds of sale, excluding VAT. The statement must be endorsed 'This payment is your share of the proceeds of sale of [insert details]. I am accounting for the full amount of VAT due on the sale under the scheme.'

(*c*) **On resale by another joint buyer (JB2)**, he must obtain the original purchase invoice from JB1, issue (and keep a copy of) a sales invoice showing all the details in 61.11 above and complete his stock book treating the purchase and sale as being made entirely by him. The purchase price is the full joint purchase price and the selling price is the full joint selling price.

JB2 must then issue a statement to the other joint buyer(s) as in (*b*) above.

JB1, the original buyer, must close the entry in his stock book stating that VAT has been accounted for by JB2 and cross-refer to the statement received from JB2.

(VAT Notice 718, paras 14.2–14.4).

61.22 **Records and accounts**

The following requirements as to records and accounts have the force of law. [*SI 1992/3122, Art 8(1); SI 1995/1268, Art 12(1); SI 1995/1269*]. They are in addition to the records generally required of all taxable persons. See 56 RECORDS.

A business selling goods under the scheme must keep the purchase invoice (see 61.6 above) and a copy of the sales invoice (see 61.11 above), together with a stock book or similar records (see 61.23 below). All records must be kept for six years but if stock includes goods obtained more than six years previously, evidence must also be retained to show eligibility to use the margin scheme at the time of sale. Failure to comply with any of the requirements renders the business liable for VAT on the full value of its sales. (VAT Notice 718, paras 3.1, 3.2). See *C & E Commrs v JH Corbitt (Numismatists) Ltd, HL [1980] STC 231 (TVC 58.1)*. The requirements as to the records to be kept do not impose an obligation on the business to verify the identity of purchasers (*Bord (VTD 9824) (TVC 58.5)*).

See, however, 61.39 *et seq* below for a simplified method of operating the margin scheme (global accounting).

Occasional sales. If a trader is not in the business of selling second-hand goods, etc but occasionally sells eligible goods in the course of his business, he need not comply with the full record-keeping requirements provided he meets the other conditions of the scheme and holds evidence of both the purchase and selling price. (VAT Notice 718, para 24.12).

Motor cars. There is an alternative special method of calculating VAT for second-hand cars where the dealer has the required information on the purchase or sale of the car but not both. See 61.35 below.

Horses and ponies. Special records are required. See 61.37 below.

61.23 *Stock book*

A stock book or similar record must be kept with separate headings for each of the following.

Purchase details
Stock number in numerical sequence
Date of purchase
Purchase invoice number
Name of seller
Any unique identification number (eg car registration)
Description of the goods (eg type, make or model)

Sales details
Date of sale
Sales invoice number
Name of buyer

Accounting details
Purchase price
Selling price or other method of disposal
Margin on sale
VAT due

The purchase price must be the price on the invoice which has been agreed between the buyer and seller and must not be altered. Separate entries must be made where purchases bought in bulk are to be sold separately (see 61.9 above).

Other information can also be included but the above details must always be shown and the stock book must be kept up-to-date.

(VAT Notice 718, paras 3.3 (which has the force of law), 4.1).

Goods on sale or return. If stock includes goods supplied to the dealer on a sale or return basis, the stock book (or a separate record) must include the following details of the goods.

Date of transfer of the goods
Description of goods including any unique identification number (eg car registration)
Name and address of dealer/person transferring the goods
Date of sale or return

Similarly, if any goods are removed from stock on a sale or return basis to another dealer's premises, stock records should be noted with the date and details of the dealer to whom the goods have been transferred.

If a dealer sells goods on behalf of a third party, and issues an invoice for those goods in his own name, he is acting as an agent for VAT purposes (see 61.26 below).

(VAT Notice 718, para 3.8 which has the force of law).

61.24 Calculation of VAT

If eligible goods are sold for the same as, or less than, the price paid, no VAT is due. The loss cannot be set against profit made on other transactions.

If eligible goods are sold for more than the price paid, VAT is chargeable on the profit margin ie the amount by which the consideration for the goods are sold exceeds the purchase price. The profit margin is regarded as being VAT-inclusive ie the VAT included is

VAT-inclusive margin × VAT fraction (currently 7/47)

Profit margin. The following rules apply for the purpose of determining the profit margin.

(*a*) The price at which the goods were obtained is calculated

- (i) where the business took possession of the goods by a supply, in the same way as the consideration for the supply would normally be calculated (see 69.2 *et seq* VALUATION);
- (ii) where the business is a sole proprietor and the goods were supplied to him in a private capacity, in the same way as the consideration for the supply to him as a private individual would be calculated;
- (iii) where the goods are a work of art which was acquired by the business from the creator or his successor in title in another EC country, in the same way as the value of the acquisition would be calculated for VAT purposes (see 69.11 VALUATION) plus the VAT chargeable on the acquisition;
- (iv) where the goods are a work of art, antique or collectors' item which the business has imported itself, in the same way as the value would be calculated for the purposes of importation (see 69.15 VALUATION) plus any VAT chargeable on their importation; and

(v) where the business took possession of the motor car or goods under a transaction treated as neither a supply or goods nor a supply of services (other than a transaction within (vi) below), the price it paid by virtue of that transaction; and

(vi) where the business took possession of the motor car or goods under a transaction treated as neither a supply or goods nor a supply of services as the result of

(1) the transfer of assets of a business as a going concern (see 8.10 BUSINESS), or

(2) on or after 1 July 2002 in the case of a bank or other financial institution, the assignment of the rights in hire purchase or conditional sale agreements

and the business has a 'relevant predecessor', the price at which its relevant predecessor in title obtained the motor car or goods. For this purpose, a '*relevant predecessor*' is the person from whom the business took possession of the motor car or goods and who himself took possession of the motor car or goods in circumstances that qualified for use of the margin scheme (see 61.4 above). Where the motor car or goods have been the subject of a succession of two or more transactions within (1) or (2) above (or both), culminating in the transaction in question, the relevant predecessor is the first person in the chain who took possession of the motor car or goods in circumstances that qualified for use of the margin scheme.

Where the above provisions apply, the business will always require the original purchase invoice to calculate the margin on the goods.

(*b*) The price at which the goods are sold is calculated in the same way as the consideration for the supply would be calculated for VAT purposes. It includes everything received for the goods whether from the buyer or a third party. It also includes incidental expenses directly linked to the sale. Optional extras charged to the buyer and disbursements do *not* form part of the selling price and should be accounted for separately outside the margin scheme. The consideration may not be wholly in money and the normal rules about value apply. See 69.2 *et seq* VALUATION.

[*SI 1992/3122, Art 8(5)(8)(9); SI 1995/1268, Art 12(5)(10)(11); SI 1995/1269; SI 1998/759; SI 1998/760; SI 2002/1502; SI 2002/1503*]. (VAT Notice 718, para 2.8).

The margin cannot be reduced by deducting expenses eg repairs, spares, overheads, cleaning, etc (VAT Notice 718, para 2.10).

Motor cars. There is an alternative special method of calculating VAT for second-hand cars where the dealer has the required information on the purchase or sale of the car but not both. See 61.35 below.

61.25 Completion of VAT return

See 2.5 *et seq* ACCOUNTING PERIODS AND RETURNS for notes on the completion of Form VAT 100. The following special rules apply to eligible goods bought and sold under the margin scheme.

Box 1	Include the output tax on all eligible goods sold in the period covered by the return.
Box 6	Include the full selling price of all eligible goods sold during the period, less any VAT.
Box 7	Include the purchase price (inclusive of VAT) of eligible goods bought in the period.

There is no requirement to include margin scheme purchases and sales in Boxes 8 and 9.

(VAT Notice 718, para 3.10 which has the force of law).

61.26 Agents

Dealers frequently sell goods for or on behalf of other dealers or private sellers. The arrangements may include retaining a percentage of the selling price or making a separate charge to the owner. In either case, the seller is acting as the agent of the dealer or individual who owns the goods and the parties must follow the rules set out below.

If different parties own shares in the goods or if different parties have bought goods jointly for resale, see 61.21 above.

An agent who acts in his own name and uses the margin scheme in relation to a supply of goods must, for VAT purposes, treat the supply as a supply to him and a supply by him. See 3.4 AGENTS. When goods are sold by an agent, the margin scheme treatment will depend on the way the agent has opted to account for his commission. The following paragraphs outline the margin scheme consequences of each option.

(*a*) **How the owner or principal calculates his margin**. If the agent sells eligible goods on the owner's behalf in his own name, the owner can still account for his sale under the margin scheme. The owner's purchase price is calculated in the normal way (see 61.24 above) but his selling price depends on the way the agent has accounted for his sale and is equivalent to the agent's purchase price.

(*b*) **How the agent calculates his margin**. An agent selling eligible goods has two options.

- *Option 1.* If the agent invoices his charges to the seller or principal separately, those charges are subject to VAT and his margin for VAT is calculated as follows.

  Purchase price = The gross amount realised by the agent before any deductions are made.

  Selling price = The total price for the goods including any incidental expenses and commission charged to the buyer. (Other optional charges not directly linked to the goods such as packing, transport and insurance costs should be charged outside the margin scheme under the normal VAT rules.)

  Margin = The difference between the purchase price and the selling price.

- *Option 2.* If the agent includes his charges to the seller in his sale of the goods, his margin for VAT is calculated as follows.

Purchase price = The gross amount realised by the agent less commission charged to the seller (and not including any charges made to the buyer).

Selling price = The total price for the goods including any incidental expenses and commission charged to the buyer. (Other optional charges not directly linked to the goods such as packing, transport and insurance costs should be charged outside the margin scheme under the normal VAT rules.)

Margin = The difference between the purchase price and the selling price.

This method mirrors the method used by auctioneers to calculate their purchase and selling prices under the auctioneers' scheme (see 61.59 below).

An agent selling goods under the margin scheme who issues an invoice in his own name must keep the records described in 61.22 above.

[*SI 1992/3122, Art 8(6); SI 1995/1268, Art 12(6); SI 1995/1269*]. (VAT Notice 718, paras 13.1–13.3).

61.27 **Second-hand cars**

Margin scheme. The normal rules and conditions of the margin scheme apply to second-hand motor cars but there are also further specific provisions which apply as outlined in 61.28 to 61.35 below. These provisions have the force of law.

Motor cars are defined in 45.1 MOTOR CARS. Only second-hand cars can be sold under the margin scheme. To be eligible, the car must have been driven on the road for business or pleasure purposes. Neither the registration of the car for road use nor the delivery mileage incurred transporting a vehicle to a dealer turn a car into a used car for the purposes of the margin scheme. See also *Lincoln Street Motors (Birmingham) Ltd (VTD 1100) (TVC 42.61)*.

The margin scheme cannot be used for any vehicle on which input tax was reclaimed on purchase. See 45.4 MOTOR CARS for sales of such cars.

'Input tax margin scheme' applying before 1 March 2000. Where a business was charged input tax on the purchase of a car and the input tax was not eligible for relief because the car was available for private use, on sale output tax only needed to be accounted for on the amount, if any, by which the selling price exceeded the VAT-inclusive purchase price. This was known as the 'input tax margin scheme' and was separate from the normal margin scheme. This scheme was abolished with effect from 1 March 2000. A business may use the general margin scheme to sell a car which was supplied to it under the input tax margin scheme before 1 March 2000.

(VAT Notice 718, para 19.1).

61.28 *Purchases from other EC countries*

Where a second-hand car is bought from a private individual, or from a registered dealer using the margin scheme, in another EC country, no VAT is due when the car is brought into the UK and the margin scheme can be used for the onward sale.

Where a second-hand car is bought outside the margin scheme from a registered dealer in another EC country, acquisition VAT is due when the car is brought into the UK and the car is not eligible for the margin scheme.

The margin scheme cannot be used for any vehicle qualifying as a new means of transport (see 23.31 EUROPEAN COMMUNITY: SINGLE MARKET).

(VAT Notice 718, para 19.1).

61.29 *Imports from outside the EC*

VAT is due at the standard rate on the importation of a second-hand car unless it meets the criteria for returned goods relief (see 34.19 IMPORTS) or it can be classified as a collector's piece. An imported car is not eligible for sale under the margin scheme unless it qualifies as a collectors' piece or antique. See 45.4 MOTOR CARS for the VAT provisions applying on sale.

Personal imports. If a dealer buys a car from an unconnected person who has personally imported it, the car may be sold under the margin scheme. Where, however, the car is imported by an employee, agent or other person connected with the trader for sale in the dealer's business, the margin scheme cannot be used for the subsequent sale.

(VAT Notice 718, para 19.2).

61.30 *VED and MOTs*

Where a car is purchased with an unexpired VED which is surrendered. A refund of VED is treated as being outside the scope of VAT. The price of the car should not be adjusted to reflect the refund.

Where a car is sold with a valid VED or a VED is offered with the car as part of the agreed sale price, there is a single supply and the selling price entered in the stock book must include the value of the VED.

Where a VED is obtained after the negotiation for the sale of a car, the VED may be treated as a separate supply provided the conditions for treatment as a disbursement are met. See 3.7 AGENTS. If those conditions cannot be met, the car and the VED are treated as a single supply and VAT must be accounted for on the margin of the total value.

Where a car is sold with an MOT, this is a single supply and the full selling price, without deduction of any value for the MOT, must be recorded in the stock book and used to calculate the margin.

(VAT Notice 718, paras 19.5, 19.6).

61.31 *Mechanical breakdown insurance and warranties*

A '*warranty*' is an undertaking or guarantee by a dealer that, if a vehicle proves to be faulty within a specified time limit or mileage, the dealer will bear the cost of repair or replacement parts.

'*Mechanical breakdown insurance*' (MBI) is a contract of insurance, between an insurer (usually someone other than the dealer) and a purchaser, providing cover against the risk of the vehicle proving faulty within a specified time limit or mileage.

(*a*) *Free warranties or MBI.* The selling price of the car includes the cost of providing the warranty or MBI. The price of the car on the invoice must be entered in the stock book. Any mention of the warranty or MBI on the invoice must show that no separate charge is being made.

(*b*) *Warranties or MBI for which a separate charge is made.* The VAT treatment depends on whether the risk covered is the dealer's or the customer's.

(i) If a dealer arranges MBI for his customer, the supply is exempt provided

- it is supplied under a contract between an insurer and the customer;
- it is the customer's risks which are insured;
- the customer is entirely free to purchase the item at the price advertised without the MBI; and
- the dealer discloses to the customer the premium and any other amount (fees or commission) being charged.

This is because there are separate supplies of the item and the MBI, each with its own consideration. The following rules must be observed.

- If the dealer subsequently negotiates with the customer a reduced price for the item (including the MBI), the price originally advertised for the MBI must be treated as the value of the exempt supply of the MBI.
- If negotiations with the customer result in the supply of an upgraded MBI, the dealer may use the separately advertised price of the upgraded MBI as the value of the exempt supply of the MBI.
- If the dealer advertises the item and the MBI at a single price (ie does not disclose to the customer the amount they are paying for the MBI) any fee or commission income the dealer would receive in relation to this insurance is standard-rated. The net value of the insurance paid to, and retained by, the insurer remains exempt.

If the insurance contract is between the dealer and the insurer and only the dealer's risk of having to repair defective items is covered, then the charge shown on the dealer's invoice for insurance is standard-rated.

(ii) If a dealer provides a warranty, the charge shown on the invoice is standard-rated.

(*c*) *Other situations.* The supply of a warranty or MBI under any other type of scheme is standard-rated. This applies, for example, to 'stop loss' arrangements under which the dealer or insurance broker sets up a fund into which amounts charged to customers for warranties or MBI are paid and from which repair claims are met. Insurance cover is then obtained from a permitted insurer against any deficiency in the fund.

Any standard-rated commission or fees under (*b*) above or, if not charged separately, standard-rated warranty charges under (*c*) above must be deducted from the vehicle's selling price before the gross margin is calculated.

(VAT Notice 718, paras 20.1–20.6, 21.1).

61.32 *Demonstration cars*

VAT may be reclaimed on the purchase, acquisition or importation of any motor car which forms part of the stock in trade of a motor dealer. See 45.3 MOTOR CARS for full details. As a result, such cars are no longer eligible for the margin scheme and, on disposal, output tax must be accounted for on the full selling price in the normal way. See 45.4 MOTOR CARS.

61.33 *Rebuilt motor cars*

If a motor car is rebuilt from one or more used cars and the Driver and Vehicle Licensing Authority (DVLA) do not require it to be re-registered, it can be sold under the margin scheme. The purchase price to be entered in the stock book is the price paid for the car for which the registration number is carried forward. If, however, the DVLA give the car a new registration number, the scheme cannot be used and VAT must be accounted for on the full selling price. (VAT Notice 718, para 19.7).

61.34 *Auctions*

See 61.53 *et seq* below for the general provisions relating to auctions.

61.35 *Calculation of VAT due*

Where all required records are held, the normal rules in 61.24 above apply.

Where records in respect of either the purchase or the sale are available (but not both), HMRC should be contacted. Where they consider that the mark-up achieved on the supply does not exceed 100%, HMRC may allow VAT to be accounted for on either

- the price paid for the car (where the necessary purchase records have been kept); or
- half the selling price (where the necessary sales records have been kept).

Otherwise the sale must be dealt with outside the scheme, accounting for VAT on the full selling price.

(VAT Notice 718, para 19.4; VAT Notice 48, ESC 3.8).

61.36 Second-hand motor-cycles

Road fund licences, Mechanical breakdown insurance and warranties and *Rebuilt motor-cycles*. The provisions applying to motor cars apply equally to motor-cycles. See 61.30, 61.31 and 61.33 above respectively.

61.37 Second-hand horses and ponies

The general rules and conditions of the margin scheme also apply to the sale of second-hand horses and ponies. This has been confirmed in *Förvaltnings AB Stenholmen v Riksskatteverket, CJEC Case C–320/02, [2004] STC 1041 (TVC 21.318)*. The following rules relate specifically to second-hand horses and ponies and have the force of law.

Horses which the trader has bred and is selling for the first time are not second-hand.

A trader using the margin scheme for horses or ponies may either

- keep the normal records and accounts; or
- keep alternative records based on special three-part forms supplied by The British Equestrian Trade Association.

Each of these options is explained below.

Normal records and accounts. If a dealer decides to keep normal margin scheme records, his stock book must include sufficient details to identify the horse or pony including colour, sex, type (eg chestnut, cob, gelding), age (if known), height, stable name (if known), and distinctive markings. (These requirements have the force of law.)

On purchase, the normal conditions in 61.6 above must be complied with. If the purchase is from another VAT-registered dealer who uses the special three-part form (see below), the other dealer will hand over Part C of that form. This can be used as the purchase invoice and appropriate details entered in the stock book.

On purchase at auction, the dealer must comply with the conditions 61.60 below. If the horse or pony is being sold at auction by another VAT-registered dealer who uses the three-part form, the auctioneer will hand over Part C of that form. This can be used as the purchase invoice and appropriate details entered in the stock book.

On sale, the normal conditions in 61.11 above must be complied with. On sale at auction the dealer must comply with the conditions set out in 61.61 below.

(VAT Notice 718, paras 22.7–22.11).

Alternative records and accounts. To sell horses and ponies under the margin scheme, as an alternative to the normal records special three-part forms (produced in numbered sets) with a VAT summary sheet at the back may be used. These are sold by

The British Equestrian Trade Association,
East Wing,
Stockeld Park,
Wetherby,
West Yorkshire
LS22 4AW

The three parts of the form are

Part A	Seller's stock record
Part B	Seller's copy sales invoice
Part C	Customer's purchase invoice

These forms are the basis of stock and sales records. No other records are required to operate the scheme. It is not necessary to keep a stock book or invoices. A separate form must be properly completed for each horse, etc or VAT becomes due on the full selling price ie the records are mandatory.

(*a*) *Purchase of a horse or pony from a private person*. After ensuring that the horse or pony is eligible for the margin scheme, the 'description' and 'written description' sections of Parts A, B and C must be completed in accordance with the standard laid down by the Royal College of Veterinary Surgeons in their booklet 'Colour and Markings of Horses' (obtainable from the Royal College of Veterinary Surgeons, 32 Belgrave Square, London SW1). If the animal is not registered with a recognised Breed Society, Stud Book or Register, then unless the purchase price is less than £500, the buyer and a vet must sign Parts A, B and C to certify that the animal is the one described on the form. If the animal is registered, the signatures are not necessary. The buyer must then give the form a stock number in numerical sequence and complete the Purchase Record section on the reverse of Part A. The buyer must retain all parts of the form which will be needed on a subsequent sale.

(*b*) *Purchase of a horse or pony from someone selling under the scheme*. Similar rules apply as in (*a*) above but the seller must give the buyer Part C of the form to be kept with the partially completed form. The seller does not have to sign the declaration on the reverse of Part A. If the animal is unregistered and has a purchase price of more than £500, the Part C from the seller should have already been signed by a vet confirming the description. The details of the vet's name, practice, etc can be copied by the buyer on to his form. There is no need for a vet to sign.

(*c*) *Sale of a horse or pony*. Check that the correct procedure was followed under (*a*) or (*b*) above on purchase. If not, the margin scheme cannot be used. If the correct procedure was followed, on sale the sales record sections on the reverse of Parts A, B and C must be completed. The seller then retains Parts A and B and gives Part C to the buyer.

The VAT record on the reverse of Part A must be completed.

(*d*) *Purchases at auction*. The normal rules for purchases under (*a*) or (*b*) above apply. If the animal is being sold under the margin scheme, the auctioneer will pass the seller's completed Part C to the buyer. The buyer must keep this with his own partially completed form. If the animal is being sold by a private person, the buyer must get the auctioneer to complete details of his name, address and Lot number on the reverse of Part A of his form.

(*e*) *Sales at auction*. The auctioneer must be told that the animal is being sold under the margin scheme and be given Parts B and C of the seller's form which must already be completed as regards his purchase. After the sale, the auctioneer must complete the sales details on the reverse of Parts B and C, adding his name and address. He then returns Part C to the buyer and Part B to the seller. The seller must then complete the sales and VAT record on the reverse of Part A.

(VAT Notice 718, paras 22.1–22.6).

61.38 Imported works of art, antiques and collectors' pieces and works of art obtained from the creators or their heirs

A business which

(*a*) imports works of art, collectors' items or antiques within 71.3(*a*)-(*c*) WORKS OF ART, ETC or

(*b*) obtains works of art (by supply in the UK or acquisition from another EC country) from the creators or their heirs,

may opt to use the margin scheme or the auctioneers' scheme (see 61.53 *et seq* below) whether or not VAT has been charged on the supply, acquisition or importation. Alternatively, VAT can be accounted for under the normal rules.

Conditions for opting. The conditions for using the margin scheme or the auctioneers' scheme are as follows.

- HMRC must be notified in writing that the option is to be taken up, specifying the date from which it will apply.
- The option must be exercised for a period of at least two years. Thereafter, it will continue to apply until HMRC are advised in writing as to when it is to cease.
- If the option is used, it must be applied to *all* transactions within (*a*) and (*b*) above, not just in respect of certain transactions or certain categories of goods.
- If, having exercised the option, the business subsequently decides to sell any goods covered by the option outside a scheme, it is not entitled to recover any input tax on those goods until the period in which VAT is accounted for on their

sale. VAT must be accounted for on the full selling price at the standard rate (unless the goods are exported and qualify for zero-rating under the normal VAT rules for export).

If the option has been exercised,

- for imports within (*a*) it covers imports at the effective 5% rate (see 71.3 WORKS OF ART, ETC). Under the margin scheme, the purchase price to be entered in the records is the value for VAT at import, plus the import VAT. For the auctioneers' scheme, the purchase price is calculated according to the normal rules for that scheme. Under both schemes, VAT is calculated on the margin at 17.5% and the import VAT cannot be reclaimed as input tax; and
- for works of art obtained under (*b*) above, any VAT charged when the items are obtained cannot be reclaimed as input tax. The purchase price to be entered in the records is the total price paid inclusive of any VAT. For acquisitions, acquisition VAT should be accounted for in Box 2 of the VAT return. The corresponding amount should not be recovered in Box 4 but added to the net purchase price for margin scheme purposes. Under the auctioneers' scheme, the purchase price is calculated according to the normal rules for that scheme. If the vendor is VAT-registered, this amount will also be their VAT-inclusive selling price. As the vendor cannot use the margin scheme, any self-billed invoice issued to the vendor must show VAT separately.

Global accounting scheme. A business opting to use the margin scheme may also use the global accounting scheme subject to the normal rules of that scheme (see 61.39 *et seq* below). Eligible taxed goods must not be entered into the global accounting scheme until documentation is received which would have allowed input tax or import/acquisition VAT to be reclaimed if the option had not been used.

(VAT Notice 718, paras 18.1–18.4).

61.39 GLOBAL ACCOUNTING SCHEME

The global accounting scheme is a simplified variation of the normal margin scheme, particularly beneficial for accounting for VAT on low value, bulk volume, margin scheme goods where it may be impractical to keep detailed records required under the normal scheme. Dealers using the global accounting scheme account for VAT on the difference between the total purchases and total sales of eligible goods in each VAT period (rather than on an item by item basis). The scheme automatically allows for a loss on one transaction to be set against the profit from others.

The provisions of the scheme as set out in 61.40–61.52 below have the force of law.

De Voil Indirect Tax Service. See V3.535.

61.40 Eligible goods

The global accounting scheme can be used for any of the eligible goods within 61.3 above other than

(*a*) motor vehicles including motor-cycles (except those broken up for scrap, see below);

(*b*) aircraft;

(*c*) boats and outboard motors;

(*d*) caravans and motor caravans;

(*e*) horses and ponies.

[*SI 1995 /1268, Art 13*].

Dealers in goods within (*a*)–(*e*) above are able to keep records on an item by item basis and can therefore use the normal margin scheme of accounting. (In any case, the cost of the majority of such goods purchased are likely to exceed £500 and would therefore be excluded from the global accounting scheme, see 61.41 below.)

Sales of scrap. Motor vehicles cannot normally be sold under the global accounting scheme. However, provided the vehicle is otherwise eligible for the margin scheme, it may be included in the global accounting scheme when broken up and sold as scrap. The normal commercial documents must be kept to show that the vehicle no longer exists in order to demonstrate that it is eligible for global accounting.

Where a motor vehicle has already been entered into a stock book under the margin scheme, the entry should be closed and the details transferred to the global accounting scheme purchase records.

If a dealer purchases a scrap motor vehicle for more than £500, he can still use the global accounting scheme for disposal of the components. But any individual component valued at over £500 must be excluded from the scheme.

(VAT Notice 718, para 5.4).

61.41 **Conditions for using the scheme**

A person who is registered for VAT may use the scheme provided the following conditions are met.

(*a*) The goods were not purchased on an invoice on which VAT was shown separately.

(*b*) Every individual item for which the scheme is used must have been obtained for a price of £500 or less. See 61.24 above for the calculation of price. See 61.44 below for bulk purchases and collections.

(*c*) The goods are not sold on a VAT invoice or similar document showing an amount as being VAT or as being attributable to VAT.

(*d*) Such records and accounts are kept as specified by HMRC.

[*SI 1995/1268, Art 13*]. (VAT Notice 718, para 5.2).

Imported works of art, etc. See 61.38 above for circumstances where imported works of art and works of art obtained from their creators or heirs can be included in the scheme despite the fact that VAT has been charged on their supply, acquisition or importation. These provisions apply also to the global accounting scheme.

61.42 **Reclaiming VAT on expenses**

Subject to the normal rules, a taxable person may reclaim any VAT he is charged on business overheads, restoration, repairs, spares, etc but must not add these costs to the purchase price of the goods for the purposes of the scheme. (VAT Notice 718, para 6.10 which has the force of law).

61.43 **Purchases**

On a purchase from a private person or an unregistered dealer who does not provide an invoice, the buyer must check that the goods are eligible for the global accounting scheme and, if so, make out a purchase invoice showing

- own name and address;
- seller's name and address;
- invoice number;
- date of transaction;
- description of the goods sufficient to enable HMRC to verify that the goods are eligible for the global accounting scheme (eg 'four tables and ten chairs' is acceptable but 'assorted goods' is not);
- total price (VAT must not be shown separately); and
- an endorsement stating 'Global accounting invoice'.

On purchase from an unregistered dealer who provides an invoice, the buyer must ensure that the invoice contains all the necessary details as above.

On purchase from a VAT-registered dealer, that dealer should make out the invoice with details as above and certify that it is not a VAT invoice.

Purchase record summary. Details of the purchase must be entered in the purchase record or summary (see 61.49 below).

(VAT Notice 718, paras 6.2, 6.3 which have the force of law).

Invoices in foreign currency. If an invoice is in a foreign currency, it must be converted into sterling using one of the methods in 69.18 VALUATION or, in the case of acquisitions from another EC country, 69.14 VALUATION. Where an invoice includes individual items with a purchase price over £500 which are not eligible for the global accounting scheme, the foreign currency value must be converted into sterling and then apportioned to exclude these items. The remaining purchase amount in sterling must be entered in the purchase records. (VAT Notice 718, para 6.11 which has the force of law).

61.44 *Bulk purchases and collections*

Bulk purchases. The scheme may be used for bulk purchases with a combined price in excess of £500 but if any individual item included has a purchase price of more than £500, it must be deducted from the total purchase price and excluded from the scheme. There is no set way to apportion total price between individual items but HMRC must be satisfied that it is fair and reasonable. Any item costing over £500 can then be sold under either the margin scheme (if eligible) or the normal VAT rules.

Collections. Collections (eg of stamps) purchased can be split and sold separately or formed into other collections for sale provided all items are eligible for the global accounting scheme. Two or more items purchased separately can also be combined to produce one item for resale (eg by using one item as a spare part for another).

But if an eligible item is purchased for £500 or more, and the item is made up of several components valued at less than £500, the global accounting scheme cannot be used if the item is sold in the same state as it was purchased.

> *Example*
>
> A tea set, including many pieces each valued at less than £500, is purchased for £750.
>
> If the item is bought and sold as a 'tea set', there is only one item and the global accounting scheme cannot be used.

(VAT Notice 718, paras 5.8, 5.9).

61.45 **Sales**

On the sale of eligible goods, the dealer must check that the rules in 61.43 above where applied on purchase.

For sales to other dealers, a dealer must issue (and keep a copy of) a sales invoice showing

- own name and address and VAT registration number;
- buyer's name and address;
- invoice number;
- date of sale;
- description of the goods sufficient to enable HMRC to verify that the goods are eligible for the global accounting scheme (eg 'four tables and ten chairs' is acceptable but 'assorted goods' is not);
- total price including VAT (but which must not be shown separately); and
- an endorsement stating 'Global accounting invoice'.

If a dealer sells an item for more than £500 but does not wish to disclose to the purchaser that he bought it under the global accounting scheme, instead of the endorsement above he may choose to use the following declaration on his sales invoice: 'Input tax deduction has not been and will not be claimed by me in respect of the goods sold on this invoice'.

All other sales should be recorded in the normal way (eg by using a cash register).

Details of the daily gross takings and/or totals of copy invoices must be entered in the sales record or summary (see 61.49 below). It is therefore essential to be able to distinguish between sales under the global accounting scheme and other types of transactions at the point of sale.

(VAT Notice 718, paras 6.4, 6.5 which have the force of law).

Invoices in foreign currency. If a global accounting scheme invoice is issued in a foreign currency, it must also show the sterling equivalent of the total value of the goods. Even if more than one item is sold on the invoice, only the total foreign currency and sterling price needs to be shown and the sterling amount should be entered in the sales records. The foreign currency value must be converted into sterling using one of the methods in 69.18 VALUATION. (VAT Notice 718, para 6.11 which has the force of law).

61.46 **Transactions with overseas persons**

The same provisions apply as for the margin scheme provided the goods in question are also eligible for the global accounting scheme.

- **Acquisitions from other EC countries**. See 61.7 above ignoring the reference to motor cars.
- **Imports from outside the EC**. See 61.8 above ignoring the references to motor cars.
- **Sales to other EC countries**. See 61.12 above.
- **Exports outside the EC**. See 61.13 above ignoring the references to motor cars and boats.

61.47 **Records and accounts**

Global accounting scheme records do not have to be kept in any set way but must be complete, up-to-date and clearly distinguishable from any other records. Records must be kept of purchases and sales (see 61.49 below) and workings used to calculate the VAT due. All scheme records must be preserved for six years.

The global accounting scheme records are in addition to those generally required of all taxable persons. See RECORDS (56).

Failure to comply with any of the requirements as to records renders the taxable person liable for VAT on the full value of his sales.

(VAT Notice 718, paras 5, 6.1).

61.48 *Stock*

Stock on hand when starting to use the global accounting scheme. Any such eligible stock can be treated in either of the following ways.

- Taken into the scheme and included in the calculations for the first accounting period. Some form of stock take or valuation will be required. Where possible, stock should be identified separately and its purchase price established from invoices. Where stock cannot be related to original purchase invoices, the purchase value must be determined in some other way. There is no set way of doing this but HMRC must be satisfied that the method used is fair and reasonable. Any documents used to establish the stock valuation must be kept for six years.
- Not taken into the scheme. If the goods are then sold under the global accounting scheme, there is no 'purchase credit' to set against the sale and VAT will be accounted for on the full selling price rather than the profit margin.

Eligible stock already included in stock records under the margin scheme can either be sold under the margin scheme or transferred to the global accounting scheme. In the latter case, the stock must be deleted from the margin scheme stock book and cross-referred to and included in the global accounting scheme records.

(VAT Notice 718, paras 5.5, 5.6).

61.49 *Purchases and sales summaries*

Summary records must be kept of purchases and sales for each accounting period. These do not have to be kept in any particular way but they must include the following details taken from any purchases invoices and any sales invoices issued.

- Invoice number.
- Date of purchase/sale.
- Description of goods sufficient to enable HMRC to verify that the goods are eligible for the global accounting scheme.
- Total price.

At the end of the VAT period, the totals of purchases and sales are used to calculate the VAT due.

(VAT Notice 718, para 6.6 which has the force of law).

61.50 **Calculation of VAT due**

VAT is chargeable on the 'total profit margin' on goods supplied during a VAT period. '*Total profit margin*' is the amount (if any) by which the total sales exceed total purchases in the VAT period. See 61.24(*a*) and (*b*) above for the rules for determining the price at which goods are purchased and sold.

The excess is the VAT-inclusive margin ie the VAT included is

VAT-inclusive margin × VAT fraction (currently 7/47)

Negative margin. If there is a negative margin (because total purchases exceed total sales), no VAT is due and the negative margin is carried forward to the following VAT period for inclusion in the calculation of the total purchases of that period. A negative margin cannot be set off against other VAT due in the same VAT period on transactions outside the global accounting scheme.

Copies of all calculations must be kept as part of the records.

[*SI 1995/1268, Art 13; SI 1999/3120*]. (VAT Notice 718, para 5.7).

Example

A dealer starts to use the global accounting scheme and values his opening stock on hand at £10,000. In the first VAT period, his total purchases from his purchase summary are £2,000 and his sales from his sales summary are £8,000.

The margin for the first VAT period is £8,000 – (£10,000 + £2,000) = (£4,000)

There is a negative margin and no VAT is due. The negative margin is carried forward to the next period in which purchases are £1,000 and sales are £7,000.

The margin for the second VAT period is £7,000 – (£4,000 + £1,000) = £2,000

VAT due = £2,000 × 7/47 = £297.87

If any of the goods sold in the period were obtained following the transfer of a business as a going concern, see 61.24 above.

61.51 **Adjustments**

Removing goods from the scheme. Where purchases are initially included in the global accounting scheme purchase records but it is subsequently decided to sell the goods outside the scheme (eg because they are zero-rated on sale for export outside the EC) or the goods cease to be eligible (eg investment gold coins purchased before 1 January 2000) the scheme records must be adjusted. In the period in which the goods are removed from the scheme, the purchase value of those goods must be deducted from the global accounting scheme purchase records. There is no set way to apportion values to individual items but it must be fair and reasonable and it must be possible to demonstrate to HMRC how the value was determined.

Goods stolen or destroyed. Any loss of goods by breakage, theft or destruction must be adjusted by the deduction of their purchase price in the global accounting scheme purchase records.

Ceasing to use the global accounting scheme. If a dealer ceases to use the global accounting scheme for any reason, he must make an adjustment to take account of purchases for which he has taken credit but which have not been sold under the scheme.

- If deregistering, in the final period of using the scheme, the dealer must add the purchase value of his closing stock to his sales figure for that period.
- If transferring goods as part of a transfer of a going concern (TOGC), the dealer should add the purchase value of goods included in the scheme to sales figure for the period in which the TOGC takes place. This adjustment is separate from the actual TOGC which is not subject to VAT.

In either case, no adjustment is required if the total VAT due on stock on hand is £1,000 or less.

(VAT Notice 718, paras 6.7–6.9 which have the force of law).

61.52 **Completion of VAT return**

See 2.5 *et seq* ACCOUNTING PERIODS AND RETURNS for notes on the completion of Form VAT 100. The following special rules apply to eligible goods bought and sold under the global accounting scheme.

Box 1	Where there is a positive margin, include the output tax calculated by reference to the difference between total purchases and total sales of eligible goods in the period covered by the return.
Box 6	Include the full selling price of all eligible goods sold under the scheme during the period, less any VAT included in that price.
Box 7	Include the purchase price (inclusive of VAT) of eligible goods bought in the period.

Any negative margins should not be included on the VAT return.

61.53 **THE AUCTIONEERS' SCHEME**

If an auctioneer sells eligible goods (see 61.3 above) and invoices in his own name he may either

- account for VAT under the auctioneers' scheme; or
- apply the rules for invoicing as an agent (see 61.26 above).

The auctioneers' scheme is a variation of the margin scheme. It allows auctioneers to account for VAT on a margin, the calculation of which involves

- adding to the hammer price the cost of the auctioneer's services charged to the buyer; and
- deducting from the hammer price the cost of the auctioneer's services charged to the seller.

The detailed provisions of the scheme are set out in 61.54 to 61.61 below and have the force of law. It is therefore important to check with the seller before the sale whether the goods are eligible for inclusion in the auctioneers' scheme.

The auctioneers' scheme and its conditions are for the purposes of calculating VAT liability and do not affect the legal status of agents or the contractual relationships between auctioneers, vendors and buyers.

(VAT Notice 718, paras 7.1, 7.2).

Tax point. Where goods are treated as supplied both to and by the auctioneer, there is a common tax point for both supplies which will normally be the earlier of

- the handing over of the goods by the auctioneer to the buyer; or
- the receipt of payment by the auctioneer.

Sales under the auctioneers' scheme to other EC countries are treated in the same way as sales within the UK. The sales are liable to VAT in the UK and no further VAT is due in the country of destination.

(VAT Notice 718, paras 7.6, 7.9).

De Voil Indirect Tax Service. See V3.533.

61.54 Conditions of the scheme

The auctioneer's scheme can be used for sales of the following goods.

(*a*) Eligible goods (see 61.3 above) provided the following conditions are met.

(i) The seller is

- not registered for VAT;
- a VAT-registered person supplying goods under the margin scheme (see 61.2 to 61.38 above) or the global accounting scheme (see 61.39 to 61.52 above);
- an insurance company selling eligible goods which they have acquired as a result of an insurance claim provided that the goods are sold at auction in the same state; or
- a finance company selling eligible goods which they have repossessed provided that they are sold at auction in the same state.

(VAT Notice 718, para 7.3).

(ii) The auctioneer complies with the invoicing requirements in 61.57 below. It is not necessary to maintain a stock book in strict accordance with the margin scheme if sufficient alternative records are retained to provide the same information (eg entry forms, sales catalogues, copies of lots and sales of the day and copies of sales and purchases invoices).

(VAT Notice 718, para 8.2 which has the force of law).

(*b*) By extra-statutory concession, all goods grown, made or produced (including bloodstock or livestock reared from birth) by unregistered (non-taxable) persons.

As a condition of the relief, the auctioneer must obtain a signed certificate from the vendor including the vendor's full name and address, a description of the goods and the date of sale, a declaration that the vendor is not registered nor required to be registered for VAT, the signature of vendor and date, and the signature of auctioneer and date. The completed certificate must be retained with the relevant records for VAT purposes. An example of an acceptable certificate is set out below.

> AUCTIONEERS' SCHEME FOR SECOND-HAND GOODS, WORKS OF ART, ANTIQUES AND COLLECTORS' ITEMS
>
> Extra-statutory Concession 3.27
>
> Vendor's Certificate for goods grown, made or produced and sold at auction on behalf of non-taxable persons
>
> I (full name)
>
> of (address)
>
> declare that I am not registered or required to be registered for VAT and that the goods detailed below are to be sold at auction on my behalf by (auctioneer's name)
>
> (Description of goods)
>
> Date of sale (to be completed by auctioneer)
>
> Signature of vendor
>
> Signature of auctioneer
>
> Date

The auctioneer may, with the agreement of HMRC, incorporate the certificate into his existing sales entry.

(VAT Notice 48, ESC 3.27; VAT Notice 718, paras 7.11, 10).

61.55 Charges to be included/excluded under the scheme

Any commission or other charges made by the auctioneer to the vendor or buyer which are dependent on the sale of the goods must be included in the auctioneers' scheme calculation as set out in 61.59 below. Treatment of other charges are as follows.

- **Incidental expenses**. Any incidental expenses (eg packing, transport and insurance) incurred and charged onward to the buyer must be included in the scheme calculations unless they are a separate supply in their own right.
- **Disbursements for VAT purposes**. Any costs passed on to the client which meet all the conditions regarding disbursements under 3.7 AGENTS can be excluded from the auctioneers' scheme.

- **Exempt supplies**. Any services supplied to the buyer or vendor which are exempt (eg making arrangements for the provision of insurance by a permitted insurer provided the disclosure requirements are complied with, see 37.13 INSURANCE) should be excluded from the scheme calculations.
- **Services to an overseas vendor**. See 64.18 to 64.31 SUPPLY for the rules relating to the place of supply of services. Where the place of supply is in the UK, any services to an overseas vendor must be included in the auctioneers' scheme calculations. Where, however, the supply is treated as taking place outside the UK (eg supplies of certain services where the recipient belongs outside the EC or is in business in another EC country, see 64.26 SUPPLY) the supply is outside the scope of UK VAT and should be excluded from the auctioneers' scheme calculations.
- **Other charges**. Charges for other supplies which are optional and not directly related to the hammer price should be excluded from the auctioneers' scheme calculations.

(VAT Notice 718, para 7.5).

61.56 Zero-rated sales

Where the auctioneers' scheme is used for the sale of zero-rated goods (eg exports), the auctioneers' margin is also zero-rated. Any charges made outside the scheme are liable to VAT in the normal way. The normal conditions for zero-rating apply. See 25.1 EXPORTS. (VAT Notice 718, paras 7.7, 7.8).

61.57 Invoicing

Auctioneers using the scheme must not itemise VAT separately on any statement or invoice issued to the vendor or buyer except where goods or services are provided in addition to, but separately from, the purchase or sale. Such non-scheme items should be invoiced under the normal VAT rules.

Purchase invoices. The auctioneer should issue to the seller of the goods an invoice or statement satisfying the conditions of a purchase invoice under 61.6 above and also showing

- the hammer price of the goods;
- any commission charges to the seller; and
- the net amount due to the seller.

The net amount due to the seller is the auctioneer's purchase price. If the seller is a VAT-registered dealer using the margin scheme, the net amount due is also his selling price. The auctioneer should therefore allocate any charges included under the auctioneers' scheme against each lot.

Sales invoices. The auctioneer should issue to the buyer of the goods an invoice or statement satisfying the conditions in 61.11 above (including the certificate regarding input tax deduction) and also showing

- the hammer price of the goods;
- any other charges for services made (eg buyer's premium); and
- the amount due from the buyer.

The amount due from the buyer is the auctioneer's selling price. If the buyer is a VAT-registered dealer using the margin scheme, the amount due is also his buying price. The auctioneer should therefore allocate any charges included under the auctioneers' scheme against each lot.

(VAT Notice 718, para 8.1 which has the force of law).

Invoices in foreign currency. Invoices issued in foreign currency under the auctioneers' scheme must show the sterling equivalent of each element of the invoice (eg hammer price of the goods and the amount of commission or other charges due) and not just the total value of supplies made. The foreign currency value must be converted into sterling using one of the methods in 69.18 VALUATION.

Scheme and non-scheme supplies. If both scheme and non-scheme supplies are made to the same customer, either separate invoices can be issued (advisable) or all supplies can be included on the same invoice. In the latter case, the invoice must clearly distinguish between the two types of supply and comply with all the relevant provisions for both. In the case of a sales invoice, it must also show clearly the amount of the selling price which will form the basis of the purchase price for the buyer's margin scheme or global accounting scheme records.

Re-invoicing. If goods have been sold under the auctioneers' scheme but the buyer subsequently decides that he wishes to treat the transaction outside the scheme (paying VAT separately on the hammer price and the other charges), the auctioneer may re-invoice for the transaction under the normal VAT rules provided

(*a*) the auctioneer can comply with all the relevant VAT regulations of the substitute transaction;

(*b*) at the time of the amendment, the auctioneer and buyer hold all the original evidence relating to the transaction;

(*c*) the auctioneer cancels the first entry in his records and cross-refers to the amended transaction; and

(*d*) any substitute document (eg a VAT invoice) issued to the buyer clearly refers to the original transaction and states that it is cancelled and that the buyer should amend his VAT records accordingly.

Re-invoicing cannot be undertaken more than three years after the due date of the VAT return on which the original supply was accounted for. This is because input tax cannot be claimed under the three-year cap rules.

(VAT Notice 718, paras 8.3–8.5).

61.58 IMPORTED WORKS OF ART, ANTIQUES AND COLLECTORS' PIECES AND WORKS OF ART OBTAINED FROM THE CREATORS OR THEIR HEIRS

Goods which have been obtained with VAT charged on their full value are normally ineligible for the auctioneers' scheme. However, auctioneers acting in their own names may opt to use the scheme to deal with

(*a*) works of art, antiques and collectors' pieces which they have imported themselves (as principals on behalf of a third party) for onward sale in their own names; and

(*b*) works of art obtained (that is supplied in the UK or acquired from another EC country) from creators or their heirs for onward sale in their own names.

In both of the foregoing cases, the scheme may be used despite VAT having already been charged on the importation, acquisition or supply of the goods provided the following conditions are met.

- HMRC must be notified in writing that the option is to be taken up, specifying the date from which it will apply.
- The option must be exercised for a period of at least two years. Thereafter it will continue to apply until HMRC are advised in writing as to when it will cease.
- If the option is used, it must be applied to all transactions within (*a*) and (*b*) above, not just in respect of certain transactions or certain categories of goods.
- If, having exercised the option, the auctioneer decides to sell outside the scheme any goods covered by the option (eg he exports the goods), he is not entitled to recover any input tax on those goods until the period in which VAT is accounted for on their sale.

If the option is not used, VAT must be accounted for in accordance with the general rules for auctioneers.

Purchase price. If the option to use the auctioneers' scheme has been exercised, the purchase price is calculated as follows.

(i) *Imported works of art, antiques and collectors' items.* The option applies to imports at a reduced rate of 5%. The auctioneer must not reclaim the import VAT as input tax. His purchase price for the auctioneers' scheme is the hammer price less any commission charges made to the seller. The import VAT incurred must not be included in the auctioneers' scheme calculations although the auctioneer may wish to recoup this amount separately from the seller.

(ii) *Works of art obtained from the creator or his heirs.* The auctioneer must not reclaim any VAT charged by the supplier and must calculate his purchase price in accordance with 61.59 below. Because the creator or heir will have to account for output tax on the full hammer price they may ask the auctioneer to sell the item under the normal margin scheme option. In such cases, any invoice issued for charges for services must show VAT at the standard rate separately. This will enable the supplier to reclaim the input tax on those charges. The auctioneer's purchase price under the normal margin scheme option is the hammer price only.

(VAT Notice 718, paras 11.1–11.4).

61.59 Calculation of VAT

The purchase price, selling price, margin and VAT due are calculated from the successful bid price (hammer price) and commission and other charges.

'*Purchase price*' is the hammer price less commission payable to the auctioneer under his contract with the seller for the sale of the goods (see 61.55 above).

'*Selling price*' is the hammer price plus the consideration for any supply of services by the auctioneer to the purchaser (eg buyer's premium) in connection with the sale of the goods (see 61.55 above).

The margin is the difference between the purchase price and the selling price. The margin is regarded as being VAT-inclusive ie the VAT included is

VAT-inclusive margin × VAT fraction (currently 7/47)

Example

Goods are sold at auction for £1,000 (the hammer price). Commission is charged to the seller at 10% net of VAT and a buyer's premium is charged of 15% net of VAT.

Commission = (£1,000 × 10%) + 17.5% VAT =	£117.50
Purchase price = £1,000 – £117.50 =	£882.50
Buyer's premium = (£1,000 × 15%) + 17.5% VAT =	£176.25
Selling price = £1,000 + £176.25 =	£1,176.25
Margin = £1,176.25 – £882.50 =	£293.75
Output tax = £293.75 × 7/47 =	£43.75

[*SI 1992/3122, Art 8(7); SI 1995/1268, Art 12(7); SI 1995/1269; SI 2001/3753; SI 2001/3754*]. (VAT Notice 718, paras 7.4, 9.1).

61.60 Dealers buying at auction

Where a taxable dealer buys goods at an auction and wishes to use either the margin scheme or the global accounting scheme for the onward sale of the goods, he should

- check that the goods will be eligible for onward sale under the chosen scheme (usually clear from the auctioneer's sales catalogue). If VAT is charged separately on the hammer price, the goods will not qualify for either scheme; and
- follow the record-keeping requirements under the chosen scheme.

The dealer's purchase price is the hammer price of the goods plus charges for services (which must not show VAT separately) and should be clearly identified on the sales invoice issued by the auctioneer. The invoice should itemise, for each lot, the hammer price of the goods and any charges for services (for example, buyer's premium). The total of these amounts (ie the amount due from the dealer to the auctioneer) is the purchase price for the purpose of the margin scheme or global accounting scheme and is the amount that the dealer must show in his stock book. Any other charges for services on which VAT is shown separately must not be included as part of the purchase price.

In some cases a dealer may receive a single invoice from the auctioneer, showing the hammer price of the goods and charges for inclusion in the scheme calculations as well as charges on which VAT is shown separately. To avoid confusion, the dealer may wish to ask the auctioneer to provide him with a separate invoice for these charges. In either case, the dealer can reclaim the VAT shown under the normal rules but must make sure that he does not add the value of these charges to his purchase price for the purposes of the margin scheme.

(VAT Notice 718, paras 12.1–12.3).

61.61 Dealers selling at auction under the margin scheme or global accounting scheme

A taxable dealer selling at auction must tell the auctioneer before the sale is due to take place exactly how he wishes to treat the sale, ie under the auctioneers' scheme, margin scheme or global accounting scheme. If the auctioneer uses the auctioneers' scheme he issues an invoice/statement which includes

- the hammer price of the goods;
- his commission charges; and
- the net amount payable to the dealer.

None of these amounts should show VAT separately. Any other charges for services should be invoiced separately with VAT, if applicable, shown on the full amount of each charge.

Alternatively, the dealer can ask the auctioneer to sell the goods under the normal margin scheme. In these circumstances, the auctioneer issues an invoice/statement which only includes the hammer price of the goods. VAT must not be shown separately on this amount. His commission charges and any other charges for his services must be invoiced separately with VAT, if applicable, shown on the full amount of each charge. The dealer can reclaim the VAT on such charges under the normal rules.

Selling price of eligible goods sold at auction. A dealer's selling price for the purpose of the margin scheme should be clearly identifiable on the invoice/statement issued by the auctioneer.

- If the auctioneer has supplied the goods under the auctioneers' scheme, the hammer price of the goods and commission charges will not show VAT separately. The dealer's selling price is the net amount, ie the hammer price less the commission charge. If the auctioneer makes other charges, these should be invoiced separately and, if applicable, VAT charged under the normal rules. The dealer must not include these charges as part of his selling price but will be able to reclaim the VAT charged, subject to the normal rules.
- If, in agreement with the auctioneer, the dealer arranges for the goods to be sold by the auctioneer under the normal margin scheme as it applies to agents, the dealer's selling price is the hammer price. Any other charges that the auctioneer makes should be invoiced or itemised separately and, if applicable, VAT charged under the normal rules.

(VAT Notice 718, paras 12.4, 12.5).

62 Self-Supply

Cross-references. See 42.12 LAND AND BUILDINGS for change of use of residential and charitable buildings; 42.30 LAND AND BUILDINGS for self-supply of certain construction services; 45.6 MOTOR CARS for self-supply of motor cars; 64.45 SUPPLY for the time of self-supply.

De Voil Indirect Tax Service. See V3.241.

62.1 SCOPE OF SELF-SUPPLY

The Treasury may, by order, provide that where specified goods are taken possession of or produced by a person (not necessarily a *taxable* person) in the course or furtherance of a business carried on by him *and*

(*a*) are neither supplied to another person nor incorporated in other goods produced in the course or furtherance of that business; *but*

(*b*) are used by him for the purpose of a business carried on by him,

the goods are treated for VAT purposes as being both supplied to him for the purpose of that business and supplied by him in the course or furtherance of it. [*VATA 1994, s 5(5)(7)*].

Such a power is aimed to prevent an advantage being gained by a person who produces for himself goods on which, if supplied externally, either input tax would be specifically denied, or on which input tax would be denied or restricted because of exempt output supplies being made by the person concerned. Specific orders have been made as regards motor cars (see 45.6 MOTOR CARS) and stationery (see 62.2 below).

Similar powers to the above as regards goods are also applied to services. [*VATA 1994, s 5(6)*]. See 42.30 LAND AND BUILDINGS for self-supply of certain construction services.

62.2 PRINTED MATTER

Supplies after 31 May 2002. The requirement to account for VAT on self-supplied printing matter is abolished (subject to the transitional provisions detailed below). [*SI 1995/1268, Art 11; SI 2002/1280*].

Supplies before 1 June 2002. Printed matter (including stationery but not anything produced by typing, duplicating or photocopying) was designated under the order-making powers in 62.1 above where

- the self-supply took place before 1 June 2002; or
- the goods in question were paid for or invoiced before 1 June 2002 but collected or delivered after that date.

The powers did *not* apply if

(*a*) the person was a fully taxable person (ie the only input tax to which he was not entitled to credit in any VAT period or longer period was input tax which was specifically excluded from credit, see 35.8 INPUT TAX);

(*b*) the value of the stationery supplies which fell to be treated as self-supplied did not make that person liable to be registered (see 59 REGISTRATION) if those supplies were the only ones made by that person; or (*c*) HMRC were satisfied that the VAT (if any) which fell to be accounted for, less corresponding input tax, was negligible and they gave a direction that the order was not to apply.

The representative member of a group of companies was deemed to be subject to the self-supply provisions for all the group members' self-supplies.

[*SI 1995/1268, Art 11 before omission*].

The effect of the above was that the self-supply provisions applied where a person could not be treated as fully taxable under the partial exemption rules and the value of self-supplies alone exceeded the VAT registration limits. The provisions applied to stationery or other printed matter consisting completely or partly of paper, paperboard or similar material. *Excluded* were such items which were supplied to third parties, either alone or incorporated with other goods, or manufactured by third parties from the person's own materials. Stationery produced by typewriting, duplicating and photocopying was also excluded.

Value of the self-supply. The value of the stationery on which VAT had to be accounted for was the price the person would have had to pay (excluding VAT), at the time of the supply, to purchase stationery *identical* in every respect to the stationery concerned. Where that value could not be ascertained, the price for the purchase of stationery *similar* to the stationery concerned had to be used. If that value was also not possible to ascertain, the cost of producing the stationery concerned at that time was to be used. [*VATA 1994, Sch 6 para 6*].

Time of self-supply. The time of supply was treated as taking place when the stationery was appropriated for business use. [*VATA 1994, s 6(11)*].

Appropriation for this purpose could not normally be said to have taken place until at least the occurrence of some overt, unconditional event that could be said to show appropriation to business use. The tax point was then the date when, by any positive and recorded action, the supplier indicated his intention to use the stationery for business purposes. A mere intention to appropriate the stationery was not normally sufficient to create a tax point in these circumstances. (VAT Notice 700, para 15.2; Internal Guidance V1–11, para 29.2).

Records of stationery produced (a statutory requirement) had to include quantity and description; tax point (see above); value for VAT purposes; and the rate and amount of VAT due.

Partial exemption calculation. If the provisions applied, a partial exemption calculation for the amount of input tax able to be reclaimed was required. All input tax incurred on goods and services used to manufacture the self-supplied stationery (eg paper, ink, machinery and its repair) was reclaimable.

Self-supplies of stationery were treated both as outputs and inputs of the business. How much of the self-charged input tax could be claimed was determined by the partial exemption method used.

- Where all self-supplied stationery was used wholly in making taxable supplies, all of the input tax was deductible.
- Where it was all used in making exempt supplies or carrying out activities other than the making of taxable supplies, none of the input tax was deductible.
- Where it was used for both purposes, the input tax had to be added to the rest of the non-attributable input tax of the business and apportioned according to the partial exemption method used.

62.2 Self-Supply

If non-attributable input tax was apportioned using the standard method, the value of the self-supplies had to be excluded from the calculation.

Example

	£
Value of standard-rated self-supplies of stationery (excluding VAT)	19,000
Value of zero-rated self-supplies of stationery	1,000
Value of taxable outputs (excluding self-supplies of stationery)	100,000
Value of exempt outputs	900,000
Other non-attributable input tax (eg on general overheads)	20,000

Assume that all self-supplied stationery is used partly for taxable supplies and partly for exempt supplies (ie it is all non-attributable)

Value of total outputs (excluding self-supplies)	£1,000,000
Percentage of taxable supplies	10%

Non-attributable input tax on self-supplies (equal to output tax on standard-rated self-supplies)	
17.5% × £19,000	3,325
Other non-attributable input tax	20,000
Total non-attributable input tax	£23,325
Claimable portion £23,325 × 10%	£2,332.50

The full input tax claim was therefore £2,332.50 *plus* all input tax on goods and services for use in the manufacture of self-supplied stationery *plus* all other input tax on supplies and imports used wholly for the making of taxable supplies.

Output tax on self-supplies had to be included on returns even if full credit for input tax was obtained for a particular accounting period because of the application of the partial exemption rules. In such circumstances an amount of input tax equal to the output tax had to be provisionally deducted from the output tax accountable on the self-supplies. The value of self-supplies had to be included in the total value of taxable outputs, whether fully taxable or not.

The self-supply provisions could only cease to be applied, on application, if the value of such supplies fell below the registration threshold limits *and* the value of other taxable supplies did not exceed the limits set for cancellation of registration.

(VAT Leaflet 706/1/92 now withdrawn).

De Voil Indirect Tax Service. See V3.243.

63 Special Schemes

The contents of this chapter are as follows.

63.1 INTRODUCTION

The following special schemes are available to VAT-registered businesses.

- **Flat-rate scheme for small businesses**. Subject to conditions, including an annual turnover limit, small businesses can opt to join a flat-rate scheme under which they calculate net VAT due by applying a flat-rate percentage to VAT-inclusive turnover. The flat-rate percentage varies with the trade sector into which the business falls. See 63.15 to 63.24 below.

- **Cash accounting scheme.** Subject to conditions, including an annual turnover limit, this scheme can be used by any business. See 63.2 to 63.8 below.

- **Annual accounting scheme.** Subject to meeting certain conditions, including an annual turnover limit, a business can apply to HMRC to prepare an annual VAT return and make payments on account during the year. See 63.9 to 63.14 below.

- **Retail schemes.** There are a number of different retail schemes designed to suit different types of retail business. See 60 RETAIL SCHEMES.

- **Second-hand schemes**. In general, VAT is charged on the full value of any goods, including second-hand goods, sold by a business. However, provided certain conditions are met, VAT can be charged on the profit margin (instead of value) on supplies of second-hand goods; works of art, antiques and collectors' items; and goods sold through an agent acting in his own name in relation to the supply. See 61 SECOND-HAND GOODS for details.

- **Tour operators' margin scheme**. All UK businesses that buy travel, hotel and holiday services, etc from third parties and resell these supplies as principals *must* use a special scheme under which VAT has to be accounted for on the difference between the VAT-inclusive purchase price and selling price. See 66 TOUR OPERATORS' MARGIN SCHEME.
- **Flat-rate scheme for farmers.** A flat-rate scheme is available to farmers as an option to registering for VAT. Once in the scheme, VAT is not accounted for on sales of goods and services within certain designated activities and input tax is not recoverable on purchases. To compensate for this the farmer charges, and retains, a fixed flat-rate addition on sales, within those activities, to VAT-registered persons. See 63.25 to 63.30 below.
- **Racehorse owners**. A special arrangement has been made between HMRC and the thoroughbred horseracing and breeding industry. See 63.31 to 63.33 below.

63.2 CASH ACCOUNTING SCHEME

A business may, subject to conditions, account for and pay VAT on the basis of cash or other consideration paid and received. The conditions are as laid down in *Regulations* and as described in VAT Notice 731 *which in certain circumstances has the force of law* (see VAT Notice 747). HMRC may vary the terms of the scheme by publishing a fresh Notice or a Notice which amends an existing Notice, but without prejudicing the right of a person to withdraw from the scheme. [*VATA 1994, s 25(1), Sch 11 para 2(7); SI 1995/2518, Regs 57, 59; SI 1997/1614, Reg 4*].

The main advantages of the scheme are automatic bad debt relief and the deferral of the time for payment of VAT where extended credit is given. The scheme will probably not be beneficial for net repayment businesses or where most sales are paid promptly or for cash. (VAT Notice 731, para 1.3).

The cash accounting scheme cannot be used at the same time as the flat-rate scheme for small businesses (see 63.15 below). [*SI 1995/2518, Reg 57A; SI 2002/1142*].

De Voil Indirect Tax Service. See V2.199.

63.3 Joining the scheme

A business may begin to operate the scheme from the beginning of any VAT period, and without applying to HMRC for permission, if it meets the following conditions.

(*a*) There are reasonable grounds for believing that the value of its taxable supplies (excluding VAT) in the period of one year then beginning will not exceed £660,000 (£600,000 before 1 April 2004). All standard and zero-rated supplies should be included except anticipated sales of capital assets previously used within the business. Exempt supplies should be excluded.

(*b*) It has made all the VAT returns which it is required to make and either

- paid over all VAT due to HMRC (including penalties and interest); or
- agreed an arrangement with HMRC for such amount as is outstanding to be paid in instalments over a specified period.

(*c*) It has not in the previous year

- been convicted of any offences in connection with VAT;
- accepted an offer to compound proceedings in connection with a VAT offence;

- been assessed to a penalty for VAT evasion involving dishonest conduct (see 52.9 PENALTIES); or
- been denied access to the scheme by HMRC or had use of the scheme withdrawn by HMRC.

A business cannot begin to operate the scheme if HMRC consider that, for the protection of the revenue, it should not be able to do so. In such circumstances, the business may ask HMRC to reconsider the decision if it can provide further relevant information or if there are facts which it thinks have not been taken fully into account. If still not satisfied, an appeal may be made to a VAT tribunal. See 5 APPEALS.

The scheme cannot be applied retrospectively to the business.

[*SI 1995/2518, Reg 58(1)(4); SI 1997/1614, Reg 3; SI 2001/677; SI 2004/767, Reg 7*]. (VAT Notice 731, para 2.1 which has the force of law).

A business may join the scheme from the start of its first period of VAT registration. However, this may not be beneficial if it defers VAT recovery on initial stocks, tools, machinery, furniture or other capital items. (VAT Notice 731, para 2.2).

VAT group treatment. The turnover limit for the cash accounting scheme applies to the VAT group as a whole. Also, it is not possible to have one or more companies in a VAT group operating cash accounting while other members use the normal invoice-based requirements. The following action is therefore required when a new member enters a VAT group.

- The new member must deregister (whether or not using the cash accounting scheme).
- If the existing group is not using the cash accounting scheme but the new member is, the new member must return to the normal method of accounting and account for outstanding VAT whilst using the scheme on its final VAT return.
- If the existing group is using the cash accounting scheme, and the turnover of the enlarged group remains within the tolerance for use of the scheme in 63.7 below, the new member must use the cash accounting scheme from the date of joining the group. (If the new member makes or receives payments, after joining the group, for sales or purchases made whilst separately registered, the associated VAT must be accounted for on its final return and should be excluded from the group's VAT account.)
- If the existing group is using the cash accounting scheme, but the new member pushes the group turnover over the scheme limits, the whole group must leave the scheme at the end of the VAT period in which the new member joins the group.

(Internal Guidance V1–23, Chapter 4 para 3.1).

63.4 Supplies to be dealt with inside and outside the scheme

Subject to the following exceptions, where the cash accounting scheme is used, it must be used for the whole of the business.

Exceptions. The following transactions must be dealt with outside the cash accounting scheme under the normal VAT rules.

- Goods bought or sold under hire purchase, lease purchase, conditional sale or credit sale agreements.

- Goods imported from outside the EC, acquired from another EC country, or removed from a Customs warehouse or free zone. The scheme can be used to account for VAT on the onward supply of these goods in the UK.
- Supplies where a VAT invoice is issued and full payment of the amount shown on the invoice is not due within six months from the date of issue of the invoice.
- Supplies in respect of which a VAT invoice is issued in advance of the delivery or making available of the goods or the performance of the services, as the case may be. This does not apply where goods have been delivered or made available in part (or, as the case may be, services have been performed in part) and the VAT invoice in question relates solely to that part.

[*SI 1995/2518, Regs 58*(*2*)(*3*)*; SI 1997/1614, Reg 3*]. (VAT Notice 731, paras 2.3, 4.3 which have the force of law).

63.5 Records

The normal requirements regarding copies of VAT invoices and evidence of input tax apply. The following additional records must also be kept.

(*a*) **Receipted invoices.**

- If payment is made in money (ie banknotes or coin) to another VAT-registered business, the copy of the purchase invoice must be receipted and dated (the other business *must* on request provide such an invoice). [*SI 1995/2518, Reg 65*(*3*)]. The VAT invoice does not have to be separately receipted if the accompanying till or similar receipt states 'cash sale' or clearly indicates that cash has been given (eg through an analysis of change given). HMRC will only question non-receipted cash purchase invoices where there is clearly no evidence of cash payment. If payment is made by cheque, the VAT invoice does not have to be receipted. (Internal Guidance V1–23, Chapter 4 para 5.1).
- If payment is received in money (ie banknotes or coin), a receipted and dated VAT invoice must be issued, if requested, and a copy retained for six years or such lesser period as HMRC allow. [*SI 1995/2518, Reg 65*(*3*)]. (VAT Notice 731, para 3.1).

(*b*) **Payment record**. To use the cash accounting scheme, payments made/received must be clearly cross-referenced to the corresponding purchase/sales invoice and to normal commercial evidence such as bank statements, cheque stubs, paying-in slips. This can be done by keeping a cash book summarising all payments made and received with a separate column for VAT. (VAT Notice 731, para 3.2 which has the force of law).

See also 63.6 below for records required for specific transactions.

63.6 Accounting for VAT

Output tax must be accounted for in the return for the VAT period in which payment or other consideration is received. [*SI 1995/2518, Regs 57, 65*]. For this purpose payment by

- *cash* (ie coins and notes) is received on the date the money is received;
- *cheque* is received on the date the cheque is received or, if later, the date on the cheque. If the cheque is not honoured, no VAT is due and an adjustment can be made if VAT has already been accounted for;

- *credit or debit card* is received on the date the sales voucher is made out (*not* the date when payment is received from the card company); and
- *giros, standing orders and direct debits* are received on the day the bank account is credited.

Where an existing VAT-registered business starts to use the scheme, it should separate in its records any payments received for transactions already accounted for under the normal method of accounting. Such payments should be excluded from the scheme records.

(VAT Notice 731, paras 2.5, 3.3 which have the force of law).

Deposits. VAT on deposits must normally be accounted for when received unless the deposit is not payment for supplies (eg deposits taken as security which are either returned or forfeited) in which case there is no requirement to account for VAT. (VAT Notice 731, para 4.1).

Payments received net of deductions. Where a net payment is received after deduction of commission/expenses, VAT should be accounted for on the full value before such deduction. Examples include

- commission deducted by a customer;
- commission or payment for expenses deducted by a factor or agent collecting monies on behalf of the business;
- commission or payment for expenses deducted by an auctioneer selling goods on behalf of the business; and
- deductions made by an employer/contractor who has deducted income tax.

(VAT Notice 731, para 4.8 which has the force of law).

Payments received in foreign currency. Where a business issues an invoice in a foreign currency (including euros), it must also show the amount of VAT due in sterling. Therefore

- if the invoice is paid in full in the foreign currency, there is no need to convert the foreign currency payment and output tax is the sterling amount of VAT due as shown on the invoice; and
- if the invoice is paid in part in the foreign currency, output tax should be determined by calculating the proportion of the total amount due in the foreign currency which has been paid and applying that proportion to the sterling amount of VAT due as shown on the invoice.

Where a business issues an invoice in sterling but is paid in a foreign currency,

- if the invoice is paid in full, the output tax is the amount of VAT due as shown on the invoice; and
- if the invoice is paid in part, the foreign currency payment must be converted into sterling at the rate appropriate at the time of supply (not the time of payment). Output tax should then be determined by calculating the proportion of the total sterling amount due that the sterling equivalent of the payment represents and applying that proportion to the VAT due as shown on the invoice. See 69.18 VALUATION for methods of converting foreign exchange.

(VAT Notice 731, paras 4.10, 4.11).

Factored debts. Where debts are sold or formally assigned to a factor (so that they become the debts of the factor), output tax must be accounted for on their full value (not any reduced value for which they are assigned) in the period in which they are sold or assigned. See also *RTI Services Ltd (VTD 18512) (TVC 10.14)*. If, at a later date, all or any part of the factored debts are formally assigned back to the business under a recourse clause, it may claim BAD DEBT RELIEF (7) on any unpaid element subject to the normal bad debt rules.

On the other hand, where a business merely uses a factor or invoice discounter as a debt collector and retains legal title to the debt, the initial advance made by the factor to the business is not a payment for the purposes of the cash accounting scheme, it is simply a loan. The business must account for output tax in the VAT period in which the customer pays the factor. This will be evident on statements issued by the factor to the business. If the payment received from the factor is less than the full value of the supply (because a commission or other charge is payable to the factor) VAT is still due on the full amount received by the factor from the customer.

(VAT Notice 731, paras 4.2, 4.5 which have the force of law; Internal Guidance V1–23, Chapter 4 para 5.3).

Exports and supplies to other EC countries. The cash accounting scheme can be used to account for VAT which becomes due on goods exported or supplied to another EC country because satisfactory evidence of export/supply has not been received within the time limit allowed for zero-rating. VAT must be accounted for when the time limit expires on all payments already received. If further payments are received, VAT must be accounted for on such payments at the time of receipt. If evidence of export is received after any VAT has been accounted for, the VAT can be adjusted in the VAT period in which the evidence is obtained. (VAT Notice 731, para 4.4).

Input tax can be reclaimed in the return for the VAT period in which payment is made or other consideration is given or in a later period as may be agreed with HMRC. [*SI 1995/2518, Regs 57, 65*]. For this purpose payment by

- *cash* (ie coins and notes) is made on the date the money is paid (although a receipted VAT invoice must be held before reclaiming VAT on purchases made in this way, see 63.5 above);
- *cheque* is made on the date the cheque is sent to the supplier or, if later, the date on the cheque. If the cheque is not honoured, no VAT is reclaimable and an adjustment must be made if VAT has already been claimed;
- *credit or debit card* is made when the supplier makes out the sales voucher (*not* the date when payment is made to the card company); and
- *giros, standing orders and direct debits* are made on the day the bank account is debited.

(VAT Notice 731, para 3.4 which has the force of law).

Using the scheme from the date of registration. Newly registered businesses may reclaim VAT on certain goods and services obtained prior to registration. See 35.10 INPUT TAX. When the cash accounting scheme is used from the date of registration, VAT on such purchases should be reclaimed on the first VAT return if paid pre-registration or otherwise in the VAT period of payment.

Existing businesses starting to use the scheme. Where an existing VAT-registered business starts to use the scheme, it should separate in its records any payments made for transactions already dealt with under the normal method of accounting. Such payments should be excluded from the scheme records.

(VAT Notice 731, paras 2.5, 3.4).

Deposits. If advance payment is made by way of deposit, VAT can be reclaimed when the payment is made unless the deposit is not payment for supplies (eg deposits given as security which are either returned or forfeited) in which case there is no entitlement to deduct VAT. (VAT Notice 731, para 4.1).

Allocation of part payments. Where a payment is made or received which is part payment of one or more invoices (which may include both standard and zero-rated supplies), the payment must be allocated to the invoices in date order (earliest first). Where VAT is not identified separately on the part payment, the payment must be treated as VAT-inclusive. In cases where the payment relates to an invoice for supplies at different rates of VAT, the part payment must be apportioned between the different rates and the amounts on which VAT is due at the standard rate or reduced rate treated as VAT-inclusive.

Example

A payment of £2,500 is made against the following two invoices.

Invoice A (dated 1/5/04)	
Standard-rated goods	1,000
VAT	175
	£1,175
Invoice B (dated 26/5/04)	
Standard-rated goods	2,000
Zero-rated goods	1,000
VAT	350
	£3,350

The payment of £2,500 is allocated as follows.

(1) Allocate £1,175 against Invoice A (the earlier invoice) ie to include VAT of £175.00

(2) The balance of the payment £1,325 (£2,500 – £1,175) should be allocated against Invoice B. The proportion of the payment relating to VAT is

1,325 ÷ 3,350 × £350 = £138.43

Total amount of VAT to be accounted for on the payment of £2,500 is £313.43 (£175.00 + £138.43). The remaining VAT of £211.57 (£350.00 – £138.43) should be accounted for when any further payment is made.

(VAT Notice 731, paras 4.7, 6.2).

Payments in kind. Where payment is partly or fully in kind (eg a part exchange or barter transaction) VAT must be accounted for on the full value of the supply. This is usually the price, excluding VAT, which would have been paid for the supply if money were the only consideration. See 69.5-69.7 VALUATION for further details. VAT must be accounted for on the 'payment' on the date the business receives/supplies the goods or services agreed in lieu of money. (VAT Notice 731, para 4.9).

See also *A-Z Electrical (VTD 10718) (TVC 10.11)* where a business using the cash accounting scheme received shares in a company in lieu of the money owed to it for supplies of goods. The tribunal held that the business should be taken to have received cash in satisfaction of the debt owed to it, and to have paid the same amount of cash for the shares. The deemed payment for the supplies was liable to VAT.

Prompt payment discount. Where this is offered, VAT is chargeable on the discounted VAT-exclusive invoice price even if the customer does not take up the offer. Where an eligible business using cash accounting offers such a discount, the VAT to be accounted for is that charged on the invoice and not the VAT fraction of the payment reflecting the invoice total (otherwise too much VAT will be accounted for). Similarly, where a business using the cash accounting scheme receives such a discount, input tax reclaimable is limited to the VAT charged on the invoice. (Internal Guidance V1–23, Chapter 4 para 5.2).

Partial exemption. A business which makes both taxable and exempt supplies may not be able to reclaim all its input tax. See 49 PARTIAL EXEMPTION. A partly-exempt business which uses the cash accounting scheme must base its partial exemption calculations on payments made and received rather than purchases and sales. (VAT Notice 731, para 4.6).

Completion of VAT returns. The amounts of VAT due and VAT deductible are based on payments received and made, not on invoices issued. Similarly, the boxes for values of outputs and inputs must be completed on the basis of payments received and made (exclusive of VAT). Where supplies are made to other EC countries, the amount to be put in Box 8 is the total VAT-exclusive value of all supplies of goods and services made and *not* the total of payments received. (VAT Notice 731, para 3.5).

63.7 **Leaving the scheme**

(*a*) **Turnover exceeding the limit**. Unless HMRC allow or direct otherwise, a business must withdraw from the cash accounting scheme at the end of a VAT period (and use the normal method of accounting for subsequent periods) if the value of its taxable supplies in the year then ending has exceeded £825,000 (£750,000 before 1 April 2004). [*SI 1995/2518, Reg 60(1)(3); SI 1997/1614, Reg 5; SI 2001/677; SI 2004/767, Reg 8*]. For the purposes of this calculation, disposals of stocks and capital assets must be included. (VAT Notice 731, paras 5.1, 5.3).

Exceptionally, HMRC may allow a business to remain in the scheme where it can demonstrate that

- this limit was exceeded because of a large 'one-off' increase in sales which has not occurred before and is not expected to recur (eg the sale of a capital asset);
- the sale arose from a genuine commercial activity; and
- there are reasonable grounds for believing that turnover in the next twelve months will be below £660,000 (£600,000 before 1 April 2004).

Application must be made to HMRC in writing and will be confirmed by them in writing.

(VAT Notice 731, para 5.2).

(*b*) **Voluntary withdrawal**. A business may withdraw from the scheme at the end of a VAT period. [*SI 1995/2518, Reg 60*(*2*)*; SI 1997/1614, Reg 5*].

(*c*) **Expulsion from the scheme**. A business is not entitled to continue to operate the scheme in the following circumstances.

- It cannot comply with the record-keeping requirements in 63.5 above.
- It has, while operating the scheme,
  (i) been convicted of an offence in connection with VAT;
  (ii) accepted an offer to compound proceedings in connection with a VAT offence; or
  (iii) been assessed to a penalty under *VATA 1994, s 60* (VAT evasion involving dishonesty).

  In such circumstances, HMRC will automatically write to the business withdrawing use of the scheme.
- The business has failed to leave the scheme as provided for in (*a*) above.
- HMRC consider it necessary for the protection of the revenue.

[*SI 1995/2518, Reg 64*(*1*)*; SI 1997/1614, Reg 9*]. (VAT Notice 731, para 2.6).

Appeals. An appeal may be made against any termination of authorisation to use the cash accounting scheme. See 5.3 APPEALS. If the appeal is against a decision by HMRC to withdraw use of the scheme for the protection of the revenue or not to allow continued use of the scheme for exceeding the turnover limit, the business must cease to use the scheme until the appeal is resolved. For other appeals, HMRC will normally allow continued use of the scheme, pending outcome of the appeal, unless it considers that an appeal facilitates manipulation of the scheme. (VAT Notice 731, paras 2.10, 2.11).

Subsequent accounting for VAT. Unless the transitional arrangements below can be applied, a business which ceases to operate the cash accounting scheme because of (*a*)–(*c*) above must, on the return for the VAT period in which it ceased to operate the scheme, account for

- all VAT that it would have been required to pay to HMRC during the time the scheme was operated if it had not been operating the scheme, minus
- all VAT accounted for and paid to HMRC in accordance with the scheme, subject to any adjustment for credit for input tax.

Transitional arrangements. Where, after 1 April 2004, a business ceases to operate the cash accounting scheme because of (*a*) or (*b*) above, then provided the value of its taxable supplies in the three months ending at the end of the VAT period in which it ceased to operate the scheme has not exceeded £660,000, it may apply transitional arrangements. This means that the business can continue to operate the scheme in respect of its 'scheme supplies' for six months after the end of the VAT period in which it ceased to operate the scheme. '*Scheme supplies*' means supplies made and received while the business operated the scheme that were not excluded from the scheme under 63.4 above and did not fall to be included in the flat-rate scheme for small businesses (see 63.15 below).

Where a business chooses to apply the transitional arrangements, it must, on the return for the first VAT period that ends six months or more after the end of the VAT period in which it ceased to operate the scheme, account for

- all VAT that it would have been required to pay to HMRC during the time the scheme was operated if it had not then been operating the scheme, minus
- all VAT accounted for and paid to HMRC in accordance with the scheme (including any VAT accounted for and paid because it applied transitional arrangements), subject to any adjustment for credit for input tax.

[*SI 1995/2518, Regs 61, 64(2); SI 1997/1614, Reg 9; SI 2004/767, Reg 9*].

There is no need to apply to or notify HMRC if the transitional arrangements are used. During the six-month period it will be necessary to keep normal cash accounting records for payments and receipts for supplies which took place while the scheme was in use and separate records under the normal VAT accounting requirements for new supplies made and received. (VAT Notice 731, paras 5.6, 5.7).

Bad debt relief. With effect from 1 April 2004, where a business accounts for and pays VAT on a supply under the above provisions, it can claim BAD DEBT RELIEF (7) on the return for the VAT period in which it ceases to use the scheme. It must satisfy all the conditions of the bad debt relief scheme *other than* the condition that it has accounted for and paid the VAT on the supply in question. Where the business has opted to use the transitional arrangements, bad debt relief can be claimed in the VAT period which ends at the end of the six months. [*SI 1995/2518, Reg 64A; SI 2004/767, Reg 10*]. (VAT Notice 731, para 5.8). Previously, by concession in cases where (*a*) or (*b*) above applied, if the above provisions would have required the business to account for VAT on bad debts, HMRC were prepared to allow the outstanding VAT to be paid and the bad debt claim to be made on the same return. All the conditions for claiming bad debt relief had to be complied with (except the condition that the business must have already accounted for and paid the VAT on the supply). The concession could not be applied if use of the cash accounting scheme was compulsorily withdrawn by HMRC (VAT Notice 731 (2002 edition), para 5.6 (now superseded)).

63.8 Cessation of business

Where a business operating the cash accounting scheme ceases trading or ceases to be registered, it must, within two months or such longer period as HMRC allow, account for and pay VAT due on all supplies made and received up to the date of cessation which has not otherwise been accounted for, subject to any adjustment for credit for input tax. [*SI 1995/2518, Reg 63(1); SI 1997/1614, Reg 8*].

In practice, where a business ceases trading, HMRC allow the business to continue to use the cash accounting scheme while any remaining stocks and assets are disposed of. Once VAT registration is cancelled, however, the final VAT return must be submitted within two months of deregistration. This applies even if the business has still not been paid for all its supplies, although where any of this relates to bad debts, the concessionary relief in 63.7 above may be applied. (VAT Notice 731, paras 5.10, 5.12).

Insolvency. Where a business operating the cash accounting scheme becomes insolvent, it must, within two months of the date of insolvency, account for VAT due on all supplies made and received up to the date of insolvency which has not otherwise been accounted for, subject to any credit for input tax. [*SI 1995/2518, Reg 62; SI 1997/1614, Reg 7*]. Where trading continues after the date of insolvency, the officeholder responsible for the business may continue to use the cash accounting scheme subject to the normal rules of the scheme. If the officeholder does continue to use the scheme, he must, from the date of insolvency, separate in the business records any payments the business makes or receives for transactions already accounted for on the pre-insolvency VAT return. (VAT Notice 731, para 5.11 which has the force of law).

Transfer of a business as a going concern. Where a business or part of a business operating the cash accounting scheme is transferred as a going concern

- if the transferee does not take over the registration number of the business, the transferor must, within two months or such longer period as HMRC allow, account for and pay VAT due on all supplies made and received which has not otherwise been accounted for, subject to any adjustment for credit for input tax; and
- if the transferee takes over the VAT registration number of the business, the transferor must advise the transferee that the scheme is being used. The transferee must continue to account for and pay VAT as if it were a business operating the scheme on supplies made and received by the transferor before the date of the transfer. The transferee can leave the scheme subject to the normal rules in 63.7 above.

[*SI 1995/2518, Reg 63(2)(3); SI 1997/1614, Reg 8*].

63.9 ANNUAL ACCOUNTING SCHEME

Under *VATA 1994, s 25(1)* regulations may be made allowing a business to account for and pay VAT for VAT periods of other than three months. The annual accounting scheme allows businesses to complete one VAT return each year, making interim payments on account (see 63.12 below). The annual VAT return must be completed and sent to HMRC, with any balancing payment, within two months of the end of the annual VAT accounting period.

The main advantages of the scheme are:

- A reduction in the number of VAT returns required, normally from four to one a year.
- Management of cash flow with more certainty by paying a set amount each month.
- An extra month to complete the annual return and account for any balance of VAT due.
- Where the business uses a retail scheme, in most cases the scheme calculations which apply to each quarter are performed once a year. The only exception to this is where the Direct Calculation Scheme 2 is used, in which case calculations under the retail scheme rules follow the rules for the annual adjustment under that scheme (see 60.18 RETAIL SCHEMES).
- Where the business is partly exempt, the date it makes its partial exemption calculation must coincide with the end of its annual accounting period. This means that it does not have to make partial exemption calculations quarterly and simply make the calculation using the figures for the whole of the annual accounting period. (Where the first accounting period is for a part year, the business must do its partial exemption calculation only at the end of that period.)
- Being able to align the VAT accounting period with the financial year end.

(VAT Notice 732, paras 1.4, 3.3, 8.2, 8.3).

De Voil Indirect Tax Service. See V2.199A.

63.10 Admission to the scheme

Conditions for admission. A business is eligible to apply to join the scheme if it meets all the following conditions.

(*a*) It has been registered for at least twelve months at the date of application. This requirement does not apply where the business has reasonable grounds for believing that the value of taxable supplies in the period of 12 months beginning on the date of its application for authorisation will not exceed £150,000 (£100,000 from 25 April 2002 to 9 April 2003).

HMRC will not penalise a business for wrongly estimating that the value of its VAT turnover will not exceed £150,000 provided it can demonstrate that there were reasonable grounds for its estimate. HMRC will normally allow the business to stay in the scheme, providing it has not become ineligible in the meantime. If HMRC judge that the estimate of turnover had no reasonable basis, they may exclude the business from the scheme immediately. It is sensible, therefore, to keep a record of how the calculation was made. (VAT Notice 732, para 2.5).

(*b*) There are reasonable grounds for believing that the value of its taxable supplies (excluding VAT) in the period of twelve months beginning at the date of application will not exceed £660,000 (£600,000 before 1 April 2004). For this purpose, all standard, reduced and zero-rated supplies should be included except supplies of capital assets previously used in the business. Exempt supplies should be excluded. (VAT Notice 732, para 2.3).

(*c*) Registration is not in the name of a group (see 31 GROUPS OF COMPANIES) or a division (see 59.37 REGISTRATION).

(*d*) The business has not ceased to operate the scheme for any reason under 63.14 below in the twelve months preceding the date of application.

HMRC may refuse to permit a business to use the scheme where they consider it necessary to do so for the protection of the revenue.

[*SI 1995/2518, Reg 52; SI 1996/542; SI 2001/677; SI 2002/1142, Reg 6; SI 2003/1069, Reg 3; SI 2004/767, Reg 4*].

A business will not be allowed to join the scheme if it is insolvent or has a rising VAT debt. Entry will not necessarily be refused if there is a small debt provided the business agrees arrangements to clear the outstanding debt with HMRC. (VAT Notice 732, para 2.6).

Application procedure. Application to use the scheme must be made on Form VAT 600 (AA) (where application is to join the annual accounting scheme alone) or Form VAT 600 (AA and FRS) (where application is to join the annual accounting scheme and the flat-rate scheme for small businesses at the same time). Both forms are reproduced at the end of VAT Notice 732 or can be printed from the internet version at

www.hmrc.gov.uk

Welsh versions are available (Form VAT 600 AA(W), VAT 600 FRS(W) and VAT 600 AA/FRS(W)). The completed form must be sent to the National Registration Service, Deansgate, 62–70 Tettenhall Road, Wolverhampton, WV1 4TZ. (Business Brief 17/03). Notes on the completion of the form are in VAT Notice 732, para 4.5.

HMRC will notify the business in writing if the application is accepted. The letter will also advise

- the amount and timing of the interim payments to be made by electronic means;
- the method of electronic payment chosen, with a bank mandate form where appropriate; and
- the due date for the annual return and balancing payment.

The business should check that the payments are set high enough to reflect its actual VAT liability. If they are set too low, it will have to make a much larger balancing payment with its annual return. If there are genuine grounds to reconsider the proposed payments at any time during the year (eg a significant upturn or downturn in business) the local VAT Business Advice Centre should be contacted. (VAT Notice 732, para 3.6).

Annual accounting year and **transitional accounting period**. A business applying to join the scheme must indicate on the application form the month to the end of which it wishes its annual accounting year to run (normally the end of its financial accounting year). It must match the partial exemption year end (if applicable). If accepted, the first accounting period under the scheme (the '*transitional accounting period*') will normally run from the first day of the accounting period in which the application is made until the chosen year end. Subsequent periods of twelve months are then '*annual accounting years*'. However, HMRC cannot normally issue a VAT return for a period longer than 12 months (the exception being where a business is applying to use the annual accounting scheme from its effective date of registration, when a period of 12 months and 30 days is possible) and do not issue returns for periods of less than 3 months under the scheme. As a result, there may be instances when a business will receive more than one short period VAT return before a full twelve-month return.

Example 1

C Ltd, currently preparing VAT returns for calendar quarters, applies to join the annual accounting scheme on 28 November 2003. It chooses 30 June as the end of its annual accounting year to tie in with the financial accounts.

If accepted, C Ltd will join the scheme with effect from 1 October 2003 and have a transitional accounting period from 1 October 2003 to 30 June 2004. Thereafter, it will have annual accounting years ending on 30 June each year.

Example 2

D Ltd, currently preparing VAT returns for calendar quarters, applies to join the annual accounting scheme on 15 January 2004. It chooses the end of February as the end of its annual accounting year to tie in with the financial accounts.

If accepted, D Ltd will join the scheme with effect from 1 January 2004. As this would otherwise create an initial period of 14 months, D Ltd will probably receive a quarterly VAT return to 31 March 2004 and then a return from 1 April 2004 until the requested end of February. Thereafter, it will be issued with a full year return to the end of February.

[*SI 1995/2518, Reg 49; SI 1996/542*]. (Internal Guidance V1–23, Chapter 1 para 2.5).

The annual accounting year can be changed after joining the scheme (eg to tie in with a change in financial year end) but this may result in the business being issued with one or two short period returns during the transition because no accounting period can be longer than 12 months. (VAT Notice 732, para 5.2).

63.11 Conditions for using the scheme

To remain within the scheme, a business must comply with the following conditions.

(*a*) Make any interim payments on account required by the notified due date. See 63.12 below.

(*b*) Submit a VAT return, together with any balancing payment of VAT due to HMRC declared on that return

- in respect of a transitional accounting period of four months or more or an annual accounting year (see 63.10 above) by the end of the second month following that period or year; and
- in respect of a transitional accounting period of less than four months by the end of the first month following that period.

[*SI 1995/2518, Reg 50(2)(b), Reg 51(a)(iii)(b); SI 1996/542*].

(*c*) Tell HMRC immediately if there is any significant change in the business after starting to use the scheme (eg a change in the VAT liability of goods supplied, the opening of a new outlet or a downturn in business). (VAT Notice 732, para 2.1).

63.12 Payments on account

A business authorised to use the annual accounting scheme must make interim payments on account as follows.

(1) *Transitional periods* (see 63.10 above).

(*a*) Where the transitional accounting period is four months or more and the business and HMRC agree to such a payment pattern,

(i) in the case of a business registered for at least 12 months immediately preceding the start of its transitional period, 25% of the total VAT due for those 12 months on the last 'working day' of the 4th, and where the period has such months, 7th and 10th months of the transitional accounting period; and

(ii) in any other case, 25% of the total amount of VAT that HMRC are satisfied the business will be liable to pay in respect of the next 12 months, again on the last 'working day' of the 4th, and where the period has such months, 7th and 10th months of the transitional accounting period.

(*b*) Where the transitional accounting period is four months or more but the business and HMRC do not agree to quarterly payments as under (*a*) above,

(i) in the case of a business registered for at least 12 months immediately preceding the start of the transitional accounting period, 10% of the total VAT due for those 12 months in equal monthly instalments on the last 'working day' of the fourth and each successive month of the transitional accounting period; and

(ii) in any other case, 10% of the total amount of VAT that HMRC are satisfied the business will be liable to pay in respect of the next 12 months in equal monthly instalments on the last 'working day' of the fourth and each successive month of the transitional accounting period.

(*c*) Where the transitional accounting period is less than four months, no interim payments are required.

(2) *Subsequent annual accounting periods.*

(*a*) Where the business and HMRC agree to such a payment pattern,

(i) in the case of a business registered for at least 12 months immediately preceding the start of the current accounting year, 25% of the total VAT due for those 12 months on the last 'working day' of the 4th, 7th and 10th months of the annual accounting year; and

(ii) in any other case, 25% of the total amount of VAT that HMRC are satisfied the business will be liable to pay in respect of the next 12 months.

(*b*) Otherwise, where (*a*) does not apply,

(i) in the case of a business registered for at least 12 months immediately preceding the start of the current accounting year, 10% of the total VAT due for those 12 months in nine equal monthly instalments starting on the last 'working day' of the fourth month of its annual accounting year; and

(ii) in any other case, 10% of the total amount of VAT that HMRC are satisfied the business will be liable to pay in respect of the next 12 months.

The normal method of payment will therefore be by monthly payments under (1)(*b*) or (2)(*b*) above unless the business and HMRC agree otherwise. If a business, therefore, wishes to pay quarterly under (1)(*a*) or (1)(*b*) it should write to its VAT Business Advice Centre. (VAT Notice 732, para 6.2).

'*Working day*' means any day of the week other than Saturday, Sunday, a bank holiday or a public holiday.

[*SI 1995/2518, Reg 49, Reg 50*(*2*)(*3*)*, Reg 51; SI 1996/542; SI 2002/1142, Regs 3–5*].

Revision of payments on account. If a business expects its liability to increase or decrease significantly, it should contact its VAT Business Advice Centre with information on how it calculates revised interim payments. If they agree, HMRC will notify the new instalment amounts. (VAT Notice 732, para 6.6).

Additional voluntary payments can be made at any time. Payments must be made by electronic means (see below) and in multiples of £5. (VAT Notice 732, para 6.12).

Method of payment. All interim payments, whether monthly or quarterly, must be made by electronic means (direct debit, standing order, bank giro credit, Bankers Automated Clearing Service (BACS) or the Clearing House Automated Payment System (CHAPS)). Final payment can be made by cheque, bank giro credit, BACS or CHAPS. (VAT Notice 732, para 6.8).

Missing a payment. HMRC will send a reminder if an interim payment on account is not received. Payment will have to be made by bank giro credit (a transfer slip will be enclosed with the reminder) or by BACS. (VAT Notice 732, para 6.10).

63.13 Accounting for VAT

The annual return is completed in the same way as a normal VAT return. It is important that the figure for the value of outputs in Box 6 is accurate as this will be used as a basis for allowing continued use of the scheme.

The figure shown in Box 5 of the return is the amount of VAT due for the year. The amount payable with the VAT return is the figure in Box 5 less the total of interim payments made during the year. If the total amount paid by interim payments is more than the net VAT payable, HMRC will refund the difference automatically. (VAT Notice 732, para 7.3).

Use of the annual accounting scheme and the flat-rate scheme for small businesses. The annual accounting scheme can be used together with the flat-rate scheme (see 63.15 *et seq.*) below by simply following the rules of the flat-rate scheme for calculating VAT liability but instead of doing this four times a year, doing it just once when the annual accounting return is due.

If a business makes a joint application to use both schemes, use will normally start together from the beginning of the period in which the annual accounting scheme applies although the application form does allow a business to request different start dates. In the latter case, two calculations are required when completing the annual accounting return.

- A calculation for the period when the business was not in the flat-rate scheme, using normal VAT accounting rules.
- A calculation for the period when the business was in the flat-rate scheme using the rules for calculating liability under the flat-rate scheme.

The total liability for the return period will be the sum of those two calculations.

Where a business already using the annual accounting scheme applies to join the flat-rate scheme in the middle of its annual accounting period, it will have to do two calculations when completing its return as explained above. To avoid two calculations, it is best to apply to use the flat-rate scheme at the beginning of an annual accounting period. If the business does not wish to wait to the end of its annual accounting year, it can change its existing annual accounting year end to an earlier date and start both schemes together. This will result in amendments to the annual accounting periods and payments to accommodate these changes.

If a business becomes ineligible for one scheme, it will normally continue in the other scheme unless it requests removal. If a business leaves the flat-rate scheme in the middle of an accounting period, it must do the two calculations as described above when completing its next VAT return.

(VAT Notice 732, paras 10.1, 10.2, 10.7, 10.8, 10.10, 10.11).

63.14 Leaving the scheme

Provided the business is still authorised to use the scheme, it must continue to use it in the next annual accounting year. [*SI 1995/2518, Reg 53*(*1*); *SI 1996/542*].

A business ceases to be authorised to use the annual accounting scheme in the following circumstances.

(*a*) **Turnover exceeding the limit.**

- After the end of any transitional accounting period (see 63.10 above) if the value of taxable supplies in that period has exceeded £825,000 (£750,000 before 1 April 2004).
- After the end of any annual accounting year if the value of taxable supplies in that year has exceeded £825,000 (£750,000 before 1 April 2004).

(*b*) **Expulsion by HMRC**. HMRC *may* terminate an authorisation to use the scheme from any date where

- a false statement has been made by or on behalf of the business in relation to the application to use the scheme;
- a business fails to make any VAT return under the scheme by the due date;
- a business fails to make any payment due under the scheme;
- a business notifies HMRC that it has reason to believe that the value of taxable supplies in the current transitional accounting period (see 63.10 above) or annual accounting year will exceed £825,000 (£750,000 before 1 April 2004) (which it must do in writing within 30 days);
- there is reason to believe that the value of taxable supplies made by a business using the scheme will exceed £825,000 (£750,000 before 1 April 2004) in the current transitional accounting period (see 63.10 above) or annual accounting year;
- it is necessary to do so for the protection of the revenue; or
- a business using the scheme has not paid over to HMRC all VAT shown as due on any return made before authorisation and all VAT shown as due on any assessment made (including interest and penalties). See, however, 63.10 above for HMRC policy where there is a small amount of VAT outstanding at the time of application to join the scheme.

HMRC's policy is to remove a business from the scheme

- if it fails to make payments of interim amounts due and the debt created is greater than 20% of the expected annual liability;
- where it has been issued four reminder letters in relation to the last six interim payments (in which case it will be removed from the scheme at the year end); and
- where it fails to submit two consecutive annual VAT returns and make the balancing payments by the due date.

(Internal Guidance V1–23, Chapter 1 para 4.3).

(*c*) **Cessation of business**. Where a business authorised to use the scheme

- becomes insolvent and ceases to trade (other than for the purposes of disposing of stocks and assets),
- ceases business or ceases to be registered, or
- if a person, dies or becomes bankrupt or incapacitated

authorisation to use the scheme terminates on the date on which any such event occurs.

(*d*) **Voluntary withdrawal**. A business authorised to use the scheme may cease to operate it of its own volition at any time. Authorisation to use the scheme terminates from the date HMRC are notified in writing.

[*SI 1995/2518, Regs 53(2), 54, 55(1); SI 1996/542; SI 2001/677; SI 2003/1069, Reg 4; SI 2004/767, Reg 5*].

Consequences of leaving the scheme. Where a business leaves the annual accounting scheme, a final return under the scheme must be made and any outstanding VAT paid within two months of the date on which its authorisation is terminated. From the day following termination, the business must account for and pay VAT in the normal way and cannot rejoin the scheme for 12 months.
[*SI 1995/2518, Reg 55(2); SI 1996/542*].

63.15 FLAT-RATE SCHEME FOR SMALL BUSINESSES

HMRC may make regulations allowing eligible businesses to calculate their VAT payment as a percentage of their total turnover. [*VATA 1994, s 26B; FA 2002, s 23*]. The conditions are as laid down in *Regulations* and as described in VAT Notice 733 *which in certain circumstances has the force of law*. HMRC may vary the terms of any method prescribed by them by publishing a fresh Notice or a Notice that amends an existing Notice. [*SI 1995/2518, Reg 55T; SI 2002/1142*].

A flat-rate scheme is open to small businesses with VAT-exclusive annual taxable turnover of up to £150,000 and VAT-exclusive annual total turnover (including the value of exempt and non-taxable income) of up to £187,500.

The aim of the scheme is to simplify the way small businesses account for VAT. Under normal VAT rules, a business must identify VAT on each sale it makes, record the value and VAT separately, and pay the VAT to HMRC as output tax. Similarly, it must identify the VAT included in its purchases, record the value and the VAT separately, and claim the VAT back from HMRC as input tax. Under the flat-rate scheme, there is no need to identify and record the VAT on sales and purchases to calculate the VAT due to HMRC. A business simply records all its business supplies, including exempt supplies, and applies a flat-rate percentage to the VAT-inclusive total in each VAT period. The result is the VAT owed to HMRC. The flat-rate percentage depends upon the trade sector into which the business falls for the purpose of the scheme.

Full details of the scheme are given in 63.16 to 63.24 below.

Deciding whether to use the scheme. The flat-rate scheme is an attempt to simplify VAT for small and growing businesses. All businesses using the scheme benefit from simpler bookkeeping but any individual business may pay more or less VAT than it would under the normal VAT rules. This is because one flat rate applies to all businesses in a particular sector. To help a business decide whether the scheme is appropriate, an online ready reckoner is available at

www.hmrc.gov.uk

If the scheme is used together with the annual accounting scheme (see 63.9 above) it can make a significant difference to the cost of complying with VAT regulations.

De Voil Indirect Tax Service. See V2.199B.

63.16 **How the scheme works**

Output tax. For any VAT period, the output tax due from a flat-rate trader in respect of his 'relevant supplies' (see below) is deemed to be the appropriate 'flat-rate percentage' of his 'relevant turnover' for that period. [*SI 1995/2518, Reg 55D; SI 2002/1142; SI 2003/1069, Reg 5; SI 2003/3220, Reg 18*].

See 63.19 below for the '*flat-rate percentage*' and 63.20 below for calculating '*relevant turnover*'.

Example

A motor repair business has a VAT-inclusive turnover of £20,000 for a VAT period. Its appropriate flat-rate percentage is 7.5% and VAT due for the period is

£20,000 × 7.5% = £1,500

Input tax. A flat-rate trader does not normally make a separate claim for input tax or for VAT on imports or acquisitions as the flat-rate percentage includes an allowance for input tax. There are, however, two exceptions to this.

(*a*) *Capital expenditure over £2,000.* For any VAT period, a flat-rate trader is entitled to credit for input tax in respect of any 'relevant purchase' (see below) of goods of a capital nature with a value, including VAT, of £2,000 or more except goods which he acquired

- for the purpose of resale or incorporation into goods supplied by him,
- for consumption by him within one year, or
- to generate income by being leased, let or hired.

In such cases, the whole of the input tax on the goods concerned is regarded as used, or to be used, by the flat-rate trader exclusively in making taxable supplies.

Nothing in the above gives an entitlement to credit for input tax where it would not otherwise be allowed by any order made under *VATA 1994, s 25(7)* (eg on the purchase of a motor car).

[*SI 1995/2518, Regs 55A, 55E; SI 2002/1142*].

Where the above applies, any input tax should be claimed on the VAT return in the normal way but where such input tax is claimed, the flat-rate trader must also account for VAT on any subsequent disposal of the asset in the normal way, ie by adding any VAT due on the disposal to the VAT calculated under the flat-rate scheme. See (4) below (VAT Notice 733, para 3.8).

Purchases of capital items under £2,000 are treated like any other purchase under the flat-rate scheme and no separate claim for input tax can be made. See 63.22 below.

(*b*) *Stocks and assets on hand at registration.* A business can recover VAT incurred before registration subject to certain conditions. See 35.10 INPUT TAX. These provisions also apply where the first VAT period for which a business is authorised to account for and pay VAT in accordance with the flat-rate scheme is the first VAT period for which it is registered (or required to be registered).

Where the above applies, the whole of the input tax on the goods or services concerned is regarded as used, or to be used, by the taxable person exclusively in making taxable supplies.

[*SI 1995/2518, Reg 55F; SI 2002/1142*].

The claim should be made on the first VAT return following registration. Where such a claim is made, any subsequent disposal of capital assets has to be accounted for in the normal way, ie by adding any VAT due on the disposal to the VAT calculated under the flat-rate scheme. See (4) below. (VAT Notice 733, para 3.7).

Relevant supplies and purchases. The following provisions apply in determining whether a purchase or supply is a relevant purchase or supply for the purposes of the flat-rate scheme.

(1) Subject to (3) and (5) below, any supply of goods or services to, or acquisition of importation of goods by, a flat-rate trader is a relevant purchase of his.

(2) Subject to (3)–(5) below, any supply made by a person when he is not a flat-rate trader is not a relevant supply of his.

(3) Subject to (4) below, where

- a supply is made to, or made by, a person at a time when he is not a flat-rate trader, and
- the operative date for VAT accounting purposes is, by virtue of the cash accounting scheme, a date when he is a flat-rate trader,

that supply is a relevant supply or a relevant purchase, as the case may be, if otherwise it would not be by virtue of (2) above.

(4) Where a person

- is entitled to any credit for input tax in respect of the supply to, or acquisition or importation by, him of capital expenditure goods,
- claims any such credit, and
- makes a supply of those capital expenditure goods,

that supply is not a relevant supply, if otherwise it would be.

(5) Where by virtue of any provision of, or made under, *VATA 1994* a supply is *treated as made* by a flat-rate trader, whether to himself or otherwise, that supply is neither a relevant supply nor a relevant purchase of his.

[*SI 1995/2518, Reg 55C; SI 2002/1142*].

Issuing VAT invoices. The normal rules apply to issuing VAT invoices, ie a flat-rate trader must issue a VAT invoice to any customer who is registered for VAT. The flat-rate scheme affects the way VAT is calculated but does not change the VAT rate applicable to supplies. This means that when a flat-rate trader issue a VAT invoice, he must charge VAT at the normal rate for the supply (not the flat-rate percentage). (VAT Notice 733, para 3.9).

Using the scheme in conjunction with other schemes. The flat-rate scheme can be used in conjunction with the annual accounting scheme. The use of both schemes can help reduce the cost of complying with VAT.

The flat-rate scheme *cannot* be used in conjunction with the following schemes.

- *Cash accounting*. Although the cash accounting scheme and the flat-rate scheme cannot be used together, the flat-rate scheme has its own cash basis which is very similar to the cash accounting scheme. See 63.20 below.

  Where a business moves from the normal cash accounting scheme to the cash-based method of calculating flat-rate income, there is no need to make the adjustment normally required on ceasing to use cash accounting. See 63.20 below.

- *Retail schemes*. Although a retail scheme and the flat-rate scheme cannot be used together, the flat-rate scheme has its own retail basis which is very similar to the ordinary retail schemes. See 63.20 below.

  Where a business wishes to leave a retail scheme to join the flat-rate scheme, it should follow the rules about ceasing to use that retail scheme. See 60 RETAIL SCHEMES under the appropriate scheme.

- *Margin scheme for second-hand goods*. Where a business sells a significant proportion of second-hand goods using a margin scheme or the auctioneers' scheme, the flat-rate scheme would be of limited value to the business. This is because the flat-rate scheme calculates VAT on the total received from sales rather than on the margin.

(VAT Notice 733, para 3.10).

63.17 Eligibility and conditions

HMRC may authorise a business to account for and pay VAT under the flat-rate scheme with effect from the beginning of its next VAT period after the date on which it notifies HMRC of its wish to use the scheme (or such earlier or later date as may be agreed between them). In practice, although starting to use the scheme from the beginning of a VAT period is simplest, HMRC will agree to any start date other than 29 February. (Internal Guidance V1–23, Chapter 6 para 3.2). The date with effect from which the business is so authorised is its '*start date*'.

HMRC may refuse to so authorise a business if they consider it is necessary for the protection of the revenue.

[*SI 1995/2518, Reg 55B(1)–(3); SI 2002/1142; SI 2003/3220, Reg 17*].

A business is eligible to account for VAT in accordance with the flat-rate scheme at any time (including with effect from its date of registration) if it satisfies the following conditions.

(*a*) There are reasonable grounds for believing that

  (i) the value of its taxable supplies (excluding VAT) in the period of one year then beginning will not exceed £150,000 (£100,000 before 10 April 2003), and

  (ii) the total value of its income (excluding VAT) in the period of one year then beginning will not exceed £187,500 (£125,000 before 10 April 2003).

  In determining the value of taxable supplies or income for these purposes

  - any supply of goods or services that are capital assets of the business in the course or furtherance of which they are supplied, and
  - any supply of services treated as made by the recipient by virtue of *VATA 1994, s 8* (reverse charge on supplies from abroad)

are disregarded.

Included in (i) above is the VAT-exclusive value of standard rate, zero rate and reduced rate supplies; the VAT-exclusive turnover from the sale of second-hand goods sold outside the margin scheme; and any sales of gold covered by the special scheme in 30.9 GOLD AND PRECIOUS METALS.

Included in (ii) above, in addition to taxable supplies within (i) above, is the value of any exempt supplies and any other income received or receivable by the business. This includes any 'non-business' income (eg income arising from charitable or educational activities). (Note that non-business income is included in the joining test because the scheme is for small businesses. Once eligible, non-business income is *not* included in the VAT-inclusive turnover to which the flat-rate applies.)

Future turnover can be forecast in any reasonable way. HMRC will not penalise a business for being wrong provided it can demonstrate that there were reasonable grounds for its forecast. It is sensible, therefore, to keep a record of how the calculation was made. If HMRC judge that the estimate of turnover had no reasonable basis, a business may be excluded from the scheme immediately or even from the date its ineligible use began.

(VAT Notice 733, paras 4.2–4.5).

(*b*) The business

- is not a tour operator,
- is not required to carry out adjustments in relation to a capital item under the CAPITAL GOODS SCHEME (10), and
- does not intend to opt to account for the VAT chargeable on a supply made by it under a margin scheme (see 61 SECOND-HAND GOODS).

(*c*) The business has not, in the period of one year preceding that time

- been convicted of any offence in connection with VAT,
- made any payment to compound proceedings in respect of VAT under *CEMA 1979, s 152*,
- been assessed to a penalty for VAT evasion under *VATA 1994, s 60* (see 52.9 PENALTIES), or
- ceased to operate the flat-rate scheme.

(*d*) The business is not and, unless HMRC are satisfied that use of the flat-rate scheme poses no risk to the revenue, has not been within the past 24 months

- eligible to be registered for VAT in the name of a group under *VATA 1994, s 43A* (see 31.2 GROUPS OF COMPANIES),
- registered for VAT in the name of a division under *VATA 1994, s 46(1)* (see 59.37 REGISTRATION), or
- 'associated with' another person.

Note that it is eligibility to be in a VAT group which is the key test, not whether the business is actually in one.

A person is '*associated with*' another person at any time if that other person makes supplies in the course or furtherance of a business carried on by him, and

- the business of one is under the dominant influence of the other, or
- the persons are closely bound to one another by financial, economic and organisational links.

HMRC regard this as a test of commercial reality rather than of legal form. A business is not associated with its customers just because it supplies them with the goods they request in the form they request them. A close connection with another business is not necessarily the same as being associated. For example, where a husband is an architect and his wife is an antiques dealer, and he rents the upper floor of her shop at a market rent to use as his office, they will not be associated. (VAT Notice 733, paras 13.5, 13.7).

(*e*) It does not usually receive repayments from HMRC. This is because the flat-rate scheme calculates VAT due to HMRC and is unsuitable where a business regularly receives payments from them. (VAT Notice 733, para 4.8)

[*SI 1995/2518, Reg 55L; SI 2002/1142; SI 2003/1069, Reg 7*].

63.18 Application to use the scheme

Application to use the flat-rate scheme can be made in any of the following ways.

- **By post**. Application should be made on Form VAT 600 (FRS). HMRC do not keep copies but the form can either be removed from the paper version of VAT Notice 733 or printed from the notice on the HMRC website at:

  www.hmrc.gov.uk.

  Guidance on completing the form is given in VAT Notice 733, para 5.2.

  When completed, the form should be sent to the National Registration Service for the region where the business operates. The correct office depends on the postcode. See 59.38 REGISTRATION. If registering for VAT at the same time, the form can be enclosed with Form VAT 1 (Application for Registration).

- **By e-mail**. The scheme application form can be downloaded from

  www.hmrc.gov.uk/business/services/vat-flat-rate.htm

  It should be completed on the computer and sent to the e-mail address for flat-rate scheme applications, ie

  frsapplications@hmrc.gov.uk

  Any queries or correspondence should be sent to the National Advice Service not this e-mail address.

- **By phone**. The National Advice Service can take application details over the phone on 0845 010 9000.

Application can be made at the time of registration for VAT or any later time. If application is made at the time of registration, a business can begin to use the scheme from the date of registration. (See 63.19 below for a 1% reduction in flat-rate % for all businesses in the first year of VAT registration.) If a business is already registered when it applies, it is best to apply as early in a VAT period as possible as authorisation to use the flat-rate scheme normally takes effect from the beginning of the VAT period after HMRC have processed the application.

HMRC will notify the business either that its application has been accepted and the date from which it can operate the flat-rate scheme, or the reason why it has not allowed it.

(VAT Notice 733, paras 5.1, 5.3, 5.5, 5.6; VAT Information Sheet 17/03, para 5.1).

See 63.13 above for joint application to join the flat-rate scheme and the annual accounting scheme.

63.19 Flat-rate percentage

Provisions applying with effect from 1 January 2004

(1) *Appropriate flat-rate percentage*

The appropriate percentage to be applied by a flat-rate trader for any VAT period (or part period) is determined in accordance with the following rules and, where appropriate, (2) and (3) below.

(*a*) For any VAT period beginning with a 'relevant date', the appropriate percentage is that specified in the Table below for the category of business that he is expected, at the relevant date, on reasonable grounds, to carry on in that period.

(*b*) For any VAT period current at his 'start date' but not beginning with his start date, the appropriate percentage is that specified in the Table below for the category of business that he is expected, at his start date, on reasonable grounds, to carry on in the remainder of the period.

(*c*) For any VAT period not falling within (*a*) or (*b*) above, the appropriate percentage is that applicable to his relevant turnover at the end of the previous VAT period.

'*Relevant date*' in relation to a flat-rate trader, means any of the following.

- His '*start date*' (ie the date from which he is authorised to use the scheme).
- The first day of the VAT period current at any anniversary of his start date.
- Any day on which he first carries on a new business activity.
- Any day on which he no longer carries on an existing business activity.
- Any day with effect from which the Table below is amended in relation to him.
- Where (2) below applies
  - (i) the day that his 'newly registered period' (see (2) below) begins, and
  - (ii) the first anniversary of his EDR (see (2) below).

But where a relevant date (other than the start date) occurs on a day other than the first day of a VAT period, the following rules apply for the remainder of that VAT period.

(A) For the 'remaining portion', the appropriate percentage is that specified in the Table below for the category of business that he is expected, at the relevant date, on reasonable grounds, to carry on in that period.

'*Remaining portion*' means that part of the VAT period in which the relevant date occurs starting with the relevant date, and ending on the last day of that prescribed accounting period.

The appropriate percentage is applied to relevant turnover in the remaining portion described.

(B) If the rules set out in (A) above apply and then another relevant date occurs in the same VAT period, then the existing remaining portion ends on the day before the latest relevant date, another remaining portion begins on the latest relevant date, and the rules in (A) above are applied again in respect of the latest remaining portion.

[*SI 1995/2518, Regs 55A, 55H; SI 2003/3220, Regs 18, 19*].

(2) *Reduced appropriate percentage for newly-registered period*

Special provisions apply where the date from which a flat-rate trader is authorised to use the scheme (his '*start date*') falls within one year of the date with effect from which he is registered for VAT (his '*EDR*').

In such a case, at any relevant date (see (1) above) on or after 1 January 2004 falling within his 'newly registered period', the Table below is to be read as if each percentage were reduced by 1% unless

- HMRC receive notification of, or otherwise become fully aware of, his liability to be registered more than one year after his EDR; or
- he ceases to be authorised to use the scheme, or the first anniversary of his EDR falls, before 1 January 2004.

A flat-rate trader's '*newly registered period*' is the period beginning with the later of

- his start date, and
- the day HMRC received notification of, or otherwise became fully aware of, his liability to be registered for VAT

and ending on the day before the first anniversary of his EDR.

The effect of this is that if a business notifies its VAT liability on time and asks to use the scheme from the date of registration, the discounted rates last for one year. But if it registers for VAT late or does not immediately join the scheme, the period will be shortened.

[*SI 1995/2518, Regs 55A, 55JB; SI 2003/3220, Regs 18, 19*].

(3) *More than one category of business*

Where, at a relevant date (see (1) above), a flat-rate trader was expected, on reasonable grounds, to carry on business in more than one category of business in the period concerned, he is regarded as being expected to carry on that category of business which is expected to be his main business activity in that period, determined by reference to turnover expected to be generated by each business activity concerned.

[*SI 1995/2518, Regs 55A, 55K; SI 2003/3220, Regs 18, 19*].

(4) *Changes in the balance between two parts of a business*

If the balance between activities changes but the business still carries on the same activities, the flat-rate trader has to continue using the percentage that was appropriate at the beginning of the year until the anniversary of joining the scheme. At the start of the VAT period which includes that anniversary, the flat-rate trader should review the balance between the parts of the business and, if this has changed (or is expected to change in the year ahead), change categories to that for the larger portion of the business (or expected business). If this also involves a change in the appropriate percentage, the new percentage should be applied from the start of the VAT period in which the anniversary date falls (not just from the anniversary to the end of the period). (VAT Notice 733, para 6.6).

(5) *Notification of changes to HMRC*

- Where at the first day of the VAT period current at any anniversary of his start date (see (1) above) the appropriate percentage to be applied by a flat-rate trader under (1)(*a*) above for the VAT period just beginning differs from that applicable to his relevant turnover at the end of the previous VAT period, he must notify HMRC of that fact within 30 days of the first day of the VAT period current at the anniversary of his start date.
- Where a flat-rate trader begins to carry on a new business activity or ceases to carry on an existing business activity, he must notify HMRC of that fact, the date of change, and the appropriate percentage to be applied to the period immediately before that relevant date and immediately after it. Notification must be within 30 days of the date of change.

[*SI 1995/2518, Reg 55N*(*1*)(*2*)(*4*)*; SI 2003/3220*].

(6) *Choice of category of business*

It is for the business to choose its appropriate category of business from the table below. In choosing the category, the words should be given their ordinary meanings. The National Advice Service can help where there is doubt. See also Internal Guidance V1–23, Chapter 6 Section 14 Table A(1) (List of trade sectors and the trades they contain) and Table A(2) (List of trades and trade sector that HMRC have put them in) for how HMRC have interpreted the various categories.

Once HMRC have approved a business to join the scheme, they will not change the category of business chosen in retrospect provided the choice was reasonable and records have been kept why it was chosen. (VAT Notice 733, paras 6.1, 6.2).

Category of business	*Appropriate % before 1.1.04*	*Appropriate % 1.1.04 onwards*
Accountancy or book-keeping	13.5	13
Advertising	11	9.5
Agricultural services	9	7.5
Animal husbandry	11	N/A
Any other activity not listed elsewhere	11	10
Architects	13.5	12.5

Category of business	*Appropriate % before 1.1.04*	*Appropriate % 1.1.04 onwards*
Boarding or care of animals	N/A	10.5
Business services that are not listed elsewhere	12.5	11
Catering services, including restaurants and takeaways	13	12
Civil and structural engineers and surveyors	N/A	12.5
Computer and IT consultancy or data processing	14.5	13
Computer repair services	13.5	11
Dealing in waste or scrap	11	9.5
Entertainment (excluding film, radio, television or video production, see below) or journalism	12	11
Estate agency or property management services	11.5	11
Farming or agriculture that is not listed elsewhere	6.5	6
Film, radio, television or video production	N/A	10.5
Financial services	12	11.5
Forestry or fishing	10	9
General building or construction services (note 1)	9	8.5
Hairdressing or other beauty treatment services	13	12
Hiring or renting goods	9.5	8.5
Hotel or accommodation	10.5	9.5
Investigation or security	11	10
Labour-only building or construction services (note 1)	14.5	13.5
Laundry or dry-cleaning services	12	11
Lawyers or legal services	13.5	13
Library, archive, museum or other cultural activities	8.5	7.5
Management consultancy	13.5	12.5
Manufacturing fabricated metal products	11	10
Manufacturing food	8.5	7.5
Manufacturing that is not listed elsewhere	10	8.5
Manufacturing yarn, textiles or clothing	9.5	8.5
Membership organisations	7	5.5
Mining or quarrying	10	9
Packaging	9	8.5
Photography	10	9.5

Category of business	*Appropriate % before 1.1.04*	*Appropriate % 1.1.04 onwards*
Post offices (note 3) (from 1 April 2004)	N/A	2
Postal and courier services (note 2) (before 1 April 2004)	6	N/A
Printing	8.5	7.5
Publishing	10	9.5
Pubs	6	5.5
Real estate activities not listed elsewhere	13	12
Repairing personal or household goods	10	8.5
Repairing vehicles	8.5	7.5
Retailing food, confectionery, tobacco, newspapers or children's clothing	5	2
Retailing pharmaceuticals, medical goods, cosmetics or toiletries	8	7
Retailing that is not listed elsewhere	7	6
Retailing vehicles or fuel	8	7
Secretarial services	11.5	11
Social work	9	8.5
Sport or recreation	8	7
Transport or storage, including courier, freight, removals and taxis (note 2)	10	9
Travel agency	10	9
Veterinary medicine	11	9.5
Wholesaling agricultural products	7	6
Wholesaling food	7	5.5
Wholesaling that is not listed elsewhere	8	7

Notes

1 'Labour-only building or construction services' means building or construction services where the value of materials supplied is less than 10% of relevant turnover from such services; any other building or construction services are 'general building or construction services'.

2 With effect from 1 April 2004, couriers must apply the 9% rate for transport. However, if a business notified HMRC that it wished to join the flat-rate scheme before 3 March 2004 and, on 1 April 2004, its main business activity in the period 1 April 2004 to 30 June 2004 was expected, on reasonable grounds, to be that of a courier, the business could use a 5.5% rate during that period (or until such date in that period that its main business activity ceased to be that of a courier).

3 With effect from 1 April 2004, a separate rate of 2% applies to post offices. Previously they fell within the category for postal and courier services.

[*SI 1995/2518, Reg 55K; SI 2003/3220, Reg 20; SI 2004/767, Regs 2, 6*].

Provisions applying before 1 January 2004

(1) *Appropriate flat-rate percentage*

The appropriate flat-rate percentage to be applied by a flat-rate trader for any VAT period (or part period) was determined in accordance with (*a*)–(*c*) below and, where appropriate (2)–(4) below.

(*a*) For the VAT period current at his '*start date*' (ie the date from which he was authorised to use the scheme), the appropriate percentage was that specified in the Table above for the category of business that he was expected, at his start date, on reasonable grounds, to carry on in that period or, if his start date was not the first day of the VAT period, in the remainder of the period.

(*b*) For any subsequent VAT period current at an anniversary of his start date, the appropriate percentage was that specified in the Table above for the category of business that he was expected, on the first day of that VAT period, on reasonable grounds, to carry on in the period.

(*c*) For any other VAT period, if any, the appropriate percentage was the same as that applicable for the VAT period that was current at his start date or the most recent anniversary of his start date, whichever was the later.

[*SI 1995/2518, Reg 55H* (*as amended*) *before substitution by SI 2003/3220*].

(2) *More than one category of business*

Where, at a 'relevant date', a flat-rate trader was expected, on reasonable grounds, to carry on business in more than one category of business in the period concerned, he was regarded as being expected to carry on that category of business which was expected to be his main business activity in that period, determined by reference to turnover expected to be generated by each business activity concerned.

The '*relevant dates*' were

- where (1)(*a*) above applied, his start date;
- where (1)(*b*) above applied, the first day of a VAT period current at an anniversary of his start date;
- where there was a change in business activity (see (3) below), the change date; and
- where there was a change in the Table (see (4) below), the amendment date.

[*SI 1995/2518, Reg 55K before amendment by SI 2003/3220*].

(3) *Change in business activities during a VAT period*

Where a flat-rate trader

- began to carry on a new business activity, or
- ceased to carry on an existing business activity,

the first day on which he did so was known as '*the change date*'.

For that part of the VAT period from the date of change until the end of the period (the '*unelapsed portion*'), the appropriate percentage was that specified in the Table above for the category of business that the flat-rate trader was expected, at the change date, on reasonable grounds, to carry on in that period.

For any VAT period that fell between the VAT period current at the change date and the VAT period current at the next anniversary of his '*start date*' (ie the date at which he was authorised to use the scheme), the appropriate percentage was that applicable for the unelapsed portion.

The appropriate percentages as so calculated were applied to the relevant turnover in the periods described.

[*SI 1995/2518, Reg 55J before substitution by SI 2003/3220*].

(4) *Change in the Table*

Where the Table above was amended and the amendment date was not, in relation to a flat-rate trader

- the first day of a VAT period current at an anniversary of his start date (in which case (1)(*b*) above applied); or
- a 'change date' (in which case the rules under (3) above applied)

then for that part of the VAT period from the amendment date until the end of the period (the '*remaining portion*'), the appropriate percentage was that specified in the Table above for the category of business that the flat-rate trader was expected, at the amendment date, on reasonable grounds, to carry on in that period.

For any VAT period that fell between the VAT period current at the amendment date and the VAT period current at the next anniversary of his 'start date' (ie the date at which he was authorised to use the scheme), the appropriate percentage was that applicable for the remaining portion.

The appropriate percentages as so calculated were applied to the relevant turnover in the periods described.

[*SI 1995/2518, Reg 55JA before substitution by SI 2003/3220*].

(5) *Notification of changes to HMRC*

Where

- for any VAT period the appropriate percentage to be applied by a flat-rate trader under (1)(*b*) above differed from that applicable for the previous VAT period, he had to notify HMRC in writing of that fact within 30 days of the first day of the VAT period current at the anniversary of his start date (see (1)(*a*) above); and
- there was a change in business activities during a VAT period, a flat-rate trader had, within 30 days of the change date, to notify HMRC in writing of that fact, the change date, and the appropriate percentages to be applied in each respective part of the VAT period current at the change date.

[*SI 1995/2518, Reg 55N(1)(2)(4) before substitution by SI 2003/3220*].

63.20 **Calculating turnover**

It is important to determine correctly the turnover to which the flat-rate percentage is to be applied. If items which are not part of the turnover are included, too much VAT will be paid and if items are omitted, too little VAT will be paid and the business could have to pay a penalty and interest.

Flat-rate turnover includes all the supplies made by the business, including

- the *VAT-inclusive* sales and takings for standard-rated, zero-rated and reduced rate supplies;
- the value of exempt supplies;
- supplies of capital assets, unless they are supplies on which VAT has to be calculated outside the flat-rate scheme in accordance see 63.16 above; and
- the value of despatches to other EC countries.

Income which can be excluded includes

- private income (eg dividends);
- proceeds from the sale of goods owned but which have not been used in the business;
- any sales of gold for which the special accounting scheme applies (see 30.9 GOLD AND PRECIOUS METALS);
- non-business income and any supplies outside the scope of VAT; and
- sales of capital assets which must be accounted for outside the scheme (see 63.16 above).

(VAT Notice 733, paras 7.2, 7.3).

Methods of calculating turnover. There are three ways of calculating turnover. Whichever method is used, it should normally be used for at least 12 months.

(1) **The basic turnover method**

Under this method, the flat-rate percentage is applied to the VAT-inclusive total of supplies with a time of supply (tax point) in the VAT period in question and is principally for those who deal mainly with other VAT-registered businesses. This method follows the normal rules about the time of supply for VAT purposes. See 64.32 to 64.57 SUPPLY. Where the business usually accounts for VAT on an invoice basis, this can be the simplest to operate. (VAT Notice 733, para 9.1).

(2) **The cash-based turnover method**

Under this method, the business applies the flat-rate percentage to the supplies for which it has been paid in the accounting period in question. This method can be helpful if the business gives extended credit or frequently incurs bad debts.

The time of supply is not changed by this method. This is not important in normal circumstances, but in the event of a change in VAT rate or liability, or in case of insolvency, the basic method tax point will determine the treatment of the supplies.

If the cash accounting system was being used immediately before the flat-rate scheme, the business should carry on as before. There is no need to calculate and pay the VAT still owed when changing schemes. It includes any payments received whilst using the flat-rate scheme in the total to which it applies the flat-rate percentage.

Time of payment under the cash basis. For the purpose of the cash basis, payment by

- *cash* (coins or notes) is received on the date the money is received;
- *cheque* is received on the date the cheque is received or, if later, the date on the cheque. If the cheque is not honoured, no VAT is due and an adjustment can be made if VAT has already been accounted for;
- *credit or debit card* is received on the date the sales voucher is made out (*not* the date when payment is received from the card company); and
- *giro, standing orders and direct debits* are received on the day the bank account is credited.

(VAT Notice 733, paras 10.1–10.3).

Payments received net of deductions. Where a net payment is received, the full value must be included before such deductions (and including VAT) in the scheme turnover. This will usually be the value shown on the sales invoice. Examples of payments that may be received net of deductions are

- payments where commission has been deducted by the customer;
- payments where commission or payment for expenses has been deducted by a factor or agent collecting money on behalf of the business;
- payments where commission or payment for expenses has been deducted by an auctioneer selling goods on behalf of the business; or
- payments made by an employer/contractor who has deducted income tax.

(VAT Notice 733, para 10.4 which has the force of law).

Payments in kind (eg barter and part exchange). Where a business is paid fully or partly in kind, it must include the value, including VAT, in its flat-rate turnover each time it makes or receives a 'payment'. Such a payment is received on the date the business receives the goods or services agreed in lieu of money. It must account for VAT on the full value of the supply, ie the price, including VAT, which a customer would have to pay for the supply if they had paid for it with money only.

(VAT Notice 733, para 10.5 which has the force of law).

Ceasing to use the cash-based method. If at any time a business ceases to use the cash-based accounting method, it must account for VAT on all the supplies made while it was using the method and for which payment has not been received. The value of the supplies has to be included in the scheme turnover in the return for the VAT period in which the business ceases to use the cash-based method. The only exception to this is if it ceases to use the flat-rate scheme but immediately starts to use the cash accounting scheme. It may be possible to balance this adjustment with a claim for relief for stocks on hand (see 63.23 below), or a claim in respect of bad debts (see 63.22 below).

(VAT Notice 733, para 10.6 which has the force of law).

(3) **The retailer's turnover method**

This is essentially the same as a retail scheme and is best if the business is a retailer selling goods to the public. The method is based on 'daily takings'. To use the method, the business must record payments as they are received from customers and total the takings daily. At the end of a VAT period, the flat-rate percentage is applied to the flat-rate turnover for that period. Flat-rate turnover is the daily gross takings plus any other items of income the business receives from outside the retail environment (eg rent from a flat above the shop). At the end of the VAT period, the flat-rate percentage is applied to the total of the daily gross takings and the VAT-inclusive amount of any other income.

See 60.8 RETAIL SCHEMES for items to be included in daily takings, adjustments which can be made and the treatment of till shortages and excesses. These provisions also apply to the retailer's turnover method, as do the other adjustments to daily takings for special transactions listed in 60.9 RETAIL SCHEMES.

(VAT Notice 733, paras 7.1, 11.1–11.6 which have the force of law).

[*SI 1995/2518, Reg 55G; SI 2002/1142*].

63.21 **Accounts and records**

Invoices. VAT invoices must still be issued to VAT-registered customers, charging VAT using the normal rate for the supply (standard rate, reduced rate or zero rate) and *not* the flat-rate percentage. Customers treat these as normal VAT invoices. (VAT Notice 733, paras 7.6, 7.7).

VAT account. A VAT account must still be kept (even if the only VAT to be accounted for is that calculated under the flat-rate scheme). In some cases, however, a business may have VAT to account for outside the flat-rate scheme (eg purchases and disposals of capital assets) and these should be entered in the VAT account in the normal way in addition to the flat-rate VAT. (VAT Notice 733, para 7.5).

Records. A record of flat-rate calculations must be kept showing

- flat-rate turnover for the VAT period;
- flat-rate percentage(s) used; and
- the VAT calculated as due.

This record must be kept with the VAT account.

(VAT Notice 733, para 7.4 which has the force of law).

Completing VAT returns. Because a business using the flat-rate scheme is calculating net VAT without reference to output tax and input tax, the rules for completing the VAT return are different. If the value for any box is none, write none in the box. Do not leave any box blank.

Box 1	Include the VAT due under the flat-rate scheme. There may be other output tax to include in this box such as sales of capital assets on which the business has taken input tax separately while using the flat-rate scheme. See 63.16 above.
Box 2	Complete in the normal way for VAT payable on acquisitions from other EC countries.
Box 3	Insert sum of boxes 1 and 2 in the normal way.

Box 4	This will normally be nil. There may be a claim if (i) capital items exceeding £2,000 are bought (see 63.16 above); or (ii) VAT can be recovered on stocks and assets on hand at registration (see 63.16 above).
Box 5	Insert the difference between Box 3 and Box 4 in the normal way.
Box 6	Enter the value of turnover to which the flat-rate scheme percentage was applied. Also include the VAT-exclusive value of any supplies accounted for outside the flat-rate scheme (eg supplies of capital assets).
Box 7	This will normally be nil except where •capital items exceeding £2,000 (including VAT) are bought and input tax is claimed in Box 4; or •goods are acquired from other EC countries.
Boxes 8 and 9	Complete as normal.

(VAT Notice 733, para 7.8).

Revenue and Customs requirements. HMRC have issued a statement clarifying the accounting and record-keeping requirements of businesses using the flat-rate scheme for both direct and indirect tax purposes.

- *No additional analysis is required for VAT purposes to prepare accounts that are satisfactory for direct tax purposes.* The main bookkeeping advantage of the flat-rate scheme is that each purchase need no longer be analysed into gross, VAT and net figures when entered into the books of the business. This would be undone if at the end of each year these figures still had to be extracted for the preparation of annual accounts acceptable for income tax or corporation tax purposes. HMRC have confirmed that for businesses that are using the flat-rate scheme, it is expected that accounts will be prepared using gross receipts less the flat-rate VAT percentage for turnover and that expenses will include the irrecoverable input VAT. This is similar in form to accounts prepared by non-VAT-registered businesses who cannot recover VAT they are charged.

- *The standard of records for direct tax purposes is the same as that for VAT.* A key benefit of the flat-rate scheme is that it removes the need to check the deductibility of VAT on purchases and even their liability to VAT. For both VAT and direct taxes, there is still a requirement to keep a record of sales and purchases. But for businesses using the flat-rate scheme, that record does not have to analyse gross, VAT and net separately. HMRC is not prescriptive about the way in which records are kept. For the simplest business, the records may be as little as a file of invoices issued and received in date order with a summary of totals although most businesses will do more than the minimum. In any case, the requirements of HMRC are that the records (whether VAT-exclusive or VAT-inclusive) are orderly and easy to follow.

- *VAT 'profits'.* There is no requirement to keep a separate account of the 'VAT profit' or 'VAT loss' arising from use of the scheme. By its very nature, a scheme based on flat rates for trade sectors leads to almost all businesses who use it paying a different amount of VAT from that they would pay if they were still using the normal system. Those who pay less VAT will have increased profits that are, in principle, taxable. Those who pay more VAT will have increased costs that, in principle, will reduce direct tax on profits.

63.22 Treatment in special circumstances

(1) Acquisitions from, and sales to, other EC countries

Income received from sales of goods to other EC countries forms part of the VAT-inclusive income to which the flat-rate percentage is applied.

VAT must also be accounted for on acquisitions from other EC countries in Box 2 of the VAT return in the normal way. This acquisition VAT is treated in the same way as input tax charged by a UK supplier and is not normally recoverable when the flat-rate scheme is being used. See, however, (3) below for an exception to this rule.

(VAT Notice 733, paras 12.2, 12.4).

(2) Bad debt relief

BAD DEBT RELIEF (7) arises if a business accounts for and pays output tax on supplies for which it is subsequently not paid. The normal rules in that chapter apply to the flat-rate scheme except that, if the business is using the cash turnover method, it does not have to have accounted for and paid VAT on the supply for which it has not been paid as set out below.

Where

- a business has made a relevant supply (see 63.16 above) under the flat-rate scheme,
- it has used the cash turnover method (see 63.20 above) to determine the value of its relevant turnover for the VAT period in which the relevant supply was made,
- it has not accounted for and paid VAT on the supply,
- the whole or any part of the consideration for the supply has been written off in its accounts as a bad debt, and
- a period of six months (beginning with the date of the supply) has elapsed

the normal bad debt relief provisions apply and the amount of refund of VAT to which the business is entitled under those provisions is the VAT chargeable on the relevant supply less the 'flat-rate amount'.

The 'flat-rate amount' is

$A \times B$

where

A = the appropriate percentage applicable for the VAT period, or part thereof, in which the relevant supply was made, and

B = the value of the relevant supply together with the VAT chargeable thereon.

[*SI 1995/2518, Reg 55V; SI 2002/1142*].

> *Example*
>
> C Ltd makes a supply under the flat-rated scheme of £1,000 plus VAT of £175. It uses the cash turnover method to calculate its relevant turnover. The invoice is not paid and C writes off the amount as a bad debt in its accounts after six months. Its flat-rate percentage is 10%.
>
> | | £ |
> |---|---|
> | VAT on the unpaid supply | 175.00 |
> | VAT which would have been paid under the flat-rate scheme if the customer had paid (£1,175 × 10%) | 117.50 |
> | Special allowance under the flat-rate scheme. | £57.50 |
>
> £57.50 should be added to the VAT deductible portion of the VAT account and included in the next VAT return

(3) **Capital assets**

Purchases. Provided the assets are not covered by the capital goods scheme, capital assets can be treated like any other purchase under the flat-rate scheme. The input tax is included in the flat-rate calculation and no separate claim for input tax is made. See, however, 63.16 above where for the purchase of certain capital assets with a VAT-inclusive value of £2,000 or more.

Disposals. The treatment of sales of capital assets under the flat-rate scheme depends on how they were treated when acquired.

- If they were acquired under the scheme and no separate claim for input tax was made, then there are no special rules. VAT-inclusive income received from the disposal is included in the VAT-inclusive turnover to which the flat-rate percentage is applied.
- If the capital assets were either

  (i) bought before joining the flat-rate scheme, or

  (ii) input tax was claimed separately on purchase (see above)

  VAT must be accounted for on the sale in the normal way. The income will not form part of the turnover to which the flat-rate percentage is applied.

(VAT Notice 733, paras 12.13, 12.14).

(4) **Disbursements**

If a business

- pays amounts to third parties as the agent for its client, and
- debits its client with the precise amount paid out

it may be able to treat the payments as disbursements.

Where genuine disbursements are made, the money received in compensation for those disbursements is not part of the turnover to which the flat-rate percentage is applied.

(VAT Notice 733, para 12.15).

See 3.7 AGENTS for further details about disbursements.

(5) **Exempt supplies**

If a business is eligible for the flat-rate scheme, it is treated as fully taxable and will not be involved in partial exemption calculations. It must, however, include its exempt income in the turnover to which it applies the flat-rate percentage

(VAT Notice 733, para 12.6).

(6) **Reverse charges**

VATA 1994, s 8 (reverse charge on supplies from abroad) does not apply to any relevant supply or relevant purchase of a flat-rate trader. [*SI 1995/2518, Reg 55U; SI 2002/1142*]. No adjustment for the reverse charge on services received from abroad (see 39.4 INTERNATIONAL SERVICES) is therefore required. Similarly, any supplies of services treated as outside the scope of UK VAT need not be counted as part of the flat-rate turnover. (VAT Notice 733, paras 12.3, 12.5).

(7) **Second-hand goods**

A business can, if it wishes, include the total from the sale of second-hand goods in its flat-rate supplies to which it applies the percentage. This is the simplest option if a business makes occasional sales of second-hand goods.

It is not possible, however, to use the flat-rate scheme and the margin scheme at the same time and a business must decide which is of the greater benefit.

(VAT Notice 733, para 12.2).

63.23 Leaving the scheme

A business using the flat-rate scheme must continue to account for VAT under the scheme until its '*end date*', ie the date with effect from which it ceases to be authorised to use the scheme under the provisions below.

Voluntary withdrawal. A business can leave the scheme voluntarily at any time (although HMRC normally expect most businesses to leave at the end of a VAT period). The business ceases to be authorised to use the scheme from the date on which HMRC are notified in writing of its decision to cease using the scheme, or such earlier or later date as is agreed between them. HMRC will confirm the date of leaving the scheme in writing. (VAT Notice 733, para 8.1).

Ceasing to be eligible. A business ceases to be eligible to use the flat-rate scheme in the following circumstances and must withdraw from the date indicated.

(*a*) At any anniversary of its start date (ie the date from which it was authorised to use the scheme) if the total value of its income in the period of one year then *ending* is more than £225,000 (£150,000 before 10 April 2003) unless HMRC are satisfied that the total value of its income in the period of one year then *beginning* will not exceed £187,500 (£125,000 before 10 April 2003).

The above figures include the VAT-inclusive income of all taxable and exempt supplies, *excluding* supplies of capital assets. See 63.20 above for further details of what is included and excluded.

If a business exceeds the eligibility limits of the scheme because of a one-off increase in turnover, it may be able to remain in the scheme with the agreement of HMRC. If a business wishes to remain in the scheme in those circumstances, it must apply in writing to HMRC, demonstrating that

- its VAT-inclusive turnover in the coming year will not exceed the entry threshold for the scheme;
- the increase was the result of unexpected business activity which has not occurred before and is not expected to recur; and
- the increase arose from a genuine commercial activity.

However, even if these conditions are met, HMRC cannot allow the business to remain in the scheme if (*b*) below applies.

(VAT Notice 733, para 7.13).

Where a business ceases to be eligible under these provisions, it must withdraw from the scheme

(i) in the case of a business using the annual accounting scheme, from the end of the annual VAT period in which the relevant anniversary occurred or the end of the month following the month in which the anniversary occurred, whichever is the earlier, or

(ii) in all other cases, the end of the VAT period in which the relevant anniversary occurred.

Example

A business starts to use annual accounting and the flat-rate scheme on 1 May 2002. Its annual accounting year runs from 1 May to 30 April. It carries out the turnover test for the flat-rate scheme on 1 May 2003 and has exceeded the income limit.

The business must leave the flat-rate scheme on the earlier of the end of its current annual VAT accounting period (30 April 2004) and the end of the month following the month in which the anniversary falls (30 June 2003), ie 30 June 2003.

(*b*) There are reasonable grounds to believe that the total value of its income in the period of 30 days then beginning will exceed £225,000 (£150,000 before 10 April 2003). The business must withdraw from the scheme from the beginning of the period of 30 days in question.

The above figures include the VAT-inclusive income of all taxable and exempt supplies, *excluding* supplies of capital assets. See 63.20 above for further details of what is included and excluded.

(*c*) It becomes a tour operator and must account for VAT under the TOUR OPERATORS' MARGIN SCHEME (66), in which case it must withdraw from that date.

(*d*) It intends to acquire, construct or otherwise obtain a capital item within the CAPITAL GOODS SCHEME (10), in which case it must withdraw from that date.

(*e*) It opts to account for VAT on a supply on the profit margin under the second-hand goods scheme or the auctioneers' scheme (see 61 SECOND-HAND GOODS), in which case it must withdraw from the beginning of the VAT period for which it makes the election.

(*f*) It becomes

(i) eligible to be registered for VAT in the name of a group under *VATA 1994, s 43A* (see 31.2 GROUPS OF COMPANIES),

(ii) registered for VAT in the name of a division under *VATA 1994, s 46(1)* (see 59.37 REGISTRATION); or

(iii) 'associated with' another person.

In either case, the business must withdraw from the scheme from the date the event occurred.

A person is '*associated with*' another person at any time if that other person makes supplies in the course or furtherance of a business carried on by him, and

- the business of one is under the dominant influence of the other, or
- the persons are closely bound to one another by financial, economic and organisational links.

HMRC regard this as a test of commercial reality rather than of legal form (VAT Notice 733, para 13.5).

(*g*) Its authorisation to use the scheme is terminated by HMRC because

- they consider it necessary to do so for the protection of the revenue, or
- a false statement was made by, or on behalf of, the business in relation to its application for authorisation

in which case the business must withdraw from the scheme from the date of issue of a notice of termination by HMRC or such earlier or later date as may be directed in the notification.

Notifying HMRC. Where any of (*a*)–(*f*) above apply, the business must notify HMRC in writing of that fact within 30 days.

Consequences of leaving the scheme. A business leaving the scheme can rejoin at a later date but will not be eligible to rejoin for a period of 12 months after leaving the scheme. The transition from the scheme back to the normal VAT rules is usually simple although there are some circumstances where adjustments must be made to make the VAT returns accurate.

(1) *Ceasing to use the flat-rate scheme in the middle of a VAT period*. A business which leaves the flat-rate scheme in the middle of a VAT period must do two calculations when completing its next VAT return, one for the period when it was in the flat-rate scheme using the rules for calculating liability under that scheme and the other for the period after leaving the scheme using the normal VAT accounting rules. VAT liability for the return period is the sum of those two calculations. (VAT Notice 733, para 8.7).

(2) *Where the cash-based method is used under the flat-rate scheme* and the business does *not* move immediately to the cash accounting scheme, it must account for

VAT on all the supplies it made while using the flat-rate scheme for which payment has not been received. The value of the supplies should be included in the scheme turnover in the return for the period in which the business ceases to use the cash-based method. (VAT Notice 733, para 10.6).

(3) *Adjustments in respect of stock on hand at withdrawal from the flat-rate scheme.* Where

- a business remains registered for VAT after leaving the flat-rate scheme,
- at the date it ceases to be authorised to use the scheme, it has stock on hand in respect of which it is not entitled to credit for input tax, and
- the value of that stock on hand exceeds the value of its stock on hand in respect of which it was entitled to credit for input tax when it started to use the scheme

the business is entitled to credit for input tax in respect of its stock on hand calculated as follows.

Step 1	Establish the VAT-exclusive value of stock on hand and on which input tax had been recovered before joining the flat-rate scheme. (If previously using the cash accounting scheme, this will be based on stock for which the business had paid.) — say	£10,000
Step 2	Establish the VAT-exclusive value of stock on hand and on which the business will be unable to recover input tax after it cease to use the flat-rate scheme — say	£20,000
Step 3	Subtract the figure at Step 1 from the total at Step 2. (If the figure at Step 1 is larger than the figure at Step 2, no adjustment can be made.)	£10,000
Step 4	Multiply the result of Step 3 by the VAT rate = £10,000 × 17.5%	£1,750

Claim the VAT calculated at Step 4 in the VAT recoverable portion of the VAT account in the first return made after leaving the flat-rate scheme.

There is no need to do a formal stock take for the purpose of the calculation, but figures must be reasonable and a record should be kept of how stock was valued in case HMRC query the figures.

(VAT Notice 733, para 8.10 which has the force of law).

(4) *Self-supply of capital assets on withdrawal from the flat-rate scheme.* Where

- a business remains registered for VAT after leaving the flat-rate scheme,
- for any VAT period for which it used the scheme it was entitled to, and claimed, credit for input tax in respect of any capital expenditure goods, and
- it did not, whilst using the scheme, make a supply of those goods,

then, on the day after it ceases to use the scheme, those goods are treated as being both supplied to the business and supplied by the business in the course or furtherance of its business.

The value of the supply is calculated as for a supply for no consideration. See 69.22 VALUATION.

[*SI 1995/2518, Regs 55B(4), 55L(c), 55M, 55N(3)(4), 55P–55S; SI 2002/1142; SI 2003/1069, Reg 7*].

Transfer of a business as a going concern. Where a business using the flat-rate scheme transfers its business as a going concern,

- if its registration number is reallocated to the transferee, flat-rate scheme treatment will continue unless the transferee requests otherwise; and
- if the registration number of the transferor is not transferred, the transferor's flat-rate scheme treatment will end (unless there is still an eligible portion of the business) and the transferee will be on normal accounting unless or until it applies to use the flat-rate scheme.

(Internal Guidance V1–23, Chapter 6 para 4.6).

63.24 Appeals

If a business disagrees with a decision of HMRC

- refusing authorisation to use the scheme,
- withdrawing authorisation to use the scheme, or
- as to the appropriate flat-rate percentage(s) that applies to the business,

it may appeal to a VAT tribunal.

Where an appeal is brought against such a decision or, to the extent that it is based on such a decision, against an assessment, the tribunal must not allow the appeal unless it considers that HMRC could not reasonably have been satisfied that there were grounds for the decision.

[*VATA 1994, ss 83(fza), 84(4ZA); FA 2002, s 23(2)(3)*].

63.25 FLAT-RATE SCHEME FOR FARMERS

The flat-rate scheme is an alternative to VAT registration for farmers. Farmers already registered for VAT may either remain registered or de-register and join the flat-rate scheme (provided the value of their non-farming activities is not above the VAT registration threshold, see below). Farmers whose turnover is below the registration limit may also use the scheme if they would otherwise qualify for voluntary registration.

A farmer has to apply to HMRC to join the scheme. HMRC may then certify him for the purposes of these provisions where satisfied that

- he is carrying on a business involving one or more designated activities (see 63.26 below); and
- he has complied with the necessary conditions for admission to the scheme (see 63.27 below).

[*VATA 1994, s 54*].

Certification. If the application is accepted, the farmer is issued with a certificate (showing a unique reference number) which is proof that he qualifies for the scheme. If application is refused, an appeal may be made to a VAT tribunal.

Where a person is so certified, goods and services supplied as part of those designated activities are disregarded in determining whether he is, has become or has ceased to become liable or entitled to be registered for VAT under *VATA 1994, Sch 1.*

[*SI 1995/2518, Reg 203*].

Flat-rate addition instead of VAT. Farmers who are certified under the flat-rate scheme do not account for VAT, or submit returns, on sales of goods and services within the designated activities to other VAT-registered customers. This means that they cannot reclaim the related input tax.

To compensate for this, on sales of designated goods and services to VAT-registered persons, farmers *may* charge a fixed flat-rate addition of 4% on top of the sales price. This applies even if some of the goods would otherwise be zero-rated. The farmer retains this addition and the registered person is able to recover it as if it were VAT (subject to the normal rules). [*VATA 1994, s 54(3)(4); SI 1992/3221; SI 1995/2518, Reg 209*].

The flat-rate addition must not be charged on supplies of goods and services which are not designated (eg sales of machinery) or on supplies to non-registered persons (eg the public or other flat-rate farmers).

Sales through farmers' groups and co-operatives. Where a farmer sells produce in this way, the goods are combined with the produce of other farmers and the buyer has no way of knowing whether any of his suppliers are flat-rate farmers. In such cases, the buyer should pay the farmer's group only the price agreed for the produce *without the flat-rate addition*. The group should pay the flat-rate addition to those farmers who have a certificate when the proceeds of sale are shared out. The farmer's group can reclaim this addition on its own VAT return as though it were input tax.

Auctioneers' sales.

- *If the auctioneer is using the auctioneers' scheme or the margin scheme and acting in his own name*, he is regarded as a principal for VAT purposes, buying and selling the goods. In such a case, a flat-rate farmer can charge the flat-rate addition to the auctioneer who can reclaim it on his VAT return. The sale by the auctioneer is subject to the normal VAT rules.
- *If the auctioneer is not using either of those schemes and not acting in his own name*, he is not regarded as purchasing and selling the goods for VAT purposes. In such a case, the flat-rate farmer cannot charge the flat-rate addition to the auctioneer but can charge it to the eventual buyer of the goods if the buyer is VAT-registered.

Sales to other EC countries. A flat-rate farmer can charge the flat-rate addition on designated sales to VAT-registered persons in other EC countries (even though no VAT would have been due on the sale). The customer in the other country can reclaim the flat-rate addition charged provided he receives a flat-rate invoice.

Buying from other EC countries. Where a VAT-registered person in the UK acquires goods or services from a farmer in another EC country who charges the flat-rate addition, this can be reclaimed but from the VAT authority in the supplier's country (and not from HMRC). HMRC can give details of the procedure to be followed.

If a flat-rate farmer acquires goods from another EC country in excess of an annual threshold, he may have to register for VAT and lose the flat-rate status. See 59.18 REGISTRATION.

Sales made outside the EC. A flat-rate farmer can charge the addition on designated goods and services to purchasers outside the EC provided the goods are used for the business purposes of the purchaser.

Other farming income. Where a farmer leases or lets some of the material assets of his farming business on a long-term basis but continues to farm under the flat-rate scheme in respect of the continued farming activity, the income from such a lease and/or letting cannot be treated as taxable under the scheme and must be taxed in the normal way (*Finanzamt Rendsburg v Harbs, CJEC Case C–321/02 (unreported) (TVC 21.311)*).

Non-farming activities. If the taxable turnover of non-farming activities (eg bed and breakfast) is less than the VAT registration threshold, a farmer can still be a flat-rate farmer. He must not charge VAT or the flat-rate addition on the non-farming activities.

If his turnover of non-farming activities is above the VAT threshold, a farmer must remain registered for VAT (or, if already in the flat-rate scheme, have his certificate cancelled and register for VAT). The farmer will not be eligible to join the flat-rate scheme unless

- the non-farming activities are zero-rated, in which case the farmer may ask for exemption from registration (see 59.6 REGISTRATION) and join the scheme; or
- the non-farming business is run as a separate business by a different legal entity (eg a farmer could run his farming activities as a sole proprietor and a bed and breakfast business in partnership with another person).

(VAT Notice 700/46/02, paras 4.1–4.4, 5.2, 6.1–6.3, 8.1, 8.2).

Deregistration. Farmers who deregister to join the flat-rate scheme do not have to account for VAT on their stocks and assets on hand, even where they have claimed input tax when purchasing them. [*VATA 1994, Sch 4 para 8*(*3*)].

De Voil Indirect Tax Service. See V2.191–198.

63.26 Designated activities

For the purposes of the scheme, a farmer is someone who engages in any of the following activities.

(*a*) **Crop production** comprising any of the following.

- *General agriculture including viticulture.* Included is turf and reeds grown as a crop (eg thatching) but not peat and top soil. Also included is the growing of grape vines and the production by vineyards of their own wine up to and including the sale of the wine.
- *Growing of fruit, vegetables, flowers and ornamental plants* (*in the open and under glass*). Included are bulbs, tubers, cut flowers, branches and foliage and plants initially seeded elsewhere but subsequently bought by flat-rate farmers to grow into mature plants for sale.
- *Production of mushrooms, spices, seeds and propagating materials.*

- *Nursery production* ie the rearing of young plants, including vegetables, fruit, trees and shrubs, for sale. Also included is the sale of these products by farmers (i) who allow members of the public to come onto their farms to pick produce to buy (pick-your-own) and (ii) in their own farm shop provided the produce has undergone no further process than being harvested, cut and put into containers on the premises (although in such cases the flat-rate addition can only be charged when the produce is sold to a VAT-registered person).

(*b*) **Stock farming** comprising any of the following.

- *General stock farming*. Included is the breeding, rearing and care of animals which are either: eaten by humans; not eaten by humans but which produce food which is eaten by humans; not eaten by humans but eaten by other animals; not eaten by humans or animals but which are farmed for their skin, fur or wool; or fall into none of these categories but are specifically used in connection with agricultural production activities, eg sheepdogs. This covers animals ranging from the normal farm animals to mink, game birds (unless raised specifically for shooting), pigeons, deer and ostriches where they are raised for food and solely for the sale of their feathers. The preparation of animals for showing at agricultural shows and the showing of animals themselves will fall within the scheme.
- *Poultry and rabbit farming*. Included is the breeding and rearing of chicken, ducks, geese, turkeys, pigeons and game birds (unless raised specifically for shooting) which are generally eaten by humans and/or animals.
- *Bee-keeping and silkworm farming* up to and including the sale of the bees or silkworm cocoons.
- *Snail farming* comprising the breeding and rearing of edible snails and their farming for any other purpose.

The following activities do not qualify.

- Raising budgerigars and other birds in aviaries purely as pets.
- Raising butterflies and any other animals or birds raised for similar purposes, for example, cats and dogs (except sheepdogs).
- Most other activities involving animals (eg pony trekking, riding lessons, hunting).
- Training animals as a specialist activity.
- Training horses bred for racing and any specialist training of horses for show-jumping or eventing.
- Training pigeons for racing (however, the breeding, rearing and care of pigeons would fall within the scheme).

(*c*) **Forestry**. This covers growing, felling and general husbandry of trees in a forest, wood or copse. Included is the conversion of felled timber into sawlogs, industrial small diameter roundwood, pitprops, cordwood, fencing material and firewood. Any activity involving any process beyond that stage is excluded.

(*d*) **Fisheries** comprising fresh-water fishing; fish farming (any fish); breeding of mussels, oysters and other molluscs and crustaceans; and frog farming.

(*e*) **Processing** by a farmer of products derived from his own activities within (*a*)–(*d*) above using only such means as are normally employed in the course of such activities. Included is the gutting of fish; drying of hops; slaughter and preparation of animals raised by the farmer for sale at the farm gate; and the picking and packaging of fruit for sale on the farm.

(*f*) **Supplies of agricultural services**, by a person who also carries out one or more other designated activities falling within (*a*)–(*e*) above, comprising

- field work, reaping and mowing, threshing, bailing, collecting, harvesting, sowing and planting;
- packing and preparation of agricultural products for market (including drying, cleaning, grinding, disinfecting and ensilaging);
- storage of agricultural products;
- stock minding, rearing and fattening of animals within (*b*) above or fish within (*d*) above;
- hiring out of equipment for use in any designated activity;
- technical assistance in relation to any designated activity (including thatching if the flat rate farmer has grown the reeds, deer management (eg culling and preventing deer going on to forestry land), vermin control and agricultural pest control);
- destruction of weeds and pests, dusting and spraying of crops and land;
- operation of irrigation and drainage equipment; and
- lopping, tree felling and other forestry services (including clearing under-growth, spraying trees, marking trees for felling, making inventories of trees suitable for felling, and creating firebreaks.

Services concerned with the sale or leasing of milk quotas (whether or not they are sold with the land) are not a designated activity.

A person cannot join the scheme if

- his primary activity is to buy and sell animals (eg a dealer or trainer); or
- he is engaged in an activity once removed from farming (eg processing farm produce).

[*SI 1992/3220*]. (VAT Notice 700/46/02, paras 1.4, 3.1–3.4; Internal Guidance V1–23, Chapter 2 Appendix A).

63.27 Admission to the scheme and changes in circumstances

HMRC must certify a person for the purposes of the flat-rate scheme if the following conditions are satisfied.

(*a*) He satisfies HMRC that he is carrying on one or more designated activities within 63.26 above.

(*b*) If he is currently registered for VAT, that registration is cancelled. See 63.25 above for the position where non-farming activities are also carried on.

(*c*) He has not, in the three years before the date of application for certification,

- been convicted of any offences in connection with VAT;

- accepted an offer to compound proceedings in connection with a VAT offence; or
- been assessed to a penalty for VAT evasion involving dishonest conduct (see 52.9 PENALTIES).

(*d*) He makes an application for certification on the correct form (Form VAT 98). The form can be obtained from the Carmarthen Registration Unit, HM Revenue and Customs, Old Station Road, Carmarthen, Dyfed SA31 1BT (tel 01267 244004/012/015).

(*e*) He satisfies HMRC that, in the year following the date of his certification, the amounts of the flat-rate additions which he charges will not exceed the amount of input tax to which he would otherwise be entitled to credit by £3,000 or more. This will always be satisfied where the estimated value of agricultural supplies (shown in Box 4 of Form VAT 98) is £75,000 or less. If that figure is greater than £75,000, HMRC will calculate 4% of the figure in Box 4 and deduct input tax claimed in the last twelve months. They will allow certification if the net figure is less than £3,000 (provided the other conditions are met). If the net figure is more than £3,000 they will normally refuse certification although where the net figure is less than £3,500 they may allow certification if satisfied that the figures used are insufficiently accurate to be successfully defended on an appeal to a VAT tribunal. (Internal Guidance V1–23, Chapter 2 Table 3).

[*SI 1995/2518, Reg 204*].

Date of admission. The certificate issued by HMRC is effective from the date on which application is received by HMRC or, if the applicant so requests, from a date 30 days or less after that date. Alternatively, it may be such earlier date as HMRC agree to. No certificate can, however, be effective before any existing VAT registration is cancelled. [*SI 1995/2518, Reg 205*].

Further certification. Where a person who has been certified under the scheme, and is no longer so certified, makes a further application, he cannot be certified for a period of three years from the date of cancellation of the previous certificate except as follows.

(i) Where he has not been registered, or required to be registered, for VAT at any time since the cancellation of his previous certificate, HMRC may certify him from the date of his further application.

(ii) Where he has been registered for VAT during that time but no VAT was due on his business assets on hand at the date of deregistration because the VAT would not have been more than £1,000 (see 59.34 REGISTRATION), HMRC may certify him on a date after the expiry of one year from the date of cancellation of his previous certificate.

[*SI 1995/2518, Reg 208*].

Changes in circumstances. The certificate issued by HMRC shows the full name of the business if the owner is a sole proprietor or company and the address of the business. In the case of a partnership, it shows the trading name of the partnership or, if it does not have one, the names of at least two partners (although, in such a case, the certificate still covers all the partners listed in the application form). HMRC must be informed of any change of name or address, any changes in the members of a partnership and if a sole proprietor takes a partner. HMRC will then reissue the certificate with the same number. In all other cases where the legal entity changes, the existing certificate must be cancelled and the new entity must apply for a new certificate. (VAT Notice 700/46/02, paras 2.3, 9.1).

63.28 Cancellation of certificates

HMRC may or, as the case may be, must cancel a person's certificate in any of the following circumstances and from the date stated.

(*a*) Where a statement false in a material particular was made by him or on his behalf in connection with his application. Cancellation is from the date HMRC discover that such a statement has been made.

(*b*) He has been convicted of, or has accepted an offer to compound proceedings in connection with, a VAT offence or has been assessed to a VAT penalty. Cancellation is from the date of conviction, date of payment of the sum to compound proceedings or 30 days after the date the assessment is notified.

(*c*) He ceases to be involved in designated activities. Cancellation is from the date of cessation.

(*d*) He dies or becomes bankrupt or incapacitated. Cancellation is from the date of death, etc. HMRC may, however, in such cases, until such time as some other person is certified in respect of those activities, treat as a certified person any person carrying on those designated activities. That person must inform HMRC in writing within 30 days of the fact that he is carrying on the activities and the date of death, bankruptcy or incapacity.

Where the certified person is a company, the reference to bankruptcy is to be construed as a reference to liquidation, receivership or administration as the case may be.

(*e*) He is liable to be registered for VAT. Cancellation is from the effective date of registration.

(*f*) He makes an application in writing for cancellation. Cancellation is from a date not less than one year after the effective date of his certificate or such earlier date as HMRC agree to.

(*g*) He makes an application in writing for voluntary VAT registration (which application is deemed to be an application for cancellation of his certificate). Cancellation is from a date not less than one year after the effective date of his certificate or such earlier date as HMRC agree to.

(*h*) HMRC consider it is necessary to do so for the protection of the revenue (eg because the farmer is found to be recovering substantially more as a flat-rate farmer than he would if registered for VAT in the normal way). Cancellation is from the date on which HMRC consider a risk to the revenue arises.

(*i*) HMRC are not satisfied that any of the grounds for cancellation of a certificate within (*a*)–(*g*) above do not apply. Cancellation is from the date in (*a*)–(*g*) as appropriate.

[*SI 1995/2518, Regs 206, 207; SI 2003/2096, Art 59*].

A flat-rate farmer who leaves the scheme to register for VAT is not entitled to claim relief for any VAT incurred on purchases whilst he was a member of the scheme. (Internal Guidance V1–23, Chapter 2 para 4.5).

63.29 **Records**

Every certified person must comply with such requirements relating to keeping, preserving and producing records as HMRC notify to him. In particular, every certified person must

(*a*) keep and preserve business and accounting records and copies of all invoices showing flat-rate additions (see 63.30 below) for six years (or such lesser period as HMRC allow); and

(*b*) upon demand by a person acting under the authority of HMRC (an '*authorised person*') produce, or cause to be produced, for inspection by that person any document within (*a*) above. The document must be produced at the principal place of business (or at such other place as may be reasonably required) at such time as may reasonably be required. The authorised person may take copies or make extracts of any document and may, at a reasonable time and for a reasonable period, remove any document. Where any document removed is reasonably required for the proper conduct of the business, a copy must be provided free of charge as soon as practicable. If any documents removed are lost or damaged, reasonable compensation must be paid.

[*SI 1995/2518, Regs 210, 211*].

63.30 **Invoices**

In order that a registered person in receipt of a supply of designated goods and services may treat the flat-rate addition as if it were input tax for VAT purposes, the farmer must issue an invoice containing the following particulars.

- An identifying invoice number.
- His name, address and certificate number.
- The name and address of the person to whom the goods or services are supplied.
- The time of the supply.
- A description of the goods or services supplied.
- The consideration of the supply excluding the flat-rate addition.
- An amount entitled 'Flat-rate Addition' or 'FRA'.

[*SI 1995/2518, Reg 209*].

See 52.12 PENALTIES for the penalty for unauthorised issue of flat-rate farming invoices.

63.31 **VAT REGISTRATION SCHEME FOR RACEHORSE OWNERS**

The VAT registration scheme (the 'scheme') for racehorse owners was introduced with the agreement of the thoroughbred horseracing and breeding industry. Subject to conditions, owners are accepted as carrying on a business and can register for VAT.

Conditions for registration. An owner of racehorses can apply for VAT registration under the Scheme if registered as an owner at Weatherbys and either

(*a*) the horses are covered by a sponsorship agreement registered at Weatherbys or by a trainer's sponsorship agreement registered at Weatherbys; or (*b*) the owner can show that he has received business income from horseracing activities (eg appearance money or sponsored number cloths) and will continue to do so.

Normal procedure applies on application for registration (see 59.5 REGISTRATION) with the additional requirement that Form D1 (owners not in partnership) or D2 (partnerships), certified as correct by Weatherbys, must be sent to HMRC with the VAT registration form(s). Forms D1 and D2 are obtained from, and must be sent for certification to, VAT Declarations, Weatherbys, Sanders Road, Wellingborough, Northants, NN8 4BX.

If registration is approved, HMRC will issue a VAT registration number and inform the owner of his effective date of registration (normally the date the completed D form was received at Weatherbys).

Only the registered owner of a racehorse at Weatherbys may register for VAT under the Scheme. The registered owner can be a sole proprietor, partnership or limited company. Where a part share only in a racehorse is owned, the part owner can register in his own name if owning at least 50% of the horse. Otherwise, he must register in partnership with the other joint owners.

If an owner leases a racehorse to a person/s for racing purposes it is the lessee/s who is able to register under The Scheme. However, if a racehorse is owned by one person and races in the name of the another without a leasing agreement, registration for VAT should normally be in the name of the owner.

Owners already VAT-registered outside the Scheme. Where an owner is already registered for VAT under the normal VAT registration rules for business activities connected with bloodstock, and his racehorse owning activities form part of that business, eg if he is

- a breeder who races colts, fillies or home bred geldings with the intention of enhancing the value of their breeding stock,
- a trainer who owns and retains horses to attract owners or buyers and to provide rides for apprentices, provided the number of horses is not disproportionate to the main activity of training, or
- a dealer who purchases and sells racehorses commercially, and who races the horses held as trading stock, provided those racehorses are available for sale,

the owner does not need to register under the Scheme.

Where the owner is registered for VAT for a business activity unconnected with bloodstock or his ownership of racehorses is not regarded as part of his normal bloodstock-related business, HMRC will normally only accept that a racehorse forms part of his existing business if he can show the horse was purchased for business purposes (eg it advertises the business). But provided all the conditions of the Scheme are met, any horses owned which are not part of the owner's normal business may still be treated as part of the owner's VAT registration.

Sponsorship. After registration:

(i) If sponsorship is lost, the owner can only remain registered if actively seeking new sponsorship. Although there is no time limit set for an owner to sign up to a new agreement, as a rule of thumb HMRC expect it to be no longer than six months after the expiry of the old agreement. If longer, HMRC will ask the owner to confirm, in writing, the steps being taken to obtain sponsorship. If not satisfied with the explanation, HMRC will consider whether the registration should be cancelled and any input tax implications.

(ii) Any horses owned which are not covered by a sponsorship agreement can still be treated as part of the Scheme but only if the owner can show that he is actively seeking sponsorship for them. If sponsorship has not been obtained after six months, HMRC will taken action as in (i) above.

(VAT Notice 700/67/02, paras 1.2, 2.1–2.3, 3.1–3.3; VAT Notice 700/57/04; Internal Guidance V1–6, paras 14.2, 14.4).

Input tax. VAT incurred on the purchase, training, upkeep, etc of a racehorse put to training (including any period when it is unable to run due to injury provided there is an expectation it will run in the future) is recoverable as input tax. All other amounts of VAT incurred by an owner in pursuit of horseracing activities can be deducted subject to the normal rules. But HMRC also give the following guidelines.

- *Meals/accommodation*. HMRC would not normally expect an owner to recover any VAT. However, if the horse is racing some distance from the principal place of business, and it is unreasonable to expect the owner to travel to and from that place in one day, exceptionally input tax can be recovered in line with the normal subsistence rules (see 35.13(21) INPUT TAX). If, for example, the reason for an overnight stay is to watch the next day's racing (the owners horse having raced the day before), any VAT incurred would not be recoverable.

  Meals/drinks taken at the racecourse should normally be treated as private consumption and/or business entertainment, and the VAT is non-recoverable.
- *Telephone*. HMRC have agreed that owners may treat 10% of VAT incurred as input tax. If an owner claims a greater business usage, they will be asked to provide evidence to support their claim.
- *Racecourse admission*. Where an owner's horse has been declared to run, the owner will usually receive free admission. If not, the VAT may be recovered provided the owner holds a VAT invoice.
- *Sponsorship of a race*. Businesses that sponsor a race usually receive a package of services (eg race named after them (advertising), badges, car parking, corporate hospitality facilities, etc). Where customers/suppliers, etc are invited,

  (i) if, on the invoice the racecourse itemises the component parts and make a separate charge for each, the input tax recovery position will be relatively straightforward, ie VAT on advertising is recoverable if there is a genuine advertising benefit to the business and VAT on most other expenditure is non-recoverable under the business entertainment provisions; and

  (ii) if the racecourse invoice this supply as a complete package called 'sponsorship' (single supply of services) for a single charge, HMRC will probably ask the trader the purpose for incurring this expenditure. If (usually the case) it is both for advertising and to take customers/suppliers for a day at the races, the input tax must be apportioned. One possible method would be to value the cost of the free admissions and other free facilities and express that as a percentage of the whole.
- *Lease of executive boxes*. Some large owners/breeders lease boxes at the premier racecourses, using them for meetings with potential customers/suppliers (to discuss purchase/sale of horses, nominations, etc) during racing as well as for their own personal use and for corporate entertaining. Where HMRC are satisfied there is genuine business use, it may allow 50% of the VAT incurred on

the lease of the box to be recovered as input tax. If the box is also sub-leased, the recoverable percentage may be increased to 60%.

(Internal Guidance V1–6, para 14.10).

Output tax.

Sponsorship income. Sponsorship income is a standard-rated supply. The normal rules for sponsorship apply. A taxable supply takes place where the owner supplies clearly identifiable benefits to their sponsor (eg advertises the sponsors name or products on their colours or reflects the sponsor in the name of the racehorse).

Prize money and appearance money. Both are treated as a standard-rated taxable supplies. These payments are distributed by Weatherbys, and are shown on monthly statements ('transaction analysis summaries') which are sent to all owners. (The statements also show certain expenditure, for example, jockeys' services, on which input tax can be reclaimed.)

Under approved self-billing arrangements, Weatherbys include on the statements VAT due on prize money (other than the refund of stakes and entry fees) and appearance money where they have been notified of the owner's VAT registration number. Where an owner has failed to notify their registration number to Weatherbys, VAT will not be shown, but nevertheless a registered owner must still account for VAT on an inclusive basis (as laid down in the Rules of Racing) on the payments received.

The value for VAT purposes of prize money is the amount calculated under the Rules of Racing as receivable by the owner less entry fees, etc collected by the racecourse. (Prize money only becomes a taxable supply once an owner is registered for VAT under the Scheme. Otherwise it is treated as outside the scope of VAT.)

Sales of whole horses are supplies of goods.

- If the horse is in the UK at the time of sale, the place of supply is the UK and VAT is due at the standard rate unless

  (i) the horse is exported outside the EC (zero-rated); or

  (ii) the horse is sold to a person registered for VAT in another EC country and is removed to that country (zero-rated in the UK with the buyer accounting for acquisition VAT in his own country).

- If the horse is in another EC country at the time of sale, VAT is, in principle, due in that country subject to the VAT rules applying there.

Sales of part shares of horses are supplies of services. If the seller belongs in the UK (see 64.19 SUPPLY) the supply of a part share is subject to UK VAT wherever the buyer belongs. If the seller belongs in another EC country, there is a supply in that country.

However, where a VAT-registered person purchases a racehorse, subsequently sells a share or shares in it, and becomes a partner in a new registration, they are not required to account for VAT on their retained share.

Gifts, etc. VAT is due on racehorses given away or put to non-business use, based on what the horse would cost at the time of its disposal, taking into account its fitness/health, etc at that time. See, however, VAT Notice 700/57/02 for an agreement between HMRC, the British Horseracing Board and the Thoroughbred Breeders Association on racehorses applied permanently to personal or non-business use.

Margin scheme. Where no VAT was charged on the purchase, the margin scheme for second-hand goods can be used and VAT accounted for on the profit margin. See 61 SECOND-HAND GOODS generally and, in particular, 61.37 for special provisions applying to horses.

(VAT Notice 700/67/02, paras 5.2, 5.4–5.6; Internal Guidance V1–6, paras 14.6, 14.9, 14.11).

De Voil Indirect Tax Service. See V2.118.

63.32 Special arrangements for point-to-point horses

An owner of a 'qualifying horse' (ie a horse with a sponsorship agreement which is entered in a hunter chase) can register for VAT under the scheme for the hunter chasing season only (January to June). Registration procedure is as in 63.31 above. If already registered for VAT (under these arrangements, under the scheme or because of other business activities) there is no requirements to apply for separate registration but Form D1 or D2 as appropriate must still be completed. After the end of the hunter chasing season, VAT registration can be retained provided

- the owner can show the intention to enter the horse in hunter chases in the following season; and
- the existing sponsorship agreement is to continue or the owner intends to obtain sponsorship before the horse competes in the first race in the new season.

If these conditions cannot be met, either registration will be cancelled or, if it is continuing for other reasons, no further input tax can be recovered in respect of the horse.

(VAT Notice 700/67/02, paras 6.1–6.4).

Input tax. Input tax cannot be recovered VAT until the horse becomes a qualifying horse. Once it does, 50% of any VAT charged on its purchase can be recovered provided it was incurred no more than three years before the date of registration. (The 50% restriction is a rule of thumb apportionment which recognises that the horse is used partly for business and partly for private purposes.)

With effect from the date of registration, VAT can be recovered on

- the training, keep and other costs of a qualifying horse (temporary periods of absences due to illness or injury can be ignored); and
- the purchase or construction of fixed assets used solely for a qualifying horse. Where, for example, a stable block or horse transporter is used for both qualifying and non-qualifying horses, the VAT must be apportioned to reflect the dual usage.

It is also possible to recover

- 50% of VAT charged on training, keep and other costs of a qualifying horse in the six months prior to registration, or the date a qualifying horse runs in a hunter chase; and
- other VAT charged before registration subject to the normal requirements in 35.10 INPUT TAX.

Output tax. In addition to the information on output tax in 63.31 above, the following rules also apply to qualifying point-to-point horses.

VAT must be charged on the sale of a qualifying horse if the owner bred the horse and recovered VAT on the breeding cost. (No VAT is due on the sale of a non-qualifying horse if no VAT has been recovered in respect of it.) If a horse ceases to be a qualifying horse (eg because it is put to a permanent non-business use), VAT must be accounted for on 50% of the open market value.

(VAT Notice 700/67/02, paras 6.5, 6.6).

63.33 VAT treatment of racing clubs, etc.

Racing clubs may take a number of forms.

(*a*) **Limited companies selling shares**. A limited company sells its shares (an exempt supply) and uses the funds to buy racehorses in the company name. Profits may be distributed to shareholders as dividends.

Unless the company has other business activities involving the making of taxable supplies, it can only register for VAT if it meets the conditions of the Scheme in 63.31 above. Any benefits available to shareholders (eg visits to trainers, free entry to racecourses, etc) are disregarded for VAT purposes.

(*b*) **Racing partnerships selling shares**. A limited company or partnership sets up a racing partnership offering for sale a specific number of shares in the venture. Proceeds from prize money, sale of racehorses, etc are distributed to the owners on termination of the partnership.

The sale of shares is outside the scope of VAT. Any benefits the owners of the shares receive (eg visits to trainers, free entry to racecourses, etc) are disregarded for VAT purposes. Unless the partnership has other business activities involving the making of taxable supplies, it can only register for VAT if it meets the conditions of the scheme in 63.31 above.

(*c*) **Members racing club raising subscriptions**. A limited company, partnership or sole proprietor calling itself a 'racing club' (or having the characteristics of a club) invites persons to become members on payment of subscriptions. The subscriptions are used to buy racehorses, etc and at the end of the year surplus income is distributed to members.

- *If members receive benefits* (eg newsletters, visits to trainers, tipping service), the club is carrying on a business. [*VATA 1994, s 94*(*2*)]. See 14.1 CLUBS AND ASSOCIATIONS. The subscription income is liable to VAT and the club must register for VAT if above the registration threshold (or otherwise may apply for voluntary registration). The scheme under 63.31 above does not apply.
- *If members receive no benefits*, the club is not in business and the subscriptions are outside the scope of VAT. The club can only register for VAT if it meets the conditions of the scheme in 63.31 above.

(VAT Notice 700/67/02, paras 7.1–7.4).

63.34 SPECIAL SCHEME FOR NON-EC SUPPLIERS OF ELECTRONICALLY SUPPLIED SERVICES

With effect from 1 July 2003, the place of supply of electronically supplied services is normally in the country where the customer belongs subject, in certain circumstances, to where the services are effectively used and enjoyed. For further details of the place of supply rules, see 64.26–64.28 SUPPLY. One effect of this would mean that a non-EC business would be required, under the normal rules, to register separately and account for VAT in each EC country in which it provided electronically supplied services to private individuals and non-business organisations.

To avoid this, a special scheme offers eligible non-EC businesses the *option* of registering electronically in a single EC country of their choice and accounting for VAT on their sales of these services to all such EC consumers. This is done on a single quarterly electronic VAT declaration which provides details of VAT due in each EC country. The declaration is submitted with payment to the tax administration in the EC country of registration which then distributes the VAT to the countries where the services are consumed.

Example

A USA business, with customers in the UK, Italy and Spain, registers for the special scheme in the UK. It charges UK VAT to its UK customers, Italian VAT to its Italian customers and Spanish VAT to its Spanish customers. The business enters the VAT for each country on the appropriate line of the electronic declaration. It sends the declaration electronically with payment to HMRC who retain the UK VAT and pass on the Italian VAT to the Italian authorities and the Spanish VAT to the Spanish authorities.

Any non-EC business which uses the scheme must comply with its conditions, including electronically registering (see 63.36 below) and accounting for and paying the VAT due at the correct time (see 63.37 below). There are no penalties under the scheme but if a business persistently fails to comply with the conditions, its registration may be cancelled. In that event, it must register under the normal rules applying in the various EC countries where its customers belong and could then be subject to any penalties which those countries apply. Similarly, if a non-EC business supplies electronic services to UK consumers and fails to register for VAT (either under the scheme or under the normal rules), it may be compulsorily registered in the UK under the normal rules and may incur a late registration penalty.

This scheme does not apply to non-EU businesses supplying broadcasting or other services. If a non-EC business chooses not to register under the special scheme, or is not eligible for it, it must register under the normal rules which apply in the relevant EC country.

(VAT Information Sheet 1/03, para 9.1; VAT Information Sheet 7/03, paras 1.1, 1.3; VAT Information Sheet 10/03, para 2.1).

For full details of the scheme, see 63.35–63.39 below.

63.35 Businesses eligible to join the scheme

A business can be registered under the special scheme in the UK if it satisfies the following conditions.

(*a*) It makes, or intends to make, 'qualifying supplies' in the course of a business.

(*b*) It has neither a business establishment nor a fixed establishment in the UK or in another EC country in relation to *any* supply of goods or services. See 64.19 SUPPLY for the interpretation of 'business establishment' and 'fixed establishment'.

(*c*) It is not

- registered under *VATA 1994*,
- identified for the purposes of VAT in accordance with the law of another EC country, or
- registered under an *Act of Tynwald* for the purposes of any tax imposed by or under an *Act of Tynwald* which corresponds to VAT.

(*d*) It is not required to be registered or identified as mentioned in (*c*) above (or if it is required to be so registered or identified, this is solely by virtue of the fact that it makes or intends to make qualifying supplies).

(*e*) It is not identified under any provision of the law of another EC country which implements *EC 6th Directive, Art 26c* (ie it has not registered under a similar special scheme in another EC country).

'*Qualifying supply*' means a supply of electronically supplied services (within the meaning of *VATA 1994, Sch 5 para 7C*, see 64.27(7C) SUPPLY) to a person who

- belongs in the UK or another EC country, and
- receives those services otherwise than for the purposes of a business carried on by him.

[*VATA 1994, Sch 3B paras 2, 3; FA 2003, Sch 2 para 4*].

Provided the above conditions are met, a non-EC business can use the special scheme if it makes supplies to business customers as well as non-business customers. In such a case, it is not required to charge and account for VAT on electronically supplied services supplied to EC businesses (including non-business organisations, such as a government department, receiving supplies for business purposes) because the EC customer accounts for any VAT due under the reverse charge mechanism. See 64.28 SUPPLY. (VAT Information Sheet 7/03, para 2.3).

63.36 Registration

Where a business satisfies HMRC that it meets the conditions in 63.35 above, on request HMRC *must* register the business under these provisions. The only exception to this is that HMRC is not required to, but *may*, register a business under these provisions where it is a '*persistent defaulter*' (ie where a previous registration under these provisions has been cancelled for persistent failure to comply with the rules of the scheme (see below) or it has been excluded under the scheme in another EC country for the same reason).

Any registration request must contain the following particulars.

(*a*) The name of the business making the request.

(*b*) Its postal address and electronic addresses (including any websites).

(*c*) Where it has been allocated a number by the tax authorities in the country in which it belongs, that number.

(*d*) The date on which it began, or intends to begin, making 'qualifying supplies' (see 63.35 above).

(*e*) A statement that it is not

(i) registered under *VATA 1994*;

(ii) identified for the purposes of VAT in accordance with the law of another EC country, or

(iii) registered under an *Act of Tynwald* for the purposes of any tax imposed by or under an *Act of Tynwald* which corresponds to VAT.

The registration request must be made by such electronic means, and in such manner, as HMRC direct.

[*VATA 1994, Sch 3B paras 4, 9; FA 2003, Sch 2 para 4*].

Businesses can register at the dedicated website https://secure.hmrc.gov.uk/ecom/voes. This is a secure site which automatically guides the applicant through an electronic registration process, including selecting a user name and password for identification purposes when completing and submitting declarations electronically.

HMRC also ask for a contact name and telephone number.

(VAT Information Sheet 7/03, paras 3.2, 3.3).

Effective date of registration. Registration takes effect from the date on which the registration request is made (or such earlier or later date as is agreed with HMRC) but in any case not before 1 July 2003. [*VATA 1994, Sch 3B para 5; FA 2003, Sch 2 para 4*].

Registration number. HMRC must allocate a registration number to each business registered under these provisions and notify the number to the business electronically. [*VATA 1994, Sch 3B para 6; FA 2003, Sch 2 para 4*]. HMRC will normally send the number by e-mail within five working days of receiving the completed electronic registration request. Registration numbers have their own unique format beginning with the prefix 'EU', followed by a nine digit number. (VAT Information Sheet 7/03, para 3.4).

Businesses already registered for VAT in the EC under the normal rules. Where a business is registered for VAT in any EC country under the normal rules, it is not eligible for the special scheme and must account for VAT on any electronically supplied services to EC consumers under those normal rules. However, from 1 July 2003, a business may switch from registration under the normal rules and apply for registration in the UK under the special scheme if, for example,

- it ceases to make supplies of goods or services to EC consumers other than electronically supplied services, or
- it initially makes supplies of electronically supplied services to consumers in a single EC country but subsequently expands its market to consumers in other EC countries

provided it cancels its VAT registration under the normal rules in the EC country concerned. (VAT Information Sheet 7/03, paras 3.6, 3.9).

Changes in business circumstances. A business which has made a registration request must notify HMRC if subsequently

- there is a change in any of the particulars contained in its request under (*a*)–(*d*) above;
- it ceases to make, or to have the intention of making, qualifying supplies; or
- it ceases to satisfy any of the conditions in 63.35(*b*)–(*e*) above.

The notification must be given, using the dedicated website above, within 30 days of the date of the change of particulars or of the cessation.

[*VATA 1994, Sch 3B para 7; FA 2003, Sch 2 para 4*]. (VAT Information Sheet 7/03, para 3.7).

Cancellation of registration. HMRC must cancel the registration of a business in the following circumstances.

- The business notifies HMRC that it has ceased to make, or to have the intention of making, 'qualifying supplies' (see 63.35 above). Cancellation then takes effect from the date on which the notification is received or such earlier or later date as is agreed with HMRC.
- HMRC otherwise determine that the business has ceased to make, or to have the intention of making, qualifying supplies. Cancellation then takes effect from the date on which the determination is made or such earlier or later date HMRC may direct.
- The business notifies HMRC that it has ceased to satisfy any of the conditions in 63.35(*b*)–(*e*) above. Cancellation then takes effect from the date on which the notification is received or such earlier or later date as is agreed with HMRC.
- HMRC otherwise determine that the business has ceased to satisfy any of the conditions in 63.35(*b*)–(*e*) above. Cancellation then takes effect from the date on which the determination is made or such earlier or later date HMRC may direct.
- HMRC determine that the business has persistently failed to comply with its obligations under these provisions. Cancellation then takes effect from the date on which the determination is made or such earlier or later date HMRC may direct.

[*VATA 1994, Sch 3B para 8; FA 2003, Sch 2 para 4*].

63.37 Accounting and records

Liability for VAT. The amount of VAT which a business is liable to pay under the special scheme on any 'qualifying supply' (see 63.35 above) is calculated as follows.

(*a*) If the qualifying supply is treated as made in the UK, the amount of VAT that would have been charged on the supply if the business had been registered under *VATA 1994* when it made the supply; and any amount so calculated is regarded as VAT charged in accordance with *VATA 1994*.

(*b*) If the qualifying supply is treated as made in another EC country, the amount of VAT that would have been charged on the supply in accordance with the law of that EC country if the business had been identified for the purposes of VAT in that country when it made the supply; and any amount so calculated in relation to another EC country is regarded for the purposes of *VATA 1994* as VAT charged in accordance with the law of that EC country.

[*VATA 1994, Sch 3B para 10; FA 2003, Sch 2 para 4*].

Obligation to submit special accounting returns. A business must submit to VAT Central Unit a special accounting return for each 'reporting period' for which it is registered under the special scheme. A '*reporting period*' is each calendar quarter for the whole or part of which the business is registered under the scheme.

The special accounting return must set out the following in sterling.

- The registration number of the business.

- For each EC country in which the business is treated as having made qualifying supplies in the reporting period:
  - (i) the total value of those qualifying supplies in sterling (excluding the VAT which it is liable to pay by virtue of these provisions);
  - (ii) the rate of VAT applicable to those supplies by virtue of (*a*) or (*b*) above, and
  - (iii) the total amount of VAT payable under these provisions in respect of those supplies.
- The total amount of VAT which the business is liable to pay under these provisions in respect of all qualifying supplies treated as made by it in all EC countries in the reporting period.

Any conversion from one currency into another for these purposes must be made using the exchange rates published by the European Central Bank for the last day of the reporting period to which the special accounting return relates (or, if no such rate is published for that day, for the next day for which such a rate is published). To avoid the need for businesses to calculate a conversion from the currency of sale into Euros and then from Euros into sterling, HMRC have published the exchange rates for the following leading currencies direct into sterling.

Country/currency	*Units of currency to £*				
	31.3.04	30.6.04	30.9.04	31.12.04	31.3.05
Australia/dollar	2.4106	2.6171	2.5061	2.4763	2.4347
Canada/dollar	2.3996	2.4365	2.2918	2.3283	2.2857
Costa Rica/colon	799.285	802.415	815.387	883.037	889.552
Hong Kong/dollar	14.3006	14.1339	14.0863	15.0175	14.6855
India/rupee	81.4548	80.4643	84.4501	83.5361	81.9154
Japan/yen	190.6743	197.3910	199.7234	198.0711	201.0748
Russia/rouble	53.6994	51.1823	53.8849	53.0421	52.7064
Singapore/dollar	3.0724	3.1161	3.0485	3.1575	3.1049
Switzerland/franc	2.3418	2.2724	2.2603	2.1884	2.2492
USA/dollar	1.8357	1.8122	1.8068	1.9319	1.8829

(VAT Information Sheets 1/04, 4/04, 6/04, 8/04, 11/04, 1/05).

Alternatively, the conversion can be calculated using the exchange rates shown at the ECB's website at:

www.ecb.int

Rates of VAT in other EC countries are published on the EC Commission's website at:

http://europa.eu.int/comm/taxation_customs/taxation/ecommerce/vat_en_faq.htm#16rate

The special accounting return must be submitted to HMRC by electronic means within 20 days after the last day of the reporting period to which it relates.

[*VATA 1994, Sch 3B paras 11, 12; FA 2003, Sch 2 para 4*]. (VAT Information Sheet 10/03, paras 3.1, 3.2).

Returns must be completed by logging on to the dedicated website

https://secure.hmrc.gov.uk/ecom/voes

and using the VAT identification number, user name and password of the business to ensure security. A return is required even if there are no qualifying supplies in the quarter.

HMRC send an on-line acknowledgment confirming that they have received the return. This acknowledgment also provides a unique reference number for each return submitted. This number should be referred to if it is necessary to contact HMRC with a query about the return. If this confirmation is not received *immediately*, the Customer Services Team should be contacted by e-mail at

voes@hmrc.gsi.gov.uk.

(VAT Information Sheet 7/03, paras 4.1, 4.6).

Payment of VAT. At the same time as submitting the special accounting return, a business must pay to HMRC, in sterling, the total amount of VAT as shown due by the return. [*VATA 1994, Sch 3B para 13; FA 2003, Sch 2 para 4*].

VAT on purchases. The special scheme provides only for payment of the VAT due on sales to EC customers, without any deductions of EC VAT incurred on purchases. However, a business may be able to reclaim VAT it has paid on goods and services used for the purpose of its taxable activities falling within the scheme, from the EC country where that VAT was paid, under the *EC 13th Directive*. See 22.49 EUROPEAN COMMUNITY LEGISLATION for the provisions of the *Directive* and 48.5 OVERSEAS TRADERS for applications to the UK for refunds.

Obligations to keep and produce records. A business registered under the special scheme in the UK must keep records of its transactions in qualifying supplies (see 63.35 above) in sufficient detail to enable the tax authorities in the EC countries in which those supplies are treated as made to determine whether any special accounting return is correct. These records include normal commercial data held for each transaction (eg transaction number, date, type (credit or debit), customer name and location, currency and values including VAT).

Any records required to be kept must, on request, be made available electronically to HMRC and the tax authorities of any EC country where the qualifying supplies were treated as made. HMRC also may request records of a business where its qualifying supplies are treated as made in the UK but it is registered under the scheme in another EC country

The records must be kept for ten years beginning with the 1st January following the date on which the transaction was entered into.

[*VATA 1994, Sch 3B paras 14, 15; FA 2003, Sch 2 para 4*]. (VAT Information Sheet 7/03, para 4.8).

Invoices. There are no special rules for issuing VAT invoices under the special scheme and consequently the normal rules apply. In the UK, a business is not required to issue VAT invoices for such supplies because its customers are not in business and cannot deduct VAT on their purchases. (VAT Information Sheet 7/03, para 4.10).

63.38 Errors in special scheme returns

Errors discovered by HMRC. If HMRC consider that a business which is, or has been, registered under the special scheme (whether in the UK or another EC country) has submitted a scheme return which understates or overstates liability to UK VAT, they may give the business a notice

- identifying the return in which they consider that the under/overstatement was made; and
- specifying the amount by which they consider that the liability to VAT has been under/overstated.

In the case of an understatement, HMRC will request the business to pay the amount understated to HMRC within 30 days of the date of the notice. There are no penalties for underdeclaring the amount of VAT due under the special scheme. However, failure to declare the full amount may make the business ineligible to use the scheme (see 63.36 above under *Cancellation of registration*).

In the case of an overstatement, HMRC must pay the business the amount specified in the notice. They will normally do this within 30 days.

Time limit. No notice under these provisions may be given more than three years after the end of the period for which the scheme return in question was made.

[*VATA 1994, Sch 3B para 16; FA 2003, Sch 2 para 4*]. (VAT Information Sheet 10/03, paras 5.2, 5.3).

Errors discovered by the non-EC supplier. If a non-EC supplier submits a declaration but subsequently discovers that it has made an error (eg entering French VAT in the line for Spain or underdeclaring UK VAT), it should contact HMRC at

voes@hmrc.gsi.gov.uk

quoting the reference number for the return in question and advising the correct amount(s) due for the EC country or countries concerned. There is no need to submit a supplementary declaration.

Where, as a result of the error, additional VAT is due, HMRC will either request that the payment is sent to them or advise that the EC country or countries concerned will contact the business to explain how it should pay the VAT due.

(VAT Information Sheet 10/03, para 4.2).

Business customers initially failing to provide VAT registration numbers. The special scheme is intended for supplies to consumers who cannot recover VAT. A business customer who fails to provide a valid VAT registration number at the time of the transaction must be charged VAT and cannot deduct that VAT as input tax. However, if it subsequently produces a valid VAT registration number and requests a credit, the non-EC supplier can refund the VAT to the business customer. (VAT Information Sheet 10/03, para 4.1).

63.39 Miscellaneous matters

(1) Appeals

An appeal can be made to a UK VAT tribunal with respect to any of the following.

- The registration or cancellation of the registration of any business under the special scheme.

- A decision of HMRC to give a notice of understatement of UK VAT liability under 63.38 above.
- The amount specified in any such notice or in a notice of overstatement of UK VAT liability under 63.38 above.

[*VATA 1994, Sch 3B para 20; FA 2003, Sch 2 para 4*].

UK VAT tribunals cannot deal with VAT matters which fall within the jurisdiction of other EC countries. If a non-EC business using the special scheme disagrees with a decision taken by another EC country about any aspect of the scheme (eg the amount of VAT owed to it), the matter should be raised with the VAT authorities in that country.

(2) **Deregistration**

Where a business which is registered under *VATA 1994 Sch 1* (registration in respect of UK supplies, see 59.1–59.10 REGISTRATION) satisfies HMRC that it intends to apply for

- registration under the special scheme in the UK, or
- identification under any provision of the law of another EC country which implements similar provisions,

they may, if the business so requests, cancel its registration under *VATA 1994 Sch 1* with effect from the day on which the request is made or from such later date as may be agreed between it and HMRC.

[*VATA 1994, Sch 3B para 18; FA 2003, Sch 2 para 4*].

(2A) **EC enlargement**

10 new countries (ie Cyprus, Czech Republic, Estonia, Hungary, Latvia, Lithuania, Malta, Poland, Slovak Republic, and Slovenia) joined the EC with effect from 1 May 2004. As a result, with effect from that date, non-EC businesses

- not already registered for the special scheme will have a greater choice of EC countries to select from in order to register under the scheme;
- registered under the special scheme but established within any of those ten countries are excluded from continuing to use the scheme; and
- registered under the special scheme but not established within any of those ten countries must extend the charging of VAT on their e-services to all non-business users who reside within those 10 countries.

(3) **Exempt supplies**

Most electronically supplied services within the EC are subject to VAT. However, certain EC countries apply an exemption to some electronically supplied services (eg gambling). If a non-EC supplier thinks that its services may qualify for an exemption, it should check with the country or countries concerned. However, unless its services are exempt from VAT in all EC countries where its customers belong, it will still be required to register and account for VAT in the EC either under the normal rules or under the special scheme. (VAT Information Sheet 10/03, para 2.3).

(4) **Registration under *VATA 1994***

Notwithstanding any provision in *VATA 1994* to the contrary, a business in the special scheme is not required to be registered under *VATA 1994* by virtue of making qualifying supplies under the special scheme. [*VATA 1994, Sch 3B para 17; FA 2003, Sch 2 para 4*].

(5) **VAT representatives**

VATA 1994, s 48(*1*) (VAT representatives, see 3.8 AGENTS) does not permit HMRC to direct a business in the special scheme to appoint a VAT representative. [*VATA 1994, Sch 3B para 19; FA 2003, Sch 2 para 4*].

However, although an agent, even an authorised one, cannot register for the special scheme on behalf of a non-EC supplier, the supplier can register itself and authorise an agent to submit declarations and, if necessary, make payments on its behalf under the scheme. But it should be noted that rules regarding agents vary between EC countries and such authorisation may render the agent jointly and severally liable for VAT in some countries. (VAT Information Sheet 10/03, para 2.3).

64 Supply

The contents of this chapter are as follows.

64.1 INTRODUCTION

A transaction is within the scope of UK VAT if the following four conditions are satisfied.

- It is a supply of goods or services.
- It takes place in the UK.
- It is made by a taxable person.
- It is made in the course or furtherance of any business carried on by that person.

[*VATA 1994, s 4(1)*].

The first three conditions are considered in this chapter.

Supplies for VAT purposes. Even before deciding whether goods or services are being supplied, it is necessary to determine whether a transaction is in fact a supply for VAT purposes by considering the following questions.

(*a*) **Is there any consideration?** Under both EC and UK law, a supply takes place for VAT purposes when something is provided or done for a consideration. [*VATA 1994, s 5(2)*]. A supply can be made in many ways, the most common being the transfer of ownership or the transfer of possession of goods, or the provision of a services by one person to another. See 64.2 below for further coverage of the meaning of supply.

Consideration for VAT purposes has a wide meaning and covers anything which might be done, given or made in exchange for something else. It does not refer only to money. It includes something exchanged in a barter transaction, such as in a part exchange, or a service performed in return for another service, or it may simply be a condition imposed upon the making of the supply. Provided there is a direct link between the supply made and the consideration given, and the consideration is capable of being expressed in money, there is a supply for VAT purposes. See 69.8 VALUATION for further coverage of the meaning of consideration.

(*b*) **If there is no consideration, is the transaction one which is deemed to be a supply for VAT purposes?** Even if there is no consideration, certain transactions made for no consideration (ie free) are deemed to be supplies of goods or services for VAT purposes. These are the

- permanent transfer/disposal of business assets (*VATA 1994, Sch 4 para 5(1)*), see 47.6 OUTPUT TAX;
- temporary use of business assets for non-business purposes (*VATA 1994, Sch 4 para 5(4)*), see 47.7 OUTPUT TAX;
- retention of certain business assets on deregistration (*VATA 1994, Sch 4 para 8*), see 59.34 REGISTRATION;
- self-supply of goods or services (by statutory instruments made under *VATA 1994, s 5(5)(6)*), see 62 SELF-SUPPLY; and
- private or other non-business use of services supplied to the business (*SI 1993/1507*), see 47.7 OUTPUT TAX.

(*c*) **Does the transaction fail to be a supply or is it a supply which is disregarded for VAT purposes?** A transaction is not a supply for VAT purposes if

- there is no consideration for the supply and it is not a deemed supply under (*b*) above;
- the transaction is within the same legal entity;

- there is a specific exclusion in VAT legislation, ie
  - (i) a business gift costing the donor £50 or less (£15 or less before 8 March 2001), unless forming part of a series or succession made to the same person (*VATA 1994, Sch 4 para 5*), see 47.6 OUTPUT TAX;
  - (ii) an industrial sample (*VATA 1994, Sch 4 para 5*), see 47.8(23) OUTPUT TAX; or
  - (iii) the transaction is deemed to be 'neither a supply of goods nor services', see 64.5 below.

Supplies of goods and services. Once it has been established that a transaction is a supply, it is then necessary to determine whether it is a supply of goods (see 64.3 below) or a supply of services (see 64.4 below). Certain transactions, although supplies, are regarded as supplies of neither goods nor services and are outside the scope of VAT (see 64.5 below).

The distinction as to whether a supply is one of goods or services is important as different rules apply to the place and time of supply. Also the treatment of the international supply of goods and services is different.

(Internal Guidance V1–3, paras 2.1–2.6).

64.2 MEANING OF SUPPLY

The legislation does not define the term 'supply'. Subject to express provisions to the contrary, supply includes all forms of supply, but not anything done otherwise than for consideration. Anything which is not a supply of goods but is done for a consideration (including, if so done, the granting, assignment or surrender of any right) is a supply of services. [*VATA 1994, s 5(2)*].

In *C & E Commrs v Oliver, QB 1979, [1980] STC 73 (TVC 60.155)*, it was held that supply of goods has a wide interpretation. It is the passing of possession in goods pursuant to an agreement whereunder the supplier agrees to part and the recipient agrees to take possession. By 'possession' is meant in this context control over the goods, in the sense of having immediate facility for their use. This may or may not involve the physical removal of the goods. See also *Carlton Lodge Club v C & E Commrs, QB [1974] STC 507 (TVC 13.29)*.

In *Tolsma v Inspecteur der Omzetbelasting Leeuwarden, CJEC [1994] STC 509 (TVC 21.59)* an individual who played a barrel organ on the public highway, and invited donations from the public, was held not to be supplying services for a consideration. There was no agreement between the parties and also 'no necessary link between the musical service and the payment to which it gave rise'.

Illegal supplies. The principle of fiscal neutrality requires that all supplies of goods for a consideration are subject to VAT unless the goods are subject to a total prohibition on circulation because they are intrinsically harmful or because all competition between a lawful economic sector and an unlawful sector is precluded. In *Witzemann v Hauptzollamt Munchen-Mitte, CJEC 1990, [1993] STC 108 (TVC 21.69)*, the Advocate-General stated that 'illegality manifests itself in many forms and there are many products that either cannot be lawfully traded or trade in which is subject to certain restrictions: drugs, counterfeit money, weapons, pornography, the pelts of certain animals, stolen goods and so forth. Not every transaction tainted with illegality will be exempt from taxation. A line must be drawn between, on the one hand, transactions that lie so clearly outside the sphere of legitimate economic activity that, instead of being taxed, they can only be the subject of criminal prosecution and, on the other hand, transactions which, though unlawful, must none the less be taxed, if only for the sake of ensuring, in the name of fiscal neutrality, that the criminal is not treated more favourably than the legitimate trader'.

Thus, the illegal sale of drugs is not a supply for VAT purposes (*Mol v Inspecteur der Invoerrechten Accijnzen, CJEC 1988, [1989] 3 CMLR 729 (TVC 21.56)*) but the supply of counterfeit perfume is. See *R v Goodwin and Unstead, CA [1997] STC 22, CJEC [1998] STC 699 (TVC 21.57)*. The prohibition on such products stems from the fact that they infringe intellectual property rights and is conditional not absolute (as in the case of drugs and counterfeit money). There is scope for competition between counterfeit perfumes and perfumes which are traded lawfully and although supply of the former is unlawful, such perfume is not liable to seizure in the hands of the final customer. The unlawful operation of a form of roulette was similarly held to be a supply for VAT purposes in *Fischer v Finanzamt Donaueschingen, CJEC [1998] STC 708 (TVC 21.248)*. However, although the unlawful playing of a game of chance is a supply, it is not taxable where the corresponding activity is exempt when carried on lawfully by a licensed casino.

In *Staatssecretaris van Financien v Coffeeshop 'Siberie vof, CJEC [1999] STC 742 (TVC 21.58)* income from renting tables for the sale of cannabis was held to be within the scope of VAT and similarly in *C & E Commrs v R & J Polok, Ch D [2002] STC 361 (TVC 60.252)* income from the running of an escort agency was held to be potentially taxable (as indeed was the income of the escorts themselves).

De Voil Indirect Tax Service. See V3.102–104.

64.3 SUPPLIES OF GOODS

EC legislation. See 22.7 EUROPEAN COMMUNITY LEGISLATION.

UK legislation. The Treasury may, by Order, deem any transaction to be a supply of services and not a supply of goods (or vice versa). [*VATA 1994, s 5(3)*]. Subject to this, the following supplies are to be treated as supplies of goods.

(*a*) **Any transfer of the whole property in goods**. [*VATA 1994, Sch 4 para 1(1)*]. This usually means transfer of both title to the goods and possession of, or control over, the goods.

If possession is transferred but title is retained (eg where goods are let out on hire) this is a supply of services (see 64.4 below). However, if possession is transferred in circumstances where title would normally pass but does not because the holder of the goods did not have good title (eg the sale of stolen goods) this is a supply of goods as if title had passed. See *C & E Commrs v Oliver, QB 1979, [1980] STC 73 (TVC 60.155)*.

(Internal Guidance V1–3, para 2.9).

The transfer of an undivided share of property is a supply of services (see 64.4 below). For the distinction, see *Sir John Astor (VTD 1030) (TVC 60.327)*.

(*b*) **The transfer of possession of goods** under an agreement for the sale of the goods or under agreements which expressly contemplate that the property also will pass at some time in the future (determined by, or ascertainable from, the agreements but in any case not later than when the goods are fully paid for). [*VATA 1994, Sch 4 para 1(2)*]. Where the conditions for future transfer are not satisfied, the supply is a supply of services (see 64.4 below).

Supplies under hire purchase contracts, conditional sale agreements and reservation of title agreements are thus supplies of goods. The simple hire or lease of goods, on the other hand, does not envisage the future transfer of title and is a supply of services. However, there a many other types of agreement where the distinction is not clear cut. In cases of doubt it is necessary to look at both the written agreement and the intention of any overall scheme operated. *EC 6th Directive, Art 5(4)* provides that there is a supply of goods where 'in the normal course of events' ownership will pass at the latest upon payment of the final instalment. Some final payments are referred to as 'option payments' where the customer has an option whether to purchase or not. Where these payments are very small, it is very unlikely that the customer would not take up the option and 'in the normal course of events' title will pass. An agreement with such an option is likely to be a single supply of goods at the outset.

(Internal Guidance V1–3, para 15.7).

(*c*) **The supply of any form of power, heat, refrigeration or ventilation**. [*VATA 1994, Sch 4 para 3*].

(*d*) **The grant, assignment or surrender of a 'major interest' in land**. [*VATA 1994, Sch 4 para 4*]. See 42.1(9) LAND AND BUILDINGS for the definition of '*major interest*'.

(*e*) **Disposal of business assets**. There is a supply of goods where goods forming part of the assets of a business are transferred or disposed of, by or under the directions of the person carrying on the business, so as no longer to form part of those assets (whether or not for consideration). [*VATA 1994, Sch 4 para 5(1)*]. This includes

- the sale of assets (eg fixed assets);
- assets permanently taken into private use; and
- assets given away.

Business gifts and industrial samples are excluded provided certain conditions are met. [*VATA 1994, Sch 4 para 5(2)(3); FA 1996, s 33; FA 1998, s 21*]. See 47.6 OUTPUT TAX for business gifts, 47.7 OUTPUT TAX for private use of business assets and 47.8(23) OUTPUT TAX for samples.

Land. Where the business assets include land,

- the grant or assignment of a major interest in the land, or
- the grant or assignment of any interest in, right over or licence to occupy the land concerned otherwise than for a consideration

is a supply of goods. Any other supply of the land is a supply of services.

[*VATA 1994, Sch 4 para 9*].

(*f*) **Transfers of own goods between EC countries**. There is a supply of goods where, in a case not falling within (*e*) above, goods forming part of the assets of any business are removed in the course of that business from one EC country by or under the directions of the person carrying on the business and taken to another EC country. This applies whether or not the removal is, or is connected with, a transaction for a consideration. [*VATA 1994, Sch 4 para 6*]. There are, however, a number of exceptions and special rules. See 23.23 EUROPEAN COMMUNITY: SINGLE MARKET for full details.

(*g*) **Sales in satisfaction of a debt**. Where in the case of a business carried on by a taxable person, goods forming part of the assets of the business are, under any power exercisable by another person, sold by the other person in or towards satisfaction of a debt owed by the taxable person, they are deemed to be supplied by the taxable person in the course or furtherance of his business. [*VATA 1994, Sch 4 para 7*]. Land forming part of the assets of the business is treated as if it were goods and any sale includes a reference to a grant or assignment of any interest in, right over or licence to occupy the land concerned. [*VATA 1994, Sch 4 para 9*].

The above provisions only apply if the creditor has the power in law to sell the goods. It does not apply, for example, where the seller has illegally repossessed (ie stolen) the goods. (Internal Guidance V1–3, para 3.1).

See 2.18 ACCOUNTING PERIODS AND RETURNS for the statement to be furnished to HMRC by the person exercising the power.

(*h*) **Deemed supplies on ceasing to be a taxable person**. Where a person ceases to be a taxable person, any goods then forming part of the assets of a business carried on by him are (subject to certain exceptions) deemed to be supplied by him in the course of furtherance of his business immediately before he ceases to be a taxable person. [*VATA 1994, Sch 4 para 8*]. See 59.34 REGISTRATION for further details.

(*i*) **Self-supplies**. Where specific goods taken possession of or produced by a person in the course or furtherance of his business are neither supplied to another person nor incorporated in other goods produced in the course or furtherance of that business but are used by him for the purpose of the business, the Treasury have power, by Order, to provide that the goods are deemed to be supplied *to* him for the purpose of the business and *by* him in the course or furtherance of it. [*VATA 1994, s 5(5), s 6(11)*]. Orders have been made in respect of printed matter (see 62.2 SELF-SUPPLY) motor cars (see 45.6 MOTOR CARS) and certain construction services (see 42.30 LAND AND BUILDINGS).

(*j*) **Water**. The supply of water insofar as it is not otherwise a supply of goods is to be treated as a supply of goods (and not services). [*SI 1989/1114*].

Returned goods and repossessions. If goods supplied are later returned to the supplier for any reason, the VAT treatment of the act of returning the goods depends on whether title to the goods has passed or not.

- *If goods are returned because they are faulty or not in accordance with the sales contract*, the original transaction may be voided. The transfer of title is cancelled and neither the original sale of the faulty or unsatisfactory goods nor their return is a supply. If the goods are replaced without further charge, this is strictly speaking a new supply although it is common practice, usually accepted by HMRC, for the original invoice to remain unaltered.

  If the faulty or unsatisfactory goods are repaired or improved for the customer and this work is performed in order to meet the original contract, the work is part of that original supply.

- *If goods are returned where title has passed* and the transfer is not cancelled as above, title passes back to the supplier and a second supply is made.

- *If an agreement within (b) above is terminated prematurely and the goods are repossessed*, such a later event cannot change the nature of a transaction. The agreement was a supply of goods for VAT purposes at the outset and this does not change. However, the repossession of the goods is neither a supply of goods (as title has not yet passed) nor a supply of services (as there is no consideration).

(Internal Guidance V1–3, paras 15.3, 15.8).

De Voil Indirect Tax Service. See V3.112.

64.4 SUPPLIES OF SERVICES

EC legislation. See 22.8 EUROPEAN COMMUNITY LEGISLATION.

UK legislation. Anything which is not a supply of goods but is done for a consideration (including, if so done, the granting, assignment or surrender of any right) is a supply of services. The Treasury may, however, by Order, deem any transaction to be treated as a supply of goods and not a supply of services (or vice versa). [*VATA 1994, s 5(2)(b)(3)*]. Subject to this, the following supplies are to be treated as supplies of services.

(*a*) **The transfer of any undivided share of the property in goods**. [*VATA 1994, Sch 4 para 1(1)*]. This refers to goods that can be owned equally by more than one person, ie where the title to the goods is shared. If all the shares in equally-owned goods are simultaneously sold to one person, there is a supply of goods, but if only one of the part shares is sold, title to the goods does not pass to the new owner of the part-share. As title does not pass, this supply is not of goods but of services. The most common example of an undivided share in property is a part-share ('nomination') in a racehorse. (Internal Guidance V1–3, para 15.4).

Unascertained (unallocated) goods. Unallocated goods are goods which remain an unidentifiable part of a larger stock of goods held by a supplier as opposed to 'allocated' goods which are set apart and earmarked as belonging to, or reserved for, a specific customer. Where goods are sold but are never allocated, title in the goods does not pass so the supply is one of services and not of goods. (Internal Guidance V1–3, para 15.12).

Fiscal warehousing. As an exception to this general rule, the transfer of any undivided share of property in eligible goods where the supply is relieved from VAT under the fiscal warehousing regime is treated as a supply of goods and not a supply of services. See 70.15 and 70.16 WAREHOUSED GOODS AND FREE ZONES.

(*b*) **The transfer of possession of goods** where the conditions in 64.3(*b*) above are not satisfied. [*VATA 1994, Sch 4 para 1(1)*]. Included is the hire, lease, rental or loan of goods.

(*c*) **Work done on another person's goods**. Any work done on another person's goods is a supply of services. Where the work produces goods, the services can be zero-rated if the goods produced are zero-rated goods. See 72.1 ZERO-RATED SUPPLIES.

(*d*) **Non-business use of goods and services**. Where, by or under the direction of a person carrying on a business, goods held or used for the purposes of the business are put to private or non-business use, whether or not for a consideration, that is a supply of services. [*VATA 1994, Sch 4 para 5(4)*]. Similarly, where a person carrying on a business puts services supplied to the business to any private or non-business use for no consideration, that is a supply of services. [*SI 1993/1507*].

See 47.7 OUTPUT TAX for further details.

(*e*) **Exchange units**. The exchange of a reconditioned article for an unserviceable article of a similar kind by a person who regularly offers, in the course or furtherance of his business, to provide a reconditioning facility by that means. [*SI 1995/1268, Art 6*]. VAT must be accounted for on the full amount charged for the exchange unit. If the charge to the customer is reduced by giving a refund when the unserviceable article is handed in, the procedure in 40.15 INVOICES should be adopted.

If the exchange is not part of the person's normal business practice (eg where, on a 'one-off' basis, a serviceable article is exchanged for an unserviceable one) or if goods are exchanged for other goods at a reduced price in any other circumstances, the transaction is a supply of goods and should be treated as a part-exchange. (VAT Notice 700, para 8.6).

(*f*) **Services received from abroad**. Where a person who belongs abroad supplies certain services to a person who belongs in the UK for the purposes of any business carried on by him and the place of supply of those services is in the UK, the same consequences apply as if the taxable person had himself supplied the services in the UK in the course or furtherance of his business and that supply were a taxable supply. See 39.4 INTERNATIONAL SERVICES.

De Voil Indirect Tax Service. See V3.113.

64.5 SUPPLIES OF NEITHER GOODS NOR SERVICES

The following transactions are treated as neither a supply of goods nor a supply of services.

(*a*) **Transfer of a business as a going concern**. The supply by a person of the assets of his business to another person to whom he transfers his business (or part thereof) as a going concern (provided certain conditions are satisfied). See 8.10 *et seq* BUSINESS.

(*b*) **The assignment of rights under a HP or conditional sales agreement**, and the goods comprised therein, by the owner to a bank or other financial institution. See 27.13 FINANCIAL SERVICES.

(*c*) **Repossession of goods**. The sale of certain goods by a person, including a finance company, who has repossessed them under the terms of a finance agreement or by an insured in settlement of a claim under an insurance policy (provided certain conditions are met). See 27.15 FINANCIAL SERVICES.

(*d*) **Groups of companies**. Where a group registration is in force, most supplies of goods or services by a member of the group to another member of the group are disregarded for VAT purposes. See 31.4 GROUPS OF COMPANIES.

(*e*) **Supplies of dutiable goods in warehouse**. Where imported goods subject to duty are supplied while warehoused in bond, the supply is disregarded for VAT purposes if the goods are supplied before payment of the duty to which they are subject. See 70.4 WAREHOUSED GOODS AND FREE ZONES.

(*f*) **Motor cars**. In addition to the sale of motor cars within (*c*) above,

- the disposal of a motor car for no consideration (eg as scrap) where, on any previous supply or importation, input tax on the motor car in question has been excluded from credit; and

- the letting on hire of a motor vehicle for less than full consideration or the making available of a motor car (otherwise than by letting) to any person for private use.

See 45.5 MOTOR CARS.

(*g*) **Companies organised in divisions**. Transactions between divisions of the same corporate body are not supplies for VAT purposes. See 59.37 REGISTRATION.

(*h*) **Supplies by pawnbrokers**. The supply by a taxable person of goods the property in which passed to him as pawnee by virtue of *Consumer Credit Act 1974, s 120(1)(a)* where the supply is to a person who was the pawnor of those goods and the supply is made not later than three months after the taxable person acquired the property in the goods. [*SI 1986/896*]. See 27.16(8) FINANCIAL SERVICES for supplies generally by pawnbrokers.

(*i*) **Temporary importations**. Sales of temporarily imported goods provided the goods remain eligible for temporary importation arrangements and the supply is to a person established outside the EC. [*SI 1992/3130*].

Additionally, the sale *by auction* of

(i) second-hand goods temporarily imported with a view to sale by auction, and

(ii) works of art temporarily imported for exhibition with a view to possible sale by auction

is treated as outside the scope of VAT. [*SI 1995/958; SI 1999/3119*]. See 34.24 IMPORTS.

(*j*) **Second-hand goods scheme**. The removal of goods to the UK under a supply to a person in the UK made by a person in another EC country who accounts for VAT there on the profit margin under the laws of that country similar to the margin scheme in the UK. [*SI 1995/1268, Art 8*]. No VAT is chargeable on such a supply in the UK and the goods may be sold under the margin scheme. See 61.7 SECOND-HAND GOODS.

(*k*) **Agents acting in their own name in relation to second-hand goods**. Services provided by an agent acting in his own name to the purchaser of second-hand goods where the consideration for the services is taken into account in calculating the price at which the agent obtained the goods. [*SI 1995/1268, Art 9*]. See 61.26 SECOND-HAND GOODS.

(*l*) **Auctioneers in relation to second-hand goods**. Services provided by an auctioneer acting in his own name to the vendor or purchaser of second-hand goods where the consideration for the services is taken into account in calculating the price at which the auctioneer obtained, or as the case may be, sold the goods. [*SI 1995/1268, Art 10*]. See 61.59 SECOND-HAND GOODS.

De Voil Indirect Tax Service. See V3.114.

64.6 SINGLE AND MULTIPLE SUPPLIES

There have always been problems in determining the correct VAT liability of transactions consisting of separately identifiable goods or services. This is particularly relevant where, if supplied on their own, some elements would be taxable and others would qualify for relief from VAT. For example, there may be a combination of two or more goods (eg zero-rated food in luxury standard-rated packaging), two or more services (eg standard-rated car hire with exempt insurance) or goods and services (eg standard-rated tuition with zero-rated books). The question is: should the different elements be treated separately for VAT purposes or are they properly part of a single overall supply?

For such transactions, it is therefore necessary to distinguish between

- a 'single' (or 'composite') supply, ie where there is one overall type of supply (either goods or services) and one VAT liability; and
- a 'multiple' (or 'mixed') supply, ie where the two or more components are separate supplies, each of which is either a supply of goods or services and each of which has its own VAT liability.

Neither UK nor EC VAT legislation provides rules to determine this. Over the years, tribunal and court decisions (or a HMRC ruling, trade agreement or statement of practice based on that litigation) have produced general guidelines on how to approach the problem but these have not provided any certainty on the issue.

More substantial guidance on the proper test for deciding if transactions constitute one or more supplies was given by the CJEC in *Card Protection Plan Ltd v C & E Commrs, CJEC [1999] STC 270 (TVC 21.223)*. The court stated that, although it is not possible to give exhaustive guidance on the approach in all cases, the following general criteria should be used.

(*a*) Following the earlier judgment in *Faaborg-Gelting Linien A/S v Finanzamt Flensburg, CJEC [1996] STC 774 (TVC 21.105)* where a transaction comprises a bundle of features and acts, regard must first be had to all the circumstances in which the transaction takes place. The essential features of the transaction must be ascertained in order to determine whether the taxable person is supplying the customer, being a typical consumer, with several distinct principal supplies or with a single supply, taking into account that

(i) it follows from *EC Sixth Directive, Art 2(1)* that a supply must normally be regarded as distinct and independent (ie it should amount to more than merely a component of the overall supply); and

(ii) a supply which comprises a single supply from an economic point of view should not be artificially split (so as not to distort the functioning of the VAT system).

> *Example*
>
> Where a garage services a customer's car, although there are different elements that go to make up a typical service, these cannot be said to be distinct or independent in the context of the overall service required by the customer. Any attempt to describe them as separate supplies would clearly be artificial.

(*b*) Where (*a*) above does distinguish separate supplies, it is necessary to consider whether each supply can be properly regarded as a principal supply or whether some of them are merely ancillary to the principal supply. There is a single supply, in particular, in cases where one or more elements are to be regarded as constituting the principal supply, whilst one or more elements are to be regarded, by contrast, as ancillary and which share the tax treatment of the principal supply. A supply must be regarded as ancillary to a principal supply if it does not constitute for customers an aim in itself, but a means of better enjoying the principal supply (see *TP Madgett & RM Baldwin (t/a Howden Court Hotel) v C & E Commrs, CJEC [1998] STC 1189 (TVC 21.314)*).

The fact that a single price is charged is not decisive. Admittedly, if what is provided to customers consists of several elements for a single price, the single price may suggest that there is a single supply. However, notwithstanding the single price, if circumstances indicate that the customers intended to purchase two distinct supplies, then it is necessary to identify the part of the single price that relates to each supply. The simplest possible method of calculation or assessment should be used for this.

Example

Catering is commonly provided together with the transport of passengers.

- In the case of in-flight catering provided to airline passengers, this is not something that the customer specifically seeks to obtain. He assumes the flight will include a meal as this is a normal feature of airline transport. The meal is provided for customers to better enjoy the transport service and, for a typical customer, is not an aim in itself. Therefore, the meal (standard-rated if supplied alone) is not liable to VAT in these circumstances because it is ancillary to the supply of zero-rated transport services. See *British Airways plc v C & E Commrs, CA [1990] STC 643 (TVC 64.8)*.
- On the other hand, where a customer books a river cruise that includes a substantial meal, the catering is more than simply an adjunct to the cruise. It is something a typical customer would regard as an end in itself. In these circumstances there are two principal supplies, comprising zero-rated transport and standard-rated catering.

HMRC accept that if a distinct service element represents 50% or more of the price of a bundle of goods and services, this will be a strong indicator that this service is not ancillary to a principal supply of any other goods or services in that bundle and that the consideration may need to be apportioned accordingly. (Business Brief 3/02).

Types of transactions that may be affected. The following list is not exhaustive but illustrates some of the areas where the issue of single and multiple supplies can have an impact.

- Delivered goods (see 47.8(18) OUTPUT TAX).
- Dispensed spectacles (see 32.3 HEALTH AND WELFARE) and dispensed hearing aids (see 32.6 HEALTH AND WELFARE).
- Membership of clubs and associations (see 14.2 CLUBS AND ASSOCIATIONS).
- Cover-mounted goods supplied with magazines (see 54.8 PRINTED MATTER, ETC).

- Admissions to sporting events, etc by programme (see 57.6 RECREATION AND SPORT).
- Books, etc supplied with correspondence courses (see 54.17 PRINTED MATTER, ETC).
- Airport parking services that include transport.
- Printed matter supplied with advertising services.
- Transport and catering (see 68.17 and 68.21 TRANSPORT AND FREIGHT).
- Installed goods.
- Programme listing magazines and broadcasting services.
- Linked promotional goods.

HMRC consider that the tests laid down in *Card Protection Plan* above will be appropriate in the great majority of cases. Businesses making supplies of the kind listed above, and which have previously relied on the outcome of earlier UK litigation (or a HMRC ruling, trade agreement or statement of practice based on that litigation), must review their VAT treatment of those supplies against the revised criteria described above. If the application of the revised criteria gives a different result, HMRC require any necessary changes in treatment to be implemented from 1 June 2001.

Single supply. Where this is established, no apportionment must be made and the supply as a whole must be considered to determine the VAT liability, if any.

Since the CJEC decision in *Card Protection Plan* above, single supplies have been held to include the following.

- The purchase of a car and its associated delivery charges (*C & E Commrs v British Telecommunications plc, HL [1999] STC 758 (TVC 42.92)*).
- The purchase of a car and free insurance (*Peugeot Motor Co plc and Another v C & E Commrs, Ch D [2003] STC 1438 (TVC 46.17)*).
- Broadcasting services and a magazine providing details of programmes (*British Sky Broadcasting Group plc (VTD 16220) (TVC 5.86)* but see *Telewest Communications* below).
- Hospitality packages offered by a football club including meals, drinks and a match programme (*Manchester United plc (VTD 17234) (TVC 5.67)*).

Earlier decisions held the following supplies to be single supplies (although these must be read in light of the tests in *Card Protection Plan*).

- Services of a launderette (which cannot be treated as separate supplies of water, heat, use of machine, etc, only the single supply of washing or drying clothes) (*Mander Laundries Ltd (VTD 31) (TVC 67.1)*).
- Services of a stud farm providing the supply of the keep of a mare with everything that is involved in maintaining her in reasonable condition and safety (a single standard-rated supply so that the supply of animal feeding stuffs included cannot be zero-rated) (*C & E Commrs v DD Scott, QB 1977, [1978] STC 191 (TVC 27.99)*).

Two-part tariff. This occurs where there are two or more payments involving apparently different transactions at different times but which amount to the purchase of a single supply. This concept was introduced in *British Railways Board v C & E*

Commrs, CA [1977] STC 221 (TVC 64.7) where there were two payments, one for a student card allowing students to buy cut-price travel tickets, and the other which the student made when obtaining the actual ticket. The court held that the two payments were both for the supply of discounted travel paid at different stages, rather than for two separate supplies (of the right to a discount and then discounted travel).

The two transactions in such cases have to be part of the composite supply, not an optional extra or subject to availability, and both payments have to be made to the same entity for the concept of 'two-part tariff' to be valid. (Internal Guidance V1–3, para 16.7).

Multiple supply. In a multiple supply, even though the supplies are often paid for together, the individual components are not integral to each other and are separate supplies.

Since the CJEC decision in *Card Protection Plan* above, multiple supplies have been held to include the following.

- Promotional/advertising services and printed brochures (*Appleby Bowers v C & E Commrs, Ch D 2000, [2001] STC 185 (TVC 5.55)*).
- Day excursions on a luxury train which included the provisions of meals (*Sea Containers Services Ltd v C & E Commrs, QB 1999, [2000] STC 82 (TVC 64.21)*).
- A monthly magazine providing details of programmes and broadcasting services where each supply was provided by a different company (*Telewest Communications plc v C & E Commrs; Telewest Communications (Publications) Ltd v C & E Commrs, CA [2005] STC 481) (TVC 60.335A)*, the court ruling that the two supplies could not be treated as a single supply merely because the customer could not enter into one transaction without the other and because there was no authority that the principles propounded in *Card Protection Plan* above could apply where there was more than one supplier.
- Ski passes including the right to transport on a funicular railway (*Cairngorm Mountain (VTD 17679) (VTD 64.22)*).
- The supply of medical services (consultation and diagnosis) by a doctor and any related supply of the provision and administration of drugs (*Dr Beynon & Partners v C & E Commrs, CA 2002, [2003] STC 169 (TVC 19.6)*).

Earlier decisions held the following supplies to be multiple supplies (although these must be read in light of the tests in *Card Protection Plan*).

- Annual subscriptions to the AA (apportionable between the benefits – a magazine, booklet, maps and information, pick-up services, repairs, etc – to which members are entitled (*C & E Commrs v The Automobile Assn, QB [1974] STC 192 (TVC 13.17)*). Membership bodies frequently treat the supply of benefits to members as multiple supplies. However, the CJEC tests in *Card Protection Plan* may mean that the supply of benefits by a number of membership bodies should be treated as a single supply of the principal benefit. In the case of non-profit making membership bodies, HMRC are considering the introduction of an extra-statutory concession whereby such bodies which supply a mixture of zero-rated, exempt and/or standard-rated benefits to members in return for their subscriptions may continue to apportion the subscriptions.
- Children's colouring books issued with felt tip pens, where the pens are not restricted in use to the book they are sold with.

- A book with an accompanying audio or video tape, each of which may be used independently of the book, and which require particular equipment for their use.
- Consideration under contracts providing for both the hire of a television set from a rental company and the insurance of the set by an insurance company within the same VAT group (*Thorn EMI plc; Granada plc (VTD 9782) (TVC 36.7)*).

Where all the supplies are liable to VAT at the same rate, there is no problem and output tax due is calculated in the normal way. Where, however, there is a mixture of zero-rated, standard-rated and/or exempt supplies, the value of each supply for VAT purposes must be calculated in order to arrive at the total output tax due. Any calculation of the apportionment of the total price must be fair and justifiable. See 47.3 OUTPUT TAX for apportionment of consideration.

De Voil Indirect Tax Service. See V3.105–107.

(Business Brief 2/01; VAT Information Sheet 2/01).

64.7 PLACE OF SUPPLY: GENERAL PROVISIONS

Having determined that a supply of goods or services has taken place, the second condition to be satisfied if the transaction is to fall within the scope of UK VAT is that the supply takes place within the UK (see 64.1 above). The place of supply rules are different for goods and for services. See 64.3-64.5 above for a consideration of what constitutes a supply of goods and a supply of services (or neither).

EC law relating to the place of supply of goods is contained in *EC 6th Directive, Arts 8, 28b(B)* (see 22.9 and 22.36 EUROPEAN COMMUNITY LEGISLATION). EC law relating to the place of supply of services is contained in *EC 6th Directive, Arts 9, 28b(C)-(F)* (see 22.10 and 22.37-22.39 EUROPEAN COMMUNITY LEGISLATION).

UK law relating to the place of supply is contained in *VATA 1994, ss 7, 9*. The Treasury are empowered to vary the normal rules by statutory instrument [*VATA 1994, s 7(11)*] and to date three main Orders have been made.

- *VAT (Tour Operators) Order 1987 (SI 1987/1806)* which relates to supplies of designated travel services by tour operators and other persons who buy in and resell travel facilities (see 66.5 TOUR OPERATORS' MARGIN SCHEME);
- *VAT (Place of Supply of Services) Order 1992 (SI 1992/3121)* which has a general impact on the place of supply of services (see 64.18 *et seq* below); and
- *VAT (Place of Supply of Goods) Order 1992 (SI 1992/3283)* which relates to supplies of goods on board ships, aircraft and trains involved in intra-EC transport (see 64.16 below).

Registration of UK suppliers in other EC countries. Where the place of supply of goods or services is outside the UK, there is no UK VAT liability. However, a UK supplier who makes supplies in another EC country may be liable to register there, subject to the registration rules applicable in that country. If they do not have an establishment there, they may have to appoint a local tax representative to account for VAT on their behalf. UK suppliers must make their own enquiries about registration in other EC countries with the authorities of the country concerned: HMRC cannot advise on the rules applicable in other countries. See 21 EUROPEAN COMMUNITY: GENERAL for the addresses of VAT authorities in other EC countries.

Registration of traders who have no place of business in the UK. Similarly, a trader belonging outside the UK with no place of business here may be liable to UK VAT registration where the place of supply of those goods or services is in the UK. See 48 OVERSEAS TRADERS for further details.

Territory of the UK and EC. The UK comprises Great Britain, Northern Ireland and the waters within twelve nautical miles of their coastlines. For VAT purposes it includes the Isle of Man but not the Channel Islands or Gibraltar. See 21.2 EUROPEAN COMMUNITY: GENERAL for the VAT territory of the EC.

64.8 PLACE OF SUPPLY OF GOODS

Subject to certain simplification procedures (see 64.17 below) and special provisions relating to warehoused goods (see 70.2 to 70.11 WAREHOUSED GOODS AND FREE ZONES), the provisions relating to the place of supply of goods are to be found in *VATA 1994, s 7* (see 64.9–64.15 below) and *The VAT* (*Place of Supply of Goods*) *Order 1992, SI 1992/3283* (see 64.16 below). It should be noted that *Sec 7* has a hierarchical structure. The place of supply of any goods may be determined by working through the rules in 64.9–64.14 below in order until one applicable to the particular supply in question is reached. [*VATA 1994, s 7(1); FA 1996, Sch 3 para 2*].

When trying to determine the place of supply of goods, the following points should be borne in mind.

- The place of supply rules can only apply if there has been a supply or a deemed supply of goods. This is particularly important when considering some intra-EC movements which are not regarded as supplies (see, for example, 23.24 EUROPEAN COMMUNITY: SINGLE MARKET for temporary movements of own goods to other EC countries).
- When applying the place of supply of goods rules, other data (eg the time of supply, invoicing routes, payment arrangements and where the parties involved belong) should be ignored.
- Different rules apply for supplies of services (see 64.18 *et seq* below).
- Where there are a number of supplies but only one movement of goods, the removal of the goods can only relate to one supply.
- EC countries have introduced simplification procedures for certain situations involving triangular trade or installed and assembled goods. These adapt the normal rules to avoid unnecessary registrations whilst achieving the desired result. See 64.17 below.

The terms 'removed' and 'removal' are used in the UK place of supply rules. They are not legally defined and should be treated as having their ordinary and everyday meaning, ie the goods are physically moved from one location to another.

(Internal Guidance V1–4, Chapter 2 paras 2.2, 2.11).

De Voil Indirect Tax Service. See V3.171–177.

64.9 Goods which do not leave or enter the UK

Where the supply of any goods does not involve their removal from or to the UK, they are treated as supplied

- in the UK if they are in the UK; and
- otherwise as supplied outside the UK.

[*VATA 1994, s 7(2)*].

The first situation covers the vast majority of transactions subject to VAT. The second situation includes sales on the high seas where the goods do not come to the UK and supplies sourced from outside the UK and delivered to a country other than the UK. In these cases it is important to disregard extraneous facts such as where the order was placed, the invoice route or how and where payment was made. (Internal Guidance V1–4, Chapter 2 para 2.3).

64.10 Installed or assembled goods

Goods whose place of supply is not determined under 64.9 above are treated as supplied

- in the UK where their supply involves their installation or assembly at a place in the UK to which they are removed; and
- outside the UK where their supply involves their installation or assembly at a place outside the UK to which they are removed.

[*VATA 1994, s 7(3)*].

By concession, where a *one-off* supply of installed or assembled goods would be treated as made in the UK, it is treated as made outside the UK if

- the supplier is not registered for VAT in the UK;
- no further UK business is anticipated;
- the goods are imported from outside the EC; and
- the customer acts as importer and shows the full value of the goods, including installation and assembly costs on the import entry.

(Business Brief 1/98).

The terms 'installation' and 'assembly' should be given their ordinary and everyday meaning. Typically, the supply will involve complex machinery or equipment requiring the expertise of the manufacturer to make it operational. However, the terms can cover a wide variety of situations, including those where the installation element by the manufacturer is minimal. It depends entirely on whether the contract between supplier and customer requires any element of installation or assembly of the goods by the supplier. Where there are separate contracts with the same supplier to supply the goods and to perform the installation or assembly, HMRC will normally treat them as being for a single supply of installed or assembled goods.

If the main supplier sub-contracts the work of installation or assembly to a third party, the place of supply for the main supplier is where the goods are installed or assembled by the subcontractor.

(Internal Guidance V1–4, Chapter 2 para 2.4).

See 64.17 below for details of a simplified procedure which eligible EC traders can use to avoid the need to register for VAT in the UK.

64.11 Distance sales to the UK

Goods whose place of supply is not determined under 64.9 or 64.10 above are treated as supplied in the UK where (*a*) the supply involves the removal of the goods to the UK by or under the direction of the supplier;

(*b*) the supply is a transaction under which the goods are acquired in the UK from another EC country by a person who is not registered or required to be registered under *VATA 1994*;

(*c*) the supplier is, or is liable to be, registered under *VATA 1994, Sch 2* by virtue of his distance sales in the UK, see 59.11 REGISTRATION (or would be so liable if he were not registrable under *VATA 1994, Sch 1* in respect of UK supplies, see 59.1 REGISTRATION); and

(*d*) the supply is neither

- a supply of goods consisting of a new means of transport (see 23.31 EUROPEAN COMMUNITY: SINGLE MARKET); nor
- anything which is treated as a supply by virtue only of *VATA 1994, Sch 4 para 5(1)* (disposal of business assets, see 64.3(*e*) above or *VATA 1994, Sch 4 para 6* (transfer of own goods between EC countries, see 23.23 EUROPEAN COMMUNITY: SINGLE MARKET).

[*VATA 1994, s 7(4)*].

The provisions in (*c*) above apply where

- the supplier has exceeded the threshold for supplies within (*a*) and (*b*) above to customers in the UK (currently £70,000) and becomes liable to register; or
- the supplier has distance sales below the threshold but has opted to become registered in the UK; or
- the goods are subject to excise duty, in which case the threshold does not apply.

(Internal Guidance V1–4, Chapter 2 para 2.5).

64.12 Distance sales from the UK

Goods whose place of supply is not determined under 64.9-64.11 above and which do not consist of a new means of transport (see 23.31 EUROPEAN COMMUNITY: SINGLE MARKET) are treated as supplied outside the UK where

(*a*) the supply involves the removal of the goods to another EC country by or under the direction of the supplier;

(*b*) the person who makes the supply is taxable in another EC country; and

(*c*) the provisions of the law of that other EC country corresponding to the provisions under 64.11(*c*) above make the supplier liable to be registered and account for VAT in that country.

This does not, however, apply where the liability under (*c*) above depends on the exercise by any person of an option in the UK corresponding to such an option made by an overseas trader under 59.12(*a*) REGISTRATION unless that person has given (and not withdrawn) a notification to HMRC that his supplies are to be treated as taking place outside the UK.

[*VATA 1994, s 7(5)*].

The provisions in (*c*) above apply where

- the supplier has exceeded the threshold for supplies within (*a*) and (*b*) above to customers in the other EC country (currently either 35,000 ECU (£24,000) or 100,000 ECU (£70,000) depending on the EC country concerned) and becomes liable to register in that country; or
- the supplier has distance sales below that threshold but has opted to become registered in that country; or
- the goods are subject to excise duty in that country in which case the threshold does not apply.

(Internal Guidance V1–4, Chapter 2 para 2.5).

64.13 **Imported goods**

Goods whose place of supply is not determined under 64.9-64.12 above are treated as supplied in the UK where

(*a*) their supply involves their being imported from a place outside the EC; and

(*b*) the supplier is the person by whom, or under whose direction, they are so imported.

[*VATA 1994, s 7(6)*].

The place of supply of imported goods is therefore determined by reference to the importer.

- Where the supplier imports the goods, the place of supply is the UK (under the above rules).
- Where the customer imports the goods, the place of supply is outside the UK (under 64.14(*b*) below).

Chain supplies. For a chain of supplies, it is necessary to determine who was responsible for importation of the goods.

> *Example*
>
> A supplies goods to B who re-supplies the goods to C who, in turn, re-supplies the goods to D. The goods are imported into the UK from a third country and remain in the UK.
>
> - If A is the importer, all three supplies are in the UK.
> - If B is the importer, the supply from A to B is outside the UK and the supplies from B to C and C to D are in the UK.
> - If C is the importer, the supplies from A to B and B to C are outside the UK and the supply from C to D is in the UK.
> - If D is the importer, all three supplies are outside the UK.

It is irrelevant where, or to whom, the goods were delivered in the UK after importation, where the goods were at the time of any of the supplies, and what were the invoice and payment dates.

(Internal Guidance V1–4, Chapter 2 para 2.6).

64.14 Other goods which leave or enter the UK

Goods whose place of supply is not determined under 64.9–64.13 above but whose supply involves their removal to or from the UK are treated

(*a*) as supplied in the UK where their supply involves their removal from the UK without also involving their previous removal to the UK; and

(*b*) as supplied outside the UK in any other case.

[*VATA 1994, s 7(7)*].

These provisions cover

- under (*a*) above,
  - (i) the removal of goods from the UK to another EC country (other than distance sales within 64.12 above); and
  - (ii) the export of goods from the UK; and
- under (*b*) above,
  - (i) the removal of goods to the UK from another EC country (other than distance sales within 64.11 above); and
  - (ii) the importation of goods from outside the EC where the UK customer is the person responsible for the importation (see 64.13 above).

Intra-EC chain supplies. Where a number of supplies are linked, it is necessary to determine which supply involved the removal of the goods from one EC country to another. Only one supply can relate to the removal and if there is doubt it should be resolved by reference to the terms of the contract.

Example

French company A supplies goods located in France to another French company B which re-supplies the goods to a UK company C which, in turn, re-supplies the goods to another UK company D. The goods physically pass direct from A in France to D in the UK.

Subject to below

- if the contract between A and B required delivery of the goods to D in the UK then
  - (i) the supply from A to B is outside the UK under (*b*) above (because it involves removal of the goods to the UK); and
  - (ii) the supplies from B to C and from C to D are in the UK under 64.9 above; and
- if the contract between B and C required B to transport the goods to the UK then
  - (i) the supply from A to B would be outside the UK under 64.9 above;
  - (ii) the supply from B to C would be outside the UK under (*b*) above; and
  - (iii) the supply from C to D would be in the UK under 64.9 above.

The time of supply, invoicing arrangements and payment, etc are not relevant when determining the place of supply. Note, however, that the above analysis gives the strict interpretation of the law. In such intra-EC situations, HMRC adopt a pragmatic approach if it gives a reasonable result. In the above scenario, if A and B are only registered in France and C and D are only registered in the UK, then they are content for the supply between B and C to be treated as the intra-EC supply whichever party was contractually bound to transport the goods to the UK. Most EC countries adopt a similarly pragmatic approach but, unlike the simplification procedures in 64.17 below, it has no statutory basis.

(Internal Guidance V1–4, Chapter 2 paras 2.7, 2.8).

64.15 Goods temporarily leaving the UK in the course of a removal to another place in the UK

For the purposes of 64.9–64.14 above, where, in the course of their removal from a place in the UK to another place in the UK, goods leave and re-enter the UK, the removal is not treated as a removal from or to the UK. [*VATA 1994, s 7(8)*]. This would occur, for example, where goods moved from Northern Ireland to England passed through Ireland.

64.16 Goods supplied on board intra-EC transport

Except for goods supplied as part of a 'pleasure cruise', goods which are supplied on board a ship, aircraft or train in the course of 'community transport' are treated as supplied at the 'point of departure' except that goods supplied for consumption on board are treated as supplied outside the EC.

'*Pleasure cruise*' includes a cruise wholly or partly for the purposes of education or training.

'*Community transport*' means transportation of passengers between a point of departure and a point of arrival in the course of which there is a stop in an EC country other than that of the point of departure and there is no stop in a country which is not an EC country.

[*SI 2004/3148, Arts 4–8*].

See also *Peninsular and Oriental Steam Navigation Co v C & E Commrs, QB [2000] STC 488 (TVC 60.436)*.

64.17 Simplification procedures

The measures outlined below may, in certain circumstances, be legitimately used to avoid unnecessary VAT registration in the UK. They do not alter the basic place of supply rules but are mechanisms to vary the normal requirements so as to achieve the desired result.

(*a*) **Import agents acting for an overseas supplier who has no place of business in the UK**. An overseas trader who imports goods into the UK for onward sale is making supplies in the UK (see 64.13 above). Where the overseas trader is not liable to register for VAT in the UK he may, as an alternative to registration, appoint a UK-resident agent who is registered for VAT to act on his behalf. See 48.4 OVERSEAS TRADERS for further details.

(*b*) **Installed or assembled goods**. The place of supply for installed or assembled goods is the place where installation or assembly takes place (see 64.10 above). To avoid an overseas person making such a supply in the UK having to register for VAT in the UK, the UK customer can account for the VAT as acquisition VAT if the following conditions are satisfied.

- The goods must be sourced from outside the UK.
- The overseas supplier must be registered for VAT in another EC country and must not be registered, or required to be registered, for VAT in the UK because of other supplies made here.
- The customer must be registered for VAT in the UK.

See 23.29 EUROPEAN COMMUNITY: SINGLE MARKET for full details including notification procedures and invoice and record requirements.

The above only applies to supplies in the UK. Traders making such supplies in other EC countries should contact the appropriate authority in that country.

(*c*) **Triangular EC trade**. In a typical triangular situation, a supplier A in one EC country supplies goods to, and invoices, an intermediary supplier B in another EC country who in turn supplies the goods to, and invoices, a customer C in a third EC country. The goods, however, pass directly from A to C. To avoid having to register for VAT in the country of destination of the goods, B can opt for C to account for the VAT due there provided

- B is not registered, or liable to be registered, in the EC country of destination of the goods but is registered in another EC country; and
- C is registered for VAT in the country of destination.

See 23.22 EUROPEAN COMMUNITY: SINGLE MARKET for full details.

(Internal Guidance V1–4, Chapter 2 paras 3.1–3.4).

64.18 PLACE OF SUPPLY OF SERVICES

Significance of place of supply. For VAT purposes, the place where a supply is deemed to be made is called the *place of supply*. This is the only place where the supply can be liable to VAT. Thus, where the place of supply of any services is in an EC country, that supply is liable to VAT (if any) in that country and in no other country. If that country is not the UK, the supply is outside the scope of UK VAT. Where the place of supply of any services is outside the EC, that supply is not liable to VAT in any EC country (although local taxes may apply). The significance for a UK business is as follows.

- **If a UK business supplies services and the place of supply is the UK,** subject to the VAT registration limits the supply is standard-rated, zero-rated or exempt (as the case may be) and any VAT due must be accounted for to HMRC. This applies regardless of where the customer belongs.
- **If a UK business supplies services and the place of supply is in another EC country**, subject to the registration limits in that country either the UK supplier or the customer is liable to account for any VAT due to the VAT authorities in that country.

(VAT Notice 741, paras 1.5, 1.6).

Place of supply rules. The rules in 64.20-64.31 below must be used to determine the place of supply of services. The basic rule is that services are made where the supplier belongs (see 64.20 below) but this is subject to a number of special rules for

- services relating to land (see 64.21 below);
- certain services which are supplied where physically carried out (see 64.22–64.25 below);
- services falling within *VATA 1994, Sch 5 paras 1-8* (see 64.26-64.28 below);
- transport services (see 64.29 below);
- the hiring of means of transport (see 64.30 below); and
- certain services of intermediaries (see 64.31 below).

In addition to these rules, special place of supply rules apply

- where travel, hotel, holiday and certain other supplies of a kind enjoyed by travellers are bought in from third parties and resold as principal under the tour operators' margin scheme (see 66.5 TOUR OPERATORS' MARGIN SCHEME); and
- in relation to sales of securities, and brokers' services in connection therewith, where the identity of the purchaser (and hence the place of belonging) is not known (see 27.2 FINANCIAL SERVICES).

Rights to services. The place of supply of a 'right to services' is the same as the place of supply of the services to which the right relates. This applies whether or not the right is exercised. A '*right to services*' includes any right, option or priority with respect to the supply of services and the supply of an interest deriving from any right to services. [*SI 1992/3121, Art 21; SI 1997/1524, Art 5*].

Anti-avoidance provisions. Where any statutory instrument made after 16 March 1998 changes the place of supply of any services to the UK with effect from a specified commencement date,

- invoices and other documents issued before the commencement date are disregarded in determining the time of supply of any services which, by virtue of the statutory instrument, would be treated as supplied in the UK if their time of supply occurred on or after the commencement date;
- any payment received by the supplier before the commencement date which relates to services performed on or after the commencement date is treated as if it were received on the commencement date;
- any payment received by the supplier on or after the commencement date which relates to services performed before the commencement date is treated as if it were received before that date; and
- a payment in respect of any services is to be taken as relating to the period of time during which those services are performed. Where a payment is received in respect of a period spanning the commencement date, an apportionment must be made on a just and reasonable basis and the payment is taken as relating to a time before that date to the extent that it is attributable to services performed before that date. The remainder of the payment (if any) is taken as relating to times on or after the commencement date.

[*VATA 1994, s 97A; FA 1998, s 22*].

Input tax recovery. Input tax attributable to certain supplies of services may be recoverable even though, under the place of supply rules, the supply is deemed to take place outside the UK and is outside the scope of UK VAT. See 35.3 INPUT TAX.

De Voil Indirect Tax Service. See V3.181–195.

64.19 Place of belonging

Services which fall under the basic place of supply rule (see 64.20 below) are supplied where the supplier belongs and services falling within *VATA 1994, Sch 5 paras 1-8* (see 64.26 below) are, in certain cases, supplied where the recipient belongs. It is therefore necessary to have rules defining the place of belonging of both the supplier and the recipient of a service.

Place of belonging of a supplier/recipient of services. If a supply of services is made to an *individual* and received by him *otherwise than for the purpose of any business carried on by him*, he is treated as belonging in whatever country he has his 'usual place of residence'.

Subject to this special rule for the recipient of services, the supplier/recipient of services is treated as belonging in a country if

(*a*) he has a 'business establishment' or some other 'fixed establishment' in that country and no such establishment elsewhere; or

(*b*) he has no such establishment (there or elsewhere) but his 'usual place of residence' is in that country; or

(*c*) he has such establishments both in that country and elsewhere and the establishment of his

- (i) in the case of a supplier of services, which is most directly concerned with the supply, or
- (ii) in the case of a recipient of services, at which, or for the purposes of which, the services are most directly used or to be used

is in that country.

A supplier/recipient of services carrying on a business through a branch or agency in any country is treated as having a business establishment there.

[*VATA 1994, s 9*].

Business establishment is not defined in the legislation but is taken by HMRC to mean the principal place of business. It is usually the head office, headquarters or 'seat' from which the business is run. There can only be one such place and it may take the form of an office, showroom or factory. Following the tribunal decision in *DFDS A/S (VTD 12588) (TVC 21.316)* which related to similar legal provisions under the Tour Operators' Margin Scheme, HMRC accept that where a trader has a headquarters in one country and other premises located in different countries, the headquarters is the 'business establishment' for the purposes of the place of supply rules, and the premises in other countries are 'other fixed establishments'. (The case was subsequently referred to the CJEC but this aspect was not disputed.)

Examples

- A business has its headquarters in the UK and branches in France, Italy and Germany. Its business establishment is in the UK.

- A company is incorporated in the UK but trades entirely from its head office in Bermuda. Its business establishment is in Bermuda.

(VAT Notice 741, paras 2.3, 2.4; Internal Guidance V1–4, Chapter 2 para 5.5).

Fixed establishment is not defined in the legislation but is taken by HMRC to mean an establishment (other than the business establishment) which has both the technical and human resources necessary for providing and receiving services on a permanent basis. A business may therefore have several fixed establishments, including a branch of the business. An agency may also be a fixed establishment but a trader is not regarded as carrying on business through an agency if it *either* acts merely as an intermediary in bringing together customer and provider but is not directly involved in the supply chain *or* supplies only incidental elements such as clerical and typing services.

Examples

- An overseas business sets up a branch comprising staff and offices in the UK to provide services. The UK branch is a fixed establishment.
- An overseas television company sends staff and equipment to the UK to film for a week. The temporary presence of human and technical resources does not create a fixed establishment in the UK.
- A company with a business establishment overseas owns a property in the UK which it leases to tenants. The property does not in itself create a fixed establishment. However, if the company has UK offices and staff or appoints a UK agency to carry on its business by managing the property, this creates a fixed establishment in the UK.
- An overseas business contracts with UK customers to provide services. It has no human or technical resources in the UK and therefore sets up a UK subsidiary to act in its name to provide those services. The overseas business has a fixed establishment in the UK created by the agency of the subsidiary.
- A company is incorporated in the UK but trades entirely overseas from its head office in the USA, which is its business establishment. The UK registered office is a fixed establishment. See *Binder Hamlyn (VTD 1439) (TVC 60.437)*.
- A UK company acts as the operating member of a consortium for offshore exploitation of oil or gas using a fixed production platform. The rig is a fixed establishment of the operating member.

(VAT Notice 741, paras 2.5, 2.6).

Usual place of residence. A *body corporate* has its usual place of residence where it is legally constituted. [*VATA 1994, s 9*(*5*)(*b*)]. HMRC interpret this as the country in which its registered office is situated. (Internal Guidance V1–4, Chapter 2 para 5.8). The usual place of residence of an *individual* is not defined in the legislation. HMRC interpret the phrase according to the ordinary usage of the words, ie normally the country where the individual has set up home with his/her family and is in full-time employment. An individual is not resident in a country if only visiting as a tourist.

Examples

- A person lives in the UK, but commutes to France daily for work. He belongs in the UK.
- Overseas forces personnel on a tour of duty in the UK live in rented accommodation with their families. They have homes overseas to which they periodically return on leave. They belong in the UK throughout their tour of duty. See *USAA Ltd (VTD 10369) (TVC 60.453)*.

(VAT Notice 741, paras 2.7, 2.8).

See also *Razzak & Mishari (VTD 15240) (TVC 60.454)* where the tribunal, distinguishing *USAA Ltd* above, held that an Indian woman, who came to the UK in 1992 and remained here until October 1996 during the course of legal proceedings against a former employer, had her usual place of residence in India throughout that period. HMRC disagree with this decision but did not appeal because of the unusual facts and the small amount of VAT involved. (Internal Guidance V1–4, Chapter 2 para 5.8).

More than one establishment. For the purposes of (*c*) above, where the supplier/recipient has establishments in more than one country, the supplies made from/received at each establishment must be considered separately. For each supply of services, the establishment which is actually providing/receiving the services is normally the one most directly connected with the supply but all facts should be considered including

- for suppliers, from which establishment the services are actually provided;
- for recipients, at which establishment the services are actually consumed, effectively used or enjoyed;
- which establishment appears on the contracts, correspondence and invoices;
- where directors or others who entered into the contract are permanently based; and
- at which establishment decisions are taken and controls are exercised over the performance of the contract.

However, where an establishment is actually providing/receiving the supply of services, it is normally that establishment which is most directly connected with the supply, even if the contractual position is different.

Where the services are not supplied from/received at a particular establishment, the place of belonging is the country where the business establishment is located.

Examples

- A company whose business establishment is in France contracts with a UK bank to provide French speaking staff for the bank's international desk in London. The French supplier has a fixed establishment in the UK created by a branch, which provides staff to other customers. The

French establishment deals directly with the bank without any involvement by the UK branch. The staff are supplied from the French establishment.

- An overseas business establishment contracts with private customers in the UK to provide information. The services are provided and invoiced by its UK branch. Customers' day-to-day contact is with the UK branch and they pay the UK branch. The services are actually supplied from the UK branch which is a fixed establishment.
- A UK supplier contracts to supply advertising services. Its customer has its business establishment in Austria and a fixed establishment in the UK created by its branch. Although day-to-day contact is between the supplier and the UK branch, the Austrian establishment takes all artistic and other decisions about the advertising. The supplies are received at the overseas establishment.
- A UK accountant supplies accountancy services to a UK incorporated company which has its business establishment abroad. However, the services are received in connection with the company's UK tax obligations and therefore the UK fixed establishment, created by the registered office, receives the supply.
- A UK company seconds staff to a customer which has its business establishment in the UK and a fixed establishment in the USA, created by its branch. The supplier is contracted by the UK establishment to provide staff to the USA branch. The supplier invoices the UK establishment and is paid by them. The services are most directly used by the USA branch.

(VAT Notice 741, paras 2.9, 2.10; Business Brief 12/98).

Agency. The key test for agency is independence as an agency cannot operate independently of its principal. In deciding independence, what matters is the reality, function and substance, and not any mere name or legal form. Particular regard should be had to the actual arrangements which exist between the *prima facie* agency and its principal, rather than any mere wording in contracts. Where there is no independence, agencies may include a subsidiary acting for its parent principal or a company acting for its associated or unrelated principal. HMRC consider that the decisions in *C & E Commrs v DFDS A/S, CJEC [1997] STC 384 (TVC 21.316)* and *C & E Commrs v The Chinese Channel (Hong Kong) Ltd, QB [1998] STC 347 (TVC 60.443)* support their policy that a UK agency creates a fixed establishment of its overseas principal where

- it is of a certain minimum size with the permanent human and technical resources necessary for providing (or receiving) services;
- it is not, in function and substance, operating independently of the overseas business; and
- it actually supplies (or receives) the services, ie does more than merely bring together customer and provider or supply incidental services such as clerical or typing services.

(Internal Guidance V1–4, Chapter 2 para 5.7; Business Brief 12/98).

VAT groups. A VAT group is treated as a single entity. This also applies when applying the 'place of belonging' rules (*Shamrock Leasing Ltd (VTD 15719) (TVC 60.455)*). As a result, a group has establishments wherever any member of the group has establishments.

> *Example*
>
> The ABC VAT group has three members. Its representative member, Company A, has its business establishment in the UK but no establishments elsewhere. Companies B and C also have their business establishments in the UK but each has a branch, respectively in the USA and Germany.
>
> The VAT group has establishments in the UK, the USA and Germany.

(Internal Guidance V1–4, Chapter 2 para 5.13).

Other case law. In *Faaborg-Gelting Linien A/S v Finanzamt Flensburg, CJEC [1996] STC 774 (TVC 21.105)* the court held that where, under *EC Sixth Directive, Art 9(1)*, a supply could be treated as taking place at the supplier's business establishment or at another fixed establishment from which the services are supplied, then the primary point of reference had to be the former unless that did not lead to a rational result or created a conflict with another EC country. In any case, services cannot be deemed to be supplied at a fixed establishment other than the place where the supplier has established his business unless that fixed establishment is of a certain minimum size and both the human and technical resources necessary for the provision of the particular services are permanently present (*Berkholz v Finanzamt Hamburg-Mitte-Altstadt, CJEC [1985] ECR 2251; [1985] 3 CMLR 667 (TVC 21.134)*). See also *ARO Lease BV v Inspecteur der Belastingdienst Grote Ondernemingen Amsterdam, CJEC [1997] STC 1272 (TVC 21.135)*.

Securities. See 27.2 FINANCIAL SERVICES for a special rule applying where a UK supplier cannot determine the place of belonging of a purchaser of securities.

64.20 Basic rule

Subject to the special rules in 64.21-64.31 below, a supply of services is treated as made

- in the UK if the supplier belongs in the UK; and
- in another country (and not the UK) if the supplier belongs in that other country.

[*VATA 1994, s 7(10)(11)*].

See 64.19 above for the place of belonging of the supplier.

The basic rule will therefore only apply if a supply of services does not fall under any of the special rules in 64.21-64.31 below. Before determining that a supply falls under the basic rule, the exact nature of the services must be identified and considered against those special rules.

Examples of services supplied where the supplier belongs

- Services described as management services where the actual services are not of a type covered by the special rules in 64.21-64.31 below (see, for example, 64.26 below in particular for consultancy, accountancy, legal and financial services).

- Clerical or secretarial services or the provision of office services.
- Archiving services involving the maintenance of documents and records.
- Entertainment services not covered by the special rules in 64.21-64.31 below (see, for example, 64.23 below for live performances). This normally includes services of production assistants, hairdressers and make-up artists for films or television.
- Veterinary services. See Business Brief 12/98.
- Broadcasting to subscribers.

(VAT Notice 741, para 3.4).

De Voil Indirect Tax Service. See V3.183.

64.21 Services relating to land

The following supplies of services are treated as made where the 'land' in connection with which the supply is made is situated.

(*a*) The grant, assignment or surrender of

- an interest in or right over land;
- a personal right to call for or be granted such an interest or right; or
- a licence to occupy land or any other contractual right exerciseable over or in relation to land.

(*b*) Any works of construction, demolition, conversion, reconstruction, alteration, enlargement, repair or maintenance of a building or civil engineering work.

(*c*) Services such as are supplied by estate agents, auctioneers, architects, surveyors, engineers and others involved in matters relating to land.

[*SI 1992/3121, Art 5*].

'*Land*' includes all forms of land and property (growing crops, buildings, walls, fences, civil engineering works and other structures fixed permanently to the land or sea bed) and plant, machinery or equipment which is an installation or edifice in its own right (eg a refinery or fixed oil/gas production platform). Machinery installed in buildings other than as a fixture is normally not regarded as land but as goods. (VAT Notice 741, para 4.3). The Channel Tunnel is land within the UK as far as its mid point (Internal Guidance V1–4, Chapter 2 para 7.2).

The services must relate *directly* to specific sites of land. It does not apply if there is only an indirect connection with land, or if the land-related service is only an incidental part of a more comprehensive service.

Examples of services relating to land

- Leases of buildings for less than 21 years.
- Options to purchase land.
- Provision of car parking.
- The supply of hotel or holiday accommodation.
- The provision of a site for a stand at an exhibition where the exhibitor obtains the right to a defined area of the exhibition hall. (If a supply of exhibition stand

space is made with the specific location of the stand allocated on arrival, this would fall to be taxed where the exhibition takes place, see 64.24 below.)

- The supply of plant or machinery, together with an operator, for work on a construction site.
- The management, conveyancing, survey or valuation of property by a solicitor or surveyor.
- Services of a loss adjuster in assessing the validity of an insurance claim relating to damage to land or buildings.
- Services connected with oil/gas/mineral exploration or exploitation relating to specific sites of land or the seabed (see 64.23 and 64.26 below where services do not relate to specific sites).
- The surveying (such as seismic, geological or geomagnetic) of land or seabed, including associated data processing services to collate the required information.
- Legal services such as conveyancing or dealing with applications for planning permission.
- Packages of property management services which may include rent collection, arranging repairs and the maintenance of financial accounts.
- Accountancy services relating to the letting of property.
- Interior designing for an hotel.

Examples of services which are not land-related

Work falling within 64.25 *below*

- Repair and maintenance of machinery which is not installed as a fixture.

Work falling within 64.26 *below*

- The hiring out of civil engineering plant on its own.
- The secondment of staff to a building site.
- The legal administration of a deceased person's estate which happens to include property.
- Advice or information relating to land prices or property markets as they do not relate to specific sites.
- Insurance of property.
- Feasibility studies assessing the potential of particular businesses or business potential in a geographic area (ie which do not relate to a specific property or site).
- Provision of a recording studio where technicians are included as part of the supply (which are engineering services).
- Design of a corporate style for an hotel chain.
- Services of an accountant in simply calculating a tax return from figures provided by a client, even when those figures relate to rental income.

(VAT Notice 741, paras 4.5–4.7; Internal Guidance V1–4, Chapter 2 paras 7.3, 7.5).

VAT registration of non-UK suppliers of land-related services in the UK. Following the decision in *WH Payne & Co (VTD 13668) (TVC 60.476)* the making of supplies of land-related services is insufficient in itself to treat the supplier as belonging where the land is situated. However, where a non-UK supplier has land in the UK, it is necessary to look closely at whether there are also human and technical resources here which are sufficient to create a fixed establishment (see 64.19 above).

- If a non-UK supplier without a business or fixed establishment in the UK makes supplies within (*a*)–(*c*) above in the UK

  (i) to a UK VAT-registered customer, the supplier may register if he wishes. If he does not, the customer must account for any VAT due under the reverse charge procedure (see 39.4 INTERNATIONAL SERVICES); and

  (ii) to unregistered customers, where the supplies are taxable, the supplier is liable to register and account for VAT in the UK (subject to the normal rules).

- If a non-UK supplier has either a business or fixed establishment in the UK (see 64.19 above) from which supplies within (*a*)–(*c*) above are made in the UK, the supplier is liable to register and account for VAT in the UK (subject to the normal rules).

VAT registration of UK suppliers of land-related services overseas. Where a UK supplier makes supplies within (*a*)–(*c*) above outside the UK,

- if the land is in another EC country (even if the customer belongs in the UK), the supplier may be liable to register in the country where the land is situated (subject to the VAT registration rules in that country). Alternatively, that other country may allow the customer (if VAT-registered) to account for VAT under the reverse charge; and
- if the land is outside the EC, the supply is outside the scope of UK and EC VAT (although it may be subject to the equivalent local indirect taxes).

(VAT Notice 741, paras 4.8, 4.9; Internal Guidance V1–4, Chapter 2 para 7.6).

De Voil Indirect Tax Service. See V3.188.

64.22 Services supplied where physically carried out

A supply of the following services is treated as made where the services are physically carried out (irrespective of where the customer belongs).

(*a*) Cultural, artistic, sporting, scientific, educational or entertainment services and any services ancillary to (including organising) any such services. See 64.23 below.

(*b*) Services relating to exhibitions, conferences or meetings and any services ancillary to (including organising) any such services. See 64.24 below.

(*c*) Valuation of, or work carried out on, any goods. See 64.25 below.

(*d*) Ancillary transport services. See 64.29 below.

Tour operators. Where supplies of services within (*a*)-(*d*) above (particularly educational services and services connected with conferences and meetings) involve the onward supply as principal of bought-in supplies of accommodation, travel, etc, the provisions of the TOUR OPERATORS' MARGIN SCHEME (66) may apply.

Overseas suppliers of services physically carried out in the UK. Where a supplier of services within (*a*)-(*d*) above belongs overseas

- if the recipient of the services is a UK VAT-registered person, the reverse charge procedure applies and the recipient is liable to account for the VAT (see 39.4 INTERNATIONAL SERVICES); and
- if the recipient of the services is not registered for UK VAT, the overseas supplier must account for any UK VAT and is liable to be registered (subject to the registration threshold).

(VAT Notice 741, paras 5.16, 5.17).

UK suppliers of services physically carried out overseas. If the services within (*a*)-(*d*) above are physically carried out in another EC country (even if the customer belongs in the UK), the supplier may be liable to register in that country. See 64.7 above. If the services are physically carried out outside the EC, the supply is outside the scope of UK and EC VAT (although it may be subject to the equivalent local indirect taxes).

De Voil Indirect Tax Service. See V3.192.

64.23 *Cultural, artistic, sporting, scientific, educational or entertainment services*

Supplies of such services and any services ancillary to (including organising) any such services are treated as made where the services are physically carried out (irrespective of where the customer belongs). [*SI 1992/3121, Art 15*(*a*)(*c*)]. Note that the place of supply of ancillary services is where the services are themselves performed which may be different from where the main services are performed.

Examples of services included

- Services of sportspersons appearing in exhibition matches, races or other forms of competition. Where, however, sponsorship or prize money is received, it is necessary to determine whether these monies are received as consideration for a supply (see 57.18 RECREATION AND SPORT) and if so, what is the nature of that supply. For example, sponsorship may be a payment for product endorsement or publicity appearances which may be advertising services within 64.26 below.
- The provision of race-prepared cars. Such packages include the hire of the car and support services to ensure optimum maintenance and operation of the car throughout a series of races.
- Scientific services of technicians carrying out tests or experiments in order to obtain data. The final compilation of the records of results, carried out in the UK, will not make the supply liable to UK VAT provided the services were otherwise performed outside the UK. However, if the services
  - — include a recommendation or conclusion based on those results, they comprise consultancy services within 64.26 below; and
  - — are connected with oil, gas or mineral exploration or exploitation and relate to specific sites of land or the seabed, they fall within 64.21 above.
- Services of an actor or singer performing before a *live* audience.
- Services of an oral interpreter at an event, eg a meeting. Written translation services, or interpreters' services which do not take place at an event, are consultancy services within 64.26 below.

- Education and training services. Such services may be exempt if made in the UK (see 20 EDUCATION). For these purposes

  — flying training is treated as supplied outside the UK provided the trainer aircraft leaves UK airspace, proceeds directly to a destination abroad and at least 12 hours' training is provided at that place; and

  — sailing training is treated as supplied outside the UK provided all the training is carried out on a vessel which clears UK territorial waters for a foreign destination and remains outside those waters for the whole of the period of training (except for proceeding directly from and returning directly to the UK).

  See also 39.6 INTERNATIONAL SERVICES for an extra-statutory concession allowing zero-rating of training services supplied in the UK to overseas Governments for the purpose of their sovereign activities.

- Services of a co-ordinator in administering arrangements for a sporting event on behalf of a promoter (but not advertising services to a sponsor by the promoter which fall within 64.26 below).

- Services ancillary to a *live* performance (eg make-up or hairdressing services or the services of a prompter) but not services ancillary to non-live entertainment (which may be consultancy services within 64.26 below or fall within the basic rule under 64.20 above).

- Services of lighting or sound technicians at a concert (including the hire of equipment included as a part of the same supply). See also *Dudda v Finanzamt Bergisch Gladbach, CJEC [1996] STC 1290 (TVC 21.145).*

(VAT Notice 741, paras 5.1, 5.3–5.6).

For a more detailed consideration of the place of supply of services provided within the entertainment industry, see the guidance notes agreed between HMRC and B.E.C.T.U. reproduced in Internal Guidance V1–4, Appendix J.

Accounting for VAT. See 64.22 above for accounting for VAT where overseas suppliers supply these services within the UK and UK suppliers supply these services abroad.

64.24 *Services relating to exhibitions, conferences or meetings*

Supplies of services relating to exhibitions, conferences and meetings and any services ancillary to (including organising) any such services are treated as made where the services are physically carried out (irrespective of where the customer belongs). [*SI 1992/3121, Art 15*(*b*)(*c*)]. Note that the place of supply of ancillary services is where the services are themselves performed which may be different from where the main services are performed.

Examples of services included

- The right to participate in an exhibition or the provision of an undefined site for a stand at an exhibition. The provision of a defined site for a stand at an exhibition falls within 64.21 above.

- Services of tradesmen such as carpenters and electricians erecting and fitting out stands at exhibition venues for organisers or exhibitors. Where a tradesman is contracted to design and build a stand in one country (eg the UK) and then transport it to another country (eg Sweden) where he erects it at the exhibition site, the place of supply of all the contracted work is where the stand is erected.

Examples of services not included

- The hiring of equipment for use at a concert without the services of technicians or operators (which falls within 64.26 below).
- Supplies of consultancy design and similar services to organisers and exhibitors (which fall within 64.26 below).

(VAT Notice 741, paras 5.1, 5.3, 5.4, 5.6; Internal Guidance V1–4, Chapter 2 paras 8.12, 8.13).

Accounting for VAT. See 64.22 above for accounting for VAT where overseas suppliers supply these services within the UK and UK suppliers supply these services abroad.

64.25 *Valuation of, or work carried out on, any goods*

Subject to the exception below, services consisting of the valuation of, or work carried out on, any goods are treated as made where the services are physically carried out. [*SI 1992/3121, Art 15(d); SI 1995/3038; SI 1996/2992*]. See 64.22 above for accounting for VAT where overseas suppliers supply these services within the UK and UK suppliers supply these services abroad.

Exception. Where

(*a*) the services are supplied to a customer registered for VAT in an EC country other than the EC country in which the services are physically carried out,

(*b*) the customer gives a valid VAT registration number to the supplier, and

(*c*) the goods are dispatched or transported out of the EC country where the services were physically carried out (but see below for repairs to containers)

the place of supply is the EC country where the customer is registered. If the customer is registered in the same EC country as the supplier, the supplier must account for any VAT due. Otherwise, the customer must account for the VAT due.

[*SI 1992/3121, Art 14; SI 1995/3038; SI 1996/2992*].

Work carried out on 'goods' is essentially any physical service carried out on another person's goods. It includes

- processing, manufacturing or assembling;
- repairs, cleaning or restoration;
- alterations, calibrations, insulating, lacquering, painting, polishing, resetting (of jewellery), sharpening, varnishing, waterproofing, etc; and
- nominations to stallions/covering (ie attempting to secure the pregnancy of mares).

'*Goods*' for this purpose include all forms of movable tangible property, covering both finished commodities and raw materials but does not include immovable property such as permanently installed goods and fixtures (for which see 64.21 above).

Examples of services included

- Services of a subcontractor installing machinery supplied by another person.
- Simple valuation of goods by loss adjusters, average adjusters, motor assessors, surveyors and other experts in connection with an insurance proposal or claim. The final compilation of a related report in a different country from the goods

will not change the place of supply from the country where valuation work is performed. Where, however, valuation forms only a part of a supply of professional services, there is a supply of consultancy services within 64.26 below.

Examples of services not included

- Work which is not mainly physical work performed on the goods themselves, eg mere inspection is not 'work on goods' although it can be 'valuation' if that is the purpose of the inspection.
- Valuation of, or work carried out on, land or property (which falls within 64.21 above).
- Testing and analysis of goods. The physical work simply provides data for the required analysis (and falls within 64.26 below).

(VAT Notice 741, paras 5.9–5.12, 6.3).

Repairs to containers for EC customers. When applying the exception above, HMRC accept that containers will be leaving the UK without requiring the repairer to obtain specific evidence and will only request commercial evidence to confirm the removal where there is specific reason to do so. (Evidence of export is still required to support zero-rating where containers will be exported outside the EC.) (Internal Guidance V1–4, Chapter 2 para 9.5).

64.26 Services falling within VATA 1994, Sch 5 paras 1–8

The place of supply of any services falling within *VATA 1994, Sch 5 paras 1–8* (see 64.27 below) is treated as taking place

(*a*) where the recipient belongs if

(i) the recipient belongs in a country outside the EC and the Isle of Man;

(ii) the recipient belongs in an EC country other than that of the supplier and the services are supplied to him for his business purposes; or

(iii) with effect from 1 July 2003 in the case of electronically supplied services falling within 64.27(7C) below, the recipient belongs in an EC country, he receives the services in a non-business or private capacity, and the services are received from a person who belongs outside the EC and the Isle of Man.

(*b*) in all other cases, where the supplier belongs under the basic rule in 64.20 above, ie if

(i) the recipient belongs in the same EC country as the supplier;

(ii) (unless (*a*)(iii) above applies) the recipient belongs in an EC country other than that of the supplier but receives the supplies in a non-business or private capacity;

(iii) the recipient is a government body, municipal authority or similar body of another EC country (unless the services are specifically required for use in a business activity); or

(iv) the supplier is unable to determine where the recipient belongs.

[*SI 1992/3121, Arts 16, 16A; SI 1995/3038; SI 2003/862, Art 3*]. (VAT Notice 741, para 11.7).

See 64.19 above for the place of belonging of a recipient and 64.28 below for additional rules relating to telecommunications services, radio or television broadcasting services, electronically supplied services and the letting on hire of goods other than means of transport. See also 27.2 FINANCIAL SERVICES for special rules applying where a UK supplier cannot determine the place of belonging of a purchaser of securities.

Accounting for VAT

- Where a UK supplier supplies services to a recipient within (*a*)(i) above, the supply is outside the scope of UK (and EC) VAT (subject to 64.28 below).
- Where a UK supplier supplies services to a recipient within (*a*)(ii) above, the place of supply is the EC country of the recipient (subject to 64.28 below). The UK supplier does not need to account for VAT in that country and the customer must do so under the reverse charge procedure.
- Where a UK-registered person *receives* services within these provisions for the purposes of business from an overseas supplier, the place of supply is the UK (subject to 64.28 below) and the reverse charge procedure applies. The UK recipient is liable to account for the VAT. See 39.4 INTERNATIONAL SERVICES.

Evidence required

(i) *General.* A UK supplier who treats services within *VATA 1994, Sch 5 paras 1–8* as supplied where the recipient belongs must hold commercial evidence that

- the services are received and used outside the UK, and,
- where (*a*)(ii) above applies, the customer is in business in another EC country.

A VAT registration number is the best evidence of this and should always be requested but alternative acceptable evidence includes a certificate from the relevant fiscal authorities, business letterheads and other commercial documents indicating the nature of the customer's business activities. Where VAT numbers are available, they should be recorded on the invoice relating to the supply. Enquiry letters in a number of foreign languages to request the correct VAT registration number from an EC customer are available on the HMRC website.

Some customers may be VAT-registered but have non-business as well as business activities (eg government departments, municipal authorities). In such circumstances the supplier must be satisfied that the services supplied are being used for the purpose of its business activities before treating the supply as taking place where the recipient belongs. In *Diversified Agency Services Ltd v C & E Commrs, QB 1995, [1996] STC 398 (TVC 60.448)*, advertising services were supplied to the Spanish Tourist Board in Spain in its capacity as a state authority and not as a commercial public body. As there was no evidence to show that the Board was treated as liable to VAT in Spain in respect of the advertising services under the reverse charge mechanism, the services were standard-rated in the UK. The Court confirmed that the burden of proof was on the company to show that the supply was outside the scope of UK VAT.

If the supplier cannot determine where his customer belongs, or cannot obtain evidence that his services are outside the scope of UK VAT, he should normally charge his customer VAT.

(ii) *Electronically supplied services.* With effect from 1 July 2003, suppliers of electronically supplied services need to verify each of the following to determine whether the supplies are subject to VAT and, if so, in which EC country.

- *Business status.* For business-to-business supplies within the EC, the evidence required at the time of the transaction would normally be the customer's VAT registration number and country identification code prefix. The number must conform to the format for the registered person's EC country. See 21.7–21.30 EUROPEAN COMMUNITY:GENERAL for format of registration numbers and country codes.

  VAT numbers should be checked where

  — a relationship has not been established with a business customer and the VAT involved exceeds £500 on a single transaction or £500 on cumulative transactions with a single customer in a VAT quarter; or

  — a business has any reason to believe that a VAT number quoted by a customer is false or is being used incorrectly.

  Where a business customer is known, it is not necessary routinely to check a VAT number quoted provided that it conforms to the correct country format.

  Businesses that supply downloaded music, games, films, etc of a kind normally made to a private consumer should challenge any VAT number quoted in what is clearly a supply to a private consumer.

  Where a customer claims to be in business but not to be VAT-registered, alternative evidence should be obtained in the form of other reasonable commercial evidence or records (eg contracts, business letterheads, a commercial website address, publicity material, certificates from fiscal authorities, etc) A digital certificate from a reputable organisation can also be used for this purpose.

  The VAT Information Exchange System (VIES) can be used to verify VAT registration numbers in EC countries. It can be accessed at

  http://europa.eu.int/comm/taxation_customs/vies/en/vieshome.htm

  Businesses may also contact the National Advice Service which can verify names and addresses as well as dates of registration and deregistration where appropriate. This advice can also be found at

  http://163.171.52.105:8016/site/eu-vat-check.htm

  If the above checks fail to confirm that the customer is in business or if there remains any doubt about the use of a VAT registration number, VAT should be charged as appropriate on all supplies to that customer (including supplies that have already been made). Any VAT that has been charged in error may be credited under the normal rules.

- *Verification of location.* Self-declaration by the customer combined with a reasonable level of verification is acceptable. Where one or other of the following practices is followed, customer self-declaration will be acceptable (without prior approval from HMRC) provided alternative evidence is sought if the test proves unsuccessful.

— Using a customer's postal address provided it has been used to send goods, catalogues, samples, CD ROMs, invoices, correspondence, etc and the correspondence has not been returned undelivered.

— Accepting payment by credit/debit card and comparing the customer's home address with the billing address.

— Accepting payment by credit/debit card and, using proprietary software, comparing the customer's country of residence with the location of the issuing bank.

— Using geo-location or proprietary software to verify where a customer belongs.

— Using systems that are configured to identify where the service is used and enjoyed (eg telecommunication suppliers). HMRC will accept the arrangement as a proxy for identifying the country where the customer belongs.

(VAT Notice 741, para 11.6; VAT Information Sheet 1/03, para 6.3; VAT Information Sheet 5/03).

Misrepresentation of status by recipient. HMRC have indicated that, where the customer wrongly represents his status, they will not hold the supplier responsible for failing to charge the correct amount of VAT provided they are satisfied that the supplier acted in good faith and made the normal and prudent checks and enquiries about the status of the customer and of any documentation of certification provided by him. (Tax Faculty of the ICAEW Guidance Notes 15/94, para 46).

De Voil Indirect Tax Service. See V3.193.

64.27 *Provisions of VATA 1994, Sch 5 paras 1–8*

(1) *Transfers and assignments of copyright, patents, licences, trademarks and similar rights.* [*VATA 1994, Sch 5 para 1*].

'Similar rights' are intellectual property rights which are capable of being legally enforced. Payments for these intellectual rights (often known as 'royalties') can be made on a regular and continuing basis or take the form of a single, one-off fee. Services which do not involve intellectual property are not covered even though they may be described as a right or licence.

Examples of services included

- The assignment of rights in a cinematographic film to a distribution company.
- The assignment of rights by a performer for his/her performance to be exploited on record, film, television, etc.
- The granting of a licence to use computer software.
- The granting of a right to carry on a particular business activity within a defined territory (such as within some franchise agreements).
- The transfer of permission to use a logo.
- The granting of a right by a photographer for one of his photographs to be published in a magazine article.

- Trading in emissions allowances under the EU Emissions Trading Scheme (EU ETS). (Business Brief 28/04).

Examples of services not included

- The supply of individual shares in goods (eg an animal or yacht) even though certain rights may be included in the supply.
- The supply of a right to obtain reduced rates for admission to conferences, meetings, etc and similar discounts on facilities available to members of clubs, associations, societies, etc in return for a subscription.
- The supply of the right to occupy land or property including hotel accommodation (which is a supply of services relating to land).

(VAT Notice 741, para 12.2).

(2) *Advertising services.* [*VATA 1994, Sch 5 para 2*].

This covers all services of publicising another person's name or products with a view to encouraging their sale. It includes supplies of advertising services in the established media, eg radio or television advertising time; of the right to place an advertisement on a hoarding; or of advertising space in any publication. It also covers promotional methods such as an entry in a telephone enquiry directory or advertising space in any electronic location.

Everything provided as part of an advertising campaign is included, even if elements of the campaign would have fallen under other place of supply rules had they been supplied in isolation.

Examples of services included

- An advertising performance or product endorsement by a personality supplied directly to the person whose products are advertised.
- The display of a sponsor's name, or product, by a sponsored person or team in return for 'sponsorship' payments (see 57.18 RECREATION AND SPORT). See also *John Village Automotive Ltd (VTD 15540) (TVC 60.468)*.
- Supplies of services that are the 'means of advertising', ie services used in connection with specific advertising, promotion or sponsorship. For example, the supply of a master advertising film, tape, record, poster, picture or photograph, or an advertisement printing block (from which copies are made).
- The devising and undertaking of a promotional campaign by an advertising agency to launch a client's new product, even where this includes trade events or demonstrations for the public in general.
- Website advertising.

Examples of services not included

- The provision of space or stands at a trade fair or exhibition (for the place of supply of which see 64.21 and 64.24 above).
- Organising a cocktail party for an advertising company where the event is part of a promotional campaign for the advertising company's own client.

(VAT Notice 741, para 12.3).

(3) *Services of consultants, engineers, consultancy bureaux, lawyers, accountants and other similar services; data processing and provision of information (but excluding from this head any services relating to land).* [*VATA 1994, Sch 5 para 3*].

Services of consultants and consultancy bureaux. Included are

- research and development;
- market research;
- written translation services or interpreters' services which do not take place at an event (eg interpreting services for a telephone conference). For oral interpreting at an event, see 64.23 above;
- testing and analysis of goods (eg drugs, chemicals and domestic electrical appliances). The essential nature of such services is analysis by experts who use the results of the testing to reach a professional conclusion, such as whether goods meet specified standards;
- writing scientific reports;
- production of customised ('bespoke' or 'specific') computer software as well as the services of adapting existing packages (some off-the-shelf software packages are treated as supplies of goods); and
- software maintenance; involving upgrades, advice and resolving any problems. The place of performance is not relevant as solutions may be provided by telephone conversations, remote links or attending a mainframe site. However, a contract for simply maintaining computer hardware relates to work on goods (and the place of supply is covered by 64.25 above).

Not included are

- services relating to specific land or property (the place of supply of which is determined under 64.21 above);
- supplies described as management services, unless they can be shown to be essentially of consultancy services although such services may fall elsewhere within *VATA 1994, Sch 5 para 3* (see, for example, *Vision Express Ltd (VTD 16848) (TVC 37.7)*);
- clerical or secretarial services, the provision of office facilities and archiving services;
- services provided by a consultant which are outside the supplier's habitual area of expertise (eg gardening carried out by a financial adviser); and
- arbitration services (see *Von Hoffmann v Finanzamt Trier, CJEC [1997] STC 1321 (TVC 21.152)* where the court held that the services of a German professor acting as arbitrator for the International Chamber of Commerce based in France were not within the equivalent provisions of *EC 6th Directive, Art 9(2)(e)*).

(VAT Notice 741, para 12.4).

Services of engineers. The services must be of a type expected of an expert or professional. Included are

- the provision of intellectual engineering advice or design. This includes overseeing the resultant physical work, provided that any such supervision is merely to ensure that the design or other advice is properly implemented; and
- services of engineers/technicians within the entertainment industry. This covers editors and sound engineers producing an edit master from which copies can be made (films, videos, compact discs or audio tapes) as well as those who exercise a degree of artistic control or influence over material.

Not included are

- services of surveyors and consultants consisting primarily of work such as design, surveying, site supervision or valuation where these directly relate to land or property (for the place of supply of which see 64.21 above); and
- services carried out by an engineer which consist wholly or mainly of physical work on goods, including installation of goods (for the place of supply of which see 64.25 above).

(VAT Notice 741, para 12.4).

Services of lawyers and accountants. Included are

- legal and accountancy services in the general administration or winding up of a deceased's estate even if that estate includes land or property; and
- services described as management services, the essential nature of which comprise accountancy or legal services.

Not included are

- services consisting primarily of work which directly relates to land or property such as property management, conveyancing, or obtaining planning consent (for the place of supply of which see 64.21 above); and
- clerical or secretarial services which include the keeping of financial records.

(VAT Notice 741, para 12.4).

Other similar services. Included are

- services of loss adjusters and assessors in assessing the validity of claims (except where these relate to land). Such services may include examination of goods to establish a value for damage or deterioration as well as negotiating a settlement amount;
- services of surveyors providing opinions which do not relate to specific sites;
- architects' services where there is no specific site of land;
- services of fiscal agents in completing VAT returns and documentation for overseas businesses (provided that the customer does not belong in the UK for the purposes of receiving these services);
- design services;
- services of specialists or technicians which are essentially creative or artistic in nature;

- services of film directors or producers, where their services are not of rights within (1) above; and
- services described as management services which comprise the exercise of corporate or strategic guidance over the running of another (usually associated) company.

Not included are

- services provided by architects and surveyors which directly relate to land or property, including surveying, site supervision, conveyancing, valuation and obtaining planning consent (for the place of supply of which see 64.21 above); and
- loss adjusting services in relation to claims on land or property (for the place of supply of which see 64.21 above) and services provided by a loss adjuster which are simply the valuation of goods (for the place of supply of which see 64.25 above).

(VAT Notice 741, para 12.4).

Data processing is the application of programmed instructions on existing data which results in the production of required information. Not included are

- services which simply include an element of data processing;
- processing data from seismic surveys where the computer analysis relates to a specified area of land or seabed (for the place of supply of which see 64.21 above); and
- simple re-formatting where there is no change to the meaning of the content.

(VAT Notice 741, para 12.4).

The provision of information covers the supplying of knowledge of any type and in any form. Information includes facts, data, figures and other material. Included are

- tourist information;
- weather forecasts;
- information supplied by a private enquiry agent;
- telephone helpdesk services (such as for computer software);
- satellite navigational and locational services; and
- provision of on-line information.

Digitised publications. Digitised publications (ie text and/or images produced in an electronic form capable of being transmitted electronically, or 'downloaded', over the Internet or a mobile telecommunications network and read either on a PC or a hand-held device, such as a mobile phone or 'reader') which are essentially non-fiction are treated as a supply of information. Some examples of non-fiction include:

- academic articles;
- arts and crafts;
- biographies;

- educational material;
- encyclopaedias;
- history;
- maps;
- news services;
- religion; and
- travel guides.

Not included as the provision of information are

- the delivery or transmission of another person's information by whatever means; and
- information relating to specific land or property (for the place of supply of which see 64.21 above).

(VAT Notice 741, para 12.4).

(4) *Acceptance of any obligation to refrain from pursuing or exercising, in whole or part, any business activity or any such rights as are referred to in (1) above*. [*VATA 1994, Sch 5 para 4*].

Examples of services included

- The vendor of a business accepting an undertaking not to compete with the purchaser.
- Agreement by the owner of a trademark to refrain from using it.

(VAT Notice 741, para 12.5).

(5) *Banking, financial and insurance services (including reinsurance, but not including the provision of safe deposit facilities)*. [*VATA 1994, Sch 5 para 5*].

Examples of services included

- Granting of mortgages and loans; selling debts.
- The storage of gold bullion or gold coins by a bank or a dealer in gold who is a subsidiary of a bank.
- The sale of securities as principal.
- The sale of unallocated precious metals (gold, silver, platinum, palladium, rhodium, ruthenium, osmium and iridium) or unallocated precious metal coins.
- Debt collection services.
- Portfolio management services.
- The supply of financial futures and financial options.
- Trustees services.
- Commodity brokers' services of arranging transactions in futures and options.

Examples of services not included

- Services of physical safe custody.
- Rent collection services (for the place of supply of which see 64.21 above).

(VAT Notice 741, para 12.6).

(5A) *The provision of access to, and of transport or transmission through, natural gas and electricity distribution systems and the provision of other directly linked services* (with effect from 1 January 2005). [*VATA 1994, Sch 5 para 5A; SI 2004/3149*].

(6) *The supply of staff.* [*VATA 1994, Sch 5 para 6*].

A supply of staff is the placing of personnel under the general control and guidance of another party as if they become employees of that other party. A clear distinction must be drawn between a supply of staff and a supply of other services by using staff. For example, the secondment, transfer or placement of a typist with a customer where the typist comes under the control and direction of that customer is the supply of staff. If typing services are supplied under a specific assignment for a customer this does not constitute the supply of staff.

Examples of services included

- The supply, secondment, loan, hire, lease or transfer as principals of personnel for a consideration by bodies such as employment or recruitment businesses or bureaux.
- The transfer for a fee by a sports club of a professional sportsman who has a contract of service with the club, eg a professional footballer.

Examples of services not included

- The supply by a freelance or other person of a specific service or services under a contract for services.
- Supplies by employment or recruitment businesses or agencies of making arrangements for the supply of staff between other parties (which fall within (8) below).

(VAT Notice 741, para 12.7).

See also *American Institute of Foreign Study (UK) Ltd (VTD 13886) (TVC 60.481)* where the services of travel couriers provided to associated companies were held to be supplies of staff rather than the supply of courier services.

(7) *The letting on hire of goods other than means of transport.* [*VATA 1994, Sch 5 para 7*].

Goods include all forms of movable property or equipment but not land and property or equipment and machinery installed as a fixture.

Examples of services included

- The hire of mobile telephone handsets (but see (7A) below if the supply is of telecommunications services).
- The hire of freight containers (but see 25.7 EXPORTS for special rules for container exports).
- The hire of computer and office equipment.

- The hire of exhibition stand furniture and equipment without any other services.

Examples of services not included

- The hire of exhibition stand space (for the place of supply of which see 64.21 and 64.24 above).
- The hire of a means of transport (for the place of supply of which see 64.21 above and 64.30 below).
- Supplies which include the services of an operator or technician (the place of supply of which depends on the nature of the services provided).

(VAT Notice 741, para 12.8).

Mobile cranes are not means of transport (*BPH Equipment Ltd (VTD 13914) (TVC 60.482)*).

(7A) *Telecommunications services*, ie services relating to the transmission, emission or reception of signals, writing, images and sounds or information of any nature by wire, radio, optical or other electromagnetic systems, including

- the related transfer or assignment of the right to use capacity for such transmission, emission or reception, and
- in relation to any services performed after 30 June 2003, the provision of access to global information networks.

[*VATA 1994, Sch 5 para 7A; SI 1997/1523, Reg 3; SI 2003/863, Art 2*].

The definition covers the sending or receiving of material by electronic or similar communications systems. This may be via cable, fibre optics, radio waves, microwaves, satellite or copper wire. It covers telephony (systems for the transmission of speech and other sound) and telegraphy (systems involving any process that provides reproduction at a distance of written, printed or pictorial matter) as well as the right to use such facilities.

Examples of services included

- telephone calls, calls delivered by cellular phones, paging, the transmission element of Electronic Data Interchange, teleconferencing and call-back services;
- switching, completion of another provider's calls, the provision of leased lines and circuits or global networks;
- telex, facsimile, multi-messaging;
- e-mail;
- basic access to the internet and World Wide Web, the provision of e-mail addresses and chatline facilities (even if related software, some information and customer support facilities are included). If a package of Internet services is supplied where the emphasis is on content rather than communication, the supply is not of pure telecommunications services and the place of supply of the package depends on the nature of the services provided. Where services are supplied separately or services are simply delivered to a customer by electronic transmission, the place of supply depends on the nature of the services provided;

- transmission or delivery of another person's material by electronic means; and
- satellite transmission services, covering transponder rental/hire and both space segments and earth segments, which includes uplinks and downlinks via land earth stations, coastal stations, outside broadcasting units or similar.

Examples of services not included

- the supply of the 'content' of a transmission, treatment of which depends on the nature of the actual services, For example, if A contracts with B to provide general advisory services and delivers the information by fax, A is providing advisory services within *VATA 1994, Sch 5 para 3* (see (3) above) not the transmission of a fax. The transmission of the fax is a supply of services within *VATA 1994, Sch 5 para 7A* above to A by a third party;
- supplies of information ordered and delivered through the Internet;
- travel information accessed by telephone;
- granting copyright to use transmitted material;
- processing of data; and
- broadcasting to subscribers.

(VAT Notice 741, para 12.9).

(7B) *Radio and television broadcasting services* (with effect from 1 July 2003). [*VATA 1994, Sch 5 para 7B; SI 2003/863, Reg 2*].

Included is broadcasting by audio and video signals, regardless of the means used (landline, line of sight or satellite link). An example of a service covered is a subscription for satellite or cable television.

Not included is the service of transmitting another person's material by electronic means. For example, if company A transmits the programmes of company B, a subscription TV company, via satellite it is supplying telecommunications services within (7A) above (although company B is supplying broadcasting to its subscribers).

(VAT Information Sheet 1/03, para 3.2).

(7C) *Electronically supplied services* (with effect from 1 July 2003). [*VATA 1994, Sch 5 para 7C; SI 2003/863, Reg 2*].

An EU guideline (agreed between EC countries although not legally binding) defines an '*electronically supplied service*' as one that

- in the first instance is delivered over the Internet or an electronic network (ie reliant on the Internet or similar network for its provision); and then
- the nature of the service in question is heavily dependent on information technology for its supply (ie the service is essentially automated, involving minimal human intervention and in the absence of information technology does not have viability).

On the basis of this two-step test, an electronically supplied service includes

- digitised products generally, such as software and changes to or upgrades of software;
- a service which provides or supports a business or personal presence on an electronic network (eg website or web-page);
- a service automatically generated from a computer, via the Internet or an electronic network, in response to specific data input by the customer; or
- other services which are automated and dependent on the Internet or an electronic network for their provision.

Examples of services included

The *EC 6th Directive* and the UK legislation list the specific supplies in (i)–(vi) below as being included. The examples within each category do not appear in the legislation but are taken from the EC guideline referred to above.

(i) Website supply, web-hosting and distance maintenance of programmes and equipment. For example:

- Website hosting and web-page hosting.
- Automated, on-line distance maintenance of programmes.
- Remote systems administration.
- On-line data warehousing (ie where specific data is stored and retrieved electronically).
- On-line supply of on-demand disc space.

(ii) The supply of software and the updating of software. For example:

- Accessing or downloading software (eg procurement/accountancy programmes, anti-virus software) plus updates.
- Bannerblockers (software to block banner adverts showing).
- Download drivers, such as software that interfaces PC with peripheral equipment (eg printers).
- On-line automated installation of filters on web sites.
- On-line automated installation of firewalls.

(iii) The supply of images, text and information, and the making available of databases. For example:

- Accessing or downloading desktop themes.
- Accessing or downloading photographic or pictorial images or screensavers.
- The digitised content of books and other electronic publications.
- Subscription to on-line newspaper and journals.
- Weblogs and website statistics.
- On-line news, traffic information and weather reports.

- On-line information generated automatically by software from specific data input by the customer, such as legal and financial data (eg continually updated stock market data).
- The provision of advertising space (eg banner ads on a website/ web-page).
- Use of search engines and Internet directories.

(iv) The supply of music, films and games (including games of chance and gambling games). For example:

- Accessing or downloading of music onto PCs, mobile phones, etc.
- Accessing or downloading of jingles, excerpts, ringtones, or other sounds.
- Accessing or downloading of films.
- Downloads of games onto PCs, mobile phones, etc.
- Accessing automated on-line games which are dependent on the Internet, or other similar electronic networks, where players are remote from one another.

(v) The supply of political, cultural, artistic, sporting, scientific and entertainment broadcasts (including broadcasts of events). For example:

- Web-based broadcasting that is only provided over the Internet or similar electronic network and is not simultaneously broadcast over a traditional radio or television network.

(vi) The supply of distance teaching. For example:

- Teaching that is automated and dependent on the Internet or similar electronic network to function, including virtual classrooms.
- Workbooks completed by pupil on-line and marked automatically, without human intervention.

But where the supplier of a service and his customer communicate via electronic mail, this does not of itself mean that the service performed is an electronically supplied service.

Other items covered (although not specifically listed in *EC 6th Directive* or the UK legislation include:

- On-line auction services (to the extent that they are not already considered to be web-hosting services under (i) above) that are dependent on automated databases and data input by the customer requiring little or no human intervention (eg an on-line market place or on-line shopping portals).
- Internet Service Packages (ISPs) in which the telecommunications component is an ancillary and subordinate part (ie a package that goes beyond mere Internet access comprising various elements, for example, content pages containing news, weather, travel information; games fora; web-hosting; access to chat-lines etc).

Examples of transactions not included

The EC guidelines referred to above list the following as example of transactions which as not electronically supplied services.

- Supplies of
  - goods where the order and processing is done electronically,
  - CD-ROMs, floppy discs and similar tangible media,
  - printed matter such as books, newsletters, newspapers or journals, and
  - CDs, audio cassettes, video cassettes, DVDs and games on CD-ROMs

  which are supplies of goods rather than services.
- Supplies of
  - services of lawyers and financial consultants, etc who advise clients through e-mail, and
  - interactive teaching services where the course content is delivered by a teacher over the Internet or an electronic network (ie via remote link)

  which are services that rely on substantial human intervention and where the Internet or electronic network is only used as a means of communication.
- Supplies of
  - physical repair services of computer equipment,
  - off-line data warehousing services,
  - advertising services, such as in newspapers, on posters and on television,
  - telephone helpdesk services,
  - teaching services involving correspondence courses such as postal courses, and
  - conventional auctioneers' services reliant on direct human intervention, irrespective of how bids are made (eg in person, Internet or telephone)

  which are services that are not delivered over the Internet and rely on substantial human intervention.
- Supplies of radio and television broadcasting services provided over the Internet or similar electronic network simultaneous to the same broadcast being provided over traditional radio or television network (which are covered by (7B) above).
- Supply of
  - videophone services (ie telephone services with a video component),
  - access to the Internet and World Wide Web,

— telephony (ie telephone service provided through the Internet)

which are supplies of telecommunication services covered by (*h*) above.

(VAT Information Sheet 4/03).

(8) *The services rendered by one person to another in procuring for the other any of the services mentioned in (1)-(7C) above.* [*VATA 1994, Sch 5 para 8; SI 1997/1523, Reg 3; SI 2003/863, Reg 2*].

Examples of services included

- Stockbroking services.
- Insurance broking services.
- Services of patent, copyright and similar agents.
- Services of advertising agents.

Examples of services not included

- Estate agents' services in arranging supplies of land or property (for the place of supply of which see 64.21 above).
- Services of only facilitating a supply within (1)–(7C) above, such as simple introduction.

(VAT Notice 741, para 12.10).

64.28 *Letting on hire of goods (other than means of transport) and telecommunications, broadcasting and electronically supplied services*

In relation to

- the letting on hire of goods (other than means of transport) within 64.27(7) above,
- telecommunication services within 64.27(7A) above,
- radio and television broadcasting services (with effect from 1 July 2003) within 64.27(7B) above, and
- electronically supplied services (with effect from 1 July 2003) within 64.27(7C) above when received by a person for the purposes of a business carried on by him

the following rules apply *in addition* to those in 64.26 above.

(*a*) Where the supply would, under 64.26(*a*) or (*b*) above, be treated as supplied in the UK, it is not to be so treated to the extent that the 'effective use and enjoyment' takes place outside the EC.

(*b*) Where the supply would, under 64.26(*a*) or (*b*) above, be treated as supplied outside the EC, it is to be treated as supplied in the UK to the extent that the effective use and enjoyment of the services takes place in the UK.

[*SI 1992/3121, Arts 17, 18; SI 1998/763; SI 2003/862, Art 5*].

'Effective use and enjoyment' takes place where a recipient actually consumes the relevant services or uses the goods. In practice, this will be where the services are physically used or the goods are physically located, irrespective of contract, payment or beneficial interest. Where services are only partly liable to UK VAT because of the use and enjoyment provisions, there is no prescribed method of determining the extent to which services are used in the UK. Any method may be adopted which produces a fair and reasonable reflection of services. Evidence of how apportionment has been made should be retained.

Examples

(1) A Canadian company hires out recording equipment to a UK private individual who uses the equipment in his UK home. The place of supply is the UK. This is because the goods are used in the UK and the place of supply would otherwise have been outside the EC under 64.26(*b*)(ii) above.

(2) An Australian tourist hires a video camera from a UK provider during a visit to the UK. The place of supply is the UK. This is because the goods are used in the UK and the place of supply would otherwise have been outside the EC under 64.26(*b*)(ii) above.

(3) A UK golf shop hires out a set of golf clubs to a UK customer for use on a holiday in the USA. The place of supply is outside the EC if the customer is able to demonstrate that the golf clubs are used only in the USA. This is because the goods are used outside the EC and the place of supply would otherwise have been the UK under 64.26(*b*)(i) above.

(4) A business traveller makes a reservation at a Hong Kong hotel from his London office using a toll-free number. The telecommunications services are supplied to, and used by, the Hong Kong hotel. The place of supply is outside the EC because the services are not effectively used and enjoyed in the UK.

(5) A UK business purchases digitised software from an Irish supplier for use only in its branch in the Channel Islands. Although the supply is received in the UK where the business belongs, it is used outside the EC and is outside the scope of UK (and EC) VAT.

(6) A UK business purchases downloaded information from another UK business for use both in its UK headquarters and its Canadian branch. Although the supply is received in the UK, to the extent it is used in Canada, it is outside the scope of UK VAT. UK VAT is due only to the extent of use by the UK headquarters.

(7) A satellite TV company established in India supplies broadcasting to UK subscribers. The services are used and enjoyed in the UK and are subject to UK VAT. The place of supply is the UK. This is because the services are used and enjoyed in the UK and the place of supply would otherwise have been outside the EC under 64.26(*b*)(ii) above.

(VAT Notice 741, paras 13.5, 13.7, 14.5, 14.6; VAT Information Sheet 1/03, paras 5.1, 5.2, 7.1, 7.2).

Summary of liabilities. The following tables summarise the UK VAT position for services subject to the use and enjoyment provisions. Each row must be read in its entirety to arrive at the correct position.

(1) *Letting on hire of goods (other than means of transport), telecommunications services and, with effect from 1 July 2003, broadcasting services*

	UK VAT position (subject to use and enjoyment provisions)	*Impact of use and enjoyment provisions*
Supplier belongs in the UK		
Customer belongs		
— in the UK	Services are supplied in the UK and the supplier accounts for UK VAT[1]	Services used outside the EC are outside the scope of UK (and EC) VAT
— in another EC country and receives services for business purposes	Services are supplied in the other EC country and are outside the scope of UK VAT	Do not apply — outside UK jurisdiction
— in another EC country and receives the services for non-business purposes	Services are supplied in the UK and the supplier accounts for UK VAT [1]	Services used outside the EC are outside the scope of UK (and EC) VAT
— outside the EC	Services are supplied outside the EC and are outside the scope of UK (and EC) VAT	Services used in the UK are supplied in the UK and the supplier accounts for UK VAT[1, 2, 3]
Supplier belongs in another EC country		
Customer belongs		
— in the UK and receives the services for business purposes	Services are supplied in the UK and the customer accounts for UK VAT by applying the reverse charge[1]	Services used outside the EC are outside the scope of UK (and EC) VAT
— in the UK and receives the services for non-business purposes	Services are supplied in the supplier's country and are outside the scope of UK VAT[4]	Do not apply — outside UK jurisdiction
— in another EC country	Services are supplied in another EC country and are outside the scopc of UK VAT	Do not apply — outside UK jurisdiction

	UK VAT position (subject to use and enjoyment provisions)	*Impact of use and enjoyment provisions*
— outside the EC	Services are supplied outside the EC and are outside the scope of UK (and EC) VAT	Services used in the UK are supplied in the UK and the supplier accounts for UK VAT[1] unless the customer provides a UK registration number and accounts for UK VAT by applying the reverse charge[2, 3]
Supplier belongs outside the EC		
Customer belongs		
— in the UK and receives the services for business purposes	Services are supplied in the UK and the customer accounts for UK VAT by applying the reverse charge[1]	Services used outside the EC are outside the scope of UK (and EC) VAT
— in the UK and receives the services for non-business purposes	Services are supplied in the supplier's country and are outside the scope of UK (and EC) VAT – use and enjoyment provisions are likely to apply	Services used in the UK are supplied in the UK and the supplier accounts for UK VAT[1]
— in another EC country and receives the services for business purposes	Services are supplied in the other EC country and are outside the scope of UK VAT	Do not apply — outside UK jurisdiction
— in another EC country and receives the services for non-business purposes	Services are supplied in the supplier's country and are outside the scope of UK (and EC) VAT	Services used in the UK are supplied in the UK and the supplier accounts for UK VAT[1]
— outside the EC	Services are supplied outside the EC and are outside the scope of UK (and EC) VAT	Services used in the UK are supplied in the UK and the supplier accounts for UK VAT[1] unless the customer provides a UK VAT registration number and accounts for UK VAT by applying the reverse charge[2, 3]

(2) *Electronically supplied services with effect from 1 July 2003*

	UK VAT position (subject to use and enjoyment provisions)	*Impact of use and enjoyment provision*
Supplier belongs in the UK		
Customer belongs		
— in the UK and receives the services for business purposes	Services are supplied in the UK and the supplier accounts for UK VAT[1]	Services used outside the EC are outside the scope of UK (and EC) VAT
— in the UK and receives the services for non-business purposes	Services are supplied in the UK and the supplier accounts for UK VAT[1]	Do not apply to non-business services[6]
— in another EC country and receives the services for business purposes	Services are supplied in the other EC country and are outside the scope of UK VAT	Do not apply — outside UK jurisdiction
— in another EC country and receives the services for non-business purposes	Services are supplied in the UK and the supplier accounts for UK VAT[1]	Do not apply to non-business services
— outside the EC and receives the services for business purposes	Services are supplied outside the EC and are outside the scope of UK (and EC) VAT	Services used in the UK are supplied in the UK and the supplier accounts for UK VAT[1, 3]
— outside the EC and receives the services for non-business purposes	Services are supplied outside the EC and are outside the scope of UK (and EC) VAT	Do not apply to non-business services[6]
Supplier belongs in another EC country		
Customer belongs		
— in the UK and receives the services for business purposes	Services are supplied in the UK and the customer accounts for UK VAT by applying the reverse charge[1]	Services used outside the EC are outside the scope of UK VAT
— in the UK and receives the services for non-business purposes	Services are supplied in the supplier's country and are outside the scope of UK VAT. Supplier accounts for any VAT due	Do not apply to non-business services

	UK VAT position (subject to use and enjoyment provisions)	*Impact of use and enjoyment provision*
— in another EC country	Services are supplied in another EC country and are outside the scope of UK VAT	Do not apply — outside UK jurisdiction
— outside the EC and receives the services for business purposes	Services are supplied outside the EC and are outside the scope of UK (and EC) VAT	Services used in the UK are supplied in the UK and the supplier accounts for UK VAT[1] unless the customer provides a UK VAT registration number and accounts for UK VAT by applying the reverse charge[3]
— outside the EC and receives the services for non-business purposes	Services are supplied outside the EC and are outside the scope of UK (and EC) VAT	Do not apply to non-business services
Supplier belongs outside the EC		
Customer belongs		
— in the UK and receives the services for business purposes	Services are supplied in the UK and the customer accounts for UK VAT due by applying the reverse charge[1]	Services used outside the EC are outside the scope of UK (and EC) VAT
— in the UK and receives the services for non-business purposes	Services are supplied in the UK and the supplier should account for any UK VAT due[5]	Do not apply to non-business services
— in another EC country	Services are supplied in another EC country and are outside the scope of UK VAT	Do not apply — outside UK jurisdiction

	UK VAT position (subject to use and enjoyment provisions)	*Impact of use and enjoyment provision*
— outside the EC and receives the services for business purposes	Services are supplied outside the EC and are outside the scope of UK (and EC) VAT	Services used in the UK are supplied in the UK and the supplier accounts for UK VAT[1] unless the customer provides a UK VAT registration number and accounts for UK VAT by applying the reverse charge[3]
— outside the EC and receives the services for non-business purposes	Services are supplied outside the EC and are outside the scope of UK (and EC) VAT	Do not apply to non-business services

Notes

1. Subject to registration threshold.

2. Any telecommunications services used in the UK by customers belonging outside the EC are supplied in the UK. Such services are therefore subject to UK VAT when used in the UK by non-EC visitors (eg public pay-phones, fax shop services and calls made from hotel rooms). As an administrative measure, the elements of telecommunications services used in the UK may be ignored if

   - simply an incidental part of an established telephone contract or account held by a customer who belongs outside the EC;
   - used by a temporary non-EC visitor; and
   - HMRC are satisfied that these conditions are not being abused.

3. Services used in other EC countries are outside the scope of UK VAT but may be within the scope of VAT of the country where used.

4. Services may be outside the scope of the supplier's EC country if used outside the EC.

5. Suppliers may opt to use the special scheme for non-EC businesses. See 63.34 SPECIAL SCHEMES.

6. *Simplification for businesses supplying telecommunication or broadcasting services as well as electronically supplied services.* HMRC recognise that, in certain situations, the place of supply would be the same whether the rules for telecommunications and broadcasting services, or those for electronically supplied services, were applied. This is because most non-business customers use and enjoy services in the same country in which they belong. Therefore where

   - a UK business supplies electronically supplied services;
   - its services are supplied to private individuals or non-business organisations; and

- its existing accounting systems are set up to tax supplies where they are effectively used and enjoyed

it can, exceptionally, opt to apply the use and enjoyment rules to its supplies of electronically supplied services. This is a simplification measure which prevents the need for businesses to adjust their systems. However, HMRC will not allow this simplification to be used in any case where they consider it leads to abuse.

(VAT Notice 741, paras 14.7, 18.1–18.4; VAT Information Sheet 1/03, para 8.1, Flowcharts 1–6).

See 39.9 INTERNATIONAL SERVICES for further coverage of telecommunications services and 39.10 INTERNATIONAL SERVICES for further coverage of broadcasting and electronically supplied services.

64.29 Transport services

Passenger transport services. Services consisting of the transport of passengers (including any accompanying luggage and/or motor vehicle) are treated as supplied in the country in which the transportation takes place (and only to the extent that it takes place in that country). [*SI 1992/3121, Arts 6, 8*]. *For sea and air passenger transport*, provided the means of transport used does not put in or land in another country on the way, any transportation as part of a journey between two points in the same country is treated as taking place wholly inside that country even where it takes place partly outside its territorial jurisdiction. This applies even if the journey is part of a longer journey involving travel to or from another country. [*SI 1992/3121, Art 7*].

Pleasure cruises. Any goods or services provided as part of a pleasure cruise are treated as supplied in the same place as the transportation of the passengers, and for this purpose a pleasure cruise is treated as a supply of passenger transport. [*SI 1992/3121, Art 8*].

See 68.15 TRANSPORT AND FREIGHT for further details and 68.14–68.23 TRANSPORT AND FREIGHT for passenger transport generally.

Overseas suppliers of passenger transport services in the UK. Where a supplier of such services belongs overseas

- if the recipient of the services is a UK VAT-registered person, the reverse charge procedure applies and the recipient is liable to account for the VAT (see 39.4 INTERNATIONAL SERVICES); and
- if the recipient of the services is not registered for UK VAT, the overseas supplier must account for any UK VAT and is liable to be registered (subject to the registration threshold).

UK suppliers of passenger transport overseas. If a UK supplier supplies passenger transport in another EC country, he may be liable to register in that country. See 64.7 above. If the services are physically carried out outside the EC, the supply is outside the scope of UK and EC VAT.

Freight transport and related services. Subject to special rules for intra-EC transport of goods below,

- freight transport services are treated as supplied in the country where the transportation takes place (and only to the extent that it takes place in that country); and

- ancillary freight transport services (loading, unloading, handling and similar activities) are treated as made where those services are physically performed.

For sea and air freight transport, provided the means of transport used does not put in or land in another country on the way, any transportation as part of a journey between two points in the same country is treated as taking place wholly inside that country even where it takes place partly outside its territorial jurisdiction. This applies even if the journey is part of a longer journey involving travel to or from another country.

[*SI 1992/3121, Arts 2, 6, 7, 9*].

Intra-EC freight transport and related services. There are special rules for 'intra-EC freight transport' and related services.

(*a*) Intra-EC freight transport is treated as supplied in the EC country where the transportation begins.

(*b*) Ancillary freight transport services are treated as made where they are physically performed.

(*c*) Intermediary services of arranging intra-EC freight transport (or any activity intended to facilitate the making of such a supply) are treated as supplied where the transportation begins.

(*d*) Intermediary services of arranging ancillary freight transport services in connection with intra-EC freight transport (or any activity intended to facilitate the making of such a supply) are treated as supplied in the same EC country where the ancillary transport services are physically performed.

However, where

- a service within (*a*)–(*d*) above is supplied to a customer registered for VAT in an EC country other than the EC country in which the supply would otherwise be treated as taking place, and
- the customer gives a valid VAT registration number to the supplier,

the place of supply is the EC country of the customer. Where the supplier and customer belong in different EC countries, the customer must account for VAT under the reverse charge procedure.

'Intra-EC freight transport' means transport which begins in one EC country and ends in another EC country.

[*SI 1992/3121, Arts 2, 10–12, 14*].

See 68.24–68.30 TRANSPORT AND FREIGHT for further details of freight transport services, ancillary freight transport services and services of intermediaries.

De Voil Indirect Tax Service. See V3.190.

64.30 Hire of means of transport

The place of supply of the letting on hire of any 'means of transport' is where the supplier belongs under the basic rule in 64.20 above *except that*

(*a*) where the supplier belongs in the UK, to the extent that the 'effective use and enjoyment' of the letting on hire takes place outside the EC, the place of supply is outside the UK (and the EC); and (*b*) where the supplier belongs outside the EC, to the extent that the effective use and enjoyment of the letting on hire takes place in the UK, the place of supply is in the UK.

[*SI 1992/3121, Arts 17, 18; SI 1997/1524, Arts 3, 4; SI 1998/763*].

'*Means of transport*' includes ships, boats, yachts, hovercraft, barges or dracones (bulk liquid barges), aircraft, cars, trucks, lorries, touring caravans, trailers, motorcycles, cycles and rolling stock but does not include freight containers, static caravans, and racing cars for racing on race tracks. Mobile cranes are not means of transport (*BPH Equipment Ltd (VTD 13914) (TVC 60.482)*). Provided the goods hired are a means of transport, their actual use is not important (eg the provisions apply to the lease of a train to a transport museum or a yacht for use in racing).

'*Effective use and enjoyment*'. HMRC do not specifically give their interpretation of 'effective use and enjoyment' in the context of the hire of means of transport. See, however, 64.28 above for their interpretation of the phrase in the context of hire of other goods.

Hire of means of transport does not cover supplies which include the services of a driver, pilot operator or crew. The place of supply of such transport-related services depend on the nature of the services supplied. For example, the supply of a ship or aircraft *without crew* under a written charter party contract is the hire of a means of transport but if supplied *with crew* the place of supply is where the supplier belongs under the basic rule in 64.20 above.

(VAT Notice 741, paras 3.5–3.8, 9.1).

Hire of means of transport in the UK from a supplier outside the EC. Where a UK-registered customer hires a means of transport in the circumstances under (*b*) above and the place of supply is in the UK, the reverse charge procedure applies. The UK recipient is required to account for the VAT. See 39.4 INTERNATIONAL SERVICES. Where the UK customer is not registered for VAT, the overseas supplier must account for any UK VAT and is liable to be registered (subject to the registration threshold).

(VAT Notice 741, paras 13.13, 13.14).

De Voil Indirect Tax Service. See V3.194.

64.31 Services of intermediaries

Special place of supply rules apply to

- services of estate agents in arranging supplies of land or property (see 64.21 above);
- making arrangements for a supply of intra-EC freight transport or related ancillary services (see 64.29 above); and
- making arrangements for services within *VATA 1994, Sch 5 para 1-8* which are covered by the provisions in 64.26 above.

Subject to the above, the place of supply of the making of arrangements for a supply by or to another person of any goods or services (or of any other activity intended to facilitate the making of such a supply) is the same place where the supply which is being arranged is deemed to take place, *except that* where the intermediary services are supplied to a customer

- registered for VAT in an EC country other than the EC country in which the services would otherwise be treated as supplied, and

- who has given a valid VAT registration number to the supplier

the services are treated as supplied in the EC country where the customer is registered.

[*SI 1992/3121, Arts 13, 14*].

The normal rules must be followed to determine the place of supply of the supply of goods or services which is being arranged. See 64.7 *et seq* above for the place of supply of goods and 64.18 *et seq* above for the place of supply of services.

Accounting for VAT on intermediary services. Whether the supplier of the intermediary services or his customer has to account for VAT, if any, depends upon whether, and if so where, the customer is registered for VAT.

- Where a UK supplier arranges a supply which is made outside the EC, the supply is outside the scope of UK VAT and any other EC VAT. However, the supplier will still be able to recover any input tax incurred in making the supply.

- Where a UK supplier arranges a supply which is made within the EC to a customer who does not give a valid EC VAT number, the supplier is responsible for accounting for the VAT in the EC country where the supply is made. If not already registered there, the supplier may be required to register to account for the VAT.

- Where a UK supplier arranges a supply which is made within the EC to a customer registered for VAT in the UK for the purposes of receiving the supply, the place of supply is the UK. The supplier must charge and account for VAT to HMRC in the normal way. The reverse charge procedure cannot be applied.

- Where a UK supplier arranges a supply which is made within the EC to a customer registered for VAT in another EC country for the purposes of receiving the supply, the place of supply is the customer's country and the customer must account for VAT there under the reverse charge procedure. The customer must provide the supplier with a valid VAT registration number under which the service is received and which the supplier must quote on his VAT invoice.

  Since the place of supply is outside the UK, the supply is outside the scope of UK VAT and the supplier need not charge UK VAT. However, he will still be able to recover any input tax incurred in making the supply.

Intermediary services received by UK customers from overseas suppliers. Where a supplier of intermediary services belongs overseas

- if the recipient of the services is a UK VAT-registered person, the place of supply is the UK and the reverse charge procedure applies with the recipient liable to account for the VAT (see 39.4 INTERNATIONAL SERVICES); and

- if the UK customer is not registered for UK VAT and the supply is treated as made in the UK, the overseas supplier must account for any UK VAT and is liable to be registered (subject to the registration threshold).

(VAT Notice 741, paras 10.7, 10.9, 10.13, 10.14).

Example

Intermediary A, who belongs in the UK, arranges a supply of goods between seller X and buyer Y. The goods pass directly from X to Y.

(*a*) Seller X and buyer Y are both UK VAT-registered.

The place of supply of the goods is the UK. Whether A acts for X or Y, A's services are supplied in the UK and A must account for the VAT due.

(*b*) Seller X is VAT-registered in Ireland and buyer Y is VAT-registered in the UK.

The place of supply of goods is Ireland.

- If A acts for X, A's services are supplied in Ireland and X must account for the VAT due there under the reverse charge procedure.
- If A acts for Y, A's services are supplied in the UK (because although the underlying supply of goods is made in Ireland, his customer is VAT-registered in a different EC country and therefore the place of supply is where the customer is registered). A must account for the VAT due.

(*c*) Seller X is located in Russia and buyer Y is VAT-registered in France.

The place of supply of goods is Russia. Whether A acts for X or Y, A's services are supplied outside the EC (where the underlying supply of goods is supplied). A has no UK VAT liability.

(*d*) Seller X is registered for VAT in the UK and buyer Y is located in Russia.

The place of supply of the goods is the UK. Whether A acts for X or Y, A's services are supplied in the UK (where the underlying supply of goods is supplied). A's supply is zero-rated under *VATA 1994, Sch 8 Group 7 Item 2* (see 39.8 INTERNATIONAL SERVICES).

(*e*) Seller X is registered for VAT in Denmark and buyer Y is registered for VAT in Spain.

The place of supply of the goods is Denmark.

- If A acts for X, A's services are supplied in Denmark (where the underlying supply of goods is supplied) and X must account for the VAT there under the reverse charge procedure.
- If A acts for Y, A's services are supplied in Spain (because although the underlying supply of goods is made in Denmark, his customer is VAT-registered in a different EC country and therefore the place of supply is where the customer is registered) and Y must account for the VAT there under the reverse charge procedure.

(*f*) Seller X is registered for VAT in Greece and buyer Y is an unregistered person belonging in the UK. X is not required to be registered in the UK in respect of distance sales.

The place of supply of the goods is Greece.

- If A acts for X, A's services are supplied in Greece (where the underlying supply of goods is supplied) and X must account for the VAT there under the reverse charge procedure.
- If A acts for Y, A's services are supplied in Greece (because the underlying supply of goods is made in Greece and his customer is not VAT-registered in a different EC country from that in which the underlying supply is made). A must account for the VAT due in

Greece and may be liable to register for VAT there (subject to the registration limits in that country).

(Internal Guidance V1–4, Chapter 3 Appendix I).

De Voil Indirect Tax Service. See V3.195.

64.32 TIME OF SUPPLY: GENERAL PROVISIONS

EC legislation. See 22.11 EUROPEAN COMMUNITY LEGISLATION.

VAT becomes due on a supply of goods or services at the time of supply. [*VATA 1994, s 1(2)*]. It is therefore necessary to have 'time of supply' rules to determine when a supply is to be treated as taking place for VAT purposes. The resultant time is often referred to as the *tax point* (although this is not a term that is used in the legislation).

VAT must normally be accounted for on the return for the period in which the tax point occurs and at the rate of VAT in force at that time. The normal tax point rules relating to the supply of goods and services are covered in 64.39 and 64.49 below respectively. HMRC have powers, at the request of a taxable person, to alter the time at which his supplies are to be treated as taking place. [*VATA 1994, s 6(10)*]. These are known as accommodation tax points. See 64.38 below.

In addition, HMRC may make regulations with respect to the time at which a supply is to be treated as taking place where

(*a*) it is a supply of goods or services for a consideration the whole or part of which is determined or payable periodically, or from time to time, or at the end of any period;

(*b*) it is a supply of goods for a consideration the whole or part of which is determined at the time when the goods are appropriated for any purpose;

(*c*) there is a supply to which *VATA 1994, s 55* applies (special scheme for gold); or

(*d*) there is a supply of services under *VATA 1994, Sch 4 para 5(4)* (non-business use of goods) or under a Treasury Order under *VATA 1994, s 5(4)*.

[*VATA 1994, s 6(14)*].

See 64.40-64.48 below for special provisions relating to goods and 64.50-64.57 below for special provisions relating to services.

Although the principal purpose of the time of supply rules is to fix the time for accounting for VAT, the rules have other uses including

- calculating turnover for VAT registration purposes;
- establishing the period to which supplies (including exempt supplies) are to be allocated for partial exemption purposes, and
- establishing when input tax may be deducted.

Exempt supplies. The time of supply for any exempt supply is determined using the normal tax point rules (see 64.39-64.57 below as appropriate) but, as an invoice issued in respect of an exempt supply is not a VAT invoice (see 64.34 below) references to the issue of a VAT invoice have no effect. Thus, for example, in the case of a single supply of exempt services, the time of supply will normally be the earlier of receipt of payment or performance of the service. (Internal Guidance V1–11, para 6.7).

Zero-rated supplies. The time of supply for any zero-rated supply is determined using the normal tax point rules (see 64.39-64.57 below as appropriate) but, subject to the special rules for the supply of zero-rated goods in the UK for acquisition by a registered trader in another EC country (see 23.16 EUROPEAN COMMUNITY: SINGLE MARKET), as an invoice issued in respect of a zero-rated supply is not a VAT invoice (see 64.34 below) references to the issue of a VAT invoice has no effect. Thus, for example, the tax point for a zero-rated supply of goods will normally be the earlier of receipt of payment or the removal/making available of those goods. (Internal Guidance V1–11, para 6.7).

Change of rate. Where there is a change in the VAT rate or a VAT liability, VAT is chargeable according to the normal tax point rules (see 64.39-64.57 below as appropriate) unless the taxpayer elects for the special change of rate provisions to apply. See 55.6 RATES OF VAT.

Retail schemes and cash accounting. The special RETAIL SCHEMES (60) and the cash accounting arrangements (see 63.2 SPECIAL SCHEMES) do not override the time of supply rules but amend the time at which VAT is accounted for on supplies that are eligible for inclusion within the schemes. This may be at a time different from the normal rules that require the VAT to be accounted for by reference to the tax point. Nevertheless, any questions concerning the time at which VAT should be accounted for by traders using either of these schemes should be considered in the context of the scheme rules and appropriate guidance rather than the normal time of supply rules. (Internal Guidance V1–11, para 1.6).

De Voil Indirect Tax Service. See V3.131–143.

64.33 Identifying the correct tax point

The following is a step-by-step guide to determine the correct tax point.

(1) Does the supply fall within the scope of an accommodation tax point granted to the person making the supply?	See 64.38
(2) Is the supply covered by an extra-statutory class concession, eg coins operated machines?	See 64.56
(3) If the supply is a supply of goods	
— is it the permanent diversion of goods to private or non-business use?	See 64.40
— is it an intra-EC supply of goods eligible for zero-rating?	See 64.41
— is it on a 'sale or return basis' or 'on approval' terms?	See 64.43
— does it involve land in that it is either (i) in connection with a compulsory purchase where the price has not been agreed; or (ii) a further 'contingency' payment in respect of an earlier supply of the freehold; or (iii) in connection with leasehold land treated as a supply of goods	See 64.44
— is it the self-supply of goods?	See 64.45
— does it involve water, gas or any form of power, heat, refrigeration or ventilation?	See 64.46

— does it involve the supplier's goods being held by the buyer pending agreement of the price?	See 64.47
— does it come within the special scheme for gold?	See 64.48
(4) If the supply is a supply of services	
— is it a continuous supply of services?	See 64.50
— does it give rise to the payment of royalties?	See 64.51
— does it involve construction services under a contract that provides for stage payments?	See 64.52
— does it involve 'reverse charge' services?	See 64.53
— does it involve the temporary use of business goods for private or non-business purposes?	See 64.54
— does it involve the free supply of services?	See 64.55
— does it consist of professional services made by a barrister or advocate?	See 64.57
(5) Does the contract provide for a retention payment?	See 64.37
(6) Has an 'actual' tax point been created because	
— the supplier received a payment or issued a VAT invoice in respect of the supply before the 'basic' tax point?	See 64.39(*b*)(i) for goods and 64.49(*b*)(i) for services
— the supplier has issued a VAT invoice within 14 days after the 'basic' tax point and has not previously elected to forgo the 14 day rule?	See 64.39(*b*)(ii) for goods and 64.49(*b*)(ii) for services
— the supplier has been granted an extension of the 14 day rule and has issued a VAT invoice within that time?	See 64.39(*b*)(ii) for goods and 64.49(*b*)(ii) for services
(7) Where none of (1)–(6) above apply, the basic tax point applies	See 64.39(*a*) for goods and 64.49(*a*) for services

(Internal Guidance V1–11, paras 6.3, 6.4).

64.34 VAT invoices and the creation of tax points

A VAT invoice can create an actual tax point under the normal rules both before and after the basic tax point occurs (see 64.39 and 64.49 below for goods and services respectively) and most of the special time of supply regulations also provide for the issue of a VAT invoice to create a tax point. In addition, in certain instances 'period' VAT invoices issued covering payments due over a period of up to one year may create tax points.

In order to establish the creation of a tax point, the following conditions must be satisfied.

(*a*) The invoice must be a proper VAT invoice which complies with the necessary requirements. See 40.3 *et seq* INVOICES. If the invoice does not conform to the requirements, it is not a VAT invoice and cannot create a tax point. See *ABB Power Ltd (VTD 9373) (TVC 60.377)* and *SR Finch (VTD 10948) (TVC 60.378)*. This also means that, as a VAT invoice cannot be issued

- in respect of a zero-rated supply (except for intra-EC supplies of goods, see 64.41 below), or
- in respect of an exempt supply, or
- by a non-registered person

invoices issued in such circumstances are disregarded for time of supply purposes.

(*b*) The VAT invoice must be issued. In *C & E Commrs v Woolfold Motor Co Ltd, QB [1983] STC 715 (TVC 60.374)* it was held that the issue of a VAT invoice required the provision to the customer of that invoice, ie the customer must physically receive it. It is not sufficient for it to simply have been prepared in order to create a tax point.

Where an invoice has in fact been issued,

- it is the date of physical issue that determines the tax point. In the case of invoices issued by electronic data interchange (EDI), an invoice is issued when the data is transmitted (provided the recipient is able to receive the data); and
- where a tax point is established, it is not invalidated because the recipient has never 'processed' the invoice, eg by disputing it (*Hurley Robinson Partnership (VTD 750) (TVC 60.118)*).

Where the issue of an invoice does create a tax point so that a supply is treated as taking place, it only does so to the extent covered by the invoice. [*SI 1995/2518, Reg 94*]. The issue of an invoice covering part only of a larger supply does not therefore create a tax point for the whole supply.

Period VAT invoices. Special time of supply rules apply to

- leasehold property (see 64.44 below),
- certain supplies of water, fuel and power (see 64.46 below), and
- continuous supplies of services (see 64.50 below)

where the supplier makes use of 'period' VAT invoices. This facility recognises that, without such arrangements, suppliers might otherwise have to issue a large volume of repetitive VAT invoices to the same customer, eg leased equipment subject to monthly rental payments. By adopting the period VAT invoicing arrangements, provided the invoice contains the required details in respect of two or more instalments due, the supplier can issue a single document showing all the payments due over a period of up to one year. The tax point then becomes the earlier of the receipt of the payment or the time when the payment falls due.

(Internal Guidance V1–11, paras 9.2–9.4).

64.35 *Self-billing*

Under an approved self-billing arrangement it is the customer who prepares the VAT invoice. See 40.6 INVOICES for further details. For time of supply purposes, not all self-billed VAT invoices can create a tax point as the law refers consistently to an invoice that has been issued by the supplier or in similar terms. A tax point is not normally created, therefore, where the invoice is issued by the customer as in the case of a self-billing arrangement. The one exception to this are self-billed invoices that fall within the scope of the 14 day rule where specific provision is included for self-billed invoices to be treated as if they were issued by the supplier (see 64.39 and 64.49 below for supplies of goods and services respectively). Therefore, a self-billed invoice issued within 14 days of the basic tax point has the same potential to create the tax point for the supply as if it had been issued by the supplier.

In all other circumstances (eg where an invoice is issued in advance of the basic tax point or is in respect of a supply covered by one of the special time of supply regulations) a tax point cannot be created by the issue of a self-billed VAT invoice.

Special arrangements for input tax deduction purposes. Because of the above, HMRC have agreed special arrangements that provide the issuer of the self-billed invoice with a notional tax point *for input tax deduction purposes only*. Under this procedure,

- the person issuing the self-billed invoice must
  - (*a*) show, on the original invoice, the date of despatch (but this must not be referred to as the tax point), and
  - (*b*) retain a copy and show on it the day following the date of issue as the notional tax point for input tax purposes; and
- the person receiving the invoice must, *on receipt of the invoice and payment*, add the date of receipt. This becomes the tax point for output tax purposes.

(Internal Guidance V1–11, paras 9.5, 20.6).

64.36 *Credit notes*

The time of supply rules do not apply in any way to the issue of credit notes. Similarly, the issue of a credit note has no direct effect on a tax point once it has been established, ie it does not cancel or expunge an existing tax point. It normally simply permits the issuer to adjust the VAT previously accounted for in response to an earlier tax point. (Internal Guidance V1–11, para 9.6).

64.37 Receipt of payment and the creation of tax points

The receipt of a payment can create an actual tax point before the basic tax point occurs (see 64.39 and 64.49 below for goods and services respectively) and most of the special time of supply regulations also provide for the receipt of a payment to create a tax point. Where the receipt of a payment does create a tax point so that a supply is treated as taking place, it only does so to the extent covered by the payment.

[*SI 1995/2518, Reg 94*]. The receipt of a payment covering part only of a larger supply does not therefore create a tax point for the whole supply.

Deposits. Deposits are frequently required either as an indication of good faith on the part of the customer or to put the supplier in funds to cover costs, etc. Depending on the contract, the deposit may be refundable in the event of the contract subsequently being cancelled or may be liable, either wholly or in part, to forfeiture.

Apart from security deposits (see below) a pre-payment or deposit normally creates a tax point when received where it is made in the expectation that it will eventually form part of the total payment for a supply that is contemplated by the parties to the payment. See, for example, *JD Fox Ltd (VTD 1012) (TVC 60.403)* (deposits for furniture), *Bethway & Moss Ltd (VTD 2667) (TVC 60.407)* (deposits for fitted kitchens) and *C & E Commrs v Richmond Theatre Management Ltd, QB [1995] STC 257 (TVC 60.397)* (advance payments of theatre tickets). This applies even if the deposit is refundable. See, for example, *C & E Commrs v Moonraker's Guest House Ltd, QB [1992] STC 544 (TVC 60.406)* (deposits for holiday accommodation) and *Clowance plc (VTD 2541) (TVC 60.395)* (advance payments for time-share accommodation). For an exception to this general rule where deposits were not held to create tax points, see *Nigel Mansell Sports Co Ltd (VTD 6116) (TVC 60.415)* (initial deposit from prospective customer in order to be placed on the waiting list for a sports car and paid before a firm order was placed for the car) although the facts in this case were unusual.

Security deposits. Deposits taken as security to ensure safe return of goods hired out, and which are refunded when the goods are safely returned or forfeited to compensate for loss or damage, do not normally create a tax point. A payment tax point can be created if, for example, hire charges are later offset against the refund of an amount originally received as a security deposit but only where this happens before the basic tax point, ie completion of the hire period.

(Internal Guidance V1–11, paras 8.4–8.7).

Third parties acting as stakeholders. Where a third party acts as a stakeholder (as opposed to an agent of the vendor) and receives a deposit in connection with a supply of property, a time of supply is not created until the money is released to the vendor. (VAT Notice 700, para 14.2). See *Double Shield Window Co Ltd (VTD 1771) (TVC 60.384)*.

Payment by cheque. Under banking law, payment can only be said to have occurred when the cheque has been presented and met by the drawer's bank. In the normal course of events it takes five working days for a cheque to complete the clearance cycle. It is common banking practice for a cheque to be credited to the payee's bank account on the date it is paid in and, therefore, unless the cheque was the subject of special clearance procedures, payment for VAT purposes will not strictly occur until the fifth working day following the date of presentation. However, where a trader's normal commercial practice is to use the date a cheque is received as the date of payment for accounting purposes, and provided the cheque is subsequently presented and cleared without undue delay, that date may be used as the payment date for VAT time of supply purposes. In the event of the cheque not being honoured, however, no payment will have occurred and any VAT accounted for on this basis may be adjusted accordingly. Where presentation of a cheque is delayed for any reason, the date of clearance is to be regarded as the date of payment. (Internal Guidance V1–11, para 8.9).

Payment by credit card, charge card, etc. Payment is not strictly received until the sum involved is paid over to the supplier by the card company. However, a trader may be permitted to treat the date of acceptance of the card as the payment tax point where this conforms with normal commercial accounting practice of the business and provided there is no unreasonable delay in processing the transaction. HMRC do not allow this in cases where the card company withholds payment pending satisfactory delivery of goods (which can occur with mail order transactions). (Internal Guidance V1–11, para 8.10).

Payment by bank transfer. Whether by standing order, direct debit, home banking facilities or other forms of electronic transfer, the time of payment for VAT purposes occurs when the amount in question is actually transferred into the recipient's bank account. (Internal Guidance V1–11, para 8.11).

Payment by book entry. A payment tax point can be created by a book entry or an adjustment to the accounting records (eg supplies between group companies may be recorded by offsetting sales and purchases ledger accounts or making entries in the inter-company current accounts). The time of payment is the date on which the appropriate entries are made in the accounting records (*Pentex Oil Ltd (VTD 7989, VTD 7991) (TVC 41.5)*). In order for there to be a payment tax point by book entry, the debt must actually have been settled or expunged. Entries that simply reflect or acknowledge an outstanding debt should not be regarded as evidence of payment for tax point purposes.

Where the value of a continuous supply of services is not agreed until the annual accounts of the business are drawn up, the date the accounts are approved may be taken to represent a payment tax point where they demonstrate that the supplies have been paid for by way of adjustment to each company's accounts.

(Internal Guidance V1–11, para 8.12).

Retention payments. Some contracts for the supply of goods or services provide for the retention of part of the consideration pending full and satisfactory performance of the contract (or of any part of it) by the supplier. This is a common feature of construction contracts and contracts for the supply and installation of plant and machinery.

Without special provisions, under the normal rules, the VAT on the retained element of the contract price would fall due at the basic tax point (see 64.39 and 64.49 below for goods and services respectively). However, in these circumstances the tax point for the retentions is delayed until either a VAT invoice is issued, or a payment is received, in respect of the retentions (whichever is the earlier). This only applies to the retained element of the contract price and the rest of the supply is subject to the normal tax point rules. In any case, the provisions do not apply to

- a supply of goods for acquisition by a taxable person in another EC country; and
- construction services under contracts providing for stage or interim payments (see 42.29 LAND AND BUILDINGS).

[*SI 1995/2518, Reg 89; SI 1997/2887, Reg 5; SI 2003/3220, Reg 16*].

Assignment of debts. A receipt of a payment, however expressed, includes a reference to receipt by a person to whom the right to receive it has been assigned. [*SI 1995/2518, Reg 94A; SI 1999/599*]. Where, therefore, a business assigns any of its debts, it must account for VAT on payments received by the person to whom the debts are assigned as if those payments were received by the business itself (rather than accounting for VAT when payments are received from the assignee). See 64.38 below for an accommodation tax point if this causes any problems.

64.38 Accommodation tax points

HMRC may, at the request of a taxable person, alter the time at which supplies are to be treated as made by him by either advancing or delaying the tax point. [*VATA 1994, s 6(10)*]. These are often referred to as accommodation tax points, the most common of which are considered below.

- **Monthly invoicing**. Many traders invoice for their supplies periodically, typically issuing a single invoice to each customer detailing the supplies made during the preceding monthly or four/five week commercial accounting period. Provided this represents the trader's normal commercial accounting practice, HMRC, on written application, may grant an accommodation tax point without the trader being required to demonstrate that the normal tax point rules cannot be complied with. Applications should state whether the accommodation tax point is to be linked to the last day of the period covered by the invoice or the date of issue of the invoice. In the latter case, this will not normally be permitted to exceed 14 days from the end of the commercial accounting period. (Internal Guidance V1–11, para 11.2).
- **Exempt supplies of credit**. Supplies of goods on credit can involve both a taxable supply of goods and an exempt supply of credit. There is also an exempt supply of credit when a loan is made for interest or for some other form of consideration. In either case, particularly with agreements subject to fixed rates of interest, traders can have difficulty in identifying the proportion of the periodical repayment attributable to the supply of credit and the element in respect of either the goods or repayment of the capital amount in the case of a loan of money.

  Application may be made to HMRC to use a single accommodation tax point for the supply of the credit provided the time nominated as the tax point is earlier than would otherwise be the case under the normal rules. For example, for supplies of credit in conjunction with a supply of goods, the accommodation tax point might be linked to the tax point for the supply of the goods. For a loan of money, a convenient tax point might be the date of the agreement or any other date before receipt of the first instalment.

  Applications should be in writing and signed by a person eligible to sign the trader's VAT returns. In the case of group registrations, the application must be made by the representative member. A suitable form of application is set out in Internal Guidance V1–11, para 12.2. Other forms of application may be accepted provided they contain the following information.

  - The identity of the supplier.
  - Details sufficient to identify precisely which supplies are intended to be covered by the direction.
  - The event to be treated as the tax point for the supply.

  Applications involving different tax points for different categories of exempt supplies of credit are acceptable provided they can be identified without difficulty.

  (Internal Guidance V1–11, para 11.3).
- **Corporate purchasing (procurement) cards**. Such cards are intended to be used as a method of payment by corporate customers with high levels of low value expenditure (eg stationery, spare parts and other expenditure delegated to individual staff members). They are designed to eliminate much of the paper-

work in the purchasing process. The practical arrangements are similar to the use of credit cards and charge cards. Under normal circumstances, suppliers do not issue invoices to card-holders, invoicing being carried out on the supplier's behalf by the card company or bank using transaction information transmitted through the purchasing card system. A difficulty arises with such cards as the supplier is unaware of the date on which the card company or bank actually issues the invoice to the purchaser.

Application may be made to HMRC by the supplier for an accommodation tax point. This allows the tax point for all purchase card transactions to be the time at which the supplier keys the transaction details into the purchasing card system (the 'transmission date') provided all transactions are keyed into the system no later than the basic tax point (the date the goods are sent to, or taken away by, the customer). Card issuers have made it a condition of membership that potential suppliers will apply to use the accommodation tax point. (VAT Notice 701/48/02, paras 1.2, 2.1–2.4; Internal Guidance V1–11, para 11.4).

- **Ministry of Defence contractors**. There can be considerable delays in agreeing contract prices in the case of supplies made by defence industry contractors to the Ministry of Defence. Where one of the centrally agreed extensions to the 14 day rule is inadequate (see 64.39 and 64.49 below for supplies of goods and services respectively) application may be made for an accommodation tax point if the difficulties are wholly as a result of delays on the part of the MoD.

  Applications should be in writing and signed by a person eligible to sign the trader's VAT returns. In the case of group registrations, the application must be made by the representative member. A suitable form of application is set out in Internal Guidance V1–11, para 12.4. If HMRC agree, in cases where the consideration under an MoD contract is ascertained or ascertainable at or before the time when the goods are removed or the services performed, the supply in question is treated as taking place on the date a VAT invoice is issued or a payment is received, to the extent covered by the invoice or payment, but in any case not later than six years after the goods are removed or the services performed.

  (Internal Guidance V1–11, para 11.5).

- **Assigned debts**. Where a business assigns any of its debts, it must account for VAT on payments received by the assignee as if those payments were received by the business itself (rather than accounting for VAT when payments are received from the assignee). See 64.37 above. Where the assignee notifies the business of amounts received from the latter's customers, the business should have no difficulty in complying with the normal payment tax point rules. Alternatively, a tax point may have already been created prior to assignment of the debt by the issue of a VAT invoice. However, HMRC recognise that occasions may arise where the assignor may not receive details of any subsequent payments and will therefore be unaware when a payment tax point has occurred. A business affected in this way can, if it wishes, apply to HMRC to bring forward the time of supply to the time of assignment, although this will mean that any VAT outstanding on the amount assigned must be accounted for at that time. (Internal Guidance V1–11, para 11.6).

- **'En primeur' wine**. 'En primeur' wine is wine that is offered for sale, whilst still lying in the producer's cellars abroad, for delivery in the UK by the wine merchant at some time in the future. Trade practice is normally to require the customer to pay the net price of the wine when submitting an order. Further charges, based on the duty and VAT payable, together with the costs of transportation, etc become due from the customer at the time of delivery.

At the time the net price is paid, it is not certain that the wine will ever actually be removed to the UK. Even if it is, the wine may be sold by the customer, before taking delivery, while it is still subject to a warehousing regime in the UK. As a result, it has been agreed that if VAT does become due, the supply may be accounted for at the time the customer is invoiced for the VAT and other charges where, in accordance with trade practice, this takes place immediately prior to delivery in the UK.

(Internal Guidance V1–11, para 35.1).

- **Services received by members of the Institute of London Underwriters**. All claims on members of the Institute of London Underwriters (ILU) are processed centrally by the ILU. When a claim has been finalised the ILU issues a 'claim closing slip' to the underwriters advising them of their share of the liability arising from the claim and including details of services received from abroad in respect of the claim which have already been paid for on the underwriters behalf. This can be the first notification the underwriter receives in respect of the claim.

  As an accommodation tax point, all supplies relating to the provision of marine and aviation insurance which are received by member companies of the ILU from abroad and which are treated as being made by them in the UK by virtue of the reverse charge procedure may be treated as taking place at the end of the day on which the claims closing advice for the related insurance claim is issued by the ILU.

  (Internal Guidance V1–11, para 24.2).

64.39 TIME OF SUPPLY OF GOODS

Subject to

- any accommodation tax points agreed under 64.38 above,
- the special cases in 64.40 to 64.48 below,
- any extra-statutory class concession,
- the provisions relating to warehoused goods (see 70 WAREHOUSED GOODS AND FREE ZONES), and
- the provisions relating to gas and electricity supplies from persons outside the UK (see 29.9 FUEL AND POWER),

a supply of goods is treated as taking place at the basic or actual tax point.

(*a*) **Basic tax point**. The basic tax point is determined as follows.

(i) *If the goods are to be removed*, the basic tax point occurs at the time of removal.

This normally occurs when the goods are delivered by, or on behalf of, the supplier or collected by, or on behalf of, the customer. Where there is more than one supply but only one movement of the goods (eg where the goods are supplied via a third party such as a finance company), it is necessary to determine to which of the supplies the removal relates (the remaining supply/supplies falling within (ii) below).

Where a single supply of goods involves delivery/collection over a period of time, provided there is genuinely a single supply (and not a succession of separate supplies) the basic tax point will not occur until the time of removal of the final consignment (although actual tax points under (*b*) below may have been created before that time).

(ii) *If the goods are not to be removed* at the time when they are made available to the customer.

The words 'if the goods are not to be removed' must be viewed in the context of the supply itself and not the nature of the goods involved. The 'made available' basic tax point is therefore not restricted to goods that are incapable of ever being moved. Examples include

- the supply of fully-assembled and installed goods on site (delivery of the components being merely a preliminary step to enable the supplier to supply what is required under the terms of the contract); and
- in the normal case of the supply of goods via a third party finance company where the finance company does not take physical delivery of the goods, the supply of the goods to the finance company by the trader.

(*b*) **Actual tax points.**

(i) *Advance payment or invoicing.* If, before the basic tax point, the supplier issues a VAT invoice or receives payment in respect of the supply, there is a tax point at the time the invoice is issued or payment is received, whichever occurs first, to the extent covered by the invoice or payment. (There will thus always be a further tax point where the amount invoiced or paid is less than the full value of the supply.)

(ii) *The 14 day rule.* If the supplier issues a VAT invoice (or a taxable person issues a document to himself under the self-billing arrangements, see 40.6 INVOICES) within 14 days *after* the basic tax point, then, unless he has notified HMRC in writing that he does not wish the rule to be applied, the tax point is the date the invoice is issued. This rule does not, however, override (*b*)(i) above.

HMRC normally expect a trader to either apply the 14 day rule to all supplies or to opt out of its use altogether. However, it may be applied selectively

- by separate companies in a VAT group registration;
- for supplies subject to the self-billing arrangements and supplies subject to conventional invoicing; or
- where a trader has a genuine need to treat some supplies differently and can easily distinguish those supplies.

Extending the 14 day rule under (*b*)(ii) above. HMRC may, at the request of the taxable person, extend the 14 day rule in respect of all or part of his supplies. They will not do this unless the taxable person is genuinely unable to issue an invoice within 14 days of the basic tax point, eg where prices cannot be determined until invoices have been received for materials or subcontractors' charges. HMRC are unlikely to grant any significant period of extension as any payment received between the basic tax point and the date when the invoice is actually issued does not create a tax point. It should also be noted that the tax point is only delayed if a VAT invoice is issued within the extended period. If, for any reason, it is not, the tax point reverts to the earlier basic tax point (rather than the date of expiry of the extended period) which may have penalty implications.

The following extensions to the 14 day rule have been centrally agreed.

1. *Members of The British Electrical and Allied Manufacturers Association, The Scientific Instruments Manufacturers Association and The Electronic Engineering Association.* If the consideration for a supply of goods made by member companies under a Government contract is not ascertained or ascertainable at or before the time when the goods are removed, the supply may be treated as taking place at the time when the member issues a VAT invoice, provided it is issued within one year of the date of removal of the goods.

2. *Government contracts.* Where a taxable person supplies goods for an agreed price under a Government contract and the supplier's invoicing is delayed due to Government procedures (eg the use of Ministry of Defence Form 640), the supply may be treated as taking place at the time a VAT invoice is issued, provided it is issued within four months of the date of removal of the goods.

3. *Local authorities.* Where a local authority supplies taxable goods in the course of business activities, the supply may be treated as taking place at the time a VAT invoice is issued, provided it is issued within two months of the date of removal of the goods.

4. *Scrap metal.* As the consideration for a supply of 'material on valuation' in the scrap metal trade is not ascertained or ascertainable at or before the time when the goods are removed, the supply may be treated as taking place at the time a VAT invoice is issued, provided it is issued within three months of removal of the goods.

5. *The Society of British Aerospace Companies Ltd* (SBAC). If the consideration for a supply of goods made by member companies of SBAC is not ascertained or ascertainable at or before the time when the goods are removed (because the price is subject to negotiation and agreement after the work has been completed), the supply may be treated as taking place at the time a VAT invoice is issued, provided it is issued within six months of the date of removal of the goods (one year in the case of a Government contract).

[*VATA 1994, s 6(1)(2)(4)–(6)(9)(10); FA 1996, Sch 3 para 1*]. (VAT Notice 700, para 14.2; Internal Guidance V1–11, paras 6.2, 6.3, 10.1, 10.2, 10.4).

64.40 Disposal of business assets

Where there is a supply of goods on the transfer or disposal of business assets under *VATA 1994, Sch 4 para 5(1)* (see 64.3(*e*) above), the supply is treated as taking place when the goods are transferred or disposed of. [*VATA 1994, s 6(12)*]. This includes goods transferred for no consideration (ie goods taken out of the business permanently for non-business use). See also 47.7 OUTPUT TAX.

64.41 Intra-EC supplies of goods

Supplies to VAT registered persons in other EC countries. Where a supply of goods involves

- the removal of the goods from the UK, and

- their acquisition in another EC country by a person who is liable for VAT on their acquisition under the provisions of that country corresponding to those in 23.3 EUROPEAN COMMUNITY: SINGLE MARKET,

the time of supply is the earlier of the 15th day of the month following that in which the goods are removed or the date of the issue of a VAT invoice (or other prescribed invoice) in respect of the supply.

[*VATA 1994, s 6(7)(8)*].

Supplies to non-VAT registered persons in other EC countries. Such supplies are subject to UK VAT and the tax point is determined under the normal rules in 64.39 above.

Acquisitions of goods by taxable persons in the UK from another EC country. The time of supply (mirroring those above for supplies from the UK to registered persons) is the earlier of the 15th day of the month following that in which the first removal of the goods occurred and the date of the issue of an invoice by the supplier or, with effect from 1 January 2004, the customer under the provisions of the law in the supplier's country corresponding to those relating the VAT invoices for UK supplies. [*VATA 1994, s 12; FA 1996, Sch 3 para 3; SI 1995/2518, Reg 83; SI 2003/3220, Reg 12*].

64.42 Hire purchase, credit sales and conditional sales

The supply of the goods. If the credit is 'self-financed', there is one supply of the goods by the trader direct to the customer. If a third party finance company is involved, there will normally be two supplies (by the trader to the finance company and by the finance company to the customer). However, this should not automatically be assumed. For example, there is unlikely to be a supply of the goods to the finance company where the finance consists of an unsecured loan.

Supplies of goods on hire purchase, credit sales and conditional sales are treated in the same way as an outright sale where title passes at the outset.

- *The basic tax point* for the supply to the customer is, in most cases, the date of delivery or collection of the goods. Where there are two supplies (see above) this is the supply by the finance company. The basic tax point for the supply by the trader to the finance company normally occurs at the time the goods are made available to the finance company. Unless the agreement indicates otherwise, this may be taken to be the time when the finance agreement comes into force, possibly at the time when the last party signs up to it.
- *A VAT invoice* issued to the customer (whether it is a conventional VAT invoice or the finance agreement adapted for the purpose) creates a tax point for the supply if it is issued in advance of, or within 14 days after, the basic tax point.
- *A deposit* paid before an agreement has come into force, or before the goods have been removed, or a VAT invoice has been issued, also normally creates a tax point.

The supply of the credit element. The tax point for the separate supply of credit is the date of payment of the interest. Where the instalments include an element attributable to the charge for credit this will mean that a tax point occurs each time that a payment is received. See, however, 64.38 above for an accommodation tax point in these circumstances.

(Internal Guidance V1–11, paras 23.1–23.5).

64.43 Goods supplied on sale or return and goods on approval

The following rules apply to sale or return agreements, ie where goods are supplied on terms whereby the customer has a right to return the goods at any point up until the time they are adopted but, in the meantime, ownership of the goods remains with the supplier. Retail supplies on these terms are generally referred to as being 'on approval'.

If goods are sent or taken on approval or sale or return (or similar terms) so that they are removed before it is known whether a supply will take place, the basic tax point is the time when it becomes certain that the supply has taken place ('adoption') or, if sooner, twelve months after the removal. If, however, before this time a supplier issues a VAT invoice in respect of the supply, the tax point for the amount invoiced is the date the invoice is issued. [*VATA 1994, s 6(2)(c)(4)*].

'Adoption' is not defined but normally occurs when the holder of the goods does something to indicate that the option to return the goods is not going to be exercised, eg

- the goods become the subject of an offer for resale by the holder;
- the holder allocates the goods to a customer;
- the goods are hired out by the holder to a customer;
- the holder uses the goods otherwise than for display purposes; or
- the goods are permanently modified or adapted by the holder or to the order of the holder.

Payment received by the supplier before the basic tax point does not, of itself, create a tax point in these circumstances although it normally indicates that the goods have been adopted and thus establishes a basic tax point at that time. However, this does not apply where it is a condition of the agreement that the recipient of the goods is required to pay an amount to the supplier in order to receive the goods in the first place. Provided this does not affect the unfettered right of the recipient subsequently to return the goods, the payment in these circumstances has no time of supply significance.

(Internal Guidance V1–11, paras 28.1–28.3).

Retail sales by mail order. In *Littlewoods Organisation plc (VTD 14977) (TVC 60.357)* the company sold goods by mail order and a dispute arose with Customs as to the time of supply of sales when the standard rate of VAT increased from 15% to 17.5%. The tribunal held that supplies were within *VATA 1994, s 6(2)(a)* and were supplied at the time of removal, ruling that *VATA 1994, s 6(2)(c)* above applied to transactions where there was no contract of sale unless and until the person concerned adopted or was deemed to have adopted the transaction, whereas *VATA 1994, s 6(2)(a)* applied to transactions where there was a contract of sale but the buyer had the right to rescind the contract if he wished.

Retail sales by internet. In *Robertson's Electrical Ltd (VTD 18765) (TVC 60.358)* the company sold electrical goods over the internet and did not account for output tax until seven days after delivery. The tribunal, declining to follow the decision in *Littlewoods Organisation* above, accepted that the goods were sold 'on approval', holding that the effect of *Consumer Protection (Distance Selling) Regulations 2000 (SI 2000/2334)* was that the customer was entitled to decline to accept the supply of the goods in question without justifying his reason for doing so. As a result, until the time for cancelling or disapproving passed, the supplier did not know whether the goods would be retained and had to accept them back.

64.44 Land and property

(1) Freehold land

The supply of freehold land is a supply of goods [*VATA 1994, Sch 4 para 4*] and the normal time of supply rules apply (see 64.39 above) subject to the rules below where the total purchase price cannot be determined at the time of the transfer.

Basic tax point. As land is incapable of removal, the basic tax point is when the land is made available to the purchaser, ie the date of the freehold conveyance (in Scotland, the time of delivery of the disposition which is known as the settlement date). If a prospective purchaser is allowed to enter the property in advance of completion (eg to carry out preliminary works or testing on the site), this does not advance the basic tax point for the sale of the freehold. See *Cumbernauld Development Corporation v C & E Commrs, CS [2002] STC 226 (TVC 60.355)* where an exchange of land in Scotland between the Corporation and a local golf club was held to take place 'at the time of the exchange of dispositions' and not at the earlier time when the land had been made available to the club.

Actual tax points. The basic tax point is subject to the creation of an actual tax point by the issue of a VAT invoice in advance of, or within 14 days after, the basic tax point or the receipt of a payment in advance of the basic tax point.

It is common for a contract for the sale of the freehold interest in land to require the payment of a deposit by the purchaser at the time contracts are exchanged. If this is payable either direct to the vendor or to a solicitor acting as the vendor's agent, the deposit creates a tax point to the extent of the amount received. If, on the other hand, the deposit is received by a third party (which can be the vendor's solicitor) acting in the capacity of a stakeholder holding the money on behalf of both parties pending satisfactory performance of the contract, the payment does not create a tax point until it is released by the stakeholder to the vendor.

(Internal Guidance V1–11, paras 26.2, 26.3).

(2) Freehold property — total purchase price not determinable at the time of supply

Where the freehold in land or a building is sold, any VAT due must generally be accounted for under the above rules. Sometimes, however, the full value of the supply is not known at this time. This would apply, for example, where the vendor is entitled to receive a further payment in the event of the purchaser later obtaining planning permission, or the final consideration is dependent on any profit from future development of the land. In these cases, a special rule allows VAT to be accounted for when the undetermined part of the consideration is received, thus avoiding the need to estimate the final value of the supply at the time of the sale.

Subject to the anti-avoidance rules below, where the total consideration cannot be determined at the time the grantor grants or assigns the freehold interest in any land, the land is treated as separately and successively supplied

- in respect of that part of the consideration which was determinable at the time of the grant or assignment, under the normal tax point rules as described above and in 64.39 above; and

- in respect of any part of the consideration not so determinable, at the earlier of the times whenever any such part is received by the grantor or the grantor issues a VAT invoice in respect of it.

[*SI 1995/2518, Reg 84(2); SI 2002/2918; SI 2003/3220, Reg 13*]. (Internal Guidance V1–11, para 26.7).

Anti-avoidance rules applying to grants or assignments made after 9 April 2003. The special rule above does not apply in relation to a grant or assignment falling within *VATA 1994, Sch 9 Group 1 Item 1(a)* (sale of new and uncompleted non-qualifying buildings and civil engineering works, see 42.3 LAND AND BUILDINGS) where any of the specified persons listed below intend or expect to occupy the land on a date within ten years of the building or civil engineering work on the land being 'completed', without being in occupation of it wholly or mainly for 'eligible purposes'.

The specified persons are

(*a*) the grantor;

(*b*) any person who, with the intention or in the expectation that occupation of the land on a date within ten years of completion of the building or civil engineering work would not be wholly or mainly for eligible purposes

  (i) 'provides finance' for the 'grantor's development of the land', or

  (ii) has entered into any agreement, arrangement or understanding (whether or not legally enforceable) to provide finance for the grantor's development of the land; and

(*c*) any person who is connected with any person falling within (*a*) or (*b*) above under *ICTA 1988, s 839*, see 69.19 VALUATION.

For these purposes:

(i) '*Completed*' in relation to a building/civil engineering work is when an architect/engineer issues a certificate of practical completion in relation to it or it is fully occupied/used, whichever happens first.

(ii) '*Occupation for eligible purposes*' means one of the following.

- Occupation by a taxable person for the purpose of making supplies which are in the course or furtherance of a business carried on by him and of such a description that he is entitled to credit for any wholly attributable input tax.
- Occupation by a specified body within *VATA 1994, s 33* (see 43.2 LOCAL AUTHORITIES AND PUBLIC BODIES) to the extent that the body occupies the land for non-business purposes.
- Occupation by a government department.

For these purposes

- where occupation is by a person who is not a taxable person but whose supplies are treated for the purposes of *VATA 1994* as made by another person who is a taxable person, those two persons are to be regarded as a single taxable person; and

- a person is taken to be in occupation of any land whether he occupies it alone or together with one or more other persons and whether he occupies all of that land or only part of it.

(iii) '*Providing finance*' is widely defined. It includes directly or indirectly providing funds *either* to meet the whole (or part) of the cost of the grantor's development of the land *or* to discharge the whole (or part) of any liability incurred in raising funds to meet that cost. It also includes directly or indirectly procuring the provision of funds by another person for either of those purposes. The funds may be provided by way of loan, guarantee or other security, consideration for a share issue used to raise the funds or any other transfer of assets or value as a consequence of which the funds are made available. However, the purchaser of the freehold grant whose treatment is in question is not providing finance simply by paying the consideration due under the grant.

(iv) '*The grantor's development of the land*' means any acquisition by the grantor of an interest in the land, building or civil engineering work and includes the construction of the building or civil engineering work.

[*SI 1995/2518, Reg 84(3)–(5); SI 2003/1069, Reg 9*].

Anti-avoidance rules applying to grants and assignments made after 27 November 2002 and before 10 April 2003. The special rule above did not apply in relation to land

- which included a 'new' building (other than a building designed as a dwelling or number of dwellings, or intended for use solely for a 'relevant residential purpose' or a 'relevant charitable purpose') or 'new' civil engineering work,
- which included a building (other than a building designed as a dwelling or number of dwellings, or intended for use solely for a 'relevant residential purpose' or a 'relevant charitable purpose') which had not been completed or a civil engineering work which had not been completed, or
- on which the 'grantor' intended or expected to construct a new building (other than a building designed as a dwelling or number of dwellings, or intended for use solely for a 'relevant residential purpose' or a 'relevant charitable purpose') or a new civil engineering work

unless the following conditions applied.

- The grantor had opted to tax the land in question and the option had effect at the time the grant or assignment was made. See 42.8 *et seq* LAND AND BUILDINGS.
- The anti-avoidance provisions in 42.9(*g*) LAND AND BUILDINGS did not prevent that election applying to supplies made under the grant or assignment. In determining whether this was the case,

  (i) the land, building or civil engineering work (as the case may be) was treated as if it were a capital item subject to capital goods scheme; and

  (ii) the grantor was treated as if he were the owner of that capital item.

  The effect of this was that the special rule could not be used at all where supplies were arranged between related parties to reduce VAT payable on buildings intended for exempt use.

A building was taken as '*new*' if it was completed less than three years before the grant and a building/civil engineering work was to be taken as '*completed*' when an architect/engineer issued a certificate of practical completion in relation to it or it was fully occupied/used, whichever happened first.

'*Grantor*' included anyone whom the grantor expected to acquire the right to receive all or part of the consideration which was not determinable at the time of the grant or assignment.

See 42.1(13) LAND AND BUILDINGS for the meaning of '*relevant charitable purpose*' and 42.1(15) LAND AND BUILDINGS for the meaning of '*relevant residential purpose*'.

[*SI 1995/2518, Reg 84(3)–(9) as inserted by SI 2002/2918 and replaced by SI 2003/1069, Reg 9*].

(3) **Long leases and tenancies**

Treatment as supply of goods. The supply of a lease or tenancy exceeding 21 years (or Scottish equivalent) is regarded as a major interest in land and is treated as a supply of goods. [*VATA 1994, Sch 4 para 4*].

General time of supply provisions. Subject to the rules below on *advance invoicing* and *anti-avoidance provisions*, if under the grant of such a lease or tenancy the whole or part of the consideration for the grant is payable periodically or from time to time, the goods are treated as separately and successively supplied each time that

- a part of the consideration is received by the supplier; or
- the supplier issues a VAT invoice relating to the grant,

whichever is the earlier. This applies to rent, ground rent and any premium received.

[*SI 1995/2518, Reg 85(1)*].

Advance invoicing. Where, at or about the beginning of any period not exceeding one year, the supplier issues a VAT invoice which, in addition to the normal requirements for a VAT invoice, shows

(*a*) the dates on which any parts of the consideration are to become due for payment in the period;

(*b*) the amount payable (excluding VAT) on each such date; and

(*c*) the rate of VAT in force at the time of issue of the VAT invoice and the amount of VAT chargeable in accordance with that rate on each payment,

the goods are to be treated as separately and successively supplied each time that a payment in respect of the tenancy or lease becomes due or is received, whichever is the earlier. If there is a change in the rate of VAT before any of the due dates for payment under (*a*) above, the invoice ceases to be treated as a VAT invoice in respect of any supplies for which payment is due after the change (and not received before the change).

[*SI 1995/2518, Reg 85(2)(3)*].

Anti-avoidance provisions. The above continuous supply provisions have enabled some suppliers to delay (sometimes indefinitely) the time at which they accounted for VAT. The following anti-avoidance provisions are designed to prevent this by imposing periodic tax points (usually based on twelve-month periods) on specified supplies between connected persons where VAT has not already been accounted for under the above provisions. The provisions apply to supplies of goods, the benefit of which is received after 1 October 2003.

In relation to supplies of goods where

(1) *either* the supplier and the recipient are '*connected persons*' (see 69.19 VALUATION) *or* both are members of a 'group undertaking' (see *Companies Act 1985, s 259*) but are not members of the same VAT group (see 31 GROUPS OF COMPANIES),

(2) the supply is taxable at a positive rate (ie the standard or reduced rate), and

(3) the supplier cannot show that the recipient is able to recover *all* the VAT on the supply

then, subject to below, to the extent that the goods in question have been 'provided' and have not already been treated as supplied under any other provisions, they are treated as separately and successively supplied

(i) in the case of supplies the provision of which commenced on or before 1 October 2003, at the end of twelve-month period after that date;

(ii) in the case of supplies the provision of which commenced after 1 October 2003, at the end of the twelve-month period after the supplies commenced; or

(iii) such earlier date falling within the period specified in (i) or (ii) above notified by the supplier to HMRC in writing and agreed by them

and thereafter at the end of each subsequent twelve-month period. For these purposes, goods are provided at the time when, and to the extent that, the recipient receives the benefit of them.

But where the supplier, within six months after the time applicable under (i)–(iii) above, either

- issues a VAT invoice in respect of it, or
- receives a payment in respect of it,

to the extent that the supply has not already been treated as taking place at some other time under any other provisions, the supply is treated as taking place at the time the invoice is issued or the payment is received. Where the supplier intends to issue a VAT invoice, or payment is due, within the six month's period, he should wait for either of those events before accounting for VAT. However, if, for whatever reason, neither of those events has materialised at the end of the six months, the tax point reverts to the annual tax point date as above. (VAT Information Sheet 14/03, para 4.5).

A supplier can exercise a number of options in relation to the provisions by writing to one of HMRC's written enquiry teams (see 15.4 CUSTOMS: ADMINISTRATION).

- He can request to vary the six-month period if there are genuine commercial reasons for doing so. Full details of why the variation is required should be given. Such a change is subject to approval by HMRC and a supplier should not therefore start using a revised date until it is formally approved.

- He can elect not to be bound by the six-month rule at any time, in which case thereafter he must account for VAT as required at each annual tax point as described above.
- He can, after the start of any annual period established as above, select an earlier alternative period end date in relation to some or all of his supplies. Provided this is approved by HMRC, the date selected establishes the end of the supplier's current and subsequent twelve-month periods. Written notice should advise HMRC of the alternative date to be adopted and *either* state that this date is to apply to all supplies to which the rules might apply *or* nominate different dates for different categories of supply. In the latter case, supplies must be identified in sufficient detail so as to be distinguishable from one another.

(VAT Information Sheet 14/03, paras 4.3, 4.5).

Where the leasing depends upon one or more other leases (the superior lease or leases), the reference to a supplier in (1) above includes a reference to any lessor of a superior lease.

Where these anti-avoidance provisions apply, the normal time of supply rules for continuous supplies detailed above do not apply to the extent that supplies have been treated as having taken place under the anti-avoidance rules.

[*SI 1995/2518, Reg 94B; SI 2003/2318, Reg 3*].

(4) **Short-term leases**

Supplies of leases not qualifying as long-term leases above are supplies of services and are normally treated as continuous supplies of services within 64.50 below.

(5) **Compulsory purchase**

In most cases of compulsory purchase, the transfer does not take place until the price has been agreed and the normal time of supply rules apply (see 64.39 above and 64.49 below for supplies of goods and services respectively). However, where, by or under any enactment, an interest in or right over land is compulsorily purchased and the person from whom the land is purchased does not know the amount of the payment he is to receive at the normal time for the supply, a supply is treated as taking place each time he receives any payment for the purchase. [*SI 1995/2518, Reg 84(1)*].

64.45 Taxable self-supplies

Where goods are treated as self-supplied by an order made under *VATA 1994, s 5(5)*, the supply is treated as taking place when they are appropriated to the use giving rise to the self-supply. [*VATA 1994, s 6(11)*].

Orders under *VATA 1994, s 5(5)* have been made in respect of motor cars (see 45.6 MOTOR CARS) and stationery (see 62.2 SELF-SUPPLY).

64.46 **Supplies of water, gas or any form of power, heat, refrigeration or ventilation**

Treatment as supplies of goods. The supply of any form of power, heat, refrigeration or ventilation is a supply of goods. [*VATA 1994, Sch 4 para 3*].

General time of supply provisions. Subject to the following provisions in this paragraph, a supply of

(*a*) water (other than distilled or deionised water or water of a similar purity and water comprised in any of the excepted items set out in *VATA 1994, Sch 8 Group 1*, see 28.8 FOOD),

(*b*) coal gas, water gas, producer gases or similar gases,

(*c*) petroleum gases, or other gaseous hydrocarbons, in a gaseous state, or

(*d*) any form of power, heat, refrigeration or ventilation,

is treated as taking place whenever a payment in respect of the supply is received or a VAT invoice is issued by the supplier, whichever is the earlier.

[*SI 1995/2518, Reg 86*(*1*)].

Supplies to other EC countries. Supplies within (*a*)–(*d*) above made to a taxable person in another EC country are treated as taking place on the day of the issue of the VAT invoice in respect of the supply. [*SI 1995/2518, Reg 86*(*5*)].

Continuous supplies. Subject to the anti-avoidance provisions below, where the whole or part of the consideration for

- a supply under (*a*)–(*c*) above, or
- a supply of power in the form of electricity

is determined or payable periodically or from time to time, the goods are treated as separately and successively supplied each time that a part of the consideration is received or the supplier issues a VAT invoice relating to the supply, whichever is the earlier.

Where such separate and successive supplies are made under an agreement which provides for successive payments and the supplier, at or about the beginning of any period not exceeding one year, issues a VAT invoice which, in addition to the normal requirements for a VAT invoice, shows

- the dates on which payments under the agreement are to become due for payment in the period,
- the amount payable (excluding VAT) on each such date; and
- the rate of VAT in force at the time of issue of the VAT invoice and the amount of VAT chargeable in accordance with that rate on each payment,

the goods are treated as separately and successively supplied each time that a payment in respect of the supply becomes due or is received, whichever is the earlier. If there is a change in the rate of VAT before any of the due dates for payment, the invoice ceases to be treated as a VAT invoice in respect of any supplies for which payments are due after the change (and not received before the change).

[*SI 1995/2518, Reg 86*(*2*)–(*4*)].

Anti-avoidance provisions. The above continuous supply provisions have enabled some suppliers to delay (sometimes indefinitely) the time at which they accounted for VAT. The following anti-avoidance provisions are designed to prevent this by imposing periodic tax points (usually based on twelve-month periods) on specified supplies between connected persons where VAT has not already been accounted for under the above provisions. The provisions apply to supplies of goods, the benefit of which is received after 1 October 2003.

In relation to supplies of goods within (*a*)–(*d*) above, where

- *either* the supplier and the recipient are '*connected persons*' (see 69.19 VALUATION) *or* both are members of a 'group undertaking' (see *Companies Act 1985, s 259*) but are not members of the same VAT group (see 31 GROUPS OF COMPANIES),
- the supply is taxable at a positive rate (ie the standard or reduced rate), and
- the supplier cannot show that the recipient is able to recover *all* the VAT on the supply

then, subject to below, to the extent that the goods in question have been 'provided' and have not already been treated as supplied under any other provisions, they are treated as separately and successively supplied

(i) in the case of supplies the provision of which commenced on or before 1 October 2003, at the end of twelve-month period after that date;

(ii) in the case of supplies the provision of which commenced after 1 October 2003, at the end of the twelve-month period after the supplies commenced; or

(iii) such earlier date falling within the period specified in (i) or (ii) above notified by the supplier to HMRC in writing and agreed by them

and thereafter at the end of each subsequent twelve-month period. For these purposes, goods are provided at the time when, and to the extent that, the recipient receives the benefit of them.

But where the supplier, within six months after the time applicable under (i)–(iii) above, either

- issues a VAT invoice in respect of it, or
- receives a payment in respect of it,

to the extent that the supply has not already been treated as taking place at some other time under any other provisions, the supply is treated as taking place at the time the invoice is issued or the payment is received. Where the supplier intends to issue a VAT invoice, or payment is due, within the six-month's period, he should wait for either of those events before accounting for VAT. However, if, for whatever reason, neither of those events has materialised at the end of the six months, the tax point reverts to the annual tax point date as above. (VAT Information Sheet 14/03, para 4.5).

A supplier can exercise a number of options in relation to the provisions by writing to one of HMRC's written enquiry teams (see 15.4 CUSTOMS: ADMINISTRATION).

- He can request to vary the six-month period if there are genuine commercial reasons for doing so. Full details of why the variation is required should be given. Such a change is subject to approval by HMRC and a supplier should not therefore start using a revised date until it is formally approved.

- He can elect not to be bound by the six-month rule at any time, in which case thereafter he must account for VAT as required at each annual tax point as described above.
- He can, after the start of any annual period established as above, select an earlier alternative period end date in relation to some or all of his supplies. Provided this is approved by HMRC, the date selected establishes the end of the supplier's current and subsequent twelve-month periods. Written notice should advise HMRC of the alternative date to be adopted and *either* state that this date is to apply to all supplies to which the rules might apply *or* nominate different dates for different categories of supply. In the latter case, supplies must be identified in sufficient detail so as to be distinguishable from one another.

Where these anti-avoidance provisions apply, the normal time of supply rules for continuous supplies detailed above do not apply to the extent that supplies have been treated as having taken place under the anti-avoidance rules.

[*SI 1995/2518, Reg 94B; SI 2003/2318, Reg 3*]. (VAT Information Sheet 14/03, paras 4.3, 4.5).

64.47 Supplier's goods in possession of buyer

Subject to below, where goods are supplied under an agreement where

- the supplier retains the property in the goods until all or part are appropriated under the agreement by the buyer, and
- the whole or part of the consideration is determined at that time,

the tax point is the earliest of

(*a*) the date of such appropriation by the buyer;

(*b*) the date when a VAT invoice is issued by the supplier; or

(*c*) the date when a payment is received by the supplier.

If, within 14 days after the appropriation under (*a*) above, the supplier issues a VAT invoice in respect of goods appropriated or, with effect from 1 January 2004, a self-billed invoice is issued by the customer (see 40.6 INVOICES), then, unless he has notified HMRC in writing that he does not wish the 14 day rule to apply, the tax point is the time that invoice is issued. This does not, however, override (*b*) or (*c*) above if earlier.

The above provisions do not apply to

- goods on sale or return (for which see 64.43 above); or
- supplier's goods in the possession of the buyer where the goods are supplied to somebody liable to account for acquisition VAT on the supply in another EC country.

[*SI 1995/2518, Reg 88*].

64.48 Gold

VATA 1994, s 55 provides a special accounting and payment system for supplies of gold. *VATA 1994, s 55*(*4*) disapplies all tax point rules apart from the basic tax point in 64.39 above and the sale or return provisions in 64.43 above. This means that the tax point for supplies covered by the scheme will normally be the date of removal of the goods. See 30.9 GOLD AND PRECIOUS METALS for further details of the scheme.

64.49 TIME OF SUPPLY OF SERVICES

Subject to

- any accommodation tax points agreed under 64.38 above,
- any extra-statutory class concession, and
- the special cases in 64.50 to 64.57 below,

a supply of services is treated as taking place at the basic or actual tax point.

(*a*) **Basic tax point**. The basic tax point for services is the time when the services are performed. This is normally taken as the date when all the work except any outstanding invoicing has been completed.

(*b*) **Actual tax points.**

(i) *Advance payment or invoicing.* If, before the basic tax point, the supplier issues a VAT invoice or receives payment in respect of the supply, there is tax point at the time the invoice is issued or payment is received, whichever occurs first, to the extent covered by the invoice or payment. (There will thus always be a further tax point where the amount invoiced or paid is less than the full value of the supply.)

(ii) *The 14 day rule.* If the supplier issues a VAT invoice (or a taxable person issues a document to himself under the self-billing arrangements, see 40.6 INVOICES) within 14 days *after* the basic tax point, then, unless he has notified HMRC in writing that he does not wish the rule to be applied, the tax point is the date the invoice is issued. This rule does not, however, override (*b*)(i) above.

HMRC normally expect a trader to either apply the 14 day rule to all supplies or to opt out of its use altogether. However, it may be applied selectively

- by separate companies in a VAT group registration;
- for supplies subject to the self-billing arrangements and supplies subject to conventional invoicing; or
- where a trader has a genuine need to treat some supplies differently and can easily distinguish those supplies.

Extending the 14 day rule under (*b*)(ii) above. HMRC may, at the request of the taxable person, extend the 14 day rule in respect of all or part of his supplies. They will not do this unless the taxable person is genuinely unable to issue an invoice within 14 days of the basic tax point, eg where prices cannot be determined until invoices have been received. HMRC are unlikely to grant any significant period of extension as any payment received between the basic tax point and the date when the invoice is actually issued does not create a tax point. It should also be noted that the tax point is only delayed if a VAT invoice is issued within the extended period. If, for any reason, it is not, the tax point reverts to the earlier basic tax point (rather than the date of expiry of the extended period) which may have penalty implications.

The following extensions to the 14 day rule have been centrally agreed.

1. *Members of The British Electrical and Allied Manufacturers Association, The Scientific Instruments Manufacturers Association and The Electronic Engineering Association*. If the consideration for a supply of services made by member companies under a Government contract is not ascertained or ascertainable at or

before the time when the services are performed, the supply may be treated as taking place at the time when the member issues a VAT invoice, provided it is issued within one year of the date of performance of the services.

2. *Government contracts.* Where a taxable person supplies services for an agreed price under a Government contract and the supplier's invoicing is delayed due to Government procedures (eg the use of Ministry of Defence Form 640) the supply may be treated as taking place at the time a VAT invoice is issued, provided it is issued within four months of the date of performance of the services.

3. *Local authorities.* Where a local authority supplies taxable services in the course of business activities, the supply may be treated as taking place at the time a VAT invoice is issued, provided it is issued within two months of the date of performance of the services.

4. *Patent agents.* If the consideration for a supply of services by a patent agent is not ascertained or ascertainable at or before the time when the services are performed, the supply may be treated as taking place at the time a VAT invoice is issued, provided it is issued within three months of the date of performance of the service.

5. *The Society of British Aerospace Companies Ltd* (SBAC). If the consideration for a supply of services made by member companies of SBAC is not ascertained or ascertainable at or before the time when the services are performed (because the price is subject to negotiation and agreement after the work has been completed), the supply may be treated as taking place at the time a VAT invoice is issued, provided it is issued within six months of the date of performance of the services (one year in the case of a Government contract).

6. *Solicitors.* If the consideration for a supply of services by a solicitor is not ascertained or ascertainable at or before the time when the services are performed, the supply may be treated as taking place at the time a VAT invoice is issued, provided that it is issued within three months of the date of performance of the services.

[*VATA 1994, s 6(3)–(6)(10), Sch 11 para 2B(4); FA 2002, s 24*]. (VAT Notice 700, para 14.2; Internal Guidance V1–11, paras 10.1, 10.2, 10.4).

64.50 Continuous supplies of services

Normal rules. Subject to

- the provisions below on *advance invoicing* and *anti-avoidance provisions*, and
- special provisions applying in the construction industry (see 64.52 below)

where services are supplied for any period for a consideration the whole or part of which is determined or payable periodically or from time to time, the services are treated as separately and successively supplied each time payment is received or a VAT invoice relating to the supply is issued by the supplier, whichever is the earlier. [*SI 1995/2518, Reg 90(1); SI 1997/2887, Reg 2*].

It is important to distinguish between supplies that fall within this category and work done over a period that culminates in a single supply (eg preparation of a client's will by a solicitor) or a series of separate supplies made over a period.

> *Example*
>
> A central heating engineer supplies services to a customer over a period of one year.
>
> (1) If the engineer is simply called out to repair the customer's boiler as and when it breaks down, there is a series of separate supplies each with basic tax point based on performance.
>
> (2) If the engineer's supplies are made under a contract to service the boiler at regular intervals and undertake repairs where necessary
>
> - where the contract is for a fixed period at a fixed price and is not renewable (eg it was secured by tender), the supply represents a single supply of services performed over an extended period; and
> - where the contract is open-ended or renewable and the amounts due under the contract are calculated or payable periodically or from time to time, the supply is a continuous supply of services.

The important elements are the existence of a contract (written, oral or implied) which commits the parties to doing something during the period and the on-going nature of the supply. An understanding that work will be undertaken should the need arise is not sufficient.

Examples of the type of supply that can meet the above criteria include

- the services of a trustee;
- regular or periodic maintenance work;
- services supplied by credit card companies to retailers;
- club membership;
- management services;
- agency services;
- long-term loans or secondments of staff; and
- hire, lease or rental of equipment.

(Internal Guidance V1–11, para 21.2).

In *B J Rice & Associates v C & E Commrs, CA [1996] STC 581 (TVC 60.418)* professional services were supplied and invoiced before registration but not paid for until after registration. The tribunal and High Court both held that, as an invoice raised before registration could not be a VAT invoice, the time of supply could only be the date payment was received and therefore VAT was due on the supply. The Court of Appeal, by a majority decision, reversed this decision holding that the provisions as to time of supply determine when, but not whether, VAT is to be charged. Liability is determined under *VATA 1994, s 4* which, *inter alia*, provides that VAT is charged where the supply is made by a taxable person. In this case, the supply was made at a time when the appellant was not a taxable person. See also *C & E Commrs v British Telecommunications plc, CA [1996] STC 818 (TVC 60.419)* for a consideration of the time of supply where customers unintentionally make overpayments. For a payment to represent consideration for a supply of services, there must be a direct link with the service provided. The inadvertent overpayment of a current debt is not a payment on account of a future liability and the recipient is under an immediate obligation to repay it.

Advance invoicing. Where separate and successive supplies of services are made under an agreement which provides for successive payments and, at or about the beginning of any period not exceeding one year, the supplier issues a VAT invoice which, in addition to the normal requirements for a VAT invoice shows

(*a*) the dates on which payments under the agreement are to become due in the period;

(*b*) the amount payable (excluding VAT) on each such date; and

(*c*) the rate of VAT in force at the time of issue of the VAT invoice and the amount of VAT chargeable in accordance with that rate on each payment,

services are to be treated as separately and successively supplied each time that a payment in respect of them becomes due or is received, whichever is the earlier. If there is a change in the rate of VAT before any of the due dates for payment under (*a*) above, the invoice ceases to be treated as a VAT invoice in respect of any supplies for which payment is due after the change.

[*SI 1995/2518, Reg 90*(*2*)(*3*)].

The customer must not reclaim, as input tax, any VAT shown on the VAT invoice until the date on which the payment is due or until payment has been received by the supplier, whichever happens first. (VAT Notice 700, para 14.3). See also *The Simkins Partnership (VTD 9705) (TVC 50.95).*

Anti-avoidance provisions. The above continuous supply provisions have enabled some suppliers to delay (sometimes indefinitely) the time at which they accounted for VAT. The following anti-avoidance provisions are designed to prevent this by imposing periodic tax points (usually based on twelve-month periods) on specified supplies between connected persons where VAT has not already been accounted for under the above provisions. The provisions apply to supplies of services, the benefit of which is received after 1 October 2003.

In relation to supplies of continuous supplies of services where

(1) *either* the supplier and the recipient are '*connected persons*' (see 69.19 VALUATION) *or* both are members of a 'group undertaking' (see *Companies Act 1985, s 259*) but are not members of the same VAT group (see 31 GROUPS OF COMPANIES),

(2) the supply is taxable at a positive rate (ie the standard or reduced rate), and

(3) the supplier cannot show that the recipient is able to recover *all* the VAT on the supply

then, subject to below, to the extent that the services in question have been 'provided' and have not already been treated as supplied under any other provisions, they are treated as separately and successively supplied

(i) in the case of supplies the provision of which commenced on or before 1 October 2003, at the end of twelve-month period after that date;

(ii) in the case of supplies the provision of which commenced after 1 October 2003, at the end of the twelve-month period after the supplies commenced; or

(iii) such earlier date falling within the period specified in (i) or (ii) above notified by the supplier to HMRC in writing and agreed by them

and thereafter at the end of each subsequent twelve-month period. For these purposes, services are provided at the time when, and to the extent that, the recipient receives the benefit of them.

But where the supplier, within six months after the time applicable under (i)–(iii) above, either

- issues a VAT invoice in respect of it, or
- receives a payment in respect of it,

to the extent that the supply has not already been treated as taking place at some other time under any other provisions, the supply is treated as taking place at the time the invoice is issued or the payment is received. Where the supplier intends to issue a VAT invoice, or payment is due, within the six-month's period, he should wait for either of those events before accounting for VAT. However, if, for whatever reason, neither of those events has materialised at the end of the six months, the tax point reverts to the annual tax point date as above. (VAT Information Sheet 14/03, para 4.5).

A supplier can exercise a number of options in relation to the provisions by writing to one of HMRC's written enquiry teams (see 15.4 CUSTOMS AND EXCISE: ADMINISTRATION).

- He can request to vary the six-month period if there are genuine commercial reasons for doing so. Full details of why the variation is required should be given. Such a change is subject to approval by HMRC and a supplier should not therefore start using a revised date until it is formally approved.
- He can elect not to be bound by the six-month rule at any time, in which case thereafter he must account for VAT as required at each annual tax point as described above.
- He can, after the start of any annual period established as above, select an earlier alternative period end date in relation to some or all of his supplies. Provided this is approved by HMRC, the date selected establishes the end of the supplier's current and subsequent twelve-month periods. Written notice should advise HMRC of the alternative date to be adopted and *either* state that this date is to apply to all supplies to which the rules might apply *or* nominate different dates for different categories of supply. In the latter case, supplies must be identified in sufficient detail so as to be distinguishable from one another.

(VAT Information Sheet 14/03, paras 4.3, 4.5).

Where the supply in question is one of letting, hiring or rental of assets however described, and that letting, etc depends upon one or more other leases of those assets (the superior lease or leases), the reference to a supplier in (1) above includes a reference to any lessor of a superior lease.

Where these anti-avoidance provisions apply, the normal time of supply rules for continuous supplies detailed above do not apply to the extent that supplies have been treated as having taken place under the anti-avoidance rules.

[*SI 1995/2518, Reg 94B; SI 2003/2318, Reg 3*].

64.51 Royalties and similar payments

The granting, assignment or surrender of the whole or part of any right is a supply of services. This can take various forms.

Licences. A licence is a supply of rights that specifically permits the licensee to do something in connection with a copyright or patent held by the licensor. It is may be issued for a set period (with or without option to renew) or for the life of the copyright or patent.

Where a licence is issued for a single payment, the supply is a single supply of services and the basic tax point occurs when the licence is granted. Where the licence agreement provides for payments to be made periodically, or from time to time, the service may be treated as a continuous supply within 64.50 above, VAT becoming due every time a payment is received or a VAT invoice is issued by the licensor, whichever is the earlier.

(Internal Guidance V1–11, paras 27.1, 27.2).

Permanent assignments. Alternatively, a supply can take the form of a permanent, outright assignment or surrender of the rights. This is normally a single supply of services to which the normal tax point rules apply. The basic tax point occurs at the time the rights are assigned.

Special provisions, however, apply if the contract provides for the assignor to receive periodic payments of royalties, repeat fees, etc where some or all of the consideration is dependent on future events (eg the level of subsequent sales or repeat broadcasts).

Where the whole amount of the consideration for the supply of services was not ascertainable at the time when the services were performed and subsequently the use of the benefit of those services by a person other than the supplier gives rise to any payment of consideration for that supply which is

- in whole or in part determined or payable periodically or from time to time or at the end of any period,
- additional to the amount, if any, already payable for the supply, and
- not a payment to which the rules relating to continuous supplies of services under 64.50 above apply,

a further supply is treated as taking place each time a payment in respect of the use of the benefit of those services is received, or a VAT invoice is issued, by the supplier, whichever is the earlier.

[*SI 1995/2518, Reg 91*]. (Internal Guidance V1–11, paras 27.1, 27.3).

HMRC take the view that *Reg 91* creates a further time of supply for the original supply. This means that the liability is determined by the VAT rate that applied to that supply at the time the rights were originally assigned. (Internal Guidance V1–11, para 27.3).

64.52 Supplies in the construction industry

The tax point for supplies in the construction industry depend upon the terms of payment under the contract for the supply.

(*a*) Where the contract provides for periodic payments to the supplier (often referred to as stage payments or interim payments) a tax point arises at the earliest of the following dates.

(i) The date a payment is received from the supplier.

(ii) The date the supplier issues a VAT invoice.

(iii) For construction services where, broadly, the building in question is occupied by a person who cannot recover VAT and the construction contractor is connected with the occupier or has been financed by the occupier to carry out the construction work, the day on which the services are performed.

[*SI 1995/2518, Reg 93; SI 1997/2887, Reg 5; SI 1999/1374*].

(*b*) Single payment contracts (even if payment of part of the price is to be delayed under a retention clause) are subject to the normal tax point rules (see 64.49 above).

See 42.29 LAND AND BUILDINGS for fuller details.

Retention payments. Where a contract within (*b*) above includes a retention clause, the tax point of the retained element is the earlier of the time when a payment is received in respect of the retention and the date the supplier issues an invoice relating to it. See 64.37 above and 42.29 LAND AND BUILDINGS for further details.

64.53 Services from outside the UK

Services which are treated as made by a person under *VATA 1994, s 8*(*1*) (reverse charge on services received from abroad, see 39.4 INTERNATIONAL SERVICES) are treated as being supplied when the supplies are paid for or, if the consideration is not in money, on the last day of the VAT period in which the services are performed. [*SI 1995/2518, Reg 82*].

See 64.38 above for an accommodation tax point for members of the Institute of London Underwriters.

64.54 Goods used for private or non-business use

Where business assets are put to any private use or are used (or made available to any person for use) for non-business purposes, a supply of services is treated as taking place under *VATA 1994, Sch 4 para 5*(*4*) (see 47.7 OUTPUT TAX). The tax point for this supply of services is when the goods are appropriated to that private or non-business use [*VATA 1994, s 6*(*13*)]. If the services are supplied for any period, the tax point is the last day of the supplier's VAT period (or of each such VAT period) in which the goods are made available or used. [*SI 1995/2518, Reg 81*(*1*)].

64.55 Free supplies of services

Where services specified in any Order made by the Treasury under *VATA 1994, s 5*(*4*) are supplied for any period, they are to be treated as supplied on the last day of the supplier's VAT period, or of each such VAT period, in which the services are performed. [*SI 1995/2518, Reg 81*(*2*)].

The only order made under these provision is the *VAT* (*Supply of Service*) *Order 1993* (*SI 1993/1507*). This covers certain services, originally acquired for business purposes, which are subsequently put to private or non-business use. See 47.7 OUTPUT TAX.

64.56 Supplies through coin-operated machines

Under the normal time of supply rules, the tax point for supplies made via coin-operated machines (eg vending machines, amusement machines and gaming machines) is the time the machine is used (or, more strictly, the time money is inserted). However, as an accounting convenience, operators may delay accounting for VAT until the takings are removed from a machine. (VAT Notice 48, ESC 3.6).

For all other purposes, the normal tax point rules apply. Therefore in the event of

- a theft of takings from a machine, VAT must still be accounted for in full on any supplies that have been made from the machine (see *Townville (Wheldale) Miners Sports and Recreation Club and Institute (VTD 719) (TVC 60.347)* where coins fraudulently extracted were subject to VAT); and
- a change in the rate of VAT, operators must revert to the normal tax point rules for the purposes of determining the VAT rates to be applied where takings removed from machines cover supplies made both before and after the rate changed (see *Glasgow Vending Services (VTD 943) (TVC 60.350)*).

(Internal Guidance V1–11, para 19.1).

64.57 Barristers and solicitors

(1) Barristers

Services supplied by a barrister (in Scotland, an advocate), acting in that capacity, are treated as taking place at whichever is the earliest of the following times.

(*a*) When the fee in respect of those services is received.

(*b*) When the barrister issues a VAT invoice in respect of them.

(*c*) The day when the barrister ceases to practise as such.

[*SI 1995/2518, Reg 92*].

These special rules were introduced because a barrister cannot sue for unpaid fees and frequently can have to wait a considerable period of time before outstanding fees are received from instructing solicitors. For most supplies by practising barristers, the tax point will be the receipt of payment under (*a*) above as the fee notes issued to solicitors normally do not become VAT invoices until they are receipted and returned to the solicitor following payment.

These rules make VAT chargeable on all outstanding fees at the time of ceasing to practice. See below, however, for a special scheme allowing a barrister to defer payment of VAT on such fees until payment is received or a VAT invoice issued in respect of them.

Ceasing to practice. Action required depends upon whether the barrister makes other taxable supplies.

- *A barrister who makes no other taxable supplies* must notify HMRC within 30 days of ceasing to practice. This can be done on Form VAT 7. A letter should be sent with the deregistration application stating whether the barrister intends to pay the VAT due on outstanding fees immediately or wishes to defer payment (see below). If deferral is approved, the barrister must still pay VAT due on fees already received, or shown on VAT invoices raised, up to the date of deregistration.

- *A barrister who continues to make other taxable supplies but can show that their value will not exceed the deregistration limit in the next twelve months* (see 59.8 REGISTRATION) may ask HMRC to cancel his registration by completing Form VAT 7. HMRC will then send a final VAT return on which the barrister must include VAT on all professional fees received, and other supplies made, between the end of the last full VAT period and the date of cancellation of registration. If he wishes to defer payment of VAT on outstanding fees (see below), he must apply to HMRC.
- *A barrister who continues to make other taxable supplies and to be registered* must include, in his normal VAT return for the quarter in which he ceased to practice, VAT on all fees received, and other supplies made, during the period. If he wishes to defer payment of VAT on outstanding fees (see below), he must apply to HMRC. VAT on other taxable supplies must be accounted for on subsequent VAT returns in the normal way and is not affected by the special procedure. VAT on professional fees outstanding at the time of ceasing to practise should be excluded from subsequent VAT returns and paid separately with Form VAT 812 (see below).

A barrister may continue to issue VAT invoices for fees which are outstanding after registration has been cancelled but

- the services must have been supplied before the date registration is cancelled;
- the tax point to be shown on the invoice is the date of ceasing to practice; and
- the rate of VAT charged must be the rate in force at that time (and not any different rate applying at the time the invoice is raised).

Deferring payment of VAT on fees outstanding on ceasing to practice. HMRC send a Form VAT 811 to a barrister who asks for deferment. On the form the barrister must list every standard-rated fee which is outstanding (or give an estimate), together with the name of the relevant case, the professional client and the date of the first fee note. The completed form should be sent to VAT Central Unit, GABS, 7th Floor SW, Alexander House, Victoria Avenue, Southend-on-Sea, SS99 1AU. A certified copy of the completed form will be returned when deferment is approved.

A copy of Form VAT 812 is then sent quarterly on which the barrister must show VAT due on any fees received, or for which a VAT invoice has been issued, during the period specified on the form. The name of the relevant case must be shown together with enough details to cross-reference the fee to the completed Form VAT 811. Form VAT 812 must also show fees for any services which were expected to be zero-rated when the Form VAT 811 was completed but which turn out to be standard-rated.

After the first year, HMRC offer the option of completing Form VAT 812 on a six-monthly basis.

When all outstanding fees have been received and the VAT due paid, the barrister must make a declaration of final payment on Form VAT 812 (with an explanation for any items shown on Form VAT 811 on which VAT has not been paid, eg because the fee has not been collected). Records must be kept for inspection for one year after the declaration of final payment.

Practising barristers who die. The deceased barrister's clerk should notify HMRC as soon as possible and the personal representatives should, within ten days of the grant of probate or order for administration, inform HMRC whether they wish to pay VAT on the barrister's outstanding professional fees straight away or to defer payment. If they choose to defer payment, the personal representatives must use the special deferment scheme outlined above. The personal representatives must give an address to which further communications should be sent and sign an adapted VAT deferment application form.

Barristers who are partly exempt for VAT purposes. Where a barrister has made exempt supplies since the beginning of the VAT year in which he ceased to practise and applies for deferment of VAT on outstanding fees, it may be necessary in due course to make a special adjustment of the input tax reclaimed. Advice should be obtained from HMRC.

(VAT Notice 700/44/02).

De Voil Indirect Tax Service. See V5.145.

(2) **Solicitors**

There are no special tax point rules for supplies made by a solicitor and, with the exception of the centrally agreed extension to the 14 day rule (see below), they are subject to the normal time of supply rules that apply to services.

Basic tax point. Most supplies by a solicitor are single supplies, even though the supply may involve work undertaken over an extended period of time (eg litigation). The basic tax point occurs when the services have been fully completed.

Where a solicitor makes supplies on a regular basis to an individual client, in most cases this represents a series of separate supplies, each of which is subject to its own basic tax point. If the solicitor bills the client periodically for all work performed or completed during the period, the basic tax point rule should be complied with for each of the separate supplies. Only in exceptional circumstances will this kind of relationship represent a continuous supply of services (eg where a solicitor is retained as the permanent legal adviser or to act as the client's legal office). However, some legal work is inherently continuous in nature (eg the supply of the services of a solicitor acting as a trustee) and such supplies normally fall within the time of supply rules for continuous supplies (see 64.50 above).

Client accounts, etc. The receipt of a payment into a client's account does not represent receipt of payment for VAT purposes, which only occurs when money is transferred from the client's account to the general office account. This does not, however, apply to the receipt of standard monthly payments for Legal Aid contracting work (see below).

Disbursements. A tax point is not created by the receipt of payments from clients in respect of expenses such as stamp duty and Land Registry fees that are accepted as disbursements for VAT purposes (see 3.7 AGENTS).

Standard monthly payments for Legal Aid contracting work. Solicitors undertaking work under what is known as the contracting arrangements receive a standard monthly payment (SMP) based on the anticipated level of this work over the forthcoming year. As individual cases are completed the fees, disbursements and VAT are 'billed' and allocated by the solicitor to the SMPs. This means that, depending on the progress of individual cases, the total amounts received from the Legal Services Commission may, at any given time, exceed the value of cases completed or there may be a shortfall.

HMRC have agreed with the Law Society that the normal tax point rules will apply to Legal Aid contracting work. As a result, unless the cash accounting scheme is used, VAT on completed cases must be accounted for at the basic tax point (the date when the supply of services is completed). VAT is due on the SMP received to the extent that it represents advance payment for cases that have not yet started or cases that have started but have not yet been completed.

In the following examples, it is assumed that the solicitor has only one case involving SMPs. In practice, an SMP will generally be for more than one client and the work undertaken for those clients is likely to be at various stages of completion. The SMPs will probably cover a combination of work not yet started, work started but not completed and work completed. However, the VAT rules used should be applied whatever the case.

Example 1

A solicitor receives an SMP of £1,175 per month on the first of each month and prepares VAT returns for calendar quarters. A case commences on 1 January and is completed on 15 March. The total fees and disbursements liable to VAT amount to £3,750 plus £656.25 VAT.

At the end of the March VAT quarter, the following tax points will have occurred with VAT to be accounted for on the return as follows.

	£
1 January	175.00
1 February	175.00
1 March	175.00
15 March	131.25
Total	£656.25

VAT due at the time of the next SMP received on 1 April will be £43.75 as £131.25 has already been accounted for on the previous return.

Example 2

A solicitor receives an SMP of £1,175 per month on the first of each month and prepares VAT returns for calendar quarters. A case commences on 1 January and is completed on 15 April. The total fees and disbursements liable to VAT amount to £1,500 plus £262.50 VAT.

At the end of the March VAT quarter, the following tax points will have occurred with VAT to be accounted for on the return as follows:

	£
1 January	175.00
1 February	175.00
1 March	175.00
Total	£525.00

When the case is completed on 15 April, the VAT due on the supply of £262.50 has already been accounted for in full against SMPs received during the previous quarter.

If a solicitor is required to repay some, or all, of an SMP to the Legal Services Commission (eg because of a fall in the amount of work undertaken), then the amount refunded ceases to be consideration for a supply. Any VAT previously accounted for on the amount to be refunded may be adjusted accordingly at that time.

HMRC take the view that the VAT treatment of SMPs is the same whether they are paid into the office account or a client account (ie they make a distinction between SMPs and payments received from privately paying clients).

Adjustments to solicitor's fees. In certain circumstances, a solicitor's fees can be subject to third party scrutiny and adjustment before acceptance. The circumstances in which this can occur, and the tax point consequences, are as follows.

- *Contentious work* (*non-Legal Aid*). If the losing party to a legal action is ordered to pay costs, the solicitor for the successful party prepares a bill which is then either agreed with the solicitor for the loser or referred to the Court for scrutiny under the taxation procedures. In such cases, settling of the costs is part of the solicitor's overall supply to the client. A basic tax point does not, therefore, occur until either the costs have been agreed between the solicitors or the taxation procedure is complete.
- *Non-contentious work* (*non-Legal Aid*). A client may ask the Law Society to scrutinise a solicitor's bill to ensure that it is fair and reasonable. The Law Society can then reduce the amount payable by the client. This procedure does not form part of the supply by the solicitor to the client and the basic tax point still occurs when all the work, except the invoicing, is completed. However, if this means that VAT is accounted for in advance of a reduction to the bill, the solicitor may subsequently adjust the amount accounted for (subject to the normal rules regarding credits).
- *Legal Aid* (*excluding contract work above*). Although relatively few bills submitted by a solicitor to the Legal Aid authorities are approved unamended, the solicitor's services are supplied to the client named in the Legal Aid Order and any action by the solicitor in connection with submitting and agreeing the amount of the bill does not form part of the supply to the client. The basic tax point occurs when all the work, except the invoicing, has been completed. Apart from the centrally negotiated extension to the 14 day rule (see below) there are no special tax point rules that apply in these circumstances. VAT must be accounted for on the basis of the normal tax point rules and adjusted later in the event of any subsequent reduction in the fee.

Extension of the '14 day' rule. Where the consideration for a supply of services by a solicitor is not ascertained or ascertainable at or before the time when the services are performed, the supply may be treated as taking place at the time when the solicitor issues an invoice in respect of the supply *provided* that the VAT invoice is issued not later than three months after the date of performance of the services. It should be noted that failure to issue a VAT invoice within the three months means that the tax point reverts to the basic tax point (and is not the end of the three-month period). This is particularly important in the case of Legal Aid work. The Legal Aid authorities are not a taxable person and therefore do not require a VAT invoice. Nevertheless, the solicitor must still issue a VAT invoice if the three-month extension is to apply.

(Internal Guidance V1–11, paras 30.1–30.5, 31.1–31.3).

64.58 SUPPLIES BY 'TAXABLE PERSONS'

EC legislation. See 22.6 EUROPEAN COMMUNITY LEGISLATION.

UK legislation. One of the four basic conditions to be satisfied for a transaction to be within the scope of UK VAT (see 64.1 above) is that it is made by a taxable person. Under *VATA 1994, s 1(2)*, VAT on any supply of goods or services is a liability of the person making the supply and under *VATA 1994, s 3(1)* a person is a taxable person while he is, or is required to be, registered for VAT purposes. It follows from this that, to decide whether a transaction meets the condition of being made by a taxable person, it is necessary to establish two facts.

(*a*) **Whether a person is required to be registered.** This is usually dependent upon the level of that person's taxable turnover; although there are special provisions covering voluntary registration, registration of intending traders and group registration. All these considerations are dealt with in the chapter REGISTRATION (59).

However, another consideration which can determine whether a person is required to be registered is employment status. There is specific provision in EC legislation for employees acting on behalf of their employers not to be considered as taxable persons. They are therefore not required to be registered and their activities are outside the scope of UK VAT. This is considered in more detail in 64.59 below.

(*b*) **Who is the person making the supply and thus liable for the VAT on that transaction.** This will, in the vast majority of cases, be self-evident but there are two key areas which frequently cause problems.

- *Agency.* An agent arranges supplies which are made by someone else, ie his principal. A principal actually makes and receives supplies in his own right. An agent is obliged to account for VAT only on the charge which he makes for his own services and can only deduct input tax relating to those services. A principal must account for VAT on the full value of the transaction, and normally can reclaim input tax on both the charges made to him for the agent's services, and the purchases made on his behalf by the agent. It is thus important to determine whether a particular transaction is a supply made by a principal or the passing on of a supply by an agent acting on the principal's behalf.

  Where certain conditions are satisfied, payments by way of disbursements made by an agent to a third party on behalf of a principal may be reimbursed to the agent by the principal without the addition of VAT.

All aspects of agency are considered in more detail in the chapter AGENTS (3).

- *Partnerships and joint ventures.* When two or more parties come together for the purpose of a specific business venture, it can be difficult to decide whether the venture itself has made a supply, or whether the venturers are supplying each other prior to one of them supplying the final product. This is considered in more detail in the chapter PARTNERSHIPS AND JOINT VENTURES (50).

Particular business areas in which problems have arisen in determining who has made a supply are considered in 64.60 below.

(Internal Guidance V1–5, Chapter 1 paras 1.2–1.4).

64.59 Employment status

The purpose of this paragraph is to help to decide whether a supply has been made by a self-employed person acting independently or by an employee acting on behalf of his or her employer.

Under *EC 6th Directive, Art 4* a taxable person means any person who *independently* carries out certain specified activities. The use of the word 'independently' specifically excludes employed and other persons from the scope of VAT in so far as they are bound to an employer by a contract of employment or by any other legal ties creating the relationship of employer and employee as regards working conditions, remuneration and the employer's liability.

The effect of this is that where employees act on behalf of their employers, they are not 'taxable persons' and such activities are therefore outside the scope of VAT.

Customs' policy on employment status. Unless there are clear reasons to do otherwise, Customs' policy is to follow the employment status given by Revenue for income tax purposes, ie they accept that a person paying income tax under the trading income provisions is self-employed and a person paying under the employment income provisions is an employee (and therefore outside the scope of VAT). If a person pays income tax under both sets of provisions, then only the gross monies earned from the work covered under trading income provisions should be considered as being potentially subject to VAT.

Exceptions to normal practice. There are, however, occasions when Customs cannot or do not follow the Revenue practice.

- The treatment by the Revenue of 'office holders' is not determinative of whether the activity is undertaken by way of business for VAT purposes. See 8.4(11) BUSINESS.
- A person may argue for a different VAT status from his Revenue tax status.
- The personal tax status of a person may be unknown or undecided.

In such cases, HMRC will examine the contracts that have been entered into in order to decide which are contracts of service (between employers and employees) and which are contracts for services (self-employed persons). In determining the relationship between the parties, all the facts must be established. There is no exhaustive list of factors to be considered and no rules about the relative weight of each factor. However, the following are some factors that the courts have found relevant in considering the status of workers.

- *Whether the individual is in business on his or her own account.*
- *The degree of control exercised.* Generally, a contract of employment gives the employer a right of control over the worker, covering what the worker has to do and where, when and how the worker has to do it.
- *Substitution rights.* Where an individual is free to hire someone to carry out his or her duties or to get substantial help from someone else, it is likely that the individual is self-employed.
- *The provision of equipment.* A self-employed contractor generally provides his or her own tools but an employee is provided by the employer with the necessary equipment to do the job.
- *Risk of loss and the prospect of profit.* An employee usually does not need to risk his own capital.
- *Basis of payment.* Typically, an employee is paid by the week or month while a self-employed contractor is paid a fixed sum.
- *Existence of sick pay, pension rights and holiday pay.* Only employees are entitled to statutory sick pay and normally membership of a firm's pension fund is only open to employees (although lack of such benefits by, for example, employees on short-term contracts does not affect their status as employees).
- *The exclusivity of the service, number of contracts held.* A typical employee works for only one employer whereas the typical self-employed contractor is ready to work for anyone and may have a number of contracts operating at once.
- *Right of dismissal.* A power to terminate an engagement by giving notice of a specified length is indicative of a contract of employment. A power to terminate only when there has been a breach of contract is more usually found in a contract for services.
- *Intention of the parties.* This is of particular relevance if other factors fail to provide an answer to the question of the workers' status.
- *The traditional structure of the trade or profession.* For rules in respect of particular trades, see 64.60 below.

(Internal Guidance V1–5, Chapter 2 paras 2.3, 2.4).

64.60 By whom a supply is made — particular problem areas

This paragraph covers particular business areas in which problems have arisen in determining who has made a supply. The list is not exhaustive and the guidance does not override the general rules on agency, partnerships and joint ventures, and employment status in 64.58 and 64.59 above.

(1) Agricultural co-operatives

Agricultural co-operatives are usually agents, selling agricultural produce for individual growers or farmers. As an agent, the agricultural co-operative should normally be accounting for VAT on the consideration for its own supply of services to its members (eg commission, haulage, storage and packing charges). It is understood that HMRC's policy in this area is under review. (Internal Guidance V1–5, Chapter 3 para 3.1).

(2) Auctioneers

See 3.15 AGENTS.

(3) **Barristers' clerks and senior clerks — employment status**

Barristers' clerks act for all the barristers in particular chambers. Customs follow the Revenue ruling on employment status. Senior barristers' clerks may be employed or self-employed depending on the terms and conditions under which they are engaged. To be self-employed, the senior clerk would operate under a contract for services to the barristers which requires him/her to provide at his/her own cost and expense a full clerking service including junior clerks and other ancillary staff. (Internal Guidance V1–5, Chapter 3 para 3.8).

(4) **Catering**

See 11.6 to 11.9 CATERING.

(5) **Direct selling or 'party plan' sales — agent or principal?**

'Direct selling' or 'party plan' is a selling method where products are sold to the public by individuals who are not registered for VAT. It is particularly common for sales of cosmetics, jewellery, and household appliances. Typically, the manufacturer sells the products on to an authorised wholesale distributor who passes the goods on to an unregistered individual to effect the final sale, often by way of a hostess party.

Whether the unregistered individuals have bought and sold the goods as principals or are acting as selling agents for the distributor depends on the facts of each case available from written contracts or agreements, letters and rules of conduct, brochures and price lists, advertisements for distributors or dealers, order forms, delivery notes, invoices, receipts, and guarantees. The principal factors which HMRC take into account in reaching any decision are as follows.

- *Title.* The unregistered individuals must obtain title to the goods if buying and selling those goods as principals. Individuals with title would be expected to replace goods at their own expense, issue refunds to customers, and bear bad debts. Where these responsibilities rest with the distributor, these are taken as indications that the individuals are merely selling agents. If the agreement or contract includes a 'Romalpa' clause which provides that the goods remain the property of the distributor until sold, this is an indication that the unregistered individual is a principal, otherwise such a clause would be unnecessary.
- *Value.* If they are principals, the unregistered individuals would have no obligation to inform the distributor of the price at which the goods are sold and would have freedom to set the retail selling price of the goods. Arrangements whereby the unregistered individuals inform the distributor of the total takings at a hostess party and are then paid a percentage of that figure indicate that they are selling agents of the distributor.
- *Separation.* If the unregistered individuals are selling agents, their fees must be identifiable and known to the distributor.

If the unregistered individuals are acting as selling agents of the distributor, the distributor must declare output tax on the full sale value. If, however, HMRC conclude that they are acting as principals, to avoid distortion of competition with taxable persons, they are likely to issue a notice of direction under *VATA 1994, Sch 6 para 2* requiring the distributor to account for VAT on the retail selling price. See 69.23 VALUATION.

(Internal Guidance V1–5, Chapter 3 paras 3.13–3.15, Appendix G).

(6) **Driving schools**

There are three possible scenarios for who is supplying driving tuition to pupils. Which scenario applies depends on the facts of each case found by examining copies of advertising and promotional material used by both the school and instructors, copies of the current agreements between school and instructors, copies of appointment cards, introductory letters, and/or offers given to the pupils by the school, and invoices/receipts given to pupils.

(*a*) **Instructors as employees**. The driving school employs its instructors under contracts of service. The school therefore makes the supply of tuition to the pupils and must account for output tax on the full value of fees received. There is no supply by the individual instructors, who are simply receiving remuneration for their services as employees.

Customs will follow any decision reached on the employment status of a driving instructor by the Revenue. If the income tax status of an instructor is disputed or undecided, Customs consider the following factors (in order of importance) in deciding whether the instructor is engaged under a contract of service (employed) or a contract for services (self-employed).

- *Chance of profit*. Where the school pays the instructor a guaranteed minimum or set weekly wage, this is strongly indicative of a contract of service as the instructor has little chance to profit.
- *Risk of loss*. A guaranteed minimum or set weekly wage is also indicative of the school, and not the instructor, bearing the risk of loss. If the school meets expenses such as insurance, vehicle repair and maintenance, and costs of petrol and oil used during tuition, these are further indicators of a contract of service as the instructor has little risk of personal loss.
- *Ownership of tools*. If the vehicle is owned by the school and no charge for its use is made to the instructor, this indicates a contract of service.
- *Control*. A high degree of control would be needed on the part of the school to support the contention that the instructors were employees under contracts of service (eg stipulating the hours the instructor works and setting fees for pupils without consulting the instructors).

For cases where instructors have been held to be employees, see *New Way School of Motoring Ltd (VTD 724) (TVC 60.205)* and *JW & MW Chalmers (VTD 1354) (TVC 60.206)*.

(*b*) The driving school engages a number of instructors as self-employed contractors under contracts for services. The instructors supply their services to the school and then act as agents of the school in making an onward supply of tuition to the pupils. The instructors need only account for output tax on their services to the school if the value exceeds the VAT registration limits. The school must account for output tax on the full value of the fees received from pupils.

(*c*) The driving instructors are self-employed principals and supply driving tuition direct to the pupils. The driving school acts as an agent in bringing pupil and instructor together. Output tax is only due on fees for driving tuition if an instructor exceeds the VAT registration limits.

Payments made by each instructor to the school are consideration for a supply of agency services by the school, and the school must declare output tax accordingly. The instructor can reclaim the input tax if registered.

Self-employed instructors. If the driving instructors are not employees of the school (so that (*a*) above cannot apply), it is necessary to determine whether they supply their services to the school under (*b*) above or the pupil under (*c*) above. This depends upon the relationship between the school and the instructor and how much control the school is able to exert.

Where (*b*) above applies, the school will provide a number of services to the instructors and maintains a relatively high degree of control over them. It will play a prominent role in setting fees to pupils and will require detailed records to be submitted by the instructors so that it can calculate what each instructor will receive. Normal practice is for fees for lessons to be passed in full to the school and only passed back to the instructors after necessary deductions have been made.

Where (*c*) above applies, the school will provide little more than a booking service and meeting place, charging a fixed fee for these services to the instructors. Instructors can work when they like and can vary their charges.

The situation will not, however, always be clear and HMRC give the following guidance to their officers in deciding whether (*b*) or (*c*) above is applicable.

Factor	*Indications that (b) above apples*	*Indications that (c) above applies*
Allocation of pupils	School usually allocates pupils to instructors who cover their geographical area	Intending pupils usually choose their own instructor by examining literature held on the school's premises (eg photographs, details of qualifications, fees charged, etc)
Fees to pupils	School plays a major role in setting fees, either dictating their level or participating at regular meetings with instructors to set uniform and binding fee structures	School either allows instructors complete freedom to decide or hold meetings to advise on levels. In practice, some instructors charge more than others

Factor	*Indications that (b) above apples*	*Indications that (c) above applies*
Ownership and costs of vehicles	School usually owns vehicles which it either lets the instructors use or hires out for a fee. School meets costs of maintaining, insuring and repairing the vehicles	Instructors provide their own cars and meet their own expenses
Fees from instructor to school	Instructors pay a variable fee to the school, retaining more of the hourly payment the more lessons they give. School makes up fees if they fall below a minimum level	Instructors pay a fee to the school which is either fixed per lesson or per week. Anything they earn above this is thus their profit
Overall advertising costs	Borne by school	Separate charge made to instructors to cover advertising costs
Payment by pupils	Cheques must be made out to the school, although they may be collected by the instructors	Pupils pay instructors direct, whether by cash or cheque
Facilities provided by school	Might extend to vehicles hire, booking service, record-keeping and training facilities	Limited to booking service, meeting room and waiting place
Division of payment	Full payment by pupils must initially pass to the school, who will then pass the balance back to the instructors after making deductions	Full payment by the pupils should initially go to the instructor, whose responsibility it is subsequently to pay the school. If cash is received by the school that cash is handed over in full to the instructor. If cheques are received, they are either held in a separate account or cashed and passed on in full to the instructor
Record keeping	School maintains detailed records of the takings and deductions of each instructor	Instructors keep their own records and appointment cards

Factor	*Indications that (b) above apples*	*Indications that (c) above applies*
Advertising on cars	All cars painted with school logo	Detachable advertising boards provided for cars; instructors under no obligation to use them
Cancelled appointments	School will arrange for another instructor to cover in the event of the original instructor cancelling	School merely passes on cancellation messages and plays no active part
Freedom of instructors	School is sole booking agent: instructors may not work elsewhere	Instructors free to work when they please and can take on pupils independently of the school
Dealing with complaints	Complaints must be forwarded to the school who might settle them if the instructor could not (eg by offering a free lesson)	Complaints entirely a matter between instructor and pupil

For cases where (*b*) above has been held to apply, see *Reeds School of Motoring (Nottingham) Ltd (VTD 4578) (TVC 60.208)*, *J Cronin (t/a Cronin's Driving School) v C & E Commrs, QB [1991] STC 333 (TVC 60.210)* and *ADI School of Motoring (VTD 11469) (TVC 60.213)*. For cases where (*c*) above has been held to apply, see *Reeds School of Motoring (Sheffield) Ltd (VTD 13404) (TVC 60.209)*, *Mr & Mrs ABC McIver (t/a Alan's School of Motoring) (VTD 5315) (TVC 60.211)* and *Fleet School of Motoring (VTD 7299) (TVC 60.212)*.

(Internal Guidance V1–5, Chapter 3 paras 3.16–3.20, Appendix I).

(7) **Employment bureaux**

See 3.13 AGENTS for employment bureaux generally.

(8) **Entertainment industry — employment status**

The Revenue now accepts that self-employment is normally more appropriate for actors, musicians and other performers in the theatre, film and television industry. This is because a typical performer is more likely to have a series of separate contracts rather than being contracted by one company or employer for a regular salary to perform in a series of productions over a period of time. Income from such contracts for services is subject to VAT where the performer's income exceeds the VAT registration limit.

There are still, however, circumstances when a contract of service applies, eg permanent members of an orchestra, ballet or theatre company. Many workers in the entertainment industry (eg ballet dancers, opera singers and orchestral players) are subject to standard contracts or agreements which have been negotiated between trade unions and management. The following standard contracts contain most of the features of a contract of employment and therefore succeed in creating a position of employment.

- Esher Standard Contract for Ballet.
- Esher Standard Contract for Opera (Opera Contract Singers).
- Touring Ballet/Opera Orchestras Agreement.
- Royal Opera House standard contract for orchestral players.
- English National Opera Ltd standard contract for orchestral players.

Customs regard services supplied under any of the above contracts, or under a contract subject to the conditions of any of the above, as being supplied by an employee to an employer and outside the scope of VAT. This applies even if the performer is taxable under trading income provisions for income tax purposes and even where minor amendments apply to the contract by virtue of a 'house' or supplementary agreement.

Services supplied under a standard contract other than those listed above should be considered as taxable for VAT purposes. This also applies to supplies made other than under a standard contract, eg

- supplies under separate contracts which principal dancers, players, soloists, 'stars', etc may have;
- supplies made by guest artists who either negotiate their own contract or retain their standard contract with another company; and
- extra payments made to principal performers when a performance is broadcast or recorded where these are made under a contract negotiated between the performer and the broadcasting or recording company. (If no such direct contract exists and, for example, the ballet or opera company makes an extra payment to the performers, Customs regard this as an overtime payment and therefore outside the scope of VAT.)

(Internal Guidance V1–5, Chapter 3 paras 3.25, 3.26).

(9) Film, television and radio industries — employment status of 'behind the camera' workers

The Revenue have agreements with various associations representing the film and video, television and radio industries. These has resulted in lists of 'behind the camera' grades in those industries whose members are accepted as self-employed for income tax purposes. Customs also accept these listed grades as self-employed for VAT purposes and they are reproduced in Internal Guidance V1–5, Appendices D (film and video), E (television) and F (radio). However, individuals in certain grades not shown on the lists may also enjoy self-employed status for income tax purposes if the Revenue accepts that they are self-employed in the light of *Lorimer v Hall, CA 1993, [1994] STC 23*. In such a case, Customs will ask for evidence that the Revenue has accepted the individual's status as self-employed before accepting self-employed status for VAT purposes. (Internal Guidance V1–5, Chapter 3 para 3.9).

(10) Hairdressing

There are three possible scenarios for who is supplying the hairdressing services to the public.

(*a*) The hairdressing salon employs its own stylists under contracts of service. The salon therefore makes the supply of hairdressing to the customers and must declare output tax on the gross takings. Monies paid by the salon to the stylist are payment for the services of that stylist as an employee and outside the scope of VAT.

Customs will only argue that the stylists are employees of the salon if there is clear documentary evidence to that effect, ie

- a contract or agreement between the salon and the stylists which states specifically that a contract of employment exists; and/or
- evidence that the stylists are taxed under the employment income rules by the Revenue.

(*b*) The hairdressing salon engages its stylists as self-employed stylists under contracts for services. The stylists supply their services to the salon and the salon then makes an onward supply of hairdressing services to its customers. The salon must account for output tax on gross takings. Monies paid by the salon to the stylist are consideration for a supply of services. The stylist must declare output tax if their supplies exceed the VAT registration limit.

(*c*) The self-employed stylists supply hairdressing services direct to the customers. The salon makes charges to the stylist to cover items such as sale of shampoos, etc or the right to use an agreed part of the salon ('chair rental'). Output tax is due on the individual gross takings of each stylist if they exceed the VAT registration limits.

Monies which the stylists pass back to the salon are consideration for supplies of services by the salon. This payment is calculated in a variety of ways, but frequently it is a fixed percentage of the stylist's takings together with a charge for any of the salon's materials (towels, shampoos, conditioners, rinses etc) used. The fixed percentage is normally referred to as a 'chair rental'. Where, under a written agreement, stylists are able to conduct their *entire* business from a designated area of the premises, such as a separate room or a partitioned area, there is likely to be an exempt supply of a licence to occupy land. However, this is unusual, especially if the salon is open-plan. *Either* there is no designated area *or* basins, hairdryers, storeroom and reception facilities are made available outside of the designated area. In such cases, there is a standard-rated supply of the general right to use the facilities of the salon as a whole. See *Simon Harris Hair Design Ltd (VTD 13939) (TVC 39.75)* where the tribunal held that, even where a space was designated, that space was economically useless without the right to use other facilities.

There have been a number of tribunal decisions on hairdressing supplies but these do not follow any discernible trend and different supply situations have been found when the facts of the respective cases do not materially differ. HMRC therefore do not base their approach on these decisions and consider each case upon its own facts. What the recorded decisions do confirm, however, is that the fact that stylists are self-employed is not conclusive that they make their supplies direct to the customer under (*c*) above. This was stated explicitly in the High Court summing up in *C & E Commrs v MacHenrys (Hairdressers) Ltd & MacHenrys, QB 1992, [1993] STC 170 (TVC 60.240)* and confirmed in *LJB Clarke (t/a Snips and Snips Hair & Beauty Salon) (VTD 14227) (TVC 60.237)*.

Self-employed stylists. To help determine whether self-employed stylists supply their services to the salon (under (*b*) above) or directly to the customer (under (*c*) above), HMRC have agreed a set of guidelines with the National Hairdressers Federation which list a number of pointers which they accept as indicating a supply of hairdressing services direct from stylist to customer. The guidelines are as follows.

1. *Status*

   The stylist must be self-employed. The business of the stylist should be independent of, and separate to, that of the salon and

   - maintain its own books and accounting records;
   - be responsible for its own taxation affairs, health and safety procedures;
   - attend to its own insurance requirements, including public liability insurance;
   - be capable of suffering losses as well as enjoying profits;
   - have complete freedom to establish its own price structure and times of opening (including closure for holidays);
   - purchase consumables and products from any source, and sell any product range;
   - be able to compete openly for clients both inside and outside the salon, and to accept or reject clients at will;
   - be free to appoint *locum tenens* as the need arises;
   - be free of restrictions about the sale, disposal or relocation of the business;
   - display a notice giving the name of the stylist and address at which documents may be served as required by *Business Names Act 1985, s 4*;
   - respond to actions brought against it by third parties;
   - have its own stationery for business letters, written orders, invoices and receipts.

2. *Access*

   - Ideally, there would be separate access to that part of the salon in which the business of the stylist is situated.
   - Stylists should have access to their business at all times, and have the ability to be open for custom at any time of their choice.

3. *Clients.*

   - The clients should be in direct contract with the stylist and be fully aware of this fact.
   - Complaints and claims from clients of the stylist should be directed to the stylist and not the salon.
   - Separate appointments (where applicable) should be maintained by or for the stylist.

- Casual clients entering the salon should themselves choose whether to patronise the stylist or salon, and should have sufficient information to make such a choice based on the name(s), and possibly portraits, displayed in the reception area; an identifiable list of specialities and price lists displayed in the reception area for each stylist; and the times to wait before receiving attention.
- The details, records, and addresses of clients who receive attention from the stylist should be the property of the stylist.

4. *Money*

- The money received from clients attended by the stylist should be the property of the stylist, whether or not it is taken centrally.
- Money collected centrally should either be handed over to the stylist or paid into an account held in the name of the stylist.
- Where money is held for and on behalf of the stylist, the salon holding such funds should account to the stylist for those funds.

5. *Salon environment*

- The salon should not exercise control over the stylist, or impose upon the stylist codes or standards relating to hygiene or behaviour unless applied equally against all parties with observance measured by an independent authority or peer pressure. Safety regulations imposed on the stylist by the salon should be no more than that required to comply with current legislation.
- The stylist should be responsible for the conduct, appearance and presentation of his or her enterprise, and in particular for behaviour, hygiene and safety matters relating to, or arising from, the its activities.
- There should be clear agreements in respect of services provided by the salon including the provision of telephone, heat, light and water; available accommodation for clients; reception, appointment booking and cash handling facilities; use of salon personnel for specific duties, and the control and discipline arrangements for such personnel; use and availability of furniture, fittings and equipment; laundry services; marketing and promotion of hairdressing services; cleaning and washing of floors and equipment; access and security; the amount to be paid by way of rent for use of space; the amount to be paid for use of services, cleaning, and maintenance of communal areas, and how such charge is to be calculated.

6. *Agreement*

The agreement should

- be a clear agreement in writing between the salon and the stylist that accurately reflects actual working practice;
- clearly state the obligations and responsibilities of the parties on termination, notice required on termination and where that notice is to be served;

- state that VAT is to be levied (when applicable) on the charge paid by the stylist for the services provided by the salon; and
- indicate that the stylist is responsible for insuring the enterprise against public and product liabilities, losses that could arise as a result of theft, fire, storm, accidental damage, etc and statutory cover in respect of staff retained by the enterprise.

If the majority of pointers are not met, HMRC will argue that (*b*) above applies. If, on the other hand, the majority of pointers are both met in the written agreement between the salon and stylist *and* confirmed in the current working practices, HMRC accept that (*c*) above applies.

(Internal Guidance V1–5, Chapter 3 paras 3.27–3.31, Appendix L; Internal Guidance V1–8, para 5.14).

(11) **Leasing**

Disposal of leases of goods. Where a business which is leasing goods to the public under lease-hire agreements disposes of its leases, HMRC still regard that business as making supplies under the leases. This applies even where, for example, the leases have been transferred to an associated company (and possibly the goods to another) and even though the original business no longer owns the goods or benefits from receiving the rental income. If the original business has de-registered, HMRC require it to re-register as a consequence. (Internal Guidance V1–5, Chapter 3 para 3.32).

(12) **Managing agents for property**

Where a landlord

- enters into a lease under which the landlord is bound to repair and maintain the property, and
- appoints a 'managing agent' who takes responsibility for the repair and maintenance (and charges the landlord a fee for his services),

any VAT on the maintenance costs relates to the landlord, and not to the managing agent. Where the managing agent is invoiced directly, he can either

- use the provisions of *VATA 1994, s 47*(*3*) (see 3.4 AGENTS) and reclaim the input tax but pass on the same sum as output tax to the landlord; or
- pass the costs on to the landlord without deducting the VAT and be reimbursed a VAT-inclusive sum.

The managing agent cannot simply deduct the input tax. See *WS Atkins (Services) Ltd (VTD 10131) (TVC 34.30)*.

(Internal Guidance V1–5, Chapter 3 paras 3.33, 3.34).

(13) **School photographers**

See 20.18 EDUCATION.

(14) **Second-hand goods retailers**

Most second-hand goods are covered by one of the margin schemes which enable the retailer to pay output tax only on the difference between purchase and sale price. See 61 SECOND-HAND GOODS. Where retailers sell goods which are not covered by such schemes (eg coins and certain goods consisting of precious metals, and precious stones) they may attempt to achieve the same result by offering goods for sale as agent of the unregistered vendor.

In deciding whether the dealer is acting as agent or is actually acting as a principal, HMRC adopt their normal approach (see 3.1 AGENTS) but place particular emphasis upon the key elements of title and value. They require all the following factors to be adhered to.

- The goods must remain the property of the vendor until sold.
- The dealer must be able to return the goods to the vendor at any time prior to sale.
- The vendor must be able to find out the full amount received by the dealer for the goods (eg from price labels in the shop) although it is not necessary for the vendor to be specifically informed of the sale price by the dealer.
- The dealer must either charge a set commission, or agree with the vendor that he will retain anything achieved in excess of the amount the vendor has agreed to accept.

In addition, agency is not normally consistent with the dealer

- paying the vendor an advance at the time the goods are left for sale,
- repairing goods at his own expense in the hope of achieving higher prices, and
- offering a guarantee to customers in his own name

and where any of these practices are present, HMRC take the view that agency can only exist if both parties have clearly agreed to these practices in writing. See also *C & E v Music and Video Exchange Ltd, QB [1992] STC 220 (TVC 1.7)*.

Accounting for VAT. If a second-hand goods retailer:

- *buys and sells as principal*, he must account for VAT on the full value of the supply unless the goods are covered by one of the margin schemes. See 61 SECOND-HAND GOODS;
- *is an agent for the vendor but is acting in his own name*, the goods must be treated as supplied to him by the vendor and onwards by him to the purchaser. See 3.4 AGENTS. Unless he uses the one of the margin schemes (see 61 SECOND-HAND GOODS), the retailer must account for VAT on the full value of the goods as well as on his own supply of services as an agent; and
- *is an agent for the vendor and is not acting in his own name*, he need not account for VAT on the sale of the goods but only on his fee or commission charged to the vendor.

(Internal Guidance V1–5, Chapter 3, paras 3.40–3.42)

(15) **Share farming and the husbandry of crops**

Landowners often reach agreements with agricultural contractors or merchants relating to the cultivation and cropping of land. These agreements fall into three broad categories.

(*a*) *Agreements which grant the contractor a right over or licence to occupy land.* If the landowner is granting the contractor or merchant exclusive occupation of the land, the landowner is making an exempt supply of land within *VATA 1994, Sch 9 Group 1 Item 1*. If the landowner makes supplies of husbandry to the contractor (eg ploughing, weeding, or the application of fertilisers which the landowner has supplied) these supplies are standard-rated where separately charged. Where the landowner charges an inclusive rental which includes a subsidiary element to cover husbandry services, the whole of the rental is exempt. The merchant markets the crop and is accountable for any VAT on that supply.

(*b*) *Agreements where the landowner engages a contractor to supply husbandry services.* In this situation there is no exempt supply of land by the landowner. The contractor makes a standard-rated supply of husbandry services to the landowner, and the landowner is accountable for any VAT on the final supply of the crop. If the contractor supplies seed or fertiliser and makes a separate charge for these, this is a separate supply of goods and taxable accordingly.

(*c*) *Share farming joint ventures.* The landowner and contractor (share farmer) share the profits from the sale of a harvested crop. The essential features which convert a share farming agreement otherwise falling within (*a*) or (*b*) above into a joint venture are

- the parties undertake to agree a farming policy and often have regular meetings to discuss it; and
- the agreement provides for a sharing of the profits and losses arising from the venture, usually achieved by the parties bearing agreed shares of the costs and sharing either the severed crops, or the proceeds of their sale, between them.

See Internal Guidance V1–5, Appendix M for a model share farming agreement devised by the Country Landowners' Association which HMRC accept as incorporating the essential features of a joint venture. Under the agreement, the share farmer does not have exclusive occupation of any part of the farm and therefore there can be no exempt supply under *VATA 1994, Sch 9 Group 1 Item 1*. Also the landowner and the share farmer are not in partnership as evidenced by the fact that they submit independent income tax and VAT returns.

Typically, at the outset of the joint venture the landowner's contribution is his land and the contractor's contribution is labour, machinery and his expertise. No money changes hands at this stage and there are no VAT implications. Later, but prior to the harvesting of the crop, the parties may reimburse each other for costs which they have borne (eg the landowner might reimburse the contractor for half of the costs of seeds, sprays, fertilisers, and chemicals). Such payments are consideration for supplies of services from one party to the other and follow the liability of the original supply. When the crop is finally harvested, whoever owns that crop must account for any VAT on its sale. Where the harvested crops are jointly owned, each party makes a supply of its agreed share and must account for VAT on that value. If, however, only one party owns the crop, that party must account for VAT on the whole amount. When a share of the proceeds of the sale is passed on to the other party, that is outside the scope of VAT.

(Internal Guidance V1–5, Chapter 3 paras 3.43–3.46).

(16) **'Shell' companies**

See 31.9 GROUPS OF COMPANIES.

(17) **Taxis and hire cars**

See 68.23 TRANSPORT AND FREIGHT.

65 Terminal Markets

Cross-reference. See 30 GOLD AND PRECIOUS METALS.

The contents of this chapter are as follows.

65.1 INTRODUCTION

The Treasury have been given wide powers to make provisions for the VAT treatment of dealings on terminal markets and transactions of people ordinarily engaged in such dealings. These include the right to

(*a*) zero-rate or exempt the supply of any goods or services;

(*b*) register any bodies representing persons ordinarily engaged in dealings on a terminal market;

(*c*) disregard such dealings *by* persons represented under (*b*) above in determining liability to REGISTRATION (59) for VAT purposes;

(*d*) disregard such dealings *between* persons represented under (*b*) above for all purposes; and

(*e*) refund input tax attributable to such dealings on a terminal market.

Different regulations may be made for different terminal markets.

[*VATA 1994, s 50*].

65.2 QUALIFYING MARKETS AND MARKET MEMBERS

Regulations have been made under *SI 1973/173* (*as amended*) for the zero-rating of certain supplies of goods and services in the course of dealings on specified terminal markets. To qualify, transactions must involve a member of the market which includes any person ordinarily engaged in dealings on the market. The following is a list of terminal markets included in the *Order* together with persons regarded by HMRC as ordinarily engaged in dealing on the markets.

Market	*Persons regarded as market members*
London Metal Exchange	Ring dealing members and other members of the London Metal Exchange.
London Rubber Market	For actuals transactions — Class P (producer members), Class A (selling agent and importer members), Class B (broker members) and Class C (dealer members) of the Rubber Trade Association of London. For futures transactions on the London Rubber Terminal Market — floor and associate members of the London Rubber Terminal Market Association.

Market	*Persons regarded as market members*
London Cocoa, Coffee, Sugar, Vegetable Oil, and Wool Markets and Soya Bean Meal Futures Market	Full and associate members of the London Cocoa, Coffee, Sugar, Vegetable Oil, Wool and GAFTA Soya Bean Meal Terminal Market Associations
International Petroleum Exchange of London	Any full or associate member.
London Potato Futures Market	Any full or associate member.
London Bullion Market	Any member of the London Bullion Market Association.
London Grain Futures Market	Any member of the Grain and Feed Trade Association.
Liverpool Barley Futures Market	Any member of the Liverpool Corn Trade Association.
London Meat Futures Market	Any full or associate member.
London Platinum and Palladium Market	Any full or associate member.
London Securities and Derivatives Exchange Ltd (OMLX) (from 1 September 1997)	Any full or associate member

[*SI 1973/173, Art 2; SI 1975/385; SI 1980/304; SI 1981/338; SI 1981/955; SI 1984/202; SI 1985/1046; SI 1987/806; SI 1997/1836; SI 1999/3117*]. (VAT Notice 701/9/02, para 4).

65.3 ZERO-RATED TRANSACTIONS

The transactions which are zero-rated are as follows.

(*a*) **Actual transactions**. A sale *by and to* a market member of any goods (other than investment gold) ordinarily dealt with on the market which results in the goods being delivered. In addition, if the market is the

- London Metal Exchange, the sale must be between members entitled to deal in the 'ring';
- London Cocoa Terminal Market, London Coffee Terminal Market, London Meat Futures Market, International Petroleum Exchange of London, London Potato Futures Market, London Soya Bean Meal Futures Market, London Sugar Terminal Market, London Vegetable Oil Terminal Market, or the London Wool Terminal Market, the sale must be registered with the International Commodities Clearing House Ltd;
- London Grain Futures Market, the sale must be registered in the Clearing House of the Grain and Feed Trade Association Ltd; and
- Liverpool Barley Futures Market, the sale must be registered at the Clearing House of the Liverpool Corn Trade Association Ltd.

(*b*) **Futures transactions**. A sale *by or to* a market member of any goods (other than investment gold) ordinarily dealt with on the market where, as a result of other dealings on the market, the sale does not lead to a delivery of the goods by the seller to the buyer.

'*Delivery*' is not defined but is regarded by HMRC as taking place when instructions are given for the goods to be physically removed from the warehouse, vault etc. If a futures transaction leads to a delivery of the goods, VAT must be accounted for on the basis of the original contract price.

Transactions between non-members. Any supply of goods between parties who are not listed in 65.2 above under a futures contract, even if it does not lead to physical delivery of the goods, is not zero-rated under these provisions. It will be subject to the normal VAT rules of the main supply (eg a futures contract for the supply of potatoes will be zero-rated as potatoes are zero-rated). (VAT Notice 701/9/02, para 3.3).

(*c*) **The grant of an option**. The grant *by or to* a market member of a right to acquire any goods (other than investment gold) ordinarily dealt with on the market where either

- the right is exercisable at a date later than that on which it is granted; or
- the sale resulting from the exercise of the right would be a sale falling within (*a*) or (*b*) above.

When an option is exercised, the resulting transaction should be considered under (*a*) or (*b*) above.

(*d*) **Investment gold**. A supply of 'investment gold' between members of the London Bullion Market Association. See 30.2 GOLD AND PRECIOUS METALS for the definition of '*investment gold*'.

A supply of investment gold by

- a member of the London Bullion Market Association to a taxable person who is not a member, or
- such a person to a member

is not zero-rated and is also excluded from the exemption applying to certain transactions in investment gold (see 30.2 GOLD AND PRECIOUS METALS). As a result, such a supply is standard-rated.

[*SI 1973/173, Arts 3, 4; SI 1975/385; SI 1981/338; SI 1984/202; SI 1999/3117*]. (VAT Notice 701/9/02, para 3.2).

De Voil Indirect Tax Service. See V4.208.

65.4 **Brokers' or agents' services**

Supplies of such services by market makers to their principals are zero-rated where the underlying transaction

(*a*) is zero-rated under 65.3(*a*)-(*d*) above; or

(*b*) involves the supply of investment gold by

- a member of the London Bullion Market Association to a taxable person who is not a member, or

- such a person to a member.

[*SI 1973/173, Art 3; SI 1999/3117*].

Brokers' services provided by a non-member are not zero-rated even if in relation to a supply of goods zero-rated under the above provisions or under *VATA 1994, Sch 8 Group 1* (relief for food). Where a person introduces business to a broker and receives from that broker a fee or share of the latter's commission or brokerage, that fee, etc is the consideration for a standard-rated supply of services, unless the person meets the conditions for zero-rating brokers' or agents' services above.

International services. In the opinion of HMRC, brokers' services of arranging transactions in futures and options are financial services within *VATA 1994, Sch 5 para 5*. See, however, *Gardner Lohman Ltd (VTD 1081) (TVC 60.478)* where the tribunal held that the grant of a purchase option to acquire cadmium through the London Metal Exchange was not a financial service within *Sch 5 para 5*. Subject to this, the supply of services within *Sch 5 para 5* is outside the scope of UK VAT where the recipient either belongs in another EC country and uses the supply for business purposes or belongs outside the EC. [*SI 1992/3121, Art 16; SI 1995/3038*].

(VAT Notice 701/9/02, paras 3.3, 3.4).

65.5 ACCOUNTING

Zero-rated supplies. Where a person (whether a market member or not) supplies goods or services zero-rated under the provisions in 65.3(*a*)–(*d*) above, he is not required to record such transactions for VAT purposes. If he does wish to include such items in a VAT return (eg to increase the proportion of input tax recoverable where exempt supplies are also made), he must record *all* of them. [*SI 1995/2518, Reg 33A; SI 1999/3114*]. (VAT Notice 701/9/02, para 3.5).

Standard-rated supplies of investment gold. Certain supplies of investment gold involving members of the London Bullion Market Association are standard-rated (see 65.3(*d*) above). The provisions of *VATA 1994, s 55(1)-(4)* normally apply to such supplies and the customer must account for VAT on the supply. However, where the non-member who makes or receives the supply is only liable to be registered for VAT under *VATA 1994, Sch 1* or *Sch 3* solely by virtue of that supply or acquisition, the non-member is not required to notify liability for registration and the London Bullion Market Association member must, on the non-member's behalf, keep a record of the transaction and pay the VAT due to HMRC. [*SI 1973/173, Arts 5-7; SI 1999/3117*]. See 30.8 GOLD AND PRECIOUS METALS for fuller details. The non-member is not required to keep VAT records or submit EC sales statements. [*SI 1995/2518, Reg 33B; SI 1999/3114*].

Agents' services. Where a supply of agents' services is not zero-rated under 65.4 above, VAT must be accounted for on the full amount of commission or brokerage charged before deduction of any part paid to third parties. (VAT Notice 701/9/02, para 3.5).

66 Tour Operators' Margin Scheme

Cross-references. See 33 HOTELS AND HOLIDAY ACCOMMODATION; 68 TRANSPORT AND FREIGHT.

De Voil Indirect Tax Service. See V3.591-V3.596.

The contents of this chapter are as follows.

66.1 INTRODUCTION

EC legislation. See 22.29 EUROPEAN COMMUNITY LEGISLATION.

UK legislation. The tour operators' margin scheme ('TOMS') is a special scheme for businesses that buy in and re-sell travel, accommodation and certain other services as principals or undisclosed agents (ie that act in their own name). In many cases, it enables VAT to be accounted for on travel supplies without businesses having to register and account for VAT in every EC country in which the services and goods are enjoyed. It does, however, apply to travel services enjoyed within the UK, within the EC but outside the UK, and wholly outside the EC.

Under the scheme:

- VAT cannot be reclaimed on margin scheme supplies bought in for resale (see 66.14 below). VAT on overheads outside the TOMS can be reclaimed in the normal way.
- A UK-based tour operator need only account for VAT on the margin, ie the difference between the amount received from customers (including any amounts paid on behalf of customers by third parties) and the amount paid to suppliers. See 66.17 *et seq* below for calculations of margins and output tax.
- There are special rules for determining the place, liability and time of margin scheme supplies (see 66.5 to 66.7 below).

- VAT invoices cannot be issued for margin scheme supplies (see 66.8 below).
- In-house supplies supplied on their own are not subject to the TOMS and are taxed under the normal VAT rules. But a mixture of in-house supplies and bought-in margin scheme supplies must all be accounted for within the TOMS. See 66.10 below.

(VAT Notice 709/5/04, paras 2.1, 2.5, 2.6, 2.13).

The relevant law is in *VATA 1994, s 53* and the *Value Added Tax* (*Tour Operators*) *Order 1987* (*SI 1987/1806*) as amended. The law gives HMRC certain powers in relation to the scheme, including specifying what goods and services are covered [*SI 1987/1806, Art 3*(*4*)] and how to work out the value of the supplies [*SI 1987/1806, Art 7*]. To that extent, the provisions in 66.19–66.22 below and certain other provisions as indicated in the text have the force of law.

66.2 WHO MUST USE THE TOMS?

The TOMS does not only apply to 'traditional' tour operators. It applies to anyone who is making the type of supplies detailed in 66.3 below, even if this is not their main business activity. For example, it must be used by

- hoteliers who buy in coach passenger transport to collect their guests at the start and end of their stay;
- coach operators who buy in hotel accommodation in order to put together a package; and
- companies that arrange conferences, including providing hotel accommodation for delegates.

(VAT Notice 709/5/04, para 2.2).

The CJEC have confirmed that to make the application of the TOMS depend upon whether a trader was formally classified as a travel agent or tour operator would create distortion of competition. Ancillary travel services which constitute 'a small proportion of the package price compared to accommodation' would not lead to a hotelier falling within the provisions but where, in return for a package price, a hotelier habitually offers his customers travel to the hotel from distant pick-up points in addition to accommodation, such services cannot be treated as purely ancillary. See *TP Madgett & RM Baldwin (t/a Howden Court Hotel) v C & E Commrs, CJEC [1998] STC 1189 (TVC 21.314).*

66.3 SUPPLIES COVERED BY THE TOMS

Subject to the exclusions in 66.9 below, the TOMS must be used by a person acting as a principal or undisclosed agent for

- 'margin scheme supplies'; and
- 'margin scheme packages' ie single transactions which include one or more margin scheme supplies possibly with other types of supplies (eg in-house supplies, see 66.10 below).

(VAT Notice 709/5/04, paras 2.3, 2.11).

'*Margin scheme supplies*' are those supplies which are

- bought in for the purpose of the business, and

- supplied for the benefit of a 'traveller' without material alteration or further processing

by a tour operator in an EC country in which he has established his business or has a fixed establishment.

[*SI 1987/1806, Art 3*(*1*)].

A '*traveller*' is a person, including a business or local authority, who receives supplies of transport and/or accommodation, other than for the purpose of re-supply.

Examples

If meeting the above conditions, the following are always treated as margin scheme supplies.

- Accommodation
- Passenger transport
- Hire of means of transport
- Use of special lounges at airports
- Trips or excursions
- Services of tour guides

Other supplies meeting the above conditions may be treated as margin scheme supplies but only if provided as part of a package with one or more of the supplies listed above. These include

- Catering
- Theatre tickets
- Sports facilities

(VAT Notice 709/5/04, paras 2.9, 2.10).

In a Dutch case, the CJEC ruled that *EC Sixth Directive, Art 26* applies to cases where only accommodation is provided, and is not restricted to cases where transport is also provided (*Beheersmaatschappij Van Ginkel Waddinxveen BV & Others v Inspecteur de Omzetbelasting Utrecht, CJEC 1992, [1996] STC 825 (TVC 21.312)*). A similar decision was reached in *Hotels Abroad Ltd (VTD 13026) (TVC 61.6)*. See also *Aer Lingus plc (VTD 8893) (TVC 61.2)* (where vouchers for accommodation or car hire provided to executive class passengers were held not integral or incidental to the supply of air transport and therefore fell within the margin scheme) and *Virgin Atlantic Airways Ltd (VTD 11096) (TVC 61.7)* (where chauffeur-driven car services provided to certain passengers on international flights were held to fall outside the scheme).

66.4 Nature of the supply

The sale of a package of margin scheme supplies is treated as a single supply for VAT purposes. [*SI 1987/1806, Reg 3*(*2*)]. The nature of the services is that of putting together the package or organising the travel services. For example, if hotel accommodation and transport is bought in to provide a tour, the single supply of a tour is made, rather than two separate supplies of transport and accommodation. (VAT Notice 709/5/04, para 4.5).

66.5 Place of supply

The application of the normal place of supply rules are varied so that margin scheme supplies are treated as supplied

- in the EC country in which the tour operator has established his business, or
- if the supply was made from a fixed establishment, in the EC country in which the fixed establishment is situated.

[*SI 1987/1806, Art 5; SI 1992/3125*].

The effect of this is as follows

(*a*) Where the supplier is established in the UK only, the place of supply is the UK.

(*b*) Where the supplier has an establishment in more than one country

- if the establishment from which the supplies are made is in the UK, the place of supply is the UK;
- if the establishment from which the supplies are made is in another EC country, the supply is outside the scope of UK VAT (but within the scope in that other EC country); and
- if the establishment from which the supplies are made is outside the EC, the supplies are not margin scheme supplies and the TOMS does not apply. The normal VAT place of supply rules apply. See 64.18 SUPPLY. [*SI 1987/1806, Art 3*].

(VAT Notice 709/5/04, para 4.6).

See 64.19 SUPPLY for a consideration of the terms 'business establishment' and 'fixed establishment'. See also *C & E Commrs v DFDS A/S, CJEC [1997] STC 384 (TVC 21.316)* where a UK subsidiary acted as agent for a Danish company and received commission on package tours sold on its behalf. On the facts, the subsidiary was held to be a fixed establishment.

Where margin scheme supplies are made from an establishment in another EC country, it may be necessary to register for VAT there.

66.6 LIABILITY OF TOMS SUPPLIES

Where margin scheme supplies are made in the UK (see 66.5 above) the whole of the margin is

- standard-rated when the supplies and enjoyed in the EC (see 21.2 EUROPEAN COMMUNITY: GENERAL for the VAT territory of the EC); and
- zero-rated when enjoyed outside the EC.

The liability of in-house supplies (see 66.10 below) is not affected by their inclusion in a margin scheme package.

Transport enjoyed inside and outside the EC. HMRC have given the following guidance.

(*a*) *Journeys without stops.* Where the journey begins or ends outside the EC, it may be treated as wholly enjoyed outside the EC. Temporary stops for 'comfort' or refuelling are not regarded as stops provided passengers cannot break their journey. Return legs should be treated in the same way as outbound journeys unless there is a material difference between the two legs (eg a stop).

(*b*) *Journeys with stops.*

(i) *General.* Where a journey involves travel both inside and outside the EC and a stop takes place in the EC, a fair and reasonable apportionment must be made between the EC and non-EC elements. This could be on the basis of EC/non-EC mileage or the number of nights spent inside/outside the EC.

(ii) *Cruises.* Apportionment on the basis of days in/out of the EC according to the itinerary is acceptable. For this purpose, the days on which the vessel leaves a non-EC port until it arrives at an EC port are regarded as outside the EC and the days on which it leaves an EC port until it reaches a non-EC port are regarded as inside the EC.

(iii) *Connected flights.* A second and/or subsequent flight is not regarded as a separate journey provided that the connection is made, in the case of an international connecting flight, within 24 hours of the scheduled arrival of the first flight and, in the case of a domestic connecting flight, within six hours of that time.

[*VATA 1994, Sch 8 Group 8, Item 12*]. (VAT Notice 709/5/04, paras 4.10–4.13).

66.7 TIME OF SUPPLY

The normal time of supply rules do not apply to TOMS supplies. Instead, one of the two methods below must be used to work out the tax point for margin scheme supplies and any in-house supplies (see 66.10 below) sold within a margin scheme package. Whichever method is chosen, it must be applied to all such supplies. Written permission from HMRC is needed to change methods but HMRC will only allow a change in exceptional circumstances and not normally during a financial year.

The two methods for working out tax points are as follows.

(*a*) The earlier of

- the date of departure of the traveller; and
- the first date on which the traveller occupies any accommodation.

(*b*) The earlier of

- the date of departure of the traveller;
- the first date on which the traveller occupies any accommodation; and
- the date of receipt of any payment by the tour operator (or a travel agent on its behalf) which

  (i) is a single payment covering the whole selling price; or

  (ii) exceeds 20% of the selling price; or

  (iii) exceeds 20% of the selling price where added to payments received to date on which VAT has not already been accounted for.

Example

A traveller buys a package holiday to Italy commencing 15 August

(1) He pays a 10% deposit on 20 January and the balance on 4 July.

The tax point is 4 July for the full selling price of the holiday. The initial deposit is less than 20% and is therefore ignored.

(2) He pays a 25% deposit on 20 January and the balance on 4 July.

There is a tax point for 25% of the selling price on 20 January and 75% on 4 July (each being payments exceeding 20% of the selling price).

(3) He pays 10% per month by direct debit commencing on 20 January and ending on 20 October.

No tax points arise on the January or February payments. There is a tax point for 30% of the selling price on 20 March (when the payments to date first exceed 20%). Again no tax points arise on the April and May payments (assuming VAT has been correctly accounted for on the March tax point). There is a second tax point for 30% of the selling price on 20 June (based on the payments for April, May and June). No tax point arises on the July payment. There is a final tax point of 40% of the selling price on 15 August (the date of departure).

Cash accounting scheme. In view of the special tax point rules above, the cash accounting scheme cannot be used for margin scheme supplies or for in-house supplies and agency supplies sold as part of a margin scheme package.

[*SI 1987/1806, Art 4*]. (VAT Notice 709/5/04, paras 4.14–4.16).

66.8 **VAT invoices**

VAT invoices cannot be raised for supplies accounted for under the TOMS. This is because, at the time of supply, the true amount of VAT due is not known and can only be determined when the year-end calculation is carried out (see 66.19 and 66.20 below). The absence of a VAT invoice does not usually matter unless the customer is entitled to claim the VAT. In such a case, it may be possible to exclude the supply from the TOMS (see 66.9 below). (VAT Notice 709/5/04, para 4.20).

66.9 SUPPLIES OUTSIDE THE TOMS

The following supplies should be dealt with outside the UK TOMS.

- Margin scheme supplies which are not made in the UK. See 66.3 above for the place of supply provisions. Note that where the place of supply is another EC country, there may be a liability to register for VAT and apply the equivalent TOMS in that country.
- Supplies which have been arranged as a disclosed agent or intermediary provided any commission received is readily identifiable. See 66.12 below.
- In-house supplies (see 66.10 below) and agency supplies (see 66.12 below) which are not packaged/supplied without margin scheme supplies.
- Supplies to business customers for subsequent resale (subject to an election to account for VAT under the TOMS) and supplies to business customers for their own consumption (where an election to exclude such supplies from the TOMS has been made). See 66.11 below.

- Educational school trips supplied to local authority which are to be enjoyed in the UK. See 66.13 below.

(VAT Notice 709/5/04, para 2.4).

Incidental supplies. The TOMS need not be used if

- no supplies of accommodation or passenger transport are bought in for resale; and
- other supplies which would normally be margin scheme supplies are bought in for resale but there are reasonable grounds for believing that the turnover from such supplies in the one year then beginning will not exceed 1% of all the supplies made in that year.

An example of such supplies might be where a hotelier buys in car hire for re-supply to hotel guests. Provided the 1% test is satisfied, a hotelier buying occasional car hire for guests would be outside the TOMS but occasional taxi trips for guests would not (because the re-supply of taxi trips is considered to be passenger transport).

[*SI 1987/1806, Art 14*]. (VAT Notice 709/5/04, para 3.6).

66.10 In-house supplies

In-house supplies are supplies which are not margin scheme supplies (see 66.3 above) or agency supplies (see 66.12 below). They therefore comprise supplies which are either

- made from own resources; or
- result from purchases which the business has materially altered or further processed so that what is supplied is substantially different from what was purchased.

Where in-house supplies are sold *without* margin scheme supplies, VAT must be accounted for outside the TOMS in the normal way.

Where in-house supplies are sold *with* margin scheme supplies as part of a package, the margin scheme calculations must be used to work out the value of all parts of the package. See 66.19 to 66.21 below.

Place of supply. The place of supply of in-house supplies, whether or not they are part of a margin scheme package, is determined using the normal VAT rules. The place of supply will therefore depend upon the nature of the services provided. See 64.18 *et seq* SUPPLY. For example, passenger transport is supplied where it takes place (see 64.29), hotel accommodation is supplied where the accommodation is situated (see 64.21) and live entertainment is supplied where it is physically performed (see 64.23). As a result, if the place of supply is in another EC country, it may be necessary to register and account for VAT in that country.

Examples of in-house supplies. HMRC give the following examples.

(*a*) *Coach/train transport* where a tour operator owns or hires a coach/train and supplies a driver, fuel, repairs, etc.

(*b*) *Air transport*. Any supplies of air transport by a business using aircraft owned by itself or a member of the same VAT group. In addition, under a special scheme the supply of a charter flight by a tour operator to a customer may be treated as an in-house supply (thus retaining the zero-rating for the provision of transport) provided the tour operator meets the following conditions.

- It charters the whole aircraft and not just a block of seats.
- It enters into a contract with the airline for the provision of the aircraft and crew for an entire season (eg slot 1 every Wednesday from May to October). A season is defined as either a summer season (May to October), a winter sun season (November to April) or a winter sport season (December to April).
- It puts its own catering facilities on board or buys them in from a separate source. This could be a separate catering company (including one set up by the charter airline) or a specialist catering broker.
- It buys in transfer journeys from a separate source.

For further details of the scheme, including implementation and accounting implications, see VAT Information Sheet 3/96 produced in co-operation with ABTA.

(*c*) *Cruises* where a tour operator

- charters a vessel from another owner including deck/engine crew but employs or engages own 'hotel'/domestic/catering staff; or
- charters a vessel from another owner for a period of two years or more whether only with deck/engine crew or with both deck/engine crew and 'hotel'/domestic/catering staff. The vessel need not necessarily be in service throughout the period but the owner must not have the right to use the vessel to make supplies to other customers during the period.

(*d*) *Accommodation* where a tour operator

- owns the hotel, etc;
- hires, leases or rents accommodation under an agreement whereby it takes responsibility for the upkeep of the property and is required to undertake any maintenance to the fabric of the building (ie not just general cleaning, changing bed linen, etc);
- rents space at a camp-site, installs its own tents or caravans, and sells accommodation in them (but not where accommodation in tents/caravans is bought in from a third party who provides both the site and tents/ accommodation or where space at a camp-site is bought in and sold to customers who provide their own tents/caravans — both of which are margin scheme supplies); or
- buys in accommodation and provides catering staff from a separate source (eg a ski chalet with a chalet-maid).

(*e*) *Tuition* where a tour operator organises training or tuition courses by putting together a number of elements such as teachers, classrooms, lecture theatres, projectors and other teaching aids, lighting, heating, etc. If a tour operator simply buys in a place on a course from a third party who has organised the course and sells this on as part of a package with transport and/or accommodation, the supply is a margin scheme supply.

(*f*) *Conferences* where the organiser hires a room and provides necessary equipment (eg microphones, projectors, hand-outs), reception staff, etc. Any refreshments served at such a conference form part of the in-house supply of an organised conference, even if purchased from an outside caterer.

Where overnight accommodation and/or passenger transport for delegates is also supplied, this is not part of an in-house organised conference and if these supplies are bought in and re-supplied without material alteration, they must be accounted for under the TOMS (but see 66.11 below where they are re-supplied to business customers). Other supplies (eg restaurant meals outside conference hours, theatre tickets) are also margin scheme supplies if supplied as part of a package with overnight accommodation/passenger transport.

(*g*) *Organised shoots* (including clay pigeons) where a number of elements (eg the right to use the land, host services, beaters, clays, etc) are brought together.

If a shoot is organised as above, but a package is created that includes one or more margin scheme supplies (eg passenger transport or accommodation) the supply of the shooting event only is an in-house supply and the passenger transport and/or accommodation are margin scheme supplies.

If a business simply buys in and sells on the right to participate in a shoot organised by someone else, this is a normal (non-TOMS) supply (unless provided in a package with one or more margin scheme supplies).

In some circumstances, shoots are not organised in the course or furtherance of a business and are therefore outside the scope of VAT. See 57.16 RECREATION AND SPORT.

(VAT Notice 709/5/04, paras 2.12, 4.7, 7.1–7.3, 7.6, 7.9, 7.11–7.14).

66.11 Supplies to business customers

Whether supplies to business customers should be accounted for under the TOMS depends upon whether those supplies are for subsequent resale or for consumption by the business.

(*a*) **Supplies to business customers for subsequent resale (wholesale supplies)**. Subject to the concession below, these supplies are outside the scope of the TOMS and should be accounted for under the normal VAT rules.

This allows a tour operator to set up an associated transport broking company to buy in transport from transport providers and sell it on to the tour operator outside the TOMS. This supply to the tour operator is zero-rated or outside the scope of UK VAT depending on the circumstances. See 68.14 TRANSPORT AND FREIGHT. The transport company cannot be in the same VAT group as the tour operator. For further details of the scheme, including implementation and accounting implications, see VAT Information Sheet 1/97 produced in co-operation with ABTA.

As a concession, a tour operator can request permission from HMRC to treat wholesale supplies as margin scheme supplies. Permission will be granted provided that

- the tour operator accounts for all its wholesale supplies under the TOMS; and
- HMRC are satisfied that the tour operator can account for VAT properly and that its own officers can readily check the accuracy of the VAT returns.

Such treatment will mean that business customers cannot reclaim any VAT on margin scheme supplies received. Also, other EC countries may not recognise the concession and may require the tour operator to register and account for VAT there.

(*b*) **Supplies to business customers for their own consumption.**

Subject to the concession below, supplies made to a business customer for use by that customer for the purposes of its business (eg for business travel) fall within the TOMS where they meet the definition of margin scheme supplies.

As a concession (which has the force of law), such supplies may be excluded from the TOMS and treated under normal VAT rules. In the case of supplies enjoyed in the UK, this enables the tour operator, with the permission of HMRC, to issue VAT invoices to business customers. In the case of any supplies enjoyed in another EC country, it is a condition that VAT on those supplies has been paid to the VAT authority in that country and evidence of this is available for HMRC.

[*SI 1987/1806, Art 3*(*3*)]. (VAT Notice 709/5/04, paras 3.1–3.3, 12(TL1)).

66.12 Supplies by agents

The TOMS does not cover:

(*a*) Supplies made by an agent or intermediary not packaged/supplied with margin scheme goods.

(*b*) Supplies made by a business acting as a disclosed agent in the making of margin scheme supplies (ie it names the provider of the margin scheme supplies). The commission and all monies for the supply arranged must be excluded from the TOMS.

But where a business acting as an agent must use the TOMS because it makes margin scheme supplies in its own name *and* it receives variable commission (or commission which is otherwise not readily identifiable) as a disclosed agent, it must include its agency income and directly-related costs in its TOMS calculations.

(VAT Notice 709/5/04, paras 2.4, 2.14, 6.6).

For the liability of arranging travel and other facilities as an agent or intermediary, see 3.14 AGENTS.

As a result of (*b*) above, a tour operator can use the 'agency option' scheme by entering into an agency arrangement, normally with a transport provider. Provided the conditions of the scheme are met, the supply of transport services is directly from the transport provider to the final customer. As the supply is not made by the tour operator, the transport services are not margin scheme supplies and fall outside the TOMS. Thus, whether supplied singly or as part of a package, the transport element and the tour operator's services of arranging the transport, are free of UK VAT (being either zero-rated or outside the scope).

Similar agency arrangements can be set up for the provision of accommodation and catering. However, as such supplies are subject to VAT at the standard rate, the related commission will normally be standard-rated and there will be no benefit in entering into these arrangements. Additionally, in respect of accommodation, if the accommodation is in another EC country and the commission is charged to a non-VAT registered person, this could give rise to a liability for the tour operator to be

VAT-registered in that country. For these reasons, it is unlikely that the 'agency option' scheme should be adopted for such supplies.

See 66.29 below for the accounting implications of using the 'agency option' scheme. For details of how to implement the scheme, see VAT Information Sheet 4/96 produced in co-operation with ABTA.

66.13 Supplies to local authorities and public bodies

Note. The provisions of this paragraph have the force of law.

Local authority schools. The provision of an educational school trip by a local authority school to its pupils is a non-business activity for VAT purposes. The local authority is entitled to a refund of any VAT incurred under *VATA 1994, s 33* (see 43.7 LOCAL AUTHORITIES AND PUBLIC BODIES). Northern Ireland Education Boards are entitled to refunds on such supplies under *VATA 1994, s 99* (see 46.1 NORTHERN IRELAND).

A business supplying trips to such bodies which are to be enjoyed in the UK can exclude the supply from the TOMS. This means that VAT invoices can be issued to the local authority or Education Board which can recover the VAT.

Colleges, universities, non-LEA schools and local authority-run youth clubs are not entitled to such refunds and therefore the exclusion from the TOMS does not apply to any supplies made to them. However, supplies to such bodies may be outside of the TOMS if they, in turn, re-supply the services provided in a business capacity (see 66.11 above). If a business is unsure whether or not a supply to a college, etc will be re-supplied, then it should use the TOMS to account for VAT.

(VAT Notice 709/5/04, paras 3.4, 12(TL2)).

66.14 INPUT TAX

Input tax cannot be reclaimed on goods or services acquired for re-supply as margin scheme supplies. *[SI 1987/1806, Art 12]*. This applies both to VAT incurred in the UK and in other EC countries.

Input tax can be reclaimed, outside the TOMS and subject to the normal rules, on

- overheads; and
- purchases relating to in-house supplies.

VAT incurred in another EC country on overheads and purchases relating to in-house supplies can be reclaimed from the tax authorities in that country under the procedure in 21.22 *et seq* EUROPEAN COMMUNITY: GENERAL. Note, however, that where supplies are made in that other EC country, it may be necessary to register for VAT there. If so, this refund procedure may not be appropriate.

(VAT Notice 709/5/04, paras 4.3, 4.4).

66.15 REGISTRATION AND DEREGISTRATION

For VAT registration and deregistration purposes, turnover is

- the total margin on taxable (including zero-rated) margin scheme supplies;
- the full value of taxable (including zero-rated) in-house supplies;
- the full value of taxable agency commission; plus

- the full value of any other taxable (including zero-rated) supplies you made in the UK.

(VAT Notice 709/5/04, para 4.1).

66.16 **VAT group treatment**

A business making margin scheme supplies cannot belong to a VAT group (see 31 GROUPS OF COMPANIES) if any other member of the proposed or existing group

- has an overseas establishment; and
- makes supplies outside the UK which would be taxable (including zero-rated) supplies if made in the UK; and
- supplies goods or services which will become, or are intended to become, margin scheme supplies (ie which are for resale, whether or not by the other member concerned).

[*SI 1987/1806, Art 13*]. (VAT Notice 709/5/04, para 4.2).

66.17 **CALCULATION OF MARGINS AND OUTPUT TAX**

Special calculations as laid down by HMRC are required under the TOMS to ensure that sales include only the margin for margin scheme supplies but the full value of any in-house supplies made. The purpose of the calculations are therefore to

- work out the total margin receieved;
- apportion the total margin between different types of supplies (ie margin scheme supplies (see 66.3 above), in-house supplies (see 66.10 above) and agency supplies (see 66.12 above));
- apportion the total margin between supplies with different VAT liabilities (eg, standard-rated, zero-rated or exempt);
- work out the output tax due on margin scheme supplies and packages; and
- work out net values for supplies with different VAT liabilities.

[*SI 1987/1806, Art 7*]. (VAT Notice 709/5/04, paras 5.1, 5.10).

As precise figures are not usually known at the time of preparing the VAT returns, the TOMS requires VAT to be accounted for each quarter (or month if monthly returns are made) using *provisional* figures. The final margins and output tax are based on an annual calculation and adjustment at the end of the '*financial year*', ie the year for which financial accounts are made up. This final calculation determines the output tax due for the preceding financial year and provides the percentage to calculate provisional output tax in the subsequent financial year. See 66.19 to 66.22 below for the methods of calculation which *must* be used.

VAT Notice 709/5/04 sets out a cost-based method of apportionment as the way of valuing in-house supplies. In *TP Madgett & RM Baldwin (t/a Howden Court Hotel) v C & E Commrs, CJEC [1998] STC 1189 (TVC 21.314)*, the CJEC held that a tour operator was entitled to use a method based on the market value of the in-house supplies when the cost-based calculation required complex sub-apportionment exercises and when it was possible to identify the in-house element of the package by a market value based method. HMRC intend to use this decision to simplify the TOMS. The timing of the changes is uncertain. (Business Brief 10/99).

66.18 Starting to use the scheme

Where a business is newly registered or an existing business starts to use the TOMS for the first time, it must calculate a provisional percentage to use during the first financial year under the scheme. Depending upon the circumstances, this may be based upon

- previous trading figures;
- projected costings and margins; or
- actual monthly/quarterly figures during the first year.

Whichever method is used, the first year-end calculation (see 66.19 below) will correct any under or over payment of VAT arising in the year.

(VAT Notice 709/5/04, para 5.11).

66.19 End of year calculation (annual adjustment)

Note. The provisions of this paragraph have the force of law. But see *My Travel plc (aka Airtours plc) v C & E Commrs (No 1), CJEC Case C–291/03 (unreported) (TVC 61.16)* where the Advocate-General has held that a tour operator is entitled to recalculate his VAT liability under the conditions laid down by national law, but that *EC Sixth Directive, Art 26* must be interpreted as meaning that the part of the package corresponding to in-house services should be identified on the basis of their market value where that value can be established. The actual cost method should only be used if the tour operator proves that it accurately reflects the actual structure of the package.

The steps listed below are those needed to make the final calculations based on the actual figures for the financial year (ie the period for which accounts are prepared), except that

- if all supplies are liable to VAT at the same rate, the simplified calculation in 66.20 below must be used; and
- it is possible, with permission, to do a separate annual calculation for supplies enjoyed wholly outside the EC. See 66.22 below.

Any adjustment must be made on the first VAT return for a VAT period ending *after* the end of the financial year. For example, if the financial year ends on 31 March, any adjustment must be made, as the case may be, on the return to 30 April, 31 May or 30 June. It may therefore be useful to bring VAT periods in line with the financial year for accounts purposes in order to give the maximum time to calculate any adjustment. It is not necessary to wait for the production of full audited accounts before making the calculation. If the audit subsequently identifies errors or adjustments, the annual calculation should be reworked and the normal procedure for correction of errors followed. See 56.11 RECORDS.

The steps cover every type of supply which might be accounted for via the TOMSs which means that, if not all of these different types of supplies are made, some steps can be omitted from the calculation.

Apportionment of the total margin calculated is based on the direct costs of supplies (but not indirect/overhead costs) and works on the principle that the same percentage margin is achieved on all elements of the package. For this reason, it is helpful if direct costs are recorded according to type and liability.

	Total sales of margin scheme packages (see 66.24 below)	
A	Add up the VAT-inclusive selling prices of margin scheme supplies and margin scheme packages supplied during the financial year	
	Purchase prices of margin scheme supplies (see 66.25 below)	
B	Add up the VAT-inclusive purchase prices of standard-rated margin scheme supplies included in A above	
C	Add up the VAT-inclusive purchase prices of zero-rated margin scheme supplies included in A above.	
	Direct costs of in-house supplies (see 66.26 below)	
D	Add up the VAT-exclusive direct costs of standard-rated in-house supplies included in A above. Add a percentage of that amount equivalent to the standard rate of VAT	
E	Add up the VAT-exclusive direct costs of zero-rated in-house supplies included in A above	
F	Add up the VAT-inclusive direct costs of exempt in-house supplies included in A above. Deduct any input tax recoverable on these costs	
G	Add up the direct costs of in-house supplies included in A above that are supplied outside the UK, exclusive of any VAT incurred on these costs that you are entitled to recover. Add to the total an uplift equivalent to the percentage VAT rate applicable to such supplies if VAT has been accounted for on these supplies to the VAT authorities in another EC country	
	'Costs' of agency supplies (see 66.29 below)	
H	Add up the VAT-inclusive amounts paid by the business to principals in respect of the agency supplies included in A above for which the consideration received is standard-rated	
I	Add up the VAT-inclusive amounts paid by the business to principals in respect of the agency supplies included in A above for which the consideration received is not standard-rated	
	Calculation of total margin	
J	Add the total of costs at B to I above inclusive.	
K	Calculate the total margin for all the supplies included in A by deducting the total at J from the total at A	
	Apportioning the margin	
	Calculate the proportion of the total margin (K) relating to each type of supply	
L	Standard-rated margin scheme supplies	B ÷ J × K
M	Zero-rated margin scheme supplies	C ÷ J × K
N	Standard-rated in-house supplies	D ÷ J × K
O	Zero-rated in-house supplies	E ÷ J × K

P	Exempt in-house supplies	F ÷ J × K
Q	In-house supplies made outside the UK	G ÷ J × K
R	Standard-rated agency supplies	H ÷ J × K
S	Non-standard-rated agency supplies	I ÷ J × K
Calculation of output tax		
On standard-rated margin scheme supplies		L × 7/47
On standard-rated in-house supplies		(D + N) × 7/47
On standard-rated agency supplies		R × 7/47
Calculation of sales value		
Standard-rated margin scheme supplies (VAT-exclusive)		L × 40/47
Standard-rated in-house supplies (VAT-exclusive)		(D + N) × 40/47
Zero-rated in-house supplies		E + O
Exempt in-house supplies		F + P
In-house supplies supplied outside the UK		G + Q

Annual adjustment. The difference between the provisional output tax which has been accounted for during the financial year on supplies included in A above and the total output tax due as calculated above is payable or deductible on the first VAT return for a VAT period ending *after* the end of the financial year.

(VAT Notice 709/5/04, paras 5.2, 5.5, 5.6, 8, 12(TL5)).

66.20 **Simplified calculation**

Note. The provisions of this paragraph have the force of law.

If all component supplies of all margin scheme packages are liable to VAT at the standard rate, the simplified method set out below must be used. It achieves the same results as the full calculation but avoids the need to work out costs of in-house supplies (if included in packages).

A	Add up the VAT-inclusive selling prices of margin scheme supplies and margin scheme packages supplied during the financial year	
B	Add up the VAT-inclusive purchase prices of the margin scheme supplies included in A above	
Output tax =		(A – B) × 7/47
VAT-exclusive value of margin scheme supplies and margin scheme packages =		(A – B) × 40/47

Annual adjustment. The difference between the provisional output tax which has been accounted for during the financial year on supplies included in A above and the total output tax due as calculated above is payable or deductible on the first VAT return for a VAT period ending *after* the end of the financial year.

(VAT Notice 709/5/04, paras 5.3, 5.5, 5.6, 10, 12(TL5)).

66.21 Provisional percentages for the next financial year

Note. The provisions of this paragraph have the force of law.

When the procedure in 66.19 or 66.20 above has been completed, provisional percentages can be obtained for use in completing VAT returns for the next financial year. Revised provisional figures must be calculated each year.

Where the method in 66.19 above is used (capital letters correspond to those used in that paragraph)

1 Calculate the VAT-inclusive amount of standard-rated margin scheme supplies and margin scheme packages for the preceding financial year as a percentage of the total selling price of all margin scheme supplies and margin scheme packages in that year

(D + L + N + R) ÷ A × 100 = s%

For each VAT period

2 Add up the VAT-inclusive selling prices of margin scheme supplies and margin scheme packages supplied during the VAT period = T

Provisional output tax = T × s% × 7/47

Where the simplified calculation in 66.20 above is used (capital letters correspond to those used in that paragraph)

1 Calculate the VAT-inclusive amount of standard-rated margin scheme supplies and margin scheme packages for the preceding financial year as a percentage of the total selling price of all margin scheme supplies and margin scheme packages in that year

(A – B) ÷ A × 100 = s%

For each VAT period

2 Add up the VAT-inclusive selling prices of margin scheme supplies and margin scheme packages supplied during the VAT period = T

Provisional output tax = T × s% × 7/47

Provisional VAT-exclusive value of supplies = (T× s%) × 40/47

(VAT Notice 709/5/04, paras 5.9, 9, 11, 12(TL5)).

66.22 Separate calculation for non-EC supplies

Note. The provisions of this paragraph have the force of law.

Where a business makes supplies (including packages) which are enjoyed outside the EC, it may elect to do separate year-end and provisional calculations for those supplies. If it so elects, it must include in the non-EC calculation all supplies which are enjoyed wholly outside the EC. But where any packages are enjoyed partly within the EC and partly outside the EC, the entire package must be included in the calculation for

EC-only supplies, the related direct costs being included in the standard-rated or zero-rated steps within the EC-only calculation depending on where the supplies are enjoyed.

A business can only change to separate calculations (or revert to a single calculation) at the start of its financial year (ie no later than the due date of its first VAT return for that financial year). Permission must be requested from the local VAT Business Advice Centre, in writing, and in advance of the financial year in question. Permission will not be granted retrospectively. This policy was confirmed as having the force of law in *C & E Commrs v Simply Travel Ltd, Ch D 2001, [2002] STC 194 (TVC 61.21).*

Permission to switch to separate calculations will only be granted if HMRC are satisfied that the records of the business for direct costs and sales are adequate to calculate accurate, but separate, sets of margins.

(VAT Notice 709/5/04, paras 5.7, 5.8, 12(TL3)).

66.23 **Records**

Whether the full or simplified calculation is made, a business must keep records of

- the total selling price for margin scheme supplies and/or packages; and
- separate records of the direct costs for margin scheme supplies and the different types of supplies within margin scheme packages, ie
  - (i) standard-rated and zero-rated margin scheme supplies;
  - (ii) standard-rated, zero-rated, exempt and outside the scope in-house supplies; and
  - (iii) standard-rated, zero-rated, exempt and outside the scope agency supplies for which its commission is not readily identifiable.

(VAT Notice 709/5/04, para 5.4).

66.24 **Working out the selling prices**

The first step in the end of year calculation (see A in 66.19 and 66.20 above) is to add up the selling prices of supplies with tax points during the financial year.

Include:

- The total VAT-inclusive selling price of all margin scheme supplies (see 66.3 above).
- The total VAT-inclusive selling price of any in-house supplies (see 66.10 above) supplied together with margin scheme supplies.
- Any Air Passenger Duty payable by the customer.
- Any surcharges made.
- Monies received from customers who fail to turn up.
- Where sales are made through agents, 'the total amount to be paid by the traveller' (even if a travel agent deducts commission and only passes over the balance).

  Where a travel agent sells a package for less than the tour operator's advertised brochure price but funds the discount itself (so that the tour operator receives the full price of the holiday but, in effect, part from the traveller and part from the travel agent), the CJEC have held that '*the total amount to be paid by the traveller*' includes the additional amount that the agent, acting as an intermediary, has to pay the tour operator in addition to the actual price paid by the traveller (*C & E Commrs v First Choice Holidays plc, CJEC [2003] STC 934 (TVC 21.317)*).

- Amounts received relating to any supplies, packaged with margin scheme supplies, which the business arranges as an agent and where its commission is not readily identifiable (see 66.29 below).

Reduce sales by:

- Any refunds made to customers for unsatisfactory service.

Do not include:

- Packages of supplies which do not include any margin scheme supplies (on which VAT must be accounted for under the normal rules).
- Forfeited deposits and cancellation fees received from customers who cancel bookings.
- Amounts collected by the business as agent if its commission is readily identifiable.
- Any discount the business agrees with its customer.

(VAT Notice 709/5/04, para 6.1).

66.25 Purchase price of margin scheme supplies

The second stage in the end of year calculation is to add up the total VAT-inclusive purchase prices of goods and services bought in for resale as margin scheme supplies. Only those purchases which relate to the financial year being calculated must be included, ie which relate to supplies included within A in 66.19 above or, as the case may be, 66.20 above.

The cost must

- take into account any discounts or price reductions received from suppliers (even if received at a later date);
- include any Air Passenger Duty payable;
- not include the cost of any supplies which do not include any margin scheme supplies; and
- not include indirect costs (see 66.27 below).

(VAT Notice 709/5/04, para 6.2).

Connected persons. Where goods or services are supplied to the tour operator by a connected person (see 69.19 VALUATION) and the value of the supply would otherwise be greater than its open market value, HMRC may direct that the value of the supply is deemed to be its open market value for the purposes of calculating the value of margin scheme supplies. The direction must be in writing to the tour operator acquiring the supply within three years of the time of supply. It may also specify that the open market value rule is to apply to subsequent supplies acquired from the same connected person. [*SI 1987/1806, Art 8*].

66.26 Direct costs of in-house supplies

It is not necessary to work out the costs of in-house supplies if all supplies included in margin scheme packages are liable to VAT at the same rate. In such a case the simplified calculation under 66.20 above must be used. Otherwise, the annual calculation under 66.19 above must include the direct costs incurred in making in-house supplies which are supplied with margin scheme supplies as part of a package.

The following are examples (not exhaustive) of costs which may be included.

Direct costs of supplying in-house passenger transport

General

- Depreciation on vehicles, aircraft, vessels (which the business or a member of its VAT group owns) calculated on the same basis as its audited accounts
- Rental or leasing of vehicles, aircraft or vessels (see 66.27 below as regards HP, leasing and finance charges)
- Crew/drivers costs (including employer's NIC)
- Subsistence paid to crew/drivers
- Fuel
- Insurance
- Repair and maintenance of vehicles, aircraft or vessels

Road or rail transport

- Garaging and parking
- Bridge and road tolls
- Ferry costs
- Road fund licences

Air transport

- Air Passenger Duty (APD)
- Landing fees

Cruises

- Berthing fees

Chartering an aircraft (see 66.10 above)

- Charter fee
- Catering charges
- Transfer journeys

Chartering a vessel (see 66.10 above)

- Charter fee
- 'Hotel'/domestic/catering staff

Only in-house passenger transport supplied with margin scheme supplies can be included in the TOMS calculation. If in-house transport is also used to supply passenger transport outside the TOMS (eg coach hire), the direct cost must be apportioned to take account of this, normally

- for road or rail transport, on a mileage basis;
- for air transport, based on hours flown; and
- for sea transport, on the basis of days used on types of supply.

If a business wishes to adopt any other basis for apportionment, it should submit its proposed method in writing to its local VAT Business Advice Centre in advance of when its year-end calculation/adjustment is due.

Direct costs of standard-rated hotel accommodation

- Depreciation of buildings, fixtures and fittings (which the business or a member of its VAT group owns) calculated on the same basis as its audited accounts
- Catering purchases
- Heating and lighting
- Rates
- Building insurance
- Rental of equipment and furniture
- Repairs, maintenance and cleaning for which the business is liable
- Staff costs (including wages and employer's NI contributions)

Only costs relating to in-house accommodation supplied with margin scheme supplies can be included in the TOMS calculation. If premises are also used to provide accommodation outside the TOMS, the annual direct costs must be apportioned to take account of this, normally on the basis of number of guests/days booked for each type of supply.

If certain parts of the premises are not used specifically to provide accommodation (eg administrative offices, public bars, owner's private accommodation, etc) costs relating to the entire premises (eg rates, insurance, light and heat) must be apportioned on the basis of floor area. Any other bases of apportionment must be agreed in writing with the local VAT Business Advice Centre in advance of when the year-end calculation/adjustment is due.

See also *The Devonshire Hotel (Torquay) Ltd (VTD 14448) (TVC 61.13)*.

Sales of assets for which depreciation has been entered as an in-house cost. Where this occurs, an appropriate adjustment must be made to in-house costs in the year-end TOMS calculation for the year in which the sale takes place.

This adjustment is

- a reduction to the relevant in-house costs in respect of any profit made on disposal, or
- an increase to the relevant in-house costs in respect of a loss made on disposal

based on book values in the accounts.

(VAT Notice 709/5/04, paras 6.4, 7.4, 7.5, 7.7, 7.8, 7.10).

66.27 Indirect costs

Indirect costs must not be included in any of the calculations. Examples of indirect costs include

- brochures
- advertising
- inspection trips made to research resorts, facilities, etc
- office expenses (telephone, IT equipment, office stationery, rent, etc)
- accountancy, legal and similar professional services
- hiring and employing representatives at airports and resorts (see 66.31 below)
- financial services including bank and foreign exchange charges
- HP, leasing and finance charges for the purchase of assets (including those used for making in-house supplies)
- market research
- commission paid to agents.

(VAT Notice 709/5/04, para 6.3).

66.28 Foreign currency purchases

Note. The provisions of this paragraph have the force of law.

If any supplies bought for resale as TOMS supplies are billed in foreign currency, these should be converted into sterling at either

(i) the rate of exchange published in the Financial Times using the Federation of Tour Operators' base rate current at the time the supplies are costed by the person from whom the business has acquired the goods or services;

(ii) the commercial rate of exchange current at the time that the supplies in the brochure were costed;

(iii) the rate published in the Financial Times on the date that the business pays for the supplies;

(iv) the rate of exchange which was applicable to the purchase by the business of the foreign currency used to pay for the supplies; or

(v) the period rate of exchange published by HMRC for customs purposes in force at the time the business pays for the supplies.

Documentary evidence relating to the purchase must be kept to show which of the rates have been used. If method (i) or (ii) is used, the rate must be published in any brochure or leaflet in which the supplies are held out for sale.

Once a method has been chosen, HMRC may allow a different method but only from the start of a financial year and if written notification is given to them no later than the due date for rendering the first VAT return for that financial year.

(VAT Notice 709/5/04, paras 6.5, 12(TL4)).

66.29 **Commission received for agency supplies arranged as part of a margin scheme package**

Where any commission received for agency supplies made by the business is readily identifiable, exclude from the TOMS calculation

- the commission received; and
- all monies paid for the supply arranged.

Where any commission is received which is not readily identifiable, include in the TOMS calculation

- the gross amount paid by the traveller (in A at 66.19 above); and
- the net amount paid to the principal (in H or I at 66.19 above).

(VAT Notice 709/5/04, para 6.6).

66.30 **Hotel and travel insurance**

The way hotel or travel insurance is treated for VAT purposes depends upon the precise contractual arrangements and whether it is the tour operator or the traveller who is the insured person.

(*a*) Where *the insurance policy issued by the permitted insurer makes the traveller the insured person* (the normal case), there is a supply of insurance from the permitted insurer to the traveller. If the tour operator arranges for the insurance to be supplied by a named company to the traveller under such an arrangement, it is acting as an agent.

- Where the commission received is readily identifiable, the full amount paid by the traveller for the insurance and the net premium passed on to the insurance company must be excluded from the TOMS calculations.
- Where the commission received is not readily identifiable, values relating to the insurance must be included in the TOMS calculation (see 66.29 above).
- Where the insurance is offered 'free' as part of a package, the full amount paid by the traveller for the package must be included in the TOMS calculation. Any costs incurred in relation to such insurance must not be included in the TOMS calculation.

(*b*) Where *the tour operator enters into an agreement with a permitted insurer under which the tour operator is the insured person*, the insurer agrees to reimburse the tour operator in respect of any claims by travellers for delay compensation, medical costs, etc. This is an indirect cost and therefore outside the TOMS. If the tour operator passes on a charge for the insurance (including any Insurance Premium Tax) to the traveller, this should be included in the selling prices in the TOMS calculation.

(VAT Notice 709/5/04 para 6.7).

66.31 **Representatives and guides**

The services of representatives at airports and resorts are not normally supplies in their own right and are therefore not regarded as in-house supplies. The costs incurred in providing these services should be treated as indirect costs for the purposes of the TOMS.

The specialist services of a guide, however, are often supplies in their own right. If the supply is made in-house, the place of supply and the liability depends on the exact nature of the service. See 66.10 above.

(VAT Notice 709/5/04 para 6.9).

66.32 **Unforeseen costs**

Where it is necessary to buy in accommodation, transport, meals, etc as a result of delays, breakdowns or other unforeseen circumstances, these costs should usually be treated as margin scheme supplies unless the cost of the additional items is

- ultimately met by someone else (eg an airline from whom air transport is bought in has agreed to meet any additional costs arising through flight delays) in which case the costs should be ignored in the TOMS calculation; or
- a direct cost of in-house supplies.

(VAT Notice 709/5/04, para 6.10).

66.33 **Bad debt relief**

See 7 BAD DEBT RELIEF generally for the rules for claiming bad debt relief and in particular paragraph 7.9 under which bad debt relief is restricted to a maximum of the VAT fraction of the profit margin.

The amount of VAT bad debt relief claimable is calculated by the formula

$B \times s\% \times 7/47$

where

B = the amount of the bad debt

s = the provisional percentage as calculated under 66.21 above for the financial year in which the supply is made

(VAT Notice 709/5/04, para 6.8).

67 Trade Promotion Schemes

The contents of this chapter are as follows.

67.1 INTRODUCTION

A large number of trade promotion schemes exist where goods or services are given as rewards to retail customers (the public) or trade customers.

These include

- schemes where goods are linked in a promotion (see 67.4 to 67.7 below);
- schemes where vouchers, coupons, etc are issued and later redeemed for cash (eg money-off coupons) or goods or services with or without further consideration (see 67.8 to 67.14 below);
- manufacturers' promotion schemes aimed at either the trade (see 67.15 below) or the public (see 67.16 below); and
- retail discount schemes (see 67.17 below).

The VAT consequences in many cases depend upon whether there has been a gift of goods or services and whether any non-monetary consideration has been given. These points are considered in 67.2 and 67.3 below.

67.2 Gifts

Free gifts of goods for no consideration. Where a business gives away goods, on which it is entitled to credit for input tax, without any monetary or non-monetary consideration (see 67.3 below), the VAT rules on gifts apply. If the VAT-exclusive cost of the goods is £50 or less, no VAT is due unless the gift forms part of a series or succession of such gifts to the same person. If the VAT-exclusive cost of the goods is more than £50, output tax must be accounted for on the price the person would have to pay (excluding VAT) at the time of supply, to purchase goods identical to the goods concerned, ie normally their cost value. See 47.6 OUTPUT TAX for further details.

Free provision of own services (eg free beauty treatment) is generally not a taxable supply. There is no restriction on input tax recovery and no output tax is due. However, if the supply makes use of goods (eg cosmetics) which cost more than £50, output tax may be due as above.

Free provision of bought-in services (eg beauty treatment provided by another business) will give rise to a VAT liability under *SI 1993/1507*. See 47.7 OUTPUT TAX. If, however, services are merely paid for by the business but supplied directly by a third party to the customer, the business makes no supply for VAT purposes but cannot deduct any VAT charged by the provider of the services (although it may be claimable by the customer).

If goods are lent or hired to a customer, there is a supply of services and, where no consideration is given, output tax is due on the cost of providing the services. Over a period of time, this is the amount of depreciation of the goods (plus any other costs related to the goods) multiplied by the proportion which the use outside the business forms to the total use. See 47.7 OUTPUT TAX for further details. Some free loans may, however, be outside the scope of VAT, see 67.17 below.

Free discounts on goods or services. If a business gives a discount freely on goods or services, it need only charge VAT on the discounted amount.

Free gifts of vouchers or coupons. See 67.11 below.

(VAT Notice 700/7/02, paras 2.1–2.4).

67.3 Non-monetary consideration

The VAT treatment of discounts and reward goods/services depends upon whether any consideration is given by the recipient.

Where payment is totally in money, that is the consideration. However, it is also possible to have non-monetary consideration where the customer agrees to do something (or not to do it) in return for a supply of goods or services. Where *any* non-monetary consideration is given, however small, VAT is due on that consideration. The value of the consideration is taken to be such amount in money as, with the addition of the VAT, is equivalent to the consideration, ie normally the price, excluding VAT, which the customer would have to pay to buy the goods or services. [*VATA 1994, s 19(3)*].

An example of non-monetary consideration is where a business offers incentive goods to its customer, either free or at a lower price, on condition that the customer provides it with a service in return. In agreeing to provide this service the customer is providing non-monetary consideration, the value of which is equivalent to the price, or reduction in price, of the goods. In *Empire Stores Ltd v C & E Commrs, CJEC [1994] STC 623 (TVC 21.160)* a company sold goods by mail order and offered new customers, and existing customers who introduced new customers, certain goods free of charge as inducements. The CJEC ruled that the goods in question were supplied to the customers in consideration for a service, namely the introduction of a new customer, and not in return for the purchase by the new customer of goods from the catalogue. The value of the goods was the amount that the company was prepared to spend to get the introduction, ie the cost of the articles to the company.

HMRC, however, accept that certain acts, including the following, are insignificant for these purposes and do not constitute non-monetary consideration.

(*a*) Having to buy one article either to get

- another article free at the same time; or
- a discount voucher redeemable against a further purchase; or
- a lottery ticket, etc (see 67.18 below).

(*b*) Employees having to exceed certain sales levels or sell most articles in a month, or other such schemes (see 67.19 below).

(*c*) The act of using an in-house credit card (see 67.18 below).

(*d*) Entering a free prize draw.

(*e*) Having to complete a slogan or give a recipe, etc on entry to a competition.

(*f*) A gift to an existing customer for their buying more than a certain amount.

In circumstances such as these, the normal rules for gifts set out in 67.2 above apply.

(VAT Notice 700/7/02, paras 3.1–3.3).

67.4 **GOODS LINKED IN A PROMOTION**

Goods (or goods and services) are sometimes offered together in one promotion for a single price (eg coffee and chocolate biscuits or a washing machine and iron). Alternatively, a number of articles may be sold in a multibuy offer, eg

- 'buy 1 get 1 free';
- 'buy three for the price of two'; or
- 'buy a sofa and get a free foot stool'.

This is a multiple supply and the amount paid covers all the goods or services offered.

If the items offered are subject to VAT at different rates, apportionment will normally be required. See 47.3 OUTPUT TAX. However, for certain small items linked with a major item which is liable to VAT at a different rate, the linked supplies concession in 67.7 below may apply.

(VAT Notice 700/7/02, para 4.1).

If the offer is made to other VAT-registered traders, see also the dealer loader scheme under 67.15 below.

67.5 **Linked goods schemes**

Theses are promotion schemes where a minor article is linked (not necessarily physically) with a main article (either goods or services) and sold with it at a single price. An example would be an empty plastic storage jar attached to a box of cereals. Where the articles are liable to VAT at the same rate, no problem arises but where they are liable at different rates, the price should normally be apportioned (see 47.3 OUTPUT TAX). However, by concession, VAT can be accounted for on the minor article at the same rate as the main article (so that the selling price need not be apportioned) provided the following conditions are satisfied.

(*a*) The minor article is not charged to the customer at a separate price.

(*b*) The minor article costs no more than

  (i) 20% of the total cost (excluding VAT) of the combined supply; and

  (ii) £1 (excluding VAT) if included with goods intended for retail sale or £5 (excluding VAT) otherwise.

Where the conditions are met, the articles need not be detailed separately on the invoice.

In all other circumstances where a VAT invoice has to be issued, details of the minor article must be shown separately.

See also 28.13 FOOD for mixtures and assortments of food and 54.18 PRINTED MATTER, ETC for promotional items in magazines.

(VAT Notice 700/7/02, para 4.2; VAT Notice 48, ESC 3.7).

67.6 *Accounting for linked supplies under retail schemes*

VAT must be accounted for as follows.

(*a*) *Point of Sale scheme and Direct Calculation Schemes 1 and 2.* Treatment depends upon whether the two articles are liable to VAT at the same rate or different rates.

(i) If both articles are liable at the same rate of VAT, there are no additional rules to follow.

(ii) If the articles are liable at different rates of VAT, subject to the linked supplies concession in 67.5 above, the selling price must be apportioned either on the basis in 47.3 OUTPUT TAX or, where the goods have been linked by the manufacturer, in accordance with the information shown on the supplier's invoice.

Where apportionment is required, the amount allocated to reduced rate or zero-rated goods must be separated from standard-rated takings before carrying out the scheme calculation.

(*b*) *Apportionment Schemes 1 and 2.* Any contribution from the supplier or sponsor must be included in daily gross takings.

Under Apportionment Scheme 1, no adjustment to purchases is required.

Under Apportionment Scheme 2, expected selling prices (ESPs) must also be adjusted as follows.

- No adjustment is required for a full contribution. Where only partial contribution is received, ESPs for the appropriate goods must be adjusted to the extent of the amount not supported by the supplier or sponsor. Where no contribution is received, an appropriate adjustment must be made to the ESPs of the promotion goods.
- If the promotion goods are liable to VAT at different rates, the ESPs must be apportioned either on the basis in 47.3 OUTPUT TAX or, where the goods have been linked by the manufacturer, in accordance with the information shown on the supplier's invoice.

  Where the linked supplies concession under 67.5 above is used, the record of purchases or ESPs of the promotion goods must be adjusted as appropriate.

(*c*) *Contributions from manufacturers or joint promoters.* Whichever scheme is used, strictly speaking, where the retailer receives a contribution from a manufacturer or joint sponsor representing partial payment for goods supplied to a customer, the retailer should account for this in the period the goods are supplied. However, by concession, the retailer may account for such contributions in the period they are received. If the manufacturer or joint sponsor makes any payment (eg towards advertising) this must be treated as consideration for a separate supply of services and dealt with outside the retail scheme.

(*d*) *Correcting ESPs*. Under Direct Calculation Schemes 1 and 2,

- if a contribution is received from a manufacturer or joint promoter for the class of goods which the retailer has marked up in the retail scheme, no ESP adjustment should be made if the supplier or sponsor makes a full contribution. If a partial contribution is received, ESPs for the appropriate goods should be adjusted to the extent of the amount *not* supported by the sponsor or manufacturer.
- Where no contribution is received from the manufacturer or sponsor, an appropriate adjustment must be made to the ESPs of the promotion goods.

(VAT Notice 727/3/02, para 7.6; VAT Notice 727/4/02, para 8.5; VAT Notice 727/5/02, para 7.5, all of which have the force of law).

67.7 Multisave promotions where the manufacturer subsidises the promotion

In some multisave promotions of the 'buy 2, get a third free' type, manufacturers make payments to retailers towards the costs of the promotions. In such cases, following the CJEC decision in *Elida Gibbs Ltd v C & E Commrs, CJEC [1996] STC 1387 (TVC 21.161)*, manufacturers can reduce their output tax by the amount paid to the retailer to support the promotion where it relates to products liable to VAT at the standard rate. The payments received by the retailer are further consideration for the supply to the customer upon which VAT is due and the amounts received should be included within retail scheme takings figures.

In *Elida Gibbs* the company manufactured toiletries and sold the products to both retailers and wholesalers. To promote retail sales, it

- issued money-off coupons which customers could present to a retailer in part payment for Elida Gibbs products and for which retailers sought reimbursement direct from the company; and
- printed cashback coupons directly onto the packaging of its products which, subject to meeting conditions, entitled any consumer to a cash refund direct from Elida Gibbs.

The company claimed a repayment of output tax which it had previously accounted for contending that the reimbursement of money-off coupons to retailers and the cashback payments to consumers constituted a retrospective discount which reduced the consideration for its supplies. The CJEC agreed, holding that the discounts allowed by the manufacturer were deductible but credit notes should not be issued to customers. This left the VAT position of wholesalers and retailers unchanged and maintained the balance of VAT due from them. Retailers should account for output tax on payments received from manufacturers as well as money paid by customers. This decision was subsequently applied in *EC Commission v Federal Republic of Germany (UK intervening), CJEC 2002, [2003] STC 301 (TVC 21.163)*. See also *Yorkshire Co-Operatives Ltd v C & E Commrs, CJEC [2003] STC 234 (TVC 21.170)*. However, if a VAT-registered customer requests a VAT invoice in respect of purchases made using money-off vouchers, this should be based only on the amount paid by the customer. This achieves fiscal neutrality as required by the judgment.

There may be cases where the manufacturer pays the retailer for providing a service, for example, in undertaking to advertise the promotion and/or products. In such cases, the retailer must charge the manufacturer VAT at the standard rate which is the input tax for the manufacturer subject to the normal rules.

(VAT Notice 700/7/02, para 4.3).

67.8 **COUPONS, VOUCHERS, TRADING STAMPS, ETC.**

The provisions in 67.9 to 67.14 below explain the VAT treatment of coupons generally. Particular care must be taken when dealing with 'face value vouchers' and manufacturers' promotions as considered in 67.15 and 67.16 below.

67.9 **Money-off coupon**

Money-off coupons are coupons used to offer to the public a reduction in the price of a future purchase. They can be issued in a variety of ways, for example

- given on the purchase of a particular item;
- given on the purchase of goods to a specified value;
- sent by mailshot or electronic means; or
- published as cut-out coupons in newspapers.

They may be issued by retailers under their own schemes or by manufacturers. In either case, it does not matter whether the coupon is attached to a product or not.

Issue of money-off coupons. In most cases, money-off coupons are regarded as issued for no payment (consideration). Even if the issue is dependent upon the purchase of goods, provided the goods are sold at their normal price, no VAT is due on their issue.

Sale of money-off coupons. Where, however, discount coupons or vouchers (or a discount card) entitling the holder to discounts on purchases are *sold*, the VAT consequences depend upon how and where the coupons, etc can be used.

- Where the coupons, etc are sold by a retailer using a retail scheme and discounts are only available from that retailer, proceeds must be included in gross takings. Unless the coupons are for a specific line of product, the VAT liability of which can be determined when the coupons are issued, retailers using the point of sale scheme may not be able, when the discount coupons are sold, to determine the liability of the goods or services against which the coupons will be redeemed. Such retailers should agree a method of how to account for VAT on such sales with HMRC, possibly on the basis of the average split of zero-rated and standard-rated sales.
- Where the coupons, etc sold can be used at several traders, this is a standard-rated supply of services. See *C & E Commrs v Granton Marketing Ltd; C & E Commrs v Wentwalk Ltd, CA [1996] STC 1049 (TVC 65.62)* where cards which entitled the holder to a complimentary meal and wine at certain restaurants were held not to be vouchers and their supply to be standard-rated.

  If a retail scheme is used,

  - under the Point of Sale Scheme, payments received should be added to standard-rated daily gross takings; and
  - under Apportionment Schemes 1 and 2 and Direct Calculation Schemes 1 and 2 payments received should be dealt with outside the scheme used.

Redemption of money-off coupons. Where a business uses a retail scheme, it should only include in its daily gross takings

- any additional payment received when the customer redeems the coupon; and

- any further payment which is due from any other source (eg from the manufacturer).

Where no retail scheme is in operation, VAT is due on the money received from the customer and the manufacturer (if any) under the normal time of supply rules.

See *Boots Co plc v C & E Commrs, CJEC [1990] STC 387 (TVC 21.176)* confirming that money-off coupons are not to be treated as consideration when used to buy other goods but are simply evidence of entitlement to discount.

Handling charges. Any further handling or service charge made to a manufacturer for handling coupons is exempt from VAT.

(VAT Notice 700/7/02, paras 5.2–5.5).

67.10 Vouchers, stamps and points schemes

Where vouchers, stamps or points can be redeemed for goods ('reward goods') or occasionally services without further payment, the redemption goods and services must be treated as supplied for no consideration. See 67.2 above. (VAT Notice 700/7/02, para 5.6). This follows the decision in *Kuwait Petroleum (GB) Ltd v C & E Commrs, CJEC [1999] STC 488 (TVC 21.109)*. In that case, the company ran a promotion scheme under which customers were offered vouchers with purchases of fuel. Whether or not customers accepted the vouchers, the price of fuel was the same. The vouchers could be redeemed for goods ('reward goods') or occasionally services without further payment. The CJEC held that the amounts paid by customers were entirely attributable to their original purchases and no part of the payments could be attributed to the supply of reward goods. The reward goods should therefore be treated as gifts and taxed accordingly. This was subsequently confirmed in the UK courts in *Kuwait Petroleum (GB) Ltd v C & E Commrs, Ch D [2000] STC 62 (TVC 21.110)*.

See 67.19 below where vouchers are used as rewards for employees.

67.11 Issue of face value vouchers

A '*face value voucher*' means a token, stamp or voucher (whether in physical or electronic form) that represents a right to receive goods or services to the value of an amount stated on it or recorded in it and '*face value*' means the amount stated on such a voucher. [*VATA 1994, Sch 10A para 1; FA 2003, Sch 1 para 2*]. Examples include gift vouchers, telephone cards, book tokens, electronic top-up cards and postage stamps.

(1) Face value vouchers issued free

Where a business issues face value vouchers entirely without payment (either monetary or non-monetary, see 67.3 above) which are to be redeemed by the business, no VAT is due at the time of issue. (VAT Notice 700/7/02, para 5.8).

(2) Face value vouchers issued for a payment on or after 9 April 2003

The *issue* of a face value voucher, or any subsequent supply of it, is a supply of services for the purposes of *VATA 1994*. [*VATA 1994, Sch 10A para 2; FA 2003, Sch 1 para 2*]. For the avoidance of doubt, HMRC regard 'issued' as meaning that the voucher has been given or acquired a value, is capable of being used because it carries a right to receive goods or services and has been issued to a third party in return for payment. (VAT Information Sheet 12/03, para 4). This allows the *sale* of the voucher to be equated to the underlying supply so that, if it is known that the voucher has been redeemed for, say, zero-rated goods or services, then an intermediate supplier in the supply chain can make an adjustment to reflect the liability of the final supply (see below).

The legislation recognises four categories of face value vouchers.

(*a*) '*Credit vouchers*', ie face value vouchers issued by a person who

- is not a person from whom goods or services may be obtained by the use of the voucher, and
- undertakes to give complete or partial reimbursement to any such person from whom goods or services are so obtained.

Credit vouchers are typically, therefore, gift vouchers that are administered by trade bodies or associations or that can be redeemed at a number of different retailers.

The consideration for *any* supply of a credit voucher (including by any intermediate supplier) is disregarded for VAT purposes unless

(i) the consideration exceeds the face value of the voucher (in which case the VAT is due on the excess); or

(ii) any of the persons from whom goods or services are obtained by the use of the voucher fails to account for any of the VAT due on the supply of those goods or services to the person using the voucher to obtain them.

These provisions retain those applying before 9 April 2003 to similar vouchers but with the addition of the tax loss provisions under (ii) above. These allow HMRC to collect any VAT due from the person who first sold the voucher (ie the issuer) in the event that the redeemer of the voucher fails to account for any VAT due. HMRC have undertaken only to enforce these provisions in the event of a deliberate attempt to avoid paying any VAT due. In cases of genuine error or insolvency, HMRC will not require the issuer to account for the VAT due and will seek to collect it from the redeemer (provided that the issuer has passed the funds to the redeemer).

[*VATA 1994, Sch 10A para 3; FA 2003, Sch 1 para 2*]. (VAT Information Sheet 12/03, para 6).

(*b*) '*Retailer vouchers*', ie face value vouchers issued by a person

- from whom goods or services may be obtained by the use of the voucher, and
- who, if there are other persons from whom goods or services may be obtained by the use of the voucher, undertakes to give complete or partial reimbursement to those from whom goods or services are so obtained.

Typical examples of retail vouchers are gift vouchers issued and redeemed by a high street retailer.

The consideration for the *issue* of a retailer voucher is disregarded for VAT purposes unless

(i) the consideration exceeds the face value of the voucher (in which case the VAT is due on the excess); or

(ii) the voucher is used to obtain goods or services from a person other than the issuer and that person fails to account for any of the VAT due on the supply of those goods or services to the person using the voucher to obtain them.

Any supply of a retailer voucher, subsequent to the first supply by the issuer, is treated in the same way as the supply of a voucher under (*d*) below.

These provisions retain those applying to the issue of similar vouchers before 9 April 2003 but with the addition of the tax loss provisions under (ii) above.

Where a retailer voucher can be used to obtain goods or services from a third party, it is the responsibility of that third party to account for VAT in respect of those goods or services. The provisions in (ii) above allow Customs to collect any VAT due from the person who first sold the voucher (ie the issuer) in the event that the redeemer of the voucher fails to account for any VAT due. HMRC have undertaken only to enforce these provisions in the event of a deliberate attempt to avoid paying any VAT due. In cases of genuine error or insolvency, HMRC will not require the issuer to account for the VAT due and will seek to collect it from the redeemer (provided that the issuer has passed the funds to the redeemer).

[*VATA 1994, Sch 10A para 4; FA 2003, Sch 1 para 2*]. (VAT Information Sheet 12/03, para 7).

(*c*) *Postage stamps.* The consideration for the supply of a postage stamp is disregarded for VAT purposes unless the consideration exceeds the face value of the stamp (in which case the VAT is due on the excess). [*VATA 1994, Sch 10A para 5; FA 2003, Sch 1 para 2*].

Postage stamps are redeemed for an exempt supply of postal services. These provision means that they can pass from the issuer through any intermediate suppliers and on to the final customer without VAT being charged. (VAT Information Sheet 12/03, para 13).

(*d*) *Other kinds of face value voucher.* A supply of a face value voucher that does not fall within (*a*)–(*c*) above (a supply by an intermediate supplier) is, subject to below, standard-rated.

An example falling within this category would be where a high street retailer sells gift vouchers to an intermediate supplier. The onward sale of the vouchers by the intermediate supplier is subject to VAT.

VAT need not be charged at the standard rate where one of the following applies.

- Where the voucher is one that can *only* be used to obtain goods or services in one particular non-standard rate category (ie reduced-rated, zero-rated or exempt and other non-taxable supplies), the supply of the voucher falls in that category. This has the effect of ensuring that such a voucher can pass through the supply chain at that non-standard rate. In practice, examples of this type of voucher are likely to be limited as vouchers that can be redeemed against non-standard-rated goods and services can often also be redeemed against standard-rated goods or services.

- Where the voucher *is* used to obtain goods or services all of which fall in one particular non-standard rate category (ie reduced-rated, zero-rated or exempt and other non-taxable supplies), the supply of the voucher falls in that category. This has the effect of allowing intermediate suppliers in the supply chain to make an adjustment to reflect the liability of the final supply (see below).
- Where the voucher is used to obtain goods or services in a number of different rate categories (ie any combination of standard-rated, reduced-rated, zero-rated or exempt and other non-taxable supplies), the supply of the voucher falls within those different categories and the value of each supply must be determined on a just and reasonable basis. This has the effect of allowing intermediate suppliers in the supply chain to make an adjustment to reflect the liability of the final supplies, to be apportioned between the different rate categories.

[*VATA 1994, Sch 10A para 6; FA 2003, Sch 1 para 2*].

Vouchers supplied free with other goods or services. Where

- a face-value voucher (other than a postage stamp) and other goods or services are supplied to the same person in a composite transaction, and
- the total consideration for the supplies is no different, or not significantly different, from what it would be if the voucher were not supplied,

the supply of the voucher is treated as being made for no consideration. This is an anti-avoidance provision to prevent businesses from artificially reducing the consideration for goods or services by issuing a face value voucher which is unlikely to be redeemed.

Examples

An hotel issues a voucher to a customer when the customer settles his bill for staying. The customer does not have the option of a price reduction in lieu of the voucher and very few customers ever redeem their vouchers.

A retailer gives customers a face value voucher on every purchase made over a certain amount. Customers do not have the option of a price reduction in lieu of the voucher and the voucher has a number of restrictions which are likely to limit the number of customers who eventually redeem the voucher.

A retailer sells a mobile phone boxed with a telephone card. The telephone card is a face value voucher. The customer does not have the option of refusing the telephone card for a reduction in the price of the phone.

[*VATA 1994, Sch 10A para 7; FA 2003, Sch 1 para 2*]. (VAT Information Sheet 12/03, para 12).

Transitional provisions — stock in hand at 9 April 2003. Where an intermediate supplier

- purchased face value vouchers before 9 April 2003 from an issuer who undertakes to redeem them, but
- does not sell them until on or after that date,

he continues to be treated under the old rules under (3) below, providing there is no VAT avoidance and all transactions in the supply chain are entirely at arms length. (VAT Information Sheet 3/03, para 12).

Where a business is unable to distinguish between vouchers issued under the old and new rules, it should contact either its designated officer or the National Advice Service for assistance. HMRC will not expect businesses to identify individual vouchers issued under either the old rules or the new rules but, instead, will agree any calculations provided that they give a just and reasonable result. (VAT Information Sheet 12/08, para 3).

Input tax recovery by intermediate suppliers. Intermediate suppliers are entitled to recover input tax, subject to the normal requirements. The liability of their sale of face value vouchers is deemed to equate to the underlying supply of goods or services (see above). If it is known that the vouchers have been redeemed for zero-rated, reduced-rated or exempt and other non-taxable goods or services, then the intermediate supplier can make an adjustment to both the output tax and the input tax to reflect the liability of the final supply. Adjustments can be based on retail scheme percentages or other global calculations, rather than tracking individual face value vouchers. Where intermediate suppliers know *in advance* that vouchers can be redeemed for zero-rated, reduced-rated or exempt and other non-taxable goods or services, they may use a percentage split from the outset and avoid the need to make later adjustments.

Where an intermediate supplier is purchasing face value vouchers from the issuer who takes on the obligation to accept them, and is not required to account for VAT until the voucher is redeemed, the intermediate supplier may treat the amount of VAT that will be due on the supply as input tax at the time the purchase is made.

Information regarding any split in liability can only be provided by the issuer who redeems the vouchers. In order to avoid the need to track individual vouchers, redeemers can base adjustment figures on retail scheme percentages or other global calculations, providing the result is fair and reasonable. If the redeemer chooses to make this information available to intermediate suppliers, they may include the percentage split on any VAT invoice they issue to an intermediate supplier. This split should be quoted on any further VAT invoices issued by intermediate suppliers in the supply chain.

(VAT Information Sheet 3/03, para 12; VAT Information Sheet 12/03, para 10).

Invoicing. Issuers of face value vouchers, which are not credit vouchers (see (*a*) above), who redeem them for goods or services must issue a full VAT invoice if the vouchers are sold to a VAT-registered intermediate supplier. As the issuer who redeems the voucher does not need to account for VAT until the voucher is redeemed, HMRC suggest that the invoice is annotated with the words: 'The issuer of the voucher will account for output tax under the face value voucher provisions in Schedule 10A VAT Act 1994'.

Intermediate suppliers of face value vouchers, which are not credit vouchers (see (*a*) above), must account for VAT on the sale of the vouchers at the time the vouchers are sold. They must issue a full VAT invoice to any further intermediate supplier in the supply chain. They can reclaim input tax on the purchase of the vouchers (see above) and the evidence for this is the VAT invoice received from their supplier.

(VAT Information Sheet 12/03, para 10).

Treatment of sales of face value vouchers by an intermediate supplier using a retail scheme. Whether an intermediate supplier under (*d*) above can include sales of face value vouchers within its retail scheme depends on the retail scheme used.

- Under the Point of Sale scheme, sales of face value vouchers should be included in daily gross takings at the appropriate rate of VAT.
- Under an apportionment scheme, output tax on the sale of vouchers should be accounted for outside the retail scheme.
- Under a direct calculation scheme, intermediate suppliers may be able to include the sale of vouchers depending on the minority goods they mark up and the rate of VAT due when the vouchers are redeemed. See 60.17 and 60.18 RETAIL SCHEMES.
- Intermediate suppliers using a bespoke scheme must agree with HMRC a fair and reasonable method for accounting for output tax on the sale of face value vouchers.

(VAT Information Sheet 12/03, para 11).

Top-up cards with no face value. Top-up vouchers and cards (eg telephone cards which allow the customer to add credit to their account) share many similarities to face value vouchers and are now treated in the same manner as face value vouchers. Therefore, issuers of top-up cards who redeem them for goods or services can account for VAT when the top-up is redeemed against goods or services. (VAT Information Sheet 3/03, para 10). See Business Brief 29/03 for VAT treatment of phone cards supplied to a UK distributor by an issuer in another EC country.

Face value vouchers given away for no consideration. Where face value vouchers are purchased by businesses in order to be given away for no consideration, (eg to employees as 'perks' or under a promotions scheme), the VAT incurred is claimable as input tax (subject to the normal rules). However, output tax is due under *SI 1993/1507* at the time the vouchers are given away (see 47.7 OUTPUT TAX). The sum due as output tax will be equal to the sum treated as input tax. (VAT Information Sheet 12/03, para 14).

(3) **Face value vouchers issued for a payment before 9 April 2003**

No VAT was due on the sale of face value vouchers unless sold for an amount exceeding the face value (in which case VAT is due on the excess). (VAT Notice 700/7/02, para 5.7).

If a customer making a specified purchase also received a gift voucher, the supply of the goods and voucher were treated as a multiple supply. VAT was due on that proportion of the payment which relates to the goods. The normal rules above applied to the proportion relating to the gift voucher and the rules in 67.12 below applied when the voucher was redeemed.

This did not apply to face value vouchers given in exchange for points (or stamps) that were redeemed by a customer within the terms of a points scheme. Although the exchange was ignored for VAT purposes, if the redemption vouchers were the supplier's own exclusive vouchers, then they were treated as discount vouchers as under 67.10 above. If the vouchers had been bought in from third parties (with whom they were redeemable), there are no further VAT implications for the supplier.

(VAT Notice 700/7/02, para 5.7).

Electronic face value vouchers. UK VAT law on face vouchers did not apply to electronic face vouchers so that, in principle, VAT was due when electronic face vouchers were sold and when they were redeemed, with a VAT adjustment having to be made after redemption to avoid double taxation. However, in the interests of equity and to avoid distortion of competition, with effect from 8 March 2001, by extra-statutory concession, electronic face vouchers could be treated in the same way as their tangible counterparts provided such treatment did not give rise to tax avoidance.

Top-up cards. Where a card could be topped up after its initial purchase (eg telephone cards which allowed the customer to add credit to their account), although no VAT was due on the original sale of the card for its face value, any top-up was not part of the original sale of the face value voucher and subject to VAT in the normal way.

(VAT Notice 48, ESC 3.32; Business Brief 5/01).

67.12 Redemption of face value vouchers

See 67.11 above for the definition of a '*face value voucher*'.

(1) Face value vouchers issued free

Where the vouchers are redeemed for goods or services

- without any payment, the VAT must be accounted for on the gift of goods or services as in 67.2 above; and
- with a payment or non-monetary consideration, VAT must be accounted for on the total amount received, including the value of any non-monetary consideration (see 67.3 above).

(VAT Notice 700/7/02, para 5.8).

(2) Face value vouchers issued for a payment

On redemption of the face value voucher for goods or services, its face value is the consideration for payment and the value for VAT purpose.

However, where the business has evidence to prove that a particular voucher was originally sold at below face value, the discounted amount can be used. This follows the decision in *Argos Distributors Ltd v C & E Commrs, CJEC [1996] STC 1359 (TVC 21.162)*. Argos operated a voucher scheme. The vouchers had a face value printed on them and customers could use the voucher to obtain goods up to the face value in Argos's showrooms. Argos also sold the vouchers either at face value or at a discounted price to other traders who could either distribute them freely to members of staff or resell them to the public at up to face value. The CJEC held that *EC Sixth Directive, Art 11*(*a*)(*1*)(*a*) was to be taken to mean that, where all or part of the consideration for a supply was represented by a face value voucher, the taxable amount attributable to the voucher is the money obtained by the supplier of the goods from the sale of the voucher (and not its face value). The court, however, stressed that the supplier was responsible for establishing the actual sale price of the voucher at the time of its redemption. HMRC accept that on redemption of vouchers by a VAT-registered customer, Argos and businesses operating similar schemes, can account for VAT on their discounted price provided, at the time of redemption, it can

- identify the price at which vouchers were sold; and
- issue accurate VAT invoices showing the VAT due on the discounted amount.

If a business cannot meet the above conditions on redemption of vouchers by VAT-registered businesses, VAT must be accounted for on the full face value of the vouchers.

(VAT Notice 700/7/02, para 5.7).

67.13 **Treatment of coupons and vouchers under retail schemes**

The VAT treatment under a retail scheme depends upon whether the promotion is funded solely by the retailer or by (or together with) a third party such as the manufacturer.

Discount vouchers. Where discount vouchers are taken as part payment, only the money received from the customer should be included in daily gross takings. If the retailer subsequently receives further payment for the voucher from another source, this payment must be included in daily gross takings. Strictly speaking, the retailer should account for this further payment in the period the goods are supplied. However, by concession, the retailer may account for such contributions in the period they are received.

Any charges by the retailer to the manufacturer for handling the vouchers is payment for an exempt supply and must be excluded from daily gross takings.

Vouchers—general. The following provisions apply to vouchers issued with no value/amounts and which are redeemable for whole items.

- *Vouchers issued by the retailer to customers making a specific purchase or purchases.* No VAT is due upon issue and no further VAT is due when the voucher is used by the customer to obtain the reward goods. Under Apportionment Scheme 2 and Direct Calculation Schemes 1 and 2, records of expected selling prices must be adjusted for the reward goods.
- *Vouchers issued freely by the retailer*. No VAT is due upon issue. When redeemed for goods, the rules in 69.2 above apply. See 60.9(4) RETAIL SCHEMES for the scheme adjustments where goods from normal stock are supplied as gifts.
- *Vouchers issued by another person (eg a manufacturer) but redeemed by the retailer.* These are likely to be subject to the terms and conditions of that person's promotion. For example, if the retailer is given certain stocks to give away on behalf of that person, these stocks must not be included in the retail scheme calculations.

See 60.9(30) RETAIL SCHEMES for sale of discount vouchers.

If such vouchers are redeemed for cash, the cash payment is outside the scope of VAT and daily gross takings must not be altered for the cash paid.

(VAT Notice 727/3/02, paras 7.1–7.5; VAT Notice 727/4/02, paras 8.1–8.4; VAT Notice 727/5/02, paras 7.1–7.4, all of which have the force of law).

67.14 Businesses selling vouchers

A business that sells vouchers to other businesses and can never receive the final benefit shown on the voucher is viewed for VAT purposes as selling a promotion scheme rather than selling vouchers. This sale is a supply of services liable to VAT at the standard rate.

All sales of holiday vouchers by a promoter (or other companies specialising in such schemes) are liable to VAT at the standard rate. The VAT charged is input tax for the purchaser subject to the normal rules. If vouchers bear a face value, the sale of these will also normally be taxable as the value shown is effectively only the value of a discount allowable, since the purchaser cannot receive goods or services without making a further payment. Also, the sale of booklets containing vouchers that can be exchanged for discounted accommodation in selected hotels in the UK is a single supply liable to VAT at the standard rate. The booklets in which such vouchers are usually issued are incidental to the supply of vouchers and not viewed as a zero-rated booklet for VAT purposes.

(VAT Notice 700/7/02, para 5.9).

67.15 MANUFACTURERS' PROMOTION SCHEMES AIMED AT THE TRADE

Vouchers and dealer loader schemes. Manufacturers often run promotions to encourage greater purchases of their 'premium' goods, ie those goods normally sold in day-to-day trading. Common promotions may be of three different types.

(*a*) **The issue of vouchers, or a 'proof of purchase'** with the sale of the premium trade goods which can be redeemed later for further goods. Under this type of promotion, the redemption goods are provided for no consideration and must be treated as gifts as in 67.2 above.

(*b*) **Dealer loader schemes**. These are schemes where rewards are offered on condition that a single trade order of a specified size is made. In such cases, HMRC accept in principle that the manufacturer, in costing the promotion, would have allowed for the cost of the redemption goods within the normal selling price of those 'premium' goods. No further VAT is due on the reward goods.

(*c*) **Trade orders made over a period of time**. Where rewards are offered on condition that trade orders are placed over a set period of time to a given level, the rewards are being provided for no consideration. If the rewards are goods which cost the manufacturer more than £50 or form part of a series or succession to the same customer, VAT is due on a cost value. Otherwise, no VAT is due. However, as a concession, HMRC will accept that these rewards may be treated as part of a multiple supply if

- the rewards are of a kind to be used in the recipient's business;
- the rewards are not intended for the personal use of the person receiving them; and
- the rewards appear on the final qualifying invoice, ie at the point at which the customer qualifies for the reward.

The same rules also apply where the manufacturer supplies the reward goods, but premium supplies may have gone via a wholesaler, for example

- the manufacturer supplies the reward direct to the customer;

- the wholesaler supplies the reward on behalf of the manufacturer from their own stock where the manufacturer either reimburses the wholesaler or replaces stock; or
- the wholesaler supplies the reward from stock provided for this purpose by the manufacturer.

(VAT Notice 700/7/02, para 6.1).

Retrospective discounts. Where a discount is given on condition that the customer reaches a target purchase level within a set time, the normal procedure would be to issue a credit note for the amount of the discount if the target is achieved. See 40.15 INVOICES.

If, on the other hand, the customer is given goods to the value of the discount earned, the discount has been used to pay for the additional goods supplied. Normally, to avoid accounting for further VAT, a credit note would have to be issued to reflect the reduced value of the qualifying supplies and an invoice raised for the reward goods showing an equal amount of VAT. Instead, provided

- all the goods are liable to VAT at the same rate,
- the reward goods are supplied to the same person and for business purposes,
- no VAT credit note is issued, and
- records are kept to satisfy HMRC of a proper audit trail,

a 'no charge' invoice can be issued without VAT for the additional goods as this achieves the same result.

(VAT Notice 700/7/02, para 6.6).

Goods or 'points' given by manufacturers to a customers' employees. Goods given free of charge by a manufacturer to customers' employees as a reward for promoting or selling goods are free supplies for no consideration. Similar VAT treatment applies where customers' employees accumulate voucher 'points' for selling a manufacturer's goods and the points are redeemable for goods. See 67.2 above. Any VAT incurred by the manufacturer on the goods is deductible (subject to the normal rules). (VAT Notice 700/7/02, paras 6.7, 6.8).

'Free' hire schemes for vending machines. See 47.8(30) OUTPUT TAX.

67.16 MANUFACTURERS' PROMOTION SCHEMES AIMED AT THE PUBLIC

Goods given away through a retailer. Where

- the public buy from a retailer and send a proof of purchase to the manufacturer to receive further goods (from the manufacturer), or coupons are included by the manufacturer inside the product or as part of the packaging and the coupons are collected and redeemed later for goods, or
- retailers of a manufacturer's products act as its agents in giving reward goods to those customers making qualifying purchases and where the manufacturer has provided the reward goods to the retailer (for no consideration) specifically for this purpose,

the manufacturer is providing the redemption/reward goods for no consideration and must account for VAT as in 67.2 above.

(VAT Notice 700/7/02, para 7.1).

Manufacturers issuing money-off coupons to the public. If a manufacturer issues a money-off coupon which is redeemable

- by the customer with the retailer at the amount stated on the coupon,
- at the manufacturer's expense,
- as part of a sales promotion where the coupon is to be accepted by the retailer in part payment for a specified item of goods,
- where the manufacturer has sold the specified item to the retailer at the original price, and
- where the retailer takes the coupon from the customer on sale of the specified item, presents it to the manufacturer and is paid the stated amount,

the manufacturer can reduce his taxable amount by the value of the voucher which is actually refunded. This does not alter the amount shown on the invoice originally issued. The retailer's position on receipt of money is covered in 67.9 above.

(VAT Notice 700/7/02, para 7.2).

'Points schemes'. Some businesses run promotion schemes that involve issuing points that they will subsequently redeem for good or services. They may allow other businesses to participate in their scheme by allowing them to issue redeeming businesses' points. If the redeeming businesses make a charge to the participant businesses, HMRC consider this to be payment for the right to participate in the redeeming business's promotions scheme. This is subject to VAT at the standard rate.

See 67.11 above for where points are exchanged for face value vouchers.

If a points scheme allows customers to donate points to schools or other institutions which can redeem the points with the manufacturer for goods (eg computer equipment) the manufacturer should account for the VAT as in 67.2 above.

(VAT Notice 700/7/02, para 7.3).

Goods given as prizes for competitions. If a manufacturer provides products as prizes for competitions, (eg in magazines, etc), any benefit received in exchange for the goods (eg a free advertisement in the magazine), is likely to constitute a barter transaction (see 67.3 above). The VAT due on the supply of the manufacturer's product is the same as it would be on the normal selling price of the product if there were no barter. However, if the prize provided is not something that the manufacturer ordinarily makes or sells, its value will be the actual cost incurred in providing the item. The magazine publisher would also then be making a supply of services to the manufacturer upon which VAT should be charged.

Where there is no exchange of benefits, there is no barter and VAT is due on a cost value subject to the normal business gift rules in 67.2 above.

(VAT Notice 700/7/02, para 7.4).

Cashback schemes. These are normally manufacturers' schemes aimed at the public but where goods are supplied through wholesalers and/or retailers. The cashback is a refund of money from the manufacturer directly to the final consumer if the consumer sends a proof of purchase, etc to the manufacturer. In these circumstances, the manufacturer can reduce his 'taxable amount', provided it has charged and accounted for UK VAT on the original supply to the wholesaler or retailer. This does not affect the value of its original supply to the wholesaler/retailer. No credit notes are to be issued and the wholesaler/retailer's input tax is unaffected. There is simply a reduction of output tax to be reflected in the manufacturers' VAT account. Where a VAT-registered trader receives a cashback, this reduces the taxable value of its purchase and it must reduce its input tax accordingly. (VAT Notice 700/7/02, para 7.5).

Newspaper promotions. If a manufacturer runs a promotion with a newspaper company whereby vouchers are printed in the newspaper along with the promotion of its product, and the public have to collect the vouchers in order to get reward goods or services, the goods/services are liable to VAT and the manufacturer should account for the VAT as in 67.2 above. If the vouchers offer a discount, the normal rules on redeeming vouchers in 67.9 above must be applied. (VAT Notice 700/7/02, para 7.6).

Goods given to publishers for use as magazine inserts. There are various VAT implications depending upon the exact nature of the particular circumstances.

- Where the goods are supplied to the publishers for a monetary consideration, VAT must be charged. When the goods are sold by the retailer with the magazine, there is normally a multiple supply which may have to be apportioned. See 47.3 OUTPUT TAX.
- Where the goods are supplied to the publisher for no consideration (monetary or otherwise) VAT is due as under 67.2 above.
- Where the goods are supplied to the publisher without monetary consideration but under a barter arrangement whereby non-monetary consideration is received (eg an advertising benefit), VAT is normally due on the value of the goods (see 67.3 above). Where the goods are not normally made or sold by the manufacturer, the value will be the cost incurred in acquiring them. However, where any non-monetary consideration is minimal, it may be ignored and VAT is then due on cost as above.
- Where the goods are not supplied to the publisher but both the publisher and newsagent act purely as agent for the manufacturer in distributing products (eg free goods for the retail customer), there is no supply of the free goods to the publisher and the free supply is therefore by the manufacturer to the public. In these circumstances, the business gift rules in 67.2 above apply. See also 47.8(23) OUTPUT TAX for free samples.

(VAT Notice 700/7/02, para 7.7).

67.17 RETAIL DISCOUNT SCHEMES

Discounts are normally treated as reductions in the consideration given so that VAT is due on the discounted price actually paid. See 69.24 VALUATION for a general consideration of discounts. The following are examples of schemes which generally fall to be treated in this way.

- **Deferred discount scheme**. This entitles a shareholder to a discount off the purchase price of goods. The discount is not deducted from the customer's payment but accumulated and paid out annually. Until the discount is paid to the customer it is to be treated as consideration for the goods supplied.
- **Special events**. In-store credit card holders are invited to preview sales and allowed special discounts, no payment usually being made by the credit company to the retailer. Alternatively, other selected groups may be offered discounts, again with no consideration being received from any other source.
- **'We will pay your VAT'**.

- **Graded promotions**. Graded discount vouchers are given which offer a percentage reduction which increases with the value of the purchases made.

(VAT Notice 700/7/02, paras 8.2, 8.4–8.6).

'Store card' discount schemes. A customer spends a minimum amount on any one purchase using a store card. This entitles the customer to a set amount of credit to be applied to their credit card account. There is no reimbursement by the retailer to the credit card company and the credit card company and retailer may, or may not, be in the same VAT group. If

- the retailer and credit card company are within the same VAT group, the group should only account for VAT on the discounted amount; and
- the retailer and credit card company are not in the same VAT group, the goods are sold by the retailer at their full value and VAT is due on this amount.

(VAT Notice 700/7/02, para 8.1).

Lottery promotion (scratch cards). Customers who purchase certain items (at normal price) are given a scratch card (for no extra charge) on which certain symbols can be scratched off revealing the details of a prize. Alternatively, there may be no purchasing requirement.

- Where the prize is a free gift of goods, these are supplies for no consideration and the rules set out in 67.2 above apply.
- Where the prize is discount vouchers for use against future purchases, these are normally evidence of entitlement to a discount and, on redemption, the rules set out in 67.9 above apply.
- Where the prize is gift vouchers, the voucher has not been issued for a consideration and on redemption the rules in 67.11 above apply.

(VAT Notice 700/7/02, para 8.3).

Minimum or false value trade-ins. These are promotions in which the customer is allowed either a minimum or a pre-determined (fixed) value for goods taken in part exchange, regardless of the condition of the exchange article (eg £50 for a customer's old cooker when buying a new model). The selling price of the goods should be treated as the full amount chargeable before any deductions for part exchange allowances. The purchase price of the goods taken in part exchange is the full amount allowed to the customer and it is this figure that should be used as the purchase price of the goods if sold under the second-hand scheme.

Where, however, it is clear that there is no barter and the promotion is purely for promotional purposes (eg '£1 off a tin of paint if you bring in an old tin') this can be treated as a discount.

(VAT Notice 700/7/02, para 8.7).

67.18 EMPLOYEE AWARDS

If an employer wishes to reward employees exceeding sales levels, etc by giving gifts of goods or services (eg free theatre tickets, restaurant meals or hotel accommodation), HMRC do not regard the services provided by the employees in return as non-monetary consideration (see 67.3 above). Input tax is deductible subject to the normal rules and output tax may be due under the rules for gifts in 67.2 above.

If the reward for the employee extends to non-employees (eg a spouse) the rules for the employee are as above but input tax in respect of non-employees may be blocked under the BUSINESS ENTERTAINMENT (9) provisions.

(VAT Notice 700/7/02, para 2.5).

68 Transport and Freight

Cross-references. See 23.31 EUROPEAN COMMUNITY: SINGLE MARKET for new means of transport; 25.7 EXPORTS for the supply or hiring of freight containers; 45 MOTOR CARS.

De Voil Indirect Tax Service. See V4.251.

The contents of this chapter are as follows.

68.1 ZERO-RATED SUPPLIES OF SHIPS

The supply of any 'qualifying ship' is zero-rated. A '*qualifying ship*' is any ship which is

(*a*) of a gross tonnage of not less than 15 tons; and

(*b*) neither designed nor adapted for use for recreation or pleasure.

[*VATA 1994, Sch 8 Group 8 Item 1 and Note A1; SI 1995/3039*].

'*Ship*' includes a submarine, hovercraft (see below), light vessel, fire float, dredger, barge or lighter, a mobile floating dock or crane and an offshore oil or gas installation used in the underwater exploitation or exploration of oil and gas resources, which is designed to be moved from place to place. *Not included* are

- fixed oil and gas installations (even though they might be transported to a site as a floating structure); and
- vessels which are permanently moored (eg as attractions) *and* not readily capable of navigation.

The sale of a hull does not qualify for zero-rating. A ship becomes a 'qualifying ship' from the time when it is seaworthy or, if it is not designed to go to sea, when it is fit to navigate the waterways for which it is designed (*QED Marine (VTD 17336) (TVC 64.6)*).

As a result of (*b*) above, private pleasure boats or yachts are not zero-rated even if supplied for residential or business purposes (eg sail training). See also *Callison (VTD 810) (TVC 64.1)* and *obiter dicta* in *Hamann v Finanzamt Hamburg-Eimsbuttel, CJEC 1989, [1991] STC 193 (TVC 21.154)*. Cruise ships are zero-rated provided they satisfy (*a*) above and are supplied for use in the business of providing recreational or pleasure cruises for fare-paying passengers. There is a specific zero-rating relief for houseboats without engines (see 42.35 LAND AND BUILDINGS). In *DG Everett; The London Tideway Harbour Co Ltd (VTD 11736) (TVC 64.3)*, houseboats with engines which were used as living accommodation were held to be zero-rated provided they satisfied the conditions in (*a*) above. The barges had not been originally designed for recreation or pleasure and it stretched the ordinary meaning of the words to say that it included a home or place of permanent habitation.

Gross tonnage is that ascertained under the *Merchant Shipping Acts*. If not so ascertained, it is determined, for VAT purposes only, by the formula

$L \times B \times D \times 0.235$

where

L = length;
B = extreme breadth; and
D = depth measured amidships
(all measurements being in metres)

(See VAT Notice 744C, Appendix A for further details).

Hovercraft. All hovercraft are zero-rated, irrespective of gross tonnage, unless designed or adapted for use for recreation or pleasure.

(VAT Notice 744C, paras 2.8, 2.9).

68.2 ZERO-RATED SUPPLIES OF AIRCRAFT

The supply of any 'qualifying aircraft' is zero-rated. A '*qualifying aircraft*' is any aircraft which is

- of a weight of not less than 8,000 kilogrammes; and
- neither designed nor adapted for use for recreation or pleasure.

[*VATA 1994, Sch 8 Group 8 Item 2 and Note A1; SI 1995/3039*].

'*Aircraft*' includes aeroplanes (civil and military), helicopters and airships but does not include space craft and satellites.

Weight is the authorised maximum take-off weight specified in the certificate of airworthiness or, for military aircraft, shown in the documents issued by the Ministry of Defence.

(VAT Notice 744C, paras 2.14, 2.15).

68.3 SHIPS AND AIRCRAFT — OTHER ZERO-RATED SUPPLIES

In addition to the supply of certain ships or aircraft (see 68.1 and 68.2 above) various other supplies and services in connection with such craft may also be zero-rated.

Parts and equipment. Zero-rating applies to

(*a*) the supply of parts and equipment, of a kind ordinarily installed or incorporated in, and to be installed or incorporated in, the propulsion, navigation or communication systems or general structure of a qualifying ship (see 68.1 above) or a qualifying aircraft (see 68.2 above); and

(*b*) the supply of life jackets, life rafts, smoke hoods and similar safety equipment for use in a qualifying ship or aircraft.

The letting on hire of goods within (*a*) or (*b*) above is also zero-rated.

Any supply to a Government department is excluded from zero-rating unless *either* the supply is in the course or furtherance of a business carried on by the department *or* the parts and equipment are to be installed or incorporated in ships or aircraft used for the purpose of providing rescue or assistance at sea.

[*VATA 1994, Sch 8 Group 8 Items 2A, 2B and Notes A1, 2 and 2A; SI 1995/3039*].

Parts and equipment include

- Anchors
- Catering and laundering equipment (industrial)
- Communications equipment used for the operation of the ship or aircraft
- Components to be fitted inside a ship or aircraft (eg electrical and navigation equipment, and video and similar entertainment equipment incorporated into airline seats)
- Cranes
- 'Expendable' parts and 'rotable' components used by the aircraft industry
- Fishing nets and equipment
- Fixed equipment to control, operate or launch weapons
- Laundering equipment (industrial)
- Lifeboats and life rafts
- Nuts, bolts, hoses, oil seals and rivets (referred to as 'consumables' by the aircraft industry)
- Propellers and rudders
- Pumps
- Radar and navigation equipment
- Safety equipment (eg escape chutes, life jackets, smoke hoods and oxygen masks)
- Sanitary fixtures
- Winches

Parts and equipment exclude

- Aircraft ground equipment
- Binoculars
- Bulk materials (eg adhesives, chemicals, fabrics, inhibitors, metals, oils, paints, solvents and thinners)
- Catering and laundering equipment (domestic)
- Crockery and cutlery
- Diving equipment
- Flight simulators or their parts

- Furniture (unfixed) and soft furnishings
- Missiles, shells, etc.
- Raw materials (eg fibre board, plastics, specialist metals)
- Ship's stores
- Telephones and televisions
- Tooling and equipment used for manufacturing parts or equipment
- Tools
- Underwater cameras
- Video tapes, video games and similar entertainment equipment

Evidence for zero-rating. Normal commercial documentation is sufficient provided the supplier is satisfied that the parts, etc qualify for zero-rating. If uncertain (eg because the parts could be used on a qualifying or non-qualifying ship or because the customer is a government department) the supplier should obtain an undertaking from the customer that the parts etc qualify. See Notice 744C, Appendix B for a suggested format.

(VAT Notice 744C, paras 4.3, 4.4, 4.6).

68.4 **Repairs and maintenance**

The repair or maintenance of a qualifying ship (see 68.1 above) or a qualifying aircraft (see 68.2 above) is zero-rated. [*VATA 1994, Sch 8 Group 8 Items 1, 2; SI 1995/3039*].

Maintenance includes testing of parts and components, cleaning, fumigation and ship's laundry (provided the articles are not personal to the crew or passengers). Parts, components and materials provided by the supplier of the repairs and maintenance are regarded as part of the zero-rated work.

Repairs and maintenance of parts and equipment can also be zero-rated provided

(*a*) in the case of a ship

- the repair is carried out on board; or
- the part or component is removed for repair and is replaced in the same ship; and

(*b*) in the case of an aircraft

- the repair is carried out on board; or
- the part or component is removed for repair and is replaced in the same aircraft; or
- following the repair or maintenance, the parts are returned to be held in stock for future use as spares in qualifying aircraft; or
- if they are unserviceable parts and equipment, they are exchanged for identical parts which have themselves been reconditioned, repaired or maintained.

Subcontracted services supplied in respect of repair and maintenance of a qualifying ship or aircraft can similarly be zero-rated. The subcontractor is advised to obtain evidence to substantiate zero-rating from the main contractor.

(VAT Notice 744C, paras 2.16, 3.1, 3.2).

68.5 Modifications and conversions

The modification or conversion of any qualifying ship (see 68.1 above) or qualifying aircraft (see 68.2 above) is zero-rated provided that, when so modified or converted, it will remain a qualifying ship or aircraft. [*VATA 1994, Sch 8 Group 8 Items 1 and 2; SI 1995/3039*]. Included are structural alterations and updating or improving serviceable equipment.

Sub-contracted services supplied in respect of modification or conversion of a qualifying ship or aircraft can similarly be zero-rated. The subcontractor is advised to obtain evidence to substantiate zero-rating from the main contractor.

(VAT Notice 744C, paras 2.16, 3.3).

Ship design services supplied in the UK are zero-rated as integral to the supply, modification or conversion of a qualifying ship only where a supplier specifically contracts with a customer to design *and* supply, modify or convert a qualifying ship. In other circumstances, design services are standard-rated.

68.6 Air navigation services

The supply of 'air navigation services' are zero-rated when

- provided for qualifying aircraft (see 68.2 above); or
- supplied to a person who receives the supply for the purposes of a business carried on by him and who belongs outside the UK (whether or not provided for qualifying aircraft).

'*Air navigation services*' have the same meaning as in *Civil Aviation Act 1982, s 105(1)*, ie they include information, directions and other facilities furnished, issued or provided in connection with the navigation or movement of aircraft, and include the control of movement of vehicles in any part of an aerodrome used for the movement of aircraft.

[*VATA 1994, Sch 8 Group 8 Items 6A, 11(b), Notes 6A and 7; SI 1995/653; SI 1995/3039*].

Air navigation services are largely provided by the Civil Aviation Authority which has been granted taxable status for its supply of these services. (Business Brief 20/94).

68.7 Charter services

The supply of services under the charter of a qualifying ship (see 68.1 above) or a qualifying aircraft (see 68.2 above) is zero-rated unless those services consist wholly of any one or more of

- the transport of passengers,
- accommodation,
- entertainment, or
- education,

being services wholly performed in the UK. [*VATA 1994, Sch 8 Group 8 Items 1, 2 and Note 1; SI 1995/3039*].

The correct VAT treatment of supplies of ships and aircraft under charter can cause difficulties. The term 'charter' is used to describe several different types of supply (including freight or passenger transport) and is also used in slightly different ways in respect of ships and aircraft. Also, there is a complex interaction between the rules on both place of supply and liability, of charter, hire, passenger transport and freight transport services.

Qualifying ships

Formal charters. The supply of a whole ship *with crew* under a written charter (normally referred to as a 'charter party' contract) is treated as a charter for place of supply and liability purposes. The place of supply is where the supplier belongs.

The supply of a whole ship *without crew* under a written charter (often referred to as a 'bareboat' charter) is treated as a hire of that ship for place of supply and liability purposes. The place of supply is where the supplier belongs but subject to the 'use and enjoyment' rules (see 64.30 SUPPLY).

Other charters. The place of supply and liability of

- a supply of a whole ship *with crew* but not under a written charter, or
- the supply of part of the cargo space or seating capacity in any ship

is usually determined according to the normal rules and exclusions for passenger transport (see 68.14 below) or, as the case may be, freight transport (see 68.24 below).

The supply of a whole ship *without crew* and not under a written charter is treated as a hire of that ship for place of supply and liability purposes. The place of supply is where the supplier belongs but subject to the 'use and enjoyment' rules (see 64.30 SUPPLY).

Liability

- The supply in the UK of a whole qualifying ship with crew under a written charter is normally zero-rated under *VATA 1994, Sch 8 Group 8 Item 1* above. Where one of the above exclusion applies, although excluded from zero-rating under *item 1* such a charter may qualify for zero-rating as domestic passenger transport under *VATA 1994, Sch 8 Group 8 Item 4* (see 68.16 below).
- The supply in the UK of a whole qualifying ship without crew, whether under a written charter or not, is zero-rated as the letting on hire of a ship (see 68.8 below).

Yachts

HMRC do not consider yachts to be qualifying ships in any circumstances, since they are designed for recreation and pleasure. Therefore, neither formal written charters for yachts with crew, informal charters without a written agreement, or hire of a yacht without crew can qualify for zero-rating under *Item 1* above. However, where a yacht is chartered with crew for the transport of passengers (eg a supply on charter by a yacht owner or operator to a holiday maker for a holiday cruise), HMRC accept that the supply amounts to a supply of passenger transport services and can qualify for relief. The place of supply and liability of yacht charters is therefore as follows.

- The place of supply of a yacht supplied with crew, for the transport of passengers (including holiday cruises), whether on formal written charter or not, is where the transport of passengers takes place. Where the place of supply is in the UK, the supply is

(i) zero-rated under 68.16(*a*) below if the yacht is designed or adapted to carry twelve or more passengers, including crew;

(ii) zero-rated under 68.14(*d*) below, irrespective of the carrying capacity of the yacht, if transporting passengers from a place within to a place outside the UK or vice-versa; and

(iii) standard-rated in all other cases.

- The supply of a yacht supplied without crew, whether on formal written charter or not, is treated as the hire of a means of transport and is supplied where the supplier belongs subject to the 'use and enjoyment' rules (see 64.30 SUPPLY). Where the place of supply is in the UK, the supply is standard-rated.

In either case, if the supply falls outside the UK, it is outside the scope of UK VAT.

Other non-qualifying ships

The same principles apply as for yachts. Their supply on charter cannot be zero-rated under *Item 1* above and the place of supply and liability will depend on the nature of the services supplied.

Aircraft

Charters. Aircraft charters are categorised as follows.

- 'Dry' charters (also known as dry leases or bare hull leases) which are effectively the hire of aircraft without crew by the owner to the charterer, with the crew provided by the charterer. A 'dry' charter is treated as the hire of a means of transport. The place of supply is where the supplier belongs subject to the 'use and enjoyment' rules (see 64.30 SUPPLY).
- 'Wet' charters (also known as wet leases) where the charterer obtains the use of the aircraft, but the crew, and sometimes other operating requirements such as fuel, are provided by the owner. They can be either 'flight' charters for specifically identified flights, or 'time' charters for specified periods of time. They are often supplied under terms known as 'ACMI', where the owner provides an 'aircraft, crew, maintenance and insurance' and the charterer pays other costs. See Internal Guidance V1–7, Chapter 8 para 11.6 for HMRC guidelines on the borderline between the supply of a qualifying aircraft under a 'wet' charter and the supply of freight transport services.

  A 'wet' charter is generally treated as a supply of an aircraft on charter and the place of supply is where the supplier belongs. However,

  (i) if a wet charter is supplied for the transport of passengers, the place of supply rules for passenger transport apply; and

  (ii) if a non-qualifying aircraft is supplied on a wet charter for purposes of freight transport, the place of supply rules for freight transport apply.

  See 64.29 SUPPLY.

Liability.

- The supply in the UK of a qualifying aircraft under dry charter is zero-rated under 68.8 below.
- The supply in the UK of a qualifying aircraft under a wet charter is zero-rated under *VATA 1994, Sch 8 Group 8 Item 2* above. Where one of the above

exclusion applies, although excluded from zero-rating under *item 2*, the wet charter of an aircraft for purposes of passenger transport can still qualify for zero-rating under 68.16(*a*) below if the aircraft is designed or adapted to carry twelve or more passengers or under 68.16(*d*) below irrespective of carrying capacity if the transport of passengers is from a place within to a place outside the UK or vice versa. However, supplies of recreational passenger transport are excluded from zero-rating and are standard-rated (see 68.18 below).

- The supply in the UK of a non-qualifying aircraft under dry charter is standard-rated.
- The supply in the UK of a non-qualifying aircraft under a wet charter is standard-rated unless
  - (i) the supply amounts to passenger transport services, in which case zero-rating applies under 68.16 below subject to the usual conditions; or
  - (ii) the supply is for the purposes of freight transport, in which case zero-rating under 68.27 below may apply if goods are being transported from a place within to a place outside the EC, or vice versa.

(Internal Guidance V1–7, Chapter 8, para 11.6).

68.8 **Letting on hire**

The letting on hire of a qualifying ship (see 68.1 above) or a qualifying aircraft (see 68.2 above) is zero-rated. [*VATA 1994, Sch 8 Group 8 Items 1, 2 and Note 2; SI 1995/3039*].

Letting on hire in this context means a supply without crew or pilot in which the customer takes possession of, and has exclusive use of, the ship or aircraft to operate himself. See 64.30 SUPPLY for the place of supply of the letting on hire of transport for use outside the EC. Subject to this, any other letting or hire of a ship or aircraft is standard-rated. (VAT Notice 744C, para 2.4).

68.9 **Handling services**

Any services provided for the handling of ships or aircraft in a 'port', 'customs and excise airport' or outside the UK are zero-rated when

- provided for qualifying ships (see 68.1 above) or qualifying aircraft (see 68.2 above); or
- supplied to a person who receives the supply for the purposes of a business carried on by him and who belongs outside the UK (whether or not provided for qualifying ships and aircraft).

The letting on hire of goods is specifically excluded.

'*Port*' means any port appointed for customs purposes and includes all seaports in the UK. At a seaport the port limits include all territorial waters but do not normally extend inland beyond the waterway of the port.

'*Customs and excise airport*' means an airport designated for the landing or departure of aircraft for the purposes of the *Customs and Excise Acts* by an Order in Council made pursuant to *Civil Aviation Act 1982, s 60*. The limit of such an airport is normally the boundary of the airport itself. The designated Customs airports are Aberdeen (Dyce), Belfast (Aldergrove), Biggin Hill, Birmingham, Blackpool, Bournemouth (Hurn), Bristol, Cambridge, Cardiff, Coventry, East Midlands, Edinburgh, Exeter, Glasgow,

Humberside (Hull), Leeds/Bradford, Liverpool, London City Airport, London Gatwick, London Heathrow, Luton, Lydd, Manchester International, Manston (Kent International), Newcastle, Norwich, Plymouth (Roborough), Prestwick, Shoreham, Southampton, Southend, Stansted, Sumburgh and Teeside.

[*VATA 1994, Sch 8 Group 8 Items 6(a), 11(b), Notes 5-7; SI 1995 No 3039*]. (VAT Notice 744C, Appendix C).

Ship handling includes port and harbour dues, dock and berth charges, conservancy charges (including the provision of local lights, buoys and beacons), graving dock charges, mooring charges, demurrage (where this is a charge for failure to load or discharge a ship within specified time), security and fire services, supply of crew members and the day-to-day management of a ship.

Aircraft handling includes aircraft landing, parking or housing fees, aircraft compass swinging fees, apron services, airport navigation service charges, security and fire services and the supply of crew members.

(VAT Notice 744C, paras 5.1–5.3).

68.10 **Surveys and classification services**

Any service supplied for, or in connection with, the surveying of any ship or aircraft or the classification of any ship or aircraft for the purposes of any register is zero-rated when

- provided in connection with any qualifying ship (see 68.1 above) or qualifying aircraft (see 68.2 above); or
- supplied to a person who receives the supply for the purposes of a business carried on by him and who belongs outside the UK (whether or not provided for qualifying ships and aircraft).

[*VATA 1994, Sch 8 Group 8 Items 9, 11(b) and Note 7; SI 1995/3039*].

Included are classification services performed by Lloyd's and other registers and survey services for aircraft in relation to the certificate of airworthiness. *Not included* are tonnage measurements or surveys of ships for registration or other purposes required by statute to be carried out by the Department of Trade (which are outside the scope of VAT) or services of arranging for the registering of ships for the purposes of the *Merchant Shipping Acts* (which are standard-rated). (VAT Notice 744C, para 7.4).

68.11 **Salvage and towage services**

Salvage and towage services supplied for shipping are zero-rated whatever the type of ship. [*VATA 1994, Sch 8 Group 8 Item 8*]. Shipping in this context includes inland waterway vessels and all floating objects. Zero-rating also covers dock gates, pier and bridge sections and buoys. It does not cover any subsequent repair work carried out (for which see 68.4 above). (VAT Notice 744C, para 7.3).

68.12 **Pilotage**

Pilotage services are zero-rated. [*VATA 1994, Sch 8 Group 8 Item 7*]. This applies to shipping only. (VAT Notice 744C, para 7.2).

68.13 **LIFEBOATS AND SLIPWAYS**

The following supplies are zero-rated.

(*a*) The supply to, and repair or maintenance for, a charity providing rescue or assistance at sea of

- any 'lifeboat';
- carriage equipment designed solely for the launching and recovery of lifeboats;
- tractors for the sole use of the launching and recovery of lifeboats; and
- winches and hauling equipment for the sole use of the recovery of lifeboats.

(*b*) The construction, modification, repair or maintenance for a charity providing rescue or assistance at sea of slipways used solely for the launching and recovery of lifeboats.

(*c*) The supply of spare parts or accessories to a charity providing rescue or assistance at sea for use in or with goods under (*a*) above or slipways within (*b*) above.

(*d*) With effect from 1 April 2002, the supply to a charity providing rescue or assistance at sea of equipment that is to be installed, incorporated or used in a lifeboat and is of a kind ordinarily installed, incorporated or used in a lifeboat.

Included is the letting on hire of qualifying goods.

'*Lifeboat*' means any vessel (whatever the tonnage) used or to be used solely for rescue or assistance at sea.

To qualify for zero-rating the recipient of the supply must, before the supply is made, give the supplier a certificate stating the name and address of the recipient and that the supply is of a description specified in *VATA 1994, Sch 8 Group 8 Item 3*. The supplier must take all reasonable steps to check the validity of the certificate and should consult HMRC if in doubt. Where, however, despite taking such steps, nonetheless the supplier fails to identify an incorrect certificate and in good faith makes the supplies concerned at the zero rate, HMRC will not seek to recover the VAT due from the supplier. (VAT Notice 48, ESC 3.11).

[*VATA 1994, Sch 8 Group 8 Item 3 and Notes 2, 3 and 4; SI 1995/3039; SI 2002/456*].

HMRC accept that any boat used by the RNLI qualifies as a lifeboat. The scope of the term is sufficiently wide to include vessels such as surf rescue craft provided they are capable of carrying persons and have some means of propulsion, eg sails, engines or oars. Craft with the character of surf boards do not qualify.

'Rescue and assistance at sea' covers not only the saving of human life or assisting ships or boats in difficulty but can also include assistance to marine life, eg beached whales. The term does not cover rescue of any kind on canals, rivers, lakes, etc.

HMRC do not stipulate that a boat must possess certain features to be eligible for zero-rating but a large sea rescue boat genuinely intended solely for sea rescue would possess

- navigational equipment;
- radar;
- oxygen resuscitation equipment;
- first aid equipment;

- a prominent indication on both sides that it is a rescue boat;
- a salvage pump;
- a blue flashing beacon; and
- special tow lines and posts.

Smaller craft for surf rescue would be less likely to have these features.

Accessories within (*c*) above include life rafts, life buoys and dinghies.

(Internal Guidance V1–9, paras 10.3–10.6).

68.14 PASSENGER TRANSPORT

De Voil Indirect Tax Service. See V3.189.

Passenger transport services are supplied when a vehicle, ship or aircraft is provided, *together with* a driver or crew, for the carriage of passengers. Incidental services may also be included. Where a vehicle, ship or aircraft is supplied *without* a driver or crew, this is not a supply of passenger transport services, but a means of transport.

To determine the correct VAT treatment of supplies of passenger transport it is necessary to

- decide whether the supply takes place in the UK (see 68.15 below); and if so
- consider whether the supply is zero-rated (see 68.16 below) or standard-rated (see 68.18 below).

Certain supplies of passenger transport cause particular problems because they can be zero-rated or standard-rated depending upon the precise nature of the services offered. See 68.19 below for transport of vehicles on ships, 68.20 below for cruises and 68.21 below for airline passengers' perks.

See 68.23 below for taxis and hire cars.

Bought-in supplies, packages and inclusive tours. Where passenger transport is bought in and re-supplied, either on its own or as part of a package or inclusive tour, VAT must normally be accounted for under the tour operators' margin scheme. Any other travel, hotel and holiday facilities which have been bought in and re-supplied must also be accounted for using the margin scheme. An 'in-house' supply of passenger transport (eg the provision of a driver plus vehicle for passenger transport) does not fall within the scheme and is dealt with in the normal way *unless* it is provided together with other travel and hotel facilities which have been bought in and re-supplied, in which case the 'in-house' transport must be included in the scheme calculation. See 66 TOUR OPERATORS' MARGIN SCHEME for further details.

68.15 Place of supply

Services consisting of the transportation of passengers are treated as supplied in the country where the transportation takes place to the extent that it takes place in that country. [*SI 1992/3121, Art 6*]. As a result, subject to the special rules below, if it takes place

- inside the UK, the supplies are all within the scope of UK VAT;
- outside the UK the supplies are outside the scope of UK VAT (see below);

- both inside and outside the UK, the element that takes place within the UK is within the scope of UK VAT and the element that takes place outside the UK is outside the scope of UK VAT.

In cases where cross-frontier transport is provided on an all-inclusive basis, the total consideration must be allocated on a pro-rata basis having regard to the distance covered (rather than the time spent) in each EC country (*Reisebüro Binder GmbH v Finanzamt Stuttgart-Körperschaften, CJEC 1997, [1998] STC 604 (TVC 21.143)*).

For sea and air passenger transport, provided the means of transport used does not put in or land in another country on the way, any transportation as part of a journey between two points in the same country is treated as taking place wholly inside that country even where it takes place partly outside its territorial jurisdiction. This applies even if the journey is part of a longer journey involving travel to or from another country. [*SI 1992/3121, Art 7*].

> *Example*
>
> A ferry transports passengers from Liverpool to Dublin via the Isle of Man.
>
> The first leg (Liverpool to the Isle of Man) is treated as taking place in the UK but the remaining part of the journey (Isle of Man to Dublin) takes place outside UK territorial waters and is outside the scope of UK VAT.

Pleasure cruises. Any goods or services provided as part of a pleasure cruise are treated as supplied in the same place as the transportation of the passengers and for this purpose a pleasure cruise is treated as a supply of passenger transport. [*SI 1992/3121, Art 8*]. The place of supply of a cruise follows the general rule above ie it is supplied in the country in which it takes place to the extent that it takes place in that country.

Luggage and/or accompanying motor vehicles. The transportation of any luggage or motor vehicle (car, motorcycle, caravan, trailer or small commercial vehicle) accompanying in either case a passenger is treated as supplied in the same place as the passenger transport [*SI 1992/3121, Art 8*] and as a single supply with it. The transportation of an *unaccompanied* vehicle is treated as a supply of freight transport (see 68.24 below).

Passenger transport supplied outside the UK. If the supply takes place:

- In another EC country, the supplier may have to register for VAT in that country and account for VAT at the relevant rate applying there. If the supplier does not have an establishment there, he may need to appoint a local tax representative to account for the VAT there on his behalf.
- In a country outside the EC, the supplier may be liable to account for any tax in that country that is applicable on passenger transport services.

Passenger transport supplied in the UK by persons belong outside the UK. Where a business belonging outside the UK is not registered for UK VAT and supplies passenger transport in the UK,

- if its customer is registered for UK VAT, the customer can account for VAT on its supplies under the reverse charge procedure (see 39.4 INTERNATIONAL SERVICES); and

- if its customer is not registered for UK VAT, it is liable to account for the VAT in the UK and must register for VAT in the UK where its supplies exceed the registration threshold (see 59.3 REGISTRATION).

(VAT Notice 744A, paras 3.1–3.4).

Services supplied on board passenger transport. Where such services are separate supplies in their own right (ie are not part of a single supply of transport) the following place of supply rules apply.

(*a*) *Services supplied to passengers for consumption on board.* There are no special place of supply rules for such services and the normal rules should be applied. There are, however, two exceptions.

- *Catering.* In *Faaborg-Gelting Linien A/S v Finanzamt Flensburg, CJEC [1996] STC 774 (TVC 21.105)*, the CJEC held that catering supplied on board a ferry travelling between Denmark and Germany was a supply of *services*, supplied where the supplier had his established place of business under *EC Sixth Directive, Art 9*(*1*). However, many EC countries, including the UK, have *not* implemented this judgment. HMRC treat catering as a supply of *goods* which is outside the scope of UK VAT when supplied for consumption on board intra-EC transport under *SI 2004/3148, Art 6*. It is also treated as outside the scope of UK VAT when supplied on other international passenger transport under *VATA 1994, s 7*(*2*).
- *Gaming machines.* In *Berkholz v Finanzamt Hamburg-Mitte-Altstadt, CJEC [1985] ECR 2251; [1985] 3 CMLR 667 (TVC 21.260)* the CJEC held that the provision of the service of playing on gaming machines is supplied where the supplier is established. Again, this decision has not been implemented in the UK and some other EC countries. HMRC has applied a 'stand still' provision allowed under *EC Sixth Directive, Art 8*(*1*)(*c*). The current position is that where a trader operates amusement or gaming machines on a passenger ship which is leaving the UK for a foreign destination (a foreign-going vessel) the supply of services is regarded as being made outside the UK, and therefore outside the scope of UK VAT. Any use of the facilities in UK territorial waters is effectively ignored provided the vessel has cleared to go foreign. Where the machines are operated on vessels which are not foreign-going, ie for coastwise journeys within the UK, the supply is made within the UK and is liable to VAT at the standard rate.

(*b*) *Services supplied by transport operators to businesses which trade independently on board.* The normal place of supply rules should be applied to such services. Where ferry operators supply the right to operate a concession to trade on board (eg a restaurant, photographer, etc) the supply falls under the basic rule and is taxable where the supplier belongs. For operators belonging in the UK, such a supply is made in the UK and is standard-rated.

(Internal Guidance V1–4, Chapter 2 para 10.8).

68.16 Zero-rating

Subject to the standard-rated supplies in 68.18 below, the supply of passenger transport in the UK is zero-rated if falling within any of the following categories.

(*a*) **In any vehicle, ship or aircraft designed or adapted to carry not less than 10 passengers**. [*VATA 1994, Sch 8 Group 8 Item 4*(*a*)].

For the purposes of determining the carrying capacity, the driver and crew should be treated as passengers. See also *G L Ashton (t/a Country Hotel Narrowboats) (VTD 14197) (TVC 64.13)*.

Included (subject to the seating rule) are

- santa flights which land in another country;
- pleasure cruises;
- cliff lifts;
- excursions by coach and train (including steam railways);
- horse-drawn buses;
- mystery coach trips and boat trips;
- sight-seeing tours; and
- the transport element of 'park-and-ride' schemes designed to reduce traffic congestion in city centres.

If the carrying capacity of the vehicle, ship or aircraft is less than ten passengers (12 before 1 April 2001), the transport is standard-rated unless it can be zero-rated under (*b*)-(*d*) below or the special rule for disabled passengers applies (see below).

(VAT Notice 744A, paras 4.1, 4.2).

Disabled passengers. Zero-rating specifically includes the transport of passengers in a vehicle

- which is designed, or substantially and permanently adapted, for the safe carriage of a person in a wheelchair (or two or more such persons), and
- which, if it were not so designed or adapted, would be capable of carrying no less than 10 passengers.

Note that, where the conditions are met, zero-rating applies whether or not the transport service is provided, in a particular case, for disabled persons.

[*VATA 1994, Sch 8 Group 8 Note (4D); SI 2001/753*]. (VAT Notice 48, ESC 3.12).

Aircraft. Because of problems arising where smaller aircraft are adaptable to take fewer passengers, it has been agreed with the General Aviation and Manufacturers Association (GAMTA) that passenger transport services may be zero-rated provided

- the aircraft is designed, according to the flight manual, to carry ten or more passengers, including crew;
- the necessary seat runners, tracks, mountings, etc for at least ten seats are permanently in place in the aircraft; and
- at least ten seats, together with their safety equipment (seat belts, life jackets, oxygen masks, etc) are maintained at all times by the operator to recognised airworthiness standards or in accordance with Ministry of Defence specifications.

Miniature and narrow-gauge railways. Passenger transport on such railways within a place of recreation or interest are standard-rated (see 68.18 below).

Where they are not in such a place, or are in a place where the public have free and unrestricted access such as a public park, zero-rating is likely to depend upon factors such as

- the overall scale of the railway (distance between stations, total length of track, etc);
- the context (whether or not one of several similar rides); and
- whether it performs a genuine passenger transport function (eg transports passengers around an area, up steep inclines, etc or whether it simply takes them on a round trip).

See *Metroland Ltd (VTD 14550) (TVC 64.29)* and *Narogauge Ltd (VTD 14680) (TVC 64.16)*.

(Internal Guidance V1–7, Chapter 8 para 2.5).

Narrowboats. In determining whether a narrowboat is designed to carry ten or more passengers, it is the space on each boat, rather than just the number of berths, which determines the carrying capacity (*GL Ashton (t/a Country Hotel Narrowboats) (VTD 14197) (TVC 64.13)*).

Cabin lifts. Each cabin in a cabin lift to a scenic headland has been held to be a separate vehicle and the transport of passengers standard-rated if the individual cabins are designed to hold less than ten people (*Llandudno Cabinlift Co Ltd (VTD 1) (TVC 64.25)*).

(*b*) **By the Post Office Company** (or any of its wholly-owned subsidiaries). [*VATA 1994, Sch 8 Group 8 Item 4*(*b*); *Postal Services Act 2000, Sch 8 para 22*] (VAT Notice 48, ESC 3.33). This applies irrespective of the type of vehicle or its carrying capacity. (VAT Notice 744A, para 7.1).

(*c*) **On any scheduled flight**. [*VATA 1994, Sch 8 Group 8 Item 4*(*c*)]. This applies irrespective of the carrying capacity of the aircraft. A scheduled flight is one that is run either according to a published timetable or so regularly or frequently as to constitute a recognisable systematic series of flights. (VAT Notice 744A, paras 5.1, 5.2).

(*d*) **From a place within to a place outside the UK** (or vice versa) to the extent that those services are supplied within the UK. [*VATA 1994, Sch 8 Group 8 Item 4*(*d*)]. This applies irrespective of the carrying capacity of the vehicle, ship or aircraft. Zero-rating applies to single and return journeys and journeys to or from an oil rig situated outside UK territorial waters. (VAT Notice 744A, para 3.2).

To qualify for zero-rating as passenger transport, the vehicle, ship or aircraft must be supplied with a driver or crew. Otherwise it is the vehicle, etc which is being supplied rather than passenger transport.

68.17 Incidental supplies

Incidental supplies are provided as part of a single transport service. Where a fare is zero-rated, then whether or not a separate charge is made, zero-rating also applies to

- accompanied domestic pets;
- accompanied luggage, including cycles and prams and excess luggage;
- accompanied vehicles and trailers (including Motorail);

- airport passenger charges and passenger load supplements;
- duplicate season tickets;
- pullman supplements;
- seat reservations;
- sleeping berths and cabins on ships (if provided in the course of ordinary transport, but see 68.21 below for cruises); and

(VAT Notice 744A, paras 9.2, 9.3; Internal Guidance V1–7, Chapter 8 para 2.10).

Catering on aircraft is an adjunct to the supply of transport and, where no separate charge is made, the consideration for the ticket need not be apportioned (*British Airways v C & E Commrs, CA [1990] STC 643 (TVC 64.8)*).

Payment for an identity card enabling the holder to travel at reduced price has been held to be consideration for the provision of rail transport (*British Railways Board (No 2) v C & E Commrs, CA [1977] STC 221 (TVC 64.7)*).

68.18 **Standard-rated supplies**

The following are specifically excluded from zero-rating and become standard-rated.

(*a*) **Passenger transport in places of entertainment or interest**. The transport of passengers in any vehicle to, from or within

(i) a place of entertainment, recreation or amusement, or

(ii) a place of cultural, scientific, historical or similar interest

by the person who supplies a right of admission to, or use of facilities at, such a place or by a person connected with him under the provisions of *ICTA 1988, s 839* (see 69.19 VALUATION) is standard-rated. [*VATA 1994, Sch 8 Group 8 Notes (4A)(4B); SI 1994/3014*]. Such transport services are standard-rated whether included in an overall admission price or made for a separate charge.

Places affected include

- fairgrounds;
- museums;
- piers;
- safari parks;
- stately homes;
- theme parks;
- water parks; and
- zoos.

However, places where the public enjoy totally free access are not affected (eg national parks, seaside resorts, historic towns and villages, geographical areas such as the Norfolk Broads, or canals and lakes).

The provisions do not apply to transport to, from or within a place of entertainment or cultural interest when provided *independently* from an operator of such a place. Such services remains zero-rated subject to the normal conditions. Examples include

- a trip by coach or rail to a football ground;
- a coach excursion to a theme park;
- ferries, canal boat trips and other round trips or excursions by boats, without other facilities, on the open sea or other waterways to which the public have free access.

(VAT Notice 744A, paras 8.1, 8.2, 8.5).

(*b*) **Transport in connection with airport car parks**. The transport of passengers in any 'motor vehicle' between a car park (or land adjacent) and an airport passenger terminal (or land adjacent) by the person who supplies the parking facilities in that car park or by a person connected with him under the provisions of *ICTA 1988, s 839* (see 69.19 VALUATION) is standard-rated. '*Motor vehicle*' means any mechanically propelled vehicle intended or adapted for use on the roads. [*VATA 1994, Sch 8 Group 8 Notes* (*4A*)-(*4C*); *SI 1994/3014*].

(*c*) **Pleasure flights**. The transport of passengers in an aircraft is standard-rated where the flight is advertised or held out to be for the purpose of

(i) providing entertainment, recreation or amusement, or

(ii) the experience of flying or the experience of flying in that particular aircraft

and not primarily for the purpose of transporting passengers from one place to another. [*VATA 1994, Sch 8 Group 8 Notes* (*4A*)(*4B*); *SI 1994/3014*].

Such flights are standard-rated even if they take off from one airport and land at another.

Standard-rated flights include

- hot air balloon rides;
- airship rides;
- 'fear of flying' flights; and
- Concorde 'flights to nowhere' and similar pleasure flights where the aircraft returns to the airport of departure or another UK airport without landing in another country.

(VAT Notice 744A, para 8.4).

Supplies not regarded as passenger transport. The following are standard-rated because they are not regarded as the transport of passengers.

- Donkey rides and similar rides.
- Novelty rides on miniature and model railways, ghost trains, roundabouts, dippers, other fairground equipment and similar attractions (see *C & E Commrs v Blackpool Pleasure Beach Co, QB [1974] STC 138 (TVC 64.28)*).

- The supply of any vehicle with or without a crew for a non-passenger service (eg to make a film or carry goods).

(VAT Notice 744A, para 2.2).

68.19 *Ancillary supplies*

Ancillary supplies, as opposed to incidental supplies (see 68.17 above) are not part of a single supply of passenger transport services but are supplied separately. The following supplies which are often provided in connection with passenger transport are standard-rated.

- Meals, snacks, sandwiches, drinks, etc provided in the course of catering *and supplied separately*.
- Car parking (but see 68.22 below when supplied as an airline passenger perk).
- Cycle storage.
- Left luggage and lost property.
- Platform tickets.
- Transportation of unaccompanied luggage, vehicles and trailers.

(VAT Notice 744A, para 9.4).

Club membership, entitling economy class passengers to certain facilities normally available only to first class passengers, is not an advance payment for supplies forming an integral part of passenger transport (*El Al Israel Airlines Ltd (VTD 12750) (TVC 64.32)*).

68.20 **Transport of vehicles on ships**

The transport of vehicles on a ship (eg a ferry) may, depending on the circumstances, be a supply of passenger transport or freight transport. HMRC's treatment is as follows.

Passenger transport

- Buses, coaches and taxis *with passengers* whether or not charged at the private car rate by the ship or ferry operator.
- Vehicles with drivers or passengers charged under the private car rate, including motorcycles, cars, caravans and trailers.
- Small commercial vehicles charged under the private car rate whether carrying passengers or freight.

Freight transport

- Unaccompanied vehicles, including buses, coaches and trailers.

(VAT Notice 744A, paras 2.3, 2.4).

68.21 **Cruises and other trips**

Cruises. This paragraph applies where a cruise operator provides cruises from own resources. It applies to all cruise operators whether supplying international and coastal holiday cruises or cruises on rivers and canals or other inland waterways, including disco, dinner, wedding reception and similar entertainment cruises. In all cases, the vessels must be designed or adapted to carry ten or more passengers, including crew, otherwise any supplies in the UK will be automatically standard-rated. However, the provisions do not affect cruises bought in and re-supplied under the TOUR OPERATORS' MARGIN SCHEME (66).

HMRC regard a business as providing a cruise from its own resources where it

- uses its own ship;
- charters a vessel from the owner for a period of two year or more whether only with deck/engine crew or with deck/engine crew and 'hotel'/domestic/catering crew. The vessel need not necessarily be in service continuously throughout the period but the owner must not have the right to use the vessel to make supplies to other customers during the period; or
- takes a vessel including deck/engine crew but employs or engages its own 'hotel'/domestic/catering staff.

A pleasure cruise is treated as a single supply of passenger transport *for the purposes of determining the place of supply*. Once the place of supply has been established under the general rules for passenger transport in 68.15 above, for UK VAT liability purposes a cruise may be a single or multiple supply depending on the facts of the cruise.

In *C & E Commrs v The Peninsular & Oriental Steam Navigation Co, QB [1996] STC 698 (TVC 64.14)* a cruise sold at an inclusive price covering transport, accommodation, catering, entertainment, etc was held to be a single supply which was zero-rated as a supply of passenger transport, the terms 'pleasure cruise' and 'passenger transport' not being necessarily mutually exclusive. The decision in that case was, however, distinguished in *Virgin Atlantic Airways Ltd (VTD 13840) (TVC 64.18)* where a company operated a river boat which it hired out with optional catering and entertainment. Invoices normally included separate charges for the different services provided. The tribunal held that the company made separate supplies of transport (the hire charge), catering and entertainment and that the supplies of transport were zero-rated.

Following the decisions in *P & O* and *Virgin Atlantic*, Customs indicated that the guidelines set out below were the main criteria they considered relevant in deciding liability. Since their issue, the CJEC in *Card Protection Plan Ltd v C & E Commrs, CJEC [1999] STC 270 (TVC 21.223)* (see 64.6 SUPPLY) have set out general criteria for deciding whether a supply should be treated as a single or multiple supply and HMRC require these to be applied in all cases from 1 June 2001. The following guidelines must therefore be read in the light of the general criteria.

Single zero-rated supply of passenger transport

- The essential nature of the supply is passenger transport and the normal conditions for the relief are met;
- all elements of the cruise are integral and it would be neither practicable nor realistic to separate them; and
- the cruise is held out for sale at a single price with no specific charges or discounts for particular services taken or not taken up.

Multiple supplies

- Different elements of the cruise arc the subject of separate negotiation and customer choice;

- there are separately identifiable obligations on the supplier, and separate charges;
- separate supplies are not integral to the main supply and could be omitted; and
- it must be practicable, reasonable and realistic to separate the elements of the cruise.

Where separate supplies of any of the individual elements of a cruise are made, these should be taxed according to their respective liabilities (eg a separate element of catering is standard-rated when supplied in the UK).

Services of intermediaries. The services of an intermediary making arrangements for the supply of a single zero-rated cruise is zero-rated to the extent that the supply takes place in the UK (see 68.30 below). Where the cruise is treated as a multiple supply, a reasonable apportionment will be accepted.

(VAT Notice 744A, paras 10.2–10.6).

Other trips. The liability of railway and other trips provided with facilities such as catering or entertainment should be determined using the principles outlined above.

In *Sea Containers Services Ltd v C & E Commrs, QB 1999, [2000] STC 82 (TVC 64.21)* a company operated a luxury train on which passengers were supplied with catering. Customs accepted that, where the train was used for transport to Continental destinations such as Venice, there was a single supply of zero-rated transport. Where, however, the train was used for UK charters, the court confirmed, distinguishing *The Peninsular & Oriental Steam Navigation Co* above, that the company was making separate supplies of transport and catering in the following circumstances.

- Where the whole train plus crew was chartered (whether catering was separately negotiated or included in a single price).
- Where round trips were sold to individual passengers which included high quality catering.
- Where a stopping trip was sold to an individual passenger who alighted before the return journey, again including catering.

HMRC consider that this decision confirms their current policy. (Business Brief 10/99).

See also *A & J Hughes (t/a Pennine Boat Trips of Skipton) (VTD 15680) (TVC 64.15)* where the tribunal held that canal boat trips providing food for parties of 30 or more people were single supplies of zero-rated transport. HMRC consider that this case is confined to the facts and will not accept claims for refunds of VAT on the basis of this decision. (Business Brief 5/99).

Depending on the circumstances 'wine and dine', 'steam and cuisine', disco cruises, dinner cruises, wedding reception cruises and other similar journeys may be standard-rated, zero-rated; or treated as mixed supplies. (VAT Notice 744A, para 9.8).

68.22 **Airline passenger perks**

In *Virgin Atlantic Airways Ltd v C & E Commrs; Canadian Airlines International Ltd v C & E Commrs, QB [1995] STC 341 (TVC 64.9, TVC 64.10)* chauffeur-driven limousine services to and from the airport, where the passenger paid one indivisible and irreducible sum for these services and the flight, were held to be part of the zero-rated supply of passenger transport. Following this decision, HMRC have agreed with the airline industry that this treatment would be extended to cover other 'passenger perks'.

To be eligible the perks must

(i) be included in the flight ticket price for the class of travel concerned, with no discount if not taken up;

(ii) form an integral part of an international flight;

(iii) not be gifts of goods (except where currently permitted, eg in-flight catering, toiletries); and

(iv) be restricted to one perk per customer (although the customer may be offered a number of options).

The following perks are treated as an integral part of an international flight.

- Limousine transport to and from the airport.
- Up to two days car hire for a one way ticket (four days for a return ticket).
- Car parking at the airport.
- Hotel or similar accommodation provided that it is for no more than one night's stay with breakfast and there is a direct connection with the zero-rated travel (eg where it is necessary to catch a connecting flight or it is required for the night prior to take-off or the night after landing).

Not included are

- restaurant meals;
- theatre trips and other entertainment provided during a trip or holiday; and
- hotel accommodation and car hire other than as specified above.

New options will not be automatically disallowed but individual prior approval must be obtained from HMRC to ensure that the services are incidental to and directly connected with the air travel.

The provision of allowable perks will not, in itself, render the airline liable to use the TOUR OPERATORS' MARGIN SCHEME (66) although the provision of non-allowable perks may well do so.

(VAT Notice 744A, paras 9.6, 9.7).

68.23 Taxis and hire cars

VAT liability of fares. Zero-rating of domestic passenger transport does not apply if the vehicle is designed to carry less than ten passengers. Taxi and hire car fares are, therefore, standard-rated and if the business provider is registrable for VAT, it must charge VAT to its customers. Extra charges for baggage, waiting time, etc are also standard-rated as are referral fees from other taxi businesses. Tips and gratuities given voluntarily are not payments for supplies and are outside the scope of VAT. VAT due is calculated by multiplying the fares, including extras, by the VAT fraction. See 47.2 OUTPUT TAX.

Invoices. Registered persons must issue VAT invoices to any customer who asks for one. See 40 INVOICES.

Types of business and VAT consequences.

(a) **Independent self-employed drivers.** If a driver has purchased or rented his own vehicle and operates it on a self-employed basis, he will normally be in business on his own account and will be making taxable supplies in the form of

- transport supplied direct to his own passengers; and/or
- services to another taxi business where he supplies them under a contract for services.

Where the driver supplies transport to his own passengers, he may use the agency services of a taxi business (see (*b*)(iii) below) or a taxi association (see below) to obtain customers. If, however, he drives for a taxi or private hire business as its employee (see (*b*)(i) below), he is not considered to be in business for VAT purposes.

A self-employed driver must register for VAT if making taxable supplies where the full amount he is paid for those supplies exceeds the VAT registration threshold. To calculate this, any amounts, such as vehicle and radio rentals or agency charges, deducted by a taxi firm must be added back to the amounts actually received.

(*b*) **Businesses which engage drivers.** This includes all types of business, whether sole proprietorship, partnership or limited company. There are three common scenarios for who is supplying the taxi and hire car services to the customers.

(i) *Drivers are employees of a cab business.* Where a cab business employs staff to drive its taxis or hire cars, the business makes the supplies to the customers and must account for output tax on

- the full amount payable by customers before deducting any payments made to drivers;
- any fares the sole proprietor, director or partner, as the case may be, receives if he drives for the firm;
- the full fares payable by passengers even if the work is sub-contracted to an independent business or owner driver; and
- any referral fee received from other taxi businesses.

The drivers are not considered to be in business for VAT purposes. Any money retained by the drivers is outside the scope of VAT as remuneration for their services as employees.

This scenario is, however, rarely the case and HMRC will only agree that this is so if a contract or agreement between the cab business and the driver clearly states that a contract of employment exists and/or there is evidence that the driver is taxed under Schedule E by the Inland Revenue.

(ii) *Drivers are self-employed and provide their services to a cab business.* The cab business will usually own the vehicles and bear expenses relating to them. Typically, there are more drivers than vehicles and the firm has to exercise control over the drivers to ensure that it is adequately covered at all times. The cab business is buying in the services of drivers and selling the taxi transport on to the final customer as principal. The cab firm must account for output tax as in (i) above. Monies retained by the drivers are consideration for a supply of services by themselves to the cab business under a contract for services (see (*a*) above).

(iii) *Drivers are self-employed and provide their services directly to the customers.* The drivers will usually own their own vehicles and bear expenses relating to them. They have far greater freedom to accept or refuse work; and conversely, they have to bear far greater financial risk. The cab business or taxi association acts as agent for the drivers, usually providing them with services such as radio hire, booking and support services in return for a commission or fee. This is a standard-rated supply of services by the business or association whether the drivers pay by periodic subscription or by deduction or offset from payments collected on their behalf. The business or association must register for VAT if the total of all such charges and any other supplies it makes (eg administration fees for services supplied to customers such as a breakdown or analysis of journeys made) exceeds the VAT registration limit. Individual drivers need only account for output tax if their supplies exceeds the VAT registration limits (see (*a*) above).

In practice it is often difficult to distinguish between (*b*)(ii) and (*b*)(iii) above. Factors which HMRC take into account include the following.

(1) *Ownership of the vehicles.* Ownership by the cab business indicates (*b*)(ii) whereas ownership by the drivers indicates (*b*)(iii).

(2) *Driver's access to vehicles where owned by the cab firm.* Vehicles kept on the business's premises with no private use indicates (*b*)(ii). Vehicles hired to drivers and available for private use indicates (*b*)(iii).

(3) *Costs and expenses.* If the cab business taxes, insures and maintains the vehicles and meets fuel costs, this indicates (*b*)(ii). If the drivers do, this indicates (*b*)(iii).

(4) *Payments by drivers to cab firm for support services.* If the drivers pay an agreed percentage, this indicates (*b*)(ii). If they pay a fixed weekly sum, this indicates (*b*)(iii).

(5) *Risk of bad debts.* If cheques from customers are made payable to the cab business and it compensates drivers if a cash customer does not pay, this indicates (*b*)(ii).

(6) *Advertising on cars.* If cabs bear the business logo, this indicates (*b*)(ii).

(7) *Control exercised by the cab business.* If the cab business draws up rosters and drivers must accept work offered and be available at set times, this indicates (*b*)(ii). If drivers work hours that suit them, this indicates (*b*)(iii).

(8) *Keeping records.* If the cab business keeps detailed records for each driver and can calculate each driver's takings, this indicates (*b*)(ii). If records are limited to who answered what call, this indicates (*b*)(iii).

(9) *Prices for customers.* If the business sets the prices and no deviation is allowed, this indicates (*b*)(ii). If the prices are only advisory and in practice drivers charge more or less, this indicates (*b*)(iii).

For cases where self-employed drivers were held to supply their services to the cab firm under (*b*)(ii) above, see *Hamiltax (VTD 8948) (TVC 60.215)* and *Knowles (t/a Rainbow Taxis) (VTD 13913) (TVC 60.216)*. For cases where the final supply to the customer was held to be by the drivers under (*b*)(iii) above, see *Triumph and Albany Car Service (VTD 977, VTD 1004) (TVC 60.219)* and *Carless v C & E Commrs, QB [1993] STC 632 (TVC 60.221)*.

Fees paid to controllers. In *Home Or Away Ltd (VTD 18195) (TVC 60.227)* a company engaged staff (which it treated as self-employed) to act as controllers. Drivers paid 10% of their fares directly to the controllers as fees. The tribunal held that, on the evidence, although the fees were paid directly to the controllers as a matter of convenience, they were paid for a supply by the company of the services of the controllers to the drivers.

Account work. Many taxi and hire car businesses engage in cash work (where customers pay cash to the driver upon completion of the journey) and account work (where regular customers, usually businesses, are allowed to settle their bills periodically). In most cases there will be no difference between the operation of the two types of business, ie both will fall within the same category under (*b*)(i)–(iii) above and VAT must be accounted for as indicated under the relevant category. Where both cash and account work falls within (*b*)(iii) above, invoices raised by the business to account customers should itemise separately

- fares collected on behalf of drivers (with the addition of VAT if the *driver* is registered); and
- any administration or similar charge by the business (with the addition of VAT if the *business* is registered).

However, there may be a genuine difference between the treatment of cash and account work with the business acting as agent for cash work under (*b*)(iii) above but principal for account work under (*b*)(ii) above. If such arrangements are adopted, the business must satisfy HMRC that

- the arrangements are reflected in the written terms agreed with the drivers; and
- there is a genuine difference in the operation of the cash and account sides of the business.

If a business operates as an agent for cash work and a principal for account work, it must still account for VAT at the standard rate on the full charge to the drivers for the rental of vehicles, radios or other services supplied to them. This applies even if the charge is

- offset when calculating the rate due to the drivers for account work they perform; or
- deducted before paying them for account journeys.

See *RJ and CA Blanks (VTD 14099) (TVC 65.125)*.

The basis of payment (eg where drivers are paid a fixed hourly rate for account work but their payment for cash work is directly related to takings) could be one indication of a contractual distinction between cash and account work. See *Triumph and Albany Car Service* and *Carless* above for cases where the cash and account customers were held not to be distinguishable; and *Camberwell Cars Ltd (VTD 10178) (TVC 60.225)* and *A Hussain (t/a Crossleys Private Hire Cars) (VTD 16194) (TVC 60.220)* where the tribunal held there was a real distinction between cash and account work.

Taxi associations. Some independent and self-employed taxi drivers form taxi associations to provide services to the individual driver members. These services can include

- operation of a booking office and radio link;
- hire of radios; and
- provision of rest facilities.

Supplies to members are always standard-rated whether they pay for them by periodic subscription or by deduction/offset from fares collected on the members' behalf. Taxi associations must be registered for VAT if the total of all such charges, together with the total charges for any other supplies they make, exceed the VAT registration threshold. Additional supplies can include an administration fee for services supplied to customers (eg providing a breakdown or analysis of journeys made).

Purchases of motor vehicles. VAT can be reclaimed on the purchase of a motor car if

- it is a qualifying motor car; and
- it is intended primarily to be used for letting on hire with a driver for the purpose of carrying passengers.

A qualifying motor car is generally either a new car or a used car where all previous owners were able to reclaim input on their purchases. See 45.3 MOTOR CARS for further details.

Fuel. Input tax is reclaimable on fuel bought for use in taxis or hire-cars by the proprietor and, for the time being at least, employees of a business. However, if the business funds private motoring, a scale charge is payable.

See 45.10–45.19 MOTOR CARS for motor expenses generally including fuel and private motoring.

Sales of taxis and hire cars. If a taxi or hire car is sold on which input tax has been previously reclaimed, VAT must be accounted for on the full selling price. If no input tax has been previously reclaimed (eg because it was purchased under the second-hand scheme or from a private individual) it may be sold under the second-hand margin scheme provided the conditions for the scheme can be met. VAT need then only be accounted for on the excess, if any, of the sales proceeds over cost. See 61 SECOND-HAND GOODS.

Where a vehicle is sold with a local authority hackney carriage licence plate, there is a single supply of goods (ie a licensed taxi). The full selling price is the total amount charged for the vehicle and licence plate. Licence fees paid to a local authority to operate a taxi cab are treated as separate supplies of services and cannot be included in the purchase price of a vehicle when working out the VAT due on sale under the second-hand margin scheme.

Where a taxi or hire car is exchanged or traded on the purchase of a replacement vehicle, VAT must be accounted for in the same way as if it had been sold at a price equal to the exchange or trade-in allowance received.

Sale of business as going concern. If a taxi or car hire business is sold as a going concern and certain conditions are met, there is no taxable supply for VAT purposes and no VAT liability on the assets sold, including any taxis or hire cars included in the price. See 8.10 BUSINESS. To be treated as such a sale, the transaction must include more than just the sale of a vehicle (eg the rights to a radio network, goodwill, lists of customers).

(VAT Notice 700/25/02). (Internal Guidance V1–5, Chapter 3 paras 3.51–3.56).

68.24 **FREIGHT TRANSPORT SERVICES**

Freight for these purposes includes

- goods/cargo;
- mail;
- documents;
- unaccompanied vehicles; and
- vehicles transported on ships which are charged at a 'driver accompanied' rate.

To determine the correct VAT treatment of supplies of freight transport or related services, it is necessary to determine

- the nature of the supply, ie whether it is domestic, intra-EC or international;
- whether the supply, or any part of it, takes place in the UK;
- who should account for any VAT due; and
- for UK supplies, whether the supplies are zero-rated or standard-rated.

Liability to register. If a business supplies freight transport services whose place of supply is in another EC country, the business may be liable to register for VAT in that country (subject to the VAT registration rules applying there). If it does not have an establishment there, the business may need to appoint a local VAT representative to account for the VAT on its behalf. This applies both to UK businesses making supplies in other EC countries and overseas suppliers making supplies in the UK.

(VAT Notice 744B, paras 1.2–1.5).

68.25 **Domestic freight transport**

'*Domestic freight transport*' is the transport of goods that takes place wholly within one country.

Place of supply. The place of supply of domestic freight transport is the country in which it takes place. [*SI 1992/3121, Art 6*]. For sea and air freight transport, provided the means of transport used does not put in or land in another country on the way, any transportation as part of a journey between two points in the same country is treated as taking place wholly inside that country even where it takes place partly outside its territorial jurisdiction. [*SI 1992/3121, Art 7*].

As a result of the above, where freight transport takes place wholly within the UK, the place of supply is the UK.

VAT liability. The supply of domestic freight transport in the UK is normally standard-rated with the following exceptions.

(*a*) The transport of goods to a place at which they are to be exported from the EC is zero-rated. [*VATA 1994, Sch 8 Group 8 Item 11*]. Any transport which is supplied in the UK may still be zero-rated even where exportation of the goods is to be from another EC country.

(*b*) The transport of goods from a place at which they have been imported into the EC is zero-rated. [*VATA 1994, Sch 8 Group 8 Item 11*].

Zero-rating applies to any transport of goods supplied in the UK in connection with a journey from the place of importation to their 'destination' either within the UK or within another EC country. '*Destination*' for this purpose is the furthest place, in the UK or other EC country, to which the goods are consigned at importation as stated on the consignment note (or other document) by means of which the goods are imported. If that place is unknown, it is the first place to which the goods are transported after importation.

Documentary evidence must be held to show entitlement to zero-rating. The main forms of documentary evidence include consignment notes, bills of lading, certificates of shipment, airwaybills or seawaybills and Customs declaration Forms C88 (SAD). Additionally, a combination (or all) of inter-company correspondence, the customer's order document, payment details, sales invoices and advice notes may provide suitable evidence.

Where zero-rating applies, it applies whether the supplier is the main contractor or a sub-contractor, and regardless of who the customer is. Included are the services of freight forwarders who buy in and supply on freight transport as principals.

See also 68.26 below for the domestic leg of an intra-EC freight transport movement.

Accounting for VAT. *Where the supplier belongs in the UK*, the supplier must account for the VAT due on domestic freight transport in the UK.

Where the supplier belongs overseas and is not VAT-registered in the UK,

- if the customer is not UK VAT-registered or is unable to provide a valid VAT number, the supplier must account for any VAT due on domestic freight transport in the UK. If not already registered in the UK, the overseas supplier is liable to register (subject to the current VAT registration threshold); and
- if the customer is UK VAT-registered, the customer must account for any VAT, as the recipient of domestic freight transport services, under the reverse charge procedure (see 39.4 INTERNATIONAL SERVICES).

(VAT Notice 744B, paras 2.1–2.4, 5.4, 5.5, 8.1, 8.2, 9.1).

68.26 Intra-EC freight transport

'*Intra-EC transport of goods*' means transportation of goods which begins in one EC country and ends in a different EC country. It includes the transport of goods

- which takes place entirely within one EC country where it is part of a single movement of goods from one EC country to another (eg road haulage from Dover to London for goods which are consigned from Paris to Edinburgh — see below under the heading *Domestic legs of an intra-EC freight transport movement*); and
- from one EC country to another where the journey goes through a non-EC country (eg transport of goods from London to Rome via Switzerland).

Place of supply. Services consisting of the intra-EC transport of goods are treated as made in the EC country in which the transportation of the goods begins. Where, however, the customer gives a valid VAT registration number to the supplier, the place of supply becomes the EC country of the customer *if and only if* that would result in the supply being treated as taking place in a different EC country.

[*SI 1992/3121, Arts 10, 14*].

Accounting for VAT. Whether the supplier or the customer has to account for VAT, if any, depends upon whether, and if so where, the customer is registered for VAT.

(*a*) *Where the customer is not registered for VAT or, if registered, fails to give a valid VAT registration number to the supplier*, the place of supply is the EC country where the transportation of the goods begins. The supplier is responsible for accounting for the VAT, if any, in that country. If not already registered there, the supplier may be required to register in order to account for the VAT.

Examples

- A French supplier supplies services to a UK customer not registered for VAT and the transportation of the goods begins in the UK. The French supplier is responsible for accounting for any VAT due in the UK.
- A UK supplier supplies services to a UK customer not registered for VAT and the transportation begins in Ireland. The UK supplier is responsible for accounting for any VAT due in the Ireland.

(*b*) *Where the customer is registered for VAT and gives a valid VAT registration number to the supplier for the purposes of the supply*, the place of supply is the EC country where the transportation of the goods begins or, if different, the EC country of the customer.

(i) If the customer is registered in the same EC country as the supplier, the supplier must charge and account for VAT at the domestic rate in the normal way. The reverse charge procedure cannot be applied.

(ii) If the customer is registered for VAT in a different EC country to the supplier, the supplier does not charge VAT and the customer accounts for VAT in his own country under the reverse charge procedure (see 39.4 INTERNATIONAL SERVICES).

Examples

- A UK supplier supplies services to a VAT-registered French business which provides a valid VAT registration number. Whether the transportation of the goods begins in the UK, France or Germany, the place of supply is France and the French business must account for any VAT due in France under the reverse charge procedure.
- A French supplier supplies services to a VAT-registered UK business which provides a valid UK VAT registration number. Whether the transportation of the goods begins in the UK, France or Germany, the place of supply is the UK and the UK business must account for any VAT due in the UK under the reverse charge procedure.
- A UK supplier supplies services to a VAT-registered UK business with the transportation of the goods beginning in the Ireland. The customer provides a valid VAT registration number and therefore the place of supply is the UK rather than the Ireland. As the supplier and customer are both registered in the UK, the supplier

must charge and account for any VAT on the supply.

Domestic legs of an intra-EC freight transport movement. HMRC treat a service consisting of a separate domestic leg of transport, which forms part of an intra-EC movement of goods, in the same way as an intra-EC movement. This means that UK suppliers of such legs need not charge UK VAT on those services supplied to a person who is registered for VAT in another EC country. Commercial evidence must be held to show that the service does form part of an intra-EC movement of goods.

> *Example*
>
> A UK supplier collects goods at Dover to transport them on the final leg of their journey from Rome to Birmingham for a French VAT-registered customer. The place of supply is France. The customer should account for the VAT under the reverse charge procedure.

(VAT Notice 744B, paras 3.1–3.9).

68.27 International freight transport

'*International freight transport*' is the transport of goods between EC and non-EC countries, or wholly outside the EC.

Place of supply. The place of supply of international freight transport is the country in which the transportation takes place to the extent that it takes place in that country. [*SI 1992/3121, Art 6*].

VAT liability. The transport of 'goods' from a place within to a place outside the EC (or vice versa) is zero-rated to the extent that the supply takes place in the UK. [*VATA 1994, Sch 8 Group 8 Item 5*]. To the extent that the transport takes place outside the UK, it is outside the scope of UK VAT. (The transport of goods between two places both outside the EC is outside the scope of UK and EC VAT.) '*Goods*' includes mail and documents.

See also 68.25(*a*) and (*b*) above for zero-rating of freight transport supplied in the UK in connection with goods which are to be exported to, or have been imported from, a place outside the EC.

Zero-rating applies whether the supplier is the main contractor or a sub-contractor, and regardless of who the customer is. Included are the services of freight forwarders who buy in and supply on freight transport as principals.

Evidence to support the fact that services form part of a supply of international freight transport include contracts or agreements, consignment notes, bills of lading, certificates of shipment, airway or seaway bills and Customs declaration Forms C88 (SAD). Additionally, a combination of inter-company correspondence, the customer's order documentation, payment details, sales invoices and advice notes may provide suitable evidence.

(VAT Notice 744B, paras 5.1–5.5).

68.28 **Ancillary freight transport services**

'*Ancillary transport services*' means loading, unloading, handling and similar activities. [*SI 1992/3121, Art 2*]. Included are the services of reloading, stowing, opening for inspection, cargo security services, preparing or amending bills of lading, airwaybills and certificates of shipment, packing necessary for transportation and storage.

Place of supply. Special rules apply for determining the place of supply of ancillary freight transport services.

- Ancillary transport services in connection with domestic freight transport (see 68.25 above) or international freight transport (see 68.27 above) are treated as supplied where the services are physically performed.
- Ancillary transport services in connection with the intra-EC freight transport (see 68.26 above) are treated as supplied where the services are physically performed. Where, however, the services are supplied to a customer

  (i) registered for VAT in an EC country other than that in which the services are physically performed, and

  (ii) who has given a valid VAT registration number to the supplier

  the services are treated as supplied in the customer's country.

[*SI 1992/3121, Arts 9, 14*].

VAT liability. Ancillary freight transport services supplied in the UK are normally standard-rated. However, the following services are zero-rated.

(*a*) The 'handling' or storage of goods carried in a ship or aircraft when provided in a 'port', land adjacent to a port, a 'customs and excise airport' or, from 1 June 2002, a 'transit shed'. The letting on hire of goods (including cranes and other lifting equipment) is specifically excluded. A '*transit shed*' is a place approved by HMRC for the deposit of goods having the status of goods in temporary storage. Goods are in temporary storage until they are assigned to a customs-approved treatment or use. An example of the latter is placing the goods under a customs procedure, such as entry to free circulation. See 68.9 above for the meaning of '*port*' and '*customs and excise airport*'.

It is not necessary for the ship or aircraft itself to qualify for zero-rating.

The UK legislation is based upon *EC 6th Directive, Art 15*(*8*)(*9*) which refers to services to meet the 'direct needs' of the ship or aircraft or its cargo. Overnight storage before loading is therefore zero-rated but not long-term storage of goods. Storage for a longer period than strictly required due to unavoidable events (eg industrial action) can be zero-rated. (Internal Guidance V1–7, Chapter 8 para 7.7).

(*b*) The 'handling' or storage of goods at the place at which they are to be exported from the EC or have been imported into the EC.

(*c*) The 'handling' or storage of goods in connection with their transport

(i) to a place at which they are to be exported from the EC; or

(ii) from a place at which they have been imported into the EC to their 'destination' in the UK or within another EC country (to the extent that those services are supplied in the UK). '*Destination*' for this purpose is the furthest place, in the UK or other EC country, to which the goods are consigned at importation as stated on the consignment note (or other document) by means of which the goods are imported. If that place is unknown, it is the first place to which the goods are transported after importation.

Documentary evidence must be held to show entitlement to zero-rating. The main forms of documentary evidence include consignment notes, bills of lading, certificates of shipment, airwaybills or seawaybills and Customs declaration Forms C88 (SAD). Additionally, a combination (or all) of inter-company correspondence, the customer's order document, payment details, sales invoices and advice notes may provide suitable evidence.

[*VATA 1994, Sch 8 Group 8 Item 6*(*b*), *Item 11*(*a*) *and Notes 5 and 7; SI 1995/3039; SI 2002/1173*].

'*Handling*' includes cargo security services; container handling for which a box charge is made; demurrage; loading stores and discharging empties; loading, unloading, reloading, stowing, securing and shifting cargo; preparing or amending bills of lading, airwaybills, seawaybills and certificates of shipment; preparing or amending customs entries; presenting goods for customs examination; sorting, opening for inspection, repairing and making good, weighing and taring, taping and sealing, erasing and re-marking, labelling and re-numbering, tallying, checking, sampling, measuring or gauging of goods; stevedoring and porterage; survey of cargo (including damaged cargo); and the movement of goods to or from a ship by lighter.

Where zero-rating applies, it applies whether the supplier is the main contractor or a sub-contractor, and regardless of who the customer is. Included are the services of freight forwarders who buy in and supply on freight transport as principals.

Accounting for VAT

(*a*) Ancillary freight transport services in connection with domestic or international freight transport. The supplier is normally responsible for any VAT due. The exception is where

- an overseas supplier not registered for VAT in the UK supplies domestic ancillary transport services that are physically performed in the UK, and
- the customer is registered for VAT in the UK

in which case the customer accounts for VAT under the reverse charge procedure (see 39.4 INTERNATIONAL SERVICES).

(*b*) *Ancillary freight transport services in connection with intra-EC freight transport.* The liability to account for VAT depends upon whether, and if so where, the customer is registered for VAT.

(i) Where the customer has given a valid VAT registration number

- if the customer is registered in the same EC country as the supplier, the supplier must charge and account for VAT in the EC country where the ancillary services are physically performed; and
- if the customer is not registered in the same EC country as the supplier, the supplier does not charge VAT and the customer accounts for VAT in his own country under the reverse charge procedure (see 39.4 INTERNATIONAL SERVICES).

(ii) Where the customer is not registered for VAT or, if registered, fails to give a valid VAT registration number to the supplier, the supplier must account for VAT in the place were the ancillary services are physically performed.

(VAT Notice 744B, paras 6.1, 6.2, 6.5, 7.1, 7.7, 8.1, 8.2, 8.4).

68.29 **The Azores and Madeira**

The supply of 'intra-Community transport services' in connection with the transport of goods

- to or from the Azores and Madeira, or
- between those places

is zero-rated to the extent that the services are treated as supplied in the United Kingdom.

'*Intra-Community transport services*' means

(*a*) the 'intra-EC transport of goods' (see 68.26 above);

(*b*) 'ancillary transport services' (see 68.28 above) which are provided in connection with the transportation of goods within (*a*) above; and

(*c*) the services of an intermediary in arranging for the supply by or to another person of a supply within (*a*) or (*b*) above or any other activity which is intended to facilitate the making of the supply

and for these purposes the Azores and Madeira are each to be treated as a separate EC country.

[*VATA 1994, Sch 8 Group 8 Item 13 and Note 9*].

See 68.26 above for the place of supply of intra-EC freight transport, 68.28 above for the place of supply of ancillary freight transport services and 68.30 below for the place of supply of services of intermediaries.

68.30 **INTERMEDIARY SERVICES**

Place of supply. Special rules apply for determining the place of supply of services by intermediaries making arrangements for passenger and freight transport services. Subject to below, the place of supply of making arrangements for

(*a*) a supply of

(i) passenger transport within 68.14 above,

(ii) domestic freight transport within 68.25 above and any related ancillary freight transport services within 68.28 above,

(iii) international freight transport within 68.27 above and any related ancillary freight transport services within 68.28 above, and

(iv) any activity intended to facilitate the making of a supply within (i)–(iii) above

is the place where the supply which is being arranged is deemed to be made;

(*b*) intra-EC freight transport within 68.26 above (or any activity intended to facilitate the making of such a supply) is the place where the transportation begins; and

(*c*) ancillary freight transport services within 68.28 above relating to a supply of intra-EC freight transport within 68.26 above (or any activity intended to facilitate the making of such a supply) is the place where the ancillary transport service is physically performed.

Where, however, the intermediary services within (*a*)-(*c*) above are supplied to a customer

- registered for VAT in an EC country other than the one where the arranged supply is made, and
- who has given a valid VAT registration number to the intermediary

the intermediary's services are treated as supplied in the EC country where the customer is registered (and the customer then is responsible for accounting for any VAT due under the reverse charge procedure).

[*SI 1992/3121, Arts 11-14*].

VAT liability. If the place of supply of the intermediary services is the UK, the supply is normally standard-rated. However, zero-rating applies to the making of arrangements for

- the supply of, or space in, a qualifying ship (see 68.1 above) or qualifying aircraft (see 68.2 above);
- the supply of any goods within 68.3 or, with effect from 1 April 2002, 68.13(*d*) above;
- the supply of any *services* within 68.4 to 68.28 above (but *not* 68.29 above) which are themselves zero-rated, and
- the supply of, or space in, a ship or aircraft to a person who receives the supply for the purposes of a business carried on by him and who belongs outside the UK (whether or not the ship or aircraft is a qualifying one).

[*VATA 1994, Sch 8 Group 8 Items 10, 11*(*b*) *and Note 7; SI 1995/3039; SI 2002/456*].

Intermediary services received in the UK from overseas suppliers. Where a UK-registered person makes use of a VAT registration number for the purpose of receiving intermediary services which consist of the making of arrangements for

- domestic freight transport, or part of international transport, which takes place in the EC, or
- intra-EC freight transport and/or related freight transport services

from an intermediary who belongs in either another EC country or a country outside the EC, the place of supply is the UK and the reverse charge procedure applies. The UK recipient is required to account for the VAT. See 39.4 INTERNATIONAL SERVICES.

(VAT Notice 744B, para 10.7).

69 Valuation

Cross-references. See 5 APPEALS for appeals regarding valuation; 47.3 OUTPUT TAX for the valuation of multiply supplies; 60.8, 60.9 RETAIL SCHEMES for valuation of gross takings of retailers; 64 SUPPLY for coverage of supplies generally and the time and place of supply; 67 TRADE PROMOTION SCHEMES for valuation of supplies made by the promoter.

De Voil Indirect Tax Service. See V3.151–166.

The contents of this chapter are as follows.

69.1 INTRODUCTION

EC legislation. See 22.12–22.14 EUROPEAN COMMUNITY LEGISLATION.

UK legislation. VAT is charged on

- the supply of goods and services in the UK;
- the acquisition of goods in the UK from another EC country; and
- the importation of goods from outside the EC.

[*VATA 1994, s 1(1)*].

Supplies of goods or services are usually made in return for money, ie for a consideration wholly in money. In such cases, the value for VAT purposes is normally, under the general rule in *VATA 1994, s 19(2)*, the price paid or payable excluding the VAT itself. See 69.3 below. The rest of this chapter deals with situations where this simple rule cannot be applied, for example

- where a single consideration is payment for supplies with different liabilities so that an apportionment is necessary (see 69.4 below);

- where the consideration is wholly or at least partly not in money (see 69.5-69.7 below); and
- where circumstances exist requiring special valuation rules to be applied which take precedence over the general rules (see 69.10-69.30 below). This includes special valuation provisions for acquisitions from other EC countries (see 69.11-69.14 below) and imports from outside the EC (see 69.15 below).

In certain cases, a special approach to valuing a supply may be required and there may be an agreement between HMRC and a particular trade or particular factors may have to be taken into account. Application of the valuation rules in particular circumstances are considered in 69.31 below.

In all cases, the application of the correct valuation rule depends upon correctly identifying the consideration given for the supply. For the meaning of 'consideration' see 69.8 below.

69.2 GENERAL VALUATION RULES

The general rules for determining the value of a supply of goods or services are to be found in

- *VATA 1994, s 19(2)* where the consideration for the supply is wholly in money (see 69.3 below); and
- *VATA 1994, s 19(3)* where the consideration is not wholly in money (see 69.5-69.7 below).

These general rules are, however, subject to any special valuation rules made by or under *VATA 1994*. [*VATA 1994, s 19(1)*]. These special rules are considered in 69.10-69.30 below.

69.3 Consideration wholly in money

If a supply is for a consideration in 'money', subject to the special valuation rules in 69.10–69.30 below, its value for VAT purposes is such amount as, with the addition of the VAT chargeable, is equal to the consideration. [*VATA 1994, s 19(2)*].

'*Money*' includes currencies other than sterling. [*VATA 1994, s 96(1)*]. See 69.14 and 69.18 below where acquisitions from other EC countries and supplies respectively are in foreign currency.

The value for VAT purposes is therefore that part of the payment which, when added to the VAT itself, gives a total equalling the payment. The VAT element of a VAT-inclusive consideration is determined by multiplying that consideration by the VAT fraction (see 47.2 OUTPUT TAX).

Example

Goods subject to standard-rated VAT are sold for a cash payment of £96.

The VAT element is 7/47 × £96 = £14.30

The value for VAT purposes is £81.70 (£96.00 – £14.30) and the consideration is £96.

Whether contract price inclusive or exclusive of VAT. Whether a price quoted is inclusive or exclusive of VAT must turn on the terms of the particular contract.

- Where a contract specifically states that a price is *VAT-inclusive*, the supplier must calculate the VAT element as in the above example.
- Where it specifically states that the price is *VAT-exclusive*, it is commonly understood that the purchaser must pay the VAT in addition to the quoted price. See *Hostgilt Ltd v Megahart Ltd, Ch D 1998, [1999] STC 141 (TVC 65.4)* and *Wynn Realisations Ltd (in administration) v Vogue Holdings Inc, CA [1999] STC 524 (TVC 65.5)*.
- Where the terms of the contract do not make it clear that a payment of the VAT is required in addition to the contract price, the supplier may be left to account for the VAT out of what he receives. See *Lancaster v Bird, CA 19 November 1998 unreported (TVC 65.3)* which was concerned, *inter alia*, with whether VAT could be charged in addition to the cash price quoted for building a stable block. It was held that, although there may well be a custom in the construction industry that prices are quoted exclusive of VAT, there was no evidence in the particular case that, on a contract between a small builder seeking payment in cash and a part-time farmer, it was an implied custom that VAT would be paid on top of the cash payments.

VAT on other taxes. Under *EC Sixth Directive, Art 11.A.2(a)* the taxable amount (equivalent to value in UK legislation) expressly includes taxes, duties, levies and charges, excluding the VAT itself. Although *VATA 1994, s 19(2)* does not expressly stipulate that other taxes are included in the value for VAT purposes, any such taxes levied on a supply form part of the purchase price and are therefore included in that part of the consideration upon which the VAT must be calculated. This does mean in certain circumstances, eg spirits and tobacco, that VAT is payable on other taxes.

Adequacy or otherwise of monetary consideration. There is no valuation provision by which an inflated payment in money can be reduced for VAT purposes. Where an artificially reduced payment in money is charged, the transaction can be treated as having a higher value for VAT purposes but only where

- it is between connected persons (see 64.19 below); or
- it relates to supplies of goods made to non-taxable persons for retail sale ('direct selling') (see 64.23 below).

However, in cases where apparently insufficient monetary payment appears to have been made, it may well be that the recipient of the supply has also provided additional consideration in a non-monetary form. For example, where a leasehold interest in a property has been granted for a nominal payment of say £1, the tenant may also have been obliged to perform certain building works or improvements to the property for the landlord's benefit. This non-monetary consideration must also be valued (see 69.5 below).

(Internal Guidance V1–12, paras 2.1, 2.2, 2.6).

69.4 *Apportionment of monetary consideration*

Where a supply of any goods or services is not the only matter to which a consideration in money relates, the supply is deemed to be for such part of the consideration as is properly attributable to it. [*VATA 1994, s 19(4)*].

Sometimes a single monetary consideration may be the payment for two or more supplies of different liabilities. In such a situation, the above provision requires the trader to allocate a fair proportion of the total payment to each of the supplies. It does not, however, stipulate how that apportionment should be made. A trader can use, and HMRC can accept, any method provided that it achieves a fair result and can be supported by a valid calculation.

For further coverage of apportionment of consideration, see 47.3 OUTPUT TAX.

69.5 Consideration not wholly in money

If a supply is for a consideration not consisting, or not wholly consisting, of money, subject to the special valuation rules in 69.10–69.30 below, its value is to be taken to be such amount in money as, with addition of the VAT chargeable, is equivalent to the consideration. [*VATA 1994, s 19(3)*]. In other words, it is necessary to

- determine the amount that would have been given in money for the supply if goods or services had not instead been used for all or part of the payment; and then
- multiply that amount by the VAT fraction (see 47.2 OUTPUT TAX) to establish how much VAT is due.

Distinguishing between non-monetary consideration and no consideration. Non-monetary consideration exists when a supply is made in return for payment in the form of goods or services. Where there is only non-monetary consideration, a barter transaction takes place (see 69.7 below). In some cases there may be both a monetary consideration and a non-monetary consideration.

When goods or services are provided for no payment in any form (monetary or non-monetary), there has been no consideration. It is then only necessary to value such a provision of goods or services where *VATA 1994* deems a taxable supply to have taken place. The commonest cases are

- private or non-business use of business assets for no consideration (see 69.20 below);
- private or non-business use of services supplied to the business (see 69.21 below);
- supplies of business goods/assets for no consideration (see 69.22 below); and
- deemed supplies of business goods/assets on hand at the time of deregistration (see 69.22 below).

(Internal Guidance V1–12, para 4.1).

Establishing the monetary equivalent of non-monetary consideration. Key principles in determining the monetary equivalent of non-monetary consideration have been established by the European Court in *Naturally Yours Cosmetics Ltd v C & E Commrs (No 2), CJEC [1988] STC 879 (TVC 21.159)* and *Empire Stores Ltd v C & E Commrs, CJEC [1994] STC 623 (TVC 21.160)*.

In *Naturally Yours Cosmetics Ltd* a company sold cosmetics at wholesale prices to beauty consultants who then resold them, at retail prices recommended by the company, at parties which the consultants had encouraged hostesses to arrange. As a reward, a consultant gave the hostess a pot of cream which had been purchased from the company for £1.50 instead of the usual wholesale price of £10.14. The CJEC held that VAT was due on £10.14. The consultants were providing the company with a service (arranging for the hostess to hold the party) in addition to the cash paid. The value of the service was £10.14 less the £1.50 payment. The fact that the price was reduced only if the party actually took place, showed that the parties *subjectively* assigned to the service provided a value corresponding to that price reduction.

The general rule deriving from the decision in *Naturally Yours Cosmetics Ltd* is that non-monetary consideration has the value of the alternative monetary payment that would normally have been given for the supply. Because this must be arrived at subjectively, it is necessary to determine what the particular recipient would have paid the particular supplier for the particular supply had the payment been in money.

In circumstances similar to *Naturally Yours Cosmetics Ltd*, the alternative monetary consideration is not difficult to establish because the normal price chargeable is self-evident from the contractual arrangement between the parties to the transaction. Alternatively, the monetary equivalent may be set out in a catalogue or price-list which shows what the recipient of the supply would have to pay when he provides no non-monetary consideration (eg where persons providing selling or introductory services to a mail-order trader are entitled to receive catalogue goods free or for a reduced cash payment).

However, this rule cannot be followed in case where the goods supplied in return for such services are not otherwise sold to the provider of the services. In *Empire Stores Ltd*, a company sold goods via mail order catalogues. New customers (under a 'self-introduction scheme') and existing customers (under an 'introduce-a-friend scheme') were entitled to select an item from a list (eg kettle, toaster or iron) free of charge once they (or, as the case may be, their friend) had been approved as a customer and placed an order for goods from the catalogues. The 'reward goods' in question were not advertised for sale in the catalogues. The CJEC held that the introductory service provided by the customer was non-monetary consideration because there was a direct link between its provision and the supply of the reward good. (The link was direct because, in the absence of the service, no reward good would be supplied.) The value of the goods had to be determined subjectively. Where the value was not a sum of money agreed between the parties (as in *Naturally Yours Cosmetics Ltd* above), in order to be subjective, it must be the value which the recipient of the services attributes to the services which he is seeking to obtain. This must correspond to the amount which he is prepared to spend for that purpose. Where, as in *Empire Stores Ltd*, the supply of goods is involved, the value can only be the price which the supplier has paid for those goods.

HMRC advise their officers that the general valuation rule in *Naturally Yours Cosmetics Ltd* should be applied where possible and only where it cannot should the rule in *Empire Stores Ltd* be followed.

(Internal Guidance V1–12, paras 4.3, 4.4).

See also *C & E Commrs v Pippa-Dee Parties Ltd, QB [1981] STC 495 (TVC 65.31)* and *Rosgill Group Ltd v C & E Commrs, CA [1997] STC 811 (TVC 65.32)* where goods were sold under the 'party plan' system but the provider of the services could choose between taking a 'cash commission' or selecting catalogue goods at a lower price. In *Rosgill Group Ltd* a company sold clothing and other goods. Self-employed 'organisers' displayed and sold the products at parties held in the homes of hostesses. In return for permitting a party to be held in her home, a hostess was entitled to take a cash payment or obtain goods from Rosgill's catalogues at a reduced price. The amounts of cash and price reduction were not equal. In the sample transaction considered by the tribunal, the hostess had the option of £2.89 in cash or purchasing goods for £20.76 that would have cost £27.99 if she had paid the listed retail price, ie a reduction of £7.23. It was held that the value of the consideration for the supply of the goods was the usual retail price, ie a monetary consideration of £20.76 plus a non-monetary consideration of £7.23, being the subjective value of the services supplied by the hostess. It was clear from the contractual terms of the transaction that, if the hostess had not provided the services, she would have had to pay the normal retail price for the goods. The fact that the hostess could have opted to take cash instead, did not prevent the usual non-monetary consideration valuation rules applying in those cases where the price reduction was selected rather than the cash option.

69.6 *Barter transactions*

A barter transaction is one in which no monetary payment is made. It may involve goods or services (or a mixture of both) being supplied in return for a supply of goods or services (or a mixture of both) from the other party. Each trader's supply constitutes the consideration he is providing in return for the supply from the other party. An example of a common barter transaction is where a publisher runs a competition in which prizes have been 'donated' but where the publisher is contractually bound to provide advertising to the donor of the prize in return.

(*a*) *Valuation when each supply has a different value*. Non-monetary consideration has to be valued by reference to a subjective value that the parties are regarded as having assigned to the consideration (see 69.5 above). A difficulty arises where each party has good reason for ascribing a different value to the consideration.

Example

An organisation owns a hall with a current open market valuation of £30,000. The local council require the land on which the hall is sited for development purposes. In order to get the land, the council build a new hall on a different site which it gives to the organisation in return for the old hall and land. The construction costs of the new hall are £100,000.

In such a situation, although there is no precedent authority, HMRC have been advised as follows.

- The value cannot simply be derived by taking the £30,000 open market value of the old hall. This would be the application of an objective value which is contrary to the principles set out in *Naturally Yours Cosmetics Ltd* and *Empire Stores Ltd* (see 69.5 above).
- The principle in *Naturally Yours Cosmetics Ltd* does not really assist in this situation because there is no clear monetary alternative that would have otherwise been paid for the supply. As such, it is necessary to fall back upon the principle in *Empire Stores Ltd*, ie to determine the amount which the recipient of the non-monetary consideration is prepared to spend for the purpose of obtaining it.
- The council was prepared to spend £100,000 to obtain the old hall because these were the costs incurred by it in constructing the new one. The council therefore should be regarded as having made a supply in return for consideration of £100,000.
- However, from the organisation's viewpoint, applying the *Empire Stores Ltd* principle to valuing the non-monetary consideration received by the organisation for its supply of the old hall gives a value of £30,000.

The question of values applying to supplies within a barter transaction has not been considered by the tribunals or courts.

(*b*) *Valuation* where *one or both supplies have no clear value*. A typical example occurs where a newspaper prints vouchers or tokens which the purchaser collects to obtain free or discounted goods or services from another trader. In return, the newspaper may have agreed to allocate a specific amount of space to advertising the other trader's name although, in many cases, no such precise terms exist. The newspaper is providing the other trader with services of advertising and promotion whilst the trader is allowing the newspaper to use its name and trading style in the promotion and may be supplying other services (eg promoting the particular newspaper) in return. Using the principle in *Empire Stores Ltd* (see 69.5 above) it is easier to identify costs incurred by the newspaper in providing the advertising service than the costs incurred by the other trader. HMRC suggest that the other trader's supplies can be treated as being of equal value.

Where neither side of a barter can be translated into a monetary equivalent, neither set of services can be regarded as having been supplied for a non-monetary consideration.

(Internal Guidance V1–12, paras 4.9, 4.10).

69.7 *Part-exchange*

Under a part-exchange transaction, goods are supplied in return for money and other goods.

General rule. Applying the principles in *Naturally Yours Cosmetics Ltd* (see 69.5 above), the general rule is that the goods taken in part-exchange are equal in value to the amount by which the price at which the goods would otherwise have been supplied has been reduced in the particular case. The value of the main supply is therefore the VAT-exclusive amount that would have been charged if no goods had been taken in part-exchange.

Example 1

A sells goods to the majority of his customers for a retail price of £100. To customers in the same line of business he offers the same goods at £95. B is a 'normal customer' and he brings in a part-exchange item which A values at £10. C is a 'trade customer' and he also brings in a part-exchange item which A values at £10.

The total value of the supply to B is £100 (monetary consideration of £90 plus non-monetary consideration of £10, ie the amount by which the goods have been reduced for him (£100 – £90). Similarly, the total value of the supply to C is £95 (£85 plus £10 (£95 – £85)).

See, however, *C & E Commrs v Ping (Europe) Ltd, CA [2002] STC 1186 (TVC 65.83)*. In that case, a company (P) sold golf clubs, some of which did not comply with the Rules of Golf and so could not be used for golf competitions. P offered to supply a new club for £22 to anyone surrendering one of the 'illegal' clubs in part-exchange. The new clubs had a normal wholesale price of £49.99 and a normal retail price of £72. Customs argued that the 'illegal' clubs had a part-exchange value of £27.99, so that P had to account for VAT on the normal wholesale price of £49.99. The tribunal held (and the Ch D and CA unanimously agreed) that that the 'illegal' clubs had no value so that output tax was only due on the consideration of £22 which P actually received. The scrap value of the old clubs could be ignored and the value of the non-monetary consideration involved was nil.

Exceptions to the general rule. There are situations in which a number of the general rules above do not apply.

(*a*) *Allowances for traded-in goods.* Where, as a sales promotion offer, a dealer offers a fixed allowance for traded-in goods, irrespective of their true value, such an allowance can be treated as a discount rather than a part-exchange in the following circumstances.

(i) If a fixed allowance is offered

- irrespective of the nature of the item traded-in;
- for any item of a particular class without regard to make, age, model or condition; or
- for an item of a particular class or make irrespective of age, model or condition provided that no attempt is made to value the traded-in goods and there is no reason for the goods to be accepted other than for trade promotion (which would not apply where prior arrangements have been made for the traded-in goods to be reconditioned or sold).

(ii) If a manufacturer or distributor advertises nationally or regionally a trade-in allowance on an 'at least' basis (eg an allowance of 'at least' £5) which would fall within (i) above if it had simply been a fixed allowance. Retailers can offer more than one minimum allowance but only to promote sales, it must not be because they value the traded-in goods at a higher level. There must be no references to the age or condition of the traded-in items.

Where (i) or (ii) above applies, the value of the supply is only the amount of actual money received.

(*b*) *Bumping.* It is common practice in the motor trade to manipulate the value of part exchange vehicles to satisfy the minimum deposit requirements of a finance company. This is referred to as 'bumping'. See 45.7 MOTOR CARS.

(*c*) *Payments made by suppliers to retailers under money-off coupon schemes or cash-back schemes.* Following the decision in *Elida Gibbs Ltd v C & E Commrs, CJEC [1996] STC 1387 (TVC 21.161)*, where payments have been made by manufacturers or distributors as a result of operating a money-off coupon or cash back scheme, those payments reduce their output tax. The manufacturer or dealer must demonstrate that the payments have been made to the retailers and consumers in the transaction chain and that the payments relate directly to successfully redeemed coupons following a retail sale of the goods. See 67.16 TRADE PROMOTION SCHEMES.

(Internal Guidance V1–12, para 4.11).

69.8 Meaning of consideration

Consideration is not defined either in *EC Sixth Directive* or *VATA 1994*. The word was defined in the *EC 2nd Directive, Annex A, para 13* as meaning 'everything received in return for the supply of goods or the provision of services, including incidental expenses (packing, transport, insurance, etc) that is to say not only the cash amounts charged, but also, for example, the value of goods received in exchange or, in the case of goods or services supplied by order of a public authority, the amount of compensation received.' Even though this *Directive* no longer exists, the definition is still sometimes used in cases brought before the CJEC.

The phrase 'in return for' the supply is interpreted to mean that there must be a direct link between the supply and the consideration. See *Staatssecretaris van Financiën v Cooperatieve Vereniging Cooperatieve Aardappelenbewaarplaats GA, CJEC [1981] 3 CMLR 337 (TVC 21.53)*, and *C & E Commrs v The Apple and Pear Development Council, HL [1986] STC 192 (TVC 21.55)*.

Consideration may be 'monetary' or 'non-monetary' (or a combination of both).

- 'Monetary' consideration includes payment by cash, cheque, credit card, bank transfer and deduction from pay, etc. Where a purchaser pays by credit card, the supplier's consideration is the total price charged to the customer and not the net sum received from the credit card company after deduction of commission in respect of services provided (*Chaussures Bally SA v Ministry of Finance (Belgium), CJEC 1993, [1997] STC 209 (TVC 21.164)*).
- 'Non-monetary consideration' is goods or services provided as payment, eg as in a barter or part-exchange transaction. Services provided include the giving up of a right, refraining from doing something, agreeing to suffer some loss, etc in return for the supply.

Payment by/to third parties. In some circumstances a person may pay for a supply to be made to someone else (eg a holding company may pay for supplies to an associated company). Provided there is an agreement between the supplier and the recipient, there is still a direct link between supply and consideration. Equally, where payment for a supply is made to a third party, such payment will usually be sufficient consideration to make a supply taxable. See *Lord Advocate v Largs Golf Club, CS [1985] STC 226 (TVC 13.6)* where payments made by club members to a trust which owned the freehold of the golf course were held to be part of the consideration for the supply of facilities to members by the club.

(Internal Guidance V1–3, paras 7.1–7.4).

De Voil Indirect Tax Service. See V3.103.

69.9 **Payments which may not be consideration**

Some payments are not consideration because they do not fulfil the conditions in 69.8 above, ie there is no direct link between the payment and the supply or there is no supply of goods or services in return for the payment. This paragraph covers areas requiring special attention.

(1) **Fines and penalty charges**. A true fine or penalty is a separate payment from the standard charge for a supply and is usually a sum of money levied as a consequence for a contravention of the terms of a contract. As such, it does not form part of the consideration for a supply and is outside the scope of VAT. This also applies to money levied to penalise an unlawful act (eg parking on yellow lines).

However, a payment may be described as a fine or penalty where it is not a payment for the breaking of terms and conditions, but a further payment for a fulfilment of terms and conditions (ie part of the consideration for the supply). In such cases, the payments follow the same liability as the supply.

> *Examples*
>
> - *Video hire fines.* Any fine by a video hire shop is an additional taxable supply for the extended use of a video. See *Leigh(t/a Moor Lane Video) (VTD 5098) (TVC 65.138).*
> - *Car park charges.* Any additional charge made by a car park for a driver overstaying the allotted time is not regarded as a penalty, but as an extra taxable charge for an extended stay in the car park. But see 43.4(2) LOCAL AUTHORITIES AND PUBLIC BODIES for penalties imposed by local authorities.

(Internal Guidance V1–3, paras 9.4, 10.7).

(2) **Grants and donations**. If freely given with no expectation of anything in return, grants and donations are not consideration for any supply and are outside the scope of VAT. They should not be confused with sponsorship which normally involves the sponsor receiving clearly identifiable benefits in return. See 57.18 RECREATION AND SPORT.

Project funding. Businesses and government departments, local authorities, etc sometimes co-sponsor a research and development project. The amounts contributed by individual sponsor depends on the cost of the project rather than on any commercial benefit to that sponsor. Provided any benefits are incidental to the primary purpose of the project and minimal in relation to the amount of the funding, the funding of the project is not seen as consideration for a supply. Such incidental benefits include the loan of items developed under a project; a levy on sales of the results of the projects as partial repayment of the funding; certain rights relating to or restricting the use of the results; and copies of technical reports on the project.

Donated services. The provision of donated services for no consideration is not a supply for VAT purposes. If the provider of the services asks for a donation to be made to a charity rather than payment for his usual fee (eg as in Will Aid), such payments can be disregarded for VAT purposes as long as it is clear to customer that the services can be obtained without the customer being obliged to pay anything. It must be left entirely up to the customer's discretion whether he wishes to pay anything to the charity. The fact that the provider may recommend an amount equivalent to the fee be paid to the charity does not, in itself, alter the donation status of the payments.

Local authority, central government and EC grants. The essential point to decide is whether the public authority or EC has derived any direct benefit (see 69.8 above). For cases relating to local authority grants, see *Trustees of the Bowthorpe Community Trust (VTD 12978) (TVC 40.14)*, *Hillingdon Legal Resource Centre Ltd (VTD 5210) (TVC 11.36)* and *Wolverhampton Citizens Advice Bureau (VTD 16411)(TVC 11.37)*. For case relating to EC grants, see *Mohr v Finanzamt Bad Segeberg, CJEC [1996] STC 328 (TVC 21.120)* and *Landboden-Agrardienste GmbH & Co KG v Finanzamt Calau, CJEC 1997, [1998] STC 171 (TVC 21.121)*.

(Internal Guidance V1–3, paras 10.2, 10.3).

(3) **Deposits including returnable containers**. Most deposit payments represent consideration. The amount paid over is intended by the parties to the contract to be offset against the purchase price once the supply has been made. Where a deposit is returned (eg if a contract is cancelled), it ceases to be consideration for a supply unless part of the supply has already been made, in which case the deposit is regarded as being consideration for that part of the supply and VAT must be accounted for accordingly. In the case where a contract is cancelled and nothing is supplied, the deposit is not consideration even if it is not returned.

Forfeit deposits are in general not consideration for any supplies because they constitute a payment for compensation for breach of contract. See 33.4 HOTELS AND HOLIDAY ACCOMMODATION.

Security deposits. A deposit taken as security (eg against the safe return of goods on hire or loan) is not consideration for a supply. Typically, the terms of the contract under which such a deposit is required specifies that the deposit is refundable on safe return of the goods, etc. In the event of the deposit being forfeited, either wholly or in part, through the customer failing to fulfil his contractual obligations, the amount retained by the supplier does not represent additional consideration for the original supply or consideration for an additional supply of goods or services.

Returnable containers. Where a charge is added to a supply of goods for the container until it is returned (eg the keg with beer), it is important to establish exactly why the charge has been raised. If it has been raised purely to ensure the safe return of the container and the charge is to be refunded on its return, it can be treated in the same way as a security deposit (see above). If, however, the charge has been raised to cover the loan, hire or use of the container, then the charge represents consideration for a supply of services, even if it is refundable when the container is returned.

(Internal Guidance V1–3, paras 9.2, 10.4).

See also 64.37 SUPPLY.

(4) **Management charges and directors services**. See 44 MANAGEMENT SERVICES AND SUPPLIES OF STAFF.

(5) **Gratuities, tips and service charges**. If these are genuinely freely given, they are outside the scope of VAT as they are not consideration for VAT purposes. This is so even if a customer expressly asks for a gratuity or tip to be shown on the bill in order to support an expenses claim or where payment is made by cheque or credit card, and the amount shown includes the tip. Where, however, the element of choice has been removed, the payment is part of the consideration for a supply.

Service charges in restaurants are part of the consideration for the underlying supply of the meals if customers are required to pay them. This applies even if they are passed on in full as bonuses to the staff (*Potters Lodge Restaurant Ltd (VTD 905) (TVC 65.131)*). If customers have a genuine option as to whether to pay the service charges, HMRC accept that they are not consideration even if the amounts appear on the invoices (*NDP Co Ltd (VTD 2653) (TVC 65.111)*). In HMRC's opinion, the important point in that case is that the terms of the menu set the contract between restaurant and customer and the bills are issued too late to affect the contractual position. Therefore, where menus state that service charges are optional or at the discretion of customers, the charges are not part of the consideration for the taxable meals.

(Internal Guidance V1–3, para 10.6).

(5A) **Disbursements**. See 3.7 AGENTS.

(6) **Salary sacrifice for use of a motor car**. See 45.18 MOTOR CARS.

(7) ***Ex gratia* payments**. An *ex gratia* payment by a customer to cover unexpected costs is outside the scope of VAT provided

- the amount is clearly additional to the price for the supply;
- the customer has no obligation to make the payment; and
- the customer would still receive the supply if the *ex gratia* payment were not made.

Where, however, the agreement between the parties provides for an additional charge, this forms part of the consideration.

(Internal Guidance V1–3, para 10.10).

(8) **Subject access fees**. Individuals are entitled, by law, to request access ('subject access') to personal data held about them from any data user. Under *Data Protection Act 1984, s 21(2)* the data user may charge for providing such information, subject to a maximum fee prescribed by Regulations. This subject access fee is merely a nominal sum to cover the expenses of complying with the statute and is not consideration as there is no supply for VAT purposes. (Internal Guidance V1–3, para 10.11).

(9) **Manufacturers' warranties**. A manufacturer's warranty covers the reliability of the item while it is still new, and expected to be sound. Where the manufacturer does a repair under this warranty, there is no supply at that time by the manufacturer (even if new parts are supplied) because the original goods were costed to allow for such repairs, and to tax the warranty repair again would result in double taxation.

This also applies where the manufacturer is an overseas manufacturer and warranty repairs are carried out by the UK importer or distributor of the goods as part of his after sales service to customers. There is no supply by the UK importer or distributor to the customer. The payment made by the overseas manufacturer to the UK importer or distributor to meet the cost of repairs is regarded as compensation and not consideration for a supply.

However, if a dealer or other third party carries out the repair on behalf of either a UK or overseas manufacturer, there is a supply by him to the manufacturer and his charge for that supply is consideration.

(Internal Guidance V1–3, para 10.15).

(10) **Retailers' warranties**. Certain retailers (eg jewellers) offer customers an 'insurance' or indemnity which provides for free repair or replacement if the goods sold are lost or damaged within a certain period of purchase. The retailer may cover the liability to replace a lost or damaged item either by obtaining insurance cover or by including the cost in the overall price. In such cases, neither a repair free-of-charge by the retailer nor the free replacement of the lost or damaged goods is a taxable supply, as the original charge covered the costs involved. (Internal Guidance V1–3, para 10.16).

(11) **Compensation payments**. Compensation payments for damage or loss are outside the scope of VAT as they are not consideration for a supply. This is because the payments are made either as a result of a Court Order or through an agreement between the two parties involved to compensate one party for suffering some inconvenience, loss or damage. See 47.8(4) OUTPUT TAX for further details.

(12) **Payments relating to land**. See 42.4 LAND AND BUILDINGS.

(13) **Overpayments**. Where, due to a mistake by the customer, a supplier receives payment twice for the same invoice, the value of the supply is not affected. The value remains the original price billed and cannot be doubled simply because of the overpayment. The overpayment is outside the scope of VAT unless, and until, it is used to pay or part-pay a future invoice of the supplier in which case it becomes consideration. (Internal Guidance V1–3, para 10.17).

69.10 SPECIAL VALUATION RULES

The general rules for determining the value of a supply of goods or services under 69.2 *et seq.* above are subject to any special valuation rules made by or under *VATA 1994*. In case of any conflict, the order of precedence of the special valuation rules is as follows.

(*a*) **Provisions other than those contained in *VATA 1994, Sch 6*.** These principally comprise the following.

- *VATA 1994, s 20, Sch 7* — acquisitions from other EC countries (see 69.11-69.14 below)
- *VATA 1994, s 21* — imports (see 69.15 below)
- *VATA 1994, s 23* — gaming machine takings (see 69.29 below)
- *SI 1993/1507* — non-business use of services supplied to a business (see 69.21 below)

(*b*) **Provisions in *VATA 1994, Sch 6*** These comprise

- *Sch 6 para 1* — transactions between connected persons (see 69.19 below)
- *Sch 6 para 1A* — use of stock in trade cars of motor manufacturers and motor dealers for less than market value (see 69.30 below)
- *Sch 6 para 2* — supplies of goods to non-taxable persons for retail sale ('direct selling') (see 69.23 below)
- *Sch 6 para 3* — imports and warehoused goods subject to excise duty (see 69.15 and 69.16 below)
- *Sch 6 para 4* — discounts (see 69.24 below)
- *Sch 6 para 5* — tokens, stamps and vouchers (see 69.25 below)
- *Sch 6 para 6* — supplies of goods for no consideration (see 69.22 below)
- *Sch 6 para 7* — non-business use of business assets (see 69.20 below)
- *Sch 6 para 8* — reverse charge services from abroad (see 69.17 below)
- *Sch 6 para 9* — long-term accommodation at reduced rates (see 69.26 below)

- *Sch 6 para 10* — supplies of catering and accommodation by employers to employees (see 69.27 below)
- *Sch 6 para 11* — supplies in foreign currencies (see 69.18 below)
- *Sch 6 para 12* — money consideration for a supply paid by a third party (see 69.28 below)

[*VATA 1994, s 19(1)*].

69.11 **Acquisitions from other EC countries**

The value of any acquisition of goods from another EC country is to be taken to be the value of the transaction in which the goods are acquired as follows.

- Where the goods are acquired from another EC country by means of a taxable supply (eg goods installed or assembled in the UK, see 23.29 EUROPEAN COMMUNITY: SINGLE MARKET) the value of that transaction is determined under the general valuation rules (see 69.2 above).
- Where the goods are acquired from another EC country otherwise than in pursuance of a taxable supply, subject to 69.12–69.14 below,
  - (i) if the transaction is for a consideration in money, its value is to be taken to be such amount as is equal to the consideration; and
  - (ii) if the transaction is for a consideration not consisting, or not wholly consisting, of money, its value is to be taken to be such amount in money as is equivalent to the consideration.

  Note that under (i) above the value is an amount equal to the consideration whereas under the general rule in 69.3 above the value is an amount which, with the addition of the VAT chargeable, is equivalent to the consideration.

[*VATA 1994, s 20(1)–(4); FA 1996, Sch 3 para 6*].

Consideration is any form of payment in money or in kind. It includes any payment made by the customer to cover the supplier's costs in making the supply (eg packing, transport or insurance) for which the supplier is responsible under the contract.

Where there is no consideration (eg when a business transfers its own goods from one EC country to another, or when goods are transferred to a customer without charge from another EC country by a person registered for VAT in that other country) the rules in 69.22 below apply.

(VAT Notice 725, paras 5.3, 5.4).

Consideration attributable to both an acquisition and other matters. Where the transaction in pursuance of which the goods are acquired from another EC country is not the only matter to which a consideration in money relates, the transaction is deemed to be for such part of the consideration as is properly attributable to it. [*VATA 1994, s 20(5)*].

Goods subject to duty. Where goods acquired in the UK from another EC country are charged in connection with their removal to the UK with a duty of excise (or any Community customs duty or EC agricultural levy having effect for transitional provisions in connection with the accession of any state to the EC), then the value of the acquisition for VAT purposes is its value apart from this provision plus the amount (if not already included) of the excise duty, Community customs duty or agricultural levy which has been or is to be paid in respect of the goods. This does not apply to any transaction relating to warehoused goods treated as taking place before the duty point (see 70.4 WAREHOUSED GOODS AND FREE ZONES).

[*VATA 1994, Sch 7 para 2; SI 1995/2518, Regs 96, 97*].

De Voil Indirect Tax Service. See V3.390.

69.12 *Transactions between connected persons*

Where in the case of any acquisition of goods from another EC country

(*a*) the value of the transaction is for a consideration in money which is less than its open market value, and

(*b*) the supplier and the person who acquires the goods are 'connected', and

(*c*) that person is not entitled under *VATA 1994, ss 25, 26* to credit for all the VAT on the acquisition,

HMRC may direct that the value of the transaction is to be taken to be its 'open market value'.

'*Open market value*' is the amount which would be taken as its value assuming the transaction was for such consideration in money as would be payable by a person standing in no such relationship with any person as would affect the consideration.

A direction is given by notice in writing to the person by whom the acquisition is made within a three year period from the time of the acquisition (or, in certain cases where that person is not a taxable person and the consideration is payable periodically, from the first relevant event for the purposes of taxing the acquisition). The direction may be varied or withdrawn by a further direction given by notice in writing. The direction may also include a direction that the value of any transaction made after the date of notice and to which the above conditions apply is to be taken to be its open market value. An appeal may be made against a direction (see 5.3(*v*) APPEALS).

See 69.19 below for the meaning of '*connected persons*'.

[*VATA 1994, Sch 7 paras 1, 5*].

De Voil Indirect Tax Service. See V3.391.

69.13 *Transfers and disposals of business assets*

Where goods are acquired from another EC country under a transaction treated as a supply of goods under 64.3(*e*)(*f*) SUPPLY, the value of the relevant transaction, in a case where there is no consideration, is to be taken to be

(*a*) such consideration in money as would be payable by the supplier if he were, at the time of the acquisition, to purchase goods *identical* in every respect (including age and condition) to the goods concerned; or

(*b*) where the value in (*a*) cannot be ascertained, such consideration in money as would be payable to purchase goods *similar* to, and of the same age and condition as, the goods concerned; or

(*c*) where the value cannot be ascertained under (*a*) or (*b*), the cost of producing the goods concerned if they were produced at that time.

Any VAT included in the purchase price or production cost is to be deducted in arriving at the value to be taxed.

[*VATA 1994, Sch 7 para 3*].

69.14 *Currencies other than sterling*

Where goods are acquired from another EC country and any sum relevant for determining the value of the transaction is expressed in a currency other than sterling, then unless one of the alternatives in (*a*)-(*c*) below is adopted, that sum is to be converted into sterling at the market selling rate for that currency at the time of acquisition. The rates published in national newspapers are acceptable as evidence of the rates at the relevant time. The following alternatives are, however, allowed.

(*a*) A business may use the period rate of exchange published by HMRC for customs purposes. Details of particular period rates are available from the National Advice Service (0845 010 9000). This alternative can be adopted in respect of all acquisitions or in respect of all acquisitions of a particular class or description. If the latter, that class or description should be noted in the business record at the time of adoption. There is no need to notify HMRC in advance if this alternative is to be adopted but, once it has been, a business cannot then change it without first obtaining the agreement of the National Advice Service.

(*b*) A business can apply in writing to the National Advice Service to use a rate, or a method of determining a rate, which it uses for commercial purposes. In considering whether to allow the application, the National Advice Service will take into account whether the proposed rate or method is determined by reference to the UK currency market, whether it is objectively verifiable, and the frequency with which the applicant proposes to update it. Forward rates or methods deriving from forward rates are not acceptable.

(*c*) By concession, if before 1 January 1993 a business used a rate authorised in writing by HMRC under the concessionary arrangements for supplies which applied up to that date, it may extend this to acquisitions without further notification, unless the rate it uses is wholly derived from currency markets other than in the UK. The continued use of concessionary rates is subject to review by HMRC.

Whatever rate or method is adopted, the appropriate rate for any supply is the one current at the time of supply.

[*VATA 1994, Sch 7 para 4*]. (VAT Notice 725, para 5.5 which has the force of law).

De Voil Indirect Tax Service. See V3.393.

69.15 **Importation of goods**

The value of goods imported from a place outside the EC is, subject to below, to be determined according to the rules for Community customs duties (whether or not the goods in question are subject to such duties). These rules are set out in *Council Regulation 2913/92* and *Commission Regulation 2454/93*. See also Customs Notice 252 *Valuation of imported goods for customs purposes, VAT and trade statistics*.

The following are included in the value (so far as not already included under the above rules).

(*a*) All taxes, duties and other charges levied outside or, by reason of importation, within the UK (but excluding VAT).

(*b*) All incidental expenses such as commission, packing, transport and insurance costs, up to the 'first destination' of the goods in the UK. '*First destination*' means the place mentioned on the consignment note or other importation document or, in the absence of such documentation, the place of the first transfer of cargo in the UK.

(*c*) If at the time of importation of the goods a further destination for the goods is known, and that destination is within the UK or another EC country, all such incidental expenses resulting from the transport of the goods to that other destination.

Subject to (*a*)–(*c*) above, where the consideration is wholly or partly in money and on terms allowing a discount for prompt payment (but not payment of the price by instalments), the value of the goods is reduced by the discount if payment is made in accordance with those terms so that the discount is allowed.

[*VATA 1994, s 21(1)–(3); FA 1995, s 22; FA 1996, s 27*].

Works of art, antiques and collectors' pieces. Special valuation provisions apply for these items which have the effect of subjecting them to VAT at an effective reduced rate of 5%. See 71.3 WORKS OF ART, ETC for full details.

Incidental expenses. In addition to the examples given above, 'incidental expenses' also covers items such as customs clearance charges, quay rent, entry fees, demurrage, handling, loading and storage costs. Costs which are taxable under the reverse charge procedure (see 39.4 INTERNATIONAL SERVICES), eg royalties and licence fees, should not be included in the value for import VAT.

Buyer and seller related. Under the customs valuation rules, where the buyer and seller of the goods are related, the price paid or payable for those goods can be accepted as long as the buyer shows that the relationship has not affected the price (see Customs Notice 252, paras 3.10, 3.11 and Section 30). The same rules apply for import VAT purposes, whether or not the goods are subject to a positive rate of customs duty.

Costs not known at time of importation. If all relevant costs cannot be established at the time the goods are entered (eg the cost of UK transport supplied by an independent haulier may not be known until some time later), HMRC will accept estimates of incidental expenses to be included in the import VAT value, based on certain nationally agreed rates. Details of the rates are available from Entry Processing Units.

(VAT Notice 702, para 3.1).

Value declaration. If goods are liable to *ad valorem* customs duty (ie a duty chargeable on the basis of value), a declaration on Form C105 (Valuation Declaration) or Form C109 (General Valuation Statement), made for duty purposes, will also generally be acceptable for VAT. However, the declaration will only provide information which helps determine the customs value of the goods, and it should not be regarded as establishing their full value for VAT purposes (see above).

Where goods are not liable to ad valorem duty but are liable to VAT at the standard rate, a valuation declaration for VAT is needed only if the value exceeds £4,000 and

- the importer is not registered for VAT; or
- the importer is registered for VAT but either the goods are for non-business purposes or input tax deduction would not be allowed (eg on motor cars); or
- the value of the goods is not being determined under Method 1 (see Customs Notice 252, Section 3).

Whether or not a valuation declaration is required for the goods, evidence of value must be produced. Acceptable evidence is a copy of the seller's invoice or other document against which payment will be made. This will include telex or similar messages used instead of invoices.

(VAT Notice 702, para 3.3).

De Voil Indirect Tax Service. See V3.321–329.

Excise duty. Where any goods whose supply involves their removal to the UK are charged in connection with their removal with a duty of excise or car tax (or any Community customs duty or EC agricultural levy having effect for transitional provisions in connection with the accession of any state to the EC), then the value of the supply for VAT purposes is its value apart from this provision plus the amount (so far as not already included) of any duty which has been or is to be paid in respect of the goods. [*VATA 1994, Sch 6 para 3*].

69.16 Warehoused goods

Where the time of supply of any dutiable goods (or goods comprising a mixture of dutiable goods and other goods) is determined under *VATA 1994, s 18*(*4*) (goods within the warehouse regime) to be at or after the duty point, then the value of the supply for VAT purposes is its value apart from this provision plus the amount (so far as not already included) of any duty which has been or is to be paid in respect of the goods. [*VATA 1994, Sch 6 para 3*].

See 70.8 WAREHOUSED GOODS AND FREE ZONES for the provisions of *VATA 1994, s 18*(*4*) and the definitions of '*dutiable goods*' and '*duty point*'.

69.17 Reverse charge services received from abroad

Where any supply of services is treated under the reverse charge provisions as made by the recipient of the services (rather than the supplier), the value of the supply is

- if the consideration for the services was a consideration in money, such amount as is equal to that consideration; and
- if the consideration did not, or did not wholly, consist of money, such amount in money as is equivalent to that consideration.

[*VATA 1994, Sch 6 para 8*].

It should be noted that under these provisions, value is derived from the consideration upon a VAT-exclusive basis. It is an amount equal to the consideration rather than, as under the general rule in 69.3 above, an amount which, when VAT is added, equals the consideration.

See 39.4 INTERNATIONAL SERVICES for situations where the reverse charge applies in the UK.

69.18 Supplies in foreign currency

EC legislation. See 22.14(*b*) EUROPEAN COMMUNITY LEGISLATION.

UK legislation. Where there is a supply of goods or services and any sum relevant for determining the value is expressed in a currency other than sterling, subject to below, that sum is to be converted into sterling at the market selling rate for that currency at the time of supply. The rates published in national newspapers are acceptable as evidence of the rates at the relevant time. The following options are, however, allowed.

- Where HMRC have published a notice specifying rates of exchange, or methods of determining rates of exchange, a person may opt to use a rate so specified or determined. This alternative may be adopted for all supplies or for all supplies of a particular class or description. If adopted only for a particular class, that class and the time of adoption should be noted in the records. There is no need to notify HMRC in advance that this alternative has been adopted but, once it has, it cannot be changed without first obtaining the agreement of HMRC.
- HMRC may allow a person to apply to them to use a different rate of exchange for the valuation of all or some of his supplies. Application should be made to HMRC in writing. In considering whether to allow the application, HMRC will take into account whether the proposed rate or method is determined by reference to the UK currency market, whether it is objectively verifiable and the frequency with which it is proposed to update it.

[*VATA 1994, Sch 6 para 11*]. (VAT Notice 700, para 7.7 which has the force of law).

Where a trader contracts to purchase foreign currency at a specified rate in advance of any supplies/acquisitions (to safeguard future exchange rate fluctuations), normally these contracted purchase rates of exchange are not acceptable for VAT purposes because they are forward rates or are determined by methods that rely upon forward rates. Forward rates are not based upon actual exchange rates but are speculative or hypothetical. Such a contracted purchase rate of exchange would only be acceptable where

(*a*) the contracted rate is one of the acceptable rates described above; and

(*b*) the actual time of supply or acquisition is no later than one month after the date of the purchase contract.

Similarly, it is not possible to value a supply/acquisition by reference to the exchange rate in use at the time the supplies were ordered or contracted for unless the conditions in (*a*) and (*b*) above are satisfied.

(Internal Guidance V1–12, para 5.25).

De Voil Indirect Tax Service. See V3.164.

69.19 Transactions between connected persons

Where all the following conditions are satisfied, then unless the supply falls within 69.27 below (supplies of accommodation and catering by employers to employees), HMRC *may* direct that the value of the supply is to be taken to be its 'open market value'.

(*a*) The value of a supply made by a taxable person for a consideration in money would otherwise be less than its open market value. A direction *cannot* therefore be made if

- part of the consideration is non-monetary (in which case the rules in 69.5 above must be followed); or
- the consideration is greater than the open market value (ie a direction cannot be issued to reduce an over-inflated consideration).

(*b*) The person making the supply and the person to whom it is made are 'connected' (see below).

(*c*) If the supply is a taxable supply, the recipient is not entitled under *VATA 1994, ss 25, 26* to credit for all of the VAT on the supply. In practice, this means that, where the supply is a taxable supply, a direction can only be issued if the recipient is not registered for VAT or is wholly or partly exempt for VAT purposes.

The provisions are specifically intended to counter tax avoidance. If a supply between connected persons is made below open market value for a legitimate reason that can be substantiated, and which is unconnected with avoidance, HMRC have a discretion not to issue a notice.

'*Open market value*' is the amount which would be taken as its value under (*a*) above assuming the supply were for such consideration in money as would be payable by a person standing in no such relationship with any person as would affect that consideration.

A direction is given by notice in writing to the person making the supply within a three year period from the time of the supply and may be varied or withdrawn by a further notice in writing. The notice may *also* include a direction that the value of any future supply satisfying the above conditions is to be taken to be its open market value (although a notice cannot cover future supplies only). An appeal may be made against a direction (see 5.3(*v*) APPEALS).

[*VATA 1994, s 19(5), Sch 6 para 1(1)–(3)(5), para 13*]. (Internal Guidance V1–12, para 5.3).

Connected persons. Persons are treated as 'connected' with another under the provisions of *ICTA 1988, s 839*. [*VATA 1994, Sch 6 para 1(4)*]. These are as follows.

(i) **An individual** is connected with his spouse, any 'relative' of himself or of his spouse, and with the spouse of any such relative. It appears that a widow or widower is no longer a spouse (*Vestey's Exors and Vestey v CIR, HL 1949, 31 TC 1*). Spouses divorced by decree nisi remain connected persons until the divorce is made absolute (*Aspden v Hildesley, Ch D 1981, [1982] STC 206*).

(ii) **A trustee of a settlement**, in his capacity as such, is connected with

- the settlor (if an individual);
- any person connected with that settlor; and
- a 'body corporate connected with the settlement'.

(iii) **Partners** are connected with each other and with each other's spouses and 'relatives' except in connection with acquisitions and disposals of partnership assets made pursuant to *bona fide* commercial arrangements.

(iv) **A 'company'** is connected with another company if

- the same person 'controls' both;
- one is controlled by a person who has control of the other in conjunction with persons connected with him;
- a person controls one company and persons connected with him control the other;
- the same group of persons controls both; or
- the companies are controlled by separate groups which can be regarded as the same by interchanging connected persons.

(v) **A company** is connected with another person who (either alone or with persons connected with him) has control of it.

(vi) **Persons acting together to secure or exercise control of a company** are treated in relation to that company as connected with each other and with any other person acting on the direction of any of them to secure or exercise such control. For the meaning of 'acting together to secure or exercise control' see *Steele v EVC International NV (formerly European Vinyls Corp (Holdings) BV), CA 1996, 69 TC 88*. Control may be 'exercised' passively. (See *Floor v Davis, HL 1979, 52 TC 609*).

'*Company*' includes any body corporate, unincorporated association or unit trust scheme. It does not include a partnership.

'*Control*' is as defined in *ICTA 1988, s 416*. See Tolley's Corporation Tax for full coverage of this definition.

'*Relative*' means brother, sister, ancestor or lineal descendant.

'*Settlement*' includes any disposition, trust, covenant, agreement, arrangement or transfer of assets. [*ICTA 1988, s 660G(1); FA 1995, Sch 17 para 1*].

'*A body corporate connected with the settlement*' is a 'close company' (or one which would be close if resident in the UK) the 'participators' in which include the trustees of the settlement, or a company of which such a close company, etc has 'control'. '*Close company*' for this purpose is as defined by *ICTA 1988, s 414*, '*participator*' is as defined by *ICTA 1988, s 417* and 'control' in this case, is as defined by *ICTA 1988, s 840*. See Tolley's Corporation Tax for full coverage of these definitions.

'*Settlor*' is any person by whom the settlement was made or who has directly or indirectly (or by a reciprocal arrangement) provided, or undertaken to provide, funds for the settlement. [*ICTA 1988, s 660G(1)(2); FA 1995, Sch 17 para 1*].

De Voil Indirect Tax Service. See V1.296; V3.161; V3.162.

69.20 Non-business use of business assets

Where there is a free supply of services by virtue of *VATA 1994, Sch 4 para 5(4)* (business goods put to a private or non-business use), then, unless 69.27 below applies (supplies of accommodation and catering by employers to employees), the value of the supply is taken to be the full cost to the taxable person of providing the services.

See 47.7 OUTPUT TAX for further details.

69.21 Non-business use of services supplied to a business

Where a person carrying on a business puts services supplied to him to any private or non-business use, he is treated as having supplied those services in the course or furtherance of the business. The value of the supply is that part of the value of the supply of the services to him as reasonably represents the cost to him of providing the services. Where the services are put to a private or non-business use on more than one occasion, the total VAT liability under these provisions cannot exceed the input tax claimed when the services were obtained. [*SI 1993/1507*].

See 47.7 OUTPUT TAX for further details.

69.22 Supplies of goods for no consideration

Where there is a supply of goods by virtue of

- a Treasury order under *VATA 1994, s 5(5)* (self-supply of goods, see 45.6 MOTOR CARS for self-supply of a motor car and 62.2 SELF-SUPPLY for self-supply of stationery),
- *VATA 1994, Sch 4 para 5(1)* (gifts of business assets, see 47.6 OUTPUT TAX),
- *VATA 1996, Sch 4 para 6* (removal of business assets from one EC country to another, see 23.2 EUROPEAN COMMUNITY: SINGLE MARKET), or
- *VATA 1994, Sch 4 para 8* (deemed supply on deregistration and termination of business, see 59.34 REGISTRATION),

then, unless 69.27 below applies (supplies of accommodation and catering by employers to employees), the value of the supply is

(*a*) such consideration in money (excluding any VAT) as would be payable by the person making the supply if he were, at the time of the supply, to purchase goods *identical* in every respect (including age and condition) to the goods concerned;

(*b*) where the value cannot be determined as under (*a*) above, such consideration in money (excluding any VAT) as would be payable by that person if he were, at that time, to purchase goods *similar* to, and of the same age and condition as, the goods concerned; and

(*c*) Where the value cannot be determined as under (*a*) or (*b*) above, the cost of producing the goods concerned if they were produced at that time.

[*VATA 1994, Sch 6 para 6*].

Note that what is relevant is what the goods would have cost to purchase or produce at the time of their disposal and not the actual historic cost to the business. Where disposal is close to the date the goods were obtained, the value may have remained unchanged. In most cases, however, depreciation or appreciation over the intervening period must be taken into account.

69.23 Supplies of goods made to non-taxable persons for retail sale ('direct selling')

In circumstances where

- the whole or part of a business carried on by a taxable person consists in supplying to a number of persons goods to be sold, whether by them or others, by retail, and
- those persons are not taxable persons,

HMRC may direct that the value of any such supply is to be taken as its open market value. The direction is given by notice in writing to the taxable person and is effective from the date of the giving of notice or a later date as specified in the notice and may be varied or withdrawn by a further direction given by notice in writing. An appeal may be made against a direction (see 5 APPEALS).

[*VATA 1994, Sch 6 paras 2, 13*].

HMRC has authority to issue such a direction in respect of direct selling cases because derogations have been obtained under *EC Sixth Directive, Art 27* (see 22.30 EUROPEAN COMMUNITY LEGISLATION). See also *Direct Cosmetics Ltd v C & E Commrs, CJEC [1985] STC 479 (TVC 21.320)* (and the subsequent appeal by *Direct Cosmetics* and *Laughton Photographs Ltd v C & E Commrs, CJEC [1988] STC 540 (TVC 21.321)*) and *Gold Star Publications Ltd v C & E Commrs, QB [1992] STC 365 (TVC 65.25)*. A direction has been held to be invalid where there was no effective means of determining the open market value of the goods sold by retail. See *Beckbell Ltd (VTD 9847) (TVC 65.28)* where the company did not fix a recommended retail price for goods by salesmen and frequently charged its salesmen different prices for identical goods. See, however, the subsequent decision of the House of Lords in *Fine Art Developments plc* below.

VATA 1994, Sch 6 para 2 is designed to avoid

- distortion of competition with traders using orthodox retail outlets; and
- loss of revenue through failure to tax the margin of the unregistered sellers.

HMRC's policy is that this power is only to be used where the direct sales are a regular feature of a trader's business. It will not normally be applied to direct sales to charitable organisations, church bazaars and the like. The types of business HMRC are concerned with is where sales are made through 'domestic outlets' by unregistered persons rather than normal '*retail outlets*', ie shops, street and market traders or mobile shops (eg ice cream vendors, fish and chip mobiles and hot dog sellers). The sales methods are party plan, door-to-door, catalogues or similar methods in which the principal's name, trading style or trademark are involved throughout the sales chain. Where party plan sales are involved, the party host will often be expected to promote the principal's tradename (eg a 'Tupperware' party). Door-to-door sales will usually involve the use of the principal's catalogue (eg Avon Cosmetics, Betterware). Some companies (mail order companies) specialise in sales through catalogues which are sent to applicants who show them to their friends, take orders and obtain the goods from the principal at a discount from the catalogue prices.

(Internal Guidance V1–12, para 5.5).

Issuing a notice of direction. HMRC officers are advised to work through the following steps when deciding whether or not to issue a notice.

(1) Does the trader

(*a*) sell to customers who take title in the goods (earning a discount); or

(*b*) sell through agents (earning a commission) who never take title to the goods?

If (*a*) applies, go to (2). If (*b*) applies, notice is not required as the trader is already liable to account for VAT on the price paid by the final customer.

(2) Is the trader a taxable person?

If Yes, go to (3). If No, the trader has no VAT liability and notice is not required.

(3) Does the trader's business consist of supplying goods to unregistered persons who will sell the goods on by retail?

If Yes, go to (4). If No, the trader's sales are presumably either to registered traders or to unregistered persons who do not sell the goods on. No notice is required and the trader must account for VAT on the price charged to the immediate customer.

(4) Is the trader's business of a kind described in Internal Guidance V1–12, para 5.5 (see above) as appropriate to the issue of a notice?

If Yes, go to (5). If No, the trader does not require notice and may therefore account for VAT on the price charged to the immediate customer.

(5) Do the trader's sales to unregistered persons for resale exceed £50,000 per annum?

If Yes, go to (6). If No, the trader is not regarded as being in a substantial way of business. Notice is not required where the £50,000 limit is not exceeded but HMRC officers are advised to monitor traders who may become eligible for notice at a later stage.

(6) The trader requires a notice of direction. Even if the trader is already accounting for VAT as though subject to a notice, HMRC will still issue a notice to formalise the position.

A notice issued under *VATA 1994, Sch 6 para* 2 cannot be made retrospective. In practice, the date from which the notice is to become operative will be at least seven days after the date upon which the notice is issued. A longer period may be allowed where the trader requests a short period of grace for administrative reasons (eg to revise accounting arrangements or update computer programmes) but HMRC will take the potential loss of revenue into account in reaching its decision.

(Internal Guidance V1–12, para 5.6).

'Open market value' on a sale by retail. This is essentially the price paid by the final customer in the supply chain, normally the recommended retail selling price (RRSP) or catalogue price of the goods. If the trader does not notify a RRSP to customers buying goods affected by the notice, the value can be taken as the actual price at which the goods (or similar goods) are sold by retail by the trader's customers or by similar retail outlets. Any discounts allowed to dealers, distributors or other intermediaries do not reduce the value at the retail level. (Internal Guidance V1–12, para 5.10).

Non-resale goods and goods applied to 'own use'. Where the non-taxable person to whom the trader sells the goods does not sell them (but, for example, keeps the goods or uses them as gifts), such goods are not covered by the notice as they have not been sold by retail. In such a case, the value of the goods is the money paid by the customer plus any non-monetary consideration which may be treated as given (eg in the form of services). Any claims by a trader that its customers do not resell by retail all of the goods they buy should be supported by evidence, eg customer surveys or trade statistics. (Internal Guidance V1–12, para 5.11).

In *Fine Art Developments plc v C & E Commrs, HL 1995, [1996] STC 246 (TVC 65.27)*, catalogues containing descriptions and pictures of goods for sale were sent to 'agents'. Some goods were retained by the agents for their own use and some were sold on at less than the catalogue price, although the majority were sold by the agents at the full catalogue price. The company argued that the direction issued under *VATA 1994, Sch 6 para 2* was invalid. It argued that it was not supplying goods to be sold by retail because at the time it made the supply to the agents, it did not know what the agents would be doing with the goods, and that even if the direction was not invalid for that reason, it was otherwise invalid because it was impossible to comply with its terms, ie to determine to which goods it was to apply. The House of Lords rejected these arguments and held that the direction was valid. As VAT was a self-assessed tax, it was the duty of the company to modify its order form so as to identify the goods earmarked for onward sale. Where the company was unable to show what the actual sale price for any item was, it was open to Customs to take the catalogue price as being the true open market value.

'Gifts', prizes and reward goods. Traders involved in direct selling frequently operate some form of promotion or incentive scheme providing for 'gifts' or rewards to representatives, salesmen or hostesses in return for rendering certain services, reaching specified sales targets or meeting some other obligation. Examples include

- goods equal in value to a percentage of the total sales at the party may be chosen by the hostess free of charge, any balance in excess of the reward being paid in full;
- an option is given to the hostess to take a cash commission which may be applied to the purchase of goods at a discount up to a limit related to the sales achieved;
- the hostess may purchase an unlimited amount of goods at a discount (using her own money) as a reward for her services; or
- a reward of goods (free of charge or at a discount or special price) may be given in return for the booking at the party of further parties (whether at the hostess's home or elsewhere).

The rewards are supplied in return for a non-monetary consideration in the form of services. VAT must be calculated under the provisions in 69.5 above on the amount that would have been given in money had the non-monetary consideration not taken its place.

(Internal Guidance V1–12, para 5.12).

De Voil Indirect Tax Service. See V3.161; V3.163.

69.24 Discounts

Prompt payment discounts. Where goods or services are supplied for a consideration in money and on terms allowing a discount for prompt payment, in valuing the supply the consideration is taken as reduced by the discount, whether or not payment is made in accordance with those terms. However, this treatment does not apply where the terms include any provision for payment by 'instalments'. [*VATA 1994, Sch 6 para 4*].

Suppliers that are required to issue a VAT invoice must show the rate of any cash discount on the invoice. Where the rate of discount has not been shown on a VAT invoice, a reduced value for VAT purposes can still be accepted if the trader can demonstrate the availability of the discount by other means (eg publications, terms of trading, price lists, other publicity materials and clauses in written contracts).

'*Instalments*' has its normal, everyday meaning and in the opinion of HMRC should be taken to include stage payments, ie payments made when certain conditions have been met under the terms of contract.

(Internal Guidance V1–12, para 5.14).

In *Saga Holidays Ltd (VTD 18591) (VTD 65.93)* S sold holidays and offered customers discounts for prompt payment. It failed to take account of such discounts and submitted a repayment claim. Customs agreed to refund the amounts which S had overpaid where customers actually received discounts but rejected the claim where discount had been offered but the customers had not actually taken advantage of it. The tribunal agreed with this treatment, observing that the legislation provided that the consideration should be taken as reduced 'by the discount' and holding that these words could more readily be interpreted as a reference to a discount that has actually come into existence than to one that was available but may never come into existence. Therefore, *Sch 6 para 4(1)* should be construed as meaning that the consideration is only reduced where the discount is achieved.

This does not appear to be the interpretation which HMRC state in their published material. In VAT Notice 700, para 7.3 and VAT Notice 701/49/02, para 5.2 they indicated that the value for VAT is the discounted amount 'whether of not the customer takes up the offer' and even more emphatically in Internal Guidance V1–12, para 5.14 they state that it is the discounted amount 'whether or not the purchaser has made his payment within the specified time limit'.

See also *Gold Star Publications Ltd v C & E Commrs, QB [1992] STC 365 (TVC 65.25)* (whether what was described as a discount for prompt payment was in fact such a discount or a commission given to demonstrators).

Unconditional discounts (eg because of the volume of supplies being made or the size and status of a customer) are given similar treatment as prompt payment discounts above.

Cash discounts (ie discounts offered when a payment is made wholly in cash). VAT is due upon the lower sum under the ordinary rule in 69.2 above because the consideration is only the sum of money that has actually been paid.

Trade and staff discounts provide special prices to particular customers, groups of customers and staff at reduced prices. VAT is due upon the discounted payments as the only consideration for the supplies is the money actually paid and therefore the general rules in 69.2 above applies.

Rentals of televisions and other domestic appliances. Where under a *yearly* rental contract rental companies allow customers who pay the year's rental in advance a discount on the amount that would have been payable if they had paid monthly instalments, VAT is only due upon the lower amount. However, for rental contracts under which payments are due more frequently (eg monthly) and each payment due covers a period of less than a year, the value for VAT purposes is the actual rental paid or due for each period.

Contingent discounts/rebates and other delayed reductions of price. These arise where a price reduction is made dependent upon some specified event taking place after the time of the supply (eg a discount may operate if a specified total value of purchases is made within a particular period). Such discounts, etc must be ignored initially for valuation purposes and only if a customer later qualifies for the discount can the amount of VAT previously accounted for be adjusted.

Whether the supplier actually chooses to adjust his VAT account is a matter for him to settle in consultation with his customer. Where he does,

- if the customer is a taxable person, the customer's VAT account must also be adjusted because his entitlement to input tax deduction is reduced. Adjustment is normally made by credit note; and
- the adjustment must be appropriate to the circumstances. For example, where a contingent rebate is earned if supplies of standard-rated and zero-rated goods taken together reach a certain level, the rebate must be attributed proportionately to those supplies. Apportionment is also required if the VAT rate has changed over the period within which the rebate was earned.

Direct selling. Where HMRC have issued a direction as under 69.23 above, the open market value of supplies at the retail stage cannot to be treated as reduced by any discounts allowed to the intermediaries who sell the goods on. Allowance can, however, still be made for any discounts available at the retail level.

Discounts allowed with part-exchange goods. See 69.7 above.

(VAT Notice 700, para 7.3; Internal Guidance V1–12, para 5.15).

'Dividend' paid to members in respect of their purchases of items from the society have been held to be discount in *Co-operative Retail Services Ltd (VTD 7527) (TVC 65.74)*.

69.25 **Tokens, stamps and vouchers**

In respect of tokens, stamps and vouchers issued before 9 April 2003, where a right to receive goods or services for an amount stated on any token, etc was granted for a consideration, the consideration was disregarded for the purposes of *VATA 1994* except to the extent (if any) that it exceeded that amount. [*VATA 1994, Sch 6 para 5*].

In respect of tokens, stamps and vouchers issued on or after 9 April 2003, the above provisions are repealed and replaced by special provisions relating to face-value vouchers in *VATA 1994, Sch 10A*.

See 67 TRADE PROMOTION SCHEMES for the treatment of coupons, vouchers and business promotion schemes generally.

69.26 **Long-term accommodation at a reduced rate**

Where accommodation in a hotel, inn, boarding house or similar establishment is

- provided to an individual for a period exceeding four weeks, and
- throughout that period the accommodation is provided for the use of the individual either alone or together with one or more persons who occupy the accommodation with him otherwise than at their own expense,

after the initial four weeks the value of the supply is reduced to that part attributable to facilities other than the right to occupy the accommodation (subject to a minimum of 20%). [*VATA 1994, Sch 6 para 9*].

See 33.2 HOTELS AND HOLIDAY ACCOMMODATION for further details.

69.27 **Supplies of catering and accommodation by employers to employees**

Where an employer makes a supply of goods or services to his employees consisting of

- food or beverages supplied in the course of catering, or
- accommodation in a hotel, inn, boarding house or similar establishment,

the value of that supply is to be taken to be the monetary consideration, if any, paid by the employee (ie the consideration is nil where there is no consideration or any consideration other than money).

[*VATA 1994, Sch 6 para 10*].

See 11.4 CATERING and 33.3 HOTELS AND HOLIDAY ACCOMMODATION for further details.

See also *Hotel Scandic Gasaback AB v Riksskatteverket, CJEC Case C–412/03, All ER(D) 170 (Jan)*.

69.28 **Money consideration for a supply paid by a third party**

HMRC have power to make regulations so as to require that, in prescribed circumstances, there is to be taken into account as constituting part of the monetary consideration for the purposes of 69.3 above (where it would not otherwise be so taken into account) money paid in respect of the supply by persons other than those to whom the supply is made. [*VATA 1994, Sch 6 para 12*]. No regulations have been made under these provisions.

69.29 Gaming machine takings

Whenever cash or tokens are removed from a gaming machine, the 'taxable take' is the amount paid by persons to play the game less the amount (if any) received by persons playing successfully. There are also rules for valuing tokens depending upon whether they are replayble tokens or non-replayable tokens. [*VATA 1994, s 23(1)-(3)*].

See 57.3 RECREATION AND SPORT for further details.

69.30 Use of stock in trade cars for less than market value

Where a motor manufacturer or a motor dealer allows an employee or his relative to use a stock in trade motor car for a consideration which is less than its open market value, HMRC may direct that the value of the supply is to be taken as the open market value.

[*VATA 1994, Sch 6 para 1A; FA 2004, s 22(2)*].

See 45.7 MOTOR CARS for full details.

69.31 APPLICATION OF VALUATION RULES IN PARTICULAR SITUATIONS

(1) **Admission fees including programmes**. Many sports meetings and other events make a charge for admission that covers the provision of a programme not sold separately.

Following the decision in *Card Protection Plan Ltd v C & E Commrs, CJEC [1999] STC 270 (TVC 21.223)* HMRC see this as a single standard-rated supply of the right of admission with the provision of the programme being ancillary to the right of admission. The programme does not constitute an aim in itself, but a means of better enjoying the principal supply.

(Internal Guidance V1–12, para 7.1). For other methods of apportionment, see 47.3 OUTPUT TAX.

(2) **Business gifts**. See 47.6 OUTPUT TAX for the treatments of gifts of goods and services generally.

Inducements. Goods or services offered as 'gifts', on condition that a purchase is made or some action is performed of benefit in return, are not true gifts but constitute supplies made in return for a non-monetary consideration. See 69.5 above. There are also special rules which apply to TRADE PROMOTION SCHEMES (67).

(3) **Caravans - removable contents**. Both new and used zero-rated caravans may be sold for a selling price that includes standard-rated removable contents. See 42.36 LAND AND BUILDINGS for suggested methods of apportionment.

(4) **Clubs - apportionment and valuation of membership benefits**. See

- 14.1 CLUBS AND ASSOCIATIONS for valuation of subscriptions paid under deed of covenant;
- 14.2 CLUBS AND ASSOCIATIONS for apportionment of subscription income where some of the membership benefits supplied are identifiable supplies of zero-rated or exempt goods and services;

- 14.5 CLUBS AND ASSOCIATIONS for the treatments of loans from members;
- 14.5 CLUBS AND ASSOCIATIONS for valuation of a 'nomination right' supplied with shares or debentures; and
- 57.12 RECREATION AND SPORT for a concessionary policy of HMRC not to require apportionment of exempt membership subscriptions in non-profit making sports clubs provided the non-sporting benefits (eg right to use the club bar) are not significant.

(5) **Commission received 'netted off' against fees charged.** In 1989, Customs announced that where a business reduced its normal fee to a client by passing on the benefit of commissions earned from third parties, it could treat the value of its supply to the client as reduced by the amount of commission 'netted off' against the fee, provided that the reduced amount shown on the invoice was specified as the fee payable. (VAT Notes (No 1) 1988/89).

Example

W, an accountant, wishes to bill a client for a fee of £400 for insurance advice but receives exempt commission of £100 from an insurance company which he proposes to pass on to the client.

If the client is charged a net fee of £300, the amount payable is

	£
Fee (net of commission)	300.00
VAT at 17.5%	52.50
	£352.50

Traders most likely to take advantage of this procedure are financial advisers, insurance brokers and solicitors. The practice should not be confused with that applicable to disbursements (see 3.7 AGENTS).

Following representations from various trade bodies and professional associations, HMRC have concluded that the above treatment is incorrect and VAT should properly be due upon the amount of fee payable before any 'netting off'. However, until any change of policy is announced, businesses may still account for VAT on the reduced value of their fees.

(Internal Guidance V1–12, para 7.5).

(6) **Construction industry**. See 42.29 LAND AND BUILDINGS for the treatment of retentions and 42.31(3) LAND AND BUILDINGS where a contractor is required to make a deduction for income tax under the Construction Industry Scheme or any deduction in respect of the Construction Industry Training Board levy.

(7) **Conversion of a vehicle into a car**. When a vehicle upon which VAT has been reclaimed is converted into a car and kept by the business, VAT must be accounted for on the current value of the vehicle at the time of the conversion,

including the cost of conversion. Where a vehicle has been converted into a car for resale, VAT is due upon the full selling price at the time of sale in the normal way. See 45.8 MOTOR CARS.

(8) **Correspondence courses — apportionment**. Correspondence courses can be single supplies of standard-rated tuition or multiply supplies (eg of zero-rated textbooks and standard-rated marking and assessment of students' work). In the latter case the course fees can be apportioned to allow for a reasonable zero-rated element. See 54.17 PRINTED MATTER, ETC and 47.3 OUTPUT TAX for apportionment of consideration generally.

(9) **'Cover-mounted' goods and promotional items in magazines**.

(*a*) *Cover-mounted items.* Where such items are linked to a magazine, the selling price of the magazine must be apportioned unless the linked goods concession can be applied. See 54.18 PRINTED MATTER, ETC.

(*b*) *Valuation of goods given to publishers for use as magazine inserts.* This depends upon whether

- the goods are supplied to the publisher for a monetary consideration, in which case the supplier pays VAT on the consideration in the normal way under 69.3 above;
- the goods are given to the publisher for no consideration, in which case the supplier will have to account for VAT on a value determined under *VATA 1994, Sch 6 para 6* relating to gifts of business assets (see 47.6 OUTPUT TAX);
- the goods are supplied for non-monetary consideration (eg as in a barter transaction where the supplier receives free advertising in return for the free goods), in which case the provisions in 69.5-69.7 above apply; or
- the publisher is acting purely as an agent in distributing the products (eg free samples for the retail customer), in which case there is normally no supply to the publisher and the free supply is from the supplier to the public directly. No VAT is due from the supplier if the goods are gifts costing £50 or less (£15 or less before 8 March 2001) (see 47.6 OUTPUT TAX) or samples (see 47.8(23) OUTPUT TAX).

(Internal Guidance V1–12, para 7.9.5).

(10) **Motor dealers and manufacturers**. Special valuation rules apply to

- self-supplies of new and used motor cars (see 45.6 MOTOR CARS);
- used cars supplied with mechanical breakdown insurance (see 61.31 SECOND-HAND GOODS); and
- use of stock in trade cars by employees for less than open market value (see 45.7 MOTOR CARS).

(11) **Opticians**. The price paid for spectacles includes two separate supplies – a standard-rated supply of goods (the spectacles) and an exempt supply of optician's services so that an apportionment of the price is necessary. See 32.3 HEALTH AND WELFARE for further details.

(12) **Racehorses**. HMRC have a long-standing Memorandum of Agreement with the Thoroughbred Breeders Association (TBA) covering agreed methods of valuation relating to

- racehorses applied permanently to personal or other non-business use;
- racehorses applied temporarily to training/racing or leased for no consideration;
- the keeping of stallions at stud; and
- exchange of nominations.

Since the introduction of the VAT registration scheme for racehorse owners (see 63.31 SPECIAL SCHEMES) there should be considerably fewer instances of racehorses being applied temporarily or permanently to non-business use. However, all of the existing agreements have been unified into a single Memorandum of Practice agreed with the TBA. See Internal Guidance V1–12, para 7.14.

(Internal Guidance V1–12, para 7.13).

(13) **Record companies.**

(*a*) *Contractual supplies to artistes*. Record production companies, when contracting the right to reproduce recordings, frequently agree to supply 'free of charge' a specified quantity of the recordings (as records or cassettes). HMRC regard this supply of records under contract as a supply for a non-monetary consideration, with the recipient providing in return the benefit of the use of the recording. The value of the supply is determined by establishing the amount of monetary consideration that would otherwise have been given for the records or cassettes. See 69.5 above. The arrangement does not apply to free copies of promotional records, cassettes and videos which are regarded as non-contractual handouts and are supplied for no consideration. (Internal Guidance V1–12, para 7.16.1).

(*b*) *Promotional records, cassettes and videos - standard VAT values*. Where record companies issue promotional records, cassettes, CDs and videos free of charge, they do not usually qualify for relief as business gifts and VAT is due on the cost of production. Standard amounts of VAT to be accounted for on these supplies have been agreed with the British Phonographic Industry Ltd. These amounts are derived from the BPI's calculations of the average production costs incurred by its members and are updated periodically. The latest agreed figures applicable from 1 April 1995 are

	VAT per copy
7 inch single play records	5p
12 inch single play records	11p
LPs	14p
Cassettes	9p
Compact discs – 5 inch singles	13p
Compact discs – 5 inch albums	17p

	VAT per copy
Videocassettes – V30	21p
Videocassettes – V60	24p

(Internal Guidance V1–12, paras 7.16.2, 7.17; VAT Notice 700/57/04).

(14) **Road fuel and company vehicles used for private purposes**. Special rules apply to

- road fuel supplied free or below cost for private motoring (see 45.16 MOTOR CARS); and
- private use of a vehicle for no payment (see 45.19 MOTOR CARS).

(15) **School photographers**. See 20.18 EDUCATION.

(16) **Self-supplies of stationery**. Businesses that are wholly or partly exempt from VAT, and which produce their own stationery or other printed matter for their own business use, can be required to account for VAT on these 'self-supplies' in certain circumstances. See 62.2 SELF-SUPPLY.

(17) **Solicitors and other professionals - disbursements**. See 3.7 AGENTS.

70 Warehoused Goods and Free Zones

De Voil Indirect Tax Service. See V3.331; V3.332; V3.383; V3.384; V5.141.

The contents of this chapter are as follows.

70.1 INTRODUCTION

This chapter considers the VAT treatment of goods entering, supplied within and removed from warehouses and free zones, together with the treatment of supplies of services associated with those goods. **It is substantially based on the legislation and VAT Notice 702/9/98. HMRC have temporarily cancelled this Notice with effect from 25 November 2003 and it will be re-written in due course. This should be borne in mind where the Notice is given as the source of the text.**

70.2 CUSTOMS, CUSTOMS AND EXCISE AND TAX WAREHOUSES

When goods are warehoused for customs and/or excise purposes, payment of any VAT is suspended. Warehoused goods can be moved from one approved warehouse to another or can be exported direct from the warehouse without payment of VAT. VAT only becomes payable when the goods are removed from the warehousing regime and supplied within the UK or transferred to another customs regime which does not provide for the suspension of VAT.

A '*warehouse*' for these purposes means any warehouse where goods may be stored in any EC country without payment of any one or more of the following.

(*a*) Community customs duty.

(*b*) Any agricultural levy of the EC.

(*c*) VAT on the importation of the goods into any EC country.

(*d*) Any duty of excise or any duty which is equivalent in another EC country to a duty of excise.

[*VATA 1994, s 18*(*6*)].

In the UK, this comprises

- Customs warehouses (of which there are several different types);
- Customs and excise warehouses, ie authorised warehouses where goods subject to both customs duty and excise duty can be stored; and
- Tax warehouses, ie authorised places where goods subject to excise duty are produced, processed, held, received or despatched under duty suspension arrangements by an authorised warehousekeeper in the course of his business. They include excise warehouses, registered premises, distilleries and refineries.

It also includes fiscal warehouses which are dealt with separately under 70.12 *et seq.* below.

Goods eligible for warehousing in the UK. The following goods are eligible for warehousing in the UK.

Customs warehouses	Third country goods of any kind except excise goods whether subject to a positive rate of duty or not
Tax warehouses (including both manufacturing premises and storage premises)	Third country goods on which customs duty has been paid Community goods UK goods comprising mineral (hydrocarbon) oils, alcohol and alcoholic beverages, manufactured tobacco
Customs and excise warehouses	Third country goods

(VAT Notice 702/9/98, paras 1.3, 1.4).

70.3 **Goods entering warehouses**

No VAT is payable when goods are placed in a warehousing regime. VAT becomes due only when goods are removed from the warehouse to home use and is normally payable together with any suspended duty by the person who removed the goods.

Imported goods. Goods which, on arrival in the UK, are placed in a customs or customs and excise warehouse are not deemed to be imported for VAT purposes until such time as they are removed from the warehouse into home use, or any customs duties become due. The importer must make an import declaration on Form C88 (Single Administrative Document) but no import VAT is payable and no evidence for input tax is issued.

Acquisitions from other EC countries

- '*Community goods*' are those produced or manufactured in the EC or goods received from outside the EC which have been put into free circulation in the EC. The only community goods which are in practice eligible for warehousing are those subject to excise duty (ie mineral oils, alcohol and alcoholic beverages and manufactured tobacco) which are received in the UK from an excise (tax) warehouse in another EC country.

  Where a UK trader acquires such goods from a registered person in another EC country and the goods are put into an approved warehouse, no import declaration (entry) is required for VAT purposes and VAT is not payable when the goods arrive in the UK.

- '*Non-community goods*' are goods received from outside the EC which have not been put into free circulation in the EC. In the context of acquisitions from other EC countries, such goods arrive in the UK from another EC country under external transit (T1) arrangements and may be warehoused in the same way as direct imports (see above).

  If a UK-registered trader acquires such goods from a EC VAT-registered trader, he does not need an import declaration (entry) solely for VAT purposes but in some circumstances may need one for customs duty purposes. In any event, VAT is not payable at this stage, and it is not necessary to account for VAT on the acquisition.

(VAT Notice 702/9/98, paras 2, 3.1; Internal Guidance V1–19, Chapter 2, para 1.1).

70.4 **Supplies within warehouses**

Supplies of goods within warehousing regimes are usually relieved from VAT at the time they take place (see 70.5 – 70.7 below). VAT becomes due only when the goods are removed from the warehouse to home use and is normally payable together with any suspended duty by the person removing the goods (see 70.8 below). Similarly, certain services connected with warehoused goods are relieved when originally supplied (through the mechanism of zero-rating), but may be taxed at the standard rate when the goods to which they relate are removed from the regime. See 70.19 below. (VAT Notice 702/9/98, para 3.1; Internal Guidance V1–19, Chapter 1 para 4).

70.5 *Imported goods*

Where

(*a*) any goods have been removed from a place outside the EC and have entered the EC,

(*b*) the 'material time' for any supply of those goods or acquisition of those goods from another EC country is while they are subject to a warehousing regime and before the 'duty point', and

(*c*) such goods are not mixed with any 'dutiable goods' which were

- produced or manufactured in the UK (in which case 70.7 below applies), or
- acquired from another EC country (in which case 70.6 below applies),

then the supply or acquisition referred to in (*b*) above is treated as taking place outside the UK and is disregarded for UK VAT purposes.

The '*material time*' for a supply or acquisition is the time of removal of the goods or, in the case of a supply, if the goods are not removed, at the time they are made available to the person to whom they are supplied.

'*Dutiable goods*' means any goods which are subject to a duty of excise (or any Community customs duty or EC agricultural levy having effect for transitional purposes in connection with the accession of any country to the EC).

'*Duty point*' means the time any excise duty becomes payable or, if the goods are not subject to excise duty, the time when any Community customs debt in respect of duty on the entry of the goods into the EC would be incurred.

[*VATA 1994, s 18(1)(6)(7)*].

The effect of the above provisions is that VAT must not be charged, and a VAT invoice showing VAT must not be issued, in respect of any supplies of imported goods made within a warehousing regime.

One of the key conditions of this EC trade facilitation provision is that the amount of VAT due once the goods leave the warehouse should correspond to the amount of VAT that would have been due had the transactions not been VAT-free. As the provisions have been exploited for tax avoidance purposes, HMRC may, by regulations, prescribe circumstances in which they do not apply so that the supplies in question become subject to normal UK supply rules and are taxed accordingly. [*VATA 1984, s 18(1A); F(No 2)A 2005, s 1*].

70.6 *Acquisitions from other EC countries*

Where

- any 'dutiable goods' are acquired from another EC country, or
- a person makes a supply of dutiable goods which were acquired from another EC country (or a mixture of such goods and other goods)

and the 'material time' for the acquisition or supply is while the goods are subject to a warehousing regime and before the 'duty point', then where the material time for any subsequent supply of those goods is also while the goods are subject to the warehousing regime and before the duty point, the acquisition or supply is treated as taking place outside the UK (and is disregarded for UK VAT purposes).

The '*material time*' for a supply or acquisition is the time of removal of the goods or, in the case of a supply, if the goods are not removed, at the time they are made available to the person to whom they are supplied.

'*Dutiable goods*' means any goods which are subject to a duty of excise (or, any Community customs duty or EC agricultural levy having effect for transitional purposes in connection with the accession of any country to the EC).

'*Duty point*' means the time any excise duty becomes payable or, if the goods are not subject to excise duty, the time when any Community customs debt in respect of duty on the entry of the goods into the EC would be incurred.

[*VATA 1994, s 18(2)(3)(6)(7)*].

The effect of this is that any supply of such goods is disregarded for VAT purposes if the supply is followed by another supply of the goods while they are still warehoused. No VAT should be charged on such disregarded supplies. (VAT Notice 702/9/98, para 3.2).

70.7 *Goods produced or manufactured in the UK subject to excise duty*

Where a person makes a supply of any 'dutiable goods' which were produced or manufactured in the UK (or a mixture of such goods and other goods) and the 'material time' for the supply is while the goods are subject to a warehousing regime and before the 'duty point', then where the material time for any subsequent supply of those goods is also while the goods are subject to the warehousing regime and before the duty point, the earlier supply is treated as taking place outside the UK (and is disregarded for UK VAT purposes).

The '*material time*' for a supply is the time of removal of the goods or, if the goods are not removed, at the time they are made available to the person to whom they are supplied.

'*Dutiable goods*' means any goods which are subject to a duty of excise.

'*Duty point*' means the time any excise duty becomes payable.

[*VATA 1994, s 18*(*2*)(*3*)(*6*)(*7*); *FA 1995, s 29*].

The effect of this is that any supply of such goods is disregarded for VAT purposes if the supply is followed by another supply of the goods while they are still warehoused. No VAT should be charged on such disregarded supplies. (VAT Notice 702/9/98, para 3.2).

70.8 **Removal of goods from warehouse**

VAT becomes due when goods are removed from a warehouse to home use and is normally payable by the person who removes the goods. The VAT due may be on the importation, acquisition or supply of the goods.

Imported goods. Where imported goods are removed from warehousing to home use in the UK, a removal declaration must be completed at the time the goods are removed. Any duty due must be paid and any VAT must be paid either in cash or under the duty deferment arrangements (see 34.5 IMPORTS). The value for VAT must include the duty paid. (VAT Notice 702/9/98, paras 3.3, 3.4).

Acquisitions from other EC countries. Where

- either
  - (i) 'dutiable goods' are acquired from another EC country, or
  - (ii) a person makes a supply of dutiable goods which were acquired from another EC country (or a mixture of such goods and other goods),
- the 'material time' for the acquisition or supply is while the goods are subject to a warehousing regime and before the 'duty point', and
- there is no subsequent acquisition or supply of those goods whilst subject to the warehouse regime and before the duty point

the acquisition or supply is treated as taking place at the earlier of the time the goods are removed from the warehouse regime and the duty point.

The '*material time*' for a supply or acquisition is the time of removal of the goods or, in the case of a supply, if the goods are not removed, at the time they are made available to the person to whom they are supplied.

'*Dutiable goods*' means any goods which are subject to a duty of excise (or any Community customs duty or EC agricultural levy having effect for transitional purposes in connection with the accession of any country to the EC).

'*Duty point*' means the time any excise duty becomes payable or, if the goods are not subject to excise duty, the time when any Community customs debt in respect of duty on the entry of the goods into the EC would be incurred.

[*VATA 1994, s 18*(*2*)–(*4*)(*6*)(*7*)].

The effect of this is that the person removing the goods to home use in the UK pays any duty and must account for acquisition VAT on the VAT return for the period covering the date of removal. This VAT can be recovered as input tax on the same return, subject to the normal rules. A removal declaration must also be completed. The value for VAT purposes includes any customs and/or excise duty payable. (VAT Notice 702/9/98, paras 3.3, 3.4).

Goods produced or manufactured in the UK subject to excise duty. Where

- a person makes a supply of any 'dutiable goods' which were produced or manufactured in the UK (or a mixture of such goods and other goods),
- the 'material time' for the supply is while the goods are subject to a warehousing regime and before the 'duty point', and
- there is no subsequent supply of those goods whilst subject to the warehousing regime and before the duty point,

the supply is treated as taking place at the earlier of the time the goods are removed from the warehouse regime and the duty point.

The '*material time*' for a supply is the time of removal of the goods or, if the goods are not removed, at the time they are made available to the person to whom they are supplied.

'*Dutiable goods*' means any goods which are subject to a duty of excise.

'*Duty point*' means the time any excise duty becomes payable.

[*VATA 1994, s 18(2)(3)(6)(7); FA 1995, s 29*].

The effect of this is that the person removing the UK-produced goods from the warehouse to home use must complete a removal declaration at the time the goods are removed and pay any duty and VAT due. The value for VAT purposes includes any customs and/or excise duty payable. (VAT Notice 702/9/98, paras 3.3, 3.4).

Goods removed from warehouse to a place outside the UK. Subject to the normal rules, any supply of goods from a warehouse for export outside the EC or for supply to a taxable person in another EC country may be zero-rated. Goods removed directly to a registered warehouse in another EC country can be disregarded for UK VAT purposes.

If non-community goods (see 70.3 above) are put into free circulation in the UK before being sent to another EC country, any import VAT and customs duty must normally be paid. Similarly, if community goods (see 70.3 above) on which excise duty is payable in the UK are removed, any VAT due must be paid at the same time.

(VAT Notice 702/9/98, para 3.5).

Note that special rules apply to deliveries of goods subject to excise duty to customers in other EC countries. If the excise duty has not been paid, the goods *must* be received by a VAT-registered person in the EC country of destination. If the goods are supplied for delivery to a customer in another EC country who is not VAT-registered in that country, the supplier must use the distance selling arrangements and register for VAT there. See 23.18 EUROPEAN COMMUNITY: SINGLE MARKET.

70.9 Evidence for input tax deduction

The owner of the goods will be issued with an import VAT certificate (C79) during the month after payment. This document is the official evidence needed to claim VAT paid on warehouse removals as input tax. Where an import VAT certificate is not received in time to complete the VAT return, alternative evidence of removal or payment may be used to claim input tax (in which case it is important to ensure that, when the import VAT certificate is received, it agrees with the input tax previously claimed). (VAT Notice 702/9/98, para 3.16).

70.10 Deficiency of warehoused goods

Any deficiencies of warehoused goods are deemed to be removed from the warehousing regime. Where deficiencies of imported goods are charged with duty, VAT not already paid on the imported goods is also to be charged. Similarly, any acquisition VAT on goods from another EC country which has not been accounted for should be accounted for when deficiencies occur. Deficiencies of home produced goods are not to be charged with VAT unless the goods have been supplied in warehouse before the loss. In each case, the VAT may be deducted as input tax, subject to the normal rules. (VAT Notice 702/9/98, para 3.17).

70.11 Summary tables

Receipt of goods into a UK warehouse and their removal for home use		
	Duty	*VAT*
1. Goods received (a) direct from a third country; or (b) from a third country via another EC country (including goods acquired from a customs or customs and excise warehouse in another EC country) and placed in customs warehouse	Customs duty and import duty: not due on receipt into warehouse but to be paid on removal Excise duty: N/A	N/A
2. Goods received (a) direct from a third country; or (b) from a third country via another EC country (including goods acquired from a customs or customs and excise warehouse in another EC country) and placed in customs and excise warehouse	Customs duty and import duty: not due on receipt into warehouse but to be paid on removal Excise duty: duty due, but suspended whilst in warehouse	N/A

Receipt of goods into a UK warehouse and their removal for home use		
	Duty	*VAT*
3. Goods received (a) direct from a third country; or (b) from a third country via another EC country that have not been entered to free circulation on which there is a nil rate of customs duty, or the customs duty is paid on arrival in the UK. Goods then placed in a tax warehouse	Customs duty: any due is paid on arrival of the goods in the UK Excise duty: duty due, but suspended whilst in warehouse Import duty: not due on receipt into warehouse and to be paid on removal	N/A
4. Goods acquired direct from another EC country which are community goods, and are placed in an excise warehouse, including goods from tax warehouse in another EC country	Customs duty and import duty: N/A Excise duty: duty due, but suspended whilst in warehouse	VAT on acquisition suspended whilst in warehouse
(a) Goods removed from warehouse by acquirer	Customs duty and import duty: N/A Excise duty: duty due on removal	VAT accounted for in return covering the removal of the goods
(b) Goods supplied in warehouse and removed by the customer	Customs duty and import duty: N/A Excise duty: duty due on removal	VAT due on the supply (or last supply if more than one) to be paid with the excise duty on removal. VAT on the acquisition is not accounted for
5. UK produced and/or manufactured goods in an excise warehouse or registered premises	Customs duty and import duty: N/A Excise duty: duty due on removal to home use	N/A

Receipt of goods into a UK warehouse and their removal for home use		
	Duty	*VAT*
6. Goods (a) removed to home use by the manufacturer; or (b) supplied in warehouse and removed to home use by the customer	Customs duty and import duty: N/A Excise duty: duty due on removal to home use	VAT due on the supply (or last supply if more than one) to be paid with the excise duty on removal

Receipt of goods from a UK warehouse other than to home use in the UK		
	Duty	*VAT*
1. Goods for (a) direct export to a country outside the EC; or (b) export to a country outside the EC in transit through another EC country from a customs warehouse	Customs duty: not paid Excise duty: N/A	Any VAT which would be due on removal to UK home use is not payable. Supplies of goods removed from the UK may be zero-rated as exports (subject to the normal rules)
2. Goods for (a) direct export to a country outside the EC; or (b) export to a country outside the EC in transit through another EC country from a customs and excise warehouse	Customs duty: not paid Excise duty: not paid	Any VAT which would be due on removal to UK home use is not payable. Supplies of goods removed from the UK may be zero-rated as exports (subject to the normal rules)
3. Goods for (a) direct export to a country outside the EC; or (b) export to a country outside the EC in transit through another EC country from a tax warehouse	Customs duty: N/A Excise duty: not paid	Any VAT which would be due on removal to UK home use is not payable. Supplies of goods removed from the UK may be zero-rated as exports (subject to the normal rules)

Receipt of goods from a UK warehouse other than to home use in the UK		
	Duty	*VAT*
4. Goods moved to another EC country under a duty suspensive regime from a customs warehouse	Customs duty: not paid Excise duty: N/A	Any VAT which would be due on removal to UK home use is not payable. Supplies direct into a customs warehouse in another EC country are outside the scope of UK VAT. Otherwise, outward movement of goods may be zero-rated (subject to the normal rules)
5. Goods moved to another EC country under a duty suspensive regime from a customs and excise warehouse	Customs duty: not paid Excise duty: not paid	Any VAT which would be due on removal to UK home use is not payable. Supplies direct into a customs warehouse in another EC country are outside the scope of UK VAT. Otherwise, outward movement of goods may be zero-rated (subject to the normal rules)
6. Goods moved to another EC country on which customs duty is paid on removal from a customs warehouse	Customs duty: paid on removal from warehouse regime Excise duty: N/A	VAT is payable but may be relieved if the goods are removed in the course of an onward zero-rated supply
7. Goods moved to another EC country on which customs duty is paid on removal from a customs and excise warehouse	Customs duty: paid on removal from warehouse regime Excise duty: not paid	VAT is payable but may be relieved if the goods are removed in the course of an onward zero-rated supply
8. Goods moved to another EC country from an excise warehouse and sent under excise duty suspension to a tax warehouse	Customs duty: N/A Excise duty: not paid	Any VAT which would be due on removal to home use is not payable. Supplies direct into an excise warehouse in another EC country are outside the scope of UK VAT

Receipt of goods from a UK warehouse other than to home use in the UK		
	Duty	*VAT*
9. Goods moved to another EC country from an excise warehouse and sent under excise duty suspension to a Registered Excise Dealer	Customs duty: N/A Excise duty: not paid	Any VAT which would be due on removal to home use is not payable. Outward movement of goods may be zero-rated (subject to the normal conditions)
10. Goods transferred to IPR suspension in the UK from a customs warehouse	Customs duty: to be paid on final removal from IPR regime Excise duty: N/A	Any import VAT due is to be paid with the customs duty. Supplies of goods under IPR are subject to the domestic VAT rules
11. Goods transferred to IPR drawback in the UK from a customs warehouse	Customs duty: to be paid on removal from warehouse regime Excise duty: N/A	Any import VAT due is to be paid with the customs duty. Supplies of goods under IPR are subject to the domestic VAT rules
12. Goods in customs and excise warehouse. Customs duty paid while goods remain under the warehousing regime	Customs duty: paid whilst in warehouse Excise duty: to be paid when goods are removed to UK home use	Any import VAT is to be paid when goods are removed to home use

(VAT Notice 702/9/98, Appendices B, C).

70.12 FISCAL WAREHOUSING

The *EC 2nd VAT Simplification Directive* enables countries to introduce a warehousing regime to operate alongside both customs warehouses and excise warehouses. In the UK, this regime is known as fiscal warehousing.

Under the fiscal warehousing regime, certain eligible goods (see 70.14 below) can be placed in a notified warehouse and can then be traded by dealers who will not be required to be VAT-registered if that is their only business activity. Supplies of goods and certain services within a fiscal warehouse and supplies of goods intended to be placed in the regime are, subject to conditions, relieved from VAT. See 70.15 and 70.16 below.

Excise and Customs warehouses (see 70.2 *et seq.* above) may also be used for fiscal warehousing but separate authorisation is required for the fiscal warehousing regime.

Retail sales are not allowed under the conditions of a fiscal warehousing regime [*VATA 1994, s 18A(3); FA 1996, Sch 3 para 5; SI 1996/1249*].

(VAT Notice 702/9/98, paras 4.1, 4.2).

70.13 Authorisation for fiscal warehousing

HMRC can, on written application, approve any registered person (including any company in a group registration) as a fiscal warehousekeeper, the approval being subject to such conditions as HMRC impose. [*VATA 1994, s 18A(1)(4)(7)(9); FA 1996, Sch 3 para 5*].

The authorisation procedure is stringent so that HMRC can rely on the operators' control procedures and records. All the following basic criteria for authorisation must be met.

- The applicant must be VAT-registered in the UK.
- All business revenue records must be of a high standard (eg VAT returns and payments must be up-to-date).
- If already authorised to operate any UK duty suspensive regime, the applicant must have a satisfactory proven records of operation.
- The applicant must be able to comply with the conditions of authorisation and with such regulations as may be laid down for the operation of the regime. This is important as penalties may be imposed for failure to comply.
- The administration and organisation of the business must be sound and strictly managed.
- The applicant must provide a list of the addresses of all storage sites which are to form part of the fiscal warehouse and any other premises where records are to be kept. Retail premises cannot be used as fiscal warehousing premises and all notified premises must meet health and safety legislation requirements.
- Accounts and stock control records must be capable of meeting the requirements in 70.18 below. In particular, they must be able to distinguish between fiscally warehoused goods and other stocks and be able to identify the location and quantity of any given item held within the fiscal warehousing regime at any stage.

Applications should be made to HMRC by completing a letter of application as described in VAT Notice 702/9/98, Appendix K. If the application is approved, authorisation will be granted in writing, conditional upon the acceptance of any conditions HMRC regard as appropriate, and without time limit. [*VATA 1994, s 18A(5)(8); FA 1996, Sch 3 para 5*]. See, however, under *Provisional authorisation* below.

Refusal of authorisation. HMRC may refuse authorisation if the criteria are not met. The basic procedure for appeal will be set out in the letter of refusal. This allows for an initial local review by a member of staff not connected with the decision and, if necessary, an appeal to a VAT tribunal.

Provisional authorisation may be given subject to meeting outstanding criteria within a specified period of time. This may happen, for example, where the necessary premises have not been secured at the time of the application. If any outstanding condition is not met within the deadline, the application will lapse and a new application will be required.

Transferring an authorisation is not permitted, even on the sale of a business as a going concern. The new owner must apply for a fresh authorisation.

Cancelling or revoking an authorisation. Authorisation can be cancelled by giving notice in writing to HMRC stating the date by which all goods will cease to be traded and removed from the warehousing regime. HMRC can also revoke an authorisation at any time for any reasonable cause (eg non-compliance with conditions of authorisation). Except in very exceptional circumstances the warehousekeeper would be notified in advance of any intended revocation, and would always have a right to appeal. Where authorisation is withdrawn, any goods held in the fiscal warehouse regime are deemed to have been removed by the proprietor at the time of withdrawal and VAT is due. See 70.17 below.

(VAT Notice 702/9/98, paras 4.4–4.10).

70.14 Qualifying conditions for goods

To be eligible for the fiscal warehousing regime, goods must be

(*a*) '*eligible goods*' for fiscal warehousing purposes ie

- aluminium, copper, iridium, lead, nickel, palladium, platinum, rhodium, silver, tin, and zinc;
- chemicals in bulk;
- cereals;
- coffee (not roasted), tea, and cocoa beans (whole or broken, raw or roasted);
- grains and seeds (including soya beans);
- mineral oils (including propane and butane and crude petroleum oils);
- nuts;
- oil seeds and oleaginous fruit;
- olives;
- potatoes;
- raw sugar;
- rubber, in primary forms or in plates, sheets or strip;
- vegetable oils and fats and their fractions (whether or not refined, but not chemically modified); and
- wool;

(*b*) in free circulation ie all duties, taxes and levies (including customs duty, import VAT, excise duty and any Common Agricultural Policy (CAP) duty due on the goods) must either have been paid or deferred; and

(*c*) entered in the fiscal warehousing records.

Non-eligible goods may be stored in a place which is a fiscal warehouse but cannot be subject to a fiscal warehousing regime or benefit from the conditions of fiscal warehousing.

[*VATA 1994, s 18B*(6), *Sch 5A; FA 1996, Sch 3 paras 5, 18*]. (VAT Notice 702/9/98, paras 4.3, 4.13).

70.15 Goods entering a fiscal warehouse

The following transactions are relieved from VAT (by being treated as taking place outside the UK) if any subsequent supply of the goods in question is made while they are subject to the fiscal warehouse regime.

(*a*) An acquisition of goods from another EC country where, after the acquisition but before any subsequent supply, the acquirer places the goods in a fiscal warehousing regime. The acquirer must, not later than the time of acquisition, prepare and keep a certificate stating that he intends to enter the goods in a fiscal warehouse.

(*b*) A supply of eligible goods (other than a retail transaction) where, after the supply in question but before any subsequent supply, the buyer places the goods in a fiscal warehousing regime. The buyer must give his supplier, not later than the time of supply, a certificate stating that he intends to enter the goods in a fiscal warehouse.

[*VATA 1994, s 18B(1)-(3); FA 1996, Sch 3 para 5*].

A supply falling within (*a*) or (*b*) above is treated as a supply of goods (and not a supply of services), even if it is the transfer of an undivided share in the goods, ie an unidentified part of a larger stock of eligible goods. [*SI 1996/1255*]. (Normally, such a transfer of an undivided share would be treated for VAT purposes as a supply of services, see 64.4(*a*) SUPPLY.)

Certificates. The certificate required under (*a*) or (*b*) above should be in the following form.

> I (full name)
> (status in company)
> of (name and address of company)
>
> declare that (name of company) intends to enter to the fiscal warehousing regime at the fiscal warehouse shown below on (insert date) or within (insert number) days commencing today, the goods indicated below:
>
> - name and address of fiscal warehouse
> - authorisation number of the fiscal warehousekeeper
> - description of goods
> - quantity of goods
>
> * I certify that the supply of goods is eligible to be relieved from VAT under VATA 1994, sections 18B(2)(d)/18B(3) (purchases)
>
> * I certify that the acquisition is eligible to be relieved from VAT under VATA 1994, sections 18B(1)(d)/18B(3) (acquisitions).
>
> * Delete as appropriate
>
> (signature)
> (date)

Where a taxable person prepares a certificate under (*a*) above or receives one under (*b*) above, he must retain it with his VAT records. Where a non-taxable person prepares a certificate under (*a*) above, he must keep it for six years and produce it to an HMRC officer on request.

[*SI 1995/2518, Reg 31(1), Reg 145B, Sch 1; SI 1996/1250, Regs 8, 13*]. (VAT Notice 702/9/98, Appendix I).

70.16 Supplies within fiscal warehouses

The following transactions are relieved from VAT (by being treated as taking place outside the UK) if any subsequent supply of the goods in question is made while they are subject to the fiscal warehouse regime.

(*a*) An acquisition of eligible goods from another EC country where the acquisition takes place while the goods are within a fiscal warehousing regime. The acquirer must, not later than the time of acquisition, prepare and keep a certificate stating that the goods are subject to a fiscal warehousing regime.

(*b*) A supply of eligible goods (other than a retail transaction) where the supply takes place while the goods are within a fiscal warehousing regime.

[*VATA 1994, s 18B(1)-(3); FA 1996, Sch 3 para 5*].

The effect of the above is that goods acquired or supplied after being entered to the fiscal warehousing regime are treated as though they are outside the UK and not subject to the normal supply rules *unless* the supply in question is the final supply whilst the goods are warehoused.

A supply falling within (*a*) or (*b*) above is treated as a supply of goods (and not a supply of services), even if it is the transfer of an undivided share in the goods, ie an unidentified part of a larger stock of eligible goods. [*SI 1996/1255*]. (Normally, such a transfer of an undivided share would be treated for VAT purposes as a supply of services, see 64.4(*a*) SUPPLY.)

Registration. If transactions falling within (*a*) or (*b*) above are a trader's only UK business activities, he will not be required to register for VAT although he may apply for voluntary registration if he wishes. Liability to register for other business activities is not affected by either the value of supplies made in a fiscal warehouse or the value of deemed supplies of relieved services accounted for by the remover of the goods (see 70.20 below). [*VATA 1994, Sch 1 para 1(9); FA 1996, Sch 3 para 13*].

70.17 Removal of goods from fiscal warehousing

With certain exceptions, a charge to VAT arises when eligible goods are removed from the fiscal warehouse regime. The amount of VAT due corresponds to

- the amount which would have been due on the transaction that caused the goods to be entered to the warehouse, or
- if the goods have been supplied within the warehouse, the amount which would have been due on the last supply.

VAT will also be due on any of the relieved supplies of services relating to the goods which have been carried out after that final supply. See 70.20 below.

The VAT due on removal is the liability of the person who causes the goods to cease to be covered by the fiscal warehousing regime and is chargeable and payable at the time of removal.

- A VAT-registered trader should account for the VAT on the return covering the date of removal.
- A non-registered remover must present Form VAT 150 *Advice of removals from fiscal warehouse by persons unregistered for VAT* to the local Entry Processing Unit

(EPU) even when no VAT is due on removal. Where the remover is not a taxable person but would be if such acquisitions or supplies were taken into account, although not required to register he must charge and account for VAT on any taxable transactions.

[*VATA 1994, s 18B(4)(5), s 18D; FA 1996, Sch 3 para 5*]. (VAT Notice 702/9/98, paras 4.14, 4.18).

Deemed removals. Where

(*a*) as a result of an operation on eligible goods in the fiscal warehousing regime, they cease to be eligible goods, or

(*b*) any person ceases to be a fiscal warehousekeeper or any premises cease to have fiscal warehouse status,

the relevant goods are treated as if they had been removed from the fiscal warehousing regime at that time by the proprietor of the goods. [*VATA 1994, s 18F(5)(6); FA 1996, Sch 3 para 5*].

VAT is not due on the following removals of goods.

- Removal for use in the UK of zero-rated goods. (VAT may be due at removal based on the value of any relieved supplies of services. See 70.20 below.)
- Removal by a person for use in the UK of his own goods (either produced or purchased VAT-paid) which he entered to fiscal warehouse and which have not been sold within the fiscal warehousing regime. (VAT may be due at removal based on the value of relieved supplies of services. See 70.20 below.)
- Goods exported outside the EC. Normal conditions for zero-rating exports apply. (Any associated relieved supplies of services are also not taxable. See 70.20 below.)
- Goods removed in the course of an intra-EC supply. Normal supply/acquisition and Intrastat rules apply for VAT-registered traders. (Any associated relieved supplies of services are also not taxable. See 70.20 below.)
- Transfers to another UK fiscal warehouse.
- Transfers to a corresponding regime to fiscal warehousing in another EC country.
- Temporary removals for repair, processing, treatment or other operations. Authorisation (general or specific) must be sought from HMRC and the goods must be returned to the original site or another covered by the same authorisation.
- Small quantities of negligible commercial value removed VAT-free for sampling.

[*SI 1995/2518, Reg 145H(2); SI 1996/1250, Reg 13*]. (VAT Notice 702/9/98, para 4.19).

Input tax. Any VAT paid as a result of the removal of goods from a fiscal warehouse can be reclaimed as input tax, subject to the normal rules. This will normally be on the same VAT return on which the VAT due on removal was declared as output tax. (VAT Notice 702/9/9, para 4.20).

70.18 Duties and responsibilities of a fiscal warehousekeeper

A fiscal warehousekeeper must record all receipts into the warehouse and keep a detailed fiscal warehousing record of stock. There are detailed provisions for recording and control over removals of goods and the transfer of goods to other UK fiscal warehouses or similar regimes in other EC countries. Records must be capable of ready use by an HMRC officer and must be readily reproducible for use off the premises. All records must be kept for six years following the transfer or removal of the goods.

[*SI 1995/2518, Regs 145E-145I, Sch 1A; SI 1996/1250, Reg 13*]. (VAT Notice 702/9/98, paras 4.11, 4.21).

The procedures are stringent so that HMRC can rely on the warehousekeeper's controls and records. Where goods are found to be missing or deficient, a warehouse-keeper may be personally liable for the VAT which would have been chargeable on their supply. [*VATA 1994, s 18E; FA 1996, Sch 3 para 5*].

70.19 SUPPLIES OF ASSOCIATED WAREHOUSE AND FISCAL WAREHOUSE SERVICES

Certain services associated with goods held in customs, customs and excise, tax and fiscal warehouses can be relieved from VAT at the time they are supplied. In certain circumstances, VAT will become due on such services when the goods concerned are subsequently removed from the regime to home use (see 70.20 below).

Zero-rating. Where a taxable person makes a supply of 'specified services' which are performed on, or in relation to, goods subject to the warehousing regime (see 70.2-70.11 above) or the fiscal warehousing regime (see 70.12-70.18 above), the supply is zero-rated if it would otherwise be taxable.

The '*specified services*' are as follows.

(*a*) Services of keeping the goods in question by an occupier of a warehouse or a fiscal warehousekeeper.

(*b*) For goods subject to a warehousing regime, services of carrying out any permitted operations on the goods.

In a customs warehouse, the services eligible for zero-rating are storage charges and the usual forms of handling which may be carried out in the warehouse. These cover

- simple operations to ensure the preservation of the goods in good condition during storage;
- operations improving the presentation or marketability of the goods; and
- preparing the goods for distribution or resale.

For a detailed list, see VAT Notice 702/9/98, Appendix F.

In a tax warehouse, services eligible are restricted to those physical services that take place in the warehouse and are directly associated with the goods held in the warehouse. These include those processes that create a new product (see VAT Notice 702/9/98, Appendix G) and others such as storage and secondary packaging.

Not included are services such as brokerage, agents' fees and transport between warehouses but any services which would be zero-rated if supplied outside the warehouse remain zero-rated when supplied inside. (VAT Notice 702/9/98, para 3.7).

(*c*) For goods subject to a fiscal warehousing regime, services of carrying out any non-prohibited physical operations on the goods. These are the same as those qualifying in a customs warehouse under (*b*) above and specified in VAT Notice 702/9/98, Appendix F. Written authority from HMRC is required to obtain relief on supplies of services which exceed those specified operations.

Certification. No certification is required for warehousekeepers' storage charges under (*a*) above to be zero-rated. The invoice issued by the warehousekeeper to enable zero-rating should include the words 'in accordance with section 18C(1) VAT Act 1994' and no VAT should be charged. If the owner of the goods prefers the storage to be standard-rated, he should notify the warehousekeeper in writing who will then issue an invoice and include VAT at the standard rate.

For zero-rating to apply under (*b*) or (*c*) above, the recipient of the services must give the supplier a certificate declaring that the relevant goods are fiscally warehoused services and that the supply of services is eligible for zero-rating. The following is an example of the certificate although any version may be prepared provided it contains all of the information shown.

I	(full name)
	(status in company)
of	(name and address of company)

declare that the goods shown below are subject to a fiscal or other warehousing regime at the place indicated below:

- description of goods
- quantity of goods
- warehouse stock number
- name and address of fiscal or other warehouse
- authorisation number of the relevant warehousekeeper/warehouse

and that the following services are to be performed on the goods in the fiscal or other warehouse:

(insert details of services)

I certify that the supply of services is eligible to be zero-rated for VAT purposes under section 18C(1) of the VAT Act 1994.

(signature)

(date)

[*VATA 1994. s 18C(1)(4); FA 1996, Sch 3 para 5; SI 1995/2518, Reg 145C; SI 1996/1250*]. (VAT Notice 702/9/98, Appendix J).

Invoicing. If the supplier of services receives a certificate as above, he must, within 30 days of the services being performed, give the recipient a VAT invoice with the following particulars (unless HMRC allow otherwise).

- An identifying number.
- The material time of the supply of the services in question.

- The date of the issue of the invoice.
- The name, address and registration number of the supplier.
- The name and an address of the person to whom the services are supplied.
- A description sufficient to identify the nature of the services supplied.
- The extent of the services and the amount payable, excluding VAT, expressed in sterling.
- The rate of any cash discount offered.
- The rate of VAT as zero per cent.
- A declaration that in respect of the supply of services in question, the requirements of *VATA 1994, s 18C(1)* (see above) will be or have been satisfied.

The supplier should retain the invoice and certificate in his records for six years (unless HMRC agree otherwise) as evidence needed to support the zero-rating of the supplies.

Where no certificate is received (because the customer fails to provide it or prefers, for administrative purposes, to have the services taxed at the time of supply) the supplier should issue a VAT invoice in the usual way including VAT (as necessary) at the standard rate.

[*SI 1985/2518, Reg 145D; SI 1996/1250*]. (VAT Notice 702/9/98, para 3.8).

De Voil Indirect Tax Service. See V3.515A.

70.20 **Subsequent taxation of previously zero-rated services**

Subject to the exceptions below, services which, at the time of supply, are zero-rated under 70.19 above are subsequently taxed at the time the goods are removed from the warehousing or fiscal warehousing regime or, if earlier, at the duty point. At that time, a taxable (and not zero-rated) supply of services, identical to the zero-rated supply of services, is treated as being made both to the recipient of the zero-rated supply of services and by him in the course or furtherance of his business. The value of the supply is the same as for the zero-rated supply of services. VAT is chargeable on the supply even if the person treated as making it is not a taxable person.

Exceptions. The self-supply charge does not apply in the following circumstances.

- Where the services create new goods.

  If the services or processes applied to existing goods change their nature to the extent that a new product is considered to have been created (eg refining crude oil into motor spirit), the new product is then treated as having been produced in the UK. See VAT Notice 702/9/98, Appendix G for a list of processes undertaken in tax warehouses which are regarded as creating a new UK product. In addition, HMRC also consider the mixing or blending of home produced goods with goods received from outside the EC or goods produced or manufactured in the EC as creating a new product if original goods lose their identity.

  Where such a service or process is carried out, no VAT is due in respect of that service (or the original goods) because the goods upon which the process has been carried out have ceased to exist and cannot therefore be removed from the warehouse. VAT will only be due if the new goods are subsequently supplied or further services are carried out which do not create a new UK product (eg secondary packaging).

- Where the goods are supplied (whilst still warehoused) after the services were provided (in which case VAT is only due on any services provided after the last supply in the warehouse).
- Where the goods are exported under duty suspension arrangements directly from the warehouse to a country outside the EC.
- Where the goods are sent under duty suspension arrangements to a customs or tax warehouse in another EC country.

[*VATA 1994, s 18C(2)(3); FA 1996, Sch 3 para 5; SI 1996/1249*]. (VAT Notice 702/9/98, paras 3.10–3.12).

Accounting for VAT. It is the responsibility of the person removing the goods to ensure that the correct amount of VAT is paid at the time of entry to home use.

- For removals from customs warehouses, any VAT due in respect of previously zero-rated services is to be accounted for together with any import VAT and customs duty payable on the relevant goods, using the import entry (C88).
- For removals from tax warehouses, VAT due on the importation, or on the last supply of goods in warehouse, must be accounted for and paid (or deferred) when the goods pass the duty point or are removed to home use. VAT due on goods acquired from another EC country is accounted for on the VAT return covering the period in which they pass the duty point or are removed. Any VAT due in respect of previously zero-rated services must be accounted for together with the VAT due on the relevant goods.
- For removals from fiscal warehouses, any VAT due must be accounted for, together with the VAT due on the relieved supply of the goods.

(VAT Notice 702/9/98, paras 3.13–3.15, 4.16).

Average throughput time for accounting for previously zero-rated services. Commercial practices in certain warehousing regimes make it difficult for some traders accurately to track specific goods and associated services, and therefore they do not know for certain which goods are removed from the warehouse regime. In such circumstances, HMRC can agree average throughput times for goods so that traders assume goods to have been removed from the regime by a certain date, at which time the VAT becomes due. Examples of when this arrangement may be used include

- where the services are performed on goods in bulk and the goods are then removed in smaller quantities; and
- when goods that have had a service performed on them are mixed with goods which have not.

These arrangements can apply in both customs and tax warehouses.

(Internal Guidance V1–19, Chapter 2 para 2.12).

70.21 FREE ZONES

A free zone is a designated, secure area in which goods from both outside and within the EC (including home produced goods) can be stored without payment of certain duties and VAT. HMRC may make regulations covering the control and operation of such zones and the movement of goods into and out of them and the charging of duty. [*FA 1984, s 8, Sch 4; SI 1984/1177*]. Free zones are currently operating at Liverpool, Prestwick, Southampton, Tilbury and Port of Sheerness.

70.22 **Goods entering free zones**

Imports. VAT is not due on goods entering the UK from places outside the EC and placed in a free zone. However, customs duties may be paid on goods without import VAT having to be accounted for at the same time.

Acquisitions from other EC countries. The acquisition of goods from a registered trader in another EC country where the goods are put into a free zone is treated in the same way as the acquisition of goods in the rest of the UK, ie VAT must be accounted for on the acquirer's VAT return for the period covering the time of acquisition (see 23.3 *et seq*. EUROPEAN COMMUNITY: SINGLE MARKET). The value for VAT must include any duty paid.

UK-produced goods. VAT is not due on goods of UK origin which are taken into a free zone.

70.23 **Supplies within free zones**

Supplies of goods (and services) within a free zone are treated as UK supplies and are subject to the normal domestic VAT rules. This applies even if the goods were originally acquired from another the EC or, subject to the concession below, imported from outside the EC.

By concession, the supply of free zone goods which were originally imported in the UK may be zero-rated if the supplier and customer agree that the customer will clear the goods for removal from the free zone to home use and will take responsibility for the import VAT. For the purposes of this concession, removal to home use includes authorised use or consumption within the zone. (VAT Notice 48, ESC 3.14). This concession has two main benefits.

- The customer purchasing the goods would otherwise have to pay, at virtually the same time, both the VAT due on the supply (to the supplier) and the VAT due on importation (to HMRC) on the removal of the goods from the free zone (see 70.24 below).
- It enables overseas traders who supply their imports in UK free zones and properly use the concession, to apply for exemption from registration in the UK.

The same goods can be the subject of a zero-rated supply only once under the concession. Supplies of free zone goods which do not meet the conditions of the concession must be treated in the same way as supplies of goods made outside free zones.

(VAT Notice 702/9/98, para 5.3).

See also 70.24 below for goods supplied within a free zone for onward export to a destination outside the EC.

Supplies to non-registered persons. Where a supply is made within a free zone to a non-registered person, the amount of VAT payable on removal of the goods from the free zone is reduced by the VAT already paid on the supply. [*SI 1984/1177, Reg 27*].

70.24 Removal of goods from free zones

Goods removed to home use in the UK. Goods used or consumed within a free zone are considered to have been removed from the free zone and must therefore be entered to free circulation.

- If the goods are 'non-community goods' from a third country, import VAT is due on removal from the free zone to home use.
- If the goods are non-community goods from a third country via another EC country (including those from another duty suspensive regime),
  - (*a*) import VAT is due on removal from the free zone to home use; and
  - (*b*) if the goods are the subject of an acquisition on arrival in the free zone, VAT must be accounted for on the acquirer's VAT return for the period in which the acquisition tax point falls.
- If the goods are 'community goods' direct from another EC country, acquisition VAT must be accounted for on the acquirer's VAT return for the period in which the acquisition tax point occurs.
- If the goods are goods from the UK, the normal UK VAT supply rules apply.

Goods removed other than to home use.

- If the goods are exported direct to a third country, the supply can be zero-rated subject to the normal export rules (see 25.1 EXPORTS). If the goods are non-community goods, there is no requirement to pay any import VAT that may otherwise have been due on the goods.

  If goods are supplied to a customer in a free zone for onward export to a destination in a third country, the supply may be zero-rated as an export provided a copy of the Single Administrative Document (Form C88) export declaration, certified at the place of export of the goods from the EC, is obtained and retained by the trader.
- If the goods are removed direct to another EC country,
  - (*a*) where the goods are non-community goods which are not put into free circulation in the UK
    - (i) import VAT is not due in the UK and will be paid with the customs duty in the EC country where that duty is paid;
    - (ii) if the goods are sold to a customer registered for VAT in another EC country, the supply can be zero-rated subject to the normal conditions for zero-rating an intra-EC supply (see 23.11 EUROPEAN COMMUNITY: SINGLE MARKET); and
    - (iii) if the goods are sold to a customer not registered for VAT, and the goods are not for onward export from the EC, the supply of the goods is liable to VAT in the UK; and
  - (*b*) where the goods are non-community goods put into free circulation on removal from the free zone,
    - (i) if customs duty is paid in the UK in the course of an onward supply to an EC recipient who will account for the VAT on their acquisition, total relief from import VAT can apply. If not, import VAT is paid with the customs duty;

(ii) if the goods are sold to a customer registered for VAT in another EC country, the supply can be zero-rated subject to the normal conditions for zero-rating an intra-EC supply (see 23.11 EUROPEAN COMMUNITY: SINGLE MARKET); and

(iii) if the goods are sold to a customer not registered for VAT, and the goods are not for onward export from the EC, the supply of the goods is liable to VAT in the UK.

(VAT Notice 702/9/98, paras 5.4, 5.5, Appendices D and E).

See 70.3 above for the meaning of '*community goods*' and '*non-community goods*'.

70.25 Deficiency of free zone goods

Where deficiencies of imported goods are charged with duty, VAT not already paid on the imported goods is also to be charged. Similarly, any acquisition VAT on goods from another EC country which has not been accounted for should be accounted for when deficiencies occur. Deficiencies of home produced goods are not to be charged with VAT unless the goods have been supplied in the free zone before the loss. In all cases, the VAT may be deducted as input tax, subject to the normal rules. (VAT Notice 702/9/98, para 5.7).

71 Works of Art, etc.

The contents of this chapter are as follows.

71.1 EXEMPTION

The disposal of a business asset is exempt from VAT in the following circumstances.

- The disposal is of 'qualifying property' by 'private treaty sale', or disposal otherwise than by sale, to an 'approved body' if estate duty, capital transfer tax, inheritance tax or capital gains tax would not thereby become chargeable.

  A '*private treaty sale*' is a privately arranged sale to one of the approved bodies which are allowed to buy objects by private treaty in accordance with the relevant legislative provisions.

  '*Approved bodies*' are listed in *IHTA 1984, Sch 3* and include The National Gallery, The British Museum and other similar national institutions, museums and art galleries maintained by local authorities or universities in the UK, The National Trust, etc.

- 'Qualifying property' is accepted in lieu of inheritance tax, capital transfer tax or estate duty. Acceptance in lieu allows a person who is liable to pay such taxes to settle part, or all, of the debt by disposing of a work of art or other object to the Board of Inland Revenue.

'*Qualifying property*' is detailed in *IHTA 1984, s 31* and includes pictures, prints, books, manuscripts, works of art, scientific objects, or collections or any of these items, which are pre-eminent for their national, scientific, historic or artistic interest. For further information about the capital tax provisions see *Tolley's Inheritance Tax*.

To support any claim to VAT exemption, a letter should be obtained from the Capital Taxes Office confirming that the private treaty sale, disposal otherwise than by sale, or acceptance in lieu, is exempt from capital taxes.

Value of the supply. This depends upon the reason for the exemption.

- In the case of a private treaty sale, the value of the exempt supply is the amount received for the object.
- In a disposal otherwise than by sale, the normal rules for supplies for no consideration apply. See 69.22 VALUATION.
- If an object is accepted in lieu, the value of the exempt supply is the amount of inheritance tax, capital transfer tax or estate duty actually satisfied.

[*VATA 1994, Sch 9 Group 11; IHTA 1984, Sch 8 para 24; FA 1985, Sch 26 para 14*]. (VAT Notice 701/12/02, paras 3.1–3.6).

The VAT exemption applies only to disposals under the limited circumstances set out above. Other sales of works of art, etc by a registered person in the course or furtherance of his business remain subject to VAT. See 71.6 below for sales from historic houses.

De Voil Indirect Tax Service. See V4.166.

71.2 SECOND-HAND GOODS

Special schemes may be operated by dealers registered for VAT, or by any other taxable persons, who acquire eligible goods and sell them in the course of business. See 61 SECOND-HAND GOODS generally and in particular 61.3 for eligible works of art, etc under the schemes.

71.3 IMPORTS — REDUCED RATE OF VAT

Goods imported from outside the EC. The value of any of the following goods is to be taken as 28.58% of what would otherwise be their value for VAT purposes unless

(i) the whole of the VAT chargeable is relieved from VAT on importation; or

(ii) before 1 November 2001, they were exported from the UK during the period of twelve months ending with the date of their importation (see below). With effect from 1 November 2001, by concession this 12 month restriction only applies where conditions have been artificially created for obtaining the advantage of the reduced rate of VAT on importation.

The effect of this is that the goods are charged to VAT on importation at an effective reduced rate of 5% (28.58% of 17.5%).

(*a*) Any '*work of art*' defined as follows.

- Any mounted or unmounted painting, drawing, collage, decorative plaque or similar picture that was executed by hand. *Excluded* is any technical drawing, map or plan, any picture comprised in a manufactured article that has been hand-decorated, and anything in the nature of scenery (including a backcloth).
- Any original engraving, lithograph or other print which was produced from one or more plates executed by hand without using any mechanical or photomechanical process. The engraving, etc must either be the only one produced from the plate or plates or must be comprised in a limited edition.
- Any original sculpture or statuary in any material.
- Any sculpture cast, produced by or under the supervision of the individual who made the mould (or became entitled to it by succession on death of that individual), which is either the only cast produced from the mould or is comprised in a limited edition. For this purpose, an edition is limited if the number produced from the same mould does not exceed eight or, where the cast was made before 1 January 1989, such greater number as HMRC allow in exceptional circumstances.
- Any tapestry or other hanging made by hand from an original design which is either the only one made from the design or is comprised in a limited edition not exceeding eight.
- Any ceramic executed by an individual and signed by him.
- Any enamel on copper, executed by hand and signed by the person who executed it or by someone on behalf of the studio where it was executed, which is either the only one made from the design in question or comprised in a limited edition. For this purpose, an edition is limited if

the number produced from the same design does not exceed eight and each item in the edition is numbered and signed. *Excluded* from this category are articles of jewellery and articles or a kind produced by goldsmiths or silversmiths.

- Any mounted or unmounted photograph, printed by or under the supervision of the photographer and signed by him, which is either the only print made from the exposure in question or comprised in a limited edition. For this purpose an edition is limited if the number produced from the same exposure does not exceed 30 and each print in the edition is numbered and signed.

(*b*) Any antique not falling within (*a*) above or (*c*) below that is more than 100 years old.

(*c*) Any collection or collector's piece that is of zoological, botanical, mineralogical, anatomical, historical, archaeological, palaeontological, ethnographic, numismatic or philatelic interest. A collector's piece is of philatelic interest if it is

- a postage stamp or revenue stamp, a postmark, a first-day cover or an item of pre-stamped stationery; and
- it is franked or (if unfranked) it is not legal tender and is not intended for use as such. Stamps which are currently valid in the UK are those in decimal currency or currently valid for 1st or 2nd class postage *or* with a value of £1 (or multiple thereof) of the present monarch's reign. (VAT Notice 718, para 25.1).

[*VATA 1994, s 21(4)-(6)(6A)-(6D); FA 1995, s 22; FA 1999, s 12*]. (VAT ESC 3.36).

See 69.15 VALUATION for the valuation of imported goods.

Anti-avoidance rules before 1 November 2001. The condition in (ii) above is an anti-avoidance measure to prevent the artificial movement of works of art, etc by people seeking to gain a tax advantage from the reduced rate of import VAT. In practice, however, such goods are sent outside the UK for legitimate commercial reasons (eg for exhibition prior to auction in the UK, or on a sale or return basis and returned unsold) and often return within 12 months. With effect from 1 November 2001, HMRC have now recognised this by means of an extra-statutory concession so that the provisions will only operate in artificially created situations. Before 1 November 2001, although there was no general extra-statutory concession, there could be specific reliefs which overrode the '12 month' rules.

- Goods which were held in temporary importation (TI) arrangements were not regarded as having been imported into the UK for VAT purposes until the customs duty debt was incurred (eg on removal from TI to home use). Consequently, goods which were removed from TI and sent outside the EC were not considered to have been exported for VAT purposes and therefore not be caught by the '12 month' rule. This covered, for example, goods held under TI, intended for sale by auction in the UK, but sent outside the EC for exhibition prior to auction.
- Returned goods relief under *SI 1995/2518, Reg 125* could apply to goods sent outside the EC 'on approval' or goods exported for sale by auction but which failed to sell and had to be returned to the UK within 12 months. See 34.19 IMPORTS. Provided all the conditions of the relief were satisfied such goods qualified for full relief from VAT on importation and were not affected by the '12 month' rule.

- Goods exported from the UK for repair or restoration work and returned to the UK within 12 months could qualify for outward processing relief under *SI 1995/2518, Reg 126* (see 34.19 IMPORTS). Provided all the conditions of the relief were satisfied such goods were not affected by the '12 month' rule (although VAT at the standard rate was due on the price charged for the repair or restoration).

For goods which were exported from the EC, sold, and imported back into the UK within 12 months, there were no VAT reliefs available and such transactions normally attracted VAT at 17.5% on importation. However, by concession, HMRC agreed that if goods were exported from the UK prior to 27 July 1999, where the business would not have known about the '12 month' rule at the time of exportation, then, where appropriate, goods still qualified for import VAT at the 5% rate following importation into the UK within the 12 month limit.

(Business Brief 3/2000).

Importation formalities. See Customs Notice 362 for details of how the goods can be imported. In all cases, the importer must provide the following

- A written age declaration stating

  'I declare that, to the best of my knowledge and belief, the articles in the form as imported were wholly manufactured or produced more than 100 years before the date of importation'.

- Evidence of age which can be

  (i) a certificate of age given by the seller or by an independent expert in the country where the goods were acquired;

  (ii) the catalogue of an auction sale; or

  (iii) a booklet or other document describing the article.

  Where the importer has no such evidence of age or the HMRC officer regards the evidence produced as unsatisfactory, an importer may get, at his own expense, a certificate of age from a recognised independent expert in the UK. An HMRC officer must agree in advance to the expert nominated and the articles must remain in HMRC's charge until examined by the expert. On receipt of a satisfactory certificate, the articles will be released free of duty, and at the reduced value for import VAT.

  Certain gold and silver antiques have to be inspected by the London Assay Office. If this happens, the importer must enter into a bond, giving security for any duty or VAT that may be payable, and send the goods at his own risk and expense to the Assay Master, Goldsmith's Hall, Gutter Lane, Cheapside, London C2V 8AQ. When the Assay Master passes antiques over 100 years old, they are released from HMRC's control at Goldsmith's Hall. Otherwise, articles will be held pending consideration by HMRC.

(Customs Notice 362, paras 2.1–2.4, 2.10).

De Voil Indirect Tax Service. See V1.298.

71.4 **Imported goods sold by auction**

Where 'works of art' are imported from outside the EC for exhibition with a view to possible sale, any sale by auction at a time when the goods are still subject to temporary importation arrangements with total exemption from import duty (see 34.24 IMPORTS) is treated as neither a supply of goods nor a supply of services. The provision of any services relating to the transfer of ownership is similarly treated.

'*Works of art*', with effect from 1 January 2000, mean any such items falling within the definition in *VATA 1994, s 21* (see 71.3(*a*) above). Before 1 January 2000, although broadly similar, works of art for these purposes were defined as

- paintings, drawings and pastels executed by hand but not comprised in manufactured articles that have been hand-painted or hand-decorated; collages and similar decorative plaques;
- original engravings, lithographs and other prints; and
- original sculptures and statuary, in any material.

[*SI 1995/958; SI 1999/3119*].

By concession, the above treatment is extended to all works of art, collectors' items and antiques falling within *EC 6th Directive, Annex 1* (which broadly corresponds to 71.3(*a*)-(*c*) above). (VAT Notice 48, ESC 3.26).

71.5 Museum and gallery exhibits imported

Certain works of art imported for a purpose other than sale by approved museums, galleries or other institutions are free of VAT. See 34.15(10) IMPORTS.

71.6 ASSETS OF HISTORIC HOUSES

Sale of assets. Assets sold from a house used as a private residence are not normally business assets and sales of these assets are outside the scope of VAT. This also applies to house clearance sales. But if charges are made for admission to the house, the house is being used for business purposes and where the owner is registered for VAT, there is a presumption that any assets (furniture, antiques, works of art, etc) on public display are business assets for VAT purposes. As such, they are within the scope of VAT when disposed of. The disposal is normally standard-rated but see 71.1 above for certain supplies which are exempt.

To avoid having an asset treated as a business asset, an owner has two options.

- *Treat an asset as a private asset when it is acquired.* If assets are acquired for both business and private purposes (eg furnishings of a historic house in which he lives), the owner can choose to keep them as private assets. If so, input tax on their purchase is not deductible but their disposal is outside the scope of VAT. To treat assets in this way, the owner should write to HMRC and notify them of those assets which he intends to treat as private assets.
- *Take an existing business asset outside the scope of VAT by reallocating it as a private asset.* The owner must be able to show that the asset is no longer used for any business purpose (eg by moving it to another part of the house used for private purposes only). He must write to HMRC at the time he decides to withdraw the asset from the business and advise them of the details.

  If the owner was entitled to any deduction of input tax on purchase of the asset, he must pay VAT when reallocating it as a private asset. The normal rules for the supply of assets for no consideration apply. See 69.22 VALUATION. If the asset was not chargeable with VAT when acquired (eg an inherited asset) no VAT is due on the reallocation.

When a reallocated asset is subsequently sold the sale is of a private asset and not liable to VAT.

Where a reallocated business assets consists partly of an item not chargeable with VAT when acquired and partly on asset on which VAT has been recovered (eg an inherited painting for which a new frame has been purchased), at the time of reallocation VAT would only payable on the frame.

Input tax. Where an owner purchases an asset wholly for taxable business purposes, he can normally deduct the VAT. If it is purchased partly for business and partly for private purposes, he can choose to

- apportion the VAT and treat as input tax only the VAT relating to business use; or
- treat all the VAT as input tax and then account for output tax, in each VAT period, on the private or non-business use (the 'Lennartz' approach').

See 35.7 INPUT TAX for further details.

No VAT is recoverable on the purchase of an asset treated as a private asset.

Repair and maintenance. Input tax can be reclaimed on repair and maintenance of an asset treated as a business asset. If a private asset is used for both business and other purposes, input tax can be reclaimed on repair or maintenance services, subject to the normal rules. Any claim must be in proportion to the extent the asset is used for business purposes. The recovery of input tax on such services does not make the future disposal of the asset itself liable to VAT.

(VAT Notice 701/12/02, paras 1.2, 1.3, 1.5, 2.1–2.5, 4.1–4.3).

72 Zero-Rated Supplies

De Voil Indirect Tax Service. See V4.201; V4.202.

The contents of this chapter are as follows.

72.1 ZERO-RATED SUPPLIES

Where a taxable person supplies goods or services and the supply is zero-rated, then, *whether or not VAT would otherwise be chargeable on the supply*, no VAT is charged but the supply in all other respects is treated as a taxable supply (except that an invoice for a zero-rated supply does not constitute a VAT invoice). [*VATA 1994, s 30(1)*]. The effects of this are as follows.

- The amount of VAT on zero-rated supplies is nil but they are still taxable supplies.
- As taxable supplies, they must be taken into consideration in determining whether registration is required.
- Input tax may be reclaimed in the same way as for standard-rated supplies.
- Where a supply could be either zero-rated or exempt, zero-rating takes priority.

Zero-rating applies to a supply of goods or services and, except as otherwise provided, the acquisition of goods from another EC country or the importation of goods from a place outside the EC, falling within one of the following categories specified in *VATA 1994, Sch 8*.

Group 1	FOOD (28)
Group 2	Water and sewerage services (see 72.2 and 72.3 below).
Group 3	Books, etc (see 54.2–54.12 PRINTED MATTER, ETC).
Group 4	Talking books for the blind and handicapped and wireless sets for the blind (see 12.7 CHARITIES).
Group 5	Construction of buildings, etc (see 42.13, 42.18–42.20 and 42.26–42.28 LAND AND BUILDINGS).
Group 6	Protected buildings (see 42.14 and 42.21 LAND AND BUILDINGS).
Group 7	International services (see 39.7 and 39.8 INTERNATIONAL SERVICES).
Group 8	Transport (see 68 TRANSPORT AND FREIGHT).
Group 9	Caravans and houseboats (see 42.35–42.37 LAND AND BUILDINGS).
Group 10	GOLD AND PRECIOUS METALS (30).

Group 11	Bank notes (see 72.4 below).
Group 12	Dispensing of drugs, reliefs for people with disabilities, etc (see 32.15 to 32.35 HEALTH AND WELFARE).
Group 13	Imports, exports, etc (see 34 IMPORTS and 25.2 EXPORTS).
Group 14	Tax-free shops before 1 July 1999 (see 23.20 EUROPEAN COMMUNITY: SINGLE MARKET).
Group 15	Charities, etc (see 12.6 and 12.7 CHARITIES).
Group 16	CLOTHING AND FOOTWEAR (13).

The items within the *Groups* are to be interpreted in accordance with the notes contained and the powers given to the Treasury to vary the *Groups* including powers to add to, delete or vary the notes. The descriptions of *Groups* (ie the headings shown above) are for ease of reference only and do not affect the interpretation of the description of items in the *Group*.

[*VATA 1994, s 30(2)–(4), s 96(9)(10)*].

Acquisitions of goods. In addition to the zero-rating for exports under *Group 13*, zero-rating also applies where goods are removed from the UK and acquired in another EC country by a person taxable in that country and liable for VAT on the acquisition under the law of that country. See 23.11 EUROPEAN COMMUNITY: SINGLE MARKET.

Work on another person's goods which produces goods. A supply of services which consists of applying a treatment or process to another person's goods is zero-rated if by doing so goods are produced and either

- those goods fall within one of the zero-rating *Groups* above; or
- a supply of those goods by the person applying the treatment to that other person would be zero-rated.

[*VATA 1994, s 30(2A); FA 1996, s 29(2)(5)*].

72.2 WATER

Supply of goods. The supply of water insofar as it is not otherwise a supply of goods is to be treated as a supply of goods (and not services). [*SI 1989/1114*].

Zero-rating. The supply of water is zero-rated [*VATA 1994, Sch 8 Group 2 Item 2*] unless falling within one of the following categories.

(*a*) The supply of water used in connection with the carrying on, in the course of a business, of a '*relevant industrial activity*' is standard-rated.

'*Relevant industrial activity*' means any activity described in any of Divisions 1 to 5 of the 1980 edition of the publication prepared by the Central Statistical Office and known as the Standard Industrial Classification. The activities within Divisions 1 to 5 are:

1. Energy and water supply industries.
2. Extraction of minerals and ores other than fuels; manufacture of metals, mineral products and chemicals.
3. Metal goods, engineering and vehicle industries.

4. Other manufacturing industries.

5. Construction.

Mixed use. Where water supplied to a customer is used for both relevant industrial activities within 1 to 5 above and other purposes, the liability of the supply depends upon the *predominant* activity of the 'customer'. Any reasonable basis may be used to determine the predominant activity (eg turnover, number of employees). Where water is supplied to a customer who has both domestic (or other non-business) and relevant industrial use, the predominant activity of that person for these purposes is the use to which most of the water is put. Once the supplier has established the predominant activity of a customer, any water supplied must be taxed accordingly without apportionment, ie the supply is wholly standard-rated or zero-rated. For example, water (for drinking, washing, toilets, etc) supplied to an office of a manufacturing company whose predominant activity falls within 1 to 5 above is standard-rated as it is used in connection with that industrial activity.

The only exception to this is where a relevant industrial customer has two or more business activities, one of which is both non-industrial and exempt for UK VAT purposes. If that exempt activity is not the predominant activity, the water supplied to the exempt business activity can be zero-rated provided

- the supply can be separately identified; and
- a separate invoice is raised.

The '*customer*' for these purposes is the person to whom the water supplier addresses the invoice, whatever the corporate structure of the business to which the customer belongs and whether or not the customer is part of, or the representative member of, a VAT group.

Determining the liability of a supply. The supplier is responsible for deciding whether the customer is an industrial customer. If in doubt, an acceptable way to make sure that the liability of the supply is correct is to obtain a written declaration from the customer confirming that its activities are outside 1 to 5 above. The supplier must take all reasonable steps to check the validity of the declaration and should consult HMRC if in doubt. Where, however, despite taking such steps, nonetheless the supplier fails to identify an incorrect declaration and in good faith makes the supplies concerned at the zero rate, HMRC will not seek to recover the VAT due from the supplier. (VAT Notice 48, ESC 3.11).

[*VATA 1994, Sch 8 Group 2 Item 2; SI 1996/1661*]. (VAT Notice 701/16/02, paras 2.2, 2.5–2.7).

(*b*) The supply of distilled water, deionized water or water of similar purity is standard-rated. [*VATA 1994, Sch 8 Group 2 Item 2*(*a*)*; SI 1996/1661*].

(*c*) The supply of water comprised in any of the excepted items in *VATA 1994, Sch 8 Group 1* (see 28.8 FOOD) is standard-rated. [*VATA 1994, Sch 8 Group 2 Item 2*(*b*)*; SI 1996/1661*]. This includes mineral, table and spa waters in bottles or similar containers held out for sale as beverages.

(*d*) Water which has been heated so that it is supplied at a temperature higher than that at which it was before it was heated. [*VATA 1994, Sch 8 Group 2 Item 2*(*c*)*; SI 1996/1661*]. Such a supply is not taxed as a supply of water but as a supply of heat and is therefore standard-rated unless supplied for domestic purposes or charity non-business use, in which case it is subject to VAT at the reduced rate. See 29.6 FUEL AND POWER.

For these purposes

- steam is treated as heated water;
- naturally occurring hot water (eg from hot springs) is not treated as heated water; and
- water deliberately heated by geo-thermal energy (eg by pumping down cold water which returns to the surface heated) and supplied heated, is treated as heated water.

(VAT Notice 701/16/02, paras 4.1–4.4; Internal Guidance V1–7, Chapter 2 para 5).

Examples of zero-rated supplies to non-industrial customers

- Ice
- Sterile water (except where additives alter the nature of the product)
- The provision of water against payment of an unmeasured charge, standing charge or other availability charge
- Charges for the abstraction of water by licence
- Specific charges for the supply of water for hosepipes, swimming pools and garden ponds, sprinklers and sprinkler licence fees
- Disconnection and reconnection charges arising as the result of non-payment of bills
- Opening and closing of stopcocks at the request of the water supplier
- Ordinary water, of a kind usually supplied by water mains, supplied in bottles as a drought alleviation or other emergency measure

(VAT Notice 701/16/02, para 2.4).

Other water-related supplies. The following water-related supplies commonly made by water providers are all standard-rated.

- Fluoridation charges
- Pressure testing of fire sprinkler systems
- Installation and repair of fire hydrants
- Temporary or permanent disconnection of, or reconnection of, a water supply at the customer's request
- Testing private pipework at the customer's request
- The opening and closing of a stopcock at the customer's request
- Rewashering ball valves and taps
- Hire of stand-pipes and water bowsers (irrespective of the liability of the water supplied)

- First time connection of an existing building, or a building converted from a non-residential to residential use, to the water or sewerage mains

(VAT Notice 701/16/02, para 5.1).

Civil engineering. Civil engineering work is normally standard-rated but works in the course of

- constructing a new dwelling, residential building or certain buildings used by charities,
- carrying out an approved alteration of a listed dwelling, residential building or certain listed buildings used by charities,
- converting a building into a dwelling or residential building,
- renovating or altering an empty dwelling; and
- developing a residential caravan park

can qualify for zero-rating or reduced-rating. See 42 LAND AND BUILDINGS for further details.

Infrastructure charges. The *Water Act 1989* allows a water company to make 'infrastructure charges' which are intended to contribute to the costs that have been, or will be, incurred on providing the means of supplying water and sewerage services (eg sewers, water mains, etc). Such charges are zero-rated (and not standard-rated as currently stated in the VAT Notice).

(VAT Notice 701/16/02, paras 5.2, 5.3).

Water meters. The following supplies are always standard-rated.

- The supply of a water meter without installation
- Meter survey fees
- Meter-testing fees at the request of the customer
- Special meter-reading charges at the request of a customer
- Separate charges for maintenance of meters

The supply *and* installation of a water meter is normally standard-rated. But, as for civil engineering work above, it may be zero-rated or reduced-rated. See 42 LAND AND BUILDINGS.

(VAT Notice 701/16/02, para 5.4).

Water, supplied as part of an overall service, eg in a launderette, is not a separate supply and is standard-rated (*Mander Laundries Ltd (VTD 31) (TVC 67.1)*).

De Voil Indirect Tax Service. See V4.271.

72.3 SEWERAGE SERVICES

Zero-rated supplies. The following supplies are zero-rated.

(*a*) *Services of reception, disposal or treatment of foul water or sewage in bulk.* [*VATA 1994, Sch 8 Group 2 Item 1*(*a*)].

Included is the provision of such sewerage services against payment of an unmeasured charge, a standing charge or other availability charge, or a specific charge (eg by reference to quantity and/or nature of the effluent). (VAT Notice 701/16/02, para 3.1).

(*b*) *Services of emptying of cesspools, septic tanks or similar receptacles.* Zero-rating does not apply if the cesspools, etc are used in connection with the carrying on in the course of a business of a 'relevant industrial activity'.

'*Relevant industrial activity*' means any activity described in any of Divisions 1 to 5 of the 1980 edition of the publication prepared by the Central Statistical Office and known as the Standard Industrial Classification.

[*VATA 1994, Sch 8 Group 2 Item 1*(*b*)].

The activities within Divisions 1 to 5 are as follows.

1. Energy and water supply industries.
2. Extraction of minerals and ores other than fuels; manufacture of metals, mineral products and chemicals.
3. Metal goods, engineering and vehicle industries.
4. Other manufacturing industries.
5. Construction.

Standard-rated supplies. Standard-rating applies to

- the cleaning, maintenance, unblocking, etc of sewers and drains;
- the emptying of cesspools, septic tanks or similar receptacles for industrial users (see (*b*) above); and
- the removal, treatment and disposal of industrial, farm, hospital, domestic or other waste *other than* foul water or sewerage.

(VAT Notice 701/16/02, para 3.1).

Connected civil engineering work. Similar provisions apply as for water under 72.2 above.

De Voil Indirect Tax Service. See V4.271.

72.4 BANK NOTES

The issue by a bank of a note payable to bearer on demand is zero-rated. [*VATA 1994, Sch 8 Group 11*]. This applies to the Bank of England, Scottish and Northern Irish bank notes. *Issue* includes reissue.

De Voil Indirect Tax Service. See V4.279.

72.5 VISITING FORCES

Provided conditions are satisfied, a UK VAT-registered business can supply certain goods and services free of VAT to:

- NATO visiting forces in the UK (see 72.6 and 72.7 below). '*Visiting forces*' are defined as a body, contingent or attachment of the armed forces of a sovereign state stationed in another sovereign state on the invitation of the host state's

Government, or a member of such a body. For these purposes, this term includes civilian staff accompanying the force.

- The NATO International Military Headquarters at Northwood and High Wycombe (see 72.8 below.
- The American Battle Monuments Commission in respect of supplies of goods and services for the maintenance of the US military cemeteries at Brookwood and Madingley (see 72.9 below).

The provisions do not apply to supplies to British forces based in the UK or visiting forces from non-NATO countries.

Relief is normally achieved by treating the supply as zero-rated (so that no VAT is charged but any related input tax can be recovered).

Under these provisions, the goods and services can also be supplied free of customs duty, excise duty, landfill tax and climate change levy. Relief is also available from CAP levies and air passenger duty.

Restrictions after supply. Goods which have been sold free of VAT (or any other duty) to a UK-based visiting force or a member of their personnel may not be sold on, given or otherwise disposed of to a person who does not enjoy the same privileges unless the VAT (or other duty) which has been relieved is paid to HMRC.

The supplier can cancel a sale and take the goods back provided he keeps a full and accurate record of the transaction.

(Customs Notice 431, paras 1.5, 2.1–2.3).

Supplies to other EC countries. See 23.21 EUROPEAN COMMUNITY: SINGLE MARKET.

72.6 **Supplies to US visiting forces**

Goods and services for official use. A UK-registered business can supply most goods and services free of VAT (and certain goods free of duty) for the official use of US visiting forces provided at least one of the following conditions apply.

(*a*) *It has a written contract or purchase order from an authorised US visiting forces contracting officer*. The contract or purchase order must have an *original* signature of an authorised contracting officer of the US forces (ie it must not be a photocopy or be approved by a rubber stamp) and must include the following statement:

'The goods and/or services listed are to be delivered at a price exclusive of VAT under arrangements agreed between the appropriate US authorities and HM Revenue and Customs (Reference PRIV 46/7). I hereby certify that these goods and/or services are being purchased for United States official purposes only.'

If the contract is for hotel accommodation:

- The relieved supply must only be for overnight accommodation, inclusive or exclusive of breakfast. Other food or drinks and other services cannot be relieved of VAT.
- The contract must include a reference to the category of personnel covered, for example Temporary Duty ('TDY') personnel.

- Every time accommodation is supplied under the contract, the force member must provide a purchase order from the base authority booking the accommodation.

(*b*) *Payment is made with a Government-Wide Purchase Card* (*GPC*). This is a VISA card with a special prefix: 4716. The buyer must give the supplier a letter from the contracting office that issued the GPC, stating that the goods or services are being bought for the official use of the US government.

The supplier must keep the credit card slip and letter as evidence that it has treated the supply as zero-rated.

(*c*) *Payment is made with a Procurement* (*PRO*) *card.* This is a Mastercard with a special prefix: 5405.The buyer must give the supplier a letter from the General Manager of the Army and Air Force Exchange Service (AAFES) stating that the goods or services are being bought for the official use of the US government. An example of this letter is shown in Customs Notice 431, section 11.

The supplier must keep the credit card slip and letter as evidence that it has treated the supply as zero-rated.

(*d*) *It is supplying goods from a Customs or excise warehouse*. See 72.11 below.

(*e*) *The goods have been imported and processed under the Inward Processing Relief.* See 34.30 IMPORTS.

Goods or services supplied to members of US forces based in the UK. The following can be supplied VAT free.

- A motor vehicle (see 72.10 below).
- Goods in a Customs warehouse (see 72.11 below).
- Other goods or services costing at least £100 (including VAT) for personal use by members of US forces or their family under the US 'VAT-free purchase scheme'. The supply must not include any supply of land nor any supply of a motor vehicle (for which see 72.10 below).

  The supplier must first provide the buyer with a written quote stating the price of the goods or services (excluding VAT). The quote, and any invoice, must be addressed to a named member of the US visiting forces. The buyer must then give the supplier a US government cheque in pounds sterling and two copies of a US Forces VAT-Free Purchase Certificate (reproduced in Customs Notice 431, section 13) which has been signed by an authorised signatory of the US visiting forces. The supplier must sign one copy of the certificate and return it to the buyer and keep the second copy of the certificate in his VAT records as evidence to support the VAT-free supply.

  This is a voluntary scheme. If a supplier does not wish to participate, it must charge and account for VAT in the usual way.

- Goods from a concession shop on a US base. If a UK-registered business is authorised to operate a US Army and Air Force Exchange Services (AAFES) concession shop on a US base, it must keep a 'Concessionaire's Daily Sales Report'. listing each purchase and include the following statement:

  '(a) I certify that this is a true and complete summary of sales made to entitled personnel for ...... (date) for and on behalf of ...... (name of concessionaire)

............(Concession manager)

(*b*) The price to be paid for the goods and/or services liable to VAT covered by this summary shall be exclusive of VAT in accordance with the arrangements agreed between the appropriate US authorities and HM Revenue and Customs (ref: PRIV 46/7).

............(Exchange manager)'

The concession manager must complete and sign the certificate and produce two copies of the report to the AAFES authorities. Their US base exchange manager must sign one copy and return it to the concession manager who must keep the certified copy of the report as evidence to support the tax-free supply of goods.

(Customs Notice 432, paras 3.1–3.4, 3.8–3.10)

See 72.5 above for restrictions on disposal after supply.

72.7 **Supplies to NATO visiting forces (other than US)**

These provisions relate to NATO visiting forces from Belgium, Canada, the Czech Republic, Denmark, France, Germany, Greece, Hungary, Iceland, Italy, Luxembourg, the Netherlands, Norway, Poland, Portugal, Spain and Turkey.

Goods and services for official use. NATO visiting forces are entitled to VAT (and duty) relief on most goods and services supplied to them for official purposes. In most cases they obtain relief by claiming a VAT (or duty) refund from HMRC by presenting evidence of payment of VAT (and/or duty).

If a UK VAT-registered business is asked to make a supply of goods and services to these visiting forces, it should make the supply inclusive of VAT (and duty) and provide them with evidence that the VAT and duty has been paid by means of a

- VAT invoice for purchases totalling £100 or more; or
- less detailed VAT invoice (see 40.7 INVOICES) for purchases of less than £100.

See 72.11 below for goods in an excise or Customs warehouse.

Goods or services supplied to members of visiting forces based in the UK. Members of visiting forces can obtain the following free of VAT.

- A motor vehicle (see 72.10 below).
- Consumer durable goods (eg domestic electrical equipment, furnishings, similar household effects, items of jewellery and clothing) and road fuel.

  The refund is obtainable from HMRC. If a UK VAT-registered business is asked to make a supply of such goods to a member of a NATO visiting force, it should make the supply inclusive of VAT and provide the customer with evidence that the VAT has been paid by means of a

  - VAT invoice for purchases totalling £100 or more; or
  - less detailed VAT invoice (see 40.7 INVOICES) for purchases of less than £100.
- Goods in a Customs warehouse (see 72.11 below).

(Customs Notice 431, paras 4.1–4.3).

See 72.5 above for restrictions on disposal after supply.

72.8 **Supplies to NATO International Military Headquarters (IMHQ)**

IMHQ are HQ organisations and outstations set up by NATO as part of its military structure. Currently, there are two NATO IMHQ in the UK: HQ CinCEASTLANT in Northwood and No 9 Combined Air Operations Centre at RAF High Wycombe.

Goods and services for official use. A UK-registered business can supply goods and services VAT (and duty) free to a NATO IMHQ for its official use provided it has an official contract or purchase order from the IMHQ authority. The contract or purchase order must

- be with a specific and named NATO IMHQ;
- be approved by an authorised signatory of the HQ; and
- have an *original* signature of an authorised signatory of the HQ (ie it must not be a photocopy or be approved by a rubber stamp) and must include the following statement:

  'I hereby certify that the goods and services listed are being purchased for official use by the North Atlantic Treaty Organisation and should be supplied free of VAT in accordance with the agreement with HM Revenue and Customs Reference PRIV 59/16'.

Any faxed order must be confirmed in writing.

The business should obtain an official receipt on completion of the supply and retain this with the contract or purchase order in its VAT records as supporting evidence for the VAT free supply.

Goods or services supplied to a member of a NATO IMHQ for personal use. US members of a NATO IMHQ can be treated in the same way as members of the US visiting forces (see 7.6 above) and other members of a NATO IMHQ can be treated in the same way as members of other NATO visiting forces (see 72.7 above).

(Customs Notice 431, paras 5.1, 5.2).

See 72.5 above for restrictions on disposal after supply.

72.9 **Supplies to the American Battle Monuments Commission**

A UK-registered business can supply any goods or services free of VAT to the American Military Cemetery and Memorial at Madingley, Cambridge or Brookwood, Surrey provided the following conditions are met.

- The goods or services must be solely used for the maintenance of those cemeteries.
- The supplier must have an official written order or contract from the American Battle Monuments Commission in Paris or from the American Military Cemetery and Memorial in Cambridge.
- The order or contract must

  (i) be signed by an official of one of those organisations; and

  (ii) certify that the goods and/or services are supplied for the maintenance of US military cemeteries in the UK.

- When the supply is complete, the supplier must obtain (and keep in his VAT records) an official receipt or a stamped certificate to show that the goods or services have been received in accordance with the terms of the contract or order.

(Customs Notice 431, paras 6.1, 6.2).

See 72.5 above for restrictions on disposal after supply.

72.10 Supplies of motor vehicles to NATO visiting force

A UK-registered business can supply a motor vehicle VAT-free to

- any NATO visiting force in the UK for its official use; or
- a member of any NATO visiting force for their personal use or for the use of their family. At any one time, a member is allowed to own one motor vehicle free of VAT plus a second if his or her spouse is present in the UK. No relief is available to anyone who is a UK national or who is permanently resident in the UK.

A VAT-free supply can be made in either of the following circumstances.

(*a*) On removal from a Customs warehouse (see 72.11 below).

(*b*) If the vehicle was manufactured in the EC or EFTA or if the supply is for the official use of US visiting forces.

The customer must demonstrate entitlement to receive a tax-free vehicle by

- if the vehicle is for the official use of US visiting forces, following the procedures described in 72.6(*a*)–(*c*) above; and
- in all other cases, providing a properly completed and authorised Form 941 (if the supply is from a Customs warehouse) or Form 941A (if not). Where the customer is from the US forces, the Pass and Registration Section of the force must have authorised the form. In other cases, the visiting force or NATO IMHQ must authorise the form. The completed form must also have been authorised by HMRC.

  If the supplier is also registering the vehicle on behalf of his customer, he should ask the customer for a further copy of the form to send to the Vehicle Registration Office.

  The supplier must keep the completed form with his records to prove entitlement to the tax relief.

Second-hand scheme. A business cannot supply NATO visiting forces with VAT-free goods under the margin scheme for SECOND-HAND GOODS (61). If a dealer has a second-hand vehicle in his margin scheme records and wishes to treat a sale as a zero-rated supply to a member of a visiting force, he must clearly record in his second-hand stock book that the vehicle has been supplied free of VAT to a member of a visiting force outside the margin scheme. He must then obtain and keep in his records a completed and authorised Form 941A.

(Customs Notice 431, paras 7.1–7.5).

See 72.5 above for restrictions on disposal after supply.

72.11 **Supplies of alcoholic drinks and tobacco products from a UK excise or Customs warehouse**

Excise warehouses. A business operating an approved excise warehouse in the UK can supply alcoholic drinks and tobacco products free of VAT (and excise duty) to a UK-based NATO visiting force (see 72.6 and 72.7 above) or NATO IMHQ (see 72.8 above) provided the following conditions are met.

- The visiting force authority must complete and present a Form C185 including full details of all the goods required by the members of the force. The form must be signed by an authorised signatory of the visiting force and must be kept with the other warehouse records.
- The warehouse operator must follow the procedures laid down in Customs Notice 197 *Excise goods: holding and movement*.

Customs warehousing. A business operating a Customs warehouse can release goods free of VAT (and duty) provided the following conditions are met.

- Where a UK-based visiting force or IMHQ removes goods for official use, it must make a Customs declaration on Form C88, using Customs Procedure Code (CPC) 40 71 20. Where a member of UK-based visiting force or IMHQ removes goods for personal use, the member must also make a Customs declaration on Form C88 but using Customs Procedure Code (CPC) 40 71 35. In either case, Box 8 of the form must show the name and TURN (Trader's Unique Reference Number) of the visiting force or IMHQ.
- In the case of goods for personal use, the operator must also receive a completed Form C2 or (for US forces only) DD1434.
- In the case of a motor vehicle, the additional requirements in 72.10 above must be met.

(Customs Notice 431, paras 8.1, 8.2).

See 72.5 above for restrictions on disposal after supply.

73 Table of Cases

A

Table of Cases

C

D

Debt Management Associates Ltd (VTD 17880)	27.29
Deutsche Ruck UK Reinsurance Co Ltd, QB [1995] STC 495	37.10
Devine (J) (VTD 15312)	42.4
Devonshire Hotel (Torquay) Ltd (The) (VTD 14448)	66.26
Devro Ltd (VTD 7570)	28.12
DFDS A/S, CJEC Case C–260/95; [1997] STC 384; [1997] 1 ECR 1005; [1997] 1 WLR 1037; [1997] AEECR 342	64.19, 66.5
DFS Furniture Co plc, CA [2004] STC 559; [2004] EWCA Civ 243	6.1, 6.5
Digwa (TS) [1978] VATTR 119 (VTD 612)	5.4
Dinaro Ltd (t/a Fairway Lodge) (VTD 17148)	33.1
Diners Club Ltd (The), CA [1989] STC 407; [1989] 2 All ER 385	27.16
Dingle v Turner, HL [1972] 1 All ER 878	12.1
Direct Cosmetics Ltd (No 1), CJEC Case 5/84; [1985] STC 479; [1985] ECR 617; [1985] 2 CMLR 145	22.2, 69.23
Dispute Resolution Services Ltd, CJEC [2003] All ER(D) 281(Nov)	32.2
Diversified Agency Services Ltd, QB 1995, [1996] STC 398	64.26
Don Pasquale, CA [1990] STC 556	6.1
Doncaster Borough Council (VTD 12458)	43.4
Dormer Builders (London) Ltd [1986] VATTR 69 (VTD 2044)	5.16
Double Shield Window Co Ltd (VTD 1771	64.37
Douros (T) (t/a Olympic Financial Services) (VTD 12454)	35.10
Doves Farm Foods Ltd (VTD 17805)	28.6
Dow Engineering (VTD 5771)	52.15
Draper (G) (Marlow) Ltd (VTD 2079)	8.11
Du Vergier (E) & Co Ltd [1973] VATTR 11 (VTD 4)	31.2
Dudda v Finanzamt Bergisch Gladbach, CJEC Case C–327/94; [1996] STC 1290; [1996] 1 ECR 4595; [1996] 3 CMLR 1063	64.23
Durham Aged Mineworkers' Homes Association, QB [1994] STC 553	44.1
Dyrham Park Country Club Ltd [1978] VATTR 244 (VTD 700)	14.5, 27.8
Dyslexia Institute Ltd (The) (VTD 12654)	32.16

E

Eagle Trust plc (VTD 12871)	36.11
Eastbourne Town Radio Cars Association, HL [2001] STC 606; [2001] UKHL 19; [2001] 1 WLR 794; [2001] 2 All ER 597	14.1
Eastwood Care Homes (Ilkeston) Ltd, CA [2001] STC 1629	59.2
Easyjet plc (VTD 18230)	49.4
EC Commission v Belgium (Kingdom of), CJEC Case 324/82; [1984] ECR 1861; [1985] 1 CMLR 364	22.2
EC Commission v French Republic, CJEC Case C–68/92; [1993] 1 ECR 5881; [1997] STC 684; [1995] 2 CMLR 1	22.10
EC Commission v Germany (Federal Republic of), CJEC Case C–427/98; [2003] STC 301	67.7
EC Commission v Germany (Federal Republic of), CJEC Case C–287/00; [2002] STC 982	20.6, 22.17
EC Commission v Italian Republic, CJEC Case C–45/95; [1997] STC 1062; [1997] 1 ECR 3605	9.7, 45.4
EC Commission v United Kingdom, CJEC Case C–353/85; [1988] STC 251; [1988] ECR 817	22.2
EC Commission v United Kingdom (No 2), CJEC Case C–416/85; [1988] STC 456; [1988] ECR 3127	22.2
EC Commission v United Kingdom (No 3), CJEC Case C–359/97; [2000] STC 777	47.8

Table of Cases

F

G

H

I

O

Y

Z

74 Table of Statutes

References are only included where the provisions are covered in the text. Casual references to *Acts* are not included.

75 Table of Statutory Instruments

References are only included where the provisions are covered in the text. Casual references to *Statutory Instruments* are not included.

Table of Statutory Instruments

76 Table of European Community Legislation

77 Index

This index is referenced to the chapter and paragraph number.

Index

Index

Index

Index

Index

Index

D

Index

Index

Index

Index

H

Index

M

S

Index

Index

Index